W9-ABI-141

———*The*———
# CHELSEA HOUSE LIBRARY
### *of* LITERARY CRITICISM

## ———The———
# CHELSEA HOUSE LIBRARY
## *of* LITERARY CRITICISM

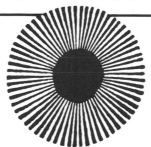

## *The*
# MAJOR AUTHORS EDITION
### *of the*
### NEW MOULTON'S LIBRARY *of* LITERARY CRITICISM

Volume 2

*William Shakespeare*

*General Editor*
## HAROLD BLOOM

1986
CHELSEA HOUSE PUBLISHERS
New York
New Haven     Philadelphia

EDITOR
S. T. Joshi

EDITORIAL COORDINATOR
Karyn Browne

EDITORIAL STAFF
Barbara Browning
Perry King
Jeffrey Kosakow

DESIGN
Susan Lusk

PICTURE RESEARCH
Juliette Dickstein
Julie Nichols

Printed and bound in the United States of
America.

10  9  8  7  6  5  4  3  2

Library of Congress Cataloging in Publication
Data

The Major authors edition of the New Moulton's library of literary criticism.
    (The Chelsea House library of literary criti-
cism)
    Includes bibliographies.
    Contents: v. 2. Shakespeare.
    1. English literature—History and criti-
cism—Collected works. American literature—History and criticism—Collected
works. I. Bloom, Harold. II. Series: Moulton's library of literary criticism.
PR85.M33  1986      820'.9
84-27426
ISBN 0-87754-816-1

# CONTENTS

The Index to this series, *The Major Authors Edition*, appears in Volume 5.

# ILLUSTRATIONS

# PREFACE

This second volume of *The Major Authors Edition* is devoted to criticism of William Shakespeare from 1592 to the turn of the twentieth century. The usual cut-off date for material in this series, 1904, has in this case been extended somewhat to incorporate material from as late as 1912, since the corresponding volume in the Chelsea House Library of Literary Criticism, *The Critical Perspective* II (devoted to twentieth-century criticism of Spenser and Shakespeare), does not include any material earlier than 1913.

The *Personal* section reprints important early biographical notices of Shakespeare as well as impressions on Shakespeare's life and character by later critics. The *General* section contains general snippets and essays on Shakespeare's work as a whole; within this large section are subsections devoted to the editing and emendation of Shakespeare's texts, to the ancient and contemporary sources of Shakespeare's plays and poems, and to the authorship controversy that emerged in the last half of the nineteenth century.

The rest of the volume is devoted to criticism of Shakespeare's individual plays and poems. The plays are arranged under the categories *Comedies*, *Histories*, *Tragedies*, and *Romances*, and chronologically (according to the chronology established by the consensus of modern opinion) within each category. The poems are divided into *Sonnets* and other poems. There is no specific discussion of the plays now considered spurious, although some mention of them will be found in the *General* section.

The aim of this volume has been to reprint the best and most important Shakespeare criticism in English up to 1912, and representative criticism in translation by French and German critics. Much has necessarily been omitted, but a list of additional readings—which also supplies information on the most important editions of Shakespeare in this period—has been provided at the end of the volume.

*The Editors*

William Shakespeare

# WILLIAM SHAKESPEARE

## 1564–1616

Few events in the life of William Shakespeare are supported by reliable evidence, and many incidents recorded by commentators of the last four centuries are either conjectural or apocryphal.

William Shakespeare was born in Stratford-on-Avon on April 22 or 23, 1564, the son of Mary Arden and the tradesman John Shakespeare. His very early education was in the hands of a tutor, for his parents were probably illiterate. At age seven he entered the Free School in Stratford, where he learned the "small Latin and less Greek" attributed to him by Ben Jonson. When not in school Shakespeare may have gone to the popular Stratford fairs and to the dramas and mystery plays performed by travelling actors.

When Shakespeare was about thirteen his father removed him from school and apprenticed him to a butcher, although it is not known how long he remained in this occupation. When he was eighteen he married Anne Hathaway; their first child, Susanna, was born six months later. A pair of twins, Hamnet and Judith, were born in February 1585. About this time Shakespeare was caught poaching deer on the estate of Sir Thomas Lucy of Cherlecot; Lucy's prosecution is said to have inspired Shakespeare to write his earliest literary work, a satire on his opponent. Shakespeare was convicted of poaching and forced to leave Stratford. He withdrew to London, leaving his family behind. He soon attached himself to the stage, initially in a menial capacity (as tender of playgoers' horses, according to one tradition), then as prompter's attendant. When the poaching furor subsided, Shakespeare returned to Stratford to join one of the many bands of itinerant actors. In the next five years he gained what little theatre training he received.

By 1592 Shakespeare was a recognized actor, and in that year he wrote and produced his first play, *1 Henry the Sixth*. Its success impelled Shakespeare soon afterward to write the second and third parts of *Henry the Sixth*. (Many early and some modern critics believe that *Love's Labour's Lost* preceded these histories as Shakespeare's earliest play, although the majority of modern scholars discount this theory.) Shakespeare's popularity provoked the jealousy of Robert Greene, as recorded in his posthumous *Groats-worth of Wit* (1592). A "Willy" mentioned in Spenser's *Teares of the Muses* (1591) was interpreted by some early writers to be the first mention of Shakespeare in extant literature, but most modern scholars disagree.

In 1593 Shakespeare published *Venus and Adonis*, based upon Ovid (or perhaps Golding's translation of Ovid's *Metamorphoses*). It was dedicated to the young Earl of Southampton—but perhaps without permission, a possible indication that Shakespeare was trying to gain the nobleman's patronage. However, the dedicatory address to Southampton in *The Rape of Lucrece* (1594) reveals Shakespeare to be on good terms with him. Many plays—such as *Titus Andronicus, The Comedy of Errors*, and *Romeo and Juliet*—were produced over the next several years, most performed by Shakespeare's troupe, the Lord Chamberlain's Company. In December 1594 Shakespeare acted in a comedy (of unknown authorship) before Queen Elizabeth; many other royal performances followed in the next decade.

In August 1596 Shakespeare's son Hamnet died. Early the next year Shakespeare bought a home, New Place, in the center of Stratford; he is said to have planted a mulberry tree in the back yard with his own hands. Shakespeare's relative prosperity is indicated by his purchasing over a hundred acres of farmland in 1602, a cottage near his estate later that year, and half-interest in the tithes of some local villages in 1605.

In September 1598 Shakespeare began his friendship with the then unknown Ben Jonson by producing his play *Every Man in His Humour*. The next year the publisher William Jaggard affixed Shakespeare's name, without his permission, to a curious medley of poems under the title *The Passionate Pilgrim*; the majority of the poems were not by Shakespeare. Two of his sonnets, however, appeared in this collection, although the 154 sonnets, with their mysterious dedication to

"Mr. W. H.," were not published as a group until 1609. Also in 1599 the Globe Theatre was built in Southwark, and Shakespeare's company began acting there. Many of Shakespeare's greatest plays, *Troilus and Cressida*, *King Lear*, *Othello*, *Macbeth*, were performed in the Globe before its destruction by fire in 1613.

The death in 1603 of Queen Elizabeth, the last of the Tudors, and the accession of the Stuart James I created anxiety throughout England. Shakespeare's fortunes, however, were unaffected, as the new monarch extended the license of Shakespeare's company to perform at the Globe. James I saw a performance of *Othello* at the court in November 1604. In October 1605 Shakespeare's company performed before the Mayor and Corporation of Oxford.

The last five years of Shakespeare's life seem void of incident; he had retired from the stage by 1613. Among the few known incidents is Shakespeare's involvement in a heated and lengthy dispute about the enclosure of common-fields around Stratford. He died on April 23, 1616, and was buried in the Church of St. Mary's in Stratford. A monument was later erected to him in the Poets' Corner of Westminster Abbey.

Numerous corrupt quarto editions of Shakespeare's plays were published during his lifetime. These editions, based either on manuscripts, prompt-books, or sometimes merely actors' recollections of the plays, were meant to capitalize on Shakespeare's renown. Other plays, now deemed wholly or largely spurious—*Edward the Third*, *The Yorkshire Tragedy*, *The Two Noble Kinsmen*, and others—were also published under Shakespeare's name during and after his lifetime. Shakespeare's plays were collected in the First Folio of 1623 by John Heminge and Henry Condell. Nine years later the Second Folio was published, and in 1640 Shakespeare's poems were collected. The first standard collected edition was by Nicholas Rowe (1709), followed by the editions of Pope (1725), Theobald (1734), Johnson (1765–68), Malone (1790), and many others.

Shakespeare's reputation, while subject to many fluctuations, was firmly established by the eighteenth century. Samuel Johnson remarked: "Perhaps it would not be easy to find any authour, except Homer, who invented so much as Shakespeare, who so much advanced the studies which he cultivated, who effused so much novelty upon his age or country. The form, the characters, the language, and the shows of the English drama are his." In France—where in the eighteenth century Voltaire had condemned Shakespeare as a barbarian who violated all the rules of dramatic art—he was hailed by Chateaubriand, Victor Hugo, and others. In Germany the criticism of Goethe, Schlegel, Tieck, and Hegel strongly influenced English and American Shakespeare studies. It was Coleridge who declared: "The Englishman who without reverence, a proud and affectionate reverence, can utter the name of William Shakspeare, stands disqualified for the office of critic. . . . Great as was the genius of Shakspeare, his judgment was at least equal to it." A. C. Bradley forms the bridge between the ancient and modern schools of criticism, and he was succeeded by T. S. Eliot, G. Wilson Knight, Northrop Frye, W. H. Auden, and many others. Such landmark editions as the New Cambridge Shakespeare (1931–66) and the New Arden Shakespeare (1951f.) have presented the text in an authoritative form and elucidated the plays with exhaustive commentaries.

# PERSONAL

Base minded men al three of you, if by my miserie ye be not warned: for vnto none of you (like me) sought those burres to cleaue: those Puppits (I meane) that speake from our mouths, those Anticks garnisht in our colours. Is it not strange that I, to whom they al haue beene beholding: is it not like that you, to whome they all haue beene beholding, shall (were ye in that case that I am now) be both at once of them forsaken? Yes, trust them not: for there is an vpstart Crow, beautified with our feathers, that with his *Tygers heart wrapt in a Players hide,* supposes he is as well able to bumbast out a blanke verse as the best of you: and being an absolute *Iohannes fac totum,* is in his owne conceit the onely Shake-scene in a countrie. O that I might intreate your rare wits to be imployed in more profitable courses: & let these Apes imitate your past excellence, and neuer more acquaint them with your admired inuentions. I know the best husband of you all will neuer proue an Vsurer, and the kindest of them all wil neuer prooue a kinde nurse: yet, whilst you may, seeke you better Maisters; for it is pittie men of such rare wits, should be subiect to the pleasures of such rude groomes.—ROBERT GREENE, *Groats-worth of Wit,* 1592

To our English Terence, Mr. Will.
Shake-speare.

Some say (good *Will*) which I, in sport, do sing,
Had'st thou not plaid some Kingly parts in sport,
Thou hadst bin a companion for a *King*;
And, beene a King among the meaner sort.
Some others raile; but, raile as they thinke fit,
Thou hast no rayling, but, a raigning Wit:
*And* honesty *thou sow'st, which they do reape,*
*So, to increase their* Stocke *which they do keepe.*

—JOHN DAVIES, *The Scourge of Folly,* c. 1611

Good frend for Iesvs sake forbeare,
To digg the dvst enclosed heare:
Bleste be y^e man y^t spares thes stones,
And cvrst be he y^t moves my bones.

—INSCRIPTION on the tablet over Shakespeare's
grave, April 25, 1616

Renowned Spencer lye a thought more nye
To learned Chaucer, and rare Beaumont lye
A little neerer Spenser, to make roome
For Shakespeare in your threefold, fowerfold Tombe.
To lodge all fowre in one bed make a shift
Vntill Doomesdaye, for hardly will a fift
Betwixt *this* day and *that* by Fate be slayne,
For whom your Curtaines may be drawn againe.
If your precedency in death doth barre
A fourth place in your sacred sepulcher,
Vnder this carued marble of thine owne,
Sleepe, rare Tragœdian, Shakespeare, sleep alone;
Thy vnmolested peace, vnshared Caue,
Possesse as Lord, not Tenant, of thy Graue,
  That vnto us & others it may be
  Honor hereafter to be layde by thee.

—WILLIAM BASSE, "On Mr. Wm. Shakespeare,"
1622

This Figure, that thou here seest put,
  It was for gentle Shakespeare cut;
Wherein the Grauer had a strife

With Nature, to out-doo the life:
O, could he but haue drawne his wit
  As well in brasse, as he hath hit
His face; the Print would then surpasse
  All, that was euer writ in brasse.
But, since he cannot, Reader, looke
  Not on his Picture, but his Booke.

—BEN JONSON, "To the Reader," *Mr. William
Shakespeares Comedies, Histories, & Tragedies,*
1623

Wee wondred (*Shake-speare*) that thou went'st so
  soone
From the Worlds-Stage, to the Graues-Tyring-
  roome.
Wee thought thee dead, but this thy printed worth,
Tels thy Spectators, that thou went'st but forth
To enter with applause. An Actors Art,
Can dye, and liue, to acte a second part.
That's but an *Exit* of Mortalitie;
This, a Re-entrance to a Plaudite.

—I. M., "To the Memorie of M. W. Shakespeare," *Mr. William Shakespeares Comedies,
Histories, & Tragedies,* 1623

Shakespear had but 2 daughters, one whereof M. Hall, y^e physitian, married, and by her had one daughter, to wit, y^e Lady Bernard of Abbingdon. . . .

I have heard y^t M^r. Shakespeare was a natural wit, without any art at all; hee frequented y^e plays all his younger time, but in his elder days lived at Stratford: and supplied y^e stage with 2 plays every year, and for y^t had an allowance so large, y^t hee spent att y^e Rate of a 1,000*l.* a year, as I have heard. . . .

Shakespear, Drayton, and Ben Jhonson, had a merry meeting, and itt seems drank too hard, for Shakespear died of a feavour there contracted. . . .

Whether Dr. Heylin does well, in reckoning up the dramatick poets which have been famous in England, to omit Shakespeare.—JOHN WARD, *Diary,* 1648–79

William Shakespeare was born at Stratford on Avon in this county ⟨Warwickshire⟩; in whom three eminent poets may seem in some sort to be compounded. 1. *Martial,* in the warlike sound of his surname (whence some may conjecture him of a military extraction) *Hasti-vibrans,* or Shake-speare. 2. *Ovid,* the most natural and witty of all poets; and hence it was that queen Elizabeth, coming into a grammar-school, made this extemporary verse,

*Persius* a crab-staffe, bawdy *Martial, Ovid* a fine
  wag.

3. *Plautus,* who was an exact comedian, yet never any scholar, as our Shakspeare (if alive) would confess himself. Add to all these, that though his genius generally was jocular, and inclining him to festivity, yet he could (when so disposed) be solemn and serious, as appears by his tragedies; so that Heraclitus himself (I mean if secret and unseen) might afford to smile at his comedies, they were so merry; and Democritus scarce forbear to sigh at his tragedies, they were so mournful.

He was an eminent instance of the truth of that rule, "Poeta non fit sed nascitur," (one is not made but born a poet.) Indeed his learning was very little; so that, as Cornish diamonds are not polished by any lapidary, but are pointed and smoothed even as they are taken out of the earth, so Nature itself was all the art which was used upon him.

Many were the wet-combats betwixt him and Ben Jonson; which two I behold like a Spanish great galleon and an English man-of-war: master Jonson (like the former) was built far higher in learning; solid, but slow, in his performances. Shakespeare, with the English man-of-war, lesser in bulk, but lighter in sailing, could turn with all tides, tack about, and take advantage of all winds, by the quickness of his wit and invention. He died anno Domini 1616, and was buried at Stratford-upon-Avon, the town of his nativity.—THOMAS FULLER, *The History of the Worthies of England*, 1662

Mr. William Shakespeare was born at Stratford upon Avon in the County of Warwick. His father was a Butcher, and I have been told heretofore by some of the neighbours, that when he was a boy he exercised his father's Trade, but when he kill'd a Calfe he would doe it in a high style, and make a Speech. There was at this time another Butcher's son in this Towne that was held not at all inferior to him for a naturall witt, his acquaintance and coetanean, byt dyed young.

This William, being inclined naturally to Poetry and acting, came to London, I guesse about 18: and was an Actor at one of the Play-houses, and did acte exceedingly well: now B. Johnson was never a good Actor, but an excellent Instructor.

He began early to make essayes at Dramatique Poetry, which at that time was very lowe; and his Playes tooke well.

He was a handsome, well-shap't man: very good company, and of a very readie and pleasant smoothe Witt.

The Humour of the Constable in *Midsomernight's Dreame*, he happened to take at Grendon, in Bucks (I thinke it was Midsomer night that he happened to lye there) which is the roade from London to Stratford, and there was living that Constable about 1642, when I first came to Oxon. Ben Johnson and he did gather Humours of men dayly where ever they came. One time as he was at the Tavern at Stratford super Avon, one Combes, an old rich Usurer, was to be buryed. He makes there this extemporary Epitaph:

> Ten in the Hundred the Devill allowes,
> But Combes will have twelve he sweares and vowes:
> If anyone askes who lies in this Tombe,
> Hoh! quoth the Devill, 'Tis my John o' Combe.

He was wont to goe to his native Countrey once a yeare. I thinke I have been told that he left 2 or 300 pounds per annum there and thereabout to a sister.

I have heard Sir William Davenant and Mr. Thomas Shadwell (who is counted the best Comoedian we have now) say that he had a most prodigious Witt, and did admire his naturall parts beyond all other Dramaticall writers.

His Comoedies will remaine witt as long as the English tongue is understood, for that he handles *mores hominum*. Now our present writers reflect so much on particular persons and coxcombeities that twenty yeares hence they will not be understood.

Though, as Ben Johnson sayes of him, that he had little Latine and lesse Greek, He understood Latine pretty well: for he had been in his younger yeares a schoolmaster in the countrey.

He was wont to say that he never blotted out a line in his life. Sayd Ben: Johnson, I wish he had blotted-out a thousand.—JOHN AUBREY, *Brief Lives*, 1669–96

---

NICHOLAS ROWE
From "Some Account of the Life, &c.
of Mr. William Shakespear"
*The Works of Mr. William Shakespear*
1709, Volume 1, pp. i–xxxvii

It seems to be a kind of Respect due to the Memory of Excellent Men, especially of those whom their Wit and Learning have made Famous, to deliver some Account of themselves, as well as their Works, to Posterity. For this Reason, how fond do we see some People of discovering any little Personal Story of the great Men of Antiquity, their Families, the common Accidents of their Lives, and even their Shape, Make and Features have been the Subject of critical Enquiries. How trifling soever this Curiosity may seem to be, it is certainly very Natural; and we are hardly satisfy'd with an Account of any remarkable Person, 'till we have heard him describ'd even to the very Cloaths he wears. As for what relates to Men of Letters, the knowledge of an Author may sometimes conduce to the better understanding his Book: And tho' the Works of Mr. *Shakespear* may seem to many not to want a Comment, yet I fancy some little Account of the Man himself may not be thought improper to go along with them.

He was the Son of Mr. *John Shakespear*, and was Born at *Stratford* upon *Avon*, in *Warwickshire*, in *April* 1564. His Family, as appears by the Register and Publick Writings relating to that Town, were of good Figure and Fashion there, and are mention'd as Gentlemen. His Father, who was a considerable Dealer in Wool, had so large a Family, ten Children in all, that tho' he was his eldest Son, he could give him no better Education than his own Employment. He had bred him, 'tis true, for some time at a Free-School, where 'tis probable he acquir'd that little *Latin* he was Master of: But the narrowness of his Circumstances, and the want of his assistance at Home, forc'd his Father to withdraw him from thence, and unhappily prevented his further Proficiency in that Language. It is without Controversie, that he had no knowledge of the Writings of the Antient Poets, not only from this Reason, but from his Works themselves, where we find no traces of any thing that looks like an Imitation of 'em; the Delicacy of his Taste, and the natural Bent of his own Great *Genius*, equal, if not superior to some of the best of theirs, would certainly have led him to Read and Study 'em with so much Pleasure, that some of their fine Images would naturally have insinuated themselves into, and been mix'd with his own Writings; so that his not copying at least something from them, may be an Argument of his never having read 'em. Whether his Ignorance of the Antients were a disadvantage to him or no, may admit of a Dispute: For tho' the knowledge of 'em might have made him more Correct, yet it is not improbable but that the Regularity and Deference for them, which would have attended that Correctness, might have restrain'd some of that Fire, Impetuosity, and even beautiful Extravagance which we admire in *Shakespear*: And I believe we are better pleas'd with those Thoughts, altogether New and Uncommon, which his own Imagination supply'd him so abundantly with, than if he had given us the most beautiful Passages out of the *Greek* and *Latin* Poets, and that in the most agreeable manner that it was possible for a Master of the *English* Language to deliver 'em. Some *Latin* without question he did know, and one may see up and down in his Plays how far his Reading that way went: In *Love's Labour Lost*, the Pedant comes out with a Verse of

*Mantuan*; and in *Titus Andronicus*, one of the *Gothick* Princes, upon reading

> Integer vitæ scelerisque purus
> Non eget Mauri jaculis nec arcu——

says, *'Tis a Verse in* Horace, *but he remembers it out of his* Grammar: Which, I suppose, was the Author's Case. Whatever *Latin* he had, 'tis certain he understood *French*, as may be observ'd from many Words and Sentences scatter'd up and down his Plays in that Language; and especially from one Scene in *Henry* the Fifth written wholly in it. Upon his leaving School, he seems to have given intirely into that way of Living which his Father propos'd to him; and in order to settle in the World after a Family manner, he thought fit to marry while he was yet very Young. His Wife was the Daughter of one *Hathaway*, said to have been a substantial Yeoman in the Neighbourhood of *Stratford*. In this kind of Settlement he continu'd for some time, 'till an Extravagance that he was guilty of, forc'd him both out of his Country and that way of Living which he had taken up; and tho' it seem'd at first to be a Blemish upon his good Manners, and a Misfortune to him, yet it afterwards happily prov'd the occasion of exerting one of the greatest *Genius's* that ever was known in Dramatick Poetry. He had, by a Misfortune common enough to young Fellows, fallen into ill Company; and amongst them, some that made a frequent practice of Deer-stealing, engag'd him with them more than once in robbing a Park that belong'd to Sir *Thomas Lucy* of *Cherlecot*, near *Stratford*. For this he was prosecuted by that Gentleman, as he thought, somewhat too severely; and in order to revenge that ill Usage, he made a Ballad upon him. And tho' this, probably the first Essay of his Poetry, be lost, yet it is said to have been so very bitter, that it redoubled the Prosecution against him to that degree, that he was oblig'd to leave his Business and Family in *Warwickshire*, for some time, and shelter himself in *London*.

It is at this Time, and upon this Accident, that he is said to have made his first Acquaintance in the Play-house. He was receiv'd into the Company then in being, at first in a very mean Rank; But his admirable Wit, and the natural Turn of it to the Stage, soon distinguish'd him, if not as an extraordinary Actor, yet as an excellent Writer. His Name is Printed, as the Custom was in those Times, amongst those of the other Players, before some old Plays, but without any particular Account of what sort of Parts he us'd to play; and tho' I have inquir'd, I could never meet with any further Account of him this way, than that the top of his Performance was the Ghost in his own *Hamlet*. I should have been much more pleas'd, to have learn'd from some certain Authority, which was the first Play he wrote; it would be without doubt a pleasure to any Man, curious in Things of this Kind, to see and know what was the first Essay of a Fancy like *Shakespear's*. Perhaps we are not to look for his Beginnings, like those of other Authors, among their least perfect Writings; Art had so little, and Nature so large a Share in what he did, that, for ought I know, the Performances of his Youth, as they were the most vigorous, and had the most fire and strength of Imagination in 'em, were the best. I would not be thought by this to mean, that his Fancy was so loose and extravagant, as to be Independent on the Rule and Government of Judgment; but that what he thought, was commonly so Great, so justly and rightly Conceiv'd in it self, that it wanted little or no Correction, and was immediately approv'd by an impartial Judgment at the first sight. Mr. *Dryden* seems to think that *Pericles* is one of his first Plays; but there is no judgment to be form'd on that, since there is good Reason to believe that the greatest part of that Play was not written by him; tho' it is own'd, some part of it certainly was, particularly

the last Act. But tho' the order of Time in which the several Pieces were written be generally uncertain, yet there are Passages in some few of them which seem to fix their Dates. So the *Chorus* in the beginning of the fifth Act of *Henry V.* by a Compliment very handsomly turn'd to the Earl of *Essex*, shews the Play to have been written when that Lord was General for the Queen in *Ireland*: And his Elogy upon Q. *Elizabeth*, and her Successor K. *James*, in the latter end of his *Henry* VIII, is a Proof of that Play's being written after the Accession of the latter of those two Princes to the Crown of *England*. Whatever the particular Times of his Writing were, the People of his Age, who began to grow wonderfully fond of Diversions of this kind, could not but be highly pleas'd to see a *Genius* arise amongst 'em of so pleasurable, so rich a Vein, and so plentifully capable of furnishing their favourite Entertainments. Besides the advantages of his Wit, he was in himself a good-natur'd Man, of great sweetness in his Manners, and a most agreeable Companion; so that it is no wonder if with so many good Qualities he made himself acquainted with the best Conversations of those Times. Queen *Elizabeth* had several of his Plays Acted before her, and without doubt gave him many gracious Marks of her Favour: It is that Maiden Princess plainly, whom he intends by

> A fair Vestal, Throned by the West.
> (*Midsummer Night's Dream*)

And that whole Passage is a Compliment very properly brought in, and very handsomly apply'd to her. She was so well pleas'd with that admirable Character of *Falstaff*, in the two Parts of *Henry* the Fourth, that she commanded him to continue it for one Play more, and to shew him in Love. This is said to be the Occasion of his Writing *The Merry Wives of* Windsor. How well she was obey'd, the Play it self is an admirable Proof. Upon this Occasion it may not be improper to observe, that this Part of *Falstaff* is said to have been written originally under the Name of *Oldcastle*; some of that Family being then remaining, the Queen was pleas'd to command him to alter it; upon which he made use of *Falstaff*. The present Offence was indeed avoided; but I don't know whether the Author may not have been somewhat to blame in his second Choice, since it is certain that Sir *John Falstaff*, who was a Knight of the Garter, and a Lieutenant-General, was a Name of distinguish'd Merit in the Wars in *France* in *Henry* the Fifth's and *Henry* the Sixth's Times. What Grace soever the Queen confer'd upon him, it was not to her only he ow'd the Fortune which the Reputation of his Wit made. He had the Honour to meet with many great and uncommon Marks of Favour and Friendship from the Earl of *Southampton*, famous in the Histories of that Time for his Friendship to the unfortunate Earl of *Essex*. It was to that Noble Lord that he Dedicated his *Venus* and *Adonis*, the only Piece of his Poetry which he ever publish'd himself, tho' many of his Plays were surreptitiously and lamely Printed in his Lifetime. There is one Instance so singular in the Magnificence of this Patron of *Shakespear's*, that if I had not been assur'd that the Story was handed down by Sir *William D'Avenant*, who was probably very well acquainted with his Affairs, I should not have ventur'd to have inserted, that my Lord *Southampton*, at one time, gave him a thousand Pounds, to enable him to go through with a Purchase which he heard he had a mind to. A Bounty very great, and very rare at any time, and almost equal to that profuse Generosity the present Age has shewn to *French* Dancers and *Italian* Eunuchs.

What particular Habitude or Friendships he contracted with private Men, I have not been able to learn, more than that every one who had a true Taste of Merit, and could distinguish Men, had generally a just Value and Esteem for him. His exceeding Candor and good Nature must certainly have inclin'd all the gentler Part of the World to love him, as the power of his Wit oblig'd the Men of the most delicate Knowledge and polite Learning to admire him. Amongst these was the incomparable Mr. *Edmond Spencer*, who speaks of him in his *Tears of the Muses*, not only with the Praises due to a good Poet, but even lamenting his Absence with the tenderness of a Friend. The Passage is in *Thalia's* Complaint for the Decay of Dramatick Poetry, and the Contempt the Stage then lay under, amongst his Miscellaneous Works.

> And he the Man, whom Nature's self had made
> To mock her self, and Truth to imitate
> With kindly Counter under mimick Shade,
> Our pleasant *Willy*, ah! is dead of late:
> With whom all Joy and jolly Merriment
> Is also deaded, and in Dolour drent.

> Instead thereof, scoffing Scurrility
> And scorning Folly with Contempt is crept,
> Rolling in Rhimes of shameless Ribaudry,
> Without Regard or due *Decorum* kept;
> Each idle Wit at will presumes to make,
> And doth the Learned's Task upon him take.

> But that same gentle Spirit, from whose Pen
> Large Streams of Honey and sweet *Nectar* flow,
> Scorning the Boldness of such base-born Men,
> Which dare their Follies forth so rashly throw;
> Doth rather choose to sit in idle Cell,
> Than so himself to Mockery to sell.

I know some People have been of Opinion, that *Shakespear* is not meant by *Willy* in the first *Stanza* of these Verses, because *Spencer's* Death happen'd twenty Years before *Shakespear's*. But, besides that the Character is not applicable to any Man of that time but himself, it is plain by the last *Stanza* that Mr. *Spencer* does not mean that he was then really Dead, but only that he had with-drawn himself from the Publick, or at least with-held his Hand from Writing, out of a disgust he had taken at the then ill taste of the Town, and the mean Condition of the Stage. Mr. *Dryden* was always of Opinion these Verses were meant of *Shakespear*; and 'tis highly probable they were so, since he was three and thirty Years old at *Spencer's* Death; and his Reputation in Poetry must have been great enough before that Time to have deserv'd what is here said of him. His Acquaintance with *Ben Johnson* began with a remarkable piece of Humanity and good Nature; Mr. *Johnson*, who was at that Time altogether unknown to the World, had offer'd one of his Plays to the Players, in order to have it Acted; and the Persons into whose Hands it was put, after having turn'd it carelessly and superciliously over, were just upon returning it to him with an ill-natur'd Answer, that it would be of no service to their Company, when *Shakespear* luckily cast his Eye upon it, and found something so well in it as to engage him first to read it through, and afterwards to recommend Mr. *Johnson* and his Writings to the Publick. After this they were profess'd Friends; tho' I don't know whether the other ever made him an equal return of Gentleness and Sincerity. *Ben* was naturally Proud and Insolent, and in the Days of his Reputation did so far take upon him the Supremacy in Wit, that he could not but look with an evil Eye upon any one that seem'd to stand in Competition with him. And if at times he has affected to commend him, it has always been with some Reserve, insinuating his Uncorrectness, a careless manner of Writing, and want of Judgment; the Praise of seldom altering or blotting out what he writ, which was given him by the Players who were the first Publishers of his Works after his Death, was what *Johnson* could not bear; he thought it impossible, perhaps, for another Man to strike out the greatest Thoughts in the finest Expression, and to reach those Excellencies of Poetry with the Ease of a first Imagination, which himself with infinite Labour and Study could but hardly attain to. *Johnson* was certainly a very good Scholar, and in that had the advantage of *Shakespear*; tho' at the same time I believe it must be allow'd, that what Nature gave the latter, was more than a Ballance for what Books had given the former; and the Judgment of a great Man upon this occasion was, I think, very just and proper. In a Conversation between Sir *John Suckling*, Sir *William D'Avenant*, *Endymion Porter*, Mr. *Hales* of *Eaton*, and *Ben Johnson*; Sir *John Suckling*, who was a profess'd Admirer of *Shakespear*, had undertaken his Defence against *Ben Johnson* with some warmth; Mr. *Hales*, who had sat still for some time, hearing *Ben* frequently reproaching him with the want of Learning, and Ignorance of the Antients, told him at last, *That if Mr.* Shakespear *had not read the Antients, he had likewise not stollen any thing from 'em*; (a Fault the other made no Conscience of) *and that if he would produce any one Topick finely treated by any of them, he would undertake to shew something upon the same Subject at least as well written by* Shakespear. *Johnson* did indeed take a large liberty, even to the transcribing and translating of whole Scenes together; and sometimes, with all Deference to so great a Name as his, not altogether for the advantage of the Authors of whom he borrow'd. And if *Augustus* and *Virgil* were really what he has made 'em in a Scene of his *Poetaster*, they are as odd an Emperor and a Poet as ever met. *Shakespear*, on the other Hand, was beholding to no body farther than the Foundation of the Tale, the Incidents were often his own, and the Writing intirely so. There is one Play of his, indeed, *The Comedy of Errors*, in a great measure taken from the *Menæchmi* of *Plautus*. How that happen'd, I cannot easily Divine, since, as I hinted before, I do not take him to have been Master of *Latin* enough to read it in the Original, and I know of no Translation of *Plautus* so Old as his Time.

As I have not propos'd to my self to enter into a Large and Compleat Criticism upon Mr. *Shakespear's* Works, so I suppose it will neither be expected that I should take notice of the severe Remarks that have been formerly made upon him by Mr. *Rhymer*. I must confess, I can't very well see what could be the Reason of his animadverting with so much Sharpness, upon the Faults of a Man Excellent on most Occasions, and whom all the World ever was and will be inclin'd to have an Esteem and Veneration for. If it was to shew his own Knowledge in the Art of Poetry, besides that there is a Vanity in making that only his Design, I question if there be not many Imperfections as well in those Schemes and Precepts he has given for the Direction of others, as well as in that Sample of Tragedy which he has written to shew the Excellency of his own *Genius*. If he had a Pique against the Man, and wrote on purpose to ruin a Reputation so well establish'd, he has had the Mortification to fail altogether in his Attempt, and to see the World at least as fond of *Shakespear* as of his Critique. But I won't believe a Gentleman, and a good-natur'd Man, capable of the last Intention. Whatever may have been his Meaning, finding fault is certainly the easiest Task of Knowledge, and commonly those Men of good Judgment, who are likewise of good and gentle Dispositions, abandon this ungrateful Province to the Tyranny of Pedants. . . .

The latter Part of his Life was spent, as all Men of good Sense will wish theirs may be, in Ease, Retirement, and the Conversation of his Friends. He had the good Fortune to gather an Estate equal to his Occasion, and, in that, to his Wish; and is said to have spent some Years before his Death at his native *Stratford*. His pleasurable Wit, and good Nature, engag'd him in the Acquaintance, and entitled him to the Friendship of the Gentlemen of the Neighbourhood. Amongst them, it is a Story almost still remember'd in that Country, that he had a particular Intimacy with Mr. *Combe*, an old Gentleman noted thereabouts for his Wealth and Usury: It happen'd, that in a pleasant Conversation amongst their common Friends, Mr. *Combe* told *Shakespear* in a laughing manner, that he fancy'd, he intended to write his Epitaph, if he happen'd to out-live him; and since he could not know what might be said of him when he was dead, he desir'd it might be done immediately: Upon which *Shakespear* gave him these four Verses.

> Ten in the Hundred lies here ingrav'd,
> 'Tis a Hundred to Ten, his Soul is not sav'd:
> If any Man ask, Who lies in this Tomb?
> Oh! ho! quoth the Devil, 'tis my *John-a-Combe*.

But the Sharpness of the Satyr is said to have stung the Man so severely, that he never forgave it.

He Dy'd in the 53d Year of his Age, and was bury'd on the North side of the Chancel, in the Great Church at *Stratford*, where a Monument, as engrav'd in the Plate, is plac'd in the Wall. On his Grave-Stone underneath is,

> Good Friend, for Jesus sake, forbear
> To dig the Dust inclosed here.
> Blest be the Man that spares these Stones,
> And Curst be he that moves my Bones.

He had three Daughters, of which two liv'd to be marry'd; *Judith*, the Elder, to one Mr. *Thomas Quiney*, by whom she had three Sons, who all dy'd without Children; and *Susannah*, who was his Favourite, to Dr. *John Hall*, a Physician of good Reputation in that Country. She left one Child only, a Daughter, who was marry'd first to *Thomas Nash*, Esq; and afterwards to Sir *John Bernard* of *Abbington*, but dy'd likewise without Issue.

## WASHINGTON IRVING
### From "Stratford-on-Avon"
*The Sketch Book of Geoffrey Crayon, Gent.*
1819–20

I had now visited the usual objects of a pilgrim's devotion, but I had a desire to see the old family seat of the Lucys at Charlecot, and to ramble through the park where Shakespeare, in company with some of the roysters of Stratford, committed his youthful offence of deer stealing. In this harebrained exploit we are told that he was taken prisoner, and carried to the keeper's lodge, where he remained all night in doleful captivity. When brought into the presence of Sir Thomas Lucy, his treatment must have been galling and humiliating; for it so wrought upon his spirit as to produce a rough pasquinade, which was affixed to the park gate at Charlecot.[1]

This flagitious attack upon the dignity of the Knight so incensed him, that he applied to a lawyer at Warwick to put the severity of the laws in force against the rhyming deer stalker. Shakespeare did not wait to brave the united puissance of a Knight of the Shire and a country attorney. He forthwith abandoned the pleasant banks of the Avon and his paternal trade; wandered away to London; became a hanger on to the theatres; then an actor; and, finally, wrote for the stage; and thus, through the persecution of Sir Thomas Lucy, Stratford lost an indifferent wool comber and the world gained an immortal poet. He retained, however, for a long time, a sense of the harsh treatment of the Lord of Charlecot, and revenged himself in his writings; but in the sportive way of a good natured mind. Sir Thomas is said to be the original of Justice Shallow, and the satire is slyly fixed upon him by the Justice's armorial bearings, which, like those of the Knight, had white luces[2] in the quarterings.

Various attempts have been made by his biographers to soften and explain away this early transgression of the poet; but I look upon it as one of those thoughtless exploits natural to his situation and turn of mind. Shakespeare, when young, had doubtless all the wildness and irregularity of an ardent, undisciplined, and undirected genius. The poetic temperament has naturally something in it of the vagabond. When left to itself it runs loosely and wildly, and delights in every thing eccentric and licentious. It is often a turn up of a die, in the gambling freaks of fate, whether a natural genius shall turn out a great rogue or a great poet; and had not Shakespeare's mind fortunately taken a literary bias, he might have as daringly transcended all civil, as he has all dramatic laws.

I have little doubt that, in early life, when running, like an unbroken colt, about the neighbourhood of Stratford, he was to be found in the company of all kinds of odd anomalous characters; that he associated with all the mad caps of the place, and was one of those unlucky urchins, at mention of whom old men shake their heads, and predict that they will one day come to the gallows. To him the poaching in Sir Thomas Lucy's park was doubtless like a foray to a Scottish Knight, and struck his eager, and as yet untamed, imagination, as something delightfully adventurous.[3]

The old mansion of Charlecot and its surrounding park still remain in the possession of the Lucy family, and are peculiarly interesting from being connected with this whimsical but eventful circumstance in the scanty history of the bard. As the house stood at little more than three miles distance from Stratford, I resolved to pay it a pedestrian visit, that I might stroll leisurely through some of those scenes from which Shakespeare must have derived his earliest ideas of rural imagery.

The country was yet naked and leafless; but English scenery is always verdant, and the sudden change in the temperature of the weather was surprising in its quickening effects upon the landscape. It was inspiring and animating to witness this first awakening of spring. To feel its warm breath stealing over the senses; to see the moist mellow earth beginning to put forth the green sprout and the tender blade; and the trees and shrubs, in their reviving tints and bursting buds, giving the promise of returning foliage and flower. The cold snow drop, that little borderer on the skirts of winter, was to be seen with its chaste white blossoms in the small gardens before the cottages. The bleating of the new dropt lambs was faintly heard from the fields. The sparrow twittered about the thatched eaves and budding hedges; the robin threw a livelier note into his late querulous wintry strain; and the lark, springing up from the reeking bosom of the meadow, towered away into the bright fleecy cloud, pouring forth torrents of melody. As I watched the little songster, mounting up higher and higher, until his body was a mere speck on the white bosom of the cloud, while the ear was still filled with his music, it called to mind Shakespeare's exquisite little song in *Cymbeline*:

> Hark! hark! the lark at heav'n's gate sings,
>    And Phœbus 'gins arise,
> His steeds to water at those springs,
>    On chaliced flowers that lies.
> And winking mary-buds begin,
>    To ope their golden eyes;

With every thing that pretty bin,
My lady sweet arise!

Indeed the whole country about here is poetic ground: every thing is associated with the idea of Shakespeare. Every old cottage that I saw, I fancied into some resort of his boyhood, where he had acquired his intimate knowledge of rustic life and manners, and heard those legendary tales and wild superstitions which he has woven like witchcraft into his dramas. For in his time, we are told, it was a popular amusement in winter evenings "to sit round the fire, and tell merry tales of errant knights, queens, lovers, lords, ladies, giants, dwarfs, thieves, cheaters, witches, fairies, goblins, and friars."[4]

*Notes*

1. The following is the only stanza extant of this lampoon:—

       A parliament member, a justice of peace,
       At home a poor scarecrow, at London an asse,
       If lowsie is Lucy, as some volke miscalle it,
       Then Lucy is lowsie, whatever befall it.
           He thinks himself great;
           Yet an asse in his state,
       We allow, by his ears, but with asses to mate.
       If Lucy is lowsie, as some volke miscall it,
       Then sing lowise Lucy whatever befall it.

2. The luce is a pike, or jack, and abounds in the Avon about Charlecot.

3. A proof of Shakespeare's random habits and associates in his youthful days, may be found in a traditionary anecdote, picked up at Stratford by the elder Ireland, and mentioned in *Picturesque Views on the Avon.*

   About seven miles from Stratford lies the thirsty little market town of Bedford, famous for its ale. Two societies of the village yeomanry used to meet, under the appellation of the Bedford topers, and to challenge the lovers of good ale of the neighbouring villages, to a contest of drinking. Among others, the people of Stratford were called out to prove the strength of their heads; and in the number of the champions was Shakespeare, who, in spite of the proverb, that "they who drink beer will think beer," was as true to his ale as Falstaff to his sack. The chivalry of Stratford was staggered at the first onset, and sounded a retreat while they had yet legs to carry them off the field. They had scarcely marched a mile, when, their legs failing them, they were forced to lie down under a crab tree, where they passed the night. It is still standing, and goes by the name of Shakespeare's tree.

   In the morning his companions awakened the bard, and proposed returning to Bedford, but he declined, saying he had had enough, having drank with

       Piping Pebworth, Dancing Marston,
       Haunted Hillbro', Hungry Grafton,
       Dudging Exhall, Papist Wicksford,
       Beggarly Broom, and Drunken Bedford.

   "The villages here alluded to," say Ireland, "still bear the epithets thus given them; the people of Pebworth are still famed for their skill on the pipe and tabor: Hillborough is now called Haunted Hillborough: and Grafton is famous for the poverty of its soil."

4. Scot, in his *Discoverie of Witchcraft*, enumerates a host of these fireside fancies. "And they have so fraid us with bull-beggers, spirits, witches, urchins, elves, hags, fairies, satyrs, pans, faunes, syrens, kit with the can'sticke, tritons, centaurs, dwarfes, giantes, imps, calcars, conjurors, nymphes, changelings, incubus, Robin-good-fellow, the spoorne, the mare, the man in the oke, the hell-waine, the fier drake, the puckle, Tom Thombe, hobgoblins, Tom Tumbler, boneless, and such other bugs, that we were afraid of our own shadowes."

## WALTER BAGEHOT
### From "Shakespeare—the Individual" (1853)
*Collected Works*, ed. Norman St. John-Stevas
1965, Volume 1, pp. 173–214

The greatest of English poets, it is often said, is but a name. 'No letter of his writing, no record of his conversation, no character of him drawn with any fulness by a contemporary,' have been extracted by antiquaries from the piles of rubbish which they have sifted. Yet of no person is there a clearer picture in the popular fancy. You seem to have known Shakespeare—to have seen Shakespeare—to have been friends with Shakespeare. We would attempt a slight delineation of the popular idea which has been formed, not from loose tradition or remote research; not from what some one says some one else said that the poet said, but from data, which are at least undoubted, from the sure testimony of his certain works.

Some extreme sceptics, we know, doubt whether it is possible to deduce anything as to an author's character from his works. Yet surely people do not keep a tame steam-engine to write their books; and if those books were really written by a man, he must have been a man who could write them; he must have had the thoughts which they express, have acquired the knowledge they contain, have possessed the style in which we read them. The difficulty is a defect of the critics. A person who knows nothing of an author he has read, will not know much of an author whom he has seen.

First of all, it may be said, that Shakespeare's works could only be produced by a first-rate imagination working on a first-rate experience. It is often difficult to make out whether the author of a poetic creation is drawing from fancy, or drawing from experience; but for art on a certain scale, the two must concur. Out of nothing, nothing can be created. Some plastic power is required, however great may be the material. And when such a work as *Hamlet* or *Othello*, still more, when both of them and others not unequal have been created by a single mind, it may be fairly said, that not only a great imagination, but a full conversancy with the world was necessary to their production. The whole powers of man under the most favourable circumstances, are not too great for such an effort. We may assume that Shakespeare had a great experience. . . .

In spiritedness, the style of Shakespeare is very like to that of Scott. The description of a charge of cavalry in Scott reads . . . as if it was written on horseback. A play by Shakespeare reads as if it were written in a playhouse. The great critics assure you, that a theatrical audience must be kept awake, but Shakespeare knew this of his own knowledge. When you read him you feel a sensation of motion, a conviction that there is something 'up,' a notion that not only is something being talked about, but also that something is being done. We do not imagine that Shakespeare owed this quality to his being a player, but rather that he became a player because he possessed this quality of mind. For after, and not withstanding everything which has, or may be said against the theatrical profession, it certainly does require from those who pursue it a certain quickness and liveliness of mind. Mimics are commonly an elastic sort of persons, and it takes a little levity of disposition to enact even the 'heavy fathers.' If a boy joins a company of strolling players, you may be sure that he is not a 'good boy;' he may be a trifle foolish, or a thought romantic, but certainly he is not slow. And this was in truth the case with Shakespeare. They say, too, that in the beginning he was a first-rate link-boy; and the tradition is affecting, though we fear it is not quite certain. Anyhow you feel about Shakespeare that he could have been a link-boy. In the same way you feel he may have been a player. You are sure at once that he could not have followed any sedentary kind of life. But wheresoever there was anything *acted* in earnest or in jest, by way of mock representation or by way of serious reality, there he found matter for his mind. If anybody could have any doubt about the liveliness of Shakespeare, let them consider the character of Falstaff. When a man has created *that* without a capacity for laughter, then a blind man may succeed in describing colours. Intense animal spirits are the single sentiment (if they be a sentiment) of the entire character. If most men were to save up all the gaiety of their whole lives, it would come about to the gaiety of one speech in Falstaff. A morose man might have amassed many jokes, might have observed many details of jovial society, might have conceived a Sir John, marked by rotundity of body, but could hardly have imagined what we call his rotundity of mind. We mean that the animal spirits of Falstaff give him an easy, vague, diffusive sagacity which is peculiar to him. A morose man, Iago, for example, may know anything, and is apt to know a good deal, but what he knows is generally all in corners. He knows number 1, number 2, number 3, and so on, but there is not anything continuous or smooth, or fluent in his knowledge. Persons conversant with the works of Hazlitt will know in a minute what we mean. Everything which he observed he seemed to observe from a certain soreness of mind; he looked at people because they offended him; he had the same vivid notion of them that a man has of objects which grate on a wound in his body. But there is nothing at all of this in Falstaff; on the contrary, everything pleases him, and everything is food for a joke. Cheerfulness and prosperity give an easy abounding sagacity of mind which nothing else does give. Prosperous people bound easily over all the surface of things which their lives present to them; very likely they keep to the surface; there are things beneath or above to which they may not penetrate or attain, but what is on any part of the surface, that they know well. 'Lift not the painted veil which those who live call life,' and they do not lift it. What is sublime or awful above, what is 'sightless and drear' beneath,—these they may not dream of. Nor is any one piece or corner of life so well impressed on them as on minds less happily constituted. It is only people who have had a tooth out, that really know the dentist's waiting-room. Yet such people, for the time at least, know nothing but that and their tooth. The easy and sympathising friend who accompanies them knows everything; hints gently at the contents of the *Times*, and would cheer you with Lord Palmerston's replies. So, on a greater scale, the man of painful experience knows but too well what has hurt him, and where and why, but the happy have a vague and rounded view of the round world, and such was the knowledge of Falstaff.

It is to be observed that these high spirits are not a mere excrescence or superficial point in an experiencing nature; on the contrary, they seem to be essential, if not to its idea or existence, at least to its exercise and employment. How are you to know people without talking to them, but how are you to talk to them without tiring yourself? A common man is exhausted in half an hour; Scott or Shakespeare could have gone on for a whole day. This is, perhaps, peculiarly necessary for a painter of English life. The basis of our national character seems to be a certain energetic humour, which may be found in full vigour in old Chaucer's time, and in great perfection in at least one of the popular writers of this age, and which is, perhaps, most easily described by the name of our greatest painter—Hogarth. It is amusing to see how entirely the efforts of critics and artists

fail to naturalise in England any other sort of painting. Their efforts are fruitless; for the people painted are not English people: they may be Italians, or Greeks, or Jews, but it is quite certain that they are foreigners. We should not fancy that modern art ought to resemble the Mediæval. So long as artists attempt the same class of paintings as Raphael, they will not only be inferior to Raphael, but they will never please, as they might please, the English people. What we want is what Hogarth gave us—a representation of ourselves. It may be that we are wrong, that we ought to prefer something of the old world, some scene in Rome or Athens, some tale from Carmel or Jerusalem; but, after all, we do not. These places are, we think, abroad, and had their greatness in former times; we wish a copy of what now exists, and of what we have seen. London we know, and Manchester we know, but where are all these? It is the same with literature, Milton excepted, and even Milton can hardly be called a popular writer: all great English writers describe English people, and in describing them, they give, as they must give, a large comic element; and, speaking generally, this is scarcely possible, except in the case of cheerful and easy-living men. There is, no doubt, a biting satire, like that of Swift, which has for its essence misanthropy. There is the mockery of Voltaire, which is based on intellectual contempt; but this is not our English humour,—it is not that of Shakespeare and Falstaff; ours is the humour of a man who laughs when he speaks, of flowing enjoyment, of an experiencing nature.

Yet it would be a great error if we gave anything like an exclusive prominence to this aspect of Shakespeare. Thus he appeared to those around him,—in some degree they knew that he was a cheerful, and humorous, and happy man; but of his higher gift they knew less than we. A great painter of men must (as has been said) have a faculty of conversing, but he must also have a capacity for solitude. There is much of mankind that a man can only learn from himself. Behind every man's external life, which he leads in company, there is another which he leads alone, and which he carries with him apart. We see but one aspect of our neighbour, as we see but one side of the moon; in either case there is also a dark half, which is unknown to us. We all come down to dinner, but each has a room to himself. And if we would study the internal lives of others, it seems essential that we should begin with our own. If we study this our *datum*, if we attain to see and feel how this influences and evolves itself in our social and (so to say) public life, then it is possible that we may find in the lives of others the same or analogous features; and if we do not, then at least we may suspect that those who want them are deficient likewise in the secret agencies which we feel produce them in ourselves. The metaphysicians assert, that people originally picked up the idea of the existence of other people in this way. It is orthodox doctrine that a baby says: 'I have a mouth, mamma has a mouth: therefore I'm the same species as mamma. I have a nose, papa has a nose, therefore papa is the same genus as me.' But whether or not this ingenious idea really does or does not represent the actual process by which we originally obtain an acquaintance with the existence of minds analogous to our own, it gives unquestionably the process by which we obtain our notion of that part of those minds which they never exhibit consciously to others, and which only becomes predominant in secrecy and solitude and to themselves. . . .

In another point also Shakespeare, as he was, must be carefully contrasted with the estimate that would be formed of him from such delineations as that of Falstaff, and that was doubtless frequently made by casual though only by casual frequenters of the Mermaid. It has been said that the mind of

Shakespeare contained within it the mind of Scott; it remains to be observed that it contained also the mind of Keats. For, beside the delineation of human life, and beside also the delineation of nature, there remains also for the poet a third subject—the delineation of *fancies*. Of course, these, be they what they may, are like to, and were originally borrowed either from man or from nature—from one or from both together. We know but two things in the simple way of direct experience, and whatever else we know, must be in some mode or manner compacted out of them. Yet 'books are a substantial world, both pure and good,' and so are fancies too. In all countries men have devised to themselves a whole series of half-divine creations—mythologies Greek and Roman, fairies, angels; beings who may be, for aught we know, but with whom, in the meantime, we can attain to no conversation. The most known of these mythologies are the Greek, and what is, we suppose, the second epoch of the Gothic, the fairies; and it so happens that Shakespeare has dealt with them both and in a remarkable manner. We are not, indeed, of those critics who profess simple and unqualified admiration for the poem of *Venus and Adonis*. It seems intrinsically, as we know it from external testimony to have been, a juvenile production, written when Shakespeare's nature might be well expected to be crude and unripened. Power is shown, and power of a remarkable kind; but it is not displayed in a manner that will please or does please the mass of men. In spite of the name of its author, the poem has never been popular—and surely this is sufficient. Nevertheless it is remarkable as a literary exercise, and as a treatment of a singular though unpleasant subject.—The fanciful class of poems differ from others in being laid, so far as their scene goes, in a perfectly unseen world. The type of such productions is Keats's *Endymion*. We mean that it is the type, not as giving the abstract perfection of this sort of art, but because it shows and embodies both its excellencies and defects in a very marked and prominent manner. In that poem there are no passions and no actions, there is no art and no life, but there is beauty, and that is meant to be enough, and to a reader of one-and-twenty it is enough and more. What are exploits or speeches? What is Cæsar or Coriolanus? What is a tragedy like *Lear*, or a real view of human life in any kind whatever, to people who do not know and do not care what human life is? In early youth it is, perhaps, not true that the passions, taken generally, are particularly violent, or that the imagination is in any remarkable degree powerful; but it is certain that the fancy (which though it be, in the last resort, but a weak stroke of that same faculty, which, when it strikes hard, we call imagination, may yet for this purpose be looked on as distinct) is particularly wakeful, and that the gentler species of passions are more absurd than they are afterwards. And the literature of this period of human life runs naturally away from the real world; away from the less ideal portion of it, from stocks and stones, and aunts and uncles, and rests on mere half-embodied sentiments, which in the hands of great poets assume a kind of semipersonality, and are, to the distinction between things and persons, 'as moonlight unto sunlight, and as water unto wine.' The 'sonnets' of Shakespeare belong exactly to the same school of poetry. They are not the sort of verses to take any particular hold upon the mind permanently and for ever, but at a certain period they take too much. For a young man to read in the spring of the year among green fields and in gentle air, they are the ideal. As first of April poetry they are perfect. . . .

Can it be made out what were Shakespeare's political views? We think it certainly can, and that without difficulty. From the English historical plays, it distinctly appears that he

accepted, like everybody then, the Constitution of his country. His lot was not cast in an age of political controversy, nor of reform. What was, was from of old. The Wars of the Roses had made it very evident how much room there was for the evils incident to an hereditary monarchy, for instance, those of a controverted succession, and the evils incident to an aristocracy, as want of public spirit and audacious selfishness, to arise and continue within the realm of England. Yet they had not repelled, and had barely disconcerted our conservative ancestors. They had not become Jacobins; they did not concur—and history, except in Shakespeare, hardly does justice to them—in Jack Cade's notion that the laws should come out of his mouth, or that the commonwealth was to be reformed by interlocutors in this scene.

> *George:* I tell thee, Jack Cade, the clothier means to dress the Commonwealth, and turn it, and set a new nap upon it.
> *John:* So he had need, for 'tis threadbare. Well, I say it was never merry world in England since gentlemen came up.
> *Geo.:* O miserable age! Virtue is not regarded in handycraftsmen.
> *John:* The nobility think scorn to go in leathern aprons.
> *Geo.:* Nay more: the king's council are no good workmen.
> *John:* True; and yet it is said, labour in thy vocation; which is as much as to say, as let the magistrates be labouring men, and therefore should we be magistrates.
> *Geo.:* Thou has hit it, for there is no better sign of a brave mind than a hard hand.
> *John:* I see them! I see them!

The English people did see them, and know them, and therefore have rejected them. An audience which, *bona fide*, entered into the merit of this scene, would never believe in everybody's suffrage. They would know that there is such a thing as nonsense, and when a man has once attained to that deep conception, you may be sure of him ever after. And though it would be absurd to say that Shakespeare originated this idea, or that the disbelief in simple democracy is owing to his teaching or suggestions, yet it may, nevertheless, be truly said, that he shared in the peculiar knowledge of men,—and also possessed the peculiar constitution of mind—which engender this effect. The author of *Coriolanus* never believed in a mob, and did something towards preventing anybody else from doing so. But this political idea was not exactly the strongest in Shakespeare's mind. We think he had two others stronger, or as strong. First, the feeling of loyalty to the ancient polity of this country—not because it was good, but because it existed. In his time, people no more thought of the origin of the monarchy than they did of the origin of the Mendip Hills. The one had always been there, and so had the other. God (such was the common notion) had made both, and one as much as the other. Everywhere, in that age, the common modes of political speech assumed the existence of certain utterly national institutions, and would have been worthless and nonsensical except on that assumption. This national habit appears as it ought to appear in our national dramatist. A great divine tells us that the Thirty-Nine Articles are 'forms of thought;' inevitable conditions of the religious understanding; in politics, 'kings, lords, and commons' are, no doubt, 'forms of thought,' to the great majority of Englishmen; in these, they live, and beyond these, they never move. You can't reason on the removal (such is the notion) of the English Channel, nor St. George's Channel, nor can you of the English Constitution in like manner. It is to most of us, and to the happiest of us, a thing immutable, and such, no doubt, it was to Shakespeare, which, if any one would have proved, let him refer at random to any page of the historical English plays.

The second peculiar tenet which we ascribe to his political creed is a disbelief in the middle classes. We fear he had no opinion of traders. In this age, we know, it is held that the keeping of a shop is equivalent to a political education. Occasionally, in country villages, where the trader sells everything, he is thought to know nothing, and has no vote; but in a town where he is a householder (as, indeed, he is in the country), and sells only one thing—there we assume that he knows everything. And this assumption is in the opinion of some observers confirmed by the fact. Sir Walter Scott used to relate, that when, after a trip to London, he returned to Tweedside, he always found the people in that district knew more of politics than the Cabinet. And so it is with the mercantile community in modern times. If you are a Chancellor of the Exchequer, it is possible that you may be acquainted with finance; but if you sell Figs it is certain that you will. Now we nowhere find this laid down in Shakespeare. On the contrary, you will generally find that when a 'citizen' is mentioned, he generally does or says something absurd. Shakespeare had a clear perception that it is possible to bribe a class as well as an individual, and that personal obscurity is but an insecure guarantee for political disinterestedness.

> Moreover, he hath left you all his walks,
> His private arbours and new-planted orchards
> On this side Tyber; he hath left them you,
> And to your heirs for ever: common pleasures,
> To walk abroad and recreate yourselves.
> Here was a Cæsar! when comes such another?

He everywhere speaks in praise of a tempered and ordered and qualified polity, in which the pecuniary classes have a certain influence, but no more, and shows in every page a keen sensibility to the large views, and high-souled energies, the gentle refinements and disinterested desires in which those classes are likely to be especially deficient. He is particularly the poet of personal nobility, though, throughout his writings, there is a sense of freedom, just as Milton is the poet of freedom, though with an underlying reference to personal nobility; indeed, we might well expect our two poets to combine the appreciation of a rude and generous liberty, with that of a delicate and refined nobleness, since it is the union of these two elements that characterises our society and their experience.

There are two things—good-tempered sense and ill-tempered sense. In our remarks on the character of Falstaff, we hope we have made it very clear, that Shakespeare had the former; we think it nearly as certain that he possessed the latter also. An instance of this might be taken from that contempt for the perspicacity of the *bourgeoisie* which we have just been mentioning. It is within the limits of what may be called malevolent sense, to take extreme and habitual pleasure in remarking the foolish opinions, the narrow notions, and fallacious deductions which seem to cling to the pompous and prosperous man of business. Ask him his opinion of the currency question, and he puts 'bill' and 'bullion' together in a sentence, and he does not seem to care what he puts between them. But a more proper instance of (what has an odd sound), the malevolence of Shakespeare is to be found in the play of *Measure for Measure*. We agree with Hazlitt, that this play seems to be written, perhaps more than any other, *con amore*, and with a relish, and this seems to be the reason why, notwithstanding the unpleasant nature of its plot, and the

absence of any very attractive character, it is yet one of the plays which take hold on the mind most easily and most powerfully. Now the entire character of Angelo, which is the expressive feature of the piece, is nothing but a successful embodiment of the pleasure, the malevolent pleasure, which a warm-blooded and expansive man takes in watching the rare, the dangerous and inanimate excesses of the constrained and cold-blooded. One seems to see Shakespeare, with his bright eyes and his large lips and buoyant face, watching with a pleasant excitement the excesses of his thin-lipped and calculating creation, as though they were the excesses of a real person. It is the complete picture of a natural hypocrite, who does not consciously disguise strong impulses, but whose very passions seem of their own accord to have disguised themselves and retreated into the recesses of the character, yet only to recur even more dangerously when their proper period is expired, when the will is cheated into security by their absence, and the world (and, it may be, the 'judicious person' himself) is impressed with a sure reliance in his chilling and remarkable rectitude.

It has, we believe, been doubted whether Shakespeare was a man much conversant with the intimate society of women. Of course no one denies that he possessed a great knowledge of them—a capital acquaintance with their excellencies, faults, and foibles; but it has been thought that this was the result rather of imagination than of society, of creative fancy rather than of perceptive experience. Now that Shakespeare possessed, among other singular qualities, a remarkable imaginative knowledge of women, is quite certain, for he was acquainted with the soliloquies of women. A woman we suppose, like a man, must be alone, in order to speak a soliloquy. After the greatest possible intimacy and experience, it must still be imagination, or fancy at least, which tells any man what a woman thinks of herself and to herself. There will still—get as near the limits of confidence or observation as you can—be a space which must be filled up from other means. Men can only divine the truth—reserve, indeed, is a part of its charm. Seeing, therefore, that Shakespeare had done what necessarily and certainly must be done without experience, we were in some doubt whether he might not have dispensed with it altogether. A grave reviewer cannot know these things. We thought indeed of reasoning that since the delineations of women in Shakespeare were admitted to be first-rate, it should follow,—at least there was a fair presumption,—that no means or aid had been wanting to their production, and that consequently we ought, in the absence of distinct evidence, to assume that personal intimacy as well as solitary imagination had been concerned in their production. And we meant to cite the 'questions about Octavia,' which Lord Byron, who thought he had the means of knowing, declared to be 'woman all over.'

But all doubt was removed and all conjecture set to rest by the coming in of an ably-dressed friend from the external world, who mentioned that the language of Shakespeare's women was essentially female language; that there were certain points and peculiarities in the English of cultivated English women, which made it a language of itself, which must be heard familiarly in order to be known. And he added, 'except a greater use of words of Latin derivation, as was natural in an age when ladies received a learned education, a few words not now proper, a few conceits that were the fashion of the time, and there is the very same English in the women's speeches in Shakespeare.' He quoted—

> Think not I love him, though I ask for him;
> 'Tis but a peevish boy:—yet he talks well;—
> But what care I for words? yet words do well,

When he that speaks them pleases those that hear.
It is a pretty youth:—not very pretty:—
But, sure, he's proud; and yet his pride becomes him;
He'll make a proper man: The best thing in him
Is his complexion; and faster than his tongue
Did make offence, his eye did heal it up.
He is not very tall; yet for his years he's tall:
His leg is but so so: and yet 'tis well.
There was a pretty redness in his lip;
A little riper and more lusty red
Than that mix'd in his cheek; 'twas just the difference
Betwixt the constant red, and mingled damask.
There be some women, Silvius, had they mark'd him
In parcels as I did, would have gone near
To fall in love with him: but, for my part,
I love him not, nor hate him not; and yet
I have more cause to hate him than to love him:
For what had he to do to chide at me?
He said, my eyes were black, and my hair black,
And, now I am remember'd, scorn'd at me:
I marvel, why I answer'd not again:
But that's all one;

and the passage of Perdita's . . . about the daffodils that—

　　take
The winds of March with beauty; violets dim,
But sweeter than the lids of Juno's eyes,
Or Cytherea's breath;

and said that these were conclusive. But we have not, ourselves, heard young ladies converse in that manner.

Perhaps it is in his power of delineating women, that Shakespeare contrasts most strikingly with the greatest master of the art of dialogue in antiquity—we mean Plato. It will, no doubt, be said that the delineation of women did not fall within Plato's plan; that men's life was in that age so separate and predominant that it could be delineated by itself and apart; and, no doubt, these remarks are very true. But what led Plato to form that plan? What led him to select that peculiar argumentative aspect of life, in which the masculine element is in so high a degree superior? We believe that he did it because he felt that he could paint that kind of scene much better than he could paint any other. If a person will consider the sort of conversation that was held in the cool summer morning, when Socrates was knocked up early to talk definitions and philosophy with Protagoras, he will feel, not only that women would fancy such dialogues to be certainly stupid, and very possibly to be without meaning, but also that the side of character which is there presented, is one from which not only the feminine but even the epicene element is nearly if not perfectly excluded. It is the intellect surveying and delineating intellectual characteristics. We have a dialogue of thinking faculties; the character of every man is delineated by showing us, not his mode of action or feeling, but his mode of thinking, alone and by itself. The pure mind, purged of all passion and affection, strives to view and describe others in like manner; and the singularity is, that the likenesses so taken are so good,—that the accurate copying of the merely intellectual effects and indications of character gives so true and so firm an impression of the whole character,—that a daguerreo-type of the mind should almost seem to be a delineation of the life. But though in the hand of a consummate artist, such a way of representation may in some sense succeed in the case of men, it would certainly seem sure to fail in the case of women. The mere intellect of a woman is a mere nothing. It originates nothing, it transmits nothing, it retains nothing; it has little life of its own, and, therefore, it can hardly be expected to attain any vigour. Of the lofty Platonic world of ideas, which the soul in the old doctrine was to arrive at by pure and continuous reasoning, women were never expected to know anything. Plato (though Mr. Grote denies that he was a practical man) was much too practical for that; he reserved his teaching for people whose belief was regulated and induced in some measure by abstract investigations; who had an interest in the pure and (as it were) geometrical truth itself; who had an intellectual character (apart from and accessory to their other character) capable of being viewed as a large and substantial existence. Shakespeare's being, like a woman's, worked as a whole. He was capable of intellectual abstractedness, but commonly he was touched with the sense of earth. One thinks of him as firmly set on our coarse world of common clay, but from it he could paint the moving essence of thoughtful feeling—which is the best refinement of the best women. Imogen and Juliet would have thought little of the conversation of Gorgias.

On few subjects has more nonsense been written than on the learning of Shakespeare. In former times, the established tenet was, that he was acquainted with the entire range of the Greek and Latin classics, and familiarly resorted to Sophocles and Æschylus as guides and models. This creed reposed not so much on any painful or elaborate criticism of Shakespeare's plays, as on one of the *à priori* assumptions permitted to the indolence of the wise old world. It was then considered clear, by all critics, that no one could write good English, who could not also write bad Latin. Questioning scepticism has rejected this axiom, and refuted with contemptuous facility the slight attempt which had been made to verify this case of it from the evidence of the plays themselves. But the new school, not content with showing that Shakespeare was no formed or elaborate scholar, propounded the idea that he was quite ignorant, just as Mr. Croker 'demonstrates' that Napoleon Bonaparte could scarcely write or read. The answer is that Shakespeare wrote his plays, and that those plays show not only a very powerful, but also a very cultivated mind. A hard student Shakespeare was not, yet he was a happy and pleased reader of interesting books. He was a natural reader; when a book was dull, he put it down, when it looked fascinating, he took it up and the consequence is, that he remembered and mastered what he read. Lively books, read with lively interest, leave strong and living recollections; the instructors, no doubt, say that they ought not to do so, and inculcate the necessity of dry reading. Yet the good sense of a busy public has practically discovered that what is read easily is recollected easily, and what is read with difficulty is remembered with more. It is certain that Shakespeare read the novels of his time, for he has founded on them the stories of his plays; he read Plutarch, for his words still live in the dialogue of the 'proud Roman' plays; and it is remarkable that Montaigne is the only philosopher that Shakespeare can be proved to have read, because, he deals more than any other philosopher with the first impressions of things which exist. On the other hand, it may be doubted if Shakespeare would have perused his commentators. . . . (W)hat would he have thought of the following speculations of an anonymous individual, whose notes have been recently published in a fine octavo by Mr. Collier, and, according to the periodical essayists, 'contribute valuable suggestions to the illustration of the immortal bard'?

THE TWO GENTLEMEN OF VERONA.
ACT I. SCENE I.
P. 92. The reading of the subsequent line has hitherto been

'Tis true; for you are over boots in love;
but the manuscript corrector of the Folio, 1632, has
changed it to

'Tis true; *but* you are over boots in love,

which seems more consistent with the course of the
dialogue; for Proteus, remarking that Leander had
been 'more than over shoes in love' with Hero,
Valentine answers, that Proteus was even more
deeply in love than Leander. Proteus observes of the
fable of Hero and Leander—

That's a deep story of a deeper love,
*For* he was more than over shoes in love.

Valentine retorts—

'Tis true; *but* you are over boots in love.

*For* instead of *but* was perhaps caught by the
compositor from the preceding line.

It is difficult to fancy Shakespeare perusing a volume of
such annotations, though we allow that we admire them
ourselves. As to the controversy on his school learning, we
have only to say, that though the alleged imitations of the
Greek tragedians are mere nonsense, yet there is clear evidence
that Shakespeare received the ordinary grammar school education of his time, and that he had derived from the pain and
suffering of several years, not exactly an acquaintance with
Greek or Latin, but like Eton boys a firm conviction that there
are such languages.

Another controversy has been raised as to whether
Shakespeare was religious. In the old editions it is commonly
enough laid down, that, when writing his plays, he had no
desire to fill the Globe Theatre, but that his intentions were of
the following description. 'In this play,' *Cymbeline,* 'Shakespeare has strongly depicted the frailties of our nature, and the
effect of vicious passions on the human mind. In the fate of the
Queen we behold the worst of perfidy justly sacrificed by the
arts she had, with unnatural ambition, prepared for others; and
in reviewing her death and that of Cloten, we may easily call to
mind the words of Scripture, &c.' And of *King Lear* it is
observed, with great confidence, that Shakespeare, '*no doubt,*
intended to mark particularly the afflicting character of
children's ingratitude to their parents, and the conduct of
Goneril and Regan to each other, *especially* in the former's
poisoning the latter, and laying hands on *herself,* we are taught
that those who want gratitude towards their parents (who gave
them their being, fed them, nurtured them to *man's* estate) will
not scruple to commit more barbarous crimes, and easily to
forget that, by destroying their body, they destroy their soul
also.' And Dr. Ulrici, a very learned and illegible writer, has
discovered that in every one of his plays Shakespeare had in
view the inculcation of the peculiar sentiments and doctrines of
the Christian religion, and considers the *Midsummer Night's
Dream* to be a specimen of the lay or amateur sermon. This is
what Dr. Ulrici thinks of Shakespeare; but what would
Shakespeare have thought of Dr. Ulrici? We believe that '*Via
goodman dull,*' is nearly the remark which the learned
professor would have received from the poet to whom his very
careful treatise is devoted. And yet, without prying into the
Teutonic mysteries, a gentleman of missionary aptitudes might
be tempted to remark, that in many points Shakespeare is
qualified to administer a rebuke to people of the prevalent
religion. Meeting a certain religionist is like striking the corner
of a wall. He is possessed of a firm and rigid persuasion that you
must leave off this and that, stop, cry, be anxious, be advised,
and, above all things, refrain from doing what you like, for
nothing is so bad for any one as that. And in quite another
quarter of the religious hemisphere, we occasionally encounter
gentlemen, who have most likely studied at the feet of Dr.

Ulrici, or at least of an equivalent Gamaliel, and who, when
we, or such as we, speaking the language of mortality, remark
of a pleasing friend, 'Nice fellow, so and so! Good fellow as
ever lived!' reply sternly, upon an unsuspecting reviewer,
with—'Sir, is he an *earnest* man?' To which, in some cases, we
are unable to return a sufficient answer. Yet Shakespeare
differing, in that respect at least, from the disciples of Carlyle,
had, we suspect, an objection to grim people, and we fear
would have liked the society of Mercutio better than that of a
dreary divine, and preferred Ophelia or '*that* Juliet' to a female
philanthropist of sinewy aspect. And, seriously, if this world is
not all evil, he who has understood and painted it best must
probably have some good. If the underlying and almighty
essence of this world be good, then it is likely that the writer
who most deeply approached to that essence, will be himself
good. There is a religion of week-days as well as of Sundays, of
'cakes and ale,' as well as of pews and altar cloths. This
England lay before Shakespeare as it lies before us all, with its
green fields, and its long hedgerows, and its many trees, and its
great towns, and its endless hamlets, and its motley society, and
its long history, and its bold exploits, and its gathering power;
and he saw that they were good. To him, perhaps, more than to
any one else, has it been given to see, that they were a great
unity, a great religious object; that if you could only descend to
the inner life, to the deep things, to the secret principles of its
noble vigour, to the essence of character, to what we know of
Hamlet, and seem to fancy of Ophelia, we might, so far as we
are capable of so doing, understand the nature which God has
made. Let us, then, think of him, not as a teacher of dry
dogmas, or a sayer of hard sayings, but as

A priest to us all,
Of the wonder and bloom of the world—

a teacher of the hearts of men and women; one from whom
may be learned something of that inmost principle that ever
modulates

with murmurs of the air,
And motions of the forest and the sea,
And voice of living beings, and woven hymns
Of night and day and the deep heart of man.

We must pause, lest our readers reject us, as the Bishop of
Durham the poor curate, because he was 'mystical and
confused.'

Yet it must be allowed that Shakespeare was worldly, and
the proof of it is, that he succeeded in the world. Possibly this is
the point on which we are most richly indebted to tradition.
We see generally indeed in Shakespeare's works the popular
author, the successful dramatist; there is a life and play in his
writings rarely to be found, except in those who have had
habitual good luck, and who, by the tact of experience, feel the
minds of their readers at every word, like a good rider feels the
mouth of his horse. But it would have been difficult quite to
make out whether the profits so accruing had been profitably
invested—whether the genius to create such illusions was
accompanied with the care and judgment necessary to put out
their proceeds properly in actual life. We could only have said,
that there was a general impression of entire calmness and
equability in his principal works, rarely to be found where there
is much pain, which usually makes gaps in the work and
dislocates the balance of the mind. But happily here, and here
almost alone, we are on sure historical ground. The reverential
nature of Englishmen has carefully preserved what they
thought the great excellence of their poet—that he made a
fortune.[1] It is certain that Shakespeare was proprietor of the
Globe Theatre—that he made money there, and invested the
same in land at Stratford-on-the-Avon, and probably no

circumstance in his life ever gave him so much pleasure. It was a great thing that he, the son of the wool-comber, the poacher, the good-for-nothing, the vagabond (for so we fear the phrase went in Shakespeare's youth), should return upon the old scene a substantial man, a person of capital, a freeholder, a gentleman to be respected, and over whom even a burgess could not affect the least superiority. The great pleasure in life is doing what people say you cannot do. Why did Mr. Disraeli take the duties of the Exchequer with so much relish? Because people said he was a novelist, and *ad captandum* man, and, *monstrum horrendum!* a Jew, that could not add up. No doubt it pleased his inmost soul to do the work of the red-tape people better than those who could do nothing else. And so with Shakespeare: it pleased him to be respected by those whom he had respected with boyish reverence, but who had rejected the imaginative man—on their own ground and in their own subject, by the only title which they would regard—in a word, as a monied man. We seem to see him eyeing the burgesses with good-humored fellowship and genial (though suppressed and half unconscious) contempt, drawing out their old stories, and acquiescing in their foolish notions, with everything in his head and easy sayings upon his tongue,—a full mind and a deep dark eye, that played upon an easy scene—now in fanciful solitude, now, in cheerful society; now occupied with deep thoughts, now and equally so, with trivial recreations, forgetting the dramatist in the man of substance, and the poet in the happy companion; beloved and even respected, with a hope for every one, and a smile for all.

### Notes

1. The only antiquarian thing which can be fairly called an anecdote of Shakespeare is, that Mrs. Alleyne, a shrewd woman in those times, and married to Mr. Alleyne, the founder of Dulwich Hospital, was one day, in the absence of her husband, applied to on some matter by a player who gave a reference to Mr. Hemminge (the 'notorious' Mr. Hemminge the commentators say) and to Mr. Shakespeare of the Globe, and that the latter, when referred to, said, 'Yes, certainly, he knew him, and he was a rascal and good-for-nothing.' The proper speech of a substantial man, such as it is worth while to give a reference to.

## NATHANIEL HAWTHORNE
### From "Recollections of a Gifted Woman"
*Our Old Home*
1863

The spire of Shakespeare's church—the Church of the Holy Trinity—begins to show itself among the trees at a little distance from Stratford. Next we see the shabby old dwellings, intermixed with mean-looking houses of modern date; and the streets being quite level, you are struck and surprised by nothing so much as the tameness of the general scene, as if Shakespeare's genius were vivid enough to have wrought pictorial splendors in the town where he was born. Here and there, however, a queer edifice meets your eye, endowed with the individuality that belongs only to the domestic architecture of times gone by; the house seems to have grown out of some odd quality in its inhabitant, as a sea-shell is moulded from within by the character of its inmate; and having been built in a strange fashion, generations ago, it has ever since been growing stranger and quainter, as old humorists are apt to do. Here, too (as so often impressed me in decayed English towns), there appeared to be a greater abundance of aged people wearing small-clothes and leaning on sticks than

you could assemble on our side of the water by sounding a trumpet and proclaiming a reward for the most venerable. I tried to account for this phenomenon by several theories: as for example, that our new towns are unwholesome for age and kill it off unseasonably; or that our old men have a subtile sense of fitness, and die of their own accord rather than live in an unseemly contrast with youth and novelty: but the secret may be, after all, that hair-dyes, false teeth, modern arts of dress, and contrivances of a skin-deep youthfulness, have not crept into these antiquated English towns, and so people grow old without the weary necessity of seeming younger than they are.

After wandering through two or three streets, I found my way to Shakespeare's birthplace, which is almost a smaller and humbler house than any description can prepare the visitor to expect; so inevitably does an august inhabitant make his abode palatial to our imaginations, receiving his guests, indeed, in a castle in the air, until we unwisely insist on meeting him among the sordid lanes and alleys of lower earth. The portion of the edifice with which Shakespeare had anything to do is hardly large enough, in the basement, to contain the butcher's stall that one of his descendants kept, and that still remains there, windowless, with the cleaver-cuts in its hacked counter, which projects into the street under a little penthouse-roof, as if waiting for a new occupant.

The upper half of the door was open, and, on my rapping at it, a young person in black made her appearance and admitted me; she was not a menial, but remarkably genteel (an American characteristic) for an English girl, and was probably the daughter of the old gentlewoman who takes care of the house. This lower room has a pavement of gray slabs of stone, which may have been rudely squared when the house was new, but are now all cracked, broken, and disarranged in a most unaccountable way. One does not see how any ordinary usage, for whatever length of time, should have so smashed these heavy stones; it is as if an earthquake had burst up through the floor, which afterwards had been imperfectly trodden down again. The room is whitewashed and very clean, but wofully shabby and dingy, coarsely built, and such as the most poetical imagination would find it difficult to idealize. In the rear of this apartment is the kitchen, a still smaller room, of a similar rude aspect: it has a great, rough fireplace, with space for a large family under the blackened opening of the chimney, and an immense passageway for the smoke, through which Shakespeare may have seen the blue sky by day and the stars glimmering down at him by night. It is now a dreary spot where the long-extinguished embers used to be. A glowing fire, even if it covered only a quarter part of the hearth, might still do much towards making the old kitchen cheerful. But we get a depressing idea of the stifled, poor, sombre kind of life that could have been lived in such a dwelling, where this room seems to have been the gathering-place of the family, with no breadth or scope, no good retirement, but old and young huddling together cheek by jowl. What a hardy plant was Shakespeare's genius, how fatal its development, since it could not be blighted in such an atmosphere! It only brought human nature the closer to him, and put more unctuous earth about his roots.

Thence I was ushered up stairs to the room in which Shakespeare is supposed to have been born: though, if you peep too curiously into the matter, you may find the shadow of an ugly doubt on this, as well as most other points of his mysterious life. It is the chamber over the butcher's shop, and is lighted by one broad window containing a great many small, irregular panes of glass. The floor is made of planks, very rudely hewn, and fitting together with little neatness; the naked beams and rafters, at the sides of the room and overhead, bear the original marks of the builder's broad-axe, with no evidence of an attempt to smooth off the job. Again we have to reconcile ourselves to the smallness of the space enclosed by these illustrious walls,—a circumstance more difficult to accept, as regards places that we have heard, read, thought, and dreamed much about, than any other disenchanting particular of a mistaken ideal. A few paces—perhaps seven or eight—take us from end to end of it. So low it is, that I could easily touch the ceiling, and might have done so without a tiptoe-stretch, had it been a good deal higher; and this humility of the chamber has tempted a vast multitude of people to write their names overhead in pencil. Every inch of the side-walls, even into the obscurest nooks and corners, is covered with a similar record; all the windowpanes, moreover, are scrawled with diamond signatures among which is said to be that of Walter Scott; but so many persons have sought to immortalize themselves in close vicinity to his name, that I really could not trace him out. Methinks it is strange that people do not strive to forget their forlorn little identities, in such situations, instead of thrusting them forward into the dazzle of a great renown, where, if noticed, they cannot but be deemed impertinent.

This room, and the entire house, so far as I saw it, are whitewashed and exceedingly clean; nor is there the aged, musty smell with which old Chester first made me acquainted, and which goes far to cure an American of his excessive predilection for antique residences. An old lady, who took charge of me up stairs, had the manners and aspect of a gentlewoman, and talked with somewhat formidable knowledge and appreciative intelligence about Shakespeare. Arranged on a table and in chairs were various prints, views of houses and scenes connected with Shakespeare's memory, together with editions of his works and local publications about his home and haunts, from the sale of which this respectable lady perhaps realizes a handsome profit. At any rate, I bought a good many of them, conceiving that it might be the civillest way of requiting her for her instructive conversation and the trouble she took in showing me the house. It cost me a pang (not a curmudgeonly, but a gentlemanly one) to offer a downright fee to the lady-like girl who had admitted me: but I swallowed my delicate scruples with some little difficulty, and she digested hers, so far as I could observe, with no difficulty at all. In fact, nobody need fear to hold out half a crown to any person with whom he has occasion to speak a word in England.

I should consider it unfair to quit Shakespeare's house without the frank acknowledgment that I was conscious of not the slightest emotion while viewing it, nor any quickening of the imagination. This has often happened to me in my visits to memorable places. Whatever pretty and apposite reflections I may have made upon the subject had either occurred to me before I ever saw Stratford, or have been elaborated since. It is pleasant, nevertheless, to think that I have seen the place; and I believe that I can form a more sensible and vivid idea of Shakespeare as a flesh-and-blood individual now that I have stood on the kitchen-hearth and in the birth-chamber; but I am not quite certain that this power of realization is altogether desirable in reference to a great poet. The Shakespeare whom I met there took various guises, but had not his laurel on. He was successively the roguish boy,—the youthful deer-stealer,—the comrade of players,—the too familiar friend of Davenant's mother,—the careful, thrifty, thriven man of property who came back from London to lend money on bond, and occupy the best house in Stratford,—the mellow, red-nosed, autumnal boon-companion of John a' Combe,—and finally (or else the Stratford gossips belied him), the victim of convivial habits,

who met his death by tumbling into a ditch on his way home from a drinking-bout, and left his second-best bed to his poor wife.

I feel, as sensibly as the reader can, what horrible impiety it is to remember these things, be they true or false. In either case, they ought to vanish out of sight on the distant ocean-line of the past, leaving a pure, white memory, even as a sail, though perhaps darkened with many stains, looks snowy white on the far horizon. But I draw a moral from these unworthy reminiscences and this embodiment of the poet, as suggested by some of the grimy actualities of his life. It is for the high interests of the world not to insist upon finding out that its greatest men are, in a certain lower sense, very much the same kind of men as the rest of us, and often a little worse; because a common mind cannot properly digest such a discovery, nor ever know the true proportion of the great man's good and evil, nor how small a part of him it was that touched our muddy or dusty earth. Thence comes moral bewilderment, and even intellectual loss, in regard to what is best of him. When Shakespeare invoked a curse on the man who should stir his bones, he perhaps meant the larger share of it for him or them who should pry into his perishing earthliness, the defects or even the merits of the character that he wore in Stratford, when he had left mankind so much to muse upon that was imperishable and divine. Heaven keep me from incurring any part of the anathema in requital for the irreverent sentences above written!

From Shakespeare's house, the next step, of course, is to visit his burial-place. The appearance of the church is most venerable and beautiful, standing amid a great green shadow of lime-trees, above which rises the spire, while the Gothic battlements and buttresses and vast arched windows are obscurely seen through the boughs. The Avon loiters past the churchyard, an exceedingly sluggish river, which might seem to have been considering which way it should flow ever since Shakespeare left off paddling in it and gathering the large forget-me-nots that grow among its flags and water-weeds.

An old man in small-clothes was waiting at the gate; and inquiring whether I wished to go in, he preceded me to the church-porch, and rapped. I could have done it quite as effectually for myself; but it seems the old people of the neighborhood haunt about the churchyard, in spite of the frowns and remonstrances of the sexton, who grudges them the half-eleemosynary sixpence which they sometimes get from visitors. I was admitted into the church by a respectable-looking and intelligent man in black, the parish-clerk, I suppose, and probably holding a richer incumbency than his vicar, if all the fees which he handles remain in his own pocket. He was already exhibiting the Shakespeare monuments to two or three visitors, and several other parties came in while I was there.

The poet and his family are in possession of what may be considered the very best burial-places that the church affords. They lie in a row, right across the breadth of the chancel, the foot of each gravestone being close to the elevated floor on which the altar stands. Nearest to the side-wall, beneath Shakespeare's bust, is a slab bearing a Latin inscription addressed to his wife, and covering her remains; then his own slab, with the old anathematizing stanza upon it; then that of Thomas Nash, who married his granddaughter; then that of Dr. Hall, the husband of his daughter Susannah; and, lastly, Susannah's own. Shakespeare's is the commonest-looking slab of all, being just such a flag-stone as Essex Street in Salem used to be paved with, when I was a boy. Moreover, unless my eyes or recollection deceive me, there is a crack across it, as if it had already undergone some such violence as the inscription deprecates. Unlike the other monuments of the family, it bears no name, nor am I acquainted with the grounds or authority on which it is absolutely determined to be Shakespeare's; although, being in a range with those of his wife and children, it might naturally be attributed to him. But, then, why does his wife, who died afterwards, take precedence of him and occupy the place next his bust? And where are the graves of another daughter and a son, who have a better right in the family row than Thomas Nash, his grandson-in-law? Might not one or both of them have been laid under the nameless stone? But it is dangerous trifling with Shakespeare's dust; so I forbear to meddle further with the grave (though the prohibition makes it tempting), and shall let whatever bones be in it rest in peace. Yet I must needs add that the inscription on the bust seems to imply that Shakespeare's grave was directly underneath it.

The poet's bust is affixed to the northern wall of the church, the base of it being about a man's height, or rather more, above the floor of the chancel. The features of this piece of sculpture are entirely unlike any portrait of Shakespeare that I have ever seen, and compel me to take down the beautiful, lofty-browed, and noble picture of him which has hitherto hung in my mental portrait-gallery. The bust cannot be said to represent a beautiful face or an eminently noble head; but it clutches firmly hold of one's sense of reality and insists upon your accepting it, if not as Shakespeare the poet, yet as the wealthy burgher of Stratford, the friend of John a' Combe, who lies yonder in the corner. I know not what the phrenologists say to the bust. The forehead is but moderately developed, and retreats somewhat, the upper part of the skull rising pyramidally; the eyes are prominent almost beyond the penthouse of the brow; the upper lip is so long that it must have been almost a deformity, unless the sculptor artistically exaggerated its length, in consideration, that, on the pedestal, it must be foreshortened by being looked at from below. On the whole, Shakespeare must have had a singular rather than a prepossessing face; and it is wonderful how, with this bust before its eyes, the world has persisted in maintaining an erroneous notion of his appearance, allowing painters and sculptors to foist their idealized nonsense on us all, instead of the genuine man. For my part, the Shakespeare of my mind's eye is henceforth to be a personage of a ruddy English complexion, with a reasonably capacious brow, intelligent and quickly observant eyes, a nose curved slightly outward, a long, queer upper lip, with the mouth a little unclosed beneath it, and cheeks considerably developed in the lower part and beneath the chin. But when Shakespeare was himself (for nine tenths of the time, according to all appearances, he was but the burgher of Stratford), he doubtless shone through this dull mask and transfigured it into the face of an angel.

Fifteen or twenty feet behind the row of Shakespeare gravestones is the great east-window of the church, now brilliant with stained glass of recent manufacture. On one side of this window, under a sculptured arch of marble, lies a full-length marble figure of John a' Combe, clad in what I take to be a robe of municipal dignity, and holding its hands devoutly clasped. It is a sturdy English figure, with coarse features, a type of ordinary man whom we smile to see immortalized in the sculpturesque material of poets and heroes; but the prayerful attitude encourages us to believe that the old usurer may not, after all, have had that grim reception in the other world which Shakespeare's squib foreboded for him. By the by, till I grew somewhat familiar with Warwickshire pronunciation, I never understood that the point of those ill-natured lines

was a pun. "'Oho!' quoth the Devil, ''t is my John a' Combe!'"—that is, "My John has come!"

Close to the poet's bust is a nameless, oblong, cubic tomb, supposed to be that of a clerical dignitary of the fourteenth century. The church has other mural monuments and altar-tombs, one or two of the latter upholding the recumbent figures of knights in armor and their dames, very eminent and worshipful personages in their day, no doubt, but doomed to appear forever intrusive and impertinent within the precincts which Shakespeare has made his own. His renown is tyrannous, and suffers nothing else to be recognized within the scope of its material presence, unless illuminated by some side-ray from himself. The clerk informed me that interments no longer take place in any part of the church. And it is better so; for methinks a person of delicate individuality, curious about his burial-place, and desirous of six feet of earth for himself alone, could never endure to lie buried near Shakespeare, but would rise up at midnight and grope his way out of the church-door, rather than sleep in the shadow of so stupendous a memory.

## JOHN RICHARD GREEN
From "The England of Shakspere"
*History of the English People*
1874, Volume 2, pp. 472–85

A few daring jests, a brawl, and a fatal stab, make up the life of Marlowe; but even details such as these are wanting to the life of William Shakspere. Of hardly any great poet indeed do we know so little. For the story of his youth we have only one or two trifling legends, and these almost certainly false. Not a single letter or characteristic saying, not one of the jests "spoken at the Mermaid," hardly a single anecdote, remain to illustrate his busy life in London. His look and figure in later age have been preserved by the bust over his tomb at Stratford, and a hundred years after his death he was still remembered in his native town; but the minute diligence of the enquirers of the Georgian time was able to glean hardly a single detail, even of the most trivial order, which could throw light upon the years of retirement before his death. It is owing perhaps to the harmony and unity of his temper that no salient peculiarity seems to have left its trace on the memory of his contemporaries; it is the very grandeur of his genius which precludes us from discovering any personal trait in his works. His supposed self-revelation in the *Sonnets* is so obscure that only a few outlines can be traced even by the boldest conjecture. In his dramas he is all his characters, and his characters range over all mankind. There is not one, or the act or word of one that we can identify personally with the poet himself.

He was born in 1564, the sixth year of Elizabeth's reign, twelve years after the birth of Spenser, three years later than the birth of Bacon. Marlowe was of the same age with Shakspere: Greene probably a few years older. His father, a glover and small farmer of Stratford-on-Avon, was forced by poverty to lay down his office of alderman as his son reached boyhood; and stress of poverty may have been the cause which drove William Shakspere, who was already married at eighteen to a wife older than himself, to London and the stage. His life in the capital can hardly have begun later than in his twenty-third year, the memorable year which followed Sidney's death, which preceded the coming of the Armada, and which witnessed the production of Marlowe's *Tamburlaine*. If we take the language of the *Sonnets* as a record of his personal feeling, his new profession as an actor stirred in him only the bitterness of self-contempt. He chides with Fortune "that did not better for my life provide than public means that public manners breed;" he writhes at the thought that he has "made himself a motley to the view" of the gaping apprentices in the pit of Blackfriars. "Thence comes it," he adds, "that my name receives a brand, and almost thence my nature is subdued to that it works in." But the application of the words is a more than doubtful one. In spite of petty squabbles with some of his dramatic rivals at the outset of his career, the genial nature of the newcomer seems to have won him a general love among his fellows. In 1592, while still a mere actor and fitter of old plays for the stage, a fellow-playwright, Chettle, answered Greene's attack on him in words of honest affection: "Myself have seen his demeanour no less civil than he excellent in the quality he professes: besides, divers of worship have reported his up-rightness of dealing, which argues his honesty, and his facetious grace in writing, that proves his art." His partner Burbage spoke of him after death as a "worthy friend and fellow;" and Jonson handed down the general tradition of his time when he described him as "indeed honest, and of an open and free nature."

His profession as an actor was at any rate of essential service to him in the poetic career which he soon undertook. Not only did it give him the sense of theatrical necessities which makes his plays so effective on the boards, but it enabled him to bring his pieces as he wrote them to the test of the stage. If there is any truth in Jonson's statement that Shakspere never blotted a line, there is no justice in the censure which it implies on his carelessness or incorrectness. The conditions of poetic publication were in fact wholly different from those of our own day. A drama remained for years in manuscript as an acting piece, subject to continual revision and amendment; and every rehearsal and representation afforded hints for change which we know the young poet was far from neglecting. The chance which has preserved an earlier edition of his *Hamlet* shows in what an unsparing way Shakspere could recast even the finest products of his genius. Five years after the supposed date of his arrival in London he was already famous as a dramatist. Greene speaks bitterly of him under the name of "Shakescene" as an "upstart crow beautified with our feathers," a sneer which points either to his celebrity as an actor or to his preparation for loftier flights by fitting pieces of his predecessors for the stage. He was soon partner in the theatre, actor, and playwright; and another nickname, that of "Johannes Factotum" or Jack-of-all-Trades, shows his readiness to take all honest work which came to hand.

With his publication in 1593 of the poem of *Venus and Adonis*, "the first heir of my invention" as Shakspere calls it, the period of independent creation fairly began. The date of its publication was a very memorable one. The *Faerie Queen* had appeared only three years before, and had placed Spenser without a rival at the head of English poetry. On the other hand the two leading dramatists of the time passed at this moment suddenly away. Greene died in poverty and self-reproach in the house of a poor shoemaker. "Doll," he wrote to the wife he had abandoned, "I charge thee, by the love of our youth and by my soul's rest, that thou wilt see this man paid; for if he and his wife had not succoured me I had died in the streets." "Oh, that a year were granted me to live," cried the young poet from his bed of death, "but I must die, of every man abhorred! Time, loosely spent, will not again be won! My time is loosely spent—and I undone!" A year later the death of Marlowe in a street brawl removed the only rival whose powers might have equalled Shakspere's own. He was now about

thirty; and the twenty-three years which elapsed between the appearance of the *Adonis* and his death were filled with a series of masterpieces. Nothing is more characteristic of his genius than its incessant activity. Through the five years which followed the publication of his early poem he seems to have produced on an average two dramas a year. When we attempt however to trace the growth and progress of the poet's mind in the order of his plays we are met in the case of many of them by an absence of certain information as to the dates of their appearance. The facts on which enquiry has to build are extremely few. *Venus and Adonis*, with the *Lucrece*, must have been written before their publication in 1593–4; the *Sonnets*, though not published till 1609, were known in some form among his private friends as early as 1598. His earlier plays are defined by a list given in the *Wit's Treasury* of Francis Meres in 1598, though the omission of a play from a casual catalogue of this kind would hardly warrant us in assuming its necessary non-existence at the time. The works ascribed to him at his death are fixed in the same approximate fashion through the edition published by his fellow-actors. Beyond these meagre facts and our knowledge of the publication of a few of his dramas in his lifetime all is uncertain; and the conclusions which have been drawn from these, and from the dramas themselves, as well as from assumed resemblances with, or references to, other plays of the period can only be accepted as approximations to the truth.

The bulk of his lighter comedies and historical dramas can be assigned with fair probability to a period from about 1593, when Shakspere was known as nothing more than an adapter, to 1598, when they are mentioned in the list of Meres. They bear on them indeed the stamp of youth. In *Love's Labour's Lost* the young playwright, fresh from his own Stratford, its "daisies pied and violets blue," with the gay bright music of its country ditties still in his ears, flings himself into the midst of the brilliant England which gathered round Elizabeth, busying himself as yet for the most part with the surface of it, with the humours and quixotisms, the wit and the whim, the unreality, the fantastic extravagance, which veiled its inner nobleness. Country-lad as he is, Shakspere shows himself master of it all; he can patter euphuism and exchange quip and repartee with the best; he is at home in their pedantries and affectations, their brag and their rhetoric, their passion for the fantastic and the marvellous. He can laugh as heartily at the romantic vagaries of the courtly world in which he finds himself as at the narrow dulness, the pompous triflings, of the country world which he has left behind him. But he laughs frankly and without malice; he sees the real grandeur of soul which underlies all this quixotry and word-play; and owns with a smile that when brought face to face with the facts of human life, with the suffering of man or the danger of England, these fops have in them the stuff of heroes. He shares the delight in existence, the pleasure in sheer living, which was so marked a feature of the age; he enjoys the mistakes, the contrasts, the adventures, of the men about him; his fun breaks almost riotously out in the practical jokes of the *Taming of the Shrew* and the endless blunderings of the *Comedy of Errors*. In these earlier efforts his work had been marked by little poetic elevation, or by passion. But the easy grace of the dialogue, the dexterous management of a complicated story, the genial gaiety of his tone, and the music of his verse promised a master of social comedy as soon as Shakspere turned from the superficial aspects of the world about him to find a new delight in the character and actions of men. The interest of human character was still fresh and vivid; the sense of individuality drew a charm from its novelty; and poet and essayist were busy alike in sketching the "humours" of mankind. Shakspere sketched with his fellows. In the *Two Gentlemen of Verona* his painting of manners was suffused by a tenderness and ideal beauty which formed an effective protest against the hard though vigorous character-painting which the first success of Ben Jonson in *Every Man in His Humour* brought at the time into fashion. But quick on these lighter comedies followed two in which his genius started fully into life. His poetic power, held in reserve till now, showed itself with a splendid profusion in the brilliant fancies of the *Midsummer Night's Dream*; and passion swept like a tide of resistless delight through *Romeo and Juliet*.

Side by side however with these passionate dreams, these delicate imaginings and piquant sketches of manners, had been appearing during this short interval of intense activity a series of dramas which mark Shakspere's relation to the new sense of patriotism, the more vivid sense of national existence, national freedom, national greatness, which gives its grandeur to the age of Elizabeth. England itself was now becoming a source of literary interest to poet and prose-writer. Warner in his *Albion's England*, Daniel in his *Civil Wars*, embalmed in verse the record of her past; Drayton in his *Polyolbion* sang the fairness of the land itself, the "tracts, mountains, forests, and other parts of this renowned isle of Britain." The national pride took its highest poetic form in the historical drama. No plays seem to have been more popular from the earliest hours of the new stage than dramatic representations of our history. Marlowe had shown in his *Edward the Second* what tragic grandeur could be reached in this favourite field; and, as we have seen, Shakspere had been led naturally towards it by his earlier occupation as an adapter of stock pieces like *Henry the Sixth* for the new requirements of the stage. He still to some extent followed in plan the older plays on the subjects he selected, but in his treatment of their themes he shook boldly off the yoke of the past. A larger and deeper conception of human character than any of the old dramatists had reached displayed itself in Richard the Third, in Falstaff, or in Hotspur; while in Constance and Richard the Second the pathos of human suffering was painted as even Marlowe had never dared to paint it.

No dramas have done so much for Shakspere's enduring popularity with his countrymen as these historical plays. They have done more than all the works of English historians to nourish in the minds of Englishmen a love of and reverence for their country's past. When Chatham was asked where he had read his English history he answered, "In the plays of Shakspere." Nowhere could he have read it so well, for nowhere is the spirit of our history so nobly rendered. If the poet's work echoes sometimes our national prejudice and unfairness of temper, it is instinct throughout with English humour, with our English love of hard fighting, our English faith in goodness and in the doom that waits upon triumphant evil, our English pity for the fallen. Shakspere is Elizabethan to the core. He stood at the meeting-point of two great epochs of our history. The age of the Renascence was passing into the age of Puritanism. Rifts which were still little were widening every hour, and threatening ruin to the fabric of Church and State which the Tudors had built up. A new political world was rising into being; a world healthier, more really national, but less picturesque, less wrapt in the mystery and splendour that poets love. Great as were the faults of Puritanism, it may fairly claim to be the first political system which recognized the grandeur of the people as a whole. As great a change was passing over the spiritual sympathies of men. A sterner Protestantism was invigorating and ennobling life by its morality, its seriousness, its intense conviction of God. But it

was at the same time hardening and narrowing it. The Bible was superseding Plutarch. The "obstinate questionings" which haunted the finer souls of the Renascence were being stereotyped into the theological formulas of the Puritan. The sense of a divine omnipotence was annihilating man. The daring which turned England into a people of "adventurers," the sense of inexhaustible resources, the buoyant freshness of youth, the intoxicating sense of beauty and joy, which created Sidney and Marlowe and Drake, were passing away before the consciousness of evil and the craving to order man's life aright before God.

From this new world of thought and feeling Shakspere stood aloof. Turn as others might to the speculations of theology, man and man's nature remained with him an inexhaustible subject of interest. Caliban was among his latest creations. It is impossible to discover whether his religious belief was Catholic or Protestant. It is hard indeed to say whether he had any religious belief or no. The religious phrases which are thinly scattered over his works are little more than expressions of a distant and imaginative reverence. But on the deeper grounds of religious faith his silence is significant. He is silent, and the doubt of Hamlet deepens his silence about the afterworld. "To die," it may be, was to him as it was to Claudio, "to go we know not whither." Often as his questionings turn to the riddle of life and death he leaves it a riddle to the last without heeding the common theological solutions around him. "We are such stuff as dreams are made of, and our little life is rounded with a sleep."

Nor were the political sympathies of the poet those of the coming time. His roll of dramas is the epic of civil war. The Wars of the Roses fill his mind, as they filled the mind of his contemporaries. It is not till we follow him through the series of plays from *Richard the Second* to *Henry the Eighth* that we realize how profoundly the memory of the struggle between York and Lancaster had moulded the temper of the people, how deep a dread of civil war, of baronial turbulence, of disputes over the succession to the throne, it had left behind it. Men had learned the horrors of the time from their fathers; they had drunk in with their childhood the lesson that such a chaos of weakness and misrule must never be risked again. From such a risk the Crown seemed the one security. With Shakspere as with his fellow-countrymen the Crown is still the centre and safeguard of the national life. His ideal England is an England grouped around a noble king, a king such as his own Henry the Fifth, devout, modest, simple as he is brave, but a lord in battle, a born ruler of men, with a loyal people about him and his enemies at his feet. Socially the poet reflects the aristocratic view of social life which was shared by all the nobler spirits of the Elizabethan time. Coriolanus is the embodiment of a great noble; and the taunts which Shakspere hurls in play after play at the rabble only echo the general temper of the Renascence. But he shows no sympathy with the struggle of feudalism against the Crown. If he paints Hotspur with a fire which proves how thoroughly he could sympathize with the rough, bold temper of the baronage, he suffers him to fall unpitied before Henry the Fourth. Apart however from the strength and justice of its rule, royalty has no charm for him. He knows nothing of the "right divine of kings to govern wrong" which became the doctrine of prelates and courtiers in the age of the Stuarts. He shows in his *Richard the Second* the doom that waits on a lawless despotism, as he denounces in his *Richard the Third* the selfish and merciless ambition that severs a ruler from his people. But the dread of misrule was a dim and distant one. Shakspere had grown up under the reign of Elizabeth; he had known no ruler save one who had cast a spell over the hearts of Englishmen. His thoughts were absorbed, as those of the country were absorbed, in the struggle for national existence which centred round the Queen. *King John* is a trumpet-call to rally round Elizabeth in her fight for England. Again a Pope was asserting his right to depose an English sovereign and to loose Englishmen from their bond of allegiance. Again political ambitions and civil discord woke at the call of religious war. Again a foreign power was threatening England at the summons of Rome, and hoping to master her with the aid of revolted Englishmen. The heat of such a struggle as this left no time for the thought of civil liberties. Shakspere casts aside the thought of the Charter to fix himself on the strife of the stranger for England itself. What he sang was the duty of patriotism, the grandeur of loyalty, the freedom of England from Pope or Spaniard, its safety within its "water-walled bulwark," if only its national union was secure. And now that the nation was at one, now that he had seen in his first years of London life Catholics as well as Protestants trooping to the muster at Tilbury and hasting down Thames to the fight in the Channel, he could thrill his hearers with the proud words that sum up the work of Elizabeth:—

> This England never did, nor never shall,
> Lie at the proud foot of a conqueror,
> But when it first did help to wound itself.
> Now that her princes are come home again,
> Come the three corners of the world in arms,
> And we shall shock them! Nought shall make us rue
> If England to itself do rest but true.

With this great series of historical and social dramas Shakspere had passed far beyond his fellows whether as a tragedian or as a writer of comedy. "The Muses," said Meres in 1598, "would speak with Shakspere's fine-filed phraze, if they would speak English." His personal popularity was now at its height. His pleasant temper and the vivacity of his wit had drawn him early into contact with the young Earl of Southampton, to whom his *Adonis* and *Lucrece* are dedicated; and the different tone of the two dedications shows how rapidly acquaintance ripened into an ardent friendship. Shakspere's wealth and influence too were growing fast. He had property both in Stratford and London, and his fellow-townsmen made him their suitor to Lord Burleigh for favours to be bestowed on Stratford. He was rich enough to aid his father, and to buy the house at Stratford which afterwards became his home. The tradition that Elizabeth was so pleased with Falstaff in *Henry the Fourth* that she ordered the poet to show her Falstaff in love—an order which produced the *Merry Wives of Windsor*—whether true or false, proves his repute as a playwright. As the group of earlier poets passed away, they found successors in Marston, Dekker, Middleton, Heywood, and Chapman, and above all in Ben Jonson. But none of these could dispute the supremacy of Shakspere. The verdict of Meres that "Shakspere among the English is the most excellent in both kinds for the stage," represented the general feeling of his contemporaries. He was at last fully master of the resources of his art. The *Merchant of Venice* marks the perfection of his development as a dramatist in the completeness of its stage effect, the ingenuity of its incidents, the ease of its movement, the beauty of its higher passages, the reserve and self-control with which its poetry is used, the conception and unfolding of character, and above all the mastery with which character and event is grouped round the figure of Shylock. Master as he is of his art, the poet's temper is still young; the *Merry Wives of Windsor* is a burst of gay laughter; and laughter more tempered, yet full of a sweeter fascination, rings round us in *As You Like It*.

But in the melancholy and meditative Jaques of the last drama we feel the touch of a new and graver mood. Youth, so full and buoyant in the poet till now, seems to have passed almost suddenly away. Though Shakspere had hardly reached forty, in one of his *Sonnets* which cannot have been written at a much later time than this there are indications that he already felt the advance of premature age. And at this moment the outer world suddenly darkened around him. The brilliant circle of young nobles whose friendship he had shared was broken up in 1601 by the political storm which burst in a mad struggle of the Earl of Essex for power. Essex himself fell on the scaffold; his friend and Shakspere's idol, Southampton, passed a prisoner into the Tower; Herbert Lord Pembroke, younger patron of the poet, was banished from the Court. While friends were thus falling and hopes fading without, Shakspere's own mind seems to have going through a phase of bitter suffering and unrest. In spite of the ingenuity of commentators, it is difficult and even impossible to derive any knowledge of Shakspere's inner history from the *Sonnets*; "the strange imagery of passion which passes over the magic mirror," it has been finely said, "has no tangible evidence before or behind it." But its mere passing is itself an evidence of the restlessness and agony within. The change in the character of his dramas gives a surer indication of his change of mood. The fresh joyousness, the keen delight in life and in man, which breathes through Shakspere's early work disappears in comedies such as *Troilus* and *Measure for Measure*. Disappointment, disillusion, a new sense of the evil and foulness that underlies so much of human life, a loss of the old frank trust in its beauty and goodness, threw their gloom over these comedies. Failure seems everywhere. In *Julius Cæsar* the virtue of Brutus is foiled by its ignorance of and isolation from mankind; in Hamlet even penetrating intellect proves helpless for want of the capacity of action; the poison of Iago taints the love of Desdemona and the grandeur of Othello; Lear's mighty passion battles helplessly against the wind and the rain; a woman's weakness of frame dashes the cup of her triumph from the hand of Lady Macbeth; lust and self-indulgence blast the heroism of Antony; pride ruins the nobleness of Coriolanus.

But the very struggle and self-introspection that these dramas betray were to give a depth and grandeur to Shakspere's work such as it had never known before. The age was one in which man's temper and powers took a new range and energy. Sidney or Raleigh lived not one but a dozen lives at once; the daring of the adventurer, the philosophy of the scholar, the passion of the lover, the fanaticism of the saint, towered into almost superhuman grandeur. Man became conscious of the immense resources that lay within him, conscious of boundless powers that seemed to mock the narrow world in which they moved. All through the age of the Renascence one feels this impress of the gigantic, this giant-like activity, this immense ambition and desire. The very bombast and extravagance of the times reveal cravings and impulses before which common speech broke down. It is this grandeur of humanity that finds its poetic expression in the later work of Shakspere. As the poet penetrated deeper and deeper into the recesses of the soul, he saw how great and wondrous a thing was man. "What a piece of work is a man," cries Hamlet; "how noble in reason; how infinite in faculty; in form and moving how express and admirable; in action how like an angel; in apprehension how like a god; the beauty of the world; the paragon of animals!" It is the wonder of man that spreads before us as the poet pictures the wide speculation of Hamlet, the awful convulsion of a great nature in Othello, the terrible storm in the soul of Lear which blends with the very storm of the heavens themselves, the awful ambition that nerved a woman's hand to dabble itself with the blood of a murdered king, the reckless lust that "flung away a world for love." Amid the terror and awe of these great dramas we learn something of the vast forces of the age from which they sprang. The passion of Mary Stuart, the ruthlessness of Alva, the daring of Drake, the chivalry of Sidney, the range of thought and action in Raleigh or Elizabeth, come better home to us as we follow the mighty series of tragedies which began in *Hamlet* and ended in *Coriolanus*.

## A. C. BRADLEY
### "Shakespeare the Man" (1904)
*Oxford Lectures on Poetry*
1909, pp. 311–57

S uch phrases as 'Shakespeare the man' or 'Shakespeare's personality' are, no doubt, open to objection. They seem to suggest that, if we could subtract from Shakespeare the mind that produced his works, the residue would be the man himself; and that his mind was some pure impersonal essence unaffected by the accidents of physique, temperament, and character. If this were so, one could but echo Tennyson's thanksgiving that we know so little of Shakespeare. But as it is assuredly not so, and as 'Shakespeare the man' really means the one indivisible Shakespeare, regarded for the time from a particular point of view, the natural desire to know whatever can be known of him is not to be repressed merely because there are people so foolish as to be careless about his works and yet curious about his private life. For my own part I confess that, though I should care nothing about the man if he had not written the works, yet, since we possess them, I would rather see and hear him for five minutes in his proper person than discover a new one. And though we may be content to die without knowing his income or even the surname of Mr. W. H., we cannot so easily resign the wish to find the man in his writings, and to form some idea of the disposition, the likes and dislikes, the character and the attitude towards life, of the human being who seems to us to have understood best our common human nature.

The answer of course will be that our biographical knowledge of Shakespeare is so small, and his writings are so completely dramatic, that this wish, however natural, is idle. But I cannot think so. Doubtless, in trying to form an idea of Shakespeare, we soon reach the limits of reasonable certainty; and it is also true that the idea we can form without exceeding them is far from being as individual as we could desire. But it is more distinct than is often supposed, and it *is* reasonably certain; and although we can add to its distinctness only by more or less probable conjectures, they are not mere guesses, they really have probability in various degrees. On this whole subject there is a tendency at the present time to an extreme scepticism, which appears to me to be justified neither by the circumstances of the particular case nor by our knowledge of human nature in general.

This scepticism is due in part to the interest excited by Mr. ⟨Sidney⟩ Lee's discussion of the Sonnets in his *Life* of Shakespeare, and to the importance rightly attached to that discussion. The Sonnets are lyrical poems of friendship and love. In them the poet ostensibly speaks in his own person and expresses his own feelings. Many critics, no doubt, had denied that he really did so; but they had not Mr. Lee's knowledge, nor had they examined the matter so narrowly as he; and therefore they had not much weakened the general belief that the

Sonnets, however conventional or exaggerated their language may sometimes be, do tell us a good deal about their author. Mr. Lee, however, showed far more fully than any previous writer that many of the themes, many even of the ideas, of these poems are commonplaces of Renaissance sonnet-writing; and he came to the conclusion that in the Sonnets Shakespeare 'unlocked,' not 'his heart,' but a very different kind of armoury, and that the sole biographical inference deducible from them is that 'at one time in his career Shakespeare disdained no weapon of flattery in an endeavour to monopolise the bountiful patronage of a young man of rank.' Now, if that inference is correct, it certainly tells us something about Shakespeare the man; but it also forbids us to take seriously what the Sonnets profess to tell us of his passionate affection, with its hopes and fears, its pain and joy; of his pride and his humility, his self-reproach and self-defence, his weariness of life and' his consciousness of immortal genius. And as, according to Mr. Lee's statement, the Sonnets alone of Shakespeare's works 'can be held to throw any illumination on a personal trait,' it seems to follow that, so far as the works are concerned (for Mr. Lee is not specially sceptical as to the external testimony), the only idea we can form of the man is contained in that single inference.

Now, I venture to surmise that Mr. Lee's words go rather beyond his meaning. But that is not our business here, nor could a brief discussion do justice to a theory to which those who disagree with it are still greatly indebted. What I wish to deny is the presupposition which seems to be frequently accepted as an obvious truth. Even if Mr. Lee's view of the Sonnets were indisputably correct, nay, if even, to go much further, the persons and the story in the Sonnets were as purely fictitious as those of *Twelfth Night*, they might and would still tell us something of the personality of their author. For however free a poet may be from the emotions which he simulates, and however little involved in the conditions which he imagines, he cannot (unless he is a mere copyist) write a hundred and fifty lyrics expressive of those simulated emotions without disclosing something of himself, something of the way in which he in particular *would* feel and behave under the imagined conditions. And the same thing holds in principle of the dramas. Is it really conceivable that a man can write some five and thirty dramas, and portray in them an enormous amount and variety of human nature, without betraying anything whatever of his own disposition and preferences? I do not believe that he could do this, even if he deliberately set himself to the task. The only question is how much of himself he would betray.

One is entitled to say this, I think, on general grounds; but we may appeal further to specific experience. Of many poets and novelists we know a good deal from external sources. And in these cases we find that the man so known to us appears also in his works, and that these by themselves would have left on us a personal impression which, though imperfect and perhaps in this or that point even false, would have been broadly true. Of course this holds of some writers much more fully than of others; but, except where the work is very scanty in amount, it seems to hold in some degree of all.[1] If so, there is an antecedent probability that it will apply to Shakespeare too. After all, he was human. We may exclaim in our astonishment that he was as universal and impartial as nature herself; but this is the language of religious rapture. If we assume that he was six times as universal as Sir Walter Scott, which is praise enough for a mortal, we may hope to form an idea of him from his plays only six times as dim as the idea of Scott that we should derive from the Waverley Novels.

And this is not all. As a matter of fact, the great majority of Shakespeare's readers—lovers of poetry untroubled by theories and questions—do form from the plays some idea of the man. Knowingly or not, they possess such an idea; and up to a certain point the idea is the same. Ask such a man whether he thinks Shakespeare was at all like Shelley, or Wordsworth, or Milton, and it will not occur to him to answer 'I have not the faintest notion'; he will answer unhesitatingly No. Ask him whether he supposes that Shakespeare was at all like Fielding or Scott, and he will probably be found to imagine that, while differing greatly from both, he did belong to the same type or class. And such answers unquestionably imply an idea which, however deficient in detail, is definite.

Again, to go a little further in the same direction, take this fact. After I had put together my notes for the present lecture, I re-read Bagehot's essay on Shakespeare the Man, and I read a book by Goldwin Smith and an essay by Leslie Stephen (who, I found, had anticipated a good deal that I meant to say).[2] These three writers, with all their variety, have still substantially the same idea of Shakespeare; and it is the idea of the competent 'general reader' more fully developed. Nor is the value of their agreement in the least diminished by the fact that they make no claim to be Shakespeare scholars. They show themselves much abler than most scholars, and if they lack the scholar's knowledge they are free from his defects. When they wrote their essays they had not wearied themselves with rival hypotheses, or pored over minutiae until they lost the broad and deep impressions which vivid reading leaves. Ultra-scepticism in this matter does not arise merely or mainly from the humility which every man of sense must feel as he creeps to and fro in Shakespeare's prodigious mind. It belongs either to the clever faddist who can see nothing straight, or it proceeds from those dangers and infirmities which the expert in any subject knows too well.

The remarks I am going to make can have an interest only for those who share the position I have tried to indicate; who believe that the most dramatic of writers must reveal in his writings something of himself, but who recognise that in Shakespeare's case we can expect a reasonable certainty only within narrow limits, which beyond them we have to trust to impressions, the value of which must depend on familiarity with his writings, on freedom from prejudice and the desire to reach any particular result, and on the amount of perception we may happen to possess. I offer my own impressions, insecure and utterly unprovable as I know them to be, simply because those of other readers have an interest for me; and I offer them for the most part without argument, because even where argument might be useful it requires more time than a lecture can afford. For the same reason I shall assume, without attempting to define it further, and without dilating on its implications, the truth of that general feeling about Shakespeare and Fielding and Scott.

But, before we come to impressions at all, we must look at the scanty store of external evidence: for we may lay down at once the canon that impressions derived from the works must supplement and not contradict this evidence, so far as it appears trustworthy. It is scanty, but it yields a decided outline.

> This figure that thou here seest put,
> It was for gentle Shakespeare cut:

—so Jonson writes of the portrait in the Folio, and the same adjective 'gentle' is used elsewhere of Shakespeare. It had not in Elizabethan English so confined a meaning as it has now; but it meant something, and I do not remember that their contemporaries called Marlowe or Jonson or Marston 'gentle.'

Next, in the earliest extant reference that we have to Shakespeare, the writer says that he himself has seen his 'demeanour' to be 'civil.'[3] It is not saying much; but it is not the first remark an acquaintance would probably have made about Ben Jonson or Samuel Johnson. The same witness adds about Shakespeare that 'divers of worship have reported his uprightness of dealing which argues his honesty.' 'Honesty' and 'honest' in an Elizabethan passage like this mean more than they would now; they answer rather to our 'honourable' or 'honour.' Lastly we have the witness borne by Jonson in the words: 'I loved the man, and do honour his memory, on this side idolatry, as much as any. He was, indeed, honest, and of an open and free nature.' With this notable phrase, to which I shall have to return, we come to an end of the testimony of eye-witnesses to Shakespeare the Man (for we have nothing to do with references to the mere actor or author). It is scanty, and insufficient to discriminate him from other persons who were gentle, civil, upright in their dealings, honourable, open, and free: but I submit that there have been not a few writers to whom all these qualities could not be truly ascribed, and that the testimony therefore does tell us something definite. To which must be added that we have absolutely no evidence which conflicts with it. Whatever Greene in his jealous embitterment might have said would carry little weight, but in fact, apart from general abuse of actors, he only says that the upstart had an over-weening opinion of his own capacities.

There remain certain traditions and certain facts; and without discussing them I will mention what seems to me to have a more or less probable significance. Stratford stories of drinking bouts may go for nothing, but not the consensus of tradition to the effect that Shakespeare was a pleasant and convivial person, 'very good company, and of a very ready and pleasant smooth wit.'[4] That after his retirement to Stratford he spent at the rate of £1000 a year is incredible, but that he spent freely seems likely enough. The tradition that as a young man he got into trouble with Sir Thomas Lucy for deer-stealing (which would probably be an escapade rather than an essay in serious poaching) is supported by his unsavoury jest about the 'luces' in Sir Robert Shallow's coat. The more general statement that in youth he was wild does not sound improbable; and, obscure as the matter is, I cannot regard as comfortable the little we know of the circumstances of his very early marriage. A contemporary story of an amorous adventure in London may well be pure invention, but we have no reason to reject it peremptorily as we should any similar gossip about Milton. Lastly, certain inferences may safely be drawn from the facts that, once securely started in London, Shakespeare soon began to prosper, and acquired, for an actor and playwright, considerable wealth; that he bought property in his native town, and was consulted sometimes by fellow-townsmen on matters of business; that he enforced the payment of certain debts; and that he took the trouble to get a coat of arms. But what cannot with any logic or any safety be inferred is that he, any more than Scott, was impelled to write simply and solely by the desire to make money and improve his social position; and the comparative abundance of business records will mislead only those who are thoughtless enough to forget that, if they buy a house or sue a debtor, the fact will be handed down, while their kind or generous deeds may be recorded, if at all, only in the statement that they were 'of an open and free nature.'

That Shakespeare was a good and perhaps keen man of business, or that he set store by a coat of arms, we could not have inferred from his writings. But we could have judged from them that he worked hard, and have guessed with some probability that he would rather have been a 'gentleman' than an actor. And most of the other characteristics that appear from the external evidence would, I think, have seemed probable from a study of the works. This should encourage us to hope that we may be right in other impressions which we receive from them. And we may begin with one on which the external evidence has a certain bearing.

Readers of Shakespeare, I believe, imagine him to have been not only sweet-tempered but modest and unassuming. I do not doubt that they are right; and, vague as the Folio portrait and the Stratford bust are, it would be difficult to believe that their subject was an irritable, boastful, or pushing person. But if we confine ourselves to the works, it is not easy to give reasons for the idea that their author was modest and unassuming; and a man is not necessarily so because he is open, free, and very good company. Perhaps we feel that a man who was not so would have allowed much more of himself to appear in his works than Shakespeare does. Perhaps again we think that anything like presumption or self-importance was incompatible with Shakespeare's sense of the ridiculous, his sublime common-sense, and his feeling of man's insignificance. And, lastly, it seems to us clear that the playwright admires and likes people who are modest, unassuming, and plain; while it may perhaps safely be said that those who lack these qualities rarely admire them in others and not seldom despise them. But, however we may justify our impression that Shakespeare possessed them, we certainly receive it; and assuming it to be as correct as the similar impression left by the Waverley Novels indubitably is, I go on to observe that the possession of them does not of necessity imply a want of spirit, or of proper self-assertion or insistence on rights.[5] It did not in Scott, and we have ground for saying that it did not in Shakespeare. If it had, he could not, being of an open and free nature, have prospered as he prospered. He took offence at Greene's attack on him, and showed that he took it. He was 'gentle,' but he liked his debts to be paid. However his attitude as to the enclosure at Welcombe may be construed, it is clear that he had to be reckoned with. It appears probable that he held himself wronged by Sir Thomas Lucy, and, pocketing up the injury because he could not resent it, gave him tit for tat after some fifteen years. The man in the Sonnets forgives his friend easily, but it is not from humility; and towards the world he is very far from humble. Oh the dedication of *The Rape of Lucrece* we cannot judge, for we do not know Shakespeare's relations with Lord Southampton at that date; but, as for the dedication of *Venus and Adonis*, could modesty and dignity be better mingled in a letter from a young poet to a great noble than they are there?

Some of Shakespeare's writings point to a strain of deep reflection and of quasi-metaphysical imagination in his nature; and a few of them seem to reveal a melancholy, at times merely sad, at times embittered or profound, if never hopeless. It is on this side mainly that we feel a decided difference between him and Fielding, and even between him and Scott. Yet nothing in the contemporary allusions or in the traditions would suggest that he was notably thoughtful or serious, and much less that he was melancholy. And although we could lay no stress on this fact if it stood alone, it is probably significant. Shakespeare's writings, on the whole, leave a strong impression that his native disposition was much more gay than grave. They seem always to have made this impression. Fuller tells us that 'though his genius generally was jocular and inclining him to festivity, yet he could, when so disposed, be solemn and serious, as appears by his tragedies.'[6] Johnson agreed with Rymer that his 'natural disposition' led him to comedy; and,

although Johnson after his manner distorts a true idea by wilful exaggeration and by perverting distinctions into antitheses, there is truth in his development of Rymer's remark. It would be easy to quote nineteenth century critics to the same effect; and the study of Shakespeare's early works leads to a similar result. It has been truly said that we feel ourselves in much closer contact with his personality in the early comedies and in *Romeo and Juliet* than in *Henry VI.* and *Richard III.* and *Titus Andronicus.* In the latter, so far as we suppose them to be his own, he seems on the whole to be following, and then improving on, an existing style, and to be dealing with subjects which engage him as a playwright without much appealing to him personally. With *Romeo and Juliet*, on the other hand, and with *Richard II.* (which seems clearly to be his first attempt to write historical tragedy in a manner entirely his own), it is different, and we feel the presence of the whole man. The stories are tragic, but it is not precisely the *tragic* aspect of them that attracts him most; and even Johnson's statement, grotesquely false of the later tragedies, that 'in tragedy he is always struggling after some occasion to be comic,' is no more than an exaggeration in respect to *Romeo and Juliet*.[7] From these tragedies, as from *Love's Labour's Lost* and the other early comedies, we should guess that the author was a young man, happy, alert, light-hearted, full of romance and poetry, but full also of fun; blessed with a keen enjoyment of absurdities, but, for all his intellectual subtlety and power, not markedly reflective, and certainly not particularly grave or much inclined to dejection. One might even suspect, I venture to think, that with such a flow of spirits and such exceeding alacrity of mind he might at present be a trifle wanting in feeling and disposed to levity. In any case, if our general impression is correct, we shall not find it hard to believe that the author of these plays and the creator of Falstaff was 'very good company' and a convivial goodfellow; and it might easily happen that he was tempted at times to 'go here and there' in society, and 'make himself a motley to the view' in a fashion that left some qualms behind.[8]

There is a tradition that Shakespeare was 'a handsome well-shaped man.' If the Stratford monument does not lie, he was not in later life a meagre man. And if our notion of his temperament has any truth, he can hardly have been physically feeble, bloodless, or inactive. Most readers probably imagine him the reverse. Even sceptical critics tell us that he was fond of field-sports; and of his familiar knowledge of them there can be no question. Yet—I can but record the impression without trying to justify it—his writings do not at all suggest to me that he was a splendidly powerful creature like Fielding, or that he greatly enjoyed bodily exertion, or was not easily tired. He says much of horses, but he does not make one think, as Scott does, that a gallop was a great delight to him. Nor again do I feel after reading him that he had a strong natural love of adventurous deeds, or longed to be an explorer or a soldier. The island of his boyish dreams—if he heard much of voyages as a boy—was, I fancy, the haunt of marmosets and hedgehogs, quaint moon-calves and flitting sprites, lovely colours, sounds and sweet airs that give delight and hurt not, less like Treasure Island than the Coral Island of Ballantyne in the original illustrations, and more full of wonders than of dangers. He would have liked the Arabian Nights better than Dumas. Of course he admired men of action, understood them, and could express their feelings; but we do not feel particularly close to his personality as we read the warrior speeches of Hotspur, Henry, Othello, Coriolanus, as we do when we read of Romeo or Hamlet, or when we feel the attraction of Henry's modesty. In the same way, I suppose nobody feels Shakespeare's personal presence in the ambition of Macbeth or the pride of Coriolanus; many feel it in Macbeth's imaginative terrors, and in the disgust of Coriolanus at the idea of recounting his exploits in order to win votes. When we seem to hear Shakespeare's voice—and we hear it from many mouths besides Romeo's or Hamlet's—it is the voice of a man with a happy, enjoying, but still contemplative and even dreamy nature, not of a man richly endowed with the impulses and feelings either of strenuous action or of self-assertion. If he had drawn a Satan, we should not have felt his personality, as we do Milton's, in Satan's pride and indomitable courage and intolerance of rule.

We know how often Shakespeare uses the antithesis of blood or passion, and judgment or reason; how he praises the due commingling of the two, or the control of the first by the second; how frequently it is the want of such control that exposes his heroes to the attack of Fortune or Fate. What, then, were the passions or the 'affections of the blood' most dangerous to himself? Not, if we have been right, those of pride or ambition; nor yet those of envy, hatred, or revenge; and still less that of avarice. But, in the first place, let us remember Jonson's words, 'he was honest and of an open and free nature,' and let me repeat an observation, made elsewhere in passing, that these words are true also of the great majority of Shakespeare's heroes, and not least of his tragic heroes. Jonson almost quotes Iago:

The Moor is of a free and open nature,
That thinks men honest that but seem to be so.

The king says that Hamlet,

being remiss,
Most generous, and free from all contrivings,
Will not peruse the foils.

The words 'open and free' apply no less eminently to Brutus, Lear, and Timon. Antony and Coriolanus are men naturally frank, liberal, and large. Prospero lost his dukedom through his trustfulness. Romeo and Troilus and Orlando, and many slighter characters, are so far of the same type. Now such a free and open nature, obviously, is specially exposed to the risks of deception, perfidy, and ingratitude. If it is also a nature sensitive and intense, but not particularly active or (if the word may be excused) volitional, such experiences will tempt it to melancholy, embitterment, anger, possibly even misanthropy. If it *is* thus active or volitional, it may become the prey of violent and destructive passion, such as that of Othello and of Coriolanus, and such as Lear's would be if he were not so old. These affections, passions, and sufferings of free and open natures are Shakespeare's favourite tragic subject; and his favouritism, surely, goes so far as to constitute a decided peculiarity, not found thus in other tragic poets. Here he painted most, one cannot but think, what his own nature was most inclined to feel. But it would rather be melancholy, embitterment, an inactive rage or misanthropy, than any destructive passion; and it would be a further question whether, and how far, he may at any time have experienced what he depicts. I am speaking here only of his disposition.[9]

That Shakespeare was as much inclined to be a lover as most poets we may perhaps safely assume; but can we conjecture anything further on this subject? I will confine myself to two points. He treats of love romantically, and tragically, and humorously. In the earlier plays especially the humorous aspect of the matter, the aspect so prominent in the *Midsummer-Night's Dream*, the changefulness, brevity, irrationality, of the feeling, is at least as much dwelt on as the romantic, and with at least as much relish:

Lord! what fools these mortals be!

Now, if there is anything peculiar in the pictures here, it is, perhaps, the special interest that Shakespeare seems to take in what we may call the unreality of the feeling of love in an imaginative nature. Romeo as he first appears, and, in a later play, Orsino, are examples of this. They are perfectly sincere, of course, but neither of them is really in love with a woman; each is in love with the state of being in love. This state is able to attach itself to a particular object, but it is not induced by the particular qualities of that object; it is more a dream than a passion, and can melt away without carrying any of the lover's heart with it; and in that sense it is unreal. This weakness, no doubt, is not confined to imaginative natures, but they may well be specially disposed to it (as Shelley was), and Shakespeare may have drawn it from his own experience. The suspicion is strengthened when we think of *Richard II*. In Richard this imaginative weakness is exhibited again, though not in relation to love. He luxuriates in images of his royal majesty, of the angels who guard his divine right, and of his own pathetic and almost sacred sufferings. The images are not insincere, and yet they are like dreams, for they refuse to touch earth and to connect themselves either with his past misdeeds or with the actions he ought now to perform. A strain of a similar weakness appears again in Hamlet, though only as one strain in a much more deep and complex nature. But this is not a common theme in poetry, much less in dramatic poetry.[10]

To come to our second question. When Shakespeare painted Cressida or described her through the mouth of Ulysses ('O these encounterers,' etc.), or, again, when he portrayed the love of Antony for Cleopatra, was he using his personal experience? To answer that he *must* have done so would be as ridiculous as to argue that Iago must be a portrait of himself; and the two plays contain nothing which, by itself, would justify us even in thinking that he probably did so. But we have the series of sonnets about the dark lady; and if we accept the sonnets to the friend as to some considerable extent based on fact and expressive of personal feelings, how can we refuse to take the others on the same footing? Even if the stories of the two series were not intertwined, we should have no ground for treating the two in different ways, unless we could say that external evidence, or the general impression we derive from Shakespeare's works, forbids us to believe that he could ever have been entangled in an intrigue like that implied in the second series, or have felt and thought in the manner there portrayed. Being unable to say this, I am compelled, most regretfully, to hold it probable that this series is, in the main, based on personal experience. And I say 'most regretfully,' not merely because one would regret to think that Shakespeare was the victim of a Cressida or even the lover of a Cleopatra, but because the story implied in these sonnets is of quite another kind. They leave, on the whole, a very disagreeable impression. We cannot compare it with the impressions produced, for example, by the 'heathen' spirit of Goethe's *Roman Elegies*, or by the passion of Shakespeare's Antony. In these two cases, widely dissimilar of course, we may speak of 'immorality,' but we are not discomfited, much less disgusted. The feeling and the attitude are poetic, whole-hearted, and in one case passionate in the extreme. But the state of mind expressed in the sonnets about the dark lady is half-hearted, often prosaic, and never worthy of the name of passion. It is uneasy, dissatisfied, distempered, the state of mind of a man who despises his 'passion' and its object and himself, but, standing intellectually far above it, still has not resolution to end it, and only pains us by his gross and joyless jests. In *Troilus and Cressida*—not at all in the portrayal of Troilus's love, but in the atmosphere of the drama—we seem to trace a similar mood of dissatisfaction, and of intellectual but practically impotent contempt.

In this connection it is natural to think of the 'unhappy period' which has so often been surmised in Shakespeare's life. There is not time here to expand the summary remarks made elsewhere on this subject; but I may refer a little more fully to a persistent impression left on my mind by writings which we have reason to assign to the years 1602–6.[11] There is surely something unusual in their tone regarding certain 'vices of the blood,' regarding drunkenness and sexual corruption. It does not lie in Shakespeare's *view* of these vices, but in an undertone of disgust. Read Hamlet's language about the habitual drunkenness of his uncle, or even Cassio's words about his casual excess; then think of the tone of *Henry IV.* or *Twelfth Night* or the *Tempest*; and ask if the difference is not striking. And if you are inclined to ascribe it wholly to the fact that *Hamlet* and *Othello* are tragedies, compare the passages in them with the scene on Pompey's galley in *Antony and Cleopatra*. The intent of that scene is terrible enough, but in the tone there is no more trace of disgust than in *Twelfth Night*. As to the other matter, what I refer to is not the transgression of lovers like Claudio and Juliet, nor even light-hearted irregularities like those of Cassio: here Shakespeare's speech has its habitual tone. But, when he is dealing with lechery and corruption, the undercurrent of disgust seems to become audible. Is it not true that in the plays from *Hamlet* to *Timon* that subject, in one shape or another, is continually before us; that the intensity of loathing in Hamlet's language about his mother's lust is unexampled in Shakespeare; that the treatment of the subject in *Measure for Measure*, though occasionally purely humorous, is on the whole quite unlike the treatment in *Henry IV.* or even in the brothel scenes of *Pericles*;[12] that while *Troilus and Cressida* is full of disgust and contempt, there is not a trace of either in *Antony and Cleopatra*, though some of the jesting there is obscene enough; that this same tone is as plainly heard in the unquestioned parts of *Timon*; and that, while it is natural in Timon to inveigh against female lechery when he speaks to Alcibiades and his harlots, there is no apparent reason why Lear in his exalted madness should choose this subject for similar invectives? 'Pah! give me an ounce of civet, good apothecary, to sweeten my imagination'—it is a fainter echo of this exclamation that one seems to hear in the plays of those years. Of course I am not suggesting that it is mainly due, or as regards drunkenness due in the least, to any private experience of Shakespeare's. It may have no connection whatever with that experience. It might well be connected with it only in so far as a man frequently wearied and depressed might be unusually sensitive to the ugly aspects of life. But, if we do not take the second series of sonnets to be purely fanciful, we shall think it probable that to some undefined extent it owed its origin to the experience depicted in them.[13]

There remain the sonnets addressed to the friend. Even if it were possible to discuss the general question about them here, it would be needless; for I accept almost wholly, and in some points am greatly indebted to, the views put forward by Mr. Beeching in his admirable edition, to which I may therefore refer my hearers.[14] I intend only to state the main reason why I believe the sonnets to be, substantially, what they purport to be, and then to touch upon one or two of the points where they seem to throw light on Shakespeare's personality.

The sonnets to the friend are, so far as we know, unique in Renaissance sonnet literature in being a prolonged and varied record of the intense affection of an older friend for a younger, and of other feelings arising from their relations. They have no real parallel in any series imitative of Virgil's second Eclogue,

or in occasional sonnets to patrons or patron-friends couched in the high-flown language of the time. The intensity of the feelings expressed, however, ought not, by itself, to convince us that they are personal. The author of the plays could, I make no doubt, have written the most intimate of these poems to a mere creature of his imagination and without ever having felt them except in imagination. Nor is there any but an aesthetic reason why he should not have done so if he had wished. But an aesthetic reason there is; and this is the decisive point. No capable poet, much less a Shakespeare, intending to produce a merely 'dramatic' series of poems, would dream of inventing a story like that of these sonnets, or, even if he did, of treating it as they treat it. The story is very odd and unattractive. Such capacities as it has are but slightly developed. It is left obscure, and some of the poems are unintelligible to us because they contain allusions of which we can make nothing. Now all this is perfectly natural if the story is substantially a real story of Shakespeare himself and of certain other persons; if the sonnets were written from time to time as the relations of the persons changed, and sometimes in reference to particular incidents; and if they were written *for* one or more of these persons (far the greater number for only one), and perhaps in a few cases for other friends,—written, that is to say, for people who knew the details and incidents of which we are ignorant. But it is all unnatural, well-nigh incredibly unnatural, if, with the most sceptical critics, we regard the sonnets as a free product of mere imagination.[15]

Assuming, then, that the persons of the story, with their relations, are real, I would add only two remarks about the friend. In the first place, Mr. Beeching seems to me right in denying that there is sufficient evidence of his standing to Shakespeare and the 'rival' poet or poets in the position of a literary patron; while, even if he did, it appears to me quite impossible to take the language of many of the sonnets as that of interested flattery. And in the second place I should be inclined to push even further Mr. Beeching's view on another point. It is clear that the young man was considerably superior to the actor-dramatist in social position; but any gentleman would be so, and there is nothing to prove that he was more than a gentleman of some note, more than plain 'Mr. W. H.' (for these, on the obvious though not compulsory interpretation of the dedication, seem to have been his initials). It is remarkable besides that, while the earlier sonnets show much deference, the later show very little, so little that, when the writer, finding that he has pained his young friend by neglecting him, begs to be forgiven, he writes almost, if not quite, as an equal. Read, for example, sonnets 109, 110, 120, and ask whether it is probable that Shakespeare is addressing here a great nobleman. It seems therefore most likely (though the question is not of much importance) that the sonnets are, to quote Meres's phrase,[16] his 'sonnets among his private friends.'

If then there is, as it appears, no obstacle of any magnitude to our taking the sonnets as substantially what they purport to be, we may naturally look in them for personal traits (and, indeed, to repeat a remark made earlier, we might still expect to find such traits even if we knew the sonnets to be purely dramatic). But in drawing inferences we have to bear in mind what is implied by the qualification 'substantially.' We have to remember that *some* of these poems may be mere exercises of art; that all of them are poems, and not letters, much less *affidavits*; that they are Elizabethan poems; that the Elizabethan language of deference, and also of affection, is to our minds habitually extravagant and fantastic;[17] and that in Elizabethan plays friends openly express their love for one another as Englishmen now rarely do. Allowance being made, however, on account of these facts, the sonnets will still leave two strong impressions—that the poet was exceedingly sensitive to the charm of beauty, and that his love for his friend was, at least at one time, a feeling amounting almost to adoration, and so intense as to be absorbing. Those who are surprised by the first of these traits must have read Shakespeare's dramas with very inactive minds, and I must add that they seem to be somewhat ignorant of human nature. We do not necessarily love best those of our relatives, friends, and acquaintances who please our eyes most; and we should look askance on anyone who regulated his behaviour chiefly by the standard of beauty; but most of us, I suppose, love any human being of either sex and of any age, the better for being beautiful, and are not the least ashamed of the fact. It is further the case that men who are beginning, like the writer of the sonnets, to feel tired and old, are apt to feel an increased and special pleasure in the beauty of the young.[18] If we remember, in addition, what some critics appear constantly to forget, that Shakespeare was a particularly poetical being, we shall hardly be surprised that the beginning of this friendship seems to have been something like a falling in love; and, if we must needs praise and blame, we should also remember that it became a 'marriage of true minds.'[19] And as to the intensity of the feeling expressed in the sonnets, we can easily believe it to be characteristic of the man who made Valentine and Proteus, Brutus and Cassius, Horatio and Hamlet; who painted that strangely moving portrait of Antonio, middle-aged, sad, and almost indifferent between life and death, but devoted to the young, brilliant spendthrift Bassanio; and who portrayed the sudden compelling enchantment exercised by the young Sebastian over the Antonio of *Twelfth Night*. 'If you will not murder me for your love, let me be your servant.' Antonio is accused of piracy: he may lose his life if he is identified:

> I have many enemies in Orsino's court,
> But, come what may, I do adore thee so
> That danger shall seem sport, and I will go.

The adoration, the 'prostration,' of the writer of the sonnets is of one kind with this.

I do not remember what critic uses the word 'prostration.' It applies to Shakespeare's attitude only in some of the sonnets, but there it does apply, unless it is taken to suggest humiliation. *That* is the term used by Hallam, but chiefly in view of a particular point, namely the failure of the poet to 'resent,' though he 'felt and bewailed,' the injury done him in 'the seduction of his mistress.' Though I think we should substitute 'resent more strongly' for the mere 'resent,' I do not deny that the poet's attitude in this matter strikes us at first as suprising as well as unpleasant to contemplate. But Hallam's explanation of it as perhaps due to the exalted position of the friend, would make it much more than unpleasant; and his language seems to show that he, like many critics, did not fully imagine the situation. It is not easy to speak of it in public with the requisite frankness; but it is necessary to realise that, whatever the friend's rank might be, he and the poet were intimate friends; that, manifestly, it was rather the mistress who seduced the friend than the friend the mistress; and that she was apparently a woman not merely of no reputation, but of such a nature that she might readily be expected to be mistress to two men at one and the same time. Anyone who realises this may call the situation 'humiliating' in one sense, and I cannot quarrel with him; but he will not call it 'humiliating' in respect of Shakespeare's relation to his friend; nor will he wonder much that the poet felt more pain than resentment at his friend's treatment of him. There is something infinitely stranger in a play of Shakespeare's, and it may be symptomatic. Ten Brink called attention to it. Proteus actually offers violence to Sylvia,

a spotless lady and the true love of his friend Valentine; and Valentine not only forgives him at once when he professes repentance, but offers to resign Sylvia to him! The incident is to us so utterly preposterous that we find it hard to imagine how the audience stood it; but, even if we conjecture that Shakespeare adopted it from the story he was using, we can hardly suppose that it was so absurd to him as it is to us.[20] And it is not the Sonnets alone which lead us to surmise that forgiveness was particularly attractive to him, and the forgiveness of a friend much easier than resentment. From the Sonnets we gather—and there is nothing in the plays or elsewhere to contradict the impression—that he would not be slow to resent the criticisms, slanders, or injuries of strangers or the world, and that he bore himself towards them with a proud, if silent, self-sufficiency. But, we surmise, for anyone whom he loved

> He carried anger as a flint bears fire;
> Who, much enforced, shows a hasty spark
> And straight is cold again;

and towards anyone so fondly loved as the friend of the Sonnets he was probably incapable of fierce or prolonged resentment.

The Sonnets must not occupy us further; and I will not dwell on the indications they afford that Shakespeare sometimes felt bitterly both the social inferiority of his position as an actor,[21] and its influence on his own character; or that (as we have already conjectured) he may sometimes have played the fool in society, sometimes felt weary of life, and often was over-tired by work. It is time to pass on to a few hesitating conjectures about what may be called his tastes.

Some passages of his about music have become household words. It is not downright impossible that, like Bottom, having only a reasonable good ear, he liked best the tongs and the bones; that he wondered, with Benedick, how sheeps-guts should hale souls out of men's bodies; and that he wrote the famous lines in the *Merchant of Venice* and in *Twelfth Night* from mere observation and imagination. But it is futile to deal with scepticism run well-nigh mad, and certainly inaccessible to argument from the cases of poets whose tastes are matter of knowledge. Assuming therefore that Shakespeare was fond of music, I may draw attention to two points. Almost always he speaks of music as having a softening, tranquillising, or pensive influence. It lulls killing care and grief of heart to sleep. It soothes the sick and weary, and even makes them drowsy. Hamlet calls for it in his hysterical excitement after the success of the play scene. When it is hoped that Lear's long sleep will have carried his madness away, music is played as he awakes, apparently to increase the desired 'temperance.' It harmonises with the still and moonlit night, and the dreamy happiness of newly-wedded lovers. Almost all the rare allusions to lively or exciting music, apart from dancing, refer, I believe, to 'the lofty instruments of *war*.' These facts would almost certainly have a personal significance if Shakespeare were a more modern poet. Whether they have any, or have much, in an Elizabethan I do not venture to judge.

The second point is diminutive, but it may be connected with the first. The Duke in *Measure for Measure* observes that music often has

> a charm
> To make bad good and good provoke to harm.

If we ask how it should provoke good to harm, we may recall what was said of the weaknesses of some poetic natures, and that no one speaks more feelingly of music than Orsino; further, how he refers to music as 'the food of love,' and who it is that almost repeats the phrase.

> Give me some music: music, moody food
> Of us that trade in love:

—the words are Cleopatra's.[22] Did Shakespeare as he wrote them remember, I wonder, the dark lady to whose music he had listened (Sonnet 128)?

We should be greatly surprised to find in Shakespeare signs of the nineteenth century feeling for mountain scenery, but we can no more doubt that within certain limits he was sensitive to the beauty of nature than that he was fond of music.[23] The only question is whether we can guess at any preferences here. It is probably inevitable that the flowers most often mentioned should be the rose and the lily;[24] but hardly that the violet should come next and not far behind, and that the fragrance of the violet should be spoken of more often even than that of the rose, and, it seems, with special affection. This may be a fancy, and it will be thought a sentimental fancy too; but poets, like other people, may have favourite flowers; that of Keats, we happen to know, was the violet.

Again, if we may draw any conclusion from the frequency and the character of the allusions, the lark held for Shakespeare the place of honour among birds; and the lines,

> Hark! hark! the lark at heaven's gate sings,
> And Phœbus gins arise,

may suggest one reason for this. The lark, as several other collocations show, was to him the bird of joy that welcomes the sun; and it can hardly be doubted that dawn and early morning was the time of day that most appealed to him. That he felt the beauty of night and of moonlight is obvious; but we find very little to match the lines in *Richard II.*,

> The setting sun, and music at the close,
> As the last taste of sweets, is sweetest last;

and still less to prove that he felt the magic of evening twilight, the 'heavenliest hour' of a famous passage in *Don Juan.* There is a wonderful line in Sonnet 132,

> And that full star that ushers in the even,

but I remember little else of the same kind. Shakespeare, as it happens, uses the word 'twilight' only once, and in an unforgettable passage:

> In me thou see'st the twilight of such day
> As after sunset fadeth in the west:
> Which by and by black night doth take away,
> Death's second self that seals up all in rest.

And this feeling, though not often so solemn, is on the whole the prevailing sentiment in the references to sunset and evening twilight. It corresponds with the analogy between the times of the day and the periods of human life. The sun sets from the weariness of age; but he rises in the strength and freshness of youth, firing the proud tops of the eastern pines, and turning the hills and the sea into burnished gold, while jocund day stands tiptoe on the misty mountain tops, and the lark sings at the gate of heaven. In almost all the familiar lines about dawn one seems to catch that 'indescribable gusto' which Keats heard in Kean's delivery of the words:

> Stir with the lark to-morrow, gentle Norfolk.

Two suggestions may be ventured as to Shakespeare's feelings towards four-footed animals. The first must be very tentative. We do not expect in a writer of that age the sympathy with animals which is so beautiful a trait in much of the poetry of the last hundred and fifty years. And I can remember in Shakespeare scarcely any sign of *fondness* for an animal,—not even for a horse, though he wrote so often of horses. But there are rather frequent, if casual, expressions of pity, in references, for example, to the hunted hare or stag, or to the spurred horse:[25] and it may be questioned whether the passage in *As You Like It* about the wounded deer is quite devoid of personal significance. No doubt Shakespeare thought the tears of Jaques

sentimental; but he put a piece of himself into Jaques. And, besides, it is not Jaques alone who dislikes the killing of the deer, but the Duke; and we may surely hear some tone of Shakespeare's voice in the Duke's speech about the life in the forest. Perhaps we may surmise that, while he enjoyed field-sports, he felt them at times to be out of tune with the harmony of nature.

On the second point, I regret to say, I can feel no doubt. Shakespeare did not care for dogs, as Homer did; he even disliked them, as Goethe did. Of course he can write eloquently about the points of hounds and the music of their voices in the chase, and humorously about Launce's love for his cur and even about the cur himself; but this is no more significant on the one side than is his conventional use of 'dog' as a term of abuse on the other. What is significant is the absence of allusion, or (to be perfectly accurate) of sympathetic allusion, to the characteristic virtues of dogs, and the abundance of allusions of an insulting kind. Shakespeare has observed and recorded, in some instances profusely, every vice that I can think of in an ill-conditioned dog. He fawns and cringes and flatters, and then bites the hand that caressed him; he is a coward who attacks you from behind, and barks at you the more the farther off you go; he knows neither charity, humanity, nor gratitude; as he flatters power and wealth, so he takes part against the poor and unfashionable, and if fortune turns against you so does he.[26] The plays swarm with these charges. Whately's exclamation—uttered after a College meeting or a meeting of Chapter, I forgot which—'The more I see of men, the more I like dogs,' would never have been echoed by Shakespeare. The things he most loathed in men he found in dogs too. And yet all this might go for nothing if we could set anything of weight against it. But what can we set? Nothing whatever, so far as I remember, except a recognition of courage in bear-baiting, bull-baiting mastiffs. For I cannot quote as favourable to the spaniel the appeal of Helena:

> I am your spaniel; and, Demetrius,
> The more you beat me I will fawn on you:
> Use me but as your spaniel, spurn me, strike me,
> Neglect me, lose me; only give me leave,
> Unworthy as I am, to follow you.

This may show that Shakespeare was alive to the baseness of a spaniel-owner, but not that he appreciated that self-less affection which he describes. It is more probable that it irritated him, as it does many men still; and, as for its implying fidelity, there is no reference, I believe, to the fidelity of the dog in the whole of his works, and he chooses the spaniel himself as a symbol of flattery and ingratitude: his Cæsar talks of

> Knee-crooked court'sies and base spaniel-fawning;

his Antony exclaims:

> the hearts
> That spaniel'd me at heels, to whom I gave
> Their wishes, do discandy, melt their sweets
> On blossoming Cæsar.

To all that he loved most in men he was blind in dogs. And then we call him universal!

This line of research into Shakespeare's tastes might be pursued a good deal further, but we must return to weightier matters. We saw that he could sympathise with anyone who erred and suffered from impulse, affections of the blood, or even such passions as were probably no danger to himself,— ambition, for instance, and pride. Can we learn anything more about him by observing virtues or types of character with which he appears to feel little sympathy, though he may approve them? He certainly does not show this imperfect sympathy towards self-control; we seem to feel even a special liking for

Brutus, and again for Horatio, who has suffered much, is quietly patient, and has mastered both himself and fortune. But, not to speak of coldly selfish natures, he seems averse to bloodless people, those who lack, or those who have deadened, the natural desires for joy and sympathy, and those who tend to be precise.[27] Nor does he appear to be drawn to men who, as we say, try to live or to act on principle; nor to those who aim habitually at self-improvement; nor yet to the saintly type of character. I mean, not that he *could* not sympathise with them, but that they did not attract him. Isabella, in *Measure for Measure*, is drawn, of course, with understanding, but, it seems to me, with little sympathy. Her readiness to abandon her pleading for Claudio, out of horror at his sin and a sense of the justice of Angelo's reasons for refusing his pardon, is doubtless in character; but if Shakespeare had sympathised more with her at this point, so should we; while, as it is, we are tempted to exclaim,

She loves him not, she wants the natural touch;

and perhaps if Shakespeare had liked her better and had not regarded her with some irony, he would not have allowed himself, for mere convenience, to degrade her by marrying her to the Duke. Brutus and Cordelia, on the other hand, are drawn with the fullest imaginative sympathy, and they, it may be said, are characters of principle; but then (even if Cordelia could be truly so described) they are also intensely affectionate, and by no means inhumanly self-controlled.

The mention of Brutus may carry us somewhat farther. Shakespeare's Brutus kills Cæsar, not because Cæsar aims at absolute power, but because Brutus fears that absolute power may make him cruel. That is not Plutarch's idea, it is Shakespeare's. He could fully sympathise with the gentleness of Brutus, with his entire superiority to private aims and almost entire freedom from personal susceptibilities, and even with his resolution to sacrifice his friend; but he could not so sympathise with mere horror of monarchy or absolute power. And now extend this a little. Can you imagine Shakespeare an enthusiast for an 'idea'; a devotee of divine right, or the rights of Parliament, or any particular form of government in Church or State; a Fifth Monarchy man, or a Quaker, or a thick-and-thin adherent of any compact, exclusive, abstract creed, even if it were as rational and noble as Mazzini's? This type of mind, even at its best, is alien from his. Scott is said, rightly or wrongly, to have portrayed the Covenanters without any deep understanding of them; it would have been the same with Shakespeare. I am not praising him, or at least not merely praising him. One may even suggest that on this side he was limited. In any age he would have been safe against fanaticism and one-sided ideas; but perhaps in no age would he have been the man to insist with the necessary emphasis on those one-sided ideas which the moment may need, or even to give his whole heart to men who join a forlorn hope or are martyred for a faith. And though it is rash to suggest that anything in the way of imagination was beyond his reach, perhaps the legend of Faust, with his longings for infinite power and knowledge and enjoyment of beauty, would have suited him less well than Marlowe; and if he had written on the subject that Cervantes took, his Don Quixote would have been at least as laughable as the hero we know, but would he have been a soul so ideally noble and a figure so profoundly pathetic?

This would be the natural place to discuss Shakespeare's politics if we were to discuss them at all. But even if the question whether he shows any interest in the political differences of his time, or any sympathies or antipathies in regard to them, admits of an answer, it could be answered only by an examination of details; and I must pass it by, and offer only the briefest remarks on a wider question. Shakespeare, as we might expect, shows no sign of believing in what is sometimes called a political 'principle'. The main ideas which, consciously or unconsciously, seem to govern or emerge from his presentation of state affairs, might perhaps be put thus. National welfare is the end of politics, and the criterion by which political actions are to be judged. It implies of necessity 'degree'; that is, differences of position and function in the members of the body politic.[28] And the first requisites of national welfare are the observance of this degree, and the concordant performance of these functions in the general interest. But there appear to be no further absolute principles than these: beyond them all is relative to the particular case and its particular conditions. We find no hint, for example, in *Julius Cæsar* that Shakespeare regarded a monarchical form of government as intrinsically better than a republican, or *vice versa*; no trace in *Richard II.* that the author shares the king's belief in his inviolable right, or regards Bolingbroke's usurpation as justifiable. We perceive, again, pretty clearly in several plays a dislike and contempt of demagogues, and an opinion that mobs are foolish, fickle, and ungrateful. But these are sentiments which the most determined of believers in democracy, if he has sense, may share; and if he thinks that the attitude of aristocrats like Volumnia and Coriolanus is inhuman and as inexcusable as that of the mob, and that a mob is as easily led right as wrong and has plenty of good nature in it, he has abundant ground for holding that Shakespeare thought so too. That Shakespeare greatly liked and admired the typical qualities of the best kind of aristocrat seems highly probable; but then this taste has always been compatible with a great variety of political opinions. It is interesting but useless to wonder what his own opinions would have been at various periods of English history: perhaps the only thing we can be pretty sure of in regard to them is that they would never have been extreme, and that he would never have supposed his opponents to be entirely wrong.

We have tried to conjecture the impulses, passions, and errors with which Shakespeare could easily sympathise, and the virtues and types of character which he may have approved without much sympathy. It remains to ask whether we can notice tendencies and vices to which he felt any special antipathy; and it is obvious and safe to point to those most alien to a gentle, open, and free nature, the vices of a cold and hard disposition, self-centred and incapable of fusion with others. Passing over, again, the plainly hideous forms or extremes of such vice, as we see them in characters like Richard III., Iago, Goneril and Regan, or the Queen in *Cymbeline*, we seem to detect a particular aversion to certain vices which have the common mark of baseness; for instance, servility and flattery (especially when deliberate and practised with a view to self-advancement), feigning in friendship, and ingratitude. Shakespeare's *animus* against the dog arises from the attribution of these vices to him, and against them in men are directed the invectives which seem to have a personal ring. There appears to be traceable also a feeling of a special, though less painful, kind against unmercifulness. I do not mean, of course, cruelty, but unforgivingness, and even the tendency to prefer justice to mercy. From no other dramatic author, probably, could there be collected such prolonged and heart-felt praises of mercy as from Shakespeare. He had not at all strongly, I think, that instinct and love of justice and retribution which in many men are so powerful; but Prospero's words,

they being penitent,
The sole drift of my purpose doth extend
Not a jot further,

came from his heart. He perceived with extreme clearness the connection of acts with their consequences; but his belief that in this sense 'the gods are just' was accompanied by the strongest feeling that forgiveness ought to follow repentance, and (if I may so put it) his favourite petition was the one that begins 'Forgive us our trespasses.' To conclude, I have fancied that he shows an unusual degree of disgust at slander and dislike of censoriousness; and where he speaks in the Sonnets of those who censured him he betrays an exceptionally decided feeling that a man's offences are his own affair and not the world's.[29]

Some of the vices which seem to have been particularly odious to Shakespeare have, we may notice, a special connection with prosperity and power. Men feign and creep and flatter to please the powerful and to win their own way to ease or power; and they envy and censure and slander their competitors in the race; and when they succeed, they are ungrateful to their friends and helpers and patrons; and they become hard and unmerciful, and despise and bully those who are now below them. So, perhaps, Shakespeare said to himself in those years when, as we imagine, melancholy and embitterment often overclouded his sky, though they did not obscure his faith in goodness and much less his intellectual vision. And prosperity and power, he may have added, come less frequently by merit than by those base arts or by mere fortune. The divorce of goodness and power was, to Shelley, the 'woe of the world'; if we substitute for 'goodness' the wider word 'merit,' we may say that this divorce, with the evil bred by power, is to Shakespeare also the root of bitterness. This fact, presented in its extreme form of the appalling cruelty of the prosperous, and the heartrending suffering of the defenceless, forms the problem of his most tremendous drama. We have no reason to surmise that his own sufferings were calamitous; and the period which seems to be marked by melancholy and embitterment was one of outward, or at least financial, prosperity; but nevertheless we can hardly doubt that he felt on the small scale of his own life the influence of that divorce of power and merit. His complaint against Fortune, who had so ill provided for his life, runs through the Sonnets. Even if we could regard as purely conventional the declarations that his verses would make his friend immortal, it is totally impossible that he can have been unaware of the gulf between his own gifts and those of others, or can have failed to feel the disproportion between his position and his mind. Hamlet had never experienced

> the spurns
> That patient merit of the unworthy takes,

and that make the patient soul weary of life; the man who had experienced them was the writer of Sonnet 66, who cried for death because he was tired with beholding

> desert a beggar born,
> And needy nothing trimmed in jollity,

—a beggarly soul flaunting in brave array. Neither had Hamlet felt in his own person 'the insolence of office'; but the actor had doubtless felt it often enough, and we can hardly err in hearing his own voice in dramatic expressions of wonder and contempt at the stupid pride of mere authority and at men's slavish respect for it. Two examples will suffice. 'Thou hast seen a farmer's dog bark at a beggar, and the creature run from the cur? There thou mightst behold the great image of authority. A dog's obeyed in office': so says Lear, when madness has cleared his vision, and indignation makes the Timon-like verses that follow. The other example is almost too famous for quotation but I have a reason for quoting it:

> man, proud man,
> Drest in a little brief authority,
> Most ignorant of what he's most assured,

His glassy essence, like an angry ape,
Plays such fantastic tricks before high heaven
As makes the angels weep; who, with our spleens,
Would all themselves laugh mortal.

It is Isabella who says that; but it is scarcely in character; Shakespeare himself is speaking.[30]

It is with great hesitation that I hazard a few words on Shakespeare's religion. Any attempt to penetrate his reserve on this subject may appear a crowning impertinence; and, since his dramas are almost exclusively secular, any impressions we may form here must be even more speculative than usual. Yet it is scarcely possible to read him much without such speculations; and there are at least some theories which may confidently be dismissed. It cannot be called absolutely impossible that Shakespeare was indifferent to music and to the beauty of Nature, and yet the idea is absurd; and in the same way it is barely possible, and yet it is preposterous, to suppose that he was an ardent and devoted atheist or Brownist or Roman Catholic, and that all the indications to the contrary are due to his artfulness and determination not to get into trouble. There is no absurdity, on the other hand, nor of necessity anything hopeless, in the question whether there are signs that he belonged to this or that church, and was inclined to one mode of thought within it rather than to another. Only the question is scarcely worth asking for our present purpose, unless there is some reason to believe that he took a keen interest in these matters. Suppose, for example, that we had ground to accept a tradition that he 'died a papist,' this would not tell us much about him unless we had also ground to think that he lived a papist, and that his faith went far into his personality. But in fact we receive from his writings, it appears to me, a rather strong impression that he concerned himself little, if at all, with differences of doctrine or church government.[31] And we may go further. Have we not reason to surmise that he was not, in the distinctive sense of the word, a religious man—a man, that is to say, whose feelings and actions are constantly and strongly influenced by thoughts of his relation to an object of worship? If Shakespeare had been such a man, is it credible that we should find nothing in tradition or in his works to indicate the fact; and is it likely that we should find in his works some things that we do find there?[32]

Venturing with much doubt a little farther I will put together certain facts and impressions without at once drawing any conclusion from them. Almost all the speeches that can be called pronouncedly religious and Christian in phraseology and spirit are placed in the mouths of persons to whom they are obviously appropriate, either from their position (*e.g.* bishops, friars, nuns), or from what Shakespeare found in histories (*e.g.* Henry IV., V., and VI.), or for some other plain reason. We cannot build, therefore, on these speeches in the least. On the other hand (except, of course, where they are hypocritical or politic), we perceive in Shakespeare's tone in regard to them not the faintest trace of dislike or contempt; nor can we find a trace anywhere of such feelings, or of irreverence, towards Christian ideas, institutions, or customs (mere humorous irreverence is not relevant here); and in the case of 'sympathetic' characters, living in Christian times but not in any decided sense religious, no disposition is visible to suppress or ignore their belief in, and use of, religious ideas. Some characters, again, Christian or heathen, who appear to be drawn with rather marked sympathy, have strong, if simple, religious convictions (*e.g.* Horatio, Edgar, Hermione); and in others, of whom so much can hardly be said, but who strike many readers, rightly or wrongly, as having a good deal of Shakespeare in them (*e.g.* Romeo and Hamlet), we observe a quiet but deep sense that they and other men are neither their own masters nor responsible only to themselves and other men, but are in the hands of 'Providence' or guiding powers 'above.'[33]

To this I will add two remarks. To every one, I suppose, certain speeches sound peculiarly personal. Perhaps others may share my feeling about Hamlet's words:

> There's a divinity that shapes our ends,
> Rough-hew them how we will;

and about those other words of his:

> There are more things in heaven and earth, Horatio,
> Than are dreamt of in your philosophy;

and about the speech of Prospero ending, 'We are such stuff as dreams are made on.'[34] On the other hand, we observe that Hamlet seems to have arrived at that conviction as to the 'divinity' after reflection, and that, while he usually speaks as one who accepts the received Christian ideas, yet, when meditating profoundly, he appears to ignore them.[35] In the same way the Duke in *Measure for Measure* is for the most part, and necessarily, a Christian; yet nobody would guess it from the great speech, 'Be absolute for death,' addressed by a supposed friar to a youth under sentence to die, yet containing not a syllable about a future life.[36]

Without adducing more of the endless but baffling material for a conclusion, I will offer the result left on my mind, and, merely for the sake of brevity, will state it with hardly any of the qualifications it doubtless needs. Shakespeare, I imagine, was not, in the sense assigned to the word some minutes ago, a religious man. Nor was it natural to him to regard good and evil, better and worse, habitually from a theological point of view. But (this appears certain) he had a lively and serious sense of 'conscience,' of the pain of self-reproach and self-condemnation, and of the torment to which this pain might rise.[37] He was not in the least disposed to regard conscience as somehow illusory or a human invention, but on the contrary thought of it (I use the most non-committal phrase I can find) as connected with the power that rules the world and is not escapable by man. He realised very fully and felt very keenly, after his youth was past and at certain times of stress, the sufferings and wrongs of men, the strength of evil, the hideousness of certain forms of it, and its apparent incurability in certain cases. And he must sometimes have felt all this as a terrible problem. But, however he may have been tempted, and may have yielded, to exasperation and even despair, he never doubted that it is best to be good; felt more and more that one must be patient and must forgive;[38] and probably maintained unbroken a conviction, practical if not formulated, that to be good is to be at peace with that unescapable power. But it is unlikely that he attempted to theorise further on the nature of the power. All was for him, in the end, mystery; and, while we have no reason whatever to attribute to him a belief in the ghosts and oracles he used in his dramas, he had no inclination to play the spy on God or to limit his power by our notions of it. That he had dreams and ponderings about the mystery such as he never put into the mouths of actors I do not doubt; but I imagine they were no more than dreams and ponderings and movings about in worlds unrealised.

Whether to this 'religion' he joined a more or less conventional acceptance of some or all of the usual Christian ideas, it is impossible to tell. There is no great improbability to me in the idea that he did not, but it is more probable to me that he did,—that, in fact, though he was never so tormented as Hamlet, his position in this matter was, at least in middle life (and he never reached old age), much like Hamlet's. If this were so it might naturally happen that, as he grew older and wearier of labour, and perhaps of the tumult of pleasure and

thought and pain, his more personal religion, the natural piety which seems to gain in weight and serenity in the latest plays, came to be more closely joined with Christian ideas. But I can find no clear indications that this did happen; and though some have believed that they discovered these ideas displayed in full, though not explicitly, in the *Tempest*, I am not able to hear there more than the stream of Shakespeare's own 'religion' moving with its fullest volume and making its deepest and most harmonious music.[39]

This lecture must end, though its subject is endless, and I will touch on only one point more,—one that may to some extent recall and connect the scattered suggestions I have offered.

If we were obliged to answer the question which of Shakespeare's plays contains, not indeed the fullest picture of his mind, but the truest expression of his nature and habitual temper, unaffected by special causes of exhilaration or gloom, I should be disposed to choose *As You Like It*. It wants, to go no further, the addition of a touch of Sir Toby or Falstaff, and the ejection of its miraculous conversions of ill-disposed characters. But the misbehaviour of Fortune, and the hardness and ingratitude of men, form the basis of its plot, and are a frequent topic of complaint. And, on the other hand, he who is reading it has a smooth brow and smiling lips, and a heart that murmurs,

> Happy is your grace,
> That can translate the stubbornness of fortune
> Into so quiet and so sweet a style.

And it is full not only of sweetness, but of romance, fun, humour of various kinds, delight in the oddities of human nature, love of modesty and fidelity and high spirit and patience, dislike of scandal and censure, contemplative curiosity, the feeling that in the end we are all merely players, together with a touch of the feeling that

> Then is there mirth in heaven
> When earthly things made even
> Atone together.

And, finally, it breathes the serene holiday mood of escape from the toil, competition, and corruption of city and court into the sun and shadow and peace of the country, where one can be idle and dream and meditate and sing, and pursue or watch the deer as the fancy takes one, and make love or smile at lovers according to one's age.[40]

If, again, the question were put to us, which of Shakespeare's characters reveals most of his personality, the majority of those who consented to give an answer would answer 'Hamlet.' This impression may be fanciful, but it is difficult to think it wholly so, and, speaking for those who share it, I will try to trace some of its sources. There is a good deal of Shakespeare that is not in Hamlet. But Hamlet, we think, is the only character in Shakespeare who could possibly have composed his plays (though it appears unlikely, from his verses to Ophelia, that he could have written the best songs). Into Hamlet's mouth are put what are evidently Shakespeare's own views on drama and acting. Hamlet alone, among the great serious characters, can be called a humorist. When in some trait of another character we seem to touch Shakespeare's personality, we are frequently reminded of Hamlet.[41] When in a profound reflective speech we hear Shakespeare's voice, we usually hear Hamlet's too, and his peculiar humour and turns of phrase appear unexpectedly in persons otherwise unlike him and unlike one another. The most melancholy group of Sonnets (71–74) recalls Hamlet at once, here and there recalls even his words; and he and the writer of Sonnet 66 both recount in a list the ills that make men long for death. And then Hamlet 'was indeed honest and of an open and free nature'; sweet-tempered and modest, yet not slow to resent calumny or injury; of a serious but not a melancholy disposition; and the lover of his friend. And, with these traits, we remember his poet ecstasy at the glory of earth and sky and the marvellous endowments of man; his eager affectionate response to everything noble or sweet in human nature; his tendency to dream and to live in the world of his own mind; his liability to sudden vehement emotion, and his admiration for men whose blood and judgment are better commingled; the overwhelming effect of disillusionment upon him; his sadness, fierceness, bitterness and cynicism. All this, and more: his sensitiveness to the call of duty; his longing to answer to it, and his anguish over his strange delay; the conviction gathering in his tortured soul that man's purposes and failures are divinely shaped to ends beyond his vision; his incessant meditation, and his sense that there are mysteries which no meditation can fathom; nay, even littler traits like his recourse to music to calm his excitement, or his feeling on the one hand that the peasant should not tread on the courtier's heels, and on the other that the mere courtier is spacious in the possession of dirt—all this, I say, corresponds with our impression of Shakespeare, or rather of characteristic traits in Shakespeare, probably here and there a good deal heightened, and mingled with others not characteristic of Shakespeare at all. And if this is more than fancy, it may explain to us why Hamlet is the most fascinating character, and the most inexhaustible, in all imaginative literature. What else should he be, if the world's greatest poet, who was able to give almost the reality of nature to creations totally unlike himself, put his own soul straight into this creation, and when he wrote Hamlet's speeches wrote down his own heart?[42]

*Notes*

1. Unquestionably it holds in a considerable degree of Browning, who in *At the Mermaid* and *House* wrote as though he imagined that neither his own work nor Shakespeare's betrayed anything of the inner man. But if we are to criticise those two poems as arguments, we must say that they involve two hopelessly false assumptions, that we have to choose between a self-revelation like Byron's and no self-revelation at all, and that the relation between a poet and his work is like that between the inside and the outside of a house.

2. Almost all Shakespearean criticism, of course, contains something bearing on our subject; but I have a practical reason for mentioning in particular Mr. Frank Harris's articles in the *Saturday Review* for 1898. A good many of Mr. Harris's views I cannot share, and I had arrived at almost all the ideas expressed in the lecture (except some on the Sonnets question) before reading his papers. But I found in them also valuable ideas which were quite new to me and would probably be so to many readers. It is a great pity that the articles are not collected and published in a book. [Mr. Harris has published, in *The Man Shakespeare*, the substance of the articles, and also matter which, in my judgment, has much less value.]

3. He is apologising for an attack made on Shakespeare in a pamphlet of which he was the publisher and Greene the writer.

4. It is said of him, indeed, in his lifetime that, had he not played some kingly parts in sport (*i.e.* on the stage), he would have been a companion for a king.

5. Nor, *vice versa*, does the possession of these latter qualities at all imply, as some writers seem to assume, the absence of the former or of gentleness.

6. Fuller may be handing down a tradition, but it is not safe to assume this. His comparison, on the other hand, of Shakespeare and Jonson, in their wit combats, to an English man-of-war and a Spanish great galleon, reads as if his own happy fancy were operating on the reports, direct or indirect, of eye-witnesses.

7. See, for example, Act IV. Sc. V., to which I know no parallel in the later tragedies.

8. I allude to Sonnet 110, Mr. Beeching's note on which seems to be unquestionably right: 'There is no reference to the poet's profession of player. The sonnet gives the confession of a favourite of society.' This applies, I think, to the whole group of sonnets (it begins with 107) in which the poet excuses his neglect of his friend, though there are *also* references to his profession and its effect on his nature and his reputation. (By a slip Mr. Beeching makes the neglect last for three years.)

9. It is perhaps most especially in his rendering of the shock and the effects of *disillusionment* in open natures that we seem to feel Shakespeare's personality. The nature of this shock is expressed in Henry's words to Lord Scroop:

> I will weep for thee;
> For this revolt of thine, methinks, is like
> Another fall of man.

10. There is nothing of this semi-reality, of course, in the *passion* of love as portrayed, for example, in men so different as Orlando, Othello, Antony, Troilus, whose love for Cressida resembles that of Romeo for Juliet. What I have said of Romeo's 'love' for Rosaline corresponds roughly with Coleridge's view; and, without subscribing to all of Coleridge's remarks, I believe he was right in finding an intentional contrast between this feeling and the passion that displaces it (though it does not follow that the feeling would not have become a genuine passion if Rosaline had been kind). Nor do I understand the notion that Coleridge's view is refuted and even rendered ridiculous by the mere fact that Shakespeare found the Rosaline story in Brooke (Halliwell-Phillipps, *Outlines*, 7th ed., illustrative note 2). Was he compelled then to use whatever he found? Was it his practice to do so? The question is always *why* he used what he found, and *how*. Coleridge's view of this matter, it need hardly be said, is far from indisputable; but it must be judged by our knowledge of Shakespeare's mind and not of his material alone. I may add, as I have referred to Halliwell-Phillipps, Shakespeare made changes in the story he found; that it is arbitrary to assume (not that it matters) that Coleridge, who read Steevens, was unaware of Shakespeare's use of Brooke; and that Brooke was by no means a 'wretched poetaster.'

11. *Hamlet, Measure for Measure, Othello, Troilus and Cressida, King Lear, Timon of Athens.* See *Shakespearean Tragedy*, pp. 79–85, 275–6. I should like to insist on the view there taken that the tragedies subsequent to *Lear* and *Timon* do not show the pressure of painful feelings.

12. It is not implied that these scenes are certainly Shakespeare's; but I see no sufficient ground for decisively rejecting them.

13. That experience, certainly in part and probably wholly, belongs to an earlier time, since sonnets 138 and 144 were printed in the *Passionate Pilgrim*. But I see no difficulty in that. What bears little fruit in a normal condition of spirits may bear abundant fruit later, in moods of discouragement and exasperation induced largely by other causes.

14. *The Sonnets of Shakespeare with an Introduction and Notes*, Ginn & Co., 1904.

15. I find that Mr. Beeching, in the Stratford Town edition of Shakespeare (1907), has also urged these considerations.

16. I do not mean to imply that Meres necessarily refers to the sonnets we possess, or that all of these are likely to have been written by 1598.

17. A fact to be remembered in regard to references to the social position of the friend.

18. Mr. Beeching's illustration of the friendship of the sonnets from the friendship of Gray and Bonstetten is worth pages of argument.

19. In 125 the poet repudiates the accusation that his friendship is too much based on beauty.

20. This does not imply that the Sonnets are as early as the *Two Gentlemen of Verona*, and much less that they are earlier.

21. This seems to be referred to in lines by John Davies of Hereford, reprinted in Ingleby's *Shakespeare's Centurie of Prayse*, second edition, pp. 58, 84, 94. In the first of these passages, dated 1603 (and perhaps in the second, 1609), there are signs that Davies had read Sonnet 111, a fact to be noted with regard to the question of the chronology of the Sonnets.

22. 'Mistress Tearsheet' too 'would fain hear some music,' and 'Sneak's noise' had to be sent for (2 *Henry IV.*, II. iv. 12).

23. It is tempting, though not safe, to infer from the *Tempest* and the great passage in *Pericles* that Shakespeare must have been in a storm at sea; but that he felt the poetry of a sea-storm is beyond all doubt. Few moments in the reading of his works are more overwhelming than that in which, after listening not without difficulty to the writer of the first two Acts of *Pericles*, suddenly, as the third opens, one hears the authentic voice:

> Thou god of this great vast, rebuke these surges
> That wash both heaven and hell. . . .
>       The seaman's whistle
> Is as a whisper in the ears of death,
> Unheard.

Knowing that this is coming, I cannot stop to read the Prologue to Act III., though I believe Shakespeare wrote it. How it can be imagined that he did more than touch up Acts I. and II. passes my comprehension.

    I may call attention to another point. Unless I mistake, there is nothing in Shakespeare's authorities, as known to us, which corresponds with the feeling of Timon's last speech, beginning,

> Come not to me again: but say to Athens,
> Timon hath made his everlasting mansion
> Upon the beached verge of the salt flood:

a feeling made more explicit in the final speech of Alcibiades.

24. The lily seems to be in almost all cases the Madonna lily. It is very doubtful whether the lily of the valley is referred to at all.

25. But there is something disappointing, and even estranging, in Sonnet 50, which, promising to show a real sympathy, cheats us in the end. I may observe, without implying that the fact has any personal significance, that the words about 'the poor beetle that we tread upon' are given to a woman (Isabella), and that it is Marina who says:

> I trod upon a worm against my will,
> But I wept for it.

26. Three times in one drama Shakespeare refers to this detestable trait. See *Shakespearean Tragedy*, p. 268, where I should like to qualify still further the sentence containing the qualification 'on the whole.' Good judges, at least, assure me that I have admitted too much against the dog.

27. Nor can I recall any sign of liking, or even approval, of that 'prudent, *cautious*, self-control' which, according to a passage in Burns, is 'wisdom's root.'

28. The *locus classicus*, of course, is *Troilus and Cressida*, I. iii. 75 ff.

29. Of all the evils inflicted by man on man those chosen for mention in the dirge in *Cymbeline*, one of the last plays, are the frown o' the great, the tyrant's stroke, slander, censure rash.

30. Having written these paragraphs, I should like to disclaim the belief that Shakespeare was habitually deeply discontented with his position in life.

31. Allusions to puritans show at most what we take almost for granted, that he did not like precisians or people hostile to the stage.

32. In the Sonnets, for example, there is an almost entire absence of definitely religious thought or feeling. The nearest approach to it is in Sonnet 146 ('Poor soul, the centre of my sinful earth'), where, however, there is no allusion to a divine law or judge. According to Sonnet 129, lust in action is

> The expense of spirit in a waste of shame;

but no word shows that it is also felt as alienation from God. It must be added that in 108 and 110 there are references to the Lord's Prayer and, perhaps, to the First Commandment, from which a decidedly religious Christian would perhaps have shrunk. Of course I am not saying that we can draw any *necessary* inference from these facts.

33. It is only this 'quiet but deep sense' that is significant. No inference can be drawn from the fact that the mere belief in powers above seems to be taken as a matter of course in practically all the characters, good and bad alike. On the other hand there may well be something symptomatic in the apparent absence of interest in theoretical disbelief in such powers and in the immortality of the soul. I have observed elsewhere that the atheism of Aaron does

not increase the probability that the conception of the character is Shakespeare's.

34. With the first compare, what to me has, though more faintly, the same ring, Hermione's

>      If powers divine
> Behold our human actions, as they do:

with the second, Helena's

> It is not so with Him that all things knows
> As 'tis with us that square our guests by shows;
> But most it is presumption in us when
> The help of heaven we count the act of men:

followed soon after by Lafeu's remark:

> They say miracles are past; and we have our philosophical persons to make modern and familiar things supernatural and causeless. Hence it is that we make trifles of terrors, ensconcing ourselves into seeming knowledge, when we should submit ourselves to an unknown fear.

35. It is worth noting that the reference, which appears in the First Quarto version of 'To be or not to be,' to 'an everlasting judge,' disappears in the revised versions.

36. The suggested inference, of course, is that this speech, thus out of character, and Hamlet's 'To be or not to be' (though that is in character), show us Shakespeare's own mind. It has force, I think, but not compulsory force. The topics of these speeches are, in the old sense of the word, commonplaces. Shakespeare may have felt, Here is my chance to show what I can do with certain feelings and thoughts of supreme interest to men of all times and places and modes of belief. It would not follow from this that they are not 'personal,' but any inference to a non-acceptance of received religious ideas would be much weakened. ('All the world's a stage' is a patent example of the suggested elaboration of a commonplace.)

37. What actions in particular *his* conscience approved and disapproved is another question and one not relevant here.

38. This does not at all imply to Shakespeare, so far as we see, that evil is never to be forcibly resisted.

39. I do not mean to reject the idea that in some passages in the *Tempest* Shakespeare, while he wrote them with a dramatic purpose, also thought of himself. It seems to me likely. And if so, there *may* have been such a thought in the words,

> And thence retire me to my Milan, where
> Every third thought shall be my grave;

and also in those lines about prayer and pardon which close the Epilogue, and to my ear come with a sudden effect of great seriousness, contrasting most strangely with their context. If they *had* a grave and personal under-meaning it cannot have been intended for the audience, which would take the prayer as addressed to itself.

40. It may be added that *As You Like It*, though idyllic, is not so falsely idyllic as some critics would make it. It is based, we may roughly say, on a contrast between court and country; but those who inhale virtue from the woodland are courtiers who bring virtue with them, and the country has its churlish masters and unkind or uncouth maidens.

41. This has been strongly urged and fully illustrated by Mr. Harris.

42. It may be suggested that, in the catalogue above, I should have mentioned that imaginative 'unreality' in love referred to on p. 326. But I do not see in Hamlet either this, or any sign that he took Ophelia for an Imogen or even a Juliet, though naturally he was less clearly aware of her deficiencies than Shakespeare.

    I may add, however, another item to the catalogue. We do not feel that the problems presented to most of the tragic heroes could have been fatal to Shakespeare himself. The immense breadth and clearness of his intellect would have saved him from the fate of Othello, Troilus, or Antony. But we do feel, I think, and he himself may have felt, that he could not have coped with Hamlet's problem; and there is no improbability in the idea that he may have experienced in some degree the melancholia of his hero.

# GENERAL

As the soule of *Euphorbus* was thought to live in *Pythagoras*: so the sweete wittie soule of *Ovid* lives in mellifluous & hony-tongued *Shakespeare*, witnes his *Venus* and *Adonis*, his *Lucrece*, his sugred Sonnets among his private friends, &c.

As *Plautus* and *Seneca* are accounted the best for Comedy and Tragedy among the Latines? so *Shakespeare* among y^e English is the most excellent in both kinds for the stage; for Comedy, witnes his *Gentlemen of Verona*, his *Errors*, his *Love labors lost*, his *Love labours wonne*, his *Midsummers night dreame*, & his *Merchant of Venice*: for Tragedy his *Richard the 2. Richard* the 3. *Henry the 4. King Iohn, Titus Andronicus* and his *Romeo and Iuliet*.

As *Epius Stolo* said, that the Muses would speake with *Plautus* tongue, if they would speak Latin: so I say that the Muses would speak with *Shakespeares* fine filed phrase, if they would speake English.—FRANCIS MERES, *Palladis Tamia,* 1598

> Honie-tong'd *Shakespeare* when I saw thine issue
> I swore *Apollo* got them and none other,
> Their rosie-tainted features cloth'd in tissue,
> Some heauen born goddesse said to be their mother:
> Rose-checkt *Adonis* with his amber tresses,
> Faire fire-hot *Venus* charming him to loue her,
> Chaste *Lucretia* virgine-like her dresses,
> Prowd lust-flung *Tarquine* seeking still to proue her:
> *Romea Richard*; more whose names I know not,
> Their sugred tongues, and power attractiue beuty
> Say they are Saints althogh that Sts they shew not
> For thousands vowes to them subiectiue dutie:
> They burn in loue thy children *Shakespear* het them,
> Go, wo thy Muse more Nymphish brood beget them.
>
> —JOHN WEEVER, "Ad Gulielmum Shakespeare,"
> *Epigrammes in the Oldest Cut and Newest Fashion,* 1599

> *Shake-speare*, at length thy pious fellowes giue
> The world thy Workes: thy Workes, by which, out-liue
> Thy Tombe, thy name must; when that stone is rent,
> And Time dissolues thy *Stratford* Moniment,
> Here we aliue shall view thee still. This Booke,
> When Brasse and Marble fade, shall make theee looke
> Fresh to all Ages: when Posteritie
> Shall loath what's new, thinke all is prodegie
> That is not *Shake-speares*; eu'ry Line, each Verse
> Here shall reuiue, redeeme thee from thy Herse.
> Nor Fire, nor cankring Age, as *Naso* said,
> Of his, thy wit-fraught Booke shall once inuade.
> Nor shall I e're beleeue, or thinke thee dead
> (Though mist) vntill our bankrout Stage be sped
> (Impossible) with some new strain t'out-do
> Passions of *Iuliet*, and her *Romeo*;
> Or till I heare a Scene more nobly take,
> Then when thy half-Sword parlying *Romans* spake.
> Till these, till any of thy Volumes rest
> Shall with more fire, more feeling be exprest,
> Be sure, our *Shake-speare*, thou canst neuer dye,
> But crown'd with Lawrell, liue eternally.
>
> —LEONARD DIGGES, "To the Memorie of the Deceased Authour Maister W. Shakespeare," *Mr. William Shakespeares Comedies, Histories, & Tragedies,* 1623

From the most able, to him that can but spell: There you are number'd. We had rather you were weighd. Especially, when the fate of all Bookes depends vpon your capacities: and not of your heads alone, but of your purses. Well! It is now publique, & you wil stand for your priuiledges wee know: to read, and censure. Do so, but buy it first. That doth best commend a Booke, the Stationer saies. Then, how odde soeuer your braines be, or your wisedomes, make your licence the same, and spare not. Iudge your sixe-pen'orth, your shillings worth, your fiue shillings worth at a time, or higher, so you rise to the iust rates, and welcome. But, what euer you do, Buy. Censure will not driue a Trade, or make the Iacke go. And though you be a Magistrate of wit, and sit on the Stage at *Black-Friers*, or the *Cock-pit*, to arraigne Playes dailie, know, these Playes haue had their triall alreadie, and stood out all Appeales; and do now come forth quitted rather by a Decree of Court, then any purchas'd Letters of commendation.

It had bene a thing, we confesse, worthie to haue bene wished, that the Author himselfe had liu'd to haue set forth, and ouerseen his owne writings; But since it hath bin ordain'd otherwise, and he by death departed from that right, we pray you do not envie his Friends, the office of their care, and paine, to haue collected & publish'd them; and so to haue publish'd them, as where (before) you were abus'd with diuerse stolne, and surreptitious copies, maimed, and deformed by the frauds and stealthes of iniurious impostors, that expos'd them: euen those, are now offer'd to your view cur'd, and perfect of their limbes; and all the rest, absolute in their numbers, as he conceiued them. Who, as he was a happie imitator of Nature, was a most gentle expresser of it. His mind and hand went together: And what he thought, he vttered with that easinesse, that wee haue scarse receiued from him a blot in his papers. But it is not our prouince, who onely gather his works, and giue them you, to praise him. It is yours that reade him. And there we hope, to your diuers capacities, you will finde enough, both to draw, and hold you: for his wit can no more lie hid, then it could be lost. Reade him, therefore; and againe, and againe: And if then you doe not like him, surely you are in some manifest danger, not to vnderstand him. And so we leaue you to other of his Friends, whom if you need, can bee your guides: if you neede them not, you can leade your selues, and others. And such Readers we wish him.—JOHN HEMINGE, HENRY CONDELL, "To the Great Variety of Readers," *Mr. William Shakespeares Comedies, Histories, & Tragedies,* 1623

> Those hands, which you so clapt, go now, and wring
> You *Britaines* braue; for done are *Shakespeares* dayes:
> His dayes are done, that made the dainty Playes,
> Which made the Globe of heau'n and earth to ring.
> Dry'de is that veine, dryd is the *Thespian* Spring,
> Turn'd all to teares, and *Phoebus* clouds his rayes:
> That corp's, that coffin now besticke those bayes,
> Which crown'd him *Poet* first, then *Poets* King.
> If *Tragedies* might any *Prologue* haue,
> All those he made, would scarse make one to this:
> Where *Fame*, now that he gone is to the graue
> (Death publique tyring-house) the *Nuncius* is.
>   For though his line of life went soone about,
>   The life yet of his lines shall neuer out.
>
> —HUGH HOLLAND, "Upon the Lines and Life of the Famous Scenicke Poet, Master William Shakespeare," *Mr. William Shakespeares Comedies, Histories, & Tragedies,* 1623

To draw no enuy (*Shakespeare*) on thy name,
　Am I thus ample to thy Booke, and Fame:
While I confesse thy writings to be such,
　As neither *Man*, nor *Muse*, can praise too much.
'Tis true, and all mens suffrage. But these wayes
　Were not the paths I meant vnto thy praise:
For seeliest Ignorance on these may light,
　Which, when it sounds at best, but eccho's right;
Or blinde Affection, which doth ne're aduance
　The truth, but gropes, and vrgeth all by chance;
Or crafty Malice, might pretend this praise,
　And thinke to ruine, where it seem'd to raise.
These are, as some infamous Baud, or Whore,
　Should praise a Matron. What could hurt her more?
But thou art proofe against them, and indeed
　Aboue th'ill fortune of them, or the need.
I, therefore will begin. Soule of the Age!
　The applause! delight! the wonder of our Stage!
My *Shakespeare*, rise; I will not lodge thee by
*Chaucer*, or *Spenser*, or bid *Beaumont* lye
A little further, to make thee a roome:
　Thou art a Moniment, without a tombe,
And art aliue still, while thy Booke doth liue,
　And we haue wits to read, and praise to giue.
That I not mixe thee so, my braine excuses;
　I meane with great, but disproportion'd *Muses*:
For, if I thought my iudgement were of yeeres,
　I should commit thee surely with thy peeres,
And tell, how farre thou didst our *Lily* out-shine,
　Or sporting *Kid*, or *Marlowes* mighty line.
And though thou hadst small *Latine*, and lesse *Greeke*,
　From thence to honour thee, I would not seeke
For names; but call forth thund'ring *Æschilus*,
*Euripides*, and *Sophocles* to vs,
*Paccuuius*, *Accius*, him of *Cordoua* dead,
　To life againe, to heare thy Buskin tread,
And shake a Stage: Or, when thy Sockes were on,
　Leaue thee alone, for the comparison
Of all, that insolent *Greece*, or haughtie *Rome*
　Sent forth, or since did from their ashes come.
Triúmph, my *Britaine*, thou hast one to showe,
　To whom all Scenes of *Europe* homage owe.
He was not of an age, but for all time!
　And all the *Muses* still were in their prime,
When like *Apollo* he came forth to warme
　Our eares, or like a *Mercury* to charme!
Nature her selfe was proud of his designes,
　And ioy'd to weare the dressing of his lines!
Which were so richly spun, and wouen so fit,
　As, since, she will vouchsafe no other Wit.
The merry *Greeke*, tart *Aristophanes*,
　Neat *Terence*, witty *Plautus*, now not please;
But antiquated, and deserted lye
　As they were not of Natures family.
Yet must I not giue Nature all: Thy Art,
　My gentle *Shakespeare*, must enioy a part.
For though the *Poets* matter, Nature be,
　His Art doth giue the fashion. And, that he,
Who casts to write a liuing line, must sweat,
　(Such as thine are) and strike the second heat
Vpon the *Muses* anuile: turne the same,
　(And himselfe with it) that he thinkes to frame;
Or for the lawrell, he may gaine a scorne,
　For a good *Poet's* made, as well as borne.
And such wert thou. Looke how the fathers face

Liues in his issue, euen so, the race
Of *Shakespeares* minde, and manners brightly shines
In his well torned, and true-filed lines:
In each of which, he seemes to shake a Lance,
　As brandish't at the eyes of Ignorance.
Sweet Swan of *Auon!* what a sight it were
　To see thee in our waters yet appeare,
And make those flights vpon the bankes of *Thames*,
　That so did take *Eliza*, and our *Iames!*
But stay, I see thee in the *Hemisphere*
　Aduanc'd, and made a Constellation there!
Shine forth, thou Starre of *Poets*, and with rage,
　Or influence, chide, or cheere the drooping Stage;
Which, since thy flight from hence, hath mourn'd like night,
　And despaires day, but for thy Volumes light.

　　　—BEN JONSON, "To the Memory of My Beloued,
　　　　the Author Mr. William Shakespeare," *Mr.*
　　　　*William Shakespeares Comedies, Histories, &*
　　　　*Tragedies*, 1623

*Shakespeare* thou hadst as smooth a Comicke vaine,
Fitting the socke, and in thy natural braine,
As strong conception, and as Cleere a rage,
As any one that trafiqu'd with the stage.

　　　—MICHAEL DRAYTON, "To My Most Dearely-
　　　　Loved Friend Henery Reynolds, Esquire, of
　　　　Poets and Poesie," *Elegies*, 1627

What needs my *Shakespear* for his honour'd Bones,
The labour of an age in piled Stones,
Or that his hallow'd reliques should be hid
Under a Star-ypointing *Pyramid?*
Dear son of memory, great heir of Fame,
What need'st thou such weak witnes of thy name?
Thou in our wonder and astonishment
Hast built thy self a live-long Monument.
For whilst to th' shame of slow-endeavouring art,
Thy easie numbers flow, and that each heart
Hath from the leaves of thy unvalu'd Book,
Those Delphick lines with deep impressions took,
Then thou our fancy of it self bereaving,
Dost make us Marble with too much conceaving;
And so Sepulcher'd in such pomp dost lie,
That Kings for such a Tomb would wish to die.

　　　—JOHN MILTON, "On Shakespear," 1630

A Mind reflecting ages past, whose cleere
And equall surface can make things appeare
Distant a Thousand yeares, and represent
Them in their lively colours just extent.
To outrun hasty time, retrive the fates,
Rowle backe the heavens, blow ope the iron gates
Of death and Lethe, where (confused) lye
Great heapes of ruinous mortalitie.
In that deepe duskie dungeon to discerne
A royall Ghost from Churles; By art to learne
The Physiognomie of shades, and give
Them suddaine birth, wondring how oft they live.
What story coldly tells, what *Poets* faine
At second hand, and picture without braine
Senselesse and soullesse showes. To give a Stage
(Ample and true with life) voyce, action, age,
As *Plato's* yeare and new Scene of the world
Them unto us, or us to them had hurld.
To raise our auncient Soveraignes from their herse
Make Kings his subjects, by exchanging verse
Enliue their pale trunkes, that the present age

Joyes in their joy, and trembles at their rage:
Yet so to temper passion, that our eares
Take pleasure in their paine; And eyes in teares
Both weepe and smile; fearefull at plots so sad,
Then, laughing at our feare; abus'd, and glad
To be abus'd, affected with that truth
Which we perceive is false; pleas'd in that ruth
At which we start; and by elaborate play
Tortur'd and tickled; by a crablike way
Time past made pastime, and in ugly sort
Disgorging up his ravaine for our sport——
——While the *Plebeian* Impe, from lofty throne,
Creates and rules a world, and workes upon
Mankind by secret engines; Now to move
A chilling pitty, then a rigorous love:
To strike up and stroake down, both joy and ire;
To steere th' affections; and by heavenly fire
Mould us anew. Stolne from ourselves——
   This, and much more which cannot be exprest,
But by himselfe, his tongue and his owne brest,
Was *Shakespeares* freehold, which his cunning braine
Improv'd by favour of the ninefold traine.
The buskind Muse, the Commicke Queene, the graund
And lowder tone of *Clio*; nimble hand,
And nimbler foote of the melodious paire,
The Silver voyced Lady; the most faire
*Calliope*, whose speaking silence daunts.
And she whose prayse the heavenly body chants.
   These joyntly woo'd him, envying one another
(Obey'd by all as Spouse, but lov'd as brother)
And wrought a curious robe of fable grave
Fresh greene, and pleasant yellow, red most brave,
And constant blew, rich purple, guiltlesse white
The lowly Russet, and the Scarlet bright;
Branch'd and embroydred like the painted Spring
Each leafe match'd with a flower, and each string
Of golden wire, each line of silke; there run
*Italian* workes whose thred the Sisters spun;
And there did sing, or seeme to sing, the choyce
Birdes of a forraine note and various voyce.
Here hangs a mossey rocke; there playes a faire
But chiding fountaine purled: Not the ayre,
Nor cloudes nor thunder, but were living drawne,
Not out of common Tiffany or Lawne.
But fine materialls, which the Muses know
And onely know the countries where they grow.
   Now, when they could no longer him enjoy
In mortall garments pent; death may destroy
They say his body, but his verse shall live
And more then nature takes, our hands shall give.
In a lesse volumne, but more strongly bound
*Shakespeare* shall breath and speake, with Laurell crown'd
Which never fades.   Fed with Ambrosian meate
In a well-lyned vesture rich and neate.
   So with this robe they cloath him, bid him weare it
   For time shall never staine, nor envy teare it.

—I. M. S., "On Worthy Master Shakespeare and
   His Poems," 1632

Poets are borne not made, when I would prove
This truth, the glad rememberance I must love
Of never dying *Shakespeare*, who alone,
Is argument enough to make that one.
First, that he was a Poet none would doubt,
That heard th' applause of what he sees set out
Imprinted; where thou hast (I will not say

Reader his Workes for to contrive a Play
To him twas none) the patterne of all wit,
Art without Art unparaleld as yet.
Next Nature onely helpt him, for looke thorow
This whole Booke, thou shalt find he doth not borrow.
One phrase from Greekes, nor Latines imitate,
Nor once from vulgar Languages Translate,
Nor Plagiari-like from others gleane,
Nor begges he from each witty friend a Scene
To peece his Acts with, all that he doth write,
Is pure his owne, plot, language exquisite,
But oh! what praise more powerfull can we give
The dead, then that by him the Kings men live,
His Players, which should they but have shar'd the Fate,
All else expir'd within the short Termes date;
How could the Globe have prospered, since through want
Of change, the Plaies and Poems had growne scant.
But happy Verse thou shalt be sung and heard,
When hungry quills shall be such honour bard.
Then vanish upstart Writers to each Stage,
You needy Poetasters of this Age,
Where *Shakespeare* liv'd or spake, Vermine forbeare,
Least with your froth you spot them, come not neere;
But if you needs must write, if poverty
So pinch, that otherwise you starve and die
On Gods name may the Bull or Cockpit have
Your lame blancke Verse, to keepe you from the grave:
Or let new Fortunes younger brethren see,
What they can picke from your leane industry.
I doe not wonder when you offer at
Blacke-Friers, that you suffer: tis the fate
Of richer veines, prime judgements that have far'd
The worse, with this deceased man compar'd.
So have I seene, when Cesar would appeare,
And on the Stage at halfe-sword parley were,
*Brutus* and *Cassius*: oh how the Audience
Were ravish'd, with what wonder they went thence,
When some new day they would not brooke a line,
Of tedious (though well laboured) *Catiline*;
*Sejanus* too was irkesome, they priz'de more
Honest *Iago*, or the jealous Moore.
And though the Fox and subtill Alchimist,
Long intermitted could not quite be mist,
Though these have sham'd all the Ancients, and might raise,
Their Authours merit with a crowne of Bayes.
Yet these sometimes, even at a friends desire
Acted, have scarce defrai'd the Seacoale fire
And doore-keepers: when let but *Falstaffe* come,
*Hall*, *Poines*, the rest you scarce shall have a roome
All is so pester'd: let but *Beatrice*
And *Benedicke* be seene, loe in a trice
The Cockpit Galleries, Boxes, all are full
To hear *Malvoglio*, that crosse garter'd Gull.
Briefe, there is nothing in his wit fraught Booke,
Whose sound we would not heare, on whose worth looke
Like old coynd gold, whose lines in every page,
Shall passe true currant to succeeding age.
But why doe I dead *Sheakspeares* praise recite,
Some second *Shakespeare* must of *Shakespeare* write;
For me tis needlesse, since an host of men,
Will pay to clap his praise, to free my Pen.

—LEONARD DIGGES, "Upon Master William
   Shakespeare, the Deceased Authour, and His
   Poems," *Shakespeare's Poems*, 1640

I remember, the players have often mentioned it as an honour to Shakspeare, that in his writing (whatsoever he penned) he never blotted out a line. My answer hath been, Would he had blotted a thousand. Which they thought a malevolent speech. I had not told posterity this, but for their ignorance, who chose that circumstance to commend their friend by, wherein he most faulted; and to justify mine own candour: for I loved the man, and do honour his memory, on this side idolatry, as much as any. He was (indeed) honest, and of an open and free nature; had an excellent phantasy, brave notions, and gentle expressions; wherein he flowed with that facility, that sometimes it was necessary he should be stopped: *Sufflaminandus erat*, as Augustus said of Haterius. His wit was in his own power, would the rule of it had been so too. Many times he fell into those things, could not escape laughter: as when he said in the person of Cæsar, one speaking to him, "Cæsar thou dost me wrong." He replied, "Cæsar did never wrong but with just cause," and such like; which were ridiculous. But he redeemed his vices with his virtues. There was ever more in him to be praised than to be pardoned.—BEN JONSON, *Timber; or Discoveries*, 1641

For Playes, *Shakespear* was one of the first, who inverted the Dramatick Stile, from dull History to quick Comedy, upon whom *Johnson* refin'd, as *Beaumont* and *Fletcher* first writ in the Heroick way, upon whom *Suckling* and others endeavoured to refine agen; one saying wittily of his *Aglaura*, that 'twas full of fine flowers, but they seem'd rather stuck, then growing there, as another of *Shakespear's* writings, that 'twas a fine Garden, but it wanted weeding.

There are few of our English Playes (excepting onely some few of *Johnsons*) without some faults or other; and if the French have fewer then our English, 'tis because they confine themselves to narrower limits, and consequently have less liberty to erre.

The chief faults of ours, are our huddling too much matter together, and making them too long and intricate; we imagining we never have intrigue enough, till we lose our selves and Auditors, who shu'd be led in a Maze, but not a Mist; and through turning and winding wayes, but so still, as they may finde their way at last.

A good Play shu'd be like a good stuff, closely and evenly wrought, without any breakes, thrums, or loose ends in 'um, or like a good Picture well painted and designed; the Plot or Contrivement, the Design, the Writing, the Coloris, and Counterplot, the Shaddowings, with other Embellishments: or finally, it shu'd be like a well contriv'd Garden, cast into its Walks and Counterwalks, betwixt an Alley and a Wilderness, neither too plain, nor too confus'd. Of all Arts, that of the Dramatick Poet is the most difficult and most subject to censure; for in all others, they write onely of some particular subject, as the Mathematician of Mathematicks, or Philosopher of Philosophy; but in that, the Poet must write of every thing, and every one undertakes to judge of it.

A Dramatick Poet is to the Stage as a Pilot to the Ship; and to the Actors, as an Architect to the Builders, or Master to his Schollars: he is to be a good moral Philosopher, but yet more learned in Men then Books. He is to be a wise, as well as a witty Man, and a good man, as well as a good Poet; and I'de allow him to be so far a good fellow too, to take a chearful cup to whet his wits, so he take not so much to dull 'um, and whet 'um quite away.

To compare our English Dramatick Poets together (without taxing them) *Shakespear* excelled in a natural Vein, *Fletcher* in Wit, and *Johnson* in Gravity and ponderousness of Style; whose onely fault was, he was too elaborate; and had he

mixt less erudition with his Playes, they had been more pleasant and delightful then they are. Comparing him with *Shakespear*, you shall see the difference betwixt Nature and Art; and with *Fletcher*, the difference betwixt Wit and Judgement: Wit being an exuberant thing, like *Nilus*, never more commendable then when it overflowes; but Judgement a stayed and reposed thing, always containing it self within its bounds and limits.—RICHARD FLECKNOE, "A Short Discourse of the English Stage," *Love's Kingdom*, 1664

*Shakespeare* . . . was the man who of all Modern, and perhaps Ancient Poets, had the largest and most comprehensive soul. All the Images of Nature were still present to him, and he drew them not laboriously, but luckily: when he describes any thing, you more than see it, you feel it too. Those who accuse him to have wanted learning, give him the greater commendation: he was naturally learn'd; he needed not the spectacles of Books to read Nature; he look'd inwards, and found her there. I cannot say he is every where alike; were he so, I should do him injury to compare him with the greatest of Mankind. He is many times flat, insipid; his Comick wit degenerating into clenches, his serious swelling into Bombast. But he is alwayes great, when some great occasion is presented to him: no man can say he ever had a fit subject for his wit, and did not then raise himself as high above the rest of Poets,

Quantum lenta solent, inter viburna cupressi.

The consideration of this made Mr. *Hales* of *Eaton* say, That there was no subject of which any Poet ever writ, but he would produce it much better done in *Shakespeare*; and however others are now generally prefer'd before him, yet the Age wherein he liv'd, which had contemporaries with him *Fletcher* and *Johnson*, never equall'd them to him in their esteem: And in the last Kings Court, when *Ben's* reputation was at highest, Sir *John Suckling*, and with him the greater part of the Courtiers, set our *Shakespeare* far above him.—JOHN DRYDEN, *An Essay of Dramatick Poesie*, 1668

The reader will easily take notice that when I speak of rejecting improper words and phrases, I mention not such as are antiquated by custom only and, as I may say, without any fault of theirs: for in this case the refinement can be but accidental; that is, when the words and phrases which are rejected happen to be improper. Neither would I be understood (when I speak of impropriety in language) either wholly to accuse the last age, or to excuse the present; and least of all myself. For all writers have their imperfections and failings. But I may safely conclude in the general, that our improprieties are less frequent, and less gross than theirs. One testimony of this is undeniable, that we are the first who have observed them. And certainly, to observe errors is a great step to the correcting of them. But malice and partiality set apart, let any man who understands English read diligently the works of Shakespeare and Fletcher; and I dare undertake that he will find in every page either some solecism of speech, or some notorious flaw in sense; and yet these men are reverenced when we are not forgiven. That their wit is great, and many times their expressions noble, envy itself cannot deny:

neque ego illi detrahere ausim
haerentem capiti multa cum laude coronam.

But the times were ignorant in which they lived. Poetry was then, if not in its infancy among us, at least not arrived to its vigour and maturity: witness the lameness of their plots; many of which, especially those which they writ first (for even that age refined itself in some measure), were made up of some ridiculous, incoherent story, which in one play many times took up the business of an age. I suppose I need not name *Pericles, Prince of Tyre*, nor the historical plays of Shakespeare. Besides many of the rest, as the *Winter's Tale*, *Love's Labour Lost*, *Measure for Measure*, which were either grounded on impossibilities, or at least so meanly written that the comedy neither caused your mirth, nor the serious part your concernment.—JOHN DRYDEN, "Defence of the Epilogue," *The Conquest of Granada*, 1672

*William Shakespeare*, the glory of the English Stage; whose nativity at *Stratford-upon-Avon* is the highest honour that town can boast of: from an *Actor* of Tragedies and Comedies he became a *Maker*: and such a *Maker*, that though some others may perhaps pretend to a more exact *decorum* and *economy*, especially in Tragedy; never any expressed a more lofty and tragic height; never any represented Nature more purely to the life: and where the polishments of Art are most wanting, as most probably his learning was not extraordinary, he pleaseth with a certain wild and native elegance: and in all his writings hath an unvulgar style; as well in his *Venus and Adonis*, his *Rape of Lucrece*, and other various poems, as in his dramatics.—EDWARD PHILLIPS, *Theatrum Poetarum Anglicanorum*, 1675

If Shakespeare be allowed, as I think he must, to have made his characters distinct, it will easily be inferred that he understood the nature of the passions: because it has been proved already that confused passions make undistinguishable characters: yet I cannot deny that he has his failings; but they are not so much in the passions themselves as in his manner of expression: he often obscures his meaning by his words, and sometimes makes it unintelligible. I will not say of so great a poet that he distinguished not the blown puffy style from true sublimity; but I may venture to maintain that the fury of his fancy often transported him beyond the bounds of judgment, either in coining of new words and phrases, or racking words which were in use into the violence of a catachresis. 'Tis not that I would explode the use of metaphors from passions, for Longinus thinks 'em necessary to raise it: but to use 'em at every word, to say nothing without a metaphor, a simile, an image, or description, is I doubt to smell a little too strongly of the buskin. I must be forced to give an example of expressing passion figuratively; but that I may do it with respect to Shakespeare, it shall not be taken from any thing of his: 'tis an exclamation against Fortune, quoted in his *Hamlet* but written by some other poet:

> Out, out, thou strumpet Fortune! all you gods,
> In general synod, take away her power;
> Break all the spokes and felleys from her wheel,
> And bowl the round nave down the hill of Heav'n,
> As low as to the fiends.

And immediately after, speaking of Hecuba, when Priam was killed before her eyes:

> The mobbled queen ran up and down,
> Threatening the flame with bisson rheum; a clout
>     about that head
> Where late the diadem stood; and for a robe,
> About her lank and all o'er-teemed loins,
> A blanket in th' alarm of fear caught up.
> Who this had seen, with tongue in venom steep'd
> 'Gainst Fortune's state would treason have pro-
>     nounced;
> But if the gods themselves did see her then,
> When she saw Pyrrhus make malicious sport
> In mincing with his sword her husband's limbs,
> The instant burst of clamour that she made

> (Unless things mortal move them not at all)
> Would have made milch the burning eyes of
>     Heaven,
> And passion in the gods.

What a pudder is here kept in raising the expression of trifling thoughts! Would not a man have thought that the poet had been bound prentice to a wheelwright, for his first rant? and had followed a ragman for the clout and blanket, in the second? Fortune is painted on a wheel, and therefore the writer, in a rage, will have poetical justice done upon every member of that engine: after this execution, he bowls the nave down hill, from Heaven to the fiends (an unreasonable long mark, a man would think); 'tis well there are no solid orbs to stop it in the way, or no element of fire to consume it: but when it came to the earth, it must be monstrous heavy, to break ground as low as to the centre. His making milch the burning eyes of Heaven was a pretty tolerable flight too: and I think no man ever drew milk out of eyes before him: yet, to make the wonder greater, these eyes were burning. Such a sight indeed were enough to have raised passion in the gods; but to excuse the effects of it, he tells you, perhaps they did not see it. Wise men would be glad to find a little sense couched under all these pompous words; for bombast is commonly the delight of that audience which loves poetry, but understands it not: and as commonly has been the practice of those writers who, not being able to infuse a natural passion into the mind, have made it their business to ply the ears and to stun their judges by the noise. But Shakespeare does not often thus; for the passions in his scene between Brutus and Cassius are extremely natural, the thoughts are such as arise from the matter, the expression of 'em not viciously figurative. I cannot leave this subject, before I do justice to that divine poet by giving you one of his passionate descriptions: 'tis of Richard the Second when he was deposed, and led in triumph through the streets of London by Henry of Bullingbrook: the painting of it is so lively, and the words so moving, that I have scarce read any thing comparable to it in any other language. Suppose you have seen already the fortunate usurper passing through the crowd, and followed by the shouts and acclamations of the people; and now behold King Richard entering upon the scene: consider the wretchedness of his condition, and his carriage in it; and refrain from pity if you can:

> As in a theatre, the eyes of men,
> After a well-graced actor leaves the stage,
> Are idly bent on him that enters next,
> Thinking his prattle to be tedious:
> Even so, or with much more contempt, men's eyes
> Did scowl on Richard: no man cried, God save him:
> No joyful tongue gave him his welcome home,
> But dust was thrown upon his sacred head,
> Which with such gentle sorrow he shook off,
> His face still combating with tears and smiles
> (The badges of his grief and patience),
> That had not God (for some strong purpose) steel'd
> The hearts of men, they must perforce have melted,
> And barbarism itself have pitied him.

To speak justly of this whole matter: 'tis neither height of thought that is discommended, nor pathetic vehemence, nor any nobleness of expression in its proper place; but 'tis a false measure of all these, something which is like 'em, and is not them; 'tis the Bristol-stone, which appears like a diamond; 'tis an extravagant thought, instead of a sublime one; 'tis roaring madness, instead of vehemence; and a sound of words, instead of sense. If Shakespeare were stripped of all the bombast in his passions, and dressed in the most vulgar words, we should find the beauties of his thoughts remaining; if his embroideries were burnt down, there would still be silver at the bottom of the melting-pot: but I fear (at least let me fear it for myself) that we who ape his sounding words have nothing of his thought, but are all outside; there is not so much as a dwarf within our giant's clothes. Therefore, let not Shakespeare suffer for our sakes; 'tis our fault, who succeed him in an age which is more refined, if we imitate him so ill that we copy his failings only, and make a virtue of that in our writings which in his was an imperfection.

For what remains, the excellency of that poet was, as I have said, in the more manly passions; Fletcher's in the softer: Shakespeare writ better betwixt man and man; Fletcher, betwixt man and woman: consequently, the one described friendship better; the other love: yet Shakespeare taught Fletcher to write love: and Juliet, and Desdemona, are originals. 'Tis true, the scholar had the softer soul; but the master had the kinder. Friendship is both a virtue and a passion essentially; love is a passion only in its nature, and is not a virtue but by accident: good nature makes friendship; but effeminacy love. Shakespeare had an universal mind, which comprehended all characters and passions; Fletcher a more confined and limited: for though he treated love in perfection, yet honour, ambition, revenge, and generally all the stronger passions, he either touched not, or not masterly. To conclude all, he was a limb of Shakespeare.—JOHN DRYDEN, "Preface" to *Troilus and Cressida*, 1679

I cannot forget the strong desire I have heard you 〈Edward Taylor〉 express to see the Common Places of our *Shakespeare*, compar'd with the most famous of the Ancients. This indeed were a Task worthy the greatest Critique. Our Learned *Hales* was wont to assert, That since the time of *Orpheus* and the Oldest Poets, no Common Place has been touch'd upon, where our Author has not perform'd as well. Our *Laureat* has thrown in his Testimony, and declar'd, That *Shakespeare* was a Man that of all Men had the largest and most comprehensive Soul.

What I have already asserted concerning the necessity of Learning to make a compleat Poet, may seem inconsistent with my reverence for our *Shakespeare*.

Cujus amor semper mihi crescit in Horas.

I confess I cou'd never yet get a true account of his Learning, and am apt to think it more than Common Report allows him. I am sure he never touches on a Roman Story, but the Persons, the Passages, the Manners, the Circumstances, the Ceremonies, all are Roman. And what Relishes yet of a more exact Knowledge, you do not only see a Roman in his Heroe, but the particular Genius of the Man, without the least mistake of his Character, given him by their best Historians. You find his *Antony* in all the Defects and Excellencies of his Mind, a Souldier, a Reveller, Amorous, sometimes Rash, sometimes Considerate, with all the various Emotions of his Mind. His *Brutus* agen has all the Constancy, Gravity, Morality, Generosity, Imaginable, without the least Mixture of private Interest or Irregular Passion. He is true to him, even in the imitation of his Oratory, the famous Speech which he makes him deliver, being exactly agreeable to his manner of expressing himself. . . .

But however it far'd with our Author for Book-Learning, 'tis evident that no man was better studied in Men and Things, the most useful Knowledge for a *Dramatic* Writer. He was a most diligent Spie upon Nature, trac'd her through her darkest Recesses, pictur'd her in her just Proportion and Colours; in which Variety 'tis impossible that all shou'd be equally pleasant, 'tis sufficient that all be proper.

Of his absolute Command of the Passions, and Mastery in distinguishing of Characters, you have a perfect Account in

〈Dryden's〉 most excellent Criticism before *Troilus and Cressida*: If any Man be a lover of *Shakespeare* and covet his Picture, there you have him drawn to the Life; but for the Eternal Plenty of his Wit on the same Theam, I will only detain you with a few instances of his Reflections on the Person, and Cruel Practices of *Richard* the Third. First of all *Henry* the Sixth bespeaks him in these words:

> The owl shriekt at thy birth, an evil sign . . .
> Thy Mother felt more than a Mothers Pain,
> And yet brought forth less than a Mothers hope;
> An indigested Lump, &c.

*Richard* afterwards makes as bold with himself, where this is part of his Soliloque.

> Cheated of Feature by dissembling Nature,
> Deform'd, unfinish'd, sent before my time
> Into this breathing world, scarce half made up. . . .

Queen *Margaret* cannot hear him mention'd without a new stream of Satyr.

> A Hell-hound that doth Hunt us all to Death,
> That Dog that had his Teeth before his Eyes,
> To worry Lambs and lap their gentle Blood, &c.

And never meets him but she presents him with his Picture;

> Hells black Intelligencer,
> Their Factour to buy *Souls* and send 'em thither.

And again,

> Thou elfish markt abortive Monster,
> Thou that wast seal'd in thy Nativity,
> The Slave of Nature and the son of Hell.
> Thou slander of thy heavy Mothers Womb.

With very many other Taunts to the same purpose.

It cannot be deny'd but he is often insipid where he is careless, many Things he wrote in hurry; but for his more elaborate Scenes, what *Cicero* spoke of the Writings of *Archias*, will hold good. *Quae vero accurate cogitateque scripsisset, ad veterum Scriptorem Laudem pervenerunt.*—NAHUM TATE, "Preface" to *The Loyal General*, 1680

What Progress soever 〈the French〉 *Criticks* have made in their Science, It's evident enough the reputation of their Authors over EUROPE is owing to them. And had we as many such, to blaze our Writers Works, and open their ordinary Beauties, sure I think they would make a different Figure in EUROPE from what they do. Our *Milton*, *Shakespear*, *Otway*, and the rest, would at least be known beyond the bounds of *Britain*. But a petty Enmity is held up between our Poets and our Criticks, which diverts the latter from their proper business and delight of dressing the Beauties of the former in engaging Colours. Whereas the *Criticks* of *France* are so kindly natured, that they cannot see a Defect in their own Authors, nor a Beauty in those of another Nation.

Can any reason be, besides the *Criticks* putting the Writers in *France*, on a certain mechanick regular Way, why their Authors are as well known to us as our own, and no sooner in the *French* than the *English* Tongue? Can any reason be besides, for our so valuing the *French*, while they won't cast an Eye on us. If by chance they mention an Author of ours, which once or twice they do thro' all their Critiques, not satisfied to put him under theirs, they will scarce allow it possible for our Nation to produce a perfect Piece. Yet methinks they should allow us ISLANDERS some little Sence, because 'tis else no Glory to surpass us. Nor do they think it much indeed; but would call it a Diminution to *Corneil* and to *Racine* to be put in compare with *Shakespear* and with *Otway*, tho' the Preference at last should fall on the *French*.

What stops, I think, the general and universal Value for

our Noblest Authors, is, Their Faults are Faults against the common known mechanick Rules of Poetry, as _Shakespear's_ Blemishes and _Otway's_ are against the Unity of Place, and mixing Comedy throughout, and the like; which are obvious to every one: Whereas how few can take the Beauties of _Shakespear_, especially in the Sentiment, which is often indeed too clouded by the Language. The _French_, on the other hand, if they can't come up to our noblest Beauties, they learn from their _Criticks_ to avoid our plainest Faults. And such Writings as are neither good nor bad, acquire the widest and the easiest Characters for good. But yet give me a dozen faults, if there's half as many noble Graces blended with 'em, before a Poem that's as regular as insipid.

'Twere too long to draw a full comparison of _Shakespear_, and _Corneil_ or _Racine_. But give me leave to appeal a little to the Judgment of the Reader.

Suppose _Shakespear_ had given _Corneil_ the Character of a fierce Savage MOOR, such as _Othello_; Then told him, that to make his Temper chaufft and fermented by Jealousie would show such a Character in the finest Light; how think ye, even then, would _Corneil_ have wrote the Play? We may guess from his own Performances. Would he have given us to the Love between the Savage and the tender Lady as _Shakespear_ has done, Or have drawn a charming Scene, where the honest old Love-Story would have been finely talkt over by 'em. How would the subtilness of _Iago_ have been shewn in working up a furious _Warriour_? But worse yet, How would he have drawn the Strugglings of a great Soul between the fiercest Hatred and the tendrest Obligations to Love? I fear He must have told us, _Othello_ had such Contests in himself. How would he have described the roughest and most open Soul in the World biting in his Wrath, and dissembling before the tender _Desdemona_? I doubt a few Monologues would have supply'd the place of that. In short, would not _Corneil_ have shewn the Grief of the innocent, surpriz'd, and gentle _Desdemona_, by a number of fine mournful Sentences between Her and a Confidant? Ay; and such a Scene would have raised a world of pity in a _French_ Audience.

Such uncommon Characters as _Othello's_, _Macbeth's_, _Hamlet's_, _Jaffeir's_, _Monomia's_, &c. are the only difficult one's to draw, the only One's that shine on the Stage, and the only One's I could never find in the _French_ writers of Tragedy.

But there is a Species in Writing which seems natural to our Nation, and inconsistent with the _French_ Vivacity; It has never yet been consider'd by any _Critick_, yet constitutes the Soul and Essence of Tragedy. I call this kind, the GLOOMY: And it consists oftner in the general scene or view, than in the Sentiment. For Instance. _Romeo_ is wandring among the Trees, and anon espy's a glimering light at _Julia's_ Window. And in King LEAR; we see LEAR under a _Hovel_ retired in the Night, while Thunder, Rain and Lightning were abroad.

All the Tragedys of _Shakespear_ which we call good, abound with the _Gloomy_. And the want of it may be one great reason why _Corneil_ and _Racine_, tho' they have so much Spirit in their Expressions, tho' their Thoughts are so rarely vitious, and their Compositions agreeable to the common and easiest Rules, yet want the Life, what shall I call it, the VIS TRAGICA, which appears in the good Tragedies of _Shakespear_ and _Otway_.

The _English_, as I said, alone have Genius's fitted for the _Gloomy_. But as we never abounded much with _Criticks_, never any has enter'd into the Nature of it. Tho' sure it deserves an entire Discourse. And so sweetly amusing it is to the Soul, That 'twill shine thro' Language even ridiculous; and alone support a Sentiment. As here,

Put out the Light, and then put out the Light.

The Language is a kind of _Pun_, and therefore to Minds that cannot take the Beauty of the Thought divested of it, the line appears absurd.

But the chief use of the GLOOMY (in the Sentiment) is in _Soliloquies_; and would a Tragick-Writer be at pains to be Master of it, he need never write, at least, a bad one. The _Soliloquies_ of _Corneil_ and _Racine_, are only such because the Person that utters 'em is alone. The Thoughts are exactly of the same kind with those in the _Dialogue_ part of the _Play_; without Solemnity or Gloominess. But what a solemn Awe do _Shakespear's_ draw over the Mind. And some of _Otway's_, as in _Venice-preserv'd_.

Jaffeir, _on the_ Rialto.
I'm here; and thus, the Shades of Night around me,
&c.

(Act 2.)

But Instances were endless; especially out of _Shakespear_. Yet 'twas the finess, I believe, of his Imagination, that fill'd his Tragedys with the GLOOMY; rather then his having 'ere sate down and consider'd the _Pleasures of the Imagination_, and then the fittest Methods to excite those Pleasures. He felt his own Mind most agreeably amused, when'ere the Gloomy overspread it; and most wrote (as was _Ovid_ and _Spencer's_ way) what most delighted him to write.

The _French_ Writers have this to offer for their wanting the Soul and Essence of Tragedy. They generally observe the Mechanick Rules, especially Unity of Place, which _Shakespear_ alway break's thro'. Now the GLOOMY, as I said, is oftnest rais'd by the general Scene or View; by leading the Mind into secret Apartments, and private Places; as PIERRE on the _Rialto every Night at twelve took his Evening's Walk of Meditation_: But if a Play-Writer would preserve the Unity of Place, it must be by laying his Scene in a Thorough-Fare, in a Palace Yard, before the Door of an House, or in a publick Hall, as _Sophocles_, _Terence_, and the _French_ Writers of Tragedy do. So that by cramping their Genius's by the observation of this Rule (which yet is necessary in the Representation) they cut themselves off from the chief Opportunity of introduceing the Gloomy. And even in the Thought, the Gloomy cannot with advantage appear, unless held up and assisted by the Scene. How could this Thought have been supported in _Romeo and Juliet_

What light is that, which breaks from yonder Window, &c.

but by _Shakespear's_ leading us, with _Romeo_, into the Secret Retirement of an _Orchat_?

Or what could have furnish'd _Othello's_ Soliloquy,

It is the Cause; It is the Cause, my Soul:
Let me not name it to you, ye chast Stars, &c.

had not _Shakespear_ lead us in into the Bed-Chamber of _Desdemona_ in the Night-time?

In short, if 'tis otherwise introduced, it must be out of the Action; as the Account of _Macbeth's_ Lady walking in her Sleep. And _Hotspur's_ Wife's relation of his talking in his Sleep with the thoughts and contrivance of a Rebellion. And the like.— THOMAS PURNEY, "Preface" to _Pastorals_; _viz. The Bashful Swain_, 1717

But Heav'n, still various in its Works, decreed
The perfect Boast of Time should last succeed.
The beauteous Union must appear at length,
Of _Tuscan_ Fancy, and _Athenian_ Strength:
One greater Muse _Eliza's_ Reign adorn,
And ev'n a _Shakespear_ to her Fame be born!
Yet ah! so bright her Morning's op'ning Ray,

In vain our *Britain* hop'd an equal Day!
No second Growth the Western Isle could bear,
At once exhausted with too rich a Year.
Too nicely *Johnson* knew the Critic's Part;
Nature in him was almost lost in Art.
Of softer Mold the gentle *Fletcher* came,
The next in Order, as the next in Name.
With pleas'd Attention 'midst his Scenes we find
Each glowing Thought, that warms the Female Mind;
Each melting Sigh, and ev'ry tender Tear,
The Lover's Wishes and the Virgin's Fear.
His ev'ry strain the *Smiles* and *Graces* own;
But stronger *Shakespear* felt for *Man* alone:
Drawn by his Pen, our ruder Passions stand
Th' unrival'd Picture of his early Hand.

. . . .

Yet He alone to ev'ry Scene could give
Th' Historian's Truth, and bid the Manners live.
Wak'd at his Call I view, with glad Surprize,
Majestic Forms of mighty Monarchs rise.
There *Henry's* Trumpets spread their loud Alarms,
And laurel'd Conquest waits her Hero's Arms.
Here gentler *Edward* claims a pitying Sigh,
Scarce born to Honours, and so soon to die!
Yet shall thy Throne, unhappy Infant, bring
No Beam of Comfort to the guilty King?
The Time shall come, when *Glo'ster's* Heart shall bleed
In Life's last Hours, with Horror of the Deed:
When dreary Visions shall at last present
Thy vengeful Image, in the midnight Tent:
Thy Hand unseen the secret Death shall bear,
Blunt the weak Sword, and break th' oppressive Spear.

Where'er we turn, by Fancy charm'd, we find
Some sweet Illusion of the cheated Mind.
Oft, wild of Wing, she calls the Soul to rove
With humbler Nature, in the rural Grove;
Where Swains contented own the quiet Scene,
And twilight Fairies tread the circled Green:
Drest by her Hand, the Woods and Vallies smile,
And Spring diffusive decks th' *enchanted Isle.*

O more than all in pow'rful Genius blest,
Come, take thine Empire o'er the willing Breast!
Whate'er the Wounds this youthful Heart shall feel,
Thy Songs support me, and thy Morals heal!
There ev'ry Thought the Poet's Warmth may raise,
There native Music dwells in all the Lays.
O might some Verse with happiest Skill persuade
Expressive Picture to adopt thine Aid!
What wond'rous Draughts might rise from ev'ry Page!
What other *Raphaels* Charm a distant Age!

Methinks ev'n now I view some free Design,
Where breathing Nature lives in ev'ry Line:
Chast and subdu'd the modest Lights decay,
Steal into Shade, and mildly melt away.
——And see, where *Anthony* in Tears approv'd,
Guards the pale Relicks of the Chief he lov'd:
O'er the cold Corse the Warrior seems to bend,
Deep sunk in Grief, and mourns his murther'd Friend!
Still as they press, he calls on all around,
Lifts the torn Robe, and points the bleeding Wound.

But who is he, whose Brows exalted bear
A Wrath impatient, and a fiercer Air?
Awake to all that injur'd Worth can feel,
On his own *Rome* he turns th'avenging Steel.
Yet shall not War's insatiate Fury fall,

(So Heav'n ordains it) on the destin'd Wall.
See the fond Mother 'midst the plaintive Train
Hung on his Knees, and prostrate on the Plain!
Touch'd to the Soul, in vain he strives to hide
The Son's Affection, in the *Roman's* Pride:
O'er all the Man conflicting Passions rise,
*Rage* grasps the Sword, while *Pity* melts the Eyes.

> —WILLIAM COLLINS, "An Epistle Addrest to Sir Thomas Hanmer on His Edition of Shakespear's Works," 1744

Far from the sun and summer-gale,
In thy green lap was Nature's Darling laid,
What time, where lucid Avon stray'd,
To Him the mighty Mother did unveil
Her aweful face: The dauntless Child
Stretch'd forth his little arms, and smiled.
This pencil take (she said) whose colours clear
Richly paint the vernal year:
Thine too these golden keys, immortal Boy!
This can unlock the gates of Joy;
Of Horrour that, and thrilling Fears,
Or ope the sacred source of sympathetic Tears.

> —THOMAS GRAY, *The Progress of Poesy*, 1754

If Shakspeare be considered as a MAN, born in a rude age, and educated in the lowest manner, without any instruction, either from the world or from books, he may be regarded as a prodigy; if represented as a poet, capable of furnishing a proper entertainment to a refined or intelligent audience, we must abate much of this eulogy. In his compositions, we regret that many irregularities, and even absurdities, should so frequently disfigure the animated and passionate scenes intermixed with them; and, at the same time, we perhaps admire the more those beauties, on account of their being surrounded with such deformities. A striking peculiarity of sentiment, adapted to a single character, he frequently hits, as it were, by inspiration; but a reasonable propriety of thought he cannot for any time uphold. Nervous and picturesque expressions as well as descriptions abound in him; but it is in vain we look either for purity or simplicity of diction. His total ignorance of all theatrical art and conduct, however material a defect, yet, as it affects the spectator rather than the reader, we can more easily excuse, than that want of taste which often prevails in his productions, and which gives way only by intervals to the irradiations of genius. A great and fertile genius he certainly possessed, and one enriched equally with a tragic and comic vein; but he ought to be cited as a proof, how dangerous it is to rely on these advantages alone for attaining an excellence in the finer arts. And there may even remain a suspicion that we overrate, if possible, the greatness of his genius; in the same manner as bodies often appear more gigantic, on account of their being disproportioned and misshapen.—DAVID HUME, "Appendix to the Reign of James I," *History of England*, 1754–62

Shakspeare mingled no water with his wine, lowered his genius by no vapid imitation. Shakspeare gave us a Shakspeare; nor could the first in ancient fame have given us more. Shakspeare is not their son, but brother; their equal, and that in spite of all his faults. Think you this too bold? Consider, in those ancients what is it the world admires? Not the fewness of their faults, but the number and brightness of their beauties; and if Shakspeare is their equal (as he doubtless is) in that which in them is admired, then is Shakspeare as great as they; and not impotence, but some other cause, must be charged with his defects. When we are setting these great men in competition, what but the comparative size of their genius is the subject of our inquiry? And a giant loses nothing of his size, though he should chance to trip in his race. But it is a compliment to those heroes of antiquity to suppose Shakspeare their equal only in dramatic powers; therefore, though his faults had been greater, the scale would still turn in his favour. There is at least as much genius on the British as on the Grecian stage, though the former is not swept so clean; so clean from violations not only of the dramatic, but moral, rule; for an honest Heathen, on reading some of our celebrated scenes, might be seriously concerned to see, that our obligations to the religion of nature were cancelled by Christianity.

Jonson, in the serious drama, is as much an imitator, as Shakspeare is an original. He was very learned, as Samson was very strong, to his own hurt. Blind to the nature of tragedy, he pulled down all antiquity on his head, and buried himself under it. We see nothing of Jonson, nor indeed of his admired (but also murdered) ancients; for what shone in the historian is a cloud on the poet; and *Catiline* might have been a good play, if Sallust had never writ.

Who knows whether Shakspeare might not have thought less, if he had read more? Who knows if he might not have laboured under the load of Jonson's learning, as Enceladus under Ætna? His mighty genius, indeed, through the most mountainous oppression would have breathed out some of his inextinguishable fire; yet, possibly, he might not have risen up into that giant, that much more than common man, at which we now gaze with amazement and delight. Perhaps he was as learned as his dramatic province required; for, whatever other learning he wanted, he was master of two books, unknown to many of the profoundly read, though books which the last conflagration alone can destroy,—the book of nature, and that of man. These he had by heart, and has transcribed many admirable pages of them into his immortal works. These are the fountain-head, whence the Castalian streams of original composition flow; and these are often mudded by other waters,—though waters, in their distinct channel, most wholesome and pure: as two chemical liquors, separately clear as crystal, grow foul by mixture, and offend the sight. So that he had not only as much learning as his dramatic province required, but perhaps, as it could safely bear. If Milton had spared some of his learning, his muse would have gained more glory than he would have lost by it.—EDWARD YOUNG, *Conjectures on Original Composition*, 1759

Shakspeare is superior to all other writers in delineating passion. It is difficult to say in what part he most excels, whether in moulding every passion to peculiarity of character, in discovering the sentiments that proceed from various tones of passion, or in expressing properly every different sentiment: he disgusts not his reader with general declamation and unmeaning words, too common in other writers: his sentiments are adjusted to the peculiar character and circumstances of the speaker: and the propriety is no less perfect between his sentiments and his diction. That this is no exaggeration, will be evident to every one of taste, upon comparing Shakspeare with other writers in similar passages. If upon any occasion he falls below himself, it is in those scenes where passion enters not: by endeavoring in that case to raise his dialogue above the style of ordinary conversation, he sometimes deviates into intricate thought and obscure expression: sometimes, to throw his language out of the familiar, he employs rhyme. But may it not, in some measure, excuse Shakspeare, I shall not say his works, that he had no pattern, in his own or in any living language, of dialogue fitted for the theatre? At the same time, it ought not to escape observation, that the stream clears in its progress, and that in his later plays he has attained the purity

and perfection of dialogue; an observation that, with greater certainty than tradition, will direct us to arrange his plays in the order of time. This ought to be considered by those who rigidly exaggerate every blemish of the finest genius for the drama ever the world enjoyed: they ought also for their own sake to consider, that it is easier to discover his blemishes, which lie generally at the surface, than his beauties, which can be truly relished by those only who dive deep into human nature. One thing must be evident to the meanest capacity, that wherever passion is to be displayed, nature shows itself mighty in him, and is conspicuous by the most delicate propriety of sentiment and expression.—HENRY HOME, LORD KAMES, *Elements of Criticism*, 1763, Ch. 17

Instances, I admit, there are, of some works that contain gross transgressions of the laws of Criticism, acquiring, nevertheless, a general, and even a lasting admiration. Such are the plays of Shakespeare, which, considered as dramatic poems, are irregular in the highest degree. But then we are to remark, that they have gained the public admiration, not by their being irregular, not by their transgressions of the rules of art, but in spite of such transgressions. They possess other beauties which are comformable to just rules; and the force of these beauties has been so great as to overpower all censure, and to give the Public a degree of satisfaction superior to the disgust arising from their blemishes. Shakespeare pleases, not by his bringing the transactions of many years into one play: not by his grotesque mixtures of Tragedy and Comedy in one piece, nor by the trained thoughts, and affected witticisms, which he sometimes employs. These we consider as blemishes, and impute them to the grossness of the age in which he lived. But he pleases by his animated and masterly representations of characters, by the liveliness of his descriptions, the force of his sentiments, and his possessing, beyond all writers, the natural language of passion: beauties which true Criticism no less teaches us to place in the highest rank, than Nature teaches us to feel.— HUGH BLAIR, *Lectures on Rhetoric and Belles-Lettres*, 1783, Lecture 3

I proceed now to the mention of Shakespear, a writer whom no ingenuous English reader can recollect without the profoundest esteem and the most unbounded admiration. His gigantic mind enabled him in a great degree to overcome the fetters in which the English language was at that period bound. In him we but rarely trace the languid and tedious formality which at that time characterised English composition. His soul was too impetuous, and his sympathy with human passions too entire, not to instruct him in the shortest road to the heart.

But Shakespear for the most part is great only, when great passions are to be expressed. In the calmer and less turbid scenes of life his genius seems in a great degree to forsake him. His wit is generally far fetched, trivial and cold. His tranquil style is perplexed, pedantical, and greatly disfigured with conceits. Of this we will exhibit some examples. They shall be taken from such of his plays as are supposed to have been written in the reign of James the first. It would not have been less easy to have detected similar faults in his earlier plays.

The following is part of the dialogue between the disguised Duke and Isabella in *Measure for Measure*, upon occasion of Angelo's atrocious proposition concerning the pardon of her brother.

> *Duk.*: The hand that hath made you faire, hath
> made you good: the goodnesse that is cheape in
> beauty, makes beauty briefe in goodnesse; but
> grace being the soule of your complexion, shall
> keepe the body of it ever faire: the assault that
> *Angelo* hath made to you, Fortune hath con-

vaid to my understanding; and, but that frailty
hath examples for his falling, I should wonder at
*Angelo*: how will you doe to content this
Substitute, and to save your brother?——

*Isab.*: Let me heare you speake farther; I have spirit to
doe any thing that appeares not foule in the
truth of my spirit.

*Duk.*: Vertue is bold, and goodness never fearfull:
Have you not heard speake of *Mariana* the sister
of *Fredericke* the great Souldier, who miscarried
at Sea?

*Isab.*: I have heard of the Lady, and good words went
with her name.

*Duk.*: She should this *Angelo* have married: was
affianced to her by oath, and the nuptial
appointed: between which time of the contract,
and limit of the solemnity, her brother *Fredericke* was wrackt at Sea, having in that perished
vessel, the dowry of his sister: but marke how
heavily this befell to the poore Gentlewoman,
there she lost a noble and renounced brother, in
his love toward her, ever most kind and naturall:
with him the portion and sinew of her fortune,
her marriage dowry: with both, her combynate-
husband, this well seeming *Angelo*.

*Isab.*: Can this be so? did *Angelo* so leave her?

*Duk.*: Left her in her teares, and dried not one of them
with his comfort: swallowed his vowes whole,
pretending in her, discoveries of dishonor: in few,
bestow'd her on her owne lamentation, which she
yet weares for his sake: and he, a marble of her
cares, is washed with them, but relents not.——
Goe you to *Angelo*, answer his requiring with a
plausible obedience, agree with his demands to the
point:——we shall advise this wronged maid to
steed up your appointment, goe in your place: if
the encounter acknowledge it selfe hereafter, it
may compell him to her recompence; and heere,
by this is your brother saved, your honor untainted, the poore *Mariana* advantaged, and the corrupt Deputy sealed.

(Edit. 1632, commonly called the second folio.)

Nothing can be of a style more quaint and uncouth, than
the letters that are from time to time introduced in different
plays of Shakespear. Take as a specimen the letter of Posthumus to Imogen in the tragedy of *Cymbeline*.

Ivstice, and your Fathers wrath (should hee take mee
in his Dominion) could not be so cruell to me, as
you, (oh the deerest of Creatures) would even renew
me with your eyes. Take notice that I am in *Cambria*
at *Milford-Haven*: what your owne Love, will out of
this advise you, follow. So he wishes you all
happinesse, that remaines loyall to his Vow, and your
encreasing in Love.

Leonatus Posthumus.

There was probably never a grander occasion of eloquence, than when Brutus ascended the rostrum to vindicate
the assassination of Cæsar. Nothing but the contagion of the
vilest taste in literature, could have led Shakespear to put into
his mouth such phrases as the following.

Be patient till the last. Romans, Countrymen, and
Lovers, heare mee for my cause, and be silent, that
you may heare. Beleeve me for mine Honor, and
have respect to mine Honor, that you may
beleeve. Censure me in your Wisedome, and awake
your Senses, that you may the better Iudge.——
There is Teares, for his Love: Ioy, for his Fortune:
Honor, for his Valour: and death for his Ambition.

I know not how far the great soul of Brutus, if he had
condescended to such poor prating as this, could have elevated
it by his enunciation; dramatic writers, well acquainted with
the stage, often err in this way, thinking rather, how feeble or
foolish things may be disguised by an admirable delivery, than
what they are in themselves. This I know, that the genuine
tendency of such expressions was to procure Brutus to be driven
out by the Roman people with hootings, execration and scorn.

We will only add to these examples, the words in which
the Duke communicates to Othello his commission for
Cyprus. One would think that no function could require
greater simplicity of language.

The Turke with a most mighty preparation makes for
Cyprus: *Othello*, the Fortitude of the place is best
knowne to you. And though we have there a
Substitute of most allowed sufficiency; yet opinion, a
more Soveraigne Mistris of Effects, throwes a more
safe voyce on you: you must therefore be content to
slubber the grosse of your new Fortunes, with this
more stubborne, and boysterous expedition.

—WILLIAM GODWIN, "Of English Style," *The
Enquirer*, 1797, pp. 388–93

The English stage might be considered equally without rule
and without model when Shakspeare arose. The effect of the
genius of an individual upon the taste of a nation is mighty; but
that genius, in its turn, is formed according to the opinions
prevalent at the period when it comes into existence. Such was
the case with Shakspeare. Had he received an education more
extensive, and possessed a taste refined by the classical models,
it is probable that he also, in admiration of the ancient Drama,
might have mistaken the form for the essence, and subscribed
to those rules which had produced such masterpieces of art.
Fortunately for the full exertion of a genius, as comprehensive
and versatile as intense and powerful, Shakspeare had no access
to any models of which the commanding merit might have
controlled and limited his own exertions. He followed the path
which a nameless crowd of obscure writers had trodden before
him; but he moved in it with the grace and majestic step of a
being of a superior order; and vindicated for ever the British
theatre from a pedantic restriction to classical rule. Nothing
went before Shakspeare which in any respect was fit to fix and
stamp the character of a national Drama; and certainly no one
will succeed him capable of establishing, by mere authority, a
form more restricted than that which Shakspeare used.

Such is the action of existing circumstances upon genius,
and the reaction of genius upon future circumstances. Shakspeare and Corneille was each the leading spirit of his age; and
the difference between them is well marked by the editor of the
latter:—"*Corneille est inégal comme Shakespeare, et plein de
genie comme lui: mais le genie de Corneille étoit à celui de
Shakespeare ce qu'un seigneur est à l'egard d'un homme de
peuple né avec le même esprit que lui.*" This distinction is
strictly accurate, and contains a compliment to the English
author which, assuredly, the critic did not intend to make.
Corneille wrote as a courtier, circumscribed within the
imaginary rules and ceremonies of a court, as a chicken is by a
circle of chalk drawn round it. Shakspeare, composing for the
amusement of the public alone, had within his province, not
only the inexhaustible field of actual life, but the whole ideal
world of fancy and superstition;—more favourable to the
display of poetical genius than even existing realities. Under
the circumstances of Corneille, Shakspeare must have been
restricted to the same dull, regular, and unvaried system. He
must have written, not according to the dictates of his own
genius, but in conformity to the mandate of some *Intendant*

*des menus plaisirs;* or of some minister of state, who, like Cardinal Richelieu, thought he could write a tragedy because he could govern a kingdom. It is not equally clear to what height Corneille might have ascended, had he enjoyed the national immunities of Shakspeare. Each pitched down a landmark in his art. The circle of Shakspeare was so extensive, that it is with advantage liable to many restrictions; that of Corneille included a narrow limit, which his successors have deemed it unlawful to enlarge.

It is not our intention, within the narrow space to which our essay is necessarily limited, to enlarge upon the character and writings of Shakspeare. We can only notice his performances as events in the history of the theatre—of a gigantic character, indeed, so far as its dignity, elevation, and importance are considered; but, in respect of the mere practice of the Drama, rather fixing and sanctioning, than altering or reforming, those rules and forms which he found already established. This we know for certain, that those historical plays or chronicles, in which Shakspeare's muse has thrown a never-fading light upon the history of his country, did, almost every one of them, exist before him in the rude shape of dry dialogue and pitiful buffoonery, stitched into scenes by the elder playwrights of the stage. His romantic Dramas exhibit the same contempt of regularity which was manifested by Marlow, and other writers; for where there was abuse or extreme license upon the stage, the example of Shakespeare may be often quoted as its sanction, never as tending to reform it.—WALTER SCOTT, "An Essay on the Drama," 1814

> Shakespeare, who's taste is never doubted,
> In a fine passage often spouted
> (I think it is in his Othello,
> Where that besotted Negro fellow
> About a 'kerchief took such fright
> And put out Desdemona's light),
> Tells us that jealousy, I ween,
> Has ghastly eyes—he calls them green;
> But save with deference to sweet Willy
> I think his green eyes rather silly,
> For jealousy, I am inclined,
> Has not green eyes but is stone blind;
> Blind as a beetle when his flight
> Goes blundering on—a summer's night,
> Into the fire or candle's light,
> And burns his nose—to mend his sight.
> (Doggerel Romaunt *By the Author.*)

Having cited as a motto to this chapter a few jingling rhymes from a doggerel poet who has rather irreverently affected to dissent from Shakespeare, I cannot resist the temptation to hazard my opinion of the genius and writings of this mighty master of the scenic art.

The English pride themselves on Shakespeare. They enthusiastically admire his plays and challenge the whole world to produce a dramatic writer of such universal preeminence. The French wits, with Voltaire as their head, have been disposed to deny to the Bard of Avon this supreme eminence and attribute the English opinion of his merits to national prejudice and to an incorrect if not a barbarous taste. No umpire has yet appeared well qualified to decide between them.

I conclude on reflection we Americans may be deemed properly qualified. Familiar with the language in which Shakespeare wrote, free from the imputation of national prejudice, and if our judgement is in any way bias'd from the not yet forgotten resentment occasioned by our revolutionary struggle and the irritation of a more recent war and the vulgar aspersions of her travellers and reviewers, it surely is not inclined to English pretentions. We, therefore, seem well suited to decide upon the claims of the dramatist and we think we ought and shall be credited when we say that the English do not estimate the genius and dramas of the immortal bard too highly.

That their enthusiastic admiration of his plays does not proceed from national prejudice or incorrect or barbarous taste, but simply from a familiarity with their vernacular tongue in which he wrote. That Shakespeare's brilliant imagination by which he repeopled the earth with the offspring of his own fancy or the splendid and noble passages so often quoted from his writings and so often vainly attempted to be translated, are but minor excellences and by far exceeded by that admirable facility and familiarity with which he penetrates the bosoms of the persons represented by his dramatis personae, making every one, whether the inmates of the palace or the cottage, of the ocean, the wilderness or the cavern, whether surrounded by domestic comforts or cast forth roofless and abandoned to bide the "peltings of the pitiless storm," whether actuated by passion or bereft of reason, whether grave or gay, drunk or sober, wise or witty, in love or in debt, pedantic or foolish, conduct just as a deep knowledge of human nature would make us conclude persons so situated would naturally act, think and talk, and frequently by some brief and unobtrusive speech making them develop a whole life of character. And all this effected in a manner so simple, so natural, and with such apparent lack of effort that the reader of his dramas is often tempted to withhold the merit of invention from the bard and to conclude it impossible for people similarly circumstanced to talk and act in any other way than they did. No, the English with all their self complacency do not estimate the genius and dramas of Shakespeare too highly, and the foreigner who can not relish his plays, tho' he may peruse the production of other English poets with pleasure, may rest assured he is still but imperfectly acquainted with the English tongue.—ROYALL TYLER, *The Bay Boy,* c. 1815, Ch. 14

The bare name of the dramatic unities is apt to excite revolting ideas of pedantry, arts of poetry, and French criticism. With none of these do I wish to annoy the reader. I conceive that it may be said of those unities as of fire and water, that they are good servants but bad masters. In perfect rigour they were never imposed by the Greeks, and they would be still heavier shackles if they were closely riveted on our own drama. It would be worse than useless to confine dramatic action literally and immoveably to one spot, or its imaginary time to the time in which it is represented. On the other hand, dramatic time and place cannot surely admit of indefinite expansion. It would be better, for the sake of illusion and probability, to change the scene from Windsor to London, than from London to Pekin; it would look more like reality of a messenger, who went and returned in the course of the play, told us of having performed a journey of ten or twenty, rather than of a thousand miles; and if the spectator had neither that, nor any other circumstance, to make him ask how so much could be performed in so short a time.

In an abstract view of dramatic art, its principles must appear to lie nearer to unity than to the opposite extreme of disunion, in our conceptions of time and place. Giving up the law of unity in its literal rigour, there is still a latitude of its application which may preserve proportion and harmony in the drama.

The brilliant and able Schlegel has traced the principles of what he denominates the romantic, in opposition to the classical drama; and conceives that Shakspeare's theatre, when tried by those principles, will be found not to have violated any of the unities, if they are largely and liberally understood. I have no doubt that Mr. Schlegel's criticism will be found to have proved this point in a considerable number of the works of our mighty poet. There are traits, however, in Shakspeare, which, I must own, appear to my humble judgment incapable of being illustrated by any system or principles of art. I do not allude to his historical plays, which, expressly from being historical, may be called a privileged class. But in those of purer fiction, it strikes me that there are licences conceded indeed to imagination's "chartered libertine," but anomalous with regard to anything which can be recognised as principles in dramatic art. When Perdita, for instance, grows from the cradle to the marriage altar in the course of the play, I can perceive no unity in the design of the piece, and take refuge in the supposition of Shakspeare's genius triumphing and trampling over art. Yet Mr. Schlegel, as far as I have observed, makes no exception to this breach of temporal unity; nor, in proving Shakspeare a regular artist on a mighty scale, does he deign to notice this circumstance, even as the *ultima Thule* of his licence. If a man contends that dramatic laws are all idle restrictions, I can understand him; or if he says that Perdita's growth on the stage is a trespass on art, but that Shakspeare's fascination over and over again redeems it, I can both understand and agree with him. But when I am left to infer that all this is right on romantic principles, I confess that those principles become too romantic for my conception. If Perdita may be born and married on the stage, why may not Webster's Duchess of Malfi lie-in between the acts, and produce a fine family of tragic children? Her Grace actually does so in Webster's drama, and he is a poet of some genius, though it is not quite so sufficient as Shakspeare's to give a "sweet oblivious antidote" to such "perilous stuff." It is not, however, either in favour of Shakspeare's or of Webster's genius that we shall be called on to make allowance, if we justify in the drama the lapse of such a number of years as may change the apparent identity of an individual. If romantic unity is to be so largely interpreted, the old Spanish dramas, where youths grow greybeards upon the stage, the mysteries and moralities, and productions teeming with the wildest anachronism, might all come in with their grave or laughable claims to romantic legitimacy:

Nam sic
Et Laberi mimos ut pulchra poemata mirer.
(*Hor.*)

On a general view, I conceive it may be said that Shakspeare nobly and legitimately enlarged the boundaries of time and place in the drama; but in extreme cases, I would rather agree with (Richard) Cumberland, to waive all mention of his name in speaking of dramatic laws, than accept of those licences for art which are not art, and designate irregularity by the name of order.—THOMAS CAMPBELL, *An Essay on English Poetry*, 1819

We discoursed upon English literature, on the greatness of Shakespeare; and on the unfavourable position held by all English dramatic authors who had appeared after that poetical giant.

"A dramatic talent of any importance," said Goethe, "could not forbear to notice Shakespeare's works; nay, could not forbear to study them. Having studied them, he must be aware that Shakespeare has already exhausted the whole of human nature in all its tendencies, in all its heights and depths, and that in fact there remains for him, the aftercomer, nothing more to do. And how get courage only to put pen to paper, if conscious, in an earnest appreciating spirit, that such unfathomable and unattainable excellences were already in existence!" . . .

I turned the conversation back to Shakespeare. "When he is disengaged from English literature," said I, "and considered as transformed into a German, his greatness seems a miracle. But in the soil of his country, and the atmosphere of his century; studied with his contemporaries and immediate successors—Ben Jonson, Massinger, Marlowe, and Beaumont and Fletcher—Shakespeare, though still a being of the most exalted magnitude, appears in some measure accessible. Much is due to the powerfully productive atmosphere of his time."

"You are right," returned Goethe. "It is with Shakespeare as with the mountains of Switzerland. Transplant Mont Blanc at once into the large plain of Luneburg Heath, and we should find no words to express our wonder at its magnitude. Seek it, however, in its gigantic home; go to it over its immense neighbours, the Jungfrau, the Finsteraarhorn, the Eiger, the Wetterhorn, St. Gothard, and Monte Rosa; Mont Blanc will indeed still remain a giant, but it will no longer produce in us such amazement.

"Besides, let him who will not believe," continued Goethe, "that much of Shakespeare's greatness appertains to his great vigorous time, only ask himself the question, whether a phenomenon so astounding would be possible in the present England of 1824, in these evil days of criticizing and hair-splitting journals?"—JOHANN PETER ECKERMANN, *Conversations with Goethe*, 1836, tr. John Oxenford

Highest among those who have exhibited human nature by means of dialogue, stands Shakspeare. His variety is like the variety of nature, endless diversity, scarcely any monstrosity. The characters of which he has given us an impression, as vivid as that which we receive from the characters of our own associates, are to be reckoned by scores. Yet in all these scores hardly one character is to be found which deviates widely from the common standard, and which we should call very eccentric if we met it in real life. The silly notion that every man has one ruling passion, and that this clue, once known, unravels all the mysteries of his conduct, finds no countenance in the plays of Shakspeare. There man appears as he is, made up of a crowd of passions, which contend for the mastery over him and govern him in turn. What is Hamlet's ruling passion? Or Othello's? Or Harry the Fifth's? Or Wolsey's? Or Lear's? Or Shylock's? Or Benedick's? Or Macbeth's? Or that of Cassius? Or that of Falconbridge? But we might go on for ever. Take a single example, Shylock. Is he so eager for money as to be indifferent to revenge? Or so eager for revenge as to be indifferent to money? Or so bent on both together as to be indifferent to the honour of his nation and the law of Moses? All his propensities are mingled with each other, so that, in trying to apportion to each its proper part, we find the same difficulty which constantly meets us in real life. A superficial critic may say, that hatred is Shylock's ruling passion. But how many passions have amalgamated to form that hatred? It is partly the result of wounded pride: Antonio has called him dog. It is partly the result of covetousness: Antonio has hindered him of half a million; and, when Antonio is gone, there will be no limit to the gains of usury. It is partly the result of national and religious feeling: Antonio has spit on the Jewish gaberdine; and the oath of revenge has been sworn by the Jewish Sabbath. We might go through all the characters which we have mentioned, and through fifty more in the same way; for it is the constant manner of Shakspeare to represent the human mind as lying, not under the absolute dominion of one despotic propensity, but under a mixed government, in which a hundred powers balance each other. Admirable as he was in all parts of his art, we most admire him for this, that while he has left us a greater number of striking portraits than all other dramatists put together, he has scarcely left us a single caricature.—THOMAS BABINGTON MACAULAY, "Madame D'Arblay" (1843), *Critical, Historical, and Miscellaneous Essays,* 1860, Vol. 5, pp. 306–7

> Others abide our question. Thou art free.
> We ask and ask—Thou smilest and art still,
> Out-topping knowledge. For the loftiest hill,
> Who to the stars uncrowns his majesty,
> Planting his stedfast footsteps in the sea,
> Making the heaven of heavens his dwelling-place,
> Spares but the cloudy border of his base
> To the foil'd searching of mortality;
> And thou, who didst the stars and sunbeams know,
> Self-school'd; self-scann'd; self-honour'd, self-secure,
> Didst tread on earth unguess'd at.—Better so!
> All pains the immortal spirit must endure,
> All weakness which impairs, all griefs which bow,
> Find their sole speech in that victorious brow.

> —MATTHEW ARNOLD, "Shakespeare" (1844),
> *Works,* 1903, Vol. 2, p. 5

There is nothing wanting either to the imagination or fancy of Shakspeare. The one is lofty, rich, affecting, palpable, subtle; the other full of grace, playfulness, and variety. He is equal to the greatest poets in grandeur of imagination; to all in diversity of it; to all in fancy; to all in everything else, except in a certain primæval intensity, such as Dante's and Chaucer's; and in narrative poetry, which (to judge from *Venus and Adonis,* and the *Rape of Lucrece*) he certainly does not appear to have had a call to write. He over-informed it with reflection. It has been supposed that when Milton spoke of Shakspeare as

*Fancy's child*
Warbling his native wood-notes wild,

the genealogy did him injustice. But the critical distinction between Fancy and Imagination was hardly determined till of late. Collins himself, in his "Ode on the Poetical Character," uses the word Fancy to imply both, even when speaking of Milton; and so did Milton, I conceive, when speaking of Shakspeare. The propriety of the words, "native wood-notes wild," is not so clear. I take them to have been hastily said by a learned man of an unlearned. But Shakspeare, though he had not a college education, was as learned as any man, in the highest sense of the word, by a scholarly intuition. He had the spirit of learning. He was aware of the education he wanted, and by some means or other supplied it. He could anticipate Milton's own Greek and Latin;

> Tortive and errant from his course of growth—
> The multitudinous seas incarnardine—
> A pudency so rosy, &c.

In fact, if Shakspeare's poetry has any fault, it is that of being too learned; too over-informed with thought and allusion. His wood-notes wild surpass Haydn and Bach. His wild roses were all twenty times double. He thinks twenty times to another man's once, and makes all his serious characters talk as well as he could himself,—with a superabundance of wit and intelligence. He knew, however, that fairies must have a language of their own; and hence, perhaps, his poetry never runs in a more purely poetical vein than when he is speaking in their persons;—I mean it is less mixed up with those heaps of comments and reflections which, however the wilful or metaphysical critic may think them suitable on all occasions, or succeed in persuading us not to wish them absent, by reason of their stimulancy to one's mental activity, are assuredly neither always proper to dramatic, still less to narrative poetry; nor yet so opposed to all idiosyncrasy on the writer's part as Mr.

Coleridge would have us believe. It is pretty manifest, on the contrary, that the over-informing intellect which Shakspeare thus carried into all his writings, must have been a personal as well as literary peculiarity; and as the events he speaks of are sometimes more interesting in their nature than even a superabundance of his comments can make them, readers may be pardoned in sometimes wishing that he had let them speak a little more briefly for themselves. Most people would prefer Ariosto's and Chaucer's narrative poetry to his; the *Griselda,* for instance, and the story of Isabel,—to the *Rape of Lucrece.* The intense passion is enough. The misery is enough. We do not want even the divinest talk about what Nature herself tends to petrify into silence. *Curæ ingentes stupent.* Our divine poet had not quite outlived the times when it was thought proper for a writer to say everything that came into his head. He was a student of Chaucer: he beheld the living fame of Spenser; and his fellow-dramatists did not help to restrain him. The players told Ben Jonson that Shakspeare never blotted a line; and Ben says he was thought invidious for observing, that he wished he had blotted a thousand. He sometimes, he says, required stopping. (*Aliquando sufflaminandus erat.*) Was this meant to apply to his conversation as well as writing? Did he manifest a like exuberance in company? Perhaps he would have done so, but for modesty and self-knowledge. To keep his eloquence altogether within bounds was hardly possible; and who could have wished it had been? Would that he had had a Boswell a hundred times as voluminous as Dr. Johnson's, to take all down! Bacon's *Essays* would have seemed like a drop out of his ocean. He would have swallowed dozens of Hobbeses by anticipation, like larks for his supper.—LEIGH HUNT, "Shakspeare," *Imagination and Fancy,* 1845

We wonder at the grandeur, the moral majesty of some of Shakespeare's characters, so far beyond what the noblest among ourselves can imitate, and at first thought we attribute it to the genius of the poet, who has outstripped nature in his creations. But we are misunderstanding the power and the meaning of poetry in attributing creativeness to it in any such sense. Shakespeare created, but only as the spirit of nature created around him, working in him as it worked abroad in those among whom he lived. The men whom he draws were such men as he saw and knew; the words they utter were such as he heard in the ordinary conversations in which he joined. At the Mermaid with Raleigh and with Sidney, and at a thousand unnamed English firesides, he found the living originals for his Prince Hals, his Orlandos, his Antonios, his Portias, his Isabellas. The closer personal acquaintance which we can form with the English of the age of Elizabeth, the more we are satisfied that Shakespeare's great poetry is no more than the rhythmic echo of the life which it depicts.—JAMES ANTHONY FROUDE, "England's Forgotten Worthies" (1852), *Short Studies on Great Subjects,* 1890, Vol. 1, pp. 445–46

Shakespeare, though he cannot be called an American poet, as he was not born here and never saw our continent, is yet a poet of the Americans. It will be granted that, if all the English were to migrate to some other region, and the French were to come in and occupy their place, Shakespeare could by no means be called a French poet, but would, by the justest title, belong to the race which had migrated. By parity of reasoning, if only a part of the English race migrate, they carry with them not only their language but its literature; they carry with them the poets who flourished before their migration, and who are as truly theirs as they are the poets of those who remain. Shakespeare died while the colonists of Jamestown, Virginia, were building their cabins; he died seven years before the first white child was born on the island now covered with the dwellings of this great city 〈New York〉; he died four years before the landing of the pilgrims on the Plymouth Rock. We Americans may therefore claim an equal property in the great English poet with those who remained in the Old World. . . .

It is common to speak of the blood of the ancestor as flowing in the veins of his descendants, and the expression has a certain truth in it. The tissues of the brain, the seat of wit and of imagination, are woven of fibres lent by our progenitors. The generation which now walks the stage of the world is the reproduction, the re-entrance, in a certain sort, of the generation which has made its exit. The blood that now warms American hearts and gushes through American arteries was once—nearly three hundred years ago, when it ran in the veins of our ancestors in the Old World, and while Shakespeare was yet alive—made to tingle by his potent words. It coursed slowly or swiftly through its purple channels at the will of that great master of the passions. It was quickened and made to glow with indignation at the conduct of Lear's ungrateful daughters; it curdled and was chilled at the sight of the ghost of the royal Dane, and of the sleep-walking murderess in *Macbeth*; it was resolved to tears at the fate of the innocent Desdemona. What American, therefore, who is willing to acknowledge that his ancestors came from the Old World, will fail to claim Shakespeare as his own poet?

It is fortunate that we have in our literature writings of such superlative excellence, so universally read and studied, and, by the exercise of memory, so incorporated into our own minds, as the dramas of Shakespeare. They keep alive the connection between the present and the remote past, and stay the hurrying process of change in certain respects in which change is undesirable. Language is an unstable thing, and, like everything dependent on usage, tends to constant variation; but this tendency has no advantage save as it is demanded by the introduction of new ideas. There are critics who affirm that the English language reached its perfection of expressiveness and copiousness in the time of Queen Elizabeth, and whoever reads the authors of that age will see little cause to wonder at this opinion. Let us congratulate ourselves that we have such an author as Shakespeare, so admired, so loved, to protect our noble language against the capricious innovations of those who read only the authors of yesterday, and that, by dwelling upon what he wrote, the speech of the master minds of his age continues familiar to our ears. There is yet another advantage—that, by tending to preserve the identity of language in regions remote from each other where English is spoken, it keeps alive the remembrance of kindred and brotherhood, and multiplies the pledges of amity and peace between the nations.—WILLIAM CULLEN BRYANT, "Shakespeare" (1870), *Prose Writings*, 1884, Vol. 2, ed. Parke Godwin, pp. 305–6

> A vision as of crowded city streets,
>    With human life in endless overflow;
>    Thunder of thoroughfares; trumpets that blow
>    To battle; clamor, in obscure retreats,
> Of sailors landed from their anchored fleets;
>    Tolling of bells in turrets, and below
>    Voices of children, and bright flowers that throw
> O'er garden-walls their intermingled sweets!
> This vision comes to me when I unfold
>    The volume of the Poet paramount,
>    Whom all the Muses loved, not one alone;—
> Into his hands they put the lyre of gold,
>    And, crowned with sacred laurel at their fount,
>    Placed him as Musagetes on their throne.

>     —HENRY WADSWORTH LONGFELLOW, "Shake-
>     speare," *A Book of Sonnets*, 1875

The transition from the second to the third period of Shake-

speare is very gradual. *All's Well That Ends Well* and *Julius Caesar* lie on the borderland. I consider the following to be as near as possible the chronological order of the third period plays; *Hamlet, Measure for Measure, Othello, Lear, Macbeth, Antony and Cleopatra, Coriolanus, Troilus and Cressida* (or perhaps after *Measure for Measure*), *Timon*. The women of the first, second and third periods have much in common. The women of the fourth period stand quite apart. They are all marked by the absence of what I would call *sweet earthliness*. Sweetness they may have and too much of it, abundance of earthliness some of them, but none of them that combination of the two which we find in Rosalind and Viola and Imogen. Here they are: Ophelia, Isabella, Desdemona, Regan, Goneril, Cordelia, Lady Macbeth, Cleopatra, Volumnia, Virgilia, Cressida. It is as if one were reading Dante.

The transition from the third to the fourth period is of startling suddenness. *Troilus and Cressida* is as incomprehensible as it is wonderful. Shakespeare seems to be pouring out all the wealth of his genius in mockery. The atmosphere of *Timon* is almost unbearable. Then in an interval of little more than a year, away from the keen irony of the *Troilus*, the fierce satire of *Timon*, and we are in the country air of Stratford in *Pericles* and *Cymbeline* and *Winter's Tale*, breathing the fragrance of flowers, looking at life with the calm far-away gaze of old age. I can't recall any more wonderful transition in literature. Shakespeare was long in attaining his maturity. He was about thirty when he reached the manhood of his genius. But half a lifetime is pressed together in the brief six years of the third period. When he wrote *The Tempest* he was old—older at 45 almost than Goethe was at 80. He takes an old man's joy in the freshness of young boyhood and girlhood; in the beauty of flowers and sunny air and peace; in the loveliness of repentance and forgiveness and reconciliation. Not that there is any trace of decay in Shakespeare's later work. He turned to the sweet Italian tales which had charmed him in youth, and touched him with a light playful touch, yet full of strength and tenderness and truth. *Cymbeline* is a lovely play. It was Hazlitt's favourite and he has criticised it admirably in his *Characters*. I always look upon Imogen as the noblest, sweetest ideal of womanhood in Shakespeare,—the woman in whom the elements of character are held in most perfect equilibrium, with indeed a certain touch of gravity that faintly recalls the third period, and yet with all the sweet earthliness of Rosalind and Viola. *The Tempest* and *The Winter's Tale* are scarcely less lovely plays.—HAVELOCK ELLIS, "William Shakespeare" (1878), *From Marlowe to Shaw*, 1950, ed. John Gawsworth, pp. 30–31

> Not if men's tongues and angels' all in one
>    Spake, might the word be said that might speak Thee.
>    Streams, winds, woods, flowers, fields, mountains, yea, the
>    sea,
> What power is in them all to praise the sun?
> His praise is this,—he can be praised of none.
>    Man, woman, child, praise God for him; but he
>    Exults not to be worshipped, but to be.
> He is; and, being, beholds his work well done.
> All joy, all glory, all sorrow, all strength, all mirth,
> Are his: without him, day were night on earth.
>    Time knows not his from time's own period.
> All lutes, all harps, all viols, all flutes, all lyres,
> Fall dumb before him ere one string suspires.
>    All stars are angels; but the sun is God.

>     —ALGERNON CHARLES SWINBURNE, "William
>     Shakespeare," *Sonnets on English Dramatic
>     Poets*, 1882

Shakspere forms a focus for all the rays of light which had emerged before his time, and that after him these rays were once more decomposed and scattered over a wide area. Thus at least we may regard the matter from our present point of survey. Yet during Shakspere's lifetime his predominance was by no means so obvious. To explain the defect of intelligence in Shakspere's contemporaries, to understand why they chose epithets like 'mellifluous,' 'sweet,' and 'gentle,' to describe the author of *King Lear, Othello*, and *Troilus and Cressida*; why they praised his 'right happy and copious industry' instead of dwelling on his interchange of tragic force and fanciful inventiveness; why the misconception of his now acknowledged place in literature extended even to Milton and to Dryden, will remain perhaps for ever impossible to every student of those times. But this intellectual obtuseness is itself instructive, when we regard Shakspere as the creature, not as the creator, of a widely diffused movement in the spirit of the nation, of which all his contemporaries were dimly conscious. They felt that behind him, as behind themselves, dwelt a motive force superior to all of them. Instead, then, of comparing him, as some have done, to the central orb of a solar system, from whom the planetary bodies take their light, it would be more correct to say that the fire of the age which burns in him so intensely, burned in them also, more dimly, but independently of him. He represents the English dramatic genius in its fullness. The subordinate playwrights bring into prominence minor qualities and special aspects of that genius. Men like Webster and Heywood, Jonson and Ford, Fletcher and Shirley, have an existence in literature outside Shakspere, and are only in an indirect sense satellites and vassals. Could Shakspere's works be obliterated from man's memory, they would still sustain the honours of the English stage with decent splendour. Still it is only when Shakspere shines among them, highest, purest, brightest of that brotherhood, that the real radiance of his epoch is discernible—that the real value and meaning of their work become apparent.

The more we study Shakspere in relation to his predecessors, the more obliged are we to reverse Dryden's famous dictum that he 'found not, but created first the stage.' The fact is, that he found dramatic form already fixed. When he began to work among the London playwrights, the Romantic Drama in its several species—Comedy, Italian Novella, Roman History, English Chronicle, Masque, Domestic Tragedy, Melodrama—had achieved its triumph over the Classical Drama of the scholars. Rhyme had been discarded, and blank verse adopted as the proper vehicle of dramatic expression. Shakspere's greatness consisted in bringing the type established by his predecessors to artistic ripeness, not in creating a new type. It may even be doubted whether Shakspere was born to be a playwright—whether it was not rather circumstance which led him to assume his place as coryphæus to the choir of dramatists. The defects of the Romantic form were accepted by him with easy acquiescence, nor did he aim at altering that form in any essential particular. He dealt with English Drama as he dealt with the materials of his plays; following an outline traced already, but glorifying each particular of style and matter; breathing into the clay-figures of a tale his own creator's breath of life, enlarging prescribed incident and vivifying suggested thought with the art of an unrivalled poet-rhetorician, raising the verse invented for him to its highest potency and beauty with inexhaustible resource and tact incomparable in the use of language.

At the same time, the more we study Shakspere in his own works, the more do we perceive that his predecessors, no less than his successors, exist for him; that without him English dramatic art would be but second rate; that he is the keystone of the arch, the justifier and interpreter of his time's striving impulses. The forms he employs are the forms he found in common usage among his fellow-craftsmen. But his method of employing them is so vastly superior, the quality of his work is so incommensurable by any standard we apply to the best of theirs, that we cannot help regarding the plays of Shakspere as not exactly different in kind, but diverse in inspiration. Without those predecessors, Shakspere would certainly not have been what he is. But having him, we might well afford to lose them. Without those successors, we should still miss much that lay implicit in the art of Shakspere. But having him, we could well dispense with them. His predecessors lead up to him, and help us to explain his method. His successors supplement his work, illustrating the breadth and length and depth and versatility of English poetry in that prolific age.

It is this twofold point of view from which Shakspere must be studied in connection with the minor dramatists, which gives them value. It appears that a whole nation laboured in those fifty years' activity to give the world one Shakspere; but it is no less manifest that Shakspere did not stand alone, without support and without lineage. He and his fellow playwrights are interdependent, mutually illustrative; and their aggregated performance is the expression of a nation's spirit.—JOHN ADDINGTON SYMONDS, "Introductory" to *Shakspere's Predecessors in the English Drama*, 1884, pp. 16–19

The most distinctive poems—the most permanently rooted and with heartiest reason for being—the copious cycle of Arthurian legends, or the almost equally copious Charlemagne cycle, or the poems of the Cid, or Scandinavian Eddas, or Nibelungen, or Chaucer, or Spenser, or *bona fide* Ossian, or Inferno—probably had their rise in the great historic perturbations, which they came in to sum up and confirm, indirectly embodying results to date. Then however precious to "culture," the grandest of those poems, it may be said, preserve and typify results offensive to the modern spirit, and long past away. To state it briefly, and taking the strongest examples, in Homer lives the ruthless military prowess of Greece, and of its special god-descended dynastic houses; in Shakspere the dragon-rancors and stormy feudal splendor of mediæval caste.

Poetry, largely consider'd, is an evolution, sending out improved and ever-expanded types—in one sense, the past, even the best of it, necessarily giving place, and dying out. For our existing world, the bases on which all the grand old poems were built have become vacuums—and even those of many comparatively modern ones are broken and half-gone. For us to-day, not their own intrinsic value, vast as that is, backs and maintains those poems—but a mountain-high growth of associations, the layers of successive ages. Everywhere—their own lands included—(is there not something terrible in the tenacity with which the one book out of millions holds its grip?)—the Homeric and Virgilian works, the interminable ballad-romances of the middle ages, the utterances of Dante, Spenser, and others, are upheld by their cumulus-entrenchment in scholarship, and as precious, always welcome, unspeakably valuable reminiscences.

Even the one who at present reigns unquestion'd—of Shakspere—for all he stands for so much in modern literature, he stands entirely for the mighty æsthetic sceptres of the past, not for the spiritual and democratic, the sceptres of the future. The inward and outward characteristics of Shakspere are his vast and rich variety of persons and themes, with his wondrous delineation of each and all—not only limitless funds of verbal and pictorial resource, but great excess, superfœtation—mannerism, like a fine, aristocratic perfume, holding a touch of musk (Euphues, his mark)—with boundless sumptuousness and adornment, real velvet and gems, not shoddy nor paste—but a good deal of bombast and fustian—(certainly some terrific mouthing in Shakspere!).

Superb and inimitable as all is, it is mostly an objective and physiological kind of power and beauty the soul finds in Shakspere—a style supremely grand of the sort, but in my opinion stopping short of the grandest sort, at any rate for fulfilling and satisfying modern and scientific and democratic American purposes. Think, not of growths as forests primeval, or Yellowstone geysers, or Colorado ravines, but of costly marble palaces, and palace rooms, and the noblest fixings and furniture, and noble owners and occupants to correspond—think of carefully built gardens from the beautiful but sophisticated gardening art at its best, with walks and bowers and artificial lakes, and appropriate statue-groups and the finest cultivated roses and lilies and japonicas in plenty—and you have the tally of Shakspere. The low characters, mechanics, even the loyal henchmen—all in themselves nothing—serve as capital foils to the aristocracy. The comedies (exquisite as they certainly are) bringing in admirably portray'd common characters, have the unmistakable hue of plays, portraits, made for the divertisement only of the élite of the castle, and from its point of view. The comedies are altogether non-acceptable to America and Democracy.

But to the deepest soul, it seems a shame to pick and choose from the riches Shakspere has left us—to criticise his infinitely royal, multiform quality—to gauge, with optic glasses, the dazzle of his sun-like beams.

The best poetic utterance, after all, can merely hint, or remind, often very indirectly, or at distant removes. Aught of real perfection, or the solution of any deep problem, or any completed statement of the moral, the true, the beautiful, eludes the greatest, deftest poet—flies away like an always uncaught bird.—WALT WHITMAN, "A Thought on Shakspere" (1886), *Prose Works*, 1964, Vol. 2, ed. Floyd Stovall, pp. 556–58

Shakespeare and Rembrandt have in common the faculty of quickening speculation and compelling the minds of men to combat and discussion. About the English poet a literature of contention has been in process of accretion ever since he was discovered to be Shakespeare; and about the Dutch painter and etcher there has gradually accumulated a literature precisely analogous in character and for the most part of equal quality. In such an age as this, when the creative faculty of the world is mainly occupied with commentary and criticism, the reason should not be far to seek. Both were giants; both were original and individual in the highest sense of the words; both were leagues ahead of their contemporaries, not merely as regards the matter of their message but also in respect of the terms of its delivery; each, moreover—and here one comes upon a capital point of contact and resemblance—each was at times prodigiously inferior to himself. Shakespeare often writes so ill that you hesitate to believe he could ever write supremely well; or, if this way of putting it seem indecorous and abominable, he very often writes so well that you are loth to believe he could ever have written thus extremely ill. There are passages in his work in which he reaches such heights of literary art as since his time no mortal has found accessible; and there are passages which few or none of us can read without a touch of that 'burning sense of shame' experienced in the presence of Mr. Poynter's *Diadumene* by the British Matron of *The Times* newspaper. Now, we have got to be so curious in ideals that we cannot away with the thought of imperfection. Our worship must have for its object something flawless, something utterly with-

out spot or blemish. We can be satisfied with nothing less than an entire and perfect chrysolite; and we cannot taste our Shakespeare at his worst without experiencing not merely the burning sense of shame aforesaid but also a frenzy of longing to father his faults upon somebody else—Marlowe for instance, or Green, or Fletcher—and a fury of proving that our divinity was absolutely incapable of them. That Shakespeare varied—that the matchless prose and the not particularly lordly verse of *As You Like It* are by the same hand; that the master to whom we owe our Hamlet is also responsible for Gertrude and King Claudius; that he who gave us the agony of Lear and the ruin of Othello did likewise perpetrate the scene of Hector's murder, in manner so poor and in spirit so cynical and vile—is beyond all belief and patience; and we have argued the point to such an extent that we are all of us in Gotham, and a mooncalf like the ascription of whatever is good in Shakespeare to Lord Bacon is no prodigy but a natural birth.—W. E. HENLEY, "Shakespeare," *Views and Reviews*, 1890, pp. 101–3

There ought certainly to be some bound beyond which the cult of favorite authors should not be suffered to go. I should keep well within the limit of that early excess now, and should not liken the creation of Shakespeare to the creation of any heavenly body bigger, say, than one of the nameless asteroids that revolve between Mars and Jupiter. Even this I do not feel to be a true means of comparison, and I think that in the case of all great men we like to let our wonder mount and mount, till it leaves the truth behind, and honesty is pretty much cast out as ballast. A wise criticism will no more magnify Shakespeare because he is already great than it will magnify any less man. But we are loaded down with the responsibility of finding him all we have been told he is, and we must do this or suspect ourselves of a want of taste, a want of sensibility. At the same time, we may really be honester than those who have led us to expect this or that of him, and more truly his friends. I wish the time might come when we could read Shakespeare, and Dante, and Homer, as sincerely and as fairly as we read any new book by the least known of our contemporaries. The course of criticism is towards this, but when I began to read Shakespeare I should not have ventured to think that he was not at every moment great. I should no more have thought of questioning the poetry of any passage in him than of questioning the proofs of holy writ. All the same, I knew very well that much which I read was really poor stuff, and the persons and positions were often preposterous. It is a great pity that the ardent youth should not be permitted and even encouraged to say this to himself, instead of falling slavishly before a great author and accepting him at all points as infallible. Shakespeare is fine enough and great enough when all the possible detractions are made, and I have no fear of saying now that he would be finer and greater for the loss of half his work, though if I had heard any one say such a thing then I should have held him as little better than one of the wicked. . . .

Probably no dramatist ever needed the stage less, and none ever brought more to it. There have been few joys for me in life comparable to that of seeing the curtain rise on *Hamlet*, and hearing the guards begin to talk about the ghost; and yet how fully this joy imparts itself without any material embodiment! It is the same in the whole range of his plays: they fill the scene, but if there is no scene they fill the soul. They are neither worse nor better because of the theatre. They are so great that it cannot hamper them; they are so vital that they enlarge it to their own proportions and endue it with something of their own living force. They make it the size of life, and yet they retire it so wholly that you think no more of it than you think of the physiognomy of one who talks importantly to you.

I have heard people say that they would rather not see Shakespeare played than to see him played ill, but I cannot agree with them. He can better afford to be played ill than any other man that ever wrote. Whoever is on the stage, it is always Shakespeare who is speaking to me, and perhaps this is the reason why in the past I can trace no discrepancy between reading his plays and seeing them.—WILLIAM DEAN HOWELLS, "Shakespeare," *My Literary Passions*, 1891, pp. 58–60

If there is no drama without action, neither is there any without character. It may be that the creation of character is the highest function of art. There is nothing which more resembles divine power than the exploit by which the poet evokes from the depths of his imagination personages who have never lived, but who thenceforward live forever, and who will take a place in our memories, in our affections, in the realities of our world, exactly as if they had been formed by the hand of the Most High. And if a single creation of this kind suffices to immortalize a writer, what shall we say of a poet who, like Shakespeare, has drawn crowds of characters, all different, all alive, uniting the most distinct physiognomy and the intensest reality to the highest quality of idealism and poetry? The English dramatist is in nothing so marvellous as in this. He is the magician who can give life to anything by his wand; or rather, he is Nature herself, capricious, prodigal, always new, always full of surprises and of profundity. His personages are not what are called heroes; there is no posing in them; there is no abstraction; the idea has become incarnate, and develops itself as a whole, with all the logic of passion, with all the spontaneity of life. The only thing which can be brought against the author is at times a too sharp change—one, so to speak, effected on the stage—in the sentiments of his characters. Aufidius, for example, passes too quickly from hatred to sorrow when he sees Coriolanus fall; and in *Richard III.* Anne accepts with too great ease the ring of the man on whom she has just spit in contempt; while Elizabeth is too quick in giving her daughter to the man who has just massacred her sons. This is certainly turning the corner too sharply, and there is a want of truth in it.

I think that something of the same kind may be said of Shakespeare's style. The language which he puts in the mouths of his characters is not always appropriate—is sometimes far from being appropriate—to the circumstances, even to the characters themselves. The poet delights too much in the expression for itself and its own sake. He dwells on it, he lingers over it, he plays with equivalents and synonyms. Menenius thus complains of the change which has occurred in Coriolanus's humor:—"The tartness of his face sours ripe grapes: when he walks he moves like an engine, and the ground shrinks before his treading: he is able to pierce a corselet with his eye: talks like a knell, and his hum is a battery. He sits in his state as a thing made for Alexander. What he bids be done is finished with his bidding. He wants nothing of a god but eternity and a heaven to throne in"—I take this quotation at random to exemplify what I mean. The form in this poet sometimes overruns in this fashion; the expression is redundant and out of proportion to the situation. This remark applies still better to the conceits and the word-plays which Shakespeare, without troubling himself about the occasion, puts in everybody's mouth. The most pathetic speeches are not free from them. It is not that the author is not conscious of the incongruity of these quips.

Do sick men play so nicely with their names?

asks Richard III. of the Duke of Lancaster, and it is certain that his last works have much fewer of these blots than his first. But if there is sometimes ill-placed wit in our poet, what verve is there in this wit, what gayety, what exuberance! With what freedom and caprice does fancy develop itself! How well (to employ an expression of Madame de Staël's) do excess and license of talent suit this unbounded invention! And we must also say at once that this wit is but one of Shakespeare's qualities. He possesses imagination and feeling in at least equal measure. He has felt everything, has understood everything. No man has lived more, has observed more, has better reproduced the outward world. And yet he is at the same time the most lyrical of poets; he expresses in finished form, in inimitable poetry, all the emotions of the heart. He says things as no one else says them, in a manner at once strange and striking. He has unbelievable depths, subtlenesses of intuition as unbelievable. There rises from his writings a kind of emanation of supreme wisdom; and it seems that their very discords melt into some transcendent harmony. Shakespeare has enlarged the domain of the mind, and, take him all in all, I do not believe that any man has added more than he has to the patrimony of mankind.—EDMOND SCHERER, "Shakespeare," *Essays on English Literature*, 1891, tr. George Saintsbury, pp. 47–50

Of Shakespeare's sonnets ⟨Tennyson⟩ would say, "Henry Hallam made a great mistake about them: they are noble. Look how beautiful such lines as these are:

> The summer flower is to the summer sweet,
> Though to itself it only live and die,

and

> And peace proclaims olives of endless age."

Of Shakespeare's blank verse he said, "Almost any prose can be cut up into blank verse, but blank verse becomes the finest vehicle of thought in the language of Shakespeare and Milton. As far as I am aware, no one has noticed what great Æschylean lines there are in Shakespeare, particularly in *King John*: for instance,

> The burning crest
> Of the old, feeble, and day-wearied sun,

or again,

> The sepulchre
> Hath oped his ponderous and marble jaws."

He would say, "There are three repartees in Shakespeare which always bring tears to my eyes from their simplicity.

"One is in *King Lear* when Lear says to Cordelia, 'So young and so untender,' and Cordelia lovingly answers, 'So young, my lord, and true.' And in *The Winter's Tale*, when Florizel takes Perdita's hand to lead her to the dance, and says, 'So turtles pair that never mean to part,' and the little Perdita answers, giving her hand to Florizel, 'I'll swear for 'em.' And in *Cymbeline*, when Imogen in tender rebuke says to her husband,

> Why did you throw your wedded lady from you?
> Think that you are upon a rock; and now
> Throw me again!

and Posthumus does not ask forgiveness, but answers, kissing her,

> Hang there like fruit, my soul,
> Till the tree die."

After reading *Pericles*, Act v. aloud:

"That is glorious Shakespeare: most of the rest of the play is poor, and not by Shakespeare, but in that act the conception of Marina's character is exquisite."

Of *Henry VI.* he said, "I am certain that *Henry VI.* is in the main not Shakespeare's, though here and there he may have put in a touch, as he undoubtedly did in *The Two Noble*

*Kinsmen.* There is a great deal of fine Shakespeare in that. Spedding insisted that Shakespeare, among the many plays that he edited for the stage, had corrected a play on Sir Thomas More in the British Museum. It is a poor play, but Spedding believed that the corrections were possibly in Shakespeare's actual handwriting.

"I have no doubt that much of *Henry VIII.* also is not Shakespeare. It is largely written by Fletcher, with passages unmistakeably by Shakespeare, notably the two first scenes in the first Act, which are sane and compact in thought, expression and simile. I could swear to Shakespeare in the *Field of the Cloth of Gold:*

> To-day the French
> All clinquant, all in gold like heathen gods,
> Shone down the English; and to-morrow they
> *Made Britain India; every man that stood*
> *Show'd like a mine.*

"*Hamlet* is the greatest creation in literature that I know of: though there may be elsewhere finer scenes and passages of poetry. Ugolino and Paolo and Francesca in Dante equal anything anywhere. It is said that Shakespeare was such a poor actor that he never got beyond his ghost in this play, but then the ghost is the most real ghost that ever was. The Queen did not think that Ophelia committed suicide, neither do I.

"Is there a more delightful love-poem than *Romeo and Juliet?* yet it is full of conceits.

"One of the most passionate things in Shakespeare is Romeo's speech:

> Amen, amen! but come what sorrow can,
> It cannot countervail the exchange of joy
> That one short minute gives me in her sight, etc.

More passionate than anything in Shelley. No one has drawn the true passion of love like Shakespeare."

For inimitably natural talk between husband and wife he would quote the scene between Hotspur and Lady Percy (*King Henry IV.*, Pt. I.), and would exclaim: "How deliciously playful is that—

> In faith, I'll break thy little finger, Harry,
> An if thou wilt not tell me all things true!

"*Macbeth* is not, as is too often represented, a noisy swash-buckler; he is a full-furnished, ambitious man. In the scene with Duncan, the excess of courtesy adds a touch to the tragedy. It is like Clytemnestra's profusion to Agamemnon; who, by the way, always strikes me as uncommonly cold and haughty to his wife whom he had not seen for years.

"*King Lear* cannot possibly be acted, it is too titanic. At the beginning of the play Lear, in his old age, has grown half mad, choleric and despotic, and therefore cannot brook Cordelia's silence. This play shows a state of society where men's passions are savage and uncurbed. No play like this anywhere—not even the *Agamemnon*—is so terrifically human.

"Actors do not comprehend that Shakespeare's greatest villains, Iago among them, have always a touch of conscience. You see the conscience working—therein lies one of Shakespeare's pre-eminences. Iago ought to be acted as the 'honest Iago,' not the stage villain; he is the essentially jealous man, not Othello."—HALLAM TENNYSON, *Alfred Lord Tennyson: A Memoir*, 1897, Vol. 2, pp. 289–92

A famous author says that there is some kind of immoral emanation from the horse, and that it affects the character of every one who has much to do with the animal. I suppose it is something like that which suspires from the earth that is thrown out in digging a canal. Perhaps it is possible to construct a short and shallow waterway without stirring up enough of this badness to corrupt "all those in authority" along the line of it, but if the enterprise is of magnitude, like the Suez or the Panama project, results most disastrous to the morals of all engaged in the work, excepting those who do it, will certainly ensue, as we may soon have the happiness to observe.

A similar phenomenon is seen in the case of Shakspeare, whose resemblance to a horse and a canal has not, I flatter myself, been heretofore pointed out. The subtle suspiration from the work of the great dramatist, however, attacks, not the morals, but the intellect. It does not prostrate the sense of right and wrong, except in so far as this is dependent on mental health; it simply lays waste the judgment by dispersing the faculties, as the shadow of a hawk squanders a flock of feeding pigeons. Some time we shall perhaps have an English-speaking critic who will be immune to Shakspearitis, but as yet Heaven has not seen fit to "raise him up." And when we have him his inaccessibility to the infection will do him no good, for we shall indubitably put him to death.

The temptation to these reflections is supplied by looking into Mr. Arlo Bates's book, *Talks on Writing English*, where I find this passage quoted from Jeffrey:

> Everything in him (Shakspeare) is in unmeasured abundance and unequaled perfection—but everything so balanced and kept in subordination as not to jostle or disturb or take the place of another. The most exquisite poetical conceptions, images and descriptions are given with such brevity and introduced with such skill as merely to adorn without loading the sense they accompany. . . . All his excellences, like those of Nature herself, are thrown out together; and, instead of interfering with, support and recommend each other.

This is so fine as to be mostly false. It is true that Shakspeare throws out his excellences in unmeasured abundance and all together; and nothing else in this passage is true. His poetical conceptions, images and descriptions are not "given" at all; they are "turned loose." They came from his brain like a swarm of bees. They race out, as shouting children from a country school. They distract, stun, confuse. So disorderly an imagination has never itself been imagined. Shakspeare had no sense of proportion, no care for the strength of restraint, no art of saying just enough, no art of any kind. He flung about him his enormous and incalculable wealth of jewels with the prodigal profusion of a drunken youth mad with the lust of spending. Only the magnificence and value of the jewels could blind us to the barbarian method of distribution. They dazzle the mind and confound all the criteria of the judgment. Small wonder that the incomparable Voltaire, French, artistic in every fiber and trained in the severe dignities of Grecian art, called this lawless and irresponsible spendthrift a drunken savage.

Of no cultivated Frenchman is the judgment on Shakspeare much milder; the man's "art," his "precision," his "perfection"—these are creations of our Teutonic imaginations, heritages of the time when in the rush-strewn baronial hall our ancestors surfeited themselves on oxen roasted whole and drank to insensibility out of wooden flagons holding a gallon each.

In literature, as in all else—in work, in love, in trade, in every kind of action or acquisition the Germanic nations are gluttons and drunkards. We want everything, as we want our food and drink, in savage profusion. And, by the same token, we rule the world.—AMBROSE BIERCE, "The Ravages of Shakspearitis" (1903), *Collected Works*, 1911, Vol. 10, pp. 109–12

MARGARET CAVENDISH,
DUCHESS OF NEWCASTLE
"Letter 123"
*CCXI Sociable Letters*
1664

MADAM,
I Wonder how that Person you mention in your Letter, could either have the Conscience, or Confidence to Dispraise *Shakespeare*'s Playes, as to say they were made up onely with Clowns, Fools, Watchmen, and the like; But to Answer that Person, though *Shakespeare*'s Wit will Answer for himself, I say, that it seems by his Judging, or Censuring, he Understands not Playes, or Wit; for to Express Properly, Rightly, Usually, and Naturally, a Clown's, or Fool's Humour, Expressions, Phrases, Garbs, Manners, Actions, Words, and Course of Life, is as Witty, Wise, Judicious, Ingenious, and Observing, as to Write and Express the Expressions, Phrases, Garbs, Manners, Actions, Words, and Course of Life, of Kings and Princes; and to Express Naturally, to the Life, a Mean Country Wench, as a Great Lady, a Courtesan, as a Chast Woman, a Mad man, as a Man in his right Reason and Senses, a Drunkard, as a Sober man, a Knave, as an Honest man, and so a Clown, as a Well-bred man, and a Fool, as a Wise man; nay, it Expresses and Declares a Greater Wit, to Express, and Deliver to Posterity, the Extravagancies of Madness, the Subtilty of Knaves, the Ignorance of Clowns, and the Simplicity of Naturals, or the Craft of Feigned Fools, than to Express Regularities, Plain Honesty, Courtly Garbs, or Sensible Discourses, for 'tis harder to Express Nonsense than Sense, and Ordinary Conversations, than that which is Unusual; and 'tis Harder, and Requires more Wit to Express a Jester, than a Grave Statesman; yet *Shakespeare* did not want Wit, to Express to the Life all Sorts of Persons, of what Quality, Profession, Degree, Breeding, or Birth soever; nor did he want Wit to Express the Divers, and Different Humours, or Natures, or Several Passions in Mankind; and so Well he hath Express'd in his Playes all Sorts of Persons, as one would think he had been Transformed into every one of those Persons he hath Described; and as sometimes one would think he was Really himself the Clown or Jester he Feigns, so one would think, he was also the King, and Privy Counsellor; also as one would think he were Really the Coward he Feigns, so one would think he were the most Valiant, and Experienced Souldier; Who would not think he had been such a man as his Sir *John Falstaff*? and who would not think he had been *Harry* the Fifth? & certainly *Julius Cæsar*, *Augustus Cæsar*, and *Antonius*, did never Really Act their parts Better, if so Well, as he hath Described them, and I believe that *Antonius* and *Brutus* did not Speak Better to the People, than he hath Feign'd them; nay, one would think that he had been Metamorphosed from a Man to a Woman, for who could Describe *Cleopatra* Better than he hath done, and many other Females of his own Creating, as *Nan Page*, Mrs. *Page*, Mrs. *Ford*, the Doctors Maid, *Beatrice*, Mrs. *Quickly*, *Doll Tearsheet*, and others, too many to Relate? and in his Tragick Vein, he Presents Passions so Naturally, and Misfortunes so Probably, as he Peirces the souls of his Readers with such a True Sense and Feeling thereof, that it Forces Tears through their Eyes, and almost Perswades them, they are Really Actors, or at least Present at those Tragedies. Who would not Swear he had been a Noble Lover, that could Woo so well? and there is not any person he hath Described in his Book, but his Readers might think they were Well acquainted with them; indeed *Shakespeare* had a Clear Judgment, a Quick Wit, a Spreading Fancy, a Subtil Observation, a Deep Apprehension, and a most Eloquent Elocution; truly, he was a Natural Orator, as well as a Natural Poet, and he was not an Orator to Speak Well only on some Subjects, as Lawyers, who can make Eloquent Orations at the Bar, and Plead Subtilly and Wittily in Law-Cases, or Divines, that can Preach Eloquent Sermons, or Dispute Subtilly and Wittily in Theology, but take them from that, and put them to other Subjects, and they will be to seek; but *Shakespeare*'s Wit and Eloquence was General, for, and upon all Subjects, he rather wanted Subjects for his Wit and Eloquence to Work on, for which he was Forced to take some of his Plots out of History, where he only took the Bare Designs, the Wit and Language being all his Own; and so much he had above others, that those, who Writ after him, were Forced to Borrow of him, or rather to Steal from him; I could mention Divers Places, that others of our Famous Poets have Borrow'd, or Stoln, but lest I should Discover the Persons, I will not Mention the Places, or Parts, but leave it to those that Read his Playes, and others, to find them out. I should not have needed to Write this to you, for his Works would have Declared the same Truth: But I believe, those that Dispraised his Playes, Dispraised them more out of Envy, than Simplicity or Ignorance, for those that could Read his Playes, could not be so Foolish to Condemn them, only the Excellency of them caused an Envy to them. By this we may perceive, Envy doth not Leave a man in the Grave, it Follows him after Death, unless a man be Buried in Oblivion, but if he Leave any thing to be Remembred, Envy and Malice will be still throwing Aspersion upon it, or striving to Pull it down by Detraction. But leaving *Shakespeare*'s Works to their own Defence, and his Detractors to their Envy, and you to your better Imployments, than Reading my Letter, I rest,

Madam,

Your faithful Friend
and humble Servant.

NICHOLAS ROWE
From "Some Account of the Life, &c.
of Mr. William Shakespear"
*The Works of Mr. William Shakespear*
1709, Volume 1, pp. xxvi–xxxv

His Plays are properly to be distinguish'd only into Comedies and Tragedies. Those which are called Histories, and even some of his Comedies, are really Tragedies, with a run or mixture of Comedy amongst 'em. That way of Trage-Comedy was the common Mistake of that Age, and is indeed become so agreeable to the *English* Tast, that tho' the severer Critiques among us cannot bear it, yet the generality of our Audiences seem to be better pleas'd with it than with an exact Tragedy. *The Merry Wives* of Windsor, *The Comedy of Errors*, and *The Taming of the Shrew*, are all pure Comedy; the rest, however they are call'd, have something of both Kinds. 'Tis not very easie to determine which way of Writing he was most Excellent in. There is certainly a great deal of Entertainment in his Comical Humours; and tho' they did not then strike at all Ranks of People, as the Satyr of the present Age has taken the Liberty to do, yet there is a pleasing and a well-distinguish'd Variety in those Characters which he thought fit to meddle with. *Falstaff* is allow'd by every body to be a

Master-piece; the Character is always well-sustain'd, tho' drawn out into the length of three Plays; and even the Account of his Death, given by his Old Landlady Mrs. *Quickly*, in the first Act of *Henry* V. tho' it be extremely Natural, is yet as diverting as any Part of his Life. If there be any Fault in the Draught he has made of this lewd old Fellow, it is, that tho' he has made him a Thief, Lying, Cowardly, Vain-glorious, and in short every way Vicious, yet he has given him so much Wit as to make him almost too agreeable; and I don't know whether some People have not, in remembrance of the Diversion he had formerly afforded 'em, been sorry to see his Friend *Hal* use him so scurvily, when he comes to the Crown in the End of the Second Part of *Henry* the Fourth. Amongst other Extravagances, in *The Merry Wives of* Windsor, he has made him a Dear-stealer, that he might at the same time remember his *Warwickshire* Prosecutor, under the Name of Justice *Shallow*; he has given him very near the same Coat of Arms which *Dugdale*, in his Antiquities of that County, describes for a Family there, and makes the *Welsh* Parson descant very pleasantly upon 'em. That whole Play is admirable; the Humours are various and well oppos'd; the main Design, which is to cure *Ford* of his unreasonable Jealousie, is extremely well conducted. *Falstaff's Billet-doux*, and Master *Slender's*

Ah! Sweet Ann Page!

are very good Expressions of Love in their Way. In *Twelfth-Night* there is something singularly Ridiculous and Pleasant in the fantastical Steward *Malvolio*. The Parasite and the Vain-glorious in *Parolles*, in *All's Well That Ends Well*, is as good as any thing of that Kind in *Plautus* or *Terence*. *Petruchio*, in *The Taming of the Shrew*, is an uncommon Piece of Humour. The Conversation of *Benedick* and *Beatrice*, in *Much Ado about Nothing*, and of *Rosalind* in *As You Like It*, have much Wit and Sprightliness all along. His Clowns, without which Character there was hardly any Play writ in that Time, are all very entertaining: And, I believe, *Thersites* in *Troilus and Cressida*, and *Apemantus* in *Timon*, will be allow'd to be Master-Pieces of ill Nature, and satyrical Snarling. To these I might add, that incomparable Character of *Shylock* the *Jew*, in *The Merchant of* Venice; but tho' we have seen that Play Receiv'd and Acted as a Comedy, and the Part of the *Jew* perform'd by an Excellent Comedian, yet I cannot but think it was design'd Tragically by the Author. There appears in it such a deadly Spirit of Revenge, such a savage Fierceness and Fellness, and such a bloody designation of Cruelty and Mischief, as cannot agree either with the Stile or Characters of Comedy. The Play it self, take it all together, seems to me to be one of the most finish'd of any of *Shakespear's*. The Tale indeed, in that Part relating to the Caskets, and the extravagant and unusual kind of Bond given by *Antonio*, is a little too much remov'd from the Rules of Probability: But taking the Fact for granted, we must allow it to be very beautifully written. There is something in the Friendship of *Antonio* to *Bassanio* very Great, Generous and Tender. The whole fourth Act, supposing, as I said, the Fact to be probable, is extremely Fine. But there are two Passages that deserve a particular Notice. The first is, what *Portia* says in praise of Mercy; and the other on the Power of Musick. The Melancholy of *Jaques*, in *As You Like It*, is as singular and odd as it is diverting. And if what *Horace* says

Difficile est proprie communia Dicere,

'Twill be a hard Task for any one to go beyond him in the Description of the several Degrees and Ages of Man's Life, tho' the Thought be old, and common enough.

All the World's a Stage,<br>And all the Men and Women meerly Players;

They have their Exits and their Entrances,<br>
And one Man in his time plays many Parts,<br>
His Acts being seven Ages. At first the Infant<br>
Mewling and puking in the Nurse's Arms:<br>
And then, the whining School-boy with his Satchel,<br>
And shining Morning-face, creeping like Snail<br>
Unwillingly to School. And then the Lover<br>
Sighing like Furnace, with a woful Ballad<br>
Made to his Mistress' Eye-brow. Then a Soldier<br>
Full of strange Oaths, and bearded like the Pard,<br>
Jealous in Honour, sudden and quick in Quarrel,<br>
Seeking the bubble Reputation<br>
Ev'n in the Cannon's Mouth. And then the Justice<br>
In fair round Belly, with good Capon lin'd,<br>
With Eyes severe, and Beard of formal Cut,<br>
Full of wise Saws and modern Instances;<br>
And so he plays his Part. The sixth Age shifts<br>
Into the lean and slipper'd Pantaloon,<br>
With Spectacles on Nose, and Pouch on Side;<br>
His youthful Hose, well sav'd, a world too wide<br>
For his shrunk Shank; and his big manly Voice<br>
Turning again tow'rd childish treble Pipes,<br>
And Whistles in his Sound. Last Scene of all,<br>
That ends this strange eventful History,<br>
Is second Childishness and meer Oblivion,<br>
Sans Teeth, sans Eyes, sans Tast, sans ev'ry thing.

His Images are indeed ev'ry where so lively, that the Thing he would represent stands full before you, and you possess ev'ry Part of it. I will venture to point out one more, which is, I think, as strong and as uncommon as any thing I ever saw; 'tis an Image of Patience. Speaking of a Maid in Love, he says,

She never told her Love,

But let Concealment, like a Worm i'th' Bud<br>
Feed on her Damask Cheek: She pin'd in Thought,<br>
And sate like *Patience* on a Monument,<br>
Smiling at *Grief*.

What an Image is here given! and what a Task would it have been for the greatest Masters of *Greece* and *Rome* to have express'd the Passions design'd by this Sketch of Statuary? The Stile of his Comedy is, in general, Natural to the Characters, and easie in it self; and the Wit most commonly sprightly and pleasing, except in those places where he runs into Dogrel Rhymes, as in *The Comedy of Errors*, and a Passage or two in some other Plays. As for his Jingling sometimes, and playing upon Words, it was the common Vice of the Age he liv'd in: And if we find it in the Pulpit, made use of as an Ornament to the Sermons of some of the Gravest Divines of those Times; perhaps it may not be thought too light for the Stage.

But certainly the greatness of this Author's Genius do's no where so much appear, as where he gives his Imagination an entire Loose, and raises his Fancy to a flight above Mankind and the Limits of the visible World. Such are his Attempts in *The Tempest, Midsummer-Night's Dream, Macbeth* and *Hamlet*. Of these, *The Tempest*, however it comes to be plac'd the first by the former Publishers of his Works, can never have been the first written by him: It seems to me as perfect in its Kind, as almost any thing we have of his. One may observe, that the Unities are kept here with an Exactness uncommon to the Liberties of his Writing: Tho' that was what, I suppose, he valu'd himself least upon, since his Excellencies were all of another Kind. I am very sensible that he do's, in this Play, depart too much from that likeness to Truth which ought to be observ'd in these sort of Writings; yet he do's it so very finely, that one is easily drawn in to have more Faith for his sake, than Reason does well allow of. His Magick has something in it very Solemn and very Poetical: And that extravagant Character of

*Caliban* is mighty well sustain'd, shews a wonderful Invention in the Author, who could strike out such a particular wild Image, and is certainly one of the finest and most uncommon Grotesques that was ever seen. The Observation, which I have been inform'd[1] three very great Men concurr'd in making upon this Part, was extremely just. *That* Shakespear *had not only found out a new Character in his* Caliban, *but had also devis'd and adapted a new manner of Language for that Character.* Among the particular Beauties of this Piece, I think one may be allow'd to point out the Tale of *Prospero* in the First Act; his Speech to *Ferdinand* in the Fourth, upon the breaking up the Masque of *Juno* and *Ceres*; and that in the Fifth, where he dissolves his Charms, and resolves to break his Magick Rod. . . .

  It is the same Magick that raises the Fairies in *Midsummer Night's Dream*, the Witches in *Macbeth*, and the Ghost in *Hamlet*, with Thoughts and Language so proper to the Parts they sustain, and so peculiar to the Talent of this Writer. But of the two last of these Plays I shall have occasion to take notice, among the Tragedies of Mr. *Shakespear*. If one undertook to examine the greatest part of these by those Rules which are establish'd by *Aristotle*, and taken from the Model of the *Grecian* Stage, it would be no very hard Task to find a great many Faults: But as *Shakespear* liv'd under a kind of mere Light of Nature, and had never been made acquainted with the Regularity of those written Precepts, so it would be hard to judge him by a Law he knew nothing of. We are to consider him as a Man that liv'd in a State of almost universal License and Ignorance: There was no establish'd Judge, but every one took the liberty to Write according to the Dictates of his own Fancy. When one considers, that there is not one Play before him of a Reputation good enough to entitle it to an Appearance on the present Stage, it cannot but be a Matter of great Wonder that he should advance Dramatick Poetry so far as he did. The Fable is what is generally plac'd the first, among those that are reckon'd the constituent Parts of a Tragick or Heroick Poem; not, perhaps, as it is the most Difficult or Beautiful, but as it is the first properly to be thought of in the Contrivance and Course of the whole; and with the Fable ought to be consider'd, the fit Disposition, Order and Conduct of its several Parts. As it is not in this Province of the *Drama* that the Strength and Mastery of *Shakespear* lay, so I shall not undertake the tedious and ill-natur'd Trouble to point out the several Faults he was guilty of in it. His Tales were seldom invented, but rather taken either from true History, or Novels and Romances: And he commonly made use of 'em in that Order, with those Incidents, and that extent of Time in which he found 'em in the Authors from whence he borrow'd them. So *The Winter's Tale*, which is taken from an old Book, call'd, *The Delectable History of* Dorastus *and* Faunia, contains the space of sixteen or seventeen Years, and the Scene is sometimes laid in *Bohemia*, and sometimes in *Sicily*, according to the original Order of the Story. Almost all his Historical Plays comprehend a great length of Time, and very different and distinct Places: And in his *Antony* and *Cleopatra*, the Scene travels over the greatest Part of the *Roman* Empire. But in Recompence for his Carelessness in this Point, when he comes to another Part of the *Drama, The Manners of his Characters, in* Acting *or* Speaking *what is proper for them, and fit to be shown by the Poet,* he may be generally justify'd, and in very many places greatly commended. For those Plays which he has taken from the *English* or *Roman* History, let any Man compare 'em, and he will find the Character as exact in the Poet as the Historian. He seems indeed so far from proposing to himself any one Action for a Subject, that the Title very often

tells you, 'tis *The Life of King* John, *King* Richard, &c. What can be more agreeable to the Idea our Historians give of *Henry* the Sixth, than the Picture *Shakespear* has drawn of him! His Manners are every where exactly the same with the Story; one finds him still describ'd with Simplicity, passive Sanctity, want of Courage, weakness of Mind, and easie Submission to the Governance of an imperious Wife, or prevailing Faction: Tho' at the same time the Poet do's Justice to his good Qualities, and moves the Pity of his Audience for him, by showing him Pious, Disinterested, a Contemner of the Things of this World, and wholly resign'd to the severest Dispensations of God's Providence. There is a short Scene in the Second Part of *Henry* VI. which I cannot but think admirable in its Kind. Cardinal *Beaufort*, who had murder'd the Duke of *Gloucester*, is shewn in the last Agonies on his Death-Bed, with the good King praying over him. There is so much Terror in one, so much Tenderness and moving Piety in the other, as must touch any one who is capable either of Fear or Pity. In his *Henry* VIII. that Prince is drawn with that Greatness of Mind, and all those good Qualities which are attributed to him in any Account of his Reign. If his Faults are not shewn in an equal degree, and the Shades in this Picture do not bear a just Proportion to the Lights, it is not that the Artist wanted either Colours or Skill in the Disposition of 'em; but the truth, I believe, might be, that he forbore doing it out of regard to Queen *Elizabeth*, since it could have been no very great Respect to the Memory of his Mistress, to have expos'd some certain Parts of her Father's Life upon the Stage. He has dealt much more freely with the Minister of that Great King, and certainly nothing was ever more justly written, than the Character of Cardinal *Wolsey*. He has shewn him Tyrannical, Cruel, and Insolent in his Prosperity; and yet, by a wonderful Address, he makes his Fall and Ruin the Subject of general Compassion. The whole Man, with his Vices and Virtues, is finely and exactly describ'd in the second Scene of the fourth Act. The Distresses likewise of Queen *Katherine*, in this Play, are very movingly touch'd; and tho' the Art of the Poet has skreen'd King *Henry* from any gross Imputation of Injustice, yet one is inclin'd to wish, the Queen had met with a Fortune more worthy of her Birth and Virtue. Nor are the Manners, proper to the Persons represented, less justly observ'd, in those Characters taken from the *Roman* History; and of this, the Fierceness and Impatience of *Coriolanus*, his Courage and Disdain of the common People, the Virtue and Philosophical Temper of *Brutus*, and the irregular Greatness of Mind in M. *Antony*, are beautiful Proofs. For the two last especially, you find 'em exactly as they are describ'd by *Plutarch*, from whom certainly *Shakespear* copy'd 'em. He has indeed follow'd his Original pretty close, and taken in several little Incidents that might have been spar'd in a Play. But, as I hinted before, his Design seems most commonly rather to describe those great Men in the several Fortunes and Accidents of their Lives, than to take any single great Action, and form his Work simply upon that. However, there are some of his Pieces, where the Fable is founded upon one Action only. Such are more especially, *Romeo* and *Juliet*, *Hamlet*, and *Othello*. The Design in *Romeo* and *Juliet*, is plainly the Punishment of their two Families, for the unreasonable Feuds and Animosities that had been so long kept up between 'em, and occasion'd the Effusion of so much Blood. In the management of this Story, he has shewn something wonderfully Tender and Passionate in the Love-part, and very Pitiful in the Distress. *Hamlet* is founded on much the same Tale with the *Electra* of Sophocles. In each of 'em a young Prince is engag'd to Revenge the Death of his Father, their Mothers are equally Guilty, are both concern'd in the Murder of their Husbands, and are afterwards married to the Murderers. There is in the first Part of the *Greek* Trajedy, something very moving in the Grief of *Electra*; but as Mr. *D'Acier* has observ'd, there is something very unnatural and shocking in the Manners he has given that Princess and *Orestes* in the latter Part. *Orestes* embrues his Hands in the Blood of his own Mother; and that barbarous Action is perform'd, tho' not immediately upon the Stage, yet so near, that the Audience hear *Clytemnestra* crying out to *Æghystus* for Help, and to her Son for Mercy: While *Electra*, her Daughter, and a Princess, both of them Characters that ought to have appear'd with more Decency, stands upon the Stage and encourages her Brother in the Parricide. What Horror does this not raise! *Clytemnestra* was a wicked Woman, and had deserv'd to Die; nay, in the truth of the Story, she was kill'd by her own Son; but to represent an Action of this Kind on the Stage, is certainly an Offence against those Rules of Manners proper to the Persons that ought to be observ'd there. On the contrary, let us only look a little on the Conduct of *Shakespear*. *Hamlet* is represented with the same Piety towards his Father, and Resolution to Revenge his Death, as *Orestes*; he has the same Abhorrence for his Mother's Guilt, which, to provoke him the more, is heighten'd by Incest: But 'tis with wonderful Art and Justness of Judgment, that the Poet restrains him from doing Violence to his Mother. To prevent any thing of that Kind, he makes his Father's Ghost forbid that part of his Vengeance.

> But howsoever thou pursu'st this Act,
> Taint not thy Mind; nor let thy Soul contrive
> Against thy Mother ought; leave her to Heav'n,
> And to those Thorns that in her Bosom lodge,
> To prick and sting her.

This is to distinguish rightly between *Horror* and *Terror*. The latter is a proper Passion of Tragedy, but the former ought always to be carefully avoided. And certainly no Dramatick Writer ever succeeded better in raising *Terror* in the Minds of an Audience than *Shakespear* has done. The whole Tragedy of *Macbeth*, but more especially the Scene where the King is murder'd, in the second Act, as well as this Play, is a noble Proof of that manly Spirit with which he writ; and both shew how powerful he was, in giving the strongest Motions to our Souls that they are capable of. I cannot leave *Hamlet*, without taking notice of the Advantage with which we have seen this Master-piece of *Shakespear* distinguish it self upon the Stage, by Mr. *Betterton's* fine Performance of that Part. A Man, who tho' he had no other good Qualities, as he has a great many, must have made his way into the Esteem of all Men of Letters, by this only Excellency. No Man is better acquainted with *Shakespear's* manner of Expression, and indeed he has study'd him so well, and is so much a Master of him, that whatever Part of his he performs he does it as if it had been written on purpose for him, and that the Author had exactly conceiv'd it as he plays it. I must own a particular Obligation to him, for the most considerable part of the Passages relating to his Life, which I have here transmitted to the Publick; his Veneration for the Memory of *Shakespear* having engag'd him to make a Journey into *Warwickshire*, on purpose to gather up what Remains he could of a Name for which he had so great a Value. Since I had at first resolv'd not to enter into any Critical Controversie, I won't pretend to enquire into the Justness of Mr. *Rhymer's* Remarks on *Othello*; he has certainly pointed out some Faults very judiciously; and indeed they are such as most People will agree, with him, to be Faults: But I wish he would likewise have observ'd some of the Beauties too; as I think it became an Exact and Equal Critique to do. It seems strange that he should allow nothing Good in the whole: If the Fable and Incidents are not to his Taste, yet the Thoughts are almost every where very Noble, and the Diction manly and proper. These last, indeed, are Parts of *Shakespear's* Praise, which it would be very hard to Dispute with him. His Sentiments and Images of Things are Great and Natural; and his Expression (tho' perhaps in some Instances a little Irregular) just, and rais'd in Proportion to his Subject and Occasion. It would be even endless to mention the particular Instances that might be given of this Kind: But his Book is in the Possession of the Publick, and 'twill be hard to dip into any Part of it, without finding what I have said of him made good.

*Notes*

1. *I.a.* Falkland, *Ld. C. J.* Vaughan, *and Mr.* Selden.

## ALEXANDER POPE
### From "The Preface of the Editor"
*The Works of Mr. William Shakespear*
1725, Volume 1, pp. i–xiii

It is not my design to enter into a Criticism upon this Author; tho' to do it effectually and not superficially, would be the best occasion that any just Writer could take, to form the judgment and taste of our nation. For of all *English* Poets *Shakespear* must be confessed to be the fairest and fullest subject for Criticism, and to afford the most numerous, as well as most conspicuous instances, both of Beauties and Faults of all sorts. But this far exceeds the bounds of a Preface, the business of which is only to give an account of the fate of his Works, and the disadvantages under which they have been transmitted to us. We shall hereby extenuate many faults which are his, and clear him from the imputation of many which are not: A design, which tho' it can be no guide to future Criticks to do him justice in one way, will at least be sufficient to prevent their doing him an injustice in the other.

I cannot however but mention some of his principal and characteristic Excellencies, for which (notwithstanding his defects) he is justly and universally elevated above all other Dramatic Writers. Not that this is the proper place of praising him, but because I would not omit any occasion of doing it.

If ever any Author deserved the name of an *Original*, it was *Shakespear*. *Homer* himself drew not his art so immediately from the fountains of Nature, it proceeded thro' *Ægyptian* strainers and channels, and came to him not without some tincture of the learning, or some cast of the models, of those before him. The Poetry of *Shakespear* was Inspiration indeed: he is not so much an Imitator, as an Instrument, of Nature; and 'tis not so just to say that he speaks from her, as that she speaks thro' him.

His *Characters* are so much Nature her self, that 'tis a sort of injury to call them by so distant a name as Copies of her. Those of other Poets have a constant resemblance, which shews that they receiv'd them from one another, and were but multiplyers of the same image: each picture like a mock-rainbow is but the reflexion of a reflexion. But every single character in *Shakespear* is as much an Individual, as those in Life itself; it is as impossible to find any two alike; and such as from their relation or affinity in any respect appear most to be Twins, will upon comparison be found remarkably distinct. To this life and variety of Character, we must add the wonderful Preservation of it; which is such throughout his plays, that had all the Speeches been printed without the very names of the Persons, I believe one might have apply'd them with certainty to every speaker.

The *Power* over our *Passions* was never possess'd in a more eminent degree, or display'd in so different instances. Yet all along, there is seen no labour, no pains to raise them; no preparation to guide our guess to the effect, or be perceiv'd to lead toward it: But the heart swells, and the tears burst out, just at the proper places: We are surpriz'd, the moment we weep; and yet upon reflection find the passion so just, that we shou'd be surpriz'd if we had not wept, and wept at that very moment.

How astonishing is it again, that the passions directly opposite to these, Laughter and Spleen, are no less at his command! that he is not more a master of the *Great*, than of the *Ridiculous* in human nature; of our noblest tendernesses, than of our vainest foibles; of our strongest emotions, than of our idlest sensations!

Nor does he only excell in the Passions: In the coolness of Reflection and Reasoning he is full as admirable. His *Sentiments* are not only in general the most pertinent and judicious upon every subject; but by a talent very peculiar, something between Penetration and Felicity, he hits upon that particular point on which the bent of each argument turns, or the force of each motive depends. This is perfectly amazing, from a man of no education or experience in those great and publick scenes of life which are usually the subject of his thoughts: So that he seems to have known the world by Intuition, to have look'd thro' humane nature at one glance, and to be the only Author that gives ground for a very new opinion, That the Philosopher and even the Man of the world, may be *Born*, as well as the Poet.

It must be own'd that with all these great excellencies, he has almost as great defects; and that as he has certainly written better, so he has perhaps written worse, than any other. But I think I can in some measure account for these defects, from several causes and accidents; without which it is hard to imagine that so large and so enlighten'd a mind could ever have been susceptible of them. That all these Contingencies should unite to his disadvantage seems to me almost as singularly unlucky, as that so many various (nay contrary) Talents should meet in one man, was happy and extraordinary.

It must be allowed that Stage-Poetry of all other, is more particularly levell'd to please the *Populace*, and its success more immediately depending upon the *Common Suffrage*. One cannot therefore wonder, if *Shakespear* having at his first appearance no other aim in his writings than to procure a subsistance, directed his endeavours solely to hit the taste and humour that then prevailed. The Audience was generally composed of the meaner sort of people; and therefore the Images of Life were to be drawn from those of their own rank: accordingly we find, that not our Author's only but almost all the old Comedies have their Scene among *Tradesmen* and *Mechanicks*: And even their Historical Plays strictly follow the common *Old Stories* or *Vulgar Traditions* of that kind of people. In Tragedy, nothing was so sure to *Surprize* and cause *Admiration*, as the most strange, unexpected, and consequently most unnatural, Events and Incidents; the most exaggerated Thoughts; the most verbose and bombast Expression; the most pompous Rhymes, and thundering Versification. In Comedy, nothing was so sure to *please*, as mean buffoonry, vile ribaldry, and unmannerly jests of fools and clowns. Yet even in these, our Author's Wit buoys up, and is born above his subject: his Genius in those low parts is like some Prince of a Romance in the disguise of a Shepherd or Peasant; a certain Greatness and Spirit now and then break out, which manifest his higher extraction and qualities.

It may be added, that not only the common Audience had no notion of the rules of writing, but few even of the better sort piqu'd themselves upon any great degree of knowledge or nicety that way; till *Ben Johnson* getting possession of the Stage, brought critical learning into vogue: And that this was not done without difficulty, may appear from those frequent lessons (and indeed almost Declamations) which he was forced to prefix to his first plays, and put into the mouth of his Actors, the *Grex*, *Chorus*, &c. to remove the prejudices, and inform the judgment of his hearers. Till then, our Authors had no thoughts of writing on the model of the Ancients: their Tragedies were only Histories in Dialogue; and their Comedies follow'd the thread of any Novel as they found it, no less implicitly than if it had been true History.

To judge therefore of *Shakespear* by *Aristotle*'s rules, is like trying a man by the Laws of one Country, who acted under those of another. He writ to the *People*; and writ at first without patronage from the better sort, and therefore without aims of pleasing them: without assistance or advice from the Learned, as without the advantage of education or acquaintance among them: without that knowledge of the best models, the Ancients, to inspire him with an emulation of them; in a word, without any views of Reputation, and of what Poets are pleas'd to call Immortality: Some or all of which have encourag'd the vanity, or animated the ambition, of other writers.

Yet it must be observ'd, that when his performances had merited the protection of his Prince, and when the encouragement of the Court had succeeded to that of the Town; the works of his riper years are manifestly raised above those of his former. The Dates of his plays sufficiently evidence that his productions improved, in proportion to the respect he had for his auditors. And I make no doubt this observation would be found true in every instance, were but Editions extant from which we might learn the exact time when every piece was composed, and whether writ for the Town, or the Court.

Another Cause (and no less strong than the former) may be deduced from our Author's being a *Player*, and forming himself first upon the judgments of that body of men whereof he was a member. They have ever had a Standard to themselves, upon other principles than those of *Aristotle*. As they live by the Majority, they know no rule but that of pleasing the present humour, and complying with the wit in fashion; a consideration which brings all their judgment to a short point. Players are just such judges of what is *right*, as Taylors are of what is *graceful*. And in this view it will be but fair to allow, that most of our Author's faults are less to be ascribed to his wrong judgment as a Poet, than to his right judgment as a Player.

By these men it was thought a praise to *Shakespear*, that he scarce ever *blotted a line*. This they industriously propagated, as appears from what we are told by *Ben Johnson* in his *Discoveries*, and from the preface of *Heminges* and *Condell* to the first folio Edition. But in reality (however it has prevailed) there never was a more groundless report, or to the contrary of which there are more undeniable evidences. As, the Comedy of the *Merry Wives* of *Windsor*, which he entirely new writ; the *History of* Henry *the 6th*, which was first published under the Title of the *Contention of* York *and* Lancaster; and that of *Henry the 5th*, extreamly improved; that of *Hamlet* enlarged to almost as much again as at first, and many others. I believe the common opinion of his want of Learning proceeded from no better ground. This too might be thought a Praise by some; and to this his Errors have as injudiciously been ascribed by others. For 'tis certain, were it true, it could concern but a small part of them; the most are such as are not properly Defects, but Superfœtations: and arise not from want of learning or reading, but from want of thinking or judging: or rather (to be more just to our Author) from a compliance to those wants in others. As to a wrong choice of the subject, a wrong conduct of the incidents, false thoughts, forc'd expressions, &c. if these are not to be ascrib'd to the foresaid accidental reasons, they must be charg'd upon the Poet himself, and there is no help for it. But I think the two Disadvantages which I have mentioned (to be obliged to please the lowest of people, and to keep the worst of company) if the consideration be extended as far as it reasonably may, will appear sufficient to mis-lead and depress the greatest Genius upon earth. Nay the more modesty with which such a one is endued, the more he is in danger of submitting and conforming to others, against his own better judgment.

But as to his *Want of Learning*, it may be necessary to say something more: There is certainly a vast difference between *Learning* and *Languages*. How far he was ignorant of the latter, I cannot determine; but 'tis plain he had much Reading at least, if they will not call it Learning. Nor is it any great matter, if a man has Knowledge, whether he has it from one language or from another. Nothing is more evident than that he had a taste of natural Philosophy, Mechanicks, ancient and modern History, Poetical learning and Mythology: We find him very knowing in the customs, rites, and manners of Antiquity. In *Coriolanus* and *Julius Cæsar*, not only the Spirit, but Manners, of the *Romans* are exactly drawn; and still a nicer distinction is shown, between the manners of the *Romans* in the time of the former, and of the latter. His reading in the ancient Historians is no less conspicuous, in many references to particular passages: and the speeches copy'd from *Plutarch* in *Coriolanus* may, I think, as well be made an instance of his learning, as those copy'd from *Cicero* in *Catiline*, of *Ben Johnson's*. The manners of other nations in general, the *Egyptians*, *Venetians*, *French*, &c. are drawn with equal propriety. Whatever object of nature, or branch of science, he either speaks of or describes; it is always with competent, if not extensive knowledge: his descriptions are still exact; all his metaphors appropriated, and remarkably drawn from the true nature and inherent qualities of each subject. When he treats of Ethic or Politic, we may constantly observe a wonderful justness of distinction, as well as extent of comprehension. No one is more a master of the Poetical story, or has more frequent allusions to the various parts of it: Mr. *Waller* (who has been celebrated for this last particular) has not shown more learning this way than *Shakespear*. We have Translations from *Ovid* published in his name, among those Poems which pass for his, and for some of which we have undoubted authority, (being published by himself, and dedicated to his noble Patron the Earl of *Southampton*:) He appears also to have been conversant in *Plautus*, from whom he has taken the plot of one of his plays: he follows the *Greek* Authors, and particularly *Dares Phrygius*, in another: (altho' I will not pretend to say in what language he read them.) The modern *Italian* writers of Novels he was manifestly acquainted with; and we may conclude him to be no less conversant with the Ancients of his own country, from the use he has made of *Chaucer* in *Troilus* and *Cressida*, and in the *Two Noble Kinsmen*, if that Play be his, as there goes a Tradition it was, (and indeed it has little resemblance of *Fletcher*, and more of our Author than some of those which have been received as genuine.)

I am inclined to think, this opinion proceeded originally from the zeal of the Partizans of our Author and *Ben Johnson*; as they endeavoured to exalt the one at the expence of the other. It is ever the nature of Parties to be in extremes; and nothing is so probable, as that because *Ben Johnson* had much the most learning, it was said on the one hand that *Shakespear* had none at all; and because *Shakespear* had much the most wit and fancy, it was retorted on the other, that *Johnson* wanted both. Because *Shakespear* borrowed nothing, it was said that *Ben Johnson* borrowed every thing. Because *Johnson* did not write extempore, he was reproached with being a year about every piece; and because *Shakespear* wrote with ease and rapidity, they cryed, he never once made a blot. Nay the spirit of opposition ran so high, that whatever those of the one side objected to the other, was taken at the rebound, and turned into Praises; as unjudiciously, as their antagonists before had made them Objections.

Poets are always afraid of Envy; but sure they have as much reason to be afraid of Admiration. They are the *Scylla* and *Charybdis* of Authors; those who escape one, often fall by the other. *Pessimum genus inimicorum Laudantes*, says *Tacitus*: and *Virgil* desires to wear a charm against those who praise a Poet without rule or reason.

> Si ultra placitum laudarit, baccare frontem
> Cingito, ne Vati noceat.

But however this contention might be carried on by the Partizans on either side, I cannot help thinking these two great Poets were good friends, and lived on amicable terms and in offices of society with each other. It is an acknowledged fact, that *Ben Johnson* was introduced upon the Stage, and his first works encouraged, by *Shakespear*. And after his death, that Author writes *To the memory of his beloved Mr.* William Shakespear, which shows as if the friendship had continued thro' life. I cannot for my own part find any thing *Invidious* or *Sparing* in those verses, but wonder Mr. *Dryden* was of that opinion. He exalts him not only above all his Contemporaries, but above *Chaucer* and *Spenser*, whom he will not allow to be great enough to be rank'd with him; and challenges the names of *Sophocles*, *Euripides*, and *Æschylus*, nay all *Greece* and *Rome* at once, to equal him. And (which is very particular) expresly vindicates him from the imputation of wanting *Art*, not enduring that all his excellencies shou'd be attributed to *Nature*. It is remarkable too, that the praise he gives him in his *Discoveries* seems to proceed from a *personal kindness*; he tells us that he lov'd the man, as well as honoured his memory; celebrates the honesty, openness, and frankness of his temper; and only distinguishes, as he reasonably ought, between the real merit of the Author, and the silly and derogatory applauses of the Players. *Ben Johnson* might indeed be sparing in his Commendations (tho' certainly he is not so in this instance) partly from his own nature, and partly from judgment. For men of judgment think they do any man more service in praising him justly, than lavishly. I say, I would fain believe they were Friends, tho' the violence and ill-breeding of their Followers and Flatterers were enough to give rise to the contrary report. I would hope that it may be with *Parties*, both in Wit and State, as with those Monsters described by the Poets; and that their *Heads* at least may have something humane, tho' their *Bodies* and *Tails* are wild beasts and serpents.

## SAMUEL JOHNSON
### From *Preface to Shakespeare*
### 1765

That praises are without reason lavished on the dead, and that the honours due only to excellence are paid to antiquity, is a complaint likely to be always continued by those, who, being able to add nothing to truth, hope for eminence from the heresies of paradox; or those, who, being forced by disappointment upon consolatory expedients, are willing to hope from posterity what the present age refuses, and flatter themselves that the regard which is yet denied by envy, will be at last bestowed by time.

Antiquity, like every other quality that attracts the notice of mankind, has undoubtedly votaries that reverence it, not from reason, but from prejudice. Some seem to admire indiscriminately whatever has been long preserved, without considering that time has sometimes co-operated with chance; all perhaps are more willing to honour past then present excellence; and the mind contemplates genius through the shades of age, as the eye surveys the sun through artificial opacity. The great contention of criticism is to find the faults of the moderns, and the beauties of the ancients. While an authour is yet living we estimate his powers by his worst performance, and when he is dead we rate them by his best.

To works, however, of which the excellence is not absolute and definite, but gradual and comparative; to works not raised upon principles demonstrative and scientifick, but appealing wholly to observation and experience, no other test can be applied than length of duration and continuance of esteem. What mankind have long possessed they have often examined and compared, and if they persist to value the possession, it is because frequent comparisons have confirmed opinion in its favour. As among the works of nature no man can properly call a river deep or a mountain high, without the knowledge of many mountains and many rivers; so in the productions of genius, nothing can be stiled excellent till it has been compared with other works of the same kind. Demonstration immediately displays its power, and has nothing to hope or fear from the flux of years; but works tentative and experimental must be estimated by their proportion to the general and collective ability of man, as it is discovered in a long succession of endeavours. Of the first building that was raised, it might be with certainty determined that it was round or square, but whether it was spacious or lofty must have been referred to time. The Pythagorean scale of numbers was at once discovered to be perfect; but the poems of Homer we yet know not to transcend the common limits of human intelligence, but by remarking, that nation after nation, and century after century, has been able to do little more than transpose his incidents, new name his characters, and paraphrase his sentiments.

The reverence due to writings that have long subsisted arises therefore not from any credulous confidence in the superior wisdom of past ages, or gloomy persuasion of the degeneracy of mankind, but is the consequence of acknowledged and indubitable positions, that what has been longest known has been most considered, and what is most considered is best understood.

The poet, of whose works I have undertaken the revision, may now begin to assume the dignity of an ancient, and claim the privilege of established fame and prescriptive veneration. He has long outlived his century, the term commonly fixed as the test of literary merit. Whatever advantages he might once derive from personal allusions, local customs, or temporary opinions, have for many years been lost; and every topick of merriment or motive of sorrow, which the modes of artificial life afforded him, now only obscure the scenes which they once illuminated. The effects of favour and competition are at an end; the tradition of his friendships and his enmities has perished; his works support no opinion with arguments, nor supply any faction with invectives; they can neither indulge vanity nor gratify malignity, but are read without any other reason than the desire of pleasure, and are therefore praised only as pleasure is obtained; yet, thus unassisted by interest or passion, they have past through variations of taste and changes of manners, and, as they devolved from one generation to another, have received new honours at every transmission.

But because human judgment, though it be gradually gaining upon certainty, never becomes infallible; and approbation, though long continued, may yet be only the approbation of prejudice or fashion; it is proper to inquire, by what peculiarities of excellence Shakespeare has gained and kept the favour of his countrymen.

Nothing can please many, and please long, but just representations of general nature. Particular manners can be known to few, and therefore few only can judge how nearly they are copied. The irregular combinations of fanciful invention may delight a-while, by that novelty of which the common satiety of life sends us all in quest; but the pleasures of sudden wonder are soon exhausted, and the mind can only repose on the stability of truth.

Shakespeare is above all writers, at least above all modern writers, the poet of nature; the poet that holds up to his readers a faithful mirrour of manners and of life. His characters are not modified by the customs of particular places, unpractised by the rest of the world; by the peculiarities of studies or professions, which can operate but upon small numbers; or by the accidents of transient fashions or temporary opinions: they are the genuine progeny of common humanity, such as the world will always supply, and observation will always find. His persons act and speak by the influence of those general passions and principles by which all minds are agitated, and the whole system of life is continued in motion. In the writings of other poets a character is too often an individual; in those of Shakespeare it is commonly a species.

It is from this wide extension of design that so much instruction is derived. It is this which fills the plays of Shakespeare with practical axioms and domestick wisdom. It was said of Euripides, that every verse was a precept; and it may be said of Shakespeare, that from his works may be collected a system of civil and œconomical prudence. Yet his real power is not shewn in the splendour of particular passages, but by the progress of his fable, and the tenour of his dialogue; and he that tries to recommend him by select quotations, will succeed like the pedant in Hierocles, who, when he offered his house to sale, carried a brick in his pocket as a specimen.

It will not easily be imagined how much Shakespeare excels in accommodating his sentiments to real life, but by comparing him with other authours. It was observed of the ancient schools of declamation, that the more diligently they were frequented, the more was the student disqualified for the world, because he found nothing there which he should ever meet in any other place. The same remark may be applied to every stage but that of Shakespeare. The theatre, when it is under any other direction, is peopled by such characters as were never seen, conversing in a language which was never heard, upon topicks which will never arise in the commerce of mankind. But the dialogue of this authour is often so evidently determined by the incident which produces it, and is pursued with so much ease and simplicity, that it seems scarcely to claim the merit of fiction, but to have been gleaned by diligent selection out of common conversation, and common occurrences.

Upon every other stage the universal agent is love, by whose power all good and evil is distributed, and every action quickened or retarded. To bring a lover, a lady and a rival into the fable; to entangle them in contradictory obligations, perplex them with oppositions of interest, and harrass them with violence of desires inconsistent with each other; to make them meet in rapture and part in agony; to fill their mouths with hyperbolical joy and outrageous sorrow; to distress them as nothing human ever was distressed; to deliver them as nothing human ever was delivered, is the business of a modern dramatist. For this, probability is violated, life is misrepresented, and language is depraved. But love is only one of many passions, and as it has no great influence upon the sum of life, it has little operation in the dramas of a poet, who caught his ideas from the living world, and exhibited only what he saw before him. He knew, that any other passion, as it was regular or exorbitant, was a cause of happiness or calamity.

Characters thus ample and general were not easily discriminated and preserved, yet perhaps no poet ever kept his personages more distinct from each other. I will not say with Pope, that every speech may be assigned to the proper speaker, because many speeches there are which have nothing characteristical; but perhaps, though some may be equally adapted to every person, it will be difficult to find any that can be properly transferred from the present possessor to another claimant. The choice is right, when there is reason for choice.

Other dramatists can only gain attention by hyperbolical or aggravated characters, by fabulous and unexampled excellence or depravity, as the writers of barbarous romances invigorated the reader by a giant and a dwarf; and he that should form his expectations of human affairs from the play, or from the tale, would be equally deceived. Shakespeare has no heroes; his scenes are occupied only by men, who act and speak as the reader thinks that he should himself have spoken or acted on the same occasion: Even where the agency is supernatural the dialogue is level with life. Other writers disguise the most natural passions and most frequent incidents; so that he who contemplates them in the book will not know them in the world: Shakespeare approximates the remote, and familiarizes the wonderful; the event which he represents will not happen, but if it were possible, its effects would probably be such as he has assigned; and it may be said, that he has not only shewn human nature as it acts in real exigences, but as it would be found in trials, to which it cannot be exposed.

This therefore is the praise of Shakespeare, that his drama is the mirrour of life; that he who has mazed his imagination, in following the phantoms which other writers raise up before him, may here be cured of his delirious extasies, by reading human sentiments in human language; by scenes from which a hermit may estimate the transactions of the world, and a confessor predict the progress of the passions.

His adherence to general nature has exposed him to the censure of criticks, who form their judgments upon narrower principles. Dennis and Rhymer think his Romans not sufficiently Roman; and Voltaire censures his kings as not completely royal. Dennis is offended, that Menenius, a senator of Rome, should play the buffoon; and Voltaire perhaps thinks decency violated when the Danish usurper is represented as a drunkard. But Shakespeare always makes nature predominate over accident; and if he preserves the essential character, is not very careful of distinctions superinduced and adventitious. His story requires Romans or kings, but he thinks only on men. He knew that Rome, like every other city, had men of all dispositions; and wanting a buffoon, he went into the senate-house for that which the senate-house would certainly have afforded him. He was inclined to shew an usurper and a murderer not only odious but despicable; he therefore added drunkenness to his other qualities, knowing that kings love wine like other men, and that wine exerts its natural power upon kings. These are the petty cavils of petty minds; a poet overlooks the casual distinction of country and condition, as a painter, satisfied with the figure, neglects the drapery.

The censure which he has incurred by mixing comick and tragick scenes, as it extends to all his works, deserves more consideration. Let the fact be first stated, and then examined.

Shakespeare's plays are not in the rigorous and critical sense either tragedies or comedies, but compositions of a distinct kind; exhibiting the real state of sublunary nature, which partakes of good and evil, joy and sorrow, mingled with endless variety of proportion and innumerable modes of combination; and expressing the course of the world, in which the loss of one is the gain of another; in which, at the same time, the reveller is hasting to his wine, and the mourner burying his friend; in which the malignity of one is sometimes defeated by the frolick of another; and many mischiefs and many benefits are done and hindered without design.

Out of this chaos of mingled purposes and casualties the ancient poets, according to the laws which custom had prescribed, selected some the crimes of men, and some their absurdities; some the momentous vicissitudes of life, and some the lighter occurrences; some the terrours of distress, and some the gayeties of prosperity. Thus rose the two modes of imitation, known by the names of tragedy and comedy, compositions intended to promote different ends by contrary means, and considered as so little allied, that I do not recollect among the Greeks or Romans a single writer who attempted both.

Shakespeare has united the powers of exciting laughter and sorrow not only in one mind but in one composition. Almost all his plays are divided between serious and ludicrous characters, and, in the successive evolutions of the design, sometimes produce seriousness and sorrow, and sometimes levity and laughter.

That this is a practice contrary to the rules of criticism will be readily allowed; but there is always an appeal open from criticism to nature. The end of writing is to instruct; the end of poetry is to instruct by pleasing. That the mingled drama may convey all the instruction of tragedy or comedy cannot be denied, because it includes both in its alternations of exhibition, and approaches nearer than either to the appearance of life, by shewing how great machinations and slender designs may promote or obviate one another, and the high and the low co-operate in the general system by unavoidable concatenation.

It is objected, that by this change of scenes the passions are interrupted in their progression, and that the principal event, being not advanced by a due graduation of preparatory incidents, wants at last the power to move, which constitutes the perfection of dramatick poetry. This reasoning is so specious, that it is received as true even by those who in daily experience feel it to be false. The interchanges of mingled scenes seldom fail to produce the intended vicissitudes of passion. Fiction cannot move so much, but that the attention may be easily transferred; and though it must be allowed that pleasing melancholy be sometimes interrupted by unwelcome levity, yet let it be considered likewise, that melancholy is often not pleasing, and that the disturbance of one man may be the relief of another; that different auditors have different habitudes; and that, upon the whole, all pleasure consists in variety.

The players, who in their edition divided our authour's works into comedies, histories, and tragedies, seem not to have distinguished the three kinds, by any very exact or definite ideas.

An action which ended happily to the principal persons, however serious or distressful through its intermediate incidents, in their opinion constituted a comedy. This idea of a comedy continued long amongst us, and plays were written, which, by changing the catastrophe, were tragedies to-day and comedies to-morrow.

Tragedy was not in those times a poem of more general dignity or elevation than comedy; it required only a calamitous conclusion, with which the common criticism of that age was satisfied, whatever lighter pleasure it afforded in its progress.

History was a series of actions, with no other than chronological succession, independent on each other, and without any tendency to introduce or regulate the conclusion. It is not always very nicely distinguished from tragedy. There is not much nearer approach to unity of action in the tragedy of *Antony and Cleopatra*, than in the history of *Richard the Second*. But a history might be continued through many plays; as it had no plan, it had no limits.

Through all these denominations of the drama, Shakespeare's mode of composition is the same; an interchange of seriousness and merriment, by which the mind is softened at one time, and exhilarated at another. But whatever be his purpose, whether to gladden or depress, or to conduct the story, without vehemence or emotion, through tracts of easy and familiar dialogue, he never fails to attain his purpose; as he commands us, we laugh or mourn, or sit silent with quiet expectation, in tranquillity without indifference.

When Shakespeare's plan is understood, most of the criticisms of Rhymer and Voltaire vanish away. The play of *Hamlet* is opened, without impropriety, by two sentinels; Iago bellows at Brabantio's window, without injury to the scheme of the play, though in terms which a modern audience would not easily endure; the character of Polonius is seasonable and useful; and the Grave-diggers themselves may be heard with applause.

Shakespeare engaged in dramatick poetry with the world open before him; the rules of the ancients were yet known to few; the publick judgment was unformed; he had no example of such fame as might force him upon imitation, nor criticks of such authority as might restrain his extravagance: He therefore indulged his natural disposition, and his disposition, as Rhymer has remarked, led him to comedy. In tragedy he often writes with great appearance of toil and study, what is written at last with little felicity; but in his comick scenes, he seems to produce without labour, what no labour can improve. In tragedy he is always struggling after some occasion to be comick, but in comedy he seems to repose, or to luxuriate, as in a mode of thinking congenial to his nature. In his tragick scenes there is always something wanting, but his comedy often surpasses expectation or desire. His comedy pleases by the thoughts and the language, and his tragedy for the greater part by incident and action. His tragedy seems to be skill, his comedy to be instinct.

The force of his comick scenes has suffered little diminution from the changes made by a century and a half, in manners or in words. As his personages act upon principles arising from genuine passion, very little modified by particular forms, their pleasures and vexations are communicable to all times and to all places; they are natural, and therefore durable; the adventitious peculiarities of personal habits, are only superficial dies, bright and pleasing for a little while, yet soon fading to a dim tinct, without any remains of former lustre; but the discriminations of true passion are the colours of nature; they pervade the whole mass, and can only perish with the body that exhibits them. The accidental compositions of heterogeneous modes are dissolved by the chance which combined them; but the uniform simplicity of primitive qualities neither admits increase, nor suffers decay. The sand heaped by one flood is scattered by another, but the rock always continues in its place. The stream of time, which is continually washing the dissoluble fabricks of other poets, passes without injury by the adamant of Shakespeare.

If there be, what I believe there is, in every nation, a stile which never becomes obsolete, a certain mode of phraseology so consonant and congenial to the analogy and principles of its respective language as to remain settled and unaltered; this stile is probably to be sought in the common intercourse of life, among those who speak only to be understood, without ambition of elegance. The polite are always catching modish innovations, and the learned depart from established forms of speech, in hope of finding or making better; those who wish for distinction forsake the vulgar, when the vulgar is right; but there is a conversation above grossness and below refinement, where propriety resides, and where this poet seems to have gathered his comick dialogue. He is therefore more agreeable to the ears of the present age than any other authour equally remote, and among his other excellencies deserves to be studied as one of the original masters of our language.

These observations are to be considered not as unexceptionably constant, but as containing general and predominant truth. Shakespeare's familiar dialogue is affirmed to be smooth and clear, yet not wholly without ruggedness or difficulty; as a country may be eminently fruitful, though it has spots unfit for cultivation: His characters are praised as natural, though their sentiments are sometimes forced, and their actions improbable; as the earth upon the whole is spherical, though its surface is varied with protuberances and cavities.

Shakespeare with his excellencies has likewise faults, and faults sufficient to obscure and overwhelm any other merit. I shall shew them in the proportion in which they appear to me, without envious malignity or superstitious veneration. No question can be more innocently discussed than a dead poet's pretensions to renown; and little regard is due to that bigotry which sets candour higher than truth.

His first defect is that to which may be imputed most of the evil in books or in men. He sacrifices virtue to convenience, and is so much more careful to please than to instruct, that he seems to write without any moral purpose. From his writings indeed a system of social duty may be selected, for he that thinks reasonably must think morally; but his precepts and axioms drop casually from him; he makes no just distribution of good or evil, nor is always careful to shew in the virtuous a disapprobation of the wicked; he carries his persons indifferently through right and wrong, and at the close dismisses them without further care, and leaves their examples to operate by chance. This fault the barbarity of his age cannot extenuate; for it is always a writer's duty to make the world better, and justice is a virtue independant on time or place.

The plots are often so loosely formed, that a very slight consideration may improve them, and so carelessly pursued, that he seems not always fully to comprehend his own design.

He omits opportunities of instructing or delighting which the train of his story seems to force upon him, and apparently rejects those exhibitions which would be more affecting, for the sake of those which are more easy.

It may be observed, that in many of his plays the latter part is evidently neglected. When he found himself near the end of his work, and in view of his reward, he shortened the labour, to snatch the profit. He therefore remits his efforts where he should most vigorously exert them, and his catastrophe is improbably produced or imperfectly represented.

He had no regard to distinction of time or place, but gives to one age or nation, without scruple, the customs, institutions, and opinions of another, at the expence not only of likelihood, but of possibility. These faults Pope has endeavoured, with more zeal than judgment, to transfer to his imagined interpolators. We need not wonder to find Hector quoting Aristotle, when we see the loves of Theseus and Hippolyta combined with the Gothick mythology of fairies. Shakespeare, indeed, was not the only violator of chronology, for in the same age Sidney, who wanted not the advantages of learning, has, in his *Arcadia*, confounded the pastoral with the feudal times, the days of innocence, quiet and security, with those of turbulence, violence and adventure.

In his comick scenes he is seldom very successful, when he engages his characters in reciprocations of smartness and contests of sarcasm; their jests are commonly gross, and their pleasantry licentious; neither his gentlemen nor his ladies have much delicacy, nor are sufficiently distinguished from his clowns by any appearance of refined manners. Whether he represented the real conversation of his time is not easy to determine; the reign of Elizabeth is commonly supposed to have been a time of stateliness, formality and reserve, yet perhaps the relaxations of that severity were not very elegant. There must, however, have been always some modes of gayety preferable to others, and a writer ought to chuse the best.

In tragedy his performance seems constantly to be worse, as his labour is more. The effusions of passion which exigence forces out are for the most part striking and energetick; but whenever he solicits his invention, or strains his faculties, the offspring of his throes is tumour, meanness, tediousness, and obscurity.

In narration he affects a disproportionate pomp of diction and a wearisome train of circumlocution, and tells the incident imperfectly in many words, which might have been more plainly delivered in few. Narration in dramatick poetry is naturally tedious, as it is unanimated and inactive, and obstructs the progress of the action; it should therefore always be rapid, and enlivened by frequent interruption. Shakespeare found it an encumbrance, and instead of lightening it by brevity, endeavoured to recommend it by dignity and splendour.

His declamations or set speeches are commonly cold and weak, for his power was the power of nature; when he endeavoured, like other tragick writers, to catch opportunities of amplification, and instead of inquiring what the occasion demanded, to show how much his stores of knowledge could supply, he seldom escapes without the pity or resentment of his reader.

It is incident to him to be now and then entangled with an unwieldy sentiment, which he cannot well express, and will not reject; he struggles with it a while, and if it continues stubborn, comprises it in words such as occur, and leaves it to be disentangled and evolved by those who have more leisure to bestow upon it.

Not that always where the language is intricate the thought is subtle, or the image always great where the line is bulky; the equality of words to things is very often neglected, and trivial sentiments and vulgar ideas disappoint the attention, to which they are recommended by sonorous epithets and swelling figures.

But the admirers of this great poet have most reason to complain when he approaches nearest to his highest excellence, and seems fully resolved to sink them in dejection, and mollify them with tender emotions by the fall of greatness, the danger of innocence, or the crosses of love. What he does best, he soon ceases to do. He is not long soft and pathetick without some idle conceit, or contemptible equivocation. He no sooner begins to move, than he counteracts himself; and terrour and pity, as they are rising in the mind, are checked and blasted by sudden frigidity.

A quibble is to Shakespeare, what luminous vapours are to the traveller; he follows it at all adventures, it is sure to lead him out of his way, and sure to engulf him in the mire. It has some malignant power over his mind, and its fascinations are irresistible. Whatever be the dignity or profundity of his disquisition, whether he be enlarging knowledge or exalting affection, whether he be amusing attention with incidents, or enchaining it in suspense, let but a quibble spring up before him, and he leaves his work unfinished. A quibble is the golden apple for which he will always turn aside from his career, or stoop from his elevation. A quibble, poor and barren as it is, gave him such delight, that he was content to purchase it, by the sacrifice of reason, propriety and truth. A quibble was to him the fatal Cleopatra for which he lost the world, and was content to lose it.

It will be thought strange, that, in enumerating the defects of this writer, I have not yet mentioned his neglect of the unities; his violation of those laws which have been instituted and established by the joint authority of poets and of criticks.

For his other deviations from the art of writing, I resign him to critical justice, without making any other demand in his favour, than that which must be indulged to all human excellence; that his virtues be rated with his failings: But, from the censure which this irregularity may bring upon him, I shall, with due reverence to that learning which I must oppose, adventure to try how I can defend him.

His histories, being neither tragedies nor comedies, are not subject to any of their laws; nothing more is necessary to all the praise which they expect, than that the changes of action be so prepared as to be understood, that the incidents be various and affecting, and the characters consistent, natural and distinct. No other unity is intended, and therefore none is to be sought.

In his other works he has well enough preserved the unity of action. He has not, indeed, an intrigue regularly perplexed and regularly unravelled; he does not endeavour to hide his design only to discover it, for this is seldom the order of real events, and Shakespeare is the poet of nature: But his plan has commonly what Aristotle requires, a beginning, a middle, and an end; one event is concatenated with another, and the conclusion follows by easy consequence. There are perhaps some incidents that might be spared, as in other poets there is much talk that only fills up time upon the stage; but the general system makes gradual advances, and the end of the play is the end of expectation.

To the unities of time and place he has shewn no regard, and perhaps a nearer view of the principles on which they stand will diminish their value, and withdraw from them the veneration which, from the time of Corneille, they have very generally received, by discovering that they have given more trouble to the poet, than pleasure to the auditor.

The necessity of observing the unities of time and place arises from the supposed necessity of making the drama credible. The criticks hold it impossible, that an action of months or years can be possibly believed to pass in three hours; or that the spectator can suppose himself to sit in the theatre, while ambassadors go and return between distant kings, while armies are levied and towns besieged, while an exile wanders and returns, or till he whom they saw courting his mistress, shall lament the untimely fall of his son. The mind revolts from evident falsehood, and fiction loses its force when it departs from the resemblance of reality.

From the narrow limitation of time necessarily arises the contraction of place. The spectator, who knows that he saw the first act at Alexandria, cannot suppose that he sees the next at Rome, at a distance to which not the dragons of Medea could, in so short a time, have transported him; he knows with certainty that he has not changed his place; and he knows that place cannot change itself; that what was a house cannot become a plain; that what was Thebes can never be Persepolis.

Such is the triumphant language with which a critick exults over the misery of an irregular poet, and exults commonly without resistance or reply. It is time therefore to tell him, by the authority of Shakespeare, that he assumes, as an unquestionable principle, a position, which, while his breath is forming it into words, his understanding pronounces to be false. It is false, that any representation is mistaken for reality; that any dramatick fable in its materiality was ever credible, or, for a single moment, was ever credited.

The objection arising from the impossibility of passing the first hour at Alexandria, and the next at Rome, supposes, that when the play opens the spectator really imagines himself at Alexandria, and believes that his walk to the theatre has been a voyage to Egypt, and that he lives in the days of Antony and Cleopatra. Surely he that imagines this may imagine more. He that can take the stage at one time for the palace of the Ptolemies, may take it in half an hour for the promontory of Actium. Delusion, if delusion be admitted, has no certain limitation; if the spectator can be once persuaded, that his old acquaintance are Alexander and Caesar, that a room illuminated with candles is the plain of Pharsalia, or the bank of Granicus, he is in a state of elevation above the reach of reason, or of truth, and from the heights of empyrean poetry, may despise the circumscriptions of terrestrial nature. There is no reason why a mind thus wandering in extasy should count the clock, or why an hour should not be a century in that calenture of the brains that can make the stage a field.

The truth is, that the spectators are always in their senses, and know, from the first act to the last, that the stage is only a stage, and that the players are only players. They come to hear a certain number of lines recited with just gesture and elegant modulation. The lines relate to some action, and an action must be in some place; but the different actions that compleat a story may be in places very remote from each other; and where is the absurdity of allowing that space to represent first Athens, and then Sicily, which was always known to be neither Sicily nor Athens, but a modern theatre.

By supposition, as place is introduced, time may be extended; the time required by the fable elapses for the most part between the acts; for, of so much of the action as is represented, the real and poetical duration is the same. If, in the first act, preparations for war against Mithridates are represented to be made in Rome, the event of the war may, without absurdity, be represented, in the catastrophe, as

happening in Pontus; we know that there is neither war, nor preparation for war; we know that we are neither in Rome nor Pontus; that neither Mithridates nor Lucullus are before us. The drama exhibits successive imitations of successive actions, and why may not the second imitation represent an action that happened years after the first; if it be so connected with it, that nothing but time can be supposed to intervene. Time is, of all modes of existence, most obsequious to the imagination; a lapse of years is as easily conceived as a passage of hours. In contemplation we easily contract the time of real actions, and therefore willingly permit it to be contracted when we only see their imitation.

It will be asked, how the drama moves, if it is not credited. It is credited with all the credit due to a drama. It is credited, whenever it moves, as a just picture of a real original; as representing to the auditor what he would himself feel, if he were to do or suffer what is there feigned to be suffered or to be done. The reflection that strikes the heart is not, that the evils before us are real evils, but that they are evils to which we ourselves may be exposed. If there be any fallacy, it is not that we fancy the players, but that we fancy ourselves unhappy for a moment; but we rather lament the possibility than suppose the presence of misery, as a mother weeps over her babe, when she remembers that death may take it from her. The delight of tragedy proceeds from our consciousness of fiction; if we thought murders and treasons real, they would please no more.

Imitations produce pain or pleasure, not because they are mistaken for realities, but because they bring realities to mind. When the imagination is recreated by a painted landscape, the trees are not supposed capable to give us shade, or the fountains coolness; but we consider, how we should be pleased with such fountains playing beside us, and such woods waving over us. We are agitated in reading the history of Henry the Fifth, yet no man takes his book for the field of Agencourt. A dramatick exhibition is a book recited with concomitants that encrease or diminish its effect. Familiar comedy is often more powerful on the theatre, than in the page; imperial tragedy is always less. The humour of Petruchio may be heightened by grimace; but what voice or what gesture can hope to add dignity or force to the soliloquy of *Cato*.

A play read, affects the mind like a play acted. It is therefore evident, that the action is not supposed to be real, and it follows that between the acts a longer or shorter time may be allowed to pass, and that no more account of space or duration is to be taken by the auditor of a drama, than by the reader of a narrative, before whom may pass in an hour the life of a hero, or the revolutions of an empire.

Whether Shakespeare knew the unities, and rejected them by design, or deviated from them by happy ignorance, it is, I think, impossible to decide, and useless to enquire. We may reasonably suppose, that, when he rose to notice, he did not want the counsels and admonitions of scholars and criticks, and that he at last deliberately persisted in a practice, which he might have begun by chance. As nothing is essential to the fable, but unity of action, and as the unities of time and place arise evidently from false assumptions, and, by circumscribing the extent of the drama, lessen its variety, I cannot think it much to be lamented, that they were not known by him, or not observed: Nor, if such another poet could arise, should I very vehemently reproach him, that his first act passed at Venice, and his next in Cyprus. Such violations of rules merely positive, become the comprehensive genius of Shakespeare, and such censures are suitable to the minute and slender criticism of Voltaire:

Non usque adeo permiscuit imis
Longus summa dies, ut non, si voce Metelli
Serventur leges, malint a Caesare tolli.

Yet when I speak thus slightly of dramatick rules, I cannot but recollect how much wit and learning may be produced against me; before such authorities I am afraid to stand, not that I think the present question one of those that are to be decided by mere authority, but because it is to be suspected, that these precepts have not been so easily received but for better reasons than I have yet been able to find. The result of my enquiries, in which it would be ludicrous to boast of impartiality, is, that the unities of time and place are not essential to a just drama, that though they may sometimes conduce to pleasure, they are always to be sacrificed to the nobler beauties of variety and instruction; and that a play, written with nice observation of critical rules, is to be contemplated as an elaborate curiosity, as the product of superfluous and ostentatious art, by which is shewn, rather what is possible, than what is necessary.

He that, without diminution of any other excellence, shall preserve all the unities unbroken, deserves the like applause with the architect, who shall display all the orders of architecture in a citadel, without any deduction from its strength; but the principal beauty of a citadel is to exclude the enemy; and the greatest graces of a play, are to copy nature and instruct life.

Perhaps, what I have here not dogmatically but deliberatively written, may recal the principles of the drama to a new examination. I am almost frighted at my own temerity; and when I estimate the fame and the strength of those that maintain the contrary opinion, am ready to sink down in reverential silence; as Æneas withdrew from the defence of Troy, when he saw Neptune shaking the wall, and Juno heading the besiegers.

Those whom my arguments cannot persuade to give their approbation to the judgment of Shakespeare, will easily, if they consider the condition of his life, make some allowance for his ignorance.

Every man's performances, to be rightly estimated, must be compared with the state of the age in which he lived, and with his own particular opportunities; and though to the reader a book be not worse or better for the circumstances of the authour, yet as there is always a silent reference of human works to human abilities, and as the enquiry, how far man may extend his designs, or how high he may rate his native force, is of far greater dignity than in what rank we shall place any particular performance, curiosity is always busy to discover the instruments, as well as to survey the workmanship, to know how much is to be ascribed to original powers, and how much to casual and adventitious help. The palaces of Peru or Mexico were certainly mean and incommodious habitations, if compared to the houses of European monarchs; yet who could forbear to view them with astonishment, who remembered that they were built without the use of iron?

The English nation, in the time of Shakespeare, was yet struggling to emerge from barbarity. The philology of Italy had been transplanted hither in the reign of Henry the Eighth; and the learned languages had been successfully cultivated by Lilly, Linacer, and More; by Pole, Cheke, and Gardiner; and afterwards by Smith, Clerk, Haddon, and Ascham. Greek was now taught to boys in the principal schools; and those who united elegance with learning, read, with great diligence, the Italian and Spanish poets. But literature was yet confined to professed scholars, or to men and women of high rank. The publick was gross and dark; and to be able to read and write, was an accomplishment still valued for its rarity.

Nations, like individuals, have their infancy. A people newly awakened to literary curiosity, being yet unacquainted with the true state of things, knows not how to judge of that which is proposed as its resemblance. Whatever is remote from common appearances is always welcome to vulgar, as to childish credulity; and of a country unenlightened by learning, the whole people is the vulgar. The study of those who then aspired to plebeian learning was laid out upon adventures, giants, dragons, and enchantments. *The Death of Arthur* was the favourite volume.

The mind, which has feasted on the luxurious wonders of fiction, has no taste of the insipidity of truth. A play which imitated only the common occurrences of the world, would, upon the admirers of *Palmerin* and *Guy of Warwick*, have made little impression; he that wrote for such an audience was under the necessity of looking round for strange events and fabulous transactions, and that incredibility, by which maturer knowledge is offended, was the chief recommendation of writings, to unskilful curiosity.

Our authour's plots are generally borrowed from novels, and it is reasonable to suppose, that he chose the most popular, such as were read by many, and related by more; for his audience could not have followed him through the intricacies of the drama, had they not held the thread of the story in their hands.

The stories, which we now find only in remoter authours, were in his time accessible and familiar. The fable of *As You Like It*, which is supposed to be copied from Chaucer's *Gamelyn*, was a little pamphlet of those times; and old Mr. Cibber remembered the tale of Hamlet in plain English prose, which the criticks have now to seek in Saxo Grammaticus.

His English histories he took from English chronicles and English ballads; and as the ancient writers were made known to his countrymen by versions, they supplied him with new subjects; he dilated some of Plutarch's lives into plays, when they had been translated by North.

His plots, whether historical or fabulous, are always crouded with incidents, by which the attention of a rude people was more easily caught than by sentiment or argumentation; and such is the power of the marvellous even over those who despise it, that every man finds his mind more strongly seized by the tragedies of Shakespeare than of any other writer; others please us by particular speeches, but he always makes us anxious for the event, and has perhaps excelled all but Homer in securing the first purpose of a writer, by exciting restless and unquenchable curiosity, and compelling him that reads his work to read it through.

The shows and bustle with which his plays abound have the same original. As knowledge advances, pleasure passes from the eye to the ear, but returns, as it declines, from the ear to the eye. Those to whom our authour's labours were exhibited had more skill in pomps or processions than in poetical language, and perhaps wanted some visible and discriminated events, as comments on the dialogue. He knew how he should most please; and whether his practice is more agreeable to nature, or whether his example has prejudiced the nation, we still find that on our stage something must be done as well as said, and inactive declamation is very coldly heard, however musical or elegant, passionate or sublime.

Voltaire expresses his wonder, that our authour's extravagances are endured by a nation, which has seen the tragedy of *Cato*. Let him be answered, that Addison speaks the language of poets, and Shakespeare, of men. We find in *Cato* innumerable beauties which enamour us of its authour, but we see nothing that acquaints us with human sentiments or human actions; we place it with the fairest and the noblest progeny which judgment propagates by conjunction with learning, but *Othello* is the vigorous and vivacious offspring of observation impregnated by genius. *Cato* affords a splendid exhibition of artificial and fictitious manners, and delivers just and noble sentiments, in diction easy, elevated and harmonious, but its hopes and fears communicate no vibration to the heart; the composition refers us only to the writer; we pronounce the name of *Cato*, but we think on Addison.

The work of a correct and regular writer is a garden accurately formed and diligently planted, varied with shades, and scented with flowers; the composition of Shakespeare is a forest, in which oaks extend their branches, and pines tower in the air, interspersed sometimes with weeds and brambles, and sometimes giving shelter to myrtles and to roses; filling the eye with awful pomp, and gratifying the mind with endless diversity. Other poets display cabinets of precious rarities, minutely finished, wrought into shape, and polished unto brightness. Shakespeare opens a mine which contains gold and diamonds in unexhaustible plenty, though clouded by incrustations, debased by impurities, and mingled with a mass of meaner minerals.

It has been much disputed, whether Shakespeare owed his excellence to his own native force, or whether he had the common helps of scholastick education, the precepts of critical science, and the examples of ancient authours.

There has always prevailed a tradition, that Shakespeare wanted learning, that he had no regular education, nor much skill in the dead languages. Johnson, his friend, affirms, that *he had small Latin, and less Greek*; who, besides that he had no imaginable temptation to falsehood, wrote at a time when the character and acquisitions of Shakespeare were known to multitudes. His evidence ought therefore to decide the controversy, unless some testimony of equal force could be opposed.

Some have imagined, that they have discovered deep learning in many imitations of old writers; but the examples which I have known urged, were drawn from books translated in his time; or were such easy coincidencies of thought, as will happen to all who consider the same subjects; or such remarks on life or axioms of morality as float in conversation, and are transmitted through the world in proverbial sentences.

I have found it remarked, that, in this important sentence, "Go before, I'll follow," we read a translation of, *I prae, sequar*. I have been told, that when Caliban, after a pleasing dream, says, "I cry'd to sleep again," the authour imitates Anacreon, who had, like every other man, the same wish on the same occasion.

There are a few passages which may pass for imitations, but so few, that the exception only confirms the rule; he obtained them from accidental quotations, or by oral communication, and as he used what he had, would have used more if he had obtained it.

The *Comedy of Errors* is confessedly taken from the *Menaechmi* of Plautus; from the only play of Plautus which was then in English. What can be more probable, than that he who copied that, would have copied more; but that those which were not translated were inaccessible?

Whether he knew the modern languages is uncertain. That his plays have some French scenes proves but little; he might easily procure them to be written, and probably, even though he had known the language in the common degree, he could not have written it without assistance. In the story of

Romeo and Juliet he is observed to have followed the English translation, where it deviates from the Italian; but this on the other part proves nothing against his knowledge of the original. He was to copy, not what he knew himself, but what was known to his audience.

It is most likely that he had learned Latin sufficiently to make him acquainted with construction, but that he never advanced to an easy perusal of the Roman authours. Concerning his skill in modern languages, I can find no sufficient ground of determination; but as no imitations of French or Italian authours have been discovered, though the Italian poetry was then high in esteem, I am inclined to believe, that he read little more than English, and chose for his fables only such tales as he found translated.

That much knowledge is scattered over his works is very justly observed by Pope, but it is often such knowledge as books did not supply. He that will understand Shakespeare, must not be content to study him in the closet, he must look for his meaning sometimes among the sports of the field, and sometimes among the manufactures of the shop.

There is however proof enough that he was a very diligent reader, nor was our language then so indigent of books, but that he might very liberally indulge his curiosity without excursion into foreign literature. Many of the Roman authours were translated, and some of the Greek; the Reformation had filled the kingdom with theological learning; most of the topicks of human disquisition had found English writers; and poetry had been cultivated, not only with diligence, but success. This was a stock of knowledge sufficient for a mind so capable of appropriating and improving it.

But the greater part of his excellence was the product of his own genius. He found the English stage in a state of the utmost rudeness; no essays either in tragedy or comedy had appeared, from which it could be discovered to what degree of delight either one or other might be carried. Neither character nor dialogue were yet understood. Shakespeare may be truly said to have introduced them both amongst us, and in some of his happier scenes to have carried them both to the utmost height.

By what gradations of improvement he proceeded, is not easily known; for the chronology of his works is yet unsettled. Rowe is of opinion, that "perhaps we are not to look for his beginning, like those of other writers, in his least perfect works; art had so little, and nature so large a share in what he did, that for ought I know," says he, "the performances of his youth, as they were the most vigorous, were the best." But the power of nature is only the power of using to any certain purpose the materials which diligence procures, or opportunity supplies. Nature gives no man knowledge, and when images are collected by study and experience, can only assist in combining or applying them. Shakespeare, however favoured by nature, could impart only what he had learned; and as he must increase his ideas, like other mortals, by gradual acquisition, he, like them, grew wiser as he grew older, could display life better, as he knew it more, and instruct with more efficacy, as he was himself more amply instructed.

There is a vigilance of observation and accuracy of distinction which books and precepts cannot confer; from this almost all original and native excellence proceeds. Shakespeare must have looked upon mankind with perspicacity, in the highest degree curious and attentive. Other writers borrow their characters from preceding writers, and diversify them only by the accidental appendages of present manners; the dress is a little varied, but the body is the same. Our authour had both matter and form to provide; for except the characters of Chaucer, to whom I think he is not much indebted, there were no writers in English, and perhaps not many in other modern languages, which shewed life its native colours.

The contest about the original benevolence or malignity of man had not yet commenced. Speculation had not yet attempted to analyse the mind, to trace the passions to their sources, to unfold the seminal principles of vice and virture, or sound the depths of the heart for the motives of action. All those enquiries, which from that time that human nature became the fashionable study, have been made sometimes with nice discernment, but often with idle subtilty, were yet unattempted. The tales, with which the infancy of learning was satisfied, exhibited only the superficial appearances of action, related the events but omitted the causes, and were formed for such as delighted in wonders rather than in truth. Mankind was not then to be studied in the closet; he that would know the world, was under the necessity of gleaning his own remarks, by mingling as he could in its business and amusements.

Boyle congratulated himself upon his high birth, because it favoured his curiosity, by facilitating his access. Shakespeare had no such advantage; he came to London a needy adventurer, and lived for a time by very mean employments. Many works of genius and learning have been performed in states of life, that appear very little favourable to thought or to enquiry; so many, that he who considers them is inclined to think that he sees enterprise and perseverance predominating over all external agency, and bidding help and hindrance vanish before them. The genius of Shakespeare was not to be depressed by the weight of poverty, nor limited by the narrow conversation to which men in want are inevitably condemned; the incumbrances of his fortune were shaken from his mind, "as dewdrops from a lion's mane."

Though he had so many difficulties to encounter, and so little assistance to surmount them, he has been able to obtain an exact knowledge of many modes of life, and many casts of native dispositions; to vary them with great multiplicity; to mark them by nice distinctions; and to shew them in full view by proper combinations. In this part of his performances he had none to imitate, but has himself been imitated by all succeeding writers; and it may be doubted, whether from all his successors more maxims of theoretical knowledge, or more rules of practical prudence, can be collected, than he alone has given to his country.

Nor was his attention confined to the actions of men; he was an exact surveyor of the inanimate world; his descriptions have always some peculiarities, gathered by contemplating things as they really exist. It may be observed, that the oldest poets of many nations preserve their reputation, and that the following generations of wit, after a short celebrity, sink into oblivion. The first, whoever they be, must take their sentiments and descriptions immediately from knowledge; the resemblance is therefore just, their descriptions are verified by every eye, and their sentiments acknowledged by every breast. Those whom their fame invites to the same studies, copy partly them, and partly nature, till the books of one age gain such authority, as to stand in the place of nature to another, and imitation, always deviating a little, becomes at last capricious and casual. Shakespeare, whether life or nature be his subject, shews plainly, that he has seen with his own eyes; he gives the image which he receives, not weakened or distorted by the intervention of any other mind; the ignorant feel his representations to be just, and the learned see that they are compleat.

Perhaps it would not be easy to find any authour, except Homer, who invented so much as Shakespeare, who so much advanced the studies which he cultivated, or effused so much novelty upon his age or country. The form, the characters, the

language, and the shows of the English drama are his. "He seems," says Dennis, "to have been the very original of our English tragical harmony, that is, the harmony of blank verse, diversified often by dissyllable and trissyllable terminations. For the diversity distinguishes it from heroick harmony, and by bringing it nearer to common use makes it more proper to gain attention, and more fit for action and dialogue. Such verse we make when we are writing prose; we make such verse in common conversation."

I know not whether this praise is rigorously just. The dissyllable termination, which the critick rightly appropriates to the drama, is to be found, though, I think, not in *Gorboduc* which is confessedly before our authour; yet in *Hieronnymo*, of which the date is not certain, but which there is reason to believe at least as old as his earliest plays. This however is certain, that he is the first who taught either tragedy or comedy to please, there being no theatrical piece of any older writer, of which the name is known, except to antiquaries and collectors of books, which are sought because they are scarce, and would not have been scarce, had they been much esteemed.

To him we must ascribe the praise, unless Spenser may divide it with him, of having first discovered to how much smoothness and harmony the English language could be softened. He has speeches, perhaps sometimes scenes, which have all the delicacy of Rowe, without his effeminacy. He endeavours indeed commonly to strike by the force and vigour of his dialogue, but he never executes his purpose better, than when he tries to sooth by softness.

Yet it must be at last confessed, that as we owe everything to him, he owes something to us; that, if much of his praise is paid by perception and judgement, much is likewise given by custom and veneration. We fix our eyes upon his graces, and turn them from his deformities, and endure in him what we should in another loath or despise. If we endured without praising, respect for the father of our drama might excuse us; but I have seen, in the book of some modern critick, a collection of anomalies, which shew that he has corrupted language by every mode of depravation, but which his admirer has accumulated as a monument of honour.

He has scenes of undoubted and perpetual excellence, but perhaps not one play, which, if it were now exhibited as the work of a contemporary writer, would be heard to the conclusion. I am indeed far from thinking, that his works were wrought to his own ideas of perfection; when they were such as would satisfy the audience, they satisfied the writer. It is seldom that authours, though more studious of fame than Shakespeare, rise much above the standard of their own age; to add a little to what is best will always be sufficient for present praise, and those who find themselves exalted into fame, are willing to credit their encomiasts, and to spare the labour of contending with themselves.

## ELIZABETH MONTAGU
### From "On the Præternatural Beings"
*An Essay on the Writings and Genius of Shakspeare*
1769

As the genius of Shakspeare, through the whole extent of the Poet's province, is the object of our enquiry, we should do him great injustice, if we did not attend to his peculiar felicity in those fictions and inventions, from which Poetry derives its highest distinction, and from whence it first assumed its pretensions to divine inspiration, and appeared the associate of Religion.

The ancient poet was admitted into the synod of the gods; he discoursed of their natures, he repeated their counsels, and, without the charge of impiety or presumption, disclosed their dissensions, and published their vices: He peopled the woods with nymphs, the rivers with deities; and, that he might still have some being within call to his assistance, he placed responsive echo in the vacant regions of air.

In the infant ages of the world, the credulity of ignorance greedily received every marvellous tale: but, as mankind increased in knowledge, and a long series of traditions had established a certain mythology and history, the poet was no longer permitted to range, uncontrolled, through the boundless dominions of fancy, but became restrained, in some measure, to things believed, or known.—Though the duty of Poetry to please and to surprize still subsisted, the means varied with the state of the world, and it soon grew necessary to make the new inventions lean on the old traditions.—The human mind delights in novelty, and is captivated by the marvellous, but, even in fable itself, requires the credible.—The poet, who can give to splendid inventions, and to fictions new and bold, the air and authority of reality and truth, is master of the genuine sources of the Castalian spring, and may justly be said to draw his inspiration from *the well-head of pure poesy*.

Shakspeare saw how useful the popular superstitions had been to the ancient poets: he felt that they were necessary to poetry itself. We need only read some modern French heroic poems, to be convinced how poorly epic poetry subsists on the pure elements of history and philosophy. Tasso, though he had a subject so popular, at the time he wrote, as the deliverance of Jerusalem, was obliged to employ the operations of magic, and the interposition of angels and dæmons, to give the marvellous, the sublime, and, I may add, that religious air to his work, which ennobles the enthusiasm, and sanctifies the fiction of the poet. Ariosto's excursive muse wanders through the regions of romance, attended by all the superb train of chivalry, giants, dwarfs, and enchanters; and however these poets, by severe and frigid critics, may have been condemned for giving ornaments not purely classical, to their works; I believe every reader of taste admires, not only the fertility of their imagination, but the judgment with which they availed themselves of the superstition of the times, and of the customs and modes of the country, in which they laid the scenes of action.

To recur, as the learned sometimes do, to the theology and fables of other ages, and other countries, has ever a poor effect: Jupiter, Minerva, and Apollo, only embellish a modern story, as a print from their statues adorns the frontispiece.—We admire indeed the art of the sculptors who give their images with grace and majesty; but no devotion is excited, no enthusiasm kindled, by the representations of characters whose divinity we do not acknowledge.

When the pagan temples ceased to be revered, and the Parnassian mount existed no longer, it would have been difficult for the poet of later times to have preserved the divinity of his muse inviolate, if the Western world too had not had its sacred fables. While there is any national superstition which credulity has consecrated, any hallowed tradition long revered by vulgar faith; to that sanctuary, that asylum, may the poet resort. Let him tread the holy ground with reverence; respect the established doctrine; exactly observe the accustomed rites, and the attributes of the object of veneration; then shall he not vainly invoke an inexorable or absent deity. Ghosts, fairies, goblins, elves, were as propitious, were as assistant to Shak-

speare, and gave as much of the sublime, and of the marvellous, to his fictions, as nymphs, satyrs, fawns, and even the triple Geryon, to the works of ancient bards. Our poet never carries his præternatural beings beyond the limits of the popular tradition. It is true, that he boldly exerts his poetic genius, and fascinating powers in that magic circle, *in which none e'er durst walk but he*: but as judicious as bold, he contains himself within it. He calls up all the stately phantoms in the regions of superstition, which our faith will receive with reverence. He throws into their manners and language a mysterious solemnity, favourable to superstition in general, with something highly characteristic of each particular being which he exhibits. His witches, his ghosts, and his fairies, seem *spirits of health or goblins damn'd; bring with them airs from heaven, or blasts from hell*. His ghosts are sullen, melancholy, and terrible. Every sentence, uttered by the witches, is a prophecy or a charm; their manners are malignant, their phrases ambiguous, their promises delusive.——The witches' cauldron is a collection of all that is most horrid, in their supposed incantations. Ariel is a spirit, mild, gentle, and sweet, possessed of supernatural powers, but subject to the command of a great magician.

The fairies are sportive and gay; the innocent artificers of harmless frauds, and mirthful delusions. Puck's enumeration of the feats of a fairy is the most agreeable recital of their supposed gambols.

To all these beings our Poet has assigned tasks, and appropriated manners adapted to their imputed dispositions and characters; which are continually developing through the whole piece, in a series of operations conducive to the catastrophe. They are not brought in as subordinate or casual agents, but lead the action, and govern the fable; in which respect our countryman has entered more into theatrical propriety than the Greek tragedians.

Every species of poetry has its distinct duties and obligations. The Drama does not, like the Epic, admit of episode, unnecessary persons, or things incredible: for, as it is observed by a critic of great ingenuity and taste[1]; "That which passes in representation, and challenges, as it were, the scrutiny of the eye, must be truth itself, or something very nearly approaching to it." It should indeed be what our imagination will adopt though our reason would reject it. Great caution and dexterity are required in the dramatic poet, to give an air of reality to fictitious existence.

In the bold attempt to give to airy nothing *a local habitation and a person*, regard must be had to fix it in such scenes, and to display it in such actions, as are agreeable to the popular opinion. Witches holding their sabbath, and saluting passengers on the blasted heath; ghosts, at the midnight hour, visiting the glimpses of the moon, and whispering a bloody secret, derive from propriety of place and action a credibility very propitious to the scheme of the poet. *Reddere personæ— convenientia cuique*, cannot be less his duty in regard to these superior and metaphysical, than to human characters. Indeed, from the invariableness of their natures, a greater consistency and uniformity is necessary; but most of all, as the belief of their intervention depends entirely on their manners and sentiments suiting with the preconceived opinion of them.

The magician Prospero raising a storm; witches performing infernal rites; or any other exertion of the supposed powers and qualities of the agent, were easily credited by the vulgar.

The genius of Shakspeare informed him that poetic fable must rise above the simple tale of the nurse; therefore he adorns the beldame, tradition, with flowers gathered on classic ground, but still wisely suffering those simples of her native soil, to which the established superstition of her country has attributed a magic spell, to be predominant. Can any thing be more poetical than Prospero's address to his attendant spirits before he dismisses them?

> Ye elves of hills, brooks, standing lakes, and groves,
> And ye that on the sands with printless foot
> Do chase the ebbing Neptune, and do fly him
> When he comes back; ye demy-puppets, that
> By the moonshine, the green sour ringlet make,
> Whereof the ewe not bites; and you, whose aid
> Is to make midnight mushrooms; that rejoice
> To hear the solemn curfew; by whose aid
> (Weak masters tho' ye be) I have bedimm'd
> The noon-tide sun, call'd forth the mutinous winds,
> And 'twixt the green-sea and the azur'd vault
> Set roaring war; to the dread rattling thunder
> Have I giv'n fire, and rifted Jove's stout oak
> With his own bolt; the strong-bas'd promontory
> Have I made shake, and by the spurs pluckt up
> The pine and cedar: graves at my command
> Have wak'd their sleepers; op'd, and let them forth,
> By my so potent art.

Here the popular stories concerning the power of magicians are agreeably collected. The incantations of the witches in *Macbeth* are more solemn and terrible than those of the Erichtho of Lucan, or of the Canidia of Horace. It may be said, indeed, that Shakspeare had an advantage derived from the more direful character of his national superstitions.

A celebrated writer, in his ingenious letters on Chivalry, has observed, that the Gothic manners, and Gothic superstitions, are more adapted to the uses of poetry, than the Grecian. The devotion of those times was gloomy and fearful, not being purged of the terrors of the Celtic fables. The Priest often availed himself of the dire inventions of his predecessor, the Druid. The church of Rome adopted many of the Celtic superstitions; others, which were not established by it, as points of faith, still maintained a traditional authority, among the vulgar. Climate, temper, modes of life, and institutions of government, seem all to have conspired to make the superstitions of the Celtic nations melancholy and terrible. Philosophy had not mitigated the austerity of ignorant devotion, or tamed the fierce spirit of enthusiasm. As the Bards, who were our philosophers and poets, pretended to be possessed of the dark secrets of magic and divination, they certainly encouraged the ignorant credulity, and anxious fears, to which such impostures owe their success and credit. The retired and gloomy scenes appointed for the most solemn rites of devotion; the austerity and rigour of Druidical discipline and jurisdiction; the fasts, the penances, the sad excommunications from the comforts and privileges of civil life; the dreadful anathema, whose vengeance pursued the wretched beyond the grave, which bounds all human power and mortal jurisdiction, must deeply imprint on the mind every form of superstition, which such an hierarchy presented. The bard, who was subservient to the Druid, had mixed them in his heroic song; in his historical annals; in his medical practice: genii assisted his heroes; dæmons decided the fate of the battle; and charms cured the sick, or the wounded. Nay, after the consecrated groves were cut down, and the temples demolished, the tales that sprung from them were still preserved, with religious reverence, in the minds of the people.

The Poet found himself happily situated amidst enchantments, ghosts, goblins; every element supposed the residence of a kind of deity; the Genius of the Mountain, the Spirit of the Floods, the oak endued with sacred prophecy, made men walk abroad with a fearful apprehension

> Of powers unseen, and mightier far than they.

On the mountains, and in the woods, stalked the angry spectre; and in the gayest and most pleasing scenes, even within the cheerful haunts of men, amongst villages and farms,

> Tripp'd the light fairies and the dapper elves.

The reader will easily perceive what resources remained for the Poet, in this visionary land of ideal forms. The general scenery of nature, considered as inanimate, only adorns the descriptive part of poetry; but being, according to the Celtic traditions, animated by a kind of intelligences, the bard could better make use of them, for his moral purposes. That awe of the immediate presence of the Deity, which, among the vulgar of other nations, is confined to temples and altars, was here diffused over every object. The Celt passed trembling through the woods, and over the mountain, and near the lakes, inhabited by these invisible powers: such apprehensions must indeed

> Deepen the murmur of the falling floods,
> And shed a browner horror on the woods;

give sadder accents to every whisper of the animate or inanimate creation, and arm every shadow with terrors.

With great reason, therefore, it has been asserted, that the Western bards had an advantage over Homer, in the superstitions of their country. The religious ceremonies of Greece were more pompous than solemn; and seemed as much a part of their civil institutions, as belonging to spiritual matters: nor did they impress so deep a sense of invisible being, and prepare the mind to catch the enthusiasm of the poet, and to receive with veneration the phantoms, he presented.

Our countryman has another kind of superiority over the Greek poets, even the earliest of them, who, having imbibed the learning of mysterious Egypt, addicted themselves to allegory; but our Gothic Bard, instead of mere amusive allegory, employs the potent agency of sacred fable. When the world becomes learned and philosophical, fable refines into allegory. But the age of fable is the golden age of poetry: when reason, and the steady lamp of inquisitive philosophy, throw their penetrating rays upon the phantoms of imagination, they discover them to have been mere shadows, formed by ignorance. The thunderbolts of Jove, forged in Cimmerian caves; the cestus of Venus, woven by the hands of the attracting Graces, cease to terrify and allure. Echo, from an amorous nymph, fades into voice, and nothing more; the very threads of Iris's scarf are untwisted; all the poet's spells are broken, his charms dissolved: deserted on his own enchanted ground, he takes refuge in the groves of Philosophy; but there his divinities evaporate in allegory, in which mystic and insubstantial state, they do but weakly assist his operations. By associating his muse to philosophy, he hopes she may establish with the learned, the worship she won from the ignorant; so he makes her quit the old traditional fable, whence she derived her first authority and power, to follow airy hypotheses, and chimerical systems. Allegory, the daughter of Fable, is admired by the fastidious wit and abstruse scholar, when her mother begins to be treated as superannuated, foolish, and doting; but however well she may please and amuse, not being worshipped as divine, she does not awe and terrify like sacred mythology, nor ever can establish the same fearful devotion, nor assume such arbitrary power over the mind. Her person is not adapted to the stage, nor her qualities to the business and end of dramatic representation. L'Abbé du Bos has judiciously distinguished the reasons, why allegory is not fit for the drama. What the critic investigated by art and study, the wisdom of nature unfolded to our unlettered Poet, or he would not have resisted the prevalent fashion of his allegorizing age; especially as Spenser's *Fairy Queen* was the admired work of the times.

Allegorical beings, performing acts of chivalry, fell in with the taste of an age that affected abstruse learning, romantic valour, and high-flown gallantry. Prince Arthur, the British Hercules, was brought from ancient ballads and romances, to be allegorized into the knight of magnanimity, at the court of Gloriana. His knights followed him thither, in the same moralized garb: and even the questynge beast received no less honour and improvement from the allegorizing art of Spenser, as has been shewn by a critic of great learning, ingenuity, and taste, in his observations on the *Fairy Queen*.

Our first theatrical entertainments, after we emerged from gross barbarism, were of the allegorical kind. The Christmas carol, and Carnival shows, the pious pastimes of our holy-days, were turned into pageantries and masques, all symbolical and allegorical. Our stage rose from hymns to the Virgin, and encomiums on the Patriarchs and Saints; as the Grecian tragedies from the hymns to Bacchus. Our early poets added narration and action to this kind of psalmody, as Æschylus had done to the song of the goat. Much more rapid indeed was the progress of the Grecian stage towards perfection—— Philosophy, poetry, eloquence, all the fine arts, were in their meridian glory, when the Drama first began to dawn at Athens, and gloriously it shone forth, illumined by every kind of intellectual light.

Shakspeare, in the dark shades of Gothic barbarism, had no resources but in the very phantoms, that walked the night of ignorance and superstition: or in touching the latent passions of civil rage and discord: sure to please best his fierce and barbarous audience, when he raised the bloody ghost, or reared the warlike standard. His choice of these subjects was judicious, if we consider the times in which he lived; his management of them so masterly, that he will be admired in all times.

In the same age, Ben Jonson, more proud of his learning than confident of his genius, was desirous to give a metaphysical air to his works. He composed many pieces of the allegorical kind, established on the Grecian mythology, and rendered his playhouse a perfect pantheon.——Shakspeare disdained these quaint devices: an admirable judge of human nature, with a capacity most extensive, and an invention most happy, he contented himself with giving dramatic manners to history, sublimity and its appropriated powers and charms to fiction; and in both these arts he is unequalled.——The *Catiline* and *Sejanus* of Jonson are cold, crude, heavy pieces; turgid where they should be great; bombast where they should be sublime; the sentiments extravagant; the manners exaggerated; and the whole undramatically conducted by long senatorial speeches, and flat plagiarisms from Tacitus and Sallust. Such of this author's pieces as he boasts to be *grounded on antiquity and solid learning, and to lay hold on removed mysteries,*[2] have neither the majesty of Shakspeare's serious fables, nor the pleasing sportfulness and poetical imagination of his fairy tales. Indeed if we compare our countryman in this respect, with the most admired writers of antiquity, we shall, perhaps, not find him inferior to them.——Æschylus, with greater impetuosity of genius than even Shakspeare, makes bold incursions into the blind chaos of mingled allegory and fable, but he is not so happy in diffusing the solemn shade; in casting the dim, religious light that should reign there. When he introduces his Furies, and other supernatural beings, he exposes them by too glaring a light; causes affright in the spectator, but never rises to the imparting that unlimited terror, which we feel when Macbeth, to his bold address,

How now! ye secret, foul, and midnight hags,
What is't ye do?

is answered,

A deed without a name.

. . . It was just now observed, that Shakspeare has an advantage over the Greek poets, in the more solemn, gloomy, and mysterious air of his national superstitions; but this avails him only with critics of deep penetration and true taste, and with whom sentiment has more sway than authority. The learned have received the popular tales of Greece from their poets; ours are derived to them from the illiterate vulgar. The phantom of Darius in the tragedy of the *Persians*, evoked by ancient rites, is beheld with reverence by the scholar, and endured by the bel esprit. To these the ghost of Hamlet is an object of contempt or ridicule. Let us candidly examine these royal shades, as exhibited to us by those great masters in the art of exciting pity and terror, Æschylus and Shakspeare; and impartially decide which poet throws most of the sublime into the præternatural character; and, also, which has the art to render it most efficient in the drama. This enquiry may be the more interesting, because the French wits have often mentioned Hamlet's ghost as an instance of the barbarism of our theatre. The *Persians*, of Æschylus, is certainly one of the most august spectacles that ever was represented on a theatre; nobly imagined, happily sustained, regularly conducted, deeply interesting to the Athenian people, and favourable to their great scheme of resisting the power of the Persian monarch. It would be absurd to depreciate this excellent piece, or to bring into a general comparison with it, a drama of so different a kind as the tragedy of *Hamlet*. But it is surely allowable to compare the Persian phantom with the Danish ghost; and to examine, whether any thing but prejudice, in favour of the ancients, protects the superstitious circumstances relative to the one, from the same ridicule with which the others have been treated. Atossa, the widow of Darius, relates to the sages of the Persian council, a dream and an omen; they advise her to consult the shade of her dead lord, upon what is to be done in the unfortunate situation of Xerxes just defeated by the Greeks. In the third act she enters offering to the manès a libation composed of milk, honey, wine, oil, &c. Upon this, Darius issues from his tomb. Let the wits, who are so smart on our ghost's disappearing at the cock's crowing, explain why, in reason, a ghost in Persia, or in Greece, should be more fond of milk and honey, than averse, in Denmark, to the crowing of a cock. Each poet adopted, in his work, the superstition relative to his subject; and the poet who does so, understands his business much better than the critic, who, in judging of that work, refuses it his attention. The phantom of Darius comes forth in his regal robes to Atossa and the satraps in council, who, in the eastern manner, pay their silent adorations to their emperor. His quality of ghost does not appear to make any impression upon them; and the satraps so exactly preserve the characters of courtiers, that they do not venture to tell him the true state of the affairs of his kingdom, and its recent disgraces: finding he cannot get any information from them, he addresses himself to Atossa, who does not break forth with that passion and tenderness one should expect, on the sight of her long-lost husband; but very calmly informs him, after some flattery on the constant prosperity of his reign, of the calamitous state of Persia under Xerxes, who has been stimulated by his courtiers, to make war upon Greece. The phantom, who was to appear ignorant of what was past, that the ear of the Athenians might be soothed and flattered with the detail of their victory at Salamis, is allowed, for the same reason, such prescience, as to foretell their future triumph at Platea. Whatever else he adds by way of counsel or reproof, either in itself, or in the mode of delivering it, is nothing more than might be expected from any experienced counsellor of state. Darius advises the old men to enjoy whatever they can, because riches are of no use in the grave. As this touches the most absurd and ridiculous foible in human nature, the increase of a greedy and solicitous desire of wealth, when the period of enjoyment of it becomes more precarious and short, the admonition has something of a comic and satirical turn, unbecoming the solemn character of the speaker, and the sad exigency upon which he was called. The intervention of this præternatural being gives nothing of the marvellous or the sublime to the piece, nor adds to, or is connected with its interest. The supernatural, divested of *the august* and *the terrible,* make but a poor figure in any species of poetry; useless and unconnected with the fable, it wants propriety, in dramatic poetry. Shakspeare had so just a taste, that he never introduced any præternatural character on the stage, that did not assist in the conduct of the drama. Indeed he had such prodigious force of talents, that he could make every being his fancy created, subservient to his designs. The uncouth, awkward monster, Caliban, is so subject to his genius, as to assist in bringing things to the proposed end and perfection. And the slight fairies, *weak masters though they be,* even in their wanton gambols and idle sports, perform great tasks by *his so potent art.*

But to return to the intended comparison between the Grecian shade, and the Danish ghost. The first propriety in the conduct of this kind of machinery seems to be, that the præternatural person be intimately connected with the fable; that he increase the interest, add to the solemnity of it, and that his efficiency, in bringing on the catastrophe, be in some measure adequate to the violence done to the ordinary course of things, in his visible interposition. These are points peculiarly important in dramatic poetry, as has been before observed. To these ends it is necessary, this being should stand acknowledged and revered by the national superstition, and thus every operation that developes the attributes, which vulgar opinion, or the nurse's legend, have taught us to ascribe to him, will augment our pleasure; whether we give the reins to our imagination, and, as spectators, willingly yield ourselves up to pleasing delusion, or, as critics, examine the merit of the composition. I hope it is not difficult to shew, that in all these capital points our author has excelled. At the solemn midnight hour, Horatio and Marcellus, the schoolfellows of young Hamlet, come to the centinels upon guard, excited by a report that a Ghost of their late Monarch had, some preceding nights, appeared to them. Horatio, not being one of the believing vulgar, gives little credit to the story, but bids Bernardo proceed in his relation.

> *Bernardo:*          Last night of all,
>   When yon same star, that's westward from the
>       pole,
>   Had made his course t'illume that part of heav'n,
>   Where now it burns, Marcellus and myself,
>   The bell then beating one——

Here enters the Ghost, after you are thus prepared. There is something solemn and sublime in thus regulating the walking of the spirit, by the course of the star: it intimates a connection and correspondence between things beyond our ken, *and above the visible diurnal sphere.* Horatio is affected with that kind of fear, which such an appearance would naturally excite. He trembles, and turns pale. When the violence of the emotion subsides, he reflects, that probably this supernatural event portends some danger lurking in the state. This suggestion gives importance to the phænomenon, and engages our attention.

Horatio's relation of the king's combat with the Norwegian, and of the forces the young Fortinbras is assembling, in order to attack Denmark, seems to point out, from what quarter the apprehended peril is to arise. Such appearances, says he, preceded the fall of mighty Julius, and the ruin of the great commonwealth; and he adds, such have often been the omens of disasters in our own state. There is great art in this conduct. The true cause of the royal Dane's discontent could not be guessed at: it was a secret which could be only revealed by himself. In the mean time, it was necessary to captivate our attention, by demonstrating, that the poet was not going to exhibit such idle and frivolous gambols, as ghosts are by the vulgar often represented to perform. The historical testimony, that antecedent to the death of Cæsar,

> The graves stood tenantless, and the sheeted dead
> Did squeak and gibber in the Roman streets,

gives credibility and importance to this phænomenon. Horatio's address to the Ghost is brief and pertinent, and the whole purport of it agreeable to the vulgar conceptions of these matters.

>               Stay, illusion!
>   If thou hast any sound, or use of voice,
>   Speak to me.
>   If there be any good thing to be done,
>   That may to thee do ease, and grace to me,
>   Speak to me.
>   If thou art privy to thy country's fate,
>   Which happily foreknowing may avoid,
>   Oh speak!
>   Or, if thou hast uphoarded in thy life
>   Extorted treasure in the womb of earth,
>   For which, they say, you spirits oft walk in death,
>   Speak of it.

Its vanishing at the crowing of the cock, is another circumstance of the established superstition.

Young Hamlet's indignation at his mother's hasty and incestuous marriage, his sorrow for his father's death, the character he gives of that prince, prepare the spectator to sympathize with his wrongs and sufferings. The son, as is natural, with much more vehement emotion than Horatio did, addresses his father's shade. Hamlet's terror, his astonishment, his vehement desire to know the cause of this visitation, are irresistibly communicated to the spectator by the following speech.

>   Angels and ministers of grace defend us!
>   Be thou a spirit of health, or goblin damn'd,
>   Bring with thee airs from heav'n or blasts from hell,
>   Be thy intents wicked or charitable,
>   Thou com'st in such a questionable shape,
>   That I will speak to thee. I'll call thee Hamlet,
>   King, father, royal Dane: oh! answer me;
>   Let me not burst in ignorance; but tell,
>   Why thy canonized bones, hearsed in death,
>   Have burst their cearments? Why the sepulchre,
>   Wherein we saw thee quietly in-urn'd,
>   Hath op'd his ponderous and marble jaws,
>   To cast thee up again? What may this mean,
>   That thou, dead corse, again, in complete steel,
>   Revisit'st thus the glimpses of the moon,
>   Making night hideous?

Never did the Grecian muse of tragedy relate a tale so full of pity and terror, as is imparted by the Ghost. Every circumstance melts us with compassion; and with what horror do we hear him say!

>               But that I am forbid
>   To tell the secrets of my prison-house,

I could a tale unfold, whose lightest word
Would harrow up thy soul, freeze thy young blood,
Make thy two eyes, like stars, start from their spheres,
Thy knotted and combined locks to part,
And each particular hair to stand on end
Like quills upon the fretful porcupine:
But this eternal blazon must not be
To ears of flesh and blood.

All that follows is solemn, sad, and deeply affecting.

*Notes*

1. Hurd, on Dramatic Imitation.
2. Prologue to the *Masque of Queens.*

### EDWARD TAYLOR (?)
### From "On Shakespear"
### *Cursory Remarks on Tragedy*
### 1774, pp. 31–51

It has been the prevailing fashion for some years past to launch out into the most extravagant praises of our countryman Shakespear, and to allot him beyond all competition the first place as a tragic writer. Compared with him, Corneille, Racine, and Voltaire, are fantastic composers, void of historical truth, imitation of character, or representation of manners; mere declaimers, without energy or fire of action, and absurdly introducing, upon all occasions, tedious, insipid, uninteresting love-scenes. But, prejudice apart, is he so transcendently their superior, and is he the glorious luminary that shines?

velut inter ignes
Luna minores.
(Hor.)

Shall I venture to proceed further, and ask, if he be in general even a good tragic writer? We have seen . . . what are some of the most material rules for dramatic compositions, as prescribed by Aristotle and other eminent masters in the art of criticism: rules consonant to reason, and calculated to deceive the spectator into a persuasion, that he is interested in a real event, whilst time, place, and action, conspire to strengthen the delusion: rules dictated by the wife, approved by the learned, and adopted by writers of judgment, genius, and taste of all nations. But these were either totally unknown to Shakespear, or wilfully neglected by him. Instead of confining the action to a limited time, he takes in the space of days, months, and even years; instead of adhering to the unity of place, by a preposterous magic he transports the spectator in the shifting of a scene, from Italy to Britain, from Venice to Cyprus, from the court of England to that of France: and shall I not be permitted to exclaim,

Quodcunque ostendis mihi sic incredulus odi.
(Hor. *de Arte Poet.*)

But Shakespear can say with the musician in Homer,

*Autodidaktos d'eimi: theos de moi en phresin oimas
Pantoias enephysen.*

Ipse autem à me sum doctus. Deus enim in mente
cantilenas
Omnigenas insevit.

(*Odys.* Lib. 22.)

His genius therefore is not to be restrained by the shackles of critic laws; his audacious fancy, his enthusiastic fire, are not to submit to the tame institutions of an Aristotle or a Quintilian. So then he is to be indulged in transgressing the bounds of nature, in neglecting to give to fiction the air of truth, and in imposing the most palpable incongruities and most striking impossibilities on the audience, because he dares. Mr. Pope's partiality seems to have gotten the better of his usual justice and candour, when he observes, that we are not to apply the rules of Aristotle to Shakespear; "for that, says he, would be like trying a man by the laws of one country, who acts under those of another." Yet surely there are laws of general society as well as of particular communities, laws that bind each individual as a citizen of the world; the infringment of which would justly excite the universal indignation and resentment of mankind. In most countries, England excepted, certain positions and rules have been holden sacred and inviolable in the literary as well as in the political word: these did the antient Greek tragedians observe and cultivate, and to these have the most eminent amongst the modern Italians and French scrupulously adhered. But our excentric English tragedian has presumed to quit the beaten track, and has boldly ventured to turn aside into the regions of the most wild, most fantastic imagination. With an unprecedented, with an unpardonable audacity, has he overleaped the pale of credibility, a boundary too confined for his romantic genius. Presented by him with impossibilities instead of the appearance of truth, we remain undeluded spectators.

Queis sic extorta voluptas
Et demtus per vim mentis gratissimus error.
(Hor.)

And although we may be affected by particular passages in any one of his plays, yet the whole of the representation cannot be very interesting on account of its extravagance. Let us not therefore approve, let us not even extenuate those faults in Shakespear, that justice, that common sense, would lead us to condemn in others. But with an impartiality that becomes every man, who dares to think for himself, let us allow him great merit as a comic writer, greater still as a poet, but little, very little, as a tragedian: for, as Quinctilian says of Seneca, Velles eum suo ingenio dixisse, alieno judicio. Digna enim fuit illa natura, quæ meliora vellet, quæ quod voluit effecit. Perhaps it will be said, that Shakespear wrote, when learning, taste, and manners were pedantic, unrefined, and illiberal; that none but such motley pieces, as his are, could please the greater part of his audience, the illiterate, low-liv'd mechanics; that some of his characters were necessitated to speak their language; and that their bursts of applause were to be purchased even at the expence of decency and common sense. When we consider his situation and circumstances, that in lieu of the

hospita musis
Otia, et exemtum curis gravioribus ævum.
(Sil. Ital. lib. 12.)

he was exposed to all the miseries of poverty and want; that to live he was constrained to write, and to adapt himself to the humour of others; it must be acknowledged, that he deserves our pity rather than our censure. But when we come to consider him as a tragic writer, and to weigh his merit as such, a standard must be established, by which our judgments are to be determined: where then are we to look for this nice criterion of merit, but in those works, that have been the delight of past ages, and are the admiration of the present.

Let it not be advanced as a merit, let it not be urged even as an excuse, that Shakespear followed nature in the busy walks of men; that he presented her, as he found her, naked and unadorned: for there are parts of nature that require concealment; there are others too that by the thin transparent veil, by the light, the careless drapery, are greatly heightened and improved; for then the roving fancy,

Ivi si spazia, ivi contempla il vero
Di tante miraviglie a parte a parte,
Poscia al desio le narra, e le descrive,
E ne fa le sue fiamme in lui più vive.
(*Gierus. lib.* canto 4.)

The scene of the grave-diggers in *Hamlet* is certainly real life, or as it is vulgarly termed, highly natural; yet how misplaced, how unworthy the tragedian:

Nec spirat tragicum satis, aut feliciter audet.
(Hor.)

To the credit of the present times indeed these puerilities are now omitted; let us hope they will not be the only ones, nor let us be afraid to reject what our ancestors, in conformity to the grosser notions then prevalent, beheld with pleasure and applause.

It is not long ago that even a comedy, which had a considerable share of merit, met with an unfavourable reception, on account of a low illiberal dialogue; though it was perfectly adapted to the persons between whom it passed. Nor has there, I believe, been found more than one haughty overgrown critic, who has dared to censure the public for expressing their disapprobation of language, that became a spunging-house indeed, but was highly improper for the stage; which even the comic muse, sportive and mirthful though she be, is not permitted to tread, but with a certain easy politeness, a certain graceful decorum.

It must be acknowledged, that Shakespear abounds in the true sublime; but it must be allowed that he abounds likewise in the low and vulgar. And who is there, that after soaring on eagle wings to unknown regions and empyreal heights, is not most sensibly mortified to be compelled the next moment to grovel in dirt and ordure. In the first case (and if he mounts with Shakespear it will frequently happen) he may chance to be dazzled with the excessive glare, even till his "eye-balls crack;" certain it is, that a person may gaze on the blazing majesty of the sun, that glorious author of light and vital warmth, when properly regarded, untill his sight shall be obscured, and himself vainly endeavour to explore his way through the intricate maze of darkness and confusion; a labyrinth in which our author is sometimes bewildered, and from which it will require an Ariadne's clue to rescue him. What a contrast there is between the sublime and the bathos! yet how closely are they united in Shakespear! Fired with the exalted sentiments of his heroes, from whose mouths virtue herself seems to dictate to mankind, we feel our hearts dilate, the current of our blood flow swifter in every vein, and our whole frame wound up to a pitch of dignity unfelt, unknown before. Although we could not expect that our enthusiasm should remain in its full energy and force, yet of itself it would subside by degrees into a benign complacency and universal philanthropy. How cruel is it then to hurry us from heroes and philosophers into a crew of plebeians, grave-diggers, and buffoons; from the bold tropes and figures of nervous and manly eloquence, from the sage lessons of morality, such as a Minerva might have inspired, or a Socrates have taught, to the obscure jest or low quibble, that base counterfeit of wit, which, like the monkey when compared with man, is rendered more disgusting by an unsightly resemblance.

Shakespear's preternatural beings seem to need little or no justification; they are such as were sanctified by tradition and vulgar credulity; he has supported them with dignity and solemnity, has made them greatly instrumental in the catastrophe of his pieces, and has in general introduced them on proper occasions: I say in general only, because in some

instances they are unnecessary, and therefore to be condemned. On the contrary the ghost in *Hamlet* is neither useless, nor introduced improperly; it comes to reveal unknown, unexpiated crimes; here is the dignus vindice nodus. But it would be fruitless to say any thing more on this point, as it has been already treated in such a masterly manner by the very ingenious author of the remarks on the writings and genius of Shakespear, to whose merit I am not the less insensible, though on many occasions I may be led to differ in opinion.

The morals of Shakespear's plays are in general extremely natural and just: yet why must innocence unnecessarily suffer? why must the hoary, the venerable Lear, be brought with sorrow to the grave? Why must Cordelia perish by an untimely fate? the amiable, the dutiful, the innocent Cordelia! She that had already felt the heart-rending anger of a much beloved, but hasty mistaken father! She that could receive, protect, and cherish a poor, infirm, weak, and despised old man, although he had showered down curses on her undeserving head! That such a melancholy catastrophe was by no means necessary, is sufficiently evinced by the manner in which the same play is now performed ⟨in the adaptation of Nahum Tate⟩. Ingratitude now meets with its proper punishment, and the audience now retire, exulting in the mutual happiness of paternal affection, and filial piety. Such, if practicable, should be the winding up of all dramatic representations, that mankind may have the most persuasive allurements to all good actions: for although virtue depressed may be amiable, virtue triumphant must be irresistable.

But it may perhaps be objected by some, that the death of the wicked cannot occasion pity; and if innocence and virtue are not to fall beneath the stroke of oppression and injustice, where is the pathos, where is the tender sympathy? To this it may be answered, in the unmerited misfortunes, in the agonizing distress of the innocent; in seeing the virtuous involuntarily led to the perpetration of some horrid crime, or in the dread apprehension of having already committed it, or tottering on the very brink of perdition. What a critical, what an interesting situation is it to the spectator, when he beholds Merope, seemingly reduced to the dreadful alternative of seeing her son perish, or of giving herself to the murderer of her husband? Again, what horror do we feel, when we see her with her arm uplifted upon the point of killing that very son, whose death she means to revenge! It is not my design to condemn those tragedies, in which innocence falls a victim to treachery or violence; we see but too many instances of it in real life; consequently it cannot be improper for the stage, which ought to represent living manners. I would be understood therefore not to reject other tragedies, but to give the preference to those, in which death, punishment, or remorse, await the guilty only. And as at all dramatic representations I am to see but an imitation of nature, let the delusion be on the side of virtue, that I may still flatter myself with the pleasing belief, that to be good is to be happy.

From contemplating the works of Shakespear, let us for a moment turn our eyes to those of Tintoret. What an enthusiasm of genius, what a boldness and impetuosity of pencil! What an hardiness of colouring, what an intelligence of light! Yet how neglectful in finishing, his attitudes how ungraceful, how extravagantly contrasted! Where shall we find in him that beautiful chasteness, that enchanting harmony of the whole, so conspicuous in the works of several other eminent artists? With such imperfections who will venture to place him on a level with his master Titian, with Raphael, Guido, or many others of the Italian schools? The resemblance between the painter and the poet is striking. In our English bard, what a glow of fancy, what a rapidity of imagination, what a sublimity in diction, what strength, what a distinction of characters, what a knowledge of the human heart! Yet how inattentive to propriety and order, how deficient in grouping, how fond of exposing disgusting as well as beautiful figures! Were we to see a statue, the several component parts of which, when detached and considered separately, would be highly just in themselves, and pleasing to the eye, yet from a want of due correctness, symmetry, and proportion to each other, the whole figure should be not only awkward and disgusting, but even unnatural and monstrous, we should not hesitate to pronounce the sculptor,

> Infelix operis summâ quia ponere totum nesciit.
> (Horat. *de Arte Poet.*)

Like such a statue are the tragedies of our author; their parts beautiful, their whole inconsistent.

And is then poor Shakespear to be excluded from the number of good tragedians? He is; but let him be banished, like Homer, from the republic of Plato, with marks of distinction and veneration; and may his forehead, like the Grecian bards, be bound with an honourable wreath of ever-blooming flowers.

## RICHARD CUMBERLAND
### From *The Observer*
#### 1786
#### No. 69

Nil intentatum nostri liquere poetæ:
Nec minimum meruere decus, vestigia Græca
Ausi deserere, et celebrare domestica facta.
(Hor. *Ars Poet.* 285.)

There are two very striking characters delineated by our great dramatic poet, which I am desirous of bringing together under one review, and these are *Macbeth* and *Richard the Third.*

The parts which these two persons sustain in their respective dramas, have a remarkable coincidence: both are actuated by the same guilty ambition in the opening of the story: both murder their lawful sovereign in the course of it: and both are defeated and slain in battle at the conclusion of it: yet these two characters, under circumstances so similar, are as strongly distinguished in every passage of their dramatic life by the art of the poet, as any two men ever were by the hand of nature.

Let us contemplate them in the three following periods; viz. The premeditation of their crime; the perpetration of it; and the catastrophe of their death.

Duncan, the reigning king of Scotland, has two sons: Edward the Fourth of England has also two sons; but these kings and their respective heirs do not affect the usurpers Macbeth and Richard in the same degree, for the latter is a prince of the blood royal, brother to the king, and next in consanguinity to the throne after the death of his elder brother the Duke of Clarence: Macbeth, on the contrary, is not in the succession—

> And to be king
> Stands not within the prospect of belief.

His views therefore being farther removed and more out of hope, a greater weight of circumstances should be thrown together to tempt and encourage him to an undertaking so much beyond *the prospect of his belief.* The art of the poet furnishes these circumstances, and the engine which his invention employs, is of a preternatural and prodigious sort. He introduces in the very opening of his scene a troop of sibyls or witches, who salute Macbeth with their divinations, and in three solemn prophetic gratulations hail him Thane of Glamis, Thane of Cawdor, and King hereafter!

> By Sinel's death I know I'm Thane of Glamis;
> But how of Cawdor?

One part of the prophecy therefore is true; the remaining promises become more deserving of belief. This is one step in the ladder of his ambition, and mark how artfully the poet has laid it in his way; no time is lost; the wonderful machinery is not suffered to stand still, for behold a verification of the second prediction, and a courtier thus addresses him from the king—

> And for an earnest of a greater honour,
> He bade me from him call thee Thane of Cawdor.

The magic now works to his heart, and he cannot wait the departure of the royal messenger before his admiration vents itself aside—

> Glamis, and Thane of Cawdor!
> The greatest is behind.

A second time he turns aside, and unable to repress the emotions, which this second confirmation of the predictions has excited, repeats the same secret observation—

> Two truths are told
> As happy prologues to the swelling act
> Of the imperial theme.

A soliloquy then ensues, in which the poet judiciously opens enough of his character to shew the spectator that these preternatural agents are not superfluously set to work upon a disposition prone to evil, but one that will have to combat many compunctious struggles, before it can be brought to yield even to oracular influence. This alone would demonstrate (if we needed demonstration) that Shakspeare, without resorting to the ancients, had the judgment of ages as it were instinctively. From this instant we are apprised that Macbeth meditates an attack upon our pity as well as upon our horror, when he puts the following question to his conscience—

> Why do I yield to that suggestion,
> Whose horrid image doth unfix my hair,
> And make my seated heart knock at my ribs
> Against the use of nature?

Now let us turn to Richard, in whose cruel heart no such remorse finds place: he needs no tempter: there is here no *dignus vindice nodus*, nor indeed any *knot* at all, for he is already practised in murder; ambition is his ruling passion, and a crown is in view, and he tells you at his very first entrance on the scene—

> I am determined to be a villain.

We are now presented with a character full formed and complete for all the savage purposes of the drama.

> Impiger, iracundus, inexorabilis acer.
> (Hor. *Ars Poet.* 121.)

The barriers of conscience are broken down, and the soul, hardened against shame, avows its own depravity—

> Plots have I laid, inductions dangerous,
> To set my brother Clarence and the king
> In deadly hate the one against the other.

He observes no gradations in guilt, expresses no hesitation, practises no refinements, but plunges into blood with the familiarity of long custom, and gives orders to his assassins to dispatch his brother Clarence with all the unfeeling tranquillity of a Nero or Caligula. Richard, having no longer any scruples to manage with his own conscience, is exactly in the predicament, which the dramatic poet Diphilus has described with such beautiful simplicity of expression—

The wretch who knows his own vile deeds, and yet
fears not himself, how should he fear another, who
knows them not.

It is manifest therefore that there is an essential difference
in the developement of these characters, and that in favour of
Macbeth: in his soul cruelty seems to dawn; it breaks out with
faint glimmerings, like a winter morning, and gathers strength
by slow degrees: in Richard it flames forth at once, mounting
like the sun between the tropics, and enters boldly on its career
without a herald. As the character of Macbeth has a moral
advantage in this distinction, so has the drama of that name a
much more interesting and affecting cast: the struggles of a
soul, naturally virtuous, whilst it holds the guilty impulse of
ambition at bay, affords the noblest theme for the drama, and
puts the creative fancy of our poet upon a resource, in which
he has been rivalled only by the great father of tragedy
Æschylus in the prophetic effusions of Cassandra, the incantations of the Persian Magi for raising the ghost of Darius, and
the imaginary terrific forms of his furies; with all which our
countryman probably had no acquaintance, or at most a very
obscure one.

When I see the names of these two great luminaries of the
dramatic sphere, so distant in time but so nearly allied in
genius, casually brought in contact by the nature of my
subject, I cannot help pausing for awhile in this place to
indulge so interesting a contemplation, in which I find my
mind balanced between two objects, that seem to have equal
claims upon me for my admiration. Æschylus is justly styled
the father of tragedy, but this is not to be interpreted as if he was
the inventor of it: Shakspeare with equal justice claims the
same title, and his originality is qualified with the same
exception: the Greek tragedy was not more rude and undigested
when Æschylus brought it into shape, than the English tragedy
was when Shakspeare began to write: if therefore it be granted
that he had no aids from the Greek theatre (and I think this is
not likely to be disputed), so far these great masters are upon
equal ground. Æschylus was a warrior of high repute, of a lofty
generous spirit, and deep, as it should seem, in the erudition of
his times: in all these particulars he has great advantage over
our countryman, who was humbly born, of the most menial
occupation, and, as it is generally thought, unlearned.
Æschylus had the whole epic of Homer in his hands, the *Iliad*,
*Odyssey*, and that prolific source of dramatic fable, the *Ilias
Minor*; he had also a great fabulous creation to resort to
amongst his own divinities, characters ready defined, and an
audience, whose superstition was prepared for every thing he
could offer; he had therefore a firmer and broader stage (if I
may be allowed the expression) under his feet, than Shakspeare
had: his fables in general are Homeric, and yet it does not
follow that we can pronounce for Shakspeare that he is more
original in his plots, for I understand that late researches have
traced him in all or nearly all: both poets added so much
machinery and invention of their own in the conduct of their
fables, that whatever might have been the source, still their
streams had little or no taste of the spring they flowed from. In
point of character we have better grounds to decide, and yet it is
but justice to observe, that it is not fair to bring a mangled poet
in comparison with one who is entire; in his divine personages,
Æschylus has the field of heaven, and indeed of hell also, to
himself; in his heroic and military characters he has never been
excelled; he had too good a model within his own bosom to fail
of making those delineations natural: in his imaginary beings
also he will be found a respectable, though not an equal rival of
our poet; but in the variety of character, in all the nicer touches
of nature, in all the extravagances of caprice and humour, from
the boldest feature down to the minutest foible, Shakspeare

stands alone: such persons as he delineates never came into the
contemplation of Æschylus as a poet; his tragedy has no
dealing with them; the simplicity of the Greek fable, and the
great portion of the drama filled up by the chorus, allow of little
variety of character; and the most which can be said of
Æschylus in this particular is, that he never offends against
nature or propriety, whether his cast is in the terrible or
pathetic, the elevated or the simple. His versification, with the
intermixture of lyric composition, is more various than that of
Shakspeare; both are lofty and sublime in the extreme,
abundantly metaphorical, and sometimes extravagant:—
    ——Nubes et inania captat.
This may be said of each poet in his turn; in each the critic, if
he is in search for defects, will readily enough discover—
    In scenam missus magno cum pondere versus.
        (Hor. *Ars Poet.* 260.)
Both were subject to be hurried on by an uncontrollable
impulse, nor could nature alone suffice for either: Æschylus
had an apt creation of imaginary beings at command—
    He could call spirits from the vasty deep,
And they *would come*—Shakspeare, having no such creation in
resource, boldly made one of his own; if Æschylus therefore
was invincible, he owed it to his armour, and that, like the
armour of Æneas, was the work of the gods: but the unassisted
invention of Shakspeare seized all and more than superstition
supplied to Æschylus.

*No. 70*

Ille profecto
Reddere personæ scit convenientia cuique.
        (Hor. *Ars Poet.* 316.)

We are now to attend Macbeth to the perpetration of the
murder, which puts him in possession of the crown of
Scotland; and this introduces a new personage on the scene, his
accomplice and wife: she thus developes her own character—

    Come, all you spirits,
That tend on mortal thoughts, unsex me here,
And fill me from the crown to the toe topful
Of direst cruelty; make thick my blood,
Stop up the access and passage to remorse,
That no compunctious visitings of nature
Shake my fell purpose, nor keep peace between
Th' effect and it. Come to my woman's breasts,
And take my milk for gall, you murth'ring ministers,
Wherever in your sightless substances
You wait on nature's mischief: come, thick night,
And pall thee in the dunnest smoke of hell!

Terrible invocation! Tragedy can speak no stronger language,
nor could any genius less than Shakspeare's support a character
of so lofty a pitch, so sublimely terrible at the very opening.

The part which Lady Macbeth fills in the drama has a
relative as well as positive importance, and serves to place the
repugnance of Macbeth in the strongest point of view; she is in
fact the auxiliary of the witches, and the natural influence,
which so high and predominant a spirit asserts over the tamer
qualities of her husband, makes those witches but secondary
agents for bringing about the main action of the drama. This is
well worth a remark; for if they, which are only artificial and
fantastic instruments, had been made the sole or even principal
movers of the great incident of the murder, Nature would have
been excluded from her share in the drama, and Macbeth
would have become the mere machine of an uncontrollable
necessity, and his character, being robbed of its free agency,
would have left no moral behind: I must take leave therefore to
anticipate a remark, which I shall hereafter repeat, that when
Lady Macbeth is urging her Lord to the murder, not a word is

dropt by either of the witches or their predictions. It is in these instances of his conduct that Shakspeare is so wonderful a study for the dramatic poet. But I proceed—

Lady Macbeth in her first scene, from which I have already extracted a passage, prepares for an attempt upon the conscience of her husband, whose nature she thus describes—

> Yet do I fear thy nature;
> It is too full o'th' milk of human kindness
> To catch the nearest way.

He arrives before she quits the scene, and she receives him with consummate address—

> Great Glamis! worthy Cawdor!
> Greater than both by the All-hail hereafter!

These are the very gratulations of the witches; she welcomes him with confirmed predictions, with the tempting salutations of ambition, not with the softening caresses of a wife—

> *Macb.*: Duncan comes here to-night.
> *Lady*: And when goes hence?
> *Macb.*: To-morrow, as he purposes.
> *Lady*: Oh never
> Shall sun that morrow see!

The rapidity of her passion hurries her into immediate explanation, and he, consistently with the character she had described, evades her precipitate solicitations with a short indecisive answer—

> We will speak further—

His reflections upon this interview, and the dreadful subject of it, are soon after given in soliloquy, in which the poet has mixed the most touching strokes of compunction with his meditations: he reasons against the villany of the act, and honour jointly with nature assails him with an argument of double force—

> He's here in double trust;
> First as I am his kinsman and his subject,
> Strong both against the deed; then as his host,
> Who should against the murtherer shut the door,
> Not bear the knife himself.

This appeal to nature, hospitality, and allegiance, was not without its impression; he again meets his lady, and immediately declares—

> We will proceed no further in this business.

This draws a retort upon him, in which his tergiversation and cowardice are satirized with so keen an edge, and interrogatory reproaches are passed so fast upon him, that, catching hold in his retreat of one small but precious fragment in the wreck of innocence and honour, he demands a truce from her attack, and, with the spirit of a combatant who has not yet yielded up his weapons, cries out—

> Pr'thee, peace;

The words are no expletives; they do not fill up a sentence, but they form one: they stand in a most important pass: they defend the breach her ambition has made in his heart; a breach in the very citadel of humanity; they mark the last dignified struggle of virtue, and they have a double reflecting power, which, in the first place, shews that nothing but the voice of authority could stem the torrent of her invective, and in the next place announces that something, worthy of the solemn audience he had demanded, was on the point to follow—and worthy it is to be a standard sentiment of moral truth expressed with proverbial simplicity, sinking into every heart that hears it—

> I dare do all that may become a man,
> Who dares do more is none.

How must every feeling spectator lament that a man should fall from virtue with such an appeal upon his lips!

"A man is not a coward because he fears to be unjust," is the sentiment of an old dramatic poet ⟨Philonides⟩.

Macbeth's principle is honour; cruelty is natural to his wife; ambition is common to both; one passion favourable to her purpose has taken place in his heart: another still hangs about it, which being adverse to her plot, is first to be expelled, before she can instil her cruelty into his nature. The sentiment above quoted had been firmly delivered, and was ushered in with an apostrophe suitable to its importance; she feels its weight; she perceives it is not to be turned aside with contempt, or laughed down by ridicule, as she had already done where weaker scruples had stood in the way: but, taking sophistry in aid, by a ready turn of argument she gives him credit for his sentiment, erects a more glittering though fallacious logic upon it, and by admitting his objection cunningly confutes it—

> What beast was't then
> That made you break this enterprise to me?
> When you durst do it, then you were a man,
> And to be more than what you were, you wou'd
> Be so much more than man.

Having thus parried his objection by a sophistry calculated to blind his reason and inflame his ambition, she breaks forth into such a vaunting display of hardened intrepidity, as presents one of the most terrific pictures that was ever imagined—

> I have given suck, and know
> How tender 'tis to love the babe that milks me;
> I wou'd, whilst it was smiling in my face,
> Have pluckt my nipple from its boneless gums,
> And dasht its brains out, had I but so sworn
> As you have done to this.

This is a note of horror, screwed to a pitch that bursts the very sinews of nature; she no longer combats with a human weapon, but seizing the flash of the lightning extinguishes her opponent with the stroke: here the controversy must end, for he must either adopt her spirit, or take her life; he sinks under the attack, and offering nothing in delay of execution but a feeble hesitation, founded in fear—"If we should fail"—he concludes with an assumed ferocity, caught from her and not springing from himself—

> I am settled, and bend up
> Each corporal agent to this terrible feat.

The strong and sublime strokes of a master impressed upon this scene make it a model of dramatic composition, and I must in this place remind the reader of the observation I have before hinted at, that no reference whatever is had to the auguries of the witches: it would be injustice to suppose that this was other than a purposed omission by the poet; a weaker genius would have resorted back to these instruments: Shakspeare had used and laid them aside for a time; he had a stronger engine at work, and he could proudly exclaim—

> We defy auguries!——

Nature was sufficient for that work, and to shew the mastery he had over nature, he took his human agent from the weaker sex.

This having passed in the first act, the murder is perpetrated in the succeeding one. The introductory soliloquy of Macbeth, the chimera of the dagger, and the signal on the bell, are awful preludes to the deed. In this dreadful interim, Lady Macbeth, the great superintending spirit, enters to support the dreadful work. It is done: and he returns appalled with sounds; he surveys his bloody hands with horror; he starts from her proposal of going back to besmear the guards of

Duncan's chamber, and she snatches the reeking daggers from his trembling hands to finish the imperfect work—

> Infirm of purpose,
> Give me the daggers!

She returns on the scene, the deed which he revolted from is performed, and with the same unshaken ferocity she vauntingly displays her bloody trophies, and exclaims—

> My hands are of your colour, but I shame
> To wear a heart so white.

Fancied noises, the throbbings of his own quailing heart, had shaken the constancy of Macbeth; real sounds, the certain signals of approaching visiters, to whom the situation of Duncan must be revealed, do not intimidate her; she is prepared for all trials, and cooly tells him—

> I hear a knocking
> At the south entry: Retire we to our chamber;
> A little water clears us of this deed.
> How easy is it then!

The several incidents thrown together in this scene of the murder of Duncan, are of so striking a sort as to need no elucidation: they are better felt than described, and my attempts point at passages of more obscurity, where the touches are thrown into shade, and the art of the author lies more out of sight.

Lady Macbeth being now retired from the scene, we may in this interval, as we did in the conclusion of the former paper, permit the genius of Æschylus to introduce a rival murderess on the stage.

Clytemnestra has received her husband Agamemnon, on his return from the capture of Troy, with studied rather than cordial congratulations. He opposes the pompous ceremonies she had devised for the display of his entry, with a magnanimous contempt of such adulation—

> Sooth me not with strains
> Of adulation, as a girl; nor raise
> As to some proud barbaric king, that loves
> Loud acclamations echoed from the mouths
> Of prostrate worshippers, a clamorous welcome:
> Spread not the streets with tapestry; 'tis invidious:
> These are the honours we should pay the gods;
> For mortal men to tread on ornaments
> Of rich embroidery—no; I dare not do it:
> Respect me as a man, not as a god.
> (Potter's *Æschylus.*)

These are heroic sentiments, but in conclusion the persuasions of the wife overcome the modest scruples of the hero, and he enters his palace in the pomp of triumph; when soon his dying groans are echoed from the interior scene, and the adultress comes forth besprinkled with the blood of her husband to avow the murder—

> I struck him twice, and twice
> He groan'd; then died: a third time as he lay
> I gor'd him with a wound; a grateful present
> To the stern god, that in the realms below
> Reigns o'er the dead: there let him take his seat.
> He lay: and spouting from his wounds a stream
> Of blood, bedew'd me with these crimson drops.
> I glory in them, like the genial earth,
> When the warm showers of heav'n descend, and wake
> The flowrets to unfold their vermeil leaves.
> Come then, ye reverend senators of Argos,
> Joy with me, if your hearts be turn'd to joy,
> And such I wish them.
> (Potter.)

*No. 71*

> Ille per extentum funem mihi posse videtur
> Ire poeta, meum qui pectus inaniter angit,
> Irritat, mulcet, falsis terroribus implet,
> Ut magus; et modò me Thebis, modò ponit Athenis.
> (Hor. *Epl.* 2, 210.)

Richard perpetrates several murders, but as the poet has not marked them with any distinguishing circumstances, they need not be enumerated on this occasion. Some of these he commits in his passage to power, others after he has seated himself on the throne. Ferociousness and hypocrisy are the prevailing features of his character, and as he has no one honourable or humane principle to combat, there is no opening for the poet to develope those secret workings of conscience, which he has so naturally done in the case of Macbeth.

The murder of Clarence, those of the queen's kinsmen, and of the young princes in the Tower, are all perpetrated in the same style of hardened cruelty. He takes the ordinary method of hiring ruffians to perform his bloody commissions, and there is nothing which particularly marks the scenes, wherein he imparts his purposes and instructions to them; a very little management serves even for Tirrel, who is not a professional murderer, but is reported to be—

> a discontented gentleman,
> Whose humble means match not his haughty spirit:

With such a spirit Richard does not hold it necessary to use much circumlocution, and seems more in dread of delay than disappointment or discovery—

> R: Is thy name Tirrel?
> T: James Tirrel, and your most obedient subject.
> R: Art thou indeed?
> T: Prove me, my gracious lord.
> R: Dar'st thou resolve to kill a friend of mine?
> T: Please you, I had rather kill two enemies.
> R: Why then thou hast it; two deep enemies,
> Foes to my rest and my sweet sleep's disturbers,
> Are they that I would have thee deal upon:
> Tirrel, I mean those bastards in the Tower.

If the reader calls to mind by what circumspect and slow degrees King John opens himself to Hubert under a similar situation with this of Richard, he will be convinced that Shakspeare considered preservation of character too important to sacrifice on any occasion to the vanity of fine writing; for the scene he has given to John, a timorous and wary prince, would ill suit the character of Richard. A close observance of nature is the first excellence of a dramatic poet, and the peculiar property of him we are reviewing.

In these two stages of our comparison, Macbeth appears with far more dramatic effect than Richard, whose first scenes present us with little else than traits of perfidiousness, one striking incident of successful hypocrisy practised on the Lady Anne, and an open unreserved display of remorseless cruelty. Impatient of any pause or interruption in his measures, a dangerous friend and a determined foe:—

> Effera torquebant avidæ præcordia curæ,
> Effugeret ne quis gladios;
> Crescebat scelerata sitis; prædæque recentis
> Incestus flagrabat amor, nullusque petendi
> Cogendive pudor: crebris perjuria nectit
> Blanditiis; sociat perituro fœdere dextras:
> Si semel et antis poscenti quisque negâsset,
> Effera prætumido quatiebat corda furore.
> (Claudian. *In Ruf.* lib. 1.)

The sole remorse his greedy heart can feel
Is if one life escapes his murdering steel;
That, which should quench, inflames his craving
    thirst,
The second draught still deepens on the first;
Shameless by force or fraud to work his way,
And no less prompt to flatter than betray:
This hour makes friendships which he breaks the
    next,
And every breach supplies a vile pretext
Basely to cancel all concessions past,
If in a thousand you deny the last.

Macbeth has now touched the goal of his ambition—

Thou hast it now; King, Cawdor, Glamis, all
The weird sisters promised—

The auguries of the witches, to which no reference had been made in the heat of the main action, are now called to mind with many circumstances of galling aggravation, not only as to the prophecy, which gave the crown to the posterity of Banquo, but also of his own safety from the gallant and noble nature of that general—

Our fears in Banquo
Stick deep, and in his royalty of nature
Reigns that which would be fear'd.

Assassins are provided to murder Banquo and his son, but this is not decided upon without much previous meditation, and he seems prompted to the act more by desperation and dread, than by any settled resolution or natural cruelty. He convenes the assassins, and in a conference of some length works round to his point, by insinuations calculated to persuade them to dispatch Banquo for injuries done to them, rather than from motives which respect himself; in which scene we discover a remarkable preservation of character in Macbeth, who by this artifice strives to blind his own conscience and throw the guilt upon theirs: in this, as in the former action, there is nothing kingly in his cruelty; in one he acted under the controlling spirit of his wife, here he plays the sycophant with hired assassins, and confesses himself under awe of the superior genius of Banquo—

Under him
My genius is rebuk'd, as it is said
Antony's was by Cæsar.

There is not a circumstance ever so minute in the conduct of this character, which does not point out to a diligent observer, how closely the poet has adhered to nature in every part of his delineation; accordingly we observe a peculiarity in the language of Macbeth, which is highly characteristic; I mean the figurative turn of his expressions, whenever his imagination strikes upon any gloomy subject—

Oh! full of scorpions is my mind, dear wife!

And in this state of self-torment every object of solemnity, though ever so familiar, becomes an object of terror! night, for instance, is not mentioned by him without an accompaniment of every melancholy attribute which a frighted fancy can annex—

Ere the bat hath flown
His cloister'd flight, ere to black Hecate's summons
The shard-born beetle with his drowsy hums
Hath rung *Night's* yawning peal, there shall be done
A deed of dreadful note.

It is the darkness of his soul that makes the night so dreadful, the *scorpions in his mind* convoke these images—but he has not yet done with it—

Come, sealing *Night!*
Scarf up the tender eye of pitiful day;
And with thy bloody and invisible hand
Cancel and tear to pieces that great bond,
Which keeps me pale. Light thickens, and the crow
Makes wing to the rooky wood.
Good things of day begin to droop and drowse,
Whilst *night's* black agents to their prey do rouse.

The critic of language will observe that here is a redundancy and crowd of metaphors, but the critic of nature will acknowledge that it is the very truth of character, and join me in the remark which points it out.

In a tragedy so replete with murder, and in the display of a character so tortured by the *scorpions of the mind*, as this of Macbeth, it is naturally to be expected that a genius like Shakspeare's will call in the dead for their share in the horror of the scene. This he has done in two several ways; first, by the apparition of Banquo, which is invisible to all but Macbeth; secondly, by the spells and incantations of the witches, who raise spirits, which in certain enigmatical predictions shadow out his fate; and these are followed by a train of unborn revelations, drawn by the power of magic from the womb of futurity before their time.

It appears that Lady Macbeth was not a party in the assassination of Banquo, and the ghost, though twice visible to the murderer, is not seen by her. This is another incident highly worthy a particular remark; for by keeping her free from any participation in the horror of the sight, the poet is enabled to make a scene aside, between Macbeth and her, which contains some of the finest speakings in the play. The ghost in *Hamlet*, and the ghost of Darius in Æschylus, are introduced by preparation and prelude; this of Banquo is an object of surprise as well as terror, and there is scarce an incident to be named of more striking and dramatic effect: it is one amongst various proofs, that must convince every man who looks critically into Shakspeare, that he was as great a master in art as in nature: how it strikes me in this point of view, I shall take the liberty of explaining more at length.

The murder of Duncan is the main incident of this tragedy; that of Banquo is subordinate: Duncan's blood was not only the first so shed by Macbeth, but the dignity of the person murdered, and the aggravating circumstances attending it, constitute a crime of the very first magnitude: for these reasons it might be expected, that the spectre most likely to haunt his imagination, would be that of Duncan; and the rather because his terror and compunction were so much more strongly excited by this first murder, perpetrated with his own hands, than by the subsequent one of Banquo, palliated by evasion, and committed to others. But when we recollect that Lady Macbeth was not only his accomplice, but in fact the first mover in the murder of the king, we see good reason why Duncan's ghost could not be called up, unless she who so deeply partook of the guilt, had also shared in the horror of the appearance; and as visitations of a peculiar sort were reserved for her in a later period of the drama, it was a point of consummate art and judgment to exclude her from the affair of Banquo's murder, and make the more susceptible conscience of Macbeth figure this apparition in his mind's eye, without any other witness to the vision.

I persuade myself these will appear very natural reasons why the poet did not raise the ghost of the king in preference, though it is reasonable to think it would have been a much more noble incident in his hands, than this of Banquo. It now remains to examine, whether this is more fully justified by the peculiar situation reserved for Lady Macbeth, to which I have before adverted.

The intrepidity of her character is so marked, that we may

well suppose no waking terrors could shake it, and in this light it must be acknowledged a very natural expedient to make her vent the agonies of her conscience in sleep. Dreams have been a dramatic expedient ever since there has been a drama; Æschylus recites the dream of Clytemnestra immediately before her son Orestes kills her; she fancies she has given birth to a dragon—

> This new-born dragon like an infant child,
> Laid in the cradle seem'd in want of food;
> And in her dream she held it to her breast:
> The milk he drew was mixed with clotted blood.
>                                    (Potter.)

This which is done by Æschylus, has been done by hundreds after him; but to introduce upon the scene the very person, walking in sleep, and giving vent to the horrid fancies that haunt her dream, in broken speeches expressive of her guilt, uttered before witnesses, and accompanied with that natural and expressive action of washing the blood from her defiled hands, was reserved for the original and bold genius of Shakspeare only. It is an incident so full of tragic horror, so daring, and at the same time so truly characteristic, that it stands out as a prominent feature in the most sublime drama in the world, and fully compensates for any sacrifices the poet might have made in the previous arrangement of his incidents.

### No. 72

Servetur ad imum
Qualis ab incepto processerit, et sibi constet.
                    (Hor. *Ars Poet.* 126.)

Macbeth now approaches towards the catastrophe; the heir of the crown is in arms, and he must defend valiantly what he has usurped villanously. His natural valour does not suffice for this trial; he resorts to the witches; he conjures them to give answer to what he shall ask, and he again runs into all those pleonasms of speech which I before remarked: the predictions he extorts from the apparitions are so couched as to seem favourable to him, at the same time that they correspond with events, which afterward prove fatal. The management of this incident has so close a resemblance to what the poet Claudian has done in the instance of Rufinus's vision, the night before his massacre, that I am tempted to insert the passage—

> Ecce videt diras alludere protinùs umbras,
> Quas dedit ipse neci; quarum quæ clarior una
> Visa loqui—Proh! surge toro; quid plurima volvis
> Anxius? hæc requiem rebus, finemque labori
> Allatura dies: Omni jam plebe redibis
> Altior, et læti manibus portabere vulgi—
> Has canit ambages. Occulto fallitur ille
> Omine, nec capitis fixi præsagia sentit.
>                     (Claud. *In Ruf.* 2, 328.)

> A ghastly vision in the dead of night,
> Of mangled, murder'd ghosts appal his sight;
> When hark! a voice from forth the shadowy train
> Cries out—Awake! what thoughts perplex thy brain?
> Awake, arise! behold the day appears,
> That ends thy labours, and dispels thy fears;
> To loftier heights thy towering head shall rise,
> And the glad crowd shall lift thee to the skies—
> Thus spake the voice: he triumphs, nor beneath
> Th' ambiguous omen sees the doom of death.

Confiding in his auguries, Macbeth now prepares for battle: by the first of these he is assured—

>                     That none of woman-born
>         Shall harm Macbeth.

By the second prediction he is told—

> Macbeth shall never vanquished be until
> Great Birnam-wood to Dunsinane's high hill
> Shall come against him.

These he calls *sweet boadments!* and concludes—

>             To sleep in spite of thunder.

This play is so replete with excellences, that it would exceed all bounds, if I were to notice every one: I pass over therefore that incomparable scene between Macbeth, the Physician, and Seyton, in which the agitations of his mind are so wonderfully expressed, and, without pausing for the death of Lady Macbeth, I conduct the reader to that crisis, when the messenger has announced the ominous approach of Birnam-wood—A burst of fury, an exclamation seconded by a blow, is the first natural explosion of a soul so stung with *scorpions* as Macbeth's: the sudden gust is no sooner discharged, than nature speaks her own language, and the still voice of conscience, like reason in the midst of madness, murmurs forth these mournful words—

> I pall in resolution, and begin
> To doubt the equivocation of the fiend,
> That lies like truth.

With what an exquisite feeling has this darling son of nature here thrown in this touching, this pathetic sentence, amidst the very whirl and eddy of conflicting passions! Here is a study for dramatic poets: this is a string for an actor's skill to touch: this will discourse sweet music to the human heart, with which it is finely unisoned when struck with the hand of a master.

The next step brings us to the last scene of Macbeth's dramatic existence. Flushed with the blood of Siward he is encountered by Macduff, who crosses him like his evil genius—Macbeth cries out—

> Of all men else I have avoided thee.

To the last moment of character the faithful poet supports him; he breaks off from single combat, and in the tremendous pause, so beautifully contrived to hang suspense and terror on the moral scene of his exit, the tyrant driven to bay, and panting with the heat and struggle of the fight, vauntingly exclaims—

> *Macb.*: As easy may'st thou the intrenchant air
>         With thy keen sword impress, as make me bleed:
>         Let fall thy blade on vulnerable crests,
>         I bear a charm'd life, which must not yield
>         To one of woman born.
> *Macd.*:             Despair thy charm!
>         And let the angel, whom thou still hast served,
>         Tell thee Macduff was from his mother's womb
>         Untimely ripp'd.
> *Macb.*: Accursed be that tongue that tells me so!
>         For it hath cowed my better part of man.

There sinks the spirit of Macbeth—

>             Behold! where stands
>     Th' usurper's cursed head!

How completely does this coincide with the passage already quoted!

Occulto fallitur ille
Omine, nec CAPITIS FIXI præsagia sentit.

Let us now approach the tent of Richard. It is matter of admiration to observe how many incidents the poet has collected in a small compass, to set the military character of his chief personage in a brilliant point of view. A succession of scouts and messengers report a variety of intelligence, all which, though generally of the most alarming nature, he meets not only with his natural gallantry, but sometimes with pleasantry, and a certain archness and repartee, which is peculiar to him throughout the drama.

It is not only a curious, but delightful task to examine by what subtle and almost imperceptible touches Shakspeare contrives to set such marks upon his characters, as give them the most living likenesses that can be conceived. In this, above all other poets that ever existed, he is a study and a model of perfection: the great distinguishing passions every poet may describe; but Shakspeare gives you their humours, their minutest foibles, those little starts and caprices, which nothing but the most intimate familiarity brings to light; other authors write characters like historians: he like the bosom friend of the person he describes. The following extracts will furnish an example of what I have been saying.

Ratcliff informs Richard that a fleet is discovered on the western coast, supposed to be the party of Richmond—

> *K. Rich.*: Some light-foot friend post to the Duke of
>     Norfolk;
>     Ratcliff, thyself; or Catesby—Where is he?
> *Cates.*: Here, my good lord.
> *K. Rich.*: Catesby, fly to the Duke.
> *Cates.*: I will, my lord, with all convenient haste.
> *K. Rich.*: Ratcliff, come hither; post to Salisbury;
>     When thou com'st thither—*Dull unmindful*
>     *villain!*
> (To Catesby.
>     Why stay'st thou here, and go'st not to the Duke?
> *Cates.*: First mighty liege, tell me your highness'
>     pleasure,
>     What from your grace I shall deliver to him.
> *K. Rich.*: Oh, true, good Catesby!

I am persuaded I need not point out to the reader's sensibility the fine turn in this expression, *Good Catesby!* How can we be surprised if such a poet makes us in love even with his villains?—Ratcliff proceeds—

> *Rat.*: What may it please you shall I do at Salisbury?
> *K. Rich.*: Why what wou'dst thou do there before I
>     go?
> *Rat.*: Your highness told me I should post before.
> *K. Rich.*: My mind is chang'd.

These fine touches can escape no man, who has an eye for nature. Lord Stanley reports to Richard—

> *Stanl.*: Richmond is on the seas.
> *K. Rich.*: There let him sink, and be the seas on him!
>     White liver'd runagate, what doth he there?

This reply is pointed with irony and invective: there are two causes in nature and character for this; first, Richard was before informed of the news; his passion was not taken by surprise, and he was enough at ease to make a play upon Stanley's words—*on the seas*—and retort *be the seas on him!*—Secondly, Stanley was a suspected subject, Richard was therefore interested to shew a contempt of his competitor, before a man of such doubtful allegiance. In the spirit of this impression he urges Stanley to give an explicit answer to the question—*What doth he there?* Stanley endeavours to evade by answering that he *knows not but by guess*: the evasion only strengthens Richard's suspicions, and he again pushes him to disclose what he only guesses—*Well as you guess*—Stanley replies—

> He makes for England here to claim the crown.
> *K. Rich.*: Is the chair empty? Is the sword unsway'd?
>     Is the king dead? the empire unpossess'd?
>     What heir of York is there alive but we?
>     And who is England's king but great York's heir?
>     Then tell me what makes he upon the sea?

What a cluster of characteristic excellences are here before us! All these interrogatories are *ad hominem*; they fit no man but Stanley, they can be uttered by no man but Richard, and they can flow from the conceptions of no poet but the poet of nature.

Stanley's whole scene ought to be investigated, for it is full of beauties; but I confess myself exhausted with the task, and language does not suffice to furnish fresh terms of admiration, which a closer scrutiny would call forth.

Other messengers succeed Lord Stanley, Richard's fiery impatience does not wait the telling, but taking the outset of the account to be ominous, he strikes the courier, who proceeding with his report, concludes with the good tidings of Buckingham's dispersion—Richard instantly retracts and says—

>     Oh! I cry thee mercy,
> There is my purse to cure that blow of thine.

This is another trait of the same cast with that of *Good Catesby*.

Battles are of the growth of modern tragedy; I am not learned enough in the old stage to know if Shakspeare is the inventor of this bold and bustling innovation; but I am sure he is unrivalled in his execution of it, and this of Bosworth-field is a masterpiece. I shall be less particular in my present description of it, because I may probably bring it under general review with other scenes of the like sort.

It will be sufficient to observe, that in the catastrophe of Richard nothing can be more glowing than the scene, nothing more brilliant than the conduct, of the chief character: he exhibits the character of a perfect general, in whom however ardent courage seems the ruling feature; he performs every part of his office with minute attention, he inquires if certain alterations are made in his armour, and even orders what particular horse he intends to charge with: he is gay with his chief officers, and even gracious to some he confides in: his gallantry is of so dazzling a quality, that we begin to feel the pride of Englishmen, and, overlooking his crimes, glory in our courageous king. Richmond is one of those civil, conscientious gentlemen, who are not very apt to captivate a spectator, and Richard, loaded as he is with enormities, rises in the comparison, and I suspect carries the good wishes of many of his audience into action, and dies with their regret.

As soon as he retires to his tent the poet begins to put in motion his great moral machinery of the ghosts. Trifles are not made for Shakspeare; difficulties, that would have plunged the spirit of any other poet, and turned his scenery into inevitable ridicule, are nothing in his way; he brings forward a long string of ghosts, and puts a speech into each of their mouths without any fear of consequences. Richard starts from his couch, and before he has shaken off the terrors of his dream, cries out—

> Give me another horse!—bind up my wounds!—
> Have mercy, Jesu!—Soft, I did but dream—
> O coward conscience—&c.

But I may conclude my subject; every reader can go on with the soliloquy, and no words of mine can be wanted to excite their admiration.

CHARLES DIBDIN
From "Shakespear"
*A Complete History of the Stage*
1795, Volume 3, pp. 14–28

Great and extraordinary objects naturally attract universal attention; unfortunately, however, human nature is composed of such various and complicate materials, that it is extremely difficult in any case to lift this attention into admiration. The fun that cheers and invigorates us, is a perpetual object of reproach. We feign to sink under those very rays that dispel the mists of contagion, that sweeten the provender for our cattle, that ripen the fruits which pamper our luxury, and that whiten the corn which composes our daily bread. We overlook the beauty, the majesty, the splendor which savages, more faithful to nature, and more ignorant of refinement, make their subject of adoration; which to enjoy cost us nothing but the trouble of opening our eyes, and the admission of a little heart-felt gratitude. All these incomparable advantages, though essentially material to our very existence, we take to ourselves as carelessly and indifferently as any other common benefit of nature, without a remark, without thanks, without emotion, while we rack invention to devise a thousand expensive operations to discover spots which in the scale of the universe are perfectly immaterial; and which, but for this restless and insatiable curiosity, would for ever have been hidden from our observation.

Shakespear whose writings are the offspring of an intuition that mocks description, that shames the schools, and that ascertains sublimity; whose knowledge of human nature was profound, penetrating and infallible; whose morality and philosophy confirm all that was good and wise in the ancients; whose words are in our mouths, and their irresistable influence in our hearts; whose eulogium may be felt but cannot be expressed, and whose own pen alone was equal to the composition of his epitaph: this Shakespear in the mouths of his fellow creatures is more known for a few inconsiderable blemishes, sprung from redundant fancy and indispensible conformity, than for innumerable beauties, delightful as truth, and commanding as inspiration.

Look at the various authors who by way of compliment to their own sagacity have deigned so far to honour biography and literature, as to point out all the blemishes, both as a man and as a writer, of him whose virtue and whose merit were either above their comprehension, or else their tingling envy would not allow them to praise. Do we hear from them a word of his polished manners that made up the delight of the court of Elizabeth; that laughed Euphuism from the circle, and that endeared him to the friends of lord Southampton, and various other patrons? Not a syllable. They just allow that he was a good kind of man, well intentioned, but they never fail, by way of a drawback, to tell you that he was a bungler at wool combing, that he was a notorious deer stealer, and that he turned out a very bad actor.

Have we any author who has had the fair disinterestedness, the noble candour, to indulge himself and gratify the world by any exclusive work that has instanced the various ways in which Shakespear so greatly commanded all the passions of the soul; in which, with a portraiture full of imagination and faithful as nature, he drew ambition, jealousy, tenderness, piety, villainy, rashness, credulity, licentiousness, and a hundred others with all their shades and gradations? Not one. We have, however, a little myriad of critics and hyper-critics who have done his memory the credit to render his works profitable

to themselves, by making holes as fast as tinkers in his reputation which, they fancy and endeavour to persuade the world they have adroitly mended by patching them up with dross of their own. Well did he say that men's perfections are written in sand their faults in marble.

In my province, I do not consider, if I were ever so inclined, that I have a right to examine the private character of any man, farther than as it may have influenced his public conduct; nor even then, unless it should relate to his connection with the drama. If, by deduction, I can shew that the world has been imposed on by a false character given in favour of any man's works through patronage procured by adulation, meanness, and the fawning arts of a sycophant, it is very fair to place the public and private sentiments of that man by the side of each other, and to appeal to the world, be this or any other the description of his mental blemishes, whether, by that criterion, they have purchased gold or been imposed on by tinsel.

If, on the contrary, I can produce any instances where meekness and modesty have been borne down by rancour and envy, it will be my duty to dwell upon the virtues of him who may have had the public misfortune and the private happiness to possess those qualities; nor can I lay a claim to impartiality, the forwardest requisite of a historian, if I neglect in such cases to deduce, from the heart of the man, the merit of the poet.

Shakespear's genius was so brilliant, his knowledge so wide and universal, his conception so true, and his sentiments so godlike, that to meditate his character is to suppose perfection. Yes, say the cavillers, but his writings are full of faults; and how, as a private man, will he be able to stand or fall upon a comparison with them. Thus quaintness, in complaisance to the time at which he wrote, temporary satire then, perhaps, excellent, now obsolete, and other venial inaccuracies, for it is extremely difficult to call them errors, which we ought not to condemn, or, if we ought, do we easily know how, are quoted to deface his monument of marble, and tortured into as many shapes as envy has snakes, to ornament a sandy heap mistaken by the ignorant for the monument of his commentators. . . .

The writings of Shakespear take in so large and so wonderful an extent of compass, that, while we acknowledge that he wrote better, we are obliged to add that he wrote more than any other dramatic writer. One voluminous author writes tragedies for which he is deservedly celebrated, that after all contain only the representations of a few passions placed in different points of view; another, equally voluminous, writes comedies, with the same just right to celebration, in which a few follies and absurdities are properly ridiculed; Shakespear goes infinitely beyond all this. He takes the whole round of the passions, bends them into every form in which they ought deservedly to be exhibited, exposes them to contempt, holds them up to ridicule, commands for them admiration, conciliates pity, excites terror, and in short displays, in his faithful portraiture of them, every effect that can unlock the anxious mind, or gratify the susceptible fancy; and, when satisfied with exploring and laying open to view the motley group of affections that characterize nature in the beings of this world, he stretches his comprehensive imagination and invents a new world, inhabited with beings the offspring of his own fancy, who in their allegorical character give a refinement to virtue, an aversion to vice, and a ridicule to folly, which no actual representation of them could have had the force or the beauty to convey.

Thus Shakespear, by having left nothing unrepresented

either as a positive and naked exhibition of nature, or a deduced and figurative description of her, has gone unequivocally beyond all other writers; and were there nothing else to sanction his astonishing merit and extend his wide fame, he would yet indisputably stand above all dramatic authors ancient and modern.

But, when we consider that there had been no school in which he might study this art, that no dramatic writer since Æschylus, whose soul seems as if it had transmigrated till it was born anew in Shakespear, had been equal to the meritorious task of restoring the glare of Melpomene's dagger and perfecting the polish on the mirror of Thalia; when we consider that the theatre in ten years, in the hands of Shakespear, attained all that perfection which it had lost for more than two thousand, and boasted additional perfection never known to it before in the course of the world, it is impossible to contemplate the character of this great man with a degree of wonder equal to its value, which I consider as the highest climax of panegyric; and yet these considerations are never afforded, and all we can learn from writers, whose geniuses would be complimented by the possession of a capacity to comprehend the genius of Shakespear, gives us no more than permission to assert, that he was an extraordinary man, when it was admitted that he had received but an indifferent education, and that, though there were passages in his works of great and wonderful beauty, there were, nevertheless, numerous faults which never ought to be permitted.

As to the faults, . . . I think it will not be very difficult to prove that they are not so numerous not of such magnitude as the world is taught to believe by the critics; I do not care much what they themselves believe on the subject, though I hope for the sake of common sense and their own reputation, they do not believe half they assert; as to the beauties, they are too indelibly impressed on the heart of every one who has heard or read them to need explanation.

But a few words as to the education of Shakespear, for though I am not writing his life I have a great pride in being the historian of his mind. He received the common advantages of learning in what is called a grammar school; that is to say, a place where a boy of any tolerable genius may learn all that the master is capable of teaching him in six months, and where boys in general study for years and at last know nothing.

Whether Shakespear learned little or much at this school makes nothing either for or against my argument. I can very willingly suppose that the scholar was very soon able to teach the master. It was not in this grammar school where he received that education which has wrought his celebrity. It was in the school of nature, who condescended to be his instructress. The lady fell in love with him; was captivated; he was her Adonis, her Endymion, and both her beauty and her chastity yielded to the irresistible impulse; while he, with all the gallantry, yet the delicacy of an honourable lover, and a faithful knight, consecrated his life to the service of his mistress, pleaded her cause, redressed her wrongs, and, with the truest constancy and most ardent gratitude, made her beauty the perpetual theme of his panegyric.

If Æschylus, when, God knows, grammar schools had nothing to do with learning, but when men were called wise because they used first so many words as served simply to express such ideas as nature taught them, and good, because their minds adopted no ideas but what tended to promote general morality: if Æschylus, studying in the school of nature, represented the great actions and glorious atchievements of his countrymen, and felt emulously and meritoriously that by that means he should render Greece and human nature a benefit,

why should we deny the same merit to Shakespear more than two thousand years afterwards, when grammar schools actually flourished. But it would wrong my cause to waste too much anxiety about it; and nothing but a necessity for strong and incontrovertible argument to cope with the opinions of men, certainly great and reputable, except in their charitable warning to the world of faults in another which are not yet, however, generally discovered, and, after all, not of the magnitude of their own, would have induced me to dwell so minutely on a theme that, with men of fair and candid discrimination, recommends itself and speaks its own eulogium.

The general merit of Shakespear manifests itself in a thousand various ways. Take any one of the passions which he has moulded at will to serve the general purpose of instruction and amusement, and see to what an astonishing pitch he has affected the human heart by a critical and interesting display of it.

Is the passion love? See how he has followed it through all its vicissitudes. The delicate tenderness, the fond impatience, the impetuous ardour, the noble constancy of Romeo and Juliet, perhaps, has not a parallel in language. To youthful love every thing is possible; and the exquisite nonsense that Shakespear has put into the mouth of the doating, enamoured, yet delicate Juliet, is full of poetic beauty, so boundlessly, so extravagant, and yet so truly natural, that we are equally captivated with her love and her innocence.

The love of Romeo is no less admirably drawn. It is impetuous, thoughtless, and rash, yet manly, noble, and generous; but its characteristic is nature. He leaps the orchard wall and braves the resentment of Juliet's relations, out of love, yet presently, out of this very love, he becomes a coward and puts up with an insult from of those relations; nor is he roused out of this apathy till called upon to revenge the death of his friend.

In the garden scene, surely nothing can be so beautiful as the enchanted, yet respectful, manner in which he listens to the unaffected tenderness, the timid honesty, the techy impatience of Juliet. His love, profound, and awful, recedes from his tongue to his heart; her's, inconsiderate and volatile, flies from her heart to her tongue, till, at length impelled to reply to her fond confession, which disdains all hypocrisy, and derides all subterfuge, they join in interchanging vows, tender and affectionate on her part, manly and honourable on his.

Absence only renders more amiable the noble and exalted minds of those lovers. His despair at hearing the sentence of banishment, his horror at the news of Juliet's death, and his solemn determination to follow her; and her resigned compliance with the friar's stratagem, her awful manner of executing it, and her destroying herself, after every hope has failed her, are masterly pictures of exquisite love.[1]

Were I to go on investigating the various ways in which Shakespear has treated this one passion, I should greatly exceed the limits I am obliged to prescribe for myself. I shall, therefore, for the present pass by the noble and persevering constancy of Imogen, the patient and endearing tenderness of Desdemona, the generous and enterprizing affection of Rosalind, the silent and devouring passion of Viola, and all those great and unexampled proofs of consummate strength of mind and profound judgment of the human heart in which Shakespear, though he may have been in one instance now and then equalled by a particular author, taking his writings on the passion of love in their full and comprehensive sense, he has clearly excelled every author.

## Notes

1. Mercier was so charmed with Romeo and Juliet, and so distressed that the lovers should become victims to the unjust and unreasonable enmity of their families, that he has given the plot a new turn. The play never was performed, but it has all the delicacy, finesse, and truth of that admirable author. Benvolio, having long foreseen the consequence of this family hatred, does his utmost to excite the love of Romeo and Juliet, in order to bring about a reconciliation. He finds both the families averse to his project, and, therefore, connives at a private marriage. Every thing happens as in Shakespear's play. Benvolio, however, in the place of the friar, having from his infancy studied chemistry, administers a potion to Juliet; and, contriving that Romeo should be informed of the death, furnishes him with another. Romeo opens the tomb and finding Juliet apparently dead, drinks the potion and falls down at her side. In the mean, Benvolio having alarmed the two fathers they presently behold their two children in this state. After reading to them a severe lecture, and reproaching them for their conduct and the dreadful consequences of their mutual enmity, he honestly confesses that he has wrought all this; tells them that this seeming death of these lovers is but a sleep; that he alone, however, knows the charm to revive them; and that, if they will discard their unjust anger and vow perpetual amity, their children shall wake and revive the double pleasure of being restored to life and to the arms of their parents; but that, if they hesitate, it will be too late. In that case he knows he shall be considered as their murderer, but that he would rather die than witness a rancour so dishonourable to themselves and such a scandal to human nature. The result is obvious. The lovers revive, and their affection is crowned with the approbation and blessing of their fathers. I shall only add that the Frenchman merely alters the story; he does not attempt to improve upon Shakespear, whose genius he reverences, and to whose productions he had upon all occasions most willingly paid a warm tribute of admiration.

AUGUST WILHELM SCHLEGEL
"Lecture XXIII"
*Lectures on Dramatic Art and Literature*
tr. John Black
1809

O ur poet's want of scholarship has been the subject of endless controversy, and yet it is surely a very easy matter to decide. Shakspeare was poor in dead school-cram, but he possessed a rich treasury of living and intuitive knowledge. He knew a little Latin, and even something of Greek, though it may be not enough to read with ease the writers in the original. With modern languages also, the French and Italian, he had, perhaps, but a superficial acquaintance. The general direction of his mind was not to the collection of words but of facts. With English books, whether original or translated, he was extensively acquainted: we may safely affirm that he had read all that his native language and literature then contained that could be of any use to him in his poetical avocations. He was sufficiently intimate with mythology to employ it, in the only manner he could wish, in the way of symbolical ornament. He had formed a correct notion of the spirit of Ancient History, and more particularly of that of the Romans; and the history of his own country was familiar to him even in detail. Fortunately for him it had not as yet been treated in a diplomatic and pragmatic spirit, but merely in the chronicle-style; in other words, it had not yet assumed the appearance of dry investigations respecting the development of political relations, diplomatic negotiations, finances, &c., but exhibited a visible image of the life and movement of an age prolific of great deeds. Shakspeare, moreover, was a nice observer of nature; he knew the technical language of mechanics and artisans; he seems to have been well travelled in the interior of his own country, while of others he inquired diligently of travelled navigators respecting their peculiarity of climate and customs. He thus became accurately acquainted with all the popular usages, opinions, and traditions which could be of use in poetry.

The proofs of his ignorance, on which the greatest stress is laid, are a few geographical blunders and anachronisms. Because in a comedy founded on an earlier tale, he makes ships visit Bohemia, he has been the subject of much laughter. But I conceive that we should be very unjust towards him, were we to conclude that he did not, as well as ourselves, possess the useful but by no means difficult knowledge that Bohemia is nowhere bounded by the sea. He could never, in that case, have looked into a map of Germany, who yet describes elsewhere, with great accuracy, the maps of both Indies, together with the discoveries of the latest navigators.[1] In such matters Shakspeare is only faithful to the details of the domestic stories. In the novels on which he worked, he avoided disturbing the associations of his audience, to whom they were known, by novelties—the correction of errors in secondary and unimportant particulars. The more wonderful the story, the more it ranged in a purely poetical region, which he transfers at will to an indefinite distance. These plays, whatever names they bear, take place in the true land of romance, and in the very century of wonderful love stories. He knew well that in the forest of Ardennes there were neither the lions and serpents of the Torrid Zone, nor the shepherdesses of Arcadia: but he transferred both to it,[2] because the design and import of his picture required them. Here he considered himself entitled to take the greatest liberties. He had not to do with a hair-splitting, hypercritical age like ours, which is always seeking in poetry for something else than poetry; his audience entered the theatre, not to learn true chronology, geography, and natural history, but to witness a vivid exhibition. I will undertake to prove that Shakspeare's anachronisms are, for the most part, committed of set purpose and deliberately. It was frequently of importance to him to move the exhibited subject out of the background of time, and bring it quite near us. Hence in *Hamlet*, though avowedly an old Northern story, there runs a tone of modish society, and in every respect the costume of the most recent period. Without those circumstantialities it would not have been allowable to make a philosophical inquirer of Hamlet, on which trait, however, the meaning of the whole is made to rest. On that account he mentions his education at a university, though, in the age of the true Hamlet of history, universities were not in existence. He makes him study at Wittenberg, and no selection of a place could have been more suitable. The name was very popular: the story of *Dr. Faustus of Wittenberg* had made it well known; it was of particular celebrity in protestant England, as Luther had taught and written there shortly before, and the very name must have immediately suggested the idea of freedom in thinking. I cannot even consider it an anachronism that Richard the Third should speak of Macchiavel. The word is here used altogether proverbially: the contents, at least, of the book entitled *Of the Prince (Del Principe,)* have been in existence ever since the existence of tyrants; Macchiavel was merely the first to commit them to writing.

That Shakspeare has accurately hit the essential costume, namely, the spirit of ages and nations, is at least acknowledged generally by the English critics; but many sins against external costume may be easily remarked. But here it is necessary to bear in mind that the Roman pieces were acted upon the stage of that day in the European dress. This was, it is true, still grand and splendid, not so silly and tasteless as it became towards the end of the seventeenth century. (Brutus and Cassius appeared in the Spanish cloak; they wore, quite contrary to the Roman custom, the sword by their side in time of peace, and, according to the testimony of an eye witness,[3] it was, in the dialogue where Brutus stimulates Cassius to the conspiracy, drawn, as if involuntarily, half out of the sheath.) This does in no way agree with our way of thinking: we are not content without the toga. The present, perhaps, is not an inappropriate place for a few general observations on costume, considered with reference to art. It has never been more accurately observed than in the present day; art has become a slop-shop for pedantic antiquities. This is because we live in a learned and critical, but by no means poetical age. The ancients before us used, when they had to represent the religions of other nations, which deviated very much from their own, to bring them into conformity with the Greek mythology. In Sculpture, again, the same dress, namely, the Phrygian, was adopted, once for all, for every barbaric tribe. Not that they did not know that there were as many different dresses as nations; but in art they merely wished to acknowledge the great contrast between barbarian and civilized: and this, they thought, was rendered most strikingly apparent in the Phrygian garb. The earlier Christian painters represent the Saviour, the Virgin Mary, the Patriarchs, and the Apostles in an ideal dress; but the subordinate actors or spectators of the action, in the dresses of their own nation and age. Here they were guided by a correct feeling: the mysterious and sacred ought to be kept at an awe-inspiring distance, but the human cannot be rightly understood if seen without its usual accompaniments. In the middle ages all heroical stories of antiquity, from Theseus and Achilles down to Alexander, were metamorphosed into true tales of chivalry. What was related to themselves spoke alone an intelligible language to them; of differences and distinctions they did not care to know. In an old manuscript of the *Iliad*, I saw a miniature illumination representing Hector's funeral procession, where the coffin is hung with noble coats of arms, and carried into a Gothic church. It is easy to make merry with this piece of simplicity, but a reflecting mind will see the subject in a very different light. A powerful consciousness of the universal validity and the solid permanency of their own manner of being, an undoubting conviction that it has always so been and will ever continue so to be in the world: these feelings of our ancestors were symptoms of a fresh fulness of life; they were the marrow of action in reality as well as in fiction. Their plain and affectionate attachment to every thing around them, handed down from their fathers, is by no means to be confounded with the obstreperous conceit of ages of mannerism, who, out of vanity, introduce the fleeting modes and fashion of the day into art, because to them everything like noble simplicity seems boorish and rude. The latter impropriety is now abolished: but, on the other hand, our poets and artists, if they would hope for our approbation, must, like servants, wear the livery of distant centuries and foreign nations. We are everywhere at home except at home. We do ourselves the justice to allow that the present mode of dressing, forms of politeness, &c., are altogether unpoetical, and art is therefore obliged to beg, as an alms, a poetical costume from the antiquaries. To that simple way of thinking, which is merely attentive to the inward truth of the composition, without stumbling at anachronisms, or other external inconsistencies, we cannot, alas! now return; but we must envy the poets to whom it offered itself; it allowed them a great breadth and freedom in the handling of their subject.

Many things in Shakspeare must be judged of according to the above principles, respecting the difference between the essential and the merely learned costume. They will also in their measure admit of an application to Calderon.

So much with respect to the spirit of the age in which Shakspeare lived, and his peculiar mental culture and knowledge. To me he appears a profound artist, and not a blind and wildly luxuriant genius. I consider, generally speaking, all that has been said on the subject a mere fable, a blind and extravagant error. In other arts the assertion refutes itself; for in them acquired knowledge is an indispensable condition of clever execution. But even in such poets, as are usually given out as careless pupils of nature, devoid of art or school discipline, I have always found, on a nearer consideration of the works of real excellence they may have produced, even a high cultivation of the mental powers, practice in art, and views both worthy in themselves and maturely considered. This applies to Homer as well as to Dante. The activity of genius is, it is true, natural to it, and, in a certain sense, unconscious; and, consequently, the person who possesses it is not always at the moment able to render an account of the course which he may have pursued; but it by no means follows, that the thinking power had not a great share in it. It is from the very rapidity and certainty of the mental process, from the utmost clearness of understanding, that thinking in a poet is not perceived as something abstracted, does not wear the appearance of reflex meditation. That notion of poetical inspiration, which many lyrical poets have brought into circulation, as if they were not in their senses, and like Pythia, when possessed by the divinity, delivered oracles unintelligible to themselves—this notion, (a mere lyrical invention,) is least of all applicable to dramatic composition, one of the most thoughtful productions of the human mind. It is admitted that Shakspeare has reflected, and deeply reflected, on character and passion, on the progress of events and human destinies, on the human constitution, on all the things and relations of the world; this is an admission which must be made, for one alone of thousands of his maxims would be a sufficient refutation of whoever should attempt to deny it. So that it was only for the structure of his own pieces that he had no thought to spare? This he left to the dominion of chance, which blew together the atoms of Epicurus. But supposing that, devoid of any higher ambition to approve himself to judicious critics and posterity, and wanting in that love of art which longs for self-satisfaction in the perfection of its works, he had merely laboured to please the unlettered crowd; still this very object alone and the pursuit of theatrical effect, would have led him to bestow attention to the structure and adherence of his pieces. For does not the impression of a drama depend in an especial manner on the relation of the parts to each other? And, however beautiful a scene may be in itself, if yet it be at variance with what the spectators have been led to expect in its particular place, so as to destroy the interest which they had hitherto felt, will it not be at once reprobated by all who possess plain common sense, and give themselves up to nature? The comic intermixtures may be considered merely as a sort of interlude, designed to relieve the straining of the mind after the stretch of the more serious parts, so long as no better purpose can be found in them; but in the progress of the main action, in the concatenation of the events, the poet must, if possible, display even more expenditure of thought than in the composition of individual character and situations, otherwise he would be like the conductor of a puppet-show who has entangled his wires, so that the puppets receive from their mechanism quite different movements from those which he actually intended.

The English critics are unanimous in their praise of the

truth and uniform consistency of his characters, of his heart-rending pathos, and his comic wit. Moreover, they extol the beauty and sublimity of his separate descriptions, images, and expressions. This last is the most superficial and cheap mode of criticising works of art. Johnson compares him who should endeavour to recommend this poet by passages unconnectedly torn from his works, to the pedant in Hierocles, who exhibited a brick as a sample of his house. And yet how little, and how very unsatisfactorily does he himself speak of the pieces considered as a whole! Let any man, for instance, bring together the short characters which he gives at the close of each play, and see if the aggregate will amount to that sum of admiration which he himself, at his outset, has stated as the correct standard for the appreciation of the poet. It was, generally speaking, the prevailing tendency of the time which preceded our own, (and which has showed itself particularly in physical science,) to consider everything having life as a mere accumulation of dead parts, to separate what exists only in connexion and cannot otherwise be conceived, instead of penetrating to the central point and viewing all the parts as so many irradiations from it. Hence nothing is so rare as a critic who can elevate himself to the comprehensive contemplation of a work of art. Shakspeare's compositions, from the very depth of purpose displayed in them, have been especially liable to the misfortune of being misunderstood. Besides, this prosaic species of criticism requires always that the poetic form should be applied to the details of execution; but when the plan of the piece is concerned, it never looks for more than the logical connexion of causes and effects, or some partial and trite moral by way of application; and all that cannot be reconciled therewith is declared superfluous, or even a pernicious appendage. On these principles we must even strike out from the Greek tragedies most of the choral songs, which also contribute nothing to the development of the action, but are merely an harmonious echo of the impressions the poet aims at conveying. In this they altogether mistake the rights of poetry and the nature of the romantic drama, which, for the very reason that it is and ought to be picturesque, requires richer accompaniments and contrasts for its main groups. In all Art and Poetry, but more especially in the romantic, the Fancy lays claims to be considered as an independent mental power governed according to its own laws.

In an essay on *Romeo and Juliet*,[4] written a number of years ago, I went through the whole of the scenes in their order, and demonstrated the inward necessity of each with reference to the whole; I showed why such a particular circle of characters and relations was placed around the two lovers; I explained the signification of the mirth here and there scattered, and justified the use of the occasional heightening given to the poetical colours. From all this it seemed to follow unquestionably, that with the exception of a few witticisms, now become unintelligible or foreign to the present taste, (imitations of the tone of society of that day,) nothing could be taken away, nothing added, nothing otherwise arranged, without mutilating and disfiguring the perfect work. I would readily undertake to do the same for all the pieces of Shakspeare's maturer years, but to do this would require a separate book. Here I am reduced to confine my observations to the tracing his great designs with a rapid pencil; but still I must previously be allowed to deliver my sentiments in a general manner on the subject of his most eminent peculiarities.

Shakspeare's knowledge of mankind has become proverbial: in this his superiority is so great, that he has justly been called the master of the human heart. A readiness to remark the mind's fainter and involuntary utterances, and the power to express with certainty the meaning of these signs, as determined by experience and reflection, constitutes "the observer of men;" but tacitly to draw from these still further conclusions, and to arrange the separate observations according to grounds of probability, into a just and valid combination, this, it may be said, is to know men. The distinguishing property of the dramatic poet who is great in characterization, is something altogether different here, and which, (take it which way we will,) either includes in it this readiness and this acuteness, or dispenses with both. It is the capability of transporting himself so completely into every situation, even the most unusual, that he is enabled, as plenipotentiary of the whole human race, without particular instructions for each separate case, to act and speak in the name of every individual. It is the power of endowing the creatures of his imagination with such self-existent energy, that they afterwards act in each conjuncture according to general laws of nature: the poet, in his dreams, institutes, as it were, experiments which are received with as much authority as if they had been made on waking objects. The inconceivable element herein, and what moreover can never be learned, is, that the characters appear neither to do nor to say any thing on the spectator's account merely; and yet that the poet simply, by means of the exhibition, and without any subsidiary explanation, communicates to his audience the gift of looking into the inmost recesses of their minds. Hence Goethe has ingeniously compared Shakspeare's characters to watches with crystalline plates and cases, which, while they point out the hours as correctly as other watches, enable us at the same time to perceive the inward springs whereby all this is accomplished.

Nothing, however, is more foreign to Shakspeare than a certain anatomical style of exhibition, which laboriously enumerates all the motives by which a man is determined to act in this or that particular manner. This rage of supplying motives, the mania of so many modern historians, might be carried at length to an extent which would abolish every thing like individuality, and resolve all character into nothing but the effect of foreign or external influences whereas we know that it often announces itself most decidedly in earliest infancy. After all, a man acts so because he is so. And what each man is, that Shakspeare reveals to us most immediately: he demands and obtains our belief, even for what is singular and deviates from the ordinary course of nature. Never perhaps was there so comprehensive a talent for characterization as Shakspeare. It not only grasps every diversity of rank, age, and sex, down to the lispings of infancy; not only do the king and the beggar, the hero and the pickpocket, the sage and the idiot, speak and act with equal truthfulness; not only does he transport himself to distant ages and foreign nations, and portray with the greatest accuracy (a few apparent violations of costume excepted) the spirit of the ancient Romans, of the French in the wars with the English, of the English themselves during a great part of their history, of the Southern Europeans (in the serious part of many comedies), the cultivated society of the day, and the rude barbarism of a Norman fore-time; his human characters have not only such depth and individuality that they do not admit of being classed under common names, and are inexhaustible even in conception: no, this Prometheus not merely forms men, he opens the gates of the magical world of spirits, calls up the midnight ghost, exhibits before us the witches with their unhallowed rites, peoples the air with sportive fairies and sylphs; and these beings, though existing only in the imagination, nevertheless possess such truth and consistency, that even with such misshapen abortions as Caliban, he extorts the assenting conviction, that were there such beings they would so conduct themselves. In a word, as he carries a bold and pregnant fancy into the kingdom of nature, on the other hand, he carries nature into the regions of fancy, which lie beyond the confines of reality. We are lost in astonishment at the close intimacy he brings us into with the extraordinary, the wonderful, and the unheard-of.

Pope and Johnson appear strangely to contradict each other, when the first says, "all the characters of Shakspeare are individuals," and the second, "they are species." And yet perhaps these opinions may admit of reconciliation. Pope's expression is unquestionably the more correct. A character which should be merely a personification of a naked general idea could neither exhibit any great depth nor any great variety. The names of genera and species are well known to be merely auxiliaries for the understanding, that we may embrace the infinite variety of nature in a certain order. The characters which Shakspeare has so thoroughly delineated have undoubtedly a number of individual peculiarities, but at the same time they possess a significance which is not applicable to them alone: they generally supply materials for a profound theory of their most prominent and distinguishing property. But even with the above correction, this opinion must still have its limitations. Characterization is merely one ingredient of the dramatic art, and not dramatic poetry itself. It would be improper in the extreme, if the poet were to draw our attention to superfluous traits of character, at a time when it ought to be his endeavour to produce other impressions. Whenever the musical or the fanciful preponderates, the characteristical necessarily falls into the background. Hence many of the figures of Shakspeare exhibit merely external designations, determined by the place which they occupy in the whole: they are like secondary persons in a public procession, to whose physiognomy we seldom pay much attention; their only importance is derived from the solemnity of their dress and the duty in which they are engaged. Shakspeare's messengers, for instance, are for the most part mere messengers, and yet not common, but poetical messengers: the messages which they have to bring is the soul which suggests to them their language. Other voices, too, are merely raised to pour forth these as melodious lamentations or rejoicings, or to dwell in reflection on what has taken place; and in a serious drama without chorus this must always be more or less the case, if we would not have it prosaical.

If Shakspeare deserves our admiration for his characters, he is equally deserving of it for his exhibition of passion, taking this word in its widest signification, as including every mental condition, every tone, from indifference or familiar mirth to the wildest rage and despair. He gives us the history of minds; he lays open to us, in a single word, a whole series of their anterior states. His passions do not stand at the same height, from first to last, as is the case with so many tragic poets, who, in the language of Lessing, are thorough masters of the legal style of love. He paints, with inimitable veracity, the gradual advance from the first origin; "he gives," as Lessing says, "a living picture of all the slight and secret artifices by which a feeling steals into our souls, of all the imperceptible advantages which it there gains, of all the stratagems by which it makes every other passion subservient to itself, till it becomes the sole tyrant of our desires and our aversions." Of all the poets, perhaps, he alone has portrayed the mental diseases, melancholy, delirium, lunacy, with such inexpressible and, in every respect, definite truth, that the physician may enrich his observations from them in the same manner as from real cases.

And yet Johnson has objected to Shakspeare that his pathos is not always natural and free from affectation. There are, it is true, passages, though comparatively speaking very few, where his poetry exceeds the bounds of actual dialogue, where a too soaring imagination, a too luxuriant wit, rendered a complete dramatic forgetfulness of himself impossible. With this exception, the censure originated in a fanciless way of thinking, to which everything appears unnatural that does not consort with its own tame insipidity. Hence an idea has been formed of simple and natural pathos, which consists in exclamations destitute of imagery and nowise elevated above every-day life. But energetical passions electrify all the mental powers, and will consequently, in highly-favoured natures, give utterance to themselves in ingenious and figurative expressions. It has been often remarked that indignation makes a man witty; and as despair occasionally breaks out into laughter, it may sometimes also give vent to itself in antithetical comparisons.

Besides, the rights of the poetical form have not been duly weighed. Shakspeare, who was always sure of his power to excite, when he wished, sufficiently powerful emotions, has occasionally, by indulging in a freer play of fancy, purposely tempered the impressions when too painful, and immediately introduced a musical softening of our sympathy.[5] He had not those rude ideas of his art which many moderns seem to have, as if the poet, like the clown in the proverb, must strike twice on the same place. An ancient rhetorician delivered a caution against dwelling too long on the excitation of pity; for nothing, he said, dries so soon as tears; and Shakspeare acted conformably to this ingenious maxim without having learned it. The paradoxical assertion of Johnson that "Shakspeare had a greater talent for comedy than tragedy, and that in the latter he has frequently displayed an affected tone," is scarcely deserving of lengthy notice. For its refutation, it is unnecessary to appeal to the great tragical compositions of the poet, which, for overpowering effect, leave far behind them almost everything that the stage has seen besides; a few of their less celebrated scenes would be quite sufficient. What to many readers might lend an appearance of truth to this assertion are the verbal witticisms, that playing upon words, which Shakspeare not unfrequently introduces into serious and sublime passages, and even into those also of a peculiarly pathetic nature.

I have already stated the point of view in which we ought to consider this sportive play upon words. I shall here, therefore, merely deliver a few observations respecting the playing upon words in general, and its poetical use. A thorough investigation would lead us too far from our subject, and too deeply into considerations on the essence of language, and its relation to poetry, or rhyme, &c.

There is in the human mind a desire that language should exhibit the object which it denotes, sensibly, by its very sound, which may be traced even as far back as in the first origin of poetry. As, in the shape in which language comes down to us, this is seldom perceptibly the case, an imagination which has been powerfully excited is fond of laying hold of any congruity in sound which may accidentally offer itself, that by such means he may, for the nonce, restore the lost resemblance between the word and the thing. For example, how common was it and is it to seek in the name of a person, however arbitrarily bestowed, a reference to his qualities and fortunes,— to convert it purposely into a significant name. Those who cry out against the play upon words as an unnatural and affected invention, only betray their own ignorance of original nature.

A great fondness for it is always evinced among children, as well as with nations of simple manners, among whom correct ideas of the derivation and affinity of words have not yet been developed, and do not, consequently, stand in the way of this caprice. In Homer we find several examples of it; the Books of Moses, the oldest written memorial of the primitive world, are, as is well known, full of them. On the other hand, poets of a very cultivated taste, like Petrarch, or orators, like Cicero, have delighted in them. Whoever, in *Richard the Second*, is disgusted with the affecting play of words of the dying John of Gaunt on his own name, should remember that the same thing occurs in the *Ajax* of Sophocles. We do not mean to say that all playing upon words is on all occasions to be justified. This must depend on the disposition of mind, whether it will admit of such a play of fancy, and whether the sallies, comparisons, and allusions, which lie at the bottom of them, possess internal solidity. Yet we must not proceed upon the principle of trying how the thought appears after it is deprived of the resemblance in sound, any more than we are to endeavour to feel the charm of rhymed versification after depriving it of its rhyme. The laws of good taste on this subject must, moreover, vary with the quality of the languages. In those which possess a great number of homonymes, that is, words possessing the same, or nearly the same, sound, though quite different in their derivation and signification, it is almost more difficult to avoid, than to fall on such a verbal play. It has, however, been feared, lest a door might be opened to puerile witticism, if they were not rigorously proscribed. But I cannot, for my part, find that Shakspeare had such an invincible and immoderate passion for this verbal witticism. It is true, he sometimes makes a most lavish use of this figure; at others, he has employed it very sparingly; and at times (for example, in *Macbeth*), I do not believe a vestige of it is to be found. Hence, in respect to the use or the rejection of the play upon words, he must have been guided by the measure of the objects, and the different style in which they required to be treated, and probably have followed here, as in every thing else, principles which, fairly examined, will bear a strict examination.

The objection that Shakspeare wounds our feelings by the open display of the most disgusting moral odiousness, unmercifully harrows up the mind, and tortures even our eyes by the exhibition of the most insupportable and hateful spectacles, is one of greater and graver importance. He has, in fact, never varnished over wild and blood-thirsty passions with a pleasing exterior—never clothed crime and want of principle with a false show of greatness of soul; and in that respect he is every way deserving of praise. Twice he has portrayed downright villains, and the masterly way in which he has contrived to elude impressions of too painful a nature may be seen in Iago and Richard the Third. I allow that the reading, and still more the sight, of some of his pieces, is not advisable to weak nerves, any more than was the *Eumenides* of Æschylus; but is the poet, who can only reach an important object by a bold and hazardous daring, to be checked by considerations for such persons? If the effeminacy of the present day is to serve as a general standard of what tragical composition may properly exhibit to human nature, we shall be forced to set very narrow limits indeed to art, and the hope of anything like powerful effect must at once and for ever be renounced. If we wish to have a grand purpose, we must also wish to have the grand means, and our nerves ought in some measure to accommodate themselves to painful impressions, if, by way of requital, our mind is thereby elevated and strengthened. The constant reference to a petty and puny race must cripple the boldness of the poet. Fortunately for his art, Shakspeare lived in an age

extremely susceptible of noble and tender impressions, but which had yet inherited enough of the firmness of a vigorous olden time, not to shrink with dismay from every strong and forcible painting. We have lived to see tragedies of which the catastrophe consists in the swoon of an enamoured princess: if Shakspeare falls occasionally into the opposite extreme, it is a noble error, originating in the fulness of a gigantic strength. And this tragical Titan, who storms the heavens and threatens to tear the world from off its hinges, who, more terrible than Æschylus, makes our hair to stand on end, and congeals our blood with horror, possessed at the same time the insinuating loveliness of the sweetest poesy; he toys with love like a child, and his songs die away on the ear like melting sighs. He unites in his soul the utmost elevation and the utmost depth; and the most opposite and even apparently irreconcilable properties subsist in him peaceably together. The world of spirits and nature have laid all their treasures at his feet: in strength a demi-god, in profundity of view a prophet, in all-seeing wisdom a guardian spirit of a higher order, he lowers himself to mortals as if unconscious of his superiority, and is as open and unassuming as a child.

If the delineation of all his characters, separately considered, is inimitably bold and correct, he surpasses even himself in so combining and contrasting them, that they serve to bring out each other's peculiarities. This is the very perfection of dramatic characterization: for we can never estimate a man's true worth if we consider him altogether abstractedly by himself; we must see him in his relations with others; and it is here that most dramatic poets are deficient. Shakspeare makes each of his principal characters the glass in which the others are reflected, and by like means enables us to discover what could not be immediately revealed to us. What in others is most profound, is with him but surface. Ill-advised should we be were we always to take men's declarations respecting themselves and others for sterling coin. Ambiguity of design with much propriety he makes to overflow with the most praiseworthy principles; and sage maxims are not unfrequently put in the mouth of stupidity, to show how easily such common-place truisms may be acquired. Nobody ever painted so truthfully as he has done the facility of self-deception, the half self-conscious hypocrisy towards ourselves, with which even noble minds attempt to disguise the almost inevitable influence of selfish motives in human nature. This secret irony of the characterization commands admiration as the profound abyss of acuteness and sagacity; but it is the grave of enthusiasm. We arrive at it only after we have had the misfortune to see human nature through and through; and when no choice remains but to adopt the melancholy truth, that "no virtue or greatness is altogether pure and genuine," or the dangerous error that "the highest perfection is attainable." Here we therefore may perceive in the poet himself, notwithstanding his power to excite the most fervent emotions, a certain cool indifference, but still the indifference of a superior mind, which has run through the whole sphere of human existence and survived feeling.

The irony in Shakspeare has not merely a reference to the separate characters, but frequently to the whole of the action. Most poets who portray human events in a narrative or dramatic form take themselves a part, and exact from their readers a blind approbation or condemnation of whatever side they choose to support or oppose. The more zealous this rhetoric is, the more certainly it fails of its effect. In every case we are conscious that the subject itself is not brought immediately before us, but that we view it through the medium of a different way of thinking. When, however, by a dexterous manœuvre, the poet allows us an occasional glance at the less brilliant reverse of the medal, then he makes, as it were, a sort of secret understanding with the select circle of the more intelligent of his readers or spectators; he shows them that he had previously seen and admitted the validity of their tacit objections; that he himself is not tied down to the represented subject, but soars freely above it; and that, if he chose, he could unrelentingly annihilate the beautiful and irresistibly attractive scenes which his magic pen has produced. No doubt, wherever the proper tragic enters every thing like irony immediately ceases; but from the avowed raillery of Comedy, to the point where the subjection of mortal beings to an inevitable destiny demands the highest degree of seriousness, there are a multitude of human relations which unquestionably may be considered in an ironical view, without confounding the eternal line of separation between good and evil. This purpose is answered by the comic characters and scenes which are interwoven with the serious parts in most of those pieces of Shakspeare where romantic fables or historical events are made the subject of a noble and elevating exhibition. Frequently an intentional parody of the serious part is not to be mistaken in them; at other times the connexion is more arbitrary and loose, and the more so the more marvellous the invention of the whole, and the more entirely it is become a light revelling of the fancy. The comic intervals everywhere serve to prevent the pastime from being converted into a business, to preserve the mind in the possession of its serenity, and to keep off that gloomy and inert seriousness which so easily steals upon the sentimental, but not tragical, drama. Most assuredly Shakspeare did not intend thereby, in defiance to his own better judgment, to humour the taste of the multitude: for in various pieces, and throughout considerable portions of others, and especially when the catastrophe is approaching, and the mind consequently is more on the stretch and no longer likely to give heed to any amusement which would distract their attention, he has abstained from all such comic intermixtures. It was also an object with him, that the clowns or buffoons should not occupy a more important place than that which he had assigned them: he expressly condemns the extemporizing with which they loved to enlarge their parts.[6] Johnson founds the justification of the species of drama in which seriousness and mirth are mixed, on this, that in real life the vulgar is found close to the sublime, that the merry and the sad usually accompany and succeed one another. But it does not follow that because both are found together, therefore they must not be separable in the compositions of art. The observation is in other respects just, and this circumstance invests the poet with a power to adopt this procedure, because every thing in the drama must be regulated by the conditions of theatrical probability; but the mixture of such dissimilar, and apparently contradictory, ingredients, in the same works, can only be justifiable on principles reconcilable with the views of art, which I have already described. In the dramas of Shakspeare the comic scenes are the antechamber of the poetry, where the servants remain; these prosaic attendants must not raise their voices so high as to deafen the speakers in the presence-chamber; however, in those intervals when the ideal society has retired they deserve to be listened to; their bold raillery, their presumption of mockery, may afford many an insight into the situation and circumstances of their masters.

Shakspeare's comic talent is equally wonderful with that which he has shown in the pathetic and tragic: it stands on an equal elevation, and possesses equal extent and profundity; in all that I have hitherto said, I only wished to guard against admitting that the former preponderated. He is highly inven-

tive in comic situations and motives: it will be hardly possible to show whence he has taken any of them, whereas, in the serious part of his dramas, he has generally laid hold of some well-known story. His comic characterization is equally true, various, and profound, with his serious. So little is he disposed to caricature, that rather, it may be said, many of his traits are almost too nice and delicate for the stage, that they can only be made available by a great actor, and fully understood by an acute audience. Not only has he delineated many kinds of folly, but even of sheer stupidity has he contrived to give a most diverting and entertaining picture. There is also in his pieces a peculiar species of the farcical, which apparently seems to be introduced more arbitrarily, but which, however, is founded on imitation of some actual custom. This is the introduction of the merrymaker, the fool with his cap and bells, and motley dress, called more commonly in England *Clown*, who appears in several comedies, though not in all, but of the tragedies in *Lear* alone, and who generally merely exercises his wit in conversation with the principal persons though he is also sometimes incorporated into the action. In those times it was not only usual for princes to have their court fools, but many distinguished families, among their other retainers, kept such an exhilarating housemate as a good antidote against the insipidity and wearisomeness of ordinary life, and as a welcome interruption of established formalities. Great statesmen, and even ecclesiastics, did not consider it beneath their dignity to recruit and solace themselves after important business with the conversation of their fools; the celebrated Sir Thomas More had his fool painted along with himself by Holbein. Shakspeare appears to have lived immediately before the time when the custom began to be abolished; in the English comic authors who succeeded him the clown is no longer to be found. The dismissal of the fool has been extolled as a proof of refinement; and our honest forefathers have been pitied for taking delight in such a coarse and farcical amusement. For my part, I am rather disposed to believe, that the practice was dropped from the difficulty in finding fools able to do full justice to their parts:[7] on the other hand, reason, with all its conceit of itself, has become too timid to tolerate such bold irony; it is always careful lest the mantle of its gravity should be disturbed in any of its folds; and rather than allow a privileged place to folly beside itself, it has unconsciously assumed the part of the ridiculous; but, alas! a heavy and cheerless ridicule.[8] It would be easy to make a collection of the excellent sallies and biting sarcasms which have been preserved of celebrated court fools. It is well known that they frequently told such truths to princes as are never now told to them.[9] Shakspeare's fools, along with somewhat of an overstraining for wit, which cannot altogether be avoided when wit becomes a separate profession, have for the most part an incomparable humour, and an infinite abundance of intellect, enough indeed to supply a whole host of ordinary wise men.

I have still a few observations to make on the diction and versification of our poet. The language is here and there somewhat obsolete, but on the whole much less so than in most of the contemporary writers, a sufficient proof of the goodness of his choice. Prose had as yet been but little cultivated, as the learned generally wrote in Latin: a favourable circumstance for the dramatic poet; for what has he to do with the scientific language of books? He had not only read, but studied the earlier English poets; but he drew his language immediately from life itself, and he possessed a masterly skill in blending the dialogical element with the highest poetical elevation. I know not what certain critics mean, when they say that Shakspeare is frequently ungrammatical. To make good their assertion, they must prove that similar constructions never occur in his contemporaries, the direct contrary of which can, however, be easily shown. In no language is every thing determined on principle; much is always left to the caprice of custom, and if this has since changed, is the poet to be made answerable for it? The English language had not then attained to that correct insipidity which has been introduced into the more recent literature of the country, to the prejudice, perhaps, of its originality. As a field when first brought under the plough produces, along with the fruitful shoots, many luxuriant weeds, so the poetical diction of the day ran occasionally into extravagance, but an extravagance originating in the exuberance of its vigour. We may still perceive traces of awkwardness, but nowhere of a laboured and spiritless display of art. In general Shakspeare's style yet remains the very best model, both ' in the vigorous and sublime, and the pleasing and tender. In his sphere he has exhausted all the means and appliances of language. On all he has impressed the stamp of his mighty spirit. His images and figures, in their unsought, nay, uncapricious singularity, have often a sweetness altogether peculiar. He becomes occasionally obscure from too great fondness for compressed brevity; but still, the labour of poring over Shakspeare's lines will invariably meet an ample requital.

The verse in all his plays is generally the rhymeless Iambic of ten or eleven syllables, occasionally only intermixed with rhymes, but more frequently alternating with prose. No one piece is written entirely in prose; for even in those which approach the most to the pure Comedy, there is always something added which gives them a more poetical hue than usually belongs to this species. Many scenes are wholly in prose, in others verse and prose succeed each other alternately. This can only appear an impropriety in the eyes of those who are accustomed to consider the lines of a drama like so many soldiers drawn up rank and file on a parade, with the same uniform, arms, and accoutrements, so that when we see one or two we may represent to ourselves thousands as being every way like them.

In the use of verse and prose Shakspeare observes very nice distinctions according to the ranks of the speakers, but still more according to their characters and disposition of mind. A noble language, elevated above the usual tone, is only suitable to a certain decorum of manners, which is thrown over both vices and virtues, and which does not even wholly disappear amidst the violence of passion. If this is not exclusively possessed by the higher ranks, it still, however, belongs naturally more to them than to the lower; and therefore in Shakspeare dignity and familiarity of language, poetry, and prose, are in this manner distributed among the characters. Hence his tradesmen, peasants, soldiers, sailors, servants, but more especially his fools and clowns, speak, almost without exception, in the tone of their actual life. However, inward dignity of sentiment, wherever it is possessed, invariably displays itself with a nobleness of its own, and stands not in need, for that end, of the artificial elegancies of education and custom; it is a universal right of man, of the highest as well as the lowest; and hence also, in Shakspeare, the nobility of nature and morality is ennobled above the artificial nobility of society. Not unfrequently also he makes the very same persons express themselves at times in the sublimest language, and at others in the lowest; and this inequality is in like manner founded in truth. Extraordinary situations, which intensely occupy the head and throw mighty passions into play, give elevation and tension to the soul: it collects together all its powers, and exhibits an unusual energy, both in its operations and in its communications by language. On the other hand,

even the greatest men have their moments of remissness, when to a certain degree they forget the dignity of their character in unreserved relaxation. This very tone of mind is necessary before they can receive amusement from the jokes of others, or what surely cannot dishonour even a hero, from passing jokes themselves. Let any person, for example, go carefully through the part of Hamlet. How bold and powerful the language of his poetry when he conjures the ghost of his father, when he spurs himself on to the bloody deed, when he thunders into the soul of his mother! How he lowers his tone down to that of common life, when he has to do with persons whose station demands from him such a line of conduct; when he makes game of Polonius and the courtiers, instructs the player, and even enters into the jokes of the grave-digger. Of all the poet's serious leading characters there is none so rich in wit and humour as Hamlet; hence he it is of all of them that makes the greatest use of the familiar style. Others, again, never do fall into it; either because they are constantly surrounded by the pomp of rank, or because a uniform seriousness is natural to them; or, in short, because through the whole piece they are under the dominion of a passion calculated to excite, and not, like the sorrow of Hamlet, to depress the mind. The choice of the one form or the other is everywhere so appropriate, and so much founded in the nature of the thing, that I will venture to assert, even where the poet in the very same speech makes the speaker leave prose for poetry, or the converse, this could not be altered without danger of injuring or destroying some beauty or other. The blank verse has this advantage, that its tone may be elevated or lowered; it admits of approximation to the familiar style of conversation, and never forms such an abrupt contrast as that, for example, between plain prose and the rhyming Alexandrines.

Shakspeare's Iambics are sometimes highly harmonious and full sounding; always varied and suitable to the subject, at one time distinguished by ease and rapidity, at another they move along with ponderous energy. They never fall out of the dialogical character, which may always be traced even in the continued discourses of individuals, excepting when the latter run into the lyrical. They are a complete model of the dramatic use of this species of verse, which, in English, since Milton, has been also used in epic poetry; but in the latter it has assumed a quite different turn. Even the irregularities of Shakspeare's versification are expressive; a verse broken off, or a sudden change of rhythmus, coincides with some pause in the progress of the thought, or the entrance of another mental disposition. As a proof that he purposely violated the mechanical rules, from a conviction that too symmetrical a versification does not suit with the drama, and on the stage has in the long run a tendency to lull the spectators asleep, we may observe that his earlier pieces are the most diligently versified, and that in the later works, when through practice he must have acquired a greater facility, we find the strongest deviations from the regular structure of the verse. As it served with him merely to make the poetical elevation perceptible, he therefore claimed the utmost possible freedom in the use of it.

The views or suggestions of feeling by which he was guided in the use of rhyme may likewise be traced with almost equal certainty. Not unfrequently scenes, or even single speeches, close with a few rhyming lines, for the purpose of more strongly marking the division, and of giving it more rounding. This was injudiciously imitated by the English tragic poets of a later date; they suddenly elevated the tone in the rhymed lines, as if the person began all at once to speak in another language. The practice was welcomed by the actors from its serving as a signal for clapping when they made their exit. In Shakspeare, on the other hand, the transitions are more easy: all changes of forms are brought about insensibly, and as if of themselves. Moreover, he is generally fond of heightening a series of ingenious and antithetical sayings by the use of rhyme. We find other passages in continued rhyme, where solemnity and theatrical pomp were suitable, as, for instance, in the mask, as it is called, *The Tempest*, and in the play introduced in Hamlet. Of other pieces, for instance, the *Midsummer Night's Dream*, and *Romeo and Juliet*, the rhymes form a considerable part; either because he may have wished to give them a glowing colour, or because the characters appropriately utter in a more musical tone their complaints or suits of love. In these cases he has even introduced rhymed strophes, which approach to the form of the sonnet, then usual in England. The assertion of Malone, that Shakspeare in his youth was fond of rhyme, but that he afterwards rejected it, is sufficiently refuted by his own chronology of the poet's works. In some of the earliest, for instance, in the Second and Third Part of *Henry the Sixth*, there are hardly any rhymes; in what is stated to be his last piece, *The Twelfth Night, or What You Will*, and in *Macbeth*, which is proved to have been composed under the reign of King James, we find them in no inconsiderable number. Even in the secondary matters of form Shakspeare was not guided by humour and accident, but, like a genuine artist, acted invariably on good and solid grounds. This we might also show of the kinds of verse which he least frequently used; for instance, of the rhyming verses of seven and eight syllables, were we not afraid of dwelling too long on merely technical peculiarities.

In England the manner of handling rhyming verse, and the opinion as to its harmony and elegance, have, in the course of two centuries, undergone a much greater change than is the case with the rhymeless Iambic or blank verse. In the former, Dryden and Pope have become models; these writers have communicated the utmost smoothing to rhyme, but they have also tied it down to a harmonious uniformity. A foreigner, to whom antiquated and new are the same, may perhaps feel with greater freedom the advantages of the more ancient manner. Certain it is, the rhyme of the present day, from the too great confinement of the couplet, is unfit for the drama. We must not estimate the rhyme of Shakspeare by the mode of subsequent times, but by a comparison with his contemporaries or with Spenser. The comparison will, without doubt, turn out to his advantage. Spenser is often diffuse; Shakspeare, though sometimes hard, is always brief and vigorous. He has more frequently been induced by the rhyme to leave out something necessary than to insert any thing superfluous. Many of his rhymes, however, are faultless: ingenious with attractive ease, and rich without false brilliancy. The songs interspersed (those, I mean, of the poet himself) are generally sweetly playful and altogether musical; in imagination, while we merely read them, we hear their melody.

The whole of Shakspeare's productions bear the certain stamp of his original genius, but yet no writer was ever farther removed from every thing like a mannerism derived from habit or personal peculiarities. Rather is he, such is the diversity of tone and colour, which varies according to the quality of his subjects he assumes, a very Proteus. Each of his compositions is like a world of its own, moving in its own sphere. They are works of art, finished in one pervading style, which revealed the freedom and judicious choice of their author. If the formation of a work throughout, even in its minutest parts, in conformity with a leading idea; if the domination of one animating spirit over all the means of execution, deserves the name of correctness (and this, excepting in matters of gram-

mar, is the only proper sense of the term); we shall then, after allowing to Shakspeare all the higher qualities which demand our admiration, be also compelled, in most cases, to concede to him the title of a correct poet.

*Notes*

1. *Twelfth Night, or What You Will*—Act iii. scene ii.
2. *As You Like It.*
3. In one of the commendatory poems in the first folio edition:

   And on the stage at *half sword parley* were
   Brutus and Cassius.

4. In the first volume of *Charakteristiken und Kritiken*, published by my brother and myself.
5. A contemporary of the poet, the author of the already-noticed poem, (subscribed I.M.S.,) tenderly felt this while he says—

   Yet so to temper passion, that our ears
   Take pleasure in their pain, and eyes in tears
   Both smile and weep.

6. In Hamlet's directions to the players. Act iii. sc. 2.
7. See Hamlet's praise of Yorick. In *The Twelfth Night*, Viola says:—

   This fellow is wise enough to play the fool,
   And to do that well craves a kind of wit;
   He must observe their mood on whom he jests,
   The quality of the persons, and the time;
   And like the haggard, check at every feather
   That comes before his eye. This is a practice
   As full of labour as a wise man's art:
   For folly that he wisely shows is fit,
   But wise men's folly fall'n quite taints their wit.

8. "Since the little wit that fools have was silenced, the little foolery that wise men have makes a greater show."—*As You Like It*. Act i., sc. 2.
9. Charles the Bold, of Burgundy, is known to have frequently boasted that he wished to rival Hannibal as the greatest general of all ages. After his defeat at Granson, his fool accompanied him in his hurried flight, and exclaimed, "Ah, your Grace, they have for once Hanniballed us!" If the Duke had given an ear to this warning raillery, he would not so soon afterwards have come to a disgraceful end.

## NATHAN DRAKE
### From *Shakspeare and His Times*
#### 1817, pp. 596–601

Of the three unities, upon which so much stress has been laid by the French critics, Shakspeare has in general, and, for the most part, very judiciously, rejected two. One of these, the unity of place, was, indeed, indissolubly connected with the tragedy of the Greeks; for as the chorus was continually on their stage, no curtain could be dropped, nor was any change of scene therefore possible; but the unity of time was most assuredly neither rigidly observed by them, nor did it constitute any essential part of their system; on the contrary, Aristotle, after remarking, "that the dramatic fable should have such a length that the connexion of the circumstances may easily be remembered," immediately afterwards declares of this very length, that "as far as regards the time of the performance and the spectators, it has no relation to the poetic art," and that "as to the natural boundary of the action, the greater it is the better, provided it be perspicuous."[1] In fact, as to unity of place, no rule was required, this limitation . . . being the inevitable consequence of the defective and insulated construction of their dramatic fable; and as to unity of time, the observation which we have just quoted from Aristotle is decisive, the circumstances attending both these supposed laws being such as fully to warrant the assertion of Mr. Twining, who, commenting on the Stagyrite, observes, that "with respect to the strict unities of time and place, no such rules were imposed on the Greek poets by the critics, or by themselves; nor are imposed on any poet, either by the nature, or the end, of the dramatic imitation itself;" and we may add, that, in as far as both have been simultaneously reduced to practice, either by the Greeks themselves, or by their still more scrupulous imitators the French, have interest and probability been proportionably sacrificed.

Whether Shakspeare, therefore, acting solely from his own judgment, rejected, or, guided merely by the usage of his day, overlooked these unities, a great point was gained for all the lovers of nature and verisimilitude. For, omitting regulations which, though generally or partially observed by the ancients, were either altogether arbitrary, or only locally necessary, he has adopted two, of which it may be said, that neither time, circumstance, nor opinion, can diminish the utility. To unity of action, the indispensable requisite of every well-constituted fable, he has added, what in him is found more perfect than in any other writer, unity of feeling, as applicable not only to individual character, but to the prevailing tone and influence of each play. Thus, while it must be confessed that the former is, in a few instances, broken in upon, by the admission of extraneous personages or occurrences, in no respect is the latter, throughout the whole range of his productions, forgotten or violated.

It is to this sedulous attention in the preservation of unity of feeling, that Shakspeare owes much of his fascination and powers of impression over the hearts and minds of his audience. It has been duly panegyrised by the critics with respect to his delineation of character; but as referable to the expression and effect of an entire drama, it has been too much overlooked. What, for example, can be more distinct than the tone of feeling which pervades every portion of *Romeo and Juliet* and *Macbeth*, and how consistently is this tone preserved throughout each! Through the first, from its opening to its close, breathe the freshness and the fragrance of youth and spring, their sweetness, their innocency, and alas! their transiency; while in the second, a tempest of more than midnight horror, and the still more turbulent strife of human vice and passion, howl for ever in our ears! Again, how delightful is the tender and philosophic melancholy, which steals upon us in every scene of *As You Like It*, and how contrasted with the bustle and vivacity, the light and effervescent wit which animate, and sparkle in, the dialogue of *Much Ado about Nothing!*—We consider this unity, by which the separate parts of a drama are rendered so strictly subservient to a single and a common object, namely, the production of a combined and uniform impression, as one of the most remarkable proofs of the depth and comprehensiveness of the mind of Shakspeare.

This excellence is the more extraordinary, as no part in the conduct of his drama is perhaps so prominent, as that mixture of seriousness and mirth, of comic and tragic effect, which springs from the very structure itself of the romantic drama. But this interchange of emotion serves only to place the intention of the poet, and the fulness of his success, more completely in our view; for he has almost always contrived, that the ludicrous personages of his play should give essential aid to the pre-determined effect of the composition as a whole; and this co-operation is even most apparent, where the impression intended to be excited is the most tragic: thus the anguish which lacerates the bosom of Lear, when deserted by his children, and driven forth amid the horrors of the tempest, is augmented almost to madness by the sarcastic drollery of the fool; developed, indeed, with an energy and strength which no other expedient could have accomplished.

These contrasts, which are, in fact, of the very essence of the romantic drama, as requiring richer and more varied accompaniments than the antique species, form, in their whole spirit and effect, a sufficient apology, were one in the least necessary, for the tragi-comic texture of our author's principal productions.

By embracing in one view the whole of the checkered scene of human existence, its joys and sorrows, its perpetually shifting circumstances and relations, and by blending these into one harmonious picture, Shakspeare has achieved a work to which the ancient world had nothing similar, and which, of all the efforts of human genius, demands perhaps the widest and profoundest exertion of intellect. It demands a knowledge of a man, both as: genus and a species; of man, as acting from himself, and of man in society under all its aspects and revolutions it demands a knowledge of what has influenced and modified his character from the earliest dawn of record; and, above all, it demands a conversancy of the most intimate kind with his constitution, moral, intellectual, and religious; so that in detaching a portion of history for the purposes of dramatic composition, the philosopher shall be as discernible in the execution as the poet.

It is this depth and comprehension of design in the conduct of his drama, this amplitude of "a mind reflecting ages past,"[2] which, while it has rendered Shakspeare an object of admiration to the intelligent student of nature, has occasioned him to be so often and so grossly misinterpreted by the narrow critic and the careless reader.

To these brief remarks on the Genius and Conduct, it will be necessary to add a few observations on the Characters, the Passions, the Comic Painting, and the Imaginative Powers, of his drama.

> To give a stage,
> Ample, and true with life,—voice, action, age,
> To story coldly told—
> To raise our ancient sovereigns from their hearse,
> To enliven their pale trunks,

and to make us

> Joy in their joy, and tremble at their rage,

is, indeed, a task of the utmost magnitude and difficulty, but one in which our poet has succeeded with a felicity altogether unparalleled. His characters live and breathe before us; we perceive not only what they say and do, but what they feel and think; and we are tempted to believe, that like some magician of old, he possessed the art of transfusing himself into the frame, and of speaking through the organs, of those whom he wished to represent; so exactly has he drawn, without deviation from the general laws and broad tract of life, each class and condition of mankind.

Whether he delineate the possessor of a throne, or the tenant of a cottage; the warrior in battle, or the statesman in debate; youth in its fervour, or old age in its repose; guilt in agony, or innocence in peace; the votaries of pleasure, or the victims of despair; we behold each character developing itself, not through the medium of self-description, but, as in actual experience, through the influence and progression of events, and through the re-action of surrounding agents. Thus, from the mutual working of conflicting interests and emotions, from their various powers of coalescence and repulsion, the characters of Shakspeare are, like those in real life, evolved with an energy and strength, with a freedom and boldness of outline which will, probably for ever, stamp them with the seal of unapproachable excellence.

Nor is he less distinguished for an illimitable sway over the Passions:—

> To move
> A chilling pity—
> To strike both joy and ire;—
> To steer the affections; and by heavenly fire
> Mould us anew,—
> Yet so to temper passion, that our ears
> Take pleasure in their pain, and eyes in tears
> Both weep and smile—

are some of the noblest attributes of the dramatic poet, and more peculiarly characteristic of Shakspeare than of any other writer. The birth and progress of the numerous passions which awaken pity and terror, he has unfolded, indeed, with such minute fidelity to nature, that it is scarcely possible, as Madame De Staël has observed, to sympathise thoroughly with Shakspeare's sufferers, without tasting also of the bitter experience of real life.

The pathos of Shakspeare is either simple or figurative, in accordancy with the character, and in proportion to the intensity of the feeling, from which it emanates. The sigh of suffering merit, or the pang of unrequited love, affects us most when clothed in the language of perfect simplicity; but the energy, the paroxysm of extreme sorrow, naturally bursts into figurative language, nay often demands that very play of imagery and words, for which our bard has been ignorantly condemned, but which, like laughter amid the horrors of madness, can alone impress us with an adequately keen sense of the overwhelming agony of the soul. Of these two modes of exciting pity, we possess very striking examples in the sufferings of Katherine in *Henry the Eighth*, and in the parental afflictions of Constance in *King John*.

The excitement, indeed, of unallayed pity must necessarily either be very short, or very painful, and it has therefore been the endeavour of dramatist, according to the language of the fine old bard just quoted,

> so to temper passion, that our ears
> Take pleasure in their pain;

and this he has effected, and often with great skill and judgment, by a transient intermixture of playful fancy or comic allusion, of which, instances without number are to be found dispersed throughout his plays.

Yet great as we acknowledge the influence of Shakspeare to have been, in eliciting the tears of pity and compassion, he has surpassed, not only others but himself, in the power and extent of his dominion over the sources and operation of terror. "It may be said of crimes painted by Shakspeare," remarks an accomplished critic, "as the Bible says of Death, that he is the KING OF TERRORS;"[3] an assertion fully warranted by an appeal to Richard, to Lear, to Hamlet, to Macbeth, where this soul-harrowing emotion, as derived from natural or supernatural causes, from remorseless cruelty, from phrenzy-stricken sorrow, from conscious guilt or withering fear, is depicted with an energy so awful and appalling as to blanch the cheek and chill the blood of every intellectual being. More especially do we pursue his creations with trembling hope and breathless apprehension, when he traces the wanderings of despair, when he presents to our view that "shipwreck of moral nature," in which "the storm of life surpasses its strength."[4]

The scenes which are necessarily required for the development of villany and its artifices, must, of course, disclose many deeds of atrocity and vice, from which the unpolluted mind recoils with shuddering astonishment; but vividly, and justly too, as these have been portrayed by our poet, in all their native deformity, he has, with only one or two exceptions, so managed the exhibition, that, unless to very feeble minds, the impression never becomes too painful to be borne. Some qualifying property in the head or heart of the offender, or some repose from the intervention of more amiable or more cheerful characters, occurs to subdue to its proper tone what would otherwise amount to torture. Thus the disgust which would be apt to arise from contemplating the gigantic iniquity of Richard the Third, is corrected by an almost involuntary admiration of his intellectual vigour; and the merciless revenge of Shylock, being perpetually broken in upon by the alleviating harmonies of love and pity in the characters of those who surround him, passes not beyond the due limits of tragic emotion.

The inimitable felicity, indeed, with which Shakspeare has intermingled the finest chords of pity and of terror, such as we listen to, with unsated rapture in his Romeo, his Lear, and his Othello, has been a subject of eulogium to thousands, but never can it meet, from mortal tongue, with praise of corresponding worth. For who shall paint the beauty of those transitions, when on a night of horror breaks the first bright ray of heaven, the dawn of light and hope; when, like the sounds of an Æolian harp amid the pauses of a tempest, the still soft voice of love succeeds the tumult of despair, and whispers to the troubled spirit accents of mercy, peace, and pardon?

It is perhaps only of Shakspeare that it can be said with truth, that his comic possesses the same unrivalled merit as his tragic drama. The force and versatility of his painting in this department, its richness, its depth, and its expression, and, more than all, the originality and fecundity of invention which it everywhere exhibits, astonish, and almost overwhelm the mind in its endeavour to form an estimate of powers so gigantic, and which may not be altogether incommensurate with its scope and comprehensiveness. Whether we consider his delineations of this kind as the product of pure fiction, or founded on the costume of his age, they alike delight us by their novelty and their adhesion to nature. Falstaff and Parolles are, in many respects, as much the birth of fancy as Caliban or Ariel; but being strictly confined within the pale of humanity, and displaying all its features with living truth and distinctness, the inventive felicity of their combination is apt to escape us through our familiarity with its component parts. His Fools, or Clowns, on the contrary, were, in his time, of daily occurrence, and not only to be found in the court of the monarch, and the castle of the baron, but in the hall of the squire, and even beneath the roof of the churchman; yet, from comparing what history has recorded of this motley tribe with the spirited sketches of our author, how has he heightened their wit and sarcasm!—to such a degree, indeed, that they have frequently become in his hands personages of poetic growth, wild and grotesque, it is true, yet powerfully original.

This pre-eminence of Shakspeare in the characterisation of his fools probably led to their dramatic extinction; for it must have been found very difficult to support their tone and spirit after such a model. Beaumont and Fletcher, it has been observed, have but rarely introduced them; Ben Jonson and Massinger never; and yet the court-fool had not ceased to exist in the reign of Charles the First, nor the domestic until the commencement of the eighteenth century.[5]

Another of the great distinctions which have elevated Shakspeare so completely above the dramatic class of poets, is the splendour and infinity of his imagination—

> To out-run hasty time, retrieve the fates,
> Roll back the heavens, blow ope the iron gates
> Of death and Lethe—by art to learn
> The physiognomy of shades, and give
> Them sudden birth—and from his lofty throne,
> Create and rule a world, and work upon
> Mankind by secret engines,

was deemed, even by his contemporaries, the peculiar destiny of our bard; a destination that has been still more thoroughly felt and acknowledged by succeeding ages, and by which, without sacrificing any of the more legitimate provinces of the drama, he has acquired for his poetry that stamp of glowing inspiration, which more than places it on a level with the daring flights of Homer, of Dante, or of Milton; while, at the same time, there exclusively belongs to him an insinuating loveliness of fancy that endears him to our feelings, and brings with it a recognition of that visionary happiness which charmed our earliest youth, when all around us breathed enchantment, and the heart alone responded to the fairy melodies of love and hope.

What contrast, for instance, of poetic power has ever exceeded that which we experience in passing from the mysterious horrors of Hamlet and Macbeth, from the visitations of the midnight spectre, and the unhallowed rites of witchcraft, to the sportive revelry of the tripping elves, and the exquisite delights of Ariel; from the fiend-like character of Iago, from the soul-harrowing distraction of Lear, and the unearthly wildness of Edgar, to that music of paradise which falls melting from the tongue of Juliet or Miranda!

Were we to lengthen this summary by any dissertation on the morality of our author's drama, it might justly be considered as a work of supererogation. So completely, indeed, does this, the most valuable result of composition, pervade every portion of his dramatic writings, that we can scarcely open a page of his best plays without being forcibly struck by its lessons of virtue and utility; such as are applicable, not only to extraordinary occasions, but to the common business and routine of life; and such as, while they must make every individual better acquainted with his own nature and conditional destiny, are calculated, beyond any other productions of unrevealed wisdom, to improve that nature, and to render that destiny more happy and exalted.

Still less it is necessary to comment on the faults of Shakspeare, for they lie immediately on the surface. When we add, that some coarsenesses and indelicacies which, however, as they excite no passion and flatter no vice, are, in a moral light, not injurious; some instances of an injudicious play on words, and a few violations, not of essential, but merely of technical, costume, form their chief amount, no little surprise, it is possible, may be excited; but let us recollect, that many of the defects which prejudice and ignorance have attributed to Shakspeare, have, on being duly weighed and investigated, assumed the character of positive excellencies. Among these, for example, it will be sufficient to mention the composite or mixed nature of his drama, and his general neglect of the unities of time and place, features in the conduct of his plays which, though they have for a long period heaped upon his head a torrent of contemptuous abuse, are, at length, acknowledged to have laid the foundation, and to have furnished the noblest model of a dramatic literature, in its principles and spirit infinitely more profound and comprehensive than that which has descended to us from the shores of Greece.

*Notes*

1. Pye's *Aristotle*, 4to, 1792, p. 22.
2. This expression, and the verses which open some of the leading subjects of this summary, are taken from a poem "On Worthy Master Shakspeare," supposed to have been the composition of Jasper Mayne, but which Mr. Godwin, if we recollect aright, for the book is not before us, is desirous of attributing, on account of its singular excellence, to the pen of Milton.—See his *Lives of E. and J. Philips*, 4to.
3. *The Influence of Literature upon Society*, by Madame De Staël-Holstein, vol. i. p. 294. Translation, 2d. edit. 1812.
4. Ibid. p. 305.

5. Of court-fools, it is observed by Mr. Douce, that "Muckle John, the fool of Charles the First, and the successor of Archee Armstrong, is perhaps the last regular personage of the kind."—*Illustrations*, vol. ii. p. 308. We also find an epitaph by Dean Swift, on Dicky Pierce, the Earl of Suffolk's fool, who was buried in Berkeley church-yard, June 18, 1728, in the same ingenious essay.

### SAMUEL TAYLOR COLERIDGE
From *Shakspeare, with Introductory Remarks on Poetry, the Drama, and the Stage* (1818)
*Literary Remains*, ed. Henry Nelson Coleridge
1836, Volume 2, pp. 53–83
*Shakspeare, a Poet Generally*

Clothed in radiant armour, and authorized by titles sure and manifold, as a poet, Shakspeare came forward to demand the throne of fame, as the dramatic poet of England. His excellencies compelled even his contemporaries to seat him on that throne, although there were giants in those days contending for the same honor. Hereafter I would fain endeavour to make out the title of the English drama as created by, and existing in, Shakspeare, and its right to the supremacy of dramatic excellence in general. But he had shown himself a poet, previously to his appearance as a dramatic poet; and had no *Lear*, no *Othello*, no *Henry IV.*, no *Twelfth Night* ever appeared, we must have admitted that Shakspeare possessed the chief, if not every, requisite of a poet,—deep feeling and exquisite sense of beauty, both as exhibited to the eye in the combinations of form, and to the ear in sweet and appropriate melody; that these feelings were under the command of his own will; that in his very first productions he projected his mind out of his own particular being, and felt, and made others feel, on subjects no way connected with himself, except by force of contemplation and that sublime faculty by which a great mind becomes that, on which it meditates. To this must be added that affectionate love of nature and natural objects, without which no man could have observed so steadily, or painted so truly and passionately, the very minutest beauties of the external world:—

> And when thou hast on foot the purblind hare,
> Mark the poor wretch; to overshoot his troubles,
> How he outruns the wind, and with what care,
> He cranks and crosses with a thousand doubles;
> The many musits through the which he goes
> Are like a labyrinth to amaze his foes.
>
> Sometimes he runs among the flock of sheep,
> To make the cunning hounds mistake their smell;
> And sometime where earth-delving conies keep,
> To stop the loud pursuers in their yell;
> And sometime sorteth with a herd of deer:
> Danger deviseth shifts, wit waits on fear.
>
> For there his smell with others' being mingled,
> The hot scent-snuffing hounds are driven to doubt,
> Ceasing their clamorous cry, till they have singled,
> With much ado, the cold fault cleanly out,
> Then do they spend their mouths; echo replies,
> As if another chase were in the skies.
>
> By this poor Wat far off, upon a hill,
> Stands on his hinder legs with listening ear,
> To hearken if his foes pursue him still:
> Anon their loud alarums he doth hear,
> And now his grief may be compared well
> To one sore-sick, that hears the passing bell.

Then shalt thou see the dew-bedabbled wretch
Turn, and return, indenting with the way:
Each envious briar his weary legs doth scratch,
Each shadow makes him stop, each murmur stay.
For misery is trodden on by many,
And being low, never relieved by any.
                                  (*Venus and Adonis.*)

And the preceding description:—

  But, lo! from forth a copse that neighbours by,
  A breeding jennet, lusty, young and proud, &c.

is much more admirable, but in parts less fitted for quotation.

Moreover Shakspeare had shown that he possessed fancy, considered as the faculty of bringing together images dissimilar in the main by some one point or more of likeness, as in such a passage as this:—

  Full gently now she takes him by the hand,
  A lily prisoned in a jail of snow,
  Or ivory in an alabaster band;
  So white a friend ingirts so white a foe!

                                                  (Ib.)

And still mounting the intellectual ladder, he had as unequivocally proved the indwelling in his mind of imagination, or the power by which one image or feeling is made to modify many others, and by a sort of fusion to force many into one;—that which afterwards showed itself in such might and energy in *Lear*, where the deep anguish of a father spreads the feeling of ingratitude and cruelty over the very elements of heaven;—and which, combining many circumstances into one moment of consciousness, tends to produce that ultimate end of all human thought and human feeling, unity, and thereby the reduction of the spirit to its principle and fountain, who is alone truly one. Various are the workings of this the greatest faculty of the human mind, both passionate and tranquil. In its tranquil and purely pleasurable operation, it acts chiefly by creating out of many things, as they would have appeared in the description of an ordinary mind, detailed in unimpassioned succession, a oneness, even as nature, the greatest of poets, acts upon us, when we open our eyes upon an extended prospect. Thus the flight of Adonis in the dusk of the evening:—

  Look! how a bright star shooteth from the sky;
  So glides he in the night from Venus' eye!

How many images and feelings are here brought together without effort and without discord, in the beauty of Adonis, the rapidity of his flight, the yearning, yet hopelessness, of the enamored gazer, while a shadowy ideal character is thrown over the whole! Or this power acts by impressing the stamp of humanity, and of human feelings, on inanimate or mere natural objects:—

  Lo! here the gentle lark, weary of rest,
  From his moist cabinet mounts up on high,
  And wakes the morning, from whose silver breast
  The sun ariseth in his majesty,
  Who doth the world so gloriously behold,
  The cedar-tops and hills seem burnish'd gold.

Or again, it acts by so carrying on the eye of the reader as to make him almost lose the consciousness of words,—to make him see every thing flashed, as Wordsworth has grandly and appropriately said,—

  *Flashed* upon that inward eye
  Which is the bliss of solitude;—

and this without exciting any painful or laborious attention, without any anatomy of description, (a fault not uncommon in descriptive poetry)—but with the sweetness and easy movement of nature. This energy is an absolute essential of poetry, and of itself would constitute a poet, though not one of the highest class;—it is, however, a most hopeful symptom, and the *Venus and Adonis* is one continued specimen of it.

In this beautiful poem there is an endless activity of thought in all the possible associations of thought with thought, thought with feeling, or with words, of feelings with feelings, and of words with words.

  Even as the sun, with purple-colour'd face,
  Had ta'en his last leave of the weeping morn,
  Rose-cheek'd Adonis hied him to the chase:
  Hunting he loved, but love he laughed to scorn.
  Sick-thoughted Venus makes amain unto him,
  And like a bold-faced suitor 'gins to woo him.

Remark the humanizing imagery and circumstances of the first two lines, and the activity of thought in the play of words in the fourth line. The whole stanza presents at once the time, the appearance of the morning, and the two persons distinctly characterized, and in six simple verses puts the reader in possession of the whole argument of the poem.

  Over one arm the lusty courser's rein,
  Under the other was the tender boy,
  Who blush'd and pouted in a dull disdain,
  With leaden appetite, unapt to toy,
  She red and hot, as coals of glowing fire,
  He red for shame, but frosty to desire:—

This stanza and the two following afford good instances of that poetic power, which I mentioned above, of making every thing present to the imagination—both the forms, and the passions which modify those forms, either actually, as in the representations of love, or anger, or other human affections; or imaginatively, by the different manner in which inanimate objects, or objects unimpassioned themselves, are caused to be seen by the mind in moments of strong excitement, and according to the kind of the excitement,—whether of jealousy, or rage, or love, in the only appropriate sense of the word, or of the lower impulses of our nature, or finally of the poetic feeling itself. It is, perhaps, chiefly in the power of producing and reproducing the latter that the poet stands distinct.

The subject of the *Venus and Adonis* is unpleasing; but the poem itself is for that very reason the more illustrative of Shakspeare. There are men who can write passages of deepest pathos and even sublimity on circumstances personal to themselves and stimulative of their own passions; but they are not, therefore, on this account poets. Read that magnificent burst of woman's patriotism and exultation, Deborah's song of victory; it is glorious, but nature is the poet there. It is quite another matter to become all things and yet remain the same,—to make the changeful god be felt in the river, the lion and the flame;—this it is, that is the true imagination. Shakspeare writes in this poem, as if he were of another planet, charming you to gaze on the movements of Venus and Adonis, as you would on the twinkling dances of two vernal butterflies.

Finally, in this poem and the *Rape of Lucrece*, Shakspeare gave ample proof of his possession of a most profound, energetic, and philosophical mind, without which he might have pleased, but could not have been a great dramatic poet. Chance and the necessity of his genius combined to lead him to the drama his proper province; in his conquest of which we should consider both the difficulties which opposed him, and the advantages by which he was assisted.

### Shakspeare's Judgment Equal to His Genius

Thus then Shakspeare appears, from his *Venus and Adonis* and *Rape of Lucrece* alone, apart from all his great works, to have possessed all the conditions of the true poet. Let me now proceed to destroy, as far as may be in my power, the popular notion that he was a great dramatist by mere instinct, that he grew immortal in his own despite, and sank below men of second or third-rate power, when he attempted aught beside the drama—even as bees construct their cells and manufacture their honey to admirable perfection; but would in vain attempt to build a nest. Now this mode of reconciling a compelled sense of inferiority with a feeling of pride, began in a few pedants, who having read that Sophocles was the great model of tragedy, and Aristotle the infallible dictator of its rules, and finding that the *Lear, Hamlet, Othello* and other master-pieces were neither in imitation of Sophocles, nor in obedience to Aristotle,—and not having (with one or two exceptions) the courage to affirm, that the delight which their country received from generation to generation, in defiance of the alterations of circumstances and habits, was wholly groundless,—took upon them, as a happy medium and refuge, to talk of Shakspeare as a sort of beautiful *lusus naturæ*, a delightful monster,—wild, indeed, and without taste or judgment, but like the inspired idiots so much venerated in the East, uttering, amid the strangest follies, the sublimest truths. In nine places out of ten in which I find his awful name mentioned, it is with some epithet of 'wild,' 'irregular,' 'pure child of nature,' &c. If all this be true, we must submit to it; though to a thinking mind it cannot but be painful to find any excellence, merely human, thrown out of all human analogy, and thereby leaving us neither rules for imitation, nor motives to imitate;—but if false, it is a dangerous falsehood;—for it affords a refuge to secret self-conceit,—enables a vain man at once to escape his reader's indignation by general swoln panegyrics, and merely by his *ipse dixit* to treat, as contemptible, what he has not intellect enough to comprehend, or soul to feel, without assigning any reason, or referring his opinion to any demonstrative principle;—thus leaving Shakspeare as a sort of grand Lama, adored indeed, and his very excrements prized as relics, but with no authority or real influence. I grieve that every late voluminous edition of his works would enable me to substantiate the present charge with a variety of facts one tenth of which would of themselves exhaust the time allotted to me. Every critic, who has or has not made a collection of black letter books—in itself a useful and respectable amusement,—puts on the seven-league boots of self-opinion, and strides at once from an illustrator into a supreme judge, and blind and deaf, fills his three-ounce phial at the waters of Niagara; and determines positively the greatness of the cataract to be neither more nor less than his three-ounce phial has been able to receive.

I think this a very serious subject. It is my earnest desire—my passionate endeavour,—to enforce at various times and by various arguments and instances the close and reciprocal connexion of just taste with pure morality. Without that acquaintance with the heart of man, or that docility and childlike gladness to be made acquainted with it, which those only can have, who dare look at their own hearts—and that with a steadiness which religion only has the power of reconciling with sincere humility;—without this, and the modesty produced by it, I am deeply convinced that no man, however wide his erudition, however patient his antiquarian researches, can possibly understand, or be worthy of understanding, the writings of Shakspeare.

Assuredly that criticism of Shakspeare will alone be genial which is reverential. The Englishman, who without reverence, a proud and affectionate reverence, can utter the name of William Shakspeare, stands disqualified for the office of critic. He wants one at least of the very senses, the language of which he is to employ, and will discourse at best, but as a blind man,

while the whole harmonious creation of light and shade with all its subtle interchange of deepening and dissolving colours rises in silence to the silent *fiat* of the uprising Apollo. However inferior in ability I may be to some who have followed me, I own I am proud that I was the first in time who publicly demonstrated to the full extent of the position, that the supposed irregularity and extravagancies of Shakspeare were the mere dreams of a pedantry that arraigned the eagle because it had not the dimensions of the swan. In all the successive courses of lectures delivered by me, since my first attempt at the Royal Institution, it has been, and it still remains, my object, to prove that in all points from the most important to the most minute, the judgment of Shakspeare is commensurate with his genius,—nay, that his genius reveals itself in his judgment, as in its most exalted form. And the more gladly do I recur to this subject from the clear conviction, that to judge aright, and with distinct consciousness of the grounds of our judgment, concerning the works of Shakspeare, implies the power and the means of judging rightly of all other works of intellect, those of abstract science alone excepted.

It is a painful truth that not only individuals, but even whole nations, are ofttimes so enslaved to the habits of their education and immediate circumstances, as not to judge disinterestedly even on those subjects, the very pleasure arising from which consists in its disinterestedness, namely, on subjects of taste and polite literature. Instead of deciding concerning their own modes and customs by any rule of reason, nothing appears rational, becoming, or beautiful to them, but what coincides with the peculiarities of their education. In this narrow circle, individuals may attain to exquisite discrimination, as the French critics have done in their own literature; but a true critic can no more be such without placing himself on some central point, from which he may command the whole, that is, some general rule, which, founded in reason, or the faculties common to all men, must therefore apply to each,—than an astronomer can explain the movements of the solar system without taking his stand in the sun. And let me remark, that this will not tend to produce despotism, but, on the contrary, true tolerance, in the critic. He will, indeed, require, as the spirit and substance of a work, something true in human nature itself, and independent of all circumstances; but in the mode of applying it, he will estimate genius and judgment according to the felicity with which the imperishable soul of intellect shall have adapted itself to the age, the place, and the existing manners. The error he will expose, lies in reversing this, and holding up the mere circumstances as perpetual to the utter neglect of the power which can alone animate them. For art cannot exist without, or apart from, nature; and what has man of his own to give to his fellow-man, but his own thoughts and feelings, and his observations so far as they are modified by his own thoughts or feelings?

Let me, then, once more submit this question to minds emancipated alike from national, or party, or sectarian prejudice:—Are the plays of Shakspeare works of rude uncultivated genius, in which the splendour of the parts compensates, if aught can compensate, for the barbarous shapelessness and irregularity of the whole?—Or is the form equally admirable with the matter, and the judgment of the great poet, not less deserving our wonder than his genius?—Or, again, to repeat the question in other words:—Is Shakspeare a great dramatic poet on account only of those beauties and excellencies which he possesses in common with the ancients, but with diminished claims to our love and honour to the full extent of his differences from them?—Or are these very differences additional proofs of poetic wisdom, at once results and symbols of living power as contrasted with lifeless mechanism—of free and rival originality as contradistinguished from servile imitation, or, more accurately, a blind copying of effects, instead of a true imitation of the essential principles?—Imagine not that I am about to oppose genius to rules. No! the comparative value of these rules is the very cause to be tried. The spirit of poetry, like all other living powers, must of necessity circumscribe itself by rules, were it only to unite power with beauty. It must embody in order to reveal itself; but a living body is of necessity an organized one; and what is organization but the connection of parts in and for a whole, so that each part is at once end and means?—This is no discovery of criticism;—it is a necessity of the human mind; and all nations have felt and obeyed it, in the invention of metre, and measured sounds, as the vehicle and *involucrum* of poetry—itself a fellow-growth from the same life,—even as the bark is to the tree!

No work of true genius dares want its appropriate form, neither indeed is there any danger of this. As it must not, so genius cannot, be lawless; for it is even this that constitutes it genius—the power of acting creatively under laws of its own origination. How then comes it that not only single *Zoili*, but whole nations have combined in unhesitating condemnation of our great dramatist, as a sort of African nature, rich in beautiful monsters,—as a wild heath where islands of fertility look the greener from the surrounding waste, where the loveliest plants now shine out among unsightly weeds, and now are choked by their parasitic growth, so intertwined that we cannot disentangle the weed without snapping the flower?—In this statement I have had no reference to the vulgar abuse of Voltaire, save as far as his charges are coincident with the decisions of Shakspeare's own commentators and (so they would tell you) almost idolatrous admirers. The true ground of the mistake lies in the confounding mechanical regularity with organic form. The form is mechanic, when on any given material we impress a pre-determined form, not necessarily arising out of the properties of the material;—as when to a mass of wet clay we give whatever shape we wish it to retain when hardened. The organic form, on the other hand, is innate; it shapes, as it developes, itself from within, and the fulness of its development is one and the same with the perfection of its outward form. Such as the life is, such is the form. Nature, the prime genial artist, inexhaustible in diverse powers, is equally inexhaustible in forms;—each exterior is the physiognomy of the being within,—its true image reflected and thrown out from the concave mirror;—and even such is the appropriate excellence of her chosen poet, of our own Shakspeare,—himself a nature humanized, a genial understanding directing self-consciously a power and an implicit wisdom deeper even than our consciousness.

I greatly dislike beauties and selections in general; but as proof positive of his unrivalled excellence, I should like to try Shakspeare by this criterion. Make out your amplest catalogue of all the human faculties, as reason or the moral law, the will, the feeling of the coincidence of the two (a feeling *sui generis et demonstratio demonstrationum*) called the conscience, the understanding or prudence, wit, fancy, imagination, judgment,—and then of the objects on which these are to be employed, as the beauties, the terrors, and the seeming caprices of nature, the realities and the capabilities, that is, the actual and the ideal, of the human mind, conceived as an individual or as a social being, as in innocence or in guilt, in a play-paradise, or in a war-field of temptation;—and then compare with Shakspeare under each of these heads all or any

of the writers in prose and verse that have ever lived! Who, that is competent to judge, doubts the result?—And ask your own hearts,—ask your own common-sense—to conceive the possibility of this man being—I say not, the drunken savage of that wretched sciolist, whom Frenchmen, to their shame, have honoured before their elder and better worthies,—but the anomalous, the wild, the irregular, genius of our daily criticism! What! are we to have miracles in sport?—Or, I speak reverently, does God choose idiots by whom to convey divine truths to man?

### Recapitulation, and Summary
### of the Characteristics of Shakspeare's Drama

In lectures, of which amusement forms a large part of the object, there are some peculiar difficulties. The architect places his foundation out of sight, and the musician tunes his instrument before he makes his appearance; but the lecturer has to try his chords in the presence of the assembly; an operation not likely, indeed, to produce much pleasure, but yet indispensably necessary to a right understanding of the subject to be developed.

Poetry in essence is as familiar to barbarous as to civilized nations. The Laplander and the savage Indian are cheered by it as well as the inhabitants of London and Paris;—its spirit takes up and incorporates surrounding materials, as a plant clothes itself with soil and climate, whilst it exhibits the working of a vital principle within independent of all accidental circumstances. And to judge with fairness of an author's works, we ought to distinguish what is inward and essential from what is outward and circumstantial. It is essential to poetry that it be simple, and appeal to the elements and primary laws of our nature; that it be sensuous, and by its imagery elicit truth at a flash; that it be impassioned, and be able to move our feelings and awaken our affections. In comparing different poets with each other, we should inquire which have brought into the fullest play our imagination and our reason, or have created the greatest excitement and produced the completest harmony. If we consider great exquisiteness of language and sweetness of metre alone, it is impossible to deny to Pope the character of a delightful writer; but whether he be a poet, must depend upon our definition of the word; and, doubtless, if every thing that pleases be poetry, Pope's satires and epistles must be poetry. This, I must say, that poetry, as distinguished from other modes of composition, does not rest in metre, and that it is not poetry, if it make no appeal to our passions or our imagination. One character belongs to all true poets, that they write from a principle within, not originating in any thing without; and that the true poet's work in its form, its shapings, and its modifications, is distinguished from all other works that assume to belong to the class of poetry, as a natural from an artificial flower, or as the mimic garden of a child from an enamelled meadow. In the former the flowers are broken from their stems and stuck into the ground; they are beautiful to the eye and fragrant to the sense, but their colours soon fade, and their odour is transient as the smile of the planter;—while the meadow may be visited again and again with renewed delight, its beauty is innate in the soil, and its bloom is of the freshness of nature.

The next ground of critical judgment, and point of comparison, will be as to how far a given poet has been influenced by accidental circumstances. As a living poet must surely write, not for the ages past, but for that in which he lives, and those which are to follow, it is, on the one hand, natural that he should not violate, and on the other, necessary that he should not depend on, the mere manners and modes of his day. See how little does Shakspeare leave us to regret that he was born in his particular age! The great æra in modern times was what is called the Restoration of Letters;—the ages preceding it are called the dark ages; but it would be more wise, perhaps, to call them the ages in which we were in the dark. It is usually overlooked that the supposed dark period was not universal, but partial and successive, or alternate; that the dark age of England was not the dark age of Italy, but that one country was in its light and vigour, whilst another was in its gloom and bondage. But no sooner had the Reformation sounded through Europe like the blast of an archangel's trumpet, than from king to peasant there arose an enthusiasm for knowledge; the discovery of a manuscript became the subject of an embassy; Erasmus read by moonlight, because he could not afford a torch, and begged a penny, not for the love of charity, but for the love of learning. The three great points of attention were religion, morals, and taste; men of genius as well as men of learning, who in this age need to be so widely distinguished, then alike became copyists of the ancients; and this, indeed, was the only way by which the taste of mankind could be improved, or their understandings informed. Whilst Dante imagined himself a humble follower of Virgil, and Ariosto of Homer, they were both unconscious of that greater power working within them, which in many points carried them beyond their supposed originals. All great discoveries bear the stamp of the age in which they are made;—hence we perceive the effects of the purer religion of the moderns, visible for the most part in their lives; and in reading their works we should not content ourselves with the mere narratives of events long since passed, but should learn to apply their maxims and conduct to ourselves.

Having intimated that times and manners lend their form and pressure to genius, let me once more draw a slight parallel between the ancient and modern stage, the stages of Greece and of England. The Greeks were polytheists; their religion was local; almost the only object of all their knowledge, art and taste, was their gods; and, accordingly, their productions were, if the expression may be allowed, statuesque, whilst those of the moderns are picturesque. The Greeks reared a structure, which in its parts, and as a whole, fitted the mind with the calm and elevated impression of perfect beauty and symmetrical proportion. The moderns also produced a whole, a more striking whole; but it was by blending materials and fusing the parts together. And as the Pantheon is to York Minster or Westminster Abbey, so is Sophocles compared with Shakspeare; in the one a completeness, a satisfaction, an excellence, on which the mind rests with complacency; in the other a multitude of interlaced materials, great and little, magnificent and mean, accompanied, indeed, with the sense of a falling short of perfection, and yet, at the same time, so promising of our social and individual progression, that we would not, if we could, exchange it for that repose of the mind which dwells on the forms of symmetry in the acquiescent admiration of grace. This general characteristic of the ancient and modern drama might be illustrated by a parallel of the ancient and modern music;—the one consisting of melody arising from a succession only of pleasing sounds,—the modern embracing harmony also, the result of combination and the effect of a whole.

I have said, and I say it again, that great as was the genius of Shakspeare, his judgment was at least equal to it. Of this any one will be convinced, who attentively considers those points in which the dramas of Greece and England differ, from the dissimilitude of circumstances by which each was modified and influenced. The Greek stage had its origin in the ceremonies of a sacrifice, such as of the goat to Bacchus, whom we most erroneously regard as merely the jolly god of wine;—for among the ancients he was venerable, as the symbol of that power

which acts without our consciousness in the vital energies of nature,—the *vinum mundi*,—as Apollo was that of the conscious agency of our intellectual being. The heroes of old under the influence of this Bacchic enthusiasm performed more than human actions;—hence tales of the favorite champions soon passed into dialogue. On the Greek stage the chorus was always before the audience; the curtain was never dropped, as we should say; and change of place being therefore, in general, impossible, the absurd notion of condemning it merely as improbable in itself was never entertained by any one. If we can believe ourselves at Thebes in one act, we may believe ourselves at Athens in the next. If a story lasts twenty-four hours or twenty-four years, it is equally improbable. There seems to be no just boundary but what the feelings prescribe. But on the Greek stage where the same persons were perpetually before the audience, great judgment was necessary in venturing on any such change. The poets never, therefore, attempted to impose on the senses by bringing places to men, but they did bring men to places, as in the well known instance in the *Eumenides*, where during an evident retirement of the chorus from the orchestra, the scene is changed to Athens, and Orestes is first introduced in the temple of Minerva, and the chorus of Furies come in afterwards in pursuit of him.

In the Greek drama there were no formal divisions into scenes and acts; there were no means, therefore, of allowing for the necessary lapse of time between one part of the dialogue and another, and unity of time in a strict sense was, of course, impossible. To overcome that difficulty of accounting for time, which is effected on the modern stage by dropping a curtain, the judgment and great genius of the ancients supplied music and measured motion, and with the lyric ode filled up the vacuity. In the story of the *Agamemnon* of Æschylus, the capture of Troy is supposed to be announced by a fire lighted on the Asiatic shore, and the transmission of the signal by successive beacons to Mycenæ. The signal is first seen at the 21st line, and the herald from Troy itself enters at the 486th, and Agamemnon himself at the 783rd line. But the practical absurdity of this was not felt by the audience, who, in imagination stretched minutes into hours, while they listened to the lofty narrative odes of the chorus which almost entirely fill up the interspace. Another fact deserves attention here, namely, that regularly on the Greek stage a drama, or acted story, consisted in reality of three dramas, called together a trilogy, and performed consecutively in the course of one day. Now you may conceive a tragedy of Shakspeare's as a trilogy connected in one single representation. Divide *Lear* into three parts, and each would be a play with the ancients; or take the three Æschylean dramas of Agamemnon, and divide them into, or call them, as many acts, and they together would be one play. The first act would comprise the usurpation of Ægisthus, and the murder of Agamemnon; the second, the revenge of Orestes, and the murder of his mother; and the third, the penance and absolution of Orestes;—occupying a period of twenty-two years.

The stage in Shakspeare's time was a naked room with a blanket for a curtain; but he made it a field for monarchs. That law of unity, which has its foundations, not in the factitious necessity of custom, but in nature itself, the unity of feeling, is every where and at all times observed by Shakspeare in his plays. Read *Romeo and Juliet*;—all is youth and spring;—youth with its follies, its virtues, its precipitancies;—spring with its odours, its flowers, and its transiency; it is one and the same feeling that commences, goes through, and ends the play. The old men, the Capulets and the Montagues, are not common old men; they have an eagerness, a heartiness, a vehemence, the effect of spring; with Romeo, his change of passion, his sudden marriage, and his rash death, are all the effects of youth;—whilst in Juliet love has all that is tender and melancholy in the nightingale, all that is voluptuous in the rose, with whatever is sweet in the freshness of spring; but it ends with a long deep sigh like the last breeze of the Italian evening. This unity of feeling and character pervades every drama of Shakspeare.

It seems to me that his plays are distinguished from those of all other dramatic poets by the following characteristics:

1. Expectation in preference to surprise. It is like the true reading of the passage;—'God said, Let there be light, and there was *light*,'—not there *was* light. As the feeling with which we startle at a shooting star, compared with that of watching the sunrise at the pre-established moment, such and so low is surprise compared with expectation.

2. Signal adherence to the great law of nature, that all opposites tend to attract and temper each other. Passion in Shakspeare generally displays libertinism, but involves morality; and if there are exceptions to this, they are, independently of their intrinsic value, all of them indicative of individual character, and, like the farewell admonitions of a parent, have an end beyond the parental relation. Thus the Countess's beautiful precepts to Bertram, by elevating her character, raise that of Helena her favorite, and soften down the point in her which Shakspeare does not mean us not to see, but to see and to forgive, and at length to justify. And so it is in Polonius, who is the personified memory of wisdom no longer actually possessed. This admirable character is always misrepresented on the stage. Shakspeare never intended to exhibit him as a buffoon; for although it was natural that Hamlet,—a young man of fire and genius, detesting formality, and disliking Polonius on political grounds, as imagining that he had assisted his uncle in his usurpation,—should express himself satirically,—yet this must not be taken as exactly the poet's conception of him. In Polonius a certain induration of character had arisen from long habits of business; but take his advice to Laertes, and Ophelia's reverence for his memory, and we shall see that he was meant to be represented as a statesman somewhat past his faculties,—his recollections of life all full of wisdom, and showing a knowledge of human nature, whilst what immediately takes place before him, and escapes from him, is indicative of weakness.

But as in Homer all the deities are in armour, even Venus; so in Shakspeare all the characters are strong. Hence real folly and dullness are made by him the vehicles of wisdom. There is no difficulty for one being a fool to imitate a fool; but to be, remain, and speak like a wise man and a great wit, and yet so as to give a vivid representation of a veritable fool,—*hic labor, hoc opus est.* A drunken constable is not uncommon, nor hard to draw; but see and examine what goes to make up a Dogberry.

3. Keeping at all times in the high road of life. Shakspeare has no innocent adulteries, no interesting incests, no virtuous vice;—he never renders that amiable which religion and reason alike teach us to detest, or clothes impurity in the garb of virtue, like Beaumont and Fletcher, the Kotzebues of the day. Shakspeare's fathers are roused by ingratitude, his husbands stung by unfaithfulness; in him, in short, the affections are wounded in those points in which all may, nay, must, feel. Let the morality of Shakspeare be contrasted with that of the writers of his own, or the succeeding, age, or of those of the present day, who boast their superiority in this respect. No one can dispute that the result of such a comparison is altogether in favour of Shakspeare;—even the letters of women of high rank in his age were often coarser than his writings. If he occasionally disgusts a keen sense of delicacy, he never injures

the mind; he neither excites, nor flatters, passion, in order to degrade the subject of it; he does not use the faulty thing for a faulty purpose, nor carries on warfare against virtue, by causing wickedness to appear as no wickedness, through the medium of a morbid sympathy with the unfortunate. In Shakspeare vice never walks as in twilight; nothing is purposely out of its place;—he inverts not the order of nature and propriety,—does not make every magistrate a drunkard or glutton, nor every poor man meek, humane, and temperate; he has no benevolent butchers, nor any sentimental rat-catchers.

4. Independence of the dramatic interest on the plot. The interest in the plot is always in fact on account of the characters, not *vice versa*, as in almost all other writers; the plot is a mere canvass and no more. Hence arises the true justification of the same stratagem being used in regard to Benedict and Beatrice,—the vanity in each being alike. Take away from the *Much Ado about Nothing* all that which is not indispensable to the plot, either as having little to do with it, or, at best, like Dogberry and his comrades, forced into the service, when any other less ingeniously absurd watchmen and night-constables would have answered the mere necessities of the action;—take away Benedict, Beatrice, Dogberry, and the reaction of the former on the character of Hero,—and what will remain? In other writers the main agent of the plot is always the prominent character; in Shakspeare it is so, or is not so, as the character is in itself calculated, or not calculated, to form the plot. Don John is the main-spring of the plot of this play; but he is merely shown and then withdrawn.

5. Independence of the interest on the story as the groundwork of the plot. Hence Shakspeare never took the trouble of inventing stories. It was enough for him to select from those that had been already invented or recorded such as had one or other, or both, of two recommendations, namely, suitableness to his particular purpose, and their being parts of popular tradition,—names of which we had often heard, and of their fortunes, and as to which all we wanted was, to see the man himself. So it is just the man himself, the Lear, the Shylock, the Richard, that Shakspeare makes us for the first time acquainted with. Omit the first scene in *Lear*, and yet every thing will remain; so the first and second scenes in the *Merchant of Venice*. Indeed it is universally true.

6. Interfusion of the lyrical—that which in its very essence is poetical—not only with the dramatic, as in the plays of Metastasio, where at the end of the scene comes the *aria* as the *exit* speech of the character,—but also in and through the dramatic. Songs in Shakspeare are introduced as songs only, just as songs are in real life, beautifully as some of them are characteristic of the person who has sung or called for them, as Desdemona's 'Willow,' and Ophelia's wild snatches, and the sweet carollings in *As You Like It*. But the whole of the *Midsummer Night's Dream* is one continued specimen of the dramatized lyrical. And observe how exquisitely the dramatic of Hotspur;—

> Marry, and I'm glad on't with all my heart;
> I had rather be a kitten and cry—mew, &c.

melts away into the lyric of Mortimer;—

> I understand thy looks: that pretty Welsh
> Which thou pourest down from these swelling heavens,
> I am too perfect in, &c.
> (Henry IV. part i. act iii. sc. i.)

7. The characters of the *dramatis personæ*, like those in real life, are to be inferred by the reader;—they are not told to him. And it is well worth remarking that Shakspeare's characters, like those in real life, are very commonly misunderstood,

and almost always understood by different persons in different ways. The causes are the same in either case. If you take only what the friends of the character say, you may be deceived, and still more so, if that which his enemies say; nay, even the character himself sees himself through the medium of his character, and not exactly as he is. Take all together, not omitting a shrewd hint from the clown or the fool, and perhaps your impression will be right; and you may know whether you have in fact discovered the poet's own idea, by all the speeches receiving light from it, and attesting its reality by reflecting it.

Lastly, in Shakspeare the heterogeneous is united, as it is in nature. You must not suppose a pressure or passion always acting on or in the character;—passion in Shakspeare is that by which the individual is distinguished from others, not that which makes a different kind of him. Shakspeare followed the main march of the human affections. He entered into no analysis of the passions or faiths of men, but assured himself that such and such passions and faiths were grounded in our common nature, and not in the mere accidents of ignorance or disease. This is an important consideration, and constitutes our Shakspeare the morning star, the guide and the pioneer, of true philosophy.

## WILLIAM HAZLITT
### From "Shakspeare and Milton"
*Lectures on the English Poets*
1818

The four greatest names in English poetry, are almost the four first we come to—Chaucer, Spenser, Shakspeare, and Milton. There are no others that can really be put in competition with these. The two last have had justice done them by the voice of common fame. Their names are blazoned in the very firmament of reputation; while the two first, (though "the fault has been more in their stars than in themselves that they are underlings") either never emerged far above the horizon, or were too soon involved in the obscurity of time. The three first of these are excluded from Dr. Johnson's *Lives of the Poets* (Shakspeare indeed is so from the dramatic form of his compositions): and the fourth, Milton, is admitted with a reluctant and churlish welcome.

In comparing these four writers together, it might be said that Chaucer excels as the poet of manners, or of real life; Spenser, as the poet of romance; Shakspeare, as the poet of nature (in the largest use of the term): and Milton, as the poet of morality. Chaucer most frequently describes things as they are; Spenser, as we wish them to be; Shakspeare, as they would be; and Milton as they ought to be. As poets, and as great poets, imagination, that is, the power of feigning things according to nature, was common to them all: but the principle or moving power, to which this faculty was most subservient in Chaucer, was habit, or inveterate prejudice; in Spenser, novelty, and the love of the marvellous; in Shakspeare, it was the force of passion, combined with every variety of possible circumstances; and in Milton, only with the highest. The characteristic of Chaucer is intensity; of Spenser, remoteness; of Milton, elevation; of Shakspeare, everything.—It has been said by some critic, that Shakspeare was distinguished from the other dramatic writers of his day only by his wit; that they had all his other qualities but that; that one writer had as much sense, another as much fancy, another as much knowledge of character, another the same depth of passion, and another as great a power of language. This statement is not true; nor is the

inference from it well-founded, even if it were. This person does not seem to have been aware that, upon his own shewing, the great distinction of Shakspeare's genius was its virtually including the genius of all the great men of his age, and not his differing from them in one accidental particular. But to have done with such minute and literal trifling.

The striking peculiarity of Shakspeare's mind was its generic quality, its power of communication with all other minds—so that it contained a universe of thought and feeling within itself, and had no one peculiar bias, or exclusive excellence more than another. He was just like any other man, but that he was like all other men. He was the least of an egotist that it was possible to be. He was nothing in himself; but he was all that others were, or that they could become. He not only had in himself the germs of every faculty and feeling, but he could follow them by anticipation, intuitively, into all their conceivable ramifications, through every change of fortune or conflict of passion, or turn of thought. He had "a mind reflecting ages past," and present:—all the people that ever lived are there. There was no respect of persons with him. His genius shone equally on the evil and on the good, on the wise and the foolish, the monarch and the beggar: "All corners of the earth, kings, queens, and states, maids, matrons, nay, the secrets of the grave," are hardly hid from his searching glance. He was like the genius of humanity, changing places with all of us at pleasure, and playing with our purposes as with his own. He turned the globe round for his amusement, and surveyed the generations of men, and the individuals as they passed, with their different concerns, passions, follies, vices, virtues, actions, and motives—as well those that they knew, as those which they did not know, or acknowledge to themselves. The dreams of childhood, the ravings of despair, were the toys of his fancy. Airy beings waited at his call, and came at his bidding. Harmless fairies "nodded to him, and did him curtesies:" and the night-hag bestrode the blast at the command of "his so potent art." The world of spirits lay open to him, like the world of real men and women: and there is the same truth in his delineations of the one as of the other; for if the preternatural characters he describes could be supposed to exist, they would speak, and feel, and act, as he makes them. He had only to think of any thing in order to become that thing, with all the circumstances belonging to it. When he conceived of a character whether real or imaginary, he not only entered into all its thoughts and feelings, but seemed instantly, and as if by touching a secret spring, to be surrounded with all the same objects, "subject to the same skyey influences," the same local, outward, and unforeseen accidents which would occur in reality. Thus the character of Caliban not only stands before us with a language and manners of its own, but the scenery and situation of the enchanted island he inhabits, the traditions of the place, its strange noises, its hidden recesses, "his frequent haunts and ancient neighbourhood," are given with a miraculous truth of nature, and with all the familiarity of an old recollection. The whole "coheres semblably together" in time, place, and circumstance. In reading this author, you do not merely learn what his characters say,—you see their persons. By something expressed or understood, you are at no loss to decypher their peculiar physiognomy, the meaning of a look, the grouping, the bye-play, as we might see it on the stage. A word, an epithet paints a whole scene, or throws us back whole years in the history of the person represented. So (as it has been ingeniously remarked) when Prospero describes himself as left alone in the boat with his daughter, the epithet which he applies to her, "Me and thy *crying* self," flings the imagination instantly back from the grown woman to the helpless condition

Anne Hathaway's cottage, Stratford-on-Avon

The Globe Theatre

# Mr. WILLIAM
# SHAKESPEARES

## COMEDIES,
## HISTORIES, &
## TRAGEDIES.

Published according to the True Originall Copies.

Martin Droeshout sculpsit London.

# LONDON
Printed by Isaac Iaggard, and Ed. Blount. 1623.

Title page, First Folio (1623)

of infancy, and places the first and most trying scene of his misfortunes before us, with all that he must have suffered in the interval. How well the silent anguish of Macduff is conveyed to the reader, by the friendly expostulation of Malcolm—"What! man, ne'er pull your hat upon your brows!" Again, Hamlet, in the scene with Rosencrans and Guildenstern, somewhat abruptly concludes his fine soliloquy on life by saying, "Man delights not me, nor woman neither, though by your smiling you seem to say so." Which is explained by their answer—"My lord, we had no such stuff in our thoughts. But we smiled to think, if you delight not in man, what lenten entertainment the players shall receive from you, whom we met on the way:"—as if while Hamlet was making this speech, his two old schoolfellows from Wittenberg had been really standing by, and he had seen them smiling by stealth, at the idea of the players crossing their minds. It is not "a combination and a form" of words, a set speech or two, a preconcerted theory of a character, that will do this: but all the persons concerned must have been present in the poet's imagination, as at a kind of rehearsal; and whatever would have passed through their minds on the occasion, and have been observed by others, passed through his, and is made known to the reader.—I may add in passing, that Shakspeare always gives the best directions for the costume and carriage of his heroes. Thus, to take one example, Ophelia gives the following account of Hamlet; and as Ophelia had seen Hamlet, I should think her word ought to be taken against that of any modern authority.

> *Ophelia*: My lord, as I was reading in my closet,
> Prince Hamlet, with his doublet all unbrac'd,
> No hat upon his head, his stockings loose,
> Ungartred, and down-gyved to his ancle,
> Pale as his shirt, his knees knocking each other,
> And with a look so piteous,
> As if he had been sent from hell
> To speak of horrors, thus he comes before me.
> *Polonius*: Mad for thy love!
> *Oph.*: My lord, I do not know,
> But truly I do fear it.
> *Pol.*:          What said he?
> *Oph.*: He took me by the wrist and held me hard.
> Then goes he to the length of all his arm;
> And with his other hand thus o'er his brow,
> He falls to such perusal of my face,
> As he would draw it: long staid he so;
> At last, a little shaking of my arm,
> And thrice his head thus waving up and down,
> He rais'd a sigh so piteous and profound,
> As it did seem to shatter all his bulk,
> And end his being. That done, he lets me go,
> And with his head over his shoulder turn'd,
> He seem'd to find his way without his eyes;
> For out of doors he went without their help,
> And to the last bended their light on me.
>                                    (Act II. Scene I.)

How after this airy, fantastic idea of irregular grace and bewildered melancholy any one can play Hamlet, as we have seen it played, with strut, and stare, and antic right-angled sharp-pointed gestures, it is difficult to say, unless it be that Hamlet is not bound, by the prompter's cue, to study the part of Ophelia. The account of Ophelia's death begins thus:

> There is a willow hanging o'er a brook,
> That shows its hoary leaves in the glassy stream.

Now this is an instance of the same unconscious power of mind which is as true to nature as itself. The leaves of the willow are, in fact, white underneath, and it is this part of them which

would appear "hoary" in the reflection in the brook. The same sort of intuitive power, the same faculty of bringing every object in nature, whether present or absent, before the mind's eye, is observable in the speech of Cleopatra, when conjecturing what were the employments of Antony in his absence:—"He's speaking now, or murmuring, where's my serpent of old Nile?" How fine to make Cleopatra have this consciousness of her own character, and to make her feel that it is this for which Antony is in love with her! She says, after the battle of Actium, when Antony has resolved to risk another fight, "It is my birthday; I had thought to have held it poor: but since my lord is Antony again, I will be Cleopatra." What other poet would have thought of such a casual resource of the imagination, or would have dared to avail himself of it? The thing happens in the play as it might have happened in fact.—That which, perhaps, more than any thing else distinguishes the dramatic productions of Shakspeare from all others, is this wonderful truth and individuality of conception. Each of his characters is as much itself, and as absolutely independent of the rest, as well as of the author, as if they were living persons, not fictions of the mind. The poet may be said, for the time, to identify himself with the character he wishes to represent, and to pass from one to another, like the same soul successively animating different bodies. By an art like that of the ventriloquist, he throws his imagination out of himself, and makes every word appear to proceed from the mouth of the person in whose name it is given. His plays alone are properly expressions of the passions, not descriptions of them. His characters are real beings of flesh and blood; they speak like men, not like authors. One might suppose that he had stood by at the time, and overheard what passed. As in our dreams we hold conversations with ourselves, make remarks, or communicate intelligence, and have no idea of the answer which we shall receive, and which we ourselves make, till we hear it: so the dialogues in Shakspeare are carried on without any consciousness of what is to follow, without any appearance of preparation or premeditation. The gusts of passion come and go like sounds of music borne on the wind. Nothing is made out by formal inference and analogy, by climax and antithesis: all comes, or seems to come, immediately from nature. Each object and circumstance exists in his mind, as it would have existed in reality: each several train of thought and feeling goes on of itself, without confusion or effort. In the world of his imagination, every thing has a life, a place, and being of its own!

Chaucer's characters are sufficiently distinct from one another, but they are too little varied in themselves, too much like identical propositions. They are consistent, but uniform; we get no new idea of them from first to last; they are not placed in different lights, nor are their subordinate *traits* brought out in new situations; they are like portraits or physiognomical studies, with the distinguishing features marked with inconceivable truth and precision, but that preserve the same unaltered air and attitude. Shakspeare's are historical figures, equally true and correct, but put into action, where every nerve and muscle is displayed in the struggle with others, with all the effect of collision and contrast, with every variety of light and shade. Chaucer's characters are narrative, Shakspeare's dramatic, Milton's epic. That is, Chaucer told only as much of his story as he pleased, as was required for a particular purpose. He answered for his characters himself. In Shakspeare they are introduced upon the stage, are liable to be asked all sorts of questions, and are forced to answer for themselves. In Chaucer we perceive a fixed essence of character. In Shakspeare there is a continual composition and decomposition of its elements, a fermentation of every particle in the whole mass, by its alternate affinity or antipathy to other principles which are brought in contact with it. Till the experiment is tried, we do not know the result, the turn which the character will take in its new circumstances. Milton took only a few simple principles of character, and raised them to the utmost conceivable grandeur, and refined them from every base alloy. His imagination, "nigh sphered in Heaven," claimed kindred only with what he saw from that height, and could raise to the same elevation with itself. He sat retired, and kept his state alone, "playing with wisdom;" while Shakspeare mingled with the crowd, and played the host, "to make society the sweeter welcome."

The passion in Shakspeare is of the same nature as his delineation of character. It is not some one habitual feeling or sentiment preying upon itself, growing out of itself, and moulding every thing to itself; it is passion modified by passion, by all the other feelings to which the individual is liable, and to which others are liable with him; subject to all the fluctuations of caprice and accident; calling into play all the resources of the understanding and all the energies of the will; irritated by obstacles or yielding to them; rising from small beginnings to its utmost height; now drunk with hope, now stung to madness, now sunk in despair, now blown to air with a breath, now raging like a torrent. The human soul is made the sport of fortune, the prey of adversity: it is stretched on the wheel of destiny, in restless ecstacy. The passions are in a state of projection. Years are melted down to moments, and every instant teems with fate. We know the results, we see the process. Thus after Iago has been boasting to himself of the effect of his poisonous suggestions on the mind of Othello, "which, with a little act upon the blood, will work like mines of sulphur," he adds—

Look where he comes! not poppy, nor mandragora,
Nor all the drowsy syrups of the East,
Shall ever medicine thee to that sweet sleep
Which thou ow'dst yesterday.

And he enters at this moment, like the crested serpent, crowned with his wrongs and raging for revenge! The whole depends upon the turn of a thought. A word, a look, blows the spark of jealousy into a flame; and the explosion is immediate and terrible as a volcano. The dialogues in *Lear*, in *Macbeth*, that between Brutus and Cassius, and nearly all those in Shakspeare, where the interest is wrought up to its highest pitch, afford examples of this dramatic fluctuation of passion. The interest in Chaucer is quite different; it is like the course of a river, strong, and full, and increasing. In Shakspeare, on the contrary, it is like the sea, agitated this way and that, and loud-lashed by furious storms; while in the still pauses of the blast, we distinguish only the cries of despair or the silence of death! Milton, on the other hand, takes the imaginative part of passion—that which remains after the event, which the mind reposes on when all is over, which looks upon circumstances from the remotest elevation of thought and fancy, and abstracts them from the world of action to that of contemplation. The objects of dramatic poetry affect us by sympathy, by their nearness to ourselves, as they take us by surprise, or force us upon action, "while rage with rage doth sympathise:" the objects of epic poetry affect us through the medium of the imagination, by magnitude and distance, by their permanence and universality. The one fill us with terror and pity, the other with admiration and delight. There are certain objects that strike the imagination, and inspire awe in the very idea of them, independently of any dramatic interest, that is, of any connection with the vicissitudes of human life. For instance, we cannot think of the pyramids of Egypt, of a Gothic ruin, or an old Roman encampment, without a certain emotion, a

sense of power and sublimity coming over the mind. The heavenly bodies that hang over our heads wherever we go, and "in their untroubled element shall shine when we are laid in dust, and all our cares forgotten," affect us in the same way. Thus Satan's address to the Sun has an epic, not a dramatic interest; for though the second person in the dialogue makes no answer and feels no concern, yet the eye of that vast luminary is upon him, like the eye of heaven, and seems conscious of what he says, like an universal presence. Dramatic poetry and epic, in their perfection, indeed, approximate to and strengthen one another. Dramatic poetry borrows aid from the dignity of persons and things, as the heroic does from human passion, but in theory they are distinct.—When Richard II. calls for the looking-glass to contemplate his faded majesty in it, and bursts into that affecting exclamation: "Oh, that I were a mockery-king of snow, to melt away before the sun of Bolingbroke," we have here the utmost force of human passion, combined with the ideas of regal splendour and fallen power. When Milton says of Satan:

His form had not yet lost
All her original brightness, nor appear'd
Less than archangel ruin'd, and th' excess
Of glory obscur'd;

the mixture of beauty, of grandeur, and pathos, from the sense of irreparable loss, of never-ending, unavailing regret, is perfect.

The great fault of a modern school of poetry is, that it is an experiment to reduce poetry to a mere effusion of natural sensibility; or what is worse, to divest it both of imaginary splendour and human passion, to surround the meanest objects with the morbid feelings and devouring egotism of the writers' own minds. Milton and Shakspeare did not so understand poetry. They gave a more liberal interpretation both to nature and art. They did not do all they could to get rid of the one and the other, to fill up the dreary void with the Moods of their own Minds. They owe their power over the human mind to their having had a deeper sense than others of what was grand in the objects of nature, or affecting in the events of human life. But to the men I speak of there is nothing interesting, nothing heroical, but themselves. To them the fall of gods or of great men is the same. They do not enter into the feeling. They cannot understand the terms. They are even debarred from the last poor, paltry consolation of an unmanly triumph over fallen greatness; for their minds reject, with a convulsive effort and intolerable loathing, the very idea that there ever was, or was thought to be, any thing superior to themselves. All that has ever excited the attention or admiration of the world they look upon with the most perfect indifference; and they are surprised to find that the world repays their indifference with scorn. "With what measure they mete, it has been meted to them again."

Shakspeare's imagination is of the same plastic kind as his conception of character or passion. "It glances from heaven to earth, from earth to heaven." Its movement is rapid and devious. It unites the most opposite extremes; or, as Puck says, in boasting of his own feats, "puts a girdle round about the earth in forty minutes." He seems always hurrying from his subject, even while describing it; but the stroke, like the lightning's, is sure as it is sudden. He takes the widest possible range, but from that very range he has his choice of the greatest variety and aptitude of materials. He brings together images the most alike, but placed at the greatest distance from each other; that is, found in circumstances of the greatest dissimilitude. From the remoteness of his combinations, and the celerity with which they are effected, they coalesce the more indissolubly together. The more the thoughts are strangers to each other, and the longer they have been kept asunder, the more intimate docs their union seem to become. Their felicity is equal to their force. Their likeness is made more dazzling by their novelty. They startle, and take the fancy prisoner in the same instant. I will mention one or two which are very striking, and not much known, out of *Troilus and Cressida*. Æneas says to Agamemnon,

> I ask that I may waken reverence,
> And on the cheek be ready with a blush
> Modest as morning, when she coldly eyes
> The youthful Phœbus.

Ulysses urging Achilles to shew himself in the field, says—

> No man is the lord of any thing,
> Till he communicate his parts to others:
> Nor doth he of himself know them for aught,
> Till he behold them formed in the applause,
> Where they're extended! which like an arch rever-
>    berates
> The voice again, or like a gate of steel,
> Fronting the sun, receives and renders back
> Its figure and its heat.

Patroclus gives the indolent warrior the same advice.

> Rouse yourself; and the weak wanton Cupid
> Shall from your neck unloose his amorous fold,
> And like a dew-drop from the lion's mane
> Be shook to air.

Shakspeare's language and versification are like the rest of him. He has a magic power over words: they come winged at his bidding; and seem to know their places. They are struck out at a heat, on the spur of the occasion, and have all the truth and vividness which arise from an actual impression of the objects. His epithets and single phrases are like sparkles, thrown off from an imagination, fired by the whirling rapidity of its own motion. His language is hieroglyphical. It translates thoughts into visible images. It abounds in sudden transitions and elliptical expressions. This is the source of his mixed metaphors, which are only abbreviated forms of speech. These, however, give no pain from long custom. They have, in fact, become idioms in the language. They are the building, and not the scaffolding to thought. We take the meaning and effect of a well-known passage entire, and no more stop to scan and spell out the particular words and phrases, than the syllables of which they are composed. In trying to recollect any other author, one sometimes stumbles, in case of failure, on a word as good. In Shakspeare, any other word but the true one, is sure to be wrong. If any body, for instance, could not recollect the words of the following description,

> Light thickens,
> And the crow makes wing to the rooky wood,

he would be greatly at a loss to substitute others for them equally expressive of the feeling. These remarks, however, are strictly applicable only to the impassioned parts of Shakspeare's language, which flowed from the warmth and originality of his imagination, and were his own. The language used for prose conversation and ordinary business is sometimes technical, and involved in the affectation of the time. Compare, for example, Othello's apology to the senate, relating "his whole course of love," with some of the preceding parts relating to his appointment, and the official dispatches from Cyprus. In this respect, "the business of the state does him offence."—His versification is no less powerful, sweet, and varied. It has every occasional excellence, of sullen intricacy, crabbed and perplexed, or of the smoothest and loftiest expansion—from the ease and familiarity of measured conversation to the lyrical sounds

> Of ditties highly penned,
> Sung by a fair queen in a summer's bower,
> With ravishing division to her lute.

It is the only blank verse in the language, except Milton's, that for itself is readable. It is not stately and uniformly swelling like his, but varied and broken by the inequalities of the ground it has to pass over in its uncertain course,

> And so by many winding nooks it strays,
> With willing sport to the wild ocean.

It remains to speak of the faults of Shakspeare. They are not so many or so great as they have been represented; what there are, are chiefly owing to the following causes:—The universality of his genius was, perhaps, a disadvantage to his single works; the variety of his resources sometimes diverting him from applying them to the most effectual purposes. He might be said to combine the powers of Æschylus and Aristophanes, of Dante and Rabelais, in his own mind. If he had been only half what he was, he would perhaps have appeared greater. The natural ease and indifference of his temper made him sometimes less scrupulous than he might have been. He is relaxed and careless in critical places; he is in earnest throughout only in *Timon*, *Macbeth*, and *Lear*. Again, he had no models of acknowledged excellence constantly in view to stimulate his efforts, and by all that appears, no love of fame. He wrote for the "great vulgar and the small," in his time, not for posterity. If Queen Elizabeth and the maids of honour laughed heartily at his worst jokes, and the catcalls in the gallery were silent at his best passages, he went home satisfied, and slept the next night well. He did not trouble himself about Voltaire's criticisms. He was willing to take advantage of the ignorance of the age in many things; and if his plays pleased others, not to quarrel with them himself. His very facility of production would make him set less value on his own excellences, and not care to distinguish nicely between what he did well or ill. His blunders in chronology and geography do not amount to above half a dozen, and they are offences against chronology and geography, not against poetry. As to the unities, he was right in setting them at defiance. He was fonder of puns than became so great a man. His barbarisms were those of his age. His genius was his own. He had no objection to float down with the stream of common taste and opinion: he rose above it by his own buoyancy, and an impulse which he could not keep under, in spite of himself or others, and "his delights did shew most dolphin-like."

He had an equal genius for comedy and tragedy; and his tragedies are better than his comedies, because tragedy is better than comedy. His female characters, which have been found fault with as insipid, are the finest in the world. Lastly, Shakspeare was the least of a coxcomb of any one that ever lived, and much of a gentleman.

## THOMAS DE QUINCEY
### From "Shakspeare" (1838)
*Collected Writings*, ed. David Masson
1889, Volume 4, pp. 70–79

I n the gravest sense it may be affirmed of Shakspeare that he is among the modern luxuries of life; that life, in fact, is a new thing, and one more to be coveted, since Shakspeare has extended the domains of human consciousness, and pushed its dark frontiers into regions not so much as dimly descried or even suspected before his time, far less illuminated (as now they are) by beauty and tropical luxuriance of life. For instance,—a single instance, indeed one which in itself is a world of new revelation,—the possible beauty of the female character had not been seen as in a dream before Shakspeare called into perfect life the radiant shapes of Desdemona, of Imogen, of Hermione, of Perdita, of Ophelia, of Miranda, and many others. The Una of Spenser, earlier by ten or fifteen years than most of these, was an idealised portrait of female innocence and virgin purity, but too shadowy and unreal for a dramatic reality. And, as to the Grecian classics, let not the reader imagine for an instant that any prototype in this field of Shakspearian power can be looked for there. The *Antigone* and the *Electra* of the tragic poets are the two leading female characters that classical antiquity offers to our respect, but assuredly not to our impassioned love, as disciplined and exalted in the school of Shakspeare. They challenge our admiration, severe, and even stern, as impersonations of filial duty, cleaving to the steps of a desolate and afflicted old man, or of sisterly affection, maintaining the rights of a brother under circumstances of peril, of desertion, and consequently of perfect self-reliance. Iphigenia, again, though not dramatically coming before us in her own person, but according to the beautiful report of a spectator, presents us with a fine statuesque model of heroic fortitude, and of one whose young heart, even in the very agonies of her cruel immolation, refused to forget, by a single indecorous gesture, or so much as a moment's neglect of her own princely descent, that she herself was "a lady in the land." These are fine marble groups, but they are not the warm breathing realities of Shakspeare; there is "no specula- tion" in their cold marble eyes; the breath of life is not in their nostrils; the fine pulses of womanly sensibilities are not throbbing in their bosoms. And, besides this immeasurable difference between the cold moony reflexes of life as exhibited by the power of Grecian art and the true sunny life of Shakspeare, it must be observed that the Antigones, &c., of the antique put forward but one single trait of character, like the aloe with its single blossom: this solitary feature is presented to us as an abstraction, and as an insulated quality; whereas in Shakspeare all is presented in the *concrete,*—that is to say, not brought forward in relief, as by some effort of an anatomical artist, but embodied and imbedded, so to speak, as by the force of a creative nature, in the complex system of a human life: a life in which all the elements move and play simultaneously, and, with something more than mere simultaneity or co- existence, acting and re-acting each upon the other—nay, even acting by each other and through each other. In Shakspeare's characters is felt for ever a real *organic* life, where each is for the whole and in the whole, and where the whole is for each and in each. They only are real incarnations.

The Greek poets could not exhibit any approximations to *female* character without violating the truth of Grecian life and shocking the feelings of the audience. The drama with the Greeks, as with us, though much less than with us, was a picture of human life; and that which could not occur in life could not wisely be exhibited on the stage. Now, in ancient Greece, women were secluded from the society of men. The conventual sequestration of the *gynaikōnitis* or female apart- ment[1] of the house, and the Mahommedan consecration of its threshold against the ingress of males, had been transplanted from Asia into Greece thousands of years perhaps before either convents or Mahommed existed. Thus barred from all open social intercourse, women could not develop or express any character by word or action. Even to *have* a character, violated,

to a Grecian mind, the ideal portrait of feminine excellence; whence, perhaps, partly the too generic, too little indi- vidualized, style of Grecian beauty. But prominently to *express* a character was impossible under the common tenor of Grecian life, unless when high tragical catastrophes tran- scended the decorums of that tenor, or for a brief interval raised the curtain which veiled it. Hence the subordinate part which women play upon the Greek stage in all but some half-dozen cases. In the paramount tragedy on that stage, the model tragedy, the *Œdipus Tyrannus* of Sophocles, there is virtually no woman at all; for Jocasta is a party to the story merely as the dead Laius or the self-murdered Sphinx was a party,—viz. by her contributions to the fatalities of the event, not by anything she does or says spontaneously. In fact, the Greek poet, if a wise poet, could not address himself genially to a task in which he must begin by shocking the sensibilities of his countrymen. And hence followed, not only the dearth of female characters in the Grecian drama, but also a second result still more favourable to the sense of a new power evolved by Shakspeare. Whenever the common law of Grecian life did give way, it was, as we have observed, to the suspending force of some great convulsion or tragical catastrophe. This for a moment (like an earthquake in a nunnery) would set at liberty even the timid, fluttering Grecian women, those doves of the dove-cot, and would call some of them into action. But which? Precisely those of energetic and masculine minds; the timid and feminine would but shrink the more from public gaze and from tumult. Thus it happened that such female characters as *were* exhibited in Greece could not but be the harsh and the severe. If a gentle Ismene appeared for a moment in contest with some energetic sister Antigone (and chiefly, perhaps, by way of drawing out the fiercer character of that sister), she was soon dismissed as unfit for scenical effect. So that not only were female characters few, but, moreover, of these few the majority were but repetitions of masculine qualities in female persons. Female agency being seldom summoned on the stage except when it had received a sort of special dispensation from its sexual character by some terrific convulsions of the house or the city, naturally it assumed the style of action suited to these circumstances. And hence it arose that not woman as she differed from man, but woman as she resembled man— woman, in short, seen under circumstances so dreadful as to abolish the effect of sexual distinction—was the woman of the Greek tragedy.[2] And hence generally arose for Shakspeare the wider field, and the more astonishing by its perfect novelty, when he first introduced female characters, not as mere varieties or echoes of masculine characters, a Medea or Clytemnestra, or a vindictive Hecuba, the mere tigress of the tragic tiger, but female characters that had the appropriate beauty of female nature; woman no longer grand, terrific, and repulsive, but woman "after her kind"—the other hemisphere of the dramatic world; woman running through the vast gamut of womanly loveliness; woman as emancipated, exalted, ennobled, under a new law of Christian morality; woman the sister and co-equal of man, no longer his slave, his prisoner, and sometimes his rebel. "It is a far cry to Loch Awe"; and from the Athenian stage to the stage of Shakspeare, it may be said, is a prodigious interval. True; but, prodigious as it is, there is really nothing between them. The Roman stage, at least the tragic stage, as is well known, was put out, as by an extinguisher, by the cruel amphitheatre, just as a candle is made pale and ridiculous by daylight. Those who were fresh from the real murders of the bloody amphitheatre regarded with contempt the mimic murders of the stage. Stimulation too coarse and too intense had its usual effect in making the sensibilities callous. Christian emperors arose at length, who abolished the amphitheatre in its bloodier features. But by that time the genius of the tragic muse had long slept the sleep of death. And that muse had no resurrection until the age of Shakspeare. So that, notwithstanding a gulf of nineteen centuries and upwards separates Shakspeare from Euripides, the last of the surviving Greek tragedians, the one is still the nearest successor of the other, just as Connaught and the islands in Clew Bay are next neighbours to America, although three thousand watery columns, each of a cubic mile in dimensions, divide them from each other.

A second reason which lends an emphasis of novelty and effective power to Shakspeare's female world is a peculiar fact of contrast which exists between that and his corresponding world of men. Let us explain. The purpose and the intention of the Grecian stage was not primarily to develop human *character*, whether in men or in women: human *fates* were its object; great tragic situations under the mighty control of a vast cloudy destiny, dimly descried at intervals, and brooding over human life by mysterious agencies, and for mysterious ends. Man, no longer the representative of an august *will*,—man, the passion-puppet of fate,—could not with any effect display what we call a character, which is a distinction between man and man, emanating originally from the will, and expressing its determinations, moving under the large variety of human impulses. The will is the central pivot of character; and this was obliterated, thwarted, cancelled, by the dark fatalism which brooded over the Grecian stage. That explanation will sufficiently clear up the reason why marked or complex variety of character was slighted by the great principles of the Greek tragedy. And every scholar who has studied that grand drama of Greece with feeling,—that drama, so magnificent, so regal, so stately,—and who has thoughtfully investigated its principles, and its difference from the English drama, will acknowledge that powerful and elaborate character,—character, for instance, that could employ the fiftieth part of that profound analysis which has been applied to Hamlet, to Falstaff, to Lear, to Othello, and applied by Mrs. Jameson so admirably to the full development of Shakspearian heroines,—would have been as much wasted, nay, would have been defeated, and interrupted the blind agencies of fate, just in the same way as it would injure the shadowy grandeur of a ghost to individualize it too much. Milton's angels are slightly touched, superficially touched, with differences of character; but they are such differences, so simple and general, as are just sufficient to rescue them from the reproach applied to Virgil's "*fortemque Gyan, fortemque Cloanthem*"; just sufficient to make them knowable apart. Pliny speaks of painters who painted in one or two colours; and, as respects the angelic characters, Milton does so; he is *monochromatic*. So, and for reasons resting upon the same ultimate philosophy, were the mighty architects of the Greek tragedy. They also were monochromatic; they also, as to the characters of their persons, painted in one colour. And so far there might have been the same novelty in Shakspeare's men as in his women. There *might* have been; but the reason why there is *not* must be sought in the fact that History, the muse of History, had there even been no such muse as Melpomene, would have forced us into an acquaintance with human character. History, as the representative of actual life, of real man, gives us powerful delineations of character in its chief agents,—that is, in men; and therefore it is that Shakspeare, the absolute creator of female character, was but the mightiest of all painters with regard to male character. Take a single instance. The Antony of Shakspeare, immortal for its execution, is found, after all, as regards the primary concep-

tion, in history: Shakspeare's delineation is but the expansion of the germ already pre-existing, by way of scattered fragments, in Cicero's *Philippics*, in Cicero's *Letters*, in Appian, &c. But Cleopatra, equally fine, is a pure creation of art: the situation and the scenic circumstances belong to history, but the character belongs to Shakspeare.

In the great world, therefore, of woman, as the interpreter of the shifting phases and the lunar varieties of that mighty changeable planet, that lovely satellite of man, Shakspeare stands not the first only, not the original only, but is yet the sole authentic oracle of truth. Woman, therefore, the beauty of the female mind, *this* is one great field of his power. The supernatural world, the world of apparitions, *that* is another: for reasons which it would be easy to give, reasons emanating from the gross mythology of the ancients, no Grecian,[3] no Roman, could have conceived a ghost. That shadowy conception, the protesting apparition, the awful projection of the human conscience, belongs to the Christian mind: and in all Christendom, who, let us ask, who, but Shakspeare, has found the power for effectually working this mysterious mode of being? In summoning back to earth "the majesty of buried Denmark," how like an awful necromancer does Shakspeare appear! All the pomps and grandeurs which religion, which the grave, which the popular superstition had gathered about the subject of apparitions, are here converted to his purpose, and bend to one awful effect. The wormy grave brought into antagonism with the scenting of the early dawn; the trumpet of resurrection suggested, and again as an antagonist idea to the crowing of the cock (a bird ennobled in the Christian mythus by the part he is made to play at the Crucifixion); its starting "as a guilty thing" placed in opposition to its majestic expression of offended dignity when struck at by the partisans of the sentinels; its awful allusions to the secrets of its prison-house; its ubiquity, contrasted with its local presence; its aerial substance, yet clothed in palpable armour; the heart-shaking solemnity of its language, and the appropriate scenery of its haunt, viz. the ramparts of a capital fortress, with no witnesses but a few gentlemen mounting guard at the dead of night,—what a mist, what a *mirage* of vapour, is here accumulated, through which the dreadful being in the centre looms upon us in far larger proportions than could have happened had it been insulated and left naked of this circumstantial pomp! In the *Tempest*, again, what new modes of life, preternatural, yet far as the poles from the spiritualities of religion. Ariel in antithesis to Caliban![4] What is most ethereal to what is most animal! A phantom of air, an abstraction of the dawn and of vesper sunlights, a bodiless sylph on the one hand; on the other a gross carnal monster, like the Miltonic Asmodai, "the fleshliest incubus" among the fiends, and yet so far ennobled into interest by his intellectual power, and by the grandeur of misanthropy! In the *Midsummer-Night's Dream*, again, we have the old traditional fairy, a lovely mode of preternatural life, remodified by Shakspeare's eternal talisman. Oberon and Titania remind us at first glance of Ariel; they approach, but how far they recede: they are like—"like, but oh, how different!" And in no other exhibition of this dreamy population of the moonlight forests and forest-lawns are the circumstantial proprieties of fairy life so exquisitely imagined, sustained, or expressed. The dialogue between Oberon and Titania is, of itself, and taken separately from its connexion, one of the most delightful poetic scenes that literature affords. The witches in *Macbeth* are another variety of supernatural life in which Shakspeare's power to enchant and to disenchant are alike portentous. The circumstances of the blasted heath, the army at a distance, the withered attire of the mysterious hags, and the choral litanies of their fiendish Sabbath, are as finely imagined in their kind as those which herald and which surround the ghost in *Hamlet*. There we see the *positive* of Shakspeare's superior power. But now turn and look to the *negative*. At a time when the trials of witches, the royal book on demonology, and popular superstition (all so far useful, as they prepared a basis of undoubting faith for the poet's serious use of such agencies) had degraded and polluted the ideas of these mysterious beings by many mean associations, Shakspeare does not fear to employ them in high tragedy (a tragedy moreover which, though not the very greatest of his efforts as an intellectual whole, nor as a struggle of passion, is *among* the greatest in any view, and positively *the* greatest for scenical grandeur, and in that respect makes the nearest approach of all English tragedies to the Grecian model); he does not fear to introduce, for the same appalling effect as that for which Æschylus introduced the Eumenides, a triad of old women, concerning whom an English wit has remarked this grotesque peculiarity in the popular creed of that day,—that, although potent over winds and storms, in league with powers of darkness, they yet stood in awe of the constable; yet, relying on his own supreme power to disenchant as well as to enchant, to create and to uncreate, he mixes these women and their dark machineries with the power of armies, with the agencies of kings, and the fortunes of martial kingdoms. Such was the sovereignty of this poet, so mighty its compass!

A third fund of Shakspeare's peculiar power lies in his teeming fertility of fine thoughts and sentiments. From his works alone might be gathered a golden bead-roll of thoughts the deepest, subtlest, most pathetic, and yet most catholic and universally intelligible; the most characteristic, also, and appropriate to the particular person, the situation, and the case, yet, at the same time, applicable to the circumstances of every human being, under all the accidents of life, and all vicissitudes of fortune. But this subject offers so vast a field of observation, it being so eminently the prerogative of Shakspeare to have thought more finely and more extensively than all other poets combined, that we cannot wrong the dignity of such a theme by doing more, in our narrow limits, than simply noticing it as one of the emblazonries upon Shakspeare's shield.

Fourthly, we shall indicate (and, as in the last case, *barely* indicate, without attempting in so vast a field to offer any inadequate illustrations) one mode of Shakspeare's dramatic excellence which hitherto has not attracted any special or separate notice. We allude to the forms of life and natural human passion as apparent in the structure of his dialogue. Among the many defects and infirmities of the French and of the Italian drama, indeed we may say of the Greek, the dialogue proceeds always by independent speeches, replying indeed to each other, but never modified in its several openings by the momentary effect of its several terminal forms immediately preceding. Now, in Shakspeare, who first set an example of that most important innovation, in all his impassioned dialogues, each reply or rejoinder seems the mere rebound of the previous speech. Every form of natural interruption, breaking through the restraints of ceremony under the impulses of tempestuous passion; every form of hasty interrogative, ardent reiteration when a question has been evaded; every form of scornful repetition of the hostile words; every impatient continuation of the hostile statement; in short, all modes and formulæ by which anger, hurry, fretfulness, scorn, impatience, or excitement under any movement whatever, can disturb or modify or dislocate the formal bookish style of commencement: these are as rife in Shakspeare's dialogue as in life itself; and how much vivacity, how profound a

verisimilitude, they add to the scenic effect as an imitation of human passion and real life, we need not say. A volume might be written illustrating the vast varieties of Shakspeare's art and power in this one field of improvement; another volume might be dedicated to the exposure of the lifeless and unnatural result from the opposite practice in the foreign stages of France and Italy. And we may truly say that, were Shakspeare distinguished from them by this single feature of nature and propriety, he would on that account alone have merited a great immortality.

*Notes*

1. *Apartment* is here used, as the reader will observe, in its true and continental acceptation, as a division or *compartment* of a house including many rooms: a suite of chambers, but a suite which is partitioned off (as in palaces); not a single chamber,—a sense so commonly and so erroneously given to this word in England.

2. And hence, by parity of reason, under the opposite circumstances, under the circumstances which, instead of abolishing, most emphatically drew forth the sexual distinctions, viz. in the *comic* aspects of social intercourse, the reason that we see no women on the Greek stage. The Greek comedy, unless when it affects the extravagant fun of farce, rejects women.

3. It may be thought, however, by some readers, that Æschylus, in his fine phantom of Darius, has approached the English ghost. As a foreign ghost, we would wish (and we are sure that our excellent readers would wish) to show every courtesy and attention to this apparition of Darius. It has the advantage of being royal, an advantage which it shares with the ghost of the royal Dane. Yet how different, how removed by a total world, from that or any of Shakspeare's ghosts! Take that of Banquo, for instance: how shadowy, how unreal, yet how real! Darius is a mere ghost—a diplomatic ghost. But Banquo—he exists only for Macbeth: the guests do not see him; yet how solemn, how real, how heart-searching he is!

4. Caliban has not yet been thoroughly fathomed. For all Shakspeare's great creations are like works of nature, subjects of unexhaustible study.

## THOMAS CARLYLE
### From "The Hero as Poet"
*On Heroes, Hero-Worship and the Heroic in History*
### 1841

As Dante, the Italian man, was sent into our world to embody musically the Religion of the Middle Ages, the Religion of our Modern Europe, its Inner Life; so Shakspeare, we may say, embodies for us the Outer Life of our Europe as developed then, its chivalries, courtesies, humours, ambitions, what practical way of thinking, acting, looking at the world, men then had. As in Homer we may still construe Old Greece; so in Shakspeare and Dante, after thousands of years, what our modern Europe was, in Faith and in Practice, will still be legible. Dante has given us the Faith or soul; Shakspeare, in a not less noble way, has given us the Practice or body. This latter also we were to have; a man was sent for it, the man Shakspeare. Just when that chivalry way of life had reached its last finish, and was on the point of breaking down into slow or swift dissolution, as we now see it everywhere, this other sovereign Poet, with his seeing eye, with his perennial singing voice, was sent to take note of it, to give long-enduring record of it. Two fit men: Dante, deep, fierce as the central fire of the world; Shakspeare, wide, placid, far-seeing, as the Sun, the upper light of the world. Italy produced the one world-voice; we English had the honour of producing the other.

Curious enough how, as it were by mere accident, this man came to us. I think always, so great, quiet, complete and self-sufficing is this Shakspeare, had the Warwickshire Squire not prosecuted him for deer-stealing, we had perhaps never heard of him as a Poet! The woods and skies, the rustic Life of Man in Stratford there, had been enough for this man! But indeed that strange outbudding of our whole English Existence, which we call the Elizabethan Era, did not it too come as of its own accord? The 'Tree Igdrasil' buds and withers by its own laws,—too deep for our scanning. Yet it does bud and wither, and every bough and leaf of it is there, by fixed eternal laws; not a Sir Thomas Lucy but comes at the hour fit for him. Curious, I say, and not sufficiently considered: how everything does coöperate with all; not a leaf rotting on the highway but is indissoluble portion of solar and stellar systems; no thought, word or act of man but has sprung withal out of all men, and works sooner or later, recognisably or irrecognisably, on all men! It is all a Tree: circulation of sap and influences, mutual communication of every minutest leaf with the lowest talon of a root, with every other greatest and minutest portion of the whole. The Tree Igdrasil, that has its roots down in the Kingdoms of Hela and Death, and whose boughs overspread the highest Heaven!—

In some sense it may be said that this glorious Elizabethan Era with its Shakspeare, as the outcome and flowerage of all which had preceded it, is itself attributable to the Catholicism of the Middle Ages. The Christian Faith, which was the theme of Dante's Song, had produced this Practical Life which Shakspeare was to sing. For Religion then, as it now and always is, was the soul of practice; the primary vital fact in men's life. And remark here, as rather curious, that Middle-Age Catholicism was abolished, so far as Acts of Parliament could abolish it, before Shakspeare, the noblest product of it, made his appearance. He did make his appearance nevertheless. Nature at her own time, with Catholicism or what else might be necessary, sent him forth; taking small thought of Acts of Parliament. King-Henrys, Queen-Elizabeths go their way; and Nature too goes hers. Acts of Parliament, on the whole, are small, notwithstanding the noise they make. What Act of Parliament, debate at St. Stephen's, on the hustings or elsewhere, was it that brought this Shakspeare into being? No dining at Freemasons' Tavern, opening subscription-lists, selling of shares, and infinite other jangling and true or false endeavouring! This Elizabethan Era, and all its nobleness and blessedness, came without proclamation, preparation of ours. Priceless Shakspeare was the free gift of Nature; given altogether silently;—received altogether silently, as if it had been a thing of little account. And yet, very literally, it is a priceless thing. One should look at that side of matters too.

Of this Shakspeare of ours, perhaps the opinion one sometimes hears a little idolatrously expressed is, in fact, the right one; I think the best judgment not of this country only, but of Europe at large, is slowly pointing to the conclusion, That Shakespeare is the chief of all Poets hitherto; the greatest intellect who, in our recorded world, has left record of himself in the way of Literature. On the whole, I know not such a power of vision, such a faculty of thought, if we take all the characters of it, in any other man. Such a calmness of depth; placid joyous strength; all things imaged in that great soul of his so true and clear, as in a tranquil unfathomable sea! It has been said, that in the constructing of Shakspeare's Dramas there is, apart from all other 'faculties' as they are called, an understanding manifested, equal to that in Bacon's *Novum Organum.* That is true; and it is not a truth that strikes every one. It would become more apparent if we tried, any of us for himself, how, out of Shakspeare's dramatic materials, *we* could fashion such a result! The built house seems all so fit,—everyway as it should be, as if it came there by its own law and the nature of

things,—we forget the rude disorderly quarry it was shaped from. The very perfection of the house, as if Nature herself had made it, hides the builder's merit. Perfect, more perfect than any other man, we may call Shakspeare in this: he discerns, knows as by instinct, what condition he works under, what his materials are, what his own force and its relation to them is. It is not a transitory glance of insight that will suffice; it is deliberate illumination of the whole matter; it is a calmly *seeing* eye; a great intellect, in short. How a man, of some wide thing that he has witnessed, will construct a narrative, what kind of picture and delineation he will give of it,—is the best measure you could get of what intellect is in the man. Which circumstance is vital and shall stand prominent; which unessential, fit to be suppressed; where is the true *beginning*, the true sequence and ending? To find out this, you task the whole force of insight that is in the man. He must *understand* the thing; according to the depth of his understanding, will the fitness of his answer be. You will try him so. Does like join itself to like; does the spirit of method stir in that confusion, so that its embroilment becomes order? Can the man say, *Fiat lux*, Let there be light; and out of chaos make a world? Precisely as there is *light* in himself, will he accomplish this.

Or indeed we may say again, it is in what I called Portrait-painting, delineating of men and things, especially of men, that Shakspeare is great. All the greatness of the man comes out decisively here. It is unexampled, I think, that calm creative perspicacity of Shakspeare. The thing he looks at reveals not this or that face of it, but its inmost heart, and generic secret: it dissolves itself as in light before him, so that he discerns the perfect structure of it. Creative, we said: poetic creation, what is this too but *seeing* the thing sufficiently? The *word* that will describe the thing, follows of itself from such clear intense sight of the thing. And is not Shakspeare's *morality*, his valour, candour, tolerance, truthfulness; his whole victorious strength and greatness, which can triumph over such obstructions, visible there too? Great as the world! No *twisted*, poor convex-concave mirror, reflecting all objects with its own convexities and concavities; a perfectly *level* mirror;—that is to say withal, if we will understand it, a man justly related to all things and men, a good man. It is truly a lordly spectacle how this great soul takes-in all kinds of men and objects, a Falstaff, an Othello, a Juliet, a Coriolanus; sets them all forth to us in their round completeness; loving, just, the equal brother of all. *Novum Organum*, and all the intellect you will find in Bacon, is of a quite secondary order; earthy, material, poor in comparison with this. Among modern men, one finds, in strictness, almost nothing of the same rank. Goethe alone, since the days of Shakspeare, reminds me of it. Of him too you say that he *saw* the object; you may say what he himself says of Shakspeare: 'His characters are like watches with dial-plates of transparent crystal; they show you the hour like others, and the inward mechanism also is all visible.'

The seeing eye! It is this that discloses the inner harmony of things; what Nature meant, what musical idea Nature has wrapped-up in these often rough embodiments. Something she did mean. To the seeing eye that something were discernible. Are they base, miserable things? You can laugh over them, you can weep over them; you can in some way or other genially relate yourself to them;—you can, at lowest, hold your peace about them, turn away your own and others' face from them, till the hour come for practically exterminating and extinguishing them! At bottom, it is the Poet's first gift, as it is all men's, that he have intellect enough. He will be a Poet if he have: a Poet in word; or failing that, perhaps still better, a Poet in act. Whether he write at all; and if so, whether in prose or in verse, will depend on accidents: who knows on what extremely trivial accidents,—perhaps on his having had a singing-master, on his being taught to sing in his boyhood! But the faculty which enables him to discern the inner heart of things, and the harmony that dwells there (for whatsoever exists has a harmony in the heart of it, or it would not hold together and exist), is not the result of habits or accidents, but the gift of Nature herself; the primary outfit for a Heroic Man in what sort soever. To the Poet, as to every other, we say first of all, *See.* If you cannot do that, it is of no use to keep stringing rhymes together, jingling sensibilities against each other, and *name* yourself a Poet; there is no hope for you. If you can, there is, in prose or verse, in action or speculation, all manner of hope. The crabbed old Schoolmaster used to ask, when they brought him a new pupil, 'But are ye sure he's *not a dunce?*' Why, really one might ask the same thing, in regard to every man proposed for whatsoever function; and consider it as the one inquiry needful: Are ye sure he's not a dunce? There is, in this world, no other entirely fatal person.

For, in fact, I say the degree of vision that dwells in a man is a correct measure of the man. If called to define Shakspeare's faculty, I should say superiority of Intellect, and think I had included all under that. What indeed are faculties? We talk of faculties as if they were distinct, things separable; as if a man had intellect, imagination, fancy, &c., as he has hands, feet, and arms. That is a capital error. Then again, we hear of a man's 'intellectual nature,' and of his 'moral nature,' as if these again were divisible, and existed apart. Necessities of language do perhaps prescribe such forms of utterance; we must speak, I am aware, in that way, if we are to speak at all. But words ought not to harden into things for us. It seems to me, our apprehension of this matter is, for most part, radically falsified thereby. We ought to know withal, and to keep forever in mind, that these divisions are at bottom but *names*; that man's spiritual nature, the vital Force which dwells in him, is essentially one and indivisible; that what we call imagination, fancy, understanding, and so forth, are but different figures of the same Power of Insight, all indissolubly connected with each other, physiognomically related; that if we knew one of them, we might know all of them. Morality itself, what we call the moral quality of a man, what is this but another *side* of the one vital Force whereby he is and works? All that a man does is physiognomical of him. You may see how a man would fight, by the way in which he sings; his courage, or want of courage, is visible in the word he utters, in the opinion he has formed, no less than in the stroke he strikes. He is *one*; and preaches the same Self abroad in all these ways.

Without hands a man might have feet; and could still walk: but, consider it,—without morality, intellect were impossible for him; a thoroughly immoral *man* could not know anything at all! To know a thing, what we can call knowing, a man must first *love* the thing, sympathise with it: that is, be *virtuously* related to it. If he have not the justice to put down his own selfishness at every turn, the courage to stand by the dangerous-true at every turn, how shall he know? His virtues, all of them, will lie recorded in his knowledge. Nature, with her truth, remains to the bad, to the selfish and the pusillanimous forever a sealed book: what such can know of Nature is mean, superficial, small; for the uses of the day merely.—But does not the very Fox know something of Nature? Exactly so: it knows where the geese lodge! The human Reynard, very frequent everywhere in the world, what more does he know but this and the like of this? Nay, it should be considered too, that if the Fox had not a certain vulpine *morality*, he could not even know where the geese were, or get at the geese! If he spent his time in splenetic atrabiliar reflections on his own misery, his ill usage by Nature, Fortune and other Foxes, and so forth; and had not courage, promptitude, practicality, and other suitable vulpine gifts and graces, he would catch no geese. We may say of the Fox too, that his morality and insight are of the same dimensions; different faces of the same internal unity of vulpine life!—These things are worth stating; for the contrary of them acts with manifold very baleful perversion, in this time: what limitations, modifications they require, your own candour will supply.

If I say, therefore, that Shakspeare is the greatest of Intellects, I have said all concerning him. But there is more in Shakspeare's intellect than we have yet seen. It is what I call an unconscious intellect; there is more virtue in it than he himself is aware of. Novalis beautifully remarks of him, that those Dramas of his are Products of Nature too, deep as Nature herself. I find a great truth in this saying. Shakspeare's Art is not Artifice; the noblest worth of it is not there by plan or precontrivance. It grows-up from the deeps of Nature, through this noble sincere soul, who is a voice of Nature. The latest generations of men will find new meanings in Shakspeare, new elucidations of their own human being; 'new harmonies with the infinite structure of the Universe; concurrences with later ideas, affinities with the higher powers and senses of man.' This well deserves meditating. It is Nature's highest reward to a true simple great soul, that he get thus to be *a part of herself.* Such a man's works, whatsoever he with utmost conscious exertion and forethought shall accomplish, grow up withal *un*consciously, from the unknown deeps in him;—as the oak-tree grows from the Earth's bosom, as the mountains and waters shape themselves; with a symmetry grounded on Nature's own laws, conformable to all Truth whatsoever. How much in Shakspeare lies hid; his sorrows, his silent struggles known to himself; much that was not known at all, not speakable at all: like *roots*, like sap and forces working underground! Speech is great; but Silence is greater.

Withal the joyful tranquillity of this man is notable. I will not blame Dante for his misery: it is as battle without victory; but true battle,—the first, indispensable thing. Yet I call Shakspeare greater than Dante, in that he fought truly, and did conquer. Doubt it not, he had his own sorrows: those *Sonnets* of his will even testify expressly in what deep waters he had waded, and swum struggling for his life;—as what man like him ever failed to have to do? It seems to me a heedless notion, our common one, that he sat like a bird on the bough; and sang forth, free and offhand, never knowing the troubles of other men. Not so; with no man is it so. How could a man travel forward from rustic deer-poaching to such tragedy-writing, and not fall-in with sorrows by the way? Or, still better, how could a man delineate a Hamlet, a Coriolanus, a Macbeth, so many suffering heroic hearts, if his own heroic heart had never suffered?—And now, in contrast with all this, observe his mirthfulness, his genuine overflowing love of laughter! You would say, in no point does he *exaggerate* but only in laughter. Fiery objurgations, words that pierce and burn, are to be found in Shakspeare; yet he is always in measure here; never what Johnson would remark as a specially 'good hater.' But his laughter seems to pour from him in floods; he heaps all manner of ridiculous nicknames on the butt he is bantering, tumbles and tosses him in all sorts of horse-play; you would say, with his whole heart laughs. And then, if not always the finest, it is always a genial laughter. Not at mere weakness, at misery or poverty; never. No man who *can* laugh, what we call laughing, will laugh at these things. It is some poor character only *desiring* to laugh, and have the credit of wit, that does so.

Laughter means sympathy; good laughter is not 'the crackling of thorns under the pot.' Even at stupidity and pretension this Shakspeare does not laugh otherwise than genially. Dogberry and Verges tickle our very hearts; and we dismiss them covered with explosions of laughter: but we like the poor fellows only the better for our laughing; and hope they will get on well there, and continue Presidents of the City-watch. Such laughter, like sunshine on the deep sea, is very beautiful to me.

We have no room to speak of Shakspeare's individual works; though perhaps there is much still waiting to be said on that head. Had we, for instance, all his plays reviewed as *Hamlet*, in *Wilhelm Meister*, is! A thing which might, one day, be done. August Wilhelm Schlegel has a remark on his Historical Plays, *Henry Fifth* and the others, which is worth remembering. He calls them a kind of National Epic. Marlborough, you recollect, said, he knew no English History but what he had learned from Shakspeare. There are really, if we look to it, few as memorable Histories. The great salient points are admirably seized; all rounds itself off, into a kind of rhythmic coherence; it is, as Schlegel says, *epic*;—as indeed all delineation by a great thinker will be. There are right beautiful things in those Pieces, which indeed together form one beautiful thing. That battle of Agincourt strikes me as one of the most perfect things, in its sort, we anywhere have of Shakspeare's. The description of the two hosts: the worn-out, jaded English; the dread hour, big with destiny, when the battle shall begin; and then that deathless valour: 'Ye good yeomen, whose limbs were made in England!' There is a noble Patriotism in it,—far other than the 'indifference' you sometimes hear ascribed to Shakspeare. A true English heart breathes, calm and strong, through the whole business; not boisterous, protrusive; all the better for that. There is a sound in it like the ring of steel. This man too had a right stroke in him, had it come to that!

But I will say, of Shakspeare's works generally, that we have no full impress of him there; even as full as we have of many men. His works are so many windows, through which we see a glimpse of the world that was in him. All his works seem, comparatively speaking, cursory, imperfect, written under cramping circumstances; giving only here and there a note of the full utterance of the man. Passages there are that come upon you like splendour out of Heaven; bursts of radiance, illuminating the very heart of the thing: you say, 'That is *true*, spoken once and forever; wheresoever and whensoever there is an open human soul, that will be recognised as true!' Such bursts, however, make us feel that the surrounding matter is not radiant; that it is, in part, temporary, conventional. Alas, Shakspeare had to write for the Globe Playhouse: his great soul had to crush itself, as it could, into that and no other mould. It was with him, then, as it is with us all. No man works save under conditions. The sculptor cannot set his own free Thought before us; but his Thought as he could translate it into the stone that was given, with the tools that were given. *Disjecta membra* are all that we find of any Poet, or of any man.

Whoever looks intelligently at this Shakspeare may recognise that he too was a *Prophet*, in his way; of an insight analogous to the Prophetic, though he took it up in another strain. Nature seemed to this man also divine; *un*speakable, deep as Tophet, high as Heaven: 'We are such stuff as Dreams are made of!' That scroll in Westminster Abbey, which few read with understanding, is of the depth of any seer. But the man sang; did not preach, except musically. We called Dante the melodious Priest of Middle-Age Catholicism. May we not call Shakspeare the still more melodious Priest of a *true*

Catholicism, the 'Universal Church' of the Future and of all times? No narrow superstition, harsh asceticism, intolerance, fanatical fierceness or perversion: a Revelation, so far as it goes, that such a thousandfold hidden beauty and divineness dwells in all Nature; which let all men worship as they can! We may say without offence, that there rises a kind of universal Psalm out of this Shakspeare too; not unfit to make itself heard among the still more sacred Psalms. Not in disharmony with these, if we understood them, but in harmony!—I cannot call this Shakspeare a 'Sceptic,' as some do; his indifference to the creeds and theological quarrels of his time misleading them. No: neither unpatriotic, though he says little about his Patriotism; nor sceptic, though he says little about his Faith. Such 'indifference' was the fruit of his greatness withal: his whole heart was in his own grand sphere of worship (we may call it such); these other controversies, vitally important to other men, were not vital to him.

But call it worship, call it what you will, is it not a right glorious thing, and set of things, this that Shakspeare has brought us? For myself, I feel that there is actually a kind of sacredness in the fact of such a man being sent into this Earth. Is he not an eye to us all; a blessed heaven-sent Bringer of Light?—And, at bottom, was it not perhaps far better that this Shakspeare, everyway an unconscious man, was *conscious* of no Heavenly message? He did not feel, like Mahomet, because he saw into those internal Splendours, that he specially was the 'Prophet of God:' and was he not greater than Mahomet in that? Greater; and also, if we compute strictly, as we did in Dante's case, more successful. It was intrinsically an error that notion of Mahomet's, of his supreme Prophethood; and has come down to us inextricably involved in error to this day; dragging along with it such a coil of fables, impurities, intolerances, as makes it a questionable step for me here and now to say, as I have done, that Mahomet was a true Speaker at all, and not rather an ambitious charlatan, perversity and simulacrum; no Speaker, but a Babbler! Even in Arabia, as I compute, Mahomet will have exhausted himself and become obsolete, while this Shakspeare, this Dante may still be young;—while this Shakspeare may still pretend to be a Priest of Mankind, of Arabia as of other places, for unlimited periods to come!

Compared with any speaker or singer one knows, even with Æschylus or Homer, why should he not, for veracity and universality, last like them? He is *sincere* as they; reaches deep down like them, to the universal and perennial. But as for Mahomet, I think it had been better for him *not* to be so conscious! Alas, poor Mahomet; all that he was *conscious* of was a mere error; a futility and triviality,—as indeed such ever is. The truly great in him too was the unconscious: that he was a wild Arab lion of the desert, and did speak-out with that great thunder-voice of his, not by words which he *thought* to be great, but by actions, by feelings, by a history which *were* great! His Koran has become a stupid piece of prolix absurdity; we do not believe, like him, that God wrote that! The Great Man here too, as always, is a Force of Nature: whatsoever is truly great in him springs-up from the *in*articulate deeps.

Well: this is our poor Warwickshire Peasant, who rose to be Manager of a Playhouse, so that he could live without begging; whom the Earl of Southampton cast some kind glances on; whom Sir Thomas Lucy, many thanks to him, was for sending to the Treadmill! We did not account him a god, like Odin, while he dwelt with us;—on which point there were much to be said. But I will say rather, or repeat: In spite of the sad state Hero-worship now lies in, consider what this Shakspeare has actually become among us. Which Englishman we ever made, in this land of ours, which million of Englishmen, would we not give-up rather than the Stratford Peasant? There is no regiment of highest Dignitaries that we would sell him for. He is the grandest thing we have yet done. For our honour among foreign nations, as an ornament to our English Household, what item is there that we would not surrender rather than him? Consider now, if they asked us, Will you give-up your Indian Empire or your Shakspeare, you English; never have had any Indian Empire, or never have had any Shakspeare? Really it were a grave question. Official persons would answer doubtless in official language; but we, for our part too, should not we be forced to answer: Indian Empire, or no Indian Empire; we cannot do without Shakspeare! Indian Empire will go, at any rate, some day; but this Shakspeare does not go, he lasts forever with us; we cannot give-up our Shakspeare!

Nay, apart from spiritualities; and considering him merely as a real, marketable, tangibly-useful possession. England, before long, this Island of ours, will hold but a small fraction of the English: in America, in New Holland, east and west to the very Antipodes, there will be a Saxondom covering great spaces of the Globe. And now, what is it that can keep all these together into virtually one Nation, so that they do not fall-out and fight, but live at peace, in brotherlike intercourse, helping one another? This is justly regarded as the greatest practical problem, the thing all manner of sovereignties and governments are here to accomplish: what is it that will accomplish this? Acts of Parliament, administrative prime-ministers cannot. America is parted from us, so far as Parliament could part it. Call it not fantastic, for there is much reality in it: Here, I say, is an English King, whom no time or chance, Parliament or combination of Parliaments, can dethrone! This King Shakspeare, does not he shine, in crowned sovereignty, over us all, as the noblest, gentlest, yet strongest of rallying-signs; *in*destructible; really more valuable in that point of view than any other means or appliance whatsoever? We can fancy him as radiant aloft over all the Nations of Englishmen, a thousand years hence. From Paramatta, from New York, wheresoever, under what sort of Parish-Constable soever, English men and women are, they will say to one another: 'Yes, this Shakspeare is ours; we produced him, we speak and think by him; we are of one blood and kind with him.' The most common-sense politician, too, if he pleases, may think of that.

Yes, truly, it is a great thing for a Nation that it get an articulate voice; that it produce a man who will speak-forth melodiously what the heart of it means! Italy, for example, poor Italy lies dismembered, scattered asunder, not appearing in any protocol or treaty as a unity at all; yet the noble Italy is actually *one*: Italy produced its Dante; Italy can speak! The Czar of all the Russias, he is strong, with so many bayonets, Cossacks, and cannons; and does a great feat in keeping such a tract of Earth politically together; but he cannot yet speak. Something great in him, but it is a dumb greatness. He has had no voice of genius, to be heard of all men and times. He must learn to speak. He is a great dumb monster hitherto. His cannons and Cossacks will all have rusted into nonentity, while that Dante's voice is still audible. The Nation that has a Dante is bound together as no dumb Russia can be.—We must here end what we had to say of the *Hero-Poet*.

## H. N. HUDSON
### From *Lectures on Shakspeare*
1848, Volume 1, pp. 64–87
#### Sensibility

Shakspeare's sensibility is in proportion with his other gifts. His heart is as great and as strong as his head. He feels the beauty and the worth of things as truly and as deeply as he discerns their relations; is alive to the slightest and equal to the strongest impression; nothing stuns and nothing eludes his sensibility. He sympathizes, calmly yet intensely, with all that he finds and all that he makes; he *loves* all things; his soul gushes out in warm virgin-like affection over all the objects of his contemplation, and embraces them in its soft, heavenly radiance. He discerns a soul, a pulse of good even in things that are evil; knows, indeed, that nothing can exist utterly divorced from good of some sort; that it must have some inward harmony to hold it in existence. To this harmony, this innate, indestructible worth, his mind is ever open. He is, therefore, a man of universal benevolence; wishes well of all things; will do his best to benefit them; not, indeed, by injuring others, but by doing them justice; by giving them their due, be they saints, or be they sinners. He is strictly and inexorably impartial, and even shows his love of perfect justice by shedding the sunshine and the rain of his genius alike on the just and on the unjust. For his feelings are the allies, not the rivals, of his other powers; exist in sympathy and reciprocity, not in antagonism with them, and therefore never try to force or tempt him from his loyalty to truth.

With most men, the head and heart will not work together; one of them is always pulling the other under: in thinking, they cease to feel, or in feeling they cease to think; so that, to borrow a figure from Coleridge, they are either like the moon, all light and no heat, or like a stove, all heat and no light. They therefore fail of true wisdom, because they are always using either the head without the heart, or the heart without the head. Shakspeare, on the contrary, everywhere exemplifies "the long pull, and strong pull, and pull altogether," of all the faculties. Though and feeling with him are always interpenetrating and interworking, and he never fails of wisdom, because he never uses head or heart alone. Notwithstanding, forasmuch as Shakspeare discovers no preference of the good characters to the bad, many think him deficient in moral sensibility; whereas, in fact, he shows the perfection of such sensibility in altogether preferring truth to them both: for there is really nothing more vicious or more vitiating than, what some people seem greatly in love with, the attempting to teach better morality than is taught by nature and Providence.

There is more, I suspect, in this matter of feeling than is generally supposed. Many people seem to have no true feelings whatever, but only sensations, which they mistake for feelings. And of the remaining portion, perhaps a majority have no feelings but of and for themselves. Like amiable sheep, they love the good shepherd only *because* he leads them into green pastures and beside the still waters. It is to be feared that even some Christians love pleasure more than they love truth; and would tell a world of lies to escape pain. If assured that Satan, though they know him the father of lies, would make them happy, there is no telling whom they would follow. Such people cannot be said to feel truth at all; nay, they can hardly be said to feel any thing save themselves; and their apparent sympathy for other things is really but a feeling of themselves or their interest in them; that is, it is but self-love diverted upon another object. There are, however, a few men, and perhaps

Shakspeare stands at their head, who truly sympathize with something out of themselves; who really feel the true, the beautiful, and the good; nay, whose feeling of these objects comparatively swallows up the feeling of themselves. Shakspeare, it is true, did not talk about his feelings, perhaps was not conscious of them; but that he had them in their truest, deepest form, seems highly probable from the fact, that instead of speaking about *them*, he spoke about the things that inspired them. His love of the true, the beautiful, and the good, was simply too deep and genuine, to be listening to its own voice, or carrying a looking-glass before itself to gaze at its own image; and such is ever the case with souls that are smitten with such objects. For it is the very nature of true feeling to interest us in something out of ourselves. And when we see a man prating about his feelings, we may know at once that he has none. In a word, it is with feeling as with religion; if a man really have any, he will have "none to speak of." Of all men, therefore, Shakspeare was perhaps the least a sentimentalist; strove not at all to reveal the truth and beauty of his feelings, but only to reveal the truth and beauty which he felt. For the sentimentalist is one who thinks he has very fine feelings and means everybody shall know it: he therefore puts his feelings on the outside, dresses himself in them, and so goes about calling on all to observe and admire them; all of which, by the way, is among the very lowest and meanest forms of conceit and selfishness.

Nor are Shakspeare's moral sympathies, his sympathy with truth and good, any more just or genuine than his mere human sympathies. He not only knows what we all know, but feels what we all feel, and utters forth the feeling with the same fidelity as he does the knowledge. The hearts of most men are so small, that they cannot fully enter into the feelings of another without ceasing to be themselves; a complete sympathy with the movements of another mind would perhaps swallow up the individuality of their own. But Shakspeare's all-embracing bosom catches and reverberates every note of man's heart. He could reproduce in their utmost depth and intensity the feelings of us all without injury to himself. His sympathies seem to have covered the extremes of human sensibility, so that the feelings of us all might, as it were, be cut out of his, and yet leave his personality entire.

Doubtless it was this omniformity of feeling, as much as any thing, that qualified him, beyond any other man, to be the representative of the whole human family. He was thus in a condition neither to withhold from a character his own, nor to yield him up another's, but simply to give him his due. Hence the strict rigid impartiality of his representations; for among all his characters, we cannot discover from the delineation itself that he had a single favourite, though of course we cannot conceive it possible for any man to regard Edmund and Edgar, for example, with the same feelings. It is as if the scenes of his dramas were forced on his observation against his will; himself, meanwhile, being under the most solemn oath to report the truth, the whole truth, and nothing but the truth. Surrounded by the angels and demons which make up the dramatic combination of Lear or Othello, though conscious the while of their inmost thoughts and feelings, such, nevertheless, is the calmness, with which he surveys them, that not the least bias comes in to distort or discolour his representation of them. He thus uniformly leaves the characters to make their own impression upon us; has no opinions or feelings of his own to promulgate through them, but simply to represent them; in a word, he is their mouth-piece, not they his; and he could be the representative of all because he would be the advocate of none. With the honour or shame, the right or wrong of their actions, he has nothing to do; that they are so and act so, is

their fault, not his; and his business is, not to reform nor deprave, to censure nor approve them, but simply to tell the truth about them, whithersoever it may lead him. Accordingly, he exhibits neither any utterly worthless, nor any utterly faultless monsters; none too good or too bad to exist; none too high to be loved, or too low to be pitied: even his worst characters (unless we except those two she-tigers, Goneril and Regan, and even their blood is red like ours) have some slight fragrance of humanity about them; some indefinable touches which redeem them from utter hatred or utter contempt, and keep them within the pale of human sympathy, or at least of human pity.

Nor does Shakspeare ever bring in any characters as the mere shadows, or instruments, or appendages of others. All the persons, great and small, contain within themselves the reason why they are there and not elsewhere, why they are so and not otherwise. None exist exclusively for others, or exclusively for themselves, but all appear, partly on their own account, with aims, and feelings, and interests of their own. None are forced in merely to supply the place of others, and so merely trifled with till the others can be got ready to resume their place; but each is treated in his turn as if he were the main character in the piece, and speaks and acts, not merely to call up and call out others, but chiefly to utter and impart himself. So true is this, that even when one character comes in as the satellite of another, he does so by a right and an impulse of his own; he is all the while but obeying or rather executing the law of his personality, and has just as much claim on the other for a primary, as the other has on him for a satellite. In a word, Shakspeare, in his mental kingdom, is a prince of absolute power, but at the same time of absolute justice, and always treats those of his subjects as the mightiest who are at the moment beneath his pen: he knows no weighty man, or rather knows no man whatever in his empire, save him who is now speaking, and knows him as such, or even at all, only while he permits him to speak. The consequence of which is, that all the characters are developed, not indeed at equal length, for they have not all the same amount to be developed, but with equal perfectness as far as they go; for to make the dwarf fill the same space as the giant, would be to dilute, not develope the dwarf.

Thus with the fruitfulness of nature Shakspeare also joined the disinterestedness of nature, who concentrates herself alike in the nettle and the oak, the night-shade and the rose, the wasp and the dove. And perhaps his greatest glory, both as a poet and as a man is, that he was no respecter of sects, or parties, or persons, but simply a teller of the truth.

Born for the universe, he shrunk not his mind,
Nor to party gave up what was meant for mankind.

He was neither Jew nor Gentile, Romanist nor Protestant, but a broad, Christian, Catholic union of them all, and threw the mantle of his genius round our universal humanity. Hence his works are always humanizing us, fusing our minds, so to speak, out of their selfish isolation, into unanimity and fellowship; in a word, they are a constant discipline of humanity, are filled with those "touches of nature," which "make the whole world kin:" at the voice of his genius the shell of individualism, into which we are so fond of retiring to "suck the paws of our own self-importance," is perpetually giving way to the ingress and egress of human sympathy. He seems indeed to have lived and worked altogether at the roots of humanity, distilling the very sap and moulding the very elements of the wonderful structure; and knew that all sects and parties were but the transient, differently-shaped leaves which the winds of time would soon blow into oblivion, while the structure itself would remain forever the same.

This universal and impartial humanity is doubtless among the highest qualities of Shakspeare's works; nay, it is among the highest possible qualities of any human productions; for it is the union and interfusion of the deepest reason and the justest feeling. The great trouble, I suspect, with most of us, is, that we dwell wholly or mostly in mere conventionalities, and personal or party peculiarities. The moment we attempt of ourselves to go out of these, we get lost amid perplexities and darkness. The result is, we are continually mistaking and substituting our individual impressions for universal truth; assuming that all people are bound to think as we think, feel as we feel, and see as we see, and concluding them very weak or very wicked, unless their opinions and feelings coincide with ours. Within the circle, indeed, of their own conventionalities, men often attain a sort of profundity; but in proportion as they become profound there, they of course become unintelligible or uninteresting to those beyond their convention. Floating merely amid some local accidents of humanity, they are therefore intelligible to, and intelligent of, those only who are within the circle of the same accidents; but should they dive to the universal attributes of humanity, they would at once become intelligible to, and intelligent of, all. Hence Shakspeare's works, the profoundest of all uninspired writings, are at the same time the most generally intelligible. Striking below the accidents of local and partial nature, he is constantly touching chords that vibrate through the universal mind of man. So exquisitely balanced were his powers, that his individual impressions coincided with universal truth, or at least instinctively adjusted themselves to it. He could, therefore, frame laws which should embrace the whole human family, instead of framing them for a particular section of mankind, and then pronouncing all others outlaws. He could not only see that others were wrong, but could see why they were wrong; why, in fact, from the constitution or condition of their minds, they could not be otherwise: he could therefore appreciate and sympathize with them, notwithstanding their errors; and, what is better, by making them known to each other and themselves, he could do something towards setting them right. Occupying, as it were, the focal point of nature, where the various coloured rays of partial truth meet and blend together into the pure white light of universal truth, he could throw them back in their integral perfection; thus giving us, along with the part of truth which we already have, and which is coloured simply because it is a part, the transparent, colourless whole which we want. If, however, we study him, as many do, with prismatic minds, we shall of course again refract the beams from him into particoloured rays, and so approve him when we find him with us, and censure him when we find him against us. But such is not the way to study him, nor, indeed, any other author worth the studying; unless, perchance, we study rather to teach him than to be taught by him.

It is for these reasons, in part, that Shakspeare's characters always affect us as those in real life. Different people, according to their respective feelings and dispositions, take up very different impressions of them. As in the case of actual persons, nothing short of a profound and subtle analysis can arrive at satisfactory conclusions respecting them. To a constant, reflecting student, they seem perpetually developing themselves, and are always undergoing apparent modifications precisely corresponding to the real modifications of the student's own character. Often they are so much addressed to the feelings, so much more is often suggested than is said, that no one can fully expound them, without completely unfolding himself. Always making the persons act and speak from what is implied, as well as from what is disclosed, the poet is perpetually sending us beyond himself to nature, and to the elements of all character. Even when the characters are seen but in part, they are yet capable of being understood and unfolded in the whole; every part being relative and inferring all the others. What is given, be it ever so little, conveys a relish of what is withheld, be it ever so much. In short, as every part of a good architectural design implies and infers the whole structure to which it belongs; so in one of Shakspeare's persons every act or word, being a result of the whole character, is significant and suggestive of the whole; involves, indeed, the seminal principle out of which the whole proceeds; and therefore supplies at once the subject and the stimulant of long meditation; contains both matter and motive for an indefinite period of thought.

From what hath been said, the perceptive, the creative, and the sensitive powers were so exquisitely balanced in Shakspeare's mind, that it is impossible to say which had the lead. That he indefinitely surpassed all other writers in something, is generally allowed; but in what particular faculty or mental activity his great superiority lay, scarce any two are agreed. And this very circumstance is probably decisive of the truth. The real secret of his superiority to all other writers, lies in his having in the highest degree the peculiar faculties of each. It is the absence of any individual preponderance or individual deficiency among his powers, that forms their united perfection; and his towering so far above the rest of mankind is sufficiently explained by the fact, that no one of his faculties towered above the others. There seems to have been an exact proportion, and equivalence, and reciprocity among all his powers, so that they worked and played together in perfect, perpetual harmony, without ever deciding, or even raising the question of precedence among themselves. In a word, the peculiarity of his mind consists in its want of peculiarities; its generic quality; its power of communicating equally with all other minds; so that "he was just like any other man, but that he was like all other men." Accordingly, wisdom, true wisdom, in the best and highest sense, seems to me the characteristic quality of his works. It is for this reason that one has to look at Shakspeare so long in order to realize his greatness; the exquisite proportion and harmony of his mind causing him to appear at first much smaller than he is.

Perhaps I cannot better close this view of Shakspeare's mind, than in the enthusiastic words of Schlegel. "This tragical Titan," says he, "who storms the heavens, and threatens to tear the world off its hinges; who, more fruitful than Eschylus, makes our hair to stand on end, and congeals our blood with horror, possessed at the same time the insinuating loveliness of the sweetest poetry; he plays with love like a child, and his songs are breathed out like melting sighs. He unites in his existence the utmost elevation and the utmost depth; the most foreign, and even apparently irreconcilable properties, in him subsist peaceably together. The world of spirits and of nature have laid their treasures at his feet: in strength a demi-god, in profundity of view a prophet, in all-seeing wisdom a protecting spirit of a higher order, he lowers himself to mortals as if unconscious of his superiority, and is as open and unassuming as a child."

## Alleged Immorality

Shakspeare's plays have been frequently charged with immoral tendencies; than which a more unfounded and injurious charge could not well be made. Like various other charges visited upon them, it has generally sprung either from a disposition to fix upon certain detached expressions, or from inability to take in the impression of a vital, organic whole. For morally, as otherwise, a work of art should be regarded in its total impression; and those who can see but one line or one sentence of a poem at once are not competent judges of its moral quality. Undoubtedly there are passages in Shakspeare's works, as indeed there are in the Bible itself, which, taken by themselves, may produce a bad effect; but there cannot be found a whole play, scarcely even a whole scene in them, whose integral impression is not altogether good. There is indeed no flower so pure and sweet but that certain reptiles will extract poison from it; even the wisest provisions of nature and the sacredest transactions of life, beauty, innocence, marriage, become to some minds the food of base, sensual desires. I have known certain lewd epicures of sin take the Bible of a Sunday, when they could not well engage in any sweeter wickedness, and glut their spirits out of its pages. What, in the name of purity, is there in the universe so pure but that such minds would draw impurity from it? Why, they would taint the very heavens themselves, and then suck back the corruption they had engendered!

It must be confessed, however, that Shakspeare's own virtue, like that of his purest characters, and like that of the purest men too, was not of that ambitious, pharisaical sort, which is always trying to bolster itself by an outrageous horror of vice, or at least the appearance of vice. Accordingly he never attires sensuality in artificial attractions, nor conceals real impurity under a wrappage of conventional decency, nor throws the drapery of affected delicacy over the movements of guilty passion. If he has occasion for a bad character, he shows him just as he is, and does not attempt to disguise his grossness, or palliate his deformity; and it is surely our own fault if we are captivated by the inward impurity of a character whose outward ugliness ought to offend even our senses. He has sometimes delineated downright villains and sensualists; but he has never volunteered to steal the robes of heaven for them to serve the devil in without offending decency. In all cases, indeed, he has most religiously kept faith with the moral sensibilities which nature has set to guard the purity of the mind, and he seldom violates even the laws of gentility save in obedience to the higher laws of morality. It is by gilding or varnishing over impurity with the superficial graces of style and sentiment, by wrapping up poison in an envelope of honey, so that it may steal a passage into the mind without offending the taste, or alarming the moral sentinels of the heart,—it is in this way that death is conveyed into the system;—a thing which no man was ever farther from doing than Shakspeare: if we wish to see it done in perfection, we had better go to the pages of Byron and Bulwer; who do indeed discover no little fondness for delineating noble, generous, magnanimous villains; gentle, amiable, sentimental cut-throats,—in a word, devils sugared over. Yet it is questionable whether even these, bad as they are, are so bad as the late importations from France, so much in favor with the more "beautiful spirits" of the time, where the laws of morality are not so much evaded by simulation of virtue as inverted by consecration of vice, and where debauchery is argued for on principles of reason, and religion itself, the sacred law of love, is urged in behalf of lewdness and lust. The truth is, there are some people whose morality seems to be all in their ears; who cannot bear to have things called by their right names; nay, who are even fond of dirty things, and will compass sea and land to come at them, provided they can have them dressed in clean words; and who are never contented unless they have something whereby to persuade themselves that they are serving God while indulging their lusts.

In Shakspeare, as in nature, virtue shows her finest lessons in contest, or in contrast with vice: if we reject the former and cleave to the latter, the fact proves our impurity, not his; and if we are corrupted by such teachings, it were surely hard to tell what can purify us. He who forsakes Isabella to follow after

Angelo, or Desdemona to follow after Iago, may be justly given up as already a spoiled egg. Under objections to such exhibitions there is often concealed a grossly impure mind, and he who goes among such examples scenting out corruption and letting loose his censure, only shows the drift of his thoughts. Such a quick susceptibility of vicious impressions often cloaks itself under a formal or verbal austerity. He who most delights to meet vice in secret, will of course be most apt to recognize and turn his back upon her in public. His fig-leaves betray him. It is the presence of powder only that makes the torch dangerous.

> So full of artless jealousy is guilt,
> It spills itself in fearing to be spilt.

In heaven's name let decency be preserved, but let it not be piled on in folds and bustles to cover up personal deformity! Obscenity is certainly bad enough, but it is infinitely better than the chaste language of a crafty seducer. It is always well for us to know whom we are with; and our best safeguard against vice, is the very indecency in which it naturally appears. In his uniform observance of these principles Shakspeare has shown a degree of moral purity of which we have few examples in literature. He is indeed sometimes gross, but never false; he may occasionally offend a sense of delicacy, but never deceives and seduces the mind into admiration of unworthy objects; and he carries on no warfare against virtue by endeavoring to entrap our sympathies by the misfortunes of vice. That he should make a Falstaff at once so delightful and so detestable; that he should so charm us with the humour, even while disgusting us with the sensuality of such a being, and so let us into the truth, without drawing us into the love of such a character; really proves the strength of his morality no less than the mastery of his genius. For my part, I dare be known to think Shakspeare's works a far better school of virtuous discipline than half the moral and religious books which are now put into the hands of youth, and of which the chief tendency seems to be, to keep them thinking continually how wise and good they are; thus dyeing them in the wool with the conceit of virtue and the cant of pietism, and laying the foundations either of spiritual pride or of rotten-hearted libertinism, in an intensely self-conscious and self-admiring morality.

Shakspeare, it is true, never lays off the poet to put on the moralist; never goes out of his way to inculcate morality in an abstract, scientific form. He does not anatomize virtue, to make us skilful casuists and dialecticians. Of that arrogant but impotent science which is always telling us what to do, but never inspiring us to do it, and which, beginning at the understanding, tries to work inwards, but never gets at the heart, he did not aspire to be a teacher. Morality comes from him as from nature, not in abstract propositions, to set our logic-mills a-going, but in a living form of beauty, to inspire us with love and noble passion. Of which method we have a beautiful example in the sweet Psalmist of Israel, who, when he found King Saul possessed by the evil spirit, took his harp and voice, and with his heavenly minstrelsy charmed the evil spirit out of him, and restored him to reason. Probably if David had undertaken to reason the devil out, he would only have strengthened the possession; for the devil, then as now, was a most expert logician, but could not stand a divine song.

Attempts enough have been made to countervail bad passions with intellectual convictions; such passions can be successfully countervailed only by awakening antagonist good passions: and herein lies the peculiar force and beauty of passion, that it represents the object as of infinite value, and so admits no selfish or prudential considerations against it. The trouble with us, is not so much a want of knowledge, as a want of love:

We see the right, but still the wrong pursue,
because we look at the right with the head only, not with the heart. What we need, therefore, is the creative faculty to imagine that which we know, and the generous impulse to act that which we imagine; in a word, we want the poetry of life, to make us feel and love the lessons which are everywhere written around and within us—lessons whose soft but irresistible appeals to the heart have been so long drowned in the logical hubbub with which science has vainly striven, and must always vainly strive, to rectify the heart through the understanding. The truth is, the process of rectification, as a certain old-fashioned Book tells us, must begin at the heart, and work the other way. This creative faculty, this generous impulse, is what Shakspeare will give us, if we be worthy to receive it. He is really the better moralist inasmuch as he never attempts to moralize. For our moral sensibilities are the most delicate elements of our constitution, and require to be touched with the utmost care, or rather, not to be touched directly at all; and if instruction be forced upon them, and crammed into them, it dulls and deadens, instead of quickening and strengthening them. It is worse than useless to feed them before they are hungry, and to anticipate the appetite with a glut is not the way to sharpen it. Hence it is, that those teachers who are always thrusting morality into the faces of their pupils, and boring them with it, and requiring them formally to study it, so seldom get them to practise it. Perhaps nothing is more common among us, than to stuff and cram people into a sort of moral dyspepsia. In a word, the true secret of success in moral instruction, is that very remoteness and reserve which distinguishes art from all other forms of expression, and which makes it as much more effective than science as example is better than precept. Moreover, by drawing the mind out of itself, and absorbing it in external objects, art instils right sentiments and principles into us without letting us know it; so that we may become virtuous, without the liability to turn our virtue into a source of moral pride and conceit, those darling vices of the age.

It should not be supposed, however, that Shakspeare is a suitable book for all readers. Probably there is no book whatsoever, whereof this can be justly affirmed. It is an old maxim, that what is one man's food is another man's poison. Whether, or how far this be physically true, I cannot say; that it is true morally and intellectually, need not be doubted. Unless we carry certain dispositions of mind and heart to the Bible even, we are liable to be injured rather than benefited by it; and it is to be feared that many have been led to eat and drink of its contents unworthily, by those who were too ambitious of doing good, to wait for proper times and occasions. In education, whether moral or intellectual, every thing depends upon wisely varying and adapting our means according to each particular subject; regard must be continually had to the special wants, conditions, inclinations, and aptitudes of individual minds, and to treat all alike, is simply to mistreat all. The wise physician is he who carefully observes and studies the peculiarities of each particular case, and frames his prescriptions accordingly; and to proceed on general prescriptions, we all understand to be quackery. The great fault in the teaching of the day is, that teachers' minds are so clogged with generalities, that they have no attention to bestow on the specialities before them. Confident in their knowledge of all, they omit to study each, and so go on *generalizing* their pupils into ignorance and imbecility. In short, babes, whether in the cradle or in the counting-room, require to be fed with milk: whereas Shakspeare is strong meat. Albeit, therefore, he is not good for all, there is no danger of his hurting any one who can truly understand him; that is, who can see particular passages in relation to the characters whence they proceed, and particular characters in relation to the others with whom they are associated.

Another item in the attempted impeachment of Shakspeare's morality is, that he does not always observe, nay, sometimes utterly disregards what are termed the laws of poetical justice; that in his exhibitions moral equity is, to say the least, but very imperfectly administered, often, indeed, not administered at all. He does not encourage virtue by making it always successful, nor discountenance vice by always defeating its aims. In short, a degree of moral confusion reigns in his plays; the innocent often fall under the machinations of the guilty; the guilty often triumph on the ruins of innocence; often both are hurried away in undistinguishable ruin.

Fortunately for Shakspeare's honour, this charge cannot be denied. This rigid dispensation of moral justice, which brings virtue and vice down to a calculation of profit and loss, however favourable it might have been to his popularity, would have been fatal to his morality. And is the not succeeding, the not getting our wages, the worst thing we fear? Most assuredly, then, it is not the worst we shall suffer, and ought to suffer. If we would not rather die as Desdemona than live and thrive as Iago, the more pity for us, and the more punishment for us too. We have ourselves lived to see virtue well-nigh banished from the fireside, and religion from the altar, by the perverse efforts of certain teachers to make out a balance of worldly motives in their favour. And how many such appeals to the selfishness of men do they think it will take to make men disinterested? Such attempts to reconcile or identify interest and duty, only encourage men to seek their interest under the mask of duty; that is, to add hypocrisy to selfishness. Conflicts of interest and duty are the very means whereby Providence tests, and enables us to test what and where our treasures are, what and where our hearts are. Truth and virtue never offer to compromise with us; to insure us success in return for our homage: lest they should make us hirelings, not subjects, they promise us simply themselves; and it is that old serpent, the devil, that promises us thrones, and kingdoms, and fat purses and fine stomachs, if we will but fall down and worship him.

The truth is, we might just about as well go into chaos in quest of harmony, as go into the present order of things in quest of moral equity. And Shakspeare knew very well,—what some wise moralists seem never to have dreamed of,—that the virtue which springs from anticipations of success, was but the offspring of Satan and selfishness; and that, standing on calculations of profit and loss, it must fall, as it deserves to fall, into the pit. Every body that has half an eye knows the rewards of this world are often obtained without being merited, and often merited without being obtained; that it is characteristic of the good, to avert evil from the bad by sacrificing themselves, and of the bad, to save themselves by diverting evil upon the good. The poetry, therefore, or the philosophy which represents virtue and vice as sure of present recompense, is a lie, and as such can only come directly or indirectly, of the father of lies. And Shakspeare was just as far from stealing the robes of Satan to serve heaven in, as from stealing the robes of heaven to serve Satan in. Accordingly, he gave his characters, good and bad, a sphere wherein to develop themselves, and then dismissed them, as nature and as God dismisses them, into a higher order of things, to receive their reward or suffer their retribution.

There is a deal of strange theology or antitheology in the world touching the question of happiness. "O happiness, our being's end and aim," says one; and many there be, who seriously maintain that happiness is the highest thing we are able to seek or required to seek. In keeping with this notion, the desire of happiness is set forth as the most original and fundamental law of our nature; one which we cannot escape from if we would, and ought not to escape from if we could. Now, I undertake to say, we have no such original desire whatever, unless as implied in original sin; that it is altogether a fallen desire; one which we ought not to act from at all, and which, God helping us, we need not act from. The truth is, happiness is in no wise a legitimate object of pursuit, though various things producing it are. Properly speaking, there is, and can be, no such thing as *love* of happiness: for happiness is altogether an inward, subjective thing, whereas love is essentially an objective sentiment; a sentiment inspired by something external to the mind; and the moment love takes happiness for its object, it degenerates into lust. For to love a thing only for the pleasure we may have of it, is the very definition of lust. Happiness, happiness, what does the word mean? Happiness, one would really think, is a thing that *happens*; a thing, too, that will not be, unless allowed to happen; so that seeking it, working for it, is the surest way to prevent its happening. There are, indeed, various susceptibilities within us, and various objects around us, answering to them; in the lawful pursuit of which objects, happiness overtakes us, falls upon us, *happens* to us, without our knowing it or before we know it; whereas the moment we go after it, we lose it, because we forsake the objects that give it. Such, as appears from the original of the word, and as all men's experience will testify, is the beautiful provision of nature, that, relatively to us, the thing called happiness must emphatically happen, else it cannot be; as if our Maker would have us owe all our happiness to Him, and so had empowered and instructed us simply to do our duty, reserving to Himself alone the power to make us happy in doing it.

On the whole, therefore, perhaps we may as well let alone our emotions; forget that we have any in the objects that inspire them; love, and seek those objects, instead of loving and seeking ourselves in them; and be happy in loving and seeking them, without knowing or caring whether we be happy or not. For it is not by love of salvation, but by love of Him who is the Way, the Truth, and the Life, that we are to be saved. In chasing the butterfly, it is not happiness, but simply the butterfly, that the child is in quest; were he seeking happiness, he would probably leave the butterfly and go to chasing sin, as the rest of us generally do, in quest of it. I know it may be urged, that happiness comes by self-sacrifice; and thus do the advocates of the theology in question, always contrive to escape among the coincidences of things. But does it follow that seeking after happiness will lead to self-sacrifice? The mischief of such teaching is, that it encourages self-sacrifice *in order to* happiness, which of course is no self-sacrifice at all. Doubtless, the profit and loss morality, so often urged against Shakspeare, is connected, either as cause or effect, with this shallow and impudent theology.

## RALPH WALDO EMERSON
### "Shakspeare; or, the Poet"
*Representative Men*
### 1850

Great men are more distinguished by range and extent than by originality. If we require the originality which consists in weaving, like a spider, their web from their own bowels; in finding clay and making bricks and building the house; no great men are original. Nor does valuable originality consist in unlikeness to other men. The hero is in the press of knights and the thick of events; and seeing what men want and sharing their desire, he adds the needful length of sight and of arm, to come at the desired point. The greatest genius is the most indebted man. A poet is no rattle-brain, saying what comes uppermost, and, because he says every thing, saying at last something good; but a heart in unison with his time and country. There is nothing whimsical and fantastic in his production, but sweet and sad earnest, freighted with the weightiest convictions and pointed with the most determined aim which any man or class knows of in his times.

The Genius of our life is jealous of individuals, and will not have any individual great, except through the general. There is no choice to genius. A great man does not wake up on some fine morning and say, 'I am full of life, I will go to sea and find an Antarctic continent: to-day I will square the circle: I will ransack botany and find a new food for man: I have a new architecture in my mind: I foresee a new mechanic power:' no, but he finds himself in the river of the thoughts and events, forced onward by the ideas and necessities of his contemporaries. He stands where all the eyes of men look one way, and their hands all point in the direction in which they should go. The Church has reared him amidst rites and pomps, and he carries out the advice which her music gave him, and builds a cathedral needed by her chants and processions. He finds a war raging: it educates him, by trumpet, in barracks, and he betters the instruction. He finds two counties groping to bring coal, or flour, or fish, from the place of production to the place of consumption, and he hits on a railroad. Every master has found his materials collected, and his power lay in his sympathy with his people and in his love of the materials he wrought in. What an economy of power! and what a compensation for the shortness of life! All is done to his hand. The world has brought him thus far on his way. The human race has gone out before him, sunk the hills, filled the hollows and bridged the rivers. Men, nations, poets, artisans, women, all have worked for him, and he enters into their labors. Choose any other thing, out of the line of tendency, out of the national feeling and history, and he would have all to do for himself: his powers would be expended in the first preparations. Great genial power, one would almost say, consists in not being original at all; in being altogether receptive; in letting the world do all, and suffering the spirit of the hour to pass unobstructed through the mind.

Shakspeare's youth fell in a time when the English people were importunate for dramatic entertainments. The court took offence easily at political allusions and attempted to suppress them. The Puritans, a growing and energetic party, and the religious among the Anglican church, would suppress them. But the people wanted them. Inn-yards, houses without roofs, and extemporaneous enclosures at country fairs were the ready theatres of strolling players. The people had tasted this new joy; and, as we could not hope to suppress newspapers now,—no, not by the strongest party,—neither then could king, prelate, or puritan, alone or united, suppress an organ which was ballad, epic, newspaper, caucus, lecture, Punch and library, at the same time. Probably king, prelate and puritan, all found their own account in it. It had become, by all causes, a national interest,—by no means conspicuous, so that some great scholar would have thought of treating it in an English history,—but not a whit less considerable because it was cheap and of no account, like a baker's-shop. The best proof of its vitality is the crowd of writers which suddenly broke into this field; Kyd, Marlow, Greene, Jonson, Chapman, Dekker, Webster, Heywood, Middleton, Peele, Ford, Massinger, Beaumont and Fletcher.

The secure possession, by the stage, of the public mind, is of the first importance to the poet who works for it. He loses no time in idle experiments. Here is audience and expectation prepared. In the case of Shakspeare there is much more. At the time when he left Stratford and went up to London, a great body of stage-plays of all dates and writers existed in manuscript and were in turn produced on the boards. Here is the *Tale of Troy*, which the audience will bear hearing some part of, every week; the *Death of Julius Cæsar*, and other stories out of Plutarch, which they never tire of; a shelf full of English history, from the chronicles of Brut and Arthur, down to the royal Henries, which men hear eagerly; and a string of doleful tragedies, merry Italian tales and Spanish voyages, which all the London 'prentices know. All the mass has been treated, with more or less skill, by every playwright, and the prompter has the soiled and tattered manuscripts. It is now no longer possible to say who wrote them first. They have been the property of the Theatre so long, and so many rising geniuses have enlarged or altered them, inserting a speech or a whole scene, or adding a song, that no man can any longer claim copyright in this work of numbers. Happily, no man wishes to. They are not yet desired in that way. We have few readers, many spectators and hearers. They had best lie where they are.

Shakspeare, in common with his comrades, esteemed the mass of old plays waste stock, in which any experiment could be freely tried. Had the *prestige* which hedges about a modern tragedy existed, nothing could have been done. The rude warm blood of the living England circulated in the play, as in street-ballads, and gave body which he wanted to his airy and majestic fancy. The poet needs a ground in popular tradition on which he may work, and which, again, may restrain his art within the due temperance. It holds him to the people, supplies a foundation for his edifice, and in furnishing so much work done to his hand, leaves him at leisure and in full strength for the audacities of his imagination. In short, the poet owes to his legend what sculpture owed to the temple. Sculpture in Egypt and in Greece grew up in subordination to architecture. It was the ornament of the temple wall: at first a rude relief carved on pediments, then the relief became bolder and a head or arm was projected from the wall; the groups being still arranged with reference to the building, which serves also as a frame to hold the figures; and when at last the greatest freedom of style and treatment was reached, the prevailing genius of architecture still enforced a certain calmness and continence in the statue. As soon as the statue was begun for itself, and with no reference to the temple or palace, the art began to decline: freak, extravagance and exhibition took the place of the old temperance. This balance-wheel, which the sculptor found in architecture, the perilous irritability of poetic talent found in the accumulated dramatic materials to which the people were already wonted, and which had a certain excellence which no single genius, however extraordinary, could hope to create.

In point of fact it appears that Shakspeare did owe debts in all directions, and was able to use whatever he found; and the amount of indebtedness may be inferred from Malone's laborious computations in regard to the first, second and third parts of *Henry VI.*, in which, "out of 6,043 lines, 1,771 were written by some author preceding Shakspeare, 2,373 by him, on the foundation laid by his predecessors, and 1,899 were entirely his own." And the proceeding investigation hardly leaves a single drama of his absolute invention. Malone's sentence is an important piece of external history. In *Henry VIII.* I think I see plainly the cropping out of the original rock on which his own finer stratum was laid. The first play was written by a superior, thoughtful man, with a vicious ear. I can

mark his lines, and know well their cadence. See Wolsey's soliloquy, and the following scene with Cromwell, where instead of the metre of Shakspeare, whose secret is that the thought constructs the tune, so that reading for the sense will best bring out the rhythm,—here the lines are constructed on a given tune, and the verse has even a trace of pulpit eloquence. But the play contains through all its length unmistakable traits of Shakspeare's hand, and some passages, as the account of the coronation, are like autographs. What is odd, the compliment to Queen Elizabeth is in the bad rhythm.

Shakspeare knew that tradition supplies a better fable than any invention can. If he lost any credit of design, he augmented his resources; and, at that day, our petulant demand for originality was not so much pressed. There was no literature for the million. The universal reading, the cheap press, were unknown. A great poet who appears in illiterate times, absorbs into his sphere all the light which is any where radiating. Every intellectual jewel, every flower of sentiment it is his fine office to bring to his people; and he comes to value his memory equally with his invention. He is therefore little solicitous whence his thoughts have been derived; whether through translation, whether through tradition, whether by travel in distant countries, whether by inspiration; from whatever source, they are equally welcome to his uncritical audience. Nay, he borrows very near home. Other men say wise things as well as he; only they say a good many foolish things, and do not know when they have spoken wisely. He knows the sparkle of the true stone, and puts it in high place, wherever he finds it. Such is the happy position of Homer perhaps; of Chaucer, of Saadi. They felt that all wit was their wit. And they are librarians and historiographers, as well as poets. Each romancer was heir and dispenser of all the hundred tales of the world,—

> Presenting Thebes' and Pelops' line
> And the tale of Troy divine.

The influence of Chaucer is conspicuous in all our early literature; and more recently not only Pope and Dryden have been beholden to him, but, in the whole society of English writers, a large unacknowledged debt is easily traced. One is charmed with the opulence which feeds so many pensioners. But Chaucer is a huge borrower. Chaucer, it seems, drew continually, through Lydgate and Caxton, from Guido di Colonna, whose Latin romance of the Trojan war was in turn a compilation from Dares Phrygius, Ovid and Statius. Then Petrarch, Boccaccio and the Provençal poets are his benefactors: the *Romaunt of the Rose* is only judicious translation from William of Lorris and John of Meung: *Troilus and Creseide*, from Lollius of Urbino: *The Cock and the Fox*, from the *Lais* of Marie: *The House of Fame*, from the French or Italian: and poor Gower he uses as if he were only a brick-kiln or stone-quarry out of which to build his house. He steals by this apology,—that what he takes has no worth where he finds it and the greatest where he leaves it. It has come to be practically a sort of rule in literature, that a man having once shown himself capable of original writing, is entitled thenceforth to steal from the writings of others at discretion. Thought is the property of him who can entertain it and of him who can adequately place it. A certain awkwardness marks the use of borrowed thoughts; but as soon as we have learned what to do with them they become our own.

Thus all originality is relative. Every thinker is retrospective. The learned member of the legislature, at Westminster or at Washington, speaks and votes for thousands. Show us the constituency, and the now invisible channels by which the senator is made aware of their wishes; the crowd of practical and knowing men, who, by correspondence or conversation, are feeding him with evidence, anecdotes and estimates, and it will bereave his fine attitude and resistance of something of their impressiveness. As Sir Robert Peel and Mr. Webster vote, so Locke and Rousseau think, for thousands; and so there were fountains all around Homer, Menu, Saadi, or Milton, from which they drew; friends, lovers, books, traditions, proverbs,— all perished—which, if seen, would go to reduce the wonder. Did the bard speak with authority? Did he feel himself overmatched by any companion? The appeal is to the consciousness of the writer. Is there at last in his breast a Delphi whereof to ask concerning any thought or thing, whether it be verily so, yea or nay? and to have answer, and to rely on that? All the debts which such a man could contract to other wit would never disturb his consciousness of originality; for the ministrations of books and of other minds are a whiff of smoke to that most private reality with which he has conversed.

It is easy to see that what is best written or done by genius in the world, was no man's work, but came by wide social labor, when a thousand wrought like one, sharing the same impulse. Our English Bible is a wonderful specimen of the strength and music of the English language. But it was not made by one man, or at one time; but centuries and churches brought it to perfection. There never was a time when there was not some translation existing. The Liturgy, admired for its energy and pathos, is an anthology of the piety of ages and nations, a translation of the prayers and forms of the Catholic church,—these collected, too, in long periods, from the prayers and meditations of every saint and sacred writer all over the world. Grotius makes the like remark in respect to the Lord's Prayer, that the single clauses of which it is composed were already in use in the time of Christ, in the Rabbinical forms. He picked out the grains of gold. The nervous language of the Common Law, the impressive forms of our courts and the precision and substantial truth of the legal distinctions, are the contribution of all the sharp-sighted, strong-minded men who have lived in the countries where these laws govern. The translation of Plutarch gets its excellence by being translation on translation. There never was a time when there was none. All the truly idiomatic and national phrases are kept, and all others successively picked out and thrown away. Something like the same process had gone on, long before, with the originals of these books. The world takes liberties with world-books. *Vedas, Æsop's Fables, Pilpay, Arabian Nights, Cid, Iliad, Robin Hood, Scottish Minstrelsy,* are not the work of single men. In the composition of such works the time thinks, the market thinks, the mason, the carpenter, the merchant, the farmer, the fop, all think for us. Every book supplies its time with one good word; every municipal law, every trade, every folly of the day; and the generic catholic genius who is not afraid or ashamed to owe his originality to the originality of all, stands with the next age as the recorder and embodiment of his own.

We have to thank the researches of antiquaries, and the Shakspeare Society, for ascertaining the steps of the English drama, from the Mysteries celebrated in churches and by churchmen, and the final detachment from the church, and the completion of secular plays, from *Ferrex and Porrex,* and *Gammer Gurton's Needle,* down to the possession of the stage by the very pieces which Shakspeare altered, remodelled and finally made his own. Elated with success and piqued by the growing interest of the problem, they have left no bookstall unsearched, no chest in a garret unopened, no file of old yellow accounts to decompose in damp and worms, so keen was the hope to discover whether the boy Shakspeare poached or not, whether he held horses at the theatre door, whether he kept school, and why he left in his will only his second-best bed to Ann Hathaway, his wife.

There is somewhat touching in the madness with which the passing age mischooses the object on which all candles shine and all eyes are turned; the care with which it registers every trifle touching Queen Elizabeth and King James, and the Essexes, Leicesters, Burleighs and Buckinghams; and lets pass without a single valuable note the founder of another dynasty, which alone will cause the Tudor dynasty to be remembered,—the man who carries the Saxon race in him by the inspiration which feeds him, and on whose thoughts the foremost people of the world are now for some ages to be nourished, and minds to receive this and not another bias. A popular player;—nobody suspected he was the poet of the human race; and the secret was kept as faithfully from poets and intellectual men as from courtiers and frivolous people. Bacon, who took the inventory of the human understanding for his times, never mentioned his name. Ben Jonson, though we have strained his few words of regard and panegyric, had no suspicion of the elastic fame whose first vibrations he was attempting. He no doubt thought the praise he has conceded to him generous, and esteemed himself, out of all question, the better poet of the two.

If it need wit to know wit, according to the proverb, Shakspeare's time should be capable of recognizing it. Sir Henry Wotton was born four years after Shakspeare, and died twenty-three years after him; and I find, among his correspondents and acquaintants, the following persons: Theodore Beza, Isaac Casaubon, Sir Philip Sidney, the Earl of Essex, Lord Bacon, Sir Walter Raleigh, John Milton, Sir Henry Vane, Isaac Walton, Dr. Donne, Abraham Cowley, Bellarmine, Charles Cotton, John Pym, John Hales, Kepler, Vieta, Albericus Gentilis, Paul Sarpi, Arminius; with all of whom exists some token of his having communicated, without enumerating many others whom doubtless he saw,— Shakspeare, Spenser, Jonson, Beaumont, Massinger, the two Herberts, Marlow, Chapman and the rest. Since the constellation of great men who appeared in Greece in the time of Pericles, there was never any such society;—yet their genius failed them to find out the best head in the universe. Our poet's mask was impenetrable. You cannot see the mountain near. It took a century to make it suspected; and not until two centuries had passed, after his death, did any criticism which we think adequate begin to appear. It was not possible to write the history of Shakspeare till now; for he is the father of German literature: it was with the introduction of Shakspeare into German, by Lessing, and the translation of his works by Wieland and Schlegel, that the rapid burst of German literature was most intimately connected. It was not until the nineteenth century, whose speculative genius is a sort of living Hamlet, that the tragedy of *Hamlet* could find such wondering readers. Now, literature, philosophy and thought, are Shakspearized. His mind is the horizon beyond which, at present, we do not see. Our ears are educated to music by his rhythm. Coleridge and Goethe are the only critics who have expressed our convictions with any adequate fidelity: but there is in all cultivated minds a silent appreciation of his superlative power and beauty, which, like Christianity, qualifies the period.

The Shakspeare Society have inquired in all directions, advertised the missing facts, offered money for any information that will lead to proof,—and with what result? Beside some important illustration of the history of the English stage, to which I have adverted, they have gleaned a few facts touching the property, and dealings in regard to property, of the poet. It appears that from year to year he owned a larger share in the

Blackfriars' Theatre: its wardrobe and other appurtenances were his: that he bought an estate in his native village with his earnings as writer and shareholder; that he lived in the best house in Stratford; was intrusted by his neighbors with their commissions in London, as of borrowing money, and the like; that he was a veritable farmer. About the time when he was writing *Macbeth*, he sues Philip Rogers, in the borough-court of Stratford, for thirty-five shillings, ten pence, for corn delivered to him at different times; and in all respects appears as a good husband, with no reputation for eccentricity or excess. He was a good-natured sort of man, an actor and shareholder in the theatre, not in any striking manner distinguished from other actors and managers. I admit the importance of this information. It was well worth the pains that have been taken to procure it.

But whatever scraps of information concerning his condition these researches may have rescued, they can shed no light upon that infinite invention which is the concealed magnet of his attraction for us. We are very clumsy writers of history. We tell the chronicle of parentage, birth, birth-place, schooling, school-mates, earning of money, marriage, publication of books, celebrity, death; and when we have come to an end of this gossip, no ray of relation appears between it and the goddess-born; and it seems as if, had we dipped at random into the *Modern Plutarch*, and read any other life there, it would have fitted the poems as well. It is the essence of poetry to spring, like the rainbow daughter of Wonder, from the invisible, to abolish the past and refuse all history. Malone, Warburton, Dyce and Collier, have wasted their oil. The famed theatres, Covent Garden, Drury Lane, the Park and Tremont have vainly assisted. Betterton, Garrick, Kemble, Kean and Macready dedicate their lives to this genius; him they crown, elucidate, obey and express. The genius knows them not. The recitation begins; one golden word leaps out immortal from all this painted pedantry and sweetly torments us with invitations to its own inaccessible homes. I remember I went once to see the Hamlet of a famed performer, the pride of the English stage; and all I then heard and all I now remember of the tragedian was that in which the tragedian had no part; simply Hamlet's question to the ghost:—

> What may this mean,
> That thou, dead corse, again in complete steel
> Revisit'st thus the glimpses of the moon?

That imagination which dilates the closet he writes in to the world's dimension, crowds it with agents in rank and order, as quickly reduces the big reality to be the glimpses of the moon. These tricks of his magic spoil for us the illusions of the green-room. Can any biography shed light on the localities into which the *Midsummer Night's Dream* admits me? Did Shakspeare confide to any notary or parish recorder, sacristan, or surrogate in Stratford, the genesis of that delicate creation? The forest of Arden, the nimble air of Scone Castle, the moonlight of Portia's villa, "the antres vast and desarts idle" of Othello's captivity,—where is the third cousin, or grand-nephew, the chancellor's file of accounts, or private letter, that has kept one word of those transcendent secrets? In fine, in this drama, as in all great works of art,—in the Cyclopæan architecture of Egypt and India, in the Phidian sculpture, the Gothic ministers, the Italian painting, the Ballads of Spain and Scotland,—the Genius draws up the ladder after him, when the creative age goes up to heaven, and gives way to a new age, which sees the works and asks in vain for a history.

Shakspeare is the only biographer of Shakspeare; and even he can tell nothing, except to the Shakspeare in us, that is, to our most apprehensive and sympathetic hour. He cannot step

from off his tripod and give us anecdotes of his inspirations. Read the antique documents extricated, analyzed and compared by the assiduous Dyce and Collier, and now read one of these skyey sentences,—aerolites,—which seem to have fallen out of heaven, and which not your experience but the man within the breast has accepted as words of fate, and tell me if they match; if the former account in any manner for the latter; or which gives the most historical insight into the man.

Hence, though our external history is so meagre, yet, with Shakspeare for biographer, instead of Aubrey and Rowe, we have really the information which is material; that which describes character and fortune, that which, if we were about to meet the man and deal with him, would most import us to know. We have his recorded convictions on those questions which knock for answer at every heart,—on life and death, on love, on wealth and poverty, on the prizes of life and the ways whereby we come at them; on the characters of men, and the influences, occult and open, which affect their fortunes; and on those mysterious and demoniacal powers which defy our science and which yet interweave their malice and their gift in our brightest hours. Who ever read the volume of the Sonnets without finding that the poet had there revealed, under masks that are no masks to the intelligent, the lore of friendship and of love; the confusion of sentiments in the most susceptible, and, at the same time, the most intellectual of men? What trait of his private mind has he hidden in his dramas? One can discern, in his ample pictures of the gentleman and the king, what forms and humanities pleased him; his delight in troops of friends, in large hospitality, in cheerful giving. Let Timon, let Warwick, let Antonio the merchant answer for his great heart. So far from Shakspeare's being the least known, he is the one person, in all modern history, known to us. What point of morals, of manners, of economy, of philosophy, of religion, of taste, of the conduct of life, has he not settled? What mystery has he not signified his knowledge of? What office, or function, or district of man's work, has he not remembered? What king has he not taught state, as Talma taught Napoleon? What maiden has not found him finer than her delicacy? What lover has he not outloved? What sage has he not outseen? What gentleman has he not instructed in the rudeness of his behavior?

Some able and appreciating critics think no criticism on Shakspeare valuable that does not rest purely on the dramatic merit; that he is falsely judged as poet and philosopher. I think as highly as these critics of his dramatic merit, but still think it secondary. He was a full man, who liked to talk; a brain exhaling thoughts and images, which, seeking vent, found the drama next at hand. Had he been less, we should have had to consider how well he filled his place, how good a dramatist he was,—and he is the best in the world. But it turns out that what he has to say is of that weight as to withdraw some attention from the vehicle; and he is like some saint whose history is to be rendered into all languages, into verse and prose, into songs and pictures, and cut up into proverbs; so that the occasion which gave the saint's meaning the form of a conversation, or of a prayer, or of a code of laws, is immaterial compared with the universality of its application. So it fares with the wise Shakspeare and his book of life. He wrote the airs for all our modern music: he wrote the text of modern life; the text of manners: he drew the man of England and Europe; the father of the man in America; he drew the man, and described the day, and what is done in it: he read the hearts of men and women, their probity, and their second thought and wiles; the wiles of innocence, and the transitions by which virtues and vices slide into their contraries: he could divide the mother's part from the father's part in the face of the child, or draw the fine demarcations of freedom and of fate: he knew the laws of repression which make the police of nature: and all the sweets and all the terrors of human lot lay in his mind as truly but as softly as the landscape lies on the eye. And the importance of this wisdom of life sinks the form, as of Drama or Epic, out of notice. 'Tis like making a question concerning the paper on which a king's message is written.

Shakspeare is as much out of the category of eminent authors, as he is out of the crowd. He is inconceivably wise; the others, conceivably. A good reader can, in a sort, nestle into Plato's brain and think from thence; but not into Shakspeare's. We are still out of doors. For executive faculty, for creation, Shakspeare is unique. No man can imagine it better. He was the farthest reach of subtlety compatible with an individual self,—the subtilest of authors, and only just within the possibility of authorship. With this wisdom of life is the equal endowment of imaginative and of lyric power. He clothed the creatures of his legend with form and sentiments as if they were people who had lived under his roof; and few real men have left such distinct characters as these fictions. And they spoke in language as sweet as it was fit. Yet his talents never seduced him into an ostentation, nor did he harp on one string. An omnipresent humanity co-ordinates all his faculties. Give a man of talents a story to tell, and his partiality will presently appear. He has certain observations, opinions, topics, which have some accidental prominence, and which he disposes all to exhibit. He crams this part and starves that other part, consulting not the fitness of the thing, but his fitness and strength. But Shakspeare has no peculiarity, no importunate topic; but all is duly given; no veins, no curiosities; no cow-painter, no bird-fancier, no mannerist is he: he has no discoverable egotism: the great he tells greatly; the small subordinately. He is wise without emphasis or assertion; he is strong, as nature is strong, who lifts the land into mountain slopes without effort and by the same rule as she floats a bubble in the air, and likes as well to do the one as the other. This makes that equality of power in farce, tragedy, narrative and love-songs; a merit so incessant that each reader is incredulous of the perception of other readers.

This power of expression, or of transferring the inmost truth of things into music and verse, makes him the type of the poet and has added a new problem to metaphysics. This is that which throws him into natural history, as a main production of the globe, and as announcing new eras, and ameliorations. Things were mirrored in his poetry without loss or blur: he could paint the fine with precision, the great with compass, the tragic and the comic indifferently and without any distortion or favor. He carried his powerful execution into minute details, to a hair point; finishes an eyelash or a dimple as firmly as he draws a mountain; and yet these, like nature's, will bear the scrutiny of the solar microscope.

In short, he is the chief example to prove that more or less of production, more or fewer pictures, is a thing indifferent. He had the power to make one picture. Daguerre learned how to let one flower etch its image on his plate of iodine, and then proceeds at leisure to etch a million. There are always objects; but there was never representation. Here is perfect representation, at last; and now let the world of figures sit for their portraits. No recipe can be given for the making of a Shakspeare; but the possibility of the translation of things into song is demonstrated.

His lyric power lies in the genius of the piece. The sonnets, though their excellence is lost in the splendor of the dramas, are as inimitable as they; and it is not a merit of lines, but a total merit of the piece; like the tone of voice of some incomparable person, so is this a speech of poetic beings, and any clause as unproducible now as a whole poem.

Though the speeches in the plays, and single lines, have a beauty which tempts the ear to pause on them for their euphuism, yet the sentence is so loaded with meaning and so linked with its foregoers and followers, that the logician is satisfied. His means are as admirable as his ends; every subordinate invention, by which he helps himself to connect some irreconcilable opposites, is a poem too. He is not reduced to dismount and walk because his horses are running off with him in some distant direction: he always rides.

The finest poetry was first experience; but the thought has suffered a transformation since it was an experience. Cultivated men often attain a good degree of skill in writing verses; but it is easy to read, through their poems, their personal history: any one acquainted with the parties can name every figure; this is Andrew and that is Rachel. The sense thus remains prosaic. It is a caterpillar with wings, and not yet a butterfly. In the poet's mind the fact has gone quite over into the new element of thought, and has lost all that is exuvial. This generosity abides with Shakspeare. We say, from the truth and closeness of his pictures, that he knows the lesson by heart. Yet there is not a trace of egotism.

One more royal trait properly belongs to the poet. I mean his cheerfulness, without which no man can be a poet,—for beauty is his aim. He loves virtue, not for its obligation but for its grace: he delights in the world, in man, in woman, for the lovely light that sparkles from them. Beauty, the spirit of joy and hilarity, he sheds over the universe. Epicurus relates that poetry hath such charms that a lover might forsake his mistress to partake of them. And the true bards have been noted for their firm and cheerful temper. Homer lies in sunshine; Chaucer is glad and erect; and Saadi says, "It was rumored abroad that I was penitent; but what had I to do with repentance?" Not less sovereign and cheerful,—much more sovereign and cheerful, is the tone of Shakspeare. His name suggests joy and emancipation to the heart of men. If he should appear in any company of human souls, who would not march in his troop? He touches nothing that does not borrow health and longevity from his festal style.

And now, how stands the account of man with this bard and benefactor, when, in solitude, shutting our ears to the reverberations of his fame, we seek to strike the balance? Solitude has austere lessons; it can teach us to spare both heroes and poets; and it weighs Shakspeare also, and finds him to share the halfness and imperfection of humanity.

Shakspeare, Homer, Dante, Chaucer, saw the splendor of meaning that plays over the visible world; knew that a tree had another use than for apples, and corn another than for meal, and the ball of the earth, than for tillage and roads: that these things bore a second and finer harvest to the mind; being emblems of its thoughts, and conveying in all their natural history a certain mute commentary on human life. Shakspeare employed them as colors to compose his picture. He rested in their beauty; and never took the step which seemed inevitable to such genius, namely to explore the virtue which resides in these symbols and imparts this power:—what is that which they themselves say? He converted the elements which waited on his command, into entertainments. He was master of the revels to mankind. Is it not as if one should have, through majestic powers of science, the comets given into his hand, or the planets and their moons, and should draw them from their orbits to glare with the municipal fireworks on a holiday night, and advertise in all towns, "Very superior pyrotechny this evening"? Are the agents of nature, and the power to understand them, worth no more than a street serenade, or the breath of a cigar? One remembers again the trumpet-text in the Koran,—"The heavens and the earth and all that is between them, think ye we have created them in jest?" As long as the question is of talent and mental power, the world of men has not his equal to show. But when the question is, to life and its materials and its auxiliaries, how does he profit me? What does it signify? It is but a *Twelfth Night,* or *Midsummer-Night's Dream,* or *Winter Evening's Tale*: what signifies another picture more or less? The Egyptian verdict of the Shakspeare Societies comes to mind; that he was a jovial actor and manager. I can not marry this fact to his verse. Other admirable men have led lives in some sort of keeping with their thought; but this man, in wide contrast. Had he been less, had he reached only the common measure of great authors, of Bacon, Milton, Tasso, Cervantes, we might leave the fact in the twilight of human fate: but that this man of men, he who gave to the science of mind a new and larger subject than had ever existed, and planted the standard of humanity some furlongs forward into Chaos,—that he should not be wise for himself;—it must even go into the world's history that the best poet led an obscure and profane life, using his genius for the public amusement.

Well, other men, priest and prophet, Israelite, German and Swede, beheld the same objects: they also saw through them that which was contained. And to what purpose? The beauty straightway vanished; they read commandments, all-excluding mountainous duty; an obligation, a sadness, as of piled mountains, fell on them, and life became ghastly, joyless, a pilgrim's progress, a probation, beleaguered round with doleful histories of Adam's fall and curse behind us; with doomsdays and purgatorial and penal fires before us; and the heart of the seer and the heart of the listener sank in them.

It must be conceded that these are half-views of half-men. The world still wants its poet-priest, a reconciler, who shall not trifle, with Shakspeare the player, nor shall grope in graves, with Swedenborg the mourner; but who shall see, speak, and act, with equal inspiration. For knowledge will brighten the sunshine; right is more beautiful than private affection; and love is compatible with universal wisdom.

## VICTOR HUGO
### From *William Shakespeare*, tr. F. T. Marzials
1864

*Part I*
*Book II. Men of Genius*
II

Shakespeare, what is he? You might almost answer, He is the earth. Lucretius is the sphere; Shakespeare is the globe. There is more and less in the globe than in the sphere. In the sphere there is the whole, on the globe there is man. Here the outer, there the inner, mystery. Lucretius is the being; Shakespeare is the existence. Thence so much shadow in Lucretius; thence so much movement in Shakespeare. Space,—*the blue,* as the Germans say,—is certainly not forbidden to Shakespeare. The earth sees and surveys heaven; the earth knows heaven under its two aspects, darkness and azure, doubt and hope. Life goes and comes in death. All life is a secret,—a sort of enigmatical parenthesis between birth and the death-throe, between the eye which opens and the eye which closes. This secret imparts its restlessness to Shakespeare. Lucretius is; Shakespeare lives. In Shakespeare the birds sing, the bushes become verdant, the hearts love, the souls suffer, the cloud wanders, it is hot, it is cold, night falls, time passes, forests and crowds speak, the vast eternal dream

hovers about. The sap and the blood, all forms of the fact multiple, the actions and the ideas, man and humanity, the living and the life, the solitudes, the cities, the religions, the diamonds and pearls, the dung-hills and the charnel-houses, the ebb and flow of beings, the steps of the comers and goers,—all, all are on Shakespeare and in Shakespeare; and this genius being the earth, the dead emerge from it. Certain sinister sides of Shakespeare are haunted by spectres. Shakespeare is a brother of Dante. The one completes the other. Dante incarnates all supernaturalism, Shakespeare all Nature; and as these two regions, Nature and supernaturalism, which appear to us so different, are really the same unity, Dante and Shakespeare, however dissimilar, commingle outwardly, and are but one innately. There is something of the Alighieri, something of the ghost in Shakespeare. The skull passes from the hands of Dante into the hands of Shakespeare. Ugolino gnaws it, Hamlet questions it; and it shows perhaps even a deeper meaning and a loftier teaching in the second than in the first. Shakespeare shakes it and makes stars fall from it. The isle of Prospero, the forest of Ardennes, the health of Armuyr, the platform of Elsinore, are not less illuminated than the seven circles of Dante's spiral by the sombre reverberation of hypothesis. The unknown—half fable, half truth—is outlined there as well as here. Shakespeare as much as Dante allows us to glimpse at the crepuscular horizon of conjecture. In the one as in the other there is the possible,—that window of the dream opening on reality. As for the real, we insist on it, Shakespeare overflows with it; everywhere the living flesh. Shakespeare possesses emotion, instinct, the true cry, the right tone, all the human multitude in his clamor. His poetry is himself, and at the same time it is you. Like Homer, Shakespeare is element. Men of genius, re-beginners,—it is the right name for them,—rise at all the decisive crises of humanity; they sum up the phases and complete the revolutions. In civilization, Homer stamps the end of Asia and the commencement of Europe, Shakespeare stamps the end of the Middle Ages. This closing of the Middle Ages, Rabelais and Cervantes have fixed also; but, being essentially satirists, they give but a partial aspect. Shakespeare's mind is a total; like Homer, Shakespeare is a cyclic man. These two geniuses, Homer and Shakespeare, close the two gates of barbarism,—the ancient door and the gothic one. That was their mission; they have fulfilled it. That was their task; they have accomplished it. The third great human crisis is the French Revolution; it is the third huge gate of barbarism, the monarchical gate, which is closing at this moment. The nineteenth century hears it rolling on its hinges. Thence for poetry, the drama, and art arises the actual era, as independent of Shakespeare as of Homer. . . .

*Part II*
*Book I. Shakespeare—His Genius*
II

A poet must at the same time, and necessarily, be a historian and a philosopher. Herodotus and Thales are included in Homer. Shakespeare, likewise, is this triple man. He is, besides, the painter, and what a painter!—the colossal painter. The poet in reality does more than relate; he exhibits. Poets have in them a reflector, observation, and a condenser, emotion; thence those grand luminous spectres which burst out from their brain, and which go on blazing forever on the gloomy human wall. These phantoms have life. To exist as much as Achilles, would be the ambition of Alexander. Shakespeare has tragedy, comedy, fairy-land, hymn, farce, grand divine laughter, terror and horror, and, to say all in one word, the drama. He touches the two poles. He belongs to Olympus and to the travelling booth. No possibility fails him.

When he grasps you, you are subdued. Do not expect from him any pity. His cruelty is pathetic. He shows you a mother,—Constance, mother of Arthur; and when he has brought you to that point of tenderness that your heart is as her heart, he kills her child. He goes farther in horror even than history, which is difficult. He does not content himself with killing Rutland and driving York to despair; he dips in the blood of the son the handkerchief with which he wipes the eyes of the father. He causes elegy to be choked by the drama, Desdemona by Othello. No attenuation in anguish. Genius is inexorable. It has its law and follows it. The mind also has its inclined planes, and these slopes determine its direction. Shakespeare glides toward the terrible. Shakespeare, Æschylus, Dante, are great streams of human emotion pouring from the depth of their cave the urn of tears.

The poet is only limited by his aim; he considers nothing but the idea to be worked out; he does not recognize any other sovereignty, any other necessity but the idea; for, art emanating from the absolute, in art, as in the absolute, the end justifies the means. This is, it may be said parenthetically, one of those deviations from the ordinary terrestrial law which make lofty criticism muse and reflect, and which reveal to it the mysterious side of art. In art, above all, is visible the *quid divinum*. The poet moves in his work as providence in its own; he excites, astounds, strikes, then exalts or depresses, often in inverse ratio to what you expected, diving into your soul through surprise. Now, consider. Art has, like the Infinite, a *Because* superior to all the *Why's*. Go and ask the wherefore of a tempest from the ocean, that great lyric. What seems to you odious or absurd has an inner reason for existing. Ask of Job why he scrapes the pus on his ulcer with a bit of glass, and of Dante why he sews with a thread of iron the eyelids of the larvas in purgatory, making the stitches trickle with fearful tears! Job continues to clean his sore with his broken glass and wipes it on his dungheap, and Dante goes on his way. The same with Shakespeare.

His sovereign horrors reign and force themselves upon you. He mingles with them, when he chooses, the charm, that august charm of the powerful, as superior to feeble sweetness, to slender attraction, to the charm of Ovid or of Tibullus, as the Venus of Milo to the Venus de Medici. The things of the unknown; the unfathomable metaphysical problems; the enigmas of the soul and of Nature, which is also a soul; the far-off intuitions of the eventual included in destiny; the amalgams of thought and event,—can be translated into delicate figures, and fill poetry with mysterious and exquisite types, the more delightful that are rather sorrowful, somewhat invisible, and at the same time very real, anxious concerning the shadow which is behind them, and yet trying to please you. Profound grace does exist.

Prettiness combined with greatness is possible (it is found in Homer; Astyanax is a type of it); but the profound grace of which we speak is something more than this epic delicacy. It is linked to a certain amount of agitation, and means the infinite without expressing it. It is a kind of light and shade radiance. The modern men of genius alone have that depth in the smile which shows elegance and depth at the same time.

Shakespeare possesses this grace, which is the very opposite to the unhealthy grace, although it resembles it, emanating as it does likewise from the grave.

Sorrow,—the great sorrow of the drama, which is nothing else but human constitution carried into art,—envelopes this grace and this horror.

Hamlet, doubt, is at the centre of his work; and at the two extremities, love,—Romeo and Othello, all the heart. There is light in the folds of the shroud of Juliet; yet nothing but darkness in the winding-sheet of Ophelia disdained and of Desdemona suspected. These two innocents, to whom love has broken faith, cannot be consoled. Desdemona sings the song of the willow under which the water bears Ophelia away. They are sisters without knowing each other, and kindred souls, although each has her separate drama. The willow trembles over them both. In the mysterious chant of the calumniated who is about to die, floats the dishevelled shadow of the drowned one.

Shakespeare in philosophy goes at times deeper than Homer. Beyond Priam there is Lear; to weep at ingratitude is worse than weeping at death. Homer meets envy and strikes it with the sceptre; Shakespeare gives the sceptre to the envious, and out of Thersites creates Richard III. Envy is exposed in its nakedness all the better for being clothed in purple; its reason for existing is then visibly altogether in itself. Envy on the throne, what more striking!

Deformity in the person of the tyrant is not enough for this philosopher; he must have it also in the shape of the valet, and he creates Falstaff. The dynasty of commonsense, inaugurated in Panurge, continued in Sancho Panza, goes wrong and miscarries in Falstaff. The rock which this wisdom splits upon is, in reality, lowness. Sancho Panza, in combination with the ass, is embodied with ignorance. Falstaff—glutton, poltroon, savage, obscene, human face and stomach, with the lower parts of the brute—walks on the four feet of turpitude; Falstaff is the centaur man and pig.

Shakespeare is, above all, an imagination. Now,—and this is a truth to which we have already alluded, and which is well known to thinkers,—imagination is depth. No faculty of the mind goes and sinks deeper than imagination; it is the great diver. Science, reaching the lowest depths, meets imagination. In conic sections, in logarithms, in the differential and integral calculus, in the calculation of probabilities, in the infinitesimal calculus, in the calculations of sonorous waves, in the application of algebra to geometry, the imagination is the co-efficient of calculation, and mathematics becomes poetry. I have no faith in the science of stupid learned men.

The poet philosophizes because he imagines. That is why Shakespeare has that sovereign management of reality which enables him to have his way with it; and his very whims are varieties of the true,—varieties which deserve meditation. Does not destiny resemble a constant whim? Nothing more incoherent in appearance, nothing less connected, nothing worse as deduction. Why crown this monster, John? Why kill that child, Arthur? Why have Joan of Arc burned? Why Monk triumphant? Why Louis XV. happy? Why Louis XVI. punished? Let the logic of God pass. It is from that logic that the fancy of the poet is drawn. Comedy bursts forth in the midst of tears; the sob rises out of laughter; figures mingle and clash; massive forms, nearly animals, pass clumsily; larvas—women perhaps, perhaps smoke—float about; souls, libellulas of darkness, flies of the twilight, quiver among all these black reeds that we call passions and events. At one pole Lady Macbeth, at the other Titania. A colossal thought, and an immense caprice.

What are the *Tempest, Troilus and Cressida, The Two Gentlemen of Verona, The Merry Wives of Windsor*, the *Midsummer Night's Dream, The Winter's Tale?* They are fancy,—arabesque work. The arabesque in art is the same phenomenon as vegetation in nature. The arabesque grows, increases, knots, exfoliates, multiplies, becomes green, blooms, branches, and creeps around every dream. The arabesque is endless; it has a strange power of extension and aggrandizement; it fills horizons, and opens up others; it intercepts the luminous deeds by innumerable intersections; and, if you mix the human figure with these entangled branches, the *ensemble* makes you giddy; it is striking. Behind the arabesque, and through its openings, all philosophy can be seen; vegetation lives; man becomes pantheist; a combination of infinite takes place in the finite; and before such work, in which are found the impossible and the true, the human soul trembles with an emotion obscure and yet supreme.

For all this, the edifice ought not to be overrun by vegetation, nor the drama by arabesque.

One of the characteristics of genius is the singular union of faculties the most distant. To draw an astragal like Ariosto, then to dive into souls like Pascal,—such is the poet. Man's inner conscience belongs to Shakespeare; he surprises you with it constantly. He extracts from conscience every unforeseen contingence that it contains. Few poets surpass him in this psychical research. Many of the strangest peculiarities of the human mind are indicated by him. He skillfully makes us feel the simplicity of the metaphysical fact under the complication of the dramatic fact. That which the human creature does not acknowledge inwardly, the obscure thing that he begins by fearing and ends by desiring—such is the point of junction and the strange place of meeting for the heart of virgins and the heart of murderers; for the soul of Juliet and the soul of Macbeth. The innocent fears and longs for love, just as the wicked one for ambition. Perilous kisses given on the sly to the phantom, smiling here, fierce there.

To all these prodigalities, analysis, synthesis, creation in flesh and bone, revery, fancy, science, metaphysics, add history,—here the history of historians, there the history of the tale; specimens of everything,—of the traitor, from Macbeth the assassin of his guest, up to Coriolanus, the assassin of his country; of the despot, from the intellectual tyrant Cæsar, to the bestial tyrant Henry VIII.; of the carnivorous, from the lion down to the usurer. One may say to Shylock: "Well bitten Jew!" And, in the background of this wonderful drama, on the desert heath, in the twilight, in order to promise crowns to murderers, three black outlines appear, in which Hesiod, through the vista of ages, perhaps recognizes the Parcæ. Inordinate force, exquisite charm, epic ferocity, pity, creative faculty, gayety (that lofty gayety unintelligible to narrow understandings), sarcasm (the cutting lash for the wicked), star-like greatness, microscopic tenuity, boundless poetry, which has a zenith and a nadir; the *ensemble* vast, the detail profound,—nothing is wanting in this mind. One feels, on approaching the work of this man, the powerful wind which would burst forth from the opening of a whole world. The radiancy of genius on every side,—that is Shakespeare. "Totus in antithesi," says Jonathan Forbes. . . .

V

If ever a man was undeserving of the good character of "he is sober," it is most certainly William Shakespeare. Shakespeare is one of the worst rakes that serious æsthetics ever had to lord over.

Shakespeare is fertility, force, exuberance, the overflowing breast, the foaming cup, the brimful tub, the overrunning sap, the overflooding lava, the whirlwind scattering germs, the universal rain of life, everything by thousands, everything by millions, no reticence, no binding, no economy, the inordinate and tranquil prodigality of the creator. To those who feel the bottom of their pocket, the inexhaustible seems insane. Will it stop soon? Never. Shakespeare is the sower of dazzling wonders. At every turn, the image; at every turn, contrast; at every turn, light and darkness.

The poet, we have said, is Nature. Subtle, minute, keen, microscopical like Nature; immense. Not discreet, not reserved, not sparing. Simply magnificent. Let us explain this word, *simple*.

Sobriety in poetry is poverty; simplicity is grandeur. To give to each thing the quantity of space which fits it, neither more nor less, is simplicity. Simplicity is justice. The whole law of taste is in that. Each thing put in its place and spoken with its own word. On the only condition that a certain latent equilibrium is maintained and a certain mysterious proportion preserved, simplicity may be found in the most stupendous complication, either in the style, or in the *ensemble*. These are the arcana of great art. Lofty criticism alone, which takes its starting-point from enthusiasm, penetrates and comprehends these learned laws. Opulence, profusion, dazzling radiancy, may be simplicity. The sun is simple.

Such simplicity does not evidently resemble the simplicity recommended by Le Batteux, the Abbé d'Aubignac, and Father Bouhours.

Whatever may be the abundance, whatever may be the entanglement, even if perplexing, confused, and inextricable, all that is true is simple. A root is simple.

That simplicity which is profound is the only one that art recognizes.

Simplicity, being true, is artless. Artlessness is the characteristic of truth. Shakespeare's simplicity is the great simplicity. He is foolishly full of it. He ignores the small simplicity.

The simplicity which is impotence, the simplicity which is meagreness, the simplicity which is shortwinded, is a case for pathology. It has nothing to do with poetry. An order for the hospital suits it better than a ride on the hippogriff.

I admit that the hump of Thersites is simple; but the breastplates of Hercules are simple also. I prefer that simplicity to the other.

The simplicity which belongs to poetry may be as bushy as the oak. Does the oak by chance produce on you the effect of a Byzantine and of a refined being? Its innumerable antitheses,—gigantic trunk and small leaves, rough bark and velvet mosses, reception of rays and shedding of shade, crowns for heroes and fruit for swine,—are they marks of affectation, corruption, subtlety and bad taste? Could the oak be too witty? Could the oak belong to the Hôtel Rambouillet? Could the oak be a *précieux ridicule*? Could the oak be tainted with Gongorism? Could the oak belong to the age of decadence? Is by chance complete simplicity, *sancta simplicitas*, condensed in the cabbage?

Refinement, excess of wit, affectation, Gongorism,—that is what they have hurled at Shakespeare's head. They say that those are the faults of littleness, and they hasten to reproach the giant with them.

But then this Shakespeare respects nothing, he goes straight on, putting out of breath those who wish to follow; he strides over proprieties; he overthrows Aristotle; he spreads havoc among the Jesuits, Methodists, the Purists, and the Puritans; he puts Loyola to flight, and upsets Wesley; he is valiant, bold, enterprising, militant, direct. His inkstand smokes like a crater. He is always laborious, ready, spirited, disposed, going forward. Pen in hand, his brow blazing, he goes on driven by the demon of genius. The stallion abuses; there are he-mules passing by to whom this is offensive. To be prolific is to be aggressive. A poet like Isaiah, like Juvenal, like Shakespeare, is, in truth, exorbitant. By all that is holy! some attention ought to be paid to others; one man has no right to everything. What! always virility, inspiration everywhere, as many metaphors as the prairie, as many antitheses as the oak, as many contrasts and depths as the universe; what! forever generation, hatching, hymen, parturition, vast *ensemble*, exquisite and robust detail, living communion, fecundation, plentitude, production! It is too much; it infringes the rights of human geldings.

For nearly three centuries Shakespeare, this poet all brimming with virility, has been looked upon by sober critics with that discontented air that certain bereaved spectators must have in the seraglio.

Shakespeare has no reserve, no discretion, no limit, no blank. What is wanting in him is that he wants nothing. No box for savings, no fast-day with him. He overflows like vegetation, like germination, like light, like flame. Yet, it does not hinder him from thinking of you, spectator or reader, from preaching to you, from giving you advice, from being your friend, like any other kind-hearted La Fontaine, and from rendering you small services. You can warm your hands at the conflagration he kindles.

Othello, Romeo, Iago, Macbeth, Shylock, Richard III., Julius Cæsar, Oberon, Puck, Ophelia, Desdemona, Juliet, Titania, men, women, witches, fairies, souls,—Shakespeare is the grand distributor; take, take, take, all of you! Do you want more? Here is Ariel, Parolles, Macduff, Prospero, Viola, Miranda, Caliban. More yet? Here is Jessica, Cordelia, Cressida, Portia, Brabantio, Polonius, Horatio, Mercutio, Imogene, Pandarus of Troy, Bottom, Theseus. *Ecce Deus!* It is the poet, he offers himself: who will have me? He gives, scatters, squanders himself; he is never empty. Why? He cannot be. Exhaustion with him is impossible. There is in him something of the fathomless. He fills up again, and spends himself; then recommences. He is the bottomless treasury of genius.

In license and audacity of language Shakespeare equals Rabelais, whom, a few days ago, a swan-like critic called a swine.

Like all lofty minds in full riot of Omnipotence, Shakespeare decants all Nature, drinks it, and makes you drink it. Voltaire reproached him for his drunkenness, and was quite right. Why on earth, we repeat, why has this Shakespeare such a temperament? He does not stop, he does not feel fatigue, he is without pity for the poor weak stomachs that are candidates for the Academy. The gastritis called "good taste," he does not labour under it. He is powerful. What is this vast intemperate song that he sings through ages,—war-song, drinking-song, love-ditty,—which passes from King Lear to Queen Mab, and from Hamlet to Falstaff, heart-rending at times as a sob, grand as the Iliad? "I have the lumbago from reading Shakespeare," said M. Auger.

His poetry has the sharp perfume of honey made by the vagabond bee without a hive. Here prose, there verse; all forms, being but receptacles for the idea, suit him. This poetry weeps and laughs. The English tongue, a language little formed, now assists, now harms him, but everywhere the deep mind gushes forth translucent. Shakespear's drama proceeds with a kind of distracted rhythm. It is so vast that it staggers; it has and gives the vertigo; but nothing is so solid as this excited grandeur. Shakespeare, shuddering, has in himself the winds, the spirits, the philters, the vibrations, the fluctuations of transient breezes, the obscure penetration of effluvia, the great unknown sap. Thence his agitation, in the depth of which is repose. It is this agitation in which Goethe is wanting, wrongly praised for his impassiveness, which is inferiority. This agitation, all minds of the first order have it. It is in Job, in Æschylus, in Alighieri. This agitation is humanity. On earth the divine must be human. It must propose to itself its own enigma and feel disturbed about it.

Inspiration being prodigy, a sacred stupor mingles with it. A certain majesty of mind resembles solitudes and is blended with astonishment. Shakespeare, like all great poets, like all great things, is absorbed by a dream. His own vegetation astounds him; his own tempest appals him. It seems at times as if Shakespeare terrified Shakespeare. He shudders at his own depth. This is the sign of supreme intellects. It is his own vastness which shakes him and imparts to him unaccountable huge oscillations. There is no genius without waves. An inebriated savage it may be. He has the wildness of the virgin forest; he has the intoxication of the high sea.

Shakespeare (the condor alone gives some idea of such gigantic gait) departs, arrives, starts again, mounts, descends, hovers, dives, sinks, rushes, plunges into the depths below, plunges into the depths above. He is one of those geniuses that God purposely leaves unbridled, so that they may go headlong and in full flight into the infinite.

From time to time comes on this globe one of these spirits. Their passage, as we have said, renews art, science, philosophy, or society.

They fill a century, then disappear. Then it is not one century alone that their light illumines, it is humanity from one end to another of time; and it is perceived that each of these men was the human mind itself contained whole in one brain, and coming, at a given moment, to give on earth an impetus to progress.

These supreme spirits, once life achieved and the work completed, go in death to rejoin the mysterious group, and are probably at home in the infinite. . . .

*Book IV. Criticism*
*I*

Every play of Shakespeare's, two excepted, *Macbeth* and *Romeo and Juliet* (thirty-four plays out of thirty-six), offers to our observation one peculiarity which seems to have escaped, up to this day, the most eminent commentators and critics,— one that the Schlegels and M. Villemain himself, in his remarkable labours, do not notice, and on which it is impossible not to give an opinion. It is a double action which traverses the drama, and reflects it on a small scale. By the side of the storm in the Atlantic, the storm in the tea-cup. Thus, Hamlet makes beneath himself a Hamlet: he kills Polonius, father of Laërtes,—and there is Laërtes opposite him exactly in the same situation he is toward Claudius. There are two fathers to avenge. There might be two ghosts. So, in *King Lear:* side by side and simultaneously, Lear, driven to despair by his daughters Goneril and Regan, and consoled by his daughter Cordelia, is reflected by Gloster, betrayed by his son Edmond, and loved by his son Edgar. The bifurcated idea, the idea echoing itself, a lesser drama copying and elbowing the principal drama, the action trailing its own shadow (a smaller action but its parallel), the unity cut asunder,—surely it is a strange fact. These twin actions have been strongly blamed by the few commentators who have pointed them out. We do not participate in their blame. Do we then approve and accept as good these twin actions? By no means. We recognize them, and this is all. The drama of Shakespeare (we said so with all our might as far back as 1827, in order to discourage all imitation),—the drama of Shakespeare is peculiar to Shakespeare. It is a drama inherent to this poet; it is his own essence; it is himself,—thence his originalities absolutely personal; thence his idiosyncrasies which exist without establishing a law.

These twin actions are purely Shakespearian. Neither Æschylus nor Molière would admit them; and we certainly would agree with Æschylus and Molière.

These twin actions are, moreover, the sign of the sixteenth

century. Each epoch has its own mysterious stamp. The centuries have a seal that they affix to *chefs-d'œuvre*, and which it is necessary to know how to decipher and recognize. The seal of the sixteenth century is not the seal of the eighteenth. The Renaissance was a subtle time,—a time of reflection. The spirit of the sixteenth century was reflected in a mirror. Every idea of the Renaissance has a double compartment. Look at the jubes in the churches. The Renaissance, with an exquisite and fantastical art, always makes the Old Testament repercussive on the New. The twin action is there in everything. The symbol explains the personage in repeating his gesture. If, in a basso-rilievo, Jehovah sacrifices his son, he has close by, in the next low relief, Abraham sacrificing his son. Jonas passes three days in the whale, and Jesus passes three days in the sepulchre; and the jaws of the monster swallowing Jonas answer to the mouth of hell engulfing Jesus.

The carver of the jube of Fécamp, so stupidly demolished, goes so far as to give for counterpart to Saint Joseph—whom? Amphitryon.

These singular results constitute one of the habits of that profound and searching high art of the sixteenth century. Nothing can be more curious in that style than the part ascribed to Saint Christopher. In the Middle Ages, and in the sixteenth century, in paintings and sculptures, Saint Christopher, the good giant martyred by Decius in 250, recorded by the Bollandists and acknowledged without a question by Baillet, is always triple,—an opportunity for the triptych. There is foremost a first Christ-bearer, a first Christophorus; that is Christopher, with the infant Jesus on his shoulders. Afterward the Virgin enceinte is a Christopher, since she carries Christ. Last, the cross is a Christopher; it also carries Christ. This treble illustration of the idea is immortalized by Rubens in the cathedral of Antwerp. The twin idea, the triple idea,—such is the seal of the sixteenth century.

Shakespeare, faithful to the spirit of his time, must needs add Laërtes avenging his father to Hamlet avenging his father, and cause Hamlet to be persecuted by Laërtes at the same time that Claudius is pursued by Hamlet; he must needs make the filial piety of Edgar a comment on the filial piety of Cordelia, and bring out in contrast, weighed down by the ingratitude of unnatural children, two wretched fathers, each bereaved of a kind light,—Lear mad, and Gloster blind. . . .

### V

Imitation is always barren and bad.

As for Shakespeare,—since Shakespeare is the poet who claims our attention now,—he is, in the highest degree, a genius human and general; but like every true genius, he is at the same time an idiosyncratic and personal mind. Axiom: the poet starts from his own inner self to come to us. It is that which makes the poet inimitable.

Examine Shakespeare, dive into him, and see how determined he is to be himself. Do not expect any concession from him. It is not egotism, but it is stubbornness. He wills it. He gives to art his orders,—of course in the limits of his work; for neither the art of Æschylus, nor the art of Aristophanes, nor the art of Plautus, nor the art of Macchiavelli, nor the art of Calderon, nor the art of Molière, nor the art of Beaumarchais, nor any of the forms of art, deriving life each of them from the special life of a genius, would obey the orders given by Shakespeare. Art, thus understood, is vast equality and profound liberty; the region of the equals is also the region of the free.

One of the grandeurs of Shakespeare consists in his impossibility to be a model. In order to realize his idiosyncrasy,

open one of his plays,—no matter which; it is always foremost and above all Shakespeare.

What more personal than *Troilus and Cressida*? A comic Troy! Here is *Much Ado about Nothing*,—a tragedy which ends with a burst of laughter. Here is the *Winter's Tale*,—a pastoral drama. Shakespeare is at home in his work. Do you wish to see true despotism: look at his fancy. What arbitrary determination to dream! What despotic resolution in his vertiginous flight! What absoluteness in his indecision and wavering! The dream fills some of his plays to that degree that man changes his nature, and is the cloud more than the man. Angelo in *Measure for Measure* is a misty tyrant. He becomes disintegrated, and wears away. Leontes in the *Winter's Tale* is an Othello who is blown away. In *Cymbeline* one thinks that Iachimo will become an Iago, but he melts down. The dream is there,—everywhere. Watch Manilius, Posthumus, Hermione, Perdita, passing by. In the *Tempest*, the Duke of Milan has "a brave son," who is like a dream in a dream. Ferdinand alone speaks of him, and no one but Ferdinand seems to have seen him. A brute becomes reasonable: witness the constable Elbow in *Measure for Measure*. An idiot is all at once witty: witness Cloten in *Cymbeline*. A King of Sicily is jealous of a King of Bohemia. Bohemia has a seashore. The shepherds pick up children there. Theseus, a duke, espouses Hippolyta, the Amazon. Oberon comes in also. For here it is Shakespeare's will to dream; elsewhere he thinks.

We say more: where he dreams he still thinks,—with a different but equal depth.

Let men of genius remain in peace in their originality. There is something wild in these mysterious civilizers. Even in their comedy, even in their buffoonery, even in their laughter, even in their smile, there is the unknown. In them is felt the sacred dread that belongs to art, and the all-powerful terror of the imaginary mixed with the real. Each of them is in his cavern, alone. They hear one another from afar, but never copy one another. We are not aware that the hippopotamus imitates the roar of the elephant, neither do lions imitate one another.

Diderot does not recast Bayle; Beaumarchais does not copy Plautus, and has no need of Davus to create Figaro. Piranesi is not inspired by Dædalus. Isaiah does not begin Moses over again.

One day, at St. Helena, M. De Las Cases said, "Sire, when you were master of Prussia, I would in your place have taken the sword of Frederick the Great, which is deposited in the tomb at Potsdam; and I would have worn it." "Fool!" replied Napoleon, "I had my own."

Shakespeare's work is absolute, sovereign, imperious, eminently solitary, unneighbourly, sublime in radiance, absurd in reflection, and must remain without a copy.

To imitate Shakespeare would be as insane as to imitate Racine would be stupid.

### JAMES RUSSELL LOWELL
#### From "Shakespeare Once More" (1868)
#### *Works*
1890, Volume 3, pp. 151–227

I t may be doubted whether any language be rich enough to maintain more than one truly great poet,—and whether there be more than one period, and that very short, in the life of a language, when such a phenomenon as a great poet is possible. It may be reckoned one of the rarest pieces of good-luck that ever fell to the share of a race, that (as was true of Shakespeare) its most rhythmic genius, its acutest intellect, its profoundest imagination, and its healthiest understanding should have been combined in one man, and that he should have arrived at the full development of his powers at the moment when the material in which he was to work—that wonderful composite called English, the best result of the confusion of tongues—was in its freshest perfection. The English-speaking nations should build a monument to the misguided enthusiasts of the Plain of Shinar; for, as the mixture of many bloods seems to have made them the most vigorous of modern races, so has the mingling of divers speeches given them a language which is perhaps the noblest vehicle of poetic thought that ever existed.

Had Shakespeare been born fifty years earlier, he would have been cramped by a book-language not yet flexible enough for the demands of rhythmic emotion, not yet sufficiently popularized for the natural and familiar expression of supreme thought, not yet so rich in metaphysical phrase as to render possible that ideal representation of the great passions which is the aim and end of Art, not yet subdued by practice and general consent to a definiteness of accentuation essential to ease and congruity of metrical arrangement. Had he been born fifty years later, his ripened manhood would have found itself in an England absorbed and angry with the solution of political and religious problems, from which his whole nature was averse, instead of in that Elizabethan social system, ordered and planetary in functions and degrees as the angelic hierarchy of the Areopagite, where his contemplative eye could crowd itself with various and brilliant picture, and whence his impartial brain—one lobe of which seems to have been Normanly refined and the other Saxonly sagacious—could draw its morals of courtly and worldly wisdom, its lessons of prudence and magnanimity. In estimating Shakespeare, it should never be forgotten, that, like Goethe, he was essentially observer and artist, and incapable of partisanship. The passions, actions, sentiments, whose character and results he delighted to watch and to reproduce, are those of man in society as it existed; and it no more occurred to him to question the right of that society to exist than to criticise the divine ordination of the seasons. His business was with men as they were, not with man as he ought to be,—with the human soul as it is shaped or twisted into character by the complex experience of life, not in its abstract essence, as something to be saved or lost. During the first half of the seventeenth century, the centre of intellectual interest was rather in the other world than in this, rather in the region of thought and principle and conscience than in actual life. It was a generation in which the poet was, and felt himself, out of place. Sir Thomas Browne, our most imaginative mind since Shakespeare, found breathing-room, for a time, among the "O altitudines!" of religious speculation, but soon descended to occupy himself with the exactitudes of science. Jeremy Taylor, who half a century earlier would have been Fletcher's rival, compels his clipped fancy to the conventual discipline of prose, (Maid Marian turned nun,) and waters his poetic wine with doctrinal eloquence. Milton is saved from making total shipwreck of his large-utteranced genius on the desolate Noman's Land of a religious epic only by the lucky help of Satan and his colleagues, with whom, as foiled rebels and republicans, he cannot conceal his sympathy. As purely poet, Shakespeare would have come too late, had his lot fallen in that generation. In mind and temperament too exoteric for a mystic, his imagination could not have at once illustrated the influence of his epoch and escaped from it, like that of Browne; the equilibrium of his judgment, essential to him as an artist,

but equally removed from propagandism, whether as enthusiast or logician, would have unfitted him for the pulpit; and his intellectual being was too sensitive to the wonder and beauty of outward life and Nature to have found satisfaction, as Milton's could, (and perhaps only by reason of his blindness,) in a world peopled by purely imaginary figures. We might fancy him becoming a great statesman, but he lacked the social position which could have opened that career to him. What we mean when we say *Shakespeare*, is something inconceivable either during the reign of Henry the Eighth, or the Commonwealth, and which would have been impossible after the Restoration.

All favorable stars seem to have been in conjunction at his nativity. The Reformation had passed the period of its vinous fermentation, and its clarified results remained as an element of intellectual impulse and exhilaration; there were small signs yet of the acetous and putrefactive stages which were to follow in the victory and decline of Puritanism. Old forms of belief and worship still lingered, all the more touching to Fancy, perhaps, that they were homeless and attainted; the light of sceptic day was baffled by depths of forest where superstitious shapes still cowered, creatures of immemorial wonder, the raw material of Imagination. The invention of printing, without yet vulgarizing letters, had made the thought and history of the entire past contemporaneous; while a crowd of translators put every man who could read in inspiring contact with the select souls of all the centuries. A new world was thus opened to intellectual adventure at the very time when the keel of Columbus had turned the first daring furrow of discovery in that unmeasured ocean which still girt the known earth with a beckoning horizon of hope and conjecture, which was still fed by rivers that flowed down out of primeval silences, and which still washed the shores of Dreamland. Under a wise, cultivated, and firm-handed monarch also, the national feeling of England grew rapidly more homogeneous and intense, the rather as the womanhood of the sovereign stimulated a more chivalric loyalty,—while the new religion, of which she was the defender, helped to make England morally, as it was geographically, insular to the continent of Europe.

If circumstances could ever make a great national poet, here were all the elements mingled at melting-heat in the alembic, and the lucky moment of projection was clearly come. If a great national poet could ever avail himself of circumstances, this was the occasion,—and, fortunately, Shakespeare was equal to it. Above all, we may esteem it lucky that he found words ready to his use, original and untarnished,—types of thought whose sharp edges were unworn by repeated impressions. In reading Hakluyt's *Voyages*, we are almost startled now and then to find that even common sailors could not tell the story of their wanderings without rising to an almost Odyssean strain, and habitually used a diction that we should be glad to buy back from desuetude at any cost. Those who look upon language only as anatomists of its structure, or who regard it as only a means of conveying abstract truth from mind to mind, as if it were so many algebraic formulæ, are apt to overlook the fact that its being alive is all that gives it poetic value. We do not mean what is technically called a living language,—the contrivance, hollow as a speaking-trumpet, by which breathing and moving bipeds, even now, sailing o'er life's solemn main, are enabled to hail each other and make known their mutual shortness of mental stores,—but one that is still hot from the hearts and brains of a people, not hardened yet, but moltenly ductile to new shapes of sharp and clear relief in the moulds of new thought. So soon as a language has become literary, so soon as there is a gap between the speech of books and that of life, the language becomes, so far as poetry is concerned, almost as dead as Latin, and (as in writing Latin verses) a mind in itself essentially original becomes in the use of such a medium of utterance unconsciously reminiscential and reflective, lunar and not solar, in expression and even in thought. For words and thoughts have a much more intimate and genetic relation, one with the other, than most men have any notion of; and it is one thing to use our mother-tongue as if it belonged to us, and another to be the puppets of an overmastering vocabulary. "Ye know not," says Ascham, "what hurt ye do to Learning, that care not for Words, but for Matter, and so make a Divorce betwixt the Tongue and the Heart." *Lingua Toscana in bocca Romana* is the Italian proverb; and that of poets should be, *The tongue of the people in the mouth of the scholar.* I imply here no assent to the early theory, or, at any rate, practice, of Wordsworth, who confounded plebeian modes of thought with rustic forms of phrase, and then atoned for his blunder by absconding into a diction more Latinized than that of any poet of his century.

Shakespeare was doubly fortunate. Saxon by the father and Norman by the mother, he was a representative Englishman. A country boy, he learned first the rough and ready English of his rustic mates, who knew how to make nice verbs and adjectives courtesy to their needs. Going up to London, he acquired the *lingua aulica* precisely at the happiest moment, just as it was becoming, in the strictest sense of the word, *modern*,—just as it had recruited itself, by fresh impressments from the Latin and Latinized languages, with new words to express the new ideas of an enlarging intelligence which printing and translation were fast making cosmopolitan,— words which, in proportion to their novelty, and to the fact that the mother-tongue and the foreign had not yet wholly mingled, must have been used with a more exact appreciation of their meaning.[1] It was in London, and chiefly by means of the stage, that a thorough amalgamation of the Saxon, Norman, and scholarly elements of English was brought about. Already, Puttenham, in his *Arte of English Poesy*, declares that the practice of the capital and the country within sixty miles of it was the standard of correct diction, the *jus et norma loquendi.* Already Spenser had almost re-created English poetry,—and it is interesting to observe, that, scholar as he was, the archaic words which he was at first over-fond of introducing are often provincialisms of purely English original. Already Marlowe had brought the English unrhymed pentameter (which had hitherto justified but half its name, by being always blank and never verse) to a perfection of melody, harmony, and variety which has never been surpassed. Shakespeare, then, found a language already to a certain extent *established*, but not yet fetlocked by dictionary and grammar mongers,—a versification harmonized, but which had not yet exhausted all its modulations, nor been set in the stocks by critics who deal judgment on refractory feet, that will dance to Orphean measures of which their judges are insensible. That the language was established is proved by its comparative uniformity as used by the dramatists, who wrote for mixed audiences, as well as by Ben Jonson's satire upon Marston's neologisms; that it at the same time admitted foreign words to the rights of citizenship on easier terms than now is in good measure equally true. What was of greater import, no arbitrary line had been drawn between high words and low; vulgar then meant simply what was common; poetry had not been aliened from the people by the establishment of an Upper House of vocables, alone entitled to move in the stately ceremonials of verse, and privileged from arrest while they forever keep the promise of meaning to the ear and break it to the sense. The hot

conception of the poet had no time to cool while he was debating the comparative respectability of this phrase or that; but he snatched what word his instinct prompted, and saw no indiscretion in making a king speak as his country nurse might have taught him.[2] It was Waller who first learned in France that to talk in rhyme alone comported with the state of royalty. In the time of Shakespeare, the living tongue resembled that tree which Father Hue saw in Tartary, whose leaves were languaged,—and every hidden root of thought, every subtilest fibre of feeling, was mated by new shoots and leafage of expression, fed from those unseen sources in the common earth of human nature.

The Cabalists had a notion, that whoever found out the mystic word for anything attained to absolute mastery over that thing. The reverse of this is certainly true of poetic expression; for he who is thoroughly possessed of his thought, who imaginatively conceives an idea or image, becomes master of the word that shall most amply and fitly utter it. Heminge and Condell tell us, accordingly, that there was scarce a blot in the manuscripts they received from Shakespeare; and this is the natural corollary from the fact that such an imagination as his is as unparalleled as the force, variety, and beauty of the phrase in which it embodied itself.[3] We believe that Shakespeare, like all other great poets, instinctively used the dialect which he found current, and that his words are not more wrested from their ordinary meaning than followed necessarily from the unwonted weight of thought or stress of passion they were called on to support. He needed not to mask familiar thoughts in the weeds of unfamiliar phraseology; for the life that was in his mind could transfuse the language of every day with an intelligent vivacity, that makes it seem lambent with fiery purpose, and at each new reading a new creation. He could say with Dante, that "no word had ever forced him to say what he would not, though he had forced many a word to say what *it* would not,"—but only in the sense that the mighty magic of his imagination had conjured out of it its uttermost secret of power or pathos. When I say that Shakespeare used the current language of his day, I mean only that he habitually employed such language as was universally comprehensible,—that he was not run away with by the hobby of any theory as to the fitness of this or that component of English for expressing certain thoughts or feelings. That the artistic value of a choice and noble diction was quite as well understood in his day as in ours is evident from the praises bestowed by his contemporaries on Drayton, and by the epithet "well-languaged" applied to Daniel, whose poetic style is as modern as that of Tennyson; but the endless absurdities about the comparative merits of Saxon and Norman-French, vented by persons incapable of distinguishing one tongue from the other, were as yet unheard of. Hasty generalizers are apt to overlook the fact, that the Saxon was never, to any great extent, a literary language. Accordingly, it held its own very well in the names of common things, but failed to answer the demands of complex ideas, derived from them. The author of *Piers Ploughman* wrote for the people,—Chaucer for the court. We open at random and count the Latin[4] words in ten verses of the *Vision* and ten of the *Romaunt of the Rose*, (a translation from the French,) and find the proportion to be seven in the former and five in the latter. . . .

Shakespeare has been sometimes taxed with the barbarism of profuseness and exaggeration. But this is to measure him by a Sophoclean scale. The simplicity of the antique tragedy is by no means that of expression, but is of form merely. In the utterance of great passions, something must be indulged to the extravagance of Nature; the subdued tones to which pathos and sentiment are limited cannot express a tempest of the soul. The range between the piteous "no more but so," in which Ophelia compresses the heart-break whose compression was to make her mad, and that sublime appeal of Lear to the elements of Nature, only to be matched, if matched at all, in the *Prometheus*, is a wide one, and Shakespeare is as truly simple in the one as in the other. The simplicity of poetry is not that of prose, nor its clearness that of ready apprehension merely. To a subtile sense, a sense heightened by sympathy, those sudden fervors of phrase, gone ere one can say it lightens, that show us Macbeth groping among the complexities of thought in his conscience-clouded mind, and reveal the intricacy rather than enlighten it, while they leave the eye darkened to the literal meaning of the words, yet make their logical sequence, the grandeur of the conception, and its truth to Nature clearer than sober daylight could. There is an obscurity of mist rising from the undrained shallows of the mind, and there is the darkness of thunder-cloud gathering its electric masses with passionate intensity from the clear element of the imagination, not at random or wilfully, but by the natural processes of the creative faculty, to brood those flashes of expression that transcend rhetoric, and are only to be apprehended by the poetic instinct.

In that secondary office of imagination, where it serves the artist, not as the reason that shapes, but as the interpreter of his conceptions into words, there is a distinction to be noticed between the higher and lower mode in which it performs its function. It may be either creative or pictorial, may body forth the thought or merely image it forth. With Shakespeare, for example, imagination seems immanent in his very consciousness; with Milton, in his memory. In the one it sends, as if without knowing it, a fiery life into the verse,

> Sei die Braut das Wort,
> Bräutigam der Geist;

in the other it elaborates a certain pomp and elevation. Accordingly, the bias of the former is toward over-intensity, of the latter toward over-diffuseness. Shakespeare's temptation is to push a willing metaphor beyond its strength, to make a passion over-inform its tenement of words; Milton cannot resist running a simile on into a fugue. One always fancies Shakespeare *in* his best verses, and Milton at the key-board of his organ. Shakespeare's language is no longer the mere vehicle of thought, it has become part of it, its very flesh and blood. The pleasure it gives us is unmixed, direct, like that from the smell of a flower or the flavor of a fruit. Milton sets everywhere his little pitfalls of bookish association for the memory. I know that Milton's manner is very grand. It is slow, it is stately, moving as in triumphal procession, with music, with historic banners, with spoils from every time and every region, and captive epithets, like huge Sicambrians, thrust their broad shoulders between us and the thought whose pomp they decorate. But it is manner, nevertheless, as is proved by the ease with which it is parodied, by the danger it is in of degenerating into mannerism whenever it forgets itself. Fancy a parody of Shakespeare,—I do not mean of his words, but of his *tone*, for that is what distinguishes the master. You might as well try it with the Venus of Melos. In Shakespeare it is always the higher thing, the thought, the fancy, that is pre-eminent; it is Cæsar that draws all eyes, and not the chariot in which he rides, or the throng which is but the reverberation of his supremacy. If not, how explain the charm with which he dominates in all tongues, even under the disenchantment of translation? Among the most alien races he is as solidly at home as a mountain seen from different sides by many lands, itself superbly solitary, yet the companion of all thoughts and domesticated in all imaginations.

In description Shakespeare is especially great, and in that instinct which gives the peculiar quality of any object of contemplation in a single happy word that colors the impression on the sense with the mood of the mind. Most descriptive poets seem to think that a hogshead of water caught at the spout will give us a livelier notion of a thunder-shower than the sullen muttering of the first big drops upon the roof. They forget that it is by suggestion, not cumulation, that profound impressions are made upon the imagination. Milton's parsimony (so rare in him) makes the success of his

> Sky lowered, and, muttering thunder, some sad drops
> Wept at completion of the mortal sin.

Shakespeare understood perfectly the charm of indirectness, of making his readers seem to discover for themselves what he means to show them. If he wishes to tell that the leaves of the willow are gray on the under side, he does not make it a mere fact of observation by bluntly saying so, but makes it picturesquely reveal itself to us as it might in Nature:—

> There is a willow grows athwart the flood,
> That shows his *hoar* leaves in the glassy stream.

Where he goes to the landscape for a comparison, he does not ransack wood and field for specialties, as if he were gathering simples, but takes one image, obvious, familiar, and makes it new to us either by sympathy or contrast with his own immediate feeling. He always looked upon Nature with the eyes of the mind. Thus he can make the melancholy of autumn or the gladness of spring alike pathetic:—

> That time of year thou mayst in me behold,
> When yellow leaves, or few, or none, do hang
> Upon those boughs that shake against the cold,
> Bare ruined choirs where late the sweet birds sang.

Or again:—

> From thee have I been absent in the spring,
> When proud-pied April, dressed in all his trim,
> Hath put a spirit of youth in everything,
> That heavy Saturn leaped and laughed with him.

But as dramatic poet, Shakespeare goes even beyond this, entering so perfectly into the consciousness of the characters he himself has created, that he sees everything through their peculiar mood, and makes every epithet, as if unconsciously, echo and re-echo it. Theseus asks Hermia,—

> Can you endure the livery of a nun,
> For aye to be in shady cloister mewed,
> To live a *barren* sister all your life,
> Chanting faint hymns to the *cold fruitless* moon?

When Romeo must leave Juliet, the private pang of the lovers becomes a property of Nature herself, and

> *Envious* streaks
> Do lace the *severing* clouds in yonder east.

But even more striking is the following instance from Macbeth:—

> The raven himself is hoarse
> That croaks the fatal enterance of Duncan
> Under your battlements.

Here Shakespeare, with his wonted tact, makes use of a vulgar superstition, of a type in which mortal presentiment is already embodied, to make a common ground on which the hearer and Lady Macbeth may meet. After this prelude we are prepared to be possessed by her emotion more fully, to feel in her ears the dull tramp of the blood that seems to make the raven's croak yet hoarser than it is, and to betray the stealthy advance of the mind to its fell purpose. For Lady Macbeth hears not so much the voice of the bodeful bird as of her own premeditated murder, and we are thus made her shuddering accomplices before the fact. Every image receives the color of the mind, every word throbs with the pulse of one controlling passion. The epithet *fatal* makes us feel the implacable resolve of the speaker, and shows us that she is tampering with her conscience by putting off the crime upon the prophecy of the Weird Sisters to which she alludes. In the word *battlements*, too, not only is the fancy led up to the perch of the raven, but a hostile image takes the place of a hospitable; for men commonly speak of receiving a guest under their roof or within their doors. That this is not over-ingenuity, seeing what is not to be seen, nor meant to be seen, is clear to me from what follows. When Duncan and Banquo arrive at the castle, their fancies, free from all suggestion of evil, call up only gracious and amiable images. The raven was but the fantastical creation of Lady Macbeth's over-wrought brain.

> This castle hath a pleasant seat, the air
> Nimbly and sweetly doth commend itself
> Unto our gentle senses.
>           This *guest* of summer,
> The *temple-haunting* martlet, doth approve
> By his *loved mansionry* that the heaven's breath
> Smells *wooingly* here; no jutty, frieze,
> Buttress, or coigne of vantage, but this bird
> Hath made his pendent bed and procreant cradle.

The contrast here cannot but be as intentional as it is marked. Every image is one of welcome, security, and confidence. The summer, one may well fancy, would be a very different hostess from her whom we have just seen expecting *them*. And why *temple-haunting*, unless because it suggests sanctuary? O *immaginativa, che si ne rubi delle cose di fuor*, how infinitely more precious are the inward ones thou givest in return! If all this be accident, it is at least one of those accidents of which only this man was ever capable. I divine something like it now and then in Æschylus, through the mists of a language which will not let me be sure of what I see, but nowhere else. Shakespeare, it is true, had, as I have said, as respects English, the privilege which only first-comers enjoy. The language was still fresh from those sources at too great a distance from which it becomes fit only for the service of prose. Wherever he dipped, it came up clear and sparkling, undefiled as yet by the drainage of literary factories, or of those dye-houses where the machine-woven fabrics of sham culture are colored up to the last desperate style of sham sentiment. Those who criticise his diction as sometimes extravagant should remember that in poetry language is something more than merely the vehicle of thought, that it is meant to convey the sentiment as much as the sense, and that, if there is a beauty of use, there is often a higher use of beauty.

What kind of culture Shakespeare had is uncertain; how much he had is disputed; that he had as much as he wanted, and of whatever kind he wanted, must be clear to whoever considers the question. Dr. Farmer has proved, in his entertaining essay, that he got everything at second-hand from translations, and that, where his translator blundered, he loyally blundered too. But Goethe, the man of widest acquirement in modern times, did precisely the same thing. In his character of poet he set as little store by useless learning as Shakespeare did. He learned to write hexameters, not from Homer, but from Voss, and Voss found them faulty; yet somehow *Hermann und Dorothea* is more readable than *Luise*. So far as all the classicism then attainable was concerned, Shakespeare got it as cheap as Goethe did, who always bought it ready-made. For such purposes of mere æsthetic nourishment Goethe always milked other minds,—if minds those ruminators and digesters of antiquity into asses' milk may be

called. There were plenty of professors who were forever assiduously browsing in vales of Enna and on Pentelican slopes among the vestiges of antiquity, slowly secreting lacteous facts, and not one of them would have raised his head from that exquisite pasturage, though Pan had made music through his pipe of reeds. Did Goethe wish to work up a Greek theme? He drove out Herr Böttiger, for example, among that fodder delicious to him for its very dryness, that sapless Arcadia of scholiasts, let him graze, ruminate, and go through all other needful processes of the antiquarian organism, then got him quietly into a corner and milked him. The product, after standing long enough, mantled over with the rich Goethean cream, from which a butter could be churned, if not precisely classic, quite as good as the ancients could have made out of the same material. But who has ever read the *Achilleis*, correct in all *un*essential particulars as it probably is?

It is impossible to conceive that a man, who, in other respects, made such booty of the world around him, whose observation of manners was so minute, and whose insight into character and motives, as if he had been one of God's spies, was so unerring that we accept it without question, as we do Nature herself, and find it more consoling to explain his confessedly immense superiority by attributing it to a happy instinct rather than to the conscientious perfecting of exceptional powers till practice made them seem to work independently of the will which still directed them,—it is impossible that such a man should not also have profited by the converse of the cultivated and quick-witted men in whose familiar society he lived, that he should not have over and over again discussed points of criticism and art with them, that he should not have had his curiosity, so alive to everything else, excited about those ancients whom university men then, no doubt, as now, extolled without too much knowledge of what they really were, that he should not have heard too much rather than too little of Aristotle's *Poetics*, Quinctilian's *Rhetoric*, Horace's *Art of Poetry*, and the *Unities*, especially from Ben Jonson,—in short, that he who speaks of himself as

> Desiring this man's art and that man's scope,
> With what he most enjoyed contented least,

and who meditated so profoundly on every other topic of human concern, should never have turned his thought to the principles of that art which was both the delight and business of his life, the bread-winner alike for soul and body. Was there no harvest of the ear for him whose eye had stocked its garners so full as wellnigh to forestall all after-comers? Did he who could so counsel the practisers of an art in which he never arrived at eminence, as in Hamlet's advice to the players, never take counsel with himself about that other art in which the instinct of the crowd, no less than the judgment of his rivals, awarded him an easy pre-eminence? If he had little Latin and less Greek, might he not have had enough of both for every practical purpose on this side pedantry? The most extraordinary, one might almost say contradictory, attainments have been ascribed to him, and yet he has been supposed incapable of what was within easy reach of every boy at Westminster School. There is a knowledge that comes of sympathy as living and genetic as that which comes of mere learning is sapless and unprocreant, and for this no profound study of the languages is needed. . . .

I have said that it was doubtful if Shakespeare had any conscious moral intention in his writings. I meant only that he was purely and primarily poet. And while he was an English poet in a sense that is true of no other, his method was thoroughly Greek, yet with this remarkable difference,—that, while the Greek dramatists took purely national themes and gave them a universal interest by their mode of treatment, he took what may be called cosmopolitan traditions, legends of human nature, and nationalized them by the infusion of his perfectly Anglican breadth of character and solidity of understanding. Wonderful as his imagination and fancy are, his perspicacity and artistic discretion are more so. This country tradesman's son, coming up to London, could set high-bred wits, like Beaumont, uncopiable lessons in drawing gentlemen such as are seen nowhere else but on the canvas of Titian; he could take Ulysses away from Homer and expand the shrewd and crafty islander into a statesman whose words are the pith of history. But what makes him yet more exceptional was his utterly unimpeachable judgment, and that poise of character which enabled him to be at once the greatest of poets and so unnoticeable a good citizen as to leave no incidents for biography. His material was never far-sought; (it is still disputed whether the fullest head of which we have record were cultivated beyond the range of grammar-school precedent!) but he used it with a poetic instinct which we cannot parallel, identified himself with it, yet remained always its born and questionless master. He finds the Clown and Fool upon the stage,—he makes them the tools of his pleasantry, his satire, and even his pathos; he finds a fading rustic superstition, and shapes out of it ideal Pucks, Titanias, and Ariels, in whose existence statesmen and scholars believe forever. Always poet, he subjects all to the ends of his art, and gives in *Hamlet* the churchyard ghost, but with the cothurnus on,—the messenger of God's revenge against murder; always philosopher, he traces in *Macbeth* the metaphysics of apparitions, painting the shadowy Banquo only on the o'erwrought brain of the murderer, and staining the hand of his wife-accomplice (because she was the more refined and higher nature) with the disgustful blood-spot that is not there. We say he had no moral intention, for the reason, that, as artist, it was not his to deal with the realities, but only with the shows of things; yet, with a temperament so just, an insight so inevitable as his, it was impossible that the moral reality, which underlies the *mirage* of the poet's vision, should not always be suggested. His humor and satire are never of the destructive kind; what he does in that way is suggestive only,—not breaking bubbles with Thor's hammer, but puffing them away with the breath of a Clown, or shivering them with the light laugh of a genial cynic. Men go about to prove the existence of God! Was it a bit of phosphorus, that brain whose creations are so real, that, mixing with them, we feel as if we ourselves were but fleeting magic-lantern shadows?

But higher even than the genius we rate the character of this unique man, and the grand impersonality of what he wrote. What has he told us of himself? In our self-exploiting nineteenth century, with its melancholy liver-complaint, how serene and high he seems! If he had sorrows, he has made them the woof of everlasting consolation to his kind; and if, as poets are wont to whine, the outward world was cold to him, its biting air did but trace itself in loveliest frost-work of fancy on the many windows of that self-centred and cheerful soul.

*Notes*

1. As where Ben Jonson is able to say,—

    Men may securely sin, but safely never.

2. "Vulgarem locutionem anpellamus eam qua infantes adsuefiunt ab adsistentibus cum primitus distinguere voces incipiunt: vel, quod brevius dici potest, vulgarem locutionem asserimus *quam sine omni regula, nutricem imitantes accepimus.*" Dante, *de Vulg. Eloquio*, Lib I. cap. i.

3. Gray, himself a painful corrector, told Nicholls that "nothing was done so well as at the first concoction,"—adding, as a reason, "We think in words." Ben Jonson said it was a pity Shakespeare had not

blotted more, for that he sometimes wrote nonsense,—and cited in proof of it the verse,

Cæsar did never wrong but with just cause.

The last four words do not appear in the passage as it now stands, and Professor Craik suggests that they were stricken out in consequence of Jonson's criticism. This is very probable; but we suspect that the pen that blotted them was in the hand of Master Heminge or his colleague. The moral confusion in the idea was surely admirably characteristic of the general who had just accomplished a successful *coup d'état*, the condemnation of which he would fancy that he read in the face of every honest man he met, and which he would therefore be forever indirectly palliating.

4. We use the word *Latin* here to express words devised either mediately or immediately from that language.

## EDWIN P. WHIPPLE
### "Shakespeare: I"
### *The Literature of the Age of Elizabeth*
### 1869, pp. 32–56

The biography of Shakespeare, if we merely look at the bulk of the books which assume to record it, is both minute and extensive; but when we subject the octavo or quarto to examination, we find a great deal that is interesting about his times, and some shrewd and some dull guessing about his probable actions and motives, but little about himself except a few dates. He was born in Stratford-on-Avon, in April, 1564, and was the son of John Shakespeare, tradesman, of that place. In 1582, in his nineteenth year, he married Anne Hathaway, aged twenty-six. About the year 1586 he went to London and became a player. In 1589 he was one of the proprietors of the Blackfriars Theatre, and in 1595 was a prominent shareholder in a larger theatre, built by the same company, called the Globe. As a playwright he seems to have served an apprenticeship; for he altered, amended, and added to the dramas of others before he produced any himself. Between the year 1591, or thereabouts, and the year 1613, or thereabouts, he wrote over thirty plays, the precise date of whose composition it is hardly possible to fix. He seems to have made yearly visits to Stratford, where his wife and children resided, and to have invested money there as he increased in wealth. Mr. Emerson has noted, that about the time he was writing *Macbeth*, perhaps the greatest tragedy of ancient or modern times, "he sued Philip Rogers, in the borough-court of Stratford, for thirty-five shillings tenpence, for corn delivered to him at various times." In 1608, Mr. Collier estimates his income at four hundred pounds a year, which, allowing for the decreased value of money, is equal to eight or nine thousand dollars at the present time. About the year 1610, he retired permanently to Stratford, though he continued to write plays for the company with which he was connected. He died on the 23d of April, 1616.

Such is essentially the meagre result of a century of research into the external life of Shakespeare. As there is hardly a page in his writings which does not shed more light upon the biography of his mind, and bring us nearer to the individuality of the man, the antiquaries in despair have been compelled to abandon him to the psychologists; and the moment the transition from external to internal facts is made, the most obscure of men passes into the most notorious. For this personality and soul we call Shakespeare, the recorded incidents of whose outward career were so few and trifling, lived a more various life—a life more crowded with ideas, passions, volitions, and *events*—than any potentate the world has ever seen. Compared with his experience, the experience of Alexander or Hannibal, of Cæsar or Napoleon, was narrow and one-sided. He had projected himself into almost all the varieties of human character, and, in imagination, had intensely realized and *lived* the life of each. From the throne of the monarch to the bench of the village alehouse, there were few positions in which he had not placed himself, and which he had not for a time identified with his own. No other man had ever seen nature and human life from so many points of view; for he had looked upon them through the eyes of Master Slender and Hamlet, of Caliban and Othello, of Dogberry and Mark Antony, of Ancient Pistol and Julius Cæsar, of Mistress Tearsheet and Imogen, of Dame Quickly and Lady Macbeth, of Robin Goodfellow and Titania, of Hecate and Ariel. No king or queen of his time had so completely felt the cares and enjoyed the dignity of the regal state as this playwright, who usurped it by his thought alone; and the freshest and simplest maiden in Europe had no innocent heart-experience which this man could not share,—escaping, in an instant, from the shattered brain of Lear, or the hag-haunted imagination of Macbeth, in order to feel the tender flutter of her soul in his own. And none of these forms, though mightier or more exquisite than the ordinary forms of humanity, could hold or imprison him a moment longer than he chose to abide in it. He was on an excursion through the world of thought and action, to seize the essence of all the excitements of human nature,—terrible, painful, criminal, rapturous, or humorous; and to do this in a short earthly career, he was compelled to condense ages into days, and lives into minutes. He exhausts, in a short time, all the glory and all the agony there is on the throne or on the couch of Henry IV., and then, wearied with royalty, is off to the Boar's Head to have a rouse with Sir John. He feels all the flaming pride and scorn of the aristocrat Coriolanus; his brain widens with the imperial ideas, and his heart beats with the measureless ambition, of the autocrat Cæsar; and anon he has donned a greasy apron, plunged into the roaring Roman mob, and is yelling against aristocrat and autocrat with all the gusto of democratic rage. He is now a prattling child, and in a second he is the murderer with the knife at its throat. Capable of *being* all that he actually or imaginatively *sees*, he enters into at will, and abandons at will, the passions that brand or blast other natures. Avarice, malice, envy, jealousy, hatred, revenge, remorse, neither in their separate nor mutual action are strong enough to fasten him; and the same may be said of love and pity and friendship and joy and ecstasy; for behind and within this multiform personality is the person Shakespeare,—serene, self-conscious, vigilant, individualizing the facts of his consciousness, and pouring his own soul into each creation, without ever parting with the personal identity which is at the heart of all, which disposes and co-ordinates all, and which dictates the impression to be left by all.

And this fact conducts us to the question of Shakespeare's individuality. We are prone to place him as a man below other great men, because we make a distinction between the man and his genius. We gather our notion of Shakespeare from the meagre details of his biography, and in his biography he appears little and commonplace,—not by any means so striking a person as Kit Marlowe or Ben Jonson. To this individuality we tack on a universal genius,—which is about as reasonable as it would be to take the controlling power of gravity from the sun and attach it to one of the asteroids. Shakespeare's genius is not something distinct *from* the man; it is the expression *of* the man, just as the sun's attraction is the result of its immense mass. The measure of a man's individuality is his creative power; and all that Shakespeare created he individually

included. We must, therefore, if we desire to grasp his greatness, discard from our minds all associations connected with the pet epithets which other authors have condescended to shower upon him, such as "Sweet Will," and "Gentle Shakespeare," and "Fancy's child,"—fond but belittling phrases, as little appropriate as would be the patronizing chatter of the planet Venus about the dear, darling little Sun;—we must discard all these from our conceptions, and consider him primarily as a vast, comprehensive, personal soul and force, that passed from eternity into time, with all the wide aptitudes and affinities for the world he entered bound up in his individual being from the beginning. These aptitudes and affinities, these quick, deep, and varied sympathies, were so many inlets of the world without him; and facts pouring into such a nature were swiftly organized into faculties. Nothing, indeed, amazes us so much, in the biography of Shakespeare's mind, as the preternatural rapidity with which he assimilated knowledge into power, and experience into insight. The night of his personality is indicated by its resistance to, as much as its breadth is evinced by its receptivity of, objects; for his force was never overwhelmed or submerged by the multiplicity of impressions that unceasingly rushed in upon it. His soul lay genially open to the world of nature and human life, to receive the objects that went streaming into it, but never parted with the power of reacting upon all it received. This would not be so marvellous had he merely taken in the forms and outside appearances of things. All his perceptions, however, were vital; and the life and force of the objects he drew into his consciousness tugged with his own life and force for the mastery, and ended in simply enriching the spirit they strove to subdue. This indestructible spiritual energy, which becomes mightier with every exercise of might; which plucks out the heart and absorbs the vitality of everything it touches; which daringly commits itself to the fiercest, and joyously to the softest passions, without losing its moral and mental sanity; which in the most terrible excitements is as "the blue dome of air" to the tempest that rages beneath it; which, aiming to include everything, refuses to be included by anything, and in the sweep of its creativeness acts with a confident audacity, as if in it nature were humanized and humanity individualized;—in short, this unexampled energy of blended sensibility, intelligence, and will, is what constitutes the man Shakespeare; and this man is no mere name for an impersonal, unconscious genius, that did its marvels by instinct, no name for a careless playwright who bundered into miracles, but is essentially a person, creating strictly within the limitations of his individuality,—within those limitations appearing to be impersonal only because he is comprehensive enough to cover a wide variety of special natures,—and, above all, a person individually as great, at least, as the sum of his whole works.

In regard to the real mystery of this man's power, both criticism and philosophy are mute. His appearance is simply a fact in the world's intellectual history, which can be connected with no preceding fact nor with the spirit of his age. "It is the nature of poetry," says Emerson, "to spring, like the rainbow daughter of Wonder, from the invisible, to abolish the past, and to refuse all history." All that we know is, that the capacities and splendors of Shakespeare's mind existed potentially in the vital germ of the spiritual nature born with him into the world; and that his works are the result of the unfolding of this. The glory of the Elizabethan age, it is absurd to call him its product, for the puzzle is not so much the peculiarities of what he assimilated as his powers of assimilation, and in any age these powers would probably have worked equal, if different effects. Take, for instance, single thoughts and imaginations of his, such as the following, and see if you can account for them by any knowledge you have of the manners and customs of the England of Elizabeth:—

> The morning steals upon the night,
> Melting the darkness.
>
> How sweet the moonlight sleeps upon this bank!
>
> The benediction of these covering heavens
> Fall on their heads like dew.
>
> [Things evil] are our outward consciences.
>
> A substitute shines brightly as a king,
> Until a king be by; and then his state
> Empties itself, as doth an inland brook
> Into the main of waters.
>
> O Westmoreland! thou art a summer bird,
> Which ever in the haunch of winter sings
> The lifting up of day.
>
> Cheer your heart:
> Be you not troubled with the time, which drives
> O'er your content these strong necessities;
> But let determined things to Destiny
> Hold unbewailed their way.

But single passages like these, though they hint of the inmost essence of the poet, and drop upon the mind, as Carlyle says, "like a splendor out of heaven,"—though they demonstrate the independence of time and place of the imagination whence they come,—are still no adequate measure of Shakespeare's power. If, however, we pass from these to what is a more decisive test of his self-conscious, self-directed creative energy, namely, to his mode of organizing a whole drama, we shall find that his method, processes, and results are different from those of the dramatists of his own age or of any other age. The materials he uses are as nothing when compared with his transformation of them into works of art. Let us, in illustration, glance at his method of creation, as successfully exerted in any one of his great dramas, say *Hamlet*, or *King Lear*, or *Macbeth*, or *Othello*.

He takes a story or a history, with which the people are familiar, the whole interest of which is narrative. He finds it a mere succession of incidents; he leaves it a combination of events. He finds the persons named in it mere commonplace sketches of humanity; he leaves them self-subsisting, individual characters, more real to the mind than the men and women we daily meet.

Now the first fact that strikes us when we compare the original story with Shakespeare's magical transformation of it is, that everything is raised from the actual world into a Shakespearian world. He alters, enlarges, expands, enriches, enlivens, informs, *recreates* everything, lifting sentiment, passion, humor, thought, action, to the level of his own nature. Through incidents and through characters is shot Shakespeare's soul,—a soul that yields itself to every mould of being, from the clown to the monarch, endows every class of character it animates with the Shakespearian felicity and certainty of speech, and, being in *all* as well as in *each*, so connects and relates the society he has called into life, that they unite to form a whole, while existing with perfect distinctness as parts. The characters are not developed by isolation, but by sympathy or collision, and the closer they come together the less they run together. They are independent of each other, and yet necessitate each other. None of them could appear in any other play without exciting disorder; yet in this play their discord conduces to the general harmony. And so tough is the hold on existence of these beings that, though thousands of millions of men and women have been born, have died, and have been forgotten since they were created, and though the actual world has strangely changed, these men and women of

Shakespeare's are still alive, and Shakespeare's world still remains untouched by time.

This drama, thus made self-existent in the free heaven of art, implies, in its conception and execution, processes analogous to those which are followed by Nature herself in the production of her works; and modern critics have not hesitated to award to Shakespeare the distinction of being an organizer after her pattern. The drama which we have been describing is, like her works, not simple, but complex. It has unity, it has the widest variety, it has unity in variety. The most diverse and seemingly heterogeneous materials all aid to form a whole, "vital in every part"; and the organization is strictly an addition to the world, with nothing in literature and nothing in nature which exactly matches it. And it is alive, and refuses to die. Nature herself is compelled to adopt it into her race,

> And give to it an equal date
> With Andes and with Ararat.

You can gaze at it as you can gaze at a natural landscape, where hills, rocks, woods, stubble, grass, clouds, sky, atmosphere, each separate, each related, combine to form one impressive effect of beauty and power.

Perhaps, however, it would be more proper to call this Shakespearian drama an approximation to an organic product, rather than a realization of one. The processes of nature are followed, but the perfection of nature is the ideal it aims at rather than reaches. Still, if we allow for human defects and imperfections, and take into view the fact that Shakespeare had to submit to conditions imposed by his audience as well as conditions imposed by his genius, his work measurably fulfils the requirements of Kant's concise definition of an organic creation, namely, "that thing in which all the parts are mutually ends and means."

Admitting, then, that the drama we are considering has organic form, and not merely mechanical regularity, the question arises, What is the inner law, the central idea, the principle of life, by which, and in obedience to which, it was organized? Perhaps the new school of philosophic critics have done almost as much injury to Shakespeare's fame, in their attempt to answer this question, as they have done good in rescuing his dramas from the old school of sciolists and commentators, who were peeking at him with their formal rules of taste. The philosophic critics very properly insisted that he should be judged by principles deduced from his own method, and not by rules generalized from the method of the Greek dramatists; that the laws by which he should be tried were the laws which he acknowledged and obeyed, the laws of his own creative imagination; and that the very originality of his dramas freed them from tests which are applicable only to the products of imitation. They thus raised Shakespeare from a breaker of the laws into a lawgiver; and the brilliant vagabond, whom every catchpole of criticism thought he could hustle about and reprimand, was all at once lifted into a dictator of law to the bench.

Having relieved Shakespeare from these policemen of letters, and substituted some reach of human vision for their rat's eyes, the new school of philosophic critics proceeded to state what *were* the ideas which formed the ground-plans and organizing principles of his works; but in doing this, they brought Shakespeare down to their own level, and made him their spokesman. Intellectual egotism supplanted intellectual interpretation. Read Schlegel, Ulrici, even Gervinus, and you are delighted as long as they confine themselves to the business of exposing the folly of the critics they supplanted; but when they come to the real problem, and attempt to state the meaning and purpose of Shakespeare in any given play, you are apt to be as much surprised as was that philanthropist, who was confidentially informed that the ultimate object Napoleon had in view in his numerous wars was the establishment of Sunday schools. They find in Shakespeare's plays certain ethical, political, or social generalities, which, it seems, they were written to illustrate, or rather from which the plays grow, as from so many roots. But causes are to be measured by effects; the effects here are marvellous structures of genius; and these do not shoot up from the withered roots of barren truisms. A whole must be greater than any of its parts; and yet the philosophic idea of a Shakespearian drama, as eliminated by the German professors, is less than the least of its parts. A single magical word in Shakespeare is often greater, and has more reach of application, than the professorial bit of wisdom which they present as the grand total of the play, and which is often too obvious in itself to make a resort to Shakespeare necessary for a perception of its truth. Their "ground ideas" of the dramas are not worth any minor Shakespearian ideas they are assumed to include.

Indeed, before we claim to understand a Shakespearian whole, we must first see if we are competent to take in one of its parts. It is evident that the most important parts are the characters, and in respect to these, and to Shakespeare's method of characterization, there is much misconception. What are these characters? Are they copies of men and women, as we see them in the world,—slightly idealized portraits of persons, witty, passionate, thoughtful, or criminal? Are they such people as Shakespeare might have seen in the streets of London in the time of Elizabeth? No, for they are plainly Shakespearian, and not merely Elizabethan. Even the court-fools are endowed with the Shakesperian quality, are perfect of their kind, and are such court-fools as Shakespeare might have conceived himself to be one of, if he had, in Mr. Weller's phrase, "been born in that station of life."

Yet these characters are certainly not individualized qualities and passions, for they are eminently natural. If their naturalness does not come from their being portraits, slightly varied and heightened, of individuals, in what does their naturalness consist?

In answer to this question, it is first to be said, that these characters prove that Shakespeare had a conception of *human nature*, abstracted from all *individuals*. He not only looked *at* individuals, and *into* individuals, but *through* individuals to their common basis in humanity. But he did not rest here. This imaginative analysis, this vital generalization, this glance into the sources of things, evinces, of course, his possession of the profoundest philosophical genius as the foundation of his dramatic genius; but it is not the genius itself, for he also surveyed human nature in action, human nature as modified by human life, by manners, customs, institutions, and beliefs, and by that primitive personality which separates men, as humanity unites them.

These characters, then, are individual natures rooted in human nature. The question then arises, Is their individuality particular or representative? The least observation shows, we think, that they stand for more than individuals. We are continually saying that this or that person of our acquaintance resembles one of Shakespeare's characters; we may even learn much about him by studying the character he resembles; but we never thoroughly identify him with the character; for the character is more powerful, more perfectly developed, acts out the law of his being with more freedom, than the actual person with whom he is compared.

Further than this,—if we are accustomed to classify the persons we know, so as to include many individuals under one type, we shall find that we can include scores of our acquaintances in one of Shakespeare's characters, and then not exhaust its full application. It is not, therefore, his mere variety of characterization, but something peculiar in each of the varieties, which makes him pre-eminently the poet of human nature. Why, for example, is not Charles Dickens as great a novelist as Shakespeare is a dramatist? Dickens has delineated as wide a variety of persons as Shakespeare, if by variety we mean the absence of repetition. There is no reason but the shortness of life why he should not people literature with new individuals, until his characters are numbered by the thousand, all in a certain sense original, all discriminated from each other, but few or none *representative*. The single character of Hamlet represents more individuals than do all the individuals Dickens has delineated.

Again, Jane Austen is placed by Macaulay next to Shakespeare for the felicity, certainty, and nicety of her portraitures of character. The most evanescent lines of distinction between persons who appear alike she seizes with wonderful tact, and indicates these differences without the least resort to caricature. If the best characterization means simply the best portrait-painting, there is no reason why Elizabeth, in *Pride and Prejudice*, should not be placed side by side with Juliet and Cordelia.

But everybody feels that neither Dickens, with his range of observation, nor Jane Austen, with her subtilty of observation, makes any approach to Shakespeare. What is the reason?

The reason is, that Shakespeare does not paint individuals, but individualizes classes. In his great nature, the processes of reason and imagination, of philosophic insight and poetic insight, worked harmoniously together. His observation of persons only supplied him with hints for his creations. He did not take up at haphazard this man and that woman, and, because of their oddity or beauty, reproduce them in his story; but he distinguished in each actual person the signs of a class nature, midway between his general nature and his individual peculiarities. He classified men as the naturalist classifies the Animal Kingdom. Agassiz is not confused by the perplexing spectacle of the myriads of animals which form the materials of his science; for the moment his eye lights upon them, they fall into certain great natural divisions, distinguished by recognized marks of structure. Under each of a few grand divisions he includes innumerable individuals. Now the difference between Agassiz and a mere observer and describer of animals is the difference between Shakespeare and Dickens, only that Shakespeare works on phenomena more complicated, and presenting more obstacles to classification, than Agassiz deals with.

In his deep, wide, and searching observation of mankind, Shakespeare detects bodies of men who agree in the general tendencies of their characters, who strive after a common ideal of good or evil, and who all fail to reach it. Through these indications and hints he seizes, by his philosophical genius, the law of the class; by his dramatic genius, he gathers up in one conception the whole multitude of individuals comprehended in the law, and embodies it in a character; and by his poetical genius he lifts this character into an ideal region of life, where all hindrances to the free and full development of its nature are removed. The character seems all the more natural because it is *perfect of its kind*, whereas the actual persons included in the conception are imperfect of their kind. Thus there are many men of the type of Falstaff, but Shakespeare's Falstaff is not an actual Falstaff. Falstaff is the ideal head of the family, the possibility which they dimly strive to realize, the person they would be if they could. Again, there are many *Iagoish* men, but only one Iago, the ideal type of them all; and by studying him we learn what they would all become if circumstances were propitious, and their loose malignant tendencies were firmly knit together in positive will and diabolically alert intelligence. And it is the same with the rest of Shakespeare's great creations. The immense domain of human nature they cover is due to the fact, not merely that they are not repetitions of individuals, but that they are not repetitions of the same types or classes of individuals. The moment we analyze them, the moment we break them up into their constituent elements, we are amazed at the wealth of wisdom and knowledge which formed the materials of each individual embodiment, and the inexhaustible interest and fulness of meaning and application revealed in the analytic scrutiny of each. Compare, for example, Shakespeare's Timon of Athens—by no means one of Shakespeare's mightiest efforts of characterization—with Lord Byron, both as man and poet, and we shall find that Timon is the highest logical result of the Byronic tendency, and that in him, rather than in Byron, the essential misanthrope is impersonated. The number of poems which Byron wrote does not affect the matter at all, because the poems are all expansions and variations of one view of life, from which Byron could not escape. Shakespeare, had he pleased, might have filled volumes with Timon's poetic misanthropy; but, being a condenser, he was contented with concentrating the idea of the whole class in one grand character, and of putting into his mouth the truest, most splendid, most terrible things which have ever been uttered from the misanthropic point of view; and then, victoriously freeing himself from the dreadful mood of mind he had imaginatively realized, he passed on to occupy other and different natures. Shakespeare is superior to Byron on Byron's own ground, because Shakespeare grasped misanthropy from its first faint beginnings in the soul to its final result on character,—clutched its inmost essence,—discerned it as one out of a hundred subjective conditions of mind,— tried it thoroughly, and found it was too weak and narrow to hold *him*. Byron was *in* it, could not escape *from* it, and never, therefore, thoroughly mastered the philosophy *of* it. Here, then, in one corner of Shakespeare's mind, we find more than ample space for so great a poet as Byron to house himself.

But Shakespeare not only in one conception thus individualizes a whole class of men, but he communicates to each character, be it little or colossal, good or evil, that peculiar Shakespearian quality which distinguishes it as his creation. This he does by being and living for the time the person he conceives. What Macaulay says of Bacon is more applicable to Shakespeare, namely, that his mind resembles the tent which the fairy gave to Prince Ahmed. "Fold it, and it seemed a toy for the hand of a lady. Spread it, and the armies of powerful sultans might repose beneath its shade." Shakespeare could run his sentiment, passion, reason, imagination, into any mould of personality he was capable of shaping, and think and speak from that. The result is that every character is a denizen of the Shakespearian World; every character, from Master Slender to Ariel, is in some sense a poet, that is, is gifted with imagination to express his whole nature, and make himself inwardly known; yet we feel throughout that the "thousand-souled" Shakespeare is still but one soul, capable of shifting into a thousand forms, but leaving its peculiar birth-mark on every individual it informs.

Now it is difficult, perhaps impossible, for a critic to reproduce synthetically in his own consciousness, or thoroughly to analyze into all its elements, any single prominent character that Shakespeare has drawn. His characters, however, are not represented apart from each other, but as acting on each other; and, great as they separately are as conceptions,

they are but integral portions of a still mightier conception, which includes the whole drama in which they appear. The value of what we call the incidents of such a drama consists in their being such incidents as would most naturally spring from the mutual action of such persons, or as would best develop their natures. The plot is of small account as disconnected from the characters, but of great moment as vitally inwrought with them, and giving coherence to the living organism which results from the combination. It is for this reason that we pay little heed to improbable incidents in the story, provided the incidents serve to bring out the persons. It is very improbable that a bond should have been given payable in a pound of flesh, and still more so that any court in Christendom could have recognized its validity; but who thinks of this in the Shakespearian society of *The Merchant of Venice*?

Now it is doubtless true that a drama of Shakespeare thus organized, with characters comprehending an immense range of human character, and yielding to analysis laws of human nature which radiate light into whole departments of human life, produces on our minds, as we read, the effect of unity in variety. We preceive it as a whole, and think therefore we preceive the whole of it. But is it true that we really receive the colossal conception of Shakespeare himself? Shakespeare, it is plain, can only convey to us what we are capable of taking in; the mind that perceives reduces greatness to its own mental stature; and persons, according to their taste, culture, experience, height of intelligence, capacity of approaching Shakespeare himself, obtain different impressions, varying in depth and breadth, of each of his great plays. Who, for instance, has stated the general conception of the play of *Hamlet*? The idea of that drama, as given by different critics, is only so much of the idea as could be got into the heads of the critics. Their interpretation at best belongs to the class of *Mémoires pour servir*;—the rounded whole is described by minds that are angular; and Shakespeare's conception is measuring them, while they are felicitating themselves that they are measuring it.

Even Goethe, the most comprehensive intelligence since Shakespeare, failed to "pluck out the heart" of Hamlet's mystery. Indeed, it is beginning to be considered, that his remarks on the character, though delicate and profound in themselves, do not touch the essential individuality of Hamlet; that his ingenuity was exercised in the wrong direction; and that, in his criticism, he resembled the sturdy and rapid walker, who checked his pace to ask a boy how far it was to Taunton. "If you go on in the way you're now going," was the reply, "it's twenty-four thousand miles; if you turn back, it's only five." But though some critics since Goethe have not been so elaborately wrong as he, Hamlet is still outside of the largest thought in the right direction. A distinguished thinker has said that there are moods of the mind in which Hamlet appears little, for what he suggests is infinitely more than what he is. This is true as to Shakespeare, but not true as to other minds; for until we have grasped the conception that Shakespeare has embodied, we have no right to suppose ourselves capable of going beyond it into that vastness of contemplation of which, from Shakespeare's height of vision, the character was an inadequate expression. Again, it is a common remark, that the school of philosophic critics, especially in their attempts to dive into the meaning of Hamlet, are continually giving Shakespeare the credit of their own thoughts. Giving Shakespeare the credit! Well might he reply, if such were the case, "Beggar that I am, I am even poor in thanks!"

Shakespeare, then, as regards his most gigantic conceptions, has probably never been adequately conceived. He must be tried by his peers; and where are his peers? We know that he grows in mental stature as our minds enlarge, and as we increase in our knowledge of him; but he has never been included by criticism as other poets have been included. The greatest and most interpretative minds which have made him their study, though they may have commenced with wielding the rod, soon found themselves seduced into taking seats on the benches, anxious to learn instead of impatient to teach; and have been compelled to admit that the poet who is the delight of the rudest urchin in the pit of the playhouse, is also the poet whose works defy the highest faculties of the philosopher thoroughly to comprehend.

### KARL ELZE
From "Shakespeare's Character and Conception
of Human Nature"
*William Shakespeare: A Literary Biography*
tr. L. Dora Schmitz
1876

Shakespeare's nature was so harmonious that it is difficult to believe that his position towards the State could have been anything else but absolutely in accordance with his position towards the Church and positive religion; in both cases we find him exhibiting the same grand objectivity; which stands as far above the different forms of state as above the different forms of faith. In taking single passages and remarks from Shakespeare's works, we can as little arrive at a general conclusion on this point as with regard to Shakespeare's religious opinions. All Shakespeare's dramatic characters speak of the various forms of government and the different estates, &c., perfectly in accordance with their own individuality, and we have no right, for instance, to assume the political views of Richard II. or of Richard III. to be the poet's own personal views; for he had no other alternative than to give expression in his histories, to the political opinions peculiar to the day and to the persons represented, and which he found in the works from which he drew his material. It is well known how closely, in this respect, Shakespeare follows Holinshed in his Histories and North's Plutarch in his Roman plays. Shakespeare was, no doubt, anything but a politician himself—"I had as lief be a Brownist as a politician." He was as far from having thought out a political system for himself as he had planned a religious system, yet he must certainly have been aware that the State is an indispensable and unavoidable means for leading both the human community and the human individual forward on the path to culture and morality, and that the right use of every form of government accomplishes this, although, of course, every form of government is liable to deteriorate. In so far, probably, monarchy and republic—from a theoretical point of view—may have been the same to him; all he demanded was that the foundations of all human existence—order and law, uprightness and faithfulness, justice and mercy—should be allowed to exert their influence; for, in his opinion, they are the pillars of the State and the Church, inasmuch as they are the basis of every moral community. Beyond these he placed weight only in one other ethical and political factor, that is, in the division and arrangement of the various grades and classes of society, which he thinks ought not to be overstepped either arrogantly or with criminal intention. He does not like to see a peasant tread on the courtier's heel,[1] and terms reverence, which makes distinction of place between high and low, "that angel of the world."[2] This can astonish us the less, as the only

form of government Shakespeare knew by experience was the monarchical form, which had worked itself out of feudalism, and was controlled more by public opinion than by parliament; hence from childhood he had been accustomed to the distinction of grades in society. In his opinion everyone ought to act in his own sphere as best he can for the good of the whole community, without venturing to grasp at things above or below him; in this way alone, the poet thinks, can the community be prosperous as a whole. This is most fully and completely brought forward in the famous speech of Ulysses in *Troilus and Cressida* (i.3). In connection with this it would seem that the poet considered the things that existed as justified by reason of their very existence. This reminds one of Hegel's proposition, that the actual is the rational form; and in this Shakespeare again shows a resemblance to Walter Scott, who resembled him in so many other respects. However, the distinction of classes Shakespeare by no means considers an exclusively monarchical institution; he makes the same demand of the republican form of government, as is proved by the opening scene in *Coriolanus*. The fable there related by Menenius Agrippa, of the various members of the body rebelling against the belly, expresses this eloquently enough. And yet here again the reverse of the case has no less its justification in Shakespeare; he attacks and condemns all prejudices respecting class, and considers rank and birth far inferior to virtue and nobility of soul. This is most distinctly taught in *All's Well That Ends Well*; and the admonitory words addressed to the young Count Rousillon (ii. 3), who despises Helena on account of the lowness of her social position, would need to be placed as *pendants* by the side of the speeches of Ulysses and Menenius Agrippa. Such objectivity is all the more confounding, as the admonitory words against class prejudice are not by any means the harangue of a democrat and revolutionist, but are spoken by a royal personage. Any form of government that is not based upon the above-mentioned foundations of all political and social life, the poet denounces and attacks with ridicule as delightful as it is withering. He introduces us to two forms of this description: to the ochlocracy of Jack Cade (in the Second Part of *Henry VI.*), and the Utopian state of nature in *The Tempest*, which is an imitation of Montaigne's idea; both forms are so admirably described that they will ever be models of their kind. W. König[3] very justly points out that Shakespeare seems to express his own opinion of these two abortions, where "the rabblement" is characterized by Jack Cade's words, "But then are we in order when we are most out of order," and where the Utopian state is despatched with Alonzo's words, "Thou dost talk nothing to me." Shakespeare denounces ochlocracy as well as the socialistic, natural state, because both speak disparagingly of culture. Jack Cade causes the Clerk of Chatham to be executed merely "because he can write, read, and cast accompt," and Lord Say because he erected schools, printing establishments, and paper-mills. The natural state advocated by Gonzalo is altogether wanting in moral foundation: he will have nothing to do with work, or property, or marriage.

Endeavours have not been wanting to represent Shakespeare as having been a good royalist and a herald of the so-called Teutonic Christian form of government; but these endeavours are precisely of the same character as those which maintain the poet to have been a strictly orthodox Christian, no matter whether Protestant or Catholic. It is no doubt true that Shakespeare has given the monarchical form of government an extremely high position, and has repeatedly praised it in enthusiastic terms as the sublime and sanctified climax of all social order; still it must not be overlooked that this praise falls from the lips of kings themselves—or, at all events, from the lips of those in their immediate surroundings—and it is not to be expected that they should have thought or spoken disparagingly of such a subject. It will be sufficient to point to the remarks of Claudio (in *Hamlet*, iv. 5) and to the speeches of Richard II. (iii. 2 and 3). But besides this, the Biblical and very poetical idea that the King rules as the Anointed of the Lord, as the representative of God on earth, corresponds absolutely with the ideas entertained in Shakespeare's day; and "His Sacred Majesty" James I. was so imbued with this idea that he would scarcely allow himself to be regarded as mortal. The same idea the poet found in Holinshed, where, for example, the Archbishop of Canterbury expresses the same opinion on the occasion of King John's coronation; in fact, the idea was part and parcel of the general current of thought of Shakespeare's day, so that even on this account it is difficult to determine how far the idea may have concealed the poet's own personal convictions. Benno Tschischwitz, in whom Shakespeare's supposed royalism has probably found its most staunch supporter, goes so far as to make the poet's feeling of reverence a principle, and has endeavoured, from the Lancastrian tetralogy, to point out that this principle of reverence, and the poet's attachment to it, forms the substance of Shakespeare's political opinions.[4] Tschischwitz arrives at these two positions, he says, first from the fact that in the Lancastrian tetralogy we find Shakespeare's fundamental political views expressed "with the full vigour of a developed and well-founded system," and secondly, because it is evident that Shakespeare considers popular absolution the ideal form of government. With neither of these two views are we able to agree. Indeed, in our opinion it would rather seem that Shakespeare entertained no greater respect for regal robes than for the robes of priests, and that the poet might very well have supplemented his remark about the hood not making the monk, by saying that neither do purple robes make a king. The cowl and the ermine are beautiful and venerable symbols, but the appearance must not belie the reality; and here again, as in every other case, the poet lays the main stress upon the man whom the regal mantle envelops. He makes his Henry V. state this very clearly (in iv. 1), where he says to John Bates, "I think the king is but a man, as I am: the violet smells to him as it doth to me; the element shows to him as it doth to me; all his senses have but human conditions; his ceremonies laid by, in his nakedness he appears but a man; and though his affections are higher mounted than ours, yet when they stoop, they stoop with the like wing."[5] These words at the same time remind us of Shylock's famous apostrophe ("Hath not a Jew eyes? Hath not a Jew hands?" &c.), and show very distinctly, when thus placed side by side, that Shakespeare recognized the rightful claims of the man in the king as well as in the Jew, in the highest as well as the lowest. Shakespeare knows that there are royal criminals, and has depicted them as such in Claudius and Richard III. He knows that royalty has important duties to perform, and he judges kings according to their ability and their endeavour to discharge these duties—and their fate, too, is made dependent upon this. The supreme freedom with which Shakespeare has not only delineated a series of the most different royal personages, but also genuine Roman republicans, makes it impossible to believe that he was an admirer of royalty *quand même*—in fact, that he can have been attached to any special political system. To what a climax an exaggerated form of royalism and absolutism may be carried is shown by an appalling example in *King Lear*. Lear himself, in his clear moments—but unfortunately too late—recognizes the fact that in a very great measure his absolute power, and the grovelling devotion and flattery of his subjects, are the cause of

his misfortunes, as, in fact, they are the cause of his downfall. Without exaggeration, it may be said that Lear is the personification of Absolutism which has lost its reason, Cæsarism gone mad, and in him it is shown that absolute power carried to excess, leads to mental aberration as a final consequence. We have here Goethe's warning about "the limitation of the human mind" in the grandest and most overwhelming form. "They flattered me like a dog," says Lear (iv. 6). "They say 'Ay' and 'No' to everything that I said!—'Ay' and 'No,' too, was no good divinity. When the rain came to wet me once, and the wind to make me chatter; when the thunder would not peace at my bidding; there I found 'em, there I smelt 'em out. Go to, they are not men o' their words; they told me I was everything; 'tis a lie, I am not ague-proof." If anywhere, the poet seems himself here to speaking through the mouths of his dramatic personages.

But the poet shows his detestation of insolence and arrogance, not only in crowned heads, but also in the king's officials; he chastises them for this at every opportunity, and even Hamlet does not omit to mention "the insolence of office" as one of the greatest plagues of life. The poet, in *Measure for Measure*, iv. 2, says that:—

> Could great men thunder
> As Jove himself does, Jove would ne'er be quiet,
> For every pelting petty officer
> Would use his heaven for thunder;
> Nothing but thunder!

And when among the lower officials conceit of office and unseemly behaviour are coupled with ignorance and stupidity, the combination is made the target of the poet's most delightful, but, at the same time, of his keenest sarcasm. Shallow, Silence, Dogberry, Verges and others, are extremely comical characters, but between the lines it is unmistakably evident what the poet's own opinion is of these caricatures of officialism. Absolutism, when carried to excess by rulers or leaders of men, ends in madness, but when carried to excess by subordinates results in absurdity. In various quarters Shakespeare has, indeed, been found fault with for the manner he has drawn these characters—for having, in fact, represented the burgher class at a disadvantage, and everywhere favoured the aristocracy. His townsfolk, it has been said, are simpletons and the heroes of Eastcheap; his country-folk, mere fools dressed as clowns; in this respect Scott—whose creations are equally numerous—is said to show an incomparably greater degree of justice. The truth, however, is that the progress of our political and social development has conferred upon the burgher class an infinitely higher position and significance than it possessed in Shakespeare's time. In his day, the lower orders had not yet succeeded in obtaining equal consideration or educational advantages; the aristocracy still formed the centre of the political, social, intellectual, and in many ways also of the literary life of the nation, whereas the burgher class in reality—and hence also in Shakespeare's dramas—occupied mostly a subordinate position. Any ambitious spirits among the burgher class (and of these there was indeed no dearth) found themselves obliged to attach themselves, in some way, to the aristocracy—who represented the *élite* of the intellect as well as of birth—and had thus, as it were, to be taken in tow. Shakespeare, however, did not fail to exhibit his all-embracing sense of justice even towards the burgher class, so far as he found it worthy of esteem and honour; this is proved by *The Merry Wives of Windsor*, which presents a picture of healthy and sterling burgher life; we here find representatives of the burgher classes who are neither simpletons nor fools, and who are at least on a par with the amusing artisans in *A Midsummer*

*Night's Dream,* or with those in *Coriolanus.* In the romantic comedies, in fact, we must not expect to find serious representatives of the burgher class; as little can we expect to find a place allotted to them in the Histories, for these dramas refer to days prior to Shakespeare's own, and hence represent an even inferior degree of development among the burgher class than was met with in Shakespeare's day. And, finally, the great tragedies move in ages and in spheres where there can be no question at all of a burgher class, in the present sense of the word.

With regard to one point in Shakespeare's character critics are happily entirely of one mind—that is, with regard to his enthusiastic love of his country, and he has given expression to this sentiment, not only in several immortal apostrophes,[6] but it is found shedding its animating and brilliant influence over all his poetry. His joyous pride of England resounds like a flourish of trumpets from every one of his dramas, and it may be said that no poet in the world surpasses him in fervent and sincere patriotism.[7] And yet he is anything but a "John Bull" *pur et simple,* and his dramatic characters are by no means, as Goethe[8] has said, "mere incarnate Englishmen." Shakespeare also allows other nationalities to assert their rights and peculiarities; prejudice and unjust one-sidedness are as far from him in this direction as everywhere else. He knows no national hatred, not even against Spain, which, as the chief representative of the Roman Catholic world, continually assumed a hostile attitude towards his native land—an attitude which brought war to its threshold, and even threatened his country with complete destruction during the very years when Shakespeare was at an age most susceptible of receiving deep and lifelong impressions. It is true that in Don Armado,[9] in *Love's Labour's Lost,* the poet has presented an extremely lifelike portrait of a specific Spanish braggart, but the sparkling wit which is provoked by this portrait exhibits neither bitterness nor sarcasm, so that it cannot offend the countrymen either of the second, or more strictly speaking, of the first Don Quixote.[10] Shakespeare is sarcastic—but not unjust—only towards the French, whose national character he perfectly understood; their vain, hollow, and unreliable nature was perfectly recognized by him, but he is ready to acknowledge that they are excellent horsemen,[11] and remarkable for the tastefulness of their attire.[12] The contrast between the French and English national character Shakespeare has described more particularly in the camp-scenes in *Henry V.* In his account of the dishonest ways of the French, which—as is said in *Henry VIII.* (i.3)— threaten to affect the English, the poet has followed Holinshed, it is true, but the two braggarts and swaggerers are altogether his own creation; they are admirably drawn characters, Frenchmen to the backbone, and so true to nature, that even in our day, after the lapse of centuries, they are absolutely correct even in the smallest features. Monsieur Lavache, Countess Rousillon's clown, in *All's Well That Ends Well,* is a Frenchman from top to toe, and a "loose fellow." It will be sufficient to mention, in addition, Monsieur Veroles in *Pericles* (iv. 2). The contrast between the reasonable, serious, and sterling perceptible character of the English is everywhere distinctly perceptible in Shakespeare. Who cannot see the Frenchman bodily before him, when Richard III.—certainly no good example of the English character—maintains (i.3):—

> Because I cannot flatter and speak fair,
> Smile in men's faces, smooth, deceive and cog,
> Duck with French nods and apish courtesy,
> I must be held a rancorous enemy.

Who can help siding with Portia when she says of her French admirer, Monsieur Le Bon: "God made him, and therefore let

him pass for a man." Only in one case does Shakespeare—according to our modern ideas—seem to have gone too far and to have been unjust, viz., in his delineation of Joan of Arc's character; but in this he has closely followed his authority, whether we assume it to have been Hall or Holinshed. La Pucelle's character was, up to the seventeenth century, a closed book even to her own countrymen, and has only in recent days by documentary evidence been revealed to us in its full purity and beauty. But even though this want of a correct knowledge of the case were not an unquestionable excuse for the poet, still his error vanishes, and appears as nothing, when compared with the filth which Voltaire—her own countryman—has cast upon the character of La Pucelle. And even though Voltaire's wit were a hundred times more poignant, it would never clear him of this wrong.

As regards the Italians, Shakespeare has, it is true, in *The Merchant of Venice* and in *Othello,* and elsewhere, succeeded in giving a reflex of the local colouring of Italy with marvellous skill and fidelity, in the same way as he has, in *The Taming of the Shrew* and elsewhere, made use—after his own fashion—of figures from Italian comedy, but we look in vain for any special delineation of the specific Italian character. The Italians introduced in his plays are by no means distinct Italians to the same extent as Parolles, Dr. Caius, and others are distinct Frenchmen. The reason of this may be found in the circumstance that the Italian national character does not present such striking traits to the eyes of a stranger as in the case of the French or even the Spanish character. Shakespeare—even though he may have visited Italy—must, therefore, have been less struck with the Italian people and with their national peculiarities, and hence was less tempted to make use of them for dramatic representation. Nevertheless, he praises Italy as the land of refined and fashionable life;[13] while, on the other hand, like his contemporaries, he too, is very well aware that it is also the land of cunning and of treachery, and more especially of poisonings.[14] Iachimo is described as a false and deceitful Italian, and himself speaks of his "Italian brain;" Posthumus (v. 5, 210) calls him the "Italian fiend." In *The Taming of the Shrew* (ii. 1, 405), Gremio calls old Vincentio "an old Italian fox."

Of Germans Shakespeare had but little occasion to speak. In *The Merchant of Venice* and in *Othello* he alludes to their love of drink, but has finally to admit that the English were their masters in the art; and, as is well known, the Danes and Dutch are referred to as their equals in this. Drunkenness and immoderate eating were a general custom in those days, throughout northern and central Europe, and accordingly the Germans need not be specially found fault with in this respect; indeed they may be the more readily reconciled to the accusation as, in the opposite scales, we have the noble testimony (uttered by the landlord of the Garter Inn, in *The Merry Wives,* iv. 5), that "Germans are honest men!"

*Notes*

1. *Hamlet,* v. 1.
2. *Cymbeline,* iv. 2, 207.
3. *Shakespeare-Jahrbuch,* vii. 194.
4. *Shakespeare's Staat und Königthum nachgewiesen an der Lancaster-Tetralogie,* by B. Tschischwitz, 1868.
5. See also Henry's monologue in the same scene: *Upon the King! Let us our lives, &c., lay on the King!*
6. Take, for instance, John of Gaunt's speech in *Richard II.* and the closing lines of *King John.*
7. The only one point which I cannot make tally with this feeling of patriotism in Shakespeare, is that Cymbeline, after a hard-won and glorious victory, declares himself ready for the sake of peace to pay tribute to Rome as before.

8. *Shakespeare und kein Ende.*
9. And may not Don Armado be an intentional allusion to the Armada? The type of the Spanish braggadocio is in fact unmistakable. Herzberg (in the Schlegel-Tieck translation of Shakespeare, vii. 262) conjectures—not without probability—that one or other of the prisoners-of-war from the Armada may have served Shakespeare as a model for the character of the Spaniard. May not the Spanish admiral, Don Pedro Valdes, whom Drake took prisoner, have been the man?
10. The first quarto of *Love's Labour Lost* belongs to the year 1598, whereas *Don Quixote* appeared first in 1606.
11. *Hamlet*, iv. 7, 82 ff.
12. *Hamlet*, i. 3, 73 ff.
13. For instance, in *King Richard II.*, ii. 1, 21 ff.
14. See *Cymbeline*, iii. 2, 4, and iii. 4, 15.

## GEORGE BERNARD SHAW
### From "Better than Shakespear?" (1897)
*Plays and Players*, ed. A. C. Ward
1952, pp. 152–57

When I saw a stage version of *The Pilgrim's Progress* (by G. G. Collingham) announced for production, I shook my head, knowing that Bunyan is far too great a dramatist for our theatre, which has never been resolute enough even in its lewdness and venality to win the respect and interest which positive, powerful wickedness always engages, much less the services of men of heroic conviction. Its greatest catch, Shakespear, wrote for the theatre because, with extraordinary artistic powers, he understood nothing and believed nothing. Thirty-six big plays in five blank verse acts, and (as Mr Ruskin, I think, once pointed out) not a single hero! Only one man in them all who believes in life, enjoys life, thinks life worth living, and has a sincere, unrhetorical tear dropped over his death-bed; and that man—Falstaff! What a crew they are— these Saturday to Monday athletic stockbroker Orlandos, these villains, fools, clowns, drunkards, cowards, intriguers, fighters, lovers, patriots, hypochondriacs who mistake themselves (and are mistaken by the author) for philosophers, princes without any sense of public duty, futile pessimists who imagine they are confronting a barren and unmeaning world when they are only contemplating their own worthlessness, self-seekers of all kinds, keenly observed and masterfully drawn from the romantic-commercial point of view. Once or twice we scent among them an anticipation of the crudest side of Ibsen's polemics on the Woman Question, as in *All's Well That Ends Well*, where the man cuts as meanly selfish a figure beside his enlightened lady doctor wife as Helmer beside Nora; or in *Cymbeline*, where Posthumus, having, as he believes, killed his wife for inconstancy, speculates for a moment on what his life would have been worth if the same standard of continence had been applied to himself. And certainly no modern study of the voluptuous temperament, and the spurious heroism and heroinism which its ecstasies produce, can add much to *Antony and Cleopatra*, unless it were some sense of the spuriousness on the author's part. But search for statesmanship, or even citizenship, or any sense of the commonwealth, material or spiritual, and you will not find the making of a decent vestryman or curate in the whole horde. As to faith, hope, courage, conviction, or any of the true heroic qualities, you find nothing but death made sensational, despair made stage-sublime, sex made romantic, and barrenness covered up by sentimentality and the mechanical lilt of blank verse.

All that you miss in Shakespear you find in Bunyan, to whom the true heroic came quite obviously and naturally. The world was to him a more terrible place than it was to Shakespear; but he saw through it a path at the end of which a man might look not only forward to the Celestial City, but back on his life and say:—'Tho' with great difficulty I am got hither, yet now I do not repent me of all the trouble I have been at to arrive where I am. My sword I give to him that shall succeed me in my pilgrimage, and my courage and skill to him that can get them.' The heart vibrates like a bell to such an utterance as this: to turn from it to 'Out, out, brief candle,' and 'The rest is silence,' and 'We are such stuff as dreams are made on, and our little life is rounded with a sleep' is to turn from life, strength, resolution, morning air and eternal youth, to the terrors of a drunken nightmare.

Let us descend now to the lower ground where Shakespear is not disabled by his inferiority in energy and elevation of spirit. Take one of his big fighting scenes, and compare its blank verse, in point of mere rhetorical strenuousness, with Bunyan's prose. Macbeth's famous cue for the fight with Macduff runs thus:—

> Yet I will try the last: before my body
> I throw my warlike shield. Lay on, Macduff,
> And damned be him that first cries Hold, enough!

Turn from this jingle, dramatically right in feeling, but silly and resourceless in thought and expression, to Apollyon's cue for the fight in the Valley of Humiliation: 'I am void of fear in this matter. Prepare thyself to die; for I swear by my infernal den that thou shalt go no farther: here will I spill thy soul.' This is the same thing done masterly. Apart from its superior grandeur, force, and appropriateness, it is better claptrap and infinitely better word-music.

Shakespear, fond as he is of describing fights, has hardly ever sufficient energy or reality of imagination to finish without betraying the paper origin of his fancies by dragging in something classical in the style of the Cyclops' hammer falling 'on Mars's armor, forged for proof eterne.' Hear how Bunyan does it: 'I fought till my sword did cleave to my hand; and when they were joined together as if the sword grew out of my arm; and when the blood run thorow my fingers, then I fought with most courage.' Nowhere in all Shakespear is there a touch like that of the blood running down through the man's fingers, and his courage rising to passion at it. Even in mere technical adaptation to the art of the actor, Bunyan's dramatic speeches are as good as Shakespear's tirades. Only a trained dramatic speaker can appreciate the terse manageableness and effectiveness of such a speech as this, with its grandiose exordium, followed up by its pointed question and its stern threat: 'By this I perceive thou art one of my subjects; for all that country is mine, and I am the Prince and the God of it. How is it then that thou hast ran away from thy King? Were it not that I hope thou mayst do me more service, I would strike thee now at one blow to the ground.' Here there is no raving and swearing and rhyming and classical allusion. The sentences go straight to their mark; and their concluding phrases soar like the sunrise, or swing and drop like a hammer, just as the actor wants them.

I might multiply these instances by the dozen; but I had rather leave dramatic students to compare the two authors at first-hand. In an article on Bunyan lately published in the *Contemporary Review*—the only article worth reading on the subject I ever saw (yes, thank you: I am quite familiar with Macaulay's patronizing prattle about *The Pilgrim's Progress*)— Mr Richard Heath, the historian of the Anabaptists, shews how Bunyan learnt his lesson, not only from his own rough pilgrimage through life, but from the tradition of many an actual journey from real Cities of Destruction (under Alva), with Interpreters' houses and convoy of Greathearts all complete. Against such a man what chance had our poor immortal William, with his 'little Latin' (would it had been less, like his Greek!), his heathen mythology, his Plutarch, his Boccaccio, his Holinshed, his circle of London literary wits, soddening their minds with books and their nerves with alcohol (quite like us), and all the rest of his Strand and Fleet Street surroundings, activities, and interests, social and professional, mentionable and unmentionable? Let us applaud him, in due measure, in that he came out of it no blackguardly Bohemian, but a thoroughly respectable snob; raised the desperation and cynicism of its outlook to something like sublimity in his tragedies; dramatized its morbid, self-centred passions and its feeble and shallow speculations with all the force that was in them; disinfected it by copious doses of romantic poetry, fun, and common sense; and gave to its perpetual sex-obsession the relief of individual character and feminine winsomeness. Also—if you are a sufficiently good Whig—that after incarnating the spirit of the whole epoch which began with the sixteenth century and is ending (I hope) with the nineteenth, he is still the idol of all well-read children. But as he never thought a noble life worth living or a great work worth doing, because the commercial profit-and-loss sheet shewed that the one did not bring happiness nor the other money, he never struck the great vein—the vein in which Bunyan told of that 'man of a very stout countenance' who went up to the keeper of the book of life and said, not 'Out, out, brief candle,' but 'Set down my name, sir,' and immediately fell on the armed men and cut his way into heaven after receiving and giving many wounds.

GEORGE SAINTSBURY
From "Shakespeare"
A *Short History of English Literature*
1898, pp. 320–29

What really is Shakespeare's earliest dramatic work is, as has been said, in the highest degree uncertain; and of the pieces which are with more or less probability ascribed to his earliest period it is not definitely known how much is his own, how much supplied by or borrowed from others. From the beginning of the play, as distinguished from the interlude, the habit seems to have established itself, in England as in other countries, of constantly reworking old pieces by new hands; and it is probably to some exceptional popularity of Shakespeare as a refashioner in this way that Greene's outburst refers. His early pieces, then, may be divided into anticipations, more or less original, of his special masterpiece, the romantic comedy, attempts in the blood-and-thunder melodrama of the time, and probably, in most cases, refashioned chronicle-plays or "histories," a kind, as we have seen, as old as Bale. To the first division belong *Love's Labour's Lost*, the *Two Gentlemen of Verona*, the *Comedy of Errors* (this touching the translated classical play), *Measure for Measure* (?), the series culminating in A *Midsummer Night's Dream*; to the second *Titus Andronicus*; to the last the majority of the great series of the English histories, while *Romeo and Juliet* stands apart as what we may call a romantic tragedy corresponding to the romantic comedy, and promising almost greater things to come.

In all this work, guessing as little as we can, and proceeding as gingerly as possible, we can see the poet's genius growing and settling itself in every possible way. In metre he begins with the lumbering fourteeners, not as yet quite spirited up even by him, the stiff blank verse which even from the first

becomes pliant in his hand, the richer but almost stiffer Marlovian hectoring style, the giant fantasies and euphusitic devices of Lyly, all frequently lapsing into rhymed couplet and even stanza. But almost from the very first there are glimpses, and very soon there are much more than glimpses, of something that we have never seen before. Such a phrase, for instance, to take but the first that occurs, as the

And shake the yoke of inauspicious stars
From this world-wearied flesh,

of *Romeo and Juliet* takes us a long way beyond Marlowe, a longer way beyond Peele. In both these masters there is a deficiency of vibration in the verse, and a certain poverty, or at least simplicity, of verbal music. "Native wood-notes wild" is rather truer of Peele than of Shakespeare. Even Shakespeare could not often outdo Marlowe in a sort of economy of majesty, the grandeur of a huge blank cliff-face, or of the empty welkin itself. But as his meaning is more complex, farther-ranging, more intricately developed than theirs, so are his versification and his form. The incomparable skill that was to achieve such things as

Peace, peace!
Dost thou not see my baby at my breast
That sucks the nurse asleep?

or the famous *Tempest* passage about "such stuff as dreams are made on," confronts us in the making (and a very rapid making) quite early. We find it in the quaint euphuisms of *Love's Labour's Lost*, in the unequal speeches of the *Two Gentlemen*, even in such a partly farcical medley as the *Comedy of Errors*, and such an ill-mingled mass of farce and tragedy as *Measure for Measure*. The real Shakespeare cannot help showing himself, if only by a flash of verse here and there; and then we are in presence of something new—of a kind of English poetry that no one has hit upon before, and which, as we cannot but feel, is revolutionising the whole structure and character of Englisli verse. He may rhyme, or he may not rhyme, or he may turn to prose; but always there is the new phrase, the new language, conceited to the despair of pedants, playing on words in a fashion maddening to dullards, not always impeccable from the stricter standpoints of taste, but always instinct with creative genius.

In respect of construction and dramatic conception these early works, as we might expect, are less advanced. The chronicle-play of its nature defies construction of the ordinary kind, though sometimes, as in Marlowe's *Edward II.* and Shakespeare's two *Richards*, the actual story may be short and central enough to give something like definite plot. It is, however, remarkable how Shakespeare contrives to infuse into these chronicles, or, as they may be not inaccurately termed, these dramatic romances, something of the unity of the regular play or dramatic epic. He will do it by the most various means—sometimes as in *King John*, by the contrasted attraction of the tragedy of Constance and Arthur and the comedy of the Bastard Falconbridge; sometimes, as in *Henry IV.*, by the inclusion of a non-historical character, like Falstaff, of the very first interest and importance, with the subsidiaries necessary to set it off; sometimes, as in *Henry V.*, by projecting an idea (in this case the patriotic idea of England) in such a fashion that the whole of the play, humours and all, imposes it on the spectator. But in the miscellaneous plays there is much less unity of construction, and, as yet, the romantic attraction of character is not quite secured. The defeat of the project of seclusion from womankind in *Love's Labour's Lost* might hardly, in any case, have been sufficient by itself, and is certainly not made sufficient; the play, agreeable as it is, loses itself in humours, and episodes, and single combats of wit and love. The central story of the *Two Gentlemen* is not more than enough for an ordinary *nouvelle*, and it may be questioned whether that of *Romeo and Juliet* is in itself much more. But this latter is quintessenced, and exalted to the heavens, by the pure and intense poetic quality of its verse, by the pity of it in the case of the hero and still more the heroine, and by the contrasted flashes of wit and gallantry in Mercutio and Tybalt and the rest. So in the other and lighter masterpiece, *A Midsummer Night's Dream*, which probably belongs to this period, the subtle fidelity to the dream-nature perhaps makes it unnecessary to give, but certainly as a matter of fact excludes, any elaborate character-drawing. Indeed, always and everywhere at this period, Shakespeare's character is far ahead of his plot. Some indeed, to whom critical adhesion can here by no means be given, would maintain that this was always the case, and that to the very last the dazzling and transcendent truth and mastery of the great personages help to blind the reader to the want of that "clockwork" excellence of construction which Jonson could perhaps already give, and was certainly to give before Shakespeare's death. Let it rather be said that Shakespeare at this time had not quite acquired the art of constructing up to his character-level; that later, when he had learnt it, he never cared to give more construction than was necessary for his characters; and that in this he was right. It may be questioned—heresy as the statement will seem to some—whether construction, pitched to the perfection of *The Silent Woman* or of *Tom Jones*, is not something of a *tour de force*, and whether it does not deserve Bacon's pleasant sneer in another matter, "you may see as good sights in tarts." Life does not consider or contrive so curiously. However this may be, Shakespeare at this time was certainly not "our best plotter"; he was already at times an almost perfect artist in character, as he was a quite perfect poet. Even in such "more rawer" work as the *Two Gentlemen*, "Who is Silvia?" does not more show us the master of lyric than Julia and Lance show us the master of the graver and the lighter, the more passionate and the more frivolous, psychology and ethology. Even in that unequal medley, *Measure for Measure*, the great scene between Isabel and Claudio so far transcends anything that English, anything that European, drama had had to show for nearly two thousand years, that in this special point of view it remains perhaps the most wonderful in Shakespeare. Marlowe has nothing like it; his greatest passages, psychologically speaking, are always monologues; he cannot even attempt the clash and play of soul with soul that is so miraculously given here. Yet, though the play (which some call a comedy!) is not known to have been acted till 1604, its general characteristics put it far earlier.

The second or middle division of plays may be said to be connected with the first by the link between *Henry IV.* and *Henry V.*,[1] the latest and most matured of the early batch, and the *Merry Wives of Windsor*, probably the first of the second. The *Merry Wives* itself is a curious study. It has failed to find favour with some, owing to a not ignoble dislike at seeing the degradation or discomfiture of Falstaff, but it must be remembered that Shakespeare, though never cruel with the morbid cruelty of the modern pessimist, is always perfectly awake to the facts of life. And, as a matter of fact, the bowls that Falstaff played involve the rubbers that are here depicted. It has also been a common saying that the play is little better than a farce. If so, it can only be said that Shakespeare very happily took or made the opportunity of showing how a farce also can pass under the species of eternity. How infinitely do the most farcical of the characters, such as Sir Hugh and Dr. Caius, excel the mere "Vices" of earlier playwrights! Who but Shakespeare had—we may almost say who but Shakespeare

has—made an immortal thing of a mere ass, a mere puff-ball of foolish froth like Slender? If Chaucer had had the dramatic as he had the narrative faculty and atmosphere he might have done Mrs. Quickly, who is a very near relative, in somewhat lower life, of the Wife of Bath, and rapidly ripening for her future experiences in Eastcheap. But Shallow is above even Chaucer, as are also the subtle differentiation between Mrs. Page and Mrs. Ford, and the half-dozen strokes which her creator judged sufficient for sweet Anne Page. As for Falstaff, it is mistaken affection which thinks him degraded, or "translated" Bottom-fashion. He is even as elsewhere, though under an unluckier star.

This completeness exhibits itself, not perhaps in more masterly fashion, but in a somewhat higher and more varied material, in the great trio of Romantic comedies which is supposed to represent the work of the last year or two of the sixteenth century—*Twelfth Night, Much Ado about Nothing,* and *As You Like It*. Whether this order represents the actual composition or not, it certainly represents an intellectual and literary progression of interest and value, though the steps between the three are not wide. *Twelfth Night*, like the *Merry Wives* though not quite to the same extent, is pure comedy with a leaning to farce. The exquisite delicacy of the character of Viola suffuses it with a more romantic tone; but the disasters of Malvolio are even less serious than Falstaff's, and the great appeal of the play lies wholly on the comical side, in the immortal characters of Sir Toby and Sir Andrew, in Feste, the first distinctly and peculiarly Shakespearian clown, in Maria the "youngest wren of nine," in the glorious fooling of the plot against the steward, and the minor Comedy of Errors put upon Viola and Sebastian. There is no touch of sadness, though the clown's final song of "The rain it raineth every day" gives a sort of warning note; the whole is sunny, and if less romantically imaginative than *A Midsummer Night's Dream*, it is almost as romantically fanciful.

*Much Ado about Nothing* changes us from pure comedy to the tragi-comic—indeed, to what threatens at one time to be tragedy undiluted. Perhaps here only, or here and in the *Winter's Tale*, Shakespeare has used tragedy to heighten his comedy, just as he habitually does the opposite; and the effect is good. But it is for the lighter side—for the peerless farce of Dogberry, the almost peerless comedy proper of Benedick and Beatrice—that we love the play. And the attraction of this couple, anticipated very early in Rosaline and Biron, is used yet again and with absolutely supreme success in *As You Like It*, one of the topmost things in Shakespeare, the masterpiece of romantic comedy, one of the great type-dramas of the world. Here, as in so many other places, Shakespeare borrowed his theme, and even no small part of his minor situations; but this matters nothing. The *Tale of Gamelyn* is pleasant and vigorous; Lodge's *Rosalynde* is ingenious and fantastically artistic. But *As You Like It* is part of the little "library of La Quinte"—of the few books exhibiting imagination and expression equally married. Rosalind and Touchstone stand, each in his or her own way, alone.

The apparent change in the subject and temper of Shakespeare's work at the beginning of the seventeenth century has been the subject of much idle talk. There is no more reason to believe that he was specially and personally merry when he wrote this group of comedies, than there is to believe that he was sad or embittered during the period which produced *Julius Caesar, Hamlet, Othello, Lear, Macbeth, Antony and Cleopatra*—to which some would add *Troilus and Cressida, Timon,* and even *Measure for Measure,* as well as *Coriolanus*. To the present writer it is pretty certain that *Measure for*

*Measure, Timon,* and *Troilus and Cressida* represent much earlier work, whether or no they had been actually produced. The three Roman plays, *Julius Caesar, Coriolanus,* and *Antony and Cleopatra,* make an interesting section to themselves, which in *Antony and Cleopatra* almost passes into that of romantic tragedy, and so joins the supreme quartette, *Hamlet, Macbeth, Othello,* and *Lear.* In all the Roman plays Shakespeare applied his English-chronicle method pretty exactly to the material that he found in North's *Plutarch,* and, since his faculties both of stage-management and of versification were now in complete maturity, with the noblest effect. But in character he does not create much, he only interprets— till we come to the "Serpent of old Nile" and her lover, who are neither the crowned wanton and besotted debauchee of uninspired history, nor the anti-Roman sorceress and victim of Horace's craven-crowing ode, but a real hero and heroine of romance, luckless though not blameless, sympathetic though not ill served.

Much, however, even of *Antony and Cleopatra* is only chronicle, and like the other two, great as they are, falls beneath the magnificent creation of the four great romantic tragedies. In each of these, of course, Shakespeare had again his authorities, and, as his wont, he sometimes followed them closely. But the interest of the four does not depend in the very least upon Cinthio or Saxo, upon Geoffrey or Holinshed. Here, as in the great companion comedies, the dramatist breaks quite free; his real themes are human passion and human action at large, caught and embodied for the nonce in individual character and fate. Nowhere else does even Shakespeare lavish his resources as he does in these four plays, and certainly in none does he manifest such power of displaying the irony of life and fate. Viewed from one standpoint, all four are as well entitled to the motto "Vanity of vanities" as Ecclesiastes itself. The love, the heroism, and the great leading qualities of Othello and Macbeth, the filial duty and intellectual subtlety of Hamlet, the generous if reckless and passionate *bonhomie* of Lear, all make shipwreck against the rocks thrown in their way by inauspicious stars, and sought out too often by their own mistakes and crimes. With that supreme genius which distinguishes him from the common playwright, Shakespeare has never made his heroes or heroines types; and this has puzzled many, and driven not a few to despairing efforts to make them out types after all. It is exactly what they are not. Shakespeare was no duped or duping preacher of the ruling passion like his second editor. *Othello* is indeed the simplest of the four; but even here the character of Iago, which is almost as complex as that of Hamlet, invites a great, from some the greater, part of the interest.

Those who would make Hamlet a mere irresolute, a mere Waverley, not only do not supply a full explanation of him even in their terms, but forget that irresolution, at least such as his, is the most complex of qualities. The inability of the will to "let itself go" is partly caused by, much more complicated with, the inability of the intellect to decide. To compare *Lear* with the wretched other play[2] on the subject, which is beyond all doubt anterior, or with Holinshed, or with Geoffrey's original, is perhaps the very best single means of appreciating the infinite variety and intricacy of Shakespeare's knowledge and expression of humanity. Although the hapless King is always in the Latin sense impotent—incapable of resisting the impulse of the moment—this fault of his is conditioned, coloured, transformed at every instant by circumstances, many of them Shakespeare's own invention, and all rearranged with new effects by him. The gifting, the unexpected fractiousness of Cordelia (and let it be remembered that Cordelia is not a

perfect character, that she is as hyper-frank as her sisters are hypocritical), the petty insults at Goneril's, the bolder outrage at Gloster's under the orders of Regan and Cornwall, the terrors of the storm, and the talk (dangerous to already tottering wits) of the sham madman, the rescue even as it is too late, the second fall into the hands of his enemies, and the final blow in the murder of Cordelia—all these engines, all these reagents, the dramatist applies to Lear's headstrong petulance with the most unvarying precision of science, the most unfailing variety of art. We have the ungovernable king and ex-king in twenty different "states," in twenty different relations and presentments, all connected by the central inexorable story. And so in *Macbeth* the hero—ambitious, uxorious, intensely under the influence of nerves and of imagination, as different from the mere "butcher" of Malcolm's insult as his greater but not less complex-souled wife is from a "fiendlike queen" passes before us whole and real, terrible but exact, before, at the crisis of, and in his criminal stage, at once with the fluttering and phantasmagoric variety of a dream, and with an utterly solid and continuous story-interest. The Macbeth who is excited by the prophecy of the witches is exactly the same Macbeth as he who shrinks from the visioned dagger, as he who is struck to a kind of numb philosophising by the cry of women that announces his wife's death.

Of the numberless and magnificent passages of our poetry which these four plays contain it were vain to attempt to speak. It must be sufficient to say that in them the Shakespearian line, which, with its absolute freedom of shifting the pause from the first syllable to the last, its almost absolute freedom of syllabic equivalence, and the infinite variety of cadence which the use of these two means (and no doubt some magic besides) allowed it to attain, is the central fact of English poetry—this line came to its very farthest. We only observe in the plays of the last six or seven years of his life one change, and that not a quite certain one, the inclination to greater indulgence in the redundant syllable which is so exceedingly noticeable in his successors in romantic drama, Beaumont and Fletcher. It is pretty certain that this license, which he had always used to some extent, would never in his hands have reached the excess which we find in them, and which in their followers simply disbands the line into loose ungirt prose, with some reminiscences of verse here and there. But it cannot be considered on the whole an improvement.

The plays of, or probably belonging to, the last period of Shakespeare's life are fewer in proportion than those of either of the preceding periods, but those of them that are certain present interesting characteristics. These are *Cymbeline,* the *Winter's Tale,* and *The Tempest,* the others being *Henry VIII.* and *Pericles.* This last play, which was not included in the first folio of 1623 by Shakespeare's friends and colleagues, Heminge and Condell, presents curious difficulties. Great part of it *must* be Shakespeare's; there is perhaps no part that *might* not be; and the general characteristics of story-management and versification are a very odd mixture of his earliest and his latest manner— a *Love's Labour's Lost* blended with a *Winter's Tale.* Nor do I at least see reason for refusing any part of *Henry VIII.* to Shakespeare, though the prominence of the redundant syllable has made many ascribe it in large part to Fletcher. But about the other three there is no doubt, and certainly there is more excuse than usual for those who read in them a special index of the author's temper in these his last days—of the "calmed and calming *mens adepta*" whereof Fulke Greville speaks. *Cymbeline* partakes somewhat of the same character as the earlier *Much Ado about Nothing.* It is very nearly a tragedy—indeed, unlike *Much Ado about Nothing,* it contains accomplished tragic incidents in the deaths of the Queen and Cloten. But as far as the interesting personages—Imogen, Iachimo, Posthumus—are concerned, the tragedy is averted, and the whole deserves the name of romantic *drame* in the French sense.

This word, indeed, exactly describes these last three plays, and with ever-increasing appropriateness. Pedants of the bookish theoric of playwright craftsmanship have found fault with the construction of *Cymbeline*, which is admittedly loose, like its fellows—a chronicle or romance rather than an epic, but perfectly sufficient for its own object and purposes. The backbone of *A Winter's Tale* is a little more carefully and distinctly vertebrated, though no doubt the action is rather improbably prolonged, and the statue-scene, in which Hermione is restored to Leontes, does not entirely atone by its extreme beauty for its equally extreme improbability. But here, as always, Shakespeare has done what he meant to do; and here, as always, it is the extremity of critical impertinence to demand from an author not what he meant to do but something that the critic thinks he might, could, should, or ought to have meant. The vivid truth of the Queen's frank courtesy, Leontes' jealous rage (so different from Othello's, yet equally lifelike), the fine lurid presentment of the "coast" of Bohemia, the exquisitely idyllic (a word much abused, yet here applicable) figure of Perdita, the inimitable *brio* of Autolycus, the pendant to Touchstone—to give all these and other things in a pleasing series was what the dramatist intended to do, and he did it.

The splendour of sunset in *The Tempest* can escape no one, and the sternest opponent of guesswork must admit the probable presence of a designed allegory in the figure of Prospero and the burying of the book, the breaking of the staff, at the close. Even if this be thought too fanciful, nowhere has Shakespeare been more prodigal of every species of his enchantment. The exquisite but contrasted grace of Miranda and Ariel, the wonderful creation of Caliban, the varied human criticism in Gonzalo and the bad brothers, the farce-comedy of Stephano and Trinculo, do not more show the illimitable fancy and creative power of the master in scene and character than the passages, not so much scattered as showered over the whole play, show his absolute supremacy in poetry. Both in the blank verse and the lyrics, in the dialogue and the set *tirades*, in long contexts and short phrases alike, he shows himself absolute, with nothing out of reach of his faculty of expression and suggestion, with every resource of verbal music and intellectual demonstration at his command.

The so-called doubtful plays[3] of Shakespeare form an interesting subject, but one which can be dealt with but briefly here. As attributed by older tradition and assertion or by modern guesswork, they amount to "some dozen or sixteen," of which only three, the *Two Noble Kinsmen*, usually printed as Beaumont and Fletcher's, *Edward III.*, and *Arden of Feversham*, have any serious claims, though some have seen such in the *Yorkshire Tragedy*, a curious little horror-piece which, however, a dozen other men might have written. Others again, *Fair Em*, *Locrine*, *Sir John Oldcastle*, have absolutely nothing but unauthoritative though pretty ancient assertion to recommend them. As for the excepted three, the *Two Noble Kinsmen*, a dramatisation of Chaucer's *Knight's Tale*, has no suggestion of Shakespeare as a whole, but in parts shows extraordinary similarity to his versification. This has tempted some to think that Shakespeare may by chance have found his younger contemporaries (Beaumont, be it remembered, died in the same year with him) working at the play, have looked at it, and have mended or patched here and there

for amusement or out of good-nature. *Edward III.* has the same similarities of versification, and in part, though a small part, of handling, but it is more suggestive of an extraordinarily clever piece of imitation or inspiration than of actual Shakespearian authorship. *Arden of Feversham*, on the other hand, has no similarities of versification, and does not, in its dealing with the murder of a husband by his wife and her baseborn paramour, suggest Shakespeare's choice of subject, but is closer in some ways than any other play to his handling in character and psychological analysis.

*Notes*

1. It is well to say nothing about *Henry VI.*, because, though I have no doubt that this trilogy is, as we have it, in the main Shakespeare's, it is also beyond all doubt, and beyond all others, a refashioning of earlier plays.
2. To be found, with other similar apparatus, in Hazlitt's *Shakespeare's Library*.
3. It was not till 1908 that a Shakespearian *Apocrypha*, containing 14 plays, was supplied by the Clarendon Press (Oxford, ed. C. F. Tucker-Brooke). Before this they were scattered in Hazlitt's *Dodsley*, Simpson's *School of Shakespeare*, and elsewhere; though there was a German edition (Halle, 1878–81) and a single vol. reprint (London, *n.d.*) of the plays added in the later folios.

## GEORGE SANTAYANA
### "The Absence of Religion in Shakespeare"
*Interpretations of Poetry and Religion*
1900, pp. 147–65

We are accustomed to think of the universality of Shakespeare as not the least of his glories. No other poet has given so many-sided an expression to human nature, or rendered so many passions and moods with such an appropriate variety of style, sentiment, and accent. If, therefore, we were asked to select one monument of human civilization that should survive to some future age, or be transported to another planet to bear witness to the inhabitants there of what we have been upon earth, we should probably choose the works of Shakespeare. In them we recognize the truest portrait and best memorial of man. Yet the archæologists of that future age, or the cosmographers of that other part of the heavens, after conscientious study of our Shakesperian autobiography, would misconceive our life in one important respect. They would hardly understand that man had had a religion.

There are, indeed, numerous exclamations and invocations in Shakespeare which we, who have other means of information, know to be evidences of current religious ideas. Shakespeare adopts these, as he adopts the rest of his vocabulary, from the society about him. But he seldom or never gives them their original value. When Iago says "'sblood," a commentator might add explanations which should involve the whole philosophy of Christian devotion; but this Christian sentiment is not in Iago's mind, nor in Shakespeare's, any more than the virtues of Heracles and his twelve labours are in the mind of every slave and pander that cries "*hercule*" in the pages of Plautus and Terence. Oaths are the fossils of piety. The geologist recognizes in them the relics of a once active devotion, but they are now only counters and pebbles tossed about in the unconscious play of expression. The lighter and more constant their use, the less their meaning.

Only one degree more inward than this survival of a religious vocabulary in profane speech is the reference we often find in Shakespeare to religious institutions and traditions.

There are monks, bishops, and cardinals; there is even mention of saints, although none is ever presented to us in person. The clergy, if they have any wisdom, have an earthly one. Friar Lawrence culls his herbs like a more benevolent Medea; and Cardinal Wolsey flings away ambition with a profoundly Pagan despair; his robe and his integrity to heaven are cold comfort to him. Juliet goes to shrift to arrange her love affairs, and Ophelia should go to a nunnery to forget hers. Even the chastity of Isabella has little in it that would have been out of place in Iphigenia. The metaphysical Hamlet himself sees a "true ghost," but so far reverts to the positivism that underlines Shakespeare's thinking as to speak soon after of that "undiscovered country from whose bourn no traveller returns."

There are only two or three short passages in the plays, and one sonnet, in which true religious feeling seems to break forth. The most beautiful of these passages is that in *Richard II*, which commemorates the death of Mowbray, Duke of Norfolk:—

> Many a time hath banished Norfolk fought
> For Jesu Christ in glorious Christian field,
> Streaming the ensign of the Christian cross
> Against black Pagans, Turks, and Saracens;
> And, toiled with works of war, retired himself
> To Italy; and there, at Venice, gave
> His body to that pleasant country's earth,
> And his pure soul unto his captain Christ,
> Under whose colours he had fought so long.

This is tender and noble, and full of an indescribable chivalry and pathos, yet even here we find the spirit of war rather than that of religion, and a deeper sense of Italy than of heaven. More unmixed is the piety of Henry V after the battle of Agincourt:—

> O God, thy arm was here;
> And not to us, but to thy arm alone,
> Ascribe was all!—When, without stratagem,
> But in plain shock and even play of battle,
> Was ever known so great and little loss,
> On one part and on the other?—Take it, God,
> For it is none but thine. . . .
> Come, go we in procession to the village,
> And be it death proclaimed through our host,
> To boast of this, or take that praise from God,
> Which is his only. . . .
>                     Do we all holy rites;
> Let there be sung *Non nobis* and *Te Deum*.

This passage is certainly a true expression of religious feeling, and just the kind that we might expect from a dramatist. Religion appears here as a manifestation of human nature and as an expression of human passion. The passion, however, is not due to Shakespeare's imagination, but is essentially historical: the poet has simply not rejected, as he usually does, the religious element in the situation he reproduces.[1]

With this dramatic representation of piety we may couple another, of a more intimate kind, from the Sonnets:—

> Poor soul, the centre of my sinful earth,
> Fooled by these rebels powers that thee array,
> Why dost thou pine within and suffer dearth,
> Painting thy outward walls so costly gay?
> Why so large cost, having so short a lease,
> Dost thou upon thy fading mansion spend?
> Shall worms, inheritors of this excess,
> Eat up thy charge? Is this thy body's end?
> Then, soul, live thou upon thy servant's loss,
> And let that pine to aggravate thy store;
> Buy terms divine by selling hours of dross,

> Within be fed, without be rich no more:
> Then shalt thou feed on death, that feeds on men,
> And death once dead, there's no more dying then.

This sonnet contains more than a natural religious emotion inspired by a single event. It contains reflection, and expresses a feeling not merely dramatically proper but rationally just. A mind that habitually ran into such thoughts would be philosophically pious; it would be spiritual. The Sonnets, as a whole, are spiritual; their passion is transmuted into discipline. Their love, which, whatever its nominal object, is hardly anything but love of beauty and youth in general, is made to triumph over time by a metaphysical transformation of the object into something eternal. At first this is the beauty of the race renewing itself by generation, then it is the description of beauty in the poet's verse, and finally it is the immortal soul enriched by the contemplation of that beauty. This noble theme is the more impressively rendered by being contrasted with another, with a vulgar love that by its nature refuses to be so transformed and transmuted. "Two loves," cries the poet, in a line that gives us the essence of the whole, "Two loves I have,—of comfort, and despair."

In all this depth of experience, however, there is still wanting any religious image. The Sonnets are spiritual, but, with the doubtful exception of the one quoted above, they are not Christian. And, of course, a poet of Shakespeare's time could not have found any other mould than Christianity for his religion. In our day, with our wide and conscientious historical sympathies, it may be possible for us to find in other rites and doctrines than those of our ancestors an expression of some ultimate truth. But for Shakespeare, in the matter of religion, the choice lay between Christianity and nothing. He chose nothing; he chose to leave his heroes and himself in the presence of life and of death with no other philosophy than that which the profane world can suggest and understand.

This positivism, we need hardly say, was not due to any grossness or sluggishness in his imagination. Shakespeare could be idealistic when he dreamed, as he could be spiritual when he reflected. The spectacle of life did not pass before his eyes as a mere phantasmagoria. He seized upon its principles; he became wise. Nothing can exceed the ripeness of his seasoned judgment, or the occasional breadth, sadness, and terseness of his reflection. The author of *Hamlet* could not be without metaphysical aptitude; *Macbeth* could not have been written without a sort of sibylline inspiration, or the Sonnets without something of the Platonic mind. It is all the more remarkable, therefore, that we should have to search through all the works of Shakespeare to find half a dozen passages that have so much as a religious sound, and that even these passages, upon examination, should prove not to be the expression of any deep religious conception. If Shakespeare had been without metaphysical capacity, or without moral maturity, we could have explained his strange insensibility to religion; but as it is, we must marvel at his indifference and ask ourselves what can be the causes of it. For, even if we should not regard the absence of religion as an imperfection in his own thought, we must admit it to be an incompleteness in his portrayal of the thought of others. Positivism may be a virtue in a philosopher, but it is a vice in a dramatist, who has to render those human passions to which the religious imagination has always given a larger meaning and a richer depth.

Those greatest poets by whose side we are accustomed to put Shakespeare did not forego this advantage. They gave us man with his piety and the world with its gods. Homer is the chief repository of the Greek religion, and Dante the faithful interpreter of the Catholic. Nature would have been inconceivable to them without the supernatural, or man without the influence and companionship of the gods. These poets live in a cosmos. In their minds, as in the mind of their age, the fragments of experience have fallen together into a perfect picture, like the bits of glass in a kaleidoscope. Their universe is a total. Reason and imagination have mastered it completely and peopled it. No chaos remains beyond, or, if it does, it is thought of with an involuntary shudder that soon passes into a healthy indifference. They have a theory of human life; they see man in his relations, surrounded by a kindred universe in which he fills his allotted place. He knows the meaning and issue of his life, and does not voyage without a chart.

Shakespeare's world, on the contrary, is only the world of human society. The cosmos eludes him; he does not seem to feel the need of framing that idea. He depicts human life in all its richness and variety, but leaves that life without a setting, and consequently without a meaning. If we asked him to tell us what is the significance of the passion and beauty he had so vividly displayed, and what is the outcome of it all, he could hardly answer in any other words than those he puts into he mouth of Macbeth:—

> To-morrow, and to-morrow, and to-morrow,
> Creeps in this petty pace from day to day,
> To the last syllable of recorded time;
> And all our yesterdays have lighted fools
> The way to dusty death. Out, out, brief candle!
> Life's but a walking shadow, a poor player
> That struts and frets his hour upon the stage
> And then is heard no more: it is a tale
> Told by an idiot, full of sound and fury,
> Signifying nothing.

How differently would Homer or Dante have answered that question! Their tragedy would have been illumined by a sense of the divinity of life and beauty, or by a sense of the sanctity of suffering and death. Their faith had enveloped the world of experience in a world of imagination, in which the ideals of the reason, of the fancy, and of the heart had a natural expression. They had caught in the reality the hint of a lovelier fable,—a fable in which that reality was completed and idealized, and made at once vaster in its extent and more intelligible in its principle. They had, as it were, dramatized the universe, and endowed it with the tragic unities. In contrast with such a luminous philosophy and so well-digested an experience, the silence of Shakespeare and his philosophical incoherence have something in them that is still heathen; something that makes us wonder whether the northern mind, even in him, did not remain morose and barbarous at its inmost core.

But before we allow ourselves such hasty and general inferences, we may well stop to consider whether there is not some simpler answer to our question. An epic poet, we might say, naturally deals with cosmic themes. He needs supernatural machinery because he depicts the movement of human affairs in their generality, as typified in the figures of heroes whose function it is to embody or overcome elemental forces. Such a poet's world is fabulous, because his inspiration is impersonal. But the dramatist renders the concrete reality of life. He has no need of a superhuman setting for his pictures. Such a setting would destroy the vitality of his creations. His plots should involve only human actors and human motives: the *deus ex machina* has always been regarded as an interloper on his stage. The passions of man are his all-sufficient material; he should weave his whole fabric out of them.

To admit the truth of all this would not, however, solve our problem. The dramatist cannot be expected to put cosmogonies on the boards. Miracle-plays become dramatic only when they become human. But the supernatural world, which the playwright does not bring before the footlights, may exist nevertheless in the minds of his characters and of his audience. He may refer to it, appeal to it, and imply it, in the actions and in the sentiments he attributes to his heroes. And if the comparison of Shakespeare with Homer or Dante on the score of religious inspiration is invalidated by the fact that he is a dramatist while they are epic poets, a comparison may yet be instituted between Shakespeare and other dramatists, from which his singular insensibility to religion will as readily appear.

Greek tragedy, as we know, is dominated by the idea of fate. Even when the gods do not appear in person, or where the service or neglect of them is not the moving cause of the whole play,—as it is in the *Bacchæ* and the *Hippolytus* of Euripides,—still the deep conviction of the limits and conditions of human happiness underlies the fable. The will of man fulfils the decrees of Heaven. The hero manifests a higher force than his own, both in success and in failure. The fates guide the willing and drag the unwilling. There is no such fragmentary view of life as we have in our romantic drama, where accidents make the meaningless happiness or unhappiness of a supersensitive adventurer. Life is seen whole, although in miniature. Its boundaries and its principles are studied more than its incidents. The human, therefore, everywhere merges with the divine. Our mortality, being sharply defined and much insisted upon, draws the attention all the more to that eternity of Nature and of law in which it is embosomed. Nor is the fact of superhuman control left for our reflection to discover; it is emphatically asserted in those oracles on which so much of the action commonly turns.

When the Greek religion was eclipsed by the Christian, the ancient way of conceiving the ultrahuman relations of human life became obsolete. It was no longer possible to speak with sincerity of the oracles and gods, of Nemesis and *hybris*. Yet for a long time it was not possible to speak in any other terms. The new ideas were without artistic definition, and literature was paralyzed. But in the course of ages, when the imagination had had time and opportunity to develop a Christian art and a Christian philosophy, the dramatic poets were ready to deal with the new themes. Only their readiness in this respect surpassed their ability, at least their ability to please those who had any memory of the ancient perfection of the arts.

The miracle-plays were the beginning. Their crudity was extreme and their levity of the frankest; but they had still, like the Greek plays, a religious excuse and a religious background. They were not without dramatic power, but their offences against taste and their demands upon faith were too great for them to survive the Renaissance. Such plays as the *Polyeucte* of Corneille and the *Devocion de la Cruz* of Calderon, with other Spanish plays that might be mentioned, are examples of Christian dramas by poets of culture; but as a whole we must say that Christianity, while it succeeded in expressing itself in painting and in architecture, failed to express itself in any adequate drama. Where Christianity was strong, the drama either disappeared or became secular; and it has never again dealt with cosmic themes successfully, except in such hands as those of Goethe and Wagner, men who either neglected Christianity altogether or used it only as an incidental ornament, having, as they say, transcended it in their philosophy.

The fact is, that art and reflection have never been able to unite perfectly the two elements of a civilization like ours, that draws its culture from one source and its religion from another.

Modern taste has ever been, and still is, largely exotic, largely a revolution in favour of something ancient or foreign. The more cultivated a period has been, the more wholly it has reverted to antiquity for its inspiration. The existence of that completer world has haunted all minds struggling for self-expression, and interfered, perhaps, with the natural development of their genius. The old art which they could not disregard distracted them from the new ideal, and prevented them from embodying this ideal outwardly; while the same idea, retaining their inward allegiance, made their revivals of ancient forms artificial and incomplete. The strange idea could thus gain admittance that art was not called to deal with everything; that its sphere was the world of polite conventions. The serious and the sacred things of life were to be left unexpressed and inarticulate; while the arts masqueraded in the forms of a Pagan antiquity, to which a triviality was at the same time attributed which in fact it had not possessed. This unfortunate separation of experience and its artistic expression betrayed itself in the inadequacy of what was beautiful and the barbarism of what was sincere.

When such are the usual conditions of artistic creation, we need not wonder that Shakespeare, a poet of the Renaissance, should have confined his representation of life to its secular aspects, and that his readers after him should rather have marvelled at the variety of the things of which he showed an understanding than have taken note of the one thing he overlooked. To omit religion was after all to omit what was not felt to be congenial to a poet's mind. The poet was to trace for us the passionate and romantic embroideries of life; he was to be artful and humane, and above all he was to be delightful. The beauty and charm of things had nothing any longer to do with those painful mysteries and contentions which made the temper of the pious so acrid and sad. In Shakespeare's time and country, to be religious already began to mean to be Puritanical; and in the divorce between the fulness of life on the one hand and the depth and unity of faith on the other, there could be no doubt to which side a man of imaginative instincts would attach himself. A world of passion and beauty without a meaning must seem to him more interesting and worthy than a world of empty principle and dogma, meagre, fanatical, and false. It was beyond the power of synthesis possessed by that age and nation to find a principle of all passion and a religion of all life.

This power of synthesis is indeed so difficult and rare that the attempt to gain it is sometimes condemned as too philosophical, and as tending to embarrass the critical eye and creative imagination with futile theories. We might say, for instance, that the absence of religion in Shakespeare was a sign of his good sense; that a healthy instinct kept his attention within the sublunary world; and that he was in that respect superior to Homer and to Dante. For, while they allowed their wisdom to clothe itself in fanciful forms, he gave us his in its immediate truth, so that he embodied what they signified. The supernatural machinery of their poems was, we might say, an accidental incumbrance, a traditional means of expression, which they only half understood, and which made their representation of life indirect and partly unreal. Shakespeare, on the other hand, had reached his poetical majority and independence. He rendered human experience no longer through symbols, but by direct imaginative representation. What I have treated as a limitation in him would, then, appear as the maturity of his strength.

There is always a class of minds in whom the spectacle of history produces a certain apathy of reason. They flatter themselves that they can escape defeat by not attempting the highest tasks. We need not here stop to discuss what value as truth a philosophical synthesis may hope to attain, nor have we to protest against the æsthetic preference for the sketch and the episode over a reasoned and unified rendering of life. Suffice it to say that the human race hitherto, whenever it has reached a phase of comparatively high development and freedom, has formed a conception of its place in Nature, no less than of the contents of its life; and that this conception has been the occasion of religious sentiments and practices; and further, that every art, whether literary or plastic, has drawn its favourite themes from this religious sphere. The poetic imagination has not commonly stopped short of the philosophical in representing a superhuman environment of man.

Shakespeare, however, is remarkable among the greater poets for being without a philosophy and without a religion. In his drama there is no fixed conception of any forces, natural or moral, dominating and transcending our mortal energies. Whether this characteristic be regarded as a merit or as a defect, its presence cannot be denied. Those who think it wise or possible to refrain from searching for general principles, and are satisfied with the successive empirical appearance of things, without any faith in their rational continuity or completeness, may well see in Shakespeare their natural prophet. For he, too, has been satisfied with the successive description of various passions and events. His world, like the earth before Columbus, extends in an indefinite plane which he is not tempted to explore.

Those of us, however, who believe in circumnavigation, and who think that both human reason and human imagination require a certain totality in our views, and who feel that the most important thing in life is the lesson of it, and its relation to its own ideal,—we can hardly find in Shakespeare all that the highest poet could give. Fulness is not necessarily wholeness, and the most profuse wealth of characterization seems still inadequate as a picture of experience, if this picture is not somehow seen from above and reduced to a dramatic unity,—to that unity of meaning that can suffuse its endless details with something of dignity, simplicity, and peace. This is the imaginative power found in several poets we have mentioned,—the power that gives certain passages in Lucretius also their sublimity, as it gives sublimity to many passages in the Bible.

For what is required for theoretic wholeness is not this or that system but some system. Its value is not the value of truth, but that of victorious imagination. Unity of conception is an æsthetic merit no less than a logical demand. A fine sense of the dignity and pathos of life cannot be attained unless we conceive somehow its outcome and its relations. Without such a conception our emotions cannot be steadfast and enlightened. Without it the imagination cannot fulfil its essential function or achieve its supreme success. Shakespeare himself, had it not been for the time and place in which he lived, when religion and imagination blocked rather than helped each other, would perhaps have allowed more of a cosmic background to appear behind his crowded scenes. If the Christian in him was not the real man, at least the Pagan would have spoken frankly. The material forces of Nature, or their vague embodiment in some northern pantheon, would then have stood behind his heroes. The various movements of events would have appeared as incidents in a larger drama to which they had at least some symbolic relation. We should have been awed as well as saddened, and purified as well as pleased, by being made to feel the dependence of human accidents upon cosmic forces and their fated evolution. Then we should not have been able to say that Shakespeare was without a religion. For the effort of religion, says Goethe, is to adjust us to the inevitable; each religion in its way strives to bring about this consummation.

*Notes*

1. "And so aboute foure of the clocke in the afternoone, the Kynge when he saw no apparaunce of enemies, caused the retreite to be blowen, and gathering his army together, gave thanks to almightie god for so happy a victory, causing his prelates and chapleines to sing this psalm, *In exitu Israell de Egipto,* and commandyng every man to kneele downe on the grounde at this verse; *Non nobis, domine, non nobis, sed nomini tuo da gloriam.* Which done, he caused *Te Deum,* with certain anthems, to be song, giving laud & praise to god, and not boasting of his owne force or any humaine power." Holinshed.

## W. B. YEATS
### From "At Stratford-on-Avon" (1901)
#### *Ideas of Good and Evil*
#### 1903, pp. 152–64

### III

In *La Peau de chagrin* Balzac spends many pages in describing a coquette, who seems the image of heartlessness, and then invents an improbable incident that her chief victim may discover how beautifully she can sing. Nobody had ever heard her sing, and yet in her singing, and in her chatter with her maid, Balzac tells us, was her true self. He would have us understand that behind the momentary self, which acts and lives in the world, and is subject to the judgment of the world, there is that which cannot be called before any mortal Judgment seat, even though a great poet, or novelist, or philosopher be sitting upon it. Great literature has always been written in a like spirit, and is, indeed, the Forgiveness of Sin, and when we find it becoming the Accusation of Sin, as in George Eliot, who plucks her Tito in pieces with as much assurance as if he had been clockwork, literature has begun to change into something else. George Eliot had a fierceness one hardly finds but in a woman turned argumentative, but the habit of mind her fierceness gave its life to was characteristic of her century, and is the habit of mind of the Shakespearian critics. They and she grew up in a century of utilitarianism, when nothing about a man seemed important except his utility to the State, and nothing so useful to the State as the actions whose effect can be weighed by the reason. The deeds of Coriolanus, Hamlet, Timon, Richard II. had no obvious use, were, indeed, no more than the expression of their personalities, and so it was thought Shakespeare was accusing them, and telling us to be careful lest we deserve the like accusations. It did not occur to the critics that you cannot know a man from his actions, because you cannot watch him in every kind of circumstance, and that men are made useless to the State as often by abundance as by emptiness, and that a man's business may at times be revelation, and not reformation. Fortinbras was, it is likely enough, a better King than Hamlet would have been, Aufidius was a more reasonable man than Coriolanus, Henry V. was a better man-at-arms than Richard II., but after all, were not those others who changed nothing for the better and many things for the worse greater in the Divine Hierarchies? Blake has said that 'the roaring of lions, the howling of wolves, the raging of the stormy sea, and the destructive sword are portions of Eternity, too great for the eye of man,' but Blake belonged by right to the ages of Faith, and thought the State of less moment than the Divine Hierarchies. Because reason can only discover completely the use of those obvious actions which everybody admires, and because every character was to be judged by efficiency in action, Shakespearian criticism became a vulgar worshipper of Success. I have turned over many books in the library at Stratford-on-Avon, and I have found in nearly all an antithesis, which grew in clearness and violence as the century grew older, between two types, whose representatives were Richard II., 'sentimental,' 'weak,' 'selfish,' 'insincere,' and Henry V., 'Shakespeare's only hero.' These books took the same delight in abasing Richard II. that school-boys do in persecuting some boy of fine temperament, who has weak muscles and a distaste for school games. And they had the admiration for Henry V. that school-boys have for the sailor or soldier hero of a romance in some boys' paper. I cannot claim any minute knowledge of these books, but I think that these emotions began among the German critics, who perhaps saw something French and Latin in Richard II., and I know that Professor Dowden, whose book I once read carefully, first made these emotions eloquent and plausible. He lived in Ireland, where everything has failed, and he meditated frequently upon the perfection of character which had, he thought, made England successful, for, as we say, 'cows beyond the water have long horns.' He forgot that England, as Gordon has said, was made by her adventurers, by her people of wildness and imagination and eccentricity; and thought that Henry V., who only seemed to be these things because he had some commonplace vices, was not only the typical Anglo-Saxon, but the model Shakespeare held up before England; and he even thought it worth while pointing out that Shakespeare himself was making a large fortune while he was writing about Henry's victories. In Professor Dowden's successors this apotheosis went further; and it reached its height at a moment of imperialistic enthusiasm, of ever-deepening conviction that the commonplace shall inherit the earth, when somebody of reputation, whose name I cannot remember, wrote that Shakespeare admired this one character alone out of all his characters. The Accusation of Sin produced its necessary fruit, hatred of all that was abundant, extravagant, exuberant, of all that sets a sail for shipwreck, and flattery of the commonplace emotions and conventional ideals of the mob, the chief Paymaster of accusation.

### IV

I cannot believe that Shakespeare looked on his Richard II. with any but sympathetic eyes, understanding indeed how ill-fitted he was to be King, at a certain moment of history, but understanding that he was lovable and full of capricious fancy, 'a wild creature' as Pater has called him. The man on whom Shakespeare modelled him had been full of French elegancies, as he knew from Hollingshead, and had given life a new luxury, a new splendour, and been 'too friendly' to his friends, 'too favourable' to his enemies. And certainly Shakespeare had these things in his head when he made his King fail, a little because he lacked some qualities that were doubtless common among his scullions, but more because he had certain qualities that are uncommon in all ages. To suppose that Shakespeare preferred the men who deposed his King is to suppose that Shakespeare judged men with the eyes of a Municipal Councillor weighing the merits of a Town Clerk; and that had he been by when Verlaine cried out from his bed, 'Sir, you have been made by the stroke of a pen, but I have been made by the breath of God,' he would have thought the Hospital Superintendent the better man. He saw indeed, as I think, in Richard II. the defeat that awaits all, whether they be Artist or Saint, who find themselves where men ask of them a rough energy and have nothing to give but some contemplative virtue, whether lyrical phantasy, or sweetness of temper, or dreamy dignity, or love of God, or love of His creatures. He saw that such a man through sheer bewilderment and impatience can become as unjust or as violent as any common man, any Bolingbroke or Prince John, and yet remain 'that sweet lovely rose.' The courtly and saintly ideals of the Middle Ages were fading, and the practical ideals of the modern age had begun to threaten the unuseful dome of the sky; Merry England was fading, and yet it was not so faded that the Poets could not watch the procession of the world with that untroubled sympathy for men as they are, as apart from all they do and seem, which is the substance of tragic irony.

Shakespeare cared little for the State, the source of all our judgments, apart from its shows and splendours, its turmoils and battles, its flamings out of the uncivilized heart. He did indeed think it wrong to overturn a King, and thereby to swamp peace in civil war, and the historical plays from *Henry IV.* to *Richard III.*, that monstrous birth and last sign of the wrath of Heaven, are a fulfilment of the prophecy of the Bishop of Carlisle, who was 'raised up by God' to make it; but he had no nice sense of utilities, no ready balance to measure deeds, like that fine instrument, with all the latest improvements, Gervinus and Professor Dowden handle so skilfully. He meditated as Solomon, not as Bentham meditated, upon blind ambitions, untoward accidents, and capricious passions, and the world was almost as empty in his eyes as it must be in the eyes of God.

> Tired with all these, for restful death I cry;—
>     As to behold desert a beggar born,
> And needy nothing trimm'd in jollity,
>     And purest faith unhappily forsworn,
> And gilded honour shamefully misplaced,
>     And maiden virtue rudely strumpeted,
> And right perfection wrongfully disgrac'd,
>     And strength by limping sway disabled,
> And Art made tongue-tied by authority,
>     And folly, doctor-like, controlling skill,
> And simple truth miscalled simplicity,
>     And captive good attending captain ill:
> Tired of all these, from these would I begone
> Save that, to die, leave I my love alone.

### V

The Greeks, a certain scholar has told me, considered that myths are the activities of the Dæmons, and that the Dæmons shape our characters and our lives. I have often had the fancy that there is some one Myth for every man, which, if we but knew it, would make us understand all he did and thought. Shakespeare's Myth, it may be, describes a wise man who was blind from very wisdom, and an empty man who thrust him from his place, and saw all that could be seen from very emptiness. It is in the story of Hamlet, who saw too great issues everywhere to play the trivial game of life, and of Fortinbras, who came from fighting battles about 'a little patch of ground' so poor that one of his Captains would not give 'six ducats' to 'farm it,' and who was yet acclaimed by Hamlet and by all as the only befitting King. And it is in the story of Richard II., that unripened Hamlet, and of Henry V., that ripened Fortinbras. To poise character against character was an element in Shakespeare's art, and scarcely a play is lacking characters that are the complement of one another, and so, having made the vessel of porcelain Richard II., he had to make the vessel of clay Henry V. He makes him the reverse of all that Richard was. He has the gross vices, the coarse nerves, of one who is to rule among violent people, and he is so little 'too friendly' to his friends that he bundles them out of doors when their time is over. He is as remorseless and undistinguished as some natural force, and the finest thing in his play is the way his old companions fall out of it broken-hearted or on their way to the gallows; and instead of that lyricism which rose out of Richard's mind like the jet of a fountain to fall again where it had risen, instead of that phantasy too enfolded in its own sincerity to make any thought the hour had need of, Shakespeare has given him a resounding rhetoric that moves men, as a leading article does to-day. His purposes are so intelligible to everybody that everybody talks of him as if he succeeded, although he fails in the end, as all men great and little fail in Shakespeare, and yet his conquests abroad are made nothing by a woman turned warrior, and that boy he and Katherine were to 'compound,' 'half French, half English,' 'that' was to 'go to Constantinople and take the Turk by the beard,' turns out a Saint, and loses all his father had built up at home and his own life.

Shakespeare watched Henry V. not indeed as he watched the greater souls in the visionary procession, but cheerfully, as one watches some handsome spirited horse, and he spoke his tale, as he spoke all tales, with tragic irony.

### LYTTON STRACHEY
#### "Shakespeare's Final Period" (1904)
*Literary Essays*
1949, pp. 1–15

The whole of the modern criticism of Shakespeare has been fundamentally affected by one important fact. The chronological order of the plays, for so long the object of the vaguest speculation, of random guesses, or at best of isolated 'points,' has been now discovered and reduced to a coherent law. It is no longer possible to suppose that *The Tempest* was written before *Romeo and Juliet*; that *Henry VI* was produced in succession to *Henry V*; or that *Antony and Cleopatra* followed close upon the heels of *Julius Caesar*. Such theories were sent to limbo for ever, when a study of those plays of whose date we have external evidence revealed the fact that, as Shakespeare's life advanced, a corresponding development took place in the metrical structure of his verse. The establishment of metrical tests, by which the approximate position and date of any play can be readily ascertained, at once followed; chaos gave way to order; and, for the first time, critics became able to judge, not only of the individual works, but of the whole succession of the works of Shakespeare.

Upon this firm foundation modern writers have been only too eager to build. It was apparent that the Plays, arranged in chronological order, showed something more than a mere development in the technique of verse—a development, that is to say, in the general treatment of characters and subjects, and in the sort of feelings which those characters and subjects were intended to arouse; and from this it was easy to draw conclusions as to the development of the mind of Shakespeare itself. Such conclusions have, in fact, been constantly drawn. But it must be noted that they all rest upon the tacit assumption, that the character of any given drama is, in fact, a true index to the state of mind of the dramatist composing it. The validity of this assumption has never been proved; it has never been shown, for instance, why we should suppose a writer of farces to be habitually merry; or whether we are really justified in concluding, from the fact that Shakespeare wrote nothing but tragedies for six years, that, during that period, more than at any other, he was deeply absorbed in the awful problems of human existence. It is not, however, the purpose of this essay to consider the question of what are the relations between the artist and his art; for it will assume the truth of the generally accepted view, that the character of the one can be inferred from that of the other. What it will attempt to discuss is whether, upon this hypothesis, the most important part of the ordinary doctrine of Shakespeare's mental development is justifiable.

What then, is the ordinary doctrine? Dr. Furnivall states it as follows:

> Shakespeare's course is thus shown to have run from the amorousness and fun of youth, through the strong patriotism of early manhood, to the wrestlings with the dark problems that beset the man of middle age, to the gloom which weighed on Shakespeare (as on so many men) in later life, when, though outwardly successful, the world seemed all against him, and his mind dwelt with sympathy on scenes of faithlessness of friends, treachery of relations and subjects, ingratitude of children, scorn of his kind; till at last, in his Stratford home again, peace came to him, Miranda and Perdita in their lovely freshness and charm greeted him, and he was laid by his quiet Avon side.

And the same writer goes on to quote with approval Professor Dowden's

> likening of Shakespeare to a ship, beaten and storm-tossed, but yet entering harbour with sails full-set, to anchor in peace.

Such, in fact, is the general opinion of modern writers upon Shakespeare; after a happy youth and a gloomy middle age he reached at last—it is the universal opinion—a state of quiet serenity in which he died. Professor Dowden's book on *Shakespeare's Mind and Art* gives the most popular expression to this view, a view which is also held by Mr. ten Brink, by Sir I. Gollancz, and, to a great extent, by Dr. Brandes. Professor Dowden, indeed, has gone so far as to label this final period with the appellation of 'On the Heights,' in opposition to the preceding one, which, he says, was passed 'In the Depths.' Sir Sidney Lee, too, seems to find, in the Plays at least, if not in Shakespeare's mind, the orthodox succession of gaiety, of tragedy, and of the serenity of meditative romance.

Now it is clear that the most important part of this version of Shakespeare's mental history is the end of it. That he did eventually attain to a state of calm content, that he did, in fact, die happy—it is this that gives colour and interest to the whole theory. For some reason or another, the end of a man's life seems naturally to afford the light by which the rest of it should be read; last thoughts do appear in some strange way to be really best and truest; and this is particularly the case when they fit in nicely with the rest of the story, and are, perhaps, just what one likes to think oneself. If it be true that Shakespeare, to quote Professor Dowden, 'did at last attain to the serene self-possession which he had sought with such persistent effort'; that, in the words of Dr. Furnivall, 'forgiven and forgiving, full of the highest wisdom and peace, at one with family and friends and foes, in harmony with Avon's flow and Stratford's level meads, Shakespeare closed his life on earth'—we have obtained a piece of knowledge which is both interesting and pleasant. But if it be not true, if, on the contrary, it can be shown that something very different was actually the case, then will it not follow that we must not only reverse our judgment as to this particular point, but also readjust our view of the whole drift and bearing of Shakespeare's 'inner life'?

The group of works which has given rise to this theory of ultimate serenity was probably entirely composed after Shakespeare's final retirement from London, and his establishment at New Place. It consists of three plays—*Cymbeline, The Winter's Tale,* and *The Tempest*—and three fragments—the Shake-

spearean parts of *Pericles, Henry VIII,* and *The Two Noble Kinsmen.* All these plays and portions of plays form a distinct group; they resemble each other in a multitude of ways, and they differ in a multitude of ways from nearly all Shakespeare's previous work.

One other complete play, however, and one other fragment, do resemble in some degree these works of the final period; for, immediately preceding them in date, they show clear traces of the beginnings of the new method, and they are themselves curiously different from the plays they immediately succeed—that great series of tragedies which began with *Hamlet* in 1601 and ended in 1608 with *Antony and Cleopatra.* In the latter year, indeed, Shakespeare's entire method underwent an astonishing change. For six years he had been persistently occupied with a kind of writing which he had himself not only invented but brought to the highest point of excellence—the tragedy of character. Every one of his master-pieces has for its theme the action of tragic situation upon character; and, without those stupendous creations in character, his greatest tragedies would obviously have lost the precise thing that has made them what they are. Yet, after *Antony and Cleopatra* Shakespeare deliberately turned his back upon the dramatic methods of all his past career. There seems no reason why he should not have continued, year after year, to produce *Othellos, Hamlets,* and *Macbeths*; instead, he turned over a new leaf, and wrote *Coriolanus.*

*Coriolanus* is certainly a remarkable, and perhaps an intolerable play: remarkable, because it shows the sudden first appearance of the Shakespeare of the final period; intolerable, because it is impossible to forget how much better it might have been. The subject is thick with situations; the conflicts of patriotism and pride, the effects of sudden disgrace following upon the very height of fortune, the struggles between family affection on the one hand and every interest of revenge and egotism on the other—these would have made a tragic and tremendous setting for some character worthy to rank with Shakespeare's best. But it pleased him to ignore completely all these opportunities; and, in the play he has given us, the situations, mutilated and degraded, serve merely as miserable props for the gorgeous clothing of his rhetoric. For rhetoric, enormously magnificent and extraordinarily elaborate, is the beginning and the middle and the end of *Coriolanus.* The hero is not a human being at all; he is the statue of a demi-god cast in bronze, which roars its perfect periods, to use a phrase of Sir Walter Raleigh's, through a melodious megaphone. The vigour of the presentment is, it is true, amazing; but it is a presentment of decoration, not of life. So far and so quickly had Shakespeare already wandered from the subtleties of *Cleopatra.* The transformation is indeed astonishing; one wonders, as one beholds it, what will happen next.

At about the same time, some of the scenes in *Timon of Athens* were in all probability composed: scenes which resemble *Coriolanus* in their lack of characterisation and abundance of rhetoric, but differ from it in the peculiar grossness of their tone. For sheer virulence of foul-mouthed abuse, some of the speeches in *Timon* are probably unsurpassed in any literature; an outraged drayman would speak so, if draymen were in the habit of talking poetry. From this whirlwind of furious ejaculation, this splendid storm of nastiness, Shakespeare, we are confidently told, passed in a moment to tranquility and joy, to blue skies, to young ladies, and to general forgiveness.

> From 1604 to 1610 [says Professor Dowden] a show of tragic figures, like the kings who pass before Macbeth, filled the vision of Shakespeare; until at last the desperate image of Timon rose before him;

when, as though unable to endure or to conceive a more lamentable ruin of man, he turned for relief to the pastoral loves of Prince Florizel and Perdita; and as soon as the tone of his mind was restored, gave expression to its ultimate mood of grave serenity in *The Tempest*, and so ended.

This is a pretty picture, but is it true? It may, indeed, be admitted at once that Prince Florizel and Perdita are charming creatures, that Prospero is 'grave,' and that Hermione is more or less 'serene'; but why is it that, in our consideration of the later plays, the whole of our attention must always be fixed upon these particular characters? Modern critics, in their eagerness to appraise everything that is beautiful and good at its proper value, seem to have entirely forgotten that there is another side to the medal; and they have omitted to point out that these plays contain a series of portraits of peculiar infamy, whose wickedness finds expression in language of extraordinary force. Coming fresh from their pages to the pages of *Cymbeline, The Winter's Tale*, and *The Tempest*, one is astonished and perplexed. How is it possible to fit into their scheme of roses and maidens that 'Italian fiend' the 'yellow Iachimo,' or Cloten, that 'thing too bad for bad report,' or the 'crafty devil,' his mother, or Leontes, or Caliban, or Trinculo? To omit these figures of discord and evil from our consideration, to banish them comfortably to the background of the stage, while Autolycus and Miranda dance before the footlights, is surely a fallacy in proportion; for the presentment of the one group of persons is every whit as distinct and vigorous as that of the other. Nowhere, indeed, is Shakespeare's violence of expression more constantly displayed than in the 'gentle utterances' of his last period; it is here that one finds Paulina, in a torrent of indignation as far from 'grave serenity' as it is from 'pastoral love,' exclaiming to Leontes:

> What studied torments, tyrant, hast for me?
> What wheels? racks? fires? what flaying? boiling
> In leads or oils? what old or newer torture
> Must I receive, whose every word deserves
> To taste of thy most worst? Thy tyranny,
> Together working with thy jealousies,
> Fancies too weak for boys, too green and idle
> For girls of nine, O! think what they have done,
> And then run mad indeed, stark mad; for all
> Thy by-gone fooleries were but spices of it.
> That thou betray'dst Polixenes, 'twas nothing;
> That did but show thee, of a fool, inconstant
> And damnable ingrateful; nor was't much
> Thou would'st have poison'd good Camillo's honour,
> To have him kill a king; poor trespasses,
> More monstrous standing by; whereof I reckon
> The casting forth to crows thy baby daughter
> To be or none or little; though a devil
> Would have shed water out of fire ere done't.
> Nor is't directly laid to thee, the death
> Of the young prince, whose honourable thoughts,
> Thoughts high for one so tender, cleft the heart
> That could conceive a gross and foolish sire
> Blemished his gracious dam.

Nowhere are the poet's metaphors more nakedly material; nowhere does he verge more often upon a sort of brutality of phrase, a cruel coarseness. Iachimo tells us how:

> The cloyed will,
> That satiate yet unsatisfied desire, that tub
> Both filled and running, ravening first the lamb,
> Longs after for the garbage.

and talks of:

> an eye
> Base and unlustrous as the smoky light
> That's fed with stinking tallow.

'The south fog rot him!' Cloten burst out to Imogen, cursing her husband in an access of hideous rage.

What traces do such passages as these show of 'serene self-possession,' of 'the highest wisdom and peace,' or of 'meditative romance'? English critics, overcome by the idea of Shakespeare's ultimate tranquillity, have generally denied to him the authorship of the brothel scenes in *Pericles*; but these scenes are entirely of a piece with the grossness of *The Winter's Tale* and *Cymbeline*.

> Is there no way for men to be, but women
> Must be half-workers?

says Posthumus when he hears of Imogen's guilty

> We are all bastards;
> And that most venerable man, which I
> Did call my father, was I know not where
> When I was stamped. Some coiner with his tools
> Made me a counterfeit; yet my mother seemed
> The Dian of that time; so doth my wife
> The nonpareil of this—O vengeance, vengeance!
> Me of my lawful pleasure she restrained
> And prayed me, oft, forbearance; did it with
> A pudency so rosy, the sweet view on't
> Might well have warmed old Saturn, that I thought
>   her
> As chaste as unsunned snow—O, all the devils!—
> This yellow Iachimo, in an hour,—was't not?
> Or less,—at first: perchance he spoke not; but,
> Like a full-acorned boar, a German one,
> Cried, oh! and mounted: found no opposition
> But what he looked for should oppose, and she
> Should from encounter guard.

And Leontes, in a similar situation, expresses himself in images no less to the point.

> There have been,
> Or I am much deceived, cuckolds ere now,
> And many a man there is, even at this present,
> Now, while I speak this, holds his wife by the arm,
> That little thinks she has been sluiced in's absence
> And his pond fished by his next neighbour, by
> Sir Smile, his neighbour: nay, there's comfort in't,
> Whiles other men have gates, and those gates
>   opened,
> As mine, against their will. Should all despair
> That have revolted wives, the tenth of mankind
> Would hang themselves. Physic for't there's none;
> It is a bawdy planet, that will strike
> Where 'tis predominant; and 'tis powerful, think it,
> From east, west, north and south: be it concluded,
> No barricado for a belly, know't;
> It will let in and out the enemy
> With bag and baggage: many thousand on's
> Have the disease, and feel't not.

It is really a little difficult, in the face of such passages, to agree with Professor Dowden's dictum: 'In these latest plays the beautiful pathetic light is always present.'

But how has it happened that the judgment of so many critics has been so completely led astray? Charm and gravity, and even serenity, are to be found in many other plays of Shakespeare. Ophelia is charming, Brutus is grave, Cordelia is serene; are we then to suppose that *Hamlet*, and *Julius Caesar*, and *King Lear* give expression to the same mood of high tranquillity which is betrayed by *Cymbeline, The Tempest*, and *The Winter's Tale*? 'Certainly not,' reply the orthodox writers, 'for you must distinguish. The plays of the last period are not tragedies; they all end happily'—'in scenes,' says Sir. I. Gollancz, 'of forgiveness, reconciliation, and peace.' Virtue, in fact, is not only virtuous, it is triumphant; what would you more?

But to this it may be retorted, that, in the case of one of Shakespeare's plays, even the final vision of virtue and beauty triumphant over ugliness and vice fails to dispel a total effect of horror and of gloom. For, in *Measure for Measure* Isabella is no whit less pure and lovely than any Perdita or Miranda, and her success is as complete; yet who would venture to deny that the atmosphere of *Measure for Measure* was more nearly one of despair than of serenity? What is it, then, that makes the difference? Why should a happy ending seem in one case futile, and in another satisfactory? Why does it sometimes matter to us a great deal, and sometimes not at all, whether virtue is rewarded or not?

The reason, in this case, is not far to seek. *Measure for Measure* is, like nearly every play of Shakespeare's before *Coriolanus*, essentially realistic. The characters are real men and women; and what happens to them upon the stage has all the effect of what happens to real men and women in actual life. Their goodness appears to be real goodness, their wickedness real wickedness; and, if their sufferings are terrible enough, we regret the fact, even though in the end they triumph, just as we regret the real sufferings of our friends. But, in the plays of the final period, all this has changed; we are no longer in the real world, but in a world of enchantment, of mystery, of wonder, a world of shifting visions; a world of hopeless anachronisms, a world in which anything may happen next. The pretences of reality are indeed usually preserved, but only the pretences. Cymbeline is supposed to be the king of a real Britain, and the real Augustus is supposed to demand tribute of him; but these are the reasons which his queen, in solemn audience with the Roman ambassador, urges to induce her husband to declare for war:

> Remember, sir, my liege,
> The Kings your ancestors, together with
> The natural bravery of your isle, which stands
> As Neptune's park, ribbed and paled in
> With rocks unscaleable and roaring waters,
> With sands that will not bear your enemies' boats,
> But suck them up to the topmast. A kind of conquest
> Caesar made here; but made not here his brag
> Of 'Came, and saw, and overcame'; with shame—
> The first that ever touched him—he was carried
> From off our coast, twice beaten; and his shipping—
> Poor ignorant baubles!—on our terrible seas,
> Like egg-shells moved upon the surges, crack'd
> As easily 'gainst our rocks; for joy whereof
> The famed Cassibelan, who was once at point—
> O giglot fortune!—to master Caesar's sword,
> Made Lud's town with rejoicing fires bright
> And Britons strut with courage.

It comes with something of a shock to remember that this medley of poetry, bombast, and myth will eventually reach the ears of no other person than the Octavius of *Antony and Cleopatra*; and the contrast is the more remarkable when one recalls the brilliant scene of negotiation and diplomacy in the latter play, which passes between Octavius, Maecenas, and Agrippa on the one side, and Antony and Enobarbus on the other, and results in the reconciliation of the rivals and the marriage of Antony and Octavia.

Thus strangely remote is the world of Shakespeare's latest period; and it is peopled, this universe of his invention, with beings equally unreal, with creatures either more or less than human, with fortunate princes and wicked step-mothers, with goblins and spirits, with lost princesses and insufferable kings.

And of course, in this sort of fairy land, it is an essential condition that everything shall end well; the prince and princess are bound to marry and live happily ever afterwards, or the whole story is unnecessary and absurd; and the villains and the goblins must naturally repent and be forgiven. But it is clear that such happy endings, such conventional closes to fantastic tales, cannot be taken as evidences of serene tranquillity on the part of their maker; they merely show that he knew, as well as anyone else, how such stories ought to end.

Yet there can be no doubt that it is this combination of charming heroines and happy endings which has blinded the eyes of modern critics to everything else. Iachimo, and Leontes, and even Caliban, are to be left out of account, as if, because in the end they repent or are forgiven, words need not be wasted on such reconciled and harmonious fiends. It is true they are grotesque; it is true that such personages never could have lived; but who, one would like to know, has ever met Miranda, or become acquainted with Prince Florizel of Bohemia? In this land of faery, is it right to neglect the goblins? In this world of dreams, are we justified in ignoring the nightmares? Is it fair to say that Shakespeare was in 'a gentle, lofty spirit, a peaceful, tranquil mood,' when he was creating the Queen in *Cymbeline*, or writing the first two acts of *The Winter's Tale*?

Attention has never been sufficiently drawn to one other characteristic of these plays, though it is touched upon both by Professor Dowden and Dr. Brandes—the singular carelessness with which great parts of them were obviously written. Could anything drag more wretchedly than the *dénouement* of *Cymbeline*? And with what perversity is the great pastoral scene in *The Winter's Tale* interspersed with long-winded intrigues, and disguises, and homilies! For these blemishes are unlike the blemishes which enrich rather than lessen the beauty of the earlier plays; they are not, like them, interesting or delightful in themselves; they are usually merely necessary to explain the action, and they are sometimes purely irrelevant. One is, it cannot be denied, often bored, and occasionally irritated, by Polixenes and Camillo and Sebastian and Gonzalo and Belarius; these personages have not even the life of ghosts; they are hardly more than speaking names, that give patient utterance to involution upon involution. What a contrast to the minor characters of Shakespeare's earlier works!

It is difficult to resist the conclusion that he was getting bored himself. Bored with people, bored with real life, bored with drama, bored, in fact, with everything except poetry and poetical dreams. He is no longer interested, one often feels, in what happens, or who says what, so long as he can find place for a faultless lyric, or a new, unimagined rhythmical effect, or a grand and mystic speech. In this mood he must have written his share in *The Two Noble Kinsmen*, leaving the plot and characters to Fletcher to deal with as he pleased, and reserving to himself only the opportunities for pompous verse. In this mood he must have broken off halfway through the tedious history of *Henry VIII*; and in this mood he must have completed, with all the resources of his rhetoric, the miserable archaic fragment of *Pericles*.

Is it not thus, then, that we should imagine him in the last years of his life? Half enchanted by visions of beauty and loveliness, and half bored to death; on the one side inspired by a soaring fancy to the singing of ethereal songs, and on the other urged by a general disgust to burst occasionally through his torpor into bitter and violent speech? If we are to learn anything of his mind from his last works, it is surely this.

And such is the conclusion which is particularly forced upon us by a consideration of the play which is in many ways most typical of Shakespeare's later work, and the one which critics most consistently point to as containing the very essence of his final benignity—*The Tempest*. There can be no doubt that the peculiar characteristics which distinguish *Cymbeline* and *The Winter's Tale* from the dramas of Shakespeare's prime, are present here in a still greater degree. In *The Tempest*, unreality has reached its apotheosis. Two of the principal characters are frankly not human beings at all; and the whole action passes, through a series of impossible occurrences, in a place which can only by courtesy be said to exist. The Enchanted Island, indeed, peopled, for a timeless moment, by this strange fantastic medley of persons and of things, has been cut adrift for ever from common sense, and floats buoyed up by a sea, not of waters, but of poetry. Never did Shakespeare's magnificence of diction reach more marvellous heights than in some of the speeches of Prospero, or his lyric art a purer beauty than in the songs of Ariel; nor is it only in these ethereal regions that the triumph of his language asserts itself. It finds as splendid a vent in the curses of Caliban:

> All the infection that the sun sucks up
> From bogs, fens, flats, on Prosper fall, and make him
> By inch-meal a disease!

and in the similes of Trinculo:

> Yond' same black cloud, yond' huge one, looks like a
> foul bombard that would shed his liquor.

The *dénouement* itself, brought about by a preposterous piece of machinery, and lost in a whirl of rhetoric, is hardly more than a peg for fine writing.

> O, it is monstrous, monstrous!
> Methought the billows spoke and told of it;
> The winds did sing it to me; and the thunder,
> That deep and dreadful organ-pipe, pronounced
> The name of Prosper; it did bass my trespass.
> Therefore my son i' th' ooze is bedded, and
> I'll seek him deeper than e'er plummet sounded,
> And with him there lie mudded.

And this gorgeous phantasm of a repentance from the mouth of the pale phantom Alonzo is a fitting climax to the whole fantastic play.

A comparison naturally suggests itself, between what was perhaps the last of Shakespeare's completed works, and that early drama which first gave undoubted proof that his imagination had taken wings. The points of resemblance between *The Tempest* and *A Midsummer Night's Dream*, their common atmosphere of romance and magic, the beautiful absurdities of their intrigues, their studied contrasts of the grotesque with the delicate, the ethereal with the earthly, the charm of their lyrics, the *verve* of the vulgar comedy—these, of course, are obvious enough; but it is the points of difference which really make the comparison striking. One thing, at any rate, is certain about the wood near Athens—it is full of life. The persons that haunt it—though most of them are hardly more than children, and some of them are fairies, and all of them are too agreeable to be true—are nevertheless substantial creatures, whose loves and jokes and quarrels receive our thorough sympathy; and the air they breathe—the lords and the ladies, no less than the mechanics and the elves—is instinct with an exquisite good-humour, which makes us as happy as the night is long. To turn from Theseus and Titania and Bottom to the Enchanted Island, is to step out of a country lane into a conservatory. The roses and the dandelions have vanished before preposterous cactuses, and fascinating orchids too delicate for the open air; and, in the artificial atmosphere, the gaiety of youth has been replaced by the disillusionment of middle age. Prospero is the central figure of *The Tempest*; and it has often been wildly asserted that he is a portrait of the author—an embodiment of that spirit of wise benevolence which is supposed to have

thrown a halo over Shakespeare's later life. But, on closer inspection, the portrait seems to be as imaginary as the original. To an irreverent eye, the ex-Duke of Milan would perhaps appear as an unpleasantly crusty personage, in whom a twelve years' monopoly of the conversation had developed an inordinate propensity for talking. These may have been the sentiments of Ariel, safe at the Bermoothes; but to state them is to risk at least ten years in the knotty entrails of an oak, and it is sufficient to point out, that if Prospero is wise, he is also self-opinionated and sour, that his gravity is often another name for pedantic severity, and that there is no character in the play to whom, during some part of it, he is not studiously disagreeable. But his Milanese countrymen are not even disagreeable; they are simply dull. 'This is the silliest stuff that e'er I heard,' remarked Hippolyta of Bottom's amateur theatricals; and one is tempted to wonder what she would have said to the dreary puns and interminable conspiracies of Alonzo, and Gonzalo, and Sebastian, and Antonio, and Adrian, and Francisco, and other shipwrecked noblemen. At all events, there can be little doubt that they would not have had the entrée at Athens.

The depth of the gulf between the two plays is, however, best measured by a comparison of Caliban and his masters with Bottom and his companions. The guileless group of English mechanics, whose sports are interrupted by the mischief of Puck, offers a strange contrast to the hideous trio of the 'jester,' the 'drunken butler,' and the 'savage and deformed slave,' whose designs are thwarted by the magic of Ariel. Bottom was the first of Shakespeare's masterpieces in characterisation, Caliban was the last: and what a world of bitterness and horror lies between them! The charming coxcomb it is easy to know and love; but the 'freckled whelp hag-born' moves us mysteriously to pity and to terror, eluding us for ever in fearful allegories, and strange coils of disgusted laughter and phantasmagorical tears. The physical vigour of the presentment is often so remorseless as to shock us. 'I left them,' says Ariel, speaking of Caliban and his crew:

> I' the filthy-mantled pool beyond your cell,
> There dancing up to the chins, that the foul lake
> O'erstunk their feet.

But at other times the great half-human shape seems to swell like the 'Pan' of Victor Hugo, into something unimaginably vast.

> You taught me language, and my profit on't
> Is, I know how to curse.

Is this Caliban addressing Prospero, or Job addressing God? It may be either; but it is not serene, nor benign, nor pastoral, nor 'On the Heights.'

## LEO TOLSTOY
### From *On Shakespeare*
trs. V. Tchertkoff and I. F. M.
1906, pp. 78–124
V

An artistic, poetic work, particularly a drama, must first of all excite in the reader or spectator the illusion that whatever the person represented is living through, or experiencing, is lived through or experienced by himself. For this purpose it is as important for the dramatist to know precisely what he should make his characters both do and say as what he should not make them say and do, so as not to destroy the illusion of the reader or spectator. Speeches, however eloquent and profound they may be, when put into the mouth of dramatic characters, if they be superfluous, or unnatural to the position and character, destroy the chief condition of dramatic art—the illusion, owing to which the reader or spectator lives in the feelings of the persons represented. Without putting an end to the illusion, one may leave much unsaid—the reader or spectator will himself fill this up, and sometimes, owing to this, his illusion is even increased, but to say what is superfluous is the same as to overthrow a statue composed of separate pieces and thereby scatter them, or to take away the lamp from a magic lantern: the attention of the reader or spectator is distracted, the reader sees the author, the spectator sees the actor, the illusion disappears, and to restore it is sometimes impossible; therefore without the feeling of measure there can not be an artist, and especially a dramatist.

Shakespeare is devoid of this feeling. His characters continually do and say what is not only unnatural to them, but utterly unnecessary. I do not cite examples of this, because I believe that he who does not himself see this striking deficiency in all Shakespeare's dramas will not be persuaded by any examples and proofs. It is sufficient to read *King Lear*, alone, with its insanity, murders, plucking out of eyes, Gloucester's jump, its poisonings, and wranglings—not to mention *Pericles, Cymbeline, The Winter's Tale, The Tempest*—to be convinced of this. Only a man devoid of the sense of measure and taste could produce such types as *Titus Andronicus* or *Troilus and Cressida*, or so mercilessly mutilate the old drama *King Leir*.

Gervinus endeavors to prove that Shakespeare possessed the feeling of beauty, "Schönheit's sinn," but all Gervinus's proofs prove only that he himself, Gervinus, is completely destitute of it. In Shakespeare everything is exaggerated: the actions are exaggerated, so are their consequences, the speeches of the characters are exaggerated, and therefore at every step the possibility of artistic impression is interfered with. Whatever people may say, however they may be enraptured by Shakespeare's works, whatever merits they may attribute to them, it is perfectly certain that he was not an artist and that his works are not artistic productions. Without the sense of measure, there never was nor can be an artist, as without the feeling of rhythm there can not be a musician. Shakespeare might have been whatever you like, but he was not an artist.

"But one should not forget the time at which Shakespeare wrote," say his admirers. "It was a time of cruel and coarse habits, a time of the then fashionable euphemism, *i.e.,* artificial way of expressing oneself—a time of forms of life strange to us, and therefore, to judge about Shakespeare, one should have in view the time when he wrote. In Homer, as in Shakespeare, there is much which is strange to us, but this does not prevent us from appreciating the beauties of Homer," say these admirers. But in comparing Shakespeare with Homer, as does Gervinus, that infinite distance which separates true poetry from its semblance manifests itself with especial force. However distant Homer is from us, we can, without the slightest effort, transport ourselves into the life he describes, and we can thus transport ourselves because, however alien to us may be the events Homer describes, he believes in what he says and speaks seriously, and therefore he never exaggerates, and the sense of measure never abandons him. This is the reason why, not to speak of the wonderfully distinct, lifelike, and beautiful characters of Achilles, Hector, Priam, Odysseus, and the eternally touching scenes of Hector's leave-taking, of Priam's embassy, of Odysseus's return, and others—the whole of the *Iliad* and still more the *Odyssey* are so humanly near to us that we feel as if we ourselves had lived, and are living, among its gods and heroes. Not so with Shakespeare. From his first words, exaggeration is seen: the exaggeration of events, the exaggeration of emotion, and the exaggeration of effects. One

sees at once that he does not believe in what he says, that it is of no necessity to him, that he invents the events he describes, and is indifferent to his characters—that he has conceived them only for the stage and therefore makes them do and say only what may strike his public; and therefore we do not believe either in the events, or in the actions, or in the sufferings of the characters. Nothing demonstrates so clearly the complete absence of esthetic feeling in Shakespeare as comparison between him and Homer. The works which we call the works of Homer are artistic, poetic, original works, lived through by the author or authors; whereas the works of Shakespeare—borrowed as they are, and, externally, like mosaics, artificially fitted together piecemeal from bits invented for the occasion—have nothing whatever in common with art and poetry. . . .

## VIII

At the beginning of the last century, when Goethe was dictator of philosophic thought and esthetic laws, a series of casual circumstances made him praise Shakespeare. The esthetic critics caught up this praise and took to writing their lengthy, misty, learned articles, and the great European public began to be enchanted with Shakespeare. The critics, answering to the popular interest, and endeavoring to compete with one another, wrote new and ever new essays about Shakespeare; the readers and spectators on their side were increasingly confirmed in their admiration, and Shakespeare's fame, like a lump of snow, kept growing and growing, until in our time it has attained that insane worship which obviously has no other foundation than "suggestion."

Shakespeare finds no rival, not even approximately, either among the old or the new writers. Here are some of the tributes paid to him.

"Poetic truth is the brightest flower in the crown of Shakespeare's merits;" "Shakespeare is the greatest moralist of all times;" "Shakespeare exhibits such many-sidedness and such objectivism that they carry him beyond the limits of time and nationality;" "Shakespeare is the greatest genius that has hitherto existed;" "For the creation of tragedy, comedy, history, idyll, idyllistic comedy, esthetic idyll, for the profoundest presentation, or for any casually thrown off, passing piece of verse, he is the only man. He not only wields an unlimited power over our mirth and our tears, over all the workings of passion, humor, thought, and observation, but he possesses also an infinite region full of the phantasy of fiction, of a horrifying and an amusing character. He possesses penetration both in the world of fiction and of reality, and above this reigns one and the same truthfulness to character and to nature, and the same spirit of humanity;" "To Shakespeare the epithet of Great comes of itself; and if one adds that independently of his greatness he has, further, become the reformer of all literature, and, moreover, has in his works not only expressed the phenomenon of life as it was in his day, but also, by the genius of thought which floated in the air has prophetically forestalled the direction that the social spirit was going to take in the future (of which we see a striking example in Hamlet),—one may, without hesitation, say that Shakespeare was not only a great poet, but the greatest of all poets who ever existed, and that in the sphere of poetic creation his only worthy rival was that same life which in his works he expressed to such perfection."

The obvious exaggeration of this estimate proves more conclusively than anything that it is the consequence, not of common sense, but of suggestion. The more trivial, the lower, the emptier a phenomenon is, if only it has become the subject of suggestion, the more supernatural and exaggerated is the significance attributed to it. The Pope is not merely saintly, but most saintly, and so forth. So Shakespeare is not merely a good writer, but the greatest genius, the eternal teacher of mankind.

Suggestion is always a deceit, and every deceit is an evil. In truth, the suggestion that Shakespeare's works are great works of genius, presenting the height of both esthetic and ethical perfection, has caused, and is causing, great injury to men.

This injury is twofold: first, the fall of the drama, and the replacement of this important weapon of progress by an empty and immoral amusement; and secondly, the direct depravation of men by presenting to them false models for imitation.

Human life is perfected only through the development of the religious consciousness, the only element which permanently unites men. The development of the religious consciousness of men is accomplished through all the sides of man's spiritual activity. One direction of this activity is in art. One section of art, perhaps the most influential, is the drama.

Therefore the drama, in order to deserve the importance attributed to it, should serve the development of religious consciousness. Such has the drama always been, and such it was in the Christian world. But upon the appearance of Protestantism in its broader sense, *i.e.*, the appearance of a new understanding of Christianity as of a teaching of life, the dramatic art did not find a form corresponding to the new understanding of Christianity, and the men of the Renaissance were carried away by the imitation of classical art. This was most natural, but the tendency was bound to pass, and art had to discover, as indeed it is now beginning to do, its new form corresponding to the change in the understanding of Christianity.

But the discovery of this new form was arrested by the teaching arising among German writers at the end of the eighteenth and beginning of the nineteenth centuries—as to so-called objective art, *i.e.*, art indifferent to good or evil—and therein the exaggerated praise of Shakespeare's dramas, which partly corresponded to the esthetic teaching of the Germans, and partly served as material for it. If there had not been exaggerated praise of Shakespeare's dramas, presenting them as the most perfect models, the men of the eighteenth and nineteenth centuries would have had to understand that the drama, to have a right to exist and to be a serious thing, must serve, as it always has served and can not but do otherwise, the development of the religious consciousness. And having understood this, they would have searched for a new form of drama corresponding to their religious understanding.

But when it was decided that the height of perfection was Shakespeare's drama, and that we ought to write as he did, not only without any religious, but even without any moral, significance, then all writers of dramas in imitation of him began to compose such empty pieces as are those of Goethe, Schiller, Hugo, and, in Russia, of Pushkin, or the chronicles of Ostrovski, Alexis Tolstoy, and an innumerable number of other more or less celebrated dramatic productions which fill all the theaters, and can be prepared wholesale by any one who happens to have the idea or desire to write a play. It is only thanks to such a low, trivial understanding of the significance of the drama that there appears among us that infinite quality of dramatic works describing men's actions, positions, characters, and frames of mind, not only void of any spiritual substance, but often of any human sense.

Let not the reader think that I exclude from this estimate of contemporary drama the theatrical pieces I have myself incidentally written. I recognize them, as well as all the rest, as not having that religious character which must form the foundation of the drama of the future.

The drama, then, the most important branch of art, has, in our time, become the trivial and immoral amusement of a trivial and immoral crowd. The worst of it is, moreover, that to dramatic art, fallen as low as it is possible to fall, is still attributed an elevated significance no longer appropriate to it. Dramatists, actors, theatrical managers, and the press—this last publishing in the most serious tone reports of theaters and operas—and the rest, are all perfectly certain that they are doing something very worthy and important.

The drama in our time is a great man fallen, who has reached the last degree of his degradation, and at the same time continues to pride himself on his past of which nothing now remains. The public of our time is like those who mercilessly amuse themselves over this man once so great and now in the lowest stage of his fall.

Such is one of the mischievous effects of the epidemic suggestion about the greatness of Shakespeare. Another deplorable result of this worship is the presentation to men of a false model for imitation. If people wrote of Shakespeare that for his time he was a good writer, that he had a fairly good turn for verse, was an intelligent actor and good stage manager—even were this appreciation incorrect and somewhat exaggerated—if only it were moderately true, people of the rising generation might remain free from Shakespeare's influence. But when every young man entering into life in our time has presented to him, as the model of moral perfection, not the religious and moral teachers of mankind, but first of all Shakespeare, concerning whom it has been decided and is handed down by learned men from generation to generation, as an incontestable truth, that he was the greatest poet, the greatest teacher of life, the young man can not remain free from this pernicious influence. When he is reading or listening to Shakespeare the question for him is no longer whether Shakespeare be good or bad, but only: In what consists that extraordinary beauty, both esthetic and ethical, of which he has been assured by learned men whom he respects, and which he himself neither sees nor feels? And constraining himself, and distorting his esthetic and ethical feeling, he tries to conform to the ruling opinion. He no longer believes in himself, but in what is said by the learned people whom he respects. I have experienced all this. Then reading critical examinations of the dramas and extracts from books with explanatory comments, he begins to imagine that he feels something of the nature of an artistic impression. The longer this continues, the more does his esthetical and ethical feeling become distorted. He ceases to distinguish directly and clearly what is artistic from an artificial imitation of art. But, above all, having assimilated the immoral view of life which penetrates all Shakespeare's writings, he loses the capacity of distinguishing good from evil. And the error of extolling an insignificant, inartistic writer—not only not moral, but directly immoral—executes its destructive work.

This is why I think that the sooner people free themselves from the false glorification of Shakespeare, the better it will be.

First, having freed themselves from this deceit, men will come to understand that the drama which has no religious element at its foundation is not only not an important and good thing, as it is now supposed to be, but the most trivial and despicable of things. Having understood this, they will have to search for, and work out, a new form of modern drama, a drama which will serve as the development and confirmation of the highest stage of religious consciousness in men.

Secondly, having freed themselves from this hypnotic state, men will understand that the trivial and immoral works of Shakespeare and his imitators, aiming merely at the recreation and amusement of the spectators, can not possibly represent the teaching of life, and that, while there is no true religious drama, the teaching of life should be sought for in other sources.

## GEORGE EDWARD WOODBERRY
"Shakspere"
*Great Writers*
1907, pp. 183–216

The primary thing in Shakspere was his sense of action. He seized all life as action in his thoughts; he led his own life as action in himself, as a career. That is his Englishry. He was a practical man; as a boy he was enterprising, in his maturity he was discreet. The traditions of his early days at Stratford show a lively, capable, eager youth, active, adventurous, expedient, quick to get into trouble, quick in marriage; and the flight from Stratford was a departure into the large scene of life, a going to London, to the field of ambition. The family had seen better days, and was in difficulties; he meant to bear up the name; he succeeded, in the end, in re-establishing the family estate in his native place. The traditions of his early days in London show the same fundamental temperament; he had no scorn of beginnings, whether he held horses at the theatre, or by whatever door of trifling service he entered on the great scene that was to be his kingdom, he would get in where he could; he accepted the terms on which life was to be led in his time and place. He learned easily because he was facile to receive; he learned much because he put what he knew to use as soon as he knew it; he was quick to experiment with his faculties and what they found to work with. The stage was developing comedy and tragedy and a verbal style proper to display them; there was a stock of plays rapidly outgrown, a public demand to be met, money to be made. He made himself apprentice to the best masters of comedy and tragedy, he tried his hand at re-making the old plays, he used what he found on the stage, adding what he could of prettiness and quibble, of grace and softness in the phrase, of heat and vivacity in the dialogue, of golden cadence, comic play, tragic thrust; and gradually he moved forward, emerged, became playwright and poet, the mark of passing and impotent malice, popular with the many, well-beloved by his comrades, successful. If the history of these days were known in detail, it would not differ from the great type shown in Scott, Cervantes; infinite interest in life, unceasing industry in work, the power to live which makes men great, and with it the apparent unconsciousness of genius, the reality of the individual life, the near regard to the private good. Whatever else there may have been, the theatre was to Shakspere a profession, a career; he made himself master and head of it by the toilsome process of daily life; and he measured his success in it, in one way at least, by the substance of what it brought him, wealth, position, a county name.

At London, where he led this career for twenty-five years, he had complete worldly success. His life there leaves two impressions on the mind. The first is that of immense labour, not only in the composition of the plays, but in the other necessary business of the stage and management, the acting, the preparation, the provincial tours, the court performances, the life of the theatre and its finances, the practical realities; it must have been a very busy life, and its wearing effects are plain in the rapid and deep maturing of his manhood, and in his comparatively early death. The second impression is of the ease, quiet and friendliness of his temperament, his companionableness and his reserve, a human and noble nature; the characteristic epithets given him that have survived from his friends' lips are the two words "gentle" and "sweet"; though a few ill-natured phrases were flung at him, he escaped with the highest good-fortune the venom that the literary life vents even on its favourites. He was helpful; his youth he befriended Jonson, and in later years he collaborated with younger men. His comrades of the theatre show him that wholesome loyalty which mixes respect and affection so that they are indistinguishable. He seems to have had by nature those unconscious, intimate, incommunicable traits that oftenest come only from breeding and make men free of the society where they are. Young Southampton was not only his patron, but his friend; and in that difficult role of poet and patron Shakspere was proud and happy in his noble friend, and gave the tribute of affectionate compliment in verse and that glory of style that lies in courtly hyberbole, and all that was due from the greatest of poets, but he gave his heart also. Shakspere accepted the conditions of the literary life with respect to rank and fortune in his day as simply as he met the state of the theatre. It is likely there was no better courtier when he went to court, as it is likely that there was no better buyer when he went to view lands and houses, no better judge of the public taste in plays. He was equal to the business of life on all sides that required worldly ability, and temperamentally as equal to it in the things of affection and comradery, of the heart, of humanity in social intercourse. The patron, the mortgage belong in his life, together with the scores of friends and the innumerable affairs to do; they are naturally there, for he was a man like others who lived the common life of man, earned and ate his bread in it, and to whom this action of life in and about and for himself was a very palpable thing. It is not a life that has left much record of itself, not diversified by adventure, not the scene of known passions; but the golden silences that lie like autumn mould upon his memory are in harmony with that thought which discovers there a life, dedicated indeed to the creative dream, but yet within the limitations of its own world distinguished by daily labour and daily kindliness, not too self-conscious, storing up provision for the future, respect from the world, the affection of friends, the things that should accompany old age—a life well-lived, well-acted, in its earthly lines. Such a life is consistent with the highest genius even in men in whom the sense of life as action is not so supreme as it was in Shakspere; in him it was born of that genius where everything set with a great tide toward reality.

Action is the core of the drama; it is what gives attractive and arresting power to the word "dramatic," focuses the attention, makes the eye look and the spirit expect at the fall of those syllables. To Shakspere, in his youth, immersed and absorbed in the dramatic movement that made a captive servant of him, mind, moods, energy, ambition, hope—that overmastered him with what was to be his fate therein, life was the object of his thoughts, but life primarily as a story. The story of life was there before him in the old plays on the stage, in the books he read, in the tales he thumbed over; at first a story of English Kings and Italian lovers, of the convulsions of state, heart-break and the words of clowns, comic confusions, tragic discords, enchanted woodlands. He found the chronicle plays in vogue, fragments of history; and here and there, beginning his art, he re-established a scene, heightened a dialogue, concentrated a passion of anger or pity; it was piecemeal work by which he came to the power at last of defining a plot, a play of his own, an interpretation and representation of the story in a way of his own. The material he used was external, given to him, persons and incidents; he did not invent them, he found them; and his manipulation of them at first was, naturally, mainly in the language, the verbal investiture of person, act, scene, that part of the work which was most flexible, most plastic, readiest for a youthful hand and most tempting for lips that had suddenly unlocked a flood of such poesy, eloquence and passion in speech, colours of nature and the heart, as had never before poured from an English fount. It is this flow of language, vehement or smooth or impassioned, reflecting natural beauty of personal graces, prone to pathos and sentiment, rhetorical, dragging along with it all the affectations of the hour, experimenting with its own powers, intoxicated with its own poetry, exuberant with its own life—it is this marvellously musical, facile, intellectual power of language, this mastery that is not merely verbal, but is of the essence of expression, poetic not purely dramatic—it is this that in the earlier works plays over the story, atmospheres it, inhabits it, and in its surplus of light, feeling and imagery, in its lyrical effusion, overflows without submerging the dramatic interest, threatens the eminence of the action. From *Love's Labour's Lost* to *A Midsummer Night's Dream*, this lyrical obsession mounts prevailing; thereafter it recedes—the tints of the morning, the bloom of spring, the hour of the bloom of life had passed. Shakspere, loosing the passion of language to the full as never English poet did, had not lost his foothold on the reality of life, on the story, the drama, the action; and, deepening in his dramatic faculty he came, in the end, to that subtle mastery of language which belongs only to the greatest genius, lords of the brief and broken phrase. Four words created light; and something of that same miracle lingers in the power of the poet who is truly divine. The gradual victory of dramatic over purely poetic diction in Shakspere reflects the victory of life itself, of the action over the illusion of life, in him.

There was a second rivalry with the dramatic instinct in Shakspere besides this of the lyrical impulse. It lay in the intellectual temptation, the power of the naked thought. What is technically called the sentiment, that is, the wise saying, the axiomatic verse in which the reflecting mind is condensed with a purely intellectual value, was an inheritance of the drama from old time; and Shakspere, particularly in his middle life, was apt at linking such counsels together or in developing them from the dialogue. It is an analogous faculty that he employs in those wit-combats of the characters that are pre-eminently intellectual in tone. The wit of Rosalind and Beatrice is more closely united to the dialogue; but in the passages of advice, from Biron's gentle sermon on love to the sage wisdom of Polonius and Ulysses, and even on to Prospero's great farewell there is a recurring interruption of the action in play after play, due to the emergence of thought in control of the scene; and as Shakspere's lyricism give to the plays that atmosphere which isolates them among the works of dramatic genius and sets them apart in an unapproached realm of creative art, so his wisdom gives to them that intellectual dilatation by which they excel all others in majesty of mind. Other dramatists have represented life with equal impressiveness in its being, but none have represented life so conscious of its own significance. Here again, as in his lyrical moment, Shakspere in his intellectual moment seems to depart from the story, the drama, the action, but he does not really depart, or if he does so it is only to bring back to the drama the offerings of all the Muses. And in a third tributary element of the drama, in the spectacle, while he uses the embellishment of the scene to the full measure of what his times allowed, he introduces the masque as an adjunct, like a song or a dance, harmonious with the scene but not an essential of the action. These three things, then, diction, sentiment and spectacle, which were the open

temptation to woo him from the essential dramatic point of view, the action, he either overcame or successfully subdued them to the enrichment and enlargement of the action; the main drift of his art, the main purpose of his mind were the same, with whatever slackening or bending of the current, toward the story of life pre-eminently, toward character and event, toward reality in its most human form. Beginning with the more intractable material of history, he came to use preferably romantic story in which his imagination was more free in creative power; and in the end, to such a height did this power reach that he seemed to create not only character and event, but also the world in which they had their being; to such a complete victory did his dramatic instinct, prevailing over all other impulses, carry him who always remained at heart a dramatist.

Shakspere was so completely a dramatist, interested in the action of life, that when he took the autobiographical mask in the Sonnets he seems transformed into his opposite, into the lyrical poet unlocking his own heart; here, it has been believed, he told his dearest secrets, his intimacies, the most sweet and bitter disgraces of his days and nights, his springs and autumns; and so inspired is the dramatic action of his mind in this play in the forms of the sonnet, if it be such, that it is only by an effort of detachment, by reflection and judgment, that one sees there only the working of that supreme faculty under the appearances of personality. The secret of the Sonnets has been so many times discovered, and escaped in the discovery, that this view, now best supported, may justly have its lease of life in turn, and the physical basis of fact on which the poet's imagination worked—such strands and suggestions of actuality as he used in the romances—may be found in Southampton's personality; but the black lady, the dear, disloyal friend, the rival poet will still wear in their faces, have in their form and moving, an insoluble mystery, because, whatever the drama, they move in a cloud of lyricism, intense with tenderness, sorrow, unavailing cries, that here all seems the form and substance of the soul itself. A dramatist who makes his own soul the scene of the drama, using the forms of personality, must necessarily leave a mysterious work; but in the Sonnets what is plain is the drama, what is obscure is only the basis of the drama, whether it be fact or convention, or mingled of both; whatever be the personal element, it is conceived, handled, developed dramatically, its truth is at bottom dramatic truth.

And if it be difficult to trace Shakspere's personality with any assured steps in the Sonnets, how much less is it to be probed in the plays proper! Those attempts that have been made to correlate the bare facts of his history with the sequence of his works, to synchronize his life-moods with the comedies and the tragedies, to make the plays render up the spiritual states of the man in his personal being, are ingenious; but the conditions of production, when Elizabeth might ask any day for a *Merry Wives of Windsor*, or some noble family desire a hymeneal spectacle like *A Midsummer Night's Dream*, or James be pleased with a Scotch theme, or the public itself, little indulgent to the moods of those who provide entertainment, might have to be recaptured to the play—such conditions are little favourable to "periods" of the private soul. The chronology of the works, too, is not convincing. Did Shakspere, in whose mind the perspective of life varied no more than the perspective of the heavens in the celestial telescope, think to have all that world of his courtesy to his private fortunes in a son's death, a friend's fall, a mistress's fickle change? Shakspere was of the objective type of genius, a trite but useful phrase for a very palpable fact. He never mistook his soul for the soul of the universe. He passed, as other men, from youth to manhood, and the deepening of his nature in the process, as it was worked out under the control of absorption in creative dramatic art is plainly discerned; he seized life in its action more logically, more ideally, more profoundly; he compassed and penetrated and filled it with omnipresent thought; height and depth, passion and fate and gloom, he laid it bare; he saw it. He passed through the disillusionment; but it was a disillusionment not of the suffering heart, but of the seeing eye; and after the disillusionment came, what comes to all, the lassitude, the indifference, the repose, the relaxed sense of fate, the concession to optimism, the fantastic world; the calm of Shakspere was the subsidence of life in him, the smoothing of the great wave of passion, the stilling of the tumultuous voices of thought.

Such a history he had, in whatever special forms of personal feeling; it is the normal life of great genius, absorbing imaginatively the passion and thought of life in the world; and from time to time, out of this continuing personal reaction on life in normal growth there would proceed modifying influences, lines of choice in subject, of intellectual direction, of creative mood, passional harmonies blending with the given theme—to such a point temperament would have its will, more or less, with the work according to time and circumstances; but such a continuing and aging mood attendant on the plays is a far different thing from "periods" determinative of the type of the plays in a sequence which makes them proceed from Shakspere's personal fortunes as a mortal spirit with changes from cheerfulness to gloom and again to equanimity. Shakspere was a dramatist by nature as well as by profession, or he became subdued to what he worked in; he was the servant of the public; and, much more, he was fascinated by life in its externality, life as it was in other men, other times, other places; he was insatiate in informing himself of its story in history, in novels and romances, in ancient and modern authors, wherever it was to be found. He was not that egotist who writes himself large and calls that the world; art in him was not self-revealing, it was the revelation of a world that had been from the foundation of being and would continue when his works were buried deeper than any plummet could sound. This objectivity, this self-effacement in art, this interest in the story of life, this absorption in life's movement, in action, is Shakspere's gift of greatness. It explains his limitations. Spirituality, properly speaking, the celestial immortality of man's nature, is not found in Shakspere either in character, thought or aspiration. The religious life sleeps in his works; and many a generation will marvel at it. He was interested in life, the action of life; and that is a thing confined to this world. He is mundane, secular, in a way scientific; he saw the spectacle as it is in time.

The second main consideration bearing on Shakspere's genius is the fact that the world he saw, dealt with and knew was an aristocratic world. It was given to him first historically, in those chronicles in which his hand learned to mould the human stuff, a kingly world of the Henrys, the Richards and John, with feudal challenge, battle incidents, the life of the council, murders in prisons or on the block, treasons, dethronements, the sorrows of queens, Norfolk, Hotspur and Falconbridge; a life focussed on aristocratic fortunes and pivoted on aristocratic power. To Shakspere the people was always the mob, and negligible. The sphere of humour, too, in which the vulgar enters, is dependent on the aristocratic sphere from the comedy of the camp-fire and the tavern to Bottom's craftsmen and the court clowns, up to Lear's Fool. Later, the Roman plays gave him the same aristocratic state in an antique form, dictatorial, imperial, with the mob of citizens though

more in evidence, more contemptible. The ordered world for him was the world of courtly life; all else, though contiguous or entering in for entertainment or service or in the mass of battle, was essentially subordinated, exteriorized, as environment. The romances, which, after the chronicles, had given him the raw material, reinforced his conception of life as an aristocratic structure by expanding it socially into a community of gentlefolk, Venetian, Veronan, Paduan, in Arden, Attica, Illyria, or on French or English meadows; a life where everything breathed civility, the sentiment of high breeding in chivalry and courtesy, the cult of phrase, the dress and behaviour, the interests, ambitions, intrigues, recreations, language, manners and customs of an aristocratic ideal. Even in those regions of the imagination, where he reared his own state in its lordliest form, with the effect of an incantation of genius, in the English realm of Lear, the Scotch court of Macbeth, the throne of Denmark, the Venetian principality of Cyprus, the Egypt of Antony, or in the woods of Cymbeline, the country-side of Perdita, the island-kingdom of Prospero, he impressed upon it aristocracy in its most majestic, noble and gentle forms as the seal of its being. Shakspere's genius is, in fact, the finest flower of the aristocratic ideal of life.

Aristocracy is, in a sense, the state of nature historically developed in society as the survival of the fittest in the selfish struggle for existence. Shakspere received it as the past of the world, contained in the forms of history and romance, the life that had always been, in which the masses, held in economic slavery under whatever name, furnished that wealth monopolized by the nobles which gave these latter liberty of the higher sphere of life, the sphere of intelligence, ambition, art, where they were enfranchised and armed for the possession of the chief goods of life. Aristocracy, so based on the enforced tribute of mankind, naturally develops individuality, the open career for those who are in command of wealth, opportunity, leisure; it spreads the scene for strong natures, highly endowed, superfluous in vital force and selfish desire; it is the breeding place of human greatness of the positive, self-assertive; world-conquering kind. Shakspere received this aristocratic ideal from the times in which life had been great, from the Greek, Roman, English periods; but he received it also at a peculiarly fortunate moment in the special movement of its historical development; he received it when the coarser, denser forms of military and tyrannic power, of feudalism, monarchy and dogma, were dissolving in the finer, milder, freer modes of rationalism, individuality, culture; he received it at a culminating moment of its excellence—from the Italian Renaissance.

Personality, the essential fruit of aristocracy, the crowning victory of nature in working out her will, came forth from the Italian Renaissance in one of its highest forms, the form of superb personal power. The idea is so native to Italy and has played so great a part in her history that it seems racial—a race-element in her greatness. It was then concentrated in the ideal of the Renaissance prince, whether as a pattern in Machiavelli, or as an illustration from history in the nobles and leaders of the Italian cities; but stripped to its essentials it is no more than the individual will to live, the dominance of that will, the ideal of conquering the world to oneself, of subduing life, of having one's way, one's will, one's desire, of the assertion of the power to live that is the thirst of great souls. The aristocratic ideal of life in the Italian Renaissance developed in the central line of its advance in history this idea of the dominance of the personal will in life, the prepotency of individuality; and in so doing it freed human faculty, energy and desire in a way and to a degree which gave to Italy its brilliant period of many-sided genius and impelled the human spirit in every civilized country and recaptured the lost provinces of Rome to the dominion of a spiritual civilization the seat of whose power is in the ideals of men. The Renaissance was so great a movement. Though not a material conquest, it was vaster in control than that of Alexander or of the elder antique Rome. Shakspere took its full impact, lived in it, fed on it, absorbed its passions, its principles, its being, became its spirit in the North, was its transcendent and overwhelming genius in literature, its greatest monument in time. This is Shakspere's position; he was the flower of the aristocratic ideal of life; he was the crest of the Renaissance; he was the incarnate spirit of that mighty power of life to live mightily which belongs to the aristocratic ideal as a right of nature and was the passion of the Renaissance in history.

The drama, it must be borne in mind, was always a European art. Shakspere's universality, which is often made the occasion of so much marvel, is in its origins closely connected with this fact. The early English drama, with its miracle-plays, moralities, school-comedies, Senecan imitations, displayed cosmopolitan traits and originals belonging to a common mental culture and a general artistic condition; and the Elizabethan drama, in its Shaksperian culmination, though locally English, proceeded out of the European mind, its general past, its ideas, principles, moods, its order of life, its accumulation of sentiment and romance, its forms of imagination; and in this Shakspere from an early point in his career was more deeply imbued than any of his contemporaries. What, then, constituted the European mind, its intellectual memory and moral passion, its conception and ideal of life, its poetic culture and means of art, was more variously, richly and profoundly present and active in him than in any other writer. He may never have been out of England; but he was the most European author then living. It is not an accident that on his stage locality ceases to exist. Italy has her immortality in the drama more in Shakspere than in her own literature. *Hamlet* is the chief literary monument of Denmark. This does not happen by the caprice of an individual, but marks that quality in Shakspere by virtue of which he is the genius of Europe. The human spirit, from time to time, detaches from the world of known geography a country of its own lying apart, a land for itself; such was Arcadia, in which Sidney and others wandered; such was the region of chivalry where Spenser and others traversed the romantic scene; and such was the realm of Shakspere's stage, the magic circle where none dared tread but he. It was a world abstracted from the great scene of life in Europe as it then lay before the thoughts of men, in its breadth out of the historic past, in its variety of living energy, its mediæval and classic garniture, its Renaissance luminousness, space, vivacity; it was this scene of the European consciousness of what life had been and was, idealized and generalized, and made to issue in poetry with the power and brilliancy of a new creation, the realm of Shakspere's art. The aristocratic ideal of life is its organic principle and determines the quality of the scene, the nature of the event, the impulse of the characters; all the flowering of phrase and fancy, of sentiment and passion, all the adornment of taste in whatever form, all that constitutes mood, temperament and atmosphere, is representative of the European fashion of courtliness, scholarship, art, the reverie and dream that belong to the Renaissance characteristically, its pastoral, dramatic, rhetorical modes, its vari-coloured romanticism; but, most cardinal of all, what is the mainspring of its life, is the human force loosed in it, that prepotency of the individual, that dominance of the personal will, which was the master-spirit of the Renaissance everywhere and finds in Shakspere's world the place of its great career. This is not a

local, a national, an English thing; it is a world-idea, and the imagination of Shakspere, mastered by its inspiration found any country a fit stage for it in that environment of an ideal courtly life which was also not local or provincial, but a great world-scene. Shakspere's universality in matter goes back to the fact that he was never anything else but cosmopolitan, in the nature of his knowledge, the ideality of his art, the sources, compass and illustrative power of his dramatic work. What is most contemporary, realistic and locally English in this work is on its fringes; in its beginnings and interludes, subordinate; in proportion as the work becomes great, profound, comprehensive, it possesses more purely the European character, it develops ideal freedom, it belongs not to Italy or Denmark or England, but to the genius of Europe.

The dawn of the Renaissance spirit, incarnating itself in English dramatic poetry, was in Marlowe, who was perhaps in his own passion of life more at one with the heart of the Renaissance than was Shakspere, but he was less nobly, less perfectly, less splendidly, at one with it in its manifold fulness of expression. Marlowe first put on the stage the career of great passions, characters of immeasurable ambition and unquenchable thirst; but in *Tamerlane*, *The Jew of Malta* and *Faustus*, the theme is not sufficiently correlated with the real play of fact and force in human affairs, it is seized with too much intellectual abstraction and presented too spectacularly and fragmentarily in the scenes; some experimenting with the modifying power of history over imagination and invention was needed before it could find its dramatic limits and free itself from fantasy, enthusiasm and exaggeration in artistic expression. Shakspere followed Marlowe in turning to English history for the material of his art. The idea of tragedy was, indeed, already defined for him in the European tradition as a thing of the fall of princes, of royal misfortune and the vicissitude of splendid fates; and in this way Shakspere's tragic course was charted out for him beforehand; but in working out dramatically the lots of the English kings he also kept a close hold on the idea of a life-force in personality determining temperament, character and the issues of the action. What in Marlowe was extravagantly set forth as the fixed idea in his characters, bearing almost the impress of madness, remains in Shakspere, but subdued to the requirements of the environment and of human nature, to probability. *Richard II* is a pathetic instance of the fall of a prince, but the story is linked with that infatuation of the idea of divine right which is the dominant idea of Richard, absorbs the eloquence, grace and chivalry of his nature and contains his fate. In *Richard III*, the prepotency of the selfish force develops its bloody way with a power to take possession of the king's soul that recalls the self-maddening tyranny of the Roman emperors, till he becomes the fiend, the enemy of society and of the state itself, whose fall clears the air like a departing thunderstorm. Romeo exhibits the mastering of passion in the youthful soul; love in him is ecstasy. The dominance of the personal will, possessed by an idea inciting it, asserting itself with unbridled desire, naturally leads to madness, and in Shakspere's great characters of this sort mania is never far off; in Macbeth there is the capital instance of the blending of the borders between reason and unreason, and, as is Shakspere's way, this elemental trait in the play permeates it, objectified in the witches, reduplicated in Lady Macbeth, but concentrated in the vivid mental action, the bodily starts and stares, the repeated challenge of fate, in Macbeth's shaking but never quite dethroned "state of man." *Timon* is a lesser illustration. *Hamlet* and *Lear* thrust this part of life into the foreground; and in *Othello*, the near neighborhood of the excess of life to madness, of the noble nature to ruin through its own power to live, to be possessed by a passion, an idea, a sorrow, is the ground of its tragic scene. The personal will is necessarily anti-social, and hence opens in its career the whole field of tragic conflict in endless ways; the drama is its natural scope in art, and there it is the most potent power to conjure with; it is, by far, the most interesting thing in the whole of that action of life which Shakspere contemplated so absorbingly. The Renaissance spirit concentrated and intensified the sense of it, carried it to the extreme, made an ideal of it, in history; Shakspere took it over into the sphere of imagination and then gave such examples of it in the transcendent forms of art that his characters became, each in its kind, the supreme models of what is possible to human nature and faculty in personal force, the types of man.

The fulness of life in all its forms, which makes the plays great, has as its underlying basis this life-force, the affirmation of life, in its energies, its desires, its revelations, in the conscious spectacle of being, and with the more brilliancy because of the transcendent idealization to which the scene of life here has been subjected. All Shakspere's male characters are self-seekers, in a true sense; the exceptions, Kent, a feudal type, and Horatio, a modern form of the Kent temperament, are also men of strength. Though with the visitation of thought, melancholy, peculiar misfortune on the scene, there is occasionally the sense of a withdrawal from life, in Hamlet, Antonio, Hermione, it is rather a forced and regretful retirement than a true withdrawal; the denial of life is truly present in Shakspere only as an unshaped suggestion. The age was one of action, of faith in life, and the ideals it projected were those of the positive, achieving, realizing kind; and in Shakspere the life-force moved in his world of art with the fruitfulness, the teeming variety, the creative overflow into being that it has in nature. Men recognize and remember this life-force in him by the immortal figures of the plays, Romeo, Hamlet, Lear, the score or more that have entered into the world's memory enduringly, eternal realities, with ideal fascination, either for their beauty or their intimacy with men's bosoms or their awe in fate or some other mode of consanguinity with man that is Shakspere's seal upon them; these figures best illustrate that power of life and will to live, in high personal forms, showing the far reach, the majesty, the pity and terror of the forces of life in the soul in their energy accomplishing the utmost possible to man unfolding his nature in the vicissitudes of fortune; but the whole Shaksperian world, no less than these, in its various planes of character, incident and plot, is the outcome and realization in art of this same life-force more widely diffused in humanity of every kind and sort. That infinite variety that so distinguishes the plays, such that each seems a fresh revelation of a new world, so embracing that they seem in their wholeness to leave no lot in life unexpressed, no mortal joy or sorrow unrecorded in its own cry, no thought almost untold,—that scene of life from the tavern-companions of Falstaff and the craftsmen of Athens up to the solitude of Cæsar in power, the solitude of Lear in grief, the solitude of Prospero in wisdom,— all this proceeds from the life-force manifesting itself with the multiplicity and abundance of humanity. Shakspere engaged his mind with the movement of life in its wholeness; he let the life-force pour through him, from clown and fool and trull up to the highest incarnations of the will in passion, wisdom, sorrow, the types of man; and this seen in imagination is the Shaksperian world. He is not an observer, bringing back word from this or that tract of life or group of mortals or peculiarity of fortune; he was a creator—his world is always whole, as entire and perfect in the Indian boy of Titania as in the Rome of Cæsar. The spirit of the Renaissance, insatiable for life,

whispered to him this secret; but in the act and passion of creation he exceeded the Renaissance and took his station with those mightiest few who are not for an age, but for all time.

The courtly sphere, the aristocratic ideal, the culmination of life in the career of great passions led up to that triumph of life which is the spectacle the Shaksperian world presents with inexhaustible profusion, splendour and vitality; but this world, though an emanation of the spirit of the Renaissance and its climax in literature, was itself sphered in a larger conception universal in the tragic art; it lies, like the antique drama, in fatality, in the mystery and under the sway of an infinity that envelops the life-force round about more profoundly and densely than the dark ether envelops the forces and imagery of nature. The prepotency of individuality, the dominance of the personal will are the great forms of life; but the power to live, however supreme in its manifestation, is a wrestling with the unseen angel of life; and to Shakspere in the long and brooding absorption of his contemplation of the action of life in mortality, what finally emerges from the strife as the master-spirit there is the dominance of fate against which the life-force is shattered. It is commonly said that fate in the antique drama is external and operates from without as destiny, and that in the modern drama it is internal and operates from within as character; the distinction brings out the larger scope of personality and its greater importance in the romantic drama of Shakspere; but in either case the fatality resides in the action, in the play of the forces determining the tragic catastrophe, in that which is essentially beyond and outside of the sphere of the personal will and operates free from its control, against its desire and to effect its ruin. The error, the weakness, the cause that initiates the play of fate may be of different degrees of ignorance or consciousness, of generosity or criminality, of responsibility or irresponsibility; but, once loosed in whatever way, fate in the end rules the issue. In what is known as Shakspere's period of tragic gloom, that is, in the plays of his manhood's maturity, in which his creative genius works with its most profound power in realizing the states of the soul, the characteristic trait is the gradual emergence in his art of the sense of fate in the world, its accumulation in his mind, its possession of his genius which then gave forth those dramas on which his fame as a master of the knowledge of life most rests and in which fate controls the scene of life in the wreck of fortune, the riving of the soul within, the catastrophe where tragic death loading the stage impresses the mind less as the penalty than as a release of the sufferer from the power of life to torture and betray, a dismissal of the soul to the peace where life is not. To Macbeth, Othello, Lear and also to Hamlet, death is welcome; and to the spectator also their death brings relief, calm, peace. Shakspere in these days pre-eminently saw fate as that against which personality is shattered, not merely dramatically by a star-crossed fortune as in Romeo, with the pathos of the death of youth, beauty and passion, but more essentially as by a law inherent in the greatness of the life-force itself to destroy it; for these are not special but typical instances of the action of life—slight changes of circumstances might have altered the fortunes of Romeo, but no change could ever have altered the fate of Macbeth, Othello, Lear, Hamlet. In these four Shakspere sets personality against fate, front to front, and the story is felt to be a universal chapter of life, of the implication of the human spirit in that vicissitude of nature and fortune which has in every tongue borne the same name and that is stronger than life.

The realization that such is the nature of human life was attended in Shakspere's mind by a storm and stress that is read not only in the great dramas, but also in the cynical acquaintance with humanity shown in *All's Well That Ends Well*, and in the savage temper toward its baseness displayed in *Troilus and Cressida*. The concentrated, intense, ideal realization of the tragedy of existence, of humanity victimized in its forms of noblest nature or of most superb power, though most brilliant in the four great tragedies, is not confined to them; it extends and spreads into many others in different planes of character, mood and thought. The action of life takes on that quality of impenetrable mystery which the face of life has always worn, in every literature, in the highest works of imagination. Mystery is an increasing element in Shakspere's dramas from the first, continuing, growing in depth, growing also in intangibility; poetically, it is etherealized in *A Midsummer Night's Dream* full of the idea of illusion in art as the wood is of moonlight; reflectively, it is precipitated in Hamlet's thought; and, at the end, as the illusion of life it fills *The Tempest*; but the finer and most secret form of mystery in Shakspere is not poetical or intellectual or metaphysical, but springs from the action itself and is dramatic. It is in Macbeth's superstitious interrogation of the witches, in Hamlet's questioning of the soul in his soliloquy, in those half-lines of tragic climax where life grows silent before the presence of fate; it is in Othello's mind-dazed question:

Will you, I pray, demand that demi-devil
Why he hath thus ensnared my soul and body,—

the mystery of the fates of man; it is in Lear's invocation of the elements:

I never gave you kingdom, called you children,—

dismissing them from the moral world as if they alone were free where all was guiltiness in the worse storm of life beating on his white, old head. It is in such passages as these, where Shakspere's dramatic faculty is at its lightning-stroke that the inner secrecy of the mystery is lighted up, shown but not revealed, in the depth of consciousness. Reason has no solvent for it, justice does not measure with it, mercy is unknown to it. The attempt to make fate ethical in Shakspere, to identify it with moral law in the universe, however it be made, fails; it was not as righteousness that he saw life; he saw it with the simpleness of his genius, as a dramatic struggle, and, emerging thence, the dominance of fate shattering life mysteriously, beyond the intelligible grasp of man's reason or the moral sense. He saw, in other words, above all else, the dramatic mystery of life.

Shakspere was thus, through and through, a dramatist; and he was the dramatist in whom the old tradition of the art, even from Æschylus, as a representative of the courtly life and a tale of the fall of princes, culminated. The idea of humanity, in the modern democratic sense, was never in his brain; the types of man that he created were, in their greatness, those of the aristocratic life; and the tragedy he set forth was not that of the spirit of life, the modern world-pain, but of the careers of individuals highly endowed by nature or fortune in a world which seemed to exist to be the theatre of their will, ambition, passion; he was the dramatist of a class-society. The aristocratic ideal of society and of action in it, however, is the will of nature, and still prevails in every state; and it makes a universal appeal to men. The ground of this appeal is little affected by the absence in Shakspere of democratic sympathy; for the scene of life which he does present includes all classes; human nature is common and constant, and the career of life in fortune, ambition, passion is now the same that he depicted; the Shaksperian world, however modern conditions may be changed, is still life as it is known to the thoughts of men. The dramatic mystery is that which is closest to mankind in daily experience, the mystery of what is done, of what happens; the

poetic, intellectual, metaphysical modes of mystery exist for the few, but the mystery of the event itself is for all, and it is seized by them in Shakspere's way as not a thing of reason or ethics, but as a fact impenetrable, leaving the soul according to its degree affected by the scene. This is the normal human attitude toward calamity, toward tragedy, of any kind; its force expends itself not in explanation, but in experience. The sense of life as action, too, and the ideal of it as lying in the prepotency of individuality, and the dominance of the personal will is natural to all men, and the thing dearest to their bosoms as their thought and desire of life; the power to live,—to loose the energies of the soul in achievement, enjoyment, experience, to affirm life in its fulness, variety, richness, intensely, extremely insatiably, to the utmost of the force that is in one— this is the impulse of self-expression, to self-realization, that drives men in their ambitions and passions of whatever nature, the action and movement of life in the world; and in this world as it lies outspread in the knowledge and thoughts of men brilliant personal force most attracts admiration, confers fame and secures imitation, oftenest without regard to moral quality. Force is the idol of life that is hardest to combat in civilizing man. In the Shaksperian world the affirmation of life in general is as broadly various as in the world of nature, and in individual types it reaches a height of beauty, power and majesty that is unrivalled in nature because seen through the ideality of art, and these types have a history and a revelation of their being such as is only possible in imagination; men, consequently, passing into this world as they read or behold the plays find there that enlargement of life and its career, that intensification and revelation of it, which, though denied to their experience, truly endows them with the greatness of life, gives them understanding of the soul and the faculties lodged in it, the heights and depths of its passion, the reaches of its thoughts, the shadows of fatality amid which it moves under the stars. The universal appeal of Shakspere lies in the power with which he has seized life in its intense forms, its richest efflorescence, its magical fantasy, its fascination and horror, its vulgar generality, its high types, its manias and humours, the whole of life, and given it back to men as an increase of their own power to live, a world in which they come to true consciousness of themselves. Life is what men desire; Shakspere gives them life, according to their own ideal, the triumph of life, yet life, which at its height is tragic and shocks them with that mystery of the actual which is the profoundest reality.

The secret of life solves the riddle of Shakspere, whose greatness has no other mystery than the mystery of the greatness of life. He is the spirit of life made manifest in its own dramatic motion, imprisoned, embodied and unveiled in art. Here are the fates of men, grotesque, heroic, terrible, or stately in prosperity with the olive crown and the sheaf of Ceres, almost as many in number as the lots set forth to be chosen by the souls at birth. It is an earthly life limited to the mortal scene; no illumination falls on it from heaven, no divinity inhabits its sphere. It is essentially Pagan in its ideal, its art and its philosophy. It is the supreme work of man's hand so rendering life in its aspects of mortality. If one were to mould in sculpture the face of life, it would be, one thinks, that over which every joy and sorrow, every thought seems to have moved—the infinite of human expression—leaving its trace in the living flesh,—the face of Shakspere. That would be, could it be won back from time, the ideal face of life, the Sphinx of our existence.

GEORGE SAINTSBURY
"Shakespeare and the Grand Style"
*Essays and Studies*, 1910, pp. 113–35

The adventure of this paper may appear extravagant, but it has seemed to me perhaps not unfitting, if not for myself, yet for the person whom the English Association has thought fit to choose for its president in the third centenary year of the publication of the *Sonnets*. Nor is the adventurer, however moderate his prowess, quite untried in the kind, at any rate, of the quest. Some years ago, at the request of the Dante Society, I wrote and read a paper, as yet unpublished, on the relation of that great poet to the mysterious entity called the Grand Style; and last year I ventured to deal with Milton in the same way, before the Royal Society of Literature. The opportunity of completing the trio was tempting, and I can only hope that I have not been tempted to too great a failure.

It is always in such a case as a ceremony desirable, though except as a ceremony it can hardly be necessary, to disclaim any intention of direct controversy. Such controversy would be, in this case, with the founder or re-founder of all recent discussion on the present subject, Mr. Matthew Arnold.[1] I do not share his views: but controversy in detail would be quite out of place in a paper at this, and, in reference to a dead antagonist, it would lack even the piquancy which, when carried on between the living, it seems to possess for many, I cannot say I think of the best, tastes. It is sufficient to remind you that Mr. Arnold could only accord to Shakespeare what I have elsewhere called a sort of 'uncovenanted' Grand Style—an occasional magnificence, chequered if not checkmated by styles the reverse of grand. It appears to me on the contrary that Shakespeare held the Grand Style in the hollow of his hand, letting it loose or withholding it as good seemed to him: and further, that the seeing almost always *was* good.

It has been often said in various forms, but hardly ever without truth, that all dispute turns upon difference of definition—and that, if people were only clear-witted enough and even-tempered enough, the arrival at definition would be the conclusion of the whole matter. For their differences of opinion would either disappear in the process, or they would be seen to be irreconcilable, and to possess no common ground on which argument is possible. My definition of the Grand Style is certainly wider than Mr. Arnold's, whose own seems to have been framed to insist upon that 'high seriousness' of his which is no doubt a grand thing. Mine would, I think, come nearer to the Longinian 'Sublime'—the perfection of expression in every direction and kind, the commonly called great and the commonly called small, the tragic and the comic, the serious, the ironic, and even to some extent the trivial (not in the worst sense, of course). Whenever this perfection of expression acquires such force that it transmutes the subject and transports the hearer or reader, then and there the Grand Style exists, for so long, and in such a degree, as the transmutation of the one and the transportation of the other lasts. It may persist, or cease, or disappear and re-appear, like a fixed or a revolving light, but there it is *in essentia* or *in potentia*. If, on the other hand, you limit the definition to the *continual* exertion of some such a transforming force, it seems to me that, in the first place, you are making an excessive and unnatural restriction, forgetful of *neque semper arcum* and other sayings of the wise, while, in the second place, as a consequence of the first error, you are preparing for yourself endless pitfalls. It is a question whether any writer, except perhaps Milton, will answer to the definition completely. Dante and Homer certainly will not—

as, to give one example in each case out of a hundred, the comparison of Adam in the *Paradiso* to an animal struggling under a cloth, which has shocked so many commentators and that passage in the *Odyssey* which shocked Longinus, will show. Further, the perpetual Grand Style of the definition which is *not* mine, can only be maintained—is only maintained by Milton himself—at the cost of an enormous *tour de force* of mannerism, which is at least questionably justifiable or artistic—which in fact itself sometimes becomes the reverse of grand. The vast region of the lighter vein must be abandoned, or clumsily handled—as it actually is by Milton when his Grand Style is once 'set'. Even in serious subjects, there must be a kind of 'second sifting' of seriousness. And, above all, there is the certainty of the arising of a spurious Grand Style—a style of mere grandiosity—a plaster imitation of the real thing, than which there has been nothing in the past, and there is likely to be nothing in the future, more detestable.

Of this there is no danger, essentially at least, under the application of that definition of the Grand Style which I prefer. It makes its appearance when it is wanted, and when the hour is come; at other times it abides apart, and possesses its strength in quietness and in confidence, not frittering it away. Of its display in this fashion I cannot remember any one in literature—not Homer, not Dante himself, not Milton certainly—who can produce such constant, such varied, such magnificent instances as Shakespeare. Even in his novitiate, when he was making his experiments, and indeed making the tools with which to make these, this Adamastor, this King of the Waves of the vasty deep of style, never fails to come when he calls on it. We do not know the exact order of his compositions; and there is dispute about some of the probably earlier items in it. Some maintain that the *Titus Andronicus* which we have is not the *Titus* that Meres attributed to him; and some that the admitted rewriting of *Love's Labour's Lost* makes it a doubtful witness; while the date of *The Two Gentlemen of Verona* is extremely uncertain. But it would, I think, be difficult so to pack a jury of competent scholars that these plays, and the *Comedy of Errors*, should not be put in the van. And though every one of them is full of crudities, the Grand Style appears in each, as it never does appear in any other probably contemporary work, except Marlowe's, and not as it appears in Marlowe himself. The central splendour of Adriana's speech in the *Errors* (II. ii. 112 ff.); the glorious 'phrase of the ring' in the fatal discovery of the murder of Bassianus in *Titus* (II iii. 226 ff.); the famous and incomparable veiled confession of Julia in the *Two Gentlemen* (IV. iv. 154 ff.); at least a dozen passages in *Love's Labour's Lost*—have the broad arrow—the royal mark—upon them unmistakably.

But, it is said, there is so much else—so much even of the close context of these very passages—which has *not* the mark! And why should it have? Poetry, and most especially dramatic poetry, is a microcosm: and it may—perhaps it should, like the macrocosm—contain wood, hay, and stubble as well as gold and silver. Again, in these plays, it is said, there are *failures* of the Grand Style—slips from it or mis-shots at it—fallings into conceit, preciousness, bombast, frigidity, what not. Is it necessary, even at this time of day, to recapitulate the classes of persons to whom, according to the adage, half-done work should not be shown? Or is there any one, not included in these classes, who really wishes that we had not got Shakespeare's half-done work? I should be sorry to think that there is—especially in this audience. But, if there be, may I suggest to him that on the calculus we are using, the fact, supposing it to be a fact, does not matter? It is not a question whether anything that is not the Grand Style exists in these plays: but whether the Grand Style itself exists there. And I profess myself unable to understand how any one can deny its presence in the passages to which I have referred, and in scores, almost hundreds, of others.

But let us come to somewhat closer quarters. What is it, in these passages themselves, which, in spite of the evident novitiate of their author, claims for them grandeur of style? It is no one thing; the sources of the Sublime in style are many—as many as the qualities and circumstances of Style itself. Whenever one of these qualities is displayed, whenever one of these circumstances is utilized, in the trasmuting and transporting fashion and degree—there is the Grand Style. In the speech of Julia, above referred to,

> She hath been fairer, Madam, than she is,

the secret lies, to a great extent, in the double meaning, and in the pathetic moderation and modulation of the disguised and deserted mistress. The language is quite plain—it is an instance, one of many, which shows that poetic diction is not a *sine qua non*, though none of these shows that it can be or ought to be wholly dispensed with. But as I am, I confess, strongly and indeed irreconcilably opposed to the doctrine that the great thought *ipso facto* makes the Great Style—that the meaning is the thing—I am particularly glad to start with an instance where the secret *does* lie mainly in the meaning.

It lies there less in the passage of the *Errors*:

> For know, my love, as easy mayst thou fall,
> A drop of water in the breaking gulf,
> And take unmingled thence that drop again,
> Without addition or diminishing,
> As take from me thyself, and not me too.

Here the meaning is good, is true, is pathetic—but it is not in it that the transport and the transmutation lie. They lie partly, as Longinus would assert, in the Figure—the vivid image of the breaking gulf, and the drop of water contrasted with and whelmed in it. They lie, I think, partly also in the actual verbal phrase by which that figure is conveyed. But to me they lie most in the management of the metre, the alternative check and rush of the rhythm of the now sundered, now overlapping, verses—the perfection of the entire phrase, prosodic and poetic.

The third passage, that in *Titus*, is more of a 'Passage Perilous'; for the evidence of the novitiate is here very strong:

> Upon his bloody finger he doth wear
> A precious ring that lightens all the hole,
> Which, like a taper in some monument,
> Doth shine upon the dead man's earthy cheeks
> And shows the ragged entrails of the pit.

After this it goes off into mere failure about Pyramus and the moon, and Cocytus, and other *gradus* matters. Even here, in the lines quoted, the expression is not thoroughly 'brought off'—it is the Grand Style in the rough, with the master's hand not yet in case to finish it. Yet the solemn splendour of the opening line, and the lights and shades and contrasts of dim outline and ghastly colour, have the right quality—or at least the promise of it.

When we come to such a play as *Romeo and Juliet* the command of these sources is far surer and more frequent, though it seems to be masqued or marred, to some spectators, by the accompanying comedy or farce, which is not, and is not intended to be, grand in any way. The famous 'Queen Mab' speech is not quite up to our mark—not at all because it is light in subject, but because Mercutio, pleasant as is his fancy, *does*, as Romeo says, 'talk of nothing' to some extent, or talk a little too much of his pleasant something. But the famous later

scenes of the play are full of the Grand Style; and Romeo's dying speeches, after he has disposed of Paris, have it in perfection and in rare volume. If anybody denies that this is the Grand Style I should like to meet him foot to foot, he taking any passage he likes from Homer, Dante, Milton, or any one else, and to fight the question out, phrase by phrase, line by line, and total impression by total impression.

It is this increasing command of the style that transmutes the subject and transports the reader, which is so characteristic of Shakespeare; joined as it is to a perfect readiness *not* to use it when he thinks it is not required. I have pointed out that I think this somewhat misled Mr. Arnold, and has misled others. They cannot conceive Apollo without the bent bow; they think that the Grand Style is a sort of panoply which the wearer, like some adventurous knights under a vow, must never take off. Once more, I cannot help thinking this is a mistake. 'Homer and the Grand Style' is a subject which would be very interesting, and which I should not be afraid to handle; but it would be quite irrelevant to say much of it here. The Homeric grandeur, whatever it is, is quite different in species from that of Dante and Milton; and though it is more like Shakespeare's, I do not think that the difference between the two is small. But it is certain that Homer does not wear his Grand Style as a continental officer wears his uniform, while Milton does this to the utmost possible extent, and Dante to an extent extremely great. Shakespeare—who is nothing if not English, except that he is also universal—is never more English than in his preference for mufti on occasion. It seems to be this preference which has, in the eyes of some, disqualified him.

And yet no one can wear his uniform with more dignity, or assume it with such lightning quickness; while no one can keep it longer fresh on duty. The *Sonnets* are, of course, the great example of this; for with the rarest exceptions the *Sonnets*, whatever else they may be or not be, are Grand Style throughout. Their subject does not, from this point of view, matter; whether Elizabethan sonnets in general, and these sonnets at a rather extraordinary particular, present rehandlings of old stuff, or not, is of no importance. Let fifty—let five hundred, or five thousand, people have moralled, poetically or prosaically, on sunrise, noon, and sunset. When the fifty-first, or the five hundred and first, writes,

> Lo! in the *orient* when the *gracious* light
> Lifts up his *burning* head,

the Grand Style appears. It is nearly as impossible to describe, meticulously, the constituents of its grandeur as to describe those of the majesty of the sun itself. There is, as Dionysius of Halicarnassus was perfectly right in holding, something mysterious in the mere word-material—the contrasted sound and structure of the words 'orient', 'gracious', 'burning'. There is much more in their juxtaposition. But there is most in the whole phrase; though with the contestable exception of 'orient' and perhaps 'Lo!' there is not a single specimen of 'poetic diction' in it; most of it is in the simplest vocabulary; and the central thought and image are as common as grass or earth. But the *attitude* of the phrase is the thing; the simple dignified *attitude* which sets off, and is set off by 'orient' and 'gracious' and 'burning', as jewels set off, and are set off by, simplicity and dignity and grace combined in the human port and bearing. It is in this that Shakespeare excels all his great competitors in quantity, and differ from all but Dante in quality. In Milton there is always something that is not exactly simple; and in Homer 'perpetual epithets', compound epithets, and the like, interfere to some extent with that every-varying yet often extraordinarily *plain* speech which we find in Shakespeare and in Dante. On the other hand, Milton is segregated from the other three by the fact that he depends less than any of them on mighty single words; it is rather (putting proper names out of the question) on the rhetorical collocation of those which he uses that he relies. The double epithets that he employs are imitations from the Greek. But Shakespeare delights in such words as 'multitudinous,' 'incarnadine,' 'unwedgable,' just as Dante does in such as *ammassiccia* and *fiammeggiante*. And yet Shakespeare can produce the Grand Style effect with five repetitions of 'never' in a single line, or with such a renunciation of emphasis, such a miracle of negative expression, as 'The rest is Silence'. I suppose the very prodigality of his use of it, the insouciance of this prodigality, like that of

> Wealthy men who care not how they give,

and above all the disconcerting way in which he gives it when people do not expect it, and are not prepared for it, account to some extent for the dubiety and discomfort with which it has been and is received, for the tendency to plead 'his time' and 'the necessities of the theatre' and the like. For it is a great mistake to suppose that the day of apologies for Shakespeare is over. The form of the apology alters, but the fact remains: and I am inclined to think that Shakespeare, though he would certainly have been amused by most of his modern assailants, would have been still more amused by some of his modern apologists. Still, the '*wilfulness*' (as his own age would have said) of this prodigality *is* no doubt disconcerting to some honest folk. People are uncomfortable at being taken by surprise. They want to be told to 'prepare to receive cavalry'; there must be a warning-bell and a voluntary, and ornaments and vestments, to put them into a proper Grand Style frame of mind. Milton provides all this, and he is recognized as a grand stylist; Shakespeare does not, and his title is questioned. A respectable but rather futile gentleman like Duke Orsino is plentifully supplied with the noblest phrase; a petulant, dishonourable, almost worthless prince like Richard II is supplied more plentifully still, and from a still nobler mint. He does not grudge it to his villains; if

> The wheel is come full circle; I am here[2]

be not in the Grand Style, I confess myself utterly ignorant what the Grand Style is. It comes sometimes, as it were, 'promiscuously' in the vulgar sense of that term. It would, for instance, be exceedingly difficult for the most expert, or the most futile, ingenuity of the commentator to assign an exact reason for the occurrence, where it occurs, of what is perhaps the grandest example of the Grand Style in all literature—the words of Prospero to Ferdinand, when the revels are ended. An excuse is wanted to break off the pretty 'vanity of his art'; to get rid of the lovers; and to punish, in defeating it, the intentionally murderous but practically idle plot of Caliban and his mates. Anything would do; and the actual pretext is anything or nothing. But Shakespeare chooses to accompany it with a 'criticism of life'—and of more than life—so all-embracing, couched in expression of such magnificence, that one knows not where to look for its like as form and matter combined. An ordinary man, if, *per impossibile*, he could have written it, would have put it at the end; an extraordinary one might have substituted it for, or added it to, the more definite announcement of abdication and change which now comes later with 'Ye elves', &c. Shakespeare puts it here.

Sometimes he will even outrage the Mrs. Grundy of criticism by almost burlesquing the Grand Style, by letting Titania, in her deluded courtship of Bottom, be not merely graceful, and fanciful, and pathetically pleading, but by making her indulge in such positive magnificence, such sheer Sublime as

> The Summer still doth tend upon my state,

which the most serious poet, telling the severest tale, might be only too happy to have invented. At other times—the examples are frequent in the probably rehandled chronicle-plays—he will take another man's phrase which is not grand at all, and 'grandee' it—equip it with the Orders of the King, and the qualifications necessary to justify them—by a stroke or two of added or altered diction. Constantly it seems as though a sort of whim took him to be grand—or as if (in the words of one of his own characters who is too graceless for the strictly Grand Style, though grand enough in his own fashion) '*grandeur* lay in his way and he found it'. Some of these characters—Hamlet for one, of course, and Macbeth for another—would speak habitually in it if they had not more grace of congruity than to do so. There is no one who has it more perfectly than Antony—unless it be Cleopatra—when either chooses; and Othello at his best excels almost all others. Once more, if his last words be not in the Grand Style, where are we to look for it?

But the old *aporia*—the old curious fallacy-objection—recurs. 'These things *are* grand—but there is so much else that is *not* grand.' To this there is, once more, only the old answer to all fallacy-objections of the kind. 'Why not?' I suspect that the fallacy arises, as so many aesthetic fallacies do, from a confusion of Arts. It is sometimes forgotten that literature, especially in some of its forms, is much more of a macrocosm than any of its sister species of Imitation. The greater epic, the novel, and especially the drama, have got to face and reproduce life, character, action, circumstance, in all their varieties, foul as well as fair, trivial as well as dignified, commonplace as well as exceptional. To attempt to clothe all this in the same Grand Style, or in the Grand Style at all, is to offend against the sumptuary laws of Art itself. The so-called classical drama of modern time has made this attempt; and the wiser judgement of the best periods of criticism has decided that it has failed. Poetry at large tried to do it for a century and a half or thereabouts, and failed even more egregiously. Prose fiction never really succeeded until it cast the attempt aside. I have boldly confessed that I do not think Dante did attempt it; and that, though Milton certainly did, and achieved perhaps the only success on record, he paid for it somewhat dearly, and could not have attained what success he did attain but for the extremely exceptional nature of his subject. Further, I think that, in certain notorious passages, he actually tried to get out of the Grand Style—without succeeding in getting into anything else good. Your short poem, like your sculpture or your picture, is all the better for being Grand Style unmixed; not so your long one, and still less your drama. Thus Shakespeare himself never deserts the Grand Style in the *Sonnets*, or indeed in any of his poems, except—and then not always—songs in the plays of such a character that grandeur would be almost or wholly out of place. In his plays themselves he suits style to subject, and so alternates Grand Style with that which is not grand.

But the grandeur of its grandeur when it is grand! And the inexhaustible variety of it, and of the means whereby it is attained! I believe I was once rash enough to assert that you could not open a double page of the *Globe* edition—which means something more than two hundred lines—(excepting of course the prose passages, the plays only partially Shakespeare's and those dealing with purely comic matter) without coming on something unmistakably in the Grand Style. To justify this boast 'at the foot of the letter' would no doubt be difficult, seeing that there are something like five hundred such page-openings. But in such experiments as I have made—and they are numerous—I have very rarely drawn the cover blank, and have frequently 'found' where, from the subject and context, finding was unlikely.

This ubiquity of the Shakespearian Grand Style, as combined and contrasted with its abstinence from continuity, is one of its most notable characteristics, and is connected in the closest degree with that absence of mannerism which has been noted. The extreme difficulty of defining or even describing Shakespeare's style has been alike the theme and the despair of the commentators; it extends to, and is intensified in the case of, his *Grand* Style. The ticketing critics who were so common in classical times, and who are not unknown in modern, would be—some of the latter have been—hopelessly 'out' with him. You cannot fix on any special collocation of words like Milton's adoption and extension of the Chaucerian epithet before and after the noun; on any tricks of grammar like Milton's apposition; on any specially favourite words such as those to be found in the most diverse writers. It seems as if he had deliberately determined that no special mould, no particular tool, no *recipe* of mixture and arrangement, should be capable of being pointed out as his secret, or even as one of his secrets, of attaining grandeur. It has been remarked already that the subject, or at least the context of subject, hardly matters. But other things matter as little. Any vocabulary; any syntax; any rhetoric, will do for Shakespeare to produce his masterpieces; and it may sometimes seem as if—like conjurors very often and chemists sometimes—he had taken a sort of whimsical delight in producing his effects with the minimum of apparatus, or with apparatus of the least formal kind.

You may find curious instances of this in the very forefront of his work as it is read, though it may have been his last completed task. Take those two well-known lines of Prospero's,

In the dark backward and abysm of Time,

and

To act her earthy and abhorred commands.

Now a hasty critic may dismiss the most obvious device by which the style is raised in these as merely the old trick, familiar for generations before Shakespeare, and already almost caricatured by men like Fisher and Berners—the trick of combining native and imported elements. But there is something much more than a mere draft on the Teutonic and Romance columns of a conveniently arranged Dictionary of Synonyms. The double source *is* drawn upon; 'backward' and 'earthy' do stand to 'abysm' and 'abhorred' as the pairs so familiar in Bible and Prayer-book do to each other. But Shakespeare is not content with this grammar-school antithesis. In the first place, he varies the meaning in 'backward' and 'abysm', giving waste horizontal stretch in the one case and unplumbed depth in the other; and he also contrasts the mere sound of the words as much as possible, while deliberately adopting the form in 'ysm' for the sake of euphony. In the second he adds to the contrast of origin and sound a complete change of point of view. 'Earthy' is a quality of the commands; 'abhorred' an attitude of the mind commanded. He has tapped not one but many of the Longinian 'sources'; he has blended the products of his tapping. And yet these are mere everyday instances, the *ordinaire*, as it were, of his cellar.

Pass from the almost certainly last to one of the certainly earliest plays, the *Two Gentlemen*, and, avoiding the apex already quoted from it, taking (at whatever may be their full value) the imperfect construction, the more imperfect characterization, the superabundant evidences of the novitiate in conceit and word-play and trifling—consider for a moment one line of its second greatest passage (I. ii. 84),

The uncertain glory of an April day.

'Quite commonplace,' says the quite commonplace reader. 'Everybody knows that April days are uncertain.' But has everybody called them so in this simplicity and consummateness of phrase? Try obvious variants:

The fickle glory of an April day,

or 'the treacherous' or 'the passing', or a dozen others, not to mention the non-obvious ones which would have commended themselves to second- or tenth-rate writers of that day and this—far-fetched and dear-bought frigidities which will suggest themselves by the dozen. Then do the same thing with 'glory,' substituting 'splendour,' 'beauty,' what you will. Put all the results of experiment beside the actual text, and you will, if you have a Grand Style ear, have very little difficulty in determining where the Grand Style lies—with Ariel and the bee, not beside the lamp and in the chemist's shop.

To go through all the plays, even by sample at fancy, would be impossible; but it may perhaps be permitted to me to give a few more of my *sortes Shakespearianae*. I shall avoid, as I have avoided, except by general reference, the most famous passages—for there is no need to have recourse to them, and the means by which their effects are achieved, though always different in individual, are never different in general character from those manifest in the smaller instances—if any can be called small. The most general touch of all is perhaps that already noticed—the *ambidexterity* with which the poet uses the most and the least unusual phrases and words. He has neither a studied grandiloquence nor a studied simplicity, nor does he specially affect that peculiar source of sublimity—that is to say, 'transport'—which consists in a sort of catachresis or deliberate misuse of words in secondary intentions, like that frequently adopted by Sir Thomas Browne. He will at one moment write a phrase 'to tear with thunder the wide cheeks of the air', which has the very sound-effect of which it speaks, and which has the largeness of the universe itself, with metrical accompaniments to match; and then he will pass in the same speech from this poetical magnificence to the plain downright scorn of

This fellow had a Volscian to his mother.[3]

He will write, using the simplest words and most familiar metre,

Fear no more the heat of the sun,
Nor the furious winter's rages,

producing, it appears, on some people the effect of 'drivel'— certainly producing on others the effect of the most perfect and poignant poetry of ordinary life. And then, within a page or two, he will sketch a picture of war in a line and a half, with a couple of images of sound and sight that could not be beaten in effect by a paragraph, or another page:

That when they hear the Roman horses neigh,
Behold their quartered fires—

where the absence of superfluity, and the presence of concentration, are equally remarkable.[4] For my part, if I had any doubt about Shakespeare having a hand in *Pericles*, one line would settle it—

A terrible childbed hast thou had, my dear.[5]

For even Middleton or Webster, the two who have come nearest to Shakespearian phraseology, could hardly have achieved this curious union of simplicity and the Grand Style; while Cyril Tourneur, who has been thought by some to have the touch, certainly could not have achieved it.

Nor is it less interesting to examine the passages which— not of the greatest as wholes; not containing any of the actual 'jewels five words long' which are so plentiful; not exempt, it may be, from the less grand marks of the form and pressure of the time, in conceit and euphuism and absence of restraint—still betray this Grand Style of Shakespeare's. Take, for instance, that in some ways most Shakespearian of all the plays *not* greatest—*Timon of Athens*. The central situation is, of course, dramatic enough; but it is not perhaps one which lends itself to effective dramatic treatment of the Shakespearian kind, because there is not sufficient development of character; while it *does* lend itself to that Shakespearian divagation and promiscuity of handling which, though they do not disturb some of us, seem to disturb others so much. But the play is simply drenched with the Grand Style—every rift is packed with Grand Style gold—not, it may be, refined to the point of the greatest, but gold unmistakable. It peeps out of the rhetorical commonplaces of the professional cynic Apemantus:

> Like madness is the glory of this life,
> As this pomp shows to a little oil and root,

where the first verse at least is perfect.[6] Alcibiades—in Shakespeare's scheme not the Admirable Crichton of some views of him, if not of history, but only a rather good specimen of professional soldier—has vouchsafed to him that splendid cadence—

> Taught thee to make vast Neptune weep for aye
> On thy low grave, on faults forgiven. Dead
> Is noble Timon.[7]

The excellent Flavius—best of servants, but certainly not most poetical of men—is made mouthpiece of that glorious line—

> O! the fierce wretchedness that glory brings us.[8]

As for Timon himself, his misfortunes make him a Shakespeare. Even the first frantic retrospect of cursing on Athens is, till the rhyme comes at least, a Grand-Style raving. The address to 'the blessed breeding sun' is greater still; and the better known demonstration of the universality of thieving is raised by the style, despite its desperate quaintness, almost to the level of the greatest things in *Hamlet*.

The fact is, ladies and gentlemen, that this Grand Style is not easily tracked or discovered by observation, unless you give yourself up primarily to the *feeling* of it. You cannot tell how it arises, and you will often have some difficulty in deciding why it goes. It is the truest, precisely because it is the most irresponsible, of the winds of the spirit—no trade wind or Etesian gale, but a breeze that rises and falls, if not exactly as *it* listeth—as the genius of the poet and the occasions of the subject list. We may recur once more—in the useful, not the useless, fashion of comparison, the fashion which appraises qualities, but does not ticket values—to the four names which, in Literature, have been most frequently associated with this Style. Homer has it in a form scarcely comparable with the others. If we had more early Greek epic—more especially if we had Antimachus—we should be much better judges of the Homeric Grand Style than we are. As it is, we see in it extraordinary and extraordinarily varied melody of verse and phrase, a use of Figure, especially of Simile, which is unsurpassed, and to which indeed all subsequent literary poetry is directly or indirectly indebted; and one great engine, the elaborate and mostly perpetual epithet, which is a great puzzle to cautious and widely experienced critics. For the ancients will not tell us exactly how these epithets affected them; and we ought to know, lest we make the same mistakes which, as we see, foreigners are constantly making about English, and which, no doubt, Englishmen as frequently make about foreign literature.

We are safer with Dante, for there we have practically all possible facilities of comparison. The language is still living; we know what those who have spoken and written it since

thought and think about it; and we have our own independent, but in this case fully informed, judgement to be the sovereign guide. We find that there is undoubtedly a *prevalent* style in Dante: and that this is of a peculiar *gravity*, the gravest style perhaps in all literature, yet in no sense stiff or stilted, and not (to some tastes) at all affected. But it seems, to some at least, that this style is very largely influenced, and even to some considerable extent produced, by the metre—which is of an intense idiosyncrasy, and though not in the least monotonous, curiously uniform in general atmosphere—much more so indeed than the Greek hexameter, and quite infinitely more so than the English blank verse. We find, further, that Dante has no exclusive preference for lofty images or even expressions: and that though he will use the most elaborate and carefully-sifted poetic-pictorial diction, his Grand Style is not so much a matter of that as of the suffused atmosphere or *aura* spoken of above. There is in fact, in the old sense of the word as applied to music, a Dantesque *mode*—pervading everything and affecting grotesque, extravagance, pedantry—(these are not *my* words, but such as others use)—almost or quite as much as the grander parts themselves. Breaking chronological order, for obvious reasons, we come to Milton, and here again we find something all-pervading. But its nature is different: and so is the nature of its pervasion. It is practically independent of metre—for the peculiarity of blank verse is that it imposes no character of its own, but takes that of its writer—'blankness' in the worst sense; the 'tumid gorgeousness' which Johnson, not without some excuse, mistook for its differentia; or a varied magnificence in the best and strictest sense of that word, which knows no limit and accepts no rule. The Miltonic style is quite above the Miltonic metre in one sense of 'above,' though hardly in another; it is perceivable almost equally, in the complicated stanza of the 'Nativity', in the octo-syllables of the early middle poems, in the rhymed blank verse of *Lycidas*, in the pure blank verse of the *Paradises*, in the dialogue and the chorics of *Samson*. It admits variety; but here also, *plus ça change, plus c'est la même chose*. I do not know that we can free it from the label of affectation; though it is affectation transcendentalized and sublimed. The proof is that it cannot descend and unbend as Dante's can. But we are not talking at length of Milton here. Suffice it to say, that this undoubted uniformity, with the less universal but somewhat similar uniformity of Dante, which no doubt patterned it, and the quite different uniformity of Homer, undoubtedly helped to create the idea of a Grand Style existing almost *ab extra*, and bound to present itself separately, at demand, everywhere, for everything.

To this idea Shakespeare is certainly rebel; if a manner so absolutely aristocratic as his can even admit the suggestion of rebellion. Milton he cannot be for many reasons, including the fact that he has to go before Milton can come; Dante he does not choose to be; Shakespeare he is. And as being Shakespeare—in order, indeed, to make what we mean by Shakespeare—he uses the Grand Style as his Attendant Spirit. He says to it, 'Come,' and it comes; he says to it, 'Go,' and it goes. It is not his master, as to some extent their styles were the masters both of Dante and of Milton. He does not make it his mistress, as not a few hardly lesser men have done—caressing it; doing homage to it; and never letting it out of his sight if he can help. Sometimes he seems almost wilfully and capriciously to give it its *congé*—to take up with inferior creatures for pastime. But this is a delusion. He knows that to employ a being so majestical for every purpose of a dramatic household is a profanation—that she is for the pageants and the passions, for the big wars and the happy or unhappy loves, for the actions and the agonies of pith and moment. For the rest, the handmaidens and the serving men, the clowns and the fools, the Osrics and the Poloniuses will do; though he will not grudge even to them, when it suits him, a touch of the higher language, a flash of the sublimer thought. To this you must make up your mind, if you go a Grand-Styling with Shakespeare.

There is no fear, as I said before, of drawing the covers blank. Take for our last instance that strange play—so puzzling in many ways, so offensive, I believe, to some good wits, such a mixture of almost the highest Shakespeare and almost the most ordinary University Wit—take *Troilus and Cressida*. Neglect, while to this or that extent acknowledging—for, if you cannot combine acknowledgement and neglect in this way, you may be an excellent neighbour and a very good bowler, but you are no critic—neglect the disappointment in the handling of some of the characters, the confused action, the uncomely patches. Neglect further—or rather do not neglect, but use only as a contrast and foil—the tale of bombasted blank verse and craggy conceited phrase as it seems to some. Postpone for consideration the jumble (I am here speaking throughout the language of the Advocatus Diaboli) of long-winded tirades and word-playing prose. What remains in your sieve—your crucible—your gold-washing cradle? Not merely the famous 'One touch of nature' which has been so frequently and so curiously misinterpreted. Not merely the less generally known but hardly inferior beauties of that same magnificent speech which begins—

Time hath, my lord, a wallet at his back,

and ends—

Made emulous missions 'mongst the Gods themselves
And drave great Mars to faction.[9]

This singular throwing into dramatic form of the ordinary Troy-books perpetually develops Grand Style; the commonplaces of Nestor and the other chiefs break into it in the same odd fashion in which an apparently quiet wave, hardly undulating the surface a little way from shore, will break on the beach itself with a sudden burst of glittering thunder. It is extraordinary how the *gnōmai* (the 'sentences', as Greek and Latin rhetoricians would have called them) of the great debating Third Scene of the First Act stick in one's memory. The play itself is never acted; never used for those official purposes which, I fear, make other parts of Shakespeare best known to us both in youth and age; nor is it in all ways seductive to private reading. Yet the Grand Style impression is made constantly: though with that singular diversity and elusiveness of means, direct and suggested, to which attention has been drawn throughout. Take this:

There is seen
The baby figure of the giant mass
Of things to come at large.[10]

That is no bad instance of what may be called the middle or average Shakespearian Grand Style—perhaps indeed it is a little below the average. It is all the better example. The poet takes, you see, the most ordinary words—the actual vocabulary of the phrase is not above even Wordsworthian proof. He takes for figure an equally ordinary antithesis—'baby' and 'giant'— though a different writer would probably have spoilt his own farther chances by using 'pygmy' or 'dwarf', instead of 'baby'. And here he gets his first hold on us; for the baby, unlike the dwarf, will grow—though whether it will grow to giant size or not, only the Future can tell. Then he thinks of something else—'figure' and 'mass' being not, like 'baby' and 'giant' contrasts of size merely, but indicating the form, the idea, that is to be impressed on the mass. And then he is not satisfied with

the limited greatness of 'giant mass' itself; but expands and flings it out into the obscure infinity of things to come, and of things to come *at large*. You have passed in some dozen or sixteen words, artfully selected, from the definite doll of the baby figure to the vast of Space and Time.

This may seem a fanciful sermon on a more fancifully selected text; but I venture to hope that it may induce some who have not yet thought on the matter to take not uninteresting views of the Grand Style in general and of Shakespeare's Grand Style in particular. They will not find these views easily exhaustible: all the less so because all really Grand Style appeals to a certain complementary gift and faculty in the person who is to appreciate it; it is a sort of infinitely varying tally, which awaits and adjusts itself to an infinite number of counter-pieces. It abides; the counter-pieces may get themselves ready as they can and will.

*Notes*

1. See the lectures *On Translating Homer.*
2. *King Lear*, v. iii. 174.
3. *Coriolanus*, v. iii. 151, 178.
4. *Cymbeline*, IV. ii. 258, iv. 17.
5. *Pericles*, III. i. 57.
6. *Timon of Athens*, I. ii. 139.
7. Ibid. v. iv. 78.
8. Ibid. IV. ii. 30.
9. *Troilus and Cressida*, III. iii. 145 ff.
10. *Troilus and Cressida*, I. iii. 345.

## J. J. JUSSERAND
From "What to Expect of Shakespeare" (1911)
*The School for Ambassadors and Other Essays*
1925, pp. 293–322

I

When Ronsard died at St. Côme, near Tours, in December, 1585, Shakespeare being then twenty-one, all France went into mourning; besides the ceremonies at St. Côme, solemn obsequies were celebrated at Paris, orations were delivered in French and in Latin by Cardinal Du Perron and others; the crowd was such that princes and magnates had to be denied admission for lack of space; not one poet of note failed to express his sorrow for the national loss; these elegies were collected under the title of "Le Tombeau de Ronsard."

On April 25, 1616, the bell of Holy Trinity Church at Stratford tolled, as we read in the register, for "William Shakespeare, Gentleman," one of the chief men of the town, wealthy, good-humored, benevolent, known to have been somebody in the capital, and to have written successful plays. A monument was raised to him with a florid inscription, such as is often granted to provincial celebrities. It was in fact a local event. "No longer mourn for me," the poet had written, "when I am dead,"

Then you shall hear the surly sullen bell
Give warning to the world that I am fled
From this vile world.

But the world knew nothing of it; the British capital paid no attention to it; not one line was written on the occasion, no poet mourned the event. "At the passing of the greatest Elizabethan the Muse shed not one tear."[1] When his plays were collected seven years after his death, they were preceded by a few eulogies, the authors whereof extolled his merits, but several went beyond what they really thought, for they had to conform to the rules of the *genre*. The friends and fellow-players of the author, who had edited the collection, apologetically offered "these trifles" to two noblemen who had been pleased to think them "something heretofore." A second edition was only wanted nine years after the first, and a third only thirty-one years after the second.

What we see now needs no description. With the single exception of the Bible, no book has been, in the same space of time, the subject of such close studies and such ardent comments as the collection of "trifles" first given to the world by Heminge and Condell in 1623. During the first five years of the present century twenty-seven new editions of Shakespeare's works were pulished; princes have played in his tragedies the part of princes, kings have tried their hand at translating his works. Some of his dramas have been acted in Japanese; his *Julius Cæsar* has been performed in the Roman theatre at Orange: a fact the knowledge of which might perhaps have restrained the maledictions of Maurice Morgann who, writing in 1777, exclaimed: "When the hand of time will have brushed off his present editors and commentators and when the very name of Voltaire and even the memory of the language in which he has written shall be no more, the Apalachian mountains, the banks of the Ohio, and the plains of Sciota shall resound with the accents of this Barbarian."[2]

Shakespeare's ideas, his sayings, the personages to whom he has given life, the scenes he has depicted, have become indeed familiar to all; men born much further than "the banks of the Ohio," nay, at the very Antipodes, will catch an allusion to a scene, a character, a word of Shakespeare's. By the middle of the last century the British Museum counted some three hundred entries under the word Shakespeare; it counts now more than five thousand.

A responsibility uncourted and unexpected by him weighs now on the poet. Books, like their authors, have their biography. They live their own lives. Some behave like honorable citizens of the world of thought, do good, propagate sound views, strengthen heart and courage, assuage, console, improve those men to whose hearths they have been invited. Others corrupt or debase, or else turn minds towards empty frivolities. In proportion to their fame, and to the degree of their perenniality is the good or evil that they do from century to century, eternal benefactors of mankind or deathless malefactors. Posted on the road followed by humanity, they help or hurt the passers-by; they deserve gratitude eternal, or levy the toll of some of our life's blood, leaving us weaker; highwaymen or good Samaritans. Some make themselves heard at once and continue to be listened to for ever; others fill the ears for one or two generations, and then begin an endless sleep; or, on the contrary, long silent or misunderstood, they awaken from their torpor, and astonished mankind discovers with surprise long-concealed treasures like those trodden upon by the unwary visitor of unexplored ruins. No works are so familiar to the nations of the world at those of Shakespeare to-day. In their continued and increasing existence what sort of life are they leading?

In the course of ages, while praise and admiration were becoming boundless, an anxious note has been sounded from time to time, the more striking that it came from admirers. Two examples will be enough to make the point clear. While stating that "the stream of time, which is continually washing the dissoluble fabrics of other poets, passes without injury by the adamant of Shakespeare," Dr. Johnson, who wanted his very dictionary to be morally useful through the examples selected by him for each word,[3] stated that Shakespeare, in spite of his beginning "to assume the dignity of an ancient, and claim the privilege of established fame," had for his "first defect that to which may be imputed most of the evils in books or in

men. He sacrifices virtue to convenience, and is so much more careful to please than to instruct that he seems to write without any moral purpose. . . . It is always a writer's duty to make the world better."[4]

Nearer our time, another, no enemy like Tolstoi, who considers that Shakespeare "has the basest and most vulgar conception of the world,"[5] but a passionate admirer, Emerson, for whom Shakespeare was not *a* poet, but *the* poet, the "representative" poet wrote: "And now, how stands the account of man with this bard and benefactor, when, in solitude, shutting our ears to the reverberations of his fame, we seek to strike the balance? Solitude has austere lessons. . . . He converted the elements, which waited on his command, into entertainments. He was master of the revels to mankind. . . . As long as the question is of talent and mental power, the world of men has not his equal to show. But when the question is as to life, and its materials, and its auxiliaries, how does it profit me? What does it signify? It is but a *Twelfth Night*, or *Midsummer-Night's Dream*, or a *Winter Evening's Tale*: what signifies another picture more or less?"[6]

So spoke Emerson in one of those Essays which Matthew Arnold went so far as to describe as "the most important work done in English prose" in the nineteenth century.

What is it then that we possess? What can we expect of Shakespeare? Is the treasure in this bewitching garden of Hesperides mere glitter, or is it real gold? Do we listen to the seer that can help solve our problems, answer our doubts, instruct our ignorance, soften the hardness of our hearts, brace our courage? Or does the great book whose fame fills the world offer us mere revels, vain dreams and tales, no moral purpose of value, virtue sacrificed to convenience, such evanescent food as was served on Prospero's table for the unworthy?

## II

Shortly after he had reached his majority, Shakespeare came to London, very poor, having received but a grammar school education, upheld by no protectors. The son of a tradesman, he reached the huge capital where one of his Stratford compatriots was established as a grocer, another as a printer. For some years he disappears, and when we hear of him again he is beginning to be known as an author. Having come to the city with no trade of his own, he had obviously soon discovered that he was better fitted to write plays than to sell groceries, and to compose books than to print them. He was apparently still in Stratford in 1585–6; six years later London dramatists are feeling jealous of the new play-mender or maker, five years after that he is a wealthy man, and purchases New Place, the finest house in Stratford, built by its most famous citizen, a former Lord Mayor of London. He was then thirty-three. Promptitude is the salient trait of such a career. When he died at fifty-two, Shakespeare left thirty-seven plays; when Racine died at sixty, only twelve.

Literary invention has been the subject in our days of minute research on the part of philosophers. Paulhan has shown[7] what different roads lead to that supreme result, a memorable book of lasting fame. One road passes through the Elysian fields, another crosses the region made doleful by Tantalus, Ixion, and Sisyphus's ceaseless groans. For that modern dramatist Dumas *fils* the labor of literary composition was accompanied, according to Binet and Passy, who went to ask him, by "a great feeling of pleasure. While he writes he is in a better humor, he eats, drinks, and sleeps more; he feels a kind of physical enjoyment through the exercising of a physical function. He does not seek isolation or silence, like those authors whose weakened inspiration vanishes at the slightest interference from external things." His manuscripts were almost without erasures. "We have never seen," his visitors say, "such neat manuscripts," in spite of his often writing at full speed; such, for instance, was the case for the *Dame aux Camélias*; he had "covered the paper with a firm and regular handwriting in which the eye looks in vain for the disorder of improvisation; page follows page without a single erasure. Mr. Dumas had moreover a horror of erasures, blots, interlineations and corrections."[8]

Others, like Rousseau, or Flaubert, had a different tale to tell: "My ideas," wrote Rousseau, "group themselves in my head with the most incredible difficulty: they move about obscurely, they ferment to the extent of upsetting me and giving me heart beats, and in the midst of all that emotion I see nothing clearly; I could not write a single word, I must wait." The same with Flaubert: "I am in a rage without knowing why: my novel, maybe, is the cause. It does not come, all goes wrong; I am more tired than if I had mountains to bear; at times I could weep. . . . I have spent four hours without being able to write a phrase. . . . Oh, Art, Art, what is that mad chimera that bites our heart, and why?"[9]

To the latter group most decidedly belongs Shakespeare's great rival, Ben Jonson. One must "labour," said he sententiously; one must be "laboured"; facility is the most dangerous of the Will-o'-the-wisps; it leads to bogs and marshes; do not follow Jack-o'-lanterns, bright as may be the lanterns; retrace your steps, "The safest is to return to our judgment and handle over again those things the easiness of which might make them justly suspected."[10]

To the first class undoubtedly belonged Shakespeare. The number of his plays and the brief interval between the composition of each, two or three plays a year being his average production during the first eight years of his authorship, show that he must have written with the "fine frenzy" attributed by his duke Theseus to the gifted ones, and flying "an eagle flight, bold and forth on," like the poet in his own "Timon." "My manuscripts," said Rousseau, "are scratched, blotted, besmeared, illegible, testifying to the trouble they have given me." Of Shakespeare, as stated before,[11] his fellow-players, who had seen him at work, said: "What he thought he uttered with that easiness that we have scarce received from him a blot in his papers." "He never blotted out a line?" grumbled Jonson; "would he had blotted a thousand!" His manuscripts obviously looked like those of Dumas *fils*, not like those of Rousseau.

He had his own ways, and rather followed, to quote him again, his own "free drift." Why take so much trouble, when what he himself expected of his plays could be reached without any of those Ixion-like agonies described by Rousseau and the others? For what he expected was simple enough, plain enough, and near at hand. What he expected he did actually attain, and his life was a successful life. His eye was on Stratford, not on posterity. His dream was to end his days a well-to-do respected citizen in his native town, and that dream was fulfilled. The idea of his being held later the Merlin of unborn times, the revealer of the unknown, the leader of men of thought and feeling, the life-giver, the pride of his country, never occurred to him, and would probably have made him laugh. His allusions to literary immortality in the *Sonnets* were only a way of speaking, which he had in common with the merest sonnet scribblers, as was well shown by Sir Sidney Lee; and since he never printed his, he cannot have cared much for an everlasting fame to be secured through them. For his poems proper he took some trouble; he published them; they were works of art; for his plays, a secondary *genre* in the common estimation and in his, he took none; they were things of no import. He never printed any; garbled copies of some of the best were issued, he did not care; he left no authentic text in view of a posterity which had never been in his thoughts; no books are mentioned in his will.

### III

Literary fame as a dramatist troubled him not, but present necessities could not be forgotten; chief among them the necessity of pleasing his public. His average public, the one he had chiefly in view, whose average heart and mind he had to touch and delight, was that of the Globe, a large, much-frequented house which drew popular audiences, and where accidentally some Ambassador might appear,[12] the fate of the play would, however, depend not upon the Ambassador's applause or some learned critic's blame, but on the impression of the crowd: a boisterous crowd, warm-hearted, full-blooded, of unbounded patriotism, a lover of extremes, now relishing the sight of tortures, now moved at the death of a fly ("How if that fly had a father and a mother?"[13]), a lover of the improbable, of unexpected changes, of coarse buffooneries, quibbles, common witticisms easy to understand, of loud noises of any sort, bells, trumpets, cannon; men, all of them, of an encyclopædic ignorance.

The part of such a public, as a contributor to Shakespeare's plays, can scarcely be over-estimated—a real contributor to whom it seemed at times as if Shakespeare had passed on the pen to scribble as it pleased, or the chalk to draw sketches on the wall. What such people would like, and what they would tolerate, is what gave those plays, which he never thought of after the performance, the unique, the marvellous, the portentous shape in which we find them. Great is the *de facto* responsibility of such a public; great that of Shakespeare too for having never denied it anything; great rather would that have been if he had not purposely intended to please only those living men, assembled in his theatre, on whom his own fortune depended; "For we," even Dr. Johnson had to acknowledge,

For we that live to please, must please to live.

From the writing of his plays, however, Shakespeare expected not one thing but two; first, immediate success with his public, and all that depended on it; second, the pleasant, happy, delightful satisfaction of a function of his brain duly exercised. This for us is the chief thing, what saved him in spite of himself: to the coarse food his groundlings wanted he added the ethereal food which has been for ages the relish of the greatest in mankind, while it had proved quite acceptable to his groundlings too. He added this as a supererogatory element because it was in him to do so, because it gave him no more trouble than to put in quibbles, jokes, or massacres, and because experience had shown him that, while it was not at all necessary to success, it did not hurt, and was received with a good grace. It was for him the exercise of a natural function, as it is for a good tree to produce good fruit.

Hence the strange nature of that work, touching all extremes, the model of all that should be aimed at, and of much that should be avoided; of actual use both ways. Prompt writing, as he had no choice (he had to live), the courting of a public whose acceptance of his work was indispensable, explain, with his prodigious, heaven-bestowed genius, how the best and the worst go together, hand in hand, in his plays, those flashes of a light that will never fade, and those concessions to the popular taste (indecencies, brutalities, mystifications, tortures, coarse jokes, over-well-explained complications), or the advantage so often taken by him of the fact that the public will not know, will not remember, will not mind. "He omits," says Dr. Johnson, "opportunities of instructing or delighting which the train of his story seems to force upon him"; the reason being that, in some cases, such opportunities did not occur to him at once and that he had little time for reconsidering; given his public, that would do. Hence also his anachronisms, his faulty geography, his indifference to real facts, so complete that he would not have stretched out his hand to take a book and verify the place of a city or the date of an event, nor would he have asked his future son-in-law, the physician, whether a human being that has been smothered can still speak. He offers to his groundlings, and not to this learned age of which he never thought and which has no right to complain, a reign of King John without *Magna Charta*, but with plenty of gunpowder and with a Duke of Austria who was dead before the play begins: Beware, says the king to the French Ambassador, "the thunder of my cannon." His Alençon, the companion in arms of Jeanne d'Arc, is prematurely described as a "notorious Machiavel." The presence of the Turks in Constantinople perturbs his Henry V, though they reached there only thirty-one years after this king's death. Shakespeare adopts, for convenience sake, two rules to which none of his hearers could be tempted to object; one is, that all antique personages having lived in antiquity are, generally speaking, contemporaries and can quote one another, so his Hector quotes Aristotle centuries before he could have been enlightened by the sage's wisdom; his Menenius has faith in Galen's prescriptions six hundred years before Galen could prescribe, and talks of Alexander a century and a half ahead of time; his Titus Lartius compares Coriolanus to unborn Cato, and so on. The other rule is that, as we have seen, all distant towns are by the seaside. Rome, Florence, Milan, Mantua, Padua, Verona, Aleppo (to say nothing of Bohemia) are by the seaside. His personages go by sea from Padua to Pisa, from Verona to Milan. Why take trouble? He wrote only for men who neither knew nor cared, composing plays not meant to survive and which had two "begetters," Shakespeare and the motley crew at the Globe.

## IV

They have survived, however; their hold on the world increases as years pass, they are famous in regions the very name of which was unknown to their author. In the calm of our study, in the corner of a railway carriage, on the deck of a ship, we open the book and read the first scene of any play: Prospero's magic works on us; we are his, ready to follow him anywhere, to feel and believe as he tells us. The sight once seen, the words once heard, so impress themselves on our mind that the mere name of the place, of the man, woman, or child cannot be pronounced henceforth without the grand or lovely landscape, the loving, hating, laughing, weeping personage from the plays, and with him all that pertains to him, his family, his enemy, his friend, his house, his dog, appearing to us in as vivid a light as if he were here alive again, and we were pacing with him the terraces at Elsinore, the moonlit garden of the Capulets, the storm-ridden, witch-haunted heath of *Lear* or *Macbeth*, the woods near Athens, the forum at Rome, the enchanted park for an enchantress at Belmont, or the real battlefields where, in bloody conflict, France and England were shaping their destinies.

So much life, such an intensity of realization are in the plays, that it is difficult to visit, in actual life, any of those places which Shakespeare sometimes merely named and did not describe, without the Shakespearean hero first appearing to us, before even we think of the real men famous there in times past. Grand or sweet figures, lovers whom death will sweep away, or leaders of armies, anxious Hamlet, scornful Coriolanus, loving Romeo, pensive Brutus, irrepressible Falstaff, and those daffodils of man's eternal spring—Portia,

Rosalind, Ophelia, Juliet, Desdemona—rise bewitching, terrible, or laughable, at the mere sound of the words Elsinore, Eastcheap, Arden, Verona, Cyprus. So long as the mirage lasts our lives seem merged into theirs. Between the true artist and the product of his brain the phenomenon is a frequent one, but between the product of his brain and the readers of the book it much more rarely happens: "A delightful thing it is," said Flaubert in one of his rare happy moods, "to write, to be no longer oneself, but to move through the whole creation one has called forth. To-day, for example, man and woman together, lover and mistress at the same time, I have ridden in a forest, during an autumnal afternoon, under yellow leaves; and I was the horses, the leaves, the wind, the words that were said, and the red sun that caused them to half close their eyelids bathed in love." This privilege of the author, Shakespeare, for better, for worse, imparts to his listener or reader.

For better or for worse? Some of his worshippers, thereby courting protest and inviting injustice of an opposite sort, have dogmatized on his perfections, his omniscience, his prescience, the safe guidance he offers in every possible trouble, and the unimpeachable solution he propounds for every difficulty.

Wiser it is perhaps to acknowledge at once, with due deference to the purest intentions, that it is not exactly so. More than one of the gravest questions that, from the beginning, have troubled mankind would be put in vain to the poet, for to them he has no answer. What he does is to place the problem before us with such force that he obliges us to think seriously of those serious questions; hence of use, though of a different use than is sometimes said.

Concerning religions he does not take sides, as is evidenced by the fact that discussions are still renewed now and then (though there is little room for doubt) as to what faith he belonged to. The lesson he gives us is, however, a great one; it was a rare one in his day, and it is summed up in the word "toleration."

No problem is put oftener and more vividly before his audience than that of death and of the hereafter. To this he has no answer. In their calmest moods his personages hope for sleep: "Our little life is rounded with a sleep." Oftener he and they (he in the sonnets, they in the plays) pore over the prospect of physical dissolution, when the time shall come to leave "this vile world, with vilest worms to dwell." It seems as if for him as an author the apologue of the sparrow, told to King Eadwine by one of his Northumbrian chiefs, had been told in vain. We still "go we know not where," and no Isabella, be she almost a nun, and bound by her part in the play to act as a consoler, has any word to clear Claudio's doubts or ours. "If I must die," says Claudio, sadly,

> I will encounter darkness as a bride,
> and hug it in mine arms.

The attitude of Shakespeare, the writer, is that of the awe-inspiring genius whom Saint-Gaudens seated in Rock Creek cemetery, sad, resigned, speechless, not of the one who carries upwards, from earth to heaven, the sacred flame of life in Bartholomé's monument on the burial ground of the poor and friendless at Père Lachaise.

As a patriot his teachings are of the common sort. Patriotism has two sides: it concerns our own country considered in itself, then our country considered in relation to others. The first kind of duty, the most natural and easiest, is admirably fulfilled by the warm-hearted, the sound, and thorough Englishman that the poet was, justly proud of the great deeds of glorious ancestors: most men feel that way without any teaching; their feeling, however, cannot but be vivified by Shakespeare's admirable lines on this "dear, dear land,"

> This precious stone set in the silver sea,
>
> . . .
>
> . . . that pale, that white-fac'd shore
> Whose foot spurns back the ocean's roaring,
> And coops from other lands her islanders.

The sons of that same dear land inspire him, as such, with the same confident pride that his Henry V felt in them:

> And you, good yeomen,
> Whose limbs were made in England, show us here
> The mettle of your pasture.

As to the other side of patriotism, Shakespeare writes not only as a man of his day, but as a man who had to echo his public's feelings: an echo can make no change. To understand that to picture the vanquished as a huge crew of cowards, traitors, and scoundrels, afraid of their own shadow, was *not* to increase the glory of a victory, proved beyond the reasoning capacity of the crowd at the Globe. The poet allows them to have their own way, to hold his pen, and write in his plays their own views of what an enemy must have been. They were his only care; unborn posterity and ratiocinating critics that would come to life long after the plays were dead, as he believed, could have on him no influence.

On those great social problems which, in this modern world of ours, fill so much space in the thoughts of all, Shakespeare again expresses himself with the force and pregnancy of a man of incomparable genius; but he speaks as a man of his time and of his *milieu*, not as a man above them. The foibles of the uneducated masses, their credulity, their fickleness, their alternate fits of enthusiasm and depression, their aptitude to cruelty, their inability to understand, are depicted with the stern accuracy of a clear-eyed, unfriendly observer. The counterpart of such vices, or the extenuating circumstances resulting from involuntary ignorance, hardship, and misery, are scarcely visible anywhere. The people, throughout the plays, are the same people, with the same faults, be they the Romans of *Coriolanus* or of *Cæsar*, or the English of Jack Cade, or even the Danes of *Hamlet* (with their selection of Laertes for a king); they are the people. Shakespeare no more hesitates to hold them up to the laughter and scorn of their brethren in the pit, than Molière hesitated to make the real court marquesses laugh at the marquesses in his comedies, or than to-day's playwrights hesitate to ask a middle-class audience to laugh at the faults and folly of middle-class characters. Shakespeare's lesson may be of use to statesmen, scarcely to the people themselves, since for a useful castigation of the many, the most efficacious factor is love.

On one more question of keen, though less general, interest, we would appeal in vain to Shakespeare the playwright; that is for information about himself. Few men (I know that contrary views have been eloquently defended) have allowed less of their personality to appear in works dealing so directly with the human passions. Shakespeare's personality was of the least obtrusive; except in Stratford where he wanted to be, and succeeded in being, a personage, his natural disposition was to *keep aloof*. This general tendency is revealed by all we know about him. In an age and a *milieu* of quarrels, fights, literary and other disputes, he avoids all chances of coming to the front. "His works," said Dr. Johnson, "support no opinion with argument, nor supply any faction with invectives." The exceedingly curious discoveries of Professor Wallace show us, as we have seen, Shakespeare unwittingly thrown by events into a quarrel; his efforts to minimize his rôle and to withdraw and disappear are the most conspicuous trait in the new-found documents. The very reverse of his friend Ben Jonson, who courted trouble and proclaimed his opinion on all problems and all people, he carefully avoided every cause of dispute. As we know, he neither printed his dramas nor claimed or denied the authorship of any play; no writer of that day published his poems without laudatory lines from his friends; Shakespeare, keeping apart, never gave nor requested any.

On rare occasions his persistence in expressing again and again certain views or feelings, or the casual inappropriateness of his personages' saying what they say, leave us no doubt that he adored music, loved the land of his birth, did not trust the mob, knew what a classical play was, objected to child-players, etc. These are exceptional occasions. The change we notice in the tone of his plays, as years pass, rather follows the curve of human life, of a life that might be almost any man's, than reveals individual peculiarities in their author. One of his chief characteristics (and merits) is, on the contrary, the free play he allows to his heroes' personality, and his care not to encumber them with his own. They go forth, fill the stage, fill the drama with their explanations and apologies, so freely, so unimpeded by the author, who seems simply to listen, that the spectator will at times remain in doubt which of them to believe and which to love. They pay no heed to Shakespeare, and they expound or contradict their maker's opinion without even knowing which. They are created independent and alive; they continue so to-day, the very reverse of so many characters in Hugo's dramas, mere spokesmen of the poet who wanted to imitate Shakespeare, but forgot to conceal, as his model had done, his own figure behind the scenes.

The *Sonnets* confirm these views; there alone Shakespeare's personality is, in a large measure, bared to the eye. But there the personage whose turn had come to speak was William Shakespeare, who used the same freedom that he had allowed to Shylock, Hamlet, Henry V, or Richard III. For him it was a kind of safety-valve giving vent to sentiments which would have been out of place anywhere else; but it was enough for him to have put them down in writing; he did not go the length of sending the sonnets to the press.

V

Far above any of those single questions rises the one of general import, propounded by Dr. Johnson, Emerson, and others: that of the permanent impression left by the plays on listeners or readers.

During the whole period to which Shakespeare belongs, and before his day too and long after, in his country and out of it, most men agreed that plays must moralize and improve mankind: they have other *raisons d'être*, but this is the chief one. Tragedy and comedy, said Ronsard, are, above all, "didascaliques et enseignantes." Sir Philip Sidney was of the same opinion. The true poet, said Ben Jonson, must be "able to inform young men to all good discipline, inflame grown men to all great virtues, keep old men in their best and supreme state," and he deplored the debasement of that sacred rôle among his contemporaries, especially in dramatic poetry. According to Corneille, the chief point is to paint virtue and vice just as they are; "and then," said he, with his austere optimism, "virtue is sure to win all hearts even in misery, and vice is sure to be hated even triumphant." "The stage," said Racine, "should be a school where virtue would be taught no less than in the schools of philosophy." Samuel Johnson deemed that a drama should cause "useful mirth and salutary woe," and he wrote his ill-fated *Irene* to show, but it turned out that no one wanted to be shown, "how heaven supports the virtuous mind . . . what anguish racks the guilty breasts," and "that peace from innocence must flow"; while Voltaire, for reasons of his own it is true, placed, in his *Babouc*, the moralizing influence of tragedies far above that of sermons.

The only shackles Shakespeare was loaded with were the needs and tastes of his public. They were heavy enough, but they were the only ones. The absence of others is so complete and so unique that this characteristic is among the most singular offered to our wonder by his works. Barring this single exception, no poet cast on the wide world a freer and clearer gaze. He wrote unhampered by traditions, rules, religious systems. He gave himself the pleasure of showing once that he knew dramatic rules existed, but he left them alone because they were "caviare to the general," and he depended on "the general." They were probably, besides, not so very sweet to him either. The final result is that, strange as it may seem, he stands much nearer Aristotle than many of Aristotle's learned followers. The great philosopher did nothing but sum up the teachings of good sense and adapt them to Greek manners. The great poet did nothing but follow the teachings of good sense, as given him by his own sound nature, and adapt them to English wants. As both were men of genius and both were excellent observers, the one taught and the other acted in similar fashion.

On the question of morality, Aristotle makes it quite evident that his own ideal is a drama in which vice is punished or even has no place; but he clearly states also that the rational end of dramatic poetry is not to moralize but to give pleasure (*pros hēdonēn*).

On this question, as on that of "rules"—mere suggestions, not "rules" in Aristotle's intentions—Shakespeare's attitude was the same. He would not go out of his way either to secure or to avoid an ethical conclusion or conformity to rules. His plays were truly written "without any moral purpose," that is, instruction was not their object. But to conclude that they do not therefore instruct at all is to wander from truth. First, in some plays the events represented are, as in real life, so full of meaning that the moral is no less obvious than in any classical tragedy with a confidant or a chorus to tell us what to think; and even, at times, the hero tells us that. No one can escape the lesson to be drawn from the fate of Macbeth, of Coriolanus, of Antony, of poor Falstaff and his wild companions. Augustus in Corneille's *Cinna* does not moralize with greater effect on his past than does Macbeth:

> Better be with the dead
> Whom we, to gain our place, have sent to peace,
> Than on the torture of the mind to lie
> In restless ecstasy.

In many cases, however, it seems as if the evil power so often at play in Greek tragedies, and in real life too, were leading the innocent to their destruction: Othello, Desdemona, Hamlet, as worthy of pity as Oedipus; fatality imposing on them tasks for which nature has not armed them, or offering them temptations to which they would not have yielded had they been less generous. Are those plays of no moral use, or is their use limited to those maxims and pregnant sayings which Corneille considered one of the chief causes of a tragedy's usefulness, and which abound in Shakespeare—

> 'Tis time to fear when tyrants seem to kiss.

> Great men may jest with Saints; 'tis wit in them,
> But in the less, foul profanation—

and others so well known that one scarcely dares to quote them?

One instinct, and only one, appears in man at his birth, that of conservation. The child eats, sleeps, does what care for his growth commands, and can no more think of anything else than a tree can think of whether its roots absorb sap that ought

to have gone to the next tree. What happens later is of immense interest: if too much of that native instinct persists and more than is strictly necessary for preservation survives, then the perverted being solidifies into a low, mean, dry-hearted egoist. To call him with Stirner an "egotheist" (*Homo sibi Deus*),[14] to deify the monster, is only to make him more monstrous, and go back to the time when stones were deities. Hearts must open. "The aim," Lord Morley has written with truth, "both in public and private life, is to secure to the utmost possible extent the victory of the social feeling over self-love, or Altruism over Egoism." The chief influences will be inherited tendencies, family tuition, early examples. Next to that will be what and whom the growing man sees, hears, reads, associates with.

For compelling hearts to expand, and making us feel for others than ourselves, for breaking the crust of inborn egoism, Shakespeare has, among playwrights, no equal. Here works that supreme power of his: to bestow life, full and real life, on whomever he pleases, to delineate character with so great a perfection that such people as he presents to us we know thoroughly, and what happens to them strikes us the more since they are of our acquaintance; not a passing acquaintance, casually made, soon forgotten, but that of men who will accompany us through life, ever reappearing on the slightest occasion or merest allusion, in tears or smiles, moving us at the remembrance of a happiness and of disasters in which we take part though they be not ours. The action on the heart is the more telling that, with his wide sympathies, the poet discovers the sacred "touch of nature" not only in great heroes, but in the humblest ones; not only in ideal heroines, but in a Shylock whom we pity, at times, to the point of not liking so very much the "learned Doctor from Padua"; even in "the poor beetle that we tread upon," and we get thinking of its pangs "as great as when a giant dies."

The fate of a Hamlet, an Ophelia, a Desdemona, an Othello, carries, to be sure, no concrete moral with it; the noblest, the purest, the most generous, sink into the dark abyss after agonizing tortures, and one can scarcely imagine what, being human, with human foibles, they could have avoided to escape their misery. Their story was undoubtedly written "without any moral purpose," but not without any moral effect. It obliges human hearts to melt, it teaches them pity.

## VI

Five thousand two hundred and sixteen entries to-day in the British Museum under the word Shakespeare (more than double the amount for Homer), against three hundred and seven in 1855; all the world reading Shakespeare: moral cannot be the only attraction, nor even the chief one. It is, in fact, as things of beauty that the works of the poet have reached their immense fame. That they are things of beauty is now admitted by all; with enthusiasm by most people, unwittingly by the rare others. Such a great writer as Tolstoi denies any merit, even of the lowest order, to Shakespeare, but having to define, in his book on art, the tests by which "real art" is to be distinguished from "its counterfeits" those he selects fit the works of Shakespeare so perfectly that, if this poet had been the typical one he had in view, he could scarcely have written otherwise.[15]

Shakespeare's plays are things of beauty, works of art; the product of an art, it is true, which cannot be learned in books—the higher for that. What is then the use of a thing of beauty, an *As You Like It*, a *Midsummer Night's Dream*, full of smiles? and all that gaiety, and all that beauty, and all those passions, and that force, and that wit, and that eloquence, and that wisdom scattered through the immense field of the thirty-seven plays? "What does it signify?" What should we expect of a thing of beauty?

No problem has been, for over a hundred years, more passionately discussed. Can art be profitable at all? Should it be profitable? Should it profit the few or the many? Is real art of a supra-terrestrial nature or not, and must it be kept above the reach and even the gaze of the lowly?

On these questions most critics have known no doubts, and they have answered without hesitation; but some have answered, Certainly yes, and others, Certainly no. "Woe," wrote d'Alembert, "to the artistic productions whose beauty is only for artists." "Here," observed the Goncourt brothers, "is one of the silliest things that was ever said." The problem continues debated and debatable, and was, some years ago, the subject of a remarkable essay by one of the best Shakespearean critics: "Poetry for Poetry's sake," by Professor Bradley.

In the course of the last century the quarrel was at its height, and it was a fierce one. For a time no vocabulary had words strong enough to express the contempt, the hatred, the indignation of artists towards those unspeakable *bourgeois* who could imagine that art might be enjoyed by any but a select few, and could be of any use: "Everything that is of any use is ugly," Théophile Gautier had decreed. The true artist must live apart, meditate, never teach, never act: action might spoil the fineness of his perceptions. He belongs to a world different from everybody else's, the world of art.

But while literary wars and revolutions were going on, other wars and other revolutions were taking place in the world and deeply influencing art theories. The revolution of 1848 made of that staunch champion of "art for art," Baudelaire, a convert to the opposite doctrine: "Art is henceforth inseparable from usefulness and morality," said he, burning what he had adored. The storm of 1870 thinned yet more the ranks of the erstwhile triumphant partisans of supra-terrestrial art. No doubt was possible, Browning was right,

The world and life's too big to pass for a dream.

Since the din and dust of the fight have abated one can get a clearer vision of the facts; and as is often the case in human quarrels, one now discovers valuable truths, though in different proportions, in the doctrine of the contending parties.

The day of the pure dilettanti saying to the world, "I am too much above thee to care for thee,"[16] is decidedly on the wane. Boutroux, with his usual acumen and sanity, has shown that their views, attitude, and success had never been a sign of progress, but of decay: "In the epochs usually called epochs of decadence or dissolution, art scornfully dissociates itself from any other object but beauty, considering that the latter displays its full power only when free from all accessory ends such as utility, truth, honesty, and is placed alone in its supreme independence and dignity." Art is, in fact, an offspring of nature; it is of course in close alliance with beauty, but it must not be cut loose from the soil under pretence of mere beauty: "Each time art has risen again from decay or has been born to a new life, it has begun by casting off vain ornaments and assigning to itself a serious and real end, closely connected with the conditions of contemporary life."[17]

But there is something true also in the theory of "art for art." If it cannot be maintained with Hegel, that art purifies all it touches, and that any kind of art is morally beneficial to mankind, it must be acknowledged to-day that art, when not wilfully perverse, is useful simply because it produces things of beauty. "All that is great," Goethe said, "contributes to our education." A tragedy, a picture, a statue, *Othello*, Rembrandt's philosopher, the Victory of Samothrace, raise us above ourselves. We cannot enjoy works of art, Paul Gaultier

has observed, without "a preliminary forgetting of our habitual preoccupations, and of the interested views which form, so to say, the woof of our lives. . . . They free us from the tyranny of interest. . . . The emotion caused by works of art acts like a preface to moral activity." The same author adds with great truth: "The morality of a work is not to be measured by the morality of the things represented, but by that of the sentiment in which they have been represented."

The influence thus exerted will be powerful and beneficial, in proportion to the perfection of the work, the depth of the emotion, and the sincerity of the artist who takes his starting-point on our real earth, allowing himself to be prompted by our real lives and our real doubts and hopes. The influence will be broad in proportion to the accessibility of the beauty represented. Without those characteristics the kind of art that may grow will be short-lived, cold, and dry, the cult will not spread; few will worship nowadays a wooden idol.

Of the former sort is Shakespeare's influence on mankind. The world is full of beauty, but with our eyes drawn to the daily task, most of it escapes us. We want the poet, the musician, the artist, to touch us with his wand and to say to us, Look. Then we see and admire what we had looked at a hundred times before, and never seen, owing to our "muddy vesture of decay."

A sunset may pass unobserved by the vulgar; it will less easily pass unobserved when arrested in its evanescence and fixed on his canvas by Claude Lorrain. For to the landscape is superadded Claude Lorrain: we have the landscape plus he; the artist changes nothing in what he sees, but he is present there with us, just to say, Look. The same with Shakespeare.

No sensible man visits that temple devoted to artistic beauty, with its innumerable recesses and shrines, where all epochs and all countries are represented, the Louvre in Paris, without leaving it a better man. The added worth may be an infinitesimal worth, it may be a considerable one; in all cases some worth will be acquired. Dormant springs of disinterested emotion will have been made to flow again, a fatigued brain will have been rested; sleepy thoughts will have been aroused, brought back to life and made to engender others. The same after a visit to Shakespeare.

Private benefactors, or the State, offer to studious youths the means of making a stay in Rome or Athens, or of journeying around the world. The belief is that they will return stronger, better armed for life, having had unusual occasions to think and consider, to store their mind. Such journeys are offered us by Shakespeare, around that microcosm, so full of wonders, and which has no secret for him, man's soul and character.

His hold both on artists and on the masses will certainly continue; on artists on account of the example given by him of taking one's stand in realities, of looking at things straight, of observing nature rather than conforming blindfolded to accepted traditions. This he does in absolute simplicity, without any touch of the pedantry of either the learned writer who worships rules because they are accepted, or the rebel who rejects them altogether, and on all occasions, because they are rules.

In Claude Lorrain's canvases we have nature, plus Claude Lorrain; in Shakespeare's plays we have nature, plus Shakespeare, plus his public. Discarding what is not his but has been contributed by his public, we find that what he adds to nature does not consist in any undue intrusion of his personality, but, on the contrary, in artistically selecting from real life what is characteristic of the individual he represents. He selects by instinct, but that instinct is genius. One might follow, step by step, a Hamlet, a nurse, a Falstaff in real life, and note every word they say, every attitude they take; and the portrait would be less life-like than the one drawn by Shakespeare. There are moments when we do not look like ourselves: such moments are often selected or occasioned by photographers, who want an image conforming to their own idea of a satisfactory picture, for which cause so many photographs made after us are not like us. The true artist is more discerning; he not only keeps his own personality apart from that of his personages, but in that of his personages he knows how to bring out what makes of them distinct individuals. That is his way of saying, Look. Boswell's portrait of Dr. Johnson is immortal simply because it was drawn in that manner.

As a trammel-breaker, Shakespeare, who played a unique rôle in that French romantic movement of the nineteenth century, the chief result of which was the awakening of French lyricism, Shakespeare who was, said Emerson, "the father of German literature," will continue to help and inspire future generations of artists. Every successful new attempt usually degenerates into a school: to imitate the successful is ever held by the many as the shortest road to success. To noisily attack yesterday's successful ones is another road habitually followed later. Old rules are thus periodically scorned and discarded; then, after a brief moment of independence and search for a different manner, the new attempt (invariably made in the name of nature) is systematized, and new rules, new shackles replace the former ones; barnacles retard the movement of the ship.

To look directly at nature; to see how Shakespeare looks at nature, to understand the amplitude of his realism, which does not, under pretense that nettles are real, discard roses, no less real; to read the parts of his plays which are truly his, and study, for example, some of his wonderful first scenes (*Romeo, Othello, Hamlet, Tempest,* etc.), will be, on such occasions, the best of cures. Human nature will have to change before the great trammel-breaker ceases to fulfil his mission.

With the masses an increase of Shakespeare's influence is to be foreseen. His plays, in their *ensemble,* were ever accessible to the many, since it was for them especially that he wrote, but the higher beauties in his works, those which he put in simply because he could not help it, because they were commanded by his nature and not because they were required by that of his hearers, will be more and more understood and enjoyed. Men's minds progress and improve.

The change in our own days has been striking; it will be greater hereafter, when owing to discoveries, to the perfecting of machinery, to a change in the conditions of life, the many will at last enjoy that chief one among the great causes of content in life, which the few now possess and the masses do not—leisure hours. For the many, as for the privileged of previous times, life will be less encumbered with matter; there will be, in their day's twenty-four hours, time for rest, for study, for a friendly book, for thoughts. Instruction and education, given in a kindly spirit as it will be (else of little advantage), will prepare them for the best use to be made of the new treasure with highest enjoyment and profit. Many, of course, as is often the case with the possessors of treasure, will squander theirs, but some will not, and their number will probably go on increasing. One of those highest enjoyments will be a better understanding of beauty, whether natural or artistic, a real sunset or a painted one.

Signs are not lacking that the influence for good of things of beauty, as such, will grow, and be more and more generally taken into account. A recent incident in far-off Colorado may be quoted as symptomatic. A commercial company there wanted, in the year 1910, to divert to its uses a stream which

formed a cascade further down; it pleaded that it had, according to the Constitution, "the right to divert waters of any natural stream unappropriated to beneficial uses." Just as if it had taken its cue from Portia, the United States Circuit Court decided that "The world delights in scenic beauty. . . . It is therefore held that the maintenance of the vegetation in Cascade Canyon by the flow and seepage and mist and spray of the stream and its falls, as it passes through the canyon, is a beneficial use of such waters within the meaning of the Constitution." Thus, with the full support of public opinion, the stream was saved as being a thing of beauty, an honest one, and therefore beneficial.

The Palace at Versailles has been transformed, as is well known, into a Museum dedicated "A toutes les gloires de la France." A visit there is for us French what a reading of *Henry V* is for the English. On Sundays the crowd is such that it is difficult to move, a crowd of the same sort that filled Shakespeare's theatre: artisans, shopkeepers, soldiers, sailors, servants, peasants come to town, and there too, now and then, a stray Ambassador. Such people are the best public, the most sincere, the one that does not look for occasions to blame and sneer, but occasions to admire, and few things are more beneficial than disinterested admiration for great deeds and noble sights. Leaving the palace once, at the hour of closure, I stood near a couple of obviously very poor and very tired country people. They had been looking for hours, and they were gazing still. "Now you must go," repeated the keeper for the second time. I wish I could render the tone and expression with which they answered: "Must we now? What a pity. It was all so beautiful." Like every man leaving with regret Shakespeare's works after having admired what is highest and truest in them, those two surely went home better people.

Let us not expect from Shakespeare what he cannot give; what he can is enough, and is of peerless value. Having come young to town, hard pressed by necessity, writing with very practical ends in view, never thinking of posterity, bound to please his public, the means of success he employed were in a way forced upon him by circumstances. He knew what ingredients his public liked, and never felt it his duty to grudge them their pleasure; he could write, and had to write, with extreme rapidity, without any preparatory study or verifying; and he did so without scruple.

But no less fully did he allow free play to that unparalleled genius of his, the extent of which was unsuspected by his contemporaries and by himself. Untrammelled, he stands, for men of letters, the model of trammel-breakers.

By the problems he obliges us to consider, the concrete moral of some of his plays, their general healthy tone, the sympathies he awakens in our hearts, the amount of beauty he offers to our gaze, as varied as the world itself, by all this he renders us the one great service of drawing us out of our paltry selves, of busying us, not superficially, but intensely, with something other than our own interests. He raises us above the plane of everyday thoughts, he improves us by fighting in us the ever-recurring danger of our original egoism.

"How does it profit me?" Emerson had said; "what does it signify? Is it but a *Twelfth Night,* or *Midsummer-Night's Dream,* or a *Winter Evening's Tale?*" Let Emerson answer Emerson, for the same thinker had said elsewhere: "All high beauty has a moral element in it."

*Notes*

1. Munro, *The Shakspere Allusion Book,* I, xiv.
2. *Essay on . . . Falstaff,* 1777. Nichol Smith, *Eighteenth Century Essays on Shakespeare,* p. 249.
3. "When I first collected these authorities, I was desirous that every

quotation should be useful to some other end than the illustration of a word. I therefore extracted from philosophers principles of science, from historians remarkable facts, from chymists complete processes, from divines striking exhortations, from poets beautiful descriptions." Preface to his *Dictionary of the English Language*, 1755.

4. *Preface to Shakspeare*, 1765. John Dennis, a passionate admirer of the poet, gave in Nov., 1719, under the title *The Invader of His Country*, a remodelled version of *Coriolanus*, with a new ending, so as to add a moral sadly lacking, he thought, in Shakespeare's play.

5. And according to whom his glory can be explained only as being one of those contagious mental diseases which now and then afflict mankind, like the crusades, the belief in sorcerers and the "passion for tulips which, at a certain time, invaded the whole of Holland." Tolstoi's *Shakespeare*, translated into French by Bienstock.

6. *Representative Men: Seven Lectures*, Boston, 1850, pp. 213, 214.

7. *Psychologie de l'invention*, 1901.

8. *Année Psychologique*, 1894, I, 79, 80.

9. Paulhan, *ut supra*, pp. 31, 32. He writes to his friend Maxime Ducamp, from Croisset, 1852: "Que je crève comme un chien plutôt que de hâter ma phrase qui ne'est pas mûre!" And again: we follow different roads, "que Dieu nous conduise où chacun demande! moi je ne cherche pas le port, mais la haute mer. Si j'y fais naufrage, je te dispense du deuil." Croisset, no date, but 1853.

10. See Jusserand, *The School for Ambassadors*, 1925, p. 274.

11. Ibid., p. 272.

12. "S. E. alla au Globe, lieu ordinaire où l'on joue les commédies, y fut représenté l'histoire du More de Venise."—Journal of the Secretary to the German Ambassador, April 30, 1610, facsimiled in Halliwell-Phillipps' *Outlines of the Life of Shakespeare*, 1893, II, p. 85.

13. *Titus Andronicus*, III, 2, a repulsive play, but one of the most successful of the period, the work of Shakespeare and others.

14. *Der Einzige und sein Eigenthum*, Leipzig, 1882, 1st ed. 1845; Bourdeau, *Les Maîtres de la pensée contemporaine*, 1904, p. 110.

15. "Il y a un signe certain et infaillible pour distinguer l'art véritable de ses contrefaçons, c'est ce que j'appellerai la contagion artistique. Si un homme, sans aucun effort de sa part, reçoit en présence de l'œuvre d'un autre homme, une émotion qui l'unit à cet autre homme et à d'autres encore recevant en même temps que lui la même impression, c'est que l'œuvre en présence de laquelle il se trouve est une œuvre d'art. Et une œuvre a beau être belle, poétique, riche d'effets, ce n'est pas une œuvre d'art si elle n'éveille pas en nous cette émotion toute particulière, la joie de nous sentir en communion d'art avec l'auteur et avec les autres hommes en compagnie de qui nous lisons, voyons, entendons l'œuvre en question." *Le Sens de l'art*, translated by T. de Wyzeva.

16. Cassagne, *L'Art pour l'art*, p. 143.

17. Preface to Paul Gaultier's *Le Sens de l'art*, 1908.

# Textual History

## ALEXANDER POPE
### From "The Preface of the Editor"
*The Works of Mr. William Shakespear*
1725, Volume 1, pp. xiv–xxiv

I shall now lay before the reader some of those almost innumerable Errors, which have risen from one source, the ignorance of the Players, both as his actors, and as his editors. When the nature and kinds of these are enumerated and considered, I dare to say that not *Shakespear* only, but *Aristotle* or *Cicero*, had their works undergone the same fate, might have appear'd to want sense as well as learning.

It is not certain that any one of his Plays was published by himself. During the time of his employment in the Theatre, several of his pieces were printed separately in Quarto. What makes me think that most of these were not publish'd by him, is the excessive carelessness of the press: every page is so scandalously false spelled, and almost all the learned or unusual words so intolerably mangled, that it's plain there either was no Corrector to the press at all, or one totally illiterate. If any were supervised by himself, I should fancy the two parts of *Henry the 4th*, and *Midsummer-Night's Dream* might have been so: because I find no other printed with any exactness; and (contrary to the rest) there is very little variation in all the subsequent editions of them. There are extant two Prefaces, to the first quarto edition of *Troilus* and *Cressida* in 1609, and to that of *Othello*; by which it appears, that the first was publish'd without his knowledge or consent, and even before it was acted, so late as seven or eight years before he died: and that the latter was not printed till after his death. The whole number of genuine plays which we have been able to find printed in his life-time, amounts but to eleven. And of some of these, we meet with two or more editions by different printers, each of which was whole heaps of trash different from

the other: which I should fancy was occasion'd, by their being taken from different copies, belonging to different Playhouses.

The folio edition (in which all the plays we now receive as his, were first collected) was published by two Players, *Heming* and *Condell*, in 1623, seven years after his decease. They declare, that all the other editions were stolen and surreptitious, and affirm theirs to be purged from the errors of the former. This is true as to the literal errors, and no other; for in all respects else it is far worse than the Quarto's:

First, because the additions of trifling and bombast passages are in this edition far more numerous. For whatever had been added, since those Quarto's, by the actors, or had stolen from their mouths into the written parts, were from thence conveyed into the printed text, and all stand charged upon the Author. He himself complained of this usage in *Hamlet*, where he wishes that *those who play the clowns wou'd speak no more than is set down for them.* (Act. 3. Sc. 4.) But as a proof that he could not escape it, in the old editions of *Romeo* and *Juliet* there is no hint of a great number of the mean conceits and ribaldries now to be found there. In others, the low scenes of Mobs, Plebeians and Clowns, are vastly shorter than at present: And I have seen one in particular (which seems to have belonged to the playhouse, by having the parts divided with lines, and the Actors names in the margin) where several of those very passages were added in a written hand, which are since to be found in the folio.

In the next place, a number of beautiful passages which are extant in the first single editions, are omitted in this: as it seems, without any other reason, than their willingness to shorten some scenes: These men (as it was said of *Procrustes*) either lopping, or stretching an Author, to make him just fit for their Stage.

This edition is said to be printed from the *Original Copies*; I believe they meant those which had lain ever since the Author's days in the playhouse, and had from time to time been cut, or added to, arbitrarily. It appears that this edition, as well as the Quarto's, was printed (at least partly) from no better copies than the *Prompter's Book*, or *Piece-meal Parts* written out for the use of the actors: For in some places their very[1] names are thro' carelessness set down instead of the *Persona Dramatis*: And in others the notes of direction to the *Property-men* for their *Moveables*, and to the *Players* for their *Entries*,[2] are inserted into the Text, thro' the ignorance of the Transcribers.

The Plays not having been before so much as distinguish'd by *Acts* and *Scenes*, they are in this edition divided according as they play'd them; often where there is no pause in the action, or where they thought fit to make a breach in it, for the sake of Musick, Masques, or Monsters.

Sometimes the scenes are transposed and shuffled backward and forward; a thing which could no otherwise happen, but by their being taken from seperate and piece-meal-written parts.

Many verses are omitted intirely, and others transposed; from whence invincible obscurities have arisen, past the guess of any Commentator to clear up, but just where the accidental glympse of an old edition enlightens us.

Some Characters were confounded and mix'd, or two put into one, for want of a competent number of actors. Thus in the Quarto edition of *Midsummer-Night's Dream*, Act. 5. *Shakespear* introduces a kind of Master of the Revels called *Philostratus*: all whose part is given to another character (that of *Ægeus*) in the subsequent editions: So also in *Hamlet* and *King Lear*. This too makes it probable that the Prompter's Books were what they call'd the Original Copies.

From liberties of this kind, many speeches also were put into the mouths of wrong persons, where the Author now seems chargeable with making them speak out of character: Or sometimes perhaps for no better reason, than that a governing Player, to have the mouthing of some favourite speech himself, would snatch it from the unworthy lips of an Underling.

Prose from verse they did not know, and they accordingly printed one for the other throughout the volume.

Having been forced to say so much of the Players, I think I ought in justice to remark, that the Judgment, as well as Condition, of that class of people was then far inferior to what it is in our days. As then the best Playhouses were Inns and Taverns (the *Globe*, the *Hope*, the *Red Bull*, the *Fortune*, &c.) so the top of the profession were then meer Players, not Gentlemen of the stage: They were led into the Buttery by the Steward, not plac'd at the Lord's table, or Lady's toilette: and consequently were intirely depriv'd of those advantages they now enjoy, in the familiar conversation of our Nobility, and an intimacy (not to say dearness) with people of the first condition.

From what has been said, there can be no question but had *Shakespear* published his works himself (especially in his latter time, and after his retreat from the stage) we should not only be certain which are genuine; but should find in those that are, the errors lessened by some thousands. If I may judge from all the distinguishing marks of his style, and his manner of thinking and writing, I make no doubt to declare that those wretched plays, *Pericles*, *Locrine*, *Sir John Oldcastle*, *Yorkshire Tragedy*, *Lord Cromwell*, *The Puritan*, and *London Prodigal*, cannot be admitted as his. And I should conjecture of some of the others, (particularly *Love's Labour Lost*, *The Winter's Tale*, and *Titus Andronicus*) that only some characters, single scenes, or perhaps a few particular passages, were of his hand. It is very probable what occasion'd some Plays to be supposed *Shakespear's* was only this; that they were pieces produced by unknown authors, or fitted up for the Theatre while it was under his administration: and no owner claiming them, they

were adjudged to him, as they give Strays to the Lord of the Manor. A mistake, which (one may also observe) it was not for the interest of the House to remove. Yet the Players themselves, *Hemings* and *Condell*, afterwards did *Shakespear* the justice to reject those eight plays in their edition; tho' they were then printed in his name, in every body's hands, and acted with some applause; (as we learn from what *Ben Johnson* says of *Pericles* in his Ode on the *New Inn*.) That *Titus Andronicus* is one of this class I am the rather induced to believe, by finding the same Author openly express his contempt of it in the *Induction* to *Bartholomew-Fair*, in the year 1614, when *Shakespear* was yet living. And there is no better authority for these latter sort, than for the former, which were equally published in his life-time.

If we give into this opinion, how many low and vicious parts and passages might no longer reflect upon this great Genius, but appear unworthily charged upon him? And even in those which are really his, how many faults may have been unjustly laid to his account from arbitrary Additions, Expunctions, Transpositions of scenes and lines, confusion of Characters and Persons, wrong application of Speeches, corruptions of innumerable Passages by the Ignorance, and wrong Corrections of 'em again by the Impertinence, of his first Editors? From one or other of these considerations, I am verily perswaded, that the greatest and the grossest part of what are thought his errors would vanish, and leave his character in a light very different from that disadvantageous one, in which it now appears to us.

This is the state in which *Shakespear's* writings lye at present; for since the above-mentioned Folio Edition, all the rest have implicitly followed it, without having recourse to any of the former, or ever making the comparison between them. It is impossible to repair the Injuries already done him; too much time has elaps'd, and the materials are too few. In what I have done I have rather given a proof of my willingness and desire, than of my ability, to do him justice. I have discharg'd the dull duty of an Editor, to my best judgment, with more labour than I expect thanks, with a religious abhorrence of all innovation, and without any indulgence to my private sense or conjecture. The method taken in this Edition will show it self. The various Readings are fairly put in the margin, so that every one may compare 'em; and those I have prefer'd into the Text are constantly *ex fide Codicum*, upon authority. The Alterations or Additions which *Shakespear* himself made, are taken notice of as they occur. Some suspected passages which are excessively bad, (and which seem Interpolations by being so inserted that one can intirely omit them without any chasm, or deficience in the context) are degraded to the bottom of the page; with an Asterisk referring to the places of their insertion. The Scenes are mark'd so distinctly that every removal of place is specify'd; which is more necessary in this Author than any other, since he shifts them more frequently: and sometimes without attending to this particular, the reader would have met with obscurities. The more obsolete or unusual words are explained. Some of the most shining passages are distinguish'd by comma's in the margin; and where the beauty lay not in particulars but in the whole, a star is prefix'd to the scene. This seems to me a shorter and less ostentatious method of performing the better half of Criticism (namely the pointing out an Author's excellencies) than to fill a whole paper with citations of fine passages, with *general Applauses*, or *empty Exclamations* at the tail of them. There is also subjoin'd a Catalogue of those first Editions by which the greater part of the various readings and of the corrected passages are authorised, (most of which are such as carry their own evidence along with them.) These Editions now hold the place of Originals, and are the only materials left to repair the deficiences or restore the corrupted sense of the Author: I can only wish that a greater number of them (if a greater were ever published) may yet be found, by a search more successful than mine, for the better accomplishment of this end.

I will conclude by saying of *Shakespear*, that with all his faults, and with all the irregularity of his *Drama*, one may look upon his works, in comparison of those that are more finish'd and regular, as upon an ancient majestick piece of *Gothick* Architecture, compar'd with a neat Modern building: The latter is more elegant and glaring, but the former is more strong and more solemn. It must be allow'd, that in one of these there are materials enough to make many of the other. It has much the greater variety, and much the nobler apartments; tho' we are often conducted to them by dark, odd, and uncouth passages. Nor does the Whole fail to strike us with greater reverence, tho' many of the Parts are childish, ill-plac'd, and unequal to its grandeur.

*Notes*

1. Much Ado about Nothing. Act 2. *Enter Prince* Leonato, Claudio, *and* Jack Wilson, *instead of* Balthasar. *And in Act* 4. Cowley, *and* Kemp, *constantly thro' a whole Scene.* (Edit. Fol. of 1623, and 1632.)
2. *Such as,*
   —My Queen is murder'd! *Ring the little Bell*—
   —His note grew as sharp as a pen, and *a table of Greenfield's,* &c.

### LEWIS THEOBALD
"Introduction"
*Shakespeare Restored*
1726, pp. i–viii

I have very often declar'd, and that in a number of Companies, that what thro' the *Indolence,* what thro' the *Ignorance* of his EDITORS, we have scarce any Book in the *English* Tongue more fertile of Errors, than the Plays of SHAKESPEARE. And, I believe, whenever I have fall'n on this subject, I have not fail'd to express my Wish, that some fine *Genius,* equal to the task, would befriend the Memory of this immortal Poet, and contribute to the Pleasure of the present and of future Times, in retrieving, as far as possible, the *original Purity* of his *Text,* and rooting out that vast Crop of *Errors,* which has almost choak'd up his *Beauties.*

IT was no small Satisfaction therefore to me, when I first heard Mr. POPE had taken upon him the Publication of SHAKESPEARE. I very reasonably expected, from his known Talents and Abilities, from his uncommon Sagacity and Discernment, and from his unwearied Diligence and Care of informing himself by an happy and extensive Conversation, we should have had our Author come out as perfect, as the want of *Manuscripts* and *original Copies* could give us a Possibility of hoping. I may dare to say, a great Number of SHAKESPEARE's Admirers, and of Mr. POPE's too, (both which I sincerely declare myself,) concurred in this Expectation: For there is a certain *curiosa fælicitas,* as was said of an eminent *Roman* Poet, in that Gentleman's Way of working, which, we presum'd, would have laid itself out largely in such a Province; and that he would not have sate down contented with performing, as he calls it himself, the *dull Duty* of an EDITOR only. SHAKESPEARE's *Works* have always appear'd to me like what he makes his *HAMLET* compare the World to, an *unweeded Garden grown to Seed:* And I am sorry there is still reason to complain, the *Weeds* in him are so very sparingly thin'd, that, not to speak out of compass, a thousand *rank* and

*unsightly* ones are left to stare us in the Face, and clog the Delight of the expected Prospect.

IT must necessarily happen, that where the Assistance of *Manuscripts* is wanting to set an Author's Meaning right, and rescue him from those Errors which have been transmitted down thro' a Series of incorrect Editions, and a long Intervention of Time, many Passages must be desperate, and past a Cure, and their true Sense irretrievable, either to Care, or the Sagacity of Conjecture.

AND there is one Unhappiness too, which generally attends the *Republication* of *English* Books, which is, That being the Property of some Persons *in Trade,* who, too often, know nothing more of their Copy than that there is a *Demand* for *reprinting* it; and who are, withal, Persons of such *commendable* Frugality, that they think every Farthing which is given for the Labour of *Revise,* to be so much Money given away for nothing: The *Press* is set to work from a *printed* Precedent, and so the more the Editions of any Book multiply, the more the Errors multiply too, and propagate out of their own Species. "Of this" (to borrow the Words and Observation of my ingenious Friend,[1] Mr. SEWEL;) Shakespeare "is a very remarkable Instance, who has been handed down, from Age to Age, very incorrect, his Errors increasing by Time, and being almost constantly republish'd to his Disgrace. Whatever were the Faults of this great Poet, the Printers have been hitherto as careful to multiply them, as if they had been real Beauties; thinking, perhaps, with the *Indians,* that the disfiguring a good Face with Scars of artificial Brutes, had improv'd the Form and Dignity of the Person."

THIS, indeed, has not been altogether the Case in the late Edition of SHAKESPEARE: The BOOKSELLER, who *farms* a Right to *some* part of this Author, and *claims* a Right to *some other* part of him, has so far *misunderstood* himself, (I mean, in Contradiction to the *Rule* of Trade,) as to be at the Expence of having his AUTHOR *revised;* and therefore we promised ourselves, this WORK would be compleat.

I HAVE so great an Esteem for Mr. POPE, and so high an Opinion of his Genius and Excellencies, that I beg to be excused from the least Intention of derogating from his Merits, in this Attempt to restore the true Reading of SHAKESPEARE. Tho' I confess a Veneration, almost rising to Idolatry, for the Writings of this inimitable Poet, I would be very loth even to do *him* Justice at the Expence of *that other* Gentleman's Character. But, I am persuaded, I shall stand as free from such a Charge in the *Execution* of this Design, as, I am sure, I am in the *Intention* of it; for I am assuming a Task here, which this learned *Editor* seems purposely (I was going to say, with too nice a Scruple) to have declined.

To explain myself, I must be obliged to make a short Quotation from Mr. POPE, in his Preface to SHAKESPEARE: "In what I have done," says he, "I have rather given a Proof of my Willingness and Desire, than of my Ability to do him Justice. I have discharg'd the dull Duty of an *Editor,* to my best Judgment, with more Labour than I expect Thanks, with a *religious* Abhorrence of all *Innovation,* and without any Indulgence to my private Sense or Conjecture." I cannot help thinking this Gentleman's *Modesty* in this Point too *nice* and *blameable;* and that what he is pleased to call a *religious* Abhorrence of *Innovation,* is downright *Superstition:* Neither can I be of Opinion, that the Writings of SHAKESPEARE are so *venerable,* as that we should be excommunicated from good Sense, for daring to *innovate properly;* or that we ought to be as cautious of altering *their* Text, as we would That of the *sacred Writings.* And yet even They, we see, have admitted of some Thousands of *various Readings;* and would have a great many more, had not Dr. BENTLEY some particular Reasons for not prosecuting his Undertaking upon the *New Testament*, as he propos'd.

CERTAINLY, that Physician would be reckon'd a very unserviceable Member in the Republick, as well as a bad Friend to himself, who would not venture to prescribe to a Patient, because not absolutely sure to cure his Distemper: As, on the other hand, he would be accounted a Man of very indifferent Morals, if he rashly tamper'd with the Health and Constitution of his Fellow-Creature, and was bold to try Conclusions only for private Information. The same Thing may be said with regard to *Attempts* upon *Books*: We should shew very little Honesty, or Wisdom, to play the Tyrants with any Author's Text; to raze, alter, innovate, and overturn, at all Adventures, and to the utter Detriment of his Sense and Meaning: But to be so very reserv'd and cautious, as to interpose no Relief or Conjecture, where it manifestly labours and cries out for Assistance, seems almost as absurd as the Indolence of that good honest *Priest*, who had for thirty Years together mistakingly, in his Breviary, read *Mumpsimus* for *Sumpsimus*; and being told of his Blunder, and solicited to correct it, "The Alteration may be just," said he; "but, however, I'll not change my old MUMPSIMUS for your new SUMPSIMUS."

FOR my own part, I don't know whether I am mistaken in Judgment, but I have always thought, that whenever a *Gentleman* and a *Scholar* turns *Editor* of any Book, he at the same Time commences *Critick* upon his *Author*; and that wherever he finds the Reading suspected, manifestly corrupted, deficient in Sense, and unintelligible, he ought to exert every Power and Faculty of the Mind to supply such a Defect, to give Light and restore Sense to the Passage, and, by a reasonable Emendation, to make that satisfactory and consistent with the Context, which before was so absurd, unintelligible, and intricate.

THIS is a *Task*, which, as I above intimated, Mr. POPE has *purposely disclaim'd*, and which I (by what Fatality, or with what Event, I know not;) have taken upon my self to prosecute. I am not insensible under what Disadvantages I must set out upon such a Work, and against such an Antagonist; *impar congressus* ACHILLI: But as I have laid it down as a Rule to myself not to be arbitrary, fantastical, or wanton, in my Conjectures upon our Author, I shall venture to aim at some little Share of Reputation, in endeavouring to restore Sense to Passages in which no Sense has hitherto been found; or, failing in that Hope, must submit to incur, which I should be very unwilling to do, the Censure of a rash and vain Pretender.

AS SHAKESPEARE stands, or at least ought to stand, in the Nature of a Classic Writer, and, indeed, he is corrupt enough to pass for one of the oldest Stamp, every one, who has a Talent and Ability this Way, is at liberty to make his Comments and Emendations upon him. This is a Palm, which (as TERENCE said, of writing Comedies) is in common to every poetical Contender:

In medio omnibus
Palmam esse positam, qui artem tractant musicam.

And he, who has the Luck to be allowed any Merit in it, does not only do a Service to the Poet, but to his Country and its Language. This Author is grown so universal a Book, that there are very few studies, or Collections of Books, tho' small, amongst which it does not hold a Place: And there is scarce a Poet, that our *English* Tongue boasts of, who is more the Subject of the Ladies Reading. But with what Pleasure can they read Passages, which the Incorrectness of the Editions will not suffer them to understand? No Vein of Pedantry, or Ostenta-

tion of useless Criticism, incited me to this Work: It is a Sacrifice to the Pleasure of SHAKESPEARE's Admirers in general; and should it fail of all the Success which I wish, it may chance to work this good Effect, That many will be tempted to read this Poet with a more diligent Eye than hitherto: The Consequence of which will be, that better Criticks will make their own Observations, with more Strength than I can pretend; and this Specimen prove only an Invitation to lead them into nobler Corrections. If, however, till that happens, where SHAKESPEARE has yet, thro' all his Editions, labour'd under flat Nonsense, and invincible Darkness, I can, by the Addition or Alteration of a single letter, or two, give him both Sense and Sentiment, who will be so unkind to say, this is a trifling or unwarrantable Attempt? Or, rather, if I may dare to flatter myself so far, what true Lover of this Poet, who shall find him so easily cur'd, will not owe his Thanks for a Passage retriev'd from Obscurity, and no Meaning? and say, SHAKESPEARE must certainly have wrote so ————? But I remember a Line in *Horace*, which ought to stop me short, and give me some Fears:

Quid dignum tanto feret hic promissor hiatu?

I am running too largely in debt, upon Promise, to my Readers, and they are calling for Payment in some Specimens of my Performance.

I am sorry that the Use and Intention of this Undertaking ties me down to the Necessity of one unpleasant Office, That of setting right the Faults in Pointing, and those meerly literal, committed by the Printer, and continued by too negligent a Revisal. This is the Drudgery of Correction, in which I could wish to have been spar'd, there being no Pleasure in the Execution of it, nor any Merit, but that of dull Diligence, when executed. But, *unpleasant* as it is, even this Part must be dispens'd with; and all that I can do, to ease myself or Readers in it, is to mark these minute Corrections with all possible Brevity, and proceed to more important Matter.

I CAN scarce suspect it will be thought, if I begin my Animadversions upon the Tragedy of HAMLET, that I have been partial to myself in picking out this Play, as one more fertile in Errors than any of the rest: On the contrary, I chose it for Reasons quite opposite. It is, perhaps, the best known, and one of the most favourite Plays of our Author: For these thirty Years last past, I believe, not a Season has elaps'd, in which it has not been perform'd on the Stage more than once; and, consequently, we might presume it the most purg'd and free from Faults and Obscurity. Yet give me Leave to say, what I am ready to prove, it is not without very gross Corruptions. Nor does it stand by itself for Faults in Mr. POPE's Edition: No, it is a Specimen only of the epidemical Corruption, if I may be allowed to use that Phrase, which runs thro' all the Work: And I cannot help saying of it, as *Æneas* does of the *Greeks* Treachery upon the Instance of *Sinon's*,

Crimine ab uno
Disce omnes:

IF *HAMLET* has its Faults, so has every other of the Plays; and I therefore only offer it as a Precedent of the same Errors, which, every body will be convinced before I have done, possess every Volume and every Play in this Impression.

BUT to proceed from Assertion to Experiment: In order to which I shall constantly be obliged, that the Emendations may stand in a fairer Light, to quote the Passages as they are read, with some part of their Context, in Mr. POPE's Edition; and likewise to prefix a short Account of the Business and Circumstances of the Scenes from which the faulty Passages are drawn; that the Readers may be inform'd at a single View, and judge of the Strength and Reason of the Emendation, without a Reference to the Plays themselves for that purpose. But this will be in no kind necessary, where Faults of the Press are only to be corrected: Where the Pointing is wrong, perhaps, That may not be alone the Fault of the Printer; and therefore I may sometimes think myself obliged to assign a Reason for my altering it.

As every Author is best expounded and explain'd in *One* Place, by his own Usage and Manner of Expression in *Others*; wherever our Poet receives an Alteration in his Text from any of my *Corrections* or *Conjectures*, I have throughout endeavour'd to support what I offer by *parallel Passages*, and *Authorities* from himself: Which, as it will be my best Justification, where my Attempts are seconded with the Concurrence of my Readers; so, it will be my best Excuse for those *Innovations*, in which I am not so happy to have them think with me.

I HAVE likewise all along, for the greater Ease and Pleasure of the Readers, distinguish'd the Nature of my Corrections by a short marginal Note to each of them, *viz. False Pointing, False Print, Various Reading, Passage omitted, Conjectural Emendation, Emendation*, and the like; so that every body will at once be appriz'd what Subject-matter to expect from every respective Division.

*Notes*

1. *In his Preface to the Seventh Volume of the Works of* SHAKESPEARE *in* Quarto.

## WILLIAM WARBURTON
### From "Preface"
### *The Works of Shakespear*
### 1747, Volume 1, pp. vii–xix

It hath been no unusual thing for Writers, when dissatisfied with the Patronage or Judgment of their own Times, to appeal to Posterity for a fair Hearing. Some have even thought fit to apply to it in the first Instance; and to decline Acquaintance with the Public till Envy and Prejudice had quite subsided. But, of all the Trusters to Futurity, commend me to the Author of the following Poems, who not only left it to Time to do him Justice as it would, but to find him out as it could. For, what between too great Attention to his Profit as a Player, and too little to his Reputation as a Poet, his Works, left to the Care of Door-keepers and Prompters, hardly escaped the common Fate of those Writings, how good soever, which are abandoned to their own Fortune, and unprotected by Party or Cabal. At length, indeed, they struggled into Light; but so disguised and travested, that no classic Author, after having run ten secular Stages thro' the blind Cloisters of Monks and Canons, ever came out in half so maimed and mangled a Condition. But for a full Account of his Disorders, I refer the Reader to the excellent Discourse which follows, and turn myself to consider the Remedies that have been applied to them.

*Shakespear's* Works, when they escaped the Players, did not fall into much better Hands when they came amongst Printers and Booksellers: who, to say the Truth, had, at first, but small Encouragement for putting him into a better Condition. The stubborn Nonsense, with which he was incrusted, occasioned his lying long neglected amongst the common Lumber of the Stage. And when that resistless Splendor, which now shoots all around him, had, by degrees, broke thro' the Shell of those Impurities, his dazzled Admirers became as suddenly insensible to the extraneous Scurf that still stuck upon him, as they had been before to the native Beauties

that lay under it. So that, as then, he was thought not to deserve a Cure, he was now supposed not to need any.

His growing Eminence, however, required that he should be used with Ceremony: And he soon had his Appointment, of an *Editor* in form. But the Bookseller, whose dealing was with Wits, having learnt of them, I know not what silly Maxim, that *none but a Poet should presume to meddle with a Poet*, engaged the ingenious Mr. *Rowe* to undertake this Employment. A Wit indeed he was; but so utterly unacquainted with the whole Business of Criticism, that he did not even collate or consult the first Editions of the Work he undertook to publish; but contented himself with giving us a meagre Account of the Author's Life, interlarded with some common-place Scraps from his Writings. The Truth is, *Shakespear's* Condition was yet but ill understood. The Nonsense, now, by consent, received for his own, was held in a kind of Reverence for its Age and Author: and thus it continued, till another great *Poet* broke the Charm; by shewing us, that the higher we went, the less of it was still to be found.

For the Proprietors, not discouraged by their first unsuccessful Effort, in due time, made a second; and, tho' they still stuck to their Poets, with infinitely more Success in their Choice of Mr. POPE. Who by the mere force of an uncommon Genius, without any particular Study or Profession of this Art, discharged the great Parts of it so well as to make his Edition the best Foundation for all further Improvements. He separated the genuine from the spurious-Plays: And, with equal Judgment, tho' not always with the same Success, attempted to clear the genuine Plays from the interpolated Scenes: He then consulted the old Editions; and, by a careful Collation of them, rectified the faulty, and supplied the imperfect Reading, in a great number of Places: And lastly, in an admirable Preface, hath drawn a general, but very lively, Sketch of *Shakespear's* poetic Character; and, in the corrected Text, marked out those peculiar Strokes of Genius which were most proper to support and illustrate that Character. Thus far Mr. POPE. And altho' much more was to be done before *Shakespear* could be restored to himself, (such as amending the corrupted Text where the printed Books afford no Assistance; explaining his licentious Phraseology and obscure Allusions; and illustrating the Beauties of his Poetry;) yet, with great Modesty and Prudence, our illustrious Editor left this to the Critic by Profession.

But nothing will give the common Reader a better Idea of the Value of Mr. *Pope's* Edition, than the two Attempts which have been since made, by Mr. *Theobald* and Sir *Thomas Hanmer*, in Opposition to it. Who, altho' they concerned themselves only in the *first* of these three Parts of Criticism, the *restoring the Text*, (without any Conception of the *second*, or venturing even to touch upon the *third*) yet succeeded so very ill in it, that they left their Author in ten times a worse Condition than they found him. But, as it was my ill Fortune to have some accidental Connexions with these two *Gentlemen*, it will be incumbent on me to be a little more particular concerning them.

The One was recommended to me as a poor Man; the Other as a poor Critic: and to each of them, at different times, I communicated a great number of Observations, which they managed, as they saw fit, to the Relief of their several Distresses. As to Mr. *Theobald*, who wanted Money, I allowed him to print what I gave him for his own Advantage: and he allowed himself in the Liberty of taking one Part for his own, and sequestering another for the Benefit, as I supposed, of some future Edition. But, as to the *Oxford Editor*, who wanted nothing, but what he might very well be without, the

Reputation of a Critic, I could not so easily forgive him for trafficking with my Papers without my Knowledge; and, when that Project fail'd, for employing a number of my Conjectures in his Edition against my express Desire not to have that Honour done unto me.

Mr. *Theobald* was naturally turned to Industry and Labour. What he read he could transcribe: but, as what he thought, if ever he did think, he could but ill express, so he read on; and, by that means got a Character of Learning, without risquing, to every Observer, the Imputation of wanting a better Talent. By a punctilious Collation of the old Books, he corrected what was manifestly wrong in the *latter* Editions, by what was manifestly right in the *earlier*. And this is his real Merit; and the whole of it. For where the Phrase was very obsolete or licentious in the *common* Books, or only slightly corrupted in the *other*, he wanted sufficient Knowledge of the Progress and various Stages of the *English* Tongue, as well as Acquaintance with the Peculiarity of *Shakespear*'s Language to understand what was right; nor had he either common Judgment to see, or critical Sagacity to amend, what was manifestly faulty. Hence he generally exerts his conjectural Talent in the wrong Place: He tampers with what is found in the *common* Books; and, in the *old* ones, omits all Notice of *Variations* the Sense of which he did not understand. .

How the *Oxford Editor* came to think himself qualified for this Office, from which his whole Course of Life had been so remote, is still more difficult to conceive. For whatever Parts he might have either of Genius or Erudition, he was absolutely ignorant of the Art of Criticism, as well as of the Poetry of that Time, and the Language of his Author. And so far from a Thought of examining the *first* Editions, that he even neglected to compare Mr. *Pope*'s, from which he printed his own, with Mr. *Theobald*'s; whereby he lost the Advantage of many fine Lines which the other had recovered from the old Quartos. Where he trusts to his own Sagacity, in what affects the Sense, his Conjectures are generally absurd and extravagant, and violating every Rule of Criticism. Tho', in this Rage of Correcting, he was not absolutely destitute of all *Art*. For, having a number of my Conjectures before him, he took as many of them as he saw fit, to work upon; and by changing them to something, he thought, synonimous or similar, he made them his own; and so became a Critic at a cheap Expence. But how well he hath succeeded in this, as likewise in his Conjectures which are properly his own, will be seen in the course of my Remarks: Tho', as he hath declined to give the Reasons for his Interpolations, he hath not afforded me so fair a hold of him as Mr. *Theobald* hath done, who was less cautious. But his principal Object was to reform his Author's Numbers; and this, which he hath done, on every Occasion, by the Insertion or Omission of a set of harmless unconcerning Expletives, makes up the gross Body of his innocent Corrections. And so, in spite of that extreme Negligence in Numbers, which distinguishes the first Dramatic Writers, he hath tricked up the old Bard, from Head to Foot, in all the finical Exactness of a modern Measurer of Syllables.

For the rest, all the Corrections which these two Editors have made on any *reasonable* Foundation, are here admitted into the Text; and carefully assigned to their respective Authors. A piece of Justice which the *Oxford Editor* never did; and which the *Other* was not always scrupulous in observing towards me. To conclude with them in a word, They separately possessed those two Qualities which, more than any other, have contributed to bring the Art of Criticism into disrepute, *Dulness of Apprehension*, and *Extravagance of Conjecture*.

I am now to give some Account of the present Undertaking. For as to all those Things, which have been published under the titles of *Essays, Remarks, Observations*, &c. on *Shakespear*, (if you except some critical Notes on *Macbeth*, given as a Specimen of a projected Edition, and written, as appears, by a Man of Parts and Genius) the rest are absolutely below a serious Notice.

The whole a Critic can do for an Author who deserves his Service, is to correct the faulty Text; to remark the Peculiarities of Language; to illustrate the obscure allusions; and to explain the Beauties and Defects of Sentiment or Composition. And surely, if ever Author had a Claim to this Service, it was our *Shakespear*: Who, widely excelling in the Knowledge of Human Nature, hath given to his infinitely varied Pictures of it, such Truth of Design, such Force of Drawing, such Beauty of Colouring, as was hardly ever equalled by any Writer, whether his Aim was the Use, or only the Entertainment of Mankind. The Notes in this Edition, therefore, take in the whole Compass of Criticism.

I. The first sort is employed in restoring the Poet's genuine Text; but in those Places only where it labours with inextricable Nonsense. In which, how much soever I may have given Scope to critical Conjecture, where the old Copies failed me, I have indulged nothing to Fancy or Imagination; but have religiously observed the severe Canons of literal Criticism; as may be seen from the Reasons accompanying every Alteration of the common Text. Nor would a different Conduct have become a Critic, whose greatest Attention, in this part, was to vindicate the established Reading from Interpolations occasioned by the fanciful Extravagancies of others. I once intended to have given the Reader a *body of Canons*, for literal Criticism, drawn out in form; as well such as concern the Art in general, as those that arise from the Nature and Circumstances of our Author's Works in particular. And this for two Reasons. First, To give the *unlearned Reader* a just Idea, and consequently a better Opinion of the Art of Criticism, now sunk very low in the popular Esteem, by the Attempts of some who would needs exercise it without either natural or acquired Talents; and by the ill Success of others, who seemed to have lost both, when they came to try them upon English Authors. Secondly, To deter the *unlearned Writer* from wantonly trifling with an Art he is a Stranger to, at the Expence of his own Reputation, and the Integrity of the Text of established Authors. But these Users may be well supplied by what is occasionally said upon the Subject, in the Course of the following Remarks.

II. The second sort of Notes consists in an Explanation of the Author's Meaning, when, by one, or more of these Causes, it becomes obscure; either from a *licentious Use of Terms*; or a *hard or ungrammatical Construction*; or lastly, from *far-fetch'd or quaint Allusions*.

I. This licentious Use of Words is almost perculiar to the Language of *Shakespear*. To common Terms he hath affixed Meanings of his own, unauthorised by Use, and not to be justified by Analogy. And this Liberty he hath taken with the noblest Parts of Speech, such as *Mixed-modes*; which, as they are most susceptible of Abuse, so their Abuse most hurts the Clearness of the Discourse. The Critics (to whom *Shakespear*'s Licence was still as much a Secret as his Meaning, which that Licence had obscured) fell into two contrary Mistakes; but equally injurious to his Reputation and his Writings. For some of them observing a Darkness, that pervaded his whole Expression, have censured him for Confusion of Ideas and Inaccuracy of reasoning. *In the Neighing of a Horse*, (says *Rymer*) *or in the Growling of a Mastiff there is a Meaning, there is a lively Expression, and, may I say, more Humanity than many times in the tragical Flights of* Shakespear. The Ignorance of which Censure is of a piece with its Brutality. The Truth is, no one thought clearer, or argued more closely than this immortal Bard. But his Superiority of Genius less needing the Intervention of Words in the Act of Thinking, when he came to draw out his Contemplations into Discourse, he took up (as he was hurried on by the Torrent of his Matter) with the first Words that lay in his way; and if, amongst these, there were two *Mixed-modes* that had but a principal Idea in common, it was enough for him; he regarded them as synonimous, and would use the one for the other without Fear or Scruple.—Again, there have been others, such as the two last Editors, who have fallen into a contrary Extreme; and regarded *Shakespear's* Anomalies (as we may call them) amongst the Corruptions of his Text; which, therefore, they have cashiered in great numbers, to make room for a Jargon of their own. This hath put me to additional Trouble; for I had not only their Interpolations to throw out again, but the genuine Text to replace, and establish in its stead; which, in many Cases, could not be done without shewing the peculiar Sense of the Terms, and explaining the Causes which led the Poet to so perverse an use of them. I had it once, indeed, in my Design, to give a general alphabetic *Glossary* of these Terms; but as each of them is explained in its proper Place, there seemed the less Occasion for such an Index.

2. The Poet's hard and unnatural Construction had a different Original. This was the Effect of mistaken Art and Design. The Public Taste was in its Infancy; and delighted, (as it always does during that State) in the high and turgid: which leads the Writer to disguise a vulgar expression with hard and forced construction, whereby the sentence frequently becomes cloudy and dark. Here, his Critics shew their modesty, and leave him to himself. For the arbitrary change of a Word doth little towards dispelling an obscurity that ariseth, not from the licentious use of a single Term, but from the unnatural arrangement of a whole Sentence. And they risqued nothing by their silence. For *Shakespear* was too clear in Fame to be suspected of a want of Meaning; and too high in fashion for any one to own he needed a Critic to find it out. Not but, in his best works, we must allow, he is often so natural and flowing, so pure and correct, that he is even a model for stile and language.

3. As to his far-fetched and quaint Allusions, these are often a cover to common thoughts; just as his hard construction is to common expression. When they are not so, the explanation of them has this further advantage, that, in clearing the Obscurity, you frequently discover some latent conceit not unworthy of his Genius.

III. The third and last sort of Notes is concerned in a critical explanation of the Author's Beauties and Defects; but chiefly of his Beauties, whether in Stile, Thought, Sentiment, Character or Composition. An odd humour of finding fault hath long prevailed amongst the Critics; as if nothing were worth *remarking* that did not, at the same time, deserve to be reproved. Whereas the public Judgment hath less need to be assisted in what it shall reject, than in what it ought to prize; Men being generally more ready at spying Faults than in discovering Beauties. Nor is the value they set upon a Work, a certain proof that they understand it. For 'tis ever seen, that half a dozen Voices of credit give the lead. And if the Publick chance to be in good humour, or the Author much in their favour, the People are sure to follow. Hence it is that the true Critic hath so frequently attached himself to Works of established reputation; not to teach the World to *admire*, which, in those circumstances, to say the truth, they are apt

enough to do of themselves; but to teach them how, *with reason to admire*: No easy matter, I will assure you, on the subject in question: For tho' it be very true, as Mr. *Pope* hath observed, that *Shakespear is the fairest and fullest subject for criticism*, yet it is not such a sort of criticism as may be raised mechanically on the Rules which *Dacier*, *Rapin* and *Bossu* have collected from Antiquity; and of which, such kind of Writers as *Rymer*, *Gildon*, *Dennis* and *Oldmixon*, have only gathered and chewed the Husks: nor on the other hand is it to be formed on the Plan of those crude and superficial Judgments, on books and things, with which a certain celebrated Paper so much abounds; too good indeed to be named with the Writers last mentioned, but being unluckily mistaken for a *Model*, because it was an *Original*, it hath given rise to a deluge of the worst sort of critical Jargon; I mean that which looks most like sense. But the kind of criticism here required is such as judgeth our Author by those only Laws and Principles on which he wrote, NATURE, and COMMON-SENSE.

## HENRY FIELDING
### From *The Covent-Garden Journal*
#### No. 31. April 18, 1752

S IR,
You are sensible, I believe, that there is nothing in this Age more fashionable, than to criticise on Shakespeare; I am indeed told, that there are not less than 200 Editions of that Author, with Commentaries, Notes, Observations, &c. now preparing for the Press; as nothing therefore is more natural than to direct one's Studies by the Humour of the Times, I have myself employed some leisure Hours on that great Poet. I here send you a short Specimen of my Labours, being some Emendations of that most celebrated Soliloquy in Hamlet, which, as I have no Intention to publish Shakespeare myself, are very much at the Service of any of the 200 Critics abovementioned.

I am, &c.

*Hamlet, Act III. Scene 2.*

To be, or not to be, that is the question.

This is certainly very intelligible; but if a slight Alteration were made in the former Part of the Line, and an easy Change was admitted in the last Word, the Sense would be greatly improved. I would propose then to read thus;

To be, or not. To be! That is the BASTION.

That is the strong Hold. The Fortress. So Addison in *Cato*.

Here will I hold——

The military Terms which follow, abundantly point out this Reading.

Whether 'tis nobler in the *Mind* to *suffer*
The *Slings* and Arrows of outragious Fortune,
Or *to take Arms against a Sea* of Troubles,
And by opposing end them.

*Suffering* is, I allow, a Christian Virtue; but I question whether it hath ever been ranked among the heroic Qualities. Shakespeare certainly wrote BUFFET; and this leads us to supply Man for Mind; Mind being alike applicable to both Sexes, whereas Hamlet is here displaying the most masculine Fortitude. *Slings* and *Arrows* in the succeeding Line, is an Impropriety which could not have come from our Author; the former being the Engine which discharges, and the latter the Weapon discharged. To the Sling, he would have opposed the Bow; or to Arrows, Stones. Read therefore WINGED

ARROWS; that is, feathered Arrows; a Figure very usual among Poets: So in the classical Ballad of *Chevy Chase*;

> The Grey-Goose Wing that was thereon
> In his Heart's Blood was wet.

The next Line is undoubtedly corrupt—to take Arms against a Sea, can give no Man, I think, an Idea; whereas by a slight Alteration and Transposition all will be set right, and the undoubted Meaning of Shakespeare restored.

> Or *tack* against an *Arm 'oth' Sea* of Troubles,
> And by composing end them.

By composing himself to Sleep, as he presently explains himself. What shall I do? says Hamlet. Shall I *buffet* the Storm, or shall I *tack* about and go to Rest?

> —*To die*, to sleep;
> No more; and by a Sleep to say we end
> The Heart-ach, and the thousand natural Shocks
> The Flesh is Heir to; 'tis a *Consummation*
> Devoutly to be wished. *To die*, to sleep;
> To sleep, perchance to dream;—

What to die first, and to go to sleep afterwards; and not only so, but to dream too?—But tho' his Commentators were dreaming of Nonsense when they read this Passage, Shakespeare was awake when he writ it. Correct it thus;

> —To lie to sleep.

*i.e.* To go to sleep, a common Expression; Hamlet himself expressly says he means *no more*; which he would hardly have said, if he had talked of Death, a Matter of the greatest and highest Nature: And is not the Context a Description of the Power of Sleep, which every one knows puts an End to the Heart-ach, the Tooth-ach, and indeed every Ach? So our Author in his *Macbeth*, speaking of this very Sleep, calls it

> Balm of hurt Minds, great Nature's *second Course*.

Where, by the bye, instead of second Course, I read SICK-EN'D DOSE; this being, indeed, the Dose which Nature chuses to apply to all her Shocks, and may be therefore well said *devoutly to be wished for*; which surely cannot be so generally said of Death.—But how can Sleep be called a *Consummation?*—The true Reading is certainly *Consultation*; the Cause for the Effect, a common Metonymy, *i.e.* When we are in any violent Pain, and a Set of Physicians are met in a *Consultation*, it is to be hoped the Consequence will be a sleeping Dose. Death, I own, is very devoutly to be apprehended, but seldom wished, I believe, at least by the Patient himself, at all such Seasons.

For natural *Shocks*, I would read *Shakes*; indeed I know only one Argument which can be brought in Justifica⟨tion⟩ of the old Reading; and this is, that *Shock* hath the same Signification, and is rather the better Word. In such Cases, the Reader must be left to his Choice.

> For in that Sleep of Death what Dreams may come,
> When we have *shuffled* off this mortal *Coil*,
> Must give us Pause——

Read and print thus:

> For in that Sleep, of Death what Dreams may come?
> When we have *scuffled* off, this mortal *Call*,
> Must give us Pause——

*i.e.* Must make us stop. *Shuffle* is a paultry Metaphor, taken from playing at Cards; whereas *scuffle* is a noble and military Word.

> The Whips and Scorns of Time.

Undoubtedly *Whips* and *Spurs*.

> When he himself might his *Quietus* make
> With a bare *Bodkin*.

With a bare *Pipkin*. The Reader will be pleased to observe, that Hamlet, as we have above proved, is here debating whether it were better to go to sleep, or to keep awake; as an Argument for the affirmative, he urges that no Man in his Senses would bear *The Whips and Scorns of Time, the Oppressor's Wrong*, &c. when he himself, without being at the Expence of an Apothecary, might make his *Quietus, or sleeping Dose*, with a bare PIPKIN, the cheapest of all Vessels, and consequently within every Man's Reach.

> —Who would Fardles bear,
> To groan and sweat under a weary Life?

Who indeed would bear any thing for such a Reward? The true Reading is

> —Who would for th' Ales bear
> To groan, &c.

Who would bear the Miseries of Life, for the Sake of the Ales. In the Days of Shakespeare, when Diversions were not arrived at that Degree of Elegance to which they have been since brought, the Assemblies of the People for Mirth were called by the Name of an ALE. This was the Drum or Rout of that Age, and was the Entertainment of the better Sort, as it is at this Day of the Vulgar. Such are the *Easter-Ales* and the *Whitsun-Ales*, at present celebrated all over the West of England. The Sentiment therefore of the Poet, is this; *Who would bear the Miseries of Life, to enjoy the Pleasures of it*; which latter Word is by no forced Metaphor called THE ALES OF LIFE.

> And makes us rather bear the Ills we have,
> Than fly to others that we know not of.

This, I own, is Sense as it stands; but the Spirit of the Passage will be improved, if we read

> Than try *some others*, &c.

> —Thus the native Hue of Resolution,
> Is sicklied o'er with the pale Cast of Thought.

Read,

> —Thus the native Blue of Resolution,
> Is pickled o'er in a stale Cask of Salt.

This restores a most elegant Sentiment; I shall leave the Relish of it therefore with the Reader, and conclude by wishing that its Taste may never be obliterated by any future Alteration of this glorious Poet.

## SAMUEL JOHNSON
*Proposals for Printing, by Subscription,*
*the Dramatick Works of William Shakespeare*
### 1756

When the works of Shakespeare are, after so many editions, again offered to the publick, it will doubtless be enquired, why Shakespeare stands in more need of critical assistance than any other of the English writers, and what are the deficiencies of the late attempts, which another editor may hope to supply.

The business of him that republishes an ancient book is, to correct what is corrupt, and to explain what is obscure. To have a text corrupt in many places, and in many doubtful, is, among the authours that have written since the use of types, almost peculiar to Shakespeare. Most writers, by publishing their own works, prevent all various readings, and preclude all conjectural criticism. Books indeed are sometimes published after the death of him who produced them, but they are better secured from corruptions than these unfortunate compositions. They subsist in a single copy, written or revised by the authour;

and the faults of the printed volume can be only faults of one descent.

But of the works of Shakespeare the condition has been far different: he sold them, not to be printed, but to be played. They were immediately copied for the actors, and multiplied by transcript after transcript, vitiated by the blunders of the penman, or changed by the affectation of the player; perhaps enlarged to introduce a jest, or mutilated to shorten the representation; and printed at last without the concurrence of the authour, without the consent of the proprietor, from compilations made by chance or by stealth out of the separate parts written for the theatre: and thus thrust into the world surreptitiously and hastily, they suffered another depravation from the ignorance and negligence of the printers, as every man who knows the state of the press in that age will readily conceive.

It is not easy for invention to bring together so many causes concurring to vitiate a text. No other authour ever gave up his works to fortune and time with so little care: no books could be left in hands so likely to injure them, as plays frequently acted, yet continued in manuscript: no other transcribers were likely to be so little qualified for their task as those who copied for the stage, at a time when the lower ranks of the people were universally illiterate: no other editions were made from fragments so minutely broken, and so fortuitously reunited; and in no other age was the art of printing in such unskilful hands.

With the causes of corruption that make the revisal of Shakespeare's dramatick pieces necessary, may be enumerated the causes of obscurity, which may be partly imputed to his age, and partly to himself.

When a writer outlives his contemporaries, and remains almost the only unforgotten name of a distant time, he is necessarily obscure. Every age has its modes of speech, and its cast of thought; which, though easily explained when there are many books to be compared with each other, become sometimes unintelligible, and always difficult, when there are no parallel passages that may conduce to their illustration. Shakespeare is the first considerable authour of sublime or familiar dialogue in our language. Of the books which he read, and from which he formed his stile, some perhaps have perished, and the rest are neglected. His imitations are therefore unnoted, his allusions are undiscovered, and many beauties, both of pleasantry and greatness, are lost with the objects to which they were united, as the figures vanish when the canvas has decayed.

It is the great excellence of Shakespeare, that he drew his scenes from nature, and from life. He copied the manners of the world then passing before him, and has more allusions than other poets to the traditions and superstition of the vulgar; which must therefore be traced before he can be understood.

He wrote at a time when our poetical language was yet unformed, when the meaning of our phrases was yet in fluctuation, when words were adopted at pleasure from the neighbouring languages, and while the Saxon was still visibly mingled in our diction. The reader is therefore embarrassed at once with dead and with foreign languages, with obsoleteness and innovation. In that age, as in all others, fashion produced phraseology, which succeeding fashion swept away before its meaning was generally known, or sufficiently authorised: and in that age, above all others, experiments were made upon our language, which distorted its combinations, and disturbed its uniformity.

If Shakespeare has difficulties above other writers, it is to be imputed to the nature of his work, which required the use of the common colloquial language, and consequently admitted many phrases allusive, elliptical, and proverbial, such as we speak and hear every hour without observing them; and of which, being now familiar, we do not suspect that they can ever grow uncouth, or that, being now obvious, they can ever seem remote.

These are the principal causes of the obscurity of Shakespeare; to which may be added that fulness of idea, which might sometimes load his words with more sentiment than they could conveniently convey, and that rapidity of imagination which might hurry him to a second thought before he had fully explained the first. But my opinion is, that very few of his lines were difficult to his audience, and that he used such expressions as were then common, though the paucity of contemporary writers makes them now seem peculiar.

Authours are often praised for improvement, or blamed for innovation, with very little justice, by those who read few other books of the same age. Addison himself has been so unsuccessful in enumerating the words with which Milton has enriched our language, as perhaps not to have named one of which Milton was the authour: and Bentley has yet more unhappily praised him as the introducer of those elisions into English poetry, which had been used from the first essays of versification among us, and which Milton was indeed the last that practised.

Another impediment, not the least vexatious to the commentator, is the exactness with which Shakespeare followed his authours. Instead of dilating his thoughts into generalities, and expressing incidents with poetical latitude, he often combines circumstances unnecessary to his main design, only because he happened to find them together. Such passages can be illustrated only by him who has read the same story in the very book which Shakespeare consulted.

He that undertakes an edition of Shakespeare, has all these difficulties to encounter, and all these obstructions to remove.

The corruptions of the text will be corrected by a careful collation of the oldest copies, by which it is hoped that many restorations may yet be made: at least it will be necessary to collect and note the variations as materials for future criticks, for it very often happens that a wrong reading has affinity to the right.

In this part all the present editions are apparently and intentionally defective. The criticks did not so much as wish to facilitate the labour of those that followed them. The same books are still to be compared; the work that has been done, is to be done again, and no single edition will supply the reader with a text on which he can rely as the best copy of the works of Shakespeare.

The edition now proposed will at least have this advantage over others. It will exhibit all the observable varieties of all the copies that can be found, that, if the reader is not satisfied with the editor's determination, he may have the means of chusing better for himself.

Where all the books are evidently vitiated, and collation can give no assistance, then begins the task of critical sagacity; and some changes may well be admitted in a text never settled by the authour, and so long exposed to caprice and ignorance. But nothing shall be imposed, as in the Oxford edition, without notice of the alteration; nor shall conjecture be wantonly or unnecessarily indulged.

It has been long found, that very specious emendations do not equally strike all minds with conviction, nor even the same mind at different times; and therefore, though perhaps many alterations may be proposed as eligible, very few will be obtruded as certain. In a language so ungrammatical as the English, and so licentious as that of Shakespeare, emendatory criticism is always hazardous; nor can it be allowed to any man who is not particularly versed in the writings of that age, and particularly studious of his authour's diction. There is danger lest peculiarities should be mistaken for corruptions, and passages rejected as unintelligible, which a narrow mind happens not to understand.

All the former criticks have been so much employed on the correction of the text, that they have not sufficiently attended to the elucidation of passages obscured by accident or time. The editor will endeavour to read the books which the authour read, to trace his knowledge to its source, and compare his copies with their originals. If in this part of his design he hopes to attain any degree of superiority to his predecessors, it must be considered, that he has the advantage of their labours; that part of the work being already done, more care is naturally bestowed on the other part; and that, to declare the truth, Mr. Rowe and Mr. Pope were very ignorant of the ancient English literature; Dr. Warburton was detained by more important studies; and Mr. Theobald, if fame be just to his memory, considered learning only as an instrument of gain, and made no further enquiry after his authour's meaning, when once he had notes sufficient to embellish his page with the expected decorations.

With regard to obsolete or peculiar diction, the editor may perhaps claim some degree of confidence, having had more motives to consider the whole extent of our language than any other man from its first formation. He hopes, that, by comparing the works of Shakespeare with those of writers who lived at the same time, immediately preceded, or immediately followed him, he shall be able to ascertain his ambiguities, disentangle his intricacies, and recover the meaning of words now lost in the darkness of antiquity.

When therefore any obscurity arises from an allusion to some other book, the passage will be quoted. When the diction is entangled, it will be cleared by a paraphrase or interpretation. When the sense is broken by the suppression of part of the sentiment in pleasantry or passion, the connection will be supplied. When any forgotten custom is hinted, care will be taken to retrieve and explain it. The meaning assigned to doubtful words will be supported by the authorities of other writers, or by parallel passages of Shakespeare himself.

The observation of faults and beauties is one of the duties of an annotator, which some of Shakespeare's editors have attempted, and some have neglected. For this part of his task, and for this only, was Mr. Pope eminently and indisputably qualified: nor has Dr. Warburton followed him with less diligence or less success. But I have never observed that mankind was much delighted or improved by their asterisks, commas, or double commas; of which the only effect is, that they preclude the pleasure of judging for ourselves, teach the young and ignorant to decide without principles; defeat curiosity and discernment, by leaving them less to discover; and at last shew the opinion of the critick, without the reasons on which it was founded, and without affording any light by which it may be examined.

The editor, though he may less delight his own vanity, will probably please his reader more, by supposing him equally able with himself to judge of beauties and faults, which require no previous acquisition of remote knowledge. A description of the obvious scenes of nature, a representation of general life, a sentiment of reflection or experience, a deduction of conclusive argument, a forcible eruption of effervescent passion, are to be considered as proportionate to common apprehension, unassisted by critical officiousness; since, to conceive them, nothing more is requisite than acquaintance with the general state of the world, and those faculties which he must always bring with him who would read Shakespeare.

But when the beauty arises from some adaptation of the sentiment to customs worn out of use, to opinions not universally prevalent, or to any accidental or minute particularity, which cannot be supplied by common understanding, or common observation, it is the duty of a commentator to lend his assistance.

The notice of beauties and faults thus limited will make no distinct part of the design, being reducible to the explanation of obscure passages.

The editor does not however intend to preclude himself from the comparison of Shakespeare's sentiments or expression with those of ancient or modern authours, or from the display of any beauty not obvious to the students of poetry; for as he hopes to leave his authour better understood, he wishes likewise to procure him more rational approbation.

The former editors have affected to slight their predecessors: but in this edition all that is valuable will be adopted from every commentator, that posterity may consider it as including all the rest, and exhibiting whatever is hitherto known of the great father of the English drama.

## CONDITIONS

I. That the book shall be elegantly printed in eight volumes in octavo.

II. That the price to subscribers shall be two guineas; one to be paid at subscribing, the other on the delivery of the book in sheets.

III. That the work shall be published on or before Christmas 1757.

## JAMES RUSSELL LOWELL
### From "Shakespeare Once More" (1868)
### *Works*
### 1890, Volume 3, pp. 166–73

T he hold which Shakespeare has acquired and maintained upon minds so many and so various, in so many vital respects utterly unsympathetic and even incapable of sympathy with his own, is one of the most noteworthy phenomena in the history of literature. That he has had the most inadequate of editors, that, as his own Falstaff was the cause of the wit, so he has been the cause of the foolishness that was in other men, (as where Malone ventured to discourse upon his metres, and Dr. Johnson on his imagination,) must be apparent to every one,— and also that his genius and its manifestations are so various, that there is no commentator but has been able to illustrate him from his own peculiar point of view or from the results of his own favorite studies. But to show that he was a good common lawyer, that he understood the theory of colors, that he was an accurate botanist, a master of the science of medicine, especially in its relation to mental disease, a profound metaphysician, and of great experience and insight in politics,—all these, while they may very well form the staple of separate treatises, and prove, that, whatever the extent of his learning, the range and accuracy of his knowledge were beyond precedent or later parallel, are really outside the province of an editor.

We doubt if posterity owe a greater debt to any two men living in 1623 than to the two obscure actors who in that year published the first folio edition of Shakespeare's plays. But for them, it is more than likely that such of his works as had remained to that time unprinted would have been irrecoverably lost, and among them were *Julius Caesar*, *The Tempest*, and

*Macbeth.* But are we to believe them when they assert that they present to us the plays which they reprinted from stolen and surreptitious copies "cured and perfect of their limbs," and those which are original in their edition "absolute in their numbers as he [Shakespeare] conceived them"? Alas, we have read too many theatrical announcements, have been taught too often that the value of the promise was in an inverse ratio to the generosity of the exclamation-marks, too easily to believe that! Nay, we have seen numberless processions of healthy kine enter our native village unheralded save by the lusty shouts of drovers, while a wretched calf, cursed by stepdame nature with two heads, was brought to us in a triumphal car, avant-couriered by a band of music as abnormal as itself, and announced as the greatest wonder of the age. If a double allowance of vituline brains deserve such honor, there are few commentators on Shakespeare that would have gone afoot, and the trumpets of Messieurs Heminge and Condell call up in our minds too many monstrous and deformed associations.

What, then, is the value of the first folio as an authority? For eighteen of the plays it is the only authority we have, and the only one also for four others in their complete form. It is admitted that in several instances Heminge and Condell reprinted the earlier quarto impressions with a few changes, sometimes for the better and sometimes for the worse; and it is most probable that copies of those editions (whether surreptitious or not) had taken the place of the original prompter's books, as being more convenient and legible. Even in these cases it is not safe to conclude that all or even any of the variations were made by the hand of Shakespeare himself. And where the players printed from manuscript, is it likely to have been that of the author? The probability is small that a writer so busy as Shakespeare must have been during his productive period should have copied out their parts for the actors himself, or that one so indifferent as he seems to have been to the immediate literary fortunes of his works should have given much care to the correction of copies, if made by others. The copies exclusively in the hands of Heminge and Condell were, it is manifest, in some cases, very imperfect, whether we account for the fact by the burning of the Globe Theatre or by the necessary wear and tear of years, and (what is worthy of notice) they are plainly more defective in some parts than in others. *Measure for Measure* is an example of this, and we are not satisfied with being told that its ruggedness of verse is intentional, or that its obscurity is due to the fact that Shakespeare grew more elliptical in his style as he grew older. Profounder in thought he doubtless became; though in a mind like his, we believe that this would imply only a more absolute supremacy in expression. But, from whatever original we suppose either the quartos or the first folio to have been printed, it is more than questionable whether the proof-sheets had the advantage of any revision other than that of the printing-office. Steevens was of opinion that authors in the time of Shakespeare never read their own proof-sheets; and Mr. Spedding, in his recent edition of Bacon, comes independently to the same conclusion.[1] We may be very sure that Heminge and Condell did not, as vicars, take upon themselves a disagreeable task which the author would have been too careless to assume.

Nevertheless, however strong a case may be made out against the Folio of 1623, whatever sins of omission we may lay to the charge of Heminge and Condell, or of commission to that of the printers, it remains the only text we have with any claims whatever to authenticity. It should be deferred to as authority in all cases where it does not make Shakespeare write bad sense, uncouth metre, or false grammar, of all which we believe him to have been more supremely incapable than any other man who ever wrote English. Yet we would not speak unkindly even of the blunders of the Folio. They have put bread into the mouth of many an honest editor, publisher, and printer for the last century and a half; and he who loves the comic side of human nature will find the serious notes of a *variorum* edition of Shakespeare as funny reading as the funny ones are serious. Scarce a commentator of them all, for more than a hundred years, but thought, as Alphonso of Castile did of Creation, that, if he had only been at Shakespeare's elbow, he could have given valuable advice; scarce one who did not know off-hand that there was never a seaport in Bohemia,—as if Shakespeare's world were one which Mercator could have projected; scarce one but was satisfied that his ten finger-tips were a sufficient key to those astronomic wonders of poise and counterpoise, of planetary law and cometary seeming-exception, in his metres; scarce one but thought he could gauge like an ale-firkin that intuition whose edging shallows may have been sounded, but whose abysses, stretching down amid the sunless roots of Being and Consciousness, mock the plummet; scarce one but could speak with condescending approval of that prodigious intelligence so utterly without congener that our baffled language must coin an adjective to qualify it, and none is so audacious as to say Shaksperian of any other. And yet, in the midst of our impatience, we cannot help thinking also of how much healthy mental activity this one man has been the occasion, how much good he has indirectly done to society by withdrawing men to investigations and habits of thought that secluded them from baser attractions, for how many he has enlarged the circle of study and reflection; since there is nothing in history or politics, nothing in art or science, nothing in physics or metaphysics, that is not sooner or later taxed for his illustration. This is partially true of all great minds, open and sensitive to truth and beauty through any large arc of their circumference; but it is true in an unexampled sense of Shakespeare, the vast round of whose balanced nature seems to have been equatorial, and to have had a southward exposure and a summer sympathy at every point, so that life, society, statecraft, serve us at last but as commentaries on him, and whatever we have gathered of thought, of knowledge, and of experience, confronted with his marvellous page, shrinks to a mere foot-note, the stepping-stone to some hitherto inaccessible verse. We admire in Homer the blind placid mirror of the world's young manhood, the bard who escapes from his misfortune in poems all memory, all life and bustle, adventure and picture; we revere in Dante that compressed force of lifelong passion which could make a private experience cosmopolitan in its reach and everlasting in its significance; we respect in Goethe the Aristotelian poet, wise by weariless observation, witty with intention, the stately *Geheimerrath* of a provincial court in the empire of Nature. As we study these, we seem in our limited way to penetrate into their consciousness and to measure and master their methods; but with Shakespeare it is just the other way; the more we have familiarized ourselves with the operations of our own consciousness, the more do we find, in reading him, that he has been beforehand with us, and that, while we have been vainly endeavouring to find the door of his being, he has searched every nook and cranny of our own. While other poets and dramatists embody isolated phases of character and work inward from the phenomenon to the special law which it illustrates, he seems in some strange way unitary with human nature itself, and his own soul to have been the law and life-giving power of which his creations are only the phenomena. We justify or criticise the characters of other writers by our memory and experience, and pronounce them natural or unnatural; but he seems to have worked in the very stuff of which memory and experience are made, and we recognize his truth to nature by an innate and unacquired sympathy, as if he alone possessed the secret of the "ideal form and universal mould," and embodied generic types rather than individuals. In this Cervantes alone has approached him; and Don Quixote and Sancho, like the men and women of Shakespeare, are the contemporaries of every generation, because they are not products of an artificial and transitory society, but because they are animated by the primeval and unchanging forces of that humanity which underlies and survives the forever-fickle creeds and ceremonials of the parochial corners which we who dwell in them sublimely call The World.

That Shakespeare did not edit his own works must be attributed, we suspect, to his premature death. That he should not have intended it is inconceivable. Is there not something of self-consciousness in the breaking of Prospero's wand and burying his book,—a sort of sad prophecy, based on self-knowledge of the nature of that man who, after such thaumaturgy, could go down to Stratford and live there for years, only collecting his dividends from the Globe Theatre, lending money on mortgage, and leaning over his gate to chat and bandy quips with neighbors? His mind had entered into every phase of human life and thought, had embodied all of them in living creations;—had he found all empty, and come at last to the belief that genius and its works were as phantasmagoric as the rest, and that fame was as idle as the rumor of the pit? However this may be, his works have come down to us in a condition of manifest and admitted corruption in some portions, while in others there is an obscurity which may be attributed either to an idiosyncratic use of words and condensation of phrase, to a depth of intuition for a proper coalescence with which ordinary language is inadequate, to a concentration of passion in a focus that consumes the lighter links which bind together the clauses of a sentence or of a process of reasoning in common parlance, or to a sense of music which mingles music and meaning without essentially confounding them. We should demand for a perfect editor, then, first, a thorough glossological knowledge of the English contemporary with Shakespeare; second, enough logical acuteness of mind and metaphysical training to enable him to follow recondite processes of thought; third, such a conviction of the supremacy of his author as always to prefer his thought to any theory of his own; fourth, a feeling for music, and so much knowledge of the practice of other poets as to understand that Shakespeare's versification differs from theirs as often in kind as in degree; fifth, an acquaintance with the world as well as with books; and last, what is, perhaps, of more importance than all, so great a familiarity with the working of the imaginative faculty in general, and of its peculiar operation in the mind of Shakespeare, as will prevent his thinking a passage dark with excess of light, and enable him to understand fully that the Gothic Shakespeare often superimposed upon the slender column of a single word, that seems to twist under it, but does not,—like the quaint shafts in cloisters,—a weight of meaning which the modern architects of sentences would consider wholly unjustifiable by correct principle.

*Notes*

1. Vol. III. p. 348, *note.* He grounds his belief, not on the misprinting of words, but on the misplacing of whole paragraphs. We were struck with the same thing in the original edition of Chapman's *Biron's Conspiracy and Tragedy.* And yet, in comparing two copies of this edition, I have found corrections which only the author could have made. One of the misprints which Mr. Spedding notices affords both a hint and a warning to the conjectural emendator. In the edition of *The Advancement of Learning* printed in 1605 occurs the word *dusinesse.* In a later edition this was conjecturally changed to *business;* but the occurrence of *vertigine* in the Latin translation enables Mr. Spedding to print rightly, *dizziness.*

## THOMAS SPENCER BAYNES
"New Shakespearian Interpretations" (1872)
*Shakespeare Studies*
1894, pp. 300–357

Mr. Gladstone, in his "Essay on the Place of Homer in Education," notices the tradition of a certain Dorotheus, who spent the whole of his life in endeavouring to elucidate the meaning of a single word in Homer, and seems to suggest that the time thus occupied was not altogether wasted. Without going quite so far as this, most critics will probably agree in his general conclusion, "that no exertion spent upon any of the great classics of the world, and attended with any amount of real result, is thrown away". Unfortunately, the greatest classic in the literatures of the world affords as much scope for this kind of labour as any of his reputed peers, not excepting the object of Mr. Gladstone's critical devotion. The oldest and most authoritative editions of Shakespeare are, it is well known, crowded with verbal errors, textual corruptions, and metrical obscurities. They include, indeed, almost every species of literary and typographical confusion which haste, ignorance, and carelessness in the multiplication and fortuitous printing of manuscript copies could produce. After a century and a half of critical labour embracing three great schools of editors and commentators, the text of these dramas is only now partially purged from the obvious blots and stains that disfigure the earliest editions. And it is only within the last ten years that the results of this prolonged critical labour have been condensed, and exhibited in a thoroughly scientific shape, by the acute and learned editors of the Cambridge *Shakespeare.*

By means of this most useful and scholarlike edition, any cultivated and intelligent reader may form some estimate of the net result and general value of Shakespearian criticism. A comparison of the best modern readings with those of the Quartos and Folios will show in what numberless instances the text has been corrected, amended, and even restored. Those who have never made such a comparison would be surprised to find how many familiar phrases and passages, some too regarded as peculiarly Shakespearian, are due to the happy conjectures of successive textual scholars. Rowe and Pope, the first critical editors, being themselves poets, are peculiarly felicitous in their suggested emendations. But even the more prosaic Theobald's single-minded and persistent devotion was surprisingly successful in the same direction. His labours were, however, still more fruitful in restoring neglected readings from the First Folio which neither of his predecessors had consulted with any care. The first school of critics, indeed, brought native sagacity rather than minute or accurate learning to the task of clearing up the difficulties of Shakespeare's text. They satisfied themselves with correcting the more obvious misprints of the Folios, and endeavouring to relieve, by conjectural emendations, some of their corruptest passages.

The second school of editors, represented by Capell, Stevens, and Malone, were diligent students of the Elizabethan literature, and found no difficulty therefore in explaining many words and phrases that had perplexed and baffled their predecessors. For elucidating the obscurities of the text, they relied more on illustration than on conjectural emendation. Many passages which the early editors, through ignorance of Elizabethan manners, usages, and allusions, had regarded as corrupt, were amply vindicated from the charge by the more exact and minute knowledge of the later. The third, and more recent schools of editors and critics, represented by Knight and Collier, Dyce and Staunton, while combining the distinctive excellences of the previous schools, have specially developed what may be regarded as the most fruitful branch of Shakespearian criticism—that of apt and illuminating illustrations from contemporary literature. The researches of Knight, Dyce, and Staunton in particular have satisfactorily explained many phrases and allusions regarded by previous editors as hopelessly ambiguous and obscure, if not altogether unintelligible. While thus working in the right direction, the modern school has, however, exemplified afresh the conflict between authority and criticism which must always prevail with regard to an original text, at once so important and so defective as that of Shakespeare's dramas. Mr. Knight, in his admiration of the First Folio, yielded a somewhat exclusive deference to authority. Mr. Collier, again, partly no doubt from the accident of possessing the Perkin's Folio, went to the other extreme, becoming the champion of conjectural emendation in its most licentious forms. Mr. Dyce and Mr. Staunton hold the balance comparatively even, but in the hands of the Cambridge editors it again inclines more decisively towards the side of authority. On the whole, the result of recent criticism and research has been to strengthen the position of the First Folio, and check the recurrent tendency to get rid of textual difficulties by ingenious, but often rash and ignorant, conjecture.

This result is in all respects a satisfactory one. Conjectural emendation is at best a double-edged instrument, to be wielded in safety only on rare occasions and by the most skillful hands. The eager Shakespearian student is, however, continually tempted to cut the Gordian knot of a difficulty by its summary use. The temptation should be steadfastly resisted, on pain, for the most part, of reading into the poet's lines a foreign and prosaic sense, instead of bringing fully out their real but latent meaning. In the majority of cases the practice of substituting his own language for the poet's simply depraves the text, and injures the finer sensibilities of the critic. Those who indulge in it too freely, however naturally gifted, soon lose that respect for the poet's words, and scrupulous care for his meaning, which is the foundation of all sound and illuminating criticism.

There is little danger of any excess in the other main department of critical labour, that of illustrating from appropriate sources the obscurer terms and allusions of Shakespeare's text. In this direction there is still ample scope, "room and verge enough," for the labours of Shakespearian students. The fact is in itself one of the most striking proofs of Shakespeare's marvellous universality. That anything should remain to be elucidated after the life-long devotion of so many learned and acute commentators is surprising enough. But Shakespeare's vision of life is so wide, his moral insight so profound, his knowledge and sympathies so vitalised and universal, and his command of language so absolute, that every part in the wide circle of contemporary learning and experience may throw some light on his pages. In particular, his birthright of pregnant speech is so imperial that he seems to appropriate by a kind of royal prerogative the more expressive elements of diction in every department of human attainment and activity. No section of life or thought is too humble for his regard; none too lofty for his sympathetic appreciation. The day-spring of his serene and glorious intellect illuminates and vivifies the whole. The more prominent features of that great world are familiar to all cultivated English readers. The order and organisation of the several parts have been diligently studied and eloquently expounded by the critics. But there are still hidden nooks and obscure recesses which even the most curious and painstaking observers have failed to explore. On these, special investigation

and persistent research may yet throw some light. Such researches are, moreover, within the reach of students who could hardly be considered Shakespearian scholars in the higher and technical sense of the term. The complete Shakespearian scholar ought to have a minute and exhaustive, but at the same time vital acquaintance with the whole Elizabethan period, its entire universe of knowledge and experience. This can only be gained by the thorough and prolonged study of its history and literature, including the most fugitive and evanescent productions, such as songs, ballads, and chap-books, squibs and letters, pamphlets and broadsides. Few even of the more devoted Shakespearian critics have reached this ideal standard. Many hands, however, make light work, and much may be done in the way of Shakespearian interpretation by the separate contributions of students who have been able to cultivate only a small portion of the wide field. The humblest labourer may add his mite to the constantly-accumulating stores of sterling commentary and illustration.

Many of the sources whence elucidations of Shakespeare's obscure passages may be drawn lie on the surface, and are well known. His writings abound, for example, with terms and phrases, similes, metaphors, and allusions derived from field sports, such as hunting and hawking; from games of chance and skill, such as cards and dice, bowls and tennis; from the military and self-defensive arts, such as archery and fencing; from fashionable pastimes, such as music and dancing; and from popular natural history—the whole folk-flora and folk-fauna of the time. The more obvious, and many of the more obscure allusions connected with these branches of popular knowledge and practice, have been amply explained by successive editors. Some, however, have been overlooked, and in the present paper we purpose giving a few illustrations of these neglected allusions. We shall offer an explanation of some passages in Shakespeare, either given up by critics and commentators as hopelessly unintelligible, or only very imperfectly and erroneously explained. So far at least as we are acquainted with Shakespearian criticism, most of the explanations now proposed of obscure terms, phrases, and allusions are new,—have not been in any way anticipated by previous writers on the subject. Even a very partial acquaintance with the wide field of Shakespearian criticism suggests, however, the propriety of some hesitation and reserve in announcing novelties of interpretation. Every persistent student of Shakespeare must have found, again and again, that what he at first imagined to be discoveries had been anticipated by previous writers, illustrious or obscure. In general, however, the best modern editions represent in a condensed form, either in notes or glossary, the main results of previous criticism. If they leave a difficulty unnoticed, or give only a vague and conjectural explanation, it may be assumed with tolerable certainty that no better solution has yet been offered. In the same way the Variorum edition gives the main results of Shakespearian criticism up to the date of its publication. In offering the following elucidations as novelties, it is meant therefore that they solve difficulties left unexplained by the Variorum edition, by modern editors, by the ablest independent critics, such as Douce, Hunter, Walker, and White, and, so far as the writer is aware, by all previous commentators on Shakespeare.

We may begin with a few illustrations from popular field sports, which in Shakespeare's day meant very much hawking and hunting. These furnish the poet with almost inexhaustible materials of imagery and allusion. In particular, the sportive warfare in the fields and woods with the nobler kinds of chase and game afforded the aptest phrases, similes, and metaphors for picturing vividly the sterner realities of martial conflict, "the pride, pomp, and circumstance of glorious war". Such references occur again and again, and many of them are even now only partially explained. In *Coriolanus*, for example, in the wonderful scene between the servants in the house of Aufidius, such an allusion occurs. While the servants who had resisted the intruder are talking together in the hall about the sudden arrival and ceremonious entertainment of their master's great enemy, a third hastily approached from the banqueting-room with the news that it has been just determined, at the suggestion of Coriolanus, to march against Rome.

> *Sec. Serv.*: Why, then we shall have a stirring world again. This peace is nothing, but to rust iron, increase tailors, and breed ballad-makers.
>
> *First Serv.*: Let me have war, say I; it exceeds peace as far as day does night; it's spritely, waking, audible, and *full of vent*. Peace is a very apoplexy, lethargy, mulled, deaf, sleepy, insensible; a getter of more bastard children than war's a destroyer of men.

Here the phrase "full of vent," the reading of the Folios, has so perplexed the critics that more than one has proposed to substitute for it "full of vaunt". The Folio text is, however, perfectly accurate, and peculiarly expressive, although it has never yet been correctly explained. The only explanation attempted is that of Johnson, repeated by subsequent editors, that "full of vent" means "full of rumour, full of materials of discourse". This, however, is a mere conjecture, and not a happy one, as it altogether misses the distinctive meaning of the phrase. Vent is a technical term in hunting to express the scenting of the game by the hounds employed in the chase. Both noun and verb are habitually used in this sense. Their exact meaning and use will be made clear by an extract or two from Turbervile's translation of *Du Fouilloux*, the popular manual of hunting in Shakespeare's day. The first extract refers to the wiles and subtleties of the hart when keenly pressed in the chase: "When a hart feeles that the hounds hold in after him, he fleeth and seeketh to beguile them with change in sundry sortes, for he will seeke other harts and deare at lare, and rowseth them before the houndes to make them hunt change; therewithall he will lie flat down upon his belly in some of their layres, and so let the houndes overshoot him, and because they should have no sent of him, nor *vent* him, he will trusse all his four feet under his belly, and will blow and breath upon the ground in some moist place, in such sort that I have seen the houndes passe by such an hart within a yard of him and never *vent* him". Further on, the author, speaking of the hart, says again expressly: "When he smelleth or *venteth* anything, we say he hath this or that in the wind". In the same way, when the hound vents anything, he pauses to verify the scent, and then, full of eager excitement, strains in the leash to be after the game that is thus perceived to be a-foot. The following extract from the rhyming report of a huntsman upon sight of a hart in pride of grease illustrates this:—

> Then if the Prince demand what head he beare,
> I answer thus with sober words and cheare:
> My Liege, I went this morning on my quest;
> My hound did sticke, and seemed to *vent* some beast.
> I held him short, and drawing after him,
> I might behold the hart was feeding trym,
> His head was high, and large in each degree,
> Well palmed eke, and seemed full sound to be.
> Of colour browne, he beareth eight and tenne,
> Of stately height, and long he seemed then.
> His beame seemd great, in good proportion led,
> Well burred and round, well pearled neare his head,
> He seemed fayre, tweene black and berrie brounde,
> He seemes well fed, by all the signes I found.

The use of the noun is exemplified in another hunting rhyme, or huntsman's soliloquy, entitled "The Blazon of the Hart," which is of special interest from the vividness of the picture it brings before us:—

> I am the hunt, which rathe and early rise,
> My bottell filled with wine in any wise,
> Two draughts I drinke, to stay my steps withall,
> For each foote one, because I would not fall.
> Then take my hound, in liam me behind,
> The stately hart in fryth or fell to find.
> And while I seeke his slott where he hath fedde,
> The sweet byrdes sing, to cheare my drowsie head.
> And when my hound doth straine upon good *vent*
> I must confesse, the same doth me content.
> But when I have my coverts walkt about,
> And harbred fast, the hart for comming out,
> Then I returne, to make a grave report.

The technical meaning and use of the word in these passages is sufficiently clear, and it will be seen how happily Shakespeare employs it. To strain at the lyam or leash "upon good vent" is in Shakespeare's phrase to be "full of vent," or in other words keenly excited, full of pluck and courage, of throbbing energy and impetuous desire, in a word, full of all the kindling stir and commotion of anticipated conflict. This is not only in harmony with the meaning of the passage, but gives point and force to the whole description. War is naturally personified as a trained hound roused to animated motion by the scent of game, giving tongue, and straining in the slips at the near prospect of the exciting chase. This explanation justifies the reading of the Folios, "*sprightly walking*, audible, full of vent," or at least affords a better explanation of it than has yet been offered. With a single exception the early reading has been rejected by all modern editors, including, strangely enough, Mr. Knight and the Cambridge editors. The exception is Mr. Staunton, who, however, while retaining the older reading, fails to understand it, and misinterprets the passage. He explains "sprightly walking" as "quick moving or marching," with evident reference to military movements, and with regard to the special phrase under review, he says boldly "vent is voice, utterance". But the previous epithet, audible, gives this feature of the description, *vent* referring not to sound at all, but to the quick perception of the game, and the signs of eagerness, such as kindled eye, dilated nostril, and muscular impatience, which keen relish for the sport produces. In such a connection "sprightly walking" would refer to the more lively and definite advance arising from the discovery of good vent as compared with the dissatisfied snuffings and uncertain progress when nothing is in view. The description thus includes quickened motion, eager tongue, and intense physical excitement. The passage finds an exact parallel in Henry V.'s spirited address to his soldiers before Harfleur:—

> And you, good yeomen,
> Whose limbs were made in England, show us here
> The mettle of your pasture; let us swear
> That you are worth your breeding: which I doubt not;
> For there is none of you so mean and base,
> That hath not noble lustre in your eyes.
> I see you stand like greyhounds in the slips,
> Straining upon the start. The game's a-foot:
> Follow your spirit; and, upon this charge,
> Cry "God for Harry, England, and Saint George!"

The same general allusion is contained in the well-known line from *Julius Cæsar*, "Cry havock, and let slip the dogs of war," as well as in several passages in other plays. In the lines just quoted, the reference to "the mettle of your pasture" is also derived from the *Noble Art of Venerie*. The colour of the stag, the size and texture of his antlers, his strength of wind and limb, and powers of endurance, depended very much upon the country in which he was reared, and especially upon the kind of pasture on which he browsed. Thus Du Fouilloux concludes a discourse on the different colours of the stag's coat, and the different descriptions of head, as follows:—

> There is another forrest about four leagues from thence called Chissay, in the which the harts beare heads cleane contrary, for they are great, red, and full of marrow, and are very light when they are dry. All these things I have thought good heere to alleadge, to let you know that harts beare their heads according to the pasture and feede of the country where they are bred; for the forrest of Merevant is altogether in mountaines, vales, and caves, whereas their feed is dry, leane, and of small substance. On that other side, the forrest of Chissay is a plaine country, environed with all good pasture and corne grounds, as wheat, peason, and such, whereupon they take good nouriture: which is the cause that their heads become so faire and well spredde.

Before leaving the subject, we may notice that the word "vent" in its technical sense is used by Shakespeare's contemporaries, especially the poets, such as Spenser and Drayton. The following extract from the graphic account of stag-hunting in the fourteenth song of the *Polyolbion* illustrates this:—

> Now when the hart doth heare
> The oft-bellowing hounds to *vent* his secret leyre,
> He rouzing rusheth out, and through the brakes doth drive,
> As though up by the roots the bushes he would rive,
> And through the cumbrous thicks, as fearefully he makes,
> Hee with his branched head, the tender saplings shakes,
> That sprinkling their moyst pearle doe seeme to him to weepe;
> When after goes the cry with yellings loud and deepe.

It need hardly be added that *vent* in this sense is, like so many of the terms of venery, taken directly from the French, to vent the game being simply to wind, or have wind of the game. Shakespeare's very expression, indeed, exists as a French phrase, and is given to illustrate the special meaning of the noun as a hunting term.

Again, Shakespeare uses the word *train* more than once in its technical hunting sense, the most striking instance of this special use being found in *Macbeth*. When Malcolm, in order to test the sincerity of Macduff's devotion, heaps vices on himself, until Macduff, in a burst of noble sorrow and indignation, renounces his enterprise in despair, Malcolm, satisfied with the result, explains the motive of his conduct as follows:—

> *Mal.:*      Macduff, this noble passion,
> Child of integrity, hath from my soul
> Wip'd the black scruples, reconciled my thoughts
> To thy good truth and honour. Devilish Macbeth
> By many of these *trains* hath sought to win me
> Into his power; and modest wisdom plucks me
> From over-credulous haste.

It has not been noticed that *trains* in this extract is a technical term both in hawking and hunting; in hawking for the lure, thrown out to reclaim a falcon given to ramble, or "rake out" as it is called, and thus in danger of escaping from the fowler; and in hunting for the bait trailed along the ground, and left exposed to tempt the animal from his lair or covert, and bring him fairly within the power of the lurking huntsman.

An extract or two from Turbervile will sufficiently exemplify this usage. The following is from a long and curious account of hunting the wolf, a common sport in France, and which in Shakespeare's day seems also to have prevailed to some extent in Ireland:—

> When a huntsman would hunt the wolfe, he must *trayne* them by these means. First, let him looke out some fayre place a mile or more from the greate woodes where there be some close standing to place a brace of good greyhounds in, if needs be, the which should be close environed, and some ponde or water by it: there shall he kill a horse or some other great beast, and take the foure legges thereof and carye them into the woods and forests adjoyning. Then let foure goode fellows take every man a legge of the beast, and drawe it at his horse tayle all alongst the pathes and wayes in the woods until they come backe againe unto the place where the dead beast lieth: there lette them lay downe their *traynes*. And when the wolves go out in the night to prey and to feede, they wil crosse upon the *trayne* and follow it untill they come at the dead carrion: there they will feede their fill. And then let the huntsman about the breake of day go thither, and leave his horse a good way off underneath the wind, and come faire and softly to the place to espie if there be any wolves feeding.

Again:—

> And when the huntsman shall by these meanes have been assured of their feeding twoo nights together, then may he make preparation to hunt them on the third day; or if they fayle to come unto the *trayne* the first or second day, then let him send out varlettes to *trayne* from about all the coverts adjoyning unto the same place: and so doing he cannot misse but draw wolves thither once within two or three nights.

The play of *Hamlet* supplies another illustration of hunting terms only partially explained. In the conversation about the players between Hamlet, Rosencrantz and Guildenstern a technical term occurs, which, though sometimes rightly understood, is often erroneously interpreted, and has never been traced or elucidated in its primary meaning and use:—

> *Ham.:* . . . . man delights not me; no, nor woman neither, though by your smiling you seem to say so.
> *Ros.:* My lord, there was no such stuff in my thoughts.
> *Ham.:* Why did you laugh, then, when I said, man delights not me?
> *Ros.:* To think, my lord, if you delight not in man, what lenten entertainment the players shall receive from you: we *coted* them on the way, and hither are they coming to offer you service.

Here *cote*, in the older spelling *coat*, is usually explained, even by modern editors, according to its etymology rather than according to its actual use, while none seem to be aware of its special technical meaning. Thus Mr. Collier interprets the phrase "we coted them" to mean "we overtook them," or, strictly, "came side by side with them," and Mr. Staunton boldly gives the latter part of this explanation as the full meaning of the term—"coted them"—"came alongside of them". Nares, again, while stating that the term is employed in coursing, gives the same erroneous interpretation, "coted," *i.e.*, "went side by side," and seems to have no real knowledge of its technical use. Mr. Dyce quotes from Caldecott a pertinent example of its use in contemporary literature, but he appears undecided as to the exact signification of the word, and unacquainted with its special secondary meaning. Both verb and noun are, however, sporting terms used in coursing of every kind, whether of the stag, the fox, or the hare. *Cote* in this technical sense is applied to a brace of greyhounds slipped together at the stag or hare, and means that one of the dogs outstrips the other and reaches the game first. In coursing the stag, it was sufficient if the foremost dog reached and pinched; in coursing the fallow deer, he was required to pinch and hold; while in coursing the hare, he had to outstrip his fellow and give the hare a turn, in order to secure the advantage of the *cote*. This will be made clear by the following extracts from Turbervile's short treatise on coursing:—

> In coursing at a Deare, if one Greyhound go endwayes by [that is beyond] another, it is accoumpted a Cote, so that he which doth so do by his fellow do reach the Deare and pinch: and in coursing of a redde Deare, that Greyhound which doth first pinch, shall winne the wager: but in coursing of a fallow Deare, your Greyhound must pinche and hold, or else he winneth not the wager.

Again, from the same treatise:—

> In coursing at the Hare, it is not materiall which dog kylleth her (which hunters call bearing of an Hare), but he that giveth most Cotes, or most turnes, winneth the wager. A Cote is when a Greyhound goeth endwayes by his fellow and giveth the Hare a turn (which is called setting a Hare about), but if he coast and so come by his fellow, that is no Cote. Likewise, if one Greyhound doe go by another, and then be not able to reach the Hare himselfe and turne her, this is but stripping and no Cote.

The definition of *cote* in the Duke of Norfolk's celebrated coursing rules, first published in Shakespeare's own day, is identical with Turbervile's; and Mr. Thacker, the best modern authority on the subject, in expounding the definition, says: "A cote is the first performance which takes place, or can be expected to take place, after the dogs are slipped at the hare. One dog outruns the other, and turns the hare, and with a good hare, and with one dog more speedy than the other, this is repeated many times in some courses." To cote is thus not simply to overtake, but to overpass, to outstrip, this being the distinctive meaning of the term. If one dog were originally behind the other, the cote would of course involve overtaking as its condition, but overtaking simply is not coting. Going beyond is the essential point, the term being usually applied under circumstances where overtaking is impossible—to dogs who start together and run abreast until the cote takes place. So Rosencrantz and Guildenstern, having coted the players in their way, reach the palace first, and have been for some time in conversation with Hamlet before the strolling company arrive. In its secondary or metaphorical use, the word uniformly retains the same distinctive meaning. In the literature of the time, to cote others in wealth, beauty, or worth, is to excel them in these respects. Thus Drant, in his translation, or rather paraphrase of Horace, published within a year or two of Shakespeare's birth, applies it to the passion of avarice, the insatiable desire to surpass all others in gain. The lines in which the verb occurs are, in fact, an expansion of the hemistich, *Hunc atque hunc superare laboret:*—

> How happeneth it, his owne estate
> That no man lyketh beste?
> But teenes, if that his neyghbour's goate
> A bygger bagge doth beare

> Than his, or yeelds her mylke sum deale
> More flowyng and more cleare:
> Nor ever will compare him selfe
> Unto the greater sorte,
> Whose state is base, and bad as his,
> Who lyves in meane apporte:
> But roves, and shoots at further marks,
> Now him he doth contende
> To passe in coyne; now him again,
> And so there is no ende.
> For he that thincks to *coate* all men
> And all to overgoe,
> In runnyng shall some ritcher fynde
> Who still will bid him hoe.

In its earlier use *cote* may, indeed, as the etymology suggests, have primarily referred to the hound's reaching the game rather than to his outstripping his fellow in the chase. But as outstripping his fellow was the necessary condition of reaching the game first, this element of meaning gradually became more prominent, until at length, as we have seen, the term, both in its technical and secondary uses, came to mean not simply to overtake but to outgo, to advance beyond, and generally to surpass or excel.

In connection with coursing, we may note the discussion that has arisen among the commentators on the meaning of *lym* or *lyam*, and *leash*, as applied to hounds. In the well-known rhyming list of dogs given by Edgar in his assumed character of Poor Tom in *King Lear*, one of the kinds specified is *lym*, or, in other words, lym-hound; and in the first part of *Henry IV.*, *leash* is used for three, in the phrase "a leash of drawers," immediately afterwards enumerated as Tom, Dick, and Francis. There has been some hesitation amongst the editors as to the exact technical meaning and use of these terms. But a single extract from the old *Art of Venerie* settles the question:—

> We finde some difference of termes between hounds and greyhounds. As of greyhounds two make a brase, and of hounds a couple. Of greyhounds three make a *lease*, and of hounds a couple and a halfe. We let slippe a greyhound, and we cast off a hound. The string wherewith we leade a greyhound is called a *lease*, and for a hound a *lyame*. The greyhound hath his collar, and the hound hath his couples. Many other differences there be, but these are most usual.

It has been conjectured with much probability that another word, *uncape*, used in the *Merry Wives of Windsor*, must have been a technical term in fox-hunting. It occurs in the humorous scene where the jealous Ford, accompanied by a posse of his friends and neighbours, arrives at his own house, resolved to hunt for the disturber of his peace, whom he declares to be harboured there by the guilty connivance of his wife. On entering the house, he meets the servants going out with the buck-basket in which Falstaff is almost smothered beneath the soiled linen:—

> *Ford:* Pray you, come near: if I suspect without cause, why then make sport at me; then let me be your jest; I deserve it. How now! whither bear you this?
>
> *Serv.:* To the laundress, forsooth.
>
> *Mrs. Ford:* Why, what have you to do whither they bear it? You were best meddle with buck-washing.
>
> *Ford:* Buck! I would I could wash myself of the buck! Buck, buck, buck! Ay buck; I warrant you, buck; and of the season too, it shall appear. [*Exeunt Servants with the basket.*] Gentle-

men, I have dreamed to-night; I'll tell you my
dream. Here, here, here, be my keys: ascend
my chambers; search, seek, find out: I'll
warrant we'll unkennel the fox. Let me stop
this way first. [*Locks the door.*] So now *uncape.*

Here it seems clear from the context that *uncape* must be a
term connected with fox-hunting, but no instance of its
technical use has been discovered, and hardly any two editors
agree as to its exact meaning. Warburton asserts, with his usual
confidence, that it means "to dig out the fox when earthed";
while Stevens maintains that the term refers to a bag-fox. "The
allusion is," he says, "to the stopping every hole at which a fox
could enter before they uncape or turn him out of the bag in
which he was brought." Hanmer substituted the reading
*uncouple*; and Nares, in support of this interpretation, and with
a special eye to Stevens' note, says that "Falstaff is the fox, and
he is supposed to be hidden, or kenneled, somewhere in the
house; no expression therefore relative to a bag-fox can be
applicable, because such a fox would be already in the hands of
the hunters. The *uncaping* is decidedly to begin the hunt after
him; when the holes for escape had been stopped." This seems
from the context to be the real meaning of the word. It must
indicate the commencement of the hunt, or, in other words,
the uncoupling of the hounds. But the text need not be altered
to bring out this signification. Though no example of its
technical use has yet been found, there can be little doubt that
uncape was a sporting term locally or colloquially employed
instead of uncouple. Nor, after all, is it very difficult to explain
its origin and use in this sense. Turbervile, after stating that
amongst other differences "the greyhound hath his collar and
the hound his couples," intimates the existence of many more
technical terms, of which those he gives are simply the most
usual. Cape might very well have been one of the terms for
collar or couple, as it undoubtedly had this meaning in
Shakespeare's day. In the sixteenth and seventeenth centuries,
while cape meant, as it still does, the top or upper part of a
garment, it was usually restricted to a much smaller portion
than the word designates now—a part encircling the neck
rather than covering the shoulders. It meant, in fact, a neck-
band, most commonly of the kind termed a falling-band; in
other words, a collar, the larger tippet, covering the shoulders,
being termed in contradistinction to the smaller cape or collar,
"a Spanish cape". Thus Minshew and Howel give us synonyms
for "the cape of a garment," French, *collet*, explained as "the
collar of a jerkin, the neck-piece of any garment"; Spanish,
*cabecón*, explained as "the neck-band of a shirt, the neck of a
doublet, the collar of a garment"; Latin, *collare*, "neck-band,
or collar". The Latin dictionaries of Wase and Coles give the
same explanation of cape as part of a dress. Shakespeare
himself uses it in the same sense—as another word for neck-
band or collar. In the *Taming of the Shrew*, amongst the
directions given to the tailor by Grumio for the making of
Katharina's robe or dress, are specified, "a loose-bodied gown
with a *small compassed cape*". Here the epithet compassed
means circular, so that the item is equivalent to a small circular
collar, or falling band around the throat. Whether cape is a
technical term in fox-hunting or not, Shakespeare was therefore perfectly entitled to use it, as he evidently does, in the
*Merry Wives of Windsor*, as a synonym for couple or collar. As
given in the old pictures, the broad, loose, indented leather
bands or collars to which the lyam or leash was attached,
completely realise the contemporary notion of a cape, and no
mistake could possibly arise from the use of the term in this
sense. The words *uncape, uncollar,* or *uncouple* would each
mean the same thing, while all would be easily, if not equally
intelligible.

We may conclude the allusions to hunting by an
illustration or two of the beautiful passage in the *Midsummer
Night's Dream*, where Theseus celebrates the music of his
hounds in full cry:—

> *The.*: Go, one of you, find out the forester:
> For now our observation is perform'd:
> And since we have the vaward of the day,
> My love shall hear the music of my hounds.—
> Uncouple in the western valley: let them go!
> Despatch, I say, and find the forester.
> We will, fair queen, up to the mountain's top
> And mark the musical confusion
> Of hounds and echo in conjunction.
> *Hip.*: I was with Hercules, and Cadmus, once,
> When in a wood of Crete they bayed the bear
> With hounds of Sparta; never did I hear
> Such gallant chiding; for, besides the groves,
> The skies, the fountains, every region near
> Seem'd all one mutual cry. I never heard
> So musical a discord, such sweet thunder.
> *The.*: My hounds are bred out of the Spartan kind,
> So flewed, so sanded; and their heads are hung
> With ears that sweep away the morning dew;
> Crook-kneed, and dew-lap'd like Thessalian bulls;
> Slow in pursuit, but matched in mouth like bells,
> Each under each. A cry more tuneable
> Was never halloo'd to, nor cheer'd with horn,
> In Crete, in Sparta, nor in Thessaly:
> Judge, when you hear.

Shakespeare might probably enough, as the commentators
suggest, have derived his knowledge of Cretan and Spartan
hounds from Golding's translation of Ovid, where they are
commemorated in the description of Actæon's tragical chase
and death. But in enumerating the points of the slow, sure,
deep-mouthed hound, it can hardly be doubted he had in view
the celebrated Talbot breed nearer home. A contemporary
writer celebrates the virtues of these hounds in terms that recall
Shakespeare's own description:—

> For the shape of your hound, it must be according to
> the climate where he is bred, and according to the
> natural composition of his body, as thus, if you
> would choose a large, heavy, slow, true Talbot-like
> hound, you must choose him which hath a round,
> big, thick head, with a short nose uprising, and large
> open nostrils, which shows that he is of a good and
> quick scent, his ears exceeding large, thin, and
> down-hanging, much lower than his chaps, and the
> flews of his upper lips almost two inches lower than
> his nether chaps; which shows a merry deep mouth
> and a loud ringer, his back strong and straight, yet
> rather rising, than inwardly yielding, which shows
> much toughness and endurance.

With regard to the other point of the hounds being "matched in
mouth like bells," it is clear that in Shakespeare's day the
greatest attention was paid to the musical quality of the cry. It
was a ruling consideration in the formation of a pack that it
should possess the musical fulness and strength of a perfect
canine quire. And hounds of good voice were selected and
arranged in the hunting chorus on the same general principles
that govern the formation of a cathedral or any other more
articulate choir. The writer already quoted brings this curious
feature fully out; and as the subject has not been illustrated by
the commentators, and is in itself of considerable interest, we
may venture on a tolerably long extract:—

> *For sweetnesse of cry.*
> If you would have your kennell for sweetness of cry,
> then you must compound it of some large dogges,

that have deepe solemne mouthes, and are swift in spending, which must, as it were, beare the base in the consort, then a double number of roaring, and loud ringing mouthes, which must beare the eounter tenor, then some hollow, plaine, sweete mouthes, which must beare the meane or middle part; and soe with these three parts of musicke you shall make your cry perfect; and heerein you shall observe that these hounds thus mixt, doe run just and even together, and not hang off loose one from another, which is the wildest sight that may be, and you shall understand that this composition is best to be made of the swiftest and largest deep mouthed dog, the slowest middle siz'd dog, and the shortest leg'd slender dog, amongst these you cast in a couple or two of small singing beagles, which as small trebles may warble amongst them; the cry will be a great deal the more sweeter.

*For lowdnesse of cry.*

If you would have your kennell for lowdnes of mouth, you shall not then choose the hollow deepe mouth, but the loud clanging mouth, which spendeth freely and sharpely, and, as it were, redoubleth in the utterance: and if you mix with them the mouth that roareth and the mouth that whineth, the crye will bee both the louder and smarter; and these hounds are for the most part of the middle size, neither extreame tail, nor extreame deepe flewed, such as for the most part your Shropshire and pure Worcestershire dogs are; and the more equally you compound these mouthes, having as many roarers as spenders, and as many whiners as of either of the other, the louder and pleasanter your crye will be, especially if it be in sounding tall woods, or under the echo of rocks.

*For deepnesse of cry.*

If you would have your kennell for depth of mouth, then you shall compound it of the largest dogges, which have the greatest mouthes, the deepest flews, such as your West Countrie, Cheshire, and Lancashire dogges are; and to five or six couple of base mouthes, you shall not adde above two couple of counter tenors, as many meanes, and not above one couple of roarers, which being heard but now and then, as at the opening or hitting of a sent, will give much sweetnesse to the solemnes and gravenesse of the crye, and the musick thereof will bee much more delightfull to the eares of every beholder.

Next to hunting, hawking was perhaps the most popular field sport in Shakespeare's day. In many parts of the country, indeed, it was more in vogue, or, at least, more habitually pursued, than hunting itself. Before the land was generally drained, the midland and eastern counties afforded peculiar facilities for the aquatic branch of hawking, which was the more exciting kind of sport. The flags of their marshy levels, their reedy hollows, the wooded banks and quiet pools of their winding streams, abounded with aquatic birds, and especially with the crane and the heron, the favourite objects of this princely recreation. The neighbourhood of Stratford itself was peculiarly favourable for aquatic falconry, the broad sweep of the tranquil Avon with is bosky margins and reedy shallows affording abundant food and inviting shelter for the larger and more important species of waterfowl. And there can be little doubt that Shakespeare in boyhood and youth had often accompanied a brilliant hawking-party, or at a little distance marked the progress of the sport, had seen the falconer spring the kingly heron from his sedgy nest, and followed with eager gaze the fortunes of the nearly-balanced conflict that en-

sued,—had watched in narrowing circles far up the sky the well-trained falcon stoop on her noble quarry until the final swoop put an end to the airy battle. However this may be, Shakespeare is perfectly familiar with the technical terms used in hawking, and his dramas abound with phrases and allusions derived from this source. We shall attempt a few illustrations of these allusions in special reference to words and phrases not as yet clearly understood or accurately explained. The first is one of the many much-disputed passages in *Measure for Measure*. It occurs in the dialogue between Claudio and Isabella, where the latter reveals the true character of Angelo:—

> This outward-sainted deputy,
> Whose settled visage and deliberate word
> Nips youth i' the head, and follies doth *emmew*
> As falcon doth the fowl, is yet a devil;
> His filth within being cast, he would appear
> A pond as deep as hell.

Here *emmew* is a term well known in falconry, the mew being the place where the hawks were kept and tended during the critical period of moulting. So long as this process lasted, while the birds were casting their feathers, they were kept close, mewed up, or emmewed. But in the passage just quoted this sense hardly seems to suit the context. Isabella is obviously describing an active policy of repression on the part of Angelo. During the lax administration of the duke, youthful vices, being virtually winked at, had been freely indulged in; and follies, fearing no check, had made head in the city until it became needful to awake the slumbering powers of the law, and carry into effect its sterner enactments. The duke dwells on this necessity in explaining the motives of his conduct:—

> *Duke:* We have strict statutes and most biting laws,—
> The needful bits and curbs to headstrong steeds,—
> Which for this fourteen years we have let sleep,
> Even like an o'ergrown lion in a cave,
> That goes not out to prey. Now, as fond fathers,
> Having bound up the threatening twigs of birch,
> Only to stick it in their children's sight
> For terror, not to use, in time the rod
> Becomes more mock'd than fear'd; so our decrees,
> Dead to infliction, to themselves are dead;
> And liberty plucks justice by the nose;
> The baby beats the nurse, and quite athwart
> Goes all decorum.

Angelo was to strike home, and we know from the earlier scenes of the play that he had at once magnified his temporary office and ridden the body politic with a tight curb and sharpened spur, putting into extreme force the more rigorous penal acts. No doubt his administration of the law would soon strike the evil-doers with terror, and make them for a time quiet enough. But in these early days he was inflicting severe penalties on convicted offenders, and it is to this feature of his policy that Isabella especially refers. Youth must have made some head before it could be nipped; and in the same way it is natural to suppose that follies must have manifested themselves before they could be actually known, or publicly dealt with by the deputy. The word *emmew* does not express this meaning, and Johnson's explanation of the phrase, "forces follies to lie in cover, without daring to show themselves," seems comparatively weak and inapplicable. From some feeling of this difficulty, probably, Mr. Keightley, in his *Shakespeare Expositor*, proposes to read *enew*, instead of *emmew*. He does this avowedly on the strength of a single passage which he quotes from Nash's *Quaternio*. This exemplifies what we have already said about fancied discoveries being often anticipated. Long before we knew of Mr. Keightley's suggestion we had ourselves marked the passage in Nash for the same purpose. After all, however,

Mr. Keightley does not really anticipate what we have to say on the subject, as he gives no reason for the proposed change, and does not understand the origin, meaning, and technical use of the verb he substitutes for *emmew*. The passage in Nash forms part of a glowing description of field sports, and is as follows:—

> And to heare an Accipitrary relate againe how he went forth in a cleare, calme, and sun-shine evening, about an houre before the sunne did usually maske himselfe, unto the river, where finding of a mallard, he whistled off his faulcon, and how shee flew from him as if shee would never have turned head againe, yet presently upon a shoote came in, how then by degrees, by little and little, by flying about and about, shee mounted so high, untill shee had lessened herselfe to the view of the beholder, to the shape of a pigeon or partridge, and had made the height of the moone the place of her flights, how presently upon the landing of the fowle, shee came down like a stone and *enewed* it, and suddenly got up againe, and suddenly upon a second landing came downe againe, and missing of it, in the downcome recovered it beyond expectation, to the admiration of the beholder, at a long flight.

The chief difficulty in the passage is as to the meaning of the verb *enew*, and this was for some time a considerable puzzle. Though freely used as a technical term in the older manuals of hawking, none of them, so far as our examinations went, afforded any explanation of the word. Thus Turbervile says: "When your falcon is accustomed to flee for it, and will lye upon you at a great gate, or at a reasonable pitch, and will come and holde in the head at your voyce, and luring, then may you goe to the river where you shall finde any fowle, and there shall it behove you to use such policie that you may cover the fowle, and get your hawke to a good gate above the fowle. And when her head is in, then lay out the fowle, and cry *hey gar, gar, gar*. And if your falcon doe stoope them, and *enew* them once or twice, then quickly thrust your hand in your hawking bagge, and make her a traine with a ducke seeled." And in the same connection, in a short chapter on "How to doe when your river hawke will take stand in a tree," the word occurs again: "If you have a falcon which (as sone as hee hath once or twice stooped and *enewed* a fowle) will take stand on a tree, you must as much as may be, eschue to flee in places where trees be". Again, Markham, in his treatise on hawking, says: "To make your hawke fly at fowle, which is called the flight at the river, you shall first whistle off an approved well quarried hawke that is a sure killer, and let her *enew* the fowle so long till she bring it to the plunge; then take her down and reward her". But while thus using the term neither Turbervile nor Markham explains its meaning. From the examples of its use, however, it soon became apparent that *enew* was restricted to aquatic falconry—"the flight at the river," as it was called—while the probable etymology connected it directly with water. When a flight at water-fowl was determined on, the falconer, advancing towards the river, whistled off his hawk up the wind at some little distance from the spot where the duck or mallard, the heron or crane, was known to be. When the hawk had attained to her gate, or, in other words, reached a tolerable pitch in her flight, the falconer, with his dogs and assistants, "made in" upon the fowl, compelling it to rise, and forcing the flight, if possible, in the direction of the land. This was technically termed "landing" the fowl, a very vital point in aquatic falconry. Then, after some preliminary wheeling on

the wing, offensive and defensive, the falcon would swiftly stoop on her prey, while the fowl, to avoid the fatal stroke, would instinctively make for the water again, where it would be for the moment comparatively safe. For in order that the falcon might stoop and strike with effect, it was necessary to have solid ground immediately below. If the fowl succeeded in swerving towards the water, she escaped with comparative impunity. In this case the hawk might stoop, and sometimes apparently even strike, without doing much damage as the blow could not be followed up, the fowl taking refuge in diving. In this case the fowl was said to be *enewed*—the hawk *enewed* the fowl; that is, forced it back to the water again, from which it had to be driven afresh by the falconer and landed before the hawk could stoop and seize, or strike and truss her quarry. The fowl was often enewed once or twice before it was landed effectively enough for the final swoop. From this explanation of its meaning the etymology of *enew* will be apparent; and in support of it we have, in Kelham's Norman Dictionary, "*Enewance de draps*, watering of cloth"; which Cotgrave gives *eneauer*, "to turn into water," and "*eneaüé*, watered, turned into water". All these points are confirmed and verified by Drayton's vivid description of the sport, where, fortunately, the word occurs accompanied by an explanatory note. In his twentieth song the poet gives a detailed account of the flight at the brook, from which we extract the closing lines:—

> Then making to the flood, to force the fowls to rise,
> The fierce and eager hawks, down thrilling from the skies,
> Make sundry cancellers ere they the fowl can reach,
> Which then to save their lives their wings do lively stretch,
> But when the whizzing bells the silent air do cleave,
> And that their greatest speed, them vainly do deceive;
> And the sharp cruel hawks, they at their backs do view,
> Themselves for very fear they instantly *ineaw*.
> The hawks get up again into their former place,
> And ranging here and there, in that their airy race;
> Still as the fearful fowl attempt to 'scape away,
> With many a stouping brave, them in again they lay.
> But when the falconers take their hawking-poles in hand,
> And crossing of the brook, do put it over land;
> The hawks gives it a souse, that makes it to rebound,
> Well near the height of man, sometimes above the ground.

Here the word *enew*, which the poets spells in his own way, has the marginal explanation, "lay the fowls again in the water". The verb occurs in the same connection, in describing the flight at the brook, in Turbervile's own curious poem "In Commendation of Hawking":—

> No fellow to the flight at brooke, that game is full of glee,
> It is a sport the stouping of a roysting Hawke to see.
> And if she misse, to marke her how she then gets up amaine,
> For best advantage, to *eneaw* the springing fowle againe,
> Who if be landed as it ought, then is it sure to die,
> Or if she slippe, a joy to see, the Hawke at randon flie.

There can be no doubt, therefore, as to the origin and technical meaning of the term. From this primary sense it seems to have acquired the secondary signification of "to check," "to drive back," and "relentlessly pursue". It would thus be naturally applied to a policy of extreme and vindictive severity, and we can have little doubt that in Isabella's speech *enew*, as the more expressive word, and the one which in all respects best harmonises with the context, should be substituted for *emmew*. The imagery is that of the penal law, or rather perhaps of despotic power in the person of the "outward-sainted deputy" pursuing its victims with reiterated strokes, and allowing them little chance of ultimate escape.

The closing lines of the passage contain another allusion to hawking, the explanation of which will throw some light on a doubtful word in *Hamlet*:—

> His filth within being cast, he would appear
> A pond as deep as hell

The reference is to the hawk when first taken out of the mew, and the result which gross feeding combined with long confinement and inaction produces. The hawk was then fat, glutted, full of grease, wholly unfit for active use, and in order to be thoroughly purged from internal filth, was subjected to a course of scouring diet. The technical name for such diet was *casting*, and as the result the hawk was said to have *cast* her filth. Again, the technical name for the whole process of cleansing the hawk from internal defilement was *enseam*. The use of this term will be made clear by an extract from Turbervile's chapter on "How you shall *enesame* a hawke or give her castings and scourings":—

> Some falcons be harder to *enseame* than some others are, for the longer that a falcon hath been in the hand, the harder she is to be *enseamed*: and an old mewed falcon of the wood which hath mewed but one cote in the falconer's handes is much easier to be *enseamed* than a yonger falcon which hath been longer in the falconer's handes: the reason is, because a hawk that preyeth for her selfe doth feede cleaner and better according to her nature, and upon more wholesome meates, than she doth when she is in man's handes; so that it is no marvaile though she bee not so fowle within when she is at her own dyet, as when another man feedeth her. For a hawke which is in our keeping doth feed greedily both on skinne, feathers, and all that comes to hand. Neyther is she mewed with so cleane and holesome feeding, nor doth endue her meate so well, nor hath such open ayre at times convenient as a hawke which is at large to prey for her selfe.

He goes on to describe the marks by which it may be known when you draw the hawk out of the mew whether she be greasy: "by the thies if they be round and fat, and also by the body if she be full in hand, and her flesh be round as high as the breast-bone". If so, she needs a course of castings. While the hawk was being enseamed it was necessary to keep the space beneath the perch clear, in order to ascertain by the result her actual state and decide when the castings had done their work. The whole process afforded striking analogies for depicting figuratively the moral and physical results of sloth, sensuality, and self-indulgence; and Shakespeare has employed these materials, not only in the passage under review, but in the closet-scene between Hamlet and his mother:—

> *Queen:*    O Hamlet, speak no more:
> Thou turn'st mine eyes into my very soul;
> And there I see such black and grainèd spots
> As will not leave their tinct.
> *Ham.:*        Nay, but to live
> In the rank sweat of an *enseamèd* bed,
> Stew'd in corruption, honeying and making love
> Over the nasty sty.
> *Queen:*    O, speak to me no more;
> These words, like daggers, enter in mine ears;
> No more, sweet Hamlet!

There has been some discussion among the commentators as to the exact signification of *enseamed* in this passage, but Dyce follows his predecessors in explaining it to mean "greasy". This, no doubt, is one meaning of the word, and it gives a sense intelligible enough. *Seam or same* is a word for lard, used locally in various parts of England, but especially in Lincolnshire. A story told of a country woman in Lincoln market illustrates this meaning of the term. Butter was often, then as now, adulterated by being mixed with lard, and a lady coming to purchase of the woman asked, "Is the butter quite pure?" to which the seller confidently but ambiguously replied, "Yes, it is the very best butter at both ends and *same* in the middle". *Seam* is moreover used by Shakespeare himself for lard in *Troilus and Cressida*. The hawking term *enseam* is traceable to this source, lard having been originally a principal ingredient in the castings or scouring diet given to the glutted falcon. Thus Turbervile says: "Within a few days after the falcon is drawn out of the mew ye must scour her and enseam her with the foresaid medicine of lard, sugar, mace, and saffron, with very little aloes, for if ye confect it with too much aloes you shall bring her over low". Though the term thus originally meant enlarding, or, on homeopathic principles, cleansing a hawk from grease by means of grease, it naturally acquired a much stronger sense, and came to mean the stirring up and casting forth of filthy matter. In this sense it is applied by Hamlet to the moral pollution of his mother's incestuous marriage, the bridal bed itself being defiled by such a union.

Again, there has been a good deal of discussion about the word *gouts* occurring in the dagger-scene in *Macbeth*. The results of this discussion are well summed up in the note on the word by the Cambridge editors in their Clarendon Press edition of the play:—

> *Gouts*, drops, from the French, *goutte*, and, according to stage-tradition, so pronounced. Stevens quotes from *The Art of Good Lyving*, 1503, "All herbys shall sweyt read goutys of water as blood". And "gowtyth" for "droppeth" occurs in an Old English MS. (Halliwell, *Archaic and Prov., Dict.*, s. v.). "Gutty," from the same root, is also used in English heraldry.

It has not been noticed, however, that the word is a technical term in falconry, and that its special sense in this art applies with peculiar force to its use in the dagger-scene soliloquy. *Gouts* is the term applied to the little knob-like swellings or indurated drops which appear at times on the legs and feet of the hawk. This will be clear by an extract from Turbervile's chapter on "The swelling in the hawk's feet we term the pin or pin-gout":—.

> Diverse times there rise up knobs upon the feet of hawks as upon the feet of capons, which some call galles, and some *gouts*. They come sometimes of the swelling of the legs and thighes, which I have spoken of before, or of other diseases that breed of the abundance of humours within the hawke, which must first be scoured with the last mentioned pilles three or four days together.

The term as thus used has peculiar force when applied, as Macbeth applies it, to the rapidly coagulating drops of blood on the blade and dudgeon of the fatal dagger.

The references to hawking may be closed by a brief illustration of a passage in the first part of *Henry VI.* that has never as yet been very satisfactorily explained. It occurs in the angry scene between the protector, Gloucester, and his rival, the Bishop of Winchester, before the Tower gates. The bishop having forbidden the warders to admit the protector, fierce taunts, menaces, and recriminations prelude the actual conflict between their followers that ensues:—

> *Win.*: How now, ambitious Humphrey! what means this?
> *Glo.*: Peel'd priest, dost thou command me be shut out?
> *Win.*: I do, thou most usurping proditor,
> And not protector of the king or realm.
> *Glo.*: Stand back, thou manifest conspirator,
> Thou that contriv'dst to murder our dear lord;
> Thou that givest whores indulgences to sin:
> I'll *canvass* thee in they broad cardinal's hat,
> If thou proceed in this thy insolence.
> *Win.*: Nay, stand thou back; I will not budge a foot:
> This be Damascus, be thou cursèd Cain,
> To slay thy brother Abel, if thou wilt.
> *Glo.*: I will not slay thee, but I'll drive thee back:
> Thy scarlet robes as a child's bearing-cloth
> I'll use to carry thee out of this place.

In this passage the phrase, "I'll canvass thee," has been variously explained. Stevens interprets it to mean, "I'll tumble thee into thy great hat, and shake thee as bran and meal are shaken in a sieve"; while Malone says: "Gloucester probably means that he will toss the cardinal in a sheet, even while he was invested with the peculiar badge of his ecclesiastical dignity". But neither of these explanations, adopted in the main by later editors, hits the distinctive allusion of the phrase, or brings out its real significance. Canvass was a technical name for the peculiarly constructed net with which wild hawks were snared by the falconer, in order to be made and manned for the fist, the flight, and the lure. At least, it was a term technically applied to catching wild hawks in this way, and to be canvassed in this sense was to be taken, trapped, or netted. The following passage from Pettie's *Palace of Pleasure*, referring to one who had been jilted in love, brings out this meaning:—

> For ever after, he fled all occasions of women's company, perswading himselfe that as hee which toucheth pitch shal be defiled therewith: so he that useth women's company shal be beguiled therewith. And as the mouse having escaped out of the trap, wil hardly be allured againe with the intising baite, or as the hawke having bin once *canvassed* in the nettes, wil make it daungerous to strike againe at the stale: so he having bin caught in the snares of crafty counterfeyting, and now having unwound himself thereout, and wonne the fields of freedome, avoided all occasions which might bring him eftsoones in bondage.

Nares gives another example, from the *Mirror for Magistrates*:—

> That restlesse I, much like the hunted hare,
> Or as the *canvist* kite doth fear the snare.

Of the word, however, Nares frankly says: "It seems to mean entrapped; but I can give no further account of it". Canvass in this sense may, however, be connected with the Italian *cannevo* and *cannevaccio*, given as alternative forms of *canapa* and *canapaccia*, and explained as "all manner of hemp, hempen halters, thread, coarse hemp and canvass, coarse hards". It could thus very naturally have the general meaning of coarse hempen netting. Or it may possibly be connected with the *canebis* or *chanvre*, against which the experienced swallow warned the small birds:—

> Il arriva qu'au temps que le *chanvre* se sème,
> Elle vit un manant en couvrir maints sillons.
> "Ceci ne me plaît pas," dit-elle aux oisillons:
> "Je vous plains; car, pour moi, dans ce péril extrême,

> Je saurai m'éloigner, ou vivre en quelque coin.
> Voyez-vous cette main qui par les airs chemine?
> Un jour viendra, qui n'est pas loin,
> Que ce qu'elle répand sera votre ruine.
> De là naitront engins à vous envelopper,
> Et lacets pour vous attraper,
> Enfin mainte et mainte machine
> Qui causera dans la saison
> Votre mort ou votre prison."

Whatever may be its origin, there can, however, be no doubt as to the special meaning and use of the term in connection with hawking, and it is, we think, clearly in this sense that Gloucester employs it in the passage quoted. The phrase has, indeed, peculiar expressiveness when applied to the broad-brimmed cardinal's hat, with its long strings knotted into net-like meshes on either side. The felicity of the phrase becomes even more apparent when the shape and working of the net in which hawks were snared are known. The apparatus for catching wild hawks consisted of a strong semi-circular bow of wood or iron, with a net attached, and fixed in the ground on either side, so as to move freely backwards and forwards. When baited for the hawk the bow was in an upright position, both the bow itself and the net attached to it being partially hidden by green twigs. The bait, stale, or lure was usually a live bird, such as a pigeon, fixed and fluttering within the sweep of the descending bow. Strings were attached to the bow on either side, and held by the falconer, concealed at a distance. By this means, when the hawk swooped on the prey the falling bow covered her with the encircling net. If the meshes happened to be too large, or the machinery were unskilfully worked, the hawk sometimes managed to escape, and hence the allusions in the passages quoted. Now, the circular sweep of the cardinal's hat with its knotted strings had a not unapt resemblance to the hawk-net machinery; and Gloucester, in saying, "I'll canvass thee in thy broad cardinal's hat," expressed his determination to trap and seize the arrogant churchman, if he persisted in his violent courses. That he really meant to abridge the cardinal's liberty by seizing his person is apparent from the context in which he says he will use the scarlet robe as a child's bearing-cloth to carry him away, the colour of the robe having reminded him of the scarlet mantle in which the children of wealthy parents were carried to the font for baptism. Even in this there is, however, an obscure reference to the imagery already employed, for the hawk when caught was carefully wrapped up, often placed in a bag, to prevent any injury to the feathers from bating. Gloucester thus expresses his determination to catch the grasping cardinal in his own trap, and mew him up where he would have no power to carry out his treasonable designs.

We shall next attempt to clear up some points still obscure connected with the natural history, rural botany, and social usages of Shakespeare's time. The first is a passage in *Hamlet*, which the critics and commentators agree, with singular unanimity, must be corrupt. It occurs in the play-scene, after the performance has been suddenly stopped by order of the king, and the listening court circle broken up "with most admired disorder," by the abrupt and excited exit of the royal party. Hamlet is left alone with Horatio, exulting in the success of his project. The play has caught effectually the conscience of the king, and in Hamlet's view he stands self-convicted of the unnatural crime. In the strange excitement produced by this complete confirmation of his worst fears, Hamlet, with a sort of assumed gaiety, indulges in snatches of verse, fragments of well-known ballads, that express in a fitful, disjointed way the feelings of the moment:—

*Ham.*: For thou dost know, O Damon dear,
    This realm dismantled was
Of Jove himself; and now reigns here
    A very, very—*Peacock*.

The readings of the Quartos and Folios are variously *pajock, pajocke,* and *paiock, paiocke*; but all agree that these are only various spellings of the same word, that word being peacock. Here, however, the real difficulty commences. The majority of critics maintain that the word, in such a connection, has no meaning, and makes nonsense of the verse. Some of the earlier editors, it is true, attempted to explain it; but the explanations were feeble, if not wholly irrelevant, and have not been generally accepted. Thus, Pope says the allusion is to the fable of the birds choosing the peacock instead of the eagle as their king. Collier, while admitting the difficulty, suggests that the fable alluded to may be that of the crow adorning itself with peacocks' feathers. Theobald rejected the word altogether, substituting for it *paddock*, or toad. Other suggested emendations are *hedgehog, padge-hawk, polack,* and, amongst the latest and strangest, that by Dr. Leo, of *hiccups*, as a stage direction. But these suggestions are only so much wasted ingenuity. The Folio word is not only the right one, but peculiarly emphatic and expressive. In discussing the passage the critics have forgotten the character assigned to the peacock in the natural history of the time, as well as in popular opinion and belief. Looked at from this point of view, the word peacock expresses in a concentrated form the odious qualities of the guilty king, the bird being, in fact, the accredited representative of inordinate pride and envy, as well as of unnatural cruelty and lust. The most popular manual of natural history in Shakespeare's day, for example, gives the following account:—

> And the pecocke is a bird that loveth not his young, for the male searcheth out the female, and seeketh out her egges for to break them, that he may so occupy him the more in his lecherie. And the female dreadeth that, and hideth busily her egges, lest the pecocke might soone find them. And Aristotle sayth that the pecocke hath an unsteadfast and evill shapen head, as it were the head of a serpent, and with a crest. And he hath a simple pace, and a small necke, and areared, and a blew breast, and a taile ful of bewty, distinguished on high of wonderfulle fairness: and he hath the foulest feet and riveled. And he wondereth at the fairnesse of his fethers, and areareth them up as it were a circle about his head, and then he looketh to his feet, and seeth the foulenesse of his feet, and lyke as he wer ashamed he leteth his fethers fall sodeinlye: and all the taile downward, as though he tooke no heed of the fairnesse of his fethers: and he hath an horrible voice. And as one sayth, he hath a voice of a feend, the head of a serpent, and the pace of a theefe. And Plinius sayth that the pecocke hath envie to man's profit, and swalloweth his owne durt: for it is full medicinable, but it is seldom found.

This last is a curiously dark touch of malevolence added to the generally repulsive character of the bird. In the whole fauna of the time, therefore, Hamlet could not have selected the name of bird or beast that expressed with greater emphasis the hateful union of corrupted passion and evil life that now usurped the throne and bed of the buried majesty of Denmark.

We turn for a moment from the popular fauna to the wild and provincial flora of Shakespeare's day. It is needless to say a word about the poet's love of flowers, and his intimate acquaintance with the richer garden varieties, as separate works have been published to illustrate this feature of his writings. But Shakespeare's fondness for wild flowers, and subtle appreci-ation of their place and influence as elements of natural scenery, are equally noteworthy. He had the keenest enjoyment of outdoor life, and in his long country rambles in the neighbourhood of Stratford the sweet wayside "nurselings of the vernal skies" had touched his imagination and his heart, and left an impression never to be effaced. Nor does he scruple at times to describe his humble favourites of the meadows, the hedgerows, and the water-courses, by the local names through which he first became familiar with them. This has been a source of some confusion and perplexity in the interpretation of his allusions. We may illustrate this point in relation to a line on which perhaps more ink has been split than on any other line of Shakespeare's dramas. It occurs on the invocation of Iris to Ceres in the Masque of the *Tempest*:—

> *Iris*: Ceres, most bounteous lady, thy rich leas
>     Of wheat, rye, barley, vetches, oats, and pease;
>     Thy turfy mountains, where live nibbling sheep,
>     And flat meads thatch'd with stover, them to keep;
>     Thy banks with *pioned* and *twilled* brims,
>     Which spongy April at thy hest betrims,
>     To make cold nymphs chaste crowns; and thy
>         broom-groves,
>     Whose shadow the dismissed bachelor loves.

Here the chief difficulties are the words italicised in the fifth line, especially the first. What *pioned* means, or can mean, has been the great crux with the commentators. An early suggested emendation was *peonied*; but the objections to this are that the peony is not a wild-flower, does not grow in marshy grounds, has, in fact, no connection with river brims, and does not bloom in April. Other emendations have, from time to time, been suggested, but, curiously enough, the one which has found as much acceptance as any, is what may be called the hedging and ditching explanation—that *pioned* means dug down, and *twilled*, ridged, or staked up, as though the river brims were rural dykes or suburban drains. Even supposing the meaning here assigned to the disputed terms were legitimate or even possible, the explanation certainly savours far more of the commentator's prose than of Shakespeare's poetry. Without noticing any of the other explanations and emendations that have been attempted, we proceed to offer an interpretation that, while preserving the Folio text, gives it a consistent and poetical meaning. The chief difficulty, as we have seen, lies in the word *pioned*, and we had long felt that the solution must be looked for in the local use of the term. We could not but believe that there must be some flower, most probably a water-flower, or one living in marshy ground, that was provincially known as a peony. In confirmation of this view, we were informed some time since by a clergyman who was for many years incumbent of a parish in the northern part of the county, that peony is the name given in Warwickshire to the marsh marygold. Knowing that he had long resided in the neighbourhood of Stratford, taking an active interest in country life, we asked if there was any wild-flower that the country people called a peony, and he promptly answered there was, and it soon appeared from the description that it must be the marsh marygold. Here was at last a ray of light. And on a little reflection it was not difficult to see why the name of the peony should have been transferred to the marsh marygold. The flowers, though differing in colour, have a remarkable similarity in general growth and shape, especially in the early stage, when the fully-formed bud is ripe for blowing. The buds of both present the unusual appearance of perfectly rounded globes or spheres at the extremity of a thick leafless stalk, the sepals being firmly locked or folded together over the substance of the flower into a bud as round as a marble. Indeed, the helibore, which belongs to the same class, having it sepals tipped with red, might easily be mistaken for a wild peony. In their early stages, moreover, when the peculiar state of the bud naturally attracts attention, the peony and marsh marygold are alike, not only in growth and form, but in colour also. The main point of agreement, however, the globular buds, is so distinctive in the marsh marygold that it has been seized on as a ground of naming the flower, and is embodied in many of its more popular designations. The garden variety, for example, differing hardly at all from its sister of the marsh, is called the globe flower. In many parts of England, again, marsh mary-golds are called *blobs*, or, from the size of the flower, horse-blobs, *blob* being an archaic word for rounded knob; only another form, in fact, of *bleb*, an older term for foam-bell or water-bubble. Thus, water-blobs is a local name for water-lilies, on account of the rounded cuplike shape of the bud. In the same way, the marsh marygold is locally the horse-blob. Clare, the Northhampton poet, for example, says:—

> Beneath the shelving banks' retreat
> The *horse-blob* swells its golden ball.

The same peculiarity of shape is embodied in the French *bassinet*, from the likeness of the flower to a small bowl or basin. Cotgrave makes *bassinet* a generic term for the buttercup tribe, including under it the "crow-foot, king-cob, gold-crap, yellow-craw, butter-flower". He adds: "There be many kinds, that which we call bachelor-buttons being one, the double one of them". *Bassinet de Marais* is the special term for the marsh marygold; but even in England, from the splendid appearance of the flower, it was sometimes called the brave bassinet. Thus Lyte, in his *Herbal*, says: "The brave bassinet or marsh marygold doth grow in most places upon the banks and borders of ditches".

From its dark green leaves and crowded discs of burnished gold the brave bassinet is one of the most striking and brilliant flowers of early spring, and as such it has been a favourite with the poets, who are minute observers of nature, from Chaucer to Tennyson. Mrs. Loudon, in describing the marsh marygold, says: "This is one of the most showy of the British plants, and it is also one of the most common, as there are few ponds or slow rivers in Great Britain that have not some of these plants growing on their banks in April and May". And Gerarde, a much more venerable authority, waxes almost eloquent in descanting on its size and beauty: "Marsh marigold hath great broad leaves, somewhat round, smooth, of a gallant greene colour, slightly indented or purld about the edges, among which rise up thicke fat stalkes, likewise greene, whereupon doe grow goodly yellow flowres, glittering like golde, and like to those of crow-foot, but greater". Parkinson, in his voluminous *Herbal*, says that another name for these flowers is *goulds*; and under this name the flower is used by Chaucer as an emblem of jealousy:—

> And jelousy,
> That wered of *yolo guldes* a garland,
> And a cukkow sittyng on hire hand.

And Gower, probably because the flower expands only in bright sunshine, and is closed or locked in cloudy weather, represents Leucothoe as turned into it by the god of day:—

> But Phebus, for the reverence
> Of that she hadde be his love,
> Hath wrought through his power above,
> That she sprong up out of the molde
> Into a flour was named *golde*,
> Which stant governed of the sonne.

Of modern poets, Mrs. Loudon quotes one who, in describing a marsh, celebrates its brightest flower under the less familiar classical name:—

> Caltha, in green and gold refulgent towers,
> And isles of splendour shine, whose radiance pours
> A glory o'er the scene.

Tennyson's line in the "May Queen" is quite familiar:—

> And the wild marsh-marigold shines like fire in
>     swamps and hollows gray.

Again, the marsh marygold is the Lucken Gowan, the locked or folded daisy, of Scotch poetry, celebrated for its beauty by northern writers from Allan Ramsay to Alexander Smith—by the former in the *Gentle Shepherd*, and by the latter in one of the most pathetic of his shorter lyrics.

We may be sure, therefore, that the marsh marygold had often caught Shakespeare's eye, and it is exactly the flower which the line we have quoted, viewed in relation to the whole context, requires in order to make the meaning complete. It haunts the watery margins as the constant associate of reeds and rushes, blooms in "spongy April," and, in common with other water-flowers, is twined with sedge "to make cold nymphs chaste crowns". With regard to the form of the word, as found in the First Folio, Shakespeare simply writes it as it was universally pronounced among those who used it. In the midland and western counties, the peony is a great favourite in rustic gardens, and is looked upon as an important element of floral decoration in all rural festivities, especially at Whitsun-tide, school-feasts, and club-walkings. And we can certify from personal experience that in these districts the word is pro-nounced as Shakespeare spells it, pi-o-ny, with a strong emphasis on the first syllable and the full English sound of the vowel, as though it were spelt pye-o-ny.

The other obscure and disputed word of the line, *twilled*, may be disposed of more rapidly. Twills is given by Halliwell as an older provincial word for reeds, and it was applied like quills to the serried rustling sedges of river reaches and marshy levels. The word is, indeed, still retained in its secondary application, being commercially used to denote the fluted or rib-like effect produced on various fabrics by a kind of ridged or corded weaving. Twilled cloth might equally be described as reeded cloth—cloth channelled or furrowed in a reed-like manner. Twilled is, therefore, the very word to describe the crowded sedges in the shallower reaches of the Avon as it winds round Stratford. It was, indeed, while watching the masses of waving sedge cutting the water-line of the Avon, not far from Stratford Church, that we first felt the peculiar force and significance of the epithet. And, although the season was too far advanced for the reeds to be brightened by the flowers of the marsh marygold, the plant was abundant enough to glorify the banks in the early spring. The whole line, therefore, gives a vivid and truthful picture of what is most characteristic of watery margins at that period of the year.

The next head of illustrations is of a miscellaneous kind, including words and phrases left unexplained, or erroneously explained, connected with the manners and customs, the social usages and appliances, of Shakespeare's day. Of these we have collected a considerable number—upwards of thirty indeed. But waning space warns us not to multiply examples, and we must be satisfied with one or two specimens at most. The first is a word that often puzzled us in the earlier days of our acquaintance with Shakespeare, but which, so far as we are aware, the commentators have not noticed. It is the word *tun* occurring in the celebrated scene between the king and the French ambassadors in *Henry V.*, where the latter delivers the "merry message" and the mocking present of the dauphin:—

> *First Amb.*: In answer of which claim, the prince our
>     master
> Says, that you savour too much of your youth;

And bids you be advis'd, there's naught in France
That can be with a nimble galliard won;
You cannot revel into dukedoms there.
He therefore sends you, meeter for your spirit,
This *tun* of treasure; and, in lieu of this,
Desires you let the dukedoms that you claim
Hear no more of you. This the Dauphin speaks.
*K. Hen.*: What treasure, uncle?
*Exe.*:                        Tennis-balls, my liege.
*K. Hen.*: We're glad the Dauphin is so pleasant with
    us;
    His present and your pains we thank you for:
    When we have match'd our rackets to these balls,
    We will, in France, by God's grace, play a set
    Shall strike his father's crown into the hazard.

Here the "tun of treasure" is evidently brought in and delivered by the ambassador, and the puzzle always was how this could be conveniently or gracefully effected, if *tun* is to be taken in its ordinary sense. The only meaning of *tun* known to our lexicographers is that of a large cask; and how a large cask filled with tennis-balls could be brought by the ambassador and delivered in the king's presence, it is not very easy to see. The difficulty is, however, removed by remembering that *tun*, or in the older spelling *tunne*, had in Shakespeare's day two widely different meanings. While the generic sense in harmony with the etymology is that which holds or contains, still the tun denoted vessels of very different sizes and uses. In addition to a large cask containing a certain measure of liquids or solids, it was applied to a goblet, chalice, or drinking-cup, more commonly a silver-gilt goblet. Thus Minshew, on the English side of his Spanish Dictionary, gives "a *tunne*, or nut to drink in, *cubiléte*," which is explained, "a drinking-cup of silver, or such a cup as juglers use to show divers tricks by". In illustration of this we may mention that in an old country town we remember an inn formerly known as "The Three Tuns," which had as its ancient painted sign three gilt goblets exactly like those used by street jugglers.[1] From a passage given by Halliwell, it would seem that *nut* or *nutte* was used like *tun* for a drinking-cup or goblet, which in wealthy houses was commonly of silver of silver-gilt. This sense of the word *tun* is further illustrated by a letter in Hakluyt's *Voyages*, describing an interview which the representatives of an English mercantile company had with the Emperor of Russia in the year 1555:—

> We came before him the tenth day; and, before we came to his presence, we went throw a great chamber, where stood many small *tunnes*, pailes, bowles, and pots of silver, I mean, like washing bowles, all *parsel gilt*; and within that another chamber, wherein sate (I thinke) neere a hundred in cloth of gold; and then into the chamber where his grace sate, and there, I thinke, were more then in the other chamber, also in cloth of gold; and we did our duty, and showed his grace our queene's grace's letters.

The silver tunnes here described were evidently vessels of the same kind as "the parcel-gilt goblet" on which the faithless Falstaff swore, "sitting in the Dolphin-chamber, at the round-table, by a sea-coal fire, upon Wednesday in Wheeson-week," to make Mistress Quickly "my lady" his wife. This distinctive meaning of the word *tun* is, however, so completely forgotten that it does not occur in any of the English dictionaries, old or new, or in any Shakespearian glossary. The only exception we are aware of is that of Mr. Halliwell, who, in his Provincial Dictionary, gives, on the authority of Kennett, "a little cup," as one meaning of *tun*. The word does not, however, occur in the bishop's published Glossary, and we presume, therefore, it must be contained in some manuscript additions that have not yet seen the light. That this is the meaning to be attached to the word as used in *Henry V.* is abundantly evident from the older play on which Shakespeare founded his drama, and from which the incident of the tennis-balls is derived. The parallel passage in the *Famous Victories of Henry the Fifth* is as follows:—

> *Archbyshop*: And it pleases your Majesty,
>     My Lord Prince Dolphin greetes you well,
>     With this present.
> [*He delivereth a* tunne *of tennis-balles*.]
> *Henry V.*: What a *guilded tunne*!
>     I pray you, my Lord of Yorke, looke what is in it.
> *Yorke*: And it pleases your Grace,
>     Here is a carpet and a *tunne* of tennis-balles.
> *Henry V.*: A *tunne* of tennis balles?
>     I pray you, good my Lord Archbishop,
>     What might the meaning thereof be?
> *Archbyshop*: And it please you, my Lord,
>     A messenger you know ought to keepe close his
>         message,
>     And specially an embassador.
> *Henry V.*: But I know that you may declare your
>         message
>     To a king, the law of armes allowes no lesse.
> *Archbyshop*: My Lord, hearing of your wildnesse
>         before your
>     Father's death, sent you this, my good Lord,
>     Meaning that you are more fitter for a tennis-court
>     Than a field, and more fitter for a carpet than the
>         campe.

Here the archbishop evidently enters the king's presence, bearing in his hand the gilded tun or chalice filled with tennis-balls, to the number probably of eight or ten, the balls being covered with a square of carpet, and at the royal direction delivers both to the Duke of York. In *Henry V.* the ambassadors who take the place of the archbishop deliver the present in the same way to the Duke of Exeter.

The last illustration we have space for is that of the phrase "unbarbed sconce," which occurs in *Coriolanus*. Those who are familiar with the drama will remember the scene in which Volumnia, Menenius, and Cominius unite in urging Coriolanus to return and speak the angry populace fair, in order to avert the impending mischief. His mother entreats him to yield for the moment, to curb his pride so far as to address the mutinous crowd, cap in hand, and with bended knee crave pardon for his previous harshness and ask their gentle loves:—

> *Enter* COMINIUS.
> *Com.*: I've been i' the market-place; and, sir, 'tis fit
>     You make strong party, or defend yourself
>     By calmness or by absence: all's in anger.
> *Men.*: Only fair speech.
> *Com.*:                        I think 'twill serve, if he
>     Can thereto frame his spirit.
> *Vol.*:                        He must, and will.—
>     Prithee now, say you will, and go about it.
> *Cor.*: Must I go show them my *unbarb'd sconce?*
>         must I
>     With my base tongue give to my noble heart
>     A lie that it must bear? Well, I'll do't:
>     Yet were there but this single plot to lose,
>     This mould of Marcius, they to dust should grind
>         it,

And throw't against the wind.—To the market-
place!—
You've put me now to such a part, which never
I shall discharge to the life.

Two main explanations of "unbarb'd sconce" have been
given: one by Stevens, to the effect that *unbarbed* means
untrimmed, unshaven, to barb a man being a common
expression for shaving him; the other by Hawkins, that
unbarbed means bare-headed. In support of this, he says
pertinently, but vaguely, that "in the times of chivalry, when a
horse was fully armed and accoutred for the encounter he was
said to be barbed". Curiously enough, of these explanations the
latter, and more correct, has been almost unanimously rejected
by modern editors and critics. Thus, Mr. Dyce explains
unbarbed, "unshorn, untrimmed"; the Cambridge editors give
the same meaning, in the Globe edition; while Todd, in his
edition of Johnson, Richardson in his Dictionary, and Nares in
his Glossary, give unbarbed as unshorn, each quoting the
passage in *Coriolanus* as the example. Mr. Staunton, it is true,
adopts Hawkins' more correct interpretation, but he does this
without a word of explanation or defence. Now, with an
erroneous rendering in almost undisputed possession of the
ground, this is hardly sufficient. It is necessary to indicate at
least the reasons that make the one interpretation right, and the
other wrong. It may be stated at the outset that the words
"barbed" and "unbarbed" are used both literally and figuratively for shaven and unshorn. But in this speech of Coriolanus the
term cannot be interpreted in this sense, as it would then have
no real meaning or relevancy at all. So far as mere personal
appearance is concerned, Coriolanus had just presented himself in the most public and official manner, both in the Capitol
and the Forum, before the senate and the citizens, with the
confidence of a proud nature, and the indifference to mere
pouncet-boxes and curling-irons proper to a soldier and a hero.
There could thus be no possible reason against his returning on
the ground of mere personal appearance. If he really were
somewhat rough and unkempt, he would surely, under the
circumstances, be the better pleased. Least of all would he
think of calling in the barber before presenting himself again to
the greasy multitude. The speech obviously refers, not to mere
personal appearance, but to the accustomed and accredited
signs of deference, humility, and respect. One of these—and
that the most eloquently submissive—was uncovering, standing bare-headed, and bowing in a lowly manner to the
assembled citizens. This the proud spirit of Coriolanus could
not stomach, and he had the greatest difficulty in forcing his
stubborn will into even momentary and simulated acquiescence. This was the bitterest element in the partial and
mocking ceremony of submission to the citizens he had just
gone through. When urged by his friends to speak to the
citizens and ask their suffrages, according to established usage,
he replies:—

I do beseech you,
Let me o'erleap that custom; for I cannot
Put on the gown, stand naked, and entreat them,
For my wounds' sake, to give their suffrage; please
you
That I may pass this doing.

Here "stand naked" cannot, of course, be literally taken,
though it might be supposed to refer indirectly to showing his
wounds. This, however, Coriolanus did not do, and the phrase
must be understood as referring primarily to the fact that he was
obliged to stand uncovered, bare-headed, before the "bisson
multitude". But his gall so rises at the degradation, that while
going through the form he cannot help flouting the citizens to
their face:—

*Third Cit.*: You have been a scourge to her enemies,
you have been a rod to her friends; you have
not, indeed, loved the common people.
*Cor.*: You should account me the more virtuous, that
I have not been common in my love. I will,
sir, flatter my sworn brother, the people, to
earn a dearer estimation of them; 'tis a condition they account gentle; and since the wisdom of their choice is rather *to have my hat*
than my heart, I will practise the insinuating
nod.

Again, Volumnia, well knowing what the chief difficulty
was, addresses herself most earnestly to this point, detailing to
her son in eager gestures the submissive actions by which he
must at once seek to regain the popular favour:—

*Vol.*: I prithee now, my son,
Go to them, with this bonnet in thy hand;
And thus far having stretch'd it,—here be with
them,—
Thy knee bussing the stones,—for in such business
Action is eloquence, and th' eyes of th' ignorant
More learned than their ears,—waving thy head,
Which often, thus, correcting thy stout heart,
Now humble as the ripest mulberry
That will not hold the handling,—say to them
Thou art their soldier, and, being bred in broils,
Hast not the soft way which, thou dost confess,
Were fit for thee to use, as they to claim,
In asking their good loves; but thou wilt frame
Thyself forsooth, hereafter theirs, so far
As thou hast power and person.

In this excited and intensely dramatic address we see
Volumnia pointing to her son's bonnet, and showing by her
own action the way in which he should use it in addressing the
citizens. At last, in reply to the reiterated and united entreaties
of mother and friends, Coriolanus impatiently exclaims:—

Must I go show them my unbarb'd sconce?

It may be easily shown that unbarbed has the meaning
which the context thus requires. A war-horse protected by head
and chest-pieces of defensive armour was technically said to be
*barbed*, *barded*, or *bard*, these being all different forms of the
same word derived from the French *bardé*, which Cotgrave
renders "barbed or trapped as a great horse". Thus Holland, in
his translation of Xenophon's *Cyropœdia*, says: "Now were they
all that attended upon Cyrus armed as he was, to wit, in purple
tabards, corslets, and head-pieces of brasse, with white crests
and with swords: every man also with a javelin of corneil wood.
Their horses were *bard*, with frontlets, poictrels, and side-
pieces of brasse." In other words, the horses were protected by
head-pieces, breast-pieces, or plates, and side-pieces of defensive armour. The terms *barb* and *barbed*, used in the same way
for horse armour, occur continually in Harrington's translation
of Ariosto, in Spenser, and generally in the chivalrous poetry of
Shakespeare's time, as well as occasionally in his own dramas.
But as the war-horse was rarely in this sense fully barbed, the
metallic armour largely increasing the weight to be carried, the
term barb came to be specially associated with the frontlet, or
head-piece, which few war-steeds were without. In this way it
was also applied, in a secondary sense, to any covering or
protection for the head, to a cap or hood, a helmet or bonnet of
almost any description. Thus Chaucer uses *barbe* for a
whimple, or a hood and cape covering the head and shoulders;
while Skelton applies the same term to a nun's hood, and also
to the cap which covered the hawk's head when carried on the
fist to the fields before being unhooded at the game. It is,
however, more to our present purpose to note that a special

form of the word was a well-known term in mediæval times for a military cap, or defensive covering for the head. Thus Ducange gives "*Barbuta*,"—"Tegminis species qua caput tegebant milites seu equites in prœliis". And Sir S. R. Meyrick quotes in illustration of *barbuta* in this sense from Hoscemius, "erant omnes armati cum *barbutis* in capite"; and from Villani, "I tutti armati di corazze e *barbute*, come cavalieri". After giving these examples Sir S. R. Meyrick adds a sentence which is tolerably decisive as to the real meaning of the term in Shakespeare's phrase: "The French call knights thus armed *barbües*, and the English *barbed*". To show an unbarbed sconce is thus to show an uncovered, unprotected sconce; in other words, to appear bare-headed.

That the word in this connection cannot possibly refer to shaving is evident from the fact that *sconce* means head, and is never applied to the face by Shakespeare or his contemporaries. Of the seven places in which the word occurs in his dramas four are in the *Comedy of Errors* where sconce is played upon in a humorous scene between Antipholus and Dromio of Syracuse. In the second scene of the first act it is synonymous with "pate"; while in the second scene of the second act it is freely punned upon by Dromio after the manner so common with Shakespeare's fools, servants, and clowns:—

> Ant. S.: If you will jest with me, know my aspect,
> And fashion your demeanour to my looks,
> Or I will beat this method on your *sconce*.

> Dro. S.: *Sconce* call you it? so you would leave battering, I had rather have it a head: and you use these blows long, I must get a *sconce* for my head, and ensconce it too; or else I shall seek my wit in my shoulders. But, I pray, sir, why am I beaten?

If our interpretation is correct, the word *sconce* is here used in three different senses: first, for head; second, for a rounded fort or blockhouse; and third, for what protects or covers the head, a cap or hood. This last sense has not been recognised by the commentators, who have interpreted "I must get me a sconce for my head" in the sense of fortification. But sconce having also the meaning of covering for the head, it is more likely that in playing on the word Dromio would use it in a different sense than that he would repeat it immediately in the same signification. The glossarists do not seem to be aware that sconce has this secondary meaning of covering for the head. But that it was really so used is apparent from the following entry in Florio's Dictionary: "Capuccio, a little round hood, or *skonce*, a cap, also a hood or a cowl, a friar's bonnet". The various significations of sconce are thus all connected with the central notion of head. It is never applied to the face; and, apart from the necessities of the context, the shaving or unshorn interpretation of the phrase is inadmissible.

Here we must close, having only partially accomplished the task proposed at the outset. Something, however, has been done. Several of the explanations we have offered vindicate on grounds of definite evidence the text of the First Folio, and we are confident there is still a good deal more to be done in the same direction. We shall hope, therefore, to find some other opportunity of returning to a subject of inexhaustible interest to the genuine lovers of literature.

*Notes*

1. See also *Cardenis Comforte*, p. 8; and Shirley's *Dramatic Works* (Dyce), vol. v. p. 49.

# C. M. INGLEBY
## "The Still Lion Discovered"
### *Shakespeare Hermeneutics*
1875, pp. 1–12

We may say of Shakespeare's text what Thomas De Quincey said of Milton's:

ON ANY ATTEMPT TO TAKE LIBERTIES WITH A PASSAGE OF *HIS*, YOU FEEL AS WHEN COMING, IN A FOREST, UPON WHAT SEEMS A DEAD LION; PERHAPS HE MAY NOT BE DEAD, BUT ONLY SLEEPING, NAY PERHAPS HE MAY NOT BE SLEEPING, BUT ONLY SHAMMING. . . . You may be put down with shame by some man reading the line otherwise,

or, we add, reading it in the light of more extended or more accurate knowledge.

Here lies the covert danger of emendation. It is true that the text of Shakespeare, as it comes down to us—"the latest seed of time"—in the folio 1623, as well as in the early quartos, is very corrupt. It is corrupt on two accounts. As to the text of the quartos, there was no proper editorial supervision, since the editions were intended merely for the accommodation of play-goers; the text was therefore imperfect not only in form but in substance as well. As to the text of the folio, the supervision of Messrs. Heminge and Condell seems to have been confined to the selection of copies for the printers, Messrs. Jaggard and Blount; and some of those were playhouse copies, which had been curtailed for representation, and certain other were copies of quarto editions; while the correction of the press was probably left to the 'reader' of the printing-house,[1] who certainly could not have exercised any extraordinary vigilance in his vocation. Accordingly we have imperfect copies at first, and a misprinted text at last.

The corrupt and mutilated condition in which the Greek and Roman Classics, especially the Greek, have been handed down to modern times is the sufficient reason for that latitude of conjectural criticism which has been brought to bear on their ancient texts. If we had to deal with an English text which bore like evidences of dilapidation, we should naturally have recourse to the same means for its correction. But such is not the case with the works of any English author who has assumed the proportions of a classic: not Chaucer, nor Shakespeare, nor Milton, is a venerable ruin demanding restoration; though Shakespeare, far more than Milton, has suffered corruption, and that by the very nature of the vehicle to which he committed his thoughts; exactly as the 'Last Supper' of Leonardo da Vinci has incurred an amount of destruction which it might have escaped had it been painted on wood or on canvass. Such corruption, however, as infects the works of Shakespeare touches but comparatively small, and often isolated, portions of the text, offering no very serious obstacle to the general reader, who is not exacting or scrupulous in the interpretation of his author's phraseology. Patches of indictable nonsense, which have hitherto defied all attempts at elucidation, there are, as we shall soon see, in some of the plays; yet it is no very violent proceeding to regard them as parts of the inferior work of a joint-author, or as interpolations by the players, or as matter adopted by Shakespeare from the older play on which his own was founded. But the critical student is naturally intolerant of every unexplored obscurity and every unresolved difficulty; and an editor who works for students as well as for general readers feels himself bound to apply to the text all the available resources of criticism. The example of the ancient Classics, and the capital success which rewarded the vigilance and invention of scholars in that field, could not fail to determine the method on which the recension of Shakespeare was to be attempted by the verbal critics.

As the natural result, the text has been subjected to a conjectural criticism which owns no restraint and systematically violates every principle of probability and of propriety. Obsolete phraseology and archaic allusion are treated as cases of corruption: the language, where corrupt, instead of being restored or amended, is modernized and *improved*: and the idiom, instead of being expounded and illustrated, is accommodated to the prevailing grammatical standard. By this means more fatuous and incapable nonsense has been manufactured for Shakespeare than can be found in any of the ancient copies of his plays.

The text of Milton, on the other hand, offers little or no holding for the conjectural critic.[2] One might have predicted that of all English texts it was the least likely to have afforded congenial sport to a classical scholar intent on havoc. But it was not so much the promise of the coverts, but the solicitations of exalted rank, that induced the combative and tenacious old Master of Trinity, when he had already earned his laurels as an editor of the Classics, and 'won his spurs' as a verbal critic of matchless resource and felicity, even in the 69th year of his age, to undertake the recension of *Paradise Lost*. As some sort of self-justification he framed the hypothesis that Milton's text had suffered through the carelessness and also the invention of the scribe to whom it had been dictated by the blind bard. Bentley was a great man, and this work of his is great in its way. He mars his author with power and splendour, and we admire his learning and talents, while we deplore their misapplication.

This reference to Milton, WHO IS ALSO A STILL LION, THRILLING INDEED WITH LIFE, BUT OFTEN DISSEMBLING HIS VITALITY, leads me to exhibit the salient contrasts between the two English classics of the seventeenth century. I will first consider the works themselves as intellectual achievements: secondly, the material vehicle of their transmission.

(1) Dramatic Literature, out of the very reason for its existence, is more within the compass of the ordinary understanding than an epic poem. Its appeal is to the common mind. If the people fail to catch the meaning of a dialogue or a soliloquy, it is a mere impertinence, how splendid soever may be its diction, or profound the reach of its thought. Shakespeare is, indeed, very strongly differenced from his contemporaries by the fervour of his imagination and his knowledge of human nature, as well as by the strength and range of his vocabulary; and certain portions of his works are pitched in as sublime a key as the epics of Milton. But on the whole the language of Shakespeare is more or less amenable to undisciplined good sense. Milton, on the contrary, 'flies an eagle's flight,' and is quite out of the blank of the general aim. He is 'caviary to the general,' and, without the poetic temperament, the strongest common sense and the most delicate ear for rhythm are quite at fault in the criticism of his greater works.

With this distinction in mind, the reason of Bentley's deplorable failure in attempting an edition of *Paradise Lost* is not far to seek. The work he had successfully done was in the field of the Greek and Latin Classics, the emendation of which, as that of our early dramatic literature, is generally within the range of that strong natural sense for which Bentley was so conspicuous: and this, complemented with his matchless ingenuity and vast book-learning, was amply sufficient for his purpose.[3] One almost wonders that he did not make the experiment on Shakespeare rather than on Milton; and it seems natural to fancy that, had he known in what relationship of marriage he stood to the Bard of Avon,[4] he would have been drawn to the recension of his great relative's works, and would

have brought to the task that reverential affection which is so conspicuously absent from his notes on Milton.

(2) The difference in the 'material vehicle' consists in the difference between Dramatic Art and Literature. We must consider this point as somewhat greater length than the former. Disallowing Bentley's pretext, as a mere device for the indulgence of licentious criticism, which especially in the case of Milton *sufflaminandus est*, it is plain that Milton's epics enjoyed the benefit of being printed, if not under the eye, at least under the direct superintendence, of their author; and we know, moreover, that in exercising that function he was fastidiously vigilant and accurate. We may be quite sure that the text contains but very few misprints, and that conjecture has no *locus standi* there. But how different was the case with the dramas of Shakespeare! Speaking of the textual vehicle only, we may be equally sure that the conjectural critic would have had 'the very cipher of a function' if those works had received the final corrections and editorial supervision of their author. They would still have been thronged with difficulties, and pestered with obscurities, taxing the utmost erudition and study of the editor, the greater number of which would have belonged to the class *historical*, consisting wholly of allusions to forgotten persons and events, and to obsolete habits and customs. Not a few, however, of those difficulties would have belonged to the class *grammatical*, demanding on the part of the expositor almost as much learning and research as the *historical* allusions in the text: for since the date of Shakespeare's *floruit* the English language has suffered no inconsiderable change, though much less than the habits and customs of the English people.

But Shakespeare died without, so far as we know, having made the attempt to collect and print his works. Of this fact an unnecessary difficulty has been made. A much more self-conscious genius than Shakespeare has himself given us the clue to its solution, a clue of which all writers, save Thomas Carlyle,[5] have failed to perceive the significance. Goethe confessed to Eckermann that he never reperused any of his poems when once it was completed and printed, unless impelled to the task by the demand for a new edition; and that he then read it with no self-complacency, but rather dissatisfaction. Why was this? Simply because he felt a *Widerwille*, or distaste, towards the offspring of his less matured self, by reason of its inadequacy to express his great ideal—the 'unbodied figure of the thought that gave 't surmised shape.' He had outgrown his own powers, in the grander sense of that phrase: never, like poor Swift, living to look back with wonder and horror on the glory of a genius that he owned no more, but prejudicially contrasting his past self with the greater present.

> 'As for what I have done,' he would repeatedly say to me, 'I take no pride in it whatever. Excellent poets have lived at the same time with myself, poets more excellent have lived before me, and others will come after me.' (*Gespräche mit Goethe*, 1836, vol. i. p. 86. Feb. 19th, 1829. Oxenford's Translation, 1850, vol. ii. p. 145.)

He also says to Falk ("with unusual rapidity and vehemence"):

> I will not hear anything of the matter; neither of the public, nor of posterity, nor of the justice, as you call it, which is hereafter to reward my efforts. I hate my *Tasso*, just because people say that it will go down to posterity; I hate *Iphigenie*; in a word, I hate everything of mine that pleases the public. I know that it belongs to the day, and the day to it; but I tell you,

once for all, I will not live for the day. (*Characteristics of Goethe*, by Sarah Austin, 1873, vol. i. p. 112.)

He had, seemingly, that very contempt for self-complacency which he attributes to Faust—

> Verflucht voraus die hohe Meinung,
> Womit der Geist sich selbst umfängt.

Now Shakespeare wrote and issued under his own eye two poems as literature, and nothing else. The rest of his works, save his sonnets and minor pieces, were written for representation on the boards, and as a simple matter of money-profit. Not faultless even as dramas, they must have fully answered his primary aim, which was mercenary, but not that grand ideal which dwelt 'deep down in his heart of hearts.' Hence he must have viewed them with some dissatisfaction, (1) as not being in the best sense Literature; (2) as being 'mere implorators of—mercenary, if not—unholy suits,' designed to catch the penny with the least pains; (3) as being often hasty and inchoate, and always imperfect, attempts to realize his own ideal. From the effort of recasting and revising them he naturally shrank. If he gave a thought to the probability of his works becoming his country's crowning glory, it might very reasonably have occurred to him that no revision would be likely to guarantee them an exemption from the common lot which was not the due of their original merits. Of one thing we may be quite sure, that Shakespeare's good sense and honesty of purpose rendered him perfectly indifferent to that vanity of vanities which Goethe, in the speech from which a citation has already been made, calls 'das Blenden der Erscheinung,' for which so many a man of letters has sacrificed the calm and comfort of his life.

Be all that as it may, it is a fact that the first collection of his plays was published six or seven years after his death; and it is a matter of certainty that the folio of 1623 was printed from inaccurate quarto editions and mutilated stagecopies. This is the 'case' of those who advocate the rights of unlimited conjecture; and we frankly make the concession, that our text needs emendation. But, before they can be permitted to conjecture, we require of them to find out where the corruptions lie. If a man's body be diseased, the seat of the disease can generally be determined, between the patient and the doctor: in some cases, however, the malady baffles alike research and experiment.

In the case of Shakespeare's text, the diagnosis is infinitely perplexed: (1) from the multitude of obscurities and difficulties that beset it: (2) from the close resemblance that often subsists between those obscurities which spring from the obsolete language or the archaic allusions, and those which are wholly due to the misreading of misprinting of the text. Our healthy parts are so like our diseased parts, that the doctor sets about the medicinal treatment of that which needs no cure; and the patient's body is so full of those seeming anomalies, that his life is endangered by the multiplicity of agencies brought to bear on his time-worn frame.

What, if there are cases in which those *kyrioi synōmotai* archaic phraseology and textual corruption, unite their powers against us? Why, in such cases, it is most likely that the critic would be utterly baffled: that he would be unable to restore the lost integrity even by the combined forces of exposition and conjecture. Now it so happens that after all that contemporary literature and conjectural criticism could do for Shakespeare's immortal works, there is a residue of about thirty-five to forty passages which have defied all attempts to cure their immortal nonsense. Does it not seem likely that the perplexity in such cases is due to the joint action of those two sources of obscurity, and our inability to *persever* or discriminate the one from the

other? We shall see. The *vintage* afforded by these remarks may be thus expressed. Conjectural criticism is legitimate; for it is needful to the perfection of the text: but no critic can be licensed to exercise it whose knowledge and culture do not guarantee these three great pre-requisites: (1) a competent knowledge of the orthography, phraseology, prosody, as well as the language of arts and customs, prevalent in the time of Shakespeare: (2) a delicate ear for the rhythm of verse and prose:[6] (3) a reverential faith in the resources of Shakespeare's genius.

The present time seems most fitting for the treatment of the question: To what extent, and in what manner, may conjectural criticism be safely exercised? For the last twenty years the text of Shakespeare has been subjected to a process, which for its wholesale destructiveness and the arrogance of its pretensions is wholly without parallel. The English press has teemed with works, from Mr. J. P. Collier's pseudo-antique Corrector down to the late Mr. Staunton's papers 'On Unsuspected Corruptions in the Text of Shakespeare,' most of which, in our judgment, have achieved no other result than that of corrupting and betraying the ancient text. We allow that some of the conjectures thus put forth are invaluable, and certain other may be entertained for careful consideration; but the mass we repudiate as impertinent and barbarous. We deny the need for any wholesale change, and impute great ignorance to the assailants:—not to insist on matters of taste, which it is proverbially difficult to make matters of controversy. We are fully able to prove the strength of our position, by showing that the passages attacked are proof against innovations by the power of their own sense. To do this at full length and in complete detail would require the dimensions of a large volume: to teach the general truth by the force of particular examples is all that we now propose to accomplish. This is our aim: to exemplify the growth of the written English language in relation to the text of Shakespeare: to point out the dangers incident to all tampering with special words and phrases in it: to examine and defend certain of its words and phrases which have suffered the wrongs of so-called emendation; and finally to discuss the general subject of the emendation of the text, and to adduce some examples of passages reclaimed or restored through this means. Having accomplished this, we shall gladly leave the old text, with its legion of archaisms and corruptions, to the tender mercies of those critics whose object is to conserve what is sound and to restore what is corrupt, and not at all to improve what, to their imperfect judgment and limited knowledge, seems unsatisfactory. To the arbitration of such critics we submit the question, whether in any particular case a word or phrase which is intelligible to the well-informed reader, however strange or uncouth, does or does not fulfil the utmost requirements of the cultivated mind, regard being had to the context, the situation, and the speaker.

*Notes*

1. Not improbably Edward Blount, Isaac Jaggard's partner. See *Notes and Queries*, 2nd S. iii. 7.
2. The *systematic* departure from the ordinary spelling of the time in the text of the *Paradise Lost* of 1667 has been noticed by De Quincey. Mr. B. M. Pickering says:

   'At the end of the first edition of *Paradise Lost* we meet with what, to a casual observer, would appear to be a very singular correction, *viz.* Lib. 2. v. 414, "For *we* read wee." Even a tolerably attentive student of the early editions of Milton might be at a loss what to make of this. It is certain that *we* is to be met with in this edition of *Paradise Lost* quite as often, or rather oftener, with a single than with a double *e*. It occurs as *we* in the very next line to that referred to in this errata. The explanation is this:—that although in ordinary cases Milton is accustomed to spell the pronouns *we, me, he, ye,* with a single *e,* whenever special emphasis is intended to be put upon them he makes a point of writing *wee, mee, hee, yee.* Many other words are differently spelt to what was then, or is now, usual, and this not in an uncertain manner, as is common in old books, but after a regular, unvarying system, deliberately formed by Milton himself, and adopted upon choice and afore-thought.' (From the Prospectus of A Reprint of the First Edition of *Paradise Lost.*)

3. See De Quincey's articles on *Bentley* and *Landor.*
4. The relationship is easily stated, though it is very remote. Shakespeare's granddaughter married (secondly) the brother of Mrs. Bentley's grandfather.
5. Consult his *Shooting Niagara, and after?*
6. The late Mr. Staunton was deficient in this. Such a symptosis as would be introduced into the text by reading, in *Macbeth,* 'Making the *green zone* red' and '*cleanse* the *clogg'd* bosom,' &c., would (to borrow De Quincey's happy phrase) 'splinter the teeth of a crocodile,' and make the adder shake her ears.

### EDMUND GOSSE
### From "The Age of Elizabeth"
*Modern English Literature: A Short History*
1897, pp. 104–7

From 1593 to 1610 . . . the volcanic forces of Elizabethan literature were pre-eminently at work. During these seventeen years Spenser was finishing the *Faerie Queen,* Bacon and Hooker were creating modern prose, Jonson was active, and Beaumont and Fletcher beginning to be prominent. These, to preserve our mountain simile, were majestic masses in the landscape, but the central cone, the truncation of which would reduce the structure to meanness, and would dwarf the entire scheme of English literature, was Shakespeare. Very briefly, we may remind ourselves of what his work for the press in those years consisted. He published no dramatic work until 1597. The plays to which his name is, with more or less propriety, attached, are thirty-eight in number; of these, sixteen appeared in small quarto form during the poet's lifetime, and the title-pages of nine or ten of these "stolen and surreptitious" editions, originally sold at sixpence each, bear his name. We have the phenomenon, therefore, of a bibliographical indifference to posterity rare even in that comparatively unlettered age. It is curious to think that, if all Shakespeare's MSS. had been destroyed when he died, we should now possess no *Macbeth* and no *Othello,* no *Twelfth Night* and no *As You Like It.* In 1623 the piety of two humble friends, Heminge and Condell—whose names deserve to be carved on the forefront of the Temple of Fame—preserved for us the famous folio text. But the conditions under which that text was prepared from what are vaguely called Shakespeare's "papers" must have been, and obviously were, highly uncritical. The folio contained neither *Pericles* nor the *Two Noble Kinsmen,* yet participation in these is plausibly claimed for Shakespeare. What other omissions were there, what intrusion of lines not genuinely his?

This question has occupied an army of investigators, whose elaborate and conflicting conjectures have not always been illuminated with common sense. More than a hundred years ago, one of the wittiest of our poets represented the indignant spirit of Shakespeare as assuring his emendators that it would be

Better to bottom tarts and cheesecakes nice
Than thus be patched and cobbled in one's grave,

and since that date whole libraries have been built over the complaining ghost. Within the last quarter of a century, systems by which to test the authenticity and the chronology of the plays have been produced with great confidence, metrical formulas which are to act as reagents and to identify the component parts of a given passage with scientific exactitude. Of these "verse-tests" and "pause-tests" no account can here be given. That the results of their employment have been curious and valuable shall not be denied; but there is already manifest in the gravest criticism a reaction against excess of confidence in them. At one time it was supposed that the "end-stopt" criterium, for instance, might be dropped, like a chemical substance, on the page of Shakespeare, and would there immediately and finally determine minute quantities of Peele or Kyd, that a fragment of Fletcher would turn purple under it, or a greenish tinge betray a layer of Rowley. It is not thus that poetry is composed; and this ultra-scientific theory showed a grotesque ignorance of the human pliability of art.

Yet, although the mechanical artifice of this class of criticism carries with it its own refutation, it cannot but have been useful for the reader of Shakespeare that this species of alchemy should be applied to his text. It has dispersed the old superstition that every word printed within the covers of the folio must certainly be Shakespeare's in the sense in which the entire text of Tennyson or of Victor Hugo belongs to those poets. We are now content to realise that much which is printed there was adapted, edited, or accepted by Shakespeare; that he worked in his youth in the studios of others, and that in middle life younger men painted on his unfinished canvases. But there must be drawn a distinction between Shakespeare's share in the general Elizabethan dramatisation of history, where anybody might lend a hand, and the creation of his own sharply individualised imaginative work. If the verse-tester comes probing in *Macbeth* for bits of Webster, we send him packing about his business; if he likes to analyse *Henry VI.* he can do no harm, and may make some curious discoveries. With the revelation of dramatic talent in England there had sprung up a desire to celebrate the dynastic glories of the country in a series of chronicle-plays. It is probable that every playwright of the period had a finger in this gallery of historical entablatures, and Shakespeare, too, a modest artisan, stood to serve his apprenticeship here before in *Richard III.* he proved that his independent brush could excel the brilliant master-worker Marlowe in Marlowe's own approved style. He proceeded to have a chronicle in hand to the close of his career, but he preserved for this class of work the laxity of evolution and lack of dramatic design which he had learned in his youth; and thus, side by side with plays the prodigious harmony of which Shakespeare alone could have conceived or executed, we have an epical fragment, like *Henry V.,* which is less a drama by one particular poet, than a fold of the vast dramatic tapestry woven to the glory of England by the combined poetic patriotism of the Elizabethans. Is the whole of what we read here implicit Shakespeare, or did another hand combine with his to decorate this portion of the gallery? It is impossible to tell, and the reply, could it be given, would have no great critical value. *Henry V.* is not *Othello.*

The Swan Theatre, London, 1596

*As You Like It* as presented in the Globe Theatre, with Shakespeare as Adam

A Shakespeare play performed ·
before Queen Elizabeth and her court

Richard Tarleton

David Garrick

Richard Burbage

# *Sources*

## JOHN DENNIS
### From *Essay on the Genius and Writings of Shakespear*
### 1712

#### *Letter I*

Shakespear was one of the greatest Genius's that the World e'er saw for the Tragick Stage. Tho' he lay under greater Disadvantages than any of his Successors, yet had he greater and more genuine Beauties than the best and greatest of them. And what makes the brightest Glory of his Character, those Beauties were entirely his own, and owing to the Force of his own Nature; whereas his Faults were owing to his Education, and to the Age that he liv'd in. One may say of him as they did of *Homer,* that he had none to imitate, and is himself inimitable. His Imaginations were often as just, as they were bold and strong. He had a natural discretion which never cou'd have been taught him, and his Judgment was strong and penetrating. He seems to have wanted nothing but Time and Leisure for Thought, to have found out those Rules of which he appears so ignorant. His Characters are always drawn justly, exactly, graphically, except where he fail'd by not knowing History or the Poetical Art. He has for the most part more fairly distinguish'd them than any of his Successors have done, who have falsified them, or confounded them, by making Love the predominant Quality in all. He had so fine a Talent for touching the Passions, and they are so lively in him, and so truly in Nature, that they often touch us more without their due Preparations, than those of other Tragick Poets, who have all the Beauty of Design and all the Advantage of Incidents. His Master-Passion was Terror, which he has often mov'd so powerfully and so wonderfully, that we may justly conclude, that if he had had the Advantage of Art and Learning, he wou'd have surpass'd the very best and strongest of the Ancients. His Paintings are often so beautiful and so lively, so graceful and so powerful, especially where he uses them in order to move Terror; that there is nothing perhaps more accomplish'd in our *English* Poetry. His Sentiments for the most part in his best Tragedies, are noble, generous, easie and natural, and adapted to the Persons who use them. His Expression is in many Places good and pure after a hundred Years; simple tho' elevated, graceful tho' bold, and easie tho' strong. He seems to have been the very Original of our *English* Tragical Harmony; that is the Harmony of Blank Verse, diversifyed often by Dissyllable and Trissyllable Terminations. For that Diversity distinguishes it from Heroick Harmony, and bringing it nearer to common Use, makes it more porper to gain Attention, and more fit for Action and Dialogue. Such Verse we make when we are writing Prose; we make such Verse in common Conversation.

If *Shakespear* had these great Qualities by Nature, what would he not have been, if he had join'd to so happy a Genius Learning and the Poetical Art. For want of the latter, our Author has sometimes made gross Mistakes in the Characters which he has drawn from History, against the Equality and Conveniency of Manners of his Dramatical Persons. Witness *Menenius* in the following Tragedy, whom he has made an errant Buffoon, which is a great Absurdity. For he might as well have imagin'd a grave majestick *Jack-Pudding,* as a Buffoon in a *Roman* Senator. *Aufidius* the General of the *Volscians* is shewn a base and a profligate Villain. He has offended against the Equality of the Manners even in his Hero himself. For *Coriolanus* who in the first part of the Tragedy is

shewn so open, so frank, so violent, and so magnanimous, is represented in the latter part by *Aufidius,* which is contradicted by no one, a flattering, fawning, cringing, insinuating Traytor.

For want of this Poetical Art, *Shakespear* has introduced things into his Tragedies, which are against the Dignity of that noble Poem, as the Rabble in *Julius Cæsar,* and that in *Coriolanus;* tho' that in *Coriolanus* offends not only against the Dignity of Tragedy, but against the Truth of History likewise, and the Customs of Ancient *Rome,* and the Majesty of the *Roman* People, as we shall have occasion to shew anon.

For want of this Art, he has Incidents less moving, less surprizing, and less wonderful. He has been so far from seeking those fine Occasions to move with which an Action furnish'd according to Art would have furnish'd him; that he seems rather to have industriously avoided them. He makes *Coriolanus,* upon his Sentence of Banishment, take his leave of his Wife and his Mother out of sight of the Audience, and so has purposely as it were avoided a great occasion to move.

If we are willing to allow, that *Shakespear* by sticking to the bare Events of History, has mov'd more than any of his Successors, yet his just Admirers must confess, that if he had had the Poetical Art, he would have mov'd ten times more. For 'tis impossible that by a bare Historical Play he could move so much as he would have done by a Fable.

We find that a Romance entertains the generality of Mankind with more Satisfaction than History, if they read only to be entertain'd; but if they read History thro' Pride or Ambition, they bring their Passions along with them, and that alters the case. Nothing is more plain than that even in an Historical Relation some Parts of it, and some Events, please more than others. And therefore a Man of Judgment, who sees why they do so, may in forming a Fable, and disposing an Action, please more than an Historian can do. For the just Fiction of a Fable moves us more than an Historical Relation can do, for the two following Reasons: First, by reason of the Communication and mutual Dependence of its Parts. For if Passion springs from Motion, then the Obstruction of that Motion or a counter Motion must obstruct and check the Passion: And therefore an Historian and a Writer of Historical Plays passing from Events of one nature to Events of another nature without a due Preparation, must of necessity stifle and confound one Passion by another. The second Reason why the Fiction of a Fable pleases us more, than an Historical Relation can do, is, because in an Historical Relation we seldom are acquainted with the true Causes of Events, whereas in a feign'd Action which is duly constituted, that is, which has a just beginning, those Causes always appear. For 'tis observable, that both in a Poetical Fiction and an Historical Relation, those Events are the most entertaining, the most surprizing, and the most wonderful, in which Providence most plainly appears. And 'tis for this Reason that the Author of a just Fable, must please more than the Writer of an Historical Relation. The Good must never fail to prosper, and the Bad must be always punish'd: Otherwise the Incidents, and particularly the Catastrophe which is the grand Incident, are liable to be imputed rather to Chance, than to Almighty Conduct and to Sovereign Justice. The want of this impartial Distribution of Justice makes the *Coriolanus* of *Shakespear* to be without Moral. 'Tis true indeed *Coriolanus* is kill'd by those Foreign Enemies with whom he had openly sided against his Country, which seems to be an Event worthy of Providence, and would look as if it were contriv'd by infinite Wisdom, and executed by supreme Justice, to make *Coriolanus* a dreadful Example to all who lead on Foreign Enemies to the Invasion of their native Country; if there were not something in the Fate of the other Characters, which gives occasion to doubt of it, and which suggests to the Sceptical Reader that this might happen by accident. For *Aufidius* the principal Murderer of *Coriolanus*, who in cold Blood gets him assassinated by Ruffians, instead of leaving him to the Law of the Country, and the Justice of the *Volscian* Senate, and who commits so black a Crime, not by any erroneous Zeal, or a mistaken publick Spirit, but thro' Jealousy, Envy, and inveterate Malice; this Assassinator not only survives, and survives unpunish'd, but seems to be rewarded for so detestable an Action; by engrossing all those Honours to himself which *Coriolanus* before had shar'd with him. But not only *Aufidius*, but the *Roman* Tribunes, *Sicinius* and *Brutus*, appear to me to cry aloud for Poetick Vengeance. For they are guilty of two Faults, neither of which ought to go unpunish'd: The first in procuring the Banishment of *Coriolanus*. If they were really jealous, that *Coriolanus* had a Design on their Liberties, when he stood for the Consulship, it was but just that they should give him a Repulse; but to get the Champion and Defender of their Country banish'd upon a pretended Jealousy was a great deal too much, and could proceed from nothing but that Hatred and Malice which they had conceiv'd against him, for opposing their Institution. Their second Fault lay in procuring this Sentence by indirect Methods, by exasperating and inflaming the People by Artifices and Insinuations, by taking a base Advantage of the Open-heartedness and Violence of *Coriolanus*, and by oppressing him with a Sophistical Argument, that he aim'd at Sovereignty, because he had not delivered into the Publick Treasury the Spoils which he had taken from the *Antiates*. As if a Design of Sovereignty could be reasonably concluded from any one Act; or any one could think of bringing to pass such a Design, by eternally favouring the Patricians, and disobliging the Populace. For we need make no doubt, but that it was among the young Patricians that *Coriolanus* distributed the Spoils which were taken from the *Antiates*; whereas nothing but caressing the Populace could enslave the *Roman* People, as Cæsar afterwards very well saw and experienc'd. So that this Injustice of the Tribunes was the original Cause of the Calamity which afterwards befel their Country, by the Invasion of the *Volscians*, under the Conduct of *Coriolanus*. And yet these Tribunes at the end of the Play, like *Aufidius*, remain unpunish'd. But indeed *Shakespear* has been wanting in the exact Distribution of Poetical Justice not only in his *Coriolanus*, but in most of his best Tragedies, in which the Guilty and the Innocent perish promiscuously; as *Duncan* and *Banquo* in *Mackbeth*, as likewise Lady *Macduffe* and her Children; *Desdemona* in *Othello*; *Cordelia*, *Kent*, and King *Lear*, in the Tragedy that bears his Name; *Brutus* and *Porcia* in *Julius Cæsar*, and young *Hamlet* in the Tragedy of *Hamlet*. For tho' it may be said in Defence of the last, that *Hamlet* had a Design to kill his Uncle who then reign'd; yet this is justify'd by no less than a Call from Heaven, and raising up one from the Dead to urge him to it. The Good and the Bad then perishing promiscuously in the best of *Shakespear*'s Tragedies, there can be either none or very weak Instruction in them: For such promiscuous Events call the Government of Providence into Question, and by Scepticks and Libertines are resolv'd into Chance. I humbly conceive therefore that this want of Dramatical Justice in the Tragedy of *Coriolanus*, gave occasion for a just Alteration, and that I was oblig'd to sacrifice to that Justice *Aufidius* and the Tribunes, as well as *Coriolanus*.

Thus have we endeavour'd to shew, that for want of the Poetical Art, *Shakespeare* lay under very great Disadvantages. At the same time we must own to his Honour, that he has often perform'd Wonders without it, in spight of the Judgment of so great a Man as *Horace*.

> Naturâ fieret laudabile carmen, an arte,
> Quæsitum est: ego nec studium sinè divite venâ,
> Nec rude quid prosit video ingenium; alterius sic
> Altera poscit opem res, & conjurat amicé.

But from this very Judgment of *Horace* we may justly conclude, that *Shakespear* would have wonderfully surpass'd himself, if Art had been join'd to Nature. There never was a greater Genius in the World than *Virgil*: He was one who seems to have been born for this glorious End, that the *Roman* Muse might exert in him the utmost Force of her Poetry: And his admirable and divine Beauties are manifestly owing to the happy Confederacy of Art and Nature. It was Art that contriv'd that incomparable Design of the *Æneis*, and it was nature that executed it. Could the greatest Genius that ever was infus'd into Earthly Mold by Heaven, if it had been unguided and unassisted by Art, have taught him to make that noble and wonderful Use of the *Pythagorean* Transmigration, which he makes in the Sixth Book of his Poem? Had *Virgil* been a circular Poet, and closely adher'd to History, how could the *Romans* have been transported with that inimitable Episode of *Dido*, which brought a-fresh into their Minds the *Carthaginian* War, and the dreadful *Hannibal*? When 'tis evident that that admirable Episode is so little owing to a faithful observance of History, and the exact order of Time, that 'tis deriv'd from a very bold but judicious Violation of these; it being undeniable that *Dido* liv'd almost 300 Years after *Æneas*. Yet is it that charming Episode that makes the chief Beauties of a third Part of the Poem. For the Destruction of *Troy* it self, which is so divinely related, is still more admirable by the Effect it produces, which is the Passion of *Dido*.

I should now proceed to shew under what Disadvantages *Shakespear* lay for want of being conversant with the Ancients. But I have already writ a long Letter, and am desirous to know how you relish what has been already said before I go any farther: For I am unwilling to take more Pains before I am sure of giving you some Pleasure. I am,

SIR,
> *Your most humble, faithful Servant.*

### Letter II

SIR,

Upon the Encouragement I have receiv'd from you, I shall proceed to shew under what Disadvantages *Shakespear* lay for want of being conversant with the Ancients. But because I have lately been in some Conversation, where they would not allow, but that he was acquainted with the Ancients, I shall endeavour to make it appear that he was not; and the shewing that in the Method in which I pretend to convince the Reader of it, will sufficiently prove, what Inconveniencies he lay under, and what Errors he committed for want of being conversant with them. But here we must distinguish between the several kinds of Acquaintance: A Man may be said to be acquainted with another who never was but twice in his Company; but that is at the best a superficial Acquaintance, from which neither very great Pleasure nor Profit can be deriv'd. Our Business is here to shew, that *Shakespear* had no familiar Acquaintance with the *Græcian* and *Roman* Authors. For if he was familiarly conversant with them, how comes it to pass that he wants Art? Is it that he studied to know them in other things; and neglected that only in them, which chiefly tends to the Advancement of the Art of the Stage? Or is it that he wanted Discernment to see the Justness, and the Greatness, and the Harmony of their Designs, and the Reasonableness of those Rules upon which those Designs are founded? Or how come his Successors to have that Discernment which he wanted, when they fall so much below him in other things? How comes he to have been guilty of the grossest Faults in Chronology, and how come we to find out those Faults? In his Tragedy of *Troylus* and *Cressida*, he introduces *Hector* speaking of *Aristotle*, who was born a thousand Years after the Death of *Hector*. In the same Play mention is made of *Milo*, which is another very great Fault in Chronology. *Alexander* is mention'd in *Coriolanus*, tho' that Conqueror of the Orient liv'd above two hundred Years after him. In this last Tragedy he has mistaken the very Names of his Dramatick Persons, if we give Credit to *Livy*. For the Mother of *Coriolanus* in the *Roman* Historian is *Vetturia*, and the Wife is *Volumnia*. Whereas in *Shakespear* the Wife is *Virgilia*, and the Mother *Volumnia*. And the *Volscian* General in *Shakespear* is *Tullus Aufidius*, and *Tullus Attius* in *Livy*. How comes it that he takes *Plutarch's* Word, who was by Birth a *Græcian*, for the Affairs of *Rome*, rather than that of the *Roman* Historian, if so be that he had read the latter? Or what Reason can be given for his not reading him, when he wrote upon a *Roman* Story, but that in *Shakespear's* time there was a Translation of *Plutarch*, and there was none of *Livy*? If *Shakespear* was familiarly conversant with the *Roman* Authors, how came he to introduce a Rabble into *Coriolanus*, in which he offended not only against the Dignity of Tragedy, but the Truth of Fact, the Authority of all the *Roman* Writers, the Customs of Ancient *Rome*, and the Majesty of the *Roman* People? By introducing a Rabble into *Julius Cæsar*, he only offended against the Dignity of Tragedy. For that part of the People who ran about the Streets upon great Festivals, or publick Calamities, or publick Rejoicings, or Revolutions in Government, are certainly the Scum of the Populace. But the Persons who in the Time of *Coriolanus*, rose in Vindication of their just Rights, and extorted from the Patricians the Institution of the Tribunes of the People, and the Persons by whom afterwards *Coriolanus* was tried, were the whole Body of the *Roman* People to the Reserve of the Patricians, which Body included the *Roman* Knights, and the wealthy substantial Citizens, who were as different from the Rabble as the Patricians themselves, as qualify'd as the latter to form a right Judgment of Things, and to contemn the vain Opinions of the Rabble. So at least *Horace* esteems them, who very well knew his Countrymen.

> Offenduntur enim, quibus est equus, aut pater, aut
> res,
> Nec si quid fricti ciceris probat aut nucis emptor,
> Æquis accipiunt animis donantve Corona?

Where we see the Knights and the substantial Citizens are rank'd in an equal Degree of Capacity with the *Roman* Senators, and are equally distinguish'd from the Rabble.

If *Shakespear* was so conversant with the Ancients, how comes he to have introduc'd some Characters into his Plays, so unlike what they are to be found in History? In the Character of *Menenius* in the following Tragedy, he has doubly offended against that Historical Resemblance. For first whereas *Menenius* was an eloquent Person, *Shakespear* has made him a downright Buffoon. And how is it possible for any Man to conceive a *Ciceronian Jack-Pudding*? Never was any Buffoon eloquent, or wise, or witty, or virtuous. All the good and ill Qualities of a Buffoon are summ'd up in one Word, and that is a Buffoon. And secondly, whereas *Shakespear* has made him a Hater and Contemner and Villifier of the People, we are assur'd by the *Roman* Historian that *Menenius* was extremely popular. He was so very far from opposing the Institution of the

Tribunes, as he is represented in *Shakespear*, that he was chiefly instrumental in it. After the People had deserted the City, and sat down upon the sacred Mountain, he was the chief of the Delegates whom the Senate deputed to them, as being look'd upon to be the Person who would be most agreeable to them. In short, this very *Menenius* both liv'd and dy'd so very much their Favourite, that dying poor he had pompous Funerals at the Expence of the *Roman* People.

Had *Shakespear* read either *Sallust* or *Cicero*, how could he have made so very little of the first and greatest of Men, as that *Cæsar* should be but a Fourth-rate Actor in his own Tragedy? How could it have been that seeing *Cæsar*, we should ask for *Cæsar*? That we should ask, where is his unequall'd Greatness of Mind, his unbounded Thirst of Glory, and that victorious Eloquence, with which he triumph'd over the Souls of both Friends, and Enemies, and with which he rivall'd *Cicero* in Genius as he did *Pompey* in Power? How fair an Occasion was there to open the Character of *Cæsar* in the first Scene between *Brutus* and *Cassius*? For when *Cassius* tells *Brutus* that *Cæsar* was but a Man like them, and had the same natural Imperfections which they had, how natural had it been for *Brutus* to reply, that *Cæsar* indeed had their Imperfections of Nature, but neither he nor *Cassius* had by any means the great Qualities of *Cæsar*: neither his Military Virtue, nor Science, nor his matchless Renown, nor his unparallell'd Victories, his unwearied Bounty to his Friends, nor his Godlike Clemency to his Foes, his Beneficence, his Munificence, his Easiness of Access to the meanest *Roman*, his indefatigable Labours, his incredible Celerity, the Plausibleness if not Justness of his Ambition, that knowing himself to be the greatest of Men, he only sought occasion to make the World confess him such. In short, if *Brutus*, after enumerating all the wonderful Qualities of *Cæsar*, had resolv'd in spight of them all to sacrifice him to publick Liberty, how had such a Proceeding heighten'd the Virtue and the Character of *Brutus*? But then indeed it would have been requisite that *Cæsar* upon his Appearance should have made all this good. And as we know no Principle of human Action but human, Sentiment only, *Cæsar* who did greater Things, and had greater Designs than the rest of the *Romans*, ought certainly to have outshin'd by many Degrees all the other Characters of his Tragedy. *Cæsar* ought particularly to have justified his Actions, and to have heighten'd his Character, by shewing that what he had done, he had done by Necessity; that the *Romans* had lost their *Agrarian*, lost their Rotation of Magistracy, and that consequently nothing but an empty Shadow of publick Liberty remain'd. That the *Gracchi* had made the last noble but unsuccessful Efforts, for the restoring the Commonwealth, that they had fail'd for want of arbitrary irresistible Power, the Restoration of the *Agrarian* requiring too vast a Retrospect to be done without it; that the Government, when *Cæsar* came to publick Affairs, was got into the Hands of a few, and that those few were factious, and were contending among themselves, and if you will pardon so mean an Expression, scrambling as it were for Power: That *Cæsar* was reduc'd to the Necessity of ruling, or himself obeying a Master; and that apprehending that another would exercise the supreme Command, without that Clemency and Moderation which he did, he had rather chosen to rule than to obey. So that *Cæsar* was faulty not so much in seizing upon the Sovereignty, which was become in a manner necessary, as in not re-establishing the Commonwealth, by restoring the *Agrarian* and the Rotation of Magistracies, after he had got absolute and uncontroulable Power. And if *Cæsar* had seiz'd upon the Sovereignty only with a View of re-establishing Liberty, he had surpass'd all Mortals in

Godlike Goodness as much as he did in the rest of his astonishing Qualities. I must confess, I do not remember that we have any Authority from the *Roman* Historians which may induce us to believe, that *Cæsar* had any such Design. Nor if he had had any such View, could he, who was the most secret, the most prudent, and the most discerning of Men, have discover'd it, before his *Parthian* Expedition was over, for fear of utterly disobliging his Veterans. And *Cæsar* believ'd that Expedition necessary for the Honour and Interest of the State, and for his own Glory. . . .

I am apt to believe that if *Shakespear* had been acquainted with all this, we had had from him quite another Character of *Cæsar* than that which we now find in him. He might then have given us a Scene something like that which *Corneille* has so happily us'd in his *Cinna*; something like that which really happen'd between *Augustus*, *Mecænas* and *Agrippa*. He might then have introduc'd *Cæsar*, consulting *Cicero* on the one side, and on the other *Anthony*, whether he should retain that absolute Sovereignty, which he had acquir'd by his Victory, or whether he should re-establish and immortalize Liberty. That would have been a Scene, which might have employ'd the finest Art and the utmost force of a Writer. That had been a Scene in which all the great Qualities of *Cæsar* might have been display'd. I will not pretend to determine here how that Scene might have been turn'd; and what I have already said on this Subject, has been spoke with the utmost Caution and Diffidence. But this I will venture to say, that if that Scene had been manag'd so, as, by the powerful Motives employ'd in it, to have shaken the Soul of *Cæsar*, and to have left room for the least Hope, for the least Doubt, that *Cæsar* would have re-establish'd Liberty, after his *Parthian* Expedition; and if this Conversation had been kept secret till the Death of *Cæsar*, and then had been discover'd by *Anthony*, then had *Cæsar* fall'n, so belov'd and lamented by the *Roman* People, so pitied and so bewail'd even by the Conspirators themselves, as never Man fell. Then there would have been a Catastrophe the most dreadful and the most deplorable that ever was beheld upon the Tragick Stage. Then had we seen the noblest of the Conspirators cursing their temerarious Act, and the most apprehensive of them, in dreadful expectation of those horrible Calamities, which fell upon the *Romans* after the Death of *Cæsar*. But, Sir, when I write this to you, I write it with the utmost Deference to the extraordinary Judgment of that great Man, who some Years ago, I hear, alter'd the *Julius Cæsar*. And I make no doubt but that his fine Discernment, and the rest of his great Qualities have amply supply'd the Defects which are found in the Character of *Shakespear*'s *Cæsar*.

I should here answer an Argument, by which some People pretend to prove, and especially those with whom I lately convers'd, that *Shakespear* was conversant with the Ancients. But besides that the Post is about to be gone, I am heartily tir'd with what I have already writ, and so doubtless are you; I shall therefore defer the rest to the next opportunity, and remain

Your, &c.

## Letter III

SIR,

I come now to the main Argument, which some People urge to prove that *Shakespear* was conversant with the Ancients. For there is, say they, among *Shakespear*'s Plays, one call'd *The Comedy of Errors*, which is undeniably an Imitation of the *Menechmi* of *Plautus*. Now *Shakespear*, say they, being conversant with *Plautus*, it undeniably follows that he was acquainted with the Ancients; because no *Roman* Author could be hard to him who had conquer'd *Plautus*. To which I answer, that the Errors which we have mention'd above are to

be accounted for no other way, but by the want of knowing the Ancients, or by downright want of Capacity. But nothing can be more absurd or more unjust than to impute it to want of Capacity. For the very Sentiments of *Shakespear* alone are sufficient to shew, that he had a great Understanding: And therefore we must account some other way for his Imitation of the *Menechmi*. I remember to have seen among the Translations of *Ovid*'s Epistles printed by Mr. *Tonson*, an Imitation of that from *Œnone* to *Paris*, which Mr. *Dryden* tells us in his Preface to those Epistles was imitated by one of the Fair Sex who understood no *Latin*, but that she had done enough to make those blush who understood it the best. There are at this day several Translators, who, as *Hudibrass* has it,

Translate from Languages of which
They understand no part of Speech.

I will not affirm that of *Shakespear*; I believe he was able to do what Pedants call construe, but that he was able to read *Plautus* without Pain and Difficulty I can never believe. Now I appeal to you, Sir, what time he had between his Writing and his Acting, to read any thing that could not be read with Ease and Pleasure. We see that our Adversaries themselves acknowledge, that if *Shakespear* was able to read *Plautus* with Ease, nothing in Latinity could be hard to him. How comes it to pass then, that he has given us no Proofs of his familiar Acquaintance with the Ancients, but this Imitation of the *Menechmi*, and a Version of two Epistles of *Ovid*? How come it that he had never read *Horace*, of a superiour Merit to either, and particularly his Epistle to the *Piso*'s, which so much concern'd his Art? Or if he had read that Epistle, how comes it that in his *Troylus* and *Cressida* [we must observe by the way, that when *Shakespear* wrote that Play, *Ben Johnson* had not as yet translated that Epistle] he runs counter to the Instructions which *Horace* has given for the forming the Character of *Achilles*?

Scriptor: Honoratum si forte reponis Achillem,
Impiger, Iracundus, Inexorablis, Acer,
Jura neget sibi nata.

Where is the *Impiger*, the *Iracundus*, or the *Acer*, in the Character of *Shakepear*'s *Achilles*? who is nothing but a drolling, lazy, conceited, overlooking Coxcomb; so far from being the honour'd *Achilles*, the Epithet that *Homer*, and *Horace* after him give him, that he is deservedly the Scorn and the Jest of the rest of the Characters, even to that Buffoon *Thersites*.

Tho' *Shakespear* succeeded very well in Comedy, yet his principal Talent and his chief Delight was Tragedy. If then *Shakespear* was qualify'd to read *Plautus* with Ease, he could read with a great deal more Ease the Translations of *Sophocles* and *Euripides*. And tho' by these Translations he would not have been able to have seen the charming colouring of those great Masters, yet would he have seen all the Harmony and the Beauty of their great and their just Designs. He would have seen enough to have stirr'd up a noble Emulation in so exalted a Soul as his. How comes it then that we hear nothing from him, of the *Œdipus*, the *Electra*, the *Antigone* of *Sophocles*, of the *Iphigenia*'s, the *Orestes*, the *Medea*, the *Hecuba* of *Euripides*? How comes it that we see nothing in the Conduct of his Pieces, that shews us that he had the least Acquaintance with any of these great Master-pieces? Did *Shakespear* appear to be so nearly touch'd with the Affliction of *Hecuba* for the Death of *Priam*, which was but daub'd and bungled by one of his Countrymen, that he could not forebear introducing it as it were by Violence into his own *Hamlet*, and would he make no Imitation, no Commendation, not the least Mention of the unparallell'd and inimitable Grief of the *Hecuba* of *Euripides*? How comes it, that we find no Imitation of any ancient Play in Him but the *Menechmi* of *Plautus*? How came he to chuse a

Comick preferably to the Tragick Poets? Or how comes he to chuse *Plautus* preferably to *Terence*, who is so much more just, more graceful, more regular, and more natural? Or how comes he to chuse the *Menechmi* of *Plautus*, which is by no means his Master-piece, before all his other Comedies? I vehemently suspect that this Imitation of the *Menechmi*, was either from a printed Translation of that Comedy which is lost, or some Version in Manuscript brought him by a Friend, or sent him perhaps by a Stranger, or from the original Play it self recommended to him, and read to him by some learned Friend. In short, I had rather account for this, by what is not absurd than by what is, or by a less Absurdity than by a greater. For nothing can be more wrong than to conclude from this that *Shakespear* was conversant with the Ancients; which contradicts the Testimony of his Contemporary, and his familiar Acquaintance *Ben Johnson*, and of his Successor *Milton*;

Lo *Shakespear*, Fancy's sweetest Child,
Warbles his native Wood-notes wild.

and of Mr. *Dryden* after them both; and which destroys the most glorious Part of *Shakespear*'s Merit immediately. For how can he be esteem'd equal by Nature, or superior to the Ancients, when he falls so far short of them in Art, tho' he had the Advantage of knowing all that they did before him? Nay it debases him below those of common Capacity, by reason of the Errors which we mention'd above. Therefore he who allows that *Shakespear* had Learning and a familiar Acquaintance with the Ancients, ought to be look'd upon as a Detractor from his extraordinary Merit, and from the Glory of *Great Britain*. For whether is it more honourable for this Island to have produc'd a Man, who without having any Acquaintance with the Ancients, or any but a slender and a superficial one, appears to be their Equal or their Superiour by the Force of Genius and Nature, or to have bred one who knowing the Ancients, falls infinitely short of them in Art, and consequently in Nature it self? *Great Britain* has but little Reason to boast of its Natives Education, since the same that they had here, they might have had in another place. But it may justly claim a very great share in their Nature and Genius; since these depend in a great measure on the Climate; and therefore *Horace* in the Instruction which he gives for the forming the Characters, advises the noble *Romans* for whose Instruction he chiefly writes to consider whether the Dramatick Person whom they introduce is

Colchus an Assyrius, Thebis nutritus an Argis?

Thus, Sir, I have endeavour'd to shew under what great Disadvantages *Shakespear* lay, for want of the Poetical Art, and for want of being conversant with the Ancients.

But besides this, he lay under other very great Inconveniencies. For he was neither Master of Time enough to consider, correct, and polish what he wrote, to alter it, to add to it, and to retrench from it, nor had he Friends to consult upon whose Capacity and Integrity he could depend. And tho' a Person of very good Judgment, may succeed very well without consulting his Friends, if he takes time enough to correct what he writes; yet even the greatest Man that Nature and Art can conspire to accomplish, can never attain to Perfection, without either employing a great deal of time, or taking the Advice of judicious Friends. Nay, 'tis the Opinion of *Horace*, that he ought to do both.

Si quid tamen olim
Scripseris, in Metii descendat Judicis aures,
Et Patris, & nostras; nonumque prematur in
Annum.

Now we know very well that *Shakespear* was an Actor, at a time when there were seven or eight Companies of Players in the Town together, who each of them did their utmost Endeavours to get the Audiences from the rest, and consequently that our Author was perpetually call'd upon, by those who had the Direction and Management of the Company to which he belong'd, for new Pieces which might be able to support them, and give them some Advantage over the rest. And 'tis easie to judge what Time he was Master of, between his laborious Employment of Acting, and his continual Hurry of Writing. As for Friends, they whom in all likelihood *Shakespear* consulted most, were two or three of his Fellow-Actors, because they had the Care of publishing his Works committed to them. Now they, as we are told by *Ben Johnson* in his *Discoveries*, were extremely pleas'd with their Friend for scarce ever making a Blot; and were very angry with *Ben*, for saying he wish'd that he had made a thousand. The Misfortune of it is, that *Horace* was perfectly of *Ben*'s mind.

Vos O,
Pompilius sanguis, carmen reprehendite, quod mon
Multa dies, & multa litura coercuit, atque
Praesectum decies non castigavit ad unguem.

And so was my Lord *Roscommon*.

Poets lose half the Praise they should have got,
Could it be known what they discreetly blot.

These Friends then of *Shakespear* were not qualify'd to advise him. As for *Ben Johnson*, besides that *Shakespear* began to know him late, and that *Ben* was not the most communicative Person in the World of the Secrets of his Art; he seems to me to have had no right Notion of Tragedy. Nay, so far from it, that he who was indeed a very great Man, and who has writ Comedies, by which he has born away the Prize of Comedy both from Ancients and Moderns, and been an Honour to *Great Britian*; and who has done this without any Rules to guide him, except what his own incomparable Talent dictated to him; This extraordinary Man has err'd so grossly in Tragedy, of which there were not only stated Rules, but Rules which he himself had often read, and had even translated, that he has chosen two Subjects, which, according to those very Rules, were utterly incapable of exciting either Compassion or Terror for the principal Characters, which yet are the chief Passions that a Tragick Poet ought to endeavour to excite. So that *Shakespear* having neither had Time to correct, nor Friends to consult, must necessarily have frequently left such faults in his Writings, for the Correction of which either a great deal of Time or a judicious and a well-natur'd Friend is indispensably necessary.

Vir bonus & prudens versus reprehendet inertes,
Culpabit duros, incomptis allinet Atrum
Transverso calamo signum, ambitiosa recidet,
Ornamenta, parum claris lucem dare coget,
Arguet ambigue dictum, mutanda notabit.

There is more than one Example of every kind of these Faults in the Tragedies of *Shakespear*, and even in the *Coriolanus*. There are Lines that are utterly void of that celestial Fire, of which *Shakespear* is sometimes Master in so great a Degree. And consequently there are Lines that are stiff and forc'd, and harsh and unmusical, tho' *Shakespear* had naturally an admirable Ear for the Numbers. But no Man ever was very musical who did not write with Fire, and no Man can always write with Fire, unless he is so far Master of his Time, as to expect those Hours when his Spirits are warm and volatile. *Shakespear* must therefore sometimes have Lines which are neither strong nor graceful: For who ever had Force or Grace that had not Spirit? There are in his *Coriolanus*, among a great many natural and admirable Beauties, three or four of those Ornaments which *Horace* would term ambitious; and which we in *English* are apt to call Fustian or Bombast. There are

Lines in some Places which are very obscure, and whole Scenes which ought to be alter'd.

I have, Sir, employ'd some Time and Pains, and that little Judgment which I have acquir'd in these Matters by a long and a faithful reading both of Ancients and Moderns, in adding, retrenching and altering several Things in the *Coriolanus* of *Shakespear*, but with what Success I must leave to be determin'd by you. I know very well that you will be surpriz'd to find, that after all that I have said in the former Part of this Letter, against *Shakespear's* introducing the Rabble into *Coriolanus*, I have not only retain'd in the second Act of the following Tragedy that Rabble which is in the Original, but deviated more from the *Roman* Customs than *Shakespear* had done before me. I desire you to look upon it as a voluntary Fault and a Trespass against Conviction: 'Tis one of those Things which are *ad Populum Phaleræ*, and by no means inserted to please such Men as you.

Thus, Sir, have I laid before you a short but impartial Account of the Beauties and Defects of *Shakespear*, with an Intention to make these Letters publick if they are approv'd by you; to teach some People to distinguish between his Beauties and his Defects, that while they imitate the one, they may with Caution avoid the other [there being nothing of more dangerous Contagion to Writers, and especially to young ones, than the Faults of great Masters] and while with *Milton* they applaud the great Qualities which *Shakespear* had by Nature, they may follow his wise Example, and form themselves as he assures us that he himself did, upon the Rules and Writings of the Ancients.

Sir, if so candid and able a Judge as your self shall happen to approve of this Essay in the main, and to excuse and correct my Errors, that Indulgence and that Correction will not only encourage me to make these Letters publick, but will enable me to bear the Reproach of those, who would fix a Brand, even upon the justest Criticism, as the Effect of Envy and Ill-nature; as if there could possibly be any Ill-nature in the doing Justice, or in the endeavouring to advance a very noble and a very useful Art, and consequently to prove beneficent to Mankind. As for those who may accuse me of the want of a due Veneration for the Merit of an Author of so establish'd a Reputation as *Shakespear*, I shall beg leave to tell them, that they chuse the wrongest time that they could possibly take for such an Accusation as that. For I appeal to you, Sir, who shews most Veneration for the Memory of *Shakespear*, he who loves and admires his Charms and makes them one of his chief Delights, who sees him and reads him over and over and still remains unsatiated, and who mentions his Faults for no other Reason but to make his Excellency the more conspicuous, or he who pretending to be his blind Admirer, shews in Effect the utmost Contempt for him, preferring empty effeminate Sound to his solid Beauties and manly Graces, and deserting him every Night for an execrable *Italian* Ballad, so vile that a Boy who should write such lamentable Dogrel, would be turn'd out of *Westminster*-School for a desperate Blockhead, too stupid to be corrected and amended by the harshest Discipline of the Place.

> I am,
> SIR,
> Yours, &c.

LEWIS THEOBALD
From "Preface"
*The Works of Shakespeare*
1734, Volume 1, pp. xxvii–xxxiii

It has been allow'd on all hands, how far our Author was indebted to *Nature*; it is not so well agreed, how much he ow'd to *Languages* and acquir'd *Learning*. The Decisions on this Subject were certainly set on Foot by the Hint from *Ben Jonson*, that he had small *Latin* and less *Greek*: And from this Tradition, as it were, Mr. *Rowe* has thought fit peremptorily to declare, that, "It is without Controversy, he had no Knowledge of the Writings of the ancient Poets, for that in his Works we find no Traces of any thing which looks like an Imitation of the Ancients. For the Delicacy of his Taste (*continues He*,) and the natural Bent of his own great Genius (equal, if not superior, to some of the Best of theirs;) would certainly have led him to read and study them with so much Pleasure, that some of their fine Images would naturally have insinuated themselves into, and been mix'd with, his own Writings; so that his not copying, at least, something from them, may be an Argument of his never having read them." I shall leave it to the Determination of my Learned Readers, from the numerous Passages, which I have occasionally quoted in my Notes, in which our Poet seems closely to have imitated the Classics, whether Mr. *Rowe's* Assertion be so absolutely to be depended on. The Result of the Controversy must certainly, either way, terminate to our Author's Honour: how happily he could imitate them, if that Point be allow'd; or how gloriously he could think like them, without owing any thing to Imitation.

Tho' I should be very unwilling to allow *Shakespeare* so poor a Scholar, as Many have labour'd to represent him, yet I shall be very cautious of declaring too positively on the other side of the Question: that is, with regard to my Opinion of his Knowledge in the dead Languages. And therefore the Passages, that I occasionally quote from the *Classics*, shall not be urged as Proofs that he knowingly imitated those Originals; but brought to shew how happily he has express'd himself upon the same Topicks. A very learned Critick of our own nation has declar'd, that a Sameness of Thought and Sameness of Expression too, in Two Writers of a different Age, can hardly happen, without a violent Suspicion of the Latter copying from his Predecessor. I shall not therefore run any great Risque of a Censure, tho' I should venture to hint, that the Resemblance, in Thought and Expression, of our Author and an Antient (which we should allow to be Imitation in One, whose Learning was not question'd) may sometimes take its Rise from Strength of Memory, and those Impressions which he ow'd to the School. And if we may allow a Possibility of This, considering that, when he quitted the School, he gave into his Father's Profession and way of Living, and had, 'tis likely, but a slender Library of Classical Learning; and considering what a Number of Translations, Romances, and Legends, started about his Time, and a little before; (most of which, 'tis very evident, he read;) I think, it may easily be reconcil'd, why he rather schemed his *Plots* and *Characters* from these more latter Informations, than went back to those Fountains, for which he might entertain a sincere Veneration, but to which he could not have so ready a Recourse.

In touching on another Part of his Learning, as it related to the Knowledge of *History* and *Books*, I shall advance something, that, at first sight, will very much wear the Appearance of a Paradox. For I shall find it no hard Matter to prove, that from the grossest Blunders in History, we are not to infer his real Ignorance of it: Nor from a greater Use of *Latin*

Words, than ever any other *English* Author used, must we infer his Knowledge of that Language.

A Reader of Taste may easily observe, that tho' *Shakespeare*, almost in every Scene of his historical Plays, commits the grossest Offences against Chronology, History, and Antient Politicks; yet This was not thro' Ignorance, as is generally supposed, but thro' the two powerful Blaze of his Imagination; which, when once raised, made all acquired Knowledge vanish and disappear before it. For Instance, in his *Timon*, he turns *Athens*, which was a perfect Democrasy, into an Aristocrasy; while he ridiculously gives a Senator the Power of banishing *Alcibiades*. On the contrary, in *Coriolanus*, he makes *Rome*, which at that time was a perfect Aristocrasy, a Democrasy full as ridiculously, by making the People choose *Coriolanus* Consul: Whereas, in Fact, it was not till the Time of *Manlius Torquatus*, that the People had a Right of choosing one Consul. But this Licence in him, as I have said, must not be imputed to Ignorance: since as often we may find him, when Occasion serves, reasoning up to the Truth of History; and throwing out Sentiments as justly adapted to the Circumstances of his Subject, as to the Dignity of his Characters, or Dictates of Nature in general.

Then, to come to his Knowledge of the *Latin* Tongue, 'tis certain, there is a surprising Effusion of *Latin* Words made *English*, far more than in any one *English* Author I have seen; but we must be cautious to imagine, this was of his own doing. For the *English* Tongue, in his Age, began extremely to suffer by an Inundation of *Latin*; and to be overlaid, as it were, by its Nurse, when it had just began to speak by her before-prudent Care and Assistance. And this, to be sure, was occasion'd by the Pedantry of those two Monarchs, *Elizabeth* and *James*, Both great *Latinists*. For it is not to be wonder'd at, if both the Court and Schools, equal Flatterers of Power, should adapt themselves to the Royal Taste. This, then, was the Condition of the *English* Tongue when *Shakespeare* took it up: like a Beggar in a rich Wardrobe. He found the pure native *English* too cold and poor to second the Heat and Abundance of his Imagination: and therefore was forc'd to dress it up in the Robes, he saw provided for it: rich in themselves, but ill-shaped; cut out to an air of Magnificence, but disproportion'd and cumbersome. To the Costliness of Ornament, he added all the Graces and Decorum of it. It may be said, this did not require, or discover a Knowledge of the *Latin*. To the first, I think, it did not; to the second, it is so far from discovering it, that, I think, it discovers the contrary. To make This more obvious by a modern Instance: The great MILTON likewise labour'd under the like Inconvenience; when he first set upon adorning his own Tongue, he likewise animated and enrich'd it with the *Latin*, but from his own Stock: and so, rather by bringing in the Phrases, than the Words: And This was natural; and will, I believe, always be the Case in the same Circumstances. His Language, especially his Prose, is full of *Latin* Words indeed, but much fuller of *Latin* Phrases: and his Mastery in the Tongue made this unavoidable. On the contrary, *Shakespeare*, who, perhaps, was not so intimately vers'd in the *Language*, abounds in the Words of it, but has few or none of its Phrases: Nor, indeed, if what I affirm be true, could He. This I take to be the truest *Criterion* to determine this long agitated Question.

It may be mention'd, tho' no certain Conclusion can be drawn from it, as a probable Argument of his having read the Antients; that He perpetually expresses the Genius of *Homer*, and other great Poets of the Old World, in animating all the Parts of his Descriptions; and, by bold and breathing Metaphors and Images, giving the Properties of Life and Action to inanimate Things. He is a Copy too of those *Greek* Masters in the infinite use of *compound* and *de-compound Epithets*. I will not, indeed, aver, but that One with *Shakespeare's* exquisite Genius and Observation might have traced these glaring Characteristics of Antiquity by reading *Homer* in *Chapman's* Version.

## PETER WHALLEY

### From *An Enquiry into the Learning of Shakespeare*
### 1748, pp. 12–84

The Glory of the *English* Drama, ⟨said⟩ *Eugenius*, appears to have been carried to its last Perfection by ⟨a⟩ *Triumvirate* of Bards. You will pardon me, I hope, the Use of this Metaphor, as I consider *Beaumont* and *Fletcher* but as one Writer. What have we that exceeds their easy and graceful Manner, and Sprightliness of Dialogue? Or does any thing surpass the Humour, Correctness, and Regularity of *Johnson*? What can we conceive more astonishing than the Genius and Imagination of *Shakespeare*? Or can we find him wanting in a single Article which is necessary to compleat the Character of a Dramatic Poet? You seem, *Eugenius*, interrupted *Neander*, to forget the Charge which hath been long brought against him, and your Affection for his Memory will not give you Leave to consider his Deficiency in a Point which is esteemed very material, and accounted a Qualification essentially belonging to a Dramatick Writer: I mean that Want of Reading which he constantly betrays, and a total Ignorance of the learned Languages. This, perhaps, returned *Eugenius*, might possibly proceed from his Concealment of that Excellence, rather than from any real Want of it. Yet I know it hath been misinterpreted into a Crime, and hath been constantly opposed to that Luxuriance of fancy so evident in the Works of *Shakespeare*; and to that extensive Command of Nature, whom he alone, of all Mankind, seems to have had entirely in his own Power. The common Accusation hath been, as you say, that he wanted Learning: Confining, I presume, the Meaning of that Word to an Acquaintance and Intimacy with the dead Languages; yet this is in Effect but a greater Commendation. *Johnson*, however, it must be owned, did not think so; not being so naturally learned, he was willing to derive the greatest Honour from his acquired Riches, and the Spoils which he had obtained from the *Greek* and *Latin* Authors: And this was good Policy in him, who, if he wanted not Imagination, was never yet reckoned to have much to spare. He placed his chief Perfection in this Article, the Fashion of the Times concurring to approve it; and what by this Means he detracted from the Sum of *Shakespeare's* Merit, was added to increase his own: For by industriously supporting this Opinion, he intended to secure the Palm to himself. I am rather, interposed *Neander*, inclined to believe, that the Partizans of the two Poets began the Opposition: For considering the honourable Testimony which *Johnson* hath left of his *beloved Shakespeare*, and the Favours he had received from him, I can hardly believe he would be guilty of that Ingratitude to diminish the Reputation of his Benefactor. However the Competition began, it certainly divided the Critics of that Age; and I think that *Johnson* himself hints at it in this Passage from one of his own Plays; "She may censure Poets, and Authors, and Stiles, and compare 'em, *Daniel* with *Spenser*, *Johnson* with the other Youth, and so forth."[1] But I have often wondered why *Beaumont* and *Fletcher* were never made Parties in this Dispute: For we may perceive as little an Appearance of Familiarity with the Classics in their Plays, as in those of *Shakespeare*.[2] As they were Gentlemen of good Families, their Learning perhaps was presumed to be inherent in the Blood, or to descend to them by Inheritance. So obliging a Presumption, interrupted *Eugenius*, smiling, would be of infinite Service to many younger Brothers of this Age, who are frequently complimented by the Courtesy of *England*, with some other Qualities, to which they have as slender a Right. And yet you cannot, but have observed, that in every Contest of this kind, our Author never wanted Advocates to maintain his Cause. Mr. *Hales* asserted in his Favour, that there was no Subject which any antient Poet had ever treated, but he would engage to shew it as well wrote by *Shakespeare*.

If you were at Leisure, I could point out some parallel Passages tending to confirm this Assertion: and I would make a previous Enquiry into the several Sources from which the Poet drew Materials to adorn his Plays. But such a Disquisition, continued *Eugenius*, would, I fear, demand more time than you can probably allow me; for undoubtedly you have many Compliments and Services from the Country to deliver, which the Ceremony of the Town must be obliged with at your first Arrival. What little Matters of that Kind, replied *Neander*, I have to do, are dispatching by a Servant; and I have *dealt* out my *Cards*, I hope, with so much Art, as to secure me your Company, if disengaged for the rest of the Day. I have no particular Appointment, returned *Eugenius*, to call me out, and, with your Leave, we may employ the rest of the Morning in our present Conversation. *Neander* acknowledging his Inclination, *Eugenius* proceeded in the following Manner.

*Shakespeare* has been deservedly esteemed the *Homer*, the Father of our Dramatic Poetry, as being the most irresistible Master of the Passions; possessed of the same creative Power of Imagination; abounding with a vast Assemblage of Ideas, and a rich Redundancy of Genius and Invention. And I think, added *Neander*, that he may be considered to deserve that Title in another Light, as having, like him, furnished many Poets and Tragedians of succeeding Times with the noblest Images and Thoughts.

> Cujusque ex ore profusos
> Omnis posteritas latices in Carmina duxit,
> Amnemque in tenues ausa est deducere rivos,
> Unius fæcunda bonis.
>
> (Manil.)

However, with all these Superiorities, and with a Dignity equal to the divinest of the Ancients, he had the Fortune to resemble them in the least desirable. Part of their Circumstances; as he met with the Fatality, peculiar almost to distinguished Writers, of being transmitted to Posterity full of Errors and Corruptions. It would appear almost incredible, that the Writings of an Author of so late a Date, should be thus extremely faulty and incorrect; and that his Works, like the Province of *Africa* to the ancient *Romans*, should yield his Commentators such a continual harvest of Victory and Triumphs; but it happens at the same time, to prevent all Surprize, that we are not only assured of the Fact, but in some measure likewise both of the Cause and Manner of it. This then being the Case, returned *Eugenius*, can it be any longer a Wonder why certain Adventurers in Criticism have so ardent an Esteem for *Shakespeare*, when he gives them the most delightful Opportunity of trying their Skill upon his Plays, and of indulging a Disposition for Guesses and Conjecture, the darling Passion of our modern Critics. Besides the Correctness of the Text, which is equally necessary to the right understanding him in common with all other Authors; it may not be improper to consider a few Particulars, which may possibly explain the Singularity of some Places, and give us a little Insight into the Learning of *Shakespeare*.

To begin with his Plots, the Ground-work and Basis of the whole: These are usually taken from some History or Novel; he follows the Thread of the Story as it lies before him, and seldom makes any Addition or Improvement to the Incidents arising from it: He copies the old Chronicles almost *verbatim*, and gives a faithful Relation of the several Characters they have left us of our Kings and Princes. It is needless to remark, how erroneous this must render the Plan of his Drama, and what Violation it must necessarily offer to the Unities, as prescribed by *Aristotle*. Yet it does not in the least abate my Veneration for our Poet, that the *French Connoisseurs* have fixed on him the Imputation of Ignorance and Barbarism. It would agree, I believe, as little with their Tempers to be freed from a sovereign Authority in the Empire of Wit and Letters, as in their civil Government. An absolute Monarch must preside over Affairs of Science, as well as over those of the Cabinet; and it is pleasant enough to observe what Pain they are put to, upon the least Appearance of offending against the Laws of the *Stagyrite*. But notwithstanding the Imperfection, and even the Absurdity of the Plots of *Shakespeare*, he continues unrivaled for his masterly Expression of the Characters and Manners; and the proper Execution of these is undoubtedly more useful, and perhaps more conducive to the Ends of Tragedy, than the Design and Conduct of the Plot. A great Part of this unjustifiable Wildness of the Fable, must be placed to the Taste and Humour of the Times; the People had been used to the Marvellous and Surprizing in all their Shews and Sports; they had seen different Kingdoms, in different Quarters of the World, engaged in the same Scene of Business, and could not be hastily confined from so unlimited a Latitude to a narrower Compass. I allow their Appetites to have been much depraved; yet probably some kind of *Regimen*, not very different from what they were before accustomed to, was the properest Method to bring them to a better. Nevertheless, were we to make a Dissection of his Plays, we should discover more Art and Judgment than we are commonly aware of, both in the Contrast and Consistency of his principal Characters, and in the different Under-parts, which are all made subservient towards carrying on the main Design; and we should observe, that still there was a Simplicity of Manner, which Nature only can give, and as wonderful a Diversity. *Homer* is admired for that Perfection of Beauty which represents Men as they are affected in Life, and shews us in the Persons of others, the Oppositions of Inclination, and the Struggles between the Passions of Self-love, and those of Honour and Virtue, which we often feel in our own Breasts.[3] This is that Excellence for which he is deservedly admired, as much as for the Variety of his Characters. May we not apply this Remark with an equal Propriety to *Shakespeare*, in whom we find as surprizing a Difference, and as natural and distinct a Preservation of his Characters? And is not this agreeable Display of Genius, interposed *Neander*, infinitely preferable to that studied Regularity and lifeless Drawing practised by our latter Poets? in whom we meet with either a constant Resemblance, or Antithesis both of Scenes and Persons; the natural Result of a confined and scanty Imagination! I am tempted to compare such Performances to that perpetual Sameness or Repetition which prevails in our modern Taste of Gardens: Where,

> Grove nods at Grove, each Ally has a Brother,
> And half the Plat-form just reflects the other.[4]

Yet I believe, however earnestly we contend for Nature, that we are neither of us inclined to exclude the Direction of Art from interposing in the Drama: It gives a heightning and *Relief* to Nature, and at the same time curbs the extravagance of Fancy, and circumscribes it within proper Bounds. All I would establish by this Remark, is the Opinion of *Longinus*, preferring a Composition with some Faults of this kind, which is wrote with Genius and Sublimity, to one of greater Regularity and Correctness, that is not animated with equal Life and Spirit. The Business and Design of Art, returned *Eugenius*, is undoubtedly to polish and improve the Beauties of Nature; and in some Cases, perhaps, it may be a more illustrious Mark of Skill, not to weaken and destroy a natural Grace, than to introduce an artificial one. Rules may probably assist and set off a Genius, tho' they can never give Perfection where that is wanting. . . .

If all the Instances, ⟨said⟩ *Eugenius*, which I shall hereafter mention, do not come fully up to the Point which we propose to settle, yet they will convince us at least that *Shakespeare* could not think like the Ancients, and express himself with an equal Simplicity: For I do not pretend to determine, that he had his Eye in every Particular upon some ancient Author. I have placed here the Volumes all before me, with some Strictures which I have made from Antiquity, and shall begin with pointing out a Passage in the *Tempest*, where the Sentiment is full in the Spirit of *Homer*. It is *Prospero's* Answer to his Daughter.

> Be collected:
> No more Amazement; tell your piteous Heart,
> There's no Harm done.
>
> (Act I. Sc. 2)

Would not you think that the Poet was imitating those Places in the other, where his Heroes are rouzing up their Courage to take Heart of Grace, and begin with a

> *Tetlathi dē Kradiē.*

We may observe also in the same Play a remarkable Example of his Knowledge in the ancient Poetic Story; when *Ceres* in the Masque speaks thus to *Iris* upon the Approach of *Juno*:

> High Queen of State,
> Great *Juno* comes; I know her by her Gait.

Here methinks now is no small Mark of the Judgment of our Author, in selecting this peculiar Circumstance for the Discovery of *Juno*. And was *Virgil* himself to have described her Motion, he would have done it in the same manner; for, probably, the *Divûm incedo Regina* of that Author, might furnish *Shakespeare* with the Hint: And his *Decorum* of the Character is perfectly consistent, and her Attendance upon the Wedding intirely agreeable to her Office.

Let us turn now to the next Play, where a Passage stops us at the very beginning. *Theseus* complains thus of the Tardiness of Time;

> Oh, methinks, how slow
> This old Moon wanes! she lingers my desires
> Like to a Stepdame, or a Dowager
> Long withering out a young Man's Revenue.
> (*Midsummer-Nights Dream*, Act I. Sc. I.)

Suppose we were to put this into a *Latin* Dress, could any Words express it more exactly, than these of *Horace*,

> Ut piger Annus
> Pupillis, quos dura premit custodia matrum,
> Sic mihi tarda fluunt, ingrataque tempora.
> (L. I. Ep. I. v. 21, & seq.)

Pass we on from these to *Measure for Measure*, where in the second Scene of the third Act, *Clodio* gives us such an Image of the intermediate State after Death, as bears a great Resemblance to the *Platonic* Purgations described by *Virgil*.

> Ay, but to die, and go we know not where;
> · · ·
> the delighted Spirit

> To bathe in fiery Floods, or to reside
> In thrilling Regions of thick-ribbed Ice,
> To be imprison'd in the viewless Winds,
> And blown with restless Violence round about
> The pendant World, &c.

> Ergo exercentur pænis, veterumque malorum
> Supplicia expendunt. Aliæ panduntur inanes
> Suspensæ ad ventos: aliis sub gurgite vasto
> Infectum eluitur scelus, aut exuritur igni.
> (*Æneid*, L. IV. 739, & seq.)

The next Instance which I have observed to demand our Notice, occurs in *Much Ado about Nothing*; where the Thought is very natural and obvious, founded on a Failing common to Human Nature.

> What we have we prize not to its worth
> Whilst we enjoy it; but being lack'd and lost,
> Why, then we rack the Value; then we find
> The Virtue that Possession would not shew us
> Whilst it was ours.
>
> (Act IV. Sc. 2.)

You may have seen, perhaps, the same Sentiment in many Classic Authors; but the most analogous, and which would almost tempt one to believe the Poet had it directly before him, is the following from *Plautus*:

> Tum denique homines nostra intelligimus bona,
> Cum quæ in potestate habuimus, ea amisimus.
> (*Captiv.* Act I. Sc. II. v. 29.)

*Shakespeare's* Translation of these Verses, if I may take the Liberty to call it so, tho' something diffused and paraphrastical, exceeds, in my humble Opinion, the Original; for the Proposition being diversified so agreeably, makes a deeper Impression on the Mind and Memory.

If we compare the Description of the wounded Stag, in *As You Like It*, with *Virgil's* Relation of the Death of the same Creature, we shall find that *Shakespeare's* is as highly finished and as masterly as the other:

> The wretched Animal heav'd forth such Groans,
> That their Discharge did stretch his Leathern Coat
> Almost to bursting; and the big round Tears
> Cours'd one another down his innocent Cheeks
> In piteous Chase.
>
> (Act II. Sc. I.)

What an exquisite Image this of dumb Distress, and of a wounded Animal languishing in the Agonies of Pain! I cannot help thinking that the Lines of *Virgil* do not reach it altogether so perfectly.

> Saucius at Quadrupes nota intra tecta refugit,
> Successitque gemens stabulis: Questuque cruentus,
> Atque imploranti similis tectum omne replevit.
> (*Æneid*, L. VII. v. 500 & seq.)

I now turn to the Tragedy of *King Lear*, where his passionate Exclamations against his Daughters, appear to have been copied from the *Thyestes* or *Seneca*,

> I will have such Revenges on you both
> That all the World shall—I will do such things,
> What they are yet I know not; but they shall be
> The Terrors of the Earth.
>
> (Act II. Sc. 2.)

> Fac quod nulla posteritas probet,
> Sed nulla taceat: aliquod audendum est nefas
> Atrox, cruentum:
>
> (Act II. v. 192, & seq.)
>
> Haud, quid sit, scio.
> Sed grande quiddam est.
>
> (Ibid. 270.)

And in the fourth Act we meet with a Passage which deserves our Attention upon a double Account. *Gloste* lamenting the Abuses which had been put both on himself and his Son *Edgar*, wishes that he might find him; and expresseth himself thus,

> O dear Son, *Edgar*,
> The Food of thy abused Father's Wrath;
> Might I but live to *see* thee in my *Touch*
> I'd say, I had Eyes again.
>
> (Act IV. Sc. I.)

To say nothing of the *Oculatæ Manus* of the Comic Poet, you may remark in these Lines a Contrariety of Metaphor equally bold and elegant; of which you may find many Examples in the ancient Tragedians, and particularly in *Æschylus*, the *Athenian Shakespeare*. The whole of it has a remarkable Affinity to the Lamentation of *Œdipus* in his Blindness, desiring that his Daughters might be brought him:

> μαλιστα μεν χεροιν
> ψαυσαι μ' εασον, κἀποκλαυσασθαι κακα.
> χερσι δ'αν θιγ'ων
> Δοκοι μ' εχειν σφας, ωσπερ ηνικ' εβλεπον.

> Oh, might I once but have them in my Touch,
> Weep o'er their Sorrows, and lament our Fate.
> With either Hand to touch their tender Forms,
> Would make me think that I had Eyes again.

There is another Passage in *King Lear*, which though not taken expressly from any particular Author, is directly the Language of the Ancients upon such Occasions. They were frequently induced by Misfortunes to deny the Justice and Equity of Heaven; and when they poured forth their Complaints, we heard of nothing but *Superûm Crimina*, & *Deorum Iniquitas*. *Claudian*, who was sceptically inclined, and questioned the Knowledge and Wisdom of Providence, at length acquitted the Gods, and was convinced by the Punishment of *Rufinus*:

> Abstulit hunc tandem Rufini pæna tumultum,
> *Absolvitque Deos.*
>
> (Claudian *in Rufin.* L. I. sub init.)

The Close of the Period in *Shakespeare* is exactly of the same kind:

> Take Physic, *Pomp*,
> Expose thy self to feel what Wretches feel,
> That thou mayest shake the Superflux to them,
> *And shew the Heavens more just.*
>
> (Act III. Sc. 5.)

The Thought in both Poets is evidently false, not being founded upon Truth and Reason, and is parallel to many of the stoical Extravagancies of *Lucan*.

By continuing our Progress, we come to the first Part of *Henry* the IVth, where we have an humorous Application of a *Greek* Proverb: "How long is't ago, *Jack*, says *Hal* to *Falstaff*, since thou saw'st thy own Knee? *Fal.* My own Knee? When I was about thy Years, *Hal*, I could have crept into any *Alderman's Thumb Ring*." Creeping through a Ring was a Phrase usually applied to such as were extremely thin; for this Reason the old Woman in *Aristophanes* makes use of it in that Sense:

> Γρ. δια δακτυλιου μεν ουν εμε γ' αν διελκυσαις.
> Χρ. ει τυγχανει ὁ δακτυλιος ων τηλια.
>
> (*Plut.* v. 1067, & seq.)

"You may draw me, says she, very easily through a Ring. Ay, replies *Chremylus*, if that Ring was about the Size of a Hoop."

From this we may proceed to the second Part of *Henry* the IVth, where we meet with a political Observation of *Warwick's*, who accounts for the Disloyalty of *Northumberland*, by observing that he had proved faithless to King *Richard*:

> There is a History in all Men's Lives,
> Figuring the Nature of the Times deceased:
> The which observ'd, a Man may prophesy
> With a near Aim of the Main Chance of things
> As yet not come to Life; which in their Seeds,
> And weak Beginnings lie intreasured,
>
> (Act III. Sc. 2.)

A Section of *Antoninus* will confirm and illustrate the Remark of *Shakespeare*: I will read it to you, as I find it translated by Mr. *Collier*. By looking back into History, and considering the Fate and Revolutions of Government, you will be able to form a Guess, and almost prophesy upon the future; for things past, present, and to come are strangely uniform and of a Colour, and are commonly cast in the same Mould. So that upon the Matter, forty Years of Human Life may serve for a Sample of ten thousand." *Lib.* VII. *Sect* 49. And such is the Character which *Pliny* gives of *Mauricus*: "Vir erat gravis, prudens, multis experimentis eruditus, & qui futura possit ex præteritis prævidere." *L. I. Epist.* 5.

The next Place remarkable which offers itself, is the Parting between *Suffolk* and Queen *Mary*, in the 2d Part of *Henry* VI. Act III. Sc. 8.

> A Wilderness is populous enough,
> So *Suffolk* had thy heavenly Company;
> For where thou art, there is the World itself,
> With every several Pleasure in the World;
> And where thou art not, Desolation.

This is the antient Language of Love and Friendship, and employed by *Tibullus* to his own Mistress.

> Sic Ego secretis possum bene vivere Silvis,
> Qua nulla humano sit via trita pede:
> Tu mihi curaram requies, tu nocte vel atrâ
> Lumen, & in solis tu mihi turba locis.
>
> (L. IV. El. 12.)

In the third Part of *Henry* VI. *Edward*, Son to the Duke of *York*, replies to his Father, who had urged to him the Oath which he had taken to the King,

> But for a Kingdom an Oath may be broken,
> I'd break a thousand Oaths to reign one Year.
>
> (Act I. Sc. 4.)

How exactly *Cæsar* and the young Nobleman could think upon the same Occasion, will appear from a Speech which the first of them used frequently to repeat from the *Phenissæ* of *Euripides*;

> Nam si violandum est Jus, regnandi Gratiâ
> Violandum est; aliis rebus pietatem colas.
>
> (Tull. *Off.* L. III. C. 21.)

The Character which *Gloucester* in *Richard* III. gives of *Hastings*, has a visible Similitude to some Lines in *Horace*; only in this latter the Thought is inverted.

> I made him my Book, wherein my Soul recorded
> The History of all her secret Thoughts.
>
> (Act III. Sc. 6.)

> Ille velut fidis arcana Sodalibus, olim
> Credebat Libris.
>
> (L. II. Sat. I. v. 30.)

When I read, interrupted *Neander*, in *Henry* VIII. Act III. Sc. I. this Speech of the Queen's to the two Cardinals;

> Would I had never trod this *English* Earth,
> Or felt the Flatteries that grow upon it:
> Ye've ANGEL's Faces, but Heaven knows your Hearts.

I have always imagined that he alluded to the well known Pun of *Gregory* the Great, upon remarking the Beauty of some *English* Youths, who were exposed to Sale at *Rome* before their Conversion to Christianity. It is the same which was afterwards made use of by the Marquis of *Villa* in his Epigram on *Milton*. . . .

I believe, ⟨said⟩ *Neander*, that not only the Riches of *Shakespeare's* Genius, prevented him from borrowing from the Ancients in many Instances, but that he was prevented as much from doing so by his Judgment likewise. For marking every Character with Sentiments which cannot possibly be applied to any other, he was under the less Necessity of having recourse to any common-place Topics; and especially to that curious Mixture of the fierce and tender; of ranting against the Gods, idolizing a Mistress, or unnaturally braving ones own Misfortunes; than all which nothing can be more dextrous, it being as easy as lying. Nor was he obliged to call out in the Style of Patriotism, on *Liberty* and *Virtue*; Sentiments which have stood many modern Poets in great stead; being suitable to every great Man, and equally proper either in the Mouth of a *Scipio*, or *Hannibal*.

It will be alledged, perhaps, that *Shakespeare* took his Hints from the Translations, which were made in the Reigns of Queen *Elizabeth* and King *James*. *Ovid* appears to have been a favourite Author with the Poet, whose Cause he pleads in the following Lines:

> Let's be no Stoics, nor no Stocks I pray,
> Or so devote to *Aristotle's* Checks,
> As *Ovid* be an out-cast quite abjured.
> (*Taming of the Shrew*, Act I. Sc. I.)

As his own Translations from this Poet prove him to be a Master of his Works, I think it may be concluded he was a competent Judge of other Authors who wrote in the same Language. These are much superior to a Translation of the *Metamorphoses* by *Author Golding*, a Person of some Eminence for Learning in those Days, who translated also *Cæsar's* Commentaries. My Edition is printed in 1603, on a black Letter, and in the same Metre with *Phaer's Virgil*. . . .

If this Inquiry into *Shakespeare's* Learning had fallen into such industrious Hands, you had probably seen more and stronger Examples than any which I am able to produce; tho' at the same time, perhaps, he would have met with more ungentle Treatment. I believe I ought to retract that Opinion; for there is no one but must be awed with Admiration in reading the Poet, whose Character is as much beyond Description, as he is above all others who have wrote in the same Art. The Judgment of *Quintilian*, with respect to *Cicero*, with a little Alteration, may faintly shadow out his Excellence; since he seems to have obtained that Honour with Posterity, that *Shakespeare* may be esteemed not so much the Name of a Man, as of Dramatic Poetry itself. And that to have a proper Relish for his Plays, is a Sign of a true and improved Taste.[5] Just as *Eugenius* had pronounced these Words, the Clock struck Two; upon which he added, turning to *Neander*, you can make no Excuse for refusing to dine with me, as the Time is near at Hand, and you informed me before that you are intirely at your own Disposal. *Neander* complied with the Invitation, on Condition that his Friend would accompany him to see the Tragedy of *Hamlet*, which was acted in the Evening, to which he readily agreed.

*Notes*

1. *Silent Woman*, Act II. Sc. 2. If this Expression is not thought applicable to *Shakespeare*, he may probably mean *Decker*, between whom and *Johnson* there was a personal Difference.
2. *Fletcher* might have properly been joined with *Shakespeare*, for never blotting out a Line, which we are informed of by good Authority. "Whatever I have seen of Mr. *Fletcher's* own Hand, is free from Interlining; and his Friends affirm he never writ any one Thing twice." *Mosely's* Pref. to Edit. 1647.

3. See *Hutcheson's Inquiry*, &c. P. 41.
4. Mr. *Pope's* Epistles to Lord *Burlington*, V. 115.
5. *Apud posteros vero id Consecutus, ut* Cicero *jam non Hominis, sed Eloquentiæ nomen habeatur. Hunc igitur Spectemus: Hoc propositum nobis sit Exemplum. Ille se profecisse sciat, cui* Cicero *valde placebit.* Quintil. *Instit. Orat. L. X. C I.*

## J. PAYNE COLLIER
### "On the Six Old Plays to Which Shakespeare Was, or Is Supposed to Have Been, Indebted"
*The History of English Dramatic Poetry*
1831, Volume 3, pp. 61–83

The six old plays on which, it is asserted by Steevens, Shakespeare 'founded' his *Measure for Measure, Comedy of Errors, Taming of the Shrew, King John, Henry the Fifth* and *King Lear* are the following:—

*The History of Promos and Cassandra*, printed in 1578.
*The Troublesome Reign of King John*, printed in 1591.
*The Famous Victories of Henry the Fifth*, acted prior to 1588, probably published in 1594, and certainly printed in 1598.
*The Taming of a Shrew*, printed in 1594.
*The Chronicle History of Leir, King of England*, probably published in 1594, and certainly printed in 1605.
*Menœchmi, taken out of Plautus*, printed in 1595.

When Steevens reprinted these pieces in 1779, he ventured upon no argument nor explanation to prove how, and to what extent Shakespeare was under obligation to their authors: with respect to the last, of which I shall speak first, it may now be taken for granted that he did not make the slightest use of it. *Menœchmi taken out of Plautus*, by W. W. (perhaps W. Warner,) did not appear, in all probability, until several years after *The Comedy of Errors* (which has been supposed to be founded upon it) had been brought upon the stage. Malone assigns *The Comedy of Errors* to 1592, and we may conclude with tolerable safety that it had its origin in that or in the following year. Although there is no trace of any similarity between it and the translation of the *Menœchmi* by W. W., yet there is little doubt that *The Comedy of Errors* was founded upon an older English play, which was an adaptation of the *Menœchmi* much anterior to 1595. On new-year's night 1576–7, the children of Paul's acted *The History of Error* at Hampton Court. This fact is recorded by Malone,[1] but he has not remarked also, that it was repeated on Twelfth-night, 1582–3; for although by mistake, in the account of the Revels at that date, it is called 'A History of *Ferrar*,' the person who made out the list of plays, writing from the sound only, meant probably the same piece as the *History of Error*. This play may have been the foundation of Shakespeare's *Comedy of Errors*, and the circumstance, that he borrowed certain parts from the old *History of Error*, will explain all that the commentators have said regarding doggrel verses, and the apparent authorship of two different persons in the same play. The doggrel fourteen-syllable verses given to the Dromios are precisely such as were used in dramatic performances not long before the period when Shakespeare began to write for the stage; and, as Malone himself has observed, he most likely obtained the designations of Antipholus *erraticus* and Antipholus *surreptus*, which are found in the old copy of the *Comedy of Errors*,[2] from this source. We may, therefore, very safely dismiss from our consideration the translation of *Menœchmi* by W. W., on the grounds, that Shakespeare did not use it, and that it was not printed until some time after he had commenced his theatrical career.

It is, I think, equally certain that the other five old plays, above enumerated, were written anterior to the date of any of Shakespeare's productions: four of them were published anonymously, and there is by no means sufficient ground for the supposition entertained by some of the German critics, that they were the juvenile works of our great dramatist, who subsequently altered and improved them. They bear no resemblance to his style, as exhibited in his undoubted performances; and nothing is more clear than that at the time when he commenced his career, and afterwards, it was the constant custom for dramatic poets to revive, amend, and make additions to, productions which had once been popular, but which required novelty and adaptation to the improvements of the age. Judging from internal and external evidence, I should be inclined to place the five old plays in the following order, with reference to the dates at which they were produced, and according to that arrangement I shall speak of each:—1. *Promos and Cassandra*. 2. *Henry the Fifth*. 3. *King John*. 4. *King Leir*. 5. *Taming of a Shrew*.

*Promos and Cassandra* was written by a poet of considerable celebrity in his day, George Whetstone, and it came from the press of Richard Jones in 1578: it is divided into a first and second part; and, perhaps, the most remarkable circumstance connected with the performance is one that has not hitherto been noticed; viz.; that the first part is entirely in rhyme, while in the second are inserted considerable portions of blank-verse, put only into the mouth of the King, as if it better suited the royal dignity. This fact might appear to militate against the position, elsewhere maintained in this work, that blank-verse was not employed upon the common, popular stage until 1586 or 1587, did we not know that *Promos and Cassandra* never was performed, either in public or private. Whetstone himself gives us this information, in his *Heptameron of Civil Discourses*, 1582: he there inserts a translation of the original novel on which he constructed his play,[3] and in a marginal note he observes: 'this Historie, for rarenes therof, is lively set out in a Comedie by the Reporter of the whole worke, but yet never presented upon stage.' It is likely that there was some interval between the penning of the first and of the second parts of *Promos and Cassandra*, and that in that interval the author had acquired a taste for blank-verse, and therefore employed it, never designing the piece for popular representation, for which on this account, among others, he might think it unfit. The year 1578 is an early date for the use of blank-verse for dramatic purposes, and a short extract will show sufficiently that Whetstone had not much improved upon the few examples already set. The King first addresses Cassandra, (who answers to Shakespeare's Isabella,) who has appealed to him, and he afterwards turns to Promos, the wicked deputy.

> Thy forced fault was free from evil intent,
> So long, no shame can blot thee any way;
> And though at full I hardly may content thee,
> Yet, as I may assure thyselfe I wyl.—
> Thou wycked man, might it not thee suffice,
> By worse then force to spoyle her chastitie,
> But, heaping sinne on sinne, against thy oth
> Hast cruelly her brother done to death?
> This over proofe ne can but make me thinke
> That many waies thou hast my subjectes wrongd;
> For how canst thou with justice use thy swaie,
> When thou thy selfe dost make thy will a lawe?
> Thy tyranny made mee this progresse make,
> How so for sport tyl nowe I colloured it,
> Unto this ende, that I might learne at large
> What other wronges by power thou hast wrought.

This quotation shows also one principal variation in the conduct of the story as related by Shakespeare. In *Promos and Cassandra*, the King sends the hero as his Viceroy into Hungary; but hearing of his tyranny and misrule, he makes a 'progress' thither, as if 'for sport,' to ascertain the truth: he does not, like the Duke in *Measure for Measure*, withdraw from his court, and in disguise watch over the administration of justice by his substitute.[4]

It has been observed that Shakespeare in no instance adopted the names of the *dramatis personæ* of Whetstone, but this will not at all establish that he did not use *Promos and Cassandra*; for Whetstone has in like manner varied from Cinthio, whose novel he professed to follow, and where the hero is called Juriste, and the heroine Epitia. It is, however, not improbable that there was another version of the Italian tale current at the time, and possibly in a dramatic form, in which Shakespeare might find the name of Vincentio inserted in his *dramatis personæ*, although throughout the play he is only called the Duke. He may have caught Isabella from Whetstone's *Heptameron*, 1582, because there a lady of that name is made the narrator of the novel in question from Cinthio.

Although the first part of *Promos and Cassandra* is in rhyme, the author has introduced variety into his measure, and he changes at will from ten-syllable to fourteen-syllable lines, making them rhyme sometimes in couplets, and sometimes alternately, two of the lines having no corresponding termination: thus, when Andrugio, the brother, recommends his sister, Cassandra, to comply with the guilty wishes of Promos, as the least of two evils, she replies, with some spirit,

> And of these evils, the least, I hold, is death,
>> To shun whose dart we can no mean devyse:
>> Yet honor lives when death hath done his worst.
>> Thus fame then lyfe is of farre more comprise.

This, however, is a comparatively rare instance, the regularity of rhyme, either in couplets or alternate, being usually observed. Besides those engaged in the serious part of the representation, Whetstone introduced many characters, parasites, cheats, pandars, bawds, prostitutes, bullies, and rustics, in order to give variety to the performance, the story of which drags heavily through the two parts to which it is extended. A person of the name of Rosko, in *Promos and Cassandra*, fills precisely the same part as the clown in *Measure for Measure*; and he is concerned in a good deal that is meant by Whetstone for comedy, though the poet has, in very few instances, accomplished anything like his intention. The most tolerable scene of this kind is between Rosko, a rustic called Grimball, and a cutpurse of the name of Rowke. Grimball, wishing to render himself amiable in the eyes of the waiting-maid to a courtesan, is carried by Rowke to Rosko (who pretends to be a barber), that he may be washed and trimmed. While this operation is performed, Rowke contrives to make off with Grimball's purse, and the countryman does not perceive his loss, until Rosko proceeds to pick his teeth. The dialogue of the comic portion of the piece possesses neither wit nor humour, but is sufficiently gross and coarse.

On the whole, although it seems clear that Shakespeare kept Whetstone's *Promos and Cassandra* in his eye, it is probable that he also made use of some other dramatic composition or novel, in which the same story was treated.

In *Measure for Measure* we have seen that Shakespeare compressed Whetstone's two plays into one, but he expanded the single play of *The famous Victories of Henry the Fifth*[5] over three performances, inserting hints from it in his two parts of *Henry IV.* and in his *Henry V.* He, however, also resorted to the chroniclers, and especially to Holinshed, for other circumstances of an historical kind, while he seems to have trusted to his own resources for most of the comic characters, scenes, and incidents. *The famous Victories of Henry the Fifth* opens with a robbery committed by Prince Henry (throughout called Henry V.) and some of his wild companions, among whom is Sir John Oldcastle, a fat knight, who also goes by the familiar name of Jockey. The question whether Shakespeare did or did not take the hint of his Falstaff from this corpulent personage, and whether in fact Falstaff was not, in the first instance, called Sir John Oldcastle, is argued at length in Malone's Shakespeare by Boswell, xvi. 410[6] &c. This point is only important, as it relates to the obligation of Shakespeare for the bare hint of such a delightful creation as Falstaff. If Shakespeare were indebted thus far, he owes little else to the old *Henry the Fifth* that can now be traced, and it certainly has not come down to us in a shape to make it probable that he would avail himself of much that he found in it. Here and there lines more or less remotely resemble, and the strongest likeness that has yet been discovered is where, in Shakespeare, (Act v. Sc. 2,) Katherine asks, 'Is it possible dat I should love the enemy of France? which runs thus in the older play, 'How should I love thee, which is my father's enemy?'

The play of *The famous Victories of Henry the Fifth* was entered on the Stationers' books in 1594, and although no copy of that date has been found, it was probably, as I have already remarked, then printed:[7] the date of its authorship was, however, more remote, and it is unquestionable that it was acted prior to 1588, because Tarleton, who is recorded to have played in it the two parts of the Judge, who was struck by Prince Henry, and Derrick, the clown, died in that year. I should be inclined to fix it not long after 1580, and it was perhaps played by the Queen's players who were selected from the companies of several noblemen in 1583, and of whom Tarleton was one. The circumstance that the whole of it is in prose deserves observation: it might be thought in 1583, or soon afterwards, that the jingle of rhyme did not well suit an historical subject on the stage, and we have learnt from Stephen Gosson, that, prior to 1579, prose plays had been acted at the Belsavage: the experiment, therefore, by the author of the old *Henry the Fifth*, was not a new one, although the present may be the earliest extant instance of an heroic story so treated.[8] Nevertheless, by the time it was printed, blank-verse had completely superseded both rhyme and prose: the publisher seems, on this account, to have chopped up much of the original prose into lines of various lengths in order to look like some kind of measure, and now and then he has contrived to find lines of ten syllables each, that run with tolerable smoothness, and as if they had been written for blank-verse. The following is a short example, the passage commencing with a regular verse terminated by a trochee: it is Prince Henry's speech in excuse for taking away the crown while his father slept—

Most soveraigne lord, and welbeloved father,
I came into your chamber to comfort the melancholy
Soule of your body, and finding you at that time
Past all recovery and dead, to my thinking,
God is my witnesse, and what should I doo
But with weeping tears lament the death of you, my
    father;
And after that, seeing the crown, I took it.
And tell me, father, who might better take it then I,
After your death? but seeing you live,
I most humbly render it into your majesties hands,
And the happiest man alive that my father live:
And live, my lord and father, for ever.

The excuse is the same in Shakespeare (*Henry IV*. Pt. ii., A. iv., Sc. 4.), but it is not necessary to show here how

differently it is urged and enforced. Among minor resemblances, which prove that Shakespeare had the old *Henry the Fifth* before him, when he wrote his play upon the events of that reign, may be noticed the refusal of the French King to allow his son, the Dauphin, to endanger his person with the English.[9] Little as Shakespeare, in the serious part of his composition, has derived from the older historical play, his obligations are still lighter with reference to the comic portions. After Prince Henry has struck the Chief Justice and has been liberated from prison, in the old *Henry the Fifth* he has a conversation with Sir John Oldcastle, Ned and Tom, his companions in his robberies at Gads-hill. Sir John Oldcastle, speaking of Henry IV., says, 'He is a good old man: God take him to his mercy;' and the Prince, addressing Ned, observes, 'So soon as I am King, the first thing I will do shall be to put my Lord Chief Justice out of office, and thou shalt be my Lord Chief Justice of England.' The reply of Ned resembles, even verbally, that of Falstaff when the Prince of Wales tells him (*Henry IV*. Pt. i., A. i., Sc. 2.) that when he is King he shall have the hanging of the thieves. Ned says, in the older play—

Shall I be Lord Chief Justice?
By Gog's wounds, I'll be the bravest Lord Chief
    Justice
That ever was in England.

The character of Derrick, the clown, runs through the whole piece, and that Tarleton was able to make anything out of such unpromising materials affords strong evidence of the original resources of that extraordinary performer.

*The Troublesome Reign of John, King of England*, is in two parts, and bears the marks of more than one hand in its composition: the first part, and especially the earlier portion of it, is full of rhymes, while in the second part they comparatively seldom occur, which may be said to establish that the one was written nearer the date when rhyme was first discarded. The blank-verse of the second part is also a decided improvement upon that of the first part: it is less cumbrous and more varied, though still monotonous in its cadences. Malone, upon conjecture only, attributed the old *King John* to Greene or Peele,[10] and some passages in the second part would do credit to either. In the opening of it is a beautiful simile, which Shakespeare might have used had he not been furnished, on the same occasion, with another from the abundant store of his own fancy: that which he employs has, perhaps, more novelty, but assuredly less grace, and both are equally appropriate. Arthur has thrown himself from the tower, and is found dead: Shakespeare calls his body

An empty casket, where the jewel of life
By some damn'd hand was robb'd and ta'en away.

The author of the second part of the old *King John* describes the dead body as a

withered flower,
Who in his life shin'd like the morning's blush,
Cast out of door.

Shakespeare may be said to have borrowed nothing from this piece beyond an unimportant historical blunder, pointed out by Steevens: as to his having 'preserved the greatest part of the conduct' of the elder production, both writers very much followed the chroniclers of the time. Our great dramatist has however displayed, as usual, his superior skill in framing the plot, and, with a single omission, he has brought into the compass of his one play the incidents that are tediously extended through the two parts of the old *King John*. That omission is the plunder of the abbey of Swinstead by Falconbridge, when he finds a nun concealed in the apartment of the Abbot, and a friar hidden in that of the Abbess.

The characters in both performances are nearly the same; but while, in the old play, they are comparatively only instruments of utterance, Shakespeare breathes a spirit of life into his historical personages, and they live again in his lines. Shakespeare may be criticised for a century, but after all we shall only arrive at this point—that we admire him above all others, because he is, more than all others, the poet of actual existence.

The story of Lear and his Daughters is full of moral impossibilities, and Shakespeare's play, founded upon it, is the triumph of sympathy over improbability. Our feelings are deeply interested from the first scene to the last; yet the events, out of which those scenes arise, could scarcely have occurred in any state of society. The old *Chronicle History of King Leir*, as it is called on the title-page, was most likely published in 1594, when it was entered for that purpose on the Stationers' books;[11] while it is probable that Shakespeare's tragedy, on the same subject, was not produced until 1605. He seems to have introduced more variance than usual in his conduct of the plot, and especially to have changed the conclusion, which, in the old play, is managed with great simplicity, and with the observance of that poetical justice which Shakespeare has been blamed by some for disregarding. In the *Chronicle History*, Lear is restored to his throne, after the defeat and exile of his two wicked daughters, while Cordella (so she is there named) and her husband, the King of France, after reposing awhile with the old King, return to their own dominions. Shakespeare has given a new interest to his performance, by the episode of Glocester and his two sons, which contributes to enforce the same moral lesson. The faithful Fool is likewise new to him; and it need not be stated how much that character adds to the effect of the awful scenes in which he is introduced. The madness of Lear is not to be traced in the old play; and I am satisfied, from the language of the ballad,[12] that it was founded upon Shakespeare's tragedy, and not, as some have supposed, Shakespeare's tragedy upon it. The hint of the part of Kent is undoubtedly taken from the Perillus of the *Chronicle History*; but the latter is a poor, spiritless lamenter over the injuries of Cordella, in the earlier scenes, and in the progress of the play, instead of contrasting with Lear, he not only partakes the sufferings, but shares the imbecilities of the old abdicated monarch. In the *Chronicle History*, one of the daughters sends a messenger, to murder her father and Perillus in a wood; and the most affecting scene in the piece is that in which the two old men so plead for their lives, that the assassin is unable to perform the duty he had undertaken. In the *Chronicle History*, the two wicked daughters are not married, until their husbands have been bribed by the offer of the division of the kingdom, and the union of Cordella with the King of France is most absurdly conducted. The King of France, with one of his nobles, visits England as a pilgrim, and meeting Cordella, driven from her father's court, they fall in love with each other on the spot, he not knowing that she is a Princess, nor she that he is a King. Old Lear puts on the dress of a shipman, when he flies to France from Ragan and Gonorill, and there is accidentally met by Cordella and her royal spouse, who are making a journey to the sea-side in disguise.

Nothing can be more tame and mechanical than the whole of the dialogue of the *Chronicle History*, which Malone, with great injustice, conjectures to have been written by Thomas Kyd.

The last of the six old plays is that to which Shakespeare was most indebted: all the principal situations, and part of the language of his *Taming of the Shrew* are to be found in the 'pleasant conceited History called the Taming of a Shrew,' a work of very considerable talent, as evinced by the conduct of the plot, the nature of the characters, and the versification of the dialogue. It was printed in 1594; and I shall give the title of this edition at length, because it was unknown to Malone, Steevens, and the rest of the modern commentators:[13] —'A pleasant conceited Historie called The taming of a Shrew. As it was sundry times acted by the Right honourable the Earle of Pembrooke his servants. Printed at London by Peter Short, and are to be sold by Cuthbert Burbie, at his shop at the Royall Exchange. 1594.' Although it is not enumerated by Meres, in 1598, among the plays Shakespeare had then written, and although in Act iv. Scene 1, it contains an allusion to Heywood's *Woman killed with Kindness*, which was not produced until after 1600, Malone finally fixed upon 1596 as the date when the *Taming of the Shrew* was produced. His earlier conjecture of 1606 seems much more probable, and his only reason for changing his mind was that the versification resembled 'the old comedies antecedent to the time' of Shakespeare, and in this notion he was certainly well-founded. I am however satisfied, that more than one hand (perhaps at distant dates) was concerned in it, and that Shakespeare had little to do with any of the scenes in which Katherine and Petruchio are not engaged. The underplot much resembles the dramatic style of William Haughton, author of an extant comedy, called *Englishmen for my Money*, which was produced prior to 1598.

Hurd gives Shakespeare great praise for 'the excellence of the moral design' of the Induction to his *Taming of the Shrew*, not being aware that the credit due on this account belongs to the author of the original comedy of 1594.[14] Shakespeare has, indeed, made very material changes, both of persons and dialogue; but the lesson enforced by the one and by the other is the same. As the copy of the old *Taming of a Shrew* of 1594 is a great curiosity,[15] and as very little attention has been hitherto paid to the Induction, as it stands in the original of Shakespeare's comedy, I shall quote from it *literatim* at greater length than usual, in order to show the nature and degree of our great dramatist's obligation.

*Enter a Tapster, beating out of his doores Slie droonken.*
*Tapster*: You whorson droonken slave, you had best be gone,
   And empty your droonken panch somewhere else,
   For in this house thou shalt not rest to night.
                                        [*Exit Tapster.*
*Slie*: Tilly vally, by crisee Tapster Ile fese you anon,
   Fil's the tother pot, and alls paid for, looke you.
   I doo drinke it of mine owne Instigation: *Omne bene.*
   Heere Ile lie a while. Why, Tapster, I say,
   Fil's a fresh cushen heere,
   Heigh ho, heer's good warme lying.
                                        [*He fals asleepe.*
*Enter a Nobleman and his men from hunting.*
*Lord*: Now that the gloomie shaddow of the night,
   Longing to view Orion's drisling lookes,
   Leapes from th' antarticke world unto the skie
   And dims the welkin with her pitchie breath,
   And darkesome night oreshades the christall heavens,
   Heere breake we off our hunting for to night.
   Cupple uppe the hounds, let us hie us home,
   And bid the huntsman see them meated well,
   For they have all deserv'd it well to daie.
   But soft, what sleepie fellow is this lies heere?
   Or is he dead, see one what he dooth lacke?·
*Servingman*: My Lord, tis nothing but a drunken sleepe.

His head is too heavie for his bodie,
And he hath drunke so much that he can go no
    furder.
*Lord:* Fie, how the slavish villaine stinkes of drinke.
    Ho, sirha, arise! What! so sound asleepe?
    Go take him uppe, and beare him to my house,
    And beare him easilie for feare he wake,
    And in my fairest chamber make a fire,
    And set a sumptuous banquet on the boord,
    And put my richest garmentes on his backe,
    Then set him at the table in a chaire.
    When that is doone, against he shall awake,
    Let heavenlie musicke play about him still.
    Go two of you awaie, and beare him hence,
    And then Ile tell you what I have devised,
    But see in any case you wake him not.
                                 [*Exeunt two with Slie.*
    Now take my cloake, and give me one of yours.
    Al fellowes now, and see you take me so,
    For we will waite upon this droonken man,
    To see his countnance when he dooth awake,
    And finde himselfe clothed in such attire.
    With heavenly musicke sounding in his eares,
    And such a banquet set before his eies,
    The fellow sure will thinke he is in heaven:
    But we will [be] about him when he wakes;
    And see you call him Lord at everie word,
    And offer thou him his horse to ride abroad,
    And thou his hawkes, and houndes to hunt the
      deere,
    And I will aske what sutes he meanes to weare,
    And what so ere he saith, see you doo not laugh,
    But still perswade him that he is a Lord.
                          *Enter one.*
*Mess.:* And it please your honour, your plaiers be
    com,
    And doo attend your honour's pleasure here.
*Lord:* The fittest time they could have chosen out.
    Bid one or two of them come hither straight;
    Now will I fit my selfe accordinglie,
    For they shall play to him when he awakes.
    *Enter two of the players with packs at their backs,*
    *and a boy.*
    Now, sirs, what store of plaies have you?
*San[der]:* Marrie, my lord, you maie have a
    Tragicall,
    Or a commoditie, or what you will.
*The other:* A Comedie thou shouldst say: souns,
    thout shame us all.
*Lord:* And what's the name of your Comedie?
*San.:* Marrie, my lord, 'tis calde The taming of a
    shrew.
    'Tis a good lesson for us, my lord, for us y$^t$ are
    married men.
*Lord:* The taming of a shrew, that's excellent sure.
    Go see that you make you readie straight,
    For you must play before a lord to-night.
    Say you are his men and I your fellow,
    Hee's something foolish, but what so ere he saies,
    See that you be not dasht out of countenance.

The reprint made by Steevens, in 1779, from the edition of the old *Taming of a Shrew,* (mentioned by Sir J. Harington in 1596,[16] will enable the reader to judge how far Shakespeare, and, as I suppose, his coadjutor, were aided by the previous drama; and as the resemblance runs through the whole performance, it is not necessary to point out particular instances. Shakespeare's *Taming of the Shrew* is deficient in the conclusion, for we there hear nothing of Sly after the play is ended. In the old piece of 1594, he is again borne to the door of the ale-house, and there left asleep: it is related in the following manner.

    *Then enter two bearing of Slie in his owne apparell,*
        *and leaves him where they found him, and then*
        *goes out: then enter the Tapster.*
*Tapster:* Now that the darkesome night is overpast,
    And dawning day appeares in cristall skie,
    Now must I haste abroade: but soft, who's this?
    What, Slie, O wondrous! hath he laine heere all
      night?
    I'le wake him: I thinke hee's starved by this,
    But that his belly was so stufft with ale.
    What now, Slie, awake for shame!
*Slie:* Sim, gives some more wine: what all the
    Players gone: am not I a Lord?
*Tapster:* A Lord, with a murrin: come, art thou
    drunken still?
*Slie:* Who's this? Tapster, O Lord sirha, I have had
    the bravest dreame to-night, that ever thou
    heardest in all thy life.
*Tapster:* I, mary, but you had best get you home,
    For your wife will course you for dreaming heere
    to-night.
*Slie:* Wil she? I know now how to tame a shrew;
    I dreamt upon it all this night till now,
    And thou hast wakt me out of the best dreame
    That ever I had in all my life: but I'le to my
    Wife presently, and tame her too, and if she anger
    me.
*Tapster:* Nay, tarry, Slie, for Ile go home with thee,
    And heare the rest that thou hast dreamt to-night.
                                 [*Exeunt omnes.*

The variations between the copies of 1594 and 1607 are not material, the latter being a reprint from the former; unless, as Reed asserts, there was an intermediate edition in 1596.[17] One circumstance has not been remarked by the commentators, viz., that the scene of the old *Taming of a Shrew* is laid in Athens, and that the names of the characters are a mixture of Greek, Latin, Italian, English, and Scotch. Shakespeare transferred it to Padua, and altered the *dramatis personæ,* observing in this particular, and some others, more dramatic propriety.

*Notes*

1. *Shakespeare* by Boswell, iv. 151.
2. It was not printed until it appeared in the folio of 1623. Meres mentions it in 1598.
3. From *La Seconda Parte de gli Hecatommithi di M. Giovanbatista Giraldi Cinthio.* Deca 8, Nov. 5 p. 415. Edit. 1565.
4. Shakespeare may have taken his title, *Measure for Measure,* from a short moral observation in Act v., Scene 4, of the first part of *Promos and Cassandra:*

    who others doth deceyve,
    Deserves himself *like measure* to receyve.
5. Malone (*Shakespeare* by Boswell, iii. 307) inserts, from Henslowe's Diary, a notice, under the date of the 26th of May, 1597, of a play called 'Harey the *fifte* Life and Death,' and in a note he adds, 'This could not have been the play already mentioned, because in that Henry does not die; nor could it have been Shakespeare's play.' His difficulty upon this point arose simply from his not being able to read the MS. of Henslowe, where it stands, as all must acknowledge who know anything of the handwriting of the time, not 'Harey the *fifte*,' but 'Harey the *firste*,' showing that there was an old historical play upon the life and death of Henry I. The play of 'Harey the V.' is entered in Henslowe's Diary as performed on the 28th of November, 1595, being then, no doubt, a revival, with improvements, of the piece

now under consideration—*The famous Victories of Henry the Fifth.*

6. Dr. Farmer (founding himself on a passage in Nathaniel Field's *Amends for Ladies*, 1618) was the first to broach this notion, and the balance of evidence seems to be decidedly in his favour: supposing the fact to be so, another question has arisen out of it, why Shakespeare subsequently made the change? It has been suggested that he did so to avoid confounding the two characters, the Sir John Oldcastle of the old *Henry the Fifth* being 'a mere pampered glutton.' The point, when he made the change, does not seem to have been examined, and at all events it is quite evident from Field's comedy that, even after the change was made, Falstaff was still known to the multitude by the name of Oldcastle. *Amends for Ladies* could not have been written before 1611, yet there Falstaff's description of honour is mentioned by a citizen of London as if it had been delivered by Sir John Oldcastle.

7. The play had, perhaps, been revived about 1592 or 1593, as Nash mentions it in his *Pierce Pennilesse*. That revival may have led Shakespeare to take up and improve the same subject; and the success of Shakespeare's play might occasion the printing of the old *Henry the Fifth* in opposition to it, or to take advantage of temporary popularity.

8. Gascoigne's *Supposes*, translated from Ariosto, we have seen was in prose; but that was only a comedy, and it was acted, not at a public theatre, but before the Society of Gray's Inn.

9. *Henry V.* Act iii. Sc. 6, and *Six Old Plays*, ii. 357.

10. In a note on Act v. Sc. 7 of *King John*, Malone cites a corresponding passage from *Lust's Dominion*, and if his reasoning were founded on fact, we might infer that Marlow, as well as Greene and Peele, was concerned in the production of the old King John. The truth, however, is that Marlow had nothing to do with the authorship of *Lust's Dominion*, although it has been invariably assigned to him, until in the last edition of Dodsley's *Old Plays* it was irrefragably proved, that Marlow had been dead five years before some of the historical events in *Lust's Dominion* occurred. *Vide* Dodsley's *Old Plays*, ii. 311. 1825.

11. It was played by Henslowe's company, as we find by his Diary, on the 6th April, 1593.

12. Malone's *Shakespeare* by Boswell, x. 297.

13. Pope seems to have had a copy of the edition of 1594, but afterwards it was lost sight of for about a century, and has only very recently been recovered. It was entered on the Stationers' books on 2d May, 1594, and, no doubt, appeared soon afterwards. Steevens reprinted from a copy dated 1607, having seen no earlier edition.

14. Unless Warton be correct in his statement (*Hist. Engl. Poet.*, iv. 118,) that it was derived from a collection of Tales by Richard Edwards (author of *Damon and Pythias*, &c.) printed in 1570, which was among the books of Collins at Chichester. No such collection is now known to be in existence.

15. It was bought by that very intelligent bookseller, Mr. T. Rodd, of Newport-street, out of the Catalogue of Longman and Co. for the year 1817; and it was subsequently sold by auction for 20*l*. It occupies forty-six quarto pages besides the title.

16. In his *Metamorphosis of Ajax* printed in that year.

17. Malone's *Shakespeare* by Boswell, ii. 341.

## PAUL STAPFER
"Shakespeare's Classical Knowledge"
*Shakespeare and Classical Antiquity*
tr. Emily J. Carey
1880, pp. 73–106

The question as to whether Molière was able to read Aristophanes, Terence and Plautus, in the original, would hardly be likely to excite a very lively interest in the mind of any Frenchman. Molière is held to be a great comic poet by his countrymen, and it may be doubted whether, if they were shown that over and above that he was also a good Greek and Latin scholar, it would greatly add to their estimation of him, or if it were proved that classical authors were only known to him through translations whether their admiration for the author of the "Misanthrope" would suffer any diminution. But in England people think and feel otherwise, and the question regarding Shakespeare's knowledge of Greek and Latin, would appear to be of vast importance in their eyes, to judge from the extraordinary eagerness with which it has generally been discussed. The combatants in this strange dispute are even more curious than the debated point itself, for—admitting for an instant the truth of the most unfavourable conclusions with regard to Shakespeare's classical learning—it is difficult to understand how such an avowal could be harmful to his glory, and that, on the contrary, it should not rather redound to his credit, and redouble our wonder and admiration for the wealth and penetrative power of a genius able, by itself alone, to furnish so many marvellous beauties that have hitherto been, to a certain extent, attributed to study and to the imitation of others. But though the controverted point has no intrinsic importance, the controversy itself is both amusing and instructive.

Great value is attached by the English, who are at heart an aristocratic people, to the distinctions inherited by noble birth and to those gained at the universities; the greatest recommendation a man can have is a title of nobility, the next is a university degree. While a democratic Frenchman, in spite of the small amount of personal merit or renown he may possess, affects as a matter of good taste to conceal his title or degree, an Englishman always proclaims and displays them; dukes and earls, those even whose talents and real worth have made them justly famous, are as exacting on this point as the obscurest of country squires; the Bachelor of Arts with his honours fresh upon him is not more careful to write after his name the initials of the degree he has just taken than are Oxford and Cambridge professors of long standing. Influenced by this national prejudice in favour of birth or, in default of that, of the certificate in due official form of a university education as a passport to a position in society, it would almost seem as if Englishmen had been a little ashamed of this poor William Shakespeare, who not only was no lord or earl, like Lord Buckhurst, but was not even a graduate of either of the universities, as Marlowe, Greene, Peele, Lyly, Lodge, Gascoigne, Richard Edwards, and, in short, as nearly all the other dramatic authors of his time were; and also as if they held it necessary for the honour of England to show that he might have been at any rate a Bachelor of Arts.

Another reason for the passionate interest with which English critics have fought over this point may be found in their evident predilection, when dealing with poets, for adding a few more units, whether great or small, to the sum of clearly ascertained biographical facts: it matters not that the discovery should be insignificant to the last degree—that it is a fact is all-sufficient. And an excellent opportunity for research of a precise and not too abstract nature, and for questions of small facts, is afforded in the measurement of the exact amount of Shakespeare's classical learning. The subject opens a fine field for erudition. Æsthetics, taste, feeling, philosophy and thought are quite unnecessary here, and all that is wanted is to ferret out and scrape together and pile up higher and higher, mountains of notes, proceeding after the manner of rats—

> Qui, les livres rongeants
> Se font savants jusques aux dents.

This is where the tribe mentioned by Voltaire in his *Temple of Taste* shines forth, Baldus, Scioppius, Lexicocrassus, Scriblerius, "a swarm of commentators who restored passages and compiled huge volumes about some word they did not understand."

> Là j'aperçus les Daciers, les Saumaises,
> Gens hérissés de savantes fadaises,
> Le teint jauni, les yeux rouges et secs,
> Le dos courbé sous un tas d'auteurs grees,
> Tout noircis d'encre et coiffés de poussière.
> Je leur criai de loin par la portière:
> "N'allez vous pas dans le Temple du Goût
> Vous décrasser? Nous, messieurs? point du tout,
> Ce n'est pas là, grace au ciel, notre étude;
> Le goût n'est rien; nous avons l'habitude
> De rédiger au long de point en point
> Ce qu'on pensa; mais nous ne pensons point."

The family of Lexicocrassus is by no means confined to England; in the present day æsthetics are everywhere supplanted by erudition, and criticism conceived as a work of art and of thought is stigmatized with the withering name of dilettanteism, by grammarians who pride themselves on possessing neither style nor ideas; while the easy-going public accepts an auctioneer's catalogue as literature. Careful research in France has recently procured for us an inventory of Molière's library, plate-chest and carpeting; and truly a knowledge of a poet's stock of household goods is not without its interest—as, for instance, to know that Malherbe's rooms were very shabbily furnished, and that, as Racine says, he had only seven or eight rush-bottomed chairs; and that Victor Hugo surrounds himself with sumptuous and artistic pieces of furniture, is not a matter of indifference to a philosophical thinker, but only on condition of his penetrating through the given facts to the general idea expressed by them, and not remaining absorbed in the contemplation of a pair of tongs, three frying-pans and a couple of chafing-dishes.

It is in this philosophical spirit that I wish to approach the task of making out the inventory of Shakespeare's intellectual furniture in the way of learning, endeavouring to extract from the mass of dry details some ideas of general interest, and taking especial care to avoid falling into the weakness of imagining that the *genius loci* can suffer either increase or diminution of glory from the riches or poverty of the house he dwells in.

It is necessary first of all to get rid of a most senseless but common confusion which has too often prevailed in the discussion touching the amount of Shakespeare's knowledge, by which the knowledge of languages has been and still is continually confounded with learning strictly so called. Yet they are assuredly two very different things. A knowledge of languages is a key wherewith to unlock the treasures of learning, but it is not learning itself. There are persons who think the key so curious that they pass their whole life in examining it, without once using it to open anything whatever,—of such are grammarians. But it is better to get into literature by a false key or by any other means, no matter what, than to rest contented with studying the ingenious mechanism of the right key; it is better to read translations of Homer and the Greek tragedians than to be satisfied with being well up in our Greek conjugations and syntax. Few men have been as learned as Goethe; few men have imbibed the Hellenic spirit and have understood it as he did, yet Goethe did not know Greek. Did Shakespeare know Greek, and did he know Latin? The whole question has been reduced to these pedantic limits, and no higher idea has been conceived of the education of a poet. While some have denied him all knowledge of classical languages, others have exaggerated his acquaintance with them,—both assertions, in spite of their contradictory nature, affording equal satisfaction to the vanity of critics; for a pedant can make as much capital by exposing the ignorance of a man

of genius, as he can by the opportunity afforded him by the learning possessed by the author under review, to display his own erudition.

The origin of the debate is to be found in a line written by Ben Jonson, in an enthusiastic epistle "to the memory of his beloved William Shakespeare," in which he exclaims that the great poet England had just lost outweighed all antiquity, though he knew "small Latin and less Greek." This line has occasioned as much wrangling and hairsplitting as any text in Perseus or Lycophron; for what, it has been asked, does Ben Jonson mean by "small Latin"? In the estimation of a mighty classical scholar like himself, a very respectable knowledge of Latin might rank as a small matter. And then, it was further remarked, he does not say "no Greek" although his metre would have perfectly allowed of his doing so, but "less Greek." Therefore—oh joy!—Shakespeare did know a little Greek.

> Du Grec, ô ciel! du grec! il sait du grec, ma sœur!
> Ah, ma nièce, du grec! du grec, quelle douceur!

And finally, in spite of the sincerely affectionate tone of Ben Jonson's epistle, it has been hinted that the "small Latin and less Greek" might have been dictated by secret jealousy; and since then it has dropped out of account.

In the eighteenth century Warburton and divers other learned commentators, finding curious points of resemblance between Shakespeare and Sophocles, Euripides, Lucian, etc., had no hesitation in concluding that he had both read and copied the Greek writers. It was in 1767 that Dr. Farmer's famous essay on the learning of Shakespeare appeared.

In comparing the text of Shakespeare's Roman tragedies with Sir Thomas North's English translation of Plutarch's *Lives* from the French of Amyot, Farmer showed that Shakespeare had borrowed entirely from that translation,—that he had copied many phrases and even whole pages from it without taking any pains to verify its accuracy by the slightest examination of the original text, as he everywhere follows the English version blindfold, even to its errors and mistranslations. For example, in the third act of *Antony and Cleopatra*, Octavius, speaking of the illustrious lovers, says—

> Unto her
> He gave the 'stablishment of Egypt; made her
> Of lower Syria, Cyprus, *Lydia*,
> Absolute Queen.

*Lydia* is a mistake for Lybia, of which Plutarch speaks, but the mistake is made both by Amyot and by North. Again, in the fourth act, Octavius, when challenged by Antony whom he had just defeated, answers—

> My messenger
> He hath whipt with rods; dares me to personal combat,
> Cæsar to Antony. Let th' old ruffian know
> I have many other ways to die; meantime,
> Laugh at his challenge."

"I have many other ways to die" is a mistranslation; Plutarch says not "I have" but "he has," that is, that Antony has many other ways to die. His sentence, translated word for word, runs thus: "After this, Antony sent to defy Cæsar to single combat, and received for answer that he might find other means of ending his life." Amyot cannot be said to be in fault here, he translates it: "And another time Antony sent to challenge Cæsar to single combat. Cæsar sent him word that he had many other ways of dying than that;" but Shakespeare was misled by the ambiguous use of the word *he*, which is also found in the English version by North, "Cæsar answered that he had many other ways to die than so."

Shakespeare's Timon composes the following epitaph for his tomb:—

Here lies a wretched corse, of wretched soul bereft:
Seek not my name; a plague consume you wicked
    caitiffs left!
Here lie I Timon; who, alive, all living men did hate:
Pass by, and curse thy fill; but pass and stay not here
    thy gait.

This epitaph is taken word for word (one word only being changed) from Sir Thomas North, who here thinks it well to follow Amyot's example of turning the lines into verse. Shakespeare's version, or that which is attributed to him, for *Timon of Athens* is full of incoherencies and doubtful passages,—presents the strange anomaly of uniting in one, two perfectly distinct epitaphs, distinguished as such by North and by Amyot, as well as by Plutarch: one is by Timon himself, the other by the poet Callimachus. It is absurd to say, "Seek not my name," and two lines further on, "Here lie I Timon." In North the passage is, "On the tomb was written this epitaph:—

Here lies a wretched corse of wretched soul bereft,
Seek not my name; a plague consume you wicked
    wretches left.

It is reported that Timon himself when he lived made this epitaph; for that which is commonly rehearsed was not his, but made by the poet Callimachus:—

Here lie I Timon, who alive all living men did hate:
Pass by and curse thy fill, but pass and stay not here
    thy gait.

Turning to *Julius Cæsar*, we find Antony (Act III. Sc. 2) saying, when reading Cæsar's will to the people:—

Moreover, he hath left you all his walks,
His private arbours, and new-planted orchards,
On *this* side Tiber.

"On this side Tiber," writes Shakespeare. Plutarch wrote *peran tou potamou*, "*across* the Tiber," but Shakespeare was misled by North, who had been misled by Amyot.

He bequeathed unto every citizen of Rome twenty-
five drachmas a man, and he left his gardens and
arbours unto the people, which he had on *this* side of
the river of Tyber.

But the most striking instances of Shakespeare borrowing from North occur in *Coriolanus*, where, in the hero's speech to Aufidius, demanding his hospitality and alliance, and in that of Volumnia to her son, in which she beseeches him not to war upon Rome,[1] Shakespeare has done little more, says Dr. Farmer, than throw the very words of North into blank verse.

The best and most conclusive part of Dr. Farmer's essay is his demonstration of the third-handedness of Shakespeare's knowledge of Plutarch, but it contains also several other curious little revelations; as, for example, that concerning the plagiarism from Anacreon that commentators have been pleased to detect in the following passages from *Timon of Athens* (Act IV., Sc. 3):—

The sun's a thief, and with his great attraction
Robs the vast sea. The moon's an arrant thief,
And her pale fire she snatches from the sun.
The sea's a thief, whose liquid surge resolves
The moon into salt tears. The earth's a thief,
That feeds and breeds by a composture stolen
From general excrement: each thing's a thief.

Dr. Farmer shows that, even supposing it impossible for Shakespeare, "who was generally able to think for himself," to have originated it, it cannot be quoted as a proof of his knowledge of Greek, seeing that Anacreon's ode had been translated several times into Latin, French, and English,

before the end of the sixteenth century, notably by Ronsard in his drinking song:—

La terre les eaux va buvant;
L'arbre la boit par la racine;
La mer salie boit le vent,
Et le soleil boit la marine.
Le soliel est bu de la lune;
Tout boit, soit en haut ou en bas;
Suivant cette règle commune,
Pourquoi donc ne boirions nous pas?

It was not only in the case of Greek authors that Shakespeare gladly availed himself of translations, for as Farmer shows, in many instances where it would have been easy for him to consult the Latin originals he preferred having recourse to English translations, as is the case, for example, with Prospero's address to his attendant spirits in the *Tempest*.

Ye elves of hills, of standing lakes, and groves,

which Warburton took to be copied from Ovid, but which a comparison of texts clearly proves to be borrowed not from the Latin poet but from the English translation by Arthur Golding in 1567.

Farmer makes some very sensible remarks on the subject of Shakespeare's frequent allusions to classical fables and memories. To infer from these allusions that Shakespeare had read Ovid, Virgil, and Homer, at any rate in English, and had himself drunk at the fountainhead of Greek and Latin antiquity, is a quite uncalled-for conclusion. The literature of the Middle Ages and of the Renaissance had popularized all the legends of antiquity, and turned them into current coin long before translations of Greek authors were in people's hands. To quote an example, Shakespeare, in the *Midsummer Night's Dream*, happens to mention Dido, and thereupon commentators carefully point out that there was no translation of Virgil's *Æneid* in Shakespeare's time. But what does that matter? "The fate of Dido had been sung very early by Gower, Chaucer, and Lydgate; Marlowe had even already introduced her to the stage."

Another passage in the *Midsummer Night's Dream* shows that Shakespeare knew of the distinction made by Ovid between Cupid's two sets of arrows, some of them being pointed with lead, and others with gold; and again the question arises whether he derived this directly from Ovid, in either Latin or English. He may possibly have done so, but still such a conclusion is perfectly unnecessary, as "Cupid's arrows appear with their characteristic differences in Surrey, in Sidney, in Spenser, and in every sonneteer of the Elizabethan period." Later on, Voltaire, when he in his turn inherited the tradition, thus describes them in the first scene of *Nanine*:—

Je vous l'ai dit, l'amour a deux carquois:
L'un est rempli de ces traits tout de flamme
Dont la douceur porte la paix dans l'âme,
Qui rend plus purs nos goûts, nos sentiments,
Nos soins plus vifs, nos plaisirs plus touchants;
L'autre n'est plein que de flèches cruelles,
Qui, répandant les soupçons, les querelles,
Rebutent l'âme, etc.

The conclusions that Dr. Farmer draws are, however, exaggerated, and overstep his premises; he is of opinion that he has proved that Shakespeare knew neither Greek nor Latin, but in reality he has only shown that the poet made use of translations from both languages as much as possible, and besides this, that independently of any translations, much of his classical knowledge may have been culled from the literature of the Middle Ages and of the Renaissance.

In criticising Shakespeare's attainments, Dr. Farmer fell

into the egregious folly of speaking in a strain of impertinent conceit; it is as if the little man—for little he must assuredly have been—was eaten up with vanity, and was bursting to show that he knew more of Greek and Latin than Shakespeare did.

Of the same order of research and of the same spirit was another equally famous work that appeared in the eighteenth century—*Illustrations of Shakespeare*, containing an essay "On the Anachronisms and Some Other Incongruities of Shakspere," by Francis Douce. In this big book, bristling with erudition but devoid of talent, and very foolish and irreverent towards Shakespeare, the poet's historical and geographical blunders are pointed out with pedantic and ponderous care, and without the least understanding of the subject; but an inquiry into Shakespeare's anachronisms, and the further criticism of Douce's book, must be reserved for another chapter.

When Shakespeare was looked upon as an "intoxicated savage," his literary learning was, naturally enough, held in small esteem, and rated lower than it really deserved; but when a complete revolution in opinion was introduced by Schlegel and Coleridge, who proclaimed that he must no longer be regarded as a mere child of nature, but as a wise and enlightened artist knowing perfectly what he was about, people fell into the opposite extreme, and entertained the most extravagant notions as to the extent and depth of his acquirements. Our own century has discovered that Shakespeare knew everything, like Dr. Pancrace, in Molière's comedy of the *Mariage Forcé*, "fables, mythology, and history, grammar, poetry, rhetoric, dialectics and sophistry; mathematics, arithmetic, optics, oneiro-criticism and physics." A legal system, a treatise on mental maladies, a complete guide-book to country life, lessons on ornithology, entomology, and botany have all been extracted from his works; while from the propriety with which he uses technical terms appertaining to military matters, to hunting and to jurisprudence, it has been concluded that he must have been a soldier, a poacher, and a lawyer. Several of his titles to the professorship of universal knowledge have escaped my memory, but those already mentioned make up a tolerably long list, in which Shakespeare figures as a doctor, a lawyer, an agriculturist, a zoologist, a botanist, a hunter and a soldier.

A complete ethnological system has also been discovered in his works by Mr. O'Connell, the author of a *New Exegesis of Shakespeare*, published in 1859, according to whom "that which constitutes the novel and peculiar greatness of Shakespeare, is that being the first to rise to a wider and, at the same time, deeper contemplation of human nature, he has depicted, not only individuals and families, but has also sketched the character of the principal European races. While Æschylus and the ancient drama limited the sphere of action to the family, the founder of the modern drama carried it further, and included larger groups in conformity with the general progress made in the knowledge of men and of nature. What Asia Minor and Hellas were to the Athenians, Europe, in its vast extent, was to the English people in the days of the Renaissance. The subjects of the Æschylean drama were the house of Pelopides and that of Labdacides; those of Shakespeare were the Germanic, Italian, and Celtic races: in this system, Iago represents the character of the Italian, Hamlet the Teutonic, and Macbeth the Celtic race."[2] It was this exaggerated notion of Shakespeare's learning and philosophy which also gave rise to the famous paradox, brought forward from time to time by some lunatic, that Shakespeare never existed, and that his name was only a fictitious one, adopted by the most learned and philosophical thinker of the time, Francis Bacon!

To rehabilitate Shakespeare as a Latin scholar was a task that lay very close to the hearts of his commentators, and they entered upon it with such eagerness and simplicity, that the disinterested observer feels quite bewildered, and tries in vain to decide which of the two sides is the more ridiculous—the one which Shakespeare's presumed ignorance rendered vainglorious of its own learning, or the other which thought the poet's glory would be enhanced by showing that he might have carried off a prize for Latin verse. As a sample of the extremely acrimonious language in which those of Coleridge's school speak of "the detractors of Shakespeare's learning," may be quoted the passage in which Knight, the well-known editor and critic of Shakespeare, expresses his appreciation of Dr. Farmer's essay:—

> He wrote an essay on the learning of Shakespeare which has not one passage of solid criticism from the first page to the last, and if the name and the works of Shakespeare were to perish, and one copy could be miraculously preserved, the only inference from the book would be, that William Shakespeare was a very obscure and ignorant man whom some misjudging admirers had been desirous to exalt into an ephemeral reputation, and that Richard Farmer was a very distinguished and learned man who had stripped the mask off the pretender.

That such a passage should ever have been written is almost inconceivable, not on account of the hard measure dealt out to Dr. Farmer, but because of the singular notion implied in it, that if Dr. Farmer were right in alleging Shakespeare's ignorance of languages, the poet would be a mere pretender to the crown of fame. For my part, I am most willing to grant Shakespeare's acquaintance with Greek and Latin, not so much for the honour of the poet, as to gratify Mr. Knight, since he takes the matter so much to heart; I believe, and will give my reasons for believing further on, that Shakespeare at all events knew Latin,—only, in truth, the strange arguments with which this view has sometimes been upheld makes one doubt whether it can possibly be the truer one.

In the second part of *Hamlet*, Polonius, in introducing the players to the Prince, praises their skill, and says, that for them, "Seneca cannot be too heavy, nor Plautus too light;" that simply is, as the German critic Delius justly remarks, "They can act with facility both the comic Plautus and the tragic Seneca." There is no hidden subtlety of meaning in the two adjectives, *heavy* and *light*. But Knight discovers in them an admirably profound and concise definition of the talent of Seneca and of Plautus.

> In *Hamlet*, Shakespeare gives in a word the characteristics of two ancient dramatists; his criticism is decisive as to his familiarity with the originals, "Seneca cannot be too heavy, nor Plautus too light."

In the *Comedy of Errors* (Act V., Sc. 1), a servant rushes in, crying—

> O mistress, mistress, shift and save yourself!
> My master and his man are both broke loose,
> Beaten the maids a-row, and bound the doctor,
> Whose beard they have singed off with brands of fire;
> And ever as it blazed they threw on him
> Great pails of puddled mire to quench the hair.

This, it appears, is an imitation of Virgil, for in the twelfth book of the *Æneid* (lines 298, and following), we read:—

> Corinæus took a lighted brand from the altar, and at the moment when Ebusus was about to strike him he threw it in his face, the flames surrounded him, and

his huge beard caught fire and burnt with a great smell of burning.

Thus, whenever the incident of a beard maliciously set on fire occurs in literature, we must go back to Virgil as its source; as, for instance, in *Tristram Shandy*, where Sterne shows us Susannah setting fire with her candle to Dr. Slop's wig (Vol. VI., Ch. III.), who, in a passion, flings in her face the cataplasm that had been prepared for little Tristram. Again, the passage in which Shakespeare, in *As You Like It*, has described the death of a stag, and "the big, round tears coursing one another down his innocent nose" (Act II., Sc. 1), must presumably be derived from the seventh book of the *Æneid;*— and yet, is it not possible that so great a poacher might have seen such a sight for himself?

But when we find Knight placing a passage in which Shakespeare puts the eulogy of blows into Dromio's mouth, side by side with one in which Cicero celebrates the praise of learning, we begin to think that we are dreaming, and rub our eyes and read the paragraph over again:—

> "When I am cold he heats me with beating; when I am warm he cools me with beating; I am waked with it when I sleep; raised with it when I sit; driven out of doors with it when I go from home; welcomed home with it when I return" (*Comedy of Errors*, Act IV., Sc. 4.): "Literature," says Cicero, "is the exercise of youth and the charm of old age; adorning fortune, it also offers in adversity a refuge and a consolation; the delight of the domestic hearth, easily enjoyed everywhere, it bears us company at night, travelling, and in the country."[3]

As to Greek authors, Knight hardly ventures to affirm positively that Shakespeare read them in the original, but he evidently wishes to intimate as much to his readers. When comparing Shakespeare's misanthrope with that of Lucian, he complacently passes in review the numberless points of resemblance between them, and significantly observes that no translation of Lucian had appeared in Shakespeare's time; as, however, the subject of Timon the Misanthrope was popular before then, and had even appeared on the stage, Knight is obliged to admit that Shakespeare may have known it in its principal details without having had recourse to the original in Greek.

In the historical drama of *Henry V.* (Act I., Sc. 2) we read:—

> While that the armed hand doth fight abroad,
> The advised head defends itself at home;
> For argument, through high, and low, and lower,
> Put into parts, doth keep in one concent;
> Congreeing in a full and natural close,
> Like music.

Then, after a very poetical comparison of the "work of honeybees" to a well-governed state, there follows a series of similes, all tending to set forth the truth that—

> So may a thousand actions, once afoot,
> End in one purpose, and be all well borne
> Without defeat.

The same idea is met with in Plato's *Republic*, as well as in a fragment, preserved by Augustine, of Cicero's long-lost treatise, *De Republica*.[4] Knight, in his edition of Shakespeare, gives the following note on this subject:—

> The words of Cicero, to which the lines of Shakespeare have so close a resemblance, form part of a fragment of that portion of his lost treatise *De Republica* which is presented to us only in the writings of St. Augustin. The first question therefore

is, Had Shakespeare read the fragment in St. Augustin? But Cicero's *De Republica* was, as far as we know, an adaptation of Plato's *Republic*, the sentence we have quoted is almost literally to be found in Plato; and what is still more curious, the lines of Shakespeare are more deeply imbued with the Platonic philosophy than the passage of Cicero. . . . They develope unquestionably the great Platonic doctrine of the Tri-unity of the three principles in man, with the idea of a state. The particular passage in Plato's *Republic* to which we refer is in Book IV., and may be thus rendered: "It is not alone wisdom and strength which make a state simply wise and strong, but it (order), like that harmony called the diapason, is diffused throughout the whole state, making both the weakest and the strongest, and the middling people concent the same melody." Again, "the harmonic power of political justice is the same as that musical concent which connects the three chords, the octave, the bass and the fifth." There was no translation of Plato in Shakespeare's time except a single dialogue by Spenser.

In a question of this kind, in which, to whatever side we may incline, it is impossible to lay claim to absolute certainty, it is well to keep within the bounds of a prudent and modest reserve; but one rule that always holds good is from among the various explanations of a fact to choose out the simplest.

What has here to be accounted for is the presence in Shakespeare's works of a passage which is imbued with the spirit of platonism, and is so beautifully expressed, and so full of an antique wisdom and philosophy that it might have been written by Plato himself. It must, in the first place, be remembered that the comparison of a well-ordered government to a concert in which every instrument plays its part, or to a bee-hive, has long since become a commonplace in literature. Ever since it was set in circulation by Plato and Cicero in their respective treatises on the *Republic*, there has probably been no ancient philosopher or poet from whose writings some analogous simile could not be quoted. In the time of the Renaissance Plato was held in the highest favour by English poets; as Coleridge tells us, "the star of serenest brilliance in the glorious constellation of Elizabeth's court, our England's Sir Philip Sidney, held high converse with Spenser on the idea of supersensual beauty." Lyly, the author of *Euphues*, borrowed the name of his hero from Plato's *Republic*, and his romance teems with comparisons between human governments and those presented to us in nature, especially in the case of bees. The tedious length of his exemplification places it far below the poetry of Shakespeare's passage, and makes it infinitely less worthy to be compared to the antique model, but it is precisely in such cases as this that we catch a glimpse of genius at work in one of its most marvellous operations, by virtue of which, diving through all the prolixity and exaggeration that a whole host of imitators have lost themselves in, it re-discovers an ancient conception, and makes it live again in all its first freshness and truth: for there is a brotherhood among all great minds, and Shakespeare happening to meet with the enfeebled expression of what had once been a thought of Plato's, was able to re-think it, almost back to its original form. A most striking example of this power or resurrection, which is the birthright of genius, is afforded in the character of Cressida, as will be seen further on. In all probability Shakespeare knew nothing of the poem of the obscure Norman trouvère who first conceived the idea of the brilliant coquette, but amidst all the more or less clumsy alterations made by numberless imitators of Benoit de

Sainte-More, he has grasped the essential features of her character with sure and unerring hand.

Amongst the many minor points of resemblance in details to the texts of classical antiquity, so abundantly offered by Shakespeare's plays, those which touch upon philosophy possess the greatest chance of being interesting, as in them we may hope to meet not only with words, but with at least a few reflected rays of thought. Professor Nebler, of the University of Berne, has dedicated one chapter of his book on Shakespeare (*Aufsätze über Shakespeare*) to pointing out all the passages in which Shakespeare alludes to the name or ideas of an ancient philosopher, and from his pages I have culled the following sentences, adding those I have gathered from my own reading of Shakespeare.

Nothing could well be more poetical than the opening of the fifth act of the *Merchant of Venice*. Jessica and Lorenzo are sitting one summer's night in Portia's garden, singing the eternal hymn of love, while the exquisite grace and charm of the duet is enhanced by the classical reminiscences more or less vague and inaccurate, which mingle with their strains:—

> *Lor.*: The moon shines bright:—in such a night as
>     this,
>     When the sweet wind did gently kiss the trees,
>     And they did make no noise,—in such a night,
>     Troilus, methinks, mounted the Trojan walls,
>     And sighed his soul toward the Grecian tents,
>     Where Cressid lay that night.[5]
> *Jes.*: In such a night
>     Did Thisbe fearfully o'ertrip the dew;
>     And saw the lion's shadow ere himself,
>     And ran dismayed away.
> *Lor.*: In such a night
>     Stood Dido with a willow in her hand[6]
>     Upon the wild sea-banks, and waft her love
>     To come again to Carthage.
> *Jes.*: In such a night
>     Medea gather'd the enchanted herbs
>     That did renew old Æson.
> *Lor.*: . . . . Look how the floor of heaven
>     Is thick inlaid with patines of bright gold,
>     There's not the smallest orb which thou behold'st
>     But in his motion like an angel sings,
>     Still quiring to the young-eyed cherubins:
>     Such harmony is in immortal souls.
>     But whilst this muddy vesture of decay
>     Doth grossly close it in, we cannot hear it.

The idea of the music of the spheres belongs primarily to the philosophy or rather to the poetry of Plato; and the same thought is finely expressed by Cicero in the fragment known under the title of *The Dream of Scipio*. In *Antony and Cleopatra*, Cleopatra, bewailing Antony's death, compares his voice to the "tunèd spheres" (Act V., Sc. 2); and in *Twelfth Night* Olivia pays the same compliment to the page in disguise, with whom she is in love. Pericles, prince of Tyre, in his ecstasy at finding his daughter Marina, suddenly hears sounds of music unheard by the others, which he calls the music of the spheres.

The name of Aristotle occurs in the first scene of the *Taming of the Shrew*, but there is a more curious mention of him in *Troilus and Cressida*, Act II., Sc. 2. In the council held by Priam, Troilus and Paris with the unreflective impetuosity of youth vote for the continuation of the war; but Hector, no less calm and prudent than brave, maintains that it would be right as well as politic to restore the wife of Menelaus to her lawful husband, and reproves his two scatter-brained brothers, saying—

> Paris and Troilus, you have both said well;
> And on the cause and question now in hand
> Have glozed,—but superficially; not much
> Unlike young men, whom Aristotle thought
> Unfit to hear moral philosophy.

For Hector to speak of Aristotle is an amusing anachronism, but it is difficult to decide whether Shakespeare fell into it intentionally or through inadvertence, the humorous licence which runs through the whole play lending probability to the former suggestion; just as Goethe, it may be remembered, has been pleased to put the name of Luther into the mouth of Faust. It would be as idle to conclude, as Gervinus does, on the strength of Hector's speech, that Shakespeare had read Aristotle's *Ethics*, as it would be to imagine that every poet of the present day who alludes to a tenet of the Cartesian philosophy or of eclecticism or of positivism has necessarily read the works of Des Cartes, of Cousin, or of Auguste Comte. In his *De Augmentis*, Bacon quotes Aristotle's same opinion of young men, and strangely enough makes precisely the same mistake that Shakespeare does; it being politics, not moral philosophy, for which the Greek philosopher deemed young men unfit.

Pythagoras is several times mentioned in Shakespeare, and always with some ironical allusion to his doctrine of the transmigration of souls. The lively Gratiano, in the *Merchant of Venice*, tells Shylock that he must have been a wolf in a former existence (Act IV., Sc. 1); Rosalind, in *As You Like It*, has a confused recollection of having once been an Irish rat (Act III., Sc. 2); and in *Twelfth Night*, the clown, when mocking and jeering at Malvolio, advises him not to kill a woodcock lest he should thereby dislodge the soul of his grandmother (Act IV., Sc. 2.). The authority of Pythagoras is invoked by name in each of these three passages.

Shakespeare alludes to Heraclitus, though without mentioning his name, in Act I., Sc. 2, of the *Merchant of Venice*, in which Portia says of one of her suitors, the melancholy and morose County Palatine, that when he grows old he will become like the weeping philosopher.

Epicurus is only treated as the voluptuous materialist of common tradition, and is thus presented in *Antony and Cleopatra* (Act II., Sc. 1); in *King Lear* (Act I., Sc. 4); in *Macbeth* (Act V., Sc. 3) and in the *Merry Wives of Windsor* (Act II., Sc. 2).

The only mention of Socrates occurs in the *Taming of the Shrew*, where, as may readily be guessed, it is not as the philosopher but as the husband that he is alluded to: Petruchio replies to his friend's report of Katharine's shrewish disposition, "Be she as curst and shrewd as Socrates' Xantippe she moves me not." (Act I., Sc. 2.)

Shakespeare, it may be noted, is fond of laughing at philosophers, which indeed is not only allowable but is in fact a highly philosophical proceeding; for if, as Pascal says, "to laugh at philosophy is really to philosophize," to laugh at philosophers is still more so. In *Much Ado about Nothing* (Act V., Sc. 1), Leonato observes that—

> There was never yet philosopher
> That could endure the toothache patiently;
> However they have writ the style of gods,
> And made a push at chance and sufferance.

In *King John*, Constance, after the loss of her son Arthur, says to Cardinal Pandulph (Act III., Sc. 4)—

> I am not mad;—I would to heaven I were!
> For then 'tis like I should forget myself;
> O, if I could, what grief should I forget!—
> Preach some philosophy to make me mad.

And King Lear calls Edgar, who is counterfeiting madness, his *philosopher*.

But Shakespeare especially makes fun of the truisms philosophers are wont to deal in—commonplace truths which noodles admire as profound thoughts and to which the seven wise men of Greece are so greatly indebted for their fame. Touchstone, in *As You Like It*, deals continually in sentences in imitation of the seven sages; as, for instance, when he gravely says to William the simple countryman, who opens his eyes wide at hearing such fine words (Act V., Sc. 1)—

> I do now remember a saying: "The fool doth think he is wise, but the wise man knows himself to be a fool." The heathen philosopher, when he had a desire to eat a grape, would open his lips when he put it into his mouth, meaning thereby, that grapes were meant to eat and lips to open.

Sir Hugh Evans, in the *Merry Wives of Windsor*, thinks with equal truth that lips are a part of the mouth, an opinion which he says he shares with many philosophers. Falstaff displays no less wisdom when, in acting the part of King Henry, he thus addresses his royal son:—

> There is a thing Harry which thou hast often heard of, and it is known to many in our land by the name of pitch; this pitch, *as ancient writers do report*, doth defile; so doth the company thou keepest. (*King Henry IV.*, Pt. I., Act. II., Sc. 4.)

Any learned scholar who took a delight in what I confess seems to me the barren and ungrateful task of pointing out all the passages in Shakespeare capable of serving as a text, or pretext, for classical quotations would have to distinguish three separate classes: first, the passages borrowed directly from ancient authors; second, those borrowed indirectly; third, mere coincidences. The distinction is not always easy to make; as, for instance, when Ophelia is buried, Laertes takes last leave of her in the touching and poetic words:—

> Lay her i' the earth;
> And from her fair and unpolluted flesh
> May violets spring!
> (Act V., Sc. 1.)

And in Persius we find—

> Non nunc e manibus istis,
> Non nunc e tumulo fortunataque favilla
> Nascentur violæ?

Did Shakespeare borrow this, or is it a mere coincidence?

Polonius says of Hamlet's madness, that "Though this be madness, yet there is method in it:" upon which a commentator remarks that this is precisely Horace's line—"Insanire paret certa ratione modoque." Yet I think that without Horace's line, Polonius's speech would be just as it is. Again, when Hamlet speaks of "the undiscovered country from whose bourn no traveller returns," it is natural to recall the fine lines of Catullus:—

> Qui nunc it per iter tenebricosum,
> Illuc, unde negant redire quemquam.

But there is not the slightest necessity to thrust in a remark that no English translation of Catullus had yet appeared; surely the imagination of both poets may have met here.

Sleep, as an image of death, is a well-known idea, and appears under various forms—in *Macbeth*, "this downy sleep, death's counterfeit;" in *Cymbeline*, "Sleep, the ape of death," and in the *Midsummer Night's Dream*, "Death counterfeiting sleep;" but a critic must have but a poor opinion of Shakespeare's imagination to suppose the comparison was suggested to him by a passage translated by Marlowe from Ovid.

Coriolanus says, "I shall be loved when I am lacked" (Act IV., Sc. 1), and the same thought occurs in Antony and Cleopatra:—

> The ebb'd man, ne'er loved till ne'er worth love,
> Comes dear'd by being lacked;

in connection with which is quoted Horace's line—

> Extinctus amabitur idem;

and to this there is no objection, but we ought also to note the old proverb: "When people are missed then they are mourned."

In the *Two Gentlemen of Verona*, when Proteus tells Silvia that Valentine is dead, she answers:—

> In his grave
> Assure thyself my love is buried.
> (Act IV., Sc. 2.)

As Dido affirms, in like manner, that Sicheus has borne her love with him into the tomb:—

> Ille habeat secum servetque sepulchro,

we are left to decide whether Shakespeare obtained Silvia's answer from Virgil, or from the natural feeling of the heart.

In the *Tempest*, Miranda says to Ferdinand (Act III., Sc. 1)—

> I am your wife, if you will marry me;
> If not I'll die your maid; to be your fellow
> You may deny me; but I'll be your servant,
> Whether you will or no. .

This is so completely the natural language of passion, while at the same time the five exquisite lines of Catullus[7] rush so irresistibly into the mind, that it is very embarrassing to decide whether we have here a coincidence or a case of borrowing.

The same thing occurs in the passage in the *Comedy of Errors*, in which Adriana says to Antipholus:—

> Come, I will fasten on this sleeve of thine:
> Thou art an elm, my husband, I, a vine;
> Whose weakness, married to thy stronger state,
> Makes me with thy strength to communicate.
> (Act II., Sc. 2.)

Shakespeare may very well have imitated Catullus:—

> Lenta, qui, velut assitas
> Vitis implicat arbores,
> Implicabitur in tuum
> Complexum;

but in Beaumont's and Fletcher's *Elder Brother*, the scholar, Charles, says to his servant, "Marry thyself to understanding, Andrew" (Act II., Sc. 4); and in the *Femmes Savantes*, Armande says to Henriette, in exactly the same spirit and in almost the same terms, "Marry yourself to philosophy, my sister," without Molière having imitated Beaumont and Fletcher.

But the quotation of classical authors would only form the easier portion of the task of drawing up a list of all the passages in Shakespeare in which some reminiscence of antiquity is evoked, for it would be requisite to show by what means the poet came to know them, whether it was from contemporaneous literature, or through translations, or from the originals. For instance, in *Troilus and Cressida*, we read—

> For to be wise and love
> Exceeds man's might; that dwells with gods above.

This thought is first met with in Publius Syrus, a Latin author of the first century before Christ, and accordingly, commentators began by saying, that Shakespeare had translated a passage direct from Publius Syrus. But later on, the discovery was made by some learned bookworm, of an English translation of Publius Syrus, by Taverner, published in 1553, at the end of a little duodecimo volume called the *Distichs of Cato*; and it then seemed more natural to suppose that it was through this translation that Shakespeare had acquired his knowledge of Publius Syrus. This is not all, however, for another learned bookworm found the same thought in Marston's play of *The Dutch Courtezan* (1605), and in Spenser's *Shepheardes Calender*; from this time the third explanation was adopted, more likely to be true than either of the two others, that Shakespeare had simply borrowed the passage of Publius Syrus from the current literature of the day. Examples of this sort are innumerable, *ab uno disce omnes*. However great a reader of ancient authors Shakespeare may have been, it will be readily admitted on all hands that the writers of his own time and country were those he knew best; and not the faintest shadow of disparagement is thrown over his fame by our agreeing with Dr. Farmer, that he was more familiar with translations than with the originals. In the *Taming of the Shrew*, for instance, we read—

> Young budding virgin, fair and fresh and sweet,
> Whither away; or where is thy abode?
> Happy the parents of so fair a child;
> Happier the man, whom favourable stars
> Allot thee for his lovely bedfellow!

The first thought of this salutation belongs to Homer; from whom it was borrowed by Ovid; Golding translated Ovid, and Shakespeare knew and imitated Golding, as is admitted, not only by Steevens, but even by Delius. It matters little whether a translation intervened or not,—the perfume of antiquity clings none the less to Shakespeare's passage, and it could not be more Homeric if he had transcribed it straight from the *Odyssey*.

There are, however, lines which, to all appearances, were translated, or imitated, from the classics by Shakespeare himself. In the *Comedy of Errors*, Ægeon begins the account of his tragic history with these words:—

> A heavier task could not have been imposed
> Than I to speak my griefs unspeakable.

This beginning resembles too closely the even then familiar and well-known "Infandum regina jubes renovare dolorem," to leave room for any doubt as to its having been directly borrowed. Further on, when speaking of the storm in which his ship perished Ægeon describes the obscured light of heaven, and how everything—

> Did but convey into our fearful minds
> A doubtful warrant of immediate death.

Virgil's line:—

> Præsentemque viris intentant omnia mortem,

is here very closely followed.

In the *Tempest* (Act IV., Sc. 1), we read—

> Highest queen of state,
> Great Juno comes; I know her by her gait,

which is evidently a recollection of the "Incedo Regina." In the *Taming of the Shrew*, Petruchio, after having said of Katharine, "Be she as curst and shrewd as Socrates' Xantippe," adds, "Were she as rough as are the swelling Adriatic seas," which is a close translation of the "Improbo iracundior Adria," in Horace's well-known ode to Lydia, "Donec gratus eram."

Shakespeare frequently introduces Latin words and phrases into his text; as, for instance, in the last-named comedy, he quotes two lines from Ovid,[8] and a line from Terence,[9] which last line does not indeed exactly tally with the text of the Latin author, and which it has been proved Shakespeare took from Lilly's Latin Grammar; but he could

have taken it with equal ease from Terence. He heads his poem of *Venus and Adonis* with a Latin epigraph, and we may rest assured that, to a nature as free from every kind of pedantry and pretence as his was, it would have been utterly repugnant to affect a knowledge he did not really possess. Shakespeare, we need not doubt, knew Latin as well as any man of his time; and in his time the educated portion of the public knew it better than they do now.

At Stratford-on-Avon, where Shakespeare was born, there was a free grammar school, which could be entered under the three conditions of residing in the town; being seven years old; and knowing how to read. Little William Shakespeare was sent by his father to the school, probably in 1571, when he had attained the age of seven, and knew how to read. The school hours were decidedly long—from daybreak to dark in winter, from six in the morning to six at night in the summer, excepting intervals for meals and recreation. Here Latin was certainly taught, and perhaps—but this is not equally certain—Greek, French, and Italian. Terence, Virgil, Cicero, Sallust and Cæsar were the principal authors read by the boys, while they learned the rules of grammar from Lilly, Donatus, or Valla. Various traditions, all agreeing on one point, relate that about 1578, that is, after about seven years of schooling, Shakespeare was removed from the school before having finished his regular course of study. His father seems at this time to have been undergoing a crisis in his pecuniary affairs, and as the family was both numerous and poor, it is hardly likely that young Shakespeare found time after leaving school to continue his studies. Added to which, he married at the age of eighteen, and by the time he was twenty-one found himself the father of a son and two daughters, and under such circumstances his hours of studious leisure must necessarily have been few. He became an actor, although as his sonnets show, not without some suffering to his pride from the humiliations attaching to the position; he touched up old plays and was ready to turn his hand to anything for which he could get paid, and thus earn a livelihood. In short, the beginning of his dramatic career was rude enough, and left him no time for any occupation of which the aim was other than present and practical utility, none consequently for the patient and thorough study which alone deserves the name. He absorbed knowledge from a thousand channels with ravenous activity, not to keep it and meditate upon it, but in order to give out again immediately whatever he had learned. As money came in, immunity from want came with it; yet even when no longer under the burden of necessity, Shakespeare's reading preserved to the end of his life the hasty character that it had at the beginning; his materials were never slowly accumulated, and carefully stored up in the memory for some grand monumental edifice in the future, but were eagerly seized upon with a view to immediate use. It was on this account that he fastened upon North's translation of Plutarch, a translation at secondhand, taken from the French of Amyot, and consequently doubly liable to inaccuracies, without troubling himself in the least as to what they would think of it at Chæronea. Capable of building up a palace out of such stones as it furnished him with, he cared little as to the intrinsic value of the raw material;—the work of transformation was no secret to him. And in the same way, it was not on account of an insufficient knowledge of Latin that he preferred to use the English translation of Ovid's *Metamorphoses* rather than the original, but because he read English more quickly, and less time was lost.

Seven years at school are enough to enable a lad to read easy passages in Latin fluently and to puzzle out the harder bits. In the sixteenth century Latin was still almost a living language; the world was only just emerging from the Middle Ages when it had been constantly spoken, and many men of letters and of learning continued to write it. It was in fact an ordinary element in the education of both men and women, and there is no shadow of reason for refusing it to Shakespeare. In all probability the *Menæchmi* of Plautus was read by him in the original, no English translation having appeared till some years after the *Comedy of Errors*. The various conjectures as to the means by which Shakespeare could have known the old comedian all proceed upon the unfounded assumption of Shakespeare's incapacity, in case of need, to get through a Latin play by himself.

Gervinus, on the other hand, affirms that Shakespeare was deeply versed in Seneca and Plautus, which is saying a good deal. It is extremely probable that he should have read, either in Latin or more likely still in English, all Seneca's plays, so well known and greatly admired as they then were, and also several of Plautus's, but Gervinus speaks of an intimate familiarity, which is not an assertion that should have been advanced without proof I know of no instance in which Shakespeare has copied Plautus except in the *Comedy of Errors*, and not even that has been completely demonstrated to be directly borrowed. In Act V., Sc. 4, of *Cymbeline*, Jupiter, seated on an eagle, descends amidst thunder and lightning and pronounces his decrees in the same antique metre that Heywood and Studley had employed in their translation of Seneca: such is the only proof given by Gervinus of Shakespeare's thorough acquaintance with the Latin tragedian. Warburton took the line in *Antony and Cleopatra* (Act IV., Sc. 10)—

Let me lodge Lichas on the horns o' the moon,

to be imitated from Seneca's *Hercules*, but Steevens deems it more likely to have been borrowed from Book IX. of the *Metamorphoses*. Gervinus adds:—

If Shakespeare had had occasion at any time to name his ideal, and to denote the highest examples of dramatic art which lay before him, he would have named none but Plautus and Seneca.

In spite of this purely gratuitous assertion, the conclusion arrived at in our preceding chapter must be repeated and maintained: that Shakespeare's feelings towards classical antiquity were those of complete indifference, that he considered it only as a rich mine of wealth, in which light it stood on exactly the same footing in his regard as the legends of the Middle Ages, and the traditions of English history.

Hallam, who advances no opinion lightly, notices the occurrence of numerous Latinisms in Shakespeare's works, "phrases, unintelligible and improper, except in the sense of their primitive roots," such as, "Things base and vile, holding no *quantity*," for value; rivers that have "overborn their *continents*," the "continente ripa" of Horace; "*compact* of imagination;" "something of great *constancy*," for consistency; "sweet Pyramis *translated* there," "the law of Athens, which by no means we may extenuate:" "expressions which it is not very likely that one, who did not understand their proper meaning, would have introduced into poetry." Hallam's remark is repeated by Gervinus; and Mr. S. Neil, the author of a very careful critical biography of Shakespeare, has no hesitation in saying that the poet's language is strongly tinged with Latinisms.

With regard to Greek, we may boldly affirm that he did not know it. Even admitting that he may have learned the declensions and verbs at school, such knowledge would have been quite insufficient to enable him to read a Greek author in the original. Every one knows that Greek is not learned at school, and Hallam declares that if in the sixteenth century men were better versed in Latin than they are now, the case was different with Greek. The extent of Shakespeare's knowledge of it may therefore fairly be measured by that of a school-boy of the present time, whose studies have been broken off unfinished, the result being the most absolute ignorance. But there was no occasion for Knight to make apologies for the great poet on this account—he is not singular in his ignorance, and even Schiller and Goethe, as their correspondence attests, read Homer, Aristotle, and the tragedians in translations.

In discussing the question of Shakespeare's learning, it must never be left out of sight, that poets are possessed of an instrument which is not in the hand of every student—the instrument of genius.

Great artists [M. Taine has well said] have no need to learn,—they guess. I have seen such an one, by means of a suit of armour, a costume, or a collection of old furniture, penetrate more deeply into the spirit of the Middle Ages than three savants put together. They rebuild, naturally and surely, in the same way that they build up, by virtue of an inspiration that lends wings to reasoning.

If we take the word "learning" in its large and liberal sense, and no longer reduce the question to a miserable pedantic wrangling over his more or less of Greek and Latin, then, of all men that ever lived, Shakespeare is one of the most learned.

Armed with indefatigable curiosity, he was an incessant reader [writes Philarète Chasles] and made himself acquainted with all the current literature of the day: Harrington's translation of Ariosto, Amyot's and North's translations of Plutarch, Fairfax's Tasso, and Florio's translation of Montaigne, were in his hands as soon as published. He read the travels of Sir Walter Raleigh, and a translation of those of Hakluyt, and of the *Week*, by Du Bartas. Stories, histories, plays, chronicles, theological works, amorous sonnets, everything printed in the sixteenth century, everything that fell into his hands, all was devoured by him, and his plays form a complete encyclopædia of his times.

Rabelais, too, he knew, a recollection of whom is found in two of his comedies.[10] And what an open door into classical antiquity he possessed in Montaigne's essays! Besides these, Pliny's *Natural History* was another book in his library; in *Antony and Cleopatra* (Act III. Sc. 7), there is a learned dissertation on the Nile, and in *Troilus and Cressida* (Act V., Sc. 3), Troilus reproaches Hector for his clemency towards the vanquished, which he says, "better fits a lion than a man,"—a notion belonging to Pliny the Elder, who observes that "the lion alone of all wild beasts is gentle to those that humble themselves before him, and will not touch any such upon their submission, but spareth what creature soever lieth prostrate before him."

Like all men of real learning, Shakespeare was fully conscious of his ignorance. The greatest stores of knowledge that any man has ever possessed are as nothing in comparison with the infinite number of things of which he is ignorant. A dark night lies all around us, and the more brightly our little torch burns, the better are we able to gauge the depth of blackness. In one of his sonnets (LXXVIII.), the image chosen by Shakespeare to describe an immense abyss is the distance that separates learning from his "rude ignorance," and elsewhere he says that ignorance is the malediction of God, and that learning is the very wing that bears us up to heaven.

Pope's reflection on this subject is very acute, in which he suggests that Shakespeare's ignorance was exaggerated for the sake of opposition and of symmetry, to form a sharper contrast with the vast learning of Ben Jonson. There is, perhaps, no more pernicious source of error in criticism than this mania for contrasting celebrated contemporaries in hard and fast lines;—because Shakespeare is full of fancy, Ben Jonson is set down as having none; and because Corneille writes with a masculine vigour, Racine, in spite of his *Athalie* and *Britannicus*, is said to be characterized by a feminine tenderness. And after all, it is childish to discuss the amount of learning possessed by an author who has taught the whole world, and from whom statesmen declare they have drawn their first notions of politics and history.

### Notes

1. "Should we be silent and not speak, etc"—Act V., Sc. 3.
2. Littré, *Littérature et histoire.*
3. Hæc studia adolescentiam agunt, senectutem oblectant secundas res ornant, adversis perfugium ac solatium præbent, delectant domi, non impediunt foris, pernoctant nobiscum, peregrinantur, rusticantur.
4. Theobald was the first of Shakespeare's commentators to whom it occurred to quote this passage, which runs as follows: "Ut in fidibus ac tibiis atque cantu ipso ac vocibus, concentus est quidam tenendus ex distinctis sonis, quem immutatum ac discrepantem aures eruditæ ferre non possunt, isque concentus ex dissimillimarum vocum moderatione concors tamen efficitur et congruens: sic ex summis et infimis et mediis interjectis ordinibus, ut sonis, moderata ratione civitas consensu dissimillimarum concinit, et quæ harmonia a musicis dicitur in cantu, ea est in civitate concordia, arctissimum atque optimum omni in republica vinculum incolumitatis: quæ sine justitia nullo pacto esse potest."
5. A recollection of Chaucer.
6. Steevens notes this passage as a proof out of many that Shakespeare was no reader of the classics.
7.    Si tibi non cordi fuerant connubia nostra
   Attamen in vestras potuisti ducere sedes
   Quæ tibi jucundo famularer serva labore,
   Candida permulcens liquidis vestigia lymphis
   Purpureave tuum consterners veste cubile.
8.    Hac ibat Simois, hic est Sigeia tellus,
   Hic steterat Priami regia celsa senis.
      (Act. III., Sc. 1.)
9.    Redime te captum, quam queas, minimo.
      (Act I., Sc. 1.)
10. In *As You Like It* (Act III., Sc. 2), Rosalind says to Celia, "Answer me in one word;" to which Celia answers, "You must borrow me Gargantua's mouth first, 'tis a word too great for any mouth of this age's size." In *Love's Labour's Lost*, the schoolmaster's name is Holofernes.

# Authorship Controversy

## DELIA BACON
### "William Shakespeare and His Plays: An Inquiry concerning Them"
*Putnam's Monthly*, January 1856, pp. 1–19

How can we undertake to account for the literary miracles of antiquity, while this great myth of the modern ages still lies at our own door, unquestioned?

This vast, magical, unexplained phenomenon which our own times have produced under our own eyes, appears to be, indeed, the only thing which our modern rationalism is not to be permitted to meddle with. For, here the critics themselves still veil their faces, filling the air with mystic utterances which seem to say, that to this shrine at least, for the footstep of the common reason and the common sense, there is yet no admittance. But how can they instruct us to take off here the sandals which they themselves have taught us to wear into the inmost *sekos* of the most ancient sanctities?

THE SHAKESPEARE DRAMA—its import, its limitations, its object and sources, its beginning and end—for the modern critic, that is surely now the question.

What, indeed, should we know of the origin of the Homeric poems? Twenty-five hundred years ago, when those mystic characters, which the learned Phenician and Egyptian had brought in vain to the singing Greek of the Heroic Ages, began, in the new modifications of national life which the later admixtures of foreign elements created, at length to be put to their true uses, that song of the nation, even in its latest form, was already old on the lips of the learned, and its origin a tradition. All the history of that wonderful individuality, wherein the inspirations of so many ages were at last united—the circumstance, the vicissitude, the poetic life that had framed that dazzling mirror of old time, and wrought in it those depths of clearness—all had gone before the art of writing and memories had found its way into Greece, or even the faculty of perceiving the actual had begun to be developed there.

And yet are the scholars of our time content to leave this matter here, where they find it! With these poetic remains in their hands, the monuments of a genius whose date is antehistorical, are they content to know of their origin only what Alexander and Plato could know, what Solon and Pisistratus were fain to content themselves with, what the Homerids themselves received of him as their ancestral patron?

No: with these works in their hands to-day, reasoning from them alone, with no collateral aids, with scarce an extant monument of the age from which they come to us, they are not afraid to fly in the face of all antiquity with their conclusions.

Have they not settled among them, already, the old dispute of the contending cities, the old dispute of the contending ages, too, for the honor of this poet's birth? Do they not take him to pieces before our eyes, this venerable Homer; and tell us how many old forgotten poets' ashes went to his formation, and trace in him the mosaic seams which eluded the scrutiny of the age of Pericles? Even Mr. Grote will tell us now, just where the *Iliad* "cuts me" the fiery Achilles "cranking in;" and what could hinder the learned Schlegel, years ago, from setting his chair in the midst of the Delian choirs, confronting the confounded children of Ion with his definitions of the term *Homeros*, and demonstrating, from the Leipsic *Iliad* in his hand that the poet's cotemporaries had, in fact, named him Homer the seer, not Homer the Blind One?

The criticism of our age found this whole question where the art of writing found it, two thousand five hundred years ago; but, because the Ionian cities, and Solon, and Pisistratus, might be presumed, beforehand, to know at least as much about it as they, or because the opinions of twenty-five centuries, in such a case, might seem to be entitled to some reverence, did the critics leave it there?

Two hundred and fifty years ago, *our* poet—our Homer—was alive in the world. Two centuries and a half ago, when the art of letters was already millenniums old in Europe, when the art of printing had already been in use a century and a half, in the midst of a cotemporary historical illumination which has its equal nowhere in history, those works were issued that have given our English life and language their imperishable claim in the earth, that have made the name in which they come to us a word by itself, in the human speech; and, to this hour, we know of their origin hardly so much as we knew of the origin of the Homeric epics, when the present discussions in regard to them commenced, *not* so much,—not a hundredth part so much, as we now know of Pharaoh's, who reigned in the valley of the Nile, ages before the invasion of the Hyksos.

But with these products of the national life in our hands, with all the cotemporary light on their implied conditions which such an age as that of Elizabeth can furnish, are we going to be able to sit still much longer, in a period of historical inquiry and criticism like this, under the gross impossibilities which the still accepted theory on this subject involves?

The age which has put back old Homer's eyes, safe, in his head again, after he had gone without them well nigh three thousand years; the age which has found, and labeled, and sent to the museum, the skull in which the pyramid of Cheops was designed, and the lions which "the mighty hunter before the Lord" ordered for his new palace on the Tigris some millenniums earlier; the age in which we have abjured our faith in Romulus and Remus, is surely one in which we may be permitted to ask this question.

Shall this crowning literary product of that great epoch, wherein these new ages have their beginning, vividly arrayed in its choicest refinements, flashing everywhere on the surface with its costliest wit, crowded everywhere with its subtlest scholasticisms, betraying, on every page, its broadest, freshest range of experience, its most varied culture, its profoundest insight, its boldest grasp of comprehension—shall this crowning result of so many preceding ages of growth and culture, with its essential, and now palpable connection with the new scientific movement of the time from which it issues, be able to conceal from us, much longer, its history?—Shall we be able to accept in explanation of it, much longer, the story of the Stratford poacher?

The popular and traditional theory of the origin of these works was received and transmitted after the extraordinary circumstances which led to its first imposition had ceased to exist, because, in fact, no one had any motive for taking the trouble to call it in question. The common disposition to receive, in good faith, a statement of this kind, however extraordinary—the natural intellectual preference of the affirmative proposition at hand, as the explanation of a given phenomenon, when the negative or the doubt compels one to launch out for himself, in search of new positions—this, alone, might serve to account for this result, at a time when criticism, as yet, was not; when the predominant mental habit, on all ordinary questions, was still that of passive acceptance, and the most extraordinary excitements, on questions of the most momentous interest, could only rouse the public mind to assume, temporarily, any other attitude.

And the impression which these works produced, even in their first imperfect mode of exhibition, was already so profound and extraordinary, as to give to all the circumstances of their attributed origin a blaze of notoriety, tending to enhance this positive force in the tradition. Propounded as a fact, not as a theory, its very boldness—its startling improbability—was made at once to contribute to its strength; covering,

beforehand, the whole ground of attack. The wonderful origin of these works was, from the first, the predominant point in the impression they made—the prominent marvel in those marvels, around which all the new wonders, that the later criticism evolved, still continued to arrange themselves.

For the discoveries of this criticism had yet no tendency to suggest any new belief on this point. In the face of all that new appreciation of the works themselves, which was involved in them, the story of that wondrous origin could still maintain its footing;—through all the ramifications of this criticism, it still grew and inwound itself, not without vital limitation, however, to the criticism thus entangled. But these new discoveries involved, for a time, conclusions altogether in keeping with the tradition.

This new force in literature, for which books contained no precedent—this new manifestation of creative energy, with its self-sustained vitalities; with its inexhaustible prodigality, mocking nature herself; with its new grasp of the whole circuit of human aims and activities;—this force, so unlike anything that scholasticism or art had ever before produced, though it came, in fact, with the sweep of all the ages—moved with all their slow accumulation—could not account for itself to those critics, as anything but a new and mystic manifestation of nature—a new upwelling of the occult vital forces, underlying our phenomenal existence—invading the historic order with one capricious leap, laughing at history, telling the laboring ages that their sweat and blood had been in vain.

And the tradition at hand was entirely in harmony with this conception. For, to this superhuman genius, bringing with it its own laws and intuitions from some outlying region of life, not subject to our natural conditions, and not to be included in our "philosophy," the differences between man and man, natural or acquired, would, of course, seem trivial. What could any culture, or any merely natural endowment accomplish, that would furnish the required explanation of this result? And, by way of defining itself as an agency wholly supernal, was it not, in fact, necessary that it should select, as its organ, one in whom the natural conditions of the highest intellectual manifestations were obviously, even grossly, wanting?

With this theory of it, no one need find it strange that it should pass in its selection those grand old cities, where learning sat enthroned with all her time-honored array of means and appliances for the development of mental resource—where the genius of England had hitherto been accomplished for all its triumphs—and that it should pass the lofty centres of church and state, and the crowded haunts of professional life, where the mental activities of the time were gathered to its conflicts; where, in hourly collision, each strong individuality was printing itself upon a thousand others, and taking in turn from all their impress; where, in the thick coming change of that "time-bettering age," in its crowding multiplicities, and varieties, and oppositions, life grew warm and in the old the new was stirring, and in the many, the one; where wit, and philosophy, and fancy, and humor, in the thickest onsets of the hour, were learning to veil, in courtly phrase, in double and triple meanings, in crowding complexities of conceits and unimagined subtleties of form, the freedoms that the time had nurtured; where genius flashed up from all her hidden sources, and the soul of the age—"the mind reflecting ages past"—was collecting itself, and ready, even then, to leap forth, "not for an age, but for all time."

And, indeed, was it not fitting that this new inspiration, which was to reveal the latent forces of nature, and her scorn of conditions—fastening her contempt for all time upon the pride of human culture at its height—was it not fitting, that it should select this moment of all others, and this locality, that it might pass by that very centre of historical influences, which the court of Elizabeth then made,—that it might involve in its perpetual eclipse that immortal group of heroes, and statesmen, and scholars, and wits, and poets, with its enthroned king of thought, taking all the past for his inheritance, and claiming the minds of men in all futurity, as the scene and limit of his dominion? Yes, even he—he, whose thought would grasp the whole, and keep his grasp on it perpetual—speaks to us still out of that cloud of mockery that fell upon him, when "Great Nature" passed him by—even him—with his immortal longings, with his world-wide aims, with his new mastery of her secrets, too, and his new sovereignty over her, to drop her crown of immortality—lit with the finest essence of that which makes his own page immortal—on the brow of the pet horse-boy at Blackfriars—the wit and good fellow of the London link-holders, the menial *attaché* and *elevé* of the play-house—the future actor, and joint proprietor, of the New Theatre on the Bankside.

Who quarrels with this movement? Who does not find it fitting and pleasant enough? Let the "thrice three muses" go into mourning as deep as they will for this desertion—as desertion it was—for we all know that to the last hour of his life, this fellow cared never a farthing for them, but only for his gains at their hands;—let learning hide as she best may, her baffled head in this disgrace—who cares?—who does not rather laugh with great creating nature in her triumph?

At least, who would be willing to admit, for a moment, that there was one in all that cotemporary circle of accomplished scholars, and men of vast and varied genius, capable of writing these plays; and who feels the least difficulty in supposing that "this player here," as Hamlet terms him—the whole force of that outburst of scorn ineffable bearing on the word, and on that which it represented to him—who doubts that this player is most abundantly and superabundantly competent to it?

Now that the deer-stealing fire has gone out of him, now that this youthful impulse has been taught its conventional social limits, sobered into the mild, sagacious, witty "Mr. Shakespeare of the Globe," distinguished for the successful management of his own fortunes, for his upright dealings with his neighbors, too, and "his facetious grace in writing," patronized by men of rank, who include his theatre among their instrumentalities for affecting the popular mind, and whose relations to him are, in fact, identical with those which Hamlet sustains to the players of *his* piece, what is to hinder this Mr. Shakespeare—the man who keeps the theatre on the Bankside—from working himself into a frenzy when he likes, and scribbling out unconsciously Lears, and Macbeths, and Hamlets, merely as the necessary dialogue to the spectacles he professionally exhibits; ay, and what is to hinder his boiling his kettle with the manuscripts, too, when he has done with them, if he chooses?

What it would be madness to suppose the most magnificently endowed men of that wondrous age could accomplish—its real men, those who have left their lives in it, woven in its web throughout—what it would be madness to suppose these men, who are but men, and known as such, could accomplish, this Mr. Shakespeare, actor and manager, of whom no one knows anything else, shall be able to do for you in "the twinkling of an eye," without so much as knowing it, and there shall be no words about it.

And are not the obscurities that involve his life, so impenetrably in fact, the true Shakespearean element? In the boundless sea of negations which surrounds that play-house, surely he can unroll himself to any length, or gather himself into any shape or attitude, which the criticism in hand may call for. There is nothing to bring up against him, with one's theories. For, here in this daylight of our modern criticism, in its noontide glare, has he not contrived to hide himself in the profoundest depths of that stuff that myths are made of? Who shall come in competition with him here? Who shall dive into the bottom of that sea to pluck his drowned honors from him?

Take, one by one, the splendid men of this Elizabethan age, and set them down with a *Hamlet* to write, and you will say beforehand, such an one can not do it, nor such an one,—nor *he*, with that profoundest insight and determination of his which taught him to put physical nature to the question that he might wring from her her secrets; but humanity, human nature, of course, has none worth noting for him;—oh no; he, with his infinite wit and invention, with his worlds of covert humor, with his driest prose, pressed, bursting with Shakspearean beauty, he could not do it; nor *he*, with his Shakespearean acquaintance with life, with his Shakespearean knowledge of men under all the differing social conditions, at home and abroad, by land and by sea, with his world-wide experiences of nature and fortune, with the rush and outbreak of his fiery mind kindling and darting through all his time; he, with his Shakespearean grace and freedom, with his versatile and profound acquirements, with his large, genial, generous, prodigal, Shakespearean soul that would comprehend all, and ally itself with all, he could not do it; neither of these men, nor both of them together, nor all the wits of the age together:—but this Mr. Shakespeare of the Globe, this mild, respectable, obliging man, this "Johannes Factotum" (as a cotemporary calls him, laughing at the idea of *his* undertaking "a blank verse,") is there any difficulty here? Oh no! None in the world: for, in the impenetrable obscurity of that illimitable green-room of his, "by the mass, he is anything, and he can do anything and that roundly too."

Is it wonderful? And is not that what we like in it? Would you make a man of him? With this miraculous inspiration of his, would you ask anything else of him? Do you not see that you touch the Shakespearean essence, with a question as to motives, and possibilities? Would he be Shakespeare still, if he should permit you to hamper him with conditions? What is the meaning of that word, then? And will you not leave him to us? Shall we have no Shakespeare? Have not we scholars enough, and wits enough, and men, of every other kind of genius, enough,—but have we many Shakespeares?—that you should wish to run this one through with your questions, this one, great, glorious, infinite impossibility, that has had us in its arms, all our lives from the beginning. If you dissolve him do you not dissolve us with him? If you take him to pieces, do you not undo us, also?

Ah, surely we did not need this master spirit of our race to tell us that there is that in the foundation of this human soul, "that loves to apprehend more than cool reason ever comprehends," nay, that there is an infinity in it, that finds her ordinances too straight, that will leap from them when it can, and shake the head at her. And have we not all lived once in regions full of people that were never compelled to give an account of themselves in any of these matters? And when, precisely, did we pass that charmed line, beyond which these phantoms cannot come? When was the word definitively spoken which told us that the childhood of the race was done, or that its grown-up children were to have henceforth no conjurors? Who yet has heard the crowing of that cock, "at whose warning, whether in earth or air, the extravagant and erring spirit hies to his confine?" The nuts, indeed, are all cracked long ago, whence of old the fairy princess, in her coach and six, drove out so freely with all her regal retinue, to crown the hero's fortunes; and the rusty lamp, that once filled the dim hut of poverty with eastern splendors, has lost its capabilities. But, when our youth robbed us of these, had it not marvels and impossibilities of its own to replace them with, yet more magical; and surely, manhood itself, the soberest maturity, can not yet be without these substitutes; and it is nature's own voice and outcry that we hear whenever one of them is taken from us.

Let him alone! We have lecturers enough and professors enough already. Let him alone! We will keep this one mighty conjuror, still, even in the place where men most do congregate, and nobody shall stir a hair on his impossible old head, or trouble him with a question. He shall stand there still, pulling interminable splendors out of places they never could have been in; that is the charm of it; he shall stand there rubbing those few sickly play-house manuscripts of his, or a few old, musty play-house novels, and wringing from them the very wine of all our life, showering from their greasy folds the gems and gold of all the ages! He shall stand there spreading, in the twinkling of an eye, for a single night in a dirty theatre, "to complete a purchase that he has a mind to," the feasts of the immortal gods; and before our lips can, by any chance, have reached even the edge of those cups, that open down into infinity, when the show has served his purpose, he shall whisk it all away again, and leave no wreck behind, except by accident; and none shall remonstrate, or say to him, "wherefore?" He shall stand there, still, for us all—the magician; nature's one, complete, incontestible, gorgeous triumph over the impossibilities of reason.

For the primary Shakespearean condition involves at present, not merely the accidental absence of those external means of intellectual enlargement and perfection, whereby the long arts of the ages are made to bring to the individual mind their last results, multiplying its single forces with the life of all;—but it requires also, the absence of all personal intellectual tastes, aims, and pursuits; it requires that this man shall be below all other men, in his sordid incapacity for appreciating intellectual values; it requires that he shall be able, not merely to witness the performance of these plays, not merely to hear them and read them for himself, but to compose them; it requires him to be able to compose the *Tempest*, and *Othello*, and *Macbeth*, without suspecting that there is anything of permanent interest in them—anything that will outlast the spectacle of the hour.

The art of writing had been already in use, twenty-five centuries in Europe, and a Shakespeare, one would think, might have been able to form some conception of its value and applications; the art of printing had been in use on the continent a century and a half, and it was already darting through every civilized corner of it, and through England, too, no uncertain intimations of its historic purport—intimations significant enough "to make bold power look pale" already—and one would think a Shakespeare might have understood its message. But no! This very spokesman of the new era it ushers in, trusted with this legacy of the new-born times; this man, whom we all so look up to, and reverence, with that inalienable treasure of ours in his hands, which even Ben Jonson knew was not for him, "nor for an age—but for all time," why this Jack Cade that he is must needs take us back three thousand years with it, and land us at the gates of Ilium! The arts of humanity and history, as they stood when Troy was burned, must save this treasure for us, and be our means of access to it! He will leave this work of his, into which the ends of the world have come to be inwrought for all the future, he will leave it where Homer left his, on the lips of the mouthing "rhapsodists!"

Apparently, indeed, he will be careful to teach these "robustious, periwig-pated fellows" their proper relations to him. He will industriously instruct them how to pronounce his dialogue, so as to give the immediate effect intended; controlling even the gesticulations, insisting on the stops, ruling out utterly the town-crier's emphasis; and, above all, protesting, with a true author's jealousy, against interpolation or any meddling with his text. Indeed, the directions to the players, which he puts into the mouth of Hamlet—involving, as they do, not merely the nice sensibility of the artist, and his nervous, instinctive, esthetic, acquaintance with his art, but a thorough scientific knowledge of its principles—these directions would have led us to infer that he would, at least, know enough of the value of his own works to avail himself of the printing press, for their preservation, and not only that, they would have led us to expect from him a most exquisitely careful revision of his proofs. But how is it? He destroys, we are given to understand, the manuscripts of his unpublished plays, and we owe to accident, and to no care of him whatever, his works as they have come to us. Did ever the human mind debase itself to the possibility of receiving such nonsense as this, on any subject, before?[1]

He had those manuscripts! He had those originals which publishers and scholars would give millions now to purchase a glimpse of; he had the original *Hamlet*, with its last finish; he had the original *Lear*, with his own final readings; he had them all—all, pointed, emphasized, directed, as they came from the gods; he had them all, all finished as the critic of *Hamlet* and *Midsummer Night's Dream* must have finished them; and he left us to wear out our youth, and squander our lifetime, in poring over and setting right the old, garbled copies of the play-house! He had those manuscripts, and the printing-press had been at its work a hundred years when he was born, but he was not ashamed to leave the best wits and scholars of all succeeding ages, with Pope and Johnson at their head, to exhaust their ingenuity, and sour their dispositions, and to waste their golden hours, year after year, in groping after and guessing out his hidden meanings!

He had those manuscripts! In the name of that sovereign reason, whose name he dares to take upon his lips so often, what did he do with them? Did he wantonly destroy them? No! Ah, no! he did not care enough for them to take that trouble. No, he did not do that! That would not have been in keeping with the character of this most respectable impersonation of the Genius of the British Isle, as it stands set up for us at present to worship. Some worthy, domestic, private, economic use, doubtless, they were put to. For, is not he a private, economical, practical man—this Shakespeare of ours—with no stuff and nonsense about him—a plain, true-blooded Englishman, who minds his own business, and leaves other people to take care of theirs? Is not this our Shakespeare? Is it not the boast of England, that he is just that, and nothing else? "What did he do with them?" He gave them to his cook, or Dr. Hale put up potions for his patients in them, or Judith, poor Judith—who signified her relationship to the author of *Lear*, and the *Tempest*, and her right to the glory of the name he left her, by the very extraordinary kind of "mark" which she affixes to legal instruments—poor Judith may have curled her hair to the day of her death with them, without dreaming of any harm.

"What did he do with them?" And whose business is it? Weren't they his own? If he chose to burn them up, or put them to some private use, had not he a perfect *right* to do it?

No! Traitor and miscreant! No! What did you do with them? You have skulked this question long enough. You will have to account for them. You will have to tell us what you did with them. The awakening ages will put you on the stand, and you will not leave it until you answer the question, "What did you do with them?"

And yet, do not the critics dare to boast to us, that he did compose these works for his own private, particular ends only? Do they not tell us, as if it were a thing to be proud of, and "a thing to thank God on," with uplifted eyes, and speechless admiration points, that he did "die, and leave the world no copy?" But who is it that insists so much, so strangely, so repetitiously, upon the wrong to humanity, the fraud done to nature, when the individual fails to render in his account to time of all that nature gives him? Who is it that writes, obscurely, indeed, so many sonnets, only to ring the changes on this very subject, singing out, point by point, not the Platonic theory, but his own fresh and beautiful study of great nature's law, and his own new and scientific doctrine of conservation and advancement? And who is it that writes, unconsciously, no doubt, and without its ever occurring to him that it was going to be printed, or to be read by any one?

> *Thyself* and *thy belongings*
> *Are not thine own* so proper, as to waste
> *Thyself upon thy virtues,* them on thee.

For here is the preacher of another doctrine, which puts the good that is private and particular where the sovereignty that is in nature puts it:

> Heaven doth with us, *as we with torches do;*
> Not light them for themselves. For if our virtues
> Did not go forth of us, 'twere all alike
> As if we had them not. Spirits are not finely touched
> But to fine issues, and nature never lends
> The smallest scruple of her excellence,
> But, like a thrifty goddess, she determines
> Herself the glory of a creditor,
> Both thanks and use.

Truly the man who writes in this style, with such poetic iteration, might put in Hamlet's plea, when his critics accuse him of unconsciousness:

> Bring me to the test
> And I the matter will reword; which madness
> Would gambol from.

What infirmity of blindness is it, then, that we charge upon this "god of our idolatry!" And what new race of Calibans are we, that we should be called upon to worship this monstrous incongruity—this Trinculo—this impersonated moral worthlessness? Oh, stupidity, past finding out! "The myriad-minded one," the light of far-off futurities was in him, and he knew it not! While the word was on his lips, and he reasoned of it, he heeded it not! He, at whose feet all men else are proud to sit, came to him, and found no reverence. The treasure for us all was put into his hands, and—he did not waste it—he did not keep it laid up in a napkin, he did not dig in the earth, and hide his lord's money; no, he used it! he used it for his own despicable and sordid ends, "to complete purchases that he had a mind to," and he left us to gather up "the arts and fragments" as best we may. And they *dare* to tell us this of him, and men believe it, and to this hour his bones are canonized, to this hour his tomb is a shrine, where the

genius of the cool, sagacious, clear-thoughted Northern Isle is worshiped, under the form of a mad, unconscious, intellectual possession—a dotard inspiration, incapable of its own designs, wanting in the essential attribute of all mental power—self-cognition.

And yet, who would be willing to spare, now, one point in that time-honored, incongruous whole? Who would be willing to dispense with the least of those contradictions, which have become, in the progressive development of our appreciation of these works, so inextricably knit together, and thereby inwrought, as it were, into our inmost life? Who can, in fact, fairly convince himself, now, that deer-stealing and link-holding, and the name of an obscure family in Stratford—common enough there, thought it means what it does to us—and bad, or indifferent performances, at a Surrey theatre, are not really, after all, essential preliminaries and concomitants to the compositon of a *Romeo and Juliet,* or a *Midsummer Night's Dream,* or a *Twelfth Night?* And what Shakespeare critic, at least, could persuade himself, now, that any other motive than the purchase of the Globe theatre, and that capital messuage or tenement in Stratford, called the New Place, with the appurtenances thereof, and the lands adjoining, and the house in Henley street, could by any possibility have originated such works as these?

And what fool would undertake to prove, now, that the fact of the deer-stealing, or any other point in the traditionary statement, may admit of question? Certainly, if we are to have an historical or traditionary Shakespeare of any kind, out of our present materials, it becomes us to protest, with the utmost severity, against the least meddling therewith. If they are not sufficiently meagre already—if the two or three historical points we have, or seem to have, and the miserable scraps and fragments of gossip, which the painful explorations of two centuries have, at length, succeeded in rescuing from the oblivion to which this man's time consigned him[2]—if these points are to be encroached upon, and impaired by criticism, we may as well throw up the question altogether. In the name of all that is tangible, leave us what there is of affirmation here. Surely we have negations enough already. If he did not steal the deer, will you tell us what one mortal thing he did do? He wrote the plays. But, did the man who wrote the plays do nothing else? Are there not some foregone conclusions in them?—some intimations, and round ones, too, that he who wrote them, be he who he may, has had experiences of some sort? Do such things as these, that the plays are full of, begin in the fingers' end? Can you find them in an ink-horn? Can you sharpen them out of a goose-quill? Has your Shakespeare wit and invention enough for that?

But the man was a player, and the manager of a playhouse, and these are plays that he writes. And what kind of play is it that you find in them—and what is the theatre—and who are the actors? Has this man's life been all *play?* Has there been no earnest in it?—no acting in his own name? Had *he* no part of his own in time, then? Has he dealt evermore with second-hand reports, unreal shadows, and mockeries of things? Has there been no personal grapple with realities, here? Ah, let him have that one living opposite. Leave him that single shot "heard round the world." Did not Eschylus fight at Salamis? Did not Scipio teach Terence how to marshal his men and wing his words? (A cotemporary and confidant of Shakespeare's thinks, from internal evidence, that the patron wrote the plays, in this case, altogether.) And was not Socrates as brave at Potidea and Delium and he was in the market-place; and did not Cæsar, the author, kill his millions? But, this giant wrestler and warrior of ours, with the essence of all the battles of all ages in his nerves—with the blood of a new Adam bubbling in his veins—he cannot be permitted to leap out of those everlasting buskins of his, long enough to have a brush with this one live deer, but the critics must have out their spectacles, and be down upon him with their objections.

And what honest man would want a Shakespeare at this hour of the day, that was not written by that same irregular, lawless, wild, reckless, facetious, law-despising, art-despising genuis of a "Will" that did steal the deer? Is not this the Shakespeare we have had on our shelves with our bibles and prayer-books, since our great grandsires' times? The next step will be to call in question Moses in the bulrushes, and Pharaoh's daughter.

And what is to become, too, under this supposition, of that exquisite specimen of the player's merciless wit, and "facetious grace in writing," which attracted the attention of his cotemporaries, and left such keen impressions on the minds of his fellow-townsmen? What is to become, in this case, of the famous lampoon on Sir Thomas Lucy, nailed up on the park gate, rivaling in Shakespearean grace and sharpness another Attic morceau from the same source—the impromptu on "John-a-Combe?" These remains of the poet, which we find accredited to him in his native village, "with likelihood of truth enough," among those who best knew him, have certainly cost the commentators too much trouble to be lightly relinquished; and, unquestionably, they do bear on the face of them most unmistakable symptoms of the player's wit and the Stratford origin.

No! no! We cannot spare the deer-stealing. As the case now stands, this one, rich, sparkling point in the tradition, can by no means be dispensed with. Take this away, and what becomes of our traditional Shakespeare? He goes! The whole fabric tumbles to pieces, or settles at once into a hopeless stolidity. But for the mercurial lightning, which this youthful reminiscence imparts to him—this single indication of a suppressed tendencey to an heroic life—how could that heavy, retired country gentleman, late manager of the Globe and the Blackfriars theatres, be made to float at any convenient distance above the earth, in the laboring conceptions of the artists whose business it is to present his apotheosis to us? Enlarge the vacant platitudes of that forehead as you will—pile up the artificial brains in the frontispiece to any height which the credulity of an awe-struck public will hesitate to pronounce idiotic—huddle the allegorical shapes about him as thickly as you will, and yet, but for the twinkle which this single reminiscence leaves, this one solitary "proof of liberty," "the flash and outbreak of a fiery mind of general assault," how could the old player and showman be made to sit the bird of Jove so comfortably as he does, on his way to the waiting Olympus?

But, after all, it is not this old actor of Elizabeth's time, who exhibited these plays at his theatre in the way of his trade, and cared for them precisely as a tradesman would—cared for them as he would have cared for tin kettles, or earthern pans and pots, if they had been in his line, instead; it is not this old tradesman; it is not this old showman and hawker of plays; it is not this old lackey, whose hand is on all our heart-strings, whose name is, of mortal names, the most awe-inspiring.

The Shakespeare of Elizabeth and James, who exhibited at his theatre as plays, among many others surpassing them in immediate theatrical success, the wonderful works which bore his name—works which were only half printed, and that surreptitiously, and in detached portions during his life-time, which, seven years after his death, were first collected and published by authority in his name, accompanied, according to the custom of the day, with eulogistic verses from surviving brother poets—this yet living theatrical Shakespeare, is a very different one from the Shakespeare of our modern criticism;—the Shakespeare, brought out, at length, by more than two centuries of readings and the best scholarly investigation of modern times, from between the two lids of that wondrous folio.

The faintly limned outlines of the nucleus which that name once included, are all gone long ago, dissolved in the splendors, dilated into the infinities which this modern Shakespeare dwells in. It is Shakespeare the author, that we now know only, the author of these worlds of profoundest art—these thought-crowded worlds, which modern reading discovers in these printed plays of his. It is the posthumous Shakespeare of the posthumous volume, that we now know only. No, not even that; it is only the work itself that we now know by that name—the phenomenon and not its beginning. For, with each new study of the printed page, further and further behind it, deeper and deeper into regions where no man so much as undertakes to follow it, retreats the power, which is for us all already, as truly as if we had confessed it to ourselves, the unknown, the unnamed.

What does this old player's name, in fact, stand for with us now? Inwrought not into all our literature merely, but into all the life of our modern time, his unlearned utterances our deepest lore, which "we are toiling all our lives to find," his mystic page, the page where each one sees his own life inscribed, point by point, deepening and deepening with each new experience from the cradle to the grave; what is he to us now? Is he the teacher of our players only? What theatres hold now his school? What actors' names stand now enrolled in its illustrious lists? Do not all our modern works incorporate his lore into their essence, are they not glittering on their surface everywhere, with ever new, unmissed jewels from his mines? Which of our statesmen, our heroes, our divines, our poets, our philosophers, has not learned of him; and in which of all their divergent and multiplying pursuits and experiences do they fail to find him still with them, still before them?

The name which has stood to us from the beginning, for all this—which has been inwrought into it, which concentrates it in its unity—cannot now be touched. It has lost its original significance. It means this, and this only to us. It has drunk in the essence of all this power, and light, and beauty, and identified itself with it. Never, perhaps, can it well mean anything else to us.

You cannot christen a world anew, though the name that was given to it at the font prove an usurper's. With all that we now know of that heroic scholar, from whose scientific dream the New World was made to emerge at last, in the face of the mockeries of his time, with all that appreciation of his work which the Old World and the New alike bestow upon it, we cannot yet separate the name of his rival from his hard-earned triumph. What name is it that has drunk into its melody, forever, all the music of that hope and promise, which the young continent of Columbus still whispers—in spite of old European evils planted there—still whispers in the troubled earth? Whose name is it that stretches its golden letters, now, from ocean to ocean, from Arctic to Antarctic, whose name now enrings the millions that are born, and live, and die, knowing no world but the world of that patient scholar's dream—no reality, but the reality of his chimera?

What matters it? Who cares? "What's in a name?" Is there any voice from that hero's own tomb, to rebuke this wrong? No. He did not toil, and struggle, and suffer, and keep his manly heart from breaking, to the end, that those millions might be called by *his* name. Ah, little know they, who thus judge of works like his, what roots such growths must spread, what broad, sweet currents they must reach and drink from. If the millions are blessed there, if, through the heat and burden of his weary day, man shall at length attain, though only after many an erring experience and fierce rebuke, in that new world, to some height of learning, to some scientific place of peace and rest, where worlds are in harmony, and men are as one, he will say, in God's name, Amen! For, on the heights of endurance and self renunciation, where the divine is possible with men, we have one name.

What have we to do with this poor peasant's name, then, so hallowed in all our hearts, now, with household memories, that we should seek to tear it from the countless fastenings which time has given it? This name, chosen at least of fortune, if not of nature, for the place it occupies, dignified with all that she can lend it—illustrious with her most lavish favoritism—has she not chosen to encircle it with honors which make poor those that she saves for her kings and heroes? Let it stand, then, and not by grace of fortune only, but by consent of one who could afford to leave it such a legacy. For he was one whom giving did not impoverish—he had wealth enough of his own and to spare, and honors that he could not part with.

"Once," but in no poet's garb, once, through the thickest of this "working-day world," "he trod" for himself, with bleeding feet, "the ways of glory here," "and sounded all the depths and shoals of honor," and, from the wrecks of lost "ambition," found to the last "the way to rise in."—

By that sin fell the angels; how can man, then,
The image of his Maker, hope to win by't?
Love thyself last: cherish the hearts that hate thee;
Still in thy right hand carry gentle peace,
To silence envious tongues. Be just, and fear not:
Let all the ends thou aim'st at, be thy country's,
Thy God's, and truth's; then, if thou fall'st, thou fall'st
A noble martyr!

Let the name stand, then, where the poet has himself left it. If he—if he himself did not scruple to forego his fairest honors, and leave his immortality in a peasant's weed; if he himself could consent to bind his own princely brows in it, though it might be for ages, why e'en let him wear it, then, as his own proudest honor. To all time let the philosophy be preached in it, which found "in a name" the heroic height whence its one great tenet could be uttered with such an emphasis, philosophy—"not harsh and crabbed as dull fools suppose, but musical as is Apollo's lute," roaming here at last in worlds of her own shaping; more rich and varied, and more intense than nature's own; where all things "echo the name of Prospero;" where, "beside the groves, the fountains, every region near seems all one mutual cry;" where even young love's own youngest melodies, from moon-lit balconies, warble its argument. Let it stand, then. Leave to it its strange honors—its unbought immortality. Let it stand, at least, till all those who have eaten in their youth of the magic tables spread in it, shall have died in the wilderness. Let it stand while it will, only let its true significance be recognized.

For, the falsity involved in it, as it now stands, has become too gross to be endured any further. The common sense cannot any longer receive it, without self-abnegation; and the relations of this question, on all sides, are now too grave and momentous to admit of any further postponement of it.

In judging of this question, we must take into account the fact that, at the time when these works were issued, all those characteristic organizations of the modern ages, for the diffusion of intellectual and moral influences, which now everywhere cross and recross, with electric fibre, the hitherto impassable social barriers, were as yet unimagined. The inventions and institutions, in which these had their origin, were then but beginning their work. To-day, there is no scholastic seclusion so profound that the allied voice and action of this mighty living age may not perpetually penetrate it. To-day, the work-shop has become *clairvoyant*. The plow and the loom are in magnetic communication with the loftiest social centres. The last results of the most exquisite culture of the world, in all its departments, are within reach of the lowest haunt, where latent genius and refinement await their summons; and there is no "smallest scruple of nature's excellence" that may not be searched out and kindled. The Englishman who but reads *The Times*, to-day, puts himself into a connection with his age, and attains thereby a means of enlargement of character and elevation of thought and aims, which, in the age of Elizabeth, was only possible to men occupying the highest official and social position.

It is necessary, too, to remember that the question here is not a question of lyric inspiration, merely; neither is it a question of dramatic genius, merely. Why, even the poor player, that Hamlet quotes so admiringly, "but in a dream of passion," his soul rapt and subdued with images of tenderness and beauty, "tears in his eyes, the color in his cheeks," even he, with his fine sensibilities, his rhythmical ear, with his living conceits, if nature has but done her part towards it, may compose you a lyric that you would bind up with "Highland Mary," or "Sir Patrick Spens," for immortality. And even this poor tinker, profane and wicked as he is, and coarse and unfurnished for the poet's mission as he seems, when once the infinities of religion, with their divine ideals, shall penetrate to the deep, sweet sources of his yet undreamed of genius, and arouse the latent soul in him, with their terrific struggles and divine triumphs, even he, from the coarse, meagre materials which his external experience furnishes to him, shall be able to compose a drama, full of immortal vigor and freshness, where all men shall hear the rushing of wings—the tread from other spheres—in their life's battle; where all men shall be able to catch voices and harpings not of this shore. But the question is not here of a Bunyan or a Burns. And it is not a Bloomfield that we have in hand here. The question is not whether nature shall be able to compose *these*, without putting into requisition the selectest instrumentalities of the ages. It is a question different in kind; how different, in the present stage of our appreciation of the works involved in it, cannot be made manifest.

It is impossible, indeed, to present any parallel to the case in question. For if we suppose a poor actor, or the manager of a theatre, or a printer, unlearned, except by the accident of his trade, to begin now to issue out of his brain, in the way of his trade, wholly bent on that, and wholly indifferent to any other result, and unconscious of any other, a body of literature, so high above anything that we now possess, in any or in all departments; so far exhausting the excellency of all, as to constitute, by universal consent, *the* literature of this time; comprehending its entire scope; based on its subtlest analysis; pronouncing everywhere its final word, even such a supposition would not begin to meet the absurdity of the case in question.

If the prince of showmen in our day, in that stately oriental retreat of his, in Connecticut, rivaling even the New Place at Stratford in literary conveniences, should begin now to conceive of something of this sort, as his crowning speculation, and should determine to undertake its execution in person, who would dare to question his ability?[3] Certainly no one would have any right to criticise, now, the motive conceded, or to put in suspicion its efficiency for the proposed result. Why, this man could not conduct his business a day, he could not even hunt through the journals for his own puffs and advertisements, without coming by accident in contact with means of moral and intellectual enlargement and stimulus, which could never have found their way, in any form, to Elizabeth's player. The railway, the magnetic telegraph, the steam-ship, the steam-press, with its journals, its magazines, its reviews, and its cheap literature of all kinds, the public library, the book-club, the popular lecture, the lyceum, the voluntary association of every kind—these are all but a part of that magnificent apparatus and means of culture which society is now putting in requisition in that great school of hers, wherein the universal man, rescued from infinite self-degradations, is now at last beginning his culture. And yet all these social instrumentalities combined cannot, even now, so supply the deficiencies in the case supposed as to make the supposition any other than a violent one, to say the least of it.

The material which nature must have contributed to the Shakespearean result, could, indeed, hardly have remained inert, under any superincumbent weight of social disadvantages. But the very first indication of its presence, under such conditions, would have been a struggle with those disadvantages. First of all, it would force its way upward, through them, to its natural element; first of all, it would make its way into the light, and possess itself of all its weapons—not spend itself in mad movements in the dark, without them. Look over the history of all the known English poets and authors of every kind, back even to the days of the Anglo-Saxon Adhelm, and Cedmon, and, no matter how humble the position in which they are born, how many will you find among them that have failed to possess themselves ultimately of the highest literary culture of the age they lived in? how many, until you come to this same Shakespeare?

Well, then, if the Genius of the British Isle turns us out such men as those from her universities; but, when she would make her Shakespeare retreat into a green-room, and send him forth from that, furnished as we find him, pull down, we say, pull down those gray old towers, for the wisdom of the Great Alfred has been laughed to scorn; undo his illustrious monument to its last Anglo-Saxon stone, and, "by our lady, build— theatres!" If not Juliet only, but her author, and Hamlet's author, too, and Lear's, and Macbeth's can be made without "philosophy," we are for Romeo's verdict, "Hang up philosophy." If such works as these, and *Julius Cæsar*, and *Coriolanus*, and *Antony*, and *Henry V.*, and *Henry VIII.*—if the *Midsummer Night's Dream*, and the *Merchant of Venice*, and the *Twelfth Night*, if Beatrice, and Benedict, and Rosalind, and Jaques, and Iago, and Othello, and all their immortal company—if these works, and all that we find in them, can be got out of Plutarch's *Lives*, and Holinshed, and a few old ballads and novels—in the name of all that is honest, give us these, and let us go about our business; and henceforth let him that can be convicted "of traitorously corrupting the youth of this realm, by erecting a grammar-school," be consigned to his victims for mercy. "Long live Lord Mortimer!" Down with the "paper-mills!" "Throw learning to the dogs! we'll none of it!"

But we are not, as yet, in a position to estimate the graver bearings of this question. For the reverence which the common theory has hitherto claimed from us, as a well-authenticated historical fact, depending apparently, indeed, on the most unimpeachable external evidence for its support, has operated, as it was intended to operate in the first instance, to prevent all that kind of reading and study of the plays which would have made its gross absurdity apparent. In accordance

with this original intention, to this hour it has constituted a barrier to the understanding of their true meaning, which no industry or perseverance could surmount; to this hour it has served to prevent, apparently, so much as a suspicion of their true source, and ultimate intention.

But let this theory, and the pre-judgment it involves, be set aside, even by an hypothesis, only long enough to permit us once to see, for ourselves, what these works do in fact contain, and no amount of historical evidence which can be produced, no art, no argument, will suffice to restore it to its present position. But it is not as a hypothesis, it is not as a theory, that the truth here indicated will be developed hereafter. It will come on other grounds. It will ask no favors.

Condemned to refer the origin of these works to the vulgar, illiterate man who kept the theatre where they were first exhibited, a person of the most ordinary character and aims, compelled to regard them as the result merely of an extraordinary talent for pecuniary speculation in this man, how could we, how could any one dare to see what is really in them? With this theory overhanging them, though we threw our most artistic lights upon it, and kept it out of sight when we could, what painful contradictory mental states, what unacknowledged internal misgivings were yet involved in our best judgments of them. How many passages were we compelled to read "trippingly," with the "mind's eye," as the players were first taught to pronounce them on the tongue; and if, in spite of all our slurring, the inner depths would open to us, if anything, which this theory could not account for, would, notwithstanding, obtrude itself upon us, we endeavored to believe that it must be the reflection of our own better learning, and so, half lying to ourselves, making a wretched compromise with our own mental integrity, we still hurried on.

Condemned to look for the author of Hamlet himself— the subtle Hamlet of the university, the courtly Hamlet, "the glass of fashion and the mould of form"—in that dirty, doggish group of players, who come into the scene summoned like a pack of hounds to his service, the very tone of his courtesy to them, with its princely condescension, with its arduous familiarity, only serving to make the great, impassable social gulf between them the more evident—compelled to look in that ignominious group, with its faithful portraiture of the players of that time (taken from the life by one who had had dealings with them), for the princely scholar himself in his author, how could we understand him—the enigmatical Hamlet, with the thought of ages in his foregone conclusions?

With such an origin, how could we see the subtlest skill of the university, not in Hamlet and Horatio only, but in the work itself, incorporated in its essence, pervading its execution? With such an origin as this, how was it possible to note, not in this play only, but in all the Shakespeare drama, what, otherwise, we could not have failed to observe, the tone of the highest Elizabethan breeding, the very loftiest tone of that peculiar courtly culture, which was then, and but *just* then, attaining its height, in the competitions among men of the highest social rank, and among the most brilliant wits and men of genius of the age, for the favor of the learned, accomplished, sagacious, wit-loving maiden queen;—a culture which required not the best acquisitions of the university merely, but acquaintance with life, practical knowledge of affairs, foreign travel and accomplishments, and, above all, the last refinements of the highest Parisian breeding. For "your courtier" must be, in fact, "your picked man of countries." He must, indeed, "get his behavior everywhere." He must be, in fact and literally, the man of "the world."

But for this prepossession, in that daring treatment of court-life which this single play of *Hamlet* involves, in the entire freedom with which its conventionalities are handled, how could we have failed to recognize the touch of one habitually practiced in its refinements? how could we have failed to recognize, not in this play only, but in all these plays, the poet whose habits and perceptions have been moulded in the atmosphere of these subtle social influences. He cannot shake off this influence when he will. He carries the court perfume with him, unconsciously, wherever he goes, among mobs of artisans that will not "keep their teeth clean;" into the ranks of "greasy citizens" and "rude mechanicals;" into country feasts and merry-makings; among "pretty low-born lasses," "the queens of curds and cheese," and into the heart of that forest, "where there is no clock." He looks into the Arden and into Eastcheap from the court stand-point, not from these into the court, and he is as much a prince with Poins and Bardolph as he is when he enters and throws open to us, without awe, without consciousness, the most delicate mysteries of the royal presence.

Compelled to refer the origin of these works to the sordid play-house, who could teach us to distinguish between the ranting, unnatural stuff and bombast which its genuine competitions elicited, in their mercenary appeals to the passions of their audience, ministering to the most vicious tastes, depraving the public conscience, and lowering the common standard of decency, getting up "scenes to tear a cat in,"—"out-Heroding Herod," and going regularly into professional fits about Hecuba and Priam and other Trojans,—who could teach us to distinguish between the tone of this original, genuine, play-house fustian, and that of the "dozen of sixteen lines" which Hamlet will at first, for some earnest purpose of his own, with the consent and privity of *one* of the players, cause to be inserted in it? Nay, thus blinded, we shall not, perhaps, be able to distinguish from this foundation that magnificent whole, with which, from such beginnings, this author will, perhaps, ultimately replace his worthless originals, altogether; that whole in which we shall see, one day, not the burning Ilium, not the old Danish court of the tenth century, but the yet living, illustrious Elizabethan age, with all its momentous interests still at stake, with its yet palpitating hopes and fears, with its new-born energies, bound but unconquerable, already heaving, and muttering through all their undertone; that magnificent whole, where we shall see, one day, "the very abstract and brief chronicle of the time," the "very body of the age, its form and pressure," under any costume of time and country, or under the drapery of any fiction, however absurd or monstrous, which this author shall find already popularized to his hands, and available for his purposes. Hard, indeed, was the time, ill bestead was the spirit of the immemorial English freedom, when the genius of works such as these, was compelled to stoop to such a scene, to find its instruments.

How could we understand from such a source, while that wretched player was still crying it for his own worthless ends, this majestic exhibition of our common human life from the highest intellectual and social stand-point of that wondrous age, letting in, on all the fripperies and affectations, the arrogance and pretension of that illustrious centre of social life, the new philosophic beam, and sealing up in it, for all time, "all the uses and customs" of the world that then was? Arrested with that transparent petrefaction, in all the rushing life of the moment, and set, henceforth, on the table of philosophic halls for scientific illustration; its gaudy butterflies impaled upon the wing, in their perpetual gold; its microscopic insects, "spacious in the possession of land and dirt," transfixed in all the swell and flutter of the moment; its fantastic apes, unrobed for inextinguishable mortal laughter and celestial tears, still playing, all unconsciously, their solemn pageants through; how could the showman explain all this to us—how could the player tell us what it meant?

How could the player's mercenary motive and the player's range of learning and experiment give us the key to this new application of the human reason to the human life, from the new vantage ground of thought, but just then rescued from the past, and built up painfully from all its wreck? How could we understand, from such a source, this new, and strange, and persevering application of thought to life, not merely to society and to her laws, but to nature, too; pursuing her to her last retreats, and holding everywhere its mirror up to her, reflecting the whole boundary of her limitations; laying bare, in its cold, clear, pure depths, in all their unpolite, undraped scientific reality, the actualities which society, as it is, can only veil, and the evils which society, as it is, can only hide and palliate?

In vain the shrieking queen remonstrates, for, it is the impersonated reason whose clutch is on her, and it says, you go not hence till you have seen the inmost part of you. But does all this tell on the thousand pounds? Is the ghost's word good for that?

No wonder that Hamlet refused to speak, or to be commanded to any utterance of harmony, let the critics listen, and entreat as they would, while this illiterate performer, who knew no touch of all that divine music of his, from its lowest note to the top of his key, was still sounding him and fretting him. We shall take another key and another interpreter with us when we begin to understand a work which comprehends, in its design, all our human aims and activities, and tracks them to their beginnings and ends; which demands the ultimate, scientific perpetual reason in all our life—a work which dares to defer the punishment of the crime that society visits with her most dreaded penalties, till all the principles of the human activity have been collected; till all the human conditions have been explored; till the only universal rational human principle is found—a work which dares to defer the punishment of the crime that society condemns, till its principle has been tracked through the crime which she tolerates; through the crime which she sanctions; through the crime which she crowns with all her honors.

We are, indeed, by no means insensible to the difference between this Shakespeare drama, and that on which it is based, and that which surrounds it. We do, indeed, already pronounce that difference, and not faintly, in our word *Shakespeare*; for that is what the word now means with us, though we received it with no such significance. Its historical development is but the next step in our progress.

Yes, there were men in England then, who had heard somewhat of those masters of the olden time, hight Eschylus and Sophocles—men who had heard of Euripides, too, and next, Aristophanes—men who had heard of Terence, and not of Terence only, but of his patrons—men who had heard of Plato, too, and of his master. There were men in England, in those days, who knew well enough what kind of an instrumentality the drama had been in its original institution, and with what voices it had then spoken; who knew, also, its permanent relations to the popular mind, and its capability for adaptation to new social exigencies; men, quick enough to perceive, and ready enough to appreciate, to the utmost, the facilities which this great organ of the wisdom of antiquity offered for effectual communication between the loftiest mind, at the height of its culture, and that mind of the world in which this, impelled by no law of its own ordaining, seeks ever its own self-completion and perpetuity.

And where had this mighty instrument of popular sway, this mechanism for moving and moulding the multitude, its first origin, but among men initiated in the profoundest religious and philosophic mysteries of their time, among men exercised in the control and administration of public affairs; men clothed even with imperial sway, the joint administrators of the government of Athens, when Athens sat on the summit of her power, the crowned mistress of the seas, the imperial ruler of "a thousand cities."

Yes, Theseus, and Solon, and Cleisthenes and Pythagoras, must be its antecedents *there*; it could not be produced there, till all Athena had been for ages in Athens, till Athena had been for ages in all; till three centuries of Olympiads had poured the Grecian life-blood through it, from Byzantium to Sicily; it could not be produced there, till the life of the state was in each true Athenian nerve, till each true Athenian's nerve was in the growing state; it could not begin to be produced there, till new religious inspirations from the east had reached, with their foreign stimulus, the deeper sources of the national life, till the secret philosophic tenet of the inner temple, had overflowed, with new gold, the ancient myth, and kindled, with new fires, the hearts of the nation's leaders. The gay summits of Homer's "every-young" Olympus, must be reached and overlaid anew from the earth's central mysteries; the Dyonisian procession must enter the temple; the road to it must cross Ægaleos; the Pnyx must empty its benches into it; Piræus must crowd its stranger's seat with her many costumes, before Eschylus or Sophocles could find an audience to command all their genius. Nay, Zeno and Anaxagoras must send their pupils thither, and Socrates must come in, and the most illustrious scholars of the Olympian cities, from Abdera to Leontium, must be found there, before all the latent resources of the Grecian drama could be unfolded.

And there were men in England, in the age of Elizabeth, who had mastered the Greek and Roman history, and not only that, but history of their own institutions—men who knew precisely what kind of crisis in human history that was which they were born to occupy. And they had seen the indigenous English drama struggling up, through the earnest, but childish, exhibitions of the cathedral—through "Miracles," and "Mysteries," and "Moralities," to be arrested, in its yet undeveloped vigor, with the unfit and unyielding forms of the finished Grecian art; and when, too, by the combined effect of institutions otherwise at variance, all that had, till then, made its life, was suddenly abstracted from it. The royal ordinances which excluded it, henceforth, from all that vital range of topics which the censorship of a capricious and timorous despotism might include among the interdicted questions of church and state, found it already expelled from the religious sanctuaries—in which not the drama only, but all that which we call art, *par excellence*, has its birth and nurture. And that was the crisis in which the pulpit began to open its new drain upon it, having only a vicious play-house, where once the indefinite priestly authority had summoned all the soul to its spectacles, and the long-drawn aisle, and fretted vault, had lent to them their sheltering sanctities; where once, as of old, the Athenian temple had pressed its scene into the heart of the Athenian hill—the holy hill—and opened its subterranean communication with Eleusis, while its centre was the altar on which the gods themselves threw incense.

And yet, there was a moment in the history of the national genius, when, roused to its utmost—stimulated to its best capability of ingenuity and invention—it found itself con-
strained to stoop at its height, even to the threshold of this same degraded play-house. There were men in England, who knew what latent capacities that debased instrument of genius yet contained within it—who knew that in the master's hand it might yet be made to yield, even then, and under those conditions, better music than any which those old Greek sons of song had known how to wake in it.

These men knew well enough the proper relation between the essence of the drama and its form. "Considering poetry in respect to the verse, and not to the argument," says one, "though men in learned languages may tie themselves to ancient measures; yet, in modern languages, it seems to me as free to make new measures as to make new dances; and, in these things, the sense is a better judge than the art." Surely, a Schlegel himself could not give us a truer Shakespearean rule than that. Indeed, if we can but catch them when the wind is south-south-west—these grave ad oracular Elizabethan wits— we shall find them putting two and two together, now and then, and drawing inferences, and making distinctions which would have much surprised their "uncle-fathers" and "aunt-mothers" at the time, if they had but noted them. But, as they themselves tell us, "in regard to the rawness and unskillfulness of the hands through which they pass, the greatest matters are sometimes carried in the weakest ciphers." Even over their own names, and in those learned tongues of theirs, if we can but once find their stops, and the skill to command them to any utterance of harmony, they will discourse to us, in spite of the disjointed times, the most eloquent music.

For, although they had, indeed, the happiness to pursue their studies under the direct personal supervision of those two matchless scholars, "Eliza and one James," whose influence in the world of letters was then so signally felt, they, nevertheless, evidently ventured to dip into antiquity a little on their own account, and that, apparently, without feeling called upon to render in a perfectly unambiguous report in full of all that they found there, for the benefit of their illustrious patrons, to whom, of course, their literary labors are dedicated. There seemed, indeed, to be no occasion for unpegging the basket on the house's top, and trying conclusions in any so summary manner.

These men distinctly postpone, not their personal reputation only, but the interpretation of their avowed works, to freer ages. There were sparrows abroad then. The tempest was already "singing in the wind," for an ear fine enough to catch it; but only invisible Ariels could dare "to play" then "*on pipe and tabor*," [stage direction]. "Thought is free," but only base Trinculos and low-born Stephanos could dare to whisper to it. "That is the tune of our catch, played by the picture of— Nobody."

Yes, there was one moment in that nation's history, wherein the costume, the fable, the scenic effect, and all the attractive and diverting appliances and concomitants of the stage, even the degradation into which it had fallen, its known subserviency to the passions of the audience, its habit of creating a spectacle merely, all combined to furnish to men, in whom the genius of the nation had attained its highest form, freer instrumentalities than the book, the pamphlet, the public document, the parliament, or the pulpit, when all alike were subject to an oppressive and despotic censorship, when all alike were forbidden to meddle with their own proper questions, when cruel maimings and tortures old and new, life-long imprisonment, and death itself, awaited, not a violation of these restrictions merely, but a suspicion of an intention, or even wish, to violate them—penalties which England's noblest men suffered, on suspicion only.

There was one moment in that history, in which the ancient drama had, in new forms, its old power; when, stamped and blazoned on its surface everywhere, with the badges of servitude it had yet leaping within the indomitable heart of its ancient freedom, the spirit of the immemorial European liberties, which Magna Charta had only recognized, and more than that, the freedom of the new ages that were then beginning, "the freedom of the chainless mind." There was one moment in which all the elements of the national genius, that are now separated and incorporated in institutions as wide apart, at least, as earth and heaven, were held together, and that in their first vigor, pressed from without into ther old Greek conjunction. That moment there was; it is chronicled; we have one word for it; we call it—Shakespeare!

Has the time come at last, or has it not yet come, in which this message of the new time can be laid open to us? This message from the lips of one endowed so wondrously, with skill to utter it; endowed, not with the speaker's melodious tones and subduing harmonies only, but with the teacher's divinely glowing heart, with the ambition that seeks its own in all, with the love that is sweeter than the tongues of men and angels. Are we, or are we not, his legatees? Surely this new summing up of all the real questions of our common life, from such an elevation in it, this new philosophy of all men's business and desires, cannot be without its perpetual vital uses. For, in all the points on which the demonstration rests, these diagrams from the dissolving views of the past are still included in the problems of the present.

And if, in this new and more earnest research into the true ends and meanings of this greatest of our teachers, the poor player who was willing enough to assume the responsibility of these works, while they were still plays—theatrical exhibitions only, and quite in his line for the time; who might, indeed, be glad enough to do it for the sake of the princely patronage that henceforth encompassed his fortunes, even to the granting of a thousand pounds at a time, if that were needed to complete his purchase—if this good man, sufficiently perplexed already with the developments which the modern criticism has by degrees already laid at his door, does here positively refuse to go any further with us on this road, why e'en let us shake hands with him and part, he as his business and desire shall point him, "for every man hath business and desire, such as it is," and not without a grateful recollection of the good service he has rendered us.

The publisher of these plays let his name go down still and to all posterity on the cover of it. They *were* his plays. He brought them out,—he and his firm. They took the scholar's text, that dull black and white, that mere ink and paper, and made of it a living, speaking, many-colored, glittering reality, which even the groundlings of that time could appreciate, in some sort. What was Hamlet to them, without his "inky cloak" and his "forest of feathers" and his "razed shoes" and "the roses" on them? And they came out of this man's bag—he was the owner of the "wardrobe" and of the other "stage properties." He was the owner of the manuscripts; and if he came honestly by them, whose business was it to inquire any further, then? If there was no one who chose, just then, to claim the authorship of them, whose else should they be? Was not the actor himself a poet, and a very facetious one, too? Witness the remains of him, the incontestible poetical remains of him, which *have* come down to us. What if his ill-natured cotemporaries, whose poetic glories he was eclipsing forever with those new plays of his, did assail him on his weak points, and call him, in the face of his time, "a *Johannes Factotum*," and held up to public ridicule his particular style of acting,

plainly intimating that it was chargeable with that very fault which the prince of Denmark directs his tragedians to omit—did not the blundering editor of that piece of offensive criticism get a decisive hint from some quarter, that he might better have withheld it; and was it not humbly retracted and hushed up directly? Some of the earlier anonymous plays, which were included in the collection published, after this player's decease, as the plays of William Shakespeare, are, indeed, known to have been produced anonymously at other theatres, and by companies with which this actor had never any connection; but the poet's company and the player's were, as it seems, two different things; and that is a fact which the criticism and history of these plays, as it stands at present, already exhibits. Several of the plays which form the nucleus of the Shakespeare drama had already been brought out, before the Stratford actor was yet in a position to assume that relation to it which proved so advantageous to his fortunes. Such as nucleus of the Shakespeare drama there was already, when the name which this actor bore, with such orthographical variations as the purpose required, began to be assumed as the name and device of that new sovereignty of genius which was then first rising and kindling behind its cloud, and dimming and overflowing with its greater glory all the less, and gilding all it shone on. The machinery of these theatrical establishments offered, indeed, the most natural and effective, as well as, at that time, on other accounts, the most convenient mode of exhibition for that particular class of subjects which the genius of this particular poet naturally inclined him to meddle with. He had the most profoundly philosophical reasons for preferring that mode of exhibiting his poems, as will be seen hereafter.

And, when we have once learned to recognize the actor's true relations to the works which have given to his name its anomalous significance, we shall be prepared, perhaps, to accept, at last, this great offer of aid in our readings of these works, which has been lying here now two hundred and thirty years, unnoticed; then, and not till then, we shall be able to avail ourselves, at last, of the aid of those "friends of his," to whom, two hundred and thirty years ago, "knowing that his wit could no more lie hid than it could be lost," the editors of the first printed collection of these works venture to refer us; "those other friends of his, whom, IF WE NEED, can be our *guides*; and, IF WE NEED THEM NOT, we are able to lead ourselves and others, and such readers they wish him."

If we had accepted either of these two conditions—if we had found ourselves with those who need this offered guidance, or with those who need it not—if we had but gone far enough in our readings of these works to feel the want of that aid, from exterior sources, which is here proffered us—there would not have been presented to the world, at this hour, the spectacle—the stupendous spectacle—of a nation referring the origin of its drama—a drama more noble, and learned, and subtle than the Greek—to the invention—the accidental, unconscious invention—of a stupid, ignorant, illiterate, third-rate play-actor.

If we had, indeed, but applied to these works the commonest rules of historical investigation and criticism, we might, ere this, have been led to inquire, on our own account, whether "this player here," who brought them out, might not possibly, in an age like that, like the player in *Hamlet*, have had some friend, or "friends," who, could, "an' if they would," or "an' if they might," explain his miracles to us, and the secret of his "poor cell."

If we had accepted this suggestion, the true Shakespeare would not have been now to seek. In the circle of that patronage with which this player's fortunes brought him in contact, in that illustrious company of wits and poets, we need not have been at a loss to find the philosopher who writes, in his prose as well, and over his own name also,

> In Nature's INFINITE BOOK OF SECRESY,
> A little I can read;—

we should have found one, at least, furnished for that last and ripest proof of learning which the drama, in the unmiraculous order of the human development, must constitute; that proof of it in which philosophy returns from history, from its noblest fields, and from her last analysis, with the secret and material of the creative synthesis—with the secret and material of art. With this direction, we should have been able to identifiy, ere this, the Philosopher who is only the Poet in disguise—the Philosopher who calls himself the New Magician—the Poet who was toiling and plotting to fill the globe with his Arts, and to make our common, everyday human life poetical—who would have *all* our life, and not a part of it, learned, artistic, beautiful, religious.

We should have found, ere this, ONE, with learning broad enough, and deep enough, and subtle enough, and comprehensive enough, one with nobility of aim and philosophic and poetic genius enough, to be able to claim his own, his own immortal progeny— undwarfed, unblinded, undeprived of one ray or dimple of that all-pervading reason that informs them; one who is able to re-claim them, even now, "cured and perfect in their limbs, and absolute in their numbers, as he conceived them."

*Notes*

1. Though the editors of the first folio profess to have access to these very papers, and boast of being able to bring out an absolutely faultless edition, to take the place of those stolen and surreptitious copies then in circulation, the edition which is actually produced, in connection with this announcement, is itself found to be full of verbal errors, and is supposed, by later editors, to have been derived from no better source than its predecessors.
2. Constituting, when well put together, precisely that historic trail which an old, defunct, indifferent, fourth-rate play-actor naturally leaves behind him, for the benefit of any antiquary who may find occasion to conduct an exploration for it.
3. It should be stated, perhaps, that the above was written two or three years since, and that no reference to Mr. Barnum's recent addition to the literature of the age was intended.

## NATHANIEL HAWTHORNE
### From "Recollections of a Gifted Woman"
#### *Our Old Home*
#### 1863

S he ⟨Delia Bacon⟩ was very communicative about her theory, and would have been much more so had I desired it; but, being conscious within myself of a sturdy unbelief, I deemed it fair and honest rather to repress than draw her out upon the subject. Unquestionably, she was a monomaniac; these overmastering ideas about the authorship of Shakespeare's Plays, and the deep political philosophy concealed beneath the surface of them, had completely thrown her off her balance; but at the same time they had wonderfully developed her intellect, and made her what she could not otherwise have become. It was a very singular phenomenon: a system of philosophy growing up in this woman's mind without her volition,—contrary, in fact, to the determined resistance of her volition,—and substituting itself in the place of everything that originally grew there. To have based such a system on fancy, and unconsciously elaborated it for herself, was almost as wonderful as really to have found it in the plays. But, in a

certain sense, she did actually find it there. Shakespeare has surface beneath surface, to an immeasurable depth, adapted to the plummet-line of every reader; his works present many phases of truth, each with scope large enough to fill a contemplative mind. Whatever you seek in him you will surely discover, provided you seek truth. There is no exhausting the various interpretation of his symbols; and a thousand years hence a world of new readers will possess a whole library of new books, as we ourselves do, in these volumes old already. I had half a mind to suggest to Miss Bacon this explanation of her theory, but forbore, because (as I could readily perceive) she had as princely a spirit as Queen Elizabeth herself, and would at once have motioned me from the room.

I had heard, long ago, that she believed that the material evidences of her dogma as to the authorship, together with the key of the new philosophy, would be found buried in Shakespeare's grave. Recently, as I understood her, this notion had been somewhat modified, and was now accurately defined and fully developed in her mind, with a result of perfect certainty. In Lord Bacon's Letters, on which she laid her finger as she spoke, she had discovered the key and clew to the whole mystery. There were definite and minute instructions how to find a will and other documents relating to the conclave of Elizabethan philosophers, which were concealed (when and by whom she did not inform me) in a hollow space in the under surface of Shakespeare's gravestone. Thus the terrible prohibition to remove the stone was accounted for. The directions, she intimated, went completely and precisely to the point, obviating all difficulties in the way of coming at the treasure, and even, if I remember right, were so contrived as to ward off any troublesome consequences likely to ensue from the interference of the parish-officers. All that Miss Bacon now remained in England for—indeed, the object for which she had come hither, and which had kept her here for three years past—was to obtain possession of these material and unquestionable proofs of the authenticity of her theory.

She communicated all this strange matter in a low, quiet tone; while, on my part, I listened as quietly, and without any expression of dissent. Controversy against a faith so settled would have shut her up at once, and that, too, without in the least weakening her belief in the existence of those treasures of the tomb; and had it been possible to convince her of their intangible nature, I apprehend that there would have been nothing left for the poor enthusiast save to collapse and die. She frankly confessed that she could no longer bear the society of those who did not at least lend a certain sympathy to her views, if not fully share in them; and meeting little sympathy or none, she had now entirely secluded herself from the world. In all these years, she had seen Mrs. Farrar a few times, but had long ago given her up; Carlyle once or twice, but not of late, although he had received her kindly; Mr. Buchanan, while Minister in England, had once called on her; and General Campbell, our Consul in London, had met her two or three times on business. With these exceptions, which she marked so scrupulously that it was preceptible what epochs they were in the monotonous passage of her days, she had lived in the profoundest solitude. She never walked out; she suffered much from ill-health; and yet, she assured me, she was perfectly happy.

I could well conceive it; for Miss Bacon imagined herself to have received (what is certainly the greatest boon ever assigned to mortals) a high mission in the world, with adequate powers for its accomplishment; and lest even these should prove insufficient, she had faith that special interpositions of Providence were forwarding her human efforts. This idea was continually coming to the surface, during our interview. She believed, for example, that she had been providentially led to her lodging-house, and put in relations with the good-natured grocer and his family; and, to say the truth, considering what a savage and stealthy tribe the London lodging-house keepers usually are, the honest kindness of this man and his household appeared to have been little less than miraculous. Evidently, too, she thought that Providence had brought me forward—a man somewhat connected with literature—at the critical juncture when she needed a negotiator with the booksellers; and, on my part, though little accustomed to regard myself as a divine minister, and though I might even have preferred that Providence should select some other instrument, I had no scruple in undertaking to do what I could for her. Her book, as I could see by turning it over, was a very remarkable one, and worthy of being offered to the public, which, if wise enough to appreciate it, would be thankful for what was good in it and merciful to its faults. It was founded on a prodigious error, but was built up from that foundation with a good many prodigious truths. And, at all events, whether I could aid her literary views or no, it would have been both rash and impertinent in me to attempt drawing poor Miss Bacon out of her delusions, which were the condition on which she lived in comfort and joy, and in the exercise of great intellectual power. So I left her to dream as she pleased about the treasures of Shakespeare's tombstone, and to form whatever designs might seem good to herself for obtaining possession of them. I was sensible of a lady-like feeling of propriety in Miss Bacon, and a New England orderliness in her character, and, in spite of her bewilderment, a sturdy common-sense, which I trusted would begin to operate at the right time, and keep her from any actual extravagance. And as regarded this matter of the tombstone, so it proved.

The interview lasted about an hour, during which she flowed out freely, as to the sole auditor, capable of any degree of intelligent sympathy, whom she had met with in a very long while. Her conversation was remarkably suggestive, alluring forth one's own ideas and fantasies from the shy places where they usually haunt. She was indeed an admirable talker, considering how long she had held her tongue for lack of a listener,—pleasant, sunny, and shadowy, often piquant, and giving glimpses of all a woman's various and readily changeable moods and humors; and beneath them all there ran a deep and powerful undercurrent of earnestness, which did not fail to produce in the listener's mind something like a temporary faith in what she herself believed so fervently. But the streets of London are not favorable to enthusiasms of this kind, nor, in fact, are they likely to flourish anywhere in the English atmosphere; so that, long before reaching Paternoster Row, I felt that it would be a difficult and doubtful matter to advocate the publication of Miss Bacon's book. Nevertheless, it did finally get published.

Months before that happened, however, Miss Bacon had taken up her residence at Stratford-on-Avon, drawn thither by the magnetism of those rich secrets which she supposed to have been hidden by Raleigh, or Bacon, or I know not whom, in Shakespeare's grave, and protected there by a curse, as pirates used to bury their gold in the guardianship of a fiend. She took a humble lodging and began to haunt the church like a ghost. But she did not condescend to any stratagem or underhand attempt to violate the grave, which, had she been capable of admitting such an idea, might possibly have been accomplished by the aid of a resurrection-man. As her first step, she made acquaintance with the clerk, and began to sound him as to the feasibility of her enterprise and his own willingness to engage in it. The clerk apparently listened with not unfavorable

ears; but as his situation (which the fees of pilgrims, more numerous than at any Catholic shrine, render lucrative) would have been forfeited by any malfeasance in office, he stipulated for liberty to consult the vicar. Miss Bacon requested to tell her own story to the reverend gentleman, and seems to have been received by him with the utmost kindness, and even to have succeeded in making a certain impression on his mind as to the desirability of the search. As their interview had been under the seal of secrecy, he asked permission to consult a friend, who, as Miss Bacon either found out or surmised, was a practitioner of the law. What the legal friend advised she did not learn; but the negotiation continued, and certainly was never broken off by an absolute refusal on the vicar's part. He, perhaps, was kindly temporizing with our poor countrywoman, whom an Englishman of ordinary mould would have sent to a lunatic asylum at once. I cannot help fancying, however, that her familiarity with the events of Shakespeare's life, and of his death and burial (of which she would speak as if she had been present at the edge of the grave), and all the history, literature, and personalities of the Elizabethan age, together with the prevailing power of her own belief, and the eloquence with which she knew how to enforce it, had really gone some little way toward making a convert of the good clergyman. If so, I honor him above all the hierarchy of England.

The affair certainly looked very hopeful. However erroneously, Miss Bacon had understood from the vicar that no obstacles would be interposed to the investigation, and that he himself would sanction it with his presence. It was to take place after nightfall; and all preliminary arrangements being made, the vicar and clerk professed to wait only her word in order to set about lifting the awful stone from the sepulchre. So, at least, Miss Bacon believed; and as her bewilderment was entirely in her own thoughts, and never disturbed her perception or accurate remembrance of external things, I see no reason to doubt it, except it be the tinge of absurdity in the fact. But, in this apparently prosperous state of things, her own convictions began to falter. A doubt stole into her mind whether she might not have mistaken the depository and mode of concealment of those historic treasures; and, after once admitting the doubt, she was afraid to hazard the shock of uplifting the stone and finding nothing. She examined the surface of the gravestone, and endeavored, without stirring it, to estimate whether it were of such thickness as to be capable of containing the archives of the Elizabethan club. She went over anew the proofs, the clews, the enigmas, the pregnant sentences, which she had discovered in Bacon's Letters and elsewhere, and now was frightened to perceive that they did not point so definitely to Shakespeare's tomb as she had heretofore supposed. There was an unmistakably distinct reference to a tomb, but it might be Bacon's, or Raleigh's, or Spenser's; and instead of the "Old Player," as she profanely called him, it might be either of those three illustrious dead, poet, warrior, or statesman, whose ashes, in Westminster Abbey, or the Tower burial-ground, or wherever they sleep, it was her mission to disturb. It is very possible, moreoever, that her acute mind may always have had a lurking and deeply latent distrust of its own fantasies, and that this now became strong enough to restrain her from a decisive step.

But she continued to hover around the church, and seems to have had full freedom of entrance in the daytime, and special license, on one occasion at least, at a late hour of the night. She went thither with a dark-lantern, which could but twinkle like a glow-worm through the volume of obscurity that filled the great dusky edifice. Groping her way up the aisle and towards the chancel, she sat down on the elevated part of the pavement above Shakespeare's grave. If the divine poet really wrote the inscription there, and cared as much about the quiet of his bones as its deprecatory earnestness would imply, it was time for those crumbling relics to bestir themselves under her sacrilegious feet. But they were safe. She made no attempt to disturb them; though, I believe, she looked narrowly into the crevices between Shakespeare's and the two adjacent stones, and in some way satisfied herself that her single strength would suffice to lift the former, in case of need. She threw the feeble ray of her lantern up towards the bust, but could not make it visible beneath the darkness of the vaulted roof. Had she been subject to superstitious terrors, it is impossible to conceive of a situation that could better entitle her to feel them, for, if Shakespeare's ghost would rise at any provocation, it must have shown itself then; but it is my sincere belief, that, if his figure had appeared within the scope of her dark-lantern, in his slashed doublet and gown, and with his eyes bent on her beneath the high, bald forehead, just as we see him in the bust, she would have met him fearlessly, and controverted his claims to the authorship of the plays, to his very face. She had taught herself to contemn "Lord Leicester's groom" (it was one of her disdainful epithets for the world's incomparable poet) so thoroughly, that even his disembodied spirit would hardly have found civil treatment at Miss Bacon's hands.

Her vigil, though it appears to have had no definite object, continued far into the night. Several times she heard a low movement in the aisles: a stealthy, dubious footfall prowling about in the darkness, now here, now there, among the pillars and ancient tombs, as if some restless inhabitant of the latter had crept forth to peep at the intruder. By and by the clerk made his appearance, and confessed that he had been watching her ever since she entered the church.

About this time it was that a strange sort of weariness seems to have fallen upon her: her toil was all but done, her great purpose, as she believed, on the very point of accomplishment, when she began to regret that so stupendous a mission had been imposed on the fragility of a woman. Her faith in the new philosophy was as mighty as ever, and so was her confidence in her own adequate development of it, now about to be given to the world; yet she wished, or fancied so, that it might never have been her duty to achieve this unparalleled task, and to stagger feebly forward under her immense burden of responsibility and renown. So far as her personal concern in the matter went, she would gladly have forfeited the reward of her patient study and labor for so many years, her exile from her country and estrangement from her family and friends, her sacrifice of health and all other interests to this one pursuit, if she could only find herself free to dwell in Stratford and be forgotten. She liked the old slumberous town, and awarded the only praise that ever I knew her to bestow on Shakespeare, the individual man, by acknowledging that his taste in a residence was good, and that he knew how to choose a suitable retirement for a person of shy, but genial temperament. And at this point, I cease to possess the means of tracing her vicissitudes of feeling any further. In consequence of some advice which I fancied it my duty to tender, as being the only confidant whom she now had in the world, I fell under Miss Bacon's most severe and passionate displeasure, and was cast off by her in the twinkling of an eye. It was a misfortune to which her friends were always particularly liable; but I think that none of them ever loved, or even respected, her most ingenuous and noble, but likewise most sensitive and tumultuous character, the less for it.

At that time her book was passing through the press. Without prejudice to her literary ability, it must be allowed that Miss Bacon was wholly unfit to prepare her own work for publication, because, among many other reasons, she was too thoroughly in earnest to know what to leave out. Every leaf and line was sacred, for all had been written under so deep a conviction of truth as to assume, in her eyes, the aspect of inspiration. A practised book-maker, with entire control of her materials, would have shaped out a duodecimo volume full of eloquent and ingenious dissertation,—criticisms which quite take the color and pungency out of other people's critical remarks on Shakespeare,—philosophic truths which she imagined herself to have found at the roots of his conceptions, and which certainly come from no inconsiderable depth somewhere. There was a great amount of rubbish, which any competent editor would have shovelled out of the way. But Miss Bacon thrust the whole bulk of inspiration and nonsense into the press in a lump, and there tumbled out a ponderous octavo volume, which fell with a dead thump at the feet of the public, and has never been picked up. A few persons turned over one or two of the leaves, as it lay there, and essayed to kick the volume deeper into the mud; for they were the hack critics of the minor periodical press in London, than whom, I suppose, though excellent fellows in their way, there are no gentlemen in the world less sensible of any sanctity in a book, or less likely to recognize an author's heart in it, or more utterly careless about bruising, if they do recognize it. It is their trade. They could not do otherwise. I never thought of blaming them. It was not for such an Englishman as one of these to get beyond the idea that an assault was meditated on England's greatest poet. From the scholars and critics of her own country, indeed, Miss Bacon might have looked for a worthier appreciation, because many of the best of them have higher cultivation, and finer and deeper literary sensibilities than all but the very profoundest and brightest of Englishmen. But they are not a courageous body of men; they dare not think a truth that has an odor of absurdity, lest they should feel themselves bound to speak it out. If any American ever wrote a word in her behalf, Miss Bacon never knew it, nor did I. Our journalists at once republished some of the most brutal vituperations of the English press, thus pelting their poor countrywoman with stolen mud, without even waiting to know whether the ignominy was deserved. And they never have known it, to this day, nor ever will.

The next intelligence that I had of Miss Bacon was by a letter from the mayor of Stratford-on-Avon. He was a medical man, and wrote both in his official and professional character, telling me that an American lady, who had recently published what the mayor called a "Shakespeare book," was afflicted with insanity. In a lucid interval she had referred to me, as a person who had some knowledge of her family and affairs. What she may have suffered before her intellect gave way, we had better not try to imagine. No author had ever hoped so confidently as she; none ever failed more utterly. A superstitious fancy might suggest that the anathema on Shakespeare's tombstone had fallen heavily on her head, in requital of even the unaccomplished purpose of disturbing the dust beneath, and that the "Old Player" had kept so quietly in his grave, on the night of her vigil, because he foresaw how soon and terribly he would be avenged. But if that benign spirit takes any care or cognizance of such things now, he has surely requited the injustice that she sought to do him—the high justice that she really did—by a tenderness of love and pity of which only he could be capable. What matters it though she called him by some other name? He had wrought a greater miracle on her than on all the world besides. This bewildered enthusiast had recognized a depth in the man whom she decried, which scholars, critics, and learned societies, devoted to the elucidation of his unrivalled scenes, had never imagined to exist there. She had paid him the loftiest honor that all these ages of renown have been able to accumulate upon his memory. And when, not many months after the outward failure of her lifelong object, she passed into the better world, I know not why we should hesitate to believe that the immortal poet may have met her on the threshold and led her in, reassuring her with friendly and comfortable words, and thanking her (yet with a smile of gentle humor in his eyes at the thought of certain mistaken speculations) for having interpreted him to mankind so well.

I believe that it has been the fate of this remarkable book never to have had more than a single reader. I myself am acquainted with it only in insulated chapters and scattered pages and paragraphs. But, since my return to America, a young man of genius and enthusiasm has assured me that he has positively read the book from beginning to end, and is completely a convert to its doctrines. It belongs to him, therefore, and not to me,—whom, in almost the last letter that I received from her, she declared unworthy to meddle with her work,—it belongs surely to this one individual, who has done her so much justice as to know what she wrote, to place Miss Bacon in her due position before the public and posterity.

## NATHANIEL HOLMES
### "Philosopher and Poet"
### *The Authorship of Shakespeare*
### 1866, pp. 589–601

S hakespeare has long been considered by all that speak the English tongue, and by the learned of other nations likewise, as the greatest of dramatic poets. The ancients had but one Homer: the moderns have but one Shakespeare. And these two have been fitly styled "the Twin Stars of Poesy" in all the world. These plays have kept the stage better than any other for nearly three centuries. They have been translated into several foreign languages; a vast amount of critical erudition has been expended upon them; and numerous editions have been printed, and countless numbers of copies have been distributed, generation after generation, increasing in a kind of geometrical progression, through all ranks and classes of society from the metropolitan palace to the frontier cabin, until it may almost be said, that if there be anywhere a family possessing but two only books, the one may be the Bible, but the other is sure to be Shakespeare.

Nevertheless, the plays have been understood and appreciated rather according to existing standards of judgment than according to all that was really in them. In general, our English minds seem to have been aware that their poet was more or less philosophical, or rather that he was a kind of universal genius; but that he was a Platonic thinker, a transcendental metaphysician and philosopher, an idealist and a realist all in one, not many seem to have discovered. Coleridge certainly had some inkling of this fact, and to Carlyle, it stood perfectly clear, that Shakespeare "does not look at a thing, but into it, through it; so that he constructively comprehends it, can take it asunder, and put it together again; the thing melts, as it were, into light under his eye, and anew *creates* itself before him." That is to say, he is a Thinker in the highest of all senses: he is a Poet. For Goethe, as for Shakespeare, the world lies all translucent, all *fusible* we might call it, encircled with WONDER; the Natural in reality the Supernatural, for to the seer's eyes both become one."[1] And so

also Gervinus concludes upon the question of "the realistic or ideal treatment," that "he is sometimes the one, sometimes the other, but in reality neither, because he is both at once."[2] Deep searching criticism, on this side of the sea, has been able to sound the depths and scale the heights of the Higher Philosophy of Bacon, and it is almost equally clear that it has discovered in it the world-streaming providence of Shakespeare. "The English shrink from a generalization," says Emerson. "They do not look abroad into universality, or they draw only a bucket-full at the fountain of the First Philosophy for their occasion, and do not go to the springhead. Bacon, who said this, is almost unique among his countrymen in that faculty, at least among the prose-writers. Milton, who was the stair or high table-land to let down the English genius from the summits of Shakespeare, used this privilege sometimes in poetry, more rarely in prose. For a long interval afterwards, it is not found."[3] We know how Bacon attained to these heights; but it is not explained how the unlearned William Shakespeare reached these same "summits" of all philosophy, otherwise than by a suggestion of "the specific gravity" of inborn genius. Have we any evidence outside of these plays, that this "dry light" of nature was greater in William Shakespeare than in Francis Bacon? In Bacon, as in the plays, we have not only the inborn genius, but a life of study, knowledge, science, philosophy, art, and the wealth of all learning. Are these things to be counted as nothing? Then we may as well abolish the universities, burn the libraries, and shut up the schools, as of no use:—

> Hang up philosophy:
> Unless philosophy can make a Juliet,
> Displant a town, reverse a Prince's doom,
> It helps not, it prevails not: talk no more.
> (*Romeo and Juliet*, Act III. Sc. 3)

For the most part, all that has been seen in Shakespeare has been considered as the product of some kind of natural genius or spontaneous inspiration. The reason has been nearly this, that since Bacon, if Berkeley be excepted, England, or the English language, has never had a philosophy at all: we have had nothing but a few sciences and a theology. Bacon's Summary Philosophy, or Philosophy itself, seems to have fallen still-born from his delivery, a dead letter to our English mind. It was not grasped, and the existence of it in his works seems to have been forgotten. No English, or American, philosopher has yet appeared to review, expound, and complete it, in any systematic manner: this work has been left to those who are said to hold dominion of the air. Some there have been, doubtless, as capable as any of undertaking to give a complete systematic statement of all philosophy; but they probably knew too well what kind of an undertaking that would be, when a perfect work might require not only a divine man, but a book as large as the Book of God's Works. The men that are called philosophers among us are occupied with physical science only. What Bacon endeavored to re-organize, and constitute anew, as methods and instruments for obtaining a broader and surer "foundation" for a higher metaphysical philosophy, they appear to have mistaken for the whole of science and the sum total of all certain knowledge, excepting only a fantastical kind of traditional supernatural knowledge, for the most part, completely ignoring metaphysics; and, as a matter of course, they have given us as little conception of a philosophy of the universe, and, with all their physical science, have had as little to give, as a Humboldt's Cosmos, or that prodigious Frenchman, M. Auguste Comte.

Besides a physical science we have had only a theology, taking old Hebrew and some later Greek literature for all divine revelation; the Mosaic cosmogony for the constitution of the universe; Usher's chronology for an account of all time on this earth; Adamic genealogy for an ethnology of the human race; Jesus of Nazareth for the creator of the whole world and sole saviour of mankind; and some five or six fantastic miracles for all the boundless and eternal wonders of the creation. These old ones are nearly worn out, and are fast becoming obsolete: indeed, they are already well-nigh extinct. It is high time they were laid up on a shelf, and labelled to be studied hereafter as fossils of the theological kingdom; and preachers, opening their eyes, should cast about for a new set, at least, out of all the universe of miracles that surround them, and henceforth found their preaching on them. There would then be much less trouble about faith, and infidelity to myths and superstitions might become fidelity to God and his truth.

And so, having no philosophy, and no conception of the possibility of any, and nothing to give the name to, our English mind has appropriated the word as a superfluous synonym for physical science, and scarcely allowed free scope to that; and among us, the Newtons, Franklins, Faradays, Brewsters, and Darwins, are called philosophers, as Hegel said. These men are certainly to be ranked among the master minds of the world as original inventors and discoverers in physics, as philosophical observers and excellent writers on physical science, with the addition, in some instances, of a considerable sprinkling of orthodox theology, and in some others, as in Newton, the younger Herschel, Agassiz, Peirce, with the addition of not a few remarkable deep-soundings into the fundamental depths of things and the hidden mysteries of creation, as it were, some prophetic flashes of the most exalted intellect across the darkness of their own age and time in dim anticipation of a coming century; as when Newton says, "Only whatever light be, I would suppose it consists of successive rays differing from one another in contingent circumstances, as bigness, force, or vigor, like as the sands of the shore, the waves of the sea, the faces of men, and all other natural things of the same kind differ, it being almost impossible for any sort of things to be formed without some contingent variety." And again, "Every soul that has perception is, though in different times and in different organs of sense and motion, still the same indivisible person. There are given successive parts in duration, co-existent parts in space, but neither the one nor the other in the person of a man, or his thinking principle; and much less can they be found in the thinking substance of God. Every man so far as he is a thing that has preception, is one and the same man during his whole life, in all and each of his organs of sense. God is the same God, always and everywhere. He is omnipresent not *virtually* only, but also *substantially*; for virtue cannot subsist without substance."[4] This is Berkeley's philosophy of a thinking substance, existing as reality, and not at all as any ideal vision of a mystical dreamer. Auguste Comte, ignoring theology and metaphysics together, calls his huge book of physical science a "Positive Philosophy": it is indeed positive enough, and in the total upshot as unphilosophical as positive;—as if a universe could be constituted and carried on by mere physics and phrenologico-biology on a basis of dead substratum, or could be conceived to go of itself as a blind perpetual-motion machine! But how shall any one, not having eyes to see, be able to see, that it goes only as the power of thought could make it go, and not otherwise? If the light within you be dark, how great is that darkness.

Among the theologians, we have had a class of writers, who have been sometimes called metaphysicians, but who were, in truth, merely metaphysical theologians, swimming, like Jean Paul's fish, in a box, and the box tied to the shore of church or state with a given length of rope; or materialistic anti-theologians, and in either case, no more metaphysicians than philosophers. Of the one sort were Locke, Reid, Brown, Stewart, and Hamilton; and of the other, Hobbes, Halley, Hume, Mill, Lewes, and Harriet Martineau. Not one of either sort appears ever to have been able to cross the threshold of that Higher Philosophy, which Bacon, following the dim light of Plato, but mainly by the help of his own Boanergic genius, endeavored to erect and constitute as the one universal science, and in which he was followed, in their own way, by Berkeley and Swedenborg. After these, Kant seems to have been the next to make a clear breach over the threshold, when prying off into the palpable obscure of the previous darkness, as a Vulcanian miner drifts into the bowels of the earth after unknown ores, or as a Columbus launches upon an unexplored ocean, believing with such as Bacon and all high philosophic genius, that beyond the pillars of Hercules there may be lands yet undiscovered, he began to make that darkness visible to some few, through the Transcendental Æsthetic of Time and Space. It has been easier, since, even for lesser lights, to follow and enlarge and clear the drift, thus roughly cut into solid darkness by the life-labor of all powerful thought; and hence that modern school of philosophy, which has done something toward a critical exegesis of the fundamental and eternal laws of thought, the true nature of substance or matter, a true knowledge of cause and "the mode of that thing which is uncaused," a sound and rational psychology, and some more scientific, intelligible, and satisfactory account of the constitution of this universe, and of the order of divine providence and the destiny of man in it:—in fine, a Universal Philosophy.

German scholars of this modern school, whether special students of this philosophy, or debtors to its results for their ideas and methods, have been filled with admiration of the super-eminent genius of Shakespeare. "The poetry of Shakespeare," says Frederick Schlegel, "has much accord with the German mind." Goethe, despairing to excel him, ranks him first among modern poets, and honors. Hamlet with a place in the *Wilhelm Meister*; and Richter, no less, discovering at once the amazing depth of his philosophy, makes him rule sovereign in the heart of his Albano,—"not through the breathing of living characters, but by lifting him up out of the loud kingdom of earth into the silent realm of infinity."[5] How wonderful, indeed, is all this! Is it, then, that we have here a born genius, to whose all-seeing vision schools and libraries, sciences and philosophies, were unnecessary,—were an idle waste of time, forsooth?—whose marvellous intuition grasped all the past and saw through all the present? whose prophetic insight spans the future ages as they roll up, measures the highest wave of the modern learning and philosophy, and follows backward the tide of civilization, arts, and letters, to the very borders of the barbaric lands?—before whose almost superhuman power, time and place seem to vanish and disappear, as if it had become with him "an everlasting Now and Here"? or, as if it had pleased the Divine Majesty to send another Messiah upon our earth, knowing all past, all present, and all future, to be leader, guide, and second Saviour of mankind? What greater miracle need be!

Being translated into German, Shakespeare became "the father of German literature," says Emerson. But it so happens, that the parts of him, which have been more especially quoted as the basis of this German appreciation, are precisely those, which have been least noticed at home, or if seen, appreciated on quite other grounds. Those transparent characters, which, said Goethe, are "like watches with crystalline plates and cases," where the whole frame and order of discovery are placed, as it were *sub oculos*, under the very eye, and those most pregnant passages, which are written, like the Faust, or the Meister, with a double aspect, whether because it was then dangerous to write otherwise, or because the highest art made such writing necessary and proper, being the highest wisdom as well as that true poetry which requires the science of sciences and "the purest of all study for knowing it," making these plays magic mirrors like "the universal world" itself, in which any looker may see as much as he is able to see and no more, have passed in the general mind for little more than ingenious poetical conceptions, powerful strokes of stage eloquence, or merely fanciful turns of expression; or if, sometimes, anything deeper may have been half discovered in them, some suspected smack of infidelity may have thrown the trammelled reader, all of a sudden, into a grim silence—a sort of moody astonishment,—very much as if he had accidentally laid his hand upon an electric eel;—as if a true man should fear to be infidel to anything but God and the eternal truth of things, or as if more credence were due to a traditional mythology of the Egyptianized, or the Grecianized, Hebrews than to the best teachings of the wisest living men and the most enlightened philosophy. It has been said, that the *Hamlet* was not discovered to be anything wonderful till within the Nineteenth Century. In truth, these new wonders of Shakespeare are precisely the parts, qualities, and characteristics of him, wherein the higher philosophy of Bacon is displayed, and which are to be understood and comprehended in their full meaning and drift by those only, who stand upon the same high cliff and platform whereon he stood alone of all his contemporaries, that topmost height and narrow strait, "where one but goes abreast," in an age, and almost without an English rival down to our time. German scholars, as well as some later English, by the help of this same higher philosophy, in the new Kantian instauration of it, have been enabled to ascend to this elevated platform; and being there, they discover the transcendent genius of Shakespeare in the philosophy, culture, science, and true art, which belonged only to Bacon. And therein and thereby is it further proven, that this "our Shakespeare" was no other than Francis Bacon himself; and William Shakespeare ceases to be that "unparelleled mortal" he has been taken for, that title being justly transferred to the man to whom it more porperly pertains. So, for the most part, in all times, has the philosopher been robbed of his glory. We worship in Jesus what belongs to Plato; in Shakespeare, what belongs to Bacon; and in many others, what belongs to the real philosopher, the actual teacher, the true saviour, and to Philosophy Herself.

All that gives peculiarity and preëminence to these plays is to be found in Bacon; vast comprehension, the profoundest philosophic depth, the subtle discrimination of differences and resemblances, matured wisdom, vigor and splendor of imagination, accurate observation of nature, extensive knowledge of men and manners, the mighty genius and the boundless wit, the brevity of expression and pregnant weight of matter, a fine æsthetic appreciation of the beautiful, the classical scholarship, familiarity with law, courts, and legal proceedings, with the metaphysic of jurisprudence, with statesmen and princes, ladies and courtiers, and that proper sense (which belonged to the age) of the dignity, sovereign duties, power and honor of the throne and king, the sovereign power in the State;—all this, and more than can be named, belongs to both writings, and therefore to one author. Here was a man that could be a Shakespeare. Coleridge, Schlegel, Goethe, Jean Paul Richter, Carlyle, Emerson, Delia Bacon, Gervinus, and, doubtless, many more, clearly saw that the real Shakespeare must have been such a man, in spite of all the biographies. "Ask your own hearts," says Coleridge, "ask your own common sense, to conceive the possibility of this man being . . . the anomalous, the wild, the irregular genius of our daily criticism! What! are we to have miracles in sport? Or, I speak reverently, does God choose idiots by whom to convey divine truths to man?"[6] And yet, even Coleridge failed to discover, that "the morning star, the guide, the pioneer of true philosophy," was not William Shakespeare, but Francis Bacon.

The last and most conclusive proof of all is that general, inwrought, and all-pervading identity, which is to be found in these writings, when carefully studied, and which, when it is looked for and seen, is appreciated and convinces, like the character of a handwriting, by an indescribable genuineness and an irresistible force of evidence. In the words of A. W. Schlegel, speaking of Shakespeare, "On all the stamp of his mighty spirit is impressed."[7] The distinguishing qualities of Bacon's prose style are precisely those which belong to the poet, namely, breadth of thought, depth of insight, weight of matter, brevity, force, and beauty of expression, brilliant metaphor, using all nature as a symbol of thought, and that supreme power of imagination that is necessary to make him an artistic creator, adding man to the universe; qualities, which mark that mind only which God hath framed "as a mirrour or glass, capable of the image of the universal world." His speeches display these qualities. The oratorical style of that day seems to have been more close and weighty than in our times: it was full of strength and earnestness. Lord Coke spoke in thunderbolts, huge, Cyclopean, tremendous: he went to the very pith and heart of the matter, at once, and his speech was always "*multum in parvo*." But in him, it was vigor without grace, power without splendor, or beauty, and ability unillumined by the divine light of genius. When we know that Bacon had been such a poet, it ceases to be a wonder that he was such an orator as he was. The mind that had been conceiving dramatic speeches, at this rate, during a period of thirty years or more, could never address a court, a parliament, or a king, otherwise than in the language, style, and imagery of poetry. In short, Bacon's prose is Shakespearean poetry, and Shakespeare's poetry is Baconian prose. Nor did these qualities altogether escape the recognition of one, who had an eye to see, an ear to hear, and a soul to comprehend: says Ben Jonson, "There happened in my time one noble speaker, who was full of gravity in his speaking. His language, where he could spare, or pass by a jest, was nobly censorious. No man ever spoke more neatly, more pressly, more weightily, or suffered less emptiness, less idleness, in what he uttered. No member of his speech but consisted of his own graces. His hearers could not cough or look aside from him without loss. He commanded where he spoke and had his judges angry and pleased at his devotion. No man had their affections more in his power. The fear of every man who heard him was lest he should make an end." And again he says, "My conceit of his person was never increased toward him by his place or honors; but I have and do reverence him for the greatness that was only proper to himself, in that he seemed to me ever by his works one of the greatest men, and most worthy of admiration that had been in many ages." Howell, another contemporary, says of him, likewise, that "he was the eloquentest that was born in this isle."

What manner of man, then, have we here for our Shakespeare? A child well born, a highly educated youth, a precocious manhood, and an all-comprehending intelligence; a retired and most diligent student, who felt that he was "fitter by nature to hold a book than play a part," and whose studies, like Plato's, or Cicero's, ended only with life; an original thinker always; a curious explorer into every branch, and a master in nearly all parts, of human learning and knowledge; a brilliant essayist, an ingenious critic, a scientific inventor, a subtle, bold, and all-grasping philosopher; an accurate and profound legal writer; a leading orator and statesman, a counsellor of sovereigns and princes, a director in the affairs of nations, and, in spite of all faults, whether his own, or of his time, or of servants whose rise was his fall, "the justest Chancellor that had been in the five changes since Sir Nicholas Bacon's time," and though frail, not having "the fountain of a corrupt heart," but being one to whose known virtue "no accident could do harm, but rather help to make it manifest"; a prodigious wit, a poetic imaginator, an artistic creator, an institutor of the art of arts and the science of sciences; a seer into the Immortal Providence, and the veritable author of the Shakespeare Drama: in truth, not (as Howell supposed) a rare exception to the fortune of an orator, a lawyer, and a philosopher, as he was, but true still to "the fortune of all poets commonly to die beggars," dying as a philosopher and a poet, "poor out of a contempt of the pelf of fortune as also out of an excess of generosity";—his life, on the whole, and to the last, a sacrifice for the benefit of all science, all future ages, and all mankind. Surely, we may exclaim with Coleridge, not without amazement still: "Merciful, wonder-making Heaven! What a man was this Shakespeare! Myriad-minded, indeed, he was."

*Notes*

1. *Essays*, III. 209.
2. *Shakespeare Comm.* (London, 1863), II. 569.
3. *English Traits*, 244.
4. *Principia*, (ed. Chittenden, N. Y. 1848,) p. 505.
5. *Titan*, by Brooks, I. 154.
6. *Notes on Shakespeare, Works*, IV. 56.
7. *Lectures on Dram. Lit.*, 302.

### JAMES SPEDDING
### "On the Authorship of the Plays Attributed to Shakespeare" (1867)
### *Reviews and Discussions*
### 1879, pp. 369–75

*From a letter to Professor Nathaniel Holmes,
15th February, 1867.*

I have read your book on the authorship of Shakespeare faithfully to the end, and if my report of the result is to be equally faithful, I must declare myself not only unconvinced, but undisturbed. To ask me to believe that the man who was accepted by all the people of his own time, to many of whom he was personally known, as the undoubted author of the best plays then going, was *not* the author of them—is like asking me to believe that Charles Dickens was not the author of *Pickwick*. To ask me to believe that a man who was famous for a variety of other accomplishments, whose life was divided between public business, the practice of a laborious profession, and private study of the art of investigating the material laws of nature,—a man of large acquaintance, of note from early manhood, and one of the busiest men of his time—but who was never suspected of wasting time in writing poetry, and is not known to have written a single blank verse in all his life,—that this man was the author of fourteen comedies, ten historical plays, and eleven tragedies, exhibiting the greatest and the greatest variety of excellence that has been attained in that kind of composition,—is like asking me to believe that Lord Brougham was the author not only of Dickens' novels, but of Thackeray's also, and of Tennyson's poems besides. That the author of *Pickwick*

was a man called Charles Dickens I know upon no better authority than that upon which I know that the author of *Hamlet* was a man called William Shakespeare. And in what respect is the one more difficult to believe than the other? A boy born and bred like Charles Dickens was unlikely *a priori* to become famous over Europe and America for a never-ending series of original stories, as a boy born and bred like William Shakespeare to become the author of the most wonderful series of dramas in the world. It is true that Shakespeare's gifts were higher and rarer; but the wonder is that *any* man should have possessed them, not that the man to whose lot they fell was the son of a poor man called John Shakespeare, and that he was christened William. That he was not a man otherwise known to the world is not strange at all. Nature's great lottery being open to everybody, the chances that the supreme prize will be drawn by an unknown man are as the numbers of the unknown to the known—millions to hundreds. It is not the famous man that becomes a great inventor; the great inventor becomes a famous man. Faraday was a bookbinder's apprentice, who in binding a copy of Mrs. Marcet's Conversations on Chemistry, was attracted to the study, got employed as an assistant to Sir Humphrey Davy—an assistant in so humble a capacity that wishing to make the acquaintance of some of the scientific men on the continent, he actually went with him to Geneva as his servant—and by his own genius, virtue, and industry, made himself the most famous man (probably) now living in England. Burns was a ploughman. Keats was a surgeon's apprentice. George Stephenson a lad employed in a colliery. Newton did not become Newton because he was sent to Cambridge; he was sent to Cambridge because he *was* Newton—because he had been endowed by nature with the singular gifts which made him Newton. But for the genius which nature gave them without any consideration of position or advantages, what would have been known of any one of these?

If Shakespeare was not trained as a scholar or a man of science, neither do the works attributed to him show traces of trained scholarship or scientific education. Given the *faculties* (which nature bestows as freely on the poor as on the rich), you will find that all the acquired knowledge, art, and dexterity which the Shakespearian plays imply, were easily attainable by a man who was labouring in his vocation and had nothing else to do. Or if you find this difficult to believe of such a man as you assume Shakespeare to have been, try Bacon. Suppose Francis Bacon, instead of being trained as a scholar, a statesman, and a lawyer, and seeking his fortune from the patronage of the great, had been turned loose into the world without means or friends, and joined a company of players as the readiest resource for a livelihood. Do you doubt that he would soon have tried his hand at writing a play? that he would have found out how to write better plays than were then the fashion? that he would have cultivated an art which he found profitable and prosperous, and sought about for such knowledge as would help him in it,—reading his Plutarch, and his Seneca, and his Hollinshead, and all the novels and play-books that came in his way; studying life and conversation by all the opportunities which his position permitted; and generally seeking to enrich his thought with observation? Do not you think that Francis Bacon would have been capable of learning in that way everything which there is any reason to think the writer of the Shakespearian plays knew? And if Francis Bacon could, why could not William Shakespeare?

If therefore your theory involved no difficulties of its own—if you merely proposed the substitution of one man for another—I should still have asked why I should doubt the tradition;—where was the difficulty which made the old story hard to believe. I see none. That which is *extraordinary* in the case, and against which therefore there lies *primâ facie* some presumption, is that *any* man should possess such a combination of faculties as must have met in the author of these plays. But that is a difficulty which cannot be avoided. There must have been *somebody* in whom the requisite combination of faculties did meet: for there the plays are: and by supposing that this somebody was a man who at the same time possessed a combination of other faculties, themselves sufficient to make him an extraordinary man too, you do not diminish the wonder but increase it. Aristotle was an extraordinary man. Plato was an extraordinary man. That two men each severally so extraordinary should have been living at the same time in the same country, was a very extraordinary thing. But would it diminish the wonder to suppose the two to be one? So I say of Bacon and Shakespeare. That a human being possessed of the faculties necessary to make a Shakespeare should exist, is extraordinary. That a human being possessed of the faculties necessary to make a Bacon should exist, is extraordinary. That two such human beings should have been living in London at the same time was more extraordinary still. But that one man should have existed possessing the faculties and opportunities necessary to make *both*, would have been the most extraordinary thing of all.

You will not deny that tradition goes for *something*: that in the absence of any reason for doubting it, the concurrent and undisputed testimony to a fact of all who had the best means of knowing it, is a reason for believing it: or at least for thinking it more probable than any other given fact, not compatible with it, which is not so supported. On this ground alone, without inquiring further, I believe that the author of the plays published in 1623 was a man called William Shakespeare. It was believed by those who had the best means of knowing: and I know no reason for doubting it. The reasons for doubting which you suggest seem all to rest upon a latent assumption that William Shakespeare could not have possessed any remarkable faculties: a fact which would no doubt settle the question if it were established. But what should make me think so? It was not the opinion of anybody who was acquainted with him, so far as we know; and why was a man of that name less likely than another to possess remarkable faculties?

With one to whom the simple story as it comes presents no difficulty, you will not expect that the other considerations which you urge should have much weight. Resemblances both in thought and language are inevitable between writers nourished upon a common literature, addressing popular audiences in a common language, and surrounded by a common atmosphere of knowledge and opinion. But to me, I confess, the resemblances between Shakespeare and Bacon are not so striking as the differences. Strange as it seems that two such minds, both so vocal, should have existed within each other's hearing without mutually affecting each other, I find so few traces of any influence exercised by Shakespeare upon Bacon, that I have great doubt whether Bacon knew any more about him than Gladstone (probably) knows about Tom Taylor (in his dramatic capacity). Shakespeare may have derived a good deal from Bacon. He had no doubt read the *Advancement of Learning* and the first edition of the *Essays*, and most likely had frequently heard him speak in the Courts and the Star Chamber. But among all the parallelisms which you have collected with such industry to illustrate the identity of the writer, I have not observed one in which I should not have inferred from the difference of style a difference of hand. Great writers, especially being contemporary, have many features in common; but if they are really great writers they write

naturally, and nature is always individual. I doubt whether there are five lines together to be found in Bacon which could be mistaken for Shakespeare, or five lines in Shakespeare which could be mistaken for Bacon, by one who was familiar with their several styles and practised in such observations. I was myself well read in Shakespeare before I began with Bacon; and I have been forced to cultivate what skill I have in distinguishing Bacon's style to a high degree; because in sifting the genuine from the spurious I had commonly nothing but the style to guide me. And to me, if it were proved that any one of the plays attributed to Shakespeare was really written by Bacon, not the least extraordinary thing about it would be the power which it would show in him of laying aside his individual peculiarities and assuming those of a different man.

If you ask me what I say to Bacon's own confession in the case of *Richard II.*, I say that your inference is founded entirely upon a misconstruction of a relative pronoun. "About the same time I remember an answer of mine in a matter which had some affinity with my lord's cause, *which* though it grew from me went after about in others' names." I say that "which" means not the *matter* but the *answer*.[1] You make it appear to refer to the "matter" only by inserting "and" (p. 251, l. 8), which is not in the original: and if so there is an end of your whole superstructure. When the queen asked him whether there was not treason in Dr. Hayward's history of the first year of Henry IV. he parried the question by an evasive answer; which was quoted afterwards and ascribed in conversation to other people, but was really his own. Even if it were possible to believe that the "matter" in question was the play of *Richard II.*, the only inference that could be drawn as to the authorship is that the ostensible author was a doctor. But for my part I can see nothing in it but a reference to Dr. Hayward's historical tract.

These are my reasons for rejecting your theory. If you had fixed upon anybody else rather than Bacon as the true author—anybody of whom I knew nothing—I should have been scarcely less incredulous; because I deny that a *primâ facie* case is made out for questioning Shakespeare's title. But if there were any reason for supposing that somebody else was the real author, I think I am in a condition to say that, whoever it was, it was not Bacon. The difficulties which such a supposition would involve would be almost innumerable and altogether insurmountable. But if what I have said does not excuse me from saying more, what I might say more would be equally ineffectual.

I ought perhaps to apologize for speaking with such confidence on the question of style in a matter where my judgment is opposed to yours. But you must remember that style is like hand-writing—not easy to recognize at first, but unmistakable when you are familiar enough with it. When some twenty-five years ago I began the work of collating the manuscripts with the printed copies, and plunged into a volume of miscellaneous letters written in the beginning of the seventeenth century, I could scarcely distinguish one hand from another, and it was some time before I discovered which was Bacon's own. But after a little of the close and continuous attention which collating and copying involves, I began to feel as if I could know it through all its varieties, from the stateliest Italian to the most sprawling black-letter, and almost swear to a semi-colon. And I am convinced that I could produce many cases in which the most expert palæographers and fac-similists would at the first view pronounce two hands different, yet find on examination that they were the same. Now it is the same with a man's manner of expressing himself. The unconscious gestures of the style, scarcely discernible at first, are scarcely mistakable after. The time may have been—I do not know—

when I could have believed the style of *Hamlet* and of the *Advancement of Learning* to be the style of the same man: and the time may yet come when you will yourself wonder that you did not perceive the difference.

*Notes*

1. Professor Holmes had assumed the "story of the first year of King Henry IV." (which was the matter in question) to be the Shakespearian play of Richard II.: and argued that, in saying that "*it* [namely the play] grew from him," Bacon confessed himself the real author. Mr. H. allows that he had misconstrued "which," and that this point of the confession must be given up, but remains otherwise satisfied that Bacon *was* the author and that the queen knew it.

## JAMES FREEMAN CLARKE
"Did Shakespeare Write Bacon's Works?"
*The North American Review*, February 1881, pp. 163–75

The greatest of English poets is Shakespeare. The greatest prose writer in English literature is probably Lord Bacon. Each of these writers, alone, is a marvel of intellectual grandeur. It is hard to understand how one man, in a few years, could have written all the masterpieces of Shakespeare,— thirty-six dramas, each a work of genius such as the world will never let die. It is a marvel that from one mind could proceed the tender charm of such poems as *Romeo and Juliet*, *As You Like It*, or *The Winter's Tale*; the wild romance of *The Tempest*, or of *The Midsummer Night's Dream*; the awful tragedies of *Lear*, *Macbeth*, and *Othello*; the profound philosophy of *Hamlet*; the perfect fun of *Twelfth Night*, and *The Merry Wives of Windsor*; and the reproductions of Roman and English history. It is another marvel that a man like Lord Bacon, immersed nearly all his life in business, a successful lawyer, an ambitious statesman, a courtier cultivating the society of the sovereign and the favorites of the sovereign, should also be the founder of a new system of philosophy, which has been the source of many inventions and new sciences down to the present day; should have critically surveyed the whole domain of knowledge, and become a master of English literary style. Each of these phenomena is a marvel; but put them together, and assume that one man did it all, and you have, not a marvel, but a miracle. Yet, this is the result which the monistic tendency of modern thought has reached. Several critics of our time have attempted to show that Lord Bacon, besides writing all the works usually attributed to him, was also the author of all of Shakespeare's plays and poems.

This theory was first publicly maintained by Miss Delia Bacon in 1857. It had been, before, in 1856, asserted by an Englishman, William Henry Smith, but only in a thin volume printed for private circulation. This book made a distinguished convert in the person of Lord Palmerston, who openly declared his conviction that Bacon was the author of Shakespeare's plays. Two papers by Appleton Morgan, written in the same sense, appeared last year in *Appleton's Journal*. But far the most elaborate and masterly work in support of this attempt to dethrone Shakespeare, and to give his seat on the summit of Parnassus to Lord Bacon, is the book by Judge Holmes, published in 1866. He has shown much ability, and brought forward every argument which has any plausibility connected with it.

Judge Holmes was, of course, obliged to admit the extreme antecedent improbability of his position. Certainly it is very difficult to believe that the author of such immortal works should have been willing, for any reason, permanently to conceal his authorship; or, if he could hide that fact, been willing to give the authorship to another; or, if willing, should have been able so effectually to conceal the substitution as to blind the eyes of all mankind down to the days of Miss Delia Bacon and Judge Holmes.

What, then, are the arguments used by Judge Holmes? The proofs he adduces are mainly these: (1st) That there are many coincidences and parallelisms of thought and expression between the works of Bacon and Shakespeare; (2d) that there is an amount of knowledge and learning in the plays, which Lord Bacon possessed, but which Shakespeare could hardly have had. Besides these principal proofs, there are many other reasons given which are of inferior weight—a phrase in a letter of Sir Tobie Matthew; another sentence of Bacon himself, which might be possibly taken as an admission that he was the author of *Richard II.*; the fact that some plays which Shakespeare certainly did not write were first published with his name or his initials. But his chief argument is that Shakespeare had neither the learning nor the time to write the plays, both of which Lord Bacon possessed; and that there are curious coincidences between the plays and the prose works.

These arguments have all been answered, and the world still believes in Shakespeare as before. But I have thought it might be interesting to show how easily another argument could be made of an exactly opposite kind—how easily all these proofs might be reversed. I am inclined to think that if we are to believe that one man was the author of the plays and the philosophy, it is much more probable that Shakespeare wrote the works of Bacon than that Bacon wrote the works of Shakespeare. For there is no evidence that Bacon was a poet as well as a philosopher; but there is ample evidence that Shakespeare was a philosopher as well as a poet. This, no doubt, assumes that Shakespeare actually wrote the plays; but this we have a right to assume, in the outset of the discussion, in order to stand on an equal ground with our opponents.

The Bacon *vs.* Shakespeare argument runs thus: "Assuming that Lord Bacon wrote the works commonly attributed to him, there is reason to believe that he also wrote the plays and poems commonly attributed to Shakespeare."

The counter argument would then be: "Assuming that Shakespeare wrote the plays and poems commonly attributed to him, there is reason to believe that he also wrote the works commonly attributed to Bacon."

This is clearly the fair basis of the discussion. What is assumed on the one side on behalf of Bacon we have a right to assume on the other on behalf of Shakespeare. But before proceeding on this basis, I must reply to the only argument of Judge Holmes which has much apparent weight. He contends that it was impossible for Shakespeare, with the opportunities he possessed, to acquire the knowledge which we find in the plays. Genius, however great, cannot give the knowledge of medical and legal terms, nor of the ancient languages. Now, it has been shown that the plays afford evidence of a great knowledge of law and medicine; and of works in Latin and Greek, French and Italian. How could such information have been obtained by a boy who had no advantages of study except at a country grammar-school, which he left at the age of fourteen, who went to London at twenty-three and became an actor, and who spent most of his life as actor, theatrical proprietor, and man of business?

This objection presents difficulties to us, and for our time, when boys sometimes spend years in the study of Latin grammar. We cannot understand the rapidity with which all sorts of knowledge were imbibed in the period of the Renaissance. Then every one studied everything. Then Greek and Latin books were read by prince and peasant, by queens and generals. Then all sciences and arts were learned by men and women, by young and old. Thus speaks Robert Burton—who was forty years old when Shakespeare died: "What a world of books offers itself, in all subjects, arts and sciences, to the sweet content and capacity of the reader! In arithmetic, geometry, perspective, opticks, astronomy, architecture, *sculptura, pictura*, of which so many and elaborate treatises have lately been written; in mechanics and their mysteries, military matters, navigation, riding of horses, fencing, swimming, gardening, planting, great tomes of husbandry, cookery, faulconry, hunting, fishing, fowling; with exquisite pictures of all sports and games. . . . What vast tomes are extant in law, physic, and divinity, for profit, pleasure, practice. . . . Some take an infinite delight to study the very languages in which these books were written: Hebrew, Greek, Syriac, Chaldee, Arabick, and the like." This was the fashion of that day, to study all languages, all subjects, all authors. A mind like that of Shakespeare could not have failed to share this universal desire for knowledge. After leaving the grammar-school, he had nine years for such studies before he went to London. As soon as he began to write plays, he had new motives for study; for the subjects of the drama in vogue were often taken from classic story.

But Shakespeare enjoyed another source of gaining knowledge besides the study of books. When he reached London, five or six play-houses were in full activity, and new plays were produced every year in vast numbers. New plays were then in constant demand, just as the new novel and new daily or weekly paper are called for now. The drama was the periodical literature of the time. Dramatic authors wrote with wonderful rapidity, borrowing their subjects from plays already on the stage, and from classic or recent history. Marlowe, Greene, Lyly, Peele, Kyd, Lodge, Nash, Chettle, Munday, Wilson, were all dramatic writers before Shakespeare. Philip Henslowe, a manager or proprietor of the theaters, bought two hundred and seventy plays in about ten years. Thomas Heywood wrote a part or the whole of two hundred and twenty plays during his dramatic career. Each acted play furnished material for some other. They were the property of the play-houses, not of the writers. One writer after another had accused Shakespeare of indifference to his reputation, because he did not publish a complete and revised edition of his works during his life. How could he do this, since they did not belong to him, but to the theater? Yet every writer was at full liberty to make use of all he could remember of other plays, as he saw them acted; and Shakespeare was not slow to use this opportunity. No doubt he gained knowledge in this way, which he afterward employed much better than the authors from whom he took it.

The first plays printed under Shakespeare's name did not appear till he had been connected with the stage eleven years. This gives time enough for him to have acquired all the knowledge to be found in his books. That he had read Latin and Greek books we are told by Ben Jonson; though that great scholar undervalued, as was natural, Shakespeare's attainments in those languages.

But Ben Jonson himself furnishes the best reply to those who think that Shakespeare could not have gained knowledge of science or literature because he did not go to Oxford or Cambridge. What opportunities had Ben Jonson? A brick-layer by trade, called back immediately from his studies to use the trowel; then running away and enlisting as a common soldier; fighting in the Low Countries; coming home at nineteen, and going on the stage; sent to prison for fighting a duel—what opportunities for study had he? He was of a strong animal

nature, combative, in perpetual quarrels, fond of drink, in pecuniary troubles, married at twenty, with a wife and children to support. Yet Jonson was celebrated for his learning. He was master of Greek and Latin literature. He took his characters from Athenæus, Libanius, Philostratus. Somehow he had found time for all this study. "Greek and Latin thought," says Taine, "were incorporated with his own, and made a part of it. He knew alchemy, and was as familiar with alembics, retorts, crucibles, etc., as if he had passed his life in seeking the philosopher's stone. He seems to have had a specialty in every branch of knowledge. He had all the methods of Latin art—possessed the brilliant conciseness of Seneca and Lucan." If Ben Jonson—a brick-layer, a soldier, a fighter, a drinker—could yet get time to acquire this vast knowledge, is there any reason why Shakespeare, with much more leisure, might not have done the like? He did not possess as much Greek and Latin lore as Ben Jonson, who, probably, had Shakespeare in his mind when he wrote the following passage in his *Poetaster*:

> His learning savors not the school-like gloss
> That most consists in echoing words and terms,
> And soonest wins a man an empty name;
> Nor any long or far-fetched circumstance
> Wrapt in the curious generalties of art—
> But a direct and analytic sum
> Of all the worth and first effects of art.
> And for his poesy, 'tis so rammed with life,
> That it shall gather strength of life with being,
> And live hereafter more admired than now.

The only other serious proof offered in support of the proposition that Lord Bacon wrote the immortal Shakespearean drama is that certain coincidences of thought and language are found in the works of the two writers. When we examine them, however, they seem very insignificant. Take, as an example, two or three, on which Judge Holmes relies, and which he thinks very striking.

Holmes says (page 48) that Bacon quotes Aristotle, who said that "young men were no fit hearers of moral philosophy," and Shakespeare says (*Troilus and Cressida*):

> Unlike young men whom Aristotle thought
> Unfit to hear moral philosophy.

But since Bacon's remark was published in 1605, and *Troilus and Cressida* did not appear until 1609, Shakespeare might have seen it there, and introduced it into his play from his recollection of the passage in the *Advancement of Learning*.

Another coincidence mentioned by Holmes is that both writers use the word "thrust": Bacon saying that a ship "thrust into Weymouth"; and Shakespeare, that "Milan was thrust from Milan." He also thinks it cannot be an accident that both frequently use the word "wilderness," though in very different ways. Both also compare Queen Elizabeth to a "star." Bacon makes Atlantis an island in mid ocean; and the island of Prospero is also in mid ocean. Both have a good deal to say about "mirrors," and "props," and like phrases.

Such reasoning as this has very little weight. You cannot prove two contemporaneous writings to have proceeded from one author by the same words and phrases being found in both; for these are in the vocabulary of the time, and are the common property of all who read and write.

My position is that if either of these writers wrote the works attributed to the other, it is much more likely that Shakespeare wrote the philosophical works of Bacon, than that Bacon wrote the poetical works of Shakespeare. Assuming then, as we have a right to do in this argument, that Shakespeare wrote the plays, what reasons are there for believing that he also wrote the philosophy?

*First.* This assumption will explain at once that hitherto insoluble problem of the utter contradiction between Bacon's character and conduct, and his works. How could he have been, at the same time, what Pope calls him—

The wisest, brightest, meanest of mankind?

He was, in his philosophy, the leader of his age, the reformer of old abuses, the friend of progress. In his conduct, he was, as Macaulay has shown, "far behind his age—far behind Sir Edward Coke; clinging to exploded abuses, withstanding the progress of improvement, struggling to push back the human mind." In his writings, he was calm, dignified, noble. In his life, he was an office-seeker through long years, seeking place by cringing subservience to men in power, made wretched to the last degree when office was denied him, addressing servile supplications to noblemen and to the sovereign. To gain and keep office he would desert his friends, attack his benefactors, and make abject apologies for any manly word he might have incautiously uttered. His philosophy rose far above earth and time, and sailed supreme in the air of universal reason. But "his desires were set on things below. Wealth, precedence, titles, patronage, the mace, the seals, the coronet, large houses, fair gardens, rich manors, massy services of plate, gay hangings," were "objects for which he stooped to everything, and endured everything." These words of Macaulay have been thought too severe. But we defy any admirer of Bacon to read his life, by Spedding, without admitting their essential truth. How was it possible for a man to spend half of his life in the meanest of pursuits, and the other half in the noblest?

This great difficulty is removed if we suppose that Bacon, the courtier and lawyer, with his other ambitions, was desirous of the fame of a great philosopher; and that he induced Shakespeare, then in the prime of his powers, to help him write the prose essays and treatises which are his chief works. He has himself admitted that he did actually ask the aid of the dramatists of his time in writing his books. This remarkable fact is stated by Bacon in a letter to Tobie Matthew, written in June, 1623, in which he says that he is devoting himself to making his writings more perfect—instancing the *Essays* and the *Advancement of Learning*—"by the help of some good pens, which forsake me not." One of these pens was that of Ben Jonson, the other might easily have been that of Shakespeare. Certainly there was no better pen in England at that time than his.

When Shakespeare's plays were being produced, Lord Bacon was fully occupied in his law practice, his parliamentary duties, and his office-seeking. The largest part of the Shakespeare drama was put on the stage, as modern research renders probable, in the ten or twelve years beginning with 1590. In 1597, Shakespeare was rich enough to buy the new place at Stratford-on-Avon, and was also lending money. In 1604, he was part owner of the Globe Theater, so that the majority of the plays which gained for him this fortune must have been produced before that time. Now these were just the busiest years of Bacon's life. In 1584, he was elected to Parliament. About the same time, he wrote his famous letter to Queen Elizabeth. In 1585, he was already seeking office from Walsingham and Burleigh. In 1586, he sat in Parliament for Taunton, and was active in debate and on committees. He became a bencher in the same year, and began to plead in the courts of Westminster. In 1589, he became queen's counsel, and member of Parliament for Liverpool. After this, he continued active, both in Parliament and at the bar. He sought, by the help of Essex, to become Attorney-General. From that period, as crown lawyer, his whole time and thought were required to trace and frustrate the conspiracies with which

the kingdom was full. It was evident that during these years he had no time to compose fifteen or twenty of the greatest works in any literature.

But how was Shakespeare occupied when Bacon's philosophy appeared? The *Advancement of Learning* was published in 1605, after most of the plays had been written, as we learn from the fact of Shakespeare's purchase of houses and lands. The *Novum Organum* was published in 1620, after Shakespeare's death. But it had been written years before; revised, altered, and copied again and again—it is said twelve times. Bacon had been engaged upon it during thirty years, and it was at last published incomplete and in fragments. If Shakespeare assisted in the composition of this work, his death in 1616 would account, at once, for its being left unfinished. And Shakespeare would have had ample time to furnish the ideas of the *Organum* in the last years of his life, when he had left the theater. In 1613, he bought a house in Black Friars, where Ben Jonson also lived. Might not this have been that they might more conveniently coöperate in assisting Bacon to write the *Novum Organum*?

When we ask whether it would have been easier for the author of the philosophy to have composed the drama, or the dramatic poet to have written the philosophy, the answer will depend on which is the greater work of the two. The greater includes the less, but the less cannot include the greater. Now the universal testimony of modern criticism in England, Germany, and France declares that no larger, deeper, or ampler intellect has ever appeared than that which produced the Shakespeare drama. This "myriad-minded" poet was also philosopher, man of the world, acquainted with practical affairs, one of those who saw the present and foresaw the future. All the ideas of the Baconian philosophy might easily have had their home in this vast intelligence. Great as are the thoughts of the *Novum Organum* they are far inferior to that world of thought which is in the drama. We can easily conceive that Shakespeare, having produced in his prime the wonders and glories of the plays, should in his after leisure have developed the leading ideas of the Baconian philosophy. But it is difficult to imagine that Bacon, while devoting his main strength to politics, to law, and to philosophy, should have, as a mere pastime for his leisure, produced in his idle moments the greatest intellectual work ever done on earth.

If the greater includes the less, then the mind of Shakespeare includes that of Bacon, and not the reverse. This will appear more plainly if we consider the quality of intellect displayed respectively in the drama and the philosophy. The one is synthetic, creative; the other analytic, critical. The one puts together, the other takes apart and examines. Now, the genius which can put together can also take apart; but it by no means follows that the power of taking apart implies that of putting together. A watch-maker, who can put a watch together, can easily take it to pieces; but many a child who has taken his watch to pieces has found it impossible to put it together again.

When we compare the Shakespeare plays and the Baconian philosophy, it is curious to see how the one is throughout a display of the synthetic intellect, and the other of the analytic. The plays are pure creation, the production of living wholes. They people our thought with a race of beings who are living persons, and not pale abstractions. These airy nothings take flesh and form, and have a name and local habitation forever on the earth. Hamlet, Desdemona, Othello, Miranda, are as real people as Queen Elizabeth or Mary of Scotland. But when we turn to the Baconian philosophy, this faculty is wholly absent. We have entered the laboratory of a great chemist, and are surrounded by retorts and crucibles, tests and re-agents, where the work done is a careful analysis of all existing things, to find what are their constituents and their qualities. Poetry creates, philosophy takes to pieces and examines.

It is, I think, an historic fact, that while those authors whose primary quality is poetic genius have often been also, on a lower plane, eminent as philosophers, there is, perhaps, not a single instance of one whose primary distinction was philosophic analysis, who has also been, on a lower plane, eminent as a poet. Milton, Petrarch, Goethe, Lucretius, Voltaire, Coleridge, were primarily and eminently poets; but all excelled, too, in a less degree, as logicians, metaphysicians, men of science, and philosophers. But what instance have we of any man like Bacon, chiefly eminent as lawyer, statesman, and philosopher, who was also distinguished, though in a less degree, as a poet? Among great lawyers, is there one eminent also as a dramatic or lyric author? Cicero tried it, but his verses are only doggerel. In Lord Campbell's list of the lord chancellors and chief-justices of England, no such instance appears. If Bacon wrote the Shakespeare drama, he is the one exception to an otherwise universal rule. But if Shakespeare coöperated in the production of the Baconian philosophy, he belongs to a class of poets who have done the same. Coleridge was one of the most imaginative of poets. His *Christabel* and *Ancient Mariner* are pure creations. But in later life he originated a new system of philosophy in England, the influence of which has not ceased to be felt to our day. The case would be exactly similar if we suppose that Shakespeare, having ranged the realm of imaginative poetry in his youth, had in his later days of leisure coöperated with Bacon and Ben Jonson in producing the *Advancement of Learning* and the *Novum Organum*. We can easily think of them as meeting, sometimes at the house of Ben Jonson, sometimes at that of Shakespeare in Black Friars, and sometimes guests at that private house built by Lord Bacon for purposes of study, near his splendid palace of Gorhambury. "A most ingeniously contrived house," says Basil Montagu, "where, in the society of his philosophical friends, he devoted himself to study and meditation." Aubrey tells us that he had the aid of Hobbes in writing down his thoughts. Lord Bacon appears to have possessed the happy gift of using other men's faculties in his service. Ben Jonson, who had been a thorough student of chemistry, alchemy, and science in all the forms then known, aided Bacon in his observations of nature. Hobbes aided him in giving clearness to his thoughts and his language. And from Shakespeare he may have derived the radical and central ideas of his philosophy. He used the help of Dr. Playfer to translate his philosophy into Latin. Tobie Matthew gives him the last argument of Galileo for the Copernican system. He sends his works to others, begging them to correct the thoughts and the style. It is evident, then, that he would have been glad of the concurrence of Shakespeare, and that could easily be had, through their common friend, Ben Jonson.

If Bacon wrote the plays of Shakespeare, it is exceedingly difficult to give any satisfactory reason for his concealment of that authorship. He had much pride, not to say vanity, in being known as an author. He had his name attached to all his other works, and sent them as presents to the universities, and to individuals, with letters calling their attention to these books. Would he have been willing to conceal permanently the fact of his being the author of the best poetry of his time? The reasons assigned by Judge Holmes for this are not satisfactory. They are: his desire to rise in the profession of the law, the low reputation of a play-writer, his wish to write more freely under an incognito, and his wish to rest his reputation on his philosophical works. But if he were reluctant to be regarded as the author of *Lear* and *Hamlet*, he was willing to be known as the writer of "Masques," and a play about Authur, exhibited by the students of Gray's Inn. It is an error to say that the reputation of a play-writer was low. Judge Holmes, himself, tells us that there was nothing remarkable in a barrister of the inns of court writing for the stage. Ford and Beaumont were both lawyers as well as eminent play-writers. Lord Backhurst, Lord Brooke, Sir Henry Wotton, all wrote plays. And we find nothing in the Shakespeare dramas which Bacon need have feared to say under his own name. It would have been ruin to Sir Philip Francis to have avowed himself the author of *Junius*. But the Shakespeare plays satirized no one, and made no enemies. If there were any reasons for concealment, they certainly do not apply to the year 1623, when the first folio appeared, which was after the death of Shakespeare and the fall of Bacon. The acknowledgment of their authorship at that time could no longer interfere with Bacon's rise. And it would be very little to the credit of his intelligence to assume that he was not then aware of the value of such works, or that he did not desire the reputation of being their author. It would have been contrary to his very nature not to have wished for the credit of that authorship.

On the other hand, there would be nothing surprising in the fact of Shakespeare's laying no claim to credit for having assisted in the composition of the *Advancement of Learning*. Shakespeare was by nature as reticent and modest as Bacon was egotistical and ostentatious. What a veil is drawn over the poet's personality in his sonnets! We read in them his inmost sentiments, but they tell us absolutely nothing of the events of his life, or the facts of his position. And if, as we assume, he was one among several who helped Lord Bacon, though he might have done the most, there was no special reason why he should proclaim that fact.

Gervinus has shown, in three striking pages, the fundamental harmony between the ideas and mental tendencies of Shakespeare and Bacon. Their philosophy of man and of life was the same. If, then, Bacon needed to be helped in thinking out his system, there was no one alive who would have given him such stimulus and encouragement as Shakespeare. This also may explain his not mentioning the name of Shakespeare in his works; for that might have called too much attention to the source from which he received this important aid.

Nevertheless, I regard the monistic theory as in the last degree improbable. We have two great authors, and not one only. But if we are compelled to accept the view which ascribes a common source to the Shakespeare drama and the Baconian philosophy, I think there are good reasons for preferring Shakespeare to Bacon as the author of both. When the plays appeared, Bacon was absorbed in pursuits and ambitions foreign to such work; his accepted writings show no sign of such creative power; he was the last man in the world not to take the credit of such a success, and had no motive to conceal his authorship. On the other hand, there was a period in Shakespeare's life when he had abundant leisure to coöperate in the literary plans of Bacon; his ample intellect was full of the ideas which took form in those works; and he was just the person neither to claim any credit for lending such assistance nor to desire it.

There is, certainly, every reason to believe that among his other ambitions, Bacon desired that of striking out a new path of discovery, and initiating a better method in the study of nature. But we know that, in doing this, he sought aid in all quarters, and especially among Shakespeare's friends and companions. It is highly probable, therefore, that he became acquainted with the great dramatist, and that Shakespeare knew of Bacon's designs and became interested in them. And if so, who could offer better suggestions than he; and who would more willingly accept them than the overworked statesman and lawyer, who wished to be also a philosopher?

Finally, we may refer those who believe that the shape of the brow and head indicates the quality of mental power, to the portraits of the two men. The head of Shakespeare, according to all the busts and pictures which remain to us, belongs to the type which antiquity has transmitted to us in the portraits of Homer and Plato. In this vast dome of thought there was room for everything. The head of Bacon is also a grand one, but less ample, less complete—less

> Teres, totus atque rotundus.

These portraits therefore agree with all we know of the writings, in showing us which, and which only, of the two minds was capable of containing the other.

## IGNATIUS DONNELLY
### "A Word Personal"
### *The Great Cryptogram: Francis Bacon's Cipher in the So-Called Shakespeare Plays*
1888, Volume 2, pp. 889–94

> Report me and my causes right
> To the unsatisfied.
>
> (*Hamlet*, v, 5.)

I began this book with an apology; I end it with another. No one can be more conscious of its defects than I am. So great a subject demanded the utmost care, deliberation and perfection; while my work has, on the other hand, been performed with the utmost haste and under many adverse circumstances.

It was my misfortune to have announced, in 1884, that I believed I had found a Cipher in the Plays. From the time I put forth that claim until the copy was placed in the hands of the publishers, I made no effort to advertise my book. But the assertion was so startling, and concerned writings of such universal interest, that it could not be suffered to fall unnoticed. I felt, at the same time, that I owed some duties to the nineteenth century, as well as to the sixteenth, and hence my work was greatly broken in upon by public affairs. After a time the reading world became clamorous for the proofs of my surprising assertion; and many were not slow to say that I was either an impostor or a lunatic. Goaded by these taunts, I made arrangements to publish before I was really ready to do so; and then set to work, under the greatest strain and the highest possible pressure, to try to keep my engagements with my publishers. But the reader can readily conceive how slowly such a Cipher work as this must have advanced, when every word was a sum in arithmetic, and had to be counted and verified again and again. In the meantime upon my poor devoted head was let loose a perfect flood-tide of denunciation, ridicule and misrepresentation from three-fourths of the newspapers of America and England. I could not pause in my work to defend myself, but had to sit, in the midst of an arctic winter, and patiently endure it all, while working from ten to twelve hours every day, at a kind of mental toil the most exhausting the human mind is capable of.

These facts will, I trust, be my excuse for all the crudeness, roughness, repetitions and errors apparent in these pages.

In the Patent Office they require the inventor to state clearly what he claims. I will follow that precedent.

I admit, as I have said before, that my workmanship in the elaboration of the Cipher is not perfect. There are one or two essential points of the Cipher rule that I have not fully worked out. I think that I see the complete rule, but I need more leisure to elaborate and verify it abundantly, and reduce my workmanship to mathematical exactness.

But I claim that, beyond a doubt, *there is a Cipher in the so-called Shakespeare Plays.*

The proofs are *cumulative.* I have shown a thousand of them.

No honest man can, I think, read this book through and say that there is nothing extraordinary, unusual and artificial in the construction of the text of *1st* and *2d Henry IV.* No honest man will, I think, deny the multitudinous evidences I present that the text, words, brackets and hyphens have been adjusted arithmetically to the necessity of matching the ends of scenes and fragments of scenes with certain root-numbers of a Cipher. No man can pretend that such words and phrases as the following could come in this, or any other book, by accident, held together in every case by the same Cipher numbers:

### THE NAMES OF PLAYS.
1. *Measure for Measure*, three times repeated.
2. *Contention of York and Lancaster*, three times repeated.
3. *The Merry Wives of Windsor*, twice repeated.
4. *Richard the Second*, twice repeated.
5. *Richard the Third*, given once.
6. *King John*, twice repeated.

### THE NAMES OF PERSONS.
1. *Shakspere*, repeated about twenty times.
2. *Marlowe*, repeated several times.
3. *Archer*, used once.
4. *Philip Henslow*, used once in full, and twice without first name.
5. *Field*, several times repeated.
6. *Cecil*, many times repeated.
7. *The Earl of Shrewsbury*, two or three times repeated.
8. *Sir Thomas Lucy*, twice repeated.
9. *Hayward*.
10. *Harry Percy*, many times repeated.
11. *Master Francis*.
12. *My Uncle Burleigh*, twice repeated.
13. *My Lord John, the Bishop of Worcester*, used twice.
14. *Dethick, King of Arms*.
15. *Ann Hathaway*.
16. *Ann Whatley*, twice repeated.
17. *King Harry, father of the present Queen*.
18. *Sir Nicholas*, twice repeated.
19. *Sir Walter*.

### NAMES OF PLACES.
1. *St. Albans*, twice repeated.
2. *The Fortune Play-house*.
3. *The Curtain Play-house*.
4. *New-Place*.
5. *Guinegate*.
6. *The Fire of Smithfield*.
7. *Holland*.
8. *The Low Countries*.
9. *The fish pond*, twice repeated.

### SIGNIFICANT PHRASES.
1. *The old jade*, many times repeated.
2. *The old termagant*, many times repeated.
3. *My cousin*, many times repeated.
4. *The royal tyrant*.
5. *The royal maiden*.
6. *The rascally knave*.

7. *A butcher's 'prentice.*
8. *Glove-making,* two or three times repeated.
9. *The King's evil.*
10. *Fifteen hundred and fifteen.*

Now I submit to all fair-minded men whether this is not an astonishing array of words to find in about a dozen pages of the text of two plays; and whether there is any other writing on earth in which, in the same space, these words can be duplicated. I cannot believe there is. But remember that not only are these significant and most necessary words found in this brief compass, but they fit exactly into sentences every word of which grows out of the same determinate Cipher number. But, in addition to all this, remember the dense packing of some columns, and the sparse condition of the adjoining columns; remember how *heart* is spelled *hart* where it refers to Shakspere's sister; remember how *and it* is spelled *an't*, and not *and't*, where allusion is had to Bacon's *aunt*; remember how *dear* is spelt *deere* when it refers to *deer*; remember how *sperato* is separated by a hair space into *sper ato*, so as to give the terminal syllable to *Shake-sper*; remember how the rare word *rabbit* is found in the text precisely cohering, arithmetically, with *hunting*. Then turn to the Cipher story on page 79 of the Folio, where not only scattered words come out, but where whole long series of words are so adjusted, with the aid of the brackets and hyphens, as to follow precisely the order of the words in the play! Then remember how every part of this Cipher story fits precisely into what we know historically to be true; and, although much of it is new, that part is, in itself, probable and reasonable.

The world will either have to admit that there is a Cipher in the Plays, or that in the construction of this narrative I have manifested an ingenuity as boundless as that which I have attributed to Bacon. But I make no such claim. No ingenuity could *create the words* necessary to tell this extraordinary story, unless they were in the text. Take Bulwer's *Richelieu*, or Byron's *Manfred*, or Goldsmith's *She Stoops to Conquer*, or any other dramatic composition of the last hundred years, and you will seek in vain for even one-tenth of the significant words found herein; and as to making any of these modern plays tell a coherent, historical tale, by counting *with the same number* from the ends of scenes and fragments of scenes, it would be altogether and absolutely impossible.

I do not blame any man for having declared *à priori* against the possibility of there being a Cipher in the Plays. On the face of it such a claim is improbable, and, viewed from our nineteenth century standpoint, and in the light of our free age, almost absurd. I could not, in the first instance, have believed it myself. I advanced to the conception slowly and reluctantly. I expected to find only a brief assertion of authorship, a word or two to a column. If any man had told me five years ago that these two plays were such an exquisite and intricate piece of microscopic mosaic-work as the facts show them to be, I should have turned from him with contempt. I could not have believed that any man would involve himself in such incalculable labor as is implied in the construction of such a Cipher. We may say the brain was abnormal that created it. But how, after all, can we judge such an intellect by the ordinary standard of mankind? If he sought immortality he certainly has achieved it, for, once the human family grasps the entirety of this inconceivable work, it will be drowned in an ocean of wonder. The Plays may lose their charm; the English language may perish; but tens of thousands of years from now, if the world and civilization endure, mankind will be talking about this extraordinary welding together of fact and fiction; this tale within a tale; this sublime and supreme triumph of the human intellect. Beside it the *Iliad* will be but as the rude song of wandering barbarians, and *Paradise Lost* a temporary offshoot of Judaism.

I trust no honest man will feel constrained, for consistency's sake, because he has judged my book unheard, to condemn it heard. It will avail nothing to assail me. I am not at issue. And you cannot pound the life out of a fact with your fists. A truth has the indestructibility of matter. It is part of God: the threads of continuity tie it to the throne of the Everlasting.

Edmund Burke said in a debate in Parliament about the population of the American colonies: "While we are disputing they grow to it." And so, even while the critics are writing their essays, to demonstrate that all I have revealed is a fortuitous combination of coincidence, keen and able minds will be taking up my imperfect clues and reducing the Cipher rule to such perfection that it will be as useless to deny the presence of the sun in the heavens as to deny the existence of the inner story in the Plays.

And what a volume of historical truths will roll out of the text of this great volume! The inner life of kings and queens, the highest, perhaps the basest, of their kind; the struggles of factions in the courts; the interior view of the birth of religions; the first colonization of the American continent, in which Bacon took an active part, and something of which is hidden in The Tempest; the death of Mary Queen of Scots; the Spanish Armada, told in *Love's Labor Lost*; the religious wars on the continent; the story of Henry of Navarre; the real biography of Essex; the real story of Bacon's career; his defense of his life, hidden in *Henry VIII.*, his own downfall, in cipher, being told in the external story of the downfall of Wolsey. What historical facts may we not expect, of which that account of the introduction of "the dreaded and incurable malady" into England is a specimen; what philosophical reflections; what disquisitions on religion; what profound and unrestrained meditations! It will be, in short, the inner story of the most important era in human history, told by the keenest observer and most powerful writer that has ever lived. And then think of the light that will be thrown upon the Plays themselves; their purposes, their history, their meaning! A great light bursting from a tomb, and covering with its royal effulgence the very cradle of English Literature.

And so I trust my long-promised book to the tender mercies of my fellow-men, saying to them in the language of the old rhyme:

> Be to its faults a little blind,
> And to its virtues very kind.

# G. K. CHESTERTON
"Sensationalism and a Cipher" (1902)
*Chesterton on Shakespeare*, ed. Dorothy Collins
1971, pp. 179–86

I

The revival of the whole astonishing Bacon-Shakespeare business is chiefly interesting to the philosophical mind as an example of the power of the letter which killeth and of how finally and murderously it kills. Baconianism is, indeed, the last wild monstrosity of literalism; it is a sort of delirium of detail. A handful of printers' types, a few alphabetical comparisons are sufficient to convince the Baconians of a proposition which is fully as fantastic historically as the proposition that the Battle of Waterloo was won by Leigh Hunt disguised as Wellington, or that the place of Queen Victoria for the last forty years of her reign was taken by Miss Frances Power

Cobbe. Both these hypotheses are logically quite possible. The dates agree; the physical similarity is practically sufficient. Briefly, in fact, there is nothing to be said against the propositions except that every sane man is convinced that they are untrue.

Let us consider for a moment the Baconian conception from the outside. A sensational theory about the position of Shakespeare was certain in the nature of things to arise. Men of small imagination have sought in every age to find a cipher in the indecipherable masterpieces of the great. Throughout the Middle Ages the whole of the *Aeneid*, full of the sad and splendid eloquence of Virgil, was used as a conjuring book. Men opened it at random, and from a few disconnected Latin words took a motto and an omen for their daily work. In the same way men in more modern times have turned to the Book of Revelation full of the terrible judgment, and yet more terrible consolation of a final moral arbitration, and found in it nothing but predictions about Napoleon Bonaparte and attacks on the English Ritualists. Everywhere, in short, we find the same general truth—the truth that facts can prove anything and that there is nothing so misleading as that which is printed in black and white. Almost everywhere and almost invariably the man who has sought a cryptogram in a great masterpiece has been highly exhilarated, logically justified, morally excited, and entirely wrong.

If, therefore, we continue to study Baconianism from the outside—a process which cannot do it or any other thesis any injustice—we shall come more and more to the conclusion that it is in itself an inevitable outcome of the circumstances of the case and the tendencies of human nature. Shakespeare was by the consent of all human beings a portent. If he had lived some thousand years earlier, people would have turned him into a god. As it is, people can apparently do nothing but attempt to turn him into a Lord Chancellor. But their great need must be served. Shakespeare must have his legend, his whisper of something more than common origin. They must at least make of him a mystery, which is as near as our century can come to a miracle. Something sensational about Shakespeare was bound ultimately to be said, for we are still the children of the ancient earth, and have myth and idolatry in our blood. But in this age of a convention of scepticism we cannot rise to an apotheosis. The nearest we can come to it is a dethronement.

So much for the *a priori* probability of a Baconian theory coming into existence. What is to be said of the *a priori* probability of the theory itself; or, rather, to take the matter in its most lucid order, what is the theory? In the time roughly covered by the latter part of the reign of Queen Elizabeth and the earlier part of the reign of James I, there arose a school of dramatists who covered their country with glory and filled libraries with their wild and wonderful plays. They differed in type and station to a certain extent: some were scholars, a few were gentlemen, most were actors and many were vagabonds. But they had a common society, common meeting-places, a common social tone. They differed in literary aim and spirit: to a certain extent some were great philosophic dramatists, some were quaint humorists, some mere scribblers of a sort of half-witted and half-inspired melodrama. But they all had a common style, a common form and vehicle, a common splendour, and a common error in their methods. Now, the Baconian theory is that one of these well-known historical figures—a man who lived their life and shared their spirit, and who happened to be the most brilliant in the cultivation of their particular form of art—was, as a matter of fact, an impostor, and that the works which his colleagues thought he

had written in the same spirit and the same circumstances in which they had written theirs, were not written by him, but by a very celebrated judge and politician of that time, whom they may sometimes have seen when his coach-wheels splashed them as he went by.

Now, what is to be said about the *a priori* probability of this view, which I stated, quite plainly and impartially above? The first thing to be said, I think, is that a man's answer to the question would be a very good test of whether he had the rudiments of a historical instinct, which is simply an instinct which is capable of realizing the way in which things happen. To many this will appear a vague and unscientific way of approaching the question. But the method I now adopt is the method which every reasonable being adopts in distinguishing between fact and fiction in real life. What would any man say if he were informed that in the private writings of Lord Rosebery that statesman claimed to have written the poems of Mr. W. B. Yeats? Certainly, he could not deny that there were very singular coincidences in detail. How remarkable, for instance, is the name Primrose, which is obviously akin to modest rose, and thus to "Secret Rose". On the top of this comes the crushing endorsement of the same idea indicated in the two words, "rose" and "bury". The remarks of the ploughman in the *Countess Kathleen* (note the rank in the peerage selected) would be anxiously scanned for some not improbable allusion to a furrow; and everything else, the statesman's abandonment of Home Rule, the poet's aversion to Imperialism, would be all parts of Lord Rosebery's cunning. But what, I repeat, would a man say if he were asked if the theory were probable? He would reply, "The theory is as near to being impossible as a natural phenomenon can be. I know Mr. W. B. Yeats, I know how he talks, I know what sort of a man he is, what sort of people he lives among, and know that he is the man to have written those poems. I know Lord Rosebery too, and what sort of a life his is, and I know that he is not."

Now, we know, almost as thoroughly as we should know the facts of this hypothetical case, the facts about Bacon and Shakespeare. We know that Shakespeare was a particular kind of man who lived with a particular kind of men, all of whom thought much as he thought and wrote much as he wrote. We know that Bacon was a man who lived in another world, who thought other thoughts, who talked with other men, who wrote another style, one might almost say another language. That Bacon wrote Shakespeare is certainly possible; but almost every other hypothesis, that Bacon never said so, that he lied when he said it, that the printers played tricks with the documents, that the Baconians played tricks with the evidence, is in its nature a hundred times more probable. Of the cipher itself, I shall speak in another article. For the moment it is sufficient to point out that the Baconian hypothesis has against it the whole weight of historical circumstance and the whole of that supra-logical realization which some of us call transcendentalism, and most of us common sense.

## II

In a previous article I drew attention to the general spirit in which the Baconian question must be approached. That spirit involves the instinct of culture which does not consist merely in knowing the fact, but in being able to imagine the truth. The Baconians imagine a vain thing, because they believe in facts. Their historical faculty is a great deal more like an ear for music. One of the matters, for example, which is most powerfully concerned in the Bacon-Shakespeare question is the question of literary style, a thing as illogical as the bouquet of a bottle of wine. It is the thing, in short, which makes us quite certain that the sentence quoted in *The Tragedy of Sir Francis Bacon* from his secret narrative, "The Queen looked pale from want of rest, but was calm and compos'd," was never written by an Elizabethan. Having explained the essentials of the method as they appear to me, I now come to the study of the mass of the Baconian details. They are set forth in a kind of résumé of various Baconian theories in *The Tragedy of Sir Francis Bacon* by Harold Bayley (Grant Richards). The work is an astonishing example of this faculty of putting out the fire of truth with the fuel of information. Mr. Bayley has collected with creditable industry an enormous number of fragmentary facts and rumours. He has looked at the water-marks in the paper used by the Rosicrucians and Jacobean dramatists. He has examined the tail-pieces and ornamental borders of German and Belgian printers. He has gone through the works of Bacon and Shakespeare and a hundred others, picking out parallel words and allusions, but all the time he is completely incapable of realizing the great and glaring truism which lies at the back of the whole question, the simple truism that a million times nought is nought. He does not see, that is, that though a million coincidences, each of which by itself has a slight value, may make up a probability, yet a million coincidences, each of which has no value in itself, make up nothing at all.

What are the sort of coincidences upon which Mr. Bayley relies? The water-mark used in some book is the design of a bunch of grapes. Bacon says, in the *Novum Organum*: "I pledge mankind in liquor pressed from countless grapes." Another water-mark represents a seal. Somebody said about Bacon that he became Lord Keeper of the Great Seal of England and of the great seal of nature. The rose and the lily were symbols used by the Rosicrucians; there are a great many allusions to roses and lilies in Shakespeare. A common printer's border consists of acorns. Bacon somewhere alludes to his fame growing like an oak tree. Does not Mr. Bayley see that no conceivable number of coincidences of this kind would make an account more probable or even more possible? Anyone in any age might talk about clusters of grapes or design clusters of grapes; anyone might make an ornament out of acorns; anyone might talk about growing like a tree. I look down at my own floor and see the Greek key pattern round the oilcloth, but it does not convince me that I am destined to open the doors of Hellenic mystery. Mr. Bayley undoubtedly produces a vast number of these parallels, but they all amount to nothing. In my previous article I took for the sake of argument the imaginary case of Lord Rosebery and Mr. W. B. Yeats. Does not Mr. Bayley see that to point out one genuine coincidence, as that Lord Rosebery paid secret cheques to Mr. Yeats, might indicate something, but to say that they both walked down Piccadilly, that they both admired Burne-Jones, that they both alluded more than once to the Irish question, in short that they both did a million things that are done by a million other people, does not approach even to having the faintest value or significance. This then, is the first thing to be said to the Baconian spirit, that it does not know how to add up a column of noughts.

The second thing to be said is rather more curious. If there is a cipher in the Shakespearian plays, it ought presumably to be a definite and unmistakable thing. It may be difficult to find, but when you have found it you have got it. But the extraordinary thing is that Mr. Bayley and most other Baconians talk about the Baconian cipher as they might talk about "a touch of pathos" in Hood's poetry, or "a flavour of cynicism" in Thackeray's novels, as if it were a thing one became faintly conscious of and suspected, without being able to point it out. If anyone thinks this unfair, let him notice the strange way in which Mr. Bayley talks about previous Baconian works. "In

1888 Mr. Ignatius Donnelly claimed to have discovered a cipher story in the first folio of Shakespeare's plays. In his much abused but little read and less refuted book, *The Great Cryptogram*, he endeavoured to convince the world of the truth of his theory. Partly by reason of the complexity of his system, the full details of which he did not reveal, and partly owing to the fact that he did not produce any definite assertion of authorship, but appeared to have stumbled into the midst of a lengthy narrative, the world was not convinced, and Mr. Donnelly was greeted with Rabelaisian laughter. He has since gone to the grave unwept, unhonoured, and unsung, and his secret has presumably died with him. The work of this writer was marred by many extravagant inferences, but *The Great Cryptogram* is nevertheless a damning indictment which has not yet been answered." Again, on the second Baconian demonstration, "Dr. Owen gave scarcely more than a hint of how his alleged cipher worked." The brain reels at all this. Why do none of the cipherists seem to be sure what the cipher is or where it is? A man publishes a huge book to prove that there is a cryptogram, and his secret dies with him. Another man devotes another huge book to giving "scarcely more than a hint of it". Are these works really so impenetrable that no one knows whether they all revealed the same cipher or different ciphers? If they pointed to the same cipher it seems odd that Mr. Bayley does not mention it. If their ciphers were different we can only conclude that the great heart of America is passionately bent on finding a cipher in Shakespeare—anyhow, anywhere, and of any kind.

Finally, there is one thing to be said about a more serious matter. In the chapter called "Mr. William Shakespeare" the author has an extraordinary theory that Shakespeare could not have been the author of the works under discussion because those works rise to the heights of mental purity, and the little we know of Shakespeare's life would seem to indicate that it was a coarse and possibly a riotous one. "Public opinion," he says solemnly, "asks us to believe that this divine stream of song, history, and philosophy sprang from so nasty and beastly a source." There is not much to be said about an argument exhibiting so strange an ignorance of human nature. The argument could equally be used to prove that Leonardo da Vinci could not paint, the Mirabeau could not speak, and that Burns's poems were written by the parson of his parish. But surely there is no need to say this to the Baconians. They should be the last people in the world to doubt the possibility of the conjunction of genius with depravity. They trace their sublime stream of song to a corrupt judge, a treacherous friend, a vulgar sycophant, a man of tawdry aims, of cowardly temper, of public and disgraceful end. He killed his benefactor for hire, and the Baconians would improve this and say that he killed his brother. We know little of Shakespeare's vices, but he might have been a scarecrow of profligacy and remained a man worthier to create Portia than the Lord Verulam whom all history knows. The matter is a matter of evidence, and sentiment has little concern with it. But if we did cherish an emotion in the matter it would certainly be a hope that "the divine stream of song" might not be traced to "so nasty and beastly a source" as Francis Bacon.

MARK TWAIN
From "Is Shakespeare Dead?" (1909)
*The Complete Essays of Mark Twain*
ed. Charles Neider
1963, pp. 407–49

*I*

Scattered here and there through the stacks of unpublished manuscript which constitute this formidable Autobiography and Diary of mine, certain chapters will in some distant future be found which deal with "Claimants"—claimants historically notorious: Satan, Claimant; the Golden Calf, Claimant; the Veiled Prophet of Khorassan, Claimant; Louis XVII., Claimant; William Shakespeare, Claimant; Authur Orton, Claimant; Mary Baker G. Eddy, Claimant—and the rest of them. Eminent Claimants, successful Claimants, defeated Claimants, royal Claimants, pleb Claimants, showy Claimants, shabby Claimants, revered Claimants, despised Claimants, twinkle star-like here and there and yonder through the mists of history and legend and tradition—and, oh, all the darling tribe are clothed in mystery and romance, and we read about them with deep interest and discuss them with loving sympathy or with rancorous resentment, according to which side we hitch ourselves to. It has always been so with the human race. There was never a Claimant that couldn't get a hearing, nor one that couldn't accumulate a rapturous following, no matter how flimsy and apparently unauthentic his claim might be. Arthur Orton's claim that he was the lost Tichborne baronet come to life again was as flimsy as Mrs. Eddy's that she wrote *Science and Health* from the direct dictation of the Deity; yet in England near forty years ago Orton had a huge army of devotees and incorrigible adherents, many of whom remained stubbornly unconvinced after their fat god had been proven an impostor and jailed as a perjurer, and to-day Mrs. Eddy's following is not only immense, but is daily augmenting in numbers and enthusiasm. Orton had many fine and educated minds among his adherents, Mrs. Eddy has had the like among hers from the beginning. Her Church is as well equipped in those particulars as is any other Church. Claimants can always count upon a following, it doesn't matter who they are, nor what they claim, nor whether they come with documents or without. It was always so. Down out of the long-vanished past, across the abyss of the ages, if you listen, you can still hear the believing multitudes shouting for Perkin Warbeck and Lambert Simnel.

A friend has sent me a new book, from England—*The Shakespeare Problem Restated*—well restated and closely reasoned; and my fifty years' interest in that matter—asleep for the last three years—is excited once more. It is an interest which was born of Delia Bacon's book—away back in that ancient day—1857, or maybe 1856. About a year later my pilot-master, Bixby, transferred me from his own steamboat to the *Pennsylvania,* and placed me under the orders and instructions of George Ealer—dead now, these many, many years. I steered for him a good many months—as was the humble duty of the pilot-apprentice: stood a daylight watch and spun the wheel under the severe superintendence and correction of the master. He was a prime chess-player and an idolater of Shakespeare. He would play chess with anybody; even with me, and it cost his official dignity something to do that. Also—quite uninvited—he would read Shakespeare to me; not just casually, but by the hour, when it was his watch and I was steering. He read well, but not profitably for me, because he constantly injected commands into the text. That broke it all up, mixed it all up, tangled it all up—to that degree, in fact, that if we were in a risky and difficult piece of river an ignorant person couldn't have told, sometimes, which observations were Shakespeare's and which were Ealer's. For instance:

What man dare, I dare!

Approach thou *what* are you laying in the leads for? what a hell of an idea! like the rugged ease her off a little, ease her off! rugged Russian bear, the armed rhinoceros or the *there* she goes! meet her, meet her! didn't you *know* she'd smell the reef if you crowded it like that? Hyrcan tiger; take any shape but that and my firm nerves she'll be in the *woods* the first you know! stop the starboard! come ahead strong on the larboard! back the starboard! . . . *Now* then, you're all right; come ahead on the starboard; straighten up and go 'long, never tremble: or be alive again, and dare me to the desert *damnation* can't you keep away from that greasy water? pull her down! snatch her! snatch her baldheaded! with thy sword; if trembling I inhabit then, lay in the leads!—no, only the starboard one, leave the other alone, protest me the baby of a girl. Hence horrible shadow! eight bells—that watchman's asleep again, I reckon, go down and call Brown yourself, unreal mockery, hence!

He certainly was a good reader, and splendidly thrilling and stormy and tragic, but it was a damage to me, because I have never since been able to read Shakespeare in a calm and sane way. I cannot rid it of his explosive interlardings, they break in everywhere with their irrelevant, "What in hell are you up to *now!* pull her down! more! *more!*—there now, steady as you go," and the other disorganizing interruptions that were always leaping from his mouth. When I read Shakespeare now I can hear them as plainly as I did in that long-departed time—fifty-one years ago. I never regarded Ealer's readings as educational. Indeed, they were a ~~detriment to me~~.

His contributions to the text seldom improved it, but barring that detail he was a good reader; I can say that much for him. He did not use the book, and did not need to; he knew his Shakespeare as well as Euclid ever knew his multiplication table.

Did he have something to say—this Shakespeare-adoring Mississippi pilot—anent Delia Bacon's book?

Yes. And he said it; said it all the time, for months—in the morning watch, the middle watch, and dog watch; and probably kept it going in his sleep. He bought the literature of the dispute as fast as it appeared, and we discussed it all through thirteen hundred miles of river four times traversed in every thirty-five days—the time required by that swift boat to achieve two round trips. We discussed, and discussed, and discussed, and disputed and disputed; at any rate, *he* did, and I got in a word now and then when he slipped a cog and there was a vacancy. He did his arguing with heat, with energy, with violence; and I did mine with the reserve and moderation of a subordinate who does not like to be flung out of a pilot-house that is perched forty feet above the water. He was fiercely loyal to Shakespeare and cordially scornful of Bacon and of all the pretensions of the Baconians. So was I—at first. And at first he was glad that that was my attitude. There were even indications that he admired it; indications dimmed, it is true, by the distance that lay between the lofty boss-pilotical altitude and my lowly one, yet perceptible to me; perceptible, and translatable into a compliment—compliment coming down from above the snow-line and not well thawed in the transit, and not likely to set anything afire, not even a cub-pilot's self-conceit; still a detectable compliment, and precious.

Naturally it flattered me into being more loyal to

Shakespeare—if possible—than I was before, and more prejudiced against Bacon—if possible—than I was before. And so we discussed and discussed, both on the same side, and were happy. For a while. Only for a while. Only for a very little while, a very, very, very little while. Then the atmosphere began to change; began to cool off.

A brighter person would have seen what the trouble was, earlier than I did, perhaps, but I saw it early enough for all practical purposes. You see, he was of an argumentative disposition. Therefore it took him but a little time to get tired of arguing with a person who agreed with everything he said and consequently never furnished him a provocative to flare up and show what he could do when it came to clear, cold, hard, rose-cut, hundred-faceted, diamond-flashing *reasoning*. That was his name for it. It has been applied since, with complacency, as many as several times, in the Bacon-Shakespeare scuffle. On the Shakespeare side.

Then the thing happened which has happened to more persons than to me when principle and personal interest found themselves in opposition to each other and a choice had to be made: I let principle go, and went over to the other side. Not the entire way, but far enough to answer the requirements of the case. That is to say, I took this attitude—to wit, I only *believed* Bacon wrote Shakespeare, whereas I *knew* Shakespeare didn't. Ealer was satisfied with that, and the war broke loose. Study, practice, experience in handling my end of the matter presently enabled me to take any new position almost seriously; a little bit later, utterly seriously; a little later still, lovingly, gratefully, devotedly; finally: fiercely, rabidly, uncompromisingly. After that I was welded to my faith, I was theoretically ready to die for it, and I looked down with compassion not unmixed with scorn upon everybody else's faith that didn't tally with mine. That faith, imposed upon me by self-interest in that ancient day, remains my faith to-day, and in it I find comfort, solace, peace, and never-failing joy. You see how curiously theological it is. The "rice Christian" of the Orient goes through the very same steps, when he is after rice and the missionary is after *him*; he goes for rice, and remains to worship.

Ealer did a lot of our "reasoning"—not to say substantially all of it. The slaves of his cult have a passion for calling it by that large name. We others do not call our inductions and deductions and reductions by any name at all. They show for themselves what they are, and we can with tranquil confidence leave the world to ennoble them with a title of its own choosing.

Now and then when Ealer had to stop to cough, I pulled my induction-talents together and hove the controversial lead myself: always getting eight feet, eight and a half, often nine, sometimes even quarter-less-twain—as *I* believed; but always "no bottom," as *he* said.

I got the best of him only once. I prepared myself. I wrote out a passage from Shakespeare—it may have been the very one I quoted awhile ago, I don't remember—and riddled it with his wild steamboatful interlardings. When an unrisky opportunity offered, one lovely summer day, when we had sounded and buoyed a tangled patch of crossings known as Hell's Half Acre, and were aboard again and he had sneaked the *Pennsylvania* triumphantly through it without once scraping sand, and the *A. T. Lacey* had followed in our wake and got stuck and he was feeling good, I showed it to him. It amused him. I asked him to fire it off—*read* it; read it, I diplomatically added, as only *he* could read dramatic poetry. The compliment touched him where he lived. He did read it; read it with surpassing fire and spirit; read it as it will never be read again;

for *he* knew how to put the right music into those thunderous interlardings and make them seem a part of the text, make them sound as if they were bursting from Shakespeare's own soul, each one of them a golden inspiration and not to be left out without damage to the massed and magnificent whole.

I waited a week, to let the incident fade; waited longer; waited until he brought up for reasonings and vituperation my pet position, my pet argument, the one which I was fondest of, the one which I prized far above all others in my ammunition-wagon—to wit, that Shakespeare couldn't have written Shakespeare's works, for the reason that the man who wrote them was limitlessly familiar with the laws, and the law-courts, and law-proceedings, and lawyer-talk, and lawyer-ways—and if Shakespeare was possessed of the infinitely divided stardust that constituted this vast wealth, *how* did he get it, and *where* and *when?*

"From books."

From books! That was always the idea. I answered as my readings of the champions of my side of the great controversy had taught me to answer: that a man can't handle glibly and easily and comfortably and successfully the argot of a trade at which he has not personally served. He will make mistakes; he will not, and cannot, get the trade-phrasings precisely and exactly right; and the moment he departs, by even a shade, from a common trade-form, the reader who has served that trade will know the writer *hasn't*. Ealer would not be convinced; he said a man could learn how to correctly handle the subtleties and mysteries and free-masonries of *any* trade by careful reading and studying. But when I got him to read again the passage from Shakespeare with the interlardings, he perceived, himself, that books couldn't teach a student a bewildering multitude of pilot-phrases so thoroughly and perfectly that he could talk them off in book and play or conversation and make no mistake that a pilot would not immediately discover. It was a triumph for me. He was silent awhile, and I knew what was happening—he was losing his temper. And I knew he would presently close the session with the same old argument that was always his stay and his support in time of need; the same old argument, the one I couldn't answer, because I dasn't—the argument that I was an ass, and better shut up. He delivered it, and I obeyed.

Oh dear, how long ago it was—how pathetically long ago! And here am I, old, forsaken, forlorn, and alone, arranging to get that argument out of somebody again.

When a man has a passion for Shakespeare, it goes without saying that he keeps company with other standard authors. Ealer always had several high-class books in the pilot-house, and he read the same ones over and over again, and did not care to change to newer and fresher ones. He played well on the flute, and greatly enjoyed hearing himself play. So did I. He had a notion that a flute would keep its health better if you took it apart when it was not standing a watch; and so, when it was not on duty it took its rest, disjointed, on the compass-shelf under the breastboard. When the *Pennsylvania* blew up and became a drifting rack-heap freighted with wounded and dying poor souls (my young brother Henry among them), pilot Brown had the watch below, and was probably asleep and never knew what killed him; but Ealer escaped unhurt. He and his pilot-house were shot up into the air; then they fell, and Ealer sank through the ragged cavern where the hurricane-deck and the boiler-deck had been, and landed in a nest of ruins on the main deck, on top of one of the unexploded boilers, where he lay prone in a fog of scald and deadly steam. But not for long. He did not lose his head—long familiarity with danger had taught him to keep it, in any and all emergencies. He held his coat-lapels to his nose with one hand, to keep out the steam, and scrabbled around with the other till he found the joints of his flute, then he took measures to save himself alive, and was successful. I was not on board. I had been put ashore in New Orleans by Captain Klinefelter. The reason—however, I have told all about it in the book called *Old Times on the Mississippi*, and it isn't important, anyway, it is so long ago. . . .

### III

How curious and interesting is the parallel—as far as poverty of biographical details is concerned—between Satan and Shakespeare. It is wonderful, it is unique, it stands quite alone, there is nothing resembling it in history, nothing resembling it in romance, nothing approaching it even in tradition. How sublime is their position, and how over-topping, how sky-reaching, how supreme—the two Great Unknowns, the two Illustrious Conjecturabilities! They are the best-known unknown persons that have ever drawn breath upon the planet.

For the instruction of the ignorant I will make a list, now, of those details of Shakespeare's history with are *facts*—verified facts, established facts, undisputed facts.

### Facts

He was born on the 23rd of April, 1564.

Of good farmer-class parents who could not read, could not write, could not sign their names.

At Stratford, a small back settlement which in that day was shabby and unclean, and densely illiterate. Of the nineteen most important men charged with the government of the town, thirteen had to "make their mark" in attesting important documents, because they could not write their names.

Of the first eighteen years of his life *nothing* is known. They are a blank.

On the 27th of November (1582) William Shakespeare took out a license to marry Anne Whateley.

Next day William Shakespeare took out a license to marry Anne Hathaway. She was eight years his senior.

William Shakespeare married Anne Hathaway. In a hurry. By grace of a reluctantly granted dispensation there was but one publication of the banns.

Within six months the first child was born.

About two (blank) years followed, during which period *nothing at all happened to Shakespeare*, so far as anybody knows.

Then came twins—1585. February.

Two blank years follow.

Then—1587—he makes a ten-year visit to London, leaving the family behind.

Five blank years follow. During this period *nothing happened to him*, as far as anybody actually knows.

Then—1592—there is mention of him as an actor.

Next year—1593—his name appears in the official list of players.

Next year—1594—he played before the queen. A detail of no consequence: other obscurities did it every year of the forty-five of her reign. And remained obscure.

Three pretty full years follow. Full of play-acting. Then In 1597 he bought New Place, Stratford.

Thirteen or fourteen busy years follow; years in which he accumulated money, and also reputation as actor and manager.

Meantime his name, liberally and variously spelt, had become associated with a number of great plays and poems, as (ostensibly) author of the same.

Some of these, in these years and later, were pirated, but he made no protest.

Then—1610–11—he returned to Stratford and settled down for good and all, and busied himself in lending money, trading in tithes, trading in land and houses; shirking a debt of forty-one shillings, borrowed by his wife during his long desertion of his family; suing debtors for shillings and coppers; being sued himself for shillings and coppers; and acting as confederate to a neighbor who tried to rob the town of its rights in a certain common, and did not succeed.

He lived five or six years—till 1616—in the joy of these elevated pursuits. Then he made a will, and signed each of its three pages with his name.

A thoroughgoing business man's will. It named in minute detail every item of property he owned in the world—houses, lands, sword, silver-gilt bowl, and so on—all the way down to his "second-best bed" and its furniture.

It carefully and calculatingly distributed his riches among the members of his family, overlooking no individual of it. Not even his wife: the wife he had been enabled to marry in a hurry by urgent grace of a special dispensation before he was nineteen; the wife whom he had left husbandless so many years; the wife who had had to borrow forty-one shillings in her need, and which the lender was never able to collect of the prosperous husband, but died at last with the money still lacking. No, even this wife was remembered in Shakespeare's will.

He left her that "second-best bed."

And *not another thing*; not even a penny to bless her lucky widowhood with.

It was eminently and conspicuously a business man's will, not a poet's.

It mentioned *not a single book*.

Books were much more precious than swords and silver-gilt bowls and second-best beds in those days, and when a departing person owned one he gave it a high place in his will.

The will mentioned *not a play, not a poem, not an unfinished literary work, not a scrap of manuscript of any kind*.

Many poets have died poor, but this is the only one in history that has died *this* poor; the others all left literary remains behind. Also a book. Maybe two.

If Shakespeare had owned a dog—but we need not go into that: we know he would have mentioned it in his will. If a good dog, Susanna would have got it; if an inferior one his wife would have got a dower interest in it. I wish he had had a dog, just so we could see how painstakingly he would have divided that dog among the family, in his careful business way.

He signed the will in three places.

In earlier years he signed two other official documents.

These five signatures still exist.

There are *no other specimens of his penmanship in existence*. Not a line.

Was he prejudiced against the art? His granddaughter, whom he loved, was eight years old when he died, yet she had had no teaching, he left no provision for her education, although he was rich, and in her mature womanhood she couldn't write and couldn't tell her husband's manuscript from anybody else's—she thought it was Shakespeare's.

When Shakespeare died in Stratford it *was not an event*. It made no more stir in England than the death of any other forgotten theater-actor would have made. Nobody came down from London; there were no lamenting poems, no eulogies, no national tears—there was merely silence, and nothing more. A striking contrast with what happened when Ben Jonson, and Francis Bacon, and Spenser, and Raleigh, and the other distinguished literary folk of Shakespeare's time passed from life! No praiseful voice was lifted for the lost Bard of Avon; even Ben Jonson waited seven years before he lifted his.

*So far as anybody actually knows and can prove,* Shakespeare of Stratford-on-Avon never wrote a play in his life.

*So far as anybody knows and can prove,* he never wrote a letter to anybody in his life.

*So far as any one knows, he received only one letter during his life.*

So far as any one *knows and can prove,* Shakespeare of Stratford wrote only one poem during his life. This one is authentic. He did write that one—a fact which stands undisputed; he wrote the whole of it; he wrote the whole of it out of his own head. He commanded that this work of art be engraved upon his tomb, and he was obeyed. There it abides to this day. This is it:

> Good friend for Iesus sake forbeare
> To digg the dust enclosed heare:
> Blest be ye man yt sparcs thes stones
> And curst be he yt moves my bones.

In the list as above set down will be found *every positively known* fact of Shakespeare's life, lean and meager as the invoice is. Beyond these details we know *not a thing* about him. All the rest of his vast history, as furnished by the biographers, is built up, course upon course, of guesses, inferences, theories, conjectures—an Eiffel Tower of artificialities rising sky-high from a very flat and very thin foundation of inconsequential facts.

## IV. *Conjectures*

The historians "suppose" that Shakespeare attended the Free School in Stratford from the time he was seven years old till he was thirteen. There is no *evidence* in existence that he ever went to school at all.

The historians "infer" that he got his Latin in that school—the school which they "suppose" he attended.

They "suppose" his father's declining fortunes made it necessary for him to leave the school they supposed he attended, and get to work and help support his parents and their ten children. But there is no evidence that he ever entered or returned from the school they suppose he attended.

They "suppose" he assisted his father in the butchering business; and that, being only a boy, he didn't have to do full-grown butchering, but only slaughtered calves. Also, that whenever he killed a calf he made a high-flown speech over it. This supposition rests upon the testimony of a man who wasn't there at the time; a man who got it from a man who could have been there, but did not say whether he was or not; and neither of them thought to mention it for decades, and decades, and decades, and two more decades after Shakespeare's death (until old age and mental decay had refreshed and vivified their memories). They hadn't two facts in stock about the long-dead distinguished citizen, but only just the one: he slaughtered calves and broke into oratory while he was at it. Curious. They had only one fact, yet the distinguished citizen had spent twenty-six years in that little town—just half his lifetime. However, rightly viewed, it was the most important fact, indeed almost the only important fact, of Shakespeare's life in Stratford. Rightly viewed. For experience is an author's most valuable asset; experience is the thing that puts the muscle and the breath and the warm blood into the book he writes. Rightly viewed, calf-butchering accounts for *Titus Andronicus,* the only play—ain't it?—that the Stratford Shakespeare ever wrote; and yet it is the only one everybody tries to chouse him out of, the Baconians included.

The historians find themselves "justified in believing" that

the young Shakespeare poached upon Sir Thomas Lucy's deer preserves and got haled before that magistrate for it. But there is no shred of respectworthy evidence that anything of the kind happened.

The historians, having argued the thing that *might* have happened into the thing that *did* happen, found no trouble in turning Sir Thomas Lucy into Mr. Justice Shallow. They have long ago convinced the world—on surmise and without trustworthy evidence—that Shallow *is* Sir Thomas.

The next addition to the young Shakespeare's Stratford history comes easy. The historian builds it out of the surmised deer-stealing, and the surmised trial before the magistrate, and the surmised vengeance-prompted satire upon the magistrate in the play: result, the young Shakespeare was a wild, wild, wild, oh, *such* a wild young scamp, and that gratuitous slander is established for all time! It is the very way Professor Osborn and I built the colossal skeleton brontosaur that stands fifty-seven feet long and sixteen feet high in the Natural History Museum, the awe and admiration of all the world, the stateliest skeleton that exists on the planet. We had nine bones, and we built the rest of him out of plaster of Paris. We ran short of plaster of Paris, or we'd have built a brontosaur that could sit down beside the Stratford Shakespeare and none but an expert could tell which was biggest or contained the most plaster.

Shakespeare pronounced *Venus and Adonis* "the first heir of his invention," apparently implying that it was his first effort at literary composition. He should not have said it. It has been an embarrassment to his historians these many, many years. They have to make him write that graceful and polished and flawless and beautiful poem before he escaped from Stratford and his family—1586 or '87—age, twenty-two, or along there; because within the next five years he wrote five great plays, and could not have found time to write another line.

It is sorely embarrassing. If he began to slaughter calves, and poach deer, and rollick around, and learn English, at the earliest likely moment—say at thirteen, when he was supposably wrenched from that school where he was supposably storing up Latin for future literary use—he had his youthful hands full, and much more than full. He must have had to put aside his Warwickshire dialect, which wouldn't be understood in London, and study English very hard. Very hard indeed; incredibly hard, almost, if the result of that labor was to be the smooth and rounded and flexible and letter-perfect English of the *Venus and Adonis* in the space of ten years; and at the same time learn great and fine and unsurpassable literary *form.*

However, it is "conjectured" that he accomplished all this and more, much more: learned law and its intricacies; and the complex procedure of the law-courts; and all about soldiering, and sailoring, and the manners and customs and ways of royal courts and aristocratic society; and likewise accumulated in his one head every kind of knowledge the learned then possessed, and every kind of humble knowledge possessed by the lowly and the ignorant; and added thereto a wider and more intimate knowledge of the world's great literatures, ancient and modern, than was possessed by any other man of his time—for he was going to make brilliant and easy and admiration-compelling use of these splendid treasures the moment he got to London. And according to the surmisers, that is what he did. Yes, although there was no one in Stratford able to teach him these things, and no library in the little village to dig them out of. His father could not read, and even the surmisers surmise that he did not keep a library.

It is surmised by the biographers that the young Shakespeare got his vast knowledge of the law and his familiar and accurate acquaintance with the manners and customs and shop-talk of lawyers through being for a time the *clerk of a*

*Stratford court*; just as a bright lad like me, reared in a village on the banks of the Mississippi, might become perfect in knowledge of the Bering Strait whale-fishery and the shop-talk of the veteran exercises of that adventure-bristling trade through catching catfish with a "trot-line" Sundays. But the surmise is damaged by the fact that there is no evidence—and not even tradition—that the young Shakespeare was ever clerk of a law-court.

It is further surmised that the young Shakespeare accumulated his law-treasures in the first years of his sojourn in London, through "amusing himself" by learning book-law in his garret and by picking up lawyer-talk and the rest of it through loitering about the law-courts and listening. But it is only surmise; there is no *evidence* that he ever did either of those things. They are merely a couple of chunks of plaster of Paris.

There is a legend that he got his bread and butter by holding horses in front of the London theaters, mornings and afternoons. Maybe he did. If he did, it seriously shortened his law-study hours and his recreation-time in the courts. In those very days he was writing great plays, and needed all the time he could get. The horse-holding legend ought to be strangled; it too formidably increases the historian's difficulty in accounting for the young Shakespeare's erudition—an erudition which he was acquiring, hunk by hunk and chunk by chunk, every day in those strenuous times, and emptying each day's catch into next day's imperishable drama.

He had to acquire a knowledge of war at the same time; and a knowledge of soldier-people and sailor-people and their ways and talk; also a knowledge of some foreign lands and their languages: for he was daily emptying fluent streams of these various knowledges, too, into his dramas. How did he acquire these rich assets?

In the usual way: by surmise. It is *surmised* that he traveled in Italy and Germany and around, and qualified himself to put their scenic and social aspects upon paper; that he perfected himself in French, Italian, and Spanish on the road; that he went in Leicester's expedition to the Low Countries, as soldier or sutler or something, for several months or years—or whatever length of time a surmiser needs in his business—and thus became familiar with soldiership and soldier-ways and soldier-talk and generalship and general-ways and general-talk, and seamanship and sailor-ways and sailor-talk.

Maybe he did all these things, but I would like to know who held the horses in the mean time; and who studied the books in the garret; and who frollicked in the law-courts for recreation. Also, who did the call-boying and the play-acting.

For he became a call-boy; and as early as '93 he became a "vagabond"—the law's ungentle term for an unlisted actor; and in '94 a "regular" and properly and officially listed member of that (in those days) lightly valued and not much respected profession.

Right soon thereafter he became a stockholder in two theaters, and manager of them. Thenceforward he was a busy and flourishing business man, and was raking in money with both hands for twenty years. Then in a noble frenzy of poetic inspiration he wrote his one poem—his only poem, his darling—and laid him down and died:

> Good friend for Iesus sake forbeare
> To digg the dust encloased heare:
> Blest be ye man yt spares thes stones
> And curst be he yt moves my bones.

He was probably dead when he wrote it. Still, this is only conjecture. We have only circumstantial evidence. Internal evidence.

Shall I set down the rest of the Conjectures which constitute the giant Biography of William Shakespeare? It would strain the Unabridged Dictionary to hold them. He is a brontosaur: nine bones and six hundred barrels of plaster of Paris.

### V. "We May Assume"

In the Assuming trade three separate and independent cults are transacting business. Two of these cults are known as the Shakespearites and the Baconians, and I am the other one—the Brontosaurian.

The Shakespearite knows that Shakespeare wrote Shakespeare's Works; the Baconian knows that Francis Bacon wrote them; the Brontosaurian doesn't really know which of them did it, but is quite composedly and contentedly sure that Shakespeare *didn't*, and strongly suspects that Bacon *did*. We all have to do a good deal of assuming, but I am fairly certain that in every case I can call to mind the Baconian assumers have come out ahead of the Shakespearites. Both parties handle the same materials, but the Baconians seem to me to get much more reasonable and rational and persuasive results out of them than is the case with the Shakespearites. The Shakespearite conducts his assuming upon a definite principle, an unchanging and immutable law: which is: 2 and 8 and 7 and 14, added together, make 165. I believe this to be an error. No matter, you cannot get a habit-sodden Shakespearite to cipher-up his materials upon any other basis. With the Baconian it is different. If you place before him the above figures and set him to adding them up, he will never in any case get more than 45 out of them, and in nine cases out of ten he will get just the proper 31.

Let me try to illustrate the two systems in a simple and homely way calculated to bring the idea within the grasp of the ignorant and unintelligent. We will suppose a case: take a lap-bred, house-fed, uneducated, inexperienced kitten; take a rugged old Tom that's scarred from stem to rudder-post with the memorials of strenuous experience, and is so cultured, so educated, so limitlessly erudite that one may say of him "all cat-knowledge is his province"; also, take a mouse. Lock the three up in a holeless, crackless, exitless prison-cell. Wait half an hour, then open the cell, introduce a Shakespearite and a Baconian, and let them cipher and assume. The mouse is missing: the question to be decided is, where it is? You can guess both verdicts beforehand. One verdict will say the kitten contains the mouse; the other will as certainly say the mouse is in the tom-cat.

The Shakespearite will Reason like this—(that is not my word, it is his). He will say the kitten *may have been* attending school when nobody was noticing; therefore *we are warranted in assuming* that it did so; also, it *could have been* training in a court-clerk's office when no one was noticing; since that could have happened, *we are justified in assuming* that it did happen; it *could have studied catology in a garret* when no one was noticing—therefore it *did*; it *could have* attended cat-assizes on the shed-roof nights, for recreation, when no one was noticing, and have harvested a knowledge of cat court-forms and cat lawyer-talk in that way: it *could* have done it, therefore without a doubt it *did*; it *could have* gone soldiering with a war-tribe when no one was noticing, and learned soldier-wiles and soldier-ways, and what to do with a mouse when opportunity offers; the plain inference, therefore, is that that is what it *did*. Since all these manifold things *could* have occurred, we have *every right to believe* they did occur. These patiently and painstakingly accumulated vast acquirements and competences needed but one thing more—opportunity—to convert themselves into triumphant action. The opportunity came, we have the result; *beyond shadow of question* the mouse is in the kitten.

It is proper to remark that when we of the three cults plant a *"We think we may assume,"* we expect it, under careful watering and fertilizing and tending, to grow up into a strong and hardy and weather-defying *"there isn't a shadow of a doubt"* at last—and it usually happens.

We know what the Baconian's verdict would be: *"There is not a rag of evidence that the kitten has had any training, any education, any experience qualifying it for the present occasion, or is indeed equipped for any achievement above lifting such unclaimed milk as comes its way; but there is abundant evidence—unassailable proof, in fact—that the other animal is equipped, to the last detail, with every qualification necessary for the event. Without shadow of doubt the tom-cat contains the mouse."*

## VI

When Shakespeare died, in 1616, great literary productions attributed to him as author had been before the London world and in high favor for twenty-four years. Yet his death was not an event. It made no stir, it attracted no attention. Apparently his eminent literary contemporaries did not realize that a celebrated poet had passed from their midst. Perhaps they knew a play-actor of minor rank had disappeared, but did not regard him as the author of his Works. "We are justified in assuming" this.

His death was not even an event in the little town of Stratford. Does this mean that in Stratford he was not regarded as a celebrity of *any* kind?

"We are privileged to assume"—no, we are indeed *obliged* to assume—that such was the case. He had spent the first twenty-two or twenty-three years of his life there, and of course knew everybody and was known by everybody of that day in the town, including the dogs and the cats and the horses. He had spent the last five or six years of his life there, diligently trading in every big and little thing that had money in it; so we are compelled to assume that many of the folk there in those said latter days knew him personally, and the rest by sight and hearsay. But not as a *celebrity*? Apparently not. For everybody soon forgot to remember any contact with him or any incident connected with him. The dozens of townspeople, still alive, who had known of him or known about him in the first twenty-three years of his life were in the same unremembering condition: if they knew of any incident connected with that period of his life they didn't tell about it. Would they if they had been asked? It is most likely. Were they asked? It is pretty apparent that they were not. Why weren't they? It is a very plausible guess that nobody there or elsewhere was interested to know.

For seven years after Shakespeare's death nobody seems to have been interested in him. Then the quarto was published, and Ben Jonson awoke out of his long indifference and sang a song of praise and put it in the front of the book. Then silence fell *again*.

For sixty years. Then inquiries into Shakespeare's Stratford life began to be made, of Stratfordians. Of Stratfordians who had known Shakespeare or had seen him? No. Then of Stratfordians who had seen people who had known or seen people who had seen Shakespeare? No. Apparently the inquiries were only made of Stratfordians who were not Stratfordians of Shakespeare's day, but later comers; and what they had learned had come to them from persons who had not seen Shakespeare; and what they had learned was not claimed as *fact*, but only as legend—dim and fading and indefinite legend; legend of the calf-slaughtering rank, and not worth remembering either as history or fiction.

Has it ever happened before—or since—that a celebrated person who had spent exactly half of a fairly long life in the village where he was born and reared, was able to slip out of this world and leave that village voiceless and gossipless behind him—utterly voiceless, utterly gossipless? And permanently so? I don't believe it has happened in any case except Shakespeare's. And couldn't and wouldn't have happened in his case if he had been regarded as a celebrity at the time of his death.

When I examine my own case—but let us do that, and see if it will not be recognizable as exhibiting a condition of things quite likely to result, most likely to result, indeed substantially *sure* to result in the case of a celebrated person, a benefactor of the human race. Like me.

My parents brought me to the village of Hannibal, Missouri, on the banks of the Mississippi, when I was two and a half years old. I entered school at five years of age, and drifted from one school to another in the village during nine and a half years. Then my father died, leaving his family in exceedingly straitened circumstances; wherefore my book-education came to a standstill forever, and I became a printer's apprentice, on board and clothes, and when the clothes failed I got a hymn-book in place of them. This for summer wear, probably. I lived in Hannibal fifteen and a half years, altogether, then ran away, according to the custom of persons who are intending to become celebrated. I never lived there afterward. Four years later I became a "cub" on a Mississippi steamboat in the St. Louis and New Orleans trade, and after a year and a half of hard study and hard work the U.S. inspectors rigorously examined me through a couple of long sittings and decided that I knew every inch of the Mississippi—thirteen hundred miles—in the dark and in the day—as well as a baby knows the way to its mother's paps day or night. So they licensed me as a pilot—knighted me, so to speak—and I rose up clothed with authority, a responsible servant of the United States Government.

Now then. Shakespeare died young—he was only fifty-two. He had lived in his native village twenty-six years, or about that. He died celebrated (if you believe everything you read in the books). Yet when he died nobody there or elsewhere took any notice of it; and for sixty years afterward no townsman remembered to say anything about him or about his life in Stratford. When the inquirer came at last he got but one fact—no, *legend*—and got that one at second hand, from a person who had only heard it as a rumor and didn't claim copyright in it as a production of his own. He couldn't, very well, for its date antedated his own birth-date. But necessarily a number of persons were still alive in Stratford who, in the days of their youth, had seen Shakespeare nearly every day in the last five years of his life, and they would have been able to tell that inquirer some first-hand things about him if he had in those last days been a celebrity and therefore a person of interest to the villagers. Why did not the inquirer hunt them up and interview them? Wasn't it worth while? Wasn't the matter of sufficient consequence? Had the inquirer an engagement to see a dog-fight and couldn't spare the time?

It all seems to mean that he never had any literary celebrity, there or elsewhere, and no considerable repute as actor and manager.

Now then, I am away along in life—my seventy-third year being already well behind me—yet *sixteen* of my Hannibal schoolmates are still alive to-day, and can tell—and do tell—inquirers dozens and dozens of incidents of their young lives and mine together; things that happened to us in the morning of life, in the blossom of our youth, in the good days, the dear days, "the days when we went gipsying, a long time ago." Most of them creditable to me, too. One child to whom I paid court when she was five years old and I eight still lives in Hannibal, and she visited me last summer, traversing the necessary ten or twelve hundred miles of railroad without damage to her patience or to her old-young vigor. Another little lassie to whom I paid attention in Hannibal when she was nine years old and I the same, is still alive—in London—and hale and hearty, just as I am. And on the few surviving steamboats— those lingering ghosts and remembrancers of great fleets that plied the big river in the beginning of my water-career—which is exactly as long ago as the whole invoice of the life-years of Shakespeare numbers—there are still findable two or three river-pilots who saw me do creditable things in those ancient days; and several white-headed engineers; and several roust-abouts and mates; and several deck-hands who used to heave the lead for me and send up on the still night air the "Six— feet—*scant!*" that made me shudder, and the "M-a-r-k— *twain!*" that took the shudder away, and presently the darling "By the d-e-e-p—*four!*" that lifted me to heaven for joy.[1] They know about me, and can tell. And so do printers, from St. Louis to New York; and so do newspaper reporters, from Nevada to San Francisco. And so do the police. If Shakespeare had really been celebrated, like me, Stratford could have told things about him; and if my experience goes for anything, they'd have done it.

## VII

If I had under my superintendence a controversy appointed to decide whether Shakespeare wrote Shakespeare or not, I believe I would place before the debaters only the one question, *Was Shakespeare ever a practising lawyer?* and leave everything else out.

It is maintained that the man who wrote the plays was not merely myriad-minded, but also myriad-accomplished: that he not only knew some thousands of things about human life in all its shades and grades, and about the hundred arts and trades and crafts and professions which men busy themselves in, but that he could *talk* about the men and their grades and trades accurately, making no mistakes. Maybe it is so, but have the experts spoken, or is it only Tom, Dick, and Harry? Does the exhibit stand upon wide, and loose, and eloquent generalizing—which is not evidence, and not proof—or upon details, particulars, statistics, illustrations, demonstrations?

Experts of unchallengeable authority have testified definitely as to only one of Shakespeare's multifarious craft-equipments, so far as my recollections of Shakespeare-Bacon talk abide with me—his law-equipment. I do not remember that Wellington or Napoleon ever examined Shakespeare's battles and sieges and strategies, and then decided and established for good and all that they were militarily flawless; I do not remember that any Nelson, or Drake, or Cook ever examined his seamanship and said it showed profound and accurate familiarity with that art; I don't remember that any king or prince or duke has ever testified that Shakespeare was letter-perfect in his handling of royal court-manners and the talk and manners of aristocracies; I don't remember that any illustrious Latinist or Grecian or Frenchman or Spaniard or Italian has proclaimed him a past-master in those languages; I don't remember—well, I don't remember that there is *testimony*—great testimony—imposing testimony—unanswerable and unattackable testimony as to any of Shakespeare's hundred specialties, except one—the law.

Other things change, with time, and the student cannot trace back with certainty the changes that various trades and

their processes and technicalities have undergone in the long stretch of a century or two and find out what their processes and technicalities were in those early days, but with the law it is different: it is mile-stoned and documented all the way back, and the master of that wonderful trade, that complex and intricate trade, that awe-compelling trade, has competent ways of knowing whether Shakespeare-law is good law or not; and whether his law-court procedure is correct or not, and whether his legal shop-talk is the shop-talk of a veteran practitioner or only a machine-made counterfeit of it gathered from books and from occasional loiterings in Westminster.

Richard H. Dana served two years before the mast, and had every experience that falls to the lot of the sailor before the mast of our day. His sailor-talk flows from his pen with the sure touch and the ease and confidence of a person who has *lived* what he is talking about, not gathered it from books and random listenings. Hear him:

> Having hove short, cast off the gaskets, and made the bunt of each sail fast by the jigger, with a man on each yard, at the word the whole canvas of the ship was loosed, and with the greatest rapidity possible everything was sheeted home and hoisted up, the anchor tripped and cat-headed, and the ship under headway.

Again:

> The royal yards were all crossed at once, and royals and skysails set, and, as we had the wind free, the booms were run out, and all were aloft, active as cats, laying out on the yards and booms, reeving the studding-sail gear; and sail after sail the captain piled upon her, until she was covered with canvas, her sails looking like a great white cloud resting upon a black speck.

Once more. A race in the Pacific:

> Our antagonist was in her best trim. Being clear of the point, the breeze became stiff, and the royal-masts bent under our sails, but we would not take them in until we saw three boys spring into the rigging of the *California*; then they were all furled at once, but with orders to our boys to stay aloft at the top-gallant mast-heads and loose them again at the word. It was my duty to furl the fore-royal; and while standing by to loose it again, I had a fine view of the scene. From where I stood, the two vessels seemed nothing but spars and sails, while their narrow decks, far below, slanting over by the force of the wind aloft, appeared hardly capable of supporting the great fabrics raised upon them. The *California* was to windward of us, and had every advantage; yet, while the breeze was stiff we held our own. As soon as it began to slacken she ranged a little ahead, and the order was given to loose the royals. In an instant the gaskets were off and the bunt dropped. "Sheet home the fore-royal!"—"Weather sheet's home!"—"Lee sheet's home!"—"Hoist away, sir!" is bawled from aloft. "Overhaul your clewlines!" shouts the mate. "Aye-aye, sir, all clear!"—"Taut leech! belay! Well the lee brace; haul taut to windward!" and the royals are set.

What would the captain of any sailing-vessel of our time say to that? He would say, "The man that wrote that didn't learn his trade out of a book, he has *been* there!" But would this same captain be competent to sit in judgment upon Shakespeare's seamanship—considering the changes in ships and ship-talk that have necessarily taken place, unrecorded, unremembered, and lost to history in the last three hundred years?

It is my conviction that Shakespeare's sailor-talk would be Choctaw to him. For instance—from *The Tempest*:

> *Master:* Boatswain!
>
> *Boatswain:* Here, master; what cheer?
>
> *Master:* Good, speak to the mariners: fall to 't, yarely, or we run ourselves to ground; bestir, bestir!
>
> (*Enter mariners.*)
>
> *Boatswain:* Heigh, my hearts! cheerly, cheerly, my hearts! yare, yare! Take in the topsail. Tend to the master's whistle. . . . Down with the topmast! yare! lower, lower! Bring her to try wi' the main course. . . . Lay her a-hold, a-hold! Set her two courses. Off to sea again; lay her off.

That will do, for the present; let us yare a little, now, for a change.

If a man should write a book and in it make one of his characters say, "Here, devil, empty the quoins into the standing galley and the imposing-stone into the hell-box; assemble the comps around the frisket and let them jeff for takes and be quick about it," I should recognize a mistake or two in the phrasing, and would know that the writer was only a printer theoretically, not practically.

I have been a quartz miner in the silver regions—a pretty hard life; I know all the palaver of that business: I know all about discovery claims and the subordinate claims; I know all about lodes, ledges, outcroppings, dips, spurs, angles, shafts, drifts, inclines, levels, tunnels, air-shafts, "horses," clay casings, granite casings; quartz mills and their batteries; arastras, and how to charge them with quicksilver and sulphate of copper; and how to clean them up, and how to reduce the resulting amalgam in the retorts, and how to cast the bullion into pigs; and finally I know how to screen tailings, and also how to hunt for something less robust to do, and find it. I know the argot of the quartz-mining and milling industry familiarly; and so whenever Bret Harte introduces that industry into a story, the first time one of his miners opens his mouth I recognize from his phrasing that Harte got the phrasing by listening—like Shakespeare—I mean the Stratford one—not by experience. No one can talk the quartz dialect correctly without learning it with pick and shovel and drill and fuse.

I have been a surface miner—gold—and I know all its mysteries, and the dialect that belongs with them; and whenever Harte introduces that industry into a story I know by the phrasing of his characters that neither he nor they have ever served that trade.

I have been a "pocket" miner—a sort of gold mining not findable in any but one little spot in the world, so far as I know. I know how, with horn and water, to find the trail of a pocket and trace it step by step and stage by stage up the mountain to its source, and find the compact little nest of yellow metal reposing in its secret home under the ground. I know the language of that trade, that capricious trade, that fascinating buried-treasure trade, and can catch any writer who tries to use it without having learned it by the sweat of his brow and the labor of his hands.

I know several other trades and the argot that goes with them; and whenever a person tries to talk the talk peculiar to any of them without having learned it at its source I can trap him always before he gets far on his road.

And so, as I have already remarked, if I were required to superintend a Bacon-Shakespeare controversy, I would narrow the matter down to a single question—the only one, so far as the previous controversies have informed me, concerning which illustrious experts of unimpeachable competency have testified: *Was the author of Shakespeare's Works a lawyer?*—a lawyer deeply read and of limitless experience? I would put aside the guesses and surmises, and perhapses, and might-have-beens, and could-have-beens, and must-have-beens, and we-are-justified-in-presumings, and the rest of those vague specters and shadows and indefinitenesses, and stand or fall, win or lose, by the verdict rendered by the jury upon that single question. If the verdict was Yes, I should feel quite convinced that the Stratford Shakespeare, the actor, manager, and trader who died so obscure, so forgotten, so destitute of even village consequence, that sixty years afterward no fellow-citizen and friend of his later days remembered to tell anything about him, did not write the Works. . . .

## IX

Did Francis Bacon write Shakespeare's Works?

Nobody knows.

We cannot say we *know* a thing when that thing has not been proved. *Know* is too strong a word to use when the evidence is not final and absolutely conclusive. We can infer, if we want to, like those slaves. . . . No, I will not write that word, it is not kind, it is not courteous. The upholders of the Stratford-Shakespeare superstition call *us* the hardest names they can think of, and they keep doing it all the time; very well, if they like to descend to that level, let them do it, but I will not so undignify myself as to follow them. I cannot call them harsh names; the most I can do is to indicate them by terms reflecting my disapproval; and this without malice, without venom.

To resume. What I was about to say was, those thugs have built their entire superstition upon *inferences*, not upon known and established facts. It is a weak method, and poor, and I am glad to be able to say our side never resorts to it while there is anything else to resort to.

But when we must, we must; and we have now arrived at a place of that sort. . . . Since the Stratford Shakespeare couldn't have written the Works, we infer that somebody did. Who was it, then? This requires some more inferring.

Ordinarily when an unsigned poem sweeps across the continent like a tidal wave whose roar and boom and thunder are made up of admiration, delight, and applause, a dozen obscure people rise up and claim the authorship. Why a dozen, instead of only one or two? One reason is, because there are a dozen that are recognizably competent to do that poem. Do you remember "Beautiful Snow"? Do you remember "Rock Me to Sleep, Mother, Rock Me to Sleep"? Do you remember "Backward, turn backward, O Time, in thy flight! Make me a child again just for to-night"? I remember them very well. Their authorship was claimed by most of the grown-up people who were alive at the time, and every claimant had one plausible argument in his favor, at least—to wit, he could have done the authoring; he was competent.

Have the Works been claimed by a dozen? They haven't. There was good reason. The world knows there was but one man on the planet at the time who was competent—not a dozen, and not two. A long time ago the dwellers in a far country used now and then to find a procession of prodigious footprints stretching across the plain—footprints that were three miles apart, each footprint a third of a mile long and a furlong deep, and with forests and villages mashed to mush in it. Was there any doubt as to who made that mighty trail? Were there a dozen claimants? Were there two? No—the people knew who it was that had been along there: there was only one Hercules.

There has been only one Shakespeare. There couldn't be two; certainly there couldn't be two at the same time. It takes ages to bring forth a Shakespeare, and some more ages to match him. This one was not matched before his time; nor during his time; and hasn't been matched since. The prospect of matching him in our time is not bright.

The Baconians claim that the Stratford Shakespeare was not qualified to write the Works, and that Francis Bacon was. They claim that Bacon possessed the stupendous equipment—both natural and acquired—for the miracle; and that no other Englishman of his day possessed the like; or, indeed, anything closely approaching it.

Macaulay, in his Essay, has much to say about the splendor and horizonless magnitude of that equipment. Also, he has synopsized Bacon's history—a thing which cannot be done for the Stratford Shakespeare, for he hasn't any history to synopsize. Bacon's history is open to the world, from his boyhood to his death in old age—a history consisting of known facts, displayed in minute and multitudinous detail; *facts*, not guesses and conjectures and might-have-beens.

Whereby it appears that he was born of a race of statesmen, and had a Lord Chancellor for his father, and a mother who was "distinguished both as a linguist and a theologian: she corresponded in Greek with Bishop Jewell, and translated his *Apologia* from the Latin so correctly that neither he nor Archbishop Parker could suggest a single alteration." It is the atmosphere we are reared in that determines how our inclinations and aspirations shall tend. The atmosphere furnished by the parents to the son in this present case was an atmosphere saturated with learning; with thinkings and ponderings upon deep subjects; and with polite culture. It had its natural effect. Shakespeare of Stratford was reared in a house which had no use for books, since its owners, his parents, were without education. This may have had an effect upon the son, but we do not know, because we have no history of him of an informing sort. There were but few books anywhere, in that day, and only the well-to-do and highly educated possessed them, they being almost confined to the dead languages. "All the valuable books then extant in all the vernacular dialects of Europe would hardly have filled a single shelf"—imagine it! The few existing books were in the Latin tongue mainly. "A person who was ignorant of it was shut out from all acquaintance—not merely with Cicero and Virgil, but with the most interesting memoirs, state papers, and pamphlets of his own time"—a literature necessary to the Stratford lad, for his fictitious reputation's sake, since the writer of his Works would begin to use it wholesale and in a most masterly way before the lad was hardly more than out of his teens and into his twenties.

At fifteen Bacon was sent to the university, and he spent three years there. Thence he went to Paris in the train of the English Ambassador, and there he mingled daily with the wise, the cultured, the great, and the aristocracy of fashion, during another three years. A total of six years spent at the sources of knowledge; knowledge both of books and of men. The three spent at the university were coeval with the second and last three spent by the little Stratford lad at Stratford school supposedly, and perhapsedly, and maybe, and by inference—with nothing to infer from. The second three of the Baconian six were "presumably" spent by the Stratford lad as apprentice to a butcher. That is, the thugs presume it—on no evidence of any kind. Which is their way, when they want a historical fact. Fact and presumption are, for business purposes, all the same to them. They know the difference, but they also know how to blink it. They know, too, that while in history-building a fact is better than a presumption, it doesn't take a presumption long to bloom into a fact when *they* have the handling of it. They know by old experience that when they get hold of a presumption-tadpole he is not going to *stay* tadpole in their history-tank; no, they know how to develop him into the giant four-legged bullfrog of *fact*, and make him sit up on his hams, and puff out of his chin, and look important and insolent and come-to-stay; and assert his genuine simon-pure authenticity with a thundering bellow that will convince everybody because it is so loud. The thug is aware that loudness convinces sixty persons where reasoning convinces but one. I wouldn't be a thug, not even if—but never mind about that, it has nothing to do with the argument, and it is not noble in spirit besides. If I am better than a thug, is the merit mine? No, it is His. Then to Him be the praise. That is the right spirit.

They "presume" the lad severed his "presumed" connection with the Stratford school to become apprentice to a butcher. They also "presume" that the butcher was his father. They don't know. There is no written record of it, nor any other actual evidence. If it would have helped their case any, they would have apprenticed him to thirty butchers, to fifty butchers, to a wilderness of butchers—all by their patented method "presumption." If it will help their case they will do it yet; and if it will further help it, they will "presume" that all those butchers were his father. And the week after, they will *say* it. Why, it is just like being the past tense of the compound reflexive adverbial incandescent hypodermic irregular accusative Noun of Multitude; which is father to the expression which the grammarians call Verb. It is like a whole ancestry, with only one posterity.

To resume. Next, the young Bacon took up the study of law, and mastered that abstruse science. From that day to the end of his life he was daily in close contact with lawyers and judges; not as a casual onlooker in intervals between holding horses in front of a theater, but as a practising lawyer—a great and successful one, a renowned one, a Launcelot of the bar, the most formidable lance in the high brotherhood of the legal Table Round; he lived in the law's atmosphere thenceforth, all his years, and by sheer ability forced his way up its difficult steeps to its supremest summit, the Lord-Chancellorship, leaving behind him no fellow-craftsman qualified to challenge his divine right to that majestic place.

When we read the praises bestowed by Lord Penzance and the other illustrious experts upon the legal condition and legal aptnesses, brilliances, profundities, and felicities so prodigally displayed in the Plays, and try to fit them to the historyless Stratford stage-manager, they sound wild, strange, incredible, ludicrous; but when we put them in the mouth of Bacon they do not sound strange, they seem in their natural and rightful place, they seem at home there. Please turn back and read them again. Attributed to Shakespeare of Stratford they are meaningless, they are inebriate extravagancies—intemperate admirations of the dark side of the moon, so to speak; attributed to Bacon, they are admirations of the golden glories of the moon's front side, the moon at the full—and not intemperate, not overwrought, but sane and right, and justified. "At every turn and point at which the author required a metaphor, simile, or illustration, his mind ever turned *first* to the law; he seems almost to have *thought* in legal phrases; the commonest legal phrases, the commonest of legal expressions, were ever at the end of his pen." That could happen to no one but a person whose *trade* was the law; it could not happen to a dabbler in it. Veteran mariners fill their conversation with sailor-phrases and draw all their similes from the ship and the sea and the storm, but no mere *passenger* ever does it, be he of Stratford or elsewhere; or could do it with anything resembling accuracy, if he were hardy enough to try. Please read again what Lord Campbell and the other great authorities have said about Bacon when they thought they were saying it about Shakespeare of Stratford.

## X. *The Rest of the Equipment*

The author of the Plays was equipped, beyond every other man of his time, with wisdom, eruditon, imagination, capaciousness of mind, grace, and majesty of expression. Every one has said it, no one doubts it. Also, he had humor, humor in rich abundance, and always wanting to break out. We have no evidence of any kind that Shakespeare of Stratford possessed any of these gifts or any of these acquirements. The only lines he ever wrote, so far as we know, are substantially barren of them—barren of all of them.

> Good friend for Iesus sake forbeare
> To digg the dust enclosed heare:
> Blest be ye man yt spares thes stones
> And curst be he yt moves my bones.

Ben Jonson says of Bacon, as orator:

> His language, *where he could spare and pass by a jest,* was nobly censorious. No man ever spoke more neatly, more pressly, more weightily, or suffered less emptiness, less idleness, in what he uttered. No member of his speech but consisted of his (its) own graces. . . . The fear of every man that heard him was lest he should make an end.

From Macaulay:

> He continued to distinguish himself in Parliament, particularly by his exertions in favor of one excellent measure on which the King's heart was set—the union of England and Scotland. It was not difficult for such an intellect to discover many irresistible arguments in favor of such a scheme. He conducted the great case of the *Post Nati* in the Exchequer Chamber; and the decision of the judges—a decision the legality of which may be questioned, but the beneficial effect of which must be acknowledged— was in a great measure attributed to his dexterous management.

Again:

> While actively engaged in the House of Commons and in the courts of law, he still found leisure for letters and philosophy. The noble treatise on the *Advancement of Learning,* which at a later period was expanded into the *De Augmentis,* appeared in 1605.
>
> The *Wisdom of the Ancients,* a work which, if it had proceeded from any other writer, would have been considered as a masterpiece of wit and learning, was printed in 1609.
>
> In the mean time the *Novum Organum* was slowly proceeding. Several distinguished men of learning had been permitted to see portions of that extraordinary book, and they spoke with the greatest admiration of his genius.
>
> Even Sir Thomas Bodley, after perusing the *Cogitata et Visa,* one of the most precious of those scattered leaves out of which the great oracular volume was afterward made up, acknowledged that "in all proposals and plots in that book, Bacon showed himself a master workman"; and that "it could not be gainsaid but all the treatise over did abound with choice conceits of the present state of learning, and with worthy comtemplations of the means to procure it."
>
> In 1612 a new edition of the *Essays* appeared, with additions surpassing the original collection both in bulk and quality.
>
> Nor did these pursuits distract Bacon's attention from a work the most arduous, the most glorious, and the most useful that even his mighty powers could have achieved, "the reducing and recompiling," to use his own phrase, "of the laws of England."

To serve the exacting and laborious offices of Attorney-General and Solicitor-General would have satisfied the appetite of any other man for hard work, but Bacon had to add the vast literary industries just described, to satisfy his. He was a born worker.

> The service which he rendered to letters during the last five years of his life, amid ten thousand distractions and vexations, increase the regret with which we think on the many years which he had wasted, to use the words of Sir Thomas Bodley, "on such study as was not worthy such a student."
>
> He commenced a digest of the laws of England, a History of England under the Princes of the House of Tudor, a body of National History, a Philosophical Romance. He made extensive and valuable additions to his Essays. He published the inestimable *Treatise De Augmentis Scientiarum.*

Did these labors of Hercules fill up his time to his contentment and quiet his appetite for work? Not entirely:

> The trifles with which he amused himself in hours of pain and languor bore the mark of his mind. *The best jest-book in the world* is that which he dictated from memory, without referring to any book, on a day on which illness had rendered him incapable of serious study.

Here are some scattered remarks (from Macaulay) which throw light upon Bacon, and seem to indicate—and maybe demonstrate—that he was competent to write the Plays and Poems:

> With great minuteness of observation he had an amplitude of comprehension such as has never yet been vouchsafed to any other human being.
>
> The *Essays* contain abundant proofs that no nice feature of character, no peculiarity in the ordering of a house, a garden, or a court-masque, could escape the notice of one whose mind was capable of taking in the whole world of knowledge.
>
> His understanding resembled the tent which the fairy Paribanou gave to Prince Ahmed: fold it, and it seemed a toy for the hand of a lady; spread it, and the armies of powerful Sultans might repose beneath its shade.
>
> The knowledge in which Bacon excelled all men was a knowledge of the mutual relations of all departments of knowledge.
>
> In a letter written when he was only thirty-one, to his uncle, Lord Burleigh, he said, "I have taken all knowledge to be my province."
>
> Though Bacon did not arm his philosophy with the weapons of logic, he adorned her profusely with all the richest decorations of rhetoric.
>
> The practical faculty was powerful in Bacon; but not, like his wit, so powerful as occasionally to usurp the place of his reason and to tyrannize over the whole man.

There are too many places in the Plays where this happens. Poor old dying John of Gaunt volleying second-rate puns at his own name, is a pathetic instance of it. "We may assume" that it is Bacon's fault, but the Stratford Shakespeare has to bear the blame.

No imagination was ever at once so strong and so thoroughly subjugated. It stopped at the first check from good sense.

In truth, much of Bacon's life was passed in a visionary world—amid things as strange as any that are described in the *Arabian Tales* . . . amid buildings more sumptuous than the palace of Aladdin, fountains more wonderful than the golden water of Parizade, conveyances more rapid than the hippogryph of Ruggiero, arms more formidable than the lance of Astolfo, remedies more eficacious than the balsam of Fierabras. Yet in his magnificent daydreams there was nothing wild—nothing but what sober reason sanctioned.

Bacon's greatest performance is the first book of the *Novum Organum*. . . . Every part of it blazes with wit, but with wit which is employed only to illustrate and decorate truth. No book ever made so great a revolution in the mode of thinking, overthrew so many prejudices, introduced so many new opinions.

But what we most admire is the vast capacity of that intellect which, without effort, takes in at once all the domains of science—all the past, the present and the future, all the errors of two thousand years, all the encouraging signs of the passing times, all the bright hopes of the coming age.

He had a wonderful talent for packing thought close and rendering it portable.

His eloquence would alone have entitled him to a high rank in literature.

It is evident that he had each and every one of the mental gifts and each and every one of the acquirements that are so prodigally displayed in the Plays and Poems, and in much higher and richer degree than any other man of his time or of any previous time. He was a genius without a mate, a prodigy not matable. There was only one of him; the planet could not produce two of him at one birth, nor in one age. He could have written anything that is in the Plays and Poems. He could have written this:

> The cloud-cap'd towers, the gorgeous palaces,
> The solemn temples, the great globe itself,
> Yea, all which it inherit, shall dissolve,
> And, like an insubstantial pageant faded,
> Leave not a rack behind. We are such stuff
> As dreams are made on, and our little life
> Is rounded with a sleep.

Also, he could have written this, but he refrained:

> Good friend for Iesus sake forbeare
> To digg the dust encloased heare:
> Blest be ye man yt spares thes stones
> And curst be he yt moves my bones.

When a person reads the noble verses about the cloud-cap'd towers, he ought not to follow it immediately with Good friend for Iesus sake forbeare, because he will find the transition from great poetry to poor prose too violent for comfort. It will give him a shock. You never notice how commonplace and unpoetic gravel is until you bite into a layer of it in a pie.

## XI

Am I trying to convince anybody that Shakespeare did not write Shakespeare's Works? Ah, now, what do you take me for? Would I be so soft as that, after having known the human race familiarly for nearly seventy-four years? It would grieve me to know that any one could think so injuriously of me, so uncomplimentarily, so unadmiringly of me. No, no, I am aware that when even the brightest mind in our world has been trained up from childhood in a superstition of any kind, it will never be possible for that mind, in its maturity, to examine sincerely, dispassionately, and conscientiously any evidence or any circumstance which shall seem to cast a doubt upon the validity of that superstition. I doubt if I could do it myself. We always get at second hand our notions about systems of government; and high tariff and low tariff; and prohibition and anti-prohibition; and the holiness of peace and the glories of war; and codes of honor and codes of morals; and approval of the duel and disapproval of it; and our beliefs concerning the nature of cats; and our ideas as to whether the murder of helpless wild animals is base or is heroic; and our preferences in the matter of religious and political parties; and our acceptance or rejection of the Shakespeares and the Arthur Ortons and the Mrs. Eddys. We get them all at second hand, we reason none of them out for ourselves. It is the way we are made. It is the way we are all made, and we can't help it, we can't change it. And whenever we have been furnished a fetish, and have been taught to believe in it, and love it and worship it, and refrain from examining it, there is no evidence, howsoever clear and strong, that can persuade us to withdraw from it our loyalty and our devotion. In morals, conduct, and beliefs we take the color of our environment and associations, and it is a color that can safely be warranted to wash. Whenever we have been furnished with a tar baby ostensibly stuffed with jewels, and warned that it will be dishonorable and irreverent to disembowel it and test the jewels, we keep our sacrilegious hands off it. We submit, not reluctantly, but rather gladly, for we are privately afraid we should find, upon examination, that the jewels are of the sort that are manufactured at North Adams, Mass.

I haven't any idea that Shakespeare will have to vacate his pedestal this side of the year 2209. Disbelief in him cannot come swiftly, disbelief in a healthy and deeply-loved tar baby has never been known to disintegrate swiftly; it is a very slow process. It took several thousand years to convince our fine race—including every splendid intellect in it—that there is no such thing as a witch; it has taken several thousand years to convince that same fine race—including every splendid intellect in it—that there is no such person as Satan; it has taken several centuries to remove perdition from the Protestant Church's program of post-mortem entertainments; it has taken a weary long time to persuade American Presbyterians to give up infant damnation and try to bear it the best they can; and it looks as if their Scotch brethren will still be burning babies in the everlasting fires when Shakespeare comes down from his perch.

We are The Reasoning Race. We can't prove it by the above examples, and we can't prove it by the miraculous "histories" built by those Stratfordolaters out of a hatful of rags and a barrel of sawdust, but there is a plenty of other things we can prove it by, if I could think of them. We are The Reasoning Race, and when we find a vague file of chipmunk-tracks stringing through the dust of Stratford village, we know by our reasoning powers that Hercules has been along there. I feel that our fetish is safe for three centuries yet. The bust, too—there in the Stratford Church. The precious bust, the priceless bust, the calm bust, the serene bust, the emotionless bust, with the dandy mustache, and the putty face, unseamed of care—that face which has looked passionlessly down upon the awed pilgrim for a hundred and fifty years and will still look down upon the awed pilgrim three hundred more, with the deep, deep, deep, subtle, subtle, subtle, expression of a bladder.

*Notes*

1. Four fathoms—twenty-four feet.

# COMEDIES

## *General*

*Shakespear* was the first that opened this Vein ⟨of humor⟩ upon our Stage, which has run so freely and so pleasantly ever since, that I have often wondered to find it appear so little upon any others, being a Subject so proper for them; since Humour is but a Picture of particular Life, as Comedy is of general.— WILLIAM TEMPLE, *On Poetry*, 1690

Shakespeare is a well-spring of characters which are saturated with the comic spirit; with more of what we will call blood-life than is to be found anywhere out of Shakespeare; and they are of this world, but they are of the world enlarged to our embrace by imagination, and by great poetic imagination. They are, as it were—I put it to suit my present comparison—creatures of the woods and wilds, not in walled towns, not grouped and toned to pursue a comic exhibition of the narrower world of society. Jaques, Falstaff and his regiment, the varied troop of Clowns, Malvolio, Sir Hugh Evans and Fluellen—marvellous Welshmen!—Benedict and Beatrice, Dogberry, and the rest, are subjects of a special study in the poetically comic.

His comedy of incredible imbroglio belongs to the literary section. One may conceive that there was a natural resemblance between him and Menander, both in the scheme and style of his lighter plays. Had Shakespeare lived in a later and less emotional, less heroical period of our history, he might have turned to the painting of manners as well as humanity. Euripides would probably, in the time of Menander, when Athens was enslaved but prosperous, have lent his hand to the composition of romantic comedy. He certainly inspired that fine genius.—GEORGE MEREDITH, "Essay on the Idea of Comedy and of the Uses of the Comic Spirit," 1877

## J. J. JUSSERAND
From "Shakespeare, His Dramatic Work"
A *Literary History of the English People*
1904, Volume 3, pp. 328–37

In real life, the comic is never very far from the tragic, nor in Shakespeare's drama either. The poet hates absolute classifications; if some characters approaching abstract types slip into his plays, they are exceptions. As a rule, his heroes are variable; they are influenced by circumstances; they do not belong to distinct categories; we shall see, as occasion offers, comic kings and tragic peasants, it is with the personages as with the plays themselves, laughable scenes will intersect a sombre drama, and serious scenes a comedy. The grave or the gay predominates according to circumstances, but neither the one nor the other is totally excluded: such is life.

A storm arises; the ship is about to sink, the fate of the sailors and passengers hangs by a thread. Those passengers are kings, princes, high dignitaries. The first scene of the *Tempest* is a whole tragedy and a whole comedy, one poignant, the other laughable, as true one as the other; and the two impressions, equally strong, are given in a few phrases; the peril is so imminent that already the equality of after death begins. The sailors have lost all respect for the great men that they have the honour of conveying: "I pray now, keep below . . . you mar our labour! Keep your cabin; you do assist the storm. . . . Hence! what care these roarers for the name of king? To cabin! silence! trouble us not.

"*Gonzalo* (who, with another, has made ill-timed remarks and asked useless questions, imagining they have encouraged the sailors, as is the case with all high personages in like occurrence). Good; yet remember whom thou hast aboard.

"*Boatswain*. None that I more love than myself."

As the tempest increases, the various characters stand out more clearly, and their inward nature shows forth. The high dignitaries remember etiquette and remain ceremonious to the last, so deeply have their functions stamped their imprint on their whole beings. But if there is in their professional punctiliousness something to smile at, there is something to admire too, for death is about to take them, and ridiculous though their courtliness may be, they have at least the courage to think of something else than their own end.

"*Gonzalo*. We split, we split, we split.

"*Antonio*. Let's all sink with the king.

"*Sebastiano*. Let's take leave of him."

As, in tragedy, Shakespeare does not want all eyes to turn to one hero, centre of the play, so, in comedy, he does not mean to unfold before us one only character, surrounded by mere accessories serving to make it more conspicuous. He shows individuals, with their good and bad qualities, their contradictions, their milieu, their relatives, their servants, their neighbours, who have also their individuality—all the bustle and agitation of the human bee-hive. In his plays, wisdom has no authorised representative; no Ariste, no Éliante. Of wisdom there remain shreds on every bramble; ours to gather it, if we choose, on the heath paced by the fool, on the highway followed by tun-bellied Falstaff, in the meadows where Autolycus has sung his song.

Wisdom has no authorised representative, the personages are individuals, not ready-found types; the *genre* itself is subject to no rule. It has no visible limits; many plays are tragedies or comedies as one pleases. The personages of merriest wit, the most burlesque caricatures, can be found in the dramas with the most terrible catastrophes: Mercutio, Peter, the nurse, in *Romeo and Juliet*. The comedies, properly so called, are made up of elements as varied as the dark dramas. There is room in them for schoolboy tricks, visions of fairyland, dances, songs, pageants, pantomimes, maidens disguised as pages to run after their lovers, tavern scenes, pastoral scenes, scenes of provincial life and of forest life in imaginary Ardens; quarrels, scoldings, indecencies, "wit-combats," the most refined pleasantry and the coarsest. We find in them traits worthy of Molière, sometimes the same as in Molière, who will re-invent them on his own account: "We are all frail," says hypocritical Angelo, forestalling Tartuffe's famous

Ah! pour être dévot, je n'en suis pas moins homme.

At other times, so great is the variety, we get a foretaste of the kind of humour *Punch* has accustomed us to: "If I be drunk, I'll be drunk with those that have the fear of God, and not with drunken knaves."[1]

The coarsest jests, the easiest of reach, the oftenest tried,

927

are found almost anywhere, even in the historical plays, where the bastard Faulconbridge, merely outlined in the model play, but shown by Shakespeare through a magnifying glass, provokes laughter by his gestures and remarks, befitting the valiant and joyous brute that he is. The stupid constable, the dullard who confuses one word with another, the clown who executes errands all wrong, for which cause they are usually entrusted to him, the Irishman, the Scotchman, the Welshman, the Frenchman, speaking each his gibberish, are infallible means of amusement; Shakespeare never wearies of employing them, nor the audience of making merry over them. The result is so certain that, in order to obtain it once more, the poet, generally so respectful of ready-made plots, goes so far as to deprive himself, in *Much Ado about Nothing*, of the great and striking effect that Bandello's tale afforded him with its church scene, in order to have an occasion for dialogues between silly watchmen saying "senseless" instead of "sensible," "statues" instead of "statutes," etc. The traitor's misdeeds are revealed to them by chance comers who, to tell their secrets, choose just the part of the street where the watchmen are seated. Spectators would laugh to their hearts' content at the misuse of words, and be delighted at these strange happenings, worth looking at precisely because so strange.

Witticisms and "merry fooling" were also of unfailing effect: we know that the public could spend a whole afternoon at impromptu "wit-combats." Still more pleasure would they take in the thrusts and parries of a Mercutio, a Rosalind, a Beatrice, a Benedick, in the flings of Kate the shrew, and of Petruchio her tamer; in Launcelot Gobbo's "trying confusions" with his old blind father;[2] even in the torrents of abuse of Apemantus or of Thersites: they found that abuse ingeniously invented; it was still, in their eyes, a kind of wit, "flytings" in the Scotch manner. Wit is the quality on which lays stress, in his flowery language, the pirate who published the play where Thersites figures: "So much and such savored salt of witte is in [this author's] commedies that they seeme, for their height of pleasure, to be borne in that sea that brought forth Venus. Amongst all there is none more witty then this."[3] The public admired all that jugglery of words and those "confusions," as it would have gaped in the street at the tricks of a mountebank. The success of *Love's Labour's Lost* had early apprised Shakespeare of the infallibility of this method. Late in his career, he saw that mediocre work of his youth brought out again: "I have sent and bene all thys morning," wrote Sir Walter Cope to Lord Cranborne, "huntyng for players, juglers and such kinde of creaturs, but fynde them harde to fynde; wherfore, leavinge notes for them to seeke me, Burbage ys come, and sayes ther ys no new playe that the Quene hath not seene, but they have revyved an olde one cawled *Love's Labore lost*, which for wytt and mirthe, he sayes, will please her excedingly. And thys ys apointed to be played to-morowe night at my Lord Sowthamptons, unless you send a wrytt to remove the *corpus cum causa* to your howse in Strande. Burbage ys my messenger ready attendyng your pleasure."[4]

Bursts of hearty laughter kept the audience in lively mood; subtle remarks (and they abound) would not have sufficed. This explains why such crackling is, to our taste, often too noisy. What was then considered crackling, what the personages of the plays themselves held as much, scarcely hiding their admiration for their own triumphs as "wit-crackers,"[5] seems to us more like fusillades; even the amiable Rosalind who makes such pretty remarks (this one for instance: "For lovers lacking matter, the cleanliest shift is to kiss") has some terribly grating notes in her voice. Beatrice discharges her wit shafts as a catapult hurls stones, and without any more heed as to who

receives them; at the very start, she takes as confidant of her sentiments for Benedick a messenger, who must think her a very impertinent hare-brained young person. To the reader of to-day she appears pretentious and cumbersome; her heavy teasing, then judged so elegant, is near recalling at times school-boys' wrangles, or the amorous punchings of country lovers.[6]

With that, shrewd traits of observation, innumerable vistas suddenly opened, sometimes by a single word revealing all that human nature contains of hidden vice or of secret grandeur, some unexpected word uttered by a servant arranging the chairs, or by one of the heroes of the drama ("Why should a man be proud?" says Ajax, pride itself), and which will stir the hearer, will be to him as a ray of light, and will leave him between laughter and tears, deeply moved. Those traits abound in *Hamlet*.

Admirable scenes, too, of middle life comedy, describing with wondrous exactitude everyday existence, everybody's habits of mind,[7] the contradictions of human natures,[8] or else quiet provincial life, the petty ambitions, the petty rivalries that break its monotony; the stir, too, produced in such a milieu by the arrival of a Falstaff.

Falstaff and his crew belong as absolutely to Shakespeare as Panurge and Gargantua to Rabelais, Don Quixote and Sancho Panza to Cervantes. The character is unique of its kind, as justly famous, and as worthy of immortality; dress, manner, turn of mind, vices, associates, everything that concerns him, the sound of his voice, the colour of his cheeks and of his beard, are put before us with incomparable vividness. Callot could not have drawn the contour of the personage with a more exact graver than has Shakespeare in one line when he represents him walking before his page "like a sow that has overwhelmed all her litter but one." As fat as Panurge is thin, he has as much wit and resourcefulness, promptitude at repartee,[9] wily ways to escape blows, to catch good bits, to leave the burden of life to others, and count happy days, surrounded by scorn to which he is indifferent, by dangers that he knows how to avoid, tippling his sack ("in potum copiose immittunt saccarum," says Hentzner of the English), handled sometimes rather roughly, but quickly consoled, and always regaining his imperturbable good-humour. No mishap makes upon him any durable impression; not even the harsh rebuffs and cruel pranks now and then inflicted on him, nor his great disappointment at the coming to the throne of his bosom friend, Prince Hal. He recovers himself at once: "I shall be sent for in private to him: look you, he must seem thus to the world. Fear not your advancement." From time to time, too, a melancholy plaint, funnier than any of his jollities: "'Sblood, I am as melancholy as a gib cat or a lugg'd bear. . . . An I have not forgotten what the inside of a church is made of, I am a peppercorn. . . . Company, villainous company, hath been the spoil of me.

"*Bardolph*. Sir John, You are so fretful, you cannot live long.

"*Falstaff*. Why, there is it:—come, sing me a bawdy song; make me merry. I was as virtuously given as a gentleman need to be. . . ."[10]

Following in his wake, we penetrate, when it suits him to leave his ignoble tavern, into the society of middle-class people, and thus we see charming corners of provincial life, depicted with the utmost exactness, though, as always, some caricatural sketches are added to life-like portraits, making these shine to better advantage—provincial life quietly spent in the land of Do-you-remember? where one never forgets the youthful days in the great city which it would be so pleasant to see again! What is going on there? Is Jane so and so still living?

and how is she? "Old, old, Master Shallow."—"Ha, cousin Silence, that thou hadst seen that that this knight and I have seen! Ha, Sir John?" The guests are detained with instant request; they are offered the best pigeons, the best joint of mutton; they sing in the garden in front of the house. Who knows? perhaps the passing guest will pull us out of our province, will have us appointed to the city—where we will find our youth again, since it is there that we left it, and it is waiting for us, may be. The passing guest is seen through rose-coloured spectacles; he comes from yonder; he knows every one; most certainly he can do all that he pleases.

In *Merry Wives*, Falstaff appears again in the foreground; but he has there to meet his match; he falls in with a set of honest folk, faithful subjects of the Queen, cheerful, sensible, hositable, well-to-do, worthy representatives of a class, the backbone of the nation, whose rôle was steadily becoming more important. Happily married, good husbands of good wives, Page and Ford, friends and neighbours, have each his own nature: the one all plain and open-minded, the other with a tendency to jealousy which makes him do many an unwise thing and places him in ridiculous situations. But he gets out of scrapes because he is no fool, frankly confesses his errors, and refrains from sulking. Anne Page, the young girl, is the beauty of the neighbourhood, the heiress with whom the whole borough is in love, even too a young gallant who has strayed from the court hard by, and, happily, turns out to be a true gentleman who will get the better, in the end, of his rich and silly rivals: so that the amiable maid will have had her romance, a pleasant and reasonable one, as it behoves, with a happy ending.

Falstaff's self-complacency, coarseness, and impecuniosity lead him to confound the good wives of Windsor with the inmates of the Boar's Head tavern. Mistress Page and Mistress Ford, close friends, tell each other about the declaration they have received; the same, word for word—

C'est une circulaire, il se moquait de nous,

writes Mr. Francis de Croisset in a play where he causes Chérubin to use again the same device.[11] "I warrant," says Mrs. Page, "he hath a thousand of these letters, writ with blank space for different names." The two ladies feel wroth at first, then laugh at the not very flattering adventure which happens to them, at their age, having always lived honest; and all owing to that whale! "What tempest, I trow, threw this whale, with so many tuns of oil in his belly, ashore at Windsor?" They will, since whale there be, fasten to their lines hooks for whales. Falstaff thrice bites at the bait; he is as severely punished as he deserves. Tricked and derided, half drowned, half roasted, but always recovering his spirits, much is forgiven him at the end because he has caused much merriment. The good wives, avenged, go home together:

Good husband, let us every one go home,
And laugh this sport o'er by a country fire;
Sir John and all.

This bohemia, like all bohemias, ends the more sadly that it has been more lawless and roisterous. Shakespeare, who does nothing by halves, hangs Nym and Bardolph, sends their women friends to die of foul diseases in the hospital, and stifles his huge Falstaff in a filthy garret at the horrible Mrs. Quickly's: "So 'a cried out," says Mrs. Quickly, "God, God, God! three or four times: now, I to comfort him, bid him 'a should not think of God; I hoped, there was no need to trouble himself with any such thoughts yet." The hour, however, had come.

*Notes*

1. *Merry Wives*, i. 1.
2. "O heavens, this is my true begotten father! who, being more than sand-blind . . . knows me not. I will try confusions with him." And he jocosely gives the old man all sorts of misleading information.—*Merchant of Venice*, ii. 2.
3. "And all such dull and heavy-witted worldlings, as were never capable of the witte of a commedie, comming by report of them to his representations, have found that witte there, that they never found in themselves, and have parted better-witted then they came."—"A never writer to an ever-reader," prefacing *The famous Historie of Troylus and Cresseid*, 1609.
4. Document of 1604-5 found in the Hatfield papers by Halliwell-Phillipps and published in his *Outlines*, ii. pp. 83, 84.
5. *Much Ado*, last scene. In *Taming*, word fencings, greatly resembling an exchange of blows, are judged by the characters in the play as examples of the prettiest wit:

    How likes Gremio these quick-witted folks?
    (v. 2.)

    Again, in *Love's Labour's Lost*:
    Their conceits have wings
    Fleeter than arrows, bullets, winds, thought, fleeter things.
    (v. 2.)

6. Beatrice will never marry. "So," says Benedick, "some gentleman or other shall 'scape a predestinate scratched face.
    "*Beatrice*. Scratching would not make it worse an 'twere such a face as yours were," etc. (*Much Ado*, i. 1). Cf. similar scenes in *Love's Labour's Lost*, between Biron and Rosaline, ii. 1; in *Two Gentlemen*, between Valentine and Thurio, ii, 4; and, quite at the other end of the poet's career, in *Tempest*, ii. 1, and in *Cymbeline*, i. 3.
7. See, for example, the exquisite first scene of *The Merchant of Venice*.
8. Witness that trait, worthy of Molière, in the otherwise inconspicuous part of Adriana. She complains bitterly of her husband: four lines of insulting epithets. But why then, says her sister, are you jealous of him?

    Ah! but I think him better than I say.
    (*Errors*, iv. 2.)

9. "*Pr. Henry*. . . . Art thou not ashamed?
    "*Falstaff*. Dost thou hear, Hal? thou know'st, in the state of innocency, Adam fell; and what should poor Jack Falstaff do, in the days of villainy? Thou seest, I have more flesh than another man; and therefore more frailty."—*I Henry IV.*, iii. 3.
10. *I Henry IV.*, i. 2, and iii. 3.
11. *Chérubin*, 1902.

## ADOLPHUS WILLIAM WARD
### From "Shakespere's Dramatic Genius"
### *A History of English Dramatic Literature*
### 1899, Volume 2, pp. 272–82

While the dramatic genius of Shakspere asserts itself with the most overwhelming power in his Tragedies, it is by means of his Comedies, if we still follow the nomenclature of the editors of the First Folio, that he more especially attained to an indisputable pre-eminence among the poets, not only of the English, but of the modern romantic drama at large. By way of illustrating the meaning of such an assertion, it may be permissible to review very briefly this branch of Shakespere's achievements as a dramatist, without going back either upon researches as to the sources of his comedies, or upon ascertained facts or speculations as to their relative chronological sequence. Certain broad distinctions may be maintainable among the plays included in the wonderfully varied group in question, which are not necessarily coincident with the considerations as to origin of subject or date of production. Thus, *The Comedy of Errors* and *The Taming of the*

*Shrew*, though probably more or less distant from one another in date, and in a very different measure respectively composite in origin, may be alike described as substantially adaptations or revisions of earlier plays. The subject of neither of these comedies was recast by Shakspere in a mould shaped by his own genius; and it would be futile to seek in either for evidence of real significance as to his conception of the actual or possible sphere of comedy.

*Love's Labour's Lost, The Two Gentlemen of Verona*, and, with a difference to be immediately noted, *A Midsummer Night's Dream*, bear the marks of a relatively early origin, and of an unmistakeable cognateness in the sources of their themes. They were, moreover, alike composed under the influence of Lyly, which reveals itself to some extent in the polished and witty dialogue, and more so in fanciful action full of allusions, at times open and at other times veiled, to contemporary incidents and situations. The influence of a prevalent demand, of which historical and literary research are only beginning to gauge the force, for 'topical' treatment of dramatic themes, and of which Lyly was probably a follower rather than the creator, is likewise discernible in these plays. At the same time, the humorous characters of *Love's Labour's Lost* are in part unmistakeable reproductions of favourite types of Italian comedy; and the delicate texture of this play, not obscured even by the crudities of form in which it abounds, must have been essentially new to the existing English stage. *The Two Gentlemen of Verona* exhibits similar features of workmanship; but the species of comedy of which these two plays may be regarded as furnishing the earliest signal examples on the English stage, in *A Midsummer Night's Dream* attains to a consummation which it had never before reached, either in our own, or in any other, dramatic literature. English romantic comedy, in a word, was now represented by an example, not of sudden (for nothing is sudden in literature), but of radiant perfection.[1]

The foreign growth which had exercised a most important influence upon the origin of English romantic comedy, without determining its ultimate development, had sprung up on Italian soil. The whole history of Italian culture from the Renascence period onwards, under its social as well as its more special literary aspect, exhibits a remarkably intimate co-operation of two activities which, for want of more precise names, may perhaps be designated as the academical and the popular. In French literature, these two elements ceased to co-operate in anything like the same measure after the Renascence period; and to this day French dramatic literature in particular, notwithstanding the signally favourable conditions under which it has continued to flourish, has not succeeded in thoroughly reuniting them. In Italy, however, it was the popular element which, as has been seen, produced the earliest efforts of the native drama, and which in the end gave rise to a dramatic form destined to survive the gradual decline of the dramatic growths derived from purely literary sources. Italian tragedy and comedy had their day, and have experienced periodical revivals; the hybrid species of the pastoral drama has flourished and has faded; the opera, which has summoned more than one sister-art to its aid, is a later, and has proved a more long-lived, variety. But the one dramatic form which has maintained itself from first to last is wholly popular in its origin.

In the middle of the sixteenth century the Italian *comedia dell' arte*, while it had contrived to preserve the characteristics of its popular origin, was at the same time largely under the influence of the Academies which were the chief representatives of the still active Renascence movement. In this quite peculiar epoch of its history, when its established figures had

been elaborated with constant care, and when at the same time a courtly and even learned tone had been given to some of its productions by the Academies, the English dramatists, and Shakespere among them, came in contact with this growth. The Italian actors who visited England about this time excited astonishment and admiration by the rapidity of their improvisations, but a special instructiveness must have been found in the variety of effect which they were able to create with a series of personages so far fixed as to preclude deeper characterisation.[2] With certain of the regular comedies of the Italian stage it is highly probable that Shakspere had in addition become acquainted, whether at second or at first hand matters little; and a considerable proportion of the literature of Italian prose-fiction was in one way or another open to him. But the wish which he must have entertained to satisfy the craving of his public for incident, and his observation of the lightness and ease with which the *commedia dell' arte* treated character, cannot but have largely helped to lead him to a species of comedy new to English, and indeed to any, dramatic literature.

These speculations may appear far-fetched; but whether or not they supply the requisite key, supposing any key to be called for, they illustrate the particular aspect to which I desire to refer in discussing this species of Shaksperean comedy.[3] This species is essentially a comedy of *incident*, although of course the element of character is not absent from it. There can be no pedantry in adopting a distinction which, whether applied to comedy or to prose-fiction, is legitimate, so long as it is not forced beyond reasonable limits. Incident, character, and manners give their names severally to those kinds of comedy in which, according to the conception of the author, any one of these elements predominates. Comedy of character most thoroughly fulfils the purpose which all comedy seeks to accomplish, because it advances towards that end more directly than comedy of incident, while moving in a both higher and wider sphere than comedy of manners. Hence we may recognise as the most perfect types of comedy those which with incomparable felicity exhibit the lasting types of ridiculous humanity, such as the litigious old gentleman in *The Wasps* or the unctuous hypocrite in *Tartuffe*. Now, of comedies of character in the stricter sense of the term it is not easy to find distinct examples among Shakspere's purely comic dramas, unless it be *The Merry Wives* or *The Taming of the Shrew*; but in the former of these the main character was given at the outset (whatever may be the truth of the apocryphal anecdote that the play was written to order), while the latter play was not original. Eminent critics have sought to tabulate Shakspere's comedies in general as comedies of character. In each they have been anxious to find a central character;—as Molière devoted one play to the Hypocrite, another to the Miser, a third to the Misanthrope, so it has been declared that Shakspere designed in his comedies to offer a gallery of various human types. These critics appear to have been deceived by the supposed analogy of the tragedies. It is impossible to read a tragedy of Shakspere (I do not include all the Histories under this term), or to see it represented on the stage, without feeling that its interest is centred in its hero. Popular instinct has given expression to this truism by converting into a proverbial saying the jest as to the performance of *Hamlet* with the part of Hamlet left out. *Romeo and Juliet* is the tragedy of impassioned devotion; its interest concentrates itself in the two characters which give their name to the play; no other personage is essential to it. *Othello* is the tragedy of the lover's jealousy; *Richard III* of ruthless ambition; *Macbeth* of moral weakness under temptations allying themselves with noble impulses as well as with superstitious fancies. And so forth. The comedies, on the other hand, as a rule contain no single personage in whom the interest absolutely centres; and it would be difficult to name one of them in which the attention of reader or spectator is not competitively engaged by at least two parallel actions.

That Shakspere's comedies are not comedies of manners, is a statement which seems self-evident. Many of them, of course, contain an element of manners, introduced with so masterly an ease and power as to leave no doubt but that, had Shakspere chosen, he might have excelled in this inferior branch of the art. As an entire play, *The Merry Wives* alone approaches the species; but its distinctive element is recognisable in *Twelfth Night* and in many other Shakesperean comedies.

In the main, then, although in no sense exclusively, the great dramatist's comedies are to be described as comedies of incident. In other words, their main interest lies not in the characters which their action develops, or in the manners which it furnishes opportunity for depicting, but in the story of the action itself. The incident to be found in these comedies is, however, of a peculiar kind; and here we arrive at a distinctive characteristic of our poet, the origin of which is due to the creative power of his genius. His comedies are *romantic* in the broadest sense of the term; *i.e.*, they treat of subjects far removed from the ordinary course of human experience, and familiar only to spheres in which the genius of the dramatic poet alone can make other minds at home like his own. The conditions of each dramatic action are thus taken out of the control of moral or even social laws of cause and consequence, although the art of the poet wins our sympathy for the personages by whom that action is conducted.[4]

This difference between the dramatist's intention in his tragedies and comedies respectively, is very clearly indicated by the titles which he gave to them, and the exception noticeable in the instance of a play so composite in its elements of dramatic effect as *The Merchant of Venice* may perhaps be held to prove the rule. Nothing could be more futile than to search for a deep meaning in the titles lightly bestowed, from personal whim or for playhouse purposes, upon these romantic comedies. Again and again Shakspere takes a story upon which he has lighted in some Italian novel or in its French or English version, combining it most usually with one or more other stories from similar sources. As with marvellous, although not infallible, dramaturgic skill he develops the action of his play, its personages frequently, though not always, become lifelike realities in his hands; the wondrous union of reading, fancy, humour, and wit is rapidly consummated; and then the result is christened by a pleasant name—*All's Well That Ends Well, As You Like It, Twelfth Night, The Winter's Tale*. He adopted or invented no pregnant phrases as titles for his tragedies, after the fashion of some of his brother-dramatists, such as Thomas Heywood; and still less sought, like Ben Jonson, to distil the essence of his comedies into their designations; yet what more appropriate than the plainness of his procedure in the one case, and in the other his airy freedom from embarrassment?

A single example will suffice to illustrate my meaning. In which of Shakspere's comedies has he more thoroughly compassed the end of all dramatic and literary art, than in *A Midsummer Night's Dream*; which other of his comedies has given delight so abundant and so perennial in the closet or on the stage? Apart from its beauties of diction—in the dialogue as well as in the lyrical passages—what is the source of its dramatic effectiveness? Is this to be sought either wholly or mainly in its characters? The marriage of Theseus and Hippolyta is, so to speak, the occasion of the action of the piece (to which some commentators have accordingly ascribed a

festive design). In these personages nothing is notable but the pleasant dignity of Duke and Duchess. The figure of Egeus again, the afflicted father of Hermia, is slightly drawn; and between the two pairs of lovers, Lysander and Hermia, Demetrius and Helena, distinctions and differences exist indeed, but are only very lightly indicated; the poet's intention manifestly was, not to mark the effect of the lovers' adventures upon their characters, but merely to produce a group of personages suitable for carrying out his eccentric plot. Next, we have the delectable company of tradesmen whose study and performance of the tragedy of Pyramus and Thisbe furnish forth the anti-masque. Surely, no serious criticism can see in these bubbles of a humorous fancy the embodiments of a deep design. The translation of Bottom invests him with a superior satirical importance, but with the situation comes to an end the humorous play of character, the opportunity for which Shakspere was certain not to neglect; and in the height of the fun which succeeds, characterisation becomes quite out of the question. Enough of realism is left in these 'mechanical' oddities to produce the designed effective contrast with the fairy world; but to suppose that Shakspere in these humorous creations intended to create types of character, is an imputation which, had it been known to him, might have caused him to stay his fantastic pen in a novel kind of wonderment.[5]

Lastly, to face the fairy world itself, as it appears before us in Oberon and Titania, with Puck and the rest of the frolicsome company. A judicious critic[6] speaks of them as 'beings without the finer feelings and without morality. The effects of the confusion which they produce cause no mental impression in themselves. They are without a higher intellectuality: they never reflect: there is no trace in them either of contemplation, or of the expression of a sentiment. They are without the higher intellectual capacities of human nature. Their joy is to couch in flowers, while the wings of butterflies fan them to rest. Their thoughts are merely directed towards the physical. Their sympathies are with butterflies and nightingales; it is upon hedgehogs, toads, and bats that they make war; their chief delights are dance, music, and song. It is only the sense of the Beautiful which elevates them above mere animal life.' Accepting this analysis, and acknowledging that the few incidents which occur within the sphere of the fairy crew neither produce, nor are intended to produce, any moral effect whatever,—what must be allowed to be the result? The whole *dramatis personae* of this play, the mainly conventional figures of the Duke and Duchess and the pairs of lovers, the realistic oddities of the jubilee tradesmen, and the fanciful impossibilities of the fairy court, stand confessed as a machinery—devised no doubt with extraordinary wit and skill—for sustaining the interest of the action. The whole play remains in substance a romantic comedy of incident; and the fancy is the faculty mainly engaged in enjoying it.

The same remark may, by way of illustration, be applied to one of Shakspere's latest plays, where, in this respect, he returned to his earlier method. In *The Winter's Tale* delineation of character as affected by the progress of the action is not the primary object of the comedy, and its characterisation is accordingly upon the whole the reverse of deep. Yet Gervinus and with him other critics call upon us to recognise in it a comedy of character; in Leontes, the jealous King, we are asked to see a counterpart of Othello. The Moor's, we are reminded, is a noble and confiding spirit; it is only the terrible fatality of his situation and the diabolical craft of his enemy which evoke the monster of jealousy in his mind. Leontes', on the other hand, is an intrinsically suspicious nature, whose master-tendency is to think itself always in the right and the rest of the world in the wrong. Undoubtedly his conduct towards his wife requires dramatic explanation; but has the poet psychologically explained it, and can the most careful actor make this character in itself satisfactory?[7] The improbable nature of the story of the play, which adds to its charm as a mere story, necessitated irrational conduct on the part of Leontes; and irrational his conduct remains,—some divinity made him mad, and some divinity heals him. But can this kind of characterisation be compared to that of Othello?

From the particular species of dramatic creation to which he afterwards incidentally recurred Shakspere had meanwhile proceeded to other dramatic forms; but even in works which may in part be ascribed to his maturer years, though still to a comparatively youthful period of his life, something of the method of his earlier comedies is to be found in combination with deeper purposes worked out by wider processes. In *The Merchant of Venice* the story of the caskets is a mere romantic tale, fraught indeed with a moral, but with no very weighty one; the characters concerned in it are, in part at least, mere shadows; no reality attaches to Morocco or to Aragon. The story of the Jew is, in its original conception, equally a romantic fancy, though embodying a moral lesson; but here Shakspere has made incident subservient to character, developing the latter with the utmost force, so that Shylock becomes not less distinct and memorable than the hero of any of the tragedies. So again, in a different way, in *Twelfth Night*, where the comic figures include types both of manners and of character, and where the story (the same which had, speaking comparatively, been treated so slightly in *The Two Gentlemen of Verona*) enables the dramatist to draw in Viola a character of all but tragic pathos.

*Notes*

1. Cf. Symonds, *Shakspere's Predecessors* (1884) p. 532. J. Payne Collier, *History of English Dramatic Poetry* (1831), vol. ii. p. 335, has some very interesting observations on the evidence as to the early existence of efforts in the direction of English romantic comedy. I say, *in the direction*, for apart from all controversies as to the personal intention of the famous passage in Spenser's *Teares of the Muses* referring to the obscured efforts of the earlier 'comic stage,' it seems to me that ideals rather than achievements inspired the beautiful lines of the poetic critic—ideals which he had perhaps himself sought to realise.
2. Cf. Burckhardt, *Die Kultur der Renaissance in Italien*, p. 253; and see Klein, *Geschichte des Dramas*, iv. 217. Thomas Heywood, in his *Apology for Actors* (*Old Shakespeare Society's Publications*, 1843), bk ii, proposes to 'omit all the doctors, zawnyes, pantaloons, harlakeenes, in which the French, but especially the Italians, have become excellent.' The power of improvisation of the Italian actors seems to be alluded to in *Antony and Cleopatra*, act v. sc. 2:

    the quick comedians
    Extemporally will stage us, and present
    Our Alexandrian revels.

3. See some remarks on this subject in an able work by C. Humbert, *Molière, Shakspeare und die deutsche Kritik* (1869).
4. Cf. the observations of Guizot (cited *ap.* Humbert, p. 278):

    'Shakspere's comedy is a fantastic and romantic work of the mind, a refuge for all those delightful improbabilities, which from indolence or whim fancy merely strings together by a thin thread, in order thence to construct a variety of manifold complications, exhilarating and interesting us, without precisely satisfying the judicial test of reason. Pleasing pictures, surprises, merry plots, curiosity stimulated, expectations deceived, mistakes of identity, witty problems entailing disguises,—such were the materials of these plays, innocent in themselves and lightly thrown together.— What wonder that Shakspere's youthful and brilliant power of

imagination loved to dwell on such materials as these; since by means of them it could, free from the severe yoke of reason, at the expense of probability produce all manner of serious and strong effects.—Shakspere was able to pour everything into his comedies; and he actually poured everything into them, with the exception of what was irreconcileable with their system, *viz.* the logical connexion which subordinates every part of the piece to the purpose of the whole, and in each detail attests the depth, greatness, and unity of the work. In Shakspere's tragedies hardly a single conception, situation, deed of passion, degree of vice or of virtue, will be found that does not recur in some one of his comedies; but what in the former reaches into the most abysmal depth, and shows itself productive of consequences of the most moving force, rigorously occupying its place in a series of causes and results, in the latter is barely suggested, being merely thrown out for the moment, so as to produce a fugitive impression, and to be merged with equal rapidity in a new complication.'
5. There is a romantic style of criticism as well as of composition; but though both are delightful, neither, if it is to be really enjoyed, must be taken too seriously. Hazlitt's analysis of Bottom may serve as an example:—

    'It has been observed that Shakespear's characters are constructed upon deep physiological principles: and there is something in this play which looks very like it. Bottom the Weaver who takes the lead of

        This crew of patches, rude mechanicals
        That work for bread upon the Athenian stalls—

    follows a sedentary trade, and he is accordingly represented as conceited, serious, and fantastical. He is ready to undertake anything and everything, as if it was as much a matter of course as the motion of his loom and shuttle. He is for playing the tyrant, the lover, the lady, the lion. "He will roar that it shall do any man's heart good to hear him;" and this being objected to as improper, he still has a resource in his good opinion of himself, and will "roar you an't were any nightingale." Snug the Joiner is the moral man of the piece, who proceeds by measurement and discretion in all things. You see him with his rule and compass in his hand. "Have you the lion's part written? Pray you, if it be, give it me, for I am slow of study." "You may do it extempore," says Quince, "for it is nothing but roaring." Starveling the Tailor keeps the peace, and objects to the lion and the drawn sword. "I believe we must leave the killing out when all's done." Starveling, however, does not start the objections himself, but seconds them when made by others, as if he had not spirit to express his fears without encouragement. *It is too much to suppose all this intentional; but it very luckily falls out so.* Nature includes all that is implied in the most subtle analytical distinctions; and the same distinctions will be found in Shakespear. Bottom, who is not only chief actor, but stage-manager for the occasion, has a device to obviate the danger of frightening the ladies. "Write me a prologue, and let the prologue seem to say, we will do no harm with our swords, and that Pyramus is not killed indeed; and for better assurance, tell them that I, Pyramus, am not Pyramus, but Bottom the Weaver; this will put them out of fear." Bottom seems to have understood the subject of dramatic illusion at least as well as any modern essayist. If our holiday mechanic rules the roast among his fellows, he is no less at home in his new character of an ass "with amiable cheeks, and fair long ears." He instinctively acquires a most learned taste, and grows fastidious in the choice of dried peas and bottled hay. He is quite familiar with his new attendants, and assigns them their part with all due gravity. "Monsieur Cobweb, good Monsieur, get your weapon in your hand, and kill me a redhipt humble-bee on the top of a thistle, and, good Monsieur, bring me your honeybag,"' &c.

    The late Mr. Phelps' inimitable representation of Bottom the Weaver was based on some such conception of the character, and to my mind, although magnificent, was not Shakspere.
6. Gervinus.
7. So at least it seemed to me, when renewing my acquaintance with *The Winter's Tale* as an acted play, and retaining at the same time a very lively remembrance of the late Mr. Charles Kean's Leontes.

Charlotte Cushman as Katherine
*(The Taming of the Shrew)*

Ada Rehan as Julia
*(The Two Gentlemen of Verona)*

Henry and Thomas Placide as the two Dromios
*(The Comedy of Errors)*

Bottom and Titania in *A Midsummer Night's Dream*
(painting by Paul Thumann)

Mr. Macklin as Shylock
*(The Merchant of Venice)*

*A*

# PLEASANT

## Conceited Comedie
### CALLED,
## Loues labors loſt.

As it vvas preſented before her Highnes
this laſt Chriſtmas.

Newly corrected and augmented
By *W. Shakeſpere.*

Imprinted at London by *W.W.*
for *Cutbert Burby.*
1598.

First Quarto of *Love's Labour's Lost* (1598)

# The Comedy of Errors

*The Comedy of Errors* is the subject of the *Menæchmi* of Plautus, entirely recast and enriched with new developments: of all the works of Shakspeare this is the only example of imitation of, or borrowing from, the ancients. To the two twin brothers of the same name are added two slaves, also twins, impossible to be distinguished from each other, and of the same name. The improbability becomes by this means doubled: but when once we have lent ourselves to the first, which certainly borders on the incredible, we shall not perhaps be disposed to cavil at the second; and if the spectator is to be entertained by mere perplexities they cannot be too much varied. In such pieces we must, to give to the senses at least an appearance of truth, always pre-suppose that the parts by which the misunderstandings are occasioned are played with masks, and this the poet no doubt observed. I cannot acquiesce in the censure that the discovery is too long deferred: so long as novelty and interest are possessed by the perplexing incidents, there is no need to be in dread of wearisomeness. And this is really the case here: matters are carried so far that one of the two brothers is first arrested for debt, then confined as a lunatic, and the other is forced to take refuge in a sanctuary to save his life. In a subject of this description it is impossible to steer clear of all sorts of low circumstances, abusive language, and blows; Shakspeare has however endeavoured to ennoble it in every possible way. A couple of scenes, dedicated to jealousy and love, interrupt the course of perplexities which are solely occasioned by the illusion of the external senses. A greater solemnity is given to the discovery from the Prince presiding, and from the re-union of the long separated parents of the twins who are still alive. The exposition, by which the spectators are previously instructed while the characters themselves are still involved in ignorance, and which Plautus artlessly conveys in a prologue, is here masterly introduced in an affecting narrative by the father. In short, this is perhaps the best of all written or possible *Menæchmi*; and if the piece be inferior in worth to other pieces of Shakspeare, it is merely because nothing more could be made of the materials.—AUGUST WILHELM SCHLEGEL, *Lectures on Dramatic Art and Literature*, 1809, tr. John Black

This comedy is taken very much from the *Menæchmi* of Plautus, and is not an improvement on it. Shakespear appears to have bestowed no great pains on it, and there are but a few passages which bear the decided stamp of his genius. He seems to have relied on his author, and on the interest arising out of the intricacy of the plot. The curiosity excited is certainly very considerable, though not of the most pleasing kind. We are teazed as with a riddle, which notwithstanding we try to solve. In reading the play, from the sameness of the names of the two Antipholises and the two Dromios, as well from their being constantly taken for each other by those who see them, it is difficult, without a painful effort of attention, to keep the characters distinct in the mind. And again, on the stage, either the complete similarity of their persons and dress must produce the same perplexity whenever they first enter, or the identity of appearance which the story supposes, will be destroyed. We still, however, having a clue to the difficulty, can tell which is which, merely from the practical contradictions which arise, as soon as the different parties begin to speak; and we are indemnified for the perplexity and blunders into which we are thown by seeing others thrown into greater and almost inextricable ones.—This play (among other considerations) leads us not to feel much regret that Shakespear was not what is called a classical scholar. We do not think his *forte* would ever have lain in imitating or improving on what others invented, so much as in inventing for himself, and perfecting what he invented,—not perhaps by the omission of faults, but by the addition of the highest excellencies. His own genius was strong enough to bear him up, and he soared longest and best on unborrowed plumes.—WILLIAM HAZLITT, *"The Comedy of Errors," Characters of Shakespear's Plays*, 1817

The myriad-minded man, our, and all men's, Shakspeare, has in this piece presented us with a legitimate farce in exactest consonance with the philosophical principles and character of farce, as distinguished from comedy and from entertainments. A proper farce is mainly distinguished from comedy by the license allowed, and even required, in the fable, in order to produce strange and laughable situations. The story need not be probable, it is enough that it is possible. A comedy would scarcely allow even the two Antipholises; because, although there have been instances of almost indistinguishable likeness in two persons, yet these are mere individual accidents, *casus ludentis naturæ*, and the *verum* will not excuse the *inverisimile*. But farce dares add the two Dromios, and is justified in so doing by the laws of its end and constitution. In a word, farces commence in a postulate, which must be granted.—SAMUEL TAYLOR COLERIDGE, *"Comedy of Errors," Shakspeare, with Introductory Remarks on Poetry, the Drama, and the Stage*, 1818

---

## RICHARD GRANT WHITE
### From "Introduction" to *The Comedy of Errors*
### *The Works of William Shakspeare*
### 1865, Volume 3, pp. 135–39

There is no doubt that *The Comedy of Errors* is an imitation of the *Menæchmi* of Plautus; but the question whether the imitation was direct or indirect has not been decided. We know, from the Record of the Revels at Court, that a play called *The History of Error* was in existence in the year 1576–7; for among the entries for that year is the following:—

"The Historie of Error, shewn at Hampton Court on New yeres daie at night, enacted by the children of Pawles."

Malone, who first directed attention to this memorandum, also pointed out a passage in the *Gesta Grayorum*—a contemporary record of the festivities at Gray's Inn, published in 1688—which shows that "a Comedy of Errors, like to Plautus his Menechmus, was played by the players" during the Christmas Revels at that venerable Inn of Court in December, 1594. In 1595 there was published in London a free translation of the *Menæchmi*.[1] Finally, Meres gives us evidence that Shakespeare's *Comedy of Errors* was written at least as early as 1597. These are all the facts on record from which we can determine the origin of this comedy or the date of its production; but as the old *History of Error* is entirely lost, and as we do not know whether the play at Gray's Inn was Shakespeare's Comedy or the older History, we are unable to decide from these data whether Shakespeare's play existed in any form before the publication of the translation from Plautus.

Of internal evidence upon this subject there is very little, and that not of much weight. *Dromio's* reply to *Antipholus*, Act III. Sc. 2, that he found France in the forehead of the globe-like dame who asserted uxorial rights over him, "armed and reverted,[2] making war against her heir," is, however, so plainly a punning allusion to the war of the League, which was closed by Henry IV.'s apostasy in 1593, that there can hardly be a doubt as to the existence of the passage before that date. For although it is true that 'heire' might be a misprint or loose spelling of 'haire,' to which it is changed in the folio of 1632, the allusion yet exists in as full force, in the otherwise senseless words "armed and reverted, making war," and the pun remains with a different spelling. The likeness between the phraseology of the translated *Menæchmi* and *The Comedy of Errors* is very slight indeed; and all other similarity is due, of course, to the original. *Adriana* says, Act II. Sc. 1, "poor I am but his stale," and the Wife in the translated *Menæchmi* says, "He makes me a stale and a laughing stock": W. W. translates,

> . . . nunc ibo in tabernam: vasa et argentum tibi Referam,

"Ile go strait to the Inne, and deliver up my accounts, and all your stuffe," and *Antipholus* of Syracuse says, "Come to the Centaur; fetch our stuff from thence;" and although 'stuff' and 'stale' were generally used in Shakespeare's time as they are here used, in these speeches they have somewhat the air of reminiscences.

That the author of *The Comedy of Errors* knew the story of the *Menæchmi*, needs, of course, no setting forth; but that he had studied it closely, either in the original or in a translation, is evident from similarity in minor points between the plays. In both the resident brother is married; in both the wife is shrewish; in both she has brought her husband a large dowry; in both the Courtesan appears; and in both the resident brother seeks refuge at her table from the jealous clamors of his wife; the incident of the chain is common to both, and is used by each dramatist, though with a difference, for the same purpose; in both the wandering brother gives his purse to his servant to be carried to the inn; in both the wife, on account of the behavior of his double, finally supposes her husband to be lunatic, and in the one case sends and in the other brings a leech to take him in charge, who in both encounters the husband himself. It is also noteworthy that in the first stage directions of the original, one *Antipholus* is called "*Errotis*" and the other "*Sereptus*,"—misprints, doubtless, for '*Erraticus*' and '*Surreptus*'—meaning 'wandering' and 'stolen.' Now, in *The Comedy of Errors* the resident brother is not stolen, but in the *Menæchmi* he is, and is designated as *Surreptus*; and the traveller, who is not called *Erraticus* in Plautus' Dramatis Personæ, but *Sosicles*, is, however, called 'the Traveller' in W. W.'s translation. This translation, although not published until 1595, had then been made and handed about for some time, as we know by the address of "The Printer to the Readers" which introduces it. In this he says, or, without doubt, the author for him,—"The writer hereof (loving Readers) having diverse of this Poettes Comedies Englished, for the use and delight of his private friends, who in Plautus owne words are not able to understand them: I have prevailed so far with him as to let this one go farther abroad," &c.

In the absence of evidence which amounts to proof, we may yet form an opinion; and my own, based upon a consideration of the facts just stated and of the play itself, is, that Shakespeare, at the very beginning of his dramatic career, wishing to supply his theatre with an amusing comedy to take the place of a rude imitation of the *Menæchmi*, already

somewhat known to the public, read that play in the original as thoroughly as his "small Latin" (small in the estimation of so complete a scholar as Jonson) enabled him to read it; that he also read W. W.'s translation in manuscript; and that then, using for the more comic parts the doggerel verse in which the elder play was written, for the passages of sentiment the alternate rhymes of which *Venus and Adonis* and *Romeo and Juliet* show his early preference and his mastery, and for the serious Scenes the blank verse which he was the first to bring to perfection, and which appears in great though not yet matured beauty in *The Two Gentlemen of Verona*, he wrote *The Comedy of Errors:* that, in the extravagant Scenes, he deliberately imitated, *populo ut placeret*, the versification of the old play, and perhaps adopted some of it with improvement; that this was done about 1589–90; and that the play thus produced may have been somewhat rewritten by him in its first and last Scenes in the long period during which it remained unprinted in the possession of the theatre.

It is to be observed that although the poetical value of *The Two Gentlemen of Verona* is much greater than that of *The Comedy of Errors*, the dramatic arrangement of the latter is much more skilful, and indicates longer theatrical experience on the part of the author.

The difference between the comedy of the Latin and that of the English dramatist is very wide, both in the way of addition and alteration; the most important addition being that of another pair of twins as attendants upon those who figure in the Latin play. The introduction of these tends greatly to complicate the confusion out of which the fun of this extravaganza arises. Whether the thought was original with Shakespeare or was taken from the old play, we have no means of ascertaining; but in the use made of the bondsmen we recognize the younger hand of him in whose maturer works his perception of the ridiculous and enjoyment of the broadest humor are no less apparent than his delight in all that is grand and beautiful in Man and Nature. Yet the very passages in which the *Dromios* are most prominent are those which seem most unmistakably the production of an inferior and more ancient writer. How difficult is it to believe that the rhyming part of Act III. Sc. 1, for instance, was written, at any time or for any purpose, by the author of the fine blank verse which precedes and follows it! It is more than possible that the two slaves were added in the older play to doubly supply the clown or buffoon, without which, on our ancient stage, a comedy was not a comedy. In the substitution of *Luciana*, the sister of *Adriana*, for the Father of the Latin comedy, we very surely have an indication of Shakespeare's dramatic skill; the expostulations which he puts into the mouth of the young woman are far more convincing and to the purpose than the reproaches which Plautus makes the old man deal out to both husband and wife. The introduction of *Luciana* also enabled the author to establish, in the relations between her and *Antipholus* of Syracuse, a new interest entirely wanting to the Latin play. The Parasite, who figures so largely in the *Menæchmi*, as in all Latin comedies, is omitted, as a character altogether foreign to the taste of an English audience, and needless to the production of that confusion which is the only motive of Shakespeare's play; in which, too, the action is more intricate than in its model, the movement more rapid, and the spirit much more lively, light, and humorous.

Concerning the place and the period of the action of this play, it seems that Shakespeare did not trouble himself to form a very accurate idea. The Ephesus of *The Comedy of Errors* is much like the Bohemia of *The Winter's Tale*—a remote, unknown place, yet with a familiar and imposing name, and therefore well suited to the purposes of one who as poet and dramatist cared much for men and little for things, and to whose perception the accidental was entirely eclipsed by the essential. Anachronisms are scattered through it with a profusion which could only be the result of entire indifference—in fact, of an absolute want of thought upon the subject. The existence of an abbey in Ephesus, however, is not to be considered as among them. For Christianity was established there about the middle of the fourth century; and Ephesus remained a Greek and Christian city till about A. D. 1313. The action of the play may, perhaps, be referred to about the middle of this period.

*Notes*

1. "A pleasant and fine Conceited Comœdie, taken out of the most excellent wittie Poet Plautus: Chosen purposely from out the rest, as least harmefull, and yet most delightfull. Written in English by W. W.—London. Printed by Tho. Creede, and are to be sold by William Barley, at his shop on Grations streete, 1595." 4to.

    This W. W. is supposed by Anthony Wood, in his *Athenæ Oxonienses*, to have been William Warner, the author of *Albion's England*, a sort of chronicle in verse, first published at London in 1586. 4to.

2. A misprint, left uncorrected here.

# The Taming of the Shrew

*The Taming of the Shrew* has the air of an Italian comedy; and indeed the love intrigue, which constitutes the main part of it, is derived mediately or immediately from a piece of Ariosto. The characters and passions are lightly sketched; the intrigue is introduced without much preparation, and in its rapid progress impeded by no sort of difficulties; while, in the manner in which Petruchio, though previously cautioned as to Katherine, still encounters the risks in marrying her, and contrives to tame her—in all this the character and peculiar humour of the English are distinctly visible. The colours are laid on somewhat coarsely, but the ground is good. That the obstinacy of a young and untamed girl, possessed by none of the attractions of her sex, and neither supported by bodily nor mental strength, must soon yield to the still rougher and more capricious but assumed self-will of a man: such a lesson can only be taught on the stage with all the perspicuity of a proverb.

The prelude is still more remarkable than the play itself: a drunken tinker, removed in his sleep to a palace, where he is deceived into the belief of being a nobleman. The invention, however, is not Shakspeare's. Holberg has handled the same subject in a masterly manner, and with inimitable truth; but he has spun it out to five acts, for which such material is hardly sufficient. He probably did not borrow from the English dramatist, but like him took the hint from a popular story. There are several comic motives of this description, which go back to a very remote age, without ever becoming antiquated. Here, as well as everywhere else, Shakspeare has proved himself a great poet: the whole is merely a slight sketch, but in elegance and delicate propriety it will hardly ever be excelled. Neither has he overlooked the irony which the subject naturally suggested: the great lord, who is driven by idleness and ennui to deceive a poor drunkard, can make no better use of his situation than the latter, who every moment relapses into his vulgar habits. The last half of this prelude, that in which the tinker, in his new state, again drinks himself out of his senses, and is transformed in his sleep into his former condition, is from some accident or other, lost. It ought to have followed at the end of the larger piece. The occasional remarks of the tinker, during the course of the representation of the comedy, might have been improvisatory; but it is hardly credible that Shakspeare should have trusted to the momentary suggestions of the players, whom he did not hold in high estimation, the conclusion, however short, of a work which he had so carefully commenced. Moreover, the only circumstance which connects the play with the prelude, is, that it belongs to the new life of the supposed nobleman to have plays acted in his castle by strolling actors. This invention of introducing spectators on the stage, who contribute to the entertainment, has been very wittily used by later English poets.—AUGUST WILHELM SCHLEGEL, *Lectures on Dramatic Art and Literature*, 1809, tr. John Black

*The Taming of the Shrew* is almost the only one of Shakespear's comedies that has a regular plot, and downright moral. It is full of bustle, animation, and rapidity of action. It shews admirably how self-will is only to be got the better of by stronger will, and how one degree of ridiculous perversity is only to be driven out by another still greater. Petruchio is a madman in his senses; a very honest fellow, who hardly speaks a word of truth, and succeeds in all his tricks and impostures. He acts his assumed character to the life, with the most fantastical extravagance, with complete presence of mind, with untired animal spirits, and without a particle of ill humour from beginning to end.—The situation of poor Katherine, worn out by his incessant persecutions, becomes at last almost as pitiable as it is ludicrous, and it is difficult to say which to admire most, the unaccountableness of his actions, or the unalterableness of his resolutions. It is a character which most husbands ought to study, unless perhaps the very audacity of Petruchio's attempt might alarm them more than his success would encourage them. What a sound must the following speech carry to some married ears!

> Think you a little din can daunt my ears?
> Have I not in my time heard lions roar?
> Have I not heard the sea, puff'd up with winds,
> Rage like an angry boar, chafed with sweat?
> Have I not heard great ordnance in the field?
> And heav'n's artillery in the skies?
> Have I not in a pitched battle heard
> Loud larums, neighing steeds, and trumpets clang?
> And do you tell me of a woman's tongue,
> That gives not half so great a blow to hear,
> As will a chesnut in a farmer's fire?

   . . . The most striking and at the same time laughable feature in the character of Petruchio throughout, is the studied approximation to the intractable character of real madness, his apparent insensibility to all external considerations, and utter indifference to every thing but the wild and extravagant freaks of his own self-will. There is no contending with a person on whom nothing makes any impression but his own purposes, and who is bent on his own whims just in proportion as they seem to want common sense. With him a thing's being plain and reasonable is a reason against it. The airs he gives himself are infinite, and his caprices as sudden as they are groundless. The whole of his treatment of his wife at home is in the same spirit of ironical attention and inverted gallantry. Every thing flies before his will, like a conjuror's wand, and he only metamorphoses his wife's temper by metamorphising her senses and all the objects she sees, at a word's speaking. Such are his insisting that it is the moon and not the sun which they see, etc. . . .

*The Taming of the Shrew* is a play within a play. It is supposed to be a play acted for the benefit of Sly the tinker, who is made to believe himself a lord, when he wakes after a drunken brawl. The character of Sly and the remarks with which he accompanies the play are as good as the play itself. His answer when he is asked how he likes it, 'Indifferent well; 'tis a good piece of work, would 'twere done,' is in good keeping, as if he were thinking of his Saturday night's job. Sly does not change his tastes with his new situation, but in the midst of splendour and luxury still calls out lustily and repeatedly 'for a pot o' the smallest ale.' He is very slow in giving up his personal identity in his sudden advancement.—'I am Christophero Sly, call not me honour nor lordship. I ne'er drank sack in my life: and if you give me my conserves, give me conserves of beef: ne'er ask me what raiment I'll wear, for I have no more doublets than backs, no more stockings than legs, nor no more shoes than feet, nay, sometimes more feet than shoes, or such shoes as my toes look through the over-leather.—What, would you make me mad? Am not I Christophero Sly, old Sly's son of Burton-heath, by birth a pedlar, by education a card-maker, by transmutation a bear-herd, and now by present profession a tinker? Ask Marian Hacket, the fat alewife of Wincot, if she know me not; if she say I am not fourteen-pence on the score for sheer ale, score me up for the lying'st knave in Christendom.'

This is honest. 'The Slies are no rogues,' as he says of himself. We have a great predilection for this representative of the family; and what makes us like him the better is, that we take him to be of kin (not many degrees removed) to Sancho Panza.—WILLIAM HAZLITT *"The Taming of the Shrew," Characters of Shakespear's Plays*, 1817

---

## CHARLOTTE CARMICHAEL STOPES
### *"The Taming of the Shrew"*
*The Athenaeum*, June 11, 1904, pp. 762–64

There are several peculiarities in this play which make it difficult to classify among Shakspeare's works. Others are comedies; this, called a history, is nearly a farce. Others have a Prologue or Chorus to introduce the action, or an Epilogue to sum it up; but this is the only one that has an Induction, which seems totally unconnected with the main action, and does not in any way illustrate its meaning. If, for a moment, we treat the Induction as the play in itself, we may find some parallels in *Hamlet*. By the flourish of trumpets the players announce their approach in both cases, as distinguished travellers would—

Belike some noble gentleman that means,
Travelling some journey, to repose him here.
(Ind. Sc. i.)

The travelling players come to offer their services in a fortunate hour. In *Hamlet* "the tragedians of the city" are forced to take the less reputable exercises of their calling in the provinces, because the "aery of children," "little eyases," are now the fashion in the metropolis (a curious incongruity, seeing Hamlet was *in the city*, and *at the Court*). In both plays they are cordially received. They have acted well before. The Lord and Hamlet each discuss some well-known parts, to prepare them to decide which play should be performed. The Lord has some

sport in hand, and wants a comedy; Hamlet has a terrible secret, and wants a tragedy. The Lord tells them, "Your cunning can assist me much"; Hamlet talks indefinitely to the players while others are present, recalling one play by its mentioning "savoury sallets," and straining his memory to fix the lines about Pyrrhus and Hecuba to confuse Polonius. As soon as the Chamberlain goes, Hamlet bids the chief player fix *The Murder of Gonzago* for the next night, adding, "You could, for a need, study a speech of some dozen or sixteen lines, which I would set down and insert in it, could you not?" Then he meditates—

The play's the thing
Wherein I'll catch the conscience of the King!

The Lord tells his servants, "Let them want nothing that my house affords"; Hamlet says to Polonius, "Good my lord, will you see the players well bestowed? . . . Do you hear? let them be well used." Polonius did not care much for players, and equivocates, "My lord, I will use them according to their deserts." To which Hamlet replies, "God's bodkin, man, much better!" Hamlet's play within the play is introduced by a dumb show, an induction to the performance, whereby the King's conscience is awakened before he has heard all. The Lord is not so particular, and he lets the players choose; but it is to be supposed that before a liberal patron they would perform their newest and their best.

The Induction is a humorous fragment rather than a play, but it is worth all the comedy it nominally initiates. The story was based on an incident in the life of Philip the Good, Duke of Burgundy, who carried into his house an artisan whom he had found lying drunk in the streets. He offered his visitor many more amusements than were laid before Sly, "after which they played a pleasant comedy," the name of which is not given, and the conclusion to the waking dreamer is the same.

*The Taming of the Shrew* is a play complete in itself, and would only suffer in length by being separated from the Induction. The question naturally rises, Why were they so connected? As far as regards Shakspeare, it may be only because they are combined in the old play which suggested his. On June 11th, 1594, Henslowe notes receipts at performance, by "my Lord Admirell and my Lord Chamberlen men," of *The Taming of a Shrew*, which, curiously enough, immediately follows a similar entry on their playing *Hamlet*, which must have been the old version. In that same year was published "A pleasant conceited historie called *The Taming of a Shrew*, as it hath been lately performed by the Earl of Pembroke's servants." This was a rival company. Could it be the same play? Mr. Charles Knight suggests that the two sets of performers might have separate renderings from some older source now lost, probably, from the style, a play written by Greene. The scene of the printed version—*i.e.*, that of Pembroke's servants—is laid in Athens. In Shakspeare's (which may have been that of the Chamberlain's men in 1594) all the names are changed except that of Kate, and the language is modified to such an extent that the editors of the First Folio saw fit to include it among his works, though it does not appear in the lists of those copies entered to them or to any other publisher, neither does Meres mention it.

Had he thought it necessary, Shakspeare might have changed the situations fundamentally. As he accepted them, we may discuss the play as his own. While he changed the scene, with much advantage, from Athens to Padua, it must not be forgotten that he also changed the scene of the Induction from *anywhere* to *somewhere*. The old Induction, though using the name of Sly (the name also of one of the company), might have represented London or anywhere else. The new Induction belongs clearly to Warwickshire. Christopher was son of the Sly of Barton-on-the-Heath, the home of Shakspeare's uncle and cousin Lambert, who foreclosed the mortgage on his maternal inheritance. There was a Stephen sly, labourer, working at Welcombe at that very time. The Hackets were well known in the district, and some of the family did keep an inn. It is quite possible that there was a personal dig at some hostess who "did bring stone jugs and no sealed quarts," who deserved to be presented at the Leet. "The Lord" is nameless now, but it is not at all certain that he was not recognizable then by his characteristics. Shakspeare changes the tapster of the old Induction into a hostess. She has evidently had within the house a hot discussion, not yet concluded when she gets him out of doors. His first words seem to be a repetition of what she has just said to him. To make her meaning clear, she adds, "A pair of stocks, you rogue!" The acceptance of this question-begging epithet would put him at once in danger of statutes concerning "rogues and vagabonds," and he was sober enough to claim immunity because he was a man of ancient family. The substitution of "Richard" for William was probably a bit of byplay, complimentary to Burbage. Why the drunken tinker should be made to use a Spanish phrase to a country alewife is not clear, unless it was intended to suggest that during his pedlar experience, his cardmaker education, or his transmutation into a bearherd, he had been to London and picked it up at the bear-baiting or bull-baiting there. The same remark applies to "denier" and "Jeronymy." This is generally read as "Go by," a phrase from the old part of Hieronomo. But it is quite certain that Sly at the time felt like swearing, and that he would have a special oath of his own, though as hazily founded as his "Richard Conqueror." I read it that he was ordering the hostess back to her house: "Go! by S. Jeronymy, go! to thy cold bed and warm thee!"[1] The hostess retorts that she must rather "go fetch the thirdborough!" or constable. Sly, confident that he could answer *him* in law, disdained to fly at the threat, and lay down where he could be at hand. There he was found, not by the thirdborough, but by the Lord, who must have lived near, as he thought of carrying the drunken man home, rather than bestowing him in the inn. The Lord paints a rough sketch of him: "O monstrous beast, how like a swine he lies." He seems in his condition "foul and loathsome." Sly took a good deal of persuading to believe that he was a lord, and only accepted his position with Prince Henry's reservation in regard to his love for a pot of small ale. The season seems to have been December, not only from allusions to the cold, but because he asks if the *commonty* is to be "a Christmas gambol or a tumbling trick." The page describes it as more pleasing stuff, a kind of history. Sly had said to his hostess, "Let the world slide." Now again he says to his dream-wife, as he settles down by her side to watch the play, provided with cates and surrounded by lords and gentlemen, "Let the world slip." For this strangely consorted audience, and not for us, as the play in *Hamlet* is not for us, but for the King, *the history* that they had selected is performed by the travelling actors.

If it had been selected for the clown, it is hard to say why the scene should have been laid at a university town in Italy, among gentlemen and scholars. Did Shakspeare, or his players, aim at the Lord? Was there anything personal or satirical in it?

The underplot is essentially Italian. Lucentio comes to the University of Padua to study, as he states, chiefly the higher philosophy of Epicurus, but before he ever matriculates, Romeo-like, he falls in love, and becomes not a student, but a tutor in the *art of love*, wins Bianca, in spite of his rivals, and secures her by a stolen marriage. The character of Kate is only possible to English comedy. Her unlady like violence of temper is, however, accounted for in the first scene. A motherless girl of high spirit, she had always taken her own way with her foolish father and her younger sister. Capable among incapables, she had expressed her mind freely among her equals, and domineered over her inferiors, even to the using of her fists. She had hitherto thought of nothing but the mood of the moment. Now a crisis had arrived in her life. Her father had made her heart bitter by a pronounced preference for her sister. Two men had come a-wooing to the house. She had not thought of a husband until then, but the idea was naturally suggested, just as she discovered that *both* of the men desired her sister. The awkwardness might have passed over; she might have consoled herself on the sour-grape theory that Gremio was too old and Hortensio too weak for her, that she would have no rival at home were but her sister married; but her unwise father, not content with having discoursed openly of her vile temper, repeats before her and others his desire to get rid of her, and offers her to either of her sister's suitors, without consulting her taste or theirs. Their insolent refusal shows them to be no gentlemen, and prevents her regretting their loss, while it shows her they reckon her influence in the house as naught, seeing she was not worth conciliating with a show of courtesy. When her father secludes her sister, ostensibly to give *her* a chance, he apologizes—

Good Bianca,
For I will love thee ne'er the less, my girl!

He bids Kate stay back, as he wished to commune with her sister; but the embittered girl follows in a passion. The two suitors see it their policy to find her a husband to get rid of her, as her father desires to do.

Here "the Presenters above speak." Sly had said to the hostess "paucas pallabris." He has found the "commonty" *nothing but words*; he finds it dull, and wishes it were done. Did Shakspeare allow him then to sink into his second sleep, or did he merely leave the part to Kemp's inspiration? We cannot help wishing that we had more of him. Akin to Grumio, to Sancho Panza, and Autolycus, he was a fit follower for Sir John Falstaff.

Scene ii. introduces Petruchio's violent temper and his severity to Grumio. He has come to Padua not to study, but "to wive and thrive." He cares not whether his bride be ugly, old, diseased, be curst or shrew,

As wealth is the burden of my wooing dance.

Hortensio tells him of Kate, young, rich, beauteous, cultured, but curst. Petruchio cares not, money covers all. The other gentlemen speak roughly of the girl; Tranio is the only one who treats the question like a gentleman, and recognizes Baptista's

Firm resolve
In the preferment of his elder daughter.

The painful scene in which Kate has bound her sister, and then strikes her through envy and jealousy, comes to a climax when her father intervenes to protect Bianca:—

She is your treasure, she must have a husband.
I must dance barefoot on her wedding-day,
And, for your love to her, *lead apes in hell.*

Many illustrations might be given of this curious phrase, commonly used of those who died old maids. But the only reference I know to the converse is from a fragment of Capt. Cox's *Old Book of Fortune:*—

Thou a stale bachelor wilt die,
And not a maiden for thee cry,
For apes that maids in hell do lead
Are men that die and will not wed.

Kate goes off to weep violently, and think of revenge, just before Petruchio comes in to ask Baptista for her hand.

The mock-tutors are sent to their pupils, Baptista invites the others to the orchard. Petruchio detains him. His suit is pressing—"Every day I cannot come to woo." His haste awakes Baptista too late to his duty, or a pretence of it—

When the special thing is well obtained,
That is, her love, for that is all in all.

Petruchio, secure of all that *he* wanted, exclaims, "That is nothing." He felt sure he could win any woman's love, if so he chose, and cure any woman's temper. He knew that he had a disposition, called politely among men "peremptory," among women impolitely "shrewish." It is only the amount of friction or opposition which determines the degree of noise made. Hortensio comes in with his head broken. Lucentio had secured Bianca with his books; Kate, in her wrathful mood, had discovered either stupidity or *sham* in the music-master. Possibly she recognized him, and had a part of her "revenge" thus. Petruchio is delighted. She had done just what he would have liked to do himself. A genuine feeling of admiration is awakened, and a desire of mastering her high spirit. Henceforth the action must be read, as Justice Madden points out in *The Diary of Master William Silence*, through the light of the language of falconry. Petruchio meant to "man a haggard" for himself rather than teach an "eyas." He has the advantage over her in being prepared. Baptista asks him whether he would come within to be introduced formally as a suitor, or whether he would like Kate sent to him—a most unfatherly suggestion. One wonders how the excited Baptista worded the message to Kate that at last a suitor had come for her, and whether he stirred her anger, pride, or joy. She had at least curiosity enough to come, doubtless slowly and with dignity, and a fierce modesty covering her heart-hunger to hear words of love. He does not even introduce himself, but with cool effrontery says, as if she had been a milkmaid, "Good morrow, Kate, for that's your name, I hear." Her temper blazed, but she controlled it courteously as she checked him justly. He rudely said she "lied," broke into nonsensical exclamations, and wound up by saying he wooed her for his wife.

Thereafter a dialogue of sharp repartee, until Kate strikes him. Then, apparently, he caught her by the wrists, and let her feel his strength: "I chafe you, if I tarry: let me go!" After mock praise of her gentleness, he cunningly suggests: "Why does the world report that Kate doth limp?" She could not walk away, as if to answer this, and therefore bids him begone. More praise, and then to business. She had not been consulted—was not to be consulted. Her father had already consented, everything was arranged: "and will you, nill you, I will marry you."

Baptista did not come alone, as he ought to have done, to inquire how matters had gone, but with a total stranger on one side, and the old Gremio, who had so scornfully refused her, on the other. Petruchio had at least not insulted her in this manner. She might have been advised, but her father's words rubbed her the wrong way, and she broke forth into reproaches for his desire to see her wed a man half lunatic. Petruchio outtalked her, and belied her words, skilfully interwove suggestions about finery and a feast next Sunday, and his audacity and lies, his praise, and perhaps his appearance, restore her maidenly pride. Here was a chance of taking the higher social level of a bride, and of leaving for ever the little daily irritations of her present life. Doubtless she was thinking deeply when she let her last chance pass of protesting, and she found herself betrothed, with due witnesses, before she knew what she was about, and Petruchio had gone to prepare for the wedding on Sunday.

Having thus got rid of his tiresome daughter to the first man who would have her, Baptista is free to sell the daughter he loves to the highest bidder. She is settling affairs for herself. Meek as she had seemed beside Kate, there is a spice of the same self-will in her (shown in Act V. sc. ii. l. 130)—

I'll not be tied to hours nor 'pointed times,
But learn my lessons as I please myself.

She had been tired of Hortensio before she offered him to her sister. She prefers literature to music, associated as it was with a new face. She bids Lucentio "presume not, but despair not."

After the whirl of preparations for the ceremony on Sunday, the "taming of the haggard" began in earnest. The bridegroom did not arrive in time, and, enforced to wait, on poor Kate there dawns a fear that she was about to be mocked in a more galling way than her father or Hortensio or Gremio had ever done. She had "been forced to give her hand without her heart," and now her betrothed did not trouble himself to come for her. Passionate tears flowed, and for the first time her father showed a kindly sympathy with her. Then the expected Petruchio comes without the garb even of a gentleman, without the manners of a gentleman, irreverent not only to his bride, her father, and their friends, but to Holy Church and its officiating minister. Well might Kate be daunted, who had never known fear before. She soon learnt the folly and ridiculousness of violence through her husband's explosions. She came to long for ordinary world-like ways and peace at any price. Her family resemblance to Bianca began to appear. She had not exercised her violent temper without a purpose. She had used it as means to an end. She wanted her own way, and, like other spoiled children, she had hitherto found that noise secured it. Now, amid her husband's storms, she found she must try another method: she must spoil him, as she had been spoiled, by humouring him. That was not sufficient. She must do that through hypocrisy and falsehood, alien to her direct nature. Petruchio made her a time-server. She had to agree that black was white, the sun the moon, old age fair youth, and then two was seven, and they started homewards. She wanted home, and thus she had her way.

Then came the famous wager, and Kate's more famous speech. The old "Kate" based her argument for women's submission on the popular derivation of "woman," for by her came woe to man in the creation. The change in Kate's argument is curious, or rather in her two arguments: one because a man is stronger than a woman, and the other because he toiled for her that "she might lie warm at home secure and safe." Kate's clear brain knew that *strength* was a variable quantity, and that the argument could not therefore *universally* apply, and in regard to the second argument, in her own case at least, that she was talking as arrant nonsense as when she praised old Vincentio as a young maiden. For she knew that Petruchio had not married her in order to toil for her, but to save him from toiling for himself; that if any were *breadwinner* it was her father, who had given sufficient to supply all her needs, without any self-sacrifice on Petruchio's part. If this argument had any force, if the *bread-provider* was to rule, *she* was more entitled to pre-eminence than he. But she outdid patient Griselda in her speech, though any critical listener might have thought, "The lady protests too much, methinks" (*Hamlet*, III. ii.). There is no real thought of such submission in Kate any more than in the young tree, that bends till the blast be past and strengthens itself meanwhile to withstand future ones.

A touch from the old play is missed in Shakspeare's. Sly said at first, "I hardly think that he can tame her"; and again, "For when he has done, she will do what she list," a suggestion caught up by John Fletcher, who was probably "the second hand" in this play, and elaborated in his *Woman's Prize; or, the Tamer Tamed*. The old Sly felt happy in the experiences he had gained. He knew now how to tame a shrew, and he named his wife one when she reproached him for his evil ways. But Sly had vanished from Shakspeare's action; the moral of the play, if moral there was, seems to have been a lesson to, or a satire for, the Lord. Did he represent some real gentleman of Warwickshire, known to the audience who heard the play performed there? It might have suggested Ludovic Greville, of Milcote, had not his violent life been closed by a tragic end in 1589. There might have been some other. But I have often thought that *this*, and not Justice Shallow, was intended as a dig at Sir Thomas Lucy. His marriage had been so long ago that few would remember the circumstances, but there might have been some amplified tradition of the action of the country-bred bridegroom of fourteen who sought his bride of twelve, as Petruchio did his, for her wealth. He might have thought it necessary betimes to assert his marital supremacy in a way which seemed only to himself to succeed.

But two *facts* are certain—that the Lady Joyce Lucy was declared, on the testimony of her son-in-law,[2] Sir Edward Aston, of Tixhall, to be *a veritable vixen*, and that when she died on February 10th, 1595/6, her laudatory epitaph reads as an apology and defence against charges known to have been made "by the envious." If it were so, the play must have been completed by 1595 at least.

It is curious that Meres does not mention it, and that there is no contemporary praise of the comedy. But there is a reference to the Induction, which shows that it was popular, in Sir Aston Cokaine's *Poems*, published 1658. Addressing his friend Mr. Clement Fisher, of Wincot, he says:—

Shakespeare your Wincot ale hath much renowned
That foxed a beggar so (by chance was founde
Sleeping) that there needed not many a word,
To make him to believe he was a Lord.
But you affirm (and in it seem most eager)
'Twill make a Lord as drunk as any beggar.
Bid Norton brew such ale as Shakespeare fancies
Did put Kit Sly into such lordly trances,
And let us meet there (for a fit of gladness)
And drink ourselves merry in sober sadness.

The play of *The Taming of the Shrew* differs entirely from Shakspeare's usual treatment of character and argument, in the basis for the providence of the *dénoûment*. It distinctly suggests some *sous-entendu* meaning, some satire, understood rather than to be explained.

Therefore it is hardly surprising that it is the only one of Shakspeare's plays which had what may be termed "a counterblast" written against it by a contemporary hand. I have noted my belief that John Fletcher was associated with the play as it appears in the First Folio, and his hand was therefore the most fit to point out the errors of the "morale" of the play. In his *Woman's Prize; or, the Tamer Tamed*, he shows that Petruchio had never really tamed Kate—that her temper remained the same—because he had never tamed *himself* and had remained a violent tyrant all his married life. He had worried Kate into her grave, and he seeks a new wife, Maria, who had always been meek and modest, and wins her from her father, for now *he* is rich. But the second wife, sympathetic with the wrongs of the first one, and warned by her fate, rebels at once in defence of her freedom. Bianca backs her up in her schemes; and the women of the town rise *en masse* to support her. Petruchio reproaches himself for marrying again:—

Was I not well warned . . .
And beaten to repentance in the days
Of my first doting?

When, as a ruse, he feigns to be dead, Maria pretends to weep, not for his loss, but

To think what this man was, to think how simple,
How far below a man, how far from reason,
From common understanding, and all gentry,
While he was living here, he walked among us.

The Epilogue tells men that

In their lives
They should not reign as tyrants o'er their wives . . .
it being aptly meant
To teach both sexes due equality,
And, as they stand bound, to love mutually.

Fletcher died in 1625, so this was written about the date of the First Folio. It was performed before the King and Queen on November 28th, 1633, as an old play, revised by Sir Henry Herbert, and "very well likt."

*Notes*

1. Cp. *King Lear*, III. iv. 49.
2. He had married, as his second wife, Anne, only daughter of Sir Thomas Lucy. But the partial testimony of sons-in-law is not always to be accepted.

# The Two Gentlemen of Verona

In this play there is a strange mixture of knowledge and ignorance, of care and negligence. The versification is often excellent, the allusions are learned and just; but the authour conveys his heroes by sea from one inland town to another in the same country; he places the Emperour at Milan and sends his young men to attend him, but never mentions him more; he makes Protheus, after an interview with Silvia, say he has only seen her picture, and, if we may credit the old copies, he has by mistaking places, left his scenery inextricable. The reason of all this confusion seems to be, that he took his story from a novel which he sometimes followed, and sometimes forsook, sometimes remembred, and sometimes forgot.

That this play is rightly attributed to Shakespeare, I have little doubt. If it be taken from him, to whom shall it be given? This question may be asked of all the disputed plays, except *Titus Andronicus*; and it will be found more credible, that Shakespeare might sometimes sink below his highest flights, than that any other should rise up to his lowest.—SAMUEL JOHNSON, *Notes on Shakespeare's Plays*, 1768

*The Two Gentlemen of Verona* paints the irresolution of love, and its infidelity to friendship, pleasantly enough, but in some degree superficially, we might almost say with the levity of mind which a passion suddenly entertained, and as suddenly given up, presupposes. The faithless lover is at last, on account of a very ambiguous repentance, forgiven without much difficulty by his first mistress; for the more serious part, the premeditated flight of the daughter of a Prince, the capture of her father along with herself by a band of robbers, of which one of the Two Gentlemen, the betrayed and banished friend, has been against his will elected captain: for all this a peaceful solution is soon found. It is as if the course of the world was obliged to accommodate itself to a transient youthful caprice, called love. Julia, who accompanies her faithless lover in the disguise of a page, is, as it were, a light sketch of the tender female figures of a Viola and an Imogen, who, in the latter pieces of Shakspeare, leave their home in similar disguises on love adventures, and to whom a peculiar charm is communicated by the display of the most virginly modesty in their hazardous and problematical situation.—AUGUST WILHELM SCHLEGEL, *Lectures on Dramatic Art and Literature*, 1809, tr. John Black

---

## MARY PRESTON
*"Two Gentlemen of Verona"*
*Studies in Shakspeare*
1869, pp. 84–102

Tennyson has done much for friendship. In that noble poem, *In Memoriam*, he has taught us that love cannot fill the place whence friendship is stricken down by death. Through many a year of prosperity this poet came, with his garland of verse, to lay it, an honored tribute, on the grave of his friend. But Shakspeare has done even more than the Poet-Laureate for that noble Something, that means all loyalty, all disinterestedness, all truth, and which we call Friendship. This Great Dramatist, not content with telling us *of* this virtue, has drawn, with no uncertain touch, its *every lineament*.

Friendship Shakspeare places upon a lofty column whose foundations are the solid rock, whose proportions are the lasting and unsullied marble. Love he traces as *merely* the sculptured ornament of the column, giving to it beauty, but not adding to its strength or its durability.

Shakspeare's Plays are very rich in illustrations of the friendships of women; in the play we now seek to study, he has dramatized and immortalized the friendship of "two gentlemen."

It is here necessary for us to consider, "What is a gentleman?" before we are capable of appreciating the friendship of such a character. A gentleman—it is the instinctive homage of the heart—is the highest style of man; because this honorary title is a degree no university can confer, no station secure, no riches purchase. "What, then, is a gentleman?" Shakspeare has answered the question. He has *defined* the character we recognize before and without definition. He has bequeathed to us a Valentine. Who can peruse this play without the conviction that in meeting "Valentine," we have met a gentleman? The most striking and obvious trait in Valentine is the exceeding *manliness* of the man. There is nothing puny or sickly even in his sentiment. There is a directness of action,—if I may so speak,—and a gallant frankness of spirit, that always addresses itself to the admiration of the beholder. Such a man is always popular without the care or the effort to be so. It is a necessary consequence of his openness of character; for all feel that in dealing with him there is no *darkness* to contend against. We see the man as he is; there is no hypocrite about him; and it is a pleasure to walk in the clear light of day. Valentine may be called the soul of honor. This word honor is often applied in a vague sense that amounts to no sense at all; but by honor I *mean* honesty in

trifles, truth in little matters, straightforwardness in ordinary as well as in great things,—perseverance in what a man considers *right* at any hazard or any cost; such honor is a man's shield, encompassing him in the hours of his temptation, his impenetrable armor in which he passes, unharmed by slander, through life; his epitaph, more lasting "than storied urn or animated bust," at death.

Valentine, then, is, in this high sense, an honorable man. He is also liberal, generous, confiding. Where he once trusts, he trusts forever, unless some shocking display of feeling dash the precious vase of trust into a thousand fragments. Valentine is ever courteous, without the mere parade which often hides from common notice a great want of courtesy. Valentine is a man capable of a love that knows no change, but loves on, until the fruition in another and a better world.

> *His* words are bonds, *his* oaths are oracles,
> *His* love sincere, *his* thoughts immaculate,
> *His* tears pure messages sent from his heart,
> *His* heart as far from fraud as earth from heaven.

Behold the gentleman, O man, and try yourself by this model, and then say, if you can, "I am a gentleman!"

Let us now notice the other principal character in this play. I prefer to speak of "Proteus" as the *susceptible gentleman*. I rather think that Shakspeare, in this instance, gives the title gentleman—as we all oftentimes do—as a matter of *mere ceremony*; as a counter, in the social exchange, *signifying nothing*. No one accepts these *indefinite applications of terms* as meaning anything *in particular*. When so used, we are flattering ourselves, rather than the *mis-named*, by the supposition that to us the man can only act as a gentleman. We are guilty, too, of the severest kind of sarcasm on all such occasions, and of giving a useful *hint* to the man of the importance of being a gentleman. Such men as Proteus are only gentlemen by courtesy. Let no Proteus suppose that Shakspeare would apply to him the title in its full significance.

With this *necessary* explanation, I attempt to trace out *the Proteus* outlines of character. The most remarkable trait in Proteus is the suffering he experiences over what may be called *too great a flow of feeling*. He is a man quite carried away by the variable tide of his emotions. He is never constant in love, in friendship, in business, in anything. And why is Proteus never constant? He does not hesitate to tell you the reason; for, strange hallucination of principle, he is proud of it,—*his feelings* won't admit of constancy. If, when the tide of his better feelings sets in, he would be

> constant, he were perfect, *that one error*
> Fills him with faults, makes him run through all
> sins.

The ebb of the tide of Proteus's emotion is so sudden, is so different from all charitable calculation, that he may be regarded almost as a being in the twilight of reason; and his friends, when they really know him, grow to regard him with a *curious* mixture of pity and of contempt. The danger of *relying* on the *susceptible gentleman* is, that you can never be *certain* of his *status* of feeling. If you are so fortunate as to launch your hopes on the stream when it seems to be following a clear and straight course, you may find too late the treachery of its waters. Suddenly, without any warning, it will turn from its peaceful bed and dash into some dark and devious direction. No trace will now be found of the placid waters, but in their stead the angry stream chafing against the rocks it has urged its way among.

Having given a general notion of the *Two Gentlemen of Verona*, I proceed to analyze the play, to see how far I am sustained in the opinions with which its *first* reading inspired me.

The *two* gentlemen—one only so by right of courtesy—are introduced to us as men *professing* for each other the warmest, the truest friendship. With Valentine it is not only profession; he is willing to *prove* his friendship by constancy, by devotion to all the true interests of Proteus. With Proteus, friendship, *like other emotions*, must depend *on the state of his feelings*; and these, as we have seen, are ever *fluctuating*. The *susceptible gentleman*, when we first meet him, is not only disguised as a friend, but he is also flaunting in the habiliments of love. A certain fair and faithful Julia has inspired Proteus with *a flow of love*. Valentine, who is at present "heart-whole and fancy-free," beholds in his friend's present character of lover much fuel for the flames of his gentlemanly wit and humor, though careful to restrain it within *friendly* bounds. Like other philosophers who have *not yet* been struck down with *the madness*, Valentine can *truly* moralize on *love:*—

> To be
> In love, where scorn is bought with groans; coy looks,
> With heart-sore sighs; one fading moment's mirth,
> With twenty watchful, weary, tedious nights;
> If haply won, perhaps a hapless gain;
> If lost, why then a glorious labor won:
> *However*, but a folly bought with wit,
> Or else, a wit by folly vanquished.

The sequel of Valentine's history teaches us the *practical use* of wise philosophy when Cupid takes his fatal aim.

The friends *part* through obedience to parental advice; Valentine, to prove his love theory in the Duke of Milan's court; Proteus, as he supposes, to follow the Julia flow of feeling which is now setting with a strong current. Julia is all faith and constancy, and judges of Proteus by herself. *She* never *doubts* the sincerity of his vows, *he* never suspects himself of lacking the determination to fulfil those vows; for *at present* he has every purpose of fulfilling them. But Proteus's father comes to the conclusion to send his son to where Valentine has gone, that the friends may together gather the instructions of a foreign city. The father of Proteus sees no reason for his son's remaining idle at home, and that son has never breathed *his Julia emotions* to parental ears. No. Proteus is secretive in his love-affairs; for he has a *sneaking* consciousness that he cannot trust to his feelings in them, therefore his wisdom teaches him to be *non-committal*. Proteus professes to Julia a wish that

> Our fathers would applaud our loves,
> To seal our happiness with their consents.

But Proteus, nevertheless, though there seems to be no reason for concealment, *does not* acquaint "our fathers" with the engagement; nay, such an *uncertain* man is Proteus, that, when his father tells him the resolve,—

> thou shalt spend some time
> With Valentinus in the Emperor's court,

Proteus lets go by the occasion for revealing the ties that fettered him to his native city. No. Just at *this crisis* Proteus is nervously apprehensive that his father may take "exception to his love." He asks "a day or two," to deliberate on the parental command. The father, seeing no occasion, and being informed of none, why his son should deliberate on such a natural request, and apparently aware of his son's *idiosyncrasy*, the father cuts off *Proteus's hesitation of* conduct with—

> Look, what thou want'st shall be sent after thee;
> No more of stay; *to-morrow thou must go.*

And now Proteus takes a farewell of Julia. Proteus's feelings on this occasion would put to blush many a truer and better man. He is so full of tenderness, of constancy, of

profession. He has such excellent *intentions*, so lover-like, Julia is persuaded that Proteus is a knight-errant of romance, *such chivalrous sentiment!* What a proud and trusting woman Julia is, to be sure; how natural she should be so, for *she believes in Proteus.*

While we have lingered over the *susceptible gentleman*, what change has come across our philosopher, our love-theorist, our scorner of Cupid, our jester at Love's follies? Valentine is still—it is *the habit* of the man—the model gentleman; but a change has come over him. What is it? Ah! Cupid, naughty boy, thou art always making mischief; thou delightest in making those who defy thee feel the incurable wound of thy arrow! Valentine is now thy victim, who was once thy railer and defier! The changes love effects, in those who become its captives, are so well set forth in the conversation of Valentine with his servant, Speed, that I transcribe it here for the edification of the reader.

*Val.*: But tell me, dost thou know my lady Silvia?
*Speed*: She that you gaze on so, as she sits at supper?
*Val.*: Hast thou observed that? even she I mean.
*Speed*: Why, sir, I know her not.
*Val.*: Dost thou know her by my gazing on her, and yet know'st her not?
*Speed*: Is she not hard-favor'd, sir?
*Val.*: Not so fair, boy, as well-favored.
*Speed*: Sir, I know that well enough.
*Val.*: What dost thou know?
*Speed*: That she is not so fair as (of you) well-favor'd.
*Val.*: I mean that her beauty is exquisite, but her favor infinite.
*Speed*: That's because the one is painted, and the other out of all count.
*Val.*: How painted? and how out of count?
*Speed*: Marry, sir, so painted to make her fair that no man counts of her beauty.
*Val.*: How esteemest thou me? I account of her beauty.
*Speed*: You never saw her since she was deformed.
*Val.*: How long hath she been deformed?
*Speed*: Ever since you loved her.
*Val.*: I have loved her ever since I saw her, and still I see her beautiful.
*Speed*: If you love her you cannot see her.
*Val.*: Why?
*Speed*: Because love is blind. Oh, that you had mine eyes, or your own had the lights they were wont to have, when you chid at Sir Proteus for going ungartered!
*Val.*: What should I see then?
*Speed*: You own present folly, and her passing deformity; for he, being in love, could not see to garter his hose; and you, being in love, cannot see to put on your hose.

The lady that has effected this change in the gentleman is worthy of such a heart. Silvia, however, is too beautiful, too amiable, too accomplished not to be the desired of others beside Valentine. There is a suitor of hers, favored by her father, a Sir Thurio, who is the cause of much jealousy and unhappy feeling in the gentleman. It is noteworthy, the high respect and chivalrous devotion which Shakspeare has made characteristics of a gentleman's love. The lady to whom Valentine offers himself, Valentine treats with all the *honourable manner* of a gentleman. He regards Silvia as

> a principality,
> *Sovereign* to all the creatures on the earth.

What a commentary on the modern style of courtship this play contains! Woman are now treated with a *freedom* of *attention* that has no sentiment of *respect in its manner*. There is, in social intercourse between gentlemen and ladies now, a *carelessness affected*, a familiarity maintained, that too often would be more appropriate in romping schoolchildren. I do not advocate stiffness or formality, but I do exclaim against too much freedom, too *great easiness*. There is a happy medium, even in social intercourse.

In all the knightly ardor of his new passion, Valentine does not lose or abate one jot or tittle of his friendship. It still burns, a clear, translucent flame, to cheer and bless with its mild lustre him who first lit the taper in his heart. Informed by the Duke, of Proteus's arrival, the heart of the gentleman throbs with pride and pleasure. Pride, at introducing such a friend as he conceives Proteus to be, to his new-found treasure; pleasure, at the thought of Proteus's sympathy in his love-affair. He gladly pours out his estimate of his friend, that the Duke and Silvia may welcome Proteus with the honors he regards due his friend. How proud and happy is Valentine to make known to each other the two most loved, most trusted; no breath of jealousy sullies Valentine's welcome and introduction of his friend. Besides, Valentine knows of Proteus's engagement to Julia, and would not degrade his friendship by a suspicion that Proteus might not keep it.

What could be baser than the betrayal of a friendship such as that which shone in Valentine? What could be viler than to be the repository of the treasures of a gentleman's love-secrets, and design to steal them for your own use? What could be meaner than the attempted rivalry of a confiding and devoted friend? What could be more unlike a gentleman than to break his sacred engagement to a lady? And yet Proteus is the man found low enough to execute such deeds! The *susceptible gentleman* cannot listen unmoved to Valentine's commendations of his lady-love or look without—well, I won't degrade the word love—envy on Silvia's attractions. Julia is not near to keep the flow of feeling in *her* direction. The *susceptible gentleman* is not given to the disagreeable task of putting a check on his emotions. No. They must run their course, despite love or friendship. He almost feels that he is not at all *responsible* for such vagaries. All that Valentine has been to Proteus, all that Proteus is in Valentine's estimation, cannot place the slightest check on the torrent of feeling that Proteus now allows to rush in the Silvia direction. All the vows that Proteus has made to Julia, all the love and confidence Julia has, and is lavishing upon him, cannot induce Proteus to make one great and worthy struggle against fickleness.

How *deceitful* is the *susceptible gentleman* during this *new rush of emotion*. He deliberately plans, or, rather, *yields* to the desire of supplanting his friend in Silvia's affections. To remove his friend out of his way, Proteus reveals his friend's plan of elopement to the Duke, who exiles him, on this account, from his court. He deceives Valentine, who esteems him as his ally; he deceives the Duke, who thinks these revelations were prompted by disinterested interest in his (the Duke's) affairs; he deceives Sir Thurio, whom he leads to regard him as anxious to make a match between him (Sir Thurio) and Silvia. But who dares say, the *susceptible gentleman* is *unprincipled*? No one; for if you were to state the case frankly to the susceptible gentleman, there is not a doubt that it would excite in him a rush of good feeling that would induce him to confess and mourn over the truth of your statement, and lead *you* to have a disagreeable sense of having done the susceptible gentleman some indefinable wrong. The susceptible gentleman is always *plausible*, and always able and willing to make all the amends for his injury consistent with his present flow of feeling. Therefore the susceptible gentleman is never without his

advocates and sympathizers. Oftentimes he feels himself, when doing most harm, the injured man. Such is his order of feeling.

Strange that weakness of principle should ever be dwelt upon with any other sense than contempt! Yet such is our nature, that if we think a man does not *design* to do wrong, but does it through momentary *impulse*, we sympathize with, we forgive him. Yes, the *susceptible* gentleman has his warm, devoted friends, though his absence of steady feeling, of control over himself, makes him incapable of friendship. It is noticeable—though often overlooked—that the *susceptible gentleman* is generally intensely selfish. Indeed, he could not be so *susceptible*, and have such *varied experiences*, if he were not selfish. The susceptible gentleman, through all the looseness of his sailing, keeps a pilot on the look-out for his personal safety and interests.

What a philosopher Proteus is, to convince himself of the propriety of his own actions. Hear him:

> To leave my Julia, shall I be forsworn;
> To love fair Silvia, shall I be forsworn;
> To wrong my friend, I shall be much forsworn;
> And even that power which gave me first my oath,
> Provokes me to this threefold perjury.
> Love bade me swear, and love bids me forswear;
> O sweet suggesting love, if thou hast sinned,
> Teach me, thy tempted subject, to excuse it.
> At first I did adore a twinkling star,
> But now I worship a celestial sun.
>
> . . .
>
> I will forget that Julia is alive,
> Remembering that my love to her is dead;
> And Valentine I'll hold an enemy,
> Aiming at Silvia as a sweeter friend.

It is, if we choose to be guided by our own inclination, quite possible to torture truth into an *apparent* complicity with falsehood. "A subtle traitor needs no sophister."

While Proteus is thus meditating perjury, and seeking to conceal its visage in the mask of words, a faithful and loving woman is planning to come to him, that—judging him by her own true self—she may comfort his heart in a strange place, with the presence, he vowed, most desired. Julia is not to be stopped,—by a doubt of her reception from Proteus, she *admits no doubts* of her lover,—for she thinks,

> A true, devoted pilgrim is not weary,
> To measure kingdoms with his feeble steps;
> Much less shall she, that hath love's wings to fly.

"No, my maid, you know not the heart of my Proteus, or you would not suggest a suspicion of his joy in welcoming me. He is perfection itself, and is incapable of fickleness. His vows are upon him, and my lover is a gentleman. I go to him assured of his love, confident of his glad welcome. The rapture I shall feel at our meeting will only be equalled by the ecstasy of my lover. His heart is calling for me; I obey the summons." With such feelings of delighted expectancy, Julia reaches Milan. What a shock must she experience; for in her disguise of a page, the very night of her arrival, Julia is an agonized witness of her lover's perjury. She hears that voice, whose music had swept across her heart and borne it away captive; she hears that voice murmuring of love to Silvia; speaking of Julia in terms calculated to drive her to desperation. Julia, however, controls herself. Her dream of giving a pleasant surprise to Proteus is over. She sees and feels herself to be a forgotten woman. Yet, with the strange inconsistency of the passion, Julia still loves the *susceptible gentleman*. Why such a woman, after such a revelation, should love such a man, is one of those mysteries of the heart even a Shakspeare has shown himself unable to fathom. Perhaps it is necessary to the existence of some women, to cling to what they have *once* loved, even if found unworthy; or, they feel the desolation of surrender would drive them into a revenge as awful as their loneliness! Whatever may be the reason of this life of love, when its hopes are dead, we can but acknowledge that such cases, if rare, are none the less genuine. The dramatist, then, in representing Julia as still attached to Proteus, after knowing his perfidy, is asking only our acknowledgment of a truth, an idiosyncrasy in human nature. Yes, Julia is willing, in her disguise of page,—assumed to protect herself from insult during her trip, without escort, to Milan,—Julia *is willing* to enter the service of Proteus, so disguised, and be his messenger to his new flame, so that she may be near him. So Julia comes to know Silvia, and to acknowledge the beauty of her character. For Silvia is no weak woman, to be swayed from constancy by the flatteries of a perjurer. She has given her heart to Valentine, and separation, entreaty, flattery, nothing can make her recall the gift. It is a great mistake to suppose that women are always *easily deceived*, or that they are never capable of exercising their own judgments, free from the influences by which their judgment is attempted to be clouded. A woman does not always, nay, very rarely, show all her knowledge. It would not be becoming in her to do so. It is enough if she checkmate what she sees deserves this fate. It is not necessary that she should proclaim on the housetops, or evince by her manner, her consciousness of all she knows. Silvia, then, though perfectly conscious of Proteus's perjury, though fully determined to check every lover-like advance on the part of Proteus, reveals neither to her father nor to any one the discoveries she has made in the *susceptible gentleman*. Silvia having conned the curious book of Proteus's heart, is fully determined to put no confidence in such a man's statements, in regard to the friend he has betrayed. When Proteus, to win Silvia's thoughts from Valentine, falsely informs her that "Valentine is dead," *the news* does not move Silvia, because she does not believe it; but to teach Proteus a lesson, Silvia quietly answers:

And so, suppose, am I; for in his grave,
Assure thyself, my love is buried.

Worried out, at last, with the disgraceful lovemaking of Proteus, Silvia determines to leave her home, under the escort of a gentleman—

Valiant, wise, pitiful, well-accomplished,

a Sir Eglamour, whose affections are buried in the grave of "a true love." Silvia, with this gentleman, determines to go to her injured and traduced lover. So Silvia reaches the woods, where she finds Valentine as the captain of a band of outlaws,—made officer by a cruel necessity, and with the intention of dignifying the office by restraining the band he commands from deeds of violence. To this wood Silvia comes, without her lover's knowledge. Banished, Valentine has felt no inclination for a city life when robbed of the only intercourse which is now most precious to him. Separated from the lady of his love, Valentine's grief—which is not fond of parade, being too true for show—is spent in nature's secluded retreats. Here, with no curious eye to note them, in these lonely woods, Valentine sheds the tears of true regret at the absence of his Silvia; here the moans of sincere love are uttered with the only sympathy near that is acceptable,—the sweet sympathies of nature.

Here can I [says Valentine] sit alone, unseen of any,
And to the nightingale's complaining notes,
Tune my distresses and record my woes.
O thou who dost inhabit in my breast,
Leave not the mansion so long tenantless,
Lest, growing ruinous, the building fall,
And leave no memory of what it was.

Silvia's flight is discovered by her father, and he sets out, as do Proteus and Julia, to find her. Proteus and Julia first meet with Silvia; and now Proteus determines to avail himself of Silvia's unprotected state, to make her his own. While he is endeavoring to persuade Silvia—who indignantly scorns him—to countenance his love-suit, Valentine has been the concealed and unhappy witness of the perjury of Proteus. Nothing but the evidence of his own senses could have persuaded Valentine that the man he called friend was not every inch a gentleman. His own eyes behold Proteus in his true colors. In an anguish of grief at his discovery, Valentine reveals himself.

*Now*, I dare not say,
I have one friend left; thou would'st disprove me.
Who should be trusted now, when one's right hand
Is perjur'd to the bosom? Proteus,
I am sorry I must never trust thee more,
But count the world a stranger for thy sake.
The private wound is deepest. O time, most curst
'Mongst all foes, that a friend should be the worst!

How shall Proteus *feel*, in the full view of friendship, wounded, bleeding, accusing? It creates in the *susceptible gentleman a contrite flow of emotion*. He expresses the deepest repentance for his villanies, though *we* have no reason to suppose such repentance was more lasting than "the early and the morning dew." How shall Valentine receive Proteus's apologies and penitence? He receives them as a gentleman always accepts the apology where it is the only recompense the offender can offer; nay, so *freely* does Valentine forgive at the view of the "shame" of Proteus, that his charity blots out the memory of injuries to friendship, and restores *the susceptible gentleman* to his old place in Valentine's heart. *The gentleman* feels a delicacy in accepting his own Silvia if it is to occasion Proteus any pain. No. His friend's happiness is dearer to Valentine than his own. Proteus shall have Silvia, and Valentine—

Will take up the burden of life again,
Saying only, It might have been!

And the *susceptible gentleman* seems quite willing to avail himself of the softening memories of friendship.

How Silvia would have agreed to *this friendly arrangement*, the dramatist has not found occasion to show; but, from her character, we can conjecture that she was not the description of woman to be immolated at a false shrine. At this crisis of Silvia's fate, Julia's love forces her to reveal herself as no page, but a forgotten lady. When Proteus finds "*this boy*" is Julia, he is overtaken with a rush of the old affection, so that he becomes again her lover, truly remarking:—

What is in Silvia's face, but I may spy
More fresh in Julia's with a constant eye.

So the curtain drops upon the "Two gentlemen of Verona" reunited in Friendship, with Love's rainbow spanning the heavens so lately dark and lowering.

# A Midsummer Night's Dream

There let Hymen oft appear
In saffron robe, with taper clear,
And pomp, and feast, and revelry,
With mask and antique pageantry;
Such sights as youthful poets dream
On summer eves by haunted stream.
Then to the well-trod stage anon,
If Jonson's learned sock be on,
Or sweetest Shakespeare, Fancy's child,
Warble his native wood-notes wild.

—JOHN MILTON, "L'Allegro," 1633

. . . and then to the King's Theatre, where we saw *Midsummer Night's Dream*, which I had never seen before, nor shall ever again, for it is the most insipid ridiculous play that ever I saw in my life. I saw, I confess, some good dancing and some handsome women, which was all my pleasure.—SAMUEL PEPYS, *Diary*, Sept. 29, 1662

*The Midsummer Night's Dream* and *The Tempest*, may be in so far compared together that in both the influence of a wonderful world of spirits is interwoven with the turmoil of human passions and with the farcical adventures of folly. *The Midsummer Night's Dream* is certainly an earlier production; but *The Tempest*, according to all appearance, was written in Shakspeare's later days: hence most critics, on the supposition that the poet must have continued to improve with increasing maturity of mind, have honoured the last piece with a marked preference. I cannot, however, altogether concur with them: the internal merit of these two works are, in my opinion, pretty nearly balanced, and a predilection for the one or the other can only be governed by personal taste. In profound and original characterization the superiority of *The Tempest* is obvious: as a whole we must always admire the masterly skill which he has here displayed in the economy of his means, and the dexterity with which he has disguised his preparations,—the scaffoldings for the wonderful aërial structure. In *The Midsummer Night's Dream*, on the other hand, there flows a luxuriant vein of the boldest and most fantastical invention; the most extraordinary combination of the most dissimilar ingredients seems to have been brought about without effort by some ingenious and lucky accident, and the colours are of such clear transparency that we think the whole of the variegated fabric may be blown away with a breath. The fairy world here described resembles those elegant pieces of arabesque, where little genii with butterfly wings rise, half embodied, above the flower-cups. Twilight, moonshine, dew, and spring perfumes, are the element of these tender spirits; they assist nature in embroidering her carpet with green leaves, many-coloured flowers, and glittering insects; in the human world they do but make sport childishly and waywardly with their beneficent or noxious influences. Their most violent rage dissolves in good-natured raillery; their passions, stripped of all earthly matter, are merely an ideal dream. To correspond with this, the loves of mortals are painted as a poetical enchantment, which, by a contrary enchantment, may be immediately suspended, and then renewed again. The different parts of the plot; the wedding of Theseus and Hippolyta, Oberon and Titania's quarrel, the flight of the two pair of lovers, and the theatrical manœuvres of the mechanics, are so lightly and happily interwoven that they seem necessary to each other for the formation of a whole. Oberon is desirous of relieving the lovers from their perplex-ities, but greatly adds to them through the mistakes of his minister, till he at last comes really to the aid of their fruitless amorous pain, their inconstancy and jealousy, and restores fidelity to its old rights. The extremes of fanciful and vulgar are united when the enchanted Titania awakes and falls in love with a coarse mechanic with an ass's head, who represents, or rather disfigures, the part of a tragical lover. The droll wonder of Bottom's transformation is merely the translation of a metaphor in its literal sense; but in his behaviour during the tender homage of the Fairy Queen we have an amusing proof how much the consciousness of such a head-dress heightens the effect of his usual folly. Theseus and Hippolyta are, as it were, a splendid frame for the picture; they take no part in the action, but surround it with a stately pomp. The discourse of the hero and his Amazon, as they course through the forest with their noisy hunting-train, works upon the imagination like the fresh breath of morning, before which the shapes of night disappear. Pyramus and Thisbe is not unmeaningly chosen as the grotesque play within the play; it is exactly like the pathetic part of the piece, a secret meeting of two lovers in the forest, and their separation by an unfortunate accident, and closes the whole with the most amusing parody.—AUGUST WILHELM SCHLEGEL, *Lectures on Dramatic Art and Literature*, 1809, tr. John Black

Bottom the Weaver is a character that has not had justice done him. He is the most romantic of mechanics. And what a list of companions he has—Quince the Carpenter, Snug the Joiner, Flute the Bellows-mender, Snout the Tinker, Starveling the Tailor; and then again, what a group of fairy attendants, Puck, Peaseblossom, Cobweb, Moth, and Mustard-seed! It has been observed that Shakespear's characters are constructed upon deep physiological principles; and there is something in this play which looks very like it. Bottom the Weaver, who takes the lead of

This crew of patches, rude mechanicals,
That work for bread upon Athenian stalls,

follows a sedentary trade, and he is accordingly represented as conceited, serious, and fantastical. He is ready to undertake any thing and every thing, as if it was as much a matter of course as the motion of his loom and shuttle. He is for playing the tyrant, the lover, the lady, the lion. 'He will roar that it shall do any man's heart good to hear him'; and this being objected to as improper, he still has a resource in his good opinion of himself, and 'will roar you an 'twere any nightingale.' Snug the Joiner is the moral man of the piece, who proceeds by measurement and discretion in all things. You see him with his rule and compasses in his hand. 'Have you the lion's part written? Pray you, if it be, give it me, for I am slow of study.'—'You may do it extempore,' says Quince, 'for it is nothing but roaring.' Starveling the Tailor keeps the peace, and objects to the lion and the drawn sword. 'I believe we must leave the killing out when all's done.' Starveling, however, does not start the objections himself, but seconds them when made by others, as if he had not spirit to express his fears without encouragement. It is too much to suppose all this intentional: but it very luckily falls out so. Nature includes all that is implied in the most subtle analytical distinctions; and the same distinctions will be found in Shakespear. Bottom, who is not only chief actor, but stage-manager for the occasion, has a device to obviate the danger of frightening the ladies: 'Write me a prologue, and let the prologue seem to say, we will do no harm with our swords, and that Pyramus is not killed indeed; and for better assurance, tell them that I, Pyramus, am not Pyramus, but Bottom the Weaver: this will put them out of fear.' Bottom seems to have understood the subject of dramatic illusion at least as well as any modern essayist. If our holiday mechanic rules the roast among his fellows, he is no less at home in his new character of an ass, 'with amiable cheeks, and fair large ears.' He instinctively acquires a most learned taste, and grows fastidious in the choice of dried peas and bottled hay. He is quite familiar with his new attendants, and assigns them their parts with all due gravity. 'Monsieur Cobweb, good Monsieur, get your weapon in your hand, and kill me a red-hipt humble bee on the top of a thistle, and, good Monsieur, bring me the honey-bag.' What an exact knowledge is here shewn of natural history!

Puck, or Robin Goodfellow, is the leader of the fairy band. He is the Ariel of the *Midsummer Night's Dream*; and yet as unlike as can be to the Ariel in *The Tempest*. No other poet could have made two such different characters out of the same fanciful materials and situations. Ariel is a minister of retribution, who is touched with the sense of pity at the woes he inflicts. Puck is a mad-cap sprite, full of wantonness and mischief, who laughs at those whom he misleads—'Lord, what fools these mortals be!' Ariel cleaves the air, and executes his mission with the zeal of a winged messenger; Puck is borne along on his fairy errand like the light and glittering gossamer before the breeze. He is, indeed, a most Epicurean little gentleman, dealing in quaint devices, and faring in dainty delights. Prospero and his world of spirits are a set of moralists: but with Oberon and his fairies we are launched at once into the empire of the butterflies. How beautifully is this race of beings contrasted with the men and women actors in the scene, by a single epithet which Titania gives to the latter, 'the human mortals!' It is astonishing that Shakespear should be considered, not only by foreigners, but by many of our own critics, as a gloomy and heavy writer, who painted nothing but 'gorgons and hydras, and chimeras dire.' His subtlety exceeds that of all other dramatic writers, insomuch that a celebrated person of the present day said that he regarded him rather as a metaphysician than a poet. His delicacy and sportive gaiety are infinite. In the *Midsummer Night's Dream* alone, we should imagine, there is more sweetness and beauty of description than in the whole range of French poetry put together. What we mean is this, that we will produce out of that single play ten passages, to which we do not think any ten passages in the works of the French poets can be opposed, displaying equal fancy and imagery. Shall we mention the remonstrance of Helena to Hermia, or Titania's description of her fairy train, or her disputes with Oberon about the Indian boy, or Puck's account of himself and his employments, or the Fairy Queen's exhortation to the elves to pay due attendance upon her favourite, Bottom; or Hippolita's description of a chace, or Theseus's answer? The two last are as heroical and spirited as the others are full of luscious tenderness. The reading of this play is like wandering in a grove by moonlight: the descriptions breathe a sweetness like odours thrown from beds of flowers.— WILLIAM HAZLITT, *"The Midsummer Night's Dream," Characters of Shakespear's Plays*, 1817

---

## G. G. GERVINUS
### *"Midsummer-Night's Dream"*
### *Shakespeare Commentaries*, tr. F. E. Bunnètt
### 1845

If *All's Well That Ends Well* be read immediately between *Love's Labour's Lost* and the *Midsummer-Night's Dream*, we feel that in the former the matured hand of the poet was at work, while the two other pieces stand in closer connection. The performance of the comic parts by the clowns affords a resemblance between the two pieces, but this resemblance appears still more plainly in the mode of diction. Apart from the fairy songs, in which Shakespeare, in a masterly manner, preserves the popular tone of the style which existed before him, the play bears prominently the stamp of the Italian school. The language—picturesque, descriptive, and florid with conceits—the too apparent alliterations, the doggrel passages which extend over the passionate and impressive scenes, and the old mythology so suited to the subject; all this places the piece in a close, or at least not remote relation, to *Love's Labour's Lost*. As in this play, the story and the original combination of the characters of ancient, religious, and historical legends with those of the popular Saxon myths, are the property and invention of the poet. As in *Love's Labour's Lost*, utterly unlike the characterisation which we have just seen in *All's Well That Ends Well*, the acting characters are distinguished only by a very general outline; the strongest distinction is that between the little pert Hermia, shrewish and irritable even at school, and the slender yielding Helena, distrustful and reproachful of herself; the distinction is less apparent between the upright open Lysander and the somewhat malicious and inconstant Demetrius. The period of the origin of the play—which like *Henry VIII.* and the *Tempest* may have been written in honour of the nuptials of some noble couple— is placed at about 1594 or 1596. The marriage of Theseus is the turning-point of the action of the piece, which comprises the clowns, fairies, and the common race of men. The piece is a masque, one of those dramas for special occasions appointed for private representation, which Ben Jonson especially brought to perfection. In England this species of drama has as little a law of its own as the historical drama; compared to the ordinary drama it exhibits, according to Halpin, an insensible transition, undistinguishable by definition. As in the historical drama, its distinction from the free drama almost entirely arises from the nature and the mass of the matter; so in the masque, it proceeds from the occasion of its origin, from its necessary reference to it, and from the allegorical elements which are introduced. These latter, it must be admitted, have given a peculiar stamp to the *Midsummer-Night's Dream* among the rest of Shakespeare's works.

Upon the most superficial reading we perceive that the actions in the *Midsummer-Night's Dream*, still more than the characters themselves, are treated quite differently to those in other plays of Shakespeare. The presence of an underlying motive—the great art and true magic wand of the poet—has here been completely disregarded. Instead of reasonable inducements, instead of natural impulses arising from character and circumstance, caprice is master here. We meet with a double pair, who are entangled in strange mistakes, the motives to which we, however, seek for in vain in the nature of the actors themselves. Demetrius, like Proteus in the *Two Gentlemen of Verona*, has left a bride, and, like Proteus, wooes the bride of his friend Lysander. This Lysander has fled with

Hermia to seek a spot where the law of Athens cannot pursue them. Secretly, we are told, they both steal away into the wood; Demetrius in fury follows them, and, impelled by love, Helena fastens herself like a burr upon the heels of the latter. Alike devoid of conscience, Hermia errs at first through want of due obedience to her father, and Demetrius through faithlessness to his betrothed Helena, Helena through treachery to her friend Hermia, and Lysander through mockery of his father-in-law. The strife in the first act, in which we cannot trace any distinct moral motives, is in the third act changed into a perfect confusion owing to influences of an entirely external character. In the fairy world a similar disorder exists between Oberon and Titania. The play of Pyramus and Thisbe, enacted by the honest citizens, forms a comic-tragic counterpart to the tragic-comic point of the plot, depicting two lovers, who behind their parents' backs 'think no scorn to woo by moonlight,' and through a mere accident come to a tragic end.

The human beings in the main plot of the piece are apparently impelled by mere amorous caprice; Demetrius is betrothed, then Helena pleases him no longer, he trifles with Hermia, and at the close he remembers this breach of faith only as the trifling of youth. External powers and not inward impulses and feelings appear as the cause of these amorous caprices. In the first place, the brain is heated by the warm season, the first night in May, the ghost-hour of the mystic powers; for even elsewhere Shakespeare occasionally calls a piece of folly the madness of a midsummer-day, or a dog-day's fever; and in the 98th sonnet he speaks of April as the time which puts 'the spirit of youth in everything,' making even the 'heavy Saturn laugh and leap with him.' Then Cupid, who appears in the background of the piece as a real character, misleading the judgment and blinding the eyes, takes delight in causing a frivolous breach of faith. And last of all we see the lovers completely in the hands of the fairies, who ensnare their senses and bring them into that tumult of confusion, the unravelling of which, like the entanglement itself, is to come from without. These delusions of blind passion, this jugglery of the senses during the sleep of reason, these changes of mind and errors of 'seething brains,' these actions without any higher centre of a mental and moral bearing, are compared, as it were, to a dream which unrolls before us with its fearful complications, and from which there is no deliverance but in awaking and in the recovery of consciousness.

The piece is called a *Midsummer-Night's Dream*; the Epilogue expresses satisfaction, if the spectator will regard the piece as a dream; for in a dream time and locality are obliterated; a certain twilight and dusk is spread over the whole; Oberon desires that all shall regard the matter as a dream, and so it is. Titania speaks of her adventure as a vision, Bottom of his metamorphosis as a dream; all the rest awake at last out of a sleep of weariness, and the events leave upon them the impression of a dream. The sober Theseus esteems their stories as nothing else than dreams and fantasies. Indeed these allusions in the play must have suggested to Coleridge and others the idea that the poet had intentionally aimed at letting the piece glide by as a dream. We only wonder that, with this opinion, they have not reached the inner kernel in which this intention of the poet really lies enshrined—an intention which has not only given a name to the piece, but has called forth as by magic a free poetic creation of the greatest value. For it is indeed to be expected from our poet, that such an intention on his side were not to be sought for in the mere shell. If this intention were only shown in those poetical externals, in that fragrant charm of rhythm and verse, in that harassing suspense, and in that dusky twilight, then this were but a shallow work of

superficial grace, by the sole use of which a poet like Shakespeare would never have dreamt of accomplishing anything worth the while.

We will now return to an examination of the play and its contents; and taking a higher and more commanding view, we will endeavour to reach the aim which Coleridge in truth only divined. We have already said that the play of amorous caprice proceeded from no inner impulse of the soul, but from external powers, from the influence of gods and fairies, among whom Cupid, the demon of the old mythology, only appears behind the scenes; while, on the other hand, the fairies, the spirits of later susperstition, occupy the main place upon the stage. If we look at the functions which the poet has committed to both, namely to the god of love and to the fairies, we find to our surprise that they are perfectly similar. The workings of each upon the passions of men are the same. The infidelity of Theseus towards his many forsaken ones—Ariadne, Æglé, Antiopa, and Perigenia—which according to the ancient myth, we should ascribe to Cupid and to the intoxication of sensuous love, are imputed in the *Midsummer-Night's Dream* to the elfin king. Even before the fairies appear in the play, Demetrius is prompted by the infatuation of blind love, and Puck expressly says that it is not he but Cupid who originated this madness of mortals; the same may be inferred also with Titania and the boy. The fairies pursue these errors still further, in the same manner as Cupid had begun them; they increase and heal them; the juice of a flower, Dian's bud, is employed to cure the perplexities of love in both Lysander and Titania; the juice of another flower (Cupid's) had caused them. This latter flower had received its wondrous power from a wound by Cupid's shaft. The power conveyed by the shaft was perceived by the elfin king, who knew how to use it; Oberon is closely initiated into the deepest secrets of the love-god, but not so his servant Puck.

The famous passage, in which Oberon orders Puck to fetch him this herb with its ensnaring charm, is as follows:

My gentle Puck, come hither; Thou remember'st
Since once I sat upon a promontory,
And heard a mermaid, on a dolphin's back,
Uttering such dulcet and harmonious breath,
That the rude sea grew civil at her song;
And certain stars shot madly from their spheres,
To hear the sea-maid's musick.
That very time I saw (*but thou could'st not*)
Flying between the cold moon and the earth,
Cupid all arm'd: a certain aim he took
At a fair vestal, throned by the west;
And loosed his love-shaft smartly from his bow,
As it should pierce a hundred thousand hearts:
But I might see young Cupid's fiery shaft
Quenched in the chaste beams of the wat'ry moon;
And the imperial vot'ress passed on,
In maiden meditation, fancy-free.
Yet marked I where the bolt of Cupid fell:
It fell upon a little western flower,—
Before milk-white; now purple with Love's wound,—
And maidens call it love-in-idleness.
Fetch me that flower.

This passage has recently, in the writings of the Shake-speare Society, received a spirited interpretation by Halpin (*Oberon's Vision*), which shows us that we can scarcely seek for too much in our poet; that even in the highest flight of his imagination, he never leaves the ground of reality; and that in every touch, however episodical it may appear, he ever inserts the profoundest allusions to his main subject. We know well that in the eyes of the dry critic this interpretation, though it has one firm basis of fact, has found little favour; to us this is not very conceivable: for every investigation has long proved how gladly this realistic poet maintained, in the smallest allusions as well as in the greatest designs, lively relations to the times and places round him; how in his freest tragic creations he loved to refer to historical circumstances, founding even the most foolish speeches and actions of his clowns, of his grave-diggers in *Hamlet*, or his patrols in *Much Ado about Nothing*, upon actual circumstances; and thus giving them by this very circumstance that value of indisputable truth to nature which distinguishes them so palpably beyond all other caricatures. Is it not natural that he should have been impelled to give to just such a sweet allegory as this the firmest possible basis of fact? To us, therefore, Halpin's interpretation of this passage is all the more unquestionable, as it gives a most definite purpose to the innermost spirit of the whole play. We must therefore, before we proceed further, first consider more narrowly this episodical narrative and its bearing upon the fundamental idea of the *Midsummer-Night's Dream*.

It has always been agreed that by the vestal, throned by the west, from whom Cupid's shaft glided off, Queen Elizabeth was intended; and the whole passage was in consequence esteemed as a delicate flattery of the maiden queen. But we see at once by this instance, that Shakespeare—extraordinary in this respect as in every other—knew how to make his courtly flatteries, of which he was on all occasions most sparing, subservient to the æsthetic or moral aims of his poetry, by the introduction of deeper poetic or moral bearings. It was thus with this passage, which has now received a much more extended interpretation. Cupid 'all armed' is referred to the Earl of Leicester's wooing of Elizabeth and to his great preparations at Kenilworth for this purpose (1575). From descriptions of these festivities (Gascoyne's *Princely Pleasures*, 1576, and Laneham's *Letter*, 1575), we know, that at the spectacles and fireworks which enlivened the rejoicings, a singing mermaid was introduced, swimming on smooth water upon a dolphin's back, amid shooting stars; these characteristics agree with those which Oberon specifies to Puck. The arrow aimed at the priestess of Diana, whose bud possesses the power of quenching love, and which had such force over Cupid's flower, rebounded. By the flower upon which it fell wounding, Halpin understands the Countess Lettice of Essex, with whom Leicester carried on a clandestine intercourse while her husband was absent in Ireland, who, apprised of the matter, returned in 1576, and was poisoned on the journey. The flower was milk-white, innocent, but purple with love's wound, which denoted her fall or the deeper blush of her husband's murder. The name is 'love in idleness,' which Halpin refers to the listlessness of her heart during the absence of her husband; for on other occasions also Shakespeare uses this popular denomination of the pansy, to denote a love which surprises and affects those who are indolent, unarmed, and devoid of all other feeling and aspiration. While Oberon declares to Puck that he marked the adventure, though the servant could not, the poet appears to denote the strict mystery which concealed this affair, and which might be known to him, because, as we may remember, the execution of his maternal relative, Edward Arden (1583), was closely connected with it; and because a son of that Lettice, the famous Robert Devereux, Earl of Essex, the favourite of Elizabeth, and subsequently the victim of her displeasure, was early a patron and protector of Shakespeare.

How significant then does this little allegorical episode become, which, even when regarded only as a poetic ornament, is full of grace and beauty! Whilst Spenser at that very time had extolled Elizabeth as the *Faerie Queen*, Shakespeare,

on the contrary, represents her rather as a being unapproachable by this world of fancy. His courtesy to the queen becomes transformed into a very serious meaning: for, contrasting with this insanity of love, emphasis is placed upon the other extreme, the victory of Diana over Cupid, of the mind over the body, of maiden contemplativeness over the jugglery of love; and even in other passages of the piece those are extolled as 'thrice blessed, that master so their blood, to undergo such maiden pilgrimage.' But with regard to the bearing of the passage upon the actual purport of the *Midsummer-Night's Dream*, the poet carries back the mind to a circumstance in real life, which, like an integral part, lies in close parallel with the story of the piece. More criminal and more dissolute acts, prompted by the blind passion of love, were at that time committed in reality than were ever represented in the drama. The ensnaring charm, embodied in a flower, has an effect upon the entanglements of the lovers in the play. And whatever this representation might lack in probability and psychological completeness (for the sweet allegory of the poet was not to be overburdened with too much of the prose of characterisation), the spectator with poetic faith may explain by the magic sap of the flower, or with pragmatic soberness may interpret by analogy with the actual circumstance which the poet has converted into this exquisite allegory.

But it is time that we should return from this digression. We have before said that the piece appears designed to be treated as a dream; not merely in outer form and colouring, but also in inner signification. The errors of that blind intoxication of the senses, which form the main point of the play, appear to us to be an allegorical picture of the errors of a life of dreams. Reason and consciousness are cast aside in that intoxicating passion as in a dream; Cupid's delight in breach of faith and Jove's merriment at the perjury of the lovers cause the actions of those who are in the power of the God of Love to appear almost as unaccountable as the sins which we commit in a dream. We find moreover that the actions and occupations of Cupid and of the fairies throughout the piece are interwoven or alternate. And this appears to us to confirm most forcibly the intention of the poet to compare allegorically the sensuous life of love with a dream-life; the exchange of functions between Cupid and the fairies is therefore the true poetic embodiment of this comparison. For the realm of dreams is assigned to Shakespeare's fairies; they are essentially nothing else than personified dream-gods, children of the fantasy, which, as Mercutio says, is not only the idle producer of dreams, but also of the caprices of superficial love.

Vaguely, as in a dream, this significance of the fairies rests in the ancient popular belief of the Teutonic races, and Shakespeare, with the instinctive touch of genius, has fashioned this idea into exquisite form. In German 'Alp' and 'Elfe' are the same; 'Alp' is universally applied in Germany to a dream-goblin (night-mare). The name of the fairy king Oberon is only Frenchified from Alberon or Alberich, a dwarfish elf, a figure early appearing in old German poems. The character of Puck, or, as he is properly called, Robin Goodfellow, is literally no other than our own *'guter Knecht Ruprecht;'* and it is curious that from this name in German the word 'Rüpel' is derived, the only one by which we can give the idea of the English *clown*, the very part which, in Shakespeare, Puck plays in the kingdom of the fairies. This belief in fairies was far more diffused through Scandinavia than through England; and again in Scotland and England it was far more actively developed than in Germany. Robin Goodfellow especially, of whom we hear in England as early as the thirteenth century, was a favourite in popular traditions, and to his name all the cunning tricks were imputed which we relate of Eulenspiegel and other nations of others. His *Mad Pranks and Merry Jests* were printed in 1628 in a popular book, which Thoms has recently prepared for his little blue library. Collier places the origin of the book at least forty years earlier, so that Shakespeare might have been acquainted with it. Unquestionably this is the main source of his fairy kingdom; the lyric parts of the *Midsummer-Night's Dream* are in tone and colour a perfect imitation of the songs contained in it. In this popular book Robin appears, although only in a passing manner, as the sender of the dreams; the fairies and Oberon, who is here his father, speak to him by dreams before he is received into their community. But that which Shakespeare thus received in the rough form of fragmentary popular belief he developed in his playful creation into a beautiful and regulated world. He here in a measure deserves the merit which Herodotus ascribes to Homer; as the Greek poet has created the great abode of the gods and its Olympic inhabitants, so Shakespeare has given form and place to the fairy kingdom, and with the natural creative power of genius he has breathed a soul into his merry little citizens, thus imparting a living centre to their nature and their office, their behaviour and their doings. He has given embodied form to the invisible and life to the dead, and has thus striven for the poet's greatest glory; and it seems as if it was not without consciousness of this his work that he wrote in a strain of self-reliance that passage in this very play:—

> The poet's eye, in a fine frenzy rolling,
> Doth glance from heaven to earth, from earth to
>     heaven;
> And as imagination bodies forth
> The forms of things unknown, the poet's pen
> Turns them to shapes, and gives to airy nothing
> A local habitation and a name.
> Such tricks hath strong imagination;
> That, if it would but apprehend some joy,
> It comprehends some bringer of that joy.

This he has here effected; he has clothed in bodily form those intangible phantoms, the bringers of dreams of provoking jugglery, of sweet soothing, and of tormenting raillery; and the task he has thus accomplished we shall only rightly estimate, when we have taken into account the severe design and inner congruity of this little world.

If it were Shakespeare's object expressly to remove from the fairies that dark ghost-like character (Act III. sc. 2), in which they appeared in Scandinavian and Scottish fable; if it were his desire to portray them as kindly beings in a merry and harmless relation to mortals; if he wished, in their essential office as bringers of dreams, to fashion them in their nature as personified dreams, he carried out this object in wonderful harmony both as regards their actions and their condition. The kingdom of the fairy beings is placed in the aromatic flower-scented Indies, in the land where mortals live in a half-dreamy state. From hence they come, 'following darkness,' as Puck says, 'like a dream.' Airy and swift, like the moon, they circle the earth; they avoid the sunlight without fearing it, and seek the darkness; they love the moon and dance in her beams; and above all they delight in the dusk and twilight, the very season for dreams, whether waking or asleep. They send and bring dreams to mortals; and we need only recall to mind the description of the fairies' midwife, Queen Mab, in *Romeo and Juliet*, a piece nearly of the same date with the *Midsummer-Night's Dream*, to discover that this is the charge essentially assigned to them, and the very means by which they influence mortals. The manner in which Shakespeare has fashioned their inner character in harmony with this outer function is full of profound thought. He depicts them as beings without delicate

feeling and without morality, just as in dreams we meet with no check to our tender sensations and are without moral impulse and responsibility. Careless and unscrupulous, they tempt mortals to infidelity; the effects of the mistakes which they have contrived make no impression on their minds; they feel no sympathy for the deep affliction of the lovers, but only delight and marvel over their mistakes and their foolish demeanour. The poet farther depicts his fairies as beings of no high intellectual development. Whoever attentively reads their parts will find that nowhere is reflection imparted to them. Only in one exception does Puck make a sentract remark upon the infidelity of man, and whoever has penetrated into the nature of these beings will immediately feel that it is out of harmony. They can make no direct inward impression upon mortals; their influence over the mind is not spiritual, but throughout material; it is effected by means of vision, metamorphosis, and imitation. Titania has no spiritual association with her friend, but mere delight in her beauty, her 'swimming gait,' and her powers of imitation. When she awakes from her vision there is no reflection: 'Methought I was enamoured of an ass,' she says. 'Oh how mine eyes do hate this visage now!' She is only affected by the idea of the actual and the visible. There is no scene of reconciliation with her husband; her resentment consists in separation, her reconciliation in a dance; there is no trace of reflection, no indication of feeling. Thus, to remind Puck of a past event no abstract date sufficed, but an accompanying indication, perceptible to the senses, was required. They are represented, these little gods, as natural souls, without the higher human capacities of minds, lords of a kingdom, not of reason and morality, but of imagination and ideas conveyed by the senses; and thus they are uniformly the vehicle of the fancy which produces the delusions of love and dreams. Their will, therefore, only extends to the corporeal. They lead a luxurious, merry life, given up to the pleasure of the senses; the secrets of nature and the powers of flowers and herbs are confided to them. To sleep in flowers, lulled with dances and songs, with the wings of painted butterflies to fan the moonbeams from their eyes, this is their pleasure; the gorgeous apparel of flowers and dewdrops is their joy. When Titania wishes to allure her beloved, she offers him honey, apricots, purple grapes, and dancing. This life of sense and nature is seasoned by the power of fancy and by desire after all that is most choice, most beautiful, and agreeable. They harmonise with nightingales and butterflies; they wage war with all ugly creatures, with hedgehogs, spiders, and bats; dancing, play, and song are their greatest pleasures; they steal lovely children, and substitute changelings; they torment decrepit old age, toothless gossips, aunts, and the awkward company of the players of Pyramus and Thisbe, but they love and recompense all that is pure and pretty. Thus was it of old in the popular traditions; their characteristic trait of favouring honesty among mortals and persecuting crime was certainly borrowed by Shakespeare from these traditions in the *Merry Wives of Windsor*, though not in this play. The sense of the beautiful is the one thing which elevates the fairies not only above the beasts but also above the ordinary mortal, when he is devoid of all fancy and uninfluenced by beauty. Thus, in the spirit of the fairies, in which this sense of the beautiful is so refined, it is intensely ludicrous that the elegant Titania should fal in love with an ass's head. The only pain which agitates these beings is jealousy, the desire of possessing the beautiful sooner than others; they shun the distorting quarrel; their steadfast aim and longing is for undisturbed enjoyment. But in this sweet jugglery they neither appear constant to mortals nor do they carry on intercourse among themselves in monotonous harmony. They are full also of wanton tricks and railleries, playing upon themselves and upon mortals, pranks which never hurt, but which often torment. This is especially the property of Puck, who "jests to Oberon," who is the "lob" at this court, a coarser goblin, represented with broom or threshing-flail, in a leathern dress, and with a dark countenance, a roguish but awkward fellow, skilful at all transformation, practised in wilful tricks, but also clumsy enough to make mistakes and blunders contrary to his intention.

We mortals are unable to form anything out of the richest treasure of the imagination without the aid of actual human circumstances and qualities. Thus, even in this case, it is not difficult to discover in society the types of human nature which Shakespeare deemed especially suitable as the original of his fairies. There are, particularly among women of the middle and upper ranks, natures which are not accessible to higher spiritual necessities, which take their way through life with no serious and profound reference to the principles of morality or to intellectual objects, yet with a decided inclination and qualification for all that is beautiful, agreeable, and graceful, though without being able to reach even here the higher attainments of art. They grasp readily as occasion offers all that is tangible; they are ready, dexterous, disposed for tricks and raillery, ever skilful at acting parts, at assuming appearances, at disguises and deceptions, seeking to give a stimulant to life only by festivities, pleasures, sport and jest. These light, agreeable, rallying, and sylph-like natures, who live from day to day and have no spiritual consciousness of a common object in life, whose existence is a playful dream, full of grace and embellishment, but never a life of higher aim, have been chosen by Shakespeare with singular tact as the originals from whose fixed characteristics he gave form and life to his airy fairies.

We can now readily perceive why, in this work, the "rude mechanicals" and clowns, and the company of actors with their burlesque comedy, are placed in such rude contrast to the tender and delicate play of the fairies. Prominence is given to both by the contrast afforded between the material and the aërial, between the awkward and the beautiful, between the utterly unimaginative and that which, itself fancy, is entirely woven out of fancy. The play acted by the clowns is, as it were, the reverse of the poet's own work, which demands all the spectator's reflective and imitative fancy to open to him this aërial world, whilst in the other nothing at all is left to the imagination of the spectator. The homely mechanics, who compose and act merely for gain, and for the sake of so many pence a day, the ignorant players, with hard hands and thick heads, whose unskilful art consists in learning their parts by heart, these men believe themselves obliged to represent Moon and Moonshine by name in order to render them evident; they supply the lack of side-scenes by persons, and all that should take place behind the scenes they explain by digressions. These rude doings are disturbed by the fairy chiefs with their utmost raillery, and the fantastical company of lovers mock at the performance. Theseus, however, draws quiet and thoughtful contemplation from these contrasts. He shrinks incredulously from the too-strange fables of love and its witchcraft; he enjoins that imagination should amend the play of the clowns, devoid as it is of all fancy. The real, that in this work of art has become "nothing," and the "airy nothing," which in the poet's hand has assumed this graceful form, are contrasted in the two extremes; in the centre is the intellectual man, who participates in both, who regards the one, namely, the stories of the lovers, the poets by nature, as art and poetry, and who receives the other, presented as art, only as a thanksworthy readiness to serve and as a simple offering.

It is the combination of these skilfully obtained contrasts into a whole which we especially admire in this work. The age subsequent to Shakespeare could not tolerate it, and divided it in twain. Thus sundered, the æsthetic fairy poetry and the burlesque caricature of the poet have made their own way. Yet in 1631 the *Midsummer-Night's Dream* appears to have been represented in its perfect form. We know that in this year it was acted at the bishop of Lincoln's house on a Sunday, and that a puritanical tribunal in consequence sentenced Bottom to sit for twelve hours in the porter's room belonging to the bishop's palace, wearing his ass's head. But even in the seventeenth century "the merry conceited humours of Bottom the weaver" were acted as a separate burlesque. The work was attributed to the actor Robert Cox, who, in the times of the civil wars, when the theatres were suppressed, wandered over the country, and, under cover of rope-dancing, provided the people thus depressed by religious hypocrisy with the enjoyment of small exhibitions, which he himself composed under the significant name of "drolls," and in which the stage returned as it were to the merry interludes of old. In the form in which Cox at this time produced the farce of Bottom, it was subsequently transplanted to Germany by our own Andreas Gryphius, the schoolmaster and pedant Squenz being the chief character. How expressive these burlesque parts of the piece must have been in Shakespeare's time to the public, who were acquainted with original drolleries of this kind, *we* now can scarcely imagine. Nor do we any longer understand how to perform them; the public at that time, on the contrary, had the types of the caricatured pageants in this play and in *Love's Labour's Lost* still existing among them.

On the other hand Shakespeare's fairy world became the source of a complete fairy literature. The kingdom of the fairies had indeed appeared, in the chivalric epics, many centuries before Shakespeare. The oldest Welsh tales and romances relate of the contact of mortals with this invisible world. The English of Shakespeare's time possessed a romance of this style written by Launfall, in a translation from the French. The romance of *Huon of Bordeaux* had been earlier (in 1570) translated by Lord Berners into English. From it, or from the popular book of *Robin Goodfellow*, Shakespeare may have borrowed the name of Oberon. From the reading of Ovid he probably gave to the fairy queen the name of Titania, while among his contemporaries, and even by Shakespeare, in *Romeo and Juliet*, she is called "Queen Mab." In those old chivalric romances, in Chaucer, in Spenser's allegorical *Faerie Queen*, the fairies are utterly different beings, without distinct character or office; they concur with the whole world of chivalry in the same monotonous description and want of character. But the Saxon fairy legends afforded Shakespeare a hold for renouncing the romantic art of the pastoral poets and for passing over to the rude popular taste of his fellow-countrymen. He could learn melodious language, descriptive art, the brilliancy of romantic pictures, and the sweetness of visionary images from Spenser's *Faerie Queen*; but he rejected his portrayal of this fairy world and grasped at the little pranks of Robin Goodfellow, where the simple faith of the people was preserved in pure and unassuming form. In a similar way in Germany, at the restoration of popular life at the time of the Reformation, the chivalric and romantic notions of the world of spirits were cast aside; men returned to popular belief, and we read nothing which reminds us so much of Shakespeare's fairy world as the theory of elementary spirits by our own Paracelsus. From the time that Shakespeare adopted the mysterious ideas of this mythology, and the homely expression of them in prose and verse, we may assert that the popular

Saxon taste became more and more predominant in him. In *Romeo and Juliet* and in the *Merchant of Venice* there is an evident leaning towards both sides, and necessarily so, as the poet is here still occupied upon subjects completely Italian. Working, moreover, at the same time upon historical subjects, settled the poet, as it were, fully in his native soil, and the delineation of the lower orders of the people in *Henry IV.* and *V.* shows that he felt at home there. From the period of these pieces we find no longer the conceit-style, the love of rhyme, the insertion of sonnets, and similar forms of the artificial lyric; and that characteristic delight in simple popular songs, which shows itself even here in the fairy choruses, takes the place of the discarded taste. The example given in Shakespeare's formation of the fairy world had, however, little effect. Lilly, Drayton, Ben Jonson, and other contemporaries and successors, took full possession of the fairy world for their poems, in part evidently influenced by Shakespeare, but none of them has understood how to follow him even upon the path already cleared. Among the many productions of this kind Drayton's "Nymphidia" is the most distinguished. The poem turns upon Oberon's jealousy of the fairy knight Pigwiggen; it paints the fury of the king with quixotic colouring, and treats of the combat between the two in the style of the chivalric romances, seeking, like them, its main charm in the descriptions of the little dwellings, implements, and weapons of the fairies. If we compare this with Shakespeare's magic creation, which derives its charm entirely from the reverent thoughtfulness with which the poet clings with his natural earnestness to popular legends, leaving intact this childlike belief and preserving its object undesecrated; if we compare the two together, we shall perceive most· clearly the immense distance at which our poet stood even from the best of his contemporaries.

We have frequently referred to the necessity of seeing Shakespeare's plays performed, in order to be able to estimate them fully, based as they are upon the joint effect of poetic and dramatic art. It will, therefore, be just to mention the representation which this most difficult of all theatrical tasks of a modern age has met with in all the great stages of Germany. And, that we may not be misunderstood, we will premise that, however strongly we insist upon this principle, we yet, in the present state of things, warn most decidedly against all overbold attempts at Shakespearian representation. If we would perform dramas in which such an independent position is assigned to the dramatic art as it is in these, we must before everything possess a histrionic art dependent and complete in itself. But this art has with us declined with poetic art, and amid the widely distracting concerns of the present time it is scarcely likely soon to revive. A rich, art-loving prince, endowed with feeling for the highest dramatic delights, and ready to make sacrifices on their behalf, could possibly effect much, were he to invite together to one place, during an annual holiday, the best artists from all theatres, and thus to re-cast the parts of a few of the Shakespearian pieces. Even then a profound judge of the poet must take the general management of the whole. If all this were done, a play like the *Midsummer-Night's Dream* might be at last attempted. This fairy play was produced upon the English stage when they had boys early trained for the

characters; without this proviso it is ridiculous to desire the representation of the most difficult parts, with powers utterly inappropriate. When a girl's high treble utters the part of Oberon, a character justly represented by painters with abundant beard, and possessing all the dignity of the calm ruler of this hovering world; when the rude goblin Puck is performed by an affected actress, when Titania and her suite appear in ball-costume, without beauty or dignity, for ever moving about in the hopping motion of the dancing chorus, in the most offensive ballet-fashion that modern unnaturalness has created —what then becomes of the sweet charm of these scenes and figures which should appear in pure aërial drapery, which in their sport should retain a certain elevated simplicity, and which in the affair between Titania and Bottom, far from unnecessarily pushing the awkward fellow forward as the principal figure, should understand how to place the ludicrous character at a modest distance, and to give the whole scene the quiet charm of a picture? If it be impossible to act these fairy forms at the present day, it is equally so with the clowns. The common nature of the mechanics when they are themselves is perhaps intelligible to our actors; but when they perform their work of art few actors of the present day possess the self-denial that would lead them to represent this most foolish of all follies with solemn importance, as if in thorough earnestness, instead of overdoing its exaggeration, self-complacently working by laughter and smiling at themselves. Unless this self-denial be observed, the first and greatest object of these scenes, that of exciting laughter, is inevitably lost. Lastly, the middle class of mortals introduced between the fairies and the clowns, the lovers driven about by bewildering delusions, what sensation do they excite, when we see them in the frenzy of passion through the wood in kid-gloves, in knightly dress, conversing after the manner of the refined world, devoid of all warmth, and without a breath of this charming poetry? How can knightly accoutrements suit Theseus, the kinsman of Hercules, and the Amazonian Hippolyta? Certain it is that in the fantastic play of an unlimited dream, from which time and place are effaced, these characters ought not to appear in the strict costume of Greek antiquity; but still less, while one fixed attire is avoided, should we pass over to the other extreme, and transport to Athens a knightly dress, and a guard of Swiss halberdiers. We can only compare with this mistake one equally great, that of adding a disturbing musical accompaniment, inopportunely impeding the rapid course of the action, and interrupting this work of fancy, this delicate and refined action, this ethereal dream, with a march of kettledrums and trumpets, just at the point where Theseus is expressing his thoughts as to the unsubstantial nature of these visions. And amid all these modern accompaniments, the simple balcony of the Shakespearian stage was retained, as if in respect to stage apparatus we were to return to those days! This simplicity moreover was combined with all the magnificence customary at the present day. Elements thus contradictory and thus injudiciously united, tasks thus beautiful and thus imperfectly discharged, must always make the friend of Shakespearian performances desire that, under existing circumstances, they were rather utterly renounced.

# Love's Labour's Lost

*Loves Labor Lost*, I once did see a Play,
Ycleped so, so called to my paine,
Which I to heare to my small Ioy did stay,
Giuing attendance on my froward Dame,
    My misgiuing minde presaging to me ill,
    Yet was I drawne to see it gainst my Will.

This *Play* no *Play*, but Plague was vnto me,
For there I lost the Loue I liked most:
And what to others seemde a Iest to be,
I, that (in earnest) found vnto my cost.
    To euery one (saue me) 'twas *Comicall*,
    Whilst *Tragick* like to me it did befall.

Each Actor plaid in cunning wise his part,
But chiefly Those entrapt in *Cupids* snare:
Yet All was fained, twas not from the hart,
They seemde to grieue, but yet they felt no care:
    T'was I that Griefe (indeed) did beare in brest,
    The others did but make a show in Iest.

Yet neither faining theirs, nor my meere Truth,
Could make her once so much as for to smile:
Whilst she (despite of pitie milde and ruth)
Did sit as skorning of my Woes the while.
    Thus did she sit to see LOVE lose his LOVE,
    Like hardned Rock that force nor power can moue.
      —ROBERT TOFTE, *The Months Minde of a*
        *Melancholy Lover*, 1598

I have sent and bene all thys morning huntyng for players Juglers & Such kind of Creaturs, but fynde them harde to finde, wherfore Leavinge notes for them to seeke me, burbage ys come, & Sayes ther ys no new playe that the quene ⟨Anne of Denmark⟩ hath not seene, but they have Revyved an olde one, Cawled *Loves Labore lost*, which for wytt & mirthe he sayes will please her excedingly. And Thys ys apointed to be playd to Morowe night at my Lord of Sowthamptons, unless yow send a wrytt to Remove the Corpus Cum Causa to your howse in strande. Burbage ys my messenger Ready attendying your pleasure.—WALTER COPE, Letter to Lord Viscount Cranborne, 1604

*Love's Labour Lost* is also numbered among the pieces of his youth. It is a humorsome display of frolic; a whole cornucopia of the most vivacious jokes is emptied into it. Youth is certainly perceivable in the lavish superfluity of labour in the execution: the unbroken succession of plays on words, and sallies of every description, hardly leave the spectator time to breathe; the sparkles of wit fly about in such profusion, that they resemble a blaze of fireworks; while the dialogue, for the most part, is in the same hurried style in which the passing masks at a carnival attempt to banter each other. The young king of Navarre, with three of his courtiers, has made a vow to pass three years in rigid retirement, and devote them to the study of wisdom; for that purpose he has banished all female society from his court, and imposed a penalty on the intercourse with women. But scarcely has he, in a pompous harangue, worthy of the most heroic achievements, announced this determination, when the daughter of the king of France appears at his court, in the name of her old and bed-ridden father, to demand the restitution of a province which he held in pledge. Compelled to give her audience, he falls immediately in love with her. Matters fare no better with his companions, who on their parts renew an old acquaintance with the princess's attendants. Each, in heart, is already false to his vow, without knowing that the wish is shared by his associates; they overhear one another, as they in turn confide their sorrows in a love-ditty to the solitary forest: every one jeers and confounds the one who follows him. Biron, who from the beginning was the most satirical among them, at last steps forth, and rallies the king and the two others, till the discovery of a love-letter forces him also to hang down his head. He extricates himself and his companions from their dilemma by ridiculing the folly of the broken vow, and, after a noble eulogy on women, invites them to swear new allegiance to the colours of love. This scene is inimitable, and the crowning beauty of the whole. The manner in which they afterwards prosecute their lovesuits in masks and disguise, and in which they are tricked and laughed at by the ladies, who are also masked and disguised, is, perhaps, spun out too long. It may be thought, too, that the poet, when he suddenly announces the death of the king of France, and makes the princess postpone her answer to the young prince's serious advances till the expiration of the period of her mourning, and impose, besides, a heavy penance on him for his levity, drops the proper comic tone. But the tone of raillery, which prevails throughout the piece, made it hardly possible to bring about a more satisfactory conclusion: after such extravagance, the characters could not return to sobriety, except under the presence of some foreign influence. The grotesque figures of Don Armado, a pompous fantastic Spaniard, a couple of pedants, and a clown, who between whiles contribute to the entertainment, are the creation of a whimsical imagination, and well adapted as foils for the wit of so vivacious a society.—AUGUST WILHELM SCHLEGEL, *Lectures on Dramatic Art and Literature*, 1809, tr. John Black

If we were to part with any of the author's comedies, it should be this. Yet we should be loth to part with Don Adriano de Armado, that mighty potentate of nonsense, or his page, that handful of wit; with Nathaniel the curate, or Holofernes the school-master, and their dispute after dinner on 'the golden cadences of poesy'; with Costard the clown, or Dull the constable. Biron is too accomplished a character to be lost to the world, and yet he could not appear without his fellow courtiers and the king: and if we were to leave out the ladies, the gentlemen would have no mistresses. So that we believe we may let the whole play stand as it is, and we shall hardly venture to 'set a mark of reprobation on it.' Still we have some objections to the style, which we think savours more of the pedantic spirit of Shakespear's time than of his own genius; more of controversial divinity, and the logic of Peter Lombard, than of the inspiration of the Muse. It transports us quite as much to the manners of the court, and the quirks of courts of law, as to the scenes of nature or the fairy-land of his own imagination. Shakespear has set himself to imitate the tone of polite conversation then prevailing among the fair, the witty, and the learned, and he has imitated it but too faithfully. It is as if the hand of Titian had been employed to give grace to the curls of a full-bottomed periwig, or Raphael had attempted to give expression to the tapestry figures in the House of Lords.—WILLIAM HAZLITT, *"Love's Labour's Lost," Characters of Shakespear's Plays*, 1817

SAMUEL TAYLOR COLERIDGE
From *"Love's Labour's Lost"*
*Shakspeare, with Introductory Remarks
on Poetry, the Drama, and the Stage*
1818

The characters in this play are either impersonated out of Shakspeare's own multiformity by imaginative self-position, or out of such as a country town and a schoolboy's observation might supply,—the curate, the schoolmaster, the Armado, (who even in my time was not extinct in the cheaper inns of North Wales) and so on. The satire is chiefly on follies of words. Biron and Rosaline are evidently the pre-existent state of Benedict and Beatrice, and so, perhaps, is Boyet of Lafeu, and Costard of the Tapster in *Measure for Measure*; and the frequency of the rhymes, the sweetness as well as the smoothness of the metre, and the number of acute and fancifully illustrated aphorisms, are all as they ought to be in a poet's youth. True genius begins by generalizing and condensing; it ends in realizing and expanding. It first collects the seeds.

Yet if this juvenile drama had been the only one extant of our Shakspeare, and we possessed the tradition only of his riper works, or accounts of them in writers who had not even mentioned this play,—how many of Shakspeare's characteristic features might we not still have discovered in *Love's Labour's Lost*, though as in a portrait taken of him in his boyhood.

I can never sufficiently admire the wonderful activity of thought throughout the whole of the first scene of the play, rendered natural, as it is, by the choice of the characters, and the whimsical determination on which the drama is founded. A whimsical determination certainly;—yet not altogether so very improbable to those who are conversant in the history of the middle ages, with their Courts of Love, and all that lighter drapery of chivalry, which engaged even mighty kings with a sort of serio-comic interest, and may well be supposed to have occupied more completely the smaller princes, at a time when the noble's or prince's court contained the only theatre of the domain or principality. This sort of story, too, was admirably suited to Shakspeare's times, when the English court was still the foster-mother of the state and the muses; and when, in consequence, the courtiers, and men of rank and fashion, affected a display of wit, point, and sententious observation, that would be deemed intolerable at present,—but in which a hundred years of controversy, involving every great political, and every dear domestic, interest, had trained all but the lowest classes to participate. Add to this the very style of the sermons of the time, and the eagerness of the Protestants to distinguish themselves by long and frequent preaching, and it will be found that, from the reign of Henry VIII. to the abdication of James II. no country ever received such a national education as England.

Hence the comic matter chosen in the first instance is a ridiculous imitation or apery of this constant striving after logical precision, and subtle opposition of thoughts, together with a making the most of every conception or image, by expressing it under the least expected property belonging to it, and this, again, rendered specially absurd by being applied to the most current subjects and occurrences. The phrases and modes of combination in argument were caught by the most ignorant from the custom of the age, and their ridiculous misapplication of them is most amusingly exhibited in Costard; whilst examples suited only to the gravest propositions and

impersonations, or apostrophes to abstract thoughts impersonated, which are in fact the natural language only of the most vehement agitations of the mind, are adopted by the coxcombry of Armado as mere artifices of ornament.

The same kind of intellectual action is exhibited in a more serious and elevated strain in many other parts of this play. Biron's speech at the end of the fourth act is an excellent specimen of it. It is logic clothed in rhetoric;—but observe how Shakspeare, in his two-fold being of poet and philosopher, avails himself of it to convey profound truths in the most lively images,—the whole remaining faithful to the character supposed to utter the lines, and the expressions themselves constituting a further developement of that character:

Other slow arts entirely keep the brain:
And therefore finding barren practisers,
Scarce shew a harvest of their heavy toil:
But love, first learned in a lady's eyes,
Lives not alone immured in the brain;
But, with the motion of all elements,
Courses as swift as thought in every power;
And gives to every power a double power,
Above their functions and their offices.
It adds a precious seeing to the eye,
A lover's eyes will gaze an eagle blind;
A lover's ear will hear the lowest sound,
When the suspicious tread of theft is stopp'd:
Love's feeling is more soft and sensible,
Than are the tender horns of cockled snails;
Love's tongue proves dainty Bacchus gross in taste;
For valour, is not love a Hercules,
Still climbing trees in the Hesperides?
Subtle as Sphinx; as sweet and musical,
As bright Apollo's lute, strung with his hair;
And when love speaks, the voice of all the gods
Makes heaven drowsy with the harmony.
Never durst poet touch a pen to write,
Until his ink were temper'd with love's sighs;
O, then his lines would ravish savage ears,
And plant in. tyrants mild humility.
From women's eyes this doctrine I derive:
They sparkle still the right Promethean fire;
They are the books, the arts, the academes,
That shew, contain, and nourish all the world;
Else, none at all in aught proves excellent;
Then fools you were these women to forswear;
Or, keeping what is sworn, you will prove fools.
For wisdom's sake, a word that all men love;
Or for love's sake, a word that loves all men;
Or for men's sake, the authors of these women;
Or women's sake, by whom we men are men;
Let us once lose our oaths, to find ourselves,
Or else we lose ourselves to keep our oaths:
It is religion, to be thus forsworn:
For charity itself fulfills the law:
And who can sever love from charity?

This is quite a study;—sometimes you see this youthful god of poetry connecting disparate thoughts purely by means of resemblances in the words expressing them,—a thing in character in lighter comedy, especially of that kind in which Shakspeare delights, namely, the purposed display of wit, though sometimes, too, disfiguring his graver scenes;—but more often you may see him doubling the natural connection or order of logical consequence in the thoughts by the introduction of an artificial and sought for resemblance in the words, as, for instance, in the third line of the play,

And then grace us in the disgrace of death;
this being a figure often having its force and propriety, as

justified by the law of passion, which, inducing in the mind an unusual activity, seeks for means to waste its superfluity,—when in the highest degree—in lyric repetitions and sublime tautology—(*at her feet he bowed, he fell, he lay down; at her feet he bowed, he fell; where he bowed, there he fell down dead*),—and, in lower degrees, in making the words themselves the subjects and materials of that surplus action, and for the same cause that agitates our limbs, and forces our very gestures into a tempest in states of high excitement.

The mere style of narration in *Love's Labour's Lost*, like that of Ægeon in the first scene of the *Comedy of Errors*, and of the Captain in the second scene of *Macbeth*, seems imitated with its defects and its beauties from Sir Philip Sidney; whose *Arcadia*, though not then published, was already well known in manuscript copies, and could hardly have escaped the notice and admiration of Shakspeare as the friend and client of the Earl of Southampton. The chief defect consists in the parentheses and parenthetic thoughts and descriptions, suited neither to the passion of the speaker, nor the purpose of the person to whom the information is to be given, but manifestly betraying the author himself,—not by way of continuous undersong, but—palpably, and so as to show themselves addressed to the general reader. However, it is not unimportant to notice how strong as presumption the diction and allusions of this play afford, that, though Shakspeare's acquirements in the dead languages might not be such as we suppose in a learned education, his habits had, nevertheless, been scholastic, and those of a student. For a young author's first work almost always bespeaks his recent pursuits, and his first observations of life are either drawn from the immediate employments of his youth, and from the characters and images most deeply impressed on his mind in the situations in which those employments had placed him;—or else they are fixed on such objects and occurrences in the world, as are easily connected with, and seem to bear upon, his studies and the hitherto exclusive subjects of his meditation. Just as Ben Jonson, who applied himself to the drama after having served in Flanders, fills his earliest plays with true or pretended soldiers, the wrongs and neglects of the former, and the absurd boasts and knavery of their counterfeits. So Lessing's first comedies are placed in the universities, and consist of events and characters conceivable in an academic life.

## WALTER PATER
### *"Love's Labours Lost"* (1878)
### *Appreciations*
### 1889

Love's *Labours Lost* is one of the earliest of Shakespeare's dramas, and has many of the peculiarities of his poems, which are also the work of his earlier life. The opening speech of the king on the immortality of fame—on the triumph of fame over death—and the nobler parts of Biron, display something of the monumental style of Shakespeare's Sonnets, and are not without their conceits of thought and expression. This connexion of *Love's Labours Lost* with Shakespeare's poems is further enforced by the actual insertion in it of three sonnets and a faultless song; which, in accordance with his practice in other plays, are inwoven into the argument of the piece and, like the golden ornaments of a fair woman, give it a peculiar air of distinction. There is merriment in it also, with choice illustrations of both wit and humour; a laughter, often exquisite, ringing, if faintly, yet as genuine laughter still, though sometimes sinking into mere burlesque, which has not

lasted quite so well. And Shakespeare brings a serious effect out of the trifling of his characters. A dainty love-making is interchanged with the more cumbrous play: below the many artifices of Biron's amorous speeches we may trace sometimes the "unutterable longing;" and the lines in which Katherine describes the blighting through love of her younger sister are one of the most touching things in older literature.[1] Again, how many echoes seem awakened by those strange words, actually said in jest!—"The sweet war-man (Hector of Troy) is dead and rotten; sweet chucks, beat not the bones of the buried: when he breathed, he was a man!"—words which may remind us of Shakespeare's own epitaph. In the last scene, an ingenious turn is given to the action, so that the piece does not conclude after the manner of other comedies.—

Our wooing doth not end like an old play;
Jack hath not Jill:

and Shakespeare strikes a passionate note across it at last, in the entrance of the messenger, who announces to the princess that the king her father is suddenly dead.

The merely dramatic interest of the piece is slight enough; only just sufficient, indeed, to form the vehicle of its wit and poetry. The scene—a park of the King of Navarre—is unaltered throughout; and the unity of the play is not so much the unity of a drama as that of a series of pictorial groups, in which the same figures reappear, in different combinations but on the same background. It is as if Shakespeare had intended to bind together, by some inventive conceit, the devices of an ancient tapestry, and give voices to its figures. On one side, a fair palace; on the other, the tents of the Princess of France, who has come on an embassy from her father to the King of Navarre; in the midst, a wide space of smooth grass. The same personages are combined over and over again into a series of gallant scenes—the princess, the three masked ladies, the quaint, pedantic king; one of those amiable kings men have never loved enough, whose serious occupation with the things of the mind seems, by contrast with the more usual forms of kingship, like frivolity or play. Some of the figures are grotesque merely, and all the male ones at least, a little fantastic. Certain objects reappearing from scene to scene—love-letters crammed with verses to the margin, and lovers' toys—hint obscurely at some story of intrigue. Between these groups, on a smaller scale, come the slighter and more homely episodes, with Sir Nathaniel the curate, the country-maid Jaquenetta, Moth or Mote the elfin-page, with Hiems and Ver, who recite "the dialogue that the two learned men have compiled in praise of the owl and the cuckoo." The ladies are lodged in tents, because the king, like the princess of the modern poet's fancy, has taken a vow

To make his court a little Academe,

and for three years' space no woman may come within a mile of it; and the play shows how this artificial attempt was broken through. For the king and his three fellow-scholars are of course soon forsworn, and turn to writing sonnets, each to his chosen lady. These fellow-scholars of the king—"quaint votaries of science" at first, afterwards "affection's men-at-arms"—three youthful knights, gallant, amorous, chivalrous, but also a little affected, sporting always a curious foppery of language, are, throughout, the leading figures in the foreground; one of them, in particular, being more carefully depicted than the others, and in himself very noticeable—a portrait with somewhat puzzling manner and expression, which at once catches the eye irresistibly and keeps it fixed.

Play is often that about which people are most serious; and the humourist may observe how, under all love of playthings, there is almost always hidden an appreciation of something really engaging and delightful. This is true always of the toys of children: it is often true of the playthings of grown-up people, their vanities, their fopperies even, their lighter loves; the cynic would add their pursuit of fame. Certainly, this is true without exception of the playthings of a past age, which to those who succeed it are always full of a pensive interest—old manners, old dresses, old houses. For what is called fashion in these matters occupies, in each age, much of the care of many of the most discerning people, furnishing them with a kind of mirror of their real inward refinements, and their capacity for selection. Such modes or fashions are, at their best, an example of the artistic predominance of form over matter; of the manner of the doing of it over the thing done; and have a beauty of their own. It is so with that old euphuism of the Elizabethan age—that pride of dainty language and curious expression, which it is very easy to ridicule, which often made itself ridiculous, but which had below in a real sense of fitness and nicety; and which, as we see in this very play, and still more clearly in the Sonnets, had some fascination for the young Shakespeare himself. It is this foppery of delicate language, this fashionable plaything of his time, with which Shakespeare is occupied in *Love's Labours Lost*. He shows us the manner in all its stages; passing from the grotesque and vulgar pedantry of Holofernes, through the extravagant but polished caricature of Armado, to become the peculiar characteristic of a real though still quaint poetry in Biron himself, who is still chargeable even at his best with just a little affectation. As Shakespeare laughs broadly at it in Holofernes or Armado, so he is the analyst of its curious charm in Biron; and this analysis involves a delicate raillery by Shakespeare himself at his own chosen manner.

This "foppery" of Shakespeare's day had, then, its really delightful side, a quality in no sense "affected," by which it satisfies a real instinct in our minds—the fancy so many of us have for an exquisite and curious skill in the use of words. Biron is the perfect flower of this manner:

A man of fire-new words, fashion's own knight:

—as he describes Armado, in terms which are really applicable to himself. In him this manner blends with a true gallantry of nature, and an affectionate complaisance and grace. He has at times some of its extravagance or caricature also, but the shades of expression by which he passes from this to the "golden cadence" of Shakespeare's own most characteristic verse, are so fine, that it is sometimes difficult to trace them. What is a vulgarity in Holofernes, and a caricature in Armado, refines itself with him into the expression of a nature truly and inwardly bent upon a form of delicate perfection, and is accompanied by a real insight into the laws which determine what is exquisite in language, and their root in the nature of things. He can appreciate quite the opposite style—

In russet yeas, and honest kersey noes;

he knows the first law of pathos, that

Honest plain words best suit the ear of grief.

He delights in his own rapidity of intuition; and, in harmony with the half-sensuous philosophy of the Sonnets, exalts, a

little scornfully, in many memorable expressions, the judgment of the senses, above all slower, more toilsome means of knowledge, scorning some who fail to see things only because they are so clear:

So ere you find where light in darkness lies,
Your light grows dark by losing of your eyes:

as with some German commentators on Shakespeare. Appealing always to actual sensation from men's affected theories, he might seem to despise learning; as, indeed, he has taken up his deep studies partly in sport, and demands always the profit of learning in renewed enjoyment. Yet he surprises us from time to time by intuitions which could come only from a deep experience and power of observation; and men listen to him, old and young, in spite of themselves. He is quickly impressible to the slightest clouding of the spirits in social intercourse, and has his moments of extreme seriousness: his trial-task may well be, as Rosaline puts it—

To enforce the pained impotent to smile.

But still, through all, he is true to his chosen manner: that gloss of dainty language is a second nature with him: even at his best he is not without a certain artifice: the trick of playing on words never deserts him; and Shakespeare, in whose own genius there is an element of this very quality, shows us in this graceful, and, as it seems, studied, portrait, his enjoyment of it.

As happens with every true dramatist, Shakespeare is for the most part hidden behind the persons of his creation. Yet there are certain of his characters in which we feel that there is something of self-portraiture. And it is not so much in his grander, more subtle and ingenious creations that we feel this—in *Hamlet* and *King Lear*—as in those slighter and more spontaneously developed figures, who, while far from playing principal parts, are yet distinguished by a peculiar happiness and delicate ease in the drawing of them; figures which possess, above all, that winning attractiveness which there is no man but would willingly exercise, and which resemble those works of art which, though not meant to be very great or imposing, are yet wrought of the choicest material. Mercutio, in *Romeo and Juliet*, belongs to this group of Shakespeare's characters—versatile, mercurial people, such as make good actors, and in whom the

Nimble spirits of the arteries,

the finer but still merely animal elements of great wit, predominate. A careful delineation of minor, yet expressive traits seems to mark them out as the characters of his predilection; and it is hard not to identify him with these more than with others. Biron, in *Love's Labours Lost*, is perhaps the most striking member of this group. In this character, which is never quite in touch, never quite on a perfect level of understanding, with the other persons of the play, we see, perhaps, a reflex of Shakespeare himself, when he had just become able to stand aside from and estimate the first period of his poetry.

*Notes*

1. Act V. Scene II.

# The Merchant of Venice

The *Merchant of Venice* is one of Shakspeare's most perfect works: popular to an extraordinary degree, and calculated to produce the most powerful effect on the stage, and at the same time a wonder of ingenuity and art for the reflecting critic. Shylock, the Jew, is one of the inimitable masterpieces of characterization which are to be found only in Shakspeare. It is easy for both poet and player to exhibit a caricature of national sentiments, modes of speaking, and gestures. Shylock, however, is everything but a common Jew: he possesses a strongly-marked and original individuality, and yet we perceive a light touch of Judaism in everything he says or does. We almost fancy we can hear a light whisper of the Jewish accent even in the written words, such as we sometimes still find in the higher classes, notwithstanding their social refinement. In tranquil moments, all that is foreign to the European blood and Christian sentiments is less perceptible, but in passion the national stamp comes out more strongly marked. All these inimitable niceties the finished art of a great actor can alone properly express. Shylock is a man of information, in his own way, even a thinker, only he has not discovered the region where human feelings dwell; his morality is founded on the disbelief in goodness and magnanimity. The desire to avenge the wrongs and indignities heaped upon his nation is, after avarice, his strongest spring of action. His hate is naturally directed chiefly against those Christians who are actuated by truly Christian sentiments: a disinterested love of our neighbour seems to him the most unrelenting persecution of the Jews. The letter of the law is his idol; he refuses to lend an ear to the voice of mercy, which, from the mouth of Portia, speaks to him with heavenly eloquence: he insists on rigid and inflexible justice, and at last it recoils on his own head: Thus he becomes a symbol of the general history of his unfortunate nation. The melancholy and self-sacrificing magnanimity of Antonio is affectingly sublime. Like a princely merchant, he is surrounded with a whole train of noble friends. The contrast which this forms to the selfish cruelty of the usurer Shylock was necessary to redeem the honour of human nature. The danger which almost to the close of the fourth act, hangs over Antonio, and which the imagination is almost afraid to approach, would fill the mind with too painful anxiety, if the poet did not also provide for its recreation and diversion. This is effected in an especial manner by the scenes at Portia's country-seat, which transport the spectator into quite another world. And yet they are closely connected with the main business by the chain of cause and effect: Bassanio's preparation for his courtship are the cause of Antonio's subscribing the dangerous bond; and Portia again, by the counsel and advice of her uncle, a famous lawyer, effects the safety of her lover's friend. But the relations of the dramatic composition are the while admirably observed in yet another respect. The trail between Shylock and Antonio is indeed recorded as being a real event, still, for all that, it must ever remain an unheard-of and singular case. Shakspeare has therefore associated it with a love intrigue not less extraordinary: the one consequently is rendered natural and probable by means of the other. A rich, beautiful and clever heiress, who can only be won by the solving the riddle— the locked caskets—the foreign princes, who come to try the venture—all this powerfully excites the imagination with the splendour of an olden tale of marvels. The two scenes in which, first the Prince of Morocco, in the language of Eastern hyperbole, and then the self-conceited Prince of Arragon, make their choice among the caskets, serve merely to raise our curiosity, and give employment to our wits; but on the third, where the two lovers stand trembling before the inevitable choice, which in one moment must unite or separate them for ever, Shakspeare has lavished all the charms of feeling—all the magic of poesy. We share in the rapture of Portia and Bassanio at the fortunate choice: we easily conceive why they are so fond of each other, for they are both most deserving of love. The judgment scene, with which the fourth act is occupied, is in itself a perfect drama, concentrating in itself the interest of the whole. The knot is now untied, and according to the common ideas of theatrical satisfaction, the curtain ought to drop. But the poet was unwilling to dismiss his audience with the gloomy impressions which Antonio's acquittal, effected with so much difficulty, and contrary to all expectation, and the condemnation of Shylock, were calculated to leave behind them; he has therefore added the fifth act by way of a musical afterlude in the piece itself. The episode of Jessica, the fugitive daughter of the Jew, in whom Shakspeare has contrived to throw a veil of sweetness over the national features, and the artifice by which Portia and her companion are enabled to rally their newly-married husbands, supply him with the necessary materials. The scene opens with the playful prattling of two lovers in a summer evening; it is followed by soft music, and a rapturous eulogy on this powerful disposer of the human mind and the world; the principal characters then make their appearance, and after a simulated quarrel, which is gracefully maintained, the whole end with the most exhilarating mirth.—AUGUST WILHELM SCHLEGEL, *Lectures on Dramatic Art and Literature*, 1809, tr. John Black

This is a play that in spite of the change of manners and prejudices still holds undisputed possession of the stage. Shakespear's malignant has outlived Mr. Cumberland's benevolent Jew. In proportion as Shylock has ceased to be a popular bugbear, 'baited with the rabble's curse,' he becomes a half-favourite with the philosophical part of the audience, who are disposed to think that Jewish revenge is at least as good as Christian injuries. Shylock is *a good hater;* 'a man no less sinned against than sinning.' If he carries his revenge too far, yet he has strong grounds for 'the lodged hate he bears Anthonio,' which he explains with equal force of eloquence and reason. He seems the depositary of the vengeance of his race; and though the long habit of brooding over daily insults and injuries has crusted over his temper with inveterate misanthropy, and hardened him against the contempt of mankind, this adds but little to the triumphant pretensions of his enemies. There is a strong, quick, and deep sense of justice mixed up with the gall and bitterness of his resentment. The constant apprehension of being burnt alive, plundered, banished, reviled, and trampled on, might be supposed to sour the most forbearing nature, and to take something from that 'milk of human kindness,' with which his persecutors contemplated his indignities. The desire of revenge is almost inseparable from the sense of wrong; and we can hardly help sympathising with the proud spirit, hid beneath his 'Jewish gaberdine,' stung to madness by repeated undeserved provocations, and labouring to throw off the load of obloquy and oppression heaped upon him and all his tribe by one desperate act of 'lawful' revenge, till the ferociousness of the means by which he is to execute his purpose, and the pertinacity with which he adheres to it, turn us against him; but even at last, when disappointed of the sanguinary revenge with which he had glutted his hopes, and exposed to beggary and contempt by the letter of the law on which he had insisted with so little remorse, we pity him, and think him hardly dealt with by his judges. In all his answers and retorts upon his adversaries, he has the best not only of the argument but of the question, reasoning on their own principles and practice. They are so far from allowing of any measure of equal dealing, of common justice or humanity between themselves and the Jew, that even when they come to ask a favour of him, and Shylock reminds them that 'on such a day they spit upon him, another spurned him, another called him dog, and for these curtesies request he'll lend them so much monies'—Anthonio, his old enemy, instead of any acknowledgment of the shrewdness and justice of his remonstrance, which would have been preposterous in a respectable Catholic merchant in those times, threatens him with a repetition of the same treatment—

> I am as like to call thee so again,
> To spit on thee again, to spurn thee too.

. . . Portia is not a very great favourite with us; neither are we in love with her maid, Nerissa. Portia has a certain degree of affectation and pedantry about her, which is very unusual in Shakespear's women, but which perhaps was a proper qualification for the office of a 'civil doctor,' which she undertakes and executes so successfully. The speech about Mercy is very well; but there are a thousand finer ones in Shakespear. We do not admire the scene of the caskets: and object entirely to the Black Prince, Morocchius. We should like Jessica better if she had not deceived and robbed her father, and Lorenzo, if he had not married a Jewess, though he thinks he has a right to wrong a Jew. The dialogue between this newly-married couple by moonlight, beginning 'On such a night,' etc. is a collection of classical elegancies. Launcelot, the Jew's man, is an honest fellow. The dilemma in which he describes himself placed between his 'conscience and the fiend,' the one of which advises him to run away from his master's service and the other to stay in it, is exquisitely humourous.—WILLIAM HAZLITT, *"The Merchant of Venice," Characters of Shakespear's Plays*, 1817

---

### G. H. RADFORD
### "Shylock"

*Shylock and Others*
1894, pp. 9–26

I t is proposed here to treat the character of Shylock as if Shakspeare was *not* an inspired writer. It is only courteous to make this announcement at the outset, so that those who do not care to read anything based on a hypothesis so gratifying to the profane may skip the remarks that follow. To such readers as remain to us we have to suggest that the people who say, or repeat the saying, that Shylock is a great creation do not for the most part know how great a creation it is. We are so familiar with the Jews as an element not to be ignored in our national life that we are apt to forget that for centuries the wisdom of our ancestors rigidly excluded them from this realm. For two centuries after the Conquest, Jews had indifferent entertainment in this country, and it was during this period that

> by way of mild reminders
> That he needed coin, the Knight
> Day by day extracted grinders
> From the howling Israelite.

But in the year 1290 Edward I. expelled them all, and it was not till the Commonwealth that the decree of banishment was rescinded. The late Mr. J. R. Green goes a little too far when he says that from the time of Edward to that of Cromwell no Jew touched English ground. Now and then during these centuries a stray Jew, protected by royal favour or stimulated by hopes of gain, found his way hither; but in Shakspeare's time the business of London (incredible as this may appear) was transacted without any help from the Jews, and it is quite likely that Shakspeare never saw a Jew in his life. It is, of course, possible that he may have met Roderigo Lopez, "a Portingale," who was chief physician to Queen Elizabeth, and was hanged in 1594 on unsatisfactory evidence for attempting to poison her. Sir Edward Coke says, with the venal scurrility of the lawyers of that day, that he was "a perjured and murdering villain and Jewish doctor worse than Judas himself;" but Gabriel Harvey, a contemporary without a professional bias, says that, though descended of Jews, he was himself a Christian. Nearly twenty years earlier Lopez was physician to Leicester, who was patron to Burbage, who was Shakspeare's "fellow," so there are links for those who want to make a chain to prove that the doctor and the dramatist may have come together.

However this may be, in presenting a Jew as one of the chief characters of the *Merchant of Venice*, Shakspeare was introducing a specimen of a species practically unknown both to the author and his audience. The Philistines among the latter no doubt held that the play was designed to inculcate by example the wisdom of our legislators in excluding the Jews from the country and the folly of the Venetians in admitting them. Frenchmen, Welshmen, and other "mountain foreigners" Shakspeare knew, and in depicting Fluellen and Dr. Caius he had numerous models on which to work; but in drawing Shylock he had to exercise his imagination, probably unassisted by any living model. Shylock is therefore a creation in the same sense that Caliban is.

But if there was no living model there was ample material to feed and stimulate imagination. Shakspeare knew the sacred writings of the Hebrews, and the traditional stories of the Jews descended from the Middle Ages. More specially suggestive material was also ready to his hand in Marlowe's *Jew of Malta*, then newly written, and the *Pecorone* of Ser Giovanni Fiorentino. The former contains a powerful delineation of a Jew turning with the fury of revenge on his Christian oppressors, and the latter has the very story which is followed in most of its details in Shakspeare's play. It is not known that there was any Elizabethan English translation of the *Pecorone*, and we are driven to the conclusion that Shakspeare had (notwithstanding his small Latin and less Greek) a facility for reading Italian, or that he had the help of a friend who had this facility. This presents an alternative that has no doubt been discussed by the New Shakspere Society, and this Society can probably inform any inquiring Hebrew whether Shakspeare read Italian, and why, among Shakspeare relics, an edition of the *Pecorone* (Milano, 1558) with Shakspeare's autograph thriftily inscribed on the title page is not yet forthcoming, and when it may be expected; and who among the poet's friends read the *Pecorone*, and which of them translated at sight for his dramatisation.

At any rate, Shakspeare had all this material out of which to construct his Shylock, and he, of course, used his material in his own masterly way. The marauding mind which possesses the English dramatist who has got hold of a likely foreign original was fully developed in Shakspeare, and no useful detail in Giovanni's story was left unappropriated. The old Jew, however, is not a portrait, but a kind of grim conjecture. If Shakspeare had had the advantage of intercourse with the Jews now possessed by every playwright and journalist he would have turned out something more lifelike and (possibly) more amiable.

But it seems that Shakspeare's aim in the _Merchant of Venice_ was not by any means solely to hold the mirror up to nature. This is one way of delighting an audience, but not the only one. To blend the agreeable with the surprising is an ancient prescription for producing the same result, and this is done in the character of Antonio, the Christian merchant who had scruples about usury and lent out his money gratis. Now, though Shakspeare did not know the Jews, he well knew the City, and that he had the City largely represented in his audience. _They_ knew the Christian merchant, but the Christian merchant with these scruples was entirely new to them, and no doubt delighted them hugely. The statute-book shows us clearly what was the practice of merchants at this time. _An Acte against Usurie_, 13 Eliz. c. 8, declares that "all usurie being forbidden by the laws of God, is sinne and detestable," but it does not make it illegal. It only declares all contracts void upon which "there shall be reserved or taken above the rate of X. pounds for the hundred for one yere." Recognising the hardness of heart of the Christian merchant, the legislature, while licensing the sin, merely sought to limit the evils of it by fixing ten per cent. as the maximum rate of interest. A house half-filled with usurers and borrowers was highly amused by the wildly improbable character of Antonio.

But the _rôle_ of Portia is still more improbable, and consequently more diverting. Allowing everything that can be demanded and granted for the indulgence of dramatic illusion, the appearance of this young lady in a Court of Justice, which (to use an Americanism) she proceeds to "run" herself, is an incident which the audience felt to be impossible, and enjoyed none the less on that account. The incident was at least as impossible in Shakspeare's time (or Giovanni's, for that matter) as it is now.

Imagine Mary Anderson, primed with lines written for her (alas, it is difficult to imagine who could write them!), having borrowed Mr. Lockwood's wig and gown, sweeping into the Lord Chief Justice's Court, gently taking the case of the injured defendant out of the hands of the benign Chief who looks on amazed but quiescent while the extortionate plaintiff is not only nonsuited but committed for trial at the Old Bailey—imagine all this, and you have a modern counterpart of the glorious day's work of the breezy Portia. Here is not realism but something much rarer and more delightful. This is not a digression, as the learned (and courteous) reader may suppose. On the contrary it is intended to lead him by the pleasantest route to the conclusion that Shylock himself is not realistic, is not, as has been foolishly said, a libel on the Jews, but a personage whose character is determined by the requirements of the plot. Shakspeare wanted a villain vindictive enough to endanger the life and peace of the virtuous members of the cast, but not sufficiently heroic to interfere with a happy _dénoûment_, and he devised just such a villain in Shylock.

Let us consider the character in broad outlines. He is a great and prosperous merchant, and he has many and excellent reasons for the hatred of Antonio, which has become his ruling passion. The two are alien in race. This is something. The saying of the old Meynell that foreigners are fools is quoted with approval by the Christian philosopher Johnson. But it is a second-rate patriotism which dubs a foreigner only a fool. Philologists tell us that _hostis_ originally meant a foreigner; but we only knew it at school as an enemy. It is all the same. This alone was reason enough for hatred, but there were other reasons. Antonio was a Christian, and the follower of one religion is ready to believe evil of the follower of another. "Some Jews are wicked, as _all_ Christians are," says Marlowe's Jew of Malta. Moreover, the Jews were but tolerated in Venice for commercial reasons, and subject to persecution and indignity which only stopped short at the point where such treatment would have deprived the Republic of the commercial advantages obtained through the Jews. Difference of race, difference of religion, persecution—this is enough to make Shylock hate _any_ Christian at sight. But there were special reasons for hating Antonio. It seems he had been accustomed to spit on Shylock. This is a practice which may violently stimulate even a slight antipathy. Antonio, too, was a rival in business, and while we do not forget the possibility of a Jewish reader, it is no breach of confidence to confess that fellow-Christians have quarrelled under such circumstances. The most galling incident of the rivalry appears to be that Antonio had cut down Shylock's profits as a usurer by lending money without interest, and so "brought down the rate of usance." We presume this is sound political economy: and there seems to be a suppressed proposition that the larger the number of borrowers at interest the higher the rate the lenders can exact. It does not matter, for an antipathy founded on an economic heresy is likely to be quite as strong as if based on a perfectly orthodox doctrine. The conclusion does not seem as obvious as that drawn by Launcelot Gobbo, who found that if Lorenzo converted his Jewish bride to Christianity, he would be damned for raising the price of pork.

This _is_ a digression. To return to Shylock's antipathy. Besides the general grounds above hinted at and those arising from personal reasons, Shylock was at the moment irritated by events for which Antonio was not to blame. His daughter Jessica had not only eloped in a tailor-made suit[1] with a detrimental Christian, but had carried with her quite a cargo of jewels and ready-money, and the young couple were living in Genoa on Shylock's money at the gorgeous rate of 80 ducats a night. With this respectable, old-established, and one may almost say reasonable hatred intensified by Jessica's conduct, Shylock suddenly finds himself in a position to take revenge. Antonio had made default in payment on the day, and Shylock is entitled to exact the forfeiture, "a pound of flesh to be by him cut off nearest the merchant's heart." He can kill his enemy, as he understands the laws of Venice, without incurring any risk of injury to himself. The temptation was great. There are several Christian merchants of blameless character (we mean they have never been in prison) at whose mercy we should be very sorry to be under similar circumstances. Shylock was ready to strike the blow. It was not murder, as he was advised, but justice. He could have Antonio's life without as much as standing an action for assault and battery. It was true that by so doing he would not recover the 3000 ducats secured by the bond, but he was ready to submit to this loss and even to forego the handsome profit held out by Antonio's friends who offered thrice the principal for his release. Shylock was avaricious, but his revenge rises superior to his avarice: he will not be balked of his revenge for money. This is the noblest point in his not very noble character. He refuses the cash and stands for the law. But it is always risky to rely on a strict view of the law when the court is dead against you on the merits. The judge, or even the jury, will lay hold of some quibble to justify a finding adverse to a suitor of whose conduct they disapprove. Such a quibble was raised by Portia on the language of the bond. It had not been drawn by an Equity draughtsman of the old school, in which case it would no doubt have stipulated that the creditor was entitled not only to the pound of flesh, but also to the epidermis, cartilages, arteries, veins, capillaries, blood or sanguinary fluid, and all other appurtenances thereunto belonging or therewith usually held and enjoyed. This careless draughtsmanship enabled the Court, in accordance with its inclinations, to hold that Shylock was entitled to no drop of blood. The plaintiff was baffled by this quibble. By shedding a drop of blood he would break the law and commit a capital offence. He was not prepared to run this risk. His desire for revenge is strong enough to make him unusually indifferent to money, but not strong enough to make him regardless of his life. This is not the revenge of tragedy, and Shylock is not a hero, though the vanity of certain modern actors has exalted the character to such a pitch that they cannot "climb down" in the fourth act without being ridiculous. But Shakspeare's Shylock climbs down without absurdity and with reasonable alacrity. He is the serviceable villain, serviceable, that is, for the action of the play, who has frightened the ladies by whetting his knife, and now gratifies them by dropping (reluctantly) all thoughts of bloodshed. Antonio must be saved. The pains and penalties with which Shylock is threatened by the Bench effectually secure this end. Then comes retribution. Both the life and fortune of Shylock, according to the laws of Venice, are held to be forfeited. But it would be distressing to

kill him, and his life is spared on condition that he becomes a Christian and gives up the bulk of his fortune. Shylock accepts the terms imposed on him. He appears only to retain a life interest in half his property, and the whole of it is to go on his death to the gentleman who lately stole his daughter. Shylock leaves the stage promising to execute the necessary documents, and we hear of him no more. What became of him subsequently is merely matter of conjecture, but his conduct in court justifies us in inferring that he accepted the inevitable and made the best of it. Had he lived in our day we might conjecturally sketch his subsequent career thus: His baptism was performed with pomp in a historic temple by a distinguished ecclesiastic who knows that there is Eternal Hope for Jews if not for publishers. His marriage later on with a Dowager Countess who largely endowed the Society for Propagation of the Gospel among the Jews made his social position impregnable, and the money he subsequently made by publishing a financial newspaper far exceeded anything ever acquired by him in his old profession of usury.

*Notes*

1. "*Salarino:* I for my part knew the tailor that made the wings she flew withal."—Act iii. Sc. 1.

# As You Like It

Of this play the fable is wild and pleasing. I know not how the ladies will approve the facility with which both Rosalind and Celia give away their hearts. To Celia much may be forgiven for the heroism of her friendship. The character of Jaques is natural and well preserved. The comick dialogue is very sprightly, with less mixture of low buffoonery than in some other plays; and the graver part is elegant and harmonious. By hastening to the end of his work Shakespeare suppressed the dialogue between the usurper and the hermit, and lost an opportunity of exhibiting a moral lesson in which he might have found matter worthy of his highest powers.—SAMUEL JOHNSON, *Notes on Shakespeare's Plays,* 1768

It would be difficult to bring the contents ⟨of *As You Like It*⟩ within the compass of an ordinary narrative; nothing takes place, or rather what is done is not so essential as what is said; even what may be called the *dénouement* is brought about pretty arbitrarily. Whoever can perceive nothing but what can as it were be counted on the fingers, will hardly be disposed to allow that it has any plan at all. Banishment and flight have assembled together, in the forest of Arden, a strange band: a Duke dethroned by his brother, who, with the faithful companions of his misfortune, lives in the wilds on the produce of the chase; two disguised Princesses, who love each other with a sisterly affection; a witty court fool; lastly, the native inhabitants of the forest, ideal and natural shepherds and shepherdesses. These light-sketched figures form a motley and diversified train; we see always the shady dark-green landscape in the background, and breathe in imagination the fresh air of the forest. The hours are here measured by no clocks, no regulated recurrence of duty or of toil: they flow on unnumbered by voluntary occupation or fanciful idleness, to which, according to his humour or disposition, every one yields himself, and this unrestrained freedom compensates them all for the lost conveniences of life. One throws himself down in solitary meditation under a tree, and indulges in melancholy reflections on the changes of fortune, the falsehood of the

world, and the self-inflicted torments of social life; others make the woods resound with social and festive songs, to the accompaniment of their hunting-horns. Selfishness, envy, and ambition, have been left behind in the city; of all the human passions, love alone has found an entrance into this wilderness, where it dictates the same language alike to the simple shepherd and the chivalrous youth, who hangs his love-ditty to a tree. A prudish shepherdess falls at first sight in love with Rosalind, disguised in men's apparel; the latter sharply reproaches her with her severity to her poor lover, and the pain of refusal, which she feels from experience in her own case, disposes her at length to compassion and requital. The fool carries his philosophical contempt of external show, and his raillery of the illusion of love so far, that he purposely seeks out the ugliest and simplest country wench for a mistress. Throughout the whole picture, it seems to be the poet's design to show that to call forth the poetry which has its indwelling in nature and the human mind, nothing is wanted but to throw off all artificial constraint, and restore both to mind and nature their original liberty. In the very progress of the piece, the dreamy carelessness of such an existence is sensibly expressed: it is even alluded to by Shakspeare in the title. Whoever affects to be displeased, if in this romantic forest the ceremonial of dramatic art is not duly observed, and ought in justice to be delivered over to the wise fool, to be led gently out of it to some prosaical region.—AUGUST WILHELM SCHLEGEL, *Lectures on Dramatic Art and Literature,* 1809, tr. John Black

Shakespear has here converted the forest of Arden into another Arcadia, where they 'fleet the time carelessly, as they did in the golden world.' It is the most ideal of any of this author's plays. It is a pastoral drama, in which the interest arises more out of the sentiments and characters than out of the actions or situations. It is not what is done, but what is said, that claims our attention. Nursed in solitude, 'under the shade of melancholy boughs,' the imagination grows soft and delicate, and the wit runs riot in idleness, like a spoiled child, that is never sent to school. Caprice and fancy reign and revel here, and stern necessity is banished to the court. The mild sentiments of humanity are strengthened with thought and leisure; the echo of the cares and noise of the world strikes upon the ear of those 'who have felt them knowingly,' softened by time and distance. 'They hear the tumult, and are still.' The very air of the place seems to breathe a spirit of philosophical poetry: to stir the thoughts, to touch the heart with pity, as the drowsy forest rustles to the sighing gale. Never was there such beautiful moralising, equally free from pedantry or petulance.

> And this their life, exempt from public haunts,
> Finds tongues in trees, books in the running brooks,
> Sermons in stones, and good in every thing.

Jaques is the only purely contemplative character in Shakespear. He thinks, and does nothing. His whole occupation is to amuse his mind, and he is totally regardless of his body and his fortunes. He is the prince of philosophical idlers; his only passion is thought; he sets no value upon any thing but as it serves as food for reflection. He can 'suck melancholy out of a song, as a weasel sucks eggs'; the motley fool, 'who morals on the time,' is the greatest prize he meets with in the forest. He resents Orlando's passion for Rosalind as some disparagement of his own passion for abstract truth; and leaves the Duke, as soon as he is restored to his sovereignty, to seek his brother out who has quitted it, and turned hermit.

> Out of these convertites
> There is much matter to be heard and learnt.

Within the sequestered and romantic glades of the forest of Arden, they find leisure to be good and wise, or to play the fool and fall in love. Rosalind's character is made up of sportive gaiety and natural tenderness: her tongue runs the faster to conceal the pressure at her heart. She talks herself out of breath, only to get deeper in love. The coquetry with which she plays with her lover in the double character which she has to support is managed with the nicest address. How full of voluble, laughing grace is all her conversation with Orlando—

> In heedless mazes running
> With wanton haste and giddy cunning.

How full of real fondness and pretended cruelty is her answer to him when he promises to love her 'For ever and a day!'

*Rosalind:* Say a day without the ever: no, no, Orlando, men are April when they woo, December when they wed: maids are May when they are maids, but the sky changes when they are wives: I will be more jealous of thee than a Barbary cock-pigeon over his hen; more clamorous than a parrot against rain; more new-fangled than an ape; more giddy in my desires than a monkey; I will weep for nothing like Diana in the fountain, and I will do that when you are disposed to be merry; I will laugh like a hyen, and that when you are inclined to sleep.
*Orlando:* But will my Rosalind do so?
*Rosalind:* By my life she will do as I do.

The silent and retired character of Celia is a necessary relief to the provoking loquacity of Rosalind, nor can anything be better conceived or more beautifully described than the mutual affection between the two cousins:

> We still have slept together,
> Rose at an instant, learn'd, play'd, eat together,
> And wheresoe'r we went, like Juno's swans,
> Still we went coupled and inseparable.

The unrequited love of Silvius for Phebe shews the perversity of this passion in the commonest scenes of life, and the rubs and stops which nature throws in its way, where fortune has placed none. Touchstone is not in love, but he will have a mistress as a subject for the exercise of his grotesque humour, and to shew his contempt for the passion, by his indifference about the person. He is a rare fellow. He is a mixture of the ancient cynic philosopher with the modern buffoon, and turns folly into wit, and wit into folly, just as the fit takes him. His courtship of Audrey not only throws a degree of ridicule on the state of wedlock itself, but he is equally an enemy to the prejudices of opinion in other respects. The lofty tone of enthusiasm, which the Duke and his companions in exile spread over the stillness and solitude of a country life, receives a pleasant shock from Touchstone's sceptical determination of the question.

*Corin:* And how like you this shepherd's life, Mr. Touchstone?
*Clown:* Truly, shepherd, in respect of itself, it is a good life; but in respect that it is a shepherd's life, it is naught. In respect that it is solitary, I like it very well; but in respect that it is private, it is a very vile life. Now in respect it is in the fields, it pleaseth me well; but in respect it is not in the court, it is tedious. As it is a spare life, look you, it fits my humour; but as there is no more plenty in it, it goes much against my stomach.

Zimmerman's celebrated work on Solitude discovers only *half* the sense of this passage.—WILLIAM HAZLITT, "As You Like It," *Characters of Shakespear's Plays,* 1817

## WILLIAM MAGINN
### "Jaques"
### *Shakespeare Papers*
### 1856, pp. 46–65

As he passed through the fields, and saw the animals around him—"Ye," said he, "are happy, and need not envy me that walk thus among you burthened with myself; nor do I, ye gentle beings, envy your felicity, for it is not the felicity of man. I have many distresses from which ye are free; I fear pain when I do not feel it; I sometimes shrink at evils recollected, and sometimes start at evils anticipated. Surely the equity of Providence has balanced peculiar sufferings with peculiar enjoyments."

With observations like these the prince amused himself as he returned, uttering them with a plaintive voice, yet with a look that discovered him to feel some complacence in his own perspicacity, and to receive some solace of the miseries of life from a consciousness of the delicacy with which he felt, and the eloquence with which he bewailed them."

(*Rasselas*, Chap. II.)

This remark of Dr. Johnson on the consolation derived by his hero from the eloquence with which he gave vent to his complaints is perfectly just, but just only in such cases as those of Rasselas. The misery that can be expressed in flowing periods can not be of more importance than that experienced by the Abyssinian prince enclosed in the Happy Valley. His greatest calamity was no more than that he could not leave a place in which all the luxuries of life were at his command, but, as old Chremes says in the *Heautontimorumenos,*

> Miserum? quem minus credere 'st?
> Quid reliqui 'st, quin habeat, quæ quidem in
>     homine dicuntur bona?
> Parentes, patriam incolumem, amicos, genu', cog-
>     natos, divitias:
> Atque hæ perinde sunt ut illius animus qui ea
>     possidet;
> Qui uti scit, ei bona; illi, qui non utitur rect, mala.[1]

On which, as

> Plain truth, dear Bentley, needs no arts of speech,

I can not do better than transcribe the commentary of Hickie, or some other grave expositor from whose pages he has transferred it to his own: " 'Tis certain that the real enjoyment arising from external advantages depends wholly upon the situation of the mind of him who possesses them; for if he chance to labor under any secret anguish, this destroys all relish; or, if he know not how to use them for valuable purposes, they are so far from being of any service to him, that they often turn to real misfortunes." It is of no consequence that this profound reflection is nothing to the purpose in the place where it appears, because Chremes is not talking of any secret anguish, but of the use or abuse made of advantages according to the disposition of the individual to whom they have been accorded; and the anguish of Clinia was by no means secret. He feared the perpetual displeasure of his father, and knew not whether absence might not have diminished or alienated the affections of the lady on whose account he had abandoned home and country; but the general proposition of the sentence can not be denied. A "fatal remembrance"—to borrow a phrase from one of the most beautiful of Moore's melodies—may render a life, apparently abounding in prosperity, wretched and unhappy, as the vitiation of a single humor of the eye casts a sickly and unnatural hue over the gladsome meadow, or turns to a lurid light the brilliancy of the sunniest skies.

Rasselas and Jaques have no secret anguish to torment them, no real cares to disturb the even current of their tempers. To get rid of the prince first:—His sorrow is no more than that of the starling in the *Sentimental Journey*. He can not get out. He is discontented, because he has not the patience of Wordsworth's nuns, who fret not in their narrow cells; or of Wordsworth's muse, which murmurs not at being cribbed and confined to a sonnet. He wants the philosophy of that most admirable of all jail-ditties—and will not reflect that

> Every island is a prison,
>     Close surrounded by the sea;
> Kings and princes, for that reason,
>     Prisoners are as well as we.

And as his calamity is, after all, very tolerable—as many a sore heart or a wearied mind, buffeting about amid the billows and breakers of the external world, would feel but too happy to exchange conditions with him in his safe haven of rest—it is no wonder that the weaving of the sonorous sentences of easily-soothed sorrow should be the extent of the mental afflictions of Rasselas, Prince of Abyssinia.

Who or what Jaques was before he makes his appearance in the forest, Shakespeare does not inform us—any farther than that he had been a *roué* of considerable note, as the Duke tells him when he proposes to

> Cleanse the foul body of the infected world,
> If they will patiently receive my medicine.
> *Duke:* Fie on thee! I can tell what thou wouldst do.
> *Jaques:* What, for a counter, would I do but good?
> *Duke:* Most mischievous foul sin, in chiding sin;
>     For thou thyself hast been a libertine

> As sensual as the brutish sting itself;
> And all the embossed sores and headed evils
> That thou with license of free foot hast caught,
> Wouldst thou disgorge into the general world.

This, and that he was one of the three or four loving lords who put themselves into voluntary exile with the old Duke, leaving their lands and revenues to enrich the new one, who therefore gave them good leave to wander, is all we know about him, until he is formally announced to us as the melancholy Jaques. The very announcement is a tolerable proof that he is not soul-stricken in any material degree. When Rosalind tells him that he is considered to be a melancholy fellow, he is hard put to it to describe in what his melancholy consists. "I have," he says:

> Neither the scholar's melancholy, which
> Is emulation; nor the musician's, which is
> Fantastical; nor the courtier's, which is proud;
> Nor the soldier's,
> Which is ambitious; nor the lawyer's, which
> Is politic; nor the lady's, which is nice;
> Nor the lover's, which is all these: but it is
> A melancholy of mine own, compounded
> Of many simples, extracted from many objects,
> And indeed
> The sundry contemplation of my travels,
> In which my often rumination wraps me
> In a most humorous sadness.[2]

He is nothing more than an idle gentleman given to musing, and making invectives against the affairs of the world, which are more remarkable for the poetry of their style and expression than the pungency of their satire. His famous description of the seven ages of man is that of a man who has seen but little to complain of in his career through life. The sorrows of his infant are of the slightest kind, and he notes that it is taken care of in a nurse's lap. The griefs of his schoolboy are confined to the necessity of going to school; and he, too, has had an anxious hand to attend to him. His shining morning face reflects the superintendence of one—probably a mother—interested in his welfare. The lover is tortured by no piercing pangs of love, his woes evaporating themselves musically in a ballad of his own composition, written not to his mistress, but fantastically addressed to her eyebrow. The soldier appears in all the pride and the swelling hopes of his spirit-stirring trade,

> Jealous in honor, sudden and quick in quarrel,
> Seeking the bubble reputation
> Even in the cannon's mouth.

The fair round belly of the justice lined with good capon lets us know how he has passed in life. He is full of ease, magisterial authority, and squirely dignity. The lean and slippered panta-loon, and the dotard sunk into second childishness, have suffered only the common lot of humanity, without any of the calamities that embitter the unavoidable malady of old age.[3] All the characters in Jaques's sketch are well taken care of. The infant is nursed; the boy educated; the youth tormented with no greater cares than the necessity of hunting after rhymes to please the ear of a lady, whose love sits so lightly upon him as to set him upon nothing more serious than such a self-amusing task; the man in prime of life is engaged in gallant deeds, brave in action, anxious for character, and ambitious of fame; the man in declining years has won the due honors of his rank, he enjoys the luxuries of the table and dispenses the terrors of the bench; the man of age still more advanced is well to do in the world. If his shank be shrunk, it is not without hose and slipper—if his eyes be dim, they are spectacled—if his years have made him lean, they have gathered for him wherewithal to fatten the pouch by his side. And when this strange eventful history is closed by the penalties paid by men who live too long, Jaques does not tell us that the helpless being,

>   Sans teeth, sans eyes, sans taste, sans everything,

is left unprotected in his helplessness.

Such pictures of life do not proceed from a man very heavy at heart. Nor can it be without design that they are introduced into this especial place. The moment before, the famished Orlando has burst in upon the sylvan meal of the Duke, brandishing a naked sword, demanding with furious threat food for himself and his helpless companion,

>   Oppressed with two weak evils, age and hunger.

The Duke, struck with his earnest appeal, can not refrain from comparing the real suffering which he witnesses in Orlando with that which is endured by himself and his co-mates, and partners in exile. Addressing Jaques, he says:—

>   Thou seest we are not all alone unhappy:
>   This wide and universal theatre
>   Presents more woful pageants than the scene
>   Wherein we play in.[4]

But the spectacle and the comment upon it lightly touch Jaques, and he starts off at once into a witty and poetic comparison of the real drama of the world with the mimic drama of the stage, in which, with the sight of well-nurtured youth driven to the savage desperation of periling his own life, and assailing that of others—and of weakly old age lying down in the feeble but equally resolved desperation of dying by the wayside, driven to this extremity by sore fatigue and hunger— he diverts himself and his audience, whether in the forest or theatre, on the stage or in the closet, with graphic descriptions of human life; not one of them, proceeding as they do from the lips of the *melancholy* Jaques, presenting a single point on which true melancholy can dwell. Mourning over what can not be avoided must be in its essence common-place: and nothing has been added to the lamentations over the ills brought by the flight of years since Moses, the man of God,[5] declared the concluding period of protracted life to be a period of labor and sorrow; since Solomon, or whoever else writes under the name of the Preacher, in a passage which, whether it is inspired or not, is a passage of exquisite beauty, warned us to provide in youth, "while the evil days come not, nor the years draw nigh when thou shalt say, I have no pleasure in them; while the sun, or the light, or the moon, or the stars be not darkened, nor the clouds return after the rain: in the day when the keepers of the house shall tremble, and the strong men shall bow themselves, and the grinders cease because they are few, and those that look out of the windows be darkened, and the doors shall be shut in the streets, when the sound of the grinding is low, and he shall rise up at the voice of the bird, and all the daughters of music shall be brought low; also when they shall be afraid of that which is high, and fears shall be in the way, and the almond-tree shall flourish, and the grasshopper shall be a burthen, and desire shall fail: because man goeth to his long home, and the mourners go about the streets: or ever the silver cord be loosed, or the golden bowl be broken, or the pitcher be broken at the fountain, or the wheel broken at the cistern;" or, to make a shorter quotation, since Homer summed up all these ills by applying to old age the epithet of *lygros*—a word which can not be translated, but the force of which must be felt. Abate these unavoidable misfortunes, and the catalogue of Jaques is that of happy conditions. In his visions there is no trace of the child doomed to wretchedness before its very birth; no hint that such a thing could occur as its being made an object of calculation, one part medical, three parts financial, to the starveling surgeon, whether by the floating of the lungs, or

other test equally fallacious and fee-producing, the miserable mother may be convicted of doing that which, before she had attempted, all that is her soul of woman must have been torn from its uttermost roots, when in an agony of shame and dread the child that was to have made her forget her labor was committed to the cesspool. No hint that the days of infancy should be devoted to the damnation of a factory, or to the tender mercies of a parish beadle. No hint that philosophy should come forward armed with the panoply offensive and defensive of logic and eloquence, to prove that the inversion of all natural relations was just and wise—that the toil of childhood was due to the support of manhood—that those hours, the very labors of which even the etymologists give to recreation, should be devoted to those wretched drudgeries which seem to split the heart of all but those who derive from them blood-stained money, or blood-bedabbled applause. Jaques sees not Greensmith squeezing his children by the throat until they die. He hears not the supplication of the hapless boy begging his still more hapless father for a moment's respite, ere the fatal handkerchief is twisted round his throat by the hand of him to whom he owed his being. Jaques thinks not of the baby deserted on the step of the inhospitable door, of the shame of the mother, of the disgrace of the parents, of the misery of the forsaken infant. His boy is at school, his soldier in the breach, his elder on the justice-seat. Are these the woes of life? Is there no neglected creature left to himself or to the worse nurture of others, whose trade it is to corrupt—who will teach him what was taught to swaggering Jack Chance, found on Newgate steps, and educated at the venerable seminary of St. Giles's Pound, where

>   They taught him to drink, and to thieve, and fight,
>   And everything else but to read and write.

Is there no stripling short of commons, but abundant in the supply of the strap or the cudgel?—no man fighting through the world in fortuneless struggles, and occupied by cares or oppressed by wants more stringent than those of love?—or in love itself does the current of that bitter passion never run less smooth than when sonnets to a lady's eyebrow are the prime objects of solicitude?—or may not even he who began with such sonneteering have found something more serious and sad, something more heart-throbbing and soul-rending, in the progress of his passion? Is the soldier melancholy in the storm and whirlwind of war? Is the gallant confronting of the cannon a matter to be complained of? The dolorous flight, the trampled battalion, the broken squadron, the lost battle, the lingering wound, the ill-furnished hospital, the unfed block-ade, hunger and thirst, and pain, and fatigue, and mutilation, and cold, and rout, and scorn, and slight—services neglected, unworthy claims preferred, life wasted, or honor tarnished— are all passed by! In peaceful life we have no deeper misfortune placed before us than that it is not unusual that a justice of peace may be prosy in remark and trite in illustration. Are there no other evils to assail us through the agony of life? And when the conclusion comes, how far less tragic is the portraiture of mental imbecility, if considered as a state of misery than as one of comparative happiness, as escaping a still worse lot! Crabbe is sadder far than Jaques, when, after his appalling description of the inmates of a workhouse—(what would Crabbe have written *now?*)—he winds up by showing to us amid its victims two persons as being

>   *happier* far than they,
>   The moping idiot, and the madman gay.

If what he here sums up as the result of his life's observations on mankind be all that calls forth the melancholy of the witty and eloquent speaker he had not much to complain of. Mr. Shandy lamenting in sweetly-modulated periods, because his son has been christened Tristram instead of Trismegistus, is as much an object of condolence. Jaques has just seen the aspect of famine, and heard the words of despair; the Duke has pointed out to him the consideration that more woful and practical calamities exist than even the exile of princes and the downfall of lords; and he breaks off into a light strain of satire, fit only for jesting comedy. Trim might have rebuked him as he rebuked the prostrate Mr. Shandy, by reminding him that there are other things to make us melancholy in the world: and nobody knew it better, or could say it better, than he in whose brain was minted the hysteric passion of Lear choked by his button—the farewell of victorious Othello to all the pomp, pride, and circumstance of glorious war—the tears of Richard over the submission of roan Barbary to Bolingbroke—the demand of Romeo that the Mantuan druggist should supply him with such soon-speeding gear that will rid him of hated life

> As violently as hasty powder fired
> Doth hurry from the fatal cannon's womb

the desolation of Antony—the mourning of Henry over sire slain by son, and son by sire—or the despair of Macbeth. I say nothing of the griefs of Constance, or Isabel, or Desdemona, or Juliet, or Ophelia, because in the sketches of Jaques he passes by all allusion to women; a fact which of itself is sufficient to prove that his melancholy was but in play—was nothing more than what Arthur remembered when he was in France, where

> Young gentlemen would be as sad as night,
> Only for wantonness.

Shakespeare well knew that there is no true pathetic, nothing that can permanently lacerate the heart, and embitter the speech, unless a woman be concerned. It is the legacy left us by Eve. The tenor of man's woe, says Milton, with a most ungallant and grisly pun, is still from *wo*-man to begin; and he who will give himself a few moments to reflect will find that the stern trigamist is right. On this, however, I shall not dilate. I may perhaps have something to say, as we go on, of the ladies of Shakespeare. For the present purpose, it is enough to remark with Trim, that there are many real griefs to make a man lie down and cry, without troubling ourselves with those which are put forward by the poetic mourner in the forest of Arden.

Different indeed is the sight set before the eyes of Adam in the great poem just referred to, when he is told to look upon the miseries which the fall of man has entailed upon his descendants. Far other than the scenes that flit across this melancholy man by profession are those evoked by Michael in the visionary lazar-house. It would be ill-befitting, indeed, that the merry note of the sweet bird warbling freely in the glade should be marred by discordant sounds of woe, cataloguing the dreary list of disease,

> All maladies
> Of ghastly spasm, or racking torture, qualms
> Of heartsick agony, all feverous kinds,
> Convulsions, epilepsies, fierce catarrhs,
> Intestine stone and ulcer, colic pangs,
> Demoniac frenzy, moping melancholy,
> Marasmus, and wide-wasting pestilence,
> Dropsies, and asthmas, and joint-racking rheums;

while, amid the dire tossing and deep groans of the sufferers,

> Despair
> Tended the sick, busiest from couch to couch;
> And over them triumphant Death his dart
> Shook, but delayed to strike.

And equally ill-befitting would be any serious allusion to those passions and feelings which in their violence or their anguish render the human bosom a lazar-house filled with maladies of the mind as racking and as wasting as those of the body, and call forth a supplication for the releasing blow of Death as the final hope, with an earnestness as desperate, and cry as loud as ever arose from the tenement, sad, noisome, and dark, which holds the joint-racked victims of physical disease. Such themes should not sadden the festive banquet in the forest. The Duke and his co-mates and partners in exile, reconciled to their present mode of life ["I would not change it," says Amiens, speaking, we may suppose, the sentiments of all], and successful in having plucked the precious jewel, Content, from the head of ugly and venomous Adversity, are ready to bestow their woodland fare upon real suffering, but in no mood to listen to the heart-rending descriptions of sorrows graver than those which form a theme for the discourses which Jaques in mimic melancholy contributes to their amusement.

Shakespeare designed him to be a maker of fine sentences—a dresser forth in sweet language of the ordinary common-places or the common-place mishaps of mankind, and he takes care to show us that he did not intend him for anything beside. With what admirable art he is confronted with Touchstone. He enters merrily laughing at the pointless philosophizing of the fool in the forest. His lungs crow like chanticleer when he hears him moralizing over his dial, and making the deep discovery that ten o'clock has succeeded nine, and will be followed by eleven. When Touchstone himself appears, we do not find in his own discourse any touches of such deep contemplation. He is shrewd, sharp, worldly, witty, keen, gibing, observant. It is plain that he has been mocking Jaques; and, as is usual, the mocked thinks himself the mocker. If one has moralized the spectacle of a wounded deer into a thousand similes, comparing his weeping into the stream to the conduct of worldlings in giving in their testaments the sum of more to that which had too much—his abandonment, to the parting of the flux of companions from misery—the sweeping by of the careless herd full of the pasture, to the desertion of the poor and broken bankrupt by the fat and greasy citizens—and so forth; if such have been the common-places of Jaques, are they not fitly matched by the common places of Touchstone upon his watch? It is as high a stretch of fancy that brings the reflection how

> from hour to hour we ripe and ripe,
> And then from hour to hour we rot and rot,
> And thereby hangs a tale,

which is scoffed at by Jaques, as that which dictates his own moralizings on the death of the deer. The motley fool is as wise as the melancholy lord whom he is parodying. The shepherd Corin, who replies to the courtly quizzing of Touchstone by such apophthegms as that "it is the property of rain to wet, and of fire to burn," is unconsciously performing the same part of the clown, as *he* had been designedly performing to Jaques. Witty nonsense is answered by dull nonsense, as the emptiness of poetry had been answered by the emptiness of prose. There was nothing sincere in the lamentation over the wounded stag. It was only used as a peg on which to hang fine conceits. Had Falstaff seen the deer, his imagination would have called up visions of haunches and pastries, preluding an everlasting series of cups of sack among the revel riot of boon companions, and he would have instantly ordered its throat to be cut. If it had fallen in the way of Friar Lawrence, the mild-hearted man of herbs would have endeavored to extract the arrow, heal the wound, and let the hart ungalled go free. Neither would have thought the hairy fool a subject for reflections, which neither relieved the wants of man nor the pains of beast. Jaques complains of the injustice and cruelty of killing deer, but unscrupulously sits down to dine upon venison, and sorrows over the suffering of the native burghers of the forest city, without doing anything farther than amusing himself with rhetorical flourishes drawn from the contemplation of the pain which he witnesses with professional coolness and unconcern.

It is evident, in short, that the happiest days of his life are those which he is spending in the forest. His raking days are over, and he is tired of city dissipation. He has shaken hands with the world, finding, with Cowley, that "he and it would never agree." To use an expression somewhat vulgar, he has had his fun for his money; and he thinks the bargain so fair and conclusive on both sides, that he has no notion of opening another. His mind is relieved of a thousand anxieties which beset him in the court, and he breathes freely in the forest. The iron has not entered into his soul; nothing has occurred to chase sleep from his eyelids; and his fantastic reflections are, as he himself takes care to tell us, but general observations on the ordinary and outward manners and feelings of mankind—a species of taxing which

> like a wild-goose flies,
> Unclaimed of any man.

Above all, in having abandoned station, and wealth, and country, to join the faithful few who have in evil report clung manfully to their prince, he knows that he has played a noble and an honorable part; and they to whose lot it may have fallen to experience the happiness of having done a generous, disinterested, or self-denying action—or sacrificed temporary interests to undying principle—or shown to the world without, that what are thought to be its great advantages can be flung aside, or laid aside, when they come in collision with the feelings and passions of the world within—will be perfectly sure that Jaques, reft of land, and banished from court, felt himself exalted in his own eyes, and therefore easy of mind, whether he was mourning in melodious blank verse, or weaving jocular parodies on the canzonets of the good-humored Amiens.

He was happy "under the greenwood tree." Addison I believe it is who says, that all mankind have an instinctive love of country and woodland scenery, and he traces it to a sort of dim recollection imprinted upon us of our original haunt, the garden of Eden. It is at all events certain, that, from the days when the cedars of Lebanon supplied images to the great poets of Jerusalem, to that in which the tall tree haunted Wordsworth "as a passion," the forest has caught a strong hold of the poetic mind. It is with reluctance that I refrain from quoting; but the passages of surpassing beauty which crowd upon me from all times and languages are too numerous. I know not which to exclude, and I have not room for all; let me then take a bit of prose from one who never indulged in poetry, and I think I shall make it a case in point. In a little book called *Statistical Sketches of Upper Canada, for the use of Emigrants, by a Backwoodsman*, now lying before me, the author, after describing the field-sports in Canada with a precision and a *goût* to be derived only from practice and zeal, concludes a chapter, most appropriately introduced by a motto from the *Lady of the Lake*,

> 'Tis merry, 'tis merry in good greenwood,
>     When the mavis and merle are singing,
> When the deer sweep by, and the hounds are in cry,
>     And the hunter's horn is ringing,

by saying:

"It is only since writing the above that I fell in with the first volume of Moore's *Life of Lord Edward Fitzgerald*; and I can not describe the pleasure I received from reading his vivid, spirited, and accurate description of the feelings as he experienced on first taking on him the life of a hunter. At an earlier period of life than Lord Edward had then attained, I made my debut in the forest, and first assumed the blanket-cloak and the rifle, the moccasin and the snow-shoe; and the ecstatic feeling of Arab-like independence, and the utter contempt for the advantage and restrictions of civilization, which he describes, I then felt in its fullest power. And even now, when my way of life, like Macbeth's, is falling 'into the sere, the yellow leaf,' and when a tropical climate, privation, disease, and thankless toil, are combining with advancing years to unstring a frame the strength of which once set hunger, cold, and fatigue at defiance, and to undermine a constitution that once appeared iron-bound, still I can not lie down by a fire in the woods without the elevating feeling which I experienced formerly returning, though in a diminished degree. This must be human nature; for it is an undoubted fact, that no man who associates with and follows the pursuits of the Indian, for any length of time, ever voluntarily returns to civilized society.

"What a companion in the woods Lord Edward must have been! and how shocking to think that, with talents which would have made him at once the idol and the ornament of his profession, and affections which must have rendered him an object of adoration in all the relations of private life—with honor, with courage, with generosity, with every trait that can at once ennoble and endear—he should never have been taught that there is a higher principle of action than the mere impulse of the passions—that he should never have learned, before plunging his country into blood and disorder, to have weighed the means he possessed with the end he proposed, or the problematical good with the certain evil!—that he should have had Tom Paine for a tutor in religion and politics, and Tom Moore for a biographer, to hold up as a pattern, instead of warning, the errors and misfortunes of a being so noble—to subserve the revolutionary purposes of a faction, who, like Samson, are pulling down a fabric which will bury both them and their enemies under it."

Never mind the aberrations of Lord Edward Fitzgerald, the religion or the politics of Tom Paine, or the biography of Tom Moore. On all these matters I may hold my own opinions, but they are not wanted now; but have we not here the feelings of Jaques? Here are the gloomy expressions of general sorrow over climate, privation, disease, thankless toil, advancing years, unstrung frame. But here also we have ecstatic emotions of Arab-like independence, generous reflections upon political adversaries, and high-minded adherence to the views and principles which in his honor and conscience he believed to be in all circumstances inflexibly right, coming from the heart of a forest, The Backwoodsman is Dunlop; and is he, in spite of this sad-sounding passage, melancholy? Not he, in good sooth. The very next page to that which I have quoted is a description of the pleasant mode of travelling in Canada, before the march of improvement had made it comfortable and convenient.[6]

Jaques was just as woe-begone as the Tiger, and no more. I remember when he—Dunlop I mean, not Jaques—used to laugh at the phrenologists of Edinburgh for saying, after a careful admeasurement, that his skull in all points was exactly that of Shakespeare—I suppose he will be equally inclined to laugh when he finds who is the double an old companion has selected for him. But no matter. His melancholy passes away not more rapidly than that of Jaques; and I venture to say that the latter, if he were existing in flesh and blood, would have no scruple in joining the doctor this moment over the bowl of punch which I am sure he is brewing, has brewed, or is about to brew, on the banks of Huron or Ontario.

Whether he would or not, he departs from the stage with the grace and easy elegance of a gentleman in heart and manners. He joins his old antagonist the usurping Duke in his fallen fortunes; he had spurned him in his prosperity: his restored friend he bequeaths to his former honor, deserved by his patience and his virtue—he compliments Oliver on his restoration to his land, and love, and great allies—wishes Silvius joy of his long-sought and well-earned marriage—cracks upon Touchstone one of those good-humored jests to which men of the world on the eve of marriage must laughingly submit—and makes his bow. Some sage critics have discovered as a great geographical fault in Shakespeare, that he introduces the tropical lion and serpent into Arden, which, it appears, they have ascertained to lie in some temperate zone. I wish them joy of their sagacity. Monsters more wonderful are to found in that forest; for never yet, since water ran and tall trees bloomed, were there gathered together such a company as those who compose the *dramatis personæ* of *As You Like It*. All the prodigies spawned by Africa, *"leonum arida nutrix,"* might well have teemed in a forest, wherever situate, that was inhabited by such creatures as Rosalind, Touchstone, and Jaques.

*Notes*

1. It may be thus attempted in something like the metre of the original, which the learned know by the sounding name of Tetrameter Iambic Acatalectic:

   *Chr.*: Does Clinia talk of misery? Believe his idle tale who can?
       What hinders it that he should have whate'er is counted good for man—
       His father's home, his native land, with wealth, and friends, and kith and kin?
       But all these blessings will be prized according to the mind within:
       Well used, the owner finds them good; if badly used, he deems them ill.
   *Cl.*: Nay, but his sire was always stern, and even now I fear him still, &c.

2. This is printed as prose, but assuredly it is blank verse. The alteration of a syllable or two, which in the corrupt state of the text of these plays is the slightest of all possible critical licenses, would make it run perfectly smooth. At all events, in the second line,

"emulation" should be "emulative," to make it agree with the other clauses of the sentence. The courtier's melancholy is not *pride*, nor the soldier's *ambition*, &c. The adjective is used throughout—*fantastical, proud, ambitious, politic, nice*.

3. "Senectus ipsa est morbus."—Ter. *Phorm*. IV. i. 9.
4. Query *on*? "Wherein we play *in*" is tautological. "Wherein we play *on*," *i.e.* "continue to play."
5. Psalm xc. "A prayer of Moses, the man of God," v. 10.
6. "Formerly, that is to say, previous to the peace of 1815, a journey between Quebec and Sandwich was an undertaking considerably more tedious and troublesome than the voyage from London to Quebec. In the first place, the commissariat of the expedition had to be cared for; and to that end every gentleman who was liable to travel had, as a part of his appointments, a provision basket, which held generally a cold round of beef, tin plates and drinking-cups, tea, sugar, biscuits, and about a gallon of brandy. These, with your wardrobe and a camp-bed, were stowed away in a batteau, or flat-bottomed boat; and off you set with a crew of seven stout, light-hearted, jolly, lively Canadians, who sung their boat-songs all the time they could spare from smoking their pipes. You were accompanied by a fleet of similar boats, called a brigade, the crews of which assisted each other up the rapids, and at night put into some creek, bay, or uninhabited island, where fires were lighted, tents made of the sails, and the song, the laugh, and the shout, were heard, with little intermission, all the night through; and if you had the felicity to have among the party a fifer or a fiddler, the dance was sometimes kept up all night—for, if a Frenchman has a fiddle, sleep ceases to be a necessary of life with him. This mode of travelling was far from being unpleasant, for there was something of romance and adventure in it; and the scenes you witnessed, both by night and day, were picturesque in the highest degree. But it was tedious; for you were in great luck if you arrived at your journey's end in a month; and if the weather were boisterous, or the wind a-head, you might be an indefinite time longer.

   "But your march of improvement is a sore destroyer of the romantic and picturesque. A gentleman about to take such a journey now-a-days, orders his servant to pack his portmanteau, and put it on board the John Molson, or any of his family; and at the stated hour he marches on board, the bell rings, the engine is put in motion, and away you go smoking, and splashing, and walloping along,.at the rate of ten knots an hour, in the ugliest species of craft that ever disfigured a marine landscape."

# Much Ado about Nothing

The main plot in *Much Ado about Nothing* is the same with the story of *Ariodante and Ginevra* in Ariosto; the secondary circumstances and development are no doubt very different. The mode in which the innocent Hero before the altar at the moment of the wedding, and in the presence of her family and many witnesses, is put to shame by a most degrading charge, false indeed, yet clothed with every appearance of truth, is a grand piece of theatrical effect in the true and justifiable sense. The impression would have been too tragical had not Shakspeare carefully softened it in order to prepare for a fortunate catastrophe. The discovery of the plot against Hero has been already partly made, though not by the persons interested; and the poet has contrived, by means of the blundering simplicity of a couple of constables and watchmen, to convert the arrest and the examination of the guilty individuals into scenes full of the most delightful amusement. There is also a second piece of theatrical effect not inferior to the first, where Claudio, now convinced of his error, and in obedience to the penance laid on his fault, thinking to give his hand to a relation of his injured bride, whom he supposes dead, discovers on her unmasking,

Hero herself. The extraordinary success of this play in Shakspeare's own day, and even since in England, is, however, to be ascribed more particularly to the parts of Benedict and Beatrice, two humoursome beings, who incessantly attack each other with all the resources of raillery. Avowed rebels to love, they are both entangled in its net by a merry plot of their friends to make them believe that each is the object of the secret passion of the other. Some one or other, not over-stocked with penetration, has objected to the same artifice being twice used in entrapping them; the drollery, however, lies in the very symmetry of the deception. Their friends attribute the whole effect to their own device; but the exclusive direction of their raillery against each other is in itself a proof of a growing inclination. Their witty vivacity does not even abandon them in the avowal of love; and their behaviour only assumes a serious appearance for the purpose of defending the slandered Hero. This is exceedingly well imagined; the lovers of jesting must fix a point beyond which they are not to indulge in their humour, if they would not be mistaken for buffoons by trade.—AUGUST WILHELM SCHLEGEL, *Lectures on Dramatic Art and Literature*, 1809, tr. John Black

## H. N. HUDSON
*"Much Ado about Nothing"*
*Shakespeare: His Life, Art, and Characters*
1872, Volume 1, pp. 314–29

As with many of the author's plays, a part of the plot and story of *Much Ado about Nothing* was borrowed. But the same matter had been so often borrowed before, and run into so many variations, that we cannot affirm with certainty to what source Shakespeare was immediately indebted. Mrs. Lennox, an uncommonly deep person, instructs us that the Poet here "borrowed just enough to show his poverty of invention, and added enough to prove his want of judgment"; a piece of criticism so choice and happy, that it ought by all means to be kept alive; though it is indeed just possible that the Poet can better afford to have such things said of him than the sayer can to have them repeated.

So much of the story as relates to Hero, Claudio, and John, bears a strong resemblance to the tale of Ariodante and Ginevra in Ariosto's *Orlando Furioso*. The Princess Ginevra, the heroine of the tale, rejects the love-suit of Duke Polinesso, and pledges her hand to Ariodante. Thereupon Polinesso engages her attendant Dalinda to personate the Princess on a balcony by moonlight, while he ascends to her chamber by a ladder of ropes; Ariodante being by previous arrangement stationed near the spot, so as to witness the supposed infidelity of his betrothed. This brings on a false charge against Ginevra, who is doomed to die unless within a month a true knight comes to do battle for her honour. Ariodante betakes himself to flight, and is reported to have perished. Polinesso now appears secure in his treachery. But Dalinda, seized with remorse for her part in the affair, and flying from her guilty paramour, meets with Rinaldo, and declares to him the truth. Then comes on the fight, in which Polinesso is slain by the champion of innocence; which done, the lover reappears to be made happy with his Princess.

Here, of course, the wicked Duke answers to the John of the play. But there is this important difference, that the motive of the former in vilifying the lady is to drive away her lover, that he may have her to himself; whereas the latter acts from a spontaneous pleasure in blasting the happiness of others.

A translation, by Peter Beverly, of that part of Ariosto's poem which contains this tale, was licensed for the press in 1565; and Warton says it was reprinted in 1600. And an English version of the whole poem, by Sir John Harrington, came out in 1591; but the play discovers no special marks of borrowing from this source. And indeed the fixing of any obligations in this quarter is the more difficult, inasmuch as the matter seems to have been borrowed by Ariosto himself. For the story of a lady betrayed to peril and disgrace by the personation of her waiting-woman was an old European tradition; it has been traced to Spain; and Ariosto interwove it with the adventures of Rinaldo, as yielding an apt occasion for his chivalrous heroism. Neither does the play show any traces of obligation to Spenser, who wrought the same tale into the variegated structure of his great poem. The story of Phedon, relating the treachery of his false friend Philemon, is in Book ii. canto 4 of *The Faerie Queene*; which Book was first published in 1590.

The connection between the play and one of Bandello's novels is much more evident, from the close similarity both of incidents and of names. Fenicia, the daughter of Lionato, a gentleman of Messina, is betrothed to Timbreo de Cardona, a friend of Piero d'Aragona. Girondo, a disappointed lover of the lady, goes to work to prevent the marriage. He insinuates to Timbreo that she is disloyal, and then to make good the charge arranges to have his own hired servant in the dress of a gentleman ascend a ladder and enter the house of Lionato at night, Timbreo being placed so as to witness the proceeding. The next morning Timbreo accuses the lady to her father, and rejects the alliance. Fenicia sinks down in a swoon; a dangerous illness follows; and, to prevent the shame of her alleged trespass, Lionato has it given out that she is dead, and a public funeral is held in confirmation of that report. Thereupon Girondo becomes so harrowed with remorse, that he confesses his villainy to Timbreo, and they both throw themselves on the mercy of the lady's family. Timbreo is easily forgiven, and the reconciliation is soon followed by the discovery that the lady is still alive, and by the marriage of the parties. Here the only particular wherein the play differs from the novel, and agrees with Ariosto's plan of the story, is, that the lady's waiting-woman personates her mistress when the villain scales her chamber-window.

It does not well appear how the Poet could have come to a knowledge of Bandello's novel, unless through the original; no translation of that time having been preserved. But the Italian was then the most generally-studied language in Europe; educated Englishmen were probably quite as apt to be familiar with it as they are with the French in our day; Shakespeare, at the time of writing this play, was thirty-five years old; and we have many indications that he knew enough of Italian to be able to read such a story as Bandello's in that language.

The foregoing account may serve to show, what is equally plain in many other cases, that Shakespeare preferred, for the material of his plots, such stories as were most commonly known, that he might have some tie of popular association and interest to work in aid of his purpose. It is to be observed, further, that the parts of Benedick and Beatrice, of Dogberry and Verges, and of several other persons, are altogether original with him; so that he stands responsible for all the wit and humour, and for nearly all the character, of the play. Then too, as is usual with him, the added portions are so made to knit in with the borrowed matter by mutual participation and interaction as to give a new life and meaning to the whole.

So that in this case, as in others, we have the soul of originality consisting in something far deeper and more essential than any mere sorting or linking of incidents so as to form an attractive story. The vital workings of nature in the development of individual character,—it is on these, and not on any thing so superficial or mechanical as a mere frame-work of incident, that the real life of the piece depends. On this point I probably cannot do better than by quoting the following remarks from Coleridge:

"The interest in the plot is on account of the characters, not *vice versa*, as in almost all other writers: the plot is a mere canvas, and no more. Take away from *Much Ado about Nothing* all that is not indispensable to the plot, either as having little to do with it, or, like Dogberry and his comrades, forced into the service, when any other less ingeniously-absurd watchmen and night-constables would have answered the mere necessities of the action; take away Benedick, Beatrice, Dogberry, and the reaction of the former on the character of Hero,—and what will remain? In other writers the main agent of the plot is always the prominent character: John is the main-spring of the plot in this play; but he is merely shown, and then withdrawn."

The style and diction of this play has little that calls for special remark. In this respect the workmanship, as before noted, is of about the same cast and grain with that of *As You Like It*; sustained and equal; easy, natural, and modest in dress and bearing; everywhere alive indeed with the exhilarations of wit or humour or poetry, but without the laboured smoothness of the Poet's earlier plays, or the penetrating energy and quick, sinewy movement of his later ones. Compared with some of its predecessors, the play shows a decided growth in what may be termed virility of mind: a wider scope, a higher reach, a firmer grasp, have been attained: the Poet has come to read Nature less through "the spectacles of books," and does not hesitate to meet her face to face, and to trust and try himself alone with her. The result of all which appears in a greater freshness and reality of delineation. Here the persons have nothing of a dim, equivocal hearsay air about them, such as marks in some measure his earlier efforts in comedy. The characters indeed are not pitched in so high a key, nor conceived in so much breadth and vigour, as in several of the plays written at earlier dates: the plan of the work did not require this, or even admit of it; nevertheless the workmanship on the whole discovers more ripeness of art and faculty than even in *The Merchant of Venice*.

One of the Poet's methods was, apparently, first to mark out or else to adopt to a given course of action, and then to conceive and work out his characters accordingly, making them such as would naturally cohere with and sustain the action, so that we feel an inward, vital, and essential relation between what they are and what they do. Thus there is nothing arbitrary or mechanical in the sorting together of persons and actions: the two stand together under a living law of human transpirations, instead of being gathered into a mere formal and outward juxtaposition. That is, in short, the persons act so because they *are* so, and not because the author *willed* to put them through such a course of action: what comes from them is truly rooted in them, and is *generated* vitally out of the nature within them; so that their deeds are the veritable pulsations of their hearts. And so it is in the play. The course of action, as we have seen, was partly borrowed. But there was no borrowing in the characteristic matter. The personal figures in the old tale are in themselves unmeaning and characterless. The actions ascribed to them have no ground or reason in any thing that they are: what they do, or rather *seem* to do,—for there is no real doing in the case,—proceeds not at all from their own natures or wills, but purely because the author chose to have it so. So that the persons and incidents are to all intents and purposes put together arbitrarily, and not under any vital law of human nature. Any other set of actions might just as well be tacked on to the same persons; any other persons might just as well be put through the same course of action. This merely outward and formal connection between the incidents and characters holds generally in the old tales from which Shakespeare borrowed his plots; while in his workmanship the connection becomes inherent and essential; there being indeed no difference in this respect, whether he first conceives the characters, and then draws out their actions, or whether he first plans a course of action, and then shapes the characters from which it is to proceed.

*Much Ado about Nothing* has a large variety of interest, now running into grotesque drollery, now bordering upon the sphere of tragic elevation, now revelling in the most sparkling brilliancy. The play indeed is rightly named: we have several nothings, each in its turn occasioning a deal of stir and perturbation: yet there is so much of real flavour and spirit stirred out into effect, that the littleness of the occasions is scarcely felt or observed; the thoughts being far more drawn to the persons who make the much ado than to the nothing about which the much ado is made. The excellences, however, both of plot and character, are rather of the striking sort, involving little of the hidden or retiring beauty which shows just enough on the surface to invite a diligent search, and then enriches the seeker with generous returns. Accordingly the play has always been very effective on the stage; the points and situations being so shaped and ordered that, with fair acting, they tell at once upon an average audience; while at the same time there is enough of solid substance beneath to justify and support the first impression; so that the stage-effect is withal legitimate and sound as well as quick and taking.

The characters of Hero and Claudio, though reasonably engaging in their simplicity and uprightness, offer no very salient points, and are indeed nowise extraordinary. It cannot quite be said that one "sees no more in them than in the ordinary of Nature's sale-work"; nevertheless they derive their interest mainly from the events that befall them; the reverse of which is generally true in Shakespeare's delineations. Perhaps we may justly say that, had the course of love run smooth with them, its voice, even if audible, had been hardly worth the hearing.

Hero is indeed kind, amiable, and discreet in her behaviour and temper: she has just that air, nay, rather just that soul of bland and modest quietness which makes the unobtrusive but enduring charm of home, such as I have seen in many a priestess of the domestic shrine; and this fitly marks her out as the centre of silent or unemphatic interest in her father's household. She is always thoughtful, never voluble; and when she speaks, there is no sting or sharpness in her tongue: she is even proud of her brilliant cousin, yet not at all emulous of her brilliancy; keenly relishes her popping and sometimes caustic wit, but covets no such gift for herself, and even shrinks from the laughing attention it wins. As Hero is altogether gentle and womanly in her ways, so she offers a sweet and inviting nestling-place for the fireside affections. The soft down of her disposition makes an admirable contrast to the bristling and emphatic yet genuine plumage of Beatrice; and there is something very pathetic and touching in her situation when she is stricken down in mute agony by the tongue of slander; while the "blushing apparitions" in her face, and the lightning in her eyes, tell us that her stillness of tongue proceeds from any thing but weakness of nature, or want of spirit. Her well-governed intelligence is aptly displayed in the part she bears in the stratagem for taming Beatrice to the gentler pace of love, and in the considerate forbearance which abstains from teasing words after the stratagem has done its work.

Claudio is both a lighter-timbered and a looser-built vessel than Hero; rather credulous, unstable, inconstant, and very much the sport of slight and trivial occasions. A very small matter suffices to upset him, though, to be sure, he is apt enough to be set right again. All this, no doubt, is partly owing to his youth and inexperience; but in truth his character is mainly that of a brave and clever upstart, somewhat intoxicated with sudden success, and not a little puffed with vanity of the Prince's favour. Notwithstanding John's ingrained, habitual, and well-known malice, he is ready to go it blind whenever John sees fit to try his art upon him; and even after he has been duped into one strain of petulant folly by his trick, and has found out the falsehood of it, he is still just as open to a second and worse duping. All this may indeed pass as indicating no more in his case than the levity of a rather pampered and over-sensitive self-love. In his unreflective and headlong techiness, he fires up at the least hint that but seems to touch his honour, without pausing, or deigning to observe the plainest conditions of a fair and prudent judgment.

But, after all the allowance that can be made on this score, it is still no little impeachment of his temper, or his understanding, that he should lend his ear to the poisonous breathings of one whose spirits are so well known to "toil in frame of villainies." As to his rash and overwrought scheme of revenge for Hero's imputed sin, his best excuse therein is, that the light-minded Prince, who is indeed such another, goes along with him; while it is somewhat doubtful whether the patron or the favourite is more at fault in thus suffering artful malice to "pull the wool over his eyes." Claudio's finical and foppish attention to dress, so amusingly ridiculed by Benedick, is a well-conceived trait of his character; as it naturally hints that his quest of the lady grows more from his seeing the advantage of the match than from any deep heart-interest in her person. And his being sprung into such an unreasonable fit of jealousy towards the Prince at the masquerade is another good instance of the Poet's skill and care in small matters. It makes an apt preparation for the far more serious blunder upon which the main part of the actions turns. A piece of conduct which the circumstances do not explain is at once explained by thus disclosing a certain irritable levity in the subject. On much the same ground we can also account very well for his sudden running into a match which at the best looks more like a freak of fancy than a resolution of love, while the same suddenness on the side of the more calm, discreet, and patient Hero is accounted for by the strong solicitation of the Prince and the prompt concurrence of her father. But even if Claudio's faults and blunders were greater than they are, still his behaviour at the last were enough to prove a real and sound basis of manhood in him. The clean taking-down of his vanity and self-love, by the exposure of the poor cheats which had so easily caught him, brings out the true staple of his character. When he is made to feel that on himself alone falls the blame and the guilt which he had been so eager to revenge on others, then his sense of honour acts in a right noble style, prompting him to avenge sternly on himself the wrong and the injury he has done to the gentle Hero and her kindred.

Critics have unnecessarily found fault with the Poet for the character of John, as if it lay without the proper circumference of truth and nature. They would prefer, apparently, the more commonplace character of a disappointed rival in love, whose guilt might be explained away into a pressure of violent motives. But Shakespeare saw deeper into human nature. And perhaps his wisest departure from the old story is in making John a morose, sullen, ill-conditioned rascal, whose innate malice renders the joy of others a pain, and the pain of others a joy, to him. The wanton and unprovoked doing of mischief is the natural luxury and pastime of such envious spirits as he is. To be sure, he assigns as his reason for plotting to blast Claudio's happiness, that the "young start-up hath all the glory of my overthrow"; but then he also adds, "If I can cross him any way, I bless myself every way"; which shows his true motive-spring to be a kind of envy-sickness. For this cause, any thing that will serve as a platform "to build mischief on" is grateful to him. He thus exemplifies in a small figure the same spontaneous malice which towers to such a stupendous height of wickedness in Iago. We may well reluct to believe in the reality of such characters; but, unhappily, human life discovers too many plots and doings that cannot be otherwise accounted for; nor need we go far to learn that men may "spin motives out of their own bowels." In pursuance of this idea, the Poet takes care to let us know that, in John's account, the having his sour and spiteful temper tied up under a pledge of fair and kindly behaviour is to be "trusted with a muzzle, and enfranchised with a clog"; that is, he thinks himself robbed of freedom when he is not allowed to bite.

Ulrici, regarding the play as setting forth the contrast between life as it is in itself and as it seems to those engaged in its struggles, looks upon Dogberry as embodying the whole idea of the piece. And, sure enough, the impressive insignificance of this man's action to the lookers-on is only equalled by its stuffed importance to himself: when he is really most absurd and ridiculous, then it is precisely that that he feels most confident and grand; the irony that is rarefied into wit and poetry in others being thus condensed into broad humour and drollery in him. The German critic is not quite right however in thinking that his blundering garrulity brings to light the infernal plot; as it rather operates to keep that plot in the dark: he is too fond of hearing himself talk to make known what he has to say, in time to prevent the evil; and amidst his tumblings of conceit the truth leaks out at last rather in spite of him than in consequence of any thing he does. Dogberry and his "neighbour Verges" are caricatures; but such caricatures as Shakespeare alone of English writers has had a heart to conceive and a hand to delineate; though perhaps Sir Walter comes near enough to him in that line to be named in the same sentence. And how bland, how benignant, how genial, how human-hearted, these caricatures are! as if the Poet felt the persons, with all their grotesque oddities, to be his own veritable flesh-and-blood kindred. There is no contempt, no mockery here; nothing that ministers an atom of food to any unbenevolent emotion: the subjects are made delicious as well as laughable; and delicious withal through the best and kindliest feelings of our nature. The Poet's sporting with them is the free, loving, whole-hearted play of a truly great, generous, simple, child-like soul. Compared to these genuine offspring of undeflowered genius, the ill-natured and cynical caricatures in which Dickens, for example, so often and so tediously indulges, seem the workmanship of quite another species of being. The part of Dogberry was often attempted to be imitated by other dramatists of Shakespeare's time; which shows it to have been a decided hit on the stage. And indeed there is no resisting the delectable humour of it: but then the thing is utterly inimitable; Shakespeare being no less unapproachable in this vein than in such delineations as Shylock and Lear and Cleopatra.

Benedick and Beatrice are must the most telling feature of the play. They have been justly ranked among the stronger and deeper of Shakespeare's minor characters. They are just about the right staple for the higher order of comic delineation; whereas several of the leading persons in what are called the Poet's comedies draw decidedly into the region of the Tragic. The delineation, however, of Benedick and Beatrice stays at all points within the proper sphere of Comedy. Both are gifted with a very piercing, pungent, and voluble wit; and pride of wit is with both a specially-prominent trait; in fact, it appears to be on all ordinary occasions their main actuating principle. The rare entertainment which others have from their displays in this kind has naturally made them quite conscious of their gift; and this consciousness has not less naturally led them to make it a matter of some pride. They study it and rely on it a good deal as their title or passport to approval and favour. Hence a *habit* of flouting and raillery has somewhat usurped the outside of their characters, insomuch as to keep their better qualities rather in the background, and even to obstruct seriously the outcome of what is best in them.

Whether for force of understanding or for solid worth of character, Benedick is vastly superior both to Claudio and to the Prince. He is really a very wise and noble fellow; of a healthy and penetrating intelligence, and with a sound under-pinning of earnest and true feeling; as appears when the course of the action surprises or inspires him out of his pride of brilliancy. When a grave occasion comes, his superficial habit of jesting is at once postponed, and the choicer parts of manhood promptly assert themselves in clear and handsome action. We are thus given to know that, however the witty and waggish companion or make-sport may have got the ascendency in him, still he is of an inward composition to forget it as soon as the cause of wronged and suffering virtue or innocence gives him a manly and generous part to perform. And when the blameless and gentle Hero is smitten down with cruel false-hood, and even her father is convinced of her guilt, he is the first to suspect that "the practice of it lies in John the bastard." With his just faith in the honour of the Prince and of Claudio, his quick judgment and native sagacity forthwith hit upon the right clew to the mystery. Much the same, all through, is to be said of Beatrice; who approves herself a thoroughly brave and generous character. The swiftness and brilliancy of wit upon which she so much prides herself are at once forgotten in resentment and vindication of her injured kinswoman. She becomes somewhat furious indeed, but it is a noble and righteous fury,—the fury of kindled strength too, and not of mere irritability, or of a passionate temper.

As pride of wit bears a main part in shaping the ordinary conduct of these persons; so the Poet aptly represents them as being specially piqued at what pinches or touches them in that point. Thus, in their wit-skirmish at the masquerade, what sticks most in Benedick is the being described as "the Prince's jester," and the hearing it said that, if his jests are "not marked, or not laughed at," it "strikes him into melancholy"; while, on the other side, Beatrice is equally stung at being told that "she had her good wit out of *The Hundred Merry Tales*." Their keen sensitiveness to whatever implies any depreciation or contempt of their faculty in this kind is exceedingly well conceived. Withal it shows, I think, that jesting, after all, is more a matter of art with them than of character.

As might be expected, the good repute of Benedick and Beatrice has been not a little perilled, not to say damaged, by their redundancy of wit. But it is the ordinary lot of persons so witty as they to suffer under the misconstructions of prejudice or partial acquaintance. Their very sparkling seems to augment the difficulty of coming to a true knowledge of them. How dangerous it is to be so gifted that way, may be seen by the impression these persons have had the ill luck to make on one whose good opinion is so desirable as Campbell's. "During one half of the play," says he, "we have a disagreeable female character in Beatrice. Her portrait, I may be told, is deeply drawn and minutely finished. It is; and so is that of Benedick, who is entirely her counterpart, except that he is less disagree-able." And again he speaks of Beatrice as an "odious woman." I am right sorry that so tasteful and genial a critic should have such hard thoughts of the lady. In support of his opinion he quotes Hero's speech, "Disdain and scorn ride sparkling in her eyes," &c.; but he seems to forget that these words are spoken with the intent that Beatrice shall hear them, and at the same time think she overhears them; that is, not as being true, but as being suited to a certain end, and as having just enough of truth to be effective for that end. And the effect which the speech has on Beatrice proves that it is not true as regards her character, however good it may be for the speaker's purpose. To the same end, the Prince, Claudio, and Leonato speak as much the other way, when they know Benedick is overhearing them; and what is there said in her favour is just a fair offset to what was before said against her. But indeed it is plain enough

that any thing thus spoken really for the ear of the subject, yet seemingly in confidence to another person, ought not to be received in evidence against her.

But the critic's disparaging thoughts in this case are well accounted for in what himself had unhappily witnessed. "I once knew such a pair," says he; "the lady was a perfect Beatrice: she railed hypocritically at wedlock before her marriage, and with bitter sincerity after it. She and her Benedick now live apart, but with entire reciprocity of sentiments; each devoutly wishing that the other may soon pass into a better world." So that the writer's strong dislike of Beatrice is a most pregnant testimony to the Poet's truth of delineation; inasmuch as it shows how our views of his characters, as of those in real life, depend less perhaps on what they are in themselves than on our own peculiar associations. Nature's and Shakespeare's men and women seem very differently to different persons, and even to the same persons at different times. Regarded, therefore, in this light, the censure of the lady infers such a tribute to the Poet, that I half suspect the author meant it as such. In reference to the subject, however, my judgment goes much rather with that of other critics: "That in the unamiable passages of their deportment Benedick and Beatrice are playing a part; that their playing is rather to conceal than to disclose their real feelings; that it is the very strength of their feelings which puts them upon this mode of disguise; and that the pointing of their raillery so much against each other is itself proof of a deep and growing mutual interest: though it must be confessed that the ability to play so well, and in that kind, is a great temptation to carry it to excess, or to use it where it may cause something else than mirth. This it is that justifies the repetition of the stratagem for drawing on a match between them; the same process being needed in both cases in order "to get rid of their reciprocal disguises, and make them straightforward and in earnest." And so the effect of the stratagem is to begin the unmasking which is so thoroughly completed by the wrongs and sufferings of Hero: they are thus disciplined out of their playing, and made to show themselves as they are: before we saw their art; now we see their virtue,— the real backbone of their characters; and it becomes manifest enough that, with all their superficial levity and caustic sportiveness, they yet have hearts rightly framed for the serious duties and interests of life.

It is very considerable, also, how their peculiar cast of self-love and their pride of wit are adroitly worked upon in the execution of the scheme for bringing them together. Both are deeply mortified at overhearing how they are blamed for their addiction to flouting, and at the same time both are highly flattered in being made each to believe that the other is secretly dying of love, and that the other is kept from showing the truth by dread of mocks and gibes. As they are both professed heretics on the score of love and marriage, so both are tamed out of their heresy in the glad persuasion that they have each proved too much for the other's pride of wit, and have each converted the other to the true faith. But indeed that heresy was all along feigned as a refuge from merry persecutions; and the virtue of the thing is, that in the belief that they have each conquered the other's assumed fastidiousness, they each lay aside their own. The case involves a highly curious interplay of various motives on either side; and it is not easy to say whether vanity or generosity, the self-regarding or the self-forgetting emotions, are uppermost in the process.

The wit of these two persons, though seeming at first view much the same, is very nicely discriminated. Beatrice, intelligent as she is, has little of reflection in her wit; but throws it off in rapid flashes whenever any object ministers a spark to her fancy. Though of the most piercing keenness and the most exquisite aptness, there is no ill-nature about it; it stings indeed, but does not poison. The offspring merely of the moment and the occasion, it catches the apprehension, but quickly slides from the memory. Its agility is infinite; wherever it may be, the instant one goes to put his hand upon it, he is sure to find it or feel somewhere else. The wit of Benedick, on the other hand, springs more from reflection, and grows with the growth of thought. With all the pungency, and nearly all the pleasantry of hers, it has less of spontaneous volubility. Hence in their skirmishes she always gets the better of him; hitting him so swiftly, and in so many spots, as to bewilder his aim. But he makes ample amends when out of her presence, trundling off jests in whole paragraphs. In short, if his wit be slower, it is also stronger than hers: not so agile of movement, more weighty in matter, it shines less, but burns more; and as it springs much less out of the occasion, so it bears repeating much better. The effect of the serious events in bringing these persons to an armistice of wit is a happy stroke of art; and perhaps some such thing was necessary, to prevent the impression of their being jesters by trade. It proves at least that Beatrice is a witty woman, and not a mere female wit. To be sure, she is rather spicy than sweet; but then there is a kind of sweetness in spice,—especially such spice as hers.

I have already referred to the apt naming of this play. The general view of life which it presents answers well to the title. The persons do indeed make or have *much ado*; but all the while to us who are in the secret, and ultimately to them also, all this much ado is plainly *about nothing*. Which is but a common difference in the aspect of things as they appear to the spectators and the partakers; it needs but an average experience to discover that real life is full of just such passages: what troubled and worried us yesterday made others laugh then, and makes us laugh to-day: what we fret or grieve at in the progress, we still smile and make merry over in the result.

# Twelfth Night

At our feast wee had a play called Twelve Night, or what you will, much like the commedy of errores, or Menechmi in Plautus, but most like and neere to that in Italian called *Inganni*. A good practise in it to make the steward beleeve his lady widdowe was in love with him, by counterfayting a letter as from his lady, in generall termes, telling him what shee liked best in him, and prescribing his gesture in smiling, his apparaile, &c., and then when he came to practise making him beleeve they tooke him to be mad.—JOHN MANNINGHAM, *Diary*, Feb. 2, 1601

. . . after dinner to the Duke's house, and there saw *Twelfth Night* acted well, though it be a silly play, and not related at all to the name or day.—SAMUEL PEPYS, *Diary*, Jan. 6, 1663

The Twelfth Night, or What you Will, unites the entertainment of an intrigue, contrived with great ingenuity, to a rich fund of comic characters and situations, and the beauteous colours of an ethereal poetry. In most of his plays, Shakspeare treats love more as an affair of the imagination than the heart; but here he has taken particular care to remind us that, in his language, the same word, *fancy*, signified both fancy and love. The love of the music-enraptured Duke for Olivia is not merely a fancy, but an imagination; Viola appears at first to fall arbitrarily in love with the Duke, whom she serves as a page, although she afterwards touches the tenderest strings of feeling; the proud Olivia is captivated by the modest and insinuating messenger of the Duke, in whom she is far from suspecting a disguised rival, and at last, by a second deception, takes the brother for the sister. To these, which I might call ideal follies, a contrast is formed by the naked absurdities to which the entertaining tricks of the ludicrous persons of the piece give rise, under the pretext also of love: the silly and profligate Knight's awkward courtship of Olivia, and her declaration of love to Viola; the imagination of the pedantic steward Malvolio, that his mistress is secretly in love with him, which carries him so far that he is at last shut up as a lunatic, and visited by the clown in the dress of a priest. These scenes are admirably conceived, and as significant as they are laughable. If this were really, as is asserted, Shakspeare's latest work, he must have enjoyed to the last the same youthful elasticity of mind, and have carried with him to the grave the undiminished fulness of his talents.—AUGUST

WILHELM SCHLEGEL, *Lectures on Dramatic Art and Literature*, 1809, tr. John Black

---

## WILLIAM HAZLITT
### From *"Twelfth Night; or, What You Will"*
### *Characters of Shakespear's Plays*
### 1817

Thus is justly considered as one of the most delightful of Shakespear's comedies. It is full of sweetness and pleasantry. It is perhaps too good-natured for comedy. It has little satire, and no spleen. It aims at the ludicrous rather than the ridiculous. It makes us laugh at the follies of mankind, not despise them, and still less bear any ill-will towards them. Shakespear's comic genius resembles rather in its power of extracting sweets from weeds or poisons, than in leaving a sting behind it. He gives the most amusing exaggeration of the prevailing foibles of his characters, but in a way that they themselves, instead of being offended at, would almost join in to humour; he rather contrives opportunities for them to shew themselves off in the happiest lights, than renders them contemptible in the perverse construction of the wit or malice of others.—There is a certain stage of society in which people become conscious of their peculiarities and absurdities, affect to disguise what they are, and set up pretensions to what they are not. This gives rise to a corresponding style of comedy, the object of which is to detect the disguises of self-love, and to make reprisals on these preposterous assumptions of vanity, by marking the contrast between the real and the affected character as severely as possible, and denying to those, who would impose on us for what they are not, even the merit which they have. This is the comedy of artificial life, of wit and satire, such as we see it in Congreve, Wycherley, Vanbrugh, etc. To this succeeds a state of society from which the same sort of affectation and pretence are banished by a greater knowledge of the world or by their successful exposure on the stage; and which by neutralising the materials of comic character, both natural and artificial, leaves no comedy at all—but *the sentimental*. Such is our modern comedy. There is a period in the progress of manners anterior to both these, in which the foibles and follies of individuals are of nature's planting, not the growth of art or study; in which they are therefore unconscious of them themselves, or care not who knows them, if they can but have their whim out; and in which, as there is no attempt at imposition, the spectators rather receive pleasure from humouring the inclinations of the persons they laugh at, than wish to give them pain by exposing their absurdity. This may be called the comedy of nature, and it is the comedy which we generally find in Shakespear.—Whether the analysis here given be just or not, the spirit of his comedies is evidently quite distinct from that of the authors above mentioned, as it is in its essence the same with that of Cervantes, and also very frequently of Molière, though he was more systematic in his extravagance than Shakespear. Shakespear's comedy is of a pastoral and poetical cast. Folly is indigenous to the soil, and shoots out with native, happy, unchecked luxuriance. Absurdity has every encouragement afforded it; and nonsense has room to flourish in. Nothing is stunted by the churlish, icy hand of indifference or severity. The poet runs riot in a conceit, and idolises a quibble. His whole object is to turn the meanest or rudest objects to a pleasurable account. The relish which he has of a pun, or of the quaint humour of a low character, does not interfere with the delight with which he describes a beautiful image, or the most refined love. The clown's forced jests do not spoil the sweetness of the character of Viola; the same house is big enough to hold Malvolio, the Countess, Maria, Sir Toby, and Sir Andrew Ague-cheek. For instance, nothing can fall much lower than this last character in intellect or morals: yet how are his weaknesses nursed and dandled by Sir Toby into something 'high fantastical,' when on Sir Andrew's commendation of himself for dancing and fencing, Sir Toby answers—'Wherefore are these things hid? Wherefore have these gifts a curtain before them? Are they like to take dust like mistress Moll's picture? Why dost thou not go to church in a galliard, and come home in a coranto? My very walk should be a jig! I would not so much as make water but in a cinque-pace. What dost thou mean? Is this a world to hide virtues in? I did think by the excellent constitution of thy leg, it was framed under the star of a galliard!'—How Sir Toby, Sir Andrew, and the Clown afterwards *chirp over their cups*, how they 'rouse the night-owl in a catch, able to draw three souls out of one weaver!' What can be better than Sir Toby's unanswerable answer to Malvolio, 'Dost thou think, because thou art virtuous, there shall be no more cakes and ale?'—In a word, the best turn is given to every thing, instead of the worst. There is a constant infusion of the romantic and enthusiastic, in proportion as the characters are natural and sincere: whereas, in the more artificial style of comedy, every thing gives way to ridicule and indifference, there being nothing left but affectation on one side, and incredulity on the other.—Much as we like Shakespear's comedies, we cannot agree with Dr. Johnson that they are better than his tragedies; nor do we like them half so well. If his inclination to comedy sometimes led him to trifle with the seriousness of tragedy, the poetical and impassioned passages are the best parts of his comedies. The great and secret charm of *Twelfth Night* is the character of Viola. Much as we like catches and cakes and ale, there is something that we like better. We have a friendship for Sir Toby; we patronise Sir Andrew; we have an understanding with the Clown, a sneaking kindness for Maria and her rogueries; we feel a regard for Malvolio, and sympathise with his gravity, his smiles, his cross garters, his yellow stockings, and imprisonment in the stocks. But there is something that excites in us a stronger feeling than all this—it is Viola's confession of her love.

*Duke:* What's her history?
*Viola: A blank, my lord, she never told her love:*
   She let concealment, like a worm i' th' bud,

   Feed on her damask cheek: she pin'd in thought,
   And with a green and yellow melancholy,
   She sat like Patience on a monument,
   Smiling at grief. *Was not this love indeed?*
   We men may say more, swear more, but indeed,
   Our shews are more than will; for still we prove
   Much in our vows, but little in our love.
*Duke:* But died thy sister of her love, my boy?
*Viola:* I am all the daughters of my father's house,
   And all the brothers too;—and yet I know not.

Shakespear alone could describe the effect of his own poetry.

   Oh, it came o'er the ear like the sweet south
   That breathes upon a bank of violets,
   Stealing and giving odour.

What we so much admire here is not the image of Patience on a monument, which has been generally quoted, but the lines before and after it. 'They give a very echo to the seat where love is throned.' How long ago it is since we first learnt to repeat them; and still, still they vibrate on the heart, like the sounds which the passing wind draws from the trembling strings of a harp left on some desert shore! There are other passages of not less impassioned sweetness. Such is Olivia's address to Sebastian, whom she supposes to have already deceived her in a promise of marriage.

   Blame not this haste of mine: if you mean well,
   Now go with me and with this holy man
   Into the chantry by: there before him,
   And underneath that consecrated roof,
   Plight me the full assurance of your faith,
   *That my most jealous and too doubtful soul
   May live at peace.*

## FRANK HARRIS
### From "Shakespeare as Lyric Poet: *Twelfth Night*"
#### *The Man Shakespeare*
#### 1909, pp. 129–38

The place of *Twelfth Night* is as clearly marked in Shakespeare's works as *Romeo and Juliet* or *The Tempest*. It stands on the dividing line between his light, joyous comedies and the great tragedies; it was all done at the topmost height of happy hours, but there are hints in it which we shall have to notice later, which show that when writing it Shakespeare had already looked into the valley of disillusion which he was about to tread. But *Twelfth Night* is written in the spirit of *As You Like It* or *Much Ado*, only it is still more personal-ingenuous and less dramatic than these; it is, indeed, a lyric of love and the joy of living.

There is no intenser delight to a lover of letters than to find Shakespeare singing, with happy unconcern, of the things he loved best—not the Shakespeare of Hamlet or Macbeth, whose intellect speaks in critical judgements of men and of life, and whose heart we are fain to divine from slight indications; nor Shakespeare the dramatist, who tried now and again to give life to puppets like Coriolanus and Iago, with whom he had little sympathy; but Shakespeare the poet, Shakespeare the lover, Shakespeare whom Ben Jonson called "the gentle," Shakespeare the sweet-hearted singer, as he lived and suffered and enjoyed. If I were asked to complete the portrait given to us by Shakespeare of himself in Hamlet-Macbeth with one single passage, I should certainly choose the first words of the Duke in *Twelfth Night*. I must transcribe the poem, though it will be in every reader's remembrance; for it contains the completest, the most characteristic, confession of Shakespeare's feelings ever given in a few lines:

> If music be the food of love, play on;
> Give me excess of it, that surfeiting
> The appetite may sicken, and so die.
> That strain again;—it had a dying fall:
> Oh, it came o'er my ear like the sweet south
> That breathes upon a bank of violets,
> Stealing and giving odour.—Enough! no more;
> 'Tis not so sweet now as it was before.

Every one will notice that Shakespeare as we know him in Romeo is here depicted again with insistence on a few salient traits; here, too, we have the poet of the Sonnets masquerading as a Duke and the protagonist of yet another play. There is still less art used in characterizing this Duke than there is in characterizing Macbeth; Shakespeare merely lets himself go and sings his feelings in the most beautiful words. This is his philosophy of music and of love:

> Give me excess of it, that surfeiting,
> The appetite may sicken, and so die;

and then:

> Enough, no more;
> 'Tis not so sweet now as it was before.

—the quick revulsion of the delicate artist-voluptuary who wishes to keep unblunted in memory the most exquisite pang of pleasure.

Speech after speech discovers the same happy freedom and absolute abandonment to the "sense of beauty." Curio proposes hunting the hart, and at once the Duke breaks out:

> Why, so I do, the noblest that I have.
> O, when mine eyes did see Olivia first,
> Methought she purged the air of pestilence.
> That instant was I turned into a hart,
> And my desires, like fell and cruel hounds,
> E'er since pursue me.

Valentine then comes to tell him that Olivia is still mourning for her brother, and the Duke seizes the opportunity for another lyric:

> O, she that hath a heart of that fine frame
> To pay this debt of love but to a brother,
> How will she love, when the rich golden shaft
> Hath killed the flock of all affections else
> That live in her; when liver, brain, and heart,
> These sovereign thrones, are all supplied and filled—
> Her sweet perfections—with one self King!—
> Away before me to sweet beds of flowers,
> Love-thoughts lie rich when canopied with bowers.

The last two lines show clearly enough that Shakespeare was not troubled with any thought of reality as he wrote: he was transported by Fancy into that enchanted country of romance where beds of flowers are couches and bowers, canopies of love. But what a sensuality there is in him!

> When liver, brain, and heart,
> These sovereign thrones, are all supplied and filled—
> Her sweet perfections—with one self King!

Of course, too, this Duke is inconstant, and swings from persistent pursuit of Olivia to love of Viola without any other reason than the discovery of Viola's sex. In the same way Romeo turns from Rosaline to Juliet at first sight. This trait has been praised by Coleridge and others as showing singular knowledge of a young man's character, but I should rather say that inconstancy was a characteristic of sensuality and belonged to Shakespeare himself, for Orsino, like Romeo, has no reason to change his love; and the curious part of the matter is that Shakespeare does not seem to think that the quick change in Orsino requires any explanation at all. Moreover, the love of Duke Orsino for Olivia is merely the desire of her bodily beauty—the counterpart of the sensual jealousy of Othello. Speaking from Shakespeare's very heart, the Duke says:

> Tell her, my love, more noble than the world,
> Prizes not quantity of dirty lands;
> The parts that Fortune hath bestowed upon her,
> Tell her, I hold as giddily as Fortune;
> But 'tis that miracle and queen of gems
> That nature pranks her in attracts my soul.

So the body wins the soul according to this Orsino, who is, I repeat again, Shakespeare in his most ingenuous and frankest mood; the contempt of wealth—"dirty lands"—and the sensuality—"that miracle and queen of gems"—are alike characteristic.

A few more touches and the portrait of this Duke will be complete; he says to the pretended Cesario when sending him as ambassador to Olivia:

> Cesario,
> Thou knowest no less but all; I have unclasped
> To thee the book even of my secret soul;
> Therefore, good youth,

and so forth.

It is a matter of course that this Duke should tell everything to his friend; a matter of course, too, that he should love books and bookish metaphors. Without being told, one knows that he delights in all beautiful things—pictures with their faërie false presentment of forms and life; the flesh-firm outline of marble, the warmth of ivory and the sea-green patine of bronze—was not the poop of the vessel beaten gold, the sails purple, the oars silver, and the very water amorous?

This Duke shows us Shakespeare's most intimate traits even when the action does not suggest the self-revelation. When sending Viola to woo Olivia for him he adds:

> Some four or five, attend him;
> All if you will; for I myself am best
> When least in company.

Like Vincentio, that other mask of Shakespeare, this Duke too loves solitude and "the life removed"; he is "best when least in company."

If there is any one who still doubts the essential identity of Duke Orsino and Shakespeare, let him consider the likeness in thought and form between the Duke's lyric effusions and the Sonnets, and if that does not convince him I might use a hitherto untried argument. When a dramatist creates a man's character he is apt to make him, as the French say, too much of a piece—too logical. But, in this instance, though Shakespeare has given the Duke only a short part, he has made him contradict himself with the charming ease that belongs peculiarly to self-revealing. The Duke tells us:

> For such as I am all true lovers are,—
> Unstaid and skittish in all motions else,
> Save in the constant image of the creature
> That is beloved.

The next moment he repeats this:

> For, boy, however we do praise ourselves,
> Our fancies are more giddy and unfirm,
> More longing, unwavering, sooner lost and won,
> Than women's are.

And the moment after he asserts:

> There is no woman's sides
> Can bide the beating of so strong a passion
> As love doth give my heart; no woman's heart
> So big, to hold so much; they lack retention.
> Alas! their love may be called appetite,

No motion of the liver, but the palate,
That suffers surfeit, cloyment, and revolt!

Hamlet contradicts himself, too: at one moment he declares that his soul is immortal, and at the next is full of despair. But Hamlet is so elaborate a portrait, built up of so many minute touches, that self-contradiction is a part, and a necessary part, of his many-sided complexity. But the Duke in *Twelfth Night* reveals himself as it were accidentally; we know little more of him than that he loves music and love, books and flowers, and that he despises wealth and company; accordingly, when he contradicts himself, we may suspect that Shakespeare is letting himself speak freely without much care for the coherence of characterization. And the result of this frankness is that he has given a more intimate, a more confidential, sketch of himself in Duke Orsino of *Twelfth Night* than he has given us in any play except perhaps *Hamlet* and *Macbeth*.

I hardly need to prove that Shakespeare in his earliest plays, as in his latest, in his Sonnets as in his darkest tragedy, loved flowers and music. In almost every play he speaks of flowers with affection and delight. One only needs to recall the song in A *Midsummer Night's Dream*, "I know a bank," or Perdita's exquisite words:

Daffodils,
That come before the swallow dares, and take
The wind of March with beauty; violets dim,
But sweeter than the lids of Juno's eyes
Or Cytherea's breath; pale primroses,
That die unmarried ere they can behold
Bright Phoebus in his strength, a malady
Most incident to maids; bold oxlips, and
The crown-imperial; lilies of all kinds,
The flower-de-luce being one;

or Arviragus' praise of Imogen:

Thou shalt not lack
The flower that's like thy face, pale primrose, nor
The azured harebell like thy veins; no, nor
The leaf of eglantine, whom not to slander
Outsweetened not thy breath.

Shakespeare praises music so frequently and so enthusiastically that we must regard the trait as characteristic of his deepest nature. Take this play which we are handling now. Not only the Duke, but both the heroines, Viola and Olivia, love music. Viola can sing "in many sorts of music," and Olivia admits that she would rather hear Viola solicit love than "music from the spheres." Romeo almost confounds music with love, as does Duke Orsino:

How silver-sweet sound lovers' tongues by night,
Like softest music to attending ears!

And again:

And let rich music's tongue
Unfold the imagin'd happiness that both
Receive in either by this dear encounter.

It is a curious and characteristic fact that Shakespeare gives almost the same words to Ferdinand in *The Tempest* that he gave ten years earlier to the Duke in *Twelfth Night*. In both passages music goes with passion to allay its madness:

This music crept by me upon the waters,
Allaying both their fury and my passion
With its sweet air

And Duke Orsino says:

That old and antique song we heard last night,
Methought it did relieve my passion much.

This confession is so peculiar; shows, too, so exquisitely fine a sensibility, that its repetition makes me regard it as Shakespeare's. The most splendid lyric on music is given to Lorenzo in *The Merchant of Venice*, and it may be remarked in passing that Lorenzo is not a character, but, like Claudio, a mere name and a mouthpiece of Shakespeare's feeling. Shakespeare was almost as well content, it appears, to play the lover as to play the Duke. I cannot help transcribing the magical verses, though they must be familiar to every lover of our English tongue:

How sweet the moonlight sleeps upon this bank!
Here will we sit, and let the sounds of music
Creep in our ears; soft stillness and the night
Become the touches of sweet harmony.
Sit, Jessica: Look how the floor of heaven
Is thick inlaid with patines of bright gold.
There's not the smallest orb which thou behold'st
But in his motion like an angel sings,
Still quiring to the young-eyed cherubims.
Such harmony is in immortal souls;
But, whilst this muddy vesture of decay
Doth grossly close it in, we cannot hear it.

The first lines of this poem are conceived in the very spirit of the poems of *Twelfth Night*, and in the last lines Shakespeare puts to use that divine imagination which lifts all his best verse into the higher air of life, and reaches its noblest in Prospero's solemn-sad lyric.

Shakespeare's love of music is so much a part of himself that he condemns those who do not share it; this argument, too, is given to Lorenzo:

The man that hath no music to himself,
Nor is not moved with concord of sweet sounds,
Is fit for treasons, stratagems, and spoils;
The motions of his spirit are dull as night,
And his affections dark as Erebus:
Let no such man be trusted.

That this view was not merely the expression of a passing mood is shown by the fact that Shakespeare lends no music to his villains; but Timon gives welcome to his friends with music, just as Hamlet welcomes the players with music and Portia calls for music while her suitors make their eventful choice. Titania and Oberon both seek the aid of music to help them in their loves, and the war-worn and time-worn Henry IV. prays for music to bring some rest to his "weary spirit"; in much the same mood Prospero desires music when he breaks his wand and resigns his magical powers.

Here, again, in *Twelfth Night* in full manhood Shakespeare shows himself to us as Romeo, in love with flowers and music and passion. True, this Orsino is a little less occupied with verbal quips, a little more frankly sensual, too, than Romeo; but then Romeo would have been more frankly sensual had he lived from twenty-five to thirty-five. As an older man, too, Orsino has naturally more of Hamlet-Shakespeare's peculiar traits than Romeo showed; the contempt of wealth and love of solitude are qualities hardly indicated in Romeo, while in Orsino as in the mature Shakespeare they are salient characteristics. To sum up: Hamlet-Macbeth gives us Shakespeare's mind; but in Romeo-Orsino he has discovered his heart and poetic temperament to us as ingenuously, though not, perhaps, so completely, as he does in the Sonnets.

Julia Dean as Beatrice
(*Much Ado about Nothing*)

*Twelfth Night*
(engraving by Fittler from a painting by Hamilton)

Mr. and Mrs. Wood as Touchstone and Audrey
(*As You Like It*)

*All's Well That Ends Well*

*Abhorson.* Truly, sir, I would desire you to clap into your prayers; for, look you, the warrant's come.
*Barnardine.* You rogue, I have been drinking all night; I am not fitted for 't.                    *Act IV. Scene III.*

*Measure for Measure*
(engraving by Peterson from a painting by Selous)

*The Merry Wives of Windsor*

# The Merry Wives of Windsor

Of this play there is a tradition preserved by Mr. Rowe, that it was written at the command of Queen Elizabeth, who was so delighted with the character of Falstaff, that she wished it to be diffused through more plays; but suspecting that it might pall by continued uniformity, directed the poet to diversify his manner, by shewing him in love. No task is harder than that of writing to the ideas of another. Shakespeare knew what the queen, if the story be true, seems not to have known, that by any real passion of tenderness, the selfish craft, the careless jollity, and the lazy luxury of Falstaff must have suffered so much abatement, that little of his former cast would have remained. Falstaff could not love, but by ceasing to be Falstaff. He could only counterfeit love, and his professions could be prompted, not by the hope of pleasure, but of money. Thus the poet approached as near as he could to the work enjoined him; yet having perhaps in the former plays completed his own idea, seems not to have been able to give Falstaff all his former power of entertainment.

This comedy is remarkable for the variety and number of the personages, who exhibit more characters appropriated and discriminated, then perhaps can be found in any other play.

Whether Shakespeare was the first that produced upon the English stage the effect of language distorted and depraved by provincial or foreign pronunciation, I cannot certainly decide. This mode of forming ridiculous characters can confer praise only on him, who originally discovered it, for it requires not much of either wit or judgment: its success must be derived almost wholly from the player, but its power in a skilful mouth, even he that despises it, is unable to resist.

The conduct of this drama is deficient; the action begins and ends often before the conclusion, and the different parts might change places without inconvenience; but its general power, that power by which all works of genius shall finally be tried, is such, that perhaps it never yet had reader or spectator, who did not think it too soon at an end.—Samuel Johnson, *Notes on Shakespeare's Plays*, 1768

Several of the comic parts of *Henry the Fourth* are continued in *The Merry Wives of Windsor*. This piece is said to have been composed by Shakspeare, in compliance with the request of Queen Elizabeth, who admired the character of Falstaff, and wished to see him exhibited once more, and in love. In love, properly speaking, Falstaff could not be; but for other purposes he could pretend to be so, and at all events imagine that he was the object of love. In the present piece accordingly he pays his court, as a favoured Knight, to two married ladies, who lay their heads together and agree to listen apparently to his addresses, for the sake of making him the butt of their just ridicule. The whole plan of the intrigue is therefore derived from the ordinary circle of Comedy, but yet richly and artificially interwoven with another love affair. The circumstance which has been so much admired in Molière's *School of Women*, that a jealous individual should be made the constant confidant of his rival's progress, had previously been introduced into this play, and certainly with much more probability. I would not, however, be understood as maintaining that it was the original invention of Shakspeare: it is one of those circumstances which must almost be considered as part of the common stock of Comedy, and everything depends on the delicacy and humour with which it is used. That Falstaff should fall so repeatedly into the snare gives us a less favourable

opinion of his shrewdness than the foregoing pieces had led us to form; still it will not be thought improbable, if once we admit the probability of the first infatuation on which the whole piece is founded, namely, that he can believe himself qualified to inspire a passion. This leads him, notwithstanding his age, his corpulency, and his dislike of personal inconveniences and dangers, to venture on an enterprise which requires the boldness and activity of youth; and the situations occasioned by this infatuation are droll beyond all description. Of all Shakspeare's pieces, this approaches the nearest to the species of pure Comedy: it is exclusively confined to the English manners of the day, and to the domestic relations; the characters are almost all comic, and the dialogue, with the exception of a couple of short love scenes, is written in prose. But we see that it was a point of principle with Shakspeare to make none of his compositions a mere imitation of the prosaic world, and to strip them of all poetical decoration: accordingly he has elevated the conclusion of the comedy by a wonderful intermixture, which suited the place where it was probably first represented. A popular superstition is made the means of a fanciful mystification of Falstaff; disguised as the Ghost of a Hunter who, with ragged horns, wanders about in the woods of Windsor, he is to wait for his frolicsome mistress; in this plight he is surprised by a chorus of boys and girls disguised like fairies, who, agreeably to the popular belief, are holding their midnight dances, and who sign a merry song as they pinch and torture him. This is the last affront put upon poor Falstaff; and with this contrivance the conclusion of the second love affair is made in a most ingenious manner to depend.—August Wilhelm Schlegel, *Lectures on Dramatic Art and Literature*, 1809, tr. John Black

*The Merry Wives of Windsor* is no doubt a very amusing play, with a great deal of humour, character, and nature in it: but we should have liked it much better, if any one else had been the hero of it, instead of Falstaff. We could have been contented if Shakespear had not been 'commanded to shew the knight in love.' Wits and philosophers, for the most part, do not shine in that character; and Sir John himself, by no means, comes off with flying colours. Many people complain of the degradation and insults to which Don Quixote is so frequently exposed in his various adventures. But what are the unconscious indignities which he suffers, compared with the sensible mortifications which Falstaff is made to bring upon himself? What are the blows and buffettings which the Don receives from the staves of the Yanguesian carriers or from Sancho Panza's more hard-hearted hands, compared with the contamination of the buck-basket, the disguise of the fat woman of Brentford, and the horns of Herne the hunter, which are discovered on Sir John's head? In reading the play, we indeed wish him well through all these discomfitures, but it would have been as well if he had not got into them. Falstaff in the *Merry Wives of Windsor* is not the man he was in the two parts of *Henry IV*. His wit and eloquence have left him. Instead of making a butt of others, he is made a butt of by them. Neither is there a single particle of love in him to excuse his follies: he is merely a designing, bare-faced knave, and an unsuccessful one. The scene with Ford as Master Brook, and that with Simple, Slender's man, who comes to ask after the Wise Woman, are almost the only ones in which his old intellectual ascendancy appears. He is like a person recalled to the stage to perform an unaccustomed and ungracious part; and in which we perceive only 'some faint sparks of those flashes of merriment, that were wont to set the hearers in a roar.' But the single scene with Doll Tearsheet, or Mrs. Quickly's account of his desiring 'to eat some of housewife Keach's prawns,' and telling her 'to be no more so familiarity with such people,' is worth the whole of the *Merry Wives of Windsor* put together. Ford's jealousy, which is the main spring of the comic incidents, is certainly very well managed. Page, on the contrary, appears to be somewhat uxorious in his disposition; and we have pretty plain indications of the effect of the characters of the husbands on the different degrees of fidelity in their wives. Mrs. Quickly makes a very lively go-between, both between Falstaff and his Dulcineas, and Anne Page and her lovers, and seems in the latter case so intent on her own interest as totally to overlook the intentions of her employers. Her master, Dr. Caius, the Frenchman, and her fellow-servant Jack Rugby, are very completely described. This last-mentioned person is rather quaintly commended by Mrs. Quickly as 'an honest, willing, kind fellow, as ever servant shall come in house withal, and I warrant you, no tell-tale, nor no breed-bate; his worst fault is, that he is given to prayer; he is something peevish that way; but nobody but has his fault.' The Welch Parson, Sir Hugh Evans (a title which in those days was given to the clergy) is an excellent character in all respects. He is as respectable as he is laughable. He has 'very good discretions, and very odd humours.' The duel-scene with Caius gives him an opportunity to shew his 'cholers and his tremblings of mind,' his valour and his melancholy, in an irresistible manner. In the dialogue, which at his mother's request he holds with his pupil, William Page, to shew his progress in learning, it is hard to say whether the simplicity of the master or the scholar is the greatest. Nym, Bardolph, and Pistol, are but the shadows of what they were; and Justice Shallow himself has little of his consequence left. But his cousin, Slender, makes up for the deficiency. He is a very potent piece of imbecility. In him the pretensions of the worthy Gloucestershire family are well kept up, and immortalised. He and his friend Sackerson and his book of songs and his love of Anne Page and his having nothing to say to her can never be forgotten. It is the only first-rate character in the play: but it is in that class. Shakespear is the only writer who was as great in describing weakness as strength.—WILLIAM HAZLITT, *"The Merry Wives of Windsor," Characters of Shakespear's Plays,* 1817

---

## DENTON J. SNIDER
### *"Merry Wives of Windsor"*
### *The Shakespearian Drama*
### 1887, Volume 1, pp. 144–71

There is more philological fun in this play than in any other work of Shakespeare. Language, the outer garment of thought, is distorted and torn, in order to make a comic drapery suitable to the characters. Most of the important persons in *Merry Wives* have some linguistic peculiarity, more or less pronounced; Sir John himself sets off the same tendency by turning critic of his mother tongue. Two foreigners, a Frenchman and a Welchman, are introduced, talking in a dialect which may well be able "to fright English out of his wits." In a different manner, Mrs. Quickly, though a native, "hacks our English" to very shreds. Ancient Pistol is full of theatrical bombast; Corporal Nym is overmastered by his one word, "humors;" mine Host of the Garter has his characteristic appellative, "bully rook." Linguistic oddities Shakespeare has

employed elsewhere, but never so many as in the present instance; the play is a curiosity of perverted human speech. In consonance with the spirit of the entire drama, language itself is turned into a caricature of language, and the people speak not merely their own character, but their own jargon. The result is, the piece, though humorous, is prose and must be written in prose. With a true instinct, and in perfect accord with the subject, the poet has employed less verse than in any other of his works. The minimum of meter and maximum of caricature very properly go together.

Usually, though not always in Shakespeare's comedies, prose is spoken by the characters with English names, and is reserved for burlesque and rollicking broad humor, while poetry, with its elevated passion, is spoken by persons with Italian or Romanic names. But in *Merry Wives* there is not an Italian name, though an Italian source has been found for some of its incidents; one stray French character is the Romanic contribution, and that is stranded in England and is caricatured. The setting and atmosphere of the play are purely English; there is through it a dash of English scenery with park, town, river, mead, and with a certain breeziness of the country. English jollity, too, we see throughout; merry England is here embodied, with its types in the merry wives, and in the men quite as merry. The world has turned to an English holiday, in whose pastimes business, work, the earnest ends of life have vanished. Yet not all England is here, but only the well-fed middle class of the country; the high and the low, the aristocracy and the populace are absent; the court and city appear faintly in the distance. On account of these narrow limits which exclude the refined and elevated part of the social system, the broad comic vein can be indulged in, and the picture, in many of its shades, turns a caricature.

English we find it in another sense; there is plenty of good eating and drinking in the play, to which no human being still in the bonds of the flesh ought to make objection. The drama at once finds "dinner on the table," whereof the attraction is stated, "a hot venison pasty," and the wine has been brought in already with which the attempt is made to "drink down all unkindness,"—a thing which in thirty throats requires quite a river of liquid. As the play begins with eating, so it ends with eating; thus says Page, comforting the Fat Knight: "Yet be cheerful, Knight; thou shalt eat a posset to-night at my house, where I will desire thee to laugh at my wife that now laughs at thee." So eating is the grand peace-maker. But what shall we say to the drinking, with Falstaff as hero? The center of Windsor is the tavern, the Garter, from which the influences radiate through the whole action. Fat, round, red-faced, merry English people are all the characters apparently, except one, Slender, who is ridiculed and nick-named because he is not like the rest; the national consciousness seems reflected in the fact that he is slender in mind, since he is slender in body. A lean man probably had a small chance of appreciation in Windsor. In this respect, too, the Fat Knight is the hero of the piece and gives tone to it throughout, by his ponderosity; verily he is the bearer, the grand embodiment of eating and drinking. For once we see that the poet has given over to his realistic tendency an entire drama, and allowed his idealism to be utterly swept out of the field.

Like all the comedies of Shakespeare, this play rests on Mediation, which is brought about mainly by the women. As in the instances of Portia, Rosalind, Hermione, and many others, the poet makes his leading female characters mediatorial, though their texture in the present case be slighter than usual. The merry wives not only maintain their honor against Falstaff, but to a degree, they mediate him; that is, they unmask and punish him, and bring him to repentance, which at least is uttered by him, and may last for a time. A husband is also cured of jealousy by their comic penalty. Anne Page, too, mediates her love conflict against father and mother. Even Mrs. Quickly has a mediatorial function, that of go-between and match-maker, wherein the high vocation falls down to caricature. So the four women of Windsor, though humble, show their kinship to Shakespeare's grand dramatic queens. Mediation now drops into the realm of low comedy, though it preserves its genuine spirit in an arabesque of laughter.

The plot is usually said to be Shakespeare's own, but it is made up of many well-known dramatic tricks and situations—the popular inheritance of the stage of all ages. The manifold disguises and concealments are changed somewhat, yet they essentially belong to the world's comic literature, be it story, legend, drama, novel. Dr. Caius pulling the messenger out of a hiding place, was not in Shakespeare's time, a new dramatic incident; Ford, the jealous husband, who in disguise gets from Falstaff's own lips, the scheme against the honor of his wife, is found under another name in Straparola, an Italian novelist; the Fat Knight hid in the buck-basket, and dressed as the old witch of Brentford, is very faintly suggested in the same quarter; the disguised Fairy World, as well as Herne the Hunter, seem to be the poet's application of a local legend sprung of English fairy lore. We must note that the marvelous here is not employed in its own right, as it is in *Midsummer Night's Dream*, but is something imitated, or in fact, burlesqued. But again we see that Shakespeare in the main borrowed his plot and incidents.

There are two very different texts of this play, that of the Quarto of 1602, and that of the Folio, of 1623. The first has about 1,400 lines, the second about 3,000; the difference in quantity is made more emphatic by a still greater difference in quality; the first compared with the second is defective in nearly every point worthy of notice. Accordingly the text in use at present is that of the Folio, with a few additions from the Quarto. The conjectures which seek to account for the above difference are mainly two: that the Quarto is a mutilated stolen copy of the complete play, and that it is the Poet's first draught, possibly the hasty product of the fourteen days which the Queen is said to have allowed him for writing his play. It makes little difference which conjecture we accept; in fact, we may accept both and unite them into a third conjecture, namely, that the Quarto is a mutilated copy of the first sketch, which sketch was afterward finished, as we see it in the Folio. The time of its composition would seem to be somewhere about 1600, in the period of *Henry IV.* and of *Henry V.*; but its exact chronological relation to those plays is not determinable. Dramatically *Merry Wives* asserts a decided independence of the cognate historical plays.

Two traditions are inseparably connected with this play, though they do not appear in print till a hundred years or more after its composition. Says John Dennis in the dedicatory epistle to the *Comical Gallant*, a drama of his founded on *Merry Wives*: "This comedy was written at her (Queen Elizabeth's) command, and by her direction, and she was so eager to see it acted, that she commanded it to be finished in fourteen days; and was afterwards, as tradition tells us, very well pleased at the representation." This was in 1702, when Dennis appealed to a living tradition. In 1709, Rowe in his *Life of Shakespeare*, adds another trait: "She (the Queen) was so well pleased with the admirable character of Falstaff in the two parts of *Henry IV.*, that she commanded him to continue it for one play more, and to show him in love; this is said to be the occasion of his writing the *Merry Wives of Windsor*." The truth

of the tradition cannot be positively affirmed, but it declares a plain fact concerning this drama. The Falstaff of *Henry the Fourth* has lost something; he is placed in a situation where his comic character cannot develop itself with its former freedom. The statement, therefore, concerning Her Majesty's interference, if it does not give the cause, is at least the consequence, of the play; the judgment of it has been embodied in the form of a tradition—the Poet has been placed under some external restraint, which crippled his artistic conception and characterization.

But it is, nevertheless, a great favorite on the stage, and also in the private study of the reader. For comic incident, it can hardly be surpassed; the tricks and schemes follow in quick succession, and with increasing interest to the close; the action is both rapid and diversified. A spirit of rollicking humor pervades the whole work—wit, caricature, and, sometimes, perhaps a touch of satire, are not wanting. The persons who participate in its scenes are of ample number, and of sufficient variety; there is no dullness or tediousness, though Falstaff is deceived thrice in quite the same manner. But the weak side of this drama is generally considered to be its characterization; the Fat Knight, who is the center of interest, has descended somewhat from his former high pedestal; the other characters are sketches, outlines, even caricatures—that is, the shapes here are not so fully individualized into human beings as is usual with the Poet; the chief stress seems to be laid upon movement and diversity. But there is a unity of theme and structure which places upon this drama the stamp of Shakespeare, who can be more truly detected by his dramatic architecture than by his characterization.

Casting a look at the external grouping, we observe that there are, in the main, four sets of people who are brought together. One is the Welsh parson and his foolish associates, Shallow and Slender; another is the two families of Windsor, which furnish the Merry Wives; the third is Sir John Falstaff and his boon companions, to whom mine Host of the Garter may be added; the fourth is Doctor Caius and his household. Fenton stands outside of them all, and is of a different mould. But the internal movement of the play does not run in these grooves; the groups just mentioned will separate and coalesce again, according to the necessity of the idea which is to be embodied. This demands mainly two threads, though somewhat complicated—that of Falstaff and his adventures, and that of Mistress Anne Page and her suitors. Dropping, therefore, the merely external side of the drama, we may proceed to develop its inner structure along with its thought and characters.

The action lies wholly in the realm of the Family, of which relation there are presented two phases—that after marriage, and that before marriage. In the first case an assault is made upon the marital bond—from without by incontinence, and from within by jealousy; in the person of the wife the integrity of domestic life is attacked, both by the libertine and by the husband. In the second case there is a violation of the fundamental condition of marriage on the part of both father and mother, who disregard the right of love in the person of their daughter. Such is the double wrong which the course of the drama must now overcome in a twofold manner. On the one hand the foolish voluptuary, as well as the jealous husband, must meet with a comic retribution for their deeds, and on the other hand the choice of the maiden must be shown triumphant against the will of the parents. Mrs. Ford and Mistress Anne Page are the heroines; the former maintains the honor of married life against a double assault, the latter maintains the honor of love against a double assault. Both, therefore, in their different spheres, uphold the essential principle of the Family against the various colliding obstacles. Thus the action starts with violation, and passes through conflict to triumph and ultimate unity in the domestic relation.

The structure of the play can be seen best by dividing it into three movements, since the division into acts is made according to theatrical requirements, and seldom corresponds to the demands of thought. The first thread of the first movement has for its central figure Sir John Falstaff, who is here shown in his transition from thief to lover. He—together with his companions, Bardolph, Nym, and Pistol—is in conflict with Shallow and Slender, who have been robbed and otherwise abused by the roguish set. Sir Hugh Evans (the Welsh Parson) and Page (the Windsor burgher) are the peacemakers. But from this occupation Sir John soon passes to love-making; he becomes infatuated with the notion that two married women, Mrs. Ford and Mrs. Page, are enamored of his portly person. The second thread has for its central figure Mistress Anne Page, who finds herself besieged by three suitors—the simpleton Slender, the fantastic Doctor Caius, and the sensible youth Fenton. From the rivalry of the first two lovers springs a duel—a challenge is sent by the French Doctor to the Welsh Parson. The second movement has also two threads, the first of which gives the adventures of Falstaff in his new occupation; he will continue to make advances to the Merry Wives, who will trick him twice, and thereby punish him—he will be cast into the Thames as dirty linen, and beaten as the old Witch of Brentford. Running parallel to the designs of the Fat Knight are the exploits of Ford, the jealous husband, who is also deluded and punished for his foolish suspicion. The second thread continues the story of Mistress Page and her three lovers—one of whom, Slender, has the consent of the father; another, the French Doctor, has the support of the mother; the third, Fenton, has the powerful assistance of Mistress Anne herself. There results a conspiracy of each against the others—who the winner will be can not be told till the end of the play. An undercurrent belonging here is the duel, which terminates in a practical joke played upon the combatants by the Host of the Garter, who afterwards has his trick brought home to himself. The third movement brings together the two previous threads—the third punishment of Falstaff is made the means for the solution of the conflict between the suitors; the schemes of both parents are defeated by the daughter, and she is joined in marriage to Fenton, who alone possesses her heart. Reciprocal affection must overcome all obstacles, as it is the true basis of the Family.

### I

The first movement, as usual in Shakespeare's comedies, portrays the wrong, the violation, which produces a tension, or possibly a disruption in the Family. Some breach in the Ethical World must be shown, in order to reveal the healing process of time's wounds. In the present instance, as before stated, the violation is double, against the marital and the ante-marital bond. Upon the former a double assault is made, that of incontinence and of jealousy; upon the latter a fourfold attack we witness, from father, mother, matchmaker and parson. This profusion of incident clusters around two organic lines, which we are now to trace.

1. Taking up the first thread, we find the rural justice, Shallow, in high dudgeon over certain wrongs which he had suffered. He evidently has a very lofty opinion of the dignity of a country squire, as well as of the rank and antiquity of his family. But these qualities are coupled with some obtuseness and considerable ignorance; the result is a grotesque compound of pomposity and absurdity. His complaint against Falstaff is

not groundless: "Knight, you have beaten my men, killed my deer, broken open my lodge;" but the Fat Hero laughs at him and his threats of legal procedure; his own folly will foil his attempt without any outside interference.

A second complaint of a similar kind is now made; it comes from Shallow's cousin, Slender, who also is a gentleman and a simpleton. He has, indeed, hardly sense enough to make a passable comic character; in him rustic simplicity quite reaches the borderland of irrationality. The portrait is vapid— even ugly. But he has money; he has rank. Our future interest in him arises entirely from the circumstances that he becomes one of the suitors of Mistress Anne Page. At present he prefers a charge "against you (Falstaff) and your cony-catching rascals, Bardolph, Nym, and Pistol. They carried me to the tavern and made me drunk, and afterwards picked my pocket." It is clear that Sir John and his band of retainers were making matters lively in the quiet neighborhood of Windsor; carousals at the inn, supported by thieving in the village, were the occupation of the jolly vagabonds.

Along with these two figures, which have a decided dash of caricature, is placed a third figure, which, in this respect, corresponds with them. It is Sir Hugh Evans, the Welsh Parson, who, in consonance with his holy calling, is made to play the part of a mediator; he tries to soothe the anger of his friend Shallow, and directs the attention of the latter into a more peaceful channel. His scheme is nothing less than to "leave our pribbles and prabbles and desire a marriage between Master Abraham (Slender) and Mistress Anne Page." In his work of reconciliation he is aided by the worthy burgher, Mr. Page, who invites the whole company to a dinner of venison pasty with wine, in order to "drink down all unkindness." The Welsh Parson is a good soul, but uses bad English. There is in him a strong leaven of sincerity—indeed, of piety; but his words and his actions never fail of some ridiculous incongruity, which forces us to laugh at him in spite of all our regard. But this laugh is his little penalty for his plan on marrying Slender to Anne Page's "seven hundred pounds," with the girl thrown in. Such a man·must speak unhappy English.

This preliminary conflict is now silenced—it drops out of the play, and we advance to the real theme. Sir John has seen Mrs. Ford, and he intends to make love to her. He has, too, beheld Mrs. Page, whom also he purposes to woo, after his fashion. He says that both have given him the wink of invitation, which we must suppose to be purely the product of his own imagination, though the very free behavior of two Merry Wives hereafter would indicate that they may have extended to him some "most judicious œiliads." The peculiar quality of Falstaff's love is plainly shown by the circumstances—it goes out towards two women, and married women at that. It, therefore, doubly violates the principle of the Family; one unmarried person of the opposite sex is evidently the ethical limit for man and for woman. Sensuality is, accordingly, the word to designate Sir John's nature. But there is another motive which appears here—the Knight, in both cases, seeks access to the husband's purse through the wife. These two elements run through the entire delineation of his character.

This change in his life brings about a dismissal of his attendants; Nym and Pistol refuse to be made the instruments of his suit, and are sent off. Bardolph had previously turned tapster. The discharged followers will take their revenge by informing the husbands of Falstaff's purpose; it is this information which weaves Ford, the man of jealousy, into the action. Thus we have witnessed Sir John's transition from thieving to wooing; but his love can only be lust. Also, we are able to account for the double motive to be observed in his future career; he carries along his desire for ill-gotten wealth into his amorous adventures; booty and beauty are his two almost equally balanced principles. In fact, his avarice seems sometimes stronger than his sensuality. The two traits consist well together—both are merely different forms of gratification of appetite against ethical subordination. Another remark ought to be made here—it is at this point that we can observe a connection between this play and *Henry the Fourth*; in the latter Falstaff is shown as the thief, whereas now he is seen changing to the lover.

2. The second thread leads us at once to "sweet Anne Page," about whom is spinning a web of marvels which rarely falls to the lot of a simple country girl. It has already been noticed that the good Welsh Parson, in the interest of peace, has proposed a match between the dear maiden and Slender; and now the latter has been conversing with her, in a manner which has effectually satisfied her mind, upon the interesting subject of hot meat and the bear, Sackerson. The Parson very reasonably deems himself unequal to the task of completing the enterprise, and he seeks the aid of Mrs. Quickly, famed throughout the community for her dexterity in such matters. The old gossip is a clearly-drawn character; she finds out the young marriageable people of the town, wins their confidence and their secrets, and kindly offers her mediation. She has become celebrated in this line of business; all three lovers in the play seek her assistance. The present enterprise, however, is one which is too great for her; general satisfaction is impossible; still, she promises her aid to each, and is not averse to taking money. But Anne Page, with an instinctive slyness, has not revealed her inclination; she, therefore, stands out of the reach of the old match-maker, and controls her own destiny.

Now Mrs. Quickly is attached to the household of the Frenchman, Dr. Caius, who, like Sir Hugh, is defective in English, and, moreover, lacks mental ballast. Volatile, irascible, always effervescing, he pops and foams like a bottle of champagne from his native land. He has, however, the pretension to courtly manners—a servant must be at his heels; he also fully recognizes the code of honor. Then the mixed fragments of language—French and English—which fly out of his mouth give the impression of a strong caricature. But the main link which connects him with the action is that he, too, is a suitor for the hand of Mistress Anne Page. Now comes the explosion. The Doctor goes to his closet and finds the messenger of Sir Hugh to Mrs. Quickly ensconced there in secret; he drags him out and the whole matter is revealed. Then results the challenge. The good Parson, in seeking to bring peace and happiness to others, has himself become involved in war, which particularly threatens destruction to the English tongue.

Such are two of the lovers; now comes a third—Master Fenton. He, too, is seeking the kind offices of Mrs. Quickly, who, of course, gives him encouragement and takes his money. It is clear that he is in some doubt about the success of his suit, and Mrs. Quickly also thinks to herself that "Anne loves him not, for I know Anne's mind as well as another does." The young girl is clearly mistress of the situation—she will dispose of herself according to the right of love, and bid defiance to the fine-spun schemes of father, mother, and match-maker. But it must not be thought that her conduct is the result of reflection; on the contrary, it is the true instinct of her womanly nature which guides her, amid so many snares, with complete success. She does not say much in the play; her love makes her act, but it does not seem to demand utterance. Sentimental scenes are,

therefore, suppressed in this drama, and, indeed, they would hardly be in unison with its general tenor.

Let us try to express the full scope of the first movement in a few words. There is unfolded a conflict with the Family in its real and in its potential forms—after marriage and before marriage. Falstaff assails two married women, and thus seeks to destroy the domestic bond already established; the parents of Mistress Anne Page violate the right of their daughter in disregarding her love, and thus they sap the foundation of marriage. Both parties, therefore, are in collision with the domestic institution, yet in very different degrees—the one party attacks it as realized, hence becomes criminal, and should be punished; the other party attempts to thwart its true realization by their individual ends, and hence, must be foiled in their endeavor.

## II

The second movement is essentially mediatorial; its process is to teach the old lecher a lesson, which will turn him from his evil ways—a lesson in which the jealous husband participates. Anne Page, too, shows herself an accomplished mediator of her own conflict. All these women are equal to the emergency, both in punishing the wrong and in vindicating the right, of the Family. Even Mrs. Quickly, the fraud and caricature of mediation, seems to attain her object, which is money.

1. The first thread continues to unfold the adventure of Sir John, who is misled in part by his vanity, for he thinks he is irresistible with women, and in part by his wicked experience, for he confounds the country freedom of the Windsor Wives with the city freedom of his London female acquaintances. The Merry Wives receive his love-letter; they are indignant, and resolve upon revenge. The retributive nature of his punishment is plainly suggested by Mrs. Ford: "I think the best way were to entertain him with hope till the wicked fire of lust have melted him in his own grease." The pith of their characters is, they are not squeamish, but they are honest. Their language can scarcely be called elegant, their jests are not always refined, and their imaginations are not remarkable for delicacy. It must be confessed that they have probably given some provocation for the attack of the old sensualist, in their intercourse with him. But their supreme comic trait is their love of fun; they forget insult and a soiled reputation in a good opportunity for some sport. The letter of Falstaff furnishes an occasion, which is seized on the spot. Dame Quickly is sent to him, and she prepares the way for a meeting at the house of Mrs. Ford.

Now appears the counterpart of Falstaff, namely, the jealous husband, Ford. He is informed of the Fat Knight's scheme by the dismissed attendants of the latter, and his suspicions are fully aroused. He disguises himself, goes to Sir John, and verifies his information. Here another incident is introduced which must not be forgotten in estimating the character of Falstaff—he is now seen acting the part of a procurer; this is the third capital fact of his career in this play. Ford is the contrast to the easy-going Page, who, however, has his foible in a different direction, namely, in disregarding the right of his daughter. But the jealous husband is the true counterpart of the seducer—the one embitters and undermines the domestic relation on its internal side, the other assails it from without. Hence Ford and Falstaff belong together in thought, and manifest separate phases of the same violation.

But the Merry Wives are equal to the occasion, particularly Mrs. Ford, who will punish both her assailants in a supreme manner. Twice is Sir John led into the trap prepared for him; twice does he receive the full penalty for his act. With dirty linen, a symbol of his own character, he is tossed into the water, which, however, will not cleanse him as it does a soiled garment. Once more he returns to his evil ways; this time he is beaten for a sorceress—the incarnation of Satan. In a parallel manner Ford makes two public raids upon the honor of his wife; besides the keen torture of jealousy—an infernal fire of itself—he is shamed by the jeers and reproaches of his neighbors. Ford at last repents, and expresses contrition to his wife; his reward is that he is henceforward admitted to share the sport which is now drawing to an end.

2. The second thread resumes the story of Mistress Anne Page and her wooing. The suitors present their claims with vigor; the father is won by the large amount of land which Slender possesses, and is ready, for such an offset, to marry his daughter to a simpleton. His motive is impure: he would sacrifice his child, and, hence, he must be thwarted in his attempt. The mother has selected Doctor Caius, being influenced thereto by the prospect of display and the hope of introduction at court, where the Doctor is known; thus her vanity is tickled, nor does she forget that he has money. Both parents manifestly violate the right of love, since they have some ground foreign to it for the marriage of their child. Mistress Anne, however, has made her own selection; it is Fenton. Not much is said of this young man, but what is said redounds to his credit. He openly declares that he seeks the hand of Anne not for her wealth—though he confesses that such was at first his object; further acquaintance, however, has revealed in her character something above all property. He has a higher position at court than Doctor Caius; he is better descended than Slender; and has, moreover, good sense, which belongs to neither of the other suitors. The Poet has, therefore, marked this pair with the unfailing sign of future union, namely, reciprocal affection. The love of each is requited—they are one in emotion, and, hence belong together.

In this connection we must note the result of the duel which sprang from the intrigue around Anne Page. The Host of the Garter was chosen to make the preparations; he first fools the combatants by sending each to a different place; then he brings them together, utters jibes at both, and finally goes away, taking along their weapons. They can do naught but become reconciled; a basis of agreement is furnished by their common grievance against the Host of the Garter; they at once unite in a resolution to be revenged upon him. "The soul-curer and the body-curer" are now fast friends; both are foreigners, and murder only English in trying to murder each other. They are both made comic in speech and in deed; their punishment is their caricature; they had no business to go counter to Anne Page's right of love; they are not only thwarted in this attempt, and befooled in the duel, but are not allowed by the Poet to speak good English. Such is the comic retribution; the wronger of love is the enemy of Anglo-Saxon. How they got even with the Host of the Garter is not expressly declared, though we may suppose they had something to do with the deceit practiced upon him in the name of the German Duke. But this is an obscure and unsatisfactory part of the drama.

### III

The third movement recounts the complete reconciliation of all the colliding elements. Two tricks are not enough to disillusion Falstaff, so strongly intrenched in him are his self-conceit and his salacity; the bait of temptation is flung before his eyes a third time, and he grasps for it, but the Devil will not allow him to sin. The grossest trick of all is played upon him, he is reached through his superstition in spite of his wit; he loses his vanity and sees that lechery leads to folly. The story of Falstaff's final deception is made the means of settling the

struggle among the suitors of Anne Page; thus the two threads run together in a common solution and need not be separately developed.

The Merry Wives induce Falstaff at midnight in the park to represent Herne, the Hunter, with horns on his head. The song of the disguised fairies declares the penalty of lust, and the thought of the whole incident is the retribution of sinful desire; the moral intended is directly expressed. At the same time Fenton and Anne Page, who are endowed with mutual love, slip away to the church and get married. She violates the will of her parents, but is true to the higher principle of the Family. Here, too, the lesson is inculcated in the plainest words, and the whole extract may be given as Shakespeare's view of his favorite collision:

> The offense is holy that she hath committed;
> And this deceit loses the name of craft,
> Of disobedience, of unduteous title,
> Since therein she doth evitiate and shun
> A thousand irreligious, cursed hours,
> Which forced marriage would have brought upon her.

In no passage has the Poet expressed more clearly his moral convictions upon this subject; disregard of parental will, in the present case, is an offense, yet a holy offense; the deception practiced by Mistress Anne is justifiable—indeed, praiseworthy; for thus she shuns all evils of a forced marriage. The true unity of the Family is more important than adherence to an abstract maxim. Formal morality, when it collides with the domestic institution of man, must be quietly circumvented. Here we touch the great practical question of life, which comes home, at times, to every individual: What is the true course of conduct in such a conflict of duties? One side or the other must be subordinated, yet both sides have their validity. Shakespeare's method is to put what he deems the lower principle under the higher, and to use the less important as a means for the more important. The danger of such a doctrine is manifest—men will be too apt to see a collision of duties when there is none, and proceed to trample upon morality from specious pretexts. But the difficulty is not removed by shutting the eyes or by calling names; it must be met by action, and must be solved by thought.

But what shall be said of the character of Falstaff as shown in this play? He is portrayed in love, but his love is mere sensuality. Its nature can be easily inferred from the fact that it is called forth by two married women. But there is added his desire for money; he tries to reach the husband's purse through the wife, and, at the same time, takes the gains of a procurer. Still, all his cash is spent for bodily gratification, and we come back to sensuality as his fundamental trait. The comic element of his portraiture consists in his retributive deception; his passion spreads the net in which he is caught. He is outwitted at his own game, tricked with his own cunning; his fine-spun intrigue simply entangles himself. But the personal trait which gave him most pleasure was his cunning, and, hence, he does not hesitate to attempt carrying out his monstrous scheme. Bitter is his confession: "See now how wit may be made a Jack-a-lent when 'tis upon ill employment." It is, indeed, his deepest humiliation that his cunning has been unable to save him from this supreme disgrace. "Have I laid my brain in the sun and dried it that it wants matter to prevent so gross o'er-reaching as this?" It has all been done, too, by rude country bumpkins, men and women, honest people, but merry. He belongs, in this play at least, to Involuntary Comedy of Character; he pursues an utter delusion without knowing it; the solution is that he be brought to a complete consciousness of what he has been doing, and of the absurd nature of his conduct. This is the comic retribution which here overtakes him. Nor does he fail to declare the moral of his story: "This is enough to be the decay of lust and late walking through the realm."

Thus the two groups have removed the obstacles which stood in the way of the family, and harmony has been attained. The Merry Wives have vindicated their integrity and punished the aggressors; particularly Mrs. Ford is the strong character who has defended her domestic honor against the assaults from within and from without. Mistress Anne Page has triumphed over the schemes of her parents, and is joined in wedlock to the chosen one of her heart. In both cases—before and after marriage—the principle of the Family is victorious. On the whole, it is a Comedy of Situation, or rather of situations; the disguise of Ford is one side of the intrigue, and the simulation of the Merry Wives is its other side; while the thread of Mistress Anne Page has also its concealments. Still, the whole action does not turn round a masked individual—it is made up of a series of tricks and deceptions.

With this drama the treatment of the Pure Comedies of Shakespeare is brought to a conclusion. It will be seen that the ethical sphere in which they all are placed is the Family, though other elements may, for a short time, shine in upon the main current of the action. The dramatic structure, too, is observed to be fundamentally the same in all; the threads and movements are the lines upon which the play must be followed if we wish to reach the conception of the Author. These are, indeed, the web and woof of which the close, yet varied, texture of the work is composed; around these must be grouped the characters, which are thus shown at once in their relation to the rest of the play and in their inner development. If the critic merely picks out and describes in succession the separate persons, the living movement of the whole and its parts are lost; the gradual evolution of individual character disappears from the mind, or is grasped as a dead result; while the structural principle of the drama utterly perishes. A critical method which leaves out any essential element of Shakespeare is manifestly imperfect; and it ought to be added that a critical method which injects any foreign element into Shakespeare is unquestionably vicious.

# *All's Well That Ends Well*

*All's Well That Ends Well* is the old story of a young maiden whose love looked much higher than her station. She obtains her lover in marriage from the hand of the King as a reward for curing him of a hopeless and lingering disease, by means of a hereditary areanum of her father, who had been in his lifetime a celebrated physician. The young man despises her virtue and beauty; concludes the marriage only in appearance, and seeks in the dangers of war, deliverance from a domestic happiness which wounds his pride. By faithful endurance and an innocent fraud, she fulfils the apparently impossible conditions on which the Count had promised to acknowledge her as his wife. Love appears here in humble guise: the wooing is on the woman's side; it is striving, unaided by a reciprocal inclination, to overcome the prejudices of birth. But as soon as Helena is united to the County by a sacred bond, though by him considered an oppressive chain, her error becomes her virtue. —She affects us by her patient suffering: the moment in which she appears to most advantage is when she accuses herself as the persecutor of her inflexible husband, and, under the pretext of a pilgrimage to atone for her error, privately leaves the house of her mother-in-law. Johnson expresses a cordial aversion for Count Bertram, and regrets that he should be allowed to come off at last with no other punishment than a temporary shame, nay, even be rewarded with the unmerited possession of a virtuous wife. But has Shakspeare ever attempted to soften the impression made by his unfeeling pride and light-hearted perversity? He has but given him the good qualities of a soldier. And does not the poet paint the true way of the world, which never makes much of man's injustice to woman, if so-called family honour is preserved? Bertram's sole justification is, that by the exercise of arbitrary power, the King thought proper to constrain him, in a matter of such delicacy and private right as the choice of a wife. Besides, this story, as well as that of Grissel and many similar ones, is intended to prove that woman's truth and patient will at last triumph over man's abuse of his superior power, while other novels and *fabliaux* are, on the other hand, true satires on woman's inconstancy and cunning. In this piece old age is painted with rare favour: the plain honesty of the King, the good-natured impetuosity of old Lafeu, the maternal indulgence of the Countess to Helena's passion for her son, seem all as it were to vie with each other in endeavours to overcome the arrogance of the young Count. The style of the whole is more sententious than imaginative: the glowing colours of fancy could not with propriety have been employed on such a subject. In the passages where the humiliating rejection of the poor Helena is most painfully affecting, the cowardly Parolles steps in to the relief of the spectator. The mystification with which his pretended valour and his shameless slanders are unmasked must be ranked among the most comic scenes that ever were invented: they contain matter enough for an excellent comedy, if Shakspeare were not always rich even to profusion. Falstaff has thrown Parolles into the shade, otherwise among the poet's comic characters he would have been still more famous.—AUGUST WILHELM SCHLEGEL, *Lectures on Dramatic Art and Literature*, 1809, tr. John Black

*All's Well That Ends Well* is one of the most pleasing of our author's comedies. The interest is however more of a serious than of a comic nature. The character of Helen is one of great sweetness and delicacy. She is placed in circumstances of the most critical kind, and has to court her husband both as a virgin and a wife: yet the most scrupulous nicety of female modesty is not once violated. There is not one thought or action that ought to bring a blush into her cheeks, or that for a moment lessens her in our esteem. Perhaps the romantic attachment of a beautiful and virtuous girl to one placed above her hopes by the circumstances of birth and fortune, was never so exquisitely expressed as in the reflections which she utters when young Roussillon leaves his mother's house, under whose protection she has been brought up with him, to repair to the French king's court.

> Oh, were that all—I think not on my father,
> And these great tears grace his remembrance more
> Than those I shed for him. What was he like?
> I have forgot him. My imagination
> Carries no favour in it, but Bertram's.
> I am undone, there is no living, none

If Bertram be away. It were all one
That I should love a bright particular star,
And think to wed it; he is so above me:
In his bright radiance and collateral light
Must I be comforted, not in his sphere.
Th' ambition in my love thus plagues itself;
The hind that would be mated by the lion,
Must die for love. 'Twas pretty, tho' a plague,
To see him every hour, to sit and draw
His arched brows, his hawking eye, his curls
In our heart's table: heart too capable
Of every line and trick of his sweet favour.
But now he's gone, and my idolatrous fancy
Must sanctify his relics.

The interest excited by this beautiful picture of a fond and innocent heart is kept up afterwards by her resolution to follow him to France, the success of her experiment in restoring the king's health, her demanding Bertram in marriage as a recompense, his leaving her in disdain, her interview with him afterwards disguised as Diana, a young lady whom he importunes with his secret addresses, and their final reconciliation when the consequences of her stratagem and the proofs of her love are fully made known. The persevering gratitude of the French king to his benefactress, who cures him of a languishing distemper by a prescription hereditary in her family, the indulgent kindness of the Countess, whose pride of birth yields, almost without a struggle, to her affection for Helen, the honesty and uprightness of the good old lord Lafeu, make very interesting parts of the picture. The wilful stubbornness and youthful petulance of Bertram are also very admirably described. The comic part of the play turns on the folly, boasting, and cowardice of Parolles, a parasite and hanger-on of Bertram's, the detection of whose false pretensions to bravery and honour forms a very amusing episode. He is first found out by the old lord Lafeu, who says, 'The soul of this man is in his clothes'; and it is proved afterwards that his heart is in his tongue, and that both are false and hollow. The adventure of 'the bringing off of his drum' has become proverbial as a satire on all ridiculous and blustering undertakings which the person never means to perform: nor can any thing be more severe than what one of the bye-standers remarks upon what Parolles says of himself, 'Is it possible he should know what he is, and be that he is?' Yet Parolles himself gives the best solution of the difficulty afterwards when he is thankful to escape with his life and the loss of character; for, so that he can live on, he is by no means squeamish about the loss of pretensions, to which he had sense enough to know he had no real claim, and which he had assumed only as a means to live.

Yet I am thankful: if my heart were great,
'Twould burst at this. Captain I'll be no more,
But I will eat and drink, and sleep as soft
As captain shall. Simply the thing I am
Shall make me live: who knows himself a braggart,
Let him fear this; for it shall come to pass,
That every braggart shall be found an ass.
Rust sword, cool blushes, and Parolles live
Safest in shame; being fool'd, by fool'ry thrive;
There's place and means for every man alive.
I'll after them.

The story of *All's Well That Ends Well*, and of several others of Shakespear's plays, is taken from Boccacio. The poet has dramatised the original novel with great skill and comic spirit, and has preserved all the beauty of character and sentiment without *improving upon* it, which was impossible. There is indeed in Boccacio's serious pieces a truth, a pathos, and an exquisite refinement of sentiment, which is hardly to be met with in any other prose writer whatever. Justice has not been done him by the world. He has in general passed for a mere narrator of lascivious tales or idle jests. This character probably originated in his obnoxious attacks on the monks, and has been kept up by the grossness of mankind, who revenged their own want of refinement on Boccacio, and only saw in his writings what suited the coarseness of their own tastes. But the truth is, that he has carried sentiment of every kind to its very highest purity and perfection. By sentiment we would here understand the habitual workings of some one powerful feeling, where the heart reposes almost entirely upon itself, without the violent excitement of opposing duties or untoward circumstances. In this way, nothing ever came up to the story of Frederigo Alberigi and his Falcon. The perseverance in attachment, the spirit of gallantry and generosity displayed in it, has no parallel in the history of heroical sacrifices. The feeling is so unconscious too, and involuntary, is brought out in such small, unlooked-for, and unostentatious circumstances, as to show it to have been woven into the very nature and soul of the author. The story of Isabella is scarcely less fine, and is more affecting in the circumstances and in the catastrophe. Dryden has done justice to the impassioned eloquence of the Tancred and Sigismunda; but has not given an adequate idea of the wild preternatural interest of the story of Honoria. Cimon and Iphigene is by no means one of the best, notwithstanding the popularity of the subject. The proof of unalterable affection given in the story of Jeronymo, and the simple touches of nature and picturesque beauty in the story of the two holiday lovers, who were poisoned by tasting of a leaf in the garden of Florence, are perfect master-pieces. The epithet of Divine was well bestowed on this great painter of the human heart. The invention implied in his different tales is immense: but we are not to infer that it is all his own. He probably availed himself of all the common traditions which were floating in his time, and which he was the first to appropriate. Homer appears the most original of all authors—probably for no other reason than that we can trace the plagiarism no farther. Boccacio has furnished subjects to numberless writers since his time, both dramatic and narrative. The story of Griselda is borrowed from his *Decameron* by Chaucer; as is the *Knight's Tale* (Palamon and Arcite) from his poem of the *Theseid*.—WILLIAM HAZLITT, *"All's Well That Ends Well," Characters of Shakespear's Plays,* 1817

---

### FRANK HARRIS
#### From *"All's Well That Ends Well"*
#### *The Women of Shakespeare*
#### 1912, pp. 134–60

*A*ll's Well That Ends Well remains, in spite of the early sketch which is its skeleton, so to speak, a work of the master's maturity. . . . ⟨I⟩t is of capital importance, for it fills a gap in our knowledge, making clear not only Herbert's view of Mary Fitton, but what is of infinitely more interest to us the way Shakespeare regarded his high-born patron, friend, and rival.

The picture of Helena in this play has been so bepraised that it demands attentive scrutiny; Coleridge called Helena "the loveliest of Shakespeare's characters" and the professor-mandarins all echo this nonsensical eulogy. It will be convenient to deal with this minor matter first; for it affords an easy entrance to the heart of the greater problem.

The features of Helena are outlined almost beyond power

of modification in the first scene of the first act. She admits she is in love with "a bright particular star" Bertram:

> my imagination
> Carries no favour in't but Bertram's.
> I am undone: there is no living, none
> If Bertram be away.

This is hardly the way a young girl confesses her love even to herself; it is needlessly emphatic.[1] Then Parolles comes to view, whom she weighs up far too correctly as a "notorious liar," a coward, and "a great way fool"; yet she engages at once with this fool and coward, in a long wordy discussion on virginity, which she admits "is weak in defence" while confessing that she wishes to lose it "to her own liking."

Then she talks of Bertram at court, and uses images in swarms to show off her word-wit, after the fashion of the time and the custom of young Shakespeare; and, lastly, she becomes thoughtful, almost philosophic, in the rhymed soliloquy that begins:

> Our remedies oft in themselves do lie,
> Which we ascribe to heaven

This monologue ends with the tawdry affected words:

> who ever strove
> To show her merit, that did miss her love?
> The King's disease—my project may deceive me,
> But my intents are fix'd, and will not leave me.

In all these eighty or a hundred lines there is hardly a hint of feminine characterization. It is as poor, as lifeless, a sketch as any of Shakespeare's early failures in the same field. Helena's best words are those in which she pictures her lover; she admires his "arched brows," "hawking eyes" and "curls." I must just note that this physical description, being very rare in Shakespeare, is important; it indicates his extraordinary interest in the character of Bertram.[2]

The chief peculiarity in Helena's character so far is coarseness in thought and words, and this coarseness is a characteristic of the majority of Shakespeare's heroines. English criticism following Coleridge has exhausted ingenuity in explaining and excusing it. The defence is simple: the whole fault lies, if you please, in the time: Shakespeare's heroines are cleaner-minded than Fletcher's, and what could one wish for more than that? But all primitive times were not coarse; Homer and Sophocles are free of the fault, and Dante's Francesca is a model of reticent delicacy of speech. It looks as if the fault were in our race, or, to speak more truly, in the author, and though we should not be far wrong if we concluded that the talk which went on among the young noblemen on the stage in Shakespeare's time was as lewd as it well could be, and nine out of ten of the young women whom he met in the theatre were quite willing to bandy obscenities with their aristocratic admirers, still the coarseness of speech found in his dramas must be ascribed to his individual preference. Sophocles and Aristophanes in this respect, though of the same period, were poles apart, and Spenser was far more mealy-mouthed than our world-poet. It is certain, too, from Mercutio and Hamlet, and the ever-famous Nurse, that Shakespeare himself enjoyed jests which in our more squeamish times would startle a club smoking-room. I find no fault with him on this account, but when he depicts pure maidens enjoying the high flavour of such discussions, I can only say that he commits an offence against Nature and an error in art. He does not make Helena more real to us by her eagerness to talk of her virginity, but less real. It has never been a characteristic of young girls to like to discuss this theme with men whom they despise. The truth, of course, is that Mary Fitton was excessively sensual, bold and free-spoken, and because of his love for her Shakespeare was

continually tempted to ascribe her qualities to his heroines. Raphael, it is said, gave the brown, almond eyes of his mistress to all his Madonnas.

When questioned by the Countess, Helena is forced to admit the secret of her love; true, she fences at first with words; but, as soon as she has brought herself to confess, her avowal becomes as frank and passionate as a young man's would have been. This long speech belongs to the later revision, and is manifestly Shakespeare's own confession. Here are some lines:

> I know I love in vain, strive against hope;
> *Yet in this captious and intenible sieve*
> *I still pour in the waters of my love*
> *And lack not to lose still: thus, Indian-like*
> Religious in mine error, I adore
> The sun[3] that looks upon his worshipper,
> But knows of him no more.

If any one doubts that this is Shakespeare speaking in his proper person of his love for Mary Fitton, let him consider the lines which I put in italics. Helena goes on:

> O! then, give pity
> To her *whose state is such, that cannot choose*
> *But lend and give where she is sure to lose;*
> That seeks not to find that her search implies,
> But riddle-like, lives sweetly where she dies!

The sad, Viola-like resignation of the last verses is untrue to Helena; for Helena has already told us that her "intents are fix'd"; already she means to cure the King and ask for Bertram's hand in recompense.

Her persuasion of the King, too, has nothing feminine in it; it is, indeed, curiously calm and rational in tone:

> What I can do, can do no hurt to try,

and when the King asks her how long the cure will take, she bursts into a parody of poetry:

> The greatest grace lending grace,
> Ere twice the horses of the sun shall bring
> Their fiery torcher his diurnal ring,
> Ere twice in murk and occidental damp
> Moist Hesperus hath quench'd his sleepy lamp.

and so forth in a way that ought to have frightened, or at least exasperated, his Majesty, instead of convincing him.

When asked "what she will venture" on the cure, she answers as a young lyric poet contemptuous of feminine modesty might answer:

> Tax of impudence,
> A strumpet's boldness, a divulged shame,
> Traduc'd by odious ballads: my maiden's name
> Sear'd otherwise; nay, worse of worst extended,
> With vilest torture let my life be ended.

The rhyme here adds a touch a exquisite comicality to such boasting as would befit Parolles or even the immortal Pistol.

Then the "pure and exquisite Helena," as Professor Herford calls her in the Eversley Edition, boldly asks in payment of her service for the husband she may select. Of course all this stuff is beneath criticism: one might as well take the miaullings of a midnight cat for eloquence as this for the dramatic presentation of a maiden's character. Helena hardly speaks at all; is, in fact, nothing more than the mouthpiece of young Shakespeare's crude opinions. A few phrases of his later writing glitter here and there; but they are embedded in a lot of rhymed nonsense and only serve to confuse our view of the girl.

As we have now reached the middle of the second act, it would be almost impossible for any art to make Helena live for us. Shakespeare, however, seems to have made up his mind to attempt the impossible, for we now meet continually the revision of his riper manhood. When asked to choose her husband, Helena suddenly forgets her boldness, and begins to talk like a girl: or rather like one of Shakespeare's girls, say Portia for choice:

> I am a simple maid; and therein wealthiest[4]
> That, I protest, I simply am a maid.
> Please it, your majesty, I have done already:
> The blushes in my cheeks thus whisper me,
> "We blush that thou shouldst choose; but be refus'd,
> Let the white death sit on thy cheek for ever:
> We'll ne'er come there again."

I do not like the second line of this excerpt, though it expresses a sentiment that Shakespeare uses a hundred times; but it is impossible not to admire the way in which the third line almost turns the fault into a beauty. Helena, however, doffs her maiden modesty as suddenly as she assumed it; evidently Shakespeare did not revise her speech to the fourth lord; this "pure" maiden says:

> You are too young, too happy, and too good
> To make yourself a son out of my blood.

Immediately afterwards she speaks again becomingly to Bertram: indeed just as Portia spoke to Bassanio; Portia says:

> her gentle spirit
> Commits itself to yours to be directed
> As from her lord, her governor, her king.

Helena says:

> I dare not say I take you; but I give
> Me, and my service, ever whilst I live,
> Into your guiding power. This is the man.

One could have wished the last four words away; but the first two lines almost save the situation.

When Bertram declares:

> I cannot love her, nor will I strive to do't,

one wonders, in view of the final reconciliation between them, why this Bertram should be so unnecessarily rude and resolved. It was this curt rudeness of Bertram as much as his "curls" and his insensate pride of birth which first made me see that Shakespeare was identifying Bertram with his faithless friend and rival, Lord William Herbert. For this rudeness of Bertram is not only exaggerated beyond the needs of the play, it is also consistent with what we know from history of Herbert's character and of the relations between him and Mary Fitton. After Mistress Fitton had borne him a child, Lord William Herbert was asked to marry her; but he refused peremptorily, "admitting the act," we are told, but denying responsibility.

Bertram's contempt is so wounding that Helena for the moment renounces her weird courtship; "Let the rest go," she cries; but the mischief's done. Moreover, she takes Bertram's hand as soon as he overcomes his unwillingness to offer it, and marries the man she knows dislikes her. Just as Helena has varied coarse pursuit with modest blushing, so now she varies humility with boldness. She says to Bertram:

> Sir, I cannot say
> But that I am your most obedient servant,

which sounds perilously like farcical exaggeration; the next moment she asks her unloving master for a kiss!

A little later we have the famous passage wherein she pictures Bertram as driven to the wars by her, and pities his "tender limbs" praying the bullets to "fly with false aim." But, good as the verses are, nothing can redeem Helena or render her credible, and the stratagem by which she makes her husband her lover is a thousand times more revolting than the compulsion she has used to make him wed her.

In his youth Shakespeare seems to have known very little about girls and nothing about their natural modesty, which fact in itself throws an evil sidelight upon his wife's character.

"All's well that ends well" is Helena's reiterated excuse. But it will not serve her. Take merely the words:

> But, O, strange men
> That can such sweet use make of what they hate.

The words "sweet use" under the circumstances are an offence: it is a boy's confession, not a girl's.

At the beginning of the play, indeed, Helena is a sort of boy wavering between absurd humility and cheeky boldness; later she becomes a woman at moments, with fine touches in her of pity and affection; the best I can say for her is that she is never more than half realized by the poet. When Dr. Brandes calls her a "patient Griselda" and says that Shakespeare has shed over her figure "a Raphael-like beauty," I excuse him as led astray by English commentators; but when Professor Dowden asserts that Shakespeare could not choose but endeavour to make beautiful and noble the entire character and action of Helena's "sacred boldness" I grin irreverently and recall Heine's contemptuous gibe at English critics.

The truth is that the character of Helena is a mere jumble of contradictions, without coherence or charm; she is not realized clearly enough or deeply enough to live.

The whole story of the play is unsuited to the character of a young girl, and perhaps no care could have made a girl charming, or even credible, who would pursue a man to such lengths or win him by such a trick.

Shakespeare probably sketched out the play early, about the time he was picturing girls running after men, but he had now identified Bertram with Lord Herbert and he could not paint Mary Fitton's love for his rival fairly.

I am glad that just as Dr. Johnson "could not reconcile his heart to Bertram" so Swinburne with as good reason "could not reconcile his instincts to Helena." But the desire to praise every work of Shakespeare was too strong for Swinburne even here, so he went on to talk of the "'sweet, serene, skylike' sanctity and attraction of adorable old age made more than ever near and dear to us in the incomparable figure of the old Countess of Rousillon." This sing-song of praise is undeserved; but a study of the old lady's portrait will bring us by the easiest way to our main thesis, the identity of Bertram with Herbert and his confession. Swinburne evidently took whatever the Countess says as characterization, whereas more often than not Shakespeare is using her as a mask to display his own wisdom.

At the very beginning she excuses Helena's passion in memorable words.

> Even so it was with me when I was young.
>   If we are nature's, these are ours; this thorn
> Doth to our rose of youth rightly belong;
>   Our blood to us, this to our blood is born;
> It is the show and seal of nature's truth,
> Where love's strong passion is impress'd in youth;
> By our remembrances of days foregone,
> Such were our faults—or then we thought them
>     none.

Nowhere else in all his work does Shakespeare try to give us his real opinion about passion, the whole unvarnished truth, as carefully as he does here. Desire belongs rightly to youth, he says, and yet condemns it as the thorn to the rose. Is it a fault? he asks: in youth we did not think so, is his half-hearted answer. Nowhere else do we see more clearly than here how anxious he was to keep a perfect balance, and Emerson's regret that Shakespeare never gave us his whole mind on the highest matters that concern man is a mere confession that Emerson could not read the dramatist. On this matter at least Shakespeare's opinion was far saner, better balanced, and nearer to the heart of truth than Emerson's cheap Puritanism. But is it true, as Shakespeare appears to think here, that passionate desire is an appanage of youth alone and wanes out with the years? It looks as if he were judging by convention and not after experience.

This speech does not paint the Countess for us. No old lady would be so anxious to keep a perfect balance. If she liked the girl, she might be inclined to smile on her love-sick passion for her son; if she did not like her, she would despise her for it. The Countess is too measured-wise. Or is Shakespeare suggesting here that an old lady would take a somewhat severe view of passion, severer than a man? I think not; that is too subtle for the dramatist: apparently we have here Shakespeare's own opinion, given most scrupulously.[5]

In the second scene of the third act, the old Countess brings us to wonder. As soon as she hears from her son that he has wedded Helena and not "bedded" her, and has sworn to make the "*not*" eternal, she calls him "rash unbridled boy," declares that she "washes his name out of her blood," and that "twenty such rude boys" might serve Helena. She begs the gentleman to go to him:

> tell him that his sword can never win
> The honour that he loses: more I'll entreat you
> Written to bear along.

What does this mean? It looks as if Shakespeare were taking Mary Fitton's side against young Herbert. In any case the condemnation is too impartial and far too emphatic in expression for a mother to use about an only son. It sets one thinking therefore. Of course Herbert's mother was "Sidney's sister" and renowned for high qualities. I think Shakespeare had this fine model in mind when drawing the old Countess Rousillon. However this may be, when he portrays a mother judging her only son too severely, he must, at least, have had very special reasons for disliking her son. In just the same way he gets the impartial Abbess in *The Comedy of Errors* to condemn his wife, Adriana, and her continual, jealous scolding. Moreover, it is astonishing that Shakespeare should have cared, in his maturity, to revise so poor a sketch as this *All's Well*. He must have known that the theme was impossible: why did he touch it? Why after working on it did he leave it in such a faulty condition? When Michelangelo leaves a statue unfinished, his *Pietà* of the Rodanini Palace for example, it is because the rough, imperfect modelling, the rude nose, and vast, sightless sockets are more expressive than perfect features would have been. Similarly if Shakespeare takes this unsatisfactory theme in hand and revises it, here carelessly, here with particular, unnecessary detail, it is surely to satisfy some personal need of self-expression. The whole play bristles with difficulties which no critic has ever tried to answer or even to face; let us see if the riddle will not solve itself.

First of all let us settle as near as we can the date of the revision. Several passages help us to this. Everyone remembers how the porter in *Macbeth* speaks of those who go "the primrose[6] way to the everlasting bonfire." The clown in the fifth scene of the fourth act of *All's Well* gives us the first sketch of that magnificent phrase: he speaks about:

> The flowery way that leads to the broad gate and the
> great fire.

Besides we have already caught distinct echoes of Portia and hints of Viola in the revision of Helena.

This revision was much earlier than *Macbeth*, yet it is evidently a product of Shakespeare's suffering. To be more exact, it is earlier, I feel sure, than *Hamlet* because it is not so bitter, and probably later than *Twelfth Night* and *Julius Cæsar*.

The time further explains why Shakespeare's revision of the character of Helena is so ineffectual. When he revised *The Two Gentlemen of Verona*, he did it all of a piece; he had before him the model which afterwards served for Portia; it was his first view of Mary Fitton from a certain distance as a great lady, and he made her credible to us because he pictured her in love with himself. But before revising *All's Well* he had been deceived by Mary Fitton and forced to realize her wantonness; he persisted in loving her, tried to rebuild his ruin'd love; he will not yet tell us the naked truth about her: he still prefers to idealize her, but he simply cannot describe her love for Herbert-Bertram with any charm or sincerity; even the revision, therefore, wavers and is unsatisfactory. For this and other reasons which will soon show themselves I place the revision of *All's Well* about the time of *Julius Cæsar* and slightly before *Hamlet*. But whether put before or after *Julius Cæsar* matters little; we are near enough to be true to Shakespeare's nature and growth, and that is perhaps better even than temporal truth.

Now let us take up the main question with this knowledge in mind, that Shakespeare revised the play about 1601, after he had been in love for some time with the "dark lady," and after Herbert had betrayed him. When Dr. Johnson condemned Bertram, he was wiser than he knew. It seems to me that Shakespeare's dislike of certain faults in the youthful Herbert comes to light in this harsh sketch of Bertram. Contrary to his custom the dramatist forces us to detest his protagonist. Moreover, though Bertram is by way of being the hero of the piece, he is allowed to speak most contemptuously of the heroine whom Shakespeare evidently intends us to admire. Every quality given to this Bertram must be weighed carefully. From sheer insensate pride of birth he holds Helena "most base," and disdains her as "a poor physician's daughter," though his mother loves her. Furthermore, not only does his mother condemn him and so alienate our sympathy from him, but Parolles speaks of him as "a foolish idle boy; but for all that very ruttish." And though he is shown as having despatched "sixteen businesses . . . a month's length apiece" in a night, and though he is praised on all hands for courage and capacity, Parolles returns to the charge, declaring that the young Count is "a dangerous and lascivious boy who is a whale to virginity and devours up all the fry it finds." Yet this lascivious Bertram refuses to "bed" Helena. These needless contradictions and the extravagantly precise and emphatic accusations of Parolles betray personal feeling. Besides all these charges agree with the contemporary portrait of young Herbert and his lechery given us by Clarendon.

Another weightier point. Shakespeare knows that he is going to end the play happily. As soon, therefore, as Bertram learns that he has slept with Helena, he must change towards her, and show her affection; he does this, declares, indeed, that he will love her "dearly, very dearly." Was it then the embracing which has made his right-about-face possible? It would have been well, one would think, at least to have passed this point over in silence, to have left it to be inferred by our imagination, but Shakespeare loathes this Bertram and makes him assert that the embracing had no effect upon him as, in fact, we know that it had no effect upon Herbert. But in art the abrupt change of feeling must be motived: why, then, does Bertram suddenly turn from hating to loving Helena? What should be an explanation is expressly ruled out and the improbable is thus made incredible! A man does not veer from hate to love without reason; but Bertram is left without a shadow of reason. But Shakespeare in his maturity does not blunder in this crude way. Such mistakes on his part are always due to personal feeling.

There is another piece of evidence which of itself should be convincing. Bertram's confession that he possessed Diana-Helena is most peculiar; it is worse than unnecessary as we shall see; it would have been better to pass the matter over in silence; yet the confession is dragged in, made circumstantial, and it damns Bertram in the reader's eyes as an unspeakable cad; puts him far lower than his mother's condemnation or Parolles' contempt. Yet, with consummate art, this accusing confession is contrived to strike us as sincere, bears indeed every imprint of truth heightened by careless, off-hand expression. Let us weigh each word of it, for it is surely Shakespeare telling us the actual truth about the connection between Herbert and Mary Fitton. Bertram says:

> certain it is I lik'd her,
> And boarded her i' the wanton way of youth.
> She knew her distance and did angle for me
> Madding my desire with her restraint,
> As all impediments in fancy's course
> Are motives of more fancy; and, in fine,
> *Her infinite cunning, with her modern grace,*
> *Subdued me to her rate:* she got the ring:
> And I got that which *any inferior might*
> *At market-price have bought.*

Here we have the plain, unvarnish'd truth at last. This is surely Herbert-Bertram's view of Mary Fitton. The lines I have put in italics are of intense interest: the "infinite cunning" with which Mary Fitton maddened eagerness, the affected self-restraint—are all used later to make Cressida and Cleopatra life-like to us; that "modern grace" was Mary Fitton's magic gift we may be sure, as native to her as the utter wantonness laid to her charge in the last two lines here, just as Shakespeare charged her with it again and again in the sonnets, and painted it for us as a vice of blood incurable in his "false Cressida."

Here, too, we have Shakespeare's frank and final judgment of Herbert. Bertram-Herbert paints himself for us to the life as the shallow, selfish, ineffably conceited, aristocrat-cad; not a single virtue in him save the common, hard virtues of vigour and courage. No wonder stout old Dr. Johnson could not stomach him. The contemptuous truth of the portrait shows that Shakespeare has at length been able to appraise the young nobleman at his proper value. Most likely, indeed, as I have said elsewhere, he saw Herbert in his true colours even earlier, but thought it too dangerous to himself to state his true opinion in his proper person in the sonnets. This elaborate self-judgment of Herbert is in perfect accord with the condemnation passed upon the "false friend" and "stealer" in *The Two Gentlemen of Verona* and in *Much Ado*. I am delighted, however, to have it here in unmistakable terms, for it not only throws new light on the relations between Herbert and Mary Fitton and his silly pride of birth, but it sets all doubt at rest as to the slight nature of the connection between Herbert and Shakespeare.

Some other indications that I am justified in thus identifying Bertram with Herbert may be given here. As I have said, it is an historic fact that when Miss Fitton bore Herbert a son he was asked to marry her and refused flatly, rudely, just as Bertram out of tune with the comedy refuses imperiously to have anything to do with Helena.

Another interesting point: when Parolles is questioned by the King, he declares that Bertram "was mad for her" and adds that he "knew of their going to bed, and other motions, as promising her marriage, and things which would derive me ill-will to speak of."

That "promising marriage" goes far by itself to establish the identity of Bertram with Herbert, for it has nothing on earth to do with the action; it contradicts indeed both the spirit and letter of the play, for Bertram is married and is to be reconciled to his wife. Shakespeare wishes us to believe that Lord Herbert had promised marriage to Mistress Fitton which the historical fact that he was asked to marry her, seems to imply. Again, the introduction of Parolles here only hems the action. Besides, what does Parolles mean by those "things which would derive me ill-will to speak of"? Is it Shakespeare confessing his own apprehensions to us, or a hint of worse things undivulged as yet on the part of Herbert or both? I think, both, and when we come to study Cressida we shall find the foul insinuation again and have our worst suspicions confirmed. Shakespeare's bitterness was so over-mastering, his dislike of Herbert so intense, that he takes Mary Fitton's side in the quarrel and tells the dangerous truth while hinting at darker secrets.

This identification of Bertram with Herbert fills up a great gap in our knowledge with curious completeness, and explains what otherwise must be regarded as the most stupid and fundamental blunders in the play.

I am especially delighted to find in Herbert-Bertram's confession the words "modern grace" applied to Mary Fitton. Some critics hold that "modern" should be read "modest," but I prefer "modern" in our sense of the word. I regard the phrase as Shakespeare's acknowledgment of Mary Fitton's novel witchery. That "modern grace" is the touch of inexplicable enchantment which I had been looking for in order to understand his "dark lady's" deathless fascination. In a later and still better portrait of Shakespeare's love, the very same quality in her is selected for praise by the coldest and most impartial of judges. In *Antony and Cleopatra*, Cæsar says of the dead Cleopatra she looks

> As she would catch another Antony
> In her strong toil of grace.

One or two words more in general on this play: Shakespeare is contemptuous of character in it. As in his latest work, so towards the end of this play, whenever he is led away by personal feeling, he spills himself into this or that character almost indifferently. Take, for example, what the First Lord says:

> The web of our life is of a mingled yarn, good and ill together: our virtues would be proud if our faults whipped them not; and our crimes would despair, if they were not cherished by our virtues.

This is certainly our gentle, fair-minded Shakespeare himself speaking without a mask.

The curious way in which Lafeu reads Parolles, is very much in the same vein as Hamlet's later reading of Guildenstern and Rosencrantz and Osric. At length Shakespeare sees the young courtier as he is: "There can be no kernel in this light nut . . ." and again "the soul of this man is his clothes."

It is probable that shortly after betraying him Herbert drew away from Shakespeare. Vain self-love generally teaches us to slight those whom we have injured, and as soon as the powerful patron began to stand aloof, others followed the great lord's example, and Shakespeare was taught what fair-weather friends are worth. The curious point is that he is not bitter at first. His bitterness is an after-growth, sustained by his ethical judgment; this Lafeu does not condemn Parolles as harshly as Hamlet condemns Guildenstern and Rosencrantz. Indeed he accepts him at the end and asks him to accompany him home; at least he will find amusement in him. Gentle Shakespeare could endure fools gladly as St. Paul advised, for he managed, as Lafeu tells us, to "make sport" with them.

Shakespeare sketched Lafeu as a wise old nobleman as a companion picture to the portrait of the old Countess, but the picture of Lafeu suffers from an all-too-close identification with Shakespeare himself. As in early manhood Shakespeare loved to picture a side of himself—especially his gaiety, wit, and talkativeness—in Biron, Gratiano, and Mercutio, so in maturity he loved to incorporate his honest loyalty in outspoken old gentlemen like Lafeu, Gonzalo, Flavius, Menenius, and Kent.

The gem of the play, however, for us is Herbert-Bertram's confession; it dates the revision; the talk is fresh; it smacks of the deed, and it finally settles the problem of Shakespeare's relations with Lord William Herbert. I can now go on to treat with perfect freedom of Shakespeare's long love-duel with Mary Fitton.

*Notes*

1. Unless, indeed, it is Shakespeare's idea of Mary Fitton's passion for Herbert.
2. The "curls" too and pride connect Bertram with the faithless young

lover whom we naturally took to be Herbert in *The Lover's Complaint*—
   His browny locks did hang in crooked curls.
3. Biron in *Love's Labour's Lost* is a mere mask of Shakespeare himself, and Biron says to Rosaline:
   Vouchsafe to show the sunshine of your face
   That we, like savages, may worship it.
But it is the "captious and intenible sieve" which convinces me that Shakespeare is here giving expression to his own regret.
4. This "therein wealthiest" reminds me of Portia's "happiest of all."
5. In *Love's Labour's Lost* the hero Biron, young Shakespeare's *alter ego*, speaks of passion in much the same way, but with two or three years' less experience:
   Young blood doth not obey an old decree;
   We cannot cross the cause why we were born.
6. Ophelia, too, in *Hamlet* speaks of "the primrose path of dalliance."

# *Measure for Measure*

The novel of Cynthio Giraldi, from which Shakespeare is supposed to have borrowed this fable, may be read in ⟨Charlotte Lennox's⟩ *Shakespear Illustrated*, elegantly translated, with remarks which will assist the enquirer to discover how much absurdity Shakespeare has admitted or avoided.

I cannot but suspect that some other had new modelled the novel of Cynthio, or written a story which in some particulars resembled it, and that Cinthio was not the authour whom Shakespeare immediately followed. The Emperour in Cinthio is named Maximine, the Duke, in Shakespeare's enumeration of the persons of the drama, is called Vincentio. This appears a very slight remark; but since the Duke has no name in the play, nor is ever mentioned but by his title, why should he be called Vincentio among the Persons, but because the name was copied from the story, and placed superfluously at the head of the list by the mere habit of transcription? It is therefore likely that there was then a story of Vincentio Duke of Vienna, different from that of Maximine Emperour of the Romans.

Of this play the light or comick part is very natural and pleasing, but the grave scenes, if a few passages be excepted, have more labour than elegance. The plot is rather intricate than artful. The time of the action is indefinite; some time, we know not how much, must have elapsed between the recess of the Duke and the imprisonment of Claudio; for he must have learned the story of Mariana in his disguise, or he delegated his power to a man already known to be corrupted. The unities of action and place are sufficiently preserved.—SAMUEL JOHNSON, *Notes on Shakespeare's Plays*, 1768

In *Measure for Measure* Shakspeare was compelled, by the nature of the subject, to make his poetry more familiar with criminal justice than is usual with him. All kinds of proceedings connected with the subject, all sorts of active or passive persons, pass in review before us: the hypocritical Lord Deputy, the compassionate Provost, and the hard-hearted Hangman; a young man of quality who is to suffer for the seduction of his mistress before marriage, loose wretches brought in by the police, nay, even a hardened criminal, whom even the preparations for his execution cannot awaken out of his callousness. But yet, notwithstanding this agitating truthfulness, how tender and mild is the pervading tone of the picture! The piece takes improperly its name from punishment;

the true significance of the whole is the triumph of mercy over strict justice; no man being himself so free from errors as to be entitled to deal it out to his equals. The most beautiful embellishment of the composition is the character of Isabella, who, on the point of taking the veil, is yet prevailed upon by sisterly affection to tread again the perplexing ways of the world, while, amid the general corruption, the heavenly purity of her mind is not even stained with one unholy thought: in the humble robes of the novice she is a very angel of light. When the cold and stern Angelo, heretofore of unblemished reputation, whom the Duke has commissioned, during his pretended absence, to restrain, by a rigid administration of the laws, the excesses of dissolute immorality, is even himself tempted by the virgin charms of Isabella, supplicating for the pardon of her brother Claudio, condemned to death for a youthful indiscretion; when at first, in timid and obscure language, he insinuates, but at last impudently avouches his readiness to grant Claudio's life to the sacrifice of her honour; when Isabella repulses his offer with a noble scorn; in her account of the interview to her brother, when the latter at first applauds her conduct, but at length, overcome by the fear of death, strives to persuade her to consent to dishonour;—in these masterly scenes, Shakspeare has sounded the depths of the human heart. The interest here reposes altogether on the represented action; curiosity contributes nothing to our delight, for the Duke, in the disguise of a Monk, is always present to watch over his dangerous representative, and to avert every evil which could possibly be apprehended; we look to him with confidence for a happy result. The Duke acts the part of the Monk naturally, even to deception; he unites in his person the wisdom of the priest and the prince. Only in his wisdom he is too fond of round-about ways; his vanity is flattered with acting invisibly like an earthly providence; he takes more pleasure in overhearing his subjects than governing them in the customary way of princes. As he ultimately extends a free pardon to all the guilty, we do not see how his original purpose, in committing the execution of the laws to other hands, of restoring their strictness, has in any wise been accomplished. The poet might have had this irony in view, that of the numberless slanders of the Duke, told him by the petulant Lucio, in ignorance of the person whom he is addressing, that at least which regarded his singularities and whims was not wholly without foundation. It is deserving of remark, that Shakspeare, amidst the rancour of religious parties, takes a delight in painting the condition of a monk, and always represents his influence as beneficial. We find in him none of the black and knavish monks, which an enthusiasm for Protestantism, rather than poetical inspiration, has suggested to some of our modern poets. Shakspeare merely gives his monks an inclination to busy themselves in the affairs of others, after renouncing the world for themselves; with respect, however, to pious frauds, he does not represent them as very conscientious. Such are the parts acted by the monk in *Romeo and Juliet*, and another in *Much Ado about Nothing*, and even by the Duke, whom, contrary to the well-known proverb, the cowl seems really to make a monk.—AUGUST WILHELM SCHLEGEL, *Lectures on Dramatic Art and Literature*, 1809, tr. John Black

This is a play as full of genius as it is of wisdom. Yet there is an original sin in the nature of the subject, which prevents us from taking a cordial interest in it. 'The height of moral argument' which the author has maintained in the intervals of passion or blended with the more powerful impulses of nature, is hardly surpassed in any of his plays. But there is in general a want of passion; the affections are at a stand; our sympathies are repulsed and defeated in all directions. The only passion which influences the story is that of Angelo; and yet he seems to have a much greater passion for hypocrisy than for his mistress. Neither are we greatly enamoured of Isabella's rigid chastity, though she could not act otherwise than she did. We do not feel the same confidence in the virtue that is 'sublimely good' at another's expense, as if it had been put to some less disinterested trial. As to the Duke, who makes a very imposing and mysterious stage-character, he is more absorbed in his own plots and gravity than anxious for the welfare of the state; more tenacious of his own character than attentive to the feelings and apprehensions of others. Claudio is the only person who feels naturally; and yet he is placed in circumstances of distress which almost preclude the wish for his deliverance. Mariana is also in love with Angelo, whom we hate. In this respect, there may be said to be a general system of cross-purposes between the feelings of the different characters and the sympathy of the reader or the audience. This principle of repugnance seems to have reached its height in the character of Master Barnardine, who not only sets at defiance the opinions of others, but has even thrown off all self-regard,—'one that apprehends death no more dreadfully but as a drunken sleep; careless, reckless, and fearless of what's past, present, and to come.' He is a fine antithesis to the morality and the hypocrisy of the other characters of the play. Barnardine is Caliban transported from Prospero's wizard island to the forests of Bohemia or the prisons of Vienna. He is the creature of bad habits as Caliban is of gross instincts. He has however a strong notion of the natural fitness of things, according to his own sensations—'He has been drinking hard all night, and he will not be hanged that day'— and Shakspear has let him off at last. We do not understand why the philosophical German critic, Schlegel, should be so severe on those pleasant persons, Lucio, Pompey, and Master Froth, as to call them 'wretches.' They appear all mighty comfortable in their occupations, and determined to pursue them, 'as the flesh and fortune should serve.' A very good exposure of the want of self-knowledge and contempt for others, which is so common in the world, is put into the mouth of Abhorson, the jailor, when the Provost proposes to associate Pompey with him in his office—'A bawd, sir? Fie upon him, he will discredit our mystery.' And the same answer will serve in nine instances out of ten to the same kind of remark, 'Go to, sir, you weigh equally; a feather will turn the scale.' Shakspear was in one sense the least moral of all writers; for morality (commonly so called) is made up of antipathies; and his talent consisted in sympathy with human nature, in all its shapes, degrees, depressions, and elevations. The object of the pedantic moralist is to find out the bad in everything: his was to shew that 'there is some soul of goodness in things evil.' Even Master Barnardine is not left to the mercy of what others think of him; but when he comes in, speaks for himself, and pleads his own cause, as well as if counsel had been assigned him. In one sense, Shakespear was no moralist at all: in another, he was the greatest of all moralists. He was a moralist in the same sense in which nature is one. He taught what he had learnt from her. He shewed the greatest knowledge of humanity with the greatest fellow-feeling for it.—WILLIAM HAZLITT, *"Measure for Measure," Characters of Shakespear's Plays*, 1817

This play, which is Shakspeare's throughout, is to me the most painful—say rather, the only painful—part of his genuine works. The comic and tragic parts equally border on the *misēteon*,— the one being disgusting, the other horrible; and the pardon and marriage of Angelo not merely baffles the strong indignant claim of justice—(for cruelty, with lust and damnable baseness, cannot be forgiven, because we cannot conceive them as being morally repented of;) but it is likewise degrading to the character of woman. Beaumont and Fletcher, who can follow Shakspeare in his errors only, have presented a still worse, because more loathsome and contradictory, instance of the same kind in the *Night-Walker*, in the marriage of Alathe to Algripe. Of the counterbalancing beauties of *Measure for Measure*, I need say nothing; for I have already remarked that the play is Shakspeare's throughout.—SAMUEL TAYLOR COLERIDGE, *"Measure for Measure," Shakspeare, with Introductory Remarks on Poetry, the Drama, and the Stage*, 1818

---

## WALTER PATER
*"Measure for Measure"* (1874)
*Appreciations*
1889

I n *Measure for Measure*, as in some other of his plays, Shakespeare has remodelled an earlier and somewhat rough composition to "finer issues," suffering much to remain as it had come from the less skilful hand, and not raising the whole of his work to an equal degree of intensity. Hence perhaps some of that depth and weightiness which make this play so impressive, as with the true seal of experience, like a fragment of life itself, rough and disjointed indeed, but forced to yield in places its profounder meaning. In *Measure for Measure*, in contrast with the flawless execution of *Romeo and Juliet*, Shakespeare has spent his art in just enough modification of the scheme of the older play to make it exponent of this purpose, adapting its terrible essential incidents, so that Coleridge found it the only painful work among Shakespeare's dramas, and leaving for the reader of to-day more than the usual number of difficult expressions; but infusing a lavish colour and a profound significance into it, so that under his touch certain select portions of it rise far above the level of all but his own best poetry, and working out of it a morality so characteristic that the play might well pass for the central expression of his moral judgments. It remains a comedy, as indeed is congruous with the bland, half-humorous equity which informs the whole composition, sinking from the heights of sorrow and terror into the rough scheme of the earlier piece; yet it is hardly less full of what is really tragic in man's existence than if Claudio had indeed "stooped to death."

Even the humorous concluding scenes have traits of special grace, retaining in less emphatic passages a stray line or word of power, as it seems, so that we watch to the end for the traces where the nobler hand has glanced along, leaving its vestiges, as if accidentally or wastefully, in the rising of the style.

The interest of *Measure for Measure*, therefore, is partly that of an old story told over again. We measure with curiosity that variety of resources which has enabled Shakespeare to refashion the original material with a higher motive; adding to the intricacy of the piece, yet so modifying its structure as to give the whole almost the unity of a single scene; lending, by the light of a philosophy which dwells much on what is complex and subtle in our nature, a true human propriety to its strange and unexpected turns of feeling and character, to incidents so difficult as the fall of Angelo, and the subsequent reconciliation of Isabella, so that she pleads successfully for his life. It was from Whetstone, a contemporary English writer, that Shakespeare derived the outline of Cinthio's "rare history" of *Promos and Cassandra*, one of that numerous class of Italian stories, like Boccaccio's *Tancred of Salerno*, in which the mere energy of southern passion has everything its own way, and which, though they may repel many a northern reader by a certain crudity in their colouring, seem to have been full of fascination for the Elizabethan age. This story, as it appears in Whetstone's endless comedy, is almost as rough as the roughest episode of actual criminal life. But the play seems never to have been acted, and some time after its publication Whetstone himself turned the thing into a tale, included in his *Heptameron of Civil Discourses*, where it still figures as a genuine piece, with touches of undesigned poetry, a quaint field-flower here and there of diction or sentiment, the whole strung up to an effective brevity, and with the fragrance of that admirable age of literature all about it. Here, then, there is something of the original Italian colour: in this narrative Shakespeare may well have caught the first glimpse of a composition with nobler proportions; and some artless sketch from his own hand, perhaps, putting together his first impressions, insinuated itself between Whetstone's work and the play as we actually read it. Out of these insignificant sources Shakespeare's play rises, full of solemn expression, and with a profoundly designed beauty, the new body of a higher, though sometimes remote and difficult poetry, escaping from the imperfect relics of the old story, yet not wholly transformed, and even as it stands but the preparation only, we might think, of a still more imposing design. For once we have in it a real example of that sort of writing which is sometimes described as *suggestive*, and which by the help of certain subtly calculated hints only, brings into distinct shape the reader's own half-developed imaginings. Often the quality is attributed to writing merely vague and unrealised, but in *Measure for Measure*, quite certainly, Shakespeare has directed the attention of sympathetic readers along certain channels of meditation beyond the immediate scope of his work.

*Measure for Measure*, therefore, by the quality of these higher designs, woven by his strange magic on a texture of poorer quality, is hardly less indicative than *Hamlet* even, of Shakespeare's reason, of his power of moral interpretation. It deals, not like *Hamlet* with the problems which beset one of exceptional temperament, but with mere human nature. It brings before us a group of persons, attractive, full of desire, vessels of the genial, seed-bearing powers of nature, a gaudy existence flowering out over the old court and city of Vienna, a spectacle of the fulness and pride of life which to some may seem to touch the verge of wantonness. Behind this group of people, behind their various action, Shakespeare inspires in us the sense of a strong tyranny of nature and circumstance. Then what shall there be on this side of it—on our side, the spectators' side, of this painted screen, with its puppets who are really glad or sorry all the time? what philosophy of life, what sort of equity?

Stimulated to read more carefully by Shakespeare's own profounder touches, the reader will note the vivid reality, the subtle interchange of light and shade, the strongly contrasted characters of this group of persons, passing across the stage so quickly. The slightest of them is at least not ill-natured: the meanest of them can put forth a plea for existence—*Truly, sir, I am a poor fellow that would live!*—they are never sure of themselves, even in the strong tower of a cold unimpressible nature: they are capable of many friendships and of a true dignity in danger, giving each other a sympathetic, if transitory, regret—one sorry that another "should be foolishly lost at a game of tick-tack." Words which seem to exhaust man's deepest sentiment concerning death and life are put on the lips of a gilded, witless youth; and the saintly Isabella feels fire creep along her, kindling her tongue to eloquence at the suggestion of shame. In places the shadow deepens: death intrudes itself on the scene, as among other things "a great disguiser," blanching the features of youth and spoiling its goodly hair, touching the fine Claudio even with its disgraceful associations. As in Orcagna's fresco at Pisa, it comes capriciously, giving many and long reprieves to Barnardine, who has been waiting for it nine years in prison, taking another thence by fever, another by mistake of judgment, embracing others in the midst of their music and song. The little mirror of existence, which reflects to each for a moment the stage on which he plays, is broken at last by a capricious accident; while all alike, in their yearning for untasted enjoyment, are really discounting their days, grasping so hastily and accepting so inexactly the precious pieces. The Duke's quaint but excellent moralising at the beginning of the third act does but express, like the chorus of a Greek play, the spirit of the passing incidents. To him in Shakespeare's play, to a few here and there in the actual world, this strange practical paradox of our life, so unwise in its eager haste, reveals itself in all its clearness.

The Duke disguised as a friar, with his curious moralising on life and death, and Isabella in her first mood of renunciation, a thing "ensky'd and sainted," come with the quiet of the cloister as a relief to this lust and pride of life: like some grey monastic picture hung on the wall of a gaudy room, their presence cools the heated air of the piece. For a moment we are within the placid conventual walls, whither they fancy at first that the Duke has come as a man crossed in love, with Friar Thomas and Friar Peter, calling each other by their homely, English names, or at the nunnery among the novices, with their little limited privileges, where

> If you speak you must not show your face,
> Or if you show your face you must not speak.

Not less precious for this relief in the general structure of the piece, than for its own peculiar graces is the episode of Mariana, a creature wholly of Shakespeare's invention, told, by way of interlude, in subdued prose. The moated grange, with its dejected mistress, its long, listless, discontented days, where we hear only the voice of a boy broken off suddenly in the midst of one of the loveliest songs of Shakespeare, or of Shakespeare's school,[1] is the pleasantest of many glimpses we get here of pleasant places—the field without the town, Angelo's garden-house, the consecrated fountain. Indirectly it has suggested two of the most perfect compositions among the poetry of our own generation. Again it is a picture within a picture, but with fainter lines and a greyer atmosphere: we have here the same passions, the same wrongs, the same continuance of affection, the same crying out upon death, as in the nearer and larger piece, though softened, and reduced to the mood of a more dreamy scene.

Of Angelo we may feel at first sight inclined to say only *guarda e passa!* or to ask whether he is indeed psychologically possible. In the old story, he figures as an embodiment of pure and unmodified evil, like "Hyliogabalus of Rome or Denis of Sicyll." But the embodiment of pure evil is no proper subject of art, and Shakespeare, in the spirit of a philosophy which dwells much on the complications of outward circumstance with men's inclinations, turns into a subtle study in casuistry this incident of the austere judge fallen suddenly into utmost corruption by a momentary contact with supreme purity. But the main interest in *Measure for Measure* is not, as in *Promos and Cassandra*, in the relation of Isabella and Angelo, but rather in the relation of Claudio and Isabella.

Greek tragedy in some of its noblest products has taken for its theme the love of a sister, a sentiment unimpassioned indeed, purifying by the very spectacle of its passionlessness, but capable of a fierce and almost animal strength if informed for a moment by pity and regret. At first Isabella comes upon the scene as a tranquillising influence in it. But Shakespeare, in the development of the action, brings quite different and unexpected qualities out of her. It is his characteristic poetry to expose this cold, chastened personality, respected even by the worldly Lucio as "something ensky'd and sainted, and almost an immortal spirit," to two sharp, shameful trials, and wring out of her a fiery, revealing eloquence. Thrown into the terrible dilemma of the piece, called upon to sacrifice that cloistral whiteness to sisterly affection, become in a moment the ground of strong, contending passions, she develops a new character and shows herself suddenly of kindred with those strangely conceived women, like Webster's Vittoria, who unite to a seductive sweetness something of a dangerous and tigerlike changefulness of feeling. The swift, vindictive anger leaps, like a white flame, into this white spirit, and, stripped in a moment of all convention, she stands before us clear, detached, columnar, among the tender frailties of the piece. Cassandra, the original of Isabella in Whetstone's tale, with the purpose of the Roman Lucretia in her mind, yields gracefully enough to the conditions of her brother's safety; and to the lighter reader of Shakespeare there may seem something harshly conceived, or psychologically impossible even, in the suddenness of the change wrought in her, as Claudio welcomes for a moment the chance of life through her compliance with Angelo's will, and he may have a sense here of flagging skill, as in words less finely handled than in the preceding scene. The play, though still not without traces of nobler handiwork, sinks down, as we know, at last into almost homely comedy, and it might be supposed that just here the grander manner deserted it. But the skill with which Isabella plays upon Claudio's well-recognised sense of honour, and endeavours by means of that to insure him beforehand from the acceptance of life on baser terms, indicates no coming laxity of hand just in this place. It was rather that there rose in Shakespeare's conception, as there may for the reader, as there certainly would in any good acting of the part, something of that terror, the seeking for which is one of the notes of romanticism in Shakespeare and his circle. The stream of ardent natural affection, poured as sudden hatred upon the youth condemned to die, adds an additional note of expression to the horror of the prison where so much of the scene takes place. It is not here only that Shakespeare has conceived of such extreme anger and pity as putting a sort of genius into simple women, so that their "lips drop eloquence,"

and their intuitions interpret that which is often too hard or fine for manlier reason; and it is Isabella with her grand imaginative diction, and that poetry laid upon the "prone and speechless dialect" there is in mere youth itself, who gives utterance to the equity, the finer judgments of the piece on men and things.

From behind this group with its subtle lights and shades, its poetry, its impressive contrasts, Shakespeare, as I said, conveys to us a strong sense of the tyranny of nature and circumstance over human action. The most powerful expressions of this side of experience might be found here. The bloodless, impassible temperament does but wait for its opportunity, for the almost accidental coherence of time with place, and place with wishing, to annul its long and patient discipline, and become in a moment the very opposite of that which under ordinary conditions it seemed to be, even to itself. The mere resolute self-assertion of the blood brings to others special temptations, temptations which, as defects or overgrowths, lie in the very qualities which make them otherwise imposing or attractive; the very advantage of men's gifts of intellect or sentiment being dependent on a balance in their use so delicate that men hardly maintain it always. Something also must be conceded to influences merely physical, to the complexion of the heavens, the skyey influences, shifting as the stars shift; as something also to the mere caprice of men exercised over each other in the dispensations of social or political order, to the chance which makes the life or death of Claudio dependent on Angelo's will.

The many veins of thought which render the poetry of this play so weighty and impressive unite in the image of Claudio, a flowerlike young man, whom, prompted by a few hints from Shakespeare, the imagination easily clothes with all the bravery of youth, as he crosses the stage before us on his way to death, coming so hastily to the end of his pilgrimage. Set in the horrible blackness of the prison, with its various forms of unsightly death, this flower seems the braver. Fallen by "prompture of the blood," the victim of a suddenly revived law against the common fault of youth like his, he finds his life forfeited as if by the chance of a lottery. With that instinctive clinging to life, which breaks through the subtlest casuistries of monk or sage apologising for an early death, he welcomes for a moment the chance of life through his sister's shame, though he revolts hardly less from the notion of perpetual imprisonment so repulsive to the buoyant energy of youth. Familiarised, by the words alike of friends and the indifferent, to the thought of death, he becomes gentle and subdued indeed, yet more perhaps through pride than real resignation, and would go down to darkness at last hard and unblinded. Called upon suddenly to encounter his fate, looking with keen and resolute profile straight before him, he gives utterance to some of the central truths of human feeling, the sincere, concentrated expression of the recoiling flesh. Thoughts as profound and poetical as Hamlet's arise in him; and but for the accidental arrest of sentence he would descend into the dust, a mere gilded, idle flower of youth indeed, but with what are perhaps the most eloquent of all Shakespeare's words upon his lips.

As Shakespeare in *Measure for Measure* has refashioned, after a nobler pattern, materials already at hand, so that the relics of other men's poetry are incorporated into his perfect work, so traces of the old "morality," that early form of dramatic composition which had for its function the inculcating of some moral theme, survive in it also, and give it a peculiar ethical interest. This ethical interest, though it can escape no attentive reader, yet, in accordance with that artistic law which demands the predominance of form everywhere over the mere matter or subject handled, is not to be wholly separated from the special circumstances, necessities, embarrassments, of these particular dramatic persons. The old "moralities" exemplified most often some rough-and-ready lesson. Here the very intricacy and subtlety of the moral world itself, the difficulty of seizing the true relations of so complex a material, the difficulty of just judgment, of judgment that shall not be unjust, are the lessons conveyed. Even in Whetstone's old story this peculiar vein of moralising comes to the surface: even there, we notice the tendency to dwell on mixed motives, the contending issues of action, the presence of virtues and vices alike in unexpected places, on "the hard choice of two evils," on the "imprisoning" of men's "real intents." *Measure for Measure* is full of expressions drawn from a profound experience of these casuistries, and that ethical interest becomes predominant in it: it is no longer *Promos and Cassandra*, but *Measure for Measure*, its new name expressly suggesting the subject of *poetical justice*. The action of the play, like the action of life itself for the keener observer, develops in us the conception of this poetical justice, and the yearning to realise it, the true justice of which Angelo knows nothing, because it lies for the most part beyond the limits of any acknowledged law. The idea of justice involves the idea of rights. But at bottom rights are equivalent to that which really is, to facts; and the recognition of his rights therefore, the justice he requires of our hands, or our thoughts, is the recognition of that which the person, in his inmost nature,

really is; and as sympathy alone can discover that which really is in matters of feeling and thought, true justice is in its essence a finer knowledge through love.

> 'Tis very pregnant:
> The jewel that we find we stoop and take it,
> Because we see it; but what we do not see
> We tread upon, and never think of it.

It is for this finer justice, a justice based on a more delicate appreciation of the true conditions of men and things, a true respect of persons in our estimate of actions, that the people in *Measure for Measure* cry out as they pass before us; and as the poetry of this play is full of the peculiarities of Shakespeare's poetry, so in its ethics it is an epitome of Shakespeare's moral judgments. They are the moral judgments of an observer, of one who sits as a spectator, and knows how the threads in the design before him hold together under the surface: they are the judgments of the humourist also, who follows with a half-amused but always pitiful sympathy, the various ways of human disposition, and sees less distance than ordinary men between what are called respectively great and little things. It is not always that poetry can be the exponent of morality; but it is this aspect of morals which it represents most naturally, for this true justice is dependent on just those finer appreciations which poetry cultivates in us the power of making, those peculiar valuations of action and its effect which poetry actually requires.

*Notes*

1. Fletcher, in the *Bloody Brother*, gives the rest of it.

# HISTORIES

## *General*

We have on the stage been used to the noon-tide of the struggle, and to its tempestuous night. It is the morning of the Plantagenets. The white rose is but just budding on the tree,—and we have known it only when it was wide dispersed and flaunting in the busy air, or when it was struck, and the leaves beat from the stem. Perhaps there is not a more interesting time in history than this pelican strife,—for it has a locality which none of us can mistake, at the same time that it relishes of romance in its wildness and chivalrous encounters. We read of royal deeds of valour and endurance, and of the personal conflicts between armed and youthful princes under waving and crested banners,—till we might almost think the most knightly days were come again;—but then we read of Tewkesbury and Gloucester,—and of cities and towns which lie all about us; and we find the most romantic occurrences realized in our minds. What might almost have been deemed an airy nothing acquires at once a local habitation and a name. The meeting with such places as the Temple Hall and Crosby House flatly contradicts the half formed notion that "'Tis but our fantasies," and we readily "let belief take hold of us." We have no doubt but that Shakespeare intended to have written a complete dramatic history of England,—for from Richard the Second to Richard the Third the links are unbroken. The three parts of *Henry the 6th* fall in between the two Richards. They are written with infinite vigour, but their regularity tied the hand of Shakespeare. Particular facts kept him in the high road, and would not suffer him to turn down leafy and winding lanes, or to break wildly and at once into the breathing fields. The poetry is for the most part ironed and manacled with a chain of facts, and cannot get free;—it cannot escape from the prison house of history, nor often move without our being disturbed with the clanking of its fetters. The poetry of Shakespeare is generally free as is the wind—a perfect thing of the elements, winged and sweetly coloured. Poetry must be free! It is of the air, not of the earth; and the higher it soars, the nearer it gets to its home. The poetry of *Romeo and Juliet*, of *Hamlet*, of *Macbeth*, is the poetry of Shakespeare's soul,—full of love and divine romance. It knows no stop in its delight, but "goeth where it listeth"—remaining, however, in all men's hearts a perpetual and golden dream. The poetry of *Lear*, *Othello*, *Cymbeline*, &c., is the poetry of human passions and affections,—made almost etherial by the power of the Poet. Again, the poetry of *Richard*, *John*, and the *Henries* is the blending of the imaginative with the historical:—it is poetry!—but oftentimes poetry wandering on the London Road. We hate to say a word against a word of Shakespeare's,—and we can only do so by comparing himself with himself. On going into the three parts of *Henry the Sixth* for themselves, we retract all dispraise and accusation, and declare them to be perfect works. Indeed, they are such. We live again in the olden time. The Duke of York plucks the pale rose before our eyes. Talbot stands before us majestic,—huge,—appalling,—"in his habit as he lived." Henry, the weak, careless, and good Henry, totters palpably under his crown. The Temple Hall is in our sight.—JOHN KEATS, "On Kean in *Richard Duke of York*" (1817), *Poetical Works and Other Writings*, 1939, Vol. 5, ed. H. Buxton Forman, pp. 234–39

The first form of poetry is the epic, the essence of which may be stated as the successive in events and characters. This must be distinguished from narration, in which there must always be a narrator, from whom the objects represented receive a coloring and a manner;—whereas in the epic, as in the so called poems of Homer, the whole is completely objective, and the representation is a pure reflection. The next form into which poetry passed was the dramatic;—both forms having a common basis with a certain difference, and that difference not consisting in the dialogue alone. Both are founded on the relation of providence to the human will; and this relation is the universal element, expressed under different points of view according to the difference of religions, and the moral and intellectual cultivation of different nations. In the epic poem fate is represented as overruling the will, and making it instrumental to the accomplishment of its designs:—

*Dios de teleieto boulē.*

In the drama, the will is exhibited as struggling with fate, a great and beautiful instance and illustration of which is the *Prometheus* of Æschylus; and the deepest effect is produced, when the fate is represented as a higher and intelligent will, and the opposition of the individual as springing from a defect.

In order that a drama may be properly historical, it is necessary that it should be the history of the people to whom it is addressed. In the composition, care must be taken that there appear no dramatic improbability, as the reality is taken for granted. It must, likewise, be poetical;—that only, I mean, must be taken which is the permanent in our nature, which is common, and therefore deeply interesting to all ages. The events themselves are immaterial, otherwise than as the clothing and manifestation of the spirit that is working within. In this mode, the unity resulting from succession is destroyed, but is supplied by a unity of a higher order, which connects the events by reference to the workers, gives a reason for them in the motives, and presents men in their causative character. It takes, therefore, that part of real history which is the least known, and infuses a principle of life and organization into the naked facts, and makes them all the framework of an animated whole.

In my happier days, while I had yet hope and onward-looking thoughts, I planned an historical drama of King Stephen, in the manner of Shakspeare. Indeed it would be desirable that some man of dramatic genius should dramatize all those omitted by Shakspeare, as far down as Henry VII. Perkin Warbeck would make a most interesting drama. A few scenes of Marlow's *Edward II.* might be preserved. After Henry VIII., the events are too well and distinctly known, to be, without plump inverisimilitude, crowded together in one night's exhibition. Whereas, the history of our ancient kings—the events of their reigns, I mean,—are like stars in the sky;—whatever the real interspaces may be, and however great, they seem close to each other. The stars—the events—strike us and remain in our eye, little modified by the difference of dates. An historic drama is, therefore, a collection of events borrowed from history, but connected together in respect of cause and time, poetically and by dramatic fiction. It would be a fine national custom to act such a series of dramatic histories in orderly succession, in the yearly Christmas holidays, and could not but tend to counteract that mock cosmopolitism, which under a positive term really implies nothing but a negation of, or indifference to, the particular love of our country. By its nationality must every nation retain its independence;—I mean a nationality *quoad* the nation. Better thus;—nationality in each individual, *quoad* his country, is equal to the sense of individuality *quoad* himself; but himself as subsensuous, and central. Patriotism is equal to the sense of individuality reflected from every other individual. There may come a higher virtue in both—just cosmopolitism. But this latter is not possible but by antecedence of the former.

Shakspeare has included the most important part of nine reigns in his historical dramas—namely—King John, Richard II.—Henry IV. (two)—Henry V.—Henry VI. (three) including Edward V. and Henry VIII., in all ten plays. There remain, therefore, to be done, with exception of a single scene or two that should be adopted from Marlow—eleven reigns—of which the first two appear the only unpromising subjects;—and those two dramas must be formed wholly or mainly of invented private stories, which, however, could not have happened except in consequence of the events and measures of these reigns, and which should furnish opportunity both of exhibiting the manners and oppressions of the times, and of narrating dramatically the great events;—if possible—the death of the two sovereigns, at least of the latter, should be made to have some influence on the finale of the story. All the rest are glorious subjects; especially Henry 1st. (being the struggle between the men of arms and of letters, in the persons of Henry and Becket,) Stephen, Richard I., Edward II., and Henry VII.—SAMUEL TAYLOR COLERIDGE, "Shakspeare's English Historical Plays," *Shakspeare, with Introductory Remarks on Poetry, the Drama, and the Stage*, 1818

I here observe that it would be foolish to look for precisely that kind of interest in Shakespeare's historical plays which could only be supplied by a dramatist whose highest aim is the clever manipulation of poetry. Shakespeare's aim was not only poetry, but history; he could not model his given subject-matter at will, he could not follow his fancy in describing events and characters, and as little as he could observe unity of time and place could he merge his entire interest in a single person or a single event. And yet in his historical plays we find richer, more powerful, and sweeter poetry than in the tragedies of those poets who either invent their own stories, or arrange them as suits their taste, whereby they obtain the strictest symmetry of form and surpass poor Shakespeare in art properly so-called, especially in the *enchaînement des scènes*.

Yes, it is a significant fact; the great Englishman is not only a poet but also a historian—he wields the sharp style of Klio as well as Melpomene's dagger. In this he resembles the earliest historians who likewise made no difference between poetry and history, and who not only gave a nomenclature to the past issuing in a dusty collection of events, but made truth more beautiful by song, producing from this harmony only the notes of truth. So-called objectivity, of which we now hear so much, is nothing but a tiresome lie; we cannot depict the past without giving it the colour of our feelings. And as the so-called objective historian always addresses the present generation, he writes unconsciously in the spirit of his own times, and this spirit of the times will become manifest in his works. In the interchange of epistolary correspondence we detect in like manner the characters of recipient and correspondent. So-called objectivity, proudly passive, taking its stand on the golgotha of events, may be regarded as untrue, because we not

only require an accurate summary of facts in dealing with historic truth, but also a certain description of the impression made on contemporaries by such events. Yet herein lies the difficulty; for we want more than an ordinary enumeration of events, we need the capacity of a poet to whom, Shakespeare says—*the very eye and body of the time*—have become manifest.

And not only the occurrences of his own time were manifest to him, but those which are contained in ancient records. We have a striking example of this in those tragedies where he gives us so true an account of Rome in its decay. Not only has he portrayed the knights of the Middle Ages; he has seen into the hearts of ancient heroes, drawing forth from them their inmost thoughts. He could always turn truth into poetry, and knew how to cast a poetic halo over the heartless Romans, this hard cold and prosaic nation, made up of vulgar greed and clever astuteness, a nation of casuistic soldiery.

But Shakespeare is stigmatised as wanting in *form*, even in his Roman tragedies. A talented writer, Dietrich Grabbe, called them *poetically adorned chronicles* wanting in every point of central interest, in which we fail to perceive who play the important and who the unimportant parts, and in which, though we may dispense with unity of time and place, there is not even unity of action. But the cleverest critics make strange mistakes! Not only the last named unity, but unities of time and place are by no means wanting in the great poet, only his conceptions are somewhat more elastic than ours. This world forms the stage, of his plays, and that is his unity of place; eternity is the period during which his plays come to pass, and that is his unity of time; and the hero of his plays, the bright central figure, representing the unity of action and conformable to the other two, is—Mankind; a hero who is always dying and always rising again, always loving, aways hating, yet in whom love is stronger than hate; now crawling like a worm, now soaring like an eagle, now deserving a fool's cap, now a laurel-wreath, or still oftener both of these at one and the same time; the great dwarf, the small giant, the homœopathically prepared divinity, in whom the divine elements may have become diluted, but which exist nevertheless. Ah! let us not overrate the heroism of this hero, for the sake of modesty and very shame!

Shakespeare is as true to nature as he is faithful in delineating history. It is often said that he holds up a mirror to nature. This is not correct, as these words convey a wrong impression concerning the relations in which a poet stands to nature. Nature is not reflected in the poet's mind; he is endowed with the innate capacity for representing nature, which representation is akin to the most faithful reflection; he comes into the world a world-wise man, and every part of the external world is immediately understood by him in its entirety when he awakens from the dreams of his childhood and attains to a knowledge of himself. For his mind bears an impress of the whole, he knows the ultimate reasons of all phenomena, which to the ordinary mind appear problematic, and which to the ordinary investigator seem difficult, if not impossible of solution. . . . Just as the mathematician can immediately explain the whole circle and its centre, if he is shown the smallest part of a circle, so also the poet, in the very act of contemplating the infinitesimal part of objective things, realises the connection between this part and all other things. He seems to know the circle of things and their centre, he sees things in their widest dimensions and to the inmost core.— HEINRICH HEINE, "Introduction" to *Notes on Shakespeare Heroines*, 1838, tr. Ida Benecke

We all know how much *mythus* there is in the Shakspere question as it stands to-day. Beneath a few foundations of proved facts are certainly engulf'd far more dim and elusive ones, of deepest importance—tantalizing and half suspected—suggesting explanations that one dare not put in plain statement. But coming at once to the point, the English historical plays are to me not only the most eminent as dramatic performances (my maturest judgment confirming the impressions of my early years, that the distinctiveness and glory of the Poet reside not in his vaunted dramas of the passions, but those founded on the contests of English dynasties, and the French wars,) but form, as we get it all, the chief in a complexity of puzzles. Conceiv'd out of the fullest heat and pulse of European feudalism—personifying in unparallel'd ways the mediæval aristocracy, its towering spirit of ruthless and gigantic caste, with its own peculiar air and arrogance (no mere imitation)—only one of the "wolfish earls" so plenteous in the plays themselves, or some born descendant and knower, might seem to be the true author of those amazing works—works in some respect greater than anything else in recorded literature.

The start and germ-stock of the pieces on which the present speculation is founded are undoubtedly (with, at the outset, no small amount of bungling work) in *Henry VI*. It is plain to me that as profound and forecasting a brain and pen as ever appear'd in literature, after floundering somewhat in the first part of that trilogy—or perhaps draughting it more or less experimentally or by accident—afterward developed and defined his plan in the Second and Third Parts, and from time to time, thenceforward, systematically enlarged it to majestic and mature proportions in *Richard II, Richard III, King John, Henry IV, Henry V*, and even in *Macbeth, Coriolanus* and *Lear*. For it is impossible to grasp the whole cluster of those plays, however wide the intervals and different circumstances of their composition, without thinking of them as, in a free sense, the result of an *essentially controling plan*. What was that plan? Or, rather, what was veil'd behind it?—for to me there was certainly something so veil'd. Even the episodes of Cade, Joan of Arc, and the like (which sometimes seem to me like interpolations allow'd,) may be meant to foil the possible sleuth, and throw any too 'cute pursuer off the scent. In the whole matter I should specially dwell on, and make much of, that inexplicable element of every highest poetic nature which causes it to cover up and involve its real purpose and meanings in folded removes and far recesses. Of this trait—hiding the nest where common seekers may never find it—the Shaksperean works afford the most numerous and mark'd illustrations known to me. I would even call that trait the leading one through the whole of those works.

All the foregoing to premise a brief statement of how and where I get my new light on Shakspere. Speaking of the special English plays, my friend William O'Connor says:

They seem simply and rudely historical in their motive, as aiming to give in the rough a tableau of warring dynasties,—and carry to me a lurking sense of being in aid of some ulterior design, probably well enough understood in that age, which perhaps time and criticism will reveal. . . . Their atmosphere is one of barbarous and tumultuous gloom,—they do not make us love the times they limn, . . . and it is impossible to believe that the greatest of the Elizabethan men could have sought to indoctrinate the age with the love of feudalism which his own drama in its entirety, if the view taken of it herein be true, certainly and subtly saps and mines.

Reading the just-specified plays in the light of Mr. O'Connor's suggestion, I defy any one to escape such new and

deep utterance-meanings, like magic ink, warm'd by the fire, and previously invisible. Will it not indeed be strange if the author of *Othello* and *Hamlet* is destin'd to live in America, in a generation or two, less as the cunning draughtsman of the passions, and more as putting on record the first full exposé—and by far the most vivid one, immeasurably ahead of doctrinaires and economists—of the political theory and results, or the reason-why and necessity for them which America has come on earth to abnegate and replace?

The summary of my suggestion would be, therefore, that while the more the rich and tangled jungle of the Shaksperean area is travers'd and studied, and the more baffled and mix'd, as so far appears, becomes the exploring student (who at last surmises everything, and remains certain of nothing,) it is possible a future age of criticism, diving deeper, mapping the land and lines freer, completer than hitherto, may discover in the plays named the scientific (Baconian?) inauguration of modern Democracy—furnishing realistic and first-class artistic portraitures of the mediæval world, the feudal personalities, institutes, in their morbid accumulations, deposits, upon politics and sociology,—may penetrate to that hard-pan, far down and back of the ostent of to-day, on which (and on which only) the progressism of the last two centuries has built this Democracy which now holds secure lodgment over the whole civilized world.

Whether such was the unconscious, or (as I think likely) the more or less conscious, purpose of him who fashion'd those marvellous architectonics, is a secondary question.—WALT WHITMAN, "What Lurks behind Shakspere's Historical Plays?" (1884), *Prose Works*, 1964, Vol. 2, ed. Floyd Stovall, pp. 554–56

---

## AUGUST WILHELM SCHLEGEL
### From *Lectures on Dramatic Art and Literature*
tr. John Black
1809

The dramas derived from the English history, ten in number, form one of the most valuable of Shakspere's works, and partly the fruit of his maturest age. I say advisedly *one* of his works, for the poet evidently intended them to form one great whole. It is, as it were, an historical heroic poem in the dramatic form, of which the separate plays constitute the rhapsodies. The principal features of the events are exhibited with such fidelity; their causes, and even their secret springs, are placed in such a clear light, that we may attain from them a knowledge of history in all its truths, while the living picture makes an impression on the imagination which can never be effaced. But this series of dramas is intended as the vehicle of a much higher and much more general instruction; it furnishes examples of the political course of the world, applicable to all times. This mirror of kings should be the manual of young princes; from it they may learn the intrinsic dignity of their hereditary vocation, but they will also learn from it the difficulties of their situation, the dangers of usurpation, the inevitable fall of tyranny, which buries itself under its attempts to obtain a firmer foundation; lastly, the ruinous consequences of the weaknesses, errors, and crimes of kings, for whole nations, and many subsequent generations. Eight of these plays, from *Richard the Second* to *Richard the Third*, are linked together in an uninterrupted succession, and embrace a most eventful period of nearly a century of English history. The events portrayed in them not only follow one another, but they are linked together in the closest and most exact connexion;

and the cycle of revolts, parties, civil and foreign wars, which began with the deposition of Richard II., first ends with the accession of Henry VII. to the throne. The careless rule of the first of these monarchs, and his injudicious treatment of his own relations, drew upon him the rebellion of Bolingbroke; his dethronement, however, was, in point of form, altogether unjust, and in no case could Bolingbroke be considered the rightful heir to the crown. This shrewd founder of the House of Lancaster never as Henry IV. enjoyed in peace the fruits of his usurpation: his turbulent Barons, the same who aided him in ascending the throne, allowed him not a moment's repose upon it. On the other hand, he was jealous of the brilliant qualities of his son, and this distrust, more than any really low inclination, induced the Prince, that he might avoid every appearance of ambition, to give himself up to dissolute society. These two circumstances form the subject-matter of the two parts of *Henry the Fourth*; the enterprises of the discontented make up the serious, and the wild youthful frolics of the heir-apparent supply the comic scenes. When this warlike Prince ascended the throne under the name of Henry V., he was determined to assert his ambiguous title; he considered foreign conquests as the best means of guarding against internal disturbances, and this gave rise to the glorious, but more ruinous than profitable, war with France, which Shakspeare has celebrated in the drama of *Henry the Fifth*. The early death of this king, the long legal minority of Henry VI., and his perpetual minority in the art of government, brought the greatest troubles on England. The dissensions of the Regents, and the consequently wretched administration, occasioned the loss of the French conquests; and there arose a bold candidate for the crown, whose title was indisputable, if the prescription of three governments may not be assumed to confer legitimacy on usurpation. Such was the origin of the wars between the Houses of York and Lancaster, which desolated the kingdom for a number of years, and ended with the victory of the House of York. All this Shakspeare has represented in the three parts of *Henry the Sixth*. Edward IV. shortened his life by excesses, and did not long enjoy the throne purchased at the expense of so many cruel deeds. His brother Richard, who had a great share in the elevation of the House of York, was not contented with the regency, and his ambition paved himself a way to the throne through treachery and violence; but his gloomy tyranny made him the object of the people's hatred, and at length drew on him the destruction which he merited. He was conquered by a descendant of the royal house unstained by the guilt of the civil wars, and what might seem defective in his title was made good by the merit of freeing his country from a monster. With the accession of Henry VII. to the throne, a new epoch of English history begins: the curse seemed at length to be expiated, and the long series of usurpations, revolts, and civil wars, occasioned by the levity with which the Second Richard sported away his crown, was now brought to a termination.

Such is the evident connexion of these eight plays with each other, but they were not, however, composed in chronological order. According to all appearance, the four last were first written; this is certain, indeed, with respect to the three parts of *Henry the Sixth*; and *Richard the Third* is not only from its subject a continuation of these, but is also composed in the same style. Shakspeare then went back to *Richard the Second*, and with the most careful art connected the second series with the first. The trilogies of the ancients have already given us an example of the possibility of forming a perfect dramatic whole, which shall yet contain allusions to something which goes before, and follows it. In like manner the most of these plays end with a very definite division in the history: *Richard the Second*, with the murder of that King; *the Second Part of Henry the Fourth*, with the accession of his son to the throne; *Henry the Fifth*, with the conclusion of peace with France; *the First Part of Henry the Sixth*, also, with a treaty of peace; the third, with the murder of Henry, and Edward's elevation to the throne; *Richard the Third*, was his overthrow and death. *The First Part of Henry the Fourth*, and *the Second of Henry the Sixth*, are rounded off in a less satisfactory manner. The revolt of the nobles was only half quelled by the overthrow of Percy, and it is therefore continued through the following part of the piece. The victory of York at St. Alban's could as little be considered a decisive event, in the war of the two houses. Shakspeare has fallen into this dramatic imperfection, if we may so call it, for the sake of advantages of much more importance. The picture of the civil war was too great and too rich in dreadful events for a single drama, and yet the uninterrupted series of events offered no more convenient resting-place. The government of Henry IV. might certainly have been comprehended in one piece, but it possesses too little tragical interest, and too little historical splendour, to be attractive, if handled in a serious manner throughout: hence Shakspeare has given to the comic characters belonging to the retinue of Prince Henry, the freest development, and the half of the space is occupied by this constant interlude between the political events.

The two other historical plays taken from the English history are chronologically separate from this series: King John reigned nearly two centuries before Richard II., and between Richard III. and Henry VIII. comes the long reign of Henry VII., which Shakspeare justly passed over as unsusceptible of dramatic interest. However, these two plays may in some measure be considered as the Prologue and the Epilogue of the other eight. In *King John*, all the political and national motives which play so great a part in the following pieces are already indicated: wars and treaties with France; a usurpation, and the tyrannical actions which it draws after it; the influence of the clergy, the factions of the nobles. *Henry the Eighth* again shows us the transition to another age; the policy of modern Europe, a refined court-life under a voluptuous monarch, the dangerous situation of favourites, who, after having assisted in effecting the fall of others, are themselves precipitated from power; in a word, despotism under a milder form, but not less unjust and cruel. By the prophecies on the birth of Elizabeth, Shakspeare has in some degree brought his great poem on English history down to his own time, as far at least as such recent events could be yet handled with security. He composed probably the two plays of *King John* and *Henry the Eighth* at a later period, as an addition to the others.

WALTER PATER

"Shakespeare's English Kings"

*Appreciations*

1889

A brittle glory shineth in this face:
As brittle as the glory is the face.

The English plays of Shakespeare needed but the completion of one unimportant interval to possess the unity of a popular chronicle from Richard the Second to Henry the Eighth, and possess, as they actually stand, the unity of a common motive in the handling of the various events and persons which they bring before us. Certain of his historic dramas, not English, display Shakespeare's mastery in the development of the heroic nature amid heroic circumstances; and had he chosen, from English history, to deal with Cœur-de-Lion or Edward the First, the innate quality of his subject would doubtless have called into play something of that profound and sombre power which in *Julius Cæsar* and *Macbeth* has sounded the depths of mighty character. True, on the whole, to fact, it is another side of kingship which he has made prominent in his English histories. The irony of kingship—average human nature, flung with a wonderfully pathetic effect into the vortex of great events; tragedy of everyday quality heightened in degree only by the conspicuous scene which does but make those who play their parts there conspicuously unfortunate; the utterance of common humanity straight from the heart, but refined like other common things for kingly uses by Shakespeare's unfailing eloquence: such, unconsciously for the most part, though palpably enough to the careful reader, is the conception under which Shakespeare has arranged the lights and shadows of the story of the English kings, emphasising merely the light and shadow inherent in it, and keeping very close to the original authorities, not simply in the general outline of these dramatic histories but sometimes in their very expression. Certainly the history itself, as he found it in Hall, Holinshed, and Stowe, those somewhat picturesque old chroniclers who had themselves an eye for the dramatic "effects" of human life, has much of this sentiment already about it. What he did not find there was the natural prerogative—such justification, in kingly, that is to say, in exceptional, qualities, of the exceptional position, as makes it practicable in the result. It is no *Henriade* he writes, and no history of the English people, but the sad fortunes of some English kings as conspicuous examples of the ordinary human condition. As in a children's story, all princes are in extremes. Delightful in the sunshine above the wall into which chance lifts the flower for a season, they can but plead somewhat more touchingly than others their everyday weakness in the storm. Such is the motive that gives unity to these unequal and intermittent contributions toward a slowly evolved dramatic chronicle, which it would have taken many days to rehearse; a not distant story from real life still well remembered in its general course, to which people might listen now and again, as long as they cared, finding human nature at least wherever their attention struck ground in it.

He begins with John, and allows indeed to the first of these English kings a kind of greatness, making the development of the play centre in the counteraction of his natural gifts—that something of heroic force about him—by a madness which takes the shape of reckless impiety, forced especially on men's attention by the terrible circumstances of his end, in the delineation of which Shakespeare triumphs, setting, with true poetic tact, this incident of the king's death, in all the horror of a violent one, amid a scene delicately suggestive of what is perennially peaceful and genial in the outward world. Like the sensual humours of Falstaff in another play, the presence of the bastard Faulconbridge, with his physical energy and his unmistakable family likeness—"those limbs which Sir Robert never holp to make"[1]—contributes to an almost coarse assertion of the force of nature, of the somewhat ironic preponderance of nature and circumstance over men's artificial arrangements, to the recognition of a certain potent natural aristocracy, which is far from being always identical with that more formal, heraldic one. And what is a coarse fact in the case of Faulconbridge becomes a motive of pathetic appeal in the wan and babyish Arthur. The magic with which nature models tiny and delicate children to the likeness of their rough fathers is nowhere more justly expressed than in the words of King Philip.—

Look here upon thy brother Geoffrey's face!
These eyes, these brows were moulded out of his:
This little abstract doth contain that large
Which died in Geoffrey; and the hand of time
Shall draw this brief into as huge a volume.

It was perhaps something of a boyish memory of the shocking end of his father that had distorted the piety of Henry the Third into superstitious terror. A frightened soul, himself touched with the contrary sort of religious madness, doting on all that was alien from his father's huge ferocity, on the genialities, the soft gilding, of life, on the genuine interests of art and poetry, to be credited more than any other person with the deep religious expression of Westminster Abbey, Henry the Third, picturesque though useless, but certainly touching, might have furnished Shakespeare, had he filled up this interval in his series, with precisely the kind of effect he tends towards in his English plays. But he found it completer still in the person and story of Richard the Second, a figure—"that sweet lovely rose"—which haunts Shakespeare's mind, as it seems long to have haunted the minds of the English people, as the most touching of all examples of the irony of kingship.

Henry the Fourth—to look for a moment beyond our immediate subject, in pursuit of Shakespeare's thought—is presented, of course, in general outline, as an impersonation of "surviving force:" he has a certain amount of kingcraft also, a real fitness for great opportunity. But still true to his leading motive, Shakespeare, in *King Henry the Fourth*, has left the high-water mark of his poetry in the soliloquy which represents royalty longing vainly for the toiler's sleep; while the popularity, the showy heroism, of Henry the Fifth, is used to give emphatic point to the old earthy commonplace about "wild oats." The wealth of homely humour in these plays, the fun coming straight home to all the world, of Fluellen especially in his unconscious interview with the king, the boisterous earthiness of Falstaff and his companions, contribute to the same effect. The keynote of Shakespeare's treatment is indeed expressed by Henry the Fifth himself, the *greatest* of Shakespeare's kings.—"Though I speak it to you," he says *incognito*, under cover of night, to a common soldier on the field, "I think the king is but a man, as I am: the violet smells to him as it doth to me: all his senses have but human conditions; and though his affections be higher mounted than ours yet when they stoop they stoop with like wing." And, in truth, the really kingly speeches which Shakespeare assigns to him, as to other kings weak enough in all but speech, are but a kind of flowers, worn for, and effective only as personal embellishment. They combine to one result with the merely outward and ceremonial ornaments of royalty, its pageantries, flaunting so naively, so credulously, in Shakespeare, as in that old medieval time. And then, the force of Hotspur is but transient youth, the common heat of youth, in him. The character of Henry the Sixth again, *roi fainéant*, with La Pucelle[2] for his counterfoil, lay in the direct course of Shakespeare's design: he has done much to fix the sentiment of the "holy Henry." Richard the Third, touched, like John, with an effect of real heroism, is spoiled like him by something of criminal madness, and reaches his highest level of tragic expression when circumstances reduce him to terms of mere human nature.—

A horse! A horse! My kingdom for a horse!

The Princes in the Tower recall to mind the lot of young Arthur:—

I'll go with thee,
And find the inheritance of this poor child,
His little kingdom of a forced grave.

And when Shakespeare comes to Henry the Eighth, it is not

the superficial though very English splendour of the king himself, but the really potent and ascendant nature of the butcher's son on the one hand, and Katharine's subdued reproduction of the sad fortunes or Richard the Second on the other, that define his central interest.[3]

With a prescience of the Wars of the Roses, of which his errors were the original cause, it is Richard who best exposes Shakespeare's own constant sentiment concerning war, and especially that sort of civil war which was then recent in English memories. The soul of Shakespeare, certainly, was not wanting in a sense of the magnanimity of warriors. The grandiose aspects of war, its magnificent apparelling, he records monumentally enough—the "dressing of the lists," the lion's heart, its unfaltering haste thither in all the freshness of youth and morning.—

> Not sick although I have to do with death—
> The sun doth gild our armour: Up, my Lords!—
> I saw young Harry with his beaver on,
> His cuisses on his thighs, gallantly arm'd,
> Rise from the ground like feather'd Mercury.

Only, with Shakespeare, the afterthought is immediate:—

> They come like sacrifices in their trim.

> —Will it never be to-day? I will trot to-morrow a
> mile, and my way shall be paved with English faces.

This sentiment Richard reiterates very plaintively, in association with the delicate sweetness of the English fields, still sweet and fresh, like London and her other fair towns in that England of Chaucer, for whose soil the exiled Bolingbroke is made to long so dangerously, while Richard on his return from Ireland salutes it—

> That pale, that white-fac'd shore,—
> As a long-parted mother with her child.—
> So, weeping, smiling, greet I thee, my earth!
> And do thee favour with my royal hands.—

Then (of Bolingbroke)

> Ere the crown he looks for live in peace,
> Ten thousand bloody crowns of mothers' sons
> Shall ill become the flower of England's face;
> Change the complexion of her maid-pale peace
> To scarlet indignation, and bedew
> My pastures' grass with faithful English blood,—
> Why have they dared to march?—

asks York,

> So many miles upon her peaceful bosom,
> Frighting her pale-fac'd visages with war?—

waking, according to Richard,

> Our peace, which in our country's cradle,
> Draws the sweet infant breath of gentle sleep:—

bedrenching "with crimson tempest"

> The fresh green lap of fair king Richard's land:—

frighting "fair peace" from "our quiet confines," laying

> The summer's dust with showers of blood,
> Rained from the wounds of slaughter'd Englishmen:

bruising

> Her flowerets with the armed hoofs
> Of hostile paces.

Perhaps it is not too fanciful to note in this play a peculiar recoil from the mere instruments of warfare, the contact of the "rude ribs," the "flint bosom," of Barkloughly Castle or Pomfret or

> Julius Cæsar's ill-erected tower:

the

> Boisterous untun'd drums
> With harsh-resounding trumpets' dreadful bray
> And grating shock of wrathful iron arms.

It is as if the lax, soft beauty of the king took effect, at least by contrast, on everything beside.

One gracious prerogative, certainly, Shakespeare's English kings possess: they are a very eloquent company, and Richard is the most sweet-tongued of them all. In no other play perhaps is there such a flush of those gay, fresh, variegated flowers of speech—colour and figure, not lightly attached to, but fused into, the very phrase itself—which Shakespeare cannot help dispensing to his characters, as in this "play of the Deposing of King Richard the Second," an exquisite poet if he is nothing else, from first to last, in light and gloom alike, able to see all things poetically, to give a poetic turn to his conduct of them, and refreshing with his golden language the tritest aspects of that ironic contrast between the pretensions of a king and the actual necessities of his destiny. What a garden of words! With him, blank verse, infinitely graceful, deliberate, musical in inflexion, becomes indeed a true "verse royal," that rhyming lapse, which to the Shakespearian ear, at least in youth, came as the last touch of refinement on it, being here doubly appropriate. His eloquence blends with that fatal beauty, of which he was so frankly aware, so amiable to his friends, to his wife, of the effects of which on the people his enemies were so much afraid, on which Shakespeare himself dwells so attentively as the "royal blood" comes and goes in the face with his rapid changes of temper. As happens with sensitive natures, it attunes him to a congruous suavity of manners, by which anger itself became flattering: it blends with his merely youthful hopefulness and high spirits, his sympathetic love for gay people, things, apparel—"his cote of gold and stone, valued at thirty thousand marks," the novel Italian fashions he preferred, as also with those real amiabilities that made people forget the darker touches of his character, but never tire of the pathetic rehearsal of his fall, the meekness of which would have seemed merely abject in a less graceful performer.

Yet it is only fair to say that in the painstaking "revival" of *King Richard the Second*, by the late Charles Kean, those who were very young thirty years ago were afforded much more than Shakespeare's play could ever have been before—that very person of the king based on the stately old portrait in Westminster Abbey, "the earliest extant contemporary likeness of any English sovereign," the grace, the winning pathos, the sympathetic voice of the player, the tasteful archæology confronting vulgar modern London with a scenic reproduction, for once really agreeable, of the London of Chaucer. In the hands of Kean the play became like an exquisite performance on the violin.

The long agony of one so gaily painted by nature's self, from his "tragic abdication" till the hour in which he

> Sluiced out his innocent soul thro' streams of blood,

was for playwrights a subject ready to hand, and became early the theme of a popular drama, of which some have fancied surviving favourite fragments in the rhymed parts of Shakespeare's work.

> The king Richard of Yngland
> Was in his flowris then regnand:
> But his flowris efter sone
> Fadyt, and ware all undone:—

says the old chronicle. Strangely enough, Shakespeare supposes him an over-confident believer in that divine right of kings, of which people in Shakespeare's time were coming to hear so much; a general right, sealed to him (so Richard is made to think) as an ineradicable personal gift by the touch—

stream rather, over head and breast and shoulders—of the "holy oil" of his consecration at Westminster; not, however, through some oversight, the genuine balm used at the coronation of his successor, given, according to legend, by the Blessed Virgin to Saint Thomas of Canterbury. Richard himself found that, it was said, among other forgotten treasures, at the crisis of his changing fortunes, and vainly sought reconsecration therewith—understood, wistfully, that it was reserved for his happier rival. And yet his coronation, by the pageantry, the amplitude, the learned care, of its order, so lengthy that the king, then only eleven years of age, and fasting, as a communicant at the ceremony, was carried away in a faint, fixed the type under which it has ever since continued. And nowhere is there so emphatic a reiteration as in *Richard the Second* of the sentiment which those singular rites were calculated to produce.

> Not all the water in the rough rude sea
> Can wash the balm from an anointed king,—

as supplementing another, almost supernatural, right.— "Edward's seven sons," of whom Richard's father was one,

> Were as seven phials of his sacred blood.

But this, too, in the hands of Shakespeare, becomes for him, like any other of those fantastic, ineffectual, easily discredited, personal graces, as capricious in its operation on men's wills as merely physical beauty, kindling himself to eloquence indeed, but only giving double pathos to insults which "barbarism itself" might have pitied—the dust in his face, as he returns, through the streets of London, a prisoner in the train of his victorious enemy.

> How soon my sorrow hath destroyed my face!

he cries, in that most poetic invention of the mirror scene, which does but reinforce again that physical charm which all confessed. The sense of "divine right" in kings is found to act not so much as a secret of power over others, as of infatuation of themselves. And of all those personal gifts the one which alone never altogether fails him is just that royal utterance, his appreciation of the poetry of his own hapless lot, an eloquent self-pity, infecting others in spite of themselves, till they too become irresistibly eloquent about him.

In the Roman Pontifical, of which the order of Coronation is really a part, there is no form for the inverse process, no rite of "degradation," such as that by which an offending priest or bishop may be deprived, if not of the essential quality of "orders," yet, one by one, of its outward dignities. It is as if Shakespeare had had in mind some such inverted rite, like those old ecclesiastical or military ones, by which human hardness, or human justice, adds the last touch of unkindness to the execution of its sentences, in the scene where Richard "deposes" himself, as in some long, agonising ceremony, reflectively drawn out, with an extraordinary refinement of intelligence and variety of piteous appeal, but also with a felicity of poetic invention, which puts these pages into a very select class, with the finest "vermeil and ivory" work of Chatterton or Keats.

> Fetch hither Richard that in common view
> He may surrender!—

And Richard more than concurs: he throws himself into the part, realises a type, falls gracefully as on the world's stage.— Why is he sent for?

> To do that office of thine own good will
> Which tired majesty did make thee offer.—
>
> Now mark me! how I will undo myself.

"Hath Bolingbroke deposed thine intellect?" the Queen asks him, on his way to the Tower:—

> Hath Bolingbroke
> Deposed thine intellect? hath he been in thy heart?

And in truth, but for that adventitious poetic gold, it would be only "plume-plucked Richard."—

> I find myself a traitor with the rest,
> For I have given here my soul's consent
> To undeck the pompous body of a king.

He is duly reminded, indeed, how

> That which in mean men we entitle patience
> Is pale cold cowardice in noble breasts.

Yet at least within the poetic bounds of Shakespeare's play, through Shakespeare's bountiful gifts, his desire seems fulfilled.—

> O! that I were as great
> As is my grief.

And his grief becomes nothing less than a central expression of all that in the revolutions of Fortune's wheel goes *down* in the world.

No! Shakespeare's kings are not, nor are meant to be, great men: rather, little or quite ordinary humanity, thrust upon greatness, with those pathetic results, the natural self-pity of the weak heightened in them into irresistible appeal to others as the net result of their royal prerogative. One after another, they seem to lie composed in Shakespeare's embalming pages, with just that touch of nature about them, making the whole world akin, which has infused into their tombs at Westminster a rare poetic grace. It is that irony of kingship, the sense that it is in its happiness child's play, in its sorrows, after all, but children's grief, which gives its finer accent to all the changeful feeling of these wonderful speeches:—the great meekness of the graceful, wild creature, tamed at last.—

> Give Richard leave to live till Richard die!

his somewhat abject fear of death, turning to acquiescence at moments of extreme weariness:—

> My large kingdom for a little grave!
> A little little grave, an obscure grave!—

his religious appeal in the last reserve, with its bold reference to the judgment of Pilate, as he thinks once more of his "anointing."

And as happens with children he attains contentment finally in the merely passive recognition of superior strength, in the naturalness of the result of the great battle as a matter of course, and experiences something of the royal prerogative of poetry to obscure, or at least to attune and soften men's griefs. As in some sweet anthem of Handel, the sufferer, who put finger to the organ under the utmost pressure of mental conflict, extracts a kind of peace at last from the mere skill with which he sets his distress to music.—

> Beshrew thee, Cousin, that didst lead me forth
> Of that sweet way I was in to despair!

"With Cain go wander through the shades of night!"— cries the new king to the gaoler Exton, dissimulating his share in the murder he is thought to have suggested; and in truth there is something of the murdered Abel about Shakespeare's Richard. The fact seems to be that he died of "waste and a broken heart:" it was by way of proof that his end had been a natural one that, stifling a real fear of the face, the face of Richard, on men's minds, with the added pleading now of all dead faces, Henry exposed the corpse to general view; and Shakespeare, in bringing it on the stage, in the last scene of his play, does but follow out the motive with which he has emphasised Richard's physical beauty all through it—that "most beauteous inn," as the Queen says quaintly, meeting him on the way to death—residence, then soon to be deserted, of that wayward, frenzied, but withal so affectionate soul. Though the body did not go to Westminster immediately, his tomb,

> That small model of the barren earth
> Which serves as paste and cover to our bones,[4]

the effigy clasping the hand of his youthful consort, was already prepared there, with "rich gilding and ornaments," monument of poetic regret, for Queen Anne of Bohemia, not of course the "Queen" of Shakespeare, who however seems to have transferred to this second wife something of Richard's wildly proclaimed affection for the first. In this way, through the connecting link of that sacred spot, our thoughts once more associate Richard's two fallacious prerogatives, his personal beauty and his "anointing."

According to Johnson, *Richard the Second* is one of those plays which Shakespeare has "apparently revised;" and how doubly delightful Shakespeare is where he seems to have revised! "Would that he had blotted a thousand"—a thousand hasty phrases, we may venture once more to say with his earlier critic, now that the tiresome German superstition has passed away which challenged us to a dogmatic faith in the plenary verbal inspiration of every one of Shakespeare's clowns. Like some melodiously contending anthem of Handel's, I said, of Richard's meek "undoing" of himself in the mirror-scene; and, in fact, the play of *Richard the Second* does, like a musical composition, possess a certain concentration of all its parts, a simple continuity, an evenness in execution, which are rare in the great dramatist. With *Romeo and Juliet*, that perfect symphony (symphony of three independent poetic forms set in a grander one[5] which it is the merit of German criticism to have detected) it belongs to a small group of plays, where, by happy birth and consistent evolution, dramatic form approaches to something like the unity of a lyrical ballad, a lyric, a song, a single strain of music. Which sort of poetry we are to account the highest, is perhaps a barren question. Yet if, in art generally, unity of impression is a note of what is perfect, then lyric poetry, which in spite of complex structure often preserves the unity of a single passionate ejaculation, would rank higher than dramatic poetry, where, especially to the reader, as

distinguished from the spectator assisting at a theatrical performance, there must always be a sense of the effort necessary to keep the various parts from flying asunder, a sense of imperfect continuity, such as the older criticism vainly sought to obviate by the rule of the dramatic "unities." It follows that a play attains artistic perfection just in proportion as it approaches that unity of lyrical effect, as if a song or ballad were still lying at the rear of it, all the various expression of the conflict of character and circumstance falling at last into the compass of a single melody, or musical theme. As, historically, the earliest classic drama arose out of the chorus, from which this or that person, this or that episode, detached itself, so, into the unity of a choric song the perfect drama ever tends to return, its intellectual scope deepened, complicated, enlarged, but still with an unmistakable singleness, or identity, in its impression on the mind. Just there, in that vivid single impression left on the mind when all is over, not in any mechanical limitation of time and place, is the secret of the "unities"—the true imaginative unity—of the drama.

*Notes*

1.  *Elinor:* Do you not read some tokens of my son [Cœur-de-Lion]
    In the large composition of this man?
2.  Perhaps the one person of *genius* in these English plays.
    The spirit of deep prophecy she hath,
    Exceeding the nine Sibyls of old Rome:
    What's past and what's to come she can descry.
3.  Proposing in this paper to trace the leading sentiment in Shakespeare's English Plays as a sort of *popular dramatic chronicle*, I have left untouched the question how much (or, in the case of *Henry the Sixth* and *Henry the Eighth*, how little) of them may be really his: how far inferior hands have contributed to a result, true on the whole to the greater, that is to say, the Shakespearian, elements in them.
4.  Perhaps a *double entendre:*—of any ordinary grave, as comprising, in effect, the whole small earth now left to its occupant: or, of such a tomb as Richard's in particular, with its actual model, or effigy, of the clay of him. Both senses are so characteristic that it would be a pity to lose either.
5.  The Sonnet: the Aubade: the Epithalamium.

# Henry VI

The three parts of *Henry VI.* are suspected, by Mr. Theobald, of being supposititious, and are declared, by Dr. Warburton, to be "certainly not Shakespeare's." Mr. Theobald's suspicion arises from some obsolete words; but the phraseology is like the rest of our authour's stile, and single words, of which however I do not observe more than two, can conclude little.

Dr. Warburton gives no reason, but I suppose him to judge upon deeper principles and more comprehensive views, and to draw his opinion from the general effect and spirit of the composition, which he thinks inferior to the other historical plays.

From mere inferiority nothing can be inferred; in the productions of wit there will be inequality. Sometimes judgment will err, and sometimes the matter itself will defeat the artist. Of every authour's works one will be the best, and one will be the worst. The colours are not equally pleasing, nor the attitudes equally graceful, in all the pictures of Titian or Reynolds.

Dissimilitude of stile and heterogeneousness of sentiment, may sufficiently show that a work does not really belong to the

reputed authour. But in these plays no such marks of spuriousness are found. The diction, the versification, and the figures, are Shakespeare's. These plays, considered, without regard to characters and incidents, merely as narratives in verse, are more happily conceived and more accurately finished than those of *King John*, *Richard II*, or the tragick scenes of *Henry IV.* and *V.* If we take these plays from Shakespeare, to whom shall they be given? What authour of that age had the same easiness of expression and fluency of numbers?

Having considered the evidence given by the plays themselves, and found it in their favour, let us now enquire what corroboration can be gained from other testimony. They are ascribed to Shakespeare by the first editors, whose attestation may be received in questions of fact, however unskilfully they superintended their edition. They seem to be declared genuine by the voice of Shakespeare himself, who refers to the second play in his epilogue to *Henry V.* and apparently connects the first act of *Richard III.* with the last of the third part of *Henry VI.* If it be objected that the plays were popular, and therefore he alluded to them as well known; it may be answered, with equal probability, that the natural passions of a poet would have disposed him to separate his own works from those of an inferior hand. And indeed if an authour's own testimony is to be overthrown by speculative criticism, no man can be any longer secure of literary reputation.

Of these three plays I think the second the best. The truth is, that they have not sufficient variety of action, for the incidents are too often of the same kind; yet many of the characters are well discriminated. King Henry, and his queen, King Edward, the Duke of Gloucester, and the Earl of Warwick, are very strongly and distinctly painted.

The old copies of the two latter parts of *Henry VI.* and of *Henry V.* are so apparently imperfect and mutilated, that there is no reason for supposing them the first draughts of Shakespeare. I am inclined to believe them copies taken by some auditor who wrote down, during the representation, what the time would permit, then perhaps filled up some of his omissions at a second or third hearing, and when he had by this method formed something like a play, sent it to the printer.— SAMUEL JOHNSON, *Notes on Shakespeare's Plays*, 1768

The three parts of *Henry the Sixth* . . . were composed much earlier than the ⟨other histories⟩. Shakspeare's choice fell first on this period of English history, so full of misery and horrors of every kind, because the pathetic is naturally more suitable than the characteristic to a young poet's mind. We do not yet find here the whole maturity of his genius, yet certainly its whole strength. Careless as to the apparent unconnectedness of contemporary events, he bestows little attention on preparation and development: all the figures follow in rapid succession, and announce themselves emphatically for what we ought to take them; from scenes where the effect is sufficiently agitating to form the catastrophe of a less extensive plan, the poet perpetually hurries us on to catastrophes still more dreadful. The First Part contains only the first forming of the parties of the White and Red Rose, under which blooming ensigns such bloody deeds were afterwards perpetrated; the varying results of the war in France principally fill the stage. The wonderful saviour of her country, Joan of Arc, is portrayed by Shakspeare with an Englishman's prejudices: yet he at first leaves it doubtful whether she has not in reality a heavenly mission; she appears in the pure glory of virgin heroism; by her supernatural eloquence (and this circumstance is of the poet's invention) she wins over the Duke of Burgundy to the French cause; afterwards, corrupted by vanity and luxury, she has recourse to hellish fiends, and comes to a miserable end. To her is opposed Talbot, a rough iron warrior, who moves us the more powerfully, as, in the moment when he is threatened with inevitable death, all his care is tenderly directed to save his son, who performs his first deeds of arms under his eye. After Talbot has in vain sacrificed himself, and the Maid of Orleans has fallen into the hands of the English, the French provinces are completely lost by an impolitic marriage; and with this the piece ends. The conversation between the aged Mortimer in prison, and Richard Plantagenet, afterwards Duke of York, contains an exposition of the claims of the latter to the throne: considered by itself it is a beautiful tragic elegy.

In the Second Part, the events more particularly prominent are the murder of the honest Protector, Gloster, and its consequences; the death of Cardinal Beaufort; the parting of the Queen from her favourite Suffolk, and his death by the hands of savage pirates; then the insurrection of Jack Cade under an assumed name, and at the instigation of the Duke of York. The short scene where Cardinal Beaufort, who is tormented by his conscience on account of the murder of

Gloster, is visited on his death-bed by Henry VI. is sublime beyond all praise. Can any other poet be named who has drawn aside the curtain of eternity at the close of this life with such overpowering and awful effect? And yet it is not mere horror with which the mind is filled, but solemn emotion; a blessing and a curse stand side by side; the pious King is an image of the heavenly mercy which, even in the sinner's last moments, labours to enter into his soul. The adulterous passion of Queen Margaret and Suffolk is invested with tragical dignity and all low and ignoble ideas carefully kept out of sight. Without attempting to gloss over the crime of which both are guilty, without seeking to remove our disapprobation of this criminal love, he still, by the magic force of expression, contrives to excite in us a sympathy with their sorrow. In the insurrection of Cade he has delineated the conduct of a popular demagogue, the fearful ludicrousness of the anarchical tumult of the people, with such convincing truth, that one would believe he was an eye-witness of many of the events of our age, which, from ignorance of history, have been considered as without example.

The civil war only begins in the Second Part; in the Third it is unfolded in its full destructive fury. The picture becomes gloomier and gloomier; and seems at last to be painted rather with blood than with colours. With horror we behold fury giving birth to fury, vengeance to vengeance, and see that when all the bonds of human society are violently torn asunder, even noble matrons became hardened to cruelty. The most bitter contempt is the portion of the unfortunate; no one affords to his enemy that pity which he will himself shortly stand in need of. With all party is family, country, and religion, the only spring of action. As York, whose ambition is coupled with noble qualities, prematurely perishes, the object of the whole contest is now either to support an imbecile king, or to place on the throne a luxurious monarch, who shortens the dear-bought possession by the gratification of an insatiable voluptuousness. For this the celebrated and magnanimous Warwick spends his chivalrous life; Clifford revenges the death of his father with blood-thirsty filial love; and Richard, for the elevation of his brother, practises those dark deeds by which he is soon after to pave the way to his own greatness. In the midst of the general misery, of which he has been the innocent cause, King Henry appears like the powerless image of a saint, in whose wonderworking influence no man any longer believes: he can but sigh and weep over the enormities which he witnesses. In his simplicity, however, the gift of prophecy is lent to this pious king: in the moment of his death, at the close of this great tragedy, he prophesies a still more dreadful tragedy with which futurity is pregnant, as much distinguished for the poisonous wiles of cold-blooded wickedness as the former for deeds of savage fury.—AUGUST WILHELM SCHLEGEL, *Lectures on Dramatic Art and Literature*, 1809, tr. John Black

---

WILLIAM HAZLITT
From "*Henry VI.*"
*Characters of Shakespear's Plays*
1817

During the time of the civil wars of York and Lancaster, England was a perfect bear-garden, and Shakespear has given us a very lively picture of the scene. The three parts of *Henry VI.* convey a picture of very little else; and are inferior to the other historical plays. They have brilliant passages; but the general ground-work is comparatively poor and meagre, the style 'flat and unraised.' There are few lines like the following:—

> Glory is like a circle in the water;
> Which never ceaseth to enlarge itself,
> Till by broad spreading it disperse to nought.

The first part relates to the wars in France after the death of Henry V. and the story of the Maid of Orleans. She is here almost as scurvily treated as in Voltaire's Pucelle. Talbot is a very magnificent sketch: there is something as formidable in this portrait of him, as there would be in a monumental figure of him or in the sight of the armour which he wore. The scene in which he visits the Countess of Auvergne, who seeks to entrap him, is a very spirited one, and his description of his own treatment while a prisoner to the French not less remarkable.

> *Salisbury:* Yet tell'st thou not how thou wert entertain'd.
> *Talbot:* With scoffs and scorns, and contumelious taunts.
> In open market-place produced they me,
> To be a public spectacle to all.
> Here, said they, is the terror of the French,
> The scarecrow that affrights our children so.
> Then broke I from the officers that led me,
> And with my nails digg'd stones out of the ground,
> To hurl at the beholders of my shame.
> My grisly countenance made others fly,
> None durst come near for fear of sudden death.
> In iron walls they deem'd me not secure:
> So great a fear my name amongst them spread,
> That they suppos'd I could rend bars of steel,
> And spurn in pieces posts of adamant.
> Wheretofore a guard of chosen shot I had:
> They walk'd about me every minute-while;
> And if I did but stir out of my bed,
> Ready they were to shoot me to the heart.

The second part relates chiefly to the contests between the nobles during the minority of Henry, and the death of Gloucester, the good Duke Humphrey. The character of Cardinal Beaufort is the most prominent in the group: the account of his death is one of our author's master-pieces. So is the speech of Gloucester to the nobles on the loss of the provinces of France by the King's marriage with Margaret of Anjou. The pretensions and growing ambition of the Duke of York, the father of Richard III., are also very ably developed. Among the episodes, the tragi-comedy of Jack Cade, and the detection of the impostor Simcox are truly edifying.

The third part describes Henry's loss of his crown: his death takes place in the last act, which is usually thrust into the common acting play of *Richard III.* The character of Gloucester, afterwards King Richard, is here very powerfully commenced, and his dangerous designs and long-reaching ambition are fully described in his soliloquy in the third act, beginning, 'Aye, Edward will use women honourably.' Henry VI. is drawn as distinctly as his high-spirited Queen, and notwithstanding the very mean figure which Henry makes as a King, we still feel more respect for him than for his wife.

. . . Shakespear was scarcely more remarkable for the force and marked contrasts of his characters than for the truth and subtlety with which he has distinguished those which approached the nearest to each other. For instance, the soul of Othello is hardly more distinct from that of Iago than that of Desdemona is shewn to be from Æmilia's; the ambition of Macbeth is as distinct from the ambition of Richard III. as it is from the meekness of Duncan; the real madness of Lear is as different from the feigned madness of Edgar[1] as from the

babbling of the fool; the contrast between wit and folly in Falstaff and Shallow is not more characteristic though more obvious than the gradations of folly, loquacious or reserved, in Shallow and Silence; and again, the gallantry of Prince Henry is as little confounded with that of Hotspur as with the cowardice of Falstaff, or as the sensual and philosophic cowardice of the Knight is with the pitiful and cringing cowardice of Parolles. All these several personages were as different in Shakespear as they would have been in themselves: his imagination borrowed from the life, and every circumstance, object, motive, passion, operated there as it would in reality, and produced a world of men and women as distinct, as true and as various as those that exist in nature. The peculiar property of Shakespear's imagination was this truth, accompanied with the unconsciousness of nature: indeed, imagination to be perfect must be unconscious, at least in production; for nature is so.—We shall attempt one example more in the characters of Richard II. and Henry VI.

The characters and situations of both these persons were so nearly alike, that they would have been completely confounded by a commonplace poet. Yet they are kept quite distinct in Shakespear. Both were kings, and both unfortunate. Both lost their crowns owing to their mismanagement and imbecility; the one from a thoughtless, wilful abuse of power, the other from an indifference to it. The manner in which they bear their misfortunes corresponds exactly to the causes which led to them. The one is always lamenting the loss of his power which he has not the spirit to regain; the other seems only to regret that he had ever been king, and is glad to be rid of the power, with the trouble; the effeminacy of the one is that of a voluptuary, proud, revengeful, impatient of contradiction, and inconsolable in his misfortunes; the effeminacy of the other is that of an indolent, good-natured mind, naturally averse to the turmoils of ambition and the cares of greatness, and who wishes to pass his time in monkish indolence and contemplation.—Richard bewails the loss of the kingly power only as it was the means of gratifying his pride and luxury; Henry regards it only as a means of doing right, and is less desirous of the advantages to be derived from possessing it than afraid of exercising it wrong. In knighting a young soldier, he gives him ghostly advice—

> Edward Plantagenet, arise a knight,
> And learn this lesson, draw thy sword in right.

Richard II. in the first speeches of the play betrays his real character. In the first alarm of his pride, on hearing of Bolingbroke's rebellion, before his presumption has met with any check, he exclaims—

> Mock not my senseless conjuration, lords:
> This earth shall have a feeling, and these stones
> Prove armed soldiers, ere her native king
> Shall faulter under proud rebellious arms.
>       . . . .
> Not all the water in the rough rude sea
> Can wash the balm from an anointed king;
> The breath of worldly man cannot depose
> The Deputy elected by the Lord.
> For every man that Bolingbroke hath prest,
> To lift sharp steel against our golden crown,
> Heaven for his Richard hath in heavenly pay
> A glorious angel; then if angels fight,
> Weak men must fall; for Heaven still guards the
>       right.

Yet, notwithstanding this royal confession of faith, on the very first news of actual disaster, all his conceit of himself as the peculiar favourite of Providence vanishes into air.

But now the blood of twenty thousand men
Did triumph in my face, and they are fled.
All souls that will be safe fly from my side;
For time hath set a blot upon my pride.

Immediately after, however, recollecting that 'cheap defence' of the divinity of kings which is to be found in opinion, he is for arming his name against his enemies.

Awake, thou coward Majesty, thou sleep'st;
Is not the King's name forty thousand names?
Arm, arm, my name: a puny subject strikes
At thy great glory.

King Henry does not make any such vapouring resistance to the loss of his crown, but lets it slip from off his head as a weight which he is neither able nor willing to bear; stands quietly by to see the issue of the contest for his kingdom, as if it were a game at push-pin, and is pleased when the odds prove against him.

*Notes*

1. There is another instance of the same distinction in Hamlet and Phelia. Hamlet's pretended madness would make a very good real madness in any other author.

## ERNEST RHYS
### "Shakespeare's *King Henry* VI"

*Harper's Monthly Magazine*
October-November 1905, pp. 720–27, 882–89

### I

At the time when the London stage was history's looking-glass, the old tragic Contention of the two famous Houses, Lancaster and York, and the preceding tragedy in which Talbot confronted Joan of Arc, could offer an afternoon's entertainment of which the playgoer never seemed to tire. Now these Henry VI. plays are rarely or never acted and little read; and this may be, in some degree, owing to their mixed authorship and the doubt of Shakespeare's real part in them. But the confusion of authors only adds piquancy to their interest once we turn from the stage to the common-room of the theatre. Then we see that, whether little or much is allotted to one playwright or another, the sheer interest of craftsmanship in them is extraordinary. In all three parts we are able to watch the hand of Marlowe spiriting Shakespeare's as it can be seen nowhere else to the like effect, and it was the subtle commerce of the two that wrought what one of their older associates might teach us to call the "second metamorphosis" of the Elizabethan stage.

That is not all. Behind Marlowe we see the figures of the two golden prodigals, Greene and Peele, and detect in their voices a natural accord with his. Some of the Shakespearian adepts hear still other notes,—Lodge's particularly; and indeed the various accents, clear or confused, which appear to be lurking in the theatre are bewildering. Behind the one formal voice we presently distinguish three or four more, and then we are tempted to refine our ears a half-tone further and imagine still others, until we arrive at something wholly confused; a hubbub innumerous as that heard by the King and Queen when the Commons pressed to the door after the good Duke Humphrey's death—the "noise of a crowd," as the stage directions say. It is as though all London had made a play, gathering up first its old wives' gossip of a Maid of Orleans and a Talbot and the whole contention between the two Houses of York and Lancaster, and then handing in this gossip's budget at the theatre door.

Every proverb, every fable of a great event at home or in France, that could help to bring two mighty monarchies into a cockpit and give the history of the reign its "great accompt," was hidden in that news-packet. Under the hands of the playwrights it kindled as a telegram from the seat of war quickens to-day in the hands of the Fleet Street conjurors.

The kind of expectation in the playgoer, on which the dramatist counted in this kindling of history, was very different to that set going by strict tragedy. In plays of the Henry VI. type, the direct dramatic interest in the tragic assay of character and human nature is eked out by a continual call upon popularly remembered and stated event. A gap in the plot, a lapse in the consistency of motive or of character, is easily mended by the writer of a history play if he will only draw a covering scene out of the immense fund of tradition open to him. This must have been a great temptation to the minor dramatist, who had to shuffle together a set of scenes in a hurry to meet some sudden demand from the playhouse. It was certainly a temptation to which the minor men who wrote the earlier drafts of the Henry VI. plays yielded to the utmost. And though the feeling of a reader of a play in a chimney-corner to-day is very unlike that of a typical early Elizabethan playgoer, yet he can yet contrive to realize something of that added sensation of history still vivid in men's minds and not merely written in books which gave a sort of sanction to many things otherwise without apparent art or excuse. Indeed, one finds, as one tries to analyze the various effect of these particular history-plays, that in reading and rereading them one is more often drawing upon one's sense of history than on one's sense of tragedy and the dramatic exigencies.

We are all nowadays more or less complex in our discrimination and in our working sense of what we can let pass and what we cannot pass, or what we can only half approve; and in this elaborate stage-epic which is called Shakespeare's and which is really Everyman's, we have full provision truly for all our critical moods, conceits, and hesitations. And between epic and dramatic, and actual history and the acted drama, we may turn leaf after leaf of this trilogy, and still remain confused, and inclined to say with the eloquent archbishop in Henry the Fifth,—

I this infer:
That many things having full reference
To one consent, may work contrariously;
As many arrows, loosed several ways,
Fly to one mark.

The triple pageant of history, painted in the Henry the Sixth plays, opens greatly to a sound of funeral music; and this commemoration of the mighty dead has its perfect scene at Westminster Abbey, in whose stone the heart of that old royalty may be said to be wrapped. The boyd of King Henry V. is brought there in state; but the dead-march is broken by the call to action and the news of French losses. The scene shifts: we are in France, before Orleans, and we have alarms and a retreat to prepare for Joan of Arc. Again we are in London at the Tower gates, and it is blue coats against tawny coats and Duke Humphrey against Winchester, and the Mayor of London to cry peace. And now the scene is Orleans again, and enter Talbot "dreadful to the French"; and there is a murderous cannon-shot to show what risks he survived and prove him all but immune, a scene to delight the 'prentices. Anon we have more fighting, and the forces of the infernal and La Pucelle start up against the Heaven-kept Captain. But Joan is acclaimed at the end by Charles the Dauphin, in a line which rings prophetical and which only recently had its fulfilment:

But Joan la Pucelle shall be France's saint.

One must dip deep into the old Chronicles of Raphael Holinshed for the first draft of Talbot's and Joan of Arc's stage cartoons. We come in Holinshed upon the very scene where Joan of Arc is first led to the Dolphin (as he calls him), in his gallerie, where Charles hides behind "other gay lords." But La Pucelle picks him out with a salutation which, says the Chronicler, mars all.[1]

A few pages further, we find the English king indignant because the French king had "by allurement of a diuelish witch" taken upon him the name, title, and dignity of King of France. Again we read how at the Siege of Paris (after St. Denis) the English "threw down Jone their great goddesse into the bottom of the towne ditch, where she lay behind the backe of an asse," sore hurt in the leg, till the time that she was drawn "all durtie out of the mire" by Guischard of Thielbrone. Holinshed does not consider the infamy of her being sold to the enemy for "five thousand pounds (French crowns) in money, and 150 crowns rent."

But anything was good enough for the brave Maid of Orleans, according to Holinshed. He tells us in one page, of her campestrall conversation with wicked spirits, and how, being "all damnablie faithlesse, she was a pernicious instrument to hostilitie and bloudshed in diuelish witchcraft and sorcerie." In short, Joan of Arc richly deserved to burn, by his reckoning. After her martyrdom, her ashes were carried without the town walls and shaken into the wind. Another page or two, and he reduces the witchcraft which he has been solemnly denouncing to the ridiculous by telling how the English captured one called "the Sheepheard, a simple man and a sillie soule," but yet of such repute, that the French believed if he merely touched the wall of any town they were besieging, it would straightway fall down.

Returning from the Chronicles to the play-books, we shall find we have travelled far into the heart of the first part and reached its second act and the fourth scene—the famous scene in the Temple Gardens—before the voice that we look for sounds in it, ample, easily accordant, instinctively dramatic. The scene of Mortimer in the Tower, which follows, is good Elizabethan commonplace, with one or two finer creative touches. The third act opens with another typical London tableau of history—at the Parliament Houses—and we have some faction-fighting before we get back to France and to Rouen. These vociferous fighting scenes where Talbot and Joan of Arc encounter were the really popular sensations in the first part of *Henry VI*. So we gather from Nash's *Piers Penniless*, published in 1592, where he speaks of the dramatic other-life of "brave Talbot,—the Terror of the French." In the fourth act and in its second scene we have Talbot broadly painted at last by the master hand: where he sets the trumpet sounding before Bordeaux. But the French General's retort, "Thou ominous and fearful owl of death," is not so convincing, not at any rate in its opening. The heroic resonance of the later lines accords much better with Talbot's stage valiancy.

The Plains of Gascony succeed; and we see a Sir William Lucy on the stage before we return to Bordeaux with the same heroic note and with the two Talbots father and son sounding it, but not to Shakespeare's setting. Then come their equally doubtful closing scenes, and the act ends with La Pucelle's meanly conceived triumph. Next act, and she too meets her doom shamefully and horribly, and the one consolation is here that Shakespeare wrote not a single word or line of it. The play ends with the tiresome eloquence of Suffolk in his rôle of queen's showman. "France is lost in this play," we are reminded by Dr. Johnson; but the stage is swept and made handsomely ready for the coming of Margaret of Anjou. And although, or because, this first play was written long after its two successors, the interest in the lady Margaret and her coming is as clearly provoked and left in suspense, as was ever a coming love-sensation by an old-fashioned serial romance. There is a distinct promise, too, not only of beauty, birth, "peerless feature," but of what is ominous enough in contrast with the young king's acknowledgment of his own insusceptibility to love and weak will—of "her valiant courage and undaunted spirit!" One's dramatic curiosity, at this point, wholly outruns what one remembers of this strangely assorted pair of royal lovers in the page of English history. For Henry's nervous eagerness is not for love's delight and the young lover's rapture, but only—sad confession!—for care's relief:

> I feel such sharp dissention in my breast,
> Such fierce alarums both of hope and fear,
> As I am sick with working of my thoughts.
> Take therefore shipping; post, my lord, to France;
> Agree to any covenants; and procure
> That lady Margaret do vouchsafe to come
> To cross the seas to England, and be crown'd
> King Henry's faithful and anointed queen: . . .
> Be gone, I say; for till you so return
> I rest perplexed with a thousand cares.

But it is not the title-character and his almost modern nervous temperament that one remembers best in this first part, fine and surely Shakespearian as are some of the indicative strokes that tell his characteristic ailment and conscious want of red blood. It is the full-blooded Talbot; and Talbot in his most martial last effect is (if you get back to the business of finding the authors concerned in the play) without a doubt Shakespeare's in that which makes him really vital. Again the scene of the Two Roses in the Temple Gardens is Shakespeare's by common consent. But elsewhere Marlowe's voice, and a voice now like Greene's, now like Peele's, speak in perplexing alternation. And there are often lines so thin and common that they are not worthy of Greene—unless he were drunk, and very drunk indeed. Even the obvious and easy imagery prompted by the Two Roses is so flat on occasion that a Lord Lytton of Elizabeth's days might have written it. And Talbot too,—the best of him is great:

> Lean famine, quartering steel, and climbing fire!

The poorest is very poor, or it tends to the rant of the buckram warrior, which Marlowe supplied in perfection to take the ears of the groundlings, redeeming it as he wrote or laughing perhaps at its crudity. There is no very redeeming note here:

> Foul fiend of France, and hag of all despite,
> Encompass'd with thy lustful paramours!
> Becomes it thee to taunt his valiant age,
> And twit with cowardice a man half-dead?
> Damsel, I'll have a bout with you again,
> Or else let Talbot perish with this shame!

Who composed this delicate piece of bravado? Who burlesqued it afterwards? We seem to hear something very like Pistol's voice:

> O braggard vile, and damned furious wight!
> The grave doth gape, and doting death is near;
> Therefore exhale.

Talbot then may serve as test-character. Whoever made the first draught, Shakespeare completed the portrait, as once a divine artist painted out and painted in and made a finished or living picture out of a student's poor study of a Dante's head.

We can use Joan of Arc, La Pucelle, as another test. She is not all of a piece, it is true; for at her first appearance she is sympathetically drawn, and the lines suggest a portrait by a gentler hand than Marlowe's; but it is not Shakespeare's.

Afterwards she grows into a formidable hag; and the workmanship is vile. One imagines to see an old English chap-book, with an ugly woodcut of the French witch and the familiars that attend her.

Only in Act III., Scene 3 in this first part, does one seem to hear Shakespeare speak—in the appeal that wins Burgundy back to France. But after the death of Talbot and his son, there can be no more stage-sympathy for her who was his monstrous rival and who survived him. Popular feeling at that day would not have borne a sympathetically treated heroine. And so, all her maid-warrior's shining colors gone, she is a hag and anybody's wanton, and the devil himself peeps over her shoulder.

## II

Although the sharp cross-fires of Talbot and Joan of Arc are extinct and dramatically forgotten before the first part of *Henry VI.* ends, there is no want of warring elements to take their place. There must be as much fighting and dying in the second and third parts of this stage-chronicle as there is of eating and drinking in the *Pickwick Papers*. The very figures of speech, the allusions from heraldry, the fierce words, the characteristic sanguinary colors, are all patently devised to eke out the idea of the old title of "the Contention" which was theirs. The Rampant Bear and the baiting curs, the hungry kite hovering over the chicken guarded by an equally avid eagle, the crocodile mournful to be cruel, the butcher red-handed over the calf, Cade's ostrich that eats iron, Margery Jourdain's fatal fiend, Beaufort's ominous keen red eyes of malice, Suffolk's "bloody pole" and Illyrian pirate, and the sea-captain's image of unnatural cannibal Sylla to whom he likens Suffolk: what an apparatus of deadly metaphor and murderous imagination it is!

But what of the one continuing and unresisting chief character, who stands like an uneasy umpire at an angry football match, and sees so many go down and has so many appeals made to his timorous authority, before his own fall closes the play; what of the nervous, disastrous king? Queen Margaret has much to say of his piety, his foolish pity too:

> But all his mind is bent to holiness,
> To number Ave-Maries on his beads;
> His champions are—the prophets and apostles;
> His weapons, holy saws of sacred writ.

The contrast with her own ardent uncompromising temper is always present in the minds of the authors, several and collective, as one perceives at every stage-crisis. Indeed, she is almost the masculine to his feminine. But apart from this, one cannot help remarking it to be strange that the mysterious ailment, congenital in Henry VI.'s blood, is not turned to more dramatic account. We know how effective a supposed malady, some smouldering fatal ailment, can be made, for we have seen it in greater plays than these. But it was enough, it seems, for those writers who first took their cue from Holinshed, that Henry should be the pious, the hesitating and delicately minded prince, who, intended for a quietist by nature, was buffeted by circumstance and dragged over endless battle-fields at the will of his disastrous queen. Before she appears, in the first part, Henry is young without the spirit of youth; while in the second part he is seen at his weakest, governed by her will, if not without an inert wisdom of his own. His nervous inability as he moves among these decided fighting lords, or stands still while his queen moves, is made there only too intelligible. In the third part, he has become the fugitive king; and then the playgoers' sympathies fly after him, even as they did after Edward II., whose dramatic setting is so curiously like to his. But Henry VI. acquiesces in the fate administered by Heaven: Edward II. is only a ruined Sybarite. The pathos of Edward II.'s

fall, as Marlowe designs it, is in his sense of what king's pleasures had been his, and are his no longer. He is sorry for himself, and he thinks of himself and not of his country:

> O hadst thou ever been a king, thy heart
> Pierced deeply with a sense of my distress
> Could not but take compassion of my state.
> Stately and proud, in riches and in train
> Whilom I was, powerful, and full of pomp.

Edward II. says, "Let me be king till night!" and Henry VI., "Let me, for this my lifetime, reign as king." The dramatic treatment is at points so similar in the two conclusions, however, that we must think the same hand drew them in their different predicament.

One cannot rehearse half the state-tableaux and battle-fields in the second and the third parts of *Henry VI.* In the second we see war drawing very close to the doors of the English people. The Duke of Gloster's house succeeds to the King's palace, and the Duchess outbraves the Queen, and sorcery is afoot; and St. Albans gives us a scene with a fillip for the miracle-mongers, which is rather like the work of Greene. We have a burlesque premonition of the great wars to follow in the drunkards' duel between Horner and Peter. There the action quickens, and the humiliation-scene of the Duchess leads on swiftly to the murder of the "good Duke Humphrey"—who was a popular favorite, though even the stage shows him a coward in his wife's hour of need. Then Marlowe speaks, and speaks at his rarest in the death-scene of the wicked Cardinal, where the second part has one of its great moments. Holinshed's "Capteine of Kent," Jack Cade, otherwise John Mend-All, brings another poor man's bone to the contention; and so ends Act IV. In Act V. we have England fairly sundered at last, York and Lancaster outfacing each other, and the piteous death of Clifford, and an unmistakable, repeated, desperate glimpse of that Richard Plantagenet who was to live and wax in strength thro' two plays more. His triumph was Henry's "day of doom,"—fit words to end a tragedy where doom impends like a dark cloud over all the royal ambitions and fatal family revenges and intrigues of its actors, shadowing an elemental creature like Richard of Gloster just as surely as a Clarence, or a little Prince Edward, or a King Edward V.

But we are forgetting Henry VI., that "ghoostlie" man, and his queen. Again it is Holinshed who gives us the colors of the play: tells of the gentleness and "overmuch mildness of the King," and then turns to contrast him with Margaret. For she, "contrariwise, is a ladie of great wit, and no lesse courage; desirous of honour, and furnished with the gifts of reason, policie and wisdome. But yet," says the Chronicler, "sometime (according to her kind) when she had been fullie bent on a matter," she was "suddenlie like a weather-cocke,—mutable and turning." We hear too, from the same page, an ominous whisper of how when Prince Edward was born "his mother sustained not a little slander and obloquie of the common people."

This whisper is clearly hinted in certain scenes of the second part of the trilogy; and indeed the treatment on the stage of the French princess who became an English queen is not all strictly of a piece, just as the treatment of the French Maid who led her country against the English was not all strictly accorded. In both cases this discrepancy arose from the same thing, the multiple authorship of the triple drama. But in the third part the character of Margaret is rather more consistent; and there her zeal for her son redeems her rage, and her unworthy, unqueenly mockery of York (which quite explains his "She Wolf of France!") is saved by her heroic maternal emotion, her soul's divorce from Henry, and her undaunted front before the terrible Richard Plantagenet. She is introduced in her full symbolic colors at the end of the third part, after Henry—"base, fearful, and despairing Henry"—has virtually given away the birthright of his son and hers. And well her entrance accords with that opening, which unrolls itself with a kind of fierce gayety to a sound of drums and the breaking in of the York faction with white roses in their hats, followed by the Lancaster men, headed by the King, with red roses in theirs.

Here was the proverbial three-sons episode of folk-lore; and the youngest, Richard, is the hero, as in folk-tales usually happens—a darling scene for the general. Battle succeeds battle then, the roses are continually dipped in blood, and we have the "Whole Contention" reduced to the simplest terms, with history written at the sword's point, and the Houses of York and Lancaster visibly overtopping one another on the stage. We follow their armies to Sandal Castle and the Yorkshire fields of war; and there young Clarence tastes the revenge he had foreseen, slaying young Richard; and there dies York, fulfilling the Queen's revenge,—

> So York may overlook the town of York!

But his death only serves to quicken the Plantagenet tune of Mortimer's Cross; and "this brave town of York," Towton and Saxton continue the martial strain until it dies away in King Henry's meditation on the shepherd's life, whose days and years

> Would bring white hairs unto a quiet grave.

The homely curds and the "cold thin drink" of the shepherd do not make the least delightful or the least classical touches in this dire Yorkshire pastoral. No doubt Marlowe wrote it, and a greater than he rewrote it.

The next act paints King Henry in retreat very much as Marlowe painted Edward II. England is everything now, and France under new aspects and King Lewis and Lady Bona hardly justify themselves dramatically while we spoil for the final bloody triumph of the House of York. The total emergence of Richard of Gloster reminds us next that without him and his elemental energy, converting all the forces, cross-purposes, and confusions of petty revenge into one crowning idea, the latter half of part three, poor as it often is, would be poor indeed.

If we try now to recall our impressions of the whole trilogy, we shall find that if one voice besides Shakespeare's is dominant, it is Marlowe's. There are lines, passages, effects, and phrases in all three parts, which he and only he could have written. It may be an echo of a stage Damascus in the siege of Orleans, or a lurking reminder of a Soldan or an Eastern prince in the mouth of a Dauphin, calling up without any specific rally of resemblances an illusion or a sentence, or some persistent, dimly reminiscent line, which must be his:—

> O Mahomet! O Sleepy Mahomet!

But from Marlowe in his careless vein it is not easy to detach Greene and Peele. Younger than they, he was that latecomer who can give the wasted night its new lease of time, enlarge its fellowship, and turn an orgy into a feast. Greene had more lyric ease, more humor too; but in the theatre he was lazy. When he felt his blank verse growing monotonous, he simply relaxed its beat, or evaded its laws by slipping a line at random. And Peele again had no end of faculty, but as a dramatist he could never get outside his own door, as the saying used to be. Marlowe had an epic imagination, and with it he had fully twice the dramatic genius of the other two. He was built for heroic song, a blow ended each line, he wrought blank verse in bars of gold or iron; but weld them malleably as his great

successor welded them, he could not; and he did not live to learn, as he must have done, that mastery.

Turn now, however, and summon up those who were lesser than he, and who undoubtedly helped to write these *Henry VI.* plays. Set Peele and Greene beside him. Which is responsible for the "statelier pyramids than Rhodope's," or the coffer of Darius? This is not the London gossip's voice, nor is it Shakespeare's.

Turn again to what you may call the "Old England" note, and the martial tune heard here, and heard still louder in *Henry V.* It was not Shakespeare who first set it going. Of what does it remind you? Of Greene's *Friar Bacon*, who will so strengthen England by his skill,—

> That if ten Cæsars lived and reign'd in Rome
> With all the legions Europe doth contain
> They should not touch a grass of English ground:
> The work that Ninus rear'd at Babylon,
> The brazen walls fram'd by Semiramis,
> Carv'd out like to the portal of the sun,
> Shall not be such as rings the English strand
> From Dover to the market-place of Rye.

Or of Peele's *Edward the First:*

> Display thy cross, old Amies of the Vie's
> Dub on your drums, tanned with India's sun
> My lusty western lads! Matrevers, thou
> Sound proudly here a perfect point of war
> In honour of thy sovereign's safe return
> Thus Longshanks bids his soldiers *Bien Venu*
>       [*use drums, trumpets, and ensigns.*
> O God, my God! the brightness of my day. . . .

Or of Marlowe's *Edward the Second:*

> But if proud Mortimer do wear this crown
> Heaven turn it to a blaze of quenchless fire!
> Or like the snaky wreath of Tisiphon,
> Engirt the temples of his hateful head;
> So shall not England's vine be perished,
> But Edward's name survive, though Edward dies.

The poetic life of any one of these passages is far greater than that of the average level of *Henry VI.* The individuality of their writers is distinct, their power unmistakable. And recognizing it, we easily understand how the scientific critic may be tempted to dissect the patchwork of the original plays, and assign a piece to this one, and a particular tag or thread or bit of color to another. But when all is marked off that can be distributed in this way, there remains in the continual texture a something of Marlowe and a something more of Shakespeare, that is not to be denied. A shred here, a sudden inflation of the lines there, though not remarkable otherwise for any extraordinary grace or force, make up with a hundred other minor details a total effect which is different to that made in any distinct play of Marlowe's, and certainly very different to anything by Greene and Peele. It is, however, like enough to the general Shakespearian effect to pass current in the popular acceptance, freely colored as it is by reflections from neighbors like *Henry V.* and *Richard III.*

And if we must attempt to recast the dramatic with the actual characters of history presented in the three parts, we shall find the portrait of Henry VI. not far out, save in the want of any direct indication of his fatefully recurring mental disorder; although he shows a decidedly idealized demeanor in the scene of his death. Margaret of Anjou is not punished for her French sympathies as we might, remembering the ghastly treatment of Joan of Arc in the first part, have supposed she would be. But the "good Duke Humphrey" is flattered out of all desert in the play: for if ever there was a designing foster-king to a troubled land, it was he. Upon the other Duke of Gloster, Richard Plantagenet, Richard III., there is no need to dwell further than to say that referred to his Marlowesque surroundings in the "Contention" he looms up more like a portrait by Marlowe than ever. His real enunciation of his future rôle at the murder of Henry is cast in a passage that has still one or two Marlowe-like iterations lingering in an unmistakably Shakespearian context. To compare this passage as it stands with its original version in the "Contention" is to see that Shakespeare's art, like that of other great artists, is to be seen almost as much by what he left out as by what he left in.

But no play, or series of plays, could give all that history must tell of that period. It was then that England exhibited at one juncture "the extraordinary spectacle of a country with two kings, both in prison." That was after Edgecote, in 1469. How fatal the period was we realize by the secret murders just as much as by the open battle-fields. Kings lived hard and recklessly on the whole, and died young. We have Edward IV., a man of "magnificent physique," as great a general in the field as his namesake the first Edward, dying at forty, with a ruined constitution. We have Edward V. reigning only a couple of months before he was murdered. But most telling of all, to declare the fatality of the time, are the words actually recorded as spoken by Clarence when he stabbed young Rutland, after the battle of Wakefield:

By God's blode, thy father slew myne, and so will I do the!

Although three plays went to this king's reign, it was necessary, if ever it was in the drama, for the dramatist to practise what Shakespeare calls elsewhere,—*jumping o'er times*. In the first part, the times are so jumped o'er that a whole generation of actual history is reduced to a sennight: in the second, ten years are disposed of dramatically in a fortnight; and in the third, twenty years, if we take Queen Margaret's final return to France as the historic end, pass in as many days. In all, Henry VI. reigned nearly forty years: and the stage in the three parts takes direct cognizance of only six weeks, although it continues the tale to his death.

Historically or dramatically, the second part is, although it lacks many of the picturesque elements of the first part, the most impressive of the three; and there we see Marlowe's hand most plainly. If the first part makes the effect of a play roughwritten by Greene and Peele, and revised by Marlowe and Shakespeare, the second part is like one designed by Marlowe and corrected by Shakespeare; then cut down and altered in a hurry by some inferior hand—at the time perhaps when the plague was raging—for a provincial tour. The text thus maltreated was never fully restored. The third part again, if designed by Marlowe, was altered and in a few passages enriched by Shakespeare; and then perhaps cut down, and left in much the same state. All three parts were much pulled about, altered for the better, altered again for the worse, and finally left to the mercy of strange editors when they reached the printer's office.

But whatever may be concluded of the share of others in the three parts, there is every temptation to believe that Marlowe was one of the two artificers in chief. A question of how much was done by his fellow prodigals, Peele and Greene, leaves us in a position to hope he did not write the worst Joan of Arc passages, which indeed are not unlike Greene at his worst. But between Marlowe and Shakespeare certainly lies the credit of all that is large in style and mould in the three parts.

*Notes*

1. The scene is painted in much the same way in Martial d'Auvergne's ballad:

Le roy par jeu si alla dire:
"A! ma mye, ee ne suis pas!"
A quoy elle respondit: "Sire,
C'estes vous, si je ne faulx pas."

### ADOLPHUS WILLIAM WARD
#### From "Part of Introduction to Shakespeare's *Henry VI*" (1907)
#### *Collected Papers*
1921, Volume 3, pp. 249–60

At the outset of the reign of Henry VI, the inherent difficulties of government and country were, as is well known, aggravated by the dissensions between those upon whom, during the sovereign's long minority, a special responsibility for the care of State affairs could not but be held to devolve. Unluckily, it was thought indispensable to entrust the preservation of the English rule in France to the Duke of Bedford, who had best claim to the chief control of affairs at home, and who, as "a sober-minded statesman of the best English type,"[1] might very possibly have exercised it with the acquiescence of those who stood next to him in birth or in service. It thus became impossible for Bedford, except by occasional intervention, to do what he might have done towards maintaining the Lancaster dynasty and averting the Wars of the Roses; while, at the same time, by no clearly assignable fault of his own, he failed in carrying out the special task allotted to him. Yet he is not wholly to be compassionated; for his character, partly no doubt because no faction in the State had any interest in traducing it, remains untarnished by the misrepresentations of either chronicler or dramatist.

Very different was the case of the two foremost representatives of the Lancastrian interest who, during Bedford's absence, disputed with one another the control of the English administration, and whom in 1425, on a visit paid by him to England for the purpose, he attempted to reconcile. Henry Beaufort and Humphrey Duke of Gloucester, though with intervals during which a *modus vivendi* obtained between them, and with one pretence of a reconciliation on the occasion just mentioned, carried on their contention, till a strange dispensation of fate ended the lives of both, within a few months in the early part of a single year (1447). Probably, no two English public men have ever been so persistently misjudged as this pair of antagonists. It is true that this misjudgment is of a very different kind, and has a very different origin, in the one and in the other instance; and it must, also, be allowed that the *Henry VI* plays do not adopt it to the same extent in both cases. On the character of Humphrey Duke of Gloucester these plays cannot be said to cast any light such as might have contributed either to a deeper or a more veracious interpretation of it; while, as to Cardinal Beaufort, they have simply contributed to heighten a prejudice already cruel enough in its injustice. Cardinal Beaufort, Bishop of Winchester, was a great ecclesiastical potentate, whose consistent aim it was to augment both his public and his private resources; for it is quite clear that he had recognised how in the age in which he lived—probably at least as much as it has been in any other period of our national life—wealth was the most effective support of political and social influence. But he was, also, a prelate of his Church who, in his life and when he was thinking of his death, was singularly awake to the beneficent ends which it has in all times been the highest privilege of wealth to seek to further.[2] Not less certain is it that

Henry Beaufort was from first to last desirous of accommodating the entire course of his action as to both Church and State to the interests of the Lancastrian dynasty, with which he was by birth connected and with whose fortunes his own were of course closely bound up; and it would be difficult to show that he at any time either misrepresented or misunderstood those interests. In Henry V's reign, he encouraged the prosecution of the French War, and was largely responsible for the conclusion of the Burgundian alliance which was essential to its success. Later, in Henry VI's days, he identified himself with the policy of peace, showing a magnanimous as well as statesmanlike contempt for the unpopularity which such a policy entailed. His relations to the Papacy are more obscure; but they concern the scheme of our trilogy very little, except in so far as Beaufort's Cardinalate (which has been called the great mistake of his life) unmistakably contributed to his unpopularity. At all events no ecclesiastical interests could with him ever take precedence over national; and this he showed, at a critical moment, by transferring, in 1429, the troops which he had levied for a Catholic crusade in Bohemia to the service of the Crown, when an endeavour was made to recover the English position in France after the fatal battle of Patay. During the last few years of his life—apparently from the conclusion of the King's marriage in 1445—the Cardinal had withdrawn from politics, in which he had been a constant factor for nearly half a century, and devoted himself to the interests of his diocese. Thus, apart from the fact of his exceptional wealth—a circumstance which seems to have irritated the popular consciousness in the 15th century very much as it does in the 20th—it would not be easy to understand why the chroniclers and dramatists of the Tudor period should have imbibed so ill-founded and vehement a prejudice against him, imputing to him even a degree of criminality which is held to be appropriately attested by self-torment in the hour of death—were it not that they were children of their times. To the Reformation ages a powerful and wealthy Cardinal (whether his name were Wolsey or Beaufort) signified an offender on a grand scale against both the human and the divine order of things.[3] Nevertheless, the perpetuation of the calumnies against Cardinal Beaufort with which the trilogy of *Henry VI* is chargeable, remains, with a single exception the worst offence against historical truth (in no trivial sense of the term) which it contains.

This exception is not the treatment of the character of Humphrey Duke of Gloucester. Here, instead of recording a blind adherence to the perversity of popular censure, we have rather to notice the neglect of elements that might have added life and variety to the kindly *unisono* of popular praise. Humphrey Duke of Gloucester—"the good Duke," as after his death he came to be called—was a prince of no very exalted character or commanding ability; and the long-enduring sentiment which attached itself to his name was probably due to pity for his supposed cruel fate, as well as to the tradition of his goodwill towards the Commons, and to an actual pleasantness of manner which, as we know, is an unfailing passport of royalty to popular favour. Neither his position nor his qualities ever secured to him a commanding influence over the policy of the State. His early projects of obtaining the inheritance of Jacqueline, the heiress of Holland and Hainault, were seen to be dictated by a desire of personal aggrandisement, and had to be dropped; nor was he chivalrous enough to remain true to his wedded wife. He afterwards favoured the policy of war in France; but he was without such resources as those which gave importance to his uncle and rival's support of the same line of action beyond the Narrow Seas, while in home affairs he confined himself to the manœuvres of selfish intrigue. Probably, no higher motive animated his activity against the Lollards, when in 1431 their flysheets were "about every good town in England" denouncing the clergy who were possessors of property, and advocating a community of goods. He laid hands on some of their leaders, and secured from the Privy Council a pecuniary recompense of his services to the orthodox religion. These earlier occurrences the dramatic version of Henry VI's reign not unnaturally ignores; but it likewise has nothing to say about Duke Humphrey's relations to learning and science, which connect his name as that of an early literary benefactor with the history of the University of Oxford, and which continue to engage the attention of modern students.[4] Our trilogy occupies itself mainly with the Duke's fall, and with the prelude to it supplied by the strange trial and cruel penance of Eleanor Cobham, Duke Humphrey's mistress, for whom, though they were probably never actually married, he had secured more or less formal recognition as his wife. The episode of her collapse is appropriately introduced into this Chronicle of violent ambitions and their consequences; although the question as to Eleanor's actual guilt, or as to the length to which her restless spirit carried her, is of course one that will never be solved. Humphrey of Gloucester was not shamed by the catastrophe of his partner, or by his inability to hold out to her a helping hand, into withdrawal from public life. But his political influence was, thenceforth, at an end, and his final downfall had become only a question of time. That it was marked by his murder seems, though a natural, to be an unproved, assumption. Humphrey was physically as well as morally an utter wreck, when he passed away, after he had been arrested for treason at the Bury Parliament (1447). The repetition of the story of the murder of the "good Duke" in the play may be regarded as one more attestation of the popularity which so long clung to his name, but which was originally due to negative rather than to positive reasons—to the fact that he was not a foreigner, not a friend to the Queen, and not a priest.[5]

At the other end of the social scale, according to a view of things which in no Elizabethan drama asserts itself more pointedly than in this trilogy, stands the popular agitation which, for a moment, obliged King Henry VI and the oligarchical factions around him to treat with it on terms of equality. To the author of the famous Jack Cade scenes the aim of the rising which he ruthlessly caricatures seemed sheer topsy-turvydom; henceforth "seven halfpenny loaves were to be sold for a penny"; all the realm was to be in common; Jack Cade the clothier was to be King; and Lord Say must lose his head because he could speak French and therefore was a traitor—moreover, had he not most treacherously corrupted the youth of the realm by erecting a grammar school?[6] As a matter of fact, the anarchy which reached its height in the insurrection of 1450 was the inevitable result of a weakness of government that had long continued. In 1441–43 there had been a series of disturbances in different counties, due in part to private feuds, in part to fanatical preaching, and in the north to a determination not to submit to the exactions of the Archbishop of York's Spiritual Courts. Early in 1450, troubles began in Kent, which communicated themselves to several southern counties. The rising headed in May by "Jack Cade," which from Kent spread into Surrey and Sussex, seems to have been something very different from a Peasants' War or Jacquerie, or from what Sir Humphrey Stafford in the play denounces as a rabblement of

> Rebellious hinds, the filth and scum of Kent,
> Mark'd for the gallows.

Whether Cade himself was or was not a physician by profession, he seems beyond doubt to have been a man of respectable position, who had not improbably seen service in France.[7] That he should have taken the name of Mortimer, alleging his kinship to the Duke of York as the natural son of the last Earl of March, was in the circumstances a very pardonable fiction; though perhaps, as in similar instances of imposture in this age, had his insurrection spread to a great distance from the manor of Cade, the pretence might have assumed bolder proportions.[8] As it was, the Yorkists seem generally to have identified themselves with Cade's attempt in its earlier stages. But, factious partisanship apart, there were among his followers many men of substance—yeomen and not a few squires; and in Kent and East Sussex the armed rising was organised on the lines of a regular county levy. Its avowed object was not the overthrow of all government, but the establishment of a strong rule, such as would in especial protect the tenure of land against the force, fraud, and chicanery which had long rendered it wholly insecure.[9] The loss of Normandy, which had been the real cause of Suffolk's catastrophe earlier in the year, was, as a matter of fact, only put forward by the insurgents as a secondary grievance; but the very circumstance that they should have shown their concern at what was regarded as a national calamity shows them to have been Englishmen animated by patriotic feelings.[10] The systematic misrepresentation in the play of the general character of "Jack Cade's" rising, which extends to the incidents of his capture, is significant of the spirit of the later Tudor age, when a strong government was strongest in the goodwill of the great body of a self-confident nation. But how deep the popular discontent had sunk in days of the greatest weakness of Henry VI's government is shown by its having been attributed at Court to the popular preachers—whose voice may be regarded as that of the people itself.[11]

I will conclude these few remarks on the treatment of historical truth in this trilogy by referring to a character in it which has naturally enough been subjected to much indignant censure. The glorious figure of Jeanne Darc, the Pucelle of history, after the most conscientious and painstaking enquiry, stands wholly free from the least of the stains which envy, hatred and malice had left upon it. While at the Court of Charles VII neither the Maid's miraculous achievements nor the ecclesiastical approval which they had earned converted those who looked askance at her to a whole-hearted acceptance of her patriotic mission. The English soldiery whom she drove out of Orleans and who fled panic-stricken before her at Patay regarded her simply as a witch, whose powers were derived direct from the Evil One; nor was it till the moment of her capture that the spell which her prowess and her faith had wrought was broken. A memorandum drawn up some years afterwards by Bedford, whose long labours this simple adversary had undone, attests his conviction that her success, the effects of which he sought in no way to underrate, was due to the lack of sound religious faith in the English soldiery opposed to her in the field, and to the misbelieving doubts caused in them by this limb of the Fiend and her use of false enchantments and sorcery.[12] In other words, while this brave and honourable Englishman himself entertained no doubts as to the diabolical origin of the Pucelle and all her doings, he believed that a manly faith in the God who masters devils would have overcome her. But Bedford did not say—though she was in English hands at the time of her imprisonment in the shameful tower which still lifts its head at Rouen, and though the power of England was an accomplice in her trial before a Spiritual Court—what was the nature of the durance and of the process

undergone by her. We know that instructions had been given by King Henry that, if she were acquitted, she should be detained in his keeping. And we know what steps were taken to avert that acquittal. In order to do her to death, foul means of every kind were employed by those who had conspired to destroy her—including the perversion of her answers, the insertion in the records of the proceedings of false and brutally injurious statements, the infliction of all the hardships of the dungeon, and the terrors of threatened torture.[13] It was virtually Bedford who sent her to her doom, though French Bishops share the responsibility of her death with the English statesman; Beaufort too is stated to have been present at her execution, and (more dubiously) to have ordered her ashes to be thrown into the Seine. We are naturally apt to overlook the craven desertion of the Pucelle by the King, who owed to her his Crown, in view of the bigoted abhorrence which was the one feeling entertained towards her by Bedford and the English Court. But it is impossible to ignore the fact that, though the prejudices of her foes might, in the unhappy episode of the Pucelle in the *First Part of Henry VI*, have led them to accept as true the monstrous fiction of her colloquy with the fiends, those who were directly responsible for her doom must have known the abominable accusations suggested in the following scene (derived, as a matter of fact, from the English chroniclers) to be themselves nothing but diabolical lies.[14]

*Notes*

1. Sir James Ramsay,: *Lancaster and York* (Oxford, 1892), vol. I. p. 323.
2. This is very forcibly shown in a lecture on *The Life and Times of Cardinal Beaufort*, published in 1880, by the present Archdeacon Fearon, the late Headmaster of Winchester. Dr Fearon gives good reason for believing that it was to Beaufort that the foundation of Eton and King's Colleges was originally due; at all events, every detail as to the new foundations was submitted to him by the King, and their endowments were increased by the Cardinal's will. I must not venture to suggest that Beaufort's interest in university life may have dated from the time when he had a chamber in Peterhouse (see J. H. Wylie in *Historical MSS.*, *First Report*, p. 78; cf. Mr Wylie's *Henry IV*, vol. III. p. 263; and also Dr T. A. Walker, *Peterhouse*, London, 1906, where it appears that Beaufort paid 20s., *pro pensione cameræ*, while in the same year a bachelor of the University paid 6s. 8d. under the same head). Mr Wylie has exploded the story of Beaufort's having been at the University of Aachen, which of course should be Oxford.
3. Compare R. Pauli's *Englische Geschichte*, vol. v. p. 286, note.
4. See the attractive chapter "Duke Humphrey of Gloucester, a fragment of a princely life in the 15th century," in Pauli's *Pictures of Old England*, English Translation by Miss Otté, 1861.
5. According to Ramsay, vol. II. p. 76, note, of the 247 books presented by the Duke to the University, three remain in the Bodleian, besides a scriptural commentary written for him by Capgrave at Oriel. He also contributed to the building of the University Schools. Bishop Bekyngton and Pecock, the liberally minded author of the *Repressor*, as well as Titus Livius, whose *Life of Henry V* is held to mark the beginning of the classical Renascence in England, were both patronised by the Duke.

   For an illustration of the attitude of the Tudor age towards historical truth, the reader may be referred to the exposition in Bishop Latimer's sermon to King Edward VI, cited below, of the merits of the contention between Winchester and Gloucester.
6. This last is a curious touch. Is it, conceivably, to be traced to memories of the Pilgrimage of Grace and the grievances connected with the Dissolution of the Monasteries?
7. There seems to be some evidence that Cade may have been a Somerset man, possibly from Bridgwater—the property of Richard Duke of York.
8. In Act IV, sc. ii, in reply to the accusation that he has been "put up" to his imposture by the Duke of York, Cade says: "He lies, for I invented it myself." Yet he had no reason for laying claim to

much originality on this score. I have often wondered why no attempt has been made to write a comparative history of this class of impostures in the later Middle Ages.

9. No more convincing evidence of the force of this fundamental grievance of the insurgents could be desired than that which is furnished in the *Paston Letters*.

10. Cf. Ramsay, vol. II. pp. 125 *seq.*; and see also Pauli, vol. v. p. 307, where the connexion is noted which is supposed to have existed between the Kentish insurgents and the sailors, whose murder of Suffolk forms one of the most impressive scenes of the play, and one in entire accordance with historical fact.

11. Lord Say, the most prominent victim of the insurrection, and other persons of influence, allowed no one to preach before the King until after submitting to them the proposed sermons.

12. Cf. Ramsay, vol. I. p. 398.

13. Cf. Pauli, vol. v. p. 224.

14. It has been well pointed out that, while English writers could not treat her memory very differently without condemning their own countrymen, Monstrelet and the Burgundians regarded her as a political machine.

# Richard III

To him that impt my fame with Clio's quill,
Whose magick rais'd me from oblivion's den;
That writ my storie on the Muses hill,
And with my actions dignifi'd his pen:
He that from Helicon sends many a rill,
Whose nectared veines, are drunke by thirstie men;
  Crown'd be his stile with fame, his head with bayes;
  And none detract, but gratulate his praise.

    —CHRISTOPHER BROOKE, *The Ghost of Richard the Third*, 1614

I came home this evening in a very pensive mood; and to divert me, took up a volume of Shakespeare, where I chanced to cast my eye upon a part in the tragedy of *Richard the Third*, which filled my mind with a very agreeable horror. It was the scene in which that bold but wicked prince is represented as sleeping in his tent the night before the battle in which he fell. The poet takes the occasion to set before him in a vision a terrible assembly of apparitions, the ghosts of all those innocent persons whom he is said to have murdered. Prince Edward, Henry VI., the Duke of Clarence, Rivers, Gray, and Vaughan, Lord Hastings, the two young princes, sons to Edward IV., his own wife, and the Duke of Buckingham rise up in their blood before him, beginning their speeches with that dreadful salutation, "Let me sit heavy on thy soul to-morrow;" and concluding with that dismal sentence, "Despair and die." This inspires the tyrant with a dream of his past guilt, and of the approaching vengeance. He anticipates the fatal day of Bosworth, fancies himself dismounted, weltering in his own blood; and in the agonies of despair (before he is thoroughly awake), starts up with the following speech:

Give me another horse—Bind up my wounds!
Have mercy, Jesu—Soft, I did but dream.
O coward Conscience! How dost thou afflict me?
The lights burn blue! Is it not dead midnight?
Cold fearful drops stand on my trembling flesh;
What do I fear? Myself! &c.

A scene written with so great strength of imagination indisposed me from further reading, and threw me into a deep contemplation. I began to reflect upon the different ends of good and bad kings: and as this was the birthday of our late renowned monarch, I could not forbear thinking on the departure of that excellent prince, whose life was crowned with glory, and his death with peace. I let my mind go so far into this thought, as to imagine to myself, what might have been the vision of his departing slumbers. He might have seen confederate kings applauding him in different languages, slaves that had been bound in fetters lifting up their hands and blessing him, and the persecuted in their several forms of worship imploring

comfort on his last moments. The reflection upon this excellent prince's mortality had been a very melancholy entertainment to me, had I not been relieved by the consideration of the glorious reign which succeeds it.—RICHARD STEELE, *The Tatler*, No. 90 (Nov. 5, 1709)

I am angry with the English. Not only have they taken Pondichéry from me, I believe, but they have just expressed in print that their Shakespeare is infinitely superior to Corneille. Their Shakespeare is infinitely inferior to Gilles. Imagine the tragedy of *Richard III*, which they compare to *Cinna*, has nine years for unity of time, a dozen cities and battlefields for unity of place, and thirty-seven principal events for unity of action. But that is nothing. In the first act, Richard says that he is a hunchback and smells, and to take his revenge against nature, he is going to be a hypocrite and a scoundrel. As he says these beautiful things, he sees a funeral procession—King Henry VI's. He stops the bier and the widow who is leading the procession. The widow cries out loudly; she reproaches him for killing her husband. Richard replies that he is delighted because he will be able to sleep with her more conveniently. The queen spits in his face; Richard thanks her and claims that nothing is as sweet as her spit. The queen calls him a toad, an ugly toad: "I wish my spit were poison." "Well, madam, kill me if you like; here is my sword." She takes it. "Hang it, I don't have the courage to kill you." "Well, then I am going to kill myself." "No, do not kill yourself since you found me pretty." She goes and buries her husband, and the two lovers do not speak of love any more for the remainder of the play. Isn't it true that if our water bearers wrote plays, they would make them more honest? I tell you all of this because I have had my fill. Isn't it sad that the same country that produced Newton has produced these monsters and admires them? Be well, madam. Try to have some pleasure. This is not an easy thing but not impossible.—FRANÇOIS MARIE AROUET DE VOLTAIRE, Letter to Marie Vichy de Chamrond, Marquise du Deffand (Dec. 9, 1760), *Selected Letters*, 1973, tr. Richard A. Brooks, p. 216

The part of Richard III. has become highly celebrated in England from its having been filled by excellent performers, and this has naturally had an influence on the admiration of the piece itself, for many readers of Shakspeare stand in want of good interpreters of the poet to understand him properly. This admiration is certainly in every respect well founded, though I cannot help thinking there is an injustice in considering the three parts of *Henry the Sixth* as of little value compared with *Richard the Third*. These four plays were undoubtedly composed in succession, as is proved by the style and the spirit in the handling of the subject: the last is definitely announced in the one which precedes it, and is also full of references to it: the same views run through the series; in a word, the whole make together only one single work. Even the deep characterization of Richard is by no means the exclusive property of the piece which bears his name: his character is very distinctly drawn in the two last parts of *Henry the Sixth*; nay, even his first speeches lead us already to form the most unfavourable anticipations of his future conduct. He lowers obliquely like a dark thundercloud on the horizon, which gradually approaches nearer and nearer, and first pours out the devastating elements with which it is charged when it hangs over the heads of mortals. Two of Richard's most significant soliloquies which enable us to draw the most important conclusions with regard to his mental temperament, are to be found in *The Last Part of Henry the Sixth*. As to the value and the justice of the actions to which passion impels us, we may be blind, but wickedness cannot mistake its own nature; Richard, as well as Iago, is a villain with full consciousness. That they should say this in so many words, is not perhaps in human nature: but the poet has the right in soliloquies to lend a voice to the most hidden thoughts, otherwise the form of the monologue would, generally speaking, be censurable. Richard's deformity is the expression of his internal malice, and perhaps in part the effect of it: for where is the ugliness that would not be softened by benevolence and openness? He, however, considers it as an iniquitous neglect of nature, which justifies him in taking his revenge on that human society from which it is the means of excluding him. Hence these sublime lines:

> And this word love, which graybeards call divine,
> Be resident in men like one another,
> And not in me. I am myself alone.

Wickedness is nothing but selfishness designedly unconscientious; however it can never do altogether without the form at least of morality, as this is the law of all thinking beings,—it must seek to found its depraved way of acting on something like principles. Although Richard is thoroughly acquainted with the blackness of his mind and his hellish mission, he yet endeavours to justify this to himself by a sophism: the happiness of being beloved is denied to him; what then remains to him but the happiness of ruling? All that stands in the way of this must be removed. This envy of the enjoyment of love is so much the more natural in Richard, as his brother Edward, who besides preceded him in the possession of the crown, was distinguished by the nobleness and beauty of his figure, and was an almost irresistible conqueror of female hearts. Notwithstanding his pretended renunciation, Richard places his chief vanity in being able to please and win over the women, if not by his figure at least by his insinuating discourse. Shakspeare here shows us, with his accustomed acuteness of observation, that human nature, even when it is altogether decided in goodness or wickeness, is still subject to petty infirmities. Richard's favourite amusement is to ridicule others, and he possesses an eminent satirical wit. He entertains at bottom a contempt for all mankind: for he is confident of his ability to deceive them, whether as his instruments or his adversaries. In hypocrisy he is particularly fond of using religious forms, as if actuated by a desire of profaning in the service of hell the religion whose blessings he had inwardly abjured.

So much for the main features of Richard's character. The play named after him embraces also the latter part of the reign of Edward IV., in the whole a period of eight years. It exhibits all the machinations by which Richard obtained the throne, and the deeds which he perpetrated to secure himself in its possession, which lasted however but two years. Shakspeare intended that terror rather than compassion should prevail throughout this tragedy: he has rather avoided than sought the pathetic scenes which he had at command. Of all the sacrifices to Richard's lust of power, Clarence alone is put to death on the stage: his dream excites a deep horror, and proves the omnipotence of the poet's fancy: his conversation with the murderers is powerfully agitating; but the earlier crimes of Clarence merited death, although not from his brother's hand. The most innocent and unspotted sacrifices are the two princes: we see but little of them, and their murder is merely related. Anne disappears without our learning any thing farther respecting her: in marrying the murderer of her husband, she had shown a weakness almost incredible. The parts of Lord Rivers, and other friends of the queen, are of too secondary a nature to excite a powerful sympathy; Hastings, from his triumph at the fall of his friend, forfeits all title to compassion; Buckingham is the satellite of the tyrant, who is afterwards consigned by him to the axe of the executioner. In the background the widowed Queen Margaret appears as the fury of the past, who invokes a curse on the future: every calamity, which her enemies draw down on each other, is a cordial to her revengeful heart. Other female voices join, from time to time, in the lamentations and imprecations. But Richard is the soul or rather the dæmon, of the whole tragedy. He fulfills the promise which he formerly made of leading the murderous Macchiavel to school. Notwithstanding the uniform aversion with which he inspires us, he still engages us in the greatest variety of ways by his profound skill in dissimulation, his wit, his prudence, his presence of mind, his quick activity, and his valour. He fights at last against Richmond like a desperado, and dies the honourable death of a hero on the field of battle. Shakspeare could not change this historical issue, and yet it is by no means satisfactory to our moral feelings, as Lessing, when speaking of a German play on the same subject, has very judiciously remarked. How has Shakspeare solved this difficulty? By a wonderful invention he opens a prospect into the other world, and shows us Richard in his last moments already branded with the stamp of reprobation. We see Richard and Richmond in the night before the battle sleeping in their tents; the spirits of the murdered victims of the tyrant ascend in succession, and pour out their curses against him, and their blessings on his adversary. These apparitions are properly but the dreams of the two generals represented visibly. It is no doubt contrary to probability that their tents should only be separated by so small a space; but Shakspeare could reckon on poetical spectators who were ready to take the breadth of the stage for the distance between two hostile camps, if for such indulgence they were to be recompensed by beauties of so sublime a nature as this series of spectres and Richard's awakening soliloquy. The castastrophe of *Richard the Third* is, in respect of the external events, very like that of *Macbeth*: we have only to compare the thorough difference of handling them to be convinced that Shakspeare has most accurately observed poetical justice in the genuine sense of the word, that is, as signifying the revelation of an invisible blessing or curse which hangs over human sentiments and actions.—AUGUST WILHELM SCHLEGEL, *Lectures on Dramatic Art and Literature*, 1809, tr. John Black

This play should be contrasted with *Richard II*. Pride of intellect is the characteristic of Richard, carried to the extent of even boasting to his own mind of his villany, whilst others are present to feed his pride of superiority; as in his first speech, act II. sc. 1. Shakspeare here, as in all his great parts, developes in a tone of sublime morality the dreadful consequences of placing the moral, in subordination to the mere intellectual, being. In Richard there is a predominance of irony, accompanied with apparently blunt manners to those immediately about him, but formalized into a more set hypocrisy towards the people as represented by their magistrates.—SAMUEL TAY-LOR COLERIDGE, *"Richard III," Shakspeare, with Introductory Remarks on Poetry, the Drama, and the Stage,* 1818

---

### EDWARD DOWDEN
### From "The English Historical Plays"
*Shakspere: A Critical Study of His Mind and Art*
### 1875, pp. 180–93

Certain qualities which make it unique among the dramas of Shakspere characterize the play of *King Richard III.* Its manner of conceiving and presenting character has a certain resemblance, not elsewhere to be found in Shakspere's writings, to the ideal manner of Marlowe. As in the plays of Marlowe, there is here one dominant figure distinguished by a few strongly marked and inordinately developed qualities. There is in the characterization no mystery, but much of a dæmonic intensity. Certain passages are entirely in the lyrical-dramatic style; an emotion which is one and the same, occupying at the same moment two or three of the personages, and obtaining utterance through them almost simultaneously, or in immediate succession; as a musical motive is interpreted by an orchestra, or taken up singly by successive instruments:—

> *Q. Eliz.:* Was never widow had so dear a loss!
> *Children:* Were never orphans had so dear a loss!
> *Duchess:* Was never mother had so dear a loss!
>     Alas! I am the mother of these griefs.

Mere verisimilitude in the play of *King Richard III.* becomes at times subordinate to effects of symphonic orchestration, or of statuesque composition. There is a Blake-like terror and beauty in the scene in which the three women,—queens and a duchess,—seat themselves upon the ground in their desolation and despair, and cry aloud in utter anguish of spirit. First by the mother of two kings, then by Edward's widow, last by the terrible Medusa-like Queen Margaret, the same attitude is assumed, and the same grief is poured forth. Misery has made them indifferent to all ceremony of queenship, and for a time to their private differences; they are seated, a rigid yet tumultuously passionate group, in the majesty of mere womanhood and supreme calamity. Readers acquainted with Blake's illustrations to the Book of Job will remember what effects, sublime and appalling, the artist produces by animating a group of figures with one common passion, which spontaneously produces in each individual the same extravagant movement of head and limbs.

The dæmonic intensity which distinguishes the play proceeds from the character of Richard, as from its source and centre. As with the chief personages of Marlowe's plays, so Richard in this play rather occupies the imagination by audacity and force, than insinuates himself through some subtle solvent, some magic and mystery of art. His character does not grow upon us; from the first it is complete. We are not curious to discover what Richard is, as we are curious to come into presence of the soul of Hamlet. We are in no doubt about Richard; but it yields us a strong sensation to observe him in various circumstances and situations; we are roused and animated by the presence of almost superhuman energy and power, even though that power and that energy be malign.

Coleridge has said of Richard that pride of intellect is his characteristic. This is true, but his dominant characteristic is not intellectual; it is rather a dæmonic energy of will. The same cause which produces tempest and shipwreck produces Richard; he is a fierce elemental power raging through the world; but this elemental power is concentrated in a human will. The need of action is with Richard an appetite to which all the other appetites are subordinate. He requires space in the world to bustle in; his will must wreak itself on men and things. All that is done in the play proceeds from Richard; there is, as has been observed by Mr Hudson, no interaction. "The drama is not so much a composition of co-operative characters, mutually developing and developed, as the prolonged yet hurried outcome of a single character, to which the other persons serve but as exponents and conductors; as if he were a volume of electricity disclosing himself by means of others, and quenching their active powers in the very process of doing so."[1]

Richard, with his distorted and withered body, his arm shrunk like "a blasted sapling," is yet a sublime figure by virtue of his energy of will and tremendous power of intellect. All obstacles give way before him;—the courage of men, and the bitter animosity of women. And Richard has a passionate scorn of men, because they are weaker and more obtuse than he, the deformed outcast of nature. He practises hypocrisy not merely for the sake of success, but because his hypocrisy is a cynical jest, or a gross insult to humanity. The Mayor of London has a *bourgeois* veneration for piety and established forms of religion. Richard advances to meet him reading a book of prayers, and supported on each side by a bishop. The grim joke, the contemptuous insult to the citizen faith in church and king, flatters his malignant sense of power. To cheat a gull, a coarse hypocrisy suffices.[2]

Towards his tool Buckingham, when occasion suits, Richard can be frankly contemptuous. Buckingham is unable to keep pace with Richard in his headlong career; he falls behind and is scant of breath:

> The deep-revolving, witty Buckingham
> No more shall be the neighbour to my counsel;
> Hath he so long held out with me untired
> And stops he now for breath?

The duke, "his other self, his counsel's consistory, his oracle, his prophet," comes before the king claiming the fulfilment of a promise, that he should receive the Earldom of Hereford. Richard becomes suddenly deaf and, contemptuously disregarding the interpellations of Buckingham, continues his talk on indifferent matters. At length he turns to "his other self;"—

> *Buck.:* My lord!
> *K. Rich.:* Ay, what's o'clock?
> *Buck.:* I am thus bold to put your Grace in mind
>     Of what you promised me.
> *K. Rich.:*                Well, but what's o'clock?
> *Buck.:* Upon the stroke of ten.
> *K. Rich.:*                Well, let it strike.
> *Buck.:* Why let it strike?
> *K. Rich.:* Because that like a Jack thou keep'st the stroke
>     Betwixt thy begging and my meditation.
>     I am not in the giving vein to-day.

Richard's cynicism and insolence have in them a kind of grim mirth; such a *bonhomie* as might be met with among the humourists of Pandemonium. His brutality is a manner of joking with a purpose. When his mother, with Queen Elizabeth, comes by "copious in exclaims," ready to "smother her damned son in the breath of bitter words," the mirthful Richard calls for a flourish of trumpets to drown these shrill female voices:

> A flourish trumpets! strike alarum, drums!
> Let not the heavens hear these tell-tale women
> Rail on the Lord's anointed. Strike, I say!

On an occasion when hypocrisy is more serviceable than brutality, Richard kneels to implore his mother's blessing, but has a characteristic word of contemptuous impiety to utter aside:

*Duchess:* God bless thee and put meekness in thy
breast,
Love, charity, obedience, and true duty.
*Richard:* Amen! and make me die a good old man!
That is the butt-end of a mother's blessing;
I marvel that her grace did leave it out.

He plays his part before his future wife, the Lady Anne, laying open his breast to the sword's point with a malicious confidence. He knows the measure of woman's frailty, and relies on the spiritual force of his audacity and dissimulation to subdue the weak hand, which tries to lift the sword. With no friends to back his suit, with nothing but "the plain devil, and dissembling looks," he wins his bride. The hideous irony of such a courtship, the mockery it implies of human love, is enough to make a man "your only jigmaker," and sends Richard's blood dancing along his veins.

While Richard is plotting for the crown, Lord Hastings threatens to prove an obstacle in the way. What is to be done? Buckingham is dubious and tentative:

Now, my lord, what shall we do, if we perceive
Lord Hastings will not yield to our complots?

With sharp detonation, quickly begun and quickly over, Richard's answer is discharged, "Chop off his head, man." There can be no beginning, middle, or end to a deed so simple and so summary. Presently Hastings making sundry small assignations for future days and weeks, goes, a murdered man, to the conference at the Tower. Richard, whose startling figure emerges from the background throughout the play with small regard for verisimilitude and always at the most effective moment, is suddenly on the spot, just as Hastings is about to give his voice in the conference as though he were the representative of the absent Duke. Richard is prepared, when the opportune instant has arrived, to spring a mine under Hastings' feet. But meanwhile a matter of equal importance concerns him,—my Lord of Ely's strawberries: the flavour of Holborn strawberries is exquisite, and the fruit must be sent for. Richard's desire to appear disengaged from sinister thought is less important to note than Richard's need of indulging a cynical contempt of human life. The explosion takes place; Hastings is seized; and the delicacies are reserved until the head of Richard's enemy is off. There is a wantonness of *diablerie* in this incident:

Talk'st thou to me of *ifs?* Thou art a traitor—
Off with his head! Now by Saint Paul I swear
I will not dine until I see the same.[3]

The fiery energy of Richard is at its simplest, unmingled with irony or dissimulation in great days of military movement and of battle. Then the force within him expends itself in a paroxysm which has all the intensity of ungovernable spasmodic action, and which is yet organised and controlled by his intellect. Then he is engaged at his truest devotions, and numbers his Ave-Maries, not with beads but with ringing strokes upon the helmets of his foes.[4] He is inspired with "the spleen of fiery dragons;" "a thousand hearts are great within his bosom." On the eve of the battle of Bosworth field, Richard, with uncontrollable eagerness, urges his enquiry into the minutiæ of preparation which may ensure success. He lacks his usual alacrity of spirit, yet a dozen subalterns would hardly suffice to receive the orders which he rapidly enunciates. He is upon the wing of "fiery expedition:"

I will not sup to-night. Give me some ink and
paper.
What, is my beaver easier than it was?
And all my armour laid within my tent?
*Catesby:* It is, my liege, and all things are in
readiness.
*K. Rich.:* Good Norfolk, hie thee to thy charge;
Use careful watch, choose trusty sentinels.
*Norfolk:* I go, my lord.
*K. Rich.:* Stir with the lark to-morrow, gentle
Norfolk.
*Norfolk:* I warrant you, my lord.
*K. Rich.:* Catesby!
*Catesby:*     My Lord?
*K. Rich.:* Send out a pursuivant at arms
To Stanley's regiment; bid him bring his power
Before sun-rising, lest his son George fall
Into the blind cave of eternal night.
Fill me a bowl of wine. Give me a watch.
                                    [*Exit Catesby.*
Saddle White Surrey for the field to-morrow.
Look that my staves be sound, and not too heavy,
Ratcliff!

And learning from Ratcliff, that Northumberland and Surrey are alert, giving his last direction that his attendant should return at midnight to help him to arm, King Richard retires into his tent.

In all his military movements, as in the whole of Richard's career, there is something else than self-seeking. It is true that Richard, like Edmund, like Iago, is solitary; he has no friend, no brother; "I am myself alone;" and all that Richard achieves tends to his own supremacy. Nevertheless, the central characteristic of Richard is not self-seeking or ambition. It is the necessity of releasing and letting loose upon the world the force within him (mere force in which there is nothing moral), the necessity of deploying before himself and others the terrible resources of his will. One human tie Shakspere attributes to Richard; contemptuous to his mother, indifferent to the life or death of Clarence and Edward, except as their life or death may serve his own attempt upon the crown, cynically loveless towards his feeble and unhappy wife, Richard admires with an enthusiastic admiration his great father:

Methinks 'tis prize enough to be his son.

And the memory of his father supplies him with a family pride which, however, does not imply attachment or loyalty to any member of his house.

But I was born so high;
Our aery buildeth in the cedar's top,
And dallies with the wind and scorns the sun.

History supplied Shakspere with the figure of his Richard. He has been accused of darkening the colours, and exaggerating the deformity of the character of the historical Richard found in More and Holinshed. The fact is precisely the contrary. The mythic Richard of the historians (and there must have been some appalling fact to originate such a myth) is made somewhat less grim and bloody by the dramatist.[5] Essentially, however, Shakspere's Richard is of the diabolical (something more dreadful than the criminal) class. He is not weak, because he is single-hearted in his devotion to evil. Richard does not serve two masters. He is not like John, a dastardly criminal; he is not like Macbeth, joyless and faithless because he has deserted loyalty and honour. He has a fierce joy, and he is an intense believer,—in the creed of hell. And therefore he is strong. He inverts the moral order of things, and tries to live in this inverted system. He does not succeed; he dashes himself to pieces against the laws of the world which he has outraged. Yet, while John is wholly despicable, we cannot refrain from yielding a certain tribute of admiration to the bolder malefactor, who ventures on the daring experiment of choosing evil for his good.

Such an experiment, Shakspere declares emphatically, as experience and history declare, must in the end fail. The ghosts of the usurper's victims rise between the camps, and are to Richard the Erinnyes, to Richmond inspirers of hope and victorious courage. At length Richard trembles on the brink of annihilation, trembles over the loveless gulf:—

> I shall despair; there is no creature loves me;
> And if I die, no soul shall pity me.

But the stir of battle restores him to resolute thoughts, "Come, bustle, bustle, caparison my horse," and he dies in a fierce paroxysm of action. Richmond conquers, and he conquers expressly as the champion and representative of the moral order of the world, which Richard had endeavoured to set aside:

> O Thou, whose captain I account myself,
> Look on my forces with a gracious eye;
> Put in their hands thy bruising irons of wrath,
> That they may crush down with a heavy fall
> The usurping helmets of our adversaries!
> Make us thy ministers of chastisement,
> That we may praise thee in thy victory.

The female figures of this play,—Queen Elizabeth, Queen Margaret, the Duchess of York, the Lady Anne; and with these the women of Shakspere's other historical plays, would form an interesting subject for a separate study. The women of the histories do not attain the best happiness of women. In the rough struggle of interests, of parties, of nations, they are defrauded of their joy, and of its objects. Like Constance, like Elizabeth, like Margaret, like the Queen of the Second Richard, like Katharine of Arragon, they mourn some the loss of children, some of husbands, some of brothers, and all of love. Or else, like Harry Percy's wife (who also lives to lament her husband's death, and to tremble for her father's fate),[6] they are the wives of men of action to whom they are dear, but "in sort or limitation," dwelling but in the suburbs of their husbands' good-pleasure,

> To keep with you at meals, comfort your bed,
> And talk with you sometimes.

The wooing of the French Katharine by King Henry V. is business-like, and soundly affectionate, but by no means of the kind which is most satisfying to the heart of a sensitive or ardent woman. That Shakspere himself loved in another fashion than that of Hotspur or Henry might be inferred, if no other sufficient evidence were forthcoming, from the admirable mockery of the love given by men of letters, and men of imagination—poets in chief—which he puts into Henry's mouth. "And while thou livest, dear Kate, take a fellow of plain and uncoined constancy; for he perforce must do thee right, because he hath not the gift to woo in other places; for these fellows of infinite tongue, that can rhyme themselves into ladies' favours, they do always reason themselves out again." Was this a skit by Shakspere against himself, or against an interpretation of himself for which he perceived there was a good deal to be said, from a point of view other than his own? While the poet was buying up land near Stratford, he could describe his courtier Osric as "very spacious in the possession of dirt." Is this a piece of irony similar in kind?

The figure of Queen Margaret is painfully persistent upon the mind's eye, and tyrannises, almost as much as the figure of King Richard himself, over the imagination. "Although ban-ished upon pain of death, she returns to England to assist at the intestine conflicts of the House of York. Shakspere personifies in her the ancient Nemesis; he gives her more than human proportions, and represents her as a sort of supernatural apparition. She penetrates freely into the palace of Edward IV., she there breathes forth her hatred in presence of the family of York, and its courtier attendants. No one dreams of arresting her, although she is an exiled woman, and she goes forth, meeting no obstacle, as she had entered. The same magic ring, which on the first occasion opened the doors of the royal mansion, opens them for her once again, when Edward IV. is dead, and his sons have been assassinated in the Tower by the order of Richard. She came, the first time, to curse her enemies; she comes now to gather the fruits of her malediction. Like an avenging Fury, or the classical Fate, she has announced to each his doom."[7]

The play must not be dismissed without one word spoken of King Edward IV. He did not interest the imagination of Shakspere. Edward is the self-indulgent, luxurious king. The one thing which Shakspere cared to say about him was, that his pleasant delusion of peace-making shortly before his death, was a poor and insufficient compensation for a life spent in ease and luxury rather than in laying the hard and strong bases of a substantial peace. A few soft words, and placing of hands in hands will not repair the ravage of fierce years, and the decay of sound human bonds during soft, effeminate years. Just as the peace-making is perfect, Richard is present on the scene:—

> There wanteth now our brother Gloster here
> To make the blessed period of our peace.

And Gloster stands before the dying king to announce that Clarence lies murdered in the Tower. This is Shakspere's comment upon and condemnation of the self-indulgent King.[8]

### Notes

1. H. N. Hudson, *Shakespeare, His Life, Art and Characters*, vol. ii., p. 156.
2. The plan originates with Buckingham, but Richard plays his part with manifest delight. Shakspere had no historical authority for the presence of the Bishops. See Skottowe's *Life of Shakspeare*, vol. i., pp. 195, 96.
3. This scene, including the incident of the dish of strawberries, is from Sir T. More's history. See Courtenay's *Commentaries on Shakspere*, vol. ii., pp. 84–87.
4. 3 *Henry VI.*, Act ii., Scene 1.
5. See the detailed study of this play by W. Oechelhäuser in *Jahrbuch der Deutschen Shakespeare-Gesellschaft*, vol. iii. pp. 37–39, and pp. 47, 53. Holinshed's treatment of the character of Richard is hardly in harmony with itself. From the death of Edward IV. onwards the Richard of Holinshed resembles Shakspere's Richard, but possesses fainter traces of humanity. "Wenn hiernach also thatsächlich zwei Holinshed'sche Versionen des Charakters und der Handlungen Richards vorliegen, so hat Shakespeare allerdings die auf More basierte, also die schwärzere gewählt; über diese ist er aber nicht, wie so vielfach behauptet wird, hinausgegangen, sondern er hat sie sogar gemildert, hat die Fäden, welche das Ungeheuer noch mit der Menschheit verknipfen, verstärkt, statt sie ganz zu lösen."
6. See the pathetic scene, 2 *Henry IV.*, Act ii., Scene 3.
7. A. Méxières, *Shakspeare, ses œuvres et ses critiques*, p. 139.
8. Otto Ludwig notices the ideal treatment of time in *King Richard III*. But does it differ from the treatment of time in other historical plays of Shakspere? "Wie in keinem anderen seiner Stücke die Begebenheiten gewaltsamer zusammengerückt sind, so ist auch in keinem anderen die Zeit so ideal behandelt als hier. Hier gibt es kein Gestern, kein Morgen, keine Uhr, und keinen Kalender."— *Shakespeare-Studien*, pp. 450, 451.

Edmund Kean as Richard III

William Macready as King John

David Garrick as Richard III

*Richard II*
(engraving by Walker from a painting by Corbould)

*Henry VIII*
(engraving by Leney from a painting by Westall)

Sir John Falstaff (painting by Edward Grützner)

# King John

In *King John* the political and warlike events are dressed out with solemn pomp, for the very reason that they possess but little of true grandeur. The falsehood and selfishness of the monarch speak in the style of a manifesto. Conventional dignity is most indispensable where personal dignity is wanting. The bastard Faulconbridge is the witty interpreter of this language: he ridicules the secret springs of politics, without disapproving of them, for he owns that he is endeavouring to make his fortune by similar means, and wishes rather to belong to the deceivers than the deceived, for in his view of the world there is no other choice. His litigation with his brother respecting the succession of his pretended father, by which he effects his acknowledgment at court as natural son of the most chivalrous king of England, Richard Cœur de Lion, forms a very entertaining and original prelude in the play itself. When, amidst so many disguises of real sentiments, and so much insincerity of expression, the poet shows us human nature without a veil, and allows us to take deep views of the inmost recesses of the mind, the impression produced is only the more deep and powerful. The short scene in which John urges Hubert to put out of the way Arthur, his young rival for the possession of the throne, is superlatively masterly: the cautious criminal hardly ventures to say to himself what he wishes the other to do. The young and amiable prince becomes a sacrifice of unprincipled ambition: his fate excites the warmest sympathy. When Hubert, about to put out his eyes with the hot iron, is softened by his prayers, our compassion would be almost overwhelming, were it not sweetened by the winning innocence of Arthur's childish speeches. Constance's maternal despair on her son's imprisonment is also of the highest beauty; and even the last moments of John—an unjust and feeble prince, whom we can neither respect nor admire—are yet so portrayed as to extinguish our displeasure with him, and fill us with serious considerations on the arbitrary deeds and the inevitable fate of mortals.—AUGUST WILHELM SCHLEGEL, *Lectures on Dramatic Art and Literature*, 1809, tr. John Black

*King John* is the last of the historical plays we shall have to speak of; and we are not sorry that it is. If we are to indulge our imaginations, we had rather do it upon an imaginary theme; if we are to find subjects for the exercise of our pity and terror, we prefer seeking them in fictitious danger and fictitious distress. It gives a *soreness* to our feelings of indignation or sympathy, when we know that in tracing the progress of sufferings and crimes, we are treading upon real ground, and recollect that the poet's dream '*denoted a foregone conclusion*'—irrevocable ills, not conjured up by fancy, but placed beyond the reach of poetical justice. That the treachery of King John, the death of Arthur, the grief of Constance, had a real truth in history, sharpens the sense of pain, while it hangs a leaden weight on the heart and the imagination. Something whispers us that we have no right to make a mock of calamities like these, or to turn the truth of things into the puppet and plaything of our fancies. 'To consider thus' may be 'to consider too curiously'; but still we think that the actual truth of the particular events, in proportion as we are conscious of it, is a drawback on the pleasure as well as the dignity of tragedy.

*King John* has all the beauties of language and all the richness of the imagination to relieve the painfulness of the subject. The character of King John himself is kept pretty much in the background; it is only marked in by comparatively slight indications. The crimes he is tempted to commit are such as are thrust upon him rather by circumstances and opportunity than of his own seeking: he is here represented as more cowardly than cruel, and as more contemptible than odious. The play embraces only a part of his history. There are however few characters on the stage that excite more disgust and loathing. He has no intellectual grandeur or strength of character to shield him from the indignation which his immediate conduct provokes: he stands naked and defenceless, in that respect, to the worst we can think of him: and besides, we are impelled to put the very worst construction on his meanness and cruelty by the tender picture of the beauty and helplessness of the object of it, as well as by the frantic and heart-rending pleadings of maternal despair. We do not forgive him the death of Arthur, because he had too late revoked his doom and tried to prevent it; and perhaps because he has himself repented of his black design, our *moral sense* gains courage to hate him the more for it. We take him at his word, and think his purposes must be odious indeed, when he himself shrinks back from them. . . .

The accompaniment of the comic character of the Bastard was well chosen to relieve the poignant agony of suffering, and the cold cowardly policy of behaviour in the principal characters of this play. Its spirit, invention, volubility of tongue and forwardness in action, are unbounded. *Aliquando sufflaminandus erat*, says Ben Jonson of Shakespear. But we should be sorry if Ben Jonson had been his licenser. We prefer the heedless magnanimity of his wit infinitely to all Jonson's laborious caution. The character of the Bastard's comic humour is the same in essence as that of other comic characters in Shakespear; they always run on with good things and are never exhausted; they are always daring and successful. They have words at will, and a flow of wit like a flow of animal spirits. The difference between Falconbridge and the others is that he is a soldier, and brings his wit to bear upon action, is courageous with his sword as well as tongue, and stimulates his gallantry by his jokes, his enemies feeling the sharpness of his blows and the sting of his sarcasms at the same time. Among his happiest sallies are his descanting on the composition of his own person, his invective against 'commodity, tickling commodity,' and his expression of contempt for the Archduke of Austria, who had killed his father, which begins in jest but ends in serious earnest. His conduct at the siege of Angiers shews that his resources were not confined to verbal retorts.—The same exposure of the policy of courts and camps, of kings, nobles, priests, and cardinals, takes place here as in the other plays we have gone through, and we shall not go into a disgusting repetition.—WILLIAM HAZLITT, "King John," *Characters of Shakespear's Plays*, 1817

---

## EDWARD ROSE

### "Shakespeare as an Adapter"

*Macmillan's Magazine*, November 1878, pp. 69–77

People have tried, at one time or another, to show that Shakespeare must have belonged to almost every conceivable trade and profession—he had so wonderful a technical knowledge, we are told of lawyering, doctoring, soldiering, even grave-digging. There is but one thing which, to the best of my knowledge, has never been attempted: which is, to prove that he was a really good stage-manager, that he had a thorough knowledge of what may be called the business part of his art.

For, as a matter of fact, very few purely literary critics see how all-important such skill is to every dramatist—what it has done, above all, for Shakespeare. The principles and details of the construction of plays for the stage, their division into acts and scenes, and the minor rules which regulate such matters as entrances, exits, and so forth, may seem but small things compared with the power which creates living characters, the genius which produces the highest poetry; yet those lesser qualities were in very truth indispensable to his universal fame. Shakespeare would never have been read as widely, nor studied as closely, as he now is by every class, had he not been acted always and everywhere. There is not an evening in the year during which at some provincial theatre in England some play of Shakespeare's is not being acted; "on an emergency," country managers will tell you, "we always put up *Hamlet.*" No other dramatist ever kept the stage for three hundred years; no other dramatist ever bore translation into every tongue; no other ever so pleased every class of audience, from the roughs of California to the most cultivated gatherings of artists, poets, critics. It cannot be his poetry, his philosophy, his drawing of character, which have thus supremely fitted him for the stage; they could hardly *tell* so through bad acting and bad translation. It is the way in which he makes the framework of his plots, in which he presents his story and his characters, that gives force to his strong "situations," and secures their effect, under however unfavourable circumstances.

And this art of effective presentation is absolutely necessary to make a tragedy or comedy a true work of art. Without it, a play cannot thoroughly interest an audience—can be only a "play for the closet," not a genuine acting drama; and plays for the closet are surely contradictions in terms; hybrids, not works of pure art. It is often said that a play ought to bear reading; how much more, then, ought it to bear acting! This is where Browning, Shelley, many other poets fail; to succeed, a man must be a practical dramatist—and thus, a man must be a practical dramatist to be a true dramatic poet.

How completely Shakespeare was this has never, I think, been sufficiently shown; and it is an omission in criticism which can hardly be supplied in half-a-dozen pages. Yet I hope that even the slightest of essays on such a subject will not be unwelcome, if it help to prove how careful, and ingenious, and skilful a playwright the great poet was.

For, if it is believed that he won his triumphs by a sort of direct inspiration—that his method of work was in no way like that of ordinary mortals—he can only gain a blank unreasoning admiration; a valueless wonder, indeed, instead of the hearty reverence and appreciation which he deserves. If, on the other hand, we believe that even he was not above the great human necessity of taking pains: if we examine him with the candid care we should give a modern man, and thoroughly test his knowledge of the stage: not only shall we appreciate many of the qualities to which in very truth he owes his lasting fame, but we shall also learn how, according to the highest authority the world has seen, plays ought to be constructed, how dramatic effects should be made, and in what way great situations should be led up to and "placed."

It is well known among dramatists that there is no more difficult task, none in which experience and stage tact are more required, than the adaptation to the actual theatre of a rough, straggling and ill-constructed play: the condensation of its never-ending purposeless talk, its crowded characters and unconnected incidents. If such a play contain a good scene, it is very likely put at the beginning, when the audience are not

properly settled down to enjoy it; if a situation of strong human interest, very likely the previous explanations necessary to make people really understand and feel it are not given clearly or fully, or it is spoilt by being prolonged beyond the period during which intense excitement can be kept up. The knowledge of stage-mechanism in all its details required to fit such a play for the stage, is every whit as important as the creative genius which must breathe into its rough sketches of character the breath of poetry and life.

One such play, which Shakespeare adapted and rewrote, has fortunately been preserved; and the differences between this rude original and his finished work are most interesting. It is the "history" of *King John,* a chronicle-play perhaps suggested by, though not founded upon, the still older *King Johan* of John Bale, Bishop of Ossory. Who was its author no one, I believe, knows—Pope, in his edition of Shakespeare, suggests Rowley, without, it would appear, any grounds whatever for doing so. If we take for consideration this anonymous play and compare it with Shakespeare's, we shall find how perfectly he understood his art; and we may learn by his example not only what dramatic material to choose, and how to shape it, but— which is by no means so usual with our poet—what to avoid; for *King John,* as it now stands, though it is in many ways a model of construction, and contains at least two of his finest characters and some of his noblest poetry, can hardly be called a successful stage-play.

The old "chronicle" of the *Troublesome Raigne of King John* is clearly the work of a man of considerable, though uncultivated, power; and it is some proof of the estimation in which it was held that three editions of it were published, in 1591, 1611, and 1612. On the title-page of the third the publisher had the impudence to place the name of Shakespeare, but that it was not by him must, I think, be evident to any man who has ever written a play or a poem. He has recast it more completely than any one ever could—or would, with a first sketch often so powerful—recast his own work. Although each scene of Shakespeare follows a scene of the original, he has not throughout the whole play copied one line nearly word for word—at least, I have not remarked one, except a list of "Volquesson, Touraine, Maine, Poitiers, and Anjou, these five provinces;" and this though he constantly found speeches as good as this:—

> I am interdicted by the Pope,
> All churches cursed, their doors are sealed up,
> And for the pleasure of the Romish priest
> The service of the Highest is neglected.
> The multitude (*a beast of many heads*)
> Do with confusion to their sovereign.
> The nobles, blinded with ambition's fumes,
> Assemble powers to beat mine empire down,
> And, more than this, elect a foreign king.
> O England, wert thou ever miserable?
> King John of England sees thee miserable.
> John, 'tis thy sins that makes it miserable!
> *Quicquid delirant reges plectuntur Achivi.*

So entirely, indeed, has the dialogue been rewritten, that one can hardly imagine Shakespeare to have known the original play except by seeing it acted, and perhaps quickly reading it through. How immensely he improved on even the best speeches of his predecessor may be seen from the quotations I shall make; while that predecessor's worst was mere schoolboy doggrell. Nor is his refined and polished versification a greater improvement than the clearness and depth of thought in his lines, which show not merely what men said and did, but the reason and the appropriateness of those deeds and speeches.

The chief faults of the old play are these: It has no hero—

there is not enough to bind the scenes together, and make an interesting whole of them. It is throughout filled with an anti-Romish spirit, violent and vulgar, and entirely out of place in a work of art, though no doubt adding much to the play's temporary popularity. The characters are mere rough outlines, wanting in fulness and consistency; and there is no one in the play, except here and there Falconbridge, in whom you can take much interest. The dialogue is rather dull, and lacking in variety and finish; and, finally, the play is much too long—its Second Part especially—and wants neatness and clearness of construction.

It is characteristic of Shakespeare that, in remedying these faults, he does not for a moment depart from the lines the original author has laid down. He does not go to history for fresh facts to strengthen his plot—he absolutely adds no word of allusion to the Great Charter, which might, one would think, have been worked up into a grand scene. Indeed, the only alteration of fact that he makes is a perversion of history; Arthur was not a mere child, but a young man, as, if we may judge by his conversation with Hubert, the original makes him.

The old play is divided into two parts, each of which is about the length of, and may have been split up into, five short acts. Although he has greatly extended almost every important scene, and has doubled the length of two leading characters, Shakespeare has compressed these ten acts into five of reasonable length; arranged, with a curious instinct which seems prophetic, in almost exact accordance with modern scenic requirements, except as regards the last act. Acts i. and ii. have but one scene apiece, acts iii. and iv. each three, of which the middle ones may well be flat or "carpenter's" scenes; and even in the fifth act the scenery is not very difficult.[1]

It is a very noticeable difference between the two plays, that while in the elder we find no systematic division (except that into two rather unequal halves), in the later Shakespeare—who I believe always paid great attention to the construction of his acts—has made the inter-acts divide the story into five complete and symmetrical parts. Act i. gives us the French king's challenge and its acceptance by John, with the story of the bastard Philip and his brother. Act ii. shows the commencement of hostilities, and the mutual attack upon Angiers; then the arrangement come to between the kings—the peace made on the marriage between Lewis and Blanch. In Act iii. the influence of Rome breaks off this peace; there is a battle in which the French are defeated, and Constance mourns the loss of her son. Act iv. brings us back to England, and gives us the remainder of Arthur's story, and the revolt of the barons at his death. Act v. shows the advance of the French in England, with their allies the rebellious lords; the murder of the king; and the final mishap to the Dauphin's army, which causes him to offer terms of peace.

In reconstructing the play, the great want which struck Shakespeare seems to have been that of a strong central figure. He was attracted by the rough, powerful nature which he could see the Bastard's must have been; almost like a modern dramatist "writing up" a part for a star actor, he introduced Falconbridge wherever it was possible, gave him the end of every act (except the third), and created, from a rude and inconsistent sketch, a character as strong, as complete, and as original as even he ever drew. Throughout a series of scenes, not otherwise very closely connected, this wonderfully real type of faulty, combative, not ignoble manhood is developed, a support and addition to the scenes in which he has least to say, a great power where he is prominent.

This is the most striking example of his development of a character, but his treatment of Constance, Arthur, Hubert,

Pandulph, and of some portions of the character of John himself, is very noticeable. The entire wonderful scene in which Constance laments the loss of her child is founded upon the seven lines:—

> My tongue is tuned to story forth mishap:
> When did I breathe to tell a pleasing tale?
> Must Constance speak? Let tears prevent her talk.
> Must I discourse? Let Dido sigh, and say
> She weeps again to hear the wrack of Troy:
> Two words will serve, and then my tale is done—
> Elinor's proud brat hath robbed me of my son!

The somewhat sinister wisdom of Pandulph is carefully and at length elaborated, and one of several indistinguishable barons (Salisbury) has been made chief spokesman of the revolt caused by the murder of Arthur. Hubert now stands out with a rough manhood which is very sympathetic; and many subtle touches are added to the King's character—of which more hereafter.

And now let us see what were the principal alterations, "cuts," and extensions which the adapter of this old play made, and why he made them—going straight through the piece, and studying each scene in which noticeable improvement has been effected by these means. I may here remark that he only omits four entire scenes, and introduces none, except the dialogue between Falconbridge and Hubert which concludes Act iv.

The plays both begin with the same incident—the King of France claiming the English crown for Arthur; but, while the earlier author opens with twenty lines about the death of Richard and the succession of John, Shakespeare dashes at once into the heart of his subject:—

> *John:* Now say, Chatillon, what would France with
>       us?
> *Chatillon:* Thus, after greeting, speaks the King of
>       France
>    In my behaviour to the majesty,
>    The *borrowed* majesty, of England here.

And throughout the play there is the same exchange of tediousness for spirit and brilliancy; very markedly in the succeeding discussion as to the legitimacy of Falconbridge, during which discussion Shakespeare, writing for an audience he was himself making tender and refined, does not bring the mother upon the stage, as did the elder dramatist. There is, in the midst of the said discussion in the original play, a long "aside" of the Bastard's, which is most interesting. Shakespeare omits it altogether, partly no doubt because it *is* a long "aside;" but how it influenced his conception of the character, and how he yet altered that character, are evident. I quote the soliloquy entire.

> *Essex:* Philip, speak, I say: who was thy father?
> *John:* Young man, how now! What, art thou in a
>       trance?
> *Elinor:* Philip, awake! The man is in a dream.
> *Philip:*[2] *Philippus atavis edite regibus.*
>    What sayst thou, Philip, sprung of ancient kings?
>    *Quo me rapit tempestas?*
>    What wind of honour blows this fury forth?
>    Or whence proceed these fumes of majesty?
>    Methinks I hear a hollow echo sound,
>    That Philip is the son unto a king:
>    The whistling leaves upon the trembling trees,
>    Whistle in comfort I am Richard's son:
>    The bubbling murmur of the waters fall
>    Records *Philippus Regis Filius:*
>    Birds in their flight make music with their wings,
>    Filling the air with glory of my birth:

Birds, bubbles, leaves, and mountains, echo, all
Ring in mine ears, that I am Richard's son.
Fond man! ah, whither art thou carried?
How are thy thoughts ywrapt in honour's heaven?
Forgetful what thou art, and whence thou camest.
Thy father's land cannot maintain these thoughts,
These thoughts are far unfitting Fauconbridge:
And well they may; for why this mounting mind
Doth soar too high to stoop to Fauconbridge.
Why, how now? Knowest thou where thou art?
And knowest thou who expects thine answer here?
Wilt thou upon a frantic madding vaine (? vein)
Go lose thy land and say thy self base-born?
No, keep thy land, though Richard were thy sire,
Whate'er thou thinkst, say thou art Fauconbridge.

However, when he is directly asked who was his father, he proudly claims Richard.

In the scenes in France, which form the second and third acts, Shakespeare has very closely followed his original in construction, though he has greatly extended some passages and compressed others. Many of the details of his workmanship are very ingenious; for example, when the treaty of marriage between Lewis and Blanch is made he keeps Constance off the stage, because, as he says, "the match made up, her presence would have interrupted much." He tells in three lines, too (Act. iii. Sc. 2, lines 5–7), a scene of the original in which Elinor is captured by the French, and afterwards rescued by Falconbridge; the representation of which would probably only have the effect of making the audience uncertain which side was winning.

Then follows perhaps the most important "cut" in the play, that of a scene in which Falconbridge carries out the raid upon the clergy, spoken of here in two lines only (Act. iii. Sc. 4, lines 171, 2). In this place, and throughout the play, Shakespeare has removed the attacks on the Church of Rome to so great an extent that the Catholics claim him for themselves; but it was probably more his hatred of vulgarity and buffoonery than of Protestantism that made him strike out the scene in which the Bastard, ransacking the monasteries, finds a nun in the abbot's chest, a priest in a nun's; and in which a pious friar, horror-stricken, remarks

Oh, I am undone! Fair Alice the nun
Hath took up her rest in the Abbot's chest.
Sancte benedicite, pardon my simplicitie!
Fie, Alice, confession will not salve this trans-
gression!

And, with regard to John's strong speeches against Popery at the end of the old play, they would probably make him more popular with the audience than Shakespeare could permit such a villain to be.

A great deal of valuable space occupied by the prophet, Peter of Pomfret, is also saved. He was originally brought on in the convent-scene (where his introduction seems to show that dramatists even then felt that it was better not to change the scene too often), and in two subsequent scenes he made long speeches to John, embodying the prophecy that he should give up his crown on Ascension Day, and embodied by Shakespeare, as far as Peter himself is concerned, in one single line (Act iv. Sc. 2, line 154), which was probably introduced because the audience had got used to their prophet, and would not have liked to part with him entirely.

The prettiness and pathos of the great scene which follows, between Hubert and Arthur, are quite lost when the prince is made a philosophic young man instead of a winning and tender boy—the sweetest, in Shakespeare's hands, of all pathetic children who have pleaded for their life in plays. Such arguments as the following, however sound and sensible, are not particularly touching:—

Advise thee, Hubert, for the case is hard—
To lose salvation for a king's reward.
*Hubert:* My lord, a subject dwelling in the land
Is tied to execute the king's command.
*Arthur:* Yet God commands, whose power reacheth
further
That no command should stand in force to
murther.
*Hubert:* But that same Essence hath ordained a law,
A death for guilt to keep the world in awe.

And so on, for a page of controversial epigrams. It is perhaps worth noticing that even so vague an expression of religious speculation as the terming God "that Essence" is hardly to be found in Shakespeare's writings.

The next scene is substantially the same as the present, Act iv. sc. 2; but the difference in the skill of their workmanship makes it worth while to examine them in detail. In the first place, using the simple stage expedient of announcing a thing as just done instead of doing it, Shakespeare makes the king come on immediately after his second coronation instead of before it—thus saving a good deal of time and losing absolutely nothing: there was no gain of pageantry in the old arrangement, and the discussion between Pembroke and the others is brought in quite as naturally now. Then, in accordanace with the modern stage-rule (which, as a French critic tells us, has taken the place of the ancient rule of the three unities), that there must be no more entrances and exits than are absolutely necessary, Falconbridge's two entrances are reduced to one. The five moons, also, which make their actual appearance in the old play, are, like some of the characters in Ben Jonson's lists of *dramatis personæ*, "only talked on;" and a few lines take the place of an entire later scene (the second of the Second Part), in which occurred the speech already quoted, describing the manifold evils which are making England miserable. Of the reduction of Peter of Pomfret I have already spoken.

But the most important alteration in this scene is the way in which the false tidings of Arthur's death are treated. In the old version, John, after his coronation, offers a boon; the barons ask for Arthur's safety, which he grants, but with amusing candour withdraws at once upon Peter's prophecies of evil. Then comes Hubert, and blurts out before them all the news that—

According to your highness' strict command,
Young Arthur's eyes are blinded and extinct.

To which John replies, still with candid tranquillity—

Why, so; then he may feel the crown but never see
it.
*Hubert:* Nor see nor feel; for the extreme pain
Within one hour gave he up the ghost.
*John:* What, is he dead?
*Hubert:* He is, my lord.
*John:* Then with him die my cares!
*Essex:* Now joy betide thy soul!
*Pembroke:* And heavens revenge thy death!
*Essex:* What have you done, my lord? Was ever
heard
A deed of more inhuman consequence?
Your foes will curse, your friends will cry revenge.
Unkindly rage, more rough than northern wind,
To clip the beauty of so sweet a flower.
What hope in us for mercy on a fault,

When kinsman dies without impeach of cause,
As you have done, so come to cheer you with,
The guilt shall never be cast in my teeth!

And the barons go. Now, Shakespeare has saved enough room elsewhere to be able to be far less jerky here. This is how he treats the above passage: Hubert enters, and John takes him apart, saying, "Hubert, what news with you?" Then—

*Pembroke:* This is the man should do the bloody
  deed:
  He showed his warrant to a friend of mine:
  The image of a wicked heinous fault
  Lives in his eye: that close aspect of his
  Does show the mood of a much troubled breast;
  And I do fearfully believe 'tis done,
  What we so fear'd he had a charge to do.
*Salisbury:* The colour of the king doth come and go
  Between his purpose and his conscience,
  Like heralds 'twixt two dreadful battles set:
  His passion is so ripe, it needs must break.
*Pembroke:* And when it breaks, I fear will issue
  thence
  The foul corruption of a sweet child's death.
*John:* We cannot hold mortality's strong hand:
  Good lords, although my will to give is living,
  The suit which you demand is gone and dead:
  He tells us Arthur is deceased to-night.
*Salisbury:* Indeed, we feared his sickness was past
  cure.
*Pembroke:* Indeed, we heard how near his death he
  was
  Before the child himself felt he was sick:
  This must be answered either here or hence.
*John:* Why do you bend such solemn brows on me?
  Think you I bear the shears of destiny?
  Have I commandment on the pulse of life?
*Salisbury:* It is apparent foul play; and 'tis shame
  That greatness should so grossly offer it:
  So thrive it in your game! and so, farewell.
*Pembroke:* Stay yet, Lord Salisbury; I'll go with thee,
  And find the inheritance of this poor child,
  His little kingdom of a forced grave.
  That blood which owed the breadth of all this isle
  Three foot of it doth hold: bad world the while!
  This must not be thus borne: this will break out
  To all our sorrows, and ere long I doubt.

Whoever will read this entire scene as it stands in Shakespeare cannot fail to find how very much he has improved it in neatness of construction, in probability, in effectiveness, and even in brevity, though he has doubled the dignity and philosophic fulness of nearly all the chief speeches. And throughout the Second Part (which begins with Arthur's death) his alterations are at least as important and successful. Arthur does not make a speech of fifteen lines after he has leapt from the walls—he is a much less "unconscionable time a-dying;" and an immense improvement has been made in the subsequent scene (Act iv. Sc. 3) between Hubert and the barons, by the introduction of Falconbridge.

In the first scene of Act v. Shakespeare repeats the stage expedient I have already spoken of—he makes John come on just as he has yielded up his crown to Pandulph; and indeed this scene and the next are altogether very neatly constructed. Instead of them we have, in the old piece, first a long scene in which John (after hanging poor Peter of Pomfret) describes his misfortunes, and, under great pressure, consents to become the Pope's vassal; then another in which are set forth most elaborately the appeal to Lewis by the English barons, their oath, and his treachery; and a third, showing John's acceptance of the crown at Pandulph's hands, and the refusal of Lewis to retire at the Pope's bidding.

The fifth and seventh scenes of this Second Part, giving the progress of the struggle between John and the French and rebels, correspond closely to the fourth and fifth of Shakespeare's Act v.; the sixth and eighth show at great length how John took refuge in Swinstead Abbey; how a certain monk, with the connivance of his abbot, poisoned the king's drink, and, tasting it first himself, with the historic cry of "Wassell!" died, remarking aside, "If the inwards of a toad be a compound of any proof—why, so: it works!" how Falconbridge, very naturally, killed the abbot; how the king died, after some long and powerful speeches, rather like those of Sir Giles Overreach, but very strongly anti-Catholic; and how, as he was dying, Henry and the revolted barons came, and John lifted his hand in token of forgiveness, and again as a sign that he died Christ's servant.

Now, these long scenes of meditated murder, and of murder itself and its reward, form a particularly unpleasant conclusion to a play which has already had quite its full share of treachery and crime; and their compression speaks as well for Shakespeare's healthy and manly feeling as for his skill as a dramatist. This skill is again displayed in the neatness with which he throws into a few lines, without change of scene, the establishment of Henry as king, which in the original play occupies a ninth scene, coming as an awkward anticlimax after the death of the hero. The "tag," given in both plays by Falconbridge, shows how commonplace verse can be converted into splendid poetry. The original lines—

  Let England live but true within itself,
  And all the world can never wrong her state;

and—

  If England's peers and people join in one,
  Not Pope, nor France, nor Spain can do them
    wrong!

are replaced by the glorious—

  This England never did, nor never shall,
  Lie at the proud foot of a conqueror
  But when it first did help to wound itself.
  Now these her princes are come home again,
  Come the three corners of the world in arms,
  And we shall shock them. Nought shall make us rue,
  If England to itself do rest but true.

Before I leave these details of construction, I should like to remark three points in which Shakespeare, in compressing the original, has left matters a little less clear than he found them.

In the first place, does it strike one why Falconbridge makes such a dead set at Austria—or Lymoges, as Shakespeare, repeating his predecessor's blunder, sometimes calls him? Are we not apt to fancy that it was chiefly because the Bastard was a bullying sort of fellow, and saw that Austria was a coward? But in the old play it is at once and fully shown that he wanted to avenge the duke's cruelty to his father, Richard I.; Austria is indeed wearing the skin of the lion which Richard killed, and which gave him his famous surname.

Then—it is a very minor matter—but one does not quite know why Falconbridge should be so much annoyed at the betrothal of Blanch to the Dauphin; nor why Blanch should have backed up Falconbridge in his apparently unjustifiable attack upon Austria. In the original, we find that Elinor had half promised Blanch's hand to the Bastard, whom the lady gave up for Lewis with some reluctance.

Lastly—and this is a good deal more important—Shakespeare does not at all explain *why* the monk poisoned King John. Has not one been rather startled, on seeing the play acted, by its sudden termination? Just when his fortunes are at their most critical point, the hero without rhyme or reason dies: some one comes in casually and says that the king is dying, murdered by an anonymous monk, who is indeed described as a "resolved villain," but who is not shown to have had any motive whatever for his deed. It is as if the Gravedigger should suddenly brain Hamlet with his pickaxe, in the midst of their conversation, and decline to give any reason for his conduct. The author of the *Troublesome Raigne*, besides giving at length the scene of the ransacking the monasteries by the king's command, tells us in so many words that the murderous monk expected to be "canonized for a holy saint" for poisoning the king that did "contemn the pope" and "never loved a friar," and shows us his conception of and preparation for the crime.

Having thus gone through the principal alterations which Shakespeare made in adapting this rough and diffuse old "history" for his own theatre, and having tried to show how greatly he improved it, even from the point of view of a modern stage-manager, I must explain why his example in this case seems to me, as I have said, a warning as well as a lesson to dramatists. What is it that has neutralised his efforts to make of *King John* a stage-play as successful and enduringly popular as, for example, *Richard III.?* It must be either the subject itself, or the way in which it has been dealt with in the original piece—which, in its broad outlines, he has not attempted to alter.

The subject is perhaps not altogether a good one. The king's great crime is so dastardly, the leading cause of his misfortunes (his quarrel with Rome about Stephen Langton) is so undramatic, and his nature breaks down so entirely at the end—when even a villain like Richard III. fights nobly and forces some sort of respect from the audience—that it may be that no poet could have made a strong play of the story of his life. As it is, in Acts i. and ii. he is a nonentity, Falconbridge filling the first act, and nobody being very prominent in the second; in the third act Constance is supreme, and in the fourth Arthur; while even in the fifth the king is not of very great importance, his death-scene being much weakened in effect (however it may gain in refinement) by the removal of his violently remorseful and Protestant speeches. Indeed, it must be confessed that the omission from the play of the constant attacks on Popery, though an improvement from a purely literary point of view, destroys to a certain extent its *raison d'être*, the spirit that helped to animate its old straggling

mass, and, as has been pointed out, the motive of its *dénoûment*.

The effort, too, to give the piece a hero in Falconbridge is a failure, because, as long experience teaches, you *cannot* force a character out of the position he would naturally occupy in a play. Falconbridge is properly little more than a chorus, a cynical critic of a wicked age—he might be entirely omitted without in the least degree altering the substance of the plot—and it is therefore impossible to make the story centre in him, as should every story in some one figure, or inseparably-connected group of figures.

Shakespeare has no doubt kept so closely to the lines of the older play because it was a favourite with his audience, and they had grown to accept its history as absolute fact; but one can hardly help thinking that had he boldly thrown aside these trammels and taken John as his hero, his great central figure; had he analysed and built up before us the mass of power, craft, passion, and devilry which made up the worst of the Plantagenets; had he dramatised the grand scene of the signing of the Charter, and shown vividly the gloom and horror which overhung the excommunicated land; had he painted John's last despairing struggles against rebels and invaders, as he has given us the fiery end of Macbeth's life—we might have had another Macbeth, another Richard, who would by his terrible personality have welded the play together, and carried us along breathless through his scenes of successive victory and defeat.

That by this means something would be lost is true—Falconbridge, for example, would certainly be lessened—but the worth of a real work of art is greater than the worth of any part of it; and Constance and Hubert probably need not suffer, while the influence of the death of Arthur might very likely be made to penetrate more thoroughly the entire play. In *Macbeth, Henry V., Richard III., Coriolanus*, everything is subordinated to the centre, the mainspring of the plot; in *King John* each act has a different hero. What could be more fatal to the interest of the whole?

To some it may seem presumptuous thus to criticise Shakespeare; but is it not indeed the only way to make sure that one really appreciates him? Of such appreciation I wish my unsparing criticism of his work to be a proof; it is a poor faith that dares not listen to and seek out every accusation against its idol.

*Notes*

1. Modern editors somewhat unnecessarily divide the third act into four scenes.
2. *Aside*, evidently.

# Richard II

This play is extracted from the Chronicle of Hollingshead, in which many passages may be found which Shakespeare has, with very little alteration, transplanted into his scenes; particularly a speech of the Bishop of Carlisle in defence of King Richard's unalienable right, and immunity from human jurisdiction.

Jonson, who, in his *Catiline* and *Sejanus*, has inserted many speeches from the Roman historians, was, perhaps, induced to that practice by the example of Shakespeare, who had condescended sometimes to copy more ignoble writers. But Shakespeare had more of his own than Jonson, and, if he sometimes was willing to spare his labour, shewed by what he performed at other times, that his extracts were made by choice or idleness rather than necessity.

This play is one of those which Shakespeare has apparently revised; but as success in works of invention is not always proportionate to labour, it is not finished at last with the happy force of some other of his tragedies, nor can be said much to affect the passions, or enlarge the understanding.—SAMUEL JOHNSON, *Notes on Shakespeare's Plays*, 1768

In *Richard the Second*, Shakespeare exhibits a noble kingly nature, at first obscured by levity and the errors of an unbridled youth, and afterwards purified by misfortune, and rendered by it more highly and splendidly illustrious. When he has lost the love and reverence of his subjects, and is on the point of losing also his throne, he then feels with a bitter enthusiasm the high vocation of the kingly dignity and its transcendental rights, independent of personal merit or changable institutions. When the earthly crown is fallen from his head, he first appears a king whose innate nobility no humiliation can annihilate. This is felt by a poor groom: he is shocked that his master's favourite horse should have carried the proud Bolingbroke to his coronation; he visits the captive king in prison, and shames the desertion of the great. The political incident of the deposition is sketched with extraordinary knowledge of the world;—the ebb of fortune, on the one hand, and on the other, the swelling tide, which carries every thing along with it. While Bolingbroke acts as a king, and his adherents behave towards him as if he really were so, he still continues to give out that he has come with an armed band merely to demand his birthright and the removal of abuses. The usurpation has been long completed, before the word is pronounced and the thing publicly avowed. The old John of Gaunt is a model of chivalrous honour: he stands there like a pillar of the olden time which he has outlived. His son, Henry IV., was altogether unlike him: his character is admirably sustained throughout the three pieces in which he appears. We see in it that mixture of hardness, moderation, and prudence, which, in fact, enabled him to secure the possession of the throne which he had violently usurped; but without openness, without true cordiality, and incapable of noble ebullitions, he was so little able to render his government beloved, that the deposed Richard was even wished back again.—AUGUST WILHELM SCHLEGEL, *Lectures on Dramatic Art and Literature*, 1809, tr. John Black

*Richard II.* is a play little known compared with *Richard III.* which last is a play that every unfledged candidate for theatrical fame chuses to strut and fret his hour upon the stage in; yet we confess that we prefer the nature and feeling of the one to the noise and bustle of the other; at least, as we are so often forced to see it acted. In *Richard II.* the weakness of the king leaves us leisure to take a greater interest in the misfortunes of the man. After the first act, in which the arbitrariness of his behaviour only proves his want of resolution, we see him staggering under the unlooked-for blows of fortune, bewailing his loss of kingly power, not preventing it, sinking under the aspiring genius of Bolingbroke, his authority trampled on, his hopes failing him, and his pride crushed and broken down under insults and injuries, which his own misconduct had provoked, but which he has not courage or manliness to resent. The change of tone and behaviour in the two competitors for the throne according to their change of fortune, from the capricious sentence of banishment passed by Richard upon Bolingbroke, the suppliant offers and modest pretensions of the latter on his return to the high and haughty tone with which he accepts Richard's resignation of the crown after the loss of all his power, the use which he makes of the deposed king to grace his triumphal progress through the streets of London, and the final intimation of his wish for his death, which immediately finds a servile executioner, is marked throughout with complete effect and without the slightest appearance of effort. The steps by which Bolingbroke mounts the throne are those by which Richard sinks into the grave. We feel neither respect nor love for the deposed monarch; for he is as wanting in energy as in principle: but we pity him, for he pities himself. His heart is by no means hardened against himself, but bleeds afresh at every new stroke of mischance, and his sensibility, absorbed in his own person, and unused to misfortune, is not only tenderly alive to its own sufferings, but without the fortitude to bear them. He is, however, human in his distresses; for to feel pain, and sorrow, weakness, disappointment, remorse and anguish, is the lot of humanity, and we sympathize with him accordingly. The sufferings of the man make us forget that he ever was a king.

The right assumed by sovereign power to trifle at its will with the happiness of others as a matter of course, or to remit its exercise as a matter of favour, is strikingly shewn in the sentence of banishment so unjustly pronounced on Bolingbroke and Mowbray, and in what Bolingbroke says when four years of his banishment are taken off, with as little reason.

> How long a time lies in one little word!
> Four lagging winters and four wanton springs
> End in a word: such is the breath of kings.

A more affecting image of the loneliness of a state of exile can hardly be given than by what Bolingbroke afterwards observes of his having 'sighed his English breath in foreign clouds'; or than that conveyed in Mowbray's complaint at being banished for life.

> The language I have learned these forty years,
> My native English, now I must forego;
> And now my tongue's use is to me no more
> Than an unstringed viol or a harp,
> Or like a cunning instrument cas'd up,
> Or being open, put into his hands
> That knows no touch to tune the harmony.
> I am too old to fawn upon a nurse,
> Too far in years to be a pupil now.—

How very beautiful is all this, and at the same time how very *English* too!—WILLIAM HAZLITT, "Richard II," *Characters of Shakespear's Plays*, 1817

I have stated that the transitional link between the epic poem and the drama is the historic drama; that in the epic poem a preannounced fate gradually adjusts and employs the will and the events as its instruments, whilst the drama, on the other hand, places fate and will in opposition to each other, and is then most perfect, when the victory of fate is obtained in consequence of imperfections in the opposing will, so as to leave a final impression that the fate itself is but a higher and a more intelligent will.

From the length of the speeches, and the circumstance that, with one exception, the events are all historical, and presented in their results, not produced by acts seen by, or taking place before, the audience, this tragedy is ill suited to our present large theatres. But in itself, and for the closet, I feel no hesitation in placing it as the first and most admirable of all Shakspeare's purely historical plays. For the two parts of *Henry IV.* form a species of themselves, which may be named the mixed drama. The distinction does not depend on the mere quantity of historical events in the play compared with the fictions; for there is as much history in *Macbeth* as in *Richard*, but in the relation of the history to the plot. In the purely historical plays, the history forms the plot; in the mixed, it directs it; in the rest, as *Macbeth, Hamlet, Cymbeline, Lear*, it subserves it. But, however unsuited to the stage this drama may be, God forbid that even there it should fall dead on the hearts of jacobinized Englishmen! Then, indeed, we might say— *præteriit gloria mundi!* For the spirit of patriotic reminiscence is the all-permeating soul of this noble work. It is, perhaps, the most purely historical of Shakspeare's dramas. There are not in it, as in the others, characters introduced merely for the purpose of giving a greater individuality and realness, as in the comic parts of *Henry IV.*, by presenting, as it were, our very selves. Shakspeare avails himself of every opportunity to effect the great object of the historic drama, that, namely, of familiarizing the people to the great names of their country, and thereby of exciting a steady patriotism, a love of just liberty, and respect for all those fundamental institutions of social life, which bind men together:—

> This royal throne of kings, this scepter'd isle,
> This earth of majesty, this seat of Mars,
> This other Eden, demi-paradise;
> This fortress, built by nature for herself,
> Against infection, and the hand of war;
> This happy breed of men, this little world;
> This precious stone set in the silver sea,
> Which serves it in the office of a wall,
> Or as a moat defensive to a home,
> Against the envy of less happier lands;
> This blessed plot, this earth, this realm, this England,
> This nurse, this teeming womb of royal kings,
> Fear'd by their breed, and famous by their birth, &c.

Add the famous passage in *King John:*—

> This England never did, nor ever shall,
> Lie at the proud foot of a conqueror,
> But when it first did help to wound itself.
> Now these her princes are come home again,
> Come the three corners of the world in arms,
> And we shall shock them: nought shall make us rue,
> If England to itself do rest but true.

And it certainly seems that Shakspeare's historic dramas produced a very deep effect on the minds of the English people, and in earlier times they were familiar even to the least informed of all ranks, according to the relation of Bishop Corbett. Marlborough, we know, was not ashamed to confess that his principal acquaintance with English history was derived from them; and I believe that a large part of the information as to our old names and achievements even now abroad is due, directly or indirectly, to Shakspeare.

Admirable is the judgment with which Shakspeare always in the first scenes prepares, yet how naturally, and with what concealment of art, for the catastrophe. Observe how he here presents the germ of all the after events in Richard's insincerity, partiality, arbitrariness, and favoritism, and in the proud, tempestuous, temperament of his barons. In the very beginning, also, is displayed that feature in Richard's character, which is never forgotten throughout the play—his attention to decorum, and high feeling of the kingly dignity. These anticipations show with what judgment Shakspeare wrote, and illustrate his care to connect the past and future, and unify them with the present by forecast and reminiscence.

It is interesting to a critical ear to compare the six opening lines of the play—

> Old John of Gaunt, time-honor'd Lancaster,
> Hast thou, according to thy oath and band, &c.

each closing at the tenth syllable, with the rhythmless metre of the verse in *Henry VI.* and *Titus Andronicus*, in order that the difference, indeed, the heterogeneity, of the two may be felt *etiam in simillimis prima superficie.* Here the weight of the single words supplies all the relief afforded by intercurrent verse, while the whole represents the mood. And compare the apparently defective metre of Bolingbroke's first line,—

> Many years of happy days befall—

with Prospero's,

> Twelve years since, Miranda! twelve years since—

The actor should supply the time by emphasis, and pause on the first syllable of each of these verses.

> To look upon my sometime master's face.
> O, how it yearn'd my heart, when I beheld,
> In London streets, that coronation day,
> When Bolingbroke rode on roan Barbary!
> That horse, that thou so often hast bestrid;
> That horse, that I so carefully have dress'd!
> K. Rich.: Rode he on Barbary?

Bolingbroke's character, in general, is an instance how Shakspeare makes one play introductory to another; for it is evidently a preparation for *Henry IV.*, as Gloster in the third part of *Henry VI.* is for *Richard III.*

I would once more remark upon the exalted idea of the only true loyalty developed in this noble and impressive play. We have neither the rants of Beaumont and Fletcher, nor the sneers of Massinger;—the vast importance of the personal character of the sovereign is distinctly enounced, whilst, at the same time, the genuine sanctity which surrounds him is attributed to, and grounded on, the position in which he stands as the convergence and exponent of the life and power of the state.

The great end of the body politic appears to be to humanize, and assist in the progressiveness of, the animal man;—but the problem is so complicated with contingencies as to render it nearly impossible to lay down rules for the formation of a state. And should we be able to form a system of government, which should so balance its different powers as to form a check upon each, and so continually remedy and correct itself, it would, nevertheless, defeat its own aim;—for man is destined to be guided by higher principles, by universal views, which can never be fulfilled in this state of existence,— by a spirit of progressiveness which can never be accomplished, for then it would cease to be. Plato's Republic is like Bunyan's Town of Man-Soul,—a description of an individual, all of whose faculties are in their proper subordination and interdependence; and this it is assumed may be the prototype of the state as one great individual. But there is this sophism in it, that it is forgotten that the human faculties, indeed, are parts and not separate things; but that you could never get chiefs who were wholly reason, ministers who were wholly understanding, soldiers all wrath, labourers all concupiscence, and so on through the rest. Each of these partakes of, and interferes with, all the others.—SAMUEL TAYLOR COLERIDGE, "Richard II.," *Shakspeare, with Introductory Remarks on Poetry, the Drama, and the Stage,* 1818

There is, as is well known, great variety of opinion as to whether the play of *Richard II.,* acted by the request of Sir Gilly Merrick the day before Essex's rising, was Shakespeare's or some other. The probabilities are, on the whole, perhaps in favour of its being Shakespeare's. As Shakespeare was intimately acquainted with Southampton, who was one of Essex's leading partisans, it is probable that those partisans would apply for any dramatic help they might want, or fancy they wanted, to the company to which Shakespeare belonged. Again, the omission of the Deposition Scene from the quartos of 1597 and 1598, though there can be little doubt it was then written, cannot but be regarded as significant of the use to which that scene might be turned. The publisher of those quartos evidently saw in it something that might be construed into a sense unfavourable to the Queen, and so welcome to her enemies. Nor, I think, can the fact of the play's being called an old play, and one that it would not pay to act, be said to counterweigh these probabilities. Others, however, and critics of judgment, may decide for themselves differently. But what I wish now to do is to recall attention to a piece of evidence brought forward years ago, but which seems to have been oddly overlooked or ignored by some recent editors—a piece of evidence which greatly increases the probability that the play was really Shakespeare's.

In a report of Attorney-General Bacon's speech in the *State Trials,* there is given the name of the actor with whom Sir Gilly Merrick negotiated. It is Phillips: and unless good reason is shown to the contrary, we can scarcely doubt that this is the Augustine Phillips who was a member of the famous Globe company, *i.e.,* one of Shakespeare's "fellows." In the licence of 1603 the names run: Lawrence Fletcher, William Shakespeare, Richard Burbage, Augustine Phillips, &c. A notice of him may be found in the *Historical Account of the English Stage,* and elsewhere.

The report is that described as "a fuller account of the Trial of Sir Christopher Blunt, Sir Charles Davers, Sir John Davis, Sir Gilly Merrick and Henry Cuffe, from a MS. purchased at a sale of the MSS. of Peter Le Neve, Esq., Norroy King-at-Arms;" and the passage that concerns us occurs on p. 1445 of the 1809 edition of *State Trials:*—

"And the story of Henry the Fourth being set forth in a play, and in that play there being set forth the killing of the

King upon a stage, the Friday before, Sir Gilly and some others of the Earl's train having a humour to see a play, they must needs have the play of *Henry the Fourth.* The players told them that was stale, they should get nothing by playing of that; but no play else would serve, and Sir Gilly gives forty shillings to Phillips the player to play this, besides whatever he could get."

The play's being called *Henry IV.* surely cannot cause any difficulty, seeing what is said of its contents. But if any one should think otherwise, there is abundant other evidence to show that the play was also called, or rather commonly called *Richard II.* See, for instance, Bacon's "Declaration of the Practices and Treasons attempted, and committed by Robert, Earl of Essex, and his complices, against her Majesty and her kingdoms," where we are told that, "it was given in evidence. . . . that the afternoon before the rebellion, Merick, with a great company of others that afterwards were all in the action, had procured to be played before them the *play of deposing Richard the Second.* Neither was it casual, but a play bespoken by Merick."

But if there could be any doubt on this point, or as to who that Phillips was, it must be all dissipated by the document of which a facsimile is given by Mr. J. O. Halliwell-Phillipps, in that vast storehouse of learning his Folio Shakespeare, now to be found also in the *Calendar of State Papers,* Domestic Series, 1591–1601, p. 578—a document surely not so much noticed and considered as it deserves. It is headed: "Examination of Augustine Phillips, servant to the Lord Chamberlain and one of his Players, before Lord Chief Justice Popham and Edward Fenner," and runs thus:—

"On Thursday or Friday sevennight Sir Charles Percy, Sir Josceline Percy, Lord Monteagle, and several others spoke to some of our players to play the deposing and killing of Richard ii., and promised to give them 40s. more than their ordinary to do so. Examinate and his fellows had determined to play some other play, holding that of King Richard as being so old, and so long out of use that they should have a small company of it; but at this request they were content to play it." We may just ask whether the above names do not suggest that some of Essex's accomplices may have nursed designs very different from his own, or at all events from those he professed? But this by the way. What is noticeable for us is that "the deposing and killing of Richard II." is exactly the subject of Shakespeare's play.

Considering now the general probabilities, and the facts that the company employed by the Essexians was that to which Shakespeare belonged, and that the play asked for answers in description to Shakespeare's *Richard II.,* must we not incline to believe that the play was indeed Shakespeare's? Is it likely that there were two plays answering to the same description "in the field" of the Globe—two plays dealing with the closing years of Richard II.?—JOHN W. HALES, "Richard II" (1875), *Notes and Essays on Shakespeare,* 1884, pp. 205–8

# Henry IV

. . . to the King's playhouse, and there saw *Henry the Fourth*: and contrary to expectation, was pleased in nothing more than in Cartwright's speaking of Falstaff's speech about 'What is Honour?'—SAMUEL PEPYS, *Diary*, Nov. 2, 1667

*Ben Johnson* shall speak for himself afterwards in the Character of a Critick; in the mean Time I shall take a Testimony or two from *Shakespear*. And here we may observe the admir'd *Falstaffe* goes off in Disappointment. He is thrown out of Favour as being a *Rake*, and dies like a Rat behind the Hangings. The Pleasure he had given, would not excuse him. The *Poet* was not so partial, as to let his Humour compound for his Lewdness. If 'tis objected that this Remark is wide of the Point, because *Falstaffe* is represented in Tragedy, where the Laws of Justice are more strictly observ'd. To this I answer, that you may call *Henry* the Fourth and Fifth, Tragedies if you please: But for all that, *Falstaffe* wears no *Buskins*, his Character is perfectly comical from End to End.—JEREMY COLLIER, *A Short View of the Immorality and Profaneness of the English Stage*, 1698

Tragical passion was the subject of the discourse where I last visited this evening; and a gentleman who knows that I am at present writing a very deep tragedy, directed his discourse in a particular manner to me. "It is the common fault," said he, "of you, gentlemen, who write in the buskin style, that you give us rather the sentiments of such who behold tragical events, than of such who bear a part in them themselves. I would advise all who pretend this way, to read Shakespeare with care, and they will soon be deterred from putting forth what is usually called 'tragedy.' The way of common writers in this kind, is rather the description, than the expression of sorrow. There is no medium in these attempts; and you must go to the very bottom of the heart, or it is all mere language; and the writer of such lines is no more a poet, than a man is a physician for knowing the names of distempers, without the causes of them. Men of sense are professed enemies to all such empty labours: for he who pretends to be sorrowful, and is not, is a wretch yet more contemptible than he who pretends to be merry, and is not. Such a tragedian is only maudlin drunk." The gentleman went on with much warmth; but all he could say had little effect upon me: but when I came hither, I so far observed his counsel, that I looked into Shakespeare. The tragedy I dipped into was, *Harry the Fourth* In the scene where Morton is preparing to tell Northumberland of his son's death, the old man does not give him time to speak, but says,

> The whiteness of thy cheeks
> Is apter than thy tongue to tell thy errand;
> Even such a man, so faint, so spiritless,
> So dull, so dead in look, so woebegone,
> Drew Priam's curtain at the dead of night,
> And would have told him half his Troy was burnt:
> But Priam found the fire, ere he his tongue,
> And I my Percy's death ere thou reportest it.

The image in this place is wonderfully noble and great; yet this man in all this is but rising towards his great affliction, and is still enough himself, as you see, to make a simile: but when he is certain of his son's death, he is lost to all patience, and gives up all the regards of this life; and since the last of evils is fallen upon him, he calls for it upon all the world.

> Now let not Nature's hand
> Keep the wild flood confined; let Order die,

> And let the world no longer be a stage,
> To feed contention in a lingering act;
> But let one spirit of the firstborn Cain
> Reign in all bosoms, that each heart being set
> On bloody courses, the wide scene may end,
> And darkness be the burier of the dead.

Reading but this one scene has convinced me, that he who describes the concern of great men, must have a soul as noble, and as susceptible of high thoughts, as they whom he represents: I shall therefore lay by my drama for some time, and turn my thoughts to cares and griefs, somewhat below that of heroes, but no less moving. A misfortune proper for me to take notice of, has too lately happened: the disconsolate Maria has three days kept her chamber for the loss of the beauteous Fidelia, her lap-dog. Lesbia herself did not shed more tears for her sparrow. What makes her the more concerned, is, that we know not whether Fidelia was killed or stolen; but she was seen in the parlour window when the train-bands went by, and never since. Whoever gives notice of her, dead or alive, shall be rewarded with a kiss of her lady.—RICHARD STEELE, *The Tatler*, No. 47 (July 28, 1709)

*Magnificence* is . . . a source of the sublime. A great profusion of things which are splendid or valuable in themselves, is *magnificent*. The starry heaven, though it occurs so very frequently to our view, never fails to excite an idea of grandeur. This cannot be owing to any thing in the stars themselves, separately considered. The number is certainly the cause. The apparent disorder augments the grandeur, for the appearance of care is highly contrary to our ideas of magnificence. Besides, the stars lye in such apparent confusion, as makes it impossible on ordinary occasions to reckon them. This gives them the advantage of a sort of infinity. In works of art, this kind of grandeur, which consists of multitude, is to be very cautiously admitted; because, a profusion of excellent things is not to be attained, or with too much difficulty; and, because in many cases this splendid confusion would destroy all use, which should be attended to in most of the works of art with the greatest care; besides it is to be considered, that unless you can produce an appearance of infinity by your disorder, you will have disorder only without magnificence. There are, however, a sort of fireworks, and some other things, that in this way succeed well, and are truly grand. There are also many descriptions in the poets and orators which owe their sublimity to a richness and profusion of images, in which the mind is so dazzled as to make it impossible to attend to that exact coherence and agreement of the allusions, which we should require on every other occasion. I do not now remember a more striking example of this, than the description which is given of the king's army in the play of Henry the fourth;

> All furnished, all in arms,
> All plumed like ostriches that with the wind
> Baited like eagles having lately bathed:
> As full of spirit as the month of May,
> And gorgeous as the sun in Midsummer,
> Wanton as youthful goats, wild as young bulls.
> I saw young Harry with his beaver on
> Rise from the ground like feathered Mercury;
> And vaulted with such ease into his seat
> As if an angel dropped down from the clouds
> To turn and wind a fiery Pegasus.

—EDMUND BURKE, "Magnificence," *A Philosophical Enquiry into the Origin of Our Ideas of the Sublime and Beautiful*, 1757

I fancy every reader, when he ends this play, cries out with Desdemona, "O most lame and impotent conclusion!" As this play was not, to our knowledge, divided into acts by the authour, I could be content to conclude it with the death of Henry the Fourth.

In that Jerusalem shall Harry dye.

These scenes which now make the fifth act of *Henry the Fourth*, might then be the first of *Henry the Fifth*; but the truth is, that they do unite very commodiously to either play. When these plays were represented, I believe they ended as they are now ended in the books; but Shakespeare seems to have designed that the whole series of action from the beginning of *Richard the Second*, to the end of *Henry the Fifth*, should be considered by the reader as one work, upon one plan, only broken into parts by the necessity of exhibition.

None of Shakespeare's plays are more read than the *First and Second Parts of Henry the Fourth*. Perhaps no authour has ever in two plays afforded so much delight. The great events are interesting, for the fate of kingdoms depends upon them; the slighter occurrences are diverting, and, except one or two, sufficiently probable; the incidents are multiplied with wonderful fertility of invention, and the characters diversified with the utmost nicety of discernment, and the profoundest skill in the nature of man.

The Prince, who is the hero both of the comick and tragick part, is a young man of great abilities and violent passions, whose sentiments are right, though his actions are wrong; whose virtues are obscured by negligence, and whose understanding is dissipated by levity. In his idle hours he is rather loose than wicked, and when the occasion forces out his latent qualities, he is great without effort, and brave without tumult. The trifler is roused into a hero, and the hero again reposes in the trifler. This character is great, original, and just.

Percy is a rugged soldier, cholerick, and quarrelsome, and has only the soldier's virtues, generosity and courage.

But Falstaff unimitated, unimitable Falstaff, how shall I describe thee? Thou compound of sense and vice; of sense which may be admired but not esteemed, of vice which may be despised, but hardly detested. Falstaff is a character loaded with faults, and with those faults which naturally produce contempt. He is a thief, and a glutton, a coward, and a boaster, always ready to cheat the weak, and prey upon the poor; to terrify the timorous and insult the defenceless. At once obsequious and malignant, he satirises in their absence those whom he lives by flattering. He is familiar with the Prince only as an agent of vice, but of this familiarity he is so proud as not only to be supercilious and haughty with common men, but to think his interest of importance to the Duke of Lancaster. Yet the man thus corrupt, thus despicable, makes himself necessary to the prince that despises him, by the most pleasing of all qualities, perpetual gaiety, by an unfailing power of exciting laughter, which is the more freely indulged, as his wit is not of the splendid or ambitious kind, but consists in easy escapes and sallies of levity, which make sport but raise no envy. It must be observed that he is stained with no enormous or sanguinary crimes, so that his licentiousness is not so offensive but that it may be borne for his mirth.

The moral to be drawn from this representation is, that no man is more dangerous than he that with a will to corrupt, hath the power to please; and that neither wit nor honesty ought to think themselves safe with such a companion when they see Henry seduced by Falstaff.—SAMUEL JOHNSON, *Notes on Shakespeare's Plays*, 1768

The first part of *Henry the Fourth* is particularly brilliant in the serious scenes, from the contrast between two young heroes, Prince Henry and Percy (with the characteristical name of Hotspur). All the amiability and attractiveness is certainly on the side of the prince: however familiar he makes himself with bad company, we can never mistake him for one of them: the ignoble does indeed touch, but it does not contaminate him; and his wildest freaks appear merely as witty tricks, by which his restless mind sought to burst through the inactivity to which he was constrained, for on the first occasion which wakes him out of his unruly levity he distinguishes himself without effort in the most chivalrous guise. Percy's boisterous valour is not without a mixture of rude manners, arrogance, and boyish obstinacy; but these errors, which prepare for him an early death, cannot disfigure the majestic image of his noble youth; we are carried away by his fiery spirit at the very moment we would most censure it. Shakespeare has admirably shown why so formidable a revolt against an unpopular and really an illegitimate prince was not attended with success: Glendower's superstitious fancies respecting himself, the effeminacy of the young Mortimer, the ungovernable disposition of Percy, who will listen to no prudent counsel, the irresolution of his older friends, the want of unity of plan and motive, are all characterized by delicate but unmistakable traits. After Percy has departed from the scene, the splendour of the enterprise is, it is true, at an end; there remain none but the subordinate participators in the revolts, who are reduced by Henry IV., more by policy than by warlike achievements. To overcome this dearth of matter, Shakspeare was in the second part obliged to employ great art, as he never allowed himself to adorn history with more arbitrary embellishments than the dramatic form rendered indispensable. The piece is opened by confused rumours from the field of battle; the powerful impression produced by Percy's fall, whose name and reputation were peculiarly adapted to be the watchword of a bold enterprise, make him in some degree an acting personage after his death. The last acts are occupied with the dying king's remorse of conscience, his uneasiness at the behaviour of the prince, and lastly, the clearing up of the misunderstanding between father and son, which make up several most affecting scenes. All this, however, would still be inadequate to fill the stage, if the serious events were not interrupted by a comedy which runs through both parts of the play, which is enriched from time to time with new figures, and which first comes to its catastrophe at the conclusion of the whole, namely, when Henry V., immediately after ascending the throne, banishes to a proper distance the companions of his youthful excesses, who had promised to themselves a rich harvest from his kingly favour.

Falstaff is the crown of Shakspeare's comic invention. He has, without exhausting himself, continued this character throughout three plays, and exhibited him in every variety of situation; the figure is drawn so definitely and individually, that even to the mere reader it conveys the clear impression of personal acquaintance. Falstaff is the most agreeable and entertaining knave that ever was portrayed. His contemptible qualities are not disguised: old, lecherous, and dissolute; corpulent beyond measure, and always intent upon cherishing his body with eating, drinking, and sleeping; constantly in debt, and anything but conscientious in his choice of means by which money is to be raised; a cowardly soldier, and a lying braggart; a flatterer of his friends before their face, and a satirist behind their backs; and yet we are never disgusted with him. We see that his tender care of himself is without any mixture of malice towards others; he will only not be disturbed in the pleasant repose of his sensuality, and this he obtains through the activity of his understanding. Always on the alert, and good-humoured, ever ready to crack jokes on others, and to enter into those of which he is himself the subject, so that he justly boasts he is not only witty himself, but the cause of wit in others, he is an admirable companion for youthful idleness and levity. Under a helpless exterior, he conceals an extremely acute mind; he has always at command some dexterous turn whenever any of his free jokes begin to give displeasure; he is shrewd in his distinctions, between those whose favour he has to win and those over whom he may assume a familiar authority. He is so convinced that the part which he plays can only pass under the cloak of wit, that even when alone he is never altogether serious, but gives the drollest colouring in his love-intrigues, his intercourse with others, and to his own sensual philosophy. Witness his inimitable soliloquies on honour, on the influence of wine on bravery, his descriptions of the beggarly vagabonds whom he enlisted, of Justice Shallow, &c. Falstaff has about him a whole court of amusing caricatures, who by turns make their appearance, without ever throwing him into the shade. The adventure in which the Prince, under the disguise of a robber, compels him to give up the spoil which he had just taken; the scene where the two act the part of the King and the Prince; Falstaff's behaviour in the field, his mode of raising recruits, his patronage of Justice Shallow, which afterwards takes such an unfortunate turn:—all this forms a series of characteristic scenes of the most original description, full of pleasantry, and replete with nice and ingenious observation; such as could only find a place in a historical play like the present.—AUGUST WILHELM SCHLEGEL, *Lectures on Dramatic Art and Literature*, 1809, tr. John Black

'Twas in a tavern that with old age stooped
And leaned rheumatic rafters o'er his head—
A blowzed, prodigious man, which talked, and stared,
And rolled, as if with purpose, a small eye
Like a sweet Cupid in a cask of wine.
I could not view his fatness for his soul,
Which peeped like harmless lightnings and was gone;
As haps to voyagers of the summer air.
And when he laughed, Time trickled down those beams,
As in a glass; and when in self-defence
He puffed that paunch, and wagged that huge, Greek head,
Nosed like a Punchinello, then it seemed
An hundred widows swept in his small voice,
Now tenor, and now bass of drummy war.
He smiled, compact of loam, this orchard man;
Mused like a midnight, webbed with moonbeam snares
Of flitting Love; woke—and a King he stood,
Whom all the world hath in sheer jest refused
For helpless laughter's sake. And then, forfend!
Bacchus and Jove reared vast Olympus there;
And Pan leaned leering from Promethean eyes.
"Lord!" sighed his aspect, weeping o'er the jest,
"What simple mouse brought such a mountain forth?"
—WALTER DE LA MARE, "Falstaff," *Characters from Shakespeare*, 1902

---

## CORBYN MORRIS

### From *An Essay towards Fixing the True Standards of Wit, Humour, Raillery, Satire, and Ridicule*

#### 1744, pp. 23–29

Humour extensively and fully understood, is *any remarkable* Oddity *or* Foible *belonging to a* Person *in* real Life; *whether this* Foible *be constitutional, habitual, or only affected; whether partial in one or two Circumstances; or tinging the whole Temper and Conduct of the* Person.

It has from hence been observ'd, that there is more HUMOUR in the *English* Comedies than in others; as we have more various odd *Characters* in real Life, than any other Nation, or perhaps than all other Nations together.

That HUMOUR gives more Delight, and leaves a more pleasurable Impression behind it, than WIT, is universally felt and established; Though the Reasons for this have not yet been assign'd.—I shall therefore beg Leave to submit the following.

1. HUMOUR is more *interesting* than WIT in general, as the *Oddities* and *Foibles* of *Persons* in *real Life* are more apt to affect our Passions, than any Oppositions or Relations between *inanimate* Objects.

2. HUMOUR is *Nature*, or what really appears in the Subject, without any Embellishments; WIT only a Stroke of *Art*, where the original Subject, being insufficient of itself, is garnished and deck'd with auxiliary Objects.

3. HUMOUR, or the Foible of a *Character* in real Life, is usually insisted upon for some Length of Time. From whence, and from the common Knowledge of the Character, it is universally felt and understood.—Whereas the Strokes of WIT are like sudden *Flashes*, vanishing in an Instant, and usually flying too fast to be sufficiently marked and pursued by the Audience.

4. HUMOUR, if the Representation of it be just, is compleat and perfect in its Kind, and entirely fair and unstrain'd.—Whereas in the Allusions of WIT, the Affinity is generally imperfect and defective in one Part or other; and even in those Points where the Affinity may be allow'd to subsist, some Nicety and Strain is usually requir'd to make it appear.

5. HUMOUR generally appears in such Foibles, as each of the Company thinks himself superior to.—Whereas WIT shews the Quickness and Abilities of the Person who discovers it, and places him superior to the rest of the Company.

6. HUMOUR, in the Representation of the *Foibles* of *Persons* in *real Life*, frequently exhibits very *generous benevolent* Sentiments of Heart; And these, tho' exerted in a particular odd Manner, justly command our Fondness and Love.—Whereas in the Allusions of WIT, *Severity, Bitterness,* and *Satire,* are frequently exhibited.—And where these are avoided, not worthy amiable Sentiments of the *Heart,* but quick unexpected Efforts of the *Fancy,* are presented.

7. The odd Adventures, and Embarrassments, which *Persons* in *real Life* are drawn into by their *Foibles,* are fit Subjects of *Mirth.*—Whereas in pure WIT, the Allusions are rather *surprizing,* than *mirthful*; and the *Agreements* or *Contrasts* which are started between Objects, without any relation to the *Foibles* of *Persons* in real Life, are more fit to be *admired* for their *Happiness* and *Propriety,* than to excite our *Laughter.*—Besides, WIT, in the frequent Repetition of it, tires the Imagination with its precipitate Sallies and Flights; and teizes the Judgment.—Whereas HUMOUR, in the Representation of it, puts no Fatigue upon the *Imagination,* and gives exquisite Pleasure to the *Judgment.*

These seem to me to be the different Powers and Effects of HUMOUR and WIT. However, the most agreeable Representations or Compositions of all others, appear not where they *separately* exist, but where they are *united* together in the same Fabric; where HUMOUR is the *Ground-work* and chief Substance, and WIT happily spread, *quickens* the whole with Embellishments.

This is the Excellency of the *Character* of Sir *John Falstaff*; the *Ground-work* is Humour, or the Representation and Detection of a bragging and vaunting *Coward* in real Life; However, this alone would only have expos'd the *Knight,* as a meer *Noll Bluff,* to the Derision of the Company; And after they had once been gratify'd with his Chastisement, he would have sunk into Infamy, and become quite odious and intolerable: But here the inimitable *Wit* of Sir *John* comes in to his Support, and gives a new *Rise* and *Lustre* to his Character; For the sake of his *Wit* you forgive his *Cowardice*; or rather, are fond of his *Cowardice* for the Occasions it gives to his *Wit*. In short, the *Humour* furnishes a Subject and Spur to the *Wit*, and the *Wit* again supports and embellishes the *Humour*.

At the *first* Entrance of the *Knight*, your good Humour and Tendency to *Mirth* are irresistibly excited by his jolly Appearance and Corpulency; you feel and acknowledge him, to be the fittest Subject imaginable for yielding *Diversion* and *Merriment*; but when you see him immediately set up for *Enterprize* and *Activity*, with his evident *Weight* and *Unweildiness*, your Attention is all call'd forth, and you are eager to watch him to the End of his Adventures; Your Imagination pointing out with a full Scope his future Embarrassments. All the while as you accompany him forwards, he *heightens* your Relish for his future Disasters, by his happy Opinion of his own Sufficiency, and the gay Vaunts which he makes of his Talents and Accomplishments; so that at last when he falls into a Scrape, your Expectation is exquisitely gratify'd, and you have the full Pleasure of seeing all his trumpeted Honour laid in the Dust. When in the midst of his Misfortunes, instead of being utterly demolish'd and sunk, he rises again by the superior Force of his *Wit*, and begins a *new* Course with fresh Spirit and Alacrity; This excites you the more to *renew* the Chace, in full View of his *second* Defeat; out of which he recovers again, and triumphs with new Pretensions and Boastings. After this he immediately starts upon a *third* Race, and so on; continually detected and caught, and yet constantly extricating himself by his inimitable *Wit* and *Invention*; thus yielding a perpetual *Round* of Sport and Diversion.

Again, the genteel *Quality* of Sir *John* is of great Use in supporting his Character; It prevents his *sinking* too low after several of his Misfortunes; Besides, you allow him, in consequence of his *Rank* and *Seniority*, the Privilege to dictate, and take the Lead, and to rebuke others upon many Occasions; By this he is sav'd from appearing too *nauseous* and *impudent*. The good *Sense* which he possesses comes also to his Aid, and saves him from being *despicable*, by forcing your Esteem for his real Abilities.—Again, the *Privilege* you allow him of rebuking and checking others, when he assumes it with proper Firmness and Superiority, helps to *settle* anew, and *compose* his Character after an Embarrassment; And reduces in some measure the *Spirit* of the Company to a proper *Level*, before he sets out again upon a fresh Adventure;—without this, they would be kept continually *strain'd*, and *wound up* to the highest Pitch, without sufficient Relief and Diversity.

It may also deserve to be remark'd of *Falstaff*, that the *Figure* of his *Person* is admirably suited to the *Turn* of his *Mind*; so that there arises before you a perpetual *Allusion* from one to the other, which forms an incessant Series of *Wit*, whether they are in *Contrast* or *Agreement* together.—When he pretends to *Activity*, there is *Wit* in the *Contrast* between his *Mind* and his *Person*,—And *Wit* in their *Agreement*, when he triumphs in *Jollity*.

To compleat the whole,—you have in this Character of *Falstaff*, not only a free Course of *Humour*, supported and embellish'd with admirable *Wit*; but this *Humour* is of a Species the most *jovial* and *gay* in all Nature.—Sir *John Falstaff* possesses Generosity, Chearfulness, Alacrity, Invention, Frolic and Fancy superior to all other Men;—The *Figure* of his *Person* is the Picture of Jollity, Mirth, and Good-nature, and banishes at once all other Ideas from your Breast; He is

happy himself, and makes you happy.—If you examine him further, he has no Fierceness, Reserve, Malice or Peevishness lurking in his Heart; His Intentions are all pointed at innocent Riot and Merriment; Nor has the Knight any inveterate Design, except against *Sack*, and that too he *loves*.—If, besides this, he desires to pass for a Man of *Activity* and *Valour*, you can easily excuse so harmless a *Foible*, which yields you the highest Pleasure in its constant *Detection*.

If you put all these together, it is impossible to *hate* honest *Jack Falstaff*; If you observe them again, it is impossible to avoid *loving* him; He is the gay, the witty, the frolicsome, happy, and fat *Jack Falstaff*, the most delightful *Swaggerer* in all Nature.—You must *love* him for your *own* sake,—At the same time you cannot but *love* him for *his own* Talents; And when you have *enjoy'd* them, you cannot but *love* him in Gratitude;—He has nothing to disgust you, and every thing to give you Joy;—His *Sense* and his *Foibles* are equally directed to advance your Pleasure; And it is impossible to be tired or unhappy in his Company.

This *jovial* and *gay* Humour, without any thing *envious*, *malicious*, *mischievous*, or *despicable*, and continually *quicken'd* and adorn'd with *Wit*, yields that peculiar Delight, without any *Alloy*, which we all feel and acknowledge in *Falstaff*'s Company.

## HENRY MACKENZIE
### From *The Lounger*
### 1786

#### No. 68. May 20, 1786

That "Poet and Creator are the same," is equally allowed in criticism as in etymology; and that, without the powers of invention and imagination, nothing great or highly delightful in poetry can be achieved.

I have often thought that the same thing holds in some measure with regard to the reader as well as the writer of poetry. Without somewhat of a congenial imagination in the former, the works of the latter will afford a very inferior degree of pleasure. The mind of him who reads should be able to imagine what the productive fancy of the poet creates and presents to his view; to look on the world of fancy set before him with a native's eye, and to hear its language with a native's ear; to acknowledge its manners, to feel its passions, and to trace, with somewhat of an instinctive glance, those characters with which the poet has peopled it.

If in the perusal of any poet this is required, *Shakspeare*, of all poets, seems to claim it the most. Of all poets, Shakspeare appears to have possessed a fancy the most prolific, an imagination the most luxuriantly fertile. In this particular he has been frequently compared to *Homer*, though those who have drawn the parallel, have done it, I know not why, with a sort of distrust of their assertion. Did we not look at the Greek with that reverential awe which his antiquity impresses, I think we might venture to affirm, that in this respect the other is more than his equal. In invention of incident, in diversity of character, in assemblage of images, we can scarcely indeed conceive Homer to be surpassed; but in the mere creation of fancy, I can discover nothing in the *Iliad* that equals the *Tempest* or the *Macbeth* of Shakspeare. The machinery of Homer is indeed stupendous; but of that machinery the materials were known; or though it should be allowed that he added something to the mythology he found, yet still the language and the manners of his deities are merely the language and the manners of men. Of Shakspeare, the machinery may be said to be produced as well as combined by himself.—Some of the beings of whom it is composed, neither tradition nor romance afforded him; and of those whom he borrowed thence, he invented the language and the manners; language and manners peculiar to themselves, for which he could draw no analogy from mankind. Though formed by fancy, however, his personages are true to nature, and a reader of that pregnant imagination which I have mentioned above, can immediately decide on the justness of his conceptions; as he who beholds the masterly expression of certain portraits, pronounces with confidence on their likeness, though unacquainted with the persons from whom they were drawn.

But it is not only in those untried regions of magic or of witchery that the creative power of Shakspeare has exerted itself. By a very singular felicity of invention, he has produced, in the beaten field of ordinary life, characters of such perfect originality, that we look on them with no less wonder at his invention, than on those preternatural beings, which "are not of this earth;" and yet they speak a language so purely that of common society, that we have but to step abroad into the world to hear every expression of which it is composed. Of this sort is the character of *Falstaff*.

On the subject of this character I was lately discoursing with a friend, who is very much endowed with that critical imagination of which I have suggested the use in the beginning of this paper. The general import of his observations may form neither a useless nor unamusing field for speculation to my readers.

Though the character of Falstaff, said my friend, is of so striking a kind as to engross almost the whole attention of the audience, in the representation of the play in which it is first introduced; yet it was probably only a secondary and incidental object with Shakspeare in composing that play. He was writing a series of historical dramas, on the most remarkable events of the English history, from the time of King *John* downwards. When he arrived at the reign of *Henry* IV. the dissipated youth and extravagant pranks of the Prince of Wales could not fail to excite his attention, as affording at once a source of moral reflection in the serious department, and a fund of infinite humour in the comic part of the drama. In providing him with associates for his hours of folly and of riot, he probably borrowed, as was his custom, from some old play, interlude, or story, the names and incidents which he has used in the first part of *Henry* IV. *Oldcastle*, we know, was the name of a character in such a play, inserted there, it is probable (in those days of the church's omnipotence in every department of writing), in odium of Sir John Oldcastle, chief of the *Lollards*, though Shakspeare afterward, in a Protestant reign, changed it to Falstaff. This leader of the gang, which the wanton extravagance of the Prince was to cherish and protect, it was necessary to endow with qualities sufficient to make the young Henry, in his society,

doff the world aside,
And bid it pass.

Shakspeare therefore has endowed him with infinite wit and humour, as well as an admirable degree of sagacity and acuteness in observing the characters of men; but has joined those qualities with a grossness of mind, which his youthful master could not but see, nor seeing but despise. With talents less conspicuous, Falstaff could not have attracted Henry; with profligacy less gross and less contemptible, he would have attached him too much. Falstaff's was just "that unyoked humour of idleness," which the Prince could "a while uphold," and then cast off for ever. The audience to which this strange compound was to be exhibited were to be in the same predicament with the Prince, to laugh and to admire while

they despised; to feel the power of his humour, the attraction of his wit, the justice of his reflections, while their contempt and their hatred attended the lowness of his manners, the grossness of his pleasures, and the unworthiness of his vice.

Falstaff is truly and literally "ex Epicuri grege porcus," placed here within the pale of this world to fatten at his leisure, neither disturbed by feeling nor restrained by virtue. He is not, however, positively much a villain, though he never starts aside in the pursuit of interest or of pleasure, when knavery comes in his way. We feel contempt, therefore, and not indignation, at his crimes, which rather promotes than hinders our enjoying the ridicule of the situation, and the admirable wit with which he expresses himself in it. As a man of this world, he is endowed with the most superior degree of good sense and discernment of character; his conceptions, equally acute and just, he delivers with the expression of a clear and vigorous understanding; and we see that he thinks like a wise man, even when he is not at the pains to talk wisely.

Perhaps, indeed, there is no quality more conspicuous throughout the writings of Shakspeare, than that of good sense, that intuitive sagacity with which he looks on the manners, the characters, and the pursuits, of mankind. The bursts of passion, the strokes of nature, the sublimity of his terrors, and the wonderful creation of his fancy, are those excellences which strike spectators the most, and are therefore most commonly enlarged on; but to an attentive peruser of his writings, his acute perception and accurate discernment of ordinary character and conduct; that skill, if I may so express it, with which he delineates the plan of common life, will, I think, appear no less striking, and perhaps rather more wonderful; more wonderful, because we cannot so easily conceive that power of genius by which it tells us what actually exists, though it has never seen it, than that by which it creates what never existed. This power, when we read the works, and consider the situation, of Shakspeare we shall allow him in a most extraordinary degree. The delineation of manners found in the Greek tragedians is excellent and just; but it consists chiefly of those general maxims which the wisdom of the schools might inculcate, which a borrowed experience might teach. That of Shakspeare marks the knowledge of intimacy with mankind. It reaches the elevation of the great, and penetrates the obscurity of the low; detects the cunning, and overtakes the bold; in short, presents that abstract of life in all its modes, and indeed in every time, which every one without experience must believe, and every one with experience must know to be true.

With this sagacity and penetration into the characters and motives of mankind, which himself possessed, Shakspeare has invested Falstaff in a remarkable degree; he never utters it, however out of character, or at a season where it might better be spared. Indeed his good sense is rather in his thoughts than in his speech; for so we may call those soliloquies in which he generally utters it. He knew what coin was most current with those he dealt with, and fashioned his discourse according to the disposition of his hearers; and he sometimes lends himself to the ridicule of his companions when he has a chance of getting any interest on the loan.

But we oftener laugh with than at him; for his humour is infinite, and his wit admirable. This quality, however, still partakes in him of that epicurean grossness which I have remarked to be the ruling characteristic of his disposition. He has neither the vanity of a wit, nor the singularity of a humourist, but indulges both talents, like any other natural propensity, without exertion of mind or warmth of enjoyment. A late excellent actor, whose loss the stage will long regret, used to represent the character of *Falstaff* in a manner different from what had been uniformly adopted from the time of *Quin* downwards. He exchanged the comic gravity of the old school, for those bursts of laughter in which sympathetic audiences have so often accompanied him. From accompanying him it was indeed impossible to refrain; yet, though the execution was masterly, I cannot agree in that idea of the character. He who laughs, is a man of feeling in merriment." Falstaff was of a very different constitution. He turned wit, as he says he did "disease, into commodity."—"Oh! it is much, that a lie with a slight oath, and a *jest with a sad brow*, will do with a fellow that never had the ache in his shoulders."

### No. 69. *May 27, 1786*

To a man of pleasure of such a constitution as Falstaff, temper and good humour were necessarily consequent. We find him therefore but once, I think, angry, and then not provoked beyond measure. He conducts himself with equal moderation towards others; his wit lightens, but does not burn; and he is not more inoffensive when the joker, than unoffended when joked upon: "I am not only witty myself, but the cause that wit is in other men." In the evenness of his humour he bears himself thus (to use his own expression), and takes in the points of all assailants without being hurt. The language of contempt, of rebuke, or of conviction, neither puts him out of liking with himself or with others. None of his passions rise beyond this control of reason, of self-interest, or of indulgence.

Queen Elizabeth, with a curiosity natural to a woman, desired Shakspeare to exhibit Falstaff as a lover: he obeyed her, and wrote the *Merry Wives of Windsor*; but Falstaff's love is only factor for his interests, and he wishes to make his mistresses "his Exchequer, his East and West Indies, to both of which he will trade."

Though I will not go so far as a paradoxical critic has done, and ascribe valour to Falstaff; yet if his cowardice is fairly examined, it will be found to be not so much a weakness as a principle. In his very cowardice there is much of the sagacity I have remarked in him; he has the sense of danger, but not the discomposure of fear. His presence of mind saves him from the sword of Douglas, where the danger was real; but he shews no sort of dread of the sheriff's visit; when he knew the Prince's company would probably bear him out; when Bardolph runs in frightened, and tells, that the sheriff, with a most monstrous watch, is at the door. "Out, you rogue! (answers he,) play out the play; I have much to say in behalf of that Falstaff." Falstaff's cowardice is only proportionate to the danger; and so would every wise man's be, did not other feelings make him valiant.

Such feelings, it is the very characteristic of Falstaff to want. The dread of disgrace, the sense of honour, and the love of fame, he neither feels, nor pretends to feel:

Like the fat weed
That roots itself at ease on Lethe's wharf,

he is contented to repose on that earthly corner of sensual indulgence in which his fate has placed him, and enjoys the pleasures of the moment, without once regarding those finer objects of delight which the children of fancy and of feeling so warmly pursue.

The greatest refinement of morals, as well as of minds, is produced by the culture and exercise of the imagination, which derives, or is taught to derive, its objects of pursuit, and its motives of action, not from the senses merely, but from future considerations which fancy anticipates and realizes. Of this either as the prompter, or the restraint of conduct, Falstaff is utterly devoid; yet his imagination is wonderfully quick and creative in the pictures of humour and the associations of wit. But the "pregnancy of his wit," according to his own phrase, "is made a tapster;" and his fancy, how vivid soever, still subjects itself to the grossness of those sensual conceptions which are familiar to his mind. We are astonished at that art by which Shakspeare leads the powers of genius, imagination, and wisdom, into captivity to this son of earth; 'tis as if, transported into the enchanted island in the *Tempest*, we saw the rebellion of *Caliban* successful, and the airy spirits of *Prospero* ministering to the brutality of his slave.

Hence, perhaps, may be derived great part of that infinite amusement which succeeding audiences have always found from the representation of Falstaff. We have not only the enjoyment of those combinations, and of that contrast, to which philosophers have ascribed the pleasure we derive from wit in general, but we have that singular combination and contrast which the gross, the sensual, and the brutish mind of Falstaff exhibits, when joined and compared with that admirable power of invention, of wit, and of humour, which his conversation perpetually displays.

In the immortal work of *Cervantes*, we find a character with a remarkable mixture of wisdom and absurdity, which in one page excites our highest ridicule, and in the next is entitled to our highest respect. *Don Quixote*, like Falstaff, is endowed with excellent discernment, sagacity, and genius; but his good sense holds fief of his diseased imagination, of his over-ruling madness for the achievements of knight-errantry, for heroic valour and heroic love. The ridicule in the character of Don Quixote consists in raising low and vulgar incidents, through the medium of his disordered fancy, to a rank of importance, dignity, and solemnity, to which in their nature they are the most opposite that can be imagined. With Falstaff it is nearly the reverse; the ridicule is produced by subjecting wisdom, honour, and other the most grave and dignified principles, to the control of grossness, buffoonery, and folly. 'Tis like the pastime of a family-masquerade, where laughter is equally excited by dressing clowns as gentlemen, or gentlemen as clowns. In Falstaff, the heroic attributes of our nature are made to wear the garb of meanness and absurdity. In Don Quixote, the common and the servile are clothed in the dresses of the dignified and the majestic; while, to heighten the ridicule, *Sancho*, in the half-deceived simplicity, and the half-discerning shrewdness, of his character, is every now and then employed to pull off the mask.

If you would not think me whimsical in the parallel, continued my friend, I should say, that Shakespeare has drawn, in one of his immediately subsequent plays, a tragic character very much resembling the comic one of Falstaff, I mean that of *Richard* III. Both are men of the world, both possess that sagacity and understanding which is fitted for its purposes, both despise those refined feelings, those motives of delicacy, those restraints of virtue, which might obstruct the course they have marked out for themselves. The hypocrisy of both costs them nothing, and they never feel that detection of it to themselves which rankles in the consciences of less determined hypocrites. Both use the weaknesses of others, as skilful players at a game do the ignorance of their opponents; they enjoy the advantage, not only without self-reproach, but with the pride of superiority. Richard, indeed, aspires to the crown of England because Richard is wicked and ambitious: Falstaff is contented with a thousand pounds of Justice Shallow's; because he is only luxurious and dissipated. Richard courts Lady Ann and the Princess Elizabeth for his purposes: Falstaff makes love to Mrs. Ford and Mrs. Page for his. Richard is witty like Falstaff, and talks of his own figure with the same sarcastic indifference.

Indeed so much does Richard, in the higher walk of villany, resemble Falstaff in the lower region of roguery and dissipation, that it were not difficult to shew in the dialogue of the two characters, however dissimilar in situation, many passages and expressions in a style of remarkable resemblance.

Of feeling and even of passion, both characters are very little susceptible: as Falstaff is the knave and the sensualist, so Richard is the villain of principle. Shakspeare has drawn one of passion in the person of *Macbeth*. Macbeth produces horror, fear, and sometimes pity; Richard detestation and abhorrence only. The first he has led amidst the gloom of sublimity, has shewn agitated by various and wavering emotions. He is sometimes more sanguinary than Richard, because he is not insensible of the weakness or the passion of revenge; whereas the cruelty of Richard is only proportionate to the object of his ambition, as the cowardice of Falstaff is proportionate to the object of his fear; but the bloody and revengeful Macbeth is yet susceptible of compassion and subject to remorse. In contemplating Macbeth, we often regret the perversion of his nature; and even when the justice of Heaven overtakes him, we almost forget our hatred at his enormities, in our pity for his misfortunes. Richard, Shakspeare has placed amidst the tangled paths of party and ambition, has represented cunning and fierce from his birth, untouched by the sense of humanity, hardly subject to remorse, and never to contrition; and his fall produces that unmixed and perfect satisfaction which we feel at the death of some savage beast that had desolated the country from instinctive fierceness and natural malignity.

The weird sisters, the gigantic deities of northern mythology, are fit agents to form Macbeth. Richard is the production of those worldly and creeping demons, who slide upon the earth their instruments of mischief to embroil and plague mankind. Falstaff is the work of *Circe*, and her swinish associates, who in some favoured hour of revelry and riot, moulded this compound of gross debauchery, acute discernment, admirable invention, and nimble wit, and sent him for a consort to England's madcap Prince; to stamp currency on idleness and vice, and to wave the flag of folly and dissipation over the seats of gravity, of wisdom, and of virtue.

## WILLIAM HAZLITT
### From *"Henry IV."*
### *Characters of Shakespear's Plays*
### 1817

I f Shakespear's fondness for the ludicrous sometimes led to faults in his tragedies (which was not often the case) he has made us amends by the character of Falstaff. This is perhaps the most substantial comic character that ever was invented. Sir John carries a most portly presence in the mind's eye; and in him, not to speak it profanely, 'we behold the fulness of the spirit of wit and humour bodily.' We are as well acquainted with his person as his mind, and his jokes come upon us with double force and relish from the quantity of flesh through which they make their way, as he shakes his fat sides with laughter, or 'lards the lean earth as he walks along.' Other comic characters seem, if we approach and handle them, to resolve themselves into air, 'into thin air'; but this is embodied and palpable to the grossest apprehension: it lies 'three fingers deep upon the ribs,' it plays about the lungs and the diaphragm with all the force of animal enjoyment. His body is like a good estate to his mind, from which he receives rents and revenues of profit and pleasure in kind, according to its extent, and the richness of the soil. Wit is often a meagre substitute for pleasurable sensation; an effusion of spleen and petty spite at

the comforts of others, from feeling none in itself. Falstaff's wit is an emanation of a fine constitution; an exuberance of good-humour and good-nature; an overflowing of his love of laughter and good-fellowship; a giving vent to his heart's ease, and over-contentment with himself and others. He would not be in character, if he were not so fat as he is; for there is the greatest keeping in the boundless luxury of his imagination and the pampered self-indulgence of his physical appetites. He manures and nourishes his mind with jests, as he does his body with sack and sugar. He carves out his jokes, as he would a capon or a haunch of venison, where there is *cut and come again*; and pours out upon them the oil of gladness. His tongue drops fatness, and in the chambers of his brain 'it snows of meat and drink.' He keeps up perpetual holiday and open house, and we live with him in a round of invitations to a rump and dozen.—Yet we are not to suppose that he was a mere sensualist. All this is as much in imagination as in reality. His sensuality does not engross and stupify his other faculties, but 'ascends me into the brain, clears away all the dull, crude vapours that environ it, and makes it full of nimble, fiery, and delectable shapes.' His imagination keeps up the ball after his senses have done with it. He seems to have even a greater enjoyment of the freedom from restraint, of good cheer, of his ease, of his vanity, in the ideal exaggerated description which he gives of them, than in fact. He never fails to enrich his discourse with allusions to eating and drinking, but we never see him at table. He carries his own larder about with him, and he is himself 'a tun of man.' His pulling out the bottle in a field of battle is a joke to shew his contempt for glory accompanied with danger, his systematic adherence to his Epicurean philosophy in the most trying circumstances. Again, such is his deliberate exaggeration of his own vices, that it does not seem quite certain whether the account of his hostess's bill, found in his pocket, with such an out-of-the-way charge for capons and sack with only one halfpenny-worth of bread, was not put there by himself as a trick to humour the jest upon his favourite propensities, and as a conscious caricature of himself. He is represented as a liar, a braggart, a coward, a glutton, etc. and yet we are not offended but delighted with him; for he is all these as much to amuse others as to gratify himself. He openly assumes all these characters to shew the humourous part of them. The unrestrained indulgence of his own ease, appetites, and convenience, has neither malice nor hypocrisy in it. In a word, he is an actor in himself almost as much as upon the stage, and we no more object to the character of Falstaff in a moral point of view than we should think of bringing an excellent comedian, who should represent him to the life, before one of the police offices. We only consider the number of pleasant lights in which he puts certain foibles (the more pleasant as they are opposed to the received rules and necessary restraints of society) and do not trouble ourselves about the consequences resulting from them, for no mischievous consequences do result. Sir John is old as well as fat, which gives a melancholy retrospective tinge to the character; and by the disparity between his inclinations and his capacity for enjoyment, makes it still more ludicrous and fantastical.

The secret of Falstaff's wit is for the most part a masterly presence of mind, an absolute self-possession, which nothing can disturb. His repartees are involuntary suggestions of his self-love; instinctive evasions of every thing that threatens to interrupt the career of his triumphant jollity and self-complacency. His very size floats him out of all his difficulties in a sea of rich conceits; and he turns round on the pivot of his convenience, with every occasion and at a moment's warning. His natural repugnance to every unpleasant thought or circumstance, of itself makes light of objections, and provokes the most extravagant and licentious answers in his own justification. His indifference to truth puts no check upon his invention, and the more improbable and unexpected his contrivances are, the more happily does he seem to be delivered of them, the anticipation of their effect acting as a stimulus to the gaiety of his fancy. The success of one adventurous sally gives him spirits to undertake another: he deals always in round numbers, and his exaggerations and excuses are 'open, palpable, monstrous as the father that begets them.' . . .

One of the topics of exulting superiority over others most common in Sir John's mouth is his corpulence and the exterior marks of good living which he carries about him, thus 'turning his vices into commodity.' He accounts for the friendship between the Prince and Poins, from 'their legs being both of a bigness'; and compares Justice Shallow to 'a man made after supper of a cheese-paring.' There cannot be a more striking gradation of character than that between Falstaff and Shallow, and Shallow and Silence. It seems difficult at first to fall lower than the squire; but this fool, great as he is, finds an admirer and humble foil in his cousin Silence. Vain of his acquaintance with Sir John, who makes a butt of him, he exclaims, 'Would, cousin Silence, that thou had'st seen that which this knight and I have seen!'—'Aye, Master Shallow, we have heard the chimes at midnight,' says Sir John. To Falstaff's observation 'I did not think Master Silence had been a man of this mettle,' Silence answers, 'Who, I? I have been merry twice and once ere now.' What an idea is here conveyed of a prodigality of living? What good husbandry and economical self-denial in his pleasures? What a stock of lively recollections? It is curious that Shakespear has ridiculed in Justice Shallow, who was 'in some authority under the king,' that disposition to unmeaning tautology which is the regal infirmity of later times, and which, it may be supposed, he acquired from talking to his cousin Silence, and receiving no answers.

> *Falstaff:* You have here a goodly dwelling, and a rich.
> *Shallow:* Barren, barren, barren; beggars all, beggars all, Sir John: marry, good air. Spread Davy, spread Davy. Well said, Davy.
> *Falstaff:* This Davy serves you for good uses.
> *Shallow:* A good varlet, a good varlet, a very good varlet. By the mass, I have drank too much sack at supper. A good varlet. Now sit down, now sit down. Come, cousin.

The true spirit of humanity, the thorough knowledge of the stuff we are made of, the practical wisdom with the seeming fooleries in the whole of the garden-scene at Shallow's country-seat, and just before in the exquisite dialogue between him and Silence on the death of old Double, have no parallel any where else. In one point of view, they are laughable in the extreme; in another they are equally affecting, if it is affecting to shew *what a little thing is human life*, what a poor forked creature man is!

The heroic and serious part of these two plays founded on the story of Henry IV. is not inferior to the comic and farcical. The characters of Hotspur and Prince Henry are two of the most beautiful and dramatic, both in themselves and from contrast, that ever were drawn. They are the essence of chivalry. We like Hotspur the best upon the whole, perhaps because he was unfortunate.—The characters of their fathers, Henry IV. and old Northumberland, are kept up equally well. Henry naturally succeeds by his prudence and caution in keeping what he has got; Northumberland fails in his enterprise from an excess of the same quality, and is caught in the web of

his own cold, dilatory policy. Owen Glendower is a masterly character. It is as bold and original as it is intelligible and thoroughly natural. The disputes between him and Hotspur are managed with infinite address and insight into nature. We cannot help pointing out here some very beautiful lines, where Hotspur describes the fight between Glendower and Mortimer.

> When on the gentle Severn's sedgy bank,
> In single opposition hand to hand,
> He did confound the best part of an hour
> In changing hardiment with great Glendower:
> Three times they breath'd, and three times did they
>       drink,
> Upon agreement, of swift Severn's flood;
> Who then affrighted with their bloody looks,
> Ran fearfully among the trembling reeds,
> And hid his crisp head in the hollow bank,
> Blood-stained with these valiant combatants.

The peculiarity and the excellence of Shakespear's poetry is, that it sems as if he made his imagination the hand-maid of nature, and nature the plaything of his imagination. He appears to have been all the characters, and in all the situations he describes. It is as if either he had had all their feelings, or had lent them all his genius to express themselves. There cannot be stronger instances of this than Hotspur's rage when Henry IV. forbids him to speak to Mortimer, his insensibility to all that his father and uncle urge to calm him, and his fine abstracted apostrophe to honour, 'By heaven methinks it were an easy leap to pluck bright honour from the moon,' etc. After all, notwithstanding the gallantry, generosity, good temper, and idle freaks of the mad-cap Prince of Wales, we should not have been sorry, if Northumberland's force had come up in time to decide the fate of the battle at Shrewsbury; at least, we always heartily sympathise with Lady Percy's grief, when she exclaims,

> Had my sweet Harry had but half their numbers,
> To-day might I (hanging on Hotspur's neck)
> Have talked of Monmouth's grave.

The truth is, that we never could forgive the Prince's treatment of Falstaff; though perhaps Shakespear knew what was best, according to the history, the nature of the times, and of the man. We speak only as dramatic critics. Whatever terror the French in those days might have of Henry v. yet, to the readers of poetry at present, Falstaff is the better man of the two. We think of him and quote him oftener.

## HENRY GILES
### From "Falstaff: A Type of Epicurean Life"
### *Lectures and Essays*
### 1850, Volume 1, pp. 29–44

Falstaff is an Epicurean, after the lowest interpretation of Epicurus; and such is the least evil form of character, which springs from mere intellect combined with the senses. Where moral principles and sympathy are inactive, it is well that irritable and ambitious passions should be so likewise, or a great intellect would become a great scourge. Indolence, therefore, and self-indulgence, sets limits to energies which would scarcely be used aright, and the love of ease becomes a safeguard against talents which the love of power would make a curse. Falstaff is of those who value each moment by what it confers of palpable enjoyment; of those who say, Let us eat and drink, for to-morrow we die; and he acted out his philosophy consistently and completely. He is true to his creed, and his practice fulfills it to the letter. He is honest and open, too, in its profession. Beyond the boundary of the actual, Falstaff discerns no reality. Out from the region of the senses he appreciates no means of happiness. Within this boundary all being exists for him; beyond it are only emptiness and death. A spiritual order of things has no hold on his convictions; and the future, which is to survive his animal economy, has no influence on his feelings. He has therefore no *sentiment*. He laughs at it. He derides it. Chivalry is to him mere vanity; glory a worthless phantom. Daring, in his view, is hot-brained folly. Danger is always to be avoided, and never to be sought. After feigning death at Shrewsbury, he thus soliloquizes: "Counterfeit? I lie. I am no counterfeit; for he is but the counterfeit of a man, who has not the life of a man; but to counterfeit dying when a man thereby liveth, is to be no counterfeit, but the true and perfect image of life indeed. The better part of valor is, discretion; in the which better part I have saved my life." His reflections upon "honor" are conceived in the same absorbing materialism: "Can honor set a leg? No. Honor hath no skill in surgery, then. What is honor? A word. What is in that word honor? Air; a trim reckoning. Who hath it? He that died o' Wednesday. Doth he feel it? No. Doth he hear it? No. Is it insensible, then? Yea, to the dead. But will it not live with the living? No. Why? Detraction will not suffer it. Therefore, I'll none of it."

Falstaff has little sympathy. He loves none, and he cares for few. He is luxuriously selfish. Constant indulgence of the passions blunts every finer sensibility, and extinguishes generosity of character. The affections are narrowed by depravity, and all that corrupts the moral nature, contracts the social. The voluptuary is by necessity selfish, and the gifted voluptuary effectively so. The vouptuary of talents is selfish by instinct, and selfish by ability; by instinct he pursues merely his own gratification, and by ability he makes others the instruments of it. Thus it is with Falstaff. All are for his use, and, except for that, he esteems them of no value. The prince is to supply his money; Dame Quickly is to provide his food; the page is for his service; and Bardolf for his jests.

Seeing that so much of the selfish and the heartless enters into this character, why is it not more odious to us? The fact is, the brilliant qualities alone of Falstaff render him attractive; and his vicious ones are not directly or aforethought inhuman. He is not in earnest for any thing; he has no enthusiasm; he admires nothing; he covets merely to live jovially, and to live at ease. Companions to his wish around him, fare to his taste before him; plenty of sack, and a sea-coal fire; no disturbances from justices or duns; and he would have the best Elysium he could conceive or picture. He does not love any, neither does he hate any. If he is wanting in affection, he is also void of malice. It is from this conviction that we tolerate him; that we laugh at his jokes, and revel in the prodigality of his fancy. Did we feel in him any positive inhumanity, his jokes would disgust, and his fancy would revolt us. And, besides, selfish though he be, there is a sort of rude friendliness about him. Though he *uses* Bardolf, he does not *abuse* him. Even when he is most exacting, he pays back more than he receives, in the humor and the wit by which he diversifies the lives of those who serve him; and this he seems to know most thoroughly, and not to set it any whit below its value. He is often grotesque, but he is never tryannical; and between himself and the page there goes on a strain of playfulness, in which his rollicking jokes appear to conceal an underlying vein of gentleness and tenderness. He is a big, fat, easy-going, easy-living man; who is not unkind, but *will* be indulged; who can bear much scolding, and yet is liked by those who scold him the loudest and with the most justice; a jovial, joyous, care-hating man, who will not

beg pardon of the world for being in it; and who, moreover, thinks that the world ought to keep him well while it has him.

As it is, then, we take him for what he is, and accept the pleasure he affords. He does not arouse our antipathies, and he does not falsify our expectations. He is open and clear to our view, and we know him as he is; we do not look for moral greatness in him, as we do not require him to walk a thousand miles successively in a thousand hours. We should never mistake him for a peripatetic philosopher, and we feel no anger because he is not. As little should we mistake him for a patriot or a philanthropist. We should have had no hope, did he live in our age, to see him volunteer in the Greek war, or a missionary to the heathens of India. We should despair to move his heart to subscribe to the Bible Society. Believing merely in this world, he would have no care beyond his own term of possession. With the Irishman in the house on fire, he would probably exclaim, What is it to me? I am but a tenant. Go to, go to, (he would say,) annoy me not with these vain disturbances; let your melancholy bipeds take such things in charge; let your lean folks see to them; let your restless, attenuated apologies for humanity, that have no appetite and no digestion, busy themselves with your spiritual irritations; but leave an honest man in peace, who understands what is good, and who knows how to use it.

To lay aside levity of expression, earnest purpose is foreign to characters of the Falstaff order. Seriousness, for good or evil, is no part of their nature; and if we laugh at their wit, it is with no approbation of their vices. We may relax with the indolent, and yet not depart from the worthy; we may contemplate a phase of human nature, and though we do not resist the mirth which it excites, neither need we turn from it without some addition to our wisdom.

And this remark applies, I think, with very peculiar force to any intelligent reflection on the character of Falstaff. What a mornful condition of humanity is presented to us in the debasement of talent to the appetites! Behold it in the picture set before us in Falstaff! Look at that gray-headed, gray-bearded old man, lolling, bloated on the dregs of life; the desires insatiate as strength declines; the senses gross, while a brilliant imagination flows in radiance over them, as the sun upon a morass; abilities, which might have exalted empires, devoted to the cooking of a capon or the merits of a sack posset; eloquence and wit lavished upon blackguards; law, honor, courage, chastity, made a jest. Laugh, it is true, you must; but, when you have laughed, turn back and think; and after thinking, you will admit that tragedy itself has not any thing more sad.

In the character of Falstaff there is a foregone conclusion, upon which every thoughtful mind will dwell. He is presented to us an old man, "written down old, with all the characters of age." We have, therefore, before us the last stage of a life, and we have its ultimate result. Were we to meet, in actual intercourse, a man with the genius and habits of Falstaff, we would know that a miserable experience lay behind it. The brilliant wit of the antiquated libertine might, for a moment, cause us to forget the purpose of existence, but soon, the bloated spectre would become to us its most solemn memento. Much, we would know, of excellent living material had been spoiled, ere the ruin which we gazed on, could exist. There was a youth to this old age. We are sure that commanding abilities enriched it, for, even in their last abuse, these abilities are yet commanding; and truth, as it is now, could not always have been a jest. By what process, we would ask, has the noble been changed into the base? By a process, alas, too often repeated ever to be strange! There was fine judgment, but it was not under the guidance of rectitude. There was imagination, but it was not chastened by purity. There was sensibility, but it fell amidst grosser pleasures, and among them it was smothered. The merely intellectual faculties kept their supremacy, and the passions went from strength to strength. In the midst of boon companions, the royalty of sheer mind was acknowledged. The discourse of a strong reason compelled respect, even through the shoutings of revelry. The corruscations of a fire-lit fancy played among the broken clouds of nightly orgies, and tinted their ragged fringes with golden light. Days there were, which excitement shortened, and nights which gaiety prolonged. While the senses had the delusion of an immortality in youth, pleasure appeared perennial; it seemed to have a fairness which could never wither, to flourish with a summer bloom which no frost could chill. Years wore on, the physical powers grew sluggish, and the mental powers selfish. At this stage of his course, let us suppose that we have such a person in the character of Falstaff. He has come to a dishonored and to a comfortless age. The world owes him no reverence. Mankind is indebted to such a man for nothing but his example; and, for his example, only as a warning. He has been untrue to the affections, and now he has no affections true to him. Old, unwieldy, infirm, wifeless, childless, friendless, he is at last alone, among the dishonest and the false.

A sad life is that which is called a life of pleasure; and it is immeasurably sad when the sons of genius enslave themselves to it. How often must remorse appal them! What alternations to them of anguish and lassitude! What nights of madness, and what days of sorrow! Oh, how terrible to think of the past, when the past is an ocean overhung with darkness, and the shipwrecked faculties tossed in fragments upon its waves! Take into your mental view some voluptuary, who might have been an ornament to his species, but whom the infatuation of the senses has destroyed. Behold him in a moment of repentance, and in solitude. Mark the wretchedness of his face, and the convulsions of his breast. Look at him in his joyless home, where ruin is gathering to its last desolation, where hearts are throbbing which must soon be broken. For a little, the man, the generous, the loving man, seems to triumph in his nature; a new life seems to spring forth in his weeping, the return of an alienated heart to its allegiance, of a wandering soul to its peace, and a light of joy begins to overspread his dwelling. Watch him again encircled by his companions; watch him, amused by the clashings of intoxicated eloquence; whirled in the mazes of a delirious imagination; the fatal spell comes over him again; he gives himself to the trance with his eyes open, and the next time he awakes, he awakes to his perdition.

The law of compensation operates with certainty, and it operates impartially. To this solemn fact our great dramatist is ever faithful. This august poet of conscience and the heart, this wonderful revealer of the passions and their struggles, this moralist of insight, almost of inspiration, never forgets the eternal principles of right and wrong. In Falstaff, even as in Macbeth, Shakspeare vindicates these principles. Falstaff is loosely related to other men; other men are, therefore, loosely related to him. He does not reap attachment where he has only sown indifference. His creed is turned on himself. He has no faith in excellence, and he gets no credit for possessing any. His practice is retorted as well as his creed. He uses his inferiors, and his superiors use *him*. They give him their presence when it is their desire to be amused, but they discard him as a worn rag when gaiety is no longer seemly. Falstaff occasions mirth, but does not gain esteem. He adds to the brightness of the revel, but when the revel is over he is paid by no gratitude. For the vile there can be no esteem. Esteem cannot be where there

is no confidence; and there can be no confidence where there is no respect. The pure cannot have respect for the vicious; and the vicious have no respect for each other. Their association precludes all reverence, for it is a cohesion in common infamy. They tolerate each other upon a mutual suppression of moral distinctions; but there are times, when the bad appear to the bad more detestable than they possibly can to the upright. The upright look not on the worst of their brethren without a touch of mercy; but the bad, under the laceration of their crimes, glare upon their compeers with unmitigated horror. The bonds which keep them together are as fragile as they are corrupt, and when low interest or depraved gratification is exhausted, always easy to be severed. The vicissitude which breaks up the combination finds in every brother of it a traitor or an enemy. When once, therefore, a man plunges into a gross existence, he will, in time, discover that even the lowest will not do him reverence. He will be rejected by the persons who basked in the radiance of his fancy, and who were electrified by the flashes of his wit. Approbation is not for great talents, but for good works. Wages belong to the laborer, not to the idler, and much less to the spendthrift. It is no matter for praise that a man has a strong intellect, which is active only in debasement; that he has an affluence of imagination, which is squandered in corruption; that he has a rich faculty of eloquence, which is dumb on every generous theme; and absent from all worthy places, which is only to be heard among inebriate debaters, and is only to be aroused by maudlin applause. No glory is for this man but shame, and shame the more burning for his genius.

The end of Falstaff may stand as a type for the close of every such life. It was without regret and without honor. There is no life so melancholy in its close, as that of a licentious wit. The companions with whom he jested abandon him; the hope of the visible world is gone, and, in the spiritual, he has no refuge. Utterly impoverished in all means of amusement and comfort, he is thrown entirely on himself; and, when he can least bear to be alone, he is delivered over to unmitigated solitude. Pleasure was the bond by which he held his former associates, and by affliction that bond is broken. The gay assembly takes no thought of him, and the place therein shall know him no more. Instead of the hilarious looks which were wont to beam around him, a crowd of ghastly images are flitting in his solitary room; instead of a board groaning under the weight of the feast, a couch is made hard with the pressure of disease; instead of the blaze of many lights, there is the dimness of a single taper; and for the song and the viol, there are the moanings of death.

Laurence Sterne had sentiment, which was often expressed with the most delicate tenderness, but he debased the finest of humor by the grossest of ribaldry. He scattered about him the wit of Rabelais, and his filth also; but when his brilliant career was run, there were none to cheer him at the end. "The last offices," Sir Walter Scott tells us, "were rendered him, not in his own house, or by kindred affection, but in an inn, and by strangers." Sir Walter also remarks, that Sterne's death strikingly resembled Falstaff's. Brinsley Sheridan was, like Falstaff, companion to a Prince of Wales. He was, also, like Falstaff, "a fellow of infinite jest, of most excellent fancy." He lavished upon this heir of kings the bounties of his humor and his eloquence, and in return for such wealth, the heir of kings abandoned the donor. When the lights went out upon the banquet, the man who threw the glory over it was no more remembered. But, when the frame sickened and the soul drooped, no royalty was at hand; when the eye had no more the lustre of wit, it looked in vain for brothers of the feast; when lips, from which there once flew winged words, feebly stammered titled names, none who bore those names were present to hear. The spendthrift, both in property and talents, was left alone with fate; and while eternity was opening for his spirit, the bailiffs were watching for his corpse.

The late Theodore Hook had vast capacities for amusing, and he, too, was a favorite with nobles and with princes. His repartees banished dullness from their parties, and his pen was the slave of their order. He was equally the champion of their politics, and the glory of their dinner tables. He was, in fact, a wit of all-work in aristocratic houses. He played, jested, conversed; tried, by every device, to make himself generally useful to his entertainers, and he was not unsuccessful. His brain was a storehouse of combustibles, out of which he played off intellectual fire-works in every caprice of oddity; his listless spectators gazed and admired, retired when the exhibition was over, and forgot the show. Meanwhile, secret wretchedness was devouring this man's life, and outward ruin was collecting on his head. He had gone through the experience of his class; he outran his means, depended on those whom he had amused, and found it was reliance upon a vapor. His comicry was all they wanted; they could afford him laughter, but not sympathy; they could join in his merriment, but they had no concern in his distress. His death was sudden, it was silent, and it was in poverty; *"He died, and made no sign!"*

This class is well embodied in Falstaff, in his life, also in his death. No death in Shakspeare is more sadly impressive to me than that of Falstaff. In the other deaths there is the sweetness of innocence, or the force of passion. Desdemona expires in her gentleness; Hamlet, with all his solemn majesty about him; Macbeth reels beneath the blow of destiny; Richard, in the tempest of his courage and his wickedness, finds a last hour conformable to his cruel soul; Lear has at once

exhausted life and misery; Othello has no more for which he can exist; but the closing moments of Falstaff are gloomy without being tragic; they are dreary and oppressive, with little to relieve the sinking of our thoughts, except it be the presence of humanity in the person of Mrs. Quickly. When prince and courtier had forsaken their associate, this humble woman remained near him. The woman, whose property he squandered, and whose good name he did not spare; this woman, easily persuaded and easily deceived, would not quit even a worthless man in his helpless hour, nor speak severely of him when that hour was ended. Here is the greatness of Shakspeare: he never forgets our nature, and in the most unpromising circumstances he compels us to feel its sacredness. The last hours even of Falstaff he enshrouds in the dignity of death; and, by a few simple and pathetic words in the mouth of his ignorant but charitable hostess, he lays bare the mysterious struggles of an expiring soul. "A parted," she says, "even just between twelve and one, e'en at the turning o' the tide; for after I saw him fumble with the sheets, and play with flowers, and smile upon his finger ends, I knew there was but one way, for his nose was sharp as a pen, and a babbled of green fields. How now, Sir John, quoth I? What, man, be of good cheer! So a cried out, God! God! God! three or four times; then all was cold."

Thus, as Shakspeare pictures, a man of pleasure died. Even upon him nature again exerts her sway; the primitive delights of childhood revisit his final dreaming; and he plays with flowers, and he babbles of green fields. And that voice of an eternal Power, which was lost in the din of the festival, must have utterance in the travail of mortality; and exclamations, which falter to the silence of the tomb, make confession of a faith which all the practice had denied.

# Henry V

This play has many scenes of high dignity, and many of easy merriment. The character of the King is well supported, except in his courtship, where he has neither the vivacity of Hal, nor the grandeur of Henry. The humour of Pistol is very happily continued; his character has perhaps been the model of all the bullies that have yet appeared on the English stage.

The lines given to the chorus have many admirers; but the truth is, that in them a little may be praised, and much must be forgiven; nor can it be easily discovered why the intelligence given by the chorus is more necessary in this play than in many others where it is omitted. The great defect of this play is the emptiness and narrowness of the last act, which a very little diligence might have easily avoided.—SAMUEL JOHNSON, *Notes on Shakespeare's Plays,* 1768

*Henry* V is a very favourite monarch with the English nation, and he appears to have been also a favourite with Shakespear, who labours hard to apologise for the actions of the king, by shewing us the character of the man, as 'the king of good fellows.' He scarcely deserves this honour. He was fond of war and low company:—we know little else of him. He was careless, dissolute, and ambitious;—idle, or doing mischief. In private, he seemed to have no idea of the common decencies of life, which he subjected to a kind of regal licence; in public affairs, he seemed to have no idea of any rule of right or wrong, but brute force, glossed over with a little religious hypocrisy and archiepiscopal advice. His principles did not change with

his situation and professions. His adventure on Gadshill was a prelude to the affair of Agincourt, only a bloodless one; Falstaff was a puny prompter of violence and outrage, compared with the pious and politic Archbishop of Canterbury, who gave the king *carte blanche,* in a genealogical tree of his family, to rob and murder in circles of latitude and longitude abroad—to save the possessions of the church at home. This appears in the speeches in Shakespear, where the hidden motives that actuate princes and their advisers in war and policy are better laid open than in speeches from the throne or woolsack. Henry, because he did not know how to govern his own kingdom, determined to make war upon his neighbours. Because his own title to the crown was doubtful, he laid claim to that of France. Because he did not know how to exercise the enormous power, which had just dropped into his hands, to any one good purpose, he immediately undertook (a cheap and obvious resource of sovereignty) to do all the mischief he could. Even if absolute monarchs had the wit to find out objects of laudable ambition, they could only 'plume up their wills' in adhering to the more sacred formula of the royal prerogative, 'the right divine of kings to govern wrong,' because will is only then triumphant when it is opposed to the will of others, because the pride of power is only then shewn, not when it consults the rights and interests of others, but when it insults and tramples on all justice and all humanity. Henry declares his resolution 'when France is his, to bend it to his awe, or break it all to pieces'—a resolution worthy of a conqueror, to destroy all that he cannot enslave; and what adds to the joke, he lays all the blame of the consequences of his ambition on those who will not submit tamely to his tyranny. Such is the history of kingly power, from the beginning to the end of the world;—with this difference, that the object of war formerly, when the people adhered to their allegiance, was to depose kings; the object latterly, since the people swerved from their allegiance, has been to restore kings, and to make common cause against mankind. The object of our late invasion and conquest of France was to restore the legitimate monarch, the descendant of Hugh Capet, to the throne: Henry V. in his time made war on and deposed the descendant of this very Hugh Capet, on the plea that he was a usurper and illegitimate. What would the great modern catspaw of legitimacy and restorer of divine right have said to the claim of Henry and the title of the descendants of Hugh Capet? Henry V., it is true, was a hero, a King of England, and the conqueror of the king of France. Yet we feel little love or admiration for him. He was a hero, that is, he was ready to sacrifice his own life for the pleasure of destroying thousands of other lives: he was a king of England, but not a constitutional one, and we only like kings according to the law; lastly, he was a conqueror of the French king, and for this we dislike him less than if he had conquered the French people. How then do we like him? We like him in the play. There he is a very amiable monster, a very splendid pageant. As we like to gaze at a panther or a young lion in their cages in the Tower, and catch a pleasing horror from their glistening eyes, their velvet paws, and dreadless roar, so we take a very romantic, heroic, patriotic, and poetical delight in the boasts and feats of our younger Harry, as they appear on the stage and are confined to lines of ten syllables; where no blood follows the stroke that wounds our ears, where no harvest bends beneath horses' hoofs, no city flames, no little child is butchered, no dead men's bodies are found piled on heaps and festering the next morning—in the orchestra!

   . . . The behaviour of the king, in the difficult and doubtful circumstances in which he is placed, is as patient and modest as it is spirited and lofty in his prosperous fortune. The character of the French nobles is also very admirably depicted; and the Dauphin's praise of his horse shews the vanity of that class of persons in a very striking point of view. Shakespear always accompanies a foolish prince with a satirical courtier, as we see in this instance. The comic parts of *Henry* V. are very inferior to those of *Henry IV.* Falstaff is dead, and without him, Pistol, Nym, and Bardolph, are satellites without a sun. Fluellen the Welchman is the most entertaining character in the piece. He is good-natured, brave, choleric, and pedantic. His parallel between Alexander and Harry of Monmouth, and his desire to have 'some disputations' with Captain Macmorris on the discipline of the Roman wars, in the heat of the battle, are never to be forgotten. His treatment of Pistol is as good as Pistol's treatment of his French prisoner. There are two other remarkable prose passages in this play: the conversation of Henry in disguise with the three sentinels on the duties of a soldier, and his courtship of Katherine in broken French. We like them both exceedingly, though the first savours perhaps too much of the king, and the last too little of the lover.— WILLIAM HAZLITT, *"Henry V.," Characters of Shakespear's Plays,* 1817

---

## AUGUST WILHELM SCHLEGEL
From *Lectures on Dramatic Art and Literature*
tr. John Black
1809

King Henry the Fifth is manifestly Shakspeare's favourite hero in English history: he paints him as endowed with every chivalrous and kingly virtue; open, sincere, affable, yet, as a sort of reminiscence of his youth, still disposed to innocent raillery, in the intervals between his perilous but glorious achievements. However, to represent on the stage his whole history subsequent to his accession to the throne, was attended with great difficulty. The conquests in France were the only distinguished event of his reign; and war is an epic rather than a dramatic object. For wherever men act in masses against each other, the appearance of chance can never wholly be avoided; whereas it is the business of the drama to exhibit to us those determinations which, with a certain necessity, issue from the reciprocal relations of different individuals, their characters and passions. In several of the Greek tragedies, it is true, combats and battles are exhibited, that is, the preparations for them and their results; and in historical plays war, as the *ultima ratio regum,* cannot altogether be excluded. Still, if we would have dramatic interest, war must only be the means by which something else is accomplished, and not the last aim and substance of the whole. For instance, in *Macbeth,* the battles which are announced at the very beginning merely serve to heighten the glory of Macbeth and to fire his ambition; and the combats which take place towards the conclusion, before the eyes of the spectator, bring on the destruction of the tyrant. It is the very same in the Roman pieces, in the most of those taken from English history, and, in short, wherever Shakspeare has introduced war in a dramatic combination. With great insight into the essence of his art, he never paints the fortune of war as a blind deity who sometimes favours one and sometimes another; without going into the details of the art of war, (though sometimes he even ventures on this), he allows us to anticipate the result from the qualities of the general, and their influence on the minds of the soldiers; sometimes, without claiming our belief for miracles, he yet exhibits the issue in the light of a higher volition: the consciousness of a just cause and reliance on the protection of Heaven give courage to the one party, while the presage of a curse hanging over their undertaking weighs down the other. In *Henry the Fifth* no opportunity was afforded Shakspeare of adopting the last mentioned course, namely, rendering the issue of the war dramatic; but he has skilfully availed himself of the first.—Before the battle of Agincourt he paints in the most lively colours the light-minded impatience of the French leaders for the moment of battle, which to them seemed infallibly the moment of victory; on the other hand, he paints the uneasiness of the English King and his army in their desperate situation, coupled with their firm determination, if they must fall, at least to fall with honour. He applies this as a general contrast between the French and English national characters; a contrast which betrays a partiality for his own nation, certainly excusable in a poet, especially when he is backed with such a glorious document as that of the memorable battle in question. He has surrounded the general events of the war with a fulness of individual, characteristic, and even sometimes comic features. A heavy Scotchman, a hot Irishman, a well-meaning, honourable, but pedantic Welchman, all speaking in their peculiar dialects, are intended to show us that the warlike genius of Henry did not merely carry the English with him, but also the other natives of the two islands, who were either not yet fully united or in no degree subject to him. Several good-for-nothing associates of Falstaff among the dregs of the army either afford an opportunity for proving Henry's strictness of discipline, or are sent home in disgrace. But all this variety still seemed to the poet insufficient to animate a play of which the subject was a conquest, and nothing but a conquest. He has, therefore, tacked a prologue (in the technical language of that day *a chorus*) to the beginning of each act. These prologues, which unite epic pomp and solemnity with lyrical sublimity, and among which the description of the two camps before the battle of Agincourt forms a most admirable night-piece, are intended to keep the spectators constantly in mind, that the peculiar grandeur of the actions described cannot be developed on a narrow stage, and that they must, therefore, supply, from their own imaginations, the deficiencies of the representation. As the matter was not properly dramatic, Shakspeare chose to wander in the form also beyond the bounds of the species, and to sing, as a poetical herald, what he could not represent to the eye, rather than to cripple the progress of the action by putting long descriptions in the mouths of the dramatic personages. The confession of the poet that "four or five most vile and ragged foils, right ill disposed, can only disgrace the name of Agincourt," (a scruple which he has overlooked in the occasion of many other great battles, and among others of that of Philippi,) brings us here naturally to the question how far, generally speaking, it may be suitable and advisable to represent wars and battles on the stage. The Greeks have uniformly renounced them: as in the whole of their theatrical system they proceeded on ideas of grandeur and dignity, a feeble and petty imitation of the unattainable would have appeared insupportable in their eyes. With them, consequently, all fighting was merely recounted. The principle of the romantic dramatists was altogether different: their wonderful pictures were infinitely larger than their theatrical means of visible execution, they were every where obliged to count on the willing imagination of the spectators, and consequently they also relied on them in this point. It is certainly laughable enough that a handful of awkward warriors in mock armour, by means of two or three swords, with which we clearly see they take especial care not to do the slightest injury to one another, should decide the fate of mighty kingdoms. But the opposite extreme is still much worse. If we in reality succeed in exhibiting the tumult of a great battle, the storming of a fort, and the like, in a manner any way calculated to deceive the eye, the power of these sensible impressions is so great that they render the spectator incapable of bestowing that attention which a poetical work of art demands; and thus the essential is sacrificed to the accessory. We have learned from experience, that whenever cavalry combats are introduced the men soon become secondary personages beside the four-footed players.[1] Fortunately, in Shakspeare's time, the art of converting the yielding boards of the theatre into a riding course had not yet been invented. He tells the spectators in the first prologue in *Henry the Fifth*:—

> Think, when we talk of horses, that you see them
> Printing their proud hoofs in the receiving earth.

When Richard the Third utters the famous exclamation,—

> A horse! a horse! my kingdom for a horse!

it is no doubt inconsistent to see him both before and afterwards constantly fighting on foot. It is however better, perhaps, that the poet and player should by overpowering impressions dispose us to forget this, than by literal exactness to expose themselves to external interruptions. With all the disadvantages which I have mentioned, Shakspeare and several

Spanish poets have contrived to derive such great beauties from the immediate representation of war, that I cannot bring myself to wish they had abstained from it. A theatrical manager of the present day will have a middle course to follow: his art must, in an especial manner, be directed to make what he shows us appear only as separate groups of an immense picture, which cannot be taken in at once by the eye; he must convince the spectators that the main action takes place behind the stage; and for this purpose he has easy means at his command in the nearer or more remote sound of warlike music and the din of arms.

However much Shakspeare celebrates the French conquest of Henry, still he has not omitted to hint, after his way, the secret springs of this undertaking. Henry was in want of foreign war to secure himself on the throne; the clergy also wished to keep him employed abroad, and made an offer of rich contributions to prevent the passing of a law which would have deprived them of the half of their revenues. His learned bishops consequently are as ready to prove to him his indisputable right to the crown of France, as he is to allow his conscience to be tranquillized by them. They prove that the Salic law is not, and never was, applicable to France; and the matter is treated in a more succinct and convincing manner than such subjects usually are in manifestoes. After his renowned battles, Henry wished to secure his conquests by marriage with a French princess; all that has reference to this is intended for irony in the play. The fruit of this union, from which two nations promised to themselves such happiness in future, was the weak and feeble Henry VI., under whom every thing was so miserably lost. It must not, therefore, be imagined that it was without the knowledge and will of the poet that a heroic drama turns out a comedy in his hands, and ends in the manner of Comedy with a marriage of convenience.

*Notes*

1. The Greeks, it is true, brought horses on the tragic stage, but only in solemn processions, not in the wild disorder of a fight. Agamemnon and Pallas, in Æschylus, make their appearance drawn in a chariot with four horses. But their theatres were built on a scale very different from ours.

## DENTON J. SNIDER
### From "*Henry the Fifth*"
*The Shakespearian Drama*
1889, Volume 3, pp. 407–30

*H*enry the Fourth, with its two parts, was occupied with the internal affairs of England; it portrays the great national transition from revolution triumphant to revolution suppressed—from civil discord to domestic harmony. The dynasty has been changed and the country has acquiesced. A great ruler has spent his lifetime in this long, wearisome, and painful struggle, the right of which and the wrong of which have torn his mind with their ever-recurring contradictions. But the work is done, and is well done; England is now a unit within herself, and not a mass of warring fragments; the spirit of rebellion has been extinguished in the blood of its noblest and most powerful representatives; no such personage as the gallant Hotspur will again arise to make it attractive with beauty and chivalrous daring.

The result is that a new national life has appeared, whose vigor is pulsating through the whole land with unparalleled energy. England is fired with the hope and ardor of youth; her inward impulse is driving her forward to some higher destiny; a narrow, insular existence has become too limited for her mighty aspiration. The nation is loudly calling for a great enterprise abroad, wherein it may realize this new spirit by enlarging the country with new territory, and may give expression, by deeds of valor, to the awakened impulse of nationality.

But the nation is chiefly fortunate in the present turn of affairs on account of having a leader, a man who embodies, in the full sense of the word, the national regeneration. Henry the Fifth is now seated on the throne; he, along with his country, has passed through the political and the moral fire which burns, yet purifies; both are one in character and aspiration. The father, Henry the Fourth, could hardly have been the successful leader of a foreign enterprise; his great vocation was to put down domestic revolution—to effect which, cunning as well as violence had to be employed. The function of the subtle politician has ended with his life; the immoral taint which infected his character must also be cleansed from the land. Henry the Fifth steps forth, the warlike champion and purified man; he has overthrown Hotspur on the one hand, and has cast off Falstaff on the other; both conquests are equally necessary to make him the true representative of his people—the outer and inner conquests of an heroic soul.

England, therefore, is seen marching under his leadership to the subjugation of a foreign foe. Nothing remains to be done at home adequate to the national ambition which is bursting forth on all sides; the pent-up energy must find a vent outwards. Into what channel will it thrust itself? Just across a narrow strip of water lies France, the hereditary enemy of the nation; on France, therefore, the storm will be likely to fall. Many an old score is now to be settled between the two peoples. Each has always been a barrier to the other; cannot that barrier be swept down by us, the English? No, not permanently, so one may give the answer here; for it is just that barrier that makes you both just what you are—two distinct nations, England and France. Remove it, and England will suffer in the end quite as much as France; indeed, if she be successful in breaking down all national boundaries, she will lose the very thing which she is so vehemently maintaining, namely, nationality.

But this reflection lies beyond the play—in fact, beyond the consciousness of the Poet. To him, Henry the Fifth seems to be the supreme type of the national hero, and the conquest of France the highest national object. Thus the Lancastrian Tetralogy comes to an end; it portrays the truly constructive epoch of English History according to the conception of Shakespeare, showing the glorious rise of the country from rebellion at home to the subjection of its ancient enemy abroad. Herein, therefore, the loftiest pinnacle of nationality is reached, and the poetical work must conclude. The Yorkian Tetralogy was written first, though it follows the Lancastrian in historical order; the Poet has, in consequence, not developed the inner ground of the Wars of the Roses. The play of *Henry the Fifth* is, hence, the culminating point of the English Historical series.

The structure of *Henry the Fifth* is without its like in Shakespeare. The employment of choruses or prologues to precede every Act, as is the case here, is unknown in any of his other works, if we except the doubtful play of *Pericles*. The object of these choruses seems, in the main, twofold; they announce the subject of the Acts which are to follow, and mark with some care the large gaps of time which are to be passed over by the mind. Thus they try to connect somewhat more closely the disjointed parts of the drama. The Poet himself clearly sees the loose texture of his work; he is full of apologies, which imply his own judgment of its main weak-

ness. He appears to feel that he has transcended quite the limits of Dramatic Art—the theme is too extensive for representation on a petty stage; he seems almost afraid of turning it into ridicule. Hence he is continually begging the spectator to use his imagination and forget the apparent caricature. In no other play is he seen to struggle so hard with his artistic form as here; he surges and frets against its bounds on every side. The great exploits of his hero are in danger of appearing farcical on the stage.

The whole action is of the moving, spectacular kind; it is a series of historical pictures selected from one great campaign, with a chorus to explain the general movement and to supply the omitted links. The play, therefore, is closely tied to the external realities of place and time, and is governed to a less extent than usual by an inner controlling thought; hence criticism, whose function it is to unfold this thought, has no very profound task at present. The result is that *Henry the Fifth*, judged by the Shakespearian standard, must be considered as one of the lesser stars of the Poet's dramatic constellation; it is lacking in unity, in concentration, in organic completeness. Still, it must not be esteemed too lightly. As the play moves in the external details of history, much has to be omitted, since the dramatic form is too narrow; such a manner of treatment demands the fullness and diversity of the Epic or of the Novel. The dramatic work must compress all into the one central, glowing point; only those events are to be taken, and only those things are to be said, which embody directly the thought.

As might be inferred from its spectacular character, the play has no inherent division into movements; indeed, the structure indicates that it is made up of five separate pictures, each of which is preceded by an explanatory prologue. Yet the entire action tends to one supreme event—the battle of Agincourt—in which single effort the conquest of France was accomplished. The drama may be externally divided into two movements. First, the preparation at home on both sides, comprising the first two Acts; secondly, the conflict and its results, terminating in the overwhelming success of Henry the Fifth. England, united within after a slight ripple of opposition, prepares herself for the struggle, passes over to the territory of her enemy, subjugates the country, and tries to confirm its possession by an alliance of marriage with the royal family of France.

The division into threads is, however, strictly maintained; they were called in *Henry the Fourth*, and still may be called, the elevated or serious thread, and the low or comic thread. The first subdivides itself, according to nationality, into two groups—the French and the English—between whom lies the conflict, which is the main theme of the play. Here we must seek for the political elements which control the work. England claims the right to the throne of France, and makes good the claim by force of arms. The second or comic thread has not less than four groups; there are the remnants of the old Falstaffian company; the three English common soldiers who have the little intrigue with the King; the group of officers representing the several British nationalities—Welsh, Scotch, Irish, English; to these must be added the French Princess in her conversation with her attendant, Alice, and with the English King. The superabundance here is manifest; it branches out into so many directions that the unity of the work is in danger of being lost—the central thought seems not to be able to control the dramatic luxuriance springing out of the subject.

I

1. Beginning with the English side of the first thread, we notice at once the remarkable change in the life of the King. He is no longer the wild Prince Harry of Eastcheap, companion of thieves and revelers, but he has become a religious man; he has truly received the new birth, which has left "his body as a paradise to envelop and contain celestial spirits." The caprice of youthful wantonness, "hydra-headed willfullness," has been completely laid aside, and there has been a full submission to the established order of the world. It is clergymen who are speaking; they praise especially his holy demeanor, and wonder ·at his sudden reformation. Indeed, the play throughout exalts the piety of the King as one of his main characteristics, and there is, perhaps, no other personage in Shakespeare's dramas who comes so near being a religious hero. The associate of Falstaff has, therefore, fully redeemed his promise of amendment.

His intellectual gifts, which were never dim, seem to be wonderfully brightened and quickened by his moral change. "Hear him but reason in divinity," says the admiring Archbishop, "you would desire the King were made a prelate;" he speaks of matters of policy with the knowledge and skill of the veteran statesman. But, when he comes to his supreme vocation, "list to his discourse of war, and you shall hear a fearful battle rendered you in music." Still greater is his genius for action; he is the true practical man, who strikes boldly, yet at the same time thinks. In fine, he is the all-sufficient hero in whom intellect and will, the speculative and the active principles of man, are blended in the happiest harmony. Neither of these powers paralyzes the other, as is often the case, but each supports and intensifies the other to a supreme degree. And also he is the stronger and better for having passed through a wild period in his youth. "Wholesome berries thrive and ripen best, neighbored by fruit of baser quality," says the worthy Bishop of him, a clerical authority to which we may reasonably submit, though not without some surprise at the source.

Next there is revealed the chief object of his ambition, the object for which his whole career has been a long preparation—in fact, the object in which the Lancastrian Tetralogy culminates, namely, the conquest of France. But he will not proceed to it without being first assured of the justice of his cause. Accordingly he calls around himself his learned religious advisers, who state in full the grounds of his claim, and vindicate his title against the French doctrine of succession. The Clergy thus requite his favors to the Church; they even urge him to conquest, who needed no incitement; the Archbishop of Canterbury addresses him: "Stand for your own, unwind your bloody flag," and bids him take as a pattern his noble ancestors who once did "forage in blood of French nobility." So speaks the primate of all England, the chief apostle of peace and good-will among men in the British isles.

It is manifest that the nation is for war; it is not merely sustaining, but even pushing, Henry to the struggle. Yet he is fired with the same ambition; he, therefore, most truly represents the spirit of the country. The Nobles are with him, the People have been always with him, now the Clergy have become the most urgent advisers of an invasion of France. All classes are in harmony; then there is the furious energy resulting from a common aspiration. It is a national enterprise, at the head of which is marching the national Hero; the outlook is ill for the object which offers resistance to their purpose.

The King organizes rapidly his powers, wisely leaving a

bulwark against the Scot "who hath been still a giddy neighbor to us." Then the reply of France is heard; to a denial of the royal claim is added a wanton insult. More impatient, then, is the cry for war. Yet even here in England there is manifested a slight reaction against the general tendency of the nation; this reaction culminates in a conspiracy against the life of the King. Still some embers of revolt remain and give out sparks; thus the old spirit of insurrection will once more appear. Three nobles, most intimate friends of Henry, were ready to thrust a dagger into his heart; but the plot is discovered and the conspirators punished. It is only a momentary gleam, passing into speedy darkness. Rebellion has been put down in the previous reign with vigor and vengeance; it cannot rise now, for other business is on hand to occupy the life of Henry the Fifth. But, after his death, will not the spirit of rebellion dart up again in the face of his successor, and will not the question of title arise once more for settlement? But let us suppress the premonition which the event excites. At present, after this slight reaction, the union is firmer than ever; England—consolidated, as it were, into one body—is eager to be hurled across the channel into the heart of France, shouting with her monarch the popular war cry:—

No King of England if not King of France.

The French group, on the other hand, are introduced discussing the threatened invasion. Their monarch, with the circumspection of age, manifests no little anxiety; he recalls the many examples of English valor enacted on the soil of his own realm. But the Dauphin, with the impetuosity of youth, is eager for the conflict, having no fear of England now, because "she is so idly kinged." But the clear-headed Constable gives a well-timed warning to the young Prince; he has carefully noted the great transformation of King Henry's character, whose

> Vanities forespent
> Were but the outside of the Roman Brutus,
> Covering discretion with a coat of folly.

Of course the French emphatically reject the claims of England, and the messenger departs with the declaration of war. Thus we are prepared for the shock of armies which is to follow—two great nations are about to grapple in a terrific struggle—though the English predilection of the Poet has given a distinct hint of the result. Such is the faint outline of the leading French characters.

2. Passing now to the comic thread, we behold the Falstaffian group without Falstaff. At the first view this omission seems quite surprising, since the Poet has distinctly promised the reappearance of the jolly Fat Knight, at the end of *Henry the Fourth*. Why he is dropped can be only conjectured; but it is manifest that the Poet changed his mind only after mature deliberation. A little reflection on the part of the reader will fully justify the same conclusion; in fact, the dramatic possibilities of the character had been exhausted in the previous plays—nothing could well be added to the portraiture. Besides, some repugnance to Falstaff must have been manifested by the more decent and moral portion of the audience, inasmuch as there are not a few persons of the present day who cannot endure his appearance and behavior. Personally, we would like to have seen his enormous bulk again on the stage and heard some of his monstrous lies, but, upon the second thought, it is well as it is; we, too, like the Prince, have had enough of his society for our own good, and should now consent to a permanent separation. Only the death of poor Jack is told; it looks as if he had experienced a hard struggle in his last hours, wrestling with repentance; and we repeat involuntarily the sigh of Prince Henry on the field of Shrewsbury: "I could have better spared a better man."

The remaining members of this comic group are brought

forward from *Henry the Fourth*, and need not be characterized in detail. It is still the reverse side of society—the immoral element—in the present case transmitted to a happier era from a period of civil discord. Its importance is much diminished; still, it is here, following in the track of war, and the whole company is about to cross the channel with the army, not for the purpose of patriotism, but of plunder. The contrast to the general feeling of the nation is most clearly seen in this group of debauched camp-followers. Every great enterprise, however righteous it may be, always has such vermin clinging to it on the outside, and trying to reach its vital juices, but they must be brushed off with the strong hand of merciless justice. The fate of these people in the present undertaking will be the same as that of the external enemy—the French.

## II

In the second movement of the play, which now follows, the scene changes to France, where the struggle at once begins. The key-note is struck by the King in his famous address to his soldiers—the fierce blast of the English war bugle:—

> Once more unto the breach, dear friends, once
>   more,
> Or close the wall up with our English dead.

The sublime theme of the speech throughout is nationality, of which Henry is the most glorious representative in English History. The same spirit permeates this entire series of plays; here is its culmination. Hitherto England had been able to master her internal difficulties; now she is to measure herself with another nation, which it is her weighty enterprise to conquer. If she succeeds, then the English nationality has won the laurel among peoples. The strong appeal is, therefore, to Englishmen, their glory and superiority; it is a battle-prologue, nerving for the conflict which is to follow.

1. Great stress is laid by the Poet upon the behavior of the two armies just before the struggle comes on. The haughty confidence and fatuitous arrogance of the French are brought out in the strongest colors. It is, indeed, the only tragic ground of their fate; they seem to defy Heaven itself to keep them from their prey; on the pinnacle of insolence they are placed, to be hurled down by an avenging Nemesis. Even the cautious Constable gives way to arrogant boasting. A herald is sent to King Henry demanding ransom before the battle is fought; the common soldiers play at dice for English captives that are not yet taken. To the entire French army the victory seems to be won before the engagement; their camp is a scene of wild frolic and impatience. Very necessary and skillful is this motive of impious arrogance, in order to detach the sympathy of the hearer or reader from the side of the French, for they are really defending their nationality, while the English are assailing it; their cause is in every way the more rightful. Indeed, the English are not only committing a wrong against a neighboring nation, but against themselves; they are logically destroying their own supreme principle in the present conflict, namely, nationality. All of which is felt by the Poet, and its effects artfully guarded against by introducing an old Greek tragic motive—human arrogance humbled by a leveling Nemesis.

In the strongest contrast to the action of the French is the conduct of the English; from the noble down to the private soldier there is a feeling of humility—indeed, of depression, though not of despair. They all think that the result will be very doubtful; gloomy forebodings haunt them; still, the staunchest resolution pervades the host. But there is one Englishman who is animated by the most exalted hope, who sees in the present emergency the greatest opportunity of his life or of his century—it is King Henry himself. He moves around among his soldiers, giving a word of encouragement to all; he is full of

religious fervor—prayer is often on his lips; nor, on the other hand, does he forget even in the most trying hour of his life to play a good joke on a common soldier. He still has some of the former Prince Hal peering out of his conduct; he has not lost his sportiveness. Once, however, in a sudden fit of anger, he gives the most cruel order that every soldier should slay his prisoners—a fact which can be reconciled with his general character only by reflecting that his highest principle is the victory and supremacy of his nation, and whatever jeopardizes this supreme end must be removed at any cost. The day of Agincourt is won; King Henry the Fifth comes out of the battle the greatest of English national heroes; at one blow he utterly overwhelms and subjugates the ancient enemy of his country.

For France naught remains but submission; one people passes under the yoke of another. It has already been frequently stated that such a condition of affairs violates in the deepest manner the principle of nationality; there can result from it only perennial strife and calamity to both States. To avoid the difficulty inherent in the situation, to cement the bond between the two nations by domestic affection, the Family is now introduced into the political relation. Henry marries Catherine, daughter of the French King; but the royal woman is not here, as is often the case, made a sacrifice to the State. The famous wooing scene shows that their marriage had its true basis of love, notwithstanding the strong comic features. But the domestic ties of the Monarchs cannot control the destinies of two great people; the Family is a very imperfect bulwark against the Nation. The political object of the present matrimonial alliance is manifest from the beautiful expressions of the Queen-mother, who gives the true ground of royal intermarriage, in her earnest appeal to the happy pair:—

> As man and wife, being two, are one in love,
> So be there 'twixt your kingdoms such a spousal
> That never may ill office or fell jealousy,
> Which troubles oft the bed of blessed marriage,
> Thrust in between the paction of these kingdoms,
> To make divorce of their incorporate league,
> That English may as French, French Englishmen,
> Received each other.

2. The comic thread of the second movement breaks up into four distinct groups. The first is composed of the old associates of Falstaff; they now meet the fit retribution of their deeds. The immoral company seems to be pretty much wiped out in the course of the war; Nym and Bardolph have been hung; "Nell is dead in the spital;" Pistol, ranter and coward, steals back in shame and punishment to England. Thus debauchery from its first prominence in *Henry the Fourth* is quite brought to an end under the heroic King at the same time with his great national victory.

A second and new comic group is made up of representatives from the four British peoples—Welsh, Scotch, Irish, and English. They are all working for the common cause, though they have their little bickerings among themselves; they show how the heroic King had united every kind of subjects in his great foreign enterprise. In compliment to the birthplace and blood of Henry, the pedantic but valorous Welshman, Fluellen, is here the leading figure. The comic effect rests mainly upon the pronunciation of the English tongue in a different fashion by each of these persons, thus indicating with a laugh the checkered variety of speech and men in the English army— a motley gathering, but with the deepest purpose.

Another group is that of the three English soldiers, quite sober when talking together of the prospect of the battle, and not at all very comic figures at any time. But the King comes along in disguise, and they converse with him reprovingly; the result is, he exchanges gloves with one of them in token of a future settlement. From this incident springs a little comic intrigue, which ends in the King discovering himself to the soldier, who is overcome with confusion, but who receives a reward for his manly behavior generally. It is such a simple story as would be told among the common people of their beloved leader.

One more comic group can be distinguished, of which the French Princess, with her broken English, is the chief character. She makes the fourth person employing a brogue in the play. This slender comic instrumentality is quite worked to death; the tendency thereby is to drop down into a farce. In this respect the present play touches the *Merry Wives of Windsor*, in which broken English, spoken by a Welshman and a Frenchman, is the source of much of the fun.

These four groups, composing the second thread, have no very rigid central thought; they manifest rather the appearance of capricious diversity. Yet they all celebrate the internal or domestic triumphs of Henry, while the great battle of Agincourt, given in the first thread, celebrates the external or national triumph of the heroic King. It will hardly be questioned, however, that four comic groups here are too many; confusion results from excessive multiplicity always, and the feeling of the artistic Whole is obscured—or, even lost—in a labyrinth of details.

Such is the conclusion of the Lancastrian Tetralogy. Indeed, the present play, as was before said, may be considered as the culminating point of the whole Historical Drama of Shakespeare; it delineates the ideal ruler in his personal, civil, and military character, and it portrays the ideal England in harmony at home and in supremacy abroad. This Tetralogy is, in the highest sense, a positive work, having a happy outcome; it begins with a revolution and passes through to final reconstruction. A Drama of the Nation it may be called, as distinct from the Drama of the Individual; for here it is a nation which after many conflicts and obstacles, reaches a happy destiny, at least for the time being.

Looking back at the entire Tetralogy, we notice that the poet has seized the essence of Universal History, and put it into a poem which rounds itself into unity. He has shown the cycle of a nation's development, taking it, so to speak, out of Time and making it eternal as a typical experience of national life. It is the account of a particular period of a particular people, but it images all peoples of all periods, past, present, and future. Thus the work is poetic in the highest sense; it has an universal meaning, which gleams out of its particular shape.

The poet has taken a time of revolution, of civil war—the most important of all wars in the development of the modern State. Such a war is not a war of conquest, not a war of glory; it is rather inglorious, whichever way it may fall out, and the nation engaged in it can only succeed in whipping itself. But this is just the interest and the worth of civil war; it is a grand discipline of the people, which they take unwillingly enough, but they have to take it anyhow; it is the process by which the nation in tears and blood has to free itself of some weak, guilty, or inadequate phase of its life. The right of rebellion and the wrong of rebellion, are two halves which, put together, make the cycle of this poem, ending in a grand total outburst of the united national spirit.

Every people at some time has to go through this discipline, in order that it may take its step in advance. Not long after Shakespeare's death, England had to pass through this process again—the process of rebellion triumphant and rebellion defeated. Our own national life is made up of these two phases; American History opens with rebellion trium-

phant, and its last great act has been rebellion defeated. The two oscillations are finally one—the pulse and ebb of historic heart of the world. The rebellion of 1776 and the rebellion of 1861 are the two halves of the one entire cycle of our national discipline; they together make really one revolution, of which the two rebellions are but moieties, which complete themselves through each other, being the positive and negative phases of the same ultimate principle. The North must digest the fact that George Washington was a rebel as well as Jefferson Davis; the South must digest the fact that the one rebel was the father of his country and triumphed, the other rebel was, as far as his deed went, the destroyer of his country and had to be put down.

Thus the deepest experience in our own national life is but another manifestation of Shakespeare's Lancastrian Tetralogy. The poem is universal, belongs to all time, yet has its setting in a certain period of time. The forms which truth takes are temporal, the truth itself is eternal. Yet it must have these forms in order to manifest itself. And the manifestation also is in a process. In the present poem feudalism is the outer setting; feudal rebellion against the head of the State on the part of the powerful lord gets a death-blow in the person of Hotspur. But the greatest English rebellion, the one not long after Shakespeare's time, proceeded not from the nobility, but from the people, against the King. The double movement of this Tetralogy may well be called the systole and diastole of Time's heart, eternally repeating itself like our own heart-beat, but also eternally moving forward to the higher goal with each pulsation.

The character of Bolingbroke is this double synthesis of rebellion; he is the right rebel, and the right destroyer of the rebel. He is the genetic character; from him springs Hotspur, the image of his political violation carried to the extreme, as well as Falstaff, the image of his moral violation carried to the extreme. But his own son, Prince Henry, completes his work by putting down political rebellion in Hotspur and moral rebellion in Falstaff, thus overarching his father and becoming the hero of the Tetralogy.

In this way we behold here portrayed two grand cycles of experience: that of the nation, England, and that of the individual Prince Henry. Both have a certain correspondence; both show an alienation, a rebellion, a fall, through which both have to pass, for the sake of discipline, whereby they attain to harmony—harmony, both national and individual, with the divine order.

But there is, behind the bright skies of *Henry the Fifth* a dark, concealed background. A violation has taken place which will in its own time bring the penalty. Nationality is the spirit of England, of these English Historical plays of Shakespeare, of the modern world as distinguished from the Roman Empire, which sought to absorb all nations. But after the anguish and struggle of a thousand years, nationality has been restored to Europe, which now consists, not of one all-devouring Empire, but of a family of Nations, of which England and France have grown to be two members, independent, self-contained, with the same ultimate right, namely, that of nationality. It is this right which England assails in assailing France; it is the highest of all rights, above the right of inheritance specially to which the counselors of Henry appeal, but which cannot stand in the way of the nation, as Shakespeare himself has shown in two revolutionary plays, *King John* and *Richard the Second*. The political principle of modern times, the World-Spirit itself, is violated. The irony of the deed at once begins to show itself; England, in the pride of nationality, marches forth to destroy nationality, and thus aims a blow at herself, at her own greatest right and achievement. She obtains a transcendent victory which in the end will turn out a terrible defeat; Agincourt is really the loss of her own deepest principle. Such is the danger lurking in all victory; in the irony of history it is apt to change to the very opposite of itself. Only a national recognition and charity can avert such a fate.

Such is the transition from the Lancastrian to the Yorkian Tetralogy in idea, though this idea transcends the consciousness of the poet, who manifestly places *Henry the Fifth* on the pinnacle of his English Histories. But we, looking back through the perspective of three hundred years, must rise above the consciousness of the poet in order to understand him.

Instinctively he wrote the Yorkian before the Lancastrian series; but we must see how the former, in thought as well as in historic continuity, comes after the latter. In *Henry the Fifth* there is a violation of the World-Spirit which Shakespeare did not consciously realize, but the penalty must be paid all the same, as we see in *Henry the Sixth*. Later in life the poet will rise into this conception of the World-Spirit as the supreme ruling power of History; such we behold it in the Roman plays, but hardly in the English ones, where the national Spirit is the highest. Success has again brought guilt, and guilt will call down retribution not only upon the individual, but also upon the nation.

# *Henry VIII*

Now, to let matters of State sleep, I will entertain you at the present with what hath happened this Week at the Banks side. The King's Players had a new Play, called *All is true*, representing some principal pieces of the Reign of *Henry* the *8th*, which was set forth with many extraordinary Circumstances of Pomp and Majesty, even to the matting of the Stage; the Knights of the Order, with their Georges and Garter, the Guards with their embroidered Coats, and the like: sufficient in truth within a while to make Greatness very familiar, if not ridiculous. Now, King *Henry* making a Masque at the Cardinal *Wolsey's* House, and certain Cannons being shot off at his entry, some of the Paper, or other stuff, wherewith one of them was stopped, did light on the Thatch, where being thought at first but an idle smoak, and their Eyes more attentive to the show, it kindled inwardly, and ran round like a train, consuming within less than an hour the whole House to the very ground.—HENRY WOTTON, Letter to Edmund Bacon (July 2, 1613), *Reliquiae Wottoniae*, 1685, pp. 425–26

The play of *Henry the Eighth* is one of those which still keeps possession of the stage, by the splendour of its pageantry. The coronation about forty years ago drew the people together in multitudes for a great part of the winter. Yet pomp is not the only merit of this play. The meek sorrows and virtuous distress of Catherine have furnished some scenes which may be justly numbered among the greatest efforts of tragedy. But the genius of Shakespeare comes in and goes out with Catherine. Every other part may be easily conceived, and easily written.— SAMUEL JOHNSON, *Notes on Shakespeare's Plays*, 1768

Shakspeare was as profound a historian as a poet; when we compare his *Henry the Eighth* with the preceding pieces, we see distinctly that the English nation during the long, peaceable, and economical reign of Henry VII., whether from the exhaustion which was the fruit of the civil wars, or from more general European influences, had made a sudden transition from the powerful confusion of the middle age, to the regular tameness of modern times. *Henry the Eighth* has, therefore, somewhat of a prosaic appearance; for Shakspeare, artist-like, adapted himself always to the quality of his materials. If others of his works, both in elevation of fancy and in energy of pathos and character, tower far above this, we have here on the other hand occasion to admire his nice powers of discrimination and his perfect knowledge of courts and the world. What tact was requisite to represent before the eyes of the queen subjects of such a delicate nature, and in which she was personally so nearly concerned, without doing violence to the truth! He has unmasked the tyrannical king, and to the intelligent observer

exhibited him such as he was actually: haughty and obstinate, voluptuous and unfeeling, extravagant in conferring favours, and revengeful under the pretext of justice; and yet the picture is so dexterously handled that a daughter might take it for favourable. The legitimacy of Elizabeth's birth depended on the invalidity of Henry's first marriage, and Shakspeare has placed the proceedings respecting his separation from Catharine of Arragon in a very doubtful light. We see clearly that Henry's scruples of conscience are no other than the beauty of Anne Boleyn. Catharine is, properly speaking, the heroine of the piece; she excites the warmest sympathy by her virtues, her defenceless misery, her mild but firm opposition, and her dignified resignation. After her, the fall of Cardinal Wolsey constitutes the principal part of the business. Henry's whole reign was not adapted for dramatic poetry. It would have merely been a repetition of the same scenes: the repudiation, or the execution of his wives, and the disgrace of his most estimable ministers, which was usually soon followed by death. Of all that distinguished Henry's life Shakspeare has given us sufficient specimens. But as, properly speaking, there is no division in the history where he breaks off, we must excuse him if he gives us a flattering compliment of the great Elizabeth for a fortunate catastrophe. The piece ends with the general joy at the birth of that princess, and with prophecies of the happiness which she was afterwards to enjoy or to diffuse. It was only by such a turn that the hazardous freedom of thought in the rest of the composition could have passed with impunity: Shakspeare was not certainly himself deceived respecting this theatrical delusion. The true conclusion is the death of Catharine, which under a feeling of this kind, he has placed earlier than was conformable to history.—AUGUST WILHELM SCHLEGEL, *Lectures on Dramatic Art and Literature*, 1809, tr. John Black

---

## WILLIAM HAZLITT
### *"Henry VIII."*
### *Characters of Shakespear's Plays*
### 1817

This play contains little action or violence of passion, yet it has considerable interest of a more mild and thoughtful cast, and some of the most striking passages in the author's works. The character of Queen Katherine is the most perfect delineation of matronly dignity, sweetness, and resignation, that can be conceived. Her appeals to the protection of the king, her remonstrances to the cardinals, her conversations with her women, shew a noble and generous spirit accompanied with the utmost gentleness of nature. What can be more affecting than her answer to Campeius and Wolsey, who come to visit her as pretended friends.

> Nay, forsooth, my friends,
> They that must weigh out my afflictions,
> They that my trust must grow to, live not here;
> They are, as all my comforts are, far hence,
> In mine own country, lords.

Dr. Johnson observes of this play, that 'the meek sorrows and virtuous distress of Katherine have furnished some scenes, which may be justly numbered among the greatest efforts of tragedy. But the genius of Shakespear comes in and goes out with Katherine. Every other part may be easily conceived and easily written.' This is easily said; but with all due deference to so great a reputed authority as that of Johnson, it is not true. For instance, the scene of Buckingham led to execution is one of the most affecting and natural in Shakespear, and one to which there is hardly an approach in any other author. Again, the character of Wolsey, the description of his pride and of his fall, are inimitable, and have, besides their gorgeousness of effect, a pathos, which only the genius of Shakespear could lend to the distresses of a proud, bad man, like Wolsey. There is a sort of child-like simplicity in the very helplessness of his situation, arising from the recollection of his past overbearing ambition. After the cutting sarcasms of his enemies on his disgrace, against which he bears up with a spirit conscious of his own superiority, he breaks out into that fine apostrophe—

> Farewell, a long farewell, to all my greatness!
> This is the state of man; to-day he puts forth
> The tender leaves of hope, to-morrow blossoms,
> And bears his blushing honours thick upon him;
> The third day comes a frost, a killing frost;
> And—when he thinks, good easy man, full surely
> His greatness is a ripening—nips his root,
> And then he falls, as I do. I have ventur'd,
> Like little wanton boys that swim on bladders,
> These many summers in a sea of glory;
> But far beyond my depth: my high-blown pride
> At length broke under me; and now has left me,
> Weary and old with service, to the mercy
> Of a rude stream; that must for ever hide me.
> Vain pomp and glory of the world, I hate ye!
> I feel my heart new open'd: O how wretched
> Is that poor man, that hangs on princes' favours!
> There is betwixt that smile we would aspire to,
> That sweet aspect of princes, and our ruin,
> More pangs and fears than war and women have;
> And when he falls, he falls like Lucifer,
> Never to hope again!

There is in this passage, as well as in the well-known dialogue with Cromwell which follows, something which stretches beyond commonplace; nor is the account which Griffiths gives of Wolsey's death less Shakespearian; and the candour with which Queen Katherine listens to the praise of 'him whom of all men while living she hated most' adds the last graceful finishing to her character.

Among other images of great individual beauty might be mentioned the description of the effect of Ann Boleyn's presenting herself to the crowd at her coronation.

> While her grace sat down
> To rest awhile, some half an hour or so,
> In a rich chair of state, opposing freely
> The beauty of her person to the people.
> Believe me, sir, she is the goodliest woman
> That ever lay by man. Which when the people
> Had the full view of, *such a noise arose*

> *As the shrouds make at sea in a stiff tempest,*
> *As loud and to as many tunes.*

The character of Henry VIII. is drawn with great truth and spirit. It is like a very disagreeable portrait, sketched by the hand of a master. His gross appearance, his blustering demeanour, his vulgarity, his arrogance, his sensuality, his cruelty, his hypocrisy, his want of common decency and common humanity, are marked in strong lines. His traditional peculiarities of expression complete the reality of the picture. The authoritative expletive, 'Ha!' with which he intimates his indignation or surprise, has an effect like the first startling sound that breaks from a thunder-cloud. He is of all the monarchs in our history the most disgusting: for he unites in himself all the vices of barbarism and refinement, without their virtues. Other kings before him (such as Richard III.) were tyrants and murderers out of ambition or necessity: they gained or established unjust power by violent means: they destroyed their enemies, or those who barred their access to the throne or made its tenure insecure. But Henry VIII.'s power is most fatal to those whom he loves: he is cruel and remorseless to pamper his luxurious appetites: bloody and voluptuous; an amorous murderer; an uxorious debauchee. His hardened insensibility to the feelings of others is strengthened by the most profligate self-indulgence. The religious hypocrisy, under which he masks his cruelty and his lust, is admirably displayed in the speech in which he describes the first misgivings of his conscience and its increasing throes and terrors, which have induced him to divorce his queen. The only thing in his favour in this play is his treatment of Cranmer: there is also another circumstance in his favour, which is his patronage of Hans Holbein.—It has been said of Shakespear—'No maid could live near such a man.' It might with as good reason be said—'No king could live near such a man.' His eye would have penetrated through the pomp of circumstance and the veil of opinion. As it is, he has represented such persons to the life—his plays are in this respect the glass of history—he has done them the same justice as if he had been a privy counsellor all his life, and in each successive reign. Kings ought never to be seen upon the stage. In the abstract, they are very disagreeable characters: it is only while living that they are 'the best of kings.' It is their power, their splendour, it is the apprehension of the personal consequences of their favour or their hatred that dazzles the imagination and suspends the judgment of their favourites or their vassals; but death cancels the bond of allegiance and of interest; and seen *as they were*, their power and their pretensions look monstrous and ridiculous. The charge brought against modern philosophy as inimical to loyalty is unjust, because it might as well be brought against other things. No reader of history can be a lover of kings. We have often wondered that Henry VIII. as he is drawn by Shakespear, and as we have seen him represented in all the bloated deformity of mind and person, is not hooted from the English stage.

## G. G. GERVINUS
### From *"Henry VIII."*
*Shakespeare Commentaries*, tr. F. E. Bunnètt
1845

In the series of Shakespeare's later works we have met with several observations which seem to betray to us that there were moments in his later years when his mental interest in his own writings declined, perhaps in consequence of physical debility. The unrefreshing character of the ethical subjects of some of the dramas of this latter period, the tardy revision of such a worthless play as *Pericles*, the æsthetic defects in *Antony*, the unfinished form of *Timon*, the mistake as to material and aim in *Troilus*, all this might indeed prepare us for the time when the poet, having so early discontinued his activity as an actor, would also renounce his vocation as a poet. It has been lately conjectured that we may lay hold, as it were, of this very moment in the production of the historical play of *Henry VIII.*, in which Shakespeare, it is supposed, at the very close of his dramatic career, left his old companions a mere sketch to be carried out in the dramatic celebration of a court festivity, an end which this same historical play must have served even in the last century. The drama, overloaded with pomp and show, is a masque written for some occasion, like the *Tempest* and the *Midsummer Night's Dream*. It was formerly believed to have originated on the occasion of the coronation of King James and his Queen Anne (July 24, 1603). The latter opinion to which we refer (*Gentleman's Magazine* 34, 115 *et seq.*) supposes that the marriage of the Princess Elizabeth (February, 1612) was the cause which may have induced Burbadge's company to obtain Shakespeare's groundwork for the play, which they elaborated into this masque, a form for which the poet himself would hardly have designed his historical drama. If the play really came from Shakespeare's hand at this period of his closing dramatic career, it would be a strange sport of fate that this last of his productions should soon, like a sad and farewell celebration of this event, cause a tragic holocaust. When on June 29, 1613 (according to a notice by Sir Henry Wotton), the play was represented by Burbadge's company under the title of *All Is True*, a title to which the prologue alludes, the theatre caught fire from the discharge of some small cannons, and the Globe, for so many years the scene of the poet's fame, was burnt to the ground.

A long time ago, Roderick, in Edward's *Canons of Criticism*, hesitated at some peculiarities in the versification of *Henry VIII.*, but never since then has the genuineness of the play been doubted, and at the most the prologue and epilogue were all that were denied as the work of the poet's pen. Indeed, the strictly logical design of the four main characters suffered no doubt to arise, as no other poet of the time could have sketched their psychological outline with such sharpness, however much assistance the historical sources (Cavendish's *Life of Wolsey*, as copied in the chronicles), and two previous dramatic works upon Wolsey by Chettle and his companions, might have afforded. In the first place, in the character of the Duke of Buckingham, we look once again upon the age of the great armed nobility, with their pretensions and rebellions, which were the soul of the history under the houses of York and Lancaster, although in our present play the physiognomy of the age appears wholly changed, compared to the character of that earlier epoch. The noise of arms has ceased, the prominent personages are men of education, mind, and well-won merit; the duke himself has kept up with the change of the time; he is not merely an ambitious man of the sword; he is learned, wise in council, rich in mind, and a fascinating orator. Nevertheless, we see him standing in the midst of a number of other nobles, partly related to him, Norfolk, Surrey, Abergavenny, who conspire to maintain the old authority of the nobles, to whom the greatness of the upstart Wolsey is a thorn in their eye, who regard it as insufferable that 'a beggar's book outworths a noble's blood,' that the scarlet robe should assume the importance of their rank, and that difference in persons should be at an end. In proud passion, in the restless haste of personal contempt, Buckingham seeks to lay a snare for the cardinal, and falls himself into the net. He imputed to the priest grasping and treasonous plans; he pried too artfully and overshot his mark; but he himself was not unversed in bold, ambitious projects, which his clever adversary knew how to turn against him as crimes. He was the next heir to the throne in the Beaufort branch of the Lancastrian house if the king died without issue. As the son of that Buckingham who assisted Richard III. to the throne, and afterwards rebelled against him, he delighted in these remembrances of the history of his house; he plays wantonly with his aspiring thoughts, and speculates upon the lack of a male heir, which caused Henry so much doubt and jealousy; he gains the love of the commonalty, he listens readily to the prophecies of silly prophets, who flatter his dreams of greatness; he expresses himself imprudently once when threatened with imprisonment:—

> If I for this had been committed,
> As, to the Tower, I thought—I would have played
> The part my father meant to act upon
> The usurper Richard; who, being at Salisbury,
> Made suit to come in his presence; which if granted,
> As he made semblance of his duty, would
> Have put his knife into him.

This is stated by his surveyor, bribed by Wolsey, and it brings the man to the scaffold, who erred rather from foolish indiscretion than from actual criminal intentions. When he is fallen, he collects himself after his sentence; he dies composed and noble, forgiving, without hatred, already 'half in heaven,' completely devoid of all pride of rank in that moment which so impressively calls to remembrance the vanity of such distinctions.

In contrast to him stands Wolsey, who, born in a lower rank, had by his own mental power raised himself to the highest positions in the church and state, to the place nearest the king and the Pope. King Henry had indeed inherited his love for this man from his father; he regarded him as one who could not err, and for such a one the cardinal knew how to make himself pass; he overloaded him with benefits and advantages, raised him to the first dignity in the kingdom, and permitted him proudly and imperiously to overlook the highest nobility of the land. Fortune, favour, and merit combined to raise the immoderate ambition of this 'great child of honour,' to advance his pride beyond measure, to quench in him every appearance of restraint and humility, to feed his covetousness and love of pomp, and to spread around him royal splendour. Ambition urges him to strive after ever greater dignities, and greater positions again stir up his ambition into a brighter flame. The means to his ends become indifferent to him; he has never known truth; dissimulation is his slave, behind which he conceals the malice of his heart; munificence without bounds, advancement and favour, chain his servants inviolably to him; bribery gains over to him the confidants of his enemies, whom he pursues with all the cunning of revenge. Half fox, half wolf, he swallows greedily the treasures of the land, oppresses the commons with enormous taxes, and, when the people rebel, he assumes the appearance of having himself diminished them. With cold arrogance he disregards the blame urged against him on this occasion, and treats it as the envious rancour of the weak and the malicious, who cannot measure his merits. He makes a systematic opposition against the nobles. No peer is uninjured by him; he ruins the class in the mass, when by arbitrary designation of the persons who are to accompany the king to the festive meeting with the King of France, and by the immense splendour which they were to display there, he consumes the fortunes of many families. And when the powerful Buckingham is aimed at, he surrounds him with spies and hirelings, and plans his future fall, while he removes his nearest and most powerful relatives to positions remote from the court. Thus striding with proud head over the highest of the land, he attempts it even with the king. He had become accustomed to rank himself with princes; his servants were audacious enough to declare that their master would sooner be waited on than any other subject, if not than the king; he made use of the formula 'Ego et rex meus,' when he wrote to foreign courts. To occupy the papal chair, to obtain a rank even superior to his king's, this is the ultimate end of his ambition. He has seized upon the higher ecclesiastical positions in the land; he next strives without the king's knowledge to become the papal legate; it is the Pope himself who stirs up his ambition. To obtain the papacy he imprudently accumulates upon himself the treasures of the country. For this object he tries to bring his king into alliance with France. He has in vain sought the archbishopric of Toledo from the emperor, he must thus rest on his adversary France. To this end that resplendent feast at the meeting of the two kings must be kept in the vale of Arde, and Buckingham and the opponents to this alliance must be put out of the way. This is not yet the extreme point to which his revenge against the emperor and his wish to unite with France drive him. He undertakes to ruin the queen herself; she is the emperor's aunt, and his enemy moreover already from her character. She has lived twenty years with the king in the happiest concord, but he, taking a wide range as ever, by means of a French ecclesiastic throws out scruples as to the lawfulness of the marriage, and what these cannot effect, the king's sensuality accomplishes. The separation is effected in order that the king, according to the cardinal's intention, may marry the Duchess of Alençon, the French king's sister. If all these aims had been obtained, if Henry VIII. had entered into so close a connection with France, if Wolsey had ascended the papal chair, we may readily believe that he would have played the part towards Henry VIII. which Thomas à Becket in the see of Canterbury acted towards his king, or that under the peaceful influence of this powerful man, who in his present position fettered the kingdom by his secret dealings, Catholicism would have been anew established in England. But the cardinal had estimated everything except the king's sensual passion. The scruple concerning the legitimacy of his marriage had no sooner been instilled into him, and the prospect of a new marriage presented to him, than he quickly cast his eyes on the beautiful Anne Bullen. His conscience now became urgent, the cardinal's delay was insupportable to him, the hesitation of the papal church irritating; and this is, thus Wolsey subsequently perceives too late, 'the weight that pulled him down.' When having ventured beyond his depth in a sea of glory, when his high-blown pride has broken under him, and he has sunk, he returns to the true value of the man within him; he acknowledges that too much honour is a heavy burden for a man who aspires to Heaven, and he warns Cromwell of the sin of ambition, by which the angels fell. He casts off at once the burden of the world and of sin, he recovers the strength of his soul in poverty, and true happiness in misery,

and in an edifying return to true self-knowledge, which the poet, resting on the testimony of history (Campian, *Hist. of Ireland*) bestows upon him, according to which this man of duplicity, severity, and malice was never happy but in his fall, he gains more honour in the hour of his death than by all the pomp of his life.

In the *King Henry VIII.* the poet had to paint a portrait which must be flattered and must yet be like; he must not shake the moral respect or excite the kingly jealousy of James I., and yet he would not be untrue to history, which presented to his view a repulsive despotic character, not even indemnified by the fearful magnitude of the crime of a Richard III. Shakespeare portrayed him, without misrepresenting or disguising his cruelty, his sensuality, his caprice, his semi-refinement united with natural coarseness, but he kept them in the background; and there is great field for an actor between the vague generality with which this portrait is sketched, and the few features of complete individual peculiarity which the poet has admitted; and indeed the character of Henry VIII., originally played by Lowin, and from his conception of it transmitted through Davenant to Betterton, has always been a favourite part for the English actor. His dependence upon flatterers, together with his jealous desire to rule alone; the ease with which he is deceived, together with his resentful bitterness when he sees himself deluded, and his deceitful dissimulation in suppressing malice and revenge; his caprice, together with his impetuosity, his unwieldy clumsy appearance, together with a certain mental refinement; his lack of feeling, together with isolated traits of good-nature; his sensuality under the transparent mask of religion and conscience; his manner, condescending even to vulgarity; all these are so many delicate contrasts, in which the player has to hit the fine line of contact. Held in magic fetters by so great a man as Wolsey, surrounded throughout by devoted instruments, and humoured in every wish and every caprice by the most yielding and devoted wife, the king appears as one of the princes who

> kiss obedience,
> So much they love it, but to stubborn spirits
> They swell, and grow as terrible as storms.

and who are implacable when crossed; he is jealous, even to bloody severity, of every threatened self-exaltation in a subject, as in Buckingham. He is the slave of his nature, and of all the passion and self-will which belong to it. This is indeed most generally the source of all tyranny; in *Henry VIII.* it is at the same time the source of his homely, condescending manner. He does not like to be troubled by any restraint; a ceremonious company of nobles, if it be more than a game with his brother-in-law, would not please him; his ostentatious cardinal would be offensive to him, if his assemblies were less worldly; his companions are for the most part upstarts out of the lower classes, scholars rather than soldiers, because he was himself trained more in learning than in arms, and was more adroit at a pastoral masque than at a tournament. Throughout, therefore, the king is peaceful, citizen-like, and familiar; he has no hesitation in taking a Cranmer for the godfather of his daughter, all the less so, because it is a mark of disdain towards his distinguished adversaries. For whenever this natural bias for the equalisation of men and the disregard of rank concurs with his provoked self-will and hostile opposition, we observe that the highest authority on earth, the papacy, stands for nothing with him; when it concerns his blind passion, he regards the love of a blameless wife as little as her royal descent, in order to unite himself to a woman of a lower order.

The two female characters between whom Henry is placed betray the same masterly manner of dramatic delineation, although one is a mere sketch. Katharine is a touching model of womanly virtue and gentleness, of conjugal devotion and love, and of Christian patience in defenceless suffering. She is surrounded by the most virtuous company; her enemy is compelled to praise in her a 'disposition gentle' and a 'wisdom o'ertopping woman's power.' She has never done evil, which must seek concealment; she was incapable of calumny and injury. Only when a natural instinct provokes her against an artful intriguer, to whom, while led away by his ambition, virtue is a folly, and when she has to take poor subjects under her protection against oppression, then only does her virtue impart to her a sting, which, however, never transgresses the limits of womanly refinement. She loves her husband 'with that excellence that angels love good men with;' almost bigoted in her love, she dreams of no joy beyond his pleasure; he himself testifies to her that she was never opposed to his wishes, that she was of wife-like government, commanding in obeying; all his caprices she bore with the most saint-like patience. To see herself divorced from him after twenty years of happiness is a load of sorrow which only the noblest of women can bear with dignity and resignation; to descend from the high position of queen is moreover painful to the royal Spaniard. But she is ready to lead a life of seclusion in homely simplicity, and to bless her faithless, cruel husband even to the hour of her death. Her soul had remained beautiful upon the throne, in her outward degradation it was more beautiful still; she goes to the grave reconciled with her true enemy and destroyer. Johnson has ranked her death scene as above any scene in any other poet; so much was he impressed with its profound effect, unaided by romantic contrivance, and apart from all unnatural bursts of poetic lamentation and the ebullitions of stormy sorrow. *One* womanly weakness the poet (in obedience to history) has imputed to her even to the brink of the grave: even in the hour of death, and after she has indeed seen Heaven open, she clings to the royal honour which belongs to her. The poet indicates in Anne Bullen the counterpart to this weakness. He has portrayed this 'fresh-fish,' the rising queen, only from a distance, he has rather declared than exhibited her beauty, her loveliness, and chastity, her completeness in mind and feature; he does not attempt to enlist us excessively in her favour, when he exhibits her so merry in the society of a Sands; moreover, all place greater stress upon the blessing which is to descend from her than upon herself. The introductory scene makes us believe that she is as free from ambitious views as she asserts; her conversation indeed with the court lady convinces us as little as the former that she could not reconcile herself to splendid honours when they were laid upon her. We see her not as queen, but we see her self-love flattered so far that we can well divine that, raised out of her lowly position, she would play the part of queen as well as Katharine did that of a domestic woman.

No one in this short explanation of the main characters of *Henry VIII.* will mistake the certain hand of our poet. It is otherwise when we approach closer to the development of the action and attentively consider the poetic diction. The impression of the whole becomes then at once strange and unrefreshing; the mere external threads seem to be lacking which ought to link the actions to each other; the interest of the feelings becomes strangely divided, it is continually drawn into new directions, and is nowhere satisfied. At first it clings to Buckingham and his designs against Wolsey; but with the second act he leaves the stage; then Wolsey attracts our attention in an increased degree, and he too disappears in the third act; in the meanwhile our sympathies are more and more strongly drawn to Katharine, who then likewise leaves the stage in the fourth act; and after we have been thus shattered through

four acts by circumstances of a purely tragic character, the fifth act closes with a merry festivity, for which we are in nowise prepared, crowning the king's base passion with victory, in which we could take no warm interest. In the course of the play, the marriage of the king and Anne Bullen is only casually linked with the person of the cardinal, who seemed outwardly as if he ought to form the connecting central point of the action, and the enmity between Cranmer and Gardiner is not at all related to this; both circumstances again apparently stand in no relation to each other. The birth and christening of Elizabeth follow at the conclusion as a new by-work, linked to the preceding merely by a natural but not æsthetic sequence, and connected with the character of Cranmer only by the christening spoons which the godfather has to give to the infant. And in this same way, as we stumble at the loose development of the action, we become doubtful also of the poetic diction, as soon as we compare it with any other of Shakespeare's plays. The English critic before quoted perceived only in single scenes (Act I. sc. 1, 2; Act II. sc. 3, 4; Act III. sc. 2; Act V. sc. 1, 2) that freshness of life and nature, that perfect freedom from all the conventional language of the stage or of books, those concise expressions, that bold and rapid turn of thought, that impatient activity of mind and imagination, which so perceptibly distinguish Shakespeare's language; and even in these scenes we fancy we can feel a certain gloss of varnish, weakening these peculiarities of Shakespeare's diction; in the remaining parts, where whole scenes appear as unnecessary stop-gaps, there often prevails a languid expression of shallow conversation, which seems in scarcely one trait to remind of Shakespeare, though all the more frequently of Beaumont's and Fletcher's style of writing. Fletcher's rhythmic manner is strikingly conspicuous throughout in these very passages of the play; verses with double endings are much more constant in the whole play than in almost any other of Shakespeare's works; in the parts that appear genuine they stand in the proportion of two weak to seven strong endings, but in the less genuine the proportion is of one to two, or two to three; the spondaic double endings, so characteristic of Fletcher's versification, are met with in many passages consecutively. All these peculiarities determined our English critic in the supposition that the play had been consigned by Shakespeare in a mere sketch to Fletcher, whose influence in the completion of the work would at once explain the want of moral and æsthetic consistency and coherence in the drama.

It is striking, and it seems to us of a deciding importance, that this result of philosophical inquiry fully accords with the result of the utterly opposite æsthetical test of the unity of idea in this historical play. Formerly, indeed, I believed that the key to the play might be found in Cranmer's prophetic speech at the christening of Elizabeth, which in broad touches predicts the blessed fruits of the queen's future government: the establishment of peace, the security of Protestantism, and the consideration of merit before birth and blood; and I have thought that the essential idea of the drama might be referred to the glorification of the house of Tudor by an historical abstraction of the main merit and value of the rule of this house. I was induced to admit that the real action, the victory of Protestantism, which the poet had for this aim placed as the central point of his play of *Henry VIII.*, he could not have ventured to represent on the stage in any deep view or detailed treatment; that this might have compelled him (and this history moreover justified) to make the casual outward causes which have had this great result for England the subject of representation in his drama, which in many passages, it seems unintentionally, hints at the experience that great results often arise from the smallest and most unexpected causes. But in this attempt to obtain for the play a unity of idea as its foundation, I have not been able to conceal from myself that, even supposing the justice of such an interpretation, the whole play would evaporate into a formal dramatic spiritualising of the subject. The action represented would in this case be only the symbolic precursor to the real aim of the piece, which would not lie in the central point of the play, but in its conclusion, in that prophesying of a period and a condition, lying far behind the present, in which the scene is placed,—in a speech for which, and for the cause of which, few indeed of the facts of the play had prepared in any tangible manner. It seems, therefore, in every way more just simply to confess the lack of dramatic unity and of an ethical focus in the play, and to explain it in the manner of the considerations we have just alleged.

# TRAGEDIES

## *General*

The English already had a theatre, as did the Spanish, when the French still had nothing but portable stages. Shakespeare, who was considered the English Corneille, flourished at about the time of Lope de Vega. He had a strong and fertile genius, full of naturalness and sublimity, without the slightest spark of good taste or the least knowledge of the rules. I am going to tell you something rash but true, namely that the excellence of this author ruined the English theatre: there are such wonderful scenes, such grand and terrible passages scattered about in his monstrous farces, which are called tragedies, that these plays have always been performed with great success. Time, which alone makes the reputation of men, ends by making their defects respectable. After two hundred years most of the outlandish and monstrous ideas of this author have acquired the right to be considered sublime, and almost all modern authors have copied him. But what succeeded in Shakespeare is booed in them and, as you can imagine, the veneration in which this Ancient is held increases as the Moderns are despised. It does not occur to people that they should not copy him, and the lack of success of their copies simply makes people think that he is inimitable.

You know that in the tragedy of the *Moor of Venice*, a most touching play, a husband strangles his wife on the stage, and while the poor woman is being strangled, she shrieks that she is dying most undeservedly. You are not unaware that in *Hamlet* gravediggers dig a grave, swallowing drinks and singing popular songs, cracking jokes typical of men of their calling about the skulls they come across. But what will surprise you is that these stupidities should have been imitated in the reign of Charles II, which was the age of politeness and the golden age of the arts.

Otway, in his *Venice Preserv'd*, introduces Senator Antonio and the courtesan Naki amid the horrors of the conspiracy of the Marquis of Bedmar. Old Senator Antonio with his courtesan goes through all the monkey tricks of an old debauchee who is impotent and out his mind; he pretends to be a bull and a dog, he bites his mistress's legs and she kicks and whips him. These buffooneries, catering for the dregs of society, have been cut from Otway's play, but in Shakespeare's *Julius Caesar* the jokes of Roman shoemakers and cobblers, introduced on the stage with Brutus and Cassius, have been left in. That is because the stupidity of Otway is modern, while Shakespeare's is ancient.

You may well complain that those who have discussed the English theatre up to now, and above all the famous Shakespeare, have so far only pointed out his errors, and that nobody has translated any of the striking passages which atone for all his faults. I will answer that it is very easy to set out the errors of a poet in prose but very difficult to translate his beautiful lines. All the scribblers who set themselves up as critics of celebrated authors compile volumes. I would prefer two pages that pointed out a few of the beauties. For I shall always hold, with men of good taste, that there is more to be gained from a dozen lines of Homer and Virgil than from all the criticisms that have ever been written about these two great men.

I have ventured to translate a few passages of the best English poets. Here is one from Shakespeare. Have pity on the copy for the sake of the original, and always bear in mind when you see a translation that you are only looking at a feeble print of a great picture.

I have chosen the monologue from the tragedy of *Hamlet* which is familiar to all and begins with this line:

> To be or not to be, that is the question.

It is Hamlet, prince of Denmark, speaking:

> Demeure; il faut choisir, et passer à l'instant
> De la vie à la mort, ou de l'être au néant.
> Dieux cruels! s'il en est, éclairez mon courage.
> Faut-il vieillir courbé sous la main qui m'outrage,
> Supporter ou finir mon malheur et mon sort?
> Qui suis-je? qui m'arrête? et qu'est-ce que la mort?
> C'est la fin de nos maux, c'est mon unique asile;
> Après de longs transports, c'est un sommeil tran-
>     quille;
> On s'endort, et tout meurt. Mais un affreux réveil
> Doit succéder peut-être aux douceurs du sommeil.
> On nous menace, on dit que cette courte vie
> De tourments éternels est aussitôt suivie.
> O mort! moment fatal! affreuse éternité!
> Tout coeur à ton seul nom se glace, épouvanté.
> Eh! qui pourrait sans toi supporter cette vie,
> De nos Prêtres menteurs bénir l'hypocrisie,
> D'une indigne maîtresse encenser les erreurs,
> Ramper sous un Ministre, adorer ses hauteurs,
> Et montrer les langueurs de son âme abattue
> A des amis ingrats qui détournent la vue?
> La mort serait trop douce en ces extrémités;
> Mais le scrupule parle, et nous crie: 'Arrêtez.'
> Il défend à nos mains cet heureux homicide,
> Et d'un Héros guerrier fait un chrétien timide, etc

Do not suppose that I have rendered the English word for word; woe to the makers of literal translations, who by rendering every word weaken the meaning! It is indeed by so doing that we can say the letter kills and the spirit gives life. . . .

It is in these isolated passages that English tragic writers have excelled so far. Their plays, almost all barbarous, quite lacking in good taste, order and plausibility, have amazing flashes amid this gloom. The style is too bombastic, too far removed from nature, too much copied from Hebrew writers who are themselves so full of Asiatic hot air. But also it must be admitted that the stilts of the figurative style upon which the English language is raised do lift the spirit very high, although with an irregular gait.—FRANÇOIS MARIE AROUET DE VOLTAIRE, "Letter 12: On Tragedy," *Letters on the English (Lettres Philosophiques)*, 1734, tr. Leonard Tancock

It only now remains to speak of the state of Tragedy in Great Britain; the general character of which is, that it is more animated and passionate than French Tragedy, but more irregular and incorrect, and less attentive to decorum and to elegance. The pathetic, it must always be remembered, is the soul of Tragedy. The English, therefore, must be allowed to have aimed at the highest species of excellence; though, in the execution, they have not always joined the other beauties that ought to accompany the pathetic.

The first object which presents itself to us on the English Theatre, is the great Shakespeare. Great he may be justly called, as the extent and force of his natural genius, both for Tragedy and Comedy, are altogether unrivalled. But, at the same time, it is genius shooting wild; deficient in just taste, and altogether unassisted by knowledge or art. Long has he been idolised by the British nation; much has been said, and much has been written concerning him; Criticism has been drawn to the very dregs, in commentaries upon his words and witticisms; and yet it remains, to this day, in doubt, whether his beauties, or his faults, be greatest. Admirable scenes, and passages, without number, there are in his Plays; passages beyond what are to be found in any other Dramatic Writer; but there is hardly any one of his Plays which can be called altogether a good one, or which can be read with uninterrupted pleasure from beginning to end. Besides extreme irregularities in conduct, and grotesque mixtures of serious and comic in one piece, we are often interrupted by unnatural thoughts, harsh expressions, a certain obscure bombast, and a play upon words, which he is fond of pursuing; and these interruptions to our pleasure too frequently occur, on occasions when we would least wish to meet with them. All these faults, however, Shakespeare redeems, by two of the greatest excellencies which any Tragic Poet can possess; his lively and diversified paintings of character; his strong and natural expressions of passion. These are his two chief virtues; on these his merit rests. Notwithstanding his many absurdities, all the while we are reading his Plays, we find ourselves in the midst of our fellows; we meet with men, vulgar perhaps in their manners, coarse or harsh in their sentiments, but still they are men; they speak with human voices, and are actuated by human passions; we are interested in what they say or do, because we feel that they are of the same nature with ourselves. It is therefore no matter of wonder, that from the more polished and regular, but more cold and artificial performances of other Poets, the Public should return with pleasure to such warm and genuine representations of human nature. Shakespeare possesses likewise the merit of having created, for himself, a sort of world of præternatural beings. His witches, ghosts, fairies, and spirits of all kinds, are described with such circumstances of awful and mysterious solemnity, and speak a language so peculiar to themselves, as strongly to affect the imagination. His two master-pieces, and in which, in my opinion, the strength of his genius chiefly appears, are Othello and Macbeth. With regard to his historical plays, they are, properly speaking, neither Tragedies nor Comedies; but a peculiar species of Dramatic Entertainment, calculated to describe the manners of the times of which he treats, to exhibit the principal characters, and to fix our imagination on the most interesting events and revolutions of our own country.—HUGH BLAIR, *Lectures on Rhetoric and Belles-Lettres*, 1783, Lecture 46

---

## CHARLES LAMB

### "On the Tragedies of Shakspeare, Considered with Reference to Their Fitness for Stage Representation" (1812)
*Works*, ed. E. V. Lucas
1903, Volume 1, pp. 97–111

Taking a turn the other day in the Abbey, I was struck with the affected attitude of a figure, which I do not remember to have seen before, and which upon examination proved to be a whole-length of the celebrated Mr. Garrick. Though I would not go so far with some good catholics abroad as to shut players

altogether out of consecrated ground, yet I own I was not a little scandalized at the introduction of theatrical airs and gestures into a place set apart to remind us of the saddest realities. Going nearer, I found inscribed under this harlequin figure the following lines:—

> To paint fair Nature, by divine command,
> Her magic pencil in his glowing hand,
> A Shakspeare rose: then to expand his fame
> Wide o'er this breathing world, a Garrick came.
> Though sunk in death the forms the Poet drew,
> The Actor's genius bade them breathe anew;
> Though, like the bard himself, in night they lay,
> Immortal Garrick call'd them back to day:
> And till ETERNITY with power sublime,
> Shall mark the mortal hour of hoary TIME,
> SHAKSPEARE and GARRICK like twin stars shall shine,
> And earth irradiate with a beam divine.

It would be an insult to my readers' understandings to attempt any thing like a criticism on this farrago of false thoughts and nonsense. But the reflection it led me into was a kind of wonder, how, from the days of the actor here celebrated to our own, it should have been the fashion to compliment every performer in his turn, that has had the luck to please the town in any of the great characters of Shakspeare, with the notion of possessing a *mind congenial with the poet's*: how people should come thus unaccountably to confound the power of originating poetical images and conceptions with the faculty of being able to read or recite the same when put into words;[1] or what connection that absolute mastery over the heart and soul of man, which a great dramatic poet possesses, has with those low tricks upon the eye and ear, which a player by observing a few general effects, which some common passion, as grief, anger, &c. usually has upon the gestures and exterior, can so easily compass. To know the internal workings and movements of a great mind, of an Othello or a Hamlet for instance, the *when* and the *why* and the *how far* they should be moved; to what pitch a passion is becoming; to give the reins and to pull in the curb exactly at the moment when the drawing in or the slackening is most graceful; seems to demand a reach of intellect of a vastly different extent from that which is employed upon the bare imitation of the signs of these passions in the countenance or gesture, which signs are usually observed to be most lively and emphatic in the weaker sort of minds, and which signs can after all but indicate some passion, as I said before, anger, or grief, generally; but of the motives and grounds of the passion, wherein it differs from the same passion in low and vulgar natures, of these the actor can give no more idea by his face or gesture than the eye (without a metaphor) can speak, or the muscles utter intelligible sounds. But such is the instantaneous nature of the impressions which we take in at the eye and ear at a playhouse, compared with the slow apprehension oftentimes of the understanding in reading, that we are apt not only to sink the play-writer in the consideration which we pay to the actor, but even to identify in our minds, in a perverse manner, the actor with the character which he represents. It is difficult for a frequent playgoer to disembarrass the idea of Hamlet from the person and voice of Mr. K. We speak of Lady Macbeth, while we are in reality thinking of Mrs. S. Nor is this confusion incidental alone to unlettered persons, who, not possessing the advantage of reading, are necessarily dependent upon the stage-player for all the pleasure which they can receive from the drama, and to whom the very idea of *what an author is* cannot be made comprehensible without some pain and perplexity of mind: the error is one from which persons otherwise not meanly lettered, find it almost impossible to extricate themselves.

Never let me be so ungrateful as to forget the very high degree of satisfaction which I received some years back from seeing for the first time a tragedy of Shakspeare performed, in which these two great performers sustained the principal parts. It seemed to embody and realize conceptions which had hitherto assumed no distinct shape. But dearly do we pay all our life after for this juvenile pleasure, this sense of distinctness. When the novelty is past, we find to our cost that instead of realizing an idea, we have only materialized and brought down a fine vision to the standard of flesh and blood. We have let go a dream, in quest of an unattainable substance.

How cruelly this operates upon the mind, to have its free conceptions thus crampt and pressed down to the measure of a strait-lacing actuality, may be judged from that delightful sensation of freshness, with which we turn to those plays of Shakspeare which have escaped being performed, and to those passages in the acting plays of the same writer which have happily been left out in performance. How far the very custom of hearing any thing *spouted*, withers and blows upon a fine passage, may be seen in those speeches from Henry the Fifth, &c. which are current in the mouths of school-boys from their being to be found in *Enfield Speakers*, and such kind of books. I confess myself utterly unable to appreciate that celebrated soliloquy in Hamlet, beginning "To be or not to be," or to tell whether it be good, bad, or indifferent, it has been so handled and pawed about by declamatory boys and men, and torn so inhumanly from its living place and principle of continuity in the play, till it is become to me a perfect dead member.

It may seem a paradox, but I cannot help being of opinion that the plays of Shakspeare are less calculated for performance on a stage, than those of almost any other dramatist whatever. Their distinguished excellence is a reason that they should be so. There is so much in them, which comes not under the province of acting, with which eye, and tone, and gesture, have nothing to do.

The glory of the scenic art is to personate passion, and the turns of passion; and the more coarse and palpable the passion is, the more hold upon the eyes and ears of the spectators the performer obviously possesses. For this reason, scolding scenes, scenes where two persons talk themselves into a fit of fury, and then in a surprising manner talk themselves out of it again, have always been the most popular upon our stage. And the reason is plain, because the spectators are here most palpably appealed to, they are the proper judges in this war of words, they are the legitimate ring that should be formed round such "intellectual prize-fighters." Talking is the direct object of the imitation here. But in all the best dramas, and in Shakspeare above all, how obvious it is, that the form of *speaking*, whether it be in soliloquy or dialogue, is only a medium, and often a highly artificial one, for putting the reader or spectator into possession of that knowledge of the inner structure and workings of mind in a character, which he could otherwise never have arrived at *in that form of composition* by any gift short of intuition. We do here as we do with novels written in the *epistolary form*. How many improprieties, perfect solecisms in letter-writing, do we put up with in Clarissa and other books, for the sake of the delight which that form upon the whole gives us.

But the practice of stage representation reduces every thing to a controversy of elocution. Every character, from the boisterous blasphemings of Bajazet to the shrinking timidity of womanhood, must play the orator. The love-dialogues of Romeo and Juliet, those silver-sweet sounds of lovers' tongues by night; the more intimate and sacred sweetness of nuptial colloquy between an Othello or a Posthumus with their married wives, all those delicacies which are so delightful in the reading, as when we read of those youthful dalliances in Paradise—

> As beseem'd
> Fair couple link'd in happy nuptial league,
> Alone:

by the inherent fault of stage representation, how are these things sullied and turned from their very nature by being exposed to a large assembly; when such speeches as Imogen addresses to her lord, come drawling out of the mouth of a hired actress, whose courtship, though nominally addressed to the personated Posthumus, is manifestly aimed at the spectators, who are to judge of her endearments and her returns of love.

The character of Hamlet is perhaps that by which, since the days of Betterton, a succession of popular performers have had the greatest ambition to distinguish themselves. The length of the part may be one of their reasons. But for the character itself, we find it in a play, and therefore we judge it a fit subject of dramatic representation. The play itself abounds in maxims and reflexions beyond any other, and therefore we consider it as a proper vehicle for conveying moral instruction. But Hamlet himself—what does he suffer meanwhile by being dragged forth as a public schoolmaster, to give lectures to the crowd! Why, nine parts in ten of what Hamlet does, are transactions between himself and his moral sense, they are the effusions of his solitary musings, which he retires to holes and corners and the most sequestered parts of the palace to pour forth; or rather, they are the silent meditations with which his bosom is bursting, reduced to *words* for the sake of the reader, who must else remain ignorant of what is passing there. These profound sorrows, these light-and-noise-abhorring ruminations, which the tongue scarce dares utter to deaf walls and chambers, how can they be represented by a gesticulating actor, who comes and mouths them out before an audience, making four hundred people his confidants at once? I say not that it is the fault of the actor so to do; he must pronounce them *ore rotundo*, he must accompany them with his eye, he must insinuate them into his auditory by some trick of eye, tone, or gesture, or he fails. *He must be thinking all the while of his appearance, because he knows that all the while the spectators are judging of it.* And this is the way to represent the shy, negligent, retiring Hamlet.

It is true that there is no other mode of conveying a vast quantity of thought and feeling to a great portion of the audience, who otherwise would never earn it for themselves by reading, and the intellectual acquisition gained this way may, for aught I know, be inestimable; but I am not arguing that Hamlet should not be acted, but how much Hamlet is made another thing by being acted. I have heard much of the wonders which Garrick performed in this part; but as I never saw him, I must have leave to doubt whether the representation of such a character came within the province of his art. Those who tell me of him, speak of his eye, of the magic of his eye, and of his commanding voice: physical properties, vastly desirable in an actor, and without which he can never insinuate meaning into an auditory,—but what have they to do with Hamlet? what have they to do with intellect? In fact, the things aimed at in theatrical representation, are to arrest the spectator's eye upon the form and the gesture, and so to gain a more favourable hearing to what is spoken: it is not what the character is, but how he looks; not what he says, but how he speaks it. I see no reason to think that if the play of Hamlet were written over again by some such writer as Banks or Lillo, retaining the process of the story, but totally omitting all the poetry of it, all the divine features of Shakspeare, his stupendous intellect; and only taking care to give us enough of passionate dialogue, which Banks or Lillo were never at a loss to furnish; I see not how the effect could be much different upon an audience, nor how the actor has it in his power to represent Shakspeare to us differently from his representation of Banks or Lillo. Hamlet would still be a youthful accomplished prince, and must be gracefully personated; he might be puzzled in his mind, wavering in his conduct, seemingly-cruel to Ophelia, he might see a ghost, and start at it, and address it kindly when he found it to be his father; all this in the poorest and most homely language of the servilest creeper after nature that ever consulted the palate of an audience; without troubling Shakspeare for the matter: and I see not but there would be room for all the power which an actor has, to display himself. All the passions and changes of passion might remain: for those are much less difficult to write or act than is thought, it is a trick easy to be attained, it is but rising or falling a note or two in the voice, a whisper with a significant foreboding look to announce its approach, and so contagious the counterfeit appearance of any emotion is, that let the words be what they will, the look and tone shall carry it off and make it pass for deep skill in the passions.

It is common for people to talk of Shakspeare's plays being *so natural*; that every body can understand him. They are natural indeed, they are grounded deep in nature, so deep that the depth of them lies out of the reach of most of us. You shall hear the same persons say that George Barnwell is very natural, and Othello is very natural, that they are both very deep; and to them they are the same kind of thing. At the one they sit and shed tears, because a good sort of young man is tempted by a naughty woman to commit *a trifling peccadillo*, the murder of an uncle or so,[2] that is all, and so comes to an untimely end, which is *so moving*; and at the other, because a blackamoor in a fit of jealousy kills his innocent white wife: and the odds are that ninety-nine out of a hundred would willingly behold the same catastrophe happen to both the heroes, and have thought the rope more due to Othello than to Barnwell. For of the texture of Othello's mind, the inward construction marvellously laid open with all its strengths and weaknesses, its heroic confidences and its human misgivings, its agonies of hate springing from the depths of love, they see no more than the spectators at a cheaper rate, who pay their pennies a-piece to look through the man's telescope in Leicester-fields, see into the inward plot and topography of the moon. Some dim thing or other they see, they see an actor personating a passion, of grief, or anger, for instance, and they recognize it as a copy of the usual external effects of such passions; or at least as being true to *that symbol of the emotion which passes current at the theatre for it*, for it is often no more than that: but of the grounds of the passion, its correspondence to a great or heroic nature, which is the only worthy object of tragedy,—that common auditors know any thing of this, or can have any such notions dinned into them by the mere strength of an actor's lungs,—that apprehensions foreign to them should be thus infused into them by storm, I can neither believe, nor understand how it can be possible.

We talk of Shakspeare's admirable observation of life, when we should feel, that not from a petty inquisition into those cheap and every-day characters which surrounded him, as they surround us, but from his own mind, which was, to borrow a phrase of Ben Jonson's, the very "sphere of humanity," he fetched those images of virtue and of knowledge, of which every one of us recognizing a part, think we comprehend in our natures the whole; and oftentimes mistake the

powers which he positively creates in us, for nothing more than indigenous faculties of our own minds, which only waited the application of corresponding virtues in him to return a full and clear echo of the same.

To return to Hamlet.—Among the distinguishing features of that wonderful character, one of the most interesting (yet painful) is that soreness of mind which makes him treat the intrusions of Polonius with harshness, and that asperity which he puts on in his interviews with Ophelia. These tokens of an unhinged mind (if they be not mixed in the latter case with a profound artifice of love, to alienate Ophelia by affected discourtesies, so to prepare her mind for the breaking off of that loving intercourse, which can no longer find a place amidst business so serious as that which he has to do) are parts of his character, which to reconcile with our admiration of Hamlet, the most patient consideration of his situation is no more than necessary; they are what we *forgive afterwards*, and explain by the whole of his character, but *at the time* they are harsh and unpleasant. Yet such is the actor's necessity of giving strong blows to the audience, that I have never seen a player in this character, who did not exaggerate and strain to the utmost these ambiguous features,—these temporary deformities in the character. They make him express a vulgar scorn at Polonius which utterly degrades his gentility, and which no explanation can render palateable; they make him shew contempt, and curl up the nose at Ophelia's father,—contempt in its very grossest and most hateful form; but they get applause by it: it is natural, people say; that is, the words are scornful, and the actor expresses scorn, and that they can judge of: but why so much scorn, and of that sort, they never think of asking.

So to Ophelia.—All the Hamlets that I have ever seen, rant and rave at her as if she had committed some great crime, and the audience are highly pleased, because the words of the part are satirical, and they are enforced by the strongest expression of satirical indignation of which the face and voice are capable. But then, whether Hamlet is likely to have put on such brutal appearances to a lady whom he loved so dearly, is never thought on. The truth is, that in all such deep affections as had subsisted between Hamlet and Ophelia, there is a stock of *supererogatory love*, (if I may venture to use the expression) which in any great grief of heart, especially where that which preys upon the mind cannot be communicated, confers a kind of indulgence upon the grieved party to express itself, even to its heart's dearest object, in the language of a temporary alienation; but it is not alienation, it is a distraction purely, and so it always makes itself to be felt by that object: it is not anger, but grief assuming the appearance of anger,—love awkwardly counterfeiting hate, as sweet countenances when they try to frown: but such sternness and fierce disgust as Hamlet is made to shew, is no counterfeit, but the real face of absolute aversion,—of irreconcileable alienation. It may be said he puts on the madman; but then he should only so far put on this counterfeit lunacy as his own real distraction will give him leave; that is, incompletely, imperfectly; not in that confirmed, practised way, like a master of his art, or, as Dame Quickly would say, "like one of those harlotry players."

I mean no disrespect to any actor, but the sort of pleasure which Shakspeare's plays give in the acting seems to me not at all to differ from that which the audience receive from those of other writers; and, *they being in themselves essentially so different from all others*, I must conclude that there is something in the nature of acting which levels all distinctions. And in fact, who does not speak indifferently of the Gamester and of Macbeth as fine stage performances, and praise the Mrs. Beverley in the same way as the Lady Macbeth of Mrs. S.?

Belvidera, and Calista, and Isabella, and Euphrasia, are they less liked than Imogen, or than Juliet, or than Desdemona? Are they not spoken of and remembered in the same way? Is not the female performer as great (as they call it) in one as in the other? Did not Garrick shine, and was he not ambitious of shining in every drawling tragedy that his wretched day produced,—the productions of the Hills and the Murphys and the Browns,—and shall he have that honour to dwell in our minds for ever as an inseparable concomitant with Shakspeare? A kindred mind! O who can read that affecting sonnet of Shakspeare which alludes to his profession as a player:—

> Oh for my sake do you with Fortune chide,
> The guilty goddess of my harmful deeds,
> That did not better for my life provide
> Than public means which public custom [manners]
>       breeds—
> Thence comes it that my name receives a brand;
> And almost thence my nature is subdued
> To what it works in, like the dyer's hand—

Or that other confession:—

> Alas! 'tis true, I have gone here and there,
> And made myself a motly to thy view,
> Gor'd mine own thoughts, sold cheap what is most
>       dear—

Who can read these instances of jealous self-watchfulness in our sweet Shakspeare, and dream of any congeniality between him and one that, by every tradition of him, appears to have been as mere a player as ever existed; to have had his mind tainted with the lowest players' vices,—envy and jealousy, and miserable cravings after applause; one who in the exercise of his profession was jealous even of the women-performers that stood in his way; a manager full of managerial tricks and stratagems and finesse: that any resemblance should be dreamed of between him and Shakspeare,—Shakspeare who, in the plenitude and consciousness of his own powers, could with that noble modesty, which we can neither imitate nor appreciate, express himself thus of his own sense of his own defects:—

> Wishing me like to one more rich in hope,
> Featur'd like him, like him with friends possest;
> Desiring *this man's art, and that man's scope.*

I am almost disposed to deny to Garrick the merit of being an admirer of Shakspeare. A true lover of his excellencies he certainly was not; for would any true lover of them have admitted into his matchless scenes such ribald trash as Tate and Cibber, and the rest of them, that

> With their darkness durst affront his light,

have foisted into the acting plays of Shakspeare? I believe it impossible that he could have had a proper reverence for Shakspeare, and have condescended to go through that interpolated scene in *Richard the Third*, in which Richard tries to break his wife's heart by telling her he loves another woman, and says, "if she survives this she is immortal." Yet I doubt not he delivered this vulgar stuff with as much anxiety of emphasis as any of the genuine parts; and for acting, it is as well calculated as any. But we have seen the part of Richard lately produce great fame to an actor by his manner of playing it, and it lets us into the secret of acting, and of popular judgments of Shakspeare derived from acting. Not one of the spectators who have witnessed Mr. C.'s exertions in that part, but has come away with a proper conviction that Richard is a very wicked man, and kills little children in their beds, with something like the pleasure which the giants and ogres in children's books are represented to have taken in that practice; moreover, that he is

very close and shrewd and devilish cunning, for you could see that by his eye.

But is in fact this the impression we have in reading the Richard of Shakspeare? Do we feel any thing like disgust, as we do at that butcher-like representation of him that passes for him on the stage? A horror at his crimes blends with the effect which we feel, but how is it qualified, how is it carried off, by the rich intellect which he displays, his resources, his wit, his buoyant spirits, his vast knowledge and insight into characters, the poetry of his part,—not an atom of all which is made perceivable in Mr. C.'s way of acting it. Nothing but his crimes, his actions, is visible; they are prominent and staring; the murderer stands out, but where is the lofty genius, the man of vast capacity,—the profound, the witty, accomplished Richard?

The truth is, the Characters of Shakspeare are so much the objects of meditation rather than of interest or curiosity as to their actions, that while we are reading any of his great criminal characters,—Macbeth, Richard, even Iago,—we think not so much of the crimes which they commit, as of the ambition, the aspiring spirit, the intellectual activity, which prompts them to overleap those moral fences. Barnwell is a wretched murderer; there is a certain fitness between his neck and the rope; he is the legitimate heir to the gallows; nobody who thinks at all can think of any alleviating circumstances in his case to make him a fit object of mercy. Or to take an instance from the higher tragedy, what else but a mere assassin in Glenalvon! Do we think of any thing but of the crime which he commits, and the rack which he deserves? That is all which we really think about him. Whereas in corresponding characters in Shakspeare so little do the actions comparatively affect us, that while the impulses, the inner mind in all its perverted greatness, solely seems real and is exclusively attended to, the crime is comparatively nothing. But when we see these things represented, the acts which they do are comparatively every thing, their impulses nothing. The state of sublime emotion into which we are elevated by those images of night and horror which Macbeth is made to utter, that solemn prelude with which he entertains the time till the bell shall strike which is to call him to murder Duncan,—when we no longer read it in a book, when we have given up that vantage-ground of abstraction which reading possesses over seeing, and come to see a man in his bodily shape before our eyes actually preparing to commit a murder, if the acting be true and impressive, as I have witnessed it in Mr. K.'s performance of that part, the painful anxiety about the act, the natural longing to prevent it while it yet seems unperpetrated, the too close pressing semblance of reality, give a pain and an uneasiness which totally destroy all the delight which the words in the book convey, where the deed doing never presses upon us with the painful sense of presence: it rather seems to belong to history,—to something past and inevitable, if it has any thing to do with time at all. The sublime images, the poetry alone, is that which is present to our minds in the reading.

So to see Lear acted,—to see an old man tottering about the stage with a walking-stick, turned out of doors by his daughters in a rainy night, has nothing in it but what is painful and disgusting. We want to take him into shelter and relieve him. That is all the feeling which the acting of Lear ever produced in me. But the Lear of Shakspeare cannot be acted. The contemptible machinery by which they mimic the storm which he goes out in, is not more inadequate to represent the horrors of the real elements, than any actor can be to represent Lear: they might more easily propose to personate the Satan of Milton upon a stage, or one of Michael Angelo's terrible figures. The greatness of Lear is not in corporal dimension, but in intellectual: the explosions of his passion are terrible as a volcano: they are storms turning up and disclosing to the bottom that sea, his mind, with all its vast riches. It is his mind which is laid bare. This case of flesh and blood seems too insignificant to be thought on; even as he himself neglects it. On the stage we see nothing but corporal infirmities and weakness, the impotence of rage; while we read it, we see not Lear, but we are Lear,—we are in his mind, we are sustained by a grandeur which baffles the malice of daughters and storms; in the aberrations of his reason, we discover a mighty irregular power of reasoning, immethodized from the ordinary purposes of life, but exerting its powers, as the wind blows where it listeth, at will upon the corruptions and abuses of mankind. What have looks, or tones, to do with that sublime identification of his age with that of the *heavens themselves*, when in his reproaches to them for conniving at the injustice of his children, he reminds them that "they themselves are old." What gesture shall we appropriate to this? What has the voice or the eye to do with such things? But the play is beyond all art, as the tamperings with it shew: it is too hard and stony; it must have love-scenes, and a happy ending. It is not enough that Cordelia is a daughter, she must shine as a lover too. Tate has put his hook in the nostrils of this Leviathan, for Garrick and his followers, the showmen of the scene, to draw the mighty beast about more easily. A happy ending!—as if the living martyrdom that Lear had gone through,—the flaying of his feelings alive, did not make a fair dismissal from the stage of life the only decorous thing for him. If he is to live and be happy after, if he could sustain this world's burden after, why all this pudder and preparation,—why torment us with all this unnecessary sympathy? As if the childish pleasure of getting his gilt robes and sceptre again could tempt him to act over again his misused station,—as if at his years, and with his experience, any thing was left but to die.

Lear is essentially impossible to be represented on a stage. But how many dramatic personages are there in Shakspeare, which though more tractable and feasible (if I may so speak) than Lear, yet from some circumstance, some adjunct to their character, are improper to be shewn to our bodily eye. Othello for instance. Nothing can be more soothing, more flattering to the nobler parts of our natures, than to read of a young Venetian lady of highest extraction, through the force of love and from a sense of merit in him whom she loved, laying aside every consideration of kindred, and country, and colour, and wedding with a *coal-black Moor*—(for such he is represented, in the imperfect state of knowledge respecting foreign countries in those days, compared with our own, or in compliance with popular notions, though the Moors are now well enough known to be by many shades less unworthy of a white woman's fancy)—it is the perfect triumph of virtue over accidents, of the imagination over the senses. She sees Othello's colour in his mind. But upon the stage, when the imagination is no longer the ruling faculty, but we are left to our poor unassisted senses, I appeal to every one that has seen Othello played, whether he did not, on the contrary, sink Othello's mind in his colour; whether he did not find something extremely revolting in the courtship and wedded caresses of Othello and Desdemona; and whether the actual sight of the thing did not over-weigh all that beautiful compromise which we make in reading;—and the reason it should do so is obvious, because there is just so much reality presented to our senses as to give a perception of disagreement, with not enough of belief in the internal motives,—all that which is unseen,—to overpower and reconcile the first and obvious prejudices.[3] What we see upon a stage

is body and bodily action; what we are conscious of in reading is almost exclusively the mind, and its movements: and this I think may sufficiently account for the very different sort of delight with which the same play so often affects us in the reading and the seeing.

It requires little reflection to perceive, that if those characters in Shakspeare which are within the precincts of nature, have yet something in them which appeals too exclusively to the imagination, to admit of their being made objects to the senses without suffering a change and a diminution,—that still stronger the objection must lie against representing another line of characters, which Shakspeare has introduced to give a wildness and a supernatural elevation to his scenes, as if to remove them still farther from that assimilation to common life in which their excellence is vulgarly supposed to consist. When we read the incantations of those terrible beings the Witches in *Macbeth*, though some of the ingredients of their hellish composition savour of the grotesque, yet is the effect upon us other than the most serious and appalling that can be imagined? Do we not feel spellbound as Macbeth was? Can any mirth accompany a sense of their presence? We might as well laugh under a consciousness of the principle of Evil himself being truly and really present with us. But attempt to bring these beings on to a stage, and you turn them instantly into so many old women, that men and children are to laugh at. Contrary to the old saying, that "seeing is believing," the sight actually destroys the faith; and the mirth in which we indulge at their expense, when we see these creatures upon a stage, seems to be a sort of indemnification which we make to ourselves for the terror which they put us in when reading made them an object of belief,—when we surrendered up our reason to the poet, as children to their nurses and their elders; and we laugh at our fears, as children who thought they saw something in the dark, triumph when the bringing in of a candle discovers the vanity of their fears. For this exposure of supernatural agents upon a stage is truly bringing in a candle to expose their own delusiveness. It is the solitary taper and the book that generates a faith in these terrors: a ghost by chandelier light, and in good company, deceives no spectators,—a ghost that can be measured by the eye, and his human dimensions made out at leisusre. The sight of a well-lighted house, and a well-dressed audience, shall arm the most nervous child against any apprehensions: as Tom Brown says of the impenetrable skin of Achilles with his impenetrable armour over it, "Bully Dawson would have fought the devil with such advantages."

Much has been said, and deservedly, in reprobation of the vile mixture which Dryden has thrown into the *Tempest*: doubtless without some such vicious alloy, the impure ears of that age would never have sate out to hear so much innocence of love as is contained in the sweet courtship of Ferdinand and Miranda. But is the *Tempest* of Shakspeare at all a subject for stage representation? It is one thing to read of an enchanter, and to believe the wondrous tale while we are reading it; but to have a conjuror brought before us in his conjuring-gown, with his spirits about him, which none but himself and some hundred of favoured spectators before the curtain are supposed to see, involves such a quantity of the *hateful incredible*, that all our reverence for the author cannot hinder us from perceiving such gross attempts upon the senses to be in the highest degree childish and inefficient. Spirits and fairies cannot be represented, they cannot even be painted,—they can only be believed. But the elaborate and anxious provision of scenery, which the luxury of the age demands, in these cases works a quite contrary effect to what is intended. That which in comedy, or plays of familiar life, adds so much to the life of the imitation, in plays which appeal to the higher faculties, positively destroys the illusion which it is introduced to aid. A parlour or a drawing-room,—a library opening into a garden,—a garden with an alcove in it,—a street, or the piazza of Covent-garden, does well enough in a scene; we are content to give as much credit to it as it demands; or rather, we think little about it,—it is little more than reading at the top of a page, "Scene, a Garden;" we do not imagine ourselves there, but we readily admit the imitation of familiar objects. But to think by the help of painted trees and caverns, which we know to be painted, to transport our minds to Prospero, and his island and his lonely cell;[4] or by the aid of a fiddle dexterously thrown in, in an interval of speaking, to make us believe that we hear those supernatural noises of which the isle was full:—the Orrery Lecturer at the Haymarket might as well hope, by his musical glasses cleverly stationed out of sight behind his apparatus, to make us believe that we do indeed hear the chrystal spheres ring out that chime, which if it were to inwrap our fancy long, Milton thinks,

> Time would run back and fetch the age of gold,
> And speckled vanity
> Would sicken soon and die,
> And leprous Sin would melt from earthly mould;
> Yea hell itself would pass away,
> And leave its dolorous mansions to the peering day.

The Garden of Eden, with our first parents in it, is not more impossible to be shewn on a stage, than the Enchanted Isle, with its no less interesting and innocent first settlers.

The subject of Scenery is closely connected with that of the Dresses, which are so anxiously attended to on our stage. I remember the last time I saw Macbeth played, the discrepancy I felt at the changes of garment which he varied,—the shiftings and re-shiftings, like a Romish priest at mass. The luxury of stage-improvements, and the importunity of the public eye, require this. The coronation robe of the Scottish monarch was fairly a counterpart to that which our King wears when he goes to the Parliament-house,—just so full and cumbersome, and set out with ermine and pearls. And if things must be represented, I see not what to find fault with in this. But in reading, what robe are we conscious of? Some dim images of royalty—a crown and sceptre, may float before our eyes, but who shall describe the fashion of it? Do we see in our mind's eye what Webb or any other robe-maker could pattern? This is the inevitable consequence of imitating every thing, to make all things natural. Whereas the reading of a tragedy is a fine abstraction. It presents to the fancy just so much of external appearances as to make us feel that we are among flesh and blood, while by far the greater and better part of our imagination is employed upon the thoughts and internal machinery of the character. But in acting, scenery, dress, the most contemptible things, call upon us to judge of their naturalness.

Perhaps it would be no bad similitude, to liken the pleasure which we take in seeing one of these fine plays acted, compared with that quiet delight which we find in the reading of it, to the different feelings with which a reviewer, and a man that is not a reviewer, reads a fine poem. The accursed critical habit,—the being called upon to judge and pronounce, must make it quite a different thing to the former. In seeing these plays acted, we are affected just as judges. When Hamlet compares the two pictures of Gertrude's first and second husband, who wants to see the pictures? But in the acting, a miniature must be lugged out; which we know not to be the picture, but only to shew how finely a miniature may be represented. This shewing of every thing, levels all things: it makes tricks, bows, and curtesies, of importance. Mrs. S. never got more fame by any thing than by the manner in which she dismisses the guests in the banquet-scene in *Macbeth*: it is as much remembered as any of her thrilling tones or impressive looks. But does such a trifle as this enter into the imaginations of the readers of that wild and wonderful scene? Does not the mind dismiss the feasters as rapidly as it can? Does it care about the gracefulness of the doing it? But by acting, and judging of acting, all these non-essentials are raised into an importance, injurious to the main interest of the play.

I have confined my observations to the tragic parts of Shakspeare. It would be no very difficult task to extend the enquiry to his comedies; and to shew why Falstaff, Shallow, Sir Hugh Evans, and the rest, are equally incompatible with stage representation. The length to which this Essay has run, will make it, I am afraid, sufficiently distasteful to the Amateurs of the Theatre, without going any deeper into the subject at present.

*Notes*

1. It is observable that we fall into this confusion only in *dramatic* recitations. We never dream that the gentleman who reads Lucretius in public with great applause, is therefore a great poet and philosopher; nor do we find that Tom Davies, the bookseller, who is recorded to have recited the *Paradise Lost* better than any man in England in his day (though I cannot help thinking there must be some mistake in this tradition) was therefore, by his intimate friends, set upon a level with Milton.

2. If this note could hope to meet the eye of any of the Managers, I would entreat and beg of them, in the name of both the Galleries, that this insult upon the morality of the common people of London should cease to be eternally repeated in the holiday weeks. Why are the 'Prentices of this famous and well-governed city, instead of an amusement, to be treated over and over again with the nauseous sermon of George Barnwell? Why *at the end of their vistoes* [*vistas*] are we to place the *gallows*? Were I an uncle, I should not much like a nephew of mine to have such an example placed before his eyes. It is really making uncle-murder too trivial to exhibit it as done upon such slight motives;—it is attributing too much to such characters as Millwood;—it is putting things into the heads of good young men, which they would never otherwise have dreamed of. Uncles that think any thing of their lives, should fairly petition the Chamberlain against it.

3. The error of supposing that because Othello's colour does not offend us in the reading, it should also not offend us in the seeing, is just such a fallacy as supposing that an Adam and Eve in a picture shall affect us just as they do in the poem. But in the poem we for a while have Paradisaical senses given us, which vanish when we see a man and his wife without clothes in the picture. The painters themselves feel this, as is apparent by the awkward shifts they have recourse to, to make them look not quite naked; by a sort of prophetic anachronism, antedating the invention of fig-leaves. So in the reading of the play, we see with Desdemona's eyes; in the seeing of it, we are forced to look with our own.

4. It will be said these things are done in pictures. But pictures and scenes are very different things. Painting is a world of itself, but in scene-painting there is the attempt to deceive; and there is the discordancy, never to be got over, between painted scenes and real people.

JOHN WILSON
"A Few Words on Shakespeare" (1819)
*Essays, Critical and Imaginative*
1856, Volume 3, pp. 420–31

Shakespeare is of no age. He speaks a language which thrills in our blood in spite of the separation of two hundred years. His thoughts, passions, feelings, strains of fancy, all are of this day, as they were of his own—and his genius may be contemporary with the mind of every generation for a thousand years to come. He, above all poets, looked upon men, and lived for mankind. His genius, universal in intellect and sympathy, could find, in no more bounded circumference, its proper sphere. It could not bear exclusion from any part of human existence. Whatever in nature and life was given to man, was given in contemplation and poetry to him also, and over the undimmed mirror of his mind passed all the shadows of our mortal world. Look through his plays, and tell what form of existence, what quality of spirit, he is most skilful to delineate? Which of all the manifold beings he has drawn, lives before our thoughts, our eyes, in most unpictured reality? Is it Othello, Shylock, Falstaff, Lear, the Wife of Macbeth, Imogen, Hamlet, Ariel? In none of the other great dramatists do we see anything like a perfected art. In their works, everything, it is true, exists in some shape or other, which can be required in a drama taking for its interest the absolute interest of human life and nature; but, after all, may not the very best of their works be looked on as sublime masses of chaotic confusion, through which the elements of our moral being appear? It was Shakespeare, the most unlearned of all our writers, who first exhibited on the stage perfect models, perfect images of all human characters, and of all human events. We cannot conceive any skill that could from his great characters remove any defect, or add to their perfect composition. Except in him, we look in vain for the entire fulness, the self-consistency, and self-completeness of perfect art. All the rest of our drama may be regarded rather as a testimony of the state of genius—of the state of mind of the country, full of great poetical disposition, and great tragic capacity and power—than as a collection of the works of an art. Of Shakespeare and Homer alone it may be averred, that we miss in them nothing of the greatness of nature. In all other poets we do; we feel the measure of their power, and the restraint under which it is held; but in Shakespeare and in Homer, all is free and unbounded as in nature; and as we travel along with them, in a car drawn by celestial steeds, our view seems ever interminable as before, and still equally far off the glorious horizon.

If we may be permitted to exceed the measure of the occasion to speak so much of Shakespeare himself, may we presume yet farther, and go from our purpose to speak of his individual works? Although there is no one of them that does not bear marks of his unequalled hand—scarcely one which is not remembered by the strong affection of love and delight towards some of its characters, yet to all his readers they seem marked by very different degrees of excellence, and a few are distinguished above all the rest. Perhaps the four that may be named, as those which have been to the popular feeling of his countrymen the principal plays of their great dramatist, and which would be recognised as his master-works by philosophical criticism, are *Macbeth, Othello, Hamlet,* and *Lear.* The first of these has the most entire tragic action of any of his plays. It has, throughout, one awful interest, which is begun, carried through, and concluded with the piece. This interest of the action is a perfect example of a most important dramatic unity,

preserved entire. The matter of the interest is one which has always held a strong sway over human sympathy, though mingled with abhorrence, the rise and fall of ambition. Men look on the darings of this passion with strong sympathy, because it is one of their strongest inherent feelings—the aspiring of the mind through its consciousness of power, shown in the highest forms of human life. But it is decidedly a historical, not a poetical interest. Shakespeare has made it poetical by two things chiefly—not the character of Macbeth, which is itself historical—but by the preternatural agencies with which the whole course of the story is involved, and by the character of Lady Macbeth. The illusion of the dagger and the sleep-walking may be added as individual circumstances tending to give a character of imagination to the whole play. The human interest of the piece is the acting of the purpose of ambition, and the fate which attends it—the high capacities of blinded desire in the soul—and the moral retribution which overrules the affairs of men. But the poetry is the intermingling of preternatural agency with the transactions of life—threads of events spun by unearthly hands—the scene of the cave which blends unreality with real life—the preparation and circumstances of midnight murder—the superhuman calmness of guilt, in its elated strength, in a woman's soul—and the dreaminess of mind which is brought on those whose spirits have drunk the cup of their lust. The language of the whole is perhaps more purely tragic than that of any other of Shakespeare's plays—it is simple, chaste, and strong—rarely breaking out into fanciful expression, but a vein of imagination always running through. The language of Macbeth himself is often exceedingly beautiful. Perhaps something may be owing to national remembrances and associations; but we have observed, that in Scotland at least, *Macbeth* produces a deeper, a more breathless, and a more perturbing passion, in the audience, than any other drama.

If *Macbeth* is the most perfect in the tragic action of the story, the most perfect in tragic passion is *Othello.* There is nothing to determine unhappiness to the lives of the two principal persons. Their love begins auspiciously; and the renown, high favour, and high character of Othello seem to promise a stability of happiness to himself and the wife of his affections. But the blood which had been scorched in the veins of his race, under the suns of Africa, bears a poison that swells up to confound the peace of the Christian marriage-bed. He is jealous; and the dreadful overmastering passion, which disturbs the steadfastness of his own mind, overflows upon his life, and hers, and consumes them from the earth. The external action of the play is nothing—the causes of events are none; the whole interest of the story, the whole course of the action, the causes of all that happens, live all in the breast of Othello. The whole destiny of those who are to perish lies in his passion. Hence the high tragic character of the play—showing one false illusory passion ruling and confounding all life. All that is below tragedy in the passion of love is taken away at once by the awful character of Othello, for such he seems to us to be designed to be. He appears never as a lover—but at once as a husband—and the relation of his love made dignified, as it is a husband's justification of his marriage, is also dignified as it is a soldier's relation of his stern and perilous life. It is a courted, not a wooing, at least unconsciously-wooing love, and though full of tenderness, yet it is but slightly expressed, as being solely the gentle affection of a strong mind, and in no wise a passion. "And I loved her that she did pity them." Indeed, he is not represented as a man of passion, but of stern, sedate, immovable mood. "I have seen the cannon, that, like the devil, from his very arm puffed his own brother—and can *he* be angry?" Montalto speaks with the same astonishment, calling him respected for wisdom and gravity. Therefore it is no love story. His love itself, as long as it is happy, is perfectly calm and serene, the protecting tenderness of a husband. It is not till it is disordered that it appears as a passion. Then is shown a power in contention with itself—a mighty being struck with death, and bringing up from all the depths of life convulsions and agonies. It is no exhibition of the power of the passion of love—but of the passion of life vitally wounded, and self-over-mastering. What was his love? He had placed all his faith in good—all his imagination of purity, all his tenderness of nature, upon one heart,—and at once that heart seems to him—an ulcer. It is that recoiling agony that shakes his whole body—that having confided with the whole power of his soul, he is utterly betrayed—that having departed from the pride and might of his life, which he held in his conquest and sovereignty over men, to rest himself upon a new and gracious affection, to build himself and his life upon one beloved heart, having found a blessed affection which he had passed through life without knowing, and having chosen in the just and pure goodness of his will to take that affection instead of all other hopes, desires, and passions, to live by, that at once he sees it sent out of existence, and a damned thing standing in its place. It is then that he feels a forfeiture of all power, and a blasting of all good. If Desdemona had been really guilty, the greatness would have been destroyed, because his love would have been unworthy—false. But she is good, and his love is most perfect, just, and good. That a man should place his perfect love on a wretched thing, is miserably debasing, and shocking to thought; but that, loving perfectly and well, he should, by hellish human circumvention, be brought to distrust, and dread, and abjure his own perfect love, is most mournful indeed—it is the infirmity of our good nature, wrestling in vain with the strong powers of evil. Moreover, he would, had Desdemona been false, have been the mere victim of fate; whereas, he is now in a manner his own victim. His happy love was heroic tenderness—his injured love is terrible passion—and disordered power engendered within itself to its own destruction, is the height of all tragedy. The character of Othello is perhaps the most greatly drawn, the most heroic of any of Shakespeare's actors, but it is, perhaps, that one also of which his reader last acquires the intelligence. The intellectual and warlike energy of his mind—his tenderness of affection—his loftiness of spirit—his frank generous magnanimity—impetuosity like a thunderbolt, and that dark fierce flood of boiling passion, polluting even his imagination, compose a character entirely original, most difficult to delineate, but perfectly delineated.

Hamlet might seem to be the intellectual offspring of Shakespeare's love. He alone, of all his offspring, has Shakespeare's own intellect. But he has given him a moral nature, that makes his character individual. Princely, gentle, and loving, full of natural gladness, but having a depth of sensibility which is no sooner touched by the harsh events of life than it is jarred, and the mind for ever overcome with melancholy. For intellect and sensibility blended throughout, and commensurate, and both ideally exalted and pure, are not able to pass through the calamity and trial of life; unless they are guarded by some angel from its shock, they perish in it, or undergo a worse change. The play is a singular example of a piece of great length, resting its interest upon the delineation of one character. For Hamlet, his discourses, and the changes of his mind, are all the play. The other persons—even his father's ghost—are important through him. And in himself, it is the variation of his mind, and not the varying events of his life, that affords the interest. In the representation, his celebrated soliloquy is perhaps the part of the play that is most expected,

even by the common audience. His interview with his mother, of which the interest is produced entirely from his mind—for about her we care nothing—is in like manner remarkable by the sympathy it excites in those for whom the most intellectual of Shakespeare's works would scarcely seem to have been written. This play is perhaps superior to any other in existence for unity in the delineation of character.

We have yet to speak of the most pathetic of the plays of Shakespeare—*Lear*. A story unnatural and irrational in its foundation, but, at the same time, a natural favourite of tradition, has become in the hands of Shakespeare a tragedy of surpassing grandeur and interest. He has seized upon that germ of interest which has already made the story a favourite of popular tradition, and unfolded it into a work for the passionate sympathy of all—young, old, rich, and poor, learned and illiterate, virtuous and depraved. The majestic form of the kingly-hearted old man—the reverend head of the broken-hearted father—"a head so old and white as this"—the royalty from which he is deposed, but of which he can never be divested—the father's heart which, rejected and trampled on by two children, and trampling on its one most young and duteous child, is, in the utmost degree, a father's still—the two characters, father and king, so high to our imagination and love, blended in the reverend image of Lear—*both* in their destitution, yet *both* in their height of greatness—the spirit blighted and yet undepressed—the wits gone, and yet the moral wisdom of a good heart left unstained, almost unobscured—the wild raging of the elements, joined with human outrage and violence to persecute the helpless, unresisting, almost unoffending sufferer; and he himself in the midst of all imaginable misery and desolation, descanting upon himself, on the whirlwinds that drive around him—and then turning in tenderness to some of the wild motley association of sufferers among whom he stands;—all this is not like what has been seen on any stage, perhaps in any reality, but it has made a world to our imagination about one single imaginary individual, such as draws the reverence and sympathy which should seem to belong properly only to living men. It is like the remembrance of some wild perturbed scene of real life. Everything is perfectly woeful in this world of woe. The very assumed madness of Edgar, which, if the story of Edgar stood alone, would be insufferable, and would utterly degrade him to us, seems, associated as he is with Lear, to come within the consecration of Lear's madness. It agrees with all that is brought together; the night—the storms—the houselessness—Glo'ster with his eyes put out—the fool—the semblance of a madman, and Lear in his madness, are all bound together by a strange kind of sympathy, confusion in the elements of nature, of human society and the human soul. Throughout all the play, is there not sublimity felt amidst the continual presence of all kinds of disorder and confusion in the natural and moral world; a continual consciousness of eternal order, law, and good? This it is that so exalts it in our eyes. There is more justness of intellect in Lear's madness than in his right senses—as if the indestructible divinity of the spirit gleamed at times more brightly through the ruins of its earthly tabernacle. The death of Cordelia and the death of Lear[1] leave on our minds, at least, neither pain nor disappointment, like a common play ending ill—but, like all the rest, they show us human life involved in darkness and conflicting with wild powers let loose to rage in the world; a life which continually seeks peace, and which can only find its good in peace—tending ever to the depth of peace, but of which the peace is not here. The feeling of the play, to those who rightly consider it, is high and calm,—because we are made to know, from and through those very passions which seem there convulsed, and that very structure of life and happiness that seems there crushed,—even in the law of those passions and that life, this eternal Truth, that evil must not be, and that good must be. The only thing intolerable was, that Lear should, by the very truth of his daughter's love, be separated from her love: and his restoration to her love, and therewith to his own perfect mind, consummates all that was essentially to be desired—a consummation, after which the rage and horror of mere matter-disturbing death, seems vain and idle. In fact, Lear's killing the slave who was hanging Cordelia—bearing her in dead in his arms—and his heart bursting over her—are no more than the full consummation of their reunited love—and there father and daughter lie in final and imperturbable peace. Cordelia, whom we at last see lying dead before us, and over whom we shed such floods of loving and approving tears, scarcely speaks or acts in the play at all— she appears but at the beginning and the end—is absent from all the impressive and memorable scenes; and to what she does say, there is not much effect given;—yet, by some divine power of conception in Shakespeare's soul, she always seems to our memory one of the principal characters—and while we read the play, she is continually present to our imagination. In her sister's ingratitude, her filial love is felt—in the hopelessness of the broken-hearted king, we are turned to that perfect hope that is reserved for him in her loving bosom—in the midst of darkness, confusion, and misery, her form is like a hovering angel, seen casting its radiance on the storm.

Turning from such noble creations as these, it is natural to ask ourselves, is the age of dramatic literature gone by, never to be restored? Certainly the whole history of our stage, from the extinction of that first great dynasty, down to this very day, shows rather a strong dramatic disposition, than a strong dramatic power; and the names of Rowe, Otway, Lee, and Lillo, are perhaps as far above the most favoured of this age, as they are beneath all those of the age of Elizabeth. It is not to be denied that the whole mind of the country is lowered since those magnificent times; and that its intellectual character has become more external. With respect to the drama, the state of society was then more favourable to it, passing from the strong and turbulent life of early times, yet having much of their native vigour, and much of their pristine shape and growth. The reality of life is seldom shown to our eyes; and each now sees, as it were, but a small part of the whole. He sees a little of one class. The dark study of the constitution of our life is no longer to our taste, nor within the measure of our capacity; and therein lie the causes of their hopelessness who believe that the tragic drama is no more. Some have thought that the vast number of standard plays is the cause why new plays are not produced. But genius does not work on a consideration of the supply in the market, of the stock on hand. In whatever way it has power to bring itself into sympathy with the heart of the people, so as to dwell in their love and delight, it will go to its work in obedience to such impulses; and surely there is always change enough from one generation to another to make a new field for dramatic composition, or for any kind of literature, so as to enable a mind of power to write more entirely to the passions of his contemporaries, than any one living before him has done.

It seems to us that the poetry of our days has not dealt enough with life and reality. They surely contain elements of poetry, if we had poets who were capable of bringing to use the more difficult materials of their art. Some critics have conceived that the matter of poetry might become exhausted; but the opinion is not likely to gain much credit amongst us. The bolder opinion, that all conditions of human life, for ever, will contain the inexhaustible matter of that art, seems more suitable to our genius. There has been a decided tendency in

our own days to prove the capacity of some apparently unfavourable states of life. But it may be questioned whether the experiment has yet found eminent success. What is wanting to poetry in ages like ours, seems to be rather the proper composition of the minds of poets, than a sufficiency of matter in the life from which they would have to paint. The minds of civilised men are too much unpoetical, because the natural play of sensitive imagination in their minds is, in early years, suppressed. They are cultivated with poetry indeed, but that is an unproductive cultivation. Every mind has, by nature, its own springs of poetry. And it may be conceived, that if nature were suffered to have a freer development in our minds, we should grow up, looking upon our own life with that kind of deep emotion with which, in earlier ages, men look upon the face of society; with something like a continuance of those strange and strong feelings with which, as children, we gazed upon the life even of our own generation. We begin in imagination; but we outgrow it. We pass into a state which is not of wisdom, but one in which imagination and natural passion are suppressed and extinct, and a sort of worldly temper and tone of mind, a substitute for wisdom, is adopted—like it, only in its immunity from youthful illusions. But wisdom retains the generosity of youth without its dreams, whereas this worldly wit of ours parts with youth and generosity together; and yet, while it dispels those pardonable dreams, does not exempt us from deceptions of its own, and from passions which have the ardour, but not the beauty of youth.

What Poet of the present day is there, who, grasping resolutely with the reality of life, such as our own age brings it forth, has produced true, simple, and powerful poetry? Two have made approaches to this kind, Cowper and Wordsworth. But the poetry of Cowper wants power. And though Wordsworth has expressly applied himself to this part of poetry, yet the strongest passion of his own mind is the passion for nature; and his most powerful poetry may be called almost contemplative. He is the poet of meditation. His sympathy with passions is very imperfect. And the poetry which he has drawn from present life, which, assuredly, he has much contemplated and studied, is more of a touching gentleness than of power. It is, moreover, human life blended, and almost lost in nature. It is nowhere the strength of life brought out to be the very being of poetry. Of those of our poetical writers, who, with some power indeed of glowing imagination, have wrought pictures of other scenes of the world, we hold it not necessary to speak. They have escaped from reality. Burns appears to us the only one who, looking steadfastly upon the life to which he was born, has depictured it, and changed it into poetry.

This appears to us the true test of the mind which is born to poetry, and is faithful to its destination. It is not born to live in antecedent worlds, but in its own; in its own world, by its own power, to discover poetry; to discover, that is, to recognise and distinguish the materials of life which belong to imagination.

Imagination discovering materials of its own action in the life present around it, ennobles that life, and connects itself with the on-goings of the world; but escaping from that life, it seems to us to fly from its duty, and to desert its place of service.

The poetry which would be produced by imagination, conversing intimately with human life, would be that of tragedy. But we have no tragic poet. Schiller is, perhaps, the only great tragic poet who has lived in the same day with ourselves. And wild and portentous as his shapes of life often are, who is there that does not feel that the strange power by which they hold us is derived from the very motions of our blood, and that the breath by which we live breathes in them? He has thrown back his scenes into other times of the world: but we find *ourselves* there. It is from real, present life, that he has borrowed that terrible spell of passion by which he shakes so inwardly the very seat of feeling and thought. The tragic poets of England, in the age of our dramatic literature, have shown the same power; and they drew it from the same source; from imagination submitted to human life, and dwelling in the midst of it.

The whole character of our life and literature seems to us to show in our cultivated classes a disposition of imagination to separate itself from real life, and to go over into works of art. It may appear to some a matter of little consequence; and perhaps they will think that it is *then* beginning to confine itself to its right province. We think there are many who will not be so easily satisfied; and to whom it will appear that such a separation, if it be indeed taking place, cannot be effected without grievous injury to the character of our minds. We think it possible that the great overflow of poetry in this age may be in part from this cause. And there seems to us already a great disappearance of imagination from the character of all our passions.

But life is still strong. And wherever men are assembled in societies, and are not swallowed up in sloth or most debasing passion, there the great elements of our nature are in action: and much as in this day, to look upon the face of life, it appears to be removed from all poetry, we cannot but believe that, in the very heart of our most civilised life—in our cities—in each great metropolis of commerce—in the midst of the most active concentration of all those relations of being which seem most at war with imagination—there the materials which imagination seeks in human life are yet to be found.

It were much to be wished, therefore, for the sake both of our literature and of our life, that imagination would again be content to dwell with life—that we had less of poetry, and that of more strength; and that imagination were again to be found as it used to be, one of the elements of life itself; a strong principle of our nature living in the midst of our affections and passions, blending with, kindling, invigorating, and exalting them all. Then might the spirit of dramatic literature be revived.

*Notes*

1. For some admirable observations on this subject, see the Essays of Charles Lamb—a writer to whose generous and benign philosophy, English dramatic literature is greatly indebted.

## VICTOR HUGO
### From *William Shakespeare*, tr. F. T. Marzials
### 1864

#### Part II
*Book II. Shakespeare—His Work—The Culminating Points*
VI

Hamlet, Macbeth, Othello, Lear,—these four figures tower upon the lofty edifice of Shakespeare. We have said what Hamlet is.

To say, "Macbeth is ambitious," is to say nothing. Macbeth is hunger. What hunger? The hunger of ten monsters, which is always possible in man. Certain souls have teeth. Do not wake up their hunger.

To bite at the apple, that is a fearful thing. The apple is called *Omnia*, says Filesac, that doctor of the Sorbonne who confessed Rabaillac. Macbeth has a wife whom the chronicle calls Gruoch. This Eve tempts this Adam. Once Macbeth has given the first bite he is lost. The first thing that Adam produces with Eve is Cain; the first thing that Macbeth accomplishes with Gruoch is murder.

Covetousness easily becoming violence, violence easily becoming crime, crime easily becoming madness,—this progression is Macbeth. Covetousness, crime, madness,—these three vampires have spoken to him in the solitude, and have invited him to the throne. The cat Graymalkin has called him: Macbeth will be cunning. The toad Paddock has called him: Macbeth will be horror. The *unsexed* being, Gruoch completes him. It is done; Macbeth is no longer a man. He is nothing more than an unconscious energy rushing wildly toward evil. Henceforth, no notion of right; appetite is everything. Transitory right, royalty; eternal right, hospitality,—Macbeth murders them all. He does more than slay them,—he ignores them. Before they fell bleeding under his hand, they already lay dead within his soul. Macbeth commences by this parricide,—the murder of Duncan, his guest; a crime so terrible that from the counter-blow in the night, when their master is stabbed, the horses of Duncan again become wild. The first step taken, the fall begins. It is the avalanche. Macbeth rolls headlong. He is precipitated. He falls and rebounds from one crime to another, always deeper and deeper. He undergoes the mournful gravitation of matter invading the soul. He is a thing that destroys. He is a stone of ruin, flame of war, beast of prey, scourge. He marches over all Scotland, king as he is, his bare legged kernes and his heavily-armed gallowglasses, devouring, pillaging, slaying. He decimates the Thanes, he kills Banquo, he kills all the Macduffs except the one who shall slay him, he kills the nobility, he kills the people, he kills his country, he kills "sleep." At length the catastrophe arrives,—the forest of Birnam moves against him. Macbeth has infringed all, burst through everything, violated everything, torn everything, and this desperation ends in arousing even Nature. Nature loses patience, Nature enters into action against Macbeth, Nature becomes soul against the man who has become brute force.

This drama has epic proportions. Macbeth represents that frightful hungry one who prowls throughout history, called brigand in the forest and on the throne conqueror. The ancestor of Macbeth is Nimrod. These men of force, are they forever furious? Let us be just; no. They have a goal, which being attained, they stop. Give to Alexander, to Cyrus, to Sesostris, to Cæsar, what?—the world; they are appeased. Geoffroy St. Hilaire said to me one day: "When the lion has eaten, he is at peace with Nature." For Cambyses, Sennacherib, and Genghis Khan, and their parallels, to have eaten is to possess all the earth. They would calm themselves down in the process of digesting the human race.

Now, what is Othello? He is night; an immense fatal figure. Night is amorous of day. Darkness loves the dawn. The African adores the white woman. Desdemona is Othello's brightness and frenzy! And then how easy to him is jealousy! He is great, he is dignified, he is majestic, he soars above all heads, he has as an escort bravery, battle, the braying of trumpets, the banner of war, renown, glory; he is radiant with twenty victories, he is studded with stars, this Othello: but he is black. And thus how soon, when jealous, the hero becomes monster, the black becomes the negro! How speedily has night beckoned to death!

By the side of Othello, who is night, there is Iago, who is evil,—evil, the other form of darkness. Night is but the night of the world; evil is the night of the soul. How deeply black are perfidy and falsehood! To have ink or treason in the veins is the same thing. Whoever has jostled against imposture and perjury knows it. One must blindly grope one's way with roguery. Pour hypocrisy upon the break of day, and you put out the sun; and this, thanks to false religions, happens to God.

Iago near Othello is the precipice near the landslip. "This way!" he says in a low voice. The snare advises blindness. The being of darkness guides the black. Deceit takes upon itself to give what light may be required by night. Jealousy uses falsehood as the blind man his dog. Othello the negro, Iago the traitor, opposed to whiteness and candour,—what can be more terrible! These ferocities of the darkness act in unison. These two incarnations of the eclipse conspire together,—the one roaring, the other sneering; the tragic extinguishment of light.

Sound this profound thing. Othello is the night, and being night, and wishing to kill, what does he take to slay with? Poison, the club, the axe, the knife? No; the pillow. To kill is to lull to sleep. Shakespeare himself perhaps did not take this into account. The creator sometimes, almost unknown to himself, yields to his type, so much is that type a power. And it is thus that Desdemona, spouse of the man Night, dies stifled by the pillow, which has had the first kiss, and which has the last sigh.

Lear is the occasion for Cordelia. Maternity of the daughter toward the father,—profound subject; maternity venerable among all other maternities, so admirably translated by the legend of that Roman girl, who, in the depth of a prison, nurses her old father. The young breast near the white beard,—there is not a spectacle more holy. This filial breast is Cordelia.

Once this figure dreamed of and found, Shakespeare created his drama. Where should he put this consoling vision? In an obscure age. Shakespeare has taken the year of the world 3105, the time when Joas was king of Judah, Aganippus, king of France, and Leir, king of England. The whole earth was at that time mysterious. Represent to yourself that epoch: the temple of Jerusalem is still quite new; the gardens of Semiramis, constructed nine hundred years previously, begin to crumble; the first gold coin appears in Ægina; the first balance is made by Phydon, tyrant of Argos; the first eclipse of the sun is calculated by the Chinese; three hundred and twelve years have passed since Orestes, accused by the Eumenides before the Areopagus, was acquitted; Hesiod is just dead; Homer, if he still lives, is a hundred years old; Lycurgus, thoughtful traveller, re-enters Sparta; and one may perceive in the depth of the sombre cloud of the East the chariot fire which carries Elias away. It is at that period that Leir—Lear—lives, and reigns over the dark islands. Jonas, Holofernes, Draco, Solon, Thespis, Nebuchadnezzar, Anaximenes who is to invent the signs of the zodiac, Cyrus, Zorobabel, Tarquin, Pythagoras, Æschylus, are not born yet. Coriolanus, Xerxes, Cincinnatus, Pericles, Socrates, Brennus, Aristotle, Timoleon, Demosthenes, Alexander, Epicurus, Hannibal, are larvæ waiting their hour to enter among men. Judas Maccabæus, Viriatus, Popilius, Jugurtha, Mithridates, Marius and Sylla, Cæsar and Pompey, Cleopatra, and Antony, are far away in the future; and at the moment when Lear is king of Brittany and of Iceland, there must pass away eight hundred and ninety-five years before Virgil says, "Penitus toto divisos orbe Britannos," and nine hundred and fifty years before Seneca says "Ultima Thule." The Picts and the Celts (the Scotch and the English) are tattooed. A redskin of the present day gives a vague idea of an Englishman then. It is this twilight that Shakespeare has chosen,—a broad night well adapted to the dream in which this inventor at his pleasure puts everything that he chooses, this King Lear, and then a King of France, a Duke of Burgundy, a Duke of Cornwall, a Duke of Albany, and Earl of Kent, and an Earl of Gloster. What does your history matter to him who has humanity? Besides, he has with him the legend, which is a kind of science also, and as true as history perhaps,

but in another point of view. Shakespeare agrees with Walter Mapes, archdeacon of Oxford,—that is something; he admits, from Brutus to Cadwalla, the ninety-nine Celtic kings who have preceded the Scandinavian Hengist and the Saxon Horsa: and since he believes in Mulmutius, Cinigisil, Ceolulf, Cassibelan, Cymbeline, Cynulphus, Arviragus, Guiderius, Escuin, Cudred, Vortigern, Arthur, Uther Pendragon, he has every right to believe in King Lear, and to create Cordelia. This land adopted, the place for the scene marked out, this foundation established, he takes everything and builds his work. Unheardof edifice. He takes tyranny, of which, at a later period, he will make weakness,—Lear; he takes treason,—Edmond; he takes devotion,—Kent; he takes ingratitude which begins with a caress, and he gives to this monster two heads,—Goneril, whom the legend calls Gornerille, and Regan, whom the legend calls Ragaü; he takes paternity; he takes royalty; he takes feudality; he takes ambition; he takes madness, which he divides into three, and he puts in presence three madmen,—the king's buffoon, madman by trade; Edgar of Gloster, mad for prudence's sake; the king mad through misery. It is at the summit of this tragic heap that he raises Cordelia.

There are some formidable cathedral towers, like, for instance, the Giralda, of Seville, which seem made all complete, with their spirals, their staircases, their sculptures, their cellars, their cœcums, their aerial cells, their sounding chambers, their bells, and their mass and their spire, and all their enormity, in order to carry an angel spreading on their summit her golden wings. Such is this drama, *King Lear*.

The father is the pretext for the daughter. This admirable human creation, Lear, serves as a support to that ineffable divine creation, Cordelia. The reason why that chaos of crimes, vices, madnesses, and miseries exists is, for the more splendid setting forth of virtue. Shakespeare, carrying Cordelia in his thoughts, created that tragedy like a god who, having an Aurora to put forward, makes a world expressly for it.

And what a figure is that father! What a caryatid! He is man bent down by weight, but shifts his burdens for others that are heavier. The more the old man becomes enfeebled, the more his load augments. He lives under an overburden. He bears at first power, then ingratitude, then isolation, then despair, then hunger and thirst, then madness, then all Nature. Clouds overcast him, forests heap shadow on him, the hurricane beats on the nape of his neck, the tempest makes his mantle heavy as lead, the rain falls on his shoulders, he walks bent and haggard as if he had the two knees of night upon his back. Dismayed and yet immense, he throws to the winds and to the hail this epic cry: "Why do you hate me, tempests? Why do you persecute me? *You are not my daughters.*" And then it is over; the light is extinguished,—reason loses courage and leaves him. Lear is in his dotage. Ah, he is childish, this old man. Very well! he requires a mother. His daughter appears,—his one daughter Cordelia; for the two others Regan and Goneril, are no longer his daughters, save to that extent which gives them a right to the name of parricides.

Cordelia approaches.—"Sir, do you know me?" "You are a spirit, I know," replies the old man, with the same sublime clairvoyance of bewilderment. From this moment the adorable nursing commences. Cordelia applies herself to nourish this old despairing soul, dying of inanition in hatred. Cordelia nourishes Lear with love, and his courage revives; she nourishes him with respect, and the smile returns; she nourishes him with hope, and confidence is restored; she nourishes him with wisdom, and reason revives. Lear, convalescent, rises again, and, step by step, returns again to life. The child becomes again an old man; the old man becomes a man again. And behold him happy, this wretched one. It is on this expansion of happiness that the catastrophe is hurled down.

Alas! there are traitors, there are perjurers, there are murderers. Cordelia dies. Nothing more heartrending than this. The old man is stunned; he no longer understands anything; and embracing the corpse, he expires. He dies on this dead one. The supreme anguish is spared him of remaining behind her among the living, a poor shadow, to feel the place in his heart empty and to seek for his soul, carried away by that sweet being who is departed. O God, those whom thou lovest thou dost not allow to survive.

To live after the flight of the angel; to be the father orphaned of his child; to be the eye which no longer has light; to be the deadened heart which has no more joy; from time to time to stretch the hands into obscurity, and try to reclasp a being who was there (where, then, can she be?); to feel himself forgotten in that departure; to have lost all reason for being here below; to be henceforth a man who goes to and fro before a sepulchre, not received, not admitted,—that would be indeed a gloomy destiny. Thou hast done well, poet, to kill this old man.

## ALGERNON CHARLES SWINBURNE
### From A *Study of Shakespeare*
#### 1880, pp. 170–92

Of all Shakespeare's plays, *King Lear* is unquestionably that in which he has come nearest to the height and to the likeness of the one tragic poet on any side greater than himself whom the world in all its ages has ever seen born of time. It is by far the most Æschylean of his works; the most elemental and primæval, the most oceanic and Titanic in conception. He deals here with no subtleties as in *Hamlet*, with no conventions as in *Othello*: there is no question of "a divided duty" or a problem half insoluble, a matter of country and connection, of family or of race; we look upward and downward, and in vain, into the deepest things of nature, into the highest things of providence; to the roots of life, and to the stars; from the roots that no God waters to the stars which give no man light; over a world full of death and life without resting-place or guidance.

But in one main point it differs radically from the work and the spirit of Æschylus. Its fatalism is of a darker and harder nature. To Prometheus the fetters of the lord and enemy of mankind were bitter; upon Orestes the hand of heaven was laid too heavily to bear; yet in the not utterly infinite or everlasting distance we see beyond them the promise of the morning on which mystery and justice shall be made one; when righteousness and omnipotence at last shall kiss each other. But on the horizon of Shakespeare's tragic fatalism we see no such twilight of atonement, such pledge of reconciliation as this. Requital, redemption, amends, equity, explanation, pity and mercy, are words without a meaning here.

As flies to wanton boys are we to the gods;
They kill us for their sport.

Here is no need of the Eumenides, children of Night everlasting; for here is very Night herself.

The words just cited are not casual or episodical; they strike the keynote of the whole poem, lay the keystone of the whole arch of thought. There is no contest of conflicting forces, no judgment so much as by casting of lots: far less is there any light of heavenly harmony or of heavenly wisdom, of Apollo or Athene from above. We have heard much and often from theologians of the light of revelation: and some such thing indeed we find in Æschylus: but the darkness of revelation is here.

For in this the most terrible work of human genius it is with the very springs and sources of nature that her student has set himself to deal. The veil of the temple of our humanity is rent in twain. Nature herself, we might say, is revealed—and revealed as unnatural. In face of such a world as this a man might be forgiven who should pray that chaos might come again. Nowhere else in Shakespeare's work or in the universe of jarring lives are the lines of character and event so broadly drawn or so sharply cut. Only the supreme self-command of this one poet could so mould and handle such types as to restrain and prevent their passing from the abnormal into the monstrous: yet even as much as this, at least in all cases but one, it surely has accomplished. In Regan alone would it be, I think, impossible to find a touch or trace of anything less vile than it was devilish. Even Goneril has her one splendid hour, her fire-flaught of hellish glory; when she treads under foot the half-hearted goodness, the wordy and windy though sincere abhorrence, which is all that the mild and impotent revolt of Albany can bring to bear against her imperious and dauntless devilhood; when she flaunts before the eyes of her "milk-livered" and "moral fool" the coming banners of France about the "plumed helm" of his slayer.

On the other side, Kent is the exception which answers to Regan on this. Cordelia, the brotherless Antigone of our stage, has one passing touch of intolerance for what her sister was afterwards to brand as indiscretion and dotage in their father, which redeems her from the charge of perfection. Like Imogen, she is not too inhumanly divine for the sense of divine irritation. Godlike though they be, their very godhead is human and feminine; and only therefore credible, and only therefore adorable. Cloten and Regan, Goneril and Iachimo, have power to stir and embitter the sweetness of their blood. But for the contrast and even the contact of antagonists as abominable as these, the gold of their spirit would be too refined, the lily of their holiness too radiant, the violet of their virtue too sweet. As it is, Shakespeare has gone down perforce among the blackest and the basest things of nature to find anything so equally exceptional in evil as properly to counter-balance and make bearable the excellence and extremity of their goodness. No otherwise could either angel have escaped the blame implied in the very attribute and epithet of blameless. But where the possible depth of human hell is so foul and unfathomable as it appears in the spirits which serve as foils to these, we may endure that in them the inner height of heaven should be no less immaculate and immeasurable.

It should be a truism wellnigh as musty as Hamlet's half cited proverb, to enlarge upon the evidence given in *King Lear* of a sympathy with the mass of social misery more wide and deep and direct and bitter and tender than Shakespeare has shown elsewhere. But as even to this day and even in respectable quarters the murmur is not quite duly extinct which would charge on Shakespeare a certain share of divine indifference to suffering, of godlike satisfaction and a less than compassionate content, it is not yet perhaps utterly superfluous to insist on the utter fallacy and falsity of their creed who whether in praise or in blame would rank him to his credit or discredit among such poets as on this side at least may be classed rather with Goethe than with Shelley and with Gautier than with Hugo. A poet of revolution he is not, as none of his country in that generation could have been: but as surely as the author of *Julius Cæsar* has approved himself in the best and highest sense of the word at least potentially a republican, so surely has the author of *King Lear* avowed himself in the only good and rational sense of the words a spiritual if not a political democrat and socialist.

It is only, I think, in this most tragic of tragedies that the sovereign lord and incarnate god of pity and terror can be said to have struck with all his strength a chord of which the resonance could excite such angry agony and heartbreak of wrath as that of the brother kings when they smote their staffs against the ground in fierce imperious anguish of agonised and rebellious compassion, at the oracular cry of Calchas for the innocent blood of Iphigenia. The doom even of Desdemona seems as much less morally intolerable as it is more logically inevitable than the doom of Cordelia. But doubtless the fatalism of *Othello* is as much darker and harder than that of any third among the plays of Shakespeare, as it is less dark and hard than the fatalism of *King Lear*. For upon the head of the very noblest man whom even omnipotence or Shakespeare could ever call to life he has laid a burden in one sense yet heavier than the burden of Lear, insomuch as the sufferer can with somewhat less confidence of universal appeal proclaim himself a man more sinned against than sinning.

And yet, if ever man after Lear might lift up his voice in that protest, it would assuredly be none other than Othello. He is in all the prosperous days of his labour and his triumph so utterly and wholly nobler than the self-centred and wayward king, that the capture of his soul and body in the unimaginable snare of Iago seems a yet blinder and more unrighteous blow

Struck by the envious wrath of man or God

than ever fell on the old white head of that child-changed father. But at least he is destroyed by the stroke of a mightier hand than theirs who struck down Lear. As surely as Othello is the noblest man of man's making, Iago is the most perfect evil-doer, the most potent demi-devil. It is of course the merest commonplace to say as much, and would be no less a waste of speech to add the half comfortable reflection that it is in any case no shame to fall by such a hand. But this subtlest and strangest work of Shakespeare's admits and requires some closer than common scrutiny. Coleridge has admirably described the first great soliloquy which opens to us the pit of hell within as "the motive-hunting of a motiveless malignity." But subtle and profound and just as is this definitive appreciation, there is more in the matter yet than even this. It is not only that Iago, so to speak, half tries to make himself half believe that Othello has wronged him, and that the thought of it gnaws him inly like a poisonous mineral: though this also be true, it is not half the truth—nor half that half again. Malignant as he is, the very subtlest and strongest component of his complex nature is not even malignity. It is the instinct of what Mr. Carlyle would call an inarticulate poet. In his immortal study on the affair of the diamond necklace, the most profound and potent humourist of his country in his century has unwittingly touched on the mainspring of Iago's character—"the very pulse of the machine." He describes his Circe de la Mothe-Valois as a practical dramatic poet or playwright at least in lieu of play-writer: while indicating how and wherefore, with all her constructive skill and rhythmic art in action, such genius as hers so differs from the genius of Shakespeare that she undeniably could not have written a *Hamlet*. Neither could Iago have written an *Othello*. (From this theorem, by the way, a reasoner or a casuist benighted enough to prefer articulate poets to inarticulate, Shakespeare to Cromwell, a fair Vittoria Colonna to a "foul Circe-Megæra," and even such a strategist as Homer to such a strategist as Frederic-William, would not illogically draw such conclusions or infer such corollaries as might result in opinions hardly consonant with the Teutonic-Titanic evangel of the preacher who supplied him with his

thesis.) "But what he can do, that he will": and if it be better to make a tragedy than to write one, to act a poem than to sing it, we must allow to Iago a station in the hierarchy of poets very far in advance of his creator's. None of the great inarticulate may more justly claim place and precedence. With all his poetic gift, he has no poetic weakness. Almost any creator but his would have given him some grain of spite or some spark of lust after Desdemona. To Shakespeare's Iago she is no more than is a rhyme to another and articulate poet.[1] His stanza must at any rate and at all costs be polished: to borrow the metaphor used by Mr. Carlyle in apologetic illustration of a royal hero's peculiar system of levying recruits for his colossal brigade. He has within him a sense or conscience of power incomparable: and this power shall not be left, in Hamlet's phrase, "to fust in him unused." A genuine and thorough capacity for human lust or hate would diminish and degrade the supremacy of his evil. He is almost as far above or beyond vice as he is beneath or beyond virtue. And this it is that makes him impregnable and invulnerable. When once he has said it, we know as well as he that thenceforth he never will speak word. We could smile almost as we can see him to have smiled at Gratiano's most ignorant and empty threat, being well assured that torments will in no wise ope his lips: that as surely and as truthfully as ever did the tortured philosopher before him, he might have told his tormentors that they did but bruise the coating, batter the crust, or break the shell of Iago. Could we imagine a far other lost spirit than Farinata degli Uberti's endowed with Farinata's might of will, and transferred from the sepulchres of fire to the dykes of Malebolge, we might conceive something of Iago's attitude in hell—of his unalterable and indomitable posture for all eternity. As though it were possible and necessary that in some one point the extremities of all conceivable good and of all imaginable evil should meet and mix together in a new "marriage of heaven and hell," the action in passion of the most devilish among all the human damned could hardly be other than that of the most godlike among all divine saviours—the figure of Iago than a reflection by hell-fire of the figure of Prometheus.

Between Iago and Othello the position of Desdemona is precisely that defined with such quaint sublimity of fancy in the old English byword—"between the devil and the deep sea." Deep and pure and strong and adorable always and terrible and pitiless on occasion as the sea is the great soul of the glorious hero to whom she has given herself; and what likeness of man's enemy from Satan down to Mephistopheles could be matched for danger and for dread against the good bluff soldierly trustworthy figure of honest Iago? The rough license of his tongue at once takes warrant from his good soldiership and again gives warrant for his honesty: so that in a double sense it does him yeoman's service, and that twice told. It is pitifully ludicrous to see him staged to the show like a member—and a very inefficient member—of the secret police. But it would seem impossible for actors to understand that he is not a would-be detective, an aspirant for the honours of a Vidocq, a candidate for the laurels of a Vautrin: that he is no less than Lepidus, or than Antony's horse, "a tried and valiant soldier." It is perhaps natural that the two deepest and subtlest of all Shakespeare's intellectual studies in good and evil should be the two most painfully misused and misunderstood alike by his commentators and his fellows of the stage: it is certainly undeniable that no third figure of his creation has ever been on both sides as persistently misconceived and misrepresented with such desperate pertinacity as Hamlet and Iago.

And it is only when Iago is justly appreciated that we can justly appreciate either Othello or Desdemona. This again should surely be no more than the truism that it sounds; but practically it would seem to be no less than an adventurous and audacious paradox. Remove or deform or diminish or modify the dominant features of the destroyer, and we have but the eternal and vulgar figures of jealousy and innocence, newly vamped and veneered and padded and patched up for the stalest purposes of puppetry. As it is, when Coleridge asks "which do we pity the most" at the fall of the curtain, we can surely answer, Othello. Noble as are the "most blessed conditions" of "the gentle Desdemona," he is yet the nobler of the two; and has suffered more in one single pang than she could suffer in life or in death.

But if *Othello* be the most pathetic, *King Lear* the most terrible, *Hamlet* the subtlest and deepest work of Shakespeare, the highest in abrupt and steep simplicity of epic tragedy is *Macbeth*. There needs no ghost come from the grave, any reader may too probably remark, to tell us this. But in the present generation such novelties have been unearthed regarding Shakespeare that the reassertion of an old truth may seem to have upon it some glittering reflection from the brazen brightness of a brand-new lie. Have not certain wise men of the east of England—Cantabrigian Magi, led by the star of their goddess Mathesis ("mad Mathesis," as a daring poet was once ill-advised enough to dub her doubtful deity in defiance of scansion rather than of truth)—have they not detected in the very heart of this tragedy the "paddling palms and pinching fingers" of Thomas Middleton?

To the simpler eyes of less learned Thebans than these—Thebes, by the way, was Dryden's irreverent name for Cambridge, the nursing mother of "his green unknowing youth," when that "renegade" was recreant enough to compliment Oxford at her expense as the chosen Athens of "his riper age"—the likelihood is only too evident that the sole text we possess of *Macbeth* has not been interpolated but mutilated. In their version of *Othello*, remarkably enough, the "player-editors," contrary to their wont, have added to the treasure-house of their text one of the most precious jewels that ever the prodigal afterthought of a great poet bestowed upon the rapture of his readers. Some of these, by way of thanksgiving, have complained with a touch of petulance that it was out of place and superfluous in the setting: nay, that it was incongruous with all the circumstances—out of tone and out of harmony and out of keeping with character and tune and time. In other lips indeed than Othello's, at the crowning minute of culminant agony, the rush of imaginative reminiscence which brings back upon his eyes and ears the lightning foam and tideless thunder of the Pontic sea might seem a thing less natural than sublime. But Othello has the passion of a poet closed in as it were and shut up behind the passion of a hero. For all his practical readiness of martial eye and ruling hand in action, he is also in his season "of imagination all compact." Therefore it is that in the face and teeth of all devils akin to Iago that hell could send forth to hiss at her election, we feel and recognise the spotless exaltation, the sublime and sunbright purity, of Desdemona's inevitable and invulnerable love. When once we likewise have seen Othello's visage in his mind, we see too how much more of greatness is in this mind than in another hero's. For such an one, even a boy may well think how thankfully and joyfully he would lay down his life. Other friends we have of Shakespeare's giving whom we love deeply and well, if hardly with such love as could weep for him all the tears of the body and all the blood of the heart: but there is none we love like Othello.

I must part from his presence again for a season, and return to my topic in the text of *Macbeth*. That it is piteously rent and ragged and clipped and garbled in some of its earlier scenes, the rough construction and the poltfoot metre, lame sense and limping verse, each maimed and mangled subject of players' and printers' most treasonable tyranny contending as it were to seem harsher than the other, combine in this contention to bear indisputable and intolerable witness. Only where the witches are, and one more potent and more terrible than all witches and all devils at their beck, can we be sure that such traitors have not robbed us of one touch from Shakespeare's hand. The second scene of the play at least bears marks of such handling as the brutal Shakespearean Hector's of the "mangled Myrmidons"; it is too visibly "noseless, handless, hacked and chipped" as it comes to us, crying on Heminge and Condell. And it is in this unlucky scene that unkindly criticism has not unsuccessfully sought for the gravest faults of language and manner to be found in Shakespeare. For certainly it cannot be cleared from the charge of a style stiffened and swollen with clumsy braid and crabbed bombast. But against the weird sisters, and her who sits above them and apart, more awful than Hecate's very self, no mangling hand has been stretched forth; no blight of mistranslation by perversion has fallen upon the words which interpret and expound the hidden things of their evil will.

To one tragedy as to one comedy of Shakespeare's, the casual or the natural union of especial popularity with especial simplicity in selection and in treatment of character makes it as superfluous as it would be difficult to attempt any application of analytical criticism. There is nothing in them of a nature so compound or so complex as to call for solution or resolution into its primal elements. Here there is some genuine ground for the generally baseless and delusive opinion of self-complacent sciolism that he who runs may read Shakespeare. These two plays it is hardly worth while to point out by name: all probable readers will know them at once for *Macbeth* and *As You Like It*. There can hardly be a single point of incident or of character on which the youngest reader will not find himself at one with the oldest, the dullest with the brightest among the scholars of Shakespeare. It would be an equal waste of working hours or of playtime if any of these should devote any part of either a whole-schoolday or a holiday to remark or to rhapsody on the character of Macbeth or of Orlando, of Rosalind or of Lady Macbeth. He that runs, let him read: and he that has ears, let him hear.

I cannot but think that enough at least of time has been spent if not wasted by able and even by eminent men on examination of *Coriolanus* with regard to its political aspect or bearing upon social questions. It is from first to last, for all its turmoil of battle and clamour of contentious factions, rather a private and domestic than a public or historical tragedy. As in *Julius Cæsar* the family had been so wholly subordinated to the state, and all personal interests so utterly dominated by the preponderance of national duties, that even the sweet and sublime figure of Portia passing in her "awful loveliness" was but as a profile half caught in the background of an episode, so here on the contrary the whole force of the final impression is not that of a conflict between patrician and plebeian, but solely that of a match of passions played out for life and death between a mother and a son. The partisans of oligarchic or democratic systems may wrangle at their will over the supposed evidences of Shakespeare's prejudice against this creed and prepossession in favour of that: a third bystander may rejoice in the proof thus established of his impartial indifference towards either: it is all nothing to the real point in hand. The subject of the whole play is not the exile's revolt, the rebel's repentance, or the traitor's reward, but above all it is the son's tragedy. The inscription on the plinth of this tragic statue is simply to Volumnia Victrix.

A loftier or a more perfect piece of man's work was never done in all the world than this tragedy of *Coriolanus*: the one fit and crowning epithet for its companion or successor is that bestowed by Coleridge—"the most wonderful." It would seem a sign or birthmark of only the greatest among poets that they should be sure to rise instantly for awhile above the very highest of their native height at the touch of a thought of Cleopatra. So was it, as we all know, with William Shakespeare: so is it, as we all see, with Victor Hugo. As we feel in the marvellous and matchless verses of *Zim-Zizimi* all the splendour and fragrance and miracle of her mere bodily presence, so from her first imperial dawn on the stage of Shakespeare to the setting of that eastern star behind a pall of undissolving cloud we feel the charm and the terror and the mystery of her absolute and royal soul. Byron wrote once to Moore, with how much truth or sincerity those may guess who would care to know, that his friend's first "confounded book" of thin prurient jingle ("we call it a mellisonant tingle-tangle," as Randolph's mock Oberon says of a stolen sheep-bell) had been the first cause of all his erratic or erotic frailties: it is not impossible that spirits of another sort may remember that to their own innocent infantine perceptions the first obscure electric revelation of what Blake calls "the Eternal Female" was given through a blind wondering thrill of childish rapture by a lightning on the baby dawn of their senses and their soul from the sunrise of Shakespeare's Cleopatra.

Never has he given such proof of his incomparable instinct for abstinence from the wrong thing as well as achievement of the right. He has utterly rejected and disdained all occasion of setting her off by means of any lesser foil than all the glory of the world with all its empires. And we need not Antony's example to show us that these are less than straws in the balance.

> Entre elle et l'univers qui s'offraient à la fois
> Il hesita, lâchant le monde dans son choix.

Even as that Roman grasp relaxed and let fall the world, so has Shakespeare's self let go for awhile his greater world of imagination, with all its all but infinite variety of life and thought and action, for love of that more infinite variety which custom could not stale. Himself a second and a yet more fortunate Antony, he has once more laid a world, and a world more wonderful than ever, at her feet. He has put aside for her sake all other forms and figures of womanhood; he, father or creator of Rosalind, of Cordelia, of Desdemona, and of Imogen, he too, like the sun-god and sender of all song, has anchored his eyes on her whom "Phœbus' amorous pinches" could not leave "black," nor "wrinkled deep in time"; on that incarnate and imperishable "spirit of sense," to whom at the very last

> The stroke of death is as a lover's pinch,
> That hurts, and is desired.

To him, as to the dying husband of Octavia, this creature of his own hand might have boasted herself that the loveliest and purest among all her sisters of his begetting,

> with her modest eyes
> And still conclusion, shall acquire no honour,
> Demurring upon me.

To sum up, Shakespeare has elsewhere given us in ideal incarnation the perfect mother, the perfect wife, the perfect daughter, the perfect mistress, or the perfect maiden: here only once for all he has given us the perfect and the everlasting woman.

And what a world of great men and great things, "high actions and high passions," is this that he has spread under her for a footcloth or hung behind her for a curtain! The descendant of that other his ancestral Alcides, late offshoot of the god whom he loved and who so long was loth to leave him, is here as in history the visible one man revealed who could grapple for a second with very Rome and seem to throw it, more lightly than he could cope with Cleopatra. And not the Roman Landor himself could see or make us see more clearly than has his fellow provincial of Warwickshire that first imperial nephew of her great first paramour, who was to his actual uncle even such a foil and counterfeit and perverse and prosperous parody as the son of Hortense Beauharnais of Saint-Leu to the son of Letizia Buonaparte of Ajaccio. For Shakespeare too, like Landor, had watched his "sweet Octavius" smilingly and frowningly "draw under nose the knuckle of forefinger" as he looked out upon the trail of innocent blood after the bright receding figure of his brave young kinsman. The fair-faced false "present God" of his poetic parasites, the smooth triumphant patron and preserver with the heart of ice and iron, smiles before us to the very life. It is of no account now to remember that

> he at Philippi kept
> His sword even like a dancer:

for the sword of Antony that struck for him is in the renegade hand of Dercetas.

I have said nothing of Enobarbus or of Eros, the fugitive once ruined by his flight and again redeemed by the death-agony of his dark and doomed repentance, or the freedman transfigured by a death more fair than freedom through the glory of the greatness of his faith: for who can speak of all things or of half that are in Shakespeare? And who can speak worthily of any?

*Notes*

1. What would at least be partly lust in another man is all but purely hatred in Iago.

> Now I do love her too:
> Not out of absolute lust, (though, peradventure,
> I stand accountant for as great a sin)
> But partly led to diet my revenge.

For "partly" read "wholly," and for "peradventure" read "assuredly," and the incarnate father of lies, made manifest in the flesh, here speaks all but all the truth for once, to himself alone.

# *Titus Andronicus*

It is also agreed, that every man heere, exercise his owne Iudgement, and not censure by *Contagion*, or upon *trust*, from anothers voice, or face. . . . Hee that will sweare *Ieronimo* or *Andronicus* are the best playes, yet shall passe unexcepted at, heere, as a man whose Iudgement shewes it is constant, and hath stood still, these five and twentie, or thirtie yeeres.—BEN JONSON, "Induction" to *Bartholomew Fayre*, 1614

I think it a greater theft to Rob the dead of their Praise, then the Living of their Money. That I may not appear Guilty of such a Crime, 'tis necessary I should acquaint you, that there is a play in Mr. *Shakespeares* Volume under the name of *Titus Andronicus*, from whence I drew part of this ⟨play⟩. I have been told by some anciently conversant with the Stage, that it was not Originally his, but brought by a private Author to be Acted, and he only gave some Master-touches to one or two of the Principal Parts or Characters; this I am apt to believe, because 'tis the most incorrect and indigested piece in all his Works, It seems rather a heap of Rubbish then a Structure.—EDWARD RAVENSCROFT, "To the Reader," *Titus Andronicus, or the Rape of Lavinia*, 1687

All the editors and criticks agree with Mr. Theobald in supposing this play spurious. I see no reason for differing from them; for the colour of the stile is wholly different from that of the other plays, and there is an attempt at regular versification, and artificial closes, not always inelegant, yet seldom pleasing. The barbarity of the spectacles, and the general massacre which are here exhibited, can scarcely be conceived tolerable to any audience; yet we are told by Jonson, that they were not only borne but praised. That Shakespeare wrote any part, though Theobald declares it "incontestable," I see no reason for believing.

The testimony produced at the beginning of this play, by which it is ascribed to Shakespeare, is by no means equal to the argument against its authenticity, arising from the total difference of conduct, language, and sentiments, by which it stands apart from all the rest. Meres had probably no other evidence than that of a title-page, which, though in our time it be sufficient, was then of no great authority; for all the plays which were rejected by the first collectors of Shakespeare's works, and admitted in later editions, and again rejected by the critical editors, had Shakespeare's name on the title, as we must suppose, by the fraudulence of the printers, who, while there were yet no gazettes, nor advertisements, nor any means of circulating literary intelligence, could usurp at pleasure any celebrated name. Nor had Shakespeare any interest in detecting the imposture, as none of his fame or profit was produced by the press.

The chronology of this play does not prove it not to be Shakespeare's. If it had been written twenty-five years, in 1614, it might have been written when Shakespeare was twenty-five years old. When he left Warwickshire I know not, but at the age of twenty-five it was rather too late to fly for deer-stealing.

Ravenscroft, who, in the reign of Charles II. revised this play, and restored it to the stage, tells us in his preface, from a theatrical tradition I suppose, which in his time might be of sufficient authority, that this play was touched in different parts by Shakespeare, but written by some other poet. I do not find Shakespeare's touches very discernible.—SAMUEL JOHNSON, *Notes On Shakespeare's Plays*, 1768

All the editors, with the exception of Capell, are unanimous in rejecting *Titus Andronicus* as unworthy of Shakspeare, though they always allow it to be printed with the other pieces, as the scape-goat, as it were, of their abusive criticism. The correct method in such an investigation is first to examine into the external grounds, evidences, &c., and to weigh their value; and then to adduce the internal reasons derived from the quality of the work. The critics of Shakspeare follow a course directly the reverse of this; they set out with a preconceived opinion against a piece, and seek, in justification of this opinion, to render the historical ground suspicious, and to set them aside. Now *Titus Andronicus* is to be found in the first folio edition of Shakspeare's works, which it is known was published by Heminge and Condell, for many years his friends and fellow-managers of the same theatre. Is it possible to persuade ourselves that they would not have known if a piece in their repertory did or did not really belong to Shakspeare? And are we to lay to the charge of these honourable men an intentional fraud in this single case, when we know that they did not show themselves so very desirous of scraping everything together which went by the name of Shakspeare, but, as it appears, merely gave those plays of which they had manuscripts in hand? Yet the following circumstance is still stronger. George Meres, a contemporary and admirer of Shakspeare, in an enumeration of his works, mentions *Titus Andronicus*, in the year 1598. Meres was personally acquainted with the poet, and so very intimately, that the latter read over to him his sonnets before they were printed. I cannot conceive that all the critical scepticism in the world would ever be able to get over such a testimony.

This tragedy, it is true, is framed according to a false idea of the tragic, which by an accumulation of cruelties and enormities, degenerates into the horrible, and yet leaves no deep impression behind: the story of Tereus and Philomela is heightened and overcharged under other names, and mixed up with the repast of Atreus and Thyestes, and many other incidents. In detail there is no want of beautiful lines, bold images, nay, even features which betray the peculiar conception of Shakspeare. Among these we may reckon the joy of the treacherous Moor at the blackness and ugliness of his adulterous offspring; and in the compassion of Titus Andronicus, grown childish through grief, for a fly which had been struck dead, while his rage afterwards, when he imagines he discovers in it his black enemy, we recognize the future poet of *Lear*. Are the critics afraid that Shakspeare's fame would be injured, were it established that in his early youth he ushered into the world a feeble and immature work? Was Rome the less the conqueror of the world, because Remus could leap over its first walls? Let any one place himself in Shakspeare's situation at the commencement of his career. He found only a few indifferent models, and yet these met with the most favourable reception, because in the novelty of an art, men are never difficult to please, before their taste has been made fastidious by choice and abundance. Must not this situation have had its influence on him before he learned to make higher demands on himself, and by digging deeper in his own mind, discovered the rich veins of noble metal that ran there? It is even highly probable that he must have made several failures before he succeeded in getting into the right path. Genius is in a certain sense infallible, and has nothing to learn; but art is to be learned, and must be acquired by practice and experience. In Shakspeare's acknowledged works we find hardly any traces of his apprenticeship, and yet apprenticeship he certainly had. This every artist must have, and especially in a period where he has not before him the examples of a school already formed. I consider it as extremely probable that Shakspeare began to write for the theatre at a much earlier period than the one which is generally stated, namely, after the year 1590. It appears that, as early as the year 1584, when only twenty years of age, he had left his paternal home and repaired to London. Can we imagine that such an active head would remain idle for six whole years without making any attempt to emerge by his talents from an uncongenial situation? That in the dedication of the poem of *Venus and Adonis* he calls it "the first heir of his invention," proves nothing against the supposition. It was the first which he printed; he might have composed it at an earlier period; perhaps, also, in this term, "heirs of his invention," he did not indulge theatrical labours, especially as they then conferred but little to his literary dignity. The earlier Shakspeare began to compose for the theatre, the less are we enabled to consider the immaturity and imperfection of a work a proof of its spuriousness in opposition to historical evidence, if only we can discern in it prominent features of his mind. Several of the works rejected as spurious may still have been produced in the period betwixt *Titus Andronicus*, and the earliest of the acknowledged pieces.—AUGUST WILHELM SCHLEGEL, *Lectures on Dramatic Art and Literature*, 1809, tr. John Black

## G. G. GERVINUS
From *"Titus Andronicus and Pericles"*
*Shakespeare Commentaries*, tr. F. E. Bunnètt
1845

It is indisputable that *Titus Andronicus*, if a work of Shakespeare's at all, is one of his earliest writings. Ben Jonson (in the introduction to *Bartholomew Fair*) said, in the year 1614, that the *Andronicus*—by which he could hardly allude to any other play—had been acted for twenty-five or thirty years; it would, therefore, in any case have been produced during the first years of Shakespeare's life in London. There are few, however, among the readers who value Shakespeare who would not wish to have it proved that this piece did not proceed from the poet's pen. This wish is met by the remark of a man named Ravenscroft, who, in 1687, remodelled this tragedy, and who had heard from an old judge of stage matters that the piece came from another author, and that Shakespeare had only added 'some master-touches to one or two of the principal characters.' Among the masters of English criticism the best opinions are divided. Collier and Knight assign it unhesitatingly to Shakespeare, and the former even thinks, in accordance with his opinion upon Marlowe, that as a poetical production the piece has not had justice done to it. Nathan Drake, Coleridge (a few passages excepted), and Ingleby, absolutely reject it, and Alex. Dyce believes that the *Yorkshire Tragedy* had more claims than *Titus* to be numbered among the Shakespeare writings.

That which we wish we willingly believe. But in this case great and important reasons in evidence of Shakespeare's authorship stand opposed to the wish and the ready belief. The express testimony of Meres, a learned contemporary, who in the year 1598 mentions a list of Shakespeare's plays, places *Titus* positively among them. The friends of Shakespeare received it in the edition of his works. Neither of these facts certainly contradicts the tradition of Ravenscroft, but at all

events they prevent the piece from being expunged as supposititious without examination.

In accordance with these contradictory external testimonies, internal evidence and the arguments deduced from it appear also to lead rather to doubt than to certainty. It is true that *Titus Andronicus* belongs in matter as well as in style entirely to the older school which was set aside by Shakespeare. Reading it in the midst of his works, we do not feel at home in it: but if the piece is perused in turn with those of Kyd and Marlowe, the reader finds himself upon the same ground. If, agitated by Shakespeare's most terrible tragedies, we enter into the accumulated horrors of this drama, we perceive without effort the difference that exists between the liberal art which sympathises with the terribleness of the evil it depicts and quickly passes over it—and which, for that reason, suffers no evil to overtake men that cannot be laid to their own guilt and nature—and the rudeness of a style which unfeelingly takes pleasure in suffering innocence, in paraded sorrow, in tongues cut out and hands hewn off, and which depicts such scenes with the most complacent diffuseness of description. He who compares the most wicked of all the characters which Shakespeare depicted with this Aaron, who cursed 'the day in which he did not some notorious ill,' will feel that in the one some remnant of humanity is ever preserved, while in the other a 'ravenous tiger' commits unnatural deeds and speaks unnatural language. But if the whole impression which we receive from this barbarous subject and its treatment speaks with almost overwhelming conviction against the Shakesperian origin of the piece, it is well also to remember all the circumstances of the poet and his time which can counterbalance this conviction. The refinement of feeling which the poet acquired in his maturity was not of necessity equally the attribute of his youth. If the play, such as it is, were the work of his youthful pen, we must conclude that a mighty, indeed almost violent revolution, early transformed his moral and æsthetic nature, and as it were with one blow. Such a change, however, took place even in the far less powerful poetic natures of our own Goethe and Schiller; it has in some more or less conspicuous degree *at any rate* taken place in Shakespeare. The question might be asked, whether, in the first impetuosity of youth, which so readily is driven to misanthropical moods, this violent expression of hatred, of revenge, and of bloodthirstiness, conspicuous throughout the piece, denotes more in such a man and at such a time, than Schiller's *Robbers* or Gerstenberg's *Ugolino* did, which were written in Germany, in the eighteenth century, for a far more civilised generation. When a poet of such self-reliance as Shakespeare ventured his first essay, he might have been tempted to compete with the most victorious of his contemporaries; this was Marlowe. To strike him with his own weapons would be the surest path to ready conquest. And how should an embryo poet disdain this path? At that period scenes of blood and horror were not so rare on the great stage of real life as with us; upon the stage of art they commended a piece to hearers to whom the stronger the stimulant the more it was agreeable. It is clear, from Ben Jonson's before-mentioned testimony, that *Titus* was a welcome piece, which continued in favour on the stage, just as much as Schiller's *Robbers*. Besides this approval of the people, the author of *Titus* could claim yet higher approbation. Whoever he might be, he was imbued just as much as the poet of *Venus* and *Lucrece* with the fresh remembrance of the classical school; Latin quotations, a predilection for Ovid and Virgil, for the tales of Troy and the Trojan party, and constant references to old mythology and history, prevail throughout the play. An allusion to Sophocles' *Ajax*, and similarity to passages of Seneca, have been discovered in it. All the tragic legends of Rome and Greece were certainly present to the poet, and we know how full they are of terrible matter. The learned poet gathered them together, in order to compose his drama and its action, from the most approved poetical material of the ancients. When Titus disguises his revenge before Tamora, he plays the part of Brutus; when he stabs his daughter, that of Virginius; the dreadful fate of Lavinia is the fable of Tereus and Progne; the revenge of Titus on the sons of Tamora, that of Atreus and Thyestes; other traits remind of Æneas and Dido, of Lucretia and Coriolanus. Forming his one fable from these shreds of many fables, and uniting the materials of many old tragedies into one, the poet might believe himself most surely to have surpassed Seneca.

The inference drawn from the subject and contents of the play concerns its form also. With Coleridge the metre and style alone decided against its authenticity. Shakespeare has nowhere else written in this regular blank verse. The diction, for the most part devoid of imagery, and without the thoughtful tendency to rare expressions, to unusual allusions, and to reflective sayings and sentences, is not like Shakespeare. The grand typhon-like bombast in the mouth of the Moor, and the exaggerated mimic play of rage, is in truth that out-heroding Herod which we find the poet so abhorring in *Hamlet*. Yet even here the objection may be raised, that it was natural for a beginner like Shakespeare to allow himself to be carried away by the false taste of the age, and that it was easy for a talent like his to imitate this heterogeneous style. If we had no testimony as to the genuineness of Shakespeare's narrative poems, scarcely anyone would have considered even them as his writing. Just as with a master's hand he could imitate the conceits of the pastorals, the lyric of the Italians, and the tone of the popular Saxon song, just as well and indeed with far more ease could he affect the noisy style of a Kyd and a Marlowe. At the same time we must confess that at least here and there the diction is not quite alien to Shakespeare. The second act possesses much of that Ovid luxuriance, of that descriptive power, and of those conceits, which we find also in *Venus* and *Lucrece*, of which indeed single passages and expressions remind us. It was in these passages that even Coleridge perceived the hand of Shakespeare, and he had in these matters the keenest perception.

Amid these conflicting doubts, these opposing considerations, we more readily acquiesce in Ravenscroft's tradition, that Shakespeare only elaborated in *Titus* an older play. The whole, indeed, sounds less like the early work of a great genius than the production of a mediocre mind, which in a certain self-satisfied security felt itself already at its apex. But that which, in our opinion, decides against its Shakespeare authorship is the coarseness of the characterisation, the lack of the most ordinary probability in the actions, and the unnatural motives assigned to them. The *style* of a young writer may be perverted, and his

*taste* almost necessarily at first goes astray; but that which lies deeper than all this exterior and ornament of art—namely, the estimate of man, the deduction of motives of action, and the general contemplation of human nature—this is the power of an innate talent, which, under the guidance of sound instinct, is usually developed at an early stage of life. Whatever piece of Shakespeare's we regard as his first, everywhere, even in his narratives, the characters are delineated with a firm hand; the lines may be weak and faint, but nowhere are they drawn, as here, with a harsh and distorted touch. And besides, Shakespeare ever knew how to devise the most natural motives for the strangest actions in the traditions which he undertook to dramatise, and this even in his earliest plays; but nowhere has he grounded, as in this piece, the story of his play upon the most apparent improbability. We need only recall to mind the leading features of the piece and its hero. Titus, by military glory placed in a position to dispose of the Imperial throne of Rome, in generous loyalty creates Saturninus emperor; against the will of his sons he gives him his daughter Lavinia, who is already betrothed to Bassianus; and in his faithful zeal he even kills one of his refractory children. At the same time he gives the new emperor the captive Gothic queen, Tamora, whose son he had just slaughtered as a sacrifice for his fallen children. The emperor sees her, leaves Lavinia, and marries Tamora; and Titus, who thus experienced the base ingratitude of him whose benefactor he had been, now expects thanks from Tamora for her elevation, when he had just before murdered her son! The revengeful woman, on the contrary, commands her own sons to slay Bassianus and to dishonour and mutilate Lavinia. The father, Titus, does not guess the author of the revengeful act. The daughter hears the authors of the deed guessed and talked over; she hears her brothers accused of having murdered her husband, Bassianus; her tongue cut out, she cannot speak, but it seems also as if she could not hear; they ask her not, she can only shake her head at all their false conjectures. At length *by accident* the way is found to put a staff in her mouth, by which she writes in the sand the names of the guilty perpetrators. The dull blusterer who hitherto has been Brutus indeed and in the literal sense of the word, now *acts* the part of Brutus, and the crafty Tamora suffers herself to be allured into the snares of revenge by the same clumsy dissimulation as that by which Titus himself had been deceived. Whoever compares this rough psychological art with the fine touches with which in the poet's first production, *Venus and Adonis*, even amid the perversion of an over-refined descriptive style, those two figures are so agreeably and truly delineated that the painter might without trouble copy them from the hand of the poet, will consider it scarcely possible that the same poet, even in his greatest errors, could have so completely deadened that finer nature which he nowhere else discards.

# *Romeo and Juliet*

. . . thence to the Opera, and there saw *Romeo and Juliet*, the first time it was ever acted; but it is a play of itself the worst that ever I heard in my life.—SAMUEL PEPYS, *Diary*, March 1, 1662

This play is one of the most pleasing of our author's performances. The scenes are busy and various, the incidents numerous and important, the catastrophe irresistibly affecting, and the process of the action carried on with such probability, at least with such congruity to popular opinions, as tragedy requires.

Here is one of the few attempts of Shakespeare to exhibit the conversation of gentlemen, to represent the airy sprightliness of juvenile elegance. Mr. Dryden mentions a tradition, which might easily reach his time, of a declaration made by Shakespeare, that "he was obliged to kill Mercutio in the third act, lest he should have been killed by him." Yet he thinks him "no such formidable person, but that he might have lived through the play, and died in his bed," without danger to a poet. Dryden well knew, had he been in quest of truth, that, in a pointed sentence, more regard is commonly had to the words than the thought, and that it is very seldom to be rigorously understood. Mercutio's wit, gaiety and courage, will always procure him friends that wish him a longer life; but his death is not precipitated, he has lived out the time allotted him in the construction of the play; nor do I doubt the ability of Shakespeare to have continued his existence, though some of his sallies are perhaps out of the reach of Dryden; whose genius was not very fertile of merriment, nor ductile to humour, but acute, argumentative, comprehensive, and sublime.

The Nurse is one of the characters in which the authour delighted: he has, with great subtilty of distinction, drawn her at once loquacious and secret, obsequious and insolent, trusty and dishonest.

His comick scenes are happily wrought, but his pathetick strains are always polluted with some unexpected depravations. His persons, however distressed, "have a conceit left them in their misery, a miserable conceit."—SAMUEL JOHNSON, *Notes on Shakespeare's Plays*, 1768

*Romeo and Juliet*, and *Othello*, differ from most of the pieces which we have hitherto examined, neither in the ingredients of the composition, nor in the manner of treating them: it is merely the direction of the whole that gives them the stamp of Tragedy. *Romeo and Juliet* is a picture of love and its pitiable fate, in a world whose atmosphere is too sharp for this the tenderest blossom of human life. Two beings created for each other feel mutual love at the first glance; every consideration disappears before the irresistible impulse to live in one another; under circumstances hostile in the highest degree to their union, they unite themselves by a secret marriage, relying simply on the protection of an invisible power. Untoward incidents following in rapid succession, their heroic constancy is within a few days put to the proof, till, forcibly separated from each other, by a voluntary death they are united in the grave to meet again in another world. All this is to be found in the beautiful story which Shakspeare has not invented, and which, however simply told, will always excite a tender sympathy: but it was reserved for Shakspeare to join in one ideal picture purity of heart with warmth of imagination; sweetness and dignity of manners with passionate intensity of feeling. Under his handling, it has become a glorious song of praise on that inexpressible feeling which ennobles the soul and gives to it its highest sublimity, and which elevates even the senses into soul, while at the same time it is a melancholy elegy on its inherent and imparted frailty; it is at once the apotheosis and the obsequies of love. It appears here a heavenly spark, that, as it descends to the earth, is converted into the lightning flash, which almost in the same moment sets on fire and consumes the mortal being on whom it lights. All that is most intoxicating in the odour of a southern spring,—all that is languishing in the song of the nightingale, or voluptuous in the first opening of the rose, all alike breathe forth from this poem. But even more rapidly than the earliest blossoms of youth and beauty decay, does it from the first timidly-bold declaration and modest return of love hurry on to the most unlimited passion, to an irrevocable union; and then hastens, amidst alternating storms of rapture and despair, to the fate of the two lovers, who yet appear enviable in their hard lot, for their love survives them, and by their death they have obtained an endless triumph over every separating power. The sweetest and the bitterest love and hatred, festive rejoicings and dark forebodings, tender embraces and sepulchral horrors, the fulness of life and self-annihilation, are here all brought close to each other; and yet these contrasts are so blended into a unity of impression, that the echo which the whole leaves behind in the mind resembles a single but endless sigh.

The excellent dramatic arrangement, the significance of every character in its place, the judicious selection of all the circumstances, even the most minute, have already been dwelt upon in detail. I shall only request attention to a trait which may serve for an example of the distance to which Shakspeare goes back to lay the preparatory foundation. The most striking and perhaps incredible circumstance in the whole story is the liquor given by the Monk to Juliet, by which she for a number of hours not merely sleeps, but fully resembles a corpse, without however receiving the least injury. How does the poet dispose us to believe that Father Lorenzo possesses such a secret?—At his first appearance he exhibits him in a garden, where he is collecting herbs and descanting on their wonderful virtues. The discourse of the pious old man is full of deep meaning: he sees everywhere in nature emblems of the moral world; the same wisdom with which he looks through her has also made him master of the human heart. In this manner a circumstance of an ungrateful appearance, has become the source of a great beauty.—AUGUST WILHELM SCHLEGEL, *Lectures on Dramatic Art and Literature*, 1809, tr. John Black

In old-world nursery vacant now of children,
With posied walls, familiar, fair, demure,
And facing southward o'er romantic streets,
Sits yet and gossips winter's dusk away
One gloomy, vast, glossy, and wise, and sly:
And at her side a cherried country cousin.
Her tongue claps ever like a ram's sweet bell;
There's not a name but calls a tale to mind—
Some marrowy patty of farce or melodram;
There's not a soldier but hath babes in view;
There's not on earth what minds not of the midwife:
"O, widowhood that left me still espoused!"
Beauty she sighs o'er, and she sighs o'er gold;
Gold will buy all things, even a sweet husband,
Else only Heaven is left and—farewell youth!

Yet, strangely, in that money-haunted head,
The sad, gemmed crucifix and incense blue
Is childhood come again. Her memory
Is like an ant-hill which a twig disturbs,
But twig stilled never. And to see her face,
Broad with sleek homely beams; her babied hands,
Ever like 'lighting doves, and her small eyes—
Blue wells a-twinkle, arch and lewd and pious—
To darken all sudden into Stygian gloom,
And paint disaster with uplifted whites,
Is life's epitome. She prates and prates—
A waterbrook of words o'er twelve small pebbles.
And when she dies—some grey, long, summer evening,
When the bird shouts of childhood through the dusk,
'Neath night's faint tapers—then her body shall
Lie stiff with silks of sixty thrifty years.

—WALTER DE LA MARE, "Juliet's Nurse,"
*Characters from Shakespeare*, 1902

---

## WILLIAM HAZLITT
### From *"Romeo and Juliet"*
### *Characters of Shakespear's Plays*
### 1817

Romeo and Juliet is the only tragedy which Shakespear has written entirely on a love-story. It is supposed to have been his first play, and it deserves to stand in that proud rank. There is the buoyant spirit of youth in every line, in the rapturous intoxication of hope, and in the bitterness of despair. It has been said of *Romeo and Juliet* by a great critic, that 'whatever is most intoxicating in the odour of a southern spring, languishing in the song of the nightingale, or voluptuous in the first opening of the rose, is to be found in this poem.' The description is true; and yet it does not answer to our idea of the play. For if it has the sweetness of the rose, it has its freshness too; if it has the languor of the nightingale's song, it has also its giddy transport; if it has the softness of a southern spring, it is as glowing and as bright. There is nothing of a sickly and sentimental cast. Romeo and Juliet are in love, but they are not love-sick. Every thing speaks the very soul of pleasure, the high and healthy pulse of the passions: the heart beats, the blood circulates and mantles throughout. Their courtship is not an insipid interchange of sentiments lip-deep, learnt at second-hand from poems and plays,—made up of beauties of the most shadowy kind, of 'fancies wan that hang the pensive head,' of evanescent smiles, and sighs that breathe not, of delicacy that shrinks from the touch, and feebleness that scarce supports itself, an elaborate vacuity of thought, and an artificial dearth of sense, spirit, truth, and nature! It is the reverse of all this. It is Shakespear all over, and Shakespear when he was young.

We have heard it objected to *Romeo and Juliet*, that it is founded on an idle passion between a boy and a girl, who have scarcely seen and can have but little sympathy or rational esteem for one another, who have had no experience of the good or ills of life, and whose raptures or despair must be therefore equally groundless and fantastical. Whoever objects to the youth of the parties in this play as 'too unripe and crude' to pluck the sweets of love, and wishes to see a first-love carried on into a good old age, and the passions taken at the rebound, when their force is spent, may find all this done in the *Stranger* and in other German plays, where they do things by contraries, and transpose nature to inspire sentiment and create philosophy. Shakespear proceeded in a more strait-forward, and, we

think, effectual way. He did not endeavour to extract beauty from wrinkles, or the wild throb of passion from the last expiring sigh of indifference. He did not 'gather grapes of thorns nor figs of thistles.' It was not his way. But he has given a picture of human life, such as it is in the order of nature. He has founded the passion of the two lovers not on the pleasures they had experienced, but on all the pleasures they had *not* experienced. All that was to come of life was theirs. At that untried source of promised happiness they slaked their thirst, and the first eager draught made them drunk with love and joy. They were in full possession of their senses and their affections. Their hopes were of air, their desires of fire. Youth is the season of love, because the heart is then first melted in tenderness from the touch of novelty, and kindled to rapture, for it knows no end of its enjoyments or its wishes. Desire has no limit but itself. Passion, the love and expectation of pleasure, is infinite, extravagant, inexhaustible, till experience comes to check and kill it. Juliet exclaims on her first interview with Romeo—

My bounty is as boundless as the sea,
My love as deep.

And why should it not? What was to hinder the thrilling tide of pleasure, which had just gushed from her heart, from flowing on without stint or measure, but experience which she was yet without? What was to abate the transport of the first sweet sense of pleasure, which her heart and her senses had just tasted, but indifference which she was yet a stranger to? What was there to check the ardour of hope, of faith, of constancy, just rising in her breast, but disappointment which she had not yet felt! As are the desires and the hopes of youthful passion, such is the keenness of its disappointments, and their baleful effect. Such is the transition in this play from the highest bliss to the lowest despair, from the nuptial couch to an untimely grave. The only evil that even in apprehension befalls the two lovers is the loss of the greatest possible felicity; yet this loss is fatal to both, for they had rather part with life than bear the thought of surviving all that had made life dear to them. In all this, Shakespear has but followed nature, which existed in his time, as well as now. The modern philosophy, which reduces the whole theory of the mind to habitual impressions, and leaves the natural impulses of passion and imagination out of the account, had not then been discovered; or if it had, would have been little calculated for the uses of poetry.

It is the inadequacy of the same false system of philosophy to account for the strength of our earliest attachments, which has led Mr. Wordsworth to indulge in the mystical visions of Platonism in his 'Ode on the Progress of Life.' He has very admirably described the vividness of our impressions in youth and childhood, and how 'they fade by degrees into the light of common day,' and he ascribes the change to the supposition of a pre-existent state, as if our early thoughts were nearer heaven, reflections of former trails of glory, shadows of our past being. This is idle. It is not from the knowledge of the past that the first impressions of things derive their gloss and splendour, but from our ignorance of the future, which fills the void to come with the warmth of our desires, with our gayest hopes, and brightest fancies. It is the obscurity spread before it that colours the prospect of life with hope, as it is the cloud which reflects the rainbow. There is no occasion to resort to any mystical union and transmission of feeling through different states of being to account for the romantic enthusiasm of youth; nor to plant the root of hope in the grave, nor to derive it from the skies. Its root is in the heart of man: it lifts its head above the stars. Desire and imagination are inmates of the human breast. The heaven 'that lies about us in our infancy' is only a new world, of which we know nothing but what we wish it to be, and believe all that we wish. In youth and boyhood, the world we live in is the world of desire, and of fancy: it is experience that brings us down to the world of reality. What is it that in youth sheds a dewy light round the evening star? That makes the daisy look so bright? That perfumes the hyacinth? That embalms the first kiss of love? It is the delight of novelty, and the seeing no end to the pleasure that we fondly believe is still in store for us. The heart revels in the luxury of its own thoughts, and is unable to sustain the weight of hope and love that presses upon it.—The effects of the passion of love alone might have dissipated Mr. Wordsworth's theory, if he means any thing more by it than an ingenious and poetical allegory. *That* at least is not a link in the chain let down from other worlds; 'the purple light of love' is not a dim reflection of the smiles of celestial bliss. It does not appear till the middle of life, and then seems like 'another morn risen on mid-day.' In this respect the soul comes into the world 'in utter nakedness.' Love waits for the ripening of the youthful blood. The sense of pleasure precedes the love of pleasure, but with the sense of pleasure, as soon as it is felt, come thronging infinite desires and hopes of pleasure, and love is mature as soon as born. It withers and it dies almost as soon!

This play presents a beautiful *coup-d'œil* of the progress of human life. In thought it occupies years, and embraces the circle of the affections from childhood to old age. Juliet has become a great girl, a young woman since we first remember her a little thing in the idle prattle of the nurse. Lady Capulet was about her age when she became a mother, and old Capulet somewhat impatiently tells his younger visitors,

> I've seen the day,
> That I have worn a visor, and could tell
> A whispering tale in a fair lady's ear,
> Such as would please: 'tis gone, 'tis gone, 'tis gone.

Thus one period of life makes way for the following, and one generation pushes another off the stage. One of the most striking passages to show the intense feeling of youth in this play is Capulet's invitation to Paris to visit his entertainment.

> At my poor house, look to behold this night
> Earth-treading stars that make dark heav'n light;
> Such comfort as do lusty young men feel
> When well-apparel'd April on the heel
> Of limping winter treads, even such delight
> Among fresh female-buds shall you this night
> Inherit at my house.

The feelings of youth and of the spring are here blended together like the breath of opening flowers. Images of vernal beauty appear to have floated before the author's mind, in writing this poem, in profusion. Here is another of exquisite beauty, brought in more by accident than by necessity. Montague declares of his son smit with a hopeless passion, which he will not reveal—

> But he, his own affection's counsellor,
> Is to himself so secret and so close,
> So far from sounding and discovery,
> As is the bud bit with an envious worm,
> Ere he can spread his sweet leaves to the air,
> Or dedicate his beauty to the sun.

This casual description is as full of passionate beauty as when Romeo dwells in frantic fondness on 'the white wonder of his Juliet's hand.' The reader may, if he pleases, contrast the exquisite pastoral simplicity of the above lines with the gorgeous description of Juliet when Romeo first sees her at her father's house, surrounded by company and artificial splendour.

> What lady's that which doth enrich the hand
> Of yonder knight?
> O she doth teach the torches to burn bright;
> Her beauty hangs upon the cheek of night,
> Like a rich jewel in an Æthiop's ear.

It would be hard to say which of the two garden scenes is the finest, that where he first converses with his love, or takes leave of her the morning after their marriage. Both are like a heaven upon earth; the blissful bowers of Paradise let down upon this lower world. We will give only one passage of these well known scenes to shew the perfect refinement and delicacy of Shakespear's conception of the female character. It is wonderful how Collins, who was a critic and a poet of great sensibility, should have encouraged the common error on this subject by saying—'But stronger Shakespear felt for man alone.' . . .

Romeo is Hamlet in love. There is the same rich exuberance of passion and sentiment in the one, that there is of thought and sentiment in the other. Both are absent and self-involved, both live out of themselves in a world of imagination. Hamlet is abstracted from every thing; Romeo is abstracted from every thing but his love, and lost in it. His 'frail thoughts dally with faint surmise,' and are fashioned out of the suggestions of hope, 'the flatteries of sleep.' He is himself only in his Juliet; she is his only reality, his heart's true home and idol. The rest of the world is to him a passing dream. How finely is this character pourtrayed where he recollects himself on seeing Paris slain at the tomb of Juliet!—

> What said my man, when my betossed soul
> Did not attend him as we rode? I think
> He told me Paris should have married Juliet.

And again, just before he hears the sudden tidings of her death—

> If I may trust the flattery of sleep,
> My dreams presage some joyful news at hand;
> My bosom's lord sits lightly on his throne,
> And all this day an unaccustom'd spirit
> Lifts me above the ground with cheerful thoughts.
> I dreamt my lady came and found me dead,
> (Strange dream! that gives a dead man leave to think)
> And breath'd such life with kisses on my lips,
> That I reviv'd and was an emperour.
> Ah me! how sweet is love itself possess'd,
> When but love's shadows are so rich in joy!

Romeo's passion for Juliet is not a first love: it succeeds and drives out his passion for another mistress, Rosaline, as the sun hides the stars. This is perhaps an artifice (not absolutely necessary) to give us a higher opinion of the lady, while the first absolute surrender of her heart to him enhances the richness of the prize. The commencement, progress, and ending of his second passion are however complete in themselves, not injured if they are not bettered by the first. The outline of the play is taken from an Italian novel; but the dramatic arrangement of the different scenes between the lovers, the more than dramatic interest in the progress of the story, the development of the characters with time and circumstances, just according to the degree and kind of interest excited, are not inferior to the expression of passion and nature. It has been ingeniously remarked among other proofs of skill in the contrivance of the fable, that the improbability of the main incident in the piece, the administering of the sleeping-potion, is softened and obviated from the beginning by the introduction of the Friar on his first appearance culling simples and descanting on their virtues. Of the passionate scenes in this tragedy, that between the Friar and Romeo when he is told of his sentence of banishment, that between Juliet and the Nurse when she hears of it, and of the death of her cousin Tybalt (which bear no proportion in her mind, when passion after the first shock of surprise throws its weight into the scale of her affections) and the last scene at the tomb, are among the most natural and overpowering. In all of these it is not merely the force of any one passion that is given, but the slightest and most unlooked-for transitions from one to another, the mingling currents of every different feeling rising up and prevailing in turn, swayed by the master-mind of the poet, as the waves undulate beneath the gliding storm. Thus when Juliet has by her complaints encouraged the Nurse to say, 'Shame come to Romeo,' she instantly repels the wish, which she had herself occasioned, by answering—

> Blister'd be thy tongue
> For such a wish! He was not born to shame.
> Upon his brow shame is ashamed to sit,
> For 'tis a throne where honour may be crown'd
> Sole monarch of the universal earth!
> O, what a beast was I to chide him so?
> *Nurse:* Will you speak well of him that kill'd your
>      cousin?
> *Juliet:* Shall I speak ill of him that is my husband?
> Ah my poor lord, what tongue shall smooth thy
>      name,
> When I, thy three-hours' wife, have mangled it?'

And then follows on the neck of her remorse and returning fondness, that wish treading almost on the brink of impiety, but still held back by the strength of her devotion to her lord, that 'father, mother, nay, or both were dead,' rather than Romeo banished. If she requires any other excuse, it is in the manner in which Romeo echoes her frantic grief and disappointment in the next scene at being banished from her.—Perhaps one of the finest pieces of acting that ever was witnessed on the stage, is Mr. Kean's manner of doing this scene and his repetition of the word, *Banished*. He treads close indeed upon the genius of his author.

## SAMUEL TAYLOR COLERIDGE
### From *"Romeo and Juliet"*
*Shakspeare, with Introductory Remarks*
*on Poetry, the Drama, and the Stage*
1818

I have previously had occasion to speak at large on the subject of the three unities of time, place, and action, as applied to the drama in the abstract, and to the particular stage for which Shakspeare wrote, as far as he can be said to have written for any stage but that of the universal mind. I hope I have in some measure succeeded in demonstrating that the former two, instead of being rules, were mere inconveniences attached to the local peculiarities of the Athenian drama; that the last alone deserved the name of a principle, and that in the preservation of this unity Shakspeare stood preeminent. Yet, instead of unity of action, I should greatly prefer the more appropriate, though scholastic and uncouth, words homogeneity, proportionateness, and totality of interest,—expressions, which involve the distinction, or rather the essential difference, betwixt the shaping skill of mechanical talent, and the creative, productive, life-power of inspired genius. In the former each part is separately conceived, and then by a succeeding act put together;—not as watches are made for wholesale,—(for there each part supposes a preconception of the whole in some mind)—but more like

pictures on a motley screen. Whence arises the harmony that strikes us in the wildest natural landscapes,—in the relative shapes of rocks, the harmony of colours in the heaths, ferns, and lichens, the leaves of the beech and the oak, the stems and rich brown branches of the birch and other mountain trees, varying from verging autumn to returning spring,—compared with the visual effect from the greater number of artificial plantations?—From this, that the natural landscape is effected, as it were, by a single energy modified *ab intra* in each component part. And as this is the particular excellence of the Shakspearian drama generally, so is it especially characteristic of the *Romeo and Juliet*.

The groundwork of the tale is altogether in family life, and the events of the play have their first origin in family feuds. Filmy as are the eyes of party-spirit, at once dim and truculent, still there is commonly some real or supposed object in view, or principle to be maintained; and though but the twisted wires on the plate of rosin in the preparation for electrical pictures, it is still a guide in some degree, an assimilation to an outline. But in family quarrels, which have proved scarcely less injurious to states, wilfulness, and precipitancy, and passion from mere habit and custom, can alone be expected. With his acustomed judgment, Shakspeare has begun by placing before us a lively picture of all the impulses of the play; and, as nature ever presents two sides, one for Heraclitus, and one for Democritus, he has, by way of prelude, shown the laughable absurdity of the evil by the contagion of it reaching the servants, who have so little to do with it, but who are under the necessity of letting the superfluity of sensoreal power fly off through the escape-valve of wit-combats, and of quarrelling with weapons of sharper edge, all in humble imitation of their masters. Yet there is a sort of unhired fidelity, an *ourishness* about all this that makes it rest pleasant on one's feelings. All the first scene, down to the conclusion of the Prince's speech, is a motley dance of all ranks and ages to one tune, as if the horn of Huon had been playing behind the scenes.

Benvolio's speech—

> Madam, an hour before the worshipp'd sun
> Peer'd forth the golden window of the east—

and, far more strikingly, the following speech of old Montague—

> Many a morning hath he there been seen
> With tears augmenting the fresh morning dew—

prove that Shakspeare meant the *Romeo and Juliet* to approach to a poem, which, and indeed its early date, may be also inferred from the multitude of rhyming couplets throughout. And if we are right, from the internal evidence, in pronouncing this one of Shakspeare's early dramas, it affords a strong instance of the fineness of his insight into the nature of the passions, that Romeo is introduced already love-bewildered. The necessity of loving creates an object for itself in man and woman; and yet there is a difference in this respect between the sexes, though only to be known by a perception of it. It would have displeased us if Juliet had been represented as already in love, or as fancying herself so;—but no one, I believe, ever experiences any shock at Romeo's forgetting his Rosaline, who had been a mere name for the yearning of his youthful imagination, and rushing into his passion for Juliet. Rosaline was a mere creation of his fancy; and we should remark the boastful positiveness of Romeo in a love of his own making, which is never shown where love is really near the heart.

> When the devout religion of mine eye
> Maintains such falsehood, then turn tears to fires!
>
> . . .
>
> One fairer than my love! the all-seeing sun
> Ne'er saw her match, since first the world begun.

The character of the Nurse is the nearest of any thing in Shakspeare to a direct borrowing from mere observation; and the reason is, that as in infancy and childhood the individual in nature is a representative of a class,—just as in describing one larch tree, you generalize a grove of them,—so it is nearly as much so in old age. The generalization is done to the poet's hand. Here you have the garrulity of age strengthened by the feelings of a long-trusted servant, whose sympathy with the mother's affections gives her privileges and rank in the household; and observe the mode of connection by accidents of time and place, and the childlike fondness of repetition in a second childhood, and also that happy, humble, ducking under, yet constant resurgence against, the check of her superiors!—

Yes, madam!—Yet I cannot choose but laugh, &c.

In the fourth scene we have Mercutio introduced to us. O! how shall I describe that exquisite ebullience and overflow of youthful life, wafted on over the laughing waves of pleasure and prosperity, as a wanton beauty that distorts the face on which she knows her lover is gazing enraptured, and wrinkles her forehead in the triumph of its smoothness! Wit ever wakeful, fancy busy and procreative as an insect, courage, an easy mind that, without cares of its own, is at once disposed to laugh away those of others, and yet to be interested in them,— these and all congenial qualities, melting into the common *copula* of them all, the man of rank and the gentleman, with all its excellencies and all its weaknesses, constitute the character of Mercutio!

EDWARD DOWDEN
From *"Romeo and Juliet"*
*Transcripts and Studies*
1888, pp. 378–405

*Vieni, a veder Montecchi e Capelletti.*
(Dante, *Purg.*, Canto VI.)

I

On a day of some year unknown, early in the sixteenth century, Luigi da Porto, a young cavalry officer in the service of the Venetian Republic, was riding, as he tells us, along the lonely road between Gradisca and Udine, in the pleasant country of Friuli. Two of his attendants had been left far behind, but one followed closer, his favourite archer, Peregrino, a man of fifty, handsome of face, courageous, skilled in the use of his bow, skilled also, like most of his fellow-townsmen of Verona, in use of his tongue, and very learned in tales of love and lovers. The young man, lost in his own thoughts, was musing sadly on the cruelty of fortune, which had given his heart to one who would not give hers in exchange, when the voice of Peregrino sounded in his ears. "Do you wish to live always a wretched life because a beautiful, cruel, and fickle one loves you but little? In your profession, Master mine, it is very unbecoming to stay long in the prison of love; so sad are almost all the ends to which love leads us that to follow him is dangerous. In proof of which, and to shorten the tedium of the way, I will, should it please you, relate a story of what happened in my country, in which you will hear how two noble lovers were led to a very sad and pitiful death."

The story of Romeo and Juliet, which Peregrino, the Veronese archer, told to the jingling of bridle-reins, if not a tradition of real events, is probably a refinement on an older tale found among the *Novelle* of Masuccio Salernitano, printed at Naples in 1476. Masuccio, of whose life little is known, calls

God to witness that the tales of his recital are not vain fictions, but true passages of history. In Siena lived a young man of good family named Mariotto Mignanelli, who loved a citizen's daughter, Giannozza Saraceni, and was loved by her in return. Fate being opposed to them, they cannot avow their love, but are secretly married by an Augustine monk. After some time Mariotto quarrels with a citizen of note, whom he has the misfortune to kill with the blow of a stick. He is condemned to perpetual exile, and, after a sorrowful parting from his beloved, flies to Alexandria, in which city his uncle is a wealthy merchant. Upon Mariotto's departure the father of Giannozza urges her to accept the hand of a suitor whom he has provided, and she, like Juliet in her distress, turns to the friar, who prepares a powder which, dissolved in water, shall cast her into a three days' slumber resembling death. Having first despatched a messenger to inform her husband, she drinks the draught, and is buried in the church of St Augustine. At night the friar delivers her from the tomb, and bears her, still unconscious, to his dwelling. Here she comes to herself at the appointed time, and disguised as a monk hastens on board a ship bound for Alexandria. Meanwhile the messenger has been captured by pirates, and tidings of the sudden deaths of Giannozza and of her father (who had really died of grief for his daughter's loss) reach Mariotto. Weary of life, he comes to Siena, disguised as a pilgrim, hurries to the church where he believes that his lady's body lies, and flings himself upon her grave. While endeavouring to open the tomb he is discovered by the sacristan, who takes him for a thief. He is seized, identified as the banished Mariotto, on the rack confesses the entire truth, and, notwithstanding the general sympathy, and especially that of all women, is condemned and beheaded. Giannozza, having arrived at Alexandria, learns to her dismay that her husband, on hearing of her reported death, has returned to Siena; she instantly follows him, only to be informed of his execution. She strives to hide her grief in a convent, and there in a short time dies of a broken heart.[1]

This tale of the "Neapolitan Boccaccio" is comparatively rude—in some features almost savage. Love is here in its might, and death in its terror; but beauty has not come to lift the tale out of the melodramatic and make it a symbol of what is most piteous and most august in human existence—the strict bounds which life sets to our purest and most ardent desires, and the boundlessness of those desires which choose rather to abandon this world than to be untrue to themselves. What, then, does Masuccio's novel need? It needs that the youth and maiden sacrificed to love should be crowned and garlanded with all that makes life lovely; that their fate should come upon them at first with a terror of great joy; that they should be swept suddenly and irresistibly into the mid stream of violent delight; that the obstacle to their happiness should be of no slight or casual kind, but broad-based on an old foundation; that hate should thus stand frowning over against love; that no hazardous wanderings from Italy to Egypt should have place in the story, but that by trivial accident the purpose of destiny should be brought about; finally, that the death of one lover should be self-sought and deliberate—outcome of desperate error—and that the other should be fleet to pursue the lost one through the gates of the grave in a rapture of anguish and of desire.

II

All that was needed to Masuccio's tale Shakspere accomplished; but before the tale reached Shakspere it had been in large measure ennobled and refined. Da Porto's version (1530–35) is sixty years later in date than that of Masuccio. In Italy, says Mr Symonds, "the key-note of the Renaissance was struck by the *Novella*, as in England by the drama." The tragic simplicity of Masuccio's tale gives place in Da Porto's *Romeo and Juliet* to the heightened effects of an artist; it is a prose poem of the Italian Renaissance. Within a narrow compass it brings together splendour and gloom, joy and misery; the banquet-hall, the bridal-chamber, and the burial-vault; while over all are cast a grace of manners, a bloom of southern life, which the earlier *Novella* lacks. In almost every essential, and in various details, Da Porto's story agrees with Shakspere's play.[2] It is early in the thirteenth century, the time of Bartolomeo della Scala, Prince of Verona—the Escalus of Shakspere. The two rival houses, Capelletti and Montecchi, wearied with continual strife, are now at length almost pacified. In the Carnival season, the head of the Capelletti, Messer Antonio, gives many entertainments night and day, to one of which, on a certain night, came in pursuit of his mistress a young man of the house of Montecchi, masked, and wearing the dress of a nymph. Having removed his mask all are amazed at his comeliness, and the eyes of the daughter of the house—who is herself "of supernatural beauty, courageous, and very charming"—encounter with those of the stranger. In the torch dance the hands of the two touch, and words of love are whispered. From that evening each thinks only of the other, and sometimes at church, sometimes at a window, Romeo catches sight of his beloved. Often at peril of his life he walks before her house, or climbs to her balcony, now while the moon shines bright, and again when the winter snow is falling thick. Considering the danger to which he is exposed, Giulietta consents to be his wife, and Friar Lorenzo of St Francis, "a great philosopher, who tried many experiments as well in natural as magical things," plans, in order to gratify his patron Romeo, and hoping to reconcile the two families, how to assist their meeting and unite them in wedlock. After their secret marriage some happy bridal nights go by, when once again the smouldering hate of the houses flames forth, and in a street quarrel Romeo, although at first careful "out of regard for his lady not to hurt any of her family," driven to desperation, rushes on Tebaldo Capelletti, strikes him dead at a blow, and puts his followers to flight. The sentence of banishment follows, as in Shakspere's play, and in the confessional at the convent a sorrowful meeting of wife and husband takes place. Giulietta implores to be allowed to accompany Romeo as a page; she will cut off her hair; no one can be a more faithful servant. But Romeo will take her from her father's home only as his wedded lady; he trusts that ere long the Prince's pardon may be obtained, and peace be concluded between their kinsfolk. Half dead with grief, he reaches Mantua; worn with weeping, she abides in her Veronese palazzo. Her mother now grows anxious at sight of her tears and pallid face, and old Capulet and his wife, taking counsel together, guess that Giulietta, who on St Euphemia's Day last completed her eighteenth year, is pining in the loneliness of maidenhood; let them find for her a husband and once more she will be cheerful. An aspirant husband is speedily found in the young Count of Lodrone, and when Giulietta vehemently opposes the marriage, her father flies into a rage, trying to overwhelm her constancy with threats. In extreme perplexity she turns to Friar Lorenzo for aid: "Give me as much poison as will free me from so great sorrow, and Romeo from so great shame; if you deny this I shall, with more pain on my part, and grief on his, plunge a dagger into my breast." For a desperate case, the good padre has in store a desperate remedy; she is too young and beautiful to die; but let her drink this powder, and she shall enter into a death-like sleep for eight-and-twenty hours; the tomb of the Capelletti is hard by the Franciscan church; he will convey her from the tomb, give her shelter in his cell, and

accompany her, disguised under a friar's hood, to Mantua. "'But tell me, will you not be afraid of the corpse of your cousin Tebaldo, who was lately buried there?' The young lady, now quite joyful, said: 'Father, if I through such means was sure of going to meet Romeo, I would without fear even pass through the infernal regions.'" Giulietta returns home joyful; some unremembered sin it was that had saddened her heart, but the best confessor in the world has brought her peace of mind. She is sent by her father to a country house, where preparations for the nuptials have been going forward; she retires for the night, undresses, rises about four in the morning, calls her chambermaid, and in her presence and that of an aunt drinks the potion, with the words, "My father shall not certainly, if I can help it, marry me against my will." The women, who are dull of apprehension, fail to understand what she has done, and they sleep again. Giulietta dresses and once more lies down, composing herself as if she were at the point of dying, and crossing her hands upon her breast.

In the morning loud are the outcries and lamentations of the women, especially of the chambermaid—almost a sister to Giulietta—on finding the bride a corpse. The physician is summoned and pronounces it death. Her mother is distracted with grief. The body, brought back to Verona, is laid in the tomb with very honourable and great obsequies. Meanwhile, Friar Lorenzo has despatched by a brother of his order a letter which Giulietta had written explaining all that was to happen; but Romeo cannot be found. Found he is, however, by Giulietta's serving-man, Pietro, who has hastened from Verona with tidings of the lady's death. "Upon hearing this, Romeo, pale and half dead, drew his sword and was going to kill himself, but, being prevented by many persons, said, 'The period of my life at any rate cannot be far off, since the better part of it exists no longer.' Dismissing Pietro, disguising himself in the garb of a peasant, and taking a phial of serpent's water in his sleeve, he comes to Verona on the night after that on which his mistress has been buried. The lid of the tomb yields to his efforts, and he enters, carrying with him a dark lantern. There lies Giulietta amidst the bones of many generations; tears and cries break from Romeo, while he kisses her eyes, her mouth, her breast; then plucking the serpent-water from his sleeve, he drains the phial, and once more turns to embrace his bride."

Here the tale of Da Porto varies with tragic power from that version of it which Shakspere has made familiar to us. While Romeo's arms are round his wife, the cold about her heart is conquered, she stirs, and "coming to herself, after a deep sigh, she said, 'Alas, where am I? who embraces me? miserable me! who kisses me?'" For a moment she fears it is Friar Lorenzo who has played her false; then the voice of Romeo fills her sense of hearing, and she would also fill with his presence her sense of sight—"pushing him a little from her, and looking him in the face, she recollected him, and, embracing him, kissed him a thousand times, saying, 'What madness has induced you to come here, running into such dangers?'" A dialogue which Shakspere might have re-created and made as full of lyric beauty as that between the lovers in the moonlit garden, or that between the new husband and new wife on the balcony at break of day, takes place between Romeo, who feels the ice of death in all his limbs, and Giulietta, in whom the tide of life has begun again to surge. "'If ever my love and faith were dear to you, live, if only to think on him who dies for your sake before your eyes.' To which the lady answered, 'Since you die on account of my feigned death, what ought not I to do for your real one?' and having pronounced these words she fell down fainting. Coming afterwards to herself, she miserably received in her beautiful mouth the last sighs of her dear lover, whose death was approaching with great strides." But now the Friar, who has observed with alarm a light within the tomb, hurries in, and discovers with horror what has taken place. With a bitter cry of "Romeo!" he rouses the almost extinguished consciousness of the unhappy youth; once more the languid eyes open, just as dawn is about to touch the world, then close for ever, and "death creeping through all his limbs, he twisted himself all over, and ended his life with a short sigh." Lorenzo turns to Giulietta, to bring her such comfort as may be; for her the cloister shall be a refuge, wherein she may pray for Romeo and for herself. But love has swifter solace than this for her stricken heart. "'What can I do,' she cried, 'without thee, my sweet lord? and what else remains for me to perform, but to die and follow thee?' Having said this, and deeply musing on her great misfortune, and the death of her dear lover, resolving to live no longer, she drew in her breath, retained it a great while, and then with a loud scream fell dead upon her lover's body."

The Friar, discovered in the tomb by officers of the podestà, and brought before the Prince, relates, after some evasions, the sorrowful series of events. By order of Della Scala the bodies of Romeo and Giulietta are taken from the tomb and placed on two carpets in the church of St Francis. There over the dead children the weeping kinsfolk forget their long enmity and embrace. "And the Prince having ordered a fair monument, on which was engraven the cause of their death, the two dead lovers were buried with very great and solemn funeral pomp, lamented and accompanied by the Prince, their kindred, and all the city."

### III

The story told by the archer Peregrino to Da Porto now took wing and wandered hither and thither. A Dominican monk, Matteo Bandello, the descendant of a noble Lombard house, on whom a French bishopric was conferred by Henri II., took up the tale, re-handled it, and included it among his somewhat unclerical *Novelle*, which appeared at Lucca in 1554. Five years later it passed the Alps—a version of Bandello's *Novella*, with variations and additions, being given to French readers by Pierre Boaistuau among his *Histoires Tragiques*.[3] In 1562, Arthur Brooke produced the English poem, *The Tragicall History of Romeus and Iuliet*, on which Shakspere founded his tragedy. Brooke speaks of having seen "the same argument lately set forth on stage;" no such drama of early Elizabethan days survives; rude indeed must have been the attempt of any playwright in England of 1562. Again five years, and Boaistuau's French paraphrase of Bandello was translated into English prose by William Painter for his *Palace of Pleasure*; this also Shakspere consulted. In Italy before the close of the sixteenth century the legend had been versified in *ottava rima*, professedly by a noble lady of Verona naming herself "Clitia"—really, it is supposed, by Gherardo Bolderi; it had been dramatised by the blind poet and actor Luigi Groto, with scene and time and names of persons changed; it had been recorded as grave matter of history by De la Corte, who states that he had many times seen the tomb or sarcophagus of the lovers, then used as a washing-trough, at the well of the orphanage of St Francis, "and," says he, "discussing this matter with the Cavalier Gerardo Boldiero, my uncle, he showed me, beside the aforesaid sepulchre, a place in the wall, on that side next the Rev. Capucini Fathers', from whence, as he assured me, he had been given to understand, this sepulchre, containing bones and ashes, had been taken many years before."[4]

In Bandello's hands the story acquired many resemblances to the Shaksperian form which are wanting in Da Porto. He dwells on Romeo's amorous fancy for a hard-hearted mistress—

Shakspere's Rosaline—to which Da Porto only alludes. An elder friend—Shakspere's Benvolio—advises the enamoured youth to "examine other beauties," and to subdue his passion. Romeo enters Capulet's mansion disguised, but no longer as a nymph. The Count of Lodrone is now first known as Paris. The ladder of ropes is now first mentioned. The sleeping-potion is taken by Juliet, not in presence of her chamber-maid and aunt, but in solitude. Friar Lorenzo's messenger to Mantua fails to deliver the letter because he is detained in a house suspected of being stricken with plague. In particular we owe to Bandello the figure of the nurse, not Shakspere's humorous creation, but a friendly old woman, who very willingly plays her part of go-between for the lovers. One more development, and all the materials of Shakspere's play are in full formation. From Bandello's mention of one Spolentino of Mantua, from whom Romeo procures the poison, Pierre Boaistuau creates the episode of the Apothecary, and it is also to this French refashioner of the story that we must trace the Shaksperian close; with him, Juliet does not wake from her sleep until Romeo has ceased to breathe; and she dies, as in our tragedy, not in a paroxysm of grief, but by her own hand, armed with her husband's dagger.

### IV

*Vieni a veder Montecchi e Capelletti*—"Come, see the Montagues and Capulets." Will the reader consent to leave Italy, and before we see them in England, view the rival houses and their children as they show themselves in Spain of the seventeenth century, and in France a century later? Some eighteen months before the birth of Shakspere in his little Warwickshire town, the most prolific of Spanish dramatists, Lope de Vega, was born at Madrid. When the Great Armada hung upon the southern coast of England in 1588, Lope, a disconsolate lover, was aboard one of the tall ships, with his musket by his side, having for wadding a plentiful supply of the verses he had written in his hard-hearted lady's praise. Among Lope's cloak and sword dramas—"Comedias de Capa y Espada"—is one entitled *Castelvines y Monteses*, in which the tragic story of the Veronese lovers undergoes a strange transformation.[5] As with all of its author's productions for the stage, the plot is a bright tangle of incidents, skilfully ravelled and skilfully unravelled; as with all, the characters are subordinate to the incidents, and of course among the characters appear "the *primer galan*, or hero, all love and honour and jealousy; the *dama*, or heroine, no less loving and jealous . . . ; the *barba*, or old man and father, ready to cover the stage with blood if the lover has even been seen in the house of the heroine;" and the inevitable *gracioso*, or droll, whose love adventures parody those of his master. Lope's drama, though it keeps upon the mere surface of life as compared with Shakspere's tragedy, is not without a genuine charm; it never flags for a moment; its movement is bright as well as rapid; the stage is always bustling with animated figures; and there is poetry enough in it to lift the play above mere melodrama or spectacle. Altogether this bright southern flower has a place of its own in the garden of art; not like Shakspere's red lily, flowering alone upon a grave, but amid its fellows in some gay parterre blown over by a sunlit breeze.

The curtain rises upon a street in Verona; we see the palace of Antonio, chief of the Castelvines, lit up for revelry. Without stand Roselo (Romeo), his comrade Anselmo, and Roselo's servant Marin, the merry-man or *gracioso*. The love of frolic comes strong upon Roselo, and even overpowers the prudent counsel of Anselmo; in spite of the danger of entering their enemy's doors, the two youths, masked and cloaked, followed close by their attendant, pass into the hall of feasting and music. The scene changes; it is the garden of Antonio's house, where, escaped from the heat indoors, masked cavaliers and ladies rest or wander to and fro, while musicians finger their instruments. As Roselo enters, Julia, the daughter of the house, is seated listening to the gallant speeches of her cousin Otavio. Her beauty on the instant transports the new comer, and while standing at gaze he is reckless enough to remove his mask. Julia's father can hardly be restrained from laying violent hands on his uninvited guest, but the lady herself, struck with his noble grace, whispers to her cousin Dorotea—

> If ever Love in masquerade should come,
> And so disguise himself and yet peep forth,
> Methinks 'twould be with such a form and face.

Presently the youth grows bold, and seats himself by Julia's side. On the other side is Otavio, and to him Julia turns her face, but, skilled in love's cunning, interprets all her encouraging words by a pressure of Roselo's hand, on which she even contrives adroitly to slip her ring. Discovering through her maid Celia, after his departure, that Roselo belongs to the rival house, she grows for a moment prudent, and is about to despatch Celia to retract her assignation for a later hour, and to reclaim her gage of love. But a lover's resolutions are not constant in cruelty, and Celia actually leaves her mistress to summon Roselo to her presence. The fête is over; Julia is in the orchard with only her cousin and her maid. The troublesome cousin is speedily dismissed to lull her father to sleep, and as he disappears, Roselo is seen leaping from the orchard wall, scaled with a ladder of rope. Julia tries for a moment to stem the advancing tide of passion, but her resistance is swept away by her lover's importunities, and with hurried words respecting marriage and Roselo's friend the holy friar, they part upon the sound of approaching footsteps.

The curtain falls, and before it rises again Julia and Roselo have been wedded by the good Friar Aurelio. The scene is the open space outside a church, and there is stir and indignation within and without, for two Monteses have insolently plucked away the chair of the Castelvine damsel, Dorotea. Her father, Teobaldo, incites Otavio, his son, who has accompanied Julia to church, to revenge the insult. Roselo passes by, telling his friend the news of his fortunate love, when a cry is heard from the church, and Roselo knows that it is his father's voice. Immediately parties of the Castelvines and the Monteses issue from the porch, prepared for furious fight, Roselo, the new-wedded husband, intervenes as a peacemaker, but in vain; the furious Otavio tilts at him with his rapier, and in self-defence Roselo strikes him dead. And now the Duke of Verona appears, inquiring into the cause of this bloody fray. All who are present bear witness in favour of Roselo, but the decree goes forth against him—not death, but banishment,[6] the Duke in the meantime inviting him to his palace as an honoured guest.

Again the scene is Antonio's orchard, where a sorrowful parting takes place between Roselo and Julia. The passionate dialogue of hero and heroine has its comic counterpart in that of man-servant and maid. Roselo offers his breast if Julia choose to strike with the poignard and avenge her cousin's death; the *gracioso*, Marin, in like manner offers his double-quilted doublet for the stroke of Celia. Julia is willing to abandon all things for her husband's love; and how can the waiting-maid care whether her linen washes white, or the glass for holding preserves be cracked, while her Marin is far away? Before pathos or play has wearied of itself, the voice of old Antonio is heard above the plash of the fountain, and Roselo with his attendant beats a retreat. Her father finds Julia weeping, but she rises to the occasion, asserting that her tears are for the dead Otavio, whom she had looked on as a husband. A husband shall be found for her, thinks Antonio, and that

forthwith—there is Count Paris who will gladly accept her as his bride; let a messenger be despatched to overtake him on the way to Ferrara, and assure him that his suit for Julia is granted.

The scene shifts, and we are on the road to Ferrara. Count Paris has fallen in with Roselo, and although a friend to the Castelvines, he offers the banished youth his good-fellowship and protection against the band of assassins hired by his enemies to waylay him. While they converse, Antonio's messenger approaches bearing a missive to the Count, who, knowing nothing of Roselo's sudden wooing and wedding, announces joyously that he is the chosen son-in-law of Julia's father, and must turn back to Verona. Roselo is silent with a trembling lip, and unable to bid adieu, hurries forward to Ferrara, filled with indignation against the perfidious heart of woman. Meanwhile, the faithful Julia is suffering persecution at her father's hands; driven to desperate straits, she resolves on death; sends secretly to the Friar for a draught of poison; then assumes a joyful bearing and gives her consent to be the wife of Paris. But when her maid enters with the phial, she half distrusts the old man's purpose—may it not be some love-philtre that he has brewed? She drinks, and is soon convinced that the drug is poison, for torpor and chill seem to creep through all her veins.

> *Julia:*     Oh, sad end to all my love!
> And yet I die consoled—we'll meet above.
> Celia, write tenderly to my husband when I'm dead;
> And—and—
> *Celia:*     What says my Julia—mistress dear?
> *Julia:* I know not what I spake. 'Tis sad to die
> So young.

To Roselo, in Ferrara, tidings are brought by his friend Anselmo of the supposed death and the burial of his wife; but, happier than Shakspere's Romeo, Roselo learns at the same time that this seeming death is only a slumber at the heart; his part is to hasten to the tomb and bear his beloved away with him to France or Spain. A new scene discloses the vault beneath the church of Verona. Julia awakes, and after a sense of vague horror, remembers the Friar's draught, and guesses her grim whereabouts. A flicker of light approaches, it is Roselo who enters with his attendant; Julia shrinks aside in sudden alarm, now fearing the unknown living more than the dead. Marin, in mortal terror among the coffin-lids and death's hands, stumbles and extinguishes the light, whereupon ensues a "tedious brief scene of very tragical mirth," the *gracioso* playing clown among the dead men with lively fooling. At length a recognition takes place between wife and husband, and they leave the chamber of death to hide themselves for awhile disguised as peasants upon a farm belonging to Julia's father.

To this same farm comes Julia's father, who, childless and heirless, has resolved to marry his niece Dorotea, and while waiting for a dispensation for this marriage from the Pope, chooses to reside in quiet upon his country estate. Scarcely has he entered the farmhouse when he stands awe-struck to hear the voice of his dead Julia. That quick-witted young lady, hidden in an upper chamber, profits by the opportunity to lecture her father, as if from the spirit-world, on his cruelty, which, she declares, has caused her death; nor does she end until the old man binds himself by a solemn vow to forgive her husband Roselo, and receive him as a son. No sooner is the vow uttered than Roselo, Anselmo, and Marin, still in peasants' attire, are brought in as prisoners by the fierce old Castelvine, Teobaldo, now exulting in the hope of vengeance for his slaughtered Otavio. But the head of the house has pledged his word to his dead daughter to protect and befriend

Roselo; he will go farther—he will even resign his intended bride, Dorotea, in Roselo's favour. At this point the spirit-wife can play her ghostly part no longer—she darts in with a cry to her husband—

> No, not so; wouldst thou, traitor,
> Wed two wives?

Explanation of the mystery of Julia, now alive from the dead, is soon given, and the drama ends with the union of the lovers sanctioned and approved, to perfect the joy of which, Roselo's friend, Anselmo, wins Dorotea for his bride, while the serving-man Marin duly pairs off with the waiting-woman Celia.

> *Antonio:* Enough, let's join their hands.
> *Marin:* And I, with all my virtues, where
> Shall I find one my cares to share;
> The fright I had upon that awful day
> When I dragged forth from death yon mortal clay.
> *Julia:* Celia is thine; a thousand ducats too.
> *Roselo:* Good senators, here, I pray 'tis understood
> The Castelvines ends in happiest moods.

Lope, says François-Victor Hugo, has parodied—Shakspere has dramatised the Italian legend. But this is hardly just to Lope. We feel at least a piquant surprise on seeing how readily the tragic tale, with a few turns from the hands of a skilful playwright, transforms itself to a lively and not ungraceful comedy of the cloak and sword.

## V

There is a second Spanish play with the same subject. Francisco de Rojas y Zorrilla succeeded Lope as a writer for the stage. In *Los Bandos de Verona* the writer departs even farther from the Italian original than Lope had cared to stray.[7] In this new variation on the theme, Romeo has a sister, Elena, the unhappy wife of Count Paris, who since the outbreak of enmity between the houses slights her as a Montague, and desires to obtain a divorce in order that he may be free to wed his wife's friend, Julia. Romeo has first seen his beloved not at ball or banquet, nor in the festal garden of Antonio, but alone in her chamber, to which he had penetrated sword in hand, seeking her father's life with a maniac's fury, only to be abashed, subdued, and stricken to the heart by her beauty shining through tears. The incident of the sleeping-potion is strangely altered. Old Capulet urges his daughter to a marriage with Paris or with his own nephew, Andrés; let her choose which she pleases; but if she rejects these for Romeo's sake, her choice must be between poignard and poison now lying upon the table. Julia, before her father can step between, has rushed forward, seized the phial, and drained its contents. Happily the servant commissioned to procure the poison, fearing that it may be intended for Julia's waiting-woman, who is dear to him, has had it prepared as a simple sleeping-draught. In the escape from the vault, by a series of misadventures and cross-purposes happening in the darkened church, Romeo carries off his sister Elena in place of Julia, while Julia clings to the cloak of her cousin Andrés. Romeo is hunted through a wood by the enraged Capulets, and at dawn in the same wood Rojas's Julia, like Lope's, startles her father as an apparition from the grave. She is immured in a fortress garrisoned by the Capulet faction, which is besieged by Romeo and the Montagues; the *gracioso*, who has done the inevitable fooling throughout the play, valiantly finding his way to the rear:

> I'll sheathe my blade,
> And leave, to such as like, the cold-steel trade.
> It is a selfish world, when all is done,
> I'll stay behind; take care of number one.

The play concludes with wedding-bells in prospect for the lovers, and with a reconciliation between Count Paris and his wife. The skilful intrigue, the graceful movement and the bright poetry of Lope's comedy are conspicuous by their absence when we pass from *Castelvines y Monteses* to *Los Bandos de Verona*.

## VI

"I shall never forget," wrote the French poet Campenon, who died an old man in 1843, "I shall never forget how, one cold day of January, when I went to Versailles to visit Ducis, I found him in his bedroom, mounted on a chair, and intent on arranging with a certain pomp around the head of the English Æschylus, a huge bunch of box, which had been brought to him. 'I shall be at your service presently,' he said, as I entered, but without changing his position. Observing that I was a little surprised at the attitude in which I found him, he went on, 'You are not aware that it is the eve of Saint William, patron saint of my Shakspere.' Then, leaning on my shoulder to get down, and having consulted me as to the effect of his bouquet—the only one, doubtless, which the winter season yielded—'My friend,' added he, with an expression of countenance which I yet remember, 'the ancients crowned with flowers the streams from which they drew.'"

Hard words have been spoken by Shaksperian enthusiasts of his eighteenth-century adapter, Ducis, and not altogether without reason; but Ducis was himself a Shaksperian enthusiast. His poetic manner betrays his age, an age before the Romantic movement had attacked the conventions of the old French theatre, and when the words *nature, virtue,* and *liberty,* inspired with a kind of supernatural power by Rousseau, were those most certain to call forth the applause of the parterre. But Ducis himself stood apart from his age; there was something rare and original in his nature; a grave majesty in his very countenance. Among philosophers he remained religious; in the neighbourhood of a Court he remained simple and almost austere. "In my poetic scale," he wrote, "are the notes of the flute and of the thunder; how do these go together? I myself do not very well know, but I know that it is so.' A soul tragic yet tender; with something in it of the Carthusian—says Sainte-Beuve—and also something gentler and better. To have foiled Bonaparte is Ducis' peculiar distinction; no bribe—not the Senate, not the Cross of the Legion—could seduce him from allegiance to his ideals. "I am," said he, "a Catholic, a poet, a republican, a solitary."

Ducis was thirty-six years old when he adapted *Hamlet* to the French stage. It had a brilliant success. Three years later, in 1772, his *Roméo et Juliette* was represented by the Royal Comedians. A second success was achieved, as brilliant as the first. But the *Hamlet* of Ducis is not Shakspere's *Hamlet*, and his *Roméo et Juliette* loses the unity of motive which characterises Shakspere's tragedy; the plot is altered and complicated; old Montague becomes a chief person, as important and interesting as either of the lovers; "the cry of paternal tenderness," as Ducis expresses it, is heard above the cry of the young, passionate hearts; and a moral lesson directed against the spirit of revenge is in new ways illustrated by the story. "I need not enlarge," says Ducis, "on my obligations to Shakspere and to Dante." With the theme of the English dramatist he links the ghastly story of Ugolino found in the thirty-third canto of the *Inferno*. His tragic "note of the thunder" overpowers his lyric "note of the flute."

Old Montaigu in Ducis' play has disappeared from Verona for more than twenty years. Retiring from the city to educate his sons in the "virtuous fields," he had been pursued and persecuted by a dreadful uncle of Juliette, now dead, who, by means of hired brigands, robbed Montaigu of his boy Romeo. With four other sons the old man, it is supposed, has taken refuge in some solitude among the Apennines. But what of Romeo? Escaped from his captors, he wandered unknown into Verona, was received into Capulet's house, has grown up from boyhood under the name of Dolvédo by the side of Juliette, who alone knows the secret of his birth; and having given her his love, and won her love in exchange, is returning to Verona, at the moment when the play opens, a famous and victorious leader, bringing with him the standards of the defeated Mantuans.

At the same moment, however, there creeps into Verona an old man, miserable, haggard, desolate, but sustained by one eager hope of revenge. A presentiment of coming evil troubles the joy of Juliette in welcoming home her triumphant Dolvédo. Rumours have reached Capulet of obscure plots and stirrings among the partisans of Montaigu, and not content with strengthening his house by the approaching marriage of his son Thébaldo, he also urges—tenderly yet firmly—an alliance between his daughter Juliette and Count Paris. Juliette, in presence of her lover, opposes her father's will; and Capulet, witless of the struggle in his daughter's heart, entrusts the cause of Paris to a strangely-chosen pleader—Dolvédo. Is he doomed to see—O heavens!—"an object full of charms" which he has "acquired by his exploits and merited by his tears," borne away by an odious rival? That Juliette is not indifferent her sobs confess; yet her resolve is made—to immolate herself to the State and to obey her father—

Je m'immole à l'Etat, j'obéis à mon père.

This Juliet is indeed another than the child of Shakspere's imagination.

Tidings are brought to Romeo that his father has entered Verona plotting mischief, and that Paris is now inclining to join the Montaigu faction, and break off his intended marriage with Juliette. Romeo flies to the Duke, entreating his mediation between the heads of the rival houses. Accordingly a meeting in the Duke's presence takes place between Montaigu and Capulet; but the fierce old Montaigu cannot restrain his hatred, and with dark allusion to some hidden horror, breaks into open threats of violence. Away with him, therefore, to prison, where his passion may find time to cool! For Dolvédo-Romeo the position is an agonising one, divided as he is between his love for Juliette and his loyalty to the old man, so woe-begone, so worn with grief, so solitary. Presently, when Montaigu's retainers rescue their chief from the tower, and are in deadly strife with the Capulets, Romeo's piety as a son carries all before it, and charging the enemy, he plunges his sword into the heart of Thébaldo, Juliette's brother and his own bosom friend.

Once again the Duke intervenes—peace in Verona there must be; above the tombs of their dead the rival chieftains must make a solemn vow of amity. Capulet gladly consents; Montaigu consents in seeming; then, leading Romeo aside, he implores his son not to defeat the one desire of his joyless life—the desire of vengeance. He bears about with him an awful secret; Romeo must know it now. It is the secret of a father whose sons, like Ugolino's, have famished in prison—a father who himself, like Ugolino, has been offered the blood of his children to stay his hunger. Can such an injury as this ever be forgiven? And does Romeo start and shrink back because he is asked to strike a dagger into the breast of Capulet's daughter.

With many entreaties to reconciliation, and some hope that sentiments of honour and magnanimity have subdued the passion for revenge, Romeo leaves the old man. The fifth act opens at the tombs of the Capulets and Montaigus. Juliette has somehow obtained possession of a written order from old Montaigu to his followers, directing them, at the moment when the false vows of peace are being sworn, to fall upon their enemies, and exterminate them. It seems to Juliette that if she offer herself a voluntary sacrifice to the vengeance of the Montaigus all may be well for those who survive—with her these dismal family feuds may die. She is alone in the dim place lit by funeral lamps; and alone she drains the poisoned cup, and waits for death. Romeo hurries in buoyed up with the deceitful hope that there is to be reconciliation, and joy for him and his beloved springing up in this place of the dead. From Juliette's lips he learns his father's bloody designs, and her own fatal deed. She implores him to live; but what is life to Romeo in a world of hate without the one being that made life precious? In a moment the faithful sword is plunged into his side, but before the lovers die upon the brink of the grave they hear from one another's lips the sacred names of "husband" and "wife":

Arrête, Roméo! la fortune jalouse
Ne doit point m'empêcher de mourir ton épouse.
Sur les bords du cercueil, puisqu'il dépend de nous,
Laisse-moi te donner le nom sacré d'époux.
Hélas! j'ai bien acquis, dans ce moment suprême,
Le droit triste et flatteur de me donner moi-même.
Pour amis, pour témoins, adoptons ces tombeaux,
Ce marbre pour autel, ces clartés pour flambeaux.

In the closing scene it only remains for the implacable Montaigu to use his poignard with swift execution against his rival at the moment of the oath of peace; then to discover the body of Juliette and pause an instant to gloat over her dying pangs; in that same instant to perceive his slaughtered Romeo by her side, and to fall lifeless—the ruin of his vindictive passion—upon the body of his son.

The haggard old man driven by extreme love for his offspring into extreme hate, fascinated the imagination of Ducis. With the lovers he concerns himself less. In a preface he offers an apology for presenting suicide upon the stage: "Doubtless it is dangerous to give in the theatre an example of suicide, but I have to depict the consequences of hereditary hatred, and it is on this object alone that I have desired to fix the attention of the spectator." Happily Shakspere was not troubled by such moral scruples, or rather it is happy that Shakspere found through his imagination the laws of a profounder morality than any which Ducis could conceive.

*Notes*

1. "Con interno dolore e sanguinose lacrime con poco cibo e niente dormire." I have followed the analyses of Masuccio's novel in Dr Schulze's article, *Shakespeare-Jahrbuch*, XI., Simrock's "Die Quellen des Shakspeare," and Daniel's Preface to Brooke and Painter (New Shakspere Society, 1878).
2. In what follows I have used *The Original Story of Romeo and Juliet, Italian text with English translation*, by. G. Pace-Sanfelice, 1868.
3. An early French form of the story is found in the dedication to a translation of Boccaccio's *Philocopo*, by Adrian Sevin, 1542, with such outlandish names for the personages as Karilio Humdrum, Halquadrich, Harriaquach, &c.
4. Daniel's Introduction to the New Shakspere Society's *Originals and Analogues, Part I*. It is by no means certain that the story of Romeo and Juliet has not an historical foundation.
5. For what follows I have used the reprint of *Los Bandos de Verona*, and *Castelvines y Monteses*, in one volume (Paris, 1839), and Mr F. W. Cosens' privately-printed translation, 1869. In Furness's edition of *Romeo and Juliet*, and in the Introduction to Fr.-Victor Hugo's translation of Shakspere's play, analyses of Lope's comedy will be found.
6. Lope de Vega was himself banished from Madrid and separated from his wife, who remained behind, in consequence of a duel in which he wounded his adversary.
7. Mr F. W. Cosens, to whom Shakspere students are much indebted, has also Englished this drama in a beautiful volume printed for private distribution, 1874.

# *Julius Caesar*

The many-headed multitude were drawne
By *Brutus* speech, that *Caesar* was ambitious,
When eloquent *Mark Antonie* had showne
His vertues, who but *Brutus* then was vicious?
   Mans memorie, with new, forgets the old,
   One tale is good, untill another s told.

     —JOHN WEEVER, *The Mirror of Martyrs*, 1601

In Country Beauties as we often see,
Something that takes in their simplicity;
Yet while they charm, they know not they are fair,
And take without the spreading of the snare;
Such Artless beauty lies in *Shakespears* wit,
'Twas well in spight of him what ere he writ.
His Excellencies came and were not sought,
His words like casual Atoms made a thought:
Drew up themselves in Rank and File, and writ,
He wondring how the Devil it was such wit.
Thus like the drunken Tinker, in his Play,
He grew a Prince, and never knew which way.
He did not know what trope or Figure meant,
But to perswade is to be eloquent,
So in this *Cæsar* which to day you see,
*Tully* ne'r spoke as he makes *Anthony*.
Those then that tax his Learning are to blame,
He knew the thing, but did not know the Name:
Great *Iohnson* did that Ignorance adore,
And though he envi'd much, admir'd him more;
The faultless *Iohnson* equally writ well,
*Shakespear* made faults; but then did more excel.
One close at Guard like some old Fencer lay,
T'other more open, but he shew'd more play.
In Imitation *Iohnsons* wit was shown,
Heaven made his men; but *Shakespear* made his own.
Wise *Iohnson's* talent in observing lay,
But others follies still made up his play.
He drew the life in each elaborate line,
But *Shakespear* like a Master did design.
*Iohnson* with skill dissected humane kind,
And show'd their faults that they their faults might find:
But then as all Anatomists must do,
He to the meanest of mankind did go,
And took from Gibbets such as he would show.
Both are so great that he must boldly dare,
Who both of 'em does judge and both compare.
If amongst Poets one more bold there be,
The man that dare attempt in either way, is he.

     —JOHN DRYDEN, "Prologue to *Iulius Caesar*,"
     1672

. . . the piece of *Julius Cæsar*, to complete the action, requires to be continued to the fall of Brutus and Cassius. Cæsar is not the hero of the piece, but Brutus. The amiable beauty of this character, his feeling and patriotic heroism, are portrayed with peculiar care. Yet the poet has pointed out with great nicety the superiority of Cassius over Brutus in independent volition and discernment in judging of human affairs; that the latter from the purity of his mind and his conscientious love of justice, is unfit to be the head of a party in a state entirely corrupted; and that these very faults give an unfortunate turn to the cause of the conspirators. In the part of Cæsar several ostentatious speeches have been censured as unsuitable. But as he never appears in action, we have no other measure of his greatness than the impression which he makes upon the rest of the characters, and his peculiar confidence in himself. In this Cæsar was by no means deficient, as we learn from history and his own writings; but he displayed it more in the easy ridicule of his enemies than in pompous discourses. The theatrical effect of this play is injured by a partial falling off of the last two acts compared with the preceding in external splendour and rapidity. The first appearance of Cæsar in festal robes, when the music stops, and all are silent whenever he opens his mouth, and when the few words which he utters are received as oracles, is truly magnificent; the conspiracy is a true conspiracy, which in stolen interviews and in the dead of night prepares the blow which is to be struck in open day, and which is to change the constitution of the world;—the confused thronging before the murder of Cæsar, the general agitation even of the perpetrators after the deed, are all portrayed with most masterly skill; with the funeral procession and the speech of Antony the effect reaches its utmost height. Cæsar's shade is more powerful to avenge his fall than he himself was to guard against it. After the overthrow of the external splendour and greatness of the conqueror and ruler of the world, the intrinsic grandeur of character of Brutus and Cassius is all that remain to fill the stage and occupy the minds of the spectators: suitably to their name, as the last of the Romans, they stand there, in some degree alone; and the forming a great and hazardous determination is more powerfully calculated to excite our expectation, than the supporting the consequences of the deed with heroic firmness.—AUGUST WILHELM SCHLEGEL, *Lectures on Dramatic Art and Literature*, 1809, tr. John Black

*Julius Cæsar* was one of three principal plays by different authors, pitched upon by the celebrated Earl of Hallifax to be brought out in a splendid manner by subscription, in the year 1707. The other two were the *King and No King* of Fletcher, and Dryden's *Maiden Queen*. There perhaps might be political reasons for this selection, as far as regards our author. Otherwise, Shakespear's *Julius Cæsar* is not equal as a whole, to either of his other plays taken from the Roman history. It is inferior in interest to *Coriolanus*, and both in interest and power to *Antony and Cleopatra*. It however abounds in admirable and affecting passages, and is remarkable for the profound knowledge of character, in which Shakespear could scarcely fail. If there is any exception to this remark, it is in the hero of the piece himself. We do not much admire the representation here given of Julius Cæsar, nor do we think it answers to the portrait given of him in his Commentaries. He makes several vapouring and rather pedantic speeches, and does nothing. Indeed, he has nothing to do. So far, the fault of the character is the fault of the plot. . . .

   Shakespear has in this play and elsewhere shown the same penetration into political character and the springs of public events as into those of every-day life. For instance, the whole design of the conspirators to liberate their country fails from the generous temper and overweening confidence of Brutus in the goodness of their cause and the assistance of others. Thus it has always been. Those who mean well themselves think well of others, and fall a prey to their security. That humanity and honesty which dispose men to resist injustice and tyranny render them unfit to cope with the cunning and power of those who are opposed to them. The friends of liberty trust to the professions of others, because they are themselves sincere, and endeavour to reconcile the public good with the least possible hurt to its enemies, who have no regard to any thing but their own unprincipled ends, and stick at nothing to accomplish them. Cassius was better cut out for a conspirator. His heart prompted his head. His watchful jealousy made him fear the worst that might happen, and his irritability of temper added to his inveteracy of purpose, and sharpened his patriotism. The mixed nature of his motives made him fitter to contend with bad men. The vices are never so well employed as in combating one another. Tyranny and servility are to be dealt with after their own fashion: otherwise, they will triumph over those who spare them, and finally pronounce their funeral panegyric, as Antony did that of Brutus.

> All the conspirators, save only he,
> Did that they did in envy of great Cæsar:
> He only in a general honest thought
> And common good to all, made one of them.

The quarrel between Brutus and Cassius is managed in a masterly way. The dramatic fluctuation of passion, the calmness of Brutus, the heat of Cassius, are admirably described; and the exclamation of Cassius on hearing of the death of Portia, which he does not learn till after their reconciliation, 'How 'scaped I killing when I crost you so?' gives double force to all that has gone before. The scene between Brutus and Portia, where she endeavours to extort the secret of the conspiracy from him, is conceived in the most heroical spirit, and the burst of tenderness in Brutus—

> You are my true and honourable wife;
> As dear to me as are the ruddy drops
> That visit my sad heart—

is justified by her whole behaviour. Portia's breathless impatience to learn the event of the conspiracy, in the dialogue with Lucius, is full of passion. The interest which Portia takes in Brutus and that which Calphurnia takes in the fate of Cæsar are discriminated with the nicest precision. Mark Antony's speech over the dead body of Cæsar has been justly admired for the mixture of pathos and artifice in it: that of Brutus certainly is not so good.

The entrance of the conspirators to the house of Brutus at midnight is rendered very impressive. In the midst of this scene, we meet with one of those careless and natural digressions which occur so frequently and beautifully in Shakespear. After Cassius has introduced his friends one by one, Brutus says—

> They are all welcome.
> What watchful cares do interpose themselves
> Betwixt your eyes and night?
> *Cassius:* Shall I entreat a word?    (*They whisper.*)
> *Decius:* Here lies the east: doth not the day break
>    here?
> *Casca:* No.
> *Cinna:* O pardon, Sir, it doth; and yon grey lines,
>    That fret the clouds, are messengers of day.
> *Casca:* You shall confess, that you are both deceiv'd:
>    Here, as I point my sword, the sun arises,
>    Which is a great way growing on the south,
>    Weighing the youthful season of the year.
>    Some two months hence, up higher toward the
>       north
>    He first presents his fire, and the high east
>    Stands as the Capitol, directly here.

We cannot help thinking this graceful familiarity better than all the fustian in the world.—The truth of history in *Julius Cæsar* is very ably worked up with dramatic effect. The councils of generals, the doubtful turns of battles, are represented to the life. The death of Brutus is worthy of him—it has the dignity of the Roman senator with the firmness of the Stoic philosopher. But what is perhaps better than either, is the little incident of his boy, Lucius, falling asleep over his instrument, as he is playing to his master in his tent, the night before the battle. Nature had played him the same forgetful trick once before on the night of the conspiracy. The humanity of Brutus is the same on both occasions.

> It is no matter:
> Enjoy the honey-heavy dew of slumber.
> Thou hast no figures nor no fantasies,
> Which busy care draws in the brains of men.
> Therefore thou sleep'st so sound.

—WILLIAM HAZLITT, "*Julius Cæsar*," *Characters of Shakespear's Plays*, 1817

## THOMAS RYMER
### From A *Short View of Tragedy*
### 1693

In ⟨*Othello*⟩, our Poet might be the bolder, the persons being all his own Creatures, and meer fiction. But here he sins not against Nature and Philosophy only, but against the most known History, and the memory of the Noblest Romans, that ought to be sacred to all Posterity. He might be familiar with *Othello* and *Jago*, as his own natural acquaintance: but *Cæsar* and *Brutus* were above his conversation: To put them in Fools Coats, and make them Jack-puddens in the *Shakespear* dress, is a *Sacriledge*, beyond any thing in *Spelman*. The Truth is, this authors head was full of villainous, unnatural images, and history has only furnish'd him with great names, thereby to recommend them to the World; by writing over them, *This is* Brutus; *this is* Cicero; *this is* Cæsar. But generally his History flies in his Face; And comes in flat contradiction to the Poets imagination. As for example: of *Brutus* says Antony, his Enemy.

> *Ant.:* His life was gentle, and the Elements
>    So mixt in him, that Nature might stand up,
>    And say to all the World, this was a Man.

And when every body jug'd it necessary to kill *Antony*, our Author in his *Laconical* way, makes *Brutus* speak thus:

> *Bru.:* Our Course will seem too bloody, *Caius*
>       *Cassius*,
>    To cut the Head off, and then hack the Limbs,
>    Like wrath in death, and envy afterwards;
>    For *Antony* is but a Limb of *Cæsar*:
>    Let's be Sacrificers, but not Butchers, *Caius*,
>    We all stand up against the Spirit of *Cæsar*,
>    And in the Spirit of man there is no blood;
>    O that we then cou'd come by *Cæsars* Spirit,
>    And not dismember *Cæsar*; but, alas!
>    *Cæsar* must bleed for it. And gentle friends,
>    Let's kill him boldly, but not wrathfully;
>    Let's carve him, as a dish fit for the Gods,
>    Not hew him, as a Carkass fit for Hounds.
>    And let our Hearts, as subtle Masters do,
>    Stir up their Servants to an act of rage,
>    And after seem to chide 'em. This shall make
>    Our purpose necessary, and not envious:
>    Which so appearing to the common eyes,
>    We shall be call'd Purgers, not murderers.
>    And for *Mark Antony* think not of him:
>    For he can do no more than *Cæsars* arm,
>    When *Cæsars* head is off.

In these two speeches we have the true character of *Brutus*, according to History. But when *Shakespear's* own blundering Maggot of self contradiction works, then must *Brutus* cry out.

> *Bru.*: Stoop, *Romans*, stoop,
> And let us bath our hands in *Cæsars* blood
> Up to the Elbows—

Had this been spoken by some King of *France*, we might remember *Villon*:

> Se fusse des hoirs Hue Capel,
> Qui fut extrait de boucherie,
> On m'eut parmy ce drapel,
> Fait boire de l'escorcherie.

And what *Dante* has recorded.

> Chiamato fui di lá Ugo ciapetta,
> Di me son Nati i Philippi, e' Loigi,
> Per cui novellamente e' Francia retta,
> Figlivol fui d'un Beccaio di Parigi—

For, indeed, that Language which *Shakespear* puts in the Mouth of *Brutus* wou'd not suit, or be convenient, unless from some son of the Shambles, or some natural offspring of the Butchery. But never any Poet so boldly and so barefac'd, flounced along from contradiction to contradiction. A little preparation and forecast might do well now and then. For his *Desdemona's* Marriage, He might have helped out the probability by feigning how that some way, or other, a Black-amoor Woman had been her Nurse, and suckl'd her: Or that once, upon a time, some *Virtuoso* had transfus'd into her Veins the Blood of a black Sheep: after which she might never be at quiet till she is, as the Poet will have it, *Tupt with an old black ram*.

But to match this pithy discourse of *Brutus*; see the weighty argumentative oration, whereby *Cassius* draws him into the Conspiracy.

> *Cas.*: *Brutus*, and *Cæsar*: what shou'd be in that
> *Cæsar*?
> Why shou'd that name be sounded more than
> yours?
> Write them together: yours is as fair a name:
> Sound them, it doth become the mouth as well.
> Weigh them, it is as heavy: conjure with them,
> *Brutus* will start a Spirit as soon as *Cæsar*.
> Now, in the names of all the Gods at once,
> Upon what meat doth this our *Cæsar* feed,
> That he is grown so great? Age, thou art sham'd;
> *Rome* thou hast lost the breed of noble bloods.
> When went there by an Age since the great flood,
> But it was fam'd with more, than with one man?
> When could they say (till now) that talk'd of *Rome*,
> That her wide Walls encompass'd but one man?
> Now it is *Rome* indeed, and room enough
> When there is in it but one only Man—

One may Note that all our Authors Senators, and his Orators had their learning and education at the same school, be they Venetians, Black-amoors, Ottamites, or noble Romans. *Brutus* and *Cassius* here, may *cap sentences*, with *Brabantio*, and the *Doge* of *Venice*, or any *Magnifico* of them all. We saw how the Venetian Senate spent their time, when, amidst their alarms, call'd to Counsel at midnight. Here the Roman Senators, the midnight before *Cæsar's* death (met in the Garden of *Brutus*, to settle the matter of their Conspiracy) are gazing up to the Stars, and have no more in their heads than to wrangle about which is the East and West.

> *Decius*: Here lies the East, doth not the day break
> here?

*Caska*: No.

*Cinna*: O, pardon, Sir, it doth, and yon grey lines,
That fret the Clouds, are Messengers of Day.

*Caska*: You shall confess, that you are both deceiv'd:
Here as I point my Sword, the Sun arises,
Which is a great way growing on the South,
Weighing the youthful season of the year,
Some two months hence, up higher toward the
North,
He first presents his fire, and the high East
Stands as the Capitol directly here.

This is directly, as *Bays* tells us, *to shew the World a Pattern here, how men shou'd talk of Business*. But it wou'd be a wrong to the Poet, not to inform the reader, that on the Stage, the Spectators see *Brutus* and *Cassius* all this while at *Whisper* together. That is the importance, that deserves all the attention. But the *grand question* wou'd be: does the *Audience hear 'em Whisper*?

> *Ush.*: Why, truly I can't tell: there's much to be said
> upon the word Whisper

Another Poet wou'd have allow'd the noble *Brutus* a Watch-Candle in his Chamber this important night, rather than have puzzel'd his man *Lucius* to grope in the dark for a Flint and Tinderbox, to get the Taper lighted. It wou'd have been no great charge to the Poet, however. Afterwards, another night, the Fiddle is in danger to be broken by this sleepy Boy.

> *Bru.*: If thou dost nod thou break'st thy Instrument.

But pass we to the famous Scene, where *Brutus* and *Cassius* are by the Poet represented acting the parts of *Mimicks*: from the Nobility and Buskins, they are made the *Planipedes*; are brought to daunce *barefoot*, for a Spectacle to the people, Two Philosophers, two generals, (*imperatores* was their title) the *ultimi Romanorum*, are to play the Bullies and Buffoon, to shew their Legerdemain, their *activity* of face, and divarication of Muscles. They are to play a prize, a tryal of skill in huffing and swaggering, like two drunken Hectors, for a two-penny reckoning.

When the Roman Mettle was somewhat more allaid, and their Stomach not so very fierce, in *Augustus's* time; *Laberius*, who was excellent at that sport, was forced once by the Emperor to shew his Talent upon the Stage: in his Prologue, he complains that

> Necessity has no law.
> It was the will of *Cæsar* brought me hither,
> What was imagin'd for me to deny
> This *Cæsar*; when the Gods deny him nothing?

But says he,

> Ego bis tricenis annis actis sine nota,
> Eques Romanus lare egressus meo,
> Domum revertor *Mimus*. Nimirum hac die
> Una plus vixi mihi quàm vivendum fuit.
>
> Twice thirty years I liv'd without blemish;
> From home I came a Roman Gentleman,
> But back shall go a *Mimick*. This one day
> Is one day longer than I shou'd have liv'd.

This may shew with what indignity our Poet treats the noblest *Romans*. But there is no other cloth in his Wardrobe. Every one must be content to wear a Fools Coat, who comes to be dressed by him. Nor is he more civil to the Ladies. *Portia*, in good manners, might have challeng'd more respect: she that shines, a glory of the first magnitude in the Gallery of Heroick Dames, is with our Poet, scarce one remove from a Natural: She is the own Cousin German, of one piece, the very same impertinent silly flesh and blood with *Desdemona*. *Shakespears* genius lay for Comedy and Humour. In Tragedy he appears quite out of his Element; his Brains are turn'd, he raves and rambles, without any coherence, any spark of reason, or any rule to controul him, or set bounds to his phrenzy. His imagination was still running after his Masters, the Coblers, and Parish Clerks, and *Old Testament Stroulers*. So he might make bold with *Portia*, as they had done with the Virgin Mary. Who, in a Church Acting their Play call'd *The Incarnation*, had usually the *Ave Mary* mumbl'd over to a stradling wench (for the blessed Virgin) straw-hatted, blew-apron'd, big-bellied, with her Immaculate Conception up to her chin.

The Italian Painters are noted for drawing the *Madonna's* by their own Wives or Mistresses; one might wonder what sort of *Betty Mackerel*, *Shakespear* found in his days, to sit for his *Portia*, and *Desdemona*; and Ladies of a rank, and dignity, for their place in Tragedy. But to him a Tragedy in *Burlesk*, a merry Tragedy was no Monster, no absurdity, nor at all preposterous: all colours are the same to a Blind man. The Thunder and Lightning, the Shouting and Battel, and alarms every where in this play, may well keep the Audience awake; otherwise no Sermon wou'd be so strong an Opiate. But since the memorable action by the *Putney Pikes*, the *Hammersmith Brigade*, and the *Chelsey Cuirassiers*: one might think, in a modest Nation, no Battel wou'd ever presume to shew upon the Stage agen, unless it were at *Perin* in *Cornwal*, where the story goes that, some time before the year 88. the *Spaniards* once were landing to burn the Town, just at the nick when a Company of *Stroulers* with their Drums and their shouting were setting *Sampson* upon the *Philistines*, which so scar'd Mr. Spaniard, that they Scampered back to their Galions, as apprehending our whole *Tilbury* Camp had lain in Ambush, and were coming souse upon them.

At *Athens* (they tell us) the Tragedies of *Æschylus*, *Sophocles, and Euripides* were enroll'd with their Laws, and made part of their Statue-Book.

We want a law for Acting the *Rehearsal* once a week, to keep us in our senses, and secure us against the Noise and Nonsense, the Farce and Fustian which, in the name of Tragedy, have so long invaded, and usurp our Theater.

*Tully* defines an Orator to be, *Vir bonus dicendique peritus*. Why must he be a *good Man*, as if a bad Man might not be a good Speaker? But what avails it to Speak well, unless a man is well heard? To gain attention *Aristotle* told us, it was necessary that an Orator be a *good Man*; therefore he that writes Tragedy should be careful that the persons of his *Drama*, be of consideration and importance, that the Audience may readily lend an Ear, and give attention to what they say, and act. Who would thrust into a crowd to hear what Mr. *Jago*, *Roderigo*, or *Cassio*, is like to say? From a Venetian Senate, or a Roman Senate one might expect great matters: But their Poet was out of sorts; he had it not for them; the Senators must be no wiser than other folk.

*Ben. Johnson*, knew to distinguish men and manners, at an other rate. In *Catiline* we find our selves in *Europe*, we are no longer in the *Land of Savages*, amongst Blackamoors, Barbarians, and Monsters.

The Scene is Rome and first on the Stage appears *Sylla's* Ghost.

Dost thou not feel me, Rome? Not yet?

One would, in reason, imagine the Ghost is in some publick open place, upon some Eminence, where Rome is all within his view: But it is a surprising thing to find that this ratling Rodomontado speech is in a dark, close, private sleeping hole of *Catiline's*.

Yet the *Chorus*, is of all wonders the strangest. The *Chorus* is always present on the Stage, privy to, and interested in all that passes, and thereupon make their Reflections to Conclude the several *Acts*.

*Sylla's* Ghost, tho' never so big, might slide in at the Key-hole; but how comes the *Chorus* into *Catilins* Cabinet?

*Aurelia* is soon after with him too, but the Poet had perhaps provided her some Truckle-bed in a dark Closet by him.

In short, it is strange that *Ben*, who understood the turn of Comedy so well; and had found the success, should thus grope in the dark, and jumble things together without head or tail, without any rule or proportion, without any reason or design. Might not the *Acts of the Apostles*, or a Life in *Plutarch*, be as well Acted, and as properly called a Tragedy, as any History of a Conspiracy?

*Corneille* tells us, in the *Examen* of his *Melite*, that when first he began to write, he thought there had been no Rules: So had no guide but a little *Common sence*, with the Example of Mr. *Hardy*, and some others, not more regular than he. This *Common sence* (says he) *which was all my rule, brought me to find out the unity of Action to imbroyl four Lovers by one and the same intreague*. *Ben. Johnson*, besides his Common sence to tell him that the *Unity of Action* was necessary; had stumbl'd. (I know not how) on a *Chorus*; which is not to be drawn through a Key-hole, to be lugg'd about, or juggl'd with an *hocus pocus* hither and thither; nor stow'd in a garret, nor put into quarters with the *Brentford* Army, so must of necessity keep the Poet to *unity of place*; And also to some Conscionable *time*, for the representation: Because the *Chorus* is not to be trusted out of sight, is not to eat or drink till they have given up their Verdict, and the *Plaudite* is over.

One would not talk of rules, or what is regular with *Shakespear*, or any followers, in the Gang of the *Strouling* Fraternity; but it is lamentable that *Ben. Johnson*, his Stone and his Tymber, however otherwise of value, must lye a miserable heap of ruins, for want of Architecture, or some Son of *Vitruvius*, to joyn them together. He had red *Horace*, had Translated that to the *Pisones*:

Nec verbum verbo curabis reddere, fidus interpres.

*Ben*: Being a Poet, thou may'st feign, create,
 Not care, as thou wouldst faithfully translate,
 To render word for word——

And this other precept.

Nec circa vilem, patulumque moraberis Orbem.

*Ben*: The vile, broad-trodden ring forsake.

What is there material in this *Catiline*, either in the *Manners*, in the *Thoughts*, or in the *Expression*, (three parts of Tragedy) which is not word for word translation? In the *Fable*, or Plot (which is the first, and principal part) what see we, but the *vile broad trodden ring*? Vile, *Horace* calls it, as a thing below, and too mean for any man of wit to busie his head withal. *Patulum*, he calls it, because it is obvious, and easie for any body to do as much as that comes to. 'Tis but to plodd along, step by step in the same tract: 'Tis drudgery only for the blind Horse in a Mill. No Creature sound of Wind and Limb, but wou'd chuse a nobler Field, and a more generous Career.

*Homer*, we find, slips sometime into a *Tract of Scripture*, but his *Pegasus* is not stabl'd there, presently up he springs, mounts aloft, is on the wing, no earthly bounds, or barriers to confine him.

For *Ben*, to sin thus against the clearest light and conviction, argues a strange stupidity: It was bad enough in him, against his Judgement and Conscience, to interlard so much fiddle faddle, Comedy, and *Apocryphal* matters in the History: Because, forsooth,

his nam plebecula gaudet.

Where the Poet has chosen a subject of importance sufficient and proper for Tragedy, there is no room for this petty interlude and diversion. Had some Princes come express from *Salankemen* (remote as it is) to give an account of the battel, whilst the story was hot and new, and made a relation accurate, and distinctly, with all the pomp, and advantage of the Theatre, wou'd the Audience have suffer'd a Tumbler or Baboon, a Bear, or Rope dancer to have withdrawn their attention; or to have interrupted the Narrative; tho' it had held as long as a Dramatick Representation. Nor at that time wou'd they thank a body for his quibbles, or wit out of season: This mans Feather, or that Captains Embroidered Coat might not be touched upon but in a very short *Parenthesis*.

It is meerly by the ill-chosen Subject, or the ill-adjusting it, that the Audience runs a gadding after what is forreign, and from the business. And when some senceless trifling tale, as that of *Othello*; or some mangl'd, abus'd, undigested, interlarded History on our Stage impiously assumes the sacred name of Tragedy, it is no wonder if the Theatre grow corrupt and scandalous, and Poetry from its Ancient Reputation and Dignity, is sunk to the utmost Contempt and Derision.

## RICHARD G. MOULTON
"Julius Caesar beside His Murderers and His Avenger:
A Study in Character-Grouping"
*Shakespeare as a Dramatic Artist*
1888, pp. 168–84

Every lover of art feels that the different fine arts form not a crowd but a family; the more familiar the mind becomes with them the more it delights to trace in them the application of common ideas to different media of expression. We are reminded of this essential unity by the way in which the arts borrow their terms from one another. 'Colour' is applied to music, 'tone' to painting; we speak of costume as 'loud,' of melody as 'bright,' of orchestration as 'massive;' 'fragrance' was applied by Schumann to Liszt's playing. Two classes of oratorical style have been distinguished as 'statuesque' and 'picturesque'; while the application of a musical term, 'harmony,' and a term of sculpture, 'relief,' to all the arts alike is so common that the transference is scarcely felt. Such usages are not the devices of a straitened vocabulary, but are significant of a single *Art* which is felt to underlie the special *arts*. So the more Drama is brought by criticism into the family of the fine arts the more it will be seen to present the common features. We have already had to notice repeatedly how the idea of pattern or design is the key to dramatic plot. We are in the present study to see how contrast of character, such as was traced in the last study between Lord and Lady Macbeth, when applied to a larger number of personages, produces an effect on the mind analogous to that of *grouping* in pictures and statuary: the different personages not only present points of contrast with one another, but their varieties suddenly fall into a unity of effect if looked at from some one point of view. An example of such Character-Grouping is seen in the play of *Julius Cæsar*, where the four leading figures, all on the grandest scale, have the elements of their characters thrown into relief by comparison with one another, and the contrast stands out boldly when the four are reviewed in relation to one single idea.

This idea is the same as that which lay at the root of the Character-Contrast in *Macbeth*—the antithesis of the practical and inner life. It is, however, applied in a totally different sphere. Instead of a simple age in which the lives coincide with the sexes we are carried to the other extreme of civilisation, the final age of Roman liberty, and all four personages are merged in the busy world of political life. Naturally, then, the contrast of the two lives takes in this play a different form. In the play of *Macbeth* the inner life was seen in the force of will which could hold down alike bad and good impulses; while the outer life was made interesting by its confinement to the training given by action, and an exhibition of it devoid of the thoughtfulness and self-control for which the life of activity has to draw upon the inner life. But there is another aspect in which the two may be regarded. The idea of the inner life is reflected in the word 'individuality,' or that which a man has not in common with others. The cultivation of the inner life implies not merely cultivation of our own individuality, but to it also belongs sympathy with the individuality of others; whereas in the sphere of practical life men fall into classes, and each person has his place as a member of these classes. Thus benevolence may take the form of enquiring into individual wants and troubles and meeting these by personal assistance; but a man has an equal claim to be called benevolent who applies himself to such sciences and political economy, studies the springs which regulate human society, and by influencing these in the right direction confers benefits upon whole classes at a time. Charity and political science are the two forms benevolence assumes correspondent to the inner life of individual sympathies and the outer life of public action. Or, if we consider the contrast from the side of rights as distinguished from duties, the supreme form in which the rights of individuals may be summed up is justice; the corresponding claim which public life makes upon us is (in the highest sense of the term) policy: wherever these two, justice and policy, seem to clash, the outer and inner life are brought into conflict. It is in this form that the conflict is raised in the play of *Julius Cæsar*. To get it in its full force, the dramatist goes to the world of antiquity, for one of the leading distinctions between ancient and modern society is that the modern world gives the fullest play to the individual, while in ancient systems the individual was treated as existing solely for the state. 'Liberty' has been a watchword in both ages; but while we mean by liberty the least amount of interference with personal activity, the liberty for which ancient patriots contended was freedom of the government from external or internal control, and the ideal republic of Plato was so contrived as to reduce individual liberty to a minimum. And this subordination of private to public was most fully carried out in Rome. 'The common weal,' says Merivale, 'was after all the grand object of the heroes of Roman story. Few of the renowned heroes of old had attained their eminence as public benefactors without steeling their hearts against the purest instincts of nature. The deeds of a Brutus or a Manlius, of a Sulla or a Cæsar, would have been branded as crimes in private citizens; it was the public character of the actors that stamped them with immortal glory in the eyes of their countrymen.' Accordingly, the opposition of outer and inner life is brought before us most keenly when, in Roman life, a public policy, the cause of republican freedom, seems to be bound up with the supreme crime against justice and the rights of the individual, assassination.

Brutus is the central figure of the group: in his character the two sides are so balanced that the antithesis disappears. This evenness of development in his nature is the thought of those who in the play gather around his corpse; giving prominence to the quality in Brutus hidden from the casual observer they say:

His life was gentle; and the elements
So mix'd in him that Nature might stand up
And say to all the world 'This was a man!'
> (V. v. 73)

Of another it would be said that he was a poet, a philosopher; of Brutus the only true description was that he was a man! It is in very few characters that force and softness are each carried to such perfection. The strong side of Brutus's character is that which has given to the whole play its characteristic tone. It is seen in the way in which he appreciates the issue at stake. Weak men sin by hiding from themselves what it is they do; Brutus is fully alive to the foulness of conspiracy at the moment in which he is conspiring.

O conspiracy,
Shamest thou to show thy dangerous brow by night,
When evils are most free? O, then by day
Where wilt thou find a cavern dark enough
To mask thy monstrous visage?
> (II. i. 77)

His high tone he carries into the darkest scenes of the play. The use of criminal means has usually an intoxicating effect upon the moral sense, and suggests to those once committed to it that it is useless to haggle over the amount of the crime until the end be obtained. Brutus resists this intoxication, setting his face against the proposal to include Antony in Cæsar's fate, and resolving that not one life shall be unnecessarily sacrificed. He scorns the refuge of suicide; and with warmth adjures his comrades not to stain—

The even virtue of our enterprise,
Nor the insuppressive mettle of our spirits,
To think that or our cause or our performance
Did need an oath; when every drop of blood
That every Roman bears, and nobly bears,
Is guilty of a several bastardy,
If he do break the smallest particle
Of any promise that hath pass'd from him.
> (II. i. 114)

The scale of Brutus's character is again brought out by his relations with other personages of the play. Casca, with all his cynical depreciation of others, has to bear unqualified testimony to Brutus's greatness:

O, he sits high in all the people's hearts;
And that which would appear offence in us,
His countenance, like richest alchemy,
Will change to virtue and to worthiness.
> (I. iii. 157)

We see Ligarius coming from a sick-bed to join in he knows not what: 'it sufficeth that Brutus leads me on.' And the hero's own thought, when at the point of death he pauses to take a moment's survey of his whole life, is of the unfailing power with which he has swayed the hearts of all around him:

My heart doth joy that yet in all my life
I found no man but he was true to me.
> (V. v. 34)

Above all, contact with Cassius throws into relief the greatness of Brutus. At the opening of the play it is Cassius that we associate with the idea of force; but his is the ruling mind only while Brutus is hesitating; as soon as Brutus has thrown in his lot with the conspirators, Cassius himself is swept along with the current of Brutus's irresistible influence. In the councils every point is decided—and, so far as success is concerned, wrongly decided—against Cassius's better judgment. In the sensational moment when Popilius Lena enters the Senate-house and is seen to whisper Cæsar, Cassius's presence of mind fails him, and he prepares in despair for suicide; Brutus retains calmness enough to *watch faces*:

Cassius, be constant:
Popilius Lena speaks not of our purposes;
For, look, he smiles, and Cæsar doth not change.
> (III. i. 19)

In the Quarrel Scene Cassius has lost all pretensions to dignity of action in the impatience sprung from a ruined cause; Brutus maintains principle in despair. Finally, at the close of the scene, when it is discovered that under all the hardness of this contest for principle Brutus has been hiding a heart broken by the loss of Portia, Cassius is forced to give way and acknowledge Brutus's superiority to himself even in his own ideal of impassiveness:

I have as much of this in art as you,
But yet my nature could not bear it so.
> (IV. iii. 194)

The force in Brutus's character is obvious: it is rather its softer side that some readers find difficulty in seeing. But this difficulty is in reality a testimony to Shakespeare's skill, for Brutus is a Stoic, and what gentleness we see in him appears in spite of himself. It may be seen in his culture of art, music, and philosophy, which have such an effect in softening the manners. Nor is this in the case of the Roman Brutus a mere conventional culture: these tastes are among his strongest passions. When all is confusion around him on the eve of the fatal battle he cannot restrain his longing for the refreshing tones of his page's lyre; and, the music over, he takes up his philosophical treatise at the page he had turned down. Again Brutus's considerateness for his dependants is in strong contrast with the harshness of Roman masters. On the same eve of the battle he insists that the men who watch in his tent shall lie down instead of standing as discipline would require. An exquisite little episode brings out Brutus's sweetness of de-meanour in dealing with his youthful page; this rises to womanly tenderness at the end when, noticing how the boy, wearied out and fallen asleep, is lying in a position to injure his instrument, he rises and disengages it without waking him.

*Bru.*: Look, Lucius, here's the book I sought for so;
I put it in the pocket of my gown.
*Luc.*: I was sure your lordship did not give it me.
*Bru.*: Bear with me, good boy; I am much forgetful.
Can'st thou hold up thy heavy eyes awhile,
And touch thy instrument a strain or two?
*Luc.*: Ay, my lord, an't please you.
*Bru.*:                It does, my boy:
I trouble thee too much, but thou art willing.
*Luc.*: It is my duty, sir.
*Bru.*: I should not urge thy duty past thy might;
I know young bloods look for a time of rest.
*Luc.*: I have slept my lord, already.
*Bru.*: It was well done; and thou shalt sleep again;
I will not hold thee long: if I do live
I will be good to thee.    [*Music and a song.*
This is a sleepy tune. O murderous slumber,
Lay'st thou thy leaden mace upon my boy,
That plays thee music? Gentle knave, good night;
I will not do thee so much wrong to wake thee.—
If thou dost nod, thou break'st thy instrument;
I'll take it from thee; and, good boy, good night.
> (IV. iii. 252)

Brutus's relations with Portia bear the same testimony. Portia is a woman with as high a spirit as Lady Macbeth, and she can inflict a wound on herself to prove her courage and her right to share her husband's secrets. But she lacks the physical nerve of Lady Macbeth; her agitation on the morning of the assassination threatens to betray the conspirators, and when these have to flee from Rome the suspense is too much for her and she commits suicide. Brutus knew his wife better than she knew herself, and was right in seeking to withhold the fatal confidence; yet he allowed himself to be persuaded: no man would be so swayed by a tender woman unless he had a tender spirit of his own. In all these ways we may trace an extreme of gentleness in Brutus. But it is of the essence of his character that this softer side is concealed behind an imperturbability of outward demeanour that belongs to his stoic religion: this struggle between inward and outward is the main feature for the actor to bring out. It is a master stroke of Shakespeare that he utilises the euphuistic prose of his age to express impassiveness in Brutus's oration. The greatest man of the world has just been assassinated; the mob are swaying with fluctuating passions; the subtlest orator of his day is at hand to turn those passions into the channel of vengeance for his friend: Brutus called on amid such surroundings to speak for the conspirators still maintains the artificial style of carefully balanced sentences, such as emotionless rhetoric builds up in the quiet of a study.

> As Cæsar loved me, I weep for him; as he was fortunate, I rejoice at it; as he was valiant, I honour him: but, as he was ambitious, I slew him. There is tears for his love; joy for his fortune; honour for his valour; and death for his ambition.
>
> (III. ii. 14)

Brutus's nature then is developed on all its sides; in his character the antithesis of the outer and inner life disappears. It reappears, however, in the action; for Brutus is compelled to balance a weighty issue, with public policy on the one side, and on the other, not only justice to individual claims, but further the claims of friendship, which is one of the fairest flowers of the inner life. And the balance dips to the wrong side. If the question were of using the weapon of assassination against a criminal too high for the ordinary law to reach, this would be a moral problem which, however doubtful to modern thought, would have been readily decided by a Stoic. But the question which presented itself to Brutus was distinctly not this. Shakespeare has been careful to represent Brutus as admitting to himself that Cæsar has done no wrong: he slays him *for what he might do*.

> The abuse of greatness is, when it disjoins
> Remorse from power: and, *to speak truth of Cæsar,*
> *I have not known when his affections sway'd*
> *More than his reason.* But 'tis a common proof,
> That lowliness is young ambition's ladder;
> Whereto the climber-upward turns his face;
> But when he once attains the upmost round,
> He then unto the ladder turns his back,
> Looks in the clouds, scorning the base degrees
> By which he did ascend. So Cæsar may.
> Then, lest he may, prevent. And *since the quarrel*
> *Will bear no colour for the thing he is,*
> Fashion it thus; that what he is, augmented,
> Would run to these and these extremities:
> And therefore think him as a serpent's egg
> Which hatch'd, would, as his kind, grow mis-
>     chievous.
> And kill him in the shell.
>
> (II. i. 18–34)

It is true that Shakespeare, with his usual 'dramatic hedging,' softens down this immoral bias in a great hero by representing him as both a Roman, of the nation which beyond all other nations exalted the state over the individual, and a Brutus, representative of the house which had risen to greatness by leading violence against tyranny. But, Brutus's own conscience

being judge, the man against whom he moves is guiltless; and so the conscious sacrifice of justice and friendship to policy is a fatal error which is source sufficient for the whole tragedy of which Brutus is the hero.

The character of Cæsar is one of the most difficult in Shakespeare. Under the influence of some of his speeches we find ourselves in the presence of one of the master spirits of mankind; other scenes in which he plays a leading part breathe nothing but the feeblest vacillation and weakness. It is the business of Character-Interpretation to harmonise this contradiction; it is not interpretation at all to ignore one side of it and be content with describing Cæsar as vacillating. The force and strength of his character is seen in the impression he makes upon forceful and strong men. The attitude of Brutus to Cæsar seems throughout to be that of looking up; and notably at one point the thought of Cæsar's greatness seems to cast a lurid gleam over the assassination plot itself, and Brutus feels that the grandeur of the victim gives a dignity to the crime:

> Let's carve him as a dish fit for the gods.
>
> (II. i. 173)

The strength and force of Antony again no one will question; and Antony, at the moment when he is alone with the corpse of Cæsar and can have no motive for hypocrisy, apostrophises it in the words—

> Thou art the ruins of the noblest man
> That ever lived in the tide of times.
>
> (III. i. 256)

And we see enough of Cæsar in the play to bear out the opinions of Brutus and Antony. Those who accept vacillation a sufficient description of Cæsar's character must explain his strong speeches as vaunting and self-assertion. But surely it must be possible for dramatic language to distinguish between the true and the assumed force; and equally surely there is a genuine ring in the speeches in which Cæsar's heroic spirit, shut out from the natural sphere of action in which it has been so often proved, leaps restlessly at every opportunity into pregnant words. We may thus feel certain of his lofty physical courage.

> Cowards die many times before their deaths;
> The valiant never taste of death but once.
> Of all the wonders that I yet have heard,
> It seems to me most strange that men should
>     fear . . .
>
> (II. ii. 32)

> Danger knows full well
> That Cæsar is more dangerous than he:
> We are two lions litter'd in one day,
> And I the elder and more terrible.
>
> (II. ii. 44)

A man must have felt the thrill of courage in search of its food, danger, before his self-assertion finds language of this kind in which to express itself. In another scene we have the perfect *fortiter in re* and *suaviter in modo* of the trained statesman exhibited in the courtesy with which Cæsar receives the conspirators, combined with his perfect readiness to 'tell graybeards the truth.' Nor could imperial firmness be more ideally painted than in the way in which Cæsar 'prevents' Cimber's intercession.

> Be not fond,
> To think that Cæsar bears such rebel blood
> That will be thaw'd from the true quality
> With that which melteth fools; I mean, sweet words,
> Low-crooked court'sies, and base spaniel-fawning.
> Thy brother by decree is banished:
> If thou dost bend and pray and fawn for him,

I spurn thee like a cur out of my way.
Know, Cæsar doth not wrong, nor without cause
Will he be satisfied.

(III. i. 35)

Commonplace authority loudly proclaims that it will never relent: the true imperial spirit feels it a preliminary condition to see first that it never does wrong.

It is the antithesis of the outer and inner life that explains this contradiction in Cæsar's character. Like Macbeth, he is the embodiment of one side and one side only of the antithesis; he is the complete type of the practical—though in special qualities he is as unlike Macbeth as his age is unlike Macbeth's age. Accordingly Cæsar appears before us perfect up to the point where his own personality comes in. The military and political spheres, in which he has been such a colossal figure, call forth practical powers, and do not involve introspection and meditation on foundation principles of thought.

Theirs not to reason why:
Theirs but to do.

The tasks of the soldier and the statesman are imposed upon them by external authority and necessities, and the faculties exercised are those which shape means to ends. But at last Cæsar comes to a crisis that does involve his personality; he attempts a task imposed on him by his own ambition. He plays in a game of which the prize is the world and the stake himself, and to estimate chances in such a game tests self-knowledge and self-command to its depths. How wanting Cæsar is in the cultivation of the inner life is brought out by his contrast with Cassius. The incidents of the flood and the fever, retained by the memory of Cassius, illustrate this. The first of these was no mere swimming-match; the flood in the Tiber was such as to reduce to nothing the difference between one swimmer and another. It was a trial of nerve: and as long as action was possible Cæsar was not only as brave as Cassius, but was the one attracted by the danger. Then some chance wave or cross current renders his chance of life hopeless, and no buffeting with lusty sinews is of any avail; that is the point at which the *passive* courage born of the inner life comes in, and gives strength to submit to the inevitable in calmness. This Cæsar lacks, and he calls for rescue: Cassius would have felt the water close over him and have sunk to the bottom and died rather than accept aid from his rival. In like manner the sick bed is a region in which the highest physical and intellectual activity is helpless; the trained self-control of a Stoic may have a sphere for exercise even here; but the god Cæsar shakes, and cries for drink like a sick girl. It is interesting to note how the two types of mind, when brought into personal contact, jar upon one another's self-consciousness. The intellectual man, judging the man of action by the test of mutual intercourse, sees nothing to explain the other's greatness, and wonders what people find in him that they so admire him and submit to his influence. On the other hand, the man of achievement is uneasily conscious of a sort of superiority in one whose intellectual aims and habits he finds it so difficult to follow—yet superiority it is not, for what has he *done*? Shakespeare has illustrated this in the play by contriving to bring Cæsar and his suite across the 'public place' in which Cassius is discoursing to Brutus. Cassius feels the usual irritation at being utterly unable to find in his old acquaintance any special qualities to explain his elevation.

Now, in the names of all the gods at once,
Upon what meat doth this our Cæsar feed,
That he is grown so great?

(I. ii. 148)

Similarly Cæsar, as he casts a passing glance at Cassius,

becomes at once uneasy. 'He thinks too much,' is the exclamation of the man of action:

He loves no plays,
As thou dost, Antony; he hears no music.

The practical man, accustomed to divide mankind into a few simple types, is always uncomfortable at finding a man he cannot classify. Finally there is a climax to the jealousy that exists between the two lives: Cæsar complains that Cassius *'looks quite through the deeds of men.'*

There is another circumstance to be taken into account in explaining the weakness of Cæsar. A change has come over the spirit of Roman political life itself—such seems to be Shakespeare's conception: Cæsar on his return has found Rome no longer the Rome he had known. Before he left for Gaul, Rome had been the ideal sphere for public life, the arena in which principles alone were allowed to combat, and from which the banishment of personal aims and passions was the first condition of virtue. In his absence Rome has gradually degenerated; the mob has become the ruling force, and introduced an element of uncertainty into political life; politics has passed from science into gambling. A new order of public men has arisen, of which Cassius and Antony are the types; personal aims, personal temptations, and personal risks are now inextricably interwoven with public action. This is a changed order of things to which the mind of Cæsar, cast in a higher mould, lacks the power to adapt itself. His vacillation is the vacillation of unfamiliarity with the new political conditions. He refuses the crown 'each time gentler than the other,' showing want of decisive reading in dealing with the fickle mob; and on his return from the Capitol he is too untrained in hypocrisy to conceal the angry spot upon his face; he has tried to use the new weapons which he does not understand, and has failed. It is a subtle touch of Shakespeare's to the same effect that Cæsar is represented as having himself undergone a change *of late*:

For he is superstitious grown of late,
Quite from the main opinion he held once
Of fantasy, of dreams and ceremonies.

(II. i. 195)

To come back to a world of which you have mastered the machinery, and to find that it is no longer governed by machinery at all, that causes no longer produce their effects—this, if anything, might well drive a strong intellect to superstition. And herein consists the pathos of Cæsar's situation. The deepest tragedy of the play is not the assassination of Cæsar, it is rather seen in such a speech as this of Decius:

If he be so resolved,
I can o'ersway him; for he loves to hear
That unicorns may be betray'd with trees,
And bears with glasses, elephants with holes,
Lions with toils and men with flatterers;
But when I tell him, he hates flatterers,
He says he does, being then most flattered.

(II. i. 202)

Assassination is a less piteous thing than to see the giant intellect by its very strength unable to contend against the low cunning of a fifth-rate intriguer.

Such, then, appears to be Shakespeare's conception of Julius Cæsar. He is the consummate type of the practical: emphatically the public man, complete in all the greatness that belongs to action. On the other hand, the knowledge of self produced by self-contemplation is wanting, and so when he comes to consider the relation of his individual self to the state he vacillates with the vacillation of a strong man moving amongst men of whose greater intellectual subtlety he is dimly conscious: no unnatural conception for a Cæsar who has been founding empires abroad while his fellows have been sharpening their wits in the party contests of a decaying state.

The remaining members of the group are Cassius and Antony. In Cassius thought and action have been equally developed, and he has the qualities belonging to both the outer and the inner life. But the side which in Brutus barely preponderated, absolutely tyrannises in Cassius; his public life has given him a grand passion to which the whole of his nature becomes subservient. Inheriting a 'rash humour' from his mother, he was specially prepared for impatience of political anomalies; republican independence has become to him an ideal dearer than life.

> I had as lief not be as live to be
> In awe of such a thing as I myself.
>                                                     (I. ii. 95)

He has thus become a professional politician. Politics is to him a game, and men are counters to be used; Cassius finds satisfaction in discovering that even Brutus's 'honourable metal may be wrought from that it is disposed.' He has the politician's low view of human nature; while Brutus talks of principles Cassius interposes appeals to interest: he says to Antony,

> Your voice shall be as strong as any man's
> In the disposing of new dignities.
>                                                     (III. i. 177)

His party spirit is, as usual, unscrupulous; he seeks to work upon his friend's unsuspecting nobility by concocted letters thrown in at his windows; and in the Quarrel Scene loses patience at Brutus's scruples.

> I'll not endure it: you forget yourself,
> To hedge me in; I am a soldier, I,
> Older in practice, abler than yourself
> To make conditions.
>                                                     (IV. iii. 29)

At the same time he has a party politician's tact; his advice throughout the play is proved by the event to have been right, and he does himself no more than justice when he says his misgiving 'still falls shrewdly to the purpose.' Antony also has all the powers that belong both to the intellectual and practical life; so far as these powers are concerned, he has them developed to a higher degree than even Brutus and Cassius. His distinguishing mark lies in the use to which these powers are put; like Cassius, he has concentrated his whole nature in one aim, but this aim is not a disinterested object of public good, it is unmitigated self-seeking. Antony has greatness enough to appreciate the greatness of Cæsar; hence in the first half of the play he has effaced himself, choosing to rise to power as the useful tool of Cæsar. Here, indeed, he is famed as a devotee of the softer studies, but it is not till his patron has fallen that his irresistible strength is put forth. There seems to be but one element in Antony that is not selfish: his attachment to Cæsar is genuine, and its force is measured in the violent imagery of the vow with which when alone for a moment with the corpse, he promises vengeance till all pity is 'choked with custom of fell deeds.' And yet this perhaps is after all the best illustration of his callousness to higher feelings; for the one tender emotion of his heart is used by him as the convenient weapon with which to fight his enemies and raise himself to power.

Such, then, is the Grouping of Characters in the play of *Julius Cæsar*. To catch it they must be contemplated in the light of the antithesis between the outer and inner life. In Brutus the antithesis disappears amid the perfect balancing of his character, to reappear in the action, when Brutus has to choose between his cause and his friend. In Cæsar the practical life only is developed, and he fails as soon as action involves the inner life. Cassius has the powers of both outer and inner life perfect, and they are fused into one master-passion, morbid but unselfish. Antony has carried to an even greater perfection the culture of both lives, and all his powers are concentrated in one purpose, which is purely selfish. In the action in which this group of personages is involved the determining fact is the change that has come over the spirit of Roman life, and introduced into its public policy the element of personal aggrandisement and personal risk. The new spirit works upon Brutus: the chance of winning political liberty by the assassination of one individual just overbalances his moral judgment, and he falls. Yet in his fall he is glorious: the one false judgment of his life brings him, what is more to him than victory, the chance of maintaining the calmness of principle amid the ruins of a falling cause, and showing how a Stoic can fail and die. The new spirit affects Cæsar and tempts him into a personal enterprise in which success demands a meanness that he lacks, and he is betrayed to his fall. Yet in his fall he is glorious: the assassins' daggers purge him from the stain of his momentary personal ambition, and the sequel shows that the Roman world was not worthy of a ruler such as Cæsar. The spirit of the age affects Cassius, and fans his passion to work itself out to his own destruction, and he falls. Yet in his fall he is glorious: we forgive him the lowered tone of his political action when we see by the spirit of the new rulers how desperate was the chance for which he played, and how Cassius and his loved cause of republican freedom expire together. The spirit of the age which has wrought upon the rest is controlled and used by Antony, and he rises on their ruins. Yet in his rise he is less glorious than they in their fall: he does all for self; he may claim therefore the prize of success, but in goodness he has no share beyond that he is permitted to be the passive instrument of punishing evil.

Brutus and Strato in *Julius Caesar*
(engraving by Noble from a painting by Westall)

Romeo and Juliet
(painting by Anselm Feuerbach)

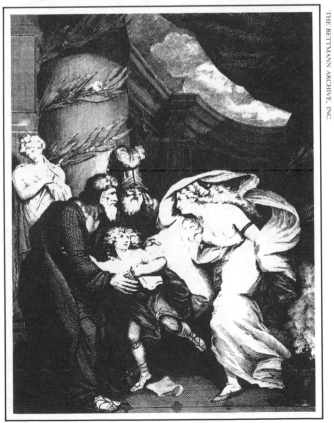

*Titus Andronicus*
(engraving by Reading from a painting by Kirk)

*Troilus and Cressida*
(engraving by Lightfoot from a painting by Opie)

Edwin Booth as Hamlet
(engraving by Linton from a painting by Hennessy)

Charles Dillon as Othello

Sarah Bernhardt as Hamlet

# Hamlet

It ⟨an "Epistle to the Reader"⟩ should be like the *Never-too-well read Arcadia*, where the *Prose* and *Verce* (*Matter* and *Words*) are like his *Mistresses* eyes, one still excelling another and without Corivall: or to come home to the vulgars *Element*, like *Friendly Shakespeare's Tragedies*, where the *Commedian* rides, when the *Tragedian* stands on Tip-toe: Faith it should please all, like Prince *Hamlet*. But in sadnesse, then it were to be feared he would runne mad: Insooth I will not be moone-sicke, to please: nor out of my wits though I displeased all.— ANTHONY SCOLOKER, "Epistle to the Reader," *Daiphantus, or the Passions of Love*, 1604

The *Poets* make *Women* speak Smuttily. Of this the Places before mention'd are sufficient Evidence: And if there was occasion they might be multiplied to a much greater Number. Indeed the *Comedies* are seldom clear of these Blemishes: And sometimes you have them in *Tragedy*. . . . For Modesty, as Mr. *Rapin* observes, is the *Character* of Women. To represent them without this Quality, is to make Monsters of them, and throw them out of their Kind. *Euripides*, who was no negligent Observer of Humane Nature, is always careful of this Decorum. Thus *Phaedra*, when possess'd with an infamous Passion, takes all imaginable Plans to conceal it. She is as regular and reserv'd in her Language as the most vertuous Matron. 'Tis true, the force of Shame and Desire; The Scandal of Satisfying, and the Difficulty of Parting with her Inclinations, disorder her to Distraction. However, her Frensy is not Lewd, she keeps her Modesty even after she has lost her Wits. Had *Shakespear* secur'd this point for his young Virgin *Ophelia*, the *Play* had been better contriv'd. Since he was resolv'd to drown the Lady like a Kitten, he should have set her a swimming a little sooner. To keep her alive only to sullen her Reputation, and discover the Rankness of her Breath, was very cruel.—JEREMY COLLIER, *A Short View of the Immorality and Profaneness of the English Stage*, 1698

The Roman philosophers had no faith in ghosts in the time of the emperors, and yet young Pompey raises one in the *Pharsalia*. The English have certainly no more belief in spirits than the Romans had, and yet they see every day with pleasure, in the tragedy of *Hamlet*, the ghost of a king, who appears nearly the same as the apparition of Ninus did at Paris. I am at the same time far from justifying the tragedy of *Hamlet* in every respect; it is a gross and barbarous piece, and would never be borne by the lowest of the rabble in France or Italy. Hamlet runs mad in the second act, and his mistress in the third; the prince kills the father of his mistress and fancies he is killing a rat; and the heroine of the play throws herself into the river. They dig her grave on the stage, and the grave-diggers, holding the dead men's skulls in their hands, talk nonsense worthy of them. Hamlet answers their abominable stuff by some whimsies not less disgusting; during this time one of the actors makes the conquest of Poland. Hamlet, his mother, and father-in-law, drink together on the stage: they sing at table, quarrel, beat and kill one another: one would think the whole piece was the product of the imagination of a drunken savage: and yet, among all these gross irregularities, which make the English theatre even at this day so absurd and barbarous, we find in *Hamlet*, which is still more strange and unaccountable, some sublime strokes worthy of the greatest genius. It seems as if nature took pleasure to unite in the head of Shakespeare all that we can imagine great and forcible, together with all that

the grossest dullness could produce of everything that is most low and detestable.

It must be acknowledged, that, among the beauties that shine forth in the midst of all these horrid extravagancies, the ghost of Hamlet's father is one of the most striking: it has always a strong effect on the English—I mean, on those who are the best judges and are most hurt by the irregularity of their old theatre. This ghost inspires more terror, even in the reading, than the apparition of Darius in the *Persians* of Æschylus: and why does it? because Darius, in Æschylus, only appears to foretell the misfortunes of his family; whereas, in Shakespeare, the ghost of Hamlet appears to demand vengeance, and to reveal secret crimes. It is neither useless, nor brought in by force, but serves to convince mankind, that there is an invisible power, the master of nature. All men have a sense of justice imprinted on their hearts, and naturally wish that heaven would interest itself in the cause of innocence: in every age, therefore, and in every nation, they will behold with pleasure, the Supreme Being engaged in the punishment of crimes which could not come within the reach of human laws: this is a consolation to the weak, and a restraint on the insolence and obstinacy of the powerful.

> Heaven
> Will oft suspend its own eternal laws
> When justice calls, reversing death's decree,
> Thus to chastise the sovereigns of the earth,
> And terrify mankind—

Thus Semiramis speaks to the high priest of Babylon, and thus the successor of Samuel might have spoken to Saul, when the ghost of Samuel came to tell him of his condemnation.

I will go still further, and venture to affirm, when an extraordinary circumstance of this kind is mentioned in the beginning of a tragedy, when it is properly prepared, when things are so situated as to render it necessary and even looked for and desired by the spectators; it ought then to be considered as perfectly natural: it is at the same time sufficiently obvious, that these bold strokes are not to be too often repeated.— FRANÇOIS MARIE AROUET DE VOLTAIRE, "Ancient and Modern Tragedy" (1749), *Works*, 1901, Vol. 19, tr. William F. Fleming, pp. 136–38

If the dramas of Shakespeare were to be characterised, each by the particular excellence which distinguishes it from the rest, we must allow to the tragedy of *Hamlet* the praise of variety. The incidents are so numerous, that the argument of the play would make a long tale. The scenes are interchangeably diversified with merriment and solemnity; with merriment that includes judicious and instructive observations, and solemnity, not strained by poetical violence above the natural sentiments of man. New characters appear from time to time in continual succession, exhibiting various forms of life and particular modes of conversation. The pretended madness of Hamlet causes much mirth, the mournful distraction of Ophelia fills the heart with tenderness, and every personage produces the effect intended, from the apparition that in the first act chills the blood with horror, to the fop in the last, that exposes affectation to just contempt.

The conduct is perhaps not wholly secure against objections. The action is indeed for the most part in continual progression, but there are some scenes which neither forward nor retard it. Of the feigned madness of Hamlet there appears no adequate cause, for he does nothing which he might not have done with the reputation of sanity. He plays the madman most, when he treats Ophelia with so much rudeness, which seems to be useless and wanton cruelty.

Hamlet is, through the whole play, rather an instrument than an agent. After he has, by the stratagem of the play, convicted the King, he makes no attempt to punish him, and his death is at last effected by an incident which Hamlet has no part in producing.

The catastrophe is not very happily produced; the exchange of weapons is rather an expedient of necessity, than a stroke of art. A scheme might easily have been formed, to kill Hamlet with the dagger, and Laertes with the bowl.

The poet is accused of having shewn little regard to poetical justice, and may be charged with equal neglect of poetical probability. The apparition left the regions of the dead to little purpose; the revenge which he demands is not obtained but by the death of him that was required to take it; and the gratification which would arise from the destruction of an usurper and a murderer, is abated by the untimely death of Ophelia, the young, the beautiful, the harmless, and the pious. . . .

Of ⟨Hamlet's⟩ celebrated soliloquy, which bursting from a man distracted with contrariety of desires, and overwhelmed with the magnitude of his own purposes, is connected rather in the speaker's mind, than on his tongue, I shall endeavour to discover the train, and to shew how one sentiment produces another.

Hamlet, knowing himself injured in the most enormous and atrocious degree, and seeing no means of redress, but such as must expose him to the extremity of hazard, meditates on his situation in this manner: "Before I can form any rational scheme of action under this pressure of distress," it is necessary to decide whether, "after our present state, we are *to be or not to be.*" That is the question, which, as it shall be answered, will determine, "whether 'tis nobler," and more suitable to the dignity of reason, "to suffer the outrages of fortune" patiently, or to take arms against, "them," and by opposing end them, "though perhaps" with the loss of life. If "to die," were "to sleep, no more, and by a sleep to end" the miseries of our nature, such a sleep were "devoutly to be wished"; but if "to sleep" in death, be "to dream," to retain our powers of sensibility, we must "pause" to consider, "in that sleep of death what dreams may come." This consideration "makes calamity" so long endured; "for who would bear" the vexations of life, which might be ended "by a bare bodkin," but that he is afraid of something in unknown futurity? This fear it is that gives efficacy to conscience, which, by turning the mind upon "this regard," chills the ardour of "resolution," checks the vigour of "enterprise," and makes the "current" to desire stagnate in inactivity.

We may suppose that he would have applied these general observations to his own case, but that he discovered Ophelia.— SAMUEL JOHNSON, *Notes on Shakespeare's Plays,* 1768

*Hamlet* is singular in its kind: a tragedy of thought inspired by continual and never-satisfied meditation on human destiny and the dark perplexity of the events of this world, and calculated to call forth the very same meditation in the minds of the spectators. This enigmatical work resembles those irrational equations in which a fraction of unknown magnitude always remains, that will in no way admit of solution. Much has been said, much written, on this piece, and yet no thinking head who anew expresses himself on it, will (in his view of the connexion and the signification of all the parts) entirely coincide with his predecessors. What naturally most astonishes

us, is the fact that with such hidden purposes, with a foundation laid in such unfathomable depth, the whole should, at a first view, exhibit an extremely popular appearance. The dread appearance of the Ghost takes possession of the mind and the imagination almost at the very commencement; then the play within the play, in which, as in a glass, we see reflected the crime, whose fruitlessly attempted punishment constitutes the subject-matter of the piece; the alarm with which it fills the King; Hamlet's pretended and Ophelia's real madness; her death and burial; the meeting of Hamlet and Laertes at her grave; their combat, and the grand determination; lastly, the appearance of the young hero Fortinbras, who, with warlike pomp, pays the last honours to an extinct family of kings; the interspersion of comic characteristic scenes with Polonius, the courtiers, and the grave-diggers, which have all of them their signification,—all this fills the stage with an animated and varied movement. The only circumstance from which this piece might be judged to be less theatrical than other tragedies of Shakespeare is, that in the last scene the main action either stands still or appears to retrograde. This, however, was inevitable, and lay in the nature of the subject. The whole is intended to show that a calculating consideration, which exhausts all the relations and possible consequences of a deed, must cripple the power of acting; as Hamlet himself expresses it:—

> And thus the native hue of resolution
> Is sicklied o'er with the pale cast of thought;
> And enterprises of great pith and moment,
> With this regard, their currents turn awry,
> And lose the name of action.

With respect to Hamlet's character: I cannot, as I understand the poet's view, pronounce altogether so favourable a sentence upon it as Goethe does. He is, it is true, of a highly cultivated mind, a prince of royal manners, endowed with the finest sense of propriety, susceptible of noble ambition, and open in the highest degree to an enthusiastic admiration of that excellence in others of which he himself is deficient. He acts the part of madness with unrivalled power, convincing the persons who are sent to examine into his supposed loss of reason, merely by telling them unwelcome truths, and rallying them with the most caustic wit. But in the resolutions which he so often embraces and always leaves unexecuted, his weakness is too apparent: he does himself only justice when he implies that there is no greater dissimilarity than between himself and Hercules. He is not solely impelled by necessity to artifice and dissimulation, he has a natural inclination for crooked ways; he is a hypocrite towards himself; his far-fetched scruples are often mere pretexts to cover his want of determination: thoughts, as he says on a different occasion, which have

> but one part wisdom
> And ever three parts coward.

He has been chiefly condemned both for his harshness in repulsing the love of Ophelia, which he himself had cherished, and for his insensibility at her death. But he is too much overwhelmed with his own sorrow to have any compassion to spare for others; besides his outward indifference gives us by no means the measure of his internal perturbation. On the other hand, we evidently perceive in him a malicious joy, when he has succeeded in getting rid of his enemies, more through necessity and accident, which alone are able to impel him to quick and decisive measures, than by the merit of his own courage, as he himself confesses after the murder of Polonius, and with respect to Rosencrantz and Guildenstern. Hamlet has no firm belief either in himself or in anything else: from expressions of religious confidence he passes over to sceptical doubts; he believes in the Ghost of his father as long as he sees it, but as soon as it has disappeared, it appears to him almost in the light of a deception. He has even gone so far as to say, "there is nothing either good or bad, but thinking makes it so;" with him the poet loses himself here in labyrinths of thought, in which neither end nor beginning is discoverable. The stars themselves, from the course of events, afford no answer to the question so urgently proposed to them. A voice from another world, commissioned it would appear, by heaven, demands vengeance for a monstrous enormity, and the demand remains without effect; the criminals are at last punished, but as it were, by an accidental blow, and not in the solemn way requisite to convey to the world a warning example of justice; irresolute foresight, cunning treachery, and impetuous rage, hurry on to a common destruction; the less guilty and the innocent are equally involved in the general ruin. The destiny of humanity is there exhibited as a gigantic Sphinx, which threatens to precipitate into the abyss of scepticism all who are unable to solve her dreadful enigmas.

As one example of the many niceties of Shakspeare which have never been understood, I may allude to the style in which the player's speech about Hecuba is conceived. It has been the subject of much controversy among the commentators, whether this was borrowed by Shakspeare from himself or from another, and whether, in the praise of the piece of which it is supposed to be a part, he was speaking seriously, or merely meant to ridicule the tragical bombast of his contemporaries. It seems never to have occurred to them that this speech must not be judged of by itself, but in connexion with the place where it is introduced. To distinguish it in the play itself as dramatic poetry, it was necessary that it should rise above the dignified poetry of the former in the same proportion that generally theatrical elevation soars above simple nature. Hence Shakspeare has composed the play in Hamlet altogether in sententious rhymes full of antitheses. But this solemn and measured tone did not suit a speech in which violent emotion ought to prevail, and the poet had no other expedient than the one of which he made choice: overcharging the pathos. The language of the speech in question is certainly falsely emphatical; but yet this fault is so mixed up with true grandeur, that a player practised in artificially calling forth in himself the emotion he is imitating, may certainly be carried away by it. Besides, it will hardly be believed that Shakspeare knew so little of his art, as not to be aware that a tragedy in which Æneas had to make a lengthy epic relation of a transaction that happened so long before as the destruction of Troy, could neither be dramatical nor theatrical.—AUGUST WILHELM SCHLEGEL, *Lectures on Dramatic Art and Literature*, 1809, tr. John Black

In all commentating upon Shakspeare, there has been a radical error, never yet mentioned. It is the error of attempting to expound his characters—to account for their actions—to reconcile his inconsistencies—not as if they were the coinage of a human brain, but as if they had been actual existences upon earth. We talk of Hamlet the man, instead of Hamlet the *dramatis persona*—of Hamlet that God, in place of Hamlet that Shakspeare created. If Hamlet had really lived, and if the tragedy were an accurate record of his deeds, from this record (with some trouble) we might, it is true, reconcile his inconsistences and settle to our satisfaction his true character. But the task becomes the purest absurdity when we deal only with a phantom. It is not (then) the inconsistencies of the acting man which we have as a subject of discussion—(although we proceed as if it were, and thus *inevitably* err,) but the whims and vacillations—the conflicting energies and

indolences of the poet. It seems to us little less than a miracle, that this obvious point should have been overlooked.

While on this topic, we may as well offer an ill-considered opinion of our own as to the *intention of the poet* in the delineation of the Dane. It must have been well known to Shakspeare, that a leading feature in certain more intense classes of intoxication, (from whatever cause,) is an almost irresistible impulse to counterfeit a farther degree of excitement than actually exists. Analogy would lead any thoughtful person to suspect the same impulse in madness—where beyond doubt, it is manifest. This, Shakspeare *felt*—not thought. He felt it through his marvellous power of *identification* with humanity at large—the ultimate source of his magical influence upon mankind. He wrote of Hamlet as if Hamlet he were; and having, in the first instance, imagined his hero excited to partial unsanity by the disclosures of the ghost—he (the poet) *felt* that it was natural he should be impelled to exaggerate the insanity.—EDGAR ALLAN POE, "William Hazlitt" (1845), *Essays and Reviews*, 1984, ed. G. R. Thompson, pp. 272–73

The *Essays* ⟨of Montaigne⟩ had already passed through many editions in French, and were known to Shakspeare in that language. Their publication in English was an event in the brilliant and intellectual London world, then keenly interested in the playhouses; and Shakspeare, in revising his *Hamlet* in 1604, gives proof of the actual occupation of his patrons with the Englished Montaigne, and confirms, too, the fact of his own occupation with the *Essays* previously.

For me the interest of this discovery does not lie in its showing that Shakspeare thought Montaigne a dangerous author, and meant to give in *Hamlet* a shocking example of what Montaigne's teaching led to. It lies in its explaining how it comes about that *Hamlet*, in spite of the prodigious mental and poetic power shown in it, is really so tantalising and ineffective a play. To the common public *Hamlet* is a famous piece by a famous poet, with crime, a ghost, battle, and carnage; and that is sufficient. To the youthful enthusiast *Hamlet* is a piece handling the mystery of the universe, and having throughout cadences, phrases, and words full of divinest Shakspearian magic; and that, too, is sufficient. To the pedant, finally, *Hamlet* is an occasion for airing his psychology; and what does pedant require more? But to the spectator who loves true and powerful drama, and can judge whether he gets it or not, *Hamlet* is a piece which opens, indeed, simply and admirably, and then: 'The rest is puzzle'!

The reason is, apparently, that Shakespeare conceived this play with his mind running on Montaigne, and placed its action and its hero in Montaigne's atmosphere and world. What is that world? It is the world of man viewed as a being *ondoyant et divers*, balancing and indeterminate, the plaything of cross motives and shifting impulses, swayed by a thousand subtle influences, physiological and pathological. Certainly the action and hero of the original Hamlet story are not such as to compel the poet to place them in this world and no other, but they admit of being placed there, Shakspeare resolved to place them there, and they lent themselves to his resolve. The resolve once taken to place the action in this world of problem, the problem became brightened by all the force of Shakspeare's faculties, of Shakspeare's subtlety. *Hamlet* thus comes at last to be not a drama followed with perfect comprehension and profoundest emotion, which is the ideal for tragedy, but a problem soliciting interpretation and solution.—MATTHEW ARNOLD, "Hamlet Once More" (1884), *Works*, 1903, Vol. 4, pp. 273–74

I know of nothing in all Drama more incomparable from the point of view of Art, or more suggestive in its subtlety of observation, than Shakespeare's drawing of Rosencrantz and

Guildenstern. They are Hamlet's college friends. They have been his companions. They bring with them memories of pleasant days together. At the moment when they come across him in the play he is staggering under the weight of a burden intolerable to one of his temperament. The dead have come armed out of the grave to impose on him a mission at once too great and too mean for him. He is a dreamer, and he is called upon to act. He has the nature of the poet and he is asked to grapple with the common complexities of cause and effect, with life in its practical realisation, of which he knows nothing, not with life in its ideal essence, of which he knows much. He has no conception of what to do, and his folly is to feign folly. Brutus used madness as a cloak to conceal the sword of his purpose, the dagger of his will, but to Hamlet madness is a mere mask for the hiding of weakness. In the making of mows and jests he sees a chance of delay. He keeps playing with action, as an artist plays with a theory. He makes himself the spy of his proper actions, and listening to his own words knows them to be but "words, words, words." Instead of trying to be the hero of his own history, he seeks to be the spectator of his own tragedy. He disbelieves in everything, including himself, and yet his doubt helps him not, as it comes not from scepticism but from a divided will.

Of all this, Guildenstern and Rosencrantz realise nothing. They bow and smirk and smile, and what the one says the other echoes with sicklier iteration. When at last, by means of the play within the play and the puppets in their dalliance, Hamlet "catches the conscience" of the King, and drives the wretched man in terror from his throne, Guildenstern and Rosencrantz see no more in his conduct than a rather painful breach of court-etiquette. That is as far as they can attain to in "the contemplation of the spectacle of life with appropriate emotions." They are close to his very secret and know nothing of it. Nor would there be any use in telling them. They are the little cups that can hold so much and no more. Towards the close it is suggested that, caught in a cunning springe set for another, they have met, or may meet with a violent and sudden death. But a tragic ending of this kind, though touched by Hamlet's humour with something of the surprise and justice of comedy, is really not for such as they. They never die. Horatio who, in order to "report Hamlet and his cause aright to the unsatisfied,"

Absents him from felicity a while

And in this harsh world draws his breath in pain,

dies, though not before an audience, and leaves no brother. But Guildenstern and Rosencrantz are as immortal as Angelo and Tartuffe, and should rank with them. They are what modern life has contributed to the antique ideal friendship. He who writes a new *De Amicitia* must find a niche for them and praise them in Tusculan prose. They are types fixed for all time. To censure them would show a lack of appreciation. They are merely out of their sphere: that is all. In sublimity of soul there is no contagion. High thoughts and high emotions are by their very existence isolated. What Ophelia herself could not understand was not to be realised by "Guildenstern and gentle Rosencrantz," by "Rosencrantz and gentle Guildenstern."—OSCAR WILDE, Letter to Lord Alfred Douglas (January-March 1897), *Selected Letters of Oscar Wilde*, 1979, ed. Rupert Hart-Davis, pp. 232–33

A recent critic enunciates a view of Hamlet which flies flat in the face of every accepted theory; he maintains that Hamlet was not irresolute, not over-intellectual, not procrastinating, not weak. The challenge, erroneous as it may be, is spirited, ingenious and well-reasoned, and it can do nothing but honour to Shakespeare. The more varied are the versions of friends and enemies, the more flatly irreconcilable are the opinions of various men about Hamlet, the more he resembles a real man. The characters of fiction, mysterious as they are, are far less mysterious than the figures of history. Men have agreed about Hamlet vastly more than they have agreed about Caesar or Mahomet or Cromwell or Mr. Gladstone or Cecil Rhodes. Nobody supposes that Mr. Gladstone was a solar myth; nobody has started the theory that Mr. Rhodes is only the hideous phantom of an idle dream. Yet hardly three men agree about either of them, hardly anyone knows that some new and suggestive view of them might not be started at any moment. If Hamlet can be thus surprised, if he can be thus taken in the rear, it is a great tribute to the solidity of the figure. If from another standpoint he appears like another statue, it shows at least that the figure is made of marble and not of cardboard. Neither the man who thinks Lord Beaconsfield a hero nor the man who thinks him a snob doubts his existence. It is a great tribute to literature if neither the man who thinks Hamlet a weakling, nor the man who thinks him a hero ever thinks of doubting Hamlet's existence.

Personally, I think the critic absolutely right in denouncing the idea that Hamlet was a "witty weakling". There is a great difference between a weakness which is at liberty and a strength which is rusted and clogged. Hamlet was not a weak man fundamentally. Shakespeare never forgets to remind us that he had an elemental force and fire in him, liable to burst out and strike everyone with terror.

Yet have I something in me dangerous
Which let thy wisdom fear.

But Hamlet was a man in whom the faculty of action had been clogged, not by the smallness of his moral nature, but by the greatness of his intellectual. Actions were really important to him, only they were not quite so dazzling and dramatic as thoughts. He belonged to a type of man which some men will never understand, the man for whom what happens inside his head does actually and literally happen; for whom ideas are adventures, for whom metaphors are living monsters, for whom an intellectual parallel has the irrevocable sanctity of a marriage ceremony. Hamlet failed, but through the greatness of his upper, not the weakness of his lower, storey. He was a giant, but he was top-heavy.

But while I warmly agree in holding that the moral greatness of Hamlet is enormously underrated, I cannot agree that Hamlet was a moral success. If this is true, indeed, the whole story loses its central meaning; if the hero was a success, the play is a failure. Surely no one who remembers Hamlet's tremendous speech, beginning:

O what a rogue and peasant slave am I,

can share the critic's conclusion:

He is not here condemning himself for inaction, there is no cause for the reproach, he is using the resources of passion and eloquence to spur himself to action.

It is difficult for me to imagine anyone reading that appalling cry out of the very hell of inutility and think that Hamlet is not condemning himself for inaction. Hamlet may, of course, be only casually mentioning that he is a moral coward; for the matter of that, the Ghost may be only cracking a joke when he says he has been murdered. But if ever there was sincerity in any human utterance, there is in the remorse of Hamlet.

The truth is that Shakespeare's Hamlet is immeasurably vaster than any mere ethical denunciation or ethical defence. Figures like this, scribbled in a few pages of pen and ink, can claim, like living human beings, to be judged by Omniscience. To call Hamlet a "witty weakling" is entirely to miss the point, which is his greatness; to call him a triumphant hero is to miss a point quite as profound. It is the business of art to seize these nameless points of greatness and littleness; the truth is not so much that art is immoral as that art has to single out sins that are not to be found in any decalogue and virtues that cannot be named in any allegory. But upon the whole it is always more indulgent than philanthropy. Falstaff was neither brave nor honest, nor chaste, nor temperate, nor clean, but he had the eighth cardinal virtue for which no name has ever been found. Hamlet was not fitted for this world; but Shakespeare does not dare to say whether he was too good or too bad for it.—G. K. CHESTERTON, "The True Hamlet" (1901), *Chesterton on Shakespeare*, 1971, ed. Dorothy Collins, pp. 41–43

There haunts in Time's bare house an active ghost,
Enamoured of his name, Polonius.
He moves small fingers much, and all his speech
Is like a sampler of precisest words,
Set in the pattern of a simpleton.
His mirth floats eerily down chill corridors;
His sigh—it is a sound that loves a keyhole;
His tenderness a faint court-tarnished thing;
His wisdom prates as from a wicker cage;
His very belly is a pompous nought;
His eye a page that hath forgot his errand.
Yet in his bran—his spiritual bran—
Lies hid a child's demure, small, silver whistle
Which, to his horror, God blows, unawares,
And sets men staring. It is sad to think,
Might he but don indeed thin flesh and blood,
And pace important to Law's inmost room,
He would see, much marvelling, one immensely wise,
Named Bacon, who, at sound of his youth's step,
Would turn and call him Cousin—for the likeness.

—WALTER DE LA MARE, "Polonius," *Characters from Shakespeare*, 1902

There runs a crisscross pattern of small leaves
Espalier, in a fading summer air,
And there Ophelia walks, an azure flower,
Whom wind, and snowflakes, and the sudden rain
Of love's wild skies have purified to heaven.
There is a beauty past all weeping now
In that sweet, crooked mouth, that vacant smile;
Only a lonely grey in those mad eyes,
Which never on earth shall learn their loneliness.
And when amid startled birds she sings lament,
Mocking in hope the long voice of the stream,
It seems her heart's lute hath a broken string.
Ivy she hath, that to old ruin clings;
And rosemary, that sees remembrance fade;
And pansies, deeper than the gloom of dreams;
But ah! if utterable, would this earth
Remain the base, unreal thing it is?
Better be out of sight of peering eyes;
Out—out of hearing of all-useless words,
Spoken of tedious tongues in heedless ears.
And lest, at last, the world should learn heart-secrets;
Lest that sweet wolf from some dim thicket steal;
Better the glassy horror of the stream.

—WALTER DE LA MARE, "Ophelia," *Characters from Shakespeare*, 1902

Umbrageous cedars murmuring symphonies
Stooped in late twilight o'er dark Denmark's Prince:
He sat, his eyes companioned with dream—
Lustrous large eyes that held the world in view

As some entrancèd child's a puppet show.
Darkness gave birth to the all-trembling stars,
And a far roar of long-drawn cataracts,
Flooding immeasurable night with sound.
He sat so still, his very thoughts took wing,
And, lightest Ariels, the stillness haunted
With midge-like measures; but, at last, even they
Sank 'neath the influences of his night.
The sweet dust shed faint perfume in the gloom;
Through all wild space the stars' bright arrows fell
On the lone Prince—the troubled son of man—
On Time's dark waters in unearthly trouble:
Then, as the roar increased, and one fair tower
Of cloud took sky and stars with majesty,
He rose, his face a parchment of old age,
Sorrow hath scribbled o'er, and o'er, and o'er.

—WALTER DE LA MARE, "Hamlet," *Characters from Shakespeare*, 1902

## JAMES DRAKE
### From *The Antient and Modern Stages Survey'd*
### 1699, pp. 201–6, 293–97

The *Modern* Tragedy is a Feild large enough for us to lose our selves in, and therefore I shall not take the Liberty of ranging thro 'em at large, but for the most part confine my self to such as Mr *Collier* has already attackt. Upon presumption therefore that these are the weakest, if these can be defended, the rest I suppose may hold out of themselves.

I shall begin with *Shakespear*, whom notwithstanding the severity of Mr *Rhimer*, and the hard usage of Mr *Collier*, I must still think the *Proto-Dramatist* of *England*, tho he fell short of the Art of *Johnson*, and the Conversation of *Beaumont* and *Fletcher*. Upon that account he wants many of their Graces, yet his Beauties make large amends for his Defects, and Nature has richly provided him with the materials, tho his unkind Fortune denied him the Art of managing them to the best Advantage.

His *Hamlet*, a Play of the first rate, has the misfortune to fall under Mr *Collier's* displeasure; and *Ophelia* who has had the luck hitherto to keep her reputation, is at last censur'd for Lightness in her Frenzy; nay, Mr *Collier* is so familiar with her, as to make an unkind discovery of the unfavouriness of her Breath, which no Body suspected before. But it may be this is a groundless surmise, and Mr *Collier* is deceived by a bad Nose, or a rotten Tooth of his own; and then he is obliged to beg the poets and the Ladies pardon for the wrong he has done 'em; But that will fall more naturally under our consideration in another place.

*Hamlet* King of *Denmark* was privately murther'd by his Brother, who immediately thereupon marry'd the Dowager, and supplanted his Nephew in the Succession of the Crown. Thus far before the proper action of the Play.

The late Kings Ghost appears to his Son young *Hamlet*, and declares how and by whom he was murther'd, and engages him to revenge it. *Hamlet* hereupon grows very much discontented, and the King very jealous of him. Hereupon he is dispatched with Ambassadors to *England*, then supposed Tributary to *Denmark*, whither a secret Commission to put him to Death, is sent by 'em: Which *Hamlet* discovering writes a new Commission, in which he inserts the names of the Ambassadors instead of his own. After this a Pirate engaging their Vessel, and *Hamlet* too eagerly boarding her is carried off, and set ashore in *Denmark* again. The Ambassadors not suspecting *Hamlet's* Trick, pursue their Voyage, and are caught in their own Trap. *Polonius*, a Councellour to the King, conveying himself as a Spy behind the Hangings, at an enterview between *Hamlet* and his Mother, is mistaken for the King, and killed by him. *Laertes* his Son, together with the King contrive the Death of *Hamlet* by a sham Match at Foyls, wherein *Laertes* uses a poyson'd unrebated Weapon. The King, not trusting to this single Treachery, prepares a poysoned Bowl for *Hamlet*, which the Queen ignorantly drinks. *Hamlet* is too hard for *Laertes*, and closes with him, and recovers the envenom'd weapon from him, but in so doing, he is hurt by, and hurts him with it. *Laertes* perceiving himself wounded, and knowing it to be mortal, confesses that it was a train laid by the King for *Hamlet's* Life, and that the foul practice is justly turn'd upon himself. The Queen at the same times cries out, that she is poysoned, whereupon *Hamlet* wounds the King with the envenom'd weapon. They all die.

Whatever defects the Criticks may find in this Fable, the Moral of it is excellent. Here was a Murther privately committed, strangely discover'd, and wonderfully punish'd. Nothing in Antiquity can rival this Plot for the admirable distribution of Poetick Justice. The criminals are not only brought to execution, but they are taken in their own Toyls, their own Stratagems recoyl upon 'em, and they are involv'd themselves in that mischief and ruine, which they had projected for *Hamlet*. *Polonius* by playing the Spy meets a Fate, which was neither expected by, nor intended for him. *Guildenstern* and *Rosencrans*, the Kings Decoys, are counter-plotted, and sent to meet that fate, to which they were trepanning the Prince. The Tyrant himself falls by his own Plot, and by the hand of the Son of that Brother, whom he had murther'd. *Laertes* suffers by his own Treachery, and dies by a Weapon of his own preparing. Thus every one's crime naturally produces his Punishment, and every one, (the Tyrant expected) commences a Wretch almost as soon as a Villain.

The Moral of all this is very obvious, it shews us, *That the Greatness of the Offender does not qualifie the Offence, and that no Humane Power, or Policy are a suffcent Guard against the Impartial Hand, and Eye of Providence, which defeats their wicked purposes, and turns their dangerous Machinations upon their own heads.* This Moral *Hamlet* himself insinuates to us, when he tells *Horatio*, that he ow'd the Discovery of the Design against his Life in *England*, to a rash indiscreet curiosity, and thence makes this Inference.

> Our Indiscretion sometimes serves as well,
>     When our dear Plots do fail, and that
>         shou'd teach us,
> There's a Divinity, that shapes our ends,
>     Rough hew'em how we will.

The Tragedies of this Author in general are Moral and Instructive, and many of 'em such, as the best of Antiquity can't equal in that respect. His *King Lear, Timon of Athens, Macbeth*, and some other are so remarkable upon that score, that 'twou'd be impertinent to trouble the Reader with a minute examination of Plays so generally known and approved. . . .

*Ophelia* was a modest young Virgin, beloved by *Hamlet*, and in Love with him. Her Passion was approv'd, and directed by her Father, and her Pretensions to a match with *Hamlet*, the heir apparent to the Crown of *Denmark*, encouraged, and supported by the Countenance and Assistance of the *King* and *Queen*. A warrantable Love, so naturally planted in so tender a Breast, so carefully nursed, so artfully manured, and so strongly forced up, must needs take very deep Root, and bear a very great head. Love, even in the most difficult Circumstances, is the Passion naturally most predominant in young Breasts but when it is encouraged and cherish'd by those of whom they stand in awe, it grows Masterly and Tyrannical, and will admit of no Check. This was poor *Ophelia's* case. *Hamlet* had sworn, her *Father* had approved, the *King* and *Queen* consented to, nay, desired the Consummation of her Wishes. Her hopes were full blown, when they were miserably blasted. *Hamlet* by mistake kills her Father, and runs mad; or, which is all one to her, counterfeits madness so well, that she is cheated into a belief of the reality of it. Here Piety and Love concur to make her Affliction piercing, and to impress her Sorrow more deep and lasting. To tear up two such passions violently by the roots, must needs make horrible Convulsions in a Mind so tender, and a Sex so weak. These Calamities distract her, and she talks incoherently; at which Mr *Collier* is amaz'd, he is downright stupified, and thinks the Woman's mad to run out of her wits. But tho she talks a little light-headed, and seems to want sleep, I don't find she needed any *Cashew* in her Mouth to correct her Breath. That's a discovery of Mr *Collier's*, (like some other of his) who perhaps is of Opinion, that the Breath and the Understanding have the same Lodging, and must needs be vitiated together. However, *Shakespear* has drown'd her at last, and Mr *Collier* is angry that he did it no sooner. He is for having Execution done upon her seriously, and in sober sadness, without the excuse of madness for Self-murther. To kill her is not sufficient with him, unless she be damn'd into the bargain. Allowing the Cause of her madness to be *Partie per Pale*, the death of her Father, and the loss of her Love, which is the utmost we can give to the latter, yet her passion is as innocent, and inoffensive in her distraction as before, tho not so reasonable and well govern'd. Mr *Collier* has not told us, what he grounds his hard censure upon, but we may guess, that if he be really so angry as he pretends, 'tis at the mad Song, which *Ophelia* sings to the Queen, which I shall venture to transcribe without fear of offending the modesty of the most chaste Ear.

> To morrow is St *Valentine's* day, all in the morn
>     betimes,
> And I a Maid at your Window to be your Valentine.
> Then up he, he arose, and don'd his Cloaths, and
>     dupt the Chamber door,
> Let in a Maid that out a Maid
>     Never departed more.
> By *Gis* and by St *Charity*:
>     Alack, and fie for shame!
> Young men will do't, if they come to't,
>     By Cock they are to blame.
> Quoth she, before you tumbled me,
>     You promis'd me to wed:
> So had I done, by yonder Sun,
>     And thou hadst not come to bed.

'Tis strange this stuff shou'd wamble so in Mr *Collier's* Stomach, and put him into such an Uproar. 'Tis silly indeed, but very harmless and inoffensive; and 'tis no great Miracle, that a Woman out of her Wits shou'd talk Nonsense, who at the soundest of her Intellects had no extraordinary Talent at Speech-making. Sure Mr *Collier's* concoctive Faculty's extreamly deprav'd, that meer Water-Pap turns to such virulent Corruption with him.

But Children and Mad Folks tell truth, they say, and he seems to discover thro her Frenzy what she wou'd be at. She was troubled for the loss of a Sweet-heart, and the breaking off her Match, Poor Soul. Not unlikely. Yet this was no Novelty in the days of our Fore-fathers; if he pleases to consult the Records, he will find even in the days of *Sophocles*, Maids had an itching the same way, and longed to know, what was what, before they died.

## WILLIAM POPPLE
*The Prompter*
No. 57. May 27, 1735

In tracing the corruption of the stage to its source, it may not be improper to take in every error that may have introduced itself and furnished its contingent to the general body. It will not therefore be foreign to my purpose to consider some characters in our dramatic pieces as they were originally designed by the poets who drew them, and as they appear to an audience from the manner in which the actor personates them.

A character falsified, like a stream of poisoned water, instead of nourishing, kills and destroys everything it runs thro'. Actors and managers have not always penetration enough to dive into the truth of character and are therefore content to receive it from tradition and misact it, as *Arlequin Astrologue* composes almanacs *de père en fils*. This branch of corruption, when it relates to old plays, is not directly chargeable on the present actors or managers but is one of those general errors which time has given a sanction to and is, for that reason, the more considerable as well as dangerous. But tho' the error of itself does not cover them with a deserved shame, the reforming of it might crown them with deserved applause and make their penetration, like the sun long eclipsed, break out to the admiration of the present age and the comfort of posterity.

I shall inforce the truth of my observation by the character of Polonius in *Hamlet*, which I shall consider in its double presentation. Polonius, according to Shakespeare, is a man of most excellent understanding and great knowledge of the world, whose ridicule arises not from any radical folly in the old gentleman's composition, but a certain affectation of formality and method, mixed with a smattering of the wit of that age (which consisted in playing upon words) which being grown up with him is *incorporated* (if I may venture the expression) with all his words and actions.

That this is the true character of Polonius the doubtful reader may be satisfied if he will give himself the trouble to peruse the scenes between Polonius, Laertes, and Ophelia, and the first scene in the second act, between Polonius and Reynaldo. To save him part of the trouble, I shall make bold to borrow a couple of speeches for the immediate confirmation of this character given of Polonius, which will both establish his good sense and knowledge of the world and his affectation of formality and method.

The first is his advice to his son.

Give thy Thoughts no Tongue;
Nor any unproportion'd Thought his Act.
Be thou *familiar*, but by no means *vulgar*.
The Friends thou hast, and their Adoption try'd,
*Grapple* them to thy Soul with *Hooks* of *Steel*.
But do not dull thy Palm with Entertainment
Of each *new-hatch'd unfledg'd* Com'rade.—Beware
Of Entrance to a Quarrel; but, being in,
Bear't, that th' Opposed may be beware of thee.
GIVE ev'ry Man thine *Ear*; but few thy *Voice*.
*Take* each Man's *Censure*; but *reserve* thy
    Judgment—
*Costly* thy *Habit*, as thy Purse can buy,
But not EXPREST in FANCY; *rich*, not *gaudy*:
FOR THE APPAREL OFT PROCLAIMS THE
    MAN.
—Neither a *Borrower*, nor a *Lender* be;

For *Loan* oft loses both itself and Friend
And borrowing dulls the Edge of Husbandry.
This, above all, TO THINE ONE SELF BE
    TRUE—
And it must follow, as the Night the Day,
Thou can'st not then be false to any Man.
Farewell, &c.

No man that was really a fool could ever make such a speech, which would become the mouth of the wisest and most experienced.

The next is where Polonius acquaints the King and Queen that he has found out the very cause of Hamlet's lunacy.

*Pol.*: My Liege and Madam, To expostulate
    What Majesty should be, what Duty is,
    Why Day is Day, Night, Night, and Time is Time,
    Were nothing but to waste Night, Day, and
        Time—
    Therefore, since Brevity's the Soul of Wit,
    And Tediousness the outward Limbs and Flour-
        ishes,
    I will be brief: Your noble Son is mad;
    *Mad* call I it; for to define true Madness,
    What is't but to be nothing else but mad?
    But let that go—

*Qu.*: More Matter, with less Art.

*Pol.*: Madam, I swear, I use no Art at all;
    That he is mad, 'tis true; 'tis true, 'tis *pitty*;
    And *pitty* 'tis, 'tis true; a foolish Figure,
    But farewel it; for I will use no Art.
    Mad let us grant him then; and now remains,
    That we find out the Cause of this Effect;
    For this EFFECT DEFECTIVE comes by
        Cause—
    Thus it remains, and the Remainder thus—
        Perpend—
    I have, &c.

Here is a visible affection of formality and method, with that particular sort of wit above mentioned, that makes the old man appear ridiculous at the same time that what he says has all the probability in the world of being the truth. If we examine the speeches of Polonius throughout the whole play, we shall find them reducible to this determinate character and to no other species of folly.

How does Polonius appear to an audience at present? He never looks or speaks but the fool stares out of his eyes and is marked in the tone of his voice. Even words that have the strongest sense, as well as beauty of sentiment and expression, lose their original stamp and dignity, as the character is now represented, and are converted into the seeming of folly. A few quotations, with the reader's recollection in what manner the speeches are delivered by Mr. Griffin and Mr. Hippisley (who perform this role in the two Theatres Royal) will illustrate this truth.

In the very first speech which Polonius makes, where I defy the most penetrating to find either a character of folly or any stamp of particular humour, or, in short, anything but a concern which the old gentleman expresses with great beauty of language and proper seriousness, at his son's going to travel and leaving him, our improving actors present us with the image of an old buffoon.

He has, My Lord, by WEARISOME Petition,
WRUNG from me my SLOW LEAVE; and at the
    last,
Upon his will, I seal'd my HARD Consent.
I do beseech you, give him Leave to go.

Here is the most simple, plain, unstudied, unaffected reply that could be given. Yet, how is this spoke and acted? The eyes are turned obliquely and dressed up in a foolish leer at the King, the words intermittently drawled out with a very strong emphasis, not to express a father's concern, which would be right, but something ridiculous to excite laughter, tho' neither the words, nor the sense, have any comic vein in them, the voice toned like the squeak of a bagpipe and the whole attitude suited to this false notion of his character.

In the scene between him and his daughter where he questions her about Hamlet's love, he fares no better. You see the figure and manner of an idiot, joined to the prudence of a parent giving advice to his daughter how to receive the addresses of a presumptive heir to the crown, a most unnatural connection which Shakespeare never thought of. The only vein of humour discoverable in the scene is a little playing on the word *Tenders*, a part of his natural character.

> Marry, I'll teach you; think yourself a Baby,
> That you have ta'en his *Tenders* for true Pay
> Which are not *Sterling: Tender* yourself more dearly
> Or (not to crack the Wind of the poor Phrase,
> Wringing it thus) you'll *tender* me a Fool.

Immediately after—

> Affection! Pugh! You speak like a green Girl
> Unsifted in such perillous Circumstance!

Every spectator of *Hamlet* will easily recollect what a horselaugh the manner of repeating these two lines never fails to occasion. Examine the sense of the language and you'll sooner find the weight and authority of a father reproving an unexperienced child who does not know in what light she ought to consider both Hamlet and his love, and acquainting her how she ought to behave for the future, than any drollery or folly. Again,

> Ay, Springes to catch *Woodcocks*; I do know
> When the *Blood boils*, how *prodigal the Soul*
> Lends the Tongue Vows.—

What can be more beautiful, as well as serious, than this sentiment! What rendered so light and ridiculous by the manner of speaking it at present!

In the first scene of the second act, where Ophelia gives Polonius an account of Hamlet's disorder, every reflection the old man makes is of the serious kind and does not give the actor the least cue for mirth or folly, yet in the representation we see a strong cast of both, without a shadow of that gravity his uncertain conjectures and reflections upon the nature of the passion he imagines the Prince possessed with should naturally give him. Those who have seen *Hamlet* will easily recollect the figure Polonius makes in this scene and the tone of voice with which he utters:

> *Pol.*: Mad for thy Love—
> *Pol.*: This is the very Ecstasy of Love.

And in the scene where Polonius comes to Hamlet with a message from the Queen, tho', 'tis evident, Polonius only flatters Hamlet's supposed lunacy and Hamlet himself tells us so.

> They fool me to the Top of my Bent—

Yet, from the manner this is acted, the audience is taught to believe that Polonius, in pure simplicity of sight, sees the cloud in the three different shapes Hamlet gives it.

It would be endless to carry *Shakespeare's* Polonius along with the *modern one* throughout the whole play in this manner. Enough has been quoted to show the judicious reader how much this character is falsified and what an intrusion of foreign false humour it labors under!

If it be said it is more entertaining now than it would be were it represented in its true humour, then the consequence will be that actors are better judges of characters than the poets who drew them, and every character will be in their power to represent as they please, which would pour a torrent of corruption on dramatic performances. It will avail them very little, as to the force of argument, to say the modern Polonius never fails to excite laughter, since neither the poet, nor the actor, should strive to please the quantity of what Shakespeare calls *barren spectators* by making the judicious grieve, *the censure of which one* (as the motto expresses it) *must outweigh a whole theatre of others*.

I have already said that this false edition of Polonius is the error of time, and no wise chargeable on the present representers, Mr. Griffin and Mr. Hippisley, who, bating some new exuberances, which I shall, in the course of this work, lop off, are the very best comic performers that we have, and that have the truest notions of the *vis comica*, which consists in bringing out the express humour of particular character, the idea of which lies *increate* in the sense of the words, 'till called forth by the penetrating genius of the actor it receives life and motion, to the delight of the judicious spectator who is ever ravished with true imagery and faithful portraiture.

But, to show that it is impossible Polonius could ever have been designed by Shakespeare the fool and idiot he appears now, we find him not only entrusted by the King with an affair of the last consequence to him (which no wise Prince would ever commit to the care of a fool) but that in his younger days he has acquired the reputation of being cunning and politic—

> Or else this Brain of mine,
> Hunts not the Trail of Policy *so sure*
> As I have us'd to do.

Again—

> *Pol.*: Has there been such a Time, I'd fain know that,
> That I have positively said, 'Tis so,
> When it prov'd otherwise.—
>
> *King*: Not that I know.—

'Tis true these are but the braggings of an old man, and he was out in his judgment in this case, but he is not the first politician, with a very good head, that has been mistaken. But, without this additional proof, the speeches quoted are sufficient to exclude folly from his composition.

One great cause of the corruption of this character of Polonius I take to lie in the obsolete language which, being very different from the phraseology of our days, the injudicious spectator takes the expressions to be what the French call *recherchees*, chosen on purpose to create laughter, as for example—

> Affection! Pugh! You speak like a green Girl,
> Unsifted in such *perillous* circumstance.—

The sense of which being only, You speak like a raw girl, unacquainted with such matters, does not create any laughter at all in this modern garb, nor with the judicious in its antique one. But by the help of the figure Polonius makes, and for want of considering the idiom of those times, it acquires, in the opinion of many, a comic turn, in spite of the serious and moral sense it contains. And so of the rest.

The compass of a half-sheet will not allow me to give any further reasons for the recovery of Polonius' true character. Those that come to plays merely to laugh, tho' at the expense of reason, will relish Polonius as he is now. Those who reflect on propriety of character, truth of circumstances, and probability of fable, cannot bear the inconsistent, ridiculous, and foolish buffoon mixed so preposterously with the man of sense. As this is not the only character that has suffered as extraordinary a metamorphosis, and others still may, I leave it to every reader's reflection, how radically this corruption affects the stage.

## THOMAS HANMER
### From *Some Remarks on the Tragedy of*
### Hamlet Prince of Denmark
### 1736

The Tragedy that is now coming under our Examination, is one of the best of his Pieces, and strikes us with a certain Awe and Seriousness of Mind, far beyond those Plays whose Whole Plot turns upon vehement and uncontroulable Love, such as are most of our modern Tragedies. These certainly have not the great Effect that others have, which turn either upon Ambition, the Love of one's Country, or Parental or Filial Tenderness. Accordingly we find, that few among the Ancients, and hardly any of our Author's Plays, are built upon the Passion of Love in a direct manner; by which I mean, that they have not the mutual Attachment of a Lover and his Mistress for their chief Basis. Love will always make a great Figure in Tragedy, if only its chief Branches be made use of; as for instance, Jealousy (as in *Othello*) or the beautiful Distress of Man and Wife (as in *Romeo* and *Juliet*) but never when the whole Play is founded upon two Lovers desiring to possess each other: And one of the Reasons for this seems to be, that this last Species of that Passion is more commonly met with than the former, and so consequently strikes us less. Add to this, that there may a suspicion arise, that the Passion of Love in a direct Manner may be more sensual than in those Branches which I have mention'd; which Suspicion is sufficient to take from its Dignity, and lessen our Veneration for it. Of all *Shakespeare's* Tragedies, none can surpass this, as to the noble Passions which it naturally raises in us. That the Reader may see what our Poet had to work upon, I shall insert the Plan of it as abridged from *Saxo-Grammaticus's Danish* History by *Mr. Theobalds.* "The Historian calls our Poet's Hero *Amlethus*, his Father *Horwendillus*, his Uncle *Fengo*, and his Mother *Gerutha.* The old king in single Combat, slew *Collerus*, King of *Norway; Fengo* makes away with his Brother *Horwendillus*, and marries his Widow *Gerutha. Amlethus*, to avoid being suspected by his Uncle of Designs, assumes a Form of utter Madness. A fine Woman is planted upon him, to try if he would yield to the Impressions of Love. *Fengo* contrives, that *Amlethus*, in order to sound him, should be closetted by his Mother. A Man is conceal'd in the Rushes to overhear their Discourse; whom *Amlethus* discovers and kills. When the Queen is frighted at this Behaviour of his; he tasks her about her criminal Course of Life, and incestuous Conversation with her former Husband's Murtherer; confesses his Madness is but counterfeited, to protect himself, and secure his Revenge for his Father; to which he injoins the Queen's Silence. *Fengo* sends *Amletlus* to *Britain:* Two of the King's Servants attend him with Letters to the *British* King, strictly pressing the Death of *Amlethus*, who, in the Night Time, coming at their Commission, over-reads it, forms a new One, and turns the Destruction designed towards himself on the Bearers of the Letters. *Amlethus* returning Home, by a Wile surprizes and kills his Uncle." I shall have Occasion to remark in the Sequel, that in one Particular he has followed the Plan so closely as to produce an Absurdity in his Plot. And I must premise also this, that in my Examination of the whole Conduct of the Play, the Reader must not be surprised, if I censure any Part of it, although it be entirely in Conformity to the Plan the Author

has chosen; because it is easy to conceive, that a Poet's Judgment is particularly shewn in chusing the proper Circumstances, and rejecting the improper Ones of the Ground-work which he raises his Play upon. In general we are to take Notice, that as History ran very low in his Days, most of his Plays are founded upon some old wretched Chronicler, or some empty *Italian* Novelist; but the more base and mean were his Materials, so much more ought we to admire His Skill, Who has been able to work up his Pieces to such Sublimity from such low Originals. Had he had the Advantages of many of his Successors, ought not we to believe, that he would have made the greatest Use of them? I shall not insist upon the Merit of those who first break through the thick Mist of *Barbarism* in Poetry, which was so strong about the time our Poet writ, because this must be easily sensible to every Reader who has the least Tincture of Letters; but thus much we must observe, that before his Time there were very few (if any) Dramatick Performances of any Tragick Writer, which deserve to be remembred; so much were all the noble Originals of Antiquity buried in Oblivion. One would think that the works of *Sophocles, Euripides, &c.* were Discoveries of the last Age only; and not that they had existed for so many Centuries. There is something very astonishing in the general Ignorance and Dulness of Taste, which for so long a Time over-spread the World, after it had been so gloriously enlighten'd by *Athens* and *Rome*; especially as so many of their excellent Masterpieces were still remaining, which one would have thought should have excited even the Brutes of those barbarous Ages to have examined them, and form'd themselves according to such Models. . . .

I shall close these Remarks with some general Observations, and shall avoid (as I have hitherto done) repeating any Thing which has been said by others, at least as much as I possibly can: Nor do I think it necessary to make an ostentatious Shew of Learning, or to draw quaint Parallels between our Author and the great Tragick Writers of Antiquity; for in Truth, this is very little to the Purpose in reviewing *Shakespeare's* Dramatick Works; since most Men are I believe convinced, that he is very little indebted to any of them; and a remarkable Instance of this is to be observed in his Tragedy of *Troilus* and *Cressida*, wherein it appears (as *Mr. Theobalds* has evidently demonstrated it,) that he has chosen an old *English* Romance concerning the *Trojan* War, as a worthier Guide than even *Homer* himself. Nature was our great Poet's Mistress; her alone has he followed as his Conductress; and therefore it has been with regard to her only, that I have considered this Tragedy. It is not to be denied, but that *Shakespeare's* Dramatick Works are in general very much mix'd; his Gold is strangely mingled with Dross in most of his Pieces. He fell too much into the low Taste of the Age he liv'd in, which delighted in miserable Punns, low Wit, and affected sententious Maxims; and what is most unpardonable in him, he has interspersed his noblest Productions with this Poorness of Thought. This I have shewn in my Remarks on this Play. Yet, notwithstanding the Defects I have Pointed out, it is I think, beyond dispute, that there is much less of this in *Hamlet* than in any of his Plays; and that the Language in the Whole, is much more pure, and much more free from Obscurity or Bombast, than any of our Author's Tragedies; for sometimes *Shakespeare* may be justly tax'd with that Fault. And we may moreover take Notice, that the Conduct of this Piece is far from being bad; it is superior in that respect (in my Opinion) to many of those Performances in which the Rules are said to be exactly kept to. The Subject, which is of the nicest Kind; is managed with great Delicacy, much beyond that Piece wherein *Agamemnon's* Death is revenged by his Son *Orestes*, so much admired by all the Lovers of Antiquity; for the Punishment of the Murderer alone by the Son of the murdered Person, is sufficient; there is something too shocking in a Mother's being put to Death by her Son, although she be never so guilty. *Shakespeare's* Management in this Particular, has been much admired by one of our greatest Writers, who takes Notice of the beautiful Caution given by the Ghost to *Hamlet*,

> But howsoever thou pursuest this Act, &c.

The making the Whole to turn upon the Appearance of a Spectre, is a great Improvement of the Plan he work'd upon; especially as he has conducted it in so sublime a Manner, and accompanied it with all the Circumstances that could make it most perfect in its kind. . . .

There is less Time employ'd in this Tragedy, as I observed else where, than in most of our Author's Pieces, and the Unity of Place is not much disturbed. But here give me leave to say, that the Critick's Rules, in respect to these two Things, if they prove any Thing, prove too much; for if our Imagination will not bear a strong Imposition, surely no Play ought to be supposed to take more Time than is really employ'd in the Acting; nor should there be any Change of Place in the least. This shews the Absurdity of such Arbitrary Rules. For how would such a Genius as *Shakespeare's* have been cramped had he thus fettered himself! But there is (in Truth) no Necessity for it. No Rules are of any Service in Poetry, of any kind, unless they add Beauties, which consist (in Tragedy) in an exact Conformity to Nature in the Conduct of the Characters, and in a sublimity of Sentiments and nobleness of Diction. If these two Things be well observed, tho' often at the Expence of Unity of Time and Place, such Pieces will always please, and never suffer us to find out the little Defects in the Plot; nay it generally happens (at least Experience has shewn it frequently) that those Pieces wherein the fantastick Rules of Criticks have been kept strictly to, have been generally flat and low. We are to consider, that no Dramatick Piece can affect us but by the Delusion of our Imagination; which, to taste true and real Pleasures at such Representations, must undergo very great Impositions, even such as in Speculation seem very gross, but which are nevertheless allowed of by the strictest Criticks. In the first Place, our Understandings are never shocked at hearing all Nations, on our Stage, speak *English*; an Absurdity one would think that should immediately revolt us; but which is, however, absolutely necessary in all Countries where Dramatick Performances are resorted to, unless the Characters be always supposed to be of each respective Nation; as for instance, in all *Shakespeare's* Historical Plays. I say, this never shocks us, nor do we find any Difficulty in believing the Stage to be *Rome*, (or *Denmark*, for instance, as in this Play;) or *Wilks* to be *Hamlet*, or *Booth* to be a Ghost, &c. These Things, I repeat it, appear difficult in Speculation; but we find, that in Reality they do go down; and must necessarily do so, or else farewell all Dramatick Performances; for unless the Distress and Woes appear to be real (which they never can, if we do not believe we actually see the Things that are represented) it is impossible our Passions should be moved. Let any one fairly judge, if these do not seem as great Impositions on our Reason, as the Change of Place, or the Length of Time, which are found fault with in our Poet. I confess there are Bounds set to this Delusion of our Imaginations, (as there are to every Thing else in this World) for this Delusion is never perform'd in direct Defiance of our Reason; on the contrary our Reason helps on the Deceit; but she will concur no farther in this Delusion, than to a certain Point which she will never pass, and that is, the Essential Difference between Plays which deceive us by the

Assistance of our Reason, and others which would impose upon our Imaginations in Despight of our Reason. It is evident by the Success our Author's Pieces have always met with for so long a Course of Time; it is, I say, certain by this general Approbation, that his Pieces are of the former, not of the latter Sort. But to go to the Bottom of this Matter, would lead me beyond what I propose.

Since therefore it is certain, that the strict Observance of the Critick's Rules might take away Beauties, but not always add any, why should our Poet be so much blamed for giving a Loose to his Fancy? The Sublimity of Sentiments in his Pieces, and that exalted Diction which is so peculiarly his own, and in time, all the Charms of his Poetry, far outweigh any little Absurdity in his Plots, which no ways disturb us in the Pleasures we reap from the above-mention'd Excellencies. And the more I read him, the more I am convinced, that as he knew his own particular Talent well, he study'd more to work up great and moving circumstances to place his chief Characters in, so as to affect our Passions strongly, he apply'd himself more to This than he did to the Means or Methods whereby he brought his Characters into those Circumstances. How far a general Vogue is the Test of the Merit of a Tragedy, has been often considered by eminent Writers, and is a subject of too complicated a Nature to discuss in these few Sheets. But I shall just hint two or three of my own Thoughts on that Head. Nature is the Basis of all Tragick Performances, and no Play that is unnatural, *i.e.* wherein the Characters act inconsistently with themselves, and in a Manner repugnant to our natural Ideas, can please at all. But a Play may be natural, and yet displease one Sett of People out of Two, of which all Audiences are composed. If a Play be built upon low Subjects, but yet carried on consistently, and has no Merit but Nature, it will please the Vulgar; by which I mean, all the unlearned and ill-educated, (as for Instance, *George Barnwell*, a Piece calculated for the Many) but it must be nauseous to the Learned, and to those of improved and exalted Understandings. So on the other Hand, a Piece which turns upon Passions, which regard those of high Station chiefly, cannot be so pleasing to the Vulgar; for tho' all Men are born with the same Passions, yet Education very much exalts and refines them. Thus the Loves and Boors and Peasants may delight the Populace, but those of better Sort must have Delicacy in that Passion to see it represented with any tolerable Patience. The same is to be said of Jealousy and Revenge, which are indeed felt by all, but in Breasts well educated are felt with sharper Pangs, and are combated with more Vehemence, and from more and greater Motives; therefore such People are fitter to judge, and more likely to be taken with noble and sublime Representations of such Incidents. I need not observe, that the Vulgar cannot judge of the Historical Propriety of a great Character, This is obvious to every one; nor can they judge of the Passion of Ambition, as it has Power with Princes and great Men, because not being versed by Reading in parallel Stories, and not being in such a Situation of Life, as to feel the Torments of such Passions, they cannot certainly tell whether such Things are represented with proper Circumstances, and proper Consequences drawn from them. And moreover, as all Men are by Nature more prone to some Passions than to others, This must cause Variety of Sentiments in relation to the same Piece. Besides all this, we may be very certain that different Education, different Degrees of Understanding, and of the Passions common to all Men, must cause a Variety of Sentiments concerning such Representations. To prove this, let us observe how the Tastes of Nations differ in relation to these Things; so much, that one would be tempted sometimes to think, that they did not all partake of the same Passions; but certainly they vary in the Degrees of them; therefore by a Parity of Reason we may justly conclude, that Difference of Education among those of the same Nation must affect their Passions and Sentiments. The better sort have (if one may so express it) some acquired Passions which the lower sort are ignorant of. Thus indeed it seems at first Sight; but on a nearer View they are found to be, as I said, the same Passions augmented or refined, and turned upon other Objects. The different Manner in which one of *Corneille's* or *Racine's* Pieces would be received by an Audience of *Turks or Russians*, and an Audience of *Frenchmen*, (supposing the former to understand the Language, and the latter to be free from any national Prejudices for the Authors) is a lively and strong Emblem of the Force of Education and Custom among Creatures, all cast in the same Mould, and endued with the same Faculties and Passions with very little real Difference. Still farther, we may observe, that even good Acting will recommend some bad Pieces, as bad Acting will take away half the Merit of Good Ones; and some National Subjects are pleasing (as the *Albion Queens* and *Earl of Essex*) to the Many, tho' they very little affect the Few. When I speak of Plays, I desire to be understood of Tragedies, in which I think the *English* excell; for I can mention very few of our Comedies with any Approbation; since in the Latter, neither the Morals of the Inhabitants of this Nation are regarded, or Nature followed. In short, not to pursue a Subject, that would carry me great Lengths, I conclude from this, that a Piece which has no Merit in it but Nature, will, please the Vulgar; whereas exalted Sentiments, and Purity and Nobleness of Diction, as well as Nature, are absolutely requisite to please those of a true Taste. And it is very possible, that a Play which turns upon some great Passion, seldom felt by the Vulgar, and wherein that Passion is treated with the greatest Delicacy and Justness; I say, it is very possible that such a Piece may please the Few, and displease the Many. And as a proof of the bad Taste of the Multitude, we find in this nation of ours, that a vile *Pantomime* Piece, full of Machinery, or a lewd blasphemous Comedy, or wretched Farce, or an empty obscure low Ballad Opera, (in all which, to the scandal of our Nation and Age, we surpass all the World) shall draw together crowded Audiences, when there is full Elbow-Room at a noble Piece of *Shakespeare's* or *Rowe's*.

Before I conclude, I must point out another Beauty in the Tragedy of Hamlet, beside those already mentioned, which does indeed arise from our Author's conforming to a Rule which he followed, (probably, without knowing it,) only because it is agreeable to Nature; and this is, that there is not one Scene in this Play but what some way or other conduces towards the *Denoüement* of the Whole; and thus the Unity of Action is indisputably kept up by every Thing tending to what we may call the main Design, and it all hangs by Consequence so close together, that no Scene can be omitted, without Prejudice to the Whole. Even *Laertes* going to *France*, and *Ophelia's* Madness, however trivial they may seem (and how much soever I dislike the Method of that last mentioned) are Incidents absolutely necessary towards the concluding of all; as will appear to any one upon due Consideration. This all holds good, notwithstanding it is my Opinion, that several of the Scenes might have been altered by our Author for the better; but as they all stand, it is, as I said, quite impossible to separate them, without a visible Prejudice to the Whole. I must add, that I am much in Doubt, whether Scenes of Prose are allowable, according to Nature and Reason, in Tragedies which are composed chiefly of Blank Verse; the Objection to them seems to be this, that as all Verse is not really in Nature, but yet Blank Verse is necessary in Tragedies, to ennoble the

Diction, and by Custom is become natural to us, Prose mixed with it serves only, methinks, to discover the Effects of Art, by the Contraste between Verse and Prose. Add to this, That it is not suitable to the Dignity of such Performances.

In short, Vice is punished in this excellent Piece, and thereby the Moral Use of it is unquestionable. And if *Hamlet's* Virtue is not rewarded as we could wish, *Mr. Addison's* Maxim ought to satisfy us, which is this, "That no Man is so thoroughly Virtuous as to claim a Reward in Tragedy, or to have Reason to repine at the Dispensations of Providence; and it is besides more Instructive to the Audience, because it abates the Insolence of Human Nature, and teaches us not to judge of Men's Merit by their Successes. And he proceeds farther, and says, that though a virtuous Man may prove unfortunate, yet a vicious Man cannot be happy in a well wrought Tragedy." This last Rule is well observed here.

Another Reason why we ought to bear with more Patience the Sufferings of a virtuous Character, is the Reflection on the future Rewards prepared for such, which is more suitable to the Moral Maxims established in a Christian Country. Besides, had it pleased our Author to have spared *Hamlet's* Life, we had been deprived of that pleasing Sensation which always (as I have else where observed) accompanies a Consciousness that we are moved as we ought to be; which we most assuredly are, when we feel Compassion rise in us for the young Prince's Death in the last Scene. I shall just touch upon one Thing more, and then I shall end these Reflections.

I am very sensible that our Nation has long been censur'd for delighting in bloody Scenes on the Stage, and our Poets have been found fault with for complying with this vicious Taste. I cannot but own, that there is a great deal of Justice in these Complaints; and must needs be of Opinion, that such Sights should never be exhibited but in order, visibly, to conduce to the Beauty of the Piece. This is sometimes so much the Case, that Action is often absolutely necessary. And to come more particularly to the Subject now in hand, I desire any unprejudiced Man, of any Nation whatever, (if such can be found) who understands our Language, to consider whether the Appearance of the Ghost, and the Deaths of the several principal Personages, (with whatever else may offend the Delicacy I mention) could possibly have that great, the noble Effect, by being told to the Audience, as they most undoubtedly have, by being brought on the Stage. If this Matter be well examined with all possible Candour, I am well perswaded that it would be found in the End, that this Piece would, by the Method I speak of, loose half its Beauty.

## HENRY MACKENZIE
### From *The Mirror*
### 1780

#### No. 99. April 18, 1780

Juvat, aut impellit ad iram,
Aut ad humum mœrore gravi deducit et angit.
(HOR. *Ars. Poet.* 109.)

Criticism, like every thing else, is subject to the prejudices of our education, or of our country. National prejudice, indeed, is, of all deviations from justice, the most common, and the most allowable; it is a near, though perhaps an illegitimate, relation of that patriotism, which has been ranked among the first virtues of characters the most eminent and illustrious. To authors, however, of a rank so elevated as to aspire to universal fame, the partiality of their countrymen has been sometimes prejudicial; in proportion as they have unreasonably applauded, the critics of other countries, from a very common sort of feeling, have unreasonably censured; and there are few great writers, whom prejudice on either side may not, from a partial view of their works, find some ground for estimating at a rate much above or much below the standard of justice.

No author, perhaps, ever existed, of whom opinion has been so various as Shakspeare. Endowed with all the sublimity, and subject to all the irregularities, of genius, his advocates have room for unbounded praise, and their opponents for frequent blame. His departure from all the common rules which criticism, somewhat arbitrarily, perhaps, has imposed, leaves no legal code by which the decision can be regulated; and in the feelings of different readers, the same passage may appear simple or mean, natural or preposterous, may excite admiration, or create disgust.

But it is not, I apprehend, from particular passages or incidents that Shakspeare is to be judged. Though his admirers frequently contend for beauty in the most distorted of the former, and probability in the most unaccountable of the latter; yet it must be owned, that, in both, there are often gross defects which criticism cannot justify, though the situation of the poet, and the time in which he wrote, may easily excuse. But we are to look for the superiority of Shakspeare in the astonishing and almost supernatural powers of his invention, his absolute command over the passions, and his wonderful knowledge of Nature. Of the structure of his stories, or the probability of his incidents, he is frequently careless; these he took at random from the legendary tale or the extravagant romance; but his intimate acquaintance with the human mind seldom or never forsake him; and admist the most fantastic and improbable situations, the persons of his drama speak in the language of the heart, and in the style of their characters.

Of all the characters of Shakspeare, that of Hamlet has been generally thought the most difficult to be reduced to any fixed or settled principle. With the strongest purposes of revenge, he is irresolute and inactive; amidst the gloom of the deepest melancholy, he is gay and jocular; and while he is described as a passionate lover, he seems indifferent about the object of his affections. It may be worth while to inquire, whether any leading idea can be found, upon which these apparent contradictions may be reconciled, and a character so pleasing in the closet, and so much applauded on the stage, rendered as unambiguous in the general as it is striking in detail? I will venture to lay before my readers some observations on this subject, though with the diffidence due to a question of which the public has doubted, and much abler critics have already written.

The basis of Hamlet's character seems to be an extreme sensibility of mind, apt to be strongly impressed by its situation, and overpowered by the feelings which that situation excites. Naturally of the most virtuous and most amiable dispositions, the circumstances in which he was placed unhinged those principles of action, which, in another situation, would have delighted mankind, and made himself happy. That kind of distress which he suffered was, beyond all others, calculated to produce this effect. His misfortunes were not the misfortunes of accident, which, though they may overwhelm at first, the mind will soon call up reflections to alleviate, and hopes to cheer; they were such as reflection only serves to irritate, such as rankle in the soul's tenderest part, her sense of virtue and feelings of natural affection: they arose from an uncle's villany, a mother's guilt, a father's murder!— Yet, amidst the gloom of melancholy and the agitation of passion, in which his calamities involve him, there are occasional breakings-out of a mind, richly endowed by nature, and cultivated by education. We perceive gentleness in his demeanour, wit in his conversation, taste in his amusements, and wisdom in his reflections.

That Hamlet's character, thus formed by nature, and thus modelled by situation, is often variable and uncertain, I am not disposed to deny. I will content myself with the supposition, that this is the very character which Shakspeare meant to allot him. Finding such a character in real life, of a person endowed with feelings so delicate as to border on weakness, with sensibility too exquisite to allow of determined action, he has placed it where it could be best exhibited, in scenes of wonder, of terror, and of indignation, where its varying emotions might be most strongly marked amidst the workings of imagination and the war of the passions.

This is the very management of the character by which, above all others, we could be interested in its behalf. Had Shakspeare made Hamlet pursue his vengeance with a steady determined purpose, had he led him through difficulties arising from accidental causes, and not from the doubts and hesitation of his own mind, the anxiety of the spectator might have been highly raised; but it would have been anxiety for the event, not for the person. As it is, we feel not only the virtues, but the weaknesses of Hamlet as our own; we see a man who, in other circumstances, would have exercised all the moral and social virtues, one whom nature had formed to be

> Th' expectancy and rose of the fair state,
> The glass of fashion, and the mould of form,
> Th' observ'd of all observers,

placed in a situation in which even the amiable qualities of his mind serve but to aggravate his distress, and to perplex his conduct. Our compassion for the first, and our anxiety for the latter, are excited in the strongest manner; and hence arises that indescribable charm in Hamlet, which attracts every reader and every spectator, which the more perfect characters of other tragedies never dispose us to feel.

The Orestes of the Greek poet, who, at his first appearance, lays down a plan of vengeance which he resolutely pursues, interests us for the accomplishment of his purpose; but of him, we think only as the instrument of that justice which we wish to overtake the murderers of Agamemnon. We feel with Orestes (or rather with Sophocles, for in such passages we always hear the poet in his hero), that "it is fit that such gross infringements of the moral law should be punished with death, in order to render wickedness less frequent;" but when Horatio exclaims on the death of his friend,

> Now cracks a noble heart!

we forget the murder of the King, the villany of Claudius, the guilt of Gertrude; our recollection dwells only on the memory of that *"sweet prince,"* the delicacy of whose feelings a milder planet should have ruled, whose gentle virtues should have bloomed through a life of felicity and usefulness.

Hamlet, from the very opening of the piece, is delineated as one under the dominion of melancholy, whose spirits were overborne by his feelings. Grief for his father's death, and displeasure at his mother's marriage, prey on his mind; and he seems, with the weakness natural to such a disposition, to yield to their control. He does not attempt to resist or combat these impressions, but is willing to fly from the contest, though it were into the grave.

> Oh! that this too solid flesh would melt, &c.

Even after his father's ghost has informed him of his murder, and commissioned him to avenge it, we find him complaining of that situation in which his fate had placed him:

The time is out of joint; oh! cursed spite,
That ever I was born to set it right!

And afterward, in the perplexity of his condition, meditating on the expediency of suicide:

To be, or not to be, that is the question.

The account he gives of his own feelings to Rosencrantz and Guildenstern, which is evidently spoken in earnest, though somewhat covered with the mist of his affected distraction, is exactly descriptive of a mind full of that weariness of life which is characteristic of low spirits;

This goodly frame, the earth, seems to me a sterile
promontory, &c.

And, indeed, he expressly delineates his own character as of the kind above-mentioned, when hesitating on the evidence of his uncle's villany, he says,

The spirit that I have seen
May be the devil, and the devil hath power
T' assume a pleasing shape; yea, and perhaps,
*Out of my weakness and my melancholy,*
Abuses me to damn me.

This doubt of the grounds on which our purpose is founded, is as often the effect, as the cause, of irresolution, which first hesitates, and then seeks out an excuse for its hesitation.

It may, perhaps, be doing Shakspeare no injustice to suppose, that he sometimes began a play, without having fixed in his mind, in any determined manner, the plan or conduct of his piece. The character of some principal person of the drama might strike his imagination strongly in the opening scenes; as he went on, this character would continue to impress itself on the conduct as well as the discourse of that person, and, it is possible, might affect the situations and incidents, especially in those romantic or legendary subjects, where history did not confine him to certain unchangeable events. In the story of Amleth, the son of Horwondil, told by Saxo-Grammaticus, from which the tragedy of Hamlet is taken, the young prince, who is to revenge the death of his father, murdered by his uncle Fengo, counterfeits madness that he may be allowed to remain about the court in safety and without suspicion. He never forgets his purposed vengeance, and acts with much more cunning towards its accomplishment than the Hamlet of Shakspeare. But Shakspeare, wishing to elevate the hero of his tragedy, and at the same time to interest the audience in his behalf, throws around him, from the beginning, the majesty of melancholy, along with that sort of weakness and irresolution which frequently attends it. The incident of the Ghost, which is entirely the poet's own, and not to be found in the Danish legend, not only produces the happiest stage effect, but is also of the greatest advantage in unfolding that character which is stamped on the young prince at the opening of the play. In the communications of such a visionary being, there is an uncertain kind of belief, and a dark unlimited horror, which are aptly suited to display the wavering purpose and varied emotions of a mind endowed with a delicacy of feeling that often shakes its fortitude, with sensibility that overpowers its strength.

### No. 100. April 22, 1780

The view of Hamlet's character, exhibited in my last Number, may, perhaps, serve to explain a difficulty which has always occurred both to the reader and the spectator on perceiving his madness, at one time, put on the appearance, not of fiction, but of reality; a difficulty by which some have been induced to suppose the distraction of the prince a strange unaccountable mixture throughout, of real insanity and counterfeit disorder.

The distraction of Hamlet, however, is clearly affected through the whole play, always subject to the control of his reason, and subservient to the accomplishment of his designs. At the grave of Ophelia, indeed, it exhibits some temporary marks of a real disorder. His mind, subject from nature to all the weakness of sensibility, agitated by the incidental misfortune of Ophelia's death, amidst the dark and permanent impression of his revenge, is thrown for awhile off its poise, and in the paroxysm of the moment breaks forth into that extravagant rhapsody which he utters to Laertes.

Counterfeited madness, in a person of the character I have ascribed to Hamlet, could not be so uniformly kept up, as not to allow the reigning impressions of his mind to shew themselves in the midst of his affected extravagance. It turned chiefly on his love to Ophelia, which he meant to hold forth as its great subject; but it frequently glanced on the wickedness of his uncle, his knowledge of which it was certainly his business to conceal.

In two of Shakspeare's tragedies are introduced, at the same time, instances of counterfeit madness, and of real distraction. In both plays the same distinction is observed, and the false discriminated from the true by similar appearances. Lear's imagination constantly runs on the ingratitude of his daughters, and the resignation of his crown; and Ophelia, after she has wasted the first ebullience of her distraction in some wild and incoherent sentences, fixes on the death of her father for the subject of her song:

They bore him bare-fac'd on the bier—
And will he not come again?
And will he not come again? &c.

But Edgar puts on a semblance as opposite as may be to his real situation and his ruling thoughts. He never ventures on any expression, bordering on the subjects of a father's cruelty, or a son's misfortune. Hamlet, in the same manner, were he as firm in mind as Edgar, would never hint any thing in his affected disorder, that might lead to a suspicion of his having discovered the villany of his uncle; but his feeling, too powerful for his prudence, often breaks through that disguise which it seems to have been his original, and ought to have continued his invariable, purpose to maintain, till an opportunity should present itself of accomplishing the revenge which he meditated.

Of the reality of Hamlet's love, doubts have also been suggested. But if that delicacy of feeling, approaching to weakness, for which I contend, be allowed him, the affected abuse, which he suffers at last to grow into scurrility, of his mistress, will, I think, be found not inconsistent with the truth of his affection for her. Feeling its real force, and beginning to play the madman on that ground, he would naturally go as far from the reality as possible. Had he not loved her at all, or slightly loved her, he might have kept up some appearance of passion amidst his feigned insanity; but really loving her, he would have been hurt by such a resemblance in the counterfeit. We can bear a downright caricature of our friend much easier than an unfavourable likeness.

It must be allowed, however, that the momentous scenes in which he is afterward engaged, seem to have smothered, if not extinguished, the feelings of his love. His total forgetfulness of Ophelia so soon after her death cannot easily be justified. It is vain, indeed, to attempt justifying Shakspeare in such particulars. "*Time,*" says Dr. Johnson, "*toil'd after him in vain.*" He seems often to forget its rights, as well in the progress of the passions, as in the business of the stage. That change of feeling and of resolution which time only can effect, he brings forth within the limits of a single scene. Whether love is to be excited, or resentment allayed, guilt to be made penitent, or sorrow cheerful, the effect is frequently produced in a space hardly sufficient for words to express it.

It has been remarked, that our great poet was not so happy in the delineation of *love* as of the other passions. Were it not treason against the majesty of Shakspeare, one might observe, that though he looked with a sort of instinctive perception into the recesses of nature, yet it was impossible for him to possess a knowledge of the refinements of delicacy, or to catch in his pictures the nicer shades of polished manners; and, without this knowledge, love can seldom be introduced on the stage, but with a degree of coarseness which will offend an audience of good taste. This observation is not meant to extend to Shakspeare's tragic scenes: in situations of deep distress or violent emotion, the *manners* are lost in the *passions*; but if we examine his *lovers*, in the lighter scenes of ordinary life, we shall generally find them trespassing against the rules of decorum, and the feelings of delicacy.

That gaiety and playfulness of deportment and of conversation, which Hamlet sometimes not only assumes, but seems actually disposed to, is, I apprehend, no contradiction to the general tone of melancholy in his character. That sort of melancholy which is the most genuine, as well as the most amiable of any, neither arising from natural sourness of temper, nor prompted by accidental chagrin, but the effect of delicate sensibility, impressed with a sense of sorrow, or a feeling of its own weakness, will, I believe, often be found indulging itself in a sportfulness of external behaviour, amidst the pressure of a sad, or even the anguish of a broken heart. Slighter emotions affect our ordinary discourse; but deep distress, sitting in the secret gloom of the soul, casts not its regard on the common occurrences of life, but suffers them to trick themselves out in the usual garb of indifference, or of gaiety, according to the fashion of the society around it, or the situation in which they chance to arise. The melancholy man feels in himself (if I may be allowed the expression) a sort of double person; one which, covered with the darkness of its imagination, looks not forth into the world, nor takes any concern in vulgar objects or frivolous pursuits; another, which he lends, as it were, to ordinary men, which can accommodate itself to their tempers and manners, and indulge, without feeling any degradation from the indulgence, a smile with the cheerful, and a laugh with the giddy.

The conversation of Hamlet with the Grave-digger seems to me to be perfectly accounted for under this supposition; and, instead of feeling it counteract the tragic effect of the story, I never see him in that scene, without receiving, from his transient jests with the clown before him, an idea of the deepest melancholy being rooted at his heart. The light point of view in which he places serious and important things, marks the power of that great impression which swallows up every thing else in his mind, which makes Cæsar and Alexander so indifferent to him, that he can trace their remains in the plaster of a cottage, or the stopper of a beer-barrel. It is from the same turn of mind, which, from the elevation of its sorrow, looks down on the bustle of ambition, and the pride of fame, that he breaks forth into the reflection, in the fourth act, on the expedition of Fortinbras.

It is with regret, as well as deference, that I accuse the judgment of Mr. Garrick, or the taste of his audience; but I cannot help thinking, that the exclusion of the scene of the Grave-digger, in his alteration of the tragedy of *Hamlet*, was not only a needless, but an unnatural violence done to the work of his favourite poet.

Shakspeare's genius attended him in all his extravagances. In the licence he took of departing from the regularity of the drama, or in his ignorance of those critical rules which might have restrained him within it, there is this advantage, that it gives him an opportunity of delineating the passions and affections of the human mind, as they exist in reality, with all the various colourings which they receive in the mixed scenes of life; not as they are accommodated by the hands of more artificial poets, to one great undivided impression, or an uninterrupted chain of congenial events. It seems therefore preposterous, to endeavour to *regularize* his plays, at the expense of depriving them of this peculiar excellence, especially as the alteration can only produce a very partial and limited improvement, and can never bring his pieces to the standard of criticism, or the form of the Aristotelian drama. Within the bounds of a pleasure-garden, we may be allowed to smooth our terraces and trim our hedge-rows; but it were equally absurd as impracticable, to apply the minute labours of the *roller* and the *pruning-knife*, to the nobler irregularity of trackless mountains and impenetrable forests.

## JOHANN WOLFGANG VON GOETHE
### From *Wilhelm Meister's Apprenticeship*
### tr. Thomas Carlyle
### 1783

#### Book IV
#### III

Seeing the ⟨drama⟩ company so favourably disposed, Wilhelm now hoped he might farther have it in his power to converse with them on the poetic merit of the pieces which might come before them. "It is not enough," said he next day, when they were all again assembled, "for the actor merely to glance over a dramatic work, to judge of it by his first impression, and thus, without investigation, to declare his satisfaction or dissatisfaction with it. Such things may be allowed in a spectator, whose purpose it is rather to be entertained and moved than formally to criticise. But the actor, on the other hand, should be prepared to give a reason for his praise or censure: and how shall he do this, if he have not taught himself to penetrate the sense, the views and feelings of his author? A common error is, to form a judgment of a drama from a single part in it; and to look upon this part itself in an isolated point of view, not in its connection with the whole. I have noticed this, within a few days, so clearly in my own conduct, that I will give you the account as an example, if you please to hear me patiently.

"You all know Shakspeare's incomparable *Hamlet*: our public reading of it at the Castle yielded every one of us the greatest satisfaction. On that occasion, we proposed to act the piece; and I, not knowing what I undertook, engaged to play the Prince's part. This I conceived that I was studying, while I began to get by heart the strongest passages, the soliloquies, and those scenes in which force of soul, vehemence and elevation of feeling have the freest scope; where the agitated heart is allowed to display itself with touching expressiveness.

"I farther conceived that I was penetrating quite into the spirit of the character, while I endeavoured as it were to take upon myself the load of deep melancholy under which my prototype was labouring, and in this humour to pursue him through the strange labyrinths of his caprices and his singularities. Thus learning, thus practising, I doubted not but I should by and by become one person with my hero.

"But the farther I advanced, the more difficult did it become for me to form any image of the whole, in its general bearings; till at last it seemed as if impossible. I next went through the entire piece, without interruption; but here too I found much that I could not away with. At one time the characters, at another time the manner of displaying them, seemed inconsistent; and I almost despaired of finding any general tint, in which I might present my whole part with all its shadings and variations. In such devious paths I toiled, and wandered long in vain; till at length a hope arose that I might reach my aim in quite a new way.

"I set about investigating every trace of Hamlet's character, as it had shown itself before his father's death: I endeavoured to distinguish what in it was independent of this mournful event; independent of the terrible events that followed; and what most probably the young man would have been, had no such thing occurred.

"Soft, and from a noble stem, this royal flower had sprung up under the immediate influences of majesty: the idea of moral rectitude with that of princely elevation, the feeling of the good and dignified with the consciousness of high birth, had in him been unfolded simultaneously. He was a prince, by birth a prince; and he wished to reign, only that good men might be good without obstruction. Pleasing in form, polished by nature, courteous from the heart, he was meant to be the pattern of youth and the joy of the world.

"Without any prominent passion, his love for Ophelia was a still presentiment of sweet wants. His zeal in knightly accomplishments was not entirely his own; it needed to be quickened and inflamed by praise bestowed on others for excelling in them. Pure in sentiment, he knew the honourable-minded, and could prize the rest which an upright spirit tastes on the bosom of a friend. To a certain degree, he had learned to discern and value the good and the beautiful in arts and sciences; the mean, the vulgar was offensive to him; and if hatred could take root in his tender soul, it was only so far as to make him properly despise the false and changeful insects of a court, and play with them in easy scorn. He was calm in his temper, artless in his conduct; neither pleased with idleness, nor too violently eager for employment. The routine of a university he seemed to continue when at court. He possessed more mirth of humour than of heart; he was a good companion, pliant, courteous, discreet, and able to forget and forgive an injury; yet never able to unite himself with those who overstept the limits of the right, the good, and the becoming.

"When we read the piece again, you shall judge whether I am yet on the proper track. I hope at least to bring forward passages that shall support my opinion in its main points." . . .

## XIII

For the first time during many months, Wilhelm felt himself in his proper element once more. Of late in talking, he had merely found submissive listeners, and even these not always; but now he had the happiness to speak with critics and artists, who not only fully understood him, but repaid his observations by others equally instructive. With wonderful vivacity they travelled through the latest pieces; with wonderful correctness judged them. The decisions of the public they could try and estimate: they speedily threw light on each other's thoughts.

Loving Shakspeare as our friend did, he failed not to lead round the conversation to the merits of that dramatist. Expressing, as he entertained, the liveliest hopes of the new epoch which these exquisite productions must form in Germany, he ere long introduced his Hamlet, who had busied him so much of late.

Serlo declared that he would long ago have played the piece, had this been possible, and that he himself would willingly engage to act Polonius. He added, with a smile: "An Ophelia, too, will certainly turn up, if we had but a Prince."

Wilhelm did not notice that Aurelia seemed a little hurt at her brother's sarcasm. Our friend was in his proper vein, becoming copious and didactic, expounding how he would have Hamlet played. He circumstantially delivered to his hearers the opinions we before saw him busied with; taking all the trouble possible to make his notion of the matter acceptable, sceptical as Serlo showed himself regarding it. "Well, then," said the latter, finally, "suppose we grant you all this, what will you explain by it?"

"Much, everything," said Wilhelm. "Conceive a prince such as I have painted him, and that his father suddenly dies. Ambition and the love of rule are not the passions that inspire him. As a king's son he would have been contented; but now he is first constrained to consider the difference which separates a sovereign from a subject. The crown was not hereditary; yet a longer possession of it by his father would have strengthened the pretensions of an only son, and secured his hopes of the succession. In place of this, he now beholds himself excluded by his uncle, in spite of specious promises, most probably forever. He is now poor in goods and favour, and a stranger in the scene which from youth he had looked upon as his inheritance. His temper here assumes its first mournful tinge. He feels that now he is not more, that he is less, than a private nobleman; he offers himself as the servant of every one; he is not courteous and condescending, he is needy and degraded.

"His past condition he remembers as a vanished dream. It is in vain that his uncle strives to cheer him, to present his situation in another point of view. The feeling of his nothingness will not leave him.

"The second stroke that came upon him wounded deeper, bowed still more. It was the marriage of his mother. The faithful tender son had yet a mother, when his father passed away. He hoped, in the company of his surviving nobleminded parent, to reverence the heroic form of the departed; but his mother too he loses, and it is something worse than death that robs him of her. The trustful image, which a good child loves to form of its parents, is gone. With the dead there is no help; on the living no hold. She also is a woman, and her name is Frailty, like that of all her sex.

"Now first does he feel himself completely bent and orphaned; and no happiness of life can repay what he has lost. Not reflective or sorrowful by nature, reflection and sorrow have become for him a heavy obligation. It is thus that we see him first enter on the scene. I do not think that I have mixed aught foreign with the piece, or overcharged a single feature of it."

Serlo looked at his sister, and said, "Did I give thee a false picture of our friend? He begins well; he has still many things to tell us, many to persuade us of." Wilhelm asseverated loudly, that he meant not to persuade, but to convince; he begged for another moment's patience.

"Figure to yourselves this youth," cried he, "this son of princes; conceive him vividly, bring his state before your eyes, and then observe him when he learns that his father's spirit walks; stand by him in the terrors of the night, when the venerable ghost itself appears before him. A horrid shudder passes over him; he speaks to the mysterious form; he sees it beckon him; he follows it, and hears. The fearful accusation of his uncle rings in his ears; the summons to revenge, and the piercing oft-repeated prayer, Remember me!

"And when the ghost has vanished, who is it that stands before us? A young hero panting for vengeance? A prince by birth, rejoicing to be called to punish the usurper of his crown? No! trouble and astonishment take hold of the solitary young man; he grows bitter against smiling villains, swears that he will not forget the spirit, and concludes with the significant ejaculation:

> The time is out of joint: O cursed spite,
> That ever I was born to set it right!

"In these words, I imagine, will be found the key to Hamlet's whole procedure. To me it is clear that Shakspeare meant, in the present case, to represent the effects of a great action laid upon a soul unfit for the performance of it. In this view the whole piece seems to me to be composed. There is an oak-tree planted in a costly jar, which should have borne only pleasant flowers in its bosom; the roots expand, the jar is shivered.

"A lovely, pure, noble and most moral nature, without the strength of nerve which forms a hero, sinks beneath a burden which it cannot bear and must not cast away. All duties are holy for him; the present is too hard. Impossibilities have been required of him; not in themselves impossibilities, but such for him. He winds, and turns, and torments himself; he advances and recoils; is ever put in mind, ever puts himself in mind; at last does all but lose his purpose from his thoughts; yet still without recovering his peace of mind."

## WILLIAM HAZLITT
### *"Hamlet"*
### *Characters of Shakespear's Plays*
### 1817

This is that Hamlet the Dane, whom we read of in our youth, and whom we may be said almost to remember in our after-years; he who made that famous soliloquy on life, who gave the advice to the players, who thought 'this goodly frame, the earth, a steril promontory, and this brave o'er-hanging firmament, the air, this majestical roof fretted with golden fire, a foul and pestilent congregation of vapours'; whom 'man delighted not, nor woman neither'; he who talked with the grave-diggers, and moralised on Yorick's skull; the school-fellow of Rosencraus and Guildenstern at Wittenberg; the friend of Horatio; the lover of Ophelia; he that was mad and sent to England; the slow avenger of his father's death; who lived at the court of Horwendillus five hundred years before we were born, but all whose thoughts we seem to know as well as we do our own, because we have read them in Shakespear.

Hamlet is a name; his speeches and sayings but the idle coinage of the poet's brain. What then, are they not real? They are as real as our own thoughts. Their reality is in the reader's mind. It is *we* who are Hamlet. This play has a prophetic truth, which is above that of history. Whoever has become thoughtful and melancholy through his own mishaps or those of others; whoever has borne about with him the clouded brow of reflection, and thought himself 'too much i' th' sun'; whoever has seen the golden lamp of day dimmed by envious mists rising in his own breast, and could find in the world before him only a dull blank with nothing left remarkable in it; whoever has known 'the pangs of despised love, the insolence of office, or the spurns which patient merit of the unworthy takes'; he who has felt his mind sink within him, and sadness cling to his heart like a malady, who has had his hopes blighted and his youth staggered by the apparitions of strange things; who cannot be well at ease, while he sees evil hovering near him like a spectre; whose powers of action have been eaten up by thought, he to whom the universe seems infinite, and himself nothing; whose bitterness of soul makes him careless of consequences, and who goes to a play as his best resource to shove off, to a second remove, the evils of life by a mock representation of them—this is the true Hamlet.

We have been so used to this tragedy that we hardly know how to criticise it any more than we should know how to describe our own faces. But we must make such observations as we can. It is the one of Shakespear's plays that we think of the oftenest, because it abounds most in striking reflections on human life, and because the distresses of Hamlet are transferred, by the turn of his mind, to the general account of humanity. Whatever happens to him we apply to ourselves, because he applies it so himself as a means of general reasoning. He is a great moraliser; and what makes him worth attending to is, that he moralises on his own feelings and experience. He is not a common-place pedant. If *Lear* is distinguished by the greatest depth of passion, *Hamlet* is the most remarkable for the ingenuity, originality, and unstudied development of character. Shakespear had more magnanimity than any other poet, and he has shewn more of it in this play than in any other. There is no attempt to force an interest: every thing is left for time and circumstances to unfold. The attention is excited without effort, the incidents succeed each other as matters of course, the characters think and speak and act just as they might do, if left entirely to themselves. There is no set purpose, no straining at a point. The observations are suggested by the passing scene—the gusts of passion come and go like sounds of music borne on the wind. The whole play is an exact transcript of what might be supposed to have taken place at the court of Denmark, at the remote period of time fixed upon, before the modern refinements in morals and manners were heard of. It would have been interesting enough to have been admitted as a by-stander in such a scene, at such a time, to have heard and witnessed something of what was going on. But here we are more than spectators. We have not only 'the outward pageants and the signs of grief'; but 'we have that within which passes shew.' We read the thoughts of the heart, we catch the passions living as they rise. Other dramatic writers give us very fine versions and paraphrases of nature; but Shakespear, together with his own comments, gives us the original text, that we may judge for ourselves. This is a very great advantage.

The character of Hamlet stands quite by itself. It is not a character marked by strength of will or even of passion, but by refinement of thought and sentiment. Hamlet is as little of the hero as a man can well be: but he is a young and princely novice, full of high enthusiasm and quick sensibility—the sport of circumstances, questioning with fortune and refining on his own feelings, and forced from the natural bias of his disposition by the strangeness of his situation. He seems incapable of deliberate action, and is only hurried into extremities on the spur of the occasion, when he has no time to reflect, as in the scene where he kills Polonius, and again, where he alters the letters which Rosencraus and Guildenstern are taking with them to England, purporting his death. At other times, when he is most bound to act, he remains puzzled, undecided, and sceptical, dallies with his purposes, till the occasion is lost, and finds out some pretence to relapse into indolence and thoughtfulness again. For this reason he refuses to kill the King when he is at his prayers, and by a refinement in malice, which is in truth only an excuse for his own want of resolution, defers his revenge to a more fatal opportunity, when he shall be engaged in some act 'that has no relish of salvation in it.'

> He kneels and prays,
> And now I'll do 't, and so he goes to heaven,
> And so am I reveng'd: *that would be scann'd.*
> He kill'd my father, and for that,
> I, his sole son, send him to heaven.

Why this is reward, not revenge.
Up sword and know thou a more horrid time,
When he is drunk, asleep, or in a rage.

He is the prince of philosophical speculators; and because he cannot have his revenge perfect, according to the most refined idea his wish can form, he declines it altogether. So he scruples to trust the suggestions of the ghost, contrives the scene of the play to have surer proof of his uncle's guilt, and then rests satisfied with this confirmation of his suspicions, and the success of his experiment, instead of acting upon it. Yet he is sensible of his own weakness, taxes himself with it, and tries to reason himself out of it.

How all occasions do inform against me,
And spur my dull revenge! What is a man,
If his chief good and market of his time
Be but to sleep and feed? A beast; no more.
Sure he that made us with such large discourse,
Looking before and after, gave us not
That capability and god-like reason
To rust in us unus'd. Now whether it be
Bestial oblivion, or some craven scruple
Of thinking too precisely on th' event,—
A thought which quarter'd, hath but one part
    wisdom,
And ever three parts coward;—I do not know
Why yet I live to say, this thing 's to do;
Sith I have cause, and will, and strength, and means
To do it. Examples gross as earth exhort me:
Witness this army of such mass and charge,
Led by a delicate and tender prince,
Whose spirit with divine ambition puff'd,
Makes mouths at the invisible event,
Exposing what is mortal and unsure
To all that fortune, death, and danger dare,
Even for an egg-shell. 'Tis not to be great
Never to stir without great argument;
But greatly to find quarrel in a straw,
When honour's at the stake. How stand I then,
That have a father kill'd, a mother stain'd,
Excitements of my reason and my blood,
And let all sleep, while to my shame I see
The imminent death of twenty thousand men,
That for a fantasy and trick of fame,
Go to their graves like beds, fight for a plot
Whereon the numbers cannot try the cause,
Which is not tomb enough and continent
To hide the slain?—O, from this time forth,
My thoughts be bloody or be nothing worth.

Still he does nothing; and this very speculation on his own infirmity only affords him another occasion for indulging it. It is not from any want of attachment to his father or of abhorrence of his murder that Hamlet is thus dilatory, but it is more to his taste to indulge his imagination in reflecting upon the enormity of the crime and refining on his schemes of vengeance, than to put them into immediate practice. His ruling passion is to think, not to act: and any vague pretext that flatters this propensity instantly diverts him from his previous purposes.

The moral perfection of this character has been called in question, we think, by those who did not understand it. It is more interesting than according to rules; amiable, though not faultless. The ethical delineations of 'that noble and liberal casuist' (as Shakespear has been well called) do not exhibit the drab-coloured quakerism of morality. His plays are not copied either from The Whole Duty of Man, or from The Academy of Compliments! We confess we are a little shocked at the want of refinement in those who are shocked at the want of refinement

in Hamlet. The neglect of punctilious exactness in his behaviour either partakes of the 'licence of the time,' or else belongs to the very excess of intellectual refinement in the character, which makes the common rules of life, as well as his own purposes, sit loose upon him. He may be said to be amenable only to the tribunal of his own thoughts, and is too much taken up with the airy world of contemplation to lay as much stress as he ought on the practical consequences of things. His habitual principles of action are unhinged and out of joint with the time. His conduct to Ophelia is quite natural in his circumstances. It is that of assumed severity only. It is the effect of disappointed hope, of bitter regrets, of affection suspended, not obliterated, by the distractions of the scene around him! Amidst the natural and preternatural horrors of his situation, he might be excused in delicacy from carrying on a regular courtship. When 'his father's spirit was in arms,' it was not a time for the son to make love in. He could neither marry Ophelia, nor wound her mind by explaining the cause of his alienation, which he durst hardly trust himself to think of. It would have taken him years to have come to a direct explanation on the point. In the harassed state of his mind, he could not have done much otherwise than he did. His conduct does not contradict what he says when he sees her funeral,

I loved Ophelia: forty thousand brothers
Could not with all their quantity of love
Make up my sum.

Nothing can be more affecting or beautiful than the Queen's apostrophe to Ophelia on throwing the flowers into the grave.

Sweets to the sweet, farewell.
I hop'd thou should'st have been my Hamlet's wife;
I thought thy bride-bed to have deck'd, sweet maid,
And not have strew'd thy grave.

Shakespear was thoroughly a master of the mixed motives of human character, and he here shews us the Queen, who was so criminal in some respects, not without sensibility and affection in other relations of life.—Ophelia is a character almost too exquisitely touching to be dwelt upon. Oh rose of May, oh flower too soon faded! Her love, her madness, her death, are described with the truest touches of tenderness and pathos. It is a character which nobody but Shakespear could have drawn in the way that he has done, and to the conception of which there is not even the smallest approach, except in some of the old romantic ballads.[1] Her brother, Laertes, is a character we do not like so well: he is too hot and choleric, and somewhat rhodomontade. Polonius is a perfect character in its kind; nor is there any foundation for the objections which have been made to the consistency of this part. It is said that he acts very foolishly and talks very sensibly. There is no inconsistency in that. Again, that he talks wisely at one time and foolishly at another; that his advice to Laertes is very excellent, and his advice to the King and Queen on the subject of Hamlet's madness very ridiculous. But he gives the one as a father, and is sincere in it; he gives the other as a mere courtier, a busy-body, and is accordingly officious, garrulous, and impertinent. In short, Shakespear has been accused of inconsistency in this and other characters, only because he has kept up the distinction which there is in nature, between the understandings and the moral habits of men, between the absurdity of their ideas and the absurdity of their motives. Polonius is not a fool, but he makes himself so. His folly, whether in his actions or speeches, comes under the head of impropriety of intention.

We do not like to see our author's plays acted, and least of all *Hamlet*. There is no play that suffers so much in being transferred to the stage. Hamlet himself seems hardly capable of being acted. Mr. Kemble unavoidably fails in this character from a want of ease and variety. The character of Hamlet is made up of undulating lines; it has the yielding flexibility of 'a wave o' th' sea.' Mr. Kemble plays it like a man in armour, with a determined inveteracy of purpose, in one undeviating straight line, which is as remote from the natural grace and refined susceptibility of the character, as the sharp angles and abrupt starts which Mr. Kean introduces into the part. Mr. Kean's Hamlet is as much too splenetic and rash as Mr. Kemble's is too deliberate and formal. His manner is too strong and pointed. He throws a severity, approaching to virulence, into the common observations and answers. There is nothing of this in Hamlet. He is, as it were, wrapped up in his reflections, and only *thinks aloud*. There should therefore be no attempt to impress what he says upon others by a studied exaggeration of emphasis or manner; no *talking at* his hearers. There should be as much of the gentleman and scholar as possible infused into the part, and as little of the actor. A pensive air of sadness should sit reluctantly upon his brow, but no appearance of fixed and sullen gloom. He is full of weakness and melancholy, but there is no harshness in his nature. He is the most amiable of misanthropes.

*Notes*

1. In the account of her death, a friend has pointed out an instance of the poet's exact observation of nature:—

> There is a willow growing o'er a brook,
> That shews its hoary leaves i' th' glassy stream.

The inside of the leaves of the willow, next the water, is of a whitish colour, and the reflection would therefore be 'hoary.'

### SAMUEL TAYLOR COLERIDGE
From *"Hamlet"*
*Shakspeare, with Introductory Remarks*
*on Poetry, the Drama, and the Stage*
1818

The seeming inconsistencies in the conduct and character of Hamlet have long exercised the conjectural ingenuity of critics: and, as we are always loth to suppose that the cause of defective apprehension is in ourselves, the mystery has been too commonly explained by the very easy process of setting it down as in fact inexplicable, and by resolving the phenomenon into a misgrowth or *lusus* of the capricious and irregular genius of Shakspeare. The shallow and stupid arrogance of these vulgar and indolent decisions I would fain do my best to expose. I believe the character of Hamlet may be traced to Shakspeare's deep and accurate science in mental philosophy. Indeed, that this character must have some connection with the common fundamental laws of our nature may be assumed from the fact, that Hamlet has been the darling of every country in which the literature of England has been fostered. In order to understand him, it is essential that we should reflect on the constitution of our own minds. Man is distinguished from the brute animals in proportion as thought prevails over sense: but in the healthy processes of the mind, a balance is constantly maintained between the impressions from outward objects and the inward operations of the intellect;—for if there be an overbalance in the contemplative faculty, man thereby becomes the creature of mere meditation, and loses his natural power of action. Now one of Shakspeare's modes of creating characters is, to conceive any one intellectual or moral faculty in morbid excess, and then to place himself, Shakspeare, thus mutilated or diseased, under given circumstances. In Hamlet he seems to have wished to exemplify the moral necessity of a due balance between our attention to the objects of our senses, and our meditation on the workings of our minds,—an *equilibrium* between the real and the imaginary worlds. In Hamlet this balance is disturbed: his thoughts, and the images of his fancy, are far more vivid than his actual perceptions, and his very perceptions, instantly passing through the *medium* of his contemplations, acquire, as they pass, a form and a colour not naturally their own. Hence we see a great, an almost enormous, intellectual activity, and a proportionate aversion to real action consequent upon it, with all its symptoms and accompanying qualities. This character Shakspeare places in circumstances, under which it is obliged to act on the spur of the moment:—Hamlet is brave and careless of death; but he vacillates from sensibility, and procrastinates from thought, and loses the power of action in the energy of resolve. Thus it is that this tragedy presents a direct contrast to that of Macbeth; the one proceeds with the utmost slowness, the other with a crowded and breathless rapidity.

The effect of this overbalance of the imaginative power is beautifully illustrated in the everlasting broodings and superfluous activities of Hamlet's mind, which, unseated from its healthy relation, is constantly occupied with the world within, and abstracted from the world without,—giving substance to shadows, and throwing a mist over all common-place actualities. It is the nature of thought to be indefinite;—definiteness belongs to external imagery alone. Hence it is that the sense of sublimity arises, not from the sight of an outward object, but from the beholder's reflection upon it;—not from the sensuous impression, but from the imaginative reflex. Few have seen a celebrated waterfall without feeling something akin to disappointment: it is only subsequently that the image comes back full into the mind, and brings with it a train of grand or beautiful associations. Hamlet feels this; his senses are in a state of trance, and he looks upon external things as hieroglyphics. His soliloquy—

> O! that this too too solid flesh would melt, &c.,

springs from that craving after the indefinite—for that which is not—which most easily besets men of genius; and the self-delusion common to this temper of mind is finely exemplified in the character which Hamlet gives of himself:—

> It cannot be
> But I am pigeon-livered, and lack gall
> To make oppression bitter.

He mistakes the seeing his chains for the breaking them, delays action till action is of no use, and dies the victim of mere circumstance and accident.

There is a great significancy in the names of Shakspeare's plays. In the *Twelfth Night, Midsummer Night's Dream, As You Like It*, and *Winter's Tale*, the total effect is produced by a co-ordination of the characters as in a wreath of flowers. But in *Coriolanus, Lear, Romeo and Juliet, Hamlet, Othello*, &c. the effect arises from the subordination of all to one, either as the prominent person, or the principal object. *Cymbeline* is the only exception; and even that has its advantages in preparing the audience for the chaos of time, place, and costume, by throwing the date back into a fabulous king's reign.

But as of more importance, so more striking, is the judgment displayed by our truly dramatic poet, as well as poet of the drama, in the management of his first scenes. With the single exception of *Cymbeline*, they either place before us at one glance both the past and the future in some effect, which implies the continuance and full agency of its cause, as in the feuds and party-spirit of the servants of the two houses in the first scene of *Romeo and Juliet*; or in the degrading passion for shews and public spectacles, and the overwhelming attachment for the newest successful war-chief in the Roman people, already become a populace, contrasted with the jealousy of the nobles in *Julius Cæsar;*—or they at once commence the action so as to excite a curiosity for the explanation in the following scenes, as in the storm of wind and waves, and the boatswain in the *Tempest*, instead of anticipating our curiosity, as in most other first scenes, and in too many other first acts;—or they act, by contrast of diction suited to the characters, at once to heighten the effect, and yet to give a naturalness to the language and rhythm of the principal personages, either as that of Prospero and Miranda by the appropriate lowness of the style,—or as in *King John*, by the equally appropriate stateliness of official harangues or narratives, so that the after blank verse seems to belong to the rank and quality of the speakers, and not to the poet;—or they strike at once the key-note, and give the predominant spirit of the play, as in the *Twelfth Night* and in *Macbeth;*—or finally, the first scene comprises all these advantages at once, as in *Hamlet*.

Compare the easy language of common life, in which this drama commences, with the direful music and wild wayward rhythm and abrupt lyrics of the opening of *Macbeth*. The tone is quite familiar;—there is no poetic description of night, no elaborate information conveyed by one speaker to another of what both had immediately before their senses—(such as the first distich in Addison's *Cato*, which is a translation into poetry of 'Past four o'clock and a dark morning!');—and yet nothing bordering on the comic on the one hand, nor any striving of the intellect on the other. It is precisely the language of sensation among men who feared no charge of effeminacy for feeling, what they had no want of resolution to bear. Yet the armour, the dead silence, the watchfulness that first interrupts it, the welcome relief of the guard, the cold, the broken expressions of compelled attention to bodily feelings still under control—all excellently accord with, and prepare for, the after gradual rise into tragedy;—but, above all, into a tragedy, the interest of which is as eminently *ad et apud intra*, as that of Macbeth is directly *ad extra*.

In all the best attested stories of ghosts and visions, as in that of Brutus, of Archbishop Cranmer, that of Benvenuto Cellini recorded by himself, and the vision of Galileo communicated by him to his favourite pupil Torricelli, the ghost-seers were in a state of cold or chilling damp from without, and of anxiety inwardly. It has been with all of them as with Francisco on his guard,—alone, in the depth and silence of the night;—'twas bitter cold, and they were sick at heart, and *not a mouse stirring.*' The attention to minute sounds,—naturally associated with the recollection of minute objects, and the more familiar and trifling, the more impressive from the unusualness of their producing any impression at all—gives a philosophic pertinency to this last image; but it has likewise its dramatic use and purpose. For its commonness in ordinary conversation tends to produce the sense of reality, and at once hides the poet, and yet approximates the reader or spectator to that state in which the highest poetry will appear, and in its component parts, though not in the whole composition, really is, the language of nature. If I should not speak it, I feel that I should be thinking it;—the voice only is the poet's,—the words are my own. That Shakspeare meant to put an effect in the actor's power in the very first words—"Who's there?"—is evident from the impatience expressed by the startled Francisco in the words that follow—"Nay, answer me: stand and unfold yourself." A brave man is never so peremptory, as when he fears that he is afraid. Observe the gradual transition from the silence and the still recent habit of listening in Francisco's—"I

think I hear them"—to the more cheerful call out, which a good actor would observe, in the—"Stand ho! Who is there?" Bernardo's inquiry after Horatio, and the repetition of his name and in his own presence indicate a respect or an eagerness that implies him as one of the persons who are in the foreground; and the scepticism attributed to him,—

> Horatio says, 'tis but our fantasy;
> And will not let belief take hold of him—

prepares us for Hamlet's after eulogy on him as one whose blood and judgment were happily commingled. The actor should also be careful to distinguish the expectation and gladness of Bernardo's "Welcome, Horatio!" from the mere courtesy of his "Welcome, good Marcellus!"

Now observe the admirable indefiniteness of the first opening out of the occasion of all this anxiety. The preparation informative of the audience is just as much as was precisely necessary, and no more;—it begins with the uncertainty appertaining to a question:—

> *Mar.:* What, has *this thing* appear'd again to-night?—

Even the word 'again' has its *credibilizing* effect. Then Horatio, the representative of the ignorance of the audience, not himself, but by Marcellus to Bernardo, anticipates the common solution—'tis but our fantasy!' upon which Marcellus rises into

> This dreaded sight, twice seen of us—

which immediately afterwards becomes 'this apparition,' and that, too, an intelligent spirit, that is, to be spoken to! Then comes the confirmation of Horatio's disbelief;—

> Tush! tush! 'twill not appear!—

and the silence, with which the scene opened, is again restored in the shivering feeling of Horatio sitting down, at such a time, and with the two eye-witnesses, to hear a story of a ghost, and that, too, of a ghost which had appeared twice before at the very same hour. In the deep feeling which Bernardo has of the solemn nature of what he is about to relate, he makes an effort to master his own imaginative terrors by an elevation of style,—itself a continuation of the effort,—and by turning off from the apparition, as from something which would force him too deeply into himself, to the outward objects, the realities of nature, which had accompanied it:—

> *Ber.:* Last night of all,
> When yon same star, that's westward from the pole,
> Had made his course to illume that part of heaven
> Where now it burns, Marcellus and myself,
> The bell then beating one—

This passage seems to contradict the critical law that what is told, makes a faint impression compared with what is beholden; for it does indeed convey to the mind more than the eye can see; whilst the interruption of the narrative at the very moment, when we are most intensely listening for the sequel, and have our thoughts diverted from the dreaded sight in expectation of the desired, yet almost dreaded, tale—this gives all the suddenness and surprise of the original appearance;—

> *Mar.:* Peace, break thee off; look, where it comes again!—

Note the judgment displayed in having the two persons present, who, as having seen the Ghost before, are naturally eager in confirming their former opinions,—whilst the sceptic is silent, and after having been twice addressed by his friends, answers with two hasty syllables—'Most like,'—and a confession of horror:

> —It harrows me with fear and wonder.

O heaven! words are wasted on those who feel, and to those who do not feel the exquisite judgment of Shakspeare in this scene, what can be said?—Hume himself could not but have had faith in this Ghost dramatically, let his antighostism have been as strong as Samson against other ghosts less powerfully raised.

## VICTOR HUGO
### From *William Shakespeare*, tr. F. T. Marzials
### 1864

#### Part II
*Book II. Shakespeare—His Work—The Culminating Points*
#### III

Two marvellous Adams, we have just said, are the man of Æschylus, Prometheus, and the man of Shakespeare, Hamlet.

Prometheus is action. Hamlet is hesitation.

In Prometheus the obstacle is exterior; in Hamlet it is interior.

In Prometheus the will is securely nailed down by nails of brass and cannot get loose; besides, it has by its side two watchers,—Force and Power. In Hamlet the will is more tied down yet; it is bound by previous meditation,—the endless chain of the undecided. Try to get out of yourself if you can! What a Gordian knot is our revery! Slavery from within, that is slavery indeed. Scale this enclosure, "to dream!" escape, if you can, from this prison, "to love!" The only dungeon is that which walls conscience in. Prometheus, in order to be free, has but a bronze collar to break and a god to conquer; Hamlet must break and conquer himself. Prometheus can raise himself upright, if he only lifts a mountain; to raise himself up, Hamlet must lift his own thoughts. If Prometheus plucks the vulture from his breast, all is said; Hamlet must tear Hamlet from his breast. Prometheus and Hamlet are two naked livers; from one runs blood, from the other doubt.

We are in the habit of comparing Æschylus and Shakespeare by Orestes and Hamlet, these two tragedies being the same drama. Never in fact was a subject more identical. The learned mark an analogy between them; the impotent, who are also the ignorant, the envious, who are also the imbeciles, have the petty joy of thinking they establish a plagiarism. It is after all a possible field for erudition and for serious criticism. Hamlet walks behind Orestes, parricide through filial love. This easy comparison, rather superficial than deep, strikes us less than the mysterious confronting of those two enchained beings, Prometheus and Hamlet.

Let us not forget that the human mind, half divine as it is, creates from time to time superhuman works. These superhuman works of man are, moreover, more numerous than it is thought, for they entirely fill art. Out of poetry, where marvels abound, there is in music Beethoven, in sculpture Phidias, in architecture Piranesi, in painting Rembrandt, and in painting, architecture, and sculpture Michael Angelo. We pass many over, and not the least.

Prometheus and Hamlet are among those more than human works.

A kind of gigantic determination; the usual measure exceeded; greatness everywhere; that which astounds ordinary intellects demonstrated when necessary by the improbable; destiny, society, law, religion, brought to trial and judgment in the name of the Unknown, the abyss of the mysterious equilibrium; the event treated as a *rôle* played out, and, on occasion, hurled as a reproach against Fatality or Providence;

passion, terrible personage, going and coming in man; the audacity and sometimes the insolence of reason; the haughty forms of a style at ease in all extremes, and at the same time a profound wisdom; the gentleness of the giant; the goodness of a softened monster; an ineffable dawn which cannot be accounted for and which lights up everything,—such are the signs of those supreme works. In certain poems there is starlight.

This light is in Æschylus and in Shakespeare.

#### IV

Nothing can be more fiercely wild than Prometheus stretched on the Caucasus. It is gigantic tragedy. The old punishment that our ancient laws of torture call extension, and which Cartouche escaped because of a hernia, Prometheus undergoes it; only, the wooden horse is a mountain. What is his crime? Right. To characterize right as crime, and movement as rebellion, is the immemorial talent of tyrants. Prometheus has done on Olympus what Eve did in Eden,—he has taken a little knowledge. Jupiter, identical with Jehovah (*Iovi, Iova*), punishes this temerity,—the desire to live. The Eginetic traditions, which localize Jupiter, deprive him of the cosmic personality of the Jehovah of Genesis. The Greek Jupiter, bad son of a bad father, in rebellion against Saturn, who has himself been a rebel against Cœlus, is a *parvenu*. The Titans are a sort of elder branch, which has its legitimists, of whom Æschylus, the avenger of Prometheus, was one. Prometheus is right conquered. Jupiter has, as is always the case, consummated the usurpation of power by the punishment of right. Olympus claims the aid of Caucasus. Prometheus is fastened there to the *carcan*. There is the Titan, fallen, prostrate, nailed down. Mercury, the friend of everybody, comes to give him such counsel as follows generally the perpetration of *coups d'état*. Mercury is the type of cowardly intellect, of every possible vice, but of vice full of wit. Mercury, the god of vice, serves Jupiter the god of crime. This fawning in evil is still marked today by the veneration of the pickpocket for the assassin. There is something of that law in the arrival of the diplomatist behind the conqueror. The *chefs-d'œuvre* are immense in this, that they are eternally present to the deeds of humanity. Prometheus on the Caucasus, is Poland after 1772; France after 1815; the Revolution after Brumaire. Mercury speaks; Prometheus listens but little. Offers of amnesty miscarry when it is the victim who alone should have the right to grant pardon. Prometheus, though conquered, scorns Mercury standing proudly above him, and Jupiter standing above Mercury, and Destiny standing above Jupiter. Prometheus jests at the vulture which gnaws at him; he shrugs disdainfully his shoulders as much as his chain allows. What does he care for Jupiter, and what good is Mercury? There is no hold on this haughty sufferer. The scorching thunderbolt causes a smart, which is a constant call upon pride. Meanwhile tears flow around him, the earth despairs, the women-clouds (the fifty Oceanides), come to worship the Titan, the forests scream, wild beasts groan, winds howl, the waves sob, the elements moan, the world suffers in Prometheus; his *carcan* chokes universal life. An immense participation in the torture of the demigod seems to be henceforth the tragic delight of all Nature; anxiety for the future mingles with it: and what is to be done now? How are we to move? What will become of us? And in the vast whole of created beings, things, men, animals, plants, rocks, all turned toward the Caucasus, is felt this inexpressible anguish,—the liberator is enchained.

Hamlet, less of a giant and more of a man, is not less grand,—Hamlet, the appalling, the unaccountable, complete in incompleteness; all, in order to be nothing. He is prince and demagogue, sagacious and extravagant, profound and frivolous, man and neuter. He has but little faith in the sceptre, rails at the throne, has a student for his comrade, converses with any one passing by, argues with the first comer, understands the people, despises the mob, hates strength, suspects success, questions obscurity, and says "thou" to mystery. He gives to others maladies which he has not himself: his false madness inoculates his mistress with true madness. He is familiar with spectres and with comedians. He jests with the axe of Orestes in his hand. He talks of literature, recites verses, composes a theatrical criticism, plays with bones in a cemetery, dumfounds his mother, avenges his father, and ends the wonderful drama of life and death by a gigantic point of interrogation. He terrifies and then disconcerts. Never has anything more overwhelming been dreamed. It is the parricide saying: "What do I know?"

Parricide? Let us pause on that word. Is Hamlet a parricide? Yes, and no. He confines himself to threatening his mother; but the threat is so fierce that the mother shudders. His words are like daggers. "What wilt thou do? Thou wilt not murder me? Help! help! ho!" And when she dies, Hamlet, without grieving for her, strikes Claudius with this tragic cry: "Follow my mother!" Hamlet is that sinister thing, the possible parricide.

In place of the northern ice which he has in his nature, let him have, like Orestes, southern fire in his veins, and he will kill his mother.

This drama is stern. In it truth doubts, sincerity lies. Nothing can be more immense, more subtle. In it man is the world, and the world is zero. Hamlet, even full of life, is not sure of his existence. In this tragedy, which is at the same time a philosophy, everything floats, hesitates, delays, staggers, becomes discomposed, scatters, and is dispersed. Thought is a cloud, will is a vapour, resolution is a crepuscule; the action blows each moment in an opposite direction; man is governed by the winds. Overwhelming and vertiginous work, in which is seen the depth of everything, in which thought oscillates only between the king murdered and Yorick buried, and in which what is best realized is royalty represented by a ghost, and mirth represented by a death's-head.

*Hamlet* is the *chef-d'œuvre* of the tragedy-dream.

## V

One of the probable causes of the feigned madness of Hamlet has not been up to the present time indicated by critics. It has been said, "Hamlet acts the madman to hide his thought, like Brutus." In fact, it is easy for apparent imbecility to hatch a great project; the supposed idiot can take aim deliberately. But the case of Brutus is not that of Hamlet. Hamlet acts the madman for his safety. Brutus screens his project, Hamlet his person. The manners of those tragic courts being known, from the moment that Hamlet, through the revelation of the ghost, is acquainted with the crime of Claudius, Hamlet is in danger. The superior historian within the poet is here manifested, and one feels the deep insight of Shakespeare into the ancient darkness of royalty. In the Middle Ages and in the Lower Empire, and even at earlier periods, woe unto him who found out a murder or a poisoning committed by a king! Ovid, according to Voltaire's conjecture, was exiled from Rome for having seen something shameful in the house of Augustus. To know that the king was an assassin was a State crime. When it pleased the prince not to have had a witness, it was a matter involving one's head to ignore everything. It was bad policy to have good eyes. A man suspected of suspicion was lost. He had but one refuge,—folly; to pass for "an innocent." He was despised, and that was all. Do you remember the advice that, in Æschylus, the Ocean gives to Prometheus: "To look a fool is

the secret of the wise man." When the Chamberlain Hugolin found the iron spit with which Edrick the Vendee had empaled Edmond II., "he hastened to put on madness," says the Saxon Chronicle of 1016, and saved himself in that way. Heraclian of Nisibe, having discovered by chance that Rhinomete was a fratricide, had himself declared mad by the doctors, and succeeded in getting himself shut up for life in a cloister. He thus lived peaceably, growing old and waiting for death with a vacant stare. Hamlet runs the same peril, and has recourse to the same means. He gets himself declared mad like Heraclian, and puts on folly like Hugolin. This does not prevent the restless Claudius from twice making an effort to get rid of him,—in the middle of the drama by the axe or the dagger in England, and toward the conclusion by poison.

The same indication is again found in *King Lear*; the Earl of Gloster's son takes refuge also in apparent lunacy. There is in that a key to open and understand Shakespeare's thought. In the eyes of the philosophy of art, the feigned folly of Edgar throws light upon the feigned folly of Hamlet.

The Amleth of Belleforest is a magician; the Hamlet of Shakespeare is a philosopher. We just now spoke of the strange reality which characterizes poetical creations. There is no more striking example than this type,—Hamlet. Hamlet has nothing belonging to an abstraction about him. He has been at the University; he has the Danish rudeness softened by Italian politeness; he is small, plump, somewhat lymphatic; he fences well with the sword, but is soon out of breath. He does not care to drink too soon during the assault of arms with Laërtes,— probably for fear of producing perspiration. After having thus supplied his personage with real life, the poet can launch him into full ideal. There is ballast enough.

Other works of the human mind equal *Hamlet*; none surpasses it. The whole majesty of melancholy is in *Hamlet*. An open sepulchre from which goes forth a drama,—this is colossal. *Hamlet* is to our mind Shakespeare's chief work.

No figure among those that poets have created is more poignant and stirring. Doubt counselled by a ghost,—that is Hamlet. Hamlet has seen his dead father and has spoken to him. Is he convinced? No, he shakes his head. What shall he do? He does not know. His hands clench, then fall by his side. Within him are conjectures, systems, monstrous apparitions, bloody recollections, veneration for the spectre, hate, tenderness, anxiety to act and not to act, his father, his mother, his duties in contradiction to each other,—a deep storm. Livid hesitation is in his mind. Shakespeare, wonderful plastic poet, makes the grandiose pallor of this soul almost visible. Like the great larva of Albert Dürer, Hamlet might be named "Melancholia." He also has above his head the bat which flies disembowelled; and at his feet science, the sphere, the compass, the hour-glass, love; and behind him in the horizon an enormous, terrible sun, which seems to make the sky but darker.

Nevertheless, at least one-half of Hamlet is anger, transport, outrage, hurricane, sarcasm to Ophelia, malediction on his mother, insult to himself. He talks with the gravediggers, nearly laughs, then clutches Laërtes by the hair in the very grave of Ophelia, and stamps furiously upon the coffin. Sword-thrusts at Polonius, sword-thrusts at Laërtes, sword-thrusts at Claudius. From time to time his inaction is torn in twain, and from the rent comes forth thunder.

He is tormented by that possible life, intermixed with reality and chimera, the anxiety of which is shared by all of us. There is in all his actions an expanded somnambulism. One might almost consider his brain as a formation; there is a layer of suffering, a layer of thought, then a layer of dreaminess. It is through this layer of dreaminess that he feels, comprehends, learns, perceives, drinks, eats, frets, mocks, weeps, and reasons. There is between life and him a transparency; it is the wall of dreams. One sees beyond, but one cannot step over it. A kind of cloudy obstacle everywhere surrounds Hamlet. Have you ever while sleeping, had the nightmare of pursuit or flight, and tried to hasten on, and felt anchylosis in the knees, heaviness in the arms, the horror of paralysed hands, the impossibility of movement? This nightmare Hamlet undergoes while waking. Hamlet is not upon the spot where his life is. He has ever the appearance of a man who talks to you from the other side of a stream. He calls to you at the same time that he questions you. He is at a distance from the catastrophe in which he takes part, from the passer-by whom he interrogates, from the thought that he carries; from the action that he performs. He seems not to touch even what he grinds. It is isolation in its highest degree. It is the loneliness of a mind, even more than the loftiness of a prince. Indecision is in fact a solitude. You have not even your will to keep you company. It is as if your own self was absent and had left you there. The burden of Hamlet is less rigid than that of Orestes, but more undulating. Orestes carries predestination; Hamlet carries fate.

And thus apart from men, Hamlet has still in him a something which represents them all. *Agnosco fratrem.* At certain hours, if we felt our own pulse, we should be conscious of his fever. His strange reality is our own reality after all. He is the mournful man that we all are in certain situations. Unhealthy as he is, Hamlet expresses a permanant condition of man. He represents the discomfort of the soul in a life which is not sufficiently adapted to it. He represents the shoe that pinches and stops our walking; the shoe is the body. Shakespeare frees him from it, and he is right. Hamlet—prince if you like, but king never—Hamlet is incapable of governing a people; he lives too much in a world beyond. On the other hand, he does better than to reign; he *is*. Take from him his family, his country, his ghost, and the whole adventure at Elsinore, and even in the form of an inactive type, he remains strangely terrible. That is the consequence of the amount of humanity and the amount of mystery that is in him. Hamlet is formidable, which does not prevent his being ironical. He has the two profiles of destiny.

Let us retract a statement made above. The chief work of Shakespeare is not *Hamlet*. The chief work of Shakespeare is all Shakespeare. That is, moreover, true of all minds of this order. They are mass, block, majesty, bible, and their solemnity is their *ensemble*.

Have you sometimes looked upon a cape prolonging itself under the clouds and jutting out, as far as the eye can go, into deep water? Each of its hillocks contributes to make it up. No one of its undulations is lost in its dimension. Its strong outline is sharply marked upon the sky, and enters as far as possible into the waves, and there is not a useless rock. Thanks to this cape, you can go amidst the boundless waters, walk among the winds, see closely the eagles soar and the monsters swim, let your humanity wander mid the eternal hum, penetrate the impenetrable. The poet renders this service to your mind. A genius is a promontory into the infinite.

## JAMES RUSSELL LOWELL
### From "Shakespeare Once More" (1868)
*Works*
1890, Volume 3, pp. 207–25

T he first demand we make upon whatever claims to be a work of art (and we have a right to make it) is that it shall be *in keeping*. Now this propriety is of two kinds, either extrinsic or intrinsic. In the first I should class whatever relates rather to the body than the soul of the work, such as fidelity to the facts of history, (wherever that is important,) congruity of costume, and the like,—in short, whatever might come under the head of *picturesque* truth, a departure from which would shock too rudely our preconceived associations. I have seen an Indian chief in French boots, and he seemed to me almost tragic; but, put upon the stage in tragedy, he would have been ludicrous. Lichtenberg, writing from London in 1775, tells us that Garrick played Hamlet in a suit of the French fashion, then commonly worn, and that he was blamed for it by some of the critics; but, he says, one hears no such criticism during the play, nor on the way home, nor at supper afterwards, nor indeed till the emotion roused by the great actor has had time to subside. He justifies Garrick, though we should not be able to endure it now. Yet nothing would be gained by trying to make Hamlet's costume true to the assumed period of the play, for the scene of it is laid in a Denmark that has no dates.

In the second and more important category, I should put, first, co-ordination of character, that is, a certain variety in harmony of the personages of a drama, as in the attitudes and coloring of the figures in a pictorial composition, so that, while mutually relieving and setting off each other, they shall combine in the total impression; second, that subordinate truth to Nature which makes each character coherent in itself; and, third, such propriety of costume and the like as shall satisfy the superhistoric sense, to which, and to which alone, the higher drama appeals. All these come within the scope of *imaginative* truth. To illustrate my third head by an example. Tieck criticises John Kemble's dressing for Macbeth in a modern Highland costume, as being ungraceful without any countervailing merit of historical exactness. I think a deeper reason for his dissatisfaction might be found in the fact, that this garb, with its purely modern and British army associations, is out of place on Fores Heath, and drags the Weird Sisters down with it from their proper imaginative remoteness in the gloom of the past to the disenchanting glare of the foot-lights. It is not the antiquarian, but the poetic conscience, that is wounded. To this, exactness, so far as concerns ideal representation, may not only not be truth, but may even be opposed to it. Anachronisms and the like are in themselves of no account, and become important only when they make a gap too wide for our illusion to cross unconsciously, that is, when they are anacoluthons to the imagination. The aim of the artist is psychologic, not historic truth. It is comparatively easy for an author to *get up* any period with tolerable minuteness in externals, but readers and audiences find more difficulty in getting them down, though oblivion swallows scores of them at a gulp. The saving truth in such matters is a truth to essential and permanent characteristics. The Ulysses of Shakespeare, like the Ulysses of Dante and Tennyson, more or less harmonizes with our ideal conception of the wary, long-considering, though adventurous son of Laertes, yet Simon Lord Lovat is doubtless nearer the original type. In *Hamlet*, though there is no Denmark of the ninth century, Shakespeare has suggested the prevailing rudeness of manners quite enough for his purpose. We see it in the single combat of Hamlet's father with the elder Fortinbras, in the vulgar wassail of the king, in the English monarch being expected to hang Rosencrantz and Guildenstern out of hand merely to oblige his cousin of Denmark, in Laertes, sent to Paris to be made a gentleman of, becoming instantly capable of any the most barbarous treachery to glut his vengeance. We cannot fancy Ragnar Lodbrog or Eric the Red matriculating at Wittenberg, but it was essential that Hamlet should be a scholar, and Shakespeare sends him thither without more ado. All through the play we get the notion of a state of society in which a savage nature has disguised itself in the externals of civilization, like a Maori deacon, who has only to strip and he becomes once more a tattooed pagan with his mouth watering for a spare-rib of his pastor. Historically, at the date of *Hamlet*, the Danes were in the habit of burning their enemies alive in their houses, with as much of their family about them as might be to make it comfortable. Shakespeare seems purposely to have dissociated his play from history by changing nearly every name in the original legend. The motive of the play—revenge as a religious duty—belongs only to a social state in which the traditions of barbarism are still operative, but, with infallible artistic judgment, Shakespeare has chosen, not untamed Nature, as he found it in history, but the period of transition, a period in which the times are always out of joint, and thus the irresolution which has its root in Hamlet's own character is stimulated by the very incompatibility of that legacy of vengeance he has inherited from the past with the new culture and refinement of which he is the representative. One of the few books which Shakespeare is known to have possessed was Florio's Montaigne, and he might well have transferred the Frenchman's motto, *Que sçais je?* to the front of his tragedy; nor can I help fancying something more than accident in the fact that Hamlet has been a student at Wittenberg, whence those new ideas went forth, of whose results in unsettling men's faith, and consequently disqualifying them for promptness in action, Shakespeare had been not only an eye-witness, but which he must actually have experienced in himself.

One other objection let me touch upon here, especially as it has been urged against *Hamlet*, and that is the introduction of low characters and comic scenes in tragedy. Even Garrick, who had just assisted at the Stratford Jubilee, where Shakespeare had been pronounced divine, was induced by this absurd outcry for the proprieties of the tragic stage to omit the grave-diggers' scene from *Hamlet*. Leaving apart the fact that Shakespeare would not have been the representative poet he is, if he had not given expression to this striking tendency of the Northern races, which shows itself constantly, not only in their literature, but even in their mythology and their architecture, the grave-diggers' scene always impresses me as one of the most pathetic in the whole tragedy. That Shakespeare introduced such scenes and characters with deliberate intention, and with a view to artistic relief and contrast, there can hardly be a doubt. We must take it for granted that a man whose works show everywhere the results of judgment sometimes acted with forethought. I find the springs of the profoundest sorrow and pity in this hardened indifference of the grave-diggers, in their careless discussion as to whether Ophelia's death was by suicide or no, in their singing and jesting at their dreary work.

> A pickaxe and a spade, a spade,
> For—and a shrouding-sheet:
> O, a pit of clay for to be made
> For such a guest is meet!

We know who is to be the guest of this earthen hospitality,—how much beauty, love, and heartbreak are to be covered in that pit of clay. All we remember of Ophelia reacts upon us with tenfold force, and we recoil from our amusement at the ghastly drollery of the two delvers with a shock of horror. That the unconscious Hamlet should stumble on *this* grave of all others, that it should be *here* that he should pause to muse humorously on death and decay,—all this prepares us for the revulsion of passion in the next scene, and for the frantic confession,—

> I loved Ophelia; forty thousand brothers
> Could not with all *their* quantity of love
> Make up my sum!

And it is only here that such an asseveration would be true even to the feeling of the moment; for it is plain from all we know of Hamlet that he could not so have loved Ophelia, that he was incapable of the self-abandonment of a true passion, that he would have analyzed this emotion as he does all others, would have peeped and botanized upon it till it became to him a mere matter of scientific interest. All this force of contrast, and this horror of surprise, were necessary so to intensify his remorseful regret that he should believe himself for once in earnest. The speech of the King, "O, he is mad, Laertes," recalls him to himself, and he at once begins to rave:—

> Zounds! show me what thou 'lt do!
> Woul't weep? woul't fight? woul't fast? woul't tear
>       thyself?
> Woul't drink up eysil? eat a crocodile?

It is easy to see that the whole plot hinges upon the character of Hamlet, that Shakespeare's conception of this was the ovum out of which the whole organism was hatched. And here let me remark, that there is a kind of genealogical necessity in the character,—a thing not altogether strange to the attentive reader of Shakespeare. Hamlet seems the natural result of the mixture of father and mother in his temperament, the resolution and persistence of the one, like sound timber wormholed and made shaky, as it were, by the other's infirmity of will and discontinuity of purpose. In natures so imperfectly mixed it is not uncommon to find vehemence of intention the prelude counterpoise of weak performance, the conscious nature striving to keep up its self-respect by a triumph in words all the more resolute that it feels assured beforehand of inevitable defeat in action. As in such slipshod housekeeping men are their own largest creditors, they find it easy to stave off utter bankruptcy of conscience by taking up one unpaid promise with another larger, and at heavier interest, till such self-swindling becomes habitual and by degrees almost painless. How did Coleridge discount his own notes of this kind with less and less specie as the figures lengthened on the paper! As with Hamlet, so it is with Ophelia and Laertes. The father's feebleness comes up again in the wasting heartbreak and gentle lunacy of the daughter, while the son shows it in a rashness of impulse and act, a kind of crankiness, of whose essential feebleness we are all the more sensible as contrasted with a nature so steady on its keel, and drawing so much water, as that of Horatio,—the foil at once, in different ways, to both him and Hamlet. It was natural, also, that the daughter of self-conceited old Polonius should have her softness stiffened with a fibre of obstinacy; for there are two kinds of weakness, that which breaks, and that which bends. Ophelia's is of the former kind; Hero is her counterpart, giving way before calamity, and rising again so soon as the pressure is removed. . . .

It is an inherent peculiarity of a mind like Hamlet's that it should be conscious of its own defect. Men of his type are forever analyzing their own emotions and motives. They cannot do anything, because they always see two ways of doing it. They cannot determine on any course of action, because they are always, as it were, standing at the cross-roads, and see too well the disadvantages of every one of them. It is not that they are incapable of resolve, but somehow the band between the motive power and the operative faculties is relaxed and loose. The engine works, but the machinery it should drive stands still. The imagination is so much in overplus, that thinking a thing becomes better than doing it, and thought with its easy perfection, capable of everything because it can accomplish everything with ideal means, is vastly more attractive and satisfactory than deed, which must be wrought at best with imperfect instruments, and always falls short of the conception that went before it. "If to do," says Portia in the *Merchant of Venice,*—"if to do were as easy as to know what 't were good to do, chapels had been churches, and poor men's cottages princes' palaces." Hamlet knows only too well what 't were good to do, but he palters with everything in a double sense: he sees the grain of good there is in evil, and the grain of evil there is in good, as they exist in the world, and, finding that he can make those feather-weighted accidents balance each other, infers that there is little to choose between the essences themselves. He is of Montaigne's mind, and says expressly that "there is nothing good or ill, but thinking makes it so." He dwells so exclusively in the world of ideas that the world of facts seems trifling, nothing is worth the while; and he has been so long objectless and purposeless, so far as actual life is concerned, that, when at last an object and an aim are forced upon him, he cannot deal with them, and gropes about vainly for a motive outside of himself that shall marshal his thoughts for him and guide his faculties into the path of action. He is the victim not so much of feebleness of will as of an intellectual indifference that hinders the will from working long in any one direction. He wishes to will, but never wills. His continual iteration of resolve shows that he has no resolution. He is capable of passionate energy where the occasion presents itself suddenly from without, because nothing is so irritable as conscious irresolution with a duty to perform. But of deliberate energy he is not capable; for there the impulse must come from within, and the blade of his analysis is so subtile that it can divide the finest hair of motive 'twixt north and northwest side, leaving him desperate to choose between them. The very consciousness of his defect is an insuperable bar to his repairing it; for the unity of purpose, which infuses every fibre of the character with will available whenever wanted, is impossible where the mind can never rest till it has resolved that unity into its component elements, and satisfied itself which on the whole is of greater value. A critical instinct so insatiable that it must turn upon itself, for lack of something else to hew and hack, becomes incapable at last of originating anything except indecision. It becomes infallible in what *not* to do. How easily he might have accomplished his task is shown by the conduct of Laertes. When *he* has a death to avenge, he raises a mob, breaks into the palace, bullies the king, and proves how weak the usurper really was.

The world is the victim of splendid parts, and is slow to accept a rounded whole, because that is something which is long in completing, still longer in demonstrating its completion. We like to be surprised into admiration, and not logically convinced that we ought to admire. We are willing to be delighted with success, though we are somewhat indifferent to the homely qualities which insure it. Our thought is so filled with the rocket's burst of momentary splendor so far above us, that we forget the poor stick, useful and unseen, that made its climbing possible. One of these homely qualities is continuity of character, and it escapes present applause because it tells chiefly, in the long run, in results. With his usual tact, Shakespeare has brought in such a character as a contrast and foil to Hamlet. Horatio is the only complete *man* in the play,—

solid, well-knit, and true; a noble, quiet nature, with that highest of all qualities, judgment, always sane and prompt; who never drags his anchors for any wind of opinion or fortune, but grips all the closer to the reality of things. He seems one of those calm, undemonstrative men whom we love and admire without asking to know why, crediting them with the capacity of great things, without any test of actual achievement, because we feel that their manhood is a constant quality, and no mere accident of circumstance and opportunity. Such men are always sure of the presence of their highest self on demand. Hamlet is continually drawing bills on the future, secured by his promise of himself to himself, which he can never redeem. His own somewhat feminine nature recognizes its complement in Horatio, and clings to it instinctively, as naturally as Horatio is attracted by that fatal gift of imagination, the absence of which makes the strength of his own character, as its overplus does the weakness of Hamlet's. It is a happy marriage of two minds drawn together by the charm of unlikeness. Hamlet feels in Horatio the solid steadiness which he misses in himself; Horatio in Hamlet that need of service and sustainment to render which gives him a consciousness of his own value. Hamlet fills the place of a woman to Horatio, revealing him to himself not only in what he says, but by a constant claim upon his strength of nature; and there is great psychological truth in making suicide the first impulse of this quiet, undemonstrative man, after Hamlet's death, as if the very reason for his being were taken away with his friend's need of him. In his grief, he for the first and only time speaks of himself, is first made conscious of himself by his loss. If this manly reserve of Horatio be true to Nature, not less so are the communicativeness of Hamlet, and his tendency to soliloquize. If self-consciousness be alien to the one, it is just as truly the happiness of the other. Like a musician distrustful of himself, he is forever tuning his instrument, first overstraining this cord a little, and then that, but unable to bring them into unison, or to profit by it if he could.

We do not believe that Horatio ever thought he "was not a pipe for Fortune's finger to play what stop she please," till Hamlet told him so. That was Fortune's affair, not his; let her try it, if she liked. He is unconscious of his own peculiar qualities, as men of decision commonly are, or they would not be men of decision. When there is a thing to be done, they go straight at it, and for the time there is nothing for them in the whole universe but themselves and their object. Hamlet, on the other hand, is always studying himself. This world and the other, too, are always present to his mind, and there in the corner is the little black kobold of a doubt making mouths at him. He breaks down the bridges before him, not behind him, as a man of action would do; but there is something more than this. He is an ingrained sceptic; though his is the scepticism, not of reason, but of feeling, whose root is want of faith in himself. In him it is passive, a malady rather than a function of the mind. We might call him insincere: not that he was in any sense a hypocrite, but only that he never was and never could be in earnest. Never could be, because no man without intense faith in something ever can. Even if he only believed in himself, that were better than nothing; for it will carry a man a great way in the outward successes of life, nay, will even sometimes give him the Archimedean fulcrum for moving the world. But Hamlet doubts everything. He doubts the immortality of the soul, just after seeing his father's spirit, and hearing from its mouth the secrets of the other world. He doubts Horatio even, and swears him to secrecy on the cross of his sword, though probably he himself has no assured belief in the sacredness of the symbol. He doubts Ophelia, and asks her, "Are you honest?" He doubts the ghost, after he has had a little time to think about it, and so gets up the play to test the guilt of the king. And how coherent the whole character is! With what perfect tact and judgment Shakespeare, in the advice to the players, makes him an exquisite critic! For just here that part of his character which would be weak in dealing with affairs is strong. A wise scepticism is the first attribute of a good critic. He must not believe that the fire-insurance offices will raise their rates of premium on Charles River, because the new volume of poems is printing at Riverside or the University Press. He must not believe so profoundly in the ancients as to think it wholly out of the question that the world has still vigor enough in its loins to beget some one who will one of these days be as good an ancient as any of them.

Another striking quality in Hamlet's nature is his perpetual inclination to irony. I think this has been generally passed over too lightly, as if it were something external and accidental, rather assumed as a mask than part of the real nature of the man. It seems to me to go deeper, to be something innate, and not merely factitious. It is nothing like the grave irony of Socrates, which was the weapon of a man thoroughly in earnest,—the *boomerang* of argument, which one throws in the opposite direction of what he means to hit, and which seems to be flying away from the adversary, who will presently find himself knocked down by it. It is not like the irony of Timon, which is but the wilful refraction of a clear mind twisting awry whatever enters it,—or of Iago, which is the slime that a nature essentially evil loves to trail over all beauty and goodness to taint them with distrust: it is the half-jest, half-earnest of an inactive temperament that has not quite made up its mind whether life is a reality or no, whether men were not made in jest, and which amuses itself equally with finding a deep meaning in trivial things and a trifling one in the profoundest mysteries of being, because the want of earnestness in its own essence infects everything else with its own indifference. If there be now and then an unmannerly rudeness and bitterness in it, as in the scenes with Polonius and Osrick, we must remember that Hamlet was just in the condition which spurs men to sallies of this kind: dissatisfied, at one neither with the world nor with himself, and accordingly casting about for something out of himself to vent his spleen upon. But even in these passages there is no hint of earnestness, of any purpose beyond the moment; they are mere cat's-paws of vexation, and not the deep-raking groundswell of passion, as we see it in the sarcasm of Lear.

The question of Hamlet's madness has been much discussed and variously decided. High medical authority has pronounced, as usual, on both sides of the question. But the induction has been drawn from too narrow premises, being based on a mere diagnosis of the *case*, and not on an appreciation of the character in its completeness. We have a case of pretended madness in the Edgar of *King Lear*; and it is certainly true that that is a charcoal sketch, coarsely outlined, compared with the delicate drawing, the lights, shades, and half-tints of the portraiture in Hamlet. But does this tend to prove that the madness of the latter, because truer to the recorded observation of experts, is real, and meant to be real, as the other to be fictitious? Not in the least, as it appears to me. Hamlet, among all the characters of Shakespeare, is the most eminently a metaphysician and psychologist. He is a close observer, continually analyzing his own nature and that of others, letting fall his little drops of acid irony on all who come near him, to make them show what they are made of. Even Ophelia is not too sacred, Osrick not too contemptible for experiment. If such a man assumed madness, he would play his part perfectly. If Shakespeare himself, without going mad, could so observe and remember all the abnormal symptoms as to be able to reproduce them in Hamlet, why should it be beyond the power of Hamlet to reproduce them in himself? If you deprive Hamlet of reason, there is no truly tragic motive left. He would be a fit subject for Bedlam, but not for the stage. We might have pathology enough, but no pathos. Ajax first becomes tragic when he recovers his wits. If Hamlet is irresponsible, the whole play is a chaos. That he is not so might be proved by evidence enough, were it not labor thrown away.

This feigned madness of Hamlet's is one of the few points in which Shakespeare has kept close to the old story on which he founded his play; and as he never decided without deliberation, so he never acted without unerring judgment. Hamlet *drifts* through the whole tragedy. He never keeps on one tack long enough to get steerage-way, even if, in a nature like his, with those electric streamers of whim and fancy forever wavering across the vault of his brain, the needle of judgment would point in one direction long enough to strike a course by. The scheme of simulated insanity is precisely the one he would have been likely to hit upon, because it enabled him to follow his own bent, and to drift with an apparent purpose, postponing decisive action by the very means he adopts to arrive at its accomplishment, and satisfying himself with the show of doing something that he may escape so much the longer the dreaded necessity of really doing anything at all. It enables him to *play* with life and duty, instead of taking them by the rougher side, where alone any firm grip is possible,—to feel that he is on the way toward accomplishing somewhat, when he is really paltering with his own irresolution. Nothing, I think, could be more finely imagined than this. Voltaire complains that he goes mad without any sufficient object or result. Perfectly true, and precisely what was most natural for him to do, and, accordingly, precisely what Shakespeare meant that he should do. It was delightful to him to indulge his imagination and humor, to prove his capacity for something by playing a part: the one thing he could not do was to bring himself to *act*, unless when surprised by a sudden impulse of suspicion,—as where he kills Polonius, and there he could not see his victim. He discourses admirably of suicide, but does not kill himself; he talks daggers, but uses none. He puts by the chance to kill the king with the excuse that he will not do it while he is praying, lest his soul be saved thereby, though it is more than doubtful whether he believed it himself. He allows himself to be packed off to England, without any motive except that it would for the time take him farther from a present duty: the more disagreeable to a nature like his because it *was* present, and not a mere matter for speculative consideration. When Goethe made his famous comparison of the acorn planted in a vase which it bursts with its growth, and says that in like manner Hamlet is a nature which breaks down under the weight of a duty too great for it to bear, he seems to have considered the character too much from one side. Had Hamlet actually killed himself to escape his too onerous commission, Goethe's conception of him would have been satisfactory enough. But Hamlet was hardly a sentimentalist, like Werther; on the contrary, he saw things only too clearly in the dry north-light of the intellect. It is chance that at last brings him to his end. It would appear rather that Shakespeare intended to show us an imaginative temperament brought face to face with actualities, into any clear relation of sympathy with which it cannot bring itself. The very means that Shakespeare makes use of to lay upon him the obligation of acting—the ghost—really seems to make it all the harder for him to act; for the spectre but gives an additional excitement to his imagination and a fresh topic for his scepticism.

I shall not attempt to evolve any high moral significance

from the play, even if I thought it possible; for that would be aside from the present purpose. The scope of the higher drama is to represent life, not everyday life, it is true, but life lifted above the plane of bread-and-butter associations, by nobler reaches of language, by the influence at once inspiring and modulating of verse, by an intenser play of passion condensing that misty mixture of feeling and reflection which makes the ordinary atmosphere of existence into flashes of thought and phrase whose brief, but terrible, illumination prints the outworn landscape of every-day upon our brains, with its little motives and mean results, in lines of tell-tale fire. The moral office of tragedy is to show us our own weaknesses idealized in grander figures and more awful results,—to teach us that what we pardon in ourselves as venial faults, if they seem to have but slight influence on our immediate fortunes, have arms as long as those of kings, and reach forward to the catastrophe of our lives, that they are dry-rotting the very fibre of will and conscience, so that, if we should be brought to the test of a great temptation or a stringent emergency, we must be involved in a ruin as sudden and complete as that we shudder at in the unreal scene of the theatre. But the primary *object* of a tragedy is not to inculcate a formal moral. Representing life, it teaches, like life, by indirection, by those nods and winks that are thrown away on us blind horses in such profusion. We may learn, to be sure, plenty of lessons from Shakespeare. We are not likely to have kingdoms to divide, crowns foretold us by weird sisters, a father's death to avenge, or to kill our wives from jealousy; but Lear may teach us to draw the line more clearly between a wise generosity and a loose-handed weakness of giving; Macbeth, how one sin involves another, and forever another, by a fatal parthenogenesis, and that the key which unlocks forbidden doors to our will or passion leaves a stain on the hand, that may not be so dark as blood, but that will not out; Hamlet, that all the noblest gifts of person, temperament, and mind slip like sand through the grasp of an infirm purpose; Othello, that the perpetual silt of some one weakness, the eddies of a suspicious temper depositing their one impalpable layer after another, may build up a shoal on which an heroic life and an otherwise magnanimous nature may bilge and go to pieces. All this we may learn, and much more, and Shakespeare was no doubt well aware of all this and more; but I do not believe that he wrote his plays with any such didactic purpose. He knew human nature too well not to know that one thorn of experience is worth a whole wilderness of warning,—that, where one man shapes his life by precept and example, there are a thousand who have it shaped for them by impulse and by circumstances. He did not mean his great tragedies for scarecrows, as if the nailing of one hawk to the barn-door would prevent the next from coming down souse into the hen-yard. No, it is not the poor bleaching victim hung up to moult its draggled feathers in the rain that he wishes to show us. He loves the hawk-nature as well as the hen-nature; and if he is unequalled in anything, it is in that sunny breadth of view, that impregnability of reason, that looks down all ranks and conditions of men, all fortune and misfortune, with the equal eye of the pure artist.

Whether I have fancied anything into Hamlet which the author never dreamed of putting there I do not greatly concern myself to inquire. Poets are always entitled to a royalty on whatever we find in their works; for these fine creations as truly build themselves up in the brain as they are built up with deliberate forethought. Praise art as we will, that which the artist did not mean to put into his work, but which found itself there by some generous process of Nature of which he was as unaware as the blue river is of its rhyme with the blue sky, has

somewhat in it that snatches us into sympathy with higher things than those which come by plot and observation. Goethe wrote his *Faust* in its earliest form without a thought of the deeper meaning which the exposition of an age of criticism was to find in it: without foremeaning it, he had impersonated in Mephistopheles the genius of his century. Shall this subtract from the debt we owe him? Not at all. If orginality were conscious of itself, it would have lost its right to be original. I believe that Shakespeare intended to impersonate in Hamlet not a mere metaphysical entity, but a man of flesh and blood: yet it is certainly curious how prophetically typical the character is of that introversion of mind which is so constant a phenomenon of these latter days, of that over-consciousness which wastes itself in analyzing the motives of action instead of acting.

The old painters had a rule, that all compositions should be pyramidal in form,—a central figure, from which the others slope gradually away on the two sides. Shakespeare probably had never heard of this rule, and, if he had, would not have been likely to respect it more than he has the so-called classical unities of time and place. But he understood perfectly the artistic advantages of gradation, contrast, and relief. Taking Hamlet as the key-note, we find in him weakness of character, which, on the one hand, is contrasted with the feebleness that springs from overweening conceit in Polonius and with frality of temperament in Ophelia, while, on the other hand, it is brought into fuller relief by the steady force of Horatio and the impulsive violence of Laertes, who is resolute from thought-lessness, just as Hamlet is irresolute from overplus of thought.

If we must draw a moral from Hamlet, it would seem to be, that Will is Fate, and that, Will once abdicating, the inevitable successor in the regency is Chance. Had Hamlet acted, instead of musing how good it would be to act, the king might have been the only victim. As it is, all the main actors in the story are the fortuitous sacrifice of his irresolution. We see how a single great vice of character at last draws to itself as allies and confederates all other weaknesses of the man, as in civil wars the timid and the selfish wait to throw themselves upon the stronger side.

> In Life's small things to be resolute and great
> To keep thy muscles trained: know'st thou when Fate
> Thy measure takes? or when she'll say to thee,
> "I find thee worthy, do this thing for me"?

### GEORGE MACDONALD
### "The Elder Hamlet" (1875)
*The Imagination and Other Essays*
1893, pp. 170–81

> 'Tis bitter cold,
> And I am sick at heart.

T he ghost in *Hamlet* is as faithfully treated as any character in the play. Next to Hamlet himself, he is to me the most interesting person of the drama.

The rumour of his appearance is wrapped in the larger rumour of war. Loud preparations for uncertain attack fill the ears of "the subject of the land." The state is troubled. The new king has hardly compassed his election before his marriage with his brother's widow swathes the court in the dust-cloud of shame, which the merriment of its forced revelry can do little to dispel. A feeling is in the moral air to which the words of Francisco, the only words of significance he utters, give the key: "'Tis bitter cold, and I am sick at heart." Into the frosty air, the pallid moonlight, the drunken shouts of Claudius and his court, the bellowing of the cannon from the rampart for the enlargement of the insane clamour that it may beat the drum of its own disgrace at the portals of heaven, glides the silent prisoner of hell, no longer a king of the day walking about his halls, "the observed of all observers," but a thrall of the night, wandering between the bell and the cock, like a jailer on each side of him. A poet tells the tale of the king who lost his garments and ceased to be a king: here is the king who has lost his body, and in the eyes of his court has ceased to be a man. Is the cold of the earth's night pleasant to him after the purging fire? What crimes had the honest ghost committed in his days of nature? He calls them foul crimes! Could such be his? Only who can tell how a ghost, with his doubled experience, may think of this thing or that? The ghost and the fire may between them distinctly recognize that as a foul crime which the man and the court regarded as a weakness at worst, and indeed in a king laudable.

Alas, poor ghost! Around the house he flits, shifting and shadowy, over the ground he once paced in ringing armour—armed still, but his very armour a shadow! It cannot keep out the arrow of the cock's cry, and the heart that pierces is no shadow. Where now is the loaded axe with which, in angry dispute, he smote the ice at his feet that cracked to the blow? Where is the arm that heaved the axe? Wasting in the marble maw of the sepulchre, and the arm he carries now—I know not what it can do, but it cannot slay his murderer. For that he seeks his son's. Doubtless his new ethereal form has its capacities and privileges. It can shift its garb at will; can appear in mail or night-gown, unaided of armourer or tailor; can pass through Hades-gates or chamber-door with equal ease; can work in the ground like mole or pioneer, and let its voice be heard from the cellarage. But there is one to whom it cannot appear, one whom the ghost can see, but to whom he cannot show himself. She has built a doorless, windowless wall between them, and sees the husband of her youth no more. Outside her heart—that is the night in which he wanders, while the palace-windows are flaring, and the low wind throbs to the wassail shouts: within, his murderer sits by the wife of his bosom, and in the orchard the spilt poison is yet gnawing at the roots of the daisies.

Twice has the ghost grown out of the night upon the eyes of the sentinels. With solemn march, slow and stately, three times each night, has he walked by them; they, jellied with fear, have uttered no challenge. They seek Horatio, who the third night speaks to him as a scholar can. To the first challenge he makes no answer, but stalks away; to the second,

> It lifted up its head, and did address
> Itself to motion, like as it would speak;

but the gaoler cock calls him, and the kingly shape

> started like a guilty thing
> Upon a fearful summons;

and then

> shrunk in haste away,
> And vanished from our sight.

Ah, that summons! at which majesty welks and shrivels, the king and soldier starts and cowers, and, armour and all, withers from the air!

But why has he not spoken before? why not now ere the cock could claim him? He cannot trust the men. His court has forsaken his memory—crowds with as eager discontent about the mildewed ear as ever about his wholesome brother, and how should he trust mere sentinels? There is but one who will heed his tale. A word to any other would but defeat his intent. Out of the multitude of courtiers and subjects, in all the land of Denmark, there is but one whom he can trust—his student-

son. Him he has not yet found—the condition of a ghost involving strange difficulties.

Or did the horror of the men at the sight of him wound and repel him? Does the sense of regal dignity, not yet exhausted for all the fasting in fires, unite with that of grievous humiliation to make him shun their speech?

But Horatio—why does the ghost not answer him ere the time of the cock is come? Does he fold the cloak of indignation around him because his son's friend has addressed him as an intruder on the night, an usurper of the form that is his own? The companions of the speaker take note that he is offended and stalks away.

Much has the kingly ghost to endure in his attempt to re-open relations with the world he has left: when he has overcome his wrath and returns, that moment Horatio again insults him, calling him an illusion. But this time he will bear it, and opens his mouth to speak. It is too late; the cock is awake, and he must go. Then alas for the buried majesty of Denmark! with upheaved halberts they strike at the shadow, and would stop it if they might—usage so grossly unfitting that they are instantly ashamed of it themselves, recognizing the offence in the majesty of the offended. But he is already gone. The proud, angry king has found himself but a thing of nothing to his body-guard—for he has lost the body which was their guard. Still, not even yet has he learned how little it lies in the power of an honest ghost to gain credit for himself or his tale! His very privileges are against him.

All this time his son is consuming his heart in the knowledge of a mother capable of so soon and so utterly forgetting such a husband, and in pity and sorrow for the dead father who has had such a wife. He is thirty years of age, an obedient, honourable son—a man of thought, of faith, of aspiration. Him now the ghost seeks, his heart burning like a coal with the sense of unendurable wrong. He is seeking the one drop that can fall cooling on that heart—the sympathy, the answering rage and grief of his boy. But when at length he finds him, the generous, loving father has to see that son tremble like an aspen-leaf in his doubtful presence. He has exposed himself to the shame of eyes and the indignities of dullness, that he may pour the pent torrent of his wrongs into his ears, but his disfranchisement from the flesh tells against him even with his son: the young Hamlet is doubtful of the identity of the apparition with his father. After all the burning words of the phantom, the spirit he has seen may yet be a devil; the devil has power to assume a pleasing shape, and is perhaps taking advantage of his melancholy to damn him.

Armed in the complete steel of a suit well known to the eyes of the sentinels, visionary none the less, with useless truncheon in hand, resuming the memory of old martial habits, but with quiet countenance, more in sorrow than in anger, troubled—not now with the thought of the hell-day to which he must sleepless return, but with that unceasing ache at the heart, which ever, as often as he is released into the cooling air of the upper world, draws him back to the region of his wrongs—where having fallen asleep in his orchard, in sacred security and old custom, suddenly, by cruel assault, he was flung into Hades, where horror upon horror awaited him—worst horror of all, the knowledge of his wife!—armed he comes, in shadowy armour but how real sorrow! Still it is not pity he seeks from his son: he needs it not—he can endure. There is no weakness in the ghost. It is but to the imperfect human sense that he is shadowy. To himself he knows his doom his deliverance; that the hell in which he finds himself shall endure but until it has burnt up the hell he has found within him—until the evil he was and is capable of shall have dropped from him into the lake of fire; he nerves himself to bear. And the cry of revenge that comes from the sorrowful lips is the cry of a king and a Dane rather than of a wronged man. It is for public justice and not individual vengeance he calls. He cannot endure that the royal bed of Denmark should be a couch for luxury and damned incest. To stay this he would bring the murderer to justice. There is a worse wrong, for which he seeks no revenge: it involves his wife; and there comes in love, and love knows no amends but amendment, seeks only the repentance tenfold more needful to the wronger than the wronged. It is not alone the father's care for the human nature of his son that warns him to take no measures against his mother; it is the husband's tenderness also for her who once lay in his bosom. The murdered brother, the dethroned king, the dishonoured husband, the tormented sinner, is yet a gentle ghost. Has suffering already begun to make him, like Prometheus, wise?

But to measure the gentleness, the forgiveness, the tenderness of the ghost, we must well understand his wrongs. The murder is plain; but there is that which went before and is worse, yet is not so plain to every eye that reads the story. There is that without which the murder had never been, and which, therefore, is a cause of all the wrong. For listen to what the ghost reveals when at length he has withdrawn his son that he may speak with him alone, and Hamlet has forestalled the disclosure of the murderer:

> Ay, that incestuous, that adulterate beast,
> With witchcraft of his wit, with traitorous gifts,
> (O wicked wit and gifts that have the power
> So to seduce!) won to his shameful lust
> The will of my most seeming virtuous queen:
> Oh, Hamlet, what a falling off was there!
> From me, whose love was of that dignity
> That it went hand in hand even with the vow
> I made to her in marriage, and to decline
> Upon a wretch, whose natural gifts were poor
> To those of mine!
> But virtue—as it never will be moved
> Though lewdness court it in a shape of heaven,
> So lust, though to a radiant angel linked,
> Will sate itself in a celestial bed,
> And prey on garbage.

Reading this passage, can any one doubt that the ghost charges his late wife with adultery, as the root of all his woes? It is true that, obedient to the ghost's injunctions, as well as his own filial instincts, Hamlet accuses his mother of no more than was patent to all the world; but unless we suppose the ghost misinformed or mistaken, we must accept this charge. And had Gertrude not yielded to the witchcraft of Claudius' wit, Claudius would never have murdered Hamlet. Through her his life was dishonoured, and his death violent and premature: unhuzled, disappointed, unaneled, he woke to the air—not of his orchard-blossoms, but of a prison-house, the lightest word of whose terrors would freeze the blood of the listener. What few men can say, he could—that his love to his wife had kept even step with the vow he made to her in marriage; and his son says of him—

> so loving to my mother
> That he might not beteem the winds of heaven
> Visit her face too roughly;

and this was her return! Yet is it thus he charges his son concerning her:

> But howsoever thou pursu'st this act,
> Taint not thy mind, nor let thy soul contrive
> Against thy mother aught; leave her to heaven,

> And to those thorns that in her bosom lodge,
> To prick and sting her.

And may we not suppose it to be for her sake in part that the ghost insists, with fourfold repetition, upon a sword-sworn oath to silence from Horatio and Marcellus?

Only once again does he show himself—not now in armour upon the walls, but in his gown and in his wife's closet.

Ever since his first appearance, that is, all the time filling the interval between the first and second acts, we may presume him to have haunted the palace unseen, waiting what his son would do. But the task has been more difficult than either had supposed. The ambassadors have gone to Norway and returned; but Hamlet has done nothing. Probably he has had no opportunity; certainly he has had no clear vision of duty. But now all through the second and third acts, together occupying, it must be remembered, only one day, something seems imminent. The play has been acted, and Hamlet has gained some assurance, yet the one chance presented of killing the king—at his prayers—he has refused. He is now in his mother's closet, whose eyes he has turned into her very soul. There, and then, the ghost once more appears—come, he says, to whet his son's almost blunted purpose. But, as I have said, he does not know all the disadvantages of one who, having forsaken the world, has yet business therein to which he would persuade; he does not know how hard it is for a man to give credence to a ghost; how thoroughly he is justified in delay, and the demand for more perfect proof. He does not know what good reasons his son has had for uncertainty, or how much natural and righteous doubt has had to do with what he takes for the blunting of his purpose. Neither does he know how much more tender his son's conscience is than his own, or how necessary it is to him to be sure before he acts. As little perhaps does he understand how hateful to Hamlet is the task laid upon him—the killing of one wretched villain in the midst of a corrupt and contemptible court, one of a world of whose women his mother may be the type!

Whatever the main object of the ghost's appearance, he has spoken but a few words concerning the matter between him and Hamlet, when he turns abruptly from it to plead with his son for his wife. The ghost sees and mistakes the terror of her looks; imagines that, either from some feeling of his presence, or from the power of Hamlet's words, her conscience is thoroughly roused, and that her vision, her conception of the facts, is now more than she can bear. She and her fighting soul are at odds. She is a kingdom divided against itself. He fears the consequences. He would not have her go mad. He would not have her die yet. Even while ready to start at the summons of that hell to which she has sold him, he forgets his vengeance on her seducer in his desire to comfort her. He dares not, if he could, manifest himself to her: what word of consolation could she hear from *his* lips? Is not the thought of him her one despair? He turns to his son for help: he cannot console his wife; his son must take his place. Alas! even now he thinks better of her than she deserves; for it is only the fancy of her son's madness that is terrifying her: he gazes on the apparition of which she sees nothing, and from his looks she anticipates an ungovernable outbreak.

> But look; amazement on thy mother sits!
> Oh; step between her and her fighting soul
> Conceit in weakest bodies strongest works.
> Speak to her, Hamlet.

The call to his son to soothe his wicked mother is the ghost's last utterance. For a few moments, sadly regardful of the two, he stands—while his son seeks in vain to reveal to his mother the presence of his father—a few moments of piteous action, all but ruining the remnant of his son's sorely-harassed self-possession—his whole concern his wife's distress, and neither his own doom nor his son's duty; then, as if lost in despair at the impassable gulf betwixt them, revealed by her utter incapacity for even the imagination of his proximity, he turns away, and steals out at the portal. Or perhaps he has heard the black cock crow, and is wanted beneath: his turn has come.

Will the fires ever cleanse *her?* Will his love ever lift him above the pain of its loss? Will eternity ever be bliss, ever be endurable to poor *King Hamlet?*

Alas! even the memory of the poor ghost is insulted. Night after night on the stage his effigy appears—cadaverous, sepulchral—no longer as Shakspere must have represented him, aërial, shadowy, gracious, the thin corporeal husk of an eternal—shall I say ineffaceable?—sorrow! It is no hollow monotone that can rightly upbear such words as his, but a sound mingled of distance and wind in the pine-tops, of agony and love, of horror and hope and loss and judgment—a voice of endless and sweetest inflection, yet with a shuddering echo in it as from the caves of memory, on whose walls are written the eternal blazon that must not be to ears of flesh and blood. The spirit that can assume form at will must surely be able to bend that form to completest and most delicate expression, and the part of the ghost in the play offers work worthy of the highest artist. The would-be actor takes from it vitality and motion, endowing it instead with the rigidity of death, as if the soul had resumed its cast-off garment, the stiffened and mouldy corpse—whose frozen deadness it could ill model to the utterance of its lively will!

## ANATOLE FRANCE
### "Hamlet at the Comédie-Française" (1886)
### *On Life and Letters, First Series*
### tr. A. W. Evans
### 1924, pp. 1–7

G ood-night, sweet prince, and flights of angels sing thee to thy rest!" That is what, on Tuesday, at midnight, we said with Horatio to young Hamlet, as we were leaving the Théâtre-Français. And, surely, we ought to wish a good-night to him who had caused us to pass so delightful an evening. Yes, Prince Hamlet is a sweet prince. He is handsome and he is unhappy; he knows everything and he can do nothing. He is to be envied and to be pitied. He is worse and better then any of us. He is a man, he is man, he is the whole of man. And there were, I swear to you, at least twenty persons in the house who had that feeling. "Good-night, sweet prince!" we cannot leave you without having our heads full of you, and for the last three days I have had no other thoughts than yours.

I felt, when I saw you, a sad joy, my Prince. And that is more than a joyous joy. I will whisper to you that the house seemed to me just a little heedless and frivolous; but we must not complain too much of that and we must not be at all astonished at it. It was a house made up of French men and French women. You were not in evening dress, you had no amorous intrigue in the world of high finance, and you did not wear a gardenia in your button-hole. That is why the ladies coughed a little, as they ate iced fruits in their boxes. Your adventures could not interest them. They are not fashionable adventures; they are only human adventures. You force people to think, and that is a wrong we will not pardon you here. However, there were here and there throughout the house some spirits whom you deeply moved. In speaking to them of yourself you spoke to them of themselves. That is why they prefer you to all the other beings who, like you, have been created by genius. A lucky chance placed me in the house beside M. Auguste Dorchain. He understands you, my Prince, just as he understands Racine, because he is a poet. I believe that I also understand you a little, because I have just come from the sea. . . . Oh! do not be afraid that I am going to say that you are two oceans. That is all words, words, and you do not care about words. No, I only mean that I understand you because, after two months of rest and quiet amidst wide horizons, I have become very simple and very accessible to what is truly beautiful, great, and profound. In our Paris, in winter, we readily acquire a taste for pretty things, for fashionable affectation, and the intricate refinements of the coteries. But one's perception is elevated and purified in the fruitful idleness of rural walks and amid the broad horizons of sea and fields. When we come back from them we are quite ready for intercourse with the wild genius of a Shakespeare. That is why you have been welcome, Prince Hamlet. It is why all your thoughts wander confusedly upon my lips, and envelop me with terror, poetry, and sadness. You saw, of course, that in the *Revue bleue* and elsewhere the question of the origin of your melancholy has been raised. It has been judged to be so deep that even the most frightful domestic catastrophes were incapable of having formed it in all its extent. A very distinguished political economist, M. Emile de Laveleye, thinks that it must be the sadness of a political economist. And he has written an article with the sole object of proving this theory. He intimates that he and his friend, Lanfrey, experienced a similar melancholy after the *coup d'état* of 1851, and that you, Prince Hamlet, must have suffered, even more than they did, from the terrible condition to which the usurper Claudius had reduced the affairs of Denmark.

In truth, I believe that you were deeply concerned for the fate of your country, and I applaud the words used by Fortinbras when he commanded four captains to bear your body like a soldier to the stage. "Had Hamlet lived," he exclaimed, "he would have proved most royally." But I do not think your melancholy was quite that of M. Emile de Laveleye. I believe that it was nobler and more intelligent. I believe that it was inspired by a keen perception of destiny. Not Denmark only, but the whole world appeared gloomy to you. You had faith in nothing, not even, as M. de Laveleye has, in the principles of public law. Let those who doubt this recall the fine and bitter prayer which left your lips when already growing cold in death.

O God! Horatio, what a wounded name,
Things standing thus unknown, shall live behind
   me.
If thou didst ever hold me in thy heart,
Absent thee from felicity awhile,
And in this harsh world draw thy breath in pain,
To tell my story.

These were your last words. He to whom they were addressed had not, like you, a family poisoned by crimes; he was not, like you, an assassin. His was an unfettered, wise, and faithful nature. He was a happy man, if such there be. But you, Prince Hamlet, knew that there never was one. You knew that all is evil in the universe. We must out with it, you are a pessimist. Doubtless, your destiny drove you to despair; it was tragic. But your nature was consonant with your destiny. That is what renders you so admirable; you were formed to taste misfortune, and you had full opportunity for exercising your taste. You were well served, Prince. And how you relish the evil in which you are steeped! What subtlety of taste! Oh! you are a connoisseur, a *gourmet* in sufferings.

Of such a nature did the great Shakespeare give you birth. And it seems to me that he was hardly an optimist himself at the time he created you. From 1601 to 1608, he, with his enchanted hands, gave life to what is, I think, a pretty large crowd of afflicted or violent shades. It was then that he showed Desdemona perishing through Iago, and the blood of a fatherly old king staining the little hands of Lady Macbeth, and poor Cordelia, and you, his favourite, and Timon of Athens.

Yes, even Timon! There is decided reason for believing that Shakespeare was a pessimist like you. What will his colleague, M. Moreau, the author of the second *Falcon*, say about it, he who, I am told, maltreats the poor pessimists so violently every evening at the Vaudeville. Oh! he gives them a bad quarter of an hour every day, I assure you. I pity them. There are, indeed, happy people everywhere who jest at them without pity. In their place I would not know where to hide myself. But Hamlet ought to give them courage. They have Job and Shakespeare on their side. That redresses the balance a little. So that M. Paul Bourget is saved this time. And it is you who have done it, Prince Hamlet.

I have under my eyes, as I write, an old German engraving, which represents you, but in which I can hardly recognise you. It represents you as you appeared in the Berlin theatre about 1780. You did not then wear that solemn mourning of which your mother speaks, that doublet, those hose, that mantle, that cap with which Delacroix so nobly clothed you when he fixed your type in his awkward but sublime drawings, and which M. Mounet-Sully wears with so virile a grace and so many poetic attitudes.

No! you appeared before the good people of Berlin in the eighteenth century in a costume which would seem very strange to us to-day. You were clad—my engraving proves it— in the latest French fashion. Your hair was elaborately dressed and powdered; you wore an embroidered collar, satin knee-breeches, silk stockings, buckled shoes, and a little mantle in the Court style, in short the whole mourning costume of the courtiers of Versailles. I was forgetting your Henri IV. hat, the true hat of the nobility in the time of the States-General. Thus equipped, with your sword at your side, you lie at Ophelia's feet, Ophelia who, upon my word, is exceedingly pretty in her hooped gown and lofty head-dress *à la* Marie-Antoinette, which is surmounted by a great plume of ostrich feathers. All the other personages are dressed in a corresponding style. They are present, with you, at the tragedy of Gonzaga and Baptista. Your beautiful Louis XV. armchair is empty and we can see all the flowers of its upholstery. Already you creep on the ground, you spy on the king's face for the mute confession of the crime which you are charged to avenge. The king also wears, just as Louis XVI. did, a splendid Henri IV. hat. Perhaps you think that I am going to smile and to scoff, and to boast about the progress of our decorations and our costumes. You are mistaken. Most certainly, if you are no longer dressed in the fashion of my old print, and no longer look like the Comte de Provence wearing mourning for the Dauphin, and if your Ophelia is no longer dressed like Mesdames, I do not regret it in the least. Far from that, I like you much better as you are now. But dress is nothing to you, you can wear any costume you please; they will all suit you if they are beautiful. You are of all times and of all countries. Your soul is of the same age as all our souls. We live together, Prince Hamlet, and you are what we are, a man in the midst of universal woe. Your words and your actions have been cavilled at. You have been shown to be inconsistent with yourself. How are we to understand this incomprehensible personage? So they have asked. He thinks in turn like a monk of the Middle Ages and like a scholar of the Renaissance; his mind is philosophic and yet it is full of impishness. He has a horror of lies and his life is only one long lie. He is irresolute, that is clear, and yet certain critics have pronounced him to be full of decision, and we cannot entirely contradict them. Lastly, my Prince, they have said that you were a warehouse of thoughts, a heap of contradictions, and not a human being. But that, on the contrary, is the sign of your profound humanity. You are prompt and slow, audacious and timid, kind and cruel; you believe and you doubt, you are wise and, above all, you are mad. In a word, you live. Which of us does not resemble you in something? Which of us thinks without contradictions and acts without incoherence? Which of us is not mad? Which of us may not say to you with a mixture of pity, sympathy, admiration, and horror: "Good-night, sweet prince!"

# *Troilus and Cressida*

Eternal reader, you have here a new play, never staled with the stage, never clapper-clawed with the palms of the vulgar, and yet passing full of the palm comical; for it is a birth of your brain that never undertook anything comical vainly. And were but the vain names of comedies changed for the titles of commodities, or of plays for pleas, you should see all those grand censors, that now style them such vanities, flock to them for the main grace of their gravities, especially this author's comedies, that are so framed to the life that they serve for the most common commentaries of all the actions of our lives, showing such a dexterity and power of wit that the most displeased with plays are pleased with his comedies. And all such dull and heavy-witted worldlings as were never capable of the wit of a comedy, coming by report of them to his representations, have found that wit there that they never found in themselves and have parted better witted than they came, feeling an edge of wit set upon them more than ever they dreamed they had brain to grind it on. So much and such savored salt of wit is in his comedies that they seem, for their height of pleasure, to be born in that sea that brought forth Venus. Amongst all there is none more witty than this: and had I time I would comment upon it, though I know it needs not, for so much as will make you think your testern well bestowed, but for so much worth as even poor I know to be stuffed in it. It deserves such a labor as well as the best comedy in Terence or Plautus. And believe this, that when he is gone and his comedies out of sale, you will scramble for them and set up a new English Inquisition. Take this for a warning, and at the peril of your pleasure's loss, and judgment's, refuse not, nor like this the less for not being sullied with the smoky breath of the multitude; but thank fortune for the 'scape it hath made amongst you, since by the grand possessors' wills I believe you should have prayed for them rather than been prayed. And so I leave all such to be prayed for, for the state of their wits' healths, that will not praise it. Vale.—WILLIAM SHAKESPEARE, "A Never Writer, to an Ever Reader: News," *Troilus and Cressida*, 1609

The original story was written by one Lollius, a Lombard, in

Latin verse, and translated by Chaucer into English; intended, I suppose, a satire on the inconstancy of women: I find nothing of it among the Ancients; not so much as the name once Cressida mentioned. Shakespeare, . . . in the apprenticeship of his writing, modelled it into that play which is now called by the name of *Troilus and Cressida*; but so lamely is it left to us, that it is not divided into acts; which fault I ascribe to the actors who printed it after Shakespeare's death; and that too so carelessly, that a more uncorrect copy I never saw. For the play itself, the author seems to have begun it with some fire; the characters of Pandarus and Thersites are promising enough; but as if he grew weary of his task, after an entrance or two, he lets 'em fall: and the later part of the tragedy is nothing but a confusion of drums and trumpets, excursions and alarms. The chief persons, who give name to the tragedy, are left alive; Cressida is false, and is not punished. Yet, after all, because the play was Shakespeare's, and that there appeared in some places of it the admirable genius of the author, I undertook to remove that heap of rubbish under which many excellent thoughts lay wholly buried. Accordingly, I new modelled the plot; threw out many unnecessary persons; improved those characters which were begun and left unfinished, as Hector, Troilus, Pandarus, and Thersites; and added that of Andromache. After this I made, with no small trouble, an order and connection of all the scenes; removing them from the places where they were inartifically set; and though it was impossible to keep 'em all unbroken, because the scene must be sometimes in the city and sometimes in the camp, yet I have so ordered them that there is a coherence of 'em with one another, and a dependence on the main design: no leaping from Troy to the Grecian tents, and thence back again in the same act; but a due proportion of time allowed for every motion. I need not say that I have refined his language, which before was obsolete; but I am willing to acknowledge that as I have often drawn his English nearer to our times, so I have sometimes conformed my own to his; and consequently, the language is not altogether so pure as it is significant. The scenes of Pandarus and Cressida, of Troilus and Pandarus, of Andromache with Hector and the Trojans, in the second act, are wholly new; together with that of Nestor and Ulysses with Thersites, and that of Thersites with Ajax and Achilles. I will not weary my reader with the scenes which are added to Pandarus and the lovers, in the third; and those of Thersites, which are wholly altered; but I cannot omit the last scene in it, which is almost half the act, betwixt Troilus and Hector. The occasion of raising it was hinted to me by Mr Betterton: the contrivance and working of it was my own. They who think to do me an injury by saying that it is an imitation of the scene betwixt Brutus and Cassius, do me an honour by supposing I could imitate the incomparable Shakespeare; but let me add that if Shakespeare's scene, or the faulty copy of it in *Amintor and Melantius*, had never been, yet Euripides had furnished me with an excellent example in his *Iphigenia*, between Agamemnon and Menelaus; and from thence, indeed, the last turn of it is borrowed. The occasion which Shakespeare, Euripides, and Fletcher have all taken is the same; grounded upon friendship: and the quarrel of two virtuous men, raised by natural degrees to the extremity of passion, is conducted in all three to the declination of the same passion, and concludes with a warm renewing of their friendship. But the particular groundwork which Shakespeare has taken is incomparably the best; because he has not only chosen two of the greatest heroes of their age, but has likewise interested the liberty of Rome, and their own honours who were the redeemers of it, in this debate. And if he has made Brutus, who was naturally a patient man, to fly into excess at

first, let it be remembered in his defence that, just before, he had received the news of Portia's death; whom the poet, on purpose neglecting a little chronology, supposes to have died before Brutus, only to give him an occasion of being more easily exasperated. Add to this that the injury he had received from Cassius had long been brooding in his mind; and that a melancholy man, upon consideration of an affront, especially from a friend, would be more eager in his passion than he who had given it, though naturally more choleric.—JOHN DRYDEN, "Preface" to *Troilus and Cressida*, 1679

This play is more correctly written than most of Shakespeare's compositions, but it is not one of those in which either the extent of his views or elevation of his fancy is fully displayed. As the story abounded with materials, he has exerted little invention; but he has diversified his characters with great variety, and preserved them with great exactness. His vicious characters sometimes disgust, but cannot corrupt, for both Cressida and Pandarus are detested and contemned. The comic characters seem to have been the favourites of the writer, they are of the superficial kind, and exhibit more of manners than nature, but they are copiously filled and powerfully impressed.

Shakespeare has in his story followed for the greater part the old book of Caxton, which was then very popular; but the character of Thersites, of which it makes no mention, is a proof that this play was written after Chapman had published his version of Homer.—SAMUEL JOHNSON, *Notes on Shakespeare's Plays*, 1768

*Troilus and Cressida* is the only play of Shakspeare which he allowed to be printed without being previously represented. It seems as if he here for once wished, without caring for theatrical effect, to satisfy the nicety of his peculiar wit, and the inclination of a certain guile, if I may say so, in the characterization. The whole is one continued irony of that crown of all heroic tales, the tale of Troy. The contemptible nature of the origin of the Trojan war, the laziness and discord with which it was carried on, so that the siege was made to last ten years, are only placed in clearer light by the noble descriptions, the sage and ingenious maxims with which the work overflows, and the high ideas which the heroes entertain of themselves and each other. Agamemnon's stately behaviour, Menelaus' irritation, Nestor's experience, Ulysses' cunning, are all productive of no effect; when they have at last arranged a single combat between the coarse braggart Ajax and Hector, the latter will not fight in good earnest, as Ajax is his cousin. Achilles is treated worst: after having long stretched himself out in arrogant idleness, and passed his time in the company of Thersites the buffoon, he falls upon Hector at a moment when he is defenceless, and kills him by means of his myrmidons. In all this let no man conceive that any indignity was intended to the venerable Homer. Shakspeare had not the *Iliad* before him, but the chivalrous romances of the Trojan war derived from *Dares Phrygius*. From this source also he took the love-intrigue of *Troilus and Cressida*, a story at one time so popular in England, that the name of Troilus had become proverbial for faithful and ill-requited love, and Cressida for female falsehood. The name of the agent between them, Pandarus, has even been adopted into the English language to signify those personages (*panders*) who dedicate themselves to similar services for inexperienced persons of both sexes. The endless contrivances of the courteous Pandarus to bring the two lovers together, who do not stand in need of him, as Cressida requires no seduction, are comic in the extreme. The manner in which this treacherous beauty excites while she refuses, and converts the virgin modesty which she pretends, into a means of seductive allurement, is portrayed in colours extremely elegant, though certainly somewhat voluptuous. Troilus, the pattern of lovers, looks patiently on, while his mistress enters into an intrigue with Diomed. No doubt, he swears that he will be revenged; but notwithstanding his violence in the fight next day, he does no harm to any one, and ends with only high-sounding threats. In a word, in this heroic comedy, where from traditional fame and the pomp of poetry, every thing seems to lay claim to admiration, Shakspeare did not wish that any room should be left, except, perhaps, in the character of Hector, for esteem and sympathy; but in this double meaning of the picture, he has afforded us the most choice entertainment.—AUGUST WILHELM SCHLEGEL, *Lectures on Dramatic Art and Literature*, 1809, tr. John Black

This is one of the most loose and desultory of our author's plays: it rambles on just as it happens, but it overtakes, together with some indifferent matter, a prodigious number of fine things in its way. Troilus himself is no character: he is merely a common lover: but Cressida and her uncle Pandarus are hit off with proverbial truth. By the speeches given to the leaders of the Grecian host, Nestor, Ulysses, Agamemnon, Achilles, Shakespear seems to have known them as well as if he had been a spy sent by the Trojans into the enemy's camp—to say nothing of their affording very lofty examples of didactic eloquence. . . .

The character of Hector, in a few slight indications which appear of it, is made very amiable. His death is sublime, and shews in a striking light the mixture of barbarity and heroism of the age. The threats of Achilles are fatal; they carry their own means of execution with them.

> Come here about me, you my myrmidons,
> Mark what I say.—Attend me where I wheel:
> Strike not a stroke, but keep yourselves in breath;
> And when I have the bloody Hector found,
> Empale him with your weapons round about,
> In fellest manner execute your arms.
> Follow me, sirs, and my proceeding eye.

He then finds Hector and slays him, as if he had been hunting down a wild beast. There is something revolting as well as terrific in the ferocious coolness with which he singles out his prey: nor does the splendour of the atchievement reconcile us to the cruelty of the means.

The characters of Cressida and Pandarus are very amusing and instructive. The disinterested willingness of Pandarus to serve his friend in an affair which lies next his heart is immediately brought forward. 'Go thy way, Troilus, go thy way; had I a sister were a grace, or a daughter was a goddess, he should take his choice. O admirable man! Paris, Paris is dirt to him, and I warrant Helen, to change, would give money to boot.' This is the language he addresses to his niece: nor is she much behindhand in coming into the plot. Her head is as light and fluttering as her heart. 'It is the prettiest villain, she fetches her breath so short as a new-ta'en sparrow.' Both characters are originals, and quite different from what they are in Chaucer. In Chaucer, Cressida is represented as a grave, sober, considerate personage (a widow—he cannot tell her age, nor whether she has children or no) who has an alternate eye to her character, her interest, and her pleasure: Shakespear's Cressida is a giddy girl, an unpractised jilt, who falls in love with Troilus, as she afterwards deserts him, from mere levity and thoughtlessness of temper. She may be wooed and won to any thing and from any thing, at a moment's warning; the other knows very well what she would be at, and sticks to it, and is more governed by substantial reasons than by caprice or vanity. Pandarus again, in Chaucer's story, is a friendly sort of go-between, tolerably

busy, officious, and forward in bringing matters to bear: but in Shakespear he has 'a stamp exclusive and professional': he wears the badge of his trade; he is a regular knight of the game. The difference of the manner in which the subject is treated arises perhaps less from intention, than from the different genius of the two poets. There is no *double entendre* in the characters of Chaucer: they are either quite serious or quite comic. In Shakespear the ludicrous and ironical are constantly blended with the stately and the impassioned. We see Chaucer's characters as they saw themselves, not as they appeared to others or might have appeared to the poet. He is as deeply implicated in the affairs of his personages as they could be themselves. He had to go a long journey with each of them, and became a kind of necessary confidant. There is little relief, or light and shade in his pictures. The conscious smile is not seen lurking under the brow of grief or impatience. Every thing with him is intense and continuous—a working out of what went before.—Shakespear never committed himself to his characters. He trifled, laughed, or wept with them as he chose. He has no prejudices for or against them; and it seems a matter of perfect indifference whether he shall be in jest or earnest. According to him 'the web of our lives is of a mingled yarn, good and ill together." His genius was dramatic, as Chaucer's was historical. He saw both sides of a question, the different views taken of it according to the different interests of the parties concerned, and he was at once an actor and spectator in the scene. If any thing, he is too various and flexible: too full of transitions, of glancing lights, of salient points. If Chaucer followed up his subject too doggedly, perhaps Shakespear was too volatile and heedless. The Muse's wing too often lifted him from off his feet. He made infinite excursions to the right and the left.

> He hath done
> Mad and fantastic execution,
> Engaging and redeeming of himself
> With such a careless force and forceless care,
> As if that luck in very spite of cunning
> Bad him win all.

Chaucer attended chiefly to the real and natural, that is, to the involuntary and inevitable impressions on the mind in given circumstances; Shakespear exhibited also the possible and the fantastical,—not only what things are in themselves, but whatever they might seem to be, their different reflections, their endless combinations. He lent his fancy, wit, invention, to others, and borrowed their feelings in return. Chaucer excelled in the force of habitual sentiment; Shakespear added to it every variety of passion, every suggestion of thought or accident. Chaucer described external objects with the eye of a painter, or he might be said to have embodied them with the hand of a sculptor, every part is so thoroughly made out, and tangible:—Shakespear's imagination threw over them a lustre

> Prouder than when blue Iris bends.

Every thing in Chaucer has a downright reality. A simile or a sentiment is as if it were given in upon evidence. In Shakespear the commonest matter-of-fact has a romantic grace about it; or seems to float with the breath of imagination in a freer element. No one could have more depth of feeling or observation than Chaucer, but he wanted resources of invention to lay open the stores of nature or the human heart with the same radiant light that Shakespear has done. However fine or profound the thought, we know what is coming, whereas the effect of reading Shakespear is 'like the eye of vassalage at unawares encountering majesty.' Chaucer's mind was consecutive, rather than discursive. He arrived at truth through a certain process; Shakespear saw every thing by intuition.

Chaucer had a great variety of power, but he could do only one thing at once. He set himself to work on a particular subject. His ideas were kept separate, labelled, ticketed and parcelled out in a set form, in pews and compartments by themselves. They did not play into one another's hands. They did not re-act upon one another, as the blower's breath moulds the yielding glass. There is something hard and dry in them. What is the most wonderful thing in Shakespear's faculties is their excessive sociability, and how they gossiped and compared notes together.—WILLIAM HAZLITT, *"Troilus and Cressida," Characters of Shakespear's Plays, 1817*

The *Troilus and Cressida* of Shakespeare can scarcely be classed with his dramas of Greek and Roman history; but it forms an intermediate link between the fictitious Greek and roman histories, which we may call legendary dramas, and the proper ancient histories; that is, between the *Pericles* or *Titus Andronicus*, and the *Coriolanus*, or *Julius Cæsar. Cymbeline* is a *congener* with *Pericles*, and distinguished from *Lear* by not having any declared prominent object. But where shall we class the *Timon of Athens?* Perhaps immediately below *Lear*. It is a *Lear* of the satirical drama; a *Lear* of domestic or ordinary life;—a local eddy of passion on the high road of society, while all around is the week-day goings on of wind and weather; a *Lear*, therefore, without its soul-searching flashes, its ear-cleaving thunderclaps, its meteoric splendors,—without the contagion and the fearful sympathies of nature, the fates, the furies, the frenzied elements, dancing in and out, now breaking through, and scattering,—now hand in hand with,—the fierce or fantastic group of human passions, crimes, and anguishes, reeling on the unsteady ground, in a wild harmony to the shock and the swell of an earthquake. But my present subject was *Troilus and Cressida*; and I suppose that, scarcely knowing what to say of it, I by a cunning of instinct ran off to subjects on which I should find it difficult not to say too much, though certain after all that I should still leave the better part unsaid, and the gleaning for others richer than my own harvest.

Indeed, there is no one of Shakspeare's plays harder to characterize. The name and the remembrances connected with it, prepare us for the representation of attachment no less faithful than fervent on the side of the youth, and of sudden and shameless inconstancy on the part of the lady. And this is, indeed, as the gold thread on which the scenes are strung, though often kept out of sight and out of mind by gems of greater value than itself. But as Shakspeare calls forth nothing from the mausoleum of history, or the catacombs of tradition, without giving, or eliciting, some permanent and general interest, and brings forward no subject which he does not moralize or intellectualize,—so here he has drawn in Cressida the portrait of a vehement passion, that, having its true origin and proper cause in warmth of temperament, fastens on, rather than fixes to, some one object by liking and temporary preference.

> There's language in her eye, her cheek, her lip,
> Nay, her foot speaks; her wanton spirits look out
> At every joint and motive of her body.

This Shakspeare has contrasted with the profound affection represented in Troilus, and alone worthy the name of love;—affection, passionate indeed,—swoln with the confluence of youthful instincts and youthful fancy, and growing in the radiance of hope newly risen, in short enlarged by the collective sympathies of nature;—but still having a depth of calmer element in a will stronger than desire, more entire than choice, and which gives permanence to its own act by converting it into faith and duty. Hence with excellent

judgment, and with an excellence higher than mere judgment can give, at the close of the play, when Cressida has sunk into infamy below retrieval and beneath hope, the same will, which had been the substance and the basis of his love, while the restless pleasures and passionate longings, like sea-waves, had tossed but on its surface,—this same moral energy is represented as snatching him aloof from all neighbourhood with her dishonour, from all lingering fondness and languishing regrets, whilst it rushes with him into other and nobler duties, and deepens the channel, which his heroic brother's death had left empty for its collected flood. Yet another secondary and subordinate purpose Shakspeare has inwoven with his delineation of these two characters,—that of opposing the inferior civilization, but purer morals, of the Trojans to the refinements, deep policy, but duplicity and sensual corruptions, of the Greeks.

To all this, however, so little comparative projection is given,—nay, the masterly group of Agamemnon, Nestor, and Ulysses, and, still more in advance, that of Achilles, Ajax, and Thersites, so manifestly occupy the foreground, that the subservience and vassalage of strength and animal courage to intellect and policy seems to be the lesson most often in our poet's view, and which he has taken little pains to connect with the former more interesting moral impersonated in the titular hero and heroine of the drama. But I am half inclined to believe, that Shakspeare's main object, or shall I rather say, his ruling impulse, was to translate the poetic heroes of paganism into the not less rude, but more intellectually vigorous, and more *featurely*, warriors of Christian chivalry,—and to substantiate the distinct and graceful profiles or outlines of the Homeric epic into the flesh and blood of the romantic drama,—in short, to give a grand history-piece in the robust style of Albert Dürer.

The character of Thersites, in particular, well deserves a more careful examination, as the Caliban of demagogic life;—the admirable portrait of intellectual power deserted by all grace, all moral principle, all not momentary impulse;—just wise enough to detect the weak head, and fool enough to provoke the armed fist of his betters;—one whom malcontent Achilles can inveigle from malcontent Ajax, under the one condition, that he shall be called on to do nothing but abuse and slander, and that he shall be allowed to abuse as much and as purulently as he likes, that is, as he can;—in short, a mule,—quarrelsome by the original discord of his nature,—a slave by tenure of his own baseness,—made to bray and be brayed at, to despise and be despicable. 'Aye, Sir, but say what you will, he is a very clever fellow, though the best friends will fall out. There was a time when Ajax thought he deserved to have a statue of gold erected to him, and handsome Achilles, at the head of the Myrmidons, gave no little credit to his *friend Thersites!*'—SAMUEL TAYLOR COLERIDGE, *"Troilus and Cressida," Shakespeare, with Introductory Remarks on Poetry, the Drama, and the Stage, 1818*

---

WILLIAM GODWIN
From *Life of Geoffrey Chaucer*
1804, Volume 1, pp. 496–515

It would be extremely unjust to quit the consideration of Chaucer's poem of *Troilus and Creseide*, without noticing the high honour it has received in having been made the foundation of one of the plays of Shakespear. There seems to have been in this respect a sort of conspiracy in the commentators upon Shakespear, against the glory of our old English bard. In what they have written concerning this play, they make a very slight mention of Chaucer; they have not consulted his poem for the purpose of illustrating this admirable drama; and they have agreed, as far as possible, to transfer to another author the honour of having supplied materials to the tragic artist. Dr. Johnson says, "Shakespeare has in his story followed, for the greater part, the old book of Caxton, which was then very popular; but the character of Thersites, of which it makes no mention, is a proof that this play was written after Chapman had published his version of Homer." Mr. Steevens asserts that "Shakspeare received the greatest part of his materials for the structure of this play from the *Troye Boke* of Lydgate." And Mr. Malone repeatedly treats the "*History of the Destruction of Troy*, translated by Caxton," as "Shakspeare's authority" in the composition of this drama.

These assertions however are far from being accurate. It would have been strange indeed if Shakespear, with a soul so poetical, and in so many respects congenial to that of Chaucer, had not been a diligent student of the works of his great predecessor. Chaucer made a much greater figure in the eyes of a reader of poetry in the sixteenth century, than it has been his fortune to do among the scholars of the eighteenth. After the death of Chaucer, the English nation experienced a long dearth of poetry, and it seemed as if the darkness introduced by the first destroyers of the Roman empire was about once more to cover our isle. Nothing worthy the name of poetry was the produce of the following century. English poets indeed existed of great reputation and merit, beside Chaucer, whose works might recommend themselves to the attention of Shakespear: Sackville, Marlow, Drayton, Donne, and Spenser. But all these were the contemporaries of Shakespear, men whom he might have seen, and with whom he had probably conversed. Chaucer was almost the only English poet in the juvenile days of Shakespear, upon whose reputation death had placed his seal; the only one whose laurels were consecrated and rendered venerable by being seen through the mild and harmonising medium of a distant age. A further direct proof that Shakespear was familiarly conversant with the works of Chaucer may be derived from an examination of the early Poems of our great dramatic bard. His *Rape of Lucrece* is written precisely; and his *Venus and Adonis* nearly, in the versification and stanza used by Chaucer in the *Troilus and Creseide* and in many other of his works. Nor is it reasonable to doubt that the idea of the luscious paintings contained in these two pieces of Shakespear, was drawn from the too great fidelity and detail with which Chaucer has entered into similar situations in the poem before us. We have already seen a striking instance in which Shakespear has imitated a passage from the *Troilus and Creseide*, in his tragedy of *Romeo and Juliet*.

The fact is, that the play of Shakespear we are here considering has for its main foundation the poem of Chaucer, and is indebted for many accessory helps to the books mentioned by the commentators. The *Troilus and Creseide* seems long to have been regarded by our ancestors in a manner somewhat similar to that in which the *Æneid* was viewed among the Romans, or the *Iliad* by the ancient Greeks. Every reader who advanced any pretensions to poetical taste, felt himself obliged to speak of it as the great classical regular English poem, which reflected the highest lustre upon our language. Shakespear therefore, as a man, felt it but a just compliment to the merits of the great father of our poetry, to introduce his characters in tangible form, and with all the advantages and allurements he could bestow upon them, before the eyes of his countrymen; and as a constructor of dramas, accustomed to consult their tastes and partialities, he conceived that he could not adopt a more promising plan, than to entertain them with a tale already familiar to their minds, which had been the associate and delight of their early years, which every man had himself praised, and had heard applauded by all the tasteful and the wise.

We are not however left to probability and conjecture as to the use made by Shakespear of the poem of Chaucer. His other sources were Chapman's translation of Homer, the *Troy Book* of Lydgate, and Caxton's *History of the Destruction of Troy*. It is well known that there is no trace of the particular story of *Troilus and Creseide* among the ancients. It occurs indeed in Lydgate and Caxton; but the name and actions of Pandarus, a very essential personage in the tale as related by Shakespear and Chaucer, are entirely wanting, except a single mention of him by Lydgate,[1] and that with an express reference to Chaucer as his authority. Shakespear has taken the story of Chaucer with all its imperfections and defects, and has copied the series of its incidents with his customary fidelity; an exactness seldom to be found in any other dramatic writer.

Since then two of the greatest writers this island has produced have treated the same story, each in his own peculiar manner, it may be neither unentertaining nor uninstructive to consider the merit of their respective modes of composition as illustrated in the present example. It has already been sufficiently seen that Chaucer's poem includes many beauties, many genuine touches of nature, and many strokes of an exquisite pathos. It is on the whole however written in that style which has unfortunately been so long imposed upon the world as dignified, classical and chaste. It is naked of incidents, of ornament, of whatever should most awaken the imagination, astound the fancy, or hurry away the soul. It has the stately march of a Dutch burgomaster as he appears in a procession, or a French poet as he shows himself in his works. It reminds one too forcibly of a tragedy of Racine. Every thing partakes of the author, as if he thought he should be everlastingly disgraced by becoming natural, inartificial and alive. We travel through a work of this sort as we travel over some of the immense downs with which our island is interspersed. All is smooth, or undulates with so gentle and slow a variation as scarcely to be adverted to by the sense. But all is homogeneous and tiresome; the mind sinks into a state of aching torpidity; and we feel as if we should never get to the end of our eternal journey.[2] What a contrast to a journey among mountains and vallies, spotted with herds of various kinds of cattle, interspersed with villages, opening ever and anon to a view of the distant ocean, and refreshed with rivulets and streams; where if the eye is ever fatigued, it is only with the boundless flood of beauty which is incessantly pouring upon it! Such is the tragedy of Shakespear.

The historical play of *Troilus and Cressida* exhibits as full a specimen of the different styles in which this wonderful writer was qualified to excel, as is to be found in any of his works. A more poetical passage, if poetry consists in sublime picturesque and beautiful imagery, neither ancient nor modern times have produced, than the exhortation addressed by Patroclus to

Achilles, to persuade him to shake off his passion for Polyxena, the daughter of Priam, and reassume the terrors of his military greatness.

> Sweet, rouse yourself; and the weak wanton Cupid
> Shall from your neck unloose his amorous fold,
> And like a dew-drop from the lion's mane,
> Be shook to air.
>
> (Act III, Scene 3.)

Never did morality hold a language more profound, persuasive and irresistible, than in Shakespear's Ulysses, who in the same scene, and engaged in the same cause with Patroclus, thus expostulates with the champion of the Grecian forces.

> For emulation hath a thousand sons,
> That one by one pursue. If you give way,
> Or hedge aside from the direct forthright,
> Like to an enter'd tide, they all rush by,
> And leave you hindmost: there you lie,
> Like to a gallant horse fallen in first rank,
> For pavement to the abject rear, o'er-run
> And trampled on. . . .
>        O, let not virtue seek
> Remuneration for the thing it was!
> For beauty, wit, high birth, desert in service,
> Love, friendship, charity, are subjects all
> To envious and calumniating time.
> One touch of nature makes the whole world kin, . . .
> That all with one consent praise new-born gauds,
> And give to dust, that is a little gilt,
> More praise than they will give to gold o'er-dusted.
> Then marvel not, thou great and complete man!
> That all the Greeks begin to worship Ajax.
>        The cry went once on thee,
> And still it might, and yet it may again,
> If thou wouldst not entomb thyself alive,
> And case thy reputation in thy tent.

But the great beauty of this play, as it is of all the genuine writings of Shakespear, beyond all didactic morality, beyond all mere flights of fancy, and beyond all sublime, a beauty entirely his own, and in which no writer ancient or modern can enter into competition with him, is that his men are men; his sentiments are living, and his characters marked with those delicate, evanescent, undefinable touches, which identify them with the great delineations of nature. The speech of Ulysses just quoted, when taken by itself, is purely an exquisite specimen of didactic morality; but when combined with the explanation given by Ulysses, before the entrance of Achilles, of the nature of his design, it becomes the attribute of a real man, and starts into life.—Achilles (says he)

>       stands in the entrance of his tent.
> Please it our general to pass strangely by him,
> As if he were forgot; and princes all,
> Lay negligent and loose regard upon him:
> I will come last: 'tis like, he'll question me,
> Why such unplausive eyes are bent, why turn'd on
>    him:
> If so, I have derision med'cinable,
> To use between your strangeness and his pride,
> Which his own will shall have desire to drink.

When we compare the plausible and seemingly affectionate manner in which Ulysses addresses himself to Achilles, with the key which he here furnishes to his meaning, and especially with the epithet "derision," we have a perfect elucidation of his character, and must allow that it is impossible to exhibit the crafty and smooth-tongued politician in a more exact or animated style. The advice given by Ulysses is in its nature sound and excellent, and in its form inoffensive and kind; the name therefore of "derision" which he gives to it, marks to a wonderful degree the cold and self-centred subtlety of his character.

The following is a most beautiful example of the genuine Shakespearian manner, such as I have been attempting to describe; where Cressida first proceeds so far as to confess to Troilus that she loves him.

> *Cres.*: Boldness comes to me now, and brings me
>     heart:—
>     Prince Troilus, I have lov'd you night and day,
>     For many weary months.
> *Tr.*: Why was my Cressid then so hard to win?
> *Cres.*: Hard to seem won; but I was won, my lord,
>     With the first glance that ever—Pardon me—
>     If I confess much, you will play the tyrant.
>     I love you now; but not, till now, so much
>     But I might master it:—in faith, I lie;
>     My thoughts were like unbridled children, grown
>     Too headstrong for their mother:—See, we fools!
>     Why have I blabb'd? Who shall be true to us,
>     When we are so unsecret to ourselves?—
>     But, though I lov'd you well, I woo'd you not;—
>     And yet, good faith, I wish'd myself a man;
>     Or that we women had men's privilege
>     Of speaking first.—Sweet, bid me hold my tongue;
>     For, in this rapture, I shall surely speak
>     The thing I shall repent.—See, see, your silence,
>     Cunning in dumbness, from my weakness draws
>     My very soul of counsel.—Stop my mouth.
>
> (Act III, Scene 2.)

What charming ingenuousness, what exquisite *naiveté*, what ravishing confusion of soul, are expressed in these words! We seem to perceive in them every fleeting thought as it rises in the mind of Cressida, at the same time that they delineate with equal skill all the beautiful timidity and innocent artifice which grace and consummate the feminine character. Other writers endeavour to conjure up before them their imaginary personages, and seek with violent effort to arrest and describe what their fancy presents to them: Shakespear alone (though not without many exceptions to this happiness) appears to have the whole train of his characters in voluntary attendance upon him, to listen to their effusions, and to commit to writing all the words, and the very words, they utter.

The whole catalogue of the *dramatis personæ* in the play of *Troilus and Cressida*, so far as they depend upon a rich and original vein of humour in the author, are drawn with a felicity which never was surpassed. The genius of Homer has been a topic of admiration to almost every generation of men since the period in which he wrote. But his characters will not bear the slightest comparison with the delineation of the same characters as they stand in Shakespear. This is a species of honour which ought by no means to be forgotten when we are making the eulogium of our immortal bard, a sort of illustration of his greatness which cannot fail to place it in a very conspicuous light. The dispositions of men perhaps had not been sufficiently unfolded in the very early period of intellectual refinement when Homer wrote; the rays of humour had not been dissected by the glass, or rendered perdurable by the pencil, of the poet. Homer's characters are drawn with a laudable portion of variety and consistency; but his Achilles, his Ajax and his Nestor are, each of them, rather a species than an individual, and can boast more of the propriety of abstraction, than of the vivacity of a moving scene of absolute life. The Achilles, the Ajax, and the various Grecian heroes of Shakespear on the other hand, are absolute men, deficient in nothing which can tend to individualise them, and already touched with the Promethean fire that might infuse a soul into what, without it, were lifeless form. From the rest perhaps the character of Thersites deserves to be selected (how cold and school-boy a sketch in Homer!) as exhibiting an appropriate vein of sarcastic humour amidst his cowardice, and a profoundness and truth in his mode of laying open the foibles of those about him, impossible to be excelled.

Before we quit this branch of Shakespear's praise, it may not be unworthy of our attention to advert to one of the methods by which he has attainted this uncommon superiority. It has already been observed that one of the most formidable adversaries of true poetry, is an attribute which is generally miscalled dignity. Shakespear possessed, no man in higher perfection, the true dignity and loftiness of the poetical afflatus, which he has displayed in many of the finest passages of his works with miraculous success. But he knew that no man ever was, or ever can be, always dignified. He knew that those subtler traits of character which identify a man, are familiar and relaxed, pervaded with passion, and not played off with an eternal eye to decorum. In this respect the peculiarities of Shakespear's genius are no where more forcibly illustrated than in the play we are here considering. The champions of Greece and Troy, from the hour in which their names were first recorded, had always worn a certain formality of attire, and marched with a slow and measured step. No poet till this time, had ever ventured to force them out of the manner which their epic creator had given them. Shakespear first suppled their limbs, took from them the classic stiffness of their gait, and enriched them with an entire set of those attributes, which might render them completely beings of the same species with ourselves.

Yet, after every degree of homage has been paid to the glorious and awful superiorities of Shakespear, it would be unpardonable in us, on the present occasion, to forget one particular in which the play of *Troilus and Cressida* does not eclipse, but on the contrary falls far short of its great archetype, the poem of Chaucer. This too is a particular, in which, as the times of Shakespear were much more enlightened and refined than those of Chaucer, the preponderance of excellence might well be expected to be found in the opposite scale. The fact

however is unquestionable, that the characters of Chaucer are much more respectable and loveworthy than the correspondent personages in Shakespear. In Chaucer Troilus is the pattern of an honourable lover, choosing rather every extremity and the loss of life, than to divulge, whether in a direct or an indirect manner, any thing which might compromise the reputation of his mistress, or lay open her name as a topic for the comments of the vulgar. Creseide, however (as Mr. Urry has observed) she proves at last a "false unconstant whore," yet in the commencement, and for a considerable time, preserves those ingenuous manners and that propriety of conduct, which are the brightest ornaments of the female character. Even Pandarus, low and dishonourable as is the part he has to play, is in Chaucer merely a friendly and kind-hearted man, so easy in his temper that, rather than not contribute to the happiness of the man he loves, he is content to overlook the odious names and construction to which his proceedings are entitled. Not so in Shakespear: his Troilus shows no reluctance to render his amour a subject of notoriety to the whole city; his Cressida (for example in the scene with the Grecian chiefs,[3] to all of whom she is a total stranger) assumes the manners of the most abandoned prostitute; and his Pandarus enters upon his vile occupation, not from any venial partiality to the desires of his friend, but from the direct and simple love of what is gross, impudent and profligate. For these reasons Shakespear's play, however enriched with a thousand various beauties, can scarcely boast of any strong claim upon our interest or affections.—It may be alleged indeed that Shakespear, having exhibited pretty much at large the whole catalogue of Greek and Trojan heroes, had by no means equal scope to interest us in the story from which the play receives its name: but this would scarcely be admitted as an adequate apology before an impartial tribunal.

*Notes*

1. *Troye Boke*, Book III, cap, xxv.
2. These remarks apply to nine-tenths of the poem, though by no means to those happier passages in which the author unfolds the sentiments of his personages.
3. Act iv, Scene 5.

# Othello

Up, and to Deptford by water, reading *Othello, Moore of Venice*, which I ever heretofore esteemed a mighty good play, but having so lately read *The Adventures of Five Houres* ⟨by Samuel Tuke⟩, it seems a mean thing.—SAMUEL PEPYS, *Diary*, Aug. 20, 1666

While mercenary Actors tread the Stage,
And hireling Scribblers lash or lull the Age,
Our's be the Task t' instruct, and entertain,
Without one Thought of Glory or of Gain.
Virtue's her own—from no external Cause—
She gives, and she demands the Self-applause:
Home to her Breast she brings the heart-felt Bays,
Heedless alike of Profit, and of Praise.
This now perhaps is wrong—yet this we know,
'Twas Sense and Truth a Century ago.
When *Britain*, with transcendant Glory crown'd,
For high Achievements, as for Wit renown'd,
Cull'd from each growing Grace the purest part,

And cropt the Flowers from every blooming Art,
Our noblest Youth would then embrace the task
Of comic Humour, or the mystic masque.
'Twas theirs t' incourage worth, and give to Bards
What now is spent in *Boxing* and in *Cards*:
Good Sense their Pleasure—Virtue still their Guide,
And *English* Magnanimity—their Pride.
Methinks I see with Fancy's magic Eye,
The Shade of *Shakespear*, in yon azure Sky.
On yon High Cloud behold the Bard advance,
Grasping all Nature with a single Glance:
In various Attitudes around him Stand
The Passions, waiting for his dread Command.
First kneeling Love before his Feet appears,
And musically sighing melts in Tears.
Near him fell Jealousy with Fury burns,
And into Storms the amorous Breathings turns
Then Hope with Heavenward looks, and Joy draws near,

While palsied Terrour trembles in the Rear.
  Such *Shakespear's* train of Horror and Delight,
And such we hope to introduce to-night.
But if, tho' just in Thought, we fail in Fact,
And good Intention ripens not to act,
Weigh our Design, your Censure still defer,
When Truth's in View 'tis glorious e'en to err.

    —CHRISTOPHER SMART, "An Occasional Prologue to *Othello*," 1751

The beauties of this play impress themselves so strongly upon the attention of the reader, that they can draw no aid from critical illustration. The fiery openness of Othello, magnanimous, artless, and credulous, boundless in his confidence, ardent in his affection, inflexible in his resolution, and obdurate in his revenge; the cool malignity of Iago, silent in his resentment, subtle in his designs, and studious at once of his interest and his vengeance; the soft simplicity of Desdemona, confident of merit, and conscious of innocence, her artless perseverance in her suit, and her slowness to suspect that she can be suspected, are such proofs of Shakespeare's skill in human nature, as, I suppose, it is vain to seek in any modern writer. The gradual progress which Iago makes in the Moor's conviction, and the circumstances which he employs to inflame him, are so artfully natural, that, though it will perhaps not be said of him as he says of himself, that he is "a man not easily jealous," yet we cannot but pity him when at last we find him "perplexed in the extreme."

There is always danger lest wickedness conjoined with abilities should steal upon esteem, though it misses of approbation: but the character of Iago is so conducted, that he is from the first scene to the last hated and despised.

Even the interiour character of this play would be very conspicuous in any other piece, not only for their justness but their strength. Cassio is brave, benevolent, and honest, ruined only by his want of stubbornness to resist an insidious invitation. Rodorigo's suspicious credulity, and impatient submission to the cheats which he sees practised upon him, and which by persuasion he suffers to be repeated, exhibit a strong picture of a weak mind betrayed by unlawful desires, to a false friend; and the virtue of Aemilia is such as we often find, worn loosely, but not cast off, easy to commit small crimes, but quickened and alarmed at atrocious villanies.

The scenes from the beginning to the end are busy, varied by happy interchanges, and regularly promoting the progression of the story; and the narrative in the end, though it tells but what is known already, yet it necessary to produce the death of Othello.

Had the scene opened in Cyprus, and the preceding incidents been occasionally related, there had been little wanting to a drama of the most exact and scrupulous regularity.—SAMUEL JOHNSON, *Notes on Shakespeare's Plays*, 1768

If *Romeo and Juliet* shines with the colours of the dawn of morning, but a dawn whose purple clouds already announce the thunder of a sultry day, *Othello* is, on the other hand, a strongly shaded picture: we might call it a tragical Rembrandt. What a fortunate mistake that the Moor (under which name in the original novel, a baptized Saracen of the Northern coast of Africa was unquestionably meant), has been made by Shakspeare in every respect a negro! We recognize in Othello the wild nature of that glowing zone which generates the most ravenous beasts of prey and the most deadly poisons, tamed only in appearance by the desire of fame, by foreign laws of honour, and by nobler and milder manners. His jealousy is not the jealousy of the heart, which is compatible with the

tenderest feeling and adoration of the beloved object; it is of that sensual kind which, in burning climes, has given birth to the disgraceful confinement of women and many other unnatural usages. A drop of this poison flows in his veins, and sets his whole blood in the wildest ferment. The Moor *seems* noble, frank, confiding, grateful for the love shown him; and he is all this, and, moreover, a hero who spurns at danger, a worthy leader of an army, a faithful servant of the state; but the mere physical force of passion puts to flight in one moment all his acquired and mere habitual virtues, and gives the upper hand to the savage over the moral man. This tyranny of the blood over the will betrays itself even in the expression of his desire of revenge upon Cassio. In his repentance, a genuine tenderness for his murdered wife, and in the presence of the damning evidence of his deed, the painful feeling of annihilated honour at last bursts forth; and in the midst of these painful emotions he assails himself with the rage wherewith a despot punishes a runaway slave. He suffers as a double man; at once in the higher and the lower sphere into which his being was divided.—While the Moor bears the nightly colour of suspicion and deceit only on his visage, Iago is black within. He haunts Othello like his evil genius, and with his light (and therefore the more dangerous,) insinuations, he leaves him no rest; it is as if by means of an unfortunate affinity, founded however in nature, this influence was by necessity more powerful over him than the voice of his good angel Desdemona. A more artful villain than this Iago was never portrayed; he spreads his nets with a skill which nothing can escape. The repugnance inspired by his aims becomes tolerable from the attention of the spectators being directed to his means: these furnish endless employment to the understanding. Cool, discontented, and morose; arrogant where he dare be so, but humble and insinuating when it suits his purposes, he is a complete master in the art of dissimulation; accessible only to selfish emotions, he is thoroughly skilled in rousing the passions of others, and of availing himself of every opening which they give him: he is as excellent an observer of men as any one can be who is unacquainted with higher motives of action from his own experience; there is always some truth in his malicious observations on them. He does not merely pretend an obdurate incredulity as to the virtue of women, he actually entertains it; and this, too, falls in with his whole way of thinking, and makes him the more fit for the execution of his purpose. As in every thing he sees merely the hateful side, he dissolves in the rudest manner the charm which the imagination casts over the relation between the two sexes: he does so for the purpose of revolting Othello's senses, whose heart otherwise might easily have convinced him of Desdemona's innocence. This must serve as an excuse for the numerous expressions in the speeches of Iago from which modesty shrinks. If Shakspeare had written in our days he would not perhaps have dared to hazard them; and yet this must certainly have greatly injured the truth of his picture. Desdemona is a sacrifice without blemish. She is not, it is true, a high ideal representation of sweetness and enthusiastic passion like Juliet; full of simplicity, softness, and humility, and so innocent, that she can hardly form to herself an idea of the possibility of infidelity, she seems calculated to make the most yielding and tenderest of wives. The female propensity wholly to resign itself to a foreign destiny has led her into the only fault of her life, that of marrying without her father's consent. Her choice seems wrong; and yet she has been gained over to Othello by that which induces the female to honour in man her protector and guide,—admiration of his determined heroism, and compassion for the sufferings which he had undergone. With great art it is so contrived, that from the very circumstance that the possibility of a suspicion of her own purity of motive never once enters her mind, she is the less reserved in her solicitations for Cassio, and thereby does but heighten more and more the jealousy of Othello. To throw out still more clearly the angelic purity of Desdemona, Shakspeare has in Emilia associated with her a companion of doubtful virtue. From the sinful levity of this woman it is also conceivable that she should not confess the abstraction of the handkerchief when Othello violently demands it back: this would otherwise be the circumstance in the whole piece the most difficult to justify. Cassio is portrayed exactly as he ought to be to excite suspicion without actual guilt,—amiable and nobly disposed, but easily seduced. The public events of the first two acts show us Othello in his most glorious aspect, as the support of Venice and the terror of the Turks: they serve to withdraw the story from the mere domestic circle, just as this is done in *Romeo and Juliet* by the dissensions between the houses of Montague and Capulet. No eloquence is capable of painting the overwhelming force of the catastrophe in *Othello*,—the pressure of feelings which measure out in a moment the abysses of eternity.—AUGUST WILHELM SCHLEGEL, *Lectures on Dramatic Art and Literature*, 1809, tr. John Black

Dr. Johnson has remarked that little or nothing is wanting to render the *Othello* a regular tragedy, but to have opened the play with the arrival of Othello in Cyprus, and to have thrown the preceding act into the form of narration. Here then is the place to determine, whether such a change would or would not be an improvement;—nay, (to throw down the glove with a full challenge) whether the tragedy would or not by such an arrangement become more regular,—that is, more consonant with the rules dictated by universal reason, on the true common-sense of mankind, in its application to the particular case. For in all acts of judgment, it can never be too often recollected, and scarcely too often repeated, that rules are means to ends, and, consequently, that the end must be determined and understood before it can be known what the rules are or ought to be. Now, from a certain species of drama, proposing to itself the accomplishment of certain ends,—these partly arising from the idea of the species itself, but in part, likewise, forced upon the dramatist by accidental circumstances beyond his power to remove or control,—three rules have been abstracted;—in other words, the means most conducive to the attainment of the proposed ends have been generalized, and prescribed under the names of the three unities,—the unity of time, the unity of place, and the unity of action,—which last would, perhaps, have been as appropriately, as well as more intelligibly, entitled the unity of interest. With this last the present question has no immediate concern: in fact, its conjunction with the former two is a mere delusion of words. It is not properly a rule, but in itself the great end not only of the drama, but of the epic poem, the lyric ode, of all poetry, down to the candle-flame cone of an epigram,—nay of poesy in general, as the proper generic term inclusive of all the fine arts as its species. But of the unities of time and place, which alone are entitled to the name of rules, the history of their origin will be their best criterion. You might take the Greek chorus to a place, but you could not bring a place to them without as palpable an equivoque as bringing Birnam wood to Macbeth at Dunsinane. It was the same, though in a less degree, with regard to the unity of time:—the positive fact, not for a moment removed from the senses, the presence, I mean, of the same identical chorus, was a continued measure of time;—and although the imagination may supersede perception, yet it must be granted to be an imperfection—however

easily tolerated —to place the two in broad contradiction to each other. In truth, it is a mere accident of terms; for the Trilogy of the Greek theatre was a drama in three acts, and notwithstanding this, what strange contrivances as to place there are in the Aristophanic *Frogs*. Besides, if the law of mere actual perception is once violated—as it repeatedly is even in the Greek tragedies—why is it more difficult to imagine three hours to be three years than to be a whole day and night?—SAMUEL TAYLOR COLERIDGE, "Notes on *Othello*," *Shakspeare, with Introductory Remarks on Poetry, the Drama, and the Stage*, 1818

> A dark lean face, a narrow, slanting eye,
> Whose deeps of blackness one pale taper's beam
> Haunts with a flitting madness of desire;
> A heart whose cinder at the breath of passion
> Glows to a momentary core of heat
> Almost beyond indifference to endure:
> So parched Iago frets his life away.
> His scorn works ever in a brain whose wit
> This world hath fools too many and gross to seek.
> Ever to live incredibly alone,
> Masked, shivering, deadly, with a simple Moor
> Of idiot gravity, and one pale flower
> Whose chill would quench in everlasting peace
> His soul's unmeasured flame—O paradox!
> Might he but learn the trick!—to wear her heart
> One fragile hour of heedless innocence,
> And then, farewell, and the incessant grave.
> "O fool! O villain!"—'tis the shuttlecock
> Wit never leaves at rest. It is his fate
> To be a needle in a world of hay,
> Where honour is the flattery of the fool;
> Sin, a tame bauble; lies, a tiresome jest;
> Virtue, a silly, whitewashed block of wood
> For words to fell. Ah! but the secret lacking,
> The secret of the child, the bird, the night,
> Faded, flouted, bespattered, in days so far
> Hate cannot bitter them, nor wrath deny;
> Else were this Desdemona. . . . Why!
> Woman a harlot is, and life a nest
> Fouled by long ages of forked fools. And God—
> Iago deals not with a tale so dull:
> To have made the world! Fie on thee, Artisan!

—WALTER DE LA MARE, "Iago," *Characters from Shakespeare*, 1902

---

## THOMAS RYMER
### From A *Short View of Tragedy*
### 1693

From all the Tragedies acted on our English Stage, *Othello* is said to bear the Bell away. The *Subject* is more of a piece, and there is indeed something like, there is, as it were, some phantom of a *Fable*. The *Fable* is always accounted the *Soul* of Tragedy. And it is the *Fable* which is properly the *Poets* part. Because the other three parts of Tragedy, to wit the *Characters* are taken from the Moral Philosopher; the *thoughts* or sence, from them that teach *Rhetorick*: And the last part, which is the *expression*, we learn from the Grammarians.

This Fable is drawn from a Novel, compos'd in Italian by *Giraldi Cinthio*, who also was a Writer of Tragedies. And to that use employ'd such of his Tales, as he judged proper for the Stage. But with this of the *Moor*, he meddl'd no farther.

*Shakespear* alters it from the Original in several particulars, but always, unfortunately, for the worse. He bestows a name on his *Moor*; and styles him the Moor of *Venice*: a Note of pre-eminence, which neither History nor Heraldry can allow him. *Cinthio*, who knew him best, and whose creature he was, calls him simply a *Moor*. We say the Piper of *Strasburgh*; the Jew of *Florence*; And, if you please, the Pindar of *Wakefield*: all upon Record, and memorable in their Places. But we see no such Cause for the *Moors* preferment to that dignity. And it is an affront to all Chroniclers, and Antiquaries, to top upon 'um a *Moor*, with that mark of renown, who yet had never faln within the Sphere of their Cognisance.

Then is the Moors *Wife*, from a simple Citizen, in *Cinthio*, dress'd up with her Top knots, and rais'd to be *Desdemona*, a Senators Daughter. All this is very strange; And therefore pleases such as reflect not on the improbability. This match might well be without the Parents Consent. Old *Horace* long ago forbad the Banes.

Sed non ut placidis Coeant immitia, non ut
Serpentes avibus geminentur, tigribus agni.

### The Fable.

Othello, *a Blackmoor Captain, by talking of his Prowess and Feats of War, makes* Desdemona *a Senators Daughter to be in love with him; and to be married to him, without her Parents knowledge; And having preferred* Cassio, *to be his Lieutenant, (a place which his Ensign* Jago *sued for)* Jago *in revenge, works the Moor into a Jealousy that* Cassio *Cuckolds him: which he effects by stealing and conveying a certain Handkerchief, which had, at the Wedding, been by the Moor presented to his Bride. Hereupon,* Othello *and* Jago *plot the Deaths of* Desdemona *and* Cassio, Othello *Murders her, and soon after is convinced of her Innocence. And as he is about to be carried to Prison, in order to be punish'd for the Murder, He kills himself.*

What ever rubs or difficulty may stick on the Bark, the Moral, sure, of this Fable is very instructive.

1. First, This may be a caution to all Maidens of Quality how, without their Parents consent, they run away with Blackamoors.

*Di non si accompagnare con huomo, cui la natura & il cielo, & il modo della vita, disgiunge da noi.* Cinthio.

Secondly, This may be a warning to all good Wives, that they look well to their Linnen.

Thirdly, This may be a lesson to Husbands, that before their Jealousie be Tragical, the proofs may be Mathematical.

*Cinthio* affirms that *She was not overcome by a Womanish Appetite, but by the Vertue of the Moor.* It must be a good-natur'd Reader that takes *Cinthio*'s word in this case, tho' in a Novel. *Shakespear*, who is accountable both to the *Eyes*, and to the *Ears*, And to convince the very heart of an Audience, shews that *Desdemona* was won, by hearing *Othello* talk,

I spake of most disastrous chances,
of Moving accidents, by flood and field;
of hair-breadth scapes i' th' imminent deadly breach;
of being taken by the insolent foe;
and sold to slavery: of my redemption thence;
and portents in my Travels History:
wherein of Antars vast, and Desarts idle,
rough Quarries, Rocks, and Hills, whose heads
    touch Heaven,
It was my hint to speak, such was my process:
and of the *Cannibals* that each others eat:
the *Anthropophagi*, and men whose heads
do grow beneath their shoulders—

This was the Charm, this was the philtre, the love-powder that took the Daughter of this Noble Venetian. This was sufficient to make the Black-amoor White, and reconcile all, tho' there had been a Cloven-foot into the bargain.

A meaner woman might be as soon taken by *Aqua Tetrachymagogon.*

*Nodes, Cataracts, Tumours, Chilblains,* Carnosity, *Shankers,* or any *Cant* in the Bill of an High-German Doctor is as good *fustian Circumstance,* and as likely to charm a Senators Daughter. But, it seems, the noble Venetians have an other sence of things. The *Doge* himself tells us;

I think this Tale wou'd win my Daughter too.

*Horace* tells us,

Intererit Multum—
Colchus an Assyrius, Thebis nutritus, an Argis.

*Shakespear* in this Play calls 'em the *supersubtle venetians.* Yet examine throughout the Tragedy there is nothing in the noble *Desdemona,* that is not below any countrey Chamber-maid with us.

And the account he gives of their Noblemen and Senate, can only be calculated for the latitude of *Gotham.*

The Character of that State is to employ strangers in their Wars; But shall a Poet thence fancy that they will set a Negro to be their General; or trust a *Moor* to defend them against the *Turk?* With us a Black-amoor might rise to be a Trumpeter; but *Shakespear* would not have him less than a Lieutenant-General. With us a *Moor* might marry some little drab, or Small-coal Wench: *Shake-spear,* would provide him the Daughter and Heir of some great Lord, or Privy-Councellor: And all the Town should reckon it a very suitable match: Yet the English are not bred up with that hatred and aversion to the *Moors,* as are the Venetians, who suffer by a perpetual Hostility from them,

Littora littoribus contraria—

Nothing is more odious in Nature than an improbable lye; And, certainly, never was any Play fraught, like this of *Othello,* with improbabilities.

The *Characters* or Manners, which are the second part in a Tragedy, are not less unnatural and improper, than the Fable was improbable and absurd.

*Othello* is made a Venetian General. We see nothing done by him, nor related concerning him, that comports with the condition of a General, or, indeed, of a Man, unless the killing himself, to avoid a death the Law was about to inflict upon him. When his Jealousy had wrought him up to a resolution of's taking revenge for the suppos'd injury, He sets *Jago* to the fighting part, to kill *Cassio*; And chuses himself to murder the silly Woman his Wife, that was like to make no resistance.

His Love and his Jealousie are no part of a Souldiers Character, unless for Comedy.

But what is most intolerable is *Jago.* He is no Black-amoor Souldier, so we may be sure he should be like other Souldiers of our acquaintance; yet never in Tragedy, nor in Comedy, nor in Nature was a Souldier with his Character; take it in the Authors own words;

Em.:        some Eternal Villain,
    Some busie, and insinuating Rogue,
    Some cogging, couzening Slave, to get some
        Office.

*Horace* Describes a Souldier otherwise:

Impiger, iracundus, inexorabilis, acer.

*Shakespear* knew his Character of *Jago* was inconsistent. In this very Play he pronounces,

If thou dost deliver more or less than Truth,
    Thou are no Souldier.

This he knew, but to entertain the Audience with something new and surprising, against common sense, and Nature, he would pass upon us a close, dissembling, false, insinuating rascal, instead of an open-hearted, frank, plain-dealing Souldier, a character constantly worn by them for some thousands of years in the World.

*Tiberius Cæsar*[1] had a Poet Arraign'd for his Life: because *Agamemnon* was brought on the Stage by him, with a character unbecoming a Souldier.

Our *Ensigns* and Subalterns, when disgusted by the Captain, throw up their Commissions, bluster, and are bare-fac'd. *Jago*, I hope, is not brought on the Stage, in a Red Coat. I know not what Livery the Venetians wear: but am sure they hold not these conditions to be *alla soldatesca*.

Non sia egli per fare la vendetta con insidie, ma con la spada in mano. (Cinthio.)

Nor is our Poet more discreet in his *Desdemona*, He had chosen a Souldier for his Knave: And a Venetian Lady is to be the Fool.

This Senators Daughter runs away to (a Carriers Inn) the *Sagittary*, with a Black-amoor: is no sooner wedded to him, but the very night she Beds him, is importuning and teizing him for a young smock-fac'd Lieutenant, *Cassio*. And tho' she perceives the *Moor* Jealous of *Cassio*, yet will she not forbear, but still rings *Cassio, Cassio* in both his Ears.

*Roderigo* is the Cully of *Jago*, brought in to be murder'd by *Jago*, that *Jago's* hands might be the more in Blood, and be yet the more abominable Villain: who without that was too wicked on all Conscience; And had more to answer for, than any Tragedy, or Furies could inflict upon him. So there can be nothing in the *characters*, either for the profit, or to delight an Audience.

The third thing to be consider'd is the *Thoughts*. But from such *Characters*, we need not expect many that are either true, or fine, or noble.

And without these, that is, without sense or meaning, the fourth part of Tragedy, which is the *expression* can hardly deserve to be treated on distinctly. The verse rumbling in our Ears are of good use to help off the action.

In the *Neighing* of an Horse, or in the *growling* of a Mastiff, there is a meaning, there is as lively expression, and, may I say, more humanity, than many times in the Tragical flights of *Shakespear*.

Step then amongst the Scenes to observe the Conduct in this Tragedy.

The first we see are *Jago* and *Roderigo*, by Night in the Streets of *Venice*. After growling a long time together, they resolve to tell *Brabantio* that his Daughter is run away with the Black-a-moor. *Jago* and *Roderigo* were not of quality to be familiar with *Brabantio*, nor had any provocation from him, to deserve a rude thing at their hands. *Brabantio* was a Noble Venetian one of the Sovereign Lords, and principal persons in the Government, Peer to the most Serene *Doge*, one attended with more state, ceremony and punctillio, than any English Duke, or Nobleman in the Government will pretend to. This misfortune in his Daughter is so prodigious, so tender a point, as might puzzle the finest Wit of the most *supersubtle* Venetian to touch upon it, or break the discovery to her Father. See then how delicately *Shakespear* minces the matter:

Rod.: What ho, *Brabantio*, Signior *Brabantio*, ho.
Jago: Awake, what ho, *Brabantio*,
    Thieves, thieves, thieves:
    Look to your House, your Daughter, and your
      Bags
    Thieves, thieves.

                    (Brabantio *at a Window.*

Bra.: What is the reason of this terrible summons?
    What is the matter there?
Rod.: Signior, is all your Family within?
Jago: Are your Doors lockt?
Bra.: Why, wherefore ask you this?
Jago: Sir, you are robb'd, for shame put on your
    Gown,
    Your Heart is burst, you have lost half your Soul,
    Even now, very now, an old black Ram
    It tupping your white Ewe: arise, arise,
    Awake the snorting Citizens with the Bell,
    Or else the Devil will make a Grandsire of you,
      arise I say.

Nor have they yet done, amongst other ribaldry, they tell him.

Jago: Sir, you are one of those that will not serve
    God, if the Devil bid you; because we come to
    do you service, you think us Ruffians, you'le
    have your Daughter covered with a Barbary
    Stallion. You'le have your Nephews neigh to
    you; you'le have Coursers for Cousins, and
    Gennets for Germans.
Bra.: What prophane wretch art thou?
Jago: I am one, Sir, that come to tell you, your
    Daughter and the Moor, are now making the
    Beast with two backs.

In former days there wont to be kept at the Courts of Princes some body in a Fools Coat, that in pure simplicity might let slip something, which made way for the ill news, and blunted the shock, which otherwise might have come too violent upon the party.

*Aristophanes* puts *Nicias* and *Demosthenes* into the disguise of Servants, that they might, without indecency, be Drunk; And Drunk he must make them that they might without reserve lay open the *Arcana* of State; And the Knavery of their *Ministers*.

After King *Francis* had been taken Prisoner at *Pavia*. *Rabelais* tells of a Drunken bout between *Gargantua* and Fryer *John*; where the valiant Fryer, bragging over his Cups, amongst his other flights, says he, *Had I liv'd in the days of Jesus Christ, I would ha' guarded* Mount Olivet *that the Jews should never ha' tane him. The Devil fetch me, if I would not have ham string'd those Mr. Apostles, that after their good Supper, ran away so scurvily and left their Master to shift for himself. I hate a Man should run away, when he should play at sharps. Pox on't, that I shou'd not be King of* France *for an hundred years or two. I wou'd curtail all our French Dogs that ran away at* Pavia.

This is address, this is truly Satyr, where the preparation is such, that the thing principally design'd, falls in, as it only were of course.

But *Shakespear* shews us another sort of address, his manners and good breeding must not be like the rest of the Civil World. *Brabantio* was not in Masquerade, was not *incognito*; *Jago* well knew his rank and dignity.

    The *Magnifico* is much beloved,
    And hath in his effect, a voice potential
    As double as the Duke—

But besides the Manners to a *Magnifico*, humanity cannot bear that an old Gentleman in his misfortune should be insulted over with such a rabble of Skoundrel language, when no cause or provocation. Yet thus it is on our Stage, this is our School of good manners, and the *Speculum Vitæ*.

But our *Magnifico* is here in the dark, nor are yet his Robes on: attend him to the Senate house, and there see the difference, see the effects of Purple.

So, by and by, we find the Duke of *Venice* with his

Senators in Councel, at Midnight, upon advice that the Turks, or Ottamites, or both together, were ready in transport Ships, put to Sea, in order to make a Descent upon *Cyprus*. This is the posture, when we see *Brabantio*, and *Othello* join them. By their Conduct and manner of talk, a body must strain hard to fancy the Scene at *Venice*; And not rather in some of our Cinq-ports, where the Baily and his Fisher-men are knocking their heads together on account of some Whale; or some terrible broil upon the Coast. But to shew them true Venetians, the Maritime affairs stick not long on their hand; the publick may sink or swim. They will sit up all night to hear a Doctors Commons, Matrimonial, Cause. And have the Merits of the Cause at large laid open to 'em, that they may decide it before they Stir. What can be pleaded to keep awake their attention so wonderfully?

Never, sure, was *form* of *pleading* so tedious and so heavy, as this whole Scene, and midnight entertainment. Take his own words: says the *Respondent*.

> Most potent, grave, and reverend Signiors,
> My very noble, and approv'd good Masters:
> That I have tane away this old mans Daughter;
> It is most true: true, I have Married her,
> The very front and head of my offending,
> Hath this extent, no more: rude I am in my speech.
> And little blest with the set phrase of peace,
> For since these Arms of mine had seven years pith,
> Till now some nine Moons wasted, they have us'd
> Their dearest action in the Tented Field:
> And little of this great World can I speak,
> More than pertains to Broils and Battail,
> And therefore little shall I grace my Cause,
> In speaking of my self; yet by your gracious patience
> I would a round unravish'd Tale deliver,
> Of my whole course of love, what drugs, what charms
> What Conjuration, and what mighty Magick,
> (for such proceedings am I charg'd withal)
> I won his Daughter.

All this is but *Preamble*, to tell the Court that He wants words. This was the Eloquence which kept them up all Night, and drew their attention, in the midst of their alarms.

One might rather think the novelty, and strangeness of the case prevail'd upon them: no, the Senators do not reckon it strange at all. Instead of starting at the Prodigy, every one is familiar with *Desdemona*, as he were her own natural Father, rejoice in her good fortune, and wish their own several Daughters as hopefully married. Should the Poet have provided such a Husband for an only Daughter of any noble Peer in *England*, the Black-amoor must have chang'd his Skin, to look our House of Lords in the Face.

*Æschylus* is noted in *Aristophanes* for letting *Niobe* be two or three *Acts* on the Stage, before she speaks. Our Noble Venetian, sure, is in the other more unnatural extreme. His words flow in abundance; no Butter-Quean can be more lavish. Nay: he is for talking of State-Affairs too, above any body:

*Bra.*: Please it your Grace, on to the State Affairs—

Yet is this *Brabantio* sensible of his affliction; before the end of the Play his Heart breaks, he dies.

*Gra.*: Poor *Desdemona*, I am glad thy Father's dead,
> Thy match was mortal to him, and pure grief
> Shore his old thread in twain—

A third part in a Tragedy is the *Thoughts*: from Venetians, Noblemen, and Senators, we may expect fine *Thoughts*. Here is a tryal of skill: for a parting blow, the *Duke*, and *Brabantio* Cap *sentences*. Where then shall we seek for the *thoughts*, if we let slip this occasion? says the Duke:

*Duke*: Let me speak like your self and lay a *Sentence*,
> Which like a greese or step, may help these lovers
> Into your favour.
> When remedies are past the grief is ended,
> By seeing the worst which late on hopes depended,
> To mourn a mischief that is past and gone,
> Is the next way to draw more mischief on;
> What cannot be preserv'd when Fortune takes,
> Patience her injury a Mocker makes.
> The rob'd that smiles, steals something from a Thief,
> He robs himself, that spends an hopeless grief.
*Bra.*: So let the Turk of *Cyprus* us beguile
> We lose it not so long as we can smile;
> He bears the sentence well, that nothing bears
> But the free comfort which from thence he hears,
> But he bears both the sentence and the sorrow,
> That to pay grief must of poor patience borrow:
> These *Sentences* to Sugar, or to Gall,
> Being strong on both sides are equivocal.
> But words are words, I never yet did hear,
> That the bruis'd Heart was pierced through the Ear.
> Beseech you now to the affairs of State.

How far wou'd the Queen of *Sheba* have travell'd to hear the Wisdom of our Noble Venetians? or is not our *Brentford*[2] a *Venetian* Colony, for methinks their talk is the very same?

What says Prince *Volscius*?

> What shall I do, what conduct shall I find
> To lead me through this twy light of my mind?

What says *Amaryllis*?

> I hope its slow beginning will portend
> A forward *exit* to all future end.

What says Prince *Pretty-man*?

> Was ever Son yet brought to this distress,
> To be, for being a Son, made Fatherless?
> Ah, you just gods, rob me not of a Father,
> The being of a Son take from me rather.

*Panurge*, sadly perplexed, and trying all the means in the World, to be well advised, in that knotty point *whether he should Marry, or no*; Amongst the rest, consults *Raminigrobis*, an old Poet; as one belonging to *Apollo*; And from whom he might expect something like an Oracle. And he was not disappointed. From *Raminigrobis* he had this Answer:

> Prenez la, ne la prenez pas.
> Si vous la prenez, c'est bien fait.
> Si ne la prenez, en effet
> Ce sera ouvre par compas.
> Gallopez, mais allez le pas.
> Reculez, entrés y de fait.
> > Prenez la, ne.
> Take, or not take her, off or on:
> Handy dandy is your Lot.
> When her name you write, you blot.
> 'Tis undone, when all is done,
> Ended, ere it is begun.
> Never Gallop whilst you Trot.
> Set not forward, when you run,
> Nor be single, tho' alone,
> Take, or not take her, off, or on.

What provocation, or cause of malice our Poet might have to Libel the most *Serene Republick*, I cannot tell: but certainly, there can be no wit in this representation.

For the *Second Act*, our Poet having dispatcht his affairs at *Venice*, shews the Action next (I know not how many leagues off) in the Island of *Cyprus*. The Audience must be there too: And yet our *Bays* had it never in his head, to make any provision of Transport Ships for them.

In the days that the *Old Testament* was Acted in *Clerkenwell*, by the *Parish Clerks* of *London*, the Israelites might pass through the *Red sea*: but alass, at this time, we have no *Moses* to bid the Waters *make way*, and to Usher us along. Well, the absurdities of this kind break no Bones. They may make Fools of us; but do not hurt our Morals.

Come a-shoar then, and observe the Countenance of the People, after the dreadful Storm, and their apprehensions from an Invasion by the Ottomites, their succour and friends scatter'd and tost, no body knew whither. The first that came to Land was *Cassio*, his first Salutation to the Governour, *Montanio*, is:

> Thanks to the valiant of this Isle:
> That so approve the Moor, and let the Heavens
> Give him defence against their Elements,
> For I have lost him on the dangerous Sea.

To him the Governour speaks, indeed, like a Man in his wits.

> Is he well Shipt?

The Lieutenant answers thus.

> His Bark is stoutly Tymber'd, and his Pilot
> Of very expert, and approv'd allowance,
> Therefore my hopes (not surfeited to death)
> Stand in bold care.

The Governours first question was very proper; his next question, in this posture of affairs, is:

> But, good Lieutenant, is our general Wiv'd?

A question so remote, so impertinent and absurd, so odd and surprising never entered *Bayes's Pericranium*. Only the answer may Tally with it.

> Most fortunately, he hath atcheiv'd a Maid,
> That Parragons description, and wild fame:
> One that excels the quirks of blasoning Pens:
> And in the essential vesture of Creation,
> Does bear an excellency—

They who like this Authors writing will not be offended to find so much repeated from him. I pretend not here to tax either the *Sense*, or the *Language*; those *Circumstances* had their proper place in the Venetian Senate. What I now cite is to shew how probable, how natural, how reasonable the Conduct is, all along.

I thought it enough that *Cassio* should be acquainted with a Virgin of that rank and consideration in *Venice*, as *Desdemona*. I wondred that in the Senate-house every one should know her so familiarly: yet, here also at *Cyprus*, every body is in a rapture at the name of *Desdemona*: except only *Montanio* who must be ignorant; that *Cassio*, who has an excellent cut in shaping an Answer, may give him the satisfaction:

> *Mont.*: What is she?
> *Cas.*: She that I spoke of: our Captains Captain,
> Left in the Conduct of the bold *Jago*,
> Whose footing here anticipates our thoughts
> A Sennets speed: great *Jove Othello* guard,
> And swell his Sail with thine own powerful breath,
> That he may bless this Bay with his Tall Ship,
> And swiftly come to *Desdemona's* Arms,
> Give renewed fire to our extincted Spirits,
> And bring all *Cyprus* comfort:
>          (*Enter Desdemona, &c.*
>    O behold,
> The riches of the Ship is come on shoar.
> Ye men of *Cyprus*, let her have your Knees:
> Hail to the Lady: and the Grace of Heaven
> Before, behind thee, and on every hand.
> Enwheel the round—

In the name of phrenzy, what means this Souldier? or would he talk thus, if he meant any thing at all? Who can say *Shakespear* is to blame in his *Character* of a Souldier? Has he not here done him reason? When cou'd our *Tramontains* talk at this rate? but our *Jarsey* and *Garnsey* Captains must not speak so fine things, nor compare with the Mediterranean, or Garrisons in *Rhodes* and *Cyprus*.

The next thing our Officer does, is to salute *Jago's* Wife, with this *Conge* to the Husband,

> *Cas.*: Good Ancient, you are welcome, welcome Mistriss,
> Let it not Gall your Patience, good *Jago*,
> That I extend my Manners, 'tis my Breeding,
> That gives me this bold shew of Curtesy.
> *Jago*: Sir, would she give you so much of her lips,
> As of her tongue she has bestow'd on me,
> You'd have enough.
> *Desd.*: Alass! she has no speech.

Now follows a long rabble of Jack-pudden farce betwixt *Jago* and *Desdemona*, that runs on with all the little plays, jingle, and trash below the patience of any Countrey Kitchin-maid with her Sweet-heart. The Venetian *Donna* is hard put to't for pastime! And this is all, when they are newly got on shoar, from a dismal Tempest, and when every moment she might expect to hear her Lord (as she calls him) that she runs so mad after, is arriv'd or lost. And moreover.

> In a Town of War,
>    . . . the peoples Hearts brimful of fear.

Never in the World had any Pagan Poet his Brains turn'd at this Monstrous rate. But the ground of all this Bedlam-Buffoonry we saw, in the case of the French *Strolers*, the Company for Acting *Christs Passion*, or the *Old Testament*, were Carpenters, Coblers, and illiterate fellows; who found that the Drolls, and Fooleries interlarded by them, brought in the rabble, and lengthened their time, so they got Money by the bargain.

Our *Shakespear*, doubtless, was a great Master in this craft. These Carpenters and Coblers were the guides he followed. And it is then no wonder that we find so much farce and *Apochryphal Matter* in his Tragedies. Thereby un-hallowing the Theatre, profaning the name of Tragedy; And instead of representing Men and Manners, turning all Morali-ty, good sence, and humanity into mockery and derision.

But pass we to something of a more serious air and Complexion. *Othello* and his Bride are the first Night, no sooner warm in Bed together, but a Drunken Quarrel happen-ing in the Garison, two Souldiers Fight; And the General rises to part the Fray: He swears.

> Now by Heaven,
> My blood begins my safer guides to rule,
> And passion, having my best judgment cool'd,
> Assays to lead the way: if once I stir,
> Or do but lift this arm, the best of you
> Shall sink in my rebuke: give me to know
> How this foul rout began; who set it on,
> And he that is approv'd in this offence,
> Tho' he had twin'd with me both at a birth,
> Should lose me: what, *in a Town of War,*
> *Yet wild, the peoples Hearts brimful of fear,*
> To manage private, and domestick quarrels,
> In Night, and on the Court, and guard of safety,
> 'Tis Monstrous, *Jago*, who began?

In the days of yore, Souldiers did not swear in this fashion. What should a Souldier say farther, when he swears, unless he blaspheme? action shou'd speak the rest. What follows must be *ex ore gladii*; He is to rap out an Oath, not Wire-draw and Spin it out: by the style one might judge that *Shakespears* Souldiers were never bred in a Camp, but rather had belong'd to some Affidavit-Office. Consider also throughout this whole Scene, how the Moorish General proceeds in examining into this *Rout*; No Justice *Clod-pate* could go on with more Phlegm and deliberation. The very first night that he lyes with the *Divine Desdemona* to be thus interrupted, might provoke a Mans Christian Patience to swear in another style. But a Negro General is a Man of strange Mettle. Only his Venetian Bride is a match for him. She understands that the Souldiers in the Garison are by th' ears together: And presently she at midnight, is in amongst them.

 *Desd.*: What's the matter there?
 *Othel.*: All's well now Sweeting—
  Come away to Bed—

In the beginning of this *second Act*, before they had lain together, *Desdemona* was said to be, *our Captains Captain*; Now they are no sooner in Bed together, but *Jago* is advising *Cassio* in these words.

 Our Generals Wife is now the General, I may say so
 in this respect, for that he hath devoted, and given up
 himself to the contemplation, mark, and devotement
 of her parts and graces. Confess your self freely to
 her, importune her; she'll help to put you in your
 place again: she is so free, so kind, so apt, so blessed a
 disposition, that she holds it a vice in her goodness,
 not to do more than she is requested. This broken
 joint between you and her Husband, intreat her to
 splinter—

And he says afterwards.

 'Tis most easie
 The inclining *Desdemona* to subdue,
 In any honest suit. She's fram'd as fruitful,
 As the free Elements: And then for her
 To win the Moor, were't to renounce his Baptism,
 All seals and symbols of redeemed sin,
 His soul is so enfetter'd to her love,
 That she may make, unmake, do what she list:
 Even as her appetite shall play the God
 With his weak function—

This kind of discourse implies an experience and long conversation, the Honey-Moon over, and a Marriage of some standing. Would any man, in his wits, talk thus of a Bridegroom and Bride the first night of their coming together?

Yet this is necessary for our Poet; it would not otherwise serve his turn. This is the source, the foundation of his Plot; hence is the spring and occasion for all the Jealousie and bluster that ensues.

Nor are we in better circumstances for *Roderigo*. The last thing said by him in the former *Act* was,

  I'll go sell all my Land.

A fair Estate is sold to *put money in his Purse*, for this adventure. And lo here, the next day.

 I do follow here in the Chace, not like a Hound that
 hunts, but one that fills up the cry: My Money is
 almost spent. I have been tonight exceedingly well
 cudgell'd, I think the issue will be, I shall have so
 much experience for my pains, and so no Money at
 all, and with a little more wit return to *Venice*.

The Venetian squire had a good riddance for his Acres. The Poet allows him just time to be once drunk, a very conscionable reckoning!

In this *Second Act*, the face of affairs could in truth be no other, than

in a Town of War,
 Yet wild, the peoples Hearts brim-ful of fear.

But nothing either in this *Act*, or in the rest that follow, shew any colour or complexion, any resemblance or proportion to that face and posture it ought to bear. Should a Painter draw any one *Scene* of this Play, and write over it, *This is a Town of War*; would any body believe that the Man were in his senses? would not a *Goose*, or *Dromedary* for it, be a name as just and suitable? And what in Painting would be absurd, can never pass upon the World of Poetry.

*Cassio* having escaped the Storm comes on shoar at *Cyprus*, that night gets Drunk, Fights, is turn'd out from his Command, grows sober again, takes advice how to be restor'd, is all Repentance and Mortification: yet before he sleeps, is in the Morning at his Generals door with a noise of Fiddles, and a Droll to introduce him to a little Mouth-speech with the Bride.

 *Cassio*: Give me advantage of some brief discourse
  With *Desdemona* alone.
 *Em.*: Pray you come in,
  I will bestow you, where you shall have time
  To speak your bosom freely.

So, they are put together: And when he had gone on a good while *speaking his bosom*, *Desdemona* answers him.

 Do not doubt that, before *Emilia* here,
 I give thee warrant of thy place; assure thee,
 If I do vow a friendship, I'll perform it,
 To the last article—

Then after a ribble rabble of fulsome impertinence, She is at her Husband slap dash:

 *Desd.*:    Good love, call him back.
 *Othel.*: Not now, sweet *Desdemona*, some other
  time.
 *Desd.*: But shall't shortly?
 *Othel.*: The sooner, sweet, for you.
 *Desd.*: Shall't be to-night at Supper?
 *Othel.*: No, not tonight.
 *Desd.*: To-morrow Dinner then?
 *Othel.*: I shall not dine at home,
  I meet the Captains at the Citadel.
 *Desd.*: Why then to morrow night, or Tuesday morn,
  Or night, or Wednesday morn?

After forty lines more, at this rate, they part, and then comes the wonderful Scene, where *Jago* by shrugs, half words, and ambiguous reflections, works *Othello* up to be Jealous. One might think, after what we have seen, that there needs no great cunning, no great poetry and address to make the *Moor* Jealous. Such impatience, such a rout for a handsome young fellow, the very morning after her Marriage must make him either to be jealous, or to take her for a *Changeling*, below his Jealousie. After this *Scene*, it might strain the Poets skill to reconcile the couple, and allay the Jealousie. *Jago* now can only *actum agere*, and vex the audience with a nauseous repetition.

Whence comes it then, that this is the top scene, the Scene that raises *Othello* above all other Tragedies on our Theatres? It is purely from the *Action*; from the Mops and the Mows, the Grimace, the Grins and Gesticulation. Such scenes as this have made all the World run after *Harlequin* and *Scaramuccio*.

The several degrees of *Action* were amongst the Ancients distinguish'd by the *Cothurnus*, the *Soccus*, and by the *Planipes*.

Had this scene been represented at old *Rome*, *Othello* and *Jago* must have quitted their Buskins; They must have played *bare-foot*: the spectators would not have been content without seeing their Podometry; And the Jealousie work at the very Toes of 'em. Words, be they Spanish, or Polish, or any inarticulate sound, have the same effect, they can only serve to distinguish, and, as it were, beat time to the *Action*. But here we see a known Language does wofully encumber, and clog the operation: as either forc'd, or heavy, or trifling, or incoherent, or improper, or most what improbable. When no words interpose to spoil the conceipt, every one interprets as he likes best. So in that memorable dispute betwixt *Panurge* and our English Philosopher in *Rabelais*, perform'd without a word speaking; The Theologians, Physicians, and Surgeons, made one inference; the Lawyers, Civilians, and Canonists, drew another conclusion more to their mind.

*Othello* the night of his arrival at *Cyprus*, is to consummate with *Desdemona*, they go to Bed. Both are rais'd and run into the Town amidst the Souldiers that were a fighting: then go to Bed again, that morning he sees *Cassio* with her; She importunes him to restore *Cassio*. *Othello* shews nothing of the Souldiers Mettle: but like a tedious, drawling, tame Goose, is gaping after any paultrey insinuation, labouring to be jealous; And catching at every blown surmize.

> *Jago*: My Lord, I see you are moved.
> *Oth.*: No, not much moved.
>   Do not think but *Desdemona* is honest.
> *Jago*: Long live she so, and long live you to think so.
> *Oth.*: And yet how Nature erring from it self,
> *Jago*: I, There's the point: as to be bold with you,
>   Not to affect many proposed Matches
>   Of her own clime, complexion, and degree,
>   Wherein we see, in all things. Nature tends,
>   Fye, we may smell in such a will most rank,
>   Foul disproportion, thoughts unnatural—

The Poet here is certainly in the right, and by consequence the foundation of the Play must be concluded to be Monstrous; And the constitution, all over, to be *most rank*,

>   Foul disproportion, thoughts unnatural.

Which instead of moving pity, or any passion Tragical and Reasonable, can produce nothing but horror and aversion, and what is odious and grievous to an Audience. After this fair Mornings work, the Bride enters, drops a Cursey.

> *Desd.*: How now, my dear *Othello*,
>   Your Dinner, and the generous Islanders
>   By you invited, do attend your presence.
> *Oth.*: I am to blame.
> *Desd.*: Why is your speech so faint? Are you not well.
> *Oth.*: I have a pain upon my Fore-head, dear.

*Michael Cassio* came not from *Venice* in the Ship with *Desdemona*, nor till this Morning could be suspected of an opportunity with her. And 'tis now but Dinner time; yet the *Moor* complains of his Fore-head. He might have set a Guard on *Cassio*, or have lockt up *Desdemona*, or have observ'd their carriage a day or two longer. He is on other occasions phlegmatick enough: this is very hasty. But after Dinner we have a wonderful flight:

>   What sense had I of her stoln hours of lust?
>   I saw't not, thought it not, it harm'd not me:
>   I slept the next night well, was free and merry,
>   I found not *Cassio*'s kisses on her lips—

A little after this, says he,

> *Oth.*: Give me a living reason that she's disloyal.
> *Jago*:     I lay with *Cassio* lately,
>   And being troubled with a raging Tooth, I could
>     not sleep;
>   There are a kind of men so loose of Soul,
>   That in their sleeps will mutter their affairs,
>   One of this kind is *Cassio*:

>   In sleep I heard him say: sweet *Desdemona*,
>   Let us be wary, let us hide our loves:
>   And then, Sir, wou'd he gripe, and wring my
>     hand,
>   Cry out, sweet Creature; and then kiss me hard,
>   As if he pluckt up kisses by the roots,
>   That grew upon my Lips, then laid his Leg
>   Over my Thigh, and sigh'd, and kiss'd, and then
>   Cry'd, cursed fate, that gave thee to the Moor.

By the Rapture of *Othello*, one might think that he raves, is not of sound Memory, forgets that he has not yet been two nights in the Matrimonial Bed with his *Desdemona*. But we find *Jago*, who should have a better memory, forging his lies after the very same Model. The very night of their Marriage at *Venice*, the Moor, and also *Cassio*, were sent away to *Cyprus*. In the *Second Act*, *Othello* and his Bride go the first time to Bed; The *Third Act* opens the next morning. The parties have been in view to this moment. We saw the opportunity which was given for *Cassio* to *speak his bosom* to her; *once*, indeed, might go a great way with a Venetian. But *once*, will not do the Poets business; The *Audience* must suppose a great many bouts, to make the plot operate. They must deny their senses, to reconcile it to common sense: or make it any way consistent, and hang together.

Nor, for the most part, are the single thoughts more consistent, than is the œconomy: The Indians do as they ought in painting the Devil White: but says *Othello*:

>   Her name that was as fresh
>   As *Dian*'s Visage, is now begrim'd and black,
>   As mine own face—

There is not a Monky but understands Nature better; not a Pug in *Barbary* that has not a truer taste of things.

>   O now for ever
>   Farewel the tranquil mind, farewel content;
>   Farewel the plumed troop, and the big Wars,
>   That make Ambition Vertue: O farewel,
>   Farewel the neighing Steed, and the shrill Trump,
>   The spirit stirring Drum, th' ear-piercing Fief,
>   The royal Banner, and all quality,
>   Pride, Pomp, and Circumstance of glorious War,
>   And O ye Mortal Engines, whose wide throats
>   Th' immortal Joves great clamours counterfeit,
>   Farewel, *Othello*'s occupation's gone.

These lines are recited here, not for any thing Poetical in them, besides the sound, that pleases. Yet this sort of imagery and amplification is extreamly taking, where it is just and natural. As in *Gorboduck*, when a young Princess on whose fancy the personal gallantry of the Kings Son then slain, had made a strong impression, thus, out of the abundance of her imagination, pours forth her grief:

>   Ah noble Prince! how oft have I beheld
>   Thee mounted on thy fierce, and trampling Steed,
>   Shining in Armour bright before the Tilt,
>   Wearing thy Mistress sleeve ty'd on thy helm.
>   Then charge thy staff, to please thy Ladies Eye,
>   That bow'd the head piece of thy friendly Foe?
>   How oft in arms, on Horse to bend the Mace,
>   How oft in arms, on foot, to break the Spear;
>   Which never now these Eyes may see agen?

Notwithstanding that this Scene had proceeded with fury and bluster sufficient to make the whole Isle ring of his Jealousy, yet is *Desdemona* diverting her self with a paultry buffoon and only solicitous in quest of *Cassio*.

> *Desd.*: Seek him, bid him come hither, tell him—
>   Where shou'd I lose that Handkerchief, *Emilia*?
>   Believe me I had rather lose my Purse,

Full of Crusado's: And but my noble Moor
Is true of mind, and made of no such baseness,
As Jealous Creatures are; it were enough
To put him to ill thinking.
*Em.*: Is he not Jealous?
*Desd.*: Who he? I think the Sun, where he was born,
Drew all such humours from him.

By this manner of speech one wou'd gather the couple had been yoak'd together a competent while, what might she say more, had they cohabited, and had been Man and Wife seven years?

She spies the Moor.

*Desd.*: I will not leave him now,
Till *Cassio* is recall'd.
I have sent to bid *Cassio* come speak with you.
*Othel.*:          Lend me thy Handkerchief.
*Desd.*:          This is a trick to put me from my suit.
I pray let *Cassio* be receiv'd agen.
*Em.*:          Is not this man Jealous?
. . . 'tis not a year or two shews us a man—

As if for the first year or two, *Othello* had not been jealous? The *third* Act begins in the morning, at noon she drops the Handkerchief, after dinner she misses it, and then follows all this outrage and horrible clutter about it. If we believe a small Damosel in the last *Scene* of this *Act*, this day is effectually seven days.

*Bianca*: What keep a week away! seven days, seven
nights,
Eightscore eight hours, and lovers absent hours,
More tedious than the Dial eightscore times.
O weary reckoning!

Our Poet is at this plunge, that whether this *Act* contains the compass of one day, of seven days, or of seven years, or of all together, the repugnance and absurdity would be the same. For *Othello*, all the while, has nothing to say or to do, but what loudly proclaim him jealous: her friend and confident *Emilia* again and again rounds her in the Ear that *the Man* is Jealous: yet this Venetian dame is neither to see, nor to hear; nor to have any sense or understanding, nor to strike any other note but *Cassio, Cassio*.

The Scotchman hearing *trut Scot, trut Scot*, when he saw it came from a Bird, checkt his Choler, and put up his *Swerd* again, with a *Braad O God, G. If thaa'dst ben a Maan, as th' art ane Green Geuse, I sud ha stuck tha' to thin heart.* *Desdemona* and that Parrot might pass for Birds of a Feather; and if *Sauney* had not been more generous than *Othello*, but continued to insult the poor Creature after this beastly example, he would have given our Poet as good stuff to work upon: And his *Tragedy of the Green Geuse*, might have deserv'd a better audience, than this of *Desdemona*, or *The Moor of Venice*.

### Act IV.
### Enter *Jago* and *Othello*
*Jago*: Will you think so?
*Othel.*: Think so, *Jago*.
*Jago*: What, to kiss in private?
*Othel.*: An unauthorised kiss.
*Jago*: Or to be naked with her friend a-bed,
An hour or more, not meaning any harm?
*Othel.*: Naked a-bed, *Jago*, and not mean harm?—

At this gross rate of trifling, our General and his Auncient March on most heroically; till the Jealous Booby has his Brains turn'd; and falls in a Trance. Would any imagine this to be the Language of Venetians, of Souldiers, and mighty Captains? no

*Bartholomew* Droll cou'd subsist upon such trash. But lo, a Stratagem never presented in Tragedy.
          Stand you a while a part—
               Incave your self;
And mark the Jeers, the Gibes, and notable scorns,
That dwell in every region of his face,
For I will make him tell the tale a new,
Where, how, how oft, how long ago, and when
He has, and is again to Cope your Wife:
I say, but mark his gesture—
With this device *Othello* withdraws. Says *Jago* aside.
Now will I question *Cassio* of *Bianca*,
A Huswife—
That doats on *Cassio*—
He when he hears of her cannot refrain
From the excess of Laughter—
As he shall smile, *Othello* shall go mad,
And his unbookish jealousy must conster
Poor *Cassio's* smiles, gesture, and light behaviour
Quite in the wrong—

So to work they go: And *Othello* is as wise a commentator, and makes his applications pat, as heart cou'd wish—but I wou'd not expect to find this Scene acted nearer than in *Southwark* Fair. But the *Hankerchief* is brought in at last, to stop all holes, and close the evidence. So now being satisfied with the proof, they come to a resolution, that the offenders shall be murdered.

*Othel.*: But yet the pity of it, *Jago*, ah the pity.
*Jago*: If you be so fond over her iniquity give her
Patent to offend.
For if it touches not you, it comes near no Boby.
Do it not with poison, strangle her in her Bed;
Even the Bed she has contaminated.
*Oth.*: Good, good, the Justice of it pleases, very
good.
*Jago*: And for *Cassio*, let me be his undertaker—

*Jago* had some pretence to be discontent with *Othello* and *Cassio*: And what passed hitherto, was the operation of revenge. *Desdemona* had never done him harm, always kind to him, and to his Wife; was his Country-woman, a Dame of quality: for him to abet her Murder, shews nothing of a Souldier, nothing of a Man, nothing of Nature in it. The *Ordinary* of *New gate* never had the like Monster to pass under his examination. Can it be any diversion to see a Rogue beyond what the Devil ever finish'd? Or wou'd it be any instruction to an Audience? *Jago* cou'd desire no better than to set *Cassio* and *Othello*, his two Enemies, by the Ears together; so he might have been reveng'd on them both at once: And chusing for his own share, the Murder of *Desdemona*, he had the opportunity to play booty, and save the poor harmless wretch. But the Poet must do every thing by contraries: to surprize the Audience still with something horrible and prodigious, beyond any human imagination. At this rate he must out-do the Devil, to be a Poet in the rank with *Shakespear*.

Soon after this, arrives from *Venice*, *Ludovico*, a noble Cousin of *Desdemona*, presently she is at him also, on the behalf of *Cassio*.

*Desd.*: Cousin there's fallen between him and my
Lord
An unkind breach, but you shall make all well.
*Lud.*: Is there division 'twixt my Lord and *Cassio*.
*Desd.*: A most unhappy one, I wou'd do much
To attone them, for the love I bear to *Cassio*.

By this time, we are to believe the couple have been a week or two Married: And *Othello's* Jealousie that had rag'd so loudly, and had been so uneasie to himself, must have reach'd her knowledge. The *Audience* have all heard him more plain with her, than was needful to a Venetian capacity: And yet she must still be impertinent in her suit for *Cassio*, well, this *Magnifico* comes from the *Doge*, and Senators, to displace *Othello*.

> *Lud.:* Deputing *Cassio* in his Government.
> *Desd.:* Trust me, I am glad on't.
> *Oth.:* Indeed.
> *Desd.:* My Lord.
> *Oth.:* I am glad to see you mad.
> *Desd.:* How, sweet *Othello*.
> *Oth.:* Devil.
> *Desd.:* I have not deserved this.
> *Oth.:* O Devil, Devil—
>   Out of my sight.
> *Desd.:* I will not stay to offend you.
> *Lud.:* Truly, an obedient Lady.
>   I do beseech your Lordship call her back.
> *Oth.:* Mistress.
> *Desd.:* My Lord.
> *Oth.:* What would you with her sir?
> *Lud.:* Who, I, my Lord?
> *Oth.:* I, you did wish that I wou'd make her turn.
>   Sir, she can turn, and turn, and yet go on,
>   And turn agen, and she can weep, Sir, weep.
>   And she is obedient, as you say, obedient:
>   Very obedient—
> *Lud.:* What strike your Wife?

Of what flesh and blood does our Poet make these noble Venetians? the men without Gall; the Women without either Brains or Sense? A Senators Daughter runs away with this Black-amoor; the Government employs this Moor to defend them against the Turks, so resent not the Moors Marriage at present, but the danger over, her Father gets the Moor Cashier'd, sends his Kinsman, Seignior *Ludovico*, to *Cyprus* with the Commission for a new General; who, at his arrival, finds the Moor calling the Lady his Kinswoman, Whore and Stumpet, and kicking her: what says the *Magnifico*?

> My Lord this would not be believ'd in *Venice*,
> Tho' I shou'd swear I saw't, 'tis very much;
> Make her amends: she weeps.

The Moor has no body to take his part, no body of his Colour: *Ludovico* has the new Governour *Cassio*, and all his Countrymen Venetians about him. What Poet wou'd give a villanous Black-amoor this Ascendant? What Tramontain could fancy the Venetians so low, so despicable, or so patient? this outrage to an injur'd Lady, the *Divine Desdemona*, might in a colder Climate have provoked some body to be her Champion: but the Italians may well conclude we have a strange Genius for Poetry. In the next Scene *Othello* is examining the supposed Bawd; then follows another storm of horrour and outrage against the poor Chicken, his Wife. Some Drayman or drunken Tinker might possibly treat his drab at this sort of rate, and mean no harm by it: but for his excellency, a My lord General, to Serenade a Senator's Daughter with such a volly of scoundrel filthy Language, is sure the most absurd Maggot that ever bred from any Poets addle Brain.

And she is in the right, who tells us,

> A Begger in his Drink,
> Cou'd not have laid such terms upon his Callet.

This is not to describe passion. *Seneca* had another notion in the Case:

> Parvæ loquuntur curæ, ingentes stupent.

And so had the Painter, who drew *Agamemnon* with his Face covered. Yet to make all worse, her Murder, and the manner of it, had before been resolv'd upon and concerted. But nothing is to provoke a Venetian; she takes all in good part; had the Scene lain in *Russia*, what cou'd we have expected more? With us a Tinkers Trull wou'd be Nettled, wou'd repartee with more spirit, and not appear so void of spleen.

> O good *Jago*,
> What shall I do to win my Lord agen?

No Woman bred out of a Pig-stye, cou'd talk so meanly. After this, she is call'd to Supper with *Othello*, *Ludovico*, &c. after that comes a filthy sort of Pastoral Scene, where the *Wedding Sheets*, and Song of *Willow*, and her Mothers Maid, poor *Barbara*, are not the least moving things in this entertainment. But that we may not be kept too long in the dumps, nor the melancholy Scenes lye too heavy, undigested on our Stomach, this *Act* gives us for a farewell, the *salsa*, *O picante*, some quibbles, and smart touches, as *Ovid* had Prophecied:

> Est & in obscœnos deflexa Tragœdia risus.

The last *Act* begins with *Jago* and *Roderigo*; Who a little before had been upon the huff:

> I say it is not very well: I will make my self known to *Desdemona*; if she will return me my Jewels, I will give over my suit, and repent my unlawful sollicitation, if not, assure your self, I'll seek satisfaction of you.

*Roderigo*, a Noble Venetian had sought *Desdemona* in Marriage, is troubled to find the Moor had got her from him, advises with *Jago*, who wheadles him to sell his Estate, and go over the Sea to *Cyprus*, in expectation to Cuckold *Othello*, there having cheated *Roderigo* of all his Money and Jewels, on pretence of presenting them to *Desdemona*, our Gallant grows angry, and would have satisfaction from *Jago*; who sets all right, by telling him *Cassio* is to be Governour, *Othello* is going with *Desdemona* into *Mauritania*: to prevent this, you are to murder *Cassio*, and then all may be well.

> He goes into *Mauritania*, and takes with him the fair *Desdemona*, unless his abode be lingred here by some accident, wherein none can be so determinate, as the removing of *Cassio*.

Had *Roderigo* been one of the *Banditi*, he might not much stick at the Murder. But why *Roderigo* should take this for payment, and risque his person where the prospect of advantage is so very uncertain and remote, no body can imagine. It had need be a *super-subtle* Venetian that this Plot will pass upon. Then after a little spurt of villany and Murder, we are brought to the most lamentable, that ever appear'd on any Stage. A noble Venetian Lady is to be murdered by our Poet; in sober sadness, purely for being a Fool. No Pagan Poet but wou'd have found some *Machine* for her deliverance. *Pegasus* wou'd have strain'd hard to have brought old *Perseus* on his back, time enough, to rescue this *Andromeda* from so foul a Monster. Has our Christian Poetry no generosity, nor bowels? Ha, Sir *Lancelot!* ha St. *George!* will no Ghost leave the shades for us in extremity, to save a distressed Damosel?

But for our comfort, however felonious is the Heart, hear with what soft language, he does approach her, with a Candle in his Hand:

> Put out the light and then put out the light;
> If I quench thee, thou flaming Minister,
> I can again thy former light restore—

Who would call him a Barbarian, Monster, Savage? Is this a Black-amoor?

> Soles occidere & redire possunt—

The very Soul and Quintessence of Sir *George Etheridge*.

One might think the General should not glory much in this action, but make an hasty work on't, and have turn'd his Eyes away from so unsouldierly an Execution: yet is he all pause and deliberation; handles her as calmly: and is as careful of her Souls health, as it had been her *Father Confessor. Have you prayed to Night,* Desdemona? But the suspence is necessary, that he might have a convenient while so to *roul his Eyes,* and so to *gnaw* his *nether lip* to the spectators. Besides the greater cruelty—*sub tam lentis maxillis.*

But hark, a most tragical thing laid to her charge.

*Oth.*: That Handkerchief, that I so lov'd, and gave thee,
  Thou gav'st to *Cassio.*
*Desd.*: No by my Life and Soul;
  Send for the man and ask him.
*Oth.*: By Heaven, I saw my Handkerchief in his hand—
  . . . I saw the Handkerchief.

So much ado, so much stress, so much passion and repetition about an Handkerchief! Why was not this call'd the *Tragedy of the Handkerchief*? What can be more absurd than (as *Quintilian* expresses it) *in parvis litibus has Tragœdias movere*? We have heard of *Fortunatus his Purse,* and of the *Invisible Cloak,* long ago worn thread bare, and stow'd up in the Wardrobe of obsolete Romances: one might think, that were a fitter place for this Handkerchief, than that it, at this time of day, be worn on the Stage, to raise every where all this clutter and turmoil. Had it been *Desdemona's* Garter, the Sagacious Moor might have smelt a Rat: but the Handkerchief is so remote a trifle, no Booby, on this side *Mauritania,* cou'd make any consequence from it.

We may learn here, that a Woman never loses her Tongue, even tho' after she is stifl'd.

*Desd.*: O falsly, falsly murder'd.
*Em.*: Sweet *Desdemona,* O sweet Mistress, speak.
*Desd.*: A guiltless death I dye.
*Em.*: O who has done the deed?
*Desd.*: No body, I my self, farewell.
  Commend me to my kind Lord, O farewell.

This *Desdemona* is a black swan; or an old Black-amoor is a bewitching Bed-fellow. If this be Nature, it is a *lascheté* below what the English Language can express.

For *Lardella,* to *make love, like an Humble Bee,* was, in the Rehearsal, thought a fancy odd enough.

But hark what follows:

  O heavy hour!
Methinks it shou'd be now a huge Eclipse
Of Sun and Moon, and that the affrighted globe
Shou'd yawn at Alteration.

This is wonderful. Here is Poetry to *elevate* and *amuse.* Here is sound All-sufficient. It wou'd be uncivil to ask *Flamstead,* if the Sun and Moon can both together be so hugely eclipsed, in any *heavy hour* whatsoever. Nor must the Spectators consult *Gresham* Colledge, whether a body is naturally *frighted* till he *Yawn* agen. The Fortune of *Greece* is not concern'd with these Matters. These are Physical circumstances a Poet may be ignorant in, with out any harm to the publick. These slips have no influence on our Manners and good Life; which are the Poets Province.

Rather may we ask here what unnatural crime *Desdemona,* or her Parents had committed, to bring this Judgment down upon her; to Wed a Black-amoor, and innocent to be thus cruelly murder'd by him. What instruction can we make out of this Catastrophe? Or whither must our reflection lead us? Is not this to envenome and sour our spirits, to make us repine and grumble at Providence; and the government of the World? If this be our end, what boots it to be Vertuous?

*Desdemona* dropt the Handkerchief, and missed it that very day after her Marriage; it might have been rumpl'd up with her Wedding sheets: And this Night that she lay in her wedding sheets, the *Fairey* Napkin (whilst *Othello* was stifling her) might have started up to disarm his fury, and stop his ungracious mouth. Then might she (in a Traunce for fear) have lain as dead. Then might he, believing her dead, touch'd with remorse, have honestly cut his own Throat, by the good leave, and with the applause of all the Spectators. Who might thereupon have gone home with a quiet mind, admiring the beauty of Providence; fairly and truly represented on the Theatre.

*Oth.*:     Why, how shou'd she be murdered?
*Em.*: Alas, who knows?
*Oth.*: You heard her say her self it was not I.
*Em.*: She did so, I must needs report a truth.
*Oth.*: She's like a liar gone to burn in Hell.
  'Twas I that did it.
*Em.*: O, the more Angel she!
  And you the blacker Devil.
*Oth.*: She turn'd to folly, and she was an Whore.
*Em.*: Thou dost belye her, and thou art a Devil.
*Oth.*: She was false as Water.
*Em.*: Thou art rash as Fire,
  To say that she was false: O she was heavenly true.

In this kind of Dialogue they continue for forty lines farther, before she bethinks her self, to cry Murder.

  Help, help, O help,
The Moor has kill'd my Mistress, murder, Murder.

But from this Scene to the end of the Play we meet with nothing but blood and butchery, described much-what to the style of *the last Speeches and Confessions of the persons executed at Tyburn*: with this difference, that there we have the *fact,* and the due course of Justice, whereas our Poet against all Justice and Reason, against all Law, Humanity and Nature, in a barbarous arbitrary way, executes and makes havock of his subjects, *Hab-nab,* as they come to hand. *Desdemona* dropt her Handkerchief; therefore she must be stifl'd. *Othello,* by law to be broken on the Wheel, by the Poets cunning escapes with cutting his own Throat. *Cassio,* for I know not what, comes off with a broken shin. *Jago* murders his Benefactor *Roderigo,* as this were poetical gratitude. *Jago* is not yet kill'd, because there never yet was such a villain alive. The Devil, if once he brings a man to be dipt in a deadly sin, lets him alone, to take his course: and now when the *Foul Fiend* has done with him, our wise Authors take the sinner into their poetical service; there to accomplish him, and do the Devils drudgery.

*Philosophy* tells us it is a principle in the Nature of Man *to be grateful.*

*History* may tell us that *John an Oaks, John a Stiles,* or *Jago* were ungrateful; *Poetry* is to follow Nature; Philosophy must be his guide: history and *fact* in particular cases of *John an Oaks,* or *John of Styles,* are no warrant or direction for a Poet. Therefore *Aristotle* is always telling us Poetry is *spoudaiōteron kai philosophōteron,* is more general and abstracted, is led more by the Philosophy, the reason and nature of things, than History: which only records things higlety, piglety, right or wrong as they happen. History might without any preamble or difficulty, say that *Jago* was ungrateful. Philosophy then calls him unnatural; But the Poet is not, without huge labour and preparation to expose the Monster; and after shew the Divine Vengeance executed upon him. The Poet is not to add wilful

Murder to his ingratitude: he has not antidote enough for the Poison: his Hell and Furies are not punishment sufficient for one single crime, of that bulk and aggravation.

> O thou dull Moor, that Handkerchief thou speakest
>     on,
> I found by Fortune, and did give my Husband:
> For often with a solemn earnestness,
> (More than indeed belong'd to such a trifle)
> He beg'd of me to steal it.

Here we see the meanest woman in the Play takes this *Handkerchief* for a *trifle* below her Husband to trouble his head about it. Yet we find, it entered into our Poets head, to make a Tragedy of this *Trifle*.

Then for the *unraveling of the Plot*, as they call it, never was old deputy Recorder in a Country Town, with his spectacles in summoning up the evidence, at such a puzzle: so blunder'd, and bedoultefied: as is our Poet, to have a good riddance: And get the *Catastrophe* off his hands.

What can remain with the Audience to carry home with them from this sort of Poetry, for their use and edification? how can it work, unless (instead of settling the mind, and purging our passions) to delude our senses, disorder our thoughts, addle our brain, pervert our affections, hair our imaginations, corrupt our appetite, and fill our head with vanity, confusion, *Tintamarre*, and Jingle-jangle, beyond what all the Parish Clarks of *London*, with their *old Testament* farces, and interludes, in *Richard* the seconds time cou'd ever pretend to? Our only hopes, for the good of their Souls, can be, that these people go to the Playhouse, as they do to Church, to sit still, look on one another, make no reflection, nor mind the Play, more than they would a Sermon.

There is in this Play, some burlesk, some humour, and ramble of Comical Wit, some shew, and some *Mimickry* to divert the spectators: but the tragical part is, plainly none other, than a Bloody Farce, without salt or savour.

*Notes*

1. Sueton. *in Tib*.
2. *Rehearsal*.

### JOHN HUGHES
#### From *The Guardian*
#### No. 37. April 23, 1713

> Me duce damnosas, homines, compescite curas.
>                     (Ovid, *Rem. Amor.* v. 69.)
> Learn, mortals, from my precepts to control
> The furious passions that disturb the soul.

It is natural for an old man to be fond of such entertainments as revive in his imagination the agreeable impressions made upon it in his youth: the set of wits and beauties he was first acquainted with, the balls and drawing-rooms in which he made an agreeable figure, the music and actors he heard and saw, when his life was fresh, and his spirits vigorous and quick, have usually the preference in his esteem to any succeeding pleasures that present themselves when his taste is grown more languid. It is for this reason I never see a picture of Sir Peter Lely's, who drew so many of my first friends and acquaintance, without a sensible delight; and I am in raptures when I reflect on the compositions of the famous Mr. Henry Lawes, long before Italian music was introduced into our nation. Above all, I am pleased in observing that the tragedies of Shakspeare, which in my youthful days have so frequently filled my eyes with tears, hold their rank still, and are the great support of our theatre.

It was with this agreeable prepossession of mind, I went, some time ago, to see the old tragedy of *Othello*, and took my female wards with me, having promised them a little before to carry them to the first play of Shakspeare's which should be acted. Mrs. Cornelia, who is a great reader, and never fails to peruse the play-bills, which are brought to her every day, gave me notice of it early in the morning. When I came to my Lady Lizard's at dinner, I found the young folks all dressed, and expecting the performance of my promise. I went with them at the proper time, placed them together in the boxes, and myself by them in a corner seat. As I have the chief scenes of the play by heart, I did not look much on the stage, but formed to myself a new satisfaction in keeping an eye on the faces of my little audience, and observing, as it were by reflection, the different passions of the play represented in their countenances. Mrs. Betty told us the names of several persons of distinction, as they took their places in their boxes, and entertained us with the history of a new marriage or two, till the curtain drew up. I soon perceived that Mrs. Jane was touched with the love of Desdemona, and in a concern to see how she would come off with her parents. Annabella had a rambling eye, and for some time was more taken up with observing what gentlemen looked at her, and with criticising the dress of the ladies, than with any thing that passed on the stage. Mrs. Cornelia, who I have often said is addicted to the study of romances, commended that speech in the play in which Othello mentions his "hair-breadth scapes in th' imminent deadly breach," and recites his travels and adventures with which he had captivated the heart of Desdemona. The Sparkler looked several times frighted: and as the distress of the play was heightened, their different attention was collected, and fixed wholly on the stage, till I saw them all, with a secret satisfaction, betrayed into tears.

I have often considered this play as a noble, but irregular, production of a genius, who had the power of animating the theatre beyond any writer we have ever known. The touches of nature in it are strong and masterly; but the economy of the fable, and in some particulars the probability, are too much neglected. If I would speak of it in the most severe terms, I should say as Waller does of the *Maid's Tragedy*,

> Great are its faults, but glorious is its flame.

But it would be poor employment in a critic to observe upon the faults, and shew no taste for the beauties, in a work that has always struck the most sensible part of our audiences in a very forcible manner.

The chief subject of this piece is the passion of jealousy, which the poet hath represented at large, in its birth, its various workings and agonies, and its horrid consequences. From this passion, and the innocence and simplicity of the person suspected, arises a very moving distress.

It is a remark, as I remember, of a modern writer, who is thought to have penetrated deeply into the nature of the passions, "that the most extravagant love is nearest to the strongest hatred." The Moor is furious in both these extremes. His love is tempestuous, and mingled with a wildness peculiar to his character, which seems very artfully to prepare for the change which is to follow.

How savage, yet how ardent, is that expression of the raptures of his heart, when, looking after Desdemona as she withdraws, he breaks out,

> Excellent wench! Perdition catch my soul,
> But I do love thee; and when I love thee not,
> Chaos is come again.

The deep and subtle villany of Iago, in working this change from love to jealousy, in so tumultuous a mind as that of Othello, prepossessed with a confidence in the disinterested affection of the man who is leading him on insensibly to his ruin, is likewise drawn with a masterly hand. Iago's broken hints, questions, and seeming care to hide the reason of them; his obscure suggestions to raise the curiosity of the Moor: his personated confusion, and refusing to explain himself while Othello is drawn on, and held in suspense till he grows impatient and angry; then his throwing in the poison, and naming to him in a caution, the passion he would raise,

—O beware of jealousy!—

are inimitable strokes of art, in that scene which has always been justly esteemed one of the best which was ever represented on the theatre.

To return to the character of Othello; his strife of passions, his starts, his returns of love, and threatenings to Iago, who had put his mind on the rack, his relapses afterward to jealousy, his rage against his wife, and his asking pardon of Iago, whom he thinks he had abused for his fidelity to him, are touches which no one can overlook that has the sentiments of human nature, or has considered the heart of man in its frailties, its penances, and all the variety of its agitations. The torments which the Moor suffers are so exquisitely drawn, as to render him as much an object of compassion, even in the barbarous action of murdering Desdemona, as the innocent person herself who falls under his hand.

But there is nothing in which the poet has more shewn his judgment in this play, than in the circumstance of the handkerchief, which is employed as a confirmation to the jealousy of Othello already raised. What I would here observe is, that the very slightness of this circumstance is the beauty of it. How finely has Shakspeare expressed the nature of jealousy in those lines, which, on this occasion, he puts into the mouth of Iago,

> Trifles light as air
> Are to the jealous, confirmation strong
> As proofs of holy writ.

It would be easy for a tasteless critic to turn any of the beauties I have here mentioned into ridicule; but such a one would only betray a mechanical judgment, formed out of borrowed rules and common-place reading, and not arising from any true discernment in human nature, and its passions.

As the moral of this tragedy is an admirable caution against hasty suspicions, and the giving way to the first transports of rage and jealousy, which may plunge a man in a few minutes into all the horrors of guilt, distraction, and ruin, I shall farther enforce it, by relating a scene of misfortunes of the like kind, which really happened some years ago in Spain; and is an instance of the most tragical hurricane of passion I have ever met with in history. It may be easily conceived, that a heart ever big with resentments of its own dignity, and never allayed by reflections which make us honour ourselves for acting with reason and equality, will take fire precipitantly. It will, on a sudden, flame too high to be extinguished. The short story I am going to tell is a lively instance of the truth of this observation, and a just warning to those of jealous honour, to look about them, and begin to possess their souls as they ought, for no man of spirit knows how terrible a creature he is, till he comes to be provoked.

Don Alonzo, a Spanish nobleman, had a beautiful and virtuous wife, with whom he had lived for some years in great tranquillity. The gentleman, however, was not free from the faults usually imputed to his nation; he was proud, suspicious, and impetuous. He kept a Moor in his house, whom, on a complaint from his lady, he had punished for a small offence with the utmost severity. The slave vowed revenge, and

communicated his resolution to one of the lady's women with whom he lived in a criminal way. This creature also hated her mistress, for she feared she was observed by her; she therefore undertook to make Don Alonzo jealous, by insinuating that the gardener was often admitted to his lady in private, and promising to make him an eye-witness of it. At a proper time agreed on between her and the Morisco, she sent a message to the gardener, that his lady, having some hasty orders to give him, would have him come that moment to her in her chamber. In the mean time she had placed Alonzo privately in an outer room, that he might observe who passed that way. It was not long before he saw the gardener appear. Alonzo had not patience, but, following him into the apartment, struck him at one blow with a dagger to the heart; then dragging his lady by the hair, without inquiring farther, he instantly killed her.

Here he paused, looked on the dead bodies with all the agitations of a demon of revenge; when the wench who had occasioned these terrors, distracted with remorse, threw herself at his feet, and in a voice of lamentation, without sense of the consequence, repeated all her guilt. Alonzo was overwhelmed with all the violent passions at one instant, and uttered the broken voices and emotions of each of them for a moment, till at last he recollected himself enough to end his agony of love, anger, disdain, revenge, and remorse, by murdering the maid, the Moor, and himself.

# WILLIAM HAZLITT
## "Othello"
### Characters of Shakespear's Plays
### 1817

It has been said that tragedy purifies the affections by terror and pity. That is, it substitutes imaginary sympathy for mere selfishness. It gives us a high and permanent interest, beyond ourselves, in humanity as such. It raises the great, the remote, and the possible to an equality with the real, the little and the near. It makes man a partaker with his kind. It subdues and softens the stubbornness of his will. It teaches him that there are and have been others like himself, by showing him as in a glass what they have felt, thought, and done. It opens the chambers of the human heart. It leaves nothing indifferent to us that can affect our common nature. It excites our sensibility by exhibiting the passions wound up to the utmost pitch by the power of imagination or the temptation of circumstances; and corrects their fatal excesses in ourselves by pointing to the greater extent of sufferings and of crimes to which they have led others. Tragedy creates a balance of the affections. It makes us thoughtful spectators in the lists of life. It is the refiner of the species; a discipline of humanity. The habitual study of poetry and works of imagination is one chief part of a well-grounded education. A taste for liberal art is necessary to complete the character of a gentleman. Science alone is hard and mechanical. It exercises the understanding upon things out of ourselves, while it leaves the affections unemployed, or engrossed with our own immediate, narrow interests.—*Othello* furnishes an illustration of these remarks. It excites our sympathy in an extraordinary degree. The moral it conveys has a closer application to the concerns of human life than that of almost any other of Shakespear's plays. 'It comes directly home to the bosoms and business of men.' The pathos in *Lear* is indeed more dreadful and overpowering: but it is less natural, and less of every day's occurrence. We have not the same degree of sympathy with the passions described in *Macbeth*.

The interest in *Hamlet* is more remote and reflex. That of *Othello* is at once equally profound and affecting.

The picturesque contrasts of character in this play are almost as remarkable as the depth of the passion. The Moor Othello, the gentle Desdemona, the villain Iago, the good-natured Cassio, the fool Roderigo, present a range and variety of character as striking and palpable as that produced by the opposition of costume in a picture. Their distinguishing qualities stand out to the mind's eye, so that even when we are not thinking of their actions or sentiments, the idea of their persons is still as present to us as ever. These characters and the images they stamp upon the mind are the farthest asunder possible, the distance between them is immense: yet the compass of knowledge and invention which the poet has shown in embodying these extreme creations of his genius is only greater than the truth and felicity with which he has identified each character with itself, or blended their different qualities together in the same story. What a contrast the character of Othello forms to that of Iago! At the same time, the force of conception with which these two figures are opposed to each other is rendered still more intense by the complete consistency with which the traits of each character are brought out in a state of the highest finishing. The making one black and the other white, the one unprincipled, the other unfortunate in the extreme, would have answered the common purposes of effect, and satisfied the ambition of an ordinary painter of character. Shakespear has laboured the finer shades of difference in both with as much care and skill as if he had had to depend on the execution alone for the success of his design. On the other hand, Desdemona and Æmilia are not meant to be opposed with anything like strong contrast to each other. Both are, to outward appearance, characters of common life, not more distinguished than women usually are, by difference of rank and situation. The difference of their thoughts and sentiments is however laid open, their minds are separated from each other by signs as plain and as little to be mistaken as the complexions of their husbands.

The movement of the passion in Othello is exceedingly different from that of Macbeth. In Macbeth there is a violent struggle between opposite feelings, between ambition and the stings of conscience, almost from first to last: in Othello, the doubtful conflict between contrary passions, though dreadful, continues only for a short time, and the chief interest is excited by the alternate ascendancy of different passions, by the entire and unforeseen change from the fondest love and most unbounded confidence to the tortures of jealousy and the madness of hatred. The revenge of Othello, after it has once taken thorough possession of his mind, never quits it, but grows stronger and stronger at every moment of its delay. The nature of the Moor is noble, confiding, tender, and generous; but his blood is of the most inflammable kind; and being once roused by a sense of his wrongs, he is stopped by no considerations of remorse or pity till he has given a loose to all the dictates of his rage and his despair. It is in working his noble nature up to this extremity through rapid but gradual transitions, in raising passion to its height from the smallest beginnings and in spite of all obstacles, in painting the expiring conflict between love and hatred, tenderness and resentment, jealousy and remorse, in unfolding the strength and the weakness of our nature, in uniting sublimity of thought with the anguish of the keenest woe, in putting in motion the various impulses that agitate this our mortal being, and at last blending them in that noble tide of deep and sustained passion, impetuous but majestic, that 'flows on to the Propontic, and knows no ebb,' that Shakespear has shown the mastery of his genius and of his power over the human heart. The third act of *Othello* is his finest display, not of knowledge or passion separately, but of the two combined, of the knowledge of character with the expression of passion, of consummate art in the keeping up of appearances with the profound workings of nature, and the convulsive movements of uncontroulable agony, of the power of inflicting torture and of suffering it. Not only is the tumult of passion in Othello's mind heaved up from the very bottom of the soul, but every the slightest undulation of feeling is seen on the surface, as it arises from the impulses of imagination or the malicious suggestions of Iago. The progressive preparation for the catastrophe is wonderfully managed from the Moor's first gallant recital of the story of his love, of 'the spells and witchcraft he had used,' from his unlooked-for and romantic success, the fond satisfaction with which he dotes on his own happiness, the unreserved tenderness of Desdemona and her innocent importunities in favour of Cassio, irritating the suspicions instilled into her husband's mind by the perfidy of Iago, and rankling there to poison, till he loses all command of himself, and his rage can only be appeased by blood. She is introduced, just before Iago begins to put his scheme in practice, pleading for Cassio with all the thoughtless gaiety of friendship and winning confidence in the love of Othello.

> What! Michael Cassio?
> That came a wooing with you, and so many a time,
> When I have spoke of you dispraisingly,
> Hath ta'en your part, to have so much to do
> To bring him in?—Why this is not a boon:
> 'Tis as I should intreat you wear your gloves,
> Or feed on nourishing meats, or keep you warm;
> Or sue to you to do a peculiar profit
> To your person. Nay, when I have a suit,
> Wherein I mean to touch your love indeed,
> It shall be full of poise, and fearful to be granted.

Othello's confidence, at first only staggered by broken hints and insinuations, recovers itself at sight of Desdemona; and he exclaims

> If she be false, O then Heav'n mocks itself:
> I'll not believe it.

But presently after, on brooding over his suspicions by himself, and yielding to his apprehensions of the worst, his smothered jealousy breaks out into open fury, and he returns to demand satisfaction of Iago like a wild beast stung with the envenomed shaft of the hunters. 'Look where he comes,' etc. In this state of exasperation and violence, after the first paroxysms of his grief and tenderness have had their vent in that passionate apostrophe, 'I felt not Cassio's kisses on her lips,' Iago, by false aspersions, and by presenting the most revolting images to his mind,[1] easily turns the storm of passion from himself against Desdemona, and works him up into a trembling agony of doubt and fear, in which he abandons all his love and hopes in a breath.

> Now do I see 'tis true. Look here, Iago,
> All my fond love thus do I blow to Heav'n. 'Tis gone.
> Arise black vengeance from the hollow hell;
> Yield up, O love, thy crown and hearted throne
> To tyrannous hate! Swell bosom with thy fraught;
> For 'tis of aspicks' tongues.

From this time, his raging thoughts 'never look back, ne'er ebb to humble love,' till his revenge is sure of its object, the painful regrets and involuntary recollections of past circumstances which cross his mind amidst the dim trances of passion, aggravating the sense of his wrongs, but not shaking his purpose. Once indeed, where Iago shows him Cassio with the handkerchief in his hand, and making sport (as he thinks) of his misfortunes, the intolerable bitterness of his feelings, the extreme sense of shame, makes him fall to praising her accomplishments and relapse into a momentary fit of weakness, 'Yet, oh the pity of it, Iago, the pity of it!' This returning fondness however only serves, as it is managed by Iago, to whet his revenge, and set his heart more against her. In his conversations with Desdemona, the persuasion of her guilt and the immediate proofs of her duplicity seem to irritate his resentment and aversion to her; but in the scene immediately preceding her death, the recollection of his love returns upon him in all its tenderness and force; and after her death, he all at once forgets his wrongs in the sudden and irreparable sense of his loss.

> My wife! My wife! What wife? I have no wife.
> Oh insupportable! Oh heavy hour!

This happens before he is assured of her innocence; but afterwards his remorse is as dreadful as his revenge has been, and yields only to fixed and death-like despair. His farewell speech, before he kills himself, in which he conveys his reasons to the senate for the murder of his wife, is equal to the first speech in which he gave them an account of his courtship of her, and 'his whole course of love.' Such an ending was alone worthy of such a commencement. . . .

The character of Desdemona is inimitable both in itself, and as it appears in contrast with Othello's groundless jealousy, and with the foul conspiracy of which she is the innocent victim. Her beauty and external graces are only indirectly glanced at: we see 'her visage in her mind'; her character every where predominates over her person.

> A maiden never bold:
> Of spirit so still and quiet, that her motion
> Blush'd at itself.

There is one fine compliment paid to her by Cassio, who exclaims triumphantly when she comes ashore at Cyprus after the storm,

> Tempests themselves, high seas, and howling winds,
> As having sense of beauty, do omit
> Their mortal natures, letting safe go by
> The divine Desdemona.

In general, as is the case with most of Shakespear's females, we lose sight of her personal charms in her attachment and devotedness to her husband. 'She is subdued even to the very quality of her lord'; and to Othello's 'honours and his valiant parts her soul and fortunes consecrates.' The lady protests so much herself, and she is as good as her word. The truth of conception, with which timidity and boldness are united in the same character, is marvellous. The extravagance of her resolutions, the pertinacity of her affections, may be said to arise out of the gentleness of her nature. They imply an unreserved reliance on the purity of her own intentions, an entire surrender of her fears to her love, a knitting of herself (heart and soul) to the fate of another. Bating the commencement of her passion, which is a little fantastical and headstrong (though even that may perhaps be consistently accounted for from her inability to resist a rising inclination[2]) her whole character consists in having no will of her own, no prompter but her obedience. Her romantic turn is only a consequence of the domestic and practical part of her disposition; and instead of following Othello to the wars, she would gladly have 'remained at home a moth of peace,' if her husband could have staid with her. Her resignation and angelic sweetness of temper do not desert her at the last. The scenes in which she laments and tries to account for Othello's estrangement from her are exquisitely beautiful. After he has struck her, and called her names, she says,

> Alas, Iago,
> What shall I do to win my lord again?
> Good friend, go to him; for by this light of heaven,
> I know not how I lost him. Here I kneel;
> If e'er my will did trespass 'gainst his love,
> Either in discourse, or thought, or actual deed,
> Or that mine eyes, mine ears, or any sense
> Delighted them on any other form;
> Or that I do not, and ever did,
> And ever will, though he do shake me off
> To beggarly divorcement, love him dearly,
> Comfort forswear me. Unkindness may do much,
> And his unkindness may defeat my life,
> But never taint my love.
> *Iago:* I pray you be content: 'tis but his humour.
> The business of the state does him offence.
> *Desdemona:* If 'twere no other!

The scene which follows with Æmilia and the song of the Willow, are equally beautiful, and show the author's extreme power of varying the expression of passion, in all its moods and in all circumstances.

> *Æmilia:* Would you had never seen him.
> *Desdemona:* So would not I: my love doth so approve
> him,
> That even his stubbornness, his checks, his
> frowns,
> Have grace and favour in them, etc.

Not the unjust suspicions of Othello, not Iago's unprovoked treachery, place Desdemona in a more amiable or interesting light than the conversation (half earnest, half jest) between her and Æmilia on the common behaviour of women to their husbands. This dialogue takes place just before the last fatal scene. If Othello had overheard it, it would have prevented the whole catastrophe; but then it would have spoiled the play.

The character of Iago is one of the supererogations of Shakespear's genius. Some persons, more nice than wise, have thought this whole character unnatural, because his villainy is *without a sufficient motive*. Shakespear, who was as good a philosopher as he was a poet, thought otherwise. He knew that the love of power, which is another name for the love of mischief, is natural to man. He would know this as well or better than if it had been demonstrated to him by a logical diagram, merely from seeing children paddle in the dirt or kill flies for sport. Iago in fact belongs to a class of character, common to Shakespear and at the same time peculiar to him; whose heads are as acute and active as their hearts are hard and callous. Iago is to be sure an extreme instance of the kind; that is to say, of diseased intellectual activity, with the most perfect indifference to moral good or evil, or rather with a decided preference of the latter, because it falls more readily in with his favourite propensity, gives greater zest to his thoughts and scope to his actions. He is quite or nearly as indifferent to his own fate as to that of others; he runs all risks for a trifling and doubtful advantage; and is himself the dupe and victim of his ruling passion—an insatiable craving after action of the most difficult and dangerous kind. 'Our ancient' is a philosopher, who fancies that a lie that kills has more point in it than an alliteration or an antithesis; who thinks a fatal experiment on the peace of a family a better thing than watching the palpitations in the heart of a flea in a microscope; who plots the ruin of his friends as an exercise for his ingenuity, and stabs men in the dark to prevent *ennui*. His gaiety, such as it is, arises from the success of his treachery; his ease from the torture he has inflicted on others. He is an amateur of tragedy in real life; and instead of employing his invention on imaginary characters, or long-forgotten incidents, he takes the bolder and more desperate course of getting up his plot at home, casts the principal parts among his nearest friends and connections, and rehearses it in downright earnest, with steady nerves and unabated resolution. We will just give an illustration or two.

One of his most characteristic speeches is that immediately after the marriage of Othello.

> *Roderigo:* What a full fortune does the thick lips owe,
>   If he can carry her thus!
> *Iago:* Call up her father:
>   Rouse him (*Othello*) make after him, poison his delight,
>   Proclaim him in the streets, incense her kinsmen,
>   And tho' he in a fertile climate dwell,
>   Plague him with flies: tho' that his joy be joy,
>   Yet throw such changes of vexation on it,
>   As it may lose some colour.

In the next passage, his imagination runs riot in the mischief he is plotting, and breaks out into the wildness and impetuosity of real enthusiasm.

> *Roderigo:* Here is her father's house: I'll call aloud.
> *Iago:* Do, with like timourous accent and dire yell
>   As when, by night and negligence, the fire
>   Is spied in populous cities.

One of his most favourite topics, on which he is rich indeed, and in descanting on which his spleen serves him for a Muse, is the disproportionate match between Desdemona and the Moor. This is a clue to the character of the lady which he is by no means ready to part with. It is brought forward in the first scene, and he recurs to it, when in answer to his insinuations against Desdemona, Roderigo says,

> I cannot believe that in her—she's full of most blest conditions.
> *Iago:* Bless'd fig's end. The wine she drinks is made of grapes. If she had been blest, she would never have married the Moor.

And again with still more spirit and fatal effect afterwards, when he turns this very suggestion arising in Othello's own breast to her prejudice.

> *Othello:* And yet how nature erring from itself—
> *Iago:* Ay, there's the point;—as to be bold with you,
>   Not to affect many proposed matches
>   Of her own clime, complexion, and degree, etc.

This is probing to the quick. Iago here turns the character of poor Desdemona, as it were, inside out. It is certain that nothing but the genius of Shakespear could have preserved the entire interest and delicacy of the part, and have even drawn an additional elegance and dignity from the peculiar circumstances in which she is placed.—The habitual licentiousness of Iago's conversation is not to be traced to the pleasure he takes in gross or lascivious images, but to his desire of finding out the worst side of everything, and of proving himself an over-match for appearances. He has none of 'the milk of human kindness' in his composition. His imagination rejects every thing that has not a strong infusion of the most unpalatable ingredients; his mind digests only poisons. Virtue or goodness or whatever has the least 'relish of salvation in it,' is, to his depraved appetite, sickly and insipid: and he even resents the good opinion entertained of his own integrity, as if it were an affront cast on the masculine sense and spirit of his character. Thus at the meeting between Othello and Desdemona, he exclaims—'Oh, you are well tuned now: but I'll set down the pegs that make this music, *as honest as I am*'—his character of *bonhommie* not sitting at all easy upon him. . . .

If Iago is detestable enough when he has business on his hands and all his engines at work, he is still worse when he has

nothing to do, and we only see into the hollowness of his heart. His indifference when Othello falls into a swoon, is perfectly diabolical.

> *Iago:* How is it, General? Have you not hurt your head?
> *Othello:* Do'st thou mock me?
> *Iago:* I mock you not, by Heaven, etc.

The part indeed would hardly be tolerated, even as a foil to the virtue and generosity of the other characters in the play, but for its indefatigable industry and inexhaustible resources, which divert the attention of the spectator (as well as his own) from the end he has in view to the means by which it must be accomplished.—Edmund the Bastard in *Lear* is something of the same character, placed in less prominent circumstances. Zanga is a vulgar caricature of it.

## JOHN QUINCY ADAMS
### "The Character of Desdemona"
*The American Monthly Magazine*, March 1836, pp. 209–17

There are critics who cannot bear to see the virtue and delicacy of Shakspeare's Desdemona called in question; who defend her on the ground that Othello is not an Ethiopian, but a Moor; that he is not black, but only tawny; and they protest against the sable mask of Othello upon the stage, and against the pictures of him in which he is always painted black. They say that prejudices have been taken against Desdemona from the slanders of Iago, from the railings of Roderigo, from the disappointed paternal rancour of Brabantio, and from the desponding concessions of Othello himself.

I have said, that since I entered upon the third of Shakspeare's seven ages, the first and chief capacity in which I have read and studied him is as a *teacher of morals*; and that I had scarcely ever seen a player of his parts who regarded him as a *moralist* at all. I further said, that in my judgment no man could understand him who did not study him preeminently as a teacher of morals. These critics say they do not incline to put Shakspeare on a level with Æsop! Sure enough *they* do not study Shakspeare as a teacher of morals. To *them*, therefore, Desdemona is a perfect character; and her love for Othello is not unnatural, because he is not a Congo negro but only a sooty Moor, and has royal blood in his veins.

My objections to the character of Desdemona arise not from what Iago, or Roderigo, or Brabantio, or Othello says of her; but from what she herself *does*. She absconds from her father's house, in the dead of night, to marry a blackamoor. She breaks a father's heart, and covers his noble house with shame, to gratify—what? Pure love, like that of Juliet or Miranda? No! unnatural passion; it cannot be named with delicacy. Her admirers now say this is criticism of 1835; that the color of Othello has nothing to do with the passion of Desdemona. No? Why, if Othello had been white, what need would there have been for her running away with him? She could have made no better match. Her father could have made no reasonable objection to it; and there could have been no tragedy. If the color of Othello is not as vital to the whole tragedy as the age of Juliet is to her character and destiny, then have I read Shakspeare in vain. The father of Desdemona charges Othello with magic arts in obtaining the affections of his daughter. Why, but because her passion for him is *unnatural*; and why is it unnatural, but because of his color? In the very first scene, in the dialogue between Roderigo and Iago, before they rouse Brabantio to inform him of his daughter's elopement, Roderigo contemptuously calls Othello "the thick lips." I cannot in decency quote here—but turn to the book, and see in what language Iago announces to her father his daughter's shameful misconduct. The language of Roderigo is more supportable. *He* is a Venitian gentleman, himself a rejected suitor of Desdemona; and who has been forbidden by her father access to his house. Roused from his repose at the dead of night by the loud cries of these two men, Brabantio spurns, with indignation and scorn, the insulting and beastly language of Iago; and sharply chides Roderigo, whom he supposes to be hovering about his house in defiance of his prohibitions and in a state of intoxication. He threatens him with punishment. Roderigo replies—

> Sir, I will answer any thing. But I beseech you,
> If't be your pleasure, and most wise consent,
> (As partly, I find, it is,) that your fair daughter
> At this odd-even and dull watch o' the night,
> Transported—with no worse nor better guard,
> But with a knave of common hire, a gondolier,—
> To the gross clasps to a lascivious Moor,—
> If this be known of you, and your allowance,
> We then have done you bold and saucy wrongs;
> But if you know not this, my manners tell me,
> We have your wrong rebuke. Do not believe,
> That, from the sense of all civility,
> I thus would play and trifle with your reverence:
> Your daughter—if you have not given her leave,—
> I say again, hath made a gross revolt;
> Tying her duty, beauty, wit, and fortunes,
> In an extravagant and wheeling stranger,
> Of here and every where: Straight satisfy yourself:
> If she be in her chamber, or your house,
> Let loose on me the justice of the state
> For thus deluding you.

Struck by this speech as by a clap of thunder, Brabantio calls up his people, remembers a portentous dream, calls for light, goes and searches with his servants, and comes back saying—

> It is too true an evil: gone she is:
> And what's to come of my despised time,
> Is nought but bitterness.

The father's heart is broken; life is no longer of any value to him; he repeats this sentiment time after time whenever he appears in the scene; and in the last scene of the play, where Desdemona lies dead, her uncle Gratiano says—

> Poor Desdemona! I am glad thy father's dead,
> Thy match was mortal to him, and pure grief
> Shore his old thread in twain.

Indeed! indeed! I must look at Shakspeare in this as in all his pictures of human life, in the capacity of a teacher of morals. I must believe that, in exhibiting a daughter of a Venitian nobleman of the highest rank eloping in the dead of the night to marry a thick-lipped wool-headed Moor, opening a train of consequences which lead to her own destruction by her husband's hands, and to that of her father by a broken heart, he did not intend to present her as an example of the perfection of female virtue. I must look first at the action, then at the motive, then at the consequences, before I inquire in what light it is received and represented by the other persons of the drama. The first action of Desdemona discards all female delicacy, all filial duty, all sense of ingenuous shame. So I consider it—and so, it is considered, by her own father. Her offence is not a mere elopement from her father's house for a clandestine marriage. I hope it requires no unreasonable rigour of morality to consider even *that* as suited to raise a prepossession rather unfavorable to the character of a young woman of refined sensibility and elevated education. But an elopement for a clandestine marriage with a blackamoor!—That is the

measure of my estimation of the character of Desdemona from the beginning; and when I have passed my judgment upon it, and find in the play that from the first moment of her father's knowledge of the act it made him loathe his life, and that it finally broke his heart, I am then in time to inquire, what was the deadly venom which inflicted the immedicable wound:— and what is it, but the color of Othello?

> Now, Roderigo,
> Where did'st thou see her?—Oh, unhappy girl!—
> *With the Moor, say'st thou?*—Who would be a
>         father?

These are the disjointed lamentations of the wretched parent when the first disclosure of his daughter's shame is made known to him. This scene is one of the inimitable pictures of human passion in the hands of Shakspeare, and that half line,

> With the *Moor* say'st thou?

comes from the deepest recesses of the soul.

Again, when Brabantio first meets Othello, he breaks out:

> O, thou foul thief, where hast thou stow'd my
>         daughter?
> Damn'd as thou art, thou hast enchanted her:
> For I'll refer me to all things of sense,
> If she, in chains of magic were not bound,
> Whether a maid so tender, fair, and happy,
> So opposite to marriage that she shunn'd
> The wealthy *curled* darlings of our nation,
> Would ever have to incur our general mock,
> Run from her guardage *to the sooty bosom*
> Of such a thing as thou; to fear, not to delight.

Several of the English commentators have puzzled themselves with the inquiry why the epithet "curled" is here applied to the wealthy darlings of the nation; and Dr. Johnson thinks it has no reference to the hair; but it evidently has. The *curled* hair is in antithetic contrast to the sooty bosom, the thick lips, and the woolly head. The contrast of color is the very hinge upon which Brabantio founds his charge of magic, counteracting the impulse of nature.

At the close of the same scene (the second of the first act) Brabantio, hearing that the duke is in council upon public business of the State, determines to carry Othello before him for trial upon the charge of magic. "Mine," says he,

> Mine's not a middle course; the duke himself
> Or any of my brothers of the state
> Cannot but feel the wrong, as 'twere their own:
> For if such actions may have passage free,
> Bond slaves and Pagans shall our statesmen be.

And Steevens, in his note on this passage, says, "He alludes to the common condition of all blacks who come from their own country, both *slaves* and *pagans*; and uses the word in contempt of Othello and his complexion. If this Moor is now suffered to escape with impunity, it will be such an encouragement to his black countrymen, that we may expect to see all the first offices of our state filled up by the Pagans and bond-slaves of Africa." Othello himself in his narrative says that he had been taken by the insolent foe and sold to slavery. He *had been* a slave.

Once more—When Desdemona pleads to the Duke and the council for permission to go with Othello to Cyprus, she says,

> That I did love the Moor, to live with him,
> My downright violence and storm of fortune
> May trumpet to the world; *my heart's subdued,*
> *Even to the very quality of my lord;*
> I saw Othello's visage in his mind;
> And to his honours and his valiant parts
> Did I my soul and fortunes consecrate.

In commenting upon this passage, Wm. Henley says, "That *quality* here signifies the Moorish *complexion* of Othello, and not his military profession (as Malone had supposed), is obvious from what immediately follows: 'I saw Othello's visage in his mind;' and also from what the Duke says to Brabantio—

> If virtue no delighted beauty lack
> Your son-in-law is far more fair than black.

The characters of Othello and Iago in this play are evidently intended as contrasted pictures of human nature, each setting off the other. They are national portraits of man—the ITALIAN and the MOOR. The Italian is *white, crafty,* and *cruel;* a consummate villain; yet, as often happens in the realities of that description whom we occasionally meet in the intercourse of life, so vain of his own artifices that he betrays himself by boasting of them and their success. Accordingly, in the very first scene he reveals to Roderigo the treachery of his own character:—

> For when my outward action doth demonstrate
> The native act and figure of my heart
> In compliment extern, 'tis not long after
> But I will wear my heart upon my sleeve
> For daws to peck at: I am not what I am.

There is a seeming inconsistency in the fact that a double dealer should disclose his own secret, which must necessarily put others upon their guard against him; but the inconsistency is in human nature, and not in the poet.

The double dealing Italian is a very intelligent man, a keen and penetrating observer, and full of ingenuity to devise and contrive base expedients. His language is coarse, rude, and obscene: his humor is caustic and bitter. Conscious of no honest principle in himself, he believes not in the existence of honesty in others. He is jealous and suspicious; quick to note every trifle light as air, and to draw from it inferences of evil as confirmed circumstances. In his dealings with the Moor, while he is even harping upon his honesty, he offers to commit any murder from extreme attachment to his person and interests. In all that Iago says of others, and especially of Desdemona, there is a mixture of truth and falsehood, blended together, in which the truth itself serves to accredit the lie; and such is the ordinary character of malicious slanders. Doctor Johnson speaks of "the soft simplicity," the "innocence," the "artlessness" of Desdemona. Iago speaks of her as a *supersubtle* Venitian; and, when kindling the sparks of jealousy in the soul of Othello, he says,

> She did deceive her father, marrying you:
> And when she seemed to shake and fear your looks,
> She loved them most.

"And so she did," answers Othello. This charge, then, was true; and Iago replies:

> Why, go to, then;
> She that so young could give out such a seeming
> To seal her father's eyes up, close as oak.—
> He thought 'twas witchcraft.

It was not witchcraft; but surely as little was it simplicity, innocence, artlessness. The effect of this suggestion upon Othello is terrible only because he knows it is true. Brabantio, on parting from him, had just given him the same warning, to which he had not then paid the slightest heed. But soon his suspicions are roused—he tries to repel them; they are fermenting in his brain: he appears vehemently moved and yet unwilling to acknowledge it. Iago, with fiend-like sagacity, seizes upon the paroxysm of emotion, and then comes the following dialogue:—

> *Iago:* My lord, I see you are mov'd.
> *Othello:*       No, not much mov'd:—
> I do not think but Desdemona's honest.
> *Iago:* Long live she so! and long live you to think so!
> *Oth.:* And yet, how nature erring from itself,—
> *Iago:* Ay, there's the point:—As,—to be bold with
>      you,—
> Not to affect many proposed matches,
> Of her own clime, complexion, and degree;
> Whereto, we see, in all things nature tends:
> Foh! one may smell, in such, a will most rank,
> Foul disproportion, thoughts unnatural.

The deadly venom of these imputations, working up to frenzy the suspicions of the Moor, consist not in their falsehood but in their truth.

I have said the character of Desdemona was deficient in delicacy. Besides the instances to which I referred in proof of this charge, observe what she says in pleading for the restoration of Cassio to his office, from which he had been cashiered by Othello for beastly drunkenness and a consequent night-brawl, in which he had stabbed Montano—the predecessor of Othello as Governor of Cypress—and nearly killed him; yet in urging Othello to restore Cassio to his office and to favor, Desdemona says—

> in faith, he's penitent;
> And yet his trespass, in our common reason,
> (Save that, they say, the wars must make examples
> Out of their best,) *is not almost a fault*
> To incur a private check.

Now, to palliate the two crimes of Cassio—his drunken fit and his stabbing of Montano—the reader knows that he has been inveigled to the commission of them by the accursed artifices of Iago; but Desdemona knows nothing of this; she has no excuse for Cassio—nothing to plead for him but his penitence. And is this the character for a woman of delicate sentiment to give of such a complicated and heinous offence as that of which Cassio has been guilty, even when pleading for his pardon? No! it is not for female delicacy to extenuate the crimes of drunkenness and bloodshed, even when performing the appropriate office of raising the soul-subduing voice for mercy.

Afterwards, in the same speech, she says—

> What! Michael Cassio,
> That came a-wooing with you; and many a time,
> When I have spoke of you dispraisingly,
> Hath ta'en your part; to have so much to do
> To bring *him* in!

I will not inquire how far this avowal that she had been in the frequent habit of speaking dispraisingly of Othello at the very time when she was so deeply enamoured with his honors and his valiant parts, was consistent with sincerity. Young ladies must be allowed a little concealment and a little disguise, even for passions of which they have no need to be ashamed. It is the rosy pudency—the irresistible charm of the sex; but the exercise of it in satirical censure upon the very object of their most ardent affections is certainly no indication of innocence, simplicity, or artlessness.

I still retain, then, the opinion—

First. That the passion of Desdemona for Othello is *unnatural,* solely and exclusively because of his color.

Second. That her elopement *to* him, and secret marriage *with* him, indicate a personal character not only very deficient in delicacy, but totally regardless of filial duty, of female modesty, and of ingenuous shame.

Third. That her deficiency in delicacy is discernible in her conduct and discourse throughout the play.

I perceive and acknowledge, indeed, the admirable address with which the part has been contrived to inspire and to warm the breast of the spectator with a deep interest in her fate; and I am well aware that my own comparative insensibility to it is not in unison with the general impression which it produces upon the stage. I shrink from the thought of slandering even a creature of the imagination. When the spectator or reader follows, on the stage or in the closet, the infernal thread of duplicity and of execrable devices with which Iago entangles his victims, it is the purpose of the dramatist to merge all the faults and vices of the sufferers in the overwhelming flood of their calamities, and in the unmingled detestation of the inhuman devil, their betrayer and destroyer. And in all this, I see not only the skill of the artist, but the power of the moral operator, the purifier of the spectator's heart by the agency of *terror* and *pity*.

The characters of Othello and Desdemona, like all the characters of men and women in real life, are of "mingled yarn," with qualities of good and bad—of virtues and vices in proportion differently composed. Iago, with a high order of intellect, is, in moral principle, the very spirit of evil. I have said the moral of the tragedy is, that the intermarriage of black and white blood is a violation of the law of nature. *That* is the lesson to be learned from the play. To exhibit all the natural consequences of their act, the poet is compelled to make the marriage secret. It must commence by an elopement, and by an outrage upon the decorum of social intercourse. He must therefore assume, for the performance of this act, persons of moral character sufficiently frail and imperfect to be capable of performing it, but in other respects endowed with pleasing and estimable qualities. Thus, the Moor is represented as of a free, and open, and generous nature; as a Christian; as a distinguished military commander in the service of the Republic of Venice; as having rendered important service to the State, and as being in the enjoyment of a splendid reputation as a warrior. The other party to the marriage is a maiden, fair, gentle, and accomplished; born and educated in the proudest rank of Venitian nobility.

Othello, setting aside his color, has every quality to fascinate and charm the female heart. Desdemona, apart from the grossness of her fault in being accessible to such a passion for such an object, is amiable and lovely; among the most attractive of her sex and condition. The faults of their characters are never brought into action excepting as they illustrate the moral principle of the whole story. Othello is not jealous by nature. On the contrary, with a strong natural understanding, and all the vigilance essential to an experienced commander, he is of a disposition so unsuspicious and confiding, that he believes in the *exceeding honesty* of Iago long after he has ample cause to suspect and distrust him. Desdemona, *supersubtle* as she is in the management of her amour with Othello; deeply as she dissembles to deceive her father; and, forward as she is in inviting the courtship of the Moor; discovers neither artifice nor duplicity from the moment that she is Othello's wife. Her innocence, in all her relations with him, is pure and spotless; her kindness for Cassio is mere untainted benevolence; and, though unguarded in her personal deportment towards him, it is far from the slightest soil of culpable impropriety. Guiltless of all conscious reproach in this part of her conduct, she never uses any of the artifices to which she had resorted to accomplish her marriage with Othello. Always feeling that she has given him no cause of suspicion, her endurance of his cruel treatment and brutal abuse of her through all its stages of violence, till he murders her in bed, is always marked with the most affecting sweetness of temper, the most perfect artlessness, and the most endearing resignation. The defects of her character have here no room for development, and the poet carefully keeps them out of sight. Hence it is that the general reader and spectator, with Dr. Johnson, give her unqualified credit for soft simplicity, artlessness, and innocence—forgetful of the qualities of a different and opposite character, stamped upon the transactions by which she effected her marriage with the Moor. The marriage, however, is the source of all her calamities; it is the primitive cause of all the tragic incidents of the play, and of its terrible catastrophe. That the moral lesson to be learned from it is of no practical utility in England, where there are no valiant Moors to steal the affections of fair and high-born dames, may be true; the lesson, however, is not the less, couched under the form of an admirable drama; nor needs it any laborious effort of the imagination to extend the moral precept resulting from the story to a salutary admonition against all ill-assorted, clandestine, and unnatural marriages.

# King Lear

You have a natural Right to this Piece, since, by your Advice, I attempted the Revival of it with Alterations. Nothing but the Power of your Perswasion, and my Zeal for all the Remains of *Shakespear*, cou'd have wrought me to so bold an Undertaking. I found that the Newmodelling of this Story, wou'd force me sometimes on the difficult Task of making the chiefest Persons speak something like their Character, on Matter whereof I had no Ground in my Author. *Lear's* real, and *Edgar's* pretended Madness have so much of extravagant *Nature* (I know not how else to express it) as cou'd never have started but from our *Shakespear's* Creating Fancy. The Images and Language are so odd and surprizing, and yet so agreeable and proper, that whilst we grant that none but *Shakespear* cou'd have form'd such Conceptions, yet we are satisfied that they were the only Things in the World that ought to be said on those Occasions. I found the whole to answer your Account of it, a Heap of Jewels, unstrung and unpolisht; yet so dazling in their Disorder, that I soon perceiv'd I had seiz'd a Treasure. 'Twas my good Fortune to light on one Expedient to rectifie what was wanting in the Regularity and Probability of the Tale, which was to run through the whole, A *Love* betwixt *Edgar* and *Cordelia*, that never chang'd word with each other in the Original. This renders *Cordelia's* Indifference and her Father's Passion in the first Scene probable. It likewise gives Countenance to *Edgar's* Disguise, making that a generous Design that was before a poor Shift to save his Life. The Distress of the Story is evidently heightned by it; and it particularly gave Occasion of a New Scene or Two, of more Success (perhaps) than Merit. This Method necessarily threw me on making the Tale conclude in a Success to the innocent distrest Persons: Otherwise I must have incumbred the Stage with dead Bodies, which Conduct makes many Tragedies conclude with unseasonable Jests. Yet was I Rackt with no small Fears for so bold a Change, till I found it well receiv'd by my Audience; and if this will not satisfie the Reader, I can produce an Authority that questionless will. *Neither is it of so Trivial an Undertaking to make a Tragedy end happily, for 'tis more difficult to Save than 'tis to Kill: The Dagger and Cup of Poyson are alwaies in Readiness; but to bring the Action to the last Extremity, and then by probable Means to recover All, will require the Art and Judgment of a Writer, and cost him many a Pang in the Performance.* ⟨Dryden⟩

I have one thing more to Apologize for, which is, that I have us'd less Quaintness of Expression even in the newest Parts of this Play. I confess 'twas Design in me, partly to comply with my Author's Style to make the Scenes of a Piece, and partly to give it some Resemblance of the Time and Persons here Represented. This, Sir, I submit wholly to you, who are both a Judge and Master of Style. Nature had exempted you before you went Abroad from the Morose Saturnine Humour of our Country, and you brought home the Refinedness of Travel without the Affectation. Many Faults I see in the following Pages, and question not but you will discover more.—NAHUM TATE, "To My Esteemed Friend Thomas Boteler, Esq.," *The History of King Lear*, 1681

> Since by Mistakes your best Delights are made,
> (For ev'n your Wives can please in Masquerade)
> 'Twere worth our While t' have drawn you in this day
> By a new Name to our old honest Play;
> But he that did this Evenings Treat prepare
> Bluntly resolv'd before-hand to declare
> Your Entertainment should be most old Fare.
> Yet hopes, since in rich *Shakespear's* soil it grew,
> 'Twill relish yet with those whose Tasts are True,
> And his Ambition is to please a Few.
> If then this Heap of Flow'rs shall chance to wear
> Fresh Beauty in the Order they now bear,
> Ev'n this *Shakespear's* Praise; each Rustick knows
> 'Mongst plenteous Flow'rs a Garland to Compose,
> Which strung by his course Hand may fairer Show,
> But 'twas a Pow'r Divine first made 'em Grow.
> Why shou'd these Scenes lie hid, in which we find
> What may at Once divert and teach the Mind?
> Morals were alwaies proper for the Stage,
> But are ev'n necessary in this Age.
> Poets must take the Churches Teaching Trade,
> Since Priests their Province of Intrigue invade;
> But We the worst in this Exchange have got,
> In vain our Poets Preach, whilst Church-men Plot.
>
> —NAHUM TATE, "Prologue" to *The History of King Lear*, 1681

The tragedy of *Lear* is deservedly celebrated among the dramas of Shakespeare. There is perhaps no play which keeps the attention so strongly fixed; which so much agitates our passions and interests our curiosity. The artful involutions of distinct interests, the striking opposition of contrary characters, the sudden changes of fortune, and the quick succession of events, fill the mind with a perpetual tumult of indignation, pity, and hope. There is no scene which does not contribute to the aggravation of the distress or conduct of the action, and scarce a line which does not conduce to the progress of the scene. So powerful is the current of the poet's imagination, that the mind, which once ventures within it, is hurried irresistibly along.

On the seeming improbability of Lear's conduct it may be observed, that he is represented according to histories at that time vulgarly received as true. And perhaps if we turn our thoughts upon the barbarity and ignorance of the age to which this story is referred, it will appear not so unlikely as while we estimate Lear's manners by our own. Such preference of one daughter to another, or resignation of dominion on such conditions, would be yet credible, if told of a petty prince of Guinea or Madagascar. Shakespeare, indeed, by the mention of his earls and dukes, has given us the idea of times more civilised, and of life regulated by softer manners; and the truth is, that though he so nicely discriminates, and so minutely describes the characters of men, he commonly neglects and confounds the characters of ages, by mingling customs ancient and modern, English and foreign.

My learned friend Mr. Warton, who has in the *Adventurer* very minutely criticised this play, remarks, that the instances of cruelty are too savage and shocking, and that the intervention of Edmund destroys the simplicity of the story. These objections may, I think, be answered, by repeating, that the cruelty of the daughters is an historical fact, to which the poet has added little, having only drawn it into a series by dialogue and action. But I am not able to apologise with equal plausibility for the extrusion of Gloucester's eyes, which seems an act too horrid to be endured in dramatick exhibition, and such as must always compel the mind to relieve its distress by incredulity. Yet let it be remembered that our authour well knew what would please the audience for which he wrote.

The injury done by Edmund to the simplicity of the action is abundantly recompensed by the addition of variety, by the art with which he is made to co-operate with the chief design, and the opportunity which he gives the poet of combining perfidy with perfidy, and connecting the wicked son with the wicked daughters, to impress this important moral, that villany is never at a stop, that crimes lead to crimes, and at last terminate in ruin.

But though this moral be incidentally enforced, Shakespeare has suffered the virtue of Cordelia to perish in a just cause, contrary to the natural ideas of justice, to the hope of the reader, and, what is yet more strange, to the faith of chronicles. Yet this conduct is justified by the Spectator, who blames Tate for giving Cordelia success and happiness in his alteration, and declares, that, in his opinion, "the tragedy has lost half its beauty." Dennis has remarked, whether justly or not, that, to secure the favourable reception of *Cato*, "the town was poisoned with much false and abominable criticism," and that endeavours had been used to discredit and decry poetical justice. A play in which the wicked prosper, and the virtuous miscarry, may doubtless be good, because it is a just representation of the common events of human life: but since all reasonable beings naturally love justice, I cannot easily be persuaded, that the observation of justice makes a play worse; or, that if other excellencies are equal, the audience will not always rise better pleased from the final triumph of persecuted virtue.

In the present case the publick has decided. Cordelia, from the time of Tate, has always retired with victory and felicity. And, if my sensations could add any thing to the general suffrage, I might relate, that I was many years ago so shocked by Cordelia's death, that I know not whether I ever endured to read again the last scenes of the play till I undertook to revise them as an editor.

There is another controversy among the cricks concerning this play. It is disputed whether the predominant image in Lear's disordered mind be the loss of his kingdom or the cruelty of his daughters. Mr. Murphy, a very judicious critick, has evinced by induction of particular passages, that the cruelty of his daughters is the primary source of his distress, and that the loss of royalty affects him only as a secondary and subordinate evil; he observes with great justness, that Lear would move our compassion but little, did we not rather consider the injured father than the degraded king.

The story of this play, except the episode of Edmund, which is derived, I think, from Sidney, is taken originally from Geoffry of Monmouth, whom Hollingshead generally copied; but perhaps immediately from an old historical ballad, of which I shall insert the greater part. My reason for believing that the play was posteriour to the ballad rather than the ballad to the play, is, that the ballad has nothing of Shakespeare's nocturnal tempest, which is too striking to have been omitted, and that it follows the chronicle; it has the rudiments of the play, but none of its amplifications: it first hinted Lear's madness, but did not array it in circumstances. The writer of the ballad added something to the history, which is a proof that he would have added more, if more had occurred to his mind, and more must have occurred if he had seen Shakespeare.— SAMUEL JOHNSON, *Notes on Shakespeare's Plays*, 1768

As in *Macbeth* terror reaches its utmost height, in *King Lear* the science of compassion is exhausted. The principal characters here are not those who act, but those who suffer. We have not in this, as in most tragedies, the picture of a calamity in which the sudden blows of fate seem still to honour the head which they strike, and where the loss is always accompanied by some flattering consolation in the memory of the former possession; but a fall from the highest elevation into the deepest abyss of misery, where humanity is stripped of all external and internal advantages, and given up a prey to naked helplessness. The threefold dignity of a king, an old man, and a father, is dishonoured by the cruel ingratitude of his unnatural daughters; the old Lear, who out of a foolish tenderness has given away every thing, is driven out to the world a wandering beggar; the childish imbecility to which he was fast advancing changes into the wildest insanity, and when he is rescued from the disgraceful destitution to which he was abandoned, it is too late: the kind consolations of filial care and attention and of true friendship are now lost on him; his bodily and mental powers are destroyed beyond all hope of recovery, and all that now remains to him of life is the capability of loving and suffering beyond measure. What a picture we have in the meeting of Lear and Edgar in a tempestuous night and in a wretched hovel! The youthful Edgar has, by the wicked arts of his brother, and through his father's blindness, fallen, as the old Lear, from the rank to which his birth entitled him; and, as the only means of escaping further persecution, is reduced to assume the disguise of a beggar tormented by evil spirits. The King's fool, notwithstanding the voluntary degradation which is implied in his situation, is, after Kent, Lear's most faithful associate, his wisest counsellor. This good-hearted fool clothes reason with the livery of his motley garb; the high-born beggar acts the part of insanity; and both were they even in reality what they seem, would still be enviable in comparison with the King, who feels that the violence of his grief threatens to overpower his reason. The meeting of Edgar with the blinded Gloster is equally heart-rending; nothing can be more affecting than to see the ejected son become the father's guide, and the good angel, who under the disguise of insanity, saves him by an ingenious and pious fraud from the horror and despair of self-murder. But who can possibly enumerate all the different combinations and situations by which our minds are here as it were stormed by the poet? Respecting the structure of the whole I will only make one observation. The story of Lear and his daughters was left by Shakspeare exactly as he found it in a fabulous tradition, with all the features characteristical of the simplicity of old times. But in that tradition there is not the slightest trace of the story of Gloster and his sons, which was derived by Shakspeare from another source. The incorporation of the two stories has been censured as destructive of the unity of action. But whatever contributes to the intrigue or the

*dénouement* must always possess unity. And with what ingenuity and skill are the two main parts of the composition dovetailed into one another! The pity felt by Gloster for the fate of Lear becomes the means which enables his son Edmund to effect his complete destruction, and affords the outcast Edgar an opportunity of being the saviour of his father. On the other hand, Edmund is active in the cause of Regan and Gonerill, and the criminal passion which they both entertain for him induces them to execute justice on each other and on themselves. The laws of the drama have therefore been sufficiently complied with; but that is the least: it is the very combination which constitutes the sublime beauty of the work. The two cases resemble each other in the main: an infatuated father is blind towards his well-disposed child, and the unnatural children, whom he prefers, requite him by the ruin of all his happiness. But all the circumstances are so different, that these stories, while they each make a correspondent impression on the heart, form a complete contrast for the imagination. Were Lear alone to suffer from his daughters, the impression would be limited to the powerful compassion felt by us for his private misfortune. But two such unheard-of examples taking place at the same time have the appearance of a great commotion in the moral world: the picture becomes gigantic, and fills us with such alarm as we should entertain at the idea that the heavenly bodies might one day fall from their appointed orbits. To save in some degree the honour of human nature, Shakspeare never wishes his spectators to forget that the story takes place in a dreary and barbarous age: he lays particular stress on the circumstance that the Britons of that day were still heathens, although he has not made all the remaining circumstances to coincide learnedly with the time which he has chosen. From this point of view we must judge of many coarsenesses in expression and manners; for instance, the immodest manner in which Gloster acknowledges his bastard, Kent's quarrel with the Steward, and more especially the cruelty personally inflicted on Gloster by the Duke of Cornwall. Even the virtue of the honest Kent bears the stamp of an iron age, in which the good and the bad display the same uncontrollable energy. Great qualities have not been superfluously assigned to the King; the poet could command our sympathy for his situation, without concealing what he had done to bring himself into it. Lear is choleric, overbearing, and almost childish from age, when he drives out his youngest daughter because she will not join in the hypocritical exaggerations of her sisters. But he has a warm and affectionate heart, which is susceptible of the most fervent gratitude; and even rays of a high and kingly disposition burst forth from the eclipse of his understanding. Of Cordelia's heavenly beauty of soul, painted in so few words, I will not venture to speak; she can only be named in the same breath with Antigone. Her death has been thought too cruel; and in England the piece is in acting so far altered that she remains victorious and happy. I must own, I cannot conceive what ideas of art and dramatic connexion those persons have who suppose that we can at pleasure tack a double conclusion to a tragedy; a melancholy one for hard-hearted spectators, and a happy one for souls of a softer mould. After surviving so many sufferings, Lear can only die; and what more truly tragic end for him than to die from grief for the death of Cordelia? and if he is also to be saved and to pass the remainder of his days in happiness, the whole loses its signification. According to Shakspeare's plan the guilty, it is true, are all punished, for wickedness destroys itself; but the virtues that would bring help and succour are everywhere too late, or overmatched by the cunning activity of malice. The persons of this drama have only such a faint belief in

Providence as heathens may be supposed to have; and the poet here wishes to show us that this belief requires a wider range than the dark pilgrimage on earth to be established in full extent.—AUGUST WILHELM SCHLEGEL, *Lectures on Dramatic Art and Literature*, 1809, tr. John Black

> O golden-tongued Romance, with serene lute!
>   Fair plumèd Syren, Queen of far-away!
>   Leave melodizing on this wintry day,
> Shut up thine olden pages, and be mute:
> Adieu! for, once again, the fierce dispute
>   Betwixt damnation and impassion'd clay
>   Must I burn through; once more humbly assay
> The bitter-sweet of this Shakespearian fruit:
> Chief Poet! and ye clouds of Albion,
>   Begetters of our deep eternal theme!
> When through the old oak Forest I am gone,
>   Let me not wander in a barren dream,
> But, when I am consumèd in the fire,
> Give me new Phœnix wings to fly at my desire.
>     —JOHN KEATS, "On Sitting Down to Read *King Lear* Once Again," 1818

The modern practice of blending comedy with tragedy, though liable to great abuse in point of practice, is undoubtedly an extension of the dramatic circle; but the comedy should be as in *King Lear*, universal, ideal, and sublime. It is perhaps the intervention of this principle which determines the balance in favour of *King Lear* against the *Œdipus Tyrannus* or the *Agamemnon*, or, if you will the trilogies with which they are connected; unless the intense power of the choral poetry, especially that of the latter, should be considered as restoring the equilibrium. *King Lear*, if it can sustain this comparison, may be judged to be the most perfect specimen of the dramatic art existing in the world; in spite of the narrow conditions to which the poet was subjected by the ignorance of the philosophy of the drama which has prevailed in modern Europe.—PERCY BYSSHE SHELLEY, *A Defence of Poetry*, 1821

---

### AARON HILL
### From *The Prompter*
No. 95. October 7, 1735

It being reasonable to suppose that the players in respect to one who was an honour to their profession would consider with partiality the opinions and instructions of Shakespeare, I took pleasure, in a late paper, to do him right against some of their notions and produced from his writings one of those beautiful pictures they abound with in proof that he must have been a most accomplished and exquisite actor. Here follows another, from the 3rd act of his *Henry the 5th*.

> In PEACE, there's nothing, so *becomes* a Man
> As *modest* Stillness—and *Humility*:
> —But, when the Blast of WAR blows in our Ears,
> Then—imitate the *Action* of the *Tyger*.
> STIFFEN the *Sinews*—Summon up the *Blood*;
> Disguise fair Nature, with *hard-favour'd* RAGE:
> Then, lend the *Eye*, a dreadful Look—and let
> The BROW O'ERHANG it, like a *jutting Rock*.—
> Now, *Set the Teeth*—and *stretch* the *Nostril wide*
> Hold *hard* the Breath—and *bend up* every Spirit,
> To his *full Height*.

Let us suppose these outlines of anger, so strongly expressed in the picture to have been understood and considered by that player of the first rate who took upon him, some time since, to act the character of King Lear to a numerous and elegant audience. What emotions of the heart, what varieties of conflicting passions, what successions of grief, pity, hatred, fear, anger and indignation would not have arisen, like whirlwinds, to agitate, transport, and convey here and there, at pleasure, the *commanded minds* of his hearers till the poet's intended impression producing its natural effects, the theatre had been shook with applause, and the thunder and lightning in the play but a faint emulation of the tempest which that actor's fine voice (so exerted) would have raised in the pit and boxes.

How happened then that all was calm and indolent, that indifference to the character left the house in but a languid attention? The reason for this was too plain. When the actor is cold, why should the audience be animated? The idea which seems to have been formed of the character was mistaken. But since it is certainly in this player's power to give us all that we missed in the part, after he shall have weighed it by the author's intention, I will lend him what light I can furnish, not without hopes to be repaid by the pleasure of assisting in his praises, which nature has qualified him to merit the next time he appears in that character.

King Lear's most distinguishing mark is the violent impatience of his temper. He is obstinate, rash, and vindictive, measuring the merit of all things by their conformity to his will. He cannot bear contradiction, catches fire at first impressions and inflames himself into a frenzy by the rage of his imagination. Hence, all his misfortunes. He has mercy, liberality, courage, wisdom, and humanity, but his virtues are eclipsed and made useless by the gusts which break out in his transports. He dotes on Cordelia yet disinherits and leaves her to misery, in the heat of an ill-grounded resentment, for a fault of no purpose or consequence, and to punish his rashness, by its effects on himself, was the moral and drift of all those wrongs which are done him.

It is plain, then, that an actor who would present him as the poet has drawn him, should preserve with the strictest care that chief point of likeness—his impatience. He should be turbulent in his passions, sharp and troubled in his voice, torn and anguished in his looks, majestically broken in his air, and discomposed, interrupted, and restless in his motions. Instead of all this, the unquickened serenity of this popular player seemed to paint him as an object of pity, not so much from the ingratitude of his unnatural daughters, as from the calmness and resignation wherewith he submitted to his sufferings. We saw in his action, we heard in his voice, the affliction of the father, without the indignation; the serenity of the monarch, without the superiority; and the wrongs of the angry man, without their resentment.

Let his provocations be weighed. They will give us a measure whereby to judge of his behaviour. After having been insulted, almost to madness, by his daughter Goneril, on whom he had newly bestowed half his kingdom, he comes (labouring with a meditated complaint) to Regan, in possession of the other half, fully convinced she would atone her sister's guilt by an excess of submission and tenderness. Here, instead of the duty he expected, he finds his first wrongs made light of and more than doubled by new ones—his messenger put in the stocks, and his daughter and her husband refusing him admission under pretence of being weary by travelling. Remember the qualities of the king thus provoked. Remember that impatience and peevishness are the marks of his character. Remember that you have seen him, but just before, casting out to destruction his most favourite and virtuous Cordelia only for expressing her apprehension that her sisters had flattered him. What storms of just rage are not now to be looked for from this violent, this ungovernable man, so beyond human patience insulted! so despised! so ill treated! See what Shakespeare makes him answer when Gloucester but puts him in mind of the Duke of Cornwall's fiery temper.

> Vengeance! Plague! Death! Confusion!
> FIERY!—*What* fiery Quality?—Breath, and Blood!
> Fiery!—the FIERY Duke!
> Go—tell the *Duke* and's *Wife*—I'd *speak* with 'em;
> Now—*presently*—Bid 'em come *forth*, and *hear* me:
> Or, at their Chamber Door, I'll *beat* the *Drum*,
> Till it cry, *Sleep to* DEATH.

When we see such starts of impetuosity hushed unfeelingly over and delivered without fire, without energy, with a look of affliction rather than astonishment, and a voice of patient restraint instead of overwhelming indignation, we may know by the calmness which we feel in our blood that the actor's is not enough agitated.

In fine, wherever King Lear called for the bass of his representor's voice, all possible justice was done him. When he mourned, prayed, repented, complained, or excited compassion, there was nothing deficient. But upon every occasion that required the sharp and the elevated, the stretched note and the exclamatory, the king *mistook*, like a dog in a dream, that does but sigh when he thinks he is barking.

I wish I could effectually recommend to so excellent yet unexerted a voice a deliberate examination into the meanings of Shakespeare in his first lines above quoted. The music and compass of an organ might be the infallible reward of his labour, did he but once accustom his nerves to that sensation which impresses (*mechanically*, and by inevitable *necessity*) the whole frame, speech, and spirit with the requisites of every character. But (I appeal to the sincerity of his own private reflection) he neither, according to the mentioned advice, stiffened the sinews, nor summoned up the blood, nor lent a terrible look to the eye, nor set the teeth, nor stretched the nostrils wide, nor held the breath hard—by which last, Shakespeare had in his view a certain out-of-breath struggle in the delivery of the words when angry, which is not only natural, but disorders and stimulates the body with the most alarming resemblance of reality.

Another thing which I must recommend to his notice is that he loses an advantage he might draw from these swellings and hurricanes of the voice in places where proper, compared with such opposite beauties as its fall, its articulate softness, its clear depth and mellowness, all which he is famed for already. These contrasts are in acting as necessary as in painting. All light, or all shade, never finished a picture.

I am loath to speak of absurdities, since I touch but upon errors, with a view to do service. Yet, in one single remark, I will indulge myself for that reason—it being an unavoidable consequence, when men *resolve* before they have *reflected*, that they must be sometimes ridiculous as well as mistaken.

The poor king, in the distraction of his spirits, amidst the agonies of ungoverned sorrow, provoked, inflamed, ashamed, astonished, and vindictive, bursts out into a succession of curses against the unnatural objects of his fury, striving to ease an over-burthened heart in the following torrent of rash wishes.

> All the *Stored Vengeances of Heaven* fall
> On her ungrateful Head—*Strike* her young Bones.
> Ye *taking* Airs, with *Lameness*—
> Ye nimble Lightnings, *dart* your blinding *Flames*,
> Into her Scornful *Eyes!*—&c.—

An actor who in this place, misled by his love of weight and composure, instead of grinding out the curses from between his teeth, amidst the rage and agitations of a man who has been wronged into madness, advances deliberately, for-ward, to the lamps in front of the pit, kneels, with elevated eyes and arms, and pronounces, with the calmness and reverence of a prayer, such a meditated string of curses in the face of heaven—that actor must destroy the pity which he labours, so injudiciously, to attract, since the audience, instead of partaking his agonies, and imputing his words to his wrongs, which they would have done, had they seen him in torture and transported out of his reason, now *mispoint* their concern, and in place of hating the daughter for reducing to such extremities a father so indulgent and generous, condemn and are scandalized at a father who with a malice so undisturbed and serene can invent all those curses for his daughter. Of such extensive importance are the mistakes of a player as even to pervert and destroy the purpose for which the poet has written!

I cannot close this paper without confessing my pleasure from the applause which that actor received who appeared in the character of Edgar. Henceforward I shall conceive warm hopes in his favour. It was once my opinion that this Edgar's voice had no bottom, and that King Lear's had no top. But Edgar has now convinced a pleased audience by the well-judged restraint of his risings (except in places where beautiful and necessary) and by a right-placed distinction in his falls, break, and tendernesses, that there is nothing we may not expect from him when he examines into nature with a view to act naturally.

I remarked, with no less delight, an unexpected and surprising improvement in Cordelia who, to a form that is soft and engaging, has, of late, added spirit, propriety, and attitude to a degree that is strikingly picturesque and delightful. I found the audience most sensible of it and *whispering* their approbation. They will *thunder* it in favour of this lady when she thinks fit to make her utterance as expressive as her gesture. She need only give us her voice, as she received it from nature, without theatric embellishment. While she aims to make it softer, she but thins and refines it till we lose its articulation and are left to guess at the sense of her speeches. Could she prevail on her modesty to speak like herself, she would speak *in her character*, but while she imitates (too humbly) some examples which mislead her, she postpones the admiration I foresee she will rise to.

## JOSEPH WARTON
### From *The Adventurer*
### 1753

*No. 113. December 4, 1753*

Ad humum mærore gravi deducit et angit.

(Hor.)

Wrings the sad soul, and bends it down to earth.

(Francis.)

One of the most remarkable differences betwixt ancient and modern tragedy, arises from the prevailing custom of describing only those distresses that are occasioned by the passion of love; a passion which, from the universality of its dominion, may doubtless justly claim a large share in representations of human life; but which, by totally engrossing the theatre, hath contributed to degrade that noble school of virtue into an academy of effeminacy.

When Racine persuaded the celebrated Arnauld to read his *Phædra*, "Why," said that severe critic to his friend, "have you falsified the manners of Hippolitus, and represented him in love?"—"Alas!" replied the poet, "without that circumstance, how would the ladies and the beaux have received my piece?" And it may well be imagined, that, to gratify so considerable and important a part of his audience, was the powerful motive that induced Corneille to enervate even the matchless and affecting story of Œdipus, by the frigid and impertinent episode of Theseus's passion for Dirce.

Shakspeare has shewn us, by his *Hamlet, Macbeth,* and *Cæsar,* and, above all, by his *Lear,* that very interesting tragedies may be written, that are not founded on gallantry and love; and that Boileau was mistaken, when he affirmed,

de l'amour la sensible peinture,
Est pour aller au cœur la route la plus sûre.

Those tender scenes that pictur'd love impart,
Ensure success, and best engage the heart.

The distresses in this tragedy are of a very uncommon nature, and are not touched upon by any other dramatic author. They are occasioned by a rash resolution of an aged monarch of strong passions and quick sensibility, to resign his crown, and to divide his kingdom amongst his three daughters; the youngest of whom, who was his favourite, not answering his sanguine expectations in expressions of affection to him, he for ever banishes, and endows her sisters with her allotted share. Their unnatural ingratitude, the intolerable affronts, indignities, and cruelties, he suffers from them, and the remorse he feels from his imprudent resignation of his power, at first inflame him with the most violent rage, and, by degrees, drive him to madness and death. This is the outline of the fable.

I shall confine myself, at present, to consider singly the judgment and art of the poet, in describing the origin and progress of the distraction of Lear; in which, I think, he has succeeded better than any other writer; even than Euripides himself, whom Longinus so highly commends for his representation of the madness of Orestes.

It is well contrived, that the first affront that is offered Lear, should be a proposal from Goneril, his eldest daughter, to lessen the number of his knights, which must needs affect and irritate a person so jealous of his rank and the respect due to it. He is, at first, astonished at the complicated impudence and ingratitude of this design; but quickly kindles into rage, and resolves to depart instantly:

Darkness and devils!
Saddle my horses, call my train together—
Degen'rate bastard! I'll not trouble thee.—

This is followed by a severe reflection upon his own folly for resigning his crown; and a solemn invocation to Nature, to heap the most horrible curses on the head of Goneril, that her own offspring may prove equally cruel and unnatural:

that she may feel,
How sharper than a serpent's tooth it is,
To have a thankless child!

When Albany demands the cause of this passion, Lear answers, "I'll tell thee!" but immediately cries out to Goneril,

Life and death! I am asham'd,
That thou hast power to shake my manhood thus.
. . . Blasts and fogs upon thee!
Th' untented woundings of a father's curse
Pierce every sense about thee!

He stops a little, and reflects:

Ha! is it come to this?
Let it be so! I have another daughter,
Who, I am sure, is kind and comfortable.
When she shall hear this of thee, with her nails,
She'll flay thy wolfish visage—

He was, however, mistaken; for the first object he encounters in the castle of the Earl of Gloucester, whither he fled to meet his other daughter, was his servant in the stocks; from whence he may easily conjecture what reception he is to meet with:

Death on my state! Wherefore
Should he sit here.

He adds immediately afterward,

O me, my heart! my rising heart!—but down.

By which single line, the inexpressible anguish of his mind, and the dreadful conflict of opposite passions with which it is agitated, are more forcibly expressed, than by the long and laboured speech, enumerating the causes of his anguish, that Rowe and other modern tragic writers would certainly have put into his mouth. But Nature, Sophocles, and Shakspeare, represent the feelings of the heart in a different manner; by a broken hint, a short exclamation, a word, or a look:

They mingle not, 'mid deep-felt sighs and groans,
Descriptions gay, or quaint comparisons,
No flowery far-fetch'd thoughts their scenes admit;
Ill suits conceit with passion, woe with wit.
Here passion prompts each short, expressive speech;
Or silence paints what words can never reach.

(J. W.)

When Jocasta, in Sophocles, has discovered that Œdipus was the murderer of her husband, she immediately leaves the stage: but in Corneille and Dryden she continues on it during a whole scene, to bewail her destiny in set speeches. I should be guilty of insensibility and injustice, if I did not take this occasion to acknowledge, that I have been more moved and delighted, by hearing this single line spoken by the only actor of the age who understands and relishes these little touches of nature, and therefore the only one qualified to personate this most difficult character of Lear, than by the most pompous declaimer of the most pompous speeches in *Cato* or *Tamerlane.*

In the next scene, the old king appears in a very distressful situation. He informs Regan, whom he believes to be still actuated by filial tenderness, of the cruelties he had suffered from her sister Goneril, in very pathetic terms:

Beloved Regan,
Thy sister's naught—O Regan! she hath tied
Sharp tooth'd unkindness, like a vulture, here,
I scarce can speak to thee—thou'lt not believe,
With how deprav'd a quality—O Regan!

It is a stroke of wonderful art in the poet to represent him incapable of specifying the particular ill usage he has received, and breaking off thus abruptly, as if his voice was choked by tenderness and resentment.

When Regan counsels him to ask her sister forgiveness, he falls on his knees with a very striking kind of irony, and asks her how such supplicating language as this becometh him:

Dear daughter, I confess that I am old;
Age is unnecessary: on my knees I beg,
That you'll vouchsafe me raiment, bed, and food.

But being again exhorted to sue for reconciliation, the advice wounds him to the quick, and forces him into execrations against Goneril, which, though they chill the soul with horror, are yet well suited to the impetuosity of his temper:

She hath abated me of half my train;
Look'd black upon me; struck me with her tongue,
Most serpent-like, upon the very heart—
All the stor'd vengeances of heaven fall
On her ungrateful top! Strike her young bones,
Ye taking airs, with lameness!
Ye nimble lightnings, dart your blinding flames
Into her scornful eyes!—

The wretched king, little imagining that he is to be outcast from Regan also, adds very movingly;

> 'Tis not in thee
> To grudge my pleasures, to cut off my train,
> To bandy hasty words, to scant my sizes,—
> Thou better know'st
> The offices of nature, bond of childhood—
> Thy half o'th' kingdom thou hast not forgot,
> Wherein I thee endow'd—.

That the hopes he had conceived of tender usage from Regan should be deceived, heightens his distress to a great degree. Yet it is still aggravated and increased by the sudden appearance of Goneril; upon the unexpected sight of whom he exclaims,

> Who comes here? O heavens!
> If you do love old men, if your sweet sway
> Allow obedience, if yourselves are old,
> Make it your cause, send down and take my part.

This address is surely pathetic beyond expression: it is scarce enough to speak of it in the cold terms of criticism. There follows a question to Goneril, that I have never read without tears:

> Ar't not asham'd to look upon this beard?

This scene abounds with many noble turns of passion; or rather conflicts of very different passions. The inhuman daughters urge him in vain, by all the sophistical and unfilial arguments they were mistresses of, to diminish the number of his train. He answers them by only four poignant words:

> I gave you all!

When Regan at last consents to receive him, but without any attendants, for that he might be served by her own domestics, he can no longer contain his disappointment and rage. First he appeals to the heavens, and points out to them a spectacle that is indeed inimitably affecting:

> You see me here, ye Gods! a poor old man,
> As full of grief as age, wretched in both:
> If it be you that stir these daughters' hearts
> Against their father, fool me not so much
> To bear it tamely!

Then suddenly he addresses Goneril and Regan in the severest terms, and with the bitterest threats:

> No, you unnatural hags!
> I will have such revenges on you both
> That all the world shall—I will do such things—
> What they are yet, I know not.

Nothing occurs to his mind severe enough for them to suffer, or him to inflict. His passion rises to a height that deprives him of articulation. He tells them that he will subdue his sorrow, though almost irresistible; and that they shall not triumph over his weakness:

> You think I'll weep!
> No! I'll not weep; I have full cause of weeping;
> But this heart shall break into a thousand flaws,
> Or e'er I'll weep!

He concludes,

> O fool—I shall go mad!

which is an artful anticipation, that judiciously prepares us for the dreadful event that is to follow in the succeeding acts.

### No. 116. December 15, 1753

> Æstuat ingens
> Imo in corde pudor, mixtoque insania luctû,
> Et furiis agitatus amor, et conscia virtus.
>
> (Virg.)

> Rage boiling from the bottom of his breast,
> And sorrow mix'd with shame his soul opprest;
> And conscious worth lay lab'ring in his thought;
> And love by jealousy to madness wrought.
>
> (Dryden.)

Thunder and a ghost have been frequently introduced into tragedy by barren and mechanical playwrights, as proper objects to impress terror and astonishment, where the distress has not been important enough to render it probable that nature would interpose for the sake of the sufferers, and where these objects themselves have not been supported by suitable sentiments. Thunder has, however, been made use of with great judgment and good effect by Shakspeare, to heighten and impress the distresses of Lear.

The venerable and wretched old king is driven out by both his daughters, without necessaries and without attendants, not only in the night, but in the midst of a most dreadful storm, and on a bleak and barren heath. On his first appearance in this situation, he draws an artful and pathetic comparison betwixt the severity of the tempest and of his daughters:

> Rumble thy belly full! spit, fire! spout, rain!
> Nor rain, wind, thunder, fire, are my daughters.
> I tax not you, ye elements, with unkindness;
> I never gave you kingdom, call'd you children;
> You owe me no subscription. Then let fall
> Your horrible pleasure. Here I stand your slave;
> A poor, infirm, weak, and despised old man!

The storm continuing with equal violence, he drops for a moment the consideration of his own miseries, and takes occasion to moralize on the terrors which such commotions of nature should raise in the breast of secret and unpunished villany:

> Tremble, thou wretch,
> That hast within thee undivulged crimes
> Unwhipt of justice! Hide thee, thou bloody hand;
> Thou perjur'd, and thou simular man of virtue
> That art incestuous!—
> Close pent-up guilts
> Rive your concealing continents and cry
> These dreadful summoners grace!—

He adds with reference to his own case,

> I am a man
> More sinn'd against, than sinning.

Kent most earnestly entreats him to enter a hovel which he had discovered on the heath; and on pressing him again and again to take shelter there, Lear exclaims,

> Wilt break my heart?

Much is contained in these four words; as if he had said, "The kindness and the gratitude of this servant exceeds that of my own children. Though I have given them a kingdom, yet have they basely discarded me, and suffered a head so old and white as mine to be exposed to this terrible tempest, while this fellow pities and would protect me from its rage. I cannot bear this kindness from a perfect stranger; it breaks my heart." All this seems to be included in that short exclamation, which another writer, less acquainted with nature, would have displayed at large: such a suppression of sentiments plainly implied, is judicious and affecting. The reflections that follow are drawn likewise from an intimate knowledge of man:

> When the mind's free,
> The body's delicate: the tempest in my mind
> Doth from my senses take all feeling else,
> Save what beats there—

Here the remembrance of his daughter's behaviour rushes

upon him, and he exclaims, full of the idea of its unparalleled cruelty,

> Filial ingratitude!
> Is it not, as this mouth should tear this hand
> For lifting food to it?

He then changes his style, and vows with impotent menaces, as if still in possession of the power he had resigned, to revenge himself on his oppressors, and to steel his breast with fortitude:

> But I'll punish home.
> No, I will weep no more!—

But the sense of his sufferings returns again, and he forgets the resolution he had formed the moment before:

> In such a night,
> To shut me out?—Pour on, I will endure—
> In such a night as this?——

At which, with a beautiful apostrophe, he suddenly addresses himself to his absent daughters, tenderly reminding them of the favours he had so lately and so liberally conferred upon them:

> O Regan, Goneril,
> Your old kind father; whose frank heart gave all!
> O that way madness lies; let me shun that;
> No more of that!

The turns of passion in these few lines are so quick and so various, that I thought they merited to be minutely pointed out by a kind of perpetual commentary.

The mind is never so sensibly disposed to pity the misfortunes of others, as when it is itself subdued and softened by calamity. Adversity diffuses a kind of sacred calm over the breast, that is the parent of thoughtfulness and meditation. The following reflections of Lear in his next speech, when his passion has subsided for a short interval, are equally proper and striking

> Poor naked wretches, wheresoe'er ye are,
> That bide the pelting of this pitiless storm!
> How shall your houseless heads, and unfed sides,
> Your loop'd and window'd raggedness, defend you
> From seasons such as these!

He concludes with a sentiment finely suited to his condition, and worthy to be written in characters of gold in the closet of every monarch upon earth:

> O! I have ta'en
> Too little care of this. Take physic, pomp!
> Expose thyself to feel what wretches feel;
> That thou may'st shake the superflux to them,
> And shew the Heavens more just!——

Lear being at last persuaded to take shelter in the hovel, the poet has artfully contrived to lodge there Edgar, the discarded son of Gloucester, who counterfeits the character and habit of a mad beggar, haunted by an evil demon, and whose supposed sufferings are enumerated with an inimitable wildness of fancy; "Whom the foul fiend hath led through fire, and through flame, through ford and whirlpool, o'er bog and quagmire; that hath laid knives under his pillow, and halters in his pew; set ratsbane by his porridge; made him proud of heart, to ride on a bay trotting horse over four inched bridges, to course his own shadow for a traitor.—Bless thy five wits, Tom's a-cold!" The assumed madness of Edgar, and the real distraction of Lear, form a judicious contrast.

Upon perceiving the nakedness and wretchedness of this figure, the poor king asks a question that I never could read without strong emotions of pity and admiration:

> What! have his daughters brought him to this pass?
> Could'st thou save nothing? Didst thou give them all?

And when Kent assures him that the beggar hath no daughters; he hastily answers;

> Death, traitor, nothing could have subdued nature
> To such a lowness, but his unkind daughters.

Afterward, upon the calm contemplation of the misery of Edgar, he breaks out into the following serious and pathetic reflection: "Thou wert better in thy grave, than to answer with thy uncovered body this extremity of the skies. Is man no more than this? Consider him well. Thou owest the worm no silk, the beast no hide, the sheep no wool, the cat no perfume. Ha! here's three of us are sophisticated. Thou art the thing itself: unaccommodated man is no more than such a poor, bare, forked animal as thou art. Off, off, you lendings! Come, unbutton here."

Shakspeare has no where exhibited more inimitable strokes of his art, then in this uncommon scene; where he has so well conducted even the natural jargon of the beggar, and the jestings of the fool, which in other hands must have sunk into burlesque, that they contribute to heighten the pathetic to a very high degree.

The heart of Lear having been agitated and torn by a conflict of such opposite and tumultuous passions, it is not wonderful that his "wits should now begin to unsettle." The first plain indication of the loss of his reason, is his calling Edgar a "learned Theban;" and telling Kent, that "he will keep still with his philosopher." When he next appears, he imagines he is punishing his daughters. The imagery is extremely strong, and chills one with horror to read it;

> To have a thousand with red burning spits
> Come hissing in upon them!

As the fancies of lunatics have an extraordinary force and liveliness, and render the objects of their frenzy as it were present to their eyes, Lear actually thinks himself suddenly restored to his kingdom, and seated in judgment to try his daughters for their cruelties:

> I'll see their trial first; bring in the evidence.
> Thou robed man of justice, take thy place;
> And thou, his yoke-fellow of equity,
> Bench by his side. You are of the commission,
> Sit you too. Arraign her first, 'tis Goneril——
> And here's another, whose warpt looks proclaim
> What store her heart is made of——

Here he imagines that Regan escapes out of his hands, and he eagerly exclaims,

> Stop her there.
> Arms, arms, sword, fire—Corruption in the place!
> False justicer, why hast thou let her 'scape?

A circumstance follows that is strangely moving indeed: for he fancies that his favourite domestic creatures, that used to fawn upon and caress him, and of which he was eminently fond, have now their tempers changed, and joined to insult him:

> The little dogs and all,
> Tray, Blanch, and Sweetheart, see! they bark at me.

He again resumes his imaginary power, and orders them to anatomize Regan; "See what breeds about her heart—Is there any cause in nature, that makes these hard hearts? You, Sir," speaking to Edgar, "I entertain for one of my hundred;" a circumstance most artfully introduced to remind us of the first affront he received, and to fix our thoughts on the causes of his distraction.

General criticism is on all subjects useless and unentertaining; but is more than commonly absurd with respect to Shakspeare, who must be accompanied step by step, and scene by scene, in his gradual developments of characters and passions, and whose finer features must be singly pointed out, if we would do complete justice to his genuine beauties. It would have been easy to have declared in general terms, "that the madness of Lear was very natural and pathetic;" and the reader might then have escaped, what he may, perhaps, call a multitude of well-known quotations; but then it had been impossible to exhibit a perfect picture of the secret workings and changes of Lear's mind, which vary in each succeeding passage, and which render an allegation of each particular sentiment absolutely necessary.

## WILLIAM HAZLITT
### From *"Lear"*
*Characters of Shakespear's Plays*
1817

W<sup>e</sup> wish that we could pass this play over, and say nothing about it. All that we can say must fall far short of the subject; or even of what we ourselves conceive of it. To attempt to give a description of the play itself or of its effect upon the mind, is mere impertinence: yet we must say something.—It is then the best of all Shakespear's plays, for it is the one in which he was the most in earnest. He was here fairly caught in the web of his own imagination. The passion which he has taken as his subject is that which strikes its root deepest into the human heart; of which the bond is the hardest to be unloosed; and the cancelling and tearing to pieces of which gives the greatest revulsion to the frame. This depth of nature, this force of passion, this tug and war of the elements of our being, this firm faith in filial piety, and the giddy anarchy and whirling tumult of the thoughts at finding this prop failing it, the contrast between the fixed, immoveable basis of natural affection, and the rapid, irregular starts of imagination, suddenly wrenched from all its accustomed holds and resting-places in the soul, this is what Shakespear has given, and what nobody else but he could give.—The mind of Lear, staggering between the weight of attachment and the hurried movements of passion, is like a tall ship driven about by the winds, buffetted by the furious waves, but that still rides above the storm, having its anchor fixed in the bottom of the sea; or it is like the sharp rock circled by the eddying whirlpool that foams and beats against it, or like the solid promontory pushed from its basis by the force of an earthquake.

The character of Lear itself is very finely conceived for the purpose. It is the only ground on which such a story could be built with the greatest truth and effect. It is his rash haste, his violent impetuosity, his blindness to every thing but the dictates of his passions or affections, that produces all his misfortunes, that aggravates his impatience of them, that enforces our pity for him. The part which Cordelia bears in the scene is extremely beautiful: the story is almost told in the first words she utters. We see at once the precipice on which the poor old king stands from his own extravagant and credulous importunity, the indiscreet simplicity of her love (which, to be sure, has a little of her father's obstinacy in it) and the hollowness of her sisters' pretensions. Almost the first burst of that noble tide of passion, which runs through the play, is in the remonstrance of Kent to his royal master on the injustice of his sentence against his youngest daughter—'Be Kent unmannerly, when Lear is mad!' This manly plainness, which draws down on him the displeasure of the unadvised king, is worthy of the fidelity with which he adheres to his fallen fortunes. The true character of the two eldest daughters, Regan and Gonerill (they are so thoroughly hateful that we do not even like to repeat their names) breaks out in their answer to Cordelia who desires them to treat their father well—'Prescribe not us our duties'—their hatred of advice being in proportion to their determination to do wrong, and to their hypocritical pretensions to do right. Their deliberate hypocrisy adds the last finishing to the odiousness of their characters. It is the absence of this detestable quality that is the only relief in the character of Edmund the Bastard, and that at times reconciles us to him. We are not tempted to exaggerate the guilt of his conduct, when he himself gives it up as a bad business, and writes himself down 'plain villain.' Nothing more can be said about it. His religious honesty in this respect is admirable. One speech of his is worth a million. His father, Gloster, whom he has just deluded with a forged story of his brother Edgar's designs against his life, accounts for his unnatural behaviour and the strange depravity of the times from the late eclipses in the sun and moon. Edmund, who is in the secret, says when he is gone—'This is the excellent foppery of the world, that when we are sick in fortune (often the surfeits of our own behaviour) we make guilty of our disasters the sun, the moon, and stars: as if we were villains on necessity; fools by heavenly compulsion; knaves, thieves, and treacherous by spherical predominance; drunkards, liars, and adulterers by an enforced obedience of planetary influence; and all that we are evil in, by a divine thrusting on. An admirable evasion of whole master man to lay his goatish disposition on the charge of a star! My father compounded with my mother under the Dragon's tail, and my nativity was under Ursa Major: so that it follows, I am rough and lecherous. Tut! I should have been what I am, had the maidenliest star in the firmament twinkled on my bastardising.'—The whole character, its careless, light-hearted villainy, contrasted with the sullen, rancorous malignity of Regan and Gonerill, its connection with the conduct of the under-plot, in which Gloster's persecution of one of his sons and the ingratitude of another, form a counterpart to the mistakes and misfortunes of Lear,—his double amour with the two sisters, and the share which he has in bringing about the fatal catastrophe, are all managed with an uncommon degree of skill and power.

It has been said, and we think justly, that the third act of *Othello* and the three first acts of *Lear*, are Shakespear's great master-pieces in the logic of passion: that they contain the highest examples not only of the force of individual passion, but of its dramatic vicissitudes and striking effects arising from the different circumstances and characters of the persons speaking. We see the ebb and flow of the feeling, its pauses and feverish starts, its impatience of opposition, its accumulating force when it has time to recollect itself, the manner in which it avails itself of every passing word or gesture, its haste to repel insinuation, the alternate contraction and dilatation of the soul, and all 'the dazzling fence of controversy' in this mortal combat with poisoned weapons, aimed at the heart, where each wound is fatal. We have seen in *Othello*, how the unsuspecting frankness and impetuous passions of the Moor are played upon and exasperated by the artful dexterity of Iago. In the present play, that which aggravates the sense of sympathy in the reader, and of uncontroulable anguish in the swoln heart of Lear, is the petrifying indifference, the cold, calculating, obdurate selfishness of his daughters. His keen passions seem whetted on their stony hearts. The contrast would be too painful, the shock too great, but for the intervention of the Fool, whose well-timed levity comes in to break the continuity of feeling when it can no longer be borne, and to bring into play again the fibres of the heart just as they are growing rigid from over-strained excitement. The imagination is glad to take refuge in the half-comic, half-serious comments of the Fool, just as the mind under the extreme anguish of a surgical operation vents itself in sallies of wit. The character was also a grotesque ornament of the barbarous times, in which alone the tragic ground-work of the story could be laid. In another point of view it is indispensable, inasmuch as while it is a diversion to the too great intensity of our disgust, it carries the pathos to the highest pitch of which it is capable, by shewing the pitiable weakness of the old king's conduct and its irretrievable consequences in the most familiar point of view. Lear may well 'beat at the gate which let his folly in,' after, as the Fool says, 'he has made his daughters his mothers.' The character is dropped in the third act to make room for the entrance of Edgar as Mad Tom, which well accords with the increasing bustle and wildness of the incidents; and nothing can be more complete than the distinction between Lear's real and Edgar's assumed madness, while the resemblance in the cause of their distresses, from the severing of the nearest ties of natural affection, keeps up a unity of interest. Shakespear's mastery over his subject, if it was not art, was owing to a knowledge of the connecting links of the passions, and their effect upon the mind, still more wonderful than any systematic adherence to rules, and that anticipated and outdid all the efforts of the most refined art, not inspired and rendered instinctive by genius. . . .

The scene in the storm, where he is exposed to all the fury of the elements, though grand and terrible, is not so fine, but the moralising scenes with Mad Tom, Kent, and Gloster, are upon a par with the former. His exclamation in the supposed trial-scene of his daughters, 'See the little dogs and all, Tray, Blanch, and Sweetheart, see they bark at me,' his issuing his orders, 'Let them anatomize Regan, see what breeds about her heart,' and his reflection when he sees the misery of Edgar, 'Nothing but his unkind daughters could have brought him to this,' are in a style of pathos, where the extremest resources of the imagination are called in to lay open the deepest movements of the heart, which was peculiar to Shakespear. In the same style and spirit is his interrupting the Fool who asks 'whether a madman be a gentleman or a yeoman,' by answering 'A king, a king.'—

The indirect part that Gloster takes in these scenes where his generosity leads him to relieve Lear and resent the cruelty of his daughters, at the very time that he is himself instigated to seek the life of his son, and suffering under the sting of his supposed ingratitude, is a striking accompaniment to the situation of Lear. Indeed, the manner in which the threads of the story are woven together is almost as wonderful in the way of art as the carrying on the tide of passion, still varying and unimpaired, is on the score of nature. Among the remarkable instances of this kind are Edgar's meeting with his old blind father; the deception he practises upon him when he pretends to lead him to the top of Dover-cliff—'Come on, sir, here's the place,' to prevent his ending his life and miseries together; his encounter with the perfidious Steward whom he kills, and his finding the letter from Gonerill to his brother upon him which leads to the final catastrophe, and brings the wheel of Justice 'full circle home' to the guilty parties. The bustle and rapid succession of events in the last scenes is surprising. But the meeting between Lear and Cordelia is by far the most affecting part of them. It has all the wildness of poetry, and all the heart-felt truth of nature. . . .

Four things have struck us in reading *Lear*:

1. That poetry is an interesting study, for this reason, that it relates to whatever is most interesting in human life.

Whoever therefore has a contempt for poetry, has a contempt for himself and humanity.

2. That the language of poetry is superior to the language of painting; because the strongest of our recollections relate to feelings, not to faces.

3. That the greatest strength of genius is shewn in describing the strongest passions: for the power of the imagination, in works of invention, must be in proportion to the force of the natural impressions, which are the subject of them.

4. That the circumstance which balances the pleasure against the pain in tragedy is, that in proportion to the greatness of the evil, is our sense and desire of the opposite good excited; and that our sympathy with actual suffering is lost in the strong impulse given to our natural affections, and carried away with the swelling tide of passion, that gushes from and relieves the heart.

## SAMUEL TAYLOR COLERIDGE
### From *"Lear"*
*Shakspeare, with Introductory Remarks*
*on Poetry, the Drama, and the Stage*
1818

O f all Shakspeare's plays *Macbeth* is the most rapid, *Hamlet* the slowest, in movement. *Lear* combines length with rapidity,—like the hurricane and the whirlpool, absorbing while it advances. It begins as a stormy day in summer, with brightness; but that brightness is lurid, and anticipates the tempest.

It was not without forethought, nor is it without its due significance, that the division of Lear's kingdom is in the first six lines of the play stated as a thing already determined in all its particulars, previously to the trial of professions, as the relative rewards of which the daughters were to be made to consider their several portions. The strange, yet by no means unnatural, mixture of selfishness, sensibility, and habit of feeling derived from, and fostered by, the particular rank and usages of the individual;—the intense desire of being intensely beloved;—selfish, and yet characteristic of the selfishness of a loving and kindly nature alone;—the self-supportless leaning for all pleasure on another's breast;—the craving after sympathy with a prodigal disinterestedness, frustrated by its own ostentation, and the mode and nature of its claims;—the anxiety, the distrust, the jealousy, which more or less accompany all selfish affections, and are amongst the surest contradistinctions of mere fondness from true love, and which originate Lear's eager wish to enjoy his daughter's violent professions, whilst the inveterate habits of sovereignty convert the wish into claim and positive right, and an incompliance with it into crime and treason;—these facts, these passions, these moral verities, on which the whole tragedy is founded, are all prepared for, and will to the retrospect be found implied, in these first four or five lines of the play. They let us know that the trial is but a trick; and that the grossness of the old king's rage is in part the natural result of a silly trick suddenly and most unexpectedly baffled and disappointed.

It may here be worthy of notice, that *Lear* is the only serious performance of Shakspeare, the interest and situations of which are derived from the assumption of a gross improbability; whereas Beaumont and Fletcher's tragedies are, almost all of them, founded on some out of the way accident and exception to the general experience of mankind. But observe the matchless judgment of our Shakspeare. First, improbable as the conduct of Lear is in the first scene, yet it was an old story rooted in the popular faith,—a thing taken for granted already, and consequently without any of the effects of improbability. Secondly, it is merely the canvass for the characters and passions,—a mere occasion for,—and not, in the manner of Beaumont and Fletcher, perpetually recurring as the cause, and *sine qua non* of,—the incidents and emotions. Let the first scene of this play have been lost, and let it only be understood that a fond father had been duped by hypocritical professions of love and duty on the part of two daughters to disinherit the third, previously, and deservedly, more dear to him;—and all the rest of the tragedy would retain its interest undiminished, and be perfectly intelligible. The accidental is no where the groundwork of the passions, but that which is catholic, which in all ages has been, and ever will be, close and native to the heart of man,—parental anguish from filial ingratitude, the genuineness of worth, though coffined in bluntness, and the execrable vileness of a smooth iniquity. Perhaps I ought to have added the *Merchant of Venice*; but here too the same remarks apply. It was an old tale; and substitute any other danger than that of the pound of flesh (the circumstance in which the improbability lies), yet all the situations and the emotions appertaining to them remain equally excellent and appropriate. Whereas take away from the *Mad Lover* of Beaumont and Fletcher the fantastic hypothesis of his engagement to cut out his own heart, and have it presented to his mistress, and all the main scenes must go with it.

Kotzebue is the German Beaumont and Fletcher, without their poetic powers, and without their *vis comica*. But, like them, he always deduces his situations and passions from marvellous accidents, and the trick of bringing one part of our moral nature to counteract another; as our pity for misfortune and admiration of generosity and courage to combat our condemnation of guilt, as in adultery, robbery, and other heinous crimes;—and, like them too, he excels in his mode of telling a story clearly and interestingly, in a series of dramatic dialogues. Only the trick of making tragedy-heroes and heroines out of shopkeepers and barmaids was too low for the age, and too unpoetic for the genius, of Beaumont and Fletcher, inferior in every respect as they are to their great predecessor and contemporary. How inferior would they have appeared, had not Shakspeare existed for them to imitate;—which in every play, more or less, they do, and in their tragedies most glaringly:—and yet—(O shame! shame!)—they miss no opportunity of sneering at the divine man, and sub-detracting from his merits!

To return to *Lear*. Having thus in the fewest words, and in a natural reply to as natural a question,—which yet answers the secondary purpose of attracting our attention to the difference or diversity between the characters of Cornwall and Albany,—provided the premises and *data*, as it were, for our after insight into the mind and mood of the person, whose character, passions, and sufferings are the main subject-matter of the play;—from Lear, the *persona patiens* of his drama, Shakspeare passes without delay to the second in importance, the chief agent and prime mover, and introduces Edmund to our acquaintance, preparing us with the same felicity of judgment, and in the same easy and natural way, for his character in the seemingly casual communication of its origin and occasion. From the first drawing up of the curtain Edmund has stood before us in the united strength and beauty of earliest manhood. Our eyes have been questioning him. Gifted as he is with high advantages of person, and further endowed by nature with a powerful intellect and a strong energetic will, even without any concurrence of circumstances and accident, pride

will necessarily be the sin that most easily besets him. But Edmund is also the known and acknowledged son of the princely Closter: he, therefore, has both the germ of pride, and the conditions best fitted to evolve and ripen it into a predominant feeling. Yet hitherto no reason appears why it should be other than the not unusual pride of person, talent, and birth,—a pride auxiliary, if not akin, to many virtues, and the natural ally of honorable impulses. But alas! in his own presence his own father takes shame to himself for the frank avowal that he is his father,—he has 'blushed so often to acknowledge him that he is now brazed to it!' Edmund hears the circumstances of his birth spoken of with a most degrading and licentious levity,—his mother described as a wanton by her own paramour, and the remembrance of the animal sting, the low criminal gratifications connected with her wantonness and prostituted beauty, assigned as the reason, why 'the whoreson must be acknowledged!' This, and the consciousness of its notoriety; the gnawing conviction that every show of respect is an effort of courtesy, which recalls, while it represses, a contrary feeling;—this is the ever trickling flow of wormwood and gall into the wounds of pride,—the corrosive *virus* which inoculates pride with a venom not its own, with envy, hatred, and a lust for that power which in its blaze of radiance would hide the dark spots on his disc,—with pangs of shame personally undeserved, and therefore felt as wrongs, and with a blind ferment of vindictive working towards the occasions and causes, especially towards a brother, whose stainless birth and lawful honours were the constant remembrancers of his own debasement, and were ever in the way to prevent all chance of its being unknown, or overlooked and forgotten. Add to this, that with excellent judgment, and provident for the claims of the moral sense,—for that which, relatively to the drama, is called poetic justice, and as the fittest means for reconciling the feelings of the spectators to the horrors of Gloster's after sufferings,—at least, of rendering them somewhat less unendurable;—(for I will not disguise my conviction, that in this one point the tragic in this play has been urged beyond the outermost mark and *ne plus ultra* of the dramatic)—Shakspeare has precluded all excuse and palliation of the guilt incurred by both the parents of the base-born Edmund, by Gloster's confession that he was at the time a married man, and already blest with a lawful heir of his fortunes. The mournful alienation of brotherly love, occasioned by the law of primogeniture in noble families, or rather by the unnecessary distinctions engrafted thereon, and this in children of the same stock, is still almost proverbial on the continent,—especially, as I know from my own observation, in the south of Europe,—and appears to have been scarcely less common in our own island before the Revolution of 1688, if we may judge from the characters and sentiments so frequent in our elder comedies. There is the younger brother, for instance, in Beaumont and Fletcher's play of the *Scornful Lady*, on the one side, and Oliver in Shakspeare's *As You Like It*, on the other. Need it be said how heavy an aggravation, in such a case, the stain of bastardy must have been, were it only that the younger brother was liable to hear his own dishonour and his mother's infamy related by his father with an excusing shrug of the shoulders, and in a tone betwixt waggery and shame!

By the circumstances here enumerated as so many predisposing causes, Edmund's character might well be deemed already sufficiently explained; and our minds prepared for it. But in this tragedy the story or fable constrained Shakspeare to introduce wickedness in an outrageous form in the persons of Regan and Goneril. He had read nature too heedfully not to know, that courage, intellect, and strength of character, are the most impressive forms of power, and that to power in itself, without reference to any moral end, an inevitable admiration and complacency appertains, whether it be displayed in the conquests of a Buonaparte or Tamerlane, or in the foam and the thunder of a cataract. But in the exhibition of such a character it was of the highest importance to prevent the guilt from passing into utter monstrosity,—which again depends on the presence or absence of causes and temptations sufficient to account for the wickedness, without the necessity of recurring to a thorough fiendishness of nature for its origination. For such are the appointed relations of intellectual power to truth, and of truth to goodness, that it becomes both morally and poetically unsafe to present what is admirable,—what our nature compels us to admire—in the mind, and what is most detestable in the heart, as co-existing in the same individual without any apparent connection, or any modification of the one by the other. That Shakspeare has in one instance, that of Iago, approached to this, and that he has done it successfully, is, perhaps, the most astonishing proof of his genius, and the opulence of its resources. But in the present tragedy, in which he was compelled to present a Goneril and a Regan, it was most carefully to be avoided;—and therefore the only one conceivable addition to the inauspicious influences on the preformation of Edmund's character is given, in the information that all the kindly counteractions to the mischievous feelings of shame, which might have been derived from co-domestication with Edgar and their common father, had been cut off by his absence from home, and foreign education from boyhood to the present time, and a prospect of its continuance, as if to preclude all risk of his interference with the father's views for the elder and legitimate son. . . .

The Fool is no comic buffoon to make the groundlings laugh,—no forced condescension of Shakspeare's genius to the taste of his audience. Accordingly the poet prepares for his introduction, which he never does with any of his common clowns and fools, by bringing him into living connection with the pathos of the play. He is as wonderful a creation as Caliban;—his wild babblings, and inspired idiocy, articulate and gauge the horrors of the scene.

The monster Goneril prepares what is necessary, while the character of Albany renders a still more maddening grievance possible, namely, Regan and Cornwall in perfect sympathy of monstrosity. Not a sentiment, not an image, which can give pleasure on its own account, is admitted; whenever these creatures are introduced, and they are brought forward as little as possible, pure horror reigns throughout. In this scene and in all the early speeches of *Lear*, the one general sentiment of filial ingratitude prevails as the main spring of the feelings;—in this early stage the outward object causing the pressure on the mind, which is not yet sufficiently familiarized with the anguish for the imagination to work upon it.

## CHARLES DICKENS
### From "The Restoration of Shakespeare's *Lear* to the Stage" (1838)
*Works*, Centenary ed.
1911, Volume 34, pp. 77–81

W hat we ventured to anticipate when Mr. Macready assumed the management of Covent Garden Theatre, has been every way realised. But the last of his well-directed efforts to vindicate the higher objects and uses of the drama has proved the most brilliant and the most successful. He has restored to the stage Shakespeare's true *Lear*, banished from it,

by impudent ignorance, for upwards of a hundred and fifty years.

A person of the name of Boteler has the infamous repute of having recommended to a notorious poet-laureate, Mr. Nahum Tate, the 'new modelling' of *Lear*. 'I found the whole,' quoth Mr. Tate, addressing the aforesaid Boteler in his dedication, 'to answer your account of it; a heap of jewels unstrung and unpolished, yet so dazzling in their disorder, that I soon perceived I had seized a treasure.' And accordingly to work set Nahum very busily indeed: strung the jewels and polished them with a vengeance; omitted the grandest things, the *Fool* among them; polished all that remained into commonplace; interlarded love-scenes; sent *Cordelia* into a comfortable cave with her lover, to dry her clothes and get warm, while her distracted and homeless old father was still left wandering without, amid all the pelting of the pitiless storm; and finally, rewarded the poor old man in his turn, and repaid him for all his suffering, by giving him back again his gilt robes and tinsel sceptre!

Betterton was the last great actor who played *Lear* before the commission of this outrage. His performances of it between the years 1663 and 1671 are recorded to have been the greatest efforts of his genius. Ten years after the latter date, Mr. Tate published his disgusting version, and this was adopted successively by Boheme, Quin, Booth, Barry, Garrick, Henderson, Kemble, Kean. Mr. Macready has now, to his lasting honour, restored the text of Shakespeare, and we shall be glad to hear of the actor foolhardy enough to attempt another restoration of the text of Mr. Tate! Mr. Macready's success has banished that disgrace from the stage for ever.

The *Fool* in the tragedy of *Lear* is one of the most wonderful creations of Shakespeare's genius. The picture of his quick and pregnant sarcasm, of his loving devotion, of his acute sensibility, of his despairing mirth, of his heartbroken silence—contrasted with the rigid sublimity of *Lear's* suffering, with the huge desolation of *Lear's* sorrow, with the vast and outraged image of *Lear's* madness—is the noblest thought that ever entered into the heart and mind of man. Nor is it a noble thought alone. Three crowded houses in Covent Garden Theatre have now proved by something better than even the deepest attention that it is for action, for representation; that it is necessary to an audience as tears are to an overcharged heart; and necessary to *Lear* himself as the recollections of his kingdom, or as the worn and faded garments of his power. We predicted some years since that this would be felt, and we have the better right to repeat it now. We take leave again to say that Shakespeare would have as soon consented to the banishment of *Lear* from the tragedy as to the banishment of his *Fool*. We may fancy him, while planning his immortal work, feeling suddenly, with an instinct of divinest genius, that its gigantic sorrows could never be presented on the stage without a suffering too frightful, a sublimity too remote, a grandeur too terrible—unless relieved by quiet pathos, and in some way brought home to the apprehensions of the audience by homely and familiar illustration. At such a moment that *Fool* rose to his mind, and not till then could he have contemplated his marvellous work in the greatness and beauty of its final completion.

The *Fool* in *Lear* is the solitary instance of such a character, in all the writings of Shakespeare, being identified with the pathos and passion of the scene. He is interwoven with *Lear*, he is the link that still associates him with *Cordelia's* love, and the presence of the regal estate he has surrendered. The rage of the wolf *Goneril* is first stirred by a report that her favourite gentleman had been struck by her father 'for chiding of his fool,'—and the first impatient questions we hear from the dethroned old man are: 'Where's my knave—my fool? Go you and call my fool hither.'—'Where's my fool? Ho! I think the world's asleep.'—'But where's my fool? I have not seen him these two days,'—'Go you and call hither my fool,'—all which prepare us for that affecting answer stammered forth at last by the knight in attendance: 'Since my young lady's going into France, sir, the fool hath much pined away.' Mr. Macready's manner of turning off at this with an expression of half impatience, half ill-repressed emotion—'No more of that, I *have noted it well'*—was inexpressibly touching. We saw him, in the secret corner of his heart, still clinging to the memory of her who was used to be his best object, the argument of his praise, balm of his age, 'most best, most dearest.' And in the same noble and affecting spirit was his manner of fondling the *Fool* when he sees him first, and asks him with earnest care, 'How now, my pretty knave? *How doest thou?'* Can there be a doubt, after this, that his love for the *Fool* is associated with *Cordelia,* who had been kind to the poor boy, and for the loss of whom he pines away? And are we not even then prepared for the sublime pathos of the close, when *Lear,* bending over the dead body of all he had left to love upon the earth, connects with her the memory of that other gentle, faithful, and loving being who had passed from his side—unites, in that moment to final agony, the two hearts that had been broken in his service, and exclaims, 'And my poor fool is hanged!'

Mr. Macready's *Lear,* remarkable before for a masterly completeness of conception, is heightened by this introduction of the *Fool* to a surprising degree. It accords exactly with the view he seeks to present of *Lear's* character. The passages we have named, for instance, had even received illustration in the first scene, where something beyond the turbulent greatness or royal impatience of *Lear* had been presented—something to redeem him from his treatment of *Cordelia.* The bewildered pause after giving his 'father's heart' away—the hurry yet hesitation of his manner as he orders *France* to be called— 'Who stirs? Call *Burgundy'*—had told us at once how much consideration he needed, how much pity, of how little of himself he was indeed the master, how crushing and irrepressible was the strength of his sharp impatience. We saw no material change in his style of playing the first great scene with *Goneril,* which fills the stage with true and appalling touches of nature. In that scene he ascends indeed with the heights of *Lear's* passion; through all its changes of agony, of anger, of impatience, of turbulent assertion, of despair, and mighty grief, till on his knees, with arms upraised and head thrown back, the tremendous Curse bursts from him amid heaving and reluctant throes of suffering and anguish. The great scene of the second act had also its great passages of power and beauty: his self-persuading utterance of 'hysterias passio'—his anxious and fearful tenderness to *Regan*—the elevated grandeur of his appeal to the heavens—his terrible suppressed efforts, his pauses, his reluctant pangs of passion, in the speech 'I will not trouble thee, my child,'—and surpassing the whole, as we think, in deep simplicity as well as agony of pathos, that noble conception of shame as he *hides his face* on the arm of *Goneril* and says—

> I'll go with thee;
> Thy fifty yet doth double five and twenty,
> And thou art twice her love!

The *Fool's* presence then enabled him to give an effect, unattempted before, to those little words which close the scene, when, in the effort of bewildering passion with which he strives to burst through the phalanx of amazed horrors that have closed him round, he feels that his intellect is shaking, and suddenly exclaims, 'O *Fool!* I shall go mad!' This is better than hitting the forehead and ranting out a self-reproach.

But the presence of the *Fool* in the storm-scene! The reader must witness this to judge its power and observe the deep impression with which it affects the audience. Every resource that the art of the painter and the mechanist can afford is called in aid of this scene—every illustration is thrown on it of which the great actor of *Lear* is capable, but these are nothing to that simple presence of the *Fool!* He has changed his character there. So long as hope existed he had sought by his hectic merriment and sarcasms to win *Lear* back to love and reason, but that half of his work is now over, and all that remains for him is to soothe and lessen the certainty of the worst. *Kent* asks who is with *Lear* in the storm, and is answered—

> None but the *Fool,* who labours to outjest
> His heart-struck injuries!

When all his attempts have failed, either to soothe or to outjest these injuries, he sings, in the shivering cold, about the necessity of 'going to bed at noon.' He leaves the stage to die in his youth, and we hear of him no more till we hear the sublime touch of pathos over the dead body of the hanged *Cordelia.*

## LEO TOLSTOY
### From *On Shakespeare*
trs. V. Tchertkoff and I. F. M.
1906, pp. 46–63

### III

For any man of our time—if he were not under the hypnotic suggestion that this drama is the height of perfection—it would be enough to read it to its end (were he to have sufficient patience for this) to be convinced that far from being the height of perfection, it is a very bad, carelessly composed production, which, if it could have been of interest to a certain public at a certain time, can not evoke among us anything but aversion and weariness. Every reader of our time, who is free from the influence of suggestion, will also receive exactly the same impression from all the other extolled dramas of Shakespeare, not to mention the senseless, dramatized tales, *Pericles, Twelfth Night, The Tempest, Cymbeline, Troilus and Cressida.*

But such free-minded individuals, not inoculated with Shakespeare-worship, are no longer to be found in our Christian society. Every man of our society and time, from the first period of his conscious life, has been inoculated with the idea that Shakespeare is a genius, a poet, and a dramatist, and that all his writings are the height of perfection. Yet, however hopeless it may seem, I will endeavor to demonstrate in the selected drama—*King Lear*—all those faults equally characteristic also of all the other tragedies and comedies of Shakespeare, on account of which he not only is not representing a model of dramatic art, but does not satisfy the most elementary demands of art recognized by all.

Dramatic art, according to the laws established by those very critics who extol Shakespeare, demands that the persons represented in the play should be, in consequence of actions proper to their characters, and owing to a natural course of events, placed in positions requiring them to struggle with the surrounding world to which they find themselves in opposition, and in this struggle should display their inherent qualities.

In *King Lear* the persons represented are indeed placed externally in opposition to the outward world, and they struggle with it. But their strife does not flow from the natural course of events nor from their own characters, but is quite arbitrarily established by the author, and therefore can not produce on the reader the illusion which represents the essential condition of art.

Lear has no necessity or motive for his abdication; also, having lived all his life with his daughters, has no reason to believe the words of the two elders and not the truthful statement of the youngest; yet upon this is built the whole tragedy of his position.

Similarly unnatural is the subordinate action: the relation of Gloucester to his sons. The positions of Gloucester and Edgar flow from the circumstance that Gloucester, just like Lear, immediately believes the coarsest untruth and does not even endeavor to inquire of his injured son whether what he is accused of be true, but at once curses and banishes him. The fact that Lear's relations with his daughters are the same as those of Gloucester to his sons makes one feel yet more strongly that in both cases the relations are quite arbitrary, and do not flow from the characters nor the natural course of events. Equally unnatural, and obviously invented, is the fact that all through the tragedy Lear does not recognize his old courtier, Kent, and therefore the realtions between Lear and Kent fail to excite the sympathy of the reader or spectator. The same, in a yet greater degree, holds true of the position of Edgar, who, unrecognized by any one, leads his blind father and persuades him that he has leapt off a cliff, when in reality Gloucester jumps on level ground.

These positions, into which the characters are placed quite arbitrarily, are so unnatural that the reader or spectator is unable not only to sympathize with their sufferings but even to be interested in what he reads or sees. This in the first place.

Secondly, in this, as in the other dramas of Shakespeare, all the characters live, think, speak, and act quite unconformably with the given time and place. The action of *King Lear* takes place 800 years B.C., and yet the characters are placed in conditions possible only in the Middle Ages: participating in the drama are kings, dukes, armies, and illegitimate children, and gentlemen, courtiers, doctors, farmers, officers, soldiers, and knights with vizors, etc. It is possible that such anachronisms (with which Shakespeare's dramas abound) did not injure the possibility of illusion in the sixteenth century and the beginning of the seventeenth, but in our time it is no longer possible to follow with interest the development of events which one knows could not take place in the conditions which the author describes in detail. The artificiality of the positions, not flowing from the natural course of events, or from the nature of the characters, and their want of conformity with time and space, is further increased by those coarse embellishments which are continually added by Shakespeare and intended to appear particularly touching. The extraordinary storm during which King Lear roams about the heath, or the grass which for some reason he puts on his head—like Ophelia in *Hamlet*—or Edgar's attire, or the fool's speeches, or the appearance of the helmeted horseman, Edgar—all these effects not only fail to enchance the impression, but produce an opposite effect. "Man sieht die Absicht und man wird verstimmt," as Goethe says. It often happens that even during these obviously intentional efforts after effect, as, for instance, the dragging out by the legs of half a dozen corpses, with which all Shakespeare's tragedies terminate, instead of feeling fear and pity, one is tempted rather to laugh.

## IV

But it is not enough that Shakespeare's characters are placed in tragic positions which are impossible, do not flow from the course of events, are inappropriate to time and space—these personages, besides this, act in a way which is out of keeping with their definite character, and is quite arbitrary. It is generally asserted that in Shakespeare's dramas the characters are specially well expressed, that, notwithstanding their vividness, they are many-sided, like those of living people; that, while exhibiting the characteristics of a given individual, they at the same time wear the features of man in general; it is usual to say that the delineation of character in Shakespeare is the height of perfection.

This is asserted with such confidence and repeated by all as indisputable truth; but however much I endeavored to find confirmation of this in Shakespeare's dramas, I always found the opposite. In reading any of Shakespeare's dramas whatever, I was, from the very first, instantly convinced that he was lacking in the most important, if not the only, means of portraying characters: individuality of language, *i.e.*, the style of speech of every person being natural to his character. This is absent from Shakespeare. All his characters speak, not their own, but always one and the same Shakespearian, pretentious, and unnatural language, in which not only they could not speak, but in which no living man ever has spoken or does speak.

No living men could or can say, as Lear says, that he would divorce his wife in the grave should Regan not receive him, or that the heavens would crack with shouting, or that the winds would burst, or that the wind wishes to blow the land into the sea, or that the curled waters wish to flood the shore, as the gentleman describes the storm, or that it is easier to bear one's grief and the soul leaps over many sufferings when grief finds fellowship, or that Lear has become childless while I am fatherless, as Edgar says, or use similar unnatural expressions with which the speeches of all the characters in all Shakespeare's dramas overflow.

Again, it is not enough that all the characters speak in a way in which no living men ever did or could speak—they all suffer from a common intemperance of language. Those who are in love, who are preparing for death, who are fighting, who are dying, all alike speak much and unexpectedly about subjects utterly inappropriate to the occasion, being evidently guided rather by consonances and play of words than by thoughts. They speak all alike. Lear raves exactly as does Edgar when feigning madness. Both Kent and the fool speak alike. The words of one of the personages might be placed in the mouth of another, and by the character of the speech it would be impossible to distinguish who speaks. If there is a difference in the speech of Shakespeare's various characters, it lies merely in the different dialogs which are pronounced for these characters—again by Shakespeare and not by themselves. Thus Shakespeare always speaks for kings in one and the same inflated, empty language. Also in one and the same Shakespearian, artificially sentimental language speak all the women who are intended to be poetic: Juliet, Desdemona, Cordelia, Imogen, Marina. In the same way, also, it is Shakespeare alone who speaks for his villains: Richard, Edmund, Iago, Macbeth, expressing for them those vicious feelings which villains never express. Yet more similar are the speeches of the madmen with their horrible words, and those of fools with their mirthless puns. So that in Shakespeare there is no language of living individuals—that language which in the drama is the chief means of setting forth character. If gesticulation be also a means of expressing character, as in ballets, this is only a secondary means. Moreover, if the characters speak at random and in a random way, and all in one and the same diction, as is the case in Shakespeare's work, then even the action of gesticulation is wasted. Therefore, whatever the blind panegyrists of Shakespeare may say, in Shakespeare there is no expression of character. Those personages who, in his dramas, stand out as characters, are characters borrowed by him from former works which have served as the foundation of his dramas, and they are mostly depicted, not by the dramatic method which consists in making each person speak with his own diction, but in the epic method of one person describing the features of another.

The perfection with which Shakespeare expresses character is asserted chiefly on the ground of the characters of Lear, Cordelia, Othello, Desdemona, Falstaff, and Hamlet. But all these characters, as well as all the others, instead of belonging to Shakespeare, are taken by him from dramas, chronicles, and romances anterior to him. All these characters not only are not rendered more powerful by him, but, in most cases, they are weakened and spoilt. This is very striking in this drama of *King Lear*, which we are examining, taken by him from the drama *King Leir*, by an unknown author. The characters of this drama, that of King Lear, and especially of Cordelia, not only were not created by Shakespeare, but have been strikingly weakened and deprived of force by him, as compared with their appearance in the older drama.

In the older drama, Leir abdicates because, having become a widower, he thinks only of saving his soul. He asks his daughters as to their love for him—that, by means of a certain device he has invented, he may retain his favorite daughter on his island. The elder daughters are betrothed, while the youngest does not wish to contract a loveless union with any of the neighboring suitors whom Leir proposes to her, and he is afraid that she may marry some distant potentate.

The device which he has invented, as he informs his courtier, Perillus (Shakespeare's Kent), is this, that when Cordelia tells him that she loves him more than any one or as much as her elder sisters do, he will tell her that she must, in proof of her love, marry the prince he will indicate on his island. All these motives for Lear's conduct are absent in Shakespeare's play. Then, when, according to the old drama, Leir asks his daughters about their love for him, Cordelia does not say, as Shakespeare has it, that she will not give her father all her love, but will love her husband, too, should she marry—which is quite unnatural—but simply says that she can not express her love in words, but hopes that her actions will prove it. Goneril and Regan remark that Cordelia's answer is not an answer, and that the father can not meekly accept such indifference, so that what is wanting in Shakespeare—*i.e.*, the explanation of Lear's anger which caused him to disinherit his youngest daughter,—exists in the old drama. Leir is annoyed by the failure of his scheme, and the poisonous words of his eldest daughters irritate him still more. After the division of the kingdom between the elder daughters, there follows in the older drama a scene between Cordelia and the King of Gaul, setting forth, instead of the colorless Cordelia of Shakespeare, a very definite and attractive character of the truthful, tender, and self-sacrificing youngest daughter. While Cordelia, without grieving that she has been deprived of a portion of the heritage, sits sorrowing at having lost her father's love, and looking forward to earn her bread by her labor, there comes the King of Gaul, who, in the disguise of a pilgrim, desires to choose a bride from among Leir's daughters. He asks Cordelia why she is sad. She tells him the cause of her grief. The King of Gaul, still in the guise of a pilgrim, falls in love with her, and

offers to arrange a marriage for her with the King of Gaul, but she says she will marry only a man whom she loves. Then the pilgrim, still disguised, offers her his hand and heart and Cordelia confesses she loves the pilgrim and consents to marry him, notwithstanding the poverty that awaits her. Then the pilgrim discloses to her that he it is who is the King of Gaul, and Cordelia marries him. Instead of this scene, Lear, according to Shakespeare, offers Cordelia's two suitors to take her without dowry, and one cynically refuses, while the other, one does not know why, accepts her. After this, in the old drama, as in Shakespeare's, Leir undergoes the insults of Goneril, into whose house he has removed, but he bears these insults in a very different way from that represented by Shakespeare: he feels that by his conduct toward Cordelia, he has deserved this, and humbly submits. As in Shakespeare's drama, so also in the older drama, the courtier, Perillus-Kent—who had interceded for Cordelia and was therefore banished—comes to Leir and assures him of his love, but under no disguise, but simply as a faithful old servant who does not abandon his king in a moment of need. Leir tells him what, according to Shakespeare, he tells Cordelia in the last scene, that, if the daughters whom he has benefited hate him, a retainer to whom he has done no good can not love him. But Perillus—Kent—assures the King of his love toward him, and Leir, pacified, goes on to Regan. In the older drama there are no tempests nor tearing out of gray hairs, but there is the weakened and humbled old man, Leir, overpowered with grief, and banished by his other daughter also, who even wishes to kill him. Turned out by his elder daughters, Leir, according to the older drama, as a last resource, goes with Perillus to Cordelia. Instead of the unnatural banishment of Lear during the tempest, and his roaming about the heath, Leir, with Perillus, in the older drama, during their journey to France, very naturally reach the last degree of destitution, sell their clothes in order to pay for their crossing over the sea, and, in the attire of fishermen, exhausted by cold and hunger, approach Cordelia's house. Here, again, instead of the unnatural combined ravings of the fool, Lear, and Edgar, as represented by Shakespeare, there follows in the older drama a natural scene of reunion between the daughter and the father. Cordelia—who, notwithstanding her happiness, has all the time been grieving about her father and praying to God to forgive her sisters who had done him so much wrong—meets her father in his extreme want, and wishes immediately to disclose herself to him, but her husband advises her not to do this, in order not to agitate her weak father. She accepts the counsel and takes Leir into her house without disclosing herself to him, and nurses him. Leir gradually revives, and then the daughter asks him who he is and how he lived formerly:

> *Leir:* If from the first I should relate the cause,
> I would make a heart of adamant to weep.
> And thou, poor soul, kind-hearted as thou art,
> Dost weep already, ere I do begin.
> *Cordelia:* For God's love tell it, and when you have done
> I'll tell the reason why I weep so soon.

And Leir relates all he has suffered from his elder daughters, and says that now he wishes to find shelter with the child who would be in the right even were she to condemn him to death. "If, however," he says, "she will receive me with love, it will be God's and her work, but not my merit." To this Cordelia says: "Oh, I know for certain that thy daughter will lovingly receive thee."—"How canst thou know this without knowing her?" says Leir. "I know," says Cordelia, "because not far from here, I had a father who acted toward me as badly as thou hast acted toward her, yet, if I were only to see his white head, I would creep to meet him on my knees."—"No, this can not be," says Leir, "for there are no children in the world so cruel as mine."—"Do not condemn all for the sins of some," says Cordelia, and falls on her knees. "Look here, dear father," she says, "look on me: I am thy loving daughter." The father recognizes her and says: "It is not for thee, but for me, to beg thy pardon on my knees for all my sins toward thee."

Is there anything approaching this exquisite scene in Shakespeare's drama?

However strange this opinion may seem to worshipers of Shakespeare, yet the whole of this old drama is incomparably and in every respect superior to Shakespeare's adaptation. It is so, first, because it has not got the utterly superfluous characters of the villain Edmund and unlifelike Gloucester and Edgar, who only distract one's attention; secondly because it

has not got the completely false "effects" of Lear running about the heath, his conversations with the fool, and all these impossible disguises, failures to recognize, and accumulated deaths; and, above all, because in this drama there is the simple, natural, and deeply touching character of Leir and the yet more touching and clearly defined character of Cordelia, both absent in Shakespeare. Therefore, there is in the older drama, instead of Shakespeare's long-drawn scene of Lear's interview with Cordelia and of Cordelia's unnecessary murder, the exquisite scene of the interview between Leir and Cordelia, unequaled by any in all Shakespeare's dramas.

The old drama also terminates more naturally and more in accordance with the moral demands of the spectator than does Shakespeare's, namely, by the King of the Gauls conquering the husbands of the elder sisters, and Cordelia, instead of being killed, restoring Leir to his former position.

# Macbeth

. . . thence to the Duke's house, and saw *Macbeth*, which, though I saw it lately, yet appears a most excellent play in all respects, but especially in divertissement, though it be a deep tragedy; which is a strange perfection in a tragedy, it being most proper here, and suitable.—SAMUEL PEPYS, *Diary*, Jan. 7, 1667

In order to make a true estimate of the abilities and merit of a writer, it is always necessary to examine the genius of his age, and the opinions of his contemporaries. A poet who should now make the whole action of his tragedy depend upon enchantment, and produce the chief events by the assistance of supernatural agents, would be censured as transgressing the bounds of probability, be banished from the theatre to the nursery, and condemned to write fairy tales instead of tragedies; but a survey of the notions that prevailed at the time when this play was written, will prove that Shakespeare was in no danger of such censures, since he only turned the system that was then universally admitted to his advantage, and was far from overburthening the credulity of his audience.

The reality of witchcraft or enchantment, which, though not strictly the same, are confounded in this play, has in all ages and countries been credited by the common people, and in most by the learned themselves. These phantoms have indeed appeared more frequently, in proportion as the darkness of ignorance has been more gross; but it cannot be shown, that the brightest gleams of knowledge have at any time been sufficient to drive them out of the world. The time in which this kind of credulity was at its height, seems to have been that of the holy war, in which the Christians imputed all their defeats to enchantments or diabolical opposition, as they ascribed their success to the assistance of their military saints; and the learned Dr. Warburton appears to believe (*Suppl. to the Introduction to Don Quixote*) that the first accounts of enchantments were brought into this part of the world by those who returned from their eastern expeditions. But there is always some distance between the birth and maturity of folly as of wickedness: this opinion had long existed, though perhaps the application of it had in no foregoing age been so frequent, nor the reception so general. Olympiodorus, in Photius's extracts, tells us of one Libanius, who practised this kind of military magic, and having promised χωρὶς ὁπλιτῶν κατὰ βαρβάρων ἐνεργεῖν, "to perform great things against the

barbarians without soldiers," was, at the instances of the Emperess Placidia, put to death, when he was about to have given proofs of his abilities. The Emperess shewed some kindness in her anger by cutting him off at a time so convenient for his reputation.

But a more remarkable proof of the antiquity of this notion may be found in St. Chrysostom's book *De Sacerdotio*, which exhibits a scene of enchantments not exceeded by any romance of the middle age: he supposes a spectator overlooking a field of battle attended by one that points out all the various objects of horror, the engines of destruction, and the arts of slaughter. Δεικνύτο δὲ ἔτι παρὰ τοῖς ἐναντίοις καὶ πετομένους ἵππους διά τινος μαγγανείας, καὶ ὁπλίτας δι' ἀέρος φερομένους, καὶ πᾶσην γοητείας δύναμιν καὶ ἰδέαν. "Let him then proceed to show him in the opposite armies horses flying by enchantment, armed men transported through the air, and every power and form of magic." Whether St. Chrysostom believed that such performances were really to be seen in a day of battle, or only endeavoured to enliven his description, by adopting the notions of the vulgar, it is equally certain, that such notions were in his time received, and that therefore they were not imported from the Saracens in a later age; the wars with the Saracens however gave occasion to their propagation, not only as bigotry naturally discovers prodigies, but as the scene of action was removed to a great distance.

The Reformation did not immediately arrive at its meridian, and tho' day was gradually encreasing upon us, the goblins of witchcraft still continued to hover in the twilight. In the time of Queen Elizabeth was the remarkable trial of the witches of Warbois, whose conviction is still commemorated in an annual sermon at Huntingdon. But in the reign of King James, in which this tragedy was written, many circumstances concurred to propagate and confirm this opinion. The King, who was much celebrated for his knowledge, had, before his arrival in England, not only examined in person a woman accused of witchcraft, but had given a very formal account of the practices and illusions of evil spirits, the compacts of witches, the ceremonies used by them, the manner of detecting them, and the justice of punishing them, in his Dialogues of *Daemonologie*, written in the Scottish dialect, and published at Edinburgh. This book was, soon after his accession, reprinted at London, and as the ready way to gain King James's favour was to flatter his speculations, the system of *Daemonologie* was

Eleonora Duse as Cordelia
*(King Lear)*

Mr. Fleming as Edgar
*(King Lear)*

Sarah Bernhardt as Lady Macbeth

Mrs. Siddons as Lady Macbeth

George Bennett as Apemantus in *Timon of Athens*
(engraving by Sherratt from a daguerreotype by Paine)

John McCullough as Coriolanus

Sarah Bernhardt as Cleopatra
in *Antony and Cleopatra*

immediately adopted by all who desired either to gain preferment or not to lose it. Thus the doctrine of witchcraft was very powerfully inculcated; and as the greatest part of mankind have no other reason for their opinions than that they are in fashion, it cannot be doubted but this persuasion made a rapid progress, since vanity and credulity co-operated in its favour. The infection soon reached the Parliament, who, in the first year of King James, made a law by which it was enacted, chap. xii. That "if any person shall use any invocation or conjuration of any evil or wicked spirit; 2. or shall consult, covenant with, entertain, employ, feed or reward any evil or cursed spirit to or for any intent or puspose; 3. or take up any dead man, woman or child out of the grave,—or the skin, bone, or any part of the dead person, to be employed or used in any manner of witchcraft, sorcery, charm, or enchantment; 4. or shall use, practise or exercise any sort of witchcraft, sorcery, charm, or enchantment; 5. whereby any person shall be destroyed, killed, wasted, consumed, pined, or lamed in any part of the body; 6. That every such person being convicted shall suffer death." This law was repealed in our own time.

Thus, in the time of Shakespeare, was the doctrine of witchcraft at once established by law and by the fashion, and it became not only unpolite, but criminal, to doubt it; and as prodigies are always seen in proportion as they are expected, witches were every day discovered, and multiplied so fast in some places, that Bishop Hall mentions a village in Lancashire, where their number was greater than that of the houses. The Jesuits and sectaries took advantage of this universal error, and endeavoured to promote the interest of their parties by pretended cures of persons afflicted by evil spirits; but they were detected and exposed by the clergy of the established church.

Upon this general infatuation Shakespeare might be easily allowed to found a play, especially since he has followed with great exactness such histories as were then thought true; nor can it be doubted that the scenes of enchantment, however they may now be ridiculed, were both by himself and his audience thought awful and affecting. . . .

This play is deservedly celebrated for the propriety of its fictions, and solemnity, grandeur, and variety of its action; but it has no nice discriminations of character, the events are too great to admit the influence of particular dispositions, and the course of the action necessarily determines the conduct of the agents.

The danger of ambition is well described; and I know not whether it may not be said in defence of some parts which now seem improbable, that, in Shakespeare's time, it was necessary to warn credulity against vain and illusive predictions.

The passions are directed to their true end. Lady Macbeth is merely detested; and though the courage of Macbeth preserves some esteem, yet every reader rejoices at his fall.—SAMUEL JOHNSON, *Notes on Shakespeare's Plays,* 1768

Of *Macbeth* I have already spoken once in passing, and who could exhaust the praises of this sublime work? Since *The Eumenides* of Æschylus, nothing so grand and terrible has ever been written. The witches are not, it is true, divine Eumenides, and are not intended to be: they are ignoble and vulgar instruments of hell. A German poet, therefore, very ill understood their meaning, when he transformed them into mongrel beings, a mixture of fates, furies, and enchantresses, and clothed them with tragic dignity. Let no man venture to lay hand on Shakspeare's works thinking to improve anything essential: he will be sure to punish himself. The bad is radically odious, and to endeavour in any manner to ennoble it, is to violate the laws of propriety. Hence, in my opinion, Dante, and even Tasso, have been much more successful in their portraiture of dæmons than Milton. Whether the age of Shakspeare still believed in ghosts and witches, is a matter of perfect indifference for the justification of the use which in *Hamlet* and *Macbeth* he has made of pre-existing traditions. No superstition can be widely diffused without having a foundation in human nature: on this the poet builds; he calls up from their hidden abysses that dread of the unknown, that presage of a dark side of nature, and a world of spirits, which philosophy now imagines it has altogether exploded. In this manner he is in some degree both the portrayer and the philosopher of superstition; that is, not the philosopher who denies and turns it into ridicule, but, what is still more difficult, who distinctly exhibits its origin in apparently irrational and yet natural opinions. But when he ventures to make arbitrary changes in these popular traditions, he altogether forfeits his right to them, and merely holds up his own idle fancies to our ridicule. Shakspeare's picture of the witches is truly magical in the short scenes where they enter, he has created for them a peculiar language, which, although composed of the usual elements, still seems to be a collection of formulæ of incantation. The sound of the words, the accumulation of rhymes, and the rhythmus of the verse, form, as it were, the hollow music of a dreary witch-dance. He has been abused for using the names of disgusting objects; but he who fancies the kettle of the witches can be made effective with agreeable aromatics, is as wise as those who desire that hell should sincerely and honestly give good advice. These repulsive things, from which the imagination shrinks, are here emblems of the hostile powers which operate in nature; and the repugnance of our senses is outweighed by the mental horror. With one another the witches discourse like women of the very lowest class; for this was the class to which witches were ordinarily supposed to belong: when, however, they address Macbeth they assume a loftier tone: their predictions, which they either themselves pronounce, or allow their apparitions to deliver, have all the obscure brevity, the majestic solemnity of oracles.

We here see that the witches are merely instruments; they are governed by an invisible spirit, or the operation of such great and dreadful events would be above their sphere. With what intent did Shakspeare assign the same place to them in his play, which they occupy in the history of Macbeth as related in the old chronicles? A monstrous crime is committed; Duncan, a venerable old man, and the best of kings, is, in defenceless sleep, under the hospitable roof, murdered by his subject, whom he has loaded with honours and rewards. Natural motives alone seem inadequate, or the perpetrator must have been portrayed as a hardened villain. Shakspeare wished to exhibit a more sublime picture: an ambitious but noble hero, yielding to a deep-laid hellish temptation; and in whom all the crimes to which, in order to secure the fruits of his first crime, he is impelled by necessity, cannot altogether eradicate the stamp of native heroism. He has, therefore, given a threefold division to the guilt of that crime. The first idea comes from that being whose whole activity is guided by a lust of wickedness. The weird sisters surprise Macbeth in the moment of intoxication of victory, when his love of glory has been gratified; they cheat his eyes by exhibiting to him as the work of fate what in reality can only be accomplished by his own deed, and gain credence for all their words by the immediate fulfilment of the first prediction. The opportunity of murdering the King immediately offers; the wife of Macbeth conjures him not to let it slip; she urges him on with a fiery eloquence, which has at command all those sophisms that serve to throw a false splendour over crime. Little more than the mere execution falls to the share of Macbeth; he is driven into it, as it were, in a tumult of fascination. Repentance immediately follows, nay, even precedes the deed, and the stings of conscience leave him rest neither night nor day. But he is now fairly entangled in the snares of hell; truly frightful is it to behold that same Macbeth, who once as a warrior could spurn at death, now that he dreads the prospect of the life to come, clinging with growing anxiety to his earthly existence the more miserable it becomes, and pitilessly removing out of the way whatever to his dark and suspicious mind seems to threaten danger. However much we may abhor his actions, we cannot altogether refuse to compassionate the state of his mind; we lament the ruin of so many noble qualities, and even in his last defence we are compelled to admire the struggle of a brave will with a cowardly conscience. We might believe that we witness in this tragedy the over-ruling destiny of the ancients represented in perfect accordance with their ideas: the whole originates in a supernatural influence, to which the subsequent events seem inevitably linked. Moreover, we even find here the same ambiguous oracles which, by their literal fulfilment, deceive those who confide in them. Yet it may be easily shown that the poet has, in his work, displayed more enlightened views. He wishes to show that the conflict of good and evil in this world can only take place by the permission of Providence, which converts the curse that individual mortals draw down on their heads into a blessing to others. An accurate scale is followed in the retaliation. Lady Macbeth, who of all the human participators in the king's murder is the most guilty, is thrown by the terrors of her conscience into a state of incurable bodily and mental disease; she dies, unlamented by her husband, with all the symptoms of reprobation. Macbeth is still found worthy to die the death of a hero on the field of battle. The noble Macduff is allowed the satisfaction of saving his country by punishing with his own hand the tyrant who had murdered his wife and children. Banquo, by an early death, atones for the ambitious curiosity which prompted the wish to know his glorious descendants, as he thereby has roused Macbeth's jealousy; but he preserved his mind pure from the evil suggestions of the witches: his name is blessed in his race, destined to enjoy for a long succession of ages that royal dignity which Macbeth could only hold for his own life. In the progress of the action, this piece is altogether the reverse of *Hamlet*: it strides forward with amazing rapidity, from the first catastrophe (for Duncan's murder may be called a catastrophe) to the last. "Thought, and done!" is the general motto; for as Macbeth says,

> The flighty purpose never is o'ertook,
> Unless the deed go with it.

In every feature we see an energetic heroic age, in the hardy North which steels every nerve. The precise duration of the action cannot be ascertained,—years perhaps, according to the story; but we know that to the imagination the most crowded time appears always the shortest. Here we can hardly conceive how so very much could ever have been compressed into so narrow a space; not merely external events,—the very inmost recesses in the minds of the dramatic personages are laid open to us. It is as if the drags were taken from the wheels of time, and they rolled along without interruption in their descent. Nothing can equal this picture in its power to excite terror. We need only allude to the circumstances attending the murder of Duncan, the dagger that hovers before the eyes of Macbeth, the vision of Banquo at the feast, the madness of Lady Macbeth; what can possibly be said on the subject that will not rather weaken the impression they naturally leave? Such scenes

stand alone, and are to be found only in this poet; otherwise the tragic muse might exchange her mask for the *head of Medusa*.

I wish merely to point out as a secondary circumstance the prudent dexterity of Shakspeare, who could still contrive to flatter a king by a work in every part of whose plan nevertheless the poetical views are evident. James the First drew his lineage from Banquo; he was the first who united the threefold sceptre of England, Scotland, and Ireland: this is foreshown in the magical vision, when a long series of glorious successors is promised to Banquo. Even the gift of the English kings to heal certain maladies by the touch, which James pretended to have inherited from Edward the Confessor, and on which he set a great value, is brought in very naturally.—With such occasional matters we may well allow ourselves to be pleased without fearing from them any danger to poetry: by similar allusions Æschylus endeavoured to recommend the Areopagus to his fellow-citizens, and Sophocles to celebrate the glory of Athens.—AUGUST WILHELM SCHLEGEL, *Lectures on Dramatic Art and Literature*, 1809, tr. John Black

In *Macbeth*, for the sake of gratifying his own enormous and teeming faculty of creation, Shakspere has introduced two murderers: and, as usual in his hands, they are remarkably discriminated: but,—though in Macbeth the strife of mind is greater than in his wife, the tiger spirit not so awake, and his feelings caught chiefly by contagion from her,—yet, as both were finally involved in the guilt of murder, the murderous mind of necessity is finally to be presumed in both. This was to be expressed; and, on its own account, as well as to make it a more proportionable antagonist to the unoffending nature of their victim, "the gracious Duncan," and adequately to expound "the deep damnation of his taking off," this was to be expressed with peculiar energy. We were to be made to feel that the human nature,—*i.e.* the divine nature of love and mercy, spread through the hearts of all creatures, and seldom utterly withdrawn from man,—was gone, vanished, extinct, and that the fiendish nature had taken its place. And, as this effect is marvellously accomplished in the *dialogues* and *soliloquies* themselves, so it is finally consummated by the expedient under consideration; and it is to this that I now solicit the reader's attention. If the reader has ever witnessed a wife, daughter, or sister in a fainting fit, he may chance to have observed that the most affecting moment in such a spectacle is *that* in which a sigh and a stirring announce the recommencement of suspended life. Or, if the reader has ever been present in a vast metropolis on the day when some great national idol was carried in funeral pomp to his grave, and, chancing to walk near the course through which it passed, has felt powerfully, in the silence and desertion of the streets, and in the stagnation of ordinary business, the deep interest which at that moment was possessing the heart of man,—if all at once he should hear the death-like stillness broken up by the sound of wheels rattling away from the scene, and making known that the transitory vision was dissolved, he will be aware that at no moment was his sense of the complete suspension and pause in ordinary human concerns so full and affecting as at that moment when the suspension ceases, and the goings-on of human life are suddenly resumed. All action in any direction is best expounded, measured, and made apprehensible, by reaction. Now, apply this to the case in *Macbeth*. Here, as I have said, the retiring of the human heart and the entrance of the fiendish heart was to be expressed and made sensible. Another world has stept in; and the murderers are taken out of the region of human things, human purposes, human desires. They are transfigured: Lady Macbeth is "unsexed"; Macbeth has forgot that he was born of woman; both are conformed to the image of devils; and the world of devils is suddenly revealed. But how shall this be conveyed and made palpable? In order that a new world may step in, this world must for a time disappear. The murderers and the murder must be insulated—cut off by an immeasurable gulf from the ordinary tide and succession of human affairs—locked up and sequestered in some deep recess; we must be made sensible that the world of ordinary life is suddenly arrested, laid asleep, tranced, racked into a dread armistice; time must be annihilated, relation to things without abolished; and all must pass self-withdrawn into a deep syncope and suspension of earthly passion. Hence it is that, when the deed is done, when the work of darkness is perfect, then the world of darkness passes away like a pageantry in the clouds: the knocking at the gate is heard, and it makes known audibly that the reaction is commenced; the human has made its reflux upon the fiendish; the pulses of life are beginning to beat again; and the re-establishment of the goings-on of the world in which we live first makes us profoundly sensible of the awful parenthesis that had suspended them.

O mighty poet! Thy works are not as those of other men, simply and merely great works of art, but are also like the phenomena of nature, like the sun and the sea, the stars and the flowers, like frost and snow, rain and dew, hail-storm and thunder, which are to be studied with entire submission of our own faculties, and in the perfect faith that in them there can be no too much or too little, nothing useless or inert, but that, the farther we press in our discoveries, the more we shall see proofs of design and self-supporting arrangement where the careless eye had seen nothing but accident!—THOMAS DE QUINCEY, "On the Knocking at the Gate in *Macbeth*" (1823), *Collected Writings*, 1890, vol. 10, ed. David Masson, pp. 392–94

"Are there not," said I, "bold strokes of artistic fiction, similar to this double light of Rubens, to be found in literature?"

"We need not go far," said Goethe, after some reflection; "I could show you a dozen of them in Shakespeare. Only take *Macbeth*. When the lady would animate her husband to the deed, she says:

> I have given suck, etc.

Whether this be true or not does not appear; but the lady says it, and she must say it, in order to give emphasis to her speech. But in the course of the piece, when Macduff hears of the account of the destruction of his family, he exclaims in wild rage:

> He has no children!

These words of Macduff contradict those of Lady Macbeth; but this does not trouble Shakespeare. The grand point with him is the force of each speech; and as the lady, in order to give the highest emphasis to her words, must say 'I have given suck,' so, for the same purpose, Macduff must say 'He has no children.'

"Generally," continued Goethe, "we must not judge too exactly and narrowly of the pencil touches of a painter, or the words of a poet; we should rather contemplate and enjoy a work of art that has been produced in a bold and free spirit, and if possible with the same spirit.

"Thus it would be foolish, if, from the words of Macbeth:

> Bring forth men children only! etc.

it were concluded that the lady was a young creature who had not yet borne any children. It would be equally foolish if we were to go still further, and say that the lady must be represented on the stage as a very youthful person.

"Shakespeare does not make Macbeth say these words to show the youth of the lady. Like those of Lady Macbeth and Macduff, which I quoted just now, they are introduced merely for rhetorical purposes, and prove nothing more than that the poet always makes his character say whatever is proper, effective, and good in each *particular place*, without troubling himself to calculate whether these words may perhaps fall into apparent contradiction with some other passage.—JOHANN PETER ECKERMANN, *Conversations with Goethe*, 1836, tr. John Oxenford

> Rose, like dim battlements, the hills and reared
> Steep crags into the fading primrose sky;
> But in the desolate valleys fell small rain,
> Mingled with drifting cloud. I saw one come,
> Like the fierce passion of that vacant place,
> His face turned glittering to the evening sky;
> His eyes, like grey despair, fixed satelessly
> On the still, rainy turrets of the storm;
> And all his armour in a haze of blue.
> He held no sword, bare was his hand and clenched,
> As if to hide the inextinguishable blood
> Murder had painted there. And his wild mouth
> Seemed spouting echoes of deluded thoughts.
> Around his head, like vipers all distort,
> His locks shook, heavy-laden, at each stride.
> If fire may burn invisible to the eye;
> O, if despair strive everlastingly;
> Then haunted here the creature of despair,
> Fanning and fanning flame to lick upon
> A soul still childish in a blackened hell.
> —WALTER DE LA MARE, "Macbeth," *Characters from Shakespeare*, 1902

> What dost thou here far from thy native place?
> What piercing influences of heaven have stirred
> Thy heart's last mansion all-corruptible to wake,
> To move, and in the sweets of wine and fire
> Sir tempting madness with unholy eyes?
> Begone, thou shuddering, pale anomaly!
> The dark presses without on yew and thorn;
> Stoops now the owl upon her lonely quest;
> The pomp runs high here, and our beauteous women
> Seek no cold witness—O, let murder cry,
> Too shrill for human ear, only to God.
> Come not in power to wreak so wild a vengeance!
> Thou knowest not now the limit of man's heart;
> He is beyond thy knowledge. Gaze not then.
> Horror enthroned lit with insanest light!
> —WALTER DE LA MARE, "Banquo," *Characters from Shakespeare*, 1902

## WILLIAM HAZLITT
### From "*Macbeth*"
### *Characters of Shakespear's Plays*
### 1817

> The poet's eye in a fine frenzy rolling
> Doth glance from heaven to earth, from earth to heaven;
> And as imagination bodies forth
> The forms of things unknown, the poet's pen
> Turns them to shape, and gives to airy nothing
> A local habitation and a name.

Macbeth and *Lear*, *Othello* and *Hamlet*, are usually reckoned Shakespear's four principal tragedies. *Lear* stands first for the profound intensity of the passion; *Macbeth* for the wildness of the imagination and the rapidity of the action; *Othello* for the progressive interest and powerful alternations of feeling; *Hamlet* for the refined development of thought and sentiment. If the force of genius shewn in each of these works is astonishing, their variety is not less so. They are like different creations of the same mind, not one of which has the slightest reference to the rest. This distinctness and originality is indeed the necessary consequence of truth and nature. Shakespear's genius alone appeared to possess the resources of nature. He is 'your only *tragedy-maker.*' His plays have the force of things upon the mind. What he represents is brought home to the bosom as a part of our experience, implanted in the memory as if we had known the places, persons, and things of which he treats. *Macbeth* is like a record of a preternatural and tragical event. It has the rugged severity of an old chronicle with all that the imagination of the poet can engraft upon traditional belief. The castle of Macbeth, round which 'the air smells wooingly,' and where 'the temple-haunting martlet builds,' has a real subsistence in the mind; the Weïrd Sisters meet us in person on 'the blasted heath'; the 'air-drawn dagger' moves slowly before our eyes; the 'gracious Duncan,' the 'blood-boultered Banquo' stand before us; all that passed through the mind of Macbeth passes, without the loss of a title, through ours. All that could actually take place, and all that is only possible to be conceived, what was said and what was done, the workings of passion, the spells of magic, are brought before us with the same absolute truth and vividness.—Shakespear excelled in the openings of his plays: that of *Macbeth* is the most striking of any. The wildness of the scenery, the sudden shifting of the situations and characters, the bustle, the expectations excited, are equally extraordinary. From the first entrance of the Witches and the description of them when they meet Macbeth,

> What are these
> So wither'd and so wild in their attire,
> That look not like the inhabitants of th' earth
> And yet are on 't?

the mind is prepared for all that follows.

This tragedy is alike distinguished for the lofty imagination it displays, and for the tumultuous vehemence of the action; and the one is made the moving principle of the other. The overwhelming pressure of preternatural agency urges on the tide of human passion with redoubled force. Macbeth himself appears driven along by the violence of his fate like a vessel drifting before a storm: he reels to and fro like a drunken man; he staggers under the weight of his own purposes and the suggestions of others; he stands at bay with his situation; and from the superstitious awe and breathless suspense into which the communications of the Weïrd Sisters throw him, is hurried on with daring impatience to verify their predictions, and with impious and bloody hand to tear aside the veil which hides the uncertainty of the future. He is not equal to the struggle with fate and conscience. He now 'bends up each corporal instrument to the terrible feat'; at other times his heart misgives him, and he is cowed and abashed by his success. 'The deed, no less than the attempt, confounds him.' His mind is assailed by the stings of remorse, and full of 'preternatural solicitings.' His speeches and soliloquies are dark riddles on human life, baffling solution, and entangling him in their labyrinths. In thought he is absent and perplexed, sudden and desperate in act, from a distrust of his own resolution. His energy springs from the anxiety and agitation of his mind. His blindly rushing forward on the objects of his ambition and revenge, or his recoiling from them, equally betrays the harassed state of his feelings.—This part of his character is admirably set off by being brought in connection with that of Lady Macbeth, whose obdurate strength of will and masculine firmness give her the

ascendancy over her husband's faultering virtue. She at once seizes on the opportunity that offers for the accomplishment of all their wished-for greatness, and never flinches from her object till all is over. The magnitude of her resolution almost covers the magnitude of her guilt. She is a great bad woman, whom we hate, but whom we fear more than we hate. She does not excite our loathing and abhorrence like Regan and Gonerill. She is only wicked to gain a great end; and is perhaps more distinguished by her commanding presence of mind and inexorable self-will, which do not suffer her to be diverted from a bad purpose, when once formed, by weak and womanly regrets, than by the hardness of her heart or want of natural affections. The impression which her lofty determination of character makes on the mind of Macbeth is well described where he exclaims,

> Bring forth men children only;
> For thy undaunted mettle should compose
> Nothing but males!

Nor do the pains she is at to 'screw his courage to the sticking-place,' the reproach to him, not to be 'lost so poorly in himself,' the assurance that 'a little water clears them of this deed,' show anything but her greater consistency in depravity. Her strong-nerved ambition furnishes ribs of steel to 'the sides of his intent'; and she is herself wound up to the execution of her baneful project with the same unshrinking fortitude in crime, that in other cricumstances she would probably have shown patience in suffering. The deliberate sacrifice of all other considerations to the gaining 'for their future days and nights sole sovereign sway and masterdom,' by the murder of Duncan, is gorgeously expressed in her invocation on hearing of 'his fatal entrance under her battlements':—

> Come all you spirits
> That tend on mortal thoughts, unsex me here:
> And fill me, from the crown to th' toe, top-full
> Of direst cruelty; make thick my blood,
> Stop up the access and passage to remorse,
> That no compunctious visitings of nature
> Shake my fell purpose, nor keep peace between
> The effect and it. Come to my woman's breasts,
> And take my milk for gall, you murthering ministers,
> Wherever in your sightless substances
> You wait on nature's mischief. Come, thick night!
> And pall thee in the dunnest smoke of hell,
> That my keen knife see not the wound it makes,
> Nor heav'n peep through the blanket of the dark,
> To cry, hold, hold!

When she first hears that 'Duncan comes here to sleep' she is so overcome by the news, which is beyond her utmost expectations, that she answers the messenger, 'Thou 'rt mad to say it': and on receiving her husband's account of the predictions of the Witches, conscious of his instability of purpose, and that her presence is necessary to goad him on to the consummation of his promised greatness, she exclaims—

> Hie thee hither,
> That I may pour my spirits in thine ear,
> And chastise with the valour of my tongue
> All that impedes thee from the golden round,
> Which fate and metaphysical aid doth seem
> To have thee crowned withal.

This swelling exultation and keen spirit of triumph, this uncontroulable eagerness of anticipation, which seems to dilate her form and take possession of all her faculties, this solid, substantial flesh and blood display of passion, exhibit a striking contrast to the cold, abstracted, gratuitous, servile malignity of the Witches, who are equally instrumental in urging Macbeth to his fate for the mere love of mischief, and from a disinterested delight in deformity and cruelty. They are hags of mischief, obscene panders to iniquity, malicious from their impotence of enjoyment, enamoured of destruction, because they are themselves unreal, abortive, half-existences— who become sublime from their exemption from all human sympathies and contempt for all human affairs, as Lady Macbeth does by the force of passion! Her fault seems to have been an excess of that strong principle of self-interest and family aggrandisement, not amenable to the common feelings of compassion and justice, which is so marked a feature in barbarous nations and times. A passing reflection of this kind, on the resemblance of the sleeping king to her father, alone prevents her from slaying Duncan with her own hand. . . .

The dramatic beauty of the character of Duncan, which excites the respect and pity even of his murderers, has been often pointed out. It forms a picture of itself. An instance of the author's power of giving a striking effect to a common reflection, by the manner of introducing it, occurs in a speech of Duncan, complaining of his having been deceived in his opinion of the Thane of Cawdor, at the very moment that he is expressing the most unbounded confidence in the loyalty and services of Macbeth.

> There is no art
> To find the mind's construction in the face:
> He was a gentleman, on whom I built
> An absolute trust.
> O worthiest cousin, (*addressing himself to Macbeth.*)
> The sin of my ingratitude e'en now
> Was great upon me, etc.

Another passage to show that Shakespear lost sight of nothing that could in any way give relief or heightening to his subject, is the conversation which takes place between Banquo and Fleance immediately before the murder-scene of Duncan.

> *Banquo:* How goes the night, boy?
> *Fleance:* The moon is down: I have not heard the clock.
> *Banquo:* And she goes down at twelve.
> *Fleance:* I take 't, 'tis later, Sir.
> *Banquo:* Hold, take my sword. There's husbandry in heav'n,
> Their candles are all out.—
> A heavy summons lies like lead upon me,
> And yet I would not sleep: Merciful Powers,
> Restrain in me the cursed thoughts that nature
> Gives way to in repose.

In like manner, a fine idea is given of the gloomy coming on of evening, just as Banquo is going to be assassinated.

> Light thickens and the crow
> Makes wing to the rooky wood.
>
> . . .
> Now spurs the lated traveller apace
> To gain the timely inn.

*Macbeth* (generally speaking) is done upon a stronger and more systematic principle of contrast than any other of Shakespear's plays. It moves upon the verge of an abyss, and is a constant struggle between life and death. The action is desperate and the reaction is dreadful. It is a huddling together of fierce extremes, a war of opposite natures which of them shall destroy the other. There is nothing but what has a violent end or violent beginnings. The lights and shades are laid on with a determined hand; the transitions from triumph to despair, from the height of terror to the repose of death, are sudden and startling; every passion brings in its fellow-contrary, and the thoughts pitch and jostle against each other as in the

dark. The whole play is an unruly chaos of strange and forbidden things, where the ground rocks under our feet. Shakespear's genius here took its full swing, and trod upon the farthest bounds of nature and passion. This circumstance will account for the abruptness and violent antitheses of the style, the throes and labour which run through the expression, and from defects will turn them into beauties. 'So fair and foul a day I have not seen,' etc. 'Such welcome and unwelcome news together.' 'Men's lives are like the flowers in their caps, dying or ere they sicken.' 'Look like the innocent flower, but be the serpent under it.' The scene before the castlegate follows the appearance of the Witches on the heath, and is followed by a midnight murder. Duncan is cut off betimes by treason leagued with witchcraft, and Macduff is ripped untimely from his mother's womb to avenge his death. Macbeth, after the death of Banquo, wishes for his presence in extravagant terms, 'To him and all we thirst,' and when his ghost appears, cries out, 'Avaunt and quit my sight,' and being gone, he is 'himself again.' Macbeth resolves to get rid of Macduff, that 'he may sleep in spite of thunder'; and cheers his wife on the doubtful intelligence of Banquo's taking-off with the encouragement— 'Then be thou jocund: ere the bat has flown his cloistered flight; ere to black Hecate's summons the shard-born beetle has rung night's yawning peal, there shall be done—a deed of dreadful note.' In Lady Macbeth's speech 'Had he not resembled my father as he slept, I had done 't,' there is murder and filial piety together; and in urging him to fulfil his vengeance against the defenceless king, her thoughts spare the blood neither of infants nor old age. The description of the Witches is full of the same contradictory principle; they 'rejoice when good kings bleed,' they are neither of the earth nor the air, but both; 'they should be women, but their beards forbid it'; they take all the pains possible to lead Macbeth on to the height of his ambition, only to betray him 'in deeper consequence,' and after showing him all the pomp of their art, discover their malignant delight in his disappointed hopes, by that bitter taunt, 'Why stands Macbeth thus amazedly?' We might multiply such instances every where.

The leading features in the character of Macbeth are striking enough, and they form what may be thought at first only a bold, rude, Gothic outline. By comparing it with other characters of the same author we shall perceive the absolute truth and identity which is observed in the midst of the giddy whirl and rapid career of events. Macbeth in Shakespear no more loses his identity of character in the fluctuations of fortune or the storm of passion, than Macbeth in himself would have lost the identity of his person. Thus he is as distinct a being from Richard III. as it is possible to imagine, though these two characters in common hands, and indeed in the hands of any other poet, would have been a repetition of the same general idea, more or less exaggerated. For both are tyrants, usurpers, murderers, both aspiring and ambitious, both courageous, cruel, treacherous. But Richard is cruel from nature and constitution. Macbeth becomes so from accidental circumstances. Richard is from his birth deformed in body and mind, and naturally incapable of good. Macbeth is full of 'the milk of human kindness,' is frank, sociable, generous. He is tempted to the commission of guilt by golden opportunities, by the instigations of his wife, and by prophetic warnings. Fate and metaphysical aid conspire against his virtue and his loyalty. Richard on the contrary needs no prompter, but wades through a series of crimes to the height of his ambition from the ungovernable violence of his temper and a reckless love of mischief. He is never gay but in the prospect or in the success of his villainies: Macbeth is full of horror at the thoughts of the murder of Duncan, which he is with difficulty prevailed on to commit, and of remorse after its perpetration. Richard has no mixture of common humanity in his composition, no regard to kindred or posterity, he owns no fellowship with others, he is 'himself alone.' Macbeth is not destitute of feelings of sympathy, is accessible to pity, is even made in some measure the dupe of his uxoriousness, ranks the loss of friends, of the cordial love of his followers, and of his good name, among the causes which have made him weary of life, and regrets that he has ever seized the crown by unjust means, since he cannot transmit it to his posterity—

> For Banquo's issue have I fil'd my mind—
> For them the gracious Duncan have I murther'd,
> To make them kings, the seed of Banquo kings.

In the agitation of his mind, he envies those whom he has sent to peace. 'Duncan is in his grave; after life's fitful fever he sleeps well.'—It is true, he becomes more callous as he plunges deeper in guilt, 'direness is thus rendered familiar to his slaughterous thoughts,' and he in the end anticipates his wife in the boldness and bloodiness of his enterprises, while she for want of the same stimulus of action, 'is troubled with thick-coming fancies that rob her of her rest,' goes mad and dies. Macbeth endeavours to escape from reflection on his crimes by repelling their consequences, and banishes remorse for the past by the meditation of future mischief. This is not the principle of Richard's cruelty, which displays the wanton malice of a fiend as much as the frailty of human passion. Macbeth is goaded on to acts of violence and retaliation by necessity; to Richard, blood is a pastime.—There are other decisive differences inherent in the two characters. Richard may be regarded as a man of the world, a plotting, hardened knave, wholly regardless of every thing but his own ends, and the means to secure them.—Not so Macbeth. The superstitions of the age, the rude state of society, the local scenery and customs, all give a wildness and imaginary grandeur to his character. From the strangeness of the events that surround him, he is full of amazement and fear; and stands in doubt between the world of reality and the world of fancy. He sees sights not shown to mortal eye, and hears unearthly music. All is tumult and disorder within and without his mind; his purposes recoil upon himself, are broken and disjointed; he is the double thrall of his passions and his evil destiny. Richard is not a character either of imagination or pathos, but of pure self-will. There is no conflict of opposite feelings in his breast. The apparitions which he sees only haunt him in his sleep; nor does he live like Macbeth in a waking dream. Macbeth has considerable energy and manliness of character; but then he is 'subject to all the skyey influences.' He is sure of nothing but the present moment. Richard in the busy turbulence of his projects never loses his self-possession, and makes use of every circumstance that happens as an instrument of his long-reaching designs. In his last extremity we can only regard him as a wild beast taken in the toils: while we never entirely lose our concern for Macbeth; and he calls back all our sympathy by that fine close of thoughtful melancholy—

> My way of life is fallen into the sear,
> The yellow leaf; and that which should accompany
>       old age,
> As honour, troops of friends, I must not look to have;
> But in their stead, curses not loud but deep,
> Mouth-honour, breath, which the poor heart
> Would fain deny, and dare not.

## SAMUEL TAYLOR COLERIDGE
### From "Notes on *Macbeth*"
*Shakspeare, with Introductory Remarks on Poetry, the Drama, and the Stage*
1818

*Macbeth* stands in contrast throughout with *Hamlet*; in the manner of opening more especially. In the latter, there is a gradual ascent from the simplest forms of conversation to the language of impassioned intellect,—yet the intellect still remaining the seat of passion: in the former, the invocation is at once made to the imagination and the emotions connected therewith. Hence the movement throughout is the most rapid of all Shakspeare's plays; and hence also, with the exception of the disgusting passage of the Porter (Act ii. sc. 3.), which I dare pledge myself to demonstrate to be an interpolation of the actors, there is not, to the best of my remembrance, a single pun or play on words in the whole drama. I have previously given an answer to the thousand times repeated charge against Shakspeare upon the subject of his punning, and I here merely mention the fact of the absence of any puns in *Macbeth*, as justifying a candid doubt at least, whether even in these figures of speech and fanciful modifications of language, Shakspeare may not have followed rules and principles that merit and would stand the test of philosophic examination. And hence, also, there is an entire absence of comedy, nay, even of irony and philosophic contemplation in *Macbeth*,—the play being wholly and purely tragic. For the same cause, there are no reasonings of equivocal morality, which would have required a more leisurely state and a consequently greater activity of mind;—no sophistry of self-delusion,—except only that previously to the dreadful act, Macbeth mistranslates the recoilings and ominous whispers of conscience into prudential and selfish reasonings, and, after the deed done, the terrors of remorse into fear from external dangers,—like delirious men who run away from the phantoms of their own brains, or, raised by terror to rage, stab the real object that is within their reach:—whilst Lady Macbeth merely endeavours to reconcile his and her own sinkings of heart by anticipations of the worst, and an affected bravado in confronting them. In all the rest, Macbeth's language is the grave utterance of the very heart, conscience-sick, even to the last faintings of moral death. It is the same in all the other characters. The variety arises from rage, caused ever and anon by disruption of anxious thought, and the quick transition of fear into it.

In *Hamlet* and *Macbeth* the scene opens with superstition; but, in each it is not merely different, but opposite. In the first it is connected with the best and holiest feelings; in the second with the shadowy, turbulent, and unsanctified cravings of the individual will. Nor is the purpose the same; in the one the object is to excite, whilst in the other it is to mark a mind already excited. Superstition, of one sort or another, is natural to victorious generals; the instances are too notorious to need mentioning. There is so much of chance in warfare, and such vast events are connected with the acts of a single individual,—the representative, in truth, of the efforts of myriads, and yet to the public and, doubtless, to his own feelings, the aggregate of all,—that the proper temperament for generating or receiving superstitious impressions is naturally produced. Hope, the master element of a commanding genius, meeting with an active and combining intellect, and an imagination of just that degree of vividness which disquiets and impels the soul to try to realize its images, greatly increases the creative power of the mind; and hence the images become a satisfying world of themselves, as is the case in every poet and original philosopher:—but hope fully gratified, and yet the elementary basis of the passion remaining, becomes fear; and, indeed, the general, who must often feel, even though he may hide it from his own consciousness, how large a share chance had in his successes, may very naturally be irresolute in a new scene, where he knows that all will depend on his own act and election.

The Wierd Sisters are as true a creation of Shakspeare's, as his Ariel and Caliban,—fates, furies, and materializing witches being the elements. They are wholly different from any representation of witches in the contemporary writers, and yet presented a sufficient external resemblance to the creatures of vulgar prejudice to act immediately on the audience. Their character consists in the imaginative disconnected from the good; they are the shadowy obscure and fearfully anomalous of physical nature, the lawless of human nature,—elemental avengers without sex or kin:

> Fair is foul, and foul is fair;
> Hover thro' the fog and filthy air.

How much it were to be wished in playing Macbeth, that an attempt should be made to introduce the flexile character-mask of the ancient pantomime;—that Flaxman would contribute his genius to the embodying and making sensuously perceptible that of Shakspeare!

The style and rhythm of the Captain's speeches in the second scene should be illustrated by reference to the interlude in *Hamlet*, in which the epic is substituted for the tragic, in order to make the latter be felt as the real-life diction. In *Macbeth*, the poet's object was to raise the mind at once to the high tragic tone, that the audience might be ready for the precipitate consummation of guilt in the early part of the play. The true reason for the first appearance of the Witches is to strike the key-note of the character of the whole drama, as is proved by their re-appearance in the third scene, after such an order of the king's as establishes their supernatural power of information. I say information,—for so it only is as to Glamis and Cawdor; the 'king hereafter' was still contingent,—still in Macbeth's moral will; although, if he should yield to the temptation, and thus forfeit his free agency, the link of cause and effect *more physico* would then commence. I need not say, that the general idea is all that can be required from the poet,— not a scholastic logical consistency in all the parts so as to meet metaphysical objectors. But O! how truly Shakspearian is the opening of Macbeth's character given in the *unpossessedness* of Banquo's mind, wholly present to the present object,—an unsullied, unscarified mirror!—And how strictly true to nature it is, that Banquo, and not Macbeth himself, directs our notice to the effect produced on Macbeth's mind, rendered temptible by previous dalliance of the fancy with ambitious thoughts:

> Good Sir, why do you start; and seem to fear
> Things that do sound so fair?

And then, again, still unintroitive, addresses the Witches:—

> I' the name of truth,
> Are ye fantastical, or that indeed
> Which outwardly ye show?

Banquo's questions are those of natural curiosity,—such as a girl would put after hearing a gipsy tell her schoolfellow's fortune;—all perfectly general, or rather planless. But Macbeth, lost in thought, raises himself to speech only by the Witches being about to depart:—

> Stay, you imperfect speakers, tell me more:—

and all that follows is reasoning on a problem already discussed in his mind,—on a hope which he welcomes, and the doubts concerning the attainment of which he wishes to have cleared up. Compare his eagerness,—the keen eye with which he has pursued the Witches' evanishing—

> Speak, I charge you!

with the easily satisfied mind of the self-uninterested Banquo:—

> The air hath bubbles, as the water has,
> And these are of them:—Whither are they vanish'd?

and then Macbeth's earnest reply,—

> Into the air; and what seem'd corporal, melted
> As breath into the wind.—*'Would they had staid!*

Is it too minute to notice the appropriateness of the simile 'as breath,' &c. in a cold climate?

Still again Banquo goes on wondering like any common spectator:

> Were such things here as we do speak about?

whilst Macbeth persists in recurring to the self-concerning:—

> Your children shall be kings.
> *Ban.*: You shall be king.
> *Macb.*: And thane of Cawdor too: went it not so?

So surely is the guilt in its germ anterior to the supposed cause, and immediate temptation! Before he can cool, the confirmation of the tempting half of the prophecy arrives, and the concatenating tendency of the imagination is fostered by the sudden coincidence:—

> Glamis, and thane of Cawdor:
> The greatest is behind.

Oppose this to Banquo's simple surprise:—

> What, can the devil speak true?

## P. W. CLAYDEN
### From "Macbeth and Lady Macbeth"
*The Fortnightly Review*, August 1867, pp. 156–68

He ⟨Shakespeare⟩ puts on the character he conceives, transfers himself in this character to the scenes he imagines, kindles within himself the emotions those scenes excite, and then utters what he feels. The force of his imagination is such that he can put off his own personality and put on another. He has in him the hero he describes. He realises in imagination heroic situations and does heroic deeds. He does not describe emotions—he expresses them. He does not write about Hamlet or Macbeth—he embodies them. Shakespeare was Hamlet when he was developing Hamlet's tragic history; he was Macbeth when he was writing Macbeth's speeches. His many-sided, comprehensive, magnificent nature has written itself upon his pages, has given in every creation an aspect of what was possible to itself, so that all his characters stand before us full of life, full of reality, and full of nature. How could it be otherwise? They live; they are real; they are Nature.

A canon of criticism, or principle of interpretation, is therefore not far to find. It is simply this,—interpret the works of genius as you would interpret Nature, a character of Shakespeare's as you would a character of history. All talk about central ideas of the character, or about the object Shakespeare had in view in making Macbeth do this or Hamlet say that, is beside the mark. Nor is it of any use to talk of what Shakespeare may have meant to teach. We can dismiss all such questions, and all that we have to ask is, What has he accomplished? He may have accomplished more than he intended, for it is sometimes the prerogative of genius to utter words the full meaning of which is hidden from the mind that utters them. A man of genius may create a man or a woman whom he does not fully understand. He feels that his delineation is true to Nature, but he cannot tell us why. He knows instinctively what the person he imagines would say and do in given circumstances, but he leaves to others—to critics and expositors who feel their painful way along a path over which he has been lightly borne upon the wings of fancy—to find reasons why he should have said and done those particular things and no other.

Macbeth and Lady Macbeth are remarkable examples in proof of all that I have said. Everybody knows that Shakespeare did not create them out of nothing, did not build up the characters around some central idea, as Goethe did those of Faust and Wilhelm Meister, but that he found them in a dead tradition and breathed into them life. We are, therefore, in an attempt to estimate them, liberated from the necessity of seeking for Shakespeare's didactic purpose. But we must equally free ourselves from prepossession by the popular view of them, which is founded on the assumption of such a purpose. Macbeth is usually regarded as his wife regards him in the opening of the play, while she herself is judged entirely by her words. He is usually represented as a tolerably good man up to the time when evil opportunity and a bad wife conspired to transform him into a villain. His murders are supposed to be done at her instigation. Her ambition, for which she had "unsexed" herself, led him away. She is said to have tempted him to crime, to have pushed him over the boundary line which divides criminality from innocence, though when once he had crossed it he became indeed a villain. But she is considered to be far worse than he. She was a born demon; he was only a man who had been sorely tempted and had awfully fallen.

Now when we come to regard Macbeth and his wife as two real characters of whom all that we know is recorded in this play, we arrive at a conclusion the very opposite of the popular one. Macbeth himself is probably an elderly man when he is introduced to us. He and his wife have had a past, and in that past the future which becomes present in the play has been prepared. Our first glance of him is indirect. The soldier describes him, Act i. Scene 2:—

> Brave Macbeth (well he deserves that name),
> Disdaining fortune, with his brandished steel,
> Which smoked with bloody execution,
> Like valour's minion,
> Carved out his passage, till he faced the slave,
> And ne'er shook hands, nor bade farewell to him,
> Till he unseamed him from the nave to the chaps,
> And fixed his head upon our battlements.

Were that our only glimpse of him, we should say that he was a brave but cruel warrior of a barbarous time.

When we first actually see him he is on the heath with Banquo meeting the witches. He is returning from the fight, just described, full of honours. It is the moment of his temptation. A diabolical suggestion comes to him—for the witches evidently do but give voice to his own unspoken thoughts. They call him "Thane of Glamis," which he already was; "Thane of Cawdor," which he was about to be; and "King," which he had dreamed of being. For this is clearly not the first time these thoughts have come to him. When he receives the suggestion that he should be king, he is at once perfectly familiar with the obstacles in his way. The witches make no suggestion to him as to the way in which the obstacles are to be removed, yet we find him saying directly after the king's messenger has told him of the rewards his sovereign had heaped upon him—

> Glamis and Thane of Cawdor:
> The greatest is behind.

And when Banquo utters a warning against ambition, Macbeth meditates thus:—

> Two truths are told
> As happy prologue to the swelling act
> Of the imperial theme. I thank you, gentlemen.
> This supernatural soliciting
> Cannot be ill, cannot be good. If ill,
> Why hath it given me earnest of success
> Commencing in a truth? I am Thane of Cawdor.
> If good, why do I yield to that suggestion
> Whose horrid image doth unfix my hair,
> And make my seated heart knock at my ribs
> Against the use of Nature? Present fears
> Are less than horrible imaginings.
> My thought, whose murder yet is but fantastical,
> Shakes so my single state of man, that function
> Is smothered in surmise, and nothing is,
> But what is not.

The plain meaning of that is, that on the very first day of his temptation, amid the very honours the king is heaping on him, he has conceived the idea of murdering him, and is frightened at it. But the fear is not moral. Conscience has nothing to do with it. He does not repel the suggestion. He does not scorn himself for being capable of receiving it. He is frightened at it, but he accepts it and bides his time.

In the fourth scene they have got to the king, who receives them nobly, and to whom Macbeth makes a fine speech. But during the interview the king names his eldest son as his heir, making him Prince of Cumberland. On this Macbeth meditates thus:—

> The Prince of Cumberland! That is a step
> On which I must fall down, or else o'erleap,
> For in my way it lies. Stars, hide your fires!
> Let not light see my black and deep desires:
> The eye wink at the hand! yet let that be
> Which the eye fears, when it is done, to see.

His mind is already made up. But conscience has no whisper against his resolution. The eye fears to see what the hand must nevertheless do; and, horrible as the thing is, he says, "Let it be." Meanwhile, he has written a letter to his wife, and she instantly conceives the same murderous purpose, and divines that her husband has done so too, although his letter does not even hint it. While their thoughts are thus full of murder the opportunity suddenly comes. The king resolves to rest under their roof, and Lady Macbeth hears of his determination to do so while she is meditating on her husband's letter. She immediately resolves that once under their roof, the king shall never leave it alive; and while she is reflecting on this, her husband arrives, and the very first sentences of their conversation reveal to each the purpose that animates both. But does not that pre-suppose some previous conversations on the subject? Could a wife and husband, while apart from each other, arrive at the same design of murder, and mention it to each other as soon as they met, had they not talked about it before, and allowed themselves to dally with the guilty thoughts and cherish the guilty ambitions their position suggested long before the moment of opportunity and temptation? Macbeth had been thought an honest man up to this time; but beneath the surface there was the villain. It is impossible that an honest man should fall at such a temptation, or should be so familiar with the thought of a fearful crime as to be able to talk it over with his wife at once. The murder must have been in his thought long before, and all that the temptation did was to transfer it suddenly from thought to purpose. He had indulged in guilty imaginings, had fed his fancy upon guilty hopes, and conscience had not rebuked them, and now they sprang to active life in guilty purposes and plans. The king came to their house on the very day on which he had greatly honoured Macbeth, and he and his wife both knew at once that he came as their victim.

The seventh scene brings Macbeth to the very verge of the accomplishment of his guilty purpose. He pauses for a moment and hesitates. In his soliloquy there is almost an echo of conscience. Still his hesitancy is rather intellectual than moral. He has no great horror of the deed. What he fears is that it should get abroad. He sees reasons against the murder; reasons which would rouse conscience, if it were possible so to do; but he sees them intellectually, and does not appreciate their moral bearing. What he says of "even-handed justice," which

> Commends the ingredients of our poisoned chalice
> To our own lips,

does not refer to the moral results of crime, but merely to the danger of rousing popular resentment against the murderer of one whose virtues plead so loud against "the deep damnation of his taking off," and to the other danger of setting an example, which may be followed when he is king:—

> We teach
> Bloody instructions, which, being taught, return
> To plague the inventor.

After the soliloquy follows the remarkable interview with his wife. In this interview he seems to come nearest to conscientiousness, but if we analyse his expressions there is no conscience in them:—

> We will proceed no further in this business.
> He hath honoured me of late, and I have bought
> Golden opinions from all sorts of people,
> Which would be worn now in their newest gloss,
> Not cast aside so soon.

This is his only objection to proceed. There is neither conscience nor pity in it, nothing but the fear of losing the good opinion he had won. Farther on he pleads:—

> I dare do all that may become a man;
> Who dares do more, is none;

and she makes him a very remarkable reply:—

> What beast was it, then,
> That made you break this enterprise to me?
> When you durst do it, then you were a man,
> And to be more than what you were you would
> Be so much more the man. Nor time, nor place,
> Did then adhere, and yet you would make both:
> They have made themselves, and that their fitness
>     now
> Does unmake you.

This is the most important passage in the play in the elucidation of Macbeth's character. The meaning is plain. It proves that they had actually talked this matter over together long before the time at which the action of the play begins. We concluded before that murder could not ripen in an honest mind so suddenly as we see it do in Macbeth's, that he must have dallied with the guilty thought and hope so long that it was quite ready to develop into purpose; and here is the proof, not only that it was so, but that the suggestion came first from him, that he had been planning and purposing some opportunity of doing this base and bloody deed, and that it was only now, when the opportunity he had sought had suddenly and unexpectedly come, that he was staggered and frightened. All experience shows this to be just what we might expect to happen. It is sometimes only by a shock and an effort that thought passes over into action—purpose into accomplishment. An opportunity for which we have worked seldom takes us by surprise, but one for which we have only watched and

waited, when it suddenly comes, finds us unprepared. Many a man has had an exceedingly happy speech to make at a public meeting. He watches for his opportunity while one after another rises to speak, but no chance seems to offer itself for him. But all at once there is silence. His opportunity has come, but with it the hesitancy sudden opportunity so often brings. He fidgets on his seat—

> Letting I dare not wait upon I would,
> Like the poor cat i' the adage;

and if he has no wife at hand to urge him to be equal to the occasion, he will most likely let the opportunity pass, and "live a coward in his own esteem." Had Macbeth gone on plotting and planning for an opportunity to murder Duncan, there would have been none of the hesitancy we see in him now. It is the sudden necessity to decide and act which makes him hesitate. He would have gone into it gradually without any hesitation. A scheme to mature to-day, a plot to lay to-morrow, a false part to play next day, would have familiarised him gradually with his position, and he would have passed easily and smoothly into crime. But here was the opportunity before him. It was now or never. A turn in his road, and there was the Rubicon. On this side "honour, love, obedience, troops of friends," but not the crown. On that side the crown, but with it possibly exposure and calamity, certainly suspicion and

> Curses not loud but deep, mouth honour, breath
> Which the poor heart would fain deny, but dare not.

No wonder at his hesitancy. Cæsar paused, and then struck across the stream. Macbeth paused. The awful grandeur of his situation came clearly before him. All its possibilities of danger and disgrace were present to his mind. It wanted but one word from conscience, one glance back to the innocence of earlier days, and the crime would never have been committed. But these did not come; and in place of them there was the evil prompting of his wife, whom he had familiarised with the thought of murder, who found it easy to urge him on, and whose taunting words so dissipate his intellectual fears that he is able to say—

> I am settled, and bend up
> Each corporal agent to this terrible feat.

But while he is afterwards waiting for the signal from his wife to commit the murder, he makes another soliloquy, addressing the dagger:—

> Is this a dagger which I see before me,
> The handle toward my hand? Come, let me clutch
>     thee.
> I have thee not, and yet I see thee still.
> Art thou not, fatal vision, sensible
> To feeling as to sight? Or art thou but
> A dagger of the mind, a false creation,
> Proceeding from the heat-oppressed brain?
> I see thee yet, in form as palpable
> As this which now I draw.
> Thou marshal'st me the way that I was going,
> And such an instrument I was to use.

Here is still further proof of his previous familiarity with the thought of crime. These thoughts are drawn from him by the fact that a situation he had long contemplated was now realised; that a position with which he had been long familiar in imagination had now become actual. The dagger he had grasped in foul and wayward fancy was now really in his hand, marshalling him the way he was to go. The situation waked his intellect, and kindled all the powers of his imagination; but did not wake his conscience, for he had none to wake.

After the murder there seem to be some gleams of remorse. But we have only to put side by side with Macbeth's exclamations the bitter reflections of Milton's Satan, and we see at once how widely different were Macbeth's fears from real remorse. Milton says of Satan—

> Now conscience wakes despair
> That slumbered; wakes the bitter memory
> Of what he was, what is, and what must be.

And Satan himself reflects—

> Ah, wherefore, he deserved no such return
> From me, whom he created what I was
> In that bright eminence, and with his good
> Upbraided none.

And again—

> Me miserable, which way shall I fly
> Infinite wrath and infinite despair?
> Which way I fly is hell; myself am hell;
> And in the lowest deep a lower deep,
> Still threatening to devour me, opens wide,
> To which the hell I suffer seems a heaven.
> Oh, then, at last relent. Is there no place
> Left for repentance, none for pardon left?

That is remorse. But how different the ring of those words from any that are uttered by Macbeth. He felt Amen stick in his throat. He heard a voice crying "Macbeth doth murder sleep." He was afraid to look on what he had done. He had become irritable and dreamy. Noises frightened him, and he saw ghosts. But there were no regrets, there was no bitter self-reproach, no longing after the peace he had slain, no looking back to the state of innocence from which he had fallen, no sense of the hell he had lighted within. It is imagination, and not conscience, which makes Macbeth afraid; and even the things invisible that alarm him are only the airy evanescent products of a morbid fancy. All his after actions strictly accord with this view of his nature. He plots the murder of Banquo, fearing his "royalty of nature," and tells the murderer—

> We wear our health but sickly in his life,
> Which in his death were perfect;

and when he hears that Fleance has escaped, he says—

> Then comes my fit again; I had else been perfect,
> Whole as the marble, founded as the rock,
> As broad and general as the casing air;
> But now I am cabined, cribbed, confined, bound in
> To saucy doubts and fears.

—but is encouraged by the assurance that "Banquo's safe." From that time an awful necessity impels him forward in his career of crime. He yields to that necessity without even a show of resistance, and earns the evil reputation which was the only thing he feared. Again he takes counsel with the witches, and his imagination permits itself to be soothed by their false words, and it is not till the last moment of his fate that he finds in what fancied security his evil arts have lulled him. He then falls back, as his last resource, on the brute courage he possessed, and though his imagination is a source of weakness even in his last fight, he dies "with the harness on his back."

The character of Macbeth is, I venture to suggest, nearly related to that of Hamlet, though so wonderfully different in its development. Hamlet is a man under the power of a tyrannous imagination, but with a sensitive conscience. Macbeth is also subject to the sway of his imagination, but he has no conscience. Hence Hamlet's imagination is a source of strength to him, but Macbeth's imagination is to him a source of weakness. Of a large intellectual nature, with vast power to do and dare, his imagination is his master. In the honest part of his life that imagination was allowed to dwell on scenes of sin, to picture to itself the means by which he might in a few sudden leaps reach the throne; and this dalliance with guilty thoughts,

this playing with a criminal design, so familiarised him with it that it grew at length to be his master, and he became a criminal at its bidding. In such a nature there must at first have been a conscience; but his imagination had smothered it, and all that remained within him now was the dim echo of a diviner voice than that of his ambition or his pride. Satisfied with a phrase, contented by a well-turned expression, silenced by a metaphor, conscience was now a merely intellectual thing, its moral function was abnegated, and its rightful authority lost. But the echo of its voice remained, and dwelling in his fancy were vague words and phrases, meaningless now, but haunting his thoughts and wandering amid his images of terror, like the ghost of that better nature he had slain. He therefore presents himself to us during the short acquaintance we have with him in the action of the play as a brave man who is a coward, a man of large poetic mind who is a murderer and a tyrant, a great soul lost, one who might have been a hero and is nothing but a villain.

The popular misunderstanding of the character of Macbeth is due, probably, to the description his wife gives of him in the first interview we have with her:—

> Thou shalt be
> What thou art promised:—Yet do I fear thy nature.
> It is too full of the milk of human kindness
> To catch the nearest way. Thou would'st be great;
> Art not without ambition, but without
> The illness should attend it. What thou would'st
>     highly
> That would'st thou holily; would'st not play false,
> And yet would'st wrongly win.

But it is obvious that so far as we see Macbeth in the play, nothing could be wider of the mark than this estimate of him. That it was the estimate his wife had formed of him, before temptation had come and turned his criminal imaginings into schemes of crime, gives us no real insight into his character, but throws much light on hers. For nothing can be farther from the truth than the popular view of Lady Macbeth. That wonderful characteristic of genius which enables it to put on the character it conceives, reaches its highest manifestation in this marvellous portrait, in which Shakespeare has realised the feelings of a woman who, with all a woman's nature, has one unwomanly passion—a great ambition in place of a great love. But all the truth and force of the delineation are lost when Lady Macbeth is regarded as a mere tempter and fiend. She is, in reality, nothing of the kind. Her part is simply that of a woman and a wife who shares her husband's ambition, and supports him in it. So far from suggesting his crimes, she distinctly declares that he broke the enterprise to her. Of Macbeth's murders, it was only that of Duncan in which she had a share, or of which she even definitely knew beforehand, and we have seen that, before he saw his wife, Macbeth had made up his mind to this first step in his career of crime. All that she does is to back him in the execution of his own design; and she does this at immense cost and by enormous effort. That first soliloquy does not describe her husband's character, but it reveals her own. Her concluding words are a self-revelation—unconscious but complete:—

> Hie thee hither,
> That I may pour my spirits in thine ear,
> And chastise with the valour of my tongue
> All that impedes thee from the gold round
> Which fate and metaphysical aid doth seem
> To have thee crowned withal.

In those words, "chastise with the valour of my tongue," we have an exact description of Lady Macbeth's attitude, not merely towards her husband, but towards herself. In her continuation of the soliloquy after its interruption by the messenger who announced the approach of the king, we find her thus "chastising" all that impedes her in her own nature:—

> Come, come, you spirits
> That tend on mortal thoughts, unsex me here,
> And fill me from the crown to the toe top full
> Of direst cruelty! Make thick my blood,
> Stop up the access and passage to remorse,
> That no compunctious visitings of nature
> Shake my fell purpose, nor keep pace between
> The effect and it. Come to my woman's breasts
> And take my milk for gall, you murd'ring ministers,
> Wherever in your sightless substances
> You wait on Nature's mischief. Come, thick night,
> And pall thee in the dunnest smoke of hell,
> That my keen knife see not the wound it makes,
> Nor heaven peep through the blanket of the dark
> To cry, Hold, hold!

These words are more frightful in their sound than any that Macbeth uses, but their whole tone and meaning are entirely different from his. He strives with external fears,—this is a fight with internal weakness. He calls to the "sure and firm set earth"—

> Hear not my steps which way they walk, for fear
> Thy very stones prate of my whereabout.

She calls to supernatural powers to help her to subdue the rising protests of her conscience, and school her better nature to submission. For that soliloquy clearly shows that hers was not a nature that was utterly without good, but that she had resolved to slay the good that was still in it. A man who feels no fear never whistles to keep up his courage. A man without compunctious visitings never talks about remorse. The utterly depraved never strive with themselves to put down their virtuous impulses; they have no such impulses to put down, no "compunctious visitings" to dread, no better part to scold into subjection. But Lady Macbeth was not utterly depraved. Her whole soul was on fire with ambition, and with a woman's energy and wholeness of devotion she gave herself up to it. She shows all a woman's wonderful self-control; but she must keep it up by using valiant words, living in public, and chastising her husband and herself "with the valour of her tongue." She had a woman's will, unswerving so long as it could keep on, but which once broken was broken for ever. It was now like a bow full-strung; but it was an immense and constant effort to keep it bent. She was afraid of her own nature. Had she been utterly unsexed, she would not have called on spirits to unsex her. Had she not feared remorse—which, indeed, did come at last and kill her—she would not have cried out to have the "access and passage" to it stopped by supernatural means. Had she not had eyes which could see the light, and some sense of Heaven's watching eye still left, she would not have called to thick night to hide her, and to "the dunnest smoke of hell" to shut out Heaven. This terrible imprecation is the expression of her will—not the ebullition of her feelings. It was indicative of a struggle. Her human, womanly nature was down beneath the fiery onset of her baser passions—throttled but not dead—held forcibly down, not slain and done with; and this language is the voice of her worse and baser part, scolding the better into silence and submission. The same thing is seen all through her character. She is not long before us, but she keeps up wonderfully. But it is emphatically what ladies call "keeping up." It is far more "the valour of her tongue" than the valour of her heart which gets expression in her speeches. Her language is everywhere that of a woman who, in screwing her husband's courage to the sticking place, as she says, is also screwing her

own. That she is so entirely successful in screwing up herself and keeping up, is not at all wonderful. In this art women excel. They "keep up" through labour, and anxiety, and trouble, through pain and loss, and keep up till the need is over, and then break down. So long as the stress remains, and there is need to wear a brave front to the public, they show no sign of failure; full-bred, they keep on like blood-horses, who will drop upon the course. Lady Macbeth is a wonderful example of a woman of this kind; keeping herself up in hideous crime, showing herself always equal to the occasion while it lasts, but when the stress is over, breaking utterly down. Through the first act she is in her heroic mood, putting down her better self, and rebuking her husband's weakness. But in the first scene of the second act she falters a little, and her words show that she has had recourse to a stimulant to keep up her courage, and that even then she can only do so by being perpetually busy.

> That which hath made them drunk hath made me
>     bold;
> What hath quenched them hath given me fire. Hark!
>     Peace!
> It was the owl that shrieked, the fatal bellman
> That gives the stern'st good night. He is about it.

There was, too, a little "compunctious visiting of nature" while she was alone, for she reflected, as only a woman would—

> Had he not resembled
> My father as he slept, I had done it.

But the presence of her husband helps her, and she is entirely herself as soon as he appears. She can completely school herself in rousing him; the friction rekindles her fire, and so long as there is anything to busy herself about, whether it is urging him or doing something herself, all her energy is at command and the valour of her tongue is perfect. She knows nothing of those outward fears which are all that Macbeth himself seems to appreciate. Chastising his fancies and chastising her own nature as well, she exclaims:—

> Infirm of purpose!
> Give me the daggers. The sleeping and the dead
> Are but as pictures; 'tis the eye of childhood
> That fears a painted devil;

and in a sudden access of fiery energy she reddens her own hands in Duncan's blood, and prints a vision of terror on her fancy from which she never after rids herself. But at the moment she feels nothing. Her husband loses his presence of mind and stands weakly lost in his thoughts. Her presence of mind never leaves her for a moment; she comprehends all the necessities of their situation in one rapid glance of intuition, and urges her husband—

> Get on your nightgown, lest occasion call us,
> And show us to be watchers. Be not lost
> So poorly in your thoughts.

But when the necessity for action is over, all her ready wit forsakes her; she faints and must be carried away when the murder is out, and she can only hear others talk about it but has nothing to say or do that will keep up her courage, and from that time she is no longer what she was. Her husband only hints Banquo's murder to her, and though she pretty well understands the hint, it is clearly a loss to her that her husband no longer needs the valour of her tongue. Her meditation just before Banquo's murder is hinted to her is very painful.

> 'Tis safer to be that which we destroy,
> Than by destruction dwell in doubtful joy;

though no sooner does her husband come in with gloom on his face than she turns upon herself in rousing him, and says:—

Things without remedy
Should be without regard. What's done is done.

Her last successful effort is at the banquet. Here she is in public, and her husband needs her, and she is quite equal to the occasion. The presence of his weakness always enables her to overcome her own. At this banquet she is truly Macbeth's helpmate, saving him by her readiness and self-possession from the consequences of his fears. But after that she breaks down, and for a time we see nothing of her. Other murders follow that of Banquo, but she knows little of them, and when we next see her it is in that awful scene where she is no longer the strong-minded woman she was; when she has felt the force of that reaction which always follows woman's wilder moods; when she can keep up no longer, but even in her broken sleep cannot avoid the awful whispers of the avenger Remorse. Even in this sad scene her words are still valiant—yet her character, as I have described it, shows itself more clearly than ever. There is the echo of her resolute language, but it is only an echo. The excitement has passed and the reaction has come. Conscience is awake. Her woman's nature has asserted itself. She could not be unsexed. The access and passage to remorse could not be stopped, and it has poured in upon her conscience and overwhelmed her reason. She had strung herself up to full tension, but had overstretched the string. Her doctor soon saw that her condition was one

More needing the divine than the physician,

and her husband described her case with far more accuracy than that with which she in her first soliloquy had described him:—

Canst thou not minister to a mind diseased,
Pluck from the memory a rooted sorrow,
Raze out the written troubles of the mind,
And with some sweet oblivious antidote
Cleanse the stuffed bosom of that perilous stuff
Which weighs upon the heart?

It weighed lightly enough on the heart of Macbeth, but it pressed the life out of his wife. It was the resurrection of her better self which really slew her. The fiend in her did not triumph, but succumbed at length, and she died of that remorse which is only possible to those who are still alive to their degradation, whose evil triumphs are the rooted sorrows of a memory which looks back to better times and better things, and on whose hearts, not yet hardened to stone, the perilous stuff of an ambition which has been gratified by crime weighs with a fatal pressure.

Macbeth and his wife were well mated. She had in her the making of a heroine, and he had the making of a hero. Ambition destroyed them both. She sustained her husband, but it was in a course he had himself chosen and in motives he had inspired. At one great crisis in his fate and hers, she not only went with him, but played the woman's part in keeping him to his chosen course, and played it only too well for his welfare and for her own. Her husband's meditation on her death is no fit epitaph for her, but is only the culminating revelation of his own less noble nature and far inferior character.

Life's but a walking shadow, a poor player
That struts and frets his hour upon the stage,
And then is heard no more. It is a tale
Told by an idiot, full of sound and fury,
Signifying nothing.

The fit reflection of such a man, put into his mouth by the instinct of genius, and telling us how life may look to those who view it from the stand-point of a career of crime. "Full of sound and fury," that is Macbeth's own character. But so far

from "signifying nothing," his life signified the danger of all dalliance with thoughts of crime and the fatal necessity by which such criminal imaginings, beneath the stimulus of opportunity, become criminal deeds. It signified, too, that the fight with conscience may be fought upon the field of fancy; that when the victory has been won by evil dreams there will be no resistance to the most evil deeds; and that to a man thus made a villain only one consolation remains, the consolation of a wild hope that the world is but a vain show, and life an idiot's tale "signifying nothing."

## HENRY IRVING
### "The Third Murderer in *Macbeth*"
#### *The Nineteenth Century*, April 1877, pp. 327–30

There have been various theories and much discussion among students of Shakspeare as to the Third Murderer in *Macbeth*. It has even been maintained that Macbeth himself was the man, and that only upon this assumption can the difficulties attending the character be solved. Anyone curious to follow out that suggestion will find it discussed in *Notes and Queries* for September 11 and November 13, 1869.

A theory on this subject has struck me, which has not, so far as I am aware, been hitherto advanced.

The stage directions in *Macbeth* concerning one particular character (who, curiously enough, is not mentioned in the *dramatis personæ* of any edition which I bear in mind) are minute, and I believe that, where such directions are so particularly given by Shakspeare, they are for a purpose, because he is generally careless about those matters, and leaves them, as it were, for the actors to carry out.

This character is described simply as 'an Attendant,' and what I wish to contend is that this 'Attendant' is the Third Murderer.

My reasons are as follows:—Macbeth utters what little he does say to this attendant in a tone of marked contempt—strangely suggestive, to my mind, of his being some wretched creature who was entirely in Macbeth's power—not an ordinary servant, but one whom he might use as a tool, and who had no courage to disobey or withstand him.

Supposing this to have been the case, such a servant (from whatever causes), in such a state of moral bondage to his master, would be just the man employed upon the work of watching without 'the palace gate' for the two murderers whose services he had, by Macbeth's orders, secured.

He need not have known the precise object of their interview with Macbeth, and I think it was probable, from the action of the scene, that he was not told of it until after Macbeth's conversation (act iii. sc. 1) with the two murderers, at the conclusion of which, I infer, he was commanded to watch them.

Now the stage direction in act iii. sc. 1 is: 'Exeunt all but Macbeth and an Attendant.' With a confidential servant, this is just what might happen without exciting notice.

The words are:

*Macb.*: Sirrah, a word with you. Attend those men
   Our pleasure?
*Attend.*: They are, my lord, without the palace gate.
*Macb.*: Bring them before us.

The tone of contempt is obvious, and also the fact that this attendant had been taken, to a certain extent, into his master's confidence, with a sort of careless assurance of his secrecy. We learn that he has been just now on the watch for the two men, and presume that he had conducted them to Macbeth the day before.

The next direction is: 'Re-enter Attendant with Two Murderers;' when Macbeth says to him, in the same tone and manner,

Now go to the door and stay there till we call.

The attendant then retires, and is not recalled by Macbeth; but the action which I am about to suggest, and which the text fully warrants, would, if carried out, afford the opportunity for Macbeth to communicate to him the undertaking of the two murderers, and give him instructions to follow and observe them. If the attendant left the chamber by one door ('Now go to the door and stay there till we call') and the murderers by another, and if Macbeth used the former egress, the suggestion would be that at this moment, while he kept the murderers waiting, and in expectation of seeing him again ('I'll call upon you straight—abide within'), he went after the attendant and gave him his instructions.

By this device Macbeth gains the object which he has been seeking. He secures to himself a check upon the two murderers in the person of this attendant, who is made an accomplice, and whose lips are sealed. A very slight and legitimate change in the accepted stage-business would make all this stratagem clear to the audience, and it fits in with my theory that the attendant was a trusty, and not a common, servant. Had he been otherwise, the most momentous and secret transaction of the play would never have been committed to him.

Coming now to the murder of Banquo (act iii. sc. 3), we find that the words prove that one man is a stranger to the other two, at any rate so far as his privity to the enterprise is concerned. But the manner in which the Second Murderer satisfies the First that the newcomer need not be mistrusted strengthens my theory. For either the Second Murderer did not recognise the stranger at all, owing to the darkness of the night, and so distrusted him until he had delivered his credentials in shape of his intimate acquaintance with the whole place and scheme, or else perhaps they did recognise him as the attendant whom they had seen before; in which case also they would have been chary of confiding in him, as they had received from Macbeth no instructions to trust him in this matter. Indeed the instant reply of the Second Murderer, in order to allay the fears and misgivings expressed by the First, would favour the assumption that the stranger was a man they already knew, and who, up to a certain point at all events, was aware of their project. His further knowledge of the matter would be less surprising to them than if shown by anybody else, and he would thus be more easily taken into comradeship. Except upon the theory that they had seen or known something of him previously, they would hardly be likely so soon to accept his mere word.

*Enter* Three Murderers.

1st *Mur.*: But who bid thee join us?
3rd *Mur.*:                              Macbeth.

2nd *Mur.*: He needs not our mistrust; since he delivers
  Our offices, and what we have to do,
  To the direction just.
1st *Mur.*:                 Then stand with us.
3rd *Mur.*: Hark! I hear horses.
*Ban.*: (*within.*) Give us a light there, hoa!
2nd *Mur.*:                          Then 'tis he; the rest
  That are within the note of expectation,
  Already are i' the court.
1st *Mur.*:                 His horses go about.
3rd *Mur.*: Almost a mile; *but he does usually,*
  *So all men do, from hence to the palace gate*
  *Make it their walk.*
2nd *Mur.*:      A light! A light!
3rd *Mur.*:                              'Tis he!

The exact familiarity which the Third Murderer shows with the surroundings of the palace and the readiness with which his information is accepted by the others, suggest that he must have been somebody quite conversant with the palace usages and approaches. This familiar knowledge may very well have been another reason in Macbeth's mind for connecting his attendant with the deed, if only by an after-thought, lest it might fail through the ignorance of the strangers as to the spot where they should post themselves, and other necessary precautions.

My theory would account for this familiar acquaintance with the locality on the part of the Third Murderer without recourse to any such violent improbability as that the Third Murderer was Macbeth himself.

It may now be considered what a difference in the usual arrangement of the banquet scene this supposition would make. We have no knowledge that it may not have been originally acted upon in the manner which I will briefly describe.

Think of the effect of the First Murderer being brought to the banquet-room by the attendant, and the latter standing by during the ghastly recital of the murder. If this expedient were adopted, there would be no intrinsic absurdity in the appearance of the strange man at the feast. He might come there with a secrecy the more effectual because of its apparent openness, for he would be in the company of one of Macbeth's chief retainers, with whom many of the guests were familiar, and with whom he might naturally, even at such a time, be obliged to speak aside a few words on some urgent and private matter. The conversation so conducted, even under the eyes, and only just out of earshot, of the whole company, might and would be no violation of probability, and need attract no special notice from the guests, even though the deadliest secret were clothed under the audacious but complete and natural disguise. But the effect upon the audience would be widely different from that of the present almost unmanageable tradition, which necessitates an improbability so absurd as almost, if not quite, to render ridiculous what might be one of the most thrilling horrors of the tragedy.

# Timon of Athens

*Timon of Athens*, of all the works of Shakspeare, possesses most the character of satire:—a laughing satire in the picture of the parasites and flatterers, and Juvenalian in the bitterness of Timon's imprecations on the ingratitude of a false world. The story is very simply treated, and is definitely divided into large masses:—in the first act the joyous life of Timon, his noble and hospitable extravagance, and around him the throng of suitors of every description; in the second and third acts his embarrassment, and the trial which he is thereby reduced to make of his supposed friends, who all desert him in the hour of need;—in the fourth and fifth acts, Timon's flight to the woods, his misanthropical melancholy, and his death. The only thing which may be called an episode is the banishment of Alcibiades, and his return by force of arms. However, they are both examples of ingratitude,—the one of a state towards its defender, and the other of private friends to their benefactor. As the merits of the General towards his fellow-citizens suppose more strength of character than those of the generous prodigal, their respective behaviours are not less different; Timon frets himself to death, Alcibiades regains his lost dignity by force. If the poet very properly sides with Timon against the common practice of the world, he is, on the other hand, by no means disposed to spare Timon. Timon was a fool in his generosity; in his discontent he is a madman: he is every where wanting in the wisdom which enables a man in all things to observe the due measure. Although the truth of his extravagant feelings is proved by his death, and though when he digs up a treasure he spurns the wealth which seems to tempt him, we yet see distinctly enough that the vanity of wishing to be singular, in both the parts that he plays, had some share in his liberal self-forgetfulness, as well as in his anchoritical seclusion. This is particularly evident in the incomparable scene where the cynic Apemantus visits Timon in the wilderness. They have a sort of competition with each other in their trade of misanthropy: the Cynic reproaches the impoverished Timon with having been merely driven by necessity to take to the way of living which he himself had long been following of his free choice, and Timon cannot bear the thought of being merely an imitator of the Cynic. In such a subject as this the due effect could only be produced by an accumulation of similar features, still, in the variety of the shades, an amazing degree of understanding has been displayed by Shakspeare. What a powerfully diversified concert of flatteries and of empty testimonies of devotedness! It is highly amusing to see the suitors, whom the ruined circumstances of their patron had dispersed, immediately flock to him again when they learn that he has been revisited by fortune. On the other hand, in the speeches of Timon, after he is undeceived, all hostile figures of speech are exhausted,—it is a dictionary of eloquent imprecations.—AUGUST WILHELM SCHLEGEL, *Lectures on Dramatic Art and Literature*, 1809, tr. John Black

*Timon of Athens* always appeared to us to be written with as intense a feeling of his subject as any one play of Shakespear. It is one of the few in which he seems to be in earnest throughout, never to trifle nor go out of his way. He does not relax in his efforts, nor lose sight of the unity of his design. It is the only play of our author in which spleen is the predominant feeling of the mind. It is as much a satire as a play: and contains some of the finest pieces of invective possible to be conceived, both in the snarling, captious answers of the cynic Apemantus,

and in the impassioned and more terrible imprecations of Timon. The latter remind the classical reader of the force and swelling impetuosity of the moral declamations in *Juvenal*, while the former have all the keenness and caustic severity of the old Stoic philosophers. The soul of Diogenes appears to have been seated on the lips of Apemantus. The churlish profession of misanthropy in the cynic is contrasted with the profound feeling of it in Timon, and also with the soldier-like and determined resentment of Alcibiades against his countrymen, who have banished him, though this forms only an incidental episode in the tragedy.

The fable consists of a single event;—of the transition from the highest pomp and profusion of artificial refinement to the most abject state of savage life, and privation of all social intercourse. The change is as rapid as it is complete; nor is the description of the rich and generous Timon, banqueting in gilded palaces, pampered by every luxury, prodigal of his hospitality, courted by crowds of flatterers, poets, painters, lords, ladies, who—

> Follow his strides, his lobbies fill with tendance,
> Rain sacrificial whisperings in his ears;
> And through him drink the free air

more striking than that of the sudden falling off of his friends and fortune, and his naked exposure in a wild forest digging roots from the earth for his sustenance, with a lofty spirit of self-denial, and bitter scorn of the world, which raise him higher in our esteem than the dazzling gloss of prosperity could do. He grudges himself the means of life, and is only busy in preparing his grave. How forcibly is the difference between what he was, and what he is, described in Apemantus's taunting questions, when he comes to reproach him with the change in his way of life!

> What, think'st thou,
> That the bleak air, thy boisterous chamberlain,
> Will put thy shirt on warm? will these moist trees
> That have outlived the eagle, page thy heels,
> And skip when thou point'st out? will the cold brook,
> Candied with ice, caudle thy morning taste
> To cure thy o'er-night's surfeit? Call the creatures,
> Whose naked natures live in all the spight
> Of wreakful heav'n, whose bare unhoused trunks,
> To the conflicting elements expos'd,
> Answer mere nature, bid them flatter thee.

The manners are every where preserved with distinct truth. The poet and painter are very skilfully played off against one another, both affecting great attention to the other, and each taken up with his own vanity, and the superiority of his own art. Shakespear has put into the mouth of the former a very lively description of the genius of poetry and of his own in particular.

> A thing slipt idly from me.
> Our poesy is as a gum, which issues
> From whence 'tis nourish'd. The fire i' th' flint
> Shews not till it be struck: our gentle flame
> Provokes itself—and like the current flies
> Each bound it chafes.

The hollow friendship and shuffling evasions of the Athenian lords, their smooth professions and pitiful ingratitude, are very satisfactorily exposed, as well as the different disguises to which the meanness of self-love resorts in such cases to hide a want of generosity and good faith. The lurking selfishness of Apemantus does not pass undetected amidst the grossness of his sarcasms and his contempt for the pretensions of others. Even the two courtezans who accompany Alcibiades to the cave of Timon are very characteristically sketched; and the thieves who come to visit him are also 'true men' in their way.—An exception to this general picture of selfish depravity is found in the old and honest steward Flavius, to whom Timon pays a full tribute of tenderness. Shakespear was unwilling to draw a picture *'ugly all over with hypocrisy.'* He owed this character to the good-natured solicitations of his Muse. His mind might well have been said to be the 'sphere of humanity.' . . .

Apemantus, it is said, 'loved few things better than to abhor himself.' This is not the case with Timon, who neither loves to abhor himself nor others. All his vehement misanthropy is forced, up-hill work. From the slippery turns of fortune, from the turmoils of passion and adversity, he wishes to sink into the quiet of the grave. On that subject his thoughts are intent, on that he finds time and place to grow romantic. He digs his own grave by the sea-shore; contrives his funeral ceremonies amidst the pomp of desolation, and builds his mausoleum of the elements.

> Come not to me again; but say to Athens,
> Timon hath made his everlasting mansion
> Upon the beached verge of the salt flood;
> Which once a-day with his embossed froth
> The turbulent surge shall cover.—Thither come,
> And let my grave-stone be your oracle.

And again, Alcibiades, after reading his epitaph, says of him,

> These well express in thee thy latter spirits:
> Though thou abhorred'st in us our human griefs,
> Scorn'd'st our brain's flow, and those our droplets, which
> From niggard nature fall; yet rich conceit
> Taught thee to make vast Neptune weep for aye
> On thy low grave

thus making the winds his funeral dirge, his mourner the murmuring ocean; and seeking in the everlasting solemnities of nature oblivion of the transitory splendour of his life-time.—WILLIAM HAZLITT, *"Timon of Athens," Characters of Shakespear's Plays*, 1817

---

### JOHN CHARLES BUCKNILL
### "Timon of Athens"
### *The Mad Folk of Shakespeare*
### 1867, pp. 236–67

I am Misanthropos, and hate mankind.

The remarkable difference between *Timon* and all the other dramas, both in construction and general idea, has been a subject of much difficulty with the literary critics. It has been generally supposed to be one of Shakespeare's latest works transmitted to us in an unfinished state; but the explanation of Mr. Knight appears far more probable, that it was originally produced by an inferior artist, and that Shakespeare remodeled it, and substituted entire scenes of his own; this substitution being almost wholly confined to the character of Timon. That of Apemantus, however, bears unmistakeable impressions of the same die.

It certainly is not like the sepia sketch of a great master, perfect so far as it goes; nor yet like an unfinished picture which shews the basis of the artist's work; nor yet like those paintings of the old masters, in which the accessories were filled in by the 'prentice hands of their pupils, while the design and prominent

figures indicated the taste and skill of high genius. It is rather an old painting, retouched perhaps in all its parts, and the prominent figures entirely remodeled by the hand of the great master, but designed and originally completed by a stranger.

Of the type of Timon's character there can be no doubt. He is unmistakeably of the family of Hamlet and Lear. The resemblance to Lear especially is close; like him at first, full of unreasoning confidence; like him at last, full of unreasoning hate. In Lear's circumstances, Timon might have followed closely in his steps. The conditions of rank and age and nation do indeed direct the course of the two in paths wide apart, but in actual development of character they are to some extent parallel.

Timon is very far from being a copy from Plutarch's sketch, "a viper, and malicious man unto mankind." He is essentially high-minded and unselfish. His prodigality is unsoiled with profligacy; indeed, it takes to a great degree the form of humane and virtuous generosity, satisfied with the pleasure of doing good, the luxury of giving, without view of recompense. Even his profuse feasting is represented as noble and dignified hospitality, alloyed by no grossness. His temper is sweet and serene; even Apemantus cannot ruffle it.

With all this goodness of heart he is no fool; his remarks on all occasions shew refined and educated intellect. He has sense on all points except two, namely, in the ability to appreciate character, and the knowledge of the relation of things, as represented by the counters which transfer them. He has all kind of sense except that which is current—common sense. How such a character could be produced in the out-of-door life of Athens, where every citizen had his wits sharpened by contact with those of his neighbours, it would be difficult indeed to conjecture; but the character of Lord Timon in his prosperity is one which may any day be found in the ranks of the English aristocracy. A young man is born to a great name and estate, he inherits a generous disposition and an ardent temper; he is brought up as a little prince, and is never allowed to feel the wholesome pain of an ungratified wish. Can it be matter of wonder that in such a hotbed the growth of mind should be luxuriant and weak. Fortunately for our golden youth they generally undergo the rough discipline of public school and college; their sensibilities are indurated, and their wits sharpened, in societies where, if they find sycophant spirits, they also find independent and even tyrannical ones. But young Crœsus, brought up at home, what must be his destiny in these latter days? When the twenty-first birthday emancipates him from mamma and the mild tutor, well for him if reckless hospitality be his worst offence against prudence; well for him if that old man of the woods, the land steward, does not suffocate him in his tenacious embrace; well for him if the turf and the card-table do not attract his green state of social initiation, devour wealth and destroy morality. Men who most need knowledge of the selfishness of their fellow men have too often the least of it. Bred up on the sunny parterres of life, they have no experience of the difficulties and dangers of the rough thicket. The human pigeon has not even the resource of fear and swift flight to save him from the accipitres of his race. The fascination of false confidence lends him a willing victim to their talons, and under the chloroform of self-esteem he does not even feel being rent and devoured. So it is with Timon: with intelligence quick enough on all other matters, he is utterly incapable of seeing his relation to men and theirs to him, of appreciating the real value of deed and motive. The kind of knowledge most imperatively needed to guide our conduct is that of relation. It is the first to which the mind opens. The child under ever recurring penalties is compelled to acquaint himself with the relation existing between his person and the physical world; he burns himself, and thereafter dreads the fire. The man under penalties more sharp and lasting must discover his moral relations in this world, must learn to estimate himself and those around him according to the actualities of motive. As the child ascertains that fire and blows cause pain, so the man must learn that flattery is not friendship, that imprudence exacts regret, that the prevalent philosophy of this selfish world is that taught by Lear's unselfish fool, "Let go thy hold when a great wheel runs down a hill, lest it break thy neck with following; but the great one that goes upward, let him draw thee after;" or by Timon's poet, who laboriously conveys the same idea that flashes from the fool:

> When Fortune in her shift and change of mood
> Spurns down her late beloved, all his dependents
> Which labour'd after him to the mountain's top
> Even on their hands and knees, let him slip down,
> Not one accompanying his declining foot.

Timon, however, takes a widely different view of life. To him society is a disinterested brotherhood in which to possess largely is but to have the greater scope for the luxury of giving, and in which want itself may be but a means to try one's friends and to learn their sterling value. His first act of bounty, not less noble than reasonable, is to pay the debt on which his friend Ventidius is imprisoned. It is done with graceful freedom, and his liberated friend is invited to him for further help in the fine sentiment, that

> 'Tis not enough to help the feeble up,
> But to support him after.

The dowry of the servant Lucilius, to satisfy the greed of the old miser whose daughter he courts, is more lavish and less reasonable. Timon will counterpoise with his fortune what the old man will give with his daughter, though he feels the burden of the task.

> To build his fortune I would strain a little,
> For 'tis a bond of men.

His inquiries are of the shortest. He has no hesitation, no suspicion, but gives away fortunes as if his means were exhaustless, and his discrimination infallible. He acts in fervent disbelief of his opinion immediately afterwards expressed, that since

> Dishonour traffics with man's nature,
> He is but outside.

Timon conducts himself as if all men on the contrary were true to the core like himself, deriving enjoyment from the happiness of others. Life to him is a poet's dream of goodness and beauty. All men are deserving of his bounty, even as he is deserving of the love and gratitude of all.

But there is more than this reasoning bounty acting upon a false estimate of man's goodness. Timon gives for the very love of giving; he scatters without motive, further than the pleasure of doing so affords.

> He outgoes the very heart of kindness,
> He pours it out; Plutus, the god of gold,
> Is but his steward; no meed, but he repays
> Sevenfold above itself.

He scatters jewels, and horses, and costly gifts among the rich, even as he distributes fortunes among the needy. He will have nothing back. Ventidius succeeds to the wealth of his father, and seeks to return the talents which freed him from prison, but Timon will have none of the gold.

> I gave it freely ever; and there's none
> Can truly say he gives, if he receives.

This squandering disposition would appear to be the converse of what phrenologists denote acquisitiveness. To coin a word, it is *disquisitiveness*, and in some men would seem to be an innate bias of the disposition. It is to give, for the pleasure of giving; to spend, for the pleasure of spending, without esteem for the things procured in return. Probably, like the opposite desire of accumulating, it is a secondary mental growth. The love of gold in itself would be as absurd as the love of iron; but after having been first esteemed for its attributes, its ability to confer pleasure and power, it becomes valued for itself, and the mere love of hoarding, without the slightest reference to the employment of the hoard, takes possession of the mind. So in the opposite mental state, the first pleasures of distributing wealth are, no doubt, derived from the gratification it affords in various ways; in contributing to the happiness of others; in purchasing esteem or the semblance of it for one's self; in apparently raising one's self above the level of those on whom the benefits are conferred, and thus gratifying vanity; or in the more direct gratification of the senses. The pleasure of enjoyment from these sources is at length unconsciously transferred to the mere act of distribution. To give and to spend for the mere pleasure of doing so, combined with the love of change, are the attributes of many a prodigal who is no profligate, of many a man who, in a stricter sense than that usually applied to the saying, is no one's enemy but his own— very strictly this can never be said, for in civilized society no man can be his own enemy without injuring others.

Such a man is Timon represented. He appears to have had no strong attachment either to men or things. The jewel recklessly purchased is lavishly thrown to the first friend he meets. His fortune is at every one's command, not only of the old friend in prison, and of the old servant aspiring to fortune, but at that of the flatterers of his own rank, empty in head and heart, who have no real wants or claims.

Timon has indeed a noble theory of friendship, but there wants in it all those heartlights which prove the reality of the thing, as it existed between Hamlet and Horatio, or Celia and Rosalind in the other sex. There is, however, a noble freedom of welcome in his introduction to his first feast:—

> Nay, my lords, ceremony was but devised at first
> To set a gloss on faint deeds, hollow welcomes,
> Recanting goodness, sorry ere 'tis shown;
> But where there is true friendship, there needs none.
> Pray, sit; more welcome are ye to my fortunes
> Than my fortunes to me.

In his table speech, his explanation of his own profuseness, and his reliance upon a return in kind from his friends, is almost communist in the expression of the idea, that the fortunes of all should be at the service of each:—

> Why, I have often wished myself poorer, that I might
> come nearer to you. We are born to do benefits: and
> what better or properer can we call our own than the
> riches of our friends? O, what a precious comfort 'tis,
> to have so many, like brothers, commanding one
> another's fortunes! O joy, e'en made away ere 't can
> be born! Mine eyes cannot hold out water, methinks:
> to forget their faults, I drink to you.

He gives more entertainment, distributes more jewels, showers presents on those who bring them and on those who do not, and, without knowing it, all "out of an empty coffer." What he bespeaks is all in debt, he owes for every word. Honest Flavius seeks to apprise him, but since "it's a word which concerns him near," he will not listen. Even Apemantus, who seems to entertain a surly liking for him, and who seeks to inspire in him some suspicion that friendship has its dregs, tenders advice which this time is not quite railing. He admits him to be honest though a fool.

Thus honest fools lay out their wealth on court'sies.

He'll not be bribed lest that should shut his mouth, and Timon would then sin the faster; Timon will give so long that soon he will give himself away in paper; but Timon will have none of his warning, it is railing on society; and Apemantus rebuffed at the only moment when he is tolerable, turns on his heel with his rejected advice:

> O, that men's ears should be
> To counsel deaf, but not to flattery!

Timon's profuseness is pourtrayed in the steward's terse account of his debts, and the ever motion of his raging waste; but the desire which prompts it is best given in his own words of farewell to his guests:

> I take all and your several visitations
> So kind to heart, 'tis not enough to give;
> Methinks I could deal kingdoms to my friends,
> And ne'er be weary.

But now the time of reckoning approaches, in which it is prophesied that

> When every feather sticks in his own wing,
> Lord Timon will be left a naked gull,
> Which flashes now a phœnix.

He is beset with the clamorous demands of creditors, and turns with reproachful enquiry to the one honest man who has been seeking so long to check the ebb of his estate and this great flow of debts; and when he at length gives ear to the importunity that can no longer be avoided, his debts double his means, and all his vast lands are engaged or forfeited. No estate could support his senseless prodigality,

> The world is but a word:
> Were it all yours to give it in a breath,
> How quickly were it gone!

Flavius, like Apemantus, refers the motive of Timon's profusion to vanity and the love of compliment:

> Who is not Timon's?
> What heart, head, sword, force, means, but is lord
>     Timon's?
> Great Timon, noble, worthy, royal Timon!
> Ah, when the means are gone that buy this praise,
> The breath is gone whereof this praise is made:
> Feast-won, fast-lost; one cloud of winter showers,
> These flies are couch'd.

This however is not quite the whole truth. There is doubtless much vanity in Timon's ostentation, but there is also a magnanimous disregard of self, and a false judgment of others founded upon it. His bounty,

> Being free itself, it thinks all other so.

Now comes the real trial, the test of man's value. Riches are gone, but the noble heart is "wealthy in his friends"; it were lack of conscience to think otherwise.

> Come, sermon me no further:
> No villanous bounty yet hath pass'd my heart;
> Unwisely, not ignobly, have I given.
> Why dost thou weep? Canst thou the conscience lack
> To think I shall lack friends? Secure thy heart;
> If I would broach the vessels of my love,
> And try the argument of hearts by borrowing,
> Men and men's fortunes could I frankly use
> As I can bid thee speak."

The trial is made, the bubble bursts; one after another the friends find characteristic and ingenious excuses. To one, bare friendship without security is nothing; another is in despair that

he hath not furnished himself against so good a time; another puts on the semblance of anger that he was not sent to first, and pretending that his honour hath thus been abated, he refuses his coin.

The world turns dark with Timon, he is struck down by his friends' desertion.

> Thy lord leans wondrously to discontent, his com-
> fortable temper has forsook him; he is much out of
> health and keeps his chamber.

The period of depression which would naturally intervene between that of confidence and enraged defiance is concealed from view, and only alluded to in the above sentence. Here, as in Lear and Constance, the poet takes care to mark the concurrence of physical with moral causes of insanity. Mere bodily disease is no subject for dramatic representation; and the fact of its existence is lightly enough indicated, but it is indicated, and that is sufficient to preserve the exact natural verisimilitude of the diseased mind's history. When Timon re-appears, the re-action of furious indignation possesses him. He rushes wildly forth from the house in which his loving servants have sought to retain him. Must his very house also be his enemy, his gaol?

> The place where I have feasted, does it now,
> Like all mankind, shew me an iron heart?

At the door he is beset with a crowd of dunning creditors, adding fuel to the flame of his rage.

*Philotus:* All our bills.
*Timon:* Knock me down with 'em: cleave me to the
    girdle.
*Luc. Serv.:* Alas, my lord,—
*Tim.:* Cut my heart in sums.
*Titus:* Mine, fifty talents.
*Tim.:* Tell out my blood.
*Luc. Serv.:* Five thousand crowns, my lord.
*Tim.:* Five thousand drops pays that.
                    What yours?—and yours?
*Tim.:* Tear me, take me, and the gods falls upon you!
*Hortensius:* 'Faith, I perceive our masters may throw
    their caps at their money: these debts may well
    be called desperate ones, for a madam owes
    'em.
            [*Timon drives them out and re-enters.*
*Tim.:* They have e'en put my breath from me, the
    slaves. Creditors?—devils.

He gives orders for his farewell feast, although Flavius reminds him of his absolute want of means, and says that in doing so

> You only speak from your distracted soul.

However, Timon and the cook will provide. The feast is toward. The expression of rage is controlled, and the infinite sarcasm of the inverted benediction is pronounced before the guests know what it means. The ambiguity of the language is of course intended to conceal for a moment its true meaning— that men are all villains and women no better; that even their piety is selfishness, so that if Gods gave all, even they would be despised like Timon; but all being amiss, let all be suitable for destruction.

The dishes uncovered are full of warm water, which Timon throws into the faces of his mock friends, whose perfect nature "is but smoke and lukewarm water." He overwhelms them with a torrent of curses by no means lukewarm, throws the dishes at them, and driving them from the hall, takes his own farewell of house and home, bursting with rage and general hate.

Burn, house! sink, Athens! henceforth hated be,
Of Timon man and all humanity!

The conclusion of the "smiling, smooth, detested parasites" is the same as that already arrived at by the servants, namely

Lord Timon's mad.

Nothing, indeed, is less safe than to adopt the opinion of some of Shakespeare's characters upon others. He makes them speak of each other according to their own light, which is often partial and perverted, obscured by ignorance, or blinded by prejudice. The spectator sees the whole field, and experiences difficulty of judgment, not from narrowness of vision, but from its extent. In Timon, as in the early parts of Lear, the psychological opinion is embarrassed by the very circumstance which constitutes the difficulty in many cases of dubious insanity, namely, that the operations of diseased mind are not retrograde to those of normal function, but merely divergent from them, in the same general direction.

Timon's eloquent declamations against his kind are identical in spirit with those of *Lear*. They are, indeed, interrupted by no vagrancy of thought, but are always true to the passion which now absorbs him, namely, intense hatred of the human race, in whom he believes baseness and wickedness inherent. Here lies his great intellectual error which may indeed be called delusion; that, because some few men have been base and thankless parasites, the whole race is steeped in infamy. His emotional being is absorbed by indignation, and this, re-acting on the intellect, represents human nature in the darkest colours of treachery and villany. It is not clearly made out to what degree Timon is influenced by spite. In the imprecation upon Athens, "Let me look back upon thee" etc., he invokes social disorder of every kind as the punishment for his own treatment, and does not represent it as actually existing, and as the cause of his fierce anger. There is some uncertainty in this passage, some confusion of thought between the depraved state of Athens which merits dire punishment, and the social disorders which in themselves constitute such punishment. The wall of Athens is thought to girdle in a mere troop of human wolves. To avenge his own injuries, he prays that the matrons may turn incontinent, that obedience may fail in children, and so forth, recognizing that the contrary has existed, and that social disorder is invoked as the punishment of demerit towards himself. He acknowledges that "degrees, observances, customs, and laws" have held their place, and that their "confounding contraries" would be a new state of things due to that human baseness which is now obvious to his distempered vision through the medium of his own wrongs. In the following scene, where he apostrophises "the blessed breeding sun" in vehement declamation, he does not so much invoke curses upon man, as describe man's actual state as in itself a curse; since he depicts moral depravity in its existing colors.

O blessed breeding sun, draw from the earth
Rotten humidity; below thy sister's orb
Infect the air! Twinn'd brothers of one womb,
Whose procreation, residence, and birth,
Scarce is dividant, touch them with several fortunes;
The greater scorns the lesser: not nature,
To whom all sores lay siege, can bear great fortune,
But by contempt of nature.
Raise me this beggar, and deny 't that lord;
The senator shall bear contempt hereditary,
The beggar native honour.
It is the pasture lards the rother's sides,

The want that makes him lean. Who dares, who
     dares,
In purity of manhood stand upright,
And say 'This man's a flatterer'? if one be,
So are they all; for every grise of fortune
Is smooth'd by that below: the learned pate
Ducks to the golden fool: all is oblique;
There's nothing level in our cursed natures,
But direct villany. Therefore, be abhorr'd
All feasts, societies, and throngs of men!
His semblable, yea, himself, Timon disdains:
Destruction fang mankind! Earth, yield me roots!

Instead of roots he finds gold, yellow, glittering, precious gold, and he comments upon it in terms which still further prove that the social curses he invokes upon the detested town he has quitted are those which he believes to exist. There is no honesty, no nobility in man, proof against this yellow slave, this damned earth which will "knit and break religions, bless the accursed, make the hoar leprosy adored, place thieves on high and give them titled approbation." This belief in the existence of man's utter unworthiness is of prime importance in estimating Timon's character. It is needful to vindicate his misanthropy from being that of miserable spite. There is no doubt a mixture of personal resentment in his feeling, but his deep-rooted disparagement and contempt of man are founded upon a fixed belief in man's utter worthlessness. If men were noble and good, or if Timon could believe them so, he would not hate them; but they are all to his distempered mind either base in themselves or base in their subserviency to baseness. "Timon Atheniensis dictus interrogatus cur omnes homines odio prosequeretur: Malos, inquit, merito odi; cæteros ob id odi, quod malos non oderint."—*Erasmus.* This is not to hate man as he ought to be, nor even as he is, but as he appears in the false colours of mental derangement.

The character of Apemantus is skilfully managed to elicit the less selfish nature of Timon's misanthropy. In the one it is the result of a bad heart, in the other that of a perverted reason. If all men were true and good they would be the more offensive to the churlish disposition of Apemantus, who is an ingrained misanthrope, and as such is recognized and abhorred by Timon himself. He seeks Timon to vex him—"always a villain's office, or a fool's." He attributes Timon's conduct to the meanest motives,—a madman before, he is now a fool:

This is in thee a nature but infected,
A poor unmanly melancholy sprung
From change of fortune.

He recommends Timon to play the part he was undone by— that of a base flatterer; and that he should turn rascal to have his wealth again, that he might again distribute it to rascals. He accuses him of being an imitator—"Thou dost affect my manners;"—of putting on the sour cold habit of nakedness and melancholy from mere want, and of the capacity to be a courtier, were he not a beggar. Timon estimates the curish spirit which thus attacks him at its true value. "Why shouldst thou hate men? they never flattered thee?" He replies,

If thou hadst not been born the worst of men,
Thou hadst been a knave and flatterer.

Apemantus, indeed, is a real misanthrope, who judges of man by his own bad heart. It was necessary to the drama that he should speak his thoughts, but naturally such a man would only express his antagonism to mankind in his actions. Such misanthropes are too common; every malevolent villain being, in fact, one of them, although selfishness in league with badness may counsel hypocrisy. Boileau recognises this in his lines on the malignant hypocrite of society:

En vain ce misanthrope, aux yeux tristes et sombres,
Veut, par un air riant, en éclaircir les ombres:
Le ris sur son visage est en mauvaise humeur;
L'agrément fuit ses traits, ses caresses font peur;
Ses mots les plus flatteurs paroissent des rudesses,
Et la vanité brille en toutes ses bassesses.

Lord Shaftesbury, in the *Characteristics*, takes a view of misanthropy, which strictly accords with the character of Apemantus. He places it among "those horrid, monstrous, and unnatural affections, to have which is to be miserable in the highest degree." He writes:

There is also among these a sort of hatred of mankind and society; a passion which has been known perfectly reigning among some men, and has had a peculiar name given to it, misanthropy. A large share of this belongs to those who have habitually indulged themselves in a habitual moroseness, or who, by force of ill-nature and ill-breeding, have contracted such a reverse of affability, and civil manners, that to see or meet a stranger is offensive. The very aspect of mankind is a disturbance to 'em, and they are sure always to hate at first sight.

Timon's contempt of the treasure of gold, which he discovers in his naked and houseless misery, marks his changed nature less than his entire disregard of the invitation of the senators to rank and power, and to captain of Athens. Riches, for their own sake, he always placed at the lowest value. He now distributes them as moral poison. To Alcibiades, whom, following Plutarch's hint, he hates less than others, he gives it to whet the sword which threatens his country. To the courtezans he gives it, because they are the infecting curses of man.

> There's more gold;
> So you damn others, and let this damn you,
> And ditches grave you all!

To Flavius he gives it tempting him to misanthropy; to the contemptible poet and painter, because they are villains; to the thieves, that in the poison of wine it may destroy them.

> Here's gold. Go, suck the subtle blood o' the grape,
> 'Till the high fever seethe your blood to froth,
> And so 'scape hanging.

Gold, which has been his own curse, has become in his eyes the curse of all. It is "the common whore of mankind." His contemptuous distribution of the "yellow slave," the "damned earth," the "strong thief," with blows and maledictions to the mean wretches who seek it from him, is the keenest satire upon the state of society, which for want of it has thrown him from its bosom.

It has been said both by Schlegel and Hazlitt that Timon is more a satire than a drama. This idea may have been derived from the limited development of character which it exhibits. Each character is placed clear and definitely formed in the page, and remains so. Timon's alone undergoes one radical change, of which we see the effect rather than the transition. During the fourth and fifth acts the movements of the drama are solely devised with the intention of bringing the several personages under Timon's withering denunciation.

There are, however, some passages which hint of change, and are more important than the more prominent and eloquent ones in affording an estimate of Timon's mental state. By the other personages he is evidently regarded as mad. Alcibiades thus excuses his anathemas on the ladies of pleasure:

> Pardon him, sweet Timandra; for his wits
> Are drown'd and lost in his calamities.

The good steward expresses wondering grief at the change in his appearance, the pregnant sign of the mind's desease:

*Flavius:* O you gods!
> Is yond despised and ruinous man my lord?
> Full of decay and failing? O monument
> And wonder of good deeds evilly bestow'd!
> What an alteration of honour
> Has desperate want made!
> What viler thing upon the earth than friends
> Who can bring noblest minds to basest ends!

Even before this, life-weariness has suggested the intention of suicide; the life-weariness of true mental disease, which is distinct from misanthropy, and has reference only to the individual. Misanthropy of opinion may be robust, egotistical, resisting, full of life. The misanthropy of melancholia is despairing and suicidal.

> I am sick of this false world, and will love nought
> But even the mere necessities upon 't.
> Then, Timon, presently prepare thy grave;
> Lie where the light foam of the sea may beat
> Thy grave-stone daily: make thine epitaph
> That death in me at others' lives may laugh.

It is, however, not certain whether Timon dies directly by his own hand, or indirectly by the misery which he inflicts upon himself. The exposure described in such noble poetry by Apemantus out of place as it seems in his churlish mouth, "What, think'st that the bleak air thy boisterous chamberlain" etc., is in itself a kind of suicide, which has many a time and oft been resorted to by the insane. Indeed, of all forms of voluntary death, that of starvation is the most frequently attempted by them. Timon, however, does not actually refuse food; he digs for roots and eats them, while he regrets the necessity

> That nature being sick of man's unkindness
> Should yet be hungry.

Although his exposure to "desperate want," which hath made him almost unrecognizable to the loving eyes of his faithful steward, may from the first have been adopted for a suicidal purpose, it seems probable that the manner of his death was still more voluntary; for, however sensibly he might feel his failing health drawing to a close, it is not likely that on the day when he supported the animated dialogue with the senators he should be able positively to foretell his death from exhaustion on the morrow.

> Why, I was writing of my epitaph;
> It will be seen to-morrow: my long sickness
> Of health and living now begins to mend,
> And nothing brings me all things.

After mocking the senators with the pretended patriotism of a public benefit, copied from the short notice to be found in Plutarch, the invitation forsooth to the Athenian citizens to stop their afflictions by hanging themselves upon his tree, Timon takes his farewell of men and their deeds, in words pointing to a voluntary death, in a predetermined time and place:

> Come not to me again: but say to Athens,
> Timon hath made his everlasting mansion
> Upon the beached verge of the salt flood;
> Who once a day with embossed froth
> The turbulent surge shall cover: thither come,
> And let my gravestone be your oracle.
> Lips, let sour words go by and language end:
> What is amiss plague and infection mend!
> Graves only be men's works and death their gain!
> Sun, hide thy beams! Timon hath done his reign.

Suicide had not that place of honour among the Greeks which it afterwards obtained among the Romans, and at the present day has among that remote and strange people, the Japanese. Yet the duty of living and bearing one's burden manfully was not fully recognized until a better religious faith instructed us that this life is but a state of preparation for another. The suicide of Timon, however, whether it is effected by exposure and want, or by more direct means, has no motive recognized even by the ancients an an excuse, and can only be attributed to the suggestions of a diseased mind.

Whether Shakespeare intended in *Timon* to describe the career of a madman is a question on which it is difficult, perhaps impossible, to come to a definite conclusion. The chief objection to the affirmative would be, that all satire upon the hollowness of the world would lose much of its point if it came from the lips of an undoubted lunatic. This objection, however, loses somewhat of its validity, when it is remembered that in *Lear* Shakespeare actually has put such satire in the mouth of the maddest of his characters during the height of the disease; and that in his devotion to the truth of nature he would have represented such misanthropy as Timon's as a monstrous growth of the mind, if it be so.

Is it possible even in a state of disease? Is it actually met with? Undoubtedly, yes. Making allowance for the difference between the adorned descriptions of poetry and plain matter of fact, putting on one side the power of eloquent declamation, which belongs indeed not to the character but to the author, the professed misanthrope in word and in deed is met with among the insane, and, probably, among the insane only. This malignant and inhuman passion, for such it is, takes divers forms. Sometimes it is mere motiveless dislike; every one is obnoxious with or without cause, like Dr. Fell in the adage. This is the malignity of Apemantus expressing itself in conduct rather than in frank confession. The explanation of it is best given by Timon himself, that

> *Ira brevis furor est,*
> But this man 's always angry.

If anger be identical with madness, except in its duration, this form of madness may be said to be a life-long and universal anger. Another form of insanity, not uncommon in and out of lunatic asylums, approaches more nearly to the misanthropy of Timon; namely, that form of chronic mental disease, whether it be called mania or melancholia, which constantly torments itself and others by attributing evil motives, not like Timon's to all ranks and classes of society, but to every individual with whom the unhappy being comes in contact. The poetical misanthropy of Timon is generalized, and cannot be said to point at any individual, unless it be Apemantus. The misanthropy of reality is individualized; it points to all persons in turn, but to one only at a time.

This form of misanthropy may, and indeed often does, exist with none of the attributes of Insanity, but as the expression of that misleading influence which evil dispositions exercise over the judgment. In not unfrequent instances, however, it passes the limits of sanity, and presents all the features of mental disease. Hate and suspicion become constant and uncontrollable emotions; belief in the misconduct of others develops into delusions, representing the commission of actual crimes; and with these mental symptoms the physical indications of brain disease are not wanting. No task of psychological diagnosis, however, is so arduous as that of determining the point at which exaggerated natural disposition of any kind becomes actual disease; but when the boundaries of sane mind are far left behind, difficulty and doubt vanish.

When sane malignity has developed into insane misan-thropy, a remarkable change is sometimes seen in the habits of the man, resembling the self-inflicted miseries of Timon. The author once knew a gentleman whose educated and acute intellect occupied itself solely in the invention of calumnies against every person with whom he was brought into contact. This habit of mind was associated with utter negligence of the proprieties of life, and indeed of personal decency, so that it became absolutely requisite, for his own sake, that he should receive the protection of an asylum. A more close approximation to the misanthropy represented by the dramatist, because more general and uninfluenced by malign feeling, was, however, presented in the case of a poor creature, in whose expulsion from that which served for his cave the author took some part. For several years he had frequently passed by a desolate-looking house, which was believed to be uninhabited. Any strange thing, accompanied by change, strikes one's attention, but stranger things not so accompanied pass by unnoticed. So it was that this house remained in this state for years, without anyone asking why it was so. At length information was received that an insane person was incarcerated within its desolate-looking walls. In company with a Justice of the Peace the author obtained admission into the house, and, by forcing a door, into the chamber of the anchorite. Here in gloomy mistrust and dislike of all mankind he had secluded himself for five years. Little of his history was known, except that he had travelled in all parts of the world, had returned to find great domestic affliction, and from that time had shut himself in one room; the bare necessaries of life being supplied to him by relatives who connived at his eccentricity, one of whom, scarcely more sane than himself, also occupied a room in this strange house. It is astonishing that, with a penurious diet and absence of all comfort, and an absolute want of fresh air and exercise, he retained health for so long a time. Had it not been for this self-inflicted misery and incarceration, it would have been difficult to certify that this poor man was insane. He disliked his fellow men, and shut himself up from them; that was all. Although not a rich man, he had property; and while it was under contemplation how he could be rescued from his voluntary misery, some relations took him under their kind protection. Had this man possessed the passionate eloquence of Timon, and been exposed to severe incitements to its use, by irritating invasions on his misan-thropic privacy, he might have declaimed as Timon did—if Timon indeed did declaim; if silence indeed is not the natural state of misanthropy, and all the eloquence of this drama that of the author rather than of the character.

The character which Shakespeare has delineated in Timon is remarkably enough the subject of the *chef d' œuvre* of French comedy. The Misanthrope of Molière, however, is in many respects a very distinct personage from that of Shake-speare. So far from being susceptible to flattery and to the blandishments of prosperity, more than half of his quarrel with society is founded upon his abhorrence of this social falsehood. Although he loudly condemns general vices, and thus accounts for his retirement from the world,

> La raison, pour mon bien, veut que je me retire;
> Je n'ai point sur ma langue un assez grand empire,

yet he detests private scandal, and reproaches his mistress for indulging in it. The dishonest praise and blame of individuals are equally hateful to his ears. The reason he assigns for his misanthropy, and its extent, are identical with those which Erasmus attributed to Timon; in his anger he says that his aversion to man admits of no exception:

> Non, elle est générale, et je hais tous les hommes;
> Les uns, parcequ'ils sont méchants et malfaisants,
> Et les autres, pour être aux méchants complaisants.

He hates all mankind, because they all come under the category of rogues or flatterers. He is, however, elevated above Timon in this, that the personal injuries he himself receives are not the cause of this hatred; on the contrary, he treats them with a noble indifference. The character of Alceste is, on the whole, that of a magnanimous, truth-loving, truth-speaking man, misplaced in a court where servility and corruption are triumphant. His very defects, his anger at vice and duplicity, and his promptness to express it, are those of a noble soul.

Rousseau has taken this view of the character in a severe criticism, to which he has exposed Molière for degrading the dramatic art, to pander to the corrupt morals of his age, in covering virtue with ridicule, and vice with false attractions. Other French writers have generally dissented from this condemnation, but Rousseau's letter to D'Alembert is a fine example of analytic criticism, not to be set aside by the sneering assertion, that he identified himself with this noble character, and felt his own vanity wounded in its unworthy treatment. Rousseau's estimate of it is irrefragably just and logical. If he has erred at all, it is in the opinion of the impression which the character of Alceste is calculated to make. His imprudent magnanimity may have been a subject of ridicule to the *parterre* of Molière's time, and doubtless was so; but this view of the character would be due less to the manner in which it is delineated, than to the corrupt morals and taste of that age. In better times it would be difficult to throw ridicule upon that which is intrinsically and morally excellent. An interesting anecdote, related by St. Simon, attests that this view of the character was even taken in Molière's own time by the person most interested in estimating it justly. The Duc de Montausier was generally recognized to be the original of the misanthrope, and was so indignant at the supposed insult that he threatened to have Molière beaten to death for it. When the king went to see the play, M. Le Duc was compelled to go with him as his governor. After the performance the Duke sent for Molière, who was with difficulty brought to him, trembling from head to foot, expecting nothing less than death. M. Montausier, however, gave him a very different reception from that which he expected; he embraced him again and again, overwhelmed him with praises and thanks, for "if he had thought of him in drawing the character of the misanthrope, which was that of the most perfectly honest man possible, he had done him an honour which was only too great, and which he should never forget."

Rousseau seems to think not only that Alceste was not a misanthrope in the proper sense of the word, but that no sane man can be such.

> One may say that the author has not ridiculed virtue in Alceste, but a true fault; that is to say, hatred of mankind. I reply, that it is not true that he has endowed his character with this hatred. The mere name of misanthrope must not be understood to imply that he who bears it is the enemy of the human race. A hatred of this kind would not be a defect, but a depravity of nature, and the greatest of all vices, since all the social virtues are connected with benevolence, and nothing is so directly contrary to them as inhumanity. The true misanthrope, if his

existence were possible, would be a monster who would not make us laugh; he would excite our horror.

The true misanthrope, in fact, is such a character as Iago, a malevolent devil, without belief in any human goodness, without human sympathies, one who has said in his heart, "evil, be thou my good." But the very nature of such inhuman hatred would impose not only silence as to evil thoughts, but hypocritical expression of humane sentiment. The honest wide-mouthed misanthropy of Timon is wholly explicable on neither of these theories. It is neither the rough garb of sincerity and virtue, as in Alceste, nor of inhuman hatred as in Iago. It is a medium between the two, inconsistent with sane mind, and explicable alone as a depravity and perversion of nature arising from disease. It is a form of insanity.

Aretæus, describing the conduct of maniacs "in the height of the disease," remarks, "some flee the haunts of men, and going into the wilderness live by themselves."

In Caius Cassius there is a fine psychological delineation of another character, who estimates man and his motives depreciatingly. Cassius is robustly sane and self-possessed, and therefore has little in common with Timon. He would approximate more closely to Jaques, did not the strong intermixture of spleen pickle him as it were from the contagion of melancholy. In Cæsar's unfriendly but graphic description he figures as the type of cynicism, except that the envy of ambition is attributed to him which the true cynic would despise.

> *Cæsar:* Let me have men about me that are fat:
> Sleek-headed men and such as sleep o'nights:
> Yond Cassius has a lean and hungry look;
> He thinks too much: such men are dangerous.
> *Antony:* Fear him not, Cæsar; he's not dangerous;
> He is a noble Roman and well given.
> *Cæs.:* Would he were fatter! But I fear him not:
> Yet if my name were liable to fear,
> I do not know the man I should avoid
> So soon as that spare Cassius. He reads much;
> He is a great observer and he looks
> Quite through the deeds of men; he loves no plays,
> As thou dost, Antony; he hears no music;
> Seldom he smiles, and smiles in such a sort
> As if he mock'd himself and scorn'd his spirit
> That could be moved to smile at any thing.
> Such men as he be never at heart's ease
> Whiles they behold a greater than themselves,
> And therefore are they very dangerous.

However true the dangerous nature of such men may be, in times when despotic power can only be attacked by conspiracy, it can scarcely be so when eloquence is the most formidable assailant of established authority. Sleep o'nights is needful to sustain the energy of the day, and a fat body is often associated with a well-nourished brain of best quality. The greatest orators and some of the greatest demagogues have at least indicated a proclivity to Falstaffian proportions; witness Danton, Fox, O'Connell, John Bright, and the Bishop of Oxford. Falstaff, indeed, himself says, "Give me spare men and spare me great ones," but this was only for soldiers.

# Antony and Cleopatra

This play keeps curiosity always busy, and the passions always interested. The continual hurry of the action, the variety of incidents, and the quick succession of one personage to another, call the mind forward without intermission from the first act to the last. But the power of delighting is derived principally from the frequent changes of the scene; for, except the feminine arts, some of which are too low, which distinguish Cleopatra, no character is very strongly discriminated. Upton, who did not easily miss what he desired to find, has discovered that the language of Antony is, with great skill and learning, made pompous and superb, according to his real practice. But I think his diction not distinguishable from that of others: the most tumid speech in the play is that which Caesar makes to Octavia.

The events, of which the principal are described according to history, are produced without any art of connection or care of disposition.—SAMUEL JOHNSON, *Notes on Shakespeare's Plays*, 1768

*Antony and Cleopatra* may, in some measure, be considered as a continuation of *Julius Cæsar*: the two principal characters of Antony and Augustus are equally sustained in both pieces. *Antony and Cleopatra* is a play of great extent; the progress is less simple than in *Julius Cæsar*. The fulness and variety of political and warlike events, to which the union of the three divisions of the Roman world under one master necessarily gave rise, were perhaps too great to admit of being clearly exhibited in one dramatic picture. In this consists the great difficulty of the historical drama:—it must be a crowded extract, and a living development of history;—the difficulty, however, has generally been successfully overcome by Shakspeare. But now many things, which are transacted in the background, are here merely alluded to, in a manner which supposes an intimate acquaintance with the history; but a work of art should contain, within itself, every thing necessary for its being fully understood. Many persons of historical importance are merely introduced in passing; the preparatory and concurring circumstances are not sufficiently collected into masses to avoid distracting our attention. The principal personages, however, are most emphatically distinguished by lineament and colouring, and powerfully arrest the imagination. In Antony we observe a mixture of great qualities, weaknesses, and vices; violent ambition and ebullitions of magnanimity; we see him now sinking into luxurious enjoyment and then nobly ashamed of his own aberrations,—manning himself to resolutions not unworthy of himself, which are always shipwrecked against the seductions of an artful woman. It is Hercules in the chains of Omphale, drawn from the fabulous heroic ages into history, and invested with the Roman costume. The seductive arts of Cleopatra are in no respect veiled over; she is an ambiguous being made up of royal pride, female vanity, luxury, inconstancy, and true attachment. Although the mutual passion of herself and Antony is without moral dignity, it still excites our sympathy as an insurmountable fascination:—they seem formed for each other, and Cleopatra is as remarkable for her seductive charms as Antony for the splendour of his deeds. As they die for each other, we forgive them for having lived for each other. The open and lavish character of Antony is admirably contrasted with the heartless littleness of Octavius, whom Shakspeare seems to have completely seen through, without allowing himself to be led astray by the fortune and the fame of Augustus.—AUGUST WILHELM SCHLEGEL, *Lectures on Dramatic Art and Literature*, 1809, tr. John Black

Shakspeare can be complimented only by comparison with himself: all other eulogies are either heterogeneous, as when they are in reference to Spenser or Milton; or they are flat truisms, as when he is gravely preferred to Corneille, Racine, or even his own immediate successors, Beaumont and Fletcher, Massinger and the rest. The highest praise, or rather form of praise, of this play, which I can offer in my own mind, is the doubt which the perusal always occasions in me, whether the *Antony and Cleopatra* is not, in all exhibitions of a giant power in its strength and vigour of maturity, a formidable rival of *Macbeth*, *Lear*, *Hamlet*, and *Othello*. *Feliciter audax* is the motto for its style comparatively with that of Shakspeare's other works, even as it is the general motto of all his works compared with those of other poets. Be it remembered, too, that this happy valiancy of style is but the representative and result of all the material excellencies so expressed.

This play should be perused in mental contrast with *Romeo and Juliet;*—as the love of passion and appetite opposed to the love of affection and instinct. But the art displayed in the character of Cleopatra is profound; in this, especially, that the sense of criminality in her passion is lessened by our insight into its depth and energy, at the very moment that we cannot but perceive that the passion itself springs out of the habitual craving of a licentious nature, and that it is supported and reinforced by voluntary stimulus and sought-for associations, instead of blossoming out of spontaneous emotion.

Of all Shakspeare's historical plays, *Antony and Cleopatra* is by far the most wonderful. There is not one in which he has followed history so minutely, and yet there are few in which he impresses the notion of angelic strength so much;—perhaps none in which he impresses it more strongly. This is greatly owing to the manner in which the fiery force is sustained throughout, and to the numerous momentary flashes of nature counteracting the historic abstraction. As a wonderful specimen of the way in which Shakspeare lives up to the very end of this play, read the last part of the concluding scene. And if you would feel the judgment as well as the genius of Shakspeare in your heart's core, compare this astonishing drama with Dryden's *All for Love*.—SAMUEL TAYLOR COLERIDGE, "*Antony and Cleopatra*," *Shakspeare, with Introductory Remarks on Poetry, the Drama, and the Stage*, 1818

---

## WILLIAM HAZLITT
### "Antony and Cleopatra"
### Characters of Shakespear's Plays
### 1817

T his is a very noble play. Though not in the first class of Shakespear's productions, it stands next to them, and is, we think, the finest of his historical plays, that is, of those in which he made poetry the organ of history, and assumed a certain tone of character and sentiment, in conformity to known facts, instead of trusting to his observations of general nature or to the unlimited indulgence of his own fancy. What he has added to the actual story, is upon a par with it. His genius was, as it were, a match for history as well as nature, and could grapple at will with either. The play is full of that pervading comprehensive power by which the poet could always make himself master of time and circumstances. It presents a fine picture of Roman pride and Eastern magnificence: and in the struggle between the two, the empire of the world seems suspended, 'like the swan's down-feather,

> That stands upon the swell at full of tide,
> And neither way inclines.'

The characters breathe, move, and live. Shakespear does not stand reasoning on what his characters would do or say, but at once *becomes* them, and speaks and acts for them. He does not present us with groups of stage-puppets or poetical machines making set speeches on human life, and acting from a calculation of problematical motives, but he brings living men and women on the scene, who speak and act from real feelings, according to the ebbs and flows of passion, without the least tincture of pedantry of logic or rhetoric. Nothing is made out by inference and analogy, by climax and antithesis, but every thing takes place just as it would have done in reality, according to the occasion.—The character of Cleopatra is a master-piece. What an extreme contrast it affords to Imogen! One would think it almost impossible for the same person to have drawn both. She is voluptuous, ostentatious, conscious, boastful of her charms, haughty, tyrannical, fickle. The luxurious pomp and gorgeous extravagance of the Egyptian queen are displayed in all their force and lustre, as well as the irregular grandeur of the soul of Mark Antony. Take only the first four lines that they speak as an example of the regal style of love-making.

*Cleopatra*: If it be love indeed, tell me how much?
*Antony*: There's beggary in the love that can be reckon'd.
*Cleopatra*: I'll set a bourn how far to be belov'd.
*Antony*: Then must thou needs find out new heav'n, new earth.

The rich and poetical description of her person beginning—

> The barge she sat in, like a burnish'd throne,
> Burnt on the water; the poop was beaten gold,
> Purple the sails, and so perfumed, that
> The winds were love-sick

seems to prepare the way for, and almost to justify the subsequent infatuation of Antony when in the sea-fight at Actium, he leaves the battle, and 'like a doating mallard' follows her flying sails.

Few things in Shakespear (and we know of nothing in any other author like them) have more of that local truth of imagination and character than the passage in which Cleopatra is represented conjecturing what were the employments of Antony in his absence—'He's speaking now, or murmuring—*Where's my serpent of old Nile?*' Or again, when she says to Antony, after the defeat at Actium, and his summoning up resolution to risk another fight—'It is my birthday; I had thought to have held it poor; but since my lord is Antony again, I will be Cleopatra.' Perhaps the finest burst of all is Antony's rage after his final defeat when he comes in, and surprises the messenger of Cæsar kissing her hand—

> To let a fellow that will take rewards,
> And say God quit you, be familiar with,
> My play-fellow, your hand; this kingly seal,
> And plighter of high hearts.

It is no wonder that he orders him to be whipped; but his low condition is not the true reason: there is another feeling which

lies deeper, though Antony's pride would not let him shew it, except by his rage; he suspects the fellow to be Cæsar's proxy.

Cleopatra's whole character is the triumph of the voluptuous, of the love of pleasure and the power of giving it, over every other consideration. Octavia is a dull foil to her, and Fulvia a shrew and shrill-tongued. What a picture do those lines give of her—

> Age cannot wither her, nor custom steal
> Her infinite variety. Other women cloy
> The appetites they feed, but she makes hungry
> Where most she satisfies.

What a spirit and fire in her conversation with Antony's messenger who brings her the unwelcome news of his marriage with Octavia! How all the pride of beauty and of high rank breaks out in her promised reward to him—

> There's gold, and here
> My bluest veins to kiss!

She had great and unpardonable faults, but the grandeur of her death almost redeems them. She learns from the depth of despair the strength of her affections. She keeps her queen-like state in the last disgrace, and her sense of the pleasurable in the last moments of her life. She tastes a luxury in death. After applying the asp, she says with fondness—

> Dost thou not see my baby at my breast,
> That sucks the nurse asleep?
> As sweet as balm, as soft as air, as gentle.
> Oh Antony!

It is worth while to observe that Shakespear has contrasted the extreme magnificence of the descriptions in this play with pictures of extreme suffering and physical horror, not less striking—partly perhaps to place the effeminate character of Mark Antony in a more favourable light, and at the same time to preserve a certain balance of feeling in the mind. Cæsar says, hearing of his rival's conduct at the court of Cleopatra,

> Antony,
> Leave thy lascivious wassels. When thou once
> Wert beaten from Mutina, where thou slew'st
> Hirtius and Pansa, consuls, at thy heel
> Did famine follow, whom thou fought'st against,
> Though daintily brought up, with patience more
> Than savages could suffer. Thou did'st drink
> The stale of horses, and the gilded puddle
> Which beast would cough at. Thy palate then did deign
> The roughest berry on the rudest hedge,
> Yea, like the stag, when snow the pasture sheets,
> The barks of trees thou browsed'st. On the Alps,
> It is reported, thou didst eat strange flesh,
> Which some did die to look on: and all this,
> It wounds thine honour, that I speak it now,
> Was borne so like a soldier, that thy cheek
> So much as lank'd not.

The passage after Antony's defeat by Augustus, where he is made to say—

> Yes, yes; he at Philippi kept
> His sword e'en like a dancer; while I struck
> The lean and wrinkled Cassius, and 'twas I
> That the mad Brutus ended

is one of those fine retrospections which show us the winding and eventful march of human life. The jealous attention which has been paid to the unities both of time and place has taken away the principle of perspective in the drama, and all the interest which objects derive from distance, from contrast, from privation, from change of fortune, from long-cherished passion; and contrasts our view of life from a strange and romantic dream, long, obscure, and infinite, into a smartly contested, three hours' inaugural disputation on its merits by the different candidates for theatrical applause.

The latter scenes of *Antony and Cleopatra* are full of the changes of accident and passion. Success and defeat follow one another with startling rapidity. Fortune sits upon her wheel more blind and giddy than usual. This precarious state and the approaching dissolution of his greatness are strikingly displayed in the dialogue of Antony with Eros.

> *Antony:* Eros, thou yet behold'st me?
> *Eros:* Ay, noble lord.
> *Antony:* Sometime we see a cloud that's dragonish,
> A vapour sometime, like a bear or lion,
> A towered citadel, a pendant rock,
> A forked mountain, or blue promontory
> With trees upon 't, that nod unto the world
> And mock our eyes with air. Thou hast seen these signs,
> They are black vesper's pageants.
> *Eros:* Ay, my lord.
> *Antony:* That which is now a horse, even with a thought
> The rack dislimns, and makes it indistinct
> As water is in water.
> *Eros:* It does, my lord.
> *Antony:* My good knave, Eros, now thy captain is
> Even such a body, etc.

This is, without doubt, one of the finest pieces of poetry in Shakespear. The splendour of the imagery, the semblance of reality, the lofty range of picturesque objects hanging over the world, their evanescent nature, the total uncertainty of what is left behind, are just like the mouldering schemes of human greatness. It is finer than Cleopatra's passionate lamentation over his fallen grandeur, because it is more dim, unstable, unsubstantial. Antony's headstrong presumption and infatuated determination to yield to Cleopatra's wishes to fight by sea instead of land, meet a merited punishment; and the extravagance of his resolutions, increasing with the desperateness of his circumstances, is well commented upon by Œnobarbus.

> I see men's judgments are
> A parcel of their fortunes, and things outward
> Do draw the inward quality after them
> To suffer all alike.

The repentance of Œnobarbus after his treachery to his master is the most affecting part of the play. He cannot recover from the blow which Antony's generosity gives him, and he dies broken-hearted, 'a master-leaver and a fugitive.'

Shakespear's genius has spread over the whole play a richness like the overflowing of the Nile.

## GEORGE BRANDES
### "The Dark Lady as a Model—The Fall of the Republic a World-Catastrophe"
*William Shakespeare: A Critical Study*
trs. William Archer and Mary Morison
1898, pp. 152–59

Assuming that it was Shakespeare's design in *Antony and Cleopatra*, as in *King Lear*, to evoke the conception of a world-catastrophe, we see that he could not in this play, as in *Macbeth* or *Othello*, focus the entire action around the leading characters alone. He could not even make the other characters completely subordinate to them; that would have rendered it

impossible for him to give the impression of majestic breadth, of an action embracing half of the then known world, which he wanted for the sake of the concluding effect.

He required in the group of figures surrounding Octavius Cæsar, and in the groups round Lepidus, Ventidius, and Sextus Pompeius, a counterpoise to Antony's group. He required the placid beauty and Roman rectitude of Octavia as a contrast to the volatile, intoxicating Egyptian. He required Enobarbus to serve as a sort of chorus and introduce an occasional touch of irony amid the high-flown passion of the play. In short, he required a throng of personages, and (in order to make us feel that the action was not taking place in some narrow precinct in a corner of Europe, but upon the stage of the world) he required a constant coming and going, sending and receiving of messengers, whose communications are awaited with anxiety, heard with bated breath, and not infrequently alter at one blow the situation of the chief characters.

The ambition which characterised Antony's past is what determines his relation to this great world; the love which has now taken such entire possession of him determines his relation to the Egyptian queen, and the consequent loss of all that his ambition had won for him. Whilst in a tragedy like Goethe's *Clavigo*, ambition plays the part of the tempter, and love is conceived as the good, the legitimate power, here it is love that is reprehensible, ambition that is proclaimed to be the great man's vocation and duty.

Thus Antony says (i. 2):

> These strong Egyptian fetters I must break,
> Or lose myself in dotage.

We saw that one element of Shakespeare's artist-nature was of use to him in his modelling of the figure of Antony. He himself had ultimately broken his fetters, or rather life had broken them for him; but as he wrote this great drama, he lived through again those years in which he himself had felt and spoken as he now made Antony feel and speak:

> A thousand groans, but thinking on thy face,
> One on another's neck, do witness bear,
> Thy black is fairest in my judgment's place.
> (*Sonnet* cxxxi.)

Day after day that woman now stood before him as his model who had been his life's Cleopatra—she to whom he had written of "lust in action":

> Mad in pursuit, and in possession so;
> Had, having, and in quest to have, extreme:
> A bliss in proof,—and prov'd, a very woe.
> (*Sonnet* cxxix.)

He had seen in her an irresistible and degrading Delilah, the Delilah whom De Vigny centuries later anathematised in a famous couplet.[1] He had bewailed, as Antony does now, that his beloved had belonged to many:

> If eyes, corrupt by over-partial looks,
> Be anchor'd in the bay where all men ride,
> . . . .
> Why should my heart think that a several plot
> Which my heart knows the wide world's common place?
> (*Sonnet* cxxxvii.)

He had, like Antony, suffered agonies from the coquetry she would lavish on any one she wanted to win. He had then burst forth in complaint, as Antony in the drama breaks out into frenzy:

> Tell me thou lov'st elsewhere; but in my sight,
> Dear heart, forbear to glance thine eye aside:

What need'st thou wound with cunning, when thy
    might
Is more than my o'er-pressed defence can 'bide?
               (*Sonnet* cxxxix.)

Now he no longer upbraided her; now he crowned her with a queenly diadem, and placed her, living, breathing, and in the largest sense true to nature, on that stage which was his world.

As in *Othello* he had made the lover-hero about as old as he was himself at the time he wrote the play, so now it interested him to represent this stately and splendid lover who was no longer young. In the Sonnets he had already dwelt upon his age. He says, for instance, in Sonnet cxxxviii.:

When my love swears that she is made of truth,
I do believe her, though I know she lies,
That she might think me some untutor'd youth,
Unlearned in the world's false subtleties.
Thus vainly thinking that she thinks me young,
Although she knows my days are past the best,
Simply I credit her false-speaking tongue.

When Antony and Cleopatra perished with each other, she was in her thirty-ninth, he in his fifty-fourth year. She was thus almost three times as old as Juliet, he more than double the age of Romeo. This correspondence with his own age pleases Shakespeare's fancy, and the fact that time has had no power to sear or wither this pair seems to hold them still farther aloof from the ordinary lot of humanity. The traces years have left upon the two have only given them a deeper beauty. All that they themselves in sadness, or others in spite, say to the contrary, signifies nothing. The contrast between their age in years and that which their beauty and passion make for them merely enhances and adds piquancy to the situation. It is in sheer malice that Pompey exclaims (ii. 1):

But all the charms of love,
Salt Cleopatra, soften thy *waned* lip!

This means no more than her own description of herself as "wrinkled." And it is on purpose to give the idea of Antony's age, of which in Plutarch there is no indication, that Shakespeare makes him dwell on the mixed colour of his own hair. He says (iii. 9):

My very hairs do mutiny; for the white
Reprove the brown for rashness, and they them
For fear and doting.

In the moment of despair he uses the expression (iii. ii): "To the boy Cæsar send this grizzled head." And again, after the last victory, he recurs to the idea in a tone of triumph. Exultingly he addresses Cleopatra (iv. 8):

What, girl! though grey
Do something mingle with our younger brown, yet
    ha' we
A brain that nourishes our nerves, and can
Get goal for goal of youth.

With a sure hand Shakespeare has depicted in Antony the mature man's fear of letting a moment pass unutilised: the vehement desire to enjoy before the hour strikes when all enjoyment must cease. Thus Antony says in one of his first speeches (i. 1):

Now, for the love of Love and her soft hours. . . .
There's not a minute of our lives should stretch
Without some pleasure now.

Then he feels the necessity of breaking his bonds. He makes Fulvia's death serve his purpose of gaining Cleopatra's consent to his departure; but even then he is not free. In order to bring out the contrast between Octavius the statesman and Antony the lover, Shakespeare emphasises the fact that Octavius has reports of the political situation brought to him every hour,

whilst Antony receives no other daily communication than the regularly arriving letters from Cleopatra which foment the longing that draws him back to Egypt.

As a means of allaying the storm and gaining peace to love his queen at leisure, he agrees to marry his opponent's sister, knowing that, when it suits him, he will neglect and repudiate her. Then vengeance overtakes him for having so contemptuously thrown away the empire over more than a third of the civilised world—vengeance for having said as he embraced Cleopatra (i. 1):

Let Rome in Tiber melt, and the wide arch
Of the ranged empire fall! Here is my space.

Rome melts through his fingers. Rome proclaims him a foe to her empire, and declares war against him. And he loses his power, his renown, his whole position, in the defeat which he so contemptibly brings upon himself at Actium. In Cleopatra flight was excusable. Her flight in the drama (which follows Plutarch and tradition) is due to cowardice; in reality it was prompted by tactical, judicious motives. But Antony was in honour bound to stay. He follows her in the tragedy (as in reality) from brainless, contemptible incapacity to remain when she has gone; leaving an army of 112,000 men and a fleet of 450 ships in the lurch, without leader or commander. Nine days did his troops await his return, rejecting every proposal of the enemy, incapable of believing in the desertion and flight of the general they admired and trusted. When at last they could no longer resist the conviction that he had sunk his soldier's honour in shame, they went over to Octavius.

After this everything turns on the mutual relation of Antony and Cleopatra, and Shakespeare has admirably depicted its ecstasies and its revulsions. Never before had they loved each other so wildly and so rapturously. Now it is not only he who openly calls her "Thou day o' the world!" She answers him with the cry, "Lord of lords! O infinite virtue!" (iv. 8)

Yet never before has their mutual distrust been so deep. She, who was at no time really great except in the arts of love and coquetry, has always felt distrustful of him, and yet never distrustful enough; for though she was prepared for a great deal, his marriage with Octavia overwhelmed her. He, knowing her past, knowing how often she has thrown herself away, and understanding her temperament, believes her false to him even when she is innocent, even when, as with Desdemona, only the vaguest of appearances are against her. In the end we see Antony develop into an Othello.

Here and there we come upon something in his character which seems to indicate that Shakespeare had been lately occupied with Macbeth. Cleopatra stimulates Anthony's voluptuousness, his sensuality, as Lady Macbeth spurred on her husband's ambition; and Antony fights his last battle with Macbeth's Berserk fury, facing with savage bravery what he knows to be invincibly superior force. But in his emotional life after the disaster of Actium it is Othello whom he more nearly resembles. He causes Octavius's messenger, Thyreus, to be whipped, simply because Cleopatra at parting has allowed him to kiss her hand. When some of her ships take to flight, he immediately believes in an alliance between her and the enemy, and heaps the coarsest invectives upon her, almost worse than those with which Othello overwhelms Desdemona. And in his monologue (iv. 10) he raves groundlessly like Othello:

Betray'd I am.
O this false soul of Egypt! this grave charm,—
Whose eye beck'd forth my wars, and call'd them
    home,
Whose bosom was my crownet, my chief end,

> Like a right gipsy, hath, at fast and loose,
> Beguil'd me to the very heart of loss.

They both, though faithless to the rest of the world, meant to be true to each other, but in the hour of trial they place no trust in each other's faithfulness. And all these strong emotions have shaken Antony's judgment. The braver he becomes in his misfortune, the more incapable is he of seeing things as they really are. Enobarbus closes the third act most felicitously with the words:

> I see still
> A diminution in our captain's brain
> Restores his heart: when valour preys on reason
> It eats the sword it fights with.

To tranquillise Antony's jealous frenzy, Cleopatra, who always finds readiest aid in a lie, sends him the false tidings of her death. In grief over her loss, he falls on his sword and mortally wounds himself. He is carried to her, and dies. She bursts forth:

> Noblest of men, woo't die?
> Hast thou no care of me? shall I abide
> In this dull world, which in they absence is
> No better than a sty?—O! see, my women,
> The crown o' the earth doth melt.

In Shakespeare, however, her first thought is not of dying herself. She endeavours to come to a compromise with Octavius, hands over to him an inventory of her treasures, and tries to trick him out of the larger half. It is only when she has ascertained that nothing, neither admiration for her beauty nor pity for her misfortunes, moves his cold sagacity, and that he is determined to exhibit her humiliation to the populace of Rome as one of the spectacles of his triumph, that she lets "the worm of Nilus" give her her death.

In these passages the poet has placed Cleopatra's behaviour in a much more unfavourable light than the Greek historian, whom he follows as far as details are concerned; and he has evidently done so wittingly and purposely, in order to complete his home-thrust at the type of woman whose dangerousness he has embodied in her. In Plutarch all these negotiations with Octavius were a feint to deceive the vigilance with which he thought to prevent her from killing herself. Suicide is her one thought, and he has baulked her in her first attempt. She pretends to cling to her treasures only to delude him into the belief that she still clings to life, and her heroic imposture is successful. Shakespeare, for whom she is ever the quintessence of the she-animal in women, disparages her intentionally by suppressing the historical explanation of her behaviour.[1]

The English critic, Arthur Symons, writes: "*Antony and Cleopatra* is the most wonderful, I think, of all Shakespeare's plays, and it is so mainly because the figure of Cleopatra is the most wonderful of Shakespeare's women. And not of Shakespeare's women only, but perhaps the most wonderful of women."

This is carrying enthusiasm almost too far. But thus much is true: the great attraction of his masterpiece lies in the unique figure of Cleopatra, elaborated as it is with all Shakespeare's human experience and artistic enthusiasm. But the greatness of the world-historic drama proceeds from the genius with which he has entwined the private relations of the two lovers with the course of history and the fate of empires. Just as Antony's ruin results from his connection with Cleopatra, so does the fall of the Roman Republic result from the contact of the simple hardihood of the West with the luxury of the East. Antony is Rome, Cleopatra is the Orient. When he perishes, a prey to the voluptuousness of the East, it seems as though Roman greatness and the Roman Republic expired with him.

Not Cæsar's ambition, nor Cæsar's assassination, but this crumbling to pieces of Roman greatness fourteen years later brings home to us the ultimate fall of the old world-republic, and impresses us with that sense of *universal annihilation* which in this play, as in *King Lear*, Shakespeare aims at begetting.

This is no tragedy of a domestic, limited nature like the conclusion of *Othello*; there is no young Fortinbras here, as in *Hamlet*, giving the promise of brighter and better times to come; the victory of Octavius brings glory to no one and promises nothing. No; the final picture is that which Shakespeare was bent on painting from the moment he felt himself attracted by this great theme—the picture of a world-catastrophe.

*Notes*

1.    Toujours ce compagnon dont le cœur n'est pas sur,
      La Femme—enfant malade et douze fois impur.
2.    Goethe has a marked imitation of Shakespeare's Cleopatra in the Adelheid of *Götz von Berlichingen*. And he has placed Weislingen between Adelheid and Maria as Antony stands between Cleopatra and Octavia—bound to the former and marrying the latter.

## M. W. MacCALLUM
### From *"Antony and Cleopatra"*
*Shakespeare's Roman Plays and Their Background*
1910, pp. 300–317

It may be taken as certain that Shakespeare did not at once set about continuing the story which he had brought to the end of one of its stages in *Julius Caesar* and of the future progress of which he had in that play given the partial programme. *Antony and Cleopatra* belongs to a different phase of his development.

Though not published, so far as we know, till it appeared in the Folio Edition of 1623, there is not much difficulty in finding its approximate date; and that, despite its close connection with *Julius Caesar* in the general march of events and in the re-employment of some of the characters, was some half-dozen years after the composition of its predecessor. The main grounds for this opinion, now almost universally accepted, are the following:

1. We learn from the *Stationers' Register* that the publisher, Edward Blount, had entered a "booke called *Antony and Cleopatra*" on May 20th, 1608. Some critics have maintained that this could not be Shakespeare's in view of the fact that in November, 1623, license was granted to the same Blount and the younger Jaggard, with whom he was now co-operating, to include in the collected edition the Shakespearian piece among sixteen plays of which the copies were "not formerly entered to other men." But the objection hardly applies, as the previous entry was in Blount's favour, and, though he is now associated with Jaggard, he may not have thought it necessary, because of a change of firm as it were, to describe himself as "another man." Even, however, if the authorship of the 1608 play be considered doubtful, its publication is significant. For, as has often been pointed out, it was customary when a piece was successful at one theatre to produce one on a similar subject at another. The mere existence, then, of an *Antony and Cleopatra* in the early months of 1608, is in so far an argument that about that time the great *Antony and Cleopatra* was attracting attention.

2. There is evidence that in the preceding years Shakespeare was occupied with and impressed by the *Life of Antony*.

*(a)* Plutarch tells how sorely Antony took to heart what he considered the disloyalty of his followers after Actium.

> He forsooke the citie and companie of his frendes, and built him a house in the sea, by the Ile of Pharos, upon certaine forced mountes which he caused to be cast into the sea, and dwelt there, as a man that banished him selfe from all mens companie; saying he would live Timons life, bicause he had the like wrong offered him, that was affore offered unto Timon: and that for the unthankefulnes of those he had done good unto, and whom he tooke to be his frendes he was angry with all men, and would trust no man.

In reference to this withdrawal of Antony's to the Timoneon, as he called his solitary house, Plutarch inserts the story of Timon of Athens, and there is reason to believe that Shakespeare made his contributions to the play of that name just before he wrote *Macbeth*, about the year 1606.[1]

*(b)* In *Macbeth* itself he has utilised the *Marcus Antonius* probably for one passage and certainly for another. In describing the scarcity of food among the Roman army in Parthia, Plutarch says:

> In the ende they were compelled to live of erbes and rootes, but they found few of them that men doe commonly eate of, and were enforced to tast of them that were never eaten before: among the which there was one that killed them, and *made them out of their witts*. For he that had once eaten of it, his memorye was gone from him, and he knewe no manner of thing.

Shakespeare is most likely thinking of this when after the disappearance of the witches, he makes Banquo exclaim in bewilderment:

> Were such things here as we do speak about?
> Or have we eaten on the insane *root*
> That *takes the reason prisoner*.
>
> (I. iii. 83.)

In any case *Macbeth* contains an unmistakable reminiscence of the soothsayer's warning to Antony.

> He . . . told Antonius plainly, that his fortune (which of it selfe was excellent good, and very great) was altogether bleamished, and obscured by Caesars fortune: and therefore he counselled him utterly to leave his company, and to get him as farre from him as he could. "For thy Demon," said he (that is to say, the good angell and spirit that kepeth thee), "is affraied of his, and being coragious and high when he is alone, becometh fearfull and timerous when he commeth neere unto the other."

Shakespeare was to make use of this in detail when he drew on the *Life* for an independent play.

> O Antony, stay not by his side:
> Thy demon, that's thy spirit which keeps thee, is
> Noble, courageous, high, unmatchable
> Where Caesar's is not; but, near him, thy angel
> Becomes a fear, as being o'erpower'd: therefore
> Make space enough between you.
>
> (II. iii. 18.)

But already in *Macbeth* it suggests a simile, when the King gives words to his mistrust of Banquo:

> There is none but he
> Whose being I do fear: and, under him,
> My Genius is rebuked; as, it is said,
> Mark Antony's was by Caesar.
>
> (III. i. 54.)

More interesting and convincing is a coincidence that

Malone pointed out in Chapman's *Bussy d' Ambois*, which was printed in 1607, but was probably written much earlier. Bussy says to Tamyra of the terrors of Sin:

> So our ignorance tames us, that we let
> His[2] shadows fright us: and like *empty clouds*
> In which our faulty apprehensions forge
> The forms of *dragons*, *lions*, elephants,
> When they *hold no proportion*, the sly charms
> Of the Witch Policy makes him like a monster.
>
> (III. i. 22.)

Compare Antony's words:

> Sometime we see a *cloud that's dragonish*:
> A vapour sometimes like a bear or lion . . .
> Here I am Antony:
> Yet *cannot hold this visible shape*.
>
> (IV. xiv. 2 and 13.)

It is hard to believe that there is no connection between these passages, and if there is Shakespeare must have been the debtor; but as *Bussy d' Ambois* was acted before 1600, this loan is without much value as a chronological indication.

3. Internal evidence likewise points to a date shortly after the composition of *Macbeth*.

*(a)* In versification especially valuable indications are furnished by the proportion of what Professor Ingram has called the light and the weak endings. By these terms he denotes the conclusion of the verse with a syllable that cannot easily or that cannot fully bear the stress which the normal scansion would lay upon it. In either case the effect is to break down the independence of the separate line as unit, and to vest the rhythm in the couplet or sequence, by forcing us on till we find an adequate resting-place. It thus has some analogy in formal prosody to enjambement, or the discrepancy between the metrical and the grammatical pause in prosody when viewed in connection with the sense. Now the employment of light and weak endings, on the one hand, and of enjambement on the other, is, generally speaking, much more frequent in the plays that are considered to be late than in those that are considered to be early. The tendency to enjambement indeed may be traced farther back and proceeds less regularly. But the laxity in regard to the endings comes with a rush and seems steadily to advance. It is first conspicuous in *Antony and Cleopatra* and reaches its maximum in *Henry VIII*. In this progress however there is one notable peculiarity. While it is unmistakable if the percentage be taken from the light and weak endings combined, or from the weak endings alone, it breaks down if the light endings be considered by themselves. Of them there is a decidedly higher proportion in *Antony and Cleopatra* than in *Coriolanus*, which nevertheless is almost universally held to be the later play. The reason probably is that the light endings mean a less revolutionary departure from the more rigid system and would therefore be the first to be attempted. When the ear had accustomed itself to them, it would be ready to accept the greater innovation. Thus the sudden outcrop of light and weak endings in *Antony and Cleopatra*, the preponderance of the light over the weak in that play, the increase in the total percentage of such endings and especially in the relative percentage of weak endings in the dramas that for various reasons are believed to be later, all confirm its position after *Macbeth* and before *Coriolanus*.

*(b)* The diction tells the same tale. Whether we admire it or no, we must admit that it is very concise, bold and difficult. Gervinus censures it as "forced, abrupt and obscure"; and it certainly makes demands on the reader. But Englishmen will rather agree with the well-known eulogy of Coleridge: "*Feliciter audax* is the motto for its style comparatively with that of

Shakspere's other works, even as it is the general motto of all his works compared with those of other poets. Be it remembered, too, that this happy valiancy of style is but the representative and result of all the material excellences so expressed." But in any case, whether to be praised or blamed, it is a typical example of Shakespeare's final manner, the manner that characterises *Coriolanus* and the Romances, and that shows itself only occasionally or incompletely in his preceding works.

4. A consideration of the tone of the tragedy yields similar results. It has been pointed out[4] that there is a gradual lightening in the atmosphere of Shakespeare's plays after the composition of *Othello* and *Lear*. In them, and especially in the latter, we move in the deepest gloom. It is to them that critics point who read in Shakespeare a message of pessimism and despair. And though there are not wanting, for those who will see them, glimpses of comfort and hope even in their horror of thick darkness, it must be owned that the misery and murder of Desdemona, the torture and remorse of Othello, the persecution of Lear, the hanging of Cordelia, are more harrowing and appalling than the heart can well endure. But we are conscious of a difference in the others of the group. Though Macbeth retains our sympathy to the last, his story does not rouse our questionings as do the stories of these earlier victims. We are well content that he should expiate his crimes, and that a cleaner hand should inherit the sceptre: we recognise the justice of the retribution and hail the dawn of better times. In *Coriolanus* the feeling is not only of assent but of exultation. True, the tragedy ends with the hero's death, but that is no unmitigated evil. He has won back something of his lost nobility and risen to the greatest height his nature could attain, in renouncing his revenge: after that what was there that he could live for either in Corioli or Rome?

*Antony and Cleopatra* has points of contact with both these plays, and shows like them that the night is on the wane. Of course in one way the view of life is still disconsolate enough. The lust of the flesh and the lust of the eye and the pride of life: ambitious egoism, uninspired craft and conventional propriety; these are the forces that clash in this gorgeous mêlée of the West and the East. At the outset passion holds the lists, then self-interest takes the lead, but principle never has a chance. We think of Lucifera's palace in the *Faerie Queene*, with the seven deadly sins passing in arrogant gala before the marble front, and with the shifting foundations beneath, the dungeons and ruins at the rear. The superb shows of life are displayed in all their superbness and in all their vanity. In the end their worshippers are exposed as their dupes. Antony is a cloud and a dream, Cleopatra no better than "a maid that milks and does the meanest chares": yet she sees that it is "paltry to be Caesar," and hears Antony mock at Caesar's luck. Whatever the goal, it is a futile one, and the objects of human desire are shown on their seamy side. We seem to lose sight of ideals, and idealism would be out of place. Even the passing reference to Shakespeare's own art shows a dissipation of the glamour. In *Julius Caesar* Brutus and Cassius had looked forward to an immortality of glory on the stage and evidently regard the theatre as equal to the highest demands, but now to Cleopatra it is only an affair of vulgar makeshifts that parodies what it presents.

> I shall see
> Some squeaking Cleopatra boy my greatness
> I' the posture of a whore.
>
> (v. ii. 219.)

In so far the impression produced is a cheerless one, and Gervinus has gone so far as to say: "There is no great or noble character among the personages, no really elevated feature in the action of this drama whether in its politics or its love affairs." This is excessive: but it is true that, as in *Timon*, the suggestion for which came from the same source and the composition of which may be dated a short time before, no very spiritual note is struck and no very dutiful figure is to the fore. And the background is a lurid one. "A world-catastrophe!" says Dr. Brandes, "(Shakespeare) has no mind now to write of anything else. What is sounding in his ears, what is filling his thoughts, is the crash of a world falling in ruins. . . . The might of Rome, stern and austere, shivered at the touch of Eastern voluptuousness. Everything sank, everything fell,—character and will, dominions and principalities, men and women. Everything was worm-eaten, serpent-bitten, poisoned by sensuality—everything tottered and collapsed."

Yet though the sultry splendours of the scenes seem to blast rather than foster, though the air is laden with pestilence, and none of the protagonists has escaped the infection, the total effect is anything but depressing. As in *Macbeth* we accept without demur the penalty exacted for the offence. As in *Coriolanus* we welcome the magnanimity that the offenders recover or achieve at the close. If there is less of acquiescence in vindicated justice than in the first, if there is less of elation at the triumph of the nobler self than in the second, there is yet something of both. In this respect too it seems to stand between them and we cannot be far wrong if we place it shortly after the one and shortly before the other, near the end of 1607.

And that means too that it comes near the end of Shakespeare's tragic period, when his four chief tragedies were already composed and when he was well aware of all the requirements of the tragic art. In his quartet of masterpieces he was free to fulfil these requirements without let or hindrance, for he was elaborating material that claimed no particular reverence from him. But now he turns once more to authorised history and in doing so once more submits to the limitations that in his practice authorised history imposed. Why he did so it is of course impossible to say. It was a famous story, accessible to the English public in some form or other from the days of Chaucer's *Legend of Good Women*, and at an early age Shakespeare was attracted by it, or at least was conversant with Cleopatra's reputation as one of the world's paragons of beauty. In *Romeo and Juliet* Mercutio includes her in his list of those, Dido, Hero, Thisbe and the rest, who in Romeo's eyes are nothing to his Rosaline; compared with that lady he finds "Cleopatra a gipsy."[5] And so indeed she was, for gipsy at first meant nothing else than Egyptian, and Skelton, in his *Garland of Laurel*, swearing by St. Mary of Egypt, exclaims:

> By Mary gipcy,
> Quod scripsi scripsi.

But in current belief the black-haired, tawny vagrants, who, from the commencement of the sixteenth century, despite cruel enactments cruelly enforced, began to swarm into England, were of Egyptian stock. And precisely in this there lay a paradox and riddle, for according to conventional ideas they were anything but comely, and yet it was a matter of common fame that a great Roman had thrown away rule, honour and duty in reckless adoration of the queen of the race. Perhaps Shakespeare had this typical instance in his mind when in *Midsummer Night's Dream* he talks of the madness of the lover who

> Sees Helen's beauty in a brow of Egypt.
>
> (v. i. II.)

For to the end the poet ignores the purity of Cleopatra's Greek descent, and seems by many touches to imagine her as one of the same type as those undesirable immigrants against whom the penal laws were of so little avail. Nevertheless he accepts the fact of her charm, and, in *As You Like It*, among the contributions which the "Heavenly Synod" levied on the supreme examples of womankind for the equipment of Rosalind, specifies "Cleopatra's majesty."[6] It is not the quality on which he was afterwards to lay stress, it is not the quality that Plutarch accentuates, nor is it likely to have been suggested by the gipsies he had seen. But there was another source on which he may have drawn. Next to the story of Julius Caesar, the story of Antony and Cleopatra was perhaps the prerogative Roman theme among the dramatists of the sixteenth century[7] and was associated with such illustrious personages as Jodelle and Garnier in France, and the Countess of Pembroke and Daniel in England. It is, as we have seen, highly probable that Shakespeare had read the versions of his compatriots at any rate, and their dignified harangues are just of the kind to produce the impression of loftiness and state.

Be that as it may, Cleopatra was a familiar name to Shakespeare when he began seriously to immerse himself in her history. We can understand how it would stir his heart as it filled in and corrected his previous vague surmises. What a revelation of her witchcraft would be that glowing picture of her progress when, careless and calculating, she condescended to obey the summons of the Roman conqueror and answer the charge that she had helped Brutus in his campaign.

> When she was sent unto by divers letters, both from Antonius him selfe and also from his frendes, she made so light of it, and mocked Antonius so much, that she disdained to set forward otherwise, but to take her barge in the river of Cydnus, the poope whereof was of gold, the sailes of purple, and the owers of silver, which kept stroke in rowing after the sounde of the musicke of flutes, howboyes, citherns, violls, and such other instruments as they played upon in the barge. And now for the person of her selfe: she was layed under a pavillion of cloth of gold of tissue, apparelled and attired like the goddesse Venus, commonly drawen in picture: and hard by her, on either hand of her, pretie faire boyes apparelled as painters doe set forth god Cupide, with little fannes in their hands, with which they fanned wind upon her. Her ladies and gentlewomen also, the fairest of them were apparelled like the nymphes Nereides (which are the mermaides of the waters) and like the Graces, some stearing the helme, others tending the tackle and ropes of the barge, out of which there came a wonderfull passing sweete savor of perfumes, that perfumed the wharfes side pestered[8] with innumerable multitudes of people. Some of them followed the barge all alongest the rivers side: others also ranne out of the citie to see her comming in. So that in thend, there ranne such multitudes of people one after an other to see her, that Antonius was left post alone in the market place, in his Imperiall seate to geve audience: and there went a rumor in the peoples mouthes that the goddesse Venus was come to play with the god Bacchus,[9] for the generall good of all Asia. When Cleopatra landed, Antonius sent to invite her to supper with him. But she sent him word againe, he should doe better rather to come and suppe with her. Antonius therefore to shew him selfe curteous unto her at her arrivall, was contented to obey her, and went to supper to her: where he found such passing sumptuous fare that no tongue can express it.

Only by a few touches has Shakespeare excelled his copy in the words of Enobarbus: but he has merely heightened and nowhere altered the effect.

> The barge she sat in, like a *burnished throne*,
> *Burn'd* on the water: the poop was beaten gold:
> Purple the sails and so perfumed that
> The winds *were love-sick* with them: the oars were
>     silver,
> Which to the tune of flutes kept stroke and made
> *The water which they beat to follow faster*,
> *As amorous of their strokes*. For her own person,
> *It beggar'd all description*: she did lie
> In her pavilion—cloth-of-gold of tissue—
> *O'er picturing* that Venus where we see
> *The fancy outwork nature*: on each side of her
> Stood pretty dimpled boys, like smiling Cupids
> With divers-colour'd fans, whose wind did seem
> To *glow the delicate cheeks which they did cool*,
> *And what they did undid.* . . .
> Her gentlewoman, like the Nereides
> So many mermaids, *tended her i' the eyes*
> And made their bends adornings: at the helm
> A seeming mermaid steers: the *silken* tackle
> *Swell with the touches of those flower-soft hands*
> That *yarely* frame the office. From the barge
> A *strange invisible* perfume hits the sense
> Of the adjacent wharfs: and Antony,
> *Enthroned i' the market-place, did sit alone*,
> *Whistling the air*: which, *but for vacancy*,
> *Had gone to gaze on Cleopatra too*,
> *And made a gap in nature.* . . .
> Upon her landing, Antony sent to her,
> Invited her to supper: she replied
> It should be better he became her guest;
> Which she entreated: our courteous Antony,
> *Whom ne'er the word of "No" woman heard speak*,
> *Being barber'd ten times o'er*, goes to the feast
> And *for his ordinary pays his heart*
> *For what his eyes eat only.*
>
>                         (II. ii. 196.)

And the impression of all this magnificence had not faded from Shakespeare's mind when in after years he wrote his *Cymbeline*. Imogen's chamber

>             is hang'd
> With tapestry of silk and silver; the story
> Proud Cleopatra, when she met her Roman,
> And Cydnus swell'd above the banks, or for
> The press of boats or pride.[10]
>
>                         (II. iv. 68.)

But it was not only the prodigality of charm that would enthral the poet. In the relation of the lovers, in the character of Cleopatra, in the nature of her ascendancy, there is something that reminds us of the story of passion enshrined in the *Sonnets*. No doubt it is uncertain whether these in detail are to be regarded as biographical, but biographical they are at the core, at least in the sense that they are authentic utterance of feelings actually experienced. No doubt, too, the balance of evidence points to their composition, at least in the parts that deal with his unknown leman, early in Shakespeare's career; but for that very reason the memories would be fitter to help him in interpreting the poetry of the historical record, for as Wordsworth says: "Poetry is emotion recollected in tranquillity." So once more Shakespeare may have been moved to "make old offences of affections new," that is, to infuse the passion of his own youth into this tale of "old unhappy far-off things." His bygone sorrows of the *Sonnets* come back to him when he is writing the drama, mirror themselves in some of the situations and sentiments, and echo in the wording of a few of the lines. It is of course easy to exaggerate the importance of these reminiscences. The Dark Lady has been described as the original of Cleopatra, but the original of Cleopatra is the Cleopatra of Plutarch, and in many ways she is unlike the temptress of the poet. She is dowered with a marvellous beauty which all from Enobarbus to Octavius acknowledge, while the other is "foul" in all eyes save those of her lover; her face "hath not the power to make love groan"; and in her there is no hint of Cleopatra's royalty of soul. Nor is the devotion of Antony the devotion of the sonneteer; it is far more absolute and unquestioning, it is also far more comrade-like and sympathetic; at first he exults in it without shame, and never till the last distracted days does suspicion or contempt enter his heart. Still less is his passing spasm of jealousy at the close like the chronic jealousy of the poet. It is a vengeful frenzy that must find other outlets as well as the self-accusing remonstrances and impotent rebukes of the lyrical complaints. The resemblance between sonnets and play is confined to the single feature that they both tell the story of an unlawful passion for a dark woman—for this was Shakespeare's fixed idea in regard to Cleopatra—whose character and reputation were stained, whose influence was pernicious, and whose fatal spells depended largely on her arts and intellect. But this was enough to give Shakespeare, as it were, a personal insight into the case, and a personal interest in it, to furnish him with the key to the situation and place him at the centre.

And there was another point of contact between the author and the hero of the tragedy. It is stated in Plutarch's account of Antony: "Some say that he lived three and fiftie yeares: and others say six and fiftie." But the action begins a decade, or (for, as we shall see, there is a jumbling of dates in the opening scenes like that which we have noted in the corresponding ones of *Julius Caesar*) more than a decade before the final catastrophe. Thus Shakespeare would imagine Antony at the outset as between forty-two and forty-six, practically on the same *niveau* of life as himself, for in 1607–1608 he was in his forty-fourth year. They had reached the same stadium in their career, had the same general outlook on the future, had their great triumphs behind them, and yet with powers hardly impaired they both could say,

> Though grey
> Do something mingle with our younger brown, yet
> ha' we
> A brain that nourishes our nerves, and can
> Get goal for goal of youth.

　　　　　　　　　　　　　　　(IV. viii. 19.)

There would be a general sympathy of attitude, and it even extends to something in the poet himself analogous to the headlong ardour of Antony. In the years that had elapsed since Shakespeare gave the first instalment of his story in *Julius Caesar*, a certain change had been proceeding in his art. The present drama belongs to a different epoch of his authorship, an epoch not of less force but of less restrained force, an epoch when he works perhaps with less austerity of stroke and less intellectualism, but—strange that it should be so in advancing years—with more abandonment to the suggestions of imagination and passion. In all these respects the fortunes of Antony and Cleopatra would offer him a fit material. In the second as compared with the first Roman play, there is certainly no decline. The subject is different, the point of view is different, the treatment is different, but subject, point of view and treatment all harmonise with each other, and the whole in its kind is as great as could be.

Perhaps some such considerations may explain why Shakespeare, after he had been for seven years expatiating on the heights of free tragic invention, yet returned for a time to a theme which, with his ideas of loyalty to recorded fact, dragged him back in some measure to the embarrassments of the chronicle history. It was all so congenial, that he was willing to face the disadvantages of an action that straggled over years and continents, of a multiplicity of short scenes that in the third act rise to a total of thirteen and in the fourth to a total of fifteen, of a number of episodic personages who appear without preparation and vanish almost without note. He had to lay his account with this if he dramatised these transactions at all, for to him they were serious matters that his fancy must not be allowed to distort. Indeed he accepts the conditions so unreservedly and makes so little effort to evade them, that his mind seems to have taken the ply, and he resorts to the meagre, episodical scene, not only when Plutarch's narrative suggests it, but when he is making additions of his own and when no very obvious advantage is to be secured. This is the only explanation that readily presents itself for the fourth scene of the second act, which in ten lines describes Lepidus' leave-taking of Mecaenas and Agrippa.[11] There is for this no authority in the *Life*; and what object does it serve? It may indicate on the one hand the punctilious deference that Octavius' minsters deem fit to show as yet to the incompetent Triumvir, and on the other his lack of efficient energy in allowing his private purposes to make him two days late at the *rendezvous* which he himself has advocated as urgent. But these hints could quite well have been conveyed in some other way, and this invented scene seems theatrically and dramatically quite otiose. Nevertheless, and this is the point to observe, it so fits into the pattern of the chronicle play that it does not force itself on one's notice as superfluous.

It is partly for this reason that *Antony and Cleopatra* holds its distinctive place among Shakespeare's masterpieces. On the one hand there is no play that springs more spontaneously out of the heart of its author, and into which he has breathed a larger portion of his inspiration; and on the other there is none that is more purely historical, so that in this respect it is comparable among the Roman dramas to *Richard II.* in the English series. This was the double characteristic that Coleridge emphasises in his *Notes on Shakespeare's Plays*: "There is not one in which he has followed history so minutely, and yet there are few in which he impresses the notion of angelic strength so much—perhaps none in which he impresses it more strongly. This is greatly owing to the manner in which the fiery force is sustained throughout, and to the numerous momentary flashes of nature counteracting the historical abstraction." The angelic strength, the fiery force, the flashes of nature are due to his complete sympathy with the facts, but that makes his close adherence to his authority all the more remarkable.

*Notes*

1. See Bradley, *Shakespearian Tragedy*.
2. I have said nothing of other possible references and loans because they seem to me irrelevant or doubtful. Thus Malone drew attention to the words of Morose in Ben Jonson's *Epicoene*: "Nay, I would sit out a play that were nothing but fights at sea, drum, trumpet and target." He thought that this remark might contain ironical allusion to the battle scenes in *Antony and Cleopatra*, for instance the stage direction at the head of Act III., Scene 10: "Canidius marcheth with his land army one way over the stage: and Taurus, the lieutenant of Caesar the other way. After their going in is heard the noise of a sea-fight." But even were this more certain than it is, it would only prove that *Antony and Cleopatra* had made so much impression as to give points to the satirist some time after its performance: it would not help us to the date. For *Epicoene* belongs to 1610, and no one would place *Antony and Cleopatra* so late.
3. *i.e.* Sin's.

4. Bradley, *Shakespearian Tragedy.*

5. II. iv. 44.

6. III. ii. 154.

7. Besides the plays discussed in the Introduction as having a possible place in the lineage of Shakespeare's, others were produced on the Continent, which in that respect are quite negligible but which serve to prove the widespread interest in the subject. Thus in 1560 Hans Sachs in Germany composed, in seven acts, one of his home-spun, well-meant dramas that were intended to edify spectator or reader. Thus in 1583 Cinthio in Italy treated the same theme, and it has been conjectured, by Klein, that his *Cleopatra* was known to Shakespeare. Certainly Shakespeare makes use of Cinthio's novels, but the particulars signalised by Klein, that are common to the English and to the Italian tragedy, which latter I have not been able to procure, are, to use Klein's own term, merely "external," and are to be explained, in so far as they are valid at all, which Moeller (*Kleopatra in der Tragödien-literatur*) disputes, by reference to Plutarch. An additional one which Moeller suggests without attaching much weight to it, is even less plausible than he supposes. He points out that Octavius' emissary, who in Plutarch is called Thyrsus, in Cinthio becomes Tireo, as in Shakespeare he similarly becomes Thyreus; but he notes that this is also the name that Shakespeare would get from North. As a matter of fact, however, in the 1623 folio of *Antony and Cleopatra* and in subsequent editions till the time of Theobald, this personage, for some reason or other as yet undiscovered, is styled Thidias; so the alleged coincidence is not so much unimportant as fallacious. A third tragedy, Montreuil's *Cléopatre*, which like Cinthio's is inaccessible to me, was published in France in 1595; but to judge from Moeller's analysis and the list of *dramatis personae*, it has no contact with Shakespeare's.

8. obstructed.

9. Antony had already been worshipped as that deity.

10. It is rather strange that Shakespeare, whose "accessories" are usually relevant, should choose such a subject for the decoration of Imogen's room. Mr. Bradley, in a note to his essay on *Antony and Cleopatra* says: "Of the 'good' heroines, Imogen is the one who has most of [Cleopatra's] spirit of fire and air." This is one of the things one sees to be true as soon as one reads it: can it be that their creator has brought them into association through some feeling, conscious or unconscious, of their kinship in this important respect?

I regret that Mr. Bradley's admirable study, which appeared when I was travelling in the Far East, escaped my notice till a few days ago, when it was too late to use it for my discussion.

11. Of course the division into scenes is not indicated in the Folio, but a new "place" is obviously required for this conversation. Of course, too, change of scene did not mean so much on the Elizabethan as on the modern stage, but it must always have counted for something. Every allowance made, the above criticism seems to me valid.

# *Coriolanus*

### WILLIAM HAZLITT
### From *"Coriolanus"*
### *Characters of Shakespear's Plays*
### 1817

Shakespear has in this play shewn himself well versed in history and state-affairs. *Coriolanus* is a store-house of political common-places. Any one who studies it may save himself the trouble of reading Burke's *Reflections*, or Paine's *Rights of Man*, or the Debates in both Houses of Parliament since the French Revolution or our own. The arguments for and against aristocracy or democracy, on the privileges of the few and the claims of the many, on liberty and slavery, power and the abuse of it, peace and war, are here very ably handled, with the spirit of a poet and the acuteness of a philosopher. Shakespear himself seems to have had a leaning to the arbitrary side of the question, perhaps from some feeling of contempt for his own origin; and to have spared no occasion of baiting the rabble. What he says of them is very true: what he says of their betters is also very true, though he dwells less upon it.—The cause of the people is indeed but little calculated as a subject for poetry: it admits of rhetoric, which goes into argument and explanation, but it presents no immediate or distinct images to the mind, 'no jutting frieze, buttress, or coigne of vantage' for poetry 'to make its pendant bed and procreant cradle in.' The language of poetry naturally falls in with the language of power. The imagination is an exaggerating and exclusive faculty: it takes from one thing to add to another: it accumulates circumstances together to give the greatest possible effect to a favourite object. The understanding is a dividing and measuring faculty: it judges of things not according to their immediate impression on the mind, but according to their relations to one another. The one is a monopolising faculty, which seeks the greatest quantity of present excitement by inequality and disproportion; the other is a distributive faculty, which seeks the greatest quantity of ultimate good, by justice and proportion. The one is an aristocratical, the other a republican faculty. The principle of poetry is a very anti-levelling principle. It aims at effect, it exists by contrast. It admits of no medium. It is every thing by excess. It rises above the ordinary standard of sufferings and crimes. It presents a dazzling appearance. It shows its head turretted, crowned, and crested. Its front is gilt and blood-stained. Before it 'it carries noise, and behind it leaves tears.' It has its altars and its victims, sacrifices, human sacrifices. Kings, priests, nobles, are its train-bearers, tyrants and slaves its executioners.—'Carnage is its daughter.'—Poetry is right-royal. It puts the individual for the species, the one above the infinite many, might before right. A lion hunting a flock of sheep or a herd of wild asses is a more poetical object than they; and we even take part with the lordly beast, because our vanity or some other feeling makes us disposed to place ourselves in the situation of the strongest party. So we feel some concern for the poor citizens of Rome when they meet together to compare their wants and grievances, till Coriolanus comes in and with blows and big words drives this set of 'poor rats,' this rascal scum, to their homes and beggary before him. There is nothing heroical in a multitude of miserable rogues not wishing to be starved, or complaining that they are like to be so: but when a single man comes forward to brave their cries and to make them submit to the last indignities, from mere pride and self-will, our admiration of his prowess is immediately converted into contempt for their pusillanimity. The insolence of power is stronger than the plea of necessity. The tame submission to usurped authority or even the natural resistance to it has nothing to excite or flatter the imagination: it is the assumption of a right to insult or oppress others that carries an imposing air of superiority with it. We had rather be the oppressor than the oppressed. The love of power in ourselves and the admiration of it in others are both natural to man: the one makes him a tyrant, the other a slave. Wrong dressed out in pride, pomp, and circumstance, has more attraction than abstract right.—Coriolanus complains of the fickleness of the people: yet, the instant he cannot gratify his pride and obstinacy at their expense, he turns his arms against his country. If his country was not worth defending, why did he build his pride on its defence? He is a conquerer and a hero; he conquers other countries, and makes this a plea for enslaving his own; and when he is prevented from doing so, he leagues with its enemies to destroy his country. He rates the poeple 'as if he were a God to punish, and not a man of their infirmity.' He scoffs at one of their tribunes for maintaining their rights and franchises: 'Mark you his absolute *shall*?' not marking his own absolute *will* to take every thing from them, his impatience of the slightest opposition to his own pretensions being in proportion to their arrogance and absurdity. If the great and powerful had the beneficence and wisdom of Gods, then all this would have been well: if with a greater knowledge of what is good for the people, they had as great a care for their interest as they have themselves, if they were seated above the world, sympathising with the welfare, but not feeling the passions of men, receiving neither good nor hurt from them, but bestowing their benefits as free gifts on them, they might then rule over them like another Providence. But this is not the case. Coriolanus is unwilling that the senate should shew their 'cares' for the people, lest their 'cares' should be construed into 'fears,' to the subversion of all due authority; and he is no sooner disappointed in his schemes to deprive the people not only of the cares of the state, but of all power to redress themselves, than Volumnia is made madly to exclaim,

> Now the red pestilence strike all trades in Rome,
> And occupations perish.

This is but natural: it is but natural for a mother to have more regard for her son than for a whole city; but then the city should be left to take some care of itself. The care of the state cannot, we here see, be safely entrusted to maternal affection, or to the domestic charities of high life. The great have private feelings of their own, to which the interests of humanity and justice must courtesy. Their interests are so far from being the same as those of the community, that they are in direct and necessary opposition to them; their power is at the expense of *our* weakness; their riches of *our* poverty; their pride of *our* degradation; their splendour of *our* wretchedness; their tyranny of *our* servitude. If they had the superior knowledge ascribed to them (which they have not) it would only render them so much more formidable; and from Gods would convert them into Devils. The whole dramatic moral of *Coriolanus* is that those who have little shall have less, and that those who have much shall take all that others have left. The people are poor; therefore they ought to be starved. They are slaves; therefore they ought to be beaten. They work hard; therefore they ought to be treated like beasts of burden. They are ignorant; therefore they ought not to be allowed to feel that they want food, or clothing, or rest, that they are enslaved, oppressed, and miserable. This is the logic of the imagination and the passions; which seek to aggrandize what excites admiration and to heap contempt on misery, to raise power into tyranny, and to make tyranny absolute; to thrust down that which is low still lower, and to make wretches desperate: to exalt magistrates into kings, kings into gods; to degrade subjects to the rank of slaves, and slaves to the condition of brutes. The history of mankind is a romance, a mask, a tragedy, constructed upon the principles of *poetical justice*; it is a noble or royal hunt, in which what is sport to the few is death to the many, and in which the spectators halloo and encourage the strong to set upon the weak, and cry havoc in the chase though they do not share in the spoil. We may depend upon it that what men delight to read in books, they will put in practice in reality.

One of the most natural traits in this play is the difference of the interest taken in the success of Coriolanus by his wife and mother. The one is only anxious for his honour; the other is fearful for his life.

> *Volumnia:* Methinks I hither hear your husband's
>      drum:
> I see him pluck Aufidius down by th' hair:
> Methinks I see him stamp thus—and call thus—
> Come on, ye cowards; ye were got in fear
> Though you were born in Rome; his bloody brow
> With his mail'd hand then wiping, forth he goes
> Like to a harvest man, that's task'd to mow
> Or all, or lose his hire.
> *Virgilia:* His bloody brow! Oh Jupiter, no blood.
> *Volumnia:* Away, you fool; it more becomes a man
> Than gilt his trophy. The breast of Hecuba,
> When she did suckle Hector, look'd not lovelier
> Than Hector's forehead, when it spit forth blood
> At Grecian swords contending.

When she hears the trumpets that proclaim her son's return, she says in the true spirit of a Roman matron,

> These are the ushers of Martius: before him
> He carries noise, and behind him he leaves tears.
> Death, that dark spirit, in's nervy arm doth lie,
> Which being advanc'd, declines, and then men die.

Coriolanus himself is a complete character: his love of reputation, his contempt of popular opinion, his pride and modesty, are consequences of each other. His pride consists in the inflexible sternness of his will; his love of glory is a determined desire to bear down all opposition, and to extort the admiration both of friends and foes. His contempt for popular favour, his unwillingness to hear his own praises, spring from the same source. He cannot contradict the praises that are bestowed upon him; therefore he is impatient at hearing them. He would enforce the good opinion of others by his actions, but does not want their acknowledgments in words.

> Pray now, no more: my mother,
> Who has a charter to extol her blood,
> When she does praise me, grieves me.

His magnanimity is of the same kind. He admires in an enemy that courage which he honours in himself; he places himself on the hearth of Aufidius with the same confidence that he would have met him in the field, and feels that by putting himself in his power, he takes from him all temptation for using it against him.

A. C. BRADLEY

*"Coriolanus"* (1912)

*A Miscellany*

1929, pp. 73–104

*C*oriolanus[1] is beyond doubt among the latest of Shakespeare's tragedies: there is some reason for thinking it the last. Like all those that succeeded *Hamlet*, it is a tragedy of vehement passion; and in none of them are more striking revolutions of fortune displayed. It is full of power, and almost every one feels it to be a noble work. We may say of it, as of its hero, that, if not one of Shakespeare's greatest creations, it is certainly one of his biggest.

Nevertheless, it is scarcely popular. It is seldom acted, and perhaps no reader ever called it his favourite play. Indeed, except for educational purposes, it is probably, after *Timon*, the least generally read of the tragedies. Even the critic who feels bound to rank it above *Romeo and Juliet*, and even above *Julius Caesar*, may add that he prefers those dramas all the same; and if he ignores his personal preferences, still we do not find him asking whether it is not the equal of the four great tragedies. He may feel this doubt as to *Antony and Cleopatra*, but not as to *Coriolanus*.

The question why this should be so will at once tell us something about the drama. We cannot say that it shows any decline in Shakespeare's powers, though in parts it may show slackness in their use. It has defects, some of which are due to the historical material; but all the tragedies have defects, and the material of *Antony and Cleopatra* was even more troublesome. There is no love-story; but then there is none in *Macbeth*, and next to none in *King Lear*. Thanks in part to the badness of the Folio text, the reader is impeded by obscurities of language and irritated by the mangling of Shakespeare's metre; yet these annoyances would not much diminish the effect of *Othello*. It may seem a more serious obstacle that the hero's faults are repellent and chill our sympathy; but Macbeth, to say nothing of his murders, is a much less noble being than Coriolanus. All this doubtless goes for something; yet there must be some further reason why this drama stands apart from the four great tragedies and *Antony and Cleopatra*. And one main reason seems to be this. Shakespeare could construe the story he found only by conceiving the hero's character in a certain way; and he had to set the whole drama in tune with that conception. In this he was, no doubt, perfectly right; but he closed the door on certain effects, in the absence of which his whole power in tragedy could not be displayed. He had to be content with something less, or rather with something else; and so have we.

Most of the great tragedies leave a certain imaginative impression of the highest value, which I describe in terms intended merely to recall it. What we witness is not the passion and doom of mere individuals. The forces that meet in the tragedy stretch far beyond the little group of figures and the tiny tract of space and time in which they appear. The darkness that covers the scene, and the light that strikes across it, are more than our common night and day. The hero's fate is, in one sense, intelligible, for it follows from his character and the conditions in which he is placed; and yet everything, character, conditions, and issue, is mystery. Now of this effect there is very little in *Coriolanus*. No doubt the story has a universal meaning, since the contending forces are permanent constituents of human nature; but that peculiar *imaginative* effect or atmosphere is hardly felt. And, thinking of the play, we notice that the means by which it is produced elsewhere are almost absent here. One of these means is the use of the supernatural; another a treatment of nature which makes her appear not merely as a background, nor even merely as a conscious witness of human feelings, sufferings, and deeds, but as a vaster fellow-actor and fellow-sufferer. Remove in fancy from *Hamlet*, *Lear*, and *Macbeth*, all that appeals to imagination through these means, and you find them utterly changed, but brought nearer to *Coriolanus*. Here Shakespeare has deliberately withdrawn his hand from those engines. He found, of course, in Plutarch allusions to the gods, and some of these he used; but he does not make us feel that the gods take part in the story. He found also wonders in the firmament, portents, a strange vision seen by a slave, a statue that spoke. He found that the Romans in their extremity sent the priests, augurs, and soothsayers to plead with Coriolanus; and that the embassy of the women which saved Rome was due to a thought which

came suddenly to Valeria, which she herself regarded as a divine inspiration, and on the nature of which Plutarch speculates. But the whole of this Shakespeare ignored. Nor would he use that other instrument I spoke of. Coriolanus was not the man to be terrified by twilight, or to feel that the stars or the wind took part against or with him. If Lear's thunderstorm had beat upon his head, he would merely have set his teeth. And not only is the mystery of nature absent; she is scarcely present even as a background. The hero's grim description of his abode in exile as "the city of kites and crows" (it is not in Plutarch) is almost all we have. In short, *Coriolanus* has scarcely more atmosphere, either supernatural or natural, than the average serious prose drama of to-day.

In Shakespeare's greatest tragedies there is a second source—in one or two the chief source—of supreme imaginative appeal, the exhibition of inward conflict, or of the outburst of one or another passion, terrible, heart-rending, or glorious to witness. At these moments the speaker becomes the greatest of poets; and yet, the dramatic convention admitted, he speaks in character. The hero in *Coriolanus* is never thus the greatest of poets, and he could not be so without a breach of more than dramatic convention. His nature is large, simple, passionate; but (except in one point, to which I will return, as it is irrelevant here) his nature is not, in any marked degree, imaginative. He feels all the rapture, but not, like Othello, all the poetry, of war. He covets honour no less than Hotspur, but he has not Hotspur's vision of honour. He meets with ingratitude, like Timon, but it does not transfigure all mankind for him. He is very eloquent, but his only free eloquence is that of vituperation and scorn. It is sometimes more than eloquence, it is splended poetry; but it is never such magical poetry as we hear in the four greatest tragedies. Then, too, it lies in his nature that his deepest and most sacred feeling, that for his mother, is almost dumb. It governs his life and leads him uncomplaining towards death, but it cannot speak. And, finally, his inward conflicts are veiled from us. The change that came when he found himself alone and homeless in exile is not exhibited. The result is partly seen in the one soliloquy of this drama, but the process is hidden. Of the passion that possesses him when his triumph seems at hand we get a far more vivid idea from the words of Cominius than from any words of his own:

> I tell you he does sit in gold, his eye
> Red as 'twould burn Rome.

In the most famous scene, when his fate is being decided, only one short sentence reveals the gradual loosening of his purpose during his mother's speech. The actor's face and hands and bearing must show it, not the hero's voice; and his submission is announced in a few quiet words, deeply moving and impressive, but destitute of the effect we know elsewhere of a lightning-flash that rends the darkness and discloses every cranny of the speaker's soul. All this we can see to be as it should be, but it does set limits to the flight of Shakespeare's imagination.

I have spoken of something that we miss in *Coriolanus*. Unfortunately there is something which a good many readers find, or think they find, and which makes it distasteful to them. A political conflict is never the centre of interest in Shakespeare's plays, but in the historical plays it is an element more or less essential, and in this one it is very prominent. Here, too, since it may be plausibly described as a conflict between people and nobles, or democracy and aristocracy, the issue is felt to be still alive. And Shakespeare, it is thought, shows an animus, and sides against the people. A hundred years ago Hazlitt, dealing with this tragedy, wrote: "Shakespeare himself seems to have had a leaning to the arbitrary side of the question, perhaps from some feeling of contempt for his own origin; and to have spared no occasion of baiting the rabble. What he says of them is very true; what he says of their betters is also very true, though he dwells less upon it." This language is very tentative and mild compared with that of some later writers. According to one, Shakespeare "loathed the common Englishman." He was a neuropath who could not endure the greasy aprons and noisome breath of mechanics, and "a snob of the purest English water." According to another, he was probably afflicted for some years with an "enormous self-esteem." A hero similarly afflicted, and a nauseous mob—behold the play!

I do not propose to join this dance, or even to ask whether any reasonable conjecture as to Shakespeare's political views and feelings could be formed from the study of this play and of others. But it may be worth while to mention certain questions which should be weighed by any one who makes the adventure. Are not the chief weaknesses and vices shown by the populace, or attributed to it by speakers, in these plays, those with which it had been habitually charged in antiquity and the Middle Ages; and did not Shakespeare find this common form, if nowhere else, in Plutarch? Again, if these traits and charges are heightened in his dramas, what else do we expect in drama, and especially in that of the Elizabethans? Granted, next, that in Shakespeare the people play a sorry political part, is that played by English nobles and Roman patricians much more glorious or beneficent; and if, in Hazlitt's phrase, Shakespeare says more of the faults of the people than of those of their betters, would we have him give to humble unlettered persons the powers of invective of lordly orators? Further, is abuse of the people ever dramatically inappropriate in Shakespeare; and is it given to Henry the Fifth, or Brutus (who had some cause for it), or, in short, to any of the most attractive characters? Is there not, besides, a great difference between his picture of the people taken as individuals, even when they talk politics, and his picture of them as a crowd or mob? Is not the former, however humorously critical, always kindly; and is a personal bias really needed to account for the latter? And, to end a catalogue easy to prolong, might not that talk, which is scarcely peculiar to Shakespeare, about greasy caps and offensive odours, have some other origin than his artistic nerves? He had, after all, some little gift of observation, and, when first he mixed with a class above his own, might he not resemble a son of the people now who, coming among his betters, observes with amusement the place held in their decalogue by the morning bath? I do not for a moment suggest that, by weighing such questions as these, we should be led to imagine Shakespeare as any more inclined to champion the populace than Spenser or Hooker or Bacon; but I think we should feel it extremely hazardous to ascribe to him any political feelings at all, and ridiculous to pretend to certainty on the subject.

Let us turn to the play. The representation of the people, whatever else it may be, is part of a dramatic design. This design is based on the main facts of the story, and these imply a certain character in the people and the hero. Since the issue is tragic, the conflict between them must be felt to be unavoidable and wellnigh hopeless. The necessity for dramatic sympathy with both sides demands that on both there should be some right and some wrong, both virtues and failings; and if the hero's monstrous purpose of destroying his native city is not to extinguish our sympathy, the provocation he receives must be great. This being so, the picture of the people is, surely, no darker than it had to be; the desired result would have been more easily secured by making it darker still. And one must go further. As regards the political situation the total effect of the

drama, it appears to me, is this. The conflict of hero and people is hopeless; but it is he alone who makes the conflict of patricians and plebeians, I do not say hopeless, but in any high degree dangerous. The people have bad faults, but no such faults as, in his absence, would prevent a constitutional development in their favour.

I will not try to describe their character, but I will illustrate this statement by comparing two accusations of their opponents with the facts shown; for these we must accept, but the accusations we must judge for ourselves. In the first scene the people are called cowards, both by the hero and by their friendly critic Menenius. Now there is no sign that they possess the kind of courage expected of gentlemen, or feel the corresponding shame if their courage fails. But if they were cowards, how could Rome be standing where we see it stand? They are the common soldiers of Rome. And when we see them in war, what do we find? One division, under Cominius, meets the Volscians in the field; the other, under Coriolanus, assaults Corioli. Both are beaten back. This is what Cominius says to his men:

> Breathe you, my friends: well fought: we are come off
> Like Romans, neither foolish in our stands,
> Nor cowardly in retire.

Nothing hints that the other division has not fought well or was cowardly in retire; but it was encouraged beforehand with threats, and, on its failure, with a torrent of curses and abuse. Nevertheless it advances again and forces the enemy to the gates, which Coriolanus enters, calling on his men to follow him.

> *First Sol.*: Fool-hardiness; not I.
> *Second Sol.*: Nor I.
> *First Sol.*: See, they have shut him in.
> *All*: To the pot, I warrant him.

Disgusting, no doubt; but the answer to threats and curses. They would not have served Cominius so; and indeed, when Lartius comes up and merely suggests to them to "fetch off" the re-appearing hero, they respond at once and take the city. These men are not cowards; but their conduct depends on their leaders. The same thing is seen when Coriolanus himself appeals to the other division for volunteers to serve in the van. For once he appeals nobly, and the whole division volunteers.

Another charge he brings against the people is that they can neither rule nor be ruled. On this his policy of "thorough" is based. Now, judging from the drama, one would certainly say that they could not rule alone,—that a pure democracy would lead to anarchy, and perhaps to foreign subjection. And one would say also that they probably could not be ruled by the patricians if all political rights were denied them. But to rule them, while granting them a place in the constitution, would seem quite feasible. They are, in fact, only too easy to guide. No doubt, collected by a mob, led by demagogues, and maddened by resentment and fear, they become wild and cruel. It is true, also, that, when their acts bear bitter fruit, they disclaim responsibility and turn on their leaders: "that we did, we did for the best; and though we willingly consented to his banishment, yet it was against our will." But they not only follow their tribunes like sheep; they receive abuse and direction submissively from any one who shows good-will. They are fundamentally good-natured, like the Englishmen they are, and have a humorous consciousness of their own weaknesses. They are, beyond doubt, mutable, and in that sense untrustworthy; but they are not by nature ungrateful, or slow to admire their bitterest enemy. False charges and mean imputations come from their leaders, not from them. If one of them blames Coriolanus for being proud, another says he cannot help his pride. They insist on the bare form of their right to name him consul, but all they want is the form, and not the whole even of that. When he asks one of them, "Well then, I pray, your price of the consulship?" the answer, "The price is to ask it kindly," ought to have melted him at once; yet when he asks it contemptuously it is still granted. Even later, when the arts of the tribunes have provoked him to such a storm of defiant and revolutionary speech that both the consulship and his life are in danger, one feels that another man might save both with no great trouble. Menenius tells him that the people

> have pardons, being ask'd, as free
> As words to little purpose.

His mother and friends urge him to deceive the people with false promises. But neither false promises nor apologies are needed, only a little humanity and some acknowledgement that the people are part of the state. He is capable of neither, and so the conflict is hopeless. But it is so not because the people, or even the tribunes, are what they are, but because he is what we call an "impossible" person.

The result is that all the force and nobility of Rome's greatest man have to be thrown away and wasted. That is tragic; and it is doubly so because it is not only his faults that make him impossible. There is bound up with them a nobleness of nature in which he surpasses every one around him.

We see this if we consider, what is not always clear to the reader, his political position. It is not shared by any of the other patricians who appear in the drama: Critics have called him a Tory or an ultra-Tory; but the tribune who calls him a "traitorous innovator" is quite as near the mark. The people have been granted tribunes. The tribunate is a part of the constitution, and it is accepted, with whatever reluctance, by the other patricians. But Coriolanus would abolish it, and that not by law but by the sword. Nor would this content him. The right of the people to control the election of the consul is no new thing; it is an old traditional right; but it too, he says, might well be taken away. The only constitution tolerable in his eyes is one where the patricians are the state, and the people a mere instrument to feed it and fight for it. It is this conviction that makes it so dangerous to appoint him consul, and also makes it impossible for him to give way. Even if he could ask pardon for his abuse of the people, he could not honestly promise to acknowledge their political rights.

Now the nobleness of his nature is at work here. He is not tyrannical; the charge brought against him of aiming at a tyranny is silly. He is an aristocrat. And Shakespeare has put decisively aside the statement of Plutarch that he was "churlish, uncivil, and altogether unfit for any man's conversation." Shakespeare's hero, though he feels his superiority to his fellow-patricians, always treats them as equals. He is never rude or over-bearing. He speaks to them with the simple directness or the bluff familiarity of a comrade. He does not resent their advice, criticism, or reproof. He shows no trace of envy or jealousy, or even of satisfaction at having surpassed them. The suggestion of the tribunes that he is willing to serve under Cominius because failure in war will be credited to Cominius, and success in war to himself, shows only the littleness of their own minds. The patricians are his fellows in a community of virtue—of a courage, fidelity, and honour, which cannot fail them because they are "true-bred," though the bright ideal of such virtue become perfect still urges them on. But the plebeians, in his eyes, are destitute of this virtue, and therefore have no place in this community. All they care for is food in peace, looting in war, flattery from their demagogues; and they will not even clean their teeth. To ask anything of them is to insult not merely himself but the virtues that he worships. To give them a real share in citizenship is treason to Rome; for Rome means these virtues. They are not Romans, they are the rats of Rome.

He is very unjust to them, and his ideal, though high, is also narrow. But he is magnificently true to it, and even when he most repels us we feel this and glory in him. He is never more true to it than when he tries to be false; and this is the scene where his superiority in nobleness is most apparent. He, who had said of his enemy, "I hate him worse than a promise-breaker," is urged to save himself and his friends by promises that he means to break. To his mother's argument that he ought no more to mind deceiving the people than outwitting an enemy in war, he cannot give the obvious answer, for he does not really count the people his fellow-countrymen; but the proposal that *he* should descend to lying or flattering astounds him. He feels that if he does so he will never be himself again; that his mind will have taken on an inherent baseness and no mere simulated one. And he is sure, as we are, that he simply cannot do what is required of him. When at last he consents to try, it is solely because his mother bids him and he cannot resist her chiding. Often he reminds us of a huge boy; and here he acts like a boy whose sense of honour is finer than his mother's, but who is too simple and too noble to frame the thought.

Unfortunately he is altogether too simple and too ignorant of himself. Though he is the proudest man in Shakespeare he seems to be unaware of his pride, and is hurt when his mother mentions it. It does not prevent him from being genuinely modest, for he never dreams that he has attained the ideal he worships; yet the sense of his own greatness is twisted round every strand of this worship. In almost all his words and deeds we are conscious of the tangle. I take a single illustration. He cannot endure to be praised. Even his mother, who has a charter to extol her blood, grieves him when she praises him. As for others,

> I had rather have one scratch my head i' the sun
> When the alarum were struck, than idly sit
> To hear my nothings monster'd.

His answer to the roar of the army hailing him "Coriolanus" is, "I will go wash." His wounds are "scratches with briars." In Plutarch he shows them to the people without demur; in Shakespeare he would rather lose his consulship. There is a greatness in all this that makes us exult. But who can assign the proportions of the elements that compose this impatience of praise: the feeling (which we are surprised to hear him express) that he, like hundreds more, has simply done what he could; the sense that it is nothing to what might be done; the want of human sympathy (for has not Shelley truly said that fame is love disguised?); the pride which makes him feel that he needs no recognition, that after all he himself could do ten times as much, and that to praise his achievement implies a limit to his power? If any one could solve this problem, Coriolanus certainly could not. To adapt a phrase in the play, he has no more introspection in him than a tiger. So he thinks that his loathing of the people is all disgust at worthlessness, and his resentment in exile all a just indignation. So too he fancies that he can stand

> As if a man were author of himself
> And knew no other kin,

while in fact public honour and home affections are the breath of his nostrils, and there is not a drop of stoic blood in his veins.

What follows on his exile depends on this self-ignorance. When he bids farewell to his mother and wife and friends he is still excited and exalted by conflict. He comforts them; he will take no companion; he will be loved when he is lacked, or at least he will be feared; while he remains alive, they shall always hear from him, and never aught but what is like him formerly. But the days go by, and no one, not even his mother, hears a word. When we see him next, he is entering Antium to offer his services against his country. If they are accepted, he knows what he will do; he will burn Rome.

As I have already remarked, Shakespeare does not exhibit to us the change of mind which issues in this frightful purpose; but from what we see and hear later we can tell how he imagined it; and the key lies in that idea of *burning* Rome. As time passes, and no suggestion of recall reaches Coriolanus, and he learns what it is to be a solitary homeless exile, his heart hardens, his pride swells to a mountainous bulk, and the wound in it becomes a fire. The fellow-patricians from whom he parted lovingly now appear to him ingrates and dastards, scarcely better than the loathsome mob. Somehow, he knows not how, even his mother and wife have deserted him. He has become nothing to Rome, and Rome shall hear nothing from him. Here in solitude he can find no relief in a storm of words; but gradually the blind intolerable chaos of resentment conceives and gives birth to a vision, not merely of battle and indiscriminate slaughter, but of the whole city one tower of flame. To see that with his bodily eyes would satisfy his soul; and the way to the sight is through the Volscians. If he is killed the moment they recognize him, he cares little: better a dead nothing than the living nothing Rome thinks him. But if he lives, she shall know what he is. He bears himself among the Volscians with something that resembles self-control; but what controls him is the vision that never leaves him and never changes, and his eye is red with its glare when he sits in his state before the doomed city.[2]

This is Shakespeare's idea, not Plutarch's. In Plutarch there is not a syllable about the burning of Rome. Coriolanus (to simplify a complicated story) intends to humiliate his country by forcing on it disgraceful terms of peace. And this, apart from its moral quality, is a reasonable design. The Romans, rather than yield to fear, decline to treat unless peace is first restored; and therefore it will be necessary to assault the city. In the play we find a single vague allusion to some unnamed conditions which, Coriolanus knows, cannot now be accepted; but everywhere, among both Romans and Volscians, we hear of the burning of Rome, and in the city there is no hope of successful resistance. What Shakespeare wanted was a simpler and more appalling situation than he found in Plutarch, and a hero enslaved by his passion and driven blindly forward. How blindly, we may judge if we ask the questions: what will happen to the hero if he disappoints the expectation he has raised among the Volscians, when their leader is preparing to accuse him even if he fulfils it: and, if the hero executes his purpose, what will happen to his mother, wife, and child: and how can it be executed by a man whom we know in his home as the most human of men, a husband who is still the lover of his wife, and a son who regards his mother not merely with devoted affection but with something like religious awe? Very likely the audience in the theatre was not expected to ask these questions, but it *was* expected to see in the hero a man totally ignorant of himself, and stumbling to the destruction either of his life or of his soul.

In speaking of the famous scene where he is confronted with Volumnia and Valeria, Virgilia and her boy, and the issue is decided, I am obliged to repeat what I have said elsewhere in print;[3] and I must speak in the first person because I do not know how far others share my view. To me the scene is one in which the tragic feelings of fear and pity have little place. Such anxiety as I feel is not for the fate of the hero or of any one else: it is, to use religious language, for the safety of his soul. And

when he yields, though I know, as he divines, that his life is lost, the emotion I feel is not pity: he is above pity and above life. And the anxiety itself is but slight: it bears no resemblance to the hopes and fears that agitate us as we approach the end in *Othello* or *King Lear*. The whole scene affects me, to exaggerate a little, more as a majestic picture of stationary figures than as the fateful climax of an action speeding to its close. And the structure of the drama seems to confirm this view. Almost throughout the first three Acts—that is, up to the banishment—we have incessant motion, excited and resounding speech, a violent oscillation of fortunes. But, after this, the dramatic tension is suddenly relaxed, and, though it increases again, it is never allowed to approach its previous height. If Shakespeare had wished it to do so in this scene, he had only to make us wait in dread of some interposition from Aufidius, at which the hero's passion might have burst into a fury fatal even to the influence of Volumnia. But our minds are crossed by no shadow of such dread. From the moment when he catches sight of the advancing figures, and the voice of nature—what he himself calls "great nature"—begins to speak in his heart long before it speaks aloud to his ear, we know the end. And all this is in harmony with that characteristic of the drama which we noticed at first,—we feel but faintly, if at all, the presence of any mysterious or fateful agency. We are witnessing only the conquest of passion by simple human feelings, and *Coriolanus* is as much a drama of reconciliation as a tragedy. That is no defect in it, but it is a reason why it cannot leave the same impression as the supreme tragedies, and should be judged by its own standard.

A tragedy it is, for the passion is gigantic, and it leads to the hero's death. But the catastrophe scarcely diminishes the influence of the great scene. Since we know that his nature, though the good in it has conquered, remains unchanged, and since his rival's plan is concerted before our eyes, we wait with little suspense, almost indeed with tranquillity, the certain end. As it approaches it is felt to be the more inevitable because the steps which lead to it are made to repeat as exactly as possible the steps which led to his exile. His task, as then, is to excuse himself, a task the most repugnant to his pride. Aufidius, like the tribunes then, knows how to render its fulfilment impossible. He hears a word of insult, the same that he heard then,— "traitor." It is followed by a sneer at the most sacred tears he ever shed, and a lying description of their effect on the bystanders; and his pride, and his loathing of falsehood and meanness, explode, as before, in furious speech. For a moment he tries to check himself and appeals to the senators; but the effort seems only to treble his rage. Though no man, since Aufidius spoke, has said a word against him, he defies the whole nation, recalling the day of its shame and his own triumph, when alone, like an eagle, he fluttered the dovecotes in Corioli. The people, who had accompanied him to the market-place, splitting the air with the noise of their enthusiasm, remember their kinsfolk whom he slaughtered, change sides, and clamour for his death. As he turns on Aufidius, the conspirators rush upon him, and in a moment, before the vision of his glory has faded from his brain, he lies dead. The instantaneous cessation of enormous energy (which is like nothing else in Shakespeare) strikes us with awe, but not with pity. As I said, the effect of the preceding scene, where he conquered something stronger than all the Volscians and escaped something worse than death, is not reversed; it is only heightened by a renewed joy in his greatness. Roman and Volscian will have peace now, and in his native city patrician and plebeian will move along the way he barred. And they are in life, and he is not. But life has suddenly shrunk and dwindled, and become a home for pygmies and not for him.[4]

Dr. Johnson observed that "the tragedy of *Coriolanus* is one of the most amusing of our author's performances." By "amusing" he did not mean "mirth-provoking"; he meant that in *Coriolanus* a lively interest is excited and sustained by the variety of the events and characters; and this is true. But we may add that the play contains a good deal that is amusing in the current sense of the word—more of this, it has been observed, than do the other Roman tragedies. When the people appear as individuals they are frequently more or less comical. Shakespeare always enjoyed the inconsequence of the uneducated mind, and its tendency to express a sound meaning in an absurd form. Again, the talk of the servants with one another and with the muffled hero, and the conversation of the sentinels with Menenius, are amusing. There is a touch of comedy in the contrast between Volumnia and Virgilia when we see them on occasions not too serious. And then, not only at the beginning, as in Plutarch, but throughout the story we meet with that pleasant and wise old gentleman Menenius, whose humour tells him how to keep the peace while he gains his point, and to say without offence what the hero cannot say without raising a storm. Perhaps no one else in the play is regarded from beginning to end with such unmingled approval, and this is not lessened when the failure of his embassy to Coriolanus makes him the subject as well as the author of mirth. If we regard the drama from this point of view we find that it differs from almost all the tragedies, though it has a certain likeness to *Antony and Cleopatra*. What is amusing in it is, for the most part, simply amusing, and has no tragic tinge. It is not like the gibes of Hamlet at Polonius, or the jokes of the clown who, we remember, is digging Ophelia's grave, or that humour of Iago which for us is full of menace; and who could dream of comparing it with the jesting of Lear's fool? Even that Shakespearean audacity, the interruption of Volumnia's speech by the hero's little son, makes one laugh almost without reserve. And all this helps to produce the characteristic tone of this tragedy.

The drawing of the character of Aufidius seems to me by far the weakest spot in the drama. At one place, where Aufidius moralizes on the banishment of the hero, Shakespeare, it appears to some critics, is himself delivering a speech which tells the audience nothing essential and ends in desperate obscurity.[5] Two other speeches have been criticized. In the first, Aufidius, after his defeat in the field, declares that, since he cannot overcome his rival in fair fight, he will do it in any way open to him, however dishonourable. The other is his lyrical cry of rapture when Coriolanus discloses himself in the house at Antium. The intention in both cases is clear. Aufidius is contrasted with the hero as a man of much slighter and less noble nature, whose lively impulses, good and bad, quickly give way before a new influence, and whose action is in the end determined by the permanent pressure of ambition and rivalry. But he is a man of straw. He was wanted merely for the plot, and in reading some passages in his talk we seem to see Shakespeare yawning as he wrote. Besides, the unspeakable baseness of his sneer at the hero's tears is an injury to the final effect. Such an emotion as mere disgust is out of place in a tragic close; but I confess I feel nothing but disgust as Aufidius speaks the last words, except some indignation with the poet who allowed him to speak them, and an unregenerate desire to see the head and body of the speaker lying on opposite sides of the stage.

Though this play is by no means a drama of destiny we might almost say that Volumnia is responsible for the hero's life and death. She trained him from the first to aim at honour in arms, to despise pain, and to

> forget that ever
> He heard the name of death;

to strive constantly to surpass himself, and to regard the populace with inhuman disdain as

> things created
> To buy and sell with groats.

Thus she led him to glory and to banishment. And it was she who, in the hour of trial, brought him to sacrifice his pride and his life.

Her sense of personal honour, we saw, was less keen than his; but she was much more patriotic. We feel this superiority even in the scene that reveals the defect; in her last scene we feel it alone. She has idolized her son; but, whatever motive she may appeal to in her effort to move him, it is not of him she thinks; her eyes look past him and are set on Rome. When, in yielding, he tells her that she has won a happy victory for her country, but a victory most dangerous, if not most mortal, to her son, she answers nothing. And her silence is sublime.

These last words would be true of Plutarch's Volumnia. But in Plutarch, though we hear of the son's devotion, and how he did great deeds to delight his mother, neither his early passion for war nor his attitude to the people is attributed to her influence, and she has no place in the action until she goes to plead with him. Hence she appears only in majesty, while Shakespeare's Volumnia has a more varied part to play. She cannot be majestic when we see her hurrying through the streets in wild exultation at the news of his triumph; and where, angrily conquering her tears, she rails at the authors of his banishment, she can hardly be called even dignified. What Shakespeare gains by her animation and vehemence in these scenes is not confined to them. He prepares for the final scene a sense of contrast which makes it doubly moving and impressive.

In Volumnia's great speech he is much indebted to Plutarch, and it is, on the whole, in the majestic parts that he keeps most close to his authority. The open appeal to affection is his own; and so are the touches of familiar language. It is his Volumnia who exclaims, "here he lets me prate like one i' the stocks," and who compares herself, as she once was, to a hen that clucks her chicken home. But then the conclusion, too, is pure Shakespeare; and if it has not majesty it has something dramatically even more potent. Volumnia, abandoning or feigning to abandon hope, turns to her companions with the words:

> Come, let us go:
> This fellow had a Volscian to his mother;
> His wife is in Corioli, and his child
> Like him by chance. Yet gives us our dispatch:
> I am hush'd until our city be a-fire,
> And then I'll speak a little.[6]

Her son's resolution has long been tottering, but now it falls at once. Throughout, it is not the substance of her appeals that moves him, but the bare fact that she appeals. And the culmination is that she ceases to appeal, and defies him. This has been observed by more than one critic. I do not know if it has been noticed[7] that on a lower level exactly the same thing happens when she tries to persuade him to go and deceive the people. The moment she stops, and says, in effect, "Well, then, follow your own will," his will gives way. Deliberately to set it against hers is beyond his power.

Ruskin, whose terms of praise and blame were never over-cautious, wrote of Virgilia as "perhaps the loveliest of Shakespeare's female characters." Others have described her as a shrinking submissive being, afraid of the very name of a wound, and much given to tears. This description is true; and,

I may remark in passing, it is pleasant to remember that the hero's letter to his mother contained a full account of his wounds, while his letter to his wife did not mention them at all. But the description of these critics can hardly be the whole truth about a woman who inflexibly rejects the repeated invitations of her formidable mother-in-law and her charming friend to leave her house; who later does what she can to rival Volumnia in rating the tribunes; and who at last quietly seconds Volumnia's assurance that Coriolanus shall only enter Rome over her body. Still these added traits do not account for the indefinable impression which Ruskin received (if he did not rightly interpret it), and which thousands of readers share. It comes in part from that kind of muteness in which Virgilia resembles Cordelia, and which is made to suggest a world of feeling in reserve. And in part it comes from the words of her husband. His greeting when he returns from the war, and she stands speechless before him:

> My gracious silence, hail!
> Wouldst thou have laugh'd had I come coffin'd
>      home,
> That weep'st to see me triumph? Ah, my dear,
> Such eyes the widows in Corioli wear,
> And mothers that lack sons:

his exclamation when he sees her approaching at their last meeting and speaks first of her and not of Volumnia:

> What is that curtsy worth, or those doves' eyes
> Which can make gods forsworn? I melt, and am not
> Of stronger earth than others;

these words envelope Virgilia in a radiance which is reflected back upon himself. And this is true also of his praise of Valeria in the lines perhaps most often quoted from this drama:

> The noble sister of Publicola,
> The moon of Rome, chaste as the icicle
> That's curdied by the frost from purest snow,
> And hangs on Dian's temple: dear Valeria!

I said that at one point the hero's nature *was* in a high degree imaginative; and it is here. In his huge violent heart there was a store, not only of tender affection, but of delicate and chivalrous poetry. And though Virgilia and Valeria evoke its expression we cannot limit its range. It extends to the widows and mothers in Corioli; and we feel that, however he might loathe and execrate the people, he was no more capable of injury or insult to a daughter of the people than Othello, or Chaucer's Knight, or Don Quixote himself.

### Postscript

Professor Case, in the Introduction to his admirable Arden edition of *Coriolanus*, while approving the interpretation suggested in this paragraph of the change in the hero's mind, withholds his assent to the stress laid in the paragraph on the particular idea of the *burning* of Rome. Instead of arguing the question I will simply describe the way in which the emphasis on that particular idea came to impress me.

When I was studying the play afresh with a view to this lecture I noticed that, as the action approached its climax, the image of fire, not present to me before, became increasingly present, persistent and vivid; and at last, when Cominius, reporting his futile embassy to the hero, exclaims,

> I tell you he does sit in gold, his eye
> Red as 'twould burn Rome

I said to myself, "Yes, *that* image of vengeance is what came to him in the solitude of his exile and has now become a possession. And, if I could have doubted this, doubt would

have vanished when I reached Volumnia's speech (v. iii. 131), and read the words, its *final* words,

> Yet give us our dispatch:
> I am hushed until our city be a-fire,
> And then I'll speak a little.

The "possession" is shattered, and the catastrophe sure—and welcome.

Dismissing imagination, I have now made a research, and some readers may be interested in the result (the references are to the Globe Shakespeare).

Throughout the greater part of the play, though there is plenty of fighting and Corioles is taken, we hear, I think, nothing of any burning of towns or cities. There is a mention of fire at II. i. 273–5, but it is the fire of contention between the hero and the people; and the "burning" and "fires" of III. ii. 24, and III. iii. 68 are those of hell; and even at IV. iii. 19–26, where the image of fire is decidedly more vivid, this fire is that of the anger of the two parties in Rome. But in IV. vi. 78, 82, 85, 115, 137, we have crowded and vivid references to the burning of the Roman territory by the army of Coriolanus, and to the prospect of his burning the city. And then, after a short scene, comes, at v. i. 14, 17, 27, 32 (where Cominius makes the report of his interview and repeats the words of Coriolanus) fire-image after fire-image, the series culminating at 63 in that of the "eye red as 'twould burn Rome." In the next scene (7, 48, 76) the series, naturally, continues; but in v. iii. where Volumnia is to appear, it ceases (for the hero is inwardly beginning to yield), until it reappears in her final words. And, after that, we have only the reference (v. v. 3) to the "triumphant fires" in the saved city.

### Notes

1. Shakespeare's treatment of his subject is often best understood through comparison with his authority, Plutarch's Life of Coriolanus in North's translation, a translation most conveniently read in the volume edited by Prof. Skeat and entitled *Shakespeare's Plutarch*. For a full development of the comparison, and, generally, for a discussion of the play much more complete than mine could be, see Prof. MacCallum's book, *Shakespeare's Roman Plays and their Background* (1910), which is admirable both for its thoroughness and for the insight and justice of its criticism. I should perhaps add that, though I read the greater part of Prof. MacCallum's book when it appeared, I was prevented from going on to the chapters on *Coriolanus*, and did so only after writing my lecture. I left untouched in the lecture the many observations which this reading confirmed, but on one or two doubtful points I have added a Postscript.
2. See Postscript.
3. *Shakespearean Tragedy*, p. 84.
4. I have tried to indicate the effect at which Shakespeare's imagination seems to have aimed. I do not say that the execution is altogether adequate. And some readers, I know, would like Coriolanus to die fighting. Shakespeare's idea is probably to be gathered from the hero's appeal to the senators to judge between Aufidius and him, and from the word "lawful" in the last speech:

   > O that I had him,
   > With six Aufidiuses, or more, his tribe,
   > To use my lawful sword!

   He is not before the people only, but before the senators, his fellow-patricians, though of another city. Besides—if I may so put it—if Coriolanus were allowed to fight at all, he would have to annihilate the whole assembly.
5. But Prof. MacCallum's defense of this passage is perhaps successful (Appendix F).
6. What she will utter, I imagine, is a mother's dying curse.
7. Yes, it is noticed by Prof. MacCallum (p. 554).

# ROMANCES

## *Pericles*

Whoever reads *Pericles* with attention readily finds that all these scenes in which there is any naturalness in the matter, or in which great passions are developed—especially the scenes in which Pericles and Marina act—stand forth with striking power from the poorness of the whole. Shakespeare's hand is here unmistakable; thus, for instance, in the fine treatment of Antiochus' crime, at the commencement of the piece; in the scene of the storm at sea (III. 1); and most especially in the last act, where the meeting of Pericles and his daughter—a scene which already in Twine's narration possesses peculiar attraction—forms a description which can rank with the best performances of the poet. The profound character of the speeches, the metaphors, the significant brevity and natural dignity, all the peculiar characteristics of Shakespeare's diction, are here exhibited. Yet these more perfect and richer scenes are only sketches; the delineation even of the two principal characters is also a sketch; but they are masterly sketches, standing in a strange contrast of delicacy with the broad details of the barbarous characters in *Titus*. It is an unusual part which Marina has to play in the house of crime. The poet found these scenes in the old narrations; it was for him to verify them in the character. As this Marina appears before us, arming envy with her charms and gifts and *disarming* persecution; as she comes forward on the stage strewing flowers for the grave of her nurse; sweet tender creature, who 'never kill'd a mouse, nor hurt a fly,' or trod upon a worm against her will and wept for it; as her father describes her as 'a palace for the crown'd truth to dwell in; as patience, smiling extremity out of act;' as we see her throughout, she is indeed a nature which appears capable of remaining unsullied amid the impurest, and, as her persecutor says, of making 'a puritan of the devil.' This character is sufficiently apparent; that of Pericles lies deeper. Nathan Drake regarded him as buoyant with hope, ardent in enterprise, a model of knighthood, the devoted servant of glory and of love. So much may praise be misplaced. This romantic sufferer exhibits far rather features of character entirely opposed to chivalrous feeling. His depth of soul and intellect and a touch of melancholy produce in him that painful sensitiveness, which indeed, as long as he is unsuspicious, leaves him indifferent to danger; but after he has once perceived the evil of men, renders him more faint-hearted than bold, and more agitated and uneasy than enterprising. The motives which induce him to venture the dangerous wooing of Antiochus' daughter have not been previously depicted by the poet, but are subsequently intimated. The man who, when he perceives the dishonour of the house into which he has fallen, recognises so quickly and acutely the danger that threatens him, who penetrates in a moment the wicked nature of the sinning father, declaring that he blushes no more for his own shame, and upon its discovery 'seem'd not to strike, but smooth;' who, modest as he is prudent, ventures not to name openly, and scarcely even to himself, the perceived connection, and who thoughtfully considers his position; the man who speaks riddles proves that he is able also to solve them. And he, whose imagination, after fear has been once excited in him, is filled with ideas of a thousand dangers, whose mind is seized with the darkest melancholy, appears also in these touches to be a nature of such prominent mental qualities that, trusting rather to these than to chance, he ventured to undertake to guess the dangerous riddle of the daughter of Antiochus. Agitation, fear, and mistrust now drive him out into the wide world, and beset him in his happiness at Pentapolis, as in his danger in Antiochia; yielding to adversity, and more noble and tender than daring, he carefully conceals himself, and in a perfectly different position fears the same snares as with Antiochus; these are without doubt intentional additions by the last elaborator, for in the story and in the English narrations of it Pericles declares at once his name and origin. The tender nature of his character, which makes him anxious in moments of quiet action, renders him excited in misfortune, and robs him of the power of resistance in suffering. The same violent emotion, the same sinking into melancholy, the same change of his innermost feelings, which he remarks in himself in the first act, after his adventure in Antiochia, we see again rising in him after the supposed death of his wife and child; as at that time he again casts himself upon the wide world and yields to immoderate grief, forgetful of men and of his duties, until the unknown daughter restores him to himself, and he at the same time recovers wife and child. The ecstatic transition from sorrow to joy is here intimated in the same masterly manner as the sudden decline from hope and happiness to melancholy and mourning was before depicted. As we said above, this is only sketched in outline; but there is a large scope left to a great actor to shape this outline into a complete form by the finishing touches of his representation. We therefore before suggested that Shakespeare may have chosen this play, in all other parts highly insignificant and trifling, only to prepare a difficult theme for his friend Burbage, who acted this character.

We should consider this almost a decided matter, if the piece had been first elaborated by Shakespeare in the year 1609, when it appeared for the first time in print, with the words 'lately presented' on the title-page. In this case we should have here discussed the play in the wrong place. Dryden, however, in a prologue, which he wrote in 1675, to the *Circe* of Charles Davenant, calls it expressly Shakespeare's first piece, and for this reason excuses its discrepancies. We must confess it is difficult to believe that, even with such a purpose as that which we have stated, Shakespeare should, at the period of his greatest maturity, have appropriated such a piece as Pericles for the first time. If we compare the revolting scenes of the fourth act with similar ones in *Measure for Measure*, a play which was written before 1609, we are reluctant to believe that Shakespeare could have prepared this over-seasoned food for the million, or even should have tolerated it from the hand of another. We should therefore prefer (with Staunton) to assume that Shakespeare appropriated the piece soon after its origin (about 1590). At the time that the play was printed with Shakespeare's name, in 1602, it may perhaps have been re-prepared for Burbage's acting, and through this it may have acquired its new fame. That at that time it excited fresh sensation is evident from the fact that the performance of the piece and Twine's version of the story gave rise to a novel, composed in 1608, by George Wilkens: 'The true history of the play of Pericles, as it was lately presented by the worthy and ancient poet John Gower.' In this publication we read the iambic verses and passages of the piece transposed into prose, but in a manner that allows us to infer that the play at that time was reprinted in a more perfect form than that in which we now read it. Shakespeare's pen—so easily is it to be distinguished—is recognised in this prose version in expressions which are not to be found in the drama, but which must have been used upon the stage. When Pericles (Act. III. sc. 1) receives the child born in the tempest, he says to it: 'Thou'rt the rudeliest welcome to this world that e'er was prince's child.' To this, the novel (p. 44, ed. Mommsen) adds the epithet: 'Poor inch of nature!' merely four words, in which everyone must recognise our poet. We the.efore probably read this drama in a form which it neither bore when Shakespeare put his hand to it for the first nor for the last time.—G. G. GERVINUS, *"Titus Andronicus and Pericles," Shakespeare Commentaries*, 1845, tr. F. E. Bunnètt

---

### CHARLES KNIGHT
*"Pericles"*
*Studies of Shakspere*
1868, pp. 52–56

The *external* testimony that Shakspere was the author of *Pericles* would appear to rest upon strong evidence; it was published with Shakspere's name as the author during his lifetime. But this evidence is not decisive. In 1600 was printed 'The first part of the true and honourable history of the Life of Sir John Oldcastle, &c. Written by William Shakespeare;'[1] and we should be entitled to receive that representation of the writer of *Sir John Oldcastle* as good evidence of the authorship, were we not in possession of a fact which entirely outweighs the bookseller's insertion of a popular name in his title-page. In the manuscript diary of Philip Henslowe, preserved at Dulwich College, is the following entry:—"This 16 of October, 99, Received by me, Thomas Downton, of Phillip Henslow, to pay Mr. Monday, Mr. Drayton, and Mr. Wilson and Hathway, for the first pte of the Lyfe of Sr Jhon Ouldcasstell, and in earnest of the Second Pte, for the use of the compayny, ten pownd, I say received 10 li."[2] The title-page of *Pericles*, in 1609, might have been as fraudulent as that of *Sir John Oldcastle* in 1600.

The play of *Pericles*, as we learn by the original title-page, was "sundry times acted by his Majesty's servants at the Globe." The proprietary interest in the play for the purposes of the stage (whoever wrote it) no doubt remained in 1623 with the proprietors of the Globe Theatre—Shakspere's fellow-share-holders. Of the popularity of *Pericles* there can be no doubt. It was printed three times separately before the publication of the folio of 1623; and it would have been to the interest of the proprietors of that edition to have included it amongst Shakspere's works. Did they reject it because they could not conscientiously affirm it to be written by him, or were they unable to make terms with those who had the right of publication?

It is a most important circumstance, with reference to the authenticity of *Titus Andronicus*, that Meres, in 1599, ascribed that play to Shakspere. We have no such testimony in the case of *Pericles*; but the tradition which assigns it to Shakspere is pretty constant. Malone has quoted a passage from 'The Times displayed, in Six Sestiads,' a poem published in 1646, and dedicated by S. Shephard to Philip, Earl of Pembroke:—

> See him, whose tragic scenes Euripides
> Doth equal, and with Sophocles we may
> Compare great Shakspeare: Aristophanes
> Never like him his fancy could display:
> Witness The Prince of Tyre, his Pericles:
> His sweet and his to be admired lay
> He wrote of lustful Tarquin's rape, shows he
> Did understand the depth of poesie.

Six years later, another writer, J. Tatham, in verses prefixed to Richard Brome's *Jovial Crew*, 1652, speaks slightingly of Shakspere, and of this particular drama:—

> But Shakespeare, the plebeian driller, was
> Founder'd in his Pericles, and must not pass.

Dryden, in his prologue to Charles Davenant's *Circe*, in 1675, has these lines:—

> Your Ben and Fletcher, in their first young flight,
> Did no Volpone, nor no Arbaces, write;
> But hopp'd about, and short excursions made
> From bough to bough, as if they were afraid,
> And each was guilty of some slighted maid.
> Shakspeare's own Muse his Pericles first bore;
> The Prince of Tyre was elder than the Moor.
> 'T is miracle to see a first good play:
> All hawthorns do not bloom on Christmas day.

The mention of Shakspere as the author of *Pericles* in the poems printed in 1646 and 1652 may in some respect be called traditionary; for the play was not printed after 1635, till it appeared in the folio of 1664. Dryden, most probably, read the play in that folio edition. Mr. Collier says, "I do not at all rely upon Dryden's evidence farther than to establish the belief as to the authorship entertained by persons engaged in theatrical affairs after the Restoration." But is such evidence wholly to be despised? and must the belief be necessarily dated "after the Restoration?" Dryden was himself forty-four years of age when he wrote "Shakspeare's own Muse," &c. He had been a writer for the stage twelve years. He was the friend of Davenant, who wrote for the stage in 1626. Of the original actors in Shakspere's plays Dryden himself might have known, when he was a young man, John Lowin, who kept the Three Pigeons Inn at Brentford, and died very old, a little before the Restoration; and Joseph Taylor, who died in 1653, although, according to the tradition of the stage, he was old enough to have played Hamlet under Shakspere's immediate instruction; and Richard Robinson, who served in the army of Charles I., and has an historical importance through having been shot to death by Harrison, after he had laid down his arms, with this exclamation from the stern republican, "Cursed is he that doth the work of the Lord negligently." It is impossible to doubt then that Dryden was a competent reporter of the traditions of the stage, and not necessarily of the traditions that survived after the Restoration. We can picture the young poet, naturally anxious to approach as closely to Shakspere as possible, taking a cheerful cup with poor Lowin in his humble inn, and listening to the old man's recital of the recollections of his youth amidst those scenes from which he was banished by the violence of civil war and the fury of puritanical intolerance. We accept, then, Dryden's assertion with little doubt; and we approach to the examination of the *internal* evidence of the authenticity of *Pericles* with the conviction that, if it be the work of Shakspere, the foundations of it were laid when his art was imperfect, and he laboured somewhat in subjection to the influence of those ruder models for which he eventually substituted his own splendid examples of dramatic excellence.

There is a very striking passage in Sidney's *Defence of*

*Poesy*, which may be taken pretty accurately to describe the infancy of the dramatic art in England, being written some four or five years before we can trace any connection of Shakspere with the stage. The passage is long, but it is deserving of attentive consideration:—

> But they will say, how then shall we set forth a story which contains both many places and many times? And do they not know that a tragedy is tied to the laws of Poesy, and not of History, not bound to follow the story, but having liberty either to feign a quite new matter, or to frame the history to the most tragical convenience? Again, many things may be told which cannot be showed: if they know the difference betwixt reporting and representing. As for example, I may speak, though I am here, of Peru, and in speech digress from that to the description of Calecut: but in action I cannot represent it without Pacolet's horse. And so was the manner the ancients took by some *Nuntius*, to recount things done in former time, or other place.
>
> Lastly, if they will represent an History, they must not (as Horace saith) begin above, but they must come to the principal point of that one action which they will represent. By example this will be best expressed. I have a story of young Polydorus, delivered, for safety's sake, with great riches, by his father Priamus, to Polymnestor, king of Thrace, in the Trojan war time. He, after some years, hearing of the overthrow of Priamus, for to make the treasure his own, murthereth the child; the body of the child is taken up; Hecuba, she, the same day, findeth a sleight to be revenged most cruelly of the tyrant. Where, now, would one of our tragedy-writers begin, but with the delivery of the child? Then should he sail over into Thrace, and to spend I know not how many years, and travel numbers of places. But where doth Euripides? Even with the finding of the body, leaving the rest to be told by the spirit of Polydorus. This needs no farther to be enlarged; the dullest wit may conceive it.

Between this notion which Sidney had formed of the propriety of a tragedy which should understand "the difference betwixt reporting and representing," there was a long space to be travelled over, before we should arrive at a tragedy which should make the whole action manifest, and keep the interest alive from the first line to the last without any "reporting" at all. When *Hamlet* and *Othello* and *Lear* were perfected, this culminating point of the dramatic art had been reached. But it is evident that Sidney described a state of things in which even the very inartificial expedient of uniting description with representation had not been thoroughly understood, or at least had not been generally practised. The "tragedy-writers" begin with the delivery of the young Polydorus, and travel on with him from place to place, till his final murder. At this point Euripides begins the story, leaving something to be told by the spirit of Polydorus. It is not difficult to conceive a young dramatic poet looking to something beyond the "tragedy-writers" of his own day, and, upon taking up a popular story, inventing a machinery for "reporting," which should emulate the ingenious device of Euripides in making the ghost of Polydorus briefly tell the history which a ruder stage would have exhibited in detail. There was a book no doubt familiar to that young poet; it was the *Confessio Amantis, the Confessyon of the Louer*, of John Gower, printed by Caxton in 1493, and by Berthelet in 1532 and 1554. That the book was popular, the fact of the publication of three editions in little more than half

a century will sufficiently manifest. That it was a book to be devoured by a youth of poetical aspirations, who can doubt? That a Chaucer and a Gower were accessible to a young man educated at the grammar-school at Stratford, we may readily believe. That was not a day of rare copies; the bountiful press of the early English printers was for the people, and the people eagerly devoured the intellectual food which that press bestowed upon them. *Appollinus, The Prince of Tyr*, is one of the most sustained, and, perhaps, altogether one of the most interesting, of the old narratives which Gower introduced into the poetical form. What did it matter to the young and enthusiastic reader that there were Latin manuscripts of this story as early as the tenth century; that there is an Anglo-Saxon version of it; that it forms one of the most elaborate stories of the *Gesta Romanorum*? What does all this matter even to us, with regard to the play before us? Mr. Collier says, "The immediate source to which Shakespeare resorted was probably Laurence Twine's version of the novel of *Appollonius, King of Tyre*, which first came out in 1576, and was afterwards several times reprinted. I have before me an edition without date, 'Imprinted at London by Valentine Simmes for the widow Newman,' which very likely was that used by our great dramatist."[3] Mr. Collier has reprinted this story of Laurence Twine with the title—*Appollonius, Prince of Tyre: upon which Shakespeare founded Pericles*. We cannot understand this. We have looked in vain throughout this story to find a single incident in *Pericles*, suggested by Twine's relation, which might not have been equally suggested by Gower's poem. We will not weary our readers, therefore, with any extracts from this narrative. That the author of *Pericles* had Gower in his thoughts, and, what is more important, that he felt that his audience were familiar with Gower, is, we think, sufficiently apparent. Upon what other principle can Gower perpetually take up the dropped threads of the action? Upon what other principle are the verses spoken by Gower, amounting to several hundred lines, formed upon a careful imitation of his style; so as to present to an audience at the latter end of the sixteenth century some notion of a poet about two centuries older? It is perfectly evident to us that Gower, and Gower only, was in the thoughts of the author of *Pericles*.

We call the play before us by the name of PERICLES, because it was so called in the first rudely printed copies, and because the contemporaries of the writer, following the printed copies, so called it in their printed books. But Malone has given us an epigram of Richard Flecknoe, 1670, *On the Play of the Life of* PYROCLES. There can be little doubt, we think, as Steevens has very justly argued, that Pyrocles was the name of the hero of this play. For who was Pyrocles? The hero of Sidney's *Arcadia*. Steevens says, "It is remarkable that many of our ancient writers were ambitious to exhibit Sidney's worthies on the stage; and, when his subordinate agents were advanced to such honour, how happened it that Pyrocles, their leader, should be overlooked?" To a young poet, who, probably, had access to the *Arcadia*, in manuscript, before its publication in 1590, the name of Pyrocles would naturally present itself as worthy to succeed the somewhat unmanageable Appollinus of Gower; and that name would recommend itself to an audience who, if they were of the privileged circles, such as the actors of the Blackfriars often addressed, were familiar with the *Arcadia* before its publication. After 1590 the *Arcadia* was the most popular work of the age.

It will be seen, then, that we advocate the belief that Pyrocles, or Pericles, was a very early work of Shakspere, in some form, however different from that which we possess. That it was an early work, we are constrained to believe; not from the evidence of particular passages, which may be deficient in power, or devoid of refinement, but from the entire construction of the dramatic action. The play is essentially one of movement, which is a great requisite for dramatic success; but that movement is not held in subjection to a unity of idea. The writer, in constructing the plot, had not arrived to a perfect conception of the principle "That a tragedy is tied to the laws of Poesy, and not of History, not bound to follow the story, but having liberty either to feign a quite new matter, or to frame the history to the most tragical convenience." But with this essential disadvantage we cannot doubt that, even with very imperfect dialogue, the action presented a succession of scenes of very absorbing interest. The introduction of Gower, however inartificial it may seem, was the result of very profound skill. The presence of Gower supplied the unity of idea which the desultory nature of the story wanted; and thus it is that, in "the true history" formed upon the play which Mr. Collier has analysed, the unity of idea is kept in the expression of the title-page, "as it was lately presented by the worthy and ancient poet, John Gower." Nevertheless, such a story we believe could not have been chosen by Shakspere in the seventeenth century, when his art was fully developed in all its wondrous powers and combinations. With his perfect mastery of the faculty of representing, instead of recording, the treatment of a story which would have required perpetual explanation and connection would have been painful to him, if not impossible.

Dr. Drake has bestowed very considerable attention upon the endeavour to prove that *Pericles* ought to be received as the indisputable work of Shakspere. Yet his arguments, after all, amount only to the establishment of the following theory:— "No play, in fact, more openly discloses the hand of Shakspeare than *Pericles*, and fortunately his share in its composition appears to have been very considerable: he may be distinctly, though not frequently, traced in the first and second acts; after which, *feeling the incompetency of his fellow-labourer*, he seems to have assumed almost the entire management of the remainder, nearly the whole of the third, fourth, and fifth acts bearing indisputable testimony to the genius and execution of the great master."[4] This theory of companionship in the production of the play is merely a repetition of the theory of Steevens: "The *purpurei panni* are Shakspeare's, and the rest the productions of some inglorious and forgotten play-wright." We have no faith whatever in this very easy mode of disposing of the authorship of a doubtful play—of leaving entirely out of view the most important part of every drama, its action, its characterization, looking at the whole merely as a collection of passages, of which the worst are to be assigned to some *âme damnée*, and the best triumphantly claimed for Shakspere. There are some, however, who judge of such matters upon broader principles. Mr. Hallam says, "*Pericles* is generally reckoned to be in part, and only in part, the work of Shakspeare. From the poverty and bad management of the fable, the want of any effective or distinguishable character (for Marina is no more than the common form of female virtue, such as all the dramatists of that age could draw), and a general feebleness of the tragedy as a whole, I should not believe the structure to have been Shakspeare's. But many passages are far

more in his manner than in that of any contemporary writer with whom I am acquainted."[5] Here "the poverty and bad management of the fable"—"the want of any effective or distinguishable character," are assigned for the belief that the structure could not have been Shakspere's. But let us accept Dryden's opinion, that

> Shakspeare's own muse his *Pericles* first bore,

with reference to the original structure of the play, and the difficulty vanishes. It was impossible that the character of the early drama should not have been impressed upon Shakspere's earliest efforts. Sidney has given us a most distinct description of that drama; and we can thus understand how the author of *Pericles* improved upon what he found. Do we therefore think that the drama, as it has come down to us, is presented in the form in which it was first written? By no means. We agree with Mr. Hallam that in parts the language seems rather that of Shakspere's "second or third manner than of his first." But this belief is not inconsistent with the opinion that the original structure was Shakspere's. No other poet that existed at the beginning of the seventeenth century—perhaps no poet that came after that period, whether Massinger, or Fletcher, or Webster—could have written the greater part of the fifth act. Coarse as the comic scenes are, there are touches in them unlike any other writer but Shakspere. Horn, with the eye of a real critic, has pointed out the deep poetical profundity of one apparently slight passage in these unpleasant scenes:—

> *Mar.*: Are you a woman?
> *Bawd*: What would you have me be, an I be not a woman?
> *Mar.*: An honest woman, or not a woman.

Touches such as these are not put into the work of other men. Who but Shakspere could have written

> The blind mole casts
> Copp'd hills towards heaven, to tell, the earth is throng'd
> By man's oppression; and the poor worm doth die for 't.

And yet this passage comes naturally enough in a speech of no very high excellence. The *purpurei panni* must be fitted to a body, as well for use as for adornment. We think that Shakspere would not have taken the trouble to produce these costly robes for the decoration of what another had essentially created. We are willing to believe that, even in the very height of his fame, he would have bestowed any amount of labour for the improvement of an early production of his own, if the taste of his audiences had from time to time demanded its continuance upon the stage. It is for this reason that we think that *Pericles*, which appears to have been in some respect a new play at the beginning of the seventeenth century, was the revival of a play written by Shakspere some twenty years earlier.

*Notes*

1. "Some of the copies have not Shakespeare's name on the title." Collier.
2. *Diary of Philip Henslowe*; edited by J. Payne Collier.
3. *Farther Particulars*, p. 36.
4. *Shakespeare and His Times*, vol. ii. p. 268.
5. *History of Literature*, vol. iii. p. 569.

# Cymbeline

*Cymbeline* is also one of Shakespeare's most wonderful compositions. He has here combined a novel of Boccacio's with traditionary tales of the ancient Britons reaching back to the times of the first Roman Emperors, and he has contrived, by the most gentle transitions, to blend together into one harmonious whole the social manners of the newest times with olden heroic deeds, and even with appearances of the gods. In the character of Imogen no one feature of female excellence is omitted: her chaste tenderness, her softness, and her virgin pride, her boundless resignation, and her magnanimity towards her mistaken husband, by whom she is unjustly persecuted, her adventures in disguise, her apparent death, and her recovery, form altogether a picture equally tender and affecting. The two Princes, Guiderius and Arviragus, both educated in the wilds, form a noble contrast to Miranda and Perdita. Shakspeare is fond of showing the superiority of the natural over the artificial. Over the art which enriches nature, he somewhere says, there is a higher art created by nature herself. As Miranda's unconscious and unstudied sweetness is more pleasing than those charms which endeavour to captivate us by the brilliant embellishments of a refined cultivation, so in these two youths, to whom the chase has given vigour and hardihood, but who are ignorant of their high destination, and have been brought up apart from human society, we are equally enchanted by a *naïve* heroism which leads them to anticipate and to dream of deeds of valour, till an occasion is offered which they are irresistibly compelled to embrace. When Imogen comes in disguise to their cave; when, with all the innocence of childhood, Guiderius and Arviragus form an impassioned friendship for the tender boy, in whom they neither suspect a female nor their own sister; when, on their return from the chase, they find her dead, then "sing her to the ground," and cover the grave with flowers:—these scenes might give to the most deadened imagination a new life for poetry. If a tragical event is only apparent, in such case, whether the spectators are already aware of it or ought merely to suspect it, Shakspeare always knows how to mitigate the impression without weakening it: he makes the mourning musical, that it may gain in solemnity what it loses in seriousness. With respect to the other parts, the wise and vigorous Belarius, who after long living as a hermit again becomes a hero, is a venerable figure; the Italian Iachimo's ready dissimulation and quick presence of mind is quite suitable to the bold treachery which he plays; Cymbeline, the father of Imogen, and even her husband Posthumus, during the first half of the piece, are somewhat sacrificed, but this could not be otherwise; the false and wicked Queen is merely an instrument of the plot; she and her stupid son Cloton (the only comic part in the piece), whose rude arrogance is portrayed with much humour, are, before the conclusion, got rid of by merited punishment. As for the heroical part of the fable, the war between the Romans and Britons, which brings on the dénouement, the poet in the extent of his plan had so little room to spare, that he merely endeavours to represent it as a mute procession. But to the last scene, where all the numerous threads of the knot are untied, he has again given its full development, that he might collect together into one focus the scattered impressions of the whole. This example and many others are a sufficient refutation of Johnson's assertion, that Shakspeare usually hurries over the conclusion of his pieces. Rather does he, from a desire to satisfy the feelings, introduce a great deal which, so far as the understanding of the *dénouement* requires, might in a strict sense be justly spared: our modern spectators are much more impatient to see the curtain drop, when there is nothing more to be determined, than those of his day could have been.— AUGUST WILHELM SCHLEGEL, *Lectures on Dramatic Art and Literature*, 1809, tr. John Black

> Even she too dead! all languor on her brow,
> All mute humanity's last simpleness,—
> And yet the roses in her cheeks unfallen!
> Can death haunt silence with a silver sound?
> Can death, that hushes all music to a close,
> Pluck one sweet wire scarce-audible that trembles,
> As if a little child, called Purity,
> Sang heedlessly on of his dear Imogen?
> Surely if some young flowers of Spring were put
> Into the tender hollow of her heart,
> 'Twould faintly answer, trembling in their petals.
> Poise but a wild bird's feather, it will stir
> On lips that even in silence wear the badge
> Only of truth. Let but a cricket wake,
> And sing of home, and bid her lids unseal
> The unspeakable hospitality of her eyes.
> O childless soul—call once her husband's name!
> And even if indeed from these green hills
> Of England, far, her spirit flits forlorn,
> Back to its youthful mansion it will turn,
> Back to the floods of sorrow these sweet locks
> Yet heavy bear in drops; and Night shall see,
> Unwearying as her stars, still Imogen,
> Pausing 'twixt death and life on one hushed word.

> —WALTER DE LA MARE, "Imogen," *Characters from Shakespeare*, 1902

## WILLIAM RICHARDSON
### "On the Character of Imogen"
*A Philosophical Analysis and Illustration of Some of Shakespeare's Remarkable Characters*
1780, pp. 177–207

Crowded theatres have applauded IMOGEN. There is a pleasing softness and delicacy in this agreeable character, that render it peculiarly interesting. Love is the ruling passion; but it is love ratified by wedlock, gentle, constant, and refined.

The strength and peculiar features of a ruling passion, and the power of other principles to influence its motions and moderate its impetuosity, are principally manifest, when it is rendered violent by fear, hope, grief, and other emotions of a like nature, excited by the concurrence of external circumstances. When love is the governing passion, those concomitant and secondary emotions are called forth by separation, the apprehension of inconstancy, and the absolute belief of disaffection. On separation, they dispose us to sorrow and regret: on the apprehension of inconstancy, they excite jealousy or solicitude: and the certainty of disaffection begets despondency. These three situations shall direct the order and arrangement of the following discourse.

I. Cymbeline, instigated against his daughter, by the insinuations of her malicious step-dame, and incensed against Posthumus Leonatus, who was secretly married to Imogen, banishes him from his court and kingdom. The lovers are overwhelmed with sorrow: and the princess, informed by Pisanio of the particular circumstances of her husband's departure, expresses herself in the following manner:

> I would have broke mine eye-strings; crack'd 'em, but
> To look upon him; till the diminution
> Of space had pointed him sharp as my needle:
> Nay, follow'd him, till he had melted from
> The smallness of a gnat to air; and then
> Have turn'd mine eye, and wept,[1]

These lines express the reluctance of the heart to part with the object of its affections, and the efforts of passion struggling with disappointment: that the sentiments they convey are natural and agreeable to the conduct of the passions, may very easily be illustrated.

Some portion of the complacency and delight we receive from the presence of those we love and admire, is annexed to their idea, or to our thoughts concerning them when they are absent. The idea of Leonatus would be, of all others, the most agreeable to Imogen; and the secret wishes and desires of her heart would for ever recal him to her remembrance. But ideas of memory and imagination, though they may be exceedingly lively, though they entertain the mind with various and unusual images, and are capable of cherishing and inflaming the most vehement passions, yield little enjoyment, compared with actual sensation. The conviction of present existence distinguishes, in an eminent manner, the ideas received from objects striking immediately on our senses, from the operations of memory, and the illusions of fancy. Fancy may dazzle and amuse: but reflection, and the consciousness of our present situation are forever intruding: and the vision vanishes at their approach. In the present instance, however, the figure of Leonatus can hardly be distinguished: and the sensation received by Imogen is imperfect, and consequently painful. This leads us to a second observation. A thought never fluctuates in the mind solitary and independent, but is connected with an assemblage, formed of thoughts depending upon one another. In every group or assemblage, some ideas are pre-eminent, and some subordinate. The principal figure makes the strongest impression; and the rest are only attended to, on account of their relation to the leading image. The mention of sun-rising, not only excites the idea of a luminous body ascending the eastern sky, but suggests the images of party-coloured clouds, meadows spangled with dew, and mists hovering on the mountains. Writers, whose works are addressed to the imagination, studying to imitate the various appearances of nature, and, at the same time, sensible that a complete enumeration of every circumstance and quality of an object would be no less tiresome than impossible, are diligent in selecting the leading and capital ideas, upon which the greatest number of other images are dependent. Discernment, in the choice of circumstances, and skill in their arrangement, are, according to Longinus, the principles of true description. Now, we observed above, that the reality of an object enhances the pleasure of the perception; and therefore that the perceptions we receive by the senses are preferred to representations merely fancied. But suppose we receive a single perception from an object exceedingly interesting; this single, and even imperfect perception, makes a lively impression, and becomes the leading idea of an assemblage. Though all the subordinate and adventitious images are the mere coinage of fancy; yet, on account of their intimate union with the primary idea, they operate on the mind, as if their architype really existed. They receive the stamp of reality from the primary perception upon which they depend; they are deemed legitimate, and are

preferred to the mere illusions of fancy. In this manner, the distant, and even imperfect view of Leonatus suggests a train of ideas more agreeable than those of memory and imagination: and it is not till this transient consolation is removed, that Imogen would have 'turned her eye and wept.'

The propriety of the following sentiments depends on the same principles with the former: for the belief that Leonatus, at certain fixed periods, was employed in discharging the tender offices of affection, would give the ideal the authority of actual perception, and its concomitant images would be cherished with romantic fondness,

> I did not take my leave of him, but had
> Most pretty things to say: ere I could tell him,
> How I would think of him at certain hours,
> Such thoughts, and such;—or have charg'd him,
> At the sixth hour of morn, at noon, at midnight,
> To encounter me with orisons, for then
> I am in heaven for him.

But why, says the critic, consume time and attention on actions so frivolous and unimportant? Can they disclose to us any of the arcana of nature? Can they reveal any of her hidden mysteries? Can they explain the wonderful mechanism of the understanding? Or discover the labyrinths of the heart?

To attend to familiar and common objects is not unworthy even of a philosopher. By observing the accidental fall of an apple, Newton explained the motions of the celestial bodies: and a principle illustrated by the easy experiment of bringing two drops of water within their sphere of attraction, accounts for the progress of vegetation. The association we have now endeavoured to explain, accounts for many strange appearances in the history and manners of mankind. It explains that amazing attachment to relicks, which forms an essential part of many modern religions, which fills the convents of Europe with more fragments of the cross than would cover mount Lebanon, and with more tears of the Blessed Virgin than would water the Holy Land. These objects confirm particular facts to the zealous votaries, and realize a train of ideas favourable to the ardour of their enthusiasm. It is not merely the handkerchief stained with the blood of Jesus, that moves, shakes, and convulses the pale and pensive nun, who, at her midnight orisons bathes it with her tears: her emotions are occasioned by the idea of particular sufferings enforced on her imagination, by the view of that melancholy object. From the same association we may deduce the passion for pilgrimage, the rage of crusades, and all the consequences of that fatal distemper. Moved by a propensity depending on the same principles, men of ingenuity, enamoured of the Muses, traverse the regions they frequented, explore every hill, and seek their footsteps in every valley. The groves of Mantua, and the cascades of Anio, are not lovelier than other groves and cascades; yet we view them with peculiar rapture. We tread as on consecrated ground, we regard those objects with veneration, which yielded ideas to the minds of Virgil and Horace; and we seem to enjoy a certain ineffable intercourse with those elegant and enlightened spirits.

Trivial, therefore, as the sentiments and expressions of Imogen may appear, by attending to the principles upon which they depend, they open the mind to the contemplation of extensive objects. Considering them in regard to character, they exhibit to us uncommon affection, sensibility, and mildness of disposition. They are not embittered with invective: she complains of the severity of Cymbeline; but does not accuse: she expresses sorrow; but not resentment: and she reflects on the injustice of the Queen as the cause of her sufferings, rather than the object of her anger. Exceedingly injured, and exceedingly afflicted, she neglects the injury, and dwells on the distress.

> Ere I could
> Give him that parting kiss, which I had set
> Betwixt two charming words; comes in my father;
> And, like the tyrannous breathing of the North,
> Shakes all our buds from growing.
> A father cruel, and a step-dame false;
> A foolish suitor to a wedded lady,
> That hath her husband banish'd:—O that husband!
> My supreme crown of grief! and those repeated
> Vexations of it.
> Most miserable
> Is the desire that's glorious.

II. We proceed, in the second place, to consider the state of Imogen's mind labouring with doubts, and pained with the apprehension of a change in the affections of Posthumus.

Nothing, in the structure of the human mind, appears more inexplicable than the seeming inconsistency of passion. Averse from believing the person we love or esteem capable of ingratitude, we are often prone to suspicion, and are alarmed with the slightest symptoms of disaffection. Whoever warns you of the treachery of a professing friend, or of the inconstancy of a smiling mistress, is treated with scorn or resentment: yet with a scrupulous and critical accuracy, you investigate the meanings of an accidental expression; you employ more sagacity and discernment than might govern a nation, to weigh the importance of a nod; and a trivial oversight or inattention will cast you into despair. The heart of Imogen, attached to Leonatus by tender and sincere affection, is yet capable of apprehension, and liable to solicitude.

Iachimo, with an intention of betraying her, sensible, at the same time, that infidelity and neglect are the only crimes unpardonable in the sight of a lover, and well aware of the address necessary to infuse suspicion into an ingenuous mind, disguises his inhuman intention with the affection of a violent and sudden emotion. He seems rapt in admiration of Imogen, and expresses sentiments of deep astonishment.

> *Ia.*: What! are men mad? hath nature given them eyes
> To see this vaulted arch, and the rich crop
> Of sea and land? which can distinguish 'twixt
> The fiery orbs above, and the twinn'd stones
> Upon the number'd beech? and can we not
> Partition make with spectacles so precious
> 'Twixt fair and foul?
> *Imo.*: What makes your admiration?
> *Ia.*: It cannot be i' th' eye; for apes and monkeys,
> 'Twixt two such she's, would chatter this way, and
> Contemn with mowes the other: nor i' the judgment;
> For idiots, in this case of favour, would
> Be wisely definite.—
> *Imo.*: What, dear Sir,
> Thus raps you? are you well?

We never feel any passion or violent emotion without a cause, either real or imagined. We are never conscious of anger, but when we apprehend ourselves injured; and never feel esteem without the conviction of excellence in the object. Sensible, as it were by intuition, of this invariable law in the conduct of our passions, we never see others very violently agitated without a conviction of their having sufficient cause, or that they are themselves convinced of it. If we see a man deeply afflicted, we are persuaded that he has suffered some dreadful calamity, or that he believes it to be so. Upon this principle, which operates instinctively, and almost without being observed, is founded that capital rule in oratorial

composition, "That he who would affect and convince his audience, ought to have his own mind convinced and affected." Accordingly, the crafty Italian, availing himself of this propensity, counterfeits admiration and astonishment: and Imogen, deceived by the specious artifice, is inclined to believe him. Moved with fearful curiosity, she inquires about Leonatus; receives an answer well calculated to alarm her; and, of consequence, betrays uneasiness.

> *Imo.*: Continues well my Lord his health, 'beseech you?
> *Ia.*: Well, Madam.
> *Imo.*: Is he dispos'd to mirth? I hope he is.
> *Ia.*: Exceeding pleasant; none a stranger there
> So merry, and so gamesome; he is called
> The Britain reveller.
> *Imo.*: When he was here,
> He did incline to sadness, and oft times
> Not knowing why.

By representing the sentiments of Leonatus as unfavourable to marriage and the fair sex, he endeavours to stimulate her disquietude.

> *Ia.*: The jolly Briton cries,
> Can my sides hold, to think, that man, who knows
> By history, report, or his own proof,
> What woman is, yea, what he cannot choose
> But must be,
> Will his free hours languish for allured bondage?
> *Imo.*: Will my Lord say so?
> *Ia.*: Ay, Madam, with his eyes in flood with laughter.
> But Heaven knows,
> Some men are much to blame.
> *Imo.*: Not he, I hope.

This expression of hope is an evident symptom of her anxiety. If we are certain of any future good, we are confident and expect: we only hope when the event is doubtful.

Iachimo practises every art; and, by expressing pity for her condition, he makes farther progress in her good opinion. Pity supposes calamity; and the imagination of Imogen, thus irritated and alarmed, conceives no other cause of compassion than the infidelity of Leonatus. The mysterious conduct of Iachimo heightens her uneasiness; for the nature and extent of her misfortune not being precisely ascertained, her apprehensions render it excessive. The reluctance he discovers, and his seeming unwillingness to accuse her husband, are evidences of his being attached to him, and give his surmises credit. Imogen, thus agitated and afflicted, is in no condition to deliberate coolly; and, as her anxiety grows vehement, she becomes credulous and unwary. Her sense of propriety, however, and the delicacy of her affections, preserve their influence, and she conceals her impatience by indirect inquiries.

> *Ia.*: Whilst I am bound to wonder, I am bound
> To pity.
> *Imo.*: What do you pity, Sir?
> *Ia.*: Two creatures, heartily.
> *Imo.*: Am I one, Sir?
> You look on me; what wreck discern you in me
> Deserves your pity?
> *Ia.*: Lamentable! what!
> To hide me from the radiant fun, and solace
> I' the dungeon by a snuff!
> *Imo.*: I pray you, Sir,
> Deliver with more openness your answers
> To my demands. Why do you pity me?

Iachimo's abrupt and impassioned demeanour, his undoubted friendship for Leonatus, the apparent interest he takes in the concerns of Imogen, and his reluctance to unfold the nature of her misfortune, adding impatience to her anxiety, and so augmenting the violence of her emotions, destroy every doubt of his sincerity, and dispose her implicitly to believe him. He, accordingly, proceeds with boldness, and, under the appearance of sorrow and indignation, hazards a more direct impeachment. To have bewailed her unhappy fate, and to have accused Leonatus in terms of bitterness and reproach, would have suited the injuries she had received, and the violence of disappointed passion. But Shakespeare, superior to all mankind in the invention of characters, hath fashioned the temper of Imogen with lineaments no less peculiar than lovely. Sentiments amiably refined, and a sense of propriety uncommonly exquisite, suppress the utterance of her sorrow, and restrain her resentment. Knowing that suspicion is allied to weakness, and unwilling to asperse the fame of her husband, she replies with a spirit of meekness and resignation.

> My Lord, I fear,
> Has forgot Britain.

Formerly she expressed hope, when the emotion she felt was fear: here she expresses fear, though fully satisfied of her misfortune.

There is a certain state of mind full of sorrow, when the approach of evil is manifest and unavoidable. Our reason is then darkened, and the soul, sinking under the apprehension of misery, suffers direful eclipse, and trembles, as at the dissolution of nature. Unable to endure the painful impression, we almost wish for annihilation, and incapable of averting the threatened danger, we endeavour, though absurdly, to be ignorant of its approach. 'Let me hear no more,' cries the Princess, convinced of her misfortune, and overwhelmed with anguish.

Iachimo, confident of success, and, persuaded that the wrongs of Imogen would naturally excite resentment, suggests the idea of revenge. Skilful to infuse suspicion, he knew not the purity of refined affection. Imogen, shocked and astonished at his infamous offer, is immediately prejudiced against his evidence: her mind recovers vigour by the renovated hope of her husband's constancy, and by indignation against the insidious informer: and she vents her displeasure with sudden unexpected vehemence.

> *Imo.*: What ho, Pisanio!—
> *Ia.*: Let me my service tender on your lips.
> *Imo.*: Away! I do condemn mine ears, that have
> So long attended thee.

This immediate transition from a dejected and desponding tone of mind, to a vigorous and animated exertion, effectuated by the infusion of hope and just indignation, is very natural and striking.

The inquietude of Imogen, softened by affection, and governed by a sense of propriety, exhibits a pattern of the most amiable and exemplary meekness. The emotions she discovers belong to solicitude rather than to jealousy. The features of solicitude are sorrowful and tender: jealousy is fierce, wrathful, and vindictive. Solicitude is the object of compassion mixed with affection; jealousy excites compassion combined with terror.

III. The same meekness and tender dejection that engage our sympathy in the interests of Imogen, and render even her suspicions amiable, preserve their character and influence, when she suffers actual calamity. Leonatus, deceived by the calumnies of Iachimo, suffers the pangs of a jealous emotion, and, in the heat of his resentment, commissions Pisanio to take away her life. But the sagacious attendant, convinced of the malignity of the accusation, disobeys his master; and, actuated

by compassion, reveals his inhuman purpose. The stroke that inflicts the deepest wound on a virtuous and ingenuous nature, is the accusation of guilt. Those who are incapable of criminal acts and intentions, instigated by a stronger abhorrence of a guilty conduct than others less virtuous than themselves, imagine, if, by any unhappy mischance, they are falsely and maliciously accused, that they are the objects of strong abhorrence. Of minds very easily affected, and susceptible of every feeling, persecuted by malice, or overwhelmed with infamy and the reproach of mankind, which they feel more severely than those who have less integrity, and, consequently, a worse opinion of others than they have, are exposed for a time to all the torment of conscious turpitude. The blush of guilty confusion often inflames the complexion of innocence, and disorders her lovely features. To be rescued from undeserved affliction, Imogen flies for relief to the review of her former conduct; and, surprised at the accusation, and indignant of the charge, she triumphs in conscious virtue.

> False to his bed! what is to be false?
> To lie in watch there, and to think on him?
> To weep 'twixt clock and clock? if sleep charge nature
> To break it with a fearful dream of him,
> And cry myself awake? That's false to his bed?

Yet resentment is so natural in cases of heinous injury, that it arises even in minds of the mildest temper. It arises, however, without any excessive or unseemly agitation: its duration is exceedingly transient. It is governed in its utterance by the memory of former friendship: and, if the blame can be transferred to any insidious or sly seducer, who may have prompted the evil we complain of, we wreck upon them the violence of our displeasure.

> I false! thy conscience witness, Iachimo—
> Thou didst accuse him of incontinency:
> Thou then look'dst like a villain: now, methinks,
> Thy favour's good enough. Some jay of Italy,[2]
> Whose mother was her painting, hath betray'd him.

The resentment of Imogen is of short continuance: it is a sudden solitary flash, extinguished instantly in her sorrow.

> Poor I am stale, a garment out of fashion.

It is not the malice of a crafty step-dame that moves the heart of Imogen to complain; nor the wrath of her incensed and deluded parent; nor that she, bred up in softness, and little accustomed to suffer hardships and sorrow, should wander amid solitary rocks and deserts, exposed to perils, famine, and death: it is, that she is forsaken, betrayed, and persecuted by him, on whose constancy she relied for protection, and to whose tenderness she entrusted her repose. Of other evils she is not insensible; but this is the 'supreme crown of her grief.' Cruelty and ingratitude are abhorred by the spectator, and resented by the sufferer. But, when the temper of the person injured is peculiarly gentle, and the author of the injury the object of confirmed affection, the mind, after the first emotion, is more apt to languish in despondency than continue inflamed with resentment. The sense of misfortune, rather than the sense of injury, rules the disposition of Imogen, and, instead of venting invective, she laments the misery of her condition.

> Poor I am stale, a garment out of fashion;
> And, for I am richer than to hang by the walls,
> I must be ript.—to pieces with me!

If a crime is committed by a person with whom we are unconnected, or who has no pretensions to pre-eminent virtue, we feel indignation against the individual; but form no conclusions against the species. The case is different, if we are connected with him by any tender affection, and regard him as of superior merit. Love and friendship, according to the immutable conduct of every passion, lead us to magnify, in our imaginations, the distinguished qualities of those we love. The rest of mankind are ranked in a lower order, and are valued no otherwise than as they resemble this illustrious model. But, perceiving depravity where we expected perfection, mortified and disappointed, that appearances of rectitude, believed by us most sincere and unchangeable, were merely specious and exterior, we become suspicious of every pretension to merit, and regard the rest of mankind, of whose integrity we have had less positive evidence, with cautious and unkind reserve.

> True honest men being heard, like false Æneas,
> Were, in his time, thought false: and Sinon's weeping
> Did scandal many a holy tear; took pity
> From most true wretchedness. So thou, Posthumus,
> Wilt lay the leaven on all proper men:
> Goodly, and gallant, shall be false and perjur'd,
> From thy great fail.

Imogen, conscious of her innocence, convinced of Leonatus's perfidy, and overwhelmed with sorrow, becomes careless of life, and offers herself a willing sacrifice to her husband's cruelty.

> Be thou honest:
> Do thou thy master's bidding: when thou seest him,
> A little witness my obedience. Look!
> I draw the sword myself: take it, and hit
> The innocent mansion of my love, my heart:
> Pr'ythee, dispatch:
> The lamb intreats the butcher. Where's thy knife?
> Thou art too slow to do thy master's bidding,
> When I desire it too.

I shall conclude these observations, by explaining more particularly, how the repulse of a ruling and habituated passion could dispose Imogen to despondency, and render her careless of life: in other words, what is the origin of despair; or, by what lamentable perversion those, who are susceptible of the pleasures of life, and in situations capable of enjoying them, become dissatisfied, and rise from the feast prematurely.

Happiness depends upon the gratification of our desires and passions. The happiness of Titus arose from the indulgence of a beneficent temper: Epaminondas reaped enjoyment from the love of his country. The love of fame was the source of Cæsar's felicity: and the gratification of groveling appetites gave delight to Vitellius. It has also been observed, that some one passion generally assumes a pre-eminence in the mind, and not only predominates over other appetites and desires; but contends with reason, and is often victorious. In proportion as one passion gains strength, the rest languish and are enfeebled. They are seldom exercised; their gratifications yield transient pleasure; they become of slight importance, are dispirited, and decay. Thus our happiness is attached to one ruling and ardent passion. But our reasonings, concerning future events, are weak and short-sighted. We form schemes of felicity that can never be realized, and cherish affections that can never be gratified. If, therefore, the disappointed passion has been long encouraged, if the gay visions of hope and imagination have long administered to its violence, if it is confined by habit in the temper and constitution, if it has superseded the operations of other active principles, and so enervated their strengths, its disappointment will be embittered; and sorrow, prevented by no other passion, will prey, unabating, on the desolate abandoned spirit. We may also observe, that none are more liable to afflictions of this sort, than those to whom nature hath given extreme sensibility: alive to every impression, their feelings are exquisite: they are eager in every pursuit: their imaginations are vigorous, and well adapted to fire them. They

live, for a time, in a state of anarchy, exposed to the inroads of every passion; and, though possessed of singular abilities, their conduct will be capricious. Glowing with the warmest affections, open, generous, and candid; yet, prone to inconstancy, they are incapable of lasting friendship. At length, by force of repeated indulgence, some one passion becomes habitual, occupies the heart, seizes the understanding, and, impatient of resistance or control, weakens or extirpates every opposing principle: disappointment ensues: no passion remains to administer comfort: and the original sensibility which promoted this disposition, will render the mind more susceptible of anguish, and yield it a prey to despondency. We ought, therefore, to beware of limiting our felicity to the gratification of any individual passion. Nature, ever wise and provident, hath endowed us with capacities for various pleasures, and hath opened to us many fountains of happiness: 'Let no tyrannous passion, let no rigid doctrine deter thee; drink of the streams, be moderate, and be grateful.'

*Notes*

1. There is a passage very familiar to this in Ovid's story of Ceyx and Halcyone.

> Sustulit illa
> Humentes oculos, stantemque in puppe recurva,
> Concussaqne manu dantem sibi signa, maritum
> Prima videt; redditque notas: ubi terra recessit
> Longius, atque oculi nequeunt cognoscere vultus,
> Dum licet, insequitur fugientem lumine pinum.
> Hæc quoque, ut haud poterat, spatio submota, videri;
> Vela tamen spectat summo fluitantia malo:
> Ut nec vela videt, vacuum petit anxia lectum;
> Seque toro ponit. Renovat lectusque locusque
> Halcyones lacrymas.

2. The word *painting* in this passage is a substantive noun, synonimous to portrait.

## WILLIAM HAZLITT
### From *"Cymbeline"*
### *Characters of Shakespear's Plays*
### 1817

*C*ymbeline is one of the most delightful of Shakespear's historical plays. It may be considered as a dramatic romance, in which the most striking parts of the story are thrown into the form of a dialogue, and the intermediate circumstances are explained by the different speakers, as occasion renders it necessary. The action is less concentrated in consequence; but the interest becomes more aerial and refined from the principle of perspective introduced into the subject by the imaginary changes of scene, as well as by the length of time it occupies. The reading of this play is like going a journey with some uncertain object at the end of it, and in which the suspense is kept up and heightened by the long intervals between each action. Though the events are scattered over such an extent of surface, and relate to such a variety of characters, yet the links which bind the different interests of the story together are never entirely broken. The most straggling and seemingly casual incidents are contrived in such a manner as to lead at last to the most complete developement of the catastrophe. The ease and conscious unconcern with which this is effected only makes the skill more wonderful. The business of the plot evidently thickens in the last act: the story moves forward with increasing rapidity at every step; its various ramifications are drawn from the most distant points to the same centre; the principal characters are brought together, and placed in very critical situations; and the fate of almost every person in the drama is made to depend on the solution of a single circumstance—the answer of Iachimo to the question of Imogen respecting the obtaining of the ring from Posthumus. Dr. Johnson is of opinion that Shakespear was generally inattentive to the winding-up of his plots. We think the contrary is true; and we might cite in proof of this remark not only the present play, but the conclusion of *Lear*, of *Romeo and Juliet*, of *Macbeth*, of *Othello*, even of *Hamlet*, and of other plays of less moment, in which the last act is crowded with decisive events brought about by natural and striking means.

The pathos in *Cymbeline* is not violent or tragical, but of the most pleasing and amiable kind. A certain tender gloom overspreads the whole. Posthumus is the ostensible hero of the piece, but its greatest charm is the character of Imogen. Posthumus is only interesting from the interest she takes in him; and she is only interesting herself from her tenderness and constancy to her husband. It is the peculiar excellence of Shakespear's heroines, that they seem to exist only in their attachment to others. They are pure abstractions of the affections. We think as little of their persons as they do themselves, because we are let into the secrets of their hearts, which are more important. We are too much interested in their affairs to stop to look at their faces, except by stealth and at intervals. No one ever hit the true perfection of the female character, the sense of weakness leaning on the strength of its affections for support, so well as Shakespear—no one ever so well painted natural tenderness free from affectation and disguise—no one else even so well shewed how delicacy and timidity, when driven to extremity, grow romantic and extravagant; for the romance of his heroines (in which they abound) is only an excess of the habitual prejudices of their sex, scrupulous of being false to their vows, truant to their affections, and taught by the force of feeling when to forego the forms of propriety for the essence of it. His women were in this respect exquisite logicians; for there is nothing so logical as passion. They knew their own minds exactly; and only followed up a favourite purpose, which they had sworn to with their tongues, and which was engraven on their hearts, into its untoward consequences. They were the prettiest little set of martyrs and confessors on record.—Cibber, in speaking of the early English stage, accounts for the want of prominence and theatrical display in Shakespear's female characters from the circumstance, that women in those days were not allowed to play the parts of women, which made it necessary to keep them a good deal in the back-ground. Does not this state of manners itself, which prevented their exhibiting themselves in public, and confined them to the relations and charities of domestic life, afford a truer explanation of the matter? His women are certainly very unlike stage-heroines; the reverse of tragedy-queens. . . .

The character of Cloten, the conceited, booby lord, and rejected lover of Imogen, though not very agreeable in itself, and at present obsolete, is drawn with much humour and quaint extravagance. The description which Imogen gives of his unwelcome addresses to her—'Whose love-suit hath been to me as fearful as a siege'—is enough to cure the most ridiculous lover of his folly. It is remarkable that though Cloten makes so poor a figure in love, he is described as assuming an air of consequence as the Queen's son in a council of state, and with all the absurdity of his person and manners, is not without shrewdness in his observations. So true is it that folly is as often owing to a want of proper sentiments as to a want of understanding! The exclamation of the ancient critic—Oh

Menander and Nature, which of you copied from the other! would not be misapplied to Shakespear.

The other characters in this play are represented with great truth and accuracy, and as it happens in most of the author's works, there is not only the utmost keeping in such separate character; but in the casting of the different parts, and their relation to one another, there is an affinity and harmony, like what we may observe in the gradations of colour in a picture. The striking and powerful contrasts in which Shakespear abounds could not escape observation; but the use he makes of the principle of analogy to reconcile the greatest diversities of character and to maintain a continuity of feeling throughout, has not been sufficiently attended to. In *Cymbeline*, for instance, the principal interest arises out of the unalterable fidelity of Imogen to her husband under the most trying circumstances. Now the other parts of the picture are filled up with subordinate examples of the same feeling, variously modified by different situations, and applied to the purposes of virtue or vice. The plot is aided by the amorous importunities of Cloten, by the persevering determination of Iachimo to conceal the defeat of his project by a daring imposture: the faithful attachment of Pisanio to his mistress is an affecting accompaniment to the whole; the obstinate adherence to his purpose in Bellarius, who keeps the fate of the young princes so long a secret in resentment for the ungrateful return to his former services, the incorrigible wickedness of the Queen, and even the blind uxorious confidence of Cymbeline, are all so many lines of the same story, tending to the same point. The effect of this coincidence is rather felt than observed; and as the impression exists unconsciously in the mind of the reader, so it probably arose in the same manner in the mind of the author, not from design, but from the force of natural association, a particular train of thought suggesting different inflections of the same predominant feeling, melting into, and strengthening one another, like chords in music.

The characters of Bellarius, Guiderius, and Arviragus, and the romantic scenes in which they appear, are a fine relief to the intrigues and artificial refinements of the court from which they are banished. Nothing can surpass the wildness and simplicity of the descriptions of the mountain life they lead. They follow the business of huntsmen, not of shepherds; and this is in keeping with the spirit of adventure and uncertainty in the rest of the story, and with the scenes in which they are afterwards called on to act. How admirably the youthful fire and impatience to emerge from their obscurity in the young princes is opposed to the cooler calculations and prudent resignation of their more experienced counsellor! How well the disadvantages of knowledge and of ignorance, of solitude and society, are placed against each other!

> *Guiderius:* Out of your proof you speak: we poor unfledg'd
> Have never wing'd from view o' th' nest; nor know not
> What air's from home. Haply this life is best,
> If quiet life is best; sweeter to you
> That have a sharper known; well corresponding
> With your stiff age: but unto it is
> A cell of ignorance; travelling a-bed,
> A prison for a debtor, that not dares
> To stride a limit.
> *Arviragus:* What should we speak of
> When we are old as you? When we shall hear
> The rain and wind beat dark December! How,
> In this our pinching cave, shall we discourse
> The freezing hours away? We have seen nothing.
> We are beastly; subtle as the fox for prey,

Like warlike as the wolf for what we eat:
Our valour is to chase what flies; our cage
We make a quire, as doth the prison'd bird,
And sing our bondage freely.

The answer of Bellarius to this expostulation is hardly satisfactory; for nothing can be an answer to hope, or the passion of the mind for unknown good, but experience.—The forest of Arden in *As You Like It* can alone compare with the mountain scenes in *Cymbeline*: yet how different the comtemplative quiet of the one from the enterprising boldness and precarious mode of subsistence in the other! Shakespear not only lets us into the minds of his characters, but gives a tone and colour to the scenes he describes from the feelings of their supposed inhabitants. He at the same time preserves the utmost propriety of action and passion, and gives all their local accompaniments. If he was equal to the greatest things, he was not above an attention to the smallest. Thus the gallant sportsmen in *Cymbeline* have to encounter the abrupt declivities of hill and valley: Touchstone and Audrey jog along a level path. The deer in *Cymbeline* are only regarded as objects of prey, 'The game's a-foot,' etc.—with Jaques they are fine subjects to moralise upon at leisure, 'under the shade of melancholy boughs.'

# The Winter's Tale

Sheakspear, in a play, brought in a number of men saying they had suffered shipwreck in Bohemia, wher ther is no sea neer by some 100 miles.—BEN JONSON, *Conversations with William Drummond*, 1618

It is evident from the conduct of Shakespeare, that the house of Tudor retained all their Lancastrian prejudices, even in the reign of queen Elizabeth. In his play of *Richard the Third*, he seems to deduce the woes of the house of York from the curses which queen Margaret had vented against them; and he could not give that weight to her curses, without supposing a right in her to utter them. This indeed is the authority which I do not pretend to combat. Shakespeare's immortal scenes will exist, when such poor arguments as mine are forgotten. Richard at least will be tried and executed on the stage, when his defence remains on some obscure shelf of a library. But while these pages may excite the curiosity of a day, it may not be unentertaining to observe, that there is another of Shakespeare's plays that may be ranked among the historic, though not one of his numerous critics and commentators have discovered the drift of it; I mean *The Winter Evening's Tale*, which was certainly intended (in compliment to queen Elizabeth) as an indirect apology for her mother Anne Boleyn. The address of the poet appears no where to more advantage. The subject was too delicate to be exhibited on the stage without a veil; and it was too recent, and touched the queen too nearly, for the bard to have ventured so home an allusion on any other ground than compliment. The unreasonable jealousy of Leontes, and his violent conduct in consequence, form a true portrait of Henry the eighth, who generally made the law the engine of his boisterous passions. Not only the general plan of the story is most applicable, but several passages are so marked, that they touch the real history nearer than the fable. Hermione on her trial says,

for honour,
'Tis a derivative from me to mine,
And only that I stand for.

This seems to be taken from the very letter of Anne Boleyn to the king before her execution, where she pleads for the infant princess his daughter. Mamillius, the young prince, an unnecessary character, dies in his infancy; but it confirms the allusion, as queen Anne, before Elizabeth, bore a stillborn son. But the most striking passage, and which had nothing to do in the tragedy, but as it pictured Elizabeth, is where Paulina, describing the new-born princess and her likeness to her father, says, *she has the very trick of his frown*. There is one sentence indeed so applicable, both to Elizabeth and her father, that I should suspect the poet inserted it after her death. Paulina, speaking of the child, tells the king,

'Tis yours;
And might we lay the old proverb to your charge,
So like you, 'tis the worse.

*The Winter Evening's Tale* was therefore in reality a second part of *Henry the Eighth*.—HORACE WALPOLE, *Historic Doubts on the Life and Reign of King Richard the Third*, 1767

*The Winter's Tale* is as appropriately named as *The Midsummer Night's Dream*. It is one of those tales which are peculiarly calculated to beguile the dreary leisure of a long winter evening, and are even attractive and intelligible to childhood, while animated by fervent truth in the delineation of character and passion, and invested with the embellishments of poetry lowering itself, as it were, to the simplicity of the subject, they transport even manhood back to the golden age of imagination. The calculation of probabilities has nothing to do with such wonderful and fleeting adventures, when all end at last in universal joy; and, accordingly, Shakspeare has here taken the greatest license of anachronisms and geographical errors; not to mention other incongruities, he opens a free navigation between Sicily and Bohemia, makes Ginlio Romano the contemporary of the Delphic oracle. The piece divides itself in some degree into two plays. Leontes becomes suddenly jealous of his royal bosom-friend Polyxenes, who is on a visit to his court; makes an attempt on his life, from which Polyxenes only saves himself by a clandestine flight;—Hermione, suspected of infidelity, is thrown into prison, and the daughter which she there brings into the world is exposed on a remote coast;—the accused Queen, declared innocent by the oracle, on learning that her infant son has pined to death on her account, falls down in a swoon, and is mourned as dead by her husband, who becomes sensible, when too late, of his error: all this makes up the three first acts. The last two are separated from these by a chasm of sixteen years; but the foregoing tragical catastrophe was only apparent, and this serves to connect the two parts. The Princess, who has been exposed on the coast of Polyxenes's kingdom, grows up among low shepherds; but her tender beauty, her noble manners, and elevation of sentiment, bespeak her descent; the Crown Prince Florizel, in the course of his hawking, falls in with her, becomes enamoured, and courts her in the disguise of a shepherd; at a rural entertainment Polyxenes discovers their attachment, and breaks out into a violent rage; the two lovers seek refuge from his persecutions at the court of Leontes in Sicily, where the discovery and general reconciliation take place. Lastly, when Leontes beholds, as he imagines, the statue of his lost wife, it descends from the niche: it is she herself, the still living Hermione, who has kept herself so long concealed; and the piece ends with universal rejoicing. The jealousy of Leontes is not, like that of Othello, developed through all its causes, symptoms and variations; it is brought forward at once full grown and mature, and is portrayed as a distempered frenzy. It is a passion whose effects the spectator is more concerned with than with its origin, and which does not produce the catastrophe, but merely ties the knot of the piece. In fact, the poet might perhaps have wished slightly to indicate that Hermione, though virtuous, was too warm in her efforts to please Polyxenes; and it appears as if this germ of inclination first attained its proper maturity in their children. Nothing can be more fresh and youthful, nothing at once so ideally pastoral and princely as the love of Florizel and Perdita; of the prince, whom love converts into a voluntary shepherd; and the princess, who betrays her exalted origin without knowing it, and in whose hands nosegays become crowns. Shakspeare has never hesitated to place ideal poetry side by side of the most vulgar prose: and in the world of reality also this is generally the case. Perdita's foster-father and his son are both made simple boors, that we may the more distinctly see how all that ennobles her belongs only to herself. Autolycus, the merry pedlar and pickpocket, so inimitably portrayed, is necessary to complete the rustic feast, which Perdita on her part seems to render meet for an assemblage of gods in disguise.—AUGUST WILHELM SCHLEGEL, *Lectures on Dramatic Art and Literature*, 1809, tr. John Black

We wonder that Mr. Pope should have entertained doubts of the genuineness of this play. He was, we suppose, shocked (as certain critic suggests) at the Chorus, Time, leaping over sixteen years with his crutch between the third and fourth act, and at Antigonus's landing with the infant Perdita on the sea-coast of Bohemia. These slips or blemishes however do not prove it not to be Shakespear's; for he was as likely to fall into them as any body; but we do not know any body but himself who could produce the beauties. The *stuff* of which the tragic passion is composed, the romantic sweetness, the comic humour, are evidently his. Even the crabbed and tortuous style of the speeches of Leontes, reasoning on his own jealousy, beset with doubts and fears, and entangled more and more in the thorny labyrinth, bears every mark of Shakespear's peculiar manner of conveying the painful struggle of different thoughts and feelings, labouring for utterance, and almost strangled in the birth. For instance:—

> Ha' not you seen, Camillo?
> (But that's past doubt; you have, or your eye-glass
> Is thicker than a cuckold's horn) or heard,
> (For to a vision so apparent, rumour
> Cannot be mute) or thought (for cogitation
> Resides not within man that does not think)
> My wife is slippery? If thou wilt, confess,
> Or else be impudently negative,
> To have nor eyes, nor ears, nor thought.

Here Leontes is confounded with his passion, and does not know which way to turn himself, to give words to the anguish, rage, and apprehension, which tug at his breast. It is only as he is worked up into a clearer conviction of his wrongs by insisting on the grounds of his unjust suspicions to Camillo, who irritates him by his opposition, that he bursts out into the following vehement strain of bitter indignation: yet even here his passion staggers, and is as it were oppressed with its own intensity.

> Is whispering nothing?
> Is leaning cheek to cheek? is meeting noses?

> Kissing with inside lip? stopping the career
> Of laughter with a sigh? (a note infallible
> Of breaking honesty!) horsing foot on foot?
> Skulking in corners? wishing clocks more swift?
> Hours, minutes? the noon, midnight? and all eyes
> Blind with the pin and web, but theirs; theirs only,
> That would, unseen, be wicked? is this nothing?
> Why then the world, and all that's in 't, is nothing,
> The covering sky is nothing, Bohemia's nothing,
> My wife is nothing!

The character of Hermione is as much distinguished by its saint-like resignation and patient forbearance, as that of Paulina is by her zealous and spirited remonstrances against the injustice done to the queen, and by her devoted attachment to her misfortunes. Hermione's restoration to her husband and her child, after her long separation from them, is as affecting in itself as it is striking in the representation. Camillo, and the old shepherd and his son, are subordinate but not uninteresting instruments in the developement of the plot, and though last, not least, comes Autolycus, a very pleasant, thriving rogue; and (what is the best feather in the cap of all knavery) he escapes with impunity in the end.—WILLIAM HAZLITT, *"The Winter's Tale," Characters of Shakespear's Plays*, 1817

Although, on the whole, this play is exquisitely respondent to its title, and even in the fault I am about to mention, still a winter's tale; yet it seems a mere indolence of the great bard not to have provided in the oracular response (Act ii. sc. 2) some ground for Hermione's seeming death and fifteen years voluntary concealment. This might have been easily effected by some obscure sentence of the oracle, as for example:—

> Nor shall he ever recover an heir, if he have a wife before that recovery.

The idea of this delightful drama is a genuine jealousy of disposition, and it should be immediately followed by the perusal of *Othello*, which is the direct contrast of it in every particular. For jealousy is a vice of the mind, a culpable tendency of the temper, having certain well known and well defined effects and concomitants, all of which are visible in Leontes, and, I boldly say, not one of which marks its presence in Othello;—such as, first, an excitability by the most inadequate causes, and an eagerness to snatch at proofs; secondly, a grossness of conception, and a disposition to degrade the object of the passion by sensual fancies and images; thirdly, a sense of shame of his own feelings exhibited in a solitary moodiness of humour, and yet from the violence of the passion forced to utter itself, and therefore catching occasions to ease the mind by ambiguities, equivoques, by talking to those who cannot, and who are known not to be able to, understand what is said to them,—in short, by soliloquy in the form of dialogue, and hence a confused, broken, and fragmentary, manner; fourthly, a dread of vulgar ridicule, as distinct from a high sense of honour, or a mistaken sense of duty; and lastly, and immediately, consequent on this, a spirit of selfish vindictiveness.—SAMUEL TAYLOR COLERIDGE, *"Notes on The Winter's Tale," Shakspeare, with Introductory Remarks on Poetry, the Drama, and the Stage*, 1818

## WILLIAM ARCHER
### *"The Winter's Tale"*
*The Nineteenth Century*, October 1887, pp. 511–21

The stage-history of this play is not so long or so full of incident as the stage-history of the great tragedies, about which volumes might be written. To trace the career of *Hamlet*, *Macbeth*, *Othello*, and *King Lear* on the stage would be, in effect, to write a history of English tragic acting. Even the more popular comedies, such as *The Merchant of Venice* or *As You Like It*, would afford matter for anecdotic annals of almost unlimited length. *The Winter's Tale* has been less popular, and consequently its record is less eventful; but it has had its fair share of vicissitudes. It suffered more than most of its fellows at the hands of the self-complacent eighteenth century, and even the nineteenth century has taken no small liberties with it.

Of *The Winter's Tale* before the Restoration little is known. It was seen by Dr. Simon Forman at the Globe on May 15, 1611, and it is plausibly argued that this must have been during its first run. Again, on August 19, 1623, Sir Henry Herbert, then Master of the Revels, enters in his notebook:—

> For the king's players. An olde playe called *Winter's Tale*, formerly allowed of by Sir George Bucke, and likewyse by mee on Mr. Hemmings his worde that there was nothing profane added or reformed, thogh the allowed booke was missinge.

The 'allowed booke' was no doubt destroyed when the Globe Theatre was burned down in 1613. In the following January (16$\frac{23}{24}$) Sir Henry Herbert notes that *The Winter's Tale* was performed at Whitehall by the King's company, 'in the kings absence.' Ten years later we find the following entry: '*The Winter's Tale* was acted on thursday night at Court, the 14 Janua. 1633, by the K. players, and likt.' It thus appears that the comedy did not, like so many of its fellows, absolutely vanish from the stage, and even that it was fairly popular.

At the Restoration, however, its popularity was forgotten, and eighty years passed before it was taken from the shelf. At last, on January 15, 1741, it was revived by Giffard at Goodman's Fields, the East End theatre to which, some nine months later, all London was attracted by the sudden fame of a young gentleman named David Garrick. Giffard himself played Leontes, and his wife Hermione—a very undistinguished pair. The Perdita was Miss Hippisley, afterwards Mrs. Green, an actress who is said to have been second only to Kitty Clive in her particular line of parts. She was now a young girl at the commencement of her career. It was not until thirty years later that she created Mrs. Hardcastle and Mrs. Malaprop. Richard Yates played Autolycus, and his wife, afterwards so famous, appeared as one of Hermione's attendants—but of them more anon. This revival was probably more or less successful, for in the following November we find the play figuring in the Covent Garden bill. The Leontes was Stephens, an actor who secured a passing success by his knack of imitating Barton Booth. Polixenes was played by Ryan, from whom Garrick is said to have borrowed many details of his Richard III. A certain Mr. and Mrs. Hale were the Florizel and Perdita—the wife a nonentity, the husband noted only for having on one occasion insisted on playing Charles I. in a full-bottomed fair wig. The Hermione was Mrs. Horton, a very handsome woman who succeeded for a time to Mrs. Oldfield's parts. Her manner, unfortunately, was that of the stilted, 'orotund' school of Quin, and we are told that 'the natural and easy dialogue of Mrs. Pritchard so captivated the public that poor Mrs. Horton was stripped of her characters one by one,' Peg Woffington, too, coming in for some of the spoils. Mrs. Pritchard on this occasion exercised her power of 'natural and easy dialogue' in the part of Paulina.

Up to this point the text presented seems to have been Shakespeare's, or something like it; but now the dauntless adaptor steps in. On March 25, 1754, a two-act piece called *The Sheep-Shearing* makes its appearance in the Covent Garden bill, which is, in fact, nothing but the fourth act of *The Winter's Tale*, torn from its context and 'written up' by a forgotten playwright named McNamara Morgan. Leontes and Hermione have, of course, disappeared from the scene, and the old Shepherd turns out to be none other than Antigonus in disguise. The part of Autolycus (spelt Autolicus) is much amplified, not to its advantage, and Sir Thomas Hanmer's sapient suggestion that 'Bohemia' must be a misprint for 'Bithyna' is accepted in all good faith. Spranger Barry, the 'harmonious Barry,' Garrick's rival in the part of Romeo, played Florizel to the Perdita of Miss Nossiter, and to the Autolicus of Ned Shuter, wit, winebibber, gambler, and 'gagger,' whom Garrick called the greatest comic genius he had ever seen. Barry must have liked the part of Florizel, for he frequently played it both in London and Dublin. At Covent Garden in 1758 his Perdita was the fair and frail George Anne Bellamy, who had played Juliet to Garrick's Romeo in the celebrated Battle of the Playhouses eight years previously. The piece may be said to have held the stage until the end of the century. It was repeated at Drury Lane in 1774, and at Covent Garden in 1790 and 1798, Florizel, Perdita, and Autolicus being played as a rule by actors who had held these parts in the unmutilated or less mutilated play. In the meantime a second maltreatment of the pastoral scenes had been perpetrated at the Haymarket by George Colman. It was in three acts, and entitled, like its predecessor, *The Sheep-Shearing*. Colman had not even gone to Shakespeare for his material, but had further mutilated Garrick's mutilation, of which we shall speak presently, introducing Leontes and Paulina into Bohemia. This execrable hotch-potch was produced unsuccessfully in 1777, and repeated in 1783, the Autolicus, on each occasion, being John Edwin, a comedian whose genuine talent was marred by an irresistible bent towards buffoonery.

We now leave *The Sheep-Shearing* and return to *The Winter's Tale*. On January 21, 1756, Garrick produced at Drury Lane *The Winter's Tale, or Florizel and Perdita*, a 'Dramatic Pastoral' in three acts. A play in which a baby grows to womanhood between the third and fourth acts was not to be tolerated by the polite public of the Georgian age. Even Shakespeare's name could not spur the imagination to a leap of sixteen years. *The Winter's Tale*, so Murphy sums the matter up, was regarded as 'the most irregular production of that great but eccentric poet,' and Garrick was the very man to shape its rough-hewn mass. It must be admitted that his enthusiasm for regularity was perfectly disinterested. He sacrificed without a qualm almost all the 'fat' (to use an expressive technicality) of his own part. The first three acts disappear at one fell slash of the cleaver. Camillo in the first scene relates to 'a gentleman' the events which took place in Sicily, and this is all that remains of the jealousy of Leontes, the despair of Hermione, the trial, and the oracle. Leontes is shipwrecked on the coast of Bohemia, whither Paulina, with Hermione in her keeping, has previously emigrated. From this the course of the action may easily be surmised, and Garrick, it must be added, has not been sparing of interpolation even where it was not strictly necessary. Yet, in his Prologue, after patronising Shakespeare at some length, he wound up with the couplet—

> *'Tis my chief Wish, my Joy, my only Plan,*
> *To lose no Drop of that immortal Man!*

Well may he add a note of admiration to this extraordinary statement, and well may Genest, in his quiet way, append the note, 'He has certainly lost a tun of him here.' One would suppose that this maltreatment of the poet could not fail to meet with loud disapprobation from the scholars of the day. Nothing could be further from the fact. 'Dear Sirs,' writes Warburton to Garrick (June 12, 1758), 'As you know me to be less an idolizer of Shakspeare than yourself, you will less suspect me of compliment when I tell you that besides your giving an elegant form to a monstrous composition, you have in your own additions written up to the best scenes in this play, so that you will easily imagine I read the *Reformed Winter's Tale* with great pleasure.' Garrick was not destined, however, to reap unmixed gratification from his *Florizel and Perdita*. One day in 1769 Mrs. Thrale happened to praise 'Garrick's talent for light gay poetry;' and in support of her praise she repeated a song he had written for Perdita, ending (as she slightly misquoted it),

> I'd smile with the simple, and feed with the poor.
>
> JOHNSON: Nay, my dear Lady, this will never do. Poor David! Smile with the simple;—What folly is that? And who would feed with the poor that can help it? No, no; let me smile with the wise, and feed with the rich!

Here was an opportunity for mischief-making which Boswell could not resist. 'I repeated this sally to Garrick,' he says, 'and wondered to find his sensibility as a writer not a little irritated by it.'[1]

The comedy, so much as was left of it, was admirably played. Of Garrick's Leontes, Davies tells us that 'his action and whole behaviour during the disinchanting of Hermione, was extremely affecting.' Mrs. Pritchard was the Hermione—the great actress of whom Johnson afterwards said to a still greater actress, 'Pritchard, in common life, was a vulgar idiot; she would talk of her *gownd*: but, when she appeared upon the stage, seemed to be inspired by gentility and understanding.' Mrs. Cibber, whose 'fascinating art Could wake the pulses of the heart,' played Perdita, converted, no doubt for her special behoof, into a singing part. It was on hearing of her death, ten years later, that Garrick cried, 'Then Tragedy is dead on one side!' Holland was the Florizel, a handsome but stiff and imitative actor. 'With truly tragic stalk,' wrote Churchill, 'He creeps—he flies. A hero should not walk.' The part of the Clown was assigned to Woodward, who on the same evening added to his laurels by playing Petruchio in Garrick's version of *The Taming of the Shrew*, then produced (as an after-piece) for the first time. Woodward was great in such parts as Bobadil and Sir Andrew Aguecheek, while as a Harlequin he almost rivalled Rich. Yates played Autolicus (so Garrick also choose to spell the name), and played it, says Davies, with marked success. Dibdin says of Yates that he 'added to chaste nature becoming respectability,' and we are assured that Churchill did him great injustice in the couplet:—

> Lo! Yates! without the least finesse of art,
> He gets applause. I wish he'd get his part.

He was as careful of money as Garrick himself, and died at the age of eighty-four, leaving a large fortune. It is said that on his wife's benefit-nights he was always to be seen in the gallery exhorting the gods to 'sit close,' and adding plaintively 'Mrs. Yates is the greatest actress in the world and has but one day.'

This quasi-Shakespearean bill—*Florizel and Perdita* and *Catherine and Petruchio*—was so attractive that it was repeated eleven times; and six years later Garrick revived the same pieces with almost the same casts. King, however, replaced Woodward as the Clown and Petruchio—King, who created Lord

Ogleby and Sir Peter Teazle, whose active life on the stage extended over fifty-four years, and of whom Lamb wrote: 'His acting left a taste on the palate, sharp and sweet, like a quince.' At Covent Garden, in 1771, Shakespeare's *Winter Tale* was revived for one night—a benefit. Leontes was played by Gentleman Smith, whose agreements with his managers always contained three stipulations—that he should not be required to blacken his face, to play in farce, or to descend through a trap. The Polixenes was Bensley, whose Malvolio and Hotspur are so warmly praised—perhaps over-praised—by Lamb. The Hermione was Mrs. Mattocks, a comic actress, who was sadly out of place in tragedy. 'She was the paragon representative,' Boaden tells us, 'of the radically *vulgar* woman.' Dubellamy, a singer of some note, played Autolycus, while the Clown and Perdita were represented by Quick and Mrs. Bulkley, who were destined, two years later, to create the parts of Tony Lumpkin and Miss Hardcastle. This was the last appearance of Shakespeare's play upon the stage for more than thirty years. In 1774 Garrick's version was revived at Covent Garden, with Smith as Leontes, Bensley as Polixenes, Quick as Autolicus, and Woodward as the Clown. The Florizel was William Lewis, who in after years was said to combine in such parts as Mercutio 'the gracefulness of Barry with the energy of Garrick.' Hermione was played by Mrs. Hartley, the lovely woman who still lives for us on the canvases of Reynolds. 'A finer creature I never saw,' said Garrick; 'her make is perfect.' Her acting, unfortunately, was quite the reverse. The Perdita was a certain (or uncertain) Miss Dayes, and the Paulina was Mrs. Green, whom we have seen, as Miss Hippisley, playing Perdita at Goodman's Fields for the first time since the Restoration. The next revival of *Florizel and Perdita*, at Drury Lane in 1779, was marked by a romantic episode. Smith again played Leontes; Bensley, Polixenes; and Mrs. Hartley, Hermione; but on the fifth night the part of Hermione was transferred to Miss Farren, afterwards Countess of Derby. Yates was the Clown, and the Autolicus was a singing comedian named Vernon, who made his chief mark in this part. Perdita was played by Mrs. Mary Robinson, a young actress who had made some success during the three previous seasons in such parts as Juliet, Ophelia, and Viola. She was a Miss Darby, daughter, according to some, of a captain in the Russian navy, according to others, of a philanthropist who wasted his substance 'in attempts to civilise the Esquimaux Indians.' She had been a pupil of Hannah More, and had made her first appearance under the auspices of Garrick. On December 3, 1779, *Florizel and Perdita* 'was acted by command of their Majesties.' 'When Mrs. Robinson,' says Genest, 'went into the green-room dressed as Perdita, Smith exclaimed, "By Jove! you will make a conquest of the Prince, for you look handsomer than ever." Smith proved a true prophet, and a few days after she received, through the hands of a Nobleman, a letter addressed to Perdita and with peculiar propriety signed Florizel.' The nobleman who carried this missive of 'peculiar propriety' was probably Viscount Malden, afterwards Earl of Essex. It is curious to reflect that his widow, formerly Miss Stephens, the celebrated singer, died so lately as 1882. The connection of Florizel and Perdita lasted only two years, after which the shepherdess was deserted by her swain. While still a young woman she was seized with paralysis, and in the *Memoirs* of Miss Hawkins we get the following pathetic glimpse of her:—

> On a table in one of the waiting-rooms of the Opera House was seated a woman of fashionable appearance, still beautiful, 'but not in the bloom of beauty's pride;' she was not noticed except by the eye of pity.

In a few minutes two liveried servants came to her, and they took from their pockets long white sleeves, which they drew on their arms; they then lifted her up and conveyed her to her carriage—it was the then helpless paralytic Perdita.

The Florizel, too, of this 1779 revival was a man of somewhat romantic destiny. His name was William Brereton. For several years he was held a hopelessly mediocre actor, until he happened to play with Mrs. Siddons, whose magnetic influence awoke him to something like genius. Before long, however, his mind gave way, and he died insane, distracted, it was said, by the hopeless passion with which the great actress had inspired him.

The subsequent revivals of *Florizel and Perdita* may be passed over rapidly. In 1783 Henderson played Leontes at Covent Garden to the Hermione of Mrs. Yates. Though Garrick sneered at him, Henderson was undoubtedly a great actor, especially in respect of versatility. His Hamlet and his Falstaff were said to be equally good. As for Mrs. Yates, all authorities agree as to her singular beauty, but there are differences of opinion as to the merits of her acting. 'Too much stumping about and too much flumping about,' said the outspoken Kitty Clive; and perhaps there was more in the criticism than a mere access of spleen. Campbell wrote of her Hermione: 'Mrs. Yates had a sculpturesque beauty that suited the statue, I have been told, as long as it stood still; but when she had to speak the charm was broken and the spectators wished her back on her pedestal.' Lewis, on this occasion, played Florizel, Quick the Clown, and Edwin Autolicus. The Perdita was Miss Satchell, afterwards Mrs. Stephen Kemble, a good actress in her day. There was a revival of the play in 1788 at Drury Lane, Miss Farren resuming the part of Hermione to the Leontes of Wroughton, 'a sterling sound, and sensible performer.' Mrs. Crouch

> Endu'd with every gentle grace,
> A voice celestial, and an angel face,

appeared as Perdita, with Barrymore, a pompous and second-rate player, as her Florizel. The clown was Dicky Suett, whom 'Shakespeare foresaw,' says Lamb, 'when he framed his fools and jesters;' and Dodd played Autolicus—a part, one would suppose, not quite within the range of 'the most perfect fopling ever placed upon the stage.' At Covent Garden in 1792 a popular singer named Mrs. Mountain chose the part of Perdita for her benefit. Harley, a tragedian of provincial fame, played Leontes to the Hermione of Mrs. Pope, an actress of the Garrick school. Of her it is said, rather pathetically, that after the retirement of Mrs. Yates and Mrs. Crawford, and but for the appearance of Mrs. Siddons, she would have been the best tragic actress on the stage. Munden, of whom more hereafter, was the Autolicus, Quick the Clown; and Holman, whose 'pavior's sighs' Lamb has immortalised, played Florizel. Three years later (1795) the play was revived at Covent Garden for the last time. The Hermione, Florizel, Autolicus, and Clown were the same as in 1792. The Leontes was Alexander Pope (the husband of Hermione), more famous as a gourmand than as an actor; and the Perdita was Miss Wallis, a promising young actress, who soon afterwards married, abandoned the stage for fifteen years, and on returning to it failed dismally.

After 1795 Garrick's *Florizel and Perdita* was heard no more. On March 25, 1802, John Philip Kemble revived Shakespeare's *Winter's Tale* at Drury Lane, borrowing from Garrick's perversion the song criticised by Johnson, and a few speeches in the last scene. He himself played Leontes to the Hermione of Mrs. Siddons, who the more readily assumed this character as 'her form was becoming too matronly for the

personation of juvenile heroines.' She looked the statue, says Campbell, 'even to literal illusion.'

The figure (says Boaden) composed something like one of the muses in profile. The drapery was ample in its folds, and seemingly stony in its texture. Upon the magical words, pronounced by Paulina, 'Musick; awake her: strike;' the sudden action of the head absolutely *startled*, as though such a miracle had really vivified the marble; and the descent from the pedestal was equally graceful and affecting.

It was on this occasion that the Muse of Tragedy narrowly escaped a tragic fate.

Whilst I was standing for the statue (she writes to her friend Mrs. Fitz Hugh) my drapery flew over the lamps that were placed behind the pedestal; it caught fire, and, had it not been for one of the scene-men, who most humanely crept on his knees and extinguished it, without my knowing anything of the matter, I might have been burnt to death, or, at all events, I should have been frightened out of my senses. Surrounded as I was with muslin, the flame would have run like wildfire. The bottom of the train was entirely burnt.

Some time afterwards she was enabled to show her gratitude to her preserver by procuring a pardon for his son, who had deserted from the army.

The play was repeated eleven nights during the season. 'Perhaps no revival,' says Boaden, 'ever drew greater crowds.' The Florizel was Charles Kemble, youngest of the family, whose Romeo, Faulconbridge, and Mark Antony are remembered by men yet living. 'The Perdita,' Boaden tells us, 'was a very delicate and pretty young lady of the name of Hickes.' It was her first appearance on any stage, and her subsequent career seems to have been undistinguished. Antigonus was played by Dowton, a 'good all round' comedian, who was excellent in Sir Anthony Absolute, and at least fair in Falstaff. Suett was the Clown, and the Autolycus was Jack Bannister, whose Ben in *Love for Love* so delighted Charles Lamb. Bannister began as a tragedian, and was considered by the stage carpenters the finest Hamlet of his time, because he got through the part twenty minutes quicker than anyone else. When he mentioned to Garrick his intention of trying comedy, the great man replied, 'Why, no, don't think of that. You may humbug the town some time longer as a tragedian; *but comedy is a serious thing*, so don't try it yet.'

Kemble twice revived *The Winter's Tale* at Covent Garden, first in 1807, then in 1811. On each occasion he himself played Leontes; his brother Charles, Florizel; and Mrs. Siddons, Hermione. 'In the assumed statue,' says a critic of the later date, 'she had as much proper dignity as the rotund state of her anatomy can allow.' Her entreaties to Polixenes, the same writer tells us, were by no means 'insinuating,' and the smile she assumed was 'more contemptuous than alluring, like Melpomene inviting Cupid to a banquet.' The Perdita of 1807 was Miss Norton, of 1811 Mrs. H. Johnston—neither an actress of any great note. The Clown in both revivals was played by the incomparable Liston; but the Autolycus of 1807 was Munden, of 1811 Fawcett. Both were great comedians, but Fawcett, according to Talfourd, 'had not the facility or richness of Munden.' 'He is not one, but legion,' said Charles Lamb of Munden; 'not so much a comedian as a company. If his name could be multiplied like his countenance it would fill a playbill.' He was an utterly ignorant man, and boasted of his ignorance. 'I never read any book but a play,' he said; 'no play but one in which I myself acted, and no portion of that play but my own scenes.' This saying was repeated to Lamb, who remarked, 'I knew Munden well, and I believe him.'

When next the play was revived (Covent Garden, 1819) Charles Young succeeded Kemble in the part of Leontes. Young was unquestionably a great tragedian. 'I flatter myself he could not act Othello as I do,' said Edmund Kean, 'yet what chance should I have in Iago after him, with his personal advantages and his d—— musical voice.' His Leontes, however, does not seem to have been very successful, for the play was only once repeated. The Hermione was Miss Somerville, afterwards the spouse of 'the poet Bunn;' the Perdita a Miss Beaumont, unknown to fame. Charles Kemble played Florizel, Fawcett Autolycus, and Liston the Clown. Young again played Leontes at Covent Garden in 1827, but only for three nights. The Hermione was Mrs. Faucit, the mother, if we were not mistaken, of Miss Helen Faucit (Lady Martin). Fawcett resumed the part of Autolycus, and Robert Keeley, a famous comedian whose no less famous wife is still among us, appeared as the Clown. In the meantime Macready, at Drury Lane, had essayed the part of Leontes in 1823, playing it twelve times. His Hermione was Mrs. Bunn, his Perdita Mrs. W. West, afterwards a noted melodramatic actress. James Wallack, the dashing and the stately, played Florizel; Mrs. Glover, an admirable comedian, appeared as Paulina; and Munden, then in the last year of his professional life, once more appeared as Autolycus.

Leontes, according to Macready's own account, was a part in which he 'produced a very strong impression.' It must evidently have been one of his favourite characters, since he chose *The Winter's Tale* as the opening production of his famous management at Covent Garden, September 30, 1837. 'Acted Leontes artist-like,' he writes in his diary, 'but not, until the last act, very effectively.' Miss Helen Faucit was the Hermione; it is to be regretted that she has not devoted to this character one of her delightful letter-studies of Shakesperean heroines. Miss Taylor (Mrs. Walter Lacy) was the Perdita, and Mr. James Anderson, a popular romantic actor in his day, made his first appearance in London as Florizel. Paulina was played by Miss Huddart, afterwards Mrs. Warner, and Mopsa by Miss P. Horton, known to this generation as Mrs. German Reed. The play was repeated at intervals under Macready's management, both at Covent Garden and at Drury Lane. On the occasion of Phelps's benefit at Drury Lane, May 30, 1843, it was given with a cast so remarkable as to be worth reproducing in full: Leontes, Macready; Polixenes, Ryder; Florizel, Anderson; Antigonus, Phelps; Camillo, Elton; Autolycus, Compton; Clown, Keeley; Hermione, Miss Helen Faucit; Paulina, Mrs. Warner; Perdita, Mrs. Nisbett; Mopsa, Mrs. Keeley; Dorcas, Miss P. Horton. At Sadler's Wells, too, during the memorable management of Phelps and Greenwood, *The Winter's Tale* stood on the stock repertory. It was first produced on November 19, 1845, with Phelps of course as Leontes, Mrs. Warner as Hermione, Miss Cooper as Perdita, and Henry Marston as Florizel. Miss Glyn afterwards replaced Mrs. Warner as Hermione.

One of the most elaborate achievements of Charles Kean's management at the Princess's was his revival of *The Winter's*

*Tale* on the 28th of April, 1856. It may be said to have reduced to absurdity the principle of spectacular archæology. The play being one into which Shakespeare has deliberately crowded every possible impossibility of time, place, and circumstance, lest anyone should mistake it for anything but a Winter's Tale, a *Wintermährchen*, Mr. Kean must needs tie it down to an historical period, correct its geography, and make it a vehicle for popular instruction in the manners and costumes of Greece. The production opened with a Syracusan feast, enlivened by a Pyrrhic dance; the trial of Hermione took place in the theatre of Syracuse; the Bithynian (not Bohemian) sheep-shearing was 'heightened into a Dionysiac orgie in which something like two hundred dancers were employed.' Now from all this the audience certainly cannot have gathered a too realistic conception of ancient Greece. The spectacle of 'thirty-six resplendently handsome young girls' dancing a Pyrrhic dance 'in shining armour' does not amount to a liberal education in Hellenics. But the intention was there—'Mamillius,' writes Oxenford, 'may not draw about a toy cart that has not its terra-cotta prototype in the British Museum.' As dirt is matter in the wrong place, so pedantry is learning in the wrong place; and it would be hard to discover a finer instance of this than Charles Kean's 'archæological fly-leaf,' describing his researches into the costume and local colour of *The Winter's Tale*. Kean himself played Leontes, and his wife (Miss Ellen Tree) was of course the Hermione. Of the minor parts, Oxenford wrote as follows:—

> Mr. Ryder is a stately Polixenes; Miss [Carlotta] Leclercq a pretty and animated Perdita; Mr. Harley a quaint Autolycus; . . . Miss Heath [the late Mrs. Wilson Barrett] an attractive Florizel; . . . and last—ay, and least too—Miss Ellen Terry plays the boy Mamillius with a vivacious precocity that proves her a worthy relative of her sister (?) Miss Kate.

The mark of interrogation is in the original.

One of the last enterprises of Mr. F. B. Chatterton's luckless management at Drury Lane was a revival of *The Winter's Tale* towards the close of 1878. Mr. Charles Dillon played Leontes; Miss Ellen Wallis, Hermione; Miss Emily Fowler, Perdita; Mr. Edward Compton, Florizel; and Mrs. Hermann Vezin, Paulina. At the same theatre, in 1881, the Meiningen Company's rendering of *Das Wintermährchen* was, next to *Julius Cæsar*, their most attractive performance. The Trial Scene afforded an excellent example of the ingenious and masterly stage-management in which their chief strength lay. Since 1881 *The Winter's Tale* has not been seen in London until its present revival at the Lyceum.

*Notes*

1. Genest hints that Garrick stole this song from Morgan's *Sheep-Shearing* and was ashamed to own the fact. This seems to be a mistake. We have been unable to procure the edition of Morgan's play said to have been published in Dublin in 1754, but the song does not appear in the edition of 1767. The popularity acquired for it by Mrs. Cibber's singing probably led to its subsequent insertion in Morgan's play. Genest had evidently not seen the 1754 edition, and jumped too hastily at the belief that it included the song.

# The Tempest

. . . resolved with Sir W. Pen to go see *The Tempest*, an old play of Shakespeare's, acted, I hear, the first day . . . the most innocent play that ever I saw; and a curious piece of musique in an echo of half sentences, the echo repeating the former half, while the man goes on to the latter; which is mighty pretty. The play has no great wit, but yet good, above ordinary plays.—SAMUEL PEPYS, *Diary*, Nov. 7, 1667

. . . and thence after dinner to the Duke of York's house, to the play, *The Tempest*, which we have often seen, but yet I was pleased again, and shall be again to see it, it is so full of variety, and particularly this day I took pleasure to learn the tune of the seaman's dance, which I have much desired to be perfect in, and have made myself so.—SAMUEL PEPYS, *Diary*, Feb. 3, 1668

The writing of prefaces to plays was probably invented by some very ambitious poet who never thought he had done enough: perhaps by some ape of the French eloquence, which uses to make a business of a letter of gallantry, an examen of a farce; and, in short, a great pomp and ostentation of words on every trifle. This is certainly the talent of that nation, and ought not to be invaded by any other. They do that out of gaiety which would be an imposition upon us.

We may satisfy ourselves with surmounting them in the scene, and safely leave them those trappings of writing and flourishes of the pen with which they adorn the borders of their plays, and which are indeed no more than good landskips to a very indifferent picture. I must proceed no farther in this argument, lest I run myself beyond my excuse for writing this. Give me leave therefore to tell you, Reader, that I do it not to set a value on any thing I have written in this play, but out of gratitude to the memory of Sir William Davenant, who did me the honour to join me with him in the alteration of it.

It was originally Shakespeare's: a poet for whom he had particularly a high veneration, and whom he first taught me to admire. The play itself had formerly been acted with success in the Blackfriars; and our excellent Fletcher had so great a value for it that he thought fit to make use of the same design, not much varied, a second time. Those who have seen his *Sea-Voyage* may easily discern that it was a copy of Shakespeare's *Tempest*: the storm, the desert island, and the woman who had never seen a man, are all sufficient testimonies of it. But Fletcher was not the only poet who made use of Shakespeare's plot: Sir John Suckling, a professed admirer of our author, has followed his footsteps in his *Goblins*, his Reginella being an open imitation of Shakespeare's Miranda; and his spirits, though counterfeit, yet are copied from Ariel. But Sir William Davenant, as he was a man of quick and piercing imagination, soon found that somewhat might be added to the design of Shakespeare of which neither Fletcher nor Suckling had ever thought: and therefore to put the last hand to it, he designed the counterpart to Shakespeare's plot, namely that of a man who had never seen a woman, that by this means those two characters of innocence and love might the more illustrate and commend each other. This excellent contrivance he was pleased to communicate to me, and to desire my assistance in it. I confess that from the very first moment it so pleased me that I never writ anything with more delight. I must likewise do him that justice to acknowledge that my writing received daily his amendments, and that is the reason why it is not so faulty as the rest, which I have done without the help or correction of so

judicious a friend. The comical parts of the sailors were also his invention and for the most part his writing, as you will easily discover by the style. In the time I writ with him, I had the opportunity to observe somewhat more nearly of him than I had formerly done when I had only a bare acquaintance with him: I found him then of so quick a fancy that nothing was proposed to him on which he could not suddenly produce a thought extremely pleasant and surprising; and those first thoughts of his, contrary to the old Latin proverb, were not always the least happy. And as his fancy was quick, so likewise were the products of it remote and new. He borrowed not of any other; and his imaginations were such as could not easily enter into any other man. His corrections were sober and judicious: and he corrected his own writings much more severely than those of another man, bestowing twice the time and labour in polishing which he used in invention. It had perhaps been easy enough for me to have arrogated more to myself than was my due in the writing of this play, and to have passed by his name with silence in the publication of it, with the same ingratitude which others have used to him, whose writings he hath not only corrected, as he has done this, but has had a greater inspection over them, and sometimes added whole scenes together, which may as easily be distinguished from the rest as true gold from counterfeit by the weight. But besides the unworthiness of the action which deterred me from it (there being nothing so base as to rob the dead of his reputation) I am satisfied I could never have received so much honour in being thought the author of any poem, how excellent soever, as I shall be from the joining my imperfections with the merit and name of Shakespeare and Sir William Davenant.—JOHN DRYDEN, "Preface" to *The Tempest, or The Enchanted Island*, 1670

As when a Tree's cut down the secret root
Lives under ground, and thence new Branches shoot;
So, from old *Shakespear's* honour'd dust, this day
Springs up and buds a new reviving Play.
*Shakespear*, who (taught by none) did first impart
To *Fletcher* Wit, to labouring *Johnson* Art.
He Monarch-like gave those his subjects law,
And is that Nature which they paint and draw.
*Fletcher* reach'd that which on his heights did grow,
Whilst *Johnson* crept and gather'd all below.
This did his Love, and this his Mirth digest:
One imitates him most, the other best.
If they have since out-writ all other men,
'Tis with the drops which fell from *Shakespear's* Pen.
The Storm which vanish'd on the Neighb'ring shore,
Was taught by *Shakespear's* Tempest first to roar.
That innocence and beauty which did smile
In *Fletcher*, grew on this *Enchanted Isle*.
But *Shakespear's* Magick could not copy'd be,
Within that Circle none durst walk but he.
I must confess 'twas bold, nor would you now,
That liberty to vulgar Wits allow,
Which works by Magick supernatural things:
But *Shakespear's* pow'r is sacred as a King's.
Those Legends from old Priest-hood were receiv'd,
And he then writ, as people then believ'd.
But, if for *Shakespear* we your grace implore,
We for our Theatre shall want it more:

Who by our dearth of Youths are forc'd t' employ
One of our Women to present a Boy.
And that's a transformation you will say
Exceeding all the Magick in the Play.
Let none expect in the last Act to find,
Her Sex transform'd from man to Woman-kind.
What e're she was before the Play began,
All you shall see of her is perfect man.
Or if your fancy will be farther led,
To find her Woman, it must be abed.

    —JOHN DRYDEN, "Prologue" to *The Tempest, or*
      *The Enchanted Island*, 1670

This Play is allowed by all Judges to be one of the strongest Testimonials of *Shakespear's* Poetic Power, and of the Force of his Imagination, which on the Doctrine of Enchantment (in his Time firmly believed) has raised so noble a Structure: And from such immoral Agents has produced such fine Lessons of Religion, and Morality as this Play abounds with.

The Plot is single; the making bad Men penitent, and manifesting that Repentance by restoring a deposed Sovereign Duke to his Dominions: With the additional Lesson, that Patience under Afflictions meets in the End its Reward, that Duke's Daughter by Marriage, being entitled to a Kingdom; the Fable being built on this simple Story.

PROSPERO, Duke of *Milan*, being fond of Knowledge in general, and particularly of *Magic* (which he never uses to any bad Purpose) that he may more closely apply to his Studies, yields up all his Power to his Brother *Anthonio*: Who, growing fond of Rule, resolves to change his deputed Authority, into an absolute Command; and to that End, enters into an Alliance with *Alonso* King of *Naples*, for his Assistance to depose *Prospero*, and substitute himself in his Place: In Consideration of which, *Milan*, (before free) is to become tributary to *Naples*.

As *Prospero* has been an excellent Sovereign to his People, they dare not destroy him, nor raise an open Rebellion against him; but *Anthonio* is to receive some *Neapolitan* Troops privately into *Milan*; then to seize *Prospero*, and *Miranda* his young Daughter, not three Years old, and carry them on Board a Bark; and when they have got them some Leagues at Sea, put them into an old and leaky Boat, without any Tackling, and commit them to the Mercy of the Waves: Which was done. But *Gonzalo*, an old *Neapolitan* Lord, who has the Management of this Affair, and is a great Friend to *Prospero*, privately furnishes the Boat with many Necessaries of Life, and especially with *Prospero's* magical Books.

*Prospero*, and his Daughter, are long lost on the Waves in a violent Tempest, but are at length brought to a desart uninhabited Island, formerly the Residence of an *Algerine* Witch, famous for her Skill in Sorcery (which she always employed to wicked Ends) named *Sycorax*; who had been banished sometime before, to this Place, where she died, leaving only *Caliban* a Monster, engendered of her by a Dæmon, (a Progeny finely imagined for such Parents;) and *Ariel*, an aeriel Spirit, (too good for her foul Works) inclosed in a Pine-Tree.

The first of these, *Prospero* instructs in Language, and other useful Knowledge, and makes his Houshold Servant, treating him with great Kindness; till he attempting to ravish *Miranda*, is confined, and used harshly, for which he meditates Revenge: The other is released from the Tree, and made useful to *Prospero* in his *Magic*.

After *Prospero* has lived twelve Years on this Island, there appears on its Coasts, *Alonso* King of *Naples*, returning from the Marriage of his Daughter *Claribel*, to the King of *Tunis* in *Barbary*: Accompanied by his Son *Ferdinand*, his Brother *Sebastian*, and many other Courtiers, amongst whom are *Anthonio*, *Prospero's* wicked Brother, and the good *Gonzalo*: *Prospero*, knowing they are on the Coast, by his Art, raises a magical *Tempest*, in which, they appear to be all shipwreck'd. With this *Tempest* the Play opens, and is named from it.

*Ferdinand*, who apprehends he saw his Father sink, is led by *Ariel* to *Prospero's Cell*; where he sees, falls in love *with*, and (she also falling in love with him) contracts himself *to Miranda*.

The King, searching for his Son, whom he thinks (not finding him) is drown'd; a Conspiracy is formed against him, by *Anthonio*, and *Sebastian*, who are prevented from assassinating him and *Gonzalo*, by *Prospero*: But he and his companions are terrified by Dæmons, and told by *Ariel*, of their wicked Behaviour to *Prospero*; that to that, they owe all their Misfortunes; which will not cease till they repent: Whereon those who are guilty run distracted.

Their Recovery; the Detection of a Plot to murther *Prospero*, framed between *Caliban*, and *Stephano*, and *Trinculo*, two Drunkards of *Alonso's* Retinue; an enchanted Masque, to celebrate the Marriage-Contract between *Ferdinand*, and *Miranda*; the Restoration of the King to his Senses, and his son; and of *Prospero* to his Dukedom; with the Discovery that all was the Effect of Magic; fill up the whole Time of Action, which is supposed to be about six Hours; *Shakespear* having observed the Unities more in this Play, than in any other he ever wrote.

The Manners are mix'd, and consequently the Sentiments, and Diction; but all proper to the Persons represented, and chiefly Moral; Teaching a Dependance upon Providence, in the utmost Danger and Distress; and the Blessings of Deliverance, and Reward, attending that Dependance.

The Language, easy in the Narrative; but where the Passions are concerned, according to this Writer's usual Method, sublimely bold, and figurative: Though now and then, something harsh in the Construction, and by that Means, obscure, to a cursory Reader.

The Characters admirably suited to their Business on the Scene, particularly *Caliban's*; which is work'd up to a Height, answerable to the Greatness of the Imagination that form'd it: And will always secure *Shakespear's* Claim to Poetic Fame, as abounding in every Part with Imagery, and Invention, which two, are the Support, and Soul of Poetry. His Language is finely adapted, nay peculiarized to his Character, as his Character is to the Fable; his Sentiments to both, and his Manners to all: His Curiosity, Avidity, Brutality, Cowardice, Vindictiveness, and Cruelty, exactly agreeing with his Ignorance, and the Origin of his Person.

The Plan mostly tragical, the Faculties being operated on, by Amazement, Fear, and Pity; but not regular, being mixed with comic Interludes, and the Catastrophe happy. The Discovery is simple, and allowing for Enchantment, very easily, and naturally brought about.

The MASQUE abovementioned, may perhaps give a Mark to guess at the Time this Play was wrote; it appearing to be a Compliment intended by the Poet, on some particular Solemnity of that Kind; and if so, none more likely, than the contracting the young Earl of *Essex*, in 1606, with the Lady *Frances Howard*; which Marriage was not attempted to be consummated, till the *Earl* returned from his Travels four Years afterwards; a Circumstance, which seems to be hinted at, in

*If thou dost break her Virgin Knot*, before
All sanctimonious Ceremonies, may
With full and holy Right be ministred, &c.

                             (Act IV. Sc. I.)

unless any one should chuse to think it designed for the Marriage of the *Palsgrave*, with the Lady *Elizabeth*, King *James*'s Daughter, in 1612. But the first seems to carry most Weight with it, as being a Testimony of the Poet's Gratitude to the then Lord *Southhampton*, a warm Patron of the Author's and as zealous a Friend to the *Essex* Family: In either Case, it will appear, 'twas one of the last Plays wrote by our Author, though it has stood the first, in all the printed Editions since 1623, which Preheminence given it by the Players, is no bad Proof of its being the last, this Author furnished them with.— JOHN HOLT, *Remarks on* The Tempest, 1749, pp. 13–18

That the character and conduct of Prospero may be understood, something must be known of the system of enchantment, which supplied all the marvellous found in the romances of the middle ages. This system seems to be founded on the opinion that the fallen spirits, having different degrees of guilt, had different habitations allotted them at their expulsion, some being confined in hell, "some," as Hooker, who delivers the opinion of our poet's age, expresses it, "dispersed in air, some on earth, some in water, others in caves, dens or minerals under the earth." Of these some were more malignant and mischievous than others. The earthy spirits seem to have been thought the most depraved, and the aerial the least vitiated. Thus Prospero observes of Ariel,

> Thou wast a spirit too delicate
> To act her *earthy* and abhorred commands.

Over these spirits a power might be obtained by certain rites performed or charms learned. This power was called the black art, or knowledge of enchantment. The enchanter being, as King James observes in his *Demonology*, one "who commands the devil, whereas the witch serves him." Those who thought best of this art, the existence of which was, I am afraid, believed very seriously, held that certain sounds and characters had a physical power over spirits, and compelled their agency; others who condemned the practice, which in reality was surely never practised, were of opinion, with more reason, that the power of charms arose *only* from compact, and was no more than the spirits voluntar(il)y allowed them for the seduction of man. The art was held by all, though not equally criminal yet unlawful, and therefore Causabon, speaking of one who had commerce with spirits, blames him, though he imagines him "one of the best kind who dealt with them by way of command." Thus Prospero repents of his art in the last scene. The spirits were always considered as in some measure enslaved to the enchanter, at least for a time, and as serving with unwillingness, therefore Ariel so often begs for liberty; and Caliban observes that the spirits serve Prospero with no good will, but "hate him rootedly."—Of these trifles enough.— SAMUEL JOHNSON, *Notes on Shakespeare's Plays*, 1768

*The Tempest* has little action or progressive movement; the union of Ferdinand and Miranda is settled at their first interview, and Prospero merely throws apparent obstacles in their way; the shipwrecked band go leisurely about the island; the attempts of Sebastian and Antonio on the life of the King of Naples, and the plot of Caliban and the drunken sailors against Prospero, are nothing but a feint, for we foresee that they will be completely frustrated by the magical skill of the latter; nothing remains therefore but the punishment of the guilty by dreadful sights which harrow up their consciences, and then the discovery and final reconciliation. Yet this want of movement is so admirably concealed by the most varied display of the fascinations of poetry, and the exhilaration of mirth, the details of the execution are so very attractive, that it requires no small degree of attention to perceive that the *dénouement* is, in

some degree, anticipated in the exposition. The history of the loves of Ferdinand and Miranda, developed in a few short scenes, is enchantingly beautiful: an affecting union of chivalrous magnanimity on the one part, and on the other of virgin openness of a heart which, brought up far from the world on an uninhabited island, has never learned to disguise its innocent movements. The wisdom of the princely hermit Prospero has a magical and mysterious air; the disagreeable impression left by the black falsehood of the two usurpers is softened by the honest gossipping of the old and faithful Gonzalo; Trinculo and Stephano, two good-for-nothing drunkards, find a worthy associate in Caliban; and Ariel hovers sweetly over the whole as the personified genius of the wonderful fable.

Caliban has become a by-word as the strange creation of a poetical imagination. A mixture of gnome and savage, half dæmon, half brute, in his behaviour we perceive at once the traces of his native disposition, and the influence of Prospero's education. The latter could only unfold his understanding, without, in the slightest degree, taming his rooted malignity: it is as if the use of reason and human speech were communicated to an awkward ape. In inclination Caliban is malicious, cowardly, false, and base; and yet he is essentially different from the vulgar knaves of a civilized world, as portrayed occasionally by Shakspeare. He is rude, but not vulgar; he never falls into the prosaic and low familiarity of his drunken associates, for he is, in his way, a poetical being; he always speaks in verse. He has picked up every thing dissonant and thorny in language to compose out of it a vocabulary of his own; and of the whole variety of nature, the hateful, repulsive, and pettily deformed, have alone been impressed on his imagination. The magical world of spirits, which the staff of Prospero has assembled on the island, casts merely a faint reflection into his mind, as a ray of light which falls into a dark cave, incapable of communicating to it either heat or illumination, serves merely to set in motion the poisonous vapours. The delineation of this monster is throughout inconceivably consistent and profound, and, notwithstanding its hatefulness, by no means hurtful to our feelings, as the honour of human nature is left untouched.

In the zephyr-like Ariel the image of air is not to be mistaken, his name even bears an allusion to it; as, on the other hand Caliban signifies the heavy element of earth. Yet they are neither of them simple, allegorical personifications but beings individually determined. In general we find in *The Midsummer Night's Dream*, in *The Tempest*, in the magical part of *Macbeth*, and wherever Shakspeare avails himself of the popular belief in the invisible presence of spirits, and the possibility of coming in contact with them, a profound view of the inward life of nature and her mysterious springs, which, it is true, can never be altogether unknown to the genuine poet, as poetry is altogether incompatible with mechanical physics, but which few have possessed in an equal degree with Dante and himself.—AUGUST WILHELM SCHLEGEL, *Lectures on Dramatic Art and Literature*, 1809, tr. John Black

There can be little doubt that Shakespear was the most universal genius that ever lived. 'Either for tragedy, comedy, history, pastoral, pastoral-comical, historical-pastoral, scene individable or poem unlimited, he is the only man. Seneca cannot be too heavy, nor Plautus too light for him.' He has not only the same absolute command over our laughter and our tears, all the resources of passion, of wit, of thought, of observation, but he has the most unbounded range of fanciful invention, whether terrible or playful, the same insight into the world of imagination that he has into the world of reality; and over all there presides the same truth of character and nature, and the same spirit of humanity. His ideal beings are as true and natural as his real characters; that is, as consistent with themselves, or if we suppose such beings to exist at all, they could not act, speak, or feel otherwise than as he makes them. He has invented for them a language, manners, and sentiments of their own, from the tremendous imprecations of the Witches in *Macbeth*, when they do 'a deed without a name,' to the sylph-like expressions of Ariel, who 'does his spiriting gently'; the mischievous tricks and gossipping of Robin Goodfellow, or the uncouth gabbling and emphatic gesticulations of Caliban in this play.

The *Tempest* is one of the most original and perfect of Shakespear's productions, and he has shewn in it all the variety of his powers. It is full of grace and grandeur. The human and imaginary characters, the dramatic and the grotesque, are blended together with the greatest art, and without any appearance of it. Though he has here given 'to airy nothing a local habitation and a name,' yet that part which is only the fantastic creation of his mind, has the same palpable texture, and coheres 'semblably' with the rest. As the preternatural part has the air of reality, and almost haunts the imagination with a sense of truth, the real characters and events partake of the wildness of a dream. The stately magician, Prospero, driven from his dukedom, but around whom (so potent is his art) airy spirits throng numberless to do his bidding; his daughter Miranda ('worthy of that name') to whom all the power of his art points, and who seems the goddess of the isle; the princely Ferdinand, cast by fate upon the haven of his happiness in this idol of his love; the delicate Ariel; the savage Caliban, half brute, half demon; the drunken ship's crew—are all connected parts of the story, and can hardly be spared from the place they fill. Even the local scenery is of a piece and character with the subject. Prospero's enchanted island seems to have risen up out of the sea; the airy music, the tempest-tost vessel, the turbulent waves, all have the effect of the landscape background of some fine picture. Shakespear's pencil is (to use an allusion of his own) 'like the dyer's hand, subdued to what it works in.' Every thing in him, though it partakes of 'the liberty of wit,' is also subjected to 'the law' of the understanding. For instance, even the drunken sailors, who are made reeling-ripe, share, in the disorder of their minds and bodies, in the tumult of the elements, and seem on shore to be as much at the mercy of chance as they were before at the mercy of the winds and waves. These fellows with their sea-wit are the least to our taste of any part of the play: but they are as like drunken sailors as they can be, and are an indirect foil to Caliban, whose figure acquires a classical dignity in the comparison.

The character of Caliban is generally thought (and justly so) to be one of the author's master-pieces. It is not indeed pleasant to see this character on the stage any more than it is to see the god Pan personated there. But in itself it is one of the wildest and most abstracted of all Shakespear's characters, whose deformity whether of body or mind is redeemed by the power and truth of the imagination displayed in it. It is the essence of grossness, but there is not a particle of vulgarity in it. Shakespear has described the brutal mind of Caliban in contact with the pure and original forms of nature; the character grows out of the soul where it is rooted, uncontrouled, uncouth and wild, uncramped by any of the meannesses of custom. It is 'of the earth, earthy.' It seems almost to have been dug out of the ground, with a soul instinctively superadded to it answering to its wants and origin. Vulgarity is not natural coarseness, but conventional coarseness, learnt from others, contrary to, or without an entire conformity of natural power and disposition;

as fashion is the common-place affectation of what is elegant and refined without any feeling of the essence of it. Schlegel, the admirable German critic on Shakespear, observes that Caliban is a poetical character, and 'always speaks in blank verse.' . . .

Shakespear has, as it were by design, drawn off from Caliban the elements of whatever is ethereal and refined, to compound them in the unearthly mould of Ariel. Nothing was ever more finely conceived than this contrast between the material and the spiritual, the gross and delicate. Ariel is imaginary power, the swiftness of thought personified. When told to make good speed by Prospero, he says, 'I drink the air before me.' This is something like Puck's boast on a similar occasion, 'I'll put a girdle round about the earth in forty minutes.' But Ariel differs from Puck in having a fellow feeling in the interests of those he is employed about. How exquisite is the following dialogue between him and Prospero!

> *Ariel:* Your charm so strongly works 'em,
>     That if you now beheld them, your affections
>     Would become tender.
> *Prospero:* Dost thou think so, spirit?
> *Ariel:* Mine would, sir, were I human.
> *Prospero:* And mine shall.
>     Hast thou, which art but air, a touch, a feeling
>     Of their afflictions, and shall not myself,
>     One of their kind, that relish all as sharply,
>     Passion'd as they, be kindlier moved than thou art?

> —WILLIAM HAZLITT, *"The Tempest," Characters of Shakespear's Plays*, 1817

If I read ⟨*The Tempest*⟩ rightly, it is an example of how a great poet should write allegory,—not embodying metaphysical abstractions, but giving us ideals abstracted from life itself, suggesting an under-meaning everywhere, forcing it upon us nowhere, tantalizing the mind with hints that imply so much and tell so little, and yet keep the attention all eye and ear with eager, if fruitless, expectation. Here the leading characters are not merely typical, but symbolical,—that is, they do not illustrate a class of persons, they belong to universal Nature. Consider the scene of the play. Shakespeare is wont to take some familiar story, to lay his scene in some place the name of which, at least, is familiar,—well knowing the reserve of power that lies in the familiar as a background, when things are set in front of it under a new and unexpected light. But in the *Tempest* the scene is laid nowhere, or certainly in no country laid down on any map. Nowhere, then? At once nowhere and anywhere,—for it is in the soul of man, that still vexed island hung between the upper and the nether world, and liable to incursions from both. There is scarce a play of Shakespeare's in which there is such variety of character, none in which character has so little to do in the carrying on and development of the story. But consider for a moment if ever the Imagination has been so embodied as in Prospero, the Fancy as in Ariel, the brute Understanding as in Caliban, who, the moment his poor wits are warmed with the glorious liquor of Stephano, plots rebellion against his natural lord, the higher Reason. Miranda is mere abstract Womanhood, as truly so before she sees Ferdinand as Eve before she was wakened to consciousness by the echo of her own nature coming back to her, the same, and yet not the same, from that of Adam. Ferdinand, again, is nothing more than Youth, compelled to drudge at something he despises, till the sacrifice of will and abnegation of self win him his ideal in Miranda. The subordinate personages are simply types; Sebastian and Antonio, of weak character and evil ambition; Gonzalo, of average sense and honesty; Adrian and Francisco, of the walking gentlemen who serve to fill up a world. They are not characters in the same sense with Iago, Falstaff, Shallow, or Leontius; and it is curious how every one of them loses his way in this enchanted island of life, all the victims of one illusion after another, except Prospero, whose ministers are purely ideal. The whole play, indeed, is a succession of illusions, winding up with those solemn words of the great enchanter who had summoned to his service every shape of merriment or passion, every figure in the great tragi-comedy of life, and who was now bidding farewell to the scene of his triumphs. For in Prospero shall we not recognize the Artist himself,—

> That did not better for his life provide
> Than public means which public manners breeds,
> Whence comes it that his name receives a brand,—

who has forfeited a shining place in the world's eye by devotion to his art, and who, turned adrift on the ocean of life in the leaky carcass of a boat, has shipwrecked on that Fortunate Island (as men always do who find their true vocation) where he is absolute lord, making all the powers of Nature serve him, but with Ariel and Caliban as special ministers? Of whom else could he have been thinking, when he says,—

> Graves, at my command,
> Have waked their sleepers, oped, and let them forth,
> By my so potent art?

> —JAMES RUSSELL LOWELL, "Shakespeare Once More" (1868), *Works*, 1890, Vol. 3, pp. 199–201

I have often thought upon the relative stations of the various classes of poetry, and am disposed to deem eminence in the grand drama the supreme eminence; and this because, at its highest, the drama includes all other forms and classes, whether considered technically or essentially. Its plot requires as much inventive and constructive faculty as any epic or other narrative. Action is its glory, and characterization must be as various and vivid as life itself. The dialogue is written in the most noble, yet flexible measure of a language; if English, in the blank verse that combines the freedom of prose with the stateliness of accentual rhythm. The gravest speech, the lightest and sweetest, find their best vehicle in our unrhymed pentameter; again, a poetic drama contains songs and other interludes which exercise the lyrical gift so captivating in the works, for example, of our English playwrights: the Elizabethans having been lions in their heroics, eagles in their wisdom, and skylarks in their rare madrigals and part-songs. Tragedy and comedy alike are unlimited with respect to contrasts of incident and utterance, light and shadow of experience; they embrace whatsoever is poetic in mirth, woe, learning, law, religion—above all, in passion and action. So that the drama is like a stately architectural structure; a cathedral that includes every part essential to minor buildings, and calls upon the entire artistic brotherhood for its shape and beauty: upon the carver and the sculptor for its reliefs and imagery; upon the painter and the decorative artist for its wall-color and stained glass; upon the moulder to fashion its altar-rail, and the founder to cast the bells that give out its knell or pæan to the land about. The drama is thus more inclusive than the epic. There is little in Homer that is not true to nature, but there is no phase of nature that is not in Shakespeare.

Analyze the components of a Shakespearian play, and you will see that I make no overstatement.

*The Tempest*, a romantic play, is as notable as any for poetic quality and varied conception. It takes elemental nature for its scenes and background, the unbarred sky, the sea in storm and calm, the enchanted flowery isle, so

full of noises,
Sounds and sweet airs that give delight and hurt not.
The personages comprise many types,—king, noble, sage, low-born sailor, boisterous vagabond, youth and maiden in the heyday of their innocent love. To them are superadded beings of the earth and air, Caliban and Ariel, creations of the purest imagination. All these reveal their natures by speech and action, with a realism impossible to the tamer method of a narrative poem. Consider the poetic thought and diction: what can excel Prospero's vision of the world's dissolution that shall leave "not a rack behind," or his stately abjuration of the magic art? Listen, here and there, to the songs of his tricksy spirit, his brave chick, Ariel: "Come unto these yellow sands," "Full fathom five thy father lies," "Where the bee sucks, there suck I." Then we have a play within a play, lightening and decorating it, the masque of Iris, Ceres, and Juno. I recapitulate these details to give a perfectly familiar illustration of the scope of the drama. True, this was Shakespeare, but the ideal should be studied in a masterpiece; and such a play as *The Tempest* shows the possibilities of invention and imagination in the most synthetic poetic form over which genius has extended its domain.—EDMUND CLARENCE STEDMAN, "Creation and Self-Expression," *The Nature and Elements of Poetry*, 1892

## JOSEPH WARTON
### From *The Adventurer*
1753

*No. 93. September 25, 1753*

Irritat, mulcet, falsis terroribus implet,
Ut Magus; et modò me Thebis, modò ponit Athenis.
(Horace.)

'Tis he who gives my breast a thousand pains,
Can make me feel each passion that he feigns;
Enrage, compose, with more than magic art;
With pity, and with terror tear my heart;
And snatch me, o'er the earth, or through the air,
To Thebes, to Athens, when he will, and where.
(Pope.)

Writers of a mixed character, that abound in transcendent beauties and in gross imperfections, are the most proper and most pregnant subjects for criticism. The regularity and correctness of a Virgil or Horace, almost confine their commentators to perpetual panegyric, and afford them few opportunities of diversifying their remarks by the detection of latent blemishes. For this reason, I am inclined to think, that a few observations on the writings of Shakspeare, will not be deemed useless or unentertaining, because he exhibits more numerous examples of excellences and faults, of every kind, than are, perhaps, to be discovered in any other author. I shall, therefore, from time to time, examine his merit as a poet, without blind admiration or wanton invective.

As Shakspeare is sometimes blamable for the conduct of his fables, which have no unity; and sometimes for his diction, which is obscure and turgid; so his characteristical excellences may possibly be reduced to these three general heads: "his lively creative imagination; his strokes of nature and passion; and his preservation of the consistency of his characters." These excellences, particularly the last, are of so much importance in the drama, that they amply compensate for his transgressions against the rules of Time and Place, which being of a more mechanical nature, are often strictly observed by a genius of the lowest order; but to pourtray characters naturally, and to preserve them uniformly, requires such an intimate knowledge of the heart of man, and is so rare a portion of felicity, as to have been enjoyed, perhaps, only by two writers, Homer and Shakspeare.

Of all the plays of Shakspeare, the *Tempest* is the most striking instance of his creative power. He has there given the reins to his boundless imagination, and has carried the romantic, the wonderful, and the wild, to the most pleasing extravagance. The scene is a desolate island; and the characters the most new and singular that can well be conceived: a prince who practises magic, an attendant spirit, a monster the son of a witch, and a young lady who had been brought to this solitude in her infancy, and had never beheld a man except her father.

As I have affirmed that Shakspeare's chief excellence is the consistency of his characters, I will exemplify the truth of this remark, by pointing out some master-strokes of this nature in the drama before us.

The poet artfully acquaints us that Prospero is a magician, by the very first words which his daughter Miranda speaks to him:

> If by your art, my dearest father, you have
> Put the wild waters in this roar, allay them:

which intimate that the tempest described in the preceding scene, was the effect of Prospero's power. The manner in which he was driven from his dukedom of Milan, and landed afterward on this solitary island, accompanied only by his daughter, is immediately introduced in a short and natural narration.

The offices of his attendant spirit, Ariel, are enumerated with amazing wildness of fancy, and yet with equal propriety: his employment is said to be,

> To tread the ooze
> Of the salt deep;
> To run upon the sharp wind of the north;
> To do—business in the veins o' th' earth,
> When it is bak'd with frost;
>         to dive into the fire; to ride
> On the curl'd clouds.

In describing the place in which he has concealed the Neapolitan ship, Ariel expresses the secrecy of its situation by the following circumstance, which artfully glances at another of his services;

> In the deep nook, where once
> Thou call'st me up at midnight, to fetch dew
> From the still-vext Bermudas.

Ariel, being one of those elves or spirits, "whose pastime is to make midnight mushrooms, and who rejoice to listen to the solemn curfew;" by whose assistance Prospero has bedimm'd the sun at noon-tide,

> And 'twixt the green sea and the azur'd vault,
> Set roaring war;

has a set of ideas and images peculiar to his station and office: a beauty of the same kind with that which is so justly admired in the Adam of Milton, whose manners and sentiments are all Paradisaical. How delightfully and how suitably to his character, are the habitations and pastimes of this invisible being pointed out in the following exquisite song!

> Where the bee sucks, there suck I:
> In a cowslip's bell I lie;
> There I couch when owls do cry.
> On the bat's back I do fly,
> After sun-set merrily.
> Merrily, merrily shall I live now,
> Under the blossom that hangs on the bough.

Mr. Pope, whose imagination has been thought by some the least of his excellences, has, doubtless, conceived and carried on the machinery in his *Rape of the Lock*, with vast exuberance of fancy. The images, customs, and employments of his Sylphs, are exactly adapted to their natures, are peculiar and appropriated, are all, if I may be allowed the expression, Sylphish. The enumeration of the punishments they were to undergo, if they neglected their charge, would, on account of its poetry and propriety, and especially the mixture of oblique satire, be superior to any circumstances in Shakspeare's Ariel, if we could suppose Pope to have been unacquainted with the *Tempest*, when he wrote this part of his accomplished poem.

> She did confine thee
> Into a cloven pine: within which rift
> Imprison'd, thou didst painfully remain
> A dozen years; within which space she died,
> And left thee there; where thou didst vent thy groans,
> As fast as mill-wheels strike.
>
> If thou more murmur'st, I will rend an oak,
> And peg thee in his knotty entrails, 'till
> Thou'st howl'd away twelve winters.
>
> For this, be sure, to-night thou shalt have cramps,
> Side-stitches that shall pen thy breath up: urchins
> Shall, for that vast of night that they may work,
> All exercise on thee; thou shalt be pinch'd
> As thick as honey-combs, each pinch more stinging
> Than bees that made 'em.
>
> If thou neglect'st or dost unwillingly
> What I command, I'll rack thee with old cramps;
> Fill all thy bones with aches: make thee roar,
> That beasts shall tremble at thy din.
>                                   (Shakespeare.)

> Whatever spirit, careless of his charge,
> Forsakes his post or leaves the fair at large,
> Shall feel sharp vengeance soon o'ertake his sins,
> Be stopp'd in vials, or transfixt with pins;
> Or plung'd in lakes of bitter washes lie,
> Or wedg'd whole ages in a bodkin's eye:
> Gums and pomatums shall his flight restrain,
> While clogg'd he beats his silken wings in vain;
> Or alum styptics with contracting pow'r,
> Shrink his thin essence like a shrivell'd flow'r:
> Or as Ixion fix'd, the wretch shall feel
> The giddy motion of the whirling wheel;
> The fumes of burning chocolate shall glow,
> And tremble at the sea that froths below!
>                                   (Pope.)

The method which is taken to induce Ferdinand to believe that his father was drowned in the late tempest is exceedingly solemn and striking. He is sitting upon a solitary rock, and weeping over-against the place where he imagined his father was wrecked, when he suddenly hears with astonishment aërial music creep by him upon the waters, and the Spirit gives him the following information in words not proper for any but a Spirit to utter:

> Full fathom five thy father lies:
>     Of his bones are coral made:
> Those are pearls that were his eyes:
>     Nothing of him that doth fade,
>     But doth suffer a sea-change,
>     Into something rich and strange.

And then follows a most lively circumstance;

> Sea-nymphs hourly ring his knell.
> Hark! now I hear them—Ding-dong-bell!

This is so truly poetical, that one can scarce forbear exclaiming with Ferdinand,

> This is no mortal business, nor no sound
> That the earth owns!

The happy versatility of Shakspeare's genius enables him to excel in lyric as well as in dramatic poesy.

But the poet rises still higher in his management of the character of Ariel, by making a moral use of it, that is, I think, incomparable, and the greatest effort of his art. Ariel informs Prospero, that he has fulfilled his orders, and punished his brother and companions so severely, that if he himself was now to behold their sufferings, he would greatly compassionate them. To which Prospero answers,

> Dost thou think so, Spirit?
> *Ariel:* Mine would, Sir, were I human.
> *Prospero:* And mine shall.

He then takes occasion, with wonderful dexterity and humanity, to draw an argument from the incorporeality of Ariel, for the justice and necessity of pity and forgiveness:

> Hast thou, which art but air, a touch, a feeling
> Of their afflictions; and shall not myself,
> One of their kind, that relish all as sharply,
> Passion'd as they, be kindlier mov'd than thou art?

The poet is a more powerful magician than his own Prospero: we are transported into fairy land; we are wrapt in a delicious dream, from which it is misery to be disturbed; all around is enchantment!

> The isle is full of noises,
> Sounds and sweet airs, that give delight and hurt not.
> Sometimes a thousand twanging instruments
> Will hum about mine ears, and sometimes voices;
> That, if I then had wak'd after long sleep,
> Will make me sleep again: and then, in dreaming,
> The clouds, methought, would open, and shew
>   riches
> Ready to drop upon me:—when I wak'd,
> I cry'd to dream again!

### No. 97. October 9, 1753

"Whoever ventures," says Horace, "to form a character totally original, let him endeavour to preserve it with uniformity and consistency; but the formation of an original character is a work of great difficulty and hazard." In this arduous and uncommon task, however, Shakspeare has wonderfully succeeded in his *Tempest:* the monster Caliban is the creature of his own imagination, in the formation of which he could derive no assistance from observation or experience.

Caliban is the son of a witch, begotten by a demon: the sorceries of his mother were so terrible, that her country-men banished her into this desert island as unfit for human society: in conformity, therefore, to this diabolical propagation, he is represented as a prodigy of cruelty, malice, pride, ignorance, idleness, gluttony, and lust. He is introduced with great propriety, cursing Prospero, and Miranda whom he had endeavoured to defile; and his execrations are artfully contrived to have reference to the occupation of his mother:

> As wicked dew, as e'er my mother brushed
> With raven's feather from unwholesome fen,
> Drop on you both!
>     All the charms
> Of Sycorax, toads, beetles, bats, light on you!

His kindness is, afterward, expressed as much in character, as his hatred, by an enumeration of offices that could be of value only in a desolate island, and in the estimation of a savage:

> I pr'ythee, let me bring thee where crabs grow;
> And I with my long nails will dig thee pig-nuts;
> Shew thee a jay's nest; and instruct thee how
> To snare the nimble marmazet. I'll bring thee
> To clust'ring filberds; and sometimes I'll get thee

> Young sea-malls from the rock . . .
> I'll shew thee the best springs; I'll pluck thee berries;
> I'll fish for thee, and get thee wood enough.

Which last is, indeed, a circumstance of great use in a place, where to be defended from the cold was neither easy nor usual; and it has a farther peculiar beauty, because the gathering wood was the occupation to which Caliban was subjected by Prospero, who, therefore, deemed it a service of high importance.

The gross ignorance of this monster is represented with delicate judgment; he knew not the names of the sun and moon, which he calls the bigger light and the less; and he believes that Stephano was the man in the moon, whom his mistress had often shewn him; and when Prospero reminds him that he first taught him to pronounce articulately, his answer is full of malevolence and rage:

> You taught me language; and my profit on't
> Is, I know how to curse:

the properest return for such a fiend to make for such a favour. The spirits whom he supposes to be employed by Prospero perpetually to torment him, and the many forms and different methods they take for this purpose, are described with the utmost liveliness and force of fancy:

> Sometimes like apes, that moe and chatter at me,
> And after bite me; then like hedge-hogs, which
> Lie tumbling in my bare-foot way, and mount
> Their pricks at my foot-fall: sometimes am I
> All wound with adders, who, with cloven tongues,
> Do hiss me into madness.

It is scarcely possible for any speech to be more expressive of the manners and sentiments, than that in which our poet has painted the brutal barbarity and unfeeling savageness of the son of Sycorax, by making him enumerate, with a kind of horrible delight, the various ways in which it was possible for the drunken sailors to surprise and kill his master:

> There thou may'st brain him,
> Having first seiz'd his books; or with a log
> Batter his skull; or paunch him with a stake;
> Or cut his wezand with thy knife.

He adds, in allusion to his own abominable attempt, "Above all, be sure to secure the daughter; whose beauty," he tells them, "is incomparable." The charms of Miranda could not be more exalted, than by extorting this testimony from so insensible a monster.

Shakspeare seems to be the only poet who possesses the power of uniting poetry with propriety of character; of which I know not an instance more striking, than the image Caliban makes use of to express silence, which is at once highly poetical, and exactly suited to the wildness of the speaker:

> Pray you tread softly, that the blind mole may not
> Hear a foot-fall.

I always lament that our author has not preseved this fierce and implacable spirit in Caliban, to the end of the play; instead of which, he has, I think, injudiciously put into his mouth, words that imply repentance and understanding.

> I'll be wise hereafter
> And seek for grace. What a thrice double ass
> Was I, to take this drunkard for a God,
> And worship this dull fool!

It must not be forgotten, that Shakspeare has artfully taken occasion from this extraordinary character, which is finely contrasted to the mildness and obedience of Ariel, obliquely to satirize the prevailing passion for new and wonderful sights, which has rendered the English so ridiculous. "Were I in

England now," says Trinculo, on first discovering Caliban, "and had but this fish painted, not a holiday-fool there but would give a piece of silver.—When they will not give a doit to relieve a lame beggar, they will lay out ten to see a dead Indian."

Such is the inexhaustible plenty of our poet's invention, that he has exhibited another character in this play, entirely his own; that of the lovely and innocent Miranda.

When Prospero first gives her a sight of Prince Ferdinand, she eagerly exclaims,

> What is't? a spirit?
> Lord, how it looks about! Believe me, Sir,
> It carries a brave form. But 'tis a spirit.

Her imagining that as he was so beautiful he must necessarily be one of her father's aërial agents, is a stroke of nature worthy admiration: as are likewise her entreaties to her father not to use him harshly, by the power of his art.

> Why speaks my father so ungently? This
> Is the third man that e'er I saw; the first
> That e'er I sigh'd for!

Here we perceive the beginning of that passion, which Prospero was desirous she should feel for the Prince; and which she afterward more fully expresses upon an occasion, which displays at once the tenderness, the innocence, and the simplicity of her character. She discovers her lover employed in the laborious task of carrying wood, which Prospero had enjoined him to perform. "Would," says she, "the lightning had burnt up those logs, that you are enjoined to pile!"

> If you'll sit down,
> I'll bear your logs the while. Pray give me that,
> I'll carry't to the pile.
> You look wearily.

It is by selecting such little, and almost imperceptible circumstances, that Shakspeare has more truly painted the passions than any other writer: affection is more powerfully expressed by this simple wish and offer of assistance, than by the unnatural eloquence and witticisms of Dryden, or the amorous declamations of Rowe.

The resentment of Prospero for the matchless cruelty and wicked usurpation of his brother; his parental affection and solicitude for the welfare of his daughter, the heiress of his dukedom; and the awful solemnity of his character, as a skilful magician; are all along preserved with equal consistency, dignity, and decorum. One part of his behaviour deserves to be particularly pointed out: during the exhibition of a mask with which he had ordered Ariel to entertain Ferdinand and Miranda, he starts suddenly, from the recollection of the conspiracy of Caliban and his confederates against his life, and dismisses his attendant spirits, who instantly vanish to a hollow and confused noise. He appears to be greatly moved; and suitably to this agitation of mind, which his danger has excited, he takes occasion, from the sudden disappearance of the visionary scene, to moralize on the dissolution of all things:

> These our actors,
> As I foretold you, were all spirits: and
> Are melted into air, into thin air.
> And, like the baseless fabric of this vision,
> The cloud-capt towers, the gorgeous palaces,
> The solemn temples, the great globe itself,
> Yeah, all which it inherit, shall dissolve;
> And, like this unsubstantial pageant faded,
> Leave not a rack behind.

To these noble images he adds a short, but comprehensive observation on human life, not excelled by any passage of the moral and sententious Euripides:

> We are such stuff
> As dreams are made of; and our little life
> Is rounded with a sleep!

Thus admirably is a uniformity of character, that leading beauty in dramatic poetry, preserved throughout the *Tempest*. And it may be farther remarked, that the unities of action, of lace, and of time, are in this play, though almost constantly violated by Shakspeare, exactly observed. The action is one, great, and entire, the restoration of Prospero to his dukedom: this business is transacted in the compass of a small island, and in or near the cave of Prospero; though, indeed, it had been more artful and regular to have confined it to this single spot: and the time which the action takes up, is only equal to that of the representation; an excellence which ought always to be aimed at in every well-conducted fable, and for the want of which a variety of the most entertaining incidents can scarcely atone.

## SAMUEL TAYLOR COLERIDGE
"Notes on *The Tempest*"
*Shakspeare, with Introductory Remarks
on Poetry, the Drama, and the Stage*
1818

There is a sort of improbability with which we are shocked in dramatic representation, not less than in a narrative of real life. Consequently, there must be rules respecting it; and as rules are nothing but means to an end previously ascertained—(inattention to which simple truth has been the occasion of all the pedantry of the French school),—we must first determine what the immediate end or object of the drama is. And here, as I have previously remarked, I find two extremes of critical decision;—the French, which evidently presupposes that a perfect delusion is to be aimed at,—an opinion which needs no fresh confutation; and the exact opposite to it, brought forward by Dr. Johnson, who supposes the auditors throughout in the full reflective knowledge of the contrary. In evincing the impossibility of delusion, he makes no sufficient allowance for an intermediate state, which I have before distinguished by the term, illusion, and have attempted to illustrate its quality and character by reference to our mental state, when dreaming. In both cases we simply do not judge the imagery to be unreal; there is a negative reality, and no more. Whatever, therefore, tends to prevent the mind from placing itself, or being placed, gradually in that state in which the images have such negative reality for the auditor, destroys this illusion, and is dramatically improbable.

Now the production of this effect—a sense of improbability—will depend on the degree of excitement in which the mind is supposed to be. Many things would be intolerable in the first scene of a play, that would not at all interrupt our enjoyment in the height of the interest, when the narrow cockpit may be made to hold

> The vasty field of France, or we may cram
> Within its wooden O, the very casques,
> That did affright the air at Agincourt.

Again, on the other hand, many obvious improbabilities will be endured, as belonging to the ground-work of the story rather than to the drama itself, in the first scenes, which would disturb or disentrance us from all illusion in the acme of our excitement; as for instance, Lear's division of his kingdom, and the banishment of Cordelia.

But, although the other excellencies of the drama besides

this dramatic probability, as unity of interest, with distinctness and subordination of the characters, and appropriateness of style, are all, so far as they tend to increase the inward excitement, means towards accomplishing the chief end, that of producing and supporting this willing illusion,—yet they do not on that account cease to be ends themselves; and we must remember that, as such, they carry their own justification with them, as long as they do not contravene or interrupt the total illusion. It is not even always, or of necessity, an objection to them, that they prevent the illusion from rising to as great a height as it might otherwise have attained;—it is enough that they are simply compatible with as high a degree of it as is requisite for the purpose. Nay, upon particular occasions, a palpable improbability may be hazarded by a great genius for the express purpose of keeping down the interest of a merely instrumental scene, which would otherwise make too great an impression for the harmony of the entire illusion. Had the panorama been invented in the time of Pope Leo X., Raffael would still, I doubt not, have smiled in contempt at the regret, that the broom-twigs and scrubby bushes at the back of some of his grand pictures were not as probable trees as those in the exhibition.

*The Tempest* is a specimen of the purely romantic drama, in which the interest is not historical, or dependent upon fidelity of portraiture, or the natural connexion of events,—but is a birth of the imagination, and rests only on the coaptation and union of the elements granted to, or assumed by, the poet. It is a species of drama which owes no allegiance to time or space, and in which, therefore, errors of chronology and geography—no mortal sins in any species—are venial faults, and count for nothing. It addresses itself entirely to the imaginative faculty; and although the illusion may be assisted by the effect on the senses of the complicated scenery and decorations of modern times, yet this sort of assistance is dangerous. For the principal and only genuine excitement ought to come from within,—from the moved and sympathetic imagination; whereas, where so much is addressed to the mere external senses of seeing and hearing, the spiritual vision is apt to languish, and the attraction from without will withdraw the mind from the proper and only legitimate interest which is intended to spring from within.

The romance opens with a busy scene admirably appropriate to the kind of drama, and giving, as it were, the key-notes to the whole harmony. It prepares and initiates the excitement required for the entire piece, and yet does not demand any thing from the spectators, which their previous habits had not fitted them to understand. It is the bustle of a tempest, from which the real horrors are abstracted;—therefore it is poetical, though not in strictness natural—(the distinction to which I have so often alluded)—and is purposely restrained from concentering the interest on itself, but used merely as an induction or tuning for what is to follow.

In the second scene, Prospero's speeches, till the entrance of Ariel, contain the finest example, I remember, of retrospective narration for the purpose of exciting immediate interest, and putting the audience in possession of all the information necessary for the understanding of the plot. Observe, too, the perfect probability of the moment chosen by Prospero (the very Shakspeare himself, as it were, of the tempest) to open out the truth to his daughter, his own romantic bearing, and how completely any thing that might have been disagreeable to us in the magician, is reconciled and shaded in the humanity and natural feelings of the father. In the very first speech of Miranda the simplicity and tenderness of her character are at once laid open;—it would have been lost in direct contact with the agitation of the first scene. The opinion once prevailed, but, happily, is now abandoned, that Fletcher alone wrote for women;—the truth is, that with very few, and those partial, exceptions, the female characters in the plays of Beaumont and Fletcher are, when of the light kind, not decent; when heroic, complete viragos. But in Shakspeare all the elements of womanhood are holy, and there is the sweet, yet dignified feeling of all that *continuates* society, as sense of ancestry and of sex, with a purity unassailable by sophistry, because it rests not in the analytic processes, but in that sane equipoise of the faculties, during which the feelings are representative of all past experience,—not of the individual only, but of all those by whom she has been educated, and their predecessors even up to the first mother that lived. Shakspeare saw that the want of prominence, which Pope notices for sarcasm, was the blessed beauty of the woman's character, and knew that it arose not from any deficiency, but from the more exquisite harmony of all the parts of the moral being constituting one living total of head and heart. He has drawn it, indeed, in all its distinctive energies of faith, patience, constancy, fortitude,—shown in all of them as following the heart, which gives its results by a nice tact and happy intuition, without the intervention of the discursive faculty,—sees all things in and by the light of the affections, and errs, if it ever err, in the exaggerations of love alone. In all the Shakspearian women there is essentially the same foundation and principle; the distinct individuality and variety are merely the result of the modification of circumstances, whether in Miranda the maiden, in Imogen the wife, or in Katharine the queen.

But to return. The appearance and characters of the super or ultra-natural servants are finely contrasted. Ariel has in every thing the airy tint which gives the name; and it is worthy of remark that Miranda is never directly brought into comparison with Ariel, lest the natural and human of the one and the supernatural of the other should tend to neutralize each other; Caliban, on the other hand, is all earth, all condensed and gross in feelings and images; he has the dawnings of understanding without reason or the moral sense, and in him, as in some brute animals, this advance to the intellectual faculties, without the moral sense, is marked by the appearance of vice. For it is in the primacy of the moral being only that man is truly human; in his intellectual powers he is certainly approached by the brutes, and, man's whole system duly considered, those powers cannot be considered other than means to an end, that is, to morality.

In this scene, as it proceeds, is displayed the impression made by Ferdinand and Miranda on each other; it is love at first sight;—

> at the first sight
> They have chang'd eyes:—

and it appears to me, that in all cases of real love, it is at one moment that it takes place. That moment may have been prepared by previous esteem, admiration, or even affection,—yet love seems to require a momentary act of volition, by which a tacit bond of devotion is imposed,—a bond not to be thereafter broken without violating what should be sacred in our nature. How finely is the true Shakspearian scene contrasted with Dryden's vulgar alteration of it, in which a mere ludicrous psychological experiment, as it were, is tried—displaying nothing but indelicacy without passion. Prospero's interruption of the courtship has often seemed to me to have no sufficient motive; still his alleged reason—

> lest too light winning
> Make the prize light—

is enough for the ethereal connexions of the romantic

imagination, although it would not be so for the historical. The whole courting scene, indeed, in the beginning of the third act, between the lovers is a masterpiece; and the first dawn of disobedience in the mind of Miranda to the command of her father is very finely drawn, so as to seem the working of the Scriptural command, *Thou shalt leave father and mother, &c.* O! with what exquisite purity this scene is conceived and executed! Shakspeare may sometimes be gross, but I boldly say that he is always moral and modest. Alas! in this our day decency is preserved at the expense of morality of heart, and delicacies for vice are allowed, whilst grossness against it is hypocritically, or at least morbidly, condemned.

In this play are admirably sketched the vices generally accompanying a low degree of civilization; and in the first scene of the second act Shakspeare has, as in many other places, shown the tendency in bad men to indulge in scorn and contemptuous expressions, as a mode of getting rid of their own uneasy feelings of inferiority to the good, and also, by making the good ridiculous, of rendering the transition of others to wickedness easy. Shakspeare never puts habitual scorn into the mouths of other than bad men, as here in the instances of Antonio and Sebastian. The scene of the intended assassination of Alonzo and Gonzalo is an exact counterpart of the scene between Macbeth and his lady, only pitched in a lower key throughout, as designed to be frustrated and concealed, and exhibiting the same profound management in the manner of familiarizing a mind, not immediately recipient, to the suggestion of guilt, by associating the proposed crime with something ludicrous or out of place,—something not habitually matter of reverence. By this kind of sophistry the imagination and fancy are first bribed to contemplate the suggested act, and at length to become acquainted with it. Observe how the effect of this scene is heightened by contrast with another counterpart of it in low life,—that between the conspirators Stephano, Caliban, and Trinculo in the second scene of the third act, in which there are the same essential characteristics.

In this play and in this scene of it are also shown the springs of the vulgar in politics,—of that kind of politics which is inwoven with human nature. In his treatment of this subject, wherever it occurs, Shakspeare is quite peculiar. In other writers we find the particular opinions of the individual; in Massinger it is rank republicanism; in Beaumont and Fletcher even *jure divino* principles are carried to excess;—but Shakspeare never promulgates any party tenets. He is always the philosopher and the moralist, but at the same time with a profound veneration for all the established institutions of society, and for those classes which form the permanent elements of the state—especially never introducing a professional character, as such, otherwise than as respectable. If he must have any name, he should be styled a philosophical aristocrat, delighting in those hereditary institutions which have a tendency to bind one age to another, and in that distinction of ranks, of which, although few may be in possession, all enjoy the advantages. Hence, again, you will observe the good nature with which he seems always to make sport with the passions and follies of a mob, as with an irrational animal. He is never angry with it, but hugely content with holding up its absurdities to its face; and sometimes you may trace a tone of almost affectionate superiority, something like that in which a father speaks of the rogueries of a child. See the good-humoured way in which he describes Stephano passing from the most licentious freedom to absolute despotism over Trinculo and Caliban. The truth is, Shakspeare's characters are all *genera* intensely individualized; the results of meditation, of which observation supplied the drapery and the colors necessary to combine them with each other. He had virtually surveyed all the great component powers and impulses of human nature,—had seen that their different combinations and subordinations were in fact the individualizers of men, and showed how their harmony was produced by reciprocal disproportions of excess or deficiency. The language in which these truths are expressed was not drawn from any set fashion, but from the profoundest depths of his moral being, and is therefore for all ages.

*The Tempest*

*The Winter's Tale*
(engraving by Neagle from a painting by Fuseli)

Imogen in the cave in *Cymbeline*
(engraving by Desvachez from a painting by Graham)

# LVCRECE.

LONDON.
Printed by Richard Field, for Iohn Harrifon; and are
to be fold at the figne of the white Greyhound
in Paules Churh yard.   **1 5 9 4.**

*The Rape of Lucrece (1594)*

# SHAKE-SPEARES

# SONNETS.

Neuer before Imprinted.

AT LONDON
By *G. Eld* for *T. T.* and are
to be folde by *Iohn Wright*, dwelling
at Chrift Church gate.
**1 6 0 9.**

*Sonnets (1609)*

This Shadowe is renowned Shakfpear's Soule of th'age
The applaufe delight! the wonder of the Stage.
Nature her felfe, was proud of his defignes
And joy'd to weare the dreffing of his lines,
The learned will Confefs, his works are fuch,
As neither man, nor Mufe, can praife to much.
For ever live thy fame, the world to tell,
Thy like, no age, shall ever paralell.
                                        W.M. fculpfit.

# POEMS:

## VVRITTEN
### BY
### WIL. SHAKE-SPEARE.
Gent.

Printed at *London* by *The. Cotes*, and are
to be fold by *Iohn Benfon*, dwelling in
S:. *Dunftans* Church-yard. **1640.**

*Poems (1640)*

# POEMS

## *General*

And *Shakespeare* thou, whose hony-flowing Vaine,
(Pleasing the World) thy Praises doth obtaine.
Whose *Venus*, and whose *Lucrece* (sweete, and chaste)
Thy name in fames immortall Booke have plac't.
   Live ever you, at least in Fame live ever:
   Well may the Bodye dye, but Fames dies never.
      —Richard Barnfield, "A Remembrance of
      Some English Poets," *Poems in Divers
      Humors*, 1598

I here presume (under favour) to present to your view, some excellent and sweetely composed Poems, of Master *William Shakespeare*, Which in Themselves appear of the same purity, the Authour himself then living avouched; they had not the fortune by reason of their Infancie in his death, to have the due accommodation of proportionable glory, with the rest of his ever-living Workes, yet the lines of themselves will afford you a more authentick approbation than my assurance any way can, to invite your allowance, in your perusall you shall finde them *Seren*, cleere and eligantly plaine, such gentle straines as shall recreate and not perplexe your braine, no intricate or cloudy stuffe to puzzell intellect, but perfect eloquence; such as will raise your admiration to his praise: this assurance I know will not differ from your acknowledgement. And certaine I am, my opinion will be seconded by the sufficiency of these ensuing Lines; I have beene some what solicitus to bring this forth to the perfect view of all men; and in so doing, glad to be serviceable for the continuance of glory to the deserved Author in these his Poems.—John Benson, "To the Reader," *Shakespeare's Poems*, 1640

Our idolatry of Shakespear (not to say our admiration) ceases with his plays. In his other productions, he was a mere author, though not a common author. It was only by representing others, that he became himself. He could go out of himself, and express the soul of Cleopatra; but in his own person, he appeared to be always waiting for the prompter's cue. In expressing the thoughts of others, he seemed inspired; in expressing his own, he was a mechanic. The licence of an assumed character was necessary to restore his genius to the privileges of nature, and to give him courage to break through the tyranny of fashion, the trammels of custom. In his plays, he was 'as broad and casing as the general air': in his poems, on the contrary, he appears to be 'cooped, and cabined in' by all the technicalities of art, by all the petty intricacies of thought and language, which poetry had learned from the controversial jargon of the schools, where words had been made a substitute for things. There was, if we mistake not, something of modesty, and a painful sense of personal propriety at the bottom of this. Shakespear's imagination, by identifying itself with the strongest characters in the most trying circumstances, grappled at once with nature, and trampled the littleness of art under his feet: the rapid changes of situation, the wide range of the universe, gave him life and spirit, and afforded full scope to his genius; but returned into his closet again, and having assumed the badge of his profession, he could only labour in his vocation, and conform himself to existing models. The

thoughts, the passions, the words which the poet's pen, 'glancing from heaven to earth, from earth to heaven,' lent to others, shook off the fetters of pedantry and affectation; while his own thoughts and feelings, standing by themselves, were seized upon as lawful prey, and tortured to death according to the established rules and practice of the day. In a word, we do not like Shakespear's poems, because we like his plays: the one, in all their excellencies, are just the reverse of the other. It has been the fashion of late to cry up our author's poems, as equal to his plays: this is the desperate cant of modern criticism. We would ask, was there the slightest comparison between Shakespear, and either Chaucer or Spenser, as mere poets? Not any.—The two poems of Venus and Adonis and of Tarquin and Lucrece appear to us like a couple of ice-houses. They are about as hard, as glittering, and as cold. The author seems all the time to be thinking of his verses, and not of his subject,—not of what his characters would feel, but of what he shall say; and as it must happen in all such cases, he always puts into their mouths those things which they would be the last to think of, and which it shews the greatest ingenuity in him to find out. The whole is laboured, up-hill work. The poet is perpetually singling out the difficulties of the art to make an exhibition of his strength and skill in wrestling with them. He is making perpetual trials of them as if his mastery over them were doubted. The images, which are often striking, are generally applied to things which they are the least like: so that they do not blend with the poem, but seem stuck upon it, like splendid patch-work, or remain quite distinct from it, like detached substances, painted and varnished over. A beautiful thought is sure to be lost in an endless commentary upon it. The speakers are like persons who have both leisure and inclination to make riddles on their own situation, and to twist and turn every object or incident into acrostics and anagrams. Everything is spun out into allegory; and a digression is always preferred to the main story. Sentiment is built up upon plays of words; the hero or heroine feels, not from the impulse of passion, but from the force of dialectics. There is besides a strange attempt to substitute the language of painting for that of poetry, to make us *see* their feelings in the faces of the persons; and again, consistently with this, in the description of the picture in Tarquin and Lucrece, those circumstances are chiefly insisted on, which it would be impossible to convey except by words. The invocation to opportunity in the Tarquin and Lucrece is full of thoughts and images, but at the same time it is overloaded by them. The concluding stanza expresses all our objections to this kind of poetry:—

   Oh! idle words, servants to shallow fools;
   Unprofitable sounds, weak arbitrators;
   Busy yourselves in skill-contending schools;
   Debate when leisure serves with dull debators;
   To trembling clients be their mediators:
   For me I force not argument a straw,
   Since that my case is past all help of law.

   The description of the horse in Venus and Adonis has been particularly admired, and not without reason:—

Round hoof'd, short jointed, fetlocks shag and long,
Broad breast, full eyes, small head, and nostril wide,
High crest, short ears, strait legs, and passing strong,
Thin mane, thick tail, broad buttock, tender hide,
Look what a horse should have, he did not lack,
Save a proud rider on so proud a back.

Now this inventory of perfections shews great knowledge of the horse; and is good matter-of-fact poetry. Let the reader but compare it with a speech in the *Midsummer Night's Dream* where Theseus describes his hounds—

And their heads are hung
With ears that sweep away the morning dew

and he will perceive at once what we mean by the difference between Shakespear's own poetry, and that of his plays. We prefer the *Passionate Pilgrim* very much to the *Lover's Complaint*. It has been doubted whether the latter poem is Shakespear's.—WILLIAM HAZLITT, "Poems and Sonnets," *Characters of Shakespear's Plays*, 1817

There were already many tuneful singers in 1593; but none of them except the master himself could raise such a pageant of voluptuous imagery, or accompany it with such a symphony of harmonious sound, as we find in *Venus and Adonis*. No one except Spenser and Sackville had evoked the rhyme-clangour of the stanza with such delicate art; no one except these two had portrayed such vivid pictures as the arrest of Adonis by Venus, the captivity of Mars, the portrait of herself by the goddess, the escape of the courser, the description of the boar and of the hare-hunt, the solitary night, the discovery of the foolish youth who has fled from Love's arms to those of Death. But while none, save these, of men living had done, or could have done, such work, there was much here which—whether either could have done it or not—neither had done.

In the first place there is, almost for the first time in English poetry since Chaucer, a directness of observation in the sketches from nature. Sackville, so far as his brief space and peculiar subjects allowed him, Spenser far more, are great painters and describers. But even the later and greater poet rather displays a magnificently decorative convention in painting than a direct re-creative or reproductive touch. Shakespeare, even in these earliest days, has this latter—the horse and the hare, though the most famous and elaborate, are only two out of many instances of it in the *Venus*. In the second place, the slow movement, which is of the essence of the poetry of Sackville and of Spenser, and which is certainly invited by the six-lined stanza in which the *Venus* is written almost as much as by the rhyme-royal and the Spenserian, cannot adjust itself to the infinite variety and the directly lyrical flow of Shakespeare's versification. It is not a mere accident which has made composers choose "Bid me discourse" and "Lo, here the gentle lark" for setting to song measures of the lightest quality; and throughout the poet shows himself—even more than Spenser, how much more then than any one else!—the absolute master of his metre, the *tregetour*, to whom all conditions of phrase and rhythm are merely *materia prima* out of which he can make whatsoever he will. And lastly, though of necessity in less measure and degree, that gift of indicating character, of opening up whole unending vistas of thought by a single phrase, which is Shakespeare's as it is hardly any one else's, is here. Of Adonis, the story forbade him to make much. But it would have been so easy to make Venus contemptible or disgusting or simply tedious; and she escapes all three fates so completely! The escape, no doubt, is effected partly, if not mainly, by the unfailing intensity of passion which the poet suffuses, but we are concerned chiefly with the means of suffusion. They are, I take it, mainly, if not wholly, comprised

in that magic of the single phrase in which Shakespeare (for this is not Spenser's gift) reminds us of no predecessor but Chaucer, and in which he outdoes Chaucer more than Chaucer outdoes others.

Ten kisses short as one, one long as twenty—
Leading him prisoner in a red-rose chain—
Love is a spirit all compact of fire—
He sees her coming and begins to glow
Even as a dying coal revives with wind—
Her two blue windows faintly she upheaveth—
Was melted like a vapour from her sight—

are mere specimens selected half at random from the things of this kind with which the piece swarms. "Conceited," "over-luscious," "unoriginal"—half a dozen other epithets the merely stop-watch critic may heap upon *Venus and Adonis*. One epithet, sometimes used in disparagement, it does deserve—it is young, but with the youth of Shakespeare.

Much of what has been said will apply to *Lucrece*, which chiefly differs from its predecessor in having a seven-line stanza, and in dealing with criminal, and not merely unhappy and tragic, passion. It is, however, on the whole, inferior; being not merely longer (and the style is not improved by length), but written with something more of an approach to the old fifteenth-century manner of allegoric and other padding. We should be sorry not to have it as well as the *Venus*, but it could not supply its companion's place.—GEORGE SAINTSBURY, *A Short History of English Literature*, 1898, pp. 317–19

---

## SIDNEY LEE
From "The First Appeal to the Reading Public"
A *Life of William Shakespeare*
1898, pp. 74–81

During the busy years (1591–4) that witnessed his first pronounced successes as a dramatist, Shakespeare came before the public in yet another literary capacity. On April 18, 1593, Richard Field, the printer, who was his fellow-townsman, obtained a license for the publication of *Venus and Adonis*, a metrical version of a classical tale of love. It was published a month or two later, without an author's name on the title-page, but Shakespeare appended his full name to the dedication, which he addressed in conventional style to Henry Wriothesley, third earl of Southampton. The Earl, who was in his twentieth year, was reckoned the handsomest man at Court, with a pronounced disposition to gallantry. He had vast possessions, was well educated, loved literature, and through life extended to men of letters a generous patronage.[1] 'I know not how I shall offend,' Shakespeare now wrote to him, 'in dedicating my unpolished lines to your lordship, nor how the world will censure me for choosing so strong a prop to support so weak a burden. . . . But if the first heir of my invention prove deformed, I shall be sorry it had so noble a godfather.' 'The first heir of my invention' implies that the poem was written, or at least designed, before Shakespeare's dramatic work. It is affluent in beautiful imagery and metrical sweetness, but imbued with a tone of license which may be held either to justify the theory that it was a precocious product of the author's youth, or to show that Shakespeare was not unready in mature years to write with a view to gratifying a patron's somewhat lascivious tastes. The title-page bears a beautiful Latin motto from Ovid's *Amores*:[2]

Vilia miretur vulgus; mihi flavus Apollo
Pocula Castalia plena ministret aqua.

The influence of Ovid, who told the story in his *Metamor-*

*phoses*, is apparent in many of the details. But the theme was doubtless first suggested to Shakespeare by a contemporary effort. Lodge's *Scillaes Metamorphosis*, which appeared in 1589, is not only written in the same metre (six-line stanzas rhyming *a b a b c c*), but narrates in the exordium the same incidents in the same spirit. There is little doubt that Shakespeare drew from Lodge some of his inspiration.[3]

A year after the issue of *Venus and Adonis*, in 1594, Shakespeare published another poem in like vein, but far more mature in temper and execution. The digression (ll. 939–59) on the destroying power of Time, especially, is in an exalted key of meditation which is not sounded in the earlier poem. The metre, too, is changed; seven-line stanzas (Chaucer's rhyme royal, *a b a b b c c*) take the place of six-line stanzas. The second poem was entered in the *Stationers' Registers* on May 9, 1594, under the title of *A Booke intitled the Ravyshement of Lucrece*, and was published in the same year under the title *Lucrece*. Richard Field printed it, and John Harrison published and sold it at the sign of the White Greyhound in St. Paul's Churchyard. The classical story of Lucretia's ravishment and suicide is briefly recorded in Ovid's *Fasti*, but Chaucer had retold it in his *Legend of Good Women*, and Shakespeare must have read it there. Again, in topic and metre, the poem reflected a contemporary poet's work. Samuel Daniel's *Complaint of Rosamond*, with its seven-line stanza (1592), stood to *Lucrece* in even closer relation than Lodge's *Scilla*, with its six-line stanza, to *Venus and Adonis*. The pathetic accents of Shakespeare's heroine are those of Daniel's heroine purified and glorified.[4] The passage on Time is elaborated from one in Watson's *Passionate Centurie of Love* (No. lxxvii).[5] Shakespeare dedicated his second volume of poetry to the Earl of Southampton, the patron of his first. He addressed him in terms of devoted friendship, which were not uncommon at the time in communications between patrons and poets, but suggest that Shakespeare's relations with the brilliant young nobleman had grown closer since he dedicated *Venus and Adonis* to him in colder language a year before. 'The love I dedicate to your lordship,' Shakespeare wrote in the opening pages of *Lucrece*, 'is without end, whereof this pamphlet without beginning is but a superfluous moiety. . . . What I have done is yours; what I have to do is yours; being part in all I have, devoted yours.'

In these poems Shakespeare made his earliest appeal to the world of readers, and the reading public welcomed his addresses with unqualified enthusiasm. The London playgoer already knew Shakespeare's name as that of a promising actor and playwright, but his dramatic efforts had hitherto been consigned in manuscript, as soon as the theatrical representation ceased, to the coffers of their owner, the playhouse manager. His early plays brought him at the outset little reputation as a man of letters. It was not as the myriad-minded dramatist, but in the restricted *rôle* of adapter for English readers of familiar Ovidian fables, that he first impressed a wide circle of his contemporaries with the fact of his mighty genius. The perfect sweetness of the verse, and the poetical imagery in *Venus and Adonis* and *Lucrece* practically silenced censure of the licentious treatment of the themes on the part of the seriously minded. Critics vied with each other in the exuberance of the eulogies in which they proclaimed that the fortunate author had gained a place in permanence on the summit of Parnassus. *Lucrece*, wrote Michael Drayton in his *Legend of Matilda* (1594), was 'revived to live another age.' In 1595 William Clerke in his *Polimanteia* gave 'all praise' to 'sweet Shakespeare' for his 'Lucrecia.' John Weever, in a sonnet addressed to 'honey-tongued Shakespeare' in his *Epi-*

*gramms* (1595), eulogised the two poems as an unmatchable achievement, although he mentioned the plays 'Romeo' and 'Richard' and 'more whose names I know not.' Richard Carew at the same time classed him with Marlowe as deserving the praises of an English Catullus.[6] Printers and publishers of the poems strained their resources to satisfy the demands of eager purchasers. No fewer than seven editions of *Venus* appeared between 1594 and 1602; an eighth followed in 1617. *Lucrece* achieved a fifth edition in the year of Shakespeare's death.

There is a likelihood, too, that Spenser, the greatest of Shakespeare's poetic contemporaries, was first drawn by the poems into the ranks of Shakespeare's admirers. It is hardly doubtful that Spenser described Shakespeare in *Colin Clouts come home againe* (completed in 1594), under the name of 'Aetion'—a familiar Greek proper name derived from *Aetos*, an eagle:

> And there, though last not least is Aetion;
> A gentler Shepheard may no where be found,
> Whose muse, full of high thought's invention,
> Doth, like himselfe, heroically sound.

The last line seems to allude to Shakespeare's surname. We may assume that the admiration was mutual. At any rate Shakespeare acknowledged acquaintance with Spenser's work in a plain reference to his *Teares of the Muses* (1591) in *Midsummer Night's Dream* (v. i. 52–3).

> The thrice three Muses, mourning for the death
> Of learning, late deceased in beggary,

is stated to be the theme of one of the dramatic entertainments wherewith it is proposed to celebrate Theseus's marriage. In Spenser's *Teares of the Muses* each of the Nine laments in turn her declining influence on the literary and dramatic effort of the age. Theseus dismisses the suggestion with the not inappropriate comment:

> That is some satire keen and critical,
> Not sorting with a nuptial ceremony.

But there is no ground for assuming that Spenser in the same poem referred figuratively to Shakespeare when he made Thalia deplore the recent death of 'our pleasant Willy.'[7] The name Willy was frequently used in contemporary literature as a term of familiarity without relation to the baptismal name of the person referred to. Sir Philip Sidney was addressed as 'Willy' by some of his elegists. A comic actor, 'dead of late' in a literal sense, was clearly intended by Spenser, and there is no reason to dispute the view of an early seventeenth-century commentator that Spenser was paying a tribute to the loss English comedy had lately sustained by the death of the comedian, Richard Tarleton.[8] Similarly the 'gentle spirit' who is described by Spenser in a later stanza as sitting 'in idle cell' rather than turn his pen to base uses cannot be reasonably identified with Shakespeare.[9]

*Notes*

1. See Sidney Lee, *A Life of William Shakespeare*, Appendix, sections iii. and iv.

2. See Ovid's *Amores*, liber i. elegy xv. ll. 35–6. Ovid's *Amores*, or Elegies of Love, were translated by Marlowe about 1589, and were first printed without a date on the title-page, probably about 1597. Marlowe's version had probably been accessible in manuscript in the eight years' interval. Marlowe rendered the lines quoted by Shakespeare thus:

   > Let base conceited wits admire vile things,
   > Fair Phœbus lead me to the Muses' springs!

3. 'Shakespeare's *Venus and Adonis* and Lodge's *Scillaes Metamorphosis*,' by James P. Reardon, in *Shakespeare Society's Papers*, iii. 143–6. Cf. Lodge's description of Venus's discovery of the wounded Adonis:

Her daintie hand addrest to dawe her deere,
Her roseall lip alied to his pale cheeke,
Her sighs and then her lookes and heavie cheere,
Her bitter threates, and then her passions meeke;
   How on his senseles corpse she lay a-crying,
   As if the boy were then but new a-dying.

In the minute description in Shakespeare's poem of the chase of the hare (ll. 673–708) there are curious resemblances to the 'Ode de la chasse' (on a stag hunt) by the French dramatist, Estienne Jodelle, in his *Œuvres et Meslanges Poétiques*, 1574.

4. Rosamond, in Daniel's poem, muses thus when King Henry challenges her honour:

But what? he is my King and may constraine me
Whether I yeeld or not, I live defamed.
The World will thinke Authoritie did gaine me,
I shall be judg'd his Love and so be shamed;
We see the faire condemn'd that never gamed,
   And if I yeeld, 'tis honourable shame.
   If not, I live disgrac'd, yet thought the same.

5. Watson makes this comment on his poem or passion on Time, (No. lxxvii): 'The chiefe contentes of this Passion are taken out of Seraphine [i.e. Serafino], Sonnet 132:

Col tempo passa[n] gli anni, i mesi, e l'hore,
Col tempo le richeze, imperio, e regno,
Col tempo fama, honor, fortezza, e ingegno,
Col tempo giouentù, con beltà more, &c.'

Watson adds that he has inverted Serafino's order for 'rimes sake,' or 'upon some other more allowable consideration.' Shakespeare was also doubtless acquainted with Giles Fletcher's similar handling of the theme in Sonnet xxviii. of his collection of sonnets called *Licia* (1593).

6. 'Excellencie of the English Tongue' in Camden's *Remaines*, p. 43.

7.    All these and all that els the Comick Stage
With seasoned wit and goodly pleasance graced,
By which mans life in his likest image
Was limned forth, are wholly now defaced . . .
And he, the man whom Nature selfe had made
To mock her selfe and Truth to imitate,
With kindly counter under mimick shade,
Our pleasant Willy, ah! is dead of late;
With whom all joy and jolly meriment
Is also deaded and in dolour drent.
                    (ll. 199–210)

8. A note to this effect, in a genuine early seventeenth-century hand, was discovered by Halliwell-Phillipps in a copy of the 1611 edition of Spenser's *Works* (cf. *Outlines*, ii. 394–5).

9.    But that same gentle spirit, from whose pen
Large streames of honnie and sweete nectar flowe,
Scorning the boldnes of such base-borne men
Which dare their follies forth so rashlie throwe,
   Doth choose to sit in idle cell
   Than so himselfe to mockerie to sell.
                    (ll. 217–22)

# Sonnets

TO THE ONLY BEGETTER OF
THESE ENSUING SONNETS
MR. W. H. ALL HAPPINESS
AND THAT ETERNITY
PROMISED
BY
OUR EVER-LIVING POET
WISHETH
THE WELL-WISHING
ADVENTURER IN
SETTING
FORTH

—THOMAS THORPE, Dedication to Shakespeare's *Sonnets*, 1609

. . . ⟨T⟩he test of a good critic is suspension of judgment in cases which are not convincingly proven.

Take the more important instance of Shakespeare's sonnets. We have all tried to wring the heart out of that mystery. We have all felt the accent of acute passion alternating with the accent of what looks like artificial compliment—the inequality of style, the inequality of emotion, the inequality of artistic handling—in those unparalleled outpourings of a mighty poet's soul. We do not doubt their genuineness. We trace the outlines of a story in them, which it is not difficult to decipher, although the import may be painful. So far we are agreed. But when it comes to deciding whether Shakespeare intended a merely dramatic series of psychological lyrics, or whether he committed his own experience from day to day to paper in the sonnets, or whether he wrote them for a friend—who Mr. W. H. was, and who the dark lady was—then at once we differ. As it seems to me, this is the point at which sound criticism diverges from criticism over-weighted with erudition or with subjective prepossession. Queen Elizabeth, Lord Southampton, Lord Pembroke, William Hughes, William Himself, have successively posed, in the schemes of constructive critics, for

Mr. W. H. I need not enlarge upon this topic, because the case of Shakespeare's sonnets is only too familiar to every student of English literature. I have adduced the instance simply because it is a crucial one—one in which the competent critic should hail every contribution made by research or formulated by a scheming brain for the solution of a sphinx-like problem, but should avoid like a hidden rock—*tanquam scopulum*—any temptation to construct a biographical romance out of elements so slender, until irrefutable facts have been presented. In a word, criticism welcomes research, welcomes discovery, welcomes constructive ingenuity. But she does not recognise these things as criticism, and holds a dubious balance until the case seems proved.—JOHN ADDINGTON SYMONDS, "On Some Principles of Criticism," *Essays Speculative and Suggestive*, 1890, Vol. 1, pp. 117–19

The *Sonnets* do not reveal to us a more exquisite or richly gifted poet than does the *Venus*; but they take us to a higher range of subject, where sensuous imagery is indeed not absent, but where the poet's absorption in it has given way to a more direct domination of the ideal, to meditation upon passion rather than realisation of it. The endless discussions on the personages probably or possibly concerned must be sought elsewhere. The famous dedication is, almost to a certainty, enigmatic of malice prepense; but there is no reason to question the fact suggested by the text throughout, and explicitly asserted once in it, that "a man right fair" and "a woman coloured ill" were the objects, either successive or simultaneous, of the poet's passionate attachment. That these two persons were live individual beings; that the passion was actually felt, but for one, two, five, or fifty other persons quite different from those adumbrated; or that the poems have no necessary connection with any particular person, will never be exclusively asserted or denied by any one acquainted with human nature.

All these theories and others are possible; none is proved; and, for the literary purpose, none is really important. What is important is that Shakespeare has here caught up the sum of love and uttered it as no poet has before or since, and that in so doing he carried poetry—that is to say, the passionate expression in verse of the sensual and intellectual facts of life—to a pitch which it had never previously reached in English, and which it has never outstepped since. The coast-line of humanity must be wholly altered, the sea must change its nature, the moon must draw it in different ways, before that tide-mark is passed.

These *Sonnets* are written in the English form, which is sometimes called from them the Shakespearian, and which, as already explained, is quite entitled to claim equality with the chief Italian or Petrarchian. Three quatrains, not connected by any necessary or usual community of rhyme, are tipped with a couplet; and, generally speaking, though not invariably, the opposition or balance of octave and sestet which the Petrarchian form naturally invites is replaced here by a steady building up of the thought through the douzain, and then either a climax or a quick antistrophe in the final couplet. The form is extraordinarily suitable to the subjects, and may be said to be, for the sonnet meditative, actually preferable to the octave-and-sestet, though the latter may have advantages for the sonnet descriptive. No such samples of the peculiar phrase beauty of the *Sonnets* can be given as those which were possible in the case of the *Venus*, simply because of their bewildering abundance. Every sonnet, and perhaps a majority of the two thousand lines or thereabouts, contains them; and among them are numbered no small proportion of the highest, the intensest, the most exquisite jewels of English poetry. But their general characteristic as verse is a steady soaring music, now lower, now higher, never exactly glad but always passionate and full, which can be found nowhere else—a harmonic of mighty heart-throbs and brain-pulsings which, once caught, never deserts the mind's ear. Like all the greatest poetry, this is almost independent of meaning though so full of it; you can attend to the sense or disregard it as you please, certain in each case of satisfaction. The thoughts are not so far-fetched, the music not quite so unearthly, as in some poems of the next generation, but they are more universal, more commanding, more human. The mastery which had been partially attained in *Venus and Adonis* is complete here. There is nothing that the poet wishes to say that he cannot say, and there is hardly a district of thought and feeling into which he does not at least cast glances of unerring vision.—GEORGE SAINTSBURY, *A Short History of English Literature*, 1898, pp. 319–20

## OSCAR WILDE
### "The Portrait of Mr. W. H." (1889)
*The Complete Shorter Fiction of Oscar Wilde*
ed. Isobel Murray
1979, pp. 139–69

I had been dining with Erskine in his pretty little house in Birdcage Walk, and we were sitting in the library over our coffee and cigarettes, when the question of literary forgeries happened to turn up in conversation. I cannot at present remember how it was that we struck upon this somewhat curious topic, as it was at that time, but I know that we had a long discussion about Macpherson, Ireland, and Chatterton, and that with regard to the last I insisted that his so-called forgeries were merely the result of an artistic desire for perfect representation; that we had no right to quarrel with an artist for the conditions under which he chooses to present his work; and that all Art being to an certain degree a mode of acting, an

attempt to realise one's own personality on some imaginative plane out of reach of the trammelling accidents and limitations of real life, to censure an artist for a forgery was to confuse an ethical with an æsthetical problem.

Erskine, who was a good deal older than I was, and had been listening to me with the amused deference of a man of forty, suddenly put his hand upon my shoulder and said to me, 'What would you say about a young man who had a strange theory about a certain work of art, believed in his theory, and committed a forgery in order to prove it?'

'Ah!, that is quite a different matter,' I answered.

Erskine remained silent for a few moments, looking at the thin grey threads of smoke that were rising from his cigarette. 'Yes,' he said, after a pause, 'quite different.'

There was something in the tone of his voice, a slight touch of bitterness perhaps, that excited my curiosity. 'Did you ever know anybody who did that?' I cried.

'Yes,' he answered, throwing his cigarette into the fire,— 'a great friend of mine, Cyril Graham. He was very fascinating, and very foolish, and very heartless. However, he left me the only legacy I ever received in my life.'

'What was that?' I exclaimed. Erskine rose from his seat, and going over to a tall inlaid cabinet that stood between the two windows, unlocked it, and came back to where I was sitting, holding in his hand a small panel picture set in an old and somewhat tarnished Elizabethan frame.

It was a full-length portrait of a young man in late sixteenth-century costume, standing by a table, with his right hand resting on an open book. He seemed about seventeen years of age, and was of quite extraordinary personal beauty, though evidently somewhat effeminate. Indeed, had it not been for the dress and the closely cropped hair, one would have said that the face, with its dreamy wistful eyes, and its delicate scarlet lips, was the face of a girl. In manner and especially in the treatment of the hands, the picture reminded one of François Clouet's later work. The black velvet doublet with its fantastically gilded points, and the peacock-blue background against which it showed up so pleasantly, and from which it gained such luminous value of colour, were quite in Clouet's style; and the two masks of Tragedy and Comedy that hung somewhat formally from the marble pedestal had that hard severity of touch—so different from the facile grace of the Italians—which even at the Court of France the great Flemish master never completely lost, and which in itself has always been a characteristic of the northern temper.

'It is a charming thing,' I cried; 'but who is this wonderful young man, whose beauty Art has so happily preserved for us?'

'This is the portrait of Mr. W. H.,' said Erskine, with a sad smile. It might have been a chance effect of light, but it seemed to me that his eyes were quite bright with tears.

'Mr. W. H!' I exclaimed; 'who was Mr. W. H.?'

'Don't you remember?' he answered; 'look at the book on which his hand is resting.'

'I see there is some writing there, but I cannot make it out,' I replied.

'Take this magnifying-glass and try,' said Erskine, with the same sad smile still playing about his mouth.

I took the glass, and moving the lamp a little nearer, I began to spell out the crabbed sixteenth-century handwriting. 'To the onlie begetter of these insuing sonnets.' . . . 'Good heavens!' I cried, 'is this Shakespeare's Mr. W. H.?'

'Cyril Graham used to say so,' muttered Erskine.

'But it is not a bit like Lord Pembroke,' I answered. 'I know the Penshurst portraits very well. I was staying near there a few weeks ago.'

'Do you really believe then that the Sonnets are addressed to Lord Pembroke?' he asked.

'I am sure of it,' I answered. 'Pembroke, Shakespeare, and Mrs. Mary Fitton are the three personages of the Sonnets; there is no doubt at all about it.'

'Well, I agree with you,' said Erskine, 'but I did not always think so. I used to believe—well, I suppose I used to believe in Cyril Graham and his theory.'

'And what was that?' I asked, looking at the wonderful portrait, which had already begun to have a strange fascination for me.

'It is a long story,' said Erskine, taking the picture away from me—rather abruptly I thought at the time—'a very long story; but if you care to hear it, I will tell it to you.'

'I love theories about the Sonnets,' I cried; 'but I don't think I am likely to be converted to any new idea. The matter has ceased to be a mystery to any one. Indeed, I wonder that it ever was a mystery.'

'As I don't believe in the theory, I am not likely to convert you to it,' said Erskine, laughing; 'but it may interest you.'

'Tell it to me, of course,' I answered. 'If it is half as delightful as the picture, I shall be more than satisfied.'

'Well,' said Erskine, lighting a cigarette, 'I must begin by telling you about Cyril Graham himself. He and I were at the same house at Eton. I was a year or two older than he was, but we were immense friends, and did all our work and all our play together. There was, of course, a good deal more play than work, but I cannot say that I am sorry for it. It is always an advantage not to have received a sound commercial education, and what I learned in the playing fields at Eton has been quite as useful to me as anything I was taught at Cambridge. I should tell you that Cyril's father and mother were both dead. They had been drowned in a horrible yachting accident off the Isle of Wight. His father had been in diplomatic service, and had married a daughter, the only daughter, in fact, of old Lord Crediton, who became Cyril's guardian after the death of his parents. I don't think that Lord Crediton cared very much for Cyril. He had never really forgiven his daughter for marrying a man who had not a title. He was an extraordinary old aristocrat, who swore like a costermonger, and had the manners of a farmer. I remember seeing him on Speech-day. He growled at me, gave me a sovereign, and told me not to grow up "a damned Radical" like my father. Cyril had very little affection for him, and was only too glad to spend most of his holidays with us in Scotland. They never really got on together at all. Cyril thought him a bear, and he thought Cyril effeminate. He was effeminate, I suppose, in some things, though he was a very good rider and a capital fencer. In fact he got the foils before he left Eton. But he was very languid in his manner, and not a little vain of his good looks, and had a strong objection to football. The two things that really gave him pleasure were poetry and acting. At Eton he was always dressing up and reciting Shakespeare, and when we went up to Trinity he became a member of the A.D.C. his first term. I remember I was always very jealous of his acting. I was absurdly devoted to him; I suppose because we were so different in some things. I was a rather awkward, weakly lad, with huge feet, and horribly freckled. Freckles run in Scotch families just as gout does in English families. Cyril used to say that of the two he preferred the gout; but he always set an absurdly high value on personal appearance, and once read a paper before our debating society to prove that it was better to be good-looking than to be good. He certainly was wonderfully handsome. People who did not like him, Philistines and college tutors, and young men reading for the Church, used to

say that he was merely pretty; but there was a great deal more in his face than mere prettiness. I think he was the most splendid creature I ever saw, and nothing could exceed the grace of his movements, the charm of his manner. He fascinated everybody who was worth fascinating, and a great many people who were not. He was often wilful and petulant, and I used to think him dreadfully insincere. It was due, I think, chiefly to his inordinate desire to please. Poor Cyril! I told him once that he was contented with very cheap triumphs, but he only laughed. He was horribly spoiled. All charming people, I fancy, are spoiled. It is the secret of their attraction.

'However, I must tell you about Cyril's acting. You know that no actresses are allowed to play at the A.D.C. At least they were not in my time. I don't know how it is now. Well, of course Cyril was always cast for the girls' parts, and when *As You Like It* was produced he played Rosalind. It was a marvellous performance. In fact, Cyril Graham was the only perfect Rosalind I have ever seen. It would be impossible to describe to you the beauty, the delicacy, the refinement of the whole thing. It made an immense sensation, and the horrid little theatre, as it was then, was crowded every night. Even when I read the play now I can't help thinking of Cyril. It might have been written for him. The next term he took his degree, and came to London to read for the diplomatic. But he never did any work. He spent his days reading Shakespeare's Sonnets, and his evenings at the theatre. He was, of course, wild to go on the stage. It was all that I and Lord Crediton could do to prevent him. Perhaps if he had gone on the stage he would be alive now. It is always a silly thing to give advice, but to give good advice is absolutely fatal. I hope you will never fall into that error. If you do, you will be sorry for it.

'Well, to come to the real point of the story, one day I got a letter from Cyril asking me to come round to his rooms that evening. He had charming chambers in Piccadilly overlooking the Green Park, and as I used to go to see him every day, I was rather surprised at his taking the trouble to write. Of course I went, and when I arrived I found him in a state of great excitement. He told me that he had at last discovered the true secret of Shakespeare's Sonnets; that all the scholars and critics had been entirely on the wrong tack; and that he was the first who, working purely by internal evidence, had found out who Mr. W. H. really was. He was perfectly wild with delight, and for a long time would not tell me his theory. Finally, he produced a bundle of notes, took his copy of the Sonnets off the mantelpiece, and sat down and gave me a long lecture on the whole subject.

'He began by pointing out that the young man to whom Shakespeare addressed these strangely passionate poems must have been somebody who was a really vital factor in the development of his dramatic art, and that this could not be said either of Lord Pembroke or Lord Southampton. Indeed, whoever he was, he could not have been anybody of high birth, as was shown very clearly by the 25th Sonnet, in which Shakespeare contrasts himself with those who are "great princes' favourites;" says quite frankly—

> Let those who are in favour with their stars
> Of public honour and proud titles boast,
> Whilst I, whom fortune of such triumph bars,
> Unlook'd for joy in that I honour most;

and ends the sonnet by congratulating himself on the mean state of him he so adored:

> Then happy I, that loved and am beloved
> Where I may not remove nor be removed.

This sonnet Cyril declared would be quite unintelligible if we fancied that it was addressed to either the Earl of Pembroke or the Earl of Southampton, both of whom were men of the highest position in England and fully entitled to be called "great princes"; and he in corroboration of his view read me Sonnets CXXIV and CXXV, in which Shakespeare tells us that his love is not "the child of state," that it "suffers not in smiling pomp," but is "builded far from accident." I listened with a good deal of interest, for I don't think the point had ever been made before; but what followed was still more curious, and seemed to me at the time to entirely dispose of Pembroke's claim. We know from Meres that the Sonnets had been written before 1598, and Sonnet CIV informs us that Shakespeare's friendship for Mr. W.H. had been already in existence for three years. Now Lord Pembroke, who was born in 1580, did not come to London till he was eighteen years of age, that is to say till 1598, and Shakespeare's acquaintance with Mr. W. H. must have begun in 1594, or at the latest in 1595. Shakespeare, accordingly, could not have known Lord Pembroke till after the Sonnets had been written.

'Cyril pointed out also that Pembroke's father did not die till 1601; whereas it was evident from the line,

You had a father, let your son say so,

that the father of Mr. W. H. was dead in 1598. Besides, it was absurd to imagine that any publisher of the time, and the preface is from the publisher's hand, would have ventured to address William Herbert, Earl of Pembroke, as Mr. W. H.; the case of Lord Buckhurst being spoken of as Mr. Sackville being not really a parallel instance, as Lord Buckhurst was not a peer, but merely the younger son of a peer, with a courtesy title, and the passage in *England's Parnassus* where he is so spoken of, is not a formal and stately dedication, but simply a casual allusion. So far for Lord Pembroke, whose supposed claims Cyril easily demolished while I sat by in wonder. With Lord Southampton Cyril had even less difficulty. Southampton became at a very early age the lover of Elizabeth Vernon, so he needed no entreaties to marry; he was not beautiful; he did not resemble his mother, as Mr. W. H. did—

Thou art thy mother's glass, and she in thee
Calls back the lovely April of her prime;

and, above all, his Christian name was Henry, whereas the punning sonnets (CXXXV and CXLIII) show that the Christian name of Shakespeare's friend was the same as his own—*Will*.

'As for the other suggestions of unfortunate commentators, that Mr. W.H. is a misprint for Mr. W.S., meaning Mr. William Shakespeare; that "Mr. W. H. all' should be read "Mr. W. Hall"; that Mr. W. H. is Mr. William Hathaway; and that a full stop should be placed after "wisheth," making Mr. W. H. the writer and not the subject of the dedication,—Cyril got rid of them in a very short time; and it is not worth while to mention his reasons, though I remember he sent me off into a fit of laughter by reading to me, I am glad to say not in the original, some extracts from a German commentator called Barnstorff, who insisted that Mr. W. H. was no less a person than "Mr. William Himself." Nor would he allow for a moment that the Sonnets are mere satires on the work of Drayton and John Davies of Hereford. To him, as indeed to me, they were poems of serious and tragic import, wrung out of the bitterness of Shakespeare's heart, and made sweet by the honey of his lips. Still less would he admit that they were merely a philosophical allegory, and that in them Shakespeare is addressing his Ideal Self, or Ideal Manhood, or the Spirit of Beauty, or the Reason, or the Divine Logos, or the Catholic Church. He felt, as indeed I think we all must feel, that the Sonnets are addressed to an individual,—to a particular young man whose personality for some reason seems to have filled the soul of Shakespeare with terrible joy and no less terrible despair.

'Having in this manner cleared the way as it were, Cyril asked me to dismiss from my mind any preconceived ideas I might have formed on the subject, and to give a fair and unbiassed hearing to his own theory. The problem he pointed out was this: Who was that young man of Shakespeare's day who, without being of noble birth or even of noble nature, was addressed by him in terms of such passionate adoration that we can but wonder at the strange worship, and are almost afraid to turn the key that unlocks the mystery of the poet's heart? Who was he whose physical beauty was such that it became the very corner-stone of Shakespeare's art; the very source of Shakespeare's inspiration; the very incarnation of Shakespeare's dreams? To look upon him as simply the object of certain love-poems is to miss the whole meaning of the poems: for the art of which Shakespeare talks in the Sonnets is not the art of the Sonnets themselves, which indeed were to him but slight and secret things—it is the art of the dramatist to which he is always alluding; and he to whom Shakespeare said—

Thou art all my art, and dost advance
As high as learning my rude ignorance,—

he to whom he promised immortality,

Where breath most breathes, even in the mouth of
men,—

was surely none other than the boy-actor for whom he created Viola and Imogen, Juliet and Rosalind, Portia and Desdemona, and Cleopatra herself. This was Cyril Graham's theory, evolved as you see purely from the Sonnets themselves, and depending for its acceptance not so much on demonstrable proof or formal evidence, but on a kind of spiritual and artistic sense, by which alone he claimed could the true meaning of the poems be discerned. I remember his reading to me that fine sonnet—

How can my Muse want subject to invent,
While thou dost breathe, that pour'st into my verse
Thine own sweet argument, too excellent
For every vulgar paper to rehearse?
O, give thyself the thanks, if aught in me
Worthy perusal stand against thy sight;
For who's so dumb that cannot write to thee,
When thou thyself dost give invention light?
Be thou the tenth Muse, ten times more in worth
Than those old nine which rhymers invocate;
And he that calls on thee, let him bring forth
Eternal numbers to outlive long date

—and pointing out how completely it corroborated his theory; and indeed he went through all the Sonnets carefully, and showed, or fancied that he showed, that, according to his new explanation of their meaning, things that had seemed obscure, or evil, or exaggerated, became clear and rational, and of high artistic import, illustrating Shakespeare's conception of the true relations between the art of the actor and the art of the dramatist.

'It is of course evident that there must have been in Shakespeare's company some wonderful boy-actor of great beauty, to whom he intrusted the presentation of his noble heroines; for Shakespeare was a practical theatrical manager as well as an imaginative poet, and Cyril Graham had actually discovered the boy-actor's name. He was Will, or, as he preferred to call him, Willie Hughes. The Christian name he found of course in the punning sonnets, CXXXV and CXLIII; the surname was, according to him, hidden in the eighth line of the 20th Sonnet, where Mr. W. H. is described as—

A man in hew, all *Hews* in his controwling.

'In the original edition of the Sonnets "Hews" is printed with a capital letter and in italics, and this, he claimed, showed clearly that a play on words was intended, his view receiving a good deal of corroboration from those sonnets in which curious puns are made on the words "use" and "usury." Of course I was converted at once, and Willie Hughes became to me as real a person as Shakespeare. The only objection I made to the theory was that the name of Willie Hughes does not occur in the list of the actors of Shakespeare's company as it is printed in the first folio. Cyril, however, pointed out that the absence of Willie Hughes's name from this list really corrorborated the theory, as it was evident from Sonnet LXXXVI that Willie Hughes had abandoned Shakespeare's company to play at a rival theatre, probably in some of Chapman's plays. It is in reference to this that in the great sonnet on Chapman Shakespeare said to Willie Hughes—

But when your countenance filled up his line,
Then lacked I matter; that enfeebled mine—

the expression "when your countenance filled up his line" referring obviously to the beauty of the young actor giving life and reality and added charm to Chapman's verse, the same idea being also put forward in the 79th Sonnet—

Whilst I alone did call upon thy aid,
My verse alone had all thy gentle grace,
But now my gracious numbers are decayed,
And my sick Muse does give another place;

and in the immediately preceding sonnet, where Shakespeare says,

Every alien pen has got my *use*
And under thee their poesy disperse,

the play upon words (use = Hughes) being of course obvious, and the phrase "under thee their poesy disperse," meaning "by your assistance as an actor bring their plays before the people."

'It was a wonderful evening, and we sat up almost till dawn reading and re-reading the Sonnets. After some time, however, I began to see that before the theory could be placed before the world in a really perfected form, it was necessary to get some independent evidence about the existence of this young actor, Willie Hughes. If this could be once established, there could be no possible doubt about his identity with Mr. W. H.; but otherwise the theory would fall to the ground. I put this forward very strongly to Cyril, who was a good deal annoyed at what he called my Philistine tone of mind, and indeed was rather bitter upon the subject. However, I made him promise that in his own interest he would not publish his discovery till he had put the whole matter beyond the reach of doubt; and for weeks and weeks we searched the registers of City churches, the Alleyn MSS. at Dulwich, the Record Office, the papers of the Lord Chamberlain—everything, in fact, that we thought might contain some allusion to Willie Hughes. We discovered nothing, of course, and every day the existence of Willie Hughes seemed to me to become more problematical. Cyril was in a dreadful state, and used to go over the whole question day after day, entreating me to believe; but I saw the one flaw in the theory, and I refused to be convinced till the actual existence of Willie Hughes, a boy-actor of Elizabethan days, had been placed beyond the reach of doubt or cavil.

'One day Cyril left town to stay with his grandfather, I thought at the time, but I afterwards heard from Lord Crediton that this was not the case; and about a fortnight afterwards I received a telegram from him, handed in at Warwick, asking me to be sure to come and dine with him that evening at eight o'clock. When I arrived, he said to me, "The only apostle who did not deserve proof was S. Thomas, and S. Thomas was the only apostle who got it." I asked him what he meant. He answered that he had not merely been able to establish the existence in the sixteenth century of a boy-actor of the name of Willie Hughes, but to prove by the most conclusive evidence that he was the Mr. W. H. of the Sonnets. He would not tell me anything more at the time; but after dinner he solemnly produced the picture I showed you, and told me that he had discovered it by the merest chance nailed to the side of an old chest that he had bought at a farmhouse in Warwickshire. The chest itself, which was a very fine example of Elizabethan work, he had, of course, brought with him, and in the centre of the front panel the initials W.H. were undoubtedly carved. It was this monogram that had attracted his attention, and he told me that it was not till he had had the chest in his possession for several days that he had thought of making any careful examination of the inside. One morning, however, he saw that one of the sides of the chest was much thicker than the other, and looking more closely, he discovered that a framed panel picture was clamped against it. On taking it out, he found it was the picture that is now lying on the sofa. It was very dirty, and covered with mould; but he managed to clean it, and, to his great joy, saw that he had fallen by mere chance on the one thing for which he had been looking. Here was an authentic portrait of Mr. W.H., with his hand resting on the dedicatory page of the Sonnets, and on the frame itself could be faintly seen the name of the young man written in black uncial letters on a faded gold ground, "Master Will. Hews."

'Well, what was I to say? It never occurred to me for a moment that Cyril Graham was playing a trick on me, or that he was trying to prove his theory by means of a forgery.'

'But is it a forgery?' I asked.

'Of course it is,' said Erskine. 'It is a very good forgery; but it is a forgery none the less. I thought at the time that Cyril was rather calm about the whole matter; but I remember he more than once told me that he himself required no proof of the kind, and that he thought the theory complete without it. I laughed at him, and told him that without it the theory would fall to the ground, and I warmly congratulated him on the marvellous discovery. We then arranged that the picture should be etched or facsimiled, and placed as the frontispiece to Cyril's edition of the Sonnets; and for three months we did nothing but go over each poem line by line, till we had settled every difficulty of text or meaning. One unlucky day I was in a print-shop in Holborn, when I saw upon the counter some extremely beautiful drawings in silver-point. I was so attracted by them that I bought them; and the proprietor of the place, a man called Rawlings, told me that they were done by a young painter of the name of Edward Merton, who was very clever, but as poor as a church mouse. I went to see Merton some days afterwards, having got his address from the printseller, and found a pale, interesting young man, with a rather common-looking wife—his model, as I subsequently learned. I told him how much I admired his drawings, at which he seemed very pleased, and I asked him if he would show me some of his other work. As we were looking over a portfolio, full of really lovely things,—for Merton had a most delicate and delightful touch,—I suddenly caught sight of a drawing of the picture of Mr. W. H. There was no doubt whatever about it. It was almost a facsimile—the only difference being that the two masks of Tragedy and Comedy were not suspended from the marble table as they are in the picture, but were lying on the floor at the young man's feet. "Where on earth did you get that?" I said. He grew rather confused, and said—"Oh, that is nothing. I did not know it was in this portfolio. It is not a thing of any value." "It is what you did for Mr. Cyril Graham," exclaimed his wife; "and if this gentleman wishes to buy it, let him have it." "For Mr. Cyril Graham?" I repeated. "Did you paint the picture of Mr. W.H.?" "I don't understand what you mean," he answered, growing very red. Well, the whole thing was quite dreadful. The wife let it all out. I gave her five pounds when I was going away. I can't bear to think of it now; but of course I was furious. I went off at once to Cyril's chambers, waited there for three hours before he came in, with that horrid lie staring me in the face, and told him I had discovered his forgery. He grew very pale and said—"I did it purely for your sake. You would not be convinced in any other way. It does not affect the truth of the theory." "The truth of the theory!" I exclaimed; "the less we talk about that the better. You never even believed in it yourself. If you had, you would not have committed a forgery to prove it." High words passed between us; we had a fearful quarrel. I daresay I was unjust. The next morning he was dead.'

'Dead!' I cried.

'Yes; he shot himself with a revolver. Some of the blood splashed upon the frame of the picture, just where the name had been painted. By the time I arrived—his servant had sent for me at once—the police were already there. He had left a letter for me, evidently written in the greatest agitation and distress of mind.'

'What was in it?' I asked.

'Oh, that he believed absolutely in Willie Hughes; that the forgery of the picture had been done simply as a concession to me, and did not in the slightest degree invalidate the truth of the theory; and that in order to show me how firm and flawless his faith in the whole thing was, he was going to offer his life as a sacrifice to the secret of the Sonnets. It was a foolish, mad letter. I remember he ended by saying that he intrusted to me the Willie Hughes theory, and that it was for me to present it to the world, and to unlock the secret of Shakespeare's heart.'

'It is a most tragic story,' I cried; 'but why have you not carried out his wishes?'

Erskine shrugged his shoulders. 'Because it is a perfectly unsound theory from beginning to end,' he answered.

'My dear Erskine,' I said, getting up from my seat, 'you are entirely wrong about the whole matter. It is the only perfect key to Shakespeare's Sonnets that has ever been made. It is complete in every detail. I believe in Willie Hughes.'

'Don't say that,' said Erskine gravely; 'I believe there is something fatal about the idea, and intellectually there is nothing to be said for it. I have gone into the whole matter, and I assure you the theory is entirely fallacious. It is plausible up to a certain point. Then it stops. For heaven's sake, my dear boy, don't take up the subject of Willie Hughes. You will break your heart over it.'

'Erskine,' I answered, 'it is your duty to give this theory to the world. If you will not do it, I will. By keeping it back you wrong the memory of Cyril Graham, the youngest and the most splendid of all the martyrs of literature. I entreat you to do him justice. He died for this thing,—don't let his death be in vain.'

Erskine looked at me in amazement. 'You are carried away by the sentiment of the whole story,' he said. 'You forget that a thing is not necessarily true because a man dies for it. I was devoted to Cyril Graham. His death was a horrible blow to me. I did not recover it for years. I don't think I have ever recovered it. But Willie Hughes? There is nothing in the idea of Willie Hughes. No such person ever existed. As for bringing the whole thing before the world—the world thinks that Cyril Graham shot himself by accident. The only proof of his suicide was contained in the letter to me, and of this letter the public

never heard anything. To the present day Lord Crediton thinks that the whole thing was accidental.'

'Cyril Graham sacrificed his life to a great idea,' I answered; 'and if you will not tell of his martyrdom, tell at least of his faith.'

'His faith,' said Erskine, 'was fixed in a thing that was false, in a thing that was unsound, in a thing that no Shakespearian scholar would accept for a moment. The theory would be laughed at. Don't make a fool of yourself, and don't follow a trail that leads nowhere. You start by assuming the existence of the very person whose existence is the thing to be proved. Besides, everybody knows that the Sonnets were addressed to Lord Pembroke. The matter is settled once for all.'

'The matter is not settled!' I exclaimed. 'I will take up the theory where Cyril Graham left it, and I will prove to the world that he was right.'

'Silly boy!' said Erskine. 'Go home: it is after two, and don't think about Willie Hughes any more. I am sorry I told you anything about it, and very sorry indeed that I should have converted you to a thing in which I don't believe.'

'You have given me the key to the greatest mystery of modern literature,' I answered; 'and I shall not rest till I have made you recognise, till I have made everybody recognise, that Cyril Graham was the most subtle Shakespearian critic of our day.'

As I walked home through St. James's Park the dawn was just breaking over London. The white swans were lying asleep on the polished lake, and the gaunt Palace looked purple against the pale-green sky. I thought of Cyril Graham, and my eyes filled with tears.

## II

It was past twelve o'clock when I awoke, and the sun was streaming in through the curtains of my room in long slanting beams of dusty gold. I told my servant that I would be at home to no one; and after I had had a cup of chocolate and a *petit-pain*, I took down from the book-shelf my copy of Shakespeare's Sonnets, and began to go carefully through them. Every poem seemed to me to corroborate Cyril Graham's theory. I felt as if I had my hand upon Shakespeare's heart, and was counting each separate throb and pulse of passion. I thought of the wonderful boy-actor, and saw his face in every line.

Two sonnets, I remember, struck me particularly: they were the 53rd and the 67th. In the first of these, Shakespeare, complimenting Willie Hughes on the versatility of his acting, on his wide range of parts, a range extending from Rosalind to Juliet, and from Beatrice to Ophelia, says to him—

> What is your substance, whereof are you made,
> That millions of strange shadows on you tend?
> Since every one hath, every one, one shade,
> And you, but one, can every shadow lend—

lines that would be unintelligible if they were not addressed to an actor, for the word 'shadow' had in Shakespeare's day a technical meaning connected with the stage. 'The best in this kind are but shadows,' says Theseus of the actors in the *Midsummer Night's Dream*, and there are many similar allusions in the literature of the day. These sonnets evidently belonged to the series in which Shakespeare discusses the nature of the actor's art, and of the strange and rare temperament that is essential to the perfect stage-player. 'How is it,' says Shakespeare to Willie Hughes, 'that you have so many personalities?' and then he goes on to point out that his beauty is such that it seems to realise every form and phase of fancy, to embody each dream of the creative imagination—an idea that is still further expanded in the sonnet that immediately follows, where, beginning with the fine thought,

> O, how much more doth beauty beauteous seem
> By that sweet ornament which *truth* doth give!

Shakespeare invites us to notice how the truth of acting, the truth of visible presentation on the stage, adds to the wonder of poetry, giving life to its loveliness, and actual reality to its ideal form. And yet, in the 67th Sonnet, Shakespeare calls upon Willie Hughes to abandon the stage with its artificiality, its false mimic life of painted face and unreal costume, its immoral influences and suggestions, its remoteness from the true world of noble action and sincere utterance.

> Ah! wherefore with infection should he live,
> And with his presence grace impiety,
> That sin by him advantage should achieve,
> And lace itself with his society?
> Why should false painting imitate his cheek
> And steal dead seeming of his living hue?
> Why should poor beauty indirectly seek
> Roses of shadow, since his rose is true?

It may seem strange that so great a dramatist as Shakespeare, who realised his own perfection as an artist and his humanity as a man on the ideal plane of stage-writing and stage-playing, should have written in these terms about the theatre; but we must remember that in sonnets CX and CXI Shakespeare shows us that he too was wearied of the world of puppets, and full of shame at having made himself 'a motley to the view.' The 111th Sonnet is especially bitter:—

> O, for my sake do you with Fortune chide
> The guilty goddess of my harmful deeds,
> That did not better for my life provide
> Than public means which public manners breeds.
> Thence comes it that my name receives a brand,
> And almost thence my nature is subdued
> To what it works in, like the dyer's hand:
> Pity me, then, and wish I were renewed—

and there are many signs elsewhere of the same feeling, signs familiar to all real students of Shakespeare.

One point puzzled me immediately as I read the Sonnets, and it was days before I struck on the true interpretation, which indeed Cyril Graham himself seems to have missed. I could not understand how it was that Shakespeare set so high a value on his young friend marrying. He himself had married young, and the result had been unhappiness, and it was not likely that he would have asked Willie Hughes to commit the same error. The boy-player of Rosalind had nothing to gain from marriage, or from the passions of real life. The early sonnets, with their strange entreaties to have children, seemed to me a jarring note. The explanation of the mystery came on me quite suddenly, and I found it in the curious dedication. It will be remembered that the dedication runs as follows:—

TO·THE·ONLIE·BEGETTER·OF·
THESE·INSUING·SONNETS·
MR. W. H. ·ALL·HAPPINESSE·
AND·THAT·ETERNITIE·
PROMISED·
BY·
OUR·EVER-LIVING·POET·
WISHETH·
THE·WELL-WISHING·
ADVENTURER·IN·
SETTING·
FORTH.
                        T. T.

Some scholars have supposed that the word 'begetter' in this dedication means simply the procurer of the Sonnets for Thomas Thorpe the publisher; but this view is now generally abandoned, and the highest authorities are quite agreed that it is to be taken in the sense of inspirer, the metaphor being drawn from the analogy of physical life. Now I saw that the same metaphor was used by Shakespeare himself all through the poems, and this set me on the right track. Finally I made my great discovery. The marriage that Shakespeare proposes for Willie Hughes is the 'marriage with his Muse,' an expression which is definitely put forward in the 82nd Sonnet, where, in the bitterness of his heart at the defection of the boy-actor for whom he had written his greatest parts, and whose beauty had indeed suggested them, he opens his complaint by saying—

> I'll grant thou wert not married to my Muse.

The children he begs him to beget are no children of flesh and blood, but more immortal children of undying fame. The whole cycle of the early sonnets is simply Shakespeare's invitation to Willie Hughes to go upon the stage and become a player. How barren and profitless a thing, he says, is this beauty of yours if it be not used:

> When forty winters shall besiege thy brow,
> And dig deep trenches in thy beauty's field,
> Thy youth's proud livery, so gazed on now,
> Will be a tattered weed, of small worth held:
> Then being asked where all thy beauty lies,
> Where all the treasure of thy lusty days,
> To say, within thine own deep-sunken eyes,
> Were an all-eating shame and thriftless praise.

You must create something in art: my verse 'is thine, and *born* of thee;' only listen to me, and I will '*bring forth* eternal numbers to outlive long date,' and you shall people with forms of your own image the imaginary world of the stage. These children that you beget, he continues, will not wither away, as mortal children do, but you shall live in them and in my plays: do but

> Make thee another self, for love of me,
> That beauty still may live in thine or thee!

I collected all the passages that seemed to me to corroborate this view, and they produced a strong impression on me, and showed me how complete Cyril Graham's theory really was. I also saw that it was quite easy to separate those lines in which he speaks of the Sonnets themselves from those in which he speaks of his great dramatic work. This was a point that had been entirely overlooked by all critics up to Cyril Graham's day. And yet it was one of the most important points in the whole series of poems. To the Sonnets Shakespeare was more or less indifferent. He did not wish to rest his fame on them. They were to him his 'slight Muse,' as he calls them, and intended, as Meres tells us, for private circulation only among a few, a very few, friends. Upon the other hand he was extremely conscious of the high artistic value of his plays, and shows a noble self-reliance upon his dramatic genius. When he says to Willie Hughes:

> But thy eternal summer shall not fade,
> Nor lose possession of that fair thou owest;
> Nor shall Death brag thou wander'st in his shade,
> When in *eternal lines* to time thou growest;
>    So long as men can breathe or eyes can see,
>    So long lives this and this gives life to thee;—

the expression 'eternal lines' clearly alludes to one of his plays that he was sending him at the time, just as the concluding couplet points to his confidence in the probability of his plays being always acted. In his address to the Dramatic Muse (Sonnets C and CI), we find the same feeling.

Where art thou, Muse, that thou forget'st so long
To speak of that which gives thee all thy might?
Spends thou thy fury on some worthless song,
Darkening thy power to lend base subjects light?

he cries, and he then proceeds to reproach the mistress of
Tragedy and Comedy for her 'neglect of Truth in Beauty dyed,'
and says—

Because he needs no praise, wilt thou be dumb?
Excuse not silence so; for 't lies in thee
To make him much outlive a gilded tomb,
And to be praised of ages yet to be.
    Then do thy office, Muse; I teach thee how
    To make him seem long hence as he shows now.

It is, however, perhaps in the 55th Sonnet that Shakespeare
gives to this idea its fullest expression. To imagine that the
'powerful rhyme' of the second line refers to the sonnet itself, is
to entirely mistake Shakespeare's meaning. It seemed to me
that it was extremely likely, from the general character of the
sonnet, that a particular play was meant, and that the play was
none other but *Romeo and Juliet*.

Not marble, nor the gilded monuments
Of princes, shall outlive this powerful rhyme;
But you shall shine more bright in these contents
Than unswept stone besmeared with sluttish time.
When wasteful wars shall statues overturn,
And broils root out of the work of masonry,
Not Mars his sword nor war's quick fire shall burn
The living record of your memory.
'Gainst death and all-oblivious enmity
Shall you pace forth; your praise shall still find room
Even in the eyes of all posterity
That wear this world out to the ending doom.
    So, till the judgment that yourself arise,
    You live in this, and dwell in lovers' eyes.

It was also extremely suggestive to note how here as elsewhere
Shakespeare promised Willie Hughes immortality in a form
that appealed to men's eyes—that is to say, in a spectacular
form, in a play that is to be looked at.

For two weeks I worked hard at the Sonnets, hardly ever
going out, and refusing all invitations. Every day I seemed to
be discovering something new, and Willie Hughes became to
me a kind of spiritual presence, an ever-dominant personality. I
could almost fancy that I saw him standing in the shadow of my
room, so well had Shakespeare drawn him, with his golden
hair, his tender flower-like grace, his dreamy deep-sunken eyes,
his delicate mobile limbs, and his white lily hands. His very
name fascinated me. Willie Hughes! Willie Hughes! How
musically it sounded! Yes; who else but he could have been the
master-mistress of Shakespeare's passion,[1] the lord of his love to
whom he was bound in vassalage,[2] the delicate minion of
pleasure,[3] the rose of the whole world,[4] the herald of the
spring[5] decked in the proud livery of youth,[6] the lovely boy
whom it was sweet music to hear,[7] and whose beauty was the
very raiment of Shakespeare's heart,[8] as it was the keystone of
his dramatic power? How bitter now seemed the whole tragedy
of his desertion and his shame!—shame that he made sweet
and lovely[9] by the mere magic of his personality, but that was
none the less shame. Yet as Shakespeare forgave him, should
not we forgive him also? I did not care to pry into the mystery of
his sin.

His abandonment of Shakespeare's theatre was a different
matter, and I investigated it at great length. Finally I came to
the conclusion that Cyril Graham had been wrong in regarding
the rival dramatist of the 80th Sonnet as Chapman. It was
obviously Marlowe who was alluded to. At the time the
Sonnets were written, such an expression as 'the proud full sail

of his great verse' could not have been used of Chapman's
work, however applicable it might have been to the style of his
later Jacobean plays. No: Marlowe was clearly the rival
dramatist of whom Shakespeare spoke in such laudatory terms;
and that

Affable familiar ghost
Which nightly gulls him with intelligence,

was the Mephistopheles of his Doctor Faustus. No doubt,
Marlowe was fascinated by the beauty and grace of the boy-
actor, and lured him away from the Blackfriars Theatre, that he
might play the Gaveston of his *Edward II*. That Shakespeare
had the legal right to retain Willie Hughes in his own company
is evident from Sonnet LXXXVII, where he says:—

Farewell! thou art too dear for my possessing,
And like enough thou know'st thy estimate:
The *charter of thy worth* gives thee releasing;
My *bonds* in thee are all determinate.
For how do I hold thee but by thy granting?
And for that riches where is my deserving?
The cause of this fair gift in me is wanting,
*And so my patent back again is swerving.*
Thyself thou gavest, thy own work then not knowing,
Or me, to whom thou gavest it, else mistaking;
So thy great gift, upon misprision growing,
Comes none again, on better judgment making.
    This have I had thee, as a dream doth flatter,
    In sleep a king, but waking no such matter.

But him whom he could not hold by love, he would not hold
by force. Willie Hughes became a member of Lord Pembroke's
company, and, perhaps in the open yard of the Red Bull
Tavern, played the part of King Edward's delicate minion. On
Marlowe's death, he seems to have returned to Shakespeare,
who, whatever his fellow-partners may have thought of the
matter, was not slow to forgive the wilfulness and treachery of
the young actor.

How well, too, had Shakespeare drawn the temperament
of the stage-player! Willie Hughes was one of those

That do not do the thing they most do show,
Who, moving others, are themselves as stone.

He could act love, but could not feel it, could mimic passion
without realising it.

In many's looks the false heart's history
Is writ in moods and frowns and wrinkles strange,

but with Willie Hughes it was not so. 'Heaven,' says Shakespeare, in a sonnet of mad idolatry—

Heaven in thy creation did decree
That in thy face sweet love should ever dwell;
Whate'er thy thoughts or thy heart's workings be,
Thy looks should nothing thence but sweetness tell.

In his 'inconstant mind' and his 'false heart,' it was easy to
recognise the insincerity and treachery that somehow seem
inseparable from the artistic nature, as in his love of praise, that
desire for immediate recognition that characterises all actors.
And yet, more fortunate in this than other actors, Willie
Hughes was to know something of immortality. Inseparably
connected with Shakespeare's plays, he was to live in them.

Your name from hence immortal life shall have,
Though I, once gone, to all the world must die:
The earth can yield me but a common grave,
When you entombed in men's eyes shall lie.
Your monument shall be my gentle verse,
Which eyes not yet created shall o'er-read,
And tongues to be your being shall rehearse
When all the breathers of this world are dead.

There were endless allusions, also, to Willie Hughes's power over his audience,—the 'gazers,' as Shakespeare calls them; but perhaps the most perfect description of his wonderful mastery over dramatic art was in *The Lover's Complaint*, where Shakespeare says of him:—

> In him a plenitude of subtle matter,
> Applied to cautels, all strange forms receives,
> Of burning blushes, or of weeping water,
> Or swooning paleness; and he takes and leaves,
> In either's aptness, as it best deceives,
> To blush at speeches rank, to weep at woes,
> Or to turn white and swoon at tragic shows.
>         . . .
> So on the tip of his subduing tongue,
> All kind of arguments and questions deep,
> All replication prompt and reason strong,
> For his advantage still did wake and sleep,
> To make the weeper laugh, the laugher weep.
>     He had the dialect and the different skill,
>     Catching all passions in his craft of will.

Once I thought that I had really found Willie Hughes in Elizabethan literature. In a wonderfully graphic account of the last days of the great Earl of Essex, his chaplain, Thomas Knell, tells us that the night before the Earl died, 'he called William Hewes, which was his musician, to play upon the virginals and to sing. "Play," said he, "my song, Will Hewes, and I will sing it to myself." So he did it most joyfully, not as the howling swan, which, still looking down, waileth her end, but as a sweet lark, lifting up his hands and casting up his eyes to his God, with this mounted the crystal skies, and reached with his unwearied tongue on the top of highest heavens.' Surely the boy who played on the virginals to the dying father of Sidney's Stella was none other but the Will Hews to whom Shakespeare dedicated the Sonnets, and whom he tells us was himself sweet 'music to hear.' Yet Lord Essex died in 1576, when Shakespeare himself was but twelve years of age. It was impossible that his musician could have been the Mr. W. H. of the Sonnets. Perhaps Shakespeare's young friend was the son of the player upon the virginals? It was at least something to have discovered that Will Hews was an Elizabethan name. Indeed the name Hews seemed to have been closely connected with music and the stage. The first English actress was the lovely Margaret Hews, whom Prince Rupert so madly loved. What more probable than that between her and Lord Essex's musician had come the boy-actor of Shakespeare's plays? But the proofs, the links—where were they? Alas! I could not find them. It seemed to me that I was always on the brink of absolute verification, but that I could never really attain to it.

From Willie Hughes's life I soon passed to thoughts of his death. I used to wonder what had been his end.

Perhaps he had been one of those English actors who in 1604 went across sea to Germany and played before the great Duke Henry Julius of Brunswick, himself a dramatist of no mean order, and at the Court of that strange Elector of Brandenburg, who was so enamoured of beauty that he was said to have bought for his weight in amber the young son of a travelling Greek merchant, and to have given pageants in honour of his slave all through that dreadful famine year of 1606–7, when the people died of hunger in the very streets of the town, and for the space of seven months there was no rain. We know at any rate that *Romeo and Juliet* was brought out at Dresden in 1613, along with *Hamlet* and *King Lear*, and it was surely to none other than Willie Hughes that in 1615 the death-mask of Shakespeare was brought by the hand of one of the suite of the English ambassador, pale token of the passing away of the great poet who had so dearly loved him. Indeed there would have been something peculiarly fitting in the idea

that the boy-actor, whose beauty had been so vital an element in the realism and romance of Shakespeare's art, should have been the first to have brought to Germany the seed of the new culture, and was in his way the precursor of that *Aufklarung* or Illumination of the eighteenth century, that splendid movement which, though begun by Lessing and Herder, and brought to its full and perfect issue by Goethe, was in no small part helped on by another actor—Friedrich Schroeder—who awoke the popular consciousness, and by means of the feigned passions and mimetic methods of the stage showed the intimate, the vital, connection between life and literature. If this was so,—and there was certainly no evidence against it,—it was not improbable that Willie Hughes was one of those English comedians (*mimæ quidam ex Britannia*, as the old chronicle calls them), who were slain at Nuremberg in a sudden uprising of the people, and were secretly buried in a little vineyard outside the city by some young men 'who had found pleasure in their performances, and of whom some had sought to be instructed in the mysteries of the new art.' Certainly no more fitting place could there be for him to whom Shakespeare said, 'thou art all my art,' than this little vineyard outside the city walls. For was it not from the sorrows of Dionysos that Tragedy sprang? Was not the light laughter of Comedy, with its careless merriment and quick replies, first heard on the lips of the Sicilian vine-dressers? Nay, did not the purple and red stain of the wine-froth on face and limbs give the first suggestion of the charm and fascination of disguise— the desire for self-concealment, the sense of the value of objectivity thus showing itself in the rude beginnings of the art? At any rate, wherever he lay—whether in the little vineyard at the gate of the Gothic town, or in some dim London churchyard amidst the roar and bustle of our great city—no gorgeous monument marked his resting-place. His true tomb, as Shakespeare saw, was the poet's verse, his true monument the permanence of the drama. So had it been with others whose beauty had given a new creative impulse to their age. The ivory body of the Bithynian slave rots in the green ooze of the Nile, and on the yellow hills of the Cerameicus is strewn the dust of the young Athenian; but Antinous lives in sculpture, and Charmides in philosophy.

### III

After three weeks had elapsed, I determined to make a strong appeal to Erskine to do justice to the memory of Cyril Graham, and to give to the world his marvellous interpretation of the Sonnets—the only interpretation that thoroughly explained the problem. I have not any copy of my letter, I regret to say, nor have I been able to lay my hand upon the original; but I remember that I went over the whole ground, and covered sheets of paper with passionate reiteration of the arguments and proofs that my study had suggested to me. It seemed to me that I was not merely restoring Cyril Graham to his proper place in literary history, but rescuing the honour of Shakespeare himself from the tedious memory of a commonplace intrigue. I put into the letter all my enthusiasm. I put into the letter all my faith.

No sooner, in fact, had I sent it off than a curious reaction came over me. It seemed to me that I had given away my capacity for belief in the Willie Hughes theory of the Sonnets, that something had gone out of me, as it were, and that I was perfectly indifferent to the whole subject. What was it that had happened? It is difficult to say. Perhaps, by finding perfect expression for a passion, I had exhausted the passion itself. Emotional forces, like the forces of physical life, have their positive limitations. Perhaps the mere effort to convert any one to a theory involves some form of renunciation of the power of credence. Perhaps I was simply tired of the whole thing, and, my enthusiasm having burnt out, my reason was left to its own unimpassioned judgment. However it came about, and I cannot pretend to explain it, there was no doubt that Willie Hughes suddenly became to me a mere myth, an idle dream, the boyish fancy of a young man who, like most ardent spirits, was more anxious to convince others than to be himself convinced.

As I had said some very unjust and bitter things to Erskine in my letter, I determined to go and see him at once, and to make my apologies to him for my behaviour. Accordingly, the next morning I drove down to Birdcage Walk, and found Erskine sitting in his library, with the forged picture of Willie Hughes in front of him.

'My dear Erskine!' I cried, 'I have come to apologise to you.'

'To apologise to me?' he said. 'What for?'

'For my letter,' I answered.

'You have nothing to regret in your letter,' he said. 'On the contrary, you have done me the greatest service in your power. You have shown me that Cyril Graham's theory is perfectly sound.'

'You don't mean to say that you believe in Willie Hughes?' I exclaimed.

'Why not?' he rejoined. 'You have proved the thing to me. Do you think I cannot estimate the value of evidence.'

'But there is no evidence at all,' I groaned, sinking into a chair. 'When I wrote to you I was under the influence of a perfectly silly enthusiasm. I had been touched by the story of Cyril Graham's death, fascinated by his romantic theory, enthralled by the wonder and novelty of the whole idea. I see now that the theory is based on a delusion. The only evidence for the existence of Willie Hughes is that picture in front of you, and the picture is a forgery. Don't be carried away by mere sentiment in this matter. Whatever romance may have to say about the Willie Hughes theory, reason is dead against it.'

'I don't understand you,' said Erskine, looking at me in amazement. 'Why, you yourself have convinced me by your letter that Willie Hughes is an absolute reality. Why have you changed your mind? Or is all that you have been saying to me merely a joke?'

'I cannot explain it to you,' I rejoined, 'but I see now that there is really nothing to be said in favour of Cyril Graham's interpretation. The Sonnets are addressed to Lord Pembroke. For heaven's sake don't waste your time in a foolish attempt to discover a young Elizabethan actor who never existed, and to make a phantom puppet the centre of the great cycle of Shakespeare's Sonnets.'

'I see that you don't understand the theory,' he replied.

'My dear Erskine,' I cried, 'not understand it! Why, I feel as if I had invented it. Surely my letter shows you that I not merely went into the whole matter, but that I contributed proofs of every kind. The one flaw in the theory is that it presupposes the existence of the person whose existence is the subject of dispute. If we grant that there was in Shakespeare's company a young actor of the name of Willie Hughes, it is not difficult to make him the object of the Sonnets. But as we know that there was no actor of this name in the company of the Globe Theatre, it is idle to pursue the investigation further.'

'But that is exactly what we don't know,' said Erskine. 'It is quite true that his name does not occur in the list given in the first folio; but, as Cyril pointed out, that is rather a proof in favour of the existence of Willie Hughes than against it, if we remember his treacherous desertion of Shakespeare for a rival dramatist.'

We argued the matter over for hours, but nothing that I could say could make Erskine surrender his faith in Cyril Graham's interpretation. He told me that he intended to devote his life to proving the theory, and that he was determined to do justice to Cyril Graham's memory. I entreated him, laughed at him, begged of him, but it was of no use. Finally we parted, not exactly in anger, but certainly with a shadow between us. He thought me shallow, I thought him foolish. When I called on him again his servant told me that he had gone to Germany.

Two years afterwards, as I was going into my club, the hall-porter handed me a letter with a foreign postmark. It was from Erskine, and written at the Hotel d'Angleterre, Cannes. When I had read it I was filled with horror, though I did not quite believe that he would be so mad as to carry his resolve into execution. The gist of the letter was that he had tried in every way to verify the Willie Hughes theory, and had failed, and that as Cyril Graham had given his life for this theory, he himself had determined to give his own life also to the same cause. The concluding words of the letter were these: 'I still believe in Willie Hughes; and by the time you receive this, I shall have died by my own hand for Willie Hughes's sake: for his sake, and for the sake of Cyril Graham, whom I drove to his death by my shallow scepticism and ignorant lack of faith. The truth was once revealed to you, and you rejected it. It comes to you now stained with the blood of two lives,—do not turn away from it.'

It was a horrible moment. I felt sick with misery, and yet I could not believe it. To die for one's theological beliefs is the worst use a man can make of his life, but to die for a literary theory! It seemed impossible.

I looked at the date. The letter was a week old. Some unfortunate chance had prevented my going to the club for several days, or I might have got it in time to save him. Perhaps it was not too late. I drove off to my rooms, packed up my things, and started by the night-mail from Charing Cross. The journey was intolerable. I thought I would never arrive.

As soon as I did I drove to the Hotel d'Angleterre. They told me that Erskine had been buried two days before, in the English cemetery. There was something horribly grotesque about the whole tragedy. I said all kinds of wild things, and the people in the hall looked curiously at me.

Suddenly Lady Erskine, in deep mourning, passed across the vestibule. When she saw me she came up to me, murmured something about her poor son, and burst into tears. I led her into her sitting-room. An elderly gentleman was there waiting for her. It was the English doctor.

We talked a great deal about Erskine, but I said nothing about his motive for committing suicide. It was evident that he had not told his mother anything about the reason that had driven him to so fatal, so mad an act. Finally Lady Erskine rose and said, 'George left you something as a memento. It was a thing he prized very much. I will get it for you.'

As soon as she had left the room I turned to the doctor and said, 'What a dreadful shock it must have been to Lady Erskine! I wonder that she bears it as well as she does.'

'Oh, she knew for months past that it was coming,' he answered.

'Knew it for months past!' I cried. 'But why didn't she stop him? Why didn't she have him watched? He must have been mad.'

The doctor stared at me. 'I don't know what you mean,' he said.

'Well,' I cried, 'if a mother knows that her son is going to commit suicide—'

'Suicide!' he answered. 'Poor Erskine did not commit

suicide. He died of consumption. He came here to die. The moment I saw him I knew that there was no hope. One lung was almost gone, and the other was very much affected. Three days before he died he asked me was there any hope. I told him frankly that there was none, and that he had only a few days to live. He wrote some letters, and was quite resigned, retaining his senses to the last.'

At that moment Lady Erskine entered the room with the fatal picture of Willie Hughes in her hand. 'When George was dying he begged me to give you this,' she said. As I took it from her, her tears fell on my hand.

The picture hangs now in my library, where it is very much admired by my artistic friends. They have decided that it is not a Clouet, but an Ouvry. I have never cared to tell them its true history. But sometimes, when I look at it, I think that there is really a great deal to be said for the Willie Hughes theory of Shakespeare's Sonnets.

*Notes*

1. Sonnet xx, 2.
2. Sonnet xxvi, i.
3. Sonnet cxxvi, 9.
4. Sonnet cix, 14.
5. Sonnet i, 10.
6. Sonnet ii, 3.
7. Sonnet viii, i.
8. Sonnet xxii, 6.
9. Sonnet xcv, i.

GEORGE BRANDES
From "Platonism in Shakespeare's
and Michael Angelo's Sonnets"
*William Shakespeare: A Critical Study*
tr. William Archer
1898, Volume 1, pp. 341–53

T he fact that the person to whom Shakespeare's Sonnets are dedicated is simply entitled "Mr. W. H." long served to divert attention from William Herbert, as it was thought that it would have been an impossible impertinence thus to address, without his title, a nobleman like the Earl of Pembroke. To us it is clear that this form of address was adopted precisely in order that Pembroke might not be exhibited to the great public as the hero of the conflict darkly adumbrated in the Sonnets. They were not, indeed, written quite without an eye to publication, as is proved by the poet's promises that they are to immortalise the memory of his friend's beauty. But it was not Shakespeare himself who gave them to the press, and bookseller Thorpe must have known very well that Lord Pembroke would not care to see himself unequivocally designated as the lover of the Dark Lady and the poet's favoured rival, especially as that dramatic episode of his youth ended in a manner which it can scarcely have been pleasant to recall.

The modern reader who takes up the Sonnets with no special knowledge of the Renaissance, its tone of feeling, its relation to Greek antiquity, its conventions and its poetic style, finds nothing in them more surprising than the language of love in which the poet addresses his young friend, the positively erotic passion for a masculine personality which here finds utterance. The friend is currently addressed as "my love." Sometimes it is stated in so many words that in the eyes of his admirer the friend combines the charms of man and woman; for instance, in Sonnet xx.:—

A woman's face, with Nature's own hand painted,
Hast thou, the master-mistress of my passion.

This Sonnet ends with a playful lament that the friend had not been born of the opposite sex; yet such is the warmth of expression in other Sonnets that one very well understands how the critics of last century supposed them to be addressed to a woman.[1]

This tone, however, is so characteristic a fashion of the age, that a number of writers, and especially those who have gone most deeply into contemporary English and Italian literature,[2] have found in it, and in other traits of mere convention, an argument for holding the circumstances set forth to be in the main imaginary, and denying to the Sonnets all direct autobiographical value.

It has been insisted that love for a beautiful youth, which the study of Plato had presented to the men of the Renaissance in its most attractive light, was a standing theme among English poets of that age, who, moreover, as in Shakespeare's case, were wont to praise the beauty of their friend above that of their mistress. The woman, too, as in this case, often enters as a disturbing element into the relation. It was an accepted part of the convention that the poet should represent himself as withered and wrinkled, whatever his real age might be; Shakespeare does so again and again, though he was at most thirty-seven. Finally, it was quite in accordance with use and wont that the fair youth should be exhorted to marry, so that his beauty might not die with him. Shakespeare had already placed such exhortations in the mouth of the Goddess of Love in *Venus and Adonis*.

Dr. Adolf Hansen, in his Danish translation of the Sonnets, has pointed out several other impersonal traits. Some of the weaker Sonnets, with their "wire-drawn and complicated imagery" (Sonnets xxiv., xlvi., xlvii.), so clearly bear the stamp of the age that they cannot be regarded as personally characteristic of Shakespeare; while others are such evident imitations that it is impossible to accept them as individual utterances. Thus the theme of Sonnets xlvi. and xlvii. is precisely that of Watson's twentieth Sonnet in *The Tears of Fancie*; Sonnets xviii. and xix. lead up to the same thought as that of Sonnet xxxix. in Daniel's *Delia*; and Sonnets lv. and lxxxi. treat of precisely the same matter as Sonnet lxix. of Spenser's *Amoretti*. Finally, the story of the two friends, one of whom robs the other of his mistress, had already appeared in Lyly's *Euphues*.

All this is ttrue, and yet there is no reasonable ground for doubting that the Sonnets stand in pretty close relation to actual facts.

The age, indeed, determines the tone, the colouring, of the expressions in which friendship clothes itself. In Germany and Denmark, at the end of the eighteenth century, friendship was a sentimental enthusiasm, just as in England and Italy during the sixteenth century it took the form of platonic love. We can clearly discern, however, that the different methods of expression answered to corresponding shades of difference in the emotion itself. The men of the Renaissance gave themselves up to an adoration of friendship and of their friend which is now unknown, except in circles where a perverted sexuality prevails. Montaigne's friendship for Estienne de la Boëtie, and Languet's passionate tenderness for the youthful Philip Sidney, are cases in point. Sir Thomas Browne writes in his *Religio Medici* (1642): "I never yet cast a true affection on a woman; but I have loved my friend as I do virtue, my soul, my God. . . . I love my friend before myself, and yet, methinks, I do not love him enough: some few months hence my multiplied affection will make me believe I have not loved him at all. When I am from him, I am dead till I be with him; when I am with him, I am not satisfied, but would still be nearer him." But the most remarkable example of a frenzied friendship in Renaissance culture and poetry is undoubtedly to be found in Michael Angelo's letters and sonnets.

Michael Angelo's relation to Messer Tommaso de' Cavalieri presents the most interesting parallel to the attitude which Shakespeare adopted towards William Herbert. We find the same expressions of passionate love from the older to the younger man; but here it is still more unquestionably certain that we have not to do with mere poetical figures of speech, since the letters are not a whit less ardent and enthusiastic than the sonnets. The expressions in the sonnets are sometimes so warm that Michael Angelo's nephew, in his edition of them, altered the word *Signiore* into *Signora*, and these poems, like Shakespeare's, were for some time supposed to have been addressed to a woman.[3]

On January 1, 1533, Michael Angelo, then fifty-seven years old, writes from Florence to Tommaso de' Cavalieri, a youth of noble Roman family, who afterwards became his favourite pupil: "If I do not possess the art of navigating the sea of your potent genius, that genius will nevertheless excuse me, and neither despise my inequality, nor demand of me that which I have it not in me to give; since that which stands alone in everything can in nothing find its counterpart. Wherefore your lordship, *the only light in our age vouchsafed to this world*, having no equal or peer, cannot find satisfaction in the work of any other hand. If, therefore, this or that in the works which I hope and promise to execute should happen to please you, I should ever feel assured that—as has been reported to me—I have given your lordship satisfaction in one thing or another, I will make a gift to you of my present and of all that the future may bring me; and it will be a great pain to me to be unable to recall the past, in order to serve you so much the longer, instead of having only the future, which cannot be long, since I am all too old. There is nothing more left for me to say. Read my heart and not my letter, for my pen cannot approach the expression of my good will."[4]

Cavalieri writes to Michael Angelo that he regards himself as born anew since he has come to know the Master; who replies, "I for my part should regard myself as not born, born dead, or deserted by heaven and earth, if your letters had not brought me the persuasion that your lordship accepts with favour certain of my works." And in a letter of the following summer to Sebastian del Piombo, he sends a greeting to Messer Tommaso, with the words: "I believe *I should instantly fall down dead* if he were no longer in my thoughts."[5]

Michael Angelo plays upon his friend's surname as Shakespeare plays upon his friend's Christian name. These are the last lines of the thirty-first sonnet:—

> Se vint' e pres' i' debb' esser beato,
> Meraviglia non è se, nud' e solo,
> Resto prigion d'un *Cavalier* armato.

> If only chains and bands can make me blest,
> No marvel if alone and bare I go
> An armed knight's captive and slave confessed.
>                               (J. A. Symonds.)

In other sonnets the tone is no less passionate than Shakespeare's—take, for example, the twenty-second:—

> More tenderly perchance than is my due,
> Your spirit sees into my heart, where rise
> The flames of holy worship, nor denies
> The grace reserved for those who humbly sue.
> Oh blessèd day when you at last are mine!
> Let time stand still, and let noon's chariot stay;
> Fixed be that moment on the dial of heaven!
> That I may clasp and keep, by grace divine—

> Clasp in these yearning arms and keep for aye
> My heart's loved lord to me desertless given.
>                               (J. A. Symonds.)

In comparison with Cavalieri, Michael Angelo could with justice call himself old. Some critics, on the other hand, have seen in the fact that Shakespeare was not really old at the time when the Sonnets were written, a proof of their conventional and unreal character. But this is to overlook the relativity of the term. As compared with a youth of eighteen, Shakespeare was in effect old, with his sixteen additional years and all his experience of life. And if we are right in assigning Sonnets lxiii. and lxxiii. to the year 1600 or 1601, Shakespeare had then reached the age of thirty-seven, an age at which (among his contemporaries) Drayton in his *Idea* dwells quite in the same spirit upon the wrinkles of age in his face, and at which, as Tyler has very aptly pointed out, Byron in his swan-song uses expressions about himself which might have been copied from Shakespeare's seventy-third Sonnet. Shakespeare says:—

> That time of year thou mayst in me behold
> When *yellow leaves*, or none, or few, do hang
> Upon those boughs which shake against the cold
> Bare ruin'd choirs, where late the sweet birds sang.

Byron thus expresses himself:—

> My days are in *the yellow leaf*,[7]
>     The flowers and fruits of love are gone,
> The worm, the canker and the grief
>     Are mine alone.

In Shakespeare we read:—

> In me thou seest *the glowing of such fire*
> That on the ashes of his youth doth lie
> As the *death-bed* whereon it must expire,
> Consum'd with that which it was nourish'd by.

Byron's words are:—

> *The fire that on my bosom preys*
>     Is lone as some volcanic isle;
> No torch is kindled at its blaze—
>     A *funeral pile*.

Thus both poets liken themselves, at this comparatively early age, to the wintry woods with their yellowing leaves, and without blossom, fruit, or the song of birds; and both compare the fire which still glows in their soul to a solitary flame which finds no nourishment from without. The ashes of my youth become its death-bed, says Shakespeare. They are a funeral pile, says Byron.

Nor is it possible to conclude, as Schück does, from the conventional style of the first seventeen Sonnets—for instance, from their almost verbal identity with a passage in Sidney's *Arcadia*—that they are quite devoid of relation to the poet's own life. We have seen that Pembroke's youth, which has been thought to render it improbable that these exhortations to marriage should have been addressed to him, in reality proves nothing to the purpose, since we have direct evidence of the fact that when he was only seventeen his parents were negotiating a marriage between him and Bridget Vere. Subsequently, when Pembroke had made the acquaintance of Mary Fitton, not only his mother but Shakespeare himself had a direct interest in seeing him married.

In short, the elements of temporary fashion and convention which appear in the Sonnets in no way prove that they were not genuine expressions of the poet's actual feelings.

They lay bare to us a side of his character which does not appear in the plays. We see in him an emotional nature with a passionate bent towards self-surrender in love and idolatry, and with a corresponding, though less excessive, yearning to be loved.

We learn from the Sonnets to what a degree Shakespeare was oppressed and tormented by his sense of the contempt in which the actor's calling was held. The scorn of ancient Rome for the mountebank, the horror of ancient Judea for whoever disguised himself in the garments of the other sex, and finally the age-old hatred of Christianity for theatres and all the temptations that follow in their train—all these habits of thought had been handed down from generation to generation, and, as Puritanism grew in strength and gained the upper hand, had begotten a contemptuous tone of public opinion under which so sensitive a nature as Shakespeare's could not but suffer keenly. He was not regarded as a poet who now and then acted, but as an actor who now and then wrote plays. It was a pain to him to feel that he belonged to a caste which had no civic status. Hence his complaint, in Sonnet xxix., of being "in disgrace with fortune and men's eyes." Hence, in Sonnet xxxvi., his assurance to his friend that he will not obtrude on others the fact of their friendship:—

> I may not evermore acknowledge thee,
> Lest my bewailèd guilt should do thee shame:
> Nor thou with public kindness honour me,
> Unless thou take that honour from thy name:
>   But do not so; I love thee in such sort,
>   As, thou being mine, mine is thy good report.

The bitter complaint in Sonnet lxxii. seems rather to refer to the writer's situation as a dramatist:—

> For I am shamed by that which I bring forth,
> And so should you, to love things nothing worth.

The melancholy which fills Sonnet cx. is occasioned by the writer's profession and his nature as a poet and artist:—

> Alas! 'tis true, I have gone here and there,
> And made myself a motley to the view;
> Gor'd mine own thoughts, sold cheap what is most
>   dear,
> Made old offences of affections new:
> Most true it is, that I have look'd on truth
> Askance and strangely; but, by all above,
> These blenches gave my heart another youth,
> And worse essays prov'd thee my best of love.

Hence, finally, his reproach to Fortune, in Sonnet cxi., that she did not "better for his life provide Than public means which public manners breeds":—

> Thence comes it that my name receives a brand;
> And almost thence my nature is subdu'd
> To what it works in, like the dyer's hand.

We must bear in mind this continual writhing under the prejudice against his calling and his art, and this indignation at the injustice of the attitude adopted towards them by a great part of the middle classes, if we would understand the high pressure of Shakespeare's feelings towards the noble youth who had approached him full of the art-loving traditions of the aristocracy, and the burning enthusiasm of the young for intellectual superiority. William Herbert, with his beauty and his personal charm, must have come to him like a very angel of light, a messenger from a higher world than that in which his lot was cast. He was a living witness to the fact that Shakespeare was not condemned to seek the applause of the multitude alone, but could win the favour of the noblest in the land, and was not excluded from a deep and almost passionate friendship which placed him on an equal footing with the bearer of an ancient name. Pembroke's great beauty no doubt made a deep impression upon the beauty-lover in Shakespeare's soul. It is very probable, too, that the young aristocrat, according to the fashion of the times, made the poet his debtor for soldier benefactions than mere friendship; and Shakespeare must thus have felt doubly painful the situation in which he was placed by the intrigue between his mistress and his friend.[8]

In any case, the affection with which Pembroke inspired Shakespeare—the passionate attachment, leading even to jealousy of other poets admired by the young nobleman—had not only a vividness, but an erotic fervour such as we never find in our century manifested between man and man. Note such an expression as this in Sonnet cx.:—

> Then give me welcome, next my haven the best,
> Even to thy pure and most most loving breast.

This exactly corresponds to Michael Angelo's recently-quoted desire to "clasp in his yearning arms his heart's loved lord." Or observe such a line as this in Sonnet lxxv.:—

> So are you to my thoughts as food to life.

We have here an exact counterpart to the following expressions in a letter from Michael Angelo to Cavalieri, dated July 1533: "I would far rather forget the food on which I live, which wretchedly sustains the body alone, than your name, which sustains both body and soul, filling both with such happiness that I can feel neither care nor fear of death while I have it in my memory."[9]

The passionate fervour of this friendship on the Platonic model is accompanied in Shakespeare, as in Michael Angelo, by a submissiveness on the part of the elder friend towards the younger, which, in these two supreme geniuses, affects the modern reader painfully. Each had put off every shred of pride in relation to his idolised young friend. How strange it seems to find Shakespeare calling himself young Herbert's "slave," and assuring him that his time, more precious than that of any other man then living, is of no value, so that his friend may let him wait or summon him to his side as his caprice and fancy dictate. In Sonnet lviii. he speaks of "that God who made me first your slave." Sonnet lvii. runs thus:—

> Being *your slave*, what should I do but tend
> Upon the hours and times of your desire?
> I have no precious time at all to spend,
> Nor services to do, till you require.
> Nor dare I chide the world-without-end hour,
> Whilst I, my sovereign, watch the clock for you,
> Nor think the bitterness of absence sour,
> When you have bid your servant once adieu;
> Nor dare I question with my jealous thought,
> Where you may be, or your affairs suppose;
> But, like a sad slave, stay and think of nought,
> Save, where you are how happy you make those.

Just as Michael Angelo spoke to Cavalieri of his works as though they were scarcely worth his friend's notice, so does Shakespeare sometimes speak of his verses. In Sonnet xxxii. he begs his friends to "re-survey" them when he is dead:—

> And though they be outstripp'd by every pen,
> Reserve them for my love, not for their rhyme,
> Exceeded by the height of happier men.

This humility becomes quite despicable when a breach is threatened between the friends. Shakespeare then repeatedly promises so to blacken himself that his friend shall reap, not shame, but honour, from his faithlessness. In Sonnet lxxxviii.:—

> With mine own weakness being best acquainted,
> Upon thy part I can set down a story
> Of faults concealed wherein I am attained,
> That thou, in losing me, shalt win much glory.

Sonnet lxxxix. is still more strongly worded:—

> Thou canst not, love, disgrace me half so ill,
> To set a form upon desirèd change,

As I'll myself disgrace; knowing thy will,
I will acquaintance strangle, and look strange:
Be absent from thy walks; and in my tongue
Thy sweet-belovèd name no more shall dwell,
Lest I (too much profane) should do it wrong,
And haply of our old acquaintance tell. ·
    For thee, against myself I'll vow debate,
    For I must ne'er love him whom thou dost hate.

We are positively surprised when, in a single passage, in
Sonnet lxii., we come upon a forcible expression of self-love;
but it does not extend beyond the first half of the Sonnet; in the
second half this self-love is already regarded as a sin, and
Shakespeare humbly effaces himself before his friend. All the
more gladly does the reader welcome the few Sonnets (lv. and
lxxxi.) in which the poet confidently predicts the immortality of
these his utterances. It is true that Shakespeare is here greatly
influenced by antiquity and by the fashion of his age; and it is
simply as records of his friend's beauty and amiability that his
verses are to be preserved through all ages to come. But no poet
without a sound and vigorous self-confidence could have
written either these lines in Sonnet lv.:—

Nor marble, nor the gilded monuments
Of princes shall outlive this powerful rhyme—

or these others in Sonnet lxxxi.:—

Your monument shall be my gentle verse,
Which eyes not yet created shall o'erread;
And tongues to be your being shall rehearse,
When all the breathers of this world are dead.

Yet, as we see, the first and last thought is always that of the
friend, his beauty, worth, and fame. And as he will live in the
future, so he has lived in the past. Shakespeare cannot
conceive existence without him. In Sonnets which have no
direct connection with each other (lix., cvi., cxxiii.) he returns
again and again to that strange thought of a perpetual cycle or
recurrence of events, which runs through the whole of the
world's history, from the Pythagoreans and Kohélet to Friedrich
Nietzsche. In view of such high-pitched idolatry, we can well
understand that the friend's faithlessness, or, if you will, the
mistress's conquest of the friend, and the sudden severance of
the bond in 1601, must have made a deep impression upon
Shakespeare's sensitive soul. The catastrophe left its mark upon
him for many a long day.

And at the same time another and purely personal
mortification was added to his troubles. Shakespeare's name
was just then involved in a degrading scandal of one sort or
another. He says so expressly in Sonnet cxii.:—

Your love and pity doth the impression fill
Which vulgar scandal stamped upon my brow.

He here avers that he cares very little "to know his shames or
praises" from the tongues of others, and that his friend's
judgment is all in all to him; but in Sonnet cxxi., where he
goes more closely into the matter, he confesses that some
"frailty" in him has given rise to these malignant rumours, and
we see that for this frailty his "sportive blood" was to blame. He
does not deny the accusation, but asks—

Why should others' false adulterate eyes
Give salutation to my sportive blood?
Or on my frailties why are frailer spies,
Which in their wills count bad what I think good?

The details of this scandal are unknown to us. We can
only conclude that it referred to Shakespeare's alleged relation
to some woman, or implication in some amorous adventure.
In discussing this point, Tyler has aptly cited two passages in
contemporary writings, though of course without absolutely
proving that they have any bearing on the matter. The first is

the above-quoted anecdote in John Manningham's Diary for
March 13, 1601 (New Style, 1602), as to Shakespeare's
forestalling Burbadge in the graces of a citizen's wife, and
announcing himself as "William the Conqueror"—an anecdote which seems to have been widely current at the time, and
no doubt arose from more or less recent events. The second
passage occurs in *The Returne from Pernassus*, dating from
December 1601, in which (iv. 3) Burbadge and Kemp are
introduced, and these words are placed in the mouth of Kemp:
"O that *Ben Ionson* is a pestilent fellow, he brought vp *Horace*
giuing the Poets a pill, but our fellow *Shakespeare* hath giuen
him a purge that made him beray his credit." The allusion is
evidently to the feud between Ben Jonson on the one hand and
Marston and Dekker on the other, which culminated in 1601
with the appearance of Ben Jonson's *Poetaster*, in which
Horace serves as the poet's mouthpiece. Dekker and Marston
retorted in the same year with *Satiromastix, or the Untrussing
of the Humorous Poet*. As Shakespeare took no direct part in
this quarrel, we can only conjecture what is meant by the
above allusion. Mr. Richard Simpson has suggested that King
William Rufus, in whose reign the action of *Satiromastix* takes
place, and who "presides over the untrussing of the humorous
poet," may be intended for William Shakespeare. Rufus, in the
play, is by no means a model of chastity, and carries off Walter
Terrill's bride very much as "William the Conqueror" in
Manningham's anecdote carries off "Richard the Third's"
mistress. Simpson thinks it probable that the spectators would
have little difficulty in recognising the William the Conqueror
of the anecdote in the William Rufus of the play, whose
nickname, indeed, might be taken as referring to Shakespeare's
complexion. If we accept this interpretation, we find in
*Satiromastix* a further proof of the notoriety of the anecdote.
Whether it be this scandal or another of the same kind to which
the Sonnets refer, Shakespeare seems to have taken greatly to
heart the besmirching of his name.

*Notes*

1. For instance, in Sonnet xxiii.:—

    O let my books be then the eloquence
    And dumb presagers of my speaking breast,
    Who plead for love, and look for recompense.

    And in Sonnet xxvi.:—

    Lord of my love, to whom in vassalage
    Thy merit hath my duty strongly knit.

2. Such as Delius and Elze in Germany and Schück in Sweden.

3. Ludwig von Scheffler: *Michel Angelo: Eine Renaissancestudie*,
    1892.

4. "E se io non àrò l'arte del navicare per l'onde del mare del vostro
    valoroso ingegno, quello mi scuserà, nè si sdegnierà del mio
    disaguagliarsigli, nè desiderrà da me quello che in me non è: perchè
    chi è solo in ogni cosa, in cosa alcuna non può aver compagni.
    Però la vostra Signoria, luce del secol nostro unica al mondo, non
    puo sodisfarsi di opera d'alcuno altro, non avendo pari nè simile à
    sè," &c.

5. "E io non nato, o vero nato morto mi reputerei, e direi in disgrazia
    del cielo e della terra, se per la vostra non avessi visto e creduto
    vostra Signoria accettare volentieri alcune delle opere mie." "Avete
    data la copia de' sopradetti Madrigali a messer Tomaso . . . che
    se m'ucissi della mente, credo che súbito cascherei morto."

6.     Accio ch' i' abbi, e non già per mie merto,
        Il desiato mio dolce signiore
        Per sempre nell' indegnie e pronte braccia.

7. This line, however, is obviously suggested by the famous passage in
    *Macbeth* (Act v.)—

        My way of life
        Is fall'n into the sere, the yellow leaf.

8. Several passages in the Sonnets suggest that Pembroke must have
    conferred substantial gifts upon Shakespeare—for example, that

expression "wealth" in Sonnet xxxvii., "your bounty" in Sonnet liii., and "your own dear-purchased right" in Sonnet cxvii.

9. "Anzi posso prima dimenticare il cibo di ch'io vivo, che nutrisce solo il corpo infelicemente, che il nome vostro, che nutrisce l'anima, riempiendo l'uno e l'altro di tanta dolcezza, che nè noia nè timor di morte, mentre la memoria mi vi serba, posso sentire."

## H. C. BEECHING
### "The Sonnets of Shakespeare"
*The Cornhill Magazine*, February 1902, pp. 244–63

The value of Shakespeare's sonnets lies, of course, in their supreme beauty, and is altogether independent of the critical and historical problems that cluster about them. These problems have, nevertheless, a perennial interest, even a fascination of their own; witness the large and ever-increasing number of volumes devoted to their investigation. Within the last few years three elaborate studies have been added to the pile, two of which, at any rate, cannot be disregarded by anyone who wishes to form a competent judgment upon the points at issue. Mr. Sidney Lee, in his monumental *Life of Shakespeare*, published in 1898, devoted four chapters and eight appendices to an examination of the general character of sonneteering in the sixteenth century, and a reinforcement of the claim of the Earl of Southampton, Shakespeare's early patron, to be the person to whom the sonnets are addressed. Of the learning displayed in that examination and the skill with which the arguments are marshalled there cannot be two opinions. I do not myself think, however, that the Southampton theory can be maintained, for reasons which will be advanced presently; and Mr. Lee's general view, which aims at formulating a scientific law of sonnet-writing, seems to me to disregard the instances—those of men of genius—which alone have any value and interest. To argue away the special characteristics of Shakespeare's sonnets on the ground that twenty contemporary sonnet-sequences do not possess them seems as illogical a course as the common habit, against which Mr. Lee protests, of ignoring the fact that Shakespeare's sonnets have literary parallels, but the new abstraction, Shakespeare being what he was, is likely to lead farther from the truth than the old. In the same year as Mr. Lee's book Mr. George Wyndham produced a handsome and scholarly edition of Shakespeare's poems, and collected into his introduction most of the historical material with which the criticism of the sonnets must deal; but the main purpose of his book, and a most praiseworthy one, was to rivet attention on the poems themselves. In the year following Mr. Samuel Butler, the author of *Erewhon*, brought out an edition of the sonnets with prolegomena; which are sufficiently good reading when they handle the absurdities and inconsistencies of his predecessors, but are negligible in their own proposals. The purpose of the present paper is not to attempt any final pronouncement on a cause which will surely go from court to court and be judged and rejudged many times yet; but simply to investigate the present position of the problem as Mr. Lee has left it, to see if any points may be taken as finally concluded, and to expose the questions remaining upon which more light is still required.

### I

Readers of the sonnets who have no theories to defend would probably agree that the friendship which the sonnets describe is an affection between an elder and a younger man, wherewith there mingles not a little admiration for his grace and charm, which, indeed, occasionally seem to get on the poet's nerves. If I may put in one word what I conceive to be the peculiar type of this affection, I should say it was a type not uncommonly found in imaginative natures. A poet, whatever else he is, is a man with keener senses and stronger emotions than other men; he is more sensitive to beauty, especially the beauty of youth; and, as the poetry of the whole world may convince us, he is especially sensitive to that beauty's decay. Hence it is not uncommon to find in poets of mature years a strong disposition to consort with young people, and a keen pleasure in their society, as though to atone for the slow sapping of youthful strength and ardour in themselves. It is well that the majority of us should stifle our dissatisfaction at the inevitable oncoming of age by doing the tasks which age lays upon us and for which youth is incompetent. The middle-aged youth or maiden is a fair theme for satire. But poets cannot be blamed if, feeling what we feel more keenly, they give to the sentiment an occasional expression; nor if they seek to keep fresh their own youthful enthusiasm by associating with younger people. There is an interesting passage in Browning's poem of 'Cleon,' where Cleon, who is a poet, writing to King Protus on the subject of joy in life, contrasts his own supposed joy in the wide outlook of age with the actual joy of living; and Browning seems there, through the mouth of Cleon, to be uttering a sentiment that many poets have felt, and which, as I believe, accounts for much in Shakespeare's sonnets:—

> The last point now: thou dost except a case,
> Holding joy not impossible to one
> With artist-gifts—to such a man as I,
> Who leave behind me living works indeed;
> For such a poem, such a painting, lives.
> What? dost thou verily trip upon a word,
> Confound the accurate view of what joy is
> (Caught somewhat clearer by my eyes than thine)
> With feeling joy? Confound the knowing how
> And showing how to live (my faculty)
> With actually living? Otherwise,
> Where is the artist's 'vantage o'er the king?
> Because in my greater epos I display
> How divers men young, strong, fair, wise can act—
> Is this as though I acted? if I paint,
> Carve the young Phœbus, am I therefore young?
> Methinks I'm older that I bowed myself
> The many years of pain that taught me art!
> Indeed, to know is something, and to prove
> How all this beauty might be enjoyed is more:
> But knowing nought, to enjoy, is something too
> Yon rower with the moulded muscles there,
> Lowering the sail, is nearer it than I.
> I can write love-odes: thy fair slave's an ode.
> I get to sing of love, when grown too grey
> For being beloved: she turns to that young man,
> The muscles all a-ripple on his back.
> I know the joy of kingship—well, thou art king!

That passage goes far to explain the attraction which many poets have found in the society of young people distinguished in some special degree for beauty, or grace, or vivacity. And, of course, there must not be forgotten another element in the problem, the peculiar sweetness of admiration and praise coming from the young. Theocritus desired to sing songs that should win the young; and the sentiment has been echoed by the most austere of our own living poets:—

> 'Twere something yet to live again among
> The gentle youth beloved, and where I learned
> My art, be there remembered for my song.

The nearest parallel I can suggest to the case of Shakespeare and his young friend is the friendship between the poet Gray and Bonstetten. Bonstetten was a Swiss youth of quality, who went to Cambridge with an introduction to Gray from his friend Norton Nicholls; and the havoc he wrought in that poet's domestic affections is visible in his correspondence. He wrote to Norton Nicholls (April 4, 1770):—

> At length, my dear sir, we have lost our poor de Bonstetten. I packed him up with my own hands in the Dover machine at four o'clock in the morning on Friday, 23rd March; the next day at seven he sailed, and reached Calais by noon, and Boulogne at night; the next night he reached Abbeville. From thence he wrote to me; and here am I again to pass my solitary evenings, which hung much lighter on my hands before I knew him. This is your fault! Pray, let the next you send me be halt and blind, dull, unapprehensive, and wrongheaded. For this (as Lady Constance says) *Was never such a gracious creature born!* and yet—

Among Gray's letters are three to Bonstetten himself; it will be sufficient to quote the shortest of them:—

> I am returned, my dear Bonstetten, from the little journey I made into Suffolk, without answering the end proposed. The thought that you might have been with me there has embittered all my hours. Your letter has made me happy—as happy as so gloomy, so solitary a being as I am is capable of being made. I know, and have too often felt the disadvantages I lay myself under, how much I hurt the little interest I have in you, by this air of sadness, so contrary to your nature and present enjoyments; but sure you will forgive, though you cannot sympathise with me. It is impossible with me to dissemble with you; such as I am I expose my heart to your view, nor wish to conceal a single thought from your penetrating eyes. All that you say to me, especially on the subject of Switzerland, is infinitely acceptable. It feels too pleasing ever to be fulfilled, and as often as I read over your truly kind letter, written long since from London, I stop at these words: 'la mort qui peut glacer nos bras avant qu'ils soient entrelacés.'

It seems to me that in these letters we have, beneath many superficial dissimilarities, a very close parallel to Shakespeare's own case as it lies before us in the sonnets. We have a companionship marked by respectful admiration and affection on the one side, on the other by a more tender sentiment. And the other letters draw the parallel closer, for one describes the pangs of absence—

> Alas! how do I every moment feel the truth of what I have somewhere read: 'Ce n'est pas le voir, que de s'en souvenir;' and yet that remembrance is the only satisfaction I have left. My life now is but a conversation with your shadow, &c.

and another warns the youth against the vices to which his youth and good looks and the example of his own class leave him peculiarly exposed. With such an actual experience to call in evidence, I do not see why we should reject as inconceivable the obvious interpretation that the sonnets put upon themselves: that Shakespeare at a certain period found the loneliness of his life in London filled up by a friendship which, not being 'equal poised,' could not last, but which was in no sense unworthy. If that were allowed, it would not, of course, follow that the sonnets could be treated as one side of an ordinary correspondence, and every statement they contain be transferred to Shakespeare's biography as literal fact. The truth at which poetry aims is a truth of feeling, not of incident. And the fact, often enough implied in the sonnets, that they were intended for publication some day (though that day was anticipated by a piratical publisher), as well as the still more cogent fact that Shakespeare was a poet, should prepare us to recognise that situations would be generalised and reduced to their common human measure.

## II

Such being, in my judgment, the view of the sonnets that will commend itself to a reader who interprets them in the light of general experience, we must see how far such a view is affected by Mr. Lee's investigation into the special conditions of Elizabethan sonnet-writing. Mr. Lee's theory is that what the ordinary reader takes for friendship in Shakespeare's sonnets is merely the conventional adulation common at the time between client and patron. 'There is nothing,' he says, 'in the vocabulary of affection which Shakespeare employed in his sonnets of friendship to conflict with the theory that they were inscribed to a literary patron, with whom the intimacy was of the kind normally subsisting at the time between literary clients and their patrons.' A new theory of this sort must, of course, stand or fall by the evidence that can be produced for it; and accordingly Mr. Lee proceeds to supply parallels. 'The tone of yearning,' he tells us, 'for a man's affection is sounded by Donne and Campion almost as plaintively in their sonnets to patrons as it was sounded by Shakespeare.' In support of this statement Mr. Lee refers to two poems (which we must presume to be the strongest instances he can find), one a verse-letter by Donne to a certain T. W., and the other a poem by Campion addressed to the young Lord Walden. The letter of Donne's must be ruled out, because it is not written to a patron at all, but to a friend. We do not know who T. W. was, but we know the names of Donne's patrons, and the initials fit none of them. In the four stanzas to Lord Walden which are prefixed, among various dedications, to one of Campion's masques, I cannot detect the least tone of yearning, or even of plaintiveness. The word 'love' certainly occurs twice, but the love meant is the general love of all the world for the young gentleman's admired virtues. As Campion's poems are not accessible except in a privately printed edition, it may be well to quote the material verses:—

> If to be sprung of high and princely blood,
>    If to inherit virtue, honour, grace,
> If to be great in all things, and yet good,
>    If to be facile, yet t' have power and place,
>       If to be just, and bountiful may get
>       The love of men, your right may challenge it.
>
> But if th' admired virtues of your youth
>    Breed such despairing to my daunted Muse
> That it can scarcely utter naked truth.
>    How shall it mount as ravished spirits use
>       Under the burden of your riper days,
>       Or hope to reach the so far distant bays?
>
> My slender Muse shall yet my love express,
>    And by the fair Thames' side of you she'll sing;
> The double streams shall bear her willing verse
>    Far hence with murmur of their ebb and spring.
>       But if you favour her light tunes, ere long
>       She'll strive to raise you with a loftier song.

I do not think that the ordinary reader unbiassed by a theory would hear in these conventional lines any tone of yearning for affection; what is too clearly audible in them is a bid for 'favour' in some more tangible shape. If Mr. Lee is to convince the world that there is nothing in Shakespeare's sonnets beyond the normal Elizabethan note of patron-worship, he must adduce by way of parallel a poem with some passion in it. Did any Elizabethan client, for example, speak of his love for his patron as keeping him awake at night, as Shakespeare says in the sixty-first sonnet that his love for his friend kept him awake?

A more specious argument is that which Mr. Lee bases on the very mysterious section of the sonnets concerned with rival poets (lxxvii.–lxxxvi.), which he interprets as an attempt on Shakespeare's part to monopolise patronage. In the sonnets Shakespeare certainly reveals some jealousy. He charges his friend with being attracted by the flattery of some other writer of verses. But it is evident that the poems in question are not dedicated to the friend, but written about him;[1] the friend is not the patron, but the subject of the rival's song; so that it is not merely patronage that Shakespeare deprecates. Indeed, how could he have done so, considering the custom of the age, with any reasonable prospect of success? I would have said, how could he have done so with decency? only Mr. Lee denies him decency. He says: 'The sole biographical inference deducible from the sonnets is that at one time in his career Shakespeare disdained no weapon of flattery in an endeavour to monopolise the bountiful patronage of a young man of rank.' The sonnets themselves, happily, lend no support to this view. It is one thing to say 'X has begun to ask your patronage for his books. I hope you will have nothing to do with him;' and quite another thing to say, as Shakespeare says, 'X has been writing verses about you in which he flatters you extravagantly. Of course you like it. And I am quite willing to own that as poetry his verses are better than mine. But for all that, mine express real affection; so don't desert me for him.' It is difficult to bring this matter to a more decisive test, because it is impossible to determine how far the complaint was serious and who this rival was; and no verses of the sort are extant. The praise of the poet's learning and the reference to the 'proud full sail of his great verse' have been thought by Professor Minto to indicate Chapman. (Those who take this view may thank me for a further argument. It is hinted in the eighty-sixth sonnet that the rival dabbled, as many Elizabethans did, in necromancy; for the reference to the familiar ghost

That nighty *gulls* him with intelligence

is not a compliment, and cannot be whittled down to a recognition of 'a touch of magic' in the poet's writing. Now we find Chapman dedicating a poem in 1598 to that celebrated Doctor Harriot of whom Marlowe had said in his 'atheistical' way, that he could juggle better than Moses.) But can we conceive of Chapman writing sentimental sonnets about any young man? With his sonnet-cycle on Philosophy before me I find it impossible to do so. A less incredible suggestion would be Ben Jonson, who was becoming known in 1597, and in that or the next year took the town by storm with *Every Man in His Humour*; and 1597–8, as I hope to show, is probably the date of a large number of the sonnets.

Mr. Lee enumerates twenty sonnets which he calls 'dedicatory' sonnets, in which he claims that the friend is 'declared without paraphrase and without disguise to be a patron of the poet's verse.' If so, Mr. Lee uses the word 'patron' in an esoteric sense. Shakespeare says again and again that his friend's beauty and constancy give his pen 'both skill and argument':—

> How can my Muse want *subject* to invent
> While thou dost breathe, that pour'st into my verse
> Thine own sweet *argument*, too excellent
> For every vulgar paper to rehearse?

Surely there is all the difference in the world between the subject and argument of a book and its patron! I do not think, then, that Mr. Lee's new and ingenious theory that the relations of the poet and his friend were simply those of client and patron, will bear the test of examination, and as the theory seriously impugns the character of Shakespeare, I for one cannot be sorry that the facts are against it.

### III

The next problem that presents itself concerns the approximate date of the sonnet-cycle: This problem is usually discussed in relation to the question whether Lord Southampton or Lord Pembroke is the friend to whom the sonnets are addressed, because a late date makes the former an impossible candidate, and an early date disposes of the latter. But it has also a bearing upon the previous question, whether we are justified in looking in the sonnets for any genuine sentiment at all. Mr. Lee in his *Life of Shakespeare* has restated with new emphasis the fact that the sonnet was a fashionable literary form in the last decade of the sixteenth century; and he has further shown, for the first time, that a large stock of ideas and images was common to the whole tribe of sonneteers. Of course it by no means follows because a poet uses a fashionable and artificial form of verse, that the emotion he puts into it is merely fashionable and artificial. It may be or it may not be. We must not forget that, although the sonnet was fashionable at this epoch, the passion of love had perhaps as great a vogue as the sonnet.[2] If, however, Shakespeare wrote a sequence of sonnets simply, as Mr. Lee thinks, to be in the mode and to please his patron, we should expect to find him turning them out as soon as he had finished *Lucrece* in 1594; for even as early as that date Sidney, Daniel, Constable, Barnes, Watson, Lodge, and Drayton—to mention only considerable people— were in the field before him. And in pursuance of his theory Mr. Lee places the bulk of Shakespeare's sonnets in 1594. But all the evidence there is points to a date considerably later. No reference to the sonnets has been traced in contemporary literature before 1598. It was not till 1599 that any of them found their way into print. And the only sonnet that can be dated with absolute certainty from internal evidence (cvii.) belongs to 1603. The evidence from style points also, for the most part, to a late date; but of that it is of no use to speak, because it convinces no one who has other reasons for not being convinced. There is, however, a line of argument hitherto neglected which, in competent hands, might yield material results—the argument from parallel passages. Every writer knows the perverse facility with which a phrase once used presents itself again; and Shakespeare seems to have been not a little liable to this human infirmity. It is not uncommon for him to use a word or a phrase twice in a single play, and never afterwards.[3] There is a strong probability, therefore, if a remarkable phrase or figure of speech occurs both in a sonnet and in a play, that the play and the sonnet belong to the same period. Now the greater number of the parallel passages hitherto recognised are to be found in *Henry IV.*, in *Love's Labour's Lost*, and in *Hamlet*; and it is certain that *Henry IV.* was written in 1597, that *Love's Labour's Lost* was revised in that same year, and that *Hamlet* is later still.[4] To take an example: the phrase 'world-without-end' makes a sufficiently remarkable epithet; but it is so used only in the fifty-seventh sonnet and in *Love's Labour's Lost* (v. 2, 799): But as it is open to anyone to reply that this and other phrases may have occurred in the original draft of that play, written several years earlier, it will be best to confine the parallels to *Henry IV.*, the date of which is beyond dispute. Compare, then, Sonnet 33—

> Anon *permit* the *basest* clouds to ride
> With ugly rack on his celestial face

with *1 Henry IV.* i. 2, 221—

The sun,
Who doth *permit* the *base* contagious clouds
To smother up his beauty from the world.

Again, compare the 52nd sonnet—

Therefore are *feasts* so *seldom* and so *rare*
Since, *seldom* coming, in the long year set
. . .
So is the time that keeps you as my chest.
Or as the wardrobe which the *robe* doth hide,
To make some special instant special blest

with '1 Henry IV.' iii. 2, 55—

My presence like a *robe* pontifical,
Ne'er seen, but wonder'd at; and so my state
*Seldom* but sumptuous, showed like a *feast*.
And won by *rareness* such solemnity,

where the concurrence of the images of a feast and a robe is very noticeable. Compare also the 64th sonnet with 2 *Henry IV.* iii. 1, 45, where the revolution of states is compared with the sea gaining on the land, and the land on the sea—an idea not found in the famous description of the works of Time in *Lucrece*. Compare also the epithet *sullen*, applied to a bell in Sonnet 71, and 2 *Henry IV.* i. 1, 102, and the phrase compounded with 'clay,' or 'dust,' found in the same sonnet and 2 *Henry IV.* iv. 5, 116. I do not wish to press this argument further than it will go, but it must be allowed that its force accumulates with every instance adduced; and, in my opinion, it is strong enough to dispose of the hypothesis that the main body of the sonnets was written in 1593 or 1594, especially as not a single argument has been brought forward for assigning them to so early a date,[5] and every indication of both internal and external evidence suggests that they were written later. One conclusion from these premisses seems to be that Shakespeare did not write his sonnets merely in pursuit of the fashion, though he recognised the fashion by introducing a sonnet occasionally into an early play, and by representing his lovers— Beatrice and Benedick, the lovesick Thurio in the *Two Gentlemen of Verona*, and the nobles in *Love's Labour's Lost*— as turning to the sonnet as the proper form in which to ease their over-burdened hearts. It may have been that the impulse to write sonnets came to Shakespeare himself from a like natural cause.

### IV

Who was Shakespeare's friend? Mr. Butler, in his edition of the sonnets referred to above, makes very merry over the popular notion that the friend must have been a peer; and to a reader who comes to the sonnets without prejudice there are a few striking passages that make the current hypothesis a little hard to believe. 'Farewell,' says the poet in the 87th sonnet; 'thou art too dear for my possessing, and *like enough* thou knowst thy estimate.' Now it is generally given to peers to know their estimate very exactly. Again, in 84 the poet says:

You to your beauteous blessings add a curse,
Being fond on praise, which makes your praises
        worse

and in 69 he says, still more rudely:

But why thy odour matcheth not thy show
The soil [solution] is this—that thou dost common
        grow.

To a mere patron such lines could never have been addressed; and hardly to an Elizabethan peer at all, unless he were very young and the friendship very intimate. But that may be the true explanation of such passages. That the friend was a person of high birth and great fortune is put beyond reasonable doubt

by the 37th sonnet. Mr. Butler attempts to get over the evidence of this sonnet by pointing to its hypothetical construction; but the whole point of the sonnet is that the friend had advantages of fortune which were denied to the poet.

As a decrepit father takes delight
To see his active child do deeds of youth,
So I, made lame by *Fortunes's* dearest spite,
Take all my comfort of thy worth and truth;

where 'worth' must be constructed in terms of what follows. And if it be replied that a private gentleman might claim 'beauty, birth, and wealth and wit' as well as a peer, the rejoinder might be that 'glory' in the twelfth line is a very strong word indeed, especially to a youth, being equivalent to 'splendour' or 'magnificence':

I in thy abundance am suffic'd,
And by a part of all thy glory live.

I admit, however, that this is the only evidence for the friend's nobility, and it is not quite convincing.

The further question, Which of the young gentlemen of the day had the honour of being Shakespeare's admired friend, is one that divides the commentators into two hostile factions— the advocates of Southampton and of Pembroke; and as I have already said that I believe the sonnets to have been written from 1597 onwards, I have implicitly given a vote against Southampton's claim; for that nobleman was born as early as 1573, and in 1597 was engaged with Essex in an expedition to the Azores. The Southampton theory has received a new lease of life from Mr. Lee's recent advocacy; but I am bold enough to think that even on Mr. Lee's own data, Southampton's claim can be disposed of. Mr. Lee, although he dates most of the sonnets in 1593-4, assigns the 107th sonnet to the year 1603;[6] it follows that the date of the Envoy (cxxvi), a poem obviously, from its exceptional form, written to conclude the series, must be at least not earlier than 1603, in which year Southampton was thirty years old. Now is it credible that anyone, even if he were the greatest peer of the realm and the most beautiful patron conceivable, should have been addressed by Shakespeare as a 'lovely boy' when thirty years of age; especially considering the fact that in the sixteenth century life began earlier than now, and ended earlier? Mr. Lee surmounts this difficulty by a theory that the Envoy is addressed not to Southampton, but to Cupid; but this does not seem to me possible. Cupid is immortal or he is nothing; and the point of the Envoy is that mortal beauty must fade at last. Nature may hold back some favourite for a while from the clutches of Time to whom all things are due, but she must at last come to the audit, and cannot secure her acquittance without surrendering her favourite:

If Nature, sovereign mistress over wrack,
As thou goest onward, still will pluck thee back,
She keeps thee to this purpose, that her skill
May Time disgrace, and envious minutes kill.
Yet fear her, O thou minion of her pleasure!
She may detain, but not still [always] keep, her
        treasure:
Her audit, though delayed, answered must be,
And her quietus is to render thee.

Mr. Lee has advanced one new argument for the Southampton theory which, if it could be maintained, would place it for ever beyond cavil. Southampton was released from prison on James's accession in 1603, and 'it is impossible,' says Mr. Lee, 'to resist the inference that Shakespeare [in the 107th sonnet] saluted his patron on the close of his days of tribulation. The inference seems to me far from irresistible. Indeed, if this sonnet were really an ode of congratulation under such circumstances, Southampton in turn could hardly have congratulated the poet on the fervour of his feelings. For there is no reference in the sonnet to any release from prison, and its crowning thought is that Shakespeare himself, not his friend, has overcome death—a curiously awkward compliment on such a remarkable occasion. Mr. Lee suggests a paraphrase of the opening quatrain which it will not bear.

> Not mine own fears, nor the prophetic soul
> Of the wide world, dreaming on things to come,
> Can yet the lease of my true love control,
> Supposed as forfeit to a confined doom.

The words 'my true love' might certainly by themselves be taken, as Mr. Lee takes them, to mean 'my true *friend*,' but 'the lease of my true love' can only mean the 'lease of my true *affection* for my friend.' All leases are for a term of years; each has a limit or 'confine' assigned to it, on which day of doom it expires. Shakespeare says that neither his own fears nor the world's prophecies of disastrous changes have justified themselves, for in the year 1603 he finds his affection fresher than ever. But to the friends of Southampton the death of Elizabeth would not have been an occasion of foreboding, but of hope.

But perhaps the most emphatic argument against the identification of Shakespeare's friend with the Earl of Southampton is the non-natural interpretation of certain words and phrases to which it compels its adherents. The publisher, Thomas Thorpe, inscribed his book to 'the only *begetter* of these insuing sonnets, Mr. W.H.'—a phrase that ninety-nine persons out of every hundred, even of those familiar with Elizabethan literature, would unhesitatingly understand to mean their inspirer. But Southampton's initials were H. W. Either, therefore, it must be assumed that the publisher inverted their order as a blind, or else some new sense must be found for 'begetter.' Boswell, the editor of the Variorum Shakespeare, who wished to relieve the poet from the imputation of having written the sonnets to any particular person, or as anything but a play of fancy, suggested for the word the sense of 'getter' (which had not occurred to either Steevens or Malone), meaning by that the person who procured the manuscript, and this interpretation has been adopted by Mr. Lee. Such a use of the word is acknowledged to be extremely rare, and the cases alleged are dubious, but it is not impossible. However, against understanding such a sense here there are several strong reasons. In the first place, it takes all meaning from the word *only*. Allowing it to be conceivable that a piratical publisher should inscribe a book of sonnets to the thief who brought him the manuscript, why should he lay stress on the fact that 'alone he did it'? Was it an enterprise of such great peril? Mr. Lee attempts to meet this and similar difficulties by depreciating Thorpe's skill in the use of language; but the examples he quotes in his interesting Appendix do not support his theory. Thorpe's words are accurately used, even to nicety, and, indeed, Mr. Lee himself owns that in another matter Thorpe showed a 'literary sense' and 'a good deal of dry humour.' I venture to affirm that this dedication also shows a fairly well-developed literary sense. In the next place, this theory of the 'procurer' obliges us to believe that Thorpe wished Mr W. H. that eternity which the poet had promised not to him, nor to men in general, but to some undesignated third party. Mr. Lee calls the words '*promised by our ever-living poet*' 'a decorative and supererogatory phrase.' That is a very mild qualification of them under the circumstances. But an examination of Thorpe's other dedications shows that his style was rather sententious than 'supererogatory.' Then, again, on this theory the epithet *well-wishing* also becomes 'supererogatory.' For what it implies is that the adventurous publisher's motive in giving the sonnets to the world without their author's consent was a good one. The person to whom they were written

might reasonably expect, though he would not necessarily credit, an assurance on this head; but what would one literary jackal care for another's good intentions? There are other points that might be urged, but these are sufficient. Only, I would add that the whole tone of the dedication, which is respectful, and the unusual absence of a qualifying phrase, such as 'his esteemed friend,' before the initials are against the theory that Mr. W. H. was on the same social level as the publisher.

There is one other point of interpretation upon which the Southampton faction are compelled by their theory to go against probabilities. There are two places in which a play is made upon the name Will, the paronomasia being indicated in the *editio princeps* by italic type, in which that edition, as Mr. Wyndham has shown at length, is very far from being lavish. In one of these places (cxliii), if the pun be allowed at all, it cannot refer to the poet's own name, but must refer to the name of his friend. In this sonnet the 'dark lady,' pursuing the poet's friend while the poet pursues her, is compared to a housewife chasing a chicken and followed by her own crying child. It concludes:

> So runn'st thou after that which flies from thee,
> Whilest I thy babe chase thee afar behind;
> But if thou catch thy hope, turn back to me,
> And play the mother's part, kiss me, be kind:
> So will I pray that thou mayst have thy *Will*,
> If thou turn back, and my loud crying still.

The word *Will* is printed here in the original text in italics, and the pun is in Shakespeare's manner. The 135th sonnet opens:

> Whoever hath her wish, thou hast thy *Will*,
> And *Will* to boot, and *Will* in overplus:
> More than enough am I that vex thee still,
> To thy sweet will making addition thus.

The third Will here must be Shakespeare, because, '*Will* in overplus' corresponds to 'more than enough am *I*'; and few critics with the 143rd sonnet also in mind would hesitate to refer the second Will to Shakespeare's friend, for whom the 'dark lady' had been laying snares. But the Southamptonites, who cannot allow that the friend's name was Will, are constrained to deny that there is any pun at all in 143, and to refer that in 135 to the distinction between 'will' in its ordinary sense and 'will' in the sense of 'desire.' But the balance of the line makes it almost necessary that, as 'Will in overplus' must be a proper name, 'Will to boot' should be a proper name also. And that there are more Wills than one concerned in the matter is made more evident still by other passages, where the poet jocosely limits his claim to the lady's favour to the fact that his Christian name is Will, acknowledging that not a few other people have as good a claim as he:

> Shall will in others seem right gracious,
> And in my will no fair acceptance shine?

and again:

> Let no unkind 'no' fair beseechers kill;
> Think all but one, and me in that one, Will.

To attempt, then, in the face of these multiplied improbabilities to maintain that Shakespeare's friend was Lord Southampton is a task worthy of a great advocate, and Mr. Lee's brilliant effort would suggest that the Bar has lost an ornament in his devotion to historical research. I own, nevertheless, that I should prefer to hear him argue the other side.

The theory that the friend addressed in the sonnets was William Herbert, afterwards third Earl of Pembroke, arose inevitably from the letters W. H. of the dedication, as soon as the sonnets themselves began to be studied; and although it cannot be said to have established itself, there are not a few arguments that may be urged in its favour. Herbert was born in 1580, so that he was sixteen years younger than Shakespeare; and he seems to have been of an intellectual temper, likely both to attract and be attracted by the poet. He wrote verses himself, and was inclined, we are told, to melancholy. Dr. Gardiner calls him the Hamlet of James's Court, and there may be more in the phrase than he intended. At any rate, the date of *Hamlet* is 1602. Pembroke's personal handsomeness is dwelt upon in a sonnet by Francis Davison, the son of Secretary Davison, who, being a gentleman, was less likely than a literary hack to say the thing that was not. In inscribing to him the *Poetical Rhapsody* in 1602 he prefixed a sonnet which opens thus:

> Great earl, whose high and noble mind is higher
> And nobler than thy noble high desire;
> Whose outward shape, *though it most lovely be*,
> Doth in fair robes a fairer soul attire. . . .

Considering that the occasion did not call for any reference to the Earl's personal appearance, Davison's statement must be received with attention. Mr. Lee denies that there is any evidence for Pembroke's beauty, and calls this sentence of Davison's 'a cautiously qualified reference'; while, on the other hand, he holds that the Virgilian tag, 'quo non formosior alter Affuit,' which an Oxford wit applied to Southampton, is a satisfactory proof that he came up to Shakespeare's ideal. Surely one passage is as good evidence as the other; and perhaps the fact that both young noblemen were admitted to Elizabeth's favour is better evidence than either. It is perhaps lucky that we have no portraits of Pembroke in youth, for the portrait that Mr. Lee prints of Southampton certainly supports his theory that Shakespeare's praises, supposing them addressed to him, were mere professional flattery. It is interesting that we should have a testimony to Pembroke's 'loveliness' as late as 1602, when he was two-and-twenty, for the use of that epithet—not, surely, a 'cautiously qualified' but a very strong one considering his age—is some argument that he is the person to whom the same epithet is applied in the 126th sonnet, and who is there stated to have retained his youthful looks beyond the usual term. Enthusiasts for the Pembroke theory, like Mr. Tyler and the Rev. W. A. Harrison, have collected from the Sidney Papers all the references they contain to the young lord, and one or two of these lend a certain additional plausibility to the theory. It is discovered, for example, that in 1597 negotiations were on foot to marry Herbert to a daughter of the Earl of Oxford, which came to nothing; and the suggestion has been made that Shakespeare was prompted to help in overcoming the youth's reluctance. It cannot be denied that the opening set of sonnets, while they are in keeping with the age, demand some such background of historical fact; though the situation is one that might have presented itself in any dozen great houses in any one year. Such a theory requires us to assume that Shakespeare was familiar at Wilton, and knew Herbert at home before he came up to London in the following spring. I do not think this so improbable as it appears to Mr. Lee, for Shakespeare had become famous three years earlier, and Lady Pembroke (Sidney's sister) was renowned for her patronage of poets; moreover Samuel Daniel, who speaks of Wilton as 'that arbour of the Muses,' was himself there at this period as tutor to the young lord; so that Shakespeare's fame is not likely to have been unsounded. As to the probability, we may ask, If Ben Jonson was welcomed at Penshurst, why should not Shakespeare have been received at Wilton? If this were allowed, it might be urged that a friendship begun at Wilton in the boy's impressionable youth was in a natural way continued in London. Of course all

this is merely conjecture; but in the extreme paucity of the records I do not think that an argument from silence is conclusive against it. A friendship is an intangible thing, and would make no stir so as to be talked about. It would be absurd to have to conclude that neither Shakespeare nor Pembroke had any friends in London because we cannot give their names. At the same time, it must not be ignored that one weak place in the Pembroke theory is the fact that some of the sonnets were certainly written before 1598, and that the young gentleman did not come to London till that year.

Another weak place in the theory is the mis-description, that it implies, of Lord Pembroke as *Mr. W. H.* It has often been alleged that a parallel case is that of the poet Lord Buckhurst, who is described on title-pages as *Mr. Sackville*; but Mr. Lee has disposed of the parallel by showing that while Lord Buckhurst was a commoner when he wrote his poems, Lord Pembroke had by courtesy always been a peer, and was known to contemporaries in his minority as Lord Herbert. It is perhaps going too far to say that this difficulty renders the Pembroke hypothesis altogether untenable; for there remain two alternative possibilities. It is possible that Thorpe found his manuscript of the Sonnets headed 'To W. H.,' and, being ignorant who W. H. was, supplied the ordinary title of respect. This would be a perfectly fair argument; though I should say that it does not answer to the impression that the terms of the dedication leave on one's mind. (The further question whether the young nobleman would have answered to the name of *Will* instead of to his family title I will not attempt to argue; to friendship all things are possible.) The alternative to Thorpe's ignorance would be that he suppressed his lordship's title by way of disguise. This also is a fairly legitimate supposition under the circumstances. Mr. Lee argues that for a publisher to have addressed any peer as plain *Mister* would have been defamation and a Star Chamber matter, as it well might if the publisher intended an insult. But in any case the peer would have to set the Star Chamber in motion; and there might be good reasons for not doing so. The terms of the dedication seem to imply that the publisher was not conscious of taking any great liberty. Hence if W. H. is to be interpreted of Pembroke, we shall have to assume that Thorpe had satisfied himself that the dedication would not be resented; for if Thorpe knew the secret, it must have been a fairly open one. If Thorpe had obtained permission to dedicate the Sonnets to Pembroke on condition that his *incognito* was respected—a somewhat difficult supposition—then it is hard to say that 'Mr. W. H.' was an impossible way of referring to him; because, though by courtesy a peer, Herbert was legally a commoner until he succeeded to the earldom in 1601. Those who on the ground of this derogation from Herbert's dignity have denied the possibility of his being the 'begetter' of the Sonnets have perhaps not always given weight enough to the impossibility of dedicating them 'To the Right Honourable William, Earle of Pembroke, Lord Chamberlaine to His Majestie, one of his most honourable Privie Counsell, and Knight of the most noble of the Garter.' Had Thorpe ventured upon such a dedication as that, I can almost conceive the Star Chamber taking action of its own accord. Still, when special pleading has done its utmost, I am bound to confess that I am not convinced. There is a smug tone about the dedication which suggests that while Mr. W. H. was far above Thorpe's own social position, he was yet something less than so magnificent a personage as the Earl of Pembroke.

The Pembroke party, however, not content with identifying the poet's friend, are determined to find a counterpart in real life to the 'dark lady' who figures so ominously in the sonnets. The number of 'dark ladies' in the capital at any time is legion, and the sonnets supply no possible clue by which the particular person can be identified. The attempt, therefore, to fix upon someone with whom Pembroke is known to have had relations is merely gratuitous; and it rejoices the heart of any sane spectator to learn that this supposed 'dark lady' turns out, when her portraits are examined, to have been conspicuously fair. Probably, as the portraits seem of unimpeachable pedigree, we shall next be told that the sonnets themselves imply that the lady dyed her hair before sitting for the portrait.

To sum up, then, the results at which the most recent Shakespearean scholarship has arrived. No new light has been gained upon the identity of the rival poet, or the friend to whom the sonnets were addressed. These mysteries remain as dark as ever. The only certain results are negative results. The poet is almost certainly not Chapman, and the friend is quite certainly not Southampton. If the friend were a peer, he must have been Herbert; if he were a commoner, he may have been any young gentleman of good family and large fortune with a taste for the theatre and the flattery of men of genius.[7] It is more important to remember that, whoever he was, we are not yet debarred by Mr. Lee's researches from regarding the sonnets as expressions of real feeling, though, in deference to his proof of the fashionableness of superlatives under Elizabeth, we may be wise to-day in transposing their key a tone lower. If superlatives trouble us, we may recollect that a sonnet, by its very nature, is a 'descant' upon a more simple 'ground.' More important still is it to remember that these sonnets contain some of the finest poetry in the world. Of that nothing has been said in this paper, because it is admitted by all critics; indeed, if it were not for their supreme beauty no one would think them worth disputing over.

### Notes

1. They may, of course, have included dedicatory poems, printed or unprinted, as the 82nd sonnet seems to imply.
2. Perhaps Mr. Lee a little overstates the case, strong as it is, for the artificiality of the emotion displayed in Elizabethan sonnets. Drayton, by calling his lady Idea, did not imply that she was merely an abstraction, but that she was his ideal. He himself identifies her with Anne Goodere. Nor does he tell his readers 'that if any sought *genuine* passion in them they had better go elsewhere.' His words are: 'Into these loves who but for passion looks, At this first sight here let him lay them by'; and he goes on to explain *passion* by 'farfetched sighs,' 'ah, me's,' and 'whining.' The point of the sonnet, which is a prefatory advertisement, is that the reader may expect variety and will not be bored. The Doctor of Divinity whom Mr. Lee quotes as warning his readers that 'a man may write of love, and not be in love,' was probably in fear of his archdeacon.
3. Examples are *discandy* (*A. and C.* iii. 13, 165; iv. 12, 22); *chare* (*A. and C.* iv. 15, 75; v. 2, 231); *bear me hard* (*J. C.* i. 3, 311; ii. 1, 215); *handsome about him* (*Much Ado.* iv. 2, 88; v. 4. 105).
4. Professor Bradley calls my attention to the series 71–74, which has not only the tone of *Hamlet* but parallelisms of phrase, especially in 74 to v. 2, 350 and i. 4, 66.
5. Mr. Lee yields a doubtful assent to the idea that Henry Willobie, in his *Avisa* (1594), refers to Shakespeare, under the initials W. S., as having escaped heart-whole from a passion in which he found himself involved. The sole ground for the conjecture is that W. S. is referred to as the 'old player.' But the love affair had been previously spoken of as 'a comedy like to end in a tragedy,' and Willobie himself is called the 'new actor.' There is, therefore, not the slightest reason for taking the one expression more literally than the other. And where, it may be asked, is there anything in the sonnets that could be referred to as a recovery from love? Another point which would be an argument for the early date of the sonnets, if it could be supported, may be referred to here. Mr. Lee thinks Sir John Davies, in a 'gulling sonnet,' was parodying Shakespeare's legal phraseology in Sonnet 26. It is possible, though, considering

the excesses in this respect of 'Zepheria,' to which Davis refers by name, it is uncertain. Mr. Lee dates Davies' sonnets in 1595 (p. 436); but they are dedicated to Sir Anthony Cooke, who, according to Grosart, was knighted at the sack of Cadiz, September 15, 1596. They must, therefore, be subsequent to that date; and they may belong to any year between 1597 and 1603, when Davies himself was knighted, for in the MSS. they are attributed to 'Mr. Davyes.'
6. It may be well to state shortly the argument for this date. The palmary line is 'The mortal moon hath her eclipse endured.' The parallel in *Antony and Cleopatra* (iii. 13, 153), 'Our terrene moon is now eclipsed,' which is applied to Cleopatra, shows that 'mortal moon' must refer to a person (and it is not easy to see what other meaning it could have), and that to '*endure* an eclipse' means to 'suffer it,' not 'to go through it and emerge.' There is no instance in Shakespeare of 'eclipse' being used with the implied notion of recovery. Mr. Lee adds other arguments from contemporary sources.
7. Tyrwhitt used to think his name was Hughes because in the 20th sonnet the word *Hews* is printed in italics for no obvious reason. As the line stands in the original edition,

　　A man in hew all *Hews* in his controwling,

it looks momentous; and there is no other word in italics between the 5th sonnet and the 53rd. But on the other hand it must be noted that what chiefly impresses us is the capital letter, and this is found with every word printed in italics throughout the sonnets, so that it is not in itself evidence of a proper name. Further, there is no pun as there is in the sonnets which contain the name 'Will.' Probably the italic is accidental. Mr. Wyndham says of *Hews*, 'if its capital and italics be a freak of the printer, they constitute the only freaks of that kind in the whole edition of 1609.' But there is another in the 104th sonnet, where 'autumn' is in italic type and both 'spring' and 'winter' in roman.

## PAUL ELMER MORE
### "Shakespeare's Sonnets"
*Shelburne Essays, Second Series*
1905, pp. 20–45

However disappointing the mass of Elizabethan sonnets in Mr. Sidney Lee's two volumes may have been, one great service at least they have performed: by contrast they have thrown the realism and human passion of Shakespeare's sonnets into a new and bold relief. They serve as a touchstone, so to speak, by means of which it is possible to tell with a kind of critical precision just where Shakespeare was juggling with the conventional commonplaces of the Renaissance, as not seldom happened, and where, on the contrary, he wrote from actual experience or native emotion. And no one, I think, can come back to these more personal sonnets after a perusal of Mr. Lee's collection without being impressed anew by the miracle of their beauty and without feeling that with this key the poet did veritably unlock his heart.

Not that they contain any rationalised philosophy or any formula of life; on the contrary, their value as a confession is bound up with the very fact that they spring directly from the experience of the writer without any attempt to shape that experience into a system after the manner of the more reflective artists. And in this they are in harmony with the spirit of the plays. I am aware of the peril of such a statement to-day, when it has become the exercise of a certain class of perfervid critics to read into the dramas some favoured idea, whether political or religious or moral or literary. Yet withal the very difficulties and contradictions that arise from the methodical interpretation of Shakespeare might have warned them that no such application of philosophy was possible. We take recourse to Matthew Arnold's saying, "Others abide our question, thou art free," or, we quote from Lord Lytton:

Each guess of others into worlds unknown
Shakespeare revolves, but keeps concealed his own;
As in the Infinite hangs poised his thought,
Surveying all things and asserting nought;—

but few of us have the courage to admit that he evades our questioning just because he has no answer to give. It is with him as the oracles of which a skeptical poet has made complaint—

That none can pierce the vast black veil uncertain,
Because there is no light beyond the curtain.

We may find the whole gamut of human emotion in Shakespeare, but we begin to darken counsel with words when we undertake to construct out of the medley of his plots any coherent vision of life such as exists in Milton or Homer or Dante or Æschylus. Other dramatists have resorted for their tragic thesis to some definite philosophy, whether of their own eliciting or of the age—to the antinomy of fate and the individual will, or the clashing of family and state, or the conflict of duty and pleasure. Shakespeare proceeds otherwise: simple passion is his theme, and his tragic exaltation is obtained by magnifying passion until it assumes the enormity of a supernatural obsession and the bearer is shattered by the excess of his own emotion. No one can have failed to observe the incongruity of the *dénouement* in most of the tragedies—the accumulated and unmeaning slaughters that bring an end to *Romeo and Juliet, Hamlet, Macbeth,* and *Lear.* The simple fact is that these gruesome conclusions, twist and turn as the system-mongers will, do not grow out of any necessity of the plot, but are the relics of a barbarous taste. The real climax lies in the frenzy of the passion-driven hero, and it is for this reason that madness forms an essential part of the greater dramas.

In this sense *Lear* may be taken as the most typical of Shakespeare's tragedies, where the very winds and clouds re-echo the hurly-burly of overwrought passion. And the summit of that passion, I think, is to be found in those scenes before Gloucester's castle and in Edgar's hovel, when the King and his little band set the world topsy-turvy with the unrestrained wildness of their pathos and mockery, through which passes Lear's cry of terror: "Oh, that way madness lies!" On the contrary, the formal conclusion of the play has no consistence in reason, and, aside from the separate passages of striking poetry, little art. The needless intrigues and the universal butchery bear no logical relation to the main theme and degrade the artistic enjoyment of the hearer. The interest of the piece lies in the excess of passion and not in any unravelling of a tragic nodus; it is a drama of character and not of plot.

And it is the same with the other plays. As the stuff of life presents itself to Shakespeare, broken and unarranged, so he reflects it in his magnifying mirror—a tale full of sound and fury, signifying nothing. I remember one warm evening in early spring standing with a friend on a balcony that overlooked the lights and the throbbing procession of Broadway. It was the hour when the theatres were closing. The scene was new to him, for he had come from a far Western town, and the odour of the city, the constant mutations of the throng, the snatches of conversation, and the occasional laughter that floated above the murmur—the mystery of this boundless activity, caught in passing glimpses, acted on his nerves as an intoxicant. It fascinated and troubled him at once; he could find no answer to the appeal of this enormous, ebullient life, and he was haunted by the feeling that each human atom of the mass was driven along in the current by some desire inexplicable to all the others—inexplicable, it might be, to himself. The whole spectacle presented itself to the eye as a tangle of passions woven on a web of illusion. "It is all new to me," he said, "yet the sensation is strangely familiar. How does it come?" And then, after a pause: "I understand. It is the world of Shakespeare, as we have just seen it on the stage. And often before, while reading his plays, I have been overwhelmed by the same feeling of infinite interacting lives and infinite illusion." And my friend knew his Shakespeare as few of us know him in these laborious days.

Only there is something to add. Though Shakespeare did not rationalise, or, in a sense, translate the events of life into an artistic design, though he gives back the crude material of emotion as he finds it, yet in another way he did have his own solution of the riddle—it may even be that his solution is, when all is said, profounder and more satisfying than that of any other poet. The passions of his play may be knit into an inextricable tangle so that no dramatic unravelling is possible, yet always when the emotion is wrought to a height beyond which human nature cannot go, always when the hearer is about to cry out, "That way madness lies; let me shun that," suddenly the poet waves aside the whole fabric of enchantment with a word of royal command. From the fitful fever of life, in the turning of a moment, he carries us into that region of eventual calm wherefrom the stage of the world seems as a little point at a mighty distance. He who created this troubled scene is no longer a partaker in its passionate perplexities; he stands a great way off, apart from it and above it, and looks down where, far beneath,

. . . the tides of day and night
With flame and darkness ridge
The void, as low as where this earth
Spins like a fretful midge.

We need not dwell on this aspect of his genius, though we may animadvert, by the way, that Taine's criticism, because it fails to recognise this other element beside the passion of Shakespeare, is finally false and shallow. Any one will recall the great moments when the curtain of disillusion falls. It is Hamlet's "The rest is silence"; or the Dauphin's "Life is as tedious as a twice-told tale Vexing the dull ear of a drowsy man"; or the Second Richard's "A brittle glory shineth in this face"; or Macbeth's "To-morrow and to-morrow and to-morrow"; or Kent's "Vex not his ghost"; or Prospero's "We are such stuff As dreams are made on, and our little life Is rounded with a sleep." More than that, there would seem to be something akin to this inner peripeteia in the development of Shakespeare's genius. The peculiar calm and beauty of *The Tempest, The Winter's Tale,* and the other late plays have often been commented upon. After the tumult of the great tragedies, those scenes of idyllic sport come like the words of Macbeth,

There's nothing serious in mortality,
All is but toys—

as if the poet, finding no significance in the thwarted fates of mankind, had turned at last to the laughter of young girls and the innocence of flowers.

No, we merely deceive ourselves if we go to Shakespeare for any philosophic systematising of life or any reshaping of the material afforded by experience into a world of artistic significance, such as we look for in the masters of Greek and French literature. What we do get from him is a sense of boundless life. Other men have suffered and enjoyed privately, but in him were brought together all the passions of mankind; he is the master of human experience, and there can come to us no pinnacle of triumph or despair, of joy or grief, no tragic melancholy or buoyant humour, no envy or hate or love or pride or shame, but we shall know that he on some day of his brief life has felt as we feel and has spoken for us better than we ourselves can speak. And so it is, I think, that we hunger for some direct word from this poet, some revelation of his own mind, more than from any other writer of the world. What had he to say of his passage through time? Was the sum of it sweet or bitter to him; did he find it a simple matter to live, or was he, too, *infelix fatis exterritus*; did he, in the sessions of silent thought, regard with complacence his contact with daily life, or was there in his memory still some touch of regret—even of shame? Just because there is here no remoulding of experience to an ideal, we believe that if he should open his heart to us in these matters he would exhibit a peculiar frankness; and because his experience was broader and deeper than that of any other man, we feel that his word would have extraordinary validity. Could Shakespeare confess, it would be, as it were, a confession of the human race.

And to a certain extent Shakespeare has confessed. I am not so rash as to suppose that here and now we shall pluck out the heart of his mystery; in the end a man of his wide-reaching vision must remain as his own Æneas says: "The secrets of nature have not more gift in taciturnity." Yet no one can compare his sonnets with those in Mr. Lee's volumes without being immediately impressed by the directness of the self-revelation they contain, nor can I conceive any reason for taking this confession otherwise than at its face value. And what has he to say for himself—this man who ran through the gamut of human emotions and made himself as it were the spokesman of the race? Alas, it is only the old story repeated. I do not see how one can read these sonnets and not feel that the sum of life to the poet of those spacious days was, as it had appeared to the Preacher of Israel long ago, *Vanity and vexation, and he that increaseth experience increaseth sorrow!* Not seldom, to be sure, there is a note of serenity or triumph, but always there is this peculiarity, that the more personal the tone becomes the sadder is its import.

He was, after all, a child of his age. There was always present with him that sense of the eternal flux of things which is so characteristic of the Renaissance, but which, curiously enough, rarely appears in the other Elizabethan sonneteers, however common it may be in the dramatists. It is safe to say that no single motive or theme recurs more persistently through the whole course of Shakespeare's works than this consciousness of the servile depredations of time, that "ceaseless lackey to eternity." As with other men of the period, this sense of brevity and mutability lay upon his mind like an obsession, and no small part of the tragic pathos in his plays arises from the jostling together of the insatiable desires of youth with the ever imminent perception of evanescence. One wonders whether Bacon could have had in recollection these apostrophes to time when he wrote in his *Essays:* "It is not good to look too long upon these turning-wheels of vicissitude, lest we become giddy."

Of the great passages in the dramas which revert to this theme I need say nothing, for they are fresh in the memory of us all. But it is just as prominent, though possibly less familiar, in the poems. In the very midst of Lucrece's agony she forgets herself awhile to rail against this power that "turn[s] the giddy round of Fortune's wheel":

> Mis-shapen Time, copesmate of ugly Night,
> Swift subtle post, carrier of grisly care!

And in the *Venus and Adonis* the thought, here in its milder aspect, is still more essential.

> The tender spring upon thy tempting lip
> Shews thee unripe yet mayst thou well be tasted;
> Make use of time, let not advantage slip;
> Beauty within itself should not be wasted:

> Fair flowers that are not gathered in their prime
> Rot and consume themselves in little time—

cries Venus to the reluctant youth, and the real charm of this first heir of Shakespeare's invention resides in a young poet's pity for what Freneau long afterwards was to call "the frail duration of a flower," and in his longing to conquer mutability by the prowess of love:

> Seeds spring from seeds and beauty breedeth beauty.

We are carried by this theme immediately to the earlier sonnets of the collection in which Shakespeare scolds his boy friend for cherishing an "unthrifty loveliness":

> Thy unused beauty must be tombed with thee.

So striking is the resemblance between these first seventeen sonnets and this part of the *Venus and Adonis* just alluded to that the poem would seem to be a mere dramatisation or objectification (if I may use the repellent word) of the more personal expression of the idea, and would afford pretty strong confirmation of the opinion that the early sonnets, at least, were written about the year 1593 (the date of *Venus and Adonis*) and were addressed to that Earl of Southampton to whom the poem was dedicated. Everything, too,—both the habit of poets in those days and the unmistakable continuity of thought running through the greater number of Shakespeare's series,—would indicate that the succeeding sonnets were meant for the same person, although some of them may have been written considerably later. Even in the more tragic part that was to come afterwards, when the hesitant friend accepted Shakespeare's advice quite too literally, he turns the theme of the *Venus and Adonis* to the culprit's exoneration:

> Gentle thou art, and therefore to be won,
> Beauteous thou art, therefore to be assailed;
> And when a woman woos what woman's son
> Will sourly leave her till she have prevailed?

Indeed, it might be a question whether the dramatisation of the subject was undertaken to confirm the earlier exhortation, or later, when the turning point of the sonnet-story occurred, to uphold the example of Adonis to the tempted, wavering youth. In either case the sonnets of both periods and the poem would seem to be written under the same inspiration and not far apart in time.

Nor is it really so difficult to explain, theoretically, the mood in which Shakespeare wrote those earlier exhortations as the mountainous controversy over them would lead one to suppose. Consider that this ambitious young poet had come up to London with a hunger for beauty unequalled perhaps in the history of literature; and that with this hunger went the haunting consciousness of the uncertainty and mutability of things which was a part also of this Renaissance inheritance. Naturally when, in the years following the first riot of youth, he fell under the sway of the noble boy, at once his patron and his love (whether it was Southampton or another)—naturally this perilous perception of beauty with its poignant regret threw an ideal colour over their friendship. And by virtue of that mingling together in England of the currents of the Renaissance and the Reformation, Shakespeare's passion for the boy took on something of the sensuousness of that relation as it was adopted in Italy from classical tradition and at the same time the moral *pudor* of the northern races. The result is thus easily explained in theory, but to most readers of to-day the realisation of this mixed sentiment is not a little baffling; the sonnets would probably leave them quite cold were it not that Shakespeare's confession deals also with larger matters. His love for the youth becomes, in fact, a beautiful symbol of that war against Time which runs through all his work. In this respect the fifteenth sonnet may be regarded as the keynote of the whole first group, although in poetic diction it cannot be ranked among the highest:

> When I consider everything that grows
> Holds in perfection but a little moment,
> That this huge stage presenteth nought but shows,
> Whereon the stars in secret influence comment;
> When I perceive that men as plants increase,
> Cheerèd and checked even by the self-same sky,
> Vaunt in their youthful sap, at height decrease,
> And wear their brave state out of memory;
> Then the conceit of this inconstant stay
> *Sets you most rich in youth before my sight,*
> *Where wasteful Time debateth with Decay,*
> To change your day of youth to sullied night;
>     *And all in war with Time for love of you,*
>     As he takes from you, I engraft you new.

He looks back to "the chronicle of wasted time," and is filled with alarm that the grace and nobility of his young friend also "among the wastes of time must go." Aided probably by some family circumstances now quite obscure to us, he appeals to the "sweet boy" to defy the heavy hand of age by the creative faculty of love, and finds it easy to write this appeal with the constant revolt of his own nature against the reign of mutability. And when, as it appears, the malicious youth let his exhortations fall unheeded, or heeded them in a manner quite foreign to the preacher's intention and desire, it was still within the range of his Renaissance training to seek to accomplish by the power of his own art what the other had failed to acquire for himself. He will eternise in his verse this "flow'ring pride, so fading and so fickle" (to use Spenser's phrase on mutability), and so put back the encroachments of decay; he is but one of many in those days who sought the "stedfast rest of all things" in such an *ære perennius*. And it soon grows evident that in the sonnets which express this hope the sense of universal vicissitude has almost driven from view his concern for the particular W. H., if those were the friend's initials:

> When I have seen by Time's fell hand defaced
> The rich proud cost of outworn buried age,
> When sometime lofty towers I see down-razed
> And brass eternal slave to mortal rage; . . .

or turning to man's estate—

> Like as the waves make towards the pebbled shore,
> So do our minutes hasten to their end;
> Each changing place with that which goes before,
> In sequent toil all forwards do contend; . . .
>     And yet to times in hope my verse shall stand,
>     Praising thy worth, despite his cruel hand.

It is only in this way, I think, by connecting Shakespeare's love for this chosen boy with the deeper current of his thought and feeling that we can understand, in part at least, the riddle of the sonnets.

But, after all, this restiveness under the hand of time, however personally expressed by Shakespeare and however strangely omitted by his compatriot sonneteers, was a commonplace of his age—of all ages poetically inspired, from Homer's "Like as the generations of leaves" down to Keats's "Forever wilt thou love and she be fair." It is possible to go beyond this in the sonnets, and to catch a note of sadness which is by no means a "topic" of the age, which is indeed now and again almost painfully intimate and individual. I am aware of the temerity of such a statement, but, taken as a whole and with all their splendours considered, these sonnets to me seem to join with the plays in forming one of the saddest human documents ever penned. There is of course humour here in abundance; but from the days of Aristophanes to the present

time humour has had a strange trick of springing luxuriantly from a bitter soil. It is common also to point to the pastoral scenes in *The Tempest, The Winter's Tale,* and the other later dramas as a proof of the large joyousness and final serenity that lay at the basis of Shakespeare's nature; and in one sense the assertion is perfectly just. Yet here, as always, it is necessary to distinguish. We may not be able to mark off the passage with mathematical precision, but no one can read the plays with such a quest in mind without feeling in a general way that at times the poet is commenting on life in the tone of his own direct experience, and that again he speaks from that far Olympian height where his own personality is forgotten and wherefrom he looks down upon the business of men as on the pretty sport of children—and then it is that the tricks of Ariel and Miranda's brave new world become a wonder equal to a dukedom, and the breath of a dim violet grows as important as the jealous rage of Leontes. This serenity is due, in part, no doubt, to the calming influence of years, and falls like the wind-swept purity of the atmosphere after a storm; it is no less the gift of genius, with its well-known faculty of dwelling alternately within and without itself.

But our concern to-day is with the poet's inner life alone, and I see no reason to question the common belief that *Hamlet* expresses more of Shakespeare's personal experience than any other play or character. So far as I know, no one has pointed out how strongly that opinion is reinforced by the similarity of tone between the dramatic utterances of *Hamlet* and the confessions of the sonnets. Compare, for instance, the list of evils pronounced by the melancholy Dane:

> The whips and scorns of time,
> The oppressor's wrong, the proud man's contumely,
> The pangs of despised love, the law's delay,
> The insolence of office, and the spurns
> That patient merit of the unworthy takes—

consider how foreign all these details are to the actual situation of Hamlet and how appropriate they are to the fortune of Shakespeare himself; consider with them the misplaced diatribe of Lucrece:

> The patient dies while the physician sleeps;
> The orphan pines while the oppressor feeds;
> Justice is feasting while the widow weeps;
> Advice is sporting while infection breeds—

and then turn to the sixty-sixth sonnet and see how clearly they express not the mere commonplace lament over the insufficiency of life, but the poet's own very personal and very bitter experience:

> Tired with all these for restful death I cry.

Indeed, as we read over the sonnets and mark the lines where he speaks his own relation to the whips and scorns of time, we may well be overwhelmed by the magnitude and the intimacy of the confession, and it is easy to understand why he never gave this work willingly to the public as he did his only other two non-dramatic poems. The one word that occurs to me as expressive of his feeling is *indignity*; if it were not for the sound of the word in connection with so revered a name I should say *shame*—indignity against the soilure that is forced upon him from contact with the world, shame for his too facile yielding to contamination. The story is best told by bringing together some of these passages without comment:—

Sonnet 29:
> When in disgrace with fortune and men's eyes,
> I all alone beweep my outcast state.

Sonnet 36:
> I may not evermore acknowledge thee,
> Lest my bewailèd guilt should do thee shame.

Sonnet 37:
>So I, made lame by fortune's dearest spite.

Sonnet 88:
>Upon my part I can set down a story
>Of faults concealed, wherein I am attained.

Sonnet 90:
>Now, while the world is bent my deeds to cross,
>Join with the spite of fortune, make me bow.

Sonnet 112:
>Your love and pity doth the impression fill
>Which vulgar scandal stamped upon my brow.

Sonnet 119:
>What potions have I drunk of Siren tears,
>Distilled from limbecs foul as hell within.

Sonnet 121:
>'T is better to be vile than vile esteemed.

These are only a few of the lines that might be quoted. Take them all together and I do not believe you will find, in the whole course of English literature, any confession comparable to them for the indignity and shame of a noble spirit outraged by the familiarity of "sluttish Time." Something of this is due, no doubt, to the peculiar position of the actor in those days. Says Casca, when he wishes to pull the great Cæsar down into the mire of common buffeted humanity: "If the tag-rag people did not clap him and hiss him according as he pleased and displeased them, as they use to do the players in the theatre, I am no true man." We do not often, while under the spell of Shakespeare's magic, consider what it must have meant to so sensitive and self-conscious a nature as his to have been exposed to the outrageous approval and disapproval of an Elizabethan audience. The groundlings, we know, paid for the discomfort of their place in the pit by boisterous assertion of their pleasure, and the comments of the nobles who sometimes sat on the stage at the very elbows of the actors must often have been as galling as the jeers of the mob below. The growing sect of the Puritans, too, gave them something worse than contempt. Thus, after the earthquake of 1580, the Lord Mayor of London writes to the Privy Council, April 12th:

>When it happened on Sundaie last that some great disorder was committed at the Theatre, I sent for the undershireve of Middlesex to understand the circumstances, to the intent that by myself or by him I might have caused such redresse to be had as in dutie and discretion I might, and therefore did also send for the plaiers to have apered afore me, and the rather because those playes doe make assembles of cittizens and there families of whome I have charge; but forasmuch as I understand that your Lordship, with other of his majesties most honourable Counsell, have entered into examination of that matter, I have surceassed to procede further, and do humbly refer the whole to your wisdomes and grave considerations; howbeit, I have further thought it my dutie to informe your Lordship, and therewith also to beseche to have in your honourable rememberance, that the players of playes which are used at the Theatre and other such places, and tumblers and such like, are a very superfluous sort of men and of suche facultie as the lawes have disalowed, and their exersise of those playes is a great hinderaunce of the service of God, who hath with His mighty hand so lately admonished us of oure earnest repentance.

Is it strange that Shakespeare should have retreated from London to the quiet of his Stratford home as soon as he was freed from the necessity of serving such a public? More than

once he shows in the sonnets how deeply the iron had entered into his heart, and how he felt the reproach of being classed among this "very superfluous sort of men." The chief passages are often quoted:

>Alas, 't is true I have gone here and there,
>And made myself a motley to the view,
>Gored mine own thoughts, sold cheap what is most
>     dear,
>Made old offences of affections new;
>Most true it is that I have looked on truth
>Askance and strangely;—

and, in the following sonnet:

>O, for my sake do you with Fortune chide,
>The guilty goddess of my harmful deeds,
>That did not better for my life provide
>Than public means which public manners breeds;
>Thence comes it that my name receives a brand, etc.

The confession is sufficiently frank and carries us far enough away from the elegant conventionalities that ruled the other Elizabethan sonneteers. It is not entirely pleasant to know that the man we reverence this side—often yonder side—idolatry, could have laid his heart open in this way even in the intimacy of friendship.

But there is a more painful element in the sonnets than mere outcry against the harshness of the guilty goddess. This man, whose knowledge of the heart enabled him, without the synthetic imagination of the other supreme poets, to build up so marvellous a literature, whose sense of passion was so profound that it took the place of tragic conflict in other dramatists—how is it with him when, laying aside the comfortable disguise of masque and cothurnus, he speaks directly for himself? We call him the master of human experience, and that is his honour to-day; but how was it with him when he stood on the stage of the Globe Theatre, a motley to the view, or indulged in the wanton life of that superfluous sort of men who were his fellows? If the hazard and spite of fortune produced in him a feeling of indignity, the subjection to the wild beast within his own heart left, for a time at least, what can only be called a stamp of shame. It is not necessary to dwell at length on the particular incident which forms the heart of this confession, nor to make any conjectures in regard to the identity and character of that "worser spirit, a woman coloured ill," who was his love "of despair." All that is essential is told only too frankly in the later sonnets. There are confessions of guilt in English—a plenty of them; but ordinarily these are made after the sinner has reached a state of grace, and when we probe the matter we are likely to find, as in the case of Bunyan, that the remembered enormities were such crimes as bell-ringing and dancing on the green. The peculiarity of Shakespeare's confession is that we see a sensitive soul actually in the toils of evil, which he deplores yet hugs to his breast. It is this association which makes the terrible one hundred and twenty-ninth sonnet unique in English—unique, so far as I know, in any language. Only the conscience of the Puritan united to the libertine fancy of a Cavalier (a phenomenon not easily conceivable outside of England) could have produced those words:

>The expense of spirit in a waste of shame
>Is lust in action. . . .
>   All this the world well knows; yet none knows well
>   To shun the heaven that leads men to this hell.

If you wish to see how much of the world's experience has entered into these lines, turn back to Horace's *Epistles* and see in what way the matter presented itself to that clear-eyed pagan.

>Sperne voluptates, nocet empta dolore voluptas,

was the height of his argument, and between that admonition and the anguish of Shakespeare have passed all the middle ages and the whole of Christianity. Or, if you care to set in relief the personal and intimate nature of the sonnet, compare it with Byron's stanza in *Childe Harold:*

> 'Tis an old lesson; Time approves it true,
> And those who know it best, deplore it most;
> When all is won that all desire to woo,
> The paltry prize is hardly worth the cost:
> Youth wasted, minds degraded, honour lost,
> These are thy fruits, successful Passion!

The thought is the same as Shakespeare's, but it is expressed by a man of the world who speaks the wisdom of his kind; there is lacking that individual conviction of sin, as the Puritans whom Shakespeare so despised would have called it.

We must not, however, forget that these sonnets were not written for the world to read, but for the privacy of one or two persons; their enigma would indeed be inexplicable were they intended for the public. And just as Shakespeare's sense of universal vicissitude is the true means of interpreting the opening appeal to the boy friend to perpetuate his beauty through the power of love, so the indignities of his public career, in his early years at least, and the remorse of submission to his own passions are the only explanation of those extravagant terms of admiration and love which he bestows on his young patron.

It is not necessary to believe all the stories of Shakespeare's irregular youth, yet we can hardly doubt that his beginnings in London were humble and not desirable in the eyes of the world. What he wrung from fortune came by struggle and by coining the experience of his life for public usage. In comparison with his own ragged honours, the brilliant person of such a child of fortune as Southampton would seem to hold as a visible symbol all that he sought and could obtain, if obtained even in part, only by paying for it in the sanctities of his own character. Southampton (or another), beautiful, proud, desired of women, rich, to whom Fortune gave all things without price, was more than a person to Shakespeare, he was an ideal; and the poet's devotion to this patron, his almost cringing submission to a boy's whims, is only comprehensible when we consider the relation between the two in this light. There is in the friendship the vicarious power of transmitting virtues:

> Thy love is better than high birth to me,
> Richer than wealth, prouder than garments' cost,
> Of more delight than hawks or horses be:
> And having thee, of all men's pride I boast.

Almost the association with this ideal of youth is able to cleanse the stains of time. Editors have been troubled by the lines in which Shakespeare speaks of his age—

> That time of year thou mayest in me behold—

and have cited them as proof that the sonnets must have been composed later than 1594, when he was only thirty. They forget that this early assumption of age was a commonplace of the Renaissance. And, apart from this, it does not appear that the difficulty is solved by making him thirty-six or thirty-eight; even at that age the ordinary man is not quite in the yellow leaf. The fact is that the very intensity of Shakespeare's passions and the depth of his experience made him feel thus old in comparison with one untried by life. And in the freshness of his friend's blossoming he would find a cloak for his own losses at the hand of Time:

> But when my glass shews me myself, indeed,
> Beated and chopt with tanned antiquity,
> Mine own self love quite contrary I read,
> Self so self-loving were iniquity.
> 'Tis thee (myself) that for myself I praise
> Painting my age with beauty of thy days.

Yet, even considered in this way, there remains something disconcerting in the peculiar tone of self-humiliation which Shakespeare assumes before a fledgling of the Court. He pays more than the ordinary adulation of the poets in those days, and pays it in a different kind:

> Is it thy spirit that thou send'st from thee
> So far from home into my deeds to prye,
> To find out shames and idle hours in me?

And the triangular comedy, in which Shakespeare and his two loves of comfort and despair play their extraordinary rôles, leaves the poet in a position not calculated to enhance his honour in the eyes of saint or worldling. Something of this whole relation between the great exemplar of human experience and his boyish patron may be accounted for by the poet's faculty of dramatising the gap in his own nature between ideal and reality; something of it is still inexplicable, an enigma never meant for our solving, and best, no doubt, left in obscurity.

And if you ask me, then, why I have attempted, so far as I could, to lay bare this darker side of Shakespeare's character, my only reply is that there is a fascination in following out what seems to one the truth. And, after all, some comfort, not of an ignoble sort I trust, abounds in knowing a little more precisely that this spokesman of mankind rose to the power and tranquillity of his vision through experiences very like our own, and that he, too, suffered the indignities of time and the remorse of his own excesses.

# Venus and Adonis

I know not how I shall offend in dedicating my unpolished lines to your Lordship, nor how the world will censure me for choosing so strong a prop to support so weak a burden; only, if your Honor seem but pleased, I account myself highly praised, and vow to take advantage of all idle hours, till I have honored you with some graver labor. But if the first heir of my invention prove deformed, I shall be sorry it had so noble a godfather, and never after ear so barren a land, for fear it yield me still so bad a harvest. I leave it to your honorable survey, and your Honor to your heart's content; which I wish may always answer your own wish and the world's hopeful expectation.—WILLIAM SHAKE-SPEARE, "To the Right Honorable Henry Wriothesley, Earl of Southampton, and Baron of Titchfield," *Venus and Adonis*, 1593

Let this duncified worlde esteeme of Spencer and Chaucer, I'le worshipp sweet Mr. Shakspeare, and to honoure him will lay his *Venus and Adonis* under my pillowe, as wee reade of one (I doe not well remember his name, but I am sure he was a kinge) slept with Homer under his bed's heade. Well, I'le bestowe a Frenche crowne in the faire writings of them out, and then I'le instructe thee about the delivery of them.—UNSIGNED, *The Return from Pernassus*, 1606, Pt. 1, Act. 4, Sc. 1

> But stay my Muse in thine owne confines keepe,
>   & wage not warre with so deere lov'd a neighbor,
> But having sung thy day song, rest and sleepe
>   preserve thy small fame and his greater favor:
> His Song was worthie merrit (*Shakspeare* hee)
> sung the faire blossome, thou the withered tree
>   *Laurell* is due to him, his art and wit
>   hath purchast it, *Cypres* thy brow will fit.

>     —WILLIAM BARKSTEAD, *Mirra, the Mother of Adonis*, 1607

## SAMUEL TAYLOR COLERIDGE
### From *Biographia Literaria*
#### 1817

In the *Venus and Adonis*, the first and most obvious excellence is the perfect sweetness of the versification; its adaptation to the subject; and the power displayed in varying the march of the words without passing into a loftier and more majestic rhythm than was demanded by the thoughts, or permitted by the propriety of preserving a sense of melody predominant. The delight in richness and sweetness of sound, even to a faulty excess, if it be evidently original, and not the result of an easily imitable mechanism, I regard as a highly favourable promise in the compositions of a young man. The man that hath not music in his soul can indeed never be a genuine poet. Imagery,—(even taken from nature, much more when transplanted from books, as travels, voyages, and works of natural history),—affecting incidents, just thoughts, interesting personal or domestic feelings, and with these the art of their combination or intertexture in the form of a poem,—may all by incessant effort be acquired as a trade, by a man of talent and much reading, who, as I once before observed, has mistaken an intense desire of poetic reputation for a natural poetic genius; the love of the arbitrary end for a possession of the peculiar means. But the sense of musical delight, with the power of producing it, is a gift of imagination; and this together with the power of reducing multitude into unity of effect, and modifying a series of thoughts by some one predominant thought or feeling, may be cultivated and improved, but can never be learned. It is in these that *"poeta nascitur non fit."*

A second promise of genius is the choice of subjects very remote from the private interests and circumstances of the writer himself. At least I have found, that where the subject is taken immediately from the author's personal sensations and experiences, the excellence of a particular poem is but an equivocal mark, and often a fallacious pledge, of genuine poetic power. We may perhaps remember the tale of the statuary, who had acquired considerable reputation for the legs of his goddesses, though the rest of the statue accorded but indifferently with ideal beauty; till his wife, elated by her husband's praises, modestly acknowledged that she had been his constant model. In the *Venus and Adonis* this proof of poetic power exists even to excess. It is throughout as if a superior spirit more intuitive, more intimately conscious, even than the characters themselves, not only of every outward look and act, but of the flux and reflux of the mind in all its subtlest thoughts and feelings, were placing the whole before our view; himself meanwhile unparticipating in the passions, and actuated only by that pleasurable excitement, which had resulted from the energetic fervour of his own spirit in so vividly exhibiting what it had so accurately and profoundly contemplated. I think, I should have conjectured from these poems, that even then the great instinct, which impelled the poet to the drama, was secretly working in him, prompting him—by a series and never broken chain of imagery, always vivid and, because unbroken, often minute; by the highest effort of the picturesque in words, of which words are capable, higher perhaps than was ever realized by any other poet, even Dante not excepted; to provide a substitute for that visual language, that constant intervention and running comment by tone, look and gesture, which in his dramatic works he was entitled to expect from the players. His Venus and Adonis seem at once the characters themselves, and the whole representation of those characters by the most consummate actors. You seem to be told nothing, but to see and hear everything. Hence it is, from the perpetual activity of attention required on the part of the reader; from the rapid flow, the quick change, and the playful nature of the thoughts and images; and above all from the alienation, and, if I may hazard such an expression, the utter *aloofness* of the poet's own feelings, from those of which he is at once the painter and the analyst;—that though the very subject cannot but detract from the pleasure of a delicate mind, yet never was poem less dangerous on a moral account. Instead of doing as Ariosto, and as, still more offensively, Wieland has done, instead of degrading and deforming passion into appetite, the trials of love into the struggles of concupiscence;—Shakespeare has here represented the animal impulse itself, so as to preclude all sympathy with it, by dissipating the reader's notice among the thousand outward images, and now beautiful, now fanciful circumstances, which form its dresses and its scenery; or by diverting our attention from the main subject by those frequent witty or profound reflections, which the poet's ever active mind has deduced from, or connected with, the imagery and the incidents. The reader is forced into too much action to sympathize with the merely passive of our nature. As little can a mind thus roused and awakened be brooded on by mean and indistinct emotion, as the low, lazy mist can creep upon the surface of a lake, while a strong gale is driving it onward in waves and billows.

It has been before observed that images, however beautiful, though faithfully copied from nature, and as accurately represented in words, do not of themselves characterize the poet. They become proofs of original genius only as far as they are modified by a predominant passion; or by associated thoughts or images awakened by that passion; or when they have the effect of reducing multitude to unity, or succession to an instant; or lastly, when a human and intellectual life is transferred to them from the poet's own spirit,

Which shoots its being through earth, sea, and air.

In the two following lines for instance, there is nothing objectionable, nothing which would preclude them from forming, in their proper place, part of a descriptive poem:

Behold yon row of pines, that shorn and bow'd
Bend from the sea-blast, seen at twilight eve.

But with a small alteration of rhythm, the same words would be equally in their place in a book of topography, or in a descriptive tour. The same image will rise into semblance of poetry if thus conveyed:

Yon row of bleak and visionary pines,
By twilight glimpse discerned, mark! how they flee
From the fierce sea-blast, all their tresses wild
Streaming before them.

. . . The last character I shall mention, which would prove indeed but little, except as taken conjointly with the former;—yet without which the former could scarce exist in a high degree, and (even if this were possible) would give promises only of transitory flashes and a meteoric power;—is depth, and energy of thought. No man was ever yet a great poet, without being at the same time a profound philosopher. For poetry is the blossom and the fragrancy of all human knowledge, human thoughts, human passions, emotions, language. In Shakespeare's poems the creative power and the intellectual energy wrestle as in a war embrace. Each in its excess of strength seems to threaten the extinction of the other. At length in the drama they were reconciled, and fought each with its shield before the breast of the other. Or like two rapid streams, that, at their first meeting within narrow and rocky banks, mutually strive to repel each other and intermix reluctantly and in tumult; but soon finding a wider channel and more yielding shores blend, and dilate, and flow on in one current and with one voice. The *Venus and Adonis* did not perhaps allow the display of the deeper passions. But the story of Lucretia seems to favour and even demand their intensest workings. And yet we find in *Shakespeare's* management of the tale neither pathos, nor any other *dramatic* quality. There is the same minute and faithful imagery as in the former poem, in the same vivid colours, inspirited by the same impetuous vigour of thought, and diverging and contracting with the same activity of the assimilative and of the modifying faculties; and with a yet larger display, a yet wider range of knowledge and reflection; and lastly, with the same perfect dominion, often domination, over the whole world of language. What then shall we say? even this; that Shakespeare, no mere child of nature; no *automaton* of genius; no passive vehicle of inspiration, possessed by the spirit, not possessing it; first studied patiently, meditated deeply, understood minutely, till knowledge, become habitual and intuitive, wedded itself to his habitual feelings, and at length gave birth to that stupendous power, by which he stands alone, with no equal or second in his own class; to that power which seated him on one of the two glory-smitten summits of the poetic mountain, with Milton as his compeer not rival. While the former darts himself forth, and passes into all the forms of human character and passion, the one Proteus of the fire and the flood; the other attracts all forms and things to himself, into the unity of his own ideal. All things and modes of action shape themselves anew in the being of Milton; while Shakespeare becomes all things, yet for ever remaining himself. O what great men hast thou not produced, England, my country!—Truly indeed—

We must be free or die, who speak the tongue,
Which Shakespeare spake; the faith and morals hold,
Which Milton held. In every thing we are sprung
Of earth's first blood, have titles manifold.

# The Rape of Lucrece

The love I dedicate to your Lordship is without end; whereof this pamphlet without beginning is but a superfluous moiety. The warrant I have of your honorable disposition, not the worth of my untutored lines, makes it assured of acceptance. What I have done is yours; what I have to do is yours; being part in all I have, devoted yours. Were my worth greater, my duty would show greater; meantime, as it is, it is bound to your Lordship, to whom I wish long life still lengthened with all happiness.—WILLIAM SHAKESPEARE, "To the Right Honorable Henry Wriothesley, Earl of Southampton, and Baron of Titchfield," *The Rape of Lucrece*, 1594

It was not so popular in its own day as its predecessor, and it does not afford the modern reader any very lively satisfaction. It shows an advance in metrical accomplishment. To the six-line stanza of *Venus and Adonis* a seventh line is added, which heightens its beauty and its dignity. The strength of *Lucrece* lies in its graphic and gorgeous descriptions, and in its sometimes microscopic psychological analysis. For the rest, its pathos consists of elaborate and far-fetched rhetoric.

The lament of the heroine after the crime has been committed is pure declamation, extremely eloquent no doubt, but copious and artificial as an oration of Cicero's, rich in apostrophes and antitheses. The sorrow of "Collatine and his consorted lords" is portrayed in laboured and quibbling speeches. Shakespeare's knowledge and mastery are most clearly seen in the reflections scattered through the narrative—such, for instance, as the following profound and exquisitely written stanza on the softness of the feminine nature:—

For men have marble, women waxen minds,
And therefore are they form'd as marble will;
The weak oppress'd, the impression of strange kinds
Is form'd in them by force, by fraud, or skill:
Then call them not the authors of their ill,
No more than wax shall be accounted evil,
Wherein is stamp'd the semblance of a devil.

In point of mere technique the most remarkable passage in the poem is the long series of stanzas (lines 1366 to 1568) describing a painting of the destruction of Troy, which Lucrece contemplates in her despair. The description is marked by such force, freshness, and naïveté as might suggest that the writer had never seen a picture before:—

> Here one man's hand leaned on another's head,
> His nose being shadowed by his neighbour's ear.

So dense is the throng of figures in the picture, so deceptive the presentation,

> That for Achilles' image stood his spear,
> Grip'd in an armed hand: himself behind
> Was left unseen, save to the eye of mind.
> A hand, a foot, a face, a leg, a head,
> Stood for the whole to be imagined.

Here, as in all other places in which Shakespeare mentions pictorial or plastic art, it is realism carried to the point of illusion that he admires and praises. The paintings in the Guild Chapel at Stratford were, doubtless, as before mentioned, the first he ever saw. He may also, during his Stratford period, have seen works of art at Kenilworth Castle or at St. Mary's Church in Coventry. In London, in the Hall belonging to the Merchants of the Steel-Yard, he had no doubt seen two greatly admired pictures by Holbein which hung there. Moreover, there were in London at that time not only numerous portraits by Dutch masters, but also a few Italian pictures. It appears, for example, from a list of "Pictures and other Works of Art" drawn up in 1613 by John Ernest, Duke of Saxe-Weimar, that there hung at Whitehall a painting of Julius Cæsar, and another of Lucretia, said to have been "very artistically executed." This picture may possibly have suggested to Shakespeare the theme of his poem. Larger compositions were no doubt familiar to him in the tapestries of the period (the hangings at Theobald's presented scenes from Roman history); and he may very likely have seen the excellent Dutch and Italian pictures at Nonsuch Palace, then in the height of its glory.

His reflections upon art led him, as aforesaid, to the conclusion that it was the artist's business to keep a close watch upon nature, to master or transcend her. Again and again he ranks truth to nature as the highest quality in art. He evidently cared nothing for allegorical or religious painting; he never so

much as mentions it. Nor, with all his love for "the concord of sweet sounds," does he ever allude to church music.

The description of the great painting of the fall of Troy is no mere irrelevant decoration of the poem; for the fall of Troy symbolises the fall of the royal house of Tarquin as a consequence of Sextus's crime. Shakespeare did not look at the event from the point of view of individual morality alone; he makes us feel that the honour of a royal family, and even its dynastic existence, are hazarded by criminal aggression upon a noble house. All the conceptions of honour belonging to mediæval chivalry are transferred to ancient Rome. "Knights, by their oaths, should right poor ladies' harms," says Lucrece, in calling upon her kinsmen to avenge her.

In his picture of the sack of Troy, Shakespeare has followed the second book of Virgil's *Æneid*; for the groundwork of his poem as a whole he has gone to the short but graceful and sympathetic rendering of the story of Lucretia in Ovid's *Fasti* (ii. 685–852).

A comparison between Ovid's style and that of Shakespeare certainly does not redound to the advantage of the modern poet. In opposition to this semi-barbarian, Ovid seems the embodiment of classic severity. Shakespeare's antithetical conceits and other lapses of taste are painfully obtrusive. Every here and there we come upon such stumbling-blocks as these:—

> Some of her blood still pure and red remain'd,
> And some look'd black, and that false Tarquin
> 　　stain'd;

or,

> If children pre-decease progenitors,
> We are their offspring, and they none of ours.

This lack of nature and of taste is not only characteristic of the age in general, but is bound up with the great excellences and rare capacities which Shakespeare was now developing with such amazing rapidity. His momentary leaning towards this style was due, in part at least, to the influence of his fellow-poets, his friends, his rivals in public favour—the influence, in short, of that artistic microscosm in whose atmosphere his genius shot up to sudden maturity.—G. G. GERVINUS, *Shakespeare Commentaries*, 1845, tr. F. E. Bunnèt

# The Passionate Pilgrim

Here likewise, I must necessarily insert a manifest injury done me in that work ⟨*The Passionate Pilgrim*⟩, by taking the two Epistles of *Paris* to *Helen*, and *Helen* to *Paris*, and printing them in a lesse volume, under the name of another, which may put the world in opinion I might steale them from him; and hee to do himselfe right, hath since published them in his owne name: but as I must acknowledge my lines not worthy his patronage, under whom he hath publisht them, so the Author ⟨Shakespeare⟩ I know much offended with M. *Jaggard* that (altogether unknown to him) presumed to make so bold with his name.—THOMAS HEYWOOD, "Epistle to Mr. Nicholas Okes," *An Apology for Actors*, 1612

## A. T. QUILLER-COUCH
From *"The Passionate Pilgrim"* (1895)
*Adventures in Criticism*
1896, pp. 29–38

This famous (or, if you like it, infamous) little anthology of thirty leaves has been singularly unfortunate in its title-pages. It was first published in 1599 as *The Passionate Pilgrime. By W. Shakespeare. At London. Printed for W. Jaggard, and are to be sold by W. Leake, at the Greyhound in Paules Churchyard.* This, of course, was disingenuous. Some of the numbers were by Shakespeare: but the authorship of some remains doubtful to this day, and others the enterprising Jaggard had boldly conveyed from Marlowe, Richard Barne-field, and Bartholomew Griffin. In short, to adapt a famous line upon a famous lexicon, "the best part was Shakespeare, the rest was not." For this, Jaggard has been execrated from time to time with sufficient heartiness. Mr. Swinburne, in his latest volume of Essays, calls him an "infamous pirate, liar, and thief." Mr. Humphreys remarks, less vivaciously, that "He was not careful and prudent, or he would not have attached the name of Shakespeare to a volume which was only partly by the bard—that was his crime. Had Jaggard foreseen the tantrums and contradictions he caused some commentators—Mr. Payne Collier, for instance—he would doubtless have substituted 'By William Shakespeare *and others*' for 'By William Shakespeare.' Thus he might have saved his reputation, and this hornets' nest which now and then rouses itself afresh around his aged ghost of three centuries ago."

That a ghost can suffer no inconvenience from hornets I take to be indisputable: but as a defence of Jaggard the above hardly seems convincing. One might as plausibly justify a forger on the ground that, had he foreseen the indignation of the prosecuting counsel, he would doubtless have saved his reputation by forbearing to forge. But before constructing a better defence, let us hear the whole tale of the alleged misdeeds. Of the second edition of *The Passionate Pilgrim* no copy exists. Nothing whatever is known of it, and the whole edition may have been but an ideal construction of Jaggard's sportive fancy. But in 1612 appeared *The Passionate Pilgrime, or certaine amorous Sonnets between Venus and Adonis, newly corrected and augmented. By W. Shakespeare. The third edition. Whereunto is newly added two Love Epistles, the first from Paris to Hellen, and Hellen's answere back again to Paris. Printed by W. Jaggard.* (These "two Love Epistles" were really by Thomas Heywood.) This title-page was very quickly cancelled, and Shakespeare's name omitted.

These are the bare facts. Now observe how they appear when set forth by Mr. Humphreys:—"Shakespeare, who, when the first edition was issued, was aged thirty-five, acted his part as a great man very well, for he with dignity took no notice of the error on the title-page of the first edition, attributing to him poems which he had never written. But when Jaggard went on sinning, and the third edition appeared under Shakespeare's name *solely*, though it had poems by Thomas Heywood, and others as well, Jaggard was promptly pulled up by both Shakespeare and Heywood. Upon this the publisher appears very properly to have printed a new title-page, omitting the name of Shakespeare."

Upon this I beg leave to observe—(1) That although it may very likely have been at Shakespeare's own request that his name was removed from the title-page of the third edition, Mr. Humphreys has no right to state this as an ascertained fact. (2) That I fail to understand, if Shakespeare acted properly in case of the third edition, why we should talk nonsense about his "acting the part of a great man very well" and "with dignity taking no notice of the error" in the first edition. In the first edition he was wrongly credited with pieces that belonged to Marlowe, Barnefield, and Griffin, and some authors unknown. In the third he was credited with these and some pieces by Heywood as well. In the name of common logic I ask why, if it were "dignified" to say nothing in the case of Marlowe and Barnefield, it suddenly became right and proper to protest in the case of Heywood? But (3) what right have we to assume that Shakespeare "took no notice of the error on the title-page of the first edition"? We know this only—that if he protested, he did not prevail as far as the first edition was concerned. That edition may have been already exhausted. It is even possible that he *did* prevail in the matter of the second edition, and that Jaggard reverted to his old courses in the third. I don't for a moment suppose this was the case. I merely suggest that where so many hypotheses will fit the scanty data known, it is best to lay down no particular hypothesis as fact.

For I imagine that anyone can, in five minutes, fit up an hypothesis quite as valuable as Mr. Humphreys'. Here is one which at least has the merit of not making Shakespeare look a fool:—W. Jaggard, publisher, comes to William Shakespeare, poet, with the information that he intends to bring out a small miscellany of verse. If the poet has an unconsidered trifle or so to spare, Jaggard will not mind giving a few shillings for them. "You may have, if you like," says Shakespeare, "the rough copies of some songs in my *Love's Labour's Lost*, published last year"; and, being further encouraged, searches among his rough MSS., and tosses Jaggard a lyric or two and a couple of sonnets. Jaggard pays his money, and departs with the verses. When the miscellany appears, Shakespeare finds his name alone upon the title-page, and remonstrates. But, of the defrauded ones, Marlowe is dead; Barnefield has retired to live the life of a country gentleman in Shropshire; Griffin dwells in Coventry (where he died, three years later). These are the men injured; and if they cannot, or will not, move in the business, Shakespeare (whose case at law would be more difficult) can hardly be expected to. So he contents himself with strong expressions at The Mermaid. But in 1612 Jaggard repeats his offence, and is indiscreet enough to add Heywood to the list of the spoiled. Heywood lives in London, on the spot; and Shakespeare, now retired to Stratford, is of more importance than he was in 1599. Armed with Shakespeare's authority Heywood goes to Jaggard and threatens; and the publisher gives way.

Whatever our hypothesis, we cannot maintain that Jaggard behaved well. On the other hand, it were foolish to judge his offence as if the man had committed it the day before yesterday. Conscience in matters of literary copy-right has been a plant of slow growth. But a year or two ago respectable citizens of the United States were publishing our books "free of authorial expenses," and even corrected our imperfect works without consulting us. We must admit that Jaggard acted up to Luther's maxim, *"Pecca fortiter."* He went so far as to include a piece so well known as Marlowe's *Live with me and be my love*—which proves at any rate his indifference to the chances of detection. But to speak of him as one would speak of a similar offender in this New Year of Grace is simply to forfeit one's claim to an historical sense.

What further palliation can we find? Mr. Swinburne calls the book "a worthless little volume of stolen and mutilated poetry, patched up and padded out with dirty and dreary doggrel, under the senseless and preposterous title of *The Passionate Pilgrim.*" On the other hand, Mr. Humphreys maintains that "Jaggard, at any rate, had very good taste. This is partly seen in the choice of a title. Few books have so charming a name as *The Passionate Pilgrim.* It is a perfect title. Jaggard also set up a good precedent, for this collection was published a year before *England's Helicon*, and, of course, very many years before any authorized collection of Shakespeare's 'Poems' was issued. We see in *The Passionate Pilgrim* a forerunner of *The Golden Treasury* and other anthologies."

Now, as for the title, if the value of a title lie in its application, Mr. Swinburne is right. It has little relevance to the verses in the volume. On the other hand, as a portly and attractive mouthful of syllables *The Passionate Pilgrim* can hardly be surpassed. If not "a perfect title," it is surely "a charming name." But Mr. Humphreys' contention that Jaggard "set up a good precedent" and produced a "forerunner" of English anthologies becomes absurd when we remember that *Tottel's Miscellany* was published in June, 1557 (just forty-two years before *The Passionate Pilgrim*), and had reached an eighth edition by 1587; that *The Paradise of Dainty Devices* appeared in 1576; *A Gorgeous Gallery of Gallant Inventions* in 1578; *A Handfull of Pleasant Delights* in 1584; and *The Phœnix' Nest* in 1593.

Almost as wide of the mark is Mr. Swinburne's description of the volume as "worthless." It contains twenty-one numbers, besides that lofty dirge, so unapproachably solemn, *The Phœnix and the Turtle.* Of these, five are undoubtedly by Shakespeare. A sixth (*Crabbed age and youth*), if not by Shakespeare, is one of the loveliest lyrics in the language, and I for my part could give it to no other man. Note also that but for Jaggard's enterprise this jewel had been irrevocably lost to us, since it is known only through *The Passionate Pilgrim.* Marlowe's *Live with me and be my love*, and Barnefield's *As it fell upon a day*, make numbers seven and eight. And I imagine that even Mr. Swinburne cannot afford to scorn *Sweet rose, fair flower, untimely pluck'd, soon vaded*—which again only occurs in *The Passionate Pilgrim.* These nine numbers, with *The Phœnix and the Turtle*, make up more than half the book. Among the rest we have the pretty and respectable lyrics, *If music and sweet poetry agree; Good night, good rest; Lord, how mine eyes throw gazes to the east. When as thine eye hath chose the dame*, and the gay little song, *It was a Lording's daughter.* There remain the *Venus and Adonis* sonnets and *My flocks feed not.* Mr. Swinburne may call these "dirty and dreary doggrel," an he list, with no more risk than of being held a somewhat over-anxious moralist. But to call the whole book worthless is mere abuse of words.

It is true, nevertheless, that one of the only two copies existing of the first edition was bought for three halfpence.

# ADDITIONAL READING

## COLLECTED WORKS

*Mr. William Shakespeares Comedies, Histories, & Tragedies.* [Edited by John Heminge and Henry Condell.] London: Printed by Isaac Jaggard and Ed. Blount, 1623 (First Folio); 1632 (Second Folio).

*The Works of Mr. William Shakespear.* Revis'd and Corrected . . . by Nicholas Rowe. London: Jacob Tonson, 1709. 6 vols.

*The Works of Mr. William Shakespear.* Collated and Corrected . . . by Alexander Pope. London: Jacob Tonson, 1723–25. 7 vols.

*The Works of Shakespeare.* Collated . . . and Corrected . . . by Lewis Theobald. London: A. Bettesworth, 1734. 7 vols.

*The Works of Shakespeare.* Carefully Revised and Corrected [by Thomas Hanmer]. Oxford: Printed at the Theatre, 1744. 6 vols.

*The Works of Shakespear.* With . . . Notes . . . by Pope and William Warburton. London: F. & P. Knapton, 1747. 8 vols.

*The Plays of William Shakespeare.* With Notes by Samuel Johnson. London: J. & R. Tonson, 1768. 8 vols.

*Twenty of the Plays of Shakespeare.* Collated . . . by George Steevens. London: J. Rivington & Sons, 1790. 10 vols.

*The Works of William Shakespeare.* Edited . . . by Richard Grant White. Boston: Little, Brown, 1857–66. 12 vols.

*A New Variorum Edition of Shakespeare.* Edited by Horace Howard Furness (and others). Philadelphia: Lippincott, 1871–1955. 27 vols.

*The Works of William Shakespeare.* Edited by William Aldis Wright. London: Macmillan, 1894–95. 9 vols. (The Cambridge Shakespeare.)

*The Tudor Shakespeare.* Edited by William Allan Neilson and Ashley Horace Thorndike. New York: Macmillan, 1911–13. 39 vols.

## PERSONAL

Calvert, George F. *Shakespeare: A Biographic Aesthetic Study.* Boston: Lee & Shepard, 1879.

Gray, Joseph William. *Shakespeare's Marriage.* London: Chapman & Hall, 1905.

Halliwell-Phillips, James O. *The Life of William Shakespeare.* London: J. R. Smith, 1848.

Kenny, Thomas. *The Life and Genius of Shakespeare.* London: Longmans, 1864.

Knight, Charles. *William Shakespeare: A Biography.* London: C. Knight, 1851.

Norris, J. Parker. *The Portraits of Shakespeare.* Philadelphia: Robert M. Lindsay, 1885.

Robinson, William Clarke. *Shakspere: The Man and His Mind.* Buffalo: C. W. Moulton, 1890.

Stopes, C. *Shakespeare's Family.* London: E. Stock, 1901.

White, Richard Grant. *Memoirs of the Life of William Shakespeare.* Boston: Little, Brown, 1865.

## GENERAL

Bradley, A. C. *Shakespearean Tragedy.* London: Macmillan, 1904.

Canning, Albert S. G. *Shakespeare Studied in Eight Plays.* London: T. Fisher Unwin, 1903.

Douce, Francis. *Illustrations of Shakespeare.* London: Thomas Tegg, 1839.

Drake, Nathan, ed. *Memorials of Shakespeare.* London: Colburn, 1828.

Egan, Maurice Francis. *The Ghost in Hamlet and Other Essays in Comparative Literature.* Chicago: McClurg, 1906.

Eschenburg, Johann Joachim. *Über W. Shakspeare.* Zurich: Orell, Gessner, Füssli, 1787.

Figgis, Darrell. *Shakespeare: A Study.* London: Dent, 1911.

Griffith, Elizabeth. *The Morality of Shakespeare's Drama.* London: T. Cadell, 1775.

Guizot, F. P. G. *Shakspeare and His Times.* New York: Harper, 1852.

Ingersoll, Robert G. *Shakespeare: A Lecture.* New York: C. P. Farrell, 1895.

Ingleby, C. M. *Shakespeare: The Man and the Book.* London: Trübner, 1877–81. 2 vols.

Lee, Sidney. *Shakespeare and the Modern Stage.* New York: Scribner's, 1906.

Lounsbury, Thomas R. *Shakespeare and Voltaire.* New York: Scribner's, 1902.

Mabie, Hamilton Wright. *William Shakespeare: Poet, Dramatist, and Man.* New York: Macmillan, 1900.

Morgann, Maurice. *An Essay on the Dramatic Character of Sir John Falstaff.* London: T. Davies, 1777.

Raleigh, Walter. *Shakespeare.* London: Macmillan, 1907.

## SOURCES

Hazlitt, W. C., ed. *Shakespeare's Library.* 2nd ed. London: Reeves & Turner, 1875. 6 vols.

Ingleby, C. M.; Smith, L. Toulmin; and Furnivall, F. J., eds. *The Shakspere Allusion-Book: 1591–1700.* Revised by John Munro. New York: Duffield, 1909. 2 vols.

Lennox, Charlotte. *Shakespear Illustrated.* London: A. Millar, 1753. 3 vols.

## AUTHORSHIP CONTROVERSY

Dixon, Theron S. E. *Francis Bacon and His Shakespeare.* Chicago: Sargent, 1895.

Edwards, William H. *Shaksper Not Shakespeare.* Cincinnati: Robert Clarke, 1900.

Greenwood, G. G. *The Shakespeare Problem Restated.* London: John Lane, 1908.

Morgan, Appleton. *The Shakespearean Myth.* Cincinnati: Robert Clarke, 1884.

Stopes, C. *The Bacon-Shakspere Question Answered.* 2nd ed. London: Trübner, 1899.

## BIBLIOGRAPHY

Bohn, Henry G. *The Biography and Bibliography of Shakespeare.* London: Privately printed, 1863.

Jaggard, William. *Shakespeare Bibliography.* Stratford-on-Avon: Shakespeare Press, 1911.

# ACKNOWLEDGMENTS

Essays and Studies. GEORGE SAINTSBURY, "Shakespeare and the Grand Style," 1910, copyright © 1910. Reprinted by permission.

Mitchell Kennerly. FRANK HARRIS, "All's Well That Ends Well," The Women of Shakespeare, copyright © 1912. Reprinted by permission.

Macmillan. A. C. BRADLEY, "Coriolanus," A Miscellany, copyright ©

1929. M. W. MACCALLUM, "Antony and Cleopatra," Shakespeare's Roman Plays and Their Background, copyright © 1910. Reprinted by permission.

G. P. Putnam's Sons. J. J. JUSSERAND, "What to Expect of Shakespeare," The School for Ambassadors and Other Essays, copyright © 1925 by J. J. Jusserand. Reprinted by permission.